CW01481437

WHO'S WHO IN SCOTLAND 2008

Who's Who

in

Scotland

2008

Carrick Media

Published by Carrick Media
32 Briar Grove, Ayr KA7 3PD
01292 283337

Copyright 2008 Carrick Media

Printed in England by Biddles Limited

British Library Cataloguing-in-Publication Data
A catalogue record for this book is available from the British Library

ISBN 978-0-9546631-6-2

Preface

Welcome to Who's Who in Scotland 2008. Firmly established as Scotland's dictionary of contemporary biography, this book first appeared in 1986. It is simultaneously a useful address book, a mine of information, and an essential guide to the establishments of Scotland (academic, ecclesiastical, legal, commercial, professional, political, artistic and literary) as well as to individuals who conform to no known category or establishment. Also, the book can be a source of amusement and miscellaneous interest.

Our thanks to all who responded to our requests for information about themselves, including and especially the hundreds of new entrants, without whose co-operation there would have been no book.

The Editors
Ayr
May 2008

THE DIRECTORY

AGRICULTURE AND HORTICULTURE

THE ROYAL HIGHLAND AND AGRICULTURAL SOCIETY OF SCOTLAND
Royal Highland Centre, Ingliston, Edinburgh EH28 8NF
Tel: 0131 335 6200 Fax: 0131 333 5236
e-mail: info@rhass.org.uk
web: www.rhass.org.uk
Contact: Ray J. Jones, Chief Executive; Adele J Thomson, Society Secretary.
The Society is Scotland's national agricultural society with over 14,000 members. Established in 1784, incorporated by Royal Charter, its principal objects are to promote Scotland's agriculture, allied and rural industries. Organiser of Scotland's premier agricultural event, the Royal Highland Show – the largest four-day single-venue event held annually in Scotland each June. Operates the Royal Highland Centre with facilities for small and large indoor and outdoor exhibitions and events, including parking for 20,000 vehicles.

SAC (THE SCOTTISH AGRICULTURAL COLLEGE)
West Mains Road, Edinburgh EH9 3JG
Tel: 0131 535 4185
e-mail: information@sac.co.uk
Contact: Mr Andrew Tibbs, Communications Manager, 0131 535 4196, communications@sac.co.uk; Dr Mike Smith, Research Manager, 0131 535 4074, mike.smith@sac.ac.uk; Ms Sonia Filby, Student Recruitment and Admissions Manager, 01292 525229, sonia.filby@sac.ac.uk; Ms Ceri Ritchie, Divisional Marketing Manager, 01224 711049, ceri.ritchie@sac.co.uk
SAC is a knowledge-based organisation which supports the development of land-based industries and communities through its specialist research and development resources, its education and training provision, and its expert advisory and consultancy services. Working within the broad areas of agriculture and related sciences, rural business development and management, food chain quality and safety, and rural resource and environmental management, SAC provides a unique Scotland-wide mechanism for the transfer of knowledge and ideas which emerge both from its own research and development and from other expert sources.

SASA
1 Roddinglaw Road, Edinburgh EH12 9FJ
Tel: 0131 244 8890 Fax: 0131 244 8940
e-mail: library@sasa.gsi.gov.uk
web: www.sasa.gov.uk
Contact: Prof. G. C. Machray, Head of SASA, 0131 244 8843; Mrs L. Clark, Librarian, 0131 244 8826, Lynda.Clark@sasa.gsi.gov.uk
The purpose of SASA, as part of Scottish Government, is to provide scientific information and advice on agricultural and horticultural crops, and aspects of the environment; to perform statutory and regulatory work in relation to national, European Union (EU) and

other international legislation and agreements on seed certification, plant health, bee health, plant variety registration, crop improvement, genetic resources, the protection of crops, food and the environment; to conduct research and development in support of statutory work undertaken above.

SCRI (SCOTTISH CROP RESEARCH INSTITUTE)
Invergowrie, Dundee DD2 5DA
Tel: 01382 562731 Fax: 01382 562426
e-mail: info@scri.ac.uk
web: www.scri.ac.uk

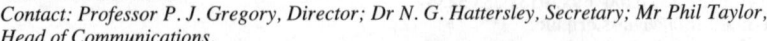

Contact: Professor P. J. Gregory, Director; Dr N. G. Hattersley, Secretary; Mr Phil Taylor, Head of Communications.
The Institute is financed principally by the Scottish Executive Environment and Rural Affairs Department and external contracts (c. £13m. per annum). It undertakes research on plants and their interactions with the environment particularly in managed ecosystems. It focuses on research on barley, potatoes and soft fruit.

ANIMALS AND WILDLIFE

ADVOCATES FOR ANIMALS
10 Queensferry Street, Edinburgh EH2 4PG
Tel: 0131 225 6039 Fax: 0131 220 6377
e-mail: info@advocatesforanimals.org
web: www.advocatesforanimals.org

Contact: Fiona Ogg, CEO.
Advocates for Animals is Scotland's leading animal protection organisation. We promote the protection of animals through investigations, high-profile campaigns, scientific reports, public education and political lobbying. We oppose all animal experiments, the exploitation of animals in entertainment and we campaign to end the barbaric practices of factory farming. We believe that Scotland's unique and diverse wildlife should be valued and respected.

DEER COMMISSION FOR SCOTLAND
Great Glen House, Leachkin Road, Inverness IV3 8NW
Tel: 01463 725000 Fax: 01463 725048
e-mail: enquiries@deercom.com
web: www.dcs.gov.uk
Contact: Professor John Milne MBE, Chairman; Nick Halfhide, Chief Executive.

The Deer Commission for Scotland is the non departmental public body charged with furthering the conservation, control and sustainable management of all species of wild deer in Scotland, and keeping under review all matters, including welfare, relating to deer.

Scotland, extending to some 65,000 Hectares. We research environmental problems and provide practical solutions. We promote opportunities for people to enjoy and learn about the natural world, running an active schools field-teaching programme. We are supported by 76,000 members and over 1,800 active volunteers in Scotland.

SCOTTISH WHITE FISH PRODUCERS ASSOCIATION LIMITED
40 Broad Street, Fraserburgh AB43 9AH
Tel: 01346 514545 Fax: 01346 518075
e-mail: george@macraestephen.co.uk
web: www.swfpa.org.uk
Contact: Mr Michael Park - Mob: 07710 504 773, e-mail: m.park@btconnect.com; MacRae Stephen & Co, Tel: 01346 514545, e-mail: george@macraestephen.co.uk; Mr John Watt - Mob: 07876 450 496, e-mail: Berachah@btinternet.com
SWFPA is the largest representative Association for fishermen in the UK and one of the largest in Europe. In value 70% of all demersal stock landings in Scotland and 50% of the UK total are landed by SWFPA members. SWFPA exists to protect and develop the political and economic interests of its members and contributes significantly to the development of EU fisheries policy both for the UK and Scotland.

SCOTTISH WILDLIFE TRUST
Cramond House, Cramond Glebe Road, Edinburgh EH4 6NS
Tel: 0131 312 7765 Fax: 0131 321 8705
e-mail: enquiries@swt.org.uk
web: www.swt.org.uk
Contact: Dennis J. N. Dick, Chairman; Simon Milne, MBE, Chief Executive.
With 30,000 members, SWT is Scotland's leading voluntary body conserving Scotland's wildlife and natural environment. SWT acquired its first wildlife reserve in 1966 and now has more than 120 reserves throughout Scotland. As well as providing homes for wildlife, these reserves are valuable places for people to interact and enjoy wildlife. Our work also has a political dimension, we influence and challenge legislation for the benefit of wildlife.

ARTISTIC AND CULTURAL

BRITISH COUNCIL, SCOTLAND
The Tun (3rd Floor), 4 Jackson's Entry,
Holyrood Road, Edinburgh EH8 8PJ
Tel: 0131 524 5700 Fax: 0131 524 5701
e-mail: britishcouncilscotland@britishcouncil.org
web: www.britishcouncil.org/scotland
Contact: Roy Cross, Director; Julia Armour, Deputy Director; Andrew Borthwick, Head of Communications.
The British Council is the UK's international organisation for educational opportunities and cultural relations. It has offices across all 4 countries of the UK and 110 countries worldwide. Its purpose is to build mutually beneficial relationships between people in the UK and other countries, and to increase appreciation of the UK's creative ideas and achievements. It operates independently from the UK government. In Scotland the British

Corporate Policy and Performance; Andrew Patience, Director of Finance and Resources.
Our vision is to be a world class museums service that informs, educates and inspires. We preserve, interpret and make accessible for all, the past and present of Scotland, of other nations and cultures, and of the natural world. The National Museums Scotland are: National Museum of Scotland and National War Museum in Edinburgh, National Museum of Flight in East Lothian, National Museum of Costume in Dumfriesshire and National Museum of Rural Life in East Kilbride.

THE ROYAL SCOTTISH ACADEMY
The Mound, Edinburgh EH2 2EL
Tel: 0131 225 6671 Fax: 0131 220 6016
e-mail: info@royalscottishacademy.org
web: www.royalscottishacademy.org
Contact: President, Professor Bill Scott, PRSA; Colin R Greenslade, Programme Director.
Founded in 1826, the RSA maintains a unique position in Scotland as an independently funded institution led by eminent artists and architects whose purpose is to promote and support the creation, understanding and enjoyment of the visual arts through exhibitions and related educational events. The RSA also administers scholarships, awards and residencies for artists in Scotland and has a historic collection of important artworks and archive of related material chronicling art and architecture in Scotland over the last 180 years.

ROYAL SCOTTISH NATIONAL ORCHESTRA
73 Claremont Street, Glasgow G3 7JB
Tel: 0141 226 3868 Fax: 0141 221 4317
e-mail: admin@rsno.org.uk

:RSNO
Royal Scottish
National Orchestra
Stéphane Denève:Music Director

Contact: Simon Woods, Chief Executive; Tom Thomson, Chairman; Stéphane Denève, Music Director.
The Royal Scottish National Orchestra is Scotland's national symphony orchestra performing a wide range of world-class music, supported by innovative community and education work, throughout Scotland and beyond.

THE SALTIRE SOCIETY
9 Fountain Close, 22 High Street, Edinburgh EH1 1TF
Tel: 0131 556 1836 Fax: 0131 557 1675
e-mail: saltire@saltiresociety.org.uk
web: www.saltiresociety.org.uk
Contact: Kathleen Munro, Administrator.

SCOTLAND
A L B A

SALTIRE
SOCIETY

The Saltire Society, founded in 1936, is a non-party political body concerned with all aspects of Scottish life and culture. Through its Awards competition, it promotes excellence in the arts and sciences. The Society has branches throughout Scotland. The branches are concerned mainly with local issues but they also liaise closely with Headquarters. Membership is open to all who support the Aims of the Society.

SCOTTISH BOOK TRUST
Sandeman House, Trunk's Close, 55 High Street, Edinburgh EH1 1SR
Tel: 0131 524 0160 Fax: 0131 524 0161
e-mail: info@scottishbooktrust.com

**THE SCOTTISH TRADITIONS OF DANCE
TRUST**
**Speirs Centre, Primrose Street, Alloa FK10
1JJ**
Tel: 01259 218444 Fax: 01259 218456
e-mail: info@stdt.org
web: www.stdt.org
Contact: Angela Dreyer-Larsen, Director, angela@stdt.org
To promote and encourage participation and enjoyment in all forms of Scottish Traditional
Dance. Support and enable people to enjoy participation in the arts. To provide
performances, workshops and events including traditional dance.

SOCIETY OF ANTIQUARIES OF SCOTLAND
National Museum of Scotland, Chambers Street, Edinburgh EH1 1JF
Tel: 0131 247 4133/4115 Fax: 0131 247 4163
e-mail: administration@socantscot.org
web: www.socantscot.org
Contact: Dr Simon Gilmour, Director.
The Society, founded in 1780, is the oldest antiquarian society in Scotland; an active body, it
organises lectures, conferences, seminars and excursions, publishes an annual *Proceedings,*
available free on the web (alongside a report series, SAIR), a twice-yearly Newsletter and a
Monograph series. It plays an important role in the cultural life and heritage of Scotland,
sponsoring archaeological and historical research. Drawing on its wide range of available
expertise, it provides an impartial and independent voice on heritage matters.

BUSINESS

GLASGOW CITY MARKETING BUREAU
11 George Square, Glasgow G2 1DY
Tel: 0141 566 0800 Fax: 0141 566 0810
e-mail: corporate@seeglasgow.com
web: www.seeglasgow.com
*Contact: Scott Taylor, Chief Executive, scott.taylor@seeglasgow.com; Nancy McLardie,
Head of Public Relations, nancy.mclardie@seeglasgow.com*
Funded by Glasgow City Council with contributions from the private sector, the Glasgow
City Marketing Bureau is the place marketing agency for the city of Glasgow. It has a staff
of 40 engaged in national and international activity comprising: conventions, incentives,
events, meetings and exhibition sales; conference and event accommodation bookings; brand
marketing and public relations. The Bureau is responsible for developing and implementing
the city branding campaign, **Glasgow: Scotland with style.**

SCOTTISH BUSINESS IN THE COMMUNITY
**Livingstone House, 43a Discovery Terrace, Heriot Watt
University Research Park, Edinburgh EH14 4AP**
Tel: 0131 4511100 Fax: 0131 4511127
e-mail: info@sbcscot.com

web: www.sbcscot.com
Contact: Samantha Barber, Chief Executive; George Borthwick, CBE, Chairman.
Scottish Business in the Community is Scotland's lead organisation in the field of Corporate Responsibility. SBC promotes CR as a mark of sound business practice, and enables companies to make their impact on society as positive and productive as possible, whilst gaining tangible business benefits. SBC is led by its member companies, a prestigious group committed to the promotion of responsible business practice in Scotland. A sophisticated network of multi sector contracts and over 25 years of experience make SBC the logical route through which the Scottish business community responds to the challenge of improving its impact on society.

CHARITABLE AND VOLUNTARY

ALZHEIMER SCOTLAND
22 Drumsheugh Gardens, Edinburgh EH3 7RN
Tel: 0131 243 1453 Fax: 0131 243 1450
e-mail: alzheimer@alzscot.org

Alzheimer Scotland
Action on Dementia

Contact: Jim Jackson, Chief Executive; Stephen Balmer, Finance Director; Rachel Guy, Fundraising and Public Relations Director.
Alzheimer Scotland is Scotland's leading dementia charity for 58,000 people with dementia and their carers. We run practical services such as day care and drop-in centres, home support, courses and support for carers on over 60 sites, and a Freephone 24-hour Dementia Helpline (0808 808 3000). We publish leaflets, booklets, reports and a quarterly newsletter, maintain a website (www.alzscot.org), campaign for better services for people with dementia and their carers, and have a research programme.

BRITISH LIMBLESS EX-SERVICE MEN'S ASSOCIATION (BLESMA)
185–187 High Road, Chadwell Heath, Romford, Essex RM6 6NA
Tel: 020 8590 1124 Fax: 020 8599 2932
e-mail: headquarters@blesma.org
web: www.blesma.org
Contact: Lt. Col. (Retd.) J.W. Church, MBE, General Secretary, as above; Lt. Cmdr Heather Nicholson, National Welfare Officer, as above; Mrs H. Kinchin-White, Manager, Ancaster BLESMA Home, Crieff, 01764 652480, crieff@blesma.org, www.blesma.org
BLESMA is a national charity formed in 1932. It supports serving and ex-service men and women who have lost limbs or the use of limbs in service. Currently there are 23 branches nationwide. It runs two care homes, one of which is in Crieff in Perthshire. It also runs a welfare service for its members and rehabilitation activities.

THE BRITISH RED CROSS SOCIETY
4 Nasmyth Place, Hillington, Glasgow G52 4PR
Tel: 0141 891 4000 Fax: 0141 891 4099
web: www.redcross.org.uk
Contact: Gerald McLaughlin; Anne O'Neill.
The British Red Cross helps people in crisis in the UK and internationally. In Scotland, 5,000 skilled volunteers train people in first aid, provide emergency response in times of disaster and care for vulnerable people through services including medical loan and transport

The Institution of Civil Engineers (ICE) is one of the pre-eminent engineering institutions in the world. Established as a learned society in 1818, it has 80,000 members worldwide, including 7,300 in Scotland and provides a voice for civil engineering, continuing professional development and promoting best practice throughout the industry.

MERCY CORPS
17 Claremont Crescent, Edinburgh EH7 4HX
Tel: 0131 558 8244 Fax: 0131 558 8288
e-mail: info@uk.mercycorps.org
web: www.mercycorps.org.uk
Registered Charity Number: SC030289
Company Registered in Scotland Number: 208829

Be the change

Contact: Mervyn Lee, Executive Director; Alison Cameron, Director of Fundraising.
Our mission is to alleviate suffering, poverty and oppression by helping people all over the world unleash their potential and win against nearly impossible odds. Mercy Corps delivers emergency relief, rehabilitation and long term development programmes in countries suffering the effects of war, natural disaster and social or economic collapse. Mercy Corps has grown to become a leading international relief and developmental organisation, headquartered in Edinburgh (Europe), Portland Oregon, Washington DC (USA) and Hong Kong. The global programmes employ 3,400 staff worldwide and reach more than 14.4 million people in over 35 countries. Over the past five years, more than 90% of the agency's resources have been allocated directly to programmes that help people in need and change lives every day.

THE ROYAL ENVIRONMENTAL HEALTH INSTITUTE OF SCOTLAND
3 Manor Place, Edinburgh EH3 7DH
Tel: 0131 225 6999 Fax: 0131 225 3993
e-mail: contact@rehis.com
web: www.rehis.org
Contact: Tom Bell, Chief Executive, tb@rehis.com; President,
Robert Howe; Senior Vice-President, Colin Wallace.
The Institute is an independent, self-financing Registered Scottish Charity whose main objectives are for the benefit of the community to promote the advancement of Environmental Health by:

a. stimulating general interest in and disseminating knowledge concerning Environmental Health;
b. promoting education and training in matters relating to Environmental Health; and
c. maintaining, by examination or otherwise, high standards of professional practice and conduct on the part of Environmental Health Officers in Scotland.

THE ROYAL SOCIETY FOR THE RELIEF OF INDIGENT GENTLEWOMEN OF SCOTLAND
14 Rutland Square, Edinburgh EH1 2BD
Tel: 0131 229 2308 Fax: 0131 229 0956
e-mail: info@igf.org
web: www.lgf.org
Contact: Mr W.F. MacTaggart, Chairman; Mr Alexander D. Mackay, Secretary.
The Society originated in 1847 to assist ladies of Scottish birth or education with professional or business backgrounds who exist on low incomes with limited capital. Applications are considered from ladies who are widowed, divorced or unmarried, aged 50 and over, who qualify by birth or education and are daughters or widows of professional or

business men. Ladies who have attained this status by their own endeavours or were prevented from doing so by devoting their lives to the care of relatives are also considered. The Society makes a regular charitable grant to ladies admitted to the roll and other grants are made for specific needs. Regular visiting and counselling is undertaken by the Society's caseworkers and representatives.

THE SCOTTISH COUNCIL FOR VOLUNTARY ORGANISATIONS (SCVO)
Mansfield Traquair Centre, 15 Mansfield Place, Edinburgh EH3 6BB
Tel: 0131 556 3882 Fax: 0131 556 0279
e-mail: enquiries@scvo.org.uk
web: www.scvo.org.uk
Contact: Martin Sime, Chief Executive; Lucy McTernan, Deputy Chief Executive; John Ferguson, Director of Development and Programmes; Paul White, Director of Networks; Tim Hencher, Director of Finance and Resources.
SCVO seeks to advance the values and interests shared by voluntary organisations by fostering co-operation, promoting best practice, and through the delivery of sustainable common services. Services include: news and current affairs, research, policy and lobbying, conferences, training courses, information, publications, software, office supplies, payroll, pensions, insurance, project development, Charity Giving Scotland and Give As You Earn, and direct links with Councils for Voluntary Service and national networks.

THE SCOTTISH GENEALOGY SOCIETY
Library and Family History Centre, 15 Victoria Terrace, Edinburgh EH1 2JL
Tel: 0131 220 3677 Fax: 0131 220 3677
e-mail: info@scotsgenealogy.com
web: www.scotsgenealogy.com
Contact: Dr. J. Cranstoun, Honorary Librarian; Ken A Nisbet, Honorary Secretary; Sales Secretary.
The aims are to promote research into Scottish family history and to collect, exchange and publish material relating to genealogy, but the Society does not engage in professional research. *The Scottish Genealogist* is published quarterly and lectures are held monthly from September until April. The library holds books, periodicals, microfilm and microfiche. Publications include transcriptions of gravestones which are a valuable adjunct to pre-1855 records.

SCOTTISH NATIONAL WAR MEMORIAL
The Castle, Edinburgh EH1 2YT
Tel: 0131 226 7393 Fax: 0131 225 8920
Contact: Lieutenant Colonel I. Shepherd, Secretary to the Trustees.
Maintains and amends the Rolls of Honour of Scots who fell in the two World Wars and Campaigns after 1945. Administers the memorial building in Edinburgh Castle.

CHILDREN

CHILDREN IN SCOTLAND
Princes House, 5 Shandwick Place,
Edinburgh EH2 4RG
Tel: 0131 228 8484 Fax: 0131 228 8585

e-mail: info@childreninscotland.org.uk
web: www.childreninscotland.org.uk
Contact: Dr Bronwen Cohen, Chief Executive.
Children in Scotland is an independent agency representing over 450 voluntary, statutory and professional organisations and individuals. It works with its members to identify and promote the interests of children, young people and their families. Its activities include information, training, policy, practice development and research, and it produces a monthly magazine and a range of publications. Children in Scotland is the English language partner in a Europe-wide network which produces a magazine simultaneously in twelve languages. Based within Children in Scotland is *Enquire*, the independent information service on additional support for learning and a number of specific development programmes. Web: www.childreninscotland.org.uk

ST. ANDREW'S CHILDREN'S SOCIETY
7 John's Place, Leith, Edinburgh
Tel: 0131 454 3370 Fax: 0131 454 3371
e-mail: info@standrews-children.org.uk
Contact: Stephen Small, Director, ssmall@standrews-children.org.uk; Claire McMahon, Administrator, cmcmahon@standrews-children.org.uk; Maureen McEvoy, Chairperson.
We offer support, advice and assistance to pregnant women considering adoption for their children. We assess couples and single people who can offer permanent and temporary homes to children through adoption and fostering. We also offer a counselling service to adopted adults and birth family members.

CONSERVATION

EDINBURGH WORLD HERITAGE
5 Charlotte Square, Edinburgh EH2 4DR
Tel: 0131 220 7720 Fax: 0131 220 7730
e-mail: info@ewht.org.uk
web: www.ewht.org.uk
Edinburgh World Heritage was set up in April 1999 to work with the City Council and the Scottish Executive in dealing with conservation issues affecting the appearance, character and integrity of the outstanding conservation areas of the Old and New Towns of Edinburgh and the World Heritage Site (WHS) lying within those areas. The Trust monitors and promotes the WHS and also administers a conservation funding programme for the repair of buildings within its area. It is funded by the City Council and Historic Scotland.

HEACS: HISTORIC ENVIRONMENT ADVISORY COUNCIL FOR SCOTLAND
Longmore House, Salisbury Place, Edinburgh
EH9 1SH
Tel: 0131 668 8810 Fax: 0131 668 8987
Contact: Olwyn Owen, Secretary; olwyn.owen@scotland.gsi.gov.uk
HEACS is an advisory, Non-Departmental Public Body which provides Scottish Ministers with strategic advice on issues affecting the historic environment. HEACS was established in 2003 under the Public Appointments and Public Bodies (Scotland) Act 2003. The Chair is Mrs Elizabeth Burns, CMG, OBE.

HISTORIC SCOTLAND
Longmore House, Salisbury Place, Edinburgh EH9 1SH
Tel: 0131 668 8600 Fax: 0131 668 8699
web: http://www.historic-scotland.gsi.gov.uk
Historic Scotland is an agency within the Scottish Government's Directorate General-Economy and Chief Economic Adviser. It is responsible for safeguarding and promoting Scotland's built heritage including listing of historic buildings and scheduling of ancient monuments, designed landscapes, grants to owners of listed buildings and ancient monuments. Historic Scotland manages a programme of rescue archaeology and is a leading authority in technical conservation and research. Historic Scotland is the country's largest operator of visitor attractions including Edinburgh Castle, Stirling Castle, Fort George and the Border Abbeys at Melrose, Dryburgh and Jedburgh.

THE NATIONAL TRUST FOR SCOTLAND
Wemyss House, 28 Charlotte Square, Edinburgh EH2 4ET
Tel: 0844 493 2100 Fax: 0131 243 9301
e-mail: information@nts.org.uk
web: www.nts.org.uk

The National Trust for Scotland

Contact: Shonaig Macpherson, Chairman; Mark Adderley, Chief Executive.
Established in 1931, The National Trust for Scotland cares for places of historic interest and natural beauty throughout Scotland. Over 100 properties are open to visitors and the Trust is supported by 300,000 members, making it Scotland's leading conservation charity.
Charity number: SC007410.

ROYAL COMMISSION ON THE ANCIENT AND HISTORICAL MONUMENTS OF SCOTLAND
John Sinclair House, 16 Bernard Terrace, Edinburgh EH8 9NX
Tel: 0131 662 1456 Fax: 0131 662 1477
e-mail: info@rcahms.gov.uk
web: www.rcahms.gov.uk
Contact: Chairman, Professor John Hume, BSc, ARCST; Diana M. Murray, MA (Cantab), FSA, FSAS, MIFA.
The aims of the Royal Commission on the Ancient and Historical Monuments of Scotland are: to survey and record the built environment of Scotland; to compile and maintain a public record of the archaeological, architectural and historical environment; to promote an understanding of this information by all appropriate means.

EDUCATION
(see also SCHOOLS)

ADAM SMITH COLLEGE
St Brycedale Avenue, Kirkcaldy, Fife KY1 1EX
Tel: 01592 223400 Fax: 01592 640225
web: www.adamsmithcollege.ac.uk

Contact: Dr Craig Thomson, Principal, 01592 223058, craigthomson@adamsmith.ac.uk; Shirley Scott, Assistant Principal, 01592 223055, shirleyscott@adamsmith.ac.uk; Beth

Dickson, Assistant Principal, 01592 223522, bethdickson@adamsmith.ac.uk
Adam Smith College works locally, nationally and internationally, delivering real benefit to students, the economy and to communities. The College has a strong presence in Fife with local learning centres throughout the region and campuses in Kirkcaldy, Glenrothes and Levenmouth. With 27,000 students, more than 800 staff and a turnover of £33 million, we are a College that can make a real difference - and we do.

ASSOCIATION OF SCOTLAND'S COLLEGES
Argyll Court, The Castle Business Park, Stirling FK9 4TY
Tel: 01786 892100 Fax: 01786 892109
e-mail: enquiries@ascol.org.uk
Contact: Howard McKenzie, Acting Chief Executive; Neil Cuthbert, Public Affairs Adviser.
The Association of Scotland's Colleges (ASC) represents colleges of further and higher education throughout Scotland. It advises Government, politicians and the media on the work and needs of colleges and on a wide range of policy on lifelong learning, training and student finance.

CARNEGIE COLLEGE
Halbeath, Dunfermline, Fife KY11 8DY
Tel: 0844 248 0115 Fax: 0844 248 0116
e-mail: info@carnegiecollege.ac.uk
web: carnegiecollege.ac.uk
Contact: Professor Bill McIntosh, Principal; Janet McCauslin MBE, Assistant Principal; Linda Greig, Commercialisation and Business Development Director.
Carnegie College is a dynamic organisation offering vocational and academic courses from introductory through to degree level, delivered through a collegiate model of 6 schools supporting education and skills for employability, wealth creation, and economic development. We offer Executive Training and Development courses in partnership with our commercial company Carnegie Enterprise Ltd. Many of these are delivered on site at our modern training and conference venue, Carnegie Conference Centre.

CENTRE FOR EDUCATION FOR RACIAL EQUALITY IN SCOTLAND
Room 2.4, Charteris Building , Faculty of Education, University of Edinburgh, Holyrood Road, Edinburgh EH8 8AQ
Tel: 0131 651 6371 Fax: 0131 651 6511
e-mail: ceres@ed.ac.uk
web: www.education.ed.ac.uk/ceres
Contact: Rowena Arshad, OBE, Director, 0131 651 6371, rowena.arshad@ed.ac.uk; Edna Sommerville, Senior Administrator, 0131 651 6371, edna.sommerville@ed.ac.uk
CERES is a Scottish Government funded initiative. Its main aim is the promotion of equity in education. Its focus is on race equity but it has also produced material on anti-sectarianism and mainstreaming equality into school education. It provides consultancy, research and public policy development on matters related to equity, anti-discrimination and mainstreaming particularly in the area of education. Visit the website for details of current work.

GIRLGUIDING SCOTLAND
16 Coates Crescent, Edinburgh
Tel: 0131 221 4511 Fax: 0131 220 4820
e-mail: administrator@girlguiding-scot.org.uk

PERTH COLLEGE
Crieff Road, Perth PH1 2NX
Tel: 01738 877000 Fax: 01738 877001
e-mail: pc.enquiries@perth.uhi.ac.uk
web: www.perth.ac.uk
Contact: Mandy Exley, Principal.
As one of Scotland's leading colleges of further and higher education, Perth College provides a wide range of education and training opportunities through its Perth campus and network of rural learning centres. It is also able to offer an increasing number of degree courses through its membership of the UHI Millennium Institute.

QUEEN MARGARET UNIVERSITY
EH21 6UU
Tel: 0131 474 0000 Fax: 0131 474 0001
e-mail: admissions@qmu.ac.uk
web: www.qmu@ac.uk
Contact: Jane Scott, Director of Marketing and Communications, e-mail: jscott@qmu.ac.uk
Queen Margaret University is an institution with approximately 5,000 students. Its courses fall into the categories of Business and Enterprise; Drama and Creative Industries; Media, Culture and Communication; Health and Social Sciences. QMU also offers a range of research and consultancy in specialist areas. QMU opened its new purpose built campus development in Autumn 2007 to the east of Edinburgh, by Musselburgh.

THE ROBERT GORDON UNIVERSITY
Schoolhill, Aberdeen AB10 1FR
Tel: 01224 262000 Fax: 01224 263000
e-mail: g.douglas-c@rgu.ac.uk
web: www.rgu.ac.uk
Contact: Professor Michael Pittilo, Principal; Ms Shona Cormack, Vice-Principal (Student Experience and External Relations); Mr Gavin Douglas, Director of Student Recruitment, 01224 262220.
The Robert Gordon University has an excellent reputation for learning and research for the real world and is highly valued in its local community. The Times Good University Guide 2008 rated it both the second best modern University in the UK and the leading Scottish University for graduate employment. The Sunday Times University Guide also acknowledged that for the second successive year, RGU has fewer than 2% of its graduates still seeking work six months after leaving, and, of these, more than four in five land graduate-level employment. Over the past decade it has invested over £100 million in existing and new buildings while the next decade promises to be just as exciting with a £140 million estates masterplan that, once completed, will give RGU the best riverside campus in Europe.

THE ROYAL SCOTTISH ACADEMY OF
MUSIC AND DRAMA
100 Renfrew Street, Glasgow G2 3DB
Tel: 0141 332 4101 Fax: 0141 332 8901
e-mail: development@rsamd.ac.uk
web: www.rsamd.ac.uk

RSAMD
The ROYAL SCOTTISH ACADEMY of MUSIC & DRAMA

Contact: John Wallace, Principal, 0141 332 4101, principal@rsamd.ac.uk; Professor Maggie Kinloch, Director of the School of Drama, 0141 332 4101, m.kinloch@rsamd.ac.uk;

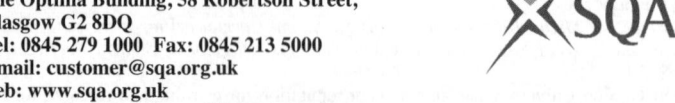

nationally through bodies such as the SNCT and GTCS. This representation is carried out for individuals as well as the whole membership, and involves shaping the future of education in Scotland as well as offering a comprehensive range of services to members.

UNIVERSITIES SCOTLAND
53 Hanover Street, Edinburgh EH2 2PJ
Tel: 0131 226 1111 Fax: 0131 226 1100
e-mail: info@universities-scotland.ac.uk
web: www.universities-scotland.ac.uk
Contact: David Caldwell, Director; Robin McAlpine, Public Affairs Manager.
"The most effective regional organisation of its kind in the UK" (Commission on Scottish Education). Universities Scotland is the official voice of the Scottish universities and higher education institutions. The Convener (2008-2010) is Professor Anton Muscatelli, Principal and Vice-Chancellor, Heriot-Watt University.

UNIVERSITY OF DUNDEE
Nethergate, Dundee DD1 4HN
Tel: 01382 383000 Fax: 01382 201604
e-mail: university@dundee.ac.uk
web: www.dundee.ac.uk
Contact: Sir Alan Langlands, FRSE, Principal and Vice Chancellor, tel: 01382 385556; Ms Joan Concannon, Director of External Relations, tel: 01382 385565; Mr James Houston, Director of Research and Innovation Services, tel: 01382 384664.
The University of Dundee has 17,900 students and 3,000 staff. It completes a £200m campus re-development programme in 2008. As a leading UK University, internationally recognised for its expertise across many disciplines, Dundee graduates more than 70% of its students into the professions while generating the 3rd highest level of research income per capita in the UK. It's ranked in the world's top five places to work by Scientist Magazine and top University in the UK for research impact by The Guardian.
University of Dundee - Aspirational, Inspirational, Exceptional.

THE UNIVERSITY OF EDINBURGH
Old College, South Bridge, Edinburgh EH8 9YL
Tel: 0131 650 1000 Fax: 0131 650 2147
web: www.ed.ac.uk
Contact: Professor Timothy O'Shea, Principal, 0131 650 2150; Melvyn Cornish, Secretary, 0131 650 2143, University.Secretary@ed.ac.uk; Ian Brian Conn, Director of Communications and External Affairs, 0131 650 2248, ian.conn@ed.ac.uk
The University of Edinburgh, with some 25,143 students and over 3,200 academic and research staff, is one of Europe's leading centres of higher education, devoted to excellence in teaching and research across a broad range of disciplines and professions. It especially values its intellectual and economic relationship with the Scottish community that forms its base and provides a wide range of research, educational, commercial and cultural services for its client groups.

UNIVERSITY
of
GLASGOW

UNIVERSITY OF GLASGOW
University Avenue, Glasgow G12 8QQ
Tel: 0141 330 2000
web: www.gla.ac.uk
Contact: Sir Muir Russell, KCB, FRSE, Principal and Vice Chancellor; Mr. David Newall, Secretary of Court.

The University of Glasgow, a top research-led university, founded 1451, had a turnover of **£312M** in **2005-06**: research income totalled **£75M**. With over **19,500** students in **nine** faculties, it employs more than **5,800** staff, including one of Europe's largest grouping of life scientists. It has one of the largest medical faculties in Europe, and is one of only four Veterinary Schools in Europe to have gained the prized **American Veterinary Medicine Association** accreditation.

UNIVERSITY OF ST. ANDREWS
College Gate, North Street, St. Andrews, Fife KY16 9AJ
Tel: 01334 462544 Fax: 01334 462543
web: www.st-andrews.ac.uk
Contact: Dr Brian Lang, Principal and Vice-Chancellor, 01334 462545, principal@st-andrews.ac.uk; Professor Keith Brown, Deputy Principal and Master, 01334 462552, deputyprincipal@st-andrews.ac.uk
Scotland's first university - world class higher education and research.

ENERGY

ENERGY ACTION SCOTLAND (EAS)
Ingram House, 227 Ingram Street, Glasgow G1 1DA
Tel: 0141 226 3064 Fax: 0141 221 2788
e-mail: eas@eas.org.uk   web: www.eas.org.uk
Contact: Norman Kerr, Director; Elizabeth Gore, PR/Information Manager and Deputy Director.
Energy Action Scotland is the national charity which aims to eliminate fuel poverty by: raising awareness of fuel poverty, particularly as it affects low income households; maintaining fuel poverty as a national issue of high priority; and working towards affordable warmth for all; identifying effective solutions which can transform cold, damp houses into warm, dry homes; researching fuel poverty and related issues in order to provide in-depth understanding of the causes and effects and to promote best practice; securing public and private investment for domestic energy efficiency initiatives. Services include publications, seminars, annual conference, consultancy and training on energy-related topics.

FINANCIAL

ADAM & COMPANY GROUP plc
22 Charlotte Square, Edinburgh EH2 4DF
Tel: 0131 225 8484 Fax: 0131 225 5136
web: www.adambank.com
Contact: David Cathie, Group Chief Executive; Harry Morgan, Managing Director, Adam & Company Investment Management Limited; John O'Donnell, Director (Glasgow).

Adam & Company is a private bank that effectively combines banking with investment management – providing a full asset and liability management service. As well as all the normal facilities expected from a bank, Adam holds in great store the old-fashioned courtesies that were a hallmark of banking in bygone days and endeavours to provide guidance in most aspects of the financial life of their clients.

AEGON
Edinburgh Park, Edinburgh EH12 9SE
Tel: 0870 600 0337 Fax: 0870 600 0338
web: www.aegon.co.uk

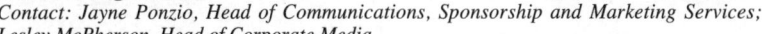

Contact: Jayne Ponzio, Head of Communications, Sponsorship and Marketing Services; Lesley McPherson, Head of Corporate Media.
AEGON is one of the world's largest pension and life insurance companies. In the UK, we own life and pensions, asset management and adviser businesses. We have £53.2 billion of assets and employ 4,900 people, including 3,000 in Edinburgh. We take a fresh approach to finance by putting our customers at the heart of what we do. Our brands include AEGON Scottish Equitable and AEGON Asset Management.

AUDITOR GENERAL FOR SCOTLAND
Audit Scotland, 110 George Street, Edinburgh EH2 4LH
Tel: 0845 146 1010 Fax: 0845 146 1009
web: www.audit-scotland.gov.uk
The Auditor General holds to account the Scottish Government and other public spending bodies (except local authorities) for the proper, efficient and effective use of public funds. The Auditor General is Robert W. Black.

AUDIT SCOTLAND
110 George Street, Edinburgh EH2 4LH
Tel: 0845 146 1010 Fax: 0845 146 1009
e-mail: info@audit-scotland.gov.uk
web: www.audit-scotland.gov.uk
Audit Scotland provides services to The Auditor General and The Accounts Commission. We support effective democratic scrutiny by providing independent, objective assurance on governance, financial stewardship and performance. We also promote continuing improvement in public services to help in securing value for money and to meet the needs of citizens.

BANK OF ENGLAND
Agency for Scotland, 177 West George Street, Glasgow G2 2LB
Tel: 0141 221 7972
e-mail: scotland@bankofengland.co.uk
web: www.bankofengland.co.uk
Contact: Tony Strachan, Agent for Scotland.
Represents the Central Bank of the United Kingdom in Scotland, reporting directly to the Bank's Monetary Policy Committee on business conditions and the Scottish economy.

THE CHARTERED INSTITUTE OF BANKERS IN SCOTLAND
Drumsheugh House, 38b Drumsheugh Gardens, Edinburgh EH3 7SW
Tel: 0131 473 7777 Fax: 0131 473 7788

e-mail: info@ciobs.org.uk
web: www.ciobs.org.uk
Contact: Mr Simon Thompson, 0131 473 7777; Colin A. Morrison, 0131 473 7791; Derek J Langley, 0131 473 7792.
The Chartered Institute of Bankers in Scotland is the professional and educational body for the Financial Services Industry. The main aims of the Institute are to: encourage the highest standards of professionalism and conduct amongst its members; improve and extend the knowledge and expertise of those engaged in the financial services industry; conduct examinations and promote the continued study of financial services; establish links, co-operate with other professional or educational bodies and represent the financial services industry both nationally and internationally. It also has a role in teaching school children about finances through the Financial Education Partnership. web: http://www.ciobs.org.uk

THE COMMITTEE OF SCOTTISH CLEARING BANKERS
Drumsheugh House, 38b Drumsheugh Gardens, Edinburgh EH3 7SW
Tel: 0131 473 7770 Fax: 0131 473 7799
e-mail: info@scotbanks.org.uk
web: www.scotbanks.org.uk
Contact: Mr J. McGuigan, Executive.
The Committee is the trade association of the four Scottish clearing banks (Bank of Scotland, The Royal Bank of Scotland plc, Clydesdale Bank PLC and Lloyds TSB Scotland plc) and represents the industry in the financial structure of Scotland. Contact is maintained with the Scottish Executive, Bank of England, Financial Services Authority and other appropriate professional and economic development organisations. The Committee addresses issues which are of specific relevance to Scotland and which are non-competitive, providing a forum in which such matters can be debated.

GEOLOGY

BRITISH GEOLOGICAL SURVEY, SCOTLAND
Murchison House, West Mains Road,
Edinburgh EH9 3LA
Tel: 0131 667 1000 Fax: 0131 668 2683
e-mail: msmi@bgs.ac.uk
web: www.bgs.ac.uk

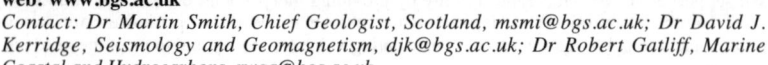

British
Geological Survey
NATURAL ENVIRONMENT RESEARCH COUNCIL

Contact: Dr Martin Smith, Chief Geologist, Scotland, msmi@bgs.ac.uk; Dr David J. Kerridge, Seismology and Geomagnetism, djk@bgs.ac.uk; Dr Robert Gatliff, Marine Coastal and Hydrocarbons, rwga@bgs.ac.uk
BGS in Scotland conducts the national geological survey for Northern Britain on land, and for the whole of the UK Continental Shelf. It builds databases for environmental surveys and research through its geochemical and groundwater divisions and is the authority for the national earthquake and geomagnetic monitoring programmes. Leading-edge research in petroleum geology and reservoir engineering supports the Scottish oil industry.

HEALTH

ARTHRITIS CARE IN SCOTLAND
Unit 25A Anniesland Business Park,
242 Netherton Road, Glasgow G13 1EU
Tel: 0141 954 7776 Fax: 0141 954 6171
e-mail: scotlandoffice@arthritiscare.org.uk
web: www.arthritiscare.org.uk/scotland

ARTHRITIS CARE
Empowering
people with arthritis.

Contact: Scotland Administrator.
Arthritis affects over 700,000 people in Scotland, and Arthritis Care is actively opening the doors to services to everyone with arthritis. It provides information and support through publications, an information helpline, a website and local information points. It delivers self-management training to enable people with arthritis to live a better quality of life, and it campaigns to ensure that arthritis becomes a priority for decision makers in Scotland.

BRITISH MEDICAL ASSOCIATION (SCOTLAND)
14 Queen Street, Edinburgh EH2 1LL
Tel: 0131 247 3000 Fax: 0131 247 3001
e-mail: bmascotland@bma.org.uk
Contact: Martin Woodrow, Scottish Secretary;
Membership Services: 0870 60 60 828;

General Enquiries: 0131 247 3000; Press Enquiries: 0131 247 3050/3052.
The British Medical Association in Scotland represents doctors from all branches of medicine. It is a voluntary professional association, independent trade union, scientific and educational body and a publishing house. The BMA and the BMJ Publishing Group, which is one of the most influential medical publishers in the world, produce a wide range of journals, reports and medical books. With a UK membership of 138,973 and 15,207 in Scotland, the BMA is regarded as the voice of the medical profession.

CHEST, HEART AND STROKE SCOTLAND
65 North Castle Street, Edinburgh EH2 3LT
Tel: 0131 225 6963 Fax: 0131 220 6313
e-mail: admin@chss.org.uk
web: www.chss.org.uk
Contact: Mr David H. Clark, Chief Executive; Dr Gavin Boyd, FRCPE, FRCPG, Chairman; Mrs Janet Buncle, Director of Public Relations.
Chest, Heart and Stroke Scotland aims to improve the quality of life for people in Scotland affected by chest, heart and stroke illness, through medical research, advice and information, and support in the community. CHSS funds research into all aspects of the prevention, treatment and social impact of chest, heart and stroke disease, and provides a network of support services for patients and carers throughout Scotland.

CLIC SARGENT
4th Floor, Mercantile Chambers, 53 Bothwell Street,
Glasgow G2 6TS
Tel: 0141 572 5700 Fax: 0141 572 5701
e-mail: glasgow@clicsargent.org.uk
web: www.clicsargent.org.uk

Caring for Children with Cancer

Every day, 10 children and young people are diagnosed with cancer or leukaemia. CLIC Sargent is the UK's largest children's charity, supporting children, young people and their families through cancer every step of the way.

During treatment - specialist nurses, doctors, play specialists, Homes from Home

In the community - specialist youth services, holidays, grants, helpline

In hospital & at home - specialist social care and family support

After treatment - helping survivors, supporting those bereaved, research

Registered Charity No.: 1107328

Private Finance Initiatives valued at approximately £220m. are currently underway, including the new Royal Infirmary of Edinburgh which opened in 2002. Lothian is one of the major clinical teaching centres in the UK, with links to three universities providing teaching and research facilities for medical and nursing staff and the allied health professions.

PAIN ASSOCIATION SCOTLAND
Cramond House, Kirk Cramond, Cramond Glebe Road, Edinburgh EH4 6NS
Tel: 0131 312 7955 Fax: 0131 312 6007
e-mail: info@painassociation.com
web: www.chronicpaininfo.org
Contact: Mr David Falconer, Director; Dr Denis Martin, Chairman.
Through a network of local peer support groups the Association offers training, education, information and a community-based pain management programme. The organisation provides support and understanding for people with chronic pain and their carers. Information, training and advice is available for health and social welfare professionals who are interested and working with people in chronic pain.

ROYAL COLLEGE OF GENERAL PRACTITIONERS (RGCP SCOTLAND)
25 Queen Street, Edinburgh EH2 1JX
Tel: 0131 260 6800 Fax: 0207 589 3145
e-mail: scottishc@rcpg.org.uk
web: www.rcgp.org.uk

RC GP — Royal College of General Practitioners

Contact: Ruth Wallace, Head of RCGP Scotland - scottishc@rcpg.org.uk; Josie Westley, Executive Affairs Coordinator - scottishc@rcgr.org.uk
The academic organisation in Scotland for General Practitioners. Encouraging and maintaining the highest standards of general medical practice.

ROYAL COLLEGE OF PHYSICIANS AND SURGEONS
232-242 St. Vincent Street, Glasgow G2 5RJ
Tel: 0141 221 6072 Fax: 0141 221 1804
web: www.rcpsg.ac.uk

Contact: Professor Brian Williams, President; Professor Paul V Knight, Honorary Secretary; Dr James A Miller, CEO, e-mail: james.miller@rcpsg.ac.uk
The College is responsible, with other Royal Colleges, for postgraduate medical, surgical and dental training in the United Kingdom. Through its examinations in medicine, surgery and dentistry, and contribution with other bodies to quality assurance processes, the College ensures that the highest standards are maintained. The College has a full programme of training courses, symposia and guest lectures on both general and specialist topics, which are attended by medical students, junior doctors, consultants, dentists and general practitioners. In addition the College offers lectures of wider interest (eg to schools) and there is an annual open day.

SCOTTISH ASSOCIATION FOR SLEEP APNOEA
26 Sinclair Way, Knightsbridge, Livingston, West Lothian EH54 8HW
Tel: 01506 433520
Contact: Mr Colin Tyler.

The Association has three main aims and objectives. These are: to raise awareness both in the general public and in the medical profession regarding the medical condition of sleep apnoea and its symptoms; to raise funds for research into sleep apnoea and the publication of such research; and to provide support to the sufferers of sleep apnoea and their families through volunteers; and where available, by local groups.

THE SCOTTISH HEALTH COUNCIL
National Office, Delta House, 50 West Nile Street,
Glasgow G1 2NP
Tel: 0141 241 6308 Fax: 0141 221 2529
e-mail: shc@scottishhealthcouncil.org
web: www.scottishhealthcouncil.org

Contact: Brian Beacom, Chairman; Richard Norris, Director; Catherine Tait, PA to Director and Chairman.
The Scottish Health Council's role is to help improve the way that people are involved in decisions about health services. As well as being a champion for patient and public involvement in the NHS in Scotland, the Scottish Health Council assesses NHS Boards to ensure they are working with, and listening to, people in their community.

HOUSING

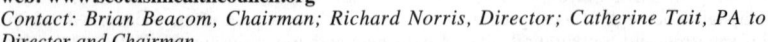

BIELD HOUSING ASSOCIATION LIMITED
79 Hopetoun Street, Edinburgh EH7 4QF
Tel: 0131 273 4000 Fax: 0131 557 6327
e-mail: info@bield.co.uk
web: www.bield.co.uk
Contact: James H Thomson, Chief Executive; Alister McDonald, Depute Chief Executive; Philip Cassidy, Director of Housing Services; Brian Logan, Director of Financial Services; Sheila McKenzie, Director of Human Resources; Stewart Clark, Director of Property Services; Charlie Dickson, Director of Care Services.
Bield's primary objective is to enable older people to live independent and fulfilling lives by being a leading and innovative provider of high quality appropriate housing care and support services. We are a non profit organisation with charitable status, governed by legislation promoting and regulating registered housing associations. We provide supported housing, community alarm services and home and day care services to approximately 15,000 older people in the Borders, Lothian, Fife, Tayside, Forth Valley and Strathclyde.

SCOTTISH FEDERATION OF HOUSING ASSOCIATIONS
4th Floor, Pegasus House, 375 West George Street, Glasgow G2 4LW
Tel: 0141 332 8113 Fax: 0141 332 9684
e-mail: sfha@sfha.co.uk
web: www.sfha.co.uk
Contact: Jacqui Watt, Chief Executive, jwatt@sfha.co.uk
The SFHA aims to contribute to the provision of high quality, affordable housing and housing related services, and to the creation of sustainable communities, by promoting, representing and providing services to housing associations in Scotland, and by campaigning on their behalf.

LAND

THE CROWN ESTATE
6 Bell's Brae, Edinburgh EH4 3BJ
Tel: 0131 260 6070 Fax: 0131 260 6090
e-mail: scotland@thecrownestate.co.uk
web: www.thecrownestate.co.uk/scotland

Contact: Alan Laidlaw; Ian Grant, Chairman.
The Crown Estate in Scotland comprises an Urban Estate in Edinburgh, five large Rural Estates, including the award-winning Glenlivet Estate in Morayshire, as well as a Marine Estate of foreshore and seabed.

Paying all of its revenue surpluses to the Treasury, for the benefit of all taxpayers, The Crown Estate uses its commercial expertise to work in partnership with many local communities in investment projects around Scotland.

The Crown Estate also leads research into the offshore renewable industry and invests in aquaculture research to ensure the long-term future of this vital Scottish industry.

JOHN MUIR TRUST
Tower House, Station Road, Pitlochry, Perthshire PH16 5AN
Tel: 01796 470080 Fax: 01796 473514
web: www.jmt.org

Contact: Nigel Hawkins, Chief Executive, 01796 470080, chiefexec@jmt.org; David Picken, Development Manager, 0131 554 0114, development@jmt.org; Helen McDade, Policy Officer, 01796 470080, policy@jmt.org
John Muir Trust is the country's leading wild land organisation and its principle aim is for wild places to be valued by all members of society. To achieve this it owns and manages some key areas of wild land and works in partnership with communities. It also seeks to influence the public about the importance of wild land and win hearts and minds through the John Muir Award.

LAW
(see also LAW FIRMS under "PROFESSIONAL SERVICES")

ADMINISTRATIVE JUSTICE AND TRIBUNALS COUNCIL, SCOTTISH COMMITTEE
George House, 126 George Street, Edinburgh EH2 4HH
Tel: 0131 271 4300 Fax: 0131 271 4309
e-mail: scajtc@gtnet.gov.uk
web: www.council-on-tribunals.gov.uk
Contact: Mrs Marjorie Macrae, Secretary.
Independent body first established in 1958 now operating under the Tribunals, Courts and Enforcement Act 2007. Statutory function to keep under review, and advise Ministers on, the administrative justice as a whole, considering how it might be made more accessible, fair

and efficient. The Council may scrutinise and comment on any legislation relating to tribunals and it must be consulted on procedural rules relating to certain listed tribunals.

THE FACULTY OF ADVOCATES
Parliament House, Edinburgh EH1 1RQ
Tel: 0131 226 5071
web: www.advocates.org.uk

The Faculty of Advocates, which has been in existence since at least 1532, is a body of independent lawyers who specialise in the preparation and presentation of cases before the courts and tribunals of Scotland. There are currently more than 460 practising advocates available to take instructions from solicitors throughout Scotland and from a number of professional bodies and individuals by means of a direct access scheme. The Faculty is a democratic body led by its Dean who is elected by a vote of the whole membership. The faculty operates a rigorous training and education programme and is also responsible for maintaining discipline and standards at the Bar.

LAW SOCIETY OF SCOTLAND
26 Drumsheugh Gardens, Edinburgh
EH3 7YR
Tel: 0131 226 7411 Fax: 0131 225 2934
e-mail: lawscot@lawscot.org.uk
web: www.lawscot.org.uk

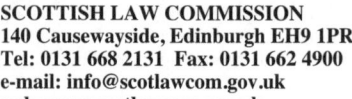

Contact: Richard Henderson, President; Douglas R. Mill, Chief Executive.
The Law Society of Scotland is the membership body of the Scottish solicitors' profession. The Society promotes the interests of solicitors and the public in relation to the Scottish solicitors profession. It regulates its members, arranges the master insurance policy for all practicing solicitors and administers the Scottish Solicitors Guarantee Fund. It provides services including: continuing legal education; advice on professional practice, European law, and a solicitor referral service. The Society promotes reform of the law in Scottish, UK and European Parliaments.

SCOTTISH LAW COMMISSION
140 Causewayside, Edinburgh EH9 1PR
Tel: 0131 668 2131 Fax: 0131 662 4900
e-mail: info@scotlawcom.gov.uk
web: www.scotlawcom.gov.uk

Contact: The Hon Lord Drummond Young, Chairman; Malcolm McMillan, Chief Executive; Lesley Young, Office Manager.
The Commission is an independent statutory body established in 1965 which is responsible to Scottish Ministers. Further information about our work can be found at www.scotlawcom.gov.uk.

LOCAL GOVERNMENT

ABERDEENSHIRE COUNCIL
Woodhill House, Westburn Road,
Aberdeen AB16 5GB
Tel: 01467 620981
e-mail: enquiries@aberdeenshire.gov.uk
web: www.aberdeenshire.gov.uk

Contact: Alan G. Campbell, CBE, Chief Executive, 01224 665400.
Aberdeenshire Council is the sixth largest of Scotland's 32 unitary authorities in population (236,260) and the fourth largest in area (6,313 sq km). The area was recently ranked as the

best place to live in Scotland, based on a series of factors including employment, the housing market, environment, education and health.

The Council is focussed on delivering an ambitious vision: "From mountain to sea, the very best of Scotland".

ANGUS COUNCIL
Angus House, Orchardbank Business Park, Forfar DD8 1AB
Tel: 08452 777 778 Fax: 01307 476140
e-mail: chiefexec@angus.gov.uk
web: www.angus.gov.uk
Angus Council is a customer and citizen focused organisation providing community leadership. We value our staff and work to deliver accessible, effective and efficient services. In a wider context we promote: active citizenship; opportunities for all; developments that last; a dynamic economy; learning throughout life; healthy, safe and caring communities; quality in our environment.

MIDLOTHIAN COUNCIL
Midlothian House, Buccleuch Street, Dalkeith EH22 1DJ
Tel: 0131 270 7500 Fax: 0131 271 3050
web: www.midlothian.gov.uk
Contact: Trevor Muir, Chief Executive.
Midlothian is situated to the south of Scotland's capital city of Edinburgh. Midlothian Council serves a population of 79,710, covering a geographical area of 35,527 hectares, incorporating the main towns of Penicuik, Bonnyrigg, Dalkeith, Mayfield and Easthouses, Loanhead and Gorebridge. The Council employs over 4,000 people.

MAPS

ORDNANCE SURVEY
Grayfield House, 5 Bankhead Avenue, Edinburgh EH11 4AA
Tel: 0131 458 8300 Fax: 0131 458 8337
e-mail: customerservices@ordnancesurvey.co.uk
web: www.ordnancesurvey.co.uk
Contact: customer helpline 08456 050505.
Ordnance Survey is Britain's national mapping agency. It is responsible for creating and updating the master map of the entire country, from which it produces and markets a range of digital data and paper maps for business, leisure and educational uses. It is a Trading Fund – a part of the Government which covers its operating costs by licensing information and selling products. Its data underpins £100bn. of economic activity across Britain.

MARINE AND COASTAL

NORTHERN LIGHTHOUSE BOARD
84 GEORGE STREET, EDINBURGH EH2 3DA
Tel: 0131 473 3100 Fax: 0131 220 2093
e-mail: enquiries@nlb.org.uk
web: www.nlb.org.uk
Contact: Roger Lockwood, Chief Executive; Lorna Hunter, Public Relations and Information Officer; Chairman: Captain George Sutherland.
The Board provides marine aids to navigation - lighthouses, buoys, beacons and a precision

satellite navigation system in Scotland and the Isle of Man. It receives no public monies and is funded entirely by light dues paid by merchant shipping and fishing vessels.

OMBUDSMAN

SPSO Scottish Public Services Ombudsman

SCOTTISH PUBLIC SERVICES OMBUDSMAN
4 Melville Street, Edinburgh EH3 7NS
Tel: 0800 377 7330 Fax: 0800 377 7331
web: www.spso.org.uk
Contact: Professor Alice Brown, Ombudsman; Eric Drake, Director of Investigations; David Robb, Director of Policy and Development.
Considers complaints which have not been resolved with the body concerned about devolved public services in Scotland, including the Scottish Government and its agencies, councils, the National Health Service, enterprise bodies, housing associations, further education and higher education.

PROFESSIONAL SERVICES

1. ACCOUNTANTS

GERBER LANDA & GEE, CHARTERED ACCOUNTANTS
11/12 Newton Terrace, Glasgow G3 7PJ
Tel: 0141 221 7446 Fax: 0141 248 2469
e-mail: mail@gerberlandagee.co.uk
web: www.gerberlandagee.co.uk
Contact: Thomas Hughes, LLB, CA, CTA; Charles Martin, CA, CTA; James Murphy, CA; Harry Seddon, FCCA; Ann McLaren, BA, CA.
Gerber Landa & Gee was formed in 1968 by an amalgamation of three practices. Since then the firm has developed a leading reputation as advisors to family business. We have assisted many businesses through their formative years and are experienced in advising the more established business to assist growth and meet the changing economic environment. Our aim is to provide a quality service to clients supported by confidentiality and integrity.

2. ARCHITECTS

SIMPSON & BROWN ARCHITECTS WITH ADDYMAN ARCHAEOLOGY
St. Ninian's Manse, Quayside Street, Edinburgh EH6 6EJ
Tel: 0131 555 4678 Fax: 0131 553 4576
e-mail: admin@simpsonandbrown.co.uk

web: www.simpsonandbrown.co.uk
Contact: James Simpson, OBE, BArch, FRIAS, RIBA, FSA Scot; A Stewart Brown, BArch (Hons), ARIAS, RIBA.
The practice is proud of its reputation for scholarly and conscientious conservation, historical and archaeological research, for green and beautiful buildings, and for caring for the needs and interests of its clients.

3. LAW FIRMS

BIGGART BAILLIE
Dalmore House, 310 St. Vincent Street,
Glasgow G2 5QR
Tel: 0141 228 8000 Fax: 0141 228 8310
7 Castle Street, Edinburgh EH2 3AP
Tel: 0131 226 5541 Fax: 0131 226 2278
e-mail: info@biggartbaillie.co.uk
web: www.biggartbaillie.co.uk

BIGGART BAILLIE
LLP

Contact: Derek Ellery, Managing Partner; Rob McInally, Director of Business Development.
Biggart Baillie provides practical commercial and corporate legal advice that counts. Areas of law that we have recognised in-depth expertise in include corporate finance, banking, pensions, energy and utilities, IT and intellectual property, construction, commercial litigation, employment and commercial property.

HARPER MACLEOD LLP
The Ca'd'oro, 45 Gordon Street, Glasgow G1 3PE
Tel: 0141 221 8888 Fax: 0141 226 4198
8 Melville Street, Edinburgh EH3 7NS
Tel: 0131 247 2500 Fax: 0131 247 2501
Alder House, Cradlehall Business Park,
Inverness IV2 5GH
Tel: 01463 798777 Fax: 01463 798787
e-mail: info@harpermacleod.co.uk
web: www.harpermacleod.co.uk

Contact: Professor Lorne D. Crerar, Chairman, 0141 227 9377, lorne.crerar@harpermacleod.co.uk; Martin Darroch, Chief Executive, 0141 227 9434, martin.darroch@harpermacleod.co.uk
Harper Macleod is one of Scotland's leading full service commercial law firms and was voted Firm of the Year 2006 at both the Scottish Legal Awards and Law Awards of Scotland. With offices in Glasgow, Edinburgh and Inverness, we have a reputation for innovation and a progressive approach to the law. The firm provides tailored legal services to clients ranging from UK and multinational companies and financial institutions to local and public authorities.

THE KELLAS PARTNERSHIP
2-6 High Street, Inverurie, Aberdeenshire AB51 3XQ
Tel: 01467 627300 Fax: 01467 622030
e-mail: info@kellas.biz
web: www.kellas.biz

The
► **KELLAS** ◄
Partnership
SOLICITORS & ESTATE AGENTS

Contact: Hamish M. Duthie, LLB, NP, hmd@kellas.biz; Louise E. Robertson, LLB, NP, ler@kellas.biz; Elizabeth A. Cobban, LLB, NP, eac@kellas.biz

Murray Beith Murray is a leading firm of solicitors based in Edinburgh, specialising in private client work.

TODS MURRAY LLP
Edinburgh Quay, 133 Fountainbridge, Edinburgh EH3 9AG
Tel: 0131 656 2000 Fax: 0131 656 2020
e-mail: maildesk@todsmurray.com
web: www.todsmurray.com

TODS MURRAY LLP
SOLICITORS

Contact: David Dunsire, Executive Partner; Ian McPake, Chairman.
Tods Murray is a leading independent Scottish law firm, providing innovative and specialist advice to businesses in both the private and public sectors and to families, individuals and charities.

We aim to be the best all service law firm in Scotland and are rated as a UK Top 100 law firm. Our services include Banking, PPP, Commercial Property, Corporate, Litigation, Recovery, Rural Property and Business and Private Client.

TURCAN CONNELL
Princes Exchange, 1 Earl Grey Street,
Edinburgh EH3 9EE
Tel: 0131 228 8111 Fax: 0131 228 8118
e-mail: enquiries@turcanconnell.com
web: www.turcanconnell.com

TURCAN CONNELL
SOLICITORS AND ASSET MANAGERS

Contact: Douglas A. Connell, dac@turcanconnell.com; Simon A Mackintosh, sam@turcanconnell.com; Ian R. Clark, irc@turcanconnell.com
Turcan Connell focuses exclusively on private clients, trusts and charities. Eighteen Partners and a staff of over 250 bring together a combination of skills and expertise unique in Scotland. These cover asset protection, land and property, succession, taxation, family law, trusts and charities, investment management, personal financial planning and employment law. The firm offers full discretionary investment management services to private individuals, trusts, charities and pension funds.

4. REPUTATION MANAGEMENT AND PUBLIC RELATIONS

INDIGO
27 Maritime Street, Leith, Edinburgh EH6 6SE
Tel: 0131 554 1230 Fax: 0131 554 1549
e-mail: enquiries@indigopr.com
web: www.indigopr.com
Indigo offers reputation management for companies and individuals. We combine media relations, public affairs and strategic marketing to create and implement intelligent communications strategies that work. Our aim is to add value as trusted advisers, working in partnership to ensure that the right messages get across to the right people at exactly the right time. Ethical, practical and always professional.

RELIGIOUS

ACTION OF CHURCHES TOGETHER IN SCOTLAND
Forrester Lodge, Inglewood, Alloa FK10 2HU
Tel: 01259 216980 Fax: 01259 215964
e-mail: ecumenical@acts-scotland.org
web: www.acts-scotland.org
ACTS is Scotland's national ecumenical body. The successor body to the Scottish Churches Council, its function is to express and to resource the ecumenical commitment of its member churches. It works in close partnership with companion bodies in Britain and Ireland and throughout Europe. ACTS' four core staff work closely with ecumenical officers at national and local level, and with colleagues recently appointed in racial justice and in interfaith work.

CHRISTIAN AID SCOTLAND
The Pentagon Centre, 36 Washington Street, Glasgow G3 8AZ
Tel: 0141 221 7475 Fax: 0141 241 6145
web: www.christianaidscotland.org.uk

 We believe in life before death

Contact: Gavin McLellan, Head of Christian Aid Scotland; Claire Shelley, Media and Communications Manager.
Christian Aid Scotland is the official agency of the Scottish churches for emergency aid and tackling of global poverty. We support partner organisations who are working to end the injustice of poverty in 50 countries, through both long-term projects and emergency response.

THE CHURCH OF SCOTLAND
121 George Street, Edinburgh EH2 4YN
Tel: 0131 225 5722 Fax: 0131 220 3113
web: www.churchofscotland.org.uk
Contact: Very Rev. Dr. Finlay A.J. Macdonald, Principal Clerk of the General Assembly.
The Church of Scotland, part of the one Holy, Catholic and Apostolic Church, is the national church in Scotland, recognised by the State but independent in spiritual matters. Trinitarian in doctrine, Reformed in tradition and Presbyterian in polity, it exists to glorify God, to work for the advancement of Christ's kingdom throughout the world and to provide religious services for the people in Scotland, through parish ministry. It co-operates with other churches in various ecumenical bodies in Scotland and beyond.

CHURCH OF SCOTLAND GUILD
121 George Street, Edinburgh EH2 4YN
Tel: 0131 225 5722 Fax: 0131 220 3113
e-mail: guild@cofscotland.org.uk
web: www.cos-guild.org.uk
The Guild is a component element of the Church of Scotland, Scottish Charity No SC011353.
Contact: Alison Twaddle, General Secretary, Ext. 218, atwaddle@cofscotland.org.uk; Fiona Punton, Information Officer, Ext. 332, fpunton@cofscotland.org.uk
The Guild is a movement within the Church of Scotland whose aim is "to invite and encourage both women and men to commit their lives to Jesus Christ and to enable them to express their faith in worship, prayer, and action". With around 1,200 groups across

Scotland, the Guild has raised over £2 million in the past ten years for projects at home and abroad. The Guild is represented on other church councils as well as other ecumenical, national and international bodies.

FREE PRESBYTERIAN CHURCH OF SCOTLAND
133 Woodlands Road, Glasgow G3 6LE
Tel: 0141 332 9283 Fax: 0141 332 4271
e-mail: fpchurch@btconnect.com
web: www.fpchurch.org.uk
Contact: Rev. J. MacLeod, Clerk of Synod, Free Presbyterian Manse, 6 Church Avenue, Sidcup, Kent DA14 6BU, Tel/Fax: 0208 309 1623, e-mail: synodclerk@fpchurch.org.uk; Mr W Campbell, General Treasurer, as above; Moderator of Synod, 2008-09: Rev. W. A. Weale, Free Presbyterian Manse, Staffa, Isle of Skye IV51 9JX.
The Free Presbyterian Church of Scotland exists to promote the biblical doctrines of the Christian faith in the UK and abroad by preaching the Gospel, administering the Sacraments and exercising ecclesiastical discipline, and by publishing and selling Christian literature and providing educational and medical facilities, along with care for the elderly and for orphans

THE SALVATION ARMY
Scotland Office and East Scotland Division:
12A Dryden Road, Loanhead, Midlothian EH20 9LZ
Tel: 0131 440 9101 Fax: 0131 440 9111
e-mail: robert.mcintyre@salvationarmy.org.uk
Contact: Major Robert McIntyre.
West Scotland Division:
4 Buchanan Court, Cumbernauld Road, Stepps, Glasgow G33 6HZ
Tel: 0141 779 5001 Fax: 0141 779 5011
Contact: Major Victor Kennedy.
North Scotland Division: Deer Road, Woodside, Aberdeen AB24 2BL
Tel: 01224 496001 Fax: 01224 496011
Contact: Major Martin Hill.
The Salvation Army is an integral part of the universal Christian church. Its message is based on the Bible, its motivation is the love of God as revealed in Jesus Christ. Its mission is to proclaim his Gospel, to persuade men and women to become his disciples and to engage in a programme of practical concern for the needs of humanity. Its ministry is offered to all, regardless of race, creed, colour or sex.

SCHOOLS

FETTES COLLEGE
Carrington Road, Edinburgh EH4 1QX
Tel: 0131 311 6701 Fax: 0131 311 6714
e-mail: enquiries@fettes.com
web: www.fettes.com
Contact: Mr Michael Spens, Headmaster.
Fettes College is one of the UK's pre-eminent co-educational boarding schools with 640

653 4570, juniorschool@loretto.com
Loretto provides an all-round education for just over 530 boys and girls - boarders, flexi-boarders and day pupils aged 3-18. Set in 85 acres of leafy campus just 6 miles from central Edinburgh it is a small friendly school well known for its relaxed family atmosphere, traditional values and emphasis on the development of the whole person, mind, body and spirit. The school is particularly renowned for its music, drama and art as well as the golf academy, which can claim to be one of the best golf schools in Britain. Over the past 5 years Loretto has produced excellent academic results.

ST. COLUMBA'S SCHOOL, KILMACOLM
Duchal Road, Kilmacolm, Renfrewshire PA13 4AU
Tel: 01505 872238 Fax: 01505 873995
e-mail: secretary@st-columbas.org
web: www.st-columbas.org
Contact: Mr D. G. Girdwood, Rector; Mrs J. Wallace, Senior Depute Rector; Mrs D. L. Cook, Head of Junior School.
Founded in 1897, St. Columba's is one of Scotland's leading independent schools with a roll of approximately 730 students. The school caters for pupils aged 3-18, is non-denominational and has equal numbers of boys and girls at all stages. It has an excellent academic reputation and, in addition, is strong musically, on the sporting front and in its participation in the Duke of Edinburgh's Award Scheme. The aim of St Columba's is to produce mannerly, mature and successful young people who have, at the same time, a care and concern for others.

ST. MARGARET'S SCHOOL FOR GIRLS
17 Albyn Place, Aberdeen AB10 1RU
Tel: 01224 584466 Fax: 01224 585600
e-mail: info@st-margaret.aberdeen.sch.uk
web: www.st-margaret.aberdeen.sch.uk
Contact: Mrs Anne Everest, Headmistress.
St. Margaret's School for Girls in Aberdeen (age range 3 to 18 years) is one of the leading girls' schools in Scotland. We value each of our pupils and our small classes allow us to treat each girl as an individual. We aim to create a challenging atmosphere in which girls learn to respect others while maturing into leadership roles. Our academic results are excellent. The full range of subjects is offered to all, and there is a wide-ranging extra-curricular programme. Music, art, debating, drama and sport are particular strengths.

TRANSPORT

FIRSTGROUP PLC
395 King Street, Aberdeen AB24 5RP
Tel: 01224 650102 Fax: 01224 650149
e-mail: contactus@firstgroup.com
web: www.firstgroup.com

Contact: Moir Lockhead, OBE, Chief Executive, 01224 650102; Avril Gill, Marketing Manager - Group Brand, 01224 650117; Paul Moore, Group Public Affairs and

Communications Director, 01224 650124; Niall Dowds, Group Public Relations Manager, 01224 650011.
FirstGroup is the world's leading transport company with an annual turnover of over £5 bn and more than 135,000 employees across the UK and North America. Based in Aberdeen, FirstGroup operates bus and passenger rail services in the UK and school buses and transit management services across the USA and Canada. First is the largest operator of school buses in North America. First is the UK's largest bus operator, running more than one in five of all local bus services with a fleet of over 9,000 vehicles. It is also the UK's largest train operator, running a balanced portfolio of inter-city, regional and commuter trains through First Great Western, First TransPennine Express, First ScotRail and First Capital Connect. In addition First operate Hull Trains, Britain's only open access operator, deliver rail freight services through FirstGBRf and operate the highly successful Croydon Tramlink on behalf of Transport for London.

FIRST SCOTRAIL
Atrium Court, 50 Waterloo Street, Glasgow G2 6HQ
Tel: 0141-335 4787 Fax: 0141-335 4345
e-mail: scotrail.enquiries@firstgroup.com
Contact: Mary Dickson, Managing Director, tel: 0141-335 4500; Steve Montgomery, Deputy Managing Director, tel: 0141-335-4422; Kenny McPhail, Finance Director, tel: 0141-335 4136; Peter Williams, Commercial Director, tel: 0141-335 4584.
First ScotRail is Scotland's national railway, operating 2100 train services daily, carrying 77m passengers a year and operating 341 stations across Scotland. We provide suburban, interurban and rural services within Scotland and also the Caledonian Sleepers linking Scotland with London. During the seven-year franchise, which commenced on 17 October 2004, First ScotRail is investing £60m in improving rail journeys for passengers. We are committed to introducing additional ticket-purchasing facilities as a customer benefit.

UNIONS

NFU SCOTLAND
Rural Centre, West Mains, Ingliston, Edinburgh EH28 8LT
Tel: 0131 472 4000 Fax: 0131 472 4010
e-mail: webmaster@nfus.org.uk
web: www.nfus.org.uk
Contact: James Withers, Chief Executive; Jim McLaren, President.
NFU Scotland represents 9,000 farmers and other rural businesses. Its aim is to promote and protect the interest of its members who play a critical role in the food industry, in environmental protection and in rural communities. NFUS influences Government, other interest groups and consumers to assist its members in developing profitable and sustainable businesses. NFUS is a key provider of information to Government, media and consumers on food, farming and rural issues.

PROSPECT
Glenorchy House, 20 Union Street, Edinburgh EH1 3LR
Tel: 0131 558 2660 Fax: 0131 558 5280
e-mail: scotland@prospect.org.uk
web: www.prospect.org.uk
Prospect is a union of more than 102,000 members representing engineers, scientists, professionals and managers. We represent staff in the Scottish parliament, across the Scottish administration, and employees of other public and private sector organisations in

Scotland. Prospect provides the UK's largest collective voice for professionals at work. Our members provide specialist services in key sectors of Scottish life – agriculture, defence, energy, the environment, aviation, health and safety and the built and natural heritage.

RCN SCOTLAND
42 South Oswald Road, Edinburgh EH9 2HH
Tel: 0131 662 1010 Fax: 0131 662 1032
e-mail: scottish.board@rcn.org.uk
web: www.rcn.org.uk/scotland

Royal College of Nursing
Scotland

Contact: Jane McCready, Chair; Theresa Fyffe, Director.
The Royal College of Nursing (RCN) is the UK's largest professional organisation and union for nurses, with over 37,000 members in Scotland. The RCN works locally, nationally and internationally to promote standards of care and the interests of patients and nurses, and of nursing as a profession. The RCN is also a major contributor to the development of nursing practice and health policy.

SCOTTISH TRADES UNION CONGRESS
333 Woodlands Road, Glasgow G3 6NG
Tel: 0141 337 8100 Fax: 0141 337 8101
e-mail: info@stuc.org.uk
Contact: Grahame Smith, General Secretary.
The STUC co-ordinates, develops and articulates the views and policies of the trade union movement in Scotland. We promote trade unionism, equality and social justice; the creation and maintenance of high quality jobs; and the public sector delivery of services.

The STUC represents over 630,000 members of 46 affiliated trade unions. We speak for trade union members across Scotland and for trade unionists that suffer discrimination in the workplace and in society.

UNISON SCOTLAND
14 West Campbell Street, Glasgow G2 6RX
Tel: 0870 7777 006 Fax: 0141 331 1203
e-mail: matt.smith@unison.co.uk
web: www.unison-scotland.org.uk
Contact: Matt Smith, Scottish Secretary, 0870 7777 006,
matt.smith@unison.co.uk; Mike Kirby, Scottish Convener, 0870 7777 006, mike@unisonscotland.freeserve.co.uk; Chris Bartter, Communications Officer, 0870 7777 006, chris.bartter@unison.org.uk
UNISON is the largest public service trade union in Scotland, representing members across local government, the health service, higher and further education, police support staff, energy and water services, and the community and voluntary sector. UNISON provides a range of membership services in addition to professional negotiation and representation. It has offices in Glasgow, Edinburgh, Aberdeen and Inverness. UNISON campaigns actively in support of public services in Scotland, against PFI and for equal opportunities.

YOUTH

THE PRINCE'S SCOTTISH YOUTH BUSINESS TRUST
15 Exchange Place, Glasgow G1 3AN
Tel: 0141 248 4999 Fax: 0141 248 4836
e-mail: team@psybt.org.uk
web: www.psybt.org.uk

Contact: Mark Strudwick, Chief Executive, 0141 243 5378, mark.strudwick@psybt.org.uk;

Biographies

An A to Z of prominent people in Scotland

A

Principal Biochemist, Aberdeen Royal Infirmary; Aberdeen City Councillor, 1988-99. Address: (b.) 825/7 Great Northern Road, Aberdeen AB24 2BR.

Abercrombie, Ian R., QC, LLB (Hons); b. 7.7.55, Bulawayo. Educ. Milton High School; Edinburgh University. Recreations: travelling; walking. Address: (h.) Tippermallo House, Methven, Perthshire PH1 3RH; T.-07779780573.

Aberdeen and Temair, June Marchioness of, CBE, DL, GCStJ, FRCM, FRSE. Musical Director, Haddo House Choral and Operatic Society. Educ. Southlands School, Harrow; Royal College of Music. Chairman: Scottish Children's League, 1969-84, NE Scotland Music School, since 1975, Advisory Council, Scottish Opera, 1979-90. Address: Haddo House, Aberdeen AB41 7EQ; T.-01651 851216.

Abernethy, Rt. Hon. Lord (John Alastair Cameron). Senator, College of Justice, 1992-2007; b. 1.2.38, Newcastle-upon-Tyne; m., Elspeth Mary Dunlop Miller; 3 s. Educ. Clergy School, Khartoum; St. Mary's School, Melrose; Glenalmond College, Perth; Pembroke College, Oxford. National Service, 2nd Lt., RASC, Aldershot and Malta, 1956-58. Called to the Bar, Inner Temple, 1963; admitted Member, Faculty of Advocates, 1966; Advocate-Depute, 1972-75; Standing Junior Counsel to Department of Energy, 1976-79, Scottish Development Department, 1978-79; QC (Scotland), 1979; Vice-Dean, Faculty of Advocates, 1983-92; President, Pensions Appeal Tribunals for Scotland, 1985-92 (Legal Chairman, 1979-85); Chairman, Faculty Services Ltd., 1983-89 (Director, 1979-83); Hon. Fellow, Pembroke College, Oxford, 1993; International Bar Association: Vice Chairman, 1993-94, Chairman, Judges' Forum, 1994-98, Member, Council, Section on Legal Practice, 1998-2002, and Member, Council, Human Rights Institute, 1998-2000 and 2002-05; Trustee, Faculty of Advocates 1985 Charitable Trust, since 1985; Member, Executive Committee, Society for the Welfare and Teaching of the Blind (Edinburgh and South East Scotland), 1979-92; Trustee, Arthur Smith Memorial Trust, 1975-2001, Chairman, 1990-2001; President, Scottish Medico-Legal Society, 1996-2000; Governor, St. Mary's School, Melrose, since 1998, Vice-Chairman, since 2004. Publications: Medical Negligence: an introduction, 1983; Reproductive Medicine and the Law (Contributor). Recreations: travel; nature conservation; Africana. Address: (b.) 4 Garscube Terrace, Edinburgh EH12 6BQ; T.-0131-337 3460.

Abram, Henry Charles, LLB, WS. Solicitor, Tods Murray WS, since 1973; b. 11.8.51, Glasgow; m., Leslie Anne Hamilton; 2 s.; 1 d. Educ. Merchiston Castle School; Aberdeen University. Articled Tods Murray WS; qualified, 1976; Partner, 1978; Chairman, Management Board, 1994-97; Chairman, 1998-2002. Member, Council, Law Society of Scotland, 1983-86; Chairman of Governors, Merchiston Castle School, 2000-07; Member, High Constables and Guard of Honour of Holyrood House; Director: Hunter Property Fund Management Ltd; Member, Finance Committee of The National Trust for Scotland. Recreations: shooting; stalking; golf; skiing; running. Address: (b.) Edinburgh Quay, 133 Fountainbridge, Edinburgh EH3 9AG; T.-0131-656-2000.
E-mail: charles.abram@todsmurray.com

Adam, Brian James, BSc, MSc. MSP (SNP), North East Scotland, 1999-2003, Aberdeen North, since 2003; b. 10.6.48, Newmill; m., Dorothy Mann; 4 s.; 1 d. Educ. Keith Grammar School; Aberdeen University. Former

Adam, Ian Clark. Non-Executive Director, Britannia Building Society, since 1998 (Non-Executive Chairman, since 2004); b. 2.9.43; m., Betty; 1 d.; 1 s. Educ. Harris Academy. Trainee Accountant, Henderson & Logie, 1962-67; Price Waterhouse: Audit Senior and Assistant Manager (Rio de Janeiro), 1967-70, Manager, Bristol, 1970-76, Partner, Edinburgh, 1976-86, Senior Partner, Scotland, 1986-95; Financial Director, Christian Salvesen plc, 1995-98; Non-Executive Director: Fishers Holdings Ltd, 1996-2004. Member, Council, Scottish Further and Higher Education Funding Council; Old Master Co of Merchants of the City of Edinburgh; Member, High Constable City of Edinburgh; MICAS 1967. Recreations: reading; golf; shooting and travel. Address: Gowanfield, 2 Cammo Road, Edinburgh EH4 8EB; T.-0131 339 6401.

Adams, Professor (Charles) David, MA, MCD, PhD, FRTPI, MRICS, FRSA. Ian Mactaggart Professor of Property and Urban Studies, University of Glasgow, since 2004; b. 10.9.54, Menston, England; m., Judith Banks; 1 s.; 1 d. Educ. Rossall School; University of Cambridge; University of Liverpool. Planning Assistant, Leeds City Council, 1978-83; Research Assistant, University of Reading, 1983-84; Lecturer, University of Manchester, 1984-93; University of Aberdeen: Senior Lecturer, 1993-95, Reader, 1995-97, Professor of Land Economy, 1997-2004. Publications: Urban Planning and the Development Process, 1994; Land for Industrial Development (Co-author), 1994; Greenfields, Brownfields and Housing Development (Co-author), 2002; Planning, Public Policy and Property Markets (Co-editor), 2005. Recreations: walking; listening to classical music. Address: (b.) Department of Urban Studies, University of Glasgow, 25 Bute Gardens, Glasgow G12 8RS.

Adams, Douglas Stewart, BA, PGCE. Headteacher, George Heriot's Junior School, Edinburgh, since 1990; b. 14.5.54, Edinburgh; m., Lindsay; 1 s.; 2 d. Educ. Daniel Stewart's College, Edinburgh; The University of Edinburgh; Moray House College of Education, Edinburgh. Class Teacher: Daniel Stewart's and Melville College/Mary Erskine's Combined Junior School, Edinburgh, 1977-80, Saltus Grammar School, Bermuda, 1980-87; Head of Junior School, Saltus Grammar School, Bermuda, 1987-90. Governor, The Compass School, East Lothian. Recreations: fly fishing; music; reading; rugby coaching; photography; road running. Address: (b.) Lauriston Place, Edinburgh EH3 9EQ; T.-0131 229 7263; e-mail: dsa@george-heriots.com

Adams, Sheenagh, MA (Hons). Managing Director, Registers of Scotland, since 2006; b. 31.8.57, Dundee; m., Peter Craig; 2 d. Educ. Harris Academy, Dundee; St. Andrews University. Welfare Rights Officer, Strathclyde Regional Council, 1979-82; Tenant Participation Officer, Clydebank Council and TPAS, 1982-85; Principal Management Officer, Falkirk District Council, 1985-90; Principal, Scottish Office, 1990-99; Secretary, Historic Buildings Council for Scotland, 1995-99; Head, Heritage Policy, Historic Scotland, 1995-99; Head, Voluntary Issues Unit, Scottish Executive, 1999-2002; Director of Heritage Policy, Historic Scotland, 2002-06. Address: (b.) Meadowbank House, 153 London Road, Edinburgh EH7 8AU; e-mail: sheenagh.adams@ros.gov.uk

Adamson, Jim, BA (Hons), BA (Humanities), PGDip. Founder and Managing Director, Speakeasy Productions, since 1993; b. 11.4.49, Perth; m., Stella. Educ. Perth Academy; Open University; Stirling University; Duncan of Jordanstone. Career History: Apprentice TV Engineer; Electronics Test Engineer; Meraldic Calligrapher; Pop Musician; Fly Dresser; Crafts Manufacturer; TV Producer. Great Scot, 1998; Director, Rehab Council; Director, SE Tayside; Director, Horse Cross Arts; Board Member, Perth College/UHI; Director, Air Service Training. Recreations: poker; reading; wine; music, guitar playing, football. Address: (h. and b.) Wildwood House, Stanley, Perth PH1 4PX; T.-01738 828524; e-mail: jim@speak.co.uk

Adderley, Mark David, MA, MEng, MBA. Chief Executive, The National Trust for Scotland, since 2007; Director, Scottish Water, since 2002; b. 15.01.65, Birmingham; m., Miranda; 4 d. Educ. King Edward's School, Birmingham; Cambridge (Emmanuel College). MAC Group/Gemini Consulting, 1988-94; The Royal Bank of Scotland, 1994-2002; Scottish Water, 2002-07. Recreations: family; outdoor activity; squash. Address: (b.) Wemyss House, 28 Charlotte Square, Edinburgh EH2 4ET; T.-0844 493 2400; e-mail: madderley@nts.org.uk

Addison, Alexander, MBE, MB, ChB, FRCGP, DObstRCOG. Senior Partner, Addison, Scott, Kane & Ferguson, 1978-95; Chairman, Lanarkshire LMC, 1989-95; Member, Scottish Committee, BMA, since 1984, and Fellow, BMA, since 1993; Member, RCCC Council, 1996-2000; Medical Officer and Anti-Drugs Officer, RCCC; b. 23.8.30, Kerala; m., Joan Wood; 3 s. Educ. Keith Grammar School; Aberdeen Grammar School; Aberdeen University. House Surgeon and Physician, Woodend General Hospital, Aberdeen, 1954-55; Captain, RAMC; Junior Medical Specialist, Cowglen MH, 1955-58; SHO, Bellshill MH, 1958-59; GP in Douglas and Physician to Lady Home Hospital, 1959-95; Member, West of Scotland Faculty of GP College, 1967-79 and of Scottish Council, 1976-78; Member, Lanarkshire LMC, since 1972, and of AMAC, since 1975; Chairman, Lanarkshire AMAC, 1982-86; Chairman, Scottish Association of General Practitioner Hospitals, 1985-87; Member, Scottish Committee of Medical Commission on Accident Prevention, 1976-98; Member, National Medical Consultative Committee, 1977-83; Honorary Surgeon, St. Andrews Ambulance Association, 1959-89. Recreations: curling; golf; reading. Address: (h.) 7 Addison Drive, Douglas, Lanarkshire ML11 0PZ; T.-01555 851302.

Agnew of Lochnaw, Sir Crispin Hamlyn. 11th Baronet (created 1629); Chief of the Agnews; Advocate 1982; Queen's Counsel (1995); Deputy Social Security Commissioner (2000); Chairman, Pension Appeal Tribunal (2002); Unicorn Pursuivant of Arms, 1981-86, Rothesay Herald of Arms, since 1986; Trustee, John Muir Trust, 1989-2005; Chairman, Crofting Law Group; b. 13.5.44, Edinburgh; m., Susan Rachel Strang Steel; 1 s.; 3 d. Educ. Uppingham School; Royal Military Academy, Sandhurst. Commissioned Royal Highland Fusiliers, 1964, as 2nd Lieutenant; Major, 1977; Retired, 1981. Member: Royal Navy Expedition to East Greenland, 1966; Joint Services Expedition to Elephant Island, Antarctica, 1970-71; Army Nuptse Himal Expedition, 1975; Army Everest Expedition, 1976; Leader: Army East Greenland Expedition, 1968; Joint Services Expedition to Chilean Patagonia, 1972-73; Army Api Himal Expedition, 1980. Publications: Licensing (Scotland) Act 1976 (5th edition 2002) (Co-author); Agricultural Law in Scotland, 1996; Connell on the Agricultural Holdings (Scotland) Acts (Co-author) 1996; Land Obligations, 1999; Crofting Law, 2000; articles in various newspapers and journals. Recreations: mountaineering; sailing. Address: 6 Palmerston Road, Edinburgh EH9 1TN; T.-0131-668 3792.

Agnew, Ian, MA (Hons) (Cantab). Rector, Perth High School, 1975-92; b. 10.5.32, Newcastle-upon-Tyne; m., Gladys Agnes Heatherill; 1 d. Educ. King's College School,

London; Pembroke College, Cambridge. Assistant Teacher of Modern Languages, Melville College, Edinburgh, 1958-63; Assistant Teacher of Modern Languages, then Principal Teacher of Russian, George Heriot's School, Edinburgh, 1964-70; Housemaster, Craigmount Secondary School, Edinburgh, 1970-73; Deputy, Liberton High School, Edinburgh, 1973-75. Non-Executive Director, Perth and Kinross Healthcare NHS Trust, 1994-98; Minute Secretary, Headteachers Association of Scotland, 1979-81; Committee Member, SCCORE; President: Perthshire Musical Festival, 1978-88, Perth Chamber Music Society, 1982-89; Past President, Rotary Club of Perth St. John's; Past Chairman: Barnton and Cramond Conservative Association and West Edinburgh Conservative and Unionist Association; Serving Officer (OStJ), Priory of Scotland of the Most Venerable Order of St. John; Member, Society of High Constables, City of Perth; Governor: Balnacraig School, Perth, 1981-2007, Kilgraston School, 1990-99, Convent of the Sacred Heart, Bridge of Earn; Secretary, Friends of Perth Festival of the Arts, 1996-99; Member, Advisory Group, Perth College Development Trust; Chairman, Friends of St. John's Kirk, Perth; Past President, Fair City Probus Club, Perth. Recreations: music (opera); reading; tennis; gardening. Address: (h.) Northwood, Heughfield Road, Bridge of Earn, Perthshire PH2 9BH; T.-01738 81 2273.

Ahmad, Bashir, MSP (SNP), Glasgow, since 2007; b. 12.2.40, India. Address: (b.) Scottish Parliament, Edinburgh EH99 1SP.

Ailsa, 8th Marquess of (Archibald Angus Charles Kennedy); b. 13.9.56; 2 d. Address: Cassillis House, Maybole KA19 7JN.

Ainslie, Allan, BSc (Hons), FRICS. Chief Valuer Scotland, since 1998; b. 16.2.51, Edinburgh; m., Jennifer Anne Park; 1 s.; 1 d. Educ. Broxburn Academy; Napier College; Edinburgh University. Valuer, Valuation Office, Inland Revenue, 1976-79; Senior Valuer, 1980-85; Principal Valuer, 1986-90; First Class Valuer, 1991-92; District Valuer (Fife and Central), 1992-95; District Valuer Scotland South East, 1996-97. Recreations: tennis; badminton; gardening. Address: (b.) 50 Frederick Street, Edinburgh EH2 1NG; T.-0131-465 0700.

Airlie, 13th Earl of (David George Coke Patrick Ogilvy), KT, GCVO, PC, KStJ, Royal Victorian Chain, JP. Former Lord Chamberlain of Queen's Household; Chancellor, University of Abertay, Dundee, since 1994; Director, Baring Stratton Investment Trust plc, since 1986; President, National Trust for Scotland, 1997-2002; Hon. President, Scottish Council, The Scout Association; Chairman, Historic Royal Palaces, 1998-2002; b. 17.5.26, London; m., Virginia Fortune Ryan; 3 s.; 3 d. Educ. Eton College. Lieutenant, Scots Guards, 1944; serving 2nd Bn., Germany, 1945; Captain, ADC to High Commissioner and C-in-C Austria, 1947-48; Malaya, 1948-49; resigned commission, 1950; Chairman, Ashdown Investment Trust Ltd., 1968-82; Director, J. Henry Schroder Wagg & Co. Ltd., 1961-84 (Chairman, 1973-77); Chairman, Schroders plc, 1977-84; Scottish and Newcastle Breweries plc, until 1983; Director, Royal Bank of Scotland Group, 1983-93; Director, Royal Bank of Scotland plc, 1991-93; Chairman, General Accident Fire & Life Assurance Corporation plc, 1987-97; Chancellor of the Royal Victorian Order, 1984-97; Trustee, Royal Collection Trust, 1993; Ensign, Queen's Body Guard for Scotland (Royal Company of Archers) (President, Council, since 2001), Captain General, 2004; Chancellor of the Most Noble and Ancient Order of the Thistle, November 13th 2007. Address: (h.) Cortachy Castle, Kirriemuir, Angus.

Airlie, Countess of (Virginia Fortune Ryan), DCVO. Lady in Waiting to HM The Queen, since 1973; Chairman, National Galleries of Scotland, 1997-2000 (Trustee since 1995); President, Angus Red Cross, since 1988; b. 9.2.33,

London; 3 s.; 3 d. Educ. Brearley School, New York City. Commissioner, Royal Fine Arts Commission; Trustee, Tate Gallery, 1983-95; Trustee, National Gallery, London, 1989-95; Member, Industrial Design Panel, British Rail, 1974-91; Trustee, American Museum in Britain, since 1985 (Chairman, since 2001); Founder/Governor, Cobham School. Address: (b.) Cortachy Castle, Kirriemuir, Angus; T.-01575 540231.

Aitchison, James Douglas, MA (Hons), MEd (Hons). Director, Scotland - Malawi School Improvement Programme, since 2005 (Adviser to Schools Inspectorate, Uganda, 2003-05); Head Teacher, Boclair Academy, Bearsden, 1991-2002; Head Teacher, Gleniffer High School, Paisley, 1984-91; b. 2.7.47, Glasgow. Educ. High School of Glasgow; Glasgow University; University of Marburg. Teacher, Lycee Faidherbe, Lille; Principal Teacher, Bearsden Academy; Assistant Head Teacher, Gryffe High School, Houston. Recreations: curling; walking; travel. Address: (h.) 44 Keystone Road, Milngavie, Glasgow G62 6QG; T.-0141-956 6693.

Aitchison, Thomas Nisbet, CBE, MA, MSc. Chief Executive, City of Edinburgh Council, since 1995; b. 24.2.51, Edinburgh; m., Kathleen Sadler; 1 s.; 2 d. Educ. Glasgow University; Heriot-Watt University. Lothian Regional Council: Corporate Planning Manager and Depute Director, Depute Chief Executive, Chief Executive. Honorary Secretary, Council, Edinburgh International Festival. Recreations: hill-walking; football; music; cycling. Address: (b.) Waverley Court, 4 East Market Street, Edinburgh EH8 8BG.

Aitken, Rev. Ewan, BA (Hons), BD (Hons). Church of Scotland Minister; Leader, Labour Group, The City of Edinburgh Council; b. 27.4.62, Paisley; m., Hilary Brown; 1 s.; 1 d. Educ. Woodmill High School, Dunfermline; University of Sussex; University of Edinburgh. Youth Worker, Ruchill Parish Church, 1980-81; Vice President (sabbatical), University of Sussex Union, 1982-83; Regional Secretary, Student Christian Movement, 1985-87; Pastor, West Avenue Presbyterian Church, Buffalo, NY, 1990-91; Assistant Minister, South Leith Parish Church, Edinburgh, 1991-93; Staff Member, St. Andrews Church of Scotland, Tiberias, Israel, 1993-94; Locum Minister, St. Andrews, Gisborne, New Zealand, 1994-95; Minister, St. Margaret's Church of Scotland, Edinburgh, 1995-2002; Elected to The City of Edinburgh Council, 1999; Executive Member for Children and Families, 2001-06; COSLA Spokesperson on Education, 2003-06; Leader, The City of Edinburgh Council, 2006-07. Recreations: following Dunfermline Athletic F.C. and Edinburgh Gunners; vegetarian cookery; laughter. Address: (b.) City Chambers, High Street, Edinburgh EH1 1YJ; T.-0131 529 3261.

Aitken, Fraser Robert, MA, BD. Minister at St. Columba Church, Ayr, since 1991; b. 8.1.53, Paisley. Educ. John Neilson Institution, Paisley; University of Glasgow. Assistant Minister, Fairmilehead Parish Church, Edinburgh, 1977-78; Minister at Neilston Parish Church, 1978-84; Minister at Girvan North Parish Church, 1984-91. Director, Glasgow-Ayrshire Society; Chaplain, Strathclyde Police 'U' Division; Trustee, Maclaurin Gallery; President, Glasgow-Ayrshire Society; Trustee, Ayr College; President, Carrick Burns Club; Honorary President, Greenock Burns' Club; Moderator of the Presbytery of Ayr, 1996-97; Convener, The Nominations Committee of The General Assembly, 2000-02. Recreations: musical theatre; reading; wining and dining; visiting Vienna and York. Address: (h.) The Manse of St. Columba, 2 Hazelwood Road, Ayr KA7 2PY; T.-01292 284177; e-mail: frasercolumba@msn.com

Aitken, Joan Nicol, SSC. Traffic Commissioner for Scotland; Solicitor; formerly Scottish Prisons Complaints Commissioner; b. 26.2.53, Glasgow; 1 d. Educ. James Gillespie's High School for Girls; Dundee University.

Solicitor in Local goverment and private practice. Council Member, Law Society of Scotland, 1988-91; Editor, Journal of Law Society of Scotland, 1991-98; former Part-time Chairman: Employment Tribunals (Scotland), Disability Appeal Tribunals, Child Support Appeal Tribunals; Member, Scottish Consumer Council, 1987-93; Member, General Dental Council; was first woman member, Society of Solicitors in the Supreme Courts of Scotland. Address: (b.) Traffic Commissioner for Scotland, J Floor, Argyle House, 3 Lady Lawson Street, Edinburgh EH3 9SE; T.-0131 200 4905; e-mail: Joan.Aitken@vosa.gov.uk

Aitken, Keith, MA (Hons). Freelance Journalist, Broadcaster and Conference Facilitator, since 1995; b. 31.10.57, Edinburgh; m., Christine Willett; 1 d. Educ. George Watson's College, Edinburgh; University of Edinburgh. The Scotsman: graduate trainee, 1979-82, Parliamentary Correspondent, 1982-85, Labour Correspondent, 1985-88, Industrial Editor, 1988-92, Economics Editor and Chief Leader Writer, 1992-95; former Columnist: The Scotsman, The Herald, Scotland on Sunday; Columnist and Crossword Compiler, Scottish Daily Express; Columnist, Holyrood Magazine; Writer and Presenter, discussion programmes and documentaries, BBC Radio Scotland, World Service and Radio 4; Video/DVD Writer and Presenter, and regular Podcaster; Trustee, Scottish Mining Museum. Awards include Business and Industry Writer of the Year, Scottish Press Awards, 1986 and 1987. Publications: The Bairns o' Adam, 1997; How Scotland's Parliament Will Work, 1999; Understanding Scotland's Parliament, 1999. Recreations: walking; collecting US political memorabilia; gardening; reading; deplorable blues guitar. Address: 25 Bridge Road, Colinton Village, Edinburgh EH13 0LH; T.-0131-441 7982; e-mail: keith@kaitken.fsnet.co.uk; website: www.keithaitken.co.uk

Aitken, Professor Robert Cairns Brown, CBE, MB, ChB, DPM, MD, DSc (Hon), FRCPEdin, FRCPsych. Chairman, Royal Infirmary of Edinburgh NHS Trust, 1994-97; Professor of Rehabilitation Studies, Edinburgh University, 1974-94 (Dean, Faculty of Medicine, 1990-91, Vice-Principal, 1991-94); Honorary Consultant in Rehabilitation Medicine, Lothian Health Board, 1974-94; b. 20.12.33, Dunoon; m., Audrey May Lunn; 1 s.; 1 d. Educ. Dunoon Grammar School; Cargilfield School, Edinburgh; Sedbergh School, Yorkshire; Glasgow University. Institute of Aviation Medicine, RAF, 1959-62; Orpington and Maudsley Hospitals, 1962-66; Senior Lecturer/Consultant Psychiatrist, Royal Infirmary and Royal Edinburgh Hospital, 1967-74. President, International College of Psychosomatic Medicine, 1985-87; Chairman, Napier Polytechnic of Edinburgh Governors, 1983-90; Member, Council for Professions Supplementary to Medicine, 1983-90; Member, General Medical Council, 1991-96; Director, Lothian Health Board, 1991-93; Editor, Journal of Psychosomatic Research, 1979-85; occasional WHO consultant; Foundation Secretary, then President, Society for Research in Rehabilitation, 1981-83; Member, Human Genetics Advisory Commission, 1996-99. Publications: papers on measurement of mood; flying phobia; management of disability. Recreations: people, places and pleasures of Edinburgh, Scotland and beyond. Address: (h.) 11 Succoth Place, Edinburgh EH12 6BJ; T.-0131-337 1550.

Aitken, William Mackie. JP, DL. MSP (Conservative), Glasgow, since 1999 (Convener, Justice Committee; Parliamentary Business Manager and Chief Whip, 2003-07; Conservative Justice Spokesman, 2001-03; Housing Spokesman, 1999-2001); b. 15.4.47, Glasgow. Educ. Allan Glen's School, Glasgow. Chairman, Scottish Young Conservatives, 1975-77; Councillor, City of Glasgow, 1976-99: Convenor, City Licensing Committee and Vice-Convenor, Personnel Committee, 1977-79; Leader of the

Opposition, City Council, 1980-84 and 1992-96, Bailie of the City, 1980-84, 1988-92, 1996-99; Depute Lord Lieutenant, City of Glasgow. Recreations: football; reading; foreign travel. Address: (h.) 35 Overnewton Square, Glasgow G3 8RW; T.-0141-357 1284.

Aitkenhead, Geoff, BSc, CEng, MICE, MCIWEM. Asset Management Director, Scottish Water, since 2002; Chairman, Scottish Water Solutions, since 2003; b. 26.9.54, Gosforth; m., Helen; 3 d. Educ. Wyndham School, Egremont; University of Newcastle Upon Tyne. Graduate engineer with Northumbrian Water engaged in environmental clean-up of the River Tyne; 3 years in Qatar, Arabian Gulf, with consulting engineers Pencol International on oil export facilities and public health projects; City of Salford, urban sewerage schemes; Borders Regional Council, Capital Planning Manager; East of Scotland Water, Strategic Operations and Customer Service roles; Scottish Water, Director of Asset Management, responsible for Business and Asset Planning, Capital Investment delivery. Chairman, WaterAid Scotland; Past-President, Institution of Water Officers. Recreations: hill walking; motorcycling; travel. Address: (b.) Castle House, 6 Castle Drive, Carnegie Campus, Dunfermline KY11 8GG; T.-01383 848471.

Aitkin, John, MBE, TD, CA. Retired Chartered Accountant; b. 10.9.33, Denholm; m., Elizabeth Charlotte Fraser; 1 s.; 1 s. (deceased); 1 d. Educ. Hawick High School. Qualified as a CA, 1956; National Service (commissioned 2nd Lt.), 1956-58; joined John J. Welch & Co., CA, Hawick, 1958, Partner, 1961-97; served in TA, 1958-73; Committee of Management, Royal British Legion Housing Association Ltd., 1978-91 (Chairman, 1986-91); National Chairman, Royal British Legion Scotland, 1995-98 (Hon. Treasurer, 1985-90); Earl Haig Fund Scotland: Member, Executive Committee, 1992-99, Director, 1999-2002; Regimental Trustee, King's Own Scottish Borderers, 1980-2004; Member, Management Committee, Ex-Services Mental Welfare Society, 1998-2002; Member, Central Advisory Committee on War Pensions, 1995-98; Member, Council, British Commonwealth Ex-Services League, 1998-2002; President, Hawick Callants Club, 1991; Member, East Scotland War Pensions Committee, 2001-04; Director, Scottish Borders Housing Association Ltd., 2001-06; Treasurer, The Gurkha Welfare Trust, Scottish Branch, since 2004. Recreations: gardening; reading; walking. Address: (h) 26 Park View, Hawick TD9 7JE; T.-01450 372424.

Akers, Fiona Moira, LLB (Hons), DipLP. Partner, Dickson Minto W.S., Solicitors, since 1999, Head of IP/Technology; b. 5.5.65, Paisley; m. Educ. Craigholme School; Edinburgh University. Trained with McGrigor Donald (now McGrigors), Partner, 1997-99. Address: (b.) 16 Charlotte Square, Edinburgh EH2 4DF; T.-0131-225-4455; e-mail: fiona.akers@dmws.com

Alba, Carlos, BA (Hons), DipJour. Editor, Sunday Times Scotland, since 2006, Deputy Editor, 2001-06; b. 28.8.65, Glasgow; m., Hilary; 1s; 2d. Educ. High School of Glasgow; University of Strathclyde. Reporter: Dumfries and Galloway Standard, 1990-92, Press and Journal, 1992-95; Chief Reporter, Edinburgh Evening News, 1995-96; Education Correspondent, The Herald, 1996-98; Scottish Political Editor, Daily Record, 1998-2000; Deputy News Editor, Sunday Times Scotland, 2000-01. Publication: Keep the Faith (Co-Author), 2001; Kane's Ladder, 2008. Recreation: shouting at Celtic defenders. Address: (b.) 124 Portman Street, Glasgow G41 1EJ; T.-0141-420 5274; e-mail: Carlos.Alba@sunday-times.co.uk

Alder, Professor Elizabeth, BSc, PhD, CPsychol, FBPsS. Professor, Faculty of Health, Life and Social Sciences, Napier University, since 2000; b. 2.11.44, St. Andrews; m., Dr. George Alder; 3 d. Educ. Edgbaston High School,

Birmingham; Aberdeen University; Edinburgh University. Lecturer, Napier College, Edinburgh, 1971-75; Senior Research Officer, MRC Reproductive Biology Unit, Edinburgh, 1975-87; Senior Lecturer, Queen Margaret College, Edinburgh, 1987-95; Senior Lecturer, Dundee University, 1995-2000. President, International Society for Psychosomatic Obstetrics and Gynaecology. Publication: The Psychology of Health, 1999. Recreations: hillwalking; skiing; gardening. Address: (b.) Faculty of Health and Life Sciences, Napier University, 74 Canaan Lane, Edinburgh EH9 2TB; T.-0131-455 5672.
E-mail: e.m.alder@napier.ac.uk

Alekseevsky, Professor Dmitri, PhD (1967), ScD (1989). Emeritus Professor, Hull University, since 2005; Visiting Professor, Edinburgh University, since 2006; b. 20.08.40, Moscow, Russia; m., Natalia; 2 s.; 2 d. Educ. 25 Kiev School; Moscow State University. Senior Researcher in Moscow Research Institute, 1967-76; Senior Lecturer and Associated Professor in Moscow Pedagogical University, 1976-90; Chief Researcher of Interim Centre, "Sophus Lie", 1990-2000; Chair, Pure Mathematics, Hull University, 2000-05. Publications: Editor of journals: Differential Geometry and its Applications, Transformation Groups, Annals of Global Analysis and Geometry, Monatshefte für Mathematik; Books: Encyclopedia of Math. Sci., Geometry I, II, vol 28, 29. Address: School of Mathematics, Edinburgh University, King's Buildings, JCMB, Edinburgh EH9 3JZ; T.-0131 6505044; e-mail: d.aleksee@ed.ac.uk

Alessi, Dario Renato, FRSE. Principal Investigator, Honorary Professor at the MRC Protein Phosphorylation Unit, University of Dundee, since 1997; b. 23.12.67, Strasbourg, France; 1 s. Educ. European School of Brussels; University of Birmingham. Discovered and characterised PDKI protein Kinase; discovered and characterised the mechanism of activation and function of the CKBI tumour suppressor; identified two physiological substrates of the WNKI and WNK4 Kinase that control blood pressure; described the mechanism by which PKB/AKT enzyme is activated; identified ERM proteins as potential substrates for the LRRK2 Parkinson's Disease Kinase. Colworth Medal, 1999; Ellendorf Young European Investigator Award, 2000; Makdougall Brisbane Prize, 2002; Philip Leverhulme Prize, 2002; Embo Gold Medal, 2005, Francis Crick Prize, 2006. Recreations: running; watching football and collecting stamps. Address: MRC Protein Phosphorylation Unit, College of Life Science, University of Dundee, Dundee DD1 5EH; T.-01382 385602; e-mail: d.r.alessi@dundee.ac.uk

Alexander, Professor Alan, MA, FRSE. Chair, Scottish Water, 2002-06 (Chair Designate, 2001-02); Chairman, West of Scotland Water Authority, 1999-2002; Professor of Local and Public Management, Strathclyde University, 1993-2000, now Emeritus Professor (Head, Department of Human Resource Management, 1993-96, Professor of Local Government, 1987-93); Visiting Professor, University of Edinburgh Management School, since 2006; b. 13.12.43, Glasgow; m., Morag MacInnes (Morag Alexander, qv); 1 s.; 1 d. Educ. Possil Secondary School, Glasgow; Albert Secondary School, Glasgow; Glasgow University. Lecturer/Assistant Professor, Political Science, Lakehead University, Ontario, 1966-71; Lecturer in Politics, Reading University, 1971-87. Member of Board, Housing Corporation, 1977-80; Member, Standing Research Committee on Local and Central Government Relations, Joseph Rowntree Memorial Trust, 1988-92; conducted inquiry into relations between Western Isles Islands Council and BCCI, 1991; Director, Scottish Local Authorities Management Centre, 1987-93; Member, Commission on Local Government and the Scottish Parliament, 1998-99; Chair, Glasgow Regeneration Fund,

1998-2001; Trustee, Quarriers, 1995-2000; Trustee, WaterAid, 2001-06; Member, Accounts Commission, since 2002; Member, Economic and Social Research Council, since 2003. President, Institution of Water Officers, 2005-06; Chair, Postwatch Scotland, since 2007; Chair, Distance Lab Ltd., since 2006. Publications: Local Government in Britain since Reorganisation, 1982; The Politics of Local Government in the UK, 1982; L'amministrazione locale in Gran Bretagna, 1984; Borough Government and Politics: Reading, 1835-1985, 1985; Managing the Fragmented Authority, 1994; The Future of DLOs/DSOs in Scotland, 1998. Recreations: theatre; cinema; walking; avoiding gardening.

Alexander, Daniel Grian (Danny). MP (Liberal Democrat), Inverness, Nairn, Badenoch and Strathspey, since 2005; b. 15.5.72. Educ. Lochaber High School, Fort William; University of Oxford. Address: (b.) House of Commons, London SW1A 0AA.

Alexander, Professor David Alan, MA (Hons), CPsychol, PhD, FBPS, FRSM, (Hon) FRCPsych. Professor of Mental Health, University of Aberdeen, since 1994 (Director, Aberdeen Centre for Trauma Research, since 1999); b. 28.8.43, Ellon. Educ. George Watson's College, Edinburgh; Morgan Academy, Dundee; University of St. Andrews; University of Dundee. MRC Research Scholar; Lecturer, then Senior Lecturer in Mental Health, then Hon. Professor of Mental Health, University of Aberdeen; Visiting Lecturer: FBI Academy, Virginia, USA, Scottish Police College; Visiting Professor to universities in USA, Russia, Croatia, Spain, West Indies and Pakistan; Member, Joint Medical Committee, Nato. Publications: co-author of three books; numerous professional articles. Recreations: badminton; squash; hill-walking. Address: (b.) Aberdeen Centre for Trauma Research, The Robert Gordon University, Garthdee Road, Aberdeen AB10 7QG.

Alexander, Major-General David Crichton, CB. Commandant, Scottish Police College, 1979-87; b. 28.11.26, Aberdour; m., 1, Diana Joyce (Jane) Fisher (deceased); 2, Elizabeth Patricia Fleming; 1 s.; 1 step-s.; 2 d. Educ. Edinburgh Academy; Staff College, Camberley; Royal College of Defence Studies. Royal Marines, 1944-77 (2nd Lieutenant to Major-General, including Equerry and Acting Treasurer to Duke of Edinburgh); Director-General, English Speaking Union, 1977-79. President, Corps of Commissionaires, 1994-97; Member, Civil Service Final Selection Board, 1978-88; Chairman, Edinburgh Academy, 1985-90; Freeman, City of London; Liveryman, Painter Stainers' Company; Member, Transport Users Consultative Committee for Scotland, 1989-93; President, SSAFA Fife, 1990-94. Recreations: fishing; golf; gardening. Address: (h.) Baldinnie, Park Place, Elie KY9 1DH; T.-01333 330882.

Alexander, Douglas, MA (Hons), LLB, DipLP. MP (Labour), Paisley and Renfrewshire South, since 2005, Paisley South, 1997-2005; Secretary of State for International Development, since 2007; Secretary of State for Scotland, 2006-07; Secretary of State for Transport, since 2006; Minister for Europe, 2005-06; Minister for Trade, 2004-05; Minister for the Cabinet Office and Chancellor of the Duchy of Lancaster, 2003-04; Minister of State, Cabinet Office, 2002-2003; Minister of State, Department of Trade and Industry, e-Commerce and Competitiveness, 2001-02; b. 26.10.67, Glasgow; m., Jacqui Christian. Educ. Park Mains High School, Erskine; University of Edinburgh; University of Pennsylvania. Speechwriter for Dr. Gordon Brown, MP, 1990; Brodies WS, Edinburgh, 1994-96; Solicitor, Digby Brown,

Edinburgh, 1996-97. Publication: New Scotland, New Britain, 1999. Recreations: running; angling. Address: House of Commons, Westminster, London SW1A 0AA; T.-020 7219 3000.

Alexander, Rev. Douglas Niven, MA, BD. Minister, Erskine Parish Church, Bishopton, 1970-99, retired; b. 8.4.35, Eaglesham; m., Dr. Joyce O. Garven; 1 s.; 2 d. Educ. Hutchesons' Boys' Grammar School, Glasgow; Glasgow University (President, SRC, 1958); Union Theological Seminary, New York. Assistant Minister, St. Ninian's Church, Greenock, 1961-62; Warden, Iona Community House, Glasgow, 1963-70. Secretary, Scottish Union of Students, 1958; Assessor to Lord Rector, Glasgow University, 1969-71; Chaplain to Erskine Hospital, since 1970; Moderator, Paisley Presbytery, 1984; Mair Memorial Lecturer, Glasgow University, 1987; Chairman, British Churches Committee for Channel 4 TV, 1986-88; Convener, Church of Scotland Board of Communication, 1987-91; Member: Scottish Committee, IBA, 1988-90; National Religious Advisory Committee, IBA, 1988-90; Central Religious Advisory Committee, 1988-92; National Religious Advisory Committee, ITC, 1991-92; Scottish Viewers Consultative Committee, ITC, 1991-92; Member, Church of Scotland Board of Social Responsibility, 1997-2001. Awarded Honorary Degree - Doctor of the University (DUniv), University of Glasgow, June 2007. Recreation: researching ways of salmon poachers! Address: West Morningside, Main Road, Langbank PA14 6XP; T.-01475 540249; e-mail: douglas.alexander@langbank.org

Alexander, Professor Michael Joseph, BA, MA (Oxon), FEA. Honorary Professor of English Literature, St. Andrews University, since 2003; b. 21.5.41, Wigan; m., 1, Eileen Mary McCall (deceased); 2, Mary Cecilia Sheahan; 1 s.; 2 d. Educ. Downside School; Trinity College, Oxford; Perugia University; Princeton University. Editor, William Collins, London, 1963-65; Lecturer, University of California, 1966-67; Editor, Andre Deutsch, London, 1967-68; Lecturer: East Anglia University, 1968-69, Stirling University, 1969; Senior Lecturer, 1977; Reader, 1985; Berry Professor of English Literature, St Andrews University, 1985-2003. Represents Scotland on Round Britain Quiz. Publications: Earliest English Poems (Translator), 1966; Beowulf (Translator), 1973; Twelve Poems, 1978; The Poetic Achievement of Ezra Pound, 1979; History of Old English Literature, 1983; Macmillan Anthology of English Literature, 1989; Beowulf (Editor), 1995; Sons of Ezra (Editor), 1995; The Canterbury Tales – The First Fragment (Editor), 1996; The Canterbury Tales: Illustrated Prologue (Editor), 1996; A History of English Literature, 2000; Medievalism: the Middle Ages in Modern England, 2007. Address: School of English, St. Andrews University, St. Andrews KY16 9AL; T.-01334 462666; e-mail: mja4@st-and.ac.uk

Alexander, Morag, BA (Hons), OBE. Scotland Commissioner, Equality and Human Rights Commission, since 2007; Lay member, General Optical Council, since 2007; Convener, Scottish Social Services Council, 2001-07; Director, Equal Opportunities Commission, Scotland, 1992-2001; b. 10.10.43, Kilwinning; m., Professor Alan Alexander (qv); 1 s.; 1 d. Educ. Lourdes Secondary School, Glasgow; Glasgow University; Lakehead University, Ontario. Research Assistant, ASTMS, 1971-73; Editor and Researcher, RIPA, 1973-82; freelance journalist and consultant, 1982-90; Founding Editor, Women in Europe, 1985-89, and UK Correspondent, Women of Europe, 1987-92; Founding Director, Training 2000 (Scotland) Ltd., Scottish Alliance for Women's Training, 1990-92; Member, Policy Committee, Children in Scotland, Chair, Early Years Advisory Group, 1995-2003; Board Member, Scottish Commission for the Regulation of Care, 2001-07; Member,

Board, Partnership for a Parliament, 1997; Member, Scottish Senate, the Windsor Meetings, 1997-2000; Member, Expert Panel on Procedures and Standing Orders, Scottish Parliament, 1997-98; Member, Committee of Inquiry into Student Finance, 1999; Member, Court, Queen Margaret University. Recreations: music; opera; visiting art galleries and museums; hill-walking. E-mail: morag.alexander@dsl.pipex.com

Alexander, Samuel, BL. Honorary Sheriff, Dumbarton, since 1983; b. Glasgow; m., Isabella Kerr Ligertwood; 2 s. Educ. Govan High School; Glasgow University. Formerly Consultant and Senior Partner, Keyden Strang & Co., Solicitors, Glasgow (historian of firm). Recreations: golf; reading. Address: (h.) 1 Hillneuk Avenue, Bearsden, Glasgow G61 3PY; T.-0141-942 4674.

Alexander, Wendy, MA (Hons), MA (Econ), MBA. MSP (Labour), Paisley North, since 1999; Leader, Scottish Labour Party, since 2007; b. 27.6.63, Glasgow; m., Prof. Brian Ashcroft; 1 s.; 1 d. Educ. Park Mains School, Erskine; Pearson College, Canada; Glasgow University; Warwick University; INSEAD, France. Research Officer, Scottish Labour Party, 1988-92; Senior Associate, Booz Allen & Hamilton Int., 1994-97; Special Adviser to Secretary of State for Scotland, 1997-98; Minister for Communities, 1999-2000; Minister for Enterprise and Lifelong Learning, 2000-01; Minister for Enterprise, Transport and Lifelong Learning, 2001-02. Visiting Professor, University of Strathclyde. Address: (b.) Scottish Parliament, Edinburgh EH99 1SP.

Allan, Alasdair James, MA, PhD. MSP (SNP), Western Isles, since 2007; b. 6.5.71, Edinburgh. Educ. Selkirk High School; University of Glasgow; University of Aberdeen. Senior Vice President, Students Representative Council, Glasgow University, 1991-92; Researcher, SNP Headquarters, 1998-99; Parliamentary Assistant: Michael Russell MSP, 1999-2002, Alex Salmond MP, 2002-03; Policy and Parliamentary Affairs Manager, Carers Scotland, 2003-04; Senior Media Relations Officer, Church of Scotland, 2004-06; Parliamentary Assistant to Angus B MacNeil MP, 2006-07. National Secretary, SNP, 2003-06; Scottish Parliament Local Government and Communities Committee, since 2007; former Vice President, Scots Language Society; serves on cross party groups including those on Gaelic and Epilepsy. Recreations: Scottish languages and literature; hill walking; travel; promoting Scottish independence. Address: (b.) 31 Bayhead, Stornoway, Isle of Lewis HS1 0JS: T.-01851 702272. E-mail: alasdair.allan.msp@scottish.parliament.uk

Allan, Angus, BSc (Hons), MBA (2002). Depute Principal, South Lanarkshire College; HM Inspector of Education; b. 28.3.60, Glasgow; m.; 3 s. Educ. Larkhall Academy; Edinburgh University. Lecturer in Agriculture, Kirkley College, Northumberland, 1982-85; farming, Ross-shire, 1985-88; Elmwood College, Cupar, 1988-2001 (latterly as Assistant Principal); Principal, Oatridge Agricultural College, 2001-02. Church of Scotland Elder. Recreation: sailing.

Allan, Charles Maitland, MA, MUniv (Aberdeen). Journalist, Economist and Farmer; b. 19.8.39, Stirling; m., Fiona Vine; 2 s.; 2 d. Educ. Dartington Hall; Aberdeen University. Lecturer in Economic History, Glasgow University, 1962-63; Lecturer in Economics, St. Andrews University, 1963-65; Lecturer and Senior Lecturer, Strathclyde University, 1965-74; Producer/Presenter, BBC, 1982-86; Managing Editor, Ardo Publishing Co. Publications: Theory of Taxation; Death of a Papermill;

Farmer's Diary I, II, III, IV, V; Neeps and Strae; The Truth Tells Twice. Recreations: cycling; turning off television sets; World Caber Tossing Champion, 1972. Address: (h.) Whinhill of Ardo, Methlick, Ellon, Aberdeenshire; T.-01651 806 218; e-mail: chas@charlieallan.com

Allan, Eric, MA (Hons). Head Teacher, St. Matthew's Academy, Saltcoats, since 2006; b. 6.9.55, Inverness; m., Elaine; 2 d. Educ. Dingwall Academy; Glasgow University; Jordanhill College. Teacher: St. Andrew's Academy, Saltcoats, St. Brendan's High School, Linwood (Principal Teacher, Geography); Assistant Head Teacher, St. Brendan's, 1987-92; Depute Head Teacher, Trinity High School, Renfrew, 1992-94; Head Teacher, St. Michael's Academy, Kilwinning, 1994-2006. Recreations: golf; supporting Kilmarnock FC; reading; music. Address: (h.) 3 Holmes Crescent, Kilmarnock; T.-01563 524199.

Allan, Gary James Graham, QC, LLB (Hons); b. 21.1.58, Aberdeen; m., Margaret Muriel Glass; 1 s.; 1 d. Educ. Aberdeen Grammar School; University of Aberdeen. Legal apprenticeship, McGrigor Donald & Co., Solicitors, Glasgow and Edinburgh; qualified as Solicitor, 1982; Hughes Dowdall, Solicitors, Glasgow: joined as Assistant Solicitor, 1982, Partner, 1986-93; Admitted as a Member of the Faculty of Advocates, 1994; Advocate Depute ad hoc, 2001-07; Appointed Queen's Counsel, 2007; Appointed Senior Advocate Depute (Crown Counsel), 2007. Executive Member, Glasgow Bar Association, 1983-93; Local Parliamentary Liaison Officer, Law Society of Scotland, 1986-88; President, Aberdeen Grammar School Former Pupils' Club, 2007-08; Director, Hillhead High School War Memorial Trust Limited, since 2000. Address: (b.) Advocates Library, Parliament House, Parliament Square, Edinburgh EH1 1RF; T.-0131-226 5071; e-mail: gary.allan@compasschambers.com

Allan, George Alexander, MA (Hons). Headmaster, Robert Gordon's College, Aberdeen, 1978-96; b. 3.2.36, Edinburgh; m., Anne Violet Veevers; 2 s. Educ. Daniel Stewart's College, Edinburgh; Edinburgh University. Teacher of Classics, Glasgow Academy, 1958-60; Daniel Stewart's College: Teacher of Classics, 1960-63, Head of Classics, 1963-73 (appointed Housemaster, 1967); Schoolmaster Fellow Commoner, Corpus Christi College, Cambridge, 1972; Deputy Headmaster, Robert Gordon's College, 1973-77. Former Chairman and former Secretary, Headmasters' Conference (Scottish Division) (Member, National Committee, 1982 and 1983); Governor, Welbeck College, 1980-89; Council Member, Scottish Council of Independent Schools, 1988-96 and 1997-2002; Director, Edinburgh Academy, 1996-2003; Governor, Longridge Towers School, Berwick-upon-Tweed, since 2004. Recreations: gardening; music. Address: 5 Abbey View, Kelso, Roxburghshire TD5 8HX.

Allan, James Morrison, FRICS, MCIArb. Chartered Surveyor; b. 1.10.43, Edinburgh; m., Elizabeth Howie Sneddon Jack; 2 s. Educ. George Watson's College; Heriot Watt College. Joined Phillips Knox & Arthur as Apprentice Quantity Surveyor, 1960; qualified ARICS, 1965; FRICS, 1975; retired from partnership, 2004; RICS: Chairman, National Junior Organisation, 1975-76; Chairman, Quantity Surveyors Committee in Scotland, 1988-89; Chairman, RICS in Scotland, 1991-92; Member, RICS Management Board, 1992-95; Chairman, RICS Business Services Ltd., 1997-2003; Honorary Secretary, RICS, since 2004. Recreations: family; caravanning and motoring; golf. Address: (h.) 4 Stevenson Way, Longniddry, East Lothian EH32 0PF; T.-01875 852377.

Allan, Sheriff John Douglas, OBE, BL, DMS. Sheriff of Lothian and Borders at Edinburgh, since 2000; b. 2.10.41, Edinburgh; m., Helen E.J. Aiton; 1 s.; 1 d. Educ. George Watson's College, Edinburgh; Edinburgh University. Solicitor in private practice, Edinburgh, 1963-67;

Procurator Fiscal Depute, Edinburgh, 1967-71; Solicitor, Crown Office, Edinburgh, 1971-76; Assistant Procurator Fiscal, then Senior Assistant Procurator Fiscal, Glasgow, 1976-79; Solicitor, Crown Office, Edinburgh, 1979-83; Procurator Fiscal for Edinburgh and Regional Procurator Fiscal for Lothians and Borders, 1983-88; Sheriff of Lanark, 1988-2000. Part-time Lecturer in Law, Napier College, Edinburgh, 1963-66; Sheriffs' Association: Secretary, 1991-97, Vice-President, 1997-2000, President, 2000-2002; Chairman, Judicial Commission, General Assembly of the Church of Scotland, 1998-2003; Member, Board, Scottish Children's Reporter Administration, 1995-2003 (Deputy Chairman, 2002-03); Regional Vice-President, Commonwealth Magistrates' and Judges' Association, since 2003 (Council Member, 2000-03); Member, Judicial Appointments Board for Scotland, since 2002; Holder, Scout "Medal of Merit". Recreations: Scouts; youth leadership; walking; Church. Address: (b.) Sheriff Court House, 27 Chambers Street, Edinburgh EH1 1LB; T.-0131-225 2525; e-mail: Sheriff.JDAllan@scotcourts.gov.uk

Allan, Terence William, BSc (Eng) (Hons), MEd. Head of Computer Education, University of Aberdeen, since 2001; b. 8.10.47, Forres; m., Linda; 1 s.; 1 d. Educ. Elgin Academy; University of Aberdeen. Lecturer: Aberdeen College of Commerce, 1970-81, Aberdeen College of Education, 1981-88; Northern College: Senior Lecturer and Depute Head of Computer Education Department, 1988-94, Head of Computer Education Department, 1994-2001. Member of Executive Committee of Scottish Table Tennis Association, 1992-94; Chairman of Disciplinary Committee of Scottish Table Tennis Association, 1993-2002. Recreations: information technologies; photography; jogging; hifi; DIY. Address: (h.) 32 Middleton Circle, Bridge of Don, Aberdeen AB22 8NZ; T.-01224 821448; e-mail: terry@allans.org

Allen, Professor John Walter, MA, FSAS, FRSE. Professor of Solid State Physics, St. Andrews University, since 1980; b. 7.3.28, Birmingham. Educ. King Edward's High School, Birmingham; Sidney Sussex College, Cambridge. RAF, 1949-51; Staff Scientist, Ericsson Telephones Ltd., 1951-56; Services Electronics Research Laboratory, 1956-68; Visiting Associate Professor, Stanford University, 1964-66; joined Department of Physics, St. Andrews University, 1968. Recreations: archaeology; country dancing. Address: (b.) Department of Physics and Astronomy, St. Andrews University, North Haugh, St. Andrews, Fife KY16 9SS; T.-01334 463029; e-mail: jwa@st-andrews.ac.uk

Allen, Martin Angus William, MA, BD (1st Class Hons), ThM. Retired Minister, Chryston Parish Church of Scotland (1977-2007); b. 5.8.42, St. Andrews; m., Ann; 2 s. Educ. St. Andrews University; Edinburgh University; Covenant Seminary, St. Louis, USA. Assistant Education and Training Officer, Scottish Gas Board, 1964-71; Student in Theology, Edinburgh University, 1971-74; Assistant Minister, Church of Scotland, Wester Hailes, Edinburgh, 1974-75; Post Graduate Student, St. Louis, USA, 1975-76. Trustee, Rutherford House, Edinburgh - Theological Study Centre; Trustee and Chairman, Crieff Trust - (Ministers' Fellowship). Recreations: golf; walking; reading. Address: (h.) Lealenge, High Barrwood Road, Kilsyth G65 0EE; T.-01236 826616; e-mail: allensall@hotmail.com

Allison, Charles William, MBChB, FRCA. Consultant Anaesthetist, Stracathro Hospital, Brechin, since 1982; Consultant, Ninewells Hospital, Dundee; Honorary Senior Lecturer, Dundee University; b. 1.7.52, Newport on Tay; m., Elspeth Stratton; 2 d. Educ. Madras College, St. Andrews; Dundee University. Training grades in anaesthesia, Dundee, 1976-81; Clinical Research Fellow, Hospital for Sick Children, Toronto, 1982. Editor, Annals of the Scottish Society of Anaesthetists, 1999-2003;

President, NESSA, 2004-05; Secretary, DMGS, since 1982; Dean, Guildry of Brechin, 2007-09. Publications: papers and book chapter. Recreations: golf; photography. Address: Summerbank House, Brechin, Angus DD9 6HL; T.-01356 623624; e-mail: charlie18h@btinternet.com

Allon, Christina Macleod, BScSocSci, DipCG, CIM, FRSA, MICG; b. 8.5.53, Stornoway; m., John Paul Allon. Educ. Nicolson Institute, Stornoway; University of Edinburgh. Careers Adviser in Highland, 1978-83; Management roles within Grampian Regional Council, 1983-90; Regional Careers Officer, Grampian Regional Council, 1990-94; 1st Chief Executive of Grampian Careers, 1994-2001; 1st Director, Careers Scotland (SE), 2001-07. Board member, Bòrd na Gàidhlig, 2008. Recreations: walking; birdwatching; music; reading. Address: (b.) 2 Beachgate, Inverbervie, Angus DD10 0QZ; e-mail: jpcallon@msn.com

Almaini, Professor A.E.A., BSc(Eng), MSc, PhD, CEng, FIEE. Professor, School of Engineering, Napier University, since 1991; b. 1.7.45, Baghdad; m., Shirley May; 2 s.; 1 d. Educ. London University; Salford University; Loughborough University. Research Scientist, Scientific Research Foundation, 1970-79; Lecturer, then Senior Lecturer, Napier University, 1980-91. Publication: Electronic Logic Systems (book); many papers published. Recreation: gardening. Address: (b.) School of Engineering, Merchiston Campus, Edinburgh EH10 5DT; T.-0131-455 2325.

Alstead, Brigadier (Francis) Allan (Littlejohns), CBE, DL, MPhil, FCILT, FCMI, FCIPD, FInstAM, FInstD, FBISA. Director, Alstead Consulting, since 2000; Chief Executive, sportscotland (formerly Scottish Sports Council), 1990-2000; Chef de Mission for Scottish Team, Commonwealth Games 2002; Chairman, Mercy Corps Scotland, since 2001; Board Member, Mercy Corps International, USA, since 2001; Board Member, CRP (Bosnia), since 2005; b. 19.6.35, Glasgow; m., Joy Veronica Edwards; 2 s. Educ. Glasgow Academy; Royal Military Academy, Sandhurst; Royal Naval Staff College; Joint Services Staff College; Edinburgh University; University of Wales, Aberystwyth. Commissioned into King's Own Scottish Borderers, 1955; commanded 1st Bn., KOSB, 1974-76 (Mention in Despatches); Military Assistant to Quarter-Master-General, 1976-79; Instructor, Army Staff College, Camberley, 1979-81; Assistant Chief of Staff, BAOR, 1981-84 (Colonel); Commander, 51st Highland Brigade, 1984-87 (Brigadier); NATO Research Fellow, Edinburgh University, 1987-88; NATO HQ Reinforcement Co-ordinator, 1988-90. Member, Royal Company of Archers (Queen's Bodyguard in Scotland); Deputy Lieutenant, City of Edinburgh; Regimental Trustee, KOSB, 1980-2006; Trustee, KOSB Association, since 2006; Trustee, Youth Sport Trust, 1992-99; Deputy Hon. Colonel, City of Edinburgh Universities OTC, 1990-99; Governor: Moray House College, 1991-97, Glasgow Academy, 1995-2001; Member, Executive, Scottish Council, Development and Industry, since 1995; Member, Lowland TAVRA; Trustee, Council for the Advancement of Arts, Recreation and Education; Director and Trustee, Seagull Trust, 1995-2007; Non-Executive Director, JRG Ltd, 1996-2007; Member, General Council, Erskine Hospital; Member, Council, National Playing Fields Association, 2001-07; President, SSAFA, Edinburgh, East and Midlothian, 1990-98 and 2003; FRSA, 1994-2002. Publications: Ten in Ten; The Reinforcement of Europe in Crisis and War. Recreations: walking; archery; tennis. Address: (h.) 49 Moray Place, Edinburgh EH3 6BQ.

Althaus-Reid, Professor Marcella Maria, BEd, BTh, PhD. Professor of Contextual Theology, Edinburgh University, since 2006; b. Rosario, Argentina. Educ. ISEDET, Buenos Aires; St. Andrews University, Scotland. University of Edinburgh: Quaker Fellow of Joseph

Rowntree Charitable Trust and Honorary Fellow of the Centre for Theology and Public Issues, 1994, Lecturer and Director of the MTh in Theology and Development, 1994-2003; Senior Lecturer, then Reader in Theology, 2001-05. Visiting Professor: Dartmouth College, New Hampshire (1998); Methodist University of Sao Paulo, Brazil (2005). Member: International Academy of Practical Theology; The American Academy of Religion (AAR); European Society of Women in Theological Research; Executive Committee and Theological Panel member of the Centre for Theology and Public Issues, Edinburgh University; Theological Advisory Panel, Metropolitan Community Church, USA; founding member of the AAR Consultation Groups: 1) Queer Theory and LGBT Studies in Religion; 2) Liberation Theology and Consultation. Honorary President of the Scottish Theological Society, 2004-05; President of the Edinburgh Queer Theology Project, 2007. Executive series editor: Gender and Spirituality (Equinox, with L Isherwood); Queer Theology (Continuum, with L Isherwood); Reclaiming Liberation Theology (SCM, with I Petrella); Controversies in Contextual Theology (SCM, with L Isherwood). Publications: Books include: Indecent Theology. Theological Perversions in Sex, Gender and Politics; La Teologia Indecente. Perversiones Teológicas en Sexualidad, Género y Teología; The Queer God; The Sexual Theologian. Address: (b.) Edinburgh University, New College, Mound Place, Edinburgh EH1 2LX; T.-0131-650-8914; e-mail: marcella.althaus-reid@ed.ac.uk

Amyes, Professor Sebastian Giles Becket, BSc, MSc, PhD, DSc, Drhc, FRCPath, FIBiol. Professor of Microbial Chemotherapy and Head of Medical Microbiology Department, Edinburgh University; b. 6.5.49, Stockton Heath; 1 s.; 1 d. Educ. Cranleigh School; University College, London. Edinburgh University, since 1977; Reader, 1988; Professor, 1992, Head of Medical Microbiology Department, 1997-2000. Royal Pharmaceutical Society annual conference award, 1984; C.L. Oakley lectureship, Pathological Society, 1987; Doctor honoris causa, Semmelweis University, Hungary, 2004; Honorary member of the Hungarian Society of Microbiology, 2007. Recreations: fishing; opera; golf; exploring parts of the world that the tour companies have not yet found. Address: (b.) Molecular Chemotherapy, Centre for Infectious Diseases, Little France, Edinburgh EH16 4SB; T.-0131 242 6652.

Anderson, Andrew Duncan, MA, LLB. Formerly Senior Partner, then Consultant, James Guthrie and Co., Solicitors, Kilmarnock; President, Scottish Law Agents Society, 2001-02; b. 23.12.41, Kilmarnock; m., Eveline; 3 s. Educ. Kilmarnock Academy; Glasgow University. Joined James Guthrie and Co., 1967 (Partner, since 1971). Council Member, Scottish Law Agents Society, 1992-2005. Chairman (part-time), Tribunals, Appeals Service; Dean, Kilmarnock Faculty of Solicitors, 1992. Recreations: golf; bridge; gardening. Address: (b.) 3 Portland Road, Kilmarnock KA1 2AN; T.-01563 525155; e-mail: Andrewdanderson@aol.com

Anderson, Professor Annie S., BSc, PhD, SRD. Professor of Food Choice, Department of Medicine, University of Dundee, Director, Centre for Public Health Nutrition Research, since 1996; b. 24.12.57, Torphins. Educ. Cults Academy, Aberdeen; RGIT; University of Aberdeen. Dietitian, Cambridge Area Health Authority, 1979-81; Research Assistant, Medical School, University of Cambridge, 1982-84; Research Dietitian, Grampian Health Board, 1985-86; Postgraduate Research Student, Department of Obstetrics, University of Aberdeen, 1987-91; Research Fellow (Human Nutrition), University of Glasgow, 1991-96; Member, Dundee University Court, 1999-2001; Editor, Journal of Human Nutrition and Dietetics; Member, Scientific Advisory Committee on Nutrition, 2001-04, 2004-08. Recreation: genealogy. Address: Mansefield House, Dundee Road, Meigle PH12 8SF; T.-01382 496442; e-mail: a.s.anderson@dundee.ac.uk

Anderson, David Alexander, BA (Hons), MEd, FCIPD. Senior Director of Operations, Scottish Enterprise Edinburgh and Lothian, since 2006; b. 2.12.54, Perth; m., Tricia; 3 s.; 1 d. Educ. Arbroath High School; University of Stirling; University of Newcastle; University of Sheffield. Graduate Management Trainee, Department of Employment; Local Office Manager, Newcastle, Department of Employment, 1980-84; Manpower Services Commission: Programme Development Manager, Newcastle, 1984-86, Policy Manager, Head Office, Sheffield, 1986-90; Operations Manager, Training Agency, Ayrshire, 1990-91; Director of Skills Development, Enterprise Ayrshire, 1991-97; Chief Executive, Scottish Enterprise Dunbartonshire, 1998-2006. Chairman, The Keynote Trust; Director: Waterfront Edinburgh Limited, since 2006, Edinburgh Chamber of Commerce Council. Recreations: golf; music; hillwalking. Address: (b.) Apex House, 99 Haymarket Terrace, Edinburgh EH12 5HD; T.-0131-313-4000.

Anderson, David Rae, MA (Hons), LLB, LLM, WS, NP. Solicitor, since 1961 (Senior Partner, Allan Grant Solicitors); Honorary Sheriff, since 1981; b. 27.1.36, Stonehaven; m., (i) Jean Strachan (deceased); (ii) Jean Elizabeth Anderstrem. Educ. Mackie Academy, Stonehaven; Aberdeen University; Edinburgh University; Australian National University, Canberra. Barrister and Solicitor of Supreme Court of Victoria, Australia, 1962; Legal Officer, Attorney-General's Department, Canberra, 1962-65; part-time research student, Law Faculty, Australian National University, Canberra, and part-time Lecturer in Legal History, 1962-65; returned to Scotland, 1965, in private legal practice, Edinburgh, 1965-67, Alloa and Central Scotland, since 1967; Interim Town Clerk, Burgh of Alva, 1973; part-time Legal Chairman, Employment (formerly Industrial) Tribunals, 1972-2006 (retired); former part-time Reporter to Secretary of State for Scotland for public enquiries; thrice Dean, Society of Solicitors of Clackmannanshire; Member, Council, Law Society of Scotland, 1984-2000; Council Member, Scottish Universities Law Institute; former Council Member and Hon. Treasurer, Commonwealth Lawyers Association; former Member, UK Delegation, Council of the Bars and Law Societies of the European Community; Member, Stirling University Conference; Elder, Church of Scotland; Parliamentary candidate, 1970 and 1971; formerly served, RNVR; Past President, Alloa Rotary Club; Past President, Alloa Burns Club. Recreations: climbing and hill-walking; reading, especially historical biography and English literature; music, especially opera; interested in current affairs, architecture, stately homes and travel. Address: (h.) Larklea, Barrack Road, Comrie, Perthshire PH6 2EQ; T.-01764 670829; 33 Buckingham Terrace, Edinburgh EH4 3AF; T.-0131 332 5164; (b.) 8 Shillinghill, Alloa FK10 1JT; T.-01259 723201.

Anderson, Dorothy Elizabeth, BSc (Hons), MB, ChB, MRCP(UK), DMRD, FRCR, FRCP(Glas). Consultant Radiologist, Glasgow Royal Infirmary, since 1981; Honorary Clinical Lecturer, then Senior Lecturer, Glasgow University, since 1982; b. 1950, Glasgow; m., David Anderson; 1 s.; 1 d. Educ. Glasgow High School for Girls; Glasgow University. Pre-registration posts, Stobhill Hospital and Glasgow Royal Infirmary; post-registration year, Respiratory Unit, Knightswood Hospital; trained in radiology, Western Infirmary, Glasgow (Registrar, then Senior Registrar). Recreation: choral singing; walking; reading; history. Address: (b.) X-Ray Department, Glasgow

Royal Infirmary, Alexandra Parade, Glasgow G31 2ER; T.-0141-211-5565.
E-mail: Dorothy.Anderson@northglasgow.scot.nhs.uk

Anderson, Douglas Kinloch, OBE, MA. Chairman, Kinloch Anderson (Holdings) Ltd., Edinburgh, since 1975; Director: Martin Currie Portfolio Investment Trust PLC; Fidelity Special Values PLC; F & C Private Equity Trust PLC; b. 19.2.39, Edinburgh; m., Deirdre Anne; 2 s.; 1 d. Educ. George Watson's Boys College; St. Andrews University. Joined Kinloch Anderson Ltd., 1962 (fifth generation in family business); Assistant on Master's Court, Edinburgh Merchant Company, 1976-79; elected Honorary Member, St. Andrew's Society of Washington DC, 1985; Board Member, Scottish Tourist Board, 1986-92; Member, Edinburgh Festival Council, 1988-90; President, Edinburgh Royal Warrant Holders Association, 1987-88; former Member, Scottish Committee, Institute of Directors; President, Edinburgh Chamber of Commerce, 1988-90; Master, Edinburgh Merchant Company, 1990-92; Deputy Chairman, Edinburgh Marketing Ltd., 1990-92; Director, Lothian and Edinburgh Enterprise Ltd., 1990-95; elected Leith High Constable, 1993; Freeman, City of London; President, Royal Warrant Holders Association. Recreations: golf; fishing; watching rugby; travel (non-business). Address: (b.) Commercial Street/Dock Street, Leith, Edinburgh EH6 6EY; T.-0131-555 1355.

Anderson, Elaine, MB, ChB, FRCSEd, MD. Clinical Director, South East Scotland Breast Screening, since 2002; Consultant Surgeon, since 1994; b. 19.10.58; m., Richard Robinson. Educ. Trinity Academy, Edinburgh; Edinburgh University. Accreditation in general surgery, 1993. Recreations: sailing; gardening; running. Address: (b.) Breast Unit, Western General Hospital, Crewe Road, Edinburgh EH4 2XU; T.-0131 537 1614.

Anderson, Gavin John, LLB (Hons), DipLP. Advocate, since 2001; b. 22.8.71, Edinburgh. Educ. St Thomas of Aquin's High School, Edinburgh; Aberdeen University. Solicitor, Anderson Strathern WS, Edinburgh, 1995; Whitten & Co., Broxburn, 1996-2000; awarded Faculty of Advocates Scholarship, 2000; admitted to Faculty, 2001. Recreations: golf; classic cars. Address: (b.) Advocates' Library, Parliament House, Edinburgh EH1 1RF; T.-0131 226 5071.

Anderson, Gordon Alexander, CBE, CA, FCMA. Chartered Accountant; b. 9.8.31, Glasgow; m., Eirene Cochrane Howie Douglas; 2 s.; 1 d. Educ. High School of Glasgow. Apprentice CA, Moores Carson & Watson, Glasgow, 1949-54; qualified CA, 1955; National Service, Royal Navy, 1955-57 (Sub Lieutenant); Partner, Moores Carson & Watson, 1958 (firm name changed to McClelland Moores, 1958, Arthur Young McClelland Moores, 1968, Arthur Young, 1985, Ernst & Young, 1989); Chairman, Arthur Young, 1987-89; Deputy Senior Partner, Ernst & Young, 1989-90; Director: Lloyds TSB Group plc, 1993-99, TSB Bank Scotland plc, 1991-99 (Chairman, 1994-99), High School of Glasgow Ltd., 1975-81 and 1990-2001 (Chairman of Governors, 1992-2001), Merchants House of Glasgow, 1996-2002; Member, Council on Tribunals and of its Scottish Committee, 1990-96; Chairman, Bitmac Ltd., 1990-96; Director: Douglas Firebrick Co. Ltd., 1960-70; Member, Scottish Milk Marketing Board, 1979-85; Institute of Chartered Accountants of Scotland: Member, Council, 1980-84, Vice President, 1984-86, President, 1986-87. Recreations: golf; gardening. Address: (h.) 4 Manse Road Gardens, Bearsden, Glasgow G61 3PJ; T.-0141-942 2803.

Anderson, Iain Buchanan, MA, DipEd, LGSM. Music Presenter/Sports Commentator, BBC, since 1985; m., Marion Elizabeth; 3 s.; 1 d. Educ. Bellahouston Academy, Glasgow; Glasgow University; Guildhall School. Lecturer in Speech and Drama, Jordanhill College, 1967; Arts Editor/Presenter, Radio Clyde, 1974. Former Rugby Correspondent, Scotland on Sunday. Address: (h.) Elmhurst, Station Road, Langbank PA14 6YA; T.-0147 554 0733.

Anderson, Ian Wilson Russell, MBChB, FRCS (Glasgow), FRCS (England), FRCS (Edinburgh), FCEM, FRCP (Glasgow), FIFEM, FRCP (London). Consultant, Accident and Emergency, Victoria Infirmary, Glasgow; Honorary Clinical Senior Lecturer, University of Glasgow; b. 4.5.51, Prestwick. Educ. Ayr Academy; University of Glasgow. House Officer posts, Glasgow; completed general professional training in surgery, 1980; completed specialist training in accident and emergency medicine and surgery, 1984; main interest in initial assessment and resuscitation of trauma. Director, Medical and Dental Defence Union of Scotland; Past President, Faculty of Accident and Emergency Medicine; Royal College of Physicians and Surgeons of Glasgow: Member, Council; Hon. Treasurer. Recreations: travel; golf; motoring. Address: Accident and Emergency Department, Victoria Infirmary, Glasgow G42 9TY; T.-0141-201 5305.

Anderson, James A., MA, MEd, MBA, DipEd. Director of Education, Angus Council, since 1995; b. 21.8.49, Aberdeen; m., Linda; 1 s.; 1 d. Educ. Aberdeen Grammar School; Aberdeen University; Edinburgh University; Stirling University. Teacher, Assistant Principal Teacher, Principal Teacher of Mathematics, 1973-84; Tayside Regional Council: Assistant Director of Education, 1984-87, Area Education Officer, 1987-91, Senior Assistant Director of Education, 1991-95, Director of Education, 1995-96. Recreations: golf; bridge. Address: (b.) Angus Council, Angus House, Orchardbank Business Park, Forfar DD8 1AE; T.-01307 476300.

Anderson, Kenneth, MBChB, MD, FRCP (Glas & Edin). Consultant Physician with special interest in respiratory medicine; b. Glasgow; m., M. Ruth Adamson. Educ. Allan Glen's School; Glasgow University. Visiting Physician, University of Colorado Hospitals, Denver. Honorary Senior Lecturer, Medicine, University of Glasgow; Member, Scottish and British Thoracic Societies. Recreations: rugby; golf; tennis; gardens. Address: Crosshouse Hospital, Kilmarnock KA2 0BE; T.-01563 577903.

Anderson, Professor Michael, OBE, MA, PhD, Dr hc, FBA, FRSE, FRHistSoc, Hon FFA. Professor of Economic History, University of Edinburgh, since 1979; b. 21.2.42, Woking; m. (1), Rosemary Elizabeth Kitching; 1 s.; 1 d.; m. (2), Elspeth MacArthur. Educ. Kingston Grammar School; Queens' College, Cambridge. University of Edinburgh: Assistant Lecturer, 1967-69, Lecturer, 1969-75, Reader, 1975-79, Dean of Faculty of Social Sciences, 1985-89, Vice-Principal, 1989-93, and 1997-2000, Acting Principal, 1994, Senior Vice-Principal, 2000-07. Member: Scottish Records Advisory Council, 1984-93, Economic and Social Research Council, 1990-94, Follett Committee on Libraries and Follett Implementation Group, 1993-97, British Library Board, 1994-2003, Council of British Academy, 1995-98; Curator, Royal Society of Edinburgh, 1997-99; Trustee, National Library of Scotland, since 1998, Chairman, since 2000; Chairman, Research Support Libraries Programme, 1998-2003. Publications: Family Structure in Nineteenth Century Lancashire, 1971; Approaches to the History of the Western Family, 1981; Population Change in North-Western Europe 1750-1850; many papers on family sociology and history and historical demography. Recreations: natural history; gardening; study of ancient civilisations. Address: (b.) School of History and Classics, University of Edinburgh, William Robertson Building, George Square, Edinburgh EH8 9JY; T.-0131-650 3844.

Anderson, Moira, OBE. Singer; b. Kirkintilloch; m., Dr. Stuart Macdonald. Educ. Ayr Academy; Royal Scottish Academy of Music, Glasgow. Began with Kirkintilloch Junior Choir, aged six; made first radio broadcast for BBC in Scotland, aged eight; was Teacher of Music in Ayr before becoming professional singer; made first professional broadcast, White Heather Club, 1960; has toured overseas, had her own radio and TV series; has introduced Stars on Sunday, ITV; appeared in summer shows, cabaret, pantomime and numerous other stage shows; several Royal Variety performances.

Anderson, Neil Robert, LLB (Hons), DipLP, NP. Partner, Biggart Baillie, Solicitors, since 2003; b. 10.5.71, Edinburgh; m., Jill Shaw Andrew. Educ. Dalkeith High School; University of Aberdeen. Trained, Fyfe Ireland WS, Edinburgh, 1994-96; Biggart Baillie, Glasgow: Assistant, 1996-99, Associate, 1999-2003. Recreations: cinema/film; orchid cultivation; travel to unusual destinations. Address: (b.) 7 Castle Street, Edinburgh EH2 3AP; T.-0131 474 2367; e-mail: nranderson@biggartbaillie.co.uk

Anderson, Peter David, MA, PhD, FSA Scot, FRHistS, FRSA. Deputy Keeper, National Archives of Scotland (formerly Scottish Record Office), since 1993; b. 10.3.47, Greenock; m., Jean Johnstone Smith; 1 d.; 1 s. (deceased). Educ. Hutchesons' Grammar School, Glasgow; St. Andrews University; Edinburgh University. Teacher of History, Cranhill Secondary School, Glasgow, 1972-73; Research Assistant, Scottish Record Office, 1974-80; Registrar, National Register of Archives (Scotland), 1980-83; Secretary, NRA(S), 1984-85; Conservation Officer, 1985-89; Head, Records Liaison Branch, 1989-93. Chair, International Council on Archives Committee on Archive Buildings and Equipment, 1996-2004; Chair, Society of Archivists, 2005-07; External Examiner, Dundee University Centre for Archive and Information Studies, since 2005; Secretary, Scottish Oral History Group, 1984-88, Deputy Convener, since 1988; Chair, Linlithgow Players, 1994-97. Publications: Robert Stewart, Earl of Orkney, Lord of Shetland, 1533-93, 1982; Black Patie, 1993. Recreations: drawing and painting; drama. Address: (b.) National Archives of Scotland, HM General Register House, Edinburgh EH1 3YY; T.-0131-535 1406.

Anderson, Robert Alexander, LLB, DipLP, NP. Solicitor, since 1983; Partner, Lindsay & Kirk, Aberdeen, since 1988; President, Aberdeen Bar Association,1996-98; b. 31.5.60, Nairn; m., Nicola Mary; 1 s.; 1 d. Educ. Nairn Academy; University of Glasgow. Trained at J.A. McGoogan & Co., Coatbridge, 1981-83, Legal Assistant, 1983-85; Legal Assistant, Lindsay & Kirk, Aberdeen, 1985-88. Involved on voluntary basis with Aberdeen Women's Aid; Tutor in Criminal Court Practice, Aberdeen University. Recreation: orienteering. Address: (b.) 39 Huntly Street, Aberdeen AB10 1TJ; T.-01224 641402.

Anderson, Robert Alexander, MA, BD (Glas), DPhil (Oxon). Minister, Blackburn and Seafield Church, since 1998; b. 3.4.47, Kilwinning; m., Christine Main; 2 step s.; 1 step d. Educ. Kilwinning High School; Irvine Royal Academy; Glasgow University; Hertford College, Oxford. Missionary of The Church of Scotland as Tutor in Theology at St. Paul's United Theological College, Limuru, Kenya, 1980-86; Head of Theology and Philosophy, 1984-86; Dean of Studies, 1982-83 and 1984-85; Minister, Overtown Parish Church, 1986-89; P/T Chaplain, Shotts Prison, 1988-89; Chaplain, Edinburgh University, 1989-94; Development Officer, Carberry Tower, 1994-96. Publications: Intimations of Love Divine, 1996; Stop The World, I Want To Think, 1998; Who Cares Wins, 2000; Changes in Spiritual Freedom in the Church of Scotland, 2005. Recreation: golf. Address: (b.) 5 MacDonald Gardens, Blackburn EH47 7RE; T.-01506 652825; e-mail: robertanderson307@btinternet.com

Anderson, Rev. Robert Scott, MA, BD (Hons), FRSA. Chief Executive, Scottish Churches World Exchange, since 1986; Principal, St. Colm's International House; b. 11.11.57, Glasgow; 1 s.; 2 d. Educ. Hutchesons' Boys' Grammar School; Glasgow University. Member: Scottish Arts Club, Royal Burgess Golfing Society; Trustee: Scottish Community Foundation; Chair: Scottish Malawi Foundation. Recreations: skiing; walking; orchid growing; reading poetry; literature; golf. Address: St. Colm's International House, 23 Inverleith Terrace, Edinburgh; e-mail: we@stcolms.org

Anderson, Very Rev. Canon William Rutherfoord Turnbull, MA, FTCL. Formerly Parish Priest, St. Francis R.C. Church, Aberdeen (retired), previously Administrator, St. Mary's R.C. Cathedral, Aberdeen; b. 7.1.31, Glasgow. Educ. George Watson's College, Edinburgh; University of Edinburgh; Sidney Sussex College, Cambridge. Curate, St. David's, Dalkeith, 1960-61; staff, St. Mary's College, Blairs, Aberdeen, 1961-69; Producer, BBC Scotland Religious Department, 1969-77; Spiritual Director, Pontifical Scots College, Rome, 1977-85; staff, St. Mary's College, Blairs, Aberdeen, 1985-86; R.C. Chaplain, University of Aberdeen, 1986-93. Canon, R.C. Diocese of Aberdeen; former Major Scholar, Sidney Sussex College, Cambridge; Poetry Society Gold Medal for verse-speaking, 1980; Preacher of the Year, The Times and College of Preachers, 1996; Warrack Lecturer, Aberdeen University, 1998; Hon. teaching fellow (Latin), Aberdeen University, since 2005. Recreations: walking; music and poetry; contributing to Press and Journal; postgraduate studies. Address: 1 Morningside Terrace, Aberdeen AB10 7NZ.

Andrew, Hugh, BA (Oxon), FSA Scot. Managing Director, Birlinn Ltd (incorporating John Donald, Polygon and Tuckwell Press); Managing Director, Seol Ltd.; Director, Compass Academic Book Sales Ltd.; b. 8.4.62. Educ. Glasgow Academy; Magdalen College, Oxford. Set up own publishing company, Birlinn Ltd., 1992; Joint Managing Director, Canongate Books, 1994-99. Recreations: reading; music; travel; archaeology; history; islands. Address: (b.) West Newington House, 10 Newington Road, Edinburgh EH9 1QS; T.-0131-668 4371; e-mail: hugh@birlinn.co.uk

Andrew, John Anthony, MA, FRICS. Chief Property Adviser, Scottish Government, since 1996; b. 10.10.52, Ormskirk; m., Mary MacLeod MacKay; 3 s. Educ. Ormskirk Grammar School; Heanor Grammar School; Downing College, University of Cambridge. Valuation Office, Inland Revenue, Cleveland North, 1976-78; Lecturer in Land Economy, University of Aberdeen, 1978-81; Valuation Office, Inland Revenue, Aberdeen and Dumfries, 1981-89; Principal Estates Surveyor, Scottish Office, 1989-92 and 1994-96; Principal, Scottish Office Agriculture and Fisheries Department, Land Use and Conservation Division, 1992-94. Vice Chairman, RICS in Scotland, 2002; Member: RICS Scottish Council, RICS Scottish Valuation Faculty Board, Castle Rock Edinvar Housing Association Ltd. Management Committee; External Examiner, Heriot-Watt University, 1999-2003, Napier University, since 2003, Aberdeen University, since 2007; Member, Editorial Advisory Board, Journal of Facilities Management; Area Coordinator, Compassion UK. Address: Scottish Government Property Advice Division, U/1 Spur, Saughton House, Broomhouse Drive, Edinburgh EH11 3XD; T.-0131-244 4521.
E-mail: anthony.andrew@scotland.gsi.gov.uk

Andrews, James Edward, BA, MA, BD, DipCG. Retired Minister and Writer; Chaplain, Army Cadet Force, since 1998; b. 2.5.45, Downpatrick; m., Margaret Elizabeth McWhirter; 2 s. Educ. Belfast Royal Academy; Magee University College Londonderry; University of Dublin (Trinity College); University of Edinburgh. Careers Officer until 1981; Licensed Presbytery of West Lothian, 1984; Assistant Minister, Jedburgh Old Parish Church; Minister,

Ardrishaig Linked with South Knapdale, 1985-91; Minister, St. Nicholas Buccleugh Parish Church, Dalkeith, 1991-2002; Chrichton West and St. Ninian's Parish Church, Cumnock, 2002-03; Minister, Armadale Parish Church, 2003-05. Moderator, Presbytery of South Argyll, 1990-91. Recreations: fishing; hunting for golf balls; reading. Address: (h.) 1a Meadowpark, Haddington EH41 4DS; T.-01620 829804; e-mail: edward.andrews@btinternet.com

Andrews, Professor June, RMN, RGN, MA(Hons). Director, Dementia Services Development Centre, University of Stirling; former Director, Centre for Change and Innovation, Health Department, Scottish Executive; b. Kilwinning. Educ. Ardrossan Academy; Glasgow University; Nottingham University. NHS nursing and management posts, Nottingham and London; Director of Nursing, Forth Valley Acute Hospitals NHS Trust; Royal College of Nursing: adviser on ethics and Aids, Assistant Director Policy and Research, Scottish Board Secretary. Address: (b.) Department of Applied Social Science, University of Stirling, Stirling FK9 4LA.

Angiolini, Elish Frances, QC, WS, LLB (Hons), DipLP. Lord Advocate, since 2006; b. 24.6.60; m.; 2 c. Educ. Notre Dame High School, Glasgow; Strathclyde University. Traineeship, Crown Office, 1983-84; Procurator Fiscal Depute, South Strathclyde, 1984-90; Crown Office: Senior Legal Assistant, Law Officers' Secretariat, 1990-92; Senior Depute Procurator Fiscal, Management Services Group, 1992-94; Senior Depute Procurator Fiscal, Solemn Unit, Procurator Fiscal's Office, Glasgow, 1994-95; Assistant Procurator Fiscal, Glasgow, 1995-97; Head, Crown Office and Procurator Fiscal Service Policy Group, 1997-2000; Regional Procurator Fiscal, Grampian, Highland and Islands, 2000-2001; Solicitor General for Scotland, 2001-06. Address: (b.) 25 Chambers Street, Edinburgh EH1 1LA.

Angus, Rae, MA (Hons), MLitt, LLD, DEd, FRSA, MCIPD. Principal, Aberdeen College, since 1993; b. 1947, Ellon; m., Alison Hay; 2 d. Educ. Peterhead Academy; Aberdeen University. Further Education Lecturer, 1975; Research Fellow, Aberdeen University, 1978-80; Aberdeen College of Commerce, 1981-90, latterly as Depute Principal; Depute Principal, Aberdeen College of Further Education, 1991-90. Recreations: reading; walking; computing. Address: (b.) Gallowgate, Aberdeen AB25 1BN; T.-01224 612000.

Annand, David Andrew, DA, ARBS, JP. Sculptor; b. 30.1.48, Insch, Aberdeenshire; m., Jean; 1 s.; 1 d. Educ. Perth Academy; Duncan of Jordanstone College of Art, Dundee. Lecturer, Sculpture Department, Duncan of Jordanstone College of Art, Dundee, 1972-74; Art Department, St. Saviour's High School, Dundee, 1975-88; full-time sculptor, since 1988; RSA Latimer Award, 1976; RSA Benno Schotz Award, 1978; RSA Ireland Alloys Award, 1982; Scottish Development Agency Dundee Technology Park Competition, 1986, "Deer Leap", Sir Otto Beit Medal, 1986; Royal Botanic Garden, Edinburgh "Ardea Cinerea", 1987; Winner, Almswall Road Sculpture Competition, Irvine Development Corporation, "The Ring", 1989; Winner, Perth High Street Sculpture Competition, Perth Partnership "Nae Day Sae Dark", 1989; Baxters of Speyside "Royal Stag" cast by Powderhall Bronze, 1993; Tranent Massacre Memorial bronze casting by Powderhall Bronze, 1995; Winner, competition to design sculpture for Lord Street, Wrexham, 1995, "Y Bwa" Civic Society Award, 1995; Winner, competition to design sculpture, Ashworth Roundabout, Blackpool, "Helter-skelter", 1995; Strathcarron Hospice composition, 1996; British High Commission Hong Kong, "Three Cranes in Flight", 1997;

Hamilton Town Square "Strongman", 1998; Aberdeen Angus Bull, Alford, 2001; The Declaration of Arbroath, Arbroath, 2001; Civic Pride, Barnet, London, 2001; other commissions completed in 2001 for BT Brentwood and Maidstone Borough Council; Winner of project to create a memorial to the poet Robert Fergusson, 2002; Sir Jimmy Shand Memorial, 2003. Recreations: music; bird watching; wine and food. Address: Pigscrave Cottage, The Wynd, Kilmany, Cupar, Fife KY15 4PT; T.-01382 330 714.

Annand, Louise Gibson, MBE, MA (Hons), AMA, DU. Artist; b. 27.5.15, Uddingston; m., 1, Alistair Matheson (deceased); 2, Roderick MacFarquhar (deceased). Educ. Hamilton Academy; Glasgow University. Teacher, primary and secondary schools, Glasgow, 1939-49; Assistant, Schools Museum Service, 1949-70; Museums Education Officer, 1970-80. Past Chairman: Scottish Educational Film Association (Glasgow Production Group); Glasgow Lady Artists Club Trust; National Vice-Chairman, Scottish Educational Media Association, 1979-84; President: Society of Scottish Women Artists, 1963-66 and 1980-85; Member, Royal Fine Art Commission for Scotland, 1979-86; President, Glasgow Society of Women Artists, 1977-79, 1988-91; Visiting Lecturer in Scottish Art, Regina University, 1982; Chairman, J.D. Fergusson Foundation, 1982-2001; Member, Business Committee, General Council, University of Glasgow, 1981-85, 1988-91; Honorary Member, Saltire Society, since 1993; DUniv, Glasgow University, 1994; exhibited widely since 1945; produced numerous 16mm films, including the first on Charles Rennie Mackintosh, 1966. Recreations: mountaineering (Ladies Scottish Climbing Club). Address: (h.) 22 Kingsborough Gardens, Glasgow G12 9NJ; T.-0141-339 8956.

Annandale and Hartfell, 11th Earl of (Patrick Andrew Wentworth Hope Johnstone of Annandale and of That Ilk). Chief, Clan Johnstone; Baron of the Barony of the Lands of the Earldom of Annandale and Hartfell, and of the Lordship of Johnstone; Hereditary Steward, Stewartry of Annandale; Hereditary Keeper, Keys of Lochmaben Castle; Deputy Lieutenant, Dumfriesshire, 1987-92, Vice-Lieutenant, since 1992; b. 19.4.41, Auldgirth, Dumfriesshire; m., Susan Josephine; 1 s.; 1 d. Educ. Stowe School; Royal Agricultural College, Cirencester. Member: Dumfriesshire County Council, 1970-75, Dumfries and Galloway Regional Council, 1975-85, Scottish Valuation Advisory Council, 1982, Solway River Purification Board, 1973-85; Underwriter, Lloyds, London, 1976-2004. Address: (b.) Annandale Estates Office, St. Anns, Lockerbie DG11 1HQ.

Anthony, Robert Brown, QC. Sheriff of Glasgow and Strathkelvin, since 2007. Admitted as a solicitor, 1984 and to the Faculty of Advocates, 1988, took silk in 2002; served as an Advocate Depute, and latterly as a senior Advocate Depute, from 2001 until 2004; appointed as a part-time sheriff, 2005. Commissioner, the Scottish Criminal Cases Review Commission, since 2007. Address: (b.) 1 Carlton Place, Glasgow G5 9DA; T.-0141-429 8888.

Anton, Alexander Elder, CBE, MA, LLB, LLD (Hon), FBA; b. 1922; m., Doris May Lawrence; 1 s. Educ. Aberdeen University. Solicitor, 1949; Lecturer, Aberdeen 1953-59; Professor of Jurisprudence, Glasgow University, 1959-73; Honorary Professor, 1984, Aberdeen University; Member, Scottish Law Commission, 1966-82; UK Delegate to Hague Conference on Private International Law, 1964-82; Chairman, Scottish Rights of Way Society, 1988-92. Publications: Private International Law, 1967 and 1990; Civil Jurisdiction in Scotland, 1984. Recreation: hill-walking. Address: (h.) 5 Seafield Drive West, Aberdeen AB15 7XA.

Arbuthnott, 16th Viscount of (John Campbell Arbuthnott), KT, CBE, DSC, FRSE, FRSA, BGCOStJ,

LLD. Lord Lieutenant, Kincardineshire, 1977-99; b. 26.10.24; m, Mary Oxley; 1 s.; 1 d. Educ. Fettes College; Gonville and Caius College, Cambridge. Served RNVR (Fleet Air Arm), 1942-46. Member, Countryside Commission for Scotland, 1967-71; Chairman, Red Deer Commission, 1969-75; Member, Aberdeen University Court, 1978-84; President, Scottish Landowners Federation, 1974-79; President, Royal Scottish Geographical Society, 1984-87; Chairman, Scottish Widows' Fund and Life Assurance Society, 1984-87; Lord High Commissioner to the General Assembly of the Church of Scotland, 1986, 1987; President, Royal Zoological Society of Scotland, 1976-96; President, Scottish Agricultural Organisation Society, 1980-83; President, Federation of Agricultural Cooperatives (UK), 1983-87; Deputy Chairman, Nature Conservancy Council, 1980-85, and Chairman, Scottish Committee, NCC; Chairman, Aberdeen and Northern Marts Ltd., 1986-91, Director, 1973-91; Director, Clydesdale Bank PLC, 1985-92 (Northern Area, 1975-85); Director, Britoil, 1988-90; Prior of Scotland, The Order of St. John, 1983-95; Member, Royal Commission on Historical Manuscripts, 1988-95; Member, BP Scottish Advisory Board, 1990-97; Hon. Air Commodore, No. 612 (County of Aberdeen) Squadron, Royal Aux. Air Force, Leuchars. Address: (h.) Arbuthnott House, by Laurencekirk, Kincardineshire AB30 1PA.

Arbuthnott, Professor Sir John Peebles, PhD, ScD, FIBiol, HonFTCD, FRSE, FIIB, FRCPath, HonFRCPSGlasg. Principal and Vice Chancellor, Strathclyde University, 1991-2000; Chairman, Greater Glasgow NHS Board, 2002-07; b. 8.4.39; m., Elinor Rutherford Smillie; 1 s.; 2 d. Educ. Glasgow University; Trinity College, Dublin. Assistant Lecturer, then Lecturer, Department of Bacteriology, Glasgow University, 1960-67; Research Fellow of the Royal Society, 1968-72; Senior Lecturer, Department of Microbiology, then Senior Lecturer, Department of Bacteriology, Glasgow University, 1972-75; Professor of Micriobiology, Trinity College, Dublin, 1976-88; Professor of Microbiology, Nottingham University, 1988-91. Secretary/Treasurer, Carnegie Trust for the Universities of Scotland, 2000-04; Member, Board, Food Standards Agency; Chairman, Scottish Food Advisory Committee, 2000-02; Chairman, National Review of Allocation of Health Resources in Scotland, 1997-99; Chairman, Standing Committee on Resource Allocation to NHS in Scotland, 2001-03; Director, Scottish Science Trust; Chairman, Wolfson Institute of Health, Medicine and the Environment, since 2000; Chairman, Commission on Voting Systems, Boundaries and Representation in Scotland, 2004-05; President, Scottish Association of Marine Science (2004); Council member, Royal Society of Edinburgh (2007). DSc: University Lodz, Poland, University Teknologi, Malaysia, Glasgow University, Glasgow Caledonian University; LLD: Queens University, Belfast, Aberdeen University; DEd, Queen Margaret University College; DUniv, Strathclyde University; Distinguished Fellowship, International Medical University, Malaysia. Recreations: bird-watching; photography; golf. Address: (h.) 9 Curlinghall, Largs KA30 8LB.

Archer, Gilbert Baird, DL. Chairman, Tods of Orkney Ltd, since 1970; former Chairman, John Dickson & Sons Ltd; b. 24.8.42, Edinburgh; m., Irene Conn; 2 d. Educ. Melville College. Vice Convenor, George Watson's College, 1978-80; Governor, Fettes College, 1986-90; Director, Scottish Council of Independent Schools, 1988-91; Council Member, Governing Bodies Association of Independent Schools, 1988-91; Governor, Napier University, 1991-97; Chairman, St. Columba's Hospice, 1998-2004; Past President, Edinburgh Chamber of Commerce & Manufactures; Past Chairman, Scottish Chambers of Commerce; former Deputy President, Association of British Chambers of Commerce; Chairman,

Edinburgh Common Purpose, 1991-94; Past Moderator, High Constabulary of the Port of Leith; Master, Worshipful Company of Gunmakers, London; Past Master, The Company of Merchants of the City of Edinburgh. Recreation: fishing. Address: (b.) 12 Broughton Place, Edinburgh EH1 3RX; T.-0131-556 4518.

Archer, John William, BA (Hons). Independent film and television producer; b. 19.9.53, Evesham; 3 s. Educ. Dean Close School, Cheltenham; University of Birmingham; University College, Cardiff. Researcher, Nationwide, 1975-77; Director, BBC TV, London: Writers and Places, Global Report, Omnibus; Producer, The Book Programme, Did You See...?; Editor, Saturday Review, A Week of British Art; Head of Music and Arts, BBC Scotland, 1989, including editing Edinburgh Nights; Executive Producer, The Bigger Picture, Billy Connolly's World Tour of Scotland/Australia; producing and directing Stevenson's Travels; BAFTA Award, best programme/ series without a category for Did You See...?, 1983; Chief Executive, Scottish Screen, 1996-2001; Managing Director, Hopscotch Films Ltd., since 2002; Producer, 'Writing Scotland'. Member, British Screen Advisory Council. Recreations: walking; tree planting; mountain biking; necessary gardening; novels. Address: (b.) Hopscotch Films, 752 Argyle Street, Glasgow G3 8UJ; T.-0141 221 2828; e-mail: john@hopscotchfilms.co.uk

Argondizza, Pauline Hazel, GMusRNCM, PPRNCM, PGDipRNCM. Principal Cellist, Royal Scottish National Orchestra, since 1989; b. 10.3.63, Chelmsford; m., Dr. Peter Argondizza; 2 c. Educ. Chelmer Valley High School; Colchester Institute; Royal Northern College of Music, Banff School of Fine Arts, Banff, Alberta, Canada. Co-Principal Cellist, English National Opera Orchestra, 1988. Address: (h.) 9, Wilmot Road, Jordanhill, Glasgow G13 1XL; T.-0141-954 9346.

Argyll, Duke of (Torquhil Ian Campbell); b. 29.5.68. Succeeded to title, 2001. Chief of Clan Campbell.

Armour, Professor Sir James, CBE, PhD, HonDU (Stirling), Dr hc Utrecht, Hon. DVM&S (Edin), HonDU (Glasgow), HonFIBiol, FRCVS, FRSE, FMedSci. Dean of Faculties, Glasgow University, 2001-04; Emeritus Professor of Veterinary Parasitology; Vice-Principal (Planning - External Relations), 1991-95; Dean, Faculty of Veterinary Medicine, 1986-90; Chairman, Glasgow Dental Hospital and School NHS Trust, 1995-99; Vice-President, Royal Society of Edinburgh, 1998-2000; b. 17.9.29, Basra, Iraq; m., 1, Irene Morris (deceased); 2, Christine Strickland; 2 s.; 2 d. Educ. Marr College, Troon; Glasgow University. Colonial veterinary service, Nigeria, 1953-60; Research Scientist, Wellcome Ltd., 1960-63; Glasgow University: Research Fellow, 1963-67, Lecturer/Senior Lecturer, 1967-73, Reader, 1973-76. Chairman, Government Committee on Animal Medicines, 1987-95; Chairman, Editorial Board, In Practice (veterinary journal), 1980-90; Chairman, Governing Body, Institute of Animal Health, 1989-97; Member, Governing Body: Moredun Research Institute, Edinburgh, 1997-2006, Institute of Aquaculture, Stirling, 1997-2003; Member, Hannah Foundation Board, since 1998; Trustee, Scottish Science Trust, 1999-2001; Chairman: Moredun Foundation for Animal Health and Welfare, 2000-04, Higher Education Funding Council Research Assessment Panels for Agriculture, Food Science and Veterinary Science, 1999-2001; Member, Royal Society of Edinburgh Inquiry into Foot and Mouth Disease in Scotland, 2001; Chairman, St. Andrews Clinics for Children in Africa, 2000-07. Awards: RCVS John Henry Steel Medal, Royal Agricultural Society Bledisloe Award, BVA Wooldridge Medal, Pfizer WAAVP Award, BVA

Chiron Award; Royal Society of Edinburgh Medal, 2002. Captain, Royal Troon GC, 1990-92, Honorary President, since 2007. Publications: joint author of textbook on veterinary parasitology; editor, two books; 150 scientific articles. Recreation: golf. Address: (h.) 4b Towans Court, Prestwick, Ayrshire; T.-01292 470869.

Armour, Julia, CAMF Dip (PR Mgmt), MA (Hons) Eng Lang & Lit (Edin). Deputy Director, British Council Scotland; Director of Secretariat, Napier University, 2006-07; Director, Group Services, Scottish Development International, 1992-2002; Assistant Director (Corporate Affairs) and Secretary to Scottish Further Education Funding Council (SHEFC), 1992-2002; Head of Corporate Affairs, Scottish Higher Education Funding Council, 1997, Clerk to the Council, 1996-97. Address: (b.) The Tun, 4 Jackson's Entry, Holyrood Road, Edinburgh EH8 8PL; T.-0131 524 5753.

Armour, Robert Malcolm, MBA, LLB (Hons), DipLP, WS, NP. General Counsel and Company Secretary, British Energy plc, since 1995; Director: Nuclear Industry Association, Scottish Council Development and Industry, British Energy International Limited, Eggborough Power Limited; b. 25.9.59, Edinburgh; m., Anne Ogilvie White. Educ. Daniel Stewart's and Melville College, Edinburgh; Edinburgh University. Solicitor, Haldanes McLaren and Scott, WS, Edinburgh, 1983-86; Partner, Wright, Johnston and MacKenzie, Edinburgh, 1986-90; Scottish Nuclear Limited: Company Secretary, 1990-95, Director, Performance Development, 1993-95; Director, Corporate Affairs, British Energy, since 1999. Recreations: golf; curling. Address: British Energy Group plc, Systems House, Alba Campus, Livingston EH54 7EG.

Armstrong, Charles Alexander, BA, CPFA, FCCA. Director of Finance, Aberdeenshire Council, since 2000; b. 17.4.48, Stirling; m., Cilla; 2 s.; 1 d. Educ. Girvan High School; Strathclyde University. Financial Co-ordinator, Dumfries and Galloway Regional Council, 1977-83; Depute Director of Finance, Wigtown District Council, 1983-87; Depute City Chamberlain, City of Aberdeen, 1987-91; Director of Finance, Gordon District Council, 1991-96; Head of Corporate Finance, Aberdeenshire Council, 1996-2000. Address: (b.) Aberdeenshire Council, Woodhill House, Westburn Road, Aberdeen AB16 5GB; T.-01224 665410.

Armstrong, Dr Ernest McAlpine, CB, FRCSEd, FRCPGlas, FRCPEd, FRCGP, FFPH. Hon. Col. 205 (S) Fd. Hosp. (V); Chairman, The Oban Hospice; Chief Medical Officer, Scottish Executive Health Department, 2001-05; b. 3.6.45, Motherwell; m., Dr Katherine Mary Dickson Armstrong; 2 s. Educ. Hamilton Academy; Glasgow University. Junior posts, medicine and surgery, Glasgow Royal and Western Infirmaries; Lecturer in Pathology, Glasgow University, 1971-74; General Practitioner, Connel, 1975-93; Secretary, British Medical Association, London, 1993-2000. Recreations: music; hill-walking; sailing. Address: (h.) 29/1 Inverleith Place, Edinburgh EH3 5QD.

Arnold, Andy, MA (Hons), DipEd. Director of Tron Theatre Glasgow, since 2008; Founder and Artistic Director, The Arches, Glasgow (1991-2008); Theatre Director, since 1980; Community Artist and Cartoonist, since 1974; b. Southend-on-Sea. Artistic Director, Theatre Workshop, Edinburgh, 1980-85; Director, Bloomsbury Theatre, London, 1986-89; directing credits include: Metropolis: The Theatre Cut, Caligari, The Devils, The Crucible, Sexual Perversity in Chicago, Waiting for Godot;

adaptations of Tam O'Shanter and Beowulf, The Caretaker, A Midsummer Night's Dream, Juno and the Paycock, Playboy of the Western World; Freelance Director, The Battle of Stirling Bridge, Stirling Castle, 1997. Two Paper Boat awards; Spirit of Mayfest Award; only Scottish-based artist shortlisted for 1999 Creative Briton Award. Honorary Doctor of Letters, Strathclyde University. Recreations: holidays; five-a-side football.

Arnold, Professor Brian, OBE, JP, BSc, MSc, DipEd, CBiol, FIBiol. Retired Head of School of Science Education, Northern College, Aberdeen (1997-2000); Honorary Sheriff at Stonehaven Court, since 2004; b. 8.7.39, Pontypridd, Wales; m., Sandra Anne; 2 s. Educ. Pontypridd Boys' Grammar; University College of Wales, Aberystwyth. Science Teacher: Bexley Grammar, 1963-64, Wagar High, Montreal, 1964-66; Acting Head of Biology, Wolverhampton Grammar, 1966-68; Lecturer in Biology, 1968-87, Coordinator of Primary Education, 1987-91, Aberdeen College of Education; Development Director, 1991-95, Head of Department of Science and Technology, 1995-97; Course Leader for BA in Professional Development Botswana, 1996-98, Northern College. Principal Examiner in Biology, 1976-80; Convener of Biology Panel, 1986-92; Convener, Higher Still Biology, 1995-97; Scottish Examination Board; External Examiner, BEd Tech, Edinburgh University, 1996-2000. Address: (h.) 2 South Headlands Crescent, Newtonhill, Stonehaven AB39 3TT; T.-01569 730581.

Arnold, James Edward, MBE, DUniv, MA (Hon), MUniv, BA, CertEd, FRSA. Director, New Lanark Conservation Trust, since 1974; b. 16.3.45, Glasgow. Educ. Caludon Castle Comprehensive School; York University; London University. Recreations: New Lanark and life. Address: (b.) Mill Number Three, New Lanark, Lanark; T.-01555 661345.

Arnott, Ian Emslie, DA, DipTP, RSA, RIBA, ARIAS, OStJ. Consultant Architect, since 1994; Chairman, Saltire Society, 2001-04; b. 7.5.29, Galashiels. Educ. Galashiels Academy; Edinburgh College of Art. Flying Officer, RAF, 1955-57; Founding Partner, then Chairman, Campbell and Arnott, 1962-94; External Examiner, Dundee University, 1989-93. RSA Gold Medal for Architecture, 1981; nine Civic Trust Awards; one RIBA Award; two EAA Awards. Recreations: music; painting; reading; swimming; resting. Address: The Rink, Gifford, East Lothian EH41 4JD; T.-01620 810278.

Aron, Michael Douglas, EU Director and Head of Scottish Government EU Office in Brussels, since 2006, on secondment from FCO; Political Counsellor, UK Permanent Representation to the EU, 2002-05; b. 22.3.59, Kuwait; m., Rachel Ann Golding Barker; 2 s.; 2 d. Educ. Exeter School; Leeds University; Polytechnic of Central London. FCO, since 1984; First Secretary (Economic and Commercial), British Embassy, Brasilia, 1988-91; First Secretary (Political) UK Mission to the UN, New York, 1993-96; Deputy Head of Mission, British Embassy, Amman, 1999-2002. Recreations: family; football; walking; holidays. Address: Scottish Government EU Office, Rond Point Schuman 6, 1040 Brussels.

Arshad, Rowena, MEd (Community Education), OBE. Director, Centre for Education for Racial Equality in Scotland (CERES), since 1994; Senior Lecturer in Equity and Rights, since 1991; Equal Opportunities Commissioner for Scotland, 2001-07; Member of the Scotland Committee of the Equality and Human Rights Commission; Member (first ever black woman Member), Scottish Trades Union

Congress General Council, 1997-2003; b. 27.4.60, Brunei Town, Brunei; m., Malcolm Quarrie Parnell; 1 s.; 1 d. Educ. Methodist Girls School, Penang, West Malaysia; Moray House Institute of Education; Edinburgh University. Education and Campaigns Organiser, Scottish Education and Action for Development, 1985-88; Director, Edinburgh Multicultural Education Centre, 1988-90. Currently, on the board of Her Majesty's Inspectorate of Education; the Scottish Funding Council; Chair of Equality Forward, first equality unit for Scottish Colleges and Universities; Member of the Scottish Advisory Group of the British Council; Member, Editorial Board of the Journal of Race Equality Teaching. Formerly, Chair of the Equality Advisory Group, COPFS (2003-05); Chair of Linknet Mentoring Initiative, Edinburgh (2000-03); Chair of the Widening Access to Council Membership Progress Group (2004-05); first Honorary President of the Institute of Contemporary Scotland; Member of the Independent Committee of Inquiry into Student Finance (Cubie Committee); Member of the Working Party on Guidelines in Sex Education in Scottish Schools (Section 2A); Convenor of the Education Institute of Scotland Anti-Racist Committee; Member, STUC Black Workers Committee; Member of the Race Equality Advisory Forum. Author of numerous chapters to publications on equality; principal writer of the first anti-sectarian education resource for teachers and youth workers in Scotland. Recreations: keen reader of crime novels; dogs and animal issues; international cuisine and baroque music. Address: (h.) CERES, Moray House Institute of Education, Room 2:4, Charteris Building, University of Edinburgh, Holyrood Road, Edinburgh EH8 8AQ; T.-0131-651 6371.

Arthur, Adrian, BL. Hon. Fellow, University of Abertay Dundee; Editor, The Courier, Dundee, 1993-2002; b. 28.9.37, Kirkcaldy; m., Patricia Mill; 1 s.; 2 d. Educ. Harris Academy, Dundee; St. Andrews University. Joined staff of People's Journal; through the editorial ranks of The Courier (Deputy Editor, 1978-93). Recreations: golf; travel; Rotary. Address: (h.) 33 Seaforth Crescent, West Ferry, Dundee DD5 1QD; T.-01382 776842.
E-mail: adrianarthur33@blueyonder.co.uk

Arthur, Alexander James, MA, MLitt, CA. Senior Lecturer, Accountancy, University of Aberdeen, since 1990; b. 18.8.53, Dingwall, Ross-shire; 4 s.; 1 d. Educ. Tain Royal Academy; Aberdeen University. Mann Judd Gordon, CA, Stornoway, 1978-81; Oil Industry, Aberdeen, 1981-90, principally Shell UK Exploration and Production and Comex UK Ltd. Treasurer, Mental Health Aberdeen; current President, University and College Union, Aberdeen Branch. Recreation: sailing. Address: (b.) University of Aberdeen Business School, Edward Wright Building, Dunbar Street, Aberdeen AB24 3QY; T.-01224 272211; e-mail: arthur@abdn.ac.uk

Arthur, Lt. General Sir Norman, KCB (1985), CVO (2007). Lord Lieutenant, Stewartry of Kirkcudbright, Dumfries and Galloway Region, 1996-2006; b. 6.3.31, London (but brought up in Ayrshire, of Scottish parents); m., Theresa Mary Hopkinson; 1 s.; 1 d.; 1 s. (deceased). Educ. Eton College; Royal Military Academy, Sandhurst. Commissioned Royal Scots Greys, 1951; commanded Royal Scots Dragoon Guards, 1972-74, 7th Armoured Brigade, 1976-77, 3rd Armoured Division, 1980-82; Director, Personal Services (Army), 1983-85; commanded Army in Scotland, and Governor of Edinburgh Castle, 1985-88; retired, 1988; Honorary Colonel, Royal Scots Dragoon Guards, 1984-92; Col. Comdt. Military Provost Staff Corps, 1983-88; Honorary Colonel, 205 (Scottish) General Hospital, Territorial Army, 1988-93; Colonel, The Scottish Yeomanry, 1992-97; mentioned in Despatches, 1974. Officer, Royal Company of Archers; President,

Scottish Conservation Projects Trust, 1989-93; Vice President, Riding for the Disabled Association, Edinburgh and the Borders, 1988-94; Chairman: Army Benevolent Fund, Scotland, 1988-2000, Leonard Cheshire Foundation, SW Scotland, 1994-2000; Member, Committee, Automobile Association, 1990-98; humanitarian aid work, Croatia and Bosnia, since 1992; President, Reserve Forces and Cadet Association, Lowlands, 2000-06; Member, British Olympic equestrian team (three-day event), 1960. Recreations: riding; country sports; country life; reading. Address: (h.) Newbarns, Dalbeattie, Kirkcudbrightshire DG5 4PY; T.-01556 630227.

Asher, Catherine Archibald, OBE, BA, RGN, SCM, RNT, DUniv. Former Chairman, National Board for Nursing, Midwifery and Health Visiting for Scotland (1982-95); b. 6.7.33, Edinburgh. Educ. Woodside School, Glasgow; Edinburgh University; Open University. Ward Sister, Glasgow Royal Infirmary, 1956-61; Nurse Teacher, Senior Tutor, Principal Nursing Officer (Teaching), Glasgow Royal Infirmary School of Nursing, 1963-74; Director of Nurse Education, Glasgow Eastern College of Nursing and Midwifery, 1974-91; Acting Principal, Glasgow College of Nursing and Midwifery, 1991-95; Governor, University of Paisley, 1996-2005 (Chairman, Court, 2002-05). Address: (h.) 73 Roman Court, Roman Road, Bearsden, Glasgow G61 2NW

Asher, Professor R. E., BA, PhD, DLitt, FRSE, FRAS. Professor of Linguistics, Edinburgh University, 1977-93, Professor Emeritus and Honorary Fellow, since 1993; b. 23.7.26, Gringley-on-the-Hill, Nottinghamshire. Educ. King Edward VI Grammar School, Retford; University College London. Assistant, Department of French, University College, London, 1951-53; Lecturer in Linguistics, then Lecturer in Tamil, School of Oriental and African Studies, London, 1953-65; joined Department of Linguistics, Edinburgh University, 1965; Dean, Faculty of Arts, 1986-89; Member, University Court, 1989-92; Vice-Principal, 1990-93; Curator of Patronage, 1991-93; Director, Centre for Speech Technology Research, 1994. Visiting appointments: Visiting Professor of Linguistics, University of Illinois, Urbana-Champaign, 1967; Visiting Professor of Tamil and Malayalam, Michigan State University, 1968; Visiting Professor of Linguistics, University of Minnesota, 1969; Chaire des Professeurs Etrangers, Collège de France, 1970; Subrahmaniya Bharati Fellow, Tamil University, Thanjavur, 1984-85; Visiting Professor, International Christian University, Tokyo, 1994-95; first occupant of Vaikom Muhammed Basheer Chair, Mahatma Gandhi University, Kottayam, Kerala, 1995-96. Medal, Collège de France, Paris, 1970; Gold Medal, Kerala Sahitya Akademi, India, 1983; Honorary Fellow, Sahitya Akademi (India's National Academy of Letters), 2007. Publications: A Tamil Prose Reader, 1971; Some Landmarks in the History of Tamil Prose, 1973; Me Grandad 'ad an Elephant! (translation), 1980; Towards a History of Phonetics (Co-Editor), 1981; Tamil, 1982; Studies on Malayalam Language and Literature, 1989; National Myths in Renaissance France: Francus, Samothes and the Druids, 1993; Scavenger's Son (translation), 1993; Atlas of the World's Languages (Co-Editor), 1994; Encyclopedia of Language and Linguistics (Editor-in-Chief), 1994; Concise History of the Language Sciences: from the Sumerians to the Cognitivists (Co-Editor), 1995; Malayalam, 1997; Basheer, Stories of the Freedom Struggle (Editor), 1998; The Novels and Stories of Vaikom Muhammed Basheer, 1999; Colloquial Tamil, 2002; What the Sufi Said (translation), 2002; Wind Flowers: Contemporary Malayalam Short Fiction (Editor and translator), 2004. Address: (b.) Linguistics and English Language, University of Edinburgh, Adam Ferguson Building, Edinburgh EH8 9LL; T.-0131-650 3484.

Ashworth, Bryan, MA, PhD, MD, FRCP(Lond), FRCP(Edin), FRSA. Honorary Senior Lecturer (Medical

History), St Andrews University, 1997-2002; Associate Lecturer, Society of Apothecaries (London), since 1998; President, Scottish Society for the History of Medicine, since 2004; Consultant Neurologist, Royal Infirmary and Western General Hospital, Edinburgh, and Senior Lecturer in Medical Neurology, Edinburgh University, 1971-92; b. 5.5.29, Oundle, Northants. Educ. Laxton School; Oundle School; St. Andrews University. National Service, Captain RAMC, Northern Nigeria, 1953-55; junior hospital posts, Manchester and Bristol; Wellcome-Swedish Travelling Research Fellow, Karolinska Hospital, Stockholm, 1965-66; Lecturer in Clinical Neurology, Manchester University, and Honorary Consultant Physician, Manchester Royal Infirmary, 1967-71; Chairman and Director (non-executive), Robert Bailey and Son, PLC, Stockport, 1978-2000; Honorary Librarian, Royal College of Physicians of Edinburgh, 1982-91. Publications: Clinical Neuro-ophthalmology, 2nd edition, 1981; Management of Neurological Disorders, 2nd edition, 1985; The Bramwells of Edinburgh, 1986; Striving Towards Elegance (Memoir), 2003. Recreations: writing; walking. Address: (h.) 13/5 Eildon Terrace, Edinburgh EH3 5NL; T.-0131-556 0547.

Aspden, Professor Richard Malcolm, PhD, DSc, FIPEM. Professor of Orthopaedic Science, Aberdeen University, since 2000; b. 23.9.55, Malta; m., Anne Maclean; 3 s.; 2 d. Educ. Bosworth College, Desford; University of York; University of Manchester (postgraduate). Research Associate, University of Manchester; Wellcome Research Fellow: University of Lund, University of Manchester, University of Aberdeen. Hon. Treasurer, Haddo Children's Theatre; European Editor, Journal of Back and Musculoskeletal Research; Editorial Consultant, Journal of Biomechanics. Publications: 2 books; 100 research papers. Recreations: woodworking; music; hill-walking. Address: (b.) University of Aberdeen, Department of Orthopaedics, IMS Building, Foresterhill, Aberdeen AB25 2ZD; T.-01224 552767.
E-mail: r.aspden@abdn.ac.uk

Atack, Alison Mary, LLB, NP, FRSA, FICS. Partner, Kidstons, Solicitors, Glasgow, since 1994; Member, Council, Law Society of Scotland (Convener: Professional Conduct Committee, Professional Practice Committee, Complaints Committee and Competence Committee; Member, Education and Training, Remuneration Guarantee Fund and Professional Practice Committees and Audit; b. 23.2.53, Richmond; m., Iain F. Atack; 1 s.; 1 d. Educ. Larbert High School; Glasgow University. Legal training and assistant, Biggart Baillie and Gifford, Glasgow. Formerly: Governor, Jordanhill College of Education. Recreations: hillwalking; skiing; gym; sailing; opera. Address: 1 Royal Bank Place, Glasgow G1 3AA; T.-0141-943 1188.
E-mail: ama@kidstons.co.uk

Atholl, 11th Duke of (John Murray); b. 19.1.29; m.; 2 s. 1 d. Succeeded to the title, 1996; lives in South Africa.

Atiyah, Michael Francis, OM, FRS, Hon FRSE, Hon DSc (Oxford, Cambridge, Harvard and others). President, Royal Society of Edinburgh, since 2005; Honorary Professor, Edinburgh University, since 1997; b. 22.4.29, London; m., Lily Jane Myles Brown; 2 s. Educ. Victoria College, Cairo; Manchester Grammar School; Trinity College, Cambridge. Fellow: Trinity College, Cambridge, 1954-58, Pembroke College, Cambridge, 1958-61; Reader/Professor, Oxford, 1961-69; Professor, Institute for Advanced Study, Princeton, USA, 1969-73; Royal Society Research Professor, Oxford, 1973-90; Master, Trinity College, Cambridge, 1990-97; President, Royal Society, 1990-95.

Fields Medal, 1966; Abel Prize, 2004; Collected Works, OUP, 1998 and 2004. Recreations: music; gardening. Address: (b.) Royal Society of Edinburgh, 22-26 George Street, Edinburgh EH2 2PQ; T.-0131-240-5022.

Atkinson, Professor The Rev. David, BSc, PhD, FIBiol, CBiol, MIEEM, ILTM, FRSA, MISoilSci. Emeritus Professor of Land Resources and former Vice Principal, Scottish Agricultural College; b. 12.9.44, Blyth; m., Elisabeth Ann Cocks; 1 s.; 2 d. Educ. Newlands County Secondary Modern School; Hull University; Newcastle-upon-Tyne University; Theological Institute of Scottish Episcopal Church (TISEC). East Malling Research Station, Maidstone, 1969-85; Macaulay Institute for Soil Research, 1985-87; Macaulay Land Use Research Institute, 1987-88; Professor of Agriculture, Aberdeen University, and Head, Land Resources Department, Scottish Agricultural College, 1988-93; Deputy Principal (R. & D.) and Dean, Edinburgh Centre, Scottish Agricultural College, 1993-2000, Vice Principal, 2000-04. Member, BCPC Council, since 1994, Vice Chairman, since 2002; Member, Advisory Group, Royal College of Physicians (Edinburgh); Member, Management Board, MRCP; Chair, ACTS Rural Committee; Ordained Deacon 2005; Priest, 2006; Associate Curate, Aberdeen Cathedral, 2005-07, Interim Priest, St Devenicks, Aberdeen, since 2007; Chair, TISEC Board of Studies, since 2007. Recreations: discussing organic agriculture and GM issues; music; reading thrillers; quotations. Address: (b.) SAC, Craibstone Estate, Bucksburn, Aberdeen AB21 9YA.

Atkinson, Elspeth. Director for Scotland and Northern Ireland, Macmillan Cancer Support, since 2005. Address: (b.) Third Floor, 132 Rose Street, Edinburgh EH2 3JD; T.-0131 260 3720.

Attwooll, Elspeth, LLB, MA. Member of the European Parliament (Liberal Democrat), since 1999; b. 1.2.43; m. Educ. St Andrews University. Recreations: reading, especially legal theory; detective fiction.

Auchincloss, Matthew, MA, LLB, DipLP, Solicitor-Advocate. Director of The Public Defence Solicitors' Office, since 2005; b. 16.10.71, Edinburgh. Educ. Sandhurst School; Linlithgow Academy; University of Glasgow. Admitted as a Solicitor in Scotland, 1997; Partner in Gordon McBain and Company, Solicitors, Edinburgh, 1999; joined Public Defence Solicitors' Office, 2003; joined the College of Justice as a Solicitor with extended rights of audience, 2005. Tutor for Central Law Training. Recreations: music; horse riding. Address: (b.) Public Defence Solicitors' Office, 37 York Place, Edinburgh EH1 3HP; T.-0131 557 1222; e-mail: mauchincloss@pdso.org.uk

Audain, Irene, MBE, MA (Hons), DipInfoScience. Chief Executive, Scottish Out of School Care Network, since 1993; b. 10.7.56, Glasgow. Educ. University of Glasgow; University of Strathclyde. Has worked in voluntary sector developing childcare, community development, campaigning on women's issues, children's rights, housing and peace education. Recreation: travel. Address: (b.) Level 2, 100 Wellington Street, Glasgow G2 6DH; T.-0141 564 1284.

Auld, Professor Alan Graeme, MA, BD, PhD, DLitt, FRSE, FSA Scot. Professor of Hebrew Bible, Edinburgh University, 1995-2007, Principal, New College, Edinburgh, 2002-08; b. 14.8.41, Aberdeen; m., Dr Sylvia Joyce Auld; 2 s.; 1 d. Educ. Robert Gordon's College,

Aberdeen; Aberdeen University; Edinburgh University. Assistant Director, British School of Archaeology in Jerusalem, 1969-72; Lecturer, then Senior Lecturer, in Hebrew and Old Testament Studies, Edinburgh University, 1972-95. Publications: Joshua, Moses and the Land; Amos; Kings Without Privilege; Joshua Retold; Samuel at the Threshold; Joshua: Jesus Son of Nauè in Codex Vaticanus. Recreations: walking; gardening; travel. Address: (b.) New College, Mound Place, Edinburgh EH1 2LX.

Auld, Douglas Oliver Urquhart Grant, BEd (Hons), DPSE, DPE. Head Teacher, Arran High School, since 2003; b. 16.2.53, Glasgow; m., Aileen; 2 s. Educ. Craigbank Secondary, Glasgow; Jordanhill College. Assistant Principal, Guidance, Eastwood High School, 1975-83; Principal Teacher, Physical Education, Braidfield High School, 1983-89; Acting Adviser, PE, Strathclyde Region, 1989-91; Assistant Head Teacher, Boclair Academy, 1991-2003. Recreations: athletics; rugby; sailing; cycling; walking; birdwatching. Address: Lamlash, Isle of Arran KA27 8NG; T.-01770 600341; e-mail: dauld@arran.n-ayrshire.sch.uk

Austin, Lloyd, BSc (Hons). Head of Conservation Policy, RSPB Scotland, since 1999; b. 5.10.60, Haddenham; divorced; 1 s.; 2 d. Educ. Peter Symond's School, Winchester; Edinburgh University. Scientific Officer, Department of Environment (NI), 1985-86; Conservation Officer: Cleveland Wildlife Trust, 1986-88, Lincolnshire Wildlife Trust, 1988-90; Conservation Planning Officer (Scotland), RSPB, 1990-99. Trustee, Scottish Environment Link, since 2000, Chair of Trustees, 2004-07. Recreations: natural history; travel; current affairs. Address: (b.) Dunedin House, 25 Ravelston Terrace, Edinburgh EH4 3TP; T.-0131-311-6500.

Axford, Nicola Dawn, BA (Hons). Arts Management Consultant; former Chief Executive, Pitlochry Festival Theatre; Drama Officer, Scottish Arts Council, 2000-01; Arts Consultant; b. London; m., Prof. Ian Brown. Educ. Bradford University. Director, Big Bird Music Theatre, 1982-86; Administrator, Major Road Theatre Company, 1986-87; Drama Finance Officer, Arts Council of Great Britain, 1987-91; Business Manager, PW Productions Ltd., 1991-92; Administrator, Manchester City of Drama 1994 Ltd., 1993-94; General Manager, Royal Lyceum Theatre Company, 1994-98. Director, Major Road Theatre Company; Board member, Scottish Enterprise Tayside. E-mail: naxford@btinternet.com

B

Bagnall, John Michael, MA (Cantab), DipLib, MCLIP. University Librarian, Dundee University, since 1987; b. 22.4.45, South Yorkshire. Educ. Mexborough Grammar School; Sidney Sussex College, Cambridge. Diploma in Librarianship, University College, London; Assistant Librarian and Sub-Librarian, Newcastle upon Tyne University. Recreations: music; bird-watching; languages. Address: University Library, Dundee DD1 4HN; T.-01382 384082.

Bailey, Professor Paul John, BA (Hons), MA, PhD, FRHS. Professor of Modern Chinese History, University of Edinburgh, since 2007; b. 7.2.50, Poole, England; m., Dawn. Educ. Leeds University; University of London (SOAS); University of British Columbia (Canada). Teacher of English Language and Literature, Lingnan College, Middle School, Hong Kong, 1973-75; British Council Postgraduate Scholar, Beijing University (China), 1980-81; Lecturer in Chinese, University of Durham, 1983-84; Teacher of History, Sevenoaks School, Kent, 1984-85; became Lecturer in East Asian History, University of Edinburgh, 1985. Publications: 7 books including: Gender and Education in China, 2007; China in the Twentieth Century, 2001. Recreations: cinema; cricket; travel; chess; swimming; classical music. Address: (b.) School of History, Classics and Archaeology, University of Edinburgh, George Square, Edinburgh EH8 9JY; T.-0131-650-3766; e-mail: paul.bailey@ed.ac.uk

Baillie, Ian David Hunter, CBE. Director, Social Care Association (Education), since 1987; non-stipendiary Minister, United Reformed Church; b. 18.12.40, Dundee; m., Margaret McCallum McFarlane; 3 d. Educ. Hutchesons Boys Grammar School. Eight years in life assurance; 35 years in social work; retired as Director of Social Work, Church of Scotland Board of Social Responsibility, 1990-2002; Director, Jeely Piece Club; Chair, Glasgow Churches Social Action Alliance, 2006. Recreations: sport (watching); reading. Address: (b.) 17 Williamwood Park West, Netherlee, Glasgow G44 3TE; T.-0141-637 7435.

Baillie, Jackie. MSP (Labour), Dumbarton, since 1999; Minister for Social Justice, 2000-01; Deputy Minister for Communities, 1999-2000; b. 15.1.64, Hong Kong; m., Stephen; 1 d. Educ. Glasgow University (part-time: to be completed). Co-ordinator, Gorbals Unemployed Workers Centre, 1987-90; Resource Centre Manager, Strathkelvin District Council, 1990-96; Community Economic Development Manager, East Dunbartonshire Council, 1996-99. Board Member, Volunteer Development Scotland, 1997-99; Chairperson, Scottish Labour Party, 1997-98. Address: (b.) Dumbarton Constituency Office, 125 College Street, Dumbarton G82 1NH; T.-01389 734214.

Baillie, Professor John, MA, CA. Visiting Professor of Accountancy: Heriot-Watt University, Edinburgh, 1989-99, University of Glasgow, since 1996; Member, Reporting Panel, Competition Commission, since 2002; Chair, Accounts Commission, since 2007; Member, Accounts Commission, 2003-07; Board Member, Audit Scotland, 2003-07; Member, Local Government Finance Review Committee, since 2004; b. 7.10.44; m., Annette Alexander; 1 s.; 1 d. Educ. Whitehill School. Johnstone-Smith Professor of Accountancy, Glasgow University, 1983-88; Partner, KPMG, 1978-92; Partner, Scott-Moncrieff, 1993-

2001. Institute of Chartered Accountants of Scotland: Convenor, Research Committee, 1994-99, member, various technical and professional affairs committees. Recreations: keeping fit; reading; music; golf. Address: (h.) The Glen, Glencairn Road, Kilmacolm, Renfrewshire; T.-Kilmacolm 3254.

Bain, Aly, MBE. Fiddler; b. 1946, Lerwick. Co-founder, Boys of the Lough, 1972; Soloist; TV and radio anchorman.

Bain, Professor Andrew David, OBE, FRSE. Member, Competition Appeals Tribunal, since 2000; b. 21.3.36, Glasgow; m., Eleanor Riches; 3 s. Educ. Glasgow Academy; Cambridge University. Various posts, Cambridge University, 1959-67; Professor of Economics: Stirling University, 1967-77, Strathclyde University, 1977-84; Group Economic Advisor, Midland Bank, 1984-90. Member: Committee to Review the Functioning of Financial Institutions, 1977-80, Monopolies and Mergers Commission, 1980-81; Visiting Professor, Glasgow University, 1991-97; Board Member, Scottish Enterprise, 1991-97; Chairman of Trustees, Scottish Enterprise Pension Scheme, 1995-2004; Member, TEC National Council, 1994-97. Publications: The Control of the Money Supply, 1970; The Economics of the Financial System (2nd Edition), 1992.

Bain, Iain Andrew, MA. Editor and Proprietor, The Nairnshire Telegraph, since 1987; b. 25.2.49, Nairn; m., Maureen Beattie; 3 d. Educ. Nairn Academy; Aberdeen University. Joined The Geographical Magazine, 1974, Editor, 1981-87. Chairman, Nairn Museum Ltd. Recreations: reading; writing; photography; golf. Address: (b.) 10 Leopold Street, Nairn IV12 4BG; T.-01667 453258.

Bain, Simon. Business Writer and Money Editor, The Herald, since 1997; b. 20.8.51, London; m., Norma; 1 s.; 1 d. Educ. St Paul's School; Christ's College, Cambridge. Reporter, The Scotsman, 1981-88; Business Editor, Scotland on Sunday, 1988-96. British Press Award winner, 1981; Scottish Press Award winner, 1986, 1992, 1998, 2000, 2007, Journalist of the Year 2000; Industrial Society Award winner, 1999; B & B Personal Finance Award winner, 1994, 1998, 2001. Address: (h.) 32 Craigleith Drive, Edinburgh; T.-0131 718 6453.

Bainbridge, Ian Paul, BSc, PhD, DMS. Chief Ecological Advisor and Deputy Director, Science Advice and Information, Rural and Environment Research and Analysis Directorate, Scottish Government, since 2001; b. 11.7.54, Derby; m., Carole Ann Rimmer. Educ. Bemrose Grammar School, Derby; Wolverhampton Polytechnic; Liverpool Polytechnic; Napier University. Conservation Liaison Officer, Northumberland Wildlife Trust, 1979-84; Forestry Policy Officer, RSPB, 1984-89; Reserves Ecologist, Scotland, RSPB, 1989-94; Head of Research, Scotland, RSPB, 1994-2001. Director, Alpines 2001 International Conference; President, Scottish Rock Garden Club, 2003-06. Recreations: Alpine plants and gardening; ornithology; food and drink. Address: (b.) 1J-77 Victoria Quay, Edinburgh EH6 6QQ; T.-0131 244 5269; e-mail: ian.bainbridge@scotland.gsi.gov.uk

Baird, Professor David Tennent, CBE, BA (Cantab), MB, ChB, MD (hc), DSc, FRCP, FRCOG, FRS(Ed), FMed.Sci. Emeritus Professor of Reproductive Endocrinology, Edinburgh University, since 2000; b. 13.3.35, Glasgow; m. 1, Frances Lichtveld (m. dissolved); 2 s.; m. 2, Anna Frances Glasier. Educ. Aberdeen Grammar School; Aberdeen University; Trinity College, Cambridge; Edinburgh University. After clinical training in endocrinology as well as obstetrics, spent three years (1965-68) as an MRC travelling Research Fellow at Worcester Foundation for Experimental Biology, Shrewsbury, Mass., USA, conducting research on reproductive endocrinology;

Deputy Director, MRC Unit of Reproductive Biology, Edinburgh, 1972-77; Professor of Obstetrics and Gynaecology, Edinburgh University, 1977-85; Medical Research Council Professor of Reproductive Endocrinology, Edinburgh University, 1985-2000; served on a number of national and international committees. Publications: four books on reproduction. Recreations: ski mountaineering, music; sport. Address· (h) Edinburgh University, Simpson Centre for Reproductive Health, 51 Little France Crescent, Edinburgh EH16 4SA; T.-0131-242 6367.

Baird, Professor James Ireland, BSc(Hons), PhD, MICE, CEng, MCIWM. Professor of Waste Management, Glasgow Caledonian University, since 1994; b. 31.10.58, Patna, Ayrshire; m., Janice McLauchlan; 1 s.; 1 d. Educ. James Hamilton Academy, Kilmarnock; University of Glasgow. Research Engineer, British Hydromechanics Research Association; Research and Development Manager, Water Research Centre, Medmenham, Bucks. General Councillor, Institute of Wastes Management. Recreation: hillwalking.

Baker, Claire. MSP (Labour), Mid Scotland and Fife, since 2007; b. 4.3.71. Address: (b.) Scottish Parliament, Edinburgh EH99 1SP.

Baker, Professor Michael John, TD, BA, BSc (Econ), DipM, CertITP (Harvard), DBA (Harvard), LLD, DUniv, FCIM, F.SCOTVEC, FCAM, FRSE, FRSA, FAM, FSQA. Professor of Marketing, Strathclyde University, 1971-99, Emeritus Professor, since 1999 (Deputy Principal, 1984-91); b. 5.11.35, Debden; m., Sheila; 1 s.; 2 d. Educ. Worksop College; Bede, Gosforth and Harvey Grammar Schools; Durham University; London University; Harvard University. Royal Artillery, 1956 (2nd Lt.); Richard Thomas & Baldwins (Sales) Ltd., 1958-64; Lecturer: Medway College of Technology, 1964-66, Hull College of Technology, 1966-68; FME Fellow, Harvard Business School, 1968-71; Member, Vice-Chairman and Chairman, SCOTBEC, 1973-85; Member, SSRC Management Committee, 1976-80; Dean, Strathclyde Business School, 1978-84; Marketing Education Group: Chairman, 1974-87, President, 1987-2005; Chairman, Institute of Marketing, 1987; Member: SHERT, 1983-96, UGC Business and Management Sub-Committee, 1986-89, Chief Scientist's Committee, 1985-96, ESRC Research Resources Board, 1994-96; Governor, CAM; Visiting Professor: Glasgow Caledonian University, Surrey University; Special Professor, Nottingham University; Honorary Professor, Aberystwyth University; Distinguished Visiting Professor, Monash University, Australia; Chairman, Westburn Publishers Ltd. Publications: Marketing New Industrial Products; Market Development; Marketing (7th edition, 2006); The Marketing Book (Editor, 6th edition, 2008); The Role of Design in International Competitiveness; Marketing and Competitive Success; Dictionary of Marketing & Advertising (3rd edition, 1998); Research for Marketing; Perspectives on Marketing Management (Editor); Marketing: Theory & Practice (Editor, 3rd edition, 1996); Marketing Strategy and Management (4th edition, 2008); Companion Encyclopedia of Marketing (2nd edition, 1999); The Marketing Manual, 1998; Product Strategy and Management (2nd edition, 2008); Marketing: Critical Perspectives (five volumes), 2001; Marketing Theory, 2002; Business and Management Research, 2003. Recreations: sailing; gardening; travel. Address: (b.) Strathclyde University, 173 Cathedral Street, Glasgow G4 ORQ; T.-0141-552 4400; e-mail: mjb@westburn.co.uk

Baker, Richard. MSP (Labour), North East Scotland, since 2003; b. 29.5.74, Edinburgh. Educ. Aberdeen University. Address: (b.) Scottish Parliament, Edinburgh EH99 1SP; T.-0131 348 5000.

Baker, Emeritus Professor Thomas Neville, BMet, PhD, DMet (Sheffield), DSc (Strathclyde), FIM, FInstP, CEng, CPhys. Professor, Department of Mechanical Engineering – Metallurgy and Engineering Materials Group, Strathclyde University; b. 11.1.34, Southport; m., Eileen May Allison. Educ. King George V School, Southport; Sheffield University. National Service, Royal Corps of Signals; Research Metallurgist, Nelson Research Laboratories, English Electric Co., Stafford, 1958-60; Scientist, Project Leader, Tube Investments Research Laboratories, Hinxton Hall, Cambridge, 1961-64; Department of Metallurgy, Strathclyde University: SRC Research Fellow, 1965, Lecturer, 1966, Senior Lecturer, 1976, Reader, 1983, Professor, 1990, Professor of Metallurgy (1886 Chair), 1992-99, Vice Dean, School of Chemical and Materials Science, 1979-82, Head, Department of Metallurgy, 1986-87, Head, Division of Metallurgy and Engineering Materials, 1988-90; President, University of Strathclyde Staff Club, 1976-77; University of Strathclyde representative as a Governor of the Renfrewshire Educational Trust, 1989-97; Committee Member, Institute of Materials, Minerals and Mining (formerly Institute of Metals), Metal Science Committee, 1980-94, Materials Technology Committee, 1994-96, Process Science and Technology Committee, 1996-99, Integrated Processing and Manufacturing Committee, 1999-2006, High Temperature Materials Committee, since 2007; Chairman, Annual Conference on Metals and Materials, 1982-92; Member, Council, Scottish Association for Metals, 1975-79 and since 1997, Vice-President, 1999-2000, President, 2001. Publications: Yield, Flow and Fracture in Polycrystals (Editor), 1983; Titanium Technology in Microalloyed Steels (Editor), 1997; over 180 learned society publications. Recreations: music; literature; creating a garden. Address: (b.) Department of Mechanical Engineering, Strathclyde University, Glasgow; T.-0141-548 3101; (h.) Clovelly, Rowantreehill Road, Kilmacolm PA13 4NW.

Balfour of Burleigh, Lord (Robert Bruce), CEng, FIEE, FRSE, Hon. D Litt (Robert Gordon), Hon. DUniv (Stirling), Hon. FRIAS. Vice Lord-Lieutenant, Clackmannan, 1995-2001; Chancellor, Stirling University, 1988-98; b. 6.1.27, London. Educ. Westminster School, London. Graduate Apprentice, English Electric Company, 1951; various positions in manufacturing mangement; started English Electric's manufacturing operations in India as General Manager of new company in Madras, 1957-64; returned to Liverpool as General Manager; appointed General Manager, D. Napier & Son, before leaving the company in 1968; joined Bank of Scotland as a Director, 1968; Deputy Governor, Bank of Scotland, 1977-91. Forestry Commissioner, 1971-74; Chairman: Scottish Arts Council, 1971-80, Federation of Scottish Bank Employers, 1977-86, The Turing Institute, 1983-92, Scottish Committee, ABSA, 1988-94, United Artists Communications (Scotland) Ltd., until 1996; Director: Scottish Investment Trust plc, 1971-96, Tarmac plc, 1981-90, William Lawson Distillers Ltd., 1984-96, Television Educational Network, 1990-96, Edinburgh Book Festival, 1981-96 (Chairman, 1981-87); Member, British Railways (Scottish) Board, 1982-92; Treasurer: Royal Society of Edinburgh, 1989-94, Royal Scottish Corporation; President, Friends of Vellore; President, Franco-Scottish Society, 1985-96; Life Member and Trustee, 1990-96, John Muir Trust; Trustee, Bletchley Park Trust, since 2000.

Balfour of Burleigh, Lady (Janet Morgan), MA, DPhil, FRSAS, Hon LLD (Strathclyde), Hon DLitt (Napier), FRSE. Writer; Company Director; b. 5.12.45, Montreal; m., Lord Balfour of Burleigh. Educ. Newbury County Girls' Grammar School; Oxford University; Sussex University; Harvard University. Member: Central Policy Review Staff, Cabinet Office, 1978-81, Board, British Council, 1989-99; Special Adviser to Director-General, BBC, 1983-86; Chairman, Cable & Wireless Flexible Resource Ltd., 1993-97; Non-Executive Director: Cable & Wireless, 1988-2004,

W.H. Smith, 1989-95, Midlands Electricity, 1990-96, Scottish American Investment Co., 1991-2008, Scottish Oriental Smaller Companies Investment Trust, since 1994, Close Ventures VCT, since 2007, The Scottish Life Assurance Company, 1995-2001, Nuclear Generation Decommissioning Fund Ltd, 1996-2005, Nuclear Liabilities Fund, since 2005, New Medical Technologies plc, 1997-2004, BPB plc, 2000-05, Stagecoach plc, since 2001, Murray International plc, since 2003, Scottish Medical Research Fund, 1992-94; Member: Scottish Museums Council Development Resource, 1988-97, Ancient Monuments Board for Scotland, 1990-97, Book Trust Scotland, 1992-99, Scottish Economic Council, 1993-95, Scottish Hospitals Endowment Research Trust, 1992-98, Dorothy Burns Charity, 1994-2002; Chairman, Scotland's Book Campaign, 1994-96, Scottish Cultural Resources Access Network, 1995-2004, Scottish Museum of the Year Award, 1999-2004; Trustee: Carnegie Endowment for the Universities of Scotland, since 1993, National Library of Scotland, since 2002, Stewart Ivory Foundation, since 2001, Trusthouse Charitable Foundation, since 2006. Publications: Diaries of a Cabinet Minister 1964-70 by Richard Crossman (4 volumes) (Editor); The Future of Broadcasting, (Co-Editor), 1982); Agatha Christie: a biography, 1984; Edwina Mountbatten: a life of her own, 1991; The Secrets of rue St. Roch, 2004. Recreations: music of JS Bach and Handel; sea bathing; pruning; ice skating out of doors.

Balfour, Ian Leslie Shaw, MA, LLB, BD, PhD, SSC, NP. Solicitor (Consultant, Balfour & Manson) since 1955; b. 16.6.32, Edinburgh; m., Joyce Margaret Ross Pryde; 3 s.; 1 d. Educ. Edinburgh Academy; Edinburgh University. Qualified as Solicitor, 1955; commissioned, RASC, 1955-57; 1959-97: Partner, then Senior Partner, Balfour & Manson; Secretary, Oliver & Son Ltd., 1959-89; Fiscal to Law Society of Scotland, 1981-2000. Baptist Union of Scotland: President, 1976-77, Law Agent, 1964-97, Secretary, Charlotte Baptist Chapel, Edinburgh, 1980-2000, Secretary, Scottish Baptist College, 1983-2003; Secretary, Elba Housing Society Ltd., 1969-92; Council, Society for Computers and Law, 1988-92; Director, Edinburgh Medical Missionary Society; Honorary Vice-President, Lawyers Christian Fellowship, 1997. Publication: Author, "Revival in Rose Street: Charlotte Baptist Chapel, 1808-2008", 2007. Recreations: gardening; home computing; lay preaching. Address: (h.) 32 Murrayfield Avenue, Edinburgh EH12 6AX; T.-0131-337 2880; e-mail: I_Balfour@msn.com

Balfour, Peter Edward Gerald, CBE. President, Scottish Council (Development and Industry), 1985-92 (Chairman, 1978-85); Director, Royal Bank of Scotland, 1972-90; Chairman, Charterhouse plc, 1985-91; b. 9.7.21, Woking; m., 1, Grizelda Ogilvy, 2, Diana Wainman; 3 s.; 2 d. Educ. Eton College. Served Scots Guards, 1940-54; joined William McEwan & Co., brewers, 1954; appointed Director, 1958; Director, Scottish Brewers, 1959; Scottish and Newcastle Breweries, 1961 (Chairman and Managing Director, 1970-83); Director and Vice Chairman, RBS Group, 1978. Recreations: farming; forestry. Address: (h.) Scadlaw House, Humbie, East Lothian.

Balfour, Robert William, DL, BSc, FRICS. Managing Partner, Balbirnie Home Farms, since 1991; Convenor, Scottish Landowners Federation, 1999-2002; b. 25.3.52, Edinburgh; m., Jessica McCrindle; 4 s. (1 deceased). Educ. Eton; Edinburgh University. Management trainee, Ocean Group, 1974-78; Surveyor, Bell-Ingram, Perth, 1978-88; Bidwells Chartered Surveyors, Perth, 1988-94, Associate Partner, 1991; Chairman, RICS RPD (Scotland), 1990-91; Member, Board of Management, Elmwood College, 2000; DL (Fife), 1994; Member, East Area Board, Scottish Natural Heritage, 2003-07, Area Advisor, 2007; Director,

Fife Coast and Countryside Trust, 2003, Chairman, 2007; Chairman, Association of Deer Management Group, 2005; Director, Paths for all Partnership, 2005; Chairman, Kettle Growers Ltd., since 2006. Elder, Markinch Parish Church; Member, Royal Company of Archers. Recreations: golf; skiing; music; arts; shooting. Address: (b.) Pitillock Farm, Freuchie KY15 7JQ; T.-01337 857437; e-mail: balfour-balbirnie@msn.com

Balfour, William Harold St. Clair. Solicitor (retired); b. 29.8.34, Edinburgh; m., 1, Patricia Waite (m. dissolved); 1 s.; 2 d.; 2, Alice Ingsay McFarlane; 2 step. d. Educ. Hillfield, Ontario; Edinburgh Academy; Edinburgh University. Partner, Balfour & Manson, 1962-98; Clerk to Admission of Notaries Public, 1971-92; Prison Visiting Committee, 1965-70; Chairman, Basic Space Dance Theatre, 1980-86; Friends of Talbot Rice Art Centre, 1982-97, Garvald Trustees, 1980-2004, Wellspring Management, 1990-97, Tekoa Trust, since 1990; Adviser, Scottish Child Psychotherapy Trust, since 2000; Council Member, Scottish Association of Marine Science, 2002-07. Recreations: sailing; walking; wine. Address: (h.) 11 Nelson Street, Edinburgh EH3 6LF; T.-0131-556 7298.

Ball, Geoffrey A., FCA. Executive Chairman, CALA Group Limited (Group Managing Director, since 1974); Non-Executive Chairman, McCarthy & Stone plc; b. 4.8.43, Bristol; m., Mary Elizabeth; 3 s.; 1 d. Educ. Cotham Grammar School, Bristol. Non-executive Director, Scottish Mortgage Investment Trust plc; Member, MCC and Honourable Company of Edinburgh Golfers. Recreations: golf; music. Address: 26 Hermitage Drive, Edinburgh EH10 6BY; T.-0131-535 5200.

Ball, Graham Edmund, FDS RCS (Eng), FDS, RCS (Edin), FFPH. Consultant in Dental Public Health, NHS Fife; Honorary Senior Lecturer, Bute Medical School, St Andrews University; b. 14.12.53; m., Carolyn Bowyer; 1 s.; 2 d. Educ. King Edward VI School, Southampton; Welsh National School of Medicine. Registrar, Oral Surgery, Portsmouth hospitals, 1979-81; general dental practice, 1984-88; Community Dental Officer, Orkney Health Board, 1988-91; Chief Administrative Dental Officer, Orkney Health Board, 1991-95; Consultant in Dental Public Health, Fife, Borders and Lothian NHS Boards, 1995-2003. Recreations: sailing; walking. Address: (b.) Fife NHS Board, Cameron House, Cameron Bridge, Leven, Fife; T.-01592 226407.

Ballantyne, Professor Colin Kerr, MA, MSc, PhD, DSc, FRSE, FRSA. Professor in Physical Geography, St. Andrews University, since 1994; b. 7.6.51, Glasgow; m., Rebecca Trengove; 1 s.; 1 d. Educ. Hutchesons' Grammar School; Glasgow University; McMaster University; Edinburgh University. Lecturer in Geography, St. Andrews University, 1980-89, Senior Lecturer in Geography and Geology, 1989-94. Gordon Warwick Award, 1987; Presidents' Medal, Royal Scottish Geographical Society, 1991; Newbigin Prize, Royal Scottish Geographical Society, 1992; Scottish Science Award, Saltire Society, 1996; Wiley Award, British Geomorphological Research Group, 1999. Visiting Professor, UNIS, Svalbard, since 2000; Erskine Fellow, University of Canterbury, New Zealand, 2003. Publications: The Quaternary of the Isle of Skye, 1991; The Periglaciation of Great Britain, 1994; Classic Landforms of the Isle of Skye, 2000; Paraglacial Geomorphology, 2002. Recreations: music; travel; mountaineering; skiing; writing. Address: (h.) Birchwood, Blebo Craigs, Fife KY15 5UF; T.-01334 850567; e-mail: ckb@st-and.ac.uk

Ballantyne, Fiona Catherine, MA, FCIM. Director, 4Consulting Ltd., since 2001; Member, Board, Queen Margaret University College, Edinburgh, 1995-2005, Vice Chair, 2002-05; Director, The Audience Business Ltd., 1998-2004; Member, Scottish Committee, Institute of

Directors, 1996-2006; Member, Audit Committee, Scottish Further and Higher Education Funding Councils, 2000-02; b. 9.7.50, Bristol; m., A. Neil Ballantyne. Educ. Marr College, Troon; Edinburgh University. Former Market Researcher and Market Research Manager; Research and Planning Manager, Thistle Hotels Ltd., 1975-77; Assistant Marketing Manager, Lloyds & Scottish Finance Group, 1977-79; Scottish Development Agency: Marketing Manager, Small Business Division, 1979-84, Head of Small Business Services, 1984-88, Director, Tayside and Fife, 1988-90; Managing Director, Ballantyne Mackay Consultants, since 1990; Vice-Chair: BBC Broadcasting Council for Scotland, 1991-96, Duncan of Jordanstone College of Art, 1988-94; Director, Edinburgh Healthcare Trust, 1994-96; Director, The Essentia Group (formerly Network Scotland Ltd.), 1991-2001, Chairman, 1997-2001; Member, Board, Scottish Campaign for Learning, 1997-98; Member, Ofcom Consumer Panel, since 2004; Board Member, Scottish Museums Council, since 2004; Chair, SMC, since 2007; Board Member, Edinburgh Printmakers, since 2004. Recreations: walking; swimming; tapestry; painting. Address: (b.) 15 Palmerston Road, Edinburgh EH9 1TL; T.-0131 668 4567.

Ballard, Mark, MA (Hons). MSP (Scottish Green Party), Lothian Region, 2003-07; Lord Rector, University of Edinburgh, 2006-09; b. 27.6.71, Leeds; m., Heather Stacey. Educ. Lawnwood Comprehensive, Leeds; Edinburgh University. Worked for European Youth Forest Action, 1994-98; Editor, Reforesting Scotland, 1998-2001; Director, EMBE Environmental Communications, 2002-03. Publication: Scotlands of the Future (Contributor). Recreations: cycling; Indian cookery.

Ballentine, Rev. Ann Marshall, MA (Hons), DipRE, DipEd, BD. Minister of Kirknewton and East Calder Church, since 1993; Minister of Airth Church, 1981-93; b. 27.12.42, Bellshill. Educ. West Calder Primary School; West Calder High School; Edinburgh University: Moray House College of Education. Teacher of English: Kingussie High School, 1966-68, Wishaw High School, 1968-69; UCCF Travelling SEC, 1969-72; Garrion Academy, Teaching English Literature and Languages, 1972-74; New College to study Divinity, 1974-76; Deaconess with Church of Scotland, Cumbernauld, 1976-81. Church of Scotland Selection School for Minister; Scottish Council for UCCF; Scottish Council for Interserve. Recreations: reading; walking in countryside; gardening. Address: 8 Manse Court, East Calder EH53 0HF; T.-01506 880 802; e-mail: annballentine@tiscali.co.uk

Band, Thomas Mollison, b. 28.3.34, Aberdeen; m., Jean McKenzie Brien; 1 s.; 2 d. Educ. Perth Academy. Principal, Tariff Division, Board of Trade, London, 1969-73; Director (Location of Industry), Department of Industry, Glasgow, 1973-76; Assistant Secretary: (Industrial Policy), Scottish Economic Planning Department, 1976-78, (Housing), Scottish Development Department, 1978-82, (Finance), Scottish Office, 1982-84; Director, Historic Buildings and Monuments, Scottish Development Department, 1984-87; Chief Executive, Scottish Tourist Board, 1987-94; Member, Board of Management, Perth Housing Association, since 1993, Chairman, since 2003; Chairman: Andersons Enterprises Ltd., 1994-99, Perth Theatre Ltd., 1995-2002, Edinburgh Europa Ltd., 1994-98, Select Line Breaks Ltd., 1995-98; Governor: Edinburgh Telford College, 1990-98, Queen Margaret College, 1995-2002; President, European Bureau Lesser Used Languages (UK), since 2003; Preses, Scots Language Society, since 2004. Recreations: gardening; skiing. Address: (h.) Heathfield, Pitcairngreen, Perthshire; T.-01738 583 403.

Banfill, Professor Phillip Frank Gower, BSc, PhD, CSci, CChem, FRSC, MCIOB, ILTM. Professor of Construction Materials, Heriot-Watt University, since 1995; b. 20.3.52, Worthing; m., Patricia; 1 s.; 1 d. Educ. Lancing College;

Southampton University; Liverpool University. Former Lecturer, Liverpool University. Publications: three books; 108 papers. Recreations: sailing; choral singing; bee-keeping. Address: (b.) School of the Built Environment, Heriot-Watt University, Riccarton, Edinburgh EH14 4AS; T.-0131-451 4648.

Banks, Christopher, MA (Oxon), MBA, FCIM, MCIPS, MIQ. Commercial Director, Scottish Water, since 2002; b. 3.1.60, Manchester; m., Isobel; 1 s.; 1 d. Educ. Manchester Grammar School; Wadham College, Oxford University. Business Development Director, Ennstone plc, 2001-02; Managing Director, Ennstone Building Products, 2000-01; Commercial Director: Scottish Coal, 1998-2000, Celtic Energy Ltd., 1995-98, George Wimpey plc, 1992-95, Wimpey Fleming Ltd., 1991-92; Managing Director, Redland plc, 1990-91. Recreations: hill walking; cricket (Level 1 ECB Cricket Coach); archaeology. Address: (b.) Castle House, 6 Castle Drive, Carnegie Campus, Dunfermline, Fife KY11 8GG; T.-01383 848459; e-mail: chris.banks@scottishwater.co.uk

Banks, Gordon., BA (Hons). MP (Labour), Ochil and Perthshire South, since 2005; b. 1955, Acomb, Northumberland; m.; 2 c. Address. (b.) House of Commons, London SW1A 0AA.

Banks, Iain M. Novelist; b. 1954. Educ. schools in North Queensferry, Gourock, Greenock; Stirling University. Hitch-hiked through Europe, Scandinavia, Morocco, 1975, later worked for British Steel and IBM, and as a costings clerk in London. Books: The Wasp Factory, 1984; Walking on Glass, 1985; The Bridge, 1986; Consider Phlebas, 1987; Espedair Street, 1987; The Player of Games, 1988; Canal Dreams, 1989; Use of Weapons, 1990; The State of the Art, 1991; The Crow Road, 1992; Against a Dark Background, 1993; Complicity, 1993 (No. 1 bestseller in paperback); Feersum Endjinn, 1994; Whit, 1995; Excession, 1996; Song of Stone, 1997; Inversions, 1998; Look to Windward, 2000; The Algebraist, 2004; The Steep Approach to Garbadale, 2007; Matter, 2008; non-fiction: Raw Spirit, 2003. Address: (b.) Little, Brown, 100 Victoria Embankment, London EC4Y 0DY.

Banks, Robert Lewis McIntyre, BL. Councillor, Argyll and Bute Council; Depute Leader, Argyll and Bute Council, 2001-07; Honorary Sheriff, Oban, since 1989; b. 24.3.32, Edinburgh; m., Ishbel Gordon. Educ. Oban High School; Edinburgh University. Partner, Anderson, Banks and Co, 1954-92 (Senior Partner, 1986-92); Dean, Oban Faculty of Solicitors, 1986-89. Hon. Secretary, RSSPCC, Oban, 1961-92; President, Comunn Gaidhealach an Obain, since 1982; Member, Executive Council, An Comunn Gaidhealach, since 1970. Recreations: hill walking; amateur drama; association football fan. Address: (h.) Gowanbrae, Ardconnel Road, Oban, Argyll PA34 5DR; T.-01631-562850.

Banks, Professor William McKerrell, BSc, MSc, PhD, CEng, FIMechE, FIMMM, FREng, FRSA, FRSE. Professor of Advanced Materials, Strathclyde University, since 1991; Director, Centre for Advanced Structural Materials; formerly Co-Director, Scottish Polymer Technology Network; Deputy President and Member, Board of Trustees, IMechE; Chairman, Qualifications and Membership Board, IMechE; Vice Chairman, Trustee Board Awards Committee, IMechE; Past Chairman and Vice Chairman, Engineering Professors' Council; former Director of Research and Training, Faraday Plastics; b. 28.3.43, Irvine; m., Martha Ruthven Hair; 3 s. Educ. Irvine Royal Academy; Strathclyde University. Senior Research

Engineer, G. & J. Weir Ltd., 1966-70; Lecturer, Senior Lecturer, Reader, Professor, Strathclyde University, since 1970. Recipient of James Alfred Ewing Medal (Royal Society and ICE), 2007. Recreations: family; Bible teaching; gardening; travel. Address: (h.) 19 Dunure Drive, Hamilton ML3 9EY; T.-01698 823730.

Barbenel, Professor Joseph Cyril, BDS, BSc, MSc, PhD, LDS RCS(Eng), CBiol, FIBiol, CPhys, FInstP, CEng, FIPEM, FRSE. Emeritus Professor, Strathclyde University, since 2001; b. 2.1.37, London; m., Lesley Mary Hyde Jowett; 2 s.; 1 d. Educ. Hackney Downs Grammar School, London; London Hospital Medical College; Queen's College, Dundee (St. Andrews University); Strathclyde University. Dental House Surgeon, London Hospital, 1960; National Service, RADC, 1960-61 (Lieutenant, 1960, Captain, 1961); general dental practice, London, 1963; student, 1963-67; Lecturer, Department of Dental Prosthetics, Dental School, Dundee, 1967-69; Senior Lecturer, Reader, Professor, Strathclyde University. Member, Council, International Union for Physics and Engineering in Medicine. Recreations: music; art; theatre. Address: (b.) University of Strathclyde, Centre for Ultrasonic Engineering, 204 George Street, Glasgow G1 1XW; T.-0141-552 4400.

Barber, Samantha, BA (Hons). Chief Executive, Scottish Business in the Community, since 2000; b. 16.10.69, Dunfermline. Educ. High School of Dundee; University of Northumbria; University of Orleans; University of Dijon; University of Nancy. Policy Advisor, European Parliament, 1994-98; Director, Business for Scotland, 1998-2000; Director, Right Track; Member of Business Advisory Board: Scottish Power, Glasgow Caledonian University. Recreations: reading; cooking; ballet. Address: (b.) Livingston House, First Floor East, 43 Discovery Terrace, Heriot-Watt University Research Pool, Edinburgh EH14 4AP.

Barbour, James Jack, OBE (1992), BA (Jt Hons Politics), MHSM. Chief Executive, Lothian NHS Board, since 2001; b. 16.1.53; partner, Julie Barnes; 1 s.; 2 d. Educ. Madras College, St. Andrews; University of Strathclyde. Graduate Management Trainee, NHS in Scotland, 1977-79; Administrator, Greater Glasgow Health Board, 1979-83; EEC Exchange scholarship in Germany, 1981; Unit Administration, Great Ormond Street Group of Hospitals, 1983-86; General Manager: Royal Manchester Children's Hospital, 1986-87; Aberdeen Royal Infirmary, 1987-92; Chief Executive: Aberdeen Royal Hospital NHS Trust, 1992-94; Central Manchester Healthcare NHS Trust, 1994-98; Sheffield Health Authority, 1998-2001. Alumnus, London Business School Development Programme, 1989. Honorary Professor, Queen Margaret University, 2002; Member of Court, University of Edinburgh, 2006; Burgess, City of Aberdeen, 1992. Recreations: spoiling my children; trying to stay fit! Club: Royal Northern (Aberdeen). Address: (b.) Lothian NHS Board, Deaconess House, 148 Pleasance, Edinburgh EH8 9RS; T.-0131 536 9000.

Barbour, Very Rev. Robert Alexander Stewart, KCVO, MC, MA, BD, STM, DD, DipEd. Minister, Church of Scotland, since 1954; Chaplain, then Extra Chaplain to the Queen in Scotland, since 1976; b. 11.5.21, Edinburgh; m., Margaret Pigot; 3 s.; 1 d. Educ. Rugby School; Balliol College, Oxford; St. Mary's College, St. Andrews. Army (Scottish Horse), 1940-45, Territorial Army, 1947-54; Editorial Assistant, Thomas Nelson & Sons, 1948-49; Secretary, Edinburgh Christian Council for Overseas Students, 1953-55; Lecturer and Senior Lecturer in New

Testament Language, Literature and Theology, New College, Edinburgh University, 1955-71; Professor of New Testament Exegesis, Aberdeen University, 1971-86; Master, Christ's College, Aberdeen, 1977-82; Prelate, Priory of Scotland, Order of St. John, 1977-93; Moderator, General Assembly of the Church of Scotland, 1979-80; Dean, Chapel Royal in Scotland, 1981-91;Honorary Secretary, Novi Testamenti Societas, 1970-77. Recreations: music; forestry; walking. Address: (h.) Old Fincastle, Pitlochry PH16 5RJ; T.-01796 473209.

Barker, Professor John Reginald, BSc, MSc, PhD, FBIS, FRAS, FRSE. Professor of Electronics, Department of Electronics and Electrical Engineering, University of Glasgow, since 1985; b. 11.11.42, Stockport; m., Elizabeth Carol; 2 s.; 1 d. Educ. New Mills Grammar School; University of Edinburgh; University of Durham; University of Warwick. University of Warwick: SRC Personal Research Fellowship, 1969-70, Lecturer in Physics, 1970-84, Senior Lecturer, 1984-85; Affiliate Professor, Colorado State University, 1979-83; Distinguished Science Lecturer, Yale University, 1992; Irvine Lectures in Chemistry, St. Andrews, 1994; broadcasting: History of the Microchip, 1982; The Magic Micro Mission, 1983. Member, various SERC/DTI committees, 1987-93: Devices Committee, Electronic Materials Committee, National Committee for Superconductivity, Materials Commission, Molecular Electronics Committee (Chairman, 1990-93). Publications: over 320 scientific papers; Physics of Non-Linear Transport in Semi-conductors (Co-Author), 1979; Granular Nanoelectronics (Co-Author), 1991. Recreations: hill-walking; astronomy; reading; cooking. Address: (b.) Nanoelectronics Research Centre, Department of Electronics and Electrical Engineering, University of Glasgow, Glasgow G12 8QQ; T.-0141-330 5221.

Barker, Ralph Fraser, MA (Hons), DipEd. Rector, Alloa Academy, since 1995; b. 10.7.51, Edinburgh; m., Suzanne; 2 s.; 1 d. Educ. Royal High School, Edinburgh; Edinburgh University. Teacher of Mathematics, then Assistant Principal Teacher, Royal High School, 1974-81; Principal Teacher, Knox Academy, 1981-84; Assistant Head Teacher, then Depute Head Teacher, Queensferry High School, 1984-94. Recreation: public transport, especially buses. Address: (b.) Claremont, Alloa FK10 2EQ; T.-01259 214979; e-mail: rbarker@clacks.gov.uk

Barlow, Nevile Robert Disney, OBE, DL, FRICS. Chartered Surveyor and Farmer; Chairman, Scottish Borders Valuation Appeal Panel, since 1995; b. 3.2.41, Bagshott, Surrey; m., Myfanwy Louise Kerr-Wilson; 3 s. Educ. Winchester College; Royal Agricultural College, Cirencester. Assistant Agent, Bathurst Estate, Cirencester, 1963-95; Resident Sub-Agent, Bletchingdon Park, 1966-67; Head Factor, National Trust for Scotland, 1986-91; Vice-President, Scottish Landowners' Federation, (Convener, 1991-94); Member, Board, East of Scotland Water, 1995-99; Member, East Region Board, Scottish Environmental Protection Agency, 1996-2000. Recreations: shooting; fishing; sailing; rowing. Address: The Park, Earlston TD4 6AB; T.-01896 849267.

Barnard, Professor Alan John, BA, MA, PhD, FSAScot. Professor of the Anthropology of Southern Africa, Edinburgh University, since 2001; Honorary Consul of Namibia in Scotland, since 2007; b. 22.2.49, Baton Rouge, USA; m., Dr Joy E. Barnard. Educ. New Providence High School; George Washington University; McMaster University; University College London. Junior Lecturer in Social Anthropology, University of Cape Town, 1972-73; Field Research with Bushmen in Botswana, 1974-75 and later; Lecturer in

Social Anthropology, University College London, 1976-78; Lecturer in Social Anthropology, 1978-90, Senior Lecturer, 1990-94, Reader, 1994-2001, Edinburgh University. Hon. Secretary, Association of Social Anthropologists, 1985-89. Publications include: Hunters and Herders of Southern Africa, 1992; Kalahari Bushmen (children's book), 1993; Encyclopaedia of Social and Cultural Anthropology (Co-Editor), 1996; History and Theory in Anthropology, 2000; Social Anthropology, 2000; The Hunter-Gatherer Peoples, 2001; Africa's Indigenous Peoples (Co-Editor), 2001; Self- and Other Images of Hunter-Gatherers (Co-Editor), 2002; Hunter-Gatherers in History (Editor), 2004; Anthropology and the Bushman, 2007. Recreations: walking; cooking; watercolour painting. Address: (b.) School of Social and Political Studies, Edinburgh University, Adam Ferguson Building, George Square, Edinburgh EH8 9LL; T.-0131-650 3938; e-mail: A.Barnard@ed.ac.uk

Barnard, Joy Elizabeth, MA (Hons), PhD, LLB, FSA Scot, WS. Partner, Morton Fraser LLP, since 2004; b. 18.12.61, Glasgow; m., Alan. Educ. Garrion Academy, Wishaw; Edinburgh University. Archaeological Research, 1983-91; Solicitor, since 1998; qualified, Joint Insolvency Examination Board, 2005; Solicitor Advocate (civil), 2006. Recreations: walking; bridge; travel; cooking. Address: (b.) 30-31 Queen Street, Edinburgh EH2 1JX; T.-0131 247 1000; e-mail: joy.barnard@morton-fraser.com

Barnes, Eddie, MA. Political Editor, Scotland on Sunday, since 2004; b. 10.6.72, Ormskirk, Lancashire; m., Malini Geeta; 1 s.; 1 d. Educ. St. Bede's Comprehensive, Ormskirk; Glasgow University. Scottish Catholic Observer Reporter, 1997, Editor, 1998-2000; Scottish Daily Mail, Political Reporter, 2000-02, Political Editor, 2002-04. Address: (b.) Scotland on Sunday, 108 Holyrood Road, Edinburgh EH10 8AS; T.-0131 620 8620; e-mail: ebarnes@scotsman.com

Barnes, James David Kentish. Director, Dobbies Garden Centres plc, 1994-2006; b. 18.4.30, Cheshire; m., 1, Julie Pinckney; 1 s.; 1 d.; m. 2, Susan Mary Leslie. Educ. Eton College; Royal Military Academy Sandhurst. Commissioned 5th Innis Dragoon Guards, 1948-57. Served Germany, Korea, Middle East. Joined John Waterer Sons & Crisp (Horticulture), 1957. Managing Director, 1968-84; Managing Director (Owner), Dobbie and Co Edinburgh, 1968-94; National Trust for Scotland member of Council and Chairman of Gardening committee, 1996-2000; Chairman, NTS Enterprise Company, 2000-05; Director, Grimsthorpe and Drummond Castle Trust Ltd., since 2005. Recreations: cricket; golf; shooting; fishing; gardening; clubs: cavalry & guards, MCC, Muirfield. Address: (h.) Biggar Park, Biggar, Lanarkshire ML12 6JS.

Barnet, James Paul, MA, LLB. Former Partner, Macbeth Currie & Co., Solicitors; Honorary Sheriff, Tayside Central and Fife, at Dunfermline; former Dean, Dunfermline District Society of Solicitors; b. 20.7.37, Darlington; m., Margaret Smart; 4 s. Educ. Dunfermline High School; Edinburgh University. Admitted as Solicitor, 1961. Council Member, Law Society of Scotland, 1985-88; Captain, Scottish Universities Golfing Society, 1980-81; President, Dunfermline Rotary Club, 1985-86. Recreations: golf (Fife Matchplay Champion, 1968); reading; quoting Dr. Johnson. Address: (h.) 33 Drumsheugh Gardens, Edinburgh EH3 7RN.

Barraclough, David Rex, BSc, DSc, MInstP, CPhys. Chairperson, Enable (formerly Scottish Society for the

Mentally Handicapped), 1998-2001; b. 7.3.40, Halifax; m., Christine; 1 s.; 1 d. Educ. Crossley and Porter Boys' School, Halifax; Imperial College, London University. Research Physicist, AEI Ltd., 1962-64; Research Assistant, Bradford University, 1964-68; Geophysicist, British Geological Survey, 1969-2000. Vice-President, Royal Astronomical Society, 1999-2000. Recreations: walking; reading; listening to music. Address: (h.) 49 Liberton Drive, Edinburgh.

Barrett, John Andrew. MP (Liberal Democrat), Edinburgh West, since 2001; b. 11.2.54, Hobart, Australia; m., Carol; 1 d. Educ. Forrester High School; Telford College; Napier Polytechnic. Company Director, ABC Productions, 1985-2001; Member, City of Edinburgh Council, 1995-2001; Director, The EDI Group, 1995-99; Board Member, Edinburgh International Film Festival, 1995-2001; Board Member, Lothian and Borders Screen Industry Office, 1998-2001; Member, Edinburgh Filmhouse Board, 1999-2001. Recreations: cinema; travel; music. Address: (b.) House of Commons, London SW1A 0AA; e-mail: barrettj@parliament.uk

Barrie, Dr Derek Andrew, MA, PhD. Scottish Council Support Officer, Association of Liberal Democrat Councillors, since 2007; Chief of Staff, Scottish Liberal Democrats, 2002-07; b. 3.8.42, Guardbridge, m., Lesley Brown. Educ. Bell-Baxter High School, Cupar; St Andrews University. Liberal candidate, East Fife, 1966; history teacher, 1968-88; various posts with Liberal Party, then Liberal Democrats, since 1989; North East Fife District Councillor, 1977-88; Chairman, NE Fife District Council, 1984-88. Recreations: golf; gardening; theatre. Address: (h.) 13 Lindsay Gardens, St Andrews KY16 8XB; T.-01334 479322.
E-mail: derekbarrie@cix.co.uk

Barrie, Ken, BA Hons (Psych), CQSW, PGDip (Alcohol Studies). Senior Lecturer, University of the West of Scotland, since 1987; b. 13.4.52, Edinburgh; m., Nancy Docherty; 1 s. Educ. Royal High School, Edinburgh; Strathclyde University; Edinburgh University; Paisley University. 1975-83: Social Worker, Strathclyde Regional Council; full range of social work tasks; specialism in addiction, Centre for Alcohol and Drug Studies, University of Paisley, since 1983. Run largest Post Graduate Course on Alcohol and Drug Studies in UK. Recreations: swimming; cycling; canoeing. Address: (b.) University of the West of Scotland, High Street, Paisley PA1 2BE; T.-0141 848 3140; e-mail: ken.barrie@paisley.ac.uk

Barron, Professor Laurence David, FRS, FRSE, DPhil, BSc, FInstP, FRSC. Gardiner Professor of Chemistry, Glasgow University; b. 12.2.44, Southampton; m., Sharon Aviva Wolf; 1 s.; 1 d. Educ. King Edward VI Grammar School, Southampton; Northern Polytechnic, London; Lincoln College, Oxford. Post-doctoral research, Cambridge University, 1969-75; Ramsay Memorial Fellow, 1974-75; Glasgow University: Lecturer in Chemistry, 1975-80, Reader, 1980-84, Professor since 1984. Corday-Morgan Medal, Chemical Society, 1977; G.M.J. Schmidt Memorial Lecturer, Weizmann Institute of Science, 1984; F.L. Conover Memorial Lecturer, Vanderbilt University, 1987; Sir Harold Thompson Award, 1992; Visiting Miller Research Professor, University of California, Berkeley, 1995; EPSRC Senior Fellow, 1995-2000. Publications: over 240 research papers and a book, Molecular Light Scattering and Optical Activity, Second Edition, 2004. Recreations: water-colour painting; walking; music; radio-controlled model aircraft. Address: (b.) Chemistry Department, The University, Glasgow G12 8QQ; T.-0141-330 5168.

Barrow, Professor Geoffrey Wallis Steuart, MA (Hons), BLitt, DLitt, FBA, FRSE, FSA, FSA Scot, FRHistS, Hon. DLitt (Glasgow and Newcastle upon Tyne). Sir William Fraser Professor of Scottish History and Palaeography,

Edinburgh University, 1979-92; b. 28.11.24, Headingley, Leeds; m., Heather Elizabeth Agnes Lownie; 1 s.; 1 d. Educ. St. Edward's School, Oxford; Inverness Royal Academy; St. Andrews University; Pembroke College, Oxford. Royal Navy and RNVR (Sub-Lieutenant), 1943-46; Lecturer in History, University College, London, 1950-61; Professor of Medieval History, Newcastle-upon-Tyne University, 1961-74; Professor of Scottish History, St. Andrews University, 1974-79. Member, Royal Commission on Historical Manuscripts, 1984-90; Royal Historical Society, Council, 1963-74; Joint Literary Director, 1964-74; Vice President, 1982-86; former Chairman: Council, Scottish History Society (President, 1973-77); President: Saltire Society, 1987-90, Scottish Record Society, 1993-97; Vice-President, Commission Internationale de Diplomatique, 1997-2005. Publications: Feudal Britain, 1956; Acts of Malcolm IV, 1960; Robert Bruce, 1965, 1988 and 2005; Acts of William I, 1971; The Kingdom of the Scots, 1973 and 2003; The Scottish Tradition (Editor), 1974; The Anglo-Norman Era in Scottish History, 1980; Kingship and Unity: Scotland 1000-1306, 1981 and 2003; Scotland and its neighbours, 1992; Charters of King David I, 1999. Recreations: visiting graveyards; travel. Address: (h.) 12A Lauder Road, Edinburgh EH9 2EL; T.-0131-668 2173.

Barstad, Professor Hans Magnus, Ctheol, Drtheol (Oslo, Norway). Professor of Hebrew Bible/Old Testament, University of Edinburgh, since 2006; Professor of Old Testament, University of Oslo, 1986-2005; b. 7.6.47, Asnes, Norway; m., Wenche; 1 s.; 1 d. Educ. University of Oslo, Norway. Studies in theology, University of Oslo; Assistant Academic Librarian, University Library, Oslo, 1971; Research Fellow (Hebrew Bible, Semitic languages) under the Norwegian Research Council, Oslo, Rome, Oxford, 1976, 1978-79; Academic Librarian and Keeper of Theological Books, University of Oslo, 1980; Fellow, Nordic Council of Ministers, Copenhagen, 1981; appointed Senior Academic Librarian, 1981; received Degree of Dr. theol. University of Oslo, 1982; Fellow, *Deutscher Akademischer Austauschdienst,* University of Tübingen, 1982; Fellow, Norwegian Ministry of Foreign Affairs, The Hebrew University, Jerusalem, 1983; appointed Keeper of Rare Books and Incunabula, Norwegian National Library, 1984; Visiting Senior Fellow, Oriel College, Oxford, 1992; Chairman of the Board of the Norwegian National Library, 1988-92. Member of the Royal Norwegian Society of Sciences and Letters; Member of the Norwegian Academy of Science and Letters. Secretary General of the Norwegian Academy, 1998-2000. Received the Nansen Award for excellence in research in 2004; Board member, Holberg Foundation, since 2003. Member of numerous international editorial boards. Publications: The Religious Polemics of Amos, 1984; A Way in the Wildnerness, 1989; Det gamle testamente, 1993; The Myth of the Empty Land, 1996; The Babylonian Captivity of the Book of Isaiah, 1997. Recreation: walking. Address: (b.) New College, Mound Place, Edinburgh EH1 2LX; T.-0131 650 8916; e-mail: h.barstad@ed.ac.uk

Bartholomew, Dorothy R. L., MA (Hons), DipEd, SQH. Head Teacher, Ross High School, Tranent, since 2006; b. 22.2.56, Edinburgh. Educ. Bo'ness Academy; University of Edinburgh; Moray House College of Education. Address: Well Wynd, Tranent, East Lothian EH33 2EQ; T.-01875 610433; e-mail: dbartholomew@ross.elcschool.org.uk

Bartlett, Professor Robert John, MA, DPhil, FRHS, FBA, FSA, FRSE. Professor of Mediaeval History, St. Andrews University, since 1992; b. 27.11.50, London; m., Honora Hickey; 1 s.; 1 d. Educ. Battersea Grammar School; Peterhouse, Cambridge; St. John's College, Oxford. Lecturer in History, Edinburgh University, 1980-86;

Professor of Medieval History, University of Chicago, 1986-92. Publications: Gerald of Wales 1146-1223, 1982; Trial by Fire and Water: the medieval judicial ordeal, 1986; The Making of Europe, 1993; England under the Norman and Angevin Kings, 2000; Medieval Panorama (Editor), 2001; The Hanged Man: A Story of Miracle, Memory and Colonization in the Middle Ages, 2004. Recreations: walking; squash. Address: (b.) Department of Mediaeval History, St. Andrews University, St. Andrews KY16 9AL; T.-01334 463308.

Barton, Professor Geoffrey John, BSc (Manchester), PhD (London). Professor of Bioinformatics, College of Life Sciences, University of Dundee, since 2001; b. 01.11.60, Glenelg, Australia; m., Julia; 3 s. Educ. Challney High School; Luton VIth Form College; University of Manchester; Birkbeck College, University of London. Imperial Cancer Research Fund Fellow, Lincoln's Inn Fields, London, 1987-89; Royal Society University Research Fellow, Laboratory of Molecular Biophysics, University of Oxford, 1989-97; Research and Development Team Leader and Head of European Macromolecular Structure Database, EMBL European Bioinformatics Institute, Hinxton, Cambridge, 1997-2001. Eighty peer reviewed publications. Recreations: family; DIY; playing the flute; playing tennis. Address: (b.) College of Life Sciences, University of Dundee, Dow Street, Dundee DD1 5EH; T.-01382 385860.
E-mail: g.j.barton@dundee.ac.uk
Web: www.compbio.dundee.ac.uk

Bartter, Christopher Richard, BA (Hons). Communications Officer, UNISON Scotland, since 1989; Chair, Board, 7:84 Theatre Company (Scotland), since 2000; b. 24.4.53, London; partner, Doreen Kean. Educ. Dorking County Grammar School; University of Strathclyde. Trainee, then Assistant Librarian, Mitchell Library, Glasgow, 1975-89; Administrative Officer, COSLA, 1989. Former Board Member, Mayfest; Member, Scottish Parliament Cross-party Group on Culture and the Media. Recreations: reading; theatre; music (rock and classical); travelling; watching cricket and football (Tottenham Hotspur supporter). Address: (b.) Unison House, 14 West Campbell Street, Glasgow G2 6RX; T.- 0870 7777 006; e-mail: c.bartter@unison.co.uk

Bashford, Caroline, BA, PGCE. Headteacher, The Edinburgh Academy Junior School; b. 12.5.55, Dundee; m., Dr. Ian Bashford; 1 s.; 2 d. Educ. St. Leonard's School, St. Andrews; Edinburgh. Gomer Junior School, Hants; St. Margaret's School, Edinburgh; Stewart's Melville/Mary Erskine JS; George Heriot's School. Recreations: tennis; golf; skiing; travel; sailing. Address: Arboretum Road, Edinburgh; T.-0131 552 3690.
E-mail: headteacher@edinburghacademy.org.uk

Baster, Jeremy, BA, MPhil, MBA, MRTPI. Director of Development Services, Orkney Islands Council, since 1996; b. 5.2.47, New York; m., Miriam Landor; 2 s.; 1 d. Educ. Leighton Park School, Reading; St. John's College, Oxford; University College, London. Early career in consultancy; Economist, Scottish Council (Development and Industry), 1975-80; Economist, Orkney Islands Council, 1980-85; Director of Economic Development, Orkney Islands Council, 1985-96. Director, Soulisquoy Printmakers Ltd. Address: (b.) Council Offices, School Place, Kirkwall KW15 1NY; T.-01856 873535.

Batchelor, Andrea Maria, BSc (Hons), TeachCert, MAppSci. Trustee, National Library of Scotland, since 2005; Head of Education (Inclusion), South Lanarkshire

Council; b. 3.11.54, Leeds; m., John Batchelor; 2 s. Educ. Edinburgh University; Jordanhill College; Glasgow University. Strathclyde Regional Council: Psychologist, 1978-83, Lanark Division; Senior Psychologist, 1983-88, Ayr Division; Depute Principal Psychologist, 1988-90, Dunbarton Division; Education Officer, 1990-93, Glasgow Division; Education Officer, 1993-96, Lanark Division. Member of Scottish Executive Action Team for Better Integrated Children's Services; Member, Advisory Council, Learning and Teaching Scotland, since 2001. Publication: "For Scotland's Children", 2001. Recreations: yoga; swimming; salsa; reading; travel. Address: (h.) 40 Buchanan Drive, Rutherglen, Glasgow G73 3PE; T.-0141 647 6302.

Batchelor, Louise Mary, BA (Hons). Environment Correspondent, BBC Scotland, since 1994; b. 23.2.53, Swanage; m., David Batchelor; 2 s. Educ. Dorchester Grammar School; Reading University. Milton Keynes Gazette, 1974; Oxford Mail, 1977; BBC Radio Scotland, 1978; Presenter/Reporter, Reporting Scotland, 1980; Presenter, Newsnight, 1981-82; Presenter, Breakfast News (Scotland), 1982-83; presenter, various programmes, including Voyager, Fringes of Faith; Presenter, Newsroom South East, 1989. Media Natura Award, 1996, for environment reporting; British Environment and Media Award for TV News and Current Affairs coverage of the environment, 2003; Director, Fair Isle Bird Observatory Trust; Member, Steering Group, Portmoak Community Woodlands. Recreations: walking; bird watching; playing cello. Address: BBC Scotland, The Tun, Holyrood Road, Edinburgh EH8 8PJ.

Bateman, Derek Walls. Presenter, BBC Radio Scotland, since 1995; b. 10.5.51, Selkirk; m., 1, Alison Edgar (deceased); 2 d.; 2, Judith Mackay. Educ. Selkirk High School; Edinburgh College of Commerce. Scotsman Publications; Glasgow Herald; BBC Scotland; Scotland on Sunday; freelance (Sunday Times, STV); BBC Scotland (Presenter, Good Morning Scotland). Publication: Unfriendly Games (Co-Author), 1986. Recreation: wine. Address: (b.) BBC Radio Scotland, 40 Pacific Quay, Glasgow G51 1DZ.

Bateman, Meg (Vivienne Margaret), MA (Hons), PhD. Gaelic poet; b. 13.4.59, Edinburgh; 1 s. Educ. Mary Erskine School, Edinburgh; University of Aberdeen. Poetry collections: Orain Ghaoil (1990); Aotromachd is Dàin Eile (Lightness and Other Poems) (1997) (both shortlisted for Scottish Book of the Year Award); Soirbheas/Fair Wind, 2006; translations of Gaelic poetry published in An Anthology of Scottish Women Poets, Gàir nan Clàrsach (The Harps' Cry); Duanaire na Sracaire/Songbook of the Pillagers, 2007. Address: (b.) Sabhal Mòr Ostaig, Sleat, Isle of Skye IV44 8RQ; T.-01471 888310; e-mail: sm00meg@groupwise.uhi.ac.uk

Bates, Damian, BA (Hons). Editor, Evening Express, Aberdeen, since 2006; b. 9.4.69, Blackpool, Lancashire; m., Jill. Educ. Cardinal Allen RC High School, Fleetwood; St. Mary's VIth Form, Blackpool; Reading University. Trainee Reporter; Business Reporter; Deputy Business Editor; Crime Reporter all Evening Gazette, Middlesbrough; Assistant News Editor; Deputy News Editor - The News, Portsmouth; News Editor; Assistant Editor (News) - Telegraph and Argus, Bradford; Deputy Editor, then Editor, Evening Express, Aberdeen. Publication: No More I Love Yous - The Nikki Conroy Story. Recreations: cooking; raising chickens; bad golf and lots of gardening. Address: (b.) AJL, Lang Stracht, Aberdeen; T.-01224 690222.

Bates, Peter James, OBE. Chair, NHS Tayside Board, 2001-07 (retired); b. 6.5.45, Birmingham; m., Ann; 1 s.; 3 d. Educ. St. Augustine's, Handsworth; Birmingham University. Depute Director of Social Work, Strathclyde; Director of Social Work, Tayside; Director of Social Work, Dundee; Acting Director with other local authorities; Management Consultant to a number of Councils; secondment to Health Department S/E. Recreations: music; reading. Address: (h.) 3 James Place, Broughty Ferry, Dundee DD5 1EE; T.-01382 774876.

Batho, Mark Thomas Scott, MA (Hons). Head, Lifelong Learning Group, Scottish Executive, since 2003; b. 10.6.56, Ashtead, Surrey; m., Vivienne Ann; 2 s.; 1 d. Educ. Glyn Grammar School, Epsom; St Andrews University. Joined Scottish Office as Administration Trainee, 1979. Non-Executive Board Member, CEiS. Address: (b.) Scottish Executive, Europa Building, 450 Argyle Street, Glasgow G2 8LG; T.-0141 242 0206.

Baughan, Mike, OBE, BEd, FEIS. Former Chief Executive, Learning and Teaching Scotland (formerly Scottish Consultative Council on the Curriculum), 2000-2004; b. 11.6.44, Dumfries; m., Anna; 1 s.; 1 d. Educ. St. Joseph's College, Dumfries; Dundee University; Dundee College of Education. RAF; brief career in industrial banking; English Teacher, secondary schools, Dundee, 1975-82; Churchill Fellow, 1977; Adviser in Education, Tayside Regional Council, 1982-87; Rector, Webster's High School, Kirriemuir, 1987-97; Scottish Consultative Council on the Curriculum: Development Fellow, 1997-98, appointed Chief Executive, 1998. Chair/Member, various national education committees; Recent Council Member, Save the Children Scotland. Recreations: hill-walking; golf; fishing; theatre; travel. Address: (b.) 6 Shepherd's Road, Newport-on-Tay, Fife DD6 8HJ.

Baverstock, Brian, CPFA. Chief Executive, APUC Ltd (Advanced Procurement Universities & Colleges), since 2006; b. 16.6.60, Haddington; divorced; 1 d. Educ. Knox Academy; Glasgow College of Technology. Administrator, then Auditor, then Senior Analyst, then Head of Branch, Scottish Executive, 1982-98; Head of Financial Appraisal, then Deputy Director, Scottish Funding Council. Recreations: golf; travel; food and wine. Address: (b.) 14 New Hart Road, Edinburgh EH14 1RL; T.-0131 442 8939; e-mail: baverstock@apuc-scot.ac.uk

Baxter, Mary Ross, MBE, MA, LRAM; b. 23.9.27, Glasgow. Educ. Park School, Glasgow; Glasgow University. John Smith & Son, Booksellers, Glasgow, 1952-56; British European Airways, Glasgow Office, 1956-60; Director, National Book League Scotland (now known as Scottish Book Trust), 1960-89; former President, International PEN Scottish Centre; Trustee, The Pushkin Prizes in Scotland. Honorary Member, Scottish Library Association. Recreations: music; books; home-decorating; cooking; gardening. Address: (h.) 18 Crown Terrace, Glasgow G12 9ES; T.-0141-357 0327; e-mail: marybaxglasgow@aol.com

Baxter, Peter R., DHE. Curator, Benmore Botanic Garden, since 1995; b. 30.6.58, Irvine; m.; 1 s.; 1 d. Address: (b.) Benmore Botanic Garden, Benmore, Dunoon PA23 8QU; e-mail: p.baxter@rbge.org.uk

Baxter, (William) Gordon, OBE, LLD, DBA, LLD. President: W.A. Baxter & Sons Ltd., since 1994 (Chairman, 1970-94); b. 8.2.18, Fochabers, Moray; m., Ena E. Robertson; 2 s.; 1 d. Educ. Ashville College, Harrogate; Aberdeen University. ICI Explosives Ltd., 1940-45 (Research and Development Manager, various military projects); joined family business, 1946; Managing Director,

1947-71; Member, British Export Council Committee for Exports to USA, 1964-72; Member, North American Advisory Group, DTI, 1979-89; former Director, Grampian Regional Board, Bank of Scotland; Lifetime Achievement Award, 2000; Entrepreneurial Exchange "Hall of Fame", 2004; Member of Council, Royal Warrant Holders Association, London; Honorary Fellow, Chartered Institute of Marketing; LLD (Aberdeen), DBA (Napier), LLD (Strathclyde). Recreations: fishing; tennis; cricket. Address: (h.) Speybank House, Fochabers, Moray; T.-01343 821234.

Baynham, John William, CBE, Doctor (honoris causa) (Edinburgh), Doctor (honoris causa) (Queen Margaret University College, BSc, PhD, DIC. Chairman, Lothian Health Board, 1990-97; Chairman, Scottish Health Board Chairmen's Group, 1995-97; b. 20.1.29, Blantyre; m., Marie B. Friel; 1 d. Educ. Bathgate Academy; Aberdeen University; Imperial College, London. Scottish Agricultural Industries PLC, 1955-87, latterly as Agribusiness Director. Member, Lothian Health Board, 1987-90; Chairman, Board of Governors, Moray House Institute of Education, Heriot Watt University, 1991-95; Governor, Queen Margaret College, 1995-99; Chairman, Salaries Committee, Conference of Scottish Centrally Funded Colleges, 1995-99. Recreations: Rotary; golf; grandchildren. Address: (h.) 'Rathmullan', 2, Somnerfield Park, Haddington, East Lothian EH41 3RX; T.-01620 825750.

Beacom, Brian MacDonald, MBE. Chairman, Scottish Health Council, since 2004; Non Executive Director, NHS QIS, since 2004; b. 24.8.43, Glasgow; m., Catherine Rorke; 2 s.; 1 d. Educ. Govan High School. Car Scheme Administrator, Britoil, 1979-93; Transport Manager, HCI Scotland Ltd., 1993-99; Manager, North Glasgow Community Health Project, 1996-2006. Member, Levern Community Council; Chairman, NATA Transport Group Glasgow; Co Secretary, North Glasgow HLC (Healthy Living Community). Recreations: golf; music; piano and organ playing. Address: (b.) Delta House, 50 West Nile Street, Glasgow G1 2NP; T.-0141-241-6308.

Bealey, Professor Frank William, BSc (Econ), DSc (Econ). Professor of Politics, Aberdeen University, 1964-90; b. 31.8.22, Bilston, Staffordshire; m., Sheila Hurst; 1 s.; 2 d. Educ. King Edward VI Grammar School, Stourbridge; London School of Economics. Able Seaman, Royal Navy, 1941-46; Extra-Mural Lecturer, Manchester University, 1951-52; Lecturer and Senior Lecturer, Keele University, 1952-64; Temporary Lecturer, Birmingham University, 1958-59. Treasurer and founder Member, Society for the Study of Labour History, 1960-63; Convener, Committee for Social Science, Aberdeen University, 1970-74 and 1986-89; Fellow, Royal Historical Society, 1971; Editorial Board, Political Studies, 1975-83; Visiting Fellow, Yale University, 1980; Organiser, Parliamentary All-Party Group, Social Science and Policy, 1984-89; Trustee, Jan Hus Educational Foundation, 1981-2000; Bailie of the Bennachie, since 1992; Co-ordinator: EC Tempus Project (Political Science, Czechoslovakia), 1990-93. Publications: Labour and Politics 1900-1906 (Co-author); Constituency Politics (Co-author); The Social and Political Thought of the British Labour Party; The Post Office Engineering Union; The Politics of Independence (Co-author); Democracy in the Contemporary State; Elements in Political Science (Co-author); A Dictionary of Political Science; Power in Business and the State. Recreations: reading poetry; eating and drinking; swimming; watching football and cricket. Address: (h.) 11 Viewforth Terrace, Edinburgh EH10 4LH.

Beamish, Sally, DMus. Composer; b. 26.8.56, London; m., Robert Irvine; 2 s.; 1 d. Educ. Camden School for Girls; Royal Northern College of Music; Staatliche Hochschule Fur Musik. Viola player until 1989 (Raphael Ensemble, Academy of St Martin's); professional composer, since 1990; Composer-in-Residence, Swedish and Scottish Chamber Orchestras, 1998-2003; several CDs on BIS label; orchestral, vocal, choral, chamber and solo works inc. opera Monster, 2002, oratorio Knotgrass Elegy; also film music; stage musical: Shenachie, 2006. Recreations: writing; painting. Address: (b.) Scottish Music Centre, City Halls, Candleriggs, Glasgow G1 1NQ; T.-0141 552 5222.
E-mail: sfbeamish@btinternet.com

Beastall, Graham Hedley, CBE, BSc, PhD, EurClinChem, FRCPath, FRCP(Glas). Top Grade Biochemist (Endocrinology), Glasgow Royal Infirmary, since 1981; Senior Lecturer, Glasgow University, since 1983; b. 11.12.47, Liverpool; m., Judith; 2 s. Educ. Liverpool Institute High School for Boys; Liverpool University. Lecturer in Biochemistry, Liverpool University, 1971-72; Lecturer in Steroid Biochemistry, Glasgow University, 1972-76; Senior Biochemist (Endocrinology), then Principal Biochemist (Endocrinology), Glasgow Royal Infirmary, 1976-81.Chairman, Association of Clinical Biochemists, 1994-97; Chairman, Conference of Clinical Scientists Organisations, 1996-98; Chairman, Scottish Affairs Committee, Royal College of Pathologists, 2000-02; Vice President, Royal College of Pathologists, 2002-05; Secretary, European Communities Confederation of Clinical Chemistry, 1996-2002. Recreations: Scouting; gardening. Address: (b.) Department of Clinical Biochemistry, Royal Infirmary, Glasgow G4 OSF; T.-0141-211 4632; e-mail: gbeastall@gri-biochem.org.uk

Beat, Janet Eveline, BMus, MA. Composer; Lecturer, Glasgow University, since 1996; Artistic Director and Founder, Soundstrata (electro-acoustic ensemble); Honorary Research Fellow, Music Department, Glasgow University; b. 17.12.37, Streetly. Educ. High School for Girls, Sutton Coldfield; Birmingham University. Freelance Orchestral Player, 1960s; Lecturer: Madeley College of Education, 1965-67; Worcester College of Education, 1967-71, Royal Scottish Academy of Music and Drama, 1972-96; founder Member and former Council Member, Scottish Society of Composers; music published by Furore Verlag, Kassel; wrote musical criticism for The Scotsman; G.D. Cunningham Award, 1962; her works have been performed throughout the UK as well as in Switzerland, Germany, Poland, North America, South America, Greece, Australia, Japan, Austria, Portugal and Spain. Recreations: travel; reading; art. Address: The Gait, Candleriggs, Glasgow G1 1NQ; T.-0141 552 5222.
E-mail: info@scottishmusiccentre.com

Beath, Professor John Arnott, MA, MPhil, FRSE, FRSA. Professor of Economics, St. Andrews University, since 1991 (Head, School of Social Sciences, 1991-98 and 2000-03); Chairman, Economic Research Institute of Northern Ireland; Member, Review Body on Doctors' and Dentists' Remuneration; b. 15.6.44, Thurso; m., Dr. Monika Schroder. Educ. Hillhead High School; St. Andrews, London, Pennsylvania and Cambridge Universities. Research Officer, Department of Applied Economics, Cambridge University; Fellow, Downing College, Cambridge; Lecturer, then Senior Lecturer in Economics, Bristol University. Member, Research Priorities Board, Economic and Social Research Council, 1996-2000; Chair, Conference of Heads of University Departments of Economics, 1997-2003; Member, Council and Executive Committee, Royal Economic Society; RAE Panellist, 1996, 2001. Publication: The Economic Theory of Product Differentiation. Recreations: gardening; golf; music. Address: (h.) Simonden, Ceres, Cupar KY15 5PP.

Beattie, Alistair Duncan, MD (Hons), FRCPGlas, FRCPLond. Consultant Physician, Southern General Hospital, Glasgow, 1976-2002; Honorary Clinical Lecturer, Glasgow University, since 1977; b. 4.4.42, Laurencekirk; m., Gillian Margaret McCutcheon; 3 s.; 2 d. Educ. Paisley Grammar School; Glasgow University. Junior hospital appointments, Royal Infirmary and Western Infirmary, Glasgow, 1965-69; Department of Materia Medica, Glasgow University: Research Fellow, 1969-73, Lecturer, 1973-74; MRC Research Fellow, Royal Free Hospital, London, 1974-75. Chairman, Medical and Dental Defence Union of Scotland. Recreations: golf; music. Address: (h.) Flat 3/2 Lauderdale Mansions, 47 Novar Drive, Glasgow G12 9UB; T.-0141-334 0101.

Beattie, Andrew Watt, LLB (Hons), DipLP, NP. Depute Scottish Parliamentary Counsel, since 1999; b. 16.11.72, Aberdeen; m., Claire Louise. Educ. Elgin Academy; Edinburgh University. Solicitor, Shepherd & Wedderburn, WS, 1995-99. Recreations: hillock-walking; squash; football. Address: (b.) Office of the Scottish Parliamentary Counsel, Victoria Quay, Edinburgh EH6 6QQ; T.-0131-244 1665.

Beattie, Bryan William, JP, BA, FRSA. Expert Adviser to Minister for Tourism, Culture and Sport, 2003-05; Chairman, Board of Governors, Eden Court Theatre, 1996-2002; Board Member, Scottish Screen, 1998-2003; b. 3.5.60, Dundee; m., Emer Leavy; 3 d.; 1 s. Educ. High School of Dundee; Stirling University. Director, Stirling Festival, 1984-86; established Stirling Writers Group, Stirling Youth Theatre; Arts Development Officer for Scotland, Scottish Council on Disability, 1986-87; Principal, Creative Services (arts consultancy), since 1992; Chairman, Scottish Youth Theatre, 1993-99; Councillor, Highland Regional Council, 1994-96, and Highland Council, 1995-99 (Chairman, Cultural and Leisure Services Committee, 1995-99); Board Member, Ross and Cromarty Enterprise, 1996-2002, Vice-Chairman, 1999-2002; Chairman: Feis Rois, since 2006, Booth Scotland, since 2007; Member, University of Highlands and Islands Foundation, 1996-99; Founder Member, Highlands and Islands Alliance, 1998; author of plays for radio and theatre; broadcaster; columnist, Press and Journal; occasional acting. Recreations: music; books; sport; regular breathing; remembering family and friends' names. Address: (h.) Drumderfit, North Kessock, by Inverness, IV1 3ZF; T.-01463 731596.
E-mail: bryan@creativeservicesscotland.co.uk

Beattie, Professor Vivien Ann, MA (Hons), PhD, CA, FRSA. Professor of Accounting, University of Glasgow, since 2004; Director of Research, Institute of Chartered Accountants of Scotland, 1998-2003; b. 9.5.58, Renfrew; 1 s. Educ. Renfrew High School; St. Andrews University. Student CA, Mann Judd Gordon, Chartered Accountants, Glasgow, 1980-83; Lecturer then Senior Lecturer, Portsmouth Polytechnic, 1983-86; Lecturer, Southampton University, 1987-93; Senior Lecturer, Reader, then Professor, Stirling University, 1993-03. Recreations: hillwalking; dogs. Address: (h.) 14 Forrester Gait, Torwood Gardens, Torwood FK5 4TB; T.-01324 563656; e-mail: V.Beattie@accfin.gla.ac.uk

Beaty, Professor Robert (Bob) Thompson, OBE, BSc (Hons), FREng, FIEE, CEng. Managing Director, GlenCon Ltd., 1996-2007; Chairman, Scottish Enterprise Renfrewshire, 1999-2003; b. 13.10.43, Kilmarnock; m., Anne Veronica; 2 s. Educ. Hamilton Academy; Glasgow University. Hoover Scholar, 1961-65; Test Engineer, Hoover Ltd., Cambuslang, 1965-68; IBM, 1968-96, latterly Director of Personal Computer Manufacturing

and Development Site at Greenock. Chair of Court, University of Paisley; former Vice-Chairman, Board of Management, James Watt College; Visiting Professor in Product Design, Glasgow University; Board Member, SIDAB. Recreations: cycling; hill-walking; golf; travel; France. Address: (h.) Glenside, 89 Newton Street, Greenock PA16 8SG; T.-01475 722027/07961 068614.
E-mail. bob.beaty@btopenworld.com

Beaumont, Nigel James Bruce, LLB. Senior Partner, Beaumont & Co., Solicitors, Edinburgh, since 1984; b. 2.3.56, Edinburgh; m., Mary E. Lee; 1 s.; 1 d. Educ. Edinburgh Academy; Edinburgh University. Apprentice Solicitor, J.C & A. Stewart, Solicitors, Edinburgh; Procurator Fiscal Depute, Inverness, Elgin, Glasgow and Edinburgh. Recreations: skiing; hillwalking; photography. Address: (b.) 31 Albany Street, Edinburgh EH1 3QN; (h.) Lime Trees, Barnton Avenue, Edinburgh; T.-0131 557 3565.

Beaumont, Professor Paul Reid, LLB, LLM. Professor of European Union and Private International Law, University of Aberdeen, since 1995 (Head, Law School, 2000-08); b. 27.10.60, Hamilton; m., Marion; 1 s.; 1 d. Educ. Claremont High School, East Kilbride; Glasgow University; Dalhousie University, Canada. University of Aberdeen: Lecturer in Public Law, 1983-91, Senior Lecturer in Public Law, 1992-95. Academic Co-ordinator, Lawyers Christian Fellowship. Author and editor of Several books. Recreations: golf; stamp collecting. Address: School of Law, University of Aberdeen, Aberdeen AB24 3UB; T.-01224 272439; e-mail: p.beaumont@abdn.ac.uk

Beaumont, Professor Phillip Barrington, BEcon (Hons), MEcon, PhD. Professor, School of Business and Management, Glasgow University, since 1990; b. 13.10.49, Melbourne, Australia; m., Patricia Mary Ann McKinlay; 2 children. Educ. Camberwell High School, Melbourne; Monash University, Melbourne; Glasgow University. Glasgow University: Research Fellow, Lecturer, 1976-84; Senior Lecturer, 1984-86; Reader, 1986-90. Visiting Professor: Massachusetts Institute of Technology, Boston, 1982, McMaster University, 1986, Case Western Reserve University, 1988, Cornell University, 1990. Publications: Bargaining in the Public Sector, 1978; Safety at Work and the Trade Unions, 1981; Job Satisfaction in Public Administration, 1983; The Decline of Trade Union Organization, 1987; Change in Industrial Relations, 1990; Public Sector Industrial Relations, 1991; Human Resource Management, 1993; The Future of Employment Management, 1995. Recreations: tennis; badminton; cricket; shooting; fishing. Address: (b.) The University, Glasgow G12 8QQ; T.-0141-339 8855.

Beaumont, Professor Steven Peter, OBE, MA, PhD, FRSE, FREng, CEng, MIET. Professor of Nanoelectronics, Department of Electronics and Electrical Engineering, Vice Principal, Research and Enterprise, University of Glasgow; b. 20.2.52, Norwich; m., Joanne Mary; 1 s.; 2 d. Educ. Norwich School; Corpus Christi College, Cambridge University. Research Fellow, Glasgow University, 1978-83; Barr and Stroud Lecturer in Electronics, Glasgow University, 1983-86, Senior Lecturer, 1986-89, Head of Department of Electronics and Electrical Engineering, 1994-98; Director: Institute for System Level Integration, 1999-2004, Intellemetrics Ltd., 1982-90, System Level Integration Ltd, Electronics Scotland, 1998-2004, Photonix Ltd, Kelvin Nanotechnology Ltd., GU Holdings Ltd. Recreations: walking; crofting. Address: (h.) 13 Kelvinside Terrace South, Glasgow G20 6DW; T.-0141-330 2112.

Bechhofer, Professor Frank, MA. University Fellow, Edinburgh University; b. 10.10.35, Nurnberg, Germany; m., Jean Barbara Conochie; 1 s.; 1 d. Educ. Nottingham High School; Queens' College, Cambridge. Junior Research Officer, Department of Applied Economics, Cambridge

University, 1962-65; Edinburgh University: Lecturer in Sociology, 1965-71, Reader in Sociology, 1971-87, Director, Research Centre for Social Sciences, 1984-97, Professor of Social Research, 1988-97. Address: (h.) 51 Barnton Park View, Edinburgh EH4 6HH; T.-0131-339 4083; e-mail: frank@bechhofer.demon.co.uk

Beckett, Rev. David Mackay, BA, BD. Minister, Greyfriars Tolbooth and Highland Kirk, Edinburgh, 1983-2002; Moderator, Presbytery of Edinburgh, 1999-2000; b. 22.3.37, Glasgow; m., Rosalie Frances Neal; 2 s. Educ. Glenalmond; Trinity Hall, Cambridge; St. Andrews University. Assistant Minister, Dundee Parish Church (St. Mary's), 1963-66; Minister, Clark Memorial Church, Largs, 1966-83. Convener, Committee on Public Worship and Aids to Devotion, General Assembly, 1978-82; President, Church Service Society, 1986-88; Secretary, General Assembly Panel on Doctrine, 1987-95. Publication: The Lord's Supper, 1984. Address: (h.) 31 (1F1) Sciennes Road, Edinburgh EH9 1NT

Beckett, John, QC. All-Scotland Floating Sheriff, since 2008; Solicitor General for Scotland, 2006-07. Educ. University of Edinburgh. Elected to the Faculty of Advocates, 1993; Advocate Depute and a Senior Advocate Depute, since 2003; Principal Advocate Depute, 2006. Address: (b.) Crown Office, 25 Chambers Street, Edinburgh EH1 1LA.

Bedell-Pearce, Keith Leonard, LLB, MSc. Chairman, The Student Loans Company Ltd., since 2001; Chairman, Norwich and Peterborough Building Society, since 2001; b. 11.3.46, Bushey; m., Gaynor (nee Trevelyan); 1 s.; 2 d. Educ. Trinity School of John Whitgift; University of Exeter; University of Warwick. Joined Prudential plc, 1972; Solicitor to the Prudential, 1978; Director, Prudential Assurance, 1988; Director, Prudential plc, 1991-2001; CEO, Prudential Financial Services, 1991; International Development Director, 1996; Chairman, Prudential Australia, 1996; Non-executive Director, F & C Asset Management plc, 2002. Honorary Professor, Warwick Business School; Member, Board of Warwick Business School; Chairman, Directgov; Member, Croydon High School Scholarship Trust; Member, Investment Advisory Committee of the Royal Society. Publication: Information Technology, 1978, 2nd ed 1980. Address: (b.) The Student Loans Co. Ltd., 100 Bothwell Street, Glasgow G2 7JD; T.-020 8660 0819; e-mail: kbp3@btinternet.com

Bedford, Professor Tim, BSc(Hons), MSc, PhD. Professor of Decision Making and Risk Analysis, Strathclyde University, since 2001; b. 14.4.60, London. Educ. Oulder Hill, Rochdale; Warwick University. Fellow, Kings College, Cambridge, 1984-87; Lecturer in Probability, Delft University of Technology, Netherlands, 1987-94; Senior Lecturer in Applications of Decision Theory, Delft University of Technology, 1994-2000. Publication: Probabilistic Risk Analysis: Foundations and Methods. Recreations: music; walking; family. Address: (b.) Department of Management Science, 40 George Street, Glasgow; T.-0141-548 2394.

Bedi, Tarlochan Singh, JP, MB, BS, FRCPsych, DPM. Consultant Psychiatrist and Honorary Clinical Senior Lecturer, Southern General Hospital, Glasgow, since 1980; b. India; m., Dr. T.H. Ratani; 1 s. Educ. Poona University, India. Junior House Officer, Aga Khan Hospital, Nairobi; Senior House Officer, Glenside and Barrow Hospital, Bristol; Registrar, Coneyhill Hospital, Gloucester; Senior Registrar, Gartnavel and Southern General Hospital,

Glasgow; Consultant Psychiatrist, Woodilee Hospital, Lenzie. Past President: Scottish Asian Action Committee, Glasgow; Indian Social and Cultural Association, Glasgow; Indian Graduates Society, Glasgow. Recreations: music; photography; culinary arts. Address: 156 Prestonfield, Milngavie G62 7QA; T.-0141-246 7160.

Beevers, Professor Clifford, OBE, BSc, PhD, MILT. Professor Emeritus, Heriot Watt University, since 2005, Professor of Mathematics, since 1993; b. 4.9.44, Castleford; m., Elizabeth Ann; 2 d. Educ. Castleford Grammar School; Manchester University. Senior Lecturer, 1985; Director, CALM, 1985; Co-Director, Scottish Centre for Research into On-Line Learning and Assessment. Past Chairman, Edinburgh Branch, British Retinitis Pigmentosa Society. Recreations: walking; jogging; music; theatre. Address: (b.) School of Mathematical and Computer Sciences, Heriot Watt University, Riccarton, Edinburgh EH14 4AS; T.-0131-451 3233; e-mail: C.E.Beevers@hw.ac.uk

Begg, Anne, MA. MP (Labour), Aberdeen South, since 1997; b. 6.12.55, Forfar. Educ. Brechin High School; University of Aberdeen; Aberdeen College of Education. Teacher of English and History, Webster's High, Kirriemuir, 1978-88; Assistant Principal Teacher, then Principal Teacher of English, Arbroath Academy, 1988-97. Disabled Scot of the Year, 1988. Recreations: cinema; theatre; reading; public speaking. Address: (b.) House of Commons, London SW1A 0AA; T.-020 7219 2140.

Begg, Professor Hugh MacKemmie, MA, MA, PhD, DipTP, FRTPI. Consultant Economist and Chartered Planner; Reporter, Scottish Executive Inquiry Reporters Unit; Visiting Professor, University of Abertay, Dundee; Associate, Cambridge Economic Associates; Member, Local Government Boundary Commission for Scotland; b. 25.10.41, Glasgow; m., Jane Elizabeth Harrison; 2 d. Educ. High School of Glasgow; St. Andrews University; University of British Columbia; Dundee University. Lecturer in Political Economy, St. Andrews University; Research Fellow, Tayside Study; Lecturer in Economics, Dundee University; Assistant Director of Planning, Tayside Regional Council; Visiting Professor, Technical University of Nova Scotia; Consultant, UN Regional Development Project, Egypt and Saudi Arabia; Consultant, Scottish Office Industry Department, Scottish Office Agriculture and Forestry Department; Head, School of Town and Regional Planning, Dundee University; Dean of Faculty of Environmental Studies, Dundee University. External Adjudicator, Scottish Enterprise; Convener, The Standards Commission for Scotland; Member, Private Legislation Procedure (Scotland) Extra-Parliamentary Panel. Recreations: local history; hill walking; rugby; puppy walking for guide dogs for the blind. Address: (h.) 4 Esplanade, Broughty Ferry, Dundee; T.-01382 779642. E-mail: hughbegg@blueyonder.co.uk

Begg, Ian McKerron, DA, FRIAS, FSA Scot, FFCS. Architect (own practice), since 1983; b. 23.6.25, Kirkcaldy; 3 d. Educ. Kirkcaldy High School; Edinburgh College of Art. Partner, Robert Hurd & Partners, 1951-83; Interim Director, Edinburgh New Town Conservation Committee; Interim Director, Edinburgh Old Town Committee for Conservation and Renewal. Honorary Member, Saltire Society. Recreations: travel, particularly to Paris; supporting Scotland's identity. Address: Ravens'Craig, Plockton, Ross-shire IV52 8UB; T.-01599 544 265.

Begg, William Kirkwood, OBE. Retired former Chairman and Managing Director, Begg, Cousland Holdings Ltd.; Former Chairman, Begg Cousland & Co. Ltd.; b. 5.2.34;

m., Thia St Clair; 2 s.; 1 d. Educ. Glenalmond College. Former Chairman, Scottish Advisory Committee on Telecommunications; former Member, CBI SME Council; former Privy Council Nominee to General Convocation, Strathclyde University; Director, Weavers' Society of Anderston; Founder Trustee, Dallas Benevolent Fund; Chairman of Trustees, James Paterson Trust; former Director (and former Vice Chairman), The Wise Group; former Director, Commercially Wise Ltd.; former Director, Merchants' House of Glasgow; former Member, Scottish Industrial Development Advisory Board; former Member, CBI Council for Scotland; Convener of Trustees, the George Craig Trust Fund. Recreations: sailing; shooting; DIY. Address: (h.) 12 Hughenden Gardens, Glasgow G12 9XW.

Beggs, Professor Jean Duthie, CBE, PhD, BSc, FRS, FRSE. Professor of Molecular Biology, Edinburgh University, since 1999; Royal Society Darwin Trust Research Professor, since 2005; b. 16.4.50, Glasgow; m., Dr Ian Beggs; 2s. Educ. Glasgow High School for Girls; Glasgow University. Post-doctoral Fellow, University of Edinburgh, 1974-77; Post-doctoral Fellow, ARC Plant Breeding Institute, Cambridge, 1977-79; Lecturer, Department of Biochemistry, Imperial College of Science and Technology, London, 1979-85; Royal Society University Research Fellow, Edinburgh University, 1985-89; Royal Society Cephalosporin Fund Senior Research Fellow, University of Edinburgh. 1989-99; Edinburgh University Professorial Research Fellow, 1994-99; Beit Memorial Fellowship, 1976-79; Elected Member, EMBO, 1991; Member various committees of Royal Society (London and Edinburgh), Biochemical Society, RNA Society; Royal Society Gabor Medal, 2003; Biochemical Society Novartis Medal, 2004; University of Edinburgh Chancellor's Award, 2005. Recreations: walking; skiing; scuba diving. Address: (b.) Institute of Cell Biology, Wellcome Trust Centre for Cell Biology, Edinburgh University, King's Buildings, Mayfield Road, Edinburgh, EH9 3JR; T.-0131-650 5351.

Belch, Professor Jill J. F., MB, ChB, FRCP, MD (Hons). Professor and Head of Vascular Diseases Research, Dundee University, Deputy Head of the Division of Medicine and Therapeutics; b. 22.10.52, Glasgow; m., Tom van der Ham; 1 s.; 3 d. Educ. Morrison's Academy, Crieff; University of Glasgow. University of Glasgow and Royal Infirmary: Research Fellow, 1980, Lecturer, 1984; University of Dundee and Ninewells Hospital: Senior Lecturer, 1987, Reader, 1990. Medical Adviser, Raynaud's and Scleroderma Association. Publications: over 200 peer-reviewed articles in scientific journals. Recreations: family; skiing. Address: (b.) University Department of Medicine, Ninewells Hospital, Dundee DD1 9SY; T.-01382 632457.

Belfall, David J., BA (Hons); b. 26.4.47, Colchester; m., Lorna McLaughlan; 1 s.; 1 d. Educ. Colchester Royal Grammar School; St. John's College, Cambridge. Home Office, 1969-88 (Private Secretary to Permanent Under Secretary of State, 1973-74); Scottish Office/Scottish Executive, 1988-2002: Under Secretary, Police and Emergency Services, 1988-91, Health Policy and Public Health, 1991-95; Head, Housing and Area Regeneration Group, 1995-2002; Chairperson, Glasgow Council for the Voluntary Sector, 2002-06. Member: Scottish Criminal Cases Review Commission, since 2002, NHS Lothian Board, since 2004. Address: (b.) SCCRC, 17 Renfield Street, Glasgow G2 5AH.

Belhaven and Stenton, 13th Lord (Robert Anthony Carmichael Hamilton); b. 27.2.27. Succeeded to title, 1961.

Bell, Sheriff Andrew Montgomery, BL. Sheriff of Lothian and Borders, at Edinburgh, 1990-2004 (Sheriff of Glasgow and Strathkelvin, at Glasgow, 1984-90); b. 21.2.40, Edinburgh; m., Ann Margaret Robinson; 1 s.; 1 d. Educ. Royal High School, Edinburgh; Edinburgh University. Solicitor, 1961-74; called to Bar, 1975; Sheriff of South Strathclyde, Dumfries and Galloway, at Hamilton, 1979-84. Address: (h.) 5 York Road, Edinburgh EH5 3EJ; T.-0131-552 3859.

Bell, Arthur J.A., CBE, BSc, FRSA, Hon FIDM. Writer and Lecturer; Marketing Consultant; former Chairman, Scotland Direct (Holdings) Ltd., and subsidiaries; b. 6.10.46, Brechin; m., G. Susan Bell; 4 c. Educ. Royal High School, Edinburgh; Edinburgh University. Chair, New Lanark Housing Association, 1979-99; Chair, New Lanark Conservation Trust, since 2003; Chairman, Caledonian Connoisseur (caleyco.com), since 2004; Chairman, Food Trust of Scotland, since 1998; President, Biggar Civic Society, since 1994; former Editor, Small Business News; Editor, History of British Direct Marketing Association; three times parliamentary candidate. Publication: Complete Edinburgh Pub Guide/A Flavour of Edinburgh (Co-author); My Chariot of Fire, 2003. Address: (h.) Newholm of Culter, Coulter, Biggar ML12 6PZ; 3 Chemin de la Serre, Haute Ville, Camares, Aveyron, France.

Bell, Christopher Philip, BMus, MMus. Conductor/Chorusmaster; Chorus Director: Edinburgh Festival Chorus, since 2007, Grant Park Music Festival, Chicago, USA, since 2001; b. 1.5.61, Belfast. Educ. Royal Belfast Academical Inst.; Edinburgh Academy. Chorus Master/Director: Edinburgh University Musical Society Choir, 1984-88, Edinburgh Royal Choral Union, 1987-90, Royal Society National Orchestra Chorus, 1989-2004, Royal Scottish National Orchestra Junior Chorus, since 1995, Belfast Philarmonic Choir, since 2005. Artistic Director: Total Aberdeen Youth Choir, 1992-96, National Youth Choir of Scotland, since 1996, Ulster Youth Choir, 1999-2003, Children's Classic Concerts, since 2002. Associate Conductor, BBC Scottish Symphony Orchestra, 1987-89; Principal Guest Conductor, State Orchestra of Victoria, Melbourne, 1997-99; Guest Conductor: New Zealand Symphony Orchestra/Wellington City Opera, 1997, Auckland Philharmonia, 1997. Publications: Author, My Voice is Changing; Co-Author: Go for Bronze; Go for Silver, Go for Gold; General Editor, SingBronze, Sing Silver, SingGold. Recordings: Mahler Symphony no 3, Chandos; Paray Joan of Arc Mass, Reference. Grammy Nomination 1999; Burns Sequence: There's Lilt in the Song, NYCoS; Holst The Planets, Naxos. Scotsman of the Year - Creative Talent, 2001; Charles Groves Prize, 2003. Address: 2F1/143 Warrender Park Road, Edinburgh EH9 1DT; T.-07712 050295; e-mail: bellman@ednet.co.uk

Bell, Colin John, MA (Hons), HonLLD (Aberdeen). Broadcaster; Journalist; Author; b. 1.4.38, London; m., Caroline Rose Bell; 1 s.; 3 d. Educ. St. Paul's School; King's College, Cambridge. Journalist, The Scotsman, 1960-62 and 1975-78; Journalist/Contributor, London Life, Sunday Times, Sunday Telegraph, Daily Mirror, Sunday Mail, etc.; Lecturer, Morley College, 1965-68; College Supervisor, King's College, Cambridge, 1968-75; Parliamentary candidate (SNP), West Edinburgh, 1979; European Parliamentary candidate (SNP), North East Scotland, 1979; Vice-Chairman, SNP, 1978-84; Campaign Director, Euro Election, 1984; a Senior Fellow, the 21st Century Trust, 1990; Rector, Aberdeen University, 1991-93. Publications: City Fathers, 1969; Boswell's Johnson, 1971; Scotch Whisky, 1985; Radical Alternative (Contributor), 1978; The Times Reports (Series) (Editor); Scotland's Century, 1999; Murder Trail, 2002. Recreations: jazz; Scottish history.

Bell, Professor Derek, BSc, MBChB, MD, FRCP(E), FRCP(L), FRCP(G). National Clinical Lead, Emergency Services Collaborative (England); National Clinical Lead, Unscheduled Care Collaborative (Scotland); Professor of Acute Medicine, Imperial College London; b. 24.3.55, Dundee; m., Sonya R Lam; 1 s.; 2 d. Educ. Morgan Academy; Edinburgh University. Qualified in medicine, Edinburgh University, 1980; trained in general and respiratory medicine, Royal Infirmary of Edinburgh, until 1988; moved to London and became a Consultant and Clinical Director of Chest Medicine and Intensive Care before returning to Edinburgh, 1996, to develop acute (emergency) medicine; President, Society for Acute Medicine (UK). Recreation: previously youth international hockey player. Address: (h.) 14 Wilton Road, Edinburgh EH16 5JX.
E-mail: d.bell@imperial.ac.uk

Bell, Patrick Ian, BA (Hons). Partner, Shepherd and Wedderburn LLP, since 2007; b. 22.3.67, Edinburgh; m., Karen Jane (nee White); 2 s.; 1 d. Educ. The Edinburgh Academy (5-12); Trinity College, Glenalmond (13-18); St. Chad's College, University of Durham; Guildford Law College. Linklaters & Paines, London: Trainee Solicitor, 1991-93, Assistant Solicitor, 1993-95; Assistant Solicitor, Linklaters & Paines, Singapore, 1995-98; Managing Associate, Linklaters & Alliance, London, 1998-2001; Partner: Linklaters, Warsaw, 2001-05, McClure Naismith, Solicitors, 2005-07. Finance Law Specialist with wide banking and capital markets experience; Member: Law Society of England and Wales (1996), Court of Directors, The Edinburgh Academy (2006), Salmon & Trout Association (Scotland) (1993), New Club (2006), Wooden Spoon Society (2007). Recreations: fishing; tennis; skiing; history. Address: (b.) Saltire Court, 20 Castle Terrace, Edinburgh EH1 2ET; T.-0131 473 5355.
E-mail: patrick.bell@shepwedd.co.uk

Bell, Robin, MA, MSc. Writer, Broadcaster and Artist; b. 4.1.45, Dundee; 2 d. Educ. Morrison's Academy, Crieff; St. Andrews University; Perugia University, Italy; Union College, New York; Columbia University, New York. Formerly: Director of Information, City University of New York, Regional Opportunity Program; Assistant Professor, John Jay College of Criminal Justice, City University of New York; Member, US Office of Education Task Force in Educational Technology; Audio-Visual Editor, Oxford University Press; Editor, Guidebook series to Ancient Monuments of Scotland; Secretary, Poetry Association of Scotland. Scottish Radio and Television Industries Award for Best Radio Feature, 1984; Sony Award, Best British Radio Documentary, 1985; Creative Scotland Award, 2005. Publications: The Invisible Mirror, 1965; Culdee, Culdee, 1966; Collected Poems of James Graham, Marquis of Montrose (Editor), 1970; Sawing Logs, 1980; Strathinver: A Portrait Album 1945-53, 1984; Radio Poems, 1989; The Best of Scottish Poetry (Editor), 1989; Bittersweet Within My Heart: collected poems of Mary Queen of Scots (Translator/Editor), 1992; Scanning the Forth Bridge, 1994; Le Château des Enfants, 2000; Chapeau!, 2001; Civil Warrior, 2002; Tethering a Horse, 2004; How To Tell Lies, 2006. Art exhibitions: My River, Your River (following the 2005 Gleneagles G8); Drawing The Tay (Travelling solo exhibition). Address: (h.) The Orchard, Muirton, Auchterarder PH3 1ND.

Bell, Tom, MSc, ChEHO MREHIS. Chief Executive, The Royal Environmental Health Institute of Scotland, since 2004; b. 15.9.58, Edinburgh; m., Angela; 2 d. Educ. Leith Academy, Edinburgh; Napier College and The University of Edinburgh. Qualified as an Environmental Health Officer, 1980; Corporate Membership of The Royal Environmental Health Institute of Scotland, 1983; gained MSc in Environmental Health, University of Edinburgh, 1993; Training Adviser to The Royal Environmental Health Institute of Scotland, 1998, Director of Professional Development, 1999; Chartered Environmental Health Officer status gained, 2004. Honorary Fellow, The University of Edinburgh, 1994-98; Member of The Scottish Parliament Cross Party Group on Tobacco Control, since 2004; Member of The Board of Examiners, The Royal Environmental Health Institute of Scotland, 1994-98; Member of The Board of Studies, Public Health Sciences, The University of Edinburgh, 1994-98; Member of The Council, The Royal Environmental Health Institute of Scotland, 1994-98; Hon. Treasurer, The Royal Environmental Health Institute of Scotland, 1995-98. Recreations: sport; travel; family life. Address: (h.) 93 Joppa Road, Edinburgh EH15 2HB; T.-0131 669 9122; e-mail: tomjoppa@aol.com

Bellany, Dr John, CBE (1994), RA; b. June, 1942, Port Seton; m., 1, Helen Margaret Percy; 2, Juliet Gray Lister (deceased); 3, for second time, Helen Margaret Bellany; 2 s.; 1 d. Educ. Cockenzie Public School; Preston Lodge, Prestonpans; Edinburgh College of Art; Royal College of Art, London. Lecturer in Fine Art, Winchester School of Art, 1969-73; Head, Faculty of Painting, Croydon College of Art, 1973-78; Visiting Lecturer in Painting, R.C.A., 1975-85; Lecturer in Fine Art, Goldsmiths College, London University, 1978-84; elected Fellow Commoner, Trinity Hall, Cambridge, 1988; lived and painted in Mexico, 1996; one-man exhibitions include: Arts Council touring show; Rosa Esman Gallery, New York; Christine Abrahams Gallery, Melbourne; Ikon Gallery, Birmingham; Walker Art Gallery, Liverpool; Roslyn Oxley Gallery, Sydney; National Portrait Gallery, London; Galerie Krikhar, Amsterdam; Fischer Fine Art, London; retrospective — Scottish National Gallery of Modern Art; Serpentine Gallery, London; Kimsthalle, Hamburg; Museum Ostral, Dortmund; Ruth Siegel Gallery, New York; Raab Gallery, Berlin; Fitzwilliam Museum, Cambridge; Kelvingrove Museum and Art Gallery (50th birthday tribute); Beaux Arts Gallery, Berkeley Square Gallery, London; Edinburgh Festival, 1997; exhibited National Gallery of China, Beijing, 2005; elected to exhibit in Beijing, Biennale, China; made 1st Freeman of East Lothian, 2005; Glasgow Mitchell Library Exhibition, 2005; Kunsthalle Ascuaffenburg Retrospective Exhibition, 2006; elected ARA, 1987; RA, 1992; Hon. RSA, 1987; elected Senior Fellow, Royal College of Art, London, 1999; joint 1st prize, Athena International Award, 1985; honorary doctorates, Edinburgh University, 1996, Heriot-Watt University, 1998; Recreation: motoring around the world in search of beauty.

Belton, Professor Valerie, PhD, MA, BSc (Hons). Professor of Management Science, University of Strathclyde, since 1999; Vice Dean (Academic), Strathclyde Business School; President Elect, EURO (European Federation of Operational Research Societies), 2008; President, UK Operational Research Society, 2004-06; b. 9.8.56, Rotherham. Educ. Wath upon Dearne School; Durham University; Lancaster University, Cambridge University. Operational Research Analyst, Civil Aviation Authority; Academic, University of Kent, 1984-88; Academic, University of Strathclyde, since 1988. Chair, International Society of Multicriteria Decision Making, 2000-04; Editor, Journal of Multicriteria Decision Analysis; author of a book and many academic articles. Recreations: orienteering; mountain biking. Address: (b.) University of Strathclyde, Management Science, 40 George Street, Glasgow G1 1QE; T.-0141-548 3615; e-mail: val.belton@strath.ac.uk

Beltrami, Joseph, SSC, BL, NP. Solicitor/Advocate (Beltrami & Co.); b. 15.5.32, Rutherglen; m., Brigid D.; 3 s. Educ. St. Aloysius College, Glasgow; Glasgow University.

Intelligence Corps, 1954-56 (Sgt.); qualified as Solicitor, 1956; specialised in criminal law; has instructed in more than 500 murder cases; closely associated with two cases of Royal Pardon; in first batch of Solicitor/Advocates to have rights of audience in High Court and Court of Criminal Appeal. Chairman, soccer testimonials: Jim Johnstone and Bobby Lennox, 1976; Danny McGrain, 1980. Publications: The Defender, 1980; Glasgow - A Celebration (Contributor), 1984; Tales of the Suspected, 1988; A Deadly Innocence, 1989; A Scottish Childhood (Contributor), 1998. Recreations: bowls; soccer; snooker; writing; boxing. Address: (h.) 12 Valence Tower, Regents Gate, Bothwell, Lanarkshire.

Bennett, David Andrew, MA, LLB, WS, NP. Consultant, Gillespie Macandrew LLP Solicitors, Edinburgh; Visiting Professor of Company Law, Edinburgh University; b. 27.3.38, Edinburgh; m., Marion Miller Park; 2 d. Educ. Melville College, Edinburgh; Fettes College, Edinburgh; Edinburgh University. Director, Jordans (Scotland) Ltd.; Member, Council, Law Society of Scotland, 1984-90. Session Clerk, Liberton Kirk, 1975-2005; Scottish Editor, Palmer's Company Law, since 1970, and Gore-Browne on Companies, since 1975. Recreations: most sports and arts. Address: (b.) 5 Atholl Crescent, Edinburgh EH3 8EJ; T.-0131 225 1677.
E-mail: david.bennett@gillespiemacandrew.co.uk

Bennett, Helen Margaret, MBE, PhD, FSA Scot. Crafts Director, Scottish Arts Council, since 1993; Group Director, Creative Arts, 1996-2001; Vice-President, World Crafts Council – Europe, 2000-06; b. 25.6.48, Newark; m., Philip Edwin Bennett; 1 d. Educ. Lilley and Stone High School for Girls, Newark; Exeter University; Edinburgh University. Edinburgh Common Purpose Graduate, 1996. Assistant Curator, Borough of Weston-super-Mare, 1969-71; Curator of Agricultural and Social History, Bristol City Museums, 1971-72; Research Assistant, Costume and Textiles, National Museum of Antiquities of Scotland, 1974-81; freelance arts administrator, 1984-88; Head of Crafts Division, Scottish Development Agency, 1989-91; freelance cultural consultant, 1991-93. Governor, Edinburgh College of Art, 1992-2000. Recreations: walking; gardening; textile crafts. Address: (b.) 12 Manor Place, Edinburgh EH3 7DD; T.-0131-226 6051; e-mail: helen.bennett@scottisharts.org.uk

Bennett, Robin Alexander George, MA, LLB, MSI. Solicitor, Bennetts, Cupar, since 1992; b. 6.6.40, Edinburgh; m., Mary Funk; 2 d. Educ. Hillhead High School, Glasgow; Glasgow University. Assistant: Harrisons and Crosfield, Malaysia and Brunei, 1965-78, Drummond Johnstone and Grosset, Cupar, 1978-80; Solicitor (Partner): Drummond Cook and Mackintosh, Cupar, 1980-90, Wallace and Bennett, 1990-92. Chairman, Tranquilliser Addiction Solicitors Group, 1988-90; Founder/Secretary, Scottish TSB Depositors Association, 1986; Chairman, Ceres and District Community Council, 1980-82 and 1993-98; Vice Convener, Scottish Legal Action Group, 1989-95; Trustee, The Lady Margaret Skiffington Trust; Honorary Sheriff, Cupar, since 1991. Recreations: hillwalking; water gardening; listening to organ music. Address: (h.) Sandakan, Curling Pond Road, Ceres, Fife KY15 5NB; T.-01334 828452.

Bennett, Sigurdur Arthur, LLB(Hons). Advocate, since 1982; b. 21.9.57, Edinburgh. Educ. Edinburgh Academy; Edinburgh University. Standing Junior Counsel, Ministry of Defence (RAF), 1991-97. Muirhead Prize for Civil Law, 1976; Member, Faculty Council, 1992-96. Publications: Divorce in the Sheriff Court; Personal Injury Damages in Scotland; Style Writs for the Sheriff Court. Address: 3 Royal Circus, Edinburgh EH3 6TL; T.-0131-225 9904.

Bennie, Norma, DipCOT, MBE. Former Vice Chairman, Mental Welfare Commission (Commissioner, 1994-2002);

General Member, Mental Health Tribunal; b. 11.11.46, Beith; m., Ernest H. Bennie; 2 s.; 1 d. Educ. Spier's School, Beith; Glasgow School of Occupational Therapy. Occupational Therapist, 1968-93. Recreations: walking; sailing; reading. Address: (h.) Oakdene, Armadale Road, Rhu, Helensburgh G84 4LG.

Bennison, Dr Jennifer Marion, MA, MBDChir, FRCGP. Assistant Director of Postgraduate General Practice Education, South East Scotland, since 2007; General Practitioner; GP Principal, Rose Garden Medical Centre, Edinburgh, since 1998; b. Essex; m., Prof. Seth Armitage; 2 s.; 2 d. Educ. Hertfordshire and Essex High School for Girls; Corpus Christi College, Cambridge; Royal Free Hospital School of Medicine, London. GP Principal, Leith Walk Surgery, Edinburgh, 1993-98; Director, Phased Evaluation Programme, RCGP Scotland, 1999-2002; former Deputy Chairman (Policy), Scottish Council, Royal College of General Practitioners. Recreations: children; walking; singing. Address: (b.) Rose Garden Medical Centre, 4 Mill Lane, Leith, Edinburgh EH6 6TL; T.-0131-554 1274; e-mail: Jenny.Bennison@lothian.scot.nhs.uk

Bentley, Professor Michael, BA, PhD, FRHistS. Professor of Modern History, St Andrews University, since 1995; b. 12.8.48, Rotherham; 1 s.; 1 d. Educ. Oakwood School, Rotherham; Sheffield University; St John's College, Cambridge. Lecturer in History, Sheffield University, 1971-95. Publications: The Liberal Mind; Politics without Democracy; Climax of Liberal Politics; Companion to Historiography; Modern Historiography; Lord Salisbury's World; Modernizing England's Past. Recreations: reading; golf. Address: (b.) Department of Modern History, St Andrews University, St Andrews KY16 9AL; T.-01334 462895.

Berry, Professor Christopher Jon, BA, PhD, FRSA, FRSE. Professor, Political Theory, Glasgow University, since 1995; Deputy Dean, Law, Business, Social Sciences, since 2006; b. 19.6.46, St. Helens; m., Christine; 2 s. Educ. Upholland Grammar School; Nottingham and LSE. Lecturer, then Senior Lecturer, then Reader, then Professor, Department of Politics, University of Glasgow. Author of 5 books and over 50 other academic publications. Recreation: contemporary literature. Address: (b.) Adam Smith Building, The University, Glasgow G12 8RT; T.-0141 330 5064; e-mail: c.berry@lbss.gla.ac.uk

Berry, Francis John, BSc, BA, MEd. Rector, St. Margaret's High School, Airdrie, since 1992; b. 10.1.50, Glasgow; m., Irene Anne; 2 s. Educ. Lourdes Secondary School, Glasgow; University of Glasgow; University of Paisley; Open University; University of Strathclyde. Teacher, Lourdes Secondary School, Glasgow, 1972-74; Principal Teacher, Mathematics, Trinity High School, Glasgow, 1974-80; Assistant Head Teacher, St. Columba's High School, Greenock, 1980-84; Deputy Head, St. Bride's High School, South Lanark, 1984-90; Head Teacher, St. Roch's Secondary School, Glasgow, 1990-92; Manager of St. Philip's Residential School, Airdrie, since 1993. Publication: Participative Management in Schools, 1987. Recreations: running; listening to music. Address: (b.) Waverley Drive, Airdrie, North Lanarkshire ML6 6EU; T.-01236 766881.

Berry, William, MA, LLB, WS, NP. Chancellor's Assessor, St. Andrews University; Director, Dawnfresh Holdings Ltd.; formerly Partner and Chairman, Murray Beith Murray, WS, Edinburgh; Director: Scottish American Investment Co. Plc, Fleming Continental European

Investment Trust Plc, Alliance Trust plc, Second Alliance Trust plc, and other companies; formerly Director (Chairman, 1993-99), Scottish Life Assurance Co.; Chairman, Inchcape Family Investments Ltd; b. 26.9.39, Newport-on-Tay; m., Elizabeth Margery Warner; 2 s. Educ. Ardvreck, Crieff; Eton College; St. Andrews University; Edinburgh University. Interests in farming, forestry, etc. Depute Chairman, Edinburgh Festival Society, 1985-89; Member Council/Board, New Town Concerts Society Ltd. Performer in three records of Scottish country dance music. Recreations: music; shooting; forestry; conservation. Address: Tayfield House, Newport-on-Tay, Fife DD6 8HA.

Bevan, John Stuart, BSc (Hons), MBChB (Hons), MD, FRCP (Edin). Consultant Physician and Endocrinologist, Aberdeen Royal Infirmary, since 1991; Honorary Senior Clinical Lecturer, Aberdeen University, since 1991, Honorary Reader in Endocrinology (2006); Member, Clinical Committee, Society for Endocrinology, since 1997; Visiting Endocrinologist to Orkney Islands, since 1994; b. 18.9.53, Portsmouth; m., Sheena Mary; 2 s.; 2 d. Educ. Portsmouth Northern Grammar School; Dunfermline High School; Edinburgh University. Registrar in Endocrinology, Radcliffe Infirmary, Oxford, 1981-83; Medical Research Council Training Fellow in Endocrinology, Oxford, 1984-86; Senior Registrar in Medicine and Endocrinology, University Hospital of Wales, Cardiff, 1987-90; Associate Editor, Clinical Endocrinology, 1994-2004, Senior European Editor, since 2008; Member, Specialist Advisory Committee for Endocrinology and Diabetes, 1998-2002; Council Member, Royal College of Physicians of Edinburgh, since 2006. Publications: papers on clinical neuroendocrinology, particularly the treatment of human pituitary tumours. Recreations: cricket; guitar; ornithology. Address: (b.) Department of Endocrinology, Aberdeen Royal Infirmary, Wards 27/28, Foresterhill, Aberdeen AB25 2ZN; T.-01224 554437; e-mail: johnbevan@nhs.net

Beveridge, Stuart Gordon Nicholas, LLB (Hons), DipLP, NP. Partner, Grant Smith Law Practice, since 2001; b. 19.3.68, Edinburgh. Educ. George Heriot's School; Daniel Stewart's and Melville College; Edinburgh University. Traineeship, Campbell Smith and Co., Solicitors, Edinburgh; Legal Adviser, Citizen's Advice Bureau, Edinburgh; Oddbins Wine Merchants; Aberdein Considine and Co., Aberdeen (Partner, 1998-2001). President, Aberdeen Bar Association, 2001-02 (Committee Member, 1995-2003). Recreations: wine; cooking; cinema; failing to finish DIY projects. Address: (b.) Amicable House, 252 Union Street, Aberdeen AB10 1TN; T.-01224 621620.

Bewsher, Colonel Harold Frederick, LVO, OBE. Vice-President, The Atlantic Salmon Trust (Chairman, 1995-2005); Vice Chairman, Association of Deer Management Groups in Scotland, since 2001 (Member, Executive Committee, since 1998); Chairman, The Airborne Initiative (Scotland) Ltd., 1995-98; Lieutenant, The Queen's Bodyguard for Scotland (Secretary, 1982-94); b. 13.1.29, Glasgow; m., Susan Elizabeth Cruickshank; 2 s. Educ. Merchiston Castle School; Royal Technical College; Glasgow University; Royal Military Academy, Sandhurst. Regular Army, The Royal Scots, 1949-72; Director-General, Scotch Whisky Association, 1973-94. Chairman, New Club, Edinburgh, 1981-82; Chairman, Scottish Society for the Employment of Ex-Regular Soldiers, Sailors and Airmen, 1973-83; Freeman, City of London, 1992; Liveryman, Worshipful Company of Distillers, 1993. Recreations: outdoors — salmon fishing, field sports. Address: (b.) 33 Blacket Place, Edinburgh EH9 1RJ; T.-0131-667 4600.

Bezuidenhout, Rev. Louis Christiaan, MA, DD. Minister: Church of Scotland, Kirkmichael, Tinwald & Torthorwald, since 2000; b. 9.7.54. Johannesburg, South Africa; m., Elsie; 1 s.; 1 d. Educ. Hartswater Secondary School, South Africa; University of Pretoria, South Africa.

Lecturer, Semitic Languages, University of Pretoria, 1977-78; Minister of Religion, Dutch Reformed Church, South Africa, 1978-84; Senior Lecturer, Semitic Languages, University of Pretoria, 1984-89; Visiting Scholar, University of St. Andrews, 1989-90; Minister of Religion, Stellenbosch, South Africa, 1990-97; Professor and Head of Department of Biblical Studies, Pretoria, 1997-2000. Published 41 scientific and popular scientific articles on Hebrew literature, Akkadian literature and theology. Recreations: painting; photography. Address: The Manse, Tinwald, Dumfries DG1 3PL; T.-01387 710246. E-mail: macbez@btinternet.com

Bhopal, Professor Raj Singh, CBE, DSc (hon), BSc, MBChB, MD, MPH, FFPH, FRCP (Edin). Bruce and John Usher Chair of Public Health, University of Edinburgh, since 1999 (Head, Division of Community Health Sciences, 2000-03); Honorary Consultant in Public Health Medicine, Lothian Health Board, since 1999; b. 10.4.53, Moga, Punjab, India; m., Roma; 4 s. Educ. University of Edinburgh; University of Glasgow. House Officer/Senior House Officer, medicine and surgery, 1978-82; Trainee GP, 1980; Registrar/Senior Registrar/Lecturer in Public Health Medicine, 1983-88; Senior Lecturer/Honorary Consultant in Public Health Medicine, 1988-91; Professor of Epidemiology and Public Health, University of Newcastle upon Tyne, 1991-99 (Head, Department of Epidemiology and Public Health); Non-Executive Director (Vice-Chairman), Newcastle and North Tyneside Health Authority, 1992-96; Non-Executive Director, Health Education Authority, 1998-99; Chairman, Steering Committee, National Resource Centre on Ethnic Minority Health, since 2002; Member, MRC Health Services Research and Public Health Board, 1999-2003. Publications: Books: Concepts of Epidemiology, 2002; Public Health, Past, Present and Future, 2004; The Epidemic of Coronary Heart Disease in South Asians, 2005; Ethnicity, race and health in multicultural societies; over 100 papers in journals and chapters in books on Legionnaires' disease, environmental epidemiology, primary care, ethnicity and health, application of epidemiology in public health and health care. Recreations: chess; golf; hill climbing; photography; travel; music; reading. Address: (b.) Public Health Sciences, University of Edinburgh, Medical School, Teviot Place, Edinburgh EH8 9AG; T.-0131-650 3216; e-mail: raj.bhopal@ed.ac.uk

Biddulph, 5th Lord (Anthony Nicholas Colin). Interior Designer and Sporting Manager; b. 8.4.59; m., Hon. Sian Gibson-Watt (divorced); 2 s. Educ. Cheltenham; RAC, Cirencester. Recreations: shooting; design; fishing; skiing; racing; painting. Address: Address: (h.) Makerstoun, Kelso TD5 7PA; T.-01573 460 234; 8 Orbel Street, London SW11 3NZ; T.-020 7228 9865.

Biggar, Donald, OBE. Chairman, Quality Meat Scotland; since 2005; m., Emma; 2 s.; 1 d. Educ. Merchiston Castle School, Edinburgh. Farmer. Address: (b.) The Rural Centre, Ingliston, Newbridge EH28 8NZ; T.-0131 472 4040.

Biggart, Thomas Norman, CBE (1984), WS, MA, LLB. Partner, Biggart Baillie & Gifford, Solicitors, Glasgow and Edinburgh, 1959-95; b. 24.1.30; m., Eileen Jean Anne Gemmell; 1 s.; 1 d. Educ. Morrison's Academy, Crieff; Glasgow University. Royal Navy, 1954-56 (Sub-Lt., RNVR). Law Society of Scotland: Council Member, 1977-86; Vice-President, 1981-82; President, 1982-83; President, Business Archives Council, Scotland, 1977-86; Member, Executive, Scottish Council (Development and Industry), 1984-94; Member: Scottish Tertiary Education Advisory Council, 1984-87, Scottish Records Advisory Council,

1985-91; Director: Clydesdale Bank, 1985-97; Independent Insurance Group, 1986-2000 (Chairman, 1989-93); Chairman, Beechwood, Glasgow, 1989-97; Trustee, Scottish Civic Trust, 1989-97; Member, Council on Tribunals (Chairman, Scottish Committee), 1990-98; Honorary Member, American Bar Association, 1982; OStJ, 1968. Recreations: golf, hill walking. Address: (h.) Gailes, Kilmacolm, Renfrewshire PA13 4LZ; T.-0150 587 2645.

Bird, Professor Colin C., CBE, Drhc (Edin), MBChB, PhD, FRCPath, FRCPE, FRCSE, FRSE, FAMS. Dean, Faculty of Medicine, Edinburgh University, 1995-2002; b. 5.3.38, Kirkintilloch; m., Ailsa M. Ross; 2 s.; 1 d. Educ. Lenzie Academy; Glasgow University. McGhie Cancer Research Scholar, Glasgow Royal Infirmary, 1962-64; Lecturer in Pathology: Glasgow University, 1964-67, Aberdeen University, 1967-72; MRC Goldsmiths Travelling Fellow, Chicago, 1970-71; Senior Lecturer in Pathology, Edinburgh University, 1972-75; Professor and Head, Department of Pathology, Leeds University, 1975-86; Professor of Pathology and Head, Department of Pathology, Edinburgh University, 1986-95. Recreations: golf; hill walking; music. Address: (h.) 45 Ann Street, Edinburgh, EH4 1PT.

Bird, Jackie. Journalist; b. 31.7.62, Bellshill; 1 s.; 1 d. Educ. Earnock High School. Music/Film/Television Editor, Jackie Magazine; Radio News Reporter and Presenter, Radio Clyde; Reporter, Evening Times; Reporter, Sun; Reporter/Presenter, TVS; Presenter, Reporting Scotland. Address: (b.) BBC Scotland, 40 Pacific Quay, Glasgow G51 1DZ.

Birley, Tim(othy) Grahame, BSc(Eng), MSc, ACGI, FRTPI, FRSA. Independent adviser on sustainable development and public policy, since 1995; b. 13.3.47, Kent; m., Catherine Anne; 1 s.; 2 d. Educ. Sir Roger Manwood's Grammar School; Imperial College, London University; Edinburgh University. Local government, 1965-71; academic appointments, 1973-81; Director, Energy and Environment Research, 1982-85; Scottish Office: Inquiry Reporter, 1985-87, Principal Inquiry Reporter, 1987-88, Deputy Director of Building, 1988-90, Head, Rural Affairs Division, 1990-95. Non-Executive Director, RPT (Scotland), 1989-91; Central Scotland Woodlands, 1991-92; Director, Centre for Human Ecology, Edinburgh University, 1995-96; Chair, Project Selection Panel, Millennium Forest for Scotland Trust, 1996-97; Board Member: Forward Scotland, Landwise, 1996-2000; Vice-President, APRS, 1998-2003; Facilitator and consultant on mainstreaming sustainable development, East of Scotland European Partnership, since 1998; Report writer for Mourne National Park Working Party, 2007. Recreation: family outings. Address: (b.) 6 Malta Terrace, Edinburgh EH4 1HR; T.-0131-332 3499.

Birss, Rev. Alan David, MA (Hons), BD (Hons). Minister, Paisley Abbey, since 1988; b. 5.6.53, Ellon; m., Carol Margaret Pearson. Educ. Glenrothes High School; St. Andrews University; Edinburgh University. Assistant Minister, Dundee Parish Church (St. Mary's), 1978-80; Minister, Inverkeithing Parish Church of St. Peter, 1982-88. Past President, Church Service Society; Member, Council, Scottish Church Society. Address: The Manse of Paisley Abbey, 15 Main Road, Castlehead, Paisley PA2 6AJ; T.-0141-889 3587.

Birt, Audrey, BSc, MPH, RGN, DipHV, DN. Director, Diabetes UK Scotland, since 2003; b. 4.2.56, Kirkcaldy, Fife; m., Andrew; 1 s.; 1 d. Educ. Glenrothes High School; University of Edinburgh; University of Glasgow. Nurse and Health Visitor in Edinburgh and Fife; Practice Nursing Sister and Nurse Manager, Helensburgh, Argyll; Service Development, Argyll and Clyde; Chair, Long Term Conditions Alliance Scotland, since 2006. Former health care professional volunteer with Diabetes UK. Recreations: walking in Scotland; interest in coaching and development. Address: (b.) Savoy House, 140 Sauchiehall Street, Glasgow G2 3DH; T.-0141 332 2700; e-mail: audrey.birt@diabetes.org.uk

Bisset, David W., FAMS, MCLIP, FSA (Scot), DEAB. Secretary, Scottish Esperanto Association, since 1997; Vice Chairman, Architectural Heritage Society of Scotland (Strathclyde); Vice President, Esperanto Association of Britain; Director of Butler Library; Trustee, Esperanto Association of Britain; b. 8.8.38, Motherwell; m., Jean; 1 s.; 1 d. Educ. Dalziel High, Motherwell; University of Strathclyde. Librarian, Coatbridge Technical College, 1962-72; Head of Library Services, Bell College of Technology, Hamilton, 1972-95. Various positions within the Esperanto Movement in Scotland and Britain; Governor, David Livingstone Trust; President, Hamilton Civic Society. Recreations: cultural tourism; town walking; architectural history. Address: (h.) 47 Airbles Crescent, Motherwell ML1 3AP; T.-01698 263199.
E-mail: david@bisset100.freeserve.co.uk

Bisset, Raymond George, OBE. Provost, Aberdeenshire Council, since 2003 (Convener, 1999-2003); Chairman, North East of Scotland Fisheries Partnership, since 2000; b. 16.8.42, Ellon; m., Heather Bisset. Educ. Inverurie Academy; Aberdeen University; College of Education. Chemistry/Physics Teacher, Ellon Academy, 1963-64; Maths/General Science Teacher, Insch School, 1965-74; Head Teacher: Keithall Primary School, 1975-76; Kintore Primary and Secondary School, 1977-81; Kintore Primary School, 1981-94. Provost, Gordon District Council, 1992-96; Member, North of Scotland Water Board, 1995-99; Chairman, Gordon Area Tourist Board, 1986-89, 1991-96; Hon. President, University for Children and Communities; former Chairman, Inverurie and District Round Table; Founder Chairman, North East Scotland Anglers' Federation; Hon. President, Inverurie Arthritis Society; Member, NHS (Grampian), since 2001; Chairman, Nestour (VisitScotland), since 2005; Chairman, Aberdeen and Grampian Tourism Strategy Group, since 2000; Present Chair of NHS (Grampian) Clinical Governance Committee. Recreations: angling; golf; hill walking; reading; amateur writing. Address: (h.) The Schoolhouse, Keithhall, Inverurie, Aberdeenshire, AB51 0LX; T.-01467 621015.

Bisset, Dr (William) Michael, BSc, MBChB, DCH, MSc, MD, FRCP, FRCPCH. Clinical Group Co-ordinator for Combined Child Health Service, NHS Grampian, since 2003; Consultant Paediatric Gastroenterologist, since 1992; b. 17.2.56, Edinburgh; m., Amanda Bisset. Educ. George Watson's College, Edinburgh; Edinburgh University; London University. Lecturer n Paediatric Gastroenterology, 1986-92. Croom Lecturer, RCPEd, 1993. Address. (b.) Royal Aberdeen Children's Hospital, Westburn Road, Aberdeen AB25 2ZG; T.-01224 554715.

Black, Rev. Archibald Tearlach, BSc. Chairman of Council, The Saltire Society, 1997-2001; retired Church of Scotland minister, formerly at Ness Bank Church, Inverness; b. 10.6.37, Edinburgh; m., Bridget Mary Baddeley; 2 s.; 1 d. Elected Member of Council, National Trust for Scotland, 1991-96, 1997-2002 and 2003-08; Chairman, Sorley MacLean Trust. Recreations: Inverness Gaelic Choir; all the arts; the enjoyment of Scotland's natural and cultural heritage. Address: (h.) 16 Elm Park, Inverness IV2 4WN; T.-01463 230588.

Black, Barbara Ann, PhD, MA (Hons). Area Director, HIE Shetland. Educ. Anderson High School, Lerwick; University of Glasgow; UHIMI. Highlands and Islands Airports Ltd, Sumburgh, Shetland: Administration Officer, 1995-97, Business Development Manager, 1997-98; Assistant Airport Manager, Sumburgh Airport, 1998-2000; Deputy Chief Executive, Shetland Enterprise, 2000-03. Chair and Director, Connect, Women Networking in Shetland; Chair, Shetland Regeneration Partnership; Director, Shetland Council of Social Services; Director, Shetland Business Innovation Centre; Trustee, Shetland College, UHIMI; Trustee, North Atlantic Fisheries College; Vice-Chair, Shetland Renewable Energy Forum. Recreations: drama; arts; travel; walking; spending time with family; gardening; antiques; restoration of old property. Address: (h.) 84 St. Olaf Street, Lerwick, Shetland ZE1 0ES; T.-01595 746813; e-mail: a.black@hient.co.uk

Black, Elspeth Catherine, LLB, NP. Solicitor, since 1973; Honorary Sheriff, Dunoon, since 1997; b. 25.10.50, Kilmarnock; m., James Anthony Black; 1 s.; 1 d. Educ. Kilmarnock Academy; Glasgow University. Apprentice, then Assistant, Wright, Johnston and McKenzie, Glasgow, 1971-74; Assistant, Messers Wm. J. Cuthbert and Hogg, Fort William, 1974-75; Assistant, then Partner, Kenneth W. Pendreich and Co. Dunoon, 1975-87; Partner, Elspeth C. Black and Co., Dunoon and Anderson Banks and Co., Oban, Fort William and Balivanich, 1987-98; Partner, Corrigall Black, Dunoon, since 1998; accredited Child Law Specialist. Honorary Solicitor to Scottish Amateur Swimming Association. Recreations: swimming coaching (Chief Coach, Dunoon ASC); running/fitness training. Address: (b.) 20 John Street, Dunoon; T.-01369 704777.

Black, James Stuart, MA (Hons), PhD. Director, Highlands and Islands Enterprise, since 2007; b. 8.2.64, Edinburgh; m., Kathleen; 3 d. Educ. Inverness High School; Edinburgh University; Glasgow University. Property Researcher, Hillier Parker, London, 1989-90; Lecturer, Department of Land Economy, Aberdeen University, 1990-96; Head of Economics, Highlands and Islands Enterprise, Inverness, 1996-2000, Director, Communities Group, 2000-03; Area Director, HIE Inverness and East Highland, 2003-07. Associate of The Royal Scottish Geographical Society. Recreations: squash; football. Address: (b.) Cowan House, Inverness Retail and Business Park, Inverness IV2 3BL; T.-01463 667217; e-mail: stuart.black@hient.co.uk

Black, Professor Robert, QC, LLB (Hons), LLM, FRSA, FRSE, FFCS. Professor of Scots Law, Edinburgh University, since 1981 (Emeritus, since 2005); Temporary Sheriff, 1981-94; b. 12.6.47, Lockerbie. Educ. Lockerbie Academy; Dumfries Academy; Edinburgh University; McGill University, Montreal. Advocate, 1972; Lecturer in Scots Law, Edinburgh University, 1972-75; Senior Legal Officer, Scottish Law Commission, 1975-78; practised at Scottish bar, 1978-81; QC, 1987; General Editor, The Laws of Scotland: Stair Memorial Encyclopaedia, 1988-96 (formerly Deputy and Joint General Editor). Publications: An Introduction to Written Pleading, 1982; Civil Jurisdiction: The New Rules, 1983; various articles on the Lockerbie disaster. Address: (h.) 6/4 Glenogle Road, Edinburgh EH3 5HW; T.-0131-557 3571; e-mail: rblackqc@gmail.com

Black, Robert William, MA (Hons, Econ), MSc (Town Planning), MSc (Public Policy), LLD. Auditor General for Scotland, since 2000; b. 6.11.46, Banff; m., Doreen Mary Riach; 3 s.; 1 d. Educ. Robert Gordon's College, Aberdeen; Aberdeen University; Heriot-Watt University; Strathclyde University. Nottinghamshire County Council, 1971-73; City

of Glasgow Corporation, 1973-75; Strathclyde Regional Council, 1975-85; Chief Executive: Stirling District Council, 1985-90, Tayside Regional Council, 1990-95; Controller of Audit, Accounts Commission for Scotland, 1995-99. Fellow, Royal Statistical Society; Hon. Doctor of Law, University of Aberdeen, 2004; Hon. Doctor of Business Administration, Queen Margaret University College, 2006; Fellow of the Royal Society of Edinburgh (FRSE), 2006. Recreations: the outdoors and the arts. Address: (b.) 110 George Street, Edinburgh EH2 4LH.

Black, Sue Margaret, OBE, BSc, PhD, DSc, FRSE. Head of The Centre for Anatomy and Human Identification, University of Dundee, since 2003; Director, Centre for International Forensic Assistance, since 2002; b. 7.5.61, Inverness; m., Tom Black; 3 d. Educ. Inverness Royal Academy; University of Aberdeen. Lecturer in Anatomy, Guy's and St. Thomas' Hospitals, 1986-92; Consultant in Forensic Anthropology, University of Glasgow, 1992-2000; Head of Profession in Kosovo for Foreign and Commonwealth Office, 1999-2000; Lead Assessor in Forensic Anthropology, CRFP; Director, Centre for International Forensic Assistance; DVI (Disaster Victim Identification) national training programme co-ordinator. Council of Royal Society of Edinburgh Young People's Committee RSE. Publications: Developmental Juvenile Osteology, 2000; The Juvenile Skeleton, 2004. Recreation: writer. Address: (b.) Centre for Anatomy and Human Identification, University of Dundee, Dundee DD1 5EH; T.-01382 385776; e-mail: s.m.black@dundee.ac.uk

Blackadder, Elizabeth, DBE, RA, RSA. Artist; Her Majesty's Painter and Limner in Scotland, since 2001; b. 24.9.31, Falkirk. Educ. Falkirk High School; Edinburgh University; Edinburgh College of Art. Lecturer, School of Drawing and Painting, Edinburgh College of Art, 1962-66; first Scottish woman painter elected full member, Royal Academy and Royal Scottish Academy. Honorary Doctorates: Heriot Watt University, University of Strathclyde, University of Edinburgh, University of Aberdeen, University of Glasgow, University of Stirling, University of St. Andrews, University of London.

Blackburn, Lucy, MA. Director of Policy, Historic Scotland, since 2006; b. 7.8.66, St. Andrews. Educ. Ysgol Friars, Bangor, Gwynedd; Oxford University; York University. Policy Officer, Association of County Councils, 1990-95; joined Scottish Office, 1995: Principal, Local Government Finance Distribution, 1995-98, Head, Constitutional Policy Branch, 1998-99; government research fellowship, 1999-2000; Head of Higher Education and Science Division, Scottish Executive, 2000-04; Head of Reducing Reoffending Division, Scottish Executive, 2004-06. Publication: Managing Conflicts After Devolution: A Toolkit for Civil Servants, 2000. Address: (b.) Historic Scotland, Longmore House, Salisbury Place, Edinburgh EH9 1SH.

Blackie, Alan John, BA, DipYCS. Director of Education and Children's Services, East Lothian, since 2003; b. 6.6.48, Haddington; 2 d. Educ. Knox Academy, Haddington; Jordanhill College, Glasgow; Open University. Community Education Service, Dunbarton County Council/Strathclyde Regional Council, 1971-79; Community Education Officer, Castlebrae High School, Edinburgh, 1979-87; Education Officer, then Assistant Director of Education, Lothian, 1987-95; Director of Education and Community Services, East Lothian, 1995-2003. President, ADES, 2002. Recreations: hill-walking; golf; skiing. Address: (h.) Byre Court, East Saltoun, EH34 5ED; T.-01875 340083.

Blackie, Professor John Walter Graham, BA (Cantab), LLB (Edin). Professor of Law, Strathclyde University, since

1991; Advocate, since 1974; b. 2.10.46, Glasgow; m., Jane Ashman. Educ. Uppingham School; Peterhouse, Cambridge; Harvard; Merton College, Oxford; Edinburgh University. Open Exhibitioner, Peterhouse, Cambridge, 1965-68; St. Andrews Society of New York Scholar, Harvard, 1968-69; practised at Scottish bar, 1974-75; Edinburgh University: Lecturer, 1975-88, Senior Lecturer in Scots Law, 1988-91. Director, Blackie & Son Ltd., publishers, 1970-93. Recreations: music; sailing. Address: (h.) The Old Coach House, 23a Russell Place, Edinburgh EH5 3HW.

Blacklock, Telfer George, MA, LLB, DipLP, NP. Partner, Blacklocks Solicitors, since 1992; b. 3.3.58, Edinburgh; m., Mairead; 4 s. Educ. St. Marks, Swaziland; George Heriots, Edinburgh; Edinburgh University. Balfour & Manson, 1982-92. Recreations: golf; bridge; cinema; cooking. Address: (b.) 89 Constitution Street, Edinburgh EH6 7AS; T.-0131 555 7500; e-mail: tgb@blacklocks.co.uk

Blackmore, Professor Stephen, BSc, PhD, FRSE, FLS, FIBiol. Regius Keeper, Royal Botanic Garden Edinburgh, since 1999; Visiting Professor, Glasgow University, since 1999, Visiting Professor, Reading University; Honorary Professor, University of Edinburgh, since 2003; Honorary Professor, Kunming Institute of Botany, since 2003; Board of Governors, Edinburgh College of Art, since 2003; Trustee, Seychelles Islands Foundation, since 1996; Trustee, Little Sparta Trust, since 2001; b. 30.7.52, Stoke on Trent; m., Patricia Jane Melrose; 1 s.; 1 d. Educ. St George's School, Hong Kong; Reading University. Royal Society Aldabra Research Station, Seychelles, 1976; Lecturer and Head of National Herbarium, University of Malawi, 1977; Palynologist, British Museum (Natural History), 1980; Keeper of Botany, Natural History Museum, 1990. Publications: author of numerous research papers on plant taxonomy and palynology. Recreations: photography; hill-walking; blues guitar music. Address: (b.) Royal Botanic Garden, 20A Inverleith Row, Edinburgh EH3 5LR; T.-0131-248 2930; e-mail: S.Blackmore@rbge.org.uk

Blackshaw, Alan, OBE, VRD. President, The International Mountaineering and Climbing Federation (UIAA, Berne, Switzerland), 2004-05; Chair, Cairngorms Recreation Forum, 1998-2004; Adviser on public access to land: Ramblers' Association Scotland, since 1994; Scottish Environment Link, 1994-2006, Central Council of Physical Recreation, 1997-2004; Academic Adviser, Highlands and Islands University Project, 1998-2004 (Chair, Tourism, Hospitality and Leisure Group, 1988-99, Member, Environment and Natural Sciences Faculty Board, 2000-2003); Management Consultant; Member, Cairngorms Partnership Advisory Panel, 1998-2003; b. 7.4.33; m., 1, Jane Elizabeth Turner (m. dissolved); 1 d.; 2, Dr. Elspeth Paterson Martin; 1 s.; 2 d. Educ. Merchant Taylors' School, Crosby; Wadham College, Oxford (MA). Royal Marines (commissioned), 1954-56, and RM Reserve, 1956-76. Entered Home Civil Service, Ministry of Power, 1956; Principal Private Secretary to Minister of Power, 1967-69; Department of Energy: Under Secretary, 1974, Offshore Supplies Office, 1974-78 (Director-General, 1977-78), Coal Division, 1978-79; Consultant, N.C.B., 1979-86; Consultant Director, Strategy International, 1980-91; Member: Scottish Council Development and Industry, 1974-78, Scottish Sports Council, 1990-96, Scottish Natural Heritage, 1992-97 (Chairman: Task Force on Access, 1992-94, Audit Committee, 1995-97); Vice-Chair, UN Inter-Governmental Conference on Sustainable Mountain Development, Trento, Italy, 1996; Member, Adventure Activities Licensing Authority, 1996-2007; Director, Moray Badenoch and Strathspey Enterprise, 1998-2000; Patron, British Mountaineering Council, since 1979 (President, 1973-76); Chairman: Standing Advisory Committee on Mountain Training Policy, 1980-86, Sports Council's National Mountain Centre, Plas y Brenin, 1986-95, Mountaineering Commission, UIAA, (Berne, Switzerland), 1989-99, Access and Conservation Working Group, UIAA, 1995-98, UK Mountain Training Board, 1991-94; President, Snowsport Scotland, 1994-2000; Honorary Adviser, Mountaineering Council of Scotland, since 1995; Director, Paths for All Partnership, 1996-97; President, Ski Club of Great Britain, 1997-2003; Council Member, Mountain Forum, Katmandu, 1999-2003; UIAA Special Representative, UN Global Mountain Partnership, 2000-04; President, The Alpine Club, 2001-04; International Olympic Committee, Lausanne, Award for voluntary service to sport and Olympism, 2001; Golden Eagle Award, Outdoor Writers' Guild, 2003; Freeman, City of London. Publication: Mountaineering, 1965. Recreations: mountaineering; sailing; skiing. Address: (h.) Rhu Grianach, Kingussie Road, Newtonmore PH20 1AY; T.-01540 673239; e-mail: alanblackshaw@hotmail.com

Blackwood, John Grahame, LLB (Hons), DLP, WS. Partner, McClure Naismith, Solicitors, since 2000, Head of Banking Unit; b. 21.11.65, Glasgow. Educ. Dundee High School; Aberdeen University. Trainee Solicitor, Alex Morison & Co.; Solicitor, then Director, Bank of Scotland. Recreations: golfing; skiing; sailing. Address: (b.) 3 Ponton Street, Edinburgh EH3 9QQ; T.-0131-272-8350; e-mail: jblackwood@mcclurenaismith.com

Blaikie, Professor Andrew, MA, PhD. Professor of Historical Sociology, University of Aberdeen, since 1999; b. 30.11.56, St. Anne's. Educ. Kirkham Grammar School; Downing College, Cambridge; Queen Mary College, London. Lecturer in Gerontology, Birkbeck College, University of London, 1986-91; Department of Sociology, University of Aberdeen: Lecturer, 1991, Senior Lecturer, 1995, Nuffield Foundation Research Fellow, 1998, Director of Research in Social Sciences and Law, 1999-2001, Head of Sociology, 2002-04; Secretary, Economic and Social History Society of Scotland, 1994-99; Executive Committee, British Sociological Association, 1997-2001 (Vice Chair). Publications: Illegitimacy, Sex and Society, 1994; Ageing and Popular Culture, 1999; Editor, Cultural Sociology. Recreations: swimming; hillwalking; travel. Address: (h.) 5 Pilot Square, Aberdeen AB11 5DS; T.-01224 588313; e-mail: a.blaikie@abdn.ac.uk

Blair, (Ann) Kay, MA (Hons), FCIM. Managing Director, Business Perceptions; business journalist; Member, Scottish Consumer Council, since 2003; Member, Consumer Panel, Financial Services Authority (FSA), since 2006; non-executive director, NHS 24, since 2007; b. 12.4.53, Edinburgh; m., William; 1 s.; 2 d. Educ. James Gillespie's High School for Girls; St. Andrews University; School of Slavonic and Eastern European Studies, London University. Journalist/ Researcher on Eastern Europe and Manager, Business Information Service, Financial Times, 1977-80; Marketing Information Manager, Scottish Development Agency, 1980-81; formerly: Marketing Columnist, The Scotsman, Non-Executive Director, Edinburgh Sick Children's NHS Trust, Board Member, Scottish Legal Aid Board; Non-Executive Director, Scottish Ambulance Service. Recreations: skiing; cinema; travel. Address: (b.) 8 Winton Terrace, Edinburgh EH10 7AP; T.-0131-477 7477; e-mail: busper@lineone.net

Blair, Anna Dempster, DPE. Writer and Lecturer; b. 12.2.27, Glasgow; m., Matthew Blair; 1 s.; 1 d. Educ. Hutchesons' Girls Grammar School, Glasgow; Dunfermline College. Novels: A Tree in the West; The Rowan on the

Ridge; Short Stories: Tales of Ayrshire; Scottish Tales; The Goose Girl of Eriska; Seed Corn; social history: Tea at Miss Cranston's; Croft and Creel; More Tea at Miss Cranston's; Old Giffnock. Recreations: film-making; travel; reading; friendship. Address: (h.) 20 Barrland Drive, Giffnock, Glasgow G46 7QD; T.-0141-638 0676.

Blair, John Samuel Greene, OBE (Mil), TD, TAVRD, KStJ, BA, Hon. DLitt (St. Andrews), ChM, FRCSEdin, FRCP, FICS, D(Obst)RCOG, FSAScot, FRHistS. Honorary Senior Teacher, Faculty of Medicine, University of Dundee, since 2004; Vice-President, International Society for the History of Medicine, 2000-04; Editorial Manager, International Journal of Medical History, 2002-06; Honorary Reader, History of Medicine and Apothecaries Lecturer, St. Andrews University, 1997-2002 (Senior Lecturer, 1993-97); Honorary Senior Lecturer in Surgery, Dundee University, 1967-90; Apothecaries Lecturer, Worshipful Society of London, since 1991; Member, Editorial Board, Vesalius, since 1994; b. 31.12.28, Wormit, Fife; m., Ailsa Jean Bowes, MBE; 2 s.; 1 d. Educ. Dundee High School (Harris Gold Medal for Dux of School, 1946); St. Andrews University (Harkness Scholar, 1946-50). National Service, RAMC, 1952-55; Tutor, Department of Anatomy, St. Salvator's College, St. Andrews, 1955; surgical and research training, Manchester, Dundee, Cambridge, London, 1957-65; Member, Court of Examiners, Royal College of Surgeons of Edinburgh, 1964-93; Consultant Surgeon, Perth Royal Infirmary, 1965-90; postgraduate Clinical Tutor, Perth, 1966-74; first North American Travelling Fellow, St. Andrews/Dundee Universities, 1971; Secretary, Tayside Area Medical Advisory Committee, 1974-83; Member, Education Advisory Committee, Association of Surgeons, 1984-88; Secretary, Perth and Kinross Division, British Medical Association, 1982-90; Member, Scottish Council and Chairman's Sub-Committee, BMA, 1985-89; Fellow of the BMA, 1990; Chairman, Armed Forces Committee, BMA, 1992-98; President: British Society for the History of Medicine, 1993-95, Scottish Society for the History of Medicine, 1990-93; Captain, Royal Perth Golf Club, 1997-99; British National Delegate, International Society for the History of Medicine, 1999-2001; Honorary Colonel (TA), RAMC; Member, Principal's Council, St Andrews University, 1984-99; Elder, Church of Scotland; Hospitaller, Priory of Scotland, Order of St. John of Jerusalem; Mitchiner Lecturer, Army Medical Services, 1994; Haldane Tait Memorial Lecturer, 1998; Osler Club Lecturer, 1998; Birmingham Medical History Society Lecturer, 1998; Douglas Guthrie Memorial Lecturer, 1998; Brigadier Ian Haywood Lecturer, 1999; Haywood Society Lecturer, 1999; Pybus Society Lecturer, 2001; International Blood Transfusion Society Lecturer, 2004; Invited Speaker, International Congress on High Technology Medicine and Doctor-Patient Relationship, Istanbul, 2006; Invited speaker, Division of Medical Humanities, University of Arkansas, 2007; Annual Osler Oration, 2007. Publications: books on medical history and anatomy including the history of medicine at St. Andrews University, 1987, the centenary history of the RAMC, 1998, The Conscript Doctors – Memories of National Service, 2001 and History of Medicine in Dundee University, 2007. Recreations: golf; travel; bridge. Address: (h.) 143 Glasgow Road, Perth; T.-Perth 623739.

Blair, Robin Leitch, MB, ChB, FRCSEdin. Head, Department of Otolaryngology, Ninewells Hospital and Medical School, Dundee, since 1984; Consultant Otolaryngologist, Tayside University Hospitals; Honorary Professor, Faculty of Medicine, Dentistry and Nursing, University of Dundee; b. 28.11.45, Gourock; 2 d. Educ. Greenock Academy; Edinburgh University; University of Toronto. House Surgeon, Royal Infirmary, Edinburgh; Lecturer, Department of Anatomy, Glasgow University; Assistant Professor, Department of Otolaryngology, University of Toronto. President, Section of Laryngology and Rhinology, Royal Society of Medicine, 2000-01; Chairman, SAC in Otolaryngology, 2000-03. Address: (b.) Department of Otolaryngology, Ninewells Hospital and Medical School, Dundee DD1 9SY; T.-01382 632162; e-mail: robinlblair@hotmail.com

Blair, Robin Orr, LVO, MA, LLB, WS. Lord Lyon King of Arms and Secretary, Order of the Thistle, 2001-07. Educ. Rugby School; St. Andrews University; Edinburgh University. Partner, Dundas & Wilson, 1967-97 (Managing Partner, 1976-83 and 1988-91); Partner, Turcan Connell WS, 1997-2000. Purse Bearer to the Lord High Commissioner to General Assembly of Church of Scotland, 1989-2002. Address: 2 Blacket Place, Edinburgh EH9 1RL; T.-0131-667 2906.

Blake, Professor Christopher, CBE, FRSE, MA, PhD. Chairman, Glenrothes Development Corporation, 1987-96; b. 28.4.26; m.; 2 s.; 2 d. Educ. Dollar Academy; St. Andrews University. Royal Navy, 1944-47; teaching posts, 1951-53; Assistant, Edinburgh University, 1953-55; Stewarts & Lloyds Ltd., 1955-60; Lecturer, then Senior Lecturer, St Andrews University, 1960-67; Dundee University: Senior Lecturer, then Professor of Economics, 1967-74; Bonar Professor of Applied Economics, 1974-88; Director, Alliance Trust plc, 1974-94; Director, William Low & Co. plc, 1980-90 (Chairman, 1985-90). Recreation: golf. Address: (h.) Westlea, 14 Wardlaw Gardens, St. Andrews, Fife, KY16 9DW.

Blakey, Rev. Ronald Stanton, MA, BD, MTh. Editor, Church of Scotland Year Book, since 2000; b. 3.7.38, Glasgow; m., Kathleen Dunbar; 1 s. Educ. Hutchesons' Boys' Grammar School, Glasgow; Glasgow University. Minister: St. Mark's, Kirkconnel, 1963-67; Bellshill West, 1967-72; Jedburgh Old Parish with Edgerston and Ancrum, 1972-81. Member, Roxburgh District Council, 1974-80 (Chairman of Council, 1977-80); Religious Adviser, Border Television, 1973-81; Member, Borders Region Children's Panel, 1974-80; JP, 1974-80; Church of Scotland: Deputy Secretary, Department of Education, 1981-88; Secretary, Assembly Council, 1988-98; Israel Project Secretary, Board of World Mission, 1998-2000. Publication: The Man in the Manse, 1978. Recreation: collecting antiquarian books on Scotland. Address: (h.) 5 Moss Side Road, Biggar, South Lanarkshire ML12 6GF.

Blanchflower, Brian William, BSc (Hons), PGCSE (Distinction). Rector, Dunfermline High School, Fife, since 2007; b. 8.1.56, Belfast; m., Karen Ann Simpson; 1 s.; 1 d. Educ. Dunfermline High School; University of Edinburgh; Moray House College of Education. Teacher of Mathematics and Geography, Inverkeithing High School, 1979-83; Assistant Principal Teacher of Geography, Buckhaven High School, 1983-84; Principal Teacher of Geography, Beath High School, 1984-87; Assistant Rector, 1987-90, Depute Rector, 1990-96, Rector, 1996-2007, Lochgelly High School. Recreations: rugby; hill-walking. Address: (b.) Dunfermline High School, St. Leonard's Place, Dunfermline, Fife KY11 3BQ; T.-01383-602402. E-mail: brian.blanchflower@fife.gov.uk

Blaxter, Professor John Harry Savage, MA (Oxon), DSc (Oxon), HonDUniv(Stirling), FIBiol, FRSE. Hon. Professor, Stirling University; b. 6.1.29, London; m., Valerie Ann McElligott; 1 s.; 1 d. Educ. Berkhamsted School; Brasenose College, Oxford. SO, then SSO, Marine Laboratory, Aberdeen, 1952-64; Lecturer, Zoology Department, Aberdeen University, 1964-69; PSO, 1969,

SPSO, 1974, DCSO, 1985-91, Hon. Research Fellow, 1992-2001, Scottish Marine Biological Association, later Scottish Association for Marine Science, Oban; Hon. Professor, St. Andrews University, 1990-99; President, Fisheries Society of the British Isles, 1992-97 (Beverton Medal, 1998); Individual Achievement Award, American Institute of Fisheries Research Biologists, 1998; Editor, Advances in Marine Biology, 1980-98; Editor, ICES Journal of Marine Science, 1991-99; Member, Editorial Board, Encyclopaedia of Ocean Sciences, 1998-2001; Trustee, Argyll Fisheries Trust, since 1999. Recreations:golf; gardening. Address: (h.) Dems Lodge, Barcaldine, Oban PA37 1SF.

Bleiman, David, MA, MBA, FCIPD. Assistant General Secretary (Scotland), University and College Union, since 1982; Member, Employment Appeal Tribunal, since 2002; Member, STUC General Council, since 1994; b. 7.8.53, Cape Town; m., Maureen McGibbon; 1 s.; 1 d. Educ. Haberdashers' Aske's School; Christ's College and King's College, Cambridge. W.E.A. Tutor, 1978; General Secretary, Scottish Further Education Association, 1979-82. Member, Independent Committee of Inquiry into Student Finance, 1999; Member, East of Scotland Water Authority, 1998-2002; President, STUC, 2001-02. Publication: Labour and Scottish Nationalism (Co-author), 1980. Recreation: collecting 78rpm records and wind-up gramophones. Address: (b.) 6 Castle Street, Edinburgh EH2 3AT; T.-0131-226 6694.

Blin, Frank, CBE, BA, CA. Head of PricewaterhouseCoopers UK Regional network, since 2002, Executive Chairman Scotland, since 1998; b. 13.5.54, Glasgow; m., Rochelle; 2 s.; 1 d. Educ. Hutchesons' Grammar School, Glasgow; University of Strathclyde. Chairman, Scottish Co-Investment Fund Advisory Board; Past Board Member: Scottish Enterprise, Scottish Financial Enterprise; Past Member, Board of Governors, Hutchesons' Grammar School; Past Board Member: CBI Scotland, Scottish Council Development & Industry; Past Member, University of Strathclyde Business School's Advisory Board. CBE, 2002 for services to Scottish Financial Sector; Strathclyde University Alumnus of the Year, 1999/2000; Business Insider Professional Adviser of the Year, 1998/99; 3i Corporate Financier of the Year, 1997/98. Recreations: sport; travel; fitness. Address: (b.) Kintyre House, 209 West George Street, Glasgow G2 2LW; T.-0141-242-7225; e-mail: frank.blin@uk.pwc.com

Bloxwich, Janet Elizabeth. Principal Bassoon, Orchestra of Scottish Opera, since 1980; b. 11.4.56, Brentwood; m., Alan J. Warhurst. Educ. Belfairs High School; Southend Technical College; Royal College of Music, London. Two years freelancing in London; on staff at Royal Scottish Academy, since 1997. Recreations: hillwalking; woodturning; instrument repairs; cooking. Address: 91 Fotheringay Road, Pollokshields, Glasgow G41 4LH; T.-0141-423 2303.

Bluck, Professor Brian John, BSc, PhD, DSc, FRSE, FGS. Emeritus Professor of Tectonics and Sedimentation, University of Glasgow; b. 29.8.35, Bridgend, S. Wales; m., Barbara Mary; 1 d. Educ. Bridgend County Grammar; University College, Wales, Swansea. Visiting Research Scholar, University of Illinois, USA, 1961; NATO Research Fellow, 1962; Assistant Lecturer, 1962, Reader, 1981, University of Glasgow. Awarded Keith Medal, Royal Society of Edinburgh, 1981; Lyell Fund, Geological Society of London, 1981; Saltire/Royal Bank of Scotland Award for contributions to geology in Scotland, 1991; Clough Medal, Geological Society of Edinburgh, 2000; Honorary Fellow, University of Glasgow, 2004. Recreations: hill-walking; music; theatre. Address: (b.) Department of Geography and Earth Sciences, University of Glasgow, Glasgow G12 8QQ; T.-0141-330 5473.

Blyth, Emeritus Professor Thomas Scott, BSc, DesSc, DSc, CMath, FIMA, FRSE, Corr. Member, Soc.Roy.Sc. Liege. Professor of Pure Mathematics, St Andrews University, since 1977; b. 3.7.38, Newburgh; m., Jane Ellen Christine Pairman; 1 d. Educ. Bell-Baxter High School, Cupar; St Andrews University. NATO Research Scholar, Sorbonne, 1960-63; St Andrews University: Lecturer in Mathematics, 1963-72, Senior Lecturer, 1972-73, Reader, 1973-77; Dean, Faculty of Science, 1994-98; Chairman, British Mathematical Colloquium, 1987; President, Edinburgh Mathematical Society, 1979-80. Publications: more than 120 research papers and ten books. Address (b.) Mathematical Institute, North Haugh, St Andrews KY16 9SS; T.-01334 463684; e-mail: tsb@st-and.ac.uk or tsblyth.prof@btinternet.com

Bolland, Alexander, QC (Scot),. BD, LLB; b. 21.11.50, Kilmarnock; m., Agnes Hunter Pate Moffat; 1 s.; 2 d. Educ. Kilmarnock Academy; St. Andrews University; Glasgow University. Admitted Faculty of Advocates, 1978; Captain, Army Legal Services, 1978-80; Standing Junior Counsel to Department of Employment in Scotland, 1988-92; QC (Scot), since 1992; Temporary Sheriff, 1988-99; part-time Chairman, Employment Tribunals, since 1992. Recreations: Hellenistics; walking; reading. Address: (h.) 60 North Street, St. Andrews, Fife; T.-01334 474599.

Bond, Maurice Samuel, BA, MSc, MTh, PhD, PGCE. Minister of St. Michael's Church, Dumfries, since 1999; Hon. Chaplain, Glasgow University, Crichton Campus, Dumfries, since 2002; Ceremonial Burgh Chaplain to Dumfries Cornet Club, since 1999; b. 25.6.52, Augher, Northern Ireland; 1 s; 1 d. Educ. Limavady High School; Universities of Nottingham, Cambridge, Dublin and Belfast. Joiner, 1967-71; Teacher, 1978-79; Minister of the Presbyterian Church in Ireland, 1981-91; Minister of the Church of Scotland, Downfield South Church, Dundee, 1991-99. Dumfries and Galloway NHS Medical Research Ethics Committee, since 2005; Research Ethics Committee of Glasgow University, Crichton Campus, since 2005. Publications: Reconciliation of Cultures in Reconciling Memories, 1998; Presence: in Theology in Scotland, 1998. Recreation: rugby. Address: St. Michael's Manse, 39 Cardoness Street, Dumfries DG1 3AL; T.-01387 253849; e-mail: maurice.bond3@tiscali.co.uk

Bond, Professor Sir Michael R., MD, PhD, FRSE, FRCSEdin, FRCA (Hon), FRCPsych, FRCPSGlas, DPM, DSc (Leics, Hon), DUniv (Glas, Hon). Emeritus Professor of Psychological Medicine, Glasgow University; President, International Association for the Study of Pain, 2002-05; b. 15.4.36, Balderton, Nottinghamshire; m., Jane; 1 s.; 1 d. Educ. Magnus Grammar School, Newark; Sheffield University. Professor of Psychological Medicine, Glasgow University, 1973-98 (former Vice-Principal, Glasgow University, former Administrative Dean, Faculty of Medicine); Member, Council, SHEFC, 1992-96; Chair, Joint Medical Advisory Committee for UK Funding Councils, 1992-95; Chairman, Medical Committee, UFC, 1989-92; former Director (former Chairman), Head Injuries Trust for Scotland; former Member, Council, St. Andrews Ambulance Association; Past President, Pain Society; former Director, Prince and Princess of Wales Hospice, Glasgow. Governor, Glasgow High School, Chairman, 2001-06; Trustee, Lloyds TSB Foundation, 1999-2005; Fellow, Royal Society of Arts; Knight Bachelor, 1995; Trade Master, Incorporation of Bakers of Glasgow, since 2007. Recreations: reading; music; painting. Address: (b.) No. 2 The Square, University of Glasgow, University

Avenue, Glasgow G12 8QQ; T.-0141-330 3692; e-mail: m.bond@admin.gla.ac.uk

Bone, Professor (James) Drummond, MA. Vice-Chancellor, University of Liverpool, since 2002; b. 11.7.47, Ayr; m., Vivian. Educ. Ayr Academy; Glasgow University; Balliol College, Oxford. Lecturer in English and Comparative Literary Studies, Warwick University; Lecturer and Senior Lecturer, English Literature, Glasgow University (Vice-Principal, 1995-99); Principal, Royal Holloway, University of London, 2000-02; President, Universities UK, 2005-07; Honorary Fellow, Royal Holloway, 2004. Academic Editor and Advisory Editor, The Byron Journal; Co-Editor, Romanticism. Recreations: music; skiing; Maseratis. Address: (h.) The Old Manse, Bow of Fife, Cupar, Fife.

Bone, Professor Thomas R., CBE, MA, MEd, PhD, FCCEA, FRSGS. Professor and Deputy Principal, Strathclyde University, until 1996; b. 2.1.35, Port Glasgow; m., Elizabeth Stewart; 1 s.; 1 d. Educ. Port Glasgow High School; Greenock High School; Glasgow University; Jordanhill College. Teacher of English, Paisley Grammar School, 1957-62; Lecturer in Education: Jordanhill College, 1962-63, Glasgow University, 1963-67; Jordanhill College: Head of Education Department, 1967-71, Principal, 1972-92. Member, Dunning Committee, 1975-77; Chairman, Educational Advisory Council, IBA, 1985-88; Vice-Chairman: Scottish Examination Board, 1977-84; Scottish Tertiary Education Advisory Council, 1984-87; Chairman: Scottish Council for Educational Technology, 1981-87, Standing Conference on Studies in Education, 1982-84, Council for National Academic Awards Board for Organisation and Management, 1983-87, Council for National Academic Awards Committee for Teacher Education, 1987-89, General Teaching Council for Scotland, 1990-91; Member, Complaints Committee, Law Society of Scotland, 1996-2000. Publication: School Inspection in Scotland, 1968; chapters in books and articles in journals. Recreations: golf; bridge. Address: (h.) 7 Marchbank Gardens, Ralston, Paisley.

Bonnar, Anne Elizabeth, MA. Director, Bonnar Keenlyside; arts management consultant; Trustee, National Galleries of Scotland; Director, National Theatre of Scotland; b. 9.10.55, St. Andrews; 2 s.; 2 d. Educ. Dumbarton Academy; Glasgow University; City University, London; Jordanhill College of Education. Publicity Officer, Citizens' Theatre, Glasgow, 1981-85; General Manager, Traverse Theatre, 1986-91. Address: (b.) 26 Southerton Gardens, Kirkcaldy KY2 5NQ; T.-01592 640460; e-mail: anne@b-k.co.uk

Bonnar, David James, OBE, FRSA. Independent arts adviser; art and craft gallery owner; b. 20.10.50, Dunfermline; m., Sally Elizabeth Armour; 2 s. Educ. Dunfermline High School. Royal Bank of Scotland, 1968-73; Theatre Royal, Glasgow, 1975-80; Theatre Royal, Newcastle upon Tyne, 1980-84; General Manager, Perth Repertory Theatre, 1984-94; Director (National Lottery), Scottish Arts Council, 1994-99; Board Member: Foxtrot Theatre Co., 2000-06, craftscotland, since 2007. Recreations: gardening; opera; architecture. Address: (h.) 12 Queen Street, Perth PH2 0EQ; T.-01738 633424.

Bonney, Professor Norman Leonard, BSc (Econ) (Hons), MA, PhD. Former Senior Research Fellow, Robert Gordon University (retired); b. 4.3.44, Great Yarmouth; 3 s. Educ. Great Yarmouth Grammar School; London School of Economics; University of Chicago. Lecturer, Senior Lecturer, Department of Sociology,

Aberdeen University, 1971-96; Professor and Head, Department of Psychology and Sociology, Napier University, 1996-2000. Councillor, Aberdeen City Council, 1974-88 (Convener, Town Planning Committee, 1981-85; Convener, Industrial Development, 1974-80); Board member, Edinburgh Community Planning Partnership; Vice-President, Association of Scottish Community Councils. Recreations: walking; swimming; tennis. Address: Schoolhill, Aberdeen AB10 1FR; e-mail: n.bonney@rgu.ac.uk

Bonnington, Alistair James, LLB (Hons), DipBusAdmin. Solicitor Advocate, BBC Scotland, since 1992; b. 28.5.52, Glasgow; m. (i), Alison Margaret (deceased); 2 s.; 1 d.; m. (ii), Fiona (Westwood). Educ. Hillhead High School, Glasgow; University of Glasgow; Bradford University. Apprentice, Biggart, Baillie and Gifford, Solicitors, Glasgow; pursued career in private practice, specialising in court work and media law. Secretary, Scottish Media Lawyers' Society; Hon. President, Scottish Young Lawyers Association. Publication: Scots Law for Journalists (Co-Author). Recreation: golf. Address: (b.) BBC Scotland, 40 Pacific Quay, Glasgow G51 1DA; T.-0141-422-6371.

Bonomy, Hon. Lord (Iain Bonomy). Senator of the College of Justice, since 1997; permanent judge of the UN International Criminal Tribunal for the Former Yugoslavia, since 2004; b. 15.1.46, Motherwell; m., Jan; 2 d. Educ. Dalziel High School; University of Glasgow. Apprentice Solicitor, East Kilbride Town Council, 1968-70; Solicitor, Ballantyne & Copland, 1970-83; Advocate, 1984-93; Queen's Counsel, 1993-96; Advocate Depute, 1990-93; Home Advocate Depute, 1993-96. Surveillance Commissioner, 1998-2004. Address: (b.) ICTY, PO Box 13888, 2501 EW The Hague, The Netherlands; T.-+31 70 5125326; e-mail: bonomy@un.org

Boon, Nicholas, MA, BChir, MD, FRCPE. Consultant Cardiologist, Royal Infirmary of Edinburgh, since 1986; Honorary Reader, University of Edinburgh, since 2004; President, British Cardiovascular Society; b. 31.12.50, London; m., Anne Robertson; 2 d. Educ. Canford School, Dorset; Gonville and Caius College, Cambridge University; Middlesex Hospital Medical School, London. Lecturer and Senior Registrar in Cardiovascular Medicine, John Radcliffe Hospital, Oxford, 1983-86; Member, Council, British Heart Foundation, since 1997. Author of scientific papers on heart disease; Co-Editor, Davidson's Principles and Practice of Medicine, 18th, 19th and 20th edition. Recreations: golf; skiing. Address: Department of Cardiology, Royal Infirmary of Edinburgh, Edinburgh EH16 4SA; T.-0131-242 1849.

Boreham, Professor Nicholas Charles, MA, PhD, CPsychol. Professor of Education and Employment, Stirling University, since 2001; b. 27.5.45, Wimbledon; m., Elizabeth Horton; 2 d. Educ. Nottingham University. Educational Researcher, Schools Council, East Anglian Examinations Board and Joint Board of Clinical Nursing Studies, 1971-76; Lecturer and Senior Lecturer in Higher Education, Manchester University, 1976-93; Professor of Education, Manchester University, 1993-2001. Address: (b.) Institute of Education, Stirling University, Stirling FK9 4LA; T.-01786 467617.

Borley, Lester, CBE, DLitt, FRSGS, FTS. Council Member, Europa Nostra; b. 7.4.31, Pontardawe, S. Wales; m., Mary Alison Pearce; 3 d. Educ. Dover County Grammar School; Queen Mary College, University of London. Joined British Travel Association, London, 1955: Assistant to General Manager (USA), New York, 1956-61, Manager,

Midwestern States (USA), Chicago, 1961-64, Manager, Australia, 1964-67, Manager, West Germany, Frankfurt, 1967-70; Chief Executive, Scottish Tourist Board, 1970-75; Chief Executive, English Tourist Board, 1975-83; Director, National Trust for Scotland, 1983-93; Secretary General, Europa Nostra, The Hague, 1992-96; Visiting Lecturer: Academia Istropolitana, Slovakia, International Cultural Centre, Cracow; Adviser, World Monuments Fund, New York; Past Chairman, Icomos (UK), Cultural Tourism Committee. Recreations: gardening; visiting museums and galleries; reading social history; music. Address: (h.) 4 Belford Place, Edinburgh EH4 3DH; T.-0131-332 2364.

Borthwick of that Ilk, Lord (John Hugh Borthwick), DL. 24th Lord Borthwick; Hereditary Falconer of Scotland to The Queen; b. 14.11.40; m. Adelaide; 2 d. Educ. Gordonstoun; Edinburgh School of Agriculture. Recreations: stalking; wild trout fishing. Address: (h.) Crookston, Heriot, Midlothian EH38 5YS.

Borthwick, Alan Charles, LLB, NP. Partner, Brechin Tindal Oatts, Solicitors, Glasgow and Edinburgh, since 1983; b. 25.4.57, Glasgow; m., Sheila; 1 d. Educ. Glasgow Academy; Glasgow University. Brechin Robb, Solicitors, 1977-81; joined Tindal Oatts & Rodger, 1981. Member, Council, Law Society of Scotland, 1995-98; Board Member, Children's Hospice Association Scotland, 1993-2005; Trustee of the following charities: Pollock Charitable Trusts; The Baird Trust. Recreations: golf; skiing; garden; family. Address: (b.) 48 St. Vincent Street, Glasgow G2 5HS; T.-0141-221 8012; e-mail: acb@bto.co.uk

Borthwick, Professor George Cooper, CBE, FRSE, CEng, DEng, DBA, BSc (Hons), FIMechE, FIET, CCMI, FRCSEd(Hon), FRCPS(Glas), FRCOG(Hon), FRCOphth (Hon). Chairman, Scottish Business in the Community, since 1999; former Chairman, Tayside Flow Technologies Ltd.; Chairman, Nova Science Ltd, since 2002; former Member, Scottish Higher Education Review Panel; Vice-Chairman, Napier University Court, since 2000; Director, Surgeons' Hall Trust Ltd, since 2005; b. 17.8.44, Glasgow; m., Milly Chalmers Redfern; 2 s.; 1 d. Educ. Lourdes Senior Secondary School, Glasgow; Strathclyde University. Worked for Ethicon for 33 years; former President, Ethicon Europe, former Managing Director, Ethicon Ltd UK, and former Member, Ethicon Global Council. Visiting Professor, Napier University, since 1993; Chairman, Breast Cancer Institute Committee, since 2001; former Lay Member, Senate of Surgery of Great Britain and Ireland; former Lay Member, Joint Committee on Higher Surgical Training; former President, European Association of the Surgical Suture Industry; Hon. Fellow, Association of Surgeons of East Africa, since 1995; Hon. Member, James IV Association of Surgeons; Patron, Royal College of Surgeons in Ireland, since 1997; Patron, Royal College of Surgeons of England; Liveryman, Worshipful Company of Needlemakers; Regent, Royal College of Surgeons of Edinburgh, since 2004; Freeman, City of London. Recreations: golf; antiques; art; theatre. Address: (h.) Hillside, 28 St John's Road, Edinburgh EH12 6NZ; T.-0131 334 6945.

Boswell, Sir Alexander, KCB, CBE, DL. Chairman, Scottish Veterans' Residences, 1991-2002; b. 3.8.28, Malaya (of Scottish parents); m., Jocelyn Pomfret; 5 s. Educ. Merchiston Castle School; RMA, Sandhurst. Enlisted in Army, 1947; commissioned Argyll & Sutherland Highlanders, 1948; regimental appointments, 1949-58; Staff College, Camberley, 1959; Military Assistant (GSO 2) to GOC Berlin, 1960-62; Company Commander, then Second in Command 1 A & SH, Malaya and Borneo, 1963-65;

Directing Staff, Staff College, Camberley, 1965-68; Commanding Officer, 1 A & SH, 1968-71; Colonel GS Army Strategic Command, 1971; Brigadier Commanding 39 Infantry Brigade, 1972-74; Chief of Staff, 1st British Corps, 1974-76; National Defence College, Canada, 1976-77; GOC 2nd Armoured Division, 1978-80; Director, Territorial Army and Cadets, 1980-82; GOC Scotland and Governor of Edinburgh Castle, 1982-85; Lieutenant Governor and Commander in Chief, Bailiwick of Guernsey, 1985-90. Address: c/o Bank of Scotland, 44 Court Street, Haddington EH41 3NP.

Bouchier, Professor Ian Arthur Dennis, CBE, MB, ChB, MD, FRCP, FRCPEdin, FFPHM, Hon. FCP (SAf), FIBiol, FMedSci, MD h.c., FRSE, FRSA. Professor of Medicine, Edinburgh University, 1986-97 (now Emeritus Professor); b. 7.9.32, Cape Town, South Africa; m., Patricia Norma Henshilwood; 2 s. Educ. Rondebosch Boys High School; Cape Town University. Instructor in Medicine, School of Medicine, Boston University, 1964; London University: Senior Lecturer in Medicine, 1965; Reader in Medicine, 1970; Professor of Medicine, Dundee University, 1973-86. Member: Court, Dundee University, Council, Royal Society, Edinburgh, Medical Research Council; former Chief Scientist, Scotland; Past President, World Organization of Gastroenterology; former Dean, Faculty of Medicine and Dentistry, Dundee University; Past President, British Society of Gastroenterology. Publications: Clinical Skills (2nd edition), 1982; Gastroenterology (3rd edition), 1982; Gastroenterology: clinical science and practice (2nd edition), 1993. Recreations: music; history of whaling; cooking. Address: (h.) 8A Merchiston Park, Edinburgh EH10 4PN.

Boulton, Professor Geoffrey Stewart, OBE, FRS, Hon DSc (Birmingham, Keele), FRSE, BSc, PhD, DSc, FGS, Hon D.Technol (Chalmers). Regius Professor of Geology and Mineralogy, Edinburgh University, since 1986 (Vice-Principal, Edinburgh University, since 1999, Provost and Dean, Faculty of Science and Engineering, 1994-99); General Secretary, Royal Society of Edinburgh, since 2007; b. 28.11.40, Stoke-on-Trent; m., Denise Bryers; 2 d. Educ. Longton High School; Birmingham University. Geological Survey of GB, 1962-64; University of Keele, 1964-65; Birmingham University, 1965-67; Water Supply Department, Kenya, 1968; University of East Anglia, 1968-81; Extraordinary Professor, University of Amsterdam, 1981-86. Kirk Bryan Award of the Geological Society of America, 1976; President, Quaternary Research Association, 1991-94; President, British Glaciological Society, 1989-91; President, Geological Society of Edinburgh, 1991-94; Member: Nature Conservancy Council for Scotland Science Board, 1991-92, Natural Environmental Research Council, 1993-98 (Chair, Earth Science and Technology Board, 1993-98), Royal Commission on Environmental Pollution, 1993-2000, Scottish Higher Education Funding Council, 1997-2003, Scottish Association for Marine Science Council, 1998-2003, Royal Society Council, 1997-99, Council for Science and Technology, since 2004; Chair, Scottish Knowledge Transfer Taskforce, since 2003. Seligman Crystal, International Glaciological Society, 2001; Scottish Science Advisory Committee, since 2002; Lyell Medal, The Geological Society, 2006; Tedford Award for Science, Institute for Contemporary Scotland, 2006; Honorary Fellow, International Union for Quaternary Research, 2007. Recreations: violin; sailing; mountaineering. Address: (b.) School of Geosciences, University of Edinburgh, Grant Institute, Kings Buildings, West Mains Road, Edinburgh EH9 3JW; e-mail: g.boulton@ed.ac.uk

Bourne, Professor Jill, BA (Hons), PGCE, DipESOL, PhD. Dean, Faculty of Education, University of

Strathclyde, since 2007, Professor, since 2007; b. 24.2.47, South Africa; m., Euan Reid; 2 s. Educ. Clark's College, Brighton; University of Liverpool. ILEA, 1980-82; Research Officer, NFER, 1984-86, Senior Research Officer, 1986-89; Lecturer, University College of Swansea, 1989-92; Senior Lecturer, Open University, 1992-98; Professor, University of Southampton, 1998-2007. RAE 2008: Member, Sub-panel 45 (Education); Board Member, TDA, 2003-06; Vice President, AILA, 1996-99; Chair, BAAL, 1997-2000. Recreations: music; theatre; walking; yoga. Address: (b.) Faculty of Education, University of Strathclyde, Glasgow; e-mail: jill.bourne@strath.ac.uk

Bowden, Frederick A.W. Chairman, Tullis Russell Group, since 2001; b. 20.1.47, Aberdeen; m., Sheila; 2 s.; 1 d. Educ. Robert Gordon's Institute of Technology. Production Management Trainee, Inveresk Paper Company, 1964-68; held several management positions, Arjo Wiggins Appleton, 1968-91; Operations Director/Managing Director/Chief Executive, Tullis Russell Group, since 1991. Address: (b.) Markinch, Glenrothes KY7 6PB.

Bowdler, Timothy John, BSc, MBA. Chief Executive, Johnston Press plc; b. 16.5.47, Wolverhampton; m., Margaretha Eklund; 2 d. Educ. Wrekin College; Birmingham University; London Business School. Recreations: golf; skiing. Address: (b.) 53 Manor Place, Edinburgh EH3 7EG; T.-0131-225 3361; tbowdler@johnstonpress.co.uk

Bowen, Sheriff Principal Edward Farquharson, TD, QC, LLB. Advocate; Sheriff Principal, Lothian and Borders, since 2005; Sheriff Principal, Glasgow and Strathkelvin, 1997-2005; Temporary Judge of the Court of Session, since 2000; Chairman, Commissioners of Northern Lighthouses, 2003-05; Visiting Professor of Law, University of Strathclyde, 1999-2004; b. 1.5.45, Edinburgh; m., Patricia Margaret Brown; 2 s.; 2 d. Educ. Melville College, Edinburgh; Edinburgh University. Admitted Solicitor, 1968; Advocate, 1970; Standing Junior Counsel, Scottish Education Department, 1976; Advocate Depute, 1979-83; Sheriff of Tayside, Central and Fife, at Dundee, 1983-90; Partner, Thorntons WS, 1990-91; resumed practice at Scottish Bar; QC, 1992; Chairman (Part-time) Industrial Tribunals, 1995-97; Member, Criminal Injuries Compensation Board, 1996-97; Governor, Dundee Institute of Technology, 1987-90. Served RAOC TA/TAVR, 1964-80. Recreation: golf. Address: (b.) Sheriff Principal's Chambers, Sheriff Court House, 27 Chambers Street, Edinburgh EH1 1LB.

Bowen, Janet, JP. Lord Lieutenant, Ross-shire, since 2007; formerly Chair, Highlands and Islands Volunteer Council of the Red Cross; m., Christopher Bowen; 2 c. Twenty-six years involvement in the voluntary sector, including 20 years serving on the Children's Panel, 5 years with Leonard Cheshire Homes as well as working with Children 1st, the Highland Hospice, WRVS and other charities. Active Member of the "church family" in the local Episcopal church.

Bowler, David P., BA, MPhil, FSA Scot, MIFA. Director, SUAT Ltd., since 1993; b. 9.12.55, Southampton. Educ. McGill University, Montreal; Lincoln College, Oxford. Address: (b.) 55 South Methven Street, Perth PH1 5NX; T.-01738 622393; e-mail: director@suat.co.uk

Bowman, Professor Adrian William, BSc (Hons), DipMathStat, PhD, FRSE. Professor of Statistics, University of Glasgow, since 1995; b. 3.1.55, Ayr; m., Janet Edith Forster; 2 s.; 1 d. Educ. Prestwick Academy; Ayr Academy; University of Glasgow; University of Cambridge. Lecturer in Mathematical Statistics, University of Manchester, 1981-86; University of Glasgow: Lecturer in Statistics, 1986-90, Senior Lecturer in Statistics, 1990-92, Reader in Statistics, 1992-95. Publications: Applied Smoothing Techniques for Data Analysis, (Co-author), 1997; Statistics and Problem Solving (Co-editor), 1999. Recreations: music, particularly singing. Address: (b.) Department of Statistics, University of Glasgow, Glasgow G12 8QQ; T.-0141-330 4046.
E-mail: adrian@stats.gla.ac.uk

Bowman, (Bernard) Neil, LLB, NP. Consultant, formerly Senior Partner, Bowman Scottish Lawyers, Solicitors, Dundee and Forfar, 1984-98; b. 11.11.43, Dundee; m., Pamela Margaret Munro Wright; 2 d. Educ. High School of Dundee; Edinburgh University; St. Andrews University. Apprenticeship, Sturrock Morrison & Gilruth, Solicitors, Dundee, 1967-69; admitted Solicitor, 1969; Notary Public, 1970; assumed Partner, Gray Robertson & Wilkie (subsequently Bowman Gray Robertson and Wilkie, now Bowman) 1971. Secretary: Dundee Institute of Architects, 1970-96, Dundee Building Trades (Employers) Association, 1970-89, Dundee Construction Industry Group Training Association, 1970-93, Tayside Construction Safety Association, 1975-89; Joint Secretary, Local Joint Council for Building Industry, 1970-89, and Local Joint Apprenticeship Committee for the Building Industry, 1970-89; Clerk, Three United Trades of Dundee and to Mason Trade, Wright Trade and Slater Trade of Dundee, 1970-2000; Lord Dean of Guild of Dundee, 1987-90; first Lord President, Court of Deans of Guild of Scotland, 1989; Director, High School of Dundee, 1980-90; Chairman, High School of Dundee Scholarship Fund, 1987-90; Co-opted Member, Law Society of Scotland Committees — Public Relations and Conference, 1982-90, Complaints, 1987-90; Member: Working Party on "Corporate Conveyancing", 1989, School Age Team Sports Enquiry, 1989; Committee Member and National Selector, Scottish Cricket Union, 1974-83; Selector, 1990; President: Scottish Counties Cricket Board, 1981, Scottish Cricket Union, 1989. Recreations: cricketophile; travel; golf. Address: (b.) 37 E. High Street, Forfar; T.-01307 468868; e-mail: bnb@ecosse.net

Bowman, Sheriff Pamela M.M., LLB. Sheriff in Glasgow Sheriff Court; b. 1.8.44, Stirling. Board Member, Scottish Children's Reporter Administration. Recreations: theatre; concerts; dancing. Address: c/o Glasgow Sheriff Court, 1 Carlton Place, Glasgow G5 9DA.

Bowman, Professor Emeritus William Cameron, BPharm, PhD, DSc, FIBiol, FRSE, FRSA, FRPharmS, HonFFARCS. Head, Department of Physiology and Pharmacology, Strathclyde University, 1966-87 and 1990-94; b. 26.4.30; m., Anne Wyllie Stafford; 1 s.; 1 d. Educ. London University. RAF (commissioned officer), 1955-57; Lecturer, then Reader in Pharmacology, London University, 1952-66, Dean, School of Pharmaceutical Sciences, Strathclyde University, 1974-77; Vice Principal, Strathclyde University, 1986-90; Visiting Professor: McGill University, Montreal; Cornell University, New York; Ohio Medical College. Member: Nomenclature Committee, BP Commission, 1964-67; Biology Committee, MOD, 1966-75; TCT and SEAR Sub-Committees, CSM, 1972-83; Biomedical Research Committee, SHHD, 1980-85; Chairman, Committee: British Pharmacological Society, 1981-84 (Foreign Secretary, 1992-97); Heads of UK Pharmacology Departments, 1990-94; Member: Executive Committee, European Federation of Pharmacologists, 1991-96, Scottish Hospital Endowments Research Trust, since

1996; Secretary General, International Union of Pharmacology, 1994-98; Director, IUPHAR Media, 1997-2005; Chairman, Science Advisory Board, Medpharma plc, since 1999. Publications: Textbook of Pharmacology, 1968, 1980; Pharmacology of Neuromuscular Function, 1980, 1990; Dictionary of Pharmacology, 1986; many research articles in scientific journals. Address: (b.) Department of Physiology and Pharmacology, Strathclyde University, Glasgow G4 0NR; T.-01556 630348; e-mail: billbowman@btinternet.com

Bownes, Professor Mary, OBE, BSc, DPhil, FIBiol, CBiol, FRES, FRSE. Vice Principal, Edinburgh University; Personal Chair of Developmental Biology, Edinburgh University, since 1994; b. 14.11.48, Drewsteignton; m., Michael J. Greaves; 1 d. Educ. Maldon Grammar School; Sussex University. Lecturer, Essex University; Lecturer, Senior Lecturer, Reader, Convener, Senatus Postgraduate Studies Committee, Edinburgh University. Publications: 100 research articles and reviews. Address: (b.) School of Biology, Edinburgh University, Darwin Building, Mayfield Road, Edinburgh EH9 3JR; T.-0131-650 5369; e-mail: Mary.Bownes@ed.ac.uk

Bowser of Argaty and the King's Lundies, David Stewart, JP, BA (Agric). Trustee, Scottish Forestry Trust, 1983-89 (Chairman, 1987); Member, Queen's Bodyguard for Scotland (Royal Company of Archers); Chairman, Dunblane Museum Trust, 1992-2003; b. 11.3.26; m.; 1 s.; 4 d. Educ. Harrow; Trinity College, Cambridge. Captain, Scots Guards, 1944-47. Member, Perth County Council, 1954-61; President, Highland Cattle Society, 1970-72; Forestry Commissioner, 1974-82; Chairman, Scottish Council, British Deer Society, 1988-94; Member, Loch Lomond and the Trossachs National Park Deer Management Forum, 2001-05. Address: Auchlyne, Killin, Perthshire FK21 8RG.

Boxer, Professor David Howell, BSc, PhD. Vice-Principal (Research and Learning), Dundee University, since 2002, Professor of Microbial Biochemistry, Professor of Biochemistry, 1991-2002, Head, Biochemistry Department, 1988-93, Dean, Science and Engineering Faculty, 1994-99, Deputy Principal, 2000-02; m., Dr. Maureen Boxer; 1 s.; 2 d. Educ. Aberdare Boys' Grammar School; Bristol University. Dundee University: Lecturer in Biochemistry, 1976, Senior Lecturer, 1985. Nuffield Research Fellow, 1983-84; Chairman, Biochemistry Biophysics Sub-Commitee, SERC, 1990-92. Recreations: travelling; skiing. Address: (b.) MSI/WTB Complex, School of Life Sciences, Dundee University, Dundee DD1 5EH.

Boyack, Sarah. MSP (Labour), Edinburgh Central, since 1999; Former lecturer in planning. Minister for Transport and Environment, 1999-2000, Minister for Transport and Planning, 2000-01; Convener, Environment and Rural Development Committee, 2003-07; Deputy Minister for Environment and Rural Development, 2007; Shadow Cabinet Secretary for Rural Development, Environment and Climate Change, since May 2007. Address: (b.) Scottish Parliament, Edinburgh EH99 1SP; T.-0131-348 5751.

Boyce, David James, MA, LLB, NP. Partner, HBJ Gateley Wareing, Solicitors, since 2007; b. 2.12.46, Coatbridge; m., Martina; 2 s. Educ. St Patrick's High School, Coatbridge; Glasgow University. Boyds: traineeship, 1971-73, Assistant, 1973-76; Partner, 1976; Senior Partner, 1992-2007. Past Chairman, Law Exchange International; Chairman, Board of Governors, St Aloysius' College, Glasgow; Director, Clyde FC. Recreations: golf; running; music; family. Address: (b.)

Thistle House, 146 West Regent Street, Glasgow G2 2RZ; T.-0141 221 8251; e-mail: dboyce@hbj-gw.com

Boyd, Alan Robb, LLB, BA, NP. Director, Public Law, McGrigors LLP (formerly McGrigor Donald), since 1997; b. 30.7.53, Glasgow; m., Frances Helen; 2 d. Educ. Irvine Royal Academy; Dundee University. Principal Solicitor, Shetland Islands Council, 1979-81; Principal Solicitor, Glenrothes Development Corporation, 1981-84; Legal Advisor, Irvine Development Corporation, 1984-97. Law Society of Scotland: Member, Council, 1985-97, Convener, Finance Committee, 1992-94, Vice-President, 1994-95, President, 1995-96; President, European Company Lawyers' Association, 1992-94; Convenor, Association for Scottish Public Affairs, 1998-2000. Recreations: golf; skiing; music. Address: (h.) 45 Craigholm Road, Ayr KA7 3LJ; T.-01292 262542.

Boyd of Duncansby, Rt Hon Lord (Colin David Boyd), PC, QC, BA (Econ), LLB, FRSA. Life Peer; Lord Advocate, 2000-06; Solicitor General for Scotland, 1997-2000; Member of the Scottish Executive, 1999-2006; Head of Public Law, Dundas & Wilson LLP; b. 7.6.53, Falkirk; m., Fiona Margaret MacLeod; 2 s.; 1 d. Educ. Wick High School; George Watson's College, Edinburgh; University of Manchester; University of Edinburgh. Solicitor, 1978-82; called to Bar, 1983; Advocate Depute, 1993-95; took Silk, 1995. Legal Associate, Royal Town Planning Institute. Publication: The Legal Aspects of Devolution (Contributor), 1997. Recreations: hill-walking; reading; watching rugby. Address: (b.) House of Lords, London SW1A 0PW; T.-020 7219 5353.

Boyd, Dr Donald MacLeod, MB, ChB, DipTheol. Medical Practitioner; Highlands and Islands Campaign Manager, Scottish Christian Party, 2006-07; Minister, Inverness Free Presbyterian Church of Scotland, 1989-2000 (Clerk, Northern Presbytery, 1991-2000); Church Tutor in Systematic Theology, 1995-2000; b. Glasgow; m., Elizabeth Schouten; 1 s.; 3 d. Educ. Glasgow Academy; Glasgow University. Southern General Hospital, 1978; Stobhill General Hospital, 1979; Vale of Leven Hospital, 1979; ordained Free Presbyterian Church of Scotland, 1983; Clerk of Religion and Morals Committee, 1984-92 and Convener, 1992-94; Deputy to Australia and New Zealand, 1988; Member, Churches Liaison Committee on AIDS, Highland Health Board, 1992-94; Member, Highland Regional Council Education Committee, 1994-96; Moderator of Synod of Free Presbyterian Church of Scotland, 1997-98. Publication: Popular History of the Origins of the Free Presbyterian Church of Scotland, 1987. Recreations: reading; writing; gardening; walking; photography; British Sign Language; historical research; advanced driving; astronomy; genealogy. Address: Inverness.

Boyd, Professor Ian L., BSc, PhD, DSc, FRSE. Professor in Biology, St Andrews University, since 2001; Director, Sea Mammal Research Unit, since 2001; Chief Executive, SMRU Ltd., since 2006; b. 9.2.57, Kilmarnock; m., Sheila M.E. Aitken; 1 s.; 2 d. Educ. George Heriot's School, Edinburgh; Aberdeen University; Cambridge University. Churchill Fellow, 1980; Institute of Terrestrial Ecology, Monks Wood, 1982-87; British Antarctic Survey, 1987-2001; Antarctic Service Medal of the United States, 1995; Bruce Medal, Royal Society of Edinburgh, 1995; Honorary Professor, Birmingham University, 1997; Scientific Medal, Zoological Society of London, 1998; Editor-in-Chief, Journal of Zoology, since 2006; Marsh Award for Marine and Freshwater Conservation, 2006. Member, Council, Hebridean Trust and Seamark Trust.

Publications: six books; 120 papers. Recreations: rugby referee; walking; photography. Address: (b.) Gatty Marine Laboratory, St Andrews University, St Andrews KY16 8LB; T.-01334 462630.

Boyd, Joe, BSc (Hons), DipEd, MEd. Headteacher, Bathgate Academy, since 2002; Headteacher, St. David's High, Dalkeith, 1997-2002; author, since 1989; b. 10.11.53, Ayr; 1 s.; 2 d.; m., Marissa Grassie. Educ. St. David's High, Dalkeith; University of St. Andrews; Moray House; University of Edinburgh. President, Students' Union, University of St. Andrews, 1975-76; teaching, various Lothian schools, including Beeslack High School, St. Augustine's High School, St. David's High School, 1977-97. Member, National Joint Working Party (Revised Higher Chemistry), 1987-90; seconded to SOEID, to work with HM Inspectorate, 1996-97; led Inservice workshops for teachers, 1983-97. Publications: co-author of 27 titles, including Understanding Science series, and Scottish Science 5-14. Recreations: cycling; hill-walking; football; sailing; skiing; reading. Address: (b.) Bathgate Academy, Edinburgh Road, Bathgate, West Lothian; T.-01506 653725.

Boyd, Rev. Ronald M. H., BD, DpTh. Minister, Portland Parish Church, Troon, since 1998; b. 1.5.67, St. Andrews. Educ. Bell Baxter High School, Cupar, Fife; St. Andrews University. Assistant Minister, New Kilpatrick Parish Church, Bearsden, Glasgow, 1991-93; Minister, Dumbarton West Kirk, 1993-98. Address: (h.) Portland Manse, 89 South Beach, Troon KA10 6EQ; T.-01292 313285; e-mail: rmhboyd@wightcablenorth.net

Boyle, Professor Alan Edward, LLD, MA, BCL. Professor of Public International Law, University of Edinburgh, since 1995; Barrister, since 1977; b. 28.3.53, Belfast; m., Caroline. Educ. Royal Belfast Academical Institution; University of Oxford (Pembroke College). Queen Mary College, University of London, Faculty of Law, 1978-94; University of Texas, School of Law, 1988 and 1994; Essex Court Chambers, London, since 2006; General Editor, International and Comparative Law Quarterly, 1998-2006. Publications: International Law and The Environment (Co-author), 1992 and 2002; The Making of International Law (Co-author), 2007. Recreations: gliding; music; theatre. Address: (b.) School of Law, University of Edinburgh, Old College, South Bridge, Edinburgh EH8 9YL.

Boyle, Rt. Rev. Mgr. Hugh Noonan, KHS, PhL, STL, FSA Scot. Canon, Chapter of Metropolitan Cathedral Church of St. Andrew, Glasgow, since 1984; Chapter Secretary, since 1991; Prelate of Honour, since 1987; Knight, Equestrian Order of the Holy Sepulchre of Jerusalem, 2002; Companion of the Order of Malta, 2003; Chaplain to the Companions, 2004; Archivist, Archdiocese of Glasgow, since 1973; b. 14.1.35, Glasgow. Educ. St. Aloysius' College, Glasgow; Glasgow University; Pontifical Scots College and Pontifical Gregorian University, Rome, 1956-63. National Service, RAF, 1954-56; ordained priest, Rome, 1962; Assistant Priest: St. Philomena's, Glasgow, 1963-66, St. Eunan's, Clydebank, 1966-76; Administrator, Metropolitan Cathedral Church of St. Andrew, Glasgow, 1983-92; Parish Priest, St. Leo's, Dumbreck, 1992-93; Chaplain, Bon Secours Convent Hospital, Glasgow, 1995-2000; Assistant Catholic Chaplain, Victoria Infirmary, Glasgow, 1995-98; Archdiocese of Glasgow: Assistant Archivist, 1967-73; Chancellor, 1976-83. Editor, Catholic Directory for Scotland and Western Catholic Calendar, issues of 1975-2006; Member: Scottish Catholic Communications Commission, 1979-87; Scottish Catholic Heritage Commission, since 1981; Patron, Hutchesons' Hospital, since 1983 (Preceptor, 2002-05). Recreations: music (listening); walking. Address: Our Holy Redeemer's, South Bank Street, Clydebank G81 1PH.

Boyle, Professor Paul Joseph, BA, PhD, FRSE. Professor of Human Geography, University of St. Andrews, since 1999; Director, Longitudinal Studies Centre - Scotland, since 2001; b. 16.11.64, Felixstowe; m., Gillian; 2 s.; 2 d. Educ. Debden High School; Lancaster University. Lecturer: University of Wales, Swansea, University of Leeds. President, British Society for Population Studies, 2007-09. Recreations: football; cricket. Address: (b.) School of Geography and Geosciences, University of St. Andrews, St. Andrews; T.-01334 462397; e-mail: p.boyle@st-andrews.ac.uk

Bradley, Rev. Dr. Ian Campbell, MA, BD, DPhil. Minister; Writer and Broadcaster; Reader in Practical Theology and Church History, St. Andrews University; Associate Minister, Holy Trinity Parish Church, St. Andrews; Honorary Church of Scotland Chaplain, St. Andrews University; b. 28.5.50, Berkhamsted; m., Lucy Patricia; 1 s.; 1 d. Educ. Tonbridge School, Kent; New College, Oxford; St. Andrews University. Research Fellow, New College, Oxford, 1971-75; Staff Journalist, The Times, 1976-82; ordained into Church of Scotland, 1990; Head, Religious Broadcasting, BBC Scotland, 1990-91; Lecturer in Practical Theology, Aberdeen University, 1992-99. Vice President: The Sullivan Society, The Stainer Society. Publications: The Call to Seriousness, 1974; William Morris and his World, 1975; The Optimists, 1976; The Penguin Annotated Gilbert & Sullivan, 1980; The Strange Rebirth of Liberal Britain, 1982; Enlightened Entrepreneurs, 1986; The Penguin Book of Hymns, 1989; God is Green, 1990; O Love That Wilt Not Let Me Go, 1990; Marching to the Promised Land, 1992; The Celtic Way, 1993; The Power of Sacrifice, 1995; The Complete Annotated Gilbert and Sullivan, 1996; Columba, Pilgrim and Penitent, 1996; Abide with Me – the World of the Victorian Hymn, 1997; Celtic Christianity: Making Myths and Chasing Dreams, 1999; The Penguin Book of Carols, 1999; Colonies of Heaven: Celtic Models for Today's Church, 2000; God Save the Queen – The Spiritual Dimension of Monarchy, 2002; You've Got to Have a Dream: The Message of the Musical, 2004; Oh Joy! Oh Rapture! The Enduring Phenomenon of Gilbert and Sullivan, 2005; The Daily Telegraph Book of Hymns, 2005; The Daily Telegraph Book of Carols, 2006; Believing in Britain, 2006. Recreations: music; walking; family; spas; tennis; singing. Address: (b.) St Mary's College, South Street, St Andrews KY16 9JU; T.-01334 462840.

Bradley, John Russell, MA, LLB, DipLP, NP. Solicitor, DLA, Edinburgh (formerly Bird Semple) since 1989; b. 20.11.62, Glasgow; 4 s. Educ. Eastbank Academy, Glasgow; Glasgow University. Trainee, Wright & Crawford, Paisley, 1987-89; Bird Semple: Assistant, 1989-94, Associate, 1994-97; Partner, since 1997. Recreations: hockey (not often enough); golf (mostly in the rough). Address: (b.) Rutland Square, Edinburgh EH1 2AA; T.-0131 242 5502.

Brady, Adrian J.B, BSc, MB, ChB, MD, FRCP (Glasg), FRCPE, FAHA. Consultant Cardiologist, Glasgow Royal Infirmary, since 1996; b. 27.5.61, Edinburgh; m., Lucy; 1 s.; 2 d. Educ. Edinburgh Academy; Scotus Academy; Edinburgh University. Trained in Cardiology at Hammersmith Hospital and National Heart and Lung Institute, London; Winner, American Heart Association Young Investigator Award, 1993; Winner, British Cardiac Society Young

Investigator Award, 1993; Chairman, Hypertension Research Group, 1992-96; Member, Committee for the British Society of Cardiovascular Research, since 1998; Faculty Member, American Heart Association. Recreations: skiing; golf; roller blading. Address: (b.) Cardiology Department, Queen Elizabeth Building, Glasgow Royal Infirmary, Glasgow, G31 2ER; T.-0141-211 4727.

Braid, Sheriff Peter John, LLB (Hons), WS. All Scotland Floating Sheriff, Kirkcaldy, since 2005; part-time Sheriff, 2001-05; Solicitor Advocate, since 1995; Partner, Morton Fraser, Solicitors, 1985-2005; b. 6.3.58, Edinburgh; m., Heather McIntosh; 2 s. Educ. George Watson's College, Edinburgh; University of Edinburgh. Recreations: golf; bridge. Address: (b.) Sheriff Court House, Whytescauseway, Kirkcaldy KY1 1AQ.

Brailsford, Hon. Lord (Sidney) Neil Brailsford. Senator of the Royal College of Justice in Scotland, since 2006; b. 15.8.54, Edinburgh; m., Elaine Nicola Robbie; 3 s. Educ. Daniel Stewart's College, Edinburgh; Stirling University; Edinburgh University. Admitted Scottish Bar, 1981, English Bar, 1990; Standing Junior Counsel, Department of Agriculture and Fisheries, 1987-92; QC, 1994; Advocate Depute, 1999-2000. Treasurer, Faculty of Advocates, 2000; Member, Court, Stirling University, 2001-05; Part-time Chairman, Discipline Committee, Institute of Chartered Accountants of Scotland, 2002-06; Senator of the College of Justice in Scotland, since 2006. Recreations: food; wine; travel; reading; American history and politics; baseball; fishing; supporting Heart of Midlothian Football Club. Address: (b.) Parliament House, Edinburgh EH1 1RF; Kidder Hill Road, Grafton, Vermont 05146, USA.

Brand, David Allan, LLB (Hons), WS. Solicitor; Senior Lecturer in Law, University of Dundee (Director of Studies, Diploma in Legal Practice; b. 4.3.50, Dundee; 1 d. Educ. Grove Academy, Broughty Ferry; Dundee University. Former Partner, Thorntons WS, Dundee. Former Member of Council, Law Society of Scotland; former Dean, Faculty of Procurators and Solicitors in Dundee. Recreations: all types of music; amateur operatics; theatre. Address: (b.) School of Law, University of Dundee, Dundee DD1 4HN; T.-01382 384459.

Brankin, Rhona, Hon. FRIBA. MSP (Labour), Midlothian, since 1999; Shadow Cabinet Secretary for Education and Lifelong Learning, since 2007; Minister for Communities, 2007; Deputy Minister for Environment and Rural Development, 2005-07; Deputy Minister for Health and Community Care, 2004-05. Educ. Aberdeen University; Northern College. Former teacher and lecturer on special educational needs; Deputy Minister for: Culture and Sport, 1999-2000, for Environment and Rural Development, 2000-01; former Chair, Scottish Labour Party; former Chair, Scottish Libraries and Information Council. Address: (b.) Scottish Parliament, Edinburgh EH99 1SP; T.-0131-348 5838; e-mail: rhona.brankin.msp@scottish.parliament.uk

Bray, Professor Francesca Anne, PhD. Professor of Social Anthropology, University of Edinburgh, since 2005; b. 18.12.48, Cairo, Egypt; m., A.F. Robertson. Educ. Collège Sévigné, Paris; Girton College, Cambridge. Research Associate, East Asian History of Science Library, Cambridge, 1973-82; Leverhulme Research Fellow, Needham Research Institute (formerly East Asian History of Science Library), Cambridge, 1982-84; Chargée de Recherche, Centre National de la Recherche Scientifique (CNRS), Paris, 1985-87; Professor of Anthropology, UCLA, 1988-93; Senior Wellcome Research Fellow, Centre

for the History of Science, Technology and Medicine, Manchester University; Professor of Anthropology, University of California Santa Barbara, 1993-2004. Prix Bordin for History, Académie des Inscriptions et Belles-Lettres, Institut Français, for Science and Civilisation in China, Vol. V1 Part 2, Agriculture, 1985; Dexter Prize (Society for the History of Technology) for Technology and Gender. Currently member of Executive Council, Society for the History of Technology; International Scientific Advisory Board, Max Planck Institute for the History of Science. Address: (b.) Social Anthropology, SSPS, Adam Ferguson Building, George Square, Edinburgh EH16 5PL; e-mail: francesca.bray@ed.ac.uk

Breaks, Michael Lenox, BA, DipLib. University Librarian, Heriot-Watt University, since 1985; b. 12.1.45, Plymouth; m., Barbara Lawson; 1 s.; 1 d. Educ. St. George's College, Weybridge; Leeds University. Assistant Librarian: University College, Swansea; York University; Social Sciences Librarian, University College, Cardiff, 1977-81; Deputy Librarian, University College, Dublin, 1981-85. Chairman, JANET National User Group, 1991-93; Non-Executive Director, UKERNA, 1994-97; Member: Board of Trustees, EduServ, SCONUL Executive Board, 1991-96, 2006-, JIS Committee on Electronic Information, 1998-2003, SLIC Management Committee, 1995-2001; President, IATUL, 2000-04; Chair, Archive Hub Steering Committee; Editor, New Review of Information Networking. Recreations: gardening; sailing; walking. Address: (h.) 2 Corrennie Gardens, Edinburgh EH10 6DG; T.-0131-451 3570; e-mail: m.l.breaks@hw.ac.uk

Brechin, George, BSc, DipCompSci, MIHM. Chief Executive, NHS Fife, since 2002; b. 21.12.49, Glasgow; m.; 1 s.; 1 d. Educ. High School of Glasgow; University of Glasgow. Chief Executive: East and Midlothian NHS Trust, 1994-96, Fife Healthcare NHS Trust, 1996-99, Fife Primary Care Trust, 1999-2002. Address: (b.) Hayfield House, Hayfield Road, Kirkcaldy KY2 5AH; T.-01592 648080; e-mail: george.brechin@nhs.net

Breeze, David John, BA, PhD, HonFSA, Scot, FRSE, FRSA, HonMIFA. Chief Inspector of Ancient Monuments, Scotland, 1989-2005; Head of Special Heritage Projects, Historic Scotland, since 2005; Visiting Professor, Department of Archaeology, Durham University, since 1993; Honorary Professor, Edinburgh University, since 1996; Honorary Professor, Newcastle University, since 2003; b. 25.7.44, Blackpool; m., Pamela Diane Silvester; 2 s. Educ. Blackpool Grammar School; Durham University. Inspector of Ancient Monuments, Scotland, 1969-88; Principal Inspector of Ancient Monuments, Scotland, 1988-89. Member: International Committee of the Congress of Roman Frontier Studies, since 1983, International Committee on Archaeological Heritage Management, since 1997, Council, Society of Antiquaries of London, 1984-86, Council, Royal Society of Edinburgh, 1997-2000; Trustee, Senhouse Roman Museum, since 1985; Chairman: 1989 and 1999 Hadrian's Wall Pilgrimages, British Archaeological Awards, since 1993; President: South Shields Archaeological and Historical Society, 1983-85, Society of Antiquaries of Scotland, 1987-90; Corresponding Member, German Archaeological Institute; Vice President: Royal Archaeological Institute, 2002-07; Cumberland and Westmorland Antiquarian and Archaeological Society, since 2002, Society of Antiquaries of Newcastle, since 2007. Publications: The Building of Hadrian's Wall, The Army of Hadrian's Wall, Hadrian's Wall, and Roman Officers and Frontiers (all Co-author); Roman Scotland: a guide to the visible remains; Roman Scotland: some recent excavations (Editor); The Romans in Scotland (Co-author); The Northern Frontiers of Roman Britain; Roman Forts in Britain; Studies in Scottish Antiquity (Editor); Hadrian's

Wall, a souvenir guide; A Queen's Progress, an introduction to the buildings associated with Mary Queen of Scots in Scotland; The Second Augustan Legion in North Britain; Service in the Roman Army (Co-editor); Invaders of Scotland (Co-author); Roman Scotland: Frontier Country; The Stone of Destiny: Symbol of Nationhood (Co-author); Historic Scotland, 5000 Years of Scotland's Heritage; Historic Scotland, People and Places; Stone of Destiny, artefact and icon (Co-editor); The Antonine Wall; Frontiers of the Roman Empire (Co-author); Handbook to the Roman Wall; Roman Frontiers in Britain. Recreations: reading; walking; travel. Address: (b.) Historic Scotland, Longmore House, Salisbury Place, Edinburgh, EH9 1SH; T.-0131-668 8724; e-mail: david.breeze@scotland.gsi.gov.uk

Bremner, Douglas, BSc (Hons); b. 18.9.38, Glasgow; m., Vivien; 3 s. Educ. Aberdeen Grammar School; Aberdeen University. Whaling Inspector, Crown Agents, South Georgia; Research Assistant, Norwood Technical College, London; Warden, Malham Tarn Field Centre, Field Studies Council; National Trust for Scotland: Principal/Chief Ranger, Culzean Country Park, Chief Ranger, Scotland, Head of Interpretation/Presentation, Regional Director, Lothians, Borders, Dumfries and Galloway Region. Publication: For the Benefit of the Nation, The National Trust for Scotland, The First Seventy Years, 2001; Sir John Stirling Maxwell, A Lad O' Pairts. Recreations: natural history; walking; gardening; painting; wildlife; sound recording. Address: (h.) Craigmore, Parton, by Castle Douglas, Kirkcudbrightshire DG7 3NL; T.-01644 470 239.

Brett, John Andrew, MA, CertMusEd, FCollP. Headmaster, St. Mary's School, Melrose, since 1998; b. 4.8.62, Sherborne; m., Clare; 3 s. Educ. King's School, Bruton; City of Leeds College of Music; University of London, Institute of Education. Direcor of Music: King's Hall, Taunton, 1989-93, Thomas's Prep. School, Battersea, 1993-98. Member of IAPS Council, 2001-04; Member of SCIS Governing Body (Scottish Council of Independent Schools). Recreations: member of MCC; listening to jazz. Address: Abbey Park, Melrose, Roxburghshire TD6 9LN; T.-01896 822517; e-mail: j.brett@btconnect.com

Brett Young, Michael Jonathan, DL. Manager, East Sutherland Village Advisory Service, 1986-99; Director: Voluntary Groups, East Sutherland, 1996-99, and since 2001, Highland Advice and Information Network Ltd., 1994-99; Deputy Lieutenant, Sutherland, since 1995; b. 18.10.37, Salisbury; m., Helen Dorothy Anne Barker; 2 s. Educ. Dartmouth. Royal Australian Navy, 1956-69; Sales and Marketing Manager, 1969-79; Senior Account Manager, 1979-84. Chairman, PR Committee, Retread Manufacturers Association, 1975-79; Executive Member, Community Organisations Group, Scotland, 1990-93; Chairman: East Sutherland Council of Social Service, 1991-94, East Sutherland Local Community Care Forum, 1993-99; Chairman, SSAFA, Sutherland; Chairman, Dornoch Cricket Club, 1991-2005. Recreations: cricket; naval history; music. Address: (h.) West Shinness Lodge, Lairg, Sutherland; T.-01549 402495.

Brettle, Raymond Patrick, BSc, MBChB, MD, FRCPEd. Consultant Physician, Regional Infectious Disease Unit, Western General Hospital, Edinburgh, since 1998; Reader in Medicine, University of Edinburgh, since 1995; b. 20.3.49, Halesowen; m., Helene Ferrier; 1 s.; 3 d. Educ. Halesowen Grammar School; Edinburgh University. Registrar, Hammersmith Hospital, London, 1977-79; Senior Registrar, City Hospital, Edinburgh, 1979-83; Fellow, Bowman Gray School of Medicine, Winston Salem, N. Carolina, 1982-83; Consultant, Regional Infectious Disease Unit, City Hospital, Edinburgh, 1983-98; Senior Lecturer,

University of Edinburgh, 1983-95. Founder Member, British HIV Association. Recreations: computing; walking; DIY. Address: RIDU, Western General Hospital, Edinburgh, EH4 2XU; T.-0131-537 2841; e-mail: raybrettle@hotmail.com

Brew, David Allan, BA, MSc. Head of Rural Communities, Scottish Government, since 2006; b. 19.2.53, Kettering. Educ. Kettering Grammar School; Heriot-Watt University; Strathclyde University; European University Institute, Florence. Administration Trainee and HEO(D), Scottish Office, 1979-81; Administrator, DGV, Commission of the EC, 1981-84; Principal, Scottish Office, Glasgow, 1984-88, Edinburgh, 1988-90; Head: Electricity Privatisation Division, 1990-91, European Funds and Co-ordination Division, 1991-95, Sea Fisheries Division,1995-98; Cabinet Office, Constitution Secretariat, 1998-99; Chief Executive, Institute of Chartered Accountants of Scotland, 2000-03; Head of Cultural Policy Division, Scottish Executive, 2004-06. Member, Court, Heriot-Watt University, 1985-91 and 2000-06; Member, AUC, since 2004. Recreations: languages; music; film; gastronomy. Address (h.) 1 Dundas Street, Edinburgh, EH3 6QG; T.-0131-556 4692.

Brewer, Professor John David, BA, MSSc, MRIA, AcSS, FRSA. Professor, University of Aberdeen, since 2004; Queen's University Belfast, 1981-2004; b. 15.9.51, Ludlow; m., Caitriona Doherty; 2 s.; 1 d. Educ. Lacon Childe School, Cleobury Mortimer; University of Nottingham; University of Birmingham. University of Natal, South Africa, 1977-80; University of East Anglia, 1980-81. Visiting appointments: Yale University, 1989, St. John's College, Oxford, 1992, Corpus Christi College, Cambridge, 2002, Australia National University, 2003; Leverhulme Research Fellow, 2007-08. Member: International Assessment Panel of the Irish Research Council for the Humanities and Social Sciences, since 2002, ESRC's Virtual Research College, since 2005, Institute of Learning and Teaching in Higher Education, since 2001. Publications include: Police, Public Order and the State (2nd edition); Anti-Catholicism in Northern Ireland 1600-1998; Ethnography; Editor, Can South Africa Survive and Restructuring South Africa; Co-Editor, the A-Z of Social Research; over 30 contributions in edited collections and 40 peer reviewed articles in journals. Recreations: fly fishing; opera; hill walking; classical music. Address: (b.) Department of Sociology, University of Aberdeen, Aberdeen AB24 3QY; T.-01224 272171; e-mail: j.brewer@abdn.ac.uk

Brewis, Marion Teresa, JP. Lord-Lieutenant for Wigtown, since 2006; m., Francis Roger MacTaggart Brewis. Educ. Convent of Sacred Heart High School, Hammersmith. Civil Servant, resigned in 1989 to move to Scotland to assist in running Ardwell Estates; Director, Ardwell Estates, since 1997. Lay Chairman, NHS Appeals Tribunal, 1993. Recreations: walking; singing; cooking. Address: Ardwell House, Ardwell, by Stranraer, Wigtownshire DG9 9LY; T.-01776 860227.

Bridges, Professor Roy Charles, BA, PhD, FRGS, FRHistS, FFCS. Emeritus Professor of History, Aberdeen University; President, Hakluyt Society; b. 26.9.32, Aylesbury; m., Jill Margaret Bridges; 2 s.; 2 d. Educ. Harrow Weald County Grammar School; Keele University; London University. Lecturer in History, Makerere University, Uganda, 1960-64; joined Aberdeen University, 1964. Council Member, Royal Historical Society, 1995-98; Treasurer, Scottish Institute of Missionary Studies; Chairman, Garioch Area, Aberdeenshire Forum of

Community Councils, 1999-2005. Publications: Africa in Times Atlas of World Exploration; Compassing the Vaste Globe of the Earth (Co-editor); 1996; Imperialism, Decolonization and Africa, 1999; People and Places in Newmachar, 2001. Recreations: cricket; geology; gardening. Address: (h.) Newmachar House, Newmachar AB21 0RD, T.-01651 863046.

Brining, James Edward, MA (Cantab) (Hons). Artistic Director/Chief Executive, Dundee Rep Theatre, since 2003; b. 10.6.68, Leeds. Educ. Leeds Grammar School; Girton College, Cambridge University. Formed Rendezvous Theatre Company 1989; Proteus Theatre Co.: Administrative Director, 1990, Artistic Director, 1992; Community Director, Orange Tree Theatre, Richmond, 1995; Artistic Director, TAG Theatre Company, 1997-2003. Chairman, Federation of Scottish Theatre. Recreations: films, music, football (playing, and watching Leeds United). Address: (b.) Dundee Rep Theatre, Tay Square, Dundee DD1 1PB.

Brink, Professor Stefan, Fil.Dr. Professor, Scandinavian Studies, University of Aberdeen, since 2005. Educ. Uppsala University. Address: (b.) Scandinavian Studies, University of Aberdeen; e-mail: s.brink@abdn.ac.uk

Brittain, Christopher Neil, MBA, BSc, MBChB, MRCGP, DRCOG, DipIMC, RCS(Edin.), FRSocMed, FFCS, MInstD. Executive Director, Scottish Science Trust, 1999-2003; b. 3.3.49, Birmingham; m., Rosemary; 1 s.; 1 d. Educ. Bishop Vesey's Grammar School, Sutton Coldfield; St. Andrews University; Dundee University; Heriot Watt University. Senior Partner, Anstruther Medical Practice, 1978-97; Co-ordinator for Scotland, Sargent Cancer Care for Children, 1997-99. Chairman, British Association of Immediate Care, 1994-97; Director, Resuscitation Council UK, 1995-1997; Member, East Board, Scottish Environment Protection Agency, 2002-07; Board Member, SSERC, 2001-04. Recreations: music; walking. Address: (h.) The White House, Smithy Brae, Kilrenny, Anstruther, Fife KY10 3JN; T.-01333 310191.

Broadfoot, John Ledingham, BA, MEd. Rector, Kelvinside Academy, since 1998; b. 16.12.48, Glasgow; m., Cecilia; 1 s.; 2 d. Educ. Merchiston Castle School; Leeds University; Stirling University. Teacher of English, Kingston College, Jamaica, 1971-73; Assistant Principal Teacher of English, Penicuik High School, 1973-78; Principal Teacher of English, Preston Lodge High School, East Lothian, 1978-87; Head of English, then Director of Studies, Strathallan School, Perthshire, 1987-98. Recreations: Scottish literature; theatre; mountaineering; sailing. Address: Kelvinside Academy, 33 Kirklee Road, Glasgow G12 OSW; T.-0141-357 3376.

Broadhurst, Paul Anthony, MBChB, MD, FRCP, FESC. Consultant Cardiologist, Aberdeen Royal Infirmary, since 2002; b. 19.12.58, Ashford, Middx; m., Amanda Jayne Powe; 2 s. Educ. Ashford Grammar School; University of Dundee. Research Fellow in Cardiology, Northwick Park Hospital, Harrow, 1987-90; Registrar then Senior Registrar in Cardiology, St. Bartholomew's Hospital, London, 1990-97; Consultant Cardiologist, Borders General Hospital and Royal Infirmary of Edinburgh, 1997-2002. Council Member, Scottish Cardiac Society. Publication: Cardiology Explained (Joint Author), 1997. Recreation: fishing. Address: Department of Cardiology, Aberdeen Royal Infirmary, Foresterhill, Aberdeen AB21 2ZB; T.-01224 559308; e-mail: Paul.Broadhurst@arh.grampian.scot.nhs.uk

Broadie, Professor Alexander, MA, PhD, DLitt, DUniv, FRSE. Professor of Logic and Rhetoric, Glasgow University. Educ. Royal High School, Edinburgh; Edinburgh University; Balliol College, Oxford. Henry Duncan Prize Lecturer in Scottish Studies, Royal Society of Edinburgh, 1990-93; Gifford Lecturer, Aberdeen University, 1994; Doctor honoris causa (Blaise Pascal). Publications: A Samaritan Philosophy, 1981; George Lokert: Late-Scholastic Logician, 1983; The Circle of John Mair, 1985; Introduction to Medieval Logic, 1987; Notion and Object, 1989; The Tradition of Scottish Philosophy, 1990; Paul of Venice: Logica Magna, 1990; Robert Kilwardby O.P.: on time and imagination, 1993; Introduction to Medieval Logic (2nd edition), 1993; The Shadow of Scotus, 1995; The Scottish Enlightenment: an anthology, 1997; Why Scottish Philosophy Matters, 2000; The Scottish Enlightenment: The Historical Age of the Historical Nation, 2001; The Cambridge Companion to the Scottish Enlightenment, 2003; George Turnbull: Principles of Moral and Christian Philosophy, 2004; Thomas Reid on Logic, Rhetoric and the Fine Arts, 2005. Address: (b.) University of Glasgow, 2 University Gardens, Glasgow G12 8QQ; T.-0141-330 4509.

Brockie, Rev. Colin Glynn Frederick, BSc (Eng), BD, SOSc. Minister, Kilmarnock: Grange, 1978-2007; Clerk to Presbytery of Irvine and Kilmarnock, since 1992; Hon. Chaplain, 327 (Kilmarnock) Squadron, Air Training Corps, since 1978; Chaplain, Glasgow and W. Scotland Wing, ATC, since 2001; b. 17.7.42, Westcliff on Sea; m., Barbara Katherine Gordon; 2 s.; 1 d. Educ. Musselburgh Grammar School; Aberdeen Grammar School; University of Aberdeen. Probationary year, Aberdeen: Mastrick, 1967-68; Minister, St. Martin's, Edinburgh, 1968-78. Recreations: billiards; photography; computing. Address: 36 Braehead Court, Kilmarnock, Ayrshire KA3 7AB; T.-01563 525311.

Brockington, Professor John Leonard, MA, DPhil, FRSE. Professor of Sanskrit, University of Edinburgh, 1998-2005 (Head, School of Asian Studies, 1998-99); Secretary General, International Association of Sanskrit Studies; b. 5.12.40, Oxford; m., Mary Fairweather; 1 s.; 1 d. Educ. Mill Hill School; Corpus Christi College, Oxford. Lecturer in Sanskrit, 1965-82, Head, Department of Sanskrit, 1975-98, Senior Lecturer, 1982-89, Reader, 1989-98. Publications: The Sacred Thread, 1981; Righteous Rama, 1984; Hinduism and Christianity, 1992; The Sanskrit Epics, 1998; Epic Threads, 2000; Rama the Steadfast, 2006 (Co-Author). Recreation: gardening. Address: (b.) School of Asian Studies, 7 Buccleuch Place, Edinburgh EH8 9LW; e-mail: J.L.Brockington@ed.ac.uk

Brocklebank, Ted. MSP (Conservative), Mid Scotland and Fife, Scottish Parliament, since 2003; Shadow Minister for Europe, External Affairs and Culture, since 2007; formerly Scottish Conservative Rural Development and Fisheries Spokesman; b. 24.9.42, St. Andrews; 2 s. Educ. Madras College, St. Andrews. D.C. Thomson, Dundee, 1960-63; Freelance Journalist, 1963-65; Scottish TV, 1965-70; Grampian Television: Reporter, 1970-76, Head of News and Current Affairs, 1977-85, Head of Documentaries and Features, 1985-95; M. D., Grey Friars Prods, St. Andrews, 1995-2003. BAFTA Award for What Price Oil?; Radio Industries Club of Scotland Special Award (Documentary) for Tale of Two Cities; Norwegian Amanda award for Oil, eight-part series on world oil business, networked on Channel 4 and throughout USA on PBS; BMA Award for Scotland the Grave. Recreations: Life Member, St. Andrews Preservation Trust; Trustee, Hamada Trust. Address: (b.) c/o Scottish Parliament, Edinburgh EH99 1SP.

Brodie of Lethen, Ewen John. Lord Lieutenant of Nairnshire, since 1999; b. 16.12.42, Inverness; m., Mariota Menzies; 3 d. Educ. Harrow School. Lt., Grenadier Guards, 1961-64; IBM (UK) Ltd., 1965-74; estate management, since 1975; Director, John Gordon & Son Ltd., since 1992. Recreation: countryside sports. Address: (h.) Dunearn Farm, Glenferness, Nairn IV12 5UR; T.-01309 651249.

Brodie, James, OBE, FFCS. National Chairman, Victim Support Scotland, 1998-2003; Director, The Ayrshire Hospice, since 1987; b. 29.4.38, Elderslie; m., Anne Tweedie; 1 s. Educ. Ayr Academy. Joined Ayrshire Constabulary, 1955, and retired as Superintendent; during career was: Chairman, West of Scotland Security Association; Chairman, Ayrshire and Arran Review Committee on Child Abuse; National Secretary, SASD; Director, Strathclyde Police Crime Prevention courses; Member, National Council, SACRO; Member, Home Office Working Party on vandalism caused by fires; Member, Secretary of State's Working Party on Police Community courses; Member, Executive Committee, Strathclyde Federation of Boys' Clubs; Member, Management Committee, Victim Support South Ayrshire; Member, West of Scotland Committee, Institute of Contemporary Scotland; Co-Chairman, Joint Management Committee, 1st Ayr Company, BB; Elder, St Columba Church. Recreations: reading; music; gardening. Address: (h.) 3 Portmark Avenue, Doonbank, Ayr KA7 4DD; T.-01292 443553.

Brodie, Peter, MA (Oxon), MA (Ed) (Kent), PGCE. Rector, The Glasgow Academy, since 2005; b. 20.5.57, Oxford. Educ. Abingdon School; St. John's College, Oxford. The King's School, Canterbury: Head of English, 1987-94, Headmaster, 1994-2005. Editor of several Longman Study Texts. Recreations: gardens; walking; reading. Address: (b.) Colebrooke Street, Glasgow G12 8HE; T.-0141 342 5485; e-mail: rector@tga.org.uk

Brodie, Hon Lord (Philip Hope Brodie); QC, LLB, LLM. Senator of the College of Justice in Scotland, since 2002; Chairman, Judicial Studies Committee; b. 14.7.50; m.; 2 s.; 1 d. Educ. Dollar Academy; Edinburgh University; University of Virginia. Address: Parliament House, Parliament Square, Edinburgh EH1 1RQ.

Brodie, Robert, CB, WS, MA, LLB. Part-time Sheriff, since 2000; Part-time Chairman, Employment Tribunals in Scotland, 2002-02; b. 9.4.38, Dundee; m., Jean Margaret McDonald; 2 s.; 2 d. Educ. Morgan Academy, Dundee; St. Andrews University; Queen's College, Dundee. Scottish Office: Legal Assistant, 1965; Senior Legal Assistant, 1970; Deputy Director, Scottish Courts Administration, 1975; Assistant Solicitor, Scottish Office, 1982; Deputy Solicitor to Secretary of State for Scotland, 1984-87; Solicitor to Secretary of State for Scotland, 1987-98. Chairman, Scottish Tourette Syndrome Support Group, 1993-98; Chair, Scottish Association of Citizens Advice Bureaux, 1999-2004; Temporary Sheriff, 1999-2000; Part-time Sheriff, 2000-08; President, Edinburgh Bach Society, since 2000. Recreations: music; hill-walking. Address: (h.) 8 York Road, Edinburgh; T.-0131-552 2028.

Broni, David Alexander Thomas, MBA. Senior Executive, Scottish Enterprise Dunbartonshire, since 2002; b. 25.10.57, Glasgow; m., Ann Frances; 1 s.; 1 d. Educ. St. Mungo's Academy. Joined civil service, 1975; Manpower Services Commission, 12 years, Training Agency, 2 years, Scottish Office Industry Department, 2 years; Head of Secretariat, Scottish Enterprise, 4 years; Scottish Development International, 7 years. Recreations: adventure racing; swimming; rugby; opera. Address: (b.) Spectrum House, 1a North Avenue, Clydebank Business Park, Clydebank G81 2DR; T.-0141 951 3009.

Brooke, (Alexander) Keith, FRAgS. Farmer. Member, Panel of Agricultural Arbiters appointed by Scottish Executive; b. 11.2.46, Minnigaff; m., Dilys K. Littlejohn; 1

s.; 3 d. Educ. George Watson's College, Edinburgh. President, Blackface Sheep Breeders Association, 1985-86, Hon. President, 1989-90 and since 2007. Awarded Connachan Salver for Services to the Breed by Blackface Sheep Breeders' Association, 2007; Director: Royal Highland and Agricultural Society of Scotland, 1986-93 and since 1994 (formerly Convener, Public Relations and Education Committee, Inaugural Chairman, Royal Highland Education Trust, 1998-2001, currently Member of Executive Committee and Chief Steward, Press Radio and Television), Animal Diseases Research Association, now Moredun Foundation for Animal Health and Welfare, 1981-96, Wallets Marts PLC, 1989-91, Scottish, English and Welsh Wool Growers Ltd., 1988-95, Wigtownshire Quality Lamb Ltd., 1991-96; Chairman, Blackface Sheep Breeders' Development Board, 1996-99; Member: Council of Awards of Royal Agricultural Societies, since 1997 and RHASS Representative on Scottish Panel; Council, British Rouge de l'Ouest Sheep Society, 1986-97 (Chairman, 1990-92, Treasurer, 1994-97); formerly Chairman of Stewartry Western District Agricultural Club; Chairman of Stewartry District Association of YFCs and Final Chairman of Old South West Area of YFCs; member of winning Scottish International Beef Judging Team, 1966, and member of winning Stewartry Team, 1970 at the Royal Highland Show Stockjudging Competition for the Glasgow Herald Trophy; member of winning team from Stewartry Western in 1966 Scottish National Beef Judging Competition. Address: (h.) Carscreugh, Glenluce, Newton Stewart, DG8 0NU; T.-01581 300334.

Brooke, Hazel, MBE, MA. Executive Director, Scottish Cot Death Trust, 1988-2005; b. 31.7.45, Forfar; m., Anthony Brooke; 2d. Educ. Inverness Royal Academy; Edinburgh University; Strathclyde University. Unilever, London; The Rank Organisation, London; Scottish Council, Development and Industry, Edinburgh; Glasgow University; Member, Merchant's House, Glasgow. Recreations: reading; wine appreciation; swimming. Address: (h.) 9 Campbell Drive, Bearsden G61 4NF; T.-0141-942 7492.

Brooks, James, DSc, PhD, MPhil, BTech, FRSC, CChem, FGS, CGeol, CSci. Senior Partner, Brooks Associates Glasgow, since 1986; President, Baptist Union of Scotland, 2002-03; Myron Sturgeon Professor in Geological Sciences, Ohio University, 2003; m., Jan Slack; 1 s.; 1 d. Educ. Salt Grammar School, Yorkshire; University of Bradford. Research Scientist, British Petroleum, 1969-75; Senior Research Fellow, Bradford University, 1975-77; Research Associate/Senior Scientist, British National Oil Corporation/Britoil PLC, 1977-86. Visiting Lecturer, Glasgow University, 1978-98; Chairman/Director, Petroleum Geology '86 Limited, 1985-99; Geological Society: Vice President, 1984-87, Secretary, 1987-90; AAPG Distinguished Achievement Award for service to petroleum geology, 1993; AAPG Distinguished Lecturer to North America, 1989-90; Geological Society Distinguished Service Award, 1999; Life Member, AAPG, 1990; Man of Achievement, 2005; Honorary Member, AAPG, 2006; Member of Research Ethics Committee for Greater Glasgow NHS, since 2006. Publications: 18 books including: "Origin and Development of Living Systems" and "Origin of Life" (awarded Golden Medallion and Order of Merit); 85 research papers. Recreations: travel; reading; writing; sport (English soccer!); Christian work. Address: (h.) 10 Langside Drive, Newlands, Glasgow G43 2EE; T.-0141-632 3068.

Broun, Janice Anne, BA. Freelance journalist and author; b. 24.3.34, Tipton; m., Canon Claud Broun; 2 s.; 1 d. Educ. Dudley Girls High School; St. Anne's College, Oxford. Publications: Conscience and Captivity: Religion in Eastern

Europe, 1988; Prague Winter, 1988; Albania: Religion in a Fortress State, 1989; Bulgaria: Religion Denied, 1989; Romania: Religion in a Hardline State, 1989; six entries in Censorship: A World Encyclopedia, 2002; frequent contributions and book reviews to Keston Institute publications: Religion, State and Society and Frontier. Recreations: swimming; cycling; music; art; history; travel; Tai-chi. Address: Martin Lodge, Ardross Place, Alness, Ross-shire, IV17 0PX; T.-01349 882442.

Brown, Alan David Gillespie, MBChB, FRCOG, FRCSEd. Emeritus Consultant Obstetrician and Gynaecologist, initially at Eastern General Hospital, then at the Royal Infirmary, Edinburgh, since 1983; b. 27.5.39, Falkirk; m., Elizabeth Ballantyne; 2 step-s; 1 step-d. Educ. Dalhousie School, Fife; Merchiston Castle School, Edinburgh; Medical Faculty, Edinburgh University. MRC Research Fellowship, Middlesex Hospital, London; appointed Senior Lecturer/Hon. Consultant in O & G, University Hospital of South Manchester, 1975; returned to Edinburgh, 1983. Previously, Hon. Gynaecologist and Vice-Chair, Caledonia Youth. Publications: over 50 articles and textbook chapters. Recreations: golf; theatre; opera; travel. Address: (h.) Arthur Lodge, Blacket Place, Edinburgh EH9 1RL; T.-0131 667 5163; e-mail: alanbrown179@btinternet.com

Brown, Professor Alice, MA, PhD, FRSE, Cipfa. Scottish Public Services Ombudsman, since 2002; b. 30.9.46, Edinburgh; m., Alan James Brown; 2 d. Educ. Boroughmuir High School, Edinburgh; Stevenson College, Edinburgh; University of Edinburgh. Lecturer in Economics, University of Stirling, 1984; University of Edinburgh: Lecturer, Departments of Economics, Continuing Education and Politics, 1985-92, Senior Lecturer in Politics, 1992-97, appointed Head of Politics Department, 1995, appointed Head, Planning Unit, 1996, Personal Chair, 1997-2002; Co-Director, Institute of Governance, 1998-2002, Vice Principal, 1992-2002. Executive Member, British and Irish Ombudsman Association (BIOA); Board Member, Architects Registration Board (ARB); Member, Lay Advisory Group, Royal College of Physicians of Edinburgh; Fellow, Sunningdale Institute. Member, Committee on Standards in Public Life, 1999-2003; ESRC Research Grants Board and other committees, 1997-2001; Board Member, Scottish Higher Education Funding Council (SHEFC), 1998-2002; Chair, Community Planning Taskforce, 2000-02; Member, Public Sector Finance Taskforce, 2001; Member, Scottish Committee, British Council, 1998-2002; Member, Hansard Society Scotland and other committees, 1998-2002; Member, Advisory Group to the EOC in Scotland, 1995-2002; Member, Advisory Group to the CRE in Scotland, 2003-07; Member, Consultative Steering Group in Scotland, 1997-98; Executive Member, Centre for Scottish Public Policy; Assistant Editor, Scottish Affairs journal. Publications: A Major Crisis? (Joint Author), 1996; Gender Equality in Scotland (Joint Author), 1997; Politics and Society in Scotland (Joint Author), 1996; The Scottish Electorate (Joint Author), 1999; New Scotland, New Politics (Joint Author), 2001. Recreations: reading; music; cooking. Address: (b.) 4 Melville Street, Edinburgh EH3 7NS; T.-0800-377 7330; e-mail: aliceb@spso.org.uk

Brown, Professor Alistair J.P., BSc, PhD, DSc, FRSE, FIBiol. Professor of Molecular and Cell Biology, Aberdeen University, since 1998; b. 5.2.55; m., Carolyn Michie; 2 s. Educ. George Watson's College, Edinburgh; University of Aberdeen. Biotechnology Lecturer, Glasgow University, 1983-89; Aberdeen University: Biotechnology Lecturer, 1989-91, Senior Lecturer, 1992-96, Reader, 1996-98. Society for General Microbiology Kathleen Barton-Wright

Prize Lecturer, 2002. Recreations: reading; Scottish rugby; his sons, Myles and Cameron. Address: (b.) Institute of Medical Sciences, Foresterhill, Aberdeen AB25 2ZD; T.-01224 555883.

Brown, Andrew Stewart, BArch (Hons), RIBA, ARIAS. Managing Partner, Simpson and Brown Architects, since 1977; b. 7.6.45, Northwood; m., Morven Islay Helen Gibson; 1 s.; 1 d. Educ. Bradfield College, Berkshire; Edinburgh University. Architect with Sir Basil Spence Glover and Ferguson, Edinburgh, 1970-73; Architect with Andrew Renton, Edinburgh, 1973-77; Founding Partner, Simpson and Brown Architects, 1977; Director and Company Secretary, Addyman Associates, Building Research, Building Archaeologists and Archaeologists. Trustee and Chairman, Executive Committee, Scotland's Churches Scheme; former Chairman, Traverse Theatre, Edinburgh. Recreations: restoring vintage motorcars and older buildings. Address: (h.) 49 Stirling Road, Edinburgh EH5 3JB; T.-(b.) 0131 555 4678; e-mail: sbrown@simpsonandbrown.co.uk

Brown, Rev. Colin Campbell, BD. Principal Clerk to General Assembly, since 2004; Minister, Darnley United Free Church, Glasgow, since 1979; Moderator, General Assembly, United Free Church of Scotland, 2002; Teacher (part-time) of Religious Education, Williamwood High School, Glasgow, since 1987; b. 30.8.54, Perth; m., Joyce; 1 s. Educ. Perth High School; University of Edinburgh; Moray House College of Education. Convener, United Free Church Youth Committee, 1985-89; Moderator, Presbytery of Glasgow and the West, 1990-91; Convener, Action of Churches Together in Scotland Education Group, 1992-94; Convener, United Free Church Ministry and Home Affairs Committee, 1997-2002; part-time Religious Education Teacher, Renfrew High School, 1980-87. Address: 2 Waukglen Drive, Southpark, Darnley, Glasgow G53 7UG; T.-0141-638 6101.

Brown, Douglas Carl Jessen, DA (Edin), DMS, MPhil, FRSA, MSDC, MIMGT, AIST, ASIC. Honorary Secretary, Commonwealth Games Council for Scotland, since 1999; Member, Board of Management, Scottish Amateur Swimming Association, 1995-2003; b. 2.10.40, Edinburgh; m., Noreen Simpson; 2 s.; 2 d. Educ. High School of Dundee; Edinburgh College of Art; Edinburgh College of Commerce; Open University. Lecturer, then Depute Head, School of Design, Edinburgh College of Art, 1964-86; Director, School of Design, Edinburgh College of Art/Heriot-Watt University, 1986-95 (retired); professional practice in design and making, silversmith and jeweller; Member, Senate, Heriot-Watt University, 1986-95; Secretary, Association of Scottish Schools of Design, 1988-90; Member, Board of Governors, Edinburgh College of Art, 1974-79, 1988-89; teaching and coaching competitive swimming at club and district levels, 1977-89; Administrative Co-ordinator for all aquatic events, Commonwealth Games, 1986; Chairman, Organising Committee, European Swimming Cup, 1988; Technical Co-ordinator, European Junior Swimming and Diving Championships, 1997; Member, Amateur Swimming Federation of Great Britain Committee, 1995-2001. Recreations: reading; photography; travel; boating; fishing. Address: (h.) 29 Hartington Place, Edinburgh EH10 4LF; T.-0131-229 6924.

Brown, Ewan, CBE, MA, LLB, DUniv, CA, FRSE, FCIBS. Chairman, Lloyds TSB Scotland Plc; Director: Lloyds TSB Group Plc, Noble Grossart Holdings Ltd.; Stagecoach Holdings Plc; James Walker (Leith) Ltd; b. 23.3.42, Perth; m., Christine; 1 s.; 1 d. Educ. Perth Academy; St. Andrews University. CA apprentice with Peat

Marwick Mitchell, 1964-67. Senior Governor of Court, St. Andrews University; Honorary Professor in Finance, Heriot Watt University; Trustee, Cove Park, since 2007; Trustee, National Youth Orchestras of Scotland; Deputy Chair, Edinburgh International Festival Society; Member, Council of Assembly, Church of Scotland, 2004-07; Council Member, Royal Society of Edinburgh; Chairman, University Court, Heriot-Watt University, 1996-2002; Master, The Company of Merchants of the City of Edinburgh, 1994-95; Lord Dean of Guild, City of Edinburgh, 1995-97; Council Member: Institute of Chartered Accountants of Scotland, 1988-91, Scottish Business School, 1974-80; Previous directorships: Scottish Transport Group, 1983-88, Scottish Development Finance, 1983-93, Harrison Lovegrove Plc, John Wood Group plc, 1983-2006, Pict Petroleum plc, 1973-95, Scottish Widows Bank plc, 1994-97; Trustee, Carnegie Trust for the Universities of Scotland, 1988-2005; Chairman: Dunedin Income Growth Investment Trust Plc, 1996-2001, Transport Initiatives Edinburgh Ltd, 2002-06, Scottish Knowledge Plc, 1997-2002; Governor, Edinburgh College of Art, 1986-89; Session Clerk, Mayfield Church, 1983-88. Recreations: family; golf; skiing; Scottish watercolours; Mah Jongg. Address: (b.) 48 Queen Street, Edinburgh; T.-0131-226 7011.

Brown, Francis Henry, BA (Hons), MHSM, DipHSM. Director of Operations, NHS Tayside, since 2004; b. 17.4.47, Falkirk; m., Marion Muir Crawford; 2 s. Educ. Falkirk High School; Strathclyde University. NHS Graduate Trainee; Principal Administrative Assistant, Borders Health Board, 1977-80; Assistant Secretary, General Administrator, Unit General Manager, Ayrshire and Arran Health Board, 1980-94; Chief Executive, Perth and Kinross Healthcare NHS Trust, 1994-99; Director of Operations, NHS Tayside Primary Care Trust, 1999-2004. Recreations: music; swimming; cycling; DIY. Address: (b.) Royal Dundee Liff Hospital, Dundee DD2 5NF; T.-01382 423115; e-mail: frankbrown@nhs.uk

Brown, Gavin. MSP (Conservative), Lothians, since 2007; Shadow Minister for Enterprise, Energy and Tourism, since 2007; b. 4.6.75, Kirkcaldy; m., Hilary Jane Brown (nee Fergus); 1 d. Educ. Fettes College; Strathclyde University. Solicitor, McGrigor Donald, 1998-2002; Director, Speak with Impact Ltd., since 2002. Economy, Energy and Tourism Committee; JCI Most Outstanding Trainer in the World Award, 2004. Recreations: tae kwon-do (1st Degree Black Belt). Address: (b.) Scottish Parliament, Edinburgh EH99 1SP; T.-0131 348 6931.
E-mail: gavin.brown.msp@scottish.parliament.uk

Brown, Gordon, BA, CA, MBA. Chairman, Scottish Enterprise Renfrewshire, since 2003; Honorary Treasurer, Scripture Union Scotland, since 2005; b. 14.5.54, Glasgow; m., Anne; 3 s. Educ. Eastwood High School; Strathclyde University; Glasgow University. Trained and qualified as a Chartered Accountant with Coopers and Lybrand and joined IBM as an Accountant in 1978; held various Financial Management Positions, including Controller of IBM's Facility at Greenock; appointed IBM Director of Business Operations in UK, Ireland, Netherlands and South Africa in 2002; retired in 2005. Non-Executive Director of Visibility; Non-Executive Director of Riverside Inverclyde Urban Regeneration Company. Address: (h.) 4 Dunure Drive, Newton Mearns, Glasgow G77 5TH; T.-0141 639 3891; e-mail: saabhotaero@hotmail.com

Brown, Hamish Macmillan, MBE, D.Litt, FRSGS. Author, Lecturer, Photographer and Mountaineer; b. 13.8.34, Colombo, Sri Lanka. Educ. several schools abroad; Dollar Academy. National Service, RAF, Middle East/East Africa; Assistant, Martyrs' Memorial Church, Paisley; first-ever full-time appointment in outdoor education (Braehead School, Fife); served many years on Scottish Mountain Leadership Board; has led expeditions world-wide for mountaineering, skiing, trekking, canoeing, botanising, etc. Publications: Hamish's Mountain Walk, 1979 (SAC award); Hamish's Groats End Walk, 1981 (Smith's Travel Prize shortlist); Time Gentlemen, Some Collected Poems, 1983; Eye to the Hills, 1982; Five Bird Stories, 1984; Poems of the Scottish Hills (Editor), 1982; Speak to the Hills (Co-Editor), 1985; Travels, 1986; The Great Walking Adventure, 1986; Hamish Brown's Scotland, 1988; Climbing the Corbetts, 1988; Great Walks Scotland (Co-author), 1989; Scotland Coast to Coast, 1990; Walking the Summits of Somerset and Avon, 1991; From the Pennines to the Highlands, 1992; The Bothy Brew & Other Stories, 1993; The Fife Coast, The Last Hundred, 1994; 25 Walks Fife; Seton Gordon's Scotland (anthology); Fort William and Glen Coe Walks, 1996; Compendium: Hamish's Mountain Walks/Climbing the Corbetts, 1997; Fife in Focus, Photographs of the Fife Coast; 25 Walks, Skye and Kintail, 2000; Billy Black's Dog/The Lost Hogmanay (stories), 2002; Travelling Hopefully (poems), 2003; Along the Fife Coastal Path, 2004; Seton Gordon's Scotland (anthology), 2005; Exploring the Edinburgh to Glasgow Canals, 2006; The Mountains Look on Marrakech, 2006 (shortlisted for Boardman-Tasker Prize, 2007). Recreations: books; music; Morocco; alpine gardening. Address: 26 Kirkcaldy Road, Burntisland, Fife, KY3 9HQ; T./Fax-01592 873546.

Brown, Professor Ian James Morris, MA (Hons), MLitt, PhD, DipEd, FRSA, FFCS. Arts and education consultant, since 2002; Playwright, since 1969; b. 28.2.45, Barnet; m., 1, Judith Sidaway; 2, Nicola Axford; 1 s.; 1 d. Educ. Dollar Academy; Edinburgh University; Crewe and Alsager College. Schoolteacher, 1967-69, 1970-71; Lecturer in Drama, Dunfermline College, 1971-76; British Council: Assistant Representative, Scotland, 1976-77, Assistant Regional Director, Istanbul, 1977-78; various posts, Crewe and Alsager College, 1978-86, latterly Leader, BA (Hons) Drama Studies; Programme Director, Alsager Arts Centre, 1980-86; Drama Director, Arts Council of Great Britain, 1986-94; Queen Margaret University College, Edinburgh: Reader, 1994-95, Professor of Drama, 1995-2002, Head, Drama Department, 1996-99, Dean, Arts Faculty, 1999-2002, Director, Scottish Centre for Cultural Management and Policy, 1996-2002. British Theatre Institute: Vice Chairman, 1983-85, Chairman, 1985-87; Member, International Advisory Committee, O'Neill Theatre Center, since 1994; Chair, Scottish Society of Playwrights, 1973-75, 1984-87, 1997-99; Scottish Society of Playwrights Council Member, 1999-2007; Chair, Highlands and Islands Theatre Network, since 2005; Visiting Professor, Centre for the Study of Media and Culture in Small Nations, University of Glamorgan; Honorary Senior Research Fellow, Department of Scottish Literature, University of Glasgow; plays include Mother Earth, The Bacchae, Carnegie, The Knife, The Fork, New Reekie, Mary, Runners, Mary Queen and the Loch Tower, Joker in the Pack, Beatrice, First Strike, The Scotch Play, Bacchai, Wasting Reality, Margaret, A Great Reckonin; books include Poems for Joan, 2001, and Journey's Beginning: the Gateway building and company, 2004; General Editor, The Edinburgh History of Scottish Literature, 2007. Recreations: theatre; sport; travel; cooking. Address: New Balghoulan, 5 Fenton Terrace, Pitlochry.

Brown, J. Craig, CBE, DUniv, BA, DipPE. Formerly Director of Football Development, Scottish Football Association; former Manager, Preston North End FC; b. 1.7.40, Glasgow; 2 s.; 1 d. Educ. Hamilton Academy. Professional footballer: Rangers F.C., 1958-60, Dundee F.C., 1960-66, Falkirk F.C., 1966-68; Assistant Manager,

Motherwell F.C., 1975-77; Manager, Clyde F.C., 1977-86; Assistant National Coach and Under-21 Coach, 1986-93; International Team Manager, 1993-2001; Vice President, Union of European Football Trainers; FIFA Instructor; Hon. Lecturer, Paisley University; Sports Photographers' Personality of the Year, 1989, 1996; City of Glasgow Sportsperson of the Year, 1997; Bells Manager of the Month, five occasions. Headteacher and Lecturer in Primary Education, 1963-86. Publications: Activity Methods in the Middle Years, 1975; Craig Brown, The Autobiography, 1998; Craig Brown, The Game of My Life, 2001. Recreation: golf.

Brown, Rt. Hon. (James) Gordon. PC, MA, PhD, MP. Prime Minister and First Lord of the Treasury, since 2007; Leader of the Labour Party, since 2007; Chancellor of the Exchequer, 1997-2007; MP (Labour), Kirkcaldy and Cowdenbeath, since 2005, Dunfermline East, 1983-2005; b. 20.2.51; m. Educ. Kirkcaldy High School; Edinburgh University. Rector, Edinburgh University, 1972-75; Temporary Lecturer, Edinburgh University, 1976; Lecturer, Glasgow College of Technology, 1976-80; Journalist and Current Affairs Editor, Scottish Television, 1980-83. Contested (Labour) South Edinburgh, 1979; Chairman, Labour Party Scottish Council, 1983-84; Opposition Chief Secretary to the Treasury, 1987; Shadow Minister for Trade and Industry, 1989. Publications: The Red Paper on Scotland (Editor), 1975; The Politics of Nationalism and Devolution (Co-Editor), 1980; Scotland: The Real Divide, 1983; Maxton, 1986; Where There is Greed, 1989. Recreations: reading and writing; football; golf; tennis. Address: (b.) House of Commons, London SW1A 0AA.

Brown, Janet Marjorie, BSc, PhD, FInstP. Chief Executive, Scottish Qualifications Authority, since 2007; b. 31.07.51, Sheffield. Educ. High Storrs Grammar School for Girls, Sheffield; University of Birmingham. Visiting Assistant Professor, University of Illinois, Urbana, IL USA, 1981-84; Member of Technical Staff, Bell Laboratories, AT & T, Murray Hill, NJ USA, 1984-90; Director of Process Architecture & Characterisation, SEMATECH, Austin, TX USA, 1990-93; Director, Reliability & Quality Assurance, Motorola, Austin, TX USA, 1993-97; European Operations Director, Smartcard Division, Motorola, East Kilbride, 1997-98; Director of Operations, Networking Systems Memories, Motorola, Austin TX, 1998-2000; Managing Director, Scottish Enterprise, Glasgow, 2000-07. Address: (b.) Scottish Qualifications Authority, The Optima Building, 58 Robertson Street, Glasgow G2 8QD; T.-0845 213 5588; e-mail: janet.brown@sqa.org.uk

Brown, Jenny, MA (Hons). Literary agent; b. 13.5.58, Manchester; m., Alexander Richardson; 4 s. Educ. George Watson's College; Aberdeen University. Assistant Administrator, Edinburgh Festival Fringe Society, 1980-82; Director, Edinburgh Book Festival, 1983-91; Presenter, Scottish Television book programmes, 1989-94; National Co-ordinator, Readiscovery Campaign, 1994-95; Head of Literature, Scottish Arts Council, 1996-2002. Commissioner, Press Complaints Commission, 1993-97; Non-Executive Director, Scottish Television (Regional) Ltd., 1998-2004; Governor, George Watson's College, 1999-2005; Board Member, Edinburgh International Book Festival, since 2003; Company Secretary, Edinburgh UNESCO City of Literature Trust, since 2004. Address: (b.) 33 Argyle Place, Edinburgh EH9 1JT; e-mail: jenny-brown@blueyonder.co.uk

Brown, Jock (John Winton), MA (Cantab), NP. Partner, Brodies LLP, Solicitors, since 2006; Football Commentator, Setanta Sports, since 2003; b. 7.5.46, Kilmarnock; m., Ishbel; 3 d. Educ. Hamilton Academy; Cambridge University (Sidney Sussex College). Journalist, The Glasgow Herald, and D.C. Thomson & Co. Ltd. (The Sunday Post), 1967-68; Assistant Secretary, The Scottish Football League, 1968-70; Journalist, D.C. Thomson & Co. Ltd. (The Sunday Post), 1970-73; Ballantyne & Copland, Solicitors, Motherwell (Partner, from 1977), 1973-93; Consultant, Ballantyne & Copland, and Director, Caledonian Television Ltd., 1993-95; Sports Law Consultant, Harper Macleod, Solicitors, Glasgow, 1995-97, General Manager, Football, Celtic F.C., 1997-98; Partner: Winton Brown, Solicitors, Hamilton, 1999-2005, Bishops Solicitors LLP, Glasgow, 2005-06. Part-Time: Sports Broadcaster, BBC Radio Scotland, 1977-80; Football Commentator: Scottish Television plc, 1980-90, BSkyB, 1989-95, BBC Scotland Television, 1990-97; Current Affairs Radio Broadcaster, Scot FM, 1999-2000; Football Commentator: ITV On Digital, 1999-2001, ntl, 2001-02. Publication: Celtic-Minded, 1999. Recreation: golf. Address: (b.) 2 Blythswood Square, Glasgow G2 4AD; T.-0141-248-4672; e-mail: jock.brown@brodies.co.uk

Brown, John Boyter, BSc (Hons). Rector, Peebles High School; b. 13.2.48, Cellardyke, Fife; m., Jennie Smith; 2 s. Educ. Waid Academy, Anstruther; Aberdeen University. Head of Maths, Mhlume School, Swaziland, 1972; Assistant Maths Teacher: St. Augustines, Edinburgh, 1973, Strathallan, Perthshire, 1974-82; APT Guidance, Berwickshire High, Duns, 1982-87; PT Maths, Portlethen Academy, Aberdeen, 1987-92; AHT, Mearns Academy, Laurencekirk, 1992-98; DHT/Acting HT, Firrhill High, Edinburgh, 1998-2003. HAS Council. Publication: O + B Foundation Maths. Recreations: running; cycling. Address: (b.) Springwood Road, Peebles EH45 9HB; T.-01721 720291; e-mail: jbrown1@scotborders.gov.uk

Brown, John Caldwell, DA, RSW. Painter; Member, Board, Leith School of Art, since 1991; b. 19.10.45, Irvine; m., Elizabeth Ann (deceased); 3 s. Educ. Ardrossan Academy; Glasgow School of Art. RSA Carnegie Travelling Scholarship and GSA Cargill Travelling Scholarship, 1968; Director of Art, Fettes College, 1971-86; Director of Art, Malvern College, 1986-88; Head of Art, Edinburgh Academy, 1988-97; former Lecturer (part-time): Edinburgh College of Art, Leith School of Art; solo exhibitions: GSA, 1970, Moray House, 1989, Torrance Gallery, 1992, Open Eye Gallery, 1996, 1998, 2000, 2002, Duncan Miller Fine Art London, 1996, 1997, 1999, 2000, 2001, 2005, 2007, John Davies Gallery, 2001, 2003; Richmond Hill Gallery, 2003, 2005; The Scottish Gallery, 2004, 2006. James Torrance Award, RGI, 1970; Scottish Arts Club Award SAAC, 1993; Scottish Provident Award, 1993; Heinzel Gallery Award SAAC, 1994; elected Member: Visual Arts Scotland, 1994, Royal Scottish Society of Painters in Watercolour, 1996; Alexander Graham Munro Award, RSW, 2004. Address: (b.) 163 Craigleith Road, Edinburgh EH4 2EH; T.-0131 332 1974.

Brown, Professor John Campbell, BSc, PhD, DSc, FRAS, FRSE, FInstP. Astronomer Royal for Scotland, since 1995; Professor of Astrophysics, Glasgow University, 1984-96, Regius Chair of Astronomy, since 1996; Honorary Professor, Edinburgh University, since 1996, Aberdeen University, since 1997; b. 4.2.47, Dumbarton; m., Dr. Margaret I. Brown; 1 s.; 1 d. Educ. Dumbarton Academy; Glasgow University. Glasgow University Astronomy Department: Research Assistant, 1968-70, Lecturer, 1970-78, Senior Lecturer, 1978-80, Reader, 1980-84; Nuffield Fellow, 1983-84; Kelvin Medallist, 1983-86; Armagh Robinson Medallist, 1998; Institute of Physics Public Awareness of Physics Award, 2002; DAAD Fellow, Tubingen University, 1971-72; ESRO/GROC Fellow, Space Research Laboratory, Utrecht, 1973-74; Visitor: Australian National University, 1975, High Altitude

Observatory, Colorado, 1977; NASA Associate Professor, Maryland University, 1980; NSF Fellow, University of California at San Diego, 1984; Brittingham Professor, University of Wisconsin, 1987; Visiting Professor: University of Amsterdam, 1999, ETH Zurich, 1999, NASA Goddard SFC, 1999, CNRS Meudan, 1999, University of Alabama, Huntsville, 2003; NASA UC Berkeley, 2006; Marlar Lectureship, Rice U, Texas, 2006; Project Astronomer, Time and Space, Natl. Maritime Museum, 2003-06; Member: SERC Solar System Committee, 1980-83, Council, Royal Astronomical Society, 1984-87, 1990-93 (Vice-President, 1986-87), Council, Royal Society of Edinburgh, 1997-2000, International Astronomical Union, since 1976; President, BAAS Physics Section, 2001. Recreations: cycling; walking; painting; lapidary; conjuring; photography; woodwork. Address: (b.) Department of Physics and Astronomy, Glasgow University, Glasgow G12 8QW; T.-0141-330 5182; e-mail: john@astro.gla.ac.uk

Brown, John Souter, MA (Hons), FCIPR. Public Relations Consultant; National Treasurer, since 2008; former Scotland Chair, Chartered Institute of Public Relations (2004-05); b. 15.10.48, Glasgow; m., Angela McGinn; 1 s.; 1 d. Educ. Kirkcaldy High School; Edinburgh University. Statistics and Information Officer, Lanark County Council, 1970-72; Senior Officer (Research, Planning Publicity), Manchester City Social Services Department, 1972-75; Press Officer, Strathclyde Regional Council, 1975-80; Journalist and Presenter, Scottish Television, 1980-82; Editor, What's Your Problem?, 1982-84; Ways and Means, 1984-86; Senior Producer (Politics), Scottish Television, 1986-91; North of Scotland TV Franchise Team, 1991; Managing Director, Lomond Television, 1992-93; Head of Public Relations, Strathclyde Regional Council, 1993-96; Head of Public Relations and Marketing, Glasgow City Council, 1996-2004. Chair, Volunteer Centre, Glasgow, 1996-98; Director, Scottish Foundation, 1990-2002; Member, BAFTA Scotland; Council and Executive Board Member, CIPR Chartered Institute of Public Relations, since 2006; Member, Church of Scotland Publications Committee, 2007-08; Trustee, CIPR Benevolent Fund/provision, since 2006; Fellow, CIPR, 2005. Address: (h.) 129 Balshagray Avenue, Glasgow G11 7EG; T.-0141 959 4380; e-mail: j.brown453@ntlworld.com

Brown, Keith James, MA (Hons). MSP (SNP), Ochil, since 2007; b. 20.12.61, Edinburgh; separated; 2 s.; 1 d. Educ. Tynecastle High School; Dundee University. Royal Marines, 1980-83; local government administrative officer, since 1988. Member, Association of Electoral Administrators. Recreations: astronomy; hill-walking; football. Address: (b.) Scottish Parliament, Edinburgh EH99 1SP.

Brown, Professor Kenneth Alexander, BSc, MSc, PhD, FRSE. Professor of Mathematics, Glasgow University; Vice-President, London Mathematical Society, 1997-99; b. 19.4.51, Ayr; m., Irene M.; 2 s. Educ. Ayr Academy; Glasgow University; Warwick University. Recreations: reading; running. Address: (b.) Mathematics Department, Glasgow University, Glasgow G12 8QW; T.-0141-330 5180; e-mail: kab@maths.gla.ac.uk

Brown, Professor Kenneth J., BSc, PhD, FRSE. Professor in Mathematics, Heriot-Watt University, since 1993; b. 20.12.45, Torphins; m., Elizabeth Lobban; 1 s.; 2 d. Educ. Banchory Academy; Robert Gordon's College; Aberdeen University; Dundee University. Lecturer in Mathematics, Heriot Watt University, 1970-81, Senior Lecturer, 1981-91, Reader, 1991-93. Publications: 50 papers. Recreations: tennis; theatre; reading. Address: (h.) 3 Highlea Grove,

Balerno, Edinburgh EH14 7HQ; T.-0131-449 5314; e-mail: k.j.brown@ma.hw.ac.uk

Brown, Leslie Armour, LLB (Hons), DipLP, DFM. Procurator Fiscal, Kilmarnock, since 2005; b. 31.7.63, Glasgow; m., Monica Anne; 3 d. Educ. Hutcheson's Grammar School, Glasgow; University of Strathclyde. Procurator Fiscal Depute, Hamilton and Glasgow, 1986-97; Principal Depute Crown Office Appeals Unit, 1997-2000; Principal Inspector, Inspectorate of Prosecution in Scotland, 2000-03; Deputy Head, High Court Unit Crown Office, 2003-05. Recreation: music. Address: (b.) Procurator Fiscal's Office, St. Marnock Street, Kilmarnock KA1 1DZ; T.-01563 548775; e-mail: les.brown@copfs.gsi.gov.uk

Brown, R. Iain F, MBE, MA, MEd, ABPsS, ChPsychol, ERC (Hon). Honorary Senior Research Fellow, Department of Psychology, Glasgow University; b. 16.1.35, Dundee; m., Catherine G.; 2 d. Educ. Daniel Stewart's College, Edinburgh; St. Andrews University; Edinburgh University; Glasgow University. Education Department, Corporation of Glasgow; Department of Psychological Medicine, Glasgow University; Senior Lecturer, Department of Psychology, Glasgow University, 1968-2000. National Training Adviser, Scottish Council on Alcohol, 1979-94; Member, Executive, Scottish Council on Alcohol, 1980-94 and Alcohol Focus Scotland, 1998-2007; Chairman, Society for the Study of Gambling, London, 1987-92; Founding Chairman, European Association for the Study of Gambling, 1992-95; Chairman, Glasgow Council on Alcohol, since 1985; Founding Chairman, Confederation of Scottish Counselling Agencies, 1989-93; Chairman, Glasgow Anniesland Lib-Dems; Candidate: Glasgow Anniesland (Holyrood) 2000, Motherwell (Westminster) 2001. Various publications, mainly on addictions, in scientific books and journals. Recreations: travel; music. Address: (h.) 13 Kirklee Terrace, Glasgow G12 0TH; T.-0141-339 7095.

Brown, Robert, LLB (Hons). MSP (Liberal Democrat), Glasgow, since 1999; Liberal Democrat Group Business Manager, 2007; Convener, Scottish Parliament Education Committee, 2003-05; Deputy Minister for Education and Young People, 2005-07; b. 1947, Newcastle upon Tyne; m.; 1 s.; 1 d. Educ. Gordon Schools, Huntly; Aberdeen University. Solicitor; former Senior Civil Partner, Ross Harper and Murphy; former Glasgow District Councillor (Leader, Lib Dem Group, 1977-92). Address: (b.) Olympic House, Suite 1, 2nd Floor; 142 Queen Street, Glasgow G1 3BU; T.-0141-243 2421; Scottish Parliament, Edinburgh EH99 1SP; T.-0131-348 5792; e-mail: robert.brown.msp.@scottish.parliament.uk

Brown, Russell Leslie. MP (Labour), Dumfries and Galloway, since 2005, Dumfries, 1997-2005; b. 17.9.51, Annan; m., Christine Margaret Calvert; 2 d. Educ. Annan Academy. Employed by ICI for 23 years in variety of positions; Local Councillor, since 1986. Recreations: walking; sport, especially football. Address: 5 Friars Vennel, Dumfries DG1 2RQ; 13 Hanover Street, Stranraer DG9 7SB; T.-01776 705254.

Brown, Samuel Jeffrey, OBE, BA (Hons). Rector, Moffat Academy, since 1990; b. 10.4.51, Airdrie; m., Elizabeth Scobbie Hamilton; 2 d. Educ. Airdrie Academy; Strathclyde University. Teacher of History/Modern Studies/Economics, Lockerbie Academy, 1974-78; Assistant Principal Teacher of Guidance, Lockerbie Academy, 1978-80; Principal Teacher of History, Dumfries High School, 1980-83; Assistant Rector with responsibility for lower school and educational needs, Stranraer Academy, 1983-88; Depute

Rector, Moffat Academy, 1988-90. Reader, Church of Scotland, since 1985; Associate Assessor, HMI Schools, since 2000; Trustee, Moffat Museum. Recreations: hillwalking; canoeing; gardening; theatre; films; music of all types; reading; travel. Address: (b.) Moffat Academy, Moffat, DG10 9DA; T.-01683 220114.

Brown, Simon Thomas David, LLB (Hons), DipLP, WS, MSI, FRSA. Partner and Head of Corporate, Anderson Strathern Solicitors, since 1997; b. 22.4.60, Edinburgh; m., Karen Ivory; 2 s.; 1 d. Educ. Royal High School, Edinburgh; Edinburgh University. Dundas and Wilson CS, 1983-89; Partner, Steedman Ramage WS, 1989-97. Director, Publishing Scotland. Recreations: golf; football; family; travel; literature. Address: (b.) 1 Rutland Court, Edinburgh EH3 8EY; T.-0131 270 7700; e-mail: simon.brown@andersonstrathern.co.uk

Brown, Professor Stewart J., BA, MA, PhD, FRHistS, FRSE. Professor of Ecclesiastical History, Edinburgh University, since 1988; Dean, Faculty of Divinity, 2000-04; b. 8.7.51, Illinois; m., Teri B. Hopkins-Brown; 1 s.; 1 d. Educ. University of Illinois; University of Chicago. Fulbright Scholar, Edinburgh University, 1976-78; Whiting Fellow in the Humanities, University of Chicago, 1979-80; Assistant to the Dean, College of Arts & Sciences, and Lecturer in History, Northwestern University, 1980-82; Associate Professor and Assistant Head, Department of History, University of Georgia, 1982-88; Visiting Lecturer, Department of Irish History, University College, Cork, 1986; Editor, Scottish Historical Review, 1993-99. Publications: Thomas Chalmers and the Godly Commonwealth in Scotland, 1982 (awarded Agnes Mure Mackenzie Prize from Saltire Society); Scotland in the Age of the Disruption (Co-author), 1993; William Robertson and the Expansion of Empire (Editor), 1997; Piety and Power in Ireland 1760-1960 (Co-editor), 2000; Scottish Christianity in the Modern World (Co-editor), 2000; The National Churches of England, Ireland and Scotland, 1801-1846, 2001; Cambridge History of Christianity, vol. 7: Enlightenment, Reawakening, and Revolution 1660-1815 (Co-editor), 2006; Providence and Empire: Religion, Politics and Society in the United Kingdom 1815-1917, 2008. Recreations: swimming; hill-walking. Address: (h.) 160 Craigleith Hill Avenue, Edinburgh EH4 2NB; T.-0131-343 1712.

Brown, Professor (Susanne) Moira, OBE, BSc, PhD, FRCPath, FRSE. Director and Chief Scientist, Crusade Laboratories Ltd., Glasgow; Professor Emeritus and Hon. Senior Research Fellow, University of Glasgow; Chairman, Medical Research Scotland; b. 21.3.46, Greenock; m., Alasdair MacDougall Brown. Educ. Greenock Academy; Strathearn School, Belfast; Queen's University, Belfast; Glasgow University. MRC Virology Unit, Glasgow, 1971-95; Wistar Institute, Philadelphia, 1977-80. Recreations: walking; travel; dogs; Christian faith. Address: (h.) 'Kilure', The Steading, Croy Cunningham, Killearn G63 9QY; T.-01360 551715; e-mail: smbrown@crusadelabs.co.uk

Brown, Rev. William David, BD, CQSW. Chairman, Children 1st, since 2000; Minister, Murrayfield Parish Church, Edinburgh, since 2001; b.21.8.48. Edinburgh; m., Shirley; 1s.; 1d. Educ. Forrester High School; Edinburgh University; Moray House College. Scottish Office, 1964-70; Royal Scottish Society for the Protection of Cruelty to Children (now Children 1st): Inspector and Project Officer, 1970-78; Development Officer, Scotland. 1978-83; New College studying for BD, 1983-87; Church of Scotland Minister, Carlisle and Longtown. Recreations: reading; walking. Address: (h.)

45 Murrayfield Gardens, Edinburgh. EH12 6DH; T.-0131-337 5431.

Browne, Desmond, MP, LLB (Hons). Labour MP, Kilmarnock and Loudoun, since 1997; Secretary of State for Defence, since 2006; Secretary of State for Scotland, since 2007; Chief Secretary to the Treasury, 2005-06; Minister for Immigration and Citizenship, 2004-05; Minister for Work, 2003-04; Under Secretary of State, Northern Ireland Office, 2001-03; b. 22.3.52; m., Maura; 2 s. Educ. St Michael's Academy, Kilwinning; Glasgow University. Partner, Ross Harper and Murphy, 1980-85; Senior Partner, McCluskey Browne, Kilmarnock, 1985-92; called to the Bar, 1993; Member, Council, Law Society of Scotland, 1988-91; Chair, Children's Rights Group, 1981-86; Member, Sheriff Court Rules Council, 1990-92; Member, Dean's Council, Faculty of Advocates, 1994-97. Recreations: football; swimming; reading. Address: (b.) House of Commons, Westminster, London SW1A 0AA.

Browning, Derek, MA, BD, DMin. Minister, Morningside Parish Church, Edinburgh, since 2001; b. 24.5.62, Edinburgh. Educ. North Berwick High School; Corpus Christi College, Oxford; St. Mary College, St. Andrews; Princeton Theological Seminary. Minister, Cupar Old Parish Church, 1987-2001; Moderator, Presbytery of St. Andrews, 1996-97; Convener, Prayer and Devotion Committee, Panel on Worship, 2000-04. Chairman, Board of Directors, Eric Liddell Centre. Recreations: reading; cooking; croquet; travel; the arts. Address: (h.) 20 Braidburn Crescent, Edinburgh EH10 6EN; T.-0131 447 1617; e-mail: derek.browning@btinternet.com

Browning, Professor George Gordon, MD, ChB, FRCS(Ed.), FRCPS(Glas). Professor of Otolaryngology, Head and Neck Surgery, University of Glasgow, 1991-2002, now Emeritus Professor; Honorary Consultant Otolaryngologist, Glasgow Royal Infirmary, since 1978; Senior Consultant Otologist to British MRC Institute of Hearing Research, 1992-2002; b. 10.1.41, Glasgow; m., Annette; 1 s.; 2 d. Educ. Kelvinside Academy; University of Glasgow. Resident House Surgeon, Western Infirmary, Glasgow, 1964-65; West of Scotland General Surgical Training Scheme, 1965-70; West of Scotland Otorhinolaryngological Training Scheme, 1970-76; MRC Wernher-Piggot Travelling Fellow, Harvard University, 1976-77. President, Otorhinolaryngological Research Society UK, 1992-94; Chairman, British Society of Academics in Otolaryngology, UK, 1995-99; Vice-Chairman, Specialist Advisory Committee in Otolaryngology, 1997-99; President, Section of Otology, Royal Society of Medicine, 1999-2000; Chairman, Academic Board, Royal Society of Medicine, 2001-03 (Vice-Chairman, 2000-01); Vice-President, Royal Society of Medicine, 2005-07; Member, Post-Graduate Examining Boards, FRCS Edinburgh, since 1997, and FRCPS Glasgow, since 1987. Publications: Updated ENT (3rd Edition), 1994; Picture Tests in Otolaryngology (Co-Author), 1998; Clinical Otology and Audiology (2nd Edition), 1998; Otoscopy – A Structured Approach (Co-Author), 1995; over 100 scientific articles. Recreations: silversmithing; skiing; swimming. Address: (b.) Department of Otolaryngology, Glasgow Royal Infirmary University NHS Trust, 16 Alexandra Parade, Glasgow G31 2ER; T.-0141-211 4695.

Brownlee, Derek. MSP (Conservative), South of Scotland, since 2005. Conservative Finance Spokesman. Address: (b.) Scottish Parliament, Edinburgh EH99 1SP.

Brownlie, Alistair Rutherford, OBE, MA, LLB, SSC, FFCS; b. 5.4.24, Edinburgh; m., Martha Barron Mounsey. Educ. George Watson's; Edinburgh University. Served as radio operator in 658 Air O.P. Squadron RAF, Europe and India; apprenticed to J. & R.A. Robertson, WS; qualified

Solicitor, 1950; in private practice; Member, Committee on Blood Grouping (House of Lords); Solicitor for the poor, 1955-64, in High Court of Justiciary; Secretary, SSC Society, 1970-95, now Archivist; former Member, Council, Law Society of Scotland; Legal Aid Central Committee; Chairman, Legal Aid Committee, Scottish Legal Aid Board, 1986-90; founder Member, Past President, now Hon. Fellow, Forensic Science Society; Member, Vice-Chairman, Scottish Council of Law Reporting, 1975-97; Chairman, Edinburgh Diabetes Research Trust; Fellow, RSA; Elder, Church of Scotland and United Reformed Church. Publications: The Universities and Scottish Legal Education; Drink, Drugs and Driving (Co-author); Crime Investigation: art or science (Editor); autobiography: "The Treasured Years"; various papers on forensic science, criminal law and legal aid. Recreations: the pen and the saw. Address: (h.) 8 Braid Mount, Edinburgh; T.-0131-447 4255.

Bruce, Alistair James, LLB, NP. Solicitor; Partner, Lows, Solicitors, Kirkwall, since 1985; b. 4.12.58, Perth; m., Jane; 2 s. Educ. Perth Academy; University of Dundee. Apprenticeship with A.C. Morrison and Richards, Advocates, Aberdeen, 1980-82; Assistant Solicitor, T.P. and J.L. Low, Kirkwall, 1982-85. Member, Council, Law Society of Scotland, 1996-98. Past President, Rotary Club of Kirkwall; Secretary, Orkney Arts Theatre. Recreations: golf; drama; St. Magnus Cathedral Choir. Address: (b.) 5 Broad Street, Kirkwall, Orkney; T.-01856 873151; e-mail: alistairb@lowsorkney.co.uk

Bruce, David, MA, FRPS, Chevalier de L'Ordre des Arts et des Lettres. Writer and Consultant; Director, Scottish Film Council, 1986-94; b. 10.6.39, Dundee; m., Barbara; 1 s.; 1 d. Educ. Dundee High School; Aberdeen Grammar School; Edinburgh University. Freelance (film), 1963; Assistant Director, Films of Scotland, 1964-66; Director, Edinburgh International Film Festival, 1965-66; Promotions Manager, Mermaid Theatre, London, 1966-67; Executive Officer, British Universities Film Council, 1967-69; joined Scottish Film Council as Assistant Director, 1969; Depute Director, SFC and Scottish Council for Educational Technology, 1977-86. Chairman, Mental Health Film Council, 1982-84; Chairman, Scottish Society for History of Photography, 1983-86 and since 2003; Chairman, Association of European Film Institutes, 1990-94; Director, David Octavius Hill Bicentenary Festival, 2002; Chairman, Glasgow Film Theatre, since 2002; Deputy Chairman, Scottish National Photography Centre, since 2003. Various publications, including Scotland–the movie, 1996. Recreations: movies; music; photo-history. Address: (h.) Rosebank, 150 West Princes Street, Helensburgh G84 8BH; e-mail: David.Bruce@ufcnet.net

Bruce, Fraser Finlayson, RD, MA (Hons), LLB, FSA(Scot). Regional Chairman, Industrial Tribunals for Scotland 1993-97 (Permanent Chairman, 1982-93); Solicitor, since 1956; b. 10.10.31, Kirkcaldy; m., Joan Gwendolen Hunter (deceased); 2 step-s. Educ. St. Andrews University. National Service, Royal Navy, 1956-58, commissioned Sub-Lieutenant, RNVR; Legal Assistant, Lanark County Council, 1958-60, Inverness County Council, 1960-66; Depute County Clerk, Argyll County Council, 1966-70, Inverness County Council, 1970-72; County Clerk, Inverness County Council, 1972-75; Joint Director of Law and Administration, Highland Regional Council, 1975-82; Temporary Sheriff, 1984-92. Served RNVR, 1956-76, retiring as Lieutenant-Commander RNR. Recreations: hill walking; reading (in philosophy and naval/military history). Address: (h.) Arlberg, Mossie Road, Grantown-on-Spey PH26 3HW; T.-01479 873969.

Bruce, Malcolm Gray, MA, MSc. MP (Liberal Democrat, formerly Liberal), Gordon, since 1983; President, Scottish Liberal Democrats, since 2000; Chair, International Development Committee; Liberal Democrat Shadow Secretary of State for the Department of Trade and Industry, 2003-05; Liberal Democrat Shadow Secretary of State for the Department of the Environment, Food and Rural Affairs, 2001-02; Liberal Democrat Treasury Spokesman, 1995-2000; Chairman, Liberal Democrat Parliamentary Party, 1999-2001; b. 17.11.44, Birkenhead; m., 1, Jane Wilson; 1 s.; 1 d; m., 2, Rosemary Vetterlein; 1 s.; 2 d. Educ. Wrekin College; St. Andrews University; Strathclyde University. Trainee Journalist, Liverpool Daily Post & Echo, 1966-67; Section Buyer, Boots the Chemist, 1968-69; Fashion Retailing Executive, A. Goldberg & Sons, 1969-70; Research and Information Officer, NESDA, 1971-75; Marketing Director, Noroil Publishing, 1975-81; Director, Aberdeen Petroleum Publishing; Editor/Publisher, Aberdeen Petroleum Report, 1981-83; Co-Editor, Scottish Petroleum Annual, 1st and 2nd editions; Called to the Bar (Gray's Inn), 1995. Vice Chairman, Political, Scottish Liberal Party, 1975-84; Rector, Dundee University, 1986-89; Privy Councillor, 2006; Chair, Globe UK - APPG dialogue on climate change, 2004-06; President, Globe International, 2004-06; Vice-Chair, Globe UK, since 2006; Vice-President, Globe International, since 2006; Chair, APPG on Deafness, since 2004; Trustee, RNID; National Vice President of National Deaf Children's Society (NDCS). Recreations: reading; music; theatre; hill-walking; cycling; travel. Address: (b.) House of Commons, London, SW1A 0AA.

Bruce, Roderick Lawrence, LLB (Hons). Partner, Dickson Minto WS, since 1986; b. 8.3.48, Edinburgh; m., Jane; 1 s.; 3 d. Educ. Boroughmuir School; Edinburgh University. Partner, Dundas and Wilson CS, 1977-86. Recreations: golf; squash; skiing; theatre. Address: (b.) 16 Charlotte Square, Edinburgh EH2 4DF; T.-0131-225 4455; e-mail: roderick.bruce@dmws.com

Bruce, Professor Steve, BA, PhD, FBA, FRSE. Professor of Sociology, Aberdeen University, since 1991; b. 1.4.54, Edinburgh; m., Elizabeth S. Duff; 1 s.; 2 d. Educ. Queen Victoria School, Dunblane; Stirling University. Variously Lecturer, Reader and Professor of Sociology, Queen's University of Belfast, 1978-91. Publications: author of numerous books on religion, and on the Northern Ireland conflict. Recreation: playing Scottish country dance music. Address: (b.) Department of Sociology, Aberdeen University, Aberdeen AB24 3QY; T.-01224 272761.

Brunt, Professor Peter William, CVO, OBE, MD, FRCP(Lond), FRCP(Edin). Consultant Physician, Aberdeen Royal Infirmary, 1970-2001; Clinical Professor of Medicine, Aberdeen University, 1996-2001; Physician to The Queen in Scotland, 1983-2001; non-stipendiary Minister in Episcopal Church of Scotland; Chairman, Alcohol Focus Scotland; Chairman, Medical Council on Alcohol; Vice-President, Royal College of Physicians, Edinburgh; b. 18.1.36, Prestatyn; m., Marina Evelyn Anne Lewis; 3 d. Educ. Manchester Grammar School; King George V School; Liverpool, London, Edinburgh and John Hopkins Universities. Recreations: mountaineering; music. Address: (h.) Flat 4, 1, Hillpark Rise, Edinburgh EH4 7BB; T.-0131-312-6687; e-mail: brunt.aberdeen@btinternet.com

Bruntisfield, 3rd Baron (Michael John George Warrender); b. 9.1.49; succeeded to title, 2007.

Brunton, Rodger James Horne, DipArch, RIBA, FRIAS, MaPS. Partner, Brunton Design Studio, since 1999; b. 11.7.51, Dundee; m., Sheila; 1 s.; 1 d. Educ. Morgan Academy, Dundee; School of Architecture, Duncan of Jordanstone College of Art. Dundee District Council, 1975-80; Robbie and Wellwood Architects, 1980-85; Brunton

Voigt Partnership, 1985-99. Past President, Dundee Institute of Architects; Secretary, Dundee Institute of Architects; Chairman, Morgan Academy Former Pupils Association; Past Chairman, School Board, Carnoustie High School. Recreations: after-dinner speaking; amateur operatics; keep fit. Address: (b.) 95 Dundee Street, Carnoustie DD7 7EW; T -01241 858153; e-mail: architects@bruntondesignstudio.co.uk

Brunton, Sandy, JP, DipY and BM. President, Mull and Iona Chamber of Commerce, since 2001; b. 22.7.59, Oban; m., Jane; 1 s.; 2 d. Educ. Oban High School; James Watt, Greenock; Southampton College of Higher Education. Shipwright/Boatbuilder, Southampton, 1983-86; Retailer and Subpostmaster, Fionnphort, Mull, since 1986. Address: The Ferry Shop, Fionnphort, Isle of Mull PA66 6BL; T.- 01681 700470; e-mail: bruntonmull@aol.com

Bryan, Amanda Jayne, BEng (Hons), MSc. Member, SNH Board, since 2004; Chairman, North Areas Board, Scottish Natural Heritage, 2004-07; Chairman, Rural Affairs Advisory Committee, BBC Scotland, 2001-07; Rural Development Consultant, trading as Aigas Associates, since 2000; b. 30.8.67, Thurso; m., Andrew Colin Leaver; 2 d. Educ. Wick High School; Heriot Watt University. Part-time research student, University of The Highlands and Islands Millennium Institute (towards a PhD in Rural Development). Address: (h.) Aigas, Beauly, Inverness-shire.

Bryan, Pauline Christina. Director, Employee Counselling Service, since 1989; b. 3.1.50, London; partner Vincent Mills. Educ. St. Edward the Confessor School; Open University. Messenger, Daily Mirror; Secretary, National Labour Press, 11 years; Development Officer, Fabian Society, 1981-86; Secretary, Local Health Council, 1986- 89. Publication: contributor to "The Red Paper on Scotland", 2005. Recreations: politics; music. Address: (b.) Savoy Tower, 77 Renfrew Street, Glasgow G2 3BZ; T.- 0141-332 9833.

Bryce, Professor Charles F.A., BSc, PhD, DipEdTech, EurBiol, CBiol, FIBiol, CSci, CChem, FRSC, FHEA. Professor and Head, School of Life Sciences, Napier University, since 1983; b. 5.9.47, Lennoxtown; m., Maureen; 2 s. Educ. Lenzie Academy; Shawlands Academy; Glasgow University; Max Planck Institute, Berlin. Former Executive Editor, Computer Applications in the Biosciences; Vice President, European Federation of Biotechnology (EFB); Member, EFB Task Group on Public Perceptions of Biotechnology; Chairman, EFB Task Group on Education and Mobility; Chairman, EFB Task Group on Innovation; Member, EFB Executive Board; Adviser to the Committee on Science and Technology in Developing Countries (India); former Chairman, UK Deans of Science Committee; Secretary General, European Association for Higher Education in Biotechnology; actively involved in quality audit and quality assessment in biomedical sciences and forensic science in UK, Bangladesh and Zambia; Visiting Professor, Zhengzhou University, China; Director, TopoSphere. Recreations: competitive bridge; collecting wine. Address: (b.) Napier University, 10 Colinton Road, Edinburgh EH10 5DT; T.-0131-455 2525.

Bryce, Colin Maxwell, DA (Edin), CertEd, FCSD, FRSA. Principal, Hunter Maxwell Associates, since 2007; Special Advisor to the Vice Principals, Napier University, 2006-08, Dean, Faculty of Arts and Social Science, 1997-2006; b. 14.9.45, Edinburgh; m., Caroline Joy; 2 s. Educ. Royal High School, Edinburgh; Edinburgh College of Art; Moray House College of Education. Art and Design Teacher,

Portobello High School, 1968-75; Head of Art and Design, Wester Hailes Education Centre, 1975-85; Education Advisory Officer/Senior Education Officer/Director, The Design Council Scotland, 1985-90; Managing Director, Quorum Graphic Design, 1990-91; Principal, Hunter Maxwell Associates, 1991-92; Head, Department of Design, Napier University, 1992-97. Board Member, Craigmillar Opportunity Trust; Director, Newbattle Abbey College; Board Member, Creative Edinburgh. Recreations: looking, listening, and talking. Address: (b.) Hunter Maxwell Associates, 126 Willowbrae Road, Edinburgh EH8 7HW; T.-0131 468 1990; e-mail: colin@hunter-maxwell.co.uk

Bryce, Professor Tom G.K., BSc, MEd, PhD, CPsychol. Professor, Department of Educational and Professional Studies, Faculty of Education, Strathclyde University, Jordanhill Campus, since 1993; Vice-Dean (Research), 1997-2002; b. 27.1.46, Glasgow; m., Karen Douglas Stewart; 1 s.; 1 d. Educ. King's Park Secondary School, Glasgow; Glasgow University. Teacher of Physics, Jordanhill College School, 1968-71; P.T. of Physics, King's Park Secondary School, 1971-73; part-time Lecturer in Psychology, Glasgow University, 1972-75; Open University Tutor, 1979-84; Lecturer, 1973, Head of Psychology, 1983, Head, Division of Education and Psychology, 1987-93, Jordanhill College of Education; Head, Department of Educational Studies, University of Strathclyde, 1993-94. Chairman, Editorial Board, Scottish Educational Review, 1988-2002. Publications include: Scottish Education (Co-Editor), 1999 (2nd edition: Post-devolution, 2003). Recreations: moutaineering (Munro completer); badminton. Address: (b.) Jordanhill Campus, Southbrae Drive, Glasgow, G13 1PP; T.-0141-950 3536.

Bryden, Professor Ian Gordon, BSc, PhD, CEng, CPhys, FIMechE, FIMarE, FInstP. Chair, Renewable Energy, University of Edinburgh, since 2006; Non Executive Director, European Marine Energy Centre (EMEC), Stromness, Orkney, since 2005; Professor and Dean of Postgraduate Studies, Robert Gordon University, 1996-2006; b. 12.9.58, Dumfries; 2 s.; 1 d. Educ. Lockerbie Academy; University of Edinburgh. Research Assistant, Heriot-Watt University; Research Engineer, BMT Ltd.; Lecturer, Heriot-Watt University; Senior Engineer, ICIT/IOE. Recreations: reading; cycling; music. Address: (b.) School of Engineering and Electronics, University of Edinburgh, Sanderson Building, The King's Buildings, Mayfield Road, Edinburgh EH9 3JL.

Bryden, Professor John Marshall, BSc (Hons), PhD, FRSA. Emeritus Professor, University of Aberdeen and Director, UHI Policy Web; Co-Director of Arkleton Institute for Rural Development Research, 1995-2004; Programme Director, Arkleton Trust, since 1980; Member, Scottish Land Fund, 1999-2006; Chairman, The International Rural Network; b. 18.12.41, Perth; m., Elspeth Anderson Mowat (divorced); 2 s.; 2 d. Educ. Edinburgh Academy; Glasgow Academy; Wrekin College; University of Glasgow; University of the West Indies; University of East Anglia. Economist, Economic Planning Staff, Ministry of Overseas Development, 1965-67; Lecturer, Overseas Development Group, University of East Anglia, 1967-72; Regional Economic Adviser, Commonwealth Caribbean, 1968-70; Head, Land Development Division, Highlands and Islands Development Board, 1972-79; Research Director, Arkleton Trust (Research) Ltd., 1985-95. Visiting Professor, University of Guelph, Canada, 1994; Member, Land Reform Policy Group and Rural Affairs Group, Scottish Office, 1997-99; Member, International Advisory Board, Polson Institute, Cornell University, since 2001; Visiting Professor, University of Missouri, Columbia, USA, 2002, and Cornell University, 2003. Publications: Tourism and Development, 1973; Agrarian Change in the Scottish Highlands (Co-author), 1976; Towards Sustainable Rural Communities, 1994; Rural Employment – An International Perspective (Co-author), 1997; A New Approach to Rural Development in Europe. Recreations: folk music; jazz; hill-walking; sailing. Address: (b.) UHI Policy Web, Great Glen House, Leachkin Road, Inverness IV3 8NW; T.-01463 3273561.

Buccleuch and Queensberry, Duke of (Richard Walter John Montagu Douglas Scott), FRSE. President, National Trust for Scotland, since 2002; Member, National Heritage Memorial Fund, 2000-05; President, Royal Scottish Geographical Society, since 2002; Member, Millennium Commission, 1994-2003; b. 14.2.54; m., Lady Elizabeth Kerr; 2 s.; 2 d. Deputy Chairman, Independent Television Commission, 1996-98. Address: (h.) Dabton, Thornhill, Dumfriesshire.

Buchan, Alistair, MA, Chartered MCIPD. Chief Executive, Orkney Islands Council, since 1997; b. 13.2.64, Aberdeen; m., Lorraine; 1 s.; 1 d. Educ. Stromness Academy, Orkney; Glasgow University; Napier College. Assistant Personnel Manager, Health Service, London; Training Manager, Argyll Group; Personnel Officer, Western Isles Islands Council; Senior Administrative Officer, then Chief Administrative Officer, then Chief Executive, Orkney Islands Council. Recreations: golf; listening to all types of music; military history. Address: (b.) Council Offices, Kirkwall, Orkney KW15 1NY; T.-01856 873535.

Buchan, Colin Alexander Mason, BComm. Director, Royal Scottish National Orchestra, since 2002; Board Member: Merrill Lynch World Mining Trust, since 2001, Standard Life Investments, since 2002, Royal Bank of Scotland Group plc, since 2002; b. 6.12.54; m., Susan, nee Monahan; 3 d. Educ. St. John's College, Johannesburg; University of the Witwatersrand. African Finance Corporation, 1980-84; Managing Director: SG Warburg, South Africa, 1984-87, SG Warburg, Far East, 1987-94; appointed Director, SG Warburg plc, 1995; Member, Executive Board, SBC Warburg, 1995; Global Head of Equities and Member, Group Management Board, UBC AG, 1999-2001. Recreations: hill walking; farming pedigree Aberdeen Angus cattle.

Buchan of Auchmacoy, Captain David William Sinclair, JP, KStJ. Chief of the Name of Buchan; b. 18.9.29; m., The Hon. Susan Blanche Fionodbhar Scott-Ellis; 4 s.; 1 d. Educ. Eton; Royal Military Academy, Sandhurst. Commissioned Gordon Highlanders, 1949; served Berlin, BAOR and Malaya; ADC to GOC-in-C, Singapore, 1951-53; retired 1955. Member, London Stock Exchange; Senior Partner, Messrs Gow and Parsons, 1963-72. Changed name from Trevor through Court of Lord Lyon King of Arms, 1949, succeeding 18th Earl of Caithness as Chief of Buchan Clan. Member: Queen's Body Guard for Scotland (Royal Company of Archers); The Pilgrims; Friends of Malta GC; Vice-President, Bucks CCC; Master, Worshipful Company of Borderers, 1992; President, Ellon Cricket Club. Address: North Court, Bampton Road, Clanfield, Oxon OX18 2RG; 30 Chipstead Street, London SW6 3SS.

Buchan-Hepburn, Sir Alastair, Bart. Chairman, Valentine Marketing Ltd., 2002-03; Chairman, Valentine Holdings Ltd., 2002-03; retired; b. 27.6.31, Hatton, Ceylon; m., Georgina Elizabeth Turner; 1 s.; 3 d. Educ. Charterhouse; St Andrews University; Royal Military Academy, Sandhurst. 1st King's Dragoon Guards, 1952-57; Captain, 1954; ADC to GOC-in-C Malaya, 1954-57;

Arthur Guinness and Son Co. Ltd., 1958-86; Director, Broughton Brewery, 1986-2001; Trustee, Dundee Industrial Heritage Trust, since 1999; Chief R&A Marshall, Open Championship, 2000 and 2005; Vice-President, Maritime Volunteer Service, since 2001; Life Member, St Andrews Preservation Trust; Member, Baronets' Trust, since 1992; Life Member, St Andrews Preservation Trust; Member, Committee, Royal British Legion, St Andrews Branch; Member: Vestry of All Saints Episcopal Church, St. Andrews; New Club, Edinburgh; Cavalry of Guards Club, London; Royal Scots Club, Edinburgh, Royal and Ancient Golf Club of St. Andrews; 1st Queen's Dragoon Guards Old Comrades Association. Recreations: travels; leading international appeal for the return of James Hepburn 4th Earl of Bothwell's remains to Scotland from Denmark; golf; tennis; shooting; gardening; fishing; reading. Address: (h.) Chagford, 60 Argyle Street, St Andrews KY16 9BU; T.-01334 472161; mobile: 07939139545. E-mail: alastair.buchan-hepburn@googlemail.com

Buchanan, Cameron R.M. Consul (Honorary) of Iceland, since 1993; Director, British Wool Marketing Board; b. Edinburgh; 2 s.; 2 d. Educ. St Edward's School, Oxford; Sorbonne, Paris. Lived and worked in France, Germany and Italy; Managing Director, Harrisons of Edinburgh, 1985-97; Entrepreneur of the Year, 1992; Textile Consultant, since 1997. High Constable of Leith; Director, United Kingdom Fashion Exports Ltd; Member, Hon. Co. Edinburgh Golfers. Recreations: skiing; tennis; golf. T.-0131 220 5775.

Buchanan, William Menzies, DA. Head of Fine Art, 1977-90, Acting Director, 1990-91, Deputy Director, 1991-92, Glasgow School of Art; b. 7.10.32, Caroni Estate, Trinidad, West Indies. Educ. Glasgow School of Art. Art Teacher, Glasgow, 1956-61; Exhibitions Officer, then Art Director, Scottish Arts Council, 1961-77. Chairman, Stills Gallery, Edinburgh, 1987-92; Member, Fine Art Board, Council for National Academic Awards, 1978-81. Publications: Scottish Art Review, 1965, 1967, 1973; Seven Scottish Painters catalogue, IBM New York, 1965; The Glasgow Boys catalogue, 1968; Joan Eardley, 1976; Mr Henry and Mr Hornel Visit Japan catalogue, 1978; Japonisme in Art (Contributor), 1980; A Companion to Scottish Culture (Contributor), 1981; The Stormy Blast catalogue, Stirling University, 1981; The Golden Age of British Photography (Contributor), 1984; The Photographic Collector (Contributor), 1985; Willie Rodger: A Retrospective (Contributor to catalogue), 1986; Scottish Photography Bulletin (Contributor), 1988; History of Photography (Contributor), 1989; Mackintosh's Masterwork (Editor), 1989 (2nd edition, 2004); British Photography in the 19th Century (Contributor), 1989; The Art of the Photographer J. Craig Annan, 1992; Photography 1900 (Contributor), 1993; J. Craig Annan: selected texts and bibliography, 1994; The Dictionary of Art (Contributor), 1995; Woven Image: Contemporary British Tapestry Catalogue (Contributor), 1996; Studies in Photography (Contributor), 1996, 2006; Charles Rennie Mackintosh: Art, Architecture and Design (CD Rom, General Editor), 1997; The Dictionary of Women Artists (Contributor), 1997; Studies in Photography (Contributor), 1997, 2003; Journal of the Scottish Society for Art History (Contributor), 2001; New Dictionary of National Biography (Contributor), 2004; The Oxford Companion to the Photograph (contributor), 2005. Recreations: gardening; cooking. Address: (h.) 6/2 Dalrymple Crescent, Edinburgh EH9 2NU; T.-0131 667 3277; e-mail: wabi.70@virgin.net

Buchanan-Jardine, Sir Andrew Rupert John, MC. Landowner; Deputy Lieutenant; b. 2.2.23, London; 1 s.; 1 d. Educ. Harrow; Royal Agricultural College. Joined Royal

Horse Guards, 1941; served NW Europe; retired as Major, 1949. Joint Master, Dumfriesshire Foxhounds, 1950-2001; JP. Recreation: country pursuits. Address: (h.) Dixons, Lockerbie, Dumfriesshire; T.-01576 202508.

Buckland, Roger, MA, MBA, MPhil. Chair of Accountancy, University of Aberdeen, since 1993; b. 22.04.51, Swallownest, England; m., Professor Lorna McKee; 2 d. Educ. Aston High School, South Yorkshire; Selwyn College, University of Cambridge. Research Assistant, University of Aston, 1972-74; Research Fellow, University of York, 1974-78; Lecturer in Finance, University of Aston, 1978-93; Visiting Professor, Bordeaux Business School, 1989-90. Address: University of Aberdeen Business School, Edward Wright Building, Dunbar Street, Old Aberdeen AB24 3QY; T.-01224 272206; e-mail: acc040@abdn.ac.uk

Buckland, Professor Stephen T., BSc, MSc, PhD, CStat. Professor of Statistics, St. Andrews University, since 1993 (Director, Centre for Research into Ecological and Environmental Modelling, 1999-2004); Co-Director, National Centre for Statistical Ecology, since 2005; b. 28.7.55, Dorchester; m., Patricia A. Peters; 1 d. Educ. Foster's School, Sherborne; Southampton University; Edinburgh University; Aberdeen University. Lecturer in Statistics, Aberdeen University, 1977-85; Senior Scientist, Tuna/Dolphin Program, Inter-American Tropical Tuna Commission, San Diego, 1985-87; Senior Consultant Statistician, Scottish Agricultural Statistics Service, 1988-93, Head, Environmental Modelling Unit, 1991-93. Publications: The Birds of North-East Scotland (Co-editor), 1990; Distance Sampling: estimating abundance of biological populations (Co-author), 1993; Introduction to Distance Sampling (Co-author), 2001; Estimating Animal Abundance (Co-author), 2002; Advanced Distance Sampling (Co-editor), 2004. Recreations: natural history; walking; reading. Address: (b.) St. Andrews University, The Observatory, Buchanan Gardens, St. Andrews KY16 9LZ; T.-01334 461841.

Buddle, (Elizabeth) Anne. Head of Exhibitions and Collections Management, National Galleries of Scotland, since 2000 (Registrar, 1993-2000); b. 4.5.51, Chatham, Kent; m., A.V.B. Norman (deceased); 1 s. (from husband's pr. m.). Educ. Christ's Hospital, Hertford. Placers Department, British Museum, 1971; Victoria and Albert Museum, 1972-93: Public Relations, 1972-73, Indian Section, 1973-78, Department of Prints, Drawings and Paintings, 1978-88, Loans Officer, 1988-89, Registrar, 1989-93. Publications: "The Tiger and The Thistle" and various collection management papers. Recreations: study of church monuments; gardening; 18th-century Scots and India. Address: (b.) National Galleries of Scotland, 75 Belford Road, Edinburgh EH4 3DR; T.-0131-624 6315.
E mail: abuddle@nationalgalleries.org

Bulfield, Professor Grahame, CBE, PhD, Hon. DSc, FIBiol, FRASE, FRSE. Vice Principal and Head, College of Science and Engineering, University of Edinburgh, since 2002; Director and Chief Executive, Roslin Institute (Edinburgh), 1993-2002; b. 12.6.41. Educ. Kings School, Macclesfield; Leeds University; Edinburgh University. Fullbright Fellow and NIH Postdoctoral Fellow, Department of Genetics, University of California, Berkeley, 1968-70; SRC Resettlement Fellow, 1970-71, and Research Associate, 1971-76, Institute of Animal Genetics, Edinburgh University; Lecturer and Convenor of Medical Genetics, Department of Genetics, Medical School and School of Biological Sciences, Leicester University, 1976-81; Head of Genetics Group, AFRC Poultry Research

Centre, Roslin, 1981-86; Head of Gene Expression Group, 1986-88, and Head of Station and Associate Director, 1988-93, Edinburgh Research Station, Institute of Animal Physiology and Genetic Research. Hon. Fellow, 1981-90, and Hon. Professor, 1990-2002, Professor of Animal Genetics, University of Edinburgh, since 2002. Non-Executive Director, Edinburgh Research and Innovation Ltd., since 2002. Recreations: fell-walking; cricket. Address: (b.) University of Edinburgh, Weir Building, The King's Buildings, West Mains Road, Edinburgh EH9 3JY; T.-0131 650 5754; e-mail: Grahame.Bulfield@ed.ac.uk

Bulloch, Douglas, CQSW, MCC, FRSA. Chair, Scottish Children's Reporter Administration, since 2002; b. 5.2.51, Hamilton; m., Irene Waddell; 1 d. Educ. Hamilton Academy; Jordanhill College; Glasgow University. Social work posts, Strathclyde Regional Council, 1976-95; Depute Director of Social Work (Community Care), East Ayrshire Council, 1995-96; Director of Social Work, East Ayrshire Council, 1996-2001; led action team on better integrated children's services, Scottish Executive, 2001-02; Chair, Scottish Social Work Best Value Network, 1998-2001; Member, Child Health Support Group, 2002-05; Expert Reference Group on Children's Services, since 2003; Steering Group for Reform of Child Protection, 2003-06; 21st Century Social Work Group, 2004-06. Publication: For Scotland's Children (principal author/editor). Address: (b.) Scottish Children's Reporter Administration, Ochil House, Springkerse Business Park, Stirling FK7 7XE; T.-01786 459501; e-mail: dbulloch@tiscali.co.uk

Bulmer, Peter Neil, DipTP, MBA (Dist.), MRTPI, MCIM. Corporate Director, Planning and Environment Services, Dumfries and Galloway Council, since 2002; b. 11.5.53. Educ. Sunderland Polytechnic; Leeds Polytechnic; Hull University. Durham County Council, 1971; Easington District Council, 1976; Newcastle City Council, 1977; Assistant Director/Director of Environmental Services, Preston City Council, 1987-2002. Recreations: family; fell-walking; football. Address: (b.) Council Offices, Kirkbank House, English Street, Dumfries DG1 2HS; T.-01387 260361.

Bunch, Antonia Janette, OBE, MA, FCLIP, FSAScot, FRSA. Freelance writer, editor, researcher; b. 13.2.37, Croydon. Educ. Notting Hill and Ealing High School; Strathclyde University. Assistant Librarian, Scottish Office; Librarian, Scottish Health Service Centre; Lecturer, Strathclyde University; Director, Scottish Science Library. Founding Chairman, Association of Scottish Health Sciences Librarians; Member: Standing Committee on Science and Technology Libraries, IFLA, 1987-91; Advisory Committee, British Library Science Reference and Information Service, 1987-96, Advisory Committee on Telematics for the Scottish Parliament, 1996-97; Chairman: Friends of St. Cecilia's Hall and the Russell Collection of Early Keyboard Instruments, 1997-2003; Trustee, Scottish Homeopathic Research and Education Trust, since 1998. Publications: Libraries in Hospitals (Co-author), 1969; Hospital and Medical Libraries in Scotland: an Historical and Sociological Study, 1975; Health Care Administration: an Information Sourcebook, 1979. Recreations: gardening; music; travelling in Italy. Address: Dove Cottage, Garvald, Haddington, East Lothian EH41 4LL.

Buncle, Tom, BA, MA. Managing Director, Yellow Railroad International Destination Consultancy; b. 25.6.53, Arbroath; m., Janet; 2 s. Educ. Trinity College, Glenalmond; Exeter University; Sheffield University; London Business School. Various overseas posts (North America, Europe, Asia), British Tourist Authority, 1978-91;

International Marketing Director, then Chief Executive, Scottish Tourist Board, 1991-2000. Board Member: Scottish Prison Service Risk Monitoring and Audit Committee, Contact Singapore Global Advisory Panel. Recreations: wind-surfing; scuba diving; cycling; sailing; hill-walking. E-mail: tom@yellowrailroad.com

Bundy, Professor Alan Richard, BSc, PhD, FRSA, FRSE, FAAAI, FECCAI, FBCS, FIEE. Professor, Edinburgh University; b. 18.5.47, Isleworth; m., D. Josephine A. Maule; 1 d. Educ. Heston Secondary Modern School; Springgrove Grammar School; Leicester University. Tutorial Assistant, Department of Mathematics, Leicester University, 1970-71; Edinburgh University: Research Fellow, Metamathematics Unit, 1971-74; Lecturer, Department of Artificial Intelligence, 1974-84; Reader, 1984-87; Professorial Fellow, 1987-90; Professor, since 1990. Editorial Board: Journal of Automated Reasoning, AJ & Society Journal. IJCAI Donald E. Walker Distinguished Service Award, 2003; IJCAI Research Excellence Award, 2007; CADE Herbrand Award, 2007. Publications: Artificial Intelligence: An Introductory Course, 1978; The Computer Modelling of Mathematical Reasoning, 1983; The Catalogue of Artificial Intelligence Tools, 1984; Rippling: Meta-level Guidance for Mathematical Reasoning. Recreations: beer making; walking. Address: (b.) School of Informatics, Edinburgh University, Appleton Tower, Crichton Street, Edinburgh EH8 9LE; T.-0131 650 2716.

Burchell, Professor Ann, BSc, PhD. Professor of Molecular Medicine, Dundee University, since 2000; b. 23.2.51, Sunderland; m., Professor Brian Burchell; 1 s.; 1 d. Educ. Harrogate Convent; Dundee University. Dundee University: Research Fellow, 1983; New Blood Lecturer, Department of Medicine, 1985-89; Senior Lecturer in Molecular Medicine, Department of Obstetrics and Gynaecology, 1989-92; Lister Institute Research Fellow, 1989-94; Reader in Molecular Medicine, 1992-2000. Member, Lister Institute of Preventative Medicine; Member, Scientific Advisory Committee, Association for Glycogen Storage Disease. Publications: 137 papers. Recreations: golf; reading. Address: (b.) Maternal and Child Health Sciences, Level 4, Ninewells Hospital, Dundee DD1 9SY; T.-01382 632445; e-mail: a.burchell@dundee.ac.uk

Burgess, William George, MA, PhD. Head of Criminal Law and Licensing Division, Scottish Government; b. 8.5.70, Aberdeen; m., Adrienne Kirk; 1 d. Educ. Keith Grammar School; Churchill College, Cambridge University. Social Work Services Group, Scottish Office, 1994-96; Finance Group, Scottish Office, 1996-97; Referendum Bill Team, Scotland Bill Team, Scotland Act Implementation, 1997-2000; Private Secretary to Deputy First Minister, 2000-02; Head of Sustainable Development Team, Scottish Executive, 2002-04. Scottish Young Scientist of the Year, 1988; CEGB Prize, Cambridge University, 1991. Recreations: choral music; historical research. Address: (b.) St. Andrew's House, Edinburgh EH1 3DG; T.-0131-244 3537.

Burgon, Robert Douglas, BA, MLitt, FPMI. Director and Secretary, Scottish & Northern Ireland Plumbing Employers' Federation, since 1988; Secretary and Pensions Manager, Plumbing Pensions (UK) Ltd., since 1988; b. 3.8.55, Haddington; m., Sheila Georgina Bryson. Educ. North Berwick High School; Heriot Watt University. SNIPEF: Assistant Industrial Relations Officer, 1978, Assistant to the Director, 1979, Secretary, 1983. Recreation:

music (church organist). Address: (b.) 2 Walker Street, Edinburgh EH3 7LB; T.-0131-225 2255.

Burley, George Elder. National Coach, Scottish Football Association, since 2008; b. 3.6.56, Cumnock. Senior Clubs played: Ipswich Town, 1973-85; Sunderland, 1985-88; Gillingham, 1988-89; Motherwell, 1989-91; Ayr United, 1991-93; Falkirk, 1993; Motherwell, 1993-94; Colchester United, 1994. Eleven appearances for National Team, 1979-82. Teams managed: Ayr United, 1991-93; Colchester United, 1994; Ipswich Town, 1994-2002; Derby County, 2003-05; Heart of Midlothian, 2005; Southampton, 2005-08. Address: (b.) Scottish Football Association, Hampden Park, Glasgow G42 9AY.

Burley, Lindsay, MBChB, FRCPE, FRCGP, FRSA, MHSM, MCIArb. Chair, National Waiting Times Centre Board; Partner, Eskhill & Co; Non Executive Director, NHS Education for Scotland; Member, Scottish Funding Council; Member, Napier University Court; formerly Chief Executive, NHS Borders; b. 2.10.50, Blackpool; m., Robin Burley. Educ. Queen Mary School, Lytham; University of Edinburgh. Lothian Health Board: Consultant Physician, Unit General Manager, Director of Planning and Development. Address: (b.) Eskhill House, 15 Inveresk Village, Musselburgh EH21 7TD; T.-0131 271 4000.

Burman, Professor Michele Jane, BA, MSc, PhD. Professor of Criminology, University of Glasgow, since 2003; Co-Director, Scottish Centre for Crime and Justice Research (SCCJR), since 2006; b. London; m., Neil Hutton; 2 d. Educ. Springfield Convent, Cape Town; University of Edinburgh. Research Officer, Criminological Research Branch, The Scottish Office, 1985-87; Research Associate, University of Edinburgh, 1987-90; Research Fellow, University of Aberdeen, 1990-92; Senior Research Officer, The Scottish Executive, 1992-94; Lecturer, Department of Sociology, University of Glasgow, 1994-98, Senior Lecturer, 1998-2003. Board Member, Ethnic Minority Law Centre. Publications: numerous papers on gender and justice. Recreations: gardening; cooking; travelling. Address: (b.) c/o Florentine House, 53 Hillhead Street, University of Glasgow; e-mail: m.burman@lbss.gla.ac.uk

Burman, Peter Ashley Thomas Insull, MBE, MA, FSA, Dr hc, Brandenburg Technical University, Cottbus, Germany. Director of Conservation & Property Services, The National Trust for Scotland, since 2003; Visiting Professor of Cultural Management, World Heritage Studies, Cottbus University, since 2007; Independent Cultural Heritage Consultant; b. 15.9.44, Solihull. Educ. Kings College, Cambridge; ICCROM, Rome. Assistant Secretary, Deputy Secretary, Secretary (Chief Executive), Church of England, Council for the Care of Churches and the Cathedrals Fabric Commission for England, 1968-90; Director, Centre of Conservation Studies, University of York, 1990-2002; Visiting Professor, Department of Fine Arts, University of Canterbury, Christchurch, New Zealand, 2002. Publications include: Books: Chapels and Churches: Who Cares?, 1977; St. Paul's Cathedral, 1987; 7 book chapters; Refereed articles: Reflections on the Lime Revival, 1995; The Ethics of Using Traditional Building Materials, 1997; The Study and Conservation of Nineteenth Century Wall Paintings, 2003. Esher Award, SPAB. Memberships include: Chairman, Fabric Advisory Committee, St Paul's Cathedral; Historic Environment Advisory Council for Scotland; Council Member and Vice Chairman, Architectural Heritage Society of Scotland and Convenor, Glasite Meeting House Trust; Companion, Guild of St. George; Furniture History Society; Garden History Society; SPAB; Ancient Monuments Society; Georgian Group; Victorian Society; Twentieth Century Society.

Recreations: music; playing keyboard instruments and recorders; walking, especially in remote upland areas of Scotland; reading, especially books relating to the Buddhist Dharma; cooking (attended one of Alastair Little's cookery courses in Umbria). Address: (h.) 39 (1F) Drummond Place, Edinburgh EH3 6NR; T.-0131-556 3876; e-mail: peterburman@btinternet.com

Burn, Lesley. Chief Executive Officer, Ladies' Golf Union, since 2006; b. 10.03.62, Sunderland. Address: (b.) The Scores, St. Andrews KY16 9AT.
E-mail: lesley.burns@lgu.org

Burnet, George Wardlaw, LVO, BA, LLB, WS, KStJ, JP. Lord Lieutenant, Midlothian, 1992-2002; b. 26.12.27, Edinburgh; m., Jane Elena Moncrieff; 2 s.; 1 d. Educ. Edinburgh Academy; Lincoln College, Oxford; Edinburgh University. Senior Partner, Murray Beith & Murray, WS, 1983-91; Chairman, Life Association of Scotland Ltd., 1985-93; Chairman, Caledonian Research Foundation, 1988-99. Captain, Queen's Bodyguard for Scotland (Royal Company of Archers); former Midlothian County Councillor, Convenor, Church of Scotland Finance Committee, 1980-83; Hon. Fellow, Royal Incorporation of Architects in Scotland. Address: (h.) Rose Court, Inveresk, Midlothian EH21 7TD.

Burnett, Charles John, KStJ, DA, AMA, FSAScot, FHSS, MLitt. Ross Herald of Arms; Chamberlain, Duff House, Banff, 1997-2004; Curator of Fine Art, Scottish United Services Museum, Edinburgh Castle, 1985-96; President, Heraldry Society of Scotland, since 2004; Vice-Patron, Genealogical Society of Queensland, since 1986; Chairman, Banff Preservation and Heritage Society, since 2002; b. 6.11.40, Sandhaven, by Fraserburgh; m., Aileen E. McIntyre; 2 s.; 1 d. Educ. Fraserburgh Academy; Gray's School of Art, Aberdeen; Aberdeen College of Education. Advertising Department, House of Fraser, Aberdeen, 1963-64; Exhibitions Division, Central Office of Information, 1964-68 (on team which planned British pavilion for World Fair, Montreal, 1967); Assistant Curator, Letchworth Museum and Art Gallery, 1968-71; Head, Design Department, National Museum of Antiquities of Scotland, 1971-85. Heraldic Adviser, Girl Guide Association in Scotland, since 1978; Librarian, Priory of the Order of St. John in Scotland, 1987-99; Vice President, Society of Antiquaries of Scotland, 1992-95; Honorary Citizen of Oklahoma, 1989; Chevalier, Orders of St. Maurice and St. Lazarus, 1999; Knight of the Royal Order of Francis I, 2002; President, 27th International Congress of Genealogical and Heraldic Sciences at St. Andrews University, 2006. Recreations: reading; visiting places of historic interest. Address: (h.) Seaview House, Portsoy, Banffshire, AB45 2RS; T.-01261 843378.

Burnett, David Anderson, DA(Edin), RIBA, FRIAS. Partner, Burnett Pollock Associates, Architects, since 1974; b. 9.6.44, Edinburgh; m., Rosemary; 3 s. Educ. George Watson's College, Edinburgh; Edinburgh College of Art, Heriot-Watt University. Chamberlin Powell and Bon, London, 1968-70; Casson Conder and Partners, London, 1970-72; Sir Basil Spence Glover and Ferguson, Edinburgh, 1973-74. Recreations: golf; writing; travel. Address: Burnett Pollock Associates, 17B Graham Street, Edinburgh EH6 5QN; T.-0131-555 3338; e-mail: dburnett@burnettpollock.co.uk

Burnett, Robert Gemmill, LLB, SSC, NP. Solicitor, since 1972; Solicitor Advocate, since 1993; b. 18.1.49, Kilmarnock; m., Patricia Margaret Masson; 1 s.; 2 d. Educ. George Heriot's School, Edinburgh; Edinburgh University.

Apprentice, then Assistant, then Partner, Drummond Miller WS; Partner, BCKM. Solicitor to General Teaching Council; Member, Criminal Law Committee, Law Society of Scotland. Recreations: golf; gardening. Address: (b.) 53 George IV Bridge, Edinburgh; T.-031-225 3456.

Burnett, Rodney Alister, MB, ChB, FRCP, FRIPHH, FRCPath. Lead Clinician in Pathology, University Department of Pathology, Western Infirmary, Glasgow, 1985-2007 (retired); b. 6.6.47, Congleton; m., Maureen Elizabeth Dunn; 2 d. Educ. Sandbach School; St. Andrews University. Lecturer in Pathology, Glasgow University, 1974-79; Consultant in administrative charge, Department of Pathology, Stobhill Hospital, Glasgow, 1979-85. Specialist Adviser, Royal Institute for Public Health and Hygiene, and Chairman, Board of Education and Examination for Anatomical Pathology Technology; Vice President, Association of Clinical Pathologists, 2001-03. Address: (h.) 77 Blairbeth Road, Burnside, Glasgow G73 4JD; T.-0141-634 4345.

Burnie, Joan Bryson. Columnist, Daily Record, since 1987, formerly Associate Editor; b. 19.12.41, Glasgow; 1 s.; 1 d. Educ. Hutchesons' Girls' Grammar School. Filed pix, Herald; married; had children; freelanced, Contributing Editor, Cosmopolitan, 1977-81; You (Mail on Sunday), 1984-90; "Just Joan", Daily Record, since 1979; hacks around the air waves for BBC Radio 5 and BBC Scotland. Publications: Scotland The Worst; Post Bus Country. Recreations: lunch; walking dogs; gardening. Address: (b.) One Central Quay, Glasgow G3 8DA.

Burns, Rt. Rev. John Joseph, PhL, STh. Vicar General, Diocese of Motherwell, since 1992; Parish Priest, St. Bride's, Bothwell, 1992-2003; Vicar General for Pastoral Care and Planning, since 1992; b. 19.2.32, Rutherglen. Educ. Our Lady's High, Motherwell; St. Joseph's College, Dumfries; Gregorian University, Rome; Scots College, Rome. Assistant Priest, Motherwell Cathedral, 1956-65; Full-time Chaplain, Our Lady's High School, Motherwell, 1965-78; Resident at St. Brendan's, Motherwell, 1971-78; Diocesan Master of Ceremonies, 1956-81; Director of Religious Education, Diocese of Motherwell, 1978-85; Resident at Diocesan Centre, Motherwell, 1978-85; Parish Priest, St. Aidan's, Wishaw, 1983-92. Publications: series of Religious Education books for pupils and teachers, S1-S5, 1979-82. Recreations: general reading; walking; watching football. Address: St. Bride's, Fallside Road, Bothwell, Lanarkshire; T.-01698 852710.

Burnside, David Melville, LLB, NP. Senior Partner, Simpson and Marwick, since 2004; b. 5.3.43, Dumfries; m., Gill; 3 s.; 2 d. Educ. Dumfries Academy; University of Edinburgh. Apprentice Solicitor, Melville & Lindsay W.S., Edinburgh, 1964-67; Assistant Solicitor: National Coal Board Legal Department, 1967-70, Clark & Wallace, Advocates, Aberdeen, 1970-71 (Partner, 1971-89); formed Burnside Advocates (later Burnside Kemp Fraser), 1989 (firm merged with Simpson and Marwick, 2004); acted for families in Chinook, Brent Spar and Cormorant Alpha helicopter crashes and Piper Alpha explosion (joint lead negotiator for Piper Alpha settlement); Member, Personal Injury Panel; Member, Executive Committee, and Scottish Convenor, Association of Personal Injury Lawyers, 1990-96; certified by Law Society of Scotland as an employment law specialist, since 1990; Treasurer, Employment Law Group; Past President: Aberdeen Bar Association, Junior Chamber, Aberdeen; Member, Board of Directors, Legal Defence Union; President, Society of Advocates in Aberdeen, 2000-01 (Treasurer, 1999-2000); Member, Edinburgh Town Council, 1967-70; Chairman, Board of Governors, Albyn School for Girls, 2001-05; Chairman,

Organising Committee, Aberdeen FC Centenary, 2003; Free Burgess and Guild Member of Burgh of Aberdeen. Recreations: family; music; theatre; following the Dons. Address: (b.) 4 Carden Terrace, Aberdeen AB10 1US; T.-01224 624924.

Burnside, John. Writer; b. 19.3.55, Dunfermline. Scottish Arts Council Book Award, 1988, 1991, 1995; shortlisted for Forward Prize, 1992; Geoffrey Faber Memorial Prize, 1994; Whitbread Poetry Prize, 2000; shortlisted for T.S. Eliot Prize, 1994; selected for New Generation Poets, 1994. Publications: poetry: The hoop, 1988; Common Knowledge, 1991; Feast Days, 1992; The myth of the twin, 1994; Swimming in the flood, 1995; A Normal Skin, 1997; The Asylum Dance, 2000; The Light Trap, 2002; The Good Neighbour, 2005; Selected Poems, 2006; Gift Songs, 2007; fiction: The Dumb House, 1997; The Mercy Boys, 1999; Burning Elvis, 2000; The Locust Room, 2001; Living Nowhere, 2003; The Devil's Footprints, 2007; memoir: A Lie About My Father, 2006. Address: (b.) c/o Jonathan Cape, Random House, 20 Vauxhall Bridge Road, London SW1V 2SA.

Burr, Malcolm, LLB (Hons), DipLP, LLM (Hons), NP. Chief Executive, Comhairle nan Eilean Siar, since 2005; b. 24.3.66, Edinburgh; m., Chrissie (nee Kennedy). Educ. George Heriot's School, Edinburgh; Edinburgh University; Cambridge University (Sidney Sussex College). Trainee Solicitor, later Solicitor, Strathclyde Regional Council, Glasgow, 1990-94; Principal Solicitor, Comhairle Nan Eilean, Stornoway, 1994-97; Orkney Islands Council, Kirkwall: Chief Administrative Officer, 1997-2000, Assistant Chief Executive, 2000-05. President, Society of Solicitors in Orkney, 2001-05. Recreations: current affairs; history; reading; walking; following football and rugby. Address: (b.) Council Offices, Sandwick Road, Stornoway, Isle of Lewis HS1 2BW; T.-01851 709500; e-mail: m.burr@cne-siar.gov.uk

Burrows, Professor Noreen, LLB, PhD, FRSA. Jean Monnet Professor of European Law, Glasgow University, since 1990; Dean, Faculty of Law and Financial Studies, since 2003; b. 22.1.51, Preston; m., Alastair Swanson; 1 s. Educ. Notre Dame High School, St Helens; Edinburgh University. Lecturer in Law, Leicester University, 1977-79; Lecturer in Law, then Senior Lecturer, 1979-90; Head, School of Law, 1990-94; Trustee, Caledonian Research Foundation; Member, Board, Scotland in Europe; Selector, VSO. Publications include: Devolution; European Social Law. Recreations: walking; family life. Address: (b.) School of Law, Glasgow University, Glasgow G12 8QQ; T.-0141-330 4172.

Burt, John Clark, OBE, MA (Hons), CertEd. Principal, Angus College, since 1996; b. 25.4.51, Dunfermline; m., Dory; 1 s.; 1 d. Educ. Dunfermline High School; Edinburgh University; Moray House College. Marketing Economist, Lloyds and Scottish Finance, 1974-76; Lecturer/Senior Lecturer in Economics and Marketing, Fife College, 1976-96. Member, Scottish Welfare to Work Advisory Task Force; Member, East of Scotland European Partnership; Director, FE Development, Scottish Further Education Funding Council (seconded); Chair of "Differences College Make Group", Scottish Executive; awarded OBE for services to Further Education in Scotland, 2006. Recreations: golf; hill-walking; running; Italian language. Address: (b.) Keptie Road, Arbroath DD11 3EA; T.-01241 432692.

Burt, Professor Steven Leslie, BA, PhD, FRSA. Professor of Retail Marketing, University of Stirling, since 1998, Deputy Principal, since 2007; b. 23.3.60, Chorley, Lancashire; m., Wendy Hayes; 2 s. Educ. Bolton School; Queen's College, Oxford University; University of Wales;

University of Stirling. University of Stirling: Research Fellow then Lecturer then Senior Lecturer, 1984-98, Head, Department of Marketing, 1993-95, 2000-03, Director, Institute for Retail Studies, 1993-96, 1999-2003; Visiting Professor, Lund University, Sweden, since 2000; Visiting Professor, Queens University, Kingston, Ontario, 2003-04. President, European Association for Education and Research in Commercial Distribution. Recreation: watching Stirling Albion Football Club. Address: (b.) University of Stirling, Stirling FK9 4LA; T.-01786 467007; e-mail: s.l.burt@stir.ac.uk

Burton, Lord (Michael Evan Victor Baillie). Landowner; b. 27.6.24, Burton-on-Trent; m., 1, Elizabeth Ursula Foster Wise (m. diss., deceased); 2, Coralie Denise Cliffe; 2 s.; 3 d. (2 d. deceased). Educ. Eton; Army. Scots Guards, 1942 (Lt., 1943); Lovat Scouts, 1948; Member, Inverness County Council, 1948-75; JP, 1961-75; Deputy Lieutenant, Inverness, 1963-65; Executive Member, Scottish Landowners Federation, 1963-92; former Member, House of Lords; has served on numerous committees. Recreations: shooting, fishing and hunting (not much time). Address: Dochgarroch Lodge, Inverness IV3 8JG; T.-01463 861252/861377.

Burton, Anthony Winston, OBE, BA (Hons). Director, Idox Information Services Ltd; b. 14.10.40, Leicester; 2 s.; 1 d. Educ. Wyggeston; Keele University. Vice Chairman, Strategic Planning Society; Deputy Chairman, Consumers' Association; Chairman, Greenbelt Group of Companies. Recreations: cooking; sailing. Address: (b.) Idox, Tontine House, 8 Gordon Street, Glasgow G1 3PL.

Busby, John Philip, NDD, DA (Edin), RSW, RSA, PPSSA; b. 2.2.28, Bradford; m., Joan; 1 s.; 2 d. Educ. Ilkley Grammar School; Leeds College of Art; Edinburgh College of Art. Lecturer in Drawing and Painting, Edinburgh College of Art, 1956-88; Founder Member, Society of Wildlife Artists; illustrated 30 books on natural history; author and illustrator: Birds in Mallorca, Drawing Birds, John Busby Nature Drawings, The Living Birds of Eric Ennion; Land Marks and Sea Wings. Recreations: music; bird-watching; travel. Address: (h.) Easter Haining, Ormiston Hall, East Lothian EH35 5NJ; T.-01875 340512.

Bush, Paul Anthony, OBE (2007), BEd, DipSC, FISC. Chief Operating Officer, EventScotland, since 2007; Chair, East of Scotland Institute of Sport, since 2007; b. 11.6.57, Leicester; m., Katriona Christine. Educ. Gateway Sixth Form College, Leicester; Borough Road College; Moray House College. Professional Swimming Coach, Bradford and Leicester; Sports/Swimming Development Officer, Leeds City Council; Technical Director, Amateur Swimming Association; Assistant Head of Development, English Sports Council; Director, Sporting Initiatives Sports Marketing and Media Consultancy. Leicestershire County Swimming Coach; Swimming Team Manager, Olympic, World, European, Commonwealth Games; Chef de Mission, BOA, European Youth Olympics; General Team Manager, Scottish Commonwealth Games Council, Manchester, 2002; Fellow, BISA; General Secretary, British Swimming Coaches Association; Member, English Sports Council Task Force – Young People and Sport; Event Director, World Cyclo Cross Championships, Leeds; school governor; Chef de Mission, Scottish Commonwealth Game Team, Melbourne, 2006. Recreations: golf; walking the dogs; sport in general; travel. Address: Ochil Paddocks, Burnfoot, Glendevon, nr. Dollar FK14 7JY.

Busuttil, Professor Anthony, OBE, MOM, KHS, MD, FRCPath, FRCP(Glasg), FRCPE, FRCS(Edin), DMJ(Path),

FRSSA, FRSM. Professor of Applied Pathology, RC Surgeons, Edinburgh; Emeritus Professor of Forensic Medicine, Edinburgh University, since 2006; Past Chairman, European Council for Legal Medicine; Honorary Consultant Pathologist, Edinburgh Universities NHS Trust, since 1976; Medical Director, Forensic Medical Examiner Service, NHS Lothian; Clinical Medical Examiner, Lothian and Borders Police Force, since 1980; b. 30.12.45, Rabat, Malta; m., Angela; 3 s. Educ. St. Aloysius' College, Malta; Royal University of Malta. Junior posts, Western Infirmary, Glasgow; Lecturer in Pathology, Glasgow University. Address: (h.) 78 Hillpark Avenue, Edinburgh EH4 7AL; T.- 0131-336 3241.

Bute, 7th Marquess of (John Colum Crichton-Stuart); b. 26.4.58; m.; 1 s.; 3 d. British Formula Three Champion, 1984; Formula One Ferrari Test Driver, 1985; JPS Lotus Grand Prix Driver, 1986; Works Driver for World Champion Sports Prototype Team Silk Cut Jaguar, 1988 (Joint Winner, Le Mans, 1988); Lead Driver for Toyota GB, World Sports Prototype Championship, 1989, 1990.

Butler, Bill. MSP (Labour), Glasgow Anniesland, since 2000; m., Patricia Ferguson (qv). Educ. Stirling University; Notre Dame College of Education. English teacher, 20 years; elected Glasgow City Councillor, 1987 (Convener, Policy and Resources (e-Glasgow) Working Group; Vice-Convener, Policy and Resources Committee; Secretary, Labour Group). Address: (b.) Constituency Advice Office, 129 Dalsetter Avenue, Glasgow G15 8SZ; e-mail: bill.butler.msp@ scottish.parliament.uk

Butlin, Ron, MA, DipAECD. Poet, Novelist, Journalist; b. 17.11.49, Edinburgh. Educ. Dumfries Academy; Edinburgh University. Writer in Residence, Lothian Region Education Authority, 1979, Edinburgh University, 1981, 1984-85; Scottish/Canadian Writing Exchange Fellow, University of New Brunswick, 1983-84; Writer in Residence for Midlothian, 1989-90; Writer in Residence, Craigmillar Literacy Trust; Novelist in Residence, St. Andrews University, 1998-99. Publications: poetry: Stretto, 1976; Creatures Tamed by Cruelty, 1979; The Exquisite Instrument, 1982 (Scottish Arts Council Book Award); Ragtime in Unfamiliar Bars, 1985 (SAC Book Award, Poetry Book Society recommendation); Histories of Desire 1995; prose: The Tilting Room (short stories), 1983 (SAC Book Award); The Sound of My Voice (novel), 1987; Blending In (play), 1989; Mauritian Voices (Editor), 1996; Night Visits (novel), 1997; When We Jump We Jump High!, 1998; Faraway Pictures (opera), 2000; Our Piece of Good Fortune (poetry), 2002; Vivaldi and the Number 3 (short stories), 2004; Without a Backward Glance - New and Selected Poems, 2005; Good Angel, Bad Angel (Opera), 2005; Belonging (novel), 2006; No More Angels (short stories), 2007; The Perfect Woman (Opera), 2008. Awarded the Prix MillePages, 2004 and the Prix Lucioles, 2005 (both for Best Foreign Novel). Recreations: music; travel. Address: (h.) 7 West Newington Place, Edinburgh EH9 1QT; T.-0131-667 0394.

Butt, Professor John, MA, PhD, FBA, FRSE, FRCO(CHM), ADCM. Gardiner Professor of Music, University of Glasgow, since 2001; b. 17.11.60, Solihull; m., Sally Cantlay; 4 s.; 1 d. Educ. Solihull School; King's College, University of Cambridge. Temporary Lecturer, University of Aberdeen, 1986-87; Research Fellow, Magdalene College, Cambridge, 1987-89; University Organist and Professor of Music, UC Berkeley, California, 1989-97; University Lecturer and Fellow, King's College Cambridge, 1997-2001. Eleven CD recordings on organ and harpsichord; Director, Dunedin Consort (Edinburgh), one

recording. Publications: five books. Recreations: reading; walking; tai chi. Address: (b.) Music Department, University of Glasgow, 14 University Gardens, Glasgow G12 8QQ; T.-0141-330 4571. E-mail: j.butt@music.gla.ac.uk

Butter, Sir David Henry, KCVO, MC. Lord Lieutenant, Perth and Kinross, 1975-95; Landowner and Company Director; b. 18.3.20, London; m., Myra Alice Wernher; 1 s.; 4 d. Educ. Eton College; Oxford University. Served in World War II, 2nd Lt., Scots Guards, 1940; served in Western Desert, North Africa, Sicily and Italy (ADC to GOC 8th Army, 1944); Temporary Major, 1946; retired, 1948; Captain, Queen's Bodyguard for Scotland (Royal Company of Archers); President, Highland TAVR, 1979-84; Member, Perth County Council, 1955-74; Deputy Lieutenant, Perthshire, 1956; Vice Lieutenant, Perthshire, 1960-71; Lord Lieutenant of County of Perth, 1971-75, of Kinross, 1974-75; Governor, Gordonstoun School, 1954-86. Recreations: golf; skiing; travel; shooting. Address: Cluniemore, Pitlochry, Perthshire PH16 5NE.

Butterworth, Neil, MA, HonFLCM. Chairman, Scottish Society of Composers, 1991-2003; Broadcaster; b. 4.9.34, Streatham, London; m., Anna Mary Barnes; 3 d. Educ. Rutlish School, Surrey; Nottingham University; London University; Guildhall School of Music, London. Lecturer, Kingston College of Technology, 1960-68; Head, Music Department, Napier College, Edinburgh, 1968-87; Music Critic, Times Educational Supplement, 1983-97. Conductor: Sutton Symphony Orchestra, 1960-64, Glasgow Orchestral Society, 1975-83, 1989-2002; Chairman: Incorporated Society of Musicians, Edinburgh Centre, 1981-86, Inveresk Preservation Society, 1988-95; Churchill Fellowship, 1975. Publications: Haydn, 1976; Dvorak, 1980; Dictionary of American Composers, 1983 (2nd edition, 2005); Aaron Copland, 1984; Vaughan Williams, 1989; Neglected Music, 1991; Samuel Barber, 1996; The American Symphony, 1998; Film Music, 2007; over 300 compositions. Recreations: autographs; collecting books and records; giant jigsaw puzzles. Address: (h.) The Lodge, East High Street, Greenlaw, Berwickshire TD10 6UF; T.-01361 810408.

Byatt, Sir Ian. Chairman, Water Industry Commission for Scotland, since 2005; Senior Associate, Frontier Economics, since 2001; Honorary Professor, Birmingham University, since 2001; Member, Public Services Productivity Panel, HM Treasury, since 2000 and Panel of Experts (Water Service), Northern Ireland, since 2003; Director General of Water Services, 1989-2000; Deputy Chief Economic Adviser to the Treasury, 1978-89. Educ. Kirkham Grammar School; St. Edmund Hall and Nuffield College, Oxford (DPhil Economics); Harvard (Commonwealth Fund/Harkness Fellow). Lecturer, Economics, Durham University, 1958-62; London School of Economics, 1964-67. Government: Economist; HM Treasury, 1962-64: Department of Education and Science, 1967-69: Ministry of Housing and Local Government, 1969-70: Department of Environment, 1970-72; Treasury, 1972-89. Boards and Committees. Economic Policy Committee of the European Communities, Chairman, 1982-85, Member, 1978-89: Economic and Social Research Council, Member, 1983-89; International Institute of Public Finance, Board of Management, 1987-90 and since 2001; Royal Economic Society, Council, 1983-92; Strategic Planning Society, Vice-President, since 1993; National Institute of Economic and Social Research, Governor, Council of Management, 1996-2002; Advisory Board, Centre for Management under Regulation, since 1996; Governor, Birkbeck College, London, 1997-2005, Chairman, F & GP, 2001-05: President, Economics and Business Education Association, 1998-2001; Boar, Regulatory Policy Institute, since 2001; Birmingham

Cathedral, Chairman, Friends, since 1999; Member, Cathedral Council, since 2003; Board of Advisors, St. Edmund Hall, 1998-2003; Trustee, Academy of Youth, 2001-05: Foundation for International Studies on Social Security, Co-Secretary-General, 2001-02: Public Utilities Research Centre, University of Florida, International Advisory Committee, since 2001. Freeman, City of London; Honorary Fellow, Chartered Institutes of Water and Environmental Management and Purchasing and Supply. Honorary Doctorates: Brunel (1994), University of Central England, 2000, Aston, 2005. Knighthood, 2000. Publications include: Managing Water for the Future: the Case of England and Wales (Eds) 2001; Managing Water Resources Past and Present, (Eds) 2004; Debat: Nationalisations et Denationalisations Entreprises et Histoire, 2004; Climate Change and Economic, Energy and Environment, 2005 (Co-Author); Regulation of Water Services, Handbook of Economic Regulation (Eds) 2005; Services of General Interest: Issues and Options, 2005; articles in learned journals on micro-economic issues. Address: Water Industry Commission for Scotland, Ochil House, Springkerse Business Park, Stirling FK7 7XE; T.-01786 430200; e-mail: ian.byatt@watercommission.co.uk

Byng, Jamie. Publisher, Canongate Books, since 1994; b. 27.6.69, Winchester; m., Whitney Osborn McVeigh (m. diss.); 1 s.; 1 d. Educ. Winchester College; Edinburgh University. Recreations: tennis; cooking; deejaying; reading; drinking. Address: (b.) 14 High Street, Edinburgh EH1 1TE; T.-0131-557 5111.

Byrne, John. Dramatist and stage designer; b. 1940, Paisley. Plays include: The Slab Boys, Cuttin' A Rug, Still Life (trilogy); Normal Service; Cara Coco; television series: Tutti Frutti; Your Cheatin' Heart.

Byrne, Kate (Kathleen) Frances, MA, MSc, CEng, MBCS, CITP. Commissioner, The Royal Commission on the Ancient and Historical Monuments of Scotland; Research in Computational Linguistics, University of Edinburgh, since 2002; b. 2.12.59, London; m., Peter Emrys Williams. Educ. St. Catherine's, Twickenham; University of Edinburgh. Various posts in the Scottish Office Computer Service, 1985-91; MIS Manager, Heriot-Watt University, 1991-92; Information Systems Manager, RCAHMS, 1992-98; Infrastructure Manager at Tullis Russell Papermakers, 1998-99; Head of Computer Services and Deputy Director of ICT, NLS (The National Library of Scotland), 1999-2002. Currently engaged in personal research towards PhD, in the School of Informatics, Edinburgh University as a member of the Language Technology Group within the Human Communication Research Centre. Director of The Scottish Gliding Union; Member of "Walking On Air" (Gliding for the Disabled). Recreations: gliding; hill-walking. Address: (h.) 5 Kirkhill Way, Penicuik EH26 8HH; T.-01968 674114; e-mail: k.byrne@ed.ac.uk

Byrne, Rosemary, Dip Ed, DipSen. MSP (Solidarity), South of Scotland, 2003-07; b. 3.3.48, Irvine; m., James; 1 s. Educ. Irvine Royal Academy; Craigie College, Ayr. Primary teacher, Ayrshire, 1977-88; Learning Support Teacher, 1988-96; Senior Teacher, North Ayrshire Network Support Team, 1996-99; Principal Teacher, Pupil Support, Ardrossan Academy, 1999-2003. Address: (h.) Williamsfield, Irvine; T.-01294 311105.

C

Cackette, Paul, LLB (Hons), DipLP, NP. Head of Civil Justice, Law Reform and International Division, Justice Directorate, Scottish Government, since 2003; b. 26.3.60, Edinburgh; m., Helen Thomson; 1 s.; 2 d. Educ. George Heriot's School, Edinburgh; Edinburgh University. Admitted as a Solicitor, 1985; Solicitor, Kirkcaldy District Council, 1985-88; Office of Solicitor to Secretary of State for Scotland, 1988-99; Office of Solicitor to the Scottish Executive, 1999-2003. Recreations: literature; athletics. Address: (b.) St. Andrews House, Edinburgh EH1 3DG; T.-0131-244 4820.

Caddy, Professor Brian, BSc, PhD, CChem, MRSC. Professor of Forensic Science, Strathclyde University, 1992-99, now Emeritus Professor; b. 26.3.37, Burslem, Stoke-on-Trent; m., Beryl Ashworth; 1 s.; 1 d. Educ. Longton High School, Stoke-on-Trent; Sheffield University. MRC Research Fellow, 1963-66; Strathclyde University: Lecturer in Forensic Science, 1966-77, Senior Lecturer in Forensic Science, 1977-92. Founder Member, European Network of Forensic Science Institutes; President, Forensic Science Society, 1999; Member, Executive Committee, Council for the Registration of Forensic Practitioners, 1999; appointed Commissioner to the Scottish Criminal Cases Review Commission, 2006; Review of the Damilola Taylor case for the Home Secretary, 2007; appointed external verifer for the Council for the Regulation of Forensic Practitioners, 2004 and 2007. Publications: three books; over 90 papers/articles. Editor, Science and Justice (Forensic Science Society journal), 1993-1999. Recreations: reading; painting; walking the dog; dining with friends; good food and wine. Address: (h.) 5 Kings Park, Torrance, Glasgow G64 4DX; T.-01360 622 358; e-mail: B.Caddy@strath.ac.uk

Cadell, Patrick Moubray, CBE, BA, FSA (Scot). Keeper of the Records of Scotland, 1991-2000; Honorary Member of the International Council on Archives; b. 17.3.41, Linlithgow; m., 1, Sarah King (d. 1996); 2 s.; 1 d.; 2, Rachel Watson. Educ. Merchiston Castle School, Edinburgh; Cambridge University; Toulouse University. Information Officer, British Museum; Assistant Keeper, Department of MSS, British Museum; Keeper of Manuscripts, National Library of Scotland, 1983-90. Bailie, Abbey Court of Holyrood; Past President, West Lothian History and Amenity Society. Recreations: walking; the French language. Address: 5 Morham Park, Edinburgh EH10 5GF.

Cadell of Grange, William Archibald, MA (Cantab), FRIAS, RIBA; b 9.3.33; m., Mary-Jean Carmichael; 3 s. Educ. Merchiston Castle; Trinity College, Cambridge; Regent Street Polytechnic. Founded William A. Cadell, Architects, 1968, retired 1995; Manager, Grange Estate, 1971-2000; Chairman, Drum Housing Development, since 1991; Commissioner, Royal Fine Art Commission for Scotland, 1992-2000; Trustee, Architectural Heritage Fund, 1997-2007. Recreations: gardening; forestry; the arts. Address: Swordie Mains, Linlithgow, West Lothian EH49 7RQ; T.-01506 842946.

Caie, Professor Graham Douglas, MA, PhD, FEA, FRSA, FRSE, FFCS. Professor of English Language, Glasgow University, since 1990; Senate Assessor, Glasgow University Court; b. 3.2.45, Aberdeen; m., Ann Pringle Abbott; 1 s.; 1 d. Educ. Aberdeen Grammar School; Aberdeen University; McMaster University, Canada. Teaching Assistant, McMaster University, 1968-72; Amanuensis and Lektor, Copenhagen University, 1972-90. Chairman, Medieval Centre, Copenhagen University, 1985-90; Visiting Professor: McMaster University, 1985-86, Guelph University, 1989; Associate Fellow, Clare Hall, Cambridge, 1977 78; Member, Scottish Arts Council Literature Panel; Vice-President, Scottish Texts Society; Secretary, European Society for the Study of English; Trustee and Vice-Chairman, National Library of Scotland; Member, Council, Dictionary of Older Scottish Tongue; Board, Scottish Language Dictionaries; English Panel, AHRC; English Panel, RAE; Board, English Subject Centre (HEA); SQA English Panel. Publications: Judgement Day II edition, The Theme of Doomsday in Old English Poetry; Beowulf; Bibliography of Junius XI MS; numerous articles. Address: (h.) 12B Upper Glenburn Road, Bearsden, Glasgow G61 4BW; T.-0141-943 1192; e-mail: G.Caie@englang.arts.gla.ac.uk

Caimbeul, Aonghas Phàdraig, MA. Sgrìobhadair; Fearnaidheachd (òraidiche agus craoladair); r. Uibhist-a-Deas; p., Liondsaidh; 1. m.; 5 n. Foghlam: Ard-Sgoil an Obain; Oilthaigh Dhùn Eideann. Treis aig: A' Phàipear Bheag, BBC Rèidio, Grampian Telebhisean; Sgrìobhaiche an t-Sabhail Mhòir, 1990-92; Oraidiche an sin on uairsin; Crìosdaidh; ag obair air nobhal mòr an-dràsda. Air foillseachadh: 2 leabhar bàrdachd; nobhal dheugairean; dà nobhal eile tighinn a-mach am bliadhna. Cuir-seachad: bhith ris an teaghlach agus leughadh Tolstoy. Seòladh: Sabhal Mòr Ostaig, An Teanga, Slèite, an t-Eilein Sgitheanach; F.-01471 844373.

Cairns, David, MP. Labour MP for Inverclyde, since 2005; Labour MP, Greenock and Inverclyde, 2001-05; Minister of State, Scotland Office, since 2007; Parliamentary Under Secretary of State, Northern Ireland Office, 2006-07; Parliamentary Under-Secretary of State, Scotland Office, 2005-07; PPS to Pensions Minister, 2003-05. Educ. Gregorian University, Rome; Franciscan Study Centre. Priest, 1991-94; Director, Christian Socialist Movement, 1994-97; researcher for MP, 1997-2001. Address: (b.) House of Commons, London SW1A 0AA.

Cairns, Professor Douglas Laidlaw, MA (Hons), PhD, FHEA. Professor of Classics, University of Edinburgh, since 2004; b. 10.1.61, Glasgow; widowed; 1 s. Educ. Eastbank Academy, Glasgow; University of Glasgow. Temporary Lecturer in Greek, University of St. Andrews, 1986; Lecturer in Classics, University of Otagao, New Zealand, 1988-92; Lecturer/Senior Lecturer in Classics: University of Leeds, 1992-99, University of Glasgow, 1999-2002. Research Fellow, Georg-August Universität, Göttingen, 1987-88, 1993-95. Publication: Author of Aidus: The Psychology and Ethics of Honour and Shame in Ancient Greek Literature, 1993. Recreations: music; travel; cinema; food and wine. Address: (b.) School of History, Classics and Archaeology, University of Edinburgh EH8 9JY; T.-0131 651 1647; e-mail: douglas.cairns@ed.ac.uk

Cairns, Very Rev. John Ballantyne, LTh, LLB. DD, LLD. Parish Minister, Aberlady and Gullane, since 2001; Chaplain to the Queen, since 1997; Dean of the Chapel Royal, since 2006; Chaplain, The Queen's Bodyguard for Scotland, Royal Company of Archers, 2007; Chaplain to the Lieutenancy of Dumbarton, since 1997; Moderator, General Assembly of the Church of Scotland, 1999-2000; General Trustee of Church of Scotland, since 1995; President, Friends of St Andrew's Jerusalem; b. 15.3.42, London; m., Dr. Elizabeth Emma Bradley; 3 s. Educ.

Sutton Valence School, Kent; Bristol University; Edinburgh University. Messrs Richards, Butler & Co., Solicitors, City of London, 1964-68; Administrative Assistant, East Lothian County Council, 1968-69; Assistant Minister, St. Giles, Elgin, 1973-75; Minister, Langholm, Ewes and Westerkirk Parish Churches, 1975-85, also linked with Canonbie, 1981-85; Clerk, Presbytery of Annandale and Eskdale, 1980-82; Minister, Riverside Church, Dumbarton, 1985-2001; Convener, Maintenance of the Ministry Committee and Joint Convener, Board of Ministry and Mission, Church of Scotland, 1984-88; Chairman, Judicial Commission of General Assembly, 1993-98; Convener, General Assembly Committee on Chaplains to Her Majesty's Forces, 1993-98; Moderator, Presbytery of Dumbarton, 1993-94; Chaplain to Moderator of General Assembly, 1995; Chaplain to Lord High Commissioner (HRH Duke of York), 2007; Divisional Chaplain, Strathclyde Police, 1987-2001; President, Dumbarton Burns Club, 2002; DD University of Aberdeen, 2003; LLD University of Bristol, 2004. Publications: Keeping Fit for Ministry, 1988; Democracy and Unwritten Constitutions, 1989. Recreations: golf; gardening; music; Robert Burns. Address: The Manse, Hummel Road, Gullane, East Lothian EH31 2BG.

Cairns, Professor John William, LLB, PhD, FRSE, FSA Scot. Professor of Legal History, University of Edinburgh, since 2000; b. 17.8.55, Crieff; partner, Donald Jardine. Educ. Hutchesons' Boys' Grammar School; University of Edinburgh. Lecturer in Jurisprudence, Queen's University of Belfast; Lecturer, Senior Lecturer, Reader, University of Edinburgh; Visiting Professor: Southern Methodist University, Dallas, 1986, Miami, 1988, 1991, 1995. Chairman, Council, The Stair Society; President, Eighteenth-Century Scottish Studies Society. Recent Publications: Beyond Dogmatics: Law and Society in the Roman World (Co-Editor), 2007; The Jury in the History of the Common Law (Co-Editor), 2002; Critical Studies in Ancient Law, Comparative Law and Legal History (Co-Editor), 2001. Recreations: cooking; reading; cinema. Address: (b.) University of Edinburgh, Faculty of Law, Old College, South Bridge, Edinburgh EH8 9YL; T.-0131-650 1000; e-mail: john.cairns@ed.ac.uk

Cairns, Richard, BA (Hons), MPhil, DipCE. Chief Executive, Glasgow Chamber of Commerce, since 2008; b. 27.5.58, Glasgow; m., Catherine; 2 s. Educ. Glasgow University; Caledonian University. Career History: Proprietor of fast food business (whilst studying at University); Community Education Worker in Coatbridge, South Lanarkshire; Manager in Community Enterprise Development Agency, Strathclyde Community Business Ltd; Seconded as specialist Adviser to Department of Employment & Training, State Government of Western Australia; Assistant Chief Executive of European Structural Funds Management Agency; Adviser to Romanian National Economic Development Agency; Private Sector Economic Development Consultant; Head of Economic & Social Initiatives, Glasgow City Council. Former member, Scottish Government Economic Consultants Panel; Board Member: Glasgow Exports Ltd, Equal Access Glasgow Ltd. Recreations: photography; camping. Address: (b.) Glasgow Chamber of Commerce, 30 George Square, Glasgow G2 1EQ; T.-0141 204 8317.
E-mail: richard.cairns@glasgowchamber.org

Cairns, Robert, MA, DipEd. Chairman, East of Scotland Water, 1998-2002; Member, City of Edinburgh Council, 1995-2007; b. 16.7.47, Dundee; 2 s. Educ. Morgan Academy; Edinburgh University; Moray House College of Education. Assistant Editor, Scottish National Dictionary, 1969-74; Parliamentary candidate (Labour), North Edinburgh, 1973, February 1974; Teacher, James Gillespie's High School, 1975-96; Member, City of

Edinburgh District Council, 1974-95 (Convener, Planning and Development Committee, 1986-95); Board Member, East Regional Board SEPA, since 2004. Recreation: walking. Address: (h.) Eastergate Cottage, Harrietfield, Logiealmond, Perthshire; T.-01738 880393.
E-mail: robert.cairns401@btinternet.com

Cairns, Professor Robert Alan, BSc, PhD, FInstP, FRSE. Professor, School of Mathematical and Computational Sciences, St. Andrews University, since 1991 (Reader, 1985-91); b. 12.3.45, Glasgow; m., Ann E. Mackay. Educ. Allan Glen's School, Glasgow; Glasgow University. Lecturer in Applied Mathematics, St. Andrews University, 1970-83; Senior Lecturer, 1983-85. Member, SERC Laser Committee, 1990-93; Member, SERC Atomic and Molecular Physics Sub-Committee, 1990-93; Chairman, Plasma Physics Group, Institute of Physics, 1999-2001 (Committee Member, 1981-84); Member, Editorial Board, Plasma Physics, 1983-85; Editor, Journal of Plasma Physics, 1995-2006. Publications: Plasma Physics, 1985; Radiofrequency heating of plasmas, 1991. Recreations: music (listening to and playing recorder and baroque flute); golf; hill-walking. Address: (b.) School of Mathematics and Statistics, St. Andrews University, North Haugh, St. Andrews, Fife KY16 9SS; T.-01334 463707.

Cairns, Tom, MA, CIPFA. Chief Executive, South Ayrshire Council, since 2004; b. 3.7.53; m., Margaret; 1 d.; 1 s. Educ. Glasgow University. Depute Director of Finance and Management Services, East Kilbride District Council, 1988-93; Director of Finance and Management Services, 1993-95; Director of Finance and Management Services, South Ayrshire Council, 1995-2001, Deputy Chief Executive, 2001-04. Chairman of Burns an a' that Festival Company; Homecoming Scotland Board Member; Past Chairman, CIPFA Scotland (1999-2000); Member of Solace (Scotland). Recreations: travel; theatre; music. Address: (b.) County Buildings, Wellington Square, Ayr KA7 1DR; T.-01292 612170.
E-mail: tom.cairns@south-ayrshire.gov.uk

Caithness, 20th Earl of (Malcolm Ian Sinclair), PC; b. 3.11.48; m.; 1 s.; 1 d. Educ. Marlborough; Royal Agricultural College, Cirencester. Succeeded to title, 1965; Paymaster General and Minister of State, HM Treasury, 1989-90; Minister of State, Foreign and Commonwealth Office, 1990-92; Department of Transport, 1992-94; Chief Executive, Clan Sinclair Trust, since 1999; elected Member, House of Lords, since 1999.

Calder, Professor Andrew Alexander, MD, FRCS (Edin), FRCP (Glas), FRCP (Edin), FRCOG, HonFCOG (SA). Professor of Obstetrics and Gynaecology, University of Edinburgh, since 1987; Head, Division of Reproductive and Developmental Sciences; Director, Jennifer Brown Research Laboratory and Tommy's Centre for Fetal and Material Health Research, Queen's Medical Research Institute; b. 17.1.45, Aberdeen; m., Valerie Anne Dugard; 1 s.; 2 d. Educ. Glasgow Academy; Glasgow University. Clinical training posts, Glasgow, 1968-72; Research Fellow, Nuffield Department of Obstetrics and Gynaecology, University of Oxford, 1972-75; Lecturer/Senior Lecturer, Obstetrics and Gynaecology, University of Glasgow, 1975-86; Consultant Obstetrician and Gynaecologist: Glasgow Royal Infirmary and Royal Maternity Hospital, 1978-86, Royal Infirmary of Edinburgh and Simpson Centre for Reproductive Health, since 1987; British Exchange Professor, University of California, Los Angeles, 1992. Blair Bell Memorial Lecturer, RCOG, 1977; WHO Travelling Fellow, Uruguay, 1985. Recreations: music; golf; curling; history of medicine. Address: Department of Obstetrics and Gynaecology, Royal Infirmary of Edinburgh, Little France, Edinburgh; e-mail: a.a.calder@ed.ac.uk

Calder, Angus Lindsay, MA, DPhil. Writer; b. 5.2.42, Sutton, Surrey; m., 1, Jennifer Daiches; 1 s.; 2 d.; 2,

Catherine Kyle; 1 s. Educ. Wallington County Grammar School; Kings College, Cambridge. Lecturer in Literature, Nairobi University, 1968-71; Visiting Lecturer, Chancellor College, Malawi University, 1978; Reader and Staff Tutor in Arts, Open University in Scotland, 1979-93; Visiting Professor of English, University of Zimbabwe, 1993; Distinguished Visiting Scholar, University of Waikato, 1995; Member, Board of Directors, Royal Lyceum Theatre Company, 1984-96; Editorial Board, Wasafiri; Member, Panel of Judges, Saltire Society Scottish Book of the Year Award, 1983-97; Member, Board, 2000 + 3 Estaitis, 1998-2004; Eric Gregory Award for Poetry, 1967. Publications: The People's War: Britain 1939-1945, 1969 (John Llewellyn Rhys Memorial Prize); Revolutionary Empire, 1981 (Scottish Arts Council Book Award); The Myth of the Blitz, 1991; Revolving Culture: notes from the Scottish Republic, 1994 (SAC Book Award); Waking in Waikato (poems), 1997; Wars (anthology), 1999; Horace in Tollcross (poems), 2000; Scotlands of the Mind, 2002; Colours of Grief (poems), 2002; Gods, Mongrels and Demons: 101 Brief But Essential Lives, 2003; Dipa's Bowl (poems), 2004; Disasters and Heroes, 2004; Sun Behind The Castle (poems), 2004. Recreations: curling; cricket. E-mail: calderboooks@yahoo.co.uk

Calder, Rev. Bryce, MA (with Merit) (Hist), BD (First Class Hons) (OT Stud). Parish Minister, St. David's Memorial Park, since 2001; b. 26.12.66, Bo'ness; m., Helen Calder (nee Miller); 1 s.; 1 d. Educ. Bo'ness Academy; Edinburgh University. Metropolitan Police Officer, 1985-87; Candidate for Church of Scotland Ministry, 1988-93; Assistant Minister of Troon: St. Medan's, 1994; Parish Minister, Buckhaven and Manager, Buckhaven Theatre, 1995-2000. Founder Member, Levenmouth YMCA; Retired Company Director, Cutting Edge Theatre Company; Chairman, Friends of SYCAM (A Charity that supported Children's Aid work in India). Recreations: football (supporter of Motherwell FC); bowls; theatre; reading; listening to music and playing bass guitar. Address: 2 Roman Road, Kirkintilloch, Glasgow G66 1EA; T.-0141-776 1434; e-mail: ministry100@aol.com

Calder, Finlay, OBE. Grain Exporter; b. 20.8.57, Haddington; m., Elizabeth; 1 s.; 1 d. Educ. Daniel Stewart's and Melville College. Played rugby for Scotland, 1986-90; captained Scotland, 1989; captained British Isles, 1989.

Calder, George, BA (Hons) (Cantab), LLB, MIPD. Secretary of KCPS Ltd., since 2007; b. 20.12.47; 2 d. Educ. George Watson's College, Edinburgh; Cambridge University; Edinburgh University. Joined Civil Service (Department of Employment), 1971; worked in European Commission (cabinet of George Thomson); Treasury, 1977-79; Manpower Services Commission, 1979-87; Scottish Office/Scottish Executive (Head of European Funds and Co-ordination Division, Head of Personnel, Head of Water Services Unit), 1987-99; Head, Scottish Executive EU Office, 1999-2004. Recreations: football; book collecting; book clubs; golf; wine; hill-walking; military history.

Calder, Jenni, BA, MPhil. Freelance Writer; b. 3.12.41, Chicago, Illinois; 1 s.; 2 d. Educ. Perse School for Girls, Cambridge; Cambridge University; London University. Freelance writer, 1966-78; taught and lectured in Scotland, England, Kenya and USA; Lecturer in English, Nairobi University, 1968-69; successively Education Officer, Head of Publications, Head of Museum of Scotland International, National Museums of Scotland, Edinburgh, 1978-2001. Publications: Chronicles of Conscience: a study of George Orwell and Arthur Koestler, 1968; Scott (with Angus Calder), 1969; There Must be a Lone Ranger: the Myth and Reality of the American West, 1974; Women and Marriage in Victorian Fiction, 1976; Brave New World and Nineteen Eighty Four, 1976; Heroes: from Byron to Guevara, 1977;

The Victorian Home, 1977; The Victorian Home from Old Photographs, 1979; RLS, A Life Study, 1980; The Robert Louis Stevenson Companion (Editor), 1980; Robert Louis Stevenson and Victorian Scotland (Editor), 1981; The Strange Case of Dr Jekyll and Mr Hyde (Editor), 1979; Kidnapped (Editor), 1981; Catriona (Editor), 1981; The Enterprising Scot (Editor), 1986; Island Landfalls (Editor), 1987; Bonny Fighters: The Story of the Scottish Soldier, 1987; Open Guide to Animal Farm and Nineteen Eighty Four, 1987; The Wealth of a Nation (Editor), 1989; St. Ives, a new ending, 1990; Scotland in Trust, 1990; Treasure Islands (Editor), 1994; Mediterranean (poems, as Jenni Daiches), 1995; Tales of the South Seas (Editor), 1996; The Nine Lives of Naomi Mitchison, 1997; Everyman's Poetry: Robert Louis Stevenson (Editor), 1997; Present Poets anthology, Editor), 1998; Translated Kingdoms (anthology, Editor), 1999; A Beleaguered City and Other Tales of the Seen and the Unseen (Editor), 2000; Scots in Canada, 2003; Not Nebuchadnezzar: In Search of Identities, 2005; Scots in the USA, 2005; Smoke (poems, as Jenni Daiches); Letters from the Great Wall (fiction, as Jenni Daiches). Recreations: music; films; walking the dog. Address: (h.) 31 Station Road, South Queensferry, West Lothian; T.-0131-331 1287.

Calder, Professor Muffy, BSc, PhD, FRSE, FIEE. Professor of Formal Methods (Computer Science), Glasgow University, since 1999; b. 21.5.58, Shawinigan, Quebec, Canada; m., David Calder. Educ. Stirling University; St Andrews University. Research Fellow, Edinburgh University and Stirling University, 1983-87; Lecturer/Senior Lecturer, Computing Science, Glasgow University, 1988-99. Recreations: road running; hill-running. Address: (b.) Department of Computer Science, Glasgow University. T.-0141-330 4969.

Calder, Robert Russell, MA. Critic, Philosophical Writer, Historian of Ideas, Poet, Freelance Journalist, Book Reviewer, Performer and Singer; b. 22.4.50, Burnbank. Educ. Hamilton Academy; Glasgow University; Edinburgh University. Co-Editor, Chapman, 1974-76 and since 1988; Editor, Lines Review, 1976-77; Theatre Critic and Feature Writer, Scot, 1983-86; Staff Writer, Popmatters (Chicago), Journal of Global Culture; Staff writer, All About Jazz. Books: A School of Thinking, 1995; Narcissism, Nihilism, Simplicity (Editor), 1992; poetry: Il Re Giovane, 1976, Ettrick & Annan, 1981; Serapion, 1996. Recreations: music - opera singing; jazz piano. Address: (h.) 23 Glenlee Street, Burnbank, Hamilton ML3 9JB; T.-01698 824244; e-mail: serapion@btinternet.com

Caldwell, David Cleland, SHNC, MA, BPhil. Director, Universities Scotland, since 2000; b. 25.2.44, Glasgow; m., Ann Scott Macrae; 1 s.; 1 d. Educ. George Watson's College, Edinburgh; St. Andrews University; Glasgow University. Warwick University: Lecturer in Politics, 1969-76, Administrative Assistant, 1976-77, Assistant Registrar, 1977-80; Registry Officer, Aberdeen University, 1980-84; Secretary, The Robert Gordon University, 1984-2000. Member: Warwick District Council, 1979-80, Grampian Regional Council, 1983-84; Parliamentary candidate (Labour), North East Fife, 1983; Member, Aberdeen Grammar School Council, 1983-88 (Chairman, 1985-88); Member, St. Andrews University Court, 1986-94 (Convener, Audit Commitee, 1990-94); Member, Board of Management, Moray College, 1995-2001; Director, Viscom (Aberdeen) Ltd., 1992-97 (Chairman, 1994-95); Director, RGIT Ltd., 1997-99. Address: (b.) Universities Scotland, 53 Hanover Street, Edinburgh EH2 2PJ; T.-0131-226 1111.

Caldwell, David Hepburn, MA, PhD, FSA, FSAScot. Keeper of Scotland and Europe and Director, Finlaggan Archaeological Project, National Museums of Scotland; b. 15.12.51, Kilwinning, Ayrshire; m., Margaret Anne McGovern; 1 s.; 2 d. Educ. Ardrossan Academy; Edinburgh

University. Joined staff, National Museum of Antiquities, 1973. Publications: The Scottish Armoury, 1979; Scottish Weapons and Fortifications, 1981; Scotland's Wars and Warriors, 1998; Islay, Jura and Colonsay, A Historical Guide, 2001. Recreation: travelling. Address: (h.) 3 James Park, Burntisland, Fife KY3 9EW; T.-872175.

Caldwell, Maren L., LLB, MICFM. Head of Regional Fundraising & Communications, RNLI; b. 20.4.47, Glasgow; m., John Caldwell; 2 s. Educ. Glasgow High School for Girls; Glasgow University. Appeal Director, Strathcarron Hospice, 1989-92; Director of Fundraising, Scottish Medical Research Fund, 1992-94; Administrator, Scottish Hospital Endowments Research Trust, 1993-94; Depute Campaign Director, Children 1st, 1994-96. Member, Business Committee, General Council, Glasgow University, 1982-92, and Convenor, Social Affairs Committee of the Business Committee, 1988-92; Trustee, University of Glasgow Trust, 1989-97. Recreations: watching rugby; gardening; opera; being a motorbike passenger; sailing. Address: Unit 3, Ruthvenfield Grove, Inveralmond Industrial Estate, Perth PH1 3GL.

Caldwell, Miller H., MA, CQSW, DipSocWk, DipRS, FFCS. Author and Film Script Writer; Camp Manager, Mundihar NWFP Pakistan 2006 Post Earthquake; former Dumfries and Galloway Authority Reporter; b. 6.10.50, Glasgow; m., Jocelyn M. France; 2d. Educ. Glasgow Academy; London University; Moray House College; Jordanhill College. Fraternal Worker, Ghana, West Africa, Overseas Council, Church of Scotland, 1972-78; Postgraduate student, 1978-80; School Social Worker, Central Regional Council, 1980-83; Kilmarnock and Loudon Reporter, 1983-88; Area Reporter, Kyle and Carrick, Cumnock and Doon Valley, 1988-92; Principal Reporter, Dumfries and Galloway, 1992-95; Regional Reporter, 1995. Past President, Dumfries and Galloway Burns Club (direct descendent of Robert Burns); Chairman, Dumfries Branch SASD; South West contact for Ghanaians in need. Publications: Operation Oboe (Historical Novel); Have You Seen My ...Umm...Memory (Self Help Memory Book); Poet's Progeny (Editor) (A line of descent from the Bard); Ponderings - poems and short stories in large print; Restless Waves (Novel); 7 Point 7 (On the Richter Scale) The Diary of the Camp Manager (Biography). Recreations: all things West African; piano; clarinet. Address: (h.) Netherholm, Edinburgh Road, Dumfries; T.-01387 263998.
E-mail: mhcaldwell@btopenworld.com; web: www.millercaldwell.org

Caldwell, Sheila Marion, BA (Hons), Fellow of Royal Geographical Society, ARSGS. Council Member, Convenor/Chair, Glasgow Centre of Royal Scottish Geographical Society; Member, Committee, Royal Scottish Geographical Society; b. England; m., Major Robert Caldwell, TD (deceased). Educ. Tunbridge Wells Grammar School; University College, London. Founder/Principal, Yejide Girls' Grammar School, Ibadan, Nigeria; first Principal, Girls' Secondary (Government) School, Lilongwe, Malawi; Depute Head, Mills Grammar School, Framlingham, Suffolk; Head, St. Columba's School, Kilmacolm, 1976-87; Treasurer, Secondary Heads' Association, Scotland, 1984-87; Public Affairs Liaison, Glasgow Association of Women Graduates. Recreations: travel; art history and architecture; music, opera and ballet; cooking. Address: (h.) 27 Oxford Road, Renfrew PA4 0SJ; T.-0141-886 2296.

Callander, Alex James, MA, FSIP. Joint Senior Partner, Baillie Gifford & Co., since 2001; b. 1.4.60, Dundee; m., Rhona; 1 s.; 1 d. Educ. Glenalmond College; St John's College, Cambridge. Baillie Gifford & Co: joined 1982; Trainee Fund Manager; Fund

Manager; Client Services Manager/Director; Manager/Head, Institutional Clients' Department. Chairman, Institute of Investment Management and Research, 1997-99. Recreations: hiking; travelling. Address: (b.) Calton Square, 1 Greenside Row, Edinburgh EH1 3AN; T.-0131 275 2000.

Calman, Professor Sir Kenneth Charles, KCB 1996, DL, MD, PhD, FRCP, FRCS, FRSE. Chancellor, University of Glasgow, since 2006; Vice-Chancellor and Warden, Durham University, 1998-2007; b. 25.12.41, Glasgow; m., Ann; 1 s.; 2 d. Educ. Allan Glen's School, Glasgow; Glasgow University. Lecturer in Surgery, Western Infirmary, Glasgow, 1968-72; MRC Clinical Research Fellow, London, 1972-73; Professor of Oncology, Glasgow University, 1974-84; Dean of Postgraduate Medicine, 1984-89; Chief Medical Officer, Scottish Home and Health Department, 1989-91; Chief Medical Officer, Department of Health, 1991-98. Chairman, Executive Board, World Health Organisation, 1998-99. Recreations: golf; gardening; cartoons; sundials. Address: (h.) 57 Kelvin Court, Glasgow G12 0AG. T.-0141-334-4443.

Cameron of Lochbroom, Rt. Hon. Lord (Kenneth John Cameron), Life Baron (1984), PC (1984), MA (Oxon), LLB, QC, FRSE, Hon. FRIAS. Senator of the College of Justice, 1989-2003; Chairman, Royal Fine Art Commission for Scotland, 1995-2005; b. 11.6.31, Edinburgh; m., Jean Pamela Murray; 2 d. Educ. Edinburgh Academy; Corpus Christi College, Oxford; Edinburgh University. Advocate, 1958; Queen's Counsel, 1972; President, Pensions Appeal Tribunal for Scotland, 1976; Chairman, Committee of Investigation Under Agricultural Marketing Act 1958, 1980; Advocate Depute, 1981; Lord Advocate, 1984; Hon. Bencher, Lincoln's Inn; Hon. Fellow, Corpus Christi College, Oxford; Hon. Fellow, RIAS; Hon Fellow, RSA. Recreation: fishing. Address: (h.) Stoneyhill House, Musselburgh.

Cameron, Alasdair, FSA Scot. Farmer and Crofter; b. 12.6.44, Dingwall; m., Jeannette Benzie; 2 d. Educ. Dingwall Academy. Hon. President, Black Isle Farmers Society; Chairman, Northern Counties Valuators Association; former Vice-Chairman, Crofters Commission; Member: Scottish Agricultural Arbiters Association, Scottish Vernacular Buildings Working Group, Historic Farm Buildings UK; Past Chairman: Highland Farming and Forestry Advisory Group, Dingwall Round Table; Director: Ross-shire Voluntary Action, Black Isle Partnership, Highland Livestock Heritage Society. Recreations: photography; industrial archaeology; local history; the countryside. Address: Wellhouse Farm, Black Isle, Muir of Ord, Ross-shire IV6 7SF; T.-01463 870416.

Cameron, Alastair Ian. Chief Executive, Scottish Churches Housing Action, since 1994; b. 3.4.53, Dundee; m., Mary Jane Elton; 2 s.; 1 d. Educ. Glasgow Academy; Lenana School, Nairobi; University of Kent at Canterbury. Neighbourhood Worker, Rochdale Metropolitan Council, 1980-85; Development Worker, Edinburgh Council for the Single Homeless, 1985-92; Housing Strategy Manager, Wester Hailes Partnership, 1992-94. Board Member, Rural Housing Service; Scots Music Group; Member, Religious Society of Friends. Recreations: traditional music; cycling; allotment gardening. Address: 3 Esplanade Terrace, Edinburgh EH15 2ES; e-mail: alastair@camell.me.uk

Cameron, Alexander, CBE, BA, CertApp SocStud, CQSW. Chairman, Parole Board for Scotland, since 2006; b. 29.4.50, Glasgow; m., Linda; 2 s. Educ. Duncanrig, East

Kilbride; Strathclyde University; Aberdeen University. Social Worker, Clackmannanshire County Council, 1973-75; Principal Officer, Central Region, 1975-81, Assistant Director of Social Work, 1981-87; Director of Social Work, Borders Region, 1987-95, Executive Director of Social Work, South Lanarkshire, 1995-2006. Chairman, Scottish Institute for Excellence in Social Work Education; Visiting Professor, Glasgow School of Social Work; Non Executive Director, The State Hospital Board; Director, Care Visions Ltd. Recreations: architecure; design; rugby; cooking; reading. Address: (b.) Parole Board for Scotland, Saughton House, Edinburgh EH11 3XD; T.-0131 244 8097.
E-mail: cameronsathome@btinternet.com

Cameron, Allan John, MBE, DL, JP. Farmer and Landowner, since 1947; b. 25.3.17, Edinburgh; m., Elizabeth Vaughan-Lee; 2 s.; 2 d. Educ. Harrow; Royal Military College. Regular officer, Queen's Own Cameron Highlanders, 1936-47 (ret. Major); Member: Ross and Cromarty County Council, 1955-75 (Chairman, Education Committee, 1962-75), Ross and Cromarty District Council, since 1975 (Convener, since 1991); former Commissioner: Red Deer Commission, Countryside Commission for Scotland; former Member, BBC Council for Scotland; President: Royal Caledonian Curling Club, 1963, International Curling Federation, 1965-69. Recreations: curling; golf; shooting; fishing; gardening. Address: (h.) Quarryfield Farmhouse, Munlochy, Ross-Shire IV8 8NZ; T.-014638 11249.

Cameron, Most Rev. Andrew Bruce. Primus of the Scottish Episcopal Church, 2000-06; Bishop of Aberdeen and Orkney, Scottish Episcopal Church, 1992-2006; b. 2.5.41, Glasgow; m., Elaine Cameron; 2 s. Educ. Eastwood Secondary School; Edinburgh Theological College. Curate, Helensburgh and Edinburgh, 1964-70; Chaplain, St. Mary's Cathedral, Edinburgh, 1970-75; Diocesan and Provincial Youth Chaplain, 1969-75; Rector, St. Mary's Church, Dalmahoy, and Anglican Chaplain, Heriot Watt University, 1975-82; Churches Development Officer, Livingston Ecumenical Parish, 1982-88; Rector, St. John's Episcopal Church, Perth, 1988-92; Convener, Mission Board, Scottish Episcopal Church, 1988-92; Resident Scholar, Bruton Parish Church, Williamsburg, USA, 2006-07. Recreations: music; theatre; various sports; gardening. Address: (h.) 2 Newbigging Grange, Coupar Angus, Perthshire PH13 9GA; T.-01821 650482; mobile: 07715 323 119; e-mail: bruce2541@gmail.com

Cameron, Rev. Charles Millar, BA, BD, PhD. Church of Scotland Minister, Darvel Parish Church, Ayrshire, since 2001; b. 31.5.51, Glasgow; m., Sharon Elizabeth Tweed; 1 s. Educ. Woodside Secondary School, Glasgow; University of Stirling; University of Glasgow. Probationer Assistant, Sherwood Church, Paisley, 1977-78; Postgraduate Study, Western Theological Seminary, Holland, Michigan, USA (Reformed Church in America), 1978-79; Minister: St. Ninians Church, Dunfermline (Church of Scotland), 1980-96, Burnside Presbyterian Church, Portstewart, Northern Ireland (Presbyterian Church in Ireland), 1996-98, Castlemilk West Church, Glasgow (Church of Scotland), 1998-2001. Publication: 'The Problem of Polarization: An Approach Based on The Writings of GC Berkouner', 1992. Address: (h. and b.) 46 West Main Street, Darvel, Ayrshire KA17 0AQ; T.-01560 322924.
E-mail: charlescameron@hotmail.co.uk

Cameron, Colin. Freelance Television Producer; Managing Director, Lion Television Scotland, 2004-07; Controller, Network Development, BBC Nations and Regions, 2001-04; b. 30.3.50; m., Christine Main; 2 s. Educ. Glasgow Academy; Duke of York School, Nairobi; Polytechnic of Central London. Journalist, Current Affairs, BBC Scotland, 1973-76; Film Director, That's Life, 1976-77; Producer/Director, Everyman and Heart of the Matter, 1977-85; Editor, Brass Tacks, BBC North, 1985-88; Head of Documentary Features, BBC Television, 1988-91; BBC Scotland: Head of Television, 1991-96, Head of Production, 1997-2000, Head of Network Programmes, 2000-01. Chair, The Research Centre; RTS International Current Affairs Award, 1984; UN Association Media Peace Prize, 1984. Recreations: canoeing; yoga; running; travelling. E-mail: colincameron@mail.com

Cameron, Colin, BL. Retired Solicitor; b. 24.8.33, Lanark; m., Rachel Weir Allison Cameron; 3 s.; 1 d. Educ. Uddingston Grammar School; Glasgow University. Solicitor, Wilson and Morgan, Blantyre, Malawi, 1957-61; Minister of Transport and Communications, Malawi, 1961-64; Solicitor, Allan Black and McCaskie, Elgin, 1964-66; Solicitor to Cumbernauld and Irvine Development Corporations, 1966-70; own Legal practice (retired). Council Member, Law Society of Scotland, 1976-82; Hon. Consul to Republic of Malawi, since 1994; Past President, Irvine Rotary Club; Past Secretary, Abbeyfield Irvine and District Society Ltd; Hon. Vice President, Clan Cameron Association. Recreations: hill-walking; swimming; music; reading; family. Address: (h.) 1 Hill Street, Irvine KA12 0DE; T.-01294 313103; Fax: 01294 279670; e-mail: accameron@btinternet.com

Cameron, David Roderick Simpson, RIBA, ARIAS, MRTPI, FSA Scot. Consultant planner and artist; retired architect; b. 2.6.41, Inverness; m., Filitsa Boulton; 1 s.; 2 d. Educ. George Watson's College; Edinburgh College of Art; Newcastle University; Leith School of Art. Depute Director of Planning, City of Edinburgh District Council, 1983-96; ECOS Project Manager for revival of Kazimierz in Krakow, 1993-96. President, Clan Cameron Association Scotland, 1999-2005 and Hon. Life President, 2006; Chairman: Saltire Society, 1990-95, Patrick Geddes Memorial Trust, 1991-99; Convener, Historic Burghs Association of Scotland, 1993-99; Hon. Secretary, Edinburgh Architectural Association, 1972-75. Member: Saltire Housing Award Panel, 1998-2003, Council, National Trust for Scotland, 1994-99, Grants Council, Scottish Community Foundation, 1996-2006, Corstorphine Community Council, 2002-06, Council, Cockburn Association, since 2003. Recreations: art; fishing; forestry; Scottish and Greek heritage. Address: (b.) Impart Enterprises, 4 Dovecot Road, Edinburgh EH12 7LE; T.-0131-539 2745.

Cameron, of Lochiel, Donald Angus, MA, FCA, JP, DL. 27th Chief of the Clan Cameron; Lord-Lieutenant of Inverness, since 2002; Director, J. Henry Schroder & Co. Limited, 1984-99; President, Highland Society of London, 1994-97; b. 2.8.46; m., Lady Cecil Kerr; 1 s. 3 d. Educ. Harrow; Christ Church, Oxford. 2nd Lieutenant, Queen's Own Cameron Highlanders (TA), 1966-68; Chartered Accountant, 1971. Address: (h.) Achnacarry, Spean Bridge, Inverness-shire.

Cameron, Rt. Rev. Douglas M. Bishop of Argyll and the Isles, 1993-2003; b. 23.3.35, Natal; m., Anne Patricia Purnell; 2 d. Educ. Eastwood Grammar School; Edinburgh Theological College; University of the South, Sewanee, Tennessee. Curate, Christ Church, Falkirk, 1962-65; Priest, Papua New Guinea, 1965-74, Archdeacon, 1972-74; Rector: St. Fillan's and St. Hilda's, Edinburgh, 1974-88, St. Mary's, Dalkeith, and St. Leonard's, Lasswade, 1988-92; Canon and Synod Clerk, Diocese of Edinburgh, 1990-92; Dean of Edinburgh, 1991-92. Recreations: hill-walking; music; cooking. Address: (h.) 23 Craigs Way, Rumford, Falkirk FK2 0EU; T.-01324 714137.

Cameron, Professor Dugald, OBE, DA, FCSD, FRSA, DSc (hc) (Strathclyde). Chairman, Glasgow Prestwick

International Airport Consultative Committee, since 2004; Director, Glasgow School of Art, 1991-99; Visiting Professor, University of Strathclyde, since 1999; Visiting Professor, Department of Aerospace Engineering, University of Glasgow, since 2000; Companion, Royal Aeronautical Society, 1996; Industrial Design Consultant, since 1965; Hon. President, R. Aero Soc. Prestwick Branch; b. 4.10.39, Glasgow; m., Nancy Inglis. Educ. Glasgow High School; Glasgow School of Art. Industrial Designer, Hard Aluminium Surfaces Ltd., 1962-65; Visiting Lecturer, Glasgow School of Art, 1963-70; Head of Product Design, Glasgow School of Art, 1970-82; Head of Design, 1982-91. Hon. Professor, Glasgow University, 1993-99; Director, Squadron Prints, 1977-2000; Member: Engineering Advisory Committee, Scottish Committee, Council of Industrial Design, since 1966, Industrial Design (Engineering) Panel and 3D Design Board, CNAA, since 1978, Scottish Committee of Higher Education, Design Council; commission RAFVR (T), 1974; Member, Railway Heritage Trust, since 2003; Patron: Universities of Glasgow and Strathclyde Air Squadron, 2001. Publications: Glasgow's Own (a history of 602 City of Glasgow Squadron, Royal Auxiliary Air Force), 1987; Glasgow's Airport, 1990; compiler of 'Central to Glasgow', 2006. Recreations: railways; flying (lapsed private pilot); aviation history (particularly Scottish). Address: (h.) Achnacraig, Skelmorlie, Ayrshire.

Cameron, Brigadier Ewen Duncan, OBE. Deputy Director, National Trust for Scotland, 1998-2000; b. 10.2.35, Bournemouth; m., Joanna Margaret Hay; 2 d. Educ. Wellington College; Royal Military Academy, Sandhurst. Commissioned The Black Watch, 1955; DS, The Staff College, 1972-75; Commanding Officer, 1st Bn., The Black Watch, 1975-78; Commander, Royal Brunei Armed Forces, 1980-82; Indian College of Defence Studies, Delhi, 1983; Divisional Brigadier, Scottish Division, 1984-86; Director of Administration and Personnel, National Trust for Scotland, 1986-98. Member, Queen's Bodyguard for Scotland (Royal Company of Archers). Recreations: opera; bridge; bird-watching; travel; gardening. Address: (h.) The Old Manse, Arngask, Glenfarg, Perth PH2 9QA; T.-01577 830394.

Cameron, Sheriff Ian Alexander, MA, LLB. Sheriff of Grampian, Highland and Islands, at Elgin, since 2001; b. 5.11.38, Elgin; m., Dr. Margaret Anne Innes; 1 s. Educ. Elgin Academy; Edinburgh University; Aberdeen University. Partner, Stewart and McIsaac, Solicitors, Elgin, 1962-86; Sheriff at Edinburgh, 1987-93, at Wick, Dornoch and Stornoway, 1993-2001. Recreation: travel. Address: Braemoray, Elgin, IV30 4NJ; T.-01343 542731; 19/4 Damside, Dean Village, Edinburgh, EH4 3BB; T.-0131-220 1548.

Cameron, Professor Rev. James Kerr, MA, BD, PhD, FRHistS. Professor of Ecclesiastical History, St. Andrews University, 1970-89; b. 5.3.24, Methven; m., Emma Leslie Birse; 1 s. Educ. Oban High School; St. Andrews University; Hartford Theological Seminary, Hartford, Connecticut. Ordained as Assistant Minister, Church of the Holy Rude, Stirling, 1953; appointed Lecturer in Church History, Aberdeen University, 1955; Lecturer, then Senior Lecturer in Ecclesiastical History, St. Andrews University, 1956-70; Dean, Faculty of Divinity, 1978-83. President: Ecclesiastical History Society, 1976-77, British Sub-Commission, Commission Internationale d'Histoire Ecclesiastique Comparee, 1979-92; Vice-President, International Association for Neo-Latin Studies, 1979-81; Honorary Fellow, Ecclesiastical History Society, 2000; Co-Editor and Contributor, Theologische Realenzyklopädie (Vol. 17 to Vol. 36). Publications: Letters of John Johnston and Robert Howie, 1963; First Book of Discipline, 1972,

reprinted 2005; Contributor to: Acta Conventus Neo-Latini Amstelodamensis, 1973; Advocates of Reform, 1953; The Scottish Tradition, 1974; Renaissance and Renewal in Christian History, 1977; Reform and Reformation: England and the Continent, 1979; Origins and Nature of the Scottish Enlightenment, 1982; A Companion to Scottish Culture, 1981; Humanism in Renaissance Scotland, 1990; The Impact of Humanism on Western Europe, 1990; Gericht Verleden, Leiden, 1991; A History of Religion in Britain, 1994; The Universities of Aberdeen and Europe, The First Three Centuries, 1995; Scotland and the Low Countries 1124–1994, 1996; Oxford DNB, 2004. A Festschrift in my honour was published by the Ecclesiastical History Society in 1991, Humanism and Reform: The Church in Europe, England and Scotland, 1400-1643, edited by James Kirk. Recreation: gardening. Address: (h.) Priorscroft, 71 Hepburn Gardens, St. Andrews KY16 9LS; T.-01334 473996; e-mail: jkc6@st-andrews.ac.uk

Cameron, J. Gordon, MA, LLB, DipLP, WS, NP. Partner, Stuart & Stuart WS, since 1987; b. 15.11.57, Edinburgh; m., Deborah Jane; 1 d. Educ. George Watson's College; Aberdeen University. Joined Stuart & Stuart WS as assistant, 1985. Hon. Secretary and Treasurer, Royal Celtic Society. Recreations: hill-running; photography; foreign travel. Address: (b.) 23 Rutland Street, Edinburgh EH1 2RN; T.-0131-228 6449.
E-mail: gcameron@stuartandstuart.co.uk

Cameron, John A. N. (Johnny), BA, MSc. Director, Chief Executive, Corporate Markets, The Royal Bank of Scotland PLC, since 2006; b. 24.06.54, Inverness; m., Julia; 2 s.; 1 d. Educ. Harrow School; Oxford University; Manipal Institute of Technology. Trade Executive, Jardine Matheson, 1976-81; Consultant, McKinsey & Co., 1981-83; various including Co-Head of Global Finance, Dresdner Kleinwort Benson, 1988-98; Royal Bank of Scotland: MD Corporate and Institutional Banking, 1998-2000, Deputy CEO, Corporate Banking and Financial Markets, 2000-01, CEO, Corporate Banking and Finacial Markets, 2001-06. Fellow of The Chartered Institute of Bankers in Scotland. Recreations: golf; tennis; sailing. Address: (b.) PO Box 31, 42 St Andrew Square, Edinburgh EH2 2YE; e-mail: john.cameron@rbs.com

Cameron, John Angus, MBChB, MRCGP, MBA. Medical Director, NHS Dumfries and Galloway, since 2003; b. Bath. Educ. Marlborough College; Edinburgh University. GP, Biggar, 1982-99; Medical Director, Dumfries and Galloway Primary Care Trust, 2001-02. Non Executive Director, Lanarkshire Health Board, 1992-99. Recreations: hill farming; hill-walking. Address: (b.) Crichton Hall, Dumfries DG1 4TG; T.-01387 244001; e-mail: anguscameron@nhs.net

Cameron, John Bell, CBE, FRAgricS, AIAgricE. Director, South West Trains, since 1995; Chairman, Scottish Beef Council, since 1997; Farmer, since 1961; b. 14.6.39, Edinburgh; m., Margaret Clapperton. Educ. Dollar Academy. Vice President, National Farmers' Union, 1976-79, President, 1979-84; Member, Agricultural Praesidium of EEC, 1979-84; Chairman, EEC Advisory Committee for Sheepmeat, 1982-90; Chairman, World Meats Group, (IFAP), since 1983; Chairman, Board of Governors, Dollar Academy, since 1985; Chairman, United Auctions Ltd., since 1985; President: Scottish Beef Cattle Association, since 2006, National Sheep Association (Scotland), since 2004; Member, Board of Governors, Macaulay Land Use Research Institute, since 1987; Chairman, British Railways (Scottish) Board, 1988-93; Member, British Railways Board, 1988-94; honorary doctorate of technology, Napier University, 1998. Long Service Award, Royal Observer

Corps. Recreations: flying; shooting; travelling. Address: (h.) Balbuthie Farm, by Leven, Fife; T.-01333 730210.

Cameron, (John Roderick) Hector, LLB, NP. Solicitor; b. 11.6.47, Glasgow; m., Rosemary Brownlee; 1 s.; 1 d. Educ. High School of Glasgow; Friends School, Wigton; St. Andrews University. Admitted Solicitor, 1971; Partner, Bishop, Milne Boyd & Co., 1973; Chairman, Glasgow Junior Chamber of Commerce, 1981; Managing Partner, Bishop & Co., 1985; Partner, Dorman Jeffrey & Co., 1990; Director, Merchants House of Glasgow, 1986; Director, Glasgow Chamber of Commerce, 1987; Partner, Hector Cameron, Solicitor, 1993; Partner, Abercrombie Capital Partners LLP, 2005. Recreations: reading; sailing. Address: (h.) 2 Lancaster Crescent, Glasgow G12 0RR.

Cameron, Rev. Dr. John Urquhart, BA, BSc, PhD, BD, ThD. Minister, Parish of Broughty Ferry, since 1974; b. 10.6.43, Dundee; m., Jill Sjoberg; 1 s.; 1 d. Educ. Falkirk High School; St. Andrews University; Edinburgh University; University of Southern California. Marketing Executive, Beechams, London, 1969-73; Assistant Minister, Wellington Church, Glasgow, 1973-74; Chaplain, Royal Naval Reserve, 1976-81; Marketing Consultant, Pergamon Press, Oxford, 1977-81; Religious Education Department, Dundee High School, 1980-87; Sports Journalist and Travel Writer, Hill Publications, Surrey, 1981-2006; Physics Department, Dundee College of Further Education, 1987-95; Moderator, Presbytery of Dundee, 1993-94; Chaplain, Royal Caledonian Curling Club, 1980-95; Chaplain, Black Watch ACF, 1994-99. National and international honours in both summer and winter sports, 1960-85; sports scholarship, University of Southern California, 1962-64. Recreations: golf; skiing; curling. Address: St. Stephen's Manse, 33 Camperdown Street, Broughty Ferry; T.-01382 477403.

Cameron, Sheriff Lewis, MA, LLB. Solicitor, since 1962; Sheriff of South Strathclyde Dumfries and Galloway at Hamilton, 1994-2002, at Dumfries, 1988-94; b. 12.8.35, Glasgow; m., Sheila Colette Gallacher; 2 s.; 2 d. Educ. St. Aloysius College; Blairs College; St. Sulpice, Paris; Glasgow University. RAF, 1954-56; admitted Solicitor, 1962. Member, Legal Aid Central Committee, 1970-80; Legal Aid Secretary, Airdrie, 1978-87; Chairman, Social Security Appeal Tribunals, 1983-88; Dean, Airdrie Society of Solicitors, 1984-85; Tutor, Strathclyde University, 1981-88; Treasurer, Monklands Victim Support Scheme, 1983-88; Chairman: Dumfries and Galloway Family Conciliation Service, 1988-92, Dumfries and Galloway, Scottish Association for the Study of Delinquency, 1988-92; Member, Scotland Committee, National Children's Homes; Trustee, Oscar Marzaroli Trust; Chairman, PHEW, 1994-2000.

Cameron, William Ross, MB, ChB. Medical Director, NHS Borders, since 2003; b. 3.7.57, Glasgow; m., Hazel; 2 s.; 1 d. Educ. Hutchesons' Grammar School; Glasgow University. GP, 1983-2003; Medical Director, Borders Primary Care Trust, 2002-03. Chair, Borders Local Health Care Co-operative, 1999-2002. Address: (b.) NHS Borders, Newstead, Melrose TD6 9DB; T.-01896 828282.

Campbell, Aileen, MA Hons (Soc Sci). MSP (SNP), South of Scotland, since 2007; b. 16.5.80, Perth. Educ. Collace PS; Perth Academy; University of Glasgow. Researcher and Presiding Officer for Shona Robison MSP and Stewart Hosie MP, 2006-07; PA to Nicola Sturgeon MSP, 2005-06; Editorial Assistant, Scottish Standard, 2005; Editor, Construction Magazine, Keystone, 2004-05. Address: (b.) Scottish Parliament, Edinburgh EH99 1SP; T.-0131 348 6707; e-mail: aileen.campbell.msp@scottishparliament.uk

Campbell, Alan Grant, CBE, LLB. Chief Executive, Aberdeenshire Council, since 1995; b. 4.12.46, Aberdeen; m., Susan Black; 1 s.; 2 d. Educ. Aberdeen Grammar School; Aberdeen University. Admitted Solicitor, Scotland, 1970; various legal appointments, Aberdeen County Council, 1968-75, Grampian Regional Council: Assistant Director of Law and Administration, 1975-79, Depute Director, 1979-84, Director of Law and Administration, 1984-91, Chief Executive, 1991-95. Chairman, SOLACE (Scotland), 1997-99; Member: McCrone Committee, 2000, 21st Century Social Work Review Group, 2004; Hon. Doctorate of Laws, Aberdeen University, 2005. Recreations: competitive cycling and following the Tour de France; photography; wine; gardening. Address: Woodhill House, Westburn Road, Aberdeen AB16 5GB; T.-01224 665400.

Campbell, Alastair James, LLB. Partner, Mitchells Roberton, Solicitors, since 1985; b. 29.12.48, Glasgow; m., Pamela Crichton; 3 s. Educ. Merchiston Castle School, Edinburgh; University of Strathclyde. Qualified as Solicitor, 1972; Partner, Mackenzie Roberton & Co. (later Mitchells Roberton), 1975. Secretary, National Burns Homes, Mauchline, Ayrshire, since 1976; Clerk, Incorporation of Coopers of Glasgow, since 1999. Recreations: golf; hill walking; curling. Address: (b.) George House, 36 North Hanover Street, Glasgow G1 2AD; T.-0141-552 3422.

Campbell of Airds, Alastair Lorne, OStJ. Former Chief Executive, Clan Campbell; Archivist, Inveraray Castle, 1984-97; H.M. Unicorn Pursuivant of Arms, Court of the Lord Lyon, since 1987; b. 11.7.37, London; m., Mary-Ann Campbell-Preston; 3 s.; 1 d. Educ. Eton; R.M.A., Sandhurst. Regular Army, 1955-63 (commissioned Argyll and Sutherland Highlanders); Reid Pye and Campbell, 1963-71 (Managing Director, 1970-71); Waverley Vintners Ltd., 1972-83 (Marketing Director, 1972, Managing Director, 1977). Member: Queen's Bodyguard for Scotland (Royal Company of Archers), Chapter of Scottish Priory, Order of St John; FSA Scot; Patron, Armorial and Heraldry Society of Australasia; Chairman, Advisory Committee on Tartan to the Lord Lyon; Member, Council, National Trust for Scotland, 1996-2001; Honorary Research Fellowship, University of Aberdeen, 1996-2001. Publications: Two Hundred Years — The Highland Society of London; The Life and Troubled Times of Sir Donald Campbell of Ardnamurchan; The History of Clan Campbell – Vol. I. Recreations: painting; fishing; walking. Address: (h.) Inverawe Barn, Taynuilt, Argyll PA35 1HU; T.-01866 822207.

Campbell, Andrew Robertson, CBE, OBE, DL, FRAGS. Convener/Leader, Dumfries and Galloway Council, 1999-2005; Vice President, COSLA, 2003-07; b. 18.06.44, Castle Douglas; m., Maureen; 1s.; 1d. Educ. Loretto School. Farmer in partnership with wife and son; Director, Royal Highland Agricultural Society; Scottish Director, NFU Mutual Insurance Society; Past President, Castle Douglas Rotary; Board Member, SNH; Fellow, Royal Agricultural Society; Councillor, Dumfries and Galloway, 1995-2007; Board Member, Dumfries and Galloway Health Board. Recreations: rugby supporter and past player; country sports. Address: (h.) Whitecraigs, Whitepark Road, Castle Douglas DG7 1EX; T.-01556 502183.

Campbell, Christopher Robert James, LLB (Hons). Director of Legal Services and Deputy General Counsel, The Royal Bank of Scotland Group; b. Edinburgh; m., Kay; 1 s.; 1 d. Educ. Daniel Stewart's and Melville College; University of Edinburgh. Joined Dundas and Wilson, 1980: Assistant Solicitor, 1982, Partner, 1987, Partner in Charge of Glasgow Office, 1991, Managing Partner, 1996; joined RBS, 2005. Honorary Professor of Commercial Law, University of Glasgow. Recreations: golf; music; football. Address: (b.) The Royal Bank of Scotland Group, Business House F, PO Box 1000, Edinburgh EH12 1HO.

Campbell, Colin MacIver, MA (Hons). MSP (SNP), West of Scotland, 1999-2003; SNP Defence Spokesperson, 1995-2003; National Secretary, SNP, 1997-99; b. 31.8.38, Ralston, Paisley; m., Evelyn; 3 s. Educ. Paisley Grammar School; Glasgow University; Jordanhill College of Education. Teacher: Hillhead High School, 1961-63, Paisley Grammar School, 1963-67; Principal Teacher, Greenock Academy, 1967-73; Depute Head Teacher, Merksworth High, 1973-77; Head Teacher, Westwood Secondary, 1977-89; Tutor (part-time), Strathclyde University Senior Studies Institute, 1995-98. Member, Renfrewshire Council, 1995-99; General Election Candidate: 1987, 1992, 1997; Euro Candidate: 1989, 1994. Elder, Church of Scotland; Former Chairman, Kilbarchan Civic Society and Kilbarchan Community Council; Former Convener, Kilbarchan SNP; Past Convener, Renfrew West SNP. Publication: co-author, Can't Shoot a Man With a Cold, 2004. Recreation: military history. Address: (h.) Braeside, Shuttle Street, Kilbarchan PA10 2PR.

Campbell, Colin Malcolm, QC (Scot), LLB. Senator of the College of Justice in Scotland, since 2007; b. 1.10.53; m. Fiona Anderson; 1 s.; 1 d (and 1 daughter deceased). Educ. Grove Academy, Broughty Ferry; University of Dundee. Passed Advocate, 1977; Lecturer, Department of Scots Law, University of Edinburgh, 1977-79; Standing Junior Counsel: to Scottish Development Department (all matters other than Planning), 1984-86; to Scottish Development Department (Planning), 1986-90. Vice-Dean, Faculty of Advocates, 1997-2001 (Dean of Faculty, 2001-04). Part-time Member, Mental Welfare Commission for Scotland, 1997-2001; Member, Judicial Appointments Board for Scotland, 2002-05.

Campbell, David Ross, CBE, CMIM, FInstD. Chairman, NHS National Services Scotland, since 2004; Chairman and Director of a number of private companies; Chairman, Health Education Board for Scotland, 1995-2001; b. 27.9.43, Glasgow; m., Moira. Educ. Whitehill Senior Secondary School, Glasgow; James Watt Memorial College, Greenock. Officer, Merchant Navy, 1961-68; Sales Executive, 1968-69; various management positions, George Outram & Co. Ltd., 1969-73; Managing Director, Scottish & Universal Newspapers Ltd., 1974-84; Executive Director, Scottish & Universal Investments Ltd.; Chief Executive, Clyde Cablevision Ltd., 1982-84; Chairman and Chief Executive, West Independent Newspapers Ltd., 1984-94; Chairman, Saltire Holdings Ltd., 1991-93. Past President: Scottish Newspaper Proprietors Association, Glasgow Chamber of Commerce; Liveryman and Freeman, City of London; Regional Chairman, PSYBT. Recreations: golf; theatre; reading. Address: (h.) Summerlea, Summerlea Road, Seamill KA23 9HP.

Campbell, Donald. Writer; b. 25.2.40, Wick; m., Jean Fairgrieve; 1 s. Educ. Boroughmuir High School, Edinburgh. Playwright, essayist, lyricist and poet; stage plays include: The Jesuit, 1976; The Widows of Clyth, 1979; Blackfriars Wynd, 1980; Till All The Seas Run Dry, 1981; Howard's Revenge, 1985; Victorian Values, 1986; The Fisher Boy and the Honest Lass, 1990; The Ould Fella, 1993, Nancy Sleekit, 1994, Glorious Hearts, 1999; also active as writer and director in a number of community projects; script co-ordinator, The Dundee Mysteries, Dundee Rep; poetry includes: Rhymes 'n Reasons, 1972; Blether, 1979; Selected Poems: 1970-1990, 1990; Homage

To Rob Donn, 2007; other work includes: A Brighter Sunshine (theatre history), 1983, Playing for Scotland (theatre history), 1996, four television plays, 50 radio programmes, Cities of the Imagination - Edinburgh, 2003 (travel writing). Fellow in Creative Writing, Dundee University, 1987-89; William Soutar Fellow, Perth, 1991-93; Royal Literary Fund Fellow, Napier University, 2000-01; awards include: three Fringe Firsts; Silver Medal, 1983 New York Radio Festival for A Clydebuilt Man; Radio Industries Club Award for The Miller's Reel, 1987. Address: (h.) 85 Spottiswoode Street, Edinburgh EH9 1BZ; T.-0131-447 2305.

Campbell, Professor Donald Murray, BSc, PhD, FRSE, FInstP, FASA. Professor of Musical Acoustics, University of Edinburgh, since 2000; b. 20.10.42, Inverness; m., Dr. Patricia Campbell; 2 s.; 1 d. Educ. Dingwall Academy; University of Edinburgh. University of Edinburgh: Demonstrator, 1968-72, Lecturer, 1972-90, Senior Lecturer, 1990-2000. Publications: Books: Co-Author, 2 textbooks on Musical Instruments and Musical Acoustics; Medaille Etrangère of French Acoustical Society, 2000. Recreations: playing and conducting music. Address: (b.) School of Physics, University of Edinburgh, James Clerk Maxwell Building, Edinburgh EH9 3JZ; T.-0131-650-5262; e-mail: d.m.campbell@ed.ac.uk

Campbell, Doris Margaret, MD, FRCOG. Reader, Obstetrics and Gynaecology and Reproductive Physiology, Aberdeen University; b. 24.1.42, Aberdeen; m., Alasdair James Campbell; 1 s.; 1 d. Educ. Aberdeen High School for Girls; Aberdeen University. Resident house officer posts, Aberdeen, 1967-69; Research Fellow, Aberdeen University, 1969-73; Registrar in Obstetrics and Gynaecology, Aberdeen Hospitals, 1973-74; Lecturer in Obstetrics and Gynaecology and Physiology, Aberdeen University, 1974-84. Former Member, Scottish Women's Hockey Council. Recreations: bridge; badminton; guiding. Address: (h.) 77 Blenheim Place, Aberdeen; T.-01224 639984; e-mail: d.m.campbell@abdn.ac.uk

Campbell, Duncan, BA (Hons), MSc, Chartered MCIPD. Director of Corporate Services, National Library of Scotland, since 2004; b. 30.11.54, Dunfermline; m., Murdina; 1 d. Educ. Dunfermline High School; Heriot Watt University; University of Strathclyde. Address: (b.) National Library of Scotland, George IV Bridge, Edinburgh EH1 1EW.

Campbell, Edward James, MA, LLB. Managing Director, Campbell's Prime Meat Ltd., 1970-2006; b. 18.3.37, Edinburgh; m., Ellen; 2 s.; 2 d. Educ. Daniel Stewart's College, Edinburgh; Edinburgh University. Worked in family business (Campbell Brothers Ltd); started Campbell's Prime Meat Ltd., 1970. Recreations: reading; cinema; bridge; travel. Address: 6 Easter Belmont Road, Edinburgh EH12 6EX;T.-0131-337 7698.

Campbell, Fiona, BA (Hons), BMus. Executive Officer, Voluntary Arts Scotland, since 2000; b. 9.10.70, Wellington, New Zealand. Educ. Wellington East Girls College; Victoria University of Wellington. Press and Marketing Officer, National Association of Youth Orchestras, 1996-97, 1999; Project Administrator, SEAD, 1998-99. Member, Scottish Civic Forum Council; Director, SEAD; Treasurer, TMSA. Postgraduate Certificate in Cultural Policy and Management (Heriot Watt University, 2004). Recreations: traditional music, song and dance; musical theatre and opera; reading; craftwork; swimming and historical interests. Address: (b.) 54 Manor Place, Edinburgh EH3 7EH; T.-0131 225 7355.

Campbell, Hugh Hall, QC, BA (Hons), MA (Oxon), LLB (Hons), FCIArb. Queen's Counsel, since 1983; b. 18.2.44, Glasgow; m., Eleanor Jane Hare; 3 s. Educ. Glasgow Academy; Trinity College, Glenalmond; Exeter College, Oxford; Edinburgh University. Called to Scottish Bar, 1969; Standing Junior Counsel to Admiralty, 1976. Recreations: carnival, wine, music. Address: (h.) 12 Ainslie Place, Edinburgh EH3 6AS; T.-0131-225 2067.

Campbell, Rev. Dr. Iain Donald, MA, BD, MTh, PhD. Minister, Back Free Church of Scotland, Isle of Lewis, since 1995; b. 20.9.63, Stornoway; m., Anne M. Davidson; 2 s.; 1 d. Educ. Nicolson Institute, Stornoway; University of Glasgow; Free Church College. Minister, Snizort Free Church, Isle of Skye, 1988-95; Editor, The Instructor (Free Church of Scotland youth magazine), 1990-96; Editor, The Monthly Record of the Free Church of Scotland, 1996-2000; Review Editor, Scottish Bulletin of Evangelical Theology, since 2003. Publications: In Thy Likeness, 1990; Heart of the Gospel (Editor), 1995; The Doctrine of Sin, 1999; The Gospel According to Ruth, 2003; Heroes and Heretics, 2004; On the First Day of the Week, 2005. Recreations: reading; walking; scootering. Address: Free Church Manse, Vatisker, Isle of Lewis HS2 0LN; T.-01851 820317; e-mail: iaind@backfreechurch.co.uk

Campbell, Professor Ian, MA, PhD. Professor of Scottish and Victorian Literature, Edinburgh University, since 1992; b. 25.8.42, Lausanne, Switzerland. Educ. Lausanne; Findochty; Buckie; Mackie Academy, Stonehaven; Aberdeen University; Edinburgh University. Joined staff, English Department, Edinburgh University, 1967; Visiting Professor, Guelph, Duke, UCLA; Europa Professor, Mainz; Visiting Lecturer, United States, Canada, France, Switzerland, Italy, Japan. Publications: editorial team of Carlyle Letters, numerous books and articles on Scottish and Victorian Literature. Recreations: music; sport. Address: (b.) Department of English, Edinburgh University, David Hume Tower, George Square, Edinburgh, EH8 9JX; T.-0131-650 4284; e-mail: Ian.Campbell@ed.ac.uk

Campbell, Sir Ian, CBE, OStJ, VRD, JP. Deputy Chairman, Heath (Scotland) Ltd., 1987-95; Chairman, Select Assured Properties PLC, 1989-96; Director, Hermiston Securities, since 1990; b. 3.2.23, Edinburgh; m., Marion Kirkhope Shiel; 1 d. Educ. Daniel Stewart's College, Edinburgh. Royal Navy, 1942-46; Royal Naval Reserve, 1946-64 (retired with rank of Commander); John Line & Sons, 1948 61 (Area Manager, West of England); Managing Director, MacGregor Wallcoverings Ltd., 1965-77; Finance Director, Scottish Conservative Party, 1977-89. Director, Travel System Ltd., 1987-90; Councillor, City of Edinburgh, 1984-88; Member, Transport Users Consultative Committee for Scotland, 1981-87; Freeman, City of Glasgow, 1991. Recreations: golf; vintage cars; water colour painting. Address: (h.) Merleton, 10 Boswall Road, Edinburgh EH5 3RH; T.-0131-552 4825.

Campbell, Sir Ilay Mark, Bt, MA (Oxon). Director, High Craigton Farming Co.; b. 29.5.27, Edinburgh; m., Margaret Minette Rohais Anderson; 2 d. Educ. Eton; Christ Church, Oxford. Christie's: Scottish Agent, 1968, Joint Scottish Agent, 1973-92; Chairman, Christie's Scotland, 1978-96; Honorary Vice-President, Scotland's Garden Scheme; Trustee: Crarae Gardens Charitable Trust, 1978-2002, Tree Register of the British Isles, 1988-2006; Chairman, Church

Buildings Renewal Trust, 1993-98 (Trustee, 1993-2001); Past President, Association for the Protection of Rural Scotland; former Convener, Church of Scotland Committee on Artistic Matters; Member, Historic Buildings Council for Scotland, 1989-98; Member, Gardens Committee, National Trust for Scotland, 1995-2001; former Scottish Representative, National Arts Collection Fund. Recreations: heraldry; genealogy; collecting heraldic bookplates. Address: (h.) Crarae Lodge, Inveraray, Argyll PA32 8YA; T.-01546 86274/370.

Campbell, John David, QC, FCIArb. QC, Scotland, since 1998; Founder, Oracle Chambers, Scotland (2007); b. 4.5.49, Inverness; 2 s.; 3 d. Educ. Gordonstoun; Edinburgh University. Former Solicitor, 1972-78; Advocate, since 1981; Arbitrator, Acc'd Mediator, Reg'd Construction Adjudicator; Vice President, Chartered Institute of Arbitrators (2006). Publication: Scottish Planning Encyclopaedia (Contributor), 2001. Recreations: family; a Border Terrier; music; tennis; gardening. Address: (b.) Oracle Chambers, Catcune Steading, Gorebridge, Midlothian EH23 4RN; T.-0131-226-5071; e-mail: jcampbellqc@oraclechambers.com

Campbell, John Ivor, FCCA. Director of Corporate Resources, Scottish Borders Council, since 2001; b. 23.8.51, Galashiels; m., Sheila; 2 d. Educ. Kelso High School. Roxburgh County Council, 1970-75; Borders Regional Council, 1975-84; Chief Accountant, Fife Regional Council, 1984-86; Depute Director of Finance, Glenrothes Development Corporation, 1986-88; Director of Finance, Roxburgh District Council, 1988-96; Director of Financial Services, Scottish Borders Council, 1995-2001. Past President, Scottish Branch, Association of Chartered Certified Accountants; Member, ACCA International Assembly, 1997-2000; Chairman, CIPFA Scottish Branch Directors of Finance Section, 2000-01; Treasurer, Scottish Borders Tourist Board, 1989-2005. Address: (b.) Council Headquarters, Newtown St. Boswells, Melrose, TD6 0SA; T.-01835 824000.

Campbell, Mary Theresa MacLeod, OBE, BA, CA. Managing Director, Blas Limited, since 2002; Member, Board of the UHI Millennium Institute; Non-executive Director, Dunfermline Building Society; b. 24.2.59, Glasgow; 2 d.; 2 s. Educ. Lochaber High School; University of Stirling. Ernst and Young,1980-86; Noble Group Limited, 1986-98; British Linen Bank Ltd., 1998-99. Founding Director, British Linen Advisers Ltd., 1999-2002; Recreations: literature; theatre; opera; Barra. Address: (b.) Blas Limited, 1 Rutland Square, Edinburgh EH1 2AS; e-mail: mary.campbell@ blaslimited.co.uk

Campbell, Melfort Andrew, OBE, FRSA. Chief Executive Officer, Imes Group Ltd., since 1997; b. 6.6.56, Exeter; m., Lucy Nickson; 3 d. Educ. Ampleforth College, York. Director, Imes Ltd and Buchan Inspection Ltd; past Chairman, CBI Scotland; Governor, RGU; Director, Scottish Enterprise Grampian. Recreations: fishing; shooting; rugby; tennis. Address: (b.) Campus 3 Science Park, Balgownie Drive, Bridge of Don AB22 8GW; T.-01224 705777; e-mail: melfort.campbell@imes-group.com

Campbell, Niall Gordon, BA. Under Secretary, Civil and Criminal Law Group, Scottish Executive Justice Department, (formerly Scottish Office Home Department) 1997-2001; b. 9.11.41, Peebles; m., Alison M. Rigg; 3 s. Educ. Edinburgh Academy; Merton College, Oxford. Entered Scottish Office 1964; Assistant Secretary, 1978; various posts in Scottish Education Department and

Scottish Development Department; Under Secretary, Social Work Services Group, 1989-97. Member, Parole Board for Scotland, since 2003; Chairman, SACRO, 2002-07; Chairman, Scottish Association for the Study of Offending, 2001-06; Council of the British Trust for Ornithology, since 2006. Address (h.) 15 Warriston Crescent, Edinburgh.

Campbell, Peter, MA (Hons), MEd. Rector, Mackie Academy, Stonehaven, since 2000; b. 30.10.53, Aberdeen; m., Isabel McIntyre; 1 s.; 1 d. Educ. Robert Gordon's College, Aberdeen; Aberdeen University. Teacher of English, Fraserburgh Academy; Learning Support Teacher, Fraserburgh Academy and South Park Primary; Principal Teacher of Learning Support, Speyside High School, Aberlour; Principal Teacher of Learning Support, Cults Academy, Aberdeen; Assistant Head Teacher, Torry Academy, Aberdeen; Depute Rector, Kemnay Academy. Elder, Peterculter Parish Church. Publication: The Environment, 1985. Recreations: reading; music; walking; chess; golf; travelling. Address: (b.) Mackie Academy, Slug Road, Stonehaven, Kincardineshire; T.-01569 762071.

Campbell, (Robert) Mungo (McCready), BA, MPhil, FRSA. Deputy Director, Hunterian Museum & Art Gallery, University of Glasgow, since 1997; b. 8.10.59, Newcastle upon Tyne; m., Teresa Margaret Green; 1 s.; 1 d. Educ. Royal Grammar School, Newcastle upon Tyne; University of Durham; University of Glasgow. Assistant Keeper, National Gallery of Scotland, Edinburgh, 1987-97; Member, Scottish Arts Council Visual Arts Committee, 1998-2003; Board Member: SCRAN, 2004-06, Scottish Museums Council; Chair, VAGA Scotland, 2005-07. Recreations: island life; walking with my children; cooking good food; eating good food. Address: (b.) Hunterian Art Gallery, 82 Hillhead Street, Glasgow G12 8QQ; T.-0141-330 4735.

Campbell, Rev. Roderick D.M., TD, BD, FSA Scot, FFCS. Minister, Parish Church of St Andrew and St George, Edinburgh, since 2003; Member, Board of World Mission, Episcopal Church of Sudan, 1999-2003; Chaplain, 3rd (Volunteer) Battalion The Royal Highland Fusiliers; Staff Chaplain, TA Army HQ, Scotland, since 1997; Member, Board of World Mission, Church of Scotland, since 1999; b. 1.8.43, Glasgow; m., Susan Norman; 2 d. Educ. Daniel Stewart's College, Edinburgh; Arbroath High School; Jordanhill College of Education; New College, Edinburgh University. Teacher, Technical Subjects, Glasgow, Tanzania and London, 1967-70; Associate Minister, St. Andrew's, Nairobi, 1975-78; Minister, Mearns Parish Church, 1979-97; Chieftain, Caledonian Society of Kenya, 1978; founder Member, Ndugu Society of Kenya, 1975. Convener, Lodging House Mission, Glasgow Presbytery, 1981-86; Convener, National Church Extension Committee, Church of Scotland, 1987-89; Deacon, Incorporation of Barbers, Trades House, Glasgow, 1992-93; Vice Chairman, Greater Glasgow Health Board, 1994-96 (Member, 1989-96); Chairman, Greater Glasgow Drug Action Team, 1995-97; Chairman, Victoria Infirmary NHS Trust, 1997-99. Recreations: swimming; horse-riding; hill-walking; fishing. Address: 22 Greenlaw Road, Newton Mearns, Glasgow G77 6ND; T.-0141 639 7328.

Campbell, Stewart, BSc, DipSH. Health and Safety Executive Director, Scotland, since 2001; b. 9.4.48, Bridge of Allan; m., Susan; 2 s. Educ. McLaren High School, Callander; Glasgow University. HM Inspector of Health and Safety, since 1973; Nuffield and Leverhulme Travelling Fellowship, 1983-84; Member: Scottish Criminal Cases Review Commission, Partnership on Health and Safety in Scotland; Trustee, Psoriasis

Association. Publication: Labour Inspection in the European Community. Recreations: golf; hill-walking; genealogy. Address: (b.) Belford House, 59 Belford Road, Edinburgh EH4 3UE; T.-0131 247 2006; e-mail: stewart.campbell@hse.gsi.gov.uk

Campbell, Thomas Ritchie, CA, MIPA, FABRP, MAE; b. 7.5.40, Dunfermline; m., Doreen; 1 s.; 1 d. Educ. Daniel Stewart's College, Edinburgh. Qualified as CA, 1963; joined T. Hunter Thomson, Edinburgh, 1966; assumed as a Partner, 1968; appointed Senior Partner, 1984; Chairman, UK 200 Group of Practising Chartered Accountants, 1994-97. President, Scottish Badminton Union, 1993-95; Member, Executive Committee, Scottish Sports Association, 1990 -2002 (Chairman, 1996-2002); Vice-President, European Badminton Union, since 2003; Member, Scottish Sports Council, 1998-2006. Elder, Church of Scotland. Recreations: golf; travel; hill-walking; reading. Address: (h.) 1 Pitbauchlie Bank, Dunfermline KY11 8DP; T.-01383 725516.

Campbell, Rt. Hon. Sir (Walter) Menzies, CBE (1987), PC, QC, MA, LLB. MP (Liberal Democrat), North East Fife, since 1987; Advocate, since 1968; Queen's Counsel, since 1982; Leader, Liberal Democrats, 2006-07; Liberal Democrat Shadow Foreign Secretary, 2001-06; Deputy Leader, Liberal Democrats, 2003-06; Member, Parliamentary Assembly of OSCE, 1992-1997; Member, North Atlantic Assembly, since 1989; b. 22.5.41, Glasgow; m., Elspeth Mary Urquhart. Educ. Hillhead High School, Glasgow; Glasgow University; Stanford University, California. President, Glasgow University Union, 1964-65; took part in Olympic Games, Tokyo, 1964; AAA 220-yards champion, 1964, 1967; Captain, UK athletics team, 1965, 1966; 1966 Commonwealth Games, Jamaica; UK 100-metres record holder, 1967-74. Advocate Depute, 1977-80; Standing Junior Counsel to the Army in Scotland, 1980-82. Parliamentary candidate (Liberal): Greenock and Port Glasgow, February, 1974, and October, 1974, East Fife, 1979, North East Fife, 1983; Chairman, Scottish Liberal Party, 1975-77; Member, Select Committee on Defence, 1992-99; Party Spokesman on Defence, Foreign Affairs and Sport, until 1997, Foreign Affairs and Defence, 1997-2001; Member: UK Sports Council, 1965-68; Scottish Sports Council, 1971-81; Chairman, Royal Lyceum Theatre, Edinburgh, 1984-87; Member, Broadcasting Council for Scotland, 1984-87. Honorary Degrees: DUniv Glasgow University, 2001; LLD Strathclyde University, 2005; LLD St. Andrews 2006; Chancellor of St. Andrews University, since 2006. Recreations: all sports; music; theatre. Address: (b.) House of Commons, London SW1A 0AA; T.-0171-219 4446.

Campbell, William Kilpatrick, MA (Hons). Director, Mainstream Publishing, since 1978; b. 1.3.51, Glasgow; 2 d. Educ. Kilmarnock Academy; Edinburgh University. Postgraduate research, Universities of Edinburgh and California; world travel, 1975; Publications Manager, Edinburgh University Student Publications, 1976-78. Publications: Alternative Edinburgh (Co-Editor), 1972; Another Edinburgh, 1976. Recreations: soccer; tennis; rugby; wine; books; people. Address: (b.) 7 Albany Street, Edinburgh EH1 3UG; T.-0131-557 2959; e-mail: bill.campbell@mainstreampublishing.com

Campbell-Gibson, Lt.Comdr. R.N. (Ret.) Hugh Desmond; b. 18.8.24; m., Deirdre Wilson; 2 s.; 1 d. Educ. Royal Naval College, Dartmouth. Naval cadet, 1937-41; served Royal Navy, 1941-60; war service convoy duties, Atlantic and Mediterranean; farmed Glenlussa, by Campbeltown, 1960-68; farmed and ran hotel, Dunmor, Seil, Argyll, 1969-83; latterly managed family woodlands at

Melfort. Recreations: gardening; fishing; local and family history. Address: (h.) Tighnamara, Melfort, Kilmelford, Argyll; T.-Kilmelford 224.

Campsie, Alistair Keith, SDA. Author, Journalist and Piper; b. 27.1.29, Inverness; m., Robbie Anderson; 2 s.; 1 d. Educ. West Sussex High School; Lanark Grammar School; West of Scotland College of Agriculture. Inspector of Agriculture, Sudan Government Service, 1949; Cocoa Survey Officer, Nigeria, 1951; experimental staff, National Institute of Agricultural Engineering (Scotland), 1953; Country Editor, Weekly Scotsman, 1954; Sub-Editor, Verse Writer, Scottish Daily Mail, 1955; Founder Editor, East African Farmer and Planter, 1956; Chief Sub-Editor, Weekly Scotsman, 1957; designed and appointed first Editor, Geneva Weekly Tribune, 1958; Chief Feature Writer, Scottish Daily Mail, 1959; Columnist, Science Correspondent and Senior Writer, Scottish Daily Express, 1962-73; founded The Piper's Press, 1988; two Scottish Arts Council writer's bursaries; two SAC publisher's awards. Publications: Poems and a Pibroch (with Hugh MacDiarmid), 1972; By Law Protected, 1976; The MacCrimmon Legend or The Madness of Angus Mackay, 1980; We Bought a County Pub (under pen-name Alan Mackinnon), 1984; Perfect Poison, 1985; Pibroch: the tangled Web (radio series), 1985; Dundas or How They Murdered Robert Burns (play): Edinburgh Festival Fringe First, 1987; The Clarinda Conspiracy, 1989; The True Story of the Ball of Kirriemuir, 1989; Cary Grant Stopped Me Smoking, 1991; Hunt Down a Prince, 1994; forced to abandon writing books, 1995-2005; Burns, The Political Prisoner, 2007; The MacCrimmon Scam, 2007; e-book (www.piperspress.com). Recreations: bagpipes (playing and composing); good whisky; self-important people. Address: No. 1 Nether Woodston Cottages, St. Cyrus, DD10 0DG; T.-01674 850838; e-mail: alistaircampsie@talktalk.net

Canavan, Dennis, BSc (Hons), DipEd. MSP (Independent), Falkirk West, 1999-2007; b. 8.8.42, Cowdenbeath. Educ. St. Bride's and St. Columba's Schools, Cowdenbeath; Edinburgh University. Principal Teacher of Mathematics, St. Modan's High School, Stirling, 1970-74; Assistant Head, Holyrood High School, Edinburgh, 1974; Leader, Labour Group, Stirling District Council, 1974; MP, West Stirlingshire, 1974-83; MP, Falkirk West, 1983-2000; Chair: Scottish Parliamentary Labour Group, 1980-81, PLP Northern Ireland Committee, 1989-97; Member: Foreign Affairs Select Committee, 1982-97, British–Irish Inter-Parliamentary Body, 1992-2000, International Development Select Committee, 1997-99; Scottish Parliament European and External Relations Committee, 1999-2007; Convener, All-Party Sports Group, Scottish Parliament, 1999-2007; President of Ramblers Scotland, since 2007; Trustee of the Scottish Mining Museum, since 2007; Honorary President, Milton Amateurs Football Club. Recreations: long distance running; hill-walking; horse riding; swimming; football (former Scottish Universities football internationalist).

Candlish, Kenneth Henry, BL, JP, DL. Retired Solicitor; Deputy Lieutenant, Berwickshire; b. 22.8.24, Edinburgh; m., Isobel Robertson-Brown; 2 d. Educ. George Watson's; Edinburgh University. Depute County Clerk, West Lothian, 1951-64; County Clerk, Berwickshire, 1964-75. Recreations: photography; music. Address: (h.) The Elms, Duns, Berwickshire; T.-Duns 883298.

Canning, Very Rev. Bernard John Canon, FSA Scot. Paisley Diocesan Archivist, since 1983; b. 30.3.32, Derry. Educ. St. Eugene's Boys' School, Derry; St. Columb's College, Derry; St. Kieran's College, Kilkenny. Ordained Priest for the Diocese of Paisley, 1956; Assistant: St.

James's, Renfrew, 1956-68, St Fergus', Paisley, 1968-74, St Laurence's, Greenock, 1974-87; Parish Priest: Christ the King, Howwood, and Our Lady of Fatima, Lochwinnoch, 1987-95, St James's, Paisley, 1995-96, St. John the Baptist's, Port Glasgow, 1996-99, St. Thomas's, Neilston, 1999-2007; retired 2007. Hon. Canon, Paisley Cathedral Chapter, 1989, full Member, 2001; Member, Editorial Board, The Parish Magazine & Journal, Glasgow, 1962-74; first Press Officer, Paisley Diocese, 1964-88; Member, Board of Governors, National Catholic Press Office, 1968-87. Publications include: Joy and Hope: St. Fergus', Paisley, 1971; A Building from God: St James's, Renfrew 1877-1977, 1977; Padraig H. Pearse and Scotland, 1979; Irish-born Secular Priests in Scotland 1829-1979, 1979; Adventure in Faith: St Ninian's, Gourock 1880-1980, 1980; The Living Stone: St Aloysius', Springburn 1882-1982, 1982; Instruments of His Work : Little Sisters of the Poor, Greenock 1884-1984, 1984; St. Mungo's, Ladyburn, Greenock 1935-1985, 1985; The Charleston Story: St Charles', Paisley, 1986; Bishops of Ireland 1870-1987, 1987; St. Fillan's, Houston 1841-1991, 1991; St. Mary's, Paisley 1891-1991, 1991; The Poor Sisters of Nazareth & Derry 1892-1992, 1992; St Colm's Church, Kilmacolm, 1992; Bishop Neil Farren, Bishop of Derry 1893-1980, 1993; St John the Baptist Parish, Port Glasgow, 1846-1996, 1996; Diocese of Paisley, 1947-1997, 2001; The Street That Is Gone But Lives On, 2001; Derry City Cemetery 1853-2003, 2003; Bishop John Keys O'Doherty of Derry, 1889-1907, 2007. Recreation: historical research. Address: (b.) 18 Royal Street, Gourock PA19 1PN.

Cannon, Steven, MA (Hons). Secretary, Aberdeen University, since 1998; b. 19.12.57, Keighley; m., Joyce. Educ. St. Bedes Grammar School, Bradford; Dundee University. Administrative Assistant, then Admissions Officer, Warwick University, 1983-86; Financial and Administration Manager, Warwick University Science Park, 1986-88; Financial Manager, Ninewells Hospital and Medical School, Dundee, 1988-93; College Secretary, Duncan of Jordanstone College of Art, 1993-94; Deputy Secretary, Dundee University, 1994-96; Secretary to the Council and Director of Finance and Central Services, Scottish Higher Education Funding Council, 1996-98. Recreations: family interests; golf; cricket; music. Address: (b.) Kings College, University of Aberdeen, Aberdeen AB24 3FX

Cantlay, Michael Brian, BA, MBA, DUniv (Stirling). Chair and Managing Director, William Glen Ltd; Convener, Loch Lomond and Trossachs National Park; Chair, Forth Valley College; President, William Glen and & Son, San Francisco; President, Cairngorm Scottish Imports, Toronto; b. 2.2.64, Galashiels; m., Linda. Educ. McLaren High School, Callander; Strathclyde University. Chair, Callander Community Council, 1992-93; Chair, Scottish Enterprise Forth Valley, 1995-2001; Advisory Board Member, Scottish Enterprise, 2000-02; Deputy Chair, VisitScotland, 2001-05. Address: Callandrade, Callander, Perthshire FK17 8HW.

Cantley, Maurice, OBE, BSc, PhD. Innovations Advisor, Innovators Counselling and Advisory Service for Scotland; b. 6.6.37, Cambuslang; m., Rosalind Diana Jones; 2 d. Educ. Bedford Modern and Bristol Grammar; Bristol University. Unilever Ltd., 1961-67; McCann Erickson Advertising, London, 1967-76; Director of Recreation and Tourism, Tayside Regional Council, 1976-82; Head of Tourism, HIDB, 1982-85; Marketing Director, Highlands and Islands Development Board, 1985-91. Director, Highlands and Islands Enterprise, 1991-99; Hon. Education Officer, Society of Cosmetic Chemists of GB, 1963-66; Chairman, Association of Directors of Recreation, Leisure and Tourism, 1980-82. Recreations: classical music; cycling; sea kayaking; crosswords. Address: (h.)

Oldshorebeg, Kinlochbervie, Sutherland IV27 4RS; T.-01971 521257; e-mail: mauricecan@cali.co.uk

Caplan, Lady (Joyce Caplan), DipEd. President, Friends of University Library, Edinburgh, since 2002; Chair, Poetry Association of Scotland, since 2002; Chair, Scottish Poetry Library, since 2004; b. 21.2.46; m.,1. David Leigh (d. 1970); 2. Lord Caplan; 1 d. Educ. Dale School, Nottingham; Clifton College, Nottingham. Primary School Teacher/Assistant Head, 1967-75; Member of Children's Panel, 1978-81; Governor, Lomond School, Helensburgh, 1985-89; Chairman: Play in Scottish Hospitals, 1990-96, Smiths Place Group, 1992-95, Scottish Play Council, 1992-95, Board, Children's Classic Concerts, since 1999; Chair, Snowball Trust, since 2000; Chairman, Couple Counselling Scotland, 1997-2001; Lecturer, Edinburgh University, since 1980. Recreations: books; music; friends; paintings; poetry. Address: (h.) Nether Liberton House, Old Mill Lane, Edinburgh EH16 5TZ.

Caplan, Hon. Lord (Philip Isaac Caplan), MA, LLB, LLD(Hon), QC. Senator of the College of Justice, 1989-2000; b. 24.2.29, Glasgow; m., Joyce Stone (2nd m.); 2 s.; 2 d. Educ. Eastwood School; Glasgow University. Solicitor, 1952-56; called to Bar, 1957; Standing Junior Counsel to Accountant of Court, 1964-70; Chairman, Plant Varieties and Seeds Tribunal, Scotland, 1977-79; Sheriff of Lothian and Borders, at Edinburgh, 1979-83; Sheriff Principal of North Strathclyde, 1983-88; Member, Sheriff Courts Rules Council, 1984-88; Commissioner, Northern Lighthouse Board, 1983-88; Chairman, Scottish Association for the Study of Delinquency, 1985-89; Honorary Life Patron, Scottish Association for the Study of Offending, since 2006; Member, Advisory Council on Messengers at Arms and Sheriff Officers, 1987-88; Chairman, Family Mediation Scotland, 1989-94; Honorary President, since 1994; Chairman, James Powell UK Trust (1992-2005), FRPS (1988), AFIAP (1985). Recreations: photography; bridge; music; reading. Address: (b.) Nether Liberton House, Old Mill Lane, Edinburgh.

Carbery, Emeritus Professor Thomas Francis, OBE, KSG, FRSA, MSc, PhD, DBA, DPA. Former Professor, Strathclyde Business School, Strathclyde University; Member, Board of Directors, Energy Action Scotland, 1996-2005; Consultant, since 2005; b. 18.1.25, Glasgow; m., Ellen Donnelly; 1 s.; 2 d. Educ. St. Aloysius' College, Glasgow; Glasgow University; Scottish College of Commerce. Cadet navigator/ meteorologist, RAF, 1943-47; civil servant, 1947-61; Lecturer, then Senior Lecturer, Scottish College of Commerce, 1961-64; Strathclyde University: Senior Lecturer in Government-Business Relations, 1964-75, Head, Department of Office Organisation, 1975-79, Professor of Office Organisation, 1979-85, Professor of Business Information, 1985-88; part-time Professor of Marketing, 1988-90. Member: Independent Broadcasting Authority, 1970-79, Broadcasting Complaints Commission, 1981-86, Royal Commission on Gambling, 1975-77, Transport Users Consultative Committee (Chairman, Scottish TUCC), 1975-81, Scottish Consumer Council (latterly Vice-Chairman), 1976-84, Scottish Legal Aid Board, 1986-92, Data Protection Tribunal, 1985-99, Church of Scotland Committee on Higher Education, 1986-87, Press Council, 1987-90; Chairman, Scottish Transport Research Group, 1983-87; Chairman, South of Scotland Consumers Committee/Office of Electricity Regulation, 1990-95; Chairman, Strathclyde University Inter-denominational Chaplaincy Committee, 1981-87; Joint Editor, Bulletin of Society for Co-operative Studies, 1967-95; Member (former Chairman), Scottish Catholic Communications Commission, 1982-2006; Member, Scottish Catholic Education Commission, 1980-93. Recreations: conversation; watching television; spectating at association football; listening to Radio 4. Address: (h.) 24 Fairfax Avenue, Glasgow, G44 5AL; T.-0141-637 0514.

Cardownie, Steve. Deputy Leader of the City of Edinburgh Council (formerly Deputy Lord Provost); b. 1.6.53, Leith; m.; 2 s. Educ. Leith Academy; Telford College. Civil service; National Executive Committee Member, CPSA, five years; Councillor, Edinburgh, since 1988; Director: Edinburgh Military Tattoo (Charities) Ltd, Edinburgh Military Tattoo Ltd, Edinburgh International Festival Council; Festival and Events Champion; Employment Tribunal Member, since 1981; Member, COSLA; Chair, Edinburgh Waterfront Ltd. Recreations: hill-walking; running; Heart of Midlothian FC; theatre; reading; fine wines and travelling. Address: (b.) City Chambers, High Street, Edinburgh; T.-0131-529 3266; e-mail: steve.cardownie@edinburgh.gov.uk

Carey, Professor Frank A., BSc, MD, FRCPath. Professor and Consultant Pathologist, since 1995; Clinical Leader, Scottish Pathology Network, since 2005; b. 5.7.61, Cork, Ireland; m., Dr Julie Curran; 1 s.; 1 d. Educ. University College, Cork. Senior House Officer, Cork University Hospital, 1986-87; Registrar in Pathology, Royal Infirmary of Edinburgh, 1987-89; Senior Registrar, Royal Infirmary of Edinburgh, 1989-95; Consultant, Tayside University Hospitals, since 1995. Member, Scottish Council, Royal College of Pathologists. Address: (b.) Department of Pathology, Ninewells Hospital and Medical School, Dundee DD1 9SY; T.-01382 632548.

Cargill, Kenneth George, MA, LLB. Director, UK Media Projects, 2003-07; Member of Court, University of Abertay; b. 17.2.47, Arbroath; m., Una Gallacher. Educ. Arbroath High School; Edinburgh University. BBC TV Scotland: Researcher, Current Affairs, 1972; Reporter, Current Account, 1973; Film Director, Public Account, 1978; Producer, Current Account, 1979, Agenda, 1981, People and Power (London), 1983; Editor of the day, Reporting Scotland, 1983; Editor, Scotland 2000, 1986-87; Deputy Editor, News and Current Affairs, Television, 1984-88; Head of TV News, Current Affairs and Sport, 1988-94, Head of News and Current Affairs, 1994-99; Project Executive, Pacific Quay Project, BBC Scotland, 1999-2002; Visiting Professor in Journalism, University of Strathclyde, 2000-05; Honorary Professor, Politics Department, University of Glasgow, 2000-05. Publication: Scotland 2000 (Editor), 1987. Recreations: Havana cigars, malt whisky; reading about UK and US politics and journalism; getting to grips with Spanish subjunctives and builders while renovating a house in Spain. E-mail: kencargill@yahoo.co.uk

Carlaw, Jackson. MSP (Conservative), West of Scotland, since 2007; b. 12.4.59. Address: (b.) Scottish Parliament, Edinburgh EH99 1SP; Constituency Office: 69 Ayr Road, Newton Mearns, Glasgow G77 6SP.

Carlisle, Elva A.M., MA. National Convener, Church of Scotland Guild, 2000-01; b. 27.5.35, Linlithgow; m., Dr J.M. Carlisle (deceased); 2 s. Educ. Marr College, Troon; Glasgow University. Teacher in Ayrshire and Glasgow until early retirement, 1992; Elder, Church of Scotland. Recreations: reading; doing crosswords; opera; visiting other countries. Address: (h.) 117 Fotheringay Road, Glasgow G41 4LG; T.-0141-423 4554.

Carloway, Hon. Lord (Colin John MacLean Sutherland). Senator of the College of Justice, since 2000; b. 20.5.54; m., Jane Alexander Turnbull; 2 s. Educ. Edinburgh Academy; Edinburgh University (LLB Hons). Advocate, 1977; Advocate Depute, 1986-89; QC (Scot), 1990. Treasurer, Faculty of Advocates, 1994-2000. Address: (b.) Parliament House, Edinburgh, EH1 1RQ.

Carlyle, Robert, OBE. Actor and Director; b. 14.4.61; m., Anastasia Shirley. Trained, RSAMD; Duncan Macrae Memorial Prize for Scots verse. Credits include: (film) The Full Monty, Carla's Song, Trainspotting, Riff Raff (European film of the year), Priest, Plunkett and MacLeane, Ravenous, The Beach, Angela's Ashes, The World Is Not Enough, There's Only One Jimmy Grimble, To End All Wars, 51st State, Once Upon a Time in the Midlands, Black and White, Dead Fish, Marilyn Hotchkiss Ballroom Dancing and Charm School, The Mighty Celt, Eragon, 28 Weeks Later, Flood, Stone of Destiny, The Meat Trade; (television) Hitler, The Rise of Evil, 2003; Gunpowder, Treason and Plot, 2004; Class of '76, 2005; Human Trafficking, 2005; Hamish Macbeth (title role), 2005; Born Equal, 2006; The Last Enemy, 2008; Flood, 2008; (theatre) Twelfth Night, Cuttin' A Rug, Othello; (television and theatre) Go Now, Face; as Director of Rain Dog Theatre Company: Wasted, One Flew Over the Cuckoo's Nest (Paper Boat Award), Conquest of the South Pole, Macbeth (Paper Boat Award); Best Actor: Evening Standard Film Awards, 1998; Film Critics' Circle Awards, 1998, Bowmore Whisky/Scottish Screen Awards, 2001, Michael Elliott Awards, 2001; David Puttnam Patrons Award. Patron of School For Life Romania, Charity No. 1062953. Address: c/o ICM, Oxford House, 76 Oxford Street, London W1N 0AX.

Carmichael, Alexander Morrison (Alistair), MP. Liberal Democrat MP, Orkney and Shetland, since 2001; b. 15.7.65; m., Kathryn Jane; 2 s. Educ. Islay High School; Aberdeen University. Hotel manager, 1984-89; Procurator Fiscal Depute, Crown Office, Edinburgh and Aberdeen, 1993-96; solicitor in private practice, 1996-2001. Address: (b.) House of Commons, London SW1A 0AA.

Carmichael, Ian Henry Buist, MA (Hons), LLB. Advocate, since 1973; b. 17.5.25, Dundee; m., Jean Davidson; 2 d. Educ. High School of Dundee; Edinburgh University. Army, 1943-47; Solicitor, Dundee, 1951-57; Advocate, 1957-60; Solicitor, Glasgow, 1960-64; Procurator Fiscal Depute, latterly Senior Depute, Glasgow, 1964-85; readmitted, Faculty of Advocates, 1973; Senior Depute in change of Deaths Unit, Glasgow, 1982-85; Advocate in private practice, 1985-2006, then non-practising. Publication: Sudden Deaths and Fatal Accident Inquiries, 3rd Edition, 2005. Recreations: music; photography. Address: (h.) 4 Fleurs Avenue, Glasgow G41 5BE.

Carmichael, (Katherine) Jane, MA (Mod Hist). Director of Collections, National Museums of Scotland, since 2003; b. 12.3.52; m., Adrian Craxton; 1 step son; 2 d.; 2 step daughters. Educ. St. Leonards; St. Andrews; Edinburgh University. Imperial War Museum, 1974-2003: Keeper of Photographic Archive, 1982-95, Director of Collections, 1995-2003. Served various committees of National Museums Directors Conf., since 1995. FRSA, 2000. Publications: 1st World War Photographers, 1989; contributed to various journal articles. Recreations: the family; country walking; going to the ballet. Address: (b.) National Museums of Scotland, Chambers Street, Edinburgh EH1 1JF; T.-0131 247 4415; e-mail: j.carmichael@nms.ac.uk

Carmichael of Carmichael (Richard John). 26th Baron of Carmichael, since 1980; 30th Chief of Name and Arms of Carmichael, since 1981; Chartered Accountant; Farmer; b. 1.12.48, Stamford; m., Patricia Margaret Branson; 1 s.; 2 d. Educ. Hyton Hill Preparatory School; Kimbolton School; Coventry College of Technology. Audit Senior, Coopers and Lybrand, Tanzania, 1972; Audit Manager, Granger Craig Tunnicliffe, Tauranga, New Zealand, 1974; ACA, 1971; FCA, 1976; Factor/Owner, Carmichael Estate, 1980; Director: Carmichael Heritage Leisure Ltd.; claims family titles: Earldom of Hyndford, Viscountcies of Inglisberry and Nemphlar, and Lordship Carmichael of Carmichael. Member, Standing Council of Scottish Chiefs; New Zealand Orienteering Champion, 1977; Senior Event Advisor, World Masters Games 2005 Orienteering. Recreations: orienteering; skiing; Clan Carmichael Association. Address: Carmichael House, Carmichael, by Biggar, Lanarkshire ML12 6PG; T.-01899 308336.

Carnegy of Lour, Baroness (Elizabeth Patricia), DL. Life Peer, since 1982; b. 28.4.25. Educ. Downham School. Cavendish Laboratory, Cambridge, 1943-46; Girl Guides Association: Training Adviser for Scotland, 1958-62 and for Commonwealth HQ, 1963-65; co-opted Angus County Council Education Committee, 1967-75; Councillor, Tayside Regional Council, 1974-82; Chairman, Education Committee, 1976-82; Chairman, Working Party on Professional Training in Community Education Scotland, 1975-77; Commissioner, Manpower Services Commission, 1979-82, and Chairman, Committee for Scotland, 1980-83; Member, Scottish Economic Council, 1980-92; President for Scotland, Girl Guides Association, 1979-89; Member, Scottish Council for Tertiary Education, 1979-84; Chairman, Scottish Council for Community Education, 1980-88; Member, Council and Finance Committee, Open University, 1984-96; Member, Court, St. Andrews University, 1991-96; Honorary Sheriff, 1969-84; Deputy Lieutenant, 1988-2001; Fellow, Royal Society of Arts, 1987; Honorary LLD: Dundee University, 1991, University of St. Andrews, 1997; Honorary DUniv, Open University, 1998. Address: (h.) Lour, Forfar, Angus DD8 2LR; T.-01307 82 237.

Carr, Professor Chris, MA, PhD, DMS, ACMA, CEng, MIMechE. Professor of Corporate Strategy, Edinburgh University, since 1999; b.13.8.51, Brentwood; m., Jennifer Munro; 1s.; 1d. Educ. Harrow; Trinity Hall, University of Cambridge; Warwick University. Early career in industry with British Aerospace, GKN; Lecturer: Buckingham University; Warwick University; Bath University; Senior Lecturer/Associate Research Director, Manchester Business School; Visiting Professor, International Business, Witten-Herdecke University, Germany; teaching posts: HEC, France; University of Carlos III, Spain; overseas teaching experience in USA, India, China, Turkey, Russia. Publications: Britain's Competitiveness, 1990; Strategic Investment Decisions, 1994; numerous articles in academic journals including the Strategic Management Journal. Recreations: politics; tennis; sailing; golf. Address: (b.) Edinburgh University Management School, William Robertson Building, 50 George Square, Edinburgh EH8 9JY; T.-0131-650 6307; e-mail: Chris.Carr@ed.ac.uk

Carr, John Roger, CBE, JP, FRICS. Chairman, Countryside Commission for Scotland, 1985-92 (Member, since 1979, Vice-Chairman, 1984-85); b. 18.1.27, Ackworth, Yorkshire; m., Catherine Elise Dickson Smith; 2 s. Educ. Ackworth & Ayton (Quaker) School. Royal Marines, 1944-47; Gordon Highlanders TA, 1950-55; Factor, Walker Scottish Estates Co., Ballater; Factor, subsequently Director and General Manager, Moray Estates

Development Co., Forres; former Convenor, Scottish Recreational Land Association; former Council Member, Scottish Landowners Federation; former District Councillor, Moray; Chairman, Scottish Committee, European Year of Environment, 1986-88 (and Member, UK Committee); Member, Macaulay Land Use Research Institute, 1987-97; Director, UK 2000 Scotland, 1990-93; Chairman, Countryside Around Towns Forum, 1991-95; Vice President, FWAG Scotland, 1993-98. Recreations: most country pursuits. Address: (b.) Goosehill, Invererne Road, Forres, Moray IV36 1DZ; T.-01309 671320.

Carradice, Professor Ian, BA, PhD, FSA, FSA Scot. Professor, School of Art History, St Andrews University, since 1989; Keeper of Museum Collections, St Andrews University, since 1989; b. 10.7.53, Kendal; m., Maria Ines Urioste; 3 d. Educ. Quarry Bank High School, Liverpool; Liverpool University; St Andrews University. Curator, British Museum, London, 1977-89 (Department of Coins and Medals); Chairman, Sylloge Nummorum Graecorum, since 1994; University Director, Scottish Museums Council, 1994-2001; Convener, University Museums in Scotland, 1999-2005. Publications (books) include: Coinage and Finances in the Reign of Domitian; Coinage in the Greek World (Co-author); Greek Coins; Roman Provincial Coinage Vol. II (Co-author). Recreations: golf; fly fishing. Address: (b.) School of Art History, St Andrews University, St Andrews KY16 9AR; T.-01334 462402.

Carruthers, Gerard Charles, BA, MPhil, PhD. Reader, University of Glasgow, since 2007, Head of Department, Scottish Literature, since 2007; b. 4.7.63, Lennoxtown, Stirlingshire. Educ. St. Andrew's High School, Clydebank; University of Strathclyde; University of Glasgow. Temporary Lecturer, Department of Scottish Literature, University of Glasgow, 1991-92; Research Fellow, Department of English, University of Aberdeen, 1993-95; Lecturer, Department of English, University of Strathclyde, 1995-2000; Lecturer, then Senior Lecturer, then Reader, Department of Scottish Literature, University of Glasgow, since 2000, Director of The Centre for Robert Burns Studies, since 2007. Publications include: Robert Burns, 2006; Editor: The Devil To Stage: Five Plays by James Bridie, 2007, Burns: Selected Poems, 2006; Co-Editor: Walter Scott, Reliquiae Trotcosienses, 2004, Beyond Scotland, 2007, English Romanticism and the Celtic World, 2003. Recreations: playing guitar; watching football. Address: Department of Scottish Literature, 7 University Gardens, University of Glasgow; T.-0141 330 4286; e-mail: gec@arts.gla.ac.uk

Carruthers, Vivian Annette, BA (Hons), DipMusStud, FMA. Senior Lecturer, University of St Andrews, since 2002, Head of School of Art History, since 2005; b. 18.7.52, Nairobi, Kenya; m., Alan Saville. Educ. Chichester High School for Girls; University of Manchester. Assistant Keeper, Decorative Art, Leicestershire Museums, 1975-83; Keeper of Museums and Keeper of Applied Art, Cheltenham Museums, 1983-90; Freelance Museum Consultant, 1990-91; Leverhulme Research Fellow, University of St. Andrews and National Museums of Scotland, 1991-94; Teaching and Research Fellow, University of St. Andrews, 1994-95, Lecturer, School of Art History, 1995. Publications: Books: Edward Barnsley and His Workshop, 1992; The Scottish Home, 1996 (Co-Author); Good Citizen's Furniture, 1994; Simplicity or Splendour, 1999. Recreations: museums and art galleries; cinema; visiting France. Address: (b.) School of Art History, University of St. Andrews, 9 The Scores, St. Andrews KY16 9AR; T.-01334 462405; e-mail: vac@st-andrews.ac.uk

Carswell, William Steven, MA, LLB. Chairman, General Trustees of the Church of Scotland, 1999-2003; Director, Association for the Relief of Incurables; Trustee, Ferguson Bequest Fund; b. 13.7.29, Manchester; m., Jean Lang Sharpe; 2 s. Educ. Hutchesons' Boys' Grammar School; Glasgow University. Legal Assistant, Dunbarton County Council, 1953-56; Legal Assistant, Stirling County Council, 1956-59; Partner, McGrigor Donald, 1960-89. Recreations: golf; walking; cycling. Address:(h.) 13 Stratton Drive, Giffnock, Glasgow G46 7AB; T.-0141-638 1286; e-mail: wscarswell@ntlworld.com

Carter, Professor Alan, DPhil (Oxon), MA (Sussex), BA Hons (Kent). Professor of Moral Philosophy, University of Glasgow, since 2005; b. 5.7.52, Lincolnshire. Educ. Monkwearmouth Grammar School; St. Cross College, Oxford. Lecturer in Political Theory, University College Dublin, 1987; Lecturer in Philosophy, Heythrop College, University of London, 1988; Professor of Philosophy and Environmental Studies, University of Colorado at Boulder, 2001. Board of Directors of Friends of The Earth Scotland. Publications: 3 books; over 50 articles in academic journals. Recreations: hiking; playing electric guitar; movies. Address: (b.) 69 Oakfield Avenue, Glasgow G12 8LT; T.-0141 330 5692; e-mail: acr@arts.gla.ac.uk

Carter, Ben, BA (Hons), MBA. Head of Strategic Relations, VisitScotland; b. 3.11.70, Edinburgh; m., Anna; 2 d. Educ. Hutchesons' Grammar School; Napier University; Strathclyde University. Commercial Manager, Ethicon Ltd., Johnson and Johnson, 1993-2004 (held a variety of other positions including - Business Manager, Sales Force Effectiveness Manager, Manufacturing Manager and Production Planning Manager); Director of Planning and Resource Management, NHS Quality Improvement Scotland, 2004-05. Non-Executive Director of Edinburgh Convention Bureau Ltd. Recreations: travel; running; listening to music. Address: (b.) VisitScotland, 4 Rothesay Terrace, Edinburgh EH3 7RY; T.-0131 473 3600. E-mail: ben.carter@visitscotland.com

Carter, Professor Sir David Craig, MB, ChB, MD, FRCSEdin, FRCPEdin, FRCSIre (Hon), FACS (Hon), FRCGP (Hon), FCS HIC (Hon), FRACS (Hon), LLD (Hon), FRSEd, FRCGP (Hon), FAcadMedSci, FFPHM, DSc (Hon), LLD (Hon). Chairman, Board for Academic Medicine, Scotland, since 2005; Chairman, BMA Board of Science, 2002-05; Vice Principal, Edinburgh University, 2000-02; Member, Scientific Executive Board, Cancer Research UK, 2002-04 (Chairman, Programmes and Projects Committees, 2002-04); Trustee, Cancer Research UK, 2004-07; Vice Chairman, Cancer Research UK, 2005-07; President, British Medical Association, 2001-02; Chief Medical Officer (Scotland), 1996-2000; Surgeon to the Queen in Scotland, 1993-97; b. 1.9.40, Penrith; m., Ilske; 2 s. Educ. St. Andrews University. Lecturer in Clinical Surgery, Edinburgh University, 1969-74; 12-month secondment as Lecturer in Surgery, Makerere University, Kampala, Uganda, 1972; Senior Lecturer in Surgery, Edinburgh University, 1974-79; 12-month secondment as Associate Professor of Surgery, University of California, 1976; St. Mungo Professor of Surgery, Glasgow University, 1979-88; Honorary Consultant, Glasgow Royal Infirmary, 1979-88; Regius Professor of Clinical Surgery, Edinburgh University, 1988-96; Honorary Consultant Surgeon, Edinburgh Royal Infirmary, 1988-96. Former Council Member, Royal College of Surgeons of Edinburgh; former Member, Broadcasting Council for Scotland; former Chairman, Scottish Council for Postgraduate Medical and Dental Education; former Co-editor, British Journal of Surgery; Member, Medical Advisory Committee, Higher

Education Funding Council, 1994-97; Non-executive Director, Lothian Health Board, 1994-96; President, Surgical Research Society, Association of Surgeons (Great Britain and Ireland), 1996-97; Vice President, Royal Society of Edinburgh, 2000-03; Chairman: The Health Foundation, since 2002, Queens Nursing Institute, Scotland, since 2002. Moynihan Prize, 1973; James IV Association of Surgeons Travelling Fellow, 1975; Royal Medal, British Medical Association, 2006; Royal Medal, Royal Society of Edinburgh, 2007. Recreations: golf; music. Address: (h.) 19 Buckingham Terrace, Edinburgh EH4 3AD.

Cartmell, Professor Matthew Phillip, BSc (Hons), PhD, CEng, FIMechE, MASME, MAIAA. James Watt Professor of Mechanical Engineering, Glasgow University, since 2006; b. 17.6.58, Altrincham, Manchester; m., Fiona C. Cartmell; 2 d. Educ. Hulme Grammar School, Oldham; Edinburgh University. Research and Development Engineer, Ferranti Ltd, 1980-81; Research Fellow, Edinburgh University, 1984-85; Lecturer, Robert Gordon Institute of Technology, Aberdeen, 1985-87; Lecturer, Aberdeen University, 1987-91; Lecturer, University of Wales, Swansea, 1991-94; Senior Lecturer, Edinburgh University, 1994-98; R.A.H. Mayers Award for Outstanding Achievement; Committee Member, IMechE, IOP. Publications: one book, invited chapters, over 100 research papers. Recreations: vintage vehicles; music; walking. Address: (b.) Department of Mechanical Engineering, James Watt Building, Glasgow University, Glasgow, G12 8QQ. T.-0141-330 4337.

Casely, Gordon, CStJ, FRSA, FSAScot. Journalist and heraldist; b. 29.6.43, Glasgow; m., Valerie Ann Thomas; 1 s. Educ. Hutchesons' Boys' Grammar School. Reporter, D.C. Thomson & Co. Ltd., Dundee, Aberdeen and Elgin, 1966-68; Evening Express, Aberdeen, 1968-73; PRO, Greater Glasgow Passenger Transport Executive, 1973-78; public affairs posts in banking, local government, offshore and energy industries, 1978-95 (Assistant Director, CBI Scotland, 1988-91). Director, Herald Strategy Ltd., since 1999; Founder Member, Heraldry Society of Scotland, 1977; Press Officer, Commonwealth Games Council for Scotland, 1989-93; Member: Scottish Commonwealth Games Team, Auckland, 1990, Guild Burgess of Aberdeen, 1992; Hon. Vice-President, Lonach Highland and Friendly Society, since 1990; President, Aberdeen Welsh Society, 1997-98; Governor, Scottish Tartans Authority, since 2003. Publications: magazine contributor and obituarist; I Belong To Glasgow (human history of the Subway), 1975; ed. Who Do You Think You Are? (heraldry in modern Scotland), 2006. Recreations: cycling the continents; veteran athletics; promoting heraldry; poking fun at ScotRail. Address: (h.) 45 Beaconsfield Place, Aberdeen AB15 4AB; T.-01224 647927; e-mail: gcasely@herald-strategy.co.uk

Cash, John David, CBE, BSc, MB, ChB, PhD, FRCPath, FRCPGlas, FRCPE, FRCSEdin, FRCP. National Medical and Scientific Director, Scottish National Blood Transfusion Service, 1979-96; Honorary Professor, Department of Medicine, Edinburgh University, 1987-96; Non-Executive Director, National Institute of Biological Standards and Control, 1996-2004; Governor, Fettes College, 1997-2003; b. 3.4.36, Reading; m., Angela Mary Thomson; 1 s.; 1 d. Educ. Ashville College, Harrogate; Edinburgh University. Edinburgh and South East Scotland Blood Transfusion Service: Deputy Director, 1969, Regional Director, 1974. President, Royal College of Physicians of Edinburgh, 1994-98. Recreations: fishing; gardening. Address: 1 Otterburn Park, Edinburgh EH14 1JX.

Caskie, Rev. J. Colin, BA, BD. Minister at Rhu and Shandon, since 2002; b. 17.8.47, Glasgow; m., Alison McDougall; 2 s.; 1 d. Educ. Knightswood Secondary School; Strathclyde University; Glasgow University. Minister, Penilee: St Andrew, 1977-83; Minister, Carnoustie, 1983-2002; Moderator, Presbytery of Angus, 1995; Chairman, The Duncan Trust, 1992-2002; Vice-Convenor, General Assembly's Board of Stewardship and Finance, 1998-2001, Convenor, 2001-05; Clerk to Presbytery of Dumbarton, 2005. Recreations: stamp collecting; gardening. Address: (h.) 11 Ardenconnel Way, Rhu, Helensburgh G84 8LX.

Cassidy, Professor James, MB, ChB, MSc, MD, FRCP (Glasgow, Edinburgh). Cancer Research UK Professor of Oncology, University of Glasgow, since 2002; Consultant Oncologist, Beatson West of Scotland Cancer Centre, since 1992; b. 28.8.58, Lennoxtown; m.; 2 s.; 1 d. Educ. St. Mirin's Academy, Paisley; University of Glasgow. General Training, Wales and Scotland MRCP (UK), 1985; Lecturer in Oncology, University of Edinburgh; Professor of Oncology, University of Aberdeen, 1994-2002. Recreations: soccer, cycling; music. Address: (b.) Cancer Research UK, Department of Medical Oncology, Alexander Stone Building, Garscube Estate, Switchback Road, Bearsden, Glasgow G61 1BD.

Cates, Professor Michael Elmhirst, MA, PhD, FRSE, FRS. Professor of Natural Philosophy, University of Edinburgh, since 1995; b. 5.5.61, Bristol. Educ. Clifton College; Trinity College, University of Cambridge. Research Fellow, Trinity College, University of Cambridge, 1985-89; Cavendish Laboratory, Cambridge: Royal Society University Research Fellow, 1988-89, University Assistant Lecturer, 1989-92, University Lecturer, 1992-94. Maxwell Medal and Prize, Institute of Physics, 1991; Prix Franco-Britannique de l'Academie des Sciences, Paris, 1994. Publications: 200 publications in scientific journals. Recreations: hill-walking; painting. Address: (b.) School of Physics, University of Edinburgh, Kings Buildings, Edinburgh EH9 3JZ; T.-0131-650 5296.

Catto, Professor Sir Graeme R.D., Kt, MB, ChB (Hons), MD (Hons), DSc, FRCP, FRCPE, FRCPGlas, FRCGP (Hon), FRSE, FMedSci, FRCSE (Hon). Professor of Medicine, University of Aberdeen, since 2005; Vice-Principal, King's College London, and Dean, Guy's, King's and St. Thomas' Hospitals Medical and Dental Schools, 2000-05; Professor of Medicine, University of London, 2000-05; Pro Vice Chancellor, University of London, 2003-05; President, General Medical Council, since 2002; Chairman, Robert Gordon's College, 1995-2005; b. 24.4.45, Aberdeen; m., Joan Sievewright; 1 s.; 1 d. Educ. Robert Gordon's College; Aberdeen University. Research Fellow/Lecturer/Senior Lecturer/Reader in Medicine, Aberdeen University, 1970-88; Harkness Fellow of Commonwealth Fund of New York, 1975-77 (Fellow in Medicine, Harvard Medical School and Peter Bent Brigham Hospital, Boston); Aberdeen University: Professor in Medicine and Therapeutics 1988-2000, Dean, Faculty of Clinical Medicine, 1992-98, Vice-Principal 1995-2000; Vice Chairman, Aberdeen Royal Hospitals NHS Trust, 1992-99; Chief Scientist, NHS in Scotland, 1997-2000; Member, Scottish Higher Education Funding Council, 1996-2002; Member, General Medical Council, Education and Standards Committee, since 1994 (Chairman, 1999-2002); Treasurer, Academy of Medical Sciences, 1998-2001; Governor, PPP Medical Foundation, 2000-02; Member, SE London Strategic Health Authority, 2002-05; Member, Council for the Regulation of Healthcare Professionals; Hon. DSc, St Andrews University, 2003; Hon. LLD, Aberdeen University, 2002; Hon. MD, University of Southampton, 2004; Hon. DSc, Robert Gordon University, 2004; Hon. FRCGP, 2000; Hon. FRCSE, 2002; Fellow, King's College London, 2005; Hon. DSc, University of Kent, 2007; Hon. DSc, South Bank University, 2007.

Recreations: hills and glens. Address: Maryfield, Glenbuchat, Strathdon, Aberdeenshire AB36 8TS; T.-0197 56 41317.

Catto, Joan, LLB, NP. Partner, Ledingham Chalmers LLP, Solicitors, since 2002; Accredited Specialist in Family Law and Child Law, since 1994; b. 30.4.46, Aberdeen; m., Sir Graeme Catto; 1 s.; 1 d. Educ. Aberdeen High School for Girls; Aberdeen University. Qualified as a solicitor in 1968; career in Aberdeen (apart from two years in the US). Court Member, Aberdeen University; Convener, Business Committee, Aberdeen University; Board Member, Mither Kirk Project; Member, Board of Friends, Aberdeen Cyrenians (charity for the homeless); Dean of Guild's Assessor, Burgesses of Aberdeen, 1999-2007; Local Chairman, RSNO Circle; Scottish Legal Group Member, British Association for Adoption & Fostering; Awards Committee Member; Aberdeen Civic Society; Member, fund-raising team, Red Cross, Aberdeen. Recreations: needlework of all kinds; English setters; R&R in Glenbuchat. Address: (h.) 4 Woodend Avenue, Aberdeen AB15 6YL; T.-01224 310509; T. (work) -01224 408618. E-mail: joancatto@btinternet.com

Catto, Simon James Dawson, LLB (Hons), DipLP, NP. Partner, HBJ Gateley Wareing, since 2006; Solicitor-Advocate, since 2007; b. 21.5.72, Aberdeen; m., Caroline; 1 d. Educ. Robert Gordon's College, Aberdeen; Edinburgh University. Ledingham Chalmers, Aberdeen: Trainee Solicitor, 1995-97, Solicitor, 1997-2002; Partner, Ledingham Chalmers, Edinburgh, 2002-06. Burgess of Guild of The City of Aberdeen. Recreations: music; sport; travel. Address: (b.) Exchange Tower, 19 Canning Street, Edinburgh EH3 8EH; T.-0131 222 9560; e-mail: scatto@hbj-gw.com

Cawdor, 7th Earl of (Colin Robert Vaughan Campbell); b. 30.6.62; m., Lady Isabella Stanhope; 1 s.; 1 d. Succeeded to title, 1993. Educ. Eton; St. Peter's College, Oxford.

Chalmers, David James, BA, MA, DipEd. Headteacher, Biggar High School, since 1995; b. 17.12.50, Falkirk; m., Isobel. Educ. Falkirk High School; Stirling University; Lancaster University; Edinburgh University. Entered teaching, 1974; taught in West Lothian, Midlothian, Tayside and South Lanarkshire; seconded to Understanding British Industry, early 1980s; involved in outdoor education. Vice-Convener, Scottish Parent Teacher Council. Recreations: walking; cycling; skiing. Address: (b.) Biggar High School, John's Loan, Biggar ML12 6AG; T.-01899 220144.

Chalmers, Douglas, MA (Hons), PhD. Lecturer, Cultural Business, Glasgow Caledonian University, since 2002; b. 22.6.57, Dundee; m., Mhairi McGowan; 2 s.; 1 d. Educ. Kirkton High School, Dundee; Dundee University. National Organiser, Young Communist League, 1981-83; General Secretary, Young Communist League, 1983-85; Scottish Organiser, Communist Party, 1985-88; Scottish Secretary, Communist Party, 1988-91; Convener, Democratic Left Scotland, 1991-95; Researcher, Glasgow Caledonian University, 1996-2002; Executive Member, Scottish Constitutional Convention, 1989-95; Member, Council, Scottish Civic Forum, 2001-05, Board Member, 2001-05; Member, Broadcasting Council for Scotland, 2005-07, Audience Council Scotland, since 2007. Recreations: politics; community; family; sport; musician; languages. Address: (b.) Glasgow Caledonian University, 70 Cowcaddens Road, Glasgow G4 0BA; T.-0141 331 3350; e-mail: d.chalmers@gcal.ac.uk web: cbs.gcal.ac.uk/content/eae/eae_staff_dchalmers.asp

Chalmers, Rev. John Pearson, BD. Pastoral Adviser and Associate Secretary, Ministries Council, Church of Scotland; Convenor, Board of Governors, Donaldson's College, since 1999; b. 5.6.52, Bothwell; m., Elizabeth; 2 s.; 1 d. Educ. Marr College; Strathclyde University; Glasgow University. Minister, Renton Trinity, 1979-86; Clerk, Dumbarton Presbytery, 1982-86; Minister, Palmerston Place, Edinburgh, 1986-95. Recreations: golf; bee-keeping. Address: (b.) 121 George Street, Edinburgh EH2 4YN; T.-0131-225 5722.

Chalmers, Roderick Thomas Alexander, MBChB, FRCSEd, MD, FRCS. Consultant Vascular Surgeon, Royal Infirmary of Edinburgh, since 1998; Honorary Senior Lecturer, Edinburgh University Medical School, since 1998; b. 18.5.63, Edinburgh; m., Clare Elizabeth Chalmers; 1 d. Educ. George Watson's College, Edinburgh; Edinburgh University. House Surgeon/Physician, Royal Infirmary, Edinburgh, 1986-87; Senior House Officer, General Surgery, South-east Scotland, 1987-89; basic surgical training rotation, South-east Scotland, 1989-92; Research Fellow in Vascular Surgery, University of Iowa, 1992-93; career registrar surgery, South-east Scotland, 1993-95; Senior Registrar/Senior Clinical Fellow, St Mary's Hospital, London, 1995-98. Director, Scottish National Service for the Treatment of Thoraco-Abdominal Aneurysms; Convener, Higher Surgical Skills Course, Royal College of Surgeons of Edinburgh. Recreations: mountaineering; golf. Address: (h.) Morar House, Braidwood Bridge, Midlothian EH26 9LW; T.-01968 678225; e-mail: rod.chalmers@luht.scot.nhs.uk

Chamberlain, April, Joint Managing Director, The Comedy Unit, since 1996; b. 21.4.59, London; m., Paul Bassett; 2 s.; 2 d. Educ. Addey and Stanhope Grammar School. Joined BBC Scotland as Business Manager, Comedy Department, 1993; The Comedy Unit, since 1996. Address: (b.) The Comedy Unit Ltd., Glasgow TV and Film Studio, 6th Floor, 53 Bothwell Street, Glasgow G2 6TS; T.-0141-220 6400; Fax: 0141-220 6444; e-mail: aprilchamberlain@comedyunit.co.uk

Chambers, Fergus Allan, FIH. Executive Director, Direct and Care Services, Glasgow City Council, since 1995; b. 20.1.56, Glasgow; m., Ruth Elizabeth; 1 s.; 1 d. Educ. Uddingston Grammar School; Glasgow College of Food Technology. Various posts, commercial catering group, 1977-82; Business Development Manager, Sutcliffe Catering, 1982-86; General Manager, Moccomat UK, 1986-88; Depute Director, Strathclyde Regional Council/Catering Direct, 1988-95. Trustee and Honorary Secretary, Hospitality Industry Trust Scotland; former Chair, A.S.S.I.S.T.; Winner: Cost Sector Catering Education Award, 1999, Catering Forum Award for Excellence, 1999, Foodservice Caterer of the Year, 1999. Recreations: golf; DIY. Address: (h.) 24 Clydeford Drive, Kylepark, Uddingston, Glasgow G71 7DJ; T.-(b.) 0141-353 9130.

Chambers, Professor Helen Elizabeth, MA, PhD. Professor of German, St Andrews University, since 1999; b. 4.3.47, Glasgow; m., Hugh Rorrison; 2 s. Educ. Hutchesons' Girls' Grammar School, Glasgow; Glasgow University; Freiburg University. Lecturer, then Senior Lecturer in German, Leeds University, 1972-99; Visiting Lecturer in German, Melbourne University, 1998. Publications: Supernatural and Irrational Elements in the Works of Theodor Fontane, 1980; Co-existent Contradictions: Joseph Roth in Retrospect (Editor), 1991; Theodor Fontane: The London Symposium (Co-Editor), 1995; T. Fontane, Effi Briest (Co-Translator), 1995; The Changing Image of Theodor Fontane, 1997; Theodor Fontane and the European Context (Co-Editor), 2001; Violence, Culture and Identity (Editor), 2006; Humor and Irony in Nineteenth-Century German

Women's Writing, 2007. Recreations: theatre; film; travel. Address: (b.) School of Modern Languages, St Andrews University, St Andrews KY16 9PH; T.: 01334 463659.

Chambers, Rev. Samuel John, OBE, BSc. Church of Scotland Minister, Ness Bank Church of Scotland, Inverness, since 1998; b. 3.4.44, Banbridge, Co. Down, Northern Ireland; m., Anne; 2 s.; 1 d. Educ. Banbridge Academy; Annadale Grammar School, Belfast; Queen's University Belfast; Presbyterian College, Belfast. Minister, Presbyterian Church in Ireland, 1972-84, Belfast, Donegal and Comber, Co. Down; Chairman, East Belfast Youth Council, 1972-73; Chief Executive, Relate, Northern Ireland, 1984-98; Chairman, International Commission on Marriage and Interpersonal Relationships, 1994-98. Contributions to Journal of Sexual and Marital Therapy. Recreations: golf; travel; hill walking. Address: (h. and b.) 15 Ballifeary Road, Inverness IV3 5PJ; T.-01463 234653; e-mail: chambers@ballifeary.freeserve.co.uk

Chaplain, Professor Mark Andrew Joseph, BSc (Hons), PhD, FRSE. Professor of Mathematical Biology, Dundee University, since 2000; b. 1.5.64, Dundee; m., Fiona; 3 s. Educ. St John's RC High School, Dundee; Dundee University. Lecturer, School of Mathematical Sciences, Bath University, 1990-96; Senior Lecturer, Department of Maths, Dundee University, 1996-98; Reader in Mathematical Biology, Dundee University, 1998-2000. Whitehead Prize, London Mathematical Society, 2000. Publication: On Growth and Form: Spatio-Temporal Pattern Formation in Biology. Publication: Polymer and Cell Dynamics: Multiscale modelling and numerical simulations. Recreations: children; golf; squash; badminton; tennis. Address: (b.) Department of Mathematics, Dundee University, Dundee DD1 4HN; T.-01382 345369.

Chapman, Francis Ian, CBE, FRSA, CIMgt, DLitt (Hon). President, Scottish Radio Holdings PLC, 1996-2001 (Chairman, 1972-96); Chairman: Media and Income Trust PLC, 2000-01, Media Zeros PLC, 2000-01, National Academy of Writing, 2000-03; Vice President, National Academy of Writing, since 2003; Chairman, Radio Trust PLC, 1997-2000; b. 26.10.25, St. Fergus, Aberdeenshire; m., Marjory Stewart Swinton; 1 s.; 1 d. Educ. Shawlands Academy, Glasgow; Ommer School of Music. War Service: RAF air crew cadet, 1943-44; National Service coal mines, 1945-47. William Collins: trainee, 1947, management trainee, New York branch, 1951, General Sales Manager, London, 1955, appointed to main operating Board as Group Sales Director, 1960; appointed to Board, William Collins (Holdings) Ltd. as Joint Managing Director, 1967; Deputy Chairman, William Collins (Holdings) Ltd , 1976; Chairman, William Collins Publishers Ltd., 1979; Chairman and Chief Executive, William Collins PLC, 1981-89; Chairman, Hatchards Ltd., 1976-89; Pan Books Ltd.: Board Member, 1962-84, Chairman, 1971-73; Chairman, Harvill Press Ltd., 1976-89; Board Member, Book Tokens Ltd., 1981-95; Member, Governing Council, SCOTBIC, since 1983; Board Member, IRN Ltd., 1983-85; President, Publishers Association, 1979-81; Trustee, Book Trade Benevolent Society, 1982-2002; Board Member, Scottish Opera Theatre Royal Ltd., 1974-79; Director, Stanley Botes Ltd., 1985-89; Non-Executive Director, Guinness PLC, 1986-91; Joint Chairman and Chief Executive, Harper and Row, New York, 1987-89; Director, United Distillers PLC, 1988-93; Chairman and Managing Director, Chapmans Publishers Ltd., 1989-94; Chairman, Guinness Publishing, 1991-96 (Deputy Chairman, 1997-99); Deputy Chairman, Orion Publishing Group, 1993-94; President, SAS Guinness

Media, Paris, 1996-99. Scottish Free Enterprise Award, 1985; Hon. DLitt, Strathclyde, 1990. Recreations: reading; golf; swimming; music; grandchildren. Address: Kenmore, 46 The Avenue, Cheam, Surrey SM2 7QE.

Chapman, Professor John N., MA, PhD, FInstP, FRSE. Professor, Physics and Astronomy, Glasgow University, since 1988; b. 21.11.47, Sheffield; m., Judith M.; 1 s.; 1 d. Educ. King Edward VII School, Sheffield; St. John's College and Fitzwilliam College, Cambridge. Research Fellow, Fitzwilliam College, Cambridge; Lecturer, Glasgow University. Recreations: photography; walking; squash. Address: (b.) Department of Physics and Astronomy, Glasgow University, Glasgow G12 8QQ; T.-0141-330 4462.

Chapman, Professor Robert, BSc, PhD, CSci, CPhys, FInstP. Professor of Physics, University of Paisley, since 1993; b. 10.8.41, Holytown; m., Norma Gilchrist Hope; 3 d. Educ. Bellshill Academy; University of Glasgow. UKAEA Research Fellow, AWRE, Aldermaston, and AERE, Harwell, 1966-70; University of Manchester: Lecturer, 1970-75, Senior Lecturer, 1975-87, Reader in Physics, 1987-93; Paisley University: Head, Department of Physics, 1993-96, Head, Department of Electronic Engineering and Physics, 1996-2000, Head, School of Information and Communication Technologies, 2000-03, Acting Vice Principal, Research and Commercialisation, 2004-06. Publications: 180 research papers. Recreations: walking; gardening; listening to music. Address: (b.) University of Paisley, Paisley PA1 2BE; T.-0141-848 3600.

Chapman, Professor Stephen Kenneth, BSc, PhD, CChem, FRSC, FRSE. Vice Principal (Planning and Resources), Edinburgh University, since 2006, Professor of Chemistry, since 1996; b. 12.05.59, Newcastle upon Tyne; m., Karen; 1 s.; 2 d. Educ. The Lakes School, Windermere; University of Newcastle upon Tyne. Nato Research Fellow, MIT, Massachusetts, USA, 1983-85; Lecturer, School of Chemistry, University of Edinburgh, 1986-92, Senior Lecturer, 1992-95, Reader, 1995-96; Head of The School of Chemistry, University of Edinburgh, 2000-05. Member of The Scottish Funding Council, Research and Knowledge Transfer Committee. Publications: 210, in leading science journals. Recreations: walking; gardening; reading; travel. Address: (b.) School of Chemistry, University of Edinburgh, West Mains Road, Edinburgh EH9 3JJ; T.-0131 650 4760; e-mail: s.k.chapman@ed.ac.uk

Charlesworth, Professor Brian, BA, PhD, FRS, FRSE. Professor and Head of Institute of Evolutionary Biology, Edinburgh University, since 2007; b. 29.4.45, Brighton; m., Deborah Maltby; 1 d. Educ. Haberdasher's Aske's Elstree School; Queens' College, Cambridge. Post-doctoral Fellow, University of Chicago, 1969-71; Lecturer, Genetics, University of Liverpool, 1971-74; Lecturer, Biology, Sussex University, 1974-82; Reader in Biology, Sussex University, 1982-84; Professor of Biology, University of Chicago, 1985-92; G.W. Beadle Distinguished Service Professor of Ecology and Evolution, University of Chicago, 1992-97; Royal Society Research Professor, Edinburgh University, 1997-2007. Darwin Medal, The Royal Society, 2000. Publications: Evolution in Age-structured Populations, 1994; co-author, Evolution: A Very Short Introduction. Recreations: walking; listening to classical music. Address: (b.) Institute of Evolutionary Biology, Edinburgh University, The King's Buildings, Edinburgh, EH9 3JT; T.-0131-650 5750.

Chatterji, Professor Monojit, BA, MA, PhD. Bonar Professor of Applied Economics, Dundee University, since 1989 (Head, Department of Economic Studies, 1993-97); Member, Advisory Group, BBC World Service; b. 15.1.51, Bombay; m., Anjum Rahmatulla; 1 s.; 2 d. Educ. Cathedral School, Bombay; St. Columba's, Delhi; Elphinstone

College, Bombay; Christ's College, Cambridge. Chairman, National Joint Council for UK Fire and Emergency Services, since 2007; Member: School Teachers Review Body, since 2004, Scottish Solicitors Discipline Tribunal, since 2001. Winner, LTSN Annual Prize. Recreations: tennis; cinema; history; theology. Address: (b.) Department of Economics, Dundee University, Dundee; T.-01382 384443.

Chester, Richard Waugh, MBE, FRAM, GRSM, ARCM, FRSA. Director and Board Member, National Youth Orchestras of Scotland, 1987-2007; b. 19.4.43, Hutton Rudby; m., Sarah Chapman-Mortimer; 1 s.; 2 d. Educ. The Friends' School, Great Ayton; Huddersfield College of Technology, Music Dept.; Royal Academy of Music. Flautist: BBC Northern Ireland, 1965, Royal Scottish National Orchestra, 1967; Conductor; Teacher; Examiner; Consultant. Chairman, Glasgow Festival Strings; Vice-Chairman, World Federation of Amateur Orchestras; Director: National Youth Choir of Scotland; Trustee: Lochaber Music School, Acting for Charities Trust, Scottish Schools Orchestra Trust. Recreations: swimming; walking; reading. Address: (h.) Milton of Cardross, Port of Menteith, Stirling FK8 3JY; T.-01877 385634; e-mail: mail@rchester.co.uk

Chesworth, Air Vice Marshal George Arthur, CB, OBE, DFC. Lord-Lieutenant of Moray, 1994-2005; b. 4.6.30; m.; 1 s. (deceased); 2 d. RAF, 1948-84; Chief Executive, Glasgow Garden Festival, 1985-98.

Chick, Jonathan Dale, MA (Cantab), MB, ChB, MPhil, DSc (Edin), FRCPE, FRCPsych. Consultant Psychiatrist, Royal Edinburgh Hospital, since 1979; part-time Senior Lecturer, Edinburgh University, since 1979; b. 23.4.45, Wallasey; 2 s. Educ. Queen Elizabeth Grammar School, Darlington; Corpus Christi College, Cambridge; Edinburgh University. Posts in Edinburgh teaching hospitals, 1971-76; scientific staff, MRC Unit for Epidemiological Studies in Psychiatry, 1976-79. Board: Int. Soc. Addiction Medicine; Chief Editor, Alcohol and Alcoholism; Hon. Life Fellow, Soc. Study Addiction; awarded Royal College of Psychiatrists Research Medal and Prize. Publications: numerous research papers; two books. Recreation: musician.

Chillingworth, David Robert, BA (Mod), TCD, MA (Oxon). Bishop of St. Andrews, Dunkeld and Dunblane, since 2005; b. 23.6.51, Dublin, Ireland; m., Alison; 2 s.; 1 d. Educ. Portora Royal School, Enniskillen; Royal Belfast Academical Institution; Trinity College, Dublin; Oriel College, Oxford. Curate Assistant, Holy Trinity, Joanmount, Belfast (Connor), 1976-79; Church of Ireland Youth Officer, 1979-83; Curate Assistant, Bangor Abbey (Down and Dromore), 1983-86; Rector, Seagoe Parish Church, Portadown, 1986-2005; Dean of Dromore, 1995-2002; Archdeacon of Dromore, 2002-05. Recreations: music; sailing; cycling; reading; travel. Address: (b.) 28A Balhousie Street, Perth PH1 5HJ; T.-01738 658075.

Chirnside, Peter Huett, BSc (Hons). National Co-ordinator, Tearfund, since 1979; b. 27.12.49, Lancaster; m., Fiona; 1 s.; 1 d. Educ. Silcoates School, Wakefield; University of Dundee. Teacher of Biology, Mackie Academy, 1973-79. Chairman, Scottish Mission Secretaries Fellowship, 1984-98; Member, Scottish Lausanne Committee, since 1995. Address: (b.) Challenge House, 29 Canal Street, Glasgow G4 0AD; e-mail: peter.chirnside@tearfund.org

Chisholm, Professor Derrick Mackenzie, BDS, PhD, FDSRCPS(Glas), FDSRCS(Edin), FFDRCS(Ire), FDSRCS(Eng), FRCPath. Boyd Professor of Dental Surgery, University of Dundee and Honorary Consultant in Oral Medicine and Pathology, 1978-2005; b. 27.3.40, Glasgow; m., June Romayne Race; 1 step-s.; 1 step-d.

Educ. Hillhead High School; University of Glasgow. Clinical Research Assistant in Oral Medicine, 1966-68; University of Glasgow: Lecturer in Oral Medicine and Pathology, 1968-76, Senior Lecturer in Oral Medicine and Pathology, 1976-78; University of Dundee: Dean of Dentistry, 1982-89, Deputy Principal, 1989-91; Vice-Principal, 1991-92. Visiting Professor of Oral Pathology, University of Illinois, USA, 1970-72; Grantholder, Dental Health Services Research Unit, SHHD, 1982-92; Member, General Dental Council, 1982-94; President, British Society for Oral Pathology, 1985; Member, Dental Committee, Medical Research Council, 1989-94; Chairman, National Dental Advisory Committee, 1990-94; Member, Board of Governors, Duncan of Jordanstone College of Art, 1993-94; Vice President, Dundee Art Society, 2003-04. Publications: Salivary Glands in Health and Disease, 1975; Introduction to Oral Medicine, 1978. Recreations: gardening; writing; oil painting. Address: Bruckley House, St. Andrews, Fife KY16 9YF; T.-01334 838375.

Chisholm, Duncan Fraser, MStJ, JP. Chairman, Duncan Chisholm & Sons Ltd., Inverness; Chairman, The Kiltmakers Association of Scotland Ltd., since 2000; Director, Inverness Project Ltd., since 2003; Director, Moray Textile Project Ltd., since 2005; b. 14.4.41, Inverness; m., Mary Rebecca MacRae; 1 s.; 1 d. Educ. Inverness High School. Member, Inverness District Council, 1984-92; Member, Board of Governors, Eden Court Theatre, Inverness, 1984-88; President, Inverness and Highland Chamber of Commerce, 1983-84 (Vice-President, 1982-83); Member, Highland TAVRA Committee, 1988-92; Vice-Chairman, Inverness, Loch Ness and Nairn Tourist Board, 1988-96; President, Clan Chisholm Society, 1978-89; Chairman, Inverness Town Twinning Committee, 1992-98; Member, Management Committee: Highland Export Club, since 1998, Inverness Town Management, since 1997; GSL, Scout Association, since 1969 (Scout Leader, 1960-69); Session Clerk, St. Columba High Church, Inverness. Recreations: swimming; music; painting. Address: (b.) 47-51 Castle Street, Inverness; T.-01463 234599.

Chisholm, Malcolm. MSP, (Labour), Edinburgh North and Leith, since 1999; Shadow Minister for Culture and External Affairs, since 2007 (Minister for Health and Community Care, 2001-04, Minister for Communities, 2004-06); MP (Labour), Edinburgh North and Leith (formerly Edinburgh Leith), 1992-2001; b. 7.3.49; m.; 2 s.; 1 d. Former teacher. Parliamentary Under-Secretary of State, Scottish Office (Minister for Local Government, Housing and Transport) 1997 (resigned over cuts). Address: (b.) Scottish Parliament, Edinburgh EH99 1SP.

Chitnis, Paul Bernard, BA (Hons). Chief Executive, Scottish Catholic International Aid Fund, since 1996; b. 29.11.60, Birmingham; m., Tracey; 3 s.; 2 d. Educ. Stonyhurst College; Nottingham University. Appeal Director and Communications Director, Handicapped Children's Pilgrimage Trust, 1986-89; Appeals Director, Sick Children's Trust, 1989-90; Head of Appeals, Christian Aid, 1990-94; Head of Fundraising, Crossroads, 1994-95. Founder and Chairman of Trustees, The Newman Trust, 1981-90; President, Coopération Internationale pour le Développement et la Solidarité. Address: (b.) 19 Park Circus, Glasgow G3 6BE; T.-0141-354 5555; e-mail: pchitnis@sciaf.org.uk

Christian, Professor Reginald Frank, MA (Oxon). Professor of Russian and Head of Department, St. Andrews University, 1966-92, now Emeritus Professor; b. 9.8.24, Liverpool; m., Rosalind Iris Napier; 1 s.; 1 d. Educ. Liverpool Institute High School; Queen's College, Oxford.

RAF, 1943-46 (aircrew), flying on 231 Sqdn. and 6 Atlantic Ferry Unit (Pilot Officer, 1944); Foreign Office (British Embassy, Moscow), 1949-50; Lecturer and Head of Russian Department, Liverpool University, 1950-55; Senior Lecturer, then Professor of Russian and Head of Department, Birmingham University, 1955-66, Visiting Professor: McGill University, Montreal, 1961-62, Institute of Foreign Languages, Moscow, 1964-65; Dean, Faculty of Arts, St. Andrews University, 1975-78; Member, University Court, 1971-73, 1981-85. President, British Universities Association of Slavists, 1967-70; Member, International Committee of Slavists, 1970-75; Honorary Vice-President, Association of Teachers of Russian; Member, UGC Arts Sub-Committee on Russian Studies. Publications: Russian Syntax (with F.M. Borras), 1959 and 1971; Korolenko's Siberia, 1954; Tolstoy's War and Peace: A Study, 1962; Russian Prose Composition (with F.M. Borras), 1964 and 1974; Tolstoy: A Critical Introduction, 1969; Tolstoy's Letters, edited, translated and annotated, 1978; Tolstoy's Diaries, edited, translated and annotated, 1985 and 1994; Alexis Aladin – The Tragedy of Exile, 1999. Recreations: music; reading. Address: (h.) 48 Lade Braes, St. Andrews, Fife; T.-01334 474407; 7, Knockard Road, Pitlochry; T.-01796 472993.

Christie, Dr. Campbell, CBE, DLitt. Honorary President, Scottish Civic Forum; b. 23.8.37, Carsluith, Kirkcudbrightshire; m., Elizabeth Brown Cameron; 2 s. Educ. Albert Senior Secondary School, Glasgow; Woolwich Polytechnic, London. Civil Servant, Department of Health and Social Security, 1954-72; National Officer, then Deputy General Secretary, Society of Civil and Public Servants, 1972-86; General Secretary, Scottish Trades Union Congress, 1986-98. Vice Chairman, British Waterways Board; Board Member, Forth Valley NHS Board; Alternate Member of the Panel on Takeovers and Mergers; Non-executive Director: South West Trains Ltd., Scottish Premier Football League (SPL); Chairman, Falkirk Football Club.

Christie, John, MTheol, DipEd. Educational consultant, since 2002; Director of Lifelong Learning, Scottish Borders Council, 2001-02 (Director of Education, 1995-2001); Non-Executive Director, Learning and Teaching Scotland, 2000-04; b. 25.12.53, Edinburgh; m., Katherine; 2 d. Educ. Daniel Stewart's College; St. Andrews University; Edinburgh University; Moray House College of Education. Teacher, 1977-83; Principal Assistant, Stockport MBC, 1983-85; Assistant Director of Education, then Depute Director of Education, Tayside Regional Council, 1985-95. Hon. Treasurer, Association of Directors of Education in Scotland, 1995-2002; Member: Health Education Board for Scotland, 1991-97, Advisory Committee on Scottish Qualification for Headship, since 1999, Scotland Against Drugs Primary School Initiative, COSLA/SEED Group on Value-Added in Schools; Non-Executive Director, Scottish Consultative Council on the Curriculum, 1995-2000. Recreation: house-building. Address: 1 Dundas Terrace, Melrose TD6 9QU; T.-01896 823980.

Christie, Rev. John Cairns., BSc, PGCertEd, CBiol. Interim Minister, Old Cumnock: Trinity; Kilmacolm: Old Kirk, since 2004; Arisaig and the Small Isles linked with Mallaig St. Columba's and Knoydart; Church of Scotland Minister, Hyndland Parish Church, Glasgow, 1990-2004; Teacher, 1972-86; b. 9.7.47, Glasgow; m., (1) Elizabeth McDonald McIntosh; 1 d.; (2) Annette Cooke Carnegie Evans (nee Hamill). Educ. Hermitage School, Helensburgh; University of Strathclyde; Jordanhill College; University of Glasgow. Teacher, Albert Secondary School, Springburn, Glasgow, 1973-76, Assistant Principal Teacher, Guidance, 1976-78; Principal Teacher of Science, Tiree High School, 1978-86; Warden, Dalneigh Hall of Residence, 1984-86; Honours Degree in New Testament and Systematic Theology, University of Glasgow, 1986-90; Probationer

Assistant Minister, Mosspark Parish Church, 1989-90. Chaplain to the Mudhook Yacht Club. Recreations: playing 5-a-side football; hill-walking; reading; radio; tv; golf (with more enthusiasm than skill); sailing; DIY; gardening. Address: (h.) 10 Cumberland Avenue, Helensburgh G84 8QG; T. 01436 674078; e-mail: rev.jcc@btinternet.com

Chrystie, Kenneth, LLB (Hons), PhD. Consultant, McClure Naismith; Chairman, Hugh Fraser Foundation, 1988; Chairman, Culture and Sport Glasgow (Trading) Ltd.; Director: Murgitroyd plc, Strathclyde University Incubator Ltd., Glasgow Science Centre; Past President, Royal Glasgow Institute of the Fine Arts; b. 24.11.46, Glasgow; m., Mary; 1 s.; 2 d. Educ. Duncanrig Senior Secondary; University of Glasgow; University of Virginia. Joined McClure Naismith, 1968. Founder Member and Director, Intellectual Property Lawyers Organisation. Publications: contributor to Encyclopedia of Scots Law, Labour Law Handbook and other legal publications. Recreations: golf; curling; tennis. Address: (b.) 292 St. Vincent Street, Glasgow G2 5TQ; T.-0141-204 2700; e-mail: kchrystie@mcclurenaismith.com

Clancy, Rev. P. Jill, BD, DipMin, Minister of Religion, St. John's Church of Scotland, Gourock, since 2000; b. 10.7.70, Irvine; m., Frank J. Clancy. Educ. Kilwinning Academy; Aberdeen University. YTS, Cunningham District Council; Rating Clerk, Northern Ireland Trailers; Distribution Assistant, Caledonian Paper Mill. Director of Board, "The Haven", Kilmacolm. Recreation: play piano. Address: (h.) 6 Barrhill Road, Gourock PA19 1JX; T.-01475 632143.

Clapham, David Charles, LLB, SSC. Solicitor (Principal, private practice, since 1984); Partner in Claphams Solicitors; Part-time Immigration Judge (formerly Adjudicator), since 2001; Part-time Sheriff, since 2007; Secretary, Glasgow, Argyll and Bute and Dunbartonshire Local Valuation Panel, since 1996; part-time Chairman, Social Security Appeal Tribunals, since 1992, and Disability Appeal Tribunals, since 2000; Legal member, Mental Health Tribunal for Scotland, since 2005; Director, Legal Defence Union; b. 16.10.58, Giffnock; m., Debra Clapham; 1 s.; 2 d. Educ. Hutchesons' Boys' Grammar School, Glasgow; Strathclyde University. Legal apprenticeship, 1979-81; admitted Solicitor, 1981; admitted Notary Public, 1982; founded own legal practice, 1984; part-time Tutor, Strathclyde University, 1984-92; part-time Lecturer, Glasgow University, 1991-94; Secretary, Strathclyde Region Local Valuation Panel, 1988-96; Glasgow Bar Association: Secretary, 1987-91, Vice President, 1991-92, President, 1992-93; Secretary, Scottish Law Agents Society, 1994-97; Council Member, Royal Faculty of Procurators in Glasgow, 1996-99; Temporary Sheriff, 1998-99; Governor, Belmont House School, 2002-04; Eastwood Rotary Club President, 2004/05. Recreations: reading; collecting books. Address: (b.) 79 West Regent Street, Glasgow G2 2AW; T.-0141-332 5537; (b.) 1B & 1C Helena House, Clarkston Toll, Glasgow G76 7RA; T.-0141-620-0800.

Clark of Calton, (Baroness M. Lynda Clark), QC, LLB, PhD. Judge, since 2006; Advocate-General for Scotland, 1999-2006; MP (Labour), Edinburgh Pentlands, 1997-2005; Life Peer; Admitted Advocate, 1977; Lecturer in Jurisprudence, Dundee University, 1973-76; Standing Junior Counsel, Department of Energy, 1984-89; called to English Bar, 1988; appointed QC, 1989; contested Fife North East (Labour), 1992. Former Member, Scottish Legal Aid Board and Edinburgh University Court. Address: (b.) House of Lords, London, SW1A 0AA.

Clark, Alex. Member, Board of Directors, Arran Theatre and Arts Trust; Trustee, James Milne Memorial Trust; Patron, Scottish Working People's Trust; b. 2.1.22, Larkhall; m., Jessie Beveridge McCulloch; 1 s.; 1 d. Educ. Larkhall Academy. Grain miller, 1936-39; coal miner,

1939-53; political organiser, 1953-69; Scottish and Northern Ireland Secretary, British Actors Equity Association, 1969-84; created the post of STUC Arts Officer, 1985-87; founder Member, Boards, Scottish Youth Theatre, Scottish Theatre Company, Royal Lyceum Theatre Company; Glasgow Jazz Festival, Mayfest (Founder); also served on Boards of Pitlochry Festival Theatre and Cumbernauld Theatre Company, Scottish Ballet, Scottish Opera, Glasgow Film Theatre; Member: Scottish Arts Council's Review Committee on Scottish Theatre Company, 1987, Working Party on a National Theatre for Scotland, 1987, STUC Entertainment and Arts Committee, 1975-94. Lord Provost's Award for services to the city of Glasgow, 1987; Winner, ABSA-Goodman & Reed Elsevier Award for Services to the Arts, 1994. Recreations: reading; music; theatre; walking; gardening. Address: (h.) Ponfeigh, 8 Strathwhillan, Brodick, Isle of Arran.

Clark, Alistair Campbell, MA, LLB, WS. Formerly Senior Partner, Blackadder, Reid, Johnston (formerly Reid, Johnston, Bell & Henderson), Solicitors, Dundee (now Blackadders); Honorary Sheriff, Tayside Central & Fife, since 1986; Trustee, Dundee Disabled Children's Association, since 1993; Chairman, Scottish Conveyancing and Executry Services Board, 1996-2003; Member, Nominations Committee, Scottish Enterprise Tayside, 1998-2002; b. 4.3.33, Dundee; m., Evelyn M. Clark; 3 s. Educ. Grove Academy, Broughty Ferry; St. Andrews University. Dean, Faculty of Procurators and Solicitors in Dundee, 1979-81, Hon. Life Member, since 1991; President, Law Society of Scotland, 1989-90 (Council Member, since 1982); founder Chairman, Broughty Ferry Round Table; Founder President, Claverhouse Rotary Club, Dundee. Recreations: family; travel; erratic golf. Address: (h.) Blythe Lodge, 85A Dundee Road, West Ferry, Dundee DD5 1LZ; T.-01382 477989.

Clark, Anita, BA (Hons). Head of Dance, Scottish Arts Council, since 2004; b. 26.11.71, Dunfermline. Educ. London College of Dance; University of Buckinghamshire. Freelance community dance artist, 1992-96; Dance co-ordinator, Glasgow City Council, 1996-97; Education Officer, Birmingham Royal Ballet, 1998-2000; Artistic Director, Citymoves Dancespace, Aberdeen, 2001-04. Lisa Ullmann Fellowship awardee in 2004. Recreations: dance and performing arts; GRF Radio team member. Address: (b.) Scottish Arts Council, 12 Manor Place, Edinburgh EH3 7DD; T.-0131 226 6051.

Clark, Bryan Malott, FC (Optom). Honorary Sheriff of Grampian Highland and Islands, since 2000; Retired Optometrist; b. 6.10.37, Orkney; m., Sheila Matheson Cusiter; 2 s.; 1 d. Educ. Kirkwall Grammar School; Stow College, Glasgow. Independent Optometrist in Orkney, 1961-2001. Past Orkney AOC Chairman; Past President, Rotary Club of Orkney; Past Chairman, Kirkwall Chamber of Commerce. Recreations: travel; gardening; golf. Address: (h.) Westwood, Berstane Road, Kirkwall, Orkney KW15 1NA; T.-01856 872659; e-mail: westwoodclark@btinternet

Clark, Professor Christopher Lacey, BSc, DipSoc Admin, DipSocWork Studies, CQSW, PhD. Dean of Postgraduate Studies, College of Humanities and Social Science, University of Edinburgh, since 2004; Professor/Lecturer in Social Work, University of Edinburgh, since 1978; b. 2.12.46, Godalming. Educ. University of Birmingham; LSE; University of Edinburgh. N. W. Regional Officer, International Voluntary Service, 1971-73; British Volunteer Programme, North Yemen, 1973-76; Community Development Officer, Wirral BC,

1976-78. Publications: Social Work Ethics, 2000; Adult day care and social inclusion, 2002. Address: (b.) Postgraduate Office, College of Humanities and Social Science, David Hume Tower, George Square, Edinburgh EH8 9JX; T.-0131 650 4084; e-mail: chris.clark@ed.ac.uk

Clark, David Findlay, OBE, DL, MA, PhD, CPsychol, FBPsS, ARPS, FFICS. Deputy Lieutenant, Banffshire, since 1992; Consulting Clinical Psychologist; former Director, Area Clinical Psychology Services, Grampian Health Board; Clinical Senior Lecturer, Department of Mental Health, Aberdeen University; b. 30.5.30, Aberdeen; m., Janet Ann Stephen; 2 d. Educ. Banff Academy; Aberdeen University. Flying Officer, RAF, 1951-53; Psychologist, Leicester Industrial Rehabilitation Unit, 1953-56; Senior, then Principal Clinical Psychologist, Leicester Area Clinical Psychology Service, and part-time Lecturer, Leicester University and Technical College, 1956-66; WHO short-term Consultant, Sri Lanka, 1977; various lecturing commitments in Canada and USA, since 1968. Honorary Sheriff, Grampian and Highlands; former Governor, Aberdeen College of Education; Member, Grampian Children's Panel, 1970-85; Safeguarder (Social Work Scotland Act, 1969 and Children (Scotland) Act, 1995), 1985-2000; Past Chairman, Clinical Division, British Psychological Society. Publications: Help, Hospitals and the Handicapped, 1984; One Boy's War, 1997; Stand By Your Beds!, 2001; Remember Who You Are!, 2007; Chancer, 2007; book chapters and technical and magazine articles. Recreations: photography; reading; writing; chess; guitar playing; painting and drawing; golf; hill-walking. Address: (h.) Glendeveron, 8 Deveron Terrace, Banff AB45 1BB; T.-01261 812624; e-mail: drdavidfindlayclark@btinternet.com

Clark, Derek John, BMus (Hons), DipMusEd (Hons), DRSAMD. Head of Music, Scottish Opera, since 1997; b. 22.8.55, Glasgow; m., Heather Fryer; 1 d. Educ. Dumbarton Academy; Royal Scottish Academy of Music and Drama; University of Durham; London Opera Centre. Debut as professional accompanist, 1976; joined music staff, Welsh National Opera, 1977, conducting debut 1982; Guest Conductor, Mid Wales Opera, 1989-92; Guest Coach and Conductor, Welsh College of Music, 1990-97; Conductor, South Wales Opera, 1994-96; Guest Coach, RSAMD and National Opera Studio, since 1997; arranger/composer since late 1980s including work for radio and television; musicals for young people; choral music (Pub: Roberton/Goodmusic). Silver Medallist, Worshipful Company of Musicians, 1976. Recreation: reading. Address: (b.) Scottish Opera, 39 Elmbank Crescent, Glasgow G2 4PT; T.-0141-248 4567.

Clark, Professor Frank, CBE, MHSM, DipHSM. Director, Strathcarron Hospice, since 1996; Chairman, Forth Valley NHS Board, 2001-02; Honorary Professor, University of Stirling, since 1997; Visiting Professor, Glasgow Caledonian University, since 1993; b. 17.10.46, Aberdeen; m., Linda Margaret; 2 d. Educ. Aberdeen Academy. Greater Glasgow Health Board: Assistant District Administrator, 1977-81, District General Administrator, 1981-83; Lanarkshire Health Board: Director of Administrative Services, 1983-84, Secretary, 1984-85; General Manager, Lanarkshire Health Board, 1985-96; Chairman, Scottish Health Board General Managers Group, 1993-95 (Vice-Chairman, 1995-97); Non-Executive Director, VAMW Homes Ltd. and VAMW Training, 1997-2006; Board Member, New Lanarkshire Ltd., 1994-98; Member, Council of Management, Scottish Partnership Agency, 1998-2001 (Deputy Chairman, 1999-2001); Chairman, Scottish Hospices, 1998-2001; Member, Help the Hospices IHRC, 1998-2001; Chairman: Central Scotland Healthcare NHS Trust, 1999, Forth Valley Primary Care NHS Trust, 1999; Chairman, Forth Valley Health Board, 1999-2000;

President, Rotary Club of Cumbernauld, 2000 and 2005; member of ministerial advisory panel reviewing management and decision-making in NHS Scotland, 2002; Honorary Treasurer, Scottish Partnership for Palliative Care, 2002-03 (Chairman, 2003-06); Chairman, Delivery Group, Scottish Academy for Health Policy and Management, 2003; Convener, Scottish Commission for the Regulation of Care, 2006; Board Member, The Scottish Social Services Council, 2006. Recreations: rotary; reading; music; gardening; driving; DIY; poetry. Address: (b.) Scottish Commission for the Regulation of Care, Compass House, Dundee.

Clark, Gregor Munro, CB, LLB. Counsel to the Scottish Law Commission, since 2006; b. 18.4.46, Glasgow; m., 1, Jane Maralyn Palmer (deceased); 2, Alexandra Groves Miller or Plumtree; 1 s.; 2 d. Educ. Queen's Park Senior Secondary School, Glasgow; Queen's College, St Andrews University. Admitted Faculty of Advocates, 1972; Lord Advocate's Department, 1974-99 (Assistant Parliamentary Draftsman, then Deputy Parliamentary Draftsman, then Parliamentary Draftsman); Counsel to the Scottish Law Commission, 1995-2000; Scottish Parliamentary Counsel, Scottish Executive, 1999-2002 and 2004-06; Scottish Parliamentary Counsel (UK), 2002-04. Recreation: piano. Address: (b.) Scottish Law Commission, 140, Causewayside, Edinburgh EH9 1PR; T.-0131 662 5219.

Clark, Guy Wyndham Nial Hamilton, FSi, JP. Vice Lord Lieutenant, Renfrewshire, 2002-07 (Deputy Lieutenant, 1987-2002); JP Inverclyde, since 1987; b. 28.3.44; m., Brighid Lovell Greene; 2 s.; 1 d. Educ. Eton. Commd. Coldstream Guards, 1962-67; Investment Manager, Murray Johnstone Ltd., Glasgow, 1973-77; Partner, R.C. Greig & Co. (Stockbrokers), Glasgow, 1977-86; Director, Greig, Middleton & Co. Ltd., 1986-97; Managing Director, Murray Johnstone Private Investors Ltd., 1997-2001; Managing Director, Aberdeen Private Investors, 2001-06; Director, Bell Lawrie Investment Management, since 2006. Member, Executive Committee, Erskine Hospital for Disabled Servicemen, 1986-97; Member, International Stock Exchange, 1983. Chairman, JP Advisory Committee, 1991-2002. Recreations: gardening and field sports. Address: (h.) Braeton, Inverkip PA16 0DU; T.-01475 520 619; e-mail: guy.clark@bell-lawrie.co.uk

Clark, Johnston Peter Campbell, LLB, DipLP, NP, MSI. Managing Partner, Blackadders, Solicitors, since 1999; b. 29.10.62, Dundee; m., Sara Elizabeth Philp; 1 s.; 1 d. Educ. High School of Dundee; Aberdeen University. Trainee Solicitor, Blackadder Gilchrist and Robertson, 1984-86; Solicitor, Blackadder Reid Johnston, 1986-88; Partner, Blackadder Reid Johnston, since 1988. Member of Council and Dean, Faculty of Procurators and Solicitors, Dundee; Secretary, Dundee Rep; Secretary, Dundee Disabled Children's Association; External Examiner, Dundee University; Director, ASIM; Deacon, Baker Incorporation of Dundee. Recreations: watching football; playing tennis; garden. Address: (b.) 34 Reform Street, Dundee DD1 1RJ; T.-01382 229222.

E-mail: johnston.clark@blackadders.co.uk

Clark, Katy. MP (Labour), North Ayrshire and Arran, since 2005; b. 3.7.67. Educ. University of Aberdeen. Address: (b.) House of Commons, London SW1A 0AA.

Clark, Robert George, BSc, PhD, MBCS, CEng, CEng, CSci, CITP. Head of Department of Computing Science and Mathematics, University of Stirling, since 2002, Senior Lecturer in Computing Science, since 1989; b. 15.09.44, Perth; m., Maureen; 1 s.; 1 d. Educ. Arbroath High School; University of St Andrews; University of Dundee. Lecturer in Computing Science, University of Stirling, 1969-89. Member, Academic Accreditation Committee, British Computer Society. Publications: Author: Comparative Programming Languages, 3rd Edition, 2001; Author: Programming in ADA, 1985. Recreations: philately; President, Stirling and District Philatelic Society, 2007-08. Address: (b.) Department of Computing Science and Mathematics, University of Stirling, Stirling FK9 4LA; T.-01786 467427; e-mail: rgc@stir.ac.uk

Clarke, Andrew David, MA, PhD. Senior Lecturer in New Testament, University of Aberdeen, since 1995; b. 3.12.64, Bradford; m., Jane; 2 s.; 1 d. Educ. Dean Close School, Cheltenham; University of Cambridge (Girton College). Research Librarian, Tyndale House, Cambridge, 1990-95; Lecturer, then Senior Lecturer, New Testament, University of Aberdeen, since 1995. Chairman of Tyndale House Council; Trustee of Universities and Colleges Christian Fellowship. Publications: A Pauline Theology of Church Leadership, 2008; Serve the Community of the Church: Christians as Leaders and Ministers (First-Century Christians in the Graeco-Roman World), 2000; Secular and Christian Leadership in Corinth: A Socio-Historical and Exegetical Study of 1 Corinthians 1-6, 2nd Edition, 2006. Address: (b.) Divinity and Religious Studies, University of Aberdeen, Aberdeen AB24 3UB.

Clarke, (Christopher) Michael, BA (Hons). Director, National Gallery of Scotland, since 2001, Deputy to The Director-General, since 2007; b. 29.8.52, York; m., Deborah Clare Cowling; 2 s.; 1 d. Educ. Felsted School, Essex; Manchester University. Art Assistant, York City Art Gallery, 1973-76; Research Assistant, British Museum, 1976-78; Assistant Keeper in charge of prints, Whitworth Art Gallery, Manchester, 1978-84; Assistant Keeper, National Gallery of Scotland, 1984-87, Keeper, 1987-2001. Visiting Fellow, Yale Center for British Art, 1985; Clark Art Institute, 2004; Chevalier de l'Ordre des Arts et des Lettres, 2004. Publications include: The Tempting Prospect; A Social History of English Watercolours; The Arrogant Connoisseur (Co-Editor); Richard Payne Knight; Lighting Up the Landscape – French Impressionism and its Origins; Corot and the Art of Landscape; Eyewitness Art – Watercolours; Corot, Courbet und die Maler von Barbizon (Co-Editor); Oxford Concise Dictionary of Art Terms; Monet: The Seine and The Sea (Co-author); The Playfair Project. Recreations: listening to music; golf. Address: (b.) National Gallery of Scotland, The Mound, Edinburgh EH2 2EL; T.-0131-624 6511.

Clarke, Eric Lionel. MP (Labour), Midlothian, 1992-2001; b. 9.4.33, Edinburgh; m., June; 2 s.; 1 d. Educ. Holy Cross Academy; W.M. Ramsey Technical College; Esk Valley Technical College. Coal miner, 1949-77; General Secretary, NUM Scottish Area, 1977-89; County Councillor, Midlothian, 1962-74; Regional Councillor, Lothian, 1974-78. Recreations: fly fishing; gardening; carpentry. Address: (h.) 32 Mortonhall Park Crescent, Edinburgh; T.-0131-664 8214.

Clarke, Kevin John, BA. Secretary, University of Stirling, since 1995; b. 8.3.52, Reading; m., Linda Susan Stewart, 2 d. Educ. Presentation College, Reading; University of Stirling. Scientific Officer, British Library Lending Division, 1975-77; Administrative Assistant, Loughborough University, 1977-83; Assistant Registrar, University of Newcastle upon Tyne, 1983-85; Clerk to the Senatus Academicus, 1985-89, Deputy Secretary, 1989-95, University of Aberdeen. Recreations: music; hill-walking; gardening. Address: (b.) University of Stirling, Stirling FK9 4LA; T.-01786 467018.

E-mail: university.secretary@stir.ac.uk

Clarke, Hon. Lord (Matthew Gerard Clarke). Senator of the College of Justice, since 2000. Educ. Holy Cross

High School, Hamilton; Glasgow University (MA, LLB). Solicitor, 1972; Lecturer, Depatment of Scots Law, Edinburgh University, 1972-78; admitted, Faculty of Advocates, 1978; QC (Scot), 1989; a Judge, Courts of Appeal of Jersey and Guernsey, 1995-2000; Leader, UK Delegation, Council of the Bars and Law Societies of EC, 1992-96; Hon. Fellow, Europa Institute, Edinburgh University, since 1995.

Clarke, Owen J., CBE. Chairman, Scottish Ambulance Service, 1997-2003; Member, Accounts Commission for Scotland, since 2003; Non-Executive Member, Programme Board, Scottish Government, since 2007; Chairman, Health Department, National Management Performance Committee, since 2006; b. 15.3.37, Edinburgh; m., Elizabeth; 2 s.; 1 d. Educ. Portobello High School, Edinburgh. Head of Inland Revenue, North of England, 1988-90; Head of Inland Revenue, Scotland, 1990-97. Trustee, Friends of Craigmillar, 1994-2001. Recreations: golf; hill-walking. Address: (h.) Dyngarth, Redholm Park, North Berwick EH39 4RA; T.-01620 892623.

Clarke, Peter, CBE, BSc, PhD, LLD (Hon), CChem, FRSC, DEd(Hon); b. 18.3.22, Mansfield; m., Ethel (deceased); 2 s. Educ. Queen Elizabeth's Grammar School, Mansfield; University College, Nottingham. Principal, Robert Gordon's Institute of Technology, Aberdeen, 1970-85. Chairman: Scottish Vocational Education Council, 1985-91, Aberdeen Enterprise Trust, 1984-92, Industrial Training Centre, Aberdeen, 1989-95; President: Association of Principals of Colleges, 1980-81, Association for Educational and Training Technology, 1993-95; Member, Science and Engineering Research Council, 1978-82; Trustee, Gordon Cook Foundation, 1988-2005. Recreation: walking. Address: (h.) 108 Whinhill Gate, Aberdeen AB11 7WF; T.-01224 587477.

Clarke, Professor Roger John, ALCM, BA, BTech, MSc, PhD, CEng, MIEE, MIEEE. Professor of Electronic Engineering, Heriot Watt University, since 1989, Emeritus Professor, since 2005; b. 1.10.40, Ewell, Surrey; m., Yvonne Clarke; 1 s. Educ. Gravesend Grammar School; Loughborough University. Development Engineer, STC Ltd., Woolwich, 1962-64; Research Associate, then Lecturer in Electrical Engineering, Loughborough University, 1964-86; Reader in Electrical Engineering, Heriot Watt University, 1986-89. Recreations: gardening; playing the cello; Shakespeare. Address: (b.) Department of Electrical, Electronic and Computer Engineering, School of Engineering and Physical Sciences, Mountbatten Building, Heriot-Watt University, Edinburgh EH14 4AS; T.-0131-451 3323.

Clarke, Rt. Hon. Thomas, CBE, JP. MP (Labour), Coatbridge and Chryston and Bellshill (formerly Monklands West); Shadow Secretary of State for Scotland, 1992-93; b. 10.1.41, Coatbridge. Educ. Columba High School, Coatbridge; Scottish College of Commerce. Former Assistant Director, Scottish Council for Educational Technology; Provost of Monklands, 1975-82; Past President, Convention of Scottish Local Authorities; MP, Coatbridge and Airdrie, 1982-83; author: Disabled Persons (Services Consultation and Representation) Act, 1986, International Development (Reporting and Transparency) Act, 2006; elected four times to Shadow Cabinet; Minister for Film and Tourism, 1997-98; director, amateur film, Give Us a Goal. Recreations: films; walking; reading. Address: (b.) Municipal Buildings, Kildonan Street, Coatbridge ML5 3LF.

Clarkson, Graeme Andrew Telford, LLB. Senior Partner, Baird & Company, Solicitors, Kirkcaldy, since 1990; b. 6.9.53, Fraserburgh; m., Moira; 3 s. Educ. High School of Dundee; Aberdeen University. Law Apprentice, Allan MacDougall & Co., Edinburgh; Assistant, Ranken & Reid,

Edinburgh; Assistant, then Partner, Baird & Company. Past Chairman, Kirkcaldy Round Table; former Council Member, Law Society of Scotland; part time Convenor, Mental Health Tribunal for Scotland. Address: (b.) 2 Park Place, Kirkcaldy Fife; T.-01592 268608.

Cleland, Ronald John, BA. Board Member, NHS Greater Glasgow & Clyde, since 1999; Chairman, Prince & Princess of Wales Hospice, since 2003; Chairman - Scotland, Odgers Ray & Berndtson, since 2006; Interim Chair, NHS Western Isles, 2006-07; Chairman, North Glasgow University Hospitals NHS Trust, 1998-2004; Chairman, West Glasgow Hospitals NHS Trust, 1997-98; Vice Chairman, Yorkhill Hospitals NHS Trust, 1992-97; Director & Partner, Thomson Partners Ltd., 1987-2006; b. 29.5.46, Glasgow; m., Sheena; 2 s.; 2 d. Educ. Allan Glen's School; Strathclyde University. Recreations: sporting interests, both actively and as spectator; reading; travel and music. Address: (b.) Odgers, Ray and Berndtson, 5th Floor, Stock Exchange Court, 77 Nelson Mandela Place, Glasgow G2 1QT; T.-0141 225 6320; e-mail: ronnie.cleland@odgers.com

Clifford, Sir Timothy (Peter Plint), Kt 2002, BA, AMA, HonLLD (St. Andrews), DLitt (Glasgow), LLD (Aberdeen), FRSE, FRSA, FSAScot. Director-General, National Galleries of Scotland, 2001-06, Director, 1984-2001; b. 26.1.46; m., Jane Olivia Paterson; 1 d. Educ. Sherborne; Perugia University; Courtauld Institute, London University. Manchester City Art Galleries: Assistant Keeper, Department of Paintings, 1968-72, Acting Keeper, 1972; Assistant Keeper, Department of Ceramics, Victoria and Albert Museum, London, 1972-76; Assistant Keeper, British Art, Department of Prints and Drawings, British Museum, London, 1976-78; Director, Manchester City Art Galleries, 1978-84. Chairman, International Committee for Museums of Fine Art (ICFA), 1980-83; Member, Museums and Galleries Commission, 1983-88; Member, Board, British Council, 1987-92; Member, Executive Committee, Scottish Museums Council, 1984-2002; National Museums Committee (CODONC), 1995-2006; President, NADFAS, 1996-2006 (Vice-President, 1990-96); Trustee: The Wallace Collection, since 2003, the former Royal Yacht Britannia, since 1998; Member, Hermitage Development Trust (Somerset House), 1999-2003, and Hermitage at Amstelhof, Amsterdam, 2000-03; Vice President, Turner Society, 1984-86 and since 1989; Vice-President, Frigate Unicorn Preservation Society, 1987-2003; British Institute of Management's Special Award, 1991; Member, Ateneo Veneto (Italy), since 1997; Grand Ufficiale della Stella della Solidarieta; Commendatore all'Ordine del Merito della Repubblica Italiana, 1988 (Cavaliere, since 1988); Member, Advisory Council, Friends of Courtauld Institute, since 1990; Patron, The Attingham Trust, since 2006; Freedom, City of London; Freeman (Liveryman, since 2006) of the Goldsmiths Company. Recreations: bird-watching; entomology. Clubs: Garrick; Beefsteak; New (Edinburgh). Address: (b.) The West Wing, Tyninghame House, Dunbar, East Lothian EH42 1XW.

Clift, Benedict, BMSc (Hons), MBChB, FRCSEd, FRCSOrth. Consultant Orthopaedic and Trauma Surgeon, Ninewells Hospital, Dundee, since 1995; Clinical Director of Musculoskeletal and A. & E. Services; Honorary Senior Lecturer, Dundee University; m., 22.7.62, Manchester; m., Alison; 1 s.; 2 d. Educ. Cardinal Langley Grammar School; Dundee University. Recreations: jazz; trees; Dante; Homer; classical piano; wrist watches. Address: (b.) Department of Orthopaedic and Trauma Surgery, Ninewells Hospital, Dundee DD1 9SY; T.-01382 660111.

Clive, Eric McCredie, CBE, MA, LLB, LLM, SJD, FRSE. Visiting Professor, Faculty of Law, Edinburgh University, since 1999; b. 24.7.38, Stranraer; m., Kay McLeman; 1 s.; 2

d. Educ. Stranraer Academy; Stranraer High School; Universities of Edinburgh, Michigan, Virginia. Lecturer, Senior Lecturer, Reader, Professor of Scots Law, Faculty of Law, Edinburgh University, 1962-81; Commissioner, Scottish Law Commission, 1981-99. Publications: The Law of Husband and Wife in Scotland (4th edition), 1997; legal articles. Address: (h.) 14 York Road, Edinburgh EH5 3EH; T.-0131-552 2875.

Closier, Michael John. Group Chief Executive, Scottish Exhibition and Conference Centre, since 1992; Chairman, Clarion Events Scotland Ltd., since 2003; b. 15.2.47, London; m., Anne-Marie; 1 s. 1 step-d. Educ. Lanchester Polytechnic. Managing Director, Compuser Ltd.; Technical Director, Centronics Ltd.; Managing Director, Bix Ltd.; Director, Peerless Control Systems. Member: IoD, CBI, ICCA, Advisory Committee, Glasgow Common Purpose; Past Chair, NAEH; Exhibition Venues Association, Business Tourism Scotland. Recreations: fell walking; gardening; opera; cooking. Address: SECC, Glasgow G3 8YW; T.-0141-275 6210; e-mail: mike.closier@secc.co.uk

Clouting, David Wallis, BDS, MSc, LDSRCS (Eng), DDPH. Specialist in dental public health; Clinical Director of Community Dental Services, Borders Primary Care NHS Trust, 2000-03, NHS Borders, since 2003; b. 29.3.53, London; m., Dr. Margaret M.C. Bacon; 3 s.; 1 d. Educ. Leyton County High School for Boys; University College Hospital Dental School, London; Institute of Dental Surgery, London; Joint Department of Dental Public Health, London Hospital Medical College and University College. Senior Dental Officer for Special Needs, East and North Hertfordshire Health Authorities, 1983-90; Chief Administrative Dental Officer, Borders Health Board, 1990-95; Community Dental Services Manager, Borders Community Health Services NHS Trust, 1995-99. Recreations: amateur radio; swimming; hill walking. Address: (b.) NHS Borders, Dental Department, Westgrove, Waverley Road, Melrose TD6 9SJ.

Clow, Robert George Menzies. Former Chairman, John Smith & Son (Glasgow) Ltd. (Managing Director (1969-94); b. 27.1.34, Sian, Shensi, North China; m., Katrina M. Watson. Educ. Eltham College, London. Trained as a Japanese as a child; National Service, RAF; trained as a bookseller, Bumpus London; worked in Geneva; joined John Smith & Son (Glasgow), 1960. Founded, with others, The New Glasgow Society, 1965 (Chairman 1967, 1968); worked for 12 years in rehabilitating St. Vincent Crescent, Glasgow, as founder member, St. Vincent Crescent Area Association; Secretary, First Glasgow Housing Association, since 1978; Past Chairman, Heritage Buildings Preservation Trust, currently Project Manager. Restored Aiket Castle, 1976-79 (winner of an Europa Nostra Merit Award, 1989; National Trust for Scotland: Member, Council 1978 and 1991, Member, Executive, 1980-90; Formerly Executive Member, Committee, Strathclyde Building Preservation Trust, 1986; Architectural Heritage Fund Council of Management, 1989-2001. Recreations: farming; bee keeping; opera; restoring old houses, swimming; skiing; reading on holiday. Address: Aiket Castle, Dunlop, Ayrshire; T.-(b.) 015604 84643.

Clugston, Carol, BSc (Hons), PhD. Secretary to the Faculty of Medicine/Head of Division of Education and Administration, University of Glasgow, since 2005; b. 26.10.62, Glasgow; m., Ewan J. Graham; 1 s. Educ. Dumbarton Academy; University of Glasgow. Research Scientist, Cancer Research Campaign Beatson Laboratories, 1989-94; Nanoelectronics Research Centre Administrator, University of Glasgow, 1994-98;

Executive Assistant to Vice-Principal (Research), University of Glasgow, 1998-2005. Community Councillor, Stepps & District. Recreations: silversmithing; painting. Address: (b.) Wolfson Medical School Building, University of Glasgow, University Avenue, Glasgow G12 8QQ; T.-0141-330-4979; e-mail: c.clugston@clinmed.gla.ac.uk

Clyde, The Rt. Hon. The Lord (James John Clyde), PC, Baron (Life Peer), DUniv (Edin), DUniv (Heriot-Watt), DLitt (Napier), BA (Oxon), LLB. Justice Oversight Commissioner (N. Ireland), 2003-06; Lord of Appeal in Ordinary, 1996-2001; Senator of the College of Justice, 1985-96; b. 29.1.32, Edinburgh; m., Ann Clunie Hoblyn; 2 s. Educ. Edinburgh Academy; Corpus Christi College, Oxford; Edinburgh University. Called to Scottish Bar, 1959; QC, 1971; Advocate Depute, 1973-74; Chancellor to Bishop of Argyll and the Isles, 1972-85; a Judge of the Courts of Appeal of Jersey and Guernsey, 1979-85; Chairman: Medical Appeal Tribunal, 1974-85, Committee of Investigation for Scotland on Agricultural Marketing, 1984-85, Scottish Valuation Advisory Council, 1987-96 (Member, since 1972); Member, UK Delegation to CCBE, 1978-84 (Leader, 1981-84); Chairman of the Inquiry into the removal of children from Orkney, 1991-92. Trustee and Manager, St. Mary's Music School, 1976-93; Convener, Children in Scotland, 2003-06; Trustee, National Library of Scotland, 1978-94; Director, Edinburgh Academy, 1979-88; Vice-President, Royal Blind Asylum and School, since 1987; President, Scottish Young Lawyers' Association, 1988-97; Chairman, St. George's School for Girls, 1989-97; Governor, Napier Polytechnic of Edinburgh, 1989-93; Chancellor's Assessor and Vice Chairman, Court, Edinburgh University, 1993-97. Recreations: music; gardening. Address: (h.) 12 Dublin Street, Edinburgh, EH1 3PP.

Clydesmuir, 3rd Baron (David Ronald Colville); b. 8.4.49; m.; 2 s.; 2 d. Educ. Charterhouse. Succeeded to title, 1996.

Coats, Adrian James Macandrew, MA, ACA, FCT. Director of Treasury and Purchasing, Scottish Power, since 2007; Non-Executive Director, Murray Income Trust plc, since 1999; b. 16.4.55, Glasgow; m., Elizabeth (Libby); 1 s.; 1 d. Educ. Eton College; University of Edinburgh. KPMG London, 1977-81; Grand Metropolitan plc, London, 1981-89; Scottish Power plc, since 1990. Trustee of Scottish Power Pension Fund. Recreations: trout and salmon fishing; shooting. Address: (b.) Scottish Power Ltd., 1 Atlantic Quay, Glasgow G2 8SP.

Cobbe, Professor Stuart Malcolm, MA, MD, FRCP, FMedSci, FRSE. Professor of Medical Cardiology, Glasgow University, since 1985; b. 2.5.48, Watford; m., Patricia Frances; 3 d. Educ. Royal Grammar School, Guildford; Cambridge University. Training in medicine, Cambridge and St. Thomas Hospital, London; qualified, 1972; specialist training in cardiology, National Heart Hospital, London, and John Radcliffe Hospital, Oxford; research work, University of Heidelberg, 1981; Consultant Cardiologist and Senior Lecturer, Oxford, 1982-85. Recreation: walking. Address: (b.) Department of Medical Cardiology, Queen Elizabeth Building, Royal Infirmary, Glasgow G31 2ER; T.-0141-211 4722.

Cochrane of Cults, 4th Baron (Ralph Henry Vere Cochrane), DL; b. 20.9.26; m.; 2 s.; succeeded to title, 1990. Educ. Eton; King's College, Cambridge.

Cockburn, David William, LLB, WS, NP. Consultant, Archibald Campbell and Harley WS; b. 4.2.43, Peebles; m., Evelyn; 1 d. Educ. Peebles High School; Edinburgh University. Apprentice, Glasgow Corporation, 1964-66; Assistant, Breeze Paterson and Chapman, Glasgow, 1966-69; Archibald Campbell and Harley, WS, since 1970; lectures widely on commercial property and planning law. Recreations: sports; hillwalking. Address: (b.) 37 Queen Street, Edinburgh EH2 1JX; T.-0131-220 3000.

Cockburn, Professor Forrester, CBE, FRSE, MD, FRCPGlas, FRCPEdin, FRCPCH (Hon), FRCSEd (Hon), DCH. Past Chairman, Yorkhill NHS Trust; Emeritus Professor and Senior Research Fellow, Department of Child Health, Royal Hospital for Sick Children, Yorkhill, Glasgow; formerly Samson Gemmell Professor of Child Health, Glasgow University; b. 13.10.34, Edinburgh; m., Alison Fisher Grieve; 2 s. Educ. Leith Academy; Edinburgh University. Early medical training, Edinburgh Royal Infirmary, Royal Hospital for Sick Children, Edinburgh, and Simpson Memorial Maternity Pavilion, Edinburgh; Research Fellow in Paediatric Metabolic Disease, Boston University; Visiting Professor, San Juan University, Puerto Rico; Nuffield Fellow, Institute for Medical Research, Oxford University; Wellcome Senior Research Fellow, then Senior Lecturer, Department of Child Life and Health, Edinburgh University. Publications: a number of textbooks on paediatric medicine, neonatal medicine, nutrition and metabolic diseases. Recreation: sailing. Address: (b.) 53, Hamilton Drive, Glasgow G12 8DP; T.-0141 339 2973.

Cockhead, Peter, BSc (Econ), MA, MSc, MRTPI. Director, North East Scotland Transport Partnership (NESTRANS), 2002-07 (retired); Teaching and Research Fellow in Land Economy, University of Aberdeen; Teaching Fellow in Town and Regional Planning, University of Dundee; Associate, BusinessLab; b. 1.12.46, Beckenham; m., Diana Douglas; 2 s.; 1 d. Educ. Beckenham Grammar School; London School of Economics; University of Witwatersrand, South Africa; University of Edinburgh. Lecturer: University of Witwatersrand, 1970-71, University of Edinburgh, 1973-74; Consultant: OECD, Paris, 1974, Percy Johnson-Marshall and Associates, Edinburgh, 1974-75; Grampian Regional Council: Assistant Director of Planning, 1975-83, Depute Director of Planning, 1983-90, Regional Planning Manager, 1990-95; Director of Planning and Strategic Development, Aberdeen City Council, 1995-2001. Chairman, Scottish Society of Directors of Planning, 1997-98; Chairman, Scottish Planning Education Forum, 1999-2001; Executive Secretary, North Sea Commission, 1992-95. Recreations: hillwalking; open water; swimming; music; VSO; family. Address: (h.) 158 Midstocket Road, Aberdeen AB15 5HT; T.-01224 625524.

Coffey, Willie, MSP (SNP), Kilmarnock and Loudon, since 2007; b. 24.5.58. Address: (b.) Scottish Parliament, Edinburgh EH99 1SP.

Cogdell, Professor Richard John, BSc, PhD, FRSE, FRS. Hooker Professor of Botany, Glasgow University, since 1993; b. 4.2.49, Guildford; m., Barbara; 1 s.; 1 d. Educ. Royal Grammar School, Guildford; Bristol University. Post-doctoral research, USA, 1973-75; Botany Department, Glasgow University, 1975-94, now Institute of Biomedical and Life Sciences. Member, Board of Governors, Scottish Crop Research Institute, 1997-2005; Chairman, Trustees, Glasgow Macintyre Begonia Trust; Member, Council of the Biochemical Society; Chairman of the Scientific Advisory Board of the Max Planck Institute for Bioinorganic Chemistry, Mülheim-an-der-Ruhr, since 2007. Recreations: cricket; aerobics; Scottish dancing; theatre. Address: (b.) Division of Biochemistry and Molecular Biology, Glasgow University, Glasgow G12 8QQ; T.-0141-330 4232; e-mail: R.Cogdell@bio.gla.ac.uk

Coggins, Professor John Richard, MA, PhD, FRSE. Professor of Molecular Enzymology and Vice Principal, Life Sciences, Medicine and Veterinary Medicine, Glasgow University, since 2006; b. 15.1.44, Bristol; m., Dr. Lesley F. Watson; 1 s.; 1 d. Educ. Bristol Grammar School; Queen's College, Oxford; Ottawa University. Post-doctoral Fellow: Biology Department, Brookhaven National Laboratory, New York, 1970-72, Biochemistry Department, Cambridge University, 1972-74; Glasgow University: Lecturer/Senior Lecturer/ Professor, Biochemistry Department, 1974-95, Director, Graduate School of Biomedical and Life Sciences, 1995-97, Head, Division of Biochemistry and Molecular Biology, 1997-98, Research Director, Institute of Biomedical and Life Sciences, 1998-2000, Director/Dean, Institute of Biomedical and Life Sciences, 2000-05. Chairman: Molecular Enzymology Group, Biochemical Society, 1982-85, Biophysics and Biochemistry Committee, SERC, 1985-88; Managing Director, Biomac Ltd., 1988-94; Member, DTI-Research Councils Biotechnology Joint Advisory Board, 1989-94; Member of Council, AFRC, 1991-94; Biochemistry Adviser to UFC, 1989-92; Governing Member, Caledonian Research Foundation, since 1994; Chairman, HEFC Research Assessment Panel for Biochemistry, 1995-96; Royal Society of Edinburgh: Research Awards Convener, 1999-2002, Vice President (Life Sciences), 2003-06; Member, Scottish Science Advisory Committee, 2002-07; Chairman, Heads of University Biological Science Departments, 2003-07; Trustee, Glasgow Science Centre, since 2004. Recreations: sailing; travelling. Address: (b.) 11 The Square, Glasgow University, Glasgow G12 8QQ; T.-0141 330 2955; e-mail: j.coggins@bio.gla.ac.uk

Cohen, Professor Anthony Paul, BA, MSc (SocSc), PhD, HonDSc (Edin), FRSE. Principal and Vice-Chancellor, Queen Margaret University, Edinburgh, since 2003; b. 3.8.46, London; m., Dr. Bronwen J. Cohen; 3 s. Educ. Whittinghame College, Brighton; Southampton University. Research Fellow, Memorial University of Newfoundland, 1968-70; Assistant Professor, Queen's University, Kingston, Ontario, 1970-71; Lecturer/Senior Lecturer in Social Anthropology, Manchester University, 1971-89; Professor of Social Anthropology, Edinburgh University, 1989-2003 (Provost of Law and Social Sciences, 1997-2002); Hon. Professor, since 2003. Convener, Scottish Forum for Graduate Education, 1996-98. Publications: The Management of Myths; The Symbolic Construction of Community; Whalsay: Symbol, Segment and Boundary in a Shetland Island Community; Self Consciousness: an alternative anthropology of identity; Belonging (Editor); Symbolising Boundaries (Editor); Humanising the City? (Co-Editor); Questions of Consciousness (Co-Editor); Signifying Identities (Editor). Recreations: occasional thinking; music; novels. Address: (b.) Queen Margaret University, Musselburgh, East Lothian EH21 6UU; T.-0131-474-0000.

Cohen, Cyril, OBE, JP, FRCPEdin, FRCPGlas. Director, Brechin Day Care Ltd.; Director, Angus Care and Repair; Director, Angus Community Care Charitable Trust; Member, Angus Carers Planning Group and Angus Older Peoples Planning Group; Member, Aberlemno Community Council; Honorary Fellow, Dundee University; retired Consultant Physician, Geriatric Medicine, and Hon. Senior Lecturer, Geriatric Medicine, Dundee University; Chairman, Angus Community Care Forum; b. 2.11.25, Manchester; m., Dr. Sarah E. Nixon; 2 s. Educ. Manchester Central High School; Victoria University, Manchester. Embarked on career in geriatric medicine, 1952. Past

President, Forfarshire Medical Association; former Chairman, Advisory Group on Health Education for Elderly People, Health Education Board for Scotland; former Chairman, Geriatric Medicine Sub-Committee, National Medical Consultative Committee; former Member/Chairman, Angus District and Tayside Area Medical Committees; Secretary/Chairman, Tayside Area Hospital Medical Services Committee; Member, Scottish and UK Central Committee, Hospital Medical Services, and Chairman, Geriatric Medicine Sub-Committee; Past Chairman, Scottish Branch, British Geriatric Society (former Council Member); Member, Panel on Nutrition of the Elderly, COMA; Honorary Vice-President, Dundee and District Branch, British Diabetic Association; Life Member, Manchester Medical Society; former Member, Chief Scientist's Committee for Research on Equipment for the Disabled and Health Services Research Committee; former Chairman, Angus Access Panel; Director, Angus Community Care Charitable Trust; Director, Angus Care and Repair; Member, Angus Joint Planning Group, Care in the Community; Previous Member, Angus SVQ Management Committee; Honorary President, Radio North Angus (Hospital Radio); former Member, Brechin and Forfar School Councils, Forfar Academy School Board and Central Committee on Primary Education; Secretary, Aberlemno Community Council; former Vice-Chairman, Angus Association of Voluntary Organisations and Director, Brechin Day Care Ltd.; former Director, Scottish Hospital Advisory Service; Past President, Montrose Burns Club and Brechin Arts Guild; Member, League of Friends, Forfar Hospitals; Past Chairman, Angus Care of the Elderly Co-ordinating Group; Member, Age Concern Angus Executive; Member, Angus Joint Management and Commissioning Group (Community Care). Publications: many on geriatric medicine and care of the elderly. Recreations: photography; short walks; being at home. Address: (h.) Mansefield, Aberlemno, Forfar DD8 3PD; T.-0130-783 259.

Cohen, Lady Patricia Townsend Wade, BSc, PhD. Professor of Molecular Biology, Dundee University, since 2001; Head of Molecular Biology and Special Appointments Scientist, Medical Research Council Protein Phosphorylation Unit, Department of Biochemistry, Dundee University; b. 3.5.44, Worsley, Lancashire; m., Professor Sir Philip Cohen (qv); 1 s.; 1 d. Educ. Bolton School; University College, London. Postdoctoral Research Fellow, Department of Medical Genetics, Washington University, Seattle, USA, 1969-71; Department of Biochemistry, Dundee University: Science Research Council Fellowship, 1971-72, Research/Teaching Fellow (part-time), 1972-83, Lecturer (part-time), 1983-90, Senior Lecturer, 1990-91, Reader, 1995. Publications: 140 papers and reviews in scientific journals. Recreations: reading; golf. Address: (h.) Inverbay II, Invergowrie, Dundee DD2 5DQ; T.-01382 562328; e-mail: p.t.w.cohen@dundee.ac.uk

Cohen, Professor Sir Philip, BSc, PhD, FRS, FRSE. Royal Society Research Professor, University of Dundee, since 1984 and Director, Wellcome Trust Biocentre, since 1997; Honorary Director, Medical Research Council Protein Phosphorylation Unit, since 1990; b. 22.7.45, London; m., Patricia Townsend Wade (qv); 1 s.; 1 d. Educ. Hendon County Grammar School; University College, London. Science Research Council/NATO postdoctoral Fellow, Department of Biochemistry, University of Washington, 1969-71; Dundee University: Lecturer in Biochemistry, 1971-78, Reader in Biochemistry, 1978-81, Professor of Enzymology, 1981-84. Publications: 480 papers and reviews, one book. Recreations: bridge; golf; natural history. Address: (h.) Inverbay II, Invergowrie, Dundee; T.-01382 562328.

Cohen, Professor Stephen Douglas, BSc, PhD. Professor of Number Theory, University of Glasgow, since 2002; b.

7.1.44, London; m., Yvonne Joy Roulet; 2 d. Educ. Allan Glen's School, Glasgow; University of Glasgow. Department of Mathematics, University of Glasgow: Lecturer, 1968, Senior Lecturer, 1988, Reader, 1992; visiting positions: Research Associate, University of Illinois, 1979, Lecturer, University of Witwatersrand, 1987, Professor, University of Limoges, France, 1994; Member, various editorial boards including: Finite Fields and Their Applications, since 1995, Applicable Algebra, since 1996, Glasgow Mathematical Journal, 1986-99 and since 2002, Proceedings of Edinburgh Mathematical Society, 1991-97. Publications: over 100 articles in mathematics research journals. Recreations: walking; music appreciation, church activities. Address: (b.) Department of Mathematics, University of Glasgow Glasgow G12 8QW; T.-0141-330 6356; e-mail: sdc@maths.gla.ac.uk

Cohn, Professor Samuel Kline, MA, PhD, FRHistS. Professor of History, Glasgow University, since 1995; b. 1949, Birmingham, Alabama; m., Genevieve Warwick; 2 s. Educ. Indian Springs School; Harvard University. Assistant Professor, Wesleyan University, Connecticut, 1978-79; Assistant Professor, Brandeis University, 1979-86; Associate Professor of History, Brandeis University, 1986-89; Visiting Professor, Brown University, 1990-91; Professor of History, Brandeis University, 1989-95. Publications include: Women in the Streets: Essays on Sex and Power in the Italian Renaissance, 1996; The Cult of Remembrance and the Black Death: Six Renaissance Cities in Central Italy, 1997; The Black Death and the Transformation of the West (Co-author), 1997; Creating the Florentine State: Peasants and Rebellion, 1348-1434, 1999; The Black Death Transformed: Disease and Culture in Early Renaissance Europe, 2002; Popular Protest in Late Medieval Europe; Lust for Liberty: The Politics of Social Revolt in Medieval Europe, 1200-1425, 2006. Recreation: hill-running. Address: (h.) 14 Hamilton Drive, Glasgow; T.-0141-330 4369.

Cole-Hamilton, Professor David John, BSc, PhD, CChem, FRSC, FRSE. Irvine Professor of Chemistry, St. Andrews University, since 1985; b. 22.5.48, Bovey Tracey; m., Elizabeth Ann Brown; 2 s.; 2 d. Educ. Haileybury and ISC; Hertford; Edinburgh University. Research Assistant, Temporary Lecturer, Imperial College, 1974-78; Lecturer, Senior Lecturer, Liverpool University, 1978-85. Sir Edward Frankland Fellow, Royal Society of Chemistry, 1984-85; Corday Morgan Medallist, 1983; President: Chemistry Section, British Association for the Advancement of Science, 1995, Chemistry Sectional Committee, Royal Society of Edinburgh, 1993-95; Vice President, Royal Society of Chemistry, Dalton Council, 1996-99. Museums and Galleries Commission Award for Innovation in Conservation, 1995 (runner-up); Royal Society of Chemistry Award for Organometallic Chemists, 1998; Tilden Lecturer, Royal Society of Chemistry, 2000-2001; Sir Geoffrey Wilkinson Prize Lecturer of the Royal Society of Chemistry, 2005-06; Scientific Editor, Journal of the Chemical Society, Dalton Transactions, 2000-03. Address: (b.) Department of Chemistry, The Purdie Building, St. Andrews, Fife KY16 9ST; T.-01334 463805.

Colella, Anton, BA (Hons), DipEd. Chief Executive, Institute of Chartered Accountants of Scotland, since 2006; Chief Executive, Scottish Qualifications Authority, 2003-06 (Director of Qualifications, 2002-03); b. 25.5.61, Glasgow; m., Angela; 2 s.; 2 d. Educ. St Mungo's Academy, Glasgow; Stirling University. Teacher of Religious Education, Holyrood Secondary School, Glasgow, 1983-87; Principal Teacher of Religious Education, St Columba's High School,

Gourock, 1987-92, Holyrood Secondary School, 1992-96; Assistant Head Teacher, Holyrood Secondary School, 1996-99; Depute Head Teacher, St Margaret Mary's Secondary, Glasgow, 1999-20001; seconded to Scottish Qualifications Authority, 2001; Board Member: Glasgow College of Nautical Studies, 2001, Quality Assurance Agency Scotland Committee, 2001, Scottish Further Education Unit, 2001. Recreations: family life; music; rugby; eating out. Address: (b.) CA House, 21 Haymarket Yards, Edinburgh EH12 5BH; T.-0141-347 0266; e-mail: acolella@icas.org.uk

Collins, Rev. Catherine E. E., MA (Hons) BD, CertEd, DipCounselling. Parish Minister, Broughty New Kirk, since 2006; b. 12.11.54, Hastings; m., Rev. David A. Collins; 2 s. Educ. Kelso High School; University of St. Andrews. Teacher of English, Full Time and Temporary in Borders and Renfrewshire, 1977-89; Parish Minister (Job Share), Greyfriars Parish Church, Lanark, 1993-2006. (Past) Moderator of Presbytery; Depute Presbytery Clerk; Convener, Pastoral Support, Church of Scotland's Board of Ministry; Currently Trustee, Housing and Loan Fund for Retired Ministers. Recreations: gardening; walking; genealogy. Address: (h./b.) 25 Ballinard Gardens, Broughty Ferry, Dundee DD5 1BZ; T.-01382 778874; e-mail: ccollins@broughtynewkirk.com

Collins, Dennis Ferguson, MA, LLB, WS, FRPSL. Senior Partner, Carlton Gilruth, Solicitors, Dundee, 1976-93; Honorary Sheriff; b. 26.3.30, Dundee; m., Elspeth Margaret Nicoll; 1 s.; 1 d. Educ. High School of Dundee; St. Andrews University. Solicitor, 1957; Part-time Lecturer in Scots Law, St. Andrews University, then Dundee University, 1960-79; Agent Consulaire for France in Dundee, 1976-96; Hon. Secretary, Dundee Society for Prevention of Cruelty to Children, 1962-90; Assessor to the Lord Dean of Guild of Dundee, since 1989; Clerk to the Guildry Incorporation of Dundee, 1993-2000; Treasurer, Dundee Congregational Church, since 1966; Past President, Dundee and District Philatelic Society; Past President, Association of Scottish Philatelic Societies; Dean, Faculty of Procurators and Solicitors in Dundee, 1987-89. Recreations: Chinese postal history; gardening; Sherlock Holmes pursuits; travelling in France. Address: (h.) Stirling Lodge, Craigiebarn Road, Dundee DD4 7PL; T.-01382 458070.

Collins, Sir Kenneth Darlingston, BSc (Hons), MSc. Chairman, Advisory Committee, SAGES (Scottish Association of Geosciences, Environment & Society), since 2008; Chairman, Scottish Environment Protection Agency, 1999-2007; Member (Labour), European Parliament, 1979-99; Ambassador for the National Asthma Campaign; b. 12.8.39, Hamilton; m., Georgina Frances Pollard; 1 s.; 1 d. Educ. St. John's Grammar School; Hamilton Academy; Glasgow University; Strathclyde University. Steelworks apprentice, 1956-59; University, 1960-65; Planning Officer, 1965-66; WEA Tutor, 1966-67; Lecturer: Glasgow College of Building, 1967-69, Paisley College of Technology, 1969-79; Member: East Kilbride Town and District Council, 1973-79, Lanark County Council, 1973-75, East Kilbride Development Corporation, 1976-79; Chairman, NE Glasgow Children's Panel, 1974-76; European Parliament: Deputy Leader, Labour Group, 1979-84, Chairman, Environment Committee, 1979-84 and 1989-99 (Vice-Chairman, 1984-87), Socialist Spokesman on Environment, Public Health and Consumer Protection, 1984-89; Fellow, Royal Scottish Geographical Society; Hon. Fellow, Chartered Institution of Water and Environmental Management; Hon. Fellow, Chartered Institution of Wastes Management; former Board Member, Institute for European Environmental Policy, London; Fellow, Industry and Parliament Trust; former Board Member, Energy Action Scotland; former Member, British Waterways Scotland Group; former Trustee, The Green Foundation; Board Member, Central Scotland Forest Trust, 2001-04 (Chairman, 1998-2001); Former Board Member, Forward Scotland; Chairman, Tak Tent Cancer Support, 1999-2002; former Member, Management Board, European Environment Agency; Honorary Vice President, National Society for Clean Air; Vice President, Royal Environmental Health Institute of Scotland; Vice President: Town and Country Planning Association, The Trading Standards Institute, The Association of Drainage Authorities; former Chairman, Health Equality Europe; Member, Advisory Board, ESRC Genomics Policy and Research Forum; Member: European Public Affairs Consultancies Association (EPACA) Professional Practices Panel, European Commission High Level Group on Competitiveness, Energy and the Environment, since 2006. Knighthood in 2003 for services to Environmental Protection; Honorary Degree of Doctor, University of Paisley, 2004. Recreations: music; boxer dogs; gardening. Address: (b.) 11 Stuarton Park, East Kilbride G74 4LA; T.-013552 37282; e-mail: ken.collins@blueyonder.co.uk

Collins, Kenneth E., MPhil, PhD, FRCGP. President, Glasgow Jewish Representative Council, 1995-98 and 2004-07 (Hon. President, 1998-2001, President, 1995-98); Chairman, Scottish Council of Jewish Communities, 1999-2003; Chairman, Scottish Jewish Archives Ccentre; b. 23.12.47, Glasgow; m., Irene Taylor; 1 s.; 3 d. Educ. High School of Glasgow; Glasgow University. General medical practitioner in Glasgow, since 1976; Medical Officer, Newark Lodge, Glasgow, since 1978; Research Fellow, Centre for the History of Medicine, Glasgow University. Past Chairman, Glasgow Board of Jewish Education. Publications: Aspects of Scottish Jewry, 1987; Go and Learn: International Story of the Jews and Medicine in Scotland, 1988; Second City Jewry, 1990; Be Well!, Jewish Immigrant Health and Welfare in Glasgow, 1860-1914, 2001. Address: (h.) 3 Glenburn Road, Giffnock, Glasgow G46 6RE.

Coltrane, Robbie, DA. Actor/Director; b. 31.3.50, Glasgow. Educ. Trinity College, Glenalmond; Glasgow School of Art. Film credits: Subway Riders, 1979, Balham Gateway to the South, 1980, Britannia Hospital, 1981, Scrubbers, 1982, Krull, 1982, Ghost Dance, 1983, Chinese Boxes, 1984, The Supergrass, 1984, Defense of the Realm, 1985, Revolution, 1985, Caravaggio, 1985, Absolute Beginners, 1985, Mona Lisa, 1985, Eat the Rich, 1987, The Fruit Machine, 1987, Slipstream, 1988, Bert Rigby, You're a Fool, 1988, Danny Champion of the World, 1988, Let It Ride, 1988, Henry V, 1988, Nuns on the Run, 1989, Perfectly Normal, 1989, Pope Must Die, 1990, Oh What A Night, 1991, Adventures of Huck Finn, 1992, Goldeneye, 1995, Buddy, 1996, Montana, 1997, Frogs for Snakes, 1997, Message in a Bottle, 1998, The World Is Not Enough, 1999, From Hell, 2000, Harry Potter and the Philosopher's Stone, 2001, Harry Potter and the Chamber of Secrets, 2002, Harry Potter and Prisoner of Azkaban, 2003, Harry Potter and the Goblet of Fire, 2004, Ocean's 12, Stormbreaker, 2005, Harry Potter and the Order of the Phoenix, 2006; The Brothers Bloom, 2007; Harry Potter and the Half Blood Prince, 2007; theatre credits: The Bug, 1976, Mr Joyce is Leaving, 1978, The Slab Boys, 1978, The Transfiguration of Benno Blimpie, 1978, The Loveliest Night of the Year, 1979-80, Dick Whittington, 1979, Snobs and Yobs, 1980, Yr Obedient Servant (one-man show), 1987, Mistero Buffo (one-man show), 1990; television credits include: roles in several The Comic Strip Presents productions, lead role in Tutti Frutti (BBC Scotland), Alive and Kicking, 1991, Coltrane in a Cadillac, 1992, Cracker, 1993, 1994, 1995, Ebbtide, 1996, Coltrane's Planes and Automobiles, 1997, Alice in Wonderland, 1998, The Plan Man, Frazier, 2004, Cracker 9:11, 2005; B Road Britain, 2007. Recreations: vintage cars; sailing; painting; reading;

movies. Address: c/o CDA, 125 Gloucester Road, London SW7 4TE.

Colville of Culross, 4th Viscount (John Mark Alexander Colville, QC); b. 19.7.33; m.; 1 s.; 4 s. by pr. m. Educ. Rugby; New College, Oxford. Barrister; Minister of State, Home Office, 1972-74; Director, Securities and Futures Authority, 1987-93; Chairman: Mental Health Act Commission, 1983-88, Alcohol Education and Research Council, 1984-90, Parole Board, 1988-92; UK Representative, UN Human Rights Commission, 1980-83; Member, UN Working Group on Disappeared Persons, 1980-84 (Chairman, 1981-84); Special Rapporteur on Human Rights in Guatemala, 1983-86; Member, UN Human Rights Committee, 1996-2000; reports on Prevention of Terrorism Act and Northern Ireland Emergency Powers Act, 1986-93; Circuit Judge, 1993-99, Assistant Surveillance Commissioner, since 2001.

Colvin, Professor Calum Munro, OBE, DA, MA (RCA), RSA. Professor of Fine Art Photography, Dundee University, since 2001; artist, since 1985; b. 26.10.61, Glasgow; m., Shirley Jean; 3 s.; 1 d. Educ. North Berwick High School; Duncan of Jordanstone College of Art and Design; Royal College of Art, London. Lecturer in Fine Art, Duncan of Jordanstone, Dundee University, from 1993; Creative Scotland Award, 2000; 13th Higashikawa Overseas Photographer Prize, 1997; has exhibited work internationally since 1986 with work in many collections; recent solo exhibitions include Scottish National Gallery of Modern Art, 1998, University of Salamanca, 1998; Kawasaki City Museum, 1998; Scottish National Portrait Gallery, 2002. Address: (h.) 1 Duddingston Park South, Edinburgh EH15 3NX; T.-0131-669 0218; e-mail: c.colvin@dundee.ac.uk

Colvin, David, CBE, DUniv (Stirling), HonSSA. Governor, St Columba's Hospice, 1998-2003; Chair, Exhibiting Societies of Scottish Artists, 1999-2008; Vice Chair, Scottish Consortium on Crime and Criminal Justice, 1998-2003; b. 31.1.31, Glasgow; m., Elma; 2 s.; 3 d. Educ. Whitehill School, Glasgow; Glasgow University; Edinburgh University. Probation Officer, Glasgow, 1955-60; Psychiatric Social Worker, Scottish Prison Service, 1960-61; Crichton Royal Hospital, Dumfries, 1961-65; Family Service Unit, Paisley, 1965-66; Adviser in Social Work, then Chief Adviser in Social Work, Scottish Office, 1966-91; Director of Social Work, Shetland, 1991. Former Chair, Dumfries Constituency Labour Party; former Chair, Scottish Marriage Council; Governor, National Institute for Social Work, 1981-91; Scottish Secretary, British Association of Social Workers, 1992-96; Scottish Chair, NCH Action for Children, 1992-97; Chair, SACRO, 1997-2002; Trustee, Scottish Disability Foundation, 1999-2003. Recreations: mountaineering; promotion of the visual arts. Address: (h.) 'Kinloch', 19 Glamis Road, Kirriemuir, Angus DD8 5BN; T.-0157-557-0965.

Comiskey, Patricia Bernadette, BSc, MSc, PhD, LLB, DipLP. Advocate, since 2001. Educ. Leicester Polytechnic; University of Minnesota; Edinburgh University. Researcher in Textile Technology, University of Minnesota, 1981-83; Lecturer in Textile Technology, Leicester Polytechnic, 1983-88; Assistant Fabric Technologist, Marks and Spencer, London, 1988-90; Menswear Buyer Manager, Jenners Ltd, Edinburgh, 1990-95. Address: (b.) Parliament House, Edinburgh EH1 1RF; e-mail: patricia.comiskey@advocates.org.uk

Comley, David John, BSc, PhD, FIH. Managing Director, Comley Consulting Ltd.; Director of Social Work Services, Glasgow City Council, 2002-07; Director of Housing Services, Glasgow City Council, 1988-2002; b. 25.4.50, Carshalton. Educ. Ashlyns School, Berkhamsted;

Birmingham University. Housing Management Trainee, then District Housing Manager, Dudley Metropolitan Borough, 1976-80; District Housing Manager, then Assistant Director of Housing, then Depute Director, then Director of Housing Services, Glasgow City Council. Recreations: jazz; classical music; hill-walking; literature; cinema; theatre. E-mail: david.comley007@btinternet.com

Conn, Stewart. Poet and playwright; b. 1936, Glasgow, brought up Kilmarnock. Educ. Glasgow University. Author of numerous stage plays, including The Burning, Herman, The Aquarium, By the Pool, Clay Bull; television work includes The Kite, Bloodhunt; recent poetry includes In the Kibble Palace, The Luncheon of the Boating Party, At the Aviary, In the Blood; Stolen Light; Distances: a personal evocation of people and places; l'Ànima del Teixidor; Ghosts at Cockcrow; The Loving-Cup; his production of Carver (by John Purser) won Gold Medal Award, International Radio Festival, 1991; left BBC, 1992; appointed to Edinburgh's poet laureateship, 2002-05. Editor, 100 Favourite Scottish Poems, 2006. E-mail: stewartconn@btinternet.com

Connal, Robert Craig, QC, LLB(Hons), SSC. Solicitor, since 1977; Partner, McGrigors, since 1980 (Head of Commercial Litigation, 2002-07); Senior Litigation Partner and UK Head of Advocacy, since 2007; Solicitor Advocate: Scotland (civil), 1996, (criminal), 2004, England and Wales, (all courts), 2006; b. 7.7.54, Brentwood; m., Mary Ferguson Bowie; 2 d. Educ. Hamilton Academy; University of Glasgow. Apprentice, Brown, Mair, Gemmill & Hislop, 1975-77; Assistant, McGrigor Donald, 1977-1980. Council Member, Royal Faculty of Procurators in Glasgow, 1995-98; appointed Scotland's first Solicitor Advocate QC, 2002; External Examiner, University of Aberdeen, 2001-05; Convenor, Law Society of Scotland Supreme Courts Training Course (Civil), since 2004. Publications: Contributor, Stair Memorial Encyclopedia; many articles in press and professional journals. Recreations: rugby referee; gardens (but not gardening). Address: (b.) Pacific House, 70 Wellington Street, Glasgow G2 6SB; T.-0141-248 6677.

Connarty, Michael, BA, DCE. MP (Labour), Linlithgow and East Falkirk, since 2005, Falkirk East, 1992-2005; Member, European Scrutiny Select Committee, since 1998; Board Member, Parliamentary Office of Science and Technology; Chair, European Scrutiny Select Committee, since 2006; Secretary, Parliamentary Offshore Oil and Gas Group; Chair, Parliamentary Jazz Appreciation Group, since 1999; Secretary, All-Party Group on Nuclear Power; Chair, All-Party Group on Peru; Board Chair (unpaid), Scottish National Jazz Orchestra; b. 3.9.47, Coatbridge; m., Margaret Doran; 1 s.; 1 d. Educ. Stirling University; Jordanhill College of Education; Glasgow University. Member, Stirling District Council, 1977-90 (Council Leader, 1980-90); Member, Convention of Scottish Local Authorities, 1980-90 (Depute Labour Leader, 1988-90); Member, Scottish Executive, Labour Party, 1981-92; Vice-Chair, Socialist Educational Association, 1983-85; Council Member, Educational Institute of Scotland, 1984-85; PPS to Tom Clarke, MP, 1987-88; Chair, Labour Party Scottish Local Government Committee, 1988-90; Vice-Chairman, Scottish MAP, 1988-95; Secretary, PLP Science and Technology Comittee, 1992-97; Member, European Directives Committee on Agriculture, Environment and Health and Safety, 1993-96; Chair, Economy, Industry and Energy Committee, Scottish PLP Group, 1993-97; Scottish Co-ordinator, Labour Crime and Drugs Campaign, 1993-97; Scottish Task Force Leader on Skills and Training in Scotland and Youth and Students, 1995-97; Member, Select Committee on the Parliamentary Commissioner for Administration, 1995-97; Chairman, Scottish Parliamentary

Labour Party Group, 1998-99. Recreations: family; hill-walking; reading; music. Address: (b.) 5 Kerse Road, Grangemouth FK3 8HQ; T.-01324 474832.

Connell, Douglas Andrew, LLB, WS. Joint Senior Partner, Turcan Connell; b. 18.5.54, Callander; m., Marjorie Elizabeth; 2 s. Educ. McLaren High School; Edinburgh University. Qualified as a solicitor, 1976; admitted as a Writer to the Signet, 1976; President, Scottish Young Lawyers Association, 1975-76; Tutor in Scots Law, Edinburgh University, 1974-76; Partner, Dundas and Wilson, 1979-97. Member, Revenue Committee, Law Society of Scotland, 1979-92; Scottish Arts Council: Member, 1994-97, Chairman, Lottery Committee, 1994-97; Member, Edinburgh Festival Council, 1997-2001; Trustee: Buildings of Scotland Trust, Historic Scotland Foundation; Patron, National Galleries of Scotland and National Museums of Scotland; Chairman, Edinburgh Book Festival, 1991-95; General Editor, Scottish Private Client Law Review, 2003-06; Member, University of St. Andrews Court, 2002-06; Chairman, Governance and Nominations Committee; Chairman, Recognition Committee of Scottish Museums Council; General Council Assessor, Court of University of Edinburgh. Recreations: books; travel; good food. Address: (b.) Princes Exchange, 1 Earl Grey Street, Edinburgh EH3 9EE; T.-0131-228 8111; e-mail: dac@turcanconnell.com

Connell, Professor John Muir Cochrane, MBChB, MD, FRCP, FAHA, FRSE, FMedSci. Professor of Endocrinology, Glasgow University, since 1996; Honorary Consultant Physician, Western Infirmary, Glasgow, since 1987; b. 10.10.54; m., Dr Lesley Connell; 3 s.; 1 d. Educ. Hutchesons' Grammar School; Glasgow University. Research Fellow, MRC Blood Pressure Unit, Western Infirmary, Glasgow; Medical Travelling Fellow, Howard Florey Institute, Melbourne, 1986-87; Senior Clinical Scientist and Hon. Consultant Phsyician, MRC Blood Pressure Unit, 1987-94; Professor in Medicine, Department of Medicine and Therapeutics, Western Infirmary, 1994-96; Clinical Director, Medicine, West Glasgow, since 2006. Honorary Secretary, Association of Physicians of Gt. Britain and Ireland, 2001-07; Member, grant-awarding committees, British Heart Foundation, etc. Recreations: family; golf. Address: (b.) BHF Glasgow Cardiovascular Research Centre, University of Glasgow, Glasgow G12 8NT; T.-0141-211 2108.

Connolly, Billy, CBE. Stand-up comedian; actor; television presenter; b. 24.11.42; m. 1., Iris (m. dissolved) 1 s.; 1 d.; 2, Pamela Stephenson; 3 d. Welder, Clyde shipyards; began showbusiness career with Gerry Rafferty as The Humblebums; first solo concert, 1971; has toured throughout the world with stand-up comedy shows; television: Androcles and the Lion, Head of the Class (USA), Billy (USA), Billy Connolly's World Tour of Scotland (Scottish BAFTA: Best Entertainment Programme), Down Among the Big Boys (Scottish BAFTA: Best Drama), The Bigger Picture (Scottish BAFTA: Best Arts Programme), The Life and Crimes of Deacon Brodie, Billy Connolly's World Tour of Australia, Return to Nose and Beak (Comic Relief special), Billy Connolly: A Scot in the Arctic; Gentleman's Relish, Billy Connolly's World Tour of England, Ireland and Wales, 2002; World Tour of New Zealand; films: Absolution, Bullshot, Water, The Big Man, Treasure Island (Muppet movie), Mrs Brown, Still Crazy, The Changeling, PAWS, The Debt Collector, The Boon Dock Saints, The Imposters, Beautiful Joe; An Everlasting Piece; Cletis Tour; Gabriel and Me; The Man Who Sued God; Timeline; The Last Samurai; Lemony Snicket A Series of Unfortunate Events, Fido, Garfield 2, voice in animated film Open Season;

appeared with Scottish Opera in Die Fledermaus; theatre: wrote The Red Runner, performed in The Beastly Beatitudes of Blathazar B; videos: Live at Hammersmith, Bite Your Bum (Music Week and Record Business Award, 1981), Hand-picked By Billy Connolly, 25 BC, Billy and Albert, An Audience with Billy Connolly, Billy Connolly Live, Live '94, World Tour of Scotland (Two Bites of), World Tour of Australia, Two Night Stand; DVD releases: Billy Connolly World Tour of England, Ireland and Wales; Billy Connolly's World Tour of New Zealand, Billy Connolly Live in New York, Billy Connolly Live - Was It Something I Said?: tribute television programme and video: Erect for 30 Years; gold disc for album Pick of Billy Connolly, 1982; UK No. 1 hit with D.I.V.O.R.C.E.; books: Gullible's Travels, 1982, Billy Connolly's World Tour of Australia, 1996. Address: c/o Tickety-boo Ltd, 2, Triq IL-Barriera, Balzan BZN06, Malta.

Connolly, Liz, BA (Hons), MBA. Senior Director Operations, Scottish Enterprise, Lanarkshire; b. 21.11.58, Glasgow. Educ. Our Lady and St. Francis School, Glasgow; Strathclyde University. Media Planner, J.F. Green Associates, 1981-83; Marketing and Economic Research, SDA, 1983-91; Planning Executive in Policy Planning Unit, S.E. National, 1991-92; Head of Strategy then Director of Strategy, LDA, 1992-98; Chief Executive, Enterprise Ayrshire, 1999-2000. Member: Board, Bell College, Board, Strathclyde European Partnership; Member, Strathclyde Partnership for Transport. Recreations: music; theatre; keep fit; socialising. Address: (b.) New Lanarkshire House, Strathclyde Business Park, Bellshill ML4.

Connon, Joyce Blair, OBE. Scottish Secretary, Workers Educational Association, since 1992; b. 11.6.47, Edinburgh; m., Neil Connon; 1 s.; 1 d. W.E.A. Tutor Organiser, Lothian, 1988; District Secretary, South-East Scotland, 1989. Chair, Learning Link Scotland; Member, Scottish European Social Fund Objective Three Programme Monitoring Committee; Director, Edinburgh's Lifelong Learning Partnership. Recreations: reading; theatre; walking. Address: (b.) W.E.A., Riddle's Court, 322 Lawnmarket, Edinburgh EH1 2PG; T.-0131-226 3456.

Connor, Professor James Michael, MD, DSc, BSc (Hons), MB, ChB (Hons), FRCP. Professor of Medical Genetics and Director, West of Scotland Regional Genetics Service, since 1987 (Wellcome Trust Senior Lecturer and Honorary Consultant in Medical Genetics, Glasgow University, 1984-87); b. 18.6.51, Grappenhall, England; m., Dr. Rachel A.C. Educ. Lymm Grammar School, Cheshire; Liverpool University. House Officer, Liverpool Royal Infirmary; Resident in Internal Medicine, Johns Hopkins Hospital, USA; University Research Fellow, Liverpool University; Instructor in Internal Medicine, Johns Hopkins Hospital, USA; Consultant in Medical Genetics, Institute of Medical Genetics, Yorkhill, Glasgow. Publications: Essential Medical Genetics (Co-author), 1984 (6th edition, 2008); Principles and Practice of Medical Genetics (Co-Editor), (5th edition, 2007); various articles on aspects of medical genetics. Recreations: mountain biking and sea kayaking. Address: (h.) East Collarie Farm, by Fenwick, Ayrshire.

Conroy, Professor James Charles, BEd, MA, PhD. Professor of Religious and Philosophical Education, University of Glasgow, since 2004, Dean of Faculty of Education, since 2005; b. 30.04.55, Portadown, Northern Ireland; m., Denise Frances (nee Meagher); 1 s.; 2 d. Educ. St. Patrick's College, Armagh; London (St. Mary's); Lancaster; VU, Amsterdam. Accounts Controller, Chase Bank of Ireland, 1973-76; Development Officer, Adult Education, Westminster Diocese, 1981-83; Teacher and Head of Department of RE, St. Brendan's VIth Form, 1983-87; Senior Lecturer, Education and Theology, St. Mary's College, Twickenham, 1987-90; Director, RE and Pastoral Care, St. Andrew's College, Bearsden, 1990-99; Head of

Department of RE, University of Glasgow, 1999-2004. 2007 Board: Learning and Teaching Scotland; President, Association For Moral Education (based in US), 2007; Publications: Catholic Education: Inside-out/Outside-in, 1999, Betwixt and Between: The Liminal Imagination, Education and Democracy, 2004. Recreations: antique furniture; gardening; cooking; family. Address: (b.) Faculty of Education, St Andrew's Building, 11 Eldon Street, Glasgow G3 6NH; T.-0141 330 3002; e-mail: j.conroy@educ.gla.ac.uk

Considine, John, MA, MEd. Rector, Inverness Royal Academy, since 1993; Director, HI Arts (Chairman, 1999-2004); b. 26.11.50, Glasgow; m., Hellen L. Campbell; 1 s.; 2 d. Educ. St. Aloysius College; Glasgow University. Teacher: St. Margaret Mary's, Glasgow, 1973, Inverness High, 1974, Millburn Academy, Inverness, 1976; Principal Teacher, then Assistant Rector, Charleston Academy, Inverness, 1978-88; Depute Rector, Woodmill High, Dunfermline, 1988-93. Member, Inverness College Board of Management, and Chair, College Personnel Sub-Committee, 1995-99; President, Highland Secondary Headteachers Association, 1997-98. Recreations: hill-walking; running; squash. Address: (b.) Inverness Royal Academy, Culduthel Road, Inverness; T.-01463 222884.

Constance, Angela. MA (Soc.Sci), MSc (Social Work). MSP (SNP), Livingston, since 2007; b. 15.7.70; m., Garry Knox; 1 s. Educ. West Calder High; Boness Academy; Glasgow University; Stirling University. Social Worker, 1997-2007; Social Worker/Mental Health Officer, 2002-07; Social Worker/Mental Health Officer/Practice Teacher, 2005-07. Executive Member, West Lothian Council, 1997-2007. Public Petitions Committee. Recreations: jogging/fun runs; marathons. Address: (b.) Scottish Parliament, Edinburgh EH99 1SP.
E-mail: angela.constance.msp@scottish.parliament.co.uk

Conti, Most Rev. Mario Joseph, KC* HS, PhL, STL, DD, FRSE. Archbishop of Glasgow, since 2002; Bishop of Aberdeen, 1977-2002; Apostolic Administrator, Paisley, 2004-05; Member, Pontifical Council for the Promotion of Christian Unity, Rome, since 1984; Member, Historic Buildings Council of Scotland, since 2000; b. 20.3.34, Elgin. Educ. St. Marie's Convent; Springfield School, Elgin; Blairs College, Aberdeen; Pontifical Scots College, Pontifical Gregorian University, Rome. Ordained priest, Rome, 1958; Curate, St. Mary's Cathedral, Aberdeen, 1959-62; Parish Priest, St. Joachim's, Wick and St. Anne's, Thurso, 1962-77. Commendatore, Order of Merit, Italian Republic; President-Treasurer, SCIAF, 1977-85; President, National Liturgy Commission, 1981-85; Member, International Commission for English in the Liturgy, 1978-87; Chairman, Scottish Catholic Heritage Commission; President, Commission for Christian Doctrine and Unity, since 1986; first Convener, Central Council, ACTS, 1990-93; Co-Moderator, Joint Working Group of the World Council of Churches and the Roman Catholic Church, 1996-2006; Head of Catholic Delegation to 8th General Assembly, World Council of Churches, Harare, 1998; a President, Churches Together in Britain and Ireland, 1999-2005; Member, Pontifical Commission for the Cultural Heritage of the Church, 1994-2004; Knight Commander of the Holy Sepulchre, 1989; Principal Chaplain to British Association of the Sovereign Military Order of Malta, 1995-2000 and since 2005; Conventual Chaplain, Grand Cross, since 2001; (Italian State honour): Grande Ufficiale (1 Classe) dell'Ordine della Stella della Solidarietà Italiana, 2007. Recreations: music; art. Address: (b.) 196 Clyde Street, Glasgow G1 4JY; Tel. 0141 226 5898.

Conway, Stephen Andrew, FCMI. Director, Strategic Planning and Performance, NHS National Services Scotland, since 2007; Chief Executive, NHS Orkney, 2004-07; b. 24.2.57, Otley, Yorkshire; m., Heather; 1 s.; 1 d. Educ. Berkhamsted School. Commissioned in

Royal Marines in September 1976, appointments included Signal Officer, Special Boat Service, Adjutant Commando Training Centre, Second in Command, Comacchio Group and Commanding Officer, Royal Marines Reserve Scotland; retired in 2002 as Lieutenant Colonel. National Emergency Planning Officer, NHS Scotland. Recreations: sailing; antique furniture restoration. Address: (h.) 89 Tay Street, Newport-on-Tay, Fife; T.-01382 540680; e-mail: steve.conway@nhs.net

Cook, Rev. James Stanley Stephen Ronald Tweedie, BD, DipPSS. Minister, Hamilton West Parish Church, 1974-2001; b. 18.8.35, Tullibody; m., Jean Douglas Maclachlan; 2 s.; 1 d. Educ. Whitehill Senior Secondary School, Glasgow; St Andrews University. Apprentice quantity surveyor, Glasgow, 1953-54; regular soldier, REME, 1954-57; Assistant Preventive Officer, Waterguard Department, HM Customs and Excise, 1957-61; Officer, HM Customs and Excise, 1961-69; studied for the ministry, 1969-74. Chairman, Cruse (Lanarkshire), 1983-93, 1994-99; Chairman, Cruse – Scotland, 1991-95, Convener, 1999-2001; Member, Council, Cruse UK, 1988-94; Member, National Training Group, Cruse, 1987-94; Member, Action Research for Crippled Child Committee, 1977-94; Substitute Provincial Grand Master, Lanarkshire (Middle Ward), 1983-88; Honorary Provincial Grand Chaplain, since 1989; founder Member, Wishaw Victim Support Scheme, 1985; President, Hamilton Rotary Club, 1994-95; Member, Hamilton Crime Prevention Panel, 1976-2000, Chairman, 1986-87; Moderator, Presbytery of Hamilton, 1999-2000; Mental Health Chaplain, since 1988. Recreations: music; photography; DIY; computer work. Address: Mansend, 137a Old Manse Road, Netherton, Wishaw ML2 0EW.

Cooke, Anthony John, BA (Hons), MA (Manchester). Chair, Scottish Urban Archaeology Trust, Perth, since 2003; Consultant, Historic Scotland, since 1996; b. 15.7.43, Salford, Lancashire; m., Judith Margaret; 2 s. Educ. Accrington Grammar School; Manchester University. Teacher, Bishops College, Carriacou, Grenada, West Indies; Lecturer, Dundee College of Commerce; Lecturer/Senior Lecturer, University of Dundee. Publications: Stanley: From Arkwright Village to Commuter Suburb, 2003; From Popular Enlightenment to Lifelong Learning, 2006. Recreations: walking; swimming; choral singing. Address: (h.) 424, Blackness Road, Dundee DD2 1TQ; T.-01382 668476; e-mail: a.j.cooke@dundee.ac.uk

Cooke, Professor David John, BSc, MSc, PhD, CPsych, FBPsS, FRSE. Professor of Forensic Clinical Psychology, Glasgow Caledonian University, since 1992; Head of Forensic Clinical Psychology, Greater Glasgow Community and Mental Health Services NHS Trust, since 1984; Glasgow University: Honorary Lecturer, since 1984, Honorary Senior Research Fellow, since 1989, Visiting Professor, 1997-2001; b. 13.7.52, Glasgow; m., Janet Ruth Salter; 2 d. Educ. Larbert High School; St. Andrews University; Newcastle-upon-Tyne University; Glasgow University. Clinical Psychologist, Gartnavel Royal Hospital, 1976-83; Cropwood Fellow, Institute of Criminology, Cambridge University, 1986; Visiting Professor, University of Bergen, since 2004. Recreations: sailing; opera; cooking. Address: (b.) Douglas Inch Centre, 2 Woodside Terrace, Glasgow G3 7UY; T.-0141-211 8000.

Cooke, Nicholas Huxley, MA (Oxon), FRSA. Independent sustainability consultant, CLEAR Services Ltd; b. 6.5.44, Godalming, Surrey; m., Anne Landon; 2 s.; 3 d. Educ.

Charterhouse School; Worcester College, Oxford. Retail management, London; chartered accountancy training, London; British International Paper, 1972-78; Director (Scotland) British Trust for Conservation Volunteers, 1978-84; Director, Scottish Conservation Projects Trust, 1984-98; Member, Scottish Committee for European Year of the Environment, 1987-88; Policy Committee Member, Scottish Council for Voluntary Organisations, 1992-2002; Board Member: Youthlink Scotland, Falkirk Environment Trust, Dundee Waste and Environment Trust, 1996-99; Member, Scottish Employer Supported Volunteering Group, 1997-2002; Chair, Scottish Committee, Voluntary Sector NTO, 1997-2001, Gowanbank Historic Village Ltd, 2001-04; Director, Rockdust Ltd., 2005-08; Secretary, Scottish Senior Alliance for Volunteering in the Environment (SSAVE), 2001-03; Managing Director, Scottish Organic Producers Association, 2003-05 (Chair, 2002-03); Secretary, Incorporated Glasgow, Stirlingshire and Sons of the Rock Society (Preses 2005); Chair, Callander Youth Project Trust (Trustee, since 2002). Recreations: fishing; field entomology; walking; marginal gardening. Address: (b.) Easter Stonefield, Port of Menteith, Stirling FK8 3RD; T.-01877 382926; e-mail: Nick@clearserv.co.uk

Cooney, Paul Francis. Managing Director, Radio Clyde, since 2000; b. 3.12.56, Blantyre, Scotland; m., Annette; 1 s.; 2 d. Educ. Holy Cross High School, Hamilton; Blairs College, Aberdeen. News Trainee, Radio Clyde, 1976-77; News Reporter/Sports Editor/News Editor, 1978-87; PR Manager, Celtic Football Club, 1987; PR Manager, Radio Clyde, 1987-91; Programme Controller, Century Radio, Dublin, 1991-92; Sports Presenter, Scottish Television, 1992-95; Director of PR, Radio Clyde, 1995-96; Managing Director, West Sound FM Ltd, 1996-2000. TRICS News/Sport Radio Journalist of the Year, 1985; New York Radio Award for Sports Programming; Sony Gold, Silver and Bronze Awards, 1986-91 and 1997. Address: (b.) Radio Clyde, Clydebank Business Park, Clydebank, Glasgow G81 2RX.

Cooper, Professor Christine, BA, MSc, PhD. Professor of Accounting, Strathclyde University, since 1999; b. 16.3.56, London; 1 d. Educ. Crown Woods, Eltham, London; Greenwich University; London School of Economics. Trustee, Association for Accountancy and Business Affairs. Address: (b.) Department of Accounting and Finance, Strathclyde University, Glasgow G4 0LN; T.-0141-548 3231; e-mail: c.cooper@strath.ac.uk

Cooper, Rev. David, BA, MPhil. Superintendent Minister, Edinburgh and Forth Circuit, since 1992; Secretary to Synod of Methodist Church in Scotland, 1995-2003; b. 6.11.49, Seaham; m., Veronica; 3 s.; 1 d. Educ. Bede Grammar School for Boys, Sunderland; University of Manchester; Hartley Victoria Methodist College. Minister: Morpeth Circuit, Newcastle District, 1977, Lerwick, North Roe and North Isles Circuit, Shetland District, 1980, Witney and Faringdon Circuit, Oxford and Leicester District, 1985. World Council of Churches Scholarship, University of Ghana, 1976-77. Recreation: music. Address: (b.) Central Hall, Tollcross, Edinburgh EH3 9BP; T.-0131-221 9029; e-mail: edinforthcircuit@btinternet.com

Cooper, Malcolm Ashton, BA (Hons), MPhil, DMS, FSA, MCMI, MIFA, FSA Scot, FRSA. Chief Inspector, Historic Scotland, since 2005; b. 28.7.59, Exeter; m., Dr Claire F. Kenwood; 1 s. Educ. University of Birmingham; North Staffordshire Polytechnic; University of Central England. Hereford and Worcester County Council, 1988-93; English Heritage, 1993-2005. Address: (b.) Longmore House, Salisbury Place, Edinburgh EH9 1SH.

Cooper, Professor Sally-Ann, BSc, MB, BS, MD, FRCPsych. Professor of Learning Disabilities, Section of

Psychological Medicine, Glasgow University, since 1999; Honorary Consultant in Learning Disabilities Psychiatry, NHS Greater Glasgow and Clyde, since 1999; b. 28.4.61, Lincoln; m., Mark Guy Venner Anderson. Educ. Medical College of St Bartholomew's Hospital, London. Address: (b.) Section of Psychological Medicine, Glasgow University, Academic Centre, Gartnavel Royal Hospital, 1055 Great Western Road, Glasgow G12 0XH; T.-0141-211 3701.

Cooper, Professor Thomas Joshua, BA, MA. Professor of Fine Art, Senior Researcher, Glasgow School of Art, since 2002; artist; b. 19.12.46, San Francisco; m., Catherine Alice Mooney; 2 d. Educ. Arcata High School, CA; University of New Mexico; Humboldt State University. Former Senior Lecturer, Trent Polytechnic, Nottingham; Head of Fine Art Photography, Glasgow School of Art, 1982-2000. Creative Scotland Award, 2005. Recreations: walking; music; wine; film; reading. Address: (b.) Glasgow School of Art, 167 Renfrew Street, Glasgow G3 6RQ; T.-0141 353 4500.

Corbett, Gavin. Policy Manager, Shelter Scotland, since 2001; b. 9.10.65, Cumnock; partner, Karen Robertson; 2 s. Educ. Cumnock Academy; Glasgow University. Joined Shelter Scotland as campaign worker, 1993-2000. Recreations: climbing hills; cycling; campaigning. Address: (h.) 28 Briarbank Terrace, Edinburgh EH11 1SU; T.-0131-337 5227.

Cormack, Arthur. Director of Fèisean nan Gàidheal, since 1992; Director of Macmeanmna Ltd., since 2004; b. 21.4.65, Portree, Isle of Skye; m., Shona (nee Macdonald); 2 s.; 1 d. Educ. Portree High School. Ran R Cormack Clothing (family business), 1985-92; established and ran EISD Music, 1987-2003; founder of Macmeanmna (Gaelic Music Recording Label) in 1987; Chairman and Co-founder of AROS Ltd in 1991; Member of Bòrd na Gàidhlig, since 2003; Gaelic Singer (professional as solo artist), since 1983. Former member of Scottish Arts Council. Recreations: music; graphic design. Address: (b.) Meall House, Portree, Isle of Skye IV51 9BZ; T.-01478 613355; e-mail: arthur@feisean.org

Cormack, James Shearer, LLB (Hons), DipLP. Solicitor, Partner, McGrigors LLP, since 2001; b. 11.11.68, Inverness; m., Samantha; 1 s.; 1 d. Educ. Lochaber High School; University of Edinburgh. Trainee Solicitor, then Qualified Assistant, McGrigor Donald, 1991-95; Member, Faculty of Advocates, 1996-2001. Recreations: family; cinema; golf. Address: (b.) McGrigors LLP, Princes Exchange, 1 Earl Grey Street, Edinburgh EH3 9AQ; T.-0131 777 7356; e-mail: jim.cormack@mcgrigors.com

Cormack, Professor Robert John, MA, FRSA. Principal, UHI Millennium Institute, since 2001; b. 14.12.46, Blantyre; m., Dr Elisabeth Cormack; 1 s.; 2 d. Educ. Montrose Academy; Aberdeen University; Brown University, USA. Queen's University of Belfast: Lecturer in Sociology, 1973-87, Senior Lecturer, 1987-92, Reader, 1992-96, Professor, 1996-2001, Head, Department of Sociology and Social Policy, 1991-93, Dean, Faculty of Economics and Social Sciences, 1993-95, Pro-Vice Chancellor, 1995-2001. Editorial Advisory Board, Widening Participation and Lifelong Learning, since 1999. Publications: numerous books and articles on Northern Ireland including Discrimination and Public Policy in Northern Ireland (Co-author). Address: (b.) UHI Millennium Institute, Executive Office, Ness Walk, Inverness IV3 5SQ; T.-01463 279212; e-mail: robert.cormack@uhi.ac.uk

Corner, David John, MA, LLD (Hon), DLitt (Hon), FRHS. Deputy Principal, St Andrews University, 2003-06; Secretary and Registrar, St. Andrews University, 1991-

2003; Honorary Lecturer, Department of Mediaeval History, St. Andrews University, since 1991; b. 24.10.47, Birmingham; m., Carol Ann; 2 s. Educ. King Edward VI Grammar School, Aston, Birmingham; Worcester College, Oxford. Prize Fellow, Magdalen College, Oxford, 1972-75; Lecturer, Department of Mediaeval History, St. Andrews University, 1975-91. Chair of Trustees of Falkland Heritage Trust, since 2006; Governor, Newbattle Abbey College, since 1991; President, St. Andrews Association of University Teachers, 1985 88. Recreations: cinema; sport. Address. St. Andrews University, College Gate, North Street, St. Andrews KY16 9AJ; T.-01334 462549.

Cornish, Melvyn David, BSc, PGCE. Secretary, Edinburgh University, since 2002; b. 29.6.48, Leighton Buzzard. Educ. Cedars Grammar School, Leighton Buzzard; Leicester University. Chemistry Teacher, Jamaica and Cumbria, 1970-73; Administrator, Leicester Polytechnic, 1973-78; Senior Administrative Officer, Assistant Secretary, Director of Planning, Deputy Secretary, Edinburgh University, 1978-2002. Recreations: hill-walking; photography; travel. Address: (b.) Old College, South Bridge, Edinburgh; T.-0131-650 2143; e-mail: university.secretary@ed.ac.uk

Cornwell, Professor John Francis, PhD, BSc, DIC, ARCS, FRSE. Professor of Theoretical Physics, St. Andrews University, 1979-2002 (Chairman, Physics Department, 1984-85); b. 28.1.37, London; m., Elizabeth Margaret Burfitt; 2 d. Educ. Ealing Grammar School; Imperial College, London. Lecturer in Applied Mathematics, Leeds University, 1961-67; St. Andrews University: Lecturer in Theoretical Physics, 1967-73, Reader, 1973-79. Publications: Group Theory in Physics, three volumes, 1984, 1989; Group Theory and Electronic Energy Bands in Solids, 1969. Recreations: sailing; hill-walking; tennis; badminton; golf. Address: (b.) Department of Physics and Astronomy, St. Andrews University, North Haugh, St. Andrews, Fife KY16 9SS; T.-01334 476161.

Cornwell, Professor Keith, BSc, PhD, DEng, FIMechE. Professor of Heat Transfer and Head of Dubai Campus, Heriot Watt University; b. 4.4.42, Abingdon; m., Sheila Joan Mott; 1 s.; 1 d. Educ. City University, London. Research Fellow, then Lecturer, Middlesex Polytechnic; Lecturer, Head of Department, Dean of Engineering, Director of Quality, and Head, School of Mathematical and Computing Science, Heriot-Watt University; appointed Head of Heriot Watt Dubai Campus, UAE, 2006. Member, UK Committee on Heat Transfer. Publications: The Flow of Heat; numerous journal papers. Recreations: classic cars; hillwalking. Address: (h.) Strathview, Templar Place, Gullane EH39 2AH.

Corrie, John Alexander. Member (Conservative), European Parliament for West Midlands Region, 1999-2004 (for Worcestershire and South Warwickshire, 1994-99); Co-ordinator, Development Committee, 1999-2004; Member, Budgets Committee, 1999-2004; Co-President, ACP/EU Joint Parliamentary Assembly, 1999-2002, now Honorary Life President; Member of North South Forum, 2002-04; Vice-President, Working Group "A", Foreign Affairs and Development, 2002-04; Delegation Leader to Dafur (Sudan), 2004; Election Monitor in Malawi, Congo, Brassaville, Solomon Isles, Madagascar, The Seychelles, Fiji and Peru, 2002-04; farms family farm in Galloway; b. 1935; m.; 1 s.; 2 d. Educ. Kirkcudbright Academy; George Watson's College, Edinburgh; Lincoln Agricultural College, New Zealand. Nuffield Farming Scholar, 1972; National Chairman, Scottish Young Conservatives, 1964; MP (Conservative): Bute and North Ayrshire, 1974-83; Cunninghame North, 1983-87; PPS to Secretary of State for Scotland, 1979-81; introduced Private Member's Bill to reduce upper limit on abortion, 1979; Member: European Assembly, 1975-76 and 1977-79, Council of Europe, 1983-87, Western European Union (Defence Committee), 1983-87; Chief Whip, Conservatives in Europe, 1997-99; Senior Instructor, British Wool Board, Agricultural Training Board, 1970-74; elected to Council, Belted Galloway Cattle Society, 1978; Chairman, Scottish Transport Users Consultative Committee, 1988-94; Vice Chairman, Central Transport Consultative Committee, 1988-94; Council Member, Royal Agricultural Society of England, 1992-2000; Industrial Fellowship with Conoco and Du Pont, USA, 1987; awarded Wilberforce Plaque for Humane Work, 1981; Belted Galloway Judge, Royal Show, 2006; Patron: Kisumu Children's Trust, Kenya, since 2006, DTI Mine Clearing and Development Initiative, since 2006; Hon. Chairman, ICCSD China, since 2006. Publications: Forestry in Europe; Fish Farming in Europe; The Importance of Forestry in the World Today; Towards a Community Rural Policy (Co-author). Address: (h.) Park House Tongland, Kirkcudbright DG6 4NE.

Corsar, Charles Herbert Kenneth, LVO, OBE, TD, JP, DL, MA. Farmer, since 1953; Secretary for Scotland, Duke of Edinburgh's Award, 1966-87; b. 13.5.26, Edinburgh; m., The Honourable Dame Mary Corsar, DBE, FRSE (qv); 2 s.; 2 d. Educ. Merchiston Castle; King's College, Cambridge. Commissioned, The Royal Scots TA, 1948; commanded 8/9 Bn.,The Royal Scots TA, 1964-67; Edinburgh and Heriot-Watt Universities OTC, 1967-72; TA Colonel, 1972-75; Hon. ADC to The Queen, 1977-81; Honorary Colonel, 1/52 Lowland Volunteers, 1975-87; Chairman, Lowland TA and VR Association, 1984-87; Zone Commissioner, Home Defence, East of Scotland; County Councillor, Midlothian, 1958-67; Deputy-Lieutenant, Midlothian; Vice President, The Boys Brigade, 1970-91 and President, Edinburgh Bn., Boys Brigade, 1969-87 (Hon. President, Edinburgh Bn.,1987-98); Chairman, Scottish Standing Conference of Voluntary Youth Organisations, 1973-78; Governor: Merchiston Castle School, Clifton Hall School; Chairman: Wellington List D School, 1978-84, Earl Haig Fund Scotland, 1984-90; Secretary, Royal Jubilee and Princes' Trusts (Lothian and Borders); Member, Scottish Sports Council, 1972-75; Elder, Church of Scotland, since 1956. Recreations: gardening; bee-keeping; shooting. Address: (h.) 85/4 South Oswald Road, Edinburgh EH9 2HH; T.-0131 662 0194.

Corsar, The Hon. Dame Mary Drummond, DBE (1993), FRSE, MA; b. 8.7.27, Edinburgh; m., Colonel Charles H.K. Corsar (qv); 2 s.; 2 d. Educ. Westbourne, Glasgow; St. Denis, Edinburgh; Edinburgh University. Chairman, Women's Royal Voluntary Service, 1988-93; Chairman, Scotland, WRVS, 1981-88; Midlothian Girl Guides: Secretary, 1951-66, County Commissioner, 1966-72; Deputy Chief Commissioner, Girl Guides Scotland, 1972-77; Member: Parole Board for Scotland, 1982-89, Executive Committee, Trefoil Centre, 1975-2002, Visiting Committee, Glenochil Detention Centre, 1976-94, Management Committee, Church of Scotland Youth Centre, Carberry, 1976-82; Chairman, Lloyds TSB Foundation Scotland, 1994-97. Recreations: countuyslde; reading; handicrafts. Address: (h.) Flat 4, 85 South Oswald Road, Edinburgh EH9 2HH; T.-0131 662 0194.

Cosgrove, Rt. Hon. Lady (Hazel Josephine Aronson), CBE, LLD. Senator of the College of Justice in Scotland, 1996-2006; b. 12.1.46, Glasgow; m., John A. Cosgrove; 1 s.; 1 d. Educ. Glasgow High School for Girls; Glasgow University. Advocate at Scottish Bar, 1968-79; Sheriff: Glasgow and Strathkelvin at Glasgow, 1979-83, Lothian and Borders at Edinburgh, 1983-96; Temporary Judge, Court of Session and High Court, 1992-96; Past Chairman, Mental Welfare Commission for Scotland; Past Chairman,

Expert Panel on Sex Offending; Past Depute Chairman, Boundaries Commission for Scotland. Recreations: swimming; walking; opera; foreign travel. Address: (b.) Parliament House, Edinburgh EH1 1RQ; T.-0131-225 2595.

Cosgrove, Stuart, PhD. Head of Programmes (Nations and Regions), Channel Four Television, since 1997; b. Perth. Educ. Hull University. Lecturer, film and television; cultural critic; Media Editor, NME; contributor, The Face, The Guardian, The Observer, Arena; regular presenter, The Late Show, BBC TV; joined Channel Four after period as independent producer; appointed Senior Commissioning Editor, then Controller of Arts and Entertainment, before returning to Scotland. Co-host, BBC Radio Scotland's popular comedy football phone-in, Off The Ball; co-host, BBC Scotland's Saturday football results show, Sportscene Results. Recreation: supporter of St Johnstone F.C. Address: (b.) 227 West George Street, Glasgow G2 2ND; T.-0141-568 7100.

Coton, Professor Frank Norman, BSc, PhD, CEng, FRAeS, AFAIAA. Professor of Low Speed Aerodynamics, Department of Aerospace Engineering, University of Glasgow, since 2003, Dean of Engineering, since 2007; b. 25.05.63, Dumbarton; m., Caroline; 1 s.; 1 d. Educ. Vale of Leven Academy; University of Glasgow. Production Engineering Apprentice, Rolls Royce Ltd., 1980-84; Glasgow University: Research Assistant, 1987-89, Lecturer, Department of Aerospace Engineering, 1986-89, Senior Lecturer, 1986-2000, Reader, 2000-03. Chair of The Aerodynamics Technical Committee of The African Institute of Aeronautics and Astronautics; Chair, The Scottish Deans of Science and Engineering. Recreation: travel. Address: (b.) Faculty of Engineering, James Watt Building, University of Glasgow, Glasgow G12 8QQ; T.-0141 330 4305; e-mail: dean@eng.gla.ac.uk

Coulsfield, Rt. Hon. Lord (John Taylor Cameron), QC, BA, LLB. Senator of the College of Justice, 1987-2002; b. 24.4.34, Dundee; m., Bridget Deirdre Sloan. Educ. Fettes College; Corpus Christi College, Oxford; Edinburgh University. Admitted to Faculty of Advocates, 1960; Queen's Counsel, 1973; Lecturer in Public Law, Edinburgh University, 1960-64; Advocate Depute, 1977-80; Keeper of the Advocates Library, 1977-87; Chairman, Medical Appeal Tribunals, 1985-87; Judge of the Appeal Courts of Jersey and Guernsey, 1986-87; Scottish Judge, Employment Appeal Tribunal, 1992-96; Chairman, Joint Standing Committee on Legal Education, 1997-2003; Trustee, National Library of Scotland, since 2000; Judge of Appeal, Botswana, since 2005; PC, 2000. Address: 17 Moray Place, Edinburgh EH3 6DT.

Coulthard, William George, LLB. Solicitor, since 1971; Honorary Sheriff, since 1988; b. 13.3.48, Whitehaven; m., Fiona Jane McQueen; 1 s.; 2 d. Educ. Glasgow Academy; Glasgow University. Partner in legal firm, since 1974; Dean, Faculty of Procurators, Stewartry of Kirkcudbright, 1986-88; Chairman, Castle Douglas High School Board, 1990-94; President, Castle Douglas Rotary Club, 1995. Recreations: rowing; jogging. Address: (h.) Netherby, Castle Douglas DG7 1BA; T.-01556 502965.

Couper, Jean, CBE, BSc, MIoD, MCMI. Member, Accounts Commission; Director: Catalyst Consulting, since 1995, The Merchants House, Glasgow, K3 Management Consultants Ltd, Mercat Law Academy, Ombudsman Services Ltd; b. 31.8.53, Kilmarnock; m., John Anderson Couper; 1 s.; 1 d. Educ. Kilmarnock Academy; University

of Glasgow. Production Engineer and Foundry Manager, Glacier Metal Co. 1974-79; Materials Manager, Levi Strauss, 1979-81; Management Consultant: Arthur Young, 1982-87, Price Waterhouse, 1987-95; Vice-Chairman, Wise Group, 1988-96; Vice Chairman, Heatwise Glasgow Ltd., 1988-96; Chairman, Scottish Legal Aid Board, 1998-2006 (Member, 1994-98); Deputy Chairman, Health Education Board for Scotland, 2000-01 (Member, 1994-2001); Member, Police Advisory Board for Scotland, 2002-06. National President, Junior Chamber Scotland, 1983; Senator, Junior Chamber International. Recreations: gardening; skiing. Address: Lismore House, 36 Sherbrooke Avenue, Pollokshields, Glasgow G41 4EP; T.-0141-427 3416.

Cousin, David Alastair Henry, BVMS, MRCVS, DBR, JP. Partner, veterinary practice, Kintyre, since 1972; Honorary Sheriff, Campbeltown Sheriff Court, since 1990; b. 19.4.44, Kincardine on Forth; m., Anne Macleod; 1 s.; 1 d. Educ. Balfron High School; Glasgow University; Liverpool University. Veterinary practice, Campbeltown: Veterinary Assistant, 1966, Junior Partner, 1972, Senior Partner, 1982. Former Commodore, Campbeltown Sailing Club, 1995. Recreations: sailing; shooting; gardening; music. Address: (h.) Southpark, Kilkerran Road, Campbeltown; T.-01586 553108.

Coutts, Alister William, DQS, BA (Hons), MBA (Dist), MSc, PhD, FRICS, FCIOB, FCMI. Partner, Head of Public Sector Services, Robinson Low Francis LLP, Construction and Property Consultants, since 2007; b. 21.12.50, Aberdeen; m., Sheelagh Anne Smith; 1 s.; 2 d. Educ. Robert Gordon's College, Aberdeen; Dundee College of Technology; Open University; University of Hong Kong; Heriot-Watt University. Armour and Partners, Chartered Quantity Surveyors: Assistant Quantity Surveyor, 1969-71, Quantity Surveyor, 1975-76; Senior Quantity Surveyor, Anderson Morgan Associates, Chartered Surveyors, 1976-78; Professional Officer, Public Works Department, Hong Kong Government, 1978-81; Project Co-ordinator, Hong Kong Mass Transit Railway Corporation, 1981-89; Project Management and Development Director, DCI (Holdings) Ltd., 1989-93; Director of Operations, Fife Health Board, 1993-98; Director of Property and Architectural Services and PPP Projects Director, The Highland Council, 1998-2007. Member, Children's Panel (Grampian), 1976-78. President, Scottish Football Association Referees (Angus and Perthshire), 1994-96. Recreations: travel; lecturing; academic research; watching soccer. Address: (h.) Mo Tien, 29 Lady Nairne Drive, Perth PH1 1RF; T.-01738 634330.

Coutts, Rev. Fred, MA, BD. Head of Spiritual Care, NHS Grampian; Moderator, Presbytery of Aberdeen, 2000-01; Healthcare Chaplaincy Training Officer (Scotland), 1997-2001; b. 13.1.47, Forfar; m., Mary Lawson Fraser Gill; 2 s.; 1 d. Educ. Brechin High School; Dollar Academy; St. Andrews University; Edinburgh University. Assistant Minister, Linwood Parish Church, 1972-74; Minister: Buckie North, 1974-84, Mastrick, Aberdeen, 1984-89. Chairman: Buckie Community Council, 1981-83, Moray Firth Community Radio Association, 1982-83. Recreations: music; photography; computing. Address: Ladebank, 1 Manse Place, Hatton, Peterhead AB24 0UQ; T.-01779 841 320; e-mail: fred.coutts@btinternet.com

Coutts, Herbert, SBStJ, AMA, FMA, FFCS, FSAScot. Director of Culture and Leisure, Edinburgh City Council, 2001-07, retired 2007; b. 9.3.44, Dundee; m., Angela E.M. Smith; 1 s.; 3 d. Educ. Morgan Academy, Dundee. Assistant Keeper of Antiquities and Bygones, Dundee City Museums, 1965-68, Keeper, 1968-71; Superintendent, Edinburgh City

Museums, 1971-73, City Curator, Edinburgh City Museums and Art Galleries, 1973-96, Head of Museums and Galleries, 1996-97, Head of Heritage and Arts, 1997-98, Director of Recreation, Edinburgh City Council, 1998-2001. Vice-President, Museum Assistants Group, 1969-70; Member: Government Committee on future of Scotland's National Museums and Galleries, 1979-80; Council, Museums Association, 1977-78, 1987-88; Council, Society of Antiquaries of Scotland, 1981-82; Board, Scottish Museums Council, 1985-88; Museums Adviser, COSLA, 1985-90; Member, Paxton House Trust, 1988-2002; Member, East Lothian Community Development Trust, since 1989; External Examiner, St. Andrews University, 1994-97. Member, Board, Museums Training Institute, 1995-2004; Contested Angus South (Lab), 1970; Trustee, East Lothian Community Development Trust, since 1995; Member, Scottish Catholic Heritage Commission, since 2006; Trustee, National Galleries of Scotland, since 2007; Trustee, Paxton House, since 2007; Board Member, Order of Malta Dial-a-Journey Ltd., since 2007; Member, Dunbar Community Council, since 2007; major projects include: City of Edinburgh Art Centre, Museum of Childhood extension, People's Story Museum, City Art Centre extension, Scott Monument restoration, Usher Hall restoration and extension. Publications: Ancient Monuments of Tayside; Tayside Before History; Edinburgh: an illustrated history; Huntly House; Lady Stair's House; The Pharaoh's Gold Mask; Gold of the Pharaohs (Editor); Dinosaurs Alive! (Editor); Sweat of the Sun — Gold of Peru (Editor); Golden Warriors of the Ukrainian Steppes (Editor); StarTrek – the exhibition (Editor); Quest for a Pirate (Editor); Gateway to the Silk Road – Relics from the Han to the Tang Dynasties from Xi'an, China (Editor); Faster, Higher, Stronger – The Story of the Olympic Movement (Editor); articles in archaeological and museums journals; Strategy Documents: Towards The New Enlightenment - A Cultural Policy for Edinburgh; Festivals Strategy; Theatre Strategy; Allotments Strategy; A Capital Commitment to Sport-Sport and Physical Recreation Strategy for Edinburgh. Recreations: family; gardening; opera; writing; reading; walking. Address: (h.) Kirkhill House, Queen's Road, Dunbar EH42 1LN; T.-01368 863113.

Coutts, (Thomas) Gordon, MA, LLB, QC, FCIArb. Queen's Counsel, since 1973; b. 5.7.33, Aberdeen; m., Winifred K. Scott; 1 s.; 1 d. Educ. Aberdeen Grammar School; Aberdeen University. Advocate, 1959; Chairman, Industrial Tribunals, 1972-2003; Chairman, Medical Appeal Tribunals, 1984; Barrister, Lincolns Inn, 1994; Vice President (Scotland), VAT and Duties Tribunals, 1996; Temporary Judge, Court of Session, 1991-2004; Special Commissioner, Income Tax, 1996-2004; Chairman, Financial Services and Markets Tribunal, 2001; Chartered Arbitrator. Recreations: travel; stamp collecting. Address: (h.) 6 Heriot Row, Edinburgh.

Cowan, Sheriff Annella Marie, LLB (Hons), MSc. Sheriff of Grampian Highland and Islands at Aberdeen since 1997; b. 14.11.53, Sheffield; m., James Temple Cowan (marriage dissolved). Educ. Elgin Academy; University of Edinburgh. Admitted Solicitor, 1978; Procurator Fiscal Depute, 1978-86; seconded to Scottish Law Commission, 1984-86; admitted Faculty of Advocates, 1987; Sheriff, Tayside Central and Fife at Stirling, 1993. Recreation: equestrianism. Address: Sheriff's Chambers, Sheriff Court, Aberdeen AB10 1WP; T.-01224 648316.

Cowan, Brigadier Colin Hunter, CBE, MA, FRSA, CEng, MICE. Chief Executive, Cumbernauld Development Corporation, 1970-85; b. 16.10.20, Edinburgh; m., 1, Elizabeth Williamson (deceased); 1 s. (deceased); 1 s.; 1 d.; 2, Mrs Janet Burnett. Educ. Wellington College; Trinity College, Cambridge. Commissioned, Royal Engineers, 1940; service in India and Burma, Royal Bombay Sappers and Miners, 1942-46; staff and regimental appointments, UK and Malta, 1951-60; commanded Field Engineer Regiment, Germany, 1960-63; Defence Adviser, UK Mission to UNO, New York, 1964-66; Chief Staff Officer to Engineer-in-Chief (Army), Ministry of Defence, 1966-68; Brigadier, Engineer Plans (Army), Ministry of Defence, 1968-70. Recreations: hill-walking; photography; music. Address: (h.) Flat 11, Varrich House, 7 Church Hill, Edinburgh EH10 4BG; T.-0131-447 9768.

Cowan, David Lockhart, MB, ChB, FRCSEdin. Consultant Otolaryngologist, City Hospital, Royal Hospital for Sick Children and Western General Hospital, Edinburgh, since 1974; Honorary Senior Lecturer, Edinburgh University; b. 30.6.41, Edinburgh; m., Eileen M. Masterton; 3 s.; 1 d. Educ. George Watson's College, Edinburgh; Trinity College, Glenalmond; Edinburgh University. Scottish Representative, Council, British Association of Otolaryngologists. Publications: Logan Turner's Diseases of the Ear, Nose and Throat (Co-author); Paediatric Otolaryngology (Co-author). Recreations: golf; all sport. Address: (h.) Kellerstane House, Gogar Station Road, Edinburgh EH12 9BS; T.-0131-339 0293.

Cowan, Rev. Gordon Leith. Retired. Former Sacristan, Iona Abbey; former Moderator, United Free Church of Scotland; b. 2.8.39, Glasgow; m., Agnes Allan Copeland; 2 s.; 2 d. Educ. Whitehill Senior Secondary School, Glasgow; Glasgow University; UF Congregational College, Edinburgh. Former Apprentice CA and book-keeper; Minister: Cumnock St. Andrews UF Church, 1968-76, Glasgow Wynd, 1976-87, Leith: Ebenezer UF Church 1987-2002. Children's Panel Member, 1972-87. Recreations: genealogy; Scotland; watching athletics. Address: (h.) 8 Morris Moodie Avenue, Stevenston, Ayrshire KA20 3NW; T.-01294 465586.

Cowan, John Mervyn, TD, MCIBS. Lt. Col. (Retd), RA/TA; President, Royal Artillery Association Scottish Region, since 2002 (Chairman, 1991-2002); b. 13.2.30, Oban; m., Marion Neilson Kidd; 1 s.; 2 d. Educ. Oban High School. National Bank of Scotland, National Commercial Bank of Scotland, Royal Bank of Scotland, 1946-90 (retired); TA commission, 1963; commanded 207 (Scottish) Battery RA(V), 1980-82; J.S.L.O., HQ Scotland, 1982-90; Chairman: The Sandilands Trust, since 1993, Earl Haig Fund (Scotland), 1993-99, SSAFA West Lothian, 2001-05; Patron, RA Council for Scotland; Trustee, 445 and City of Edinburgh RA Regimental Trusts. Recreations: travel; charitable works; sport. Address: (h.) 39 Kinloch View, Blackness Road, Linlithgow, West Lothian EH49 7HT; T.-01506 671718.

Cowan, Margaret Morton (Lady Cowan), MA, JP. Member, Council, National Trust for Scotland, 1989-94 and 1997-2002; former Member of Executive and of Highland Committee; b. 4.11.33, Newmilns; m., Sir Robert Cowan ; 2 d. Educ. St. George's School for Girls, Edinburgh; Edinburgh University. British Petroleum Company, 1955-59; Teacher, West Midlands Education Authority, 1965-76; Consultant and Lecturer in Use of Language, Hong Kong, 1976-81; Member, Justice of the Peace Committee, Inverness, 1985-2000; Member, Scottish Committee, British Council, 1991-2000; Convener, Highland Festival, 1992-97. Address: (h.) 1 Eyre Crescent, Edinburgh EH3 5ET; T.-0131-556 3379.

Cowie, Alan. Freelance television producer, journalist and broadcaster; Head, Current Affairs, Grampian Television,

1998-2000; b. 28.4.48, Aberdeen; m., Evelyn; 2 d. Educ. Aberdeen Grammar School; Central College, London; Jordanhill College of Education, Glasgow. Teacher, Glasgow, 1971-72; Reporter/Presenter, Radio Scotland, 1972-75; joined Grampian Television as News Reporter, 1975; Programme Editor, 1988. Burgess, City of Aberdeen. Recreations: Scottish art; music; fishing; e-mail: alancowietv@aol.com

Cowie, Rev. James Morton, BD, CCE, DipFam. Associate Minister of Elgin: St. Giles and St. Columba's, since 2007; b. 17.7.48, Aberdeen; m., Margaret Adams Davidson; 1 s.; 1 d. Educ. Aberdeen Academy; Aberdeen University; UTS, USA; New College, Edinburgh. Youth Director, St. Ninian's, Crieff, 1976-78; Minister, Fordyce Parish Church, 1978-84; Minister, Burnfoot, Hawick, 1984-96; Chaplain, Thistle Foundation and Community Minister, Craigmillar, 1996-2002; Minister of St. Mary's Church, Haddington, 2002-07. Convener, Board of Social Responsibility, 2001-05; Member, International Church Leaders Group for L'Arche, since 1999. Recreations: walking; reading. Address: (b.) St. Giles Church, High Street, Elgin; St. Columba's South Church, Moss Street, Elgin.

Cowie, Professor John McKenzie Grant, BSc, PhD, DSc, CChem, FRSC, FRSE. Professor Emeritus, Heriot-Watt University, since 1998; b. 31.5.33, Edinburgh; m., Agnes Neilson; 1 s.; 1 d. Educ. Royal High School Edinburgh; Edinburgh University. Assistant Lecturer, Edinburgh University, 1956-58; Associate Research Officer, National Research Council, Canada, 1958-67; Lecturer, Essex University, 1967-69; Senior Lecturer, Stirling University, 1969-73; Professor of Chemistry, Stirling University, 1973-88; Founding Professor of Chemistry and Materials, Heriot-Watt University, 1988-98; Hon. President, Stirling Voluntary Organisations and Stirling Council of Disabilities; Past Chairman and Vice-Chairman, Spinal Injuries, Scotland; Past Vice-Chairman, Disability Scotland; Past Chairman: Macrogroup UK; British High Polymer Forum; Macro Group (UK) medalist, 2001. Honorary DSc, Heriot-Watt University, 2005. Publications: Polymers, Chemistry and Physics of Modern Materials. Recreations: reading; music; painting. Address: (h.) Traquair, 50 Back Road, Dollar, Clackmannanshire, FK14 7EA; T.-01259 742031.

Cowie, Rev. Marian, MA, BD, MTh. Minister, Midstocket Church, Aberdeen, since 2006; Associate Lecturer, Open University, since 2002; b. 31.8.63, Malta; m., George Cowie; 1 s.; 1 d. Educ. Glenwood High School, Glenrothes, Fife; University of Glasgow. Netherlee Church, Glasgow: Probationer Minister, 1989-90, Ordained Assistant, 1990-91; Hospital Chaplain, Kirkcaldy, Victoria, 1992-94; Counsellor Manager with Mental Health Charity, 1994-96; Associate Minister, Howe of Fife, 1996-99; Counsellor Manager, Alcohol Advisory and Counselling, Aberdeen, 2000-03; Hospital Chaplain, Aberdeen, 2003-06. Convener, Aberdeen Bipolar Charity, since 2000. Recreations: swimming; walking; theatre; travel. Address: 54 Woodstock Road, Aberdeen AB15 5JF; T.-01224 208001; e-mail: mcowieou@aol.com

Cowie, Hon. Lord (William Lorn Kerr Cowie), MA (Cantab), LLB (Glas). Senator of the College of Justice in Scotland, 1977-94; Botswana Court of Appeal, 1995-98; b. 1.6.26, Glasgow; m., Camilla Henrietta Grizel Hoyle; 2 s.; 2 d. Educ. Fettes College, Edinburgh; Clare College, Cambridge; Glasgow University. RNVR, 1944-47 (Sub. Lt.); Member, Faculty of Advocates, 1952; QC, 1967.

Scottish rugby internationalist, 1953. Recreation: fishing. Address: (h.) 20 Blacket Place, Edinburgh.

Cowley of Innerwick, Col. Victor Charles Vereker, TD, DL; b. 4.4.18, Glasgow; m., Moyra McClure; 1 s.; 2 d. Educ. St. Mary's, Melrose; Merchiston Castle School. Young master printer, 1937; commissioned, RATA, 1939; served France, North Africa, Sicily, Italy, Burma, Indo China; Col. Depute CRA 51st Highland Division; Chairman, Brownlie Scandrett and Graham Ltd. (retired 1960); Vice Chairman, East Lothian County Council, 1973; Regional Councillor, Lothian, 1975; Commissioner of Income Tax, East Lothian, 1965-87. Address: Crowhill, Innerwick, Dunbar EH42 1QT; T.-01368 840279.

Cox, Derek, MBChB, MRCP(UK), MFPHM. Director of Public Health, Dumfries and Galloway Health Board, since 1999; b. 29.7.45, Glasgow. Educ. Hutchesons' Boys Grammar School; Glasgow University. Research Fellow, Cardiology, Glasgow University; Senior House Officer/Registrar in Cardiology, Glasgow Royal Infirmary; Medical Officer/Senior Medical Officer, Falkland Islands Government Medical Department; Registrar, General Surgery, Bignold Hospital, Wick; GP, Walls, Shetland; Director of Public Health, Shetland Health Board, 1990-99. Address: (h.) Aitkenmoor, Annan Water, Moffat DG10 9LS; T.-01683 220600.

Cox, Gilbert Kirkwood, MBE, JP. Lord Lieutenant of Lanarkshire, since 2000; Honorary Sheriff, since 2002; Board Member, New Lanarkshire plc; Board Member, Lanarkshire, Prince's Trust, Scotland; Director/Trustee, Airdrie Savings Bank, since 1987 (President, 1996-98); retired General Manager Scotland, Associated Perforators & Weavers Ltd.; b. 24.8.35, Chapelhall, Airdrie; m., Marjory Moir Ross Taylor; 2 s.; 1 d. Educ. Airdrie Academy. National Coal Board, 1953-63; David A. McPhail & Sons Ltd., 1963-68; D.A. Monteith Holdings, 1968-71. Chair, Board of Management, Coatbridge College, 1997-2000; founder Member and Past President, Monklands Rotary Club. Recreations: golf; gardening; walking. Address: (h.) Bedford House, Commonhead Street, Airdrie ML6 6NS; T.-01236 763331; e-mail: coxgk@globalnet.co.uk

Cox, Sheriff Principal Graham Loudon, QC, MA, LLB, Sheriff Principal of South Strathclyde Dumfries and Galloway, 1993-2000; b. 22.12.33, Newcastle-upon-Tyne; m., Jean Nelson; 3 c. by pr. m. Educ. Hamilton Academy; Grove Academy; Edinburgh University. Army 1956-61 (latterly Major, Directorate of Army Legal Services); called to the Bar, 1962; Advocate-Depute, 1966-68; Sheriff of Tayside Central and Fife, at Dundee, 1968-93; QC, 1993; President, Sheriffs' Association, 1991-93. Address: (h.) Crail House, Crail, Fife, KY10 3SJ; T.-01333 450270; e-mail: coxcrail@aol.com

Cox, Roy Frederick. Chairman, Sense Scotland; Partner, Old Mill Chimneys, since 1990; b. 4.11.49, Leicester; m., Elizabeth; 1 s.; 1 d. Educ. New Parks Boys School; College of Textiles, Leicester. Engineering apprenticeship, Mellor Bromley; textile mechanical engineer, Corar's. Past President, Clydebank Rotary Club. Recreations: golf; gardening; travelling. Address: Duntiglennan Farm, Farm Road, Duntocher, Clydebank G81 6RS; T.-01389 876061; e-mail: enquiries@scottishchimneys-omh.com

Craig, Gordon. Chairperson, State Hospitals Board for Scotland, since 2001; b. 12.9.47, Huntly; m., Linda May; 2 s. Educ. Gordon Schools, Huntly. Health Service technician, 1964-70; Research Officer, Scottish Trades Union Congress, 1970-77; Trade Union Officer, 1977-86; Depute Director Personnel, Glasgow City Council, 1987-95; Depute Director, Cleansing, 1995-98. Recreations: golf; football. Address: (b.) State Hospital, Carstairs, Lanark ML11 8RP; T.-01555 842001.

Craig, Emeritus Professor Gordon Younger, BSc, PhD, CGeol, FRSE. Emeritus Professor of Geology, Edinburgh University, since 1984; b. 17.1.25, Milngavie; m., Mary Thornton; 2 s.; 2 step s.; 1 step d. Educ. Hillhead High School; Bearsden Academy; Glasgow University. Edinburgh University: Lecturer, 1947; James Hutton Professor of Geology, 1967-84. Visiting Professor, University of Colorado, 1958-59, UCLA, 1959, 1965; Leverhulme Fellow, ANU, Canberra, 1978; Distinguished Foreign Scholar, Mid-America State Universities, 1980; Green Professor, University of British Columbia, 1977, Texas Christian University, 1994; President: Edinburgh Geological Society, 1967-69, International Commission on the History of the Geological Sciences, 1984-89; Trustee, Dynamic Earth Charitable Trust, 1995-2001; Clough Medal, Edinburgh Geological Society, 1987; History of Geology Division Award, Geological Society of America, 1990. Publications: Geology of Scotland (Editor), 1991 (3rd ed.); James Hutton: The Lost Drawings (Co-author), 1997; A Geological Miscellany (Co-author), 1982. Recreations: golf; gardening. Address: (h.) 14 Kevock Road, Lasswade, Edinburgh EH18 1HT; T.-0131-663 8275.

Craig, Rev. Maxwell, MA, BD, ThM. Minister, St. Andrew's Scots Church, Jerusalem, 1999-2000; Chaplain to the Queen in Scotland, since 1986; b. 25.12.31; m., Janet Margaret Macgregor; 1 s.; 3 d. Educ. Oriel College, Oxford; Edinburgh University. National Service, 1st Bn., Argyll and Sutherland Highlanders (2nd Lt.), 1954-56. Assistant Principal, Ministry of Labour, 1957-61; Parish Minister, Falkirk, Glasgow and Aberdeen, 1966-91; General Secretary, Action of Churches Together in Scotland, 1990-98. Convener, Church and Nation Committee, Church of Scotland, 1984-88; Chairman, Scottish Churches Housing Action, 2000-06. Recreations: hill-walking; choral singing. Address: (h.) 3 Queens Road, Stirling, FK8 2QY; T.-01786 472319.

Craigie, Cathie. MSP (Labour), Cumbernauld and Kilsyth, since 1999; b. 1954, Stirling; m.; 2 c. Councillor, Cumbernauld and Kilsyth District Council, 1984-96 (Council Leader, 1994-96); Member, North Lanarkshire Council, 1995-99; former Chair, Cumbernauld Housing Partnership. Address: (b.) Scottish Parliament, Edinburgh EH99 1SP.

Cramb, Auslan, MA (Hons). Scottish Correspondent, Daily Telegraph since 1994; b. 6.10.56, Dunoon; m., Catriona; 1 s.; 1 d. Educ. Perth Academy; Aberdeen University. Reporter, Press and Journal, 1979-82; Reporter, Press Association, Glasgow, 1982-85; The Herald, Glasgow, 1985-90; Environment Correspondent, The Scotsman, 1990-94. Scottish Specialist Writer of the Year, 1992 and 1993. Publications: Who Owns Scotland Now?, 1996; Fragile Land, 1998. Address: (b.) Daily Telegraph, 5 Coates Crescent, Edinburgh, EH3 7AL.

Cramb, Rev. Erik McLeish, LTh. Former National Co-ordinator, Scottish Churches Industrial Mission; Convener, Church of Scotland Committee on Ecumenical Relations; b. 26.12.39, Glasgow; m., Elizabeth McLean; 2 s.; 3 d. Educ. Woodside Secondary School, Glasgow; Glasgow University and Trinity College. Minister: St. Thomas' Gallowgate, Glasgow, 1973-81, St. Paul's United Church, Kingston, Jamaica, 1981-84, Yoker, Glasgow, 1984-89; Organiser for Tayside, Scottish Churches International Mission, 1989-97. Socialist; Member, Iona Community; former Chairman, Church Action on Poverty; Hon. Fellow, Al Maktoum Institute. Recreation: supports Partick Thistle.

Address: (h.) Flat 35, Braehead, Methven Walk, Dundee DD2 3FJ; T.-01382 526196.
E-mail: erikcramb@blueyonder.co.uk

Cramond, Ronald Duncan, CBE (1987), MA, FIMgt, FSA (Scot).Secretary, Intellectual Access Trust, since 1995; b. 22.3.27, Leith; m., 1, Constance MacGregor (deceased); 1 s.; 1 d; m., 2, Ann Rayner. Educ. George Heriot's School; Edinburgh University. Commissioned Royal Scots, 1950; entered War Office, 1951; Private Secretary to Parliamentary Under Secretary of State, Scottish Office, 1956; Principal, Department of Health for Scotland, 1957; Mactaggart Fellow, Glasgow University, 1962; Haldane Medallist in Public Administration, 1964; Assistant Secretary, Scottish Development Department, 1966; Under Secretary, 1973; Under Secretary, Department of Agriculture and Fisheries for Scotland, 1977. Deputy Chairman, Highlands and Islands Development Board, 1983-88; Member, Scottish Tourist Board, 1985-88; Trustee: National Museums of Scotland, 1985-96, Cromarty Arts Trust, 1988-91, Bo'ness Heritage Trust, 1989-97, Scottish Civic Trust, 1988-95; Vice President, Architectural Heritage Society of Scotland, 1989-94; Chairman, Scottish Museums Council, 1990-93; Commissioner, Countryside Commission for Scotland, 1988-92; Chairman, Scottish Greenbelt Foundation, 1992-2000. Recreations: reading history; visiting museums and galleries; testing a plastic hip. Address: (b.) Intact, 1-8 Dunard Garden, Edinburgh EH9 2HZ.

Crampsey, Robert A. McN., MA (Hons), ARCM, DUniv (Stirling). Scottish football historian, author and retired broadcaster; b. 8.7.30, Glasgow; m., Dr. Veronica R. Carson; 4 d. Educ. Holyrood School, Glasgow; Glasgow University; London University (External). RAF, 1952-55 (demobilised in rank of Flt. Lt.); Head of History Department, St. Aloysius College, Glasgow, 1967-71; Assistant Head Teacher, Holyrood Secondary School, 1971-74; Rector, St. Ambrose High School, Coatbridge, 1974-86. Winner, Brain of Britain, BBC, 1965; Churchill Fellow, 1970; semi-finalist, Mastermind, 1972-73; BBC Sports Commentator. Publications: History of Queen's Park FC; Puerto Rico; The Manager; The Scottish Footballer; The Edinburgh Pirate (Arts Council Award); The Run Out; Mr Stein (a biography); The Young Civilian; The Glasgow Golf Club 1787-1987; The Empire Exhibition; The Somerset Cricket Quiz Book; The Surrey Cricket Quiz Book; Ranfurly Castle Golf Club — a centenary history; The Official Centenary History of the Scottish Football League; Scottish Railway Connections; The King's Grocer – a Life of Sir Thomas Lipton. Recreations: travel; things Hispanic; listening to good music; cricket.

Cranstoun of That Ilk and Corehouse, David Alexander Somerville, TD, MA, MSc, PhD, DL. Member, Queen's Bodyguard for Scotland (Royal Company of Archers); b. 19.12.43, Washington DC; m., Dr. iur. M.M. Glättli; 2 s. Educ. Winchester College; Trinity College, Oxford. National List Trials Officer, ESCA, 1973; Emeritus Fellow, SAC, 2003. Director, Scottish Quality Cereals; Director, Crop Evaluation Ltd; Cereal Specialist, SAC, 1982-2003; Chairman, Scottish Society for Crop Research, 1996-2000; Hon. Director, Lord Roberts Workshops (Edinburgh); Vice Chairman, SSAFA Forces Help (Lanark); Commissioned Queens Own Lowland Yeomanry (TA), 1964, Lt. Col., 1982; Comd District Specialist Training Team, 1988, TA Col. Lowlands, 1990; Hon. Col. Glasgow and Lanarkshire Bn. ACF, 2001-06. Recreation: forestry. Address: (h.) Corehouse, Lanark ML11 9TQ.

Craven, Professor Alan James, MA, PhD, FInstP, CPhys. Professor of Physics, University of Glasgow, since 1998; b. 18.4.47, St. Helens; m., Rosalind; 1 s.; 1 d. Educ. Prescot Grammar School; Emmanuel College, Cambridge University. Cavendish Laboratory, Cambridge: Research Student, 1969-75, Post-doctoral Research Assistant, 1975-

78; Department of Physics and Astronomy, University of Glasgow: Lecturer, 1978-89, Senior Lecturer, 1989-91, Reader in Physics, 1991-98. Address: Department of Physics and Astronomy, University of Glasgow, Glasgow G12 8QQ; T.-0141-330 5892.

Crawford, Barbara Elizabeth, MA (Hons), PhD. Honorary Reader in Medieval History, St. Andrews University, since 2001; Hon. Director, Strathmartine Centre for Scottish History; b. 5.4.40, Barnsley; m., Robert M.M. Crawford; 1 s. Educ. Queen Margaret's School; St. Andrews University. Carnegie Senior Scholarship, 1968; Temporary Lecturer, Department of History, Aberdeen University, 1969; Lecturer in Medieval History, St. Andrews University, 1972. Elected Fellow, Society of Antiquaries London, 1973; Fellow Society of Antiquaries of Scotland, 1964; Member Norwegian Academy of Science and Letters, 1997; Fellow, Royal Society of Edinburgh, 2001; Leverhulme Research Fellow, 2000-01. Publications: Scandinavian Scotland, 1987; The Biggings, Papa Stour, Shetland, 1999. Recreations: exploring areas of Viking settlement in Scotland and North Atlantic. Address: (b.) The Strathmartine Centre, 2, Kinburn Place, St. Andrews KY16 9DT; T.-01334 478644.
E-mail: office@strathmartine.demon.co.uk

Crawford, Professor Dorothy H., OBE, MBBS, PhD, MD, DSc, FRCPath, FRSE, FAcadMedSci. Professor of Medical Microbiology, University of Edinburgh, since 1997; b. 13.4.45, Glasgow; m., Dr. W.D. Alexander; 2 s. Educ. St. Thomas's Hospital Medical School. Senior Lecturer then Reader, Royal Post-graduate Medical School, London, 1985-90; Professor of Medical Microbiology, London School of Hygiene and Tropical Medicine, 1990-97. Address: (b.) Clinical and Molecular Virology, University of Edinburgh, Summerhall, Edinburgh EH9 1QH.

Crawford, Douglas James, LLB, DipLP, NP, CF. Partner, Dundas & Wilson, since 1997; b. 28.2.65, Ayr; m., Alison; 1 s.; 2 d. Educ. Belmont Academy, Ayr; Edinburgh University. Trained, Shepherd & Wedderburn WS, 1987-89; Assistant, Associate, Partner, Maclay Murray & Spens, 1989-97. Recreations: golf; sailing; winter sports. Address: (b.) 20 Castle Terrace, Edinburgh EH1 2EN; T.-07798 855 290; e-mail: douglas.crawford@dundas-wilson.com

Crawford, Professor Elizabeth Bryden, LLB (Hons), PhD. Professor of International Private Law, University of Glasgow, since 2006; b. 20.04.49, Glasgow; m., Robin Crawford; 1 s.; 1 d. Educ. Laurel Bank School, Glasgow; University of Glasgow. Admitted as Solicitor, 1994; successively since 1976, Lecturer, then Senior Lecturer, then Reader in the Conflict of Laws, then Professor, University of Glasgow. Publications include: International Private Law in Scotland (1st ed 1998) and 2nd ed (Co-Author), 2006. Recreations: golf; cooking. Address: (b.) School of Law, Stair Building, University of Glasgow, Glasgow G12 8QQ; T.-0141-330 4729.
E-mail: e.crawford@law.gla.ac.uk

Crawford, Hugh William Jack, BArch, DipTP, RIBA, FRIAS, FRTPI. Principal, Sir Frank Mears Associates, since 1985; Part-time Inquiry Reporter (Local Plans), Scottish Executive, 1982-2005; b. 19.1.38, Dalry; m., Catherine Mary McIntyre; 1 s.; 2 d. Educ. Dalry High School; University of Strathclyde. Partner, Sir Frank Mears and Partners, 1965-85. Scottish Chairman, Royal Town Planning Institute, 1979, 1980, 1992; Past President, Committee of Liaison for Planning Practitioners in Member Countries of the European Union; President of Honour,

European Council of Town Planners, Brussels, since 1985; former National Vice-President, Pedestrians Association; President, Association of Mediators. Recreations: walking; visiting historic buildings and towns; art galleries and museums. Address: (b.) 24 Minto Street, Edinburgh EH9 1SB; T.-0131-662 9922.
E-mail: h.crawford@btinternet.com

Crawford, Professor Robert, MA, DPhil, FRSE, FEA. Professor of Modern Scottish Literature, School of English, St. Andrews University, since 1995 (Head of School, 2002-05); Associate Director, St. Andrews Scottish Studies Centre, since 1993; Poet and Critic; b. 23.2.59, Bellshill; m., Alice Wales; 1 s.; 1 d. Educ. Hutchesons' Grammar School, Glasgow; Glasgow University; Balliol College, Oxford. Snell Exhibitioner & Carnegie Scholar, Balliol College, Oxford, 1981-84; Elizabeth Wordsworth Junior Research Fellow, St. Hugh's College, Oxford, 1984-87; British Academy Postdoctoral Fellow, Department of English Literature, Glasgow University, 1987-89; Lecturer in Modern Scottish Literature, School of English, St. Andrews University, 1989-95. Former Co-Editor, Verse Magazine; Co-Editor, Scottish Studies Review, 1999-2004. Publications: The Savage and the City in the Work of T.S. Eliot, 1987; A Scottish Assembly, 1990; Sharawaggi (Co-author), 1990; About Edwin Morgan (Co-Editor), 1990; Other Tongues: young Scottish poets in English, Scots and Gaelic (Editor), 1990; The Arts of Alasdair Gray (Co-Editor), 1991; Devolving English Literature, 1992; Talkies, 1992; Reading Douglas Dunn (Co-Editor), 1992; Identifying Poets, 1993; Liz Lochhead's Voices (Co-Editor), 1993; Twentieth Century Literature of Scotland: a selected bibliography, 1995; Talking Verse (Co-Editor), 1995; Masculinity, 1996; Penguin Modern Poets 9 (Co-Author), 1996; Robert Burns and Cultural Authority (Editor), 1997; Launch-site for English Studies: Three Centuries of Literary Studies at the University of St. Andrews (Editor), 1997; Impossibility, 1998; The Scottish Invention of English Literature (Editor), 1998; The Penguin Book of Poetry from Britain and Ireland since 1945 (Co-Editor), 1998; Spirit Machines, 1999; The New Penguin Book of Scottish Verse (Co-Editor), 2000; Scottish Religious Poetry (Co-Editor), 2000; The Modern Poet, 2001; Heaven-Taught Fergusson, 2002; The Tip of My Tongue, 2003; Selected Poems, 2005; The Book of St. Andrews (Editor), 2005; Apollos of the North, 2006; Contemporary Poetry and Contemporary Science, 2006 (Editor); Scotland's Books, 2007; Full Volume, 2008. Recreation: mischief. Address: (b.) School of English, St. Andrews University, St. Andrews, KY16 9AL; T.-01334 476161, Ext. 2666.

Crawford, 29th Earl of, and Balcarres, 12th Earl of (Robert Alexander Lindsay), KT, GCVO, PC. Premier Earl of Scotland; Head of House of Lindsay; b. 5.3.27; m., Ruth Beatrice Meyer; 2 s.; 2 d. Educ. Eton; Trinity College, Cambridge. Grenadier Guards, 1945-49; MP (Conservative), Hertford, 1955-74, Welwyn and Hatfield, February to September, 1974; Opposition Front Bench Spokesman on Health and Social Security, 1967-70; Minister of State for Defence, 1970-72; Minister of State for Foreign and Commonwealth Affairs, 1972-74; Chairman, Lombard North Central Bank, 1976-80; Director, National Westminster Bank, 1975-88; Director, Scottish American Investment Co., 1978-88; Vice-Chairman, Sun Alliance & London Insurance Group, 1975-91; President, Rural District Councils Association, 1959-65; Chairman, National Association of Mental Health, 1963-70; Chairman, Historic Buildings Council for Scotland, 1976-83; Chairman, Royal Commission on Ancient and Historical Monuments of Scotland, 1985-95; First Crown Estate Commissioner, 1980-85; former Deputy Lieutenant, Fife; Chairman, National Library of Scotland, 1990-2000; Lord Chamberlain to HM Queen Elizabeth The Queen

Mother, 1992-2002. Address: (h.) Balcarres, Colinsburgh, Fife KY9 1HN.

Crawford, Robert Caldwell. Composer; b. 18.4.25, Edinburgh; m., Alison Braedine Orr; 1 s.; 1 d. Educ. Melville College, Edinburgh; Keswick Grammar School; Guildhall School of Music, London. Freelance Composer and Critic until 1970; BBC Music Producer, 1970-85; Chairman, Music Advisory Committee for Sir James Caird's Travelling Scholarships Trust, 1978-93. Recreations: carpentry; hill-walking; gardening; beekeeping. Address: (h.) 12 Inverleith Terrace, Edinburgh EH3 5NS; T.-0131-556 3600.

Crawford, Robert Hardie Bruce, JP. MSP (SNP), Stirling, since 2007, Mid Scotland and Fife, 1999-2007; Minister for Parliamentary Business, since 2007; Chairman, SNP, 2004-07; Shadow Minister for Parliament, 2003-04; Shadow Minister, Environment and Energy, 2001-03; Shadow Minister, Transport and the Environment, 2000-01; Chief Whip, SNP Scottish Parliamentary Group, 1999-2001; b. 16.2.55, Perth; m., Jacqueline; 3 s. Educ. Kinross High School; Perth High School. Civil servant, Scottish Office, 1974-99; Leader, Perth and Kinross Council, 1995-99; Chairman, Kinross-shire Partnership Ltd., 1997-99; Chairman, Perth and Kinross Recreation Facilities Ltd, 1995-99; Member: Perthshire Tourist Board, Scottish Enterprise Tayside, Perth College, 1995-99. Recreations: golf, watching Dunfermline Athletic. Address: (h.) 12 Douglas Crescent, Kinross; T.-01577 863531.

Crawford, Robert MacKay, CBE, PhD, BA (Hons). Executive Director, Glasgow Caledonian University, since 2006; Director of Strategy, Wood Group PLC (Gas Turbine Services - GTS); CEO, Mersey Partnership; Chief Executive, Scottish Enterprise, 2000-04; b. 14.6.51, Scotland; 1 s.; 1 d. Educ. Glasgow University; Harvard University; Strathclyde University. Director, Locate In Scotland, 1991-94; Managing Director, Operations, Scottish Enterprise, 1994-96; World Bank Washington D.C., USA, 1996-98; Partner, Foreign Investment, Ernst and Young, 1998-2000. Recreations: running; reading, especially history and biography. Address: (b.) Cowcaddens Road, Glasgow G4 0BA; T.-0141-331-8060; e-mail: Robert.Crawford@gcal.ac.uk

Crawford, Robin, LLB, CA. Chairman, Scottish Business Crime Centre Ltd.; Member of Court, Strathclyde University; Member of Executive Committee, Erskine; Vice-Captain, Glasgow Golf Club; Partner, KPMG, 1979-2003; b. 2.10.48, Greenock; m., Elizabeth; 1 s.; 1 d. Educ. Greenock Academy; Glasgow University. Governor, then Vice-Chairman, Laurel Bank and Laurel Park Schools, 1988-98; Member, Council, CBI Scotland, 2000-06. Recreations: golf; fly fishing; hillwalking. E-mail: robert.crawford3@ntlworld.com

Crawford, Ruth, LLB (Hons), DipLP. Admitted Faculty of Advocates, 1993; b. 17.7.65, Glasgow. Educ. Cranley School for Girls; George Heriot's School; Aberdeen University. Standing Junior Counsel to Keeper of the Registers of Scotland, 1998-2002; Second Standing Junior Counsel to Scottish Executive, since 2002. Address: Advocate's Library, Parliament House, Parliament Square, Edinburgh EH1 1RF; T.-0131-226 5071.

Crawford, Thomas, MA. Former Reader in English, Aberdeen University; b. 6.7.20, Dundee; m., Jean Rennie McBride; 1 s.; 1 d. Educ. Dunfermline High School; Edinburgh University; University of Auckland. University of Auckland: Lecturer in English, 1953-60, Senior Lecturer, 1960-62, Associate Professor, 1963-65; Lecturer in English, Edinburgh University, 1965; Commonwealth Research Fellow, Hamilton, Ontario, 1966; Senior Lecturer in English, then Reader, Aberdeen University, 1967-85; Warnock Fellow, Yale University, various times, since

1978. Past President, Association for Scottish Literary Studies; former Editor, Scottish Literary Journal. Publications: Burns: a study of the poems and songs, 1960; Scott, 1965; Scott, selected poems (Editor), 1972; Love, Labour, and Liberty, 1976; Society and the Lyric, 1980; Boswell, Burns and the French Revolution, 1990; Correspondence of James Boswell and William Johnson Temple 1756 1795, Vol I. (Editor), 1997; Boswell in Scotland and Beyond (Editor), 1997. Recreations: walking and rambling; music. Address: (h.) 34 Summerhill Terrace, Aberdeen AB15 6HE; T.-01224 311764.

Crawley, David Jonathan, MA (Oxon). Retired Senior Civil Servant. Board Member, Scottish Natural Heritage, since 2006; HM Commissioner, Queen Victoria School, since 2006; Chair, Wales Office Audit Committee, since 2006; Director, Central Scotland Forest Trust, since 2007; EU Director, Scottish Executive, 2005-06; Head of Scotland Office, 2002-05; Head of Food and Agriculture Group, Scottish Executive, 1999-2002; b. 6.5.51, Barnet; m., Anne Anderson; 1 s.; 2 d. Educ. Chichester High School; Christ Church, Oxford. Scottish Office, 1972-81, 1984-90 and 1994-99; Department of Energy, 1981-84; Principal Private Secretary to Secretary of State for Scotland, 1987-89; Counsellor, UK Permanent Representation to European Communities, Brussels, 1990-94. Recreations: family; walking; gardening. Address: (h.) 18 Braid Avenue, Edinburgh EH10 6EE.

Creally, Eugene P., LLB (Hons), DipLP, PhD. Clerk of Faculty, Faculty of Advocates, 1999-2003; b. 3.2.61, Dungannon, Co. Tyrone; 1 s. Educ. St Patrick's Academy, Dungannon; Queens University, Belfast; Edinburgh University. Admitted to Faculty of Advocates, 1993. Address: (b.) Advocates Library, Parliament House, Edinburgh EH1 1RF; T.-0131-226 5071.

Crerar, Lorne Donald, LLB (Hons), NP FCIBS. Founding Partner and Chairman, Harper Macleod LLP, since 1987; Chair in Banking Law, University of Glasgow, since 1997; b. 29.07.54, Renfrew. Educ. Kelvinside Academy, Glasgow; University of Glasgow. Partner in Mackenzie Robertson & Co., 1979-87. Chairman, Discipline for Scottish Rugby Union, since 1995; International Rugby Board Judicial Officer, since 1995; Chairman, Discipline for European Rugby Cup Limited, since 1999; Chairman, Discipline for 6 Nations Limited, since 1999; Deputy Chairman, Scottish Enterprise Glasgow, 2000-03; Chairman, Sub-Group, Housing Improvement Task Force, 2001-03; Convener, Standards Commission for Scotland, 2003-07; Non-Executive Director, Scottish Government Justice Department, since 2004; Independent Member of the Purchasers Information Advisory Group, 2005-08; Chairman, Independent Review of Audit, Inspection, Regulation and Complaints Handling in the Public Sector ("The Crerar Review") (1 July 2006-August 2008). On Editorial Board of "World Sports Law Report"; elected a "Fellow" of the Chartered Institute of Bankers, June 1999; listed in "Chambers Guide to the Legal Profession" as one of Scotland's very few "Sports Law Experts". Publications: "The Law of Banking in Scotland", 2nd ed. 2007; commissioned author for Stair Memorial Encyclopedia (the leading Scottish Text) for financial institutions, banking and currency (published, December 2000). Recreations: The West Highlands of Scotland and its history; hillwalking; fishing; travel. Address: (b.) Harper Macleod LLP, The Ca'd'oro, 45 Gordon Street, Glasgow G1 3PE; T.-0141 227 9377.
E-mail: lorne.crerar@harpermacleod.co.uk

Cresswell, Lyell Richard, BMus (Hons), MusM, PhD. Composer; b. 13.10.44, Wellington, New Zealand; m., Catherine Mawson. Educ. Victoria University of Wellington; Toronto University; Aberdeen University. Music Organiser, Chapter Arts Centre, Cardiff; Forman Fellow, Edinburgh University, 1980-82; Canadian

Commonwealth scholarship, 1969-70; Dutch Government bursary, 1974-75; Ian Whyte Award, 1978; APRA Silver Scroll, 1979; Cramb Fellow, Glasgow University, 1982-85; Winner, Scottish Arts Council Creative Scotland Award, 2001; Inaugural Elgar Bursary, 2002; Hon. DMus, Victoria University of Wellington, New Zealand, 2002; New Zealand School of Music/Creative New Zealand Composer in Residence, 2006-07. Address: (h.) 4 Leslie Place, Edinburgh EH4 1NQ; T.-0131-332 9181; e-mail: elsie@elsie.fsworld.co.uk

Crewe, Martin Alistair, BSc, PhD, MBA, MSc. Director, Barnardo's Scotland, since 2007; b. 13.07.60, London; m., Jane; 3 s.; 1 d. Educ. Alleyn's School, London; Exeter University; Nottingham-Trent University; Stirling University. Regional Manager, NSPCC, 1989-97; Finance Director, Barnardo's Scotland, 1997-2007. Board Member, Office of The Scottish Charity Regulator (OSCR), since 2006. Recreation: bringing up children. Address: (b.) 235 Corstorphine Road, Edinburgh EH12 7AR; T.-0131 334 9893; e-mail: martin.crewe@barnardos.org.uk

Crichton, John Hugh McDiarmid, BMedSci (Hons), BMBS, PhD, MRCPsych, FHEA. Consultant Forensic Psychiatrist, since 2000; Honorary Fellow in Law, since 2000; Medical Director, Forensic Mental Health Services managed Care Network and State Hospital's Board for Scotland, 2005-06; b. 8.9.66, Edinburgh; m., Dr. Anne-Marie Crichton; 3 d. Educ. Edinburgh Academy; Nottingham University; Trinity Hall, Cambridge. Nightingale Research Scholar, Institute of Criminology, Cambridge University, 1993; Lecturer in Developmental Psychiatry, Cambridge University, 1997; Lecturer in Forensic Psychiatry, Edinburgh University, 1998. Publication: Psychiatric Patient Violence: Risk and Response, 1995. Recreation: gardening. Address: (b.) Orchard Clinic, Royal Edinburgh Hospital, Edinburgh EH10 5HF; T.-0131-537 5858; e-mail: john.crichton@lpct.scot.nhs.uk

Crichton, Robin, FRAI. Retired film producer and director; b. 14.5.40, Bournemouth; m., 1, Trish Dorrell, 2, Flora Maxwell Stuart; 3 d. Educ. Sherborne; Paris; Edinburgh. Built Scotland's first independent film studio, 1968; started film training scheme, now Napier University M.A., 1970; founded first animation studio in Scotland; managed first independent outside broadcast unit in Scotland; Founder Member: Scottish ACTT Committee, Scottish Film Archive; former UK Vice-Chair and Scottish Chair, Independent Programme Producers' Association; former Co-ordinator, Working Party, Scottish Screen; co-initiated Annual Co-production Conference; organised Scottish stand at international TV television markets; Churchill Fellowship, 1990 (to study models for Scottish Screen); Co-production Consultant to various European broadcasters and producers; former Project Leader, Eureka Audiovisual Federation; founder Director, Scottish Screen Locations; Consultant Programme Buyer, Gaelic Television Committee; President, L'Association Charles Rennie Mackintosh en Roussillon. Publications: Monsieur Mackintosh; Sara; The Curious Case of Santa Claus; Christmas Mouse. Recreations: writing; DIY. Address: Keeper's House, Traquair, by Innerleithen, Peeblishire EH44 6PP; T.-01896 831188.

Criddle, Byron John, BA (Keele), MA (Leicester). Emeritus Reader in Politics, University of Aberdeen, since 2007; Honorary Research Fellow, University of Swansea, since 2007; b. 23.03.42, Stroud, Gloucestershire; m., Professor Janet Askham; 1 s.; 1 d. Educ. The Judd School, Tonbridge, Kent; University of Keele; University of Leicester. Assistant History Master, Newarke Girls' School, Leicester, 1964-66; Assistant Lecturer in Politics, University of Aberdeen, 1968-69, Lecturer in Politics, 1969-84; Visiting Professor of Political Science, University of Massachusetts, 1984-85; Senior Lecturer in Politics, University of Aberdeen, 1985-95, Reader in Politics, 1995-2007. Publications: Socialists and European Integration: A Study of the French Socialist Party (1969); The French Socialist Party: Resurgence and Victory (Co-Author), 1984; The French Socialist Party: Resurgence of a Party of Government, 1988; The French Communist Party in the Fifth Republic, 1994; The Almanac of British Politics (Co-Author), 1996, 1999, 2002, 2007 editions; Parliamentary Profiles (Co-Author), various editions from 1997. Recreations: book accumulation: occasional broadcasting; hymnology. Address: (h.) 1 Cardigan Mansions, 19 Richmond Hill, Richmond, Surrey TW10 6RD and 121 Blenheim Place, Aberdeen AB25 2DL; T.-020 8940 4863; e-mail: b.criddle@abdn.ac.uk

Croan, Sheriff Thomas Malcolm, MA, LLB. Sheriff of North Strathclyde at Kilmarnock, 1983-2004; b. 7.8.32, Edinburgh; m., Joan Kilpatrick Law; 1 s.; 3 d. Educ. St. Joseph's College, Dumfries; Edinburgh University. Admitted to Faculty of Advocates, 1956; Standing Junior Counsel, Scottish Development Department, 1964-65 and (for highways work), 1967-69; Advocate Depute, 1965-66; Sheriff of Grampian, Highland and Islands at Banff and Peterhead, 1969-83. Recreation: sailing. Address: (h.) Overdale, 113 Bentinck Drive, Troon, Ayrshire.

Croft, Trevor Anthony, BSc, DipTRP, MRTPI, ARSGS, FRSA, FFCS. Reporter, Scottish Government Directorate for Planning and Environmental Appeals, since 2002; Consultant, The National Trust for Scotland, 2001-03; Director, The National Trust for Scotland, 1997-2001; b. 9.6.48, Bradford; m., Janet Frances Halley; 2 d. Educ. Belle Vue Boys Grammar School, Bradford; Hull University; Sheffield University. Senior Assistant Planning Officer, N. Ireland Government, 1971-72; Assistant Planning Officer, Countryside Commission for Scotland, 1972-75; Physical Planning Officer, Office of the President, Malawi Government, 1976-78; Parks Planning Officer, Department of National Parks and Wildlife, Malawi Government, 1978-82; Planning Officer, then Head of Policy Research, then Regional Director, then Deputy Director/Director of Countryside, National Trust for Scotland, 1982-96. Member, Forestry Commission, South Conservancy Regional Advisory Committee, 1987-90; Member, Council, Royal Scottish Geographical Society, 1998-2001 and 2002-05, and of Finance Committee, since 2003 (Chairman, Dunfermline Branch, 1993-96); Member, Council, Europa Nostra, 1999-2001; Treasurer, European Network of National Heritage Organisations, 2000-01; Chairman, British Equestrian Vaulting Ltd., 2002-03; Board Member, British Equestrian Federation, 2002-03; Convenor, Kinross Civic Trust Awards Committee, since 2005. Recreations: sailing; travel; motor-cycling; hill-walking. Address: (h.) Glenside, Tillyrie, Milnathort, Kinross KY13 0RW; T.-01577 864105.

Crofton, Sir John Wenman, KB, MA, MD, Dr h.c. Bordeaux, DSc hc, FRCP, FRCPE, Hon FRSE; b. 27.3.12, Dublin; m., Eileen Chris Mercer, MBE; 2 s.; 3 d. Educ. Tonbridge; Sidney Sussex College, Cambridge. Professor of Respiratory Diseases, Edinburgh University, 1952-77; Dean, Faculty of Medicine, 1963-66; Vice-Principal, 1969-70; President, Royal College of Physicians of Edinburgh, 1973-76; Vice-Chairman, Scottish Committee, Chest, Heart and Stroke Association, 1976-90; Chairman: Scottish Health Education Co-ordinating Committee, SHHD, 1981-

86, Tobacco and Health Committee, International Union Against Tuberculosis and Lung Disease, 1984-88; Edinburgh Medal for Science and Society, 1995; Galen Medal for Therapeutics, Society of Apothecaries, 2001; DSc hc, Imperial College, London University; World Health Organisation Medal for Tobacco Work, 1988; International Union against Tuberculosis and Lung Disease: Union Medal 2005 for Tuberculosis and Tobacco Work. Recreations: history; music; reading science; mountains. Address: (h.) 13 Spylaw Bank Road, Edinburgh EH13 0JW; T.-0131-441 3730; eapretty@breathemail.net

Crofts, Roger Stanley, CBE, BA, MLitt, CertEd, FRSE, FRSGS, Hon DSc (St Andrews). Adviser, lecturer and writer; Chief Executive, Scottish Natural Heritage, 1991-2002; Honorary Professor in Geography and Environment, University of Aberdeen; Visiting Professor in Geoscience, University of Edinburgh; b. 17.1.44, Leicester; m. Lindsay Manson; 1 s.; 1 d. Educ. Hinckley Grammar School; Liverpool University; Leicester University. Research Assistant in Geography: Aberdeen University, 1966-72, University College, London, 1972-74; entered Scottish Office, 1974; Senior Research Officer, 1974-78; Principal Research Officer, 1978-84; Assistant Secretary, Highlands and Tourism Division, Industry Department, 1984-88; Assistant Secretary, Rural Affairs Division, Scottish Development Department, 1988-91. Chairman, IUCN UK Committee, 1999-2002; Chair, World Commission on Protected Areas (Europe), since 2001; Chairman, Plantlife International; Board Member: Scottish Agricultural College, National Trust for Scotland, Fieldfare Ecological Development; Convenor, Conservation Committee, National Trust for Scotland; Patron, Scottish Association of Geography Teachers. Recreations: gardening; choral singing; hill-walking; wildflower photography. Address: (h.) 6 Old Church Lane, Duddingston Village, Edinburgh EH15 3PX; T.-0131-661 7858.

Cromartie, Earl of (John Ruaridh Grant Mackenzie), MIExpE. Land manager, since 1989; Executive Member, Mountaineering Council of Scotland, since 1990, and President, 2003-07; Explosives Consultant, since 1979; b. 12.6.48, Inverness; m., Janet Clare Harley; 2 s. Educ. Rannoch School; Strathclyde University. Research Geologist, New Quebec, 1970s; Chief of the Clan Mackenzie and as such do (unpaid) visits to USA, Canada, Australia, as unofficial ambassador for Scotland; many articles on mountaineering; co-author of guide books on mountaineering. Recreations: mountaineering; geology; art. Address: (h.) Castle Leod, Strathpeffer IV14 9AA; T.-01997 421264.

Crompton, Professor David William Thomasson, OBE, MA, PhD, ScD, BSc (Open), FRSE. Managing Director, St Andrew's Clinics for Children, since 1992; b. 5.12.37, Bolton; m., Effie Mary Marshall; 1 s.; 2 d. Educ. Bolton School; Sidney Sussex College, University of Cambridge; Fellow, Sidney Sussex College, Cambridge, 1964-85; Lecturer, Parasitology, Cambridge University, 1968-85; Adjunct Professor, Nutritional Sciences, Cornell University, 1981-2004; John Graham Kerr Professor of Zoology, Glasgow University, 1985-2000; Visiting Professor, University of Nebraska, 1982; Chairman, Company of Biologists Ltd., 1994-2000; Scientific Medal, Zoological Society of London, 1977; Member, WHO Expert Committee on Parasitology; Hon. Member: Slovak Society of Parasitologists, 1999, American Society of Parasitologists, 2001, Helminthological Society of Washington, 2002. Honorary Fellow, University of Glasgow, 2005. Publications: author/editor,10 books; Co-editor, Parasitology, 1972- 82; author/co-editor, 250

scientific papers, Recreations: books; gardening; terriers especially bull terriers. Address: (h.) Melrose Cottage, Tyndrum, Perthshire, FK20 8SA; T.-01838 400203; e-mail: dwtc@tyndrum.demon.co.uk

Crook, Professor Jonathan Nicholas, BA, MSc(Econ). Professor of Business Economics, Management School and Economics, Edinburgh University; Director, Credit Research Centre, Edinburgh University, since 1997; b. 2.5.53, Clevedon; m., Kate Vincent; 2 d. Educ. Cheltenham Grammar School; Lancaster University; University College, Cardiff. Research Assistant, Sheffield University, 1977-79; Lecturer, then Senior Lecturer, then Reader, Department of Business Studies, Edinburgh University, 1979-2002 (Director of Research, Department of Business Studies, 1999-2001); Head of Management Science and Business Economics Group, since 2005. Joint winner, Goodeve Medal (OR Society). Fellow, Wharton Financial Institutions Center, University of Pennsylvania, USA; External Fellow, Centre for Finance and Credit, University of Nottingham. Publications: Managerial Economics (Co-author); Economics of Modern Business (Co-author); Credit Scoring and its Applications (Co-author); Credit Scoring and Credit Control (Co-editor); Readings in Credit Scoring (Co-editor). Recreations: singing; walking; enjoying family. Address: (b.) Credit Research Centre, Management School and Economics, Edinburgh University, 50 George Square, Edinburgh EH8 9JY; T.-0131 650 3802; e-mail: j.crook@ed.ac.uk

Crooks, James Crawford, BA. Principal, Elmwood College, since 2007; b. 24.7.59. Baillieston, Lanarkshire; m., Elzbeth; 1 s. Educ. Uddingtston Grammar School; The Robert Gordon's University, Aberdeen. The Accounts Commission for Scotland, 1981-84; Highland Regional Council, 1984-88; Dumfries and Galloway College, 1988-2004; Upper Bann Institute of Further and Higher Education, 2004-07. Address: (b.) Elmwood College, Carslogie Road, Cupar, Fife KY15 4JB; T.-01334 658801; e-mail: jcrooks@elmwood.ac.uk

Crory, Peter George, BA, DMS, JP. National General Secretary, YMCA Scotland, since 2000; b. 6.4.64, Newry; m., Pauline; 1 s. 1 d. Educ. Methodist College, Belfast; Queen's University, Belfast. General Secretary, YMCA Lisburn, 1988-2000; Director, Modus Management Services, 1998-2000; Member, Childrens Panel Advisory Committee, Scottish Borders, 2004/05; Director: Y Care International, 2005-07, George Williams College, London, 2004-07; Chairman, Voluntary Organisations Chief Officers Group, Youthlink Scotland, 2007. Address: (b.) 11 Rutland Street, Edinburgh EH11 2AE; T.-0131-228 1464.

Crosfield, Rev. Canon George Philip Chorley, OBE, MA (Cantab). Provost, St. Mary's Cathedral, Edinburgh, 1970-90; Hon. Canon, St. Mary's Cathedral, since 1991; b. 9.9.24, London; m., Susan Mary Jullion; 1 s.; 2 d. Educ. George Watson's College, Edinburgh; Selwyn College, Cambridge. Royal Artillery, 1942-46 (Captain); Priest, 1952; Assistant Curate: St. David's, Pilton, Edinburgh, 1951-53, St. Andrew's, St. Andrews, 1953-55; Rector, St. Cuthbert's, Hawick, 1955-60; Chaplain, Gordonstoun School, 1960-68; Canon and Vice-Provost, St. Mary's Cathedral, Edinburgh, 1968-70. Recreations: gardening; walking. Address: (h.) 21 Biggar Road, Silverburn, near Penicuik EH26 9LQ; Tel.-01968 676607.

Cross, Professor Rod, BSc(Econ), BPhil. Professor of Economics, University of Strathclyde, since 1991; Visiting Professor, University of Aix-Marseille, since 2003; b. 27.3.51, Wigan. Educ. Wigan Grammar School; London School of Economics; University of York. Research Assistant, University of Manchester, 1972-74; Temporary

Lecturer, Queen Mary College, University of London, 1974-75; Lecturer, University of St. Andrews, 1975-91. Adviser to Governor, Polish National Bank, 1990-92; Occasional Member, H.M. Treasury Academic Panel. Publications: Economic Theory and Policy in the UK, 1982; Unemployment Hysteresis and the Natural Rate Hypothesis (Editor), 1988; The Natural Rate of Unemployment, 1995. Recreations: hillwalking; rugby league and union, fiction. Address: (b.) Department of Economics, University of Strathclyde, Sir William Duncan Building, 130 Rottenrow, Glasgow G4 0GE; T.-0141-548 3855/4555.

Cross, Roy, MA, PGCE (Cantab), RSA, DipTEFL, MA (Lancaster). Director, British Council Scotland, since 2005; m., Slobodonna Slade-Cross; 2 s. Previous postings with British Council in Zagreb, London, Bucharest, Berlin, Baghdad and Munich. Address: (b.) The Tun, 4 Jackson's Entry, Holyrood Road, Edinburgh EH8 8PJ; T.-0131 524 5711.
E-mail: roy.cross@britishcouncil.org

Crowe, Sheriff Frank Richard, LLB, SSC. Director of the Judicial Studies Committee; Solicitor Advocate; b. 15.3.52, Kirkcaldy; m., Alison Margaret Purdom (separated); partner, Margaret Elizabeth Scott, QC; 2 d.; 1 s. Educ. Kirkcaldy High School; Royal High School, Edinburgh; University of Dundee. Law Apprentice, North of Scotland Hydro-Electric Board, 1973-75; Procurator Fiscal Depute: Dundee, 1975-78, Glasgow 1978-81; Senior Legal Assistant, Crown Office, 1981-83; Senior Depute Procurator Fiscal, Edinburgh 1983-87; Senior Depute i/c Crown Office Fraud Unit, 1987-88; Assistant Solicitor i/c High Court Unit, Crown Office, 1988-91; Procurator Fiscal, Kirkcaldy, 1991-96; Regional Procurator Fiscal, South Strathclyde, Dumfries and Galloway, 1996-99; Procurator Fiscal, Hamilton, 1996-99; Deputy Crown Agent, Crown Office, 1999-2001; Sheriff of Tayside Central and Fife at Dundee, 2001-04. Member: Management Committee, Lothian Victim Support Scheme, 1983-89, Training Advisory Committee, Victim Support Scotland, 1994-98, Council, Law Society of Scotland, 1996-99, Scottish Executive Stephen Lawrence Steering Group, 1999-2001; Chairman, Advisory Committee, Zone Project Dundee, 2003-04; Consultant to Justice Oversight Commission for Northern Ireland, 2003-06; Member and latterly Chairman of Stockbridge Primary School Board, Edinburgh, 2003-07. Recreations: golf; cycling; racing; music. Address: (b.) Judicial Studies Committee, Bearford House, 39 Hanover Street, Edinburgh EH2 2PJ.

Crowe, Victoria Elizabeth, OBE, MA (RCA), RSA, RSW. Artist, Painter and Printmaker; b. 8.5.45, Kingston-on-Thames; m., Michael Walton; 1 s. (deceased); 1 d. Educ. Ursuline Convent Grammar School, London; Kingston College of Art; Royal College of Art. Part-time Lecturer, Drawing and Painting, Edinburgh College of Art, 1968-98; solo exhibitions: Scottish Gallery, Edinburgh, 1970, 1973, 1977, 1982, 1995, 1998, 2001, 2004; Thackeray Gallery, London, 1983, 1985, 1987, 1989, 1991, 1994, 1999, 2001, 2003, 2005, 2007; Bruton Gallery, Bath and Leeds, 1989, 1993, 1998; Plant memory: Royal Scottish Academy, 2007; A Shepherd's Life, retrospective, Scottish National Portrait Gallery, 2000, touring throughout Scotland and to Mercer Art Gallery, Harrogate, and Hatton Art Gallery, Newcastle upon Tyne, 2001-02; exhibited throughout Europe and USA with Artists for Nature Foundation; work in public and private collections, 2003-07; Senior Visiting Scholar, St. Catherine's College, Cambridge University. Recreation: travel. Address: (h.) Bank House, Main Street, West Linton, Peeblesshire EH46 7EE.

Crowther, Professor Margaret Anne, BA, DPhil, FRHS, FRSE. Senior Research Fellow in Social History, University of Glasgow, since 1994; Chairman, Scottish Records Advisory Council, 1995-2001; b. 1.11.43, Adelaide, South Australia; m., John McCauley Crowther; 1 s. Educ. Walford Grammar School; Adelaide University; Oxford University. Publications: The Workhouse System, 1981; On Soul and Conscience, 1988; Medical Lives in the Age of the Surgical Revolution, 2007. Recreation: gardening. Address: (b.) Centre for the History of Medicine, University of Glasgow, Glasgow G12 8RT; T.-0141-330 6071.

Cruickshank, Alastair Harvey, LLB, WS, NP, DL. Retired Solicitor and Consultant; b. 10.8.43, Perth; m., Moira E. Pollock (deceased); 2 s. Educ. Perth Academy; Edinburgh University. Apprentice, then Assistant, Shepherd & Wedderburn, WS, Edinburgh, 1964-67; Assistant, then Partner, then Consultant, Condie Mackenzie & Co. (now Condies), since 1967. Diocese of Brechin: Registrar, 1974-99, Chancellor, 2000-03; Member, Perth Society of High Constables; Captain, Royal Perth Golfing Society, 2001-2003; Deputy Lieutenant, Perth and Kinross, since 1995. Recreations: hill-walking; sailing; chamber music, opera and classical music generally. Address: (b.) 8 Kincarrathie Crescent, Perth PH2 7HH; T.-01738 628484.

Cruickshank, Alastair Booth, MA, FRSGS, FRCGS, DL; b. 3.8.31, Dumfries; m., Sheena Carlin Brown (qv); 2 s.; 1 d. Educ. High School of Stirling; Glasgow University; Georgia University. RAF, 1956-58; Glasgow University, 1958-61; Nottingham University, 1961-65; Glasgow University, 1965-86. Director, Royal Scottish Geographical Society, 1986-96; ordained Auxiliary Minister, Church of Scotland, 1991. Recreations: fly fishing; peoples and places.

Cruickshank, Sheena Carlin, JP. Lord Lieutenant, County of Clackmannan, since 2001; b. 26.3.36, Stirling; m., Alistair Booth Cruickshank; (qv); 2 s.; 1 d. Educ. High School of Stirling. Honorary Sheriff. Recreation: quilting. Address: c/o Clerk to The Lieutenancy, Howie & Caesar, 27 Mar Street, Alloa; T.-01259 723408.

Cubie, Andrew, CBE, FRSE, LLD (Glasgow, Glasgow Caledonian), DUniv (Edinburgh), DBA (QMUC), FRCPS (Glas) (Hon), LLB, NP, WS, FRSA. Consultant to Fyfe Ireland LLP; Partner from 1994; Chairman, Bird Semple Fyfe Ireland WS, 1991-94; b. 24.8.46, Northallerton; m., Professor Heather Ann Cubie; 1 s.; 2 d. Educ. Dollar Academy; Edinburgh University. Partner, Fyfe Ireland & Co., WS, 1971; non-executive Director: Crown Place VCT, Blas Ltd., ESPC Ltd., Kinloch Anderson Ltd., and a number of other private companies; Vice Chairman, Northern Lighthouse Board; Board Member, HMIE; Chairman: Committee of University Chairmen for the UK (CUC), VSO, UK, Quality Scotland Foundation, Napier University Court, Scottish Credit and Qualification Framework, British Council, Scotland, RNLI Scotland, Centre for Healthy Working Lives, Scotland's Garden Trust, WS Society Education Committee; Vice President and Deputy Chairman, Fundraising and Communications Committee, RNLI; Trustee of RNLI, VSO, Scottish Chamber Orchestra and Common Purpose; sometime Chairman, Independent Committee of Inquiry into Student Finance; Member: Ministerial Action Group on Standards in Scottish Schools, Independent Commission on Local Government and the Scottish Parliament, Consultative Steering Group on the Scottish Parliament; former Chairman: CBI Scotland, Governing Council George Watson's College. Recreations: sailing; gardening. Address: (b.) The Garden Flat, 14 Moray Place, Edinburgh EH3 6DT; e-mail: andrew@cubie-edinburgh.com

Cubie, Professor Heather Ann, BSc, MSc, PhD, FRCPath. Consultant Clinical Scientist in Virology; Research and Development Director, NHS Lothian

Health Board; b. 8.12.46, Dunfermline; m., Andrew Cubie; 1 s.; 2 d. Educ. Dunfermline High School; Edinburgh University. Honorary Professor of Research and Research Management, College of Medicine and Veterinary Medicine, University of Edinburgh, 2006; National Assessor for Clinical Microbiologists, since 1994; Head of Service, Scottish Training Scheme for Clinical Scientists in Microbiology, since 1997, Chairman, Association of Clinical Microbiologists, 1999-2002; Member, Scientific Committee, Scottish Cot Death Trust, since 1998; Member, Pregnancy and Newborn Screening Group, Clinical Standards Board for Scotland, 2002; MRC College of Experts, Health Services and Public Health Research Board, 2006. Publications: in field of Human Papilloma Virus (HPV) and molecular diagnostics in clinical virology. Recreations: gardening; travel; walking. Address: (b.) ACCORD Office, Queens Medical Research Institute, 47 Little France Crescent, Edinburgh EH16 4TJ; T.-0131 242 3331; e-mail: Heather.Cubie@luht.scot.nhs.uk

Cullen, Paul B., LLB (Hons), QC. Queen's Counsel, since 1995; b. 11.3.57, Gosforth; m., Joyce Nicol; 2 s.; 1 d. Educ. St Augustine's High School, Edinburgh; Edinburgh University. Clerk, Faculty of Advocates, 1986-91; Standing Junior Counsel, Department of the Environment in Scotland, 1988-91; Advocate Depute, 1992-95; Solicitor General for Scotland, 1995-97; Consultative Steering Group on the Scottish Parliament, 1998-99; Chairman, Public Inquiry into Gilmerton Limestone Emergency, 2001-2002; Chairman, Appeal Committee of the Institute of Chartered Accountants of Scotland; Chairman, Police Appeals Tribunal; Chairman, Scottish Conservative Party Disciplinary Panel; Vice President, Edinburgh South Conservatives. Recreations: tennis; bridge. Address: (b.) Advocates' Library, Parliament House, Edinburgh EH1 1RF; T.-0131-226 5071.

Cullen of Whitekirk, Rt. Hon. Lord (William Douglas Cullen), PC, LLD, DUniv, FRSE, HonFREng. Lord President and Lord Justice General, 2001-05; b. 18.11.35, Edinburgh; m., Rosamond Mary Downer; 2 s.; 2 d. Educ. Dundee High School; St. Andrews University (MA); Edinburgh University (LLB). Called to the Scottish Bar, 1960; QC, 1973; Advocate-Depute, 1977-81; Lord Justice Clerk, 1997-2001; PC, 1997; Life Peer, 2003; Justice of Civil and Commercial Court of Qatar Financial Centre, since 2007; Chairman: Inquiry into the Piper Alpha Disaster, 1988-90, Inquiry into the Shootings at Dunblane Primary School, 1996, Ladbroke Grove Rail Inquiry, 1999-2001. Member, Royal Commission on the Ancient and Historical Monuments of Scotland, 1987-97; Member, Napier University Court, 1996-2005; Chairman: Cockburn Association, 1984-86, Board of Governors, St. Margaret's School, Edinburgh, 1994-2001; Honorary President, SACRO, since 2000; President, Saltire Society, since 2005. Recreations: gardening; natural history. Address: (b.) House of Lords, London SW1A 0PW.

Culley, Ron, MSc, CQSW, CSW, DipYCS. Chief Executive, Strathclyde Partnership for Transport, since 2006; Director General, Strathclyde Passenger Transport Executive, since 2006; Chief Executive, Scottish Enterprise Glasgow, 2000-06; b. 2.2.50, Glasgow; m., 1, Margaret Ferguson; 2 s.; m., 2, Jean Pollock; 2 s. Educ. Craigbank Comprehensive School; Jordanhill College of Education; Moray House College of Education; Strathclyde University. Social work and social policy development posts, Strathclyde Regional Council, 1975-87; Govan Initiative Ltd: Assistant Chief Executive, 1987-88, Chief Executive, 1988-2001. Founding Board

Member, Scottish Urban Regeneration Forum; Secretary, Ibrox Community Trust, 1987-2000; Board Member, Strathclyde European Partnership, 1987-2000; Chairman, Glasgow Local Economic Development Network, 1996-2000; Panel Member, Investors In People Scotland, 1998-2000; Board Member, Quality Scotland, 1999-2001; Leader, Task Force on Upper Clyde Shipbuilding, 2001-02; Governor, Scottish Police Training College, 2001-05; Board Member: Police Advisory Board for Scotland, Glasgow Alliance, 2000-06, Princes Trust, Glasgow, 2003-04, Glasgow Local Economic Forum, Glasgow Community Planning Partnership, Clyde Valley Community Planning Partnership; Board Member, Wise Group; Secretary, Govan Honours Society; Candidate (Labour), Scotland SW Region, Scottish Parliamentary election, 1999. Publications: Merkat Forces (Co-Author), 1994; The New Guards, 1999. Recreations: family and friends; playing guitar; watching association football; irreverance; fair weather gardening; convivial temulence; reading biographies; American politics; Irish politics. Address: (b) Consort House, 12, West George Street, Glasgow G2 1HN; T.-0141 333 3100; e-mail: ron.culley@spt.co.uk

Cumming, Lt. Col. Alaistair Michael, OBE; b. 22.12.41, Singapore; m., Hilary Katharine Gray; 2 d. Educ. Bradfield College, Berkshire. Cadet, RMA Sandhurst, 1960-61; commissioned into The Gordon Highlanders, 1961; Naval and Military Attache, Poland, 1989-92; retired, 1995; Regimental Secretary to The Highlanders (Seaforth, Gordons and Camerons), 1995-2006. President, SSAFA Inverness and Western Isles; Hon. Col., The Highlanders ACF, 2005. Recreations: golf; shooting; skiing. Address: (h.) Cantraybruich House, Culloden Moor, Inverness IV2 5EG.

Cumming, Alexander James, MA (Hons), CIMA, IPFA. Chief Executive Officer, IMMPACT (The International Maternal Mortality Project), since 2004; b. 7.3.47, Aberdeen; m., Margaret Callan; 1 s.; 2 d. Educ. Fordyce Academy; Robert Gordon's College; Aberdeen University. VSO, 1968-70; Accountant, Company Secretary, Chief Accountant, 1970-75; joined Grampian Health Board, 1975; Chief Executive, Grampian University Hospitals NHS Trust, 1994-2004. Address: (b.) University of Aberdeen, Regent Walk, Aberdeen AB24 3FX.

Cumming, Professor Allan David, BSc, MBChB, MD, FRCPE. Professor of Medical Education and Director of Learning and Teaching, College of Medicine and Veterinary Medicine, University of Edinburgh, since 1998; Consultant Physician, Renal Medicine, Lothian University Hospitals Division, since 1989; b. 12.2.51, Buenos Aires, Argentina; m., Lindsay Cumming (nee Galloway); 1 s.; 1 d. Educ. Nairn Academy; University of Edinburgh. Training posts in medicine/nephrology, 1975-89; Clinical research fellowship, University of Western Ontario, 1984-85; Senior Lecturer/Honorary Consultant in Renal Medicine, 1989-98; now responsible for teaching and learning in medicine, University of Edinburgh; ongoing clinical responsibilties in renal medicine; active in research and development in medical education. Chancellor's Award for teaching, University of Edinburgh, 2004; Member of Executive and Council, Association for Study of Medical Education. Recreations: golf; curling; music. Address: (b.) Medical School, Royal Infirmary of Edinburgh, 47 Little France Crescent, Edinburgh EH16 4TJ; T.-0131 242 9311; e-mail: allanc@staffmail.ed.ac.uk

Cumming, Andrew John, BSc (Hons), ACIB, FCIBS. Senior Sanctioning Director, Wholesale and International Banking, Lloyds TSB Scotland plc, since 2003; b. 17.6.54, London; 2 s.; 1 d. Educ. Cray Valley THS; Polytechnic of Central London. Various roles culminating in position of

Senior Credit Officer, Head Office, National Westminster Bank, Lothbury, 1975-86; Senior Advances Manager, Corporate, TSB Group, 1986-88; Assistant Director, Corporate, Hill Samuel, 1988-90; Director, Group Banking Services Division, TSB Group, 1991-96; Lloyds TSB: Risk Management Director, Corporate and Commercial, 1997-2000, Group Credit Director, 2001-03. Board Member, Lloyds TSB Scotland plc; Member of Steering Group for 2012 Olympics. Recreations: Member, Melrose RFC; marathon running; gym work; skiing. Address: (b.) Lloyds TSB Scotland, Henry Duncan House, 120 George Street, Edinburgh EH2 4TS.
E-mail: andy.cumming@lloydstsb.co.uk

Cumming, Grant Philip, BSc (Hons), MD, MBChB, FRCOG. Consultant, Obstetrician and Gynaecologist, Dr. Grays Hospital, Elgin, since 2000; Honorary Senior Lecturer, Grampian University Hospitals NHS Trust, since 2000; b. 8.5.61, Derby; m., Fiona; 1 s.; 2 d. Educ. George Heriots School, Edinburgh; St. Andrews University; Victoria University, Manchester. Aberdeen Royal Infirmary and Maternity Hospital, 1996-2000. Medical Director, The Menopause and You (CD Rom); Non-executive Director: menopausematters.co.uk, babyfeedingmatters.co.uk. Recreations: golf; conjuring. Address: (b.) Dr Grays Hospital, Elgin, Moray; T.-01343 543131; e-mail: grant.cumming@arh. grampian.scot.nhs.uk

Cumming, Robert Currie, BL, FCIBS, ACIB, FRCSEdin (Hon.), FRSGS; b. 21.5.21, Strathaven; m., Mary Jean McDonald Crombie. Educ. Hutchesons' Grammar School, Glasgow; Glasgow University. Former Executive Director, Royal Bank of Scotland Group PLC and Royal Bank of Scotland PLC; Chairman, English Speaking Union — Scotland, 1984-90; Trustee, Royal Scottish Geographical Society. Recreations: fishing; golf; walking. Address: (h.) 11, The Hermitage, 1, Kinellan Road, Edinburgh EH12 6ES; T.-0131-337 1910.

Cumming, Sandy, CBE, BSc (Hons). Chief Executive, Highlands and Islands Enterprise, since 2000; b. 30.10.52, Dingwall; m., Rosemary; 2 d. Educ. Dingwall Academy; University of Edinburgh. Highlands and Islands Development Board, 1973-75 and 1976-91; White Fish Authority, 1975-76; Highlands and Islands Enterprise since 1991 (Chief Executive, Ross and Cromarty Enterprise, 1993-98). Address: (b.) Cowan House, Inverness Retail and Business Park, Inverness IV2 7GF; T.-01463 244204; e-mail: sandy.cumming@hient.co.uk

Cummings, Peter Joseph, MBA, FCIBS. Chief Executive (Corporate), Bank of Scotland, since 2006; b. 19.7.55, Dumbarton; m., Margaret. Educ. St. Patrick's High School, Dumbarton; Glasgow College of Technology; University of Strathclyde. Bank of Scotland, since 1973. Recreations: scuba diving; swimming; football; music. Address: (b.) Bank of Scotland, The Mound, Edinburgh EH1 1YZ; T.-0131 243 7033.
E-mail: peter_cummings@bankofscotland.co.uk

Cunningham, David Kenneth, CBE, BEd, MEd (Hons), FRSA. Head Teacher, Hillhead High School, Glasgow, since 1993; b. 19.4.48, Saltcoats; m., Marion S. Shedden; 2 d. Educ. Ardrossan Academy; Glasgow University; Jordanhill College of Education. Principal Teacher of English, North Kelvinside Secondary, 1976-80; Assistant Head Teacher, Garthamlock Secondary, 1980-82; Adviser in English, Dunbarton Division, 1982-90, Education Officer (Acting), 1989-90; Inspector, Quality Assurance Unit, Strathclyde Regional Council, 1990-93; Examiner, Setter,

Principal Examiner, SEB, 1979-90; Member, Board, Glasgow Area, Young Enterprise Scotland; Vice-Chair, Glasgow Board, Young Enterprise Scotland; Director, National Board, Young Enterprise Scotland; Headteachers Association of Scotland: Executive Member, 1997-2005, Vice President, 2000-01, President, 2001-02; Member, UCAS Standing Committee, 1997-2007; Director, Notre Dame Centre for Children, Young People and Families, since 1999; Associate Assessor, HMI; Member, New National Qualifications Steering Group, 2001-04; Member, Ministerial Task Group New National Qualifications; Chair, English and Communications Higher Still Revision Group; Vice-Chair, Educational Broadcasting Council for Scotland, 2002-07, Chair, since 2007; Member, Minister's Group on Race Relations Amendment Act, 2002; Member, SQA Qualifications Committee, since 2003; Member, SFEU Core Skills Advisory Group. Publications: Reading for 'S' Grade English, 1988. Recreations: various sports; reading; photography; travel; family. Address: (h.) 7 Waterfoot Road, Newton Mearns, Glasgow; T.-0141-639 3367.

Cunningham, Professor Ian M.M., CBE, FRSE, FIBiol, FRAgS, Hon. Assoc. RCVS, Bsc, PhD, FRSGS, Dr hc (Edin); b. 30.9.25, Kirknewton; m., Agnes Whitelaw Frew. Educ. Lanark Grammar School; Edinburgh University. Assistant Economist, West of Scotland Agricultural College, 1946-47; Lecturer in Agriculture, Durham School of Agriculture, 1947-50; Lecturer, then Senior Lecturer, Edinburgh University, 1950-68; Director, Hill Farming Research Organisation, 1968-80; Professor of Agriculture, Glasgow University, and Principal, West of Scotland Agricultural College, 1980-87. Former Member: Farm Animal Welfare Council, Hill Farming Advisory Committee, Scotland, Agricultural Food Research Council, Court, University of Edinburgh; Chairman, Board, Macaulay Land Use Research Institute, 1987-95; Chairman, National Trust for Scotland, 1998-2000; former Chairman, Advisory Committee on Sites of Special Scientific Interest; former Governor, Royal Agricultural Society of England; George Hedley Memorial Award for services to the sheep industry; Massey Ferguson Award for services to British agriculture; Sir William Young Award for services to livestock production in Scotland. Address: (h.) 5 The Bridges, Peebles EH45 8BP.

Cunningham, Right Reverend John, JCD, RC. Bishop of Galloway, since 2004; b. 22.2.38, Paisley. Educ. St. Mary's Primary, Paisley; St. Mary's College, Blairs, Aberdeen; St. Peter's College, Cardross; Scots College and Gregorian University, Rome. Assistant Priest, Our Lady of Lourdes, Bishopton, 1964-69; Professor of Canon Law, St. Peter's College, Cardross and Newlands (Glasgow), 1967-81; Advocate of the Roman Catholic Scottish National Tribunal, 1970-82; Assistant Priest, St. Columba's, Renfrew, 1974-86; Judicial Vicar, Roman Catholic National Tribunal, 1986-92; Parish Priest, St. Patrick's Greenock, 1992-2004; Nominated Papal Chaplain in 1994; Vicar-General, Diocese of Paisley, 1997-2004; Nominated Prelate of Honour in 1999. Address: 8 Corsehill Road, Ayr KA7 2ST.

Cunningham, Maggie. Joint Head of Programmes and Services for BBC Scotland, since 2005; Head of Radio, Scotland, 2000-05; m.; 2 c. Producer, BBC Highland, 1979; freelance journalist, 1982-89; BBC Radio nan Gaidheal: Executive Producer, 1989; Editor, 1992; BBC Scotland: Secretary, 1995, returned to production to set up BBC Scotland's Talent Pool, 1997, Head of Features, Education and Religion, 1999; current board member, Scotland Venezuela music project.

Cunningham, Robert Ritchie, MA (Hons). Rector, Inverness High School, since 1991; b. 22.5.53, Stirling; m., Linda; 2s. Educ. Friends Grammar School, Lisburn, Northern Ireland; Lenzie Academy; Glasgow University. Teacher, Geography/Economics/Geology, Cumbernauld

High School, 1977-80; Principal Teacher, Geography, John Nelson High School, Paisley, 1989-84; Field Development Officer, Scottish Examinations Board, 1984-86; Adviser, Social Studies, Highland Council, 1986-91; Director, Inverness and Nairn Enterprise, 1998-2004; Director, Inverness Project, since 2002; Governor, UHI Millennium Institute, 2002 04; Governor, Inverness College, since 2003. Publications: co-author of over 20 publications including 4 textbooks. Recreations: golf; salsa; Rotary. Address; (b.) Inverness High School, Montague Row, Inverness, IV3 5DZ; T.-01463 233586; e-mail: ritchie.cunningham@highland.gov.uk

Cunningham, Roseanna. MSP (SNP), Perth, since 1999 (SNP Deputy Leader, 2000-04; Shadow Minister for Rural Affairs, Envronment, Culture and Sport, 2003-04; Shadow Minister for Justice, 1999-2003; Convener, Rural Affairs and Environment Committee, since 2007; Convener, Health Committee, 2004-07; Convener, Justice and Home Affairs Committee, 1999-2000; MP (SNP), Perth, 1995-2001; b. 27.7.51, Glasgow. Educ. University of Western Australia. SNP Research Department, 1977-79; law degree, Edinburgh University; Trainee Solicitor, Dumbarton District Council, 1983-84; Solicitor, Dumbarton, 1984-86; Solicitor, Glasgow, 1986-89; called to the Scottish Bar, 1990. Recreations: folk festivals; reading; cinema; cats; novice hill-walker. Address: (b.) Scottish Parliament, Edinburgh EH99 1SP.

Cunningham-Jardine, Ronald Charles. Lord Lieutenant, Dumfries, 1991-2006 (retired); Farmer; b. 19.9.31, Edinburgh; m., Constance Mary Teresa Inglis; 1 s.; 1 d. Educ. Ludgrove; Eton; Royal Military Academy, Sandhurst. Royal Scots Greys (retired as Captain), 1950-58. Recreations: all country sports. Address: (h.) Fourmerkland, Lockerbie, Dumfriesshire DG11 1EH; T.-01387 810226.

Curran, Frances. MSP (SSP), West of Scotland, 2003-07; b. 21.5.61, Glasgow. Educ. St Andrews Secondary School, Glasgow.

Curran, Margaret. MSP (Labour), Glasgow Baillieston, since 1999; Minister for Parliament, Scottish Executive, 2004-07, Minister for Communities, 2002-04. Educ. Glasgow University. Former Lecturer in Community Education; Deputy Minister for Social Justice, Scottish Executive, 2001. Address: (b.) Scottish Parliament, Edinburgh EH99 1SP; T.-0131-348 5842.

Currie, Rev. Ian Samuel, MBE, BD. Minister of the United Church of Bute, since 2005; Minister, Oakshaw Trinity Church, Paisley, 1991-2005; b. 14.8.43, Glasgow; m., Jennifer; 1 s.; 1 d. Educ. Bellahouston Academy; Trinity College; University of Glasgow; Minister: Blairhill Dundyvan Church, Coatbridge, 1975-80, St John's Church, Paisley, 1980-91. Chair, Victim Support Scotland, 1993-98; Director, Wynd Centre, Paisley. Recreation: chess. Address: (b.) The Manse, 10 Bishop Terrace, Rothesay, Isle of Bute PA20 9HF; T.-01700 504502.

Currie, James McGill, MA. Non-Executive Director: Royal Bank of Scotland, since 2001, Total UK, since 2004; Associate Professor of Law, Georgetown Law Centre, Washington DC, since 1997; b. 17.11.41; m., Evelyn; 1 s.; 1 d. Educ. St Joseph's School, Kilmarnock; Blairs College, Aberdeen; Royal Scots College, Valladolid, Spain; University of Glasgow. Civil Servant; Assistant Principal: Scottish Home and Health Department, 1968-72, Scottish Education Department, 1972-75; Assistant Secretary: Transport Policy, 1977-80, Industrial Development, 1981-82; Counsellor for Social Affairs and Transport, UK Permanent Representation to EEC in Brussels, 1982-86; Director, European Regional Development Fund, European Commission (Brussels), 1987-89; Chef de Cabinet to Sir Leon Brittan, 1989 92; Deputy Ambassador, EC Delegation to US in Washington, 1993-96; DG Customs and Indirect Taxation, 1996-97; DG Environment, 1997-2001. Recreations: guitar; tennis; golf; good food.

Currie, Ken. Painter; b. 1960, North Shields. Educ. Paisley College; Glasgow School of Art. Worked on two films about Glasgow and Clyde shipbuilding, 1983-85; specialises in political realism, including a series of murals for the People's Palace Museum, Glasgow, on the socialist history of the city.

Curtice, Professor John Kevin, MA (Oxon). Professor of Politics, Strathclyde University, since 1998; Research Consultant, Scottish Centre for Social Research, since 2001; b. 10.12.53, Redruth; m., Lisa; 1 d. Educ. Truro School; Magdalen and Nuffield Colleges, Oxford. Research Fellow, Nuffield College, Oxford; Lecturer in Politics, Liverpool University; Fellow, Netherlands Institute for Advanced Study, 1988-89; Senior Lecturer in Politics, Strathclyde University, 1989-96; Reader in Politics, Strathclyde University, 1997-98. FRSA 1992; FRSE 2004. Publications include: How Britain Votes; Understanding Political Change; Labour's Last Chance; On Message; New Scotland, New Politics; The Rise of New Labour; New Scotland, New Society; British Social Attitudes; Devolution – Scottish Answers to Scottish Questions?; Has Devolution Delivered? Recreations: music; gardening. Address: (b.) Department of Government, Strathclyde University, 16 Richmond Street, Glasgow G1 1XQ; T.-0141-548 4223.

Curtis, Professor Adam Sebastian Genevieve, MA, PhD. Professor of Cell Biology, Glasgow University, 1967-2004; Director, Centre for Cell Engineering, 1996-2004; Emeritus Professor and Hon. Senior Research Fellow, since 2004; President, Tissue and Cell Engineering Society, 2002-03; b. 3.1.34, London; m., Ann Park; 2 d. Educ. Aldenham School; Kings College, Cambridge. University College, London: Honorary Research Assistant, 1957-62, Lecturer in Zoology, 1962-67. Director, Company of Biologists Ltd., 1961-99; Governor, Westbourne School, 1985-90; Council Member, Royal Society of Edinburgh, 1983-86; President, Society of Experimental Biology, 1991-93; Editor, IEEE Transactions in Nanobioscience, since 2002; FBSE 2005; Editor, Scottish Diver magazine, 1978-91, and 1994-97; President, Scottish Sub-Aqua Club, 1972-76. Recreations: sports diving; gardening. Address: (h.) 2 Kirklee Circus, Glasgow G12 OTW; T.-0141-339 2152.

Cuschieri, Professor Sir Alfred, MD, DM (Hon), MD (Hon), ChM, FRSE, FMed Sci, FIBiol, FRCSEng, FRCSEd, FRCSI (Hon), FRCPSGlas (Hon). Co-Director, Institute of Medical Science and Technology, Universities of Dundee and St Andrews; Professor of Surgery, Scuola Superiore S'Anna di Studi Universitari Pisa, since 2003; b. 30.9.38, Malta; m., Dr. M.P. Holley; 3 d. Educ. St. Aloysius College; Royal University of Malta; Liverpool University. Professor and Head of Department of Surgery and Molecular Oncology, Dundee University, 1976-2003; Lecturer/Senior Lecturer/Reader in Surgery, Liverpool University. Previous President, British Association of Surgical Oncology, Academic Departments of Surgery in Europe, International Hepato-biliary Pancreatic Association, European Association of Endoscopic Surgery.

Previous Director, Minimal Access Therapy Training Unit for Scotland (MATTUS) and Surgical Skills Unit, Ninewells Hospital & Medical School, University of Dundee. Recreations: fishing; painting; carving; music; gardening. Address: (h.) Denbrae Mill, Strathkinness Low Road, St Andrews, Fife KY16 9TY.

Cusine, Sheriff Douglas James, LLB. Sheriff, Grampian, Highland and Islands at Aberdeen, since 2001; All-Scotland Floating Sheriff based at Peterhead, 2000-01; b. 2.9.46, Glasgow; m., Marilyn Calvert Ramsay; 1 s.; 1 d. Educ. Hutchesons' Boys' Grammar School; Glasgow University. Solicitor, 1971, Lecturer in Private Law, Glasgow University, 1974-76; Aberdeen University: Lecturer in Private Law, 1977-82, Senior Lecturer, 1982-90, Professor, Department of Conveyancing and Professional Practice of Law, 1990-2000. Member: Council, Law Society of Scotland, 1988-99, Lord President's Advisory Council on Messengers-at-Arms and Sheriff Officers, 1989-97; Member, UK Delegation to CCBE, 1997-2000; Member, Council of the Sheriffs Association, since 2006. Publications: Marine Pollution: Law and Practice (Co-Editor), 1980; Cases and Materials in Commercial Law (Co-Editor), 1987; A Scots Conveyancing Miscellany (Editor), 1987; New Reproductive Techniques: A Legal Perspective, 1988; Law and Practice of Diligence (Co-Author), 1989; Reproductive Medicine and the Law (Co-Editor), 1990; Standard Securities, 1990, 2nd ed., (Co-Author), 2002; Missives (Co-Author), 1993, 2nd ed., 1999; Requirements of Writing (Co-Author), 1995; Servitudes and Rights of Way (Co-Author), 1998; various articles on medico-legal issues and conveyancing. Recreations: swimming; walking; bird-watching. Address: Sheriff Court House, Castle Street, Aberdeen AB10 1WP.

Cuthbertson, Brian H., MB, ChB, FRCA, MD. Clinical Senior Lecturer in Critical Care, since 2000; Honorary Consultant in Anaesthesia and Intensive Care, since 2000; b. 8.1.68, Edinburgh; m., Susan; 2 d. Educ. Galashiels Academy; University of Aberdeen. Address: Health Services Research Unit, University of Aberdeen, Foresterhill, Aberdeen; T.-01224 552730; e-mail: b.h.cuthbertson@abdn.ac.uk

Cuthbertson, Iain, MA (Hons), FRSAMD. Actor; b. 4.1.30. Educ. Glasgow Academy; Aberdeen Grammar School; Aberdeen University. General Manager/Director of Productions, Citizens' Theatre, Glasgow, 1962-65; Associate Director, Royal Court Theatre, London, 1965; Director, Perth Theatre, 1967-68; sometime Administrator, Playhouse Theatre, Nottingham; stage performances include title roles in Armstrong's Last Goodnight (Citizens'), The Wallace (Edinburgh Festival); Serjeant Musgrave's Dance (Royal Court), Sutherland's Law (TV series); 1,500 broadcasts; TV work includes Budgie, Charles Endell Esq.; premiere of A Drunk Man Looks at the Thistle, set to music and dance; Hon. LLD, Aberdeen University; former Board Member, Scottish Theatre Company; former Hon. President, SCDA; Visiting Stage Director and Tutor, Royal Scottish Academy of Music and Drama. Recreations: countryside; sailing. Address: (b.) Janet Welch, Personal Management, Old Orchard, The Street, Ubley, Bristol BS40 6PJ.

Cuthbertson, Ian Jardine, LLB, NP, FIPA, FABRP, FInstD. Solicitor, Notary Public and Licensed Insolvency Practitioner; Partner, Dundas & Wilson, Solicitors, Glasgow, Edinburgh and London, since 1979; b. 8.5.51, Glasgow; m., Sally Jane; 1 s.; 2 d. Educ. Jordanhill College School, Glasgow; Glasgow University. Apprenticeship, Messrs Boyds; admitted as Solicitor, 1974; Partner, Messrs Boyds, 1978; jointly founded firm of Dorman Jeffrey &

Co., 1979, merged with Dundas & Wilson, 1997. Recreations: watching football and rugby. Address: (b.) 191 West George Street, Glasgow; T.-0141-222 2200; Saltire Court, Castle Terrace, Edinburgh; T.-0131-228 8000; Northwest Wing, Bush House, Aldwych, London; T.-0207 240 2401.

Cuthbertson, Rev. Malcolm, BA, BD (Hons). Minister, Easterhouse: St. George's and St. Peter's Church of Scotland, since 1984; b. 3.4.56, Glasgow; m., Rena Fennel; 1 s.; 2 d. Educ. Grangemouth High School; Stirling University; Aberdeen University. Probationer Assistant, Crown Court Church, London, 1983-84. Recreations: eating out; reading theology. Address: 3 Barony Gardens, Glasgow G69 6TS; T.-0141-573 8200; e-mail: malcuth@aol.com

Cuthell, Rev. Thomas Cuthbertson, MA, BD. Minister Emeritus, St. Cuthbert's Parish Church, Edinburgh, since 2007 (retired); b. 18.2.41, Falkirk. Educ. Bo'ness Academy; University of Edinburgh. Assistant Minister, St. Giles Cathedral, Edinburgh; Minister, North Church, Uphall. Recreations: travel; music; sailing. Address: Flat 10, 2 Kingsburgh Crescent, Edinburgh EH5 1JF.

Cutler, Timothy Robert (Robin), CBE, BSc, DSc. b. 24.7.34, India; m., Ishbel W.M.; 1 s.; 1 d. Educ. Banff Academy; Aberdeen University. Colonial Forest Service, Kenya, 1958-64; New Zealand Government Forestry, 1964-90, latterly Chief Executive, New Zealand Ministry of Forestry; Director General, Forestry Commission, 1990-95. Recreations: tennis; golf; travel. Address: 14 Swanston Road, Edinburgh EH10 7BB; T.-0131-445 5437.

Czerkawska, Catherine Lucy, MA (Hons); MA (postgraduate). Novelist and Playwright; b. 3.12.50, Leeds; m., Alan Lees; 1 s. Educ. Queen Margaret's Academy, Ayr; St. Michael's Academy, Kilwinning; Edinburgh University; Leeds University. Wrote and published two books of poetry (White Boats and a Book of Men); taught EFL in Finland and Poland; thereafter, full-time freelance writer working on novels including The Curiosity Cabinet, 2005, radio, television and stage plays; Pye Award for Best Radio Play of 1980, O Flower of Scotland; Scottish Radio Industries Club Award, 1983, for Bonnie Blue Hen; Wormwood, and Quartz produced Traverse Theatre, Edinburgh, 1997 and 2000; God's Islanders. A History of The People of Gigha, Birlinn, 2006. Recreations: antique textiles; local history; gardening. website: www.wordarts.co.uk; e-mail: catherine@wordarts.co.uk

D

Dalby, Martin, BMus, ARCM. Composer; freelance music/recording producer; music lecturer; Chairman, Composers' Guild of Great Britain, 1995-98; Founding Director: British Music Rights, 1999-2001, British Academy of Composers and Songwriters, 1998-2000; Warden of Performers and Composers Section, ISM, 2001; Chairman, ISM (Incorporated Society of Musicians) SW Scotland Centre, since 2004; b. 25.4.42, Aberdeen; m., Hilary. Educ. Aberdeen Grammar School; Royal College of Music. Music Producer, BBC Radio 3, 1965-71; Cramb Research Fellow in Composition, Glasgow University, 1971-72; Head of Music, BBC Scotland, 1972-91; Executive Music Producer, BBC Scotland, 1991-93. Recreations: flying; railways; bird-watching; hill-walking. Address: (h.) 23 Muirpark Way, Drymen, Stirlingshire G63 0DX; T.-01360 660427; Fax: 01360 660397; e-mail: martindalby@btinternet.com; website: www.impulse-music.co.uk/dalby/

Dale, Brian Graeme, LLB, WS, NP. Partner, Brooke & Brown, WS, Dunbar, since 1974; b. 20.11.46, London; m., Judith Gail de Beaufort Franklin; 4 s.; 2 d. Educ. Bristol Grammar School; Aberdeen University. Diocese of Edinburgh, Scottish Episcopal Church: Treasurer, 1971-2000, Secretary, 1974-90, Registrar, 1974-2001, Chancellor, 2001-07; Registrar and Lay Clerk to the Episcopal Synod; Honorary Secretary, Abbeyfield Society (Dunbar) Ltd. Recreations: music; bridge; singing; family life. Address: (h.) 5 The Doon, Spott, Dunbar, East Lothian; T.-Dunbar 862059.

Dale, Professor John Egerton, BSc, PhD, FRSE, FIBiol. Emeritus Professor of Plant Physiology, Edinburgh University, since 1993; b. 13.2.32, London; m., Jacqueline Joyce Benstock (deceased) 1 s.; 2 d.; m. (2), Kay. Educ. City of London School; Kings College, London. Plant Physiologist, Empire Cotton Growing Corporation, Uganda, 1956-61; Edinburgh University: Lecturer in Botany, then Reader, 1961-85, Professor of Plant Physiology, 1985-93, Head, Division of Biological Sciences, 1990-93. Secretary, Society for Experimental Biology, 1974-79; Secretary General, Federation of European Societies of Plant Physiology, 1978-84; Trustee, Peter Potter Gallery, 1994-99; Institute of Biology: Chairman, Scottish Branch, 1999-2001, Member, Council, since 2000; Scottish Wildlife Trust: Acting Chairman, 2002, Vice Chairman, 1999-2002, Convener, Conservation Strategy Committee. Publications: 100 papers on growth of leaves and related topics. Recreations: the arts; travel; gardening. Address: (h.) The Old Bothy, Drem, North Berwick, EH39 5AP; T.-01620 850394.

Dalgarno, James, MA, SQH. Headteacher, Oldmachar Academy, since 2004; b. 1.5.50, Aberdeen; m., Jennifer; 2 d. Educ. Robert Gordon's College, Aberdeen; Aberdeen University. Kincorth Academy, 1973-78; Bankhead Academy, 1978-82; Oldmachar Academy, since 1982. Recreations: sport; reading; travel. Address: (b.) Oldmachar Academy, Jesmond Drive, Bridge of Don, Aberdeen AB22 8UR; T.-01224 820887; e-mail: jdalgarno@oldmachar.aberdeen.sch.uk

Dalhousie, Earl of (James Hubert Ramsay), DL, OStJ. Chairman: Jamestown Investments Ltd., Dunedin Smaller Companies Investment Trust plc, Brechin Castle Centre Ltd.; President: Caledonian Club, British Deer Society; Vice-Chairman, Game and Wildlife Conservation Trust; Director, Scottish Woodlands, 1993-2005; b. 17.1.48, London; m., Marilyn; 1 s.; 2 d. Educ. Ampleforth College. Commissioned, Coldstream Guards, 1968-71; Hambros Bank Ltd (Director, 1981); Co-Founder, Jamestown Investments, 1987. Lieutenant, Royal Company of Archers; Vice Lord Lieutenant, County of Angus; Chairman, Governors, Unicorn Preservation Society; President, Angus Branch, Order of St John; Board Member, Deer Commission Scotland, since 2005. Address: (b.) Dalhousie Estates Office, Brechin DD9 6SG; T.-01356 624566.

Dallas, Garry, BA (Hons), DipTP, MSc, MRTPI. Director, Development and Environmental Services, Clackmannanshire Council, since 2001; b. 15.8.59, Kirkcaldy; m., Ruth. Educ. Glenrothes High School; Strathclyde University; Heriot-Watt University. Planning Officer, Principal Planner, Planning Manager, Property Development Manager, Head of Planning and Property Development, Clackmannan District Council, 1983-95; Executive Director, Development Services, Clackmannanshire Council, 1995-2001. Founding Director, Alloa Tower Building Preservation Trust. Recreations: motor sports; swimming; golf Address: (b.) Clackmannanshire Council, Kilncraigs, Greenside Street, Alloa FK10 1EB; T.-01259 452531.

Dalrymple, Sir Hew (Fleetwood) Hamilton-, 10th Bt (created 1697), GCVO, 2001 (KCVO, 1985, CVO, 1974). Lord Lieutenant, East Lothian, 1987-2001; Captain General, Queen's Bodyguard for Scotland (Royal Company of Archers); Gold Stick for Scotland, 1996-2004; b. 9.4.26; m., Lady Anne-Louise Mary Keppel; 4 s. Educ. Ampleforth; Staff College, Camberley, 1957. Commissioned Grenadier Guards, 1944; DAAG HQ 3rd Division, 1958-60; Regimental Adjt., Grenadier Guards, 1960-62; retired, 1962; Vice-Chairman, Scottish & Newcastle Breweries, 1983-86 (Director, 1967-86); Chairman, Scottish American Investment Co., 1985-91 (Director, 1967-94); DL, East Lothian, 1964; JP, 1987. Address: Leuchie, North Berwick, East Lothian; T.-North Berwick 2903.

Dalrymple Hamilton, North John Frederick, OBE, TD, MA (Hons), DL. Farmer and Estate Manager; b. 7.5.50, Edinburgh; m., Sally Anne How; 2 s.; 1 d. Educ. Eton College; Aberdeen University. Scottish and Newcastle Breweries, 1972-82; certificate of farming practice, East of Scotland College of Agriculture, 1982-84; farming of Bargany Estate, since 1984. TA Commission, 1967-95; Member, Queen's Bodyguard for Scotland; Vice Lieutenant for Ayrshire and Arran; President, RBL(S), Maybole Branch; Chair, Lowland RFCA, 2003-07. Address: (h.) Lovestone, Girvan, Ayrshire KA26 9RF.

Dalyell, Kathleen Mary, DL, MA, FRSAS, OBE. Chairman, Royal Commission on Ancient and Historical Monuments of Scotland, 2000-05; Administrator, The Binns; Director, Heritage Education Trust, 1987-2005; Director, Weslo Housing Association, 1994-2003; Director, Carmont Settlement Trust, since 1997; Deputy Lieutenant, West Lothian; b. 17.11.37, Edinburgh; m., Tam Dalyell; 1 s.; 1 d. Educ. Convent of Sacred Heart, Aberdeen; Edinburgh University; Craiglockhart Teacher Training College. Teacher of History, St. Augustine's Secondary School, Glasgow, 1961-62; James Gillespie's High School for Girls, Edinburgh, 1962-63; Member, Historic Buildings Council for Scotland, 1975-87; Member, Lady Provost of Edinburgh's Delegation to China, 1987; Member, National Committee of Architectural Heritage Society for Scotland, 1983-89 (Vice-Chair, 1986-89); Chairman, Bo'ness Heritage Trust, 1988-93; Trustee, Paxton Trust, 1988-92;

Member, Ancient Monuments Board for Scotland, 1989-2000; Member, Royal Fine Art Commission for Scotland, 1992-2000; Member, Lord Mackay's Panel on Governance, NTS, 2003; Member, Court of University of Stirling, since 2002; Trustee, Hopetoun Preservation Trust, since 2005; Hon. Degree, University of Edinburgh, 2006; Trustee, National Museums of Scotland Charitable Trust. Recreations: reading; travel; hillwalking; chess. Address: The Binns, Linlithgow EH49 7NA; T.-01506 83 4255.

Dalyell, Tam. MP (Labour), Linlithgow (formerly West Lothian), 1962-2005; Father of House of Commons, 2001-05; Weekly Columnist, New Scientist, 1967-2005; Chairman, All-Party Latin America Group, since 1998; Rector, Edinburgh University, since 2003; President, Scottish Council for Development and Industry, since 2004; b. 9.8.32, Edinburgh; m., Kathleen Wheatley; 1 s.; 1 d. Educ. Edinburgh Academy; Harecroft; Eton; King's College, Cambridge; Moray House, Edinburgh. National Service, Scots Greys; Teacher, Bo'ness Academy, 1957-61; Deputy Director of Studies, Ship-School Dunera, 1961-62; Member, Public Accounts Committee, 1962-66; PPS to R.H.S. Crossman, 1964-70; Vice-Chairman, Parliamentary Labour Party, 1974-76; Member, European Parliament, 1975-78; Member: National Executive Committee, Labour Party, 1986-87, Advisory Council on Biological Sciences, Edinburgh University; a Vice-President, Research Defence Society; led Parliamentary Delegation to: Libya, 2001, Bolivia, 2000, Peru, 1999, Brazil, 1976. Hon. Doctor of Science, Edinburgh University, 1994; Hon. Doctor, City University, London, 1998; Hon. Doctor, St. Andrews University, 2003; Hon. Doctor, Napier University, Edinburgh, 2004; Hon. Doctor, University of Stirling, 2006; Hon. Doctor, Open University, 2006; Hon. President, Classical Association of Scotland, since 2006. Publications: Case for Ship Schools, 1959; Ship-School Dunera, 1961; Devolution: the end of Britain?, 1978; A Science Policy for Britain, 1983; One Man's Falklands, 1983; Misrule, 1987; Dick Crossman: a portrait, 1989. Address: (h.) The Binns, Linlithgow EH49 7NA; T.-01506-834255.

Dalziel, Graeme Davies, BA, CA. Chief Executive, Dunfermline Building Society, since 2001; b. 25.11.56, Glasgow; m., Anne; 2 s.; 1 d. Educ. Eastwood High School; University of Strathclyde. Finance Director, Dunfermline Building Society, 1998-2001; Finance Director of the Year, 2001; Past Chairman, Lauder Group Board, Lauder College; Director, Enterprise Lauder Ltd; Qualified as CA with Thornton Baker, Chartered Accountants, Glasgow, 1977-81; Scottish Equitable Life Assurance Society, 1981-94: Group Chief Accountant, Director, Scottish Equitable Fund Managers Ltd.; Scottish Widows, 1994-98: Head of Finance, Director, Scottish Widows Fund Management, Scottish Widows Property Management, Pensions Management (SWF) Ltd. Member, CBI Scotland; Member of Council of the Building Societies Association. Recreations: family; golf; gardening Address: (b.) Caledonia House, Carnegie Avenue, Dunfermline KY11 8PJ; T.-01383 627727.
E-mail: graeme.dalziel@dunfermline-bs.co.uk

Dane, Graham Charles, BSc, BA, MEd, MCIL, MInstP, CPhys, CSci, FEIS. Principal Teacher of Physics, St. Augustine's High School, Edinburgh, since 1983, seconded to International Relations Unit, Scottish Executive Education Department, 2002-03; b. 19.7.50. Educ. St. Andrews University. Teacher of Science, Merksworth High School, Paisley, 1973-75; Information Scientist, The Electricity Council, London, 1975-77; Teacher of Physics, Forrester High School, Edinburgh, 1978-80; Assistant Principal Teacher of Science, Deans Community High School, Livingston, 1980-83. Elected Member, General Teaching Council for Scotland (Convener, Committee on

Exceptional Admission to the Register), 1995-2001; holder of numerous trade union positions over the years, mainly in the EIS (Member, EIS Council); Member, Board, SCRE, 1992-98; Chair, Currie Community Council; Vice-Chair, Socialist Educational Association Scotland; Governor, Donaldson's College, 1996-2005. Recreations: learning new things; meeting people he likes; enjoying the arts. Address: (h.) 25 Thomson Road, Edinburgh EH14 5HT.

Daniel, Ronald (Ron), Advanced DipIM, Avon Prizeman, CMCIPD, past CMCMI, past MIQA. National Chairman, Victim Support Scotland, since 2003; Chairman, Moving On (Edinburgh) Ltd., 2002-07; b. 22.4.36; m., Cecilia; 2 d. Educ. Dunfermline High School, Lauder; Glenrothes and Kirkcaldy Tech Colleges. Civil Service, 1958-86; Senior Advisor, The Industrial Society, 1986-90; Director, Human Resources, Baillie Gifford, 1990-96; Management Consultant, 1996-2005; Chairman, Institute of Professional Civil Servants, Rosyth, 1967-78; Chairman, Royal Dockyards IPCS Committee, 1975-78. Councillor on Dunfermline Town Council and Fife County Council, 1967-73; Chairman of Health, Planning and Industrial Development Committees, 1969-73; Magistrate, 1969-73; Chairman, Whitley Council, Rosyth, 1975-78; Chairman, Dunfermline Civic Week Committee, 1975-88; Group Chairman, IIM, 1976-79; Chairman, Dunfermline Sound Talking Newspaper for the Blind, 1976-2005; Part time Lecturer in Management and Industrial Relations, 1979-82; Chairman, Victim Support Fife, 1997-2002; Vice Chairman, Victim Support Scotland, 2002-03. Recreations: bad golf; good wine; voluntary work. Address: 4 Coldingham Place, Dunfermline, Fife KY12 7XL; T.-01383 738730; e-mail: ron.daniel@btinternet.com

Dareau, Margaret Grace (Marace), MA. Principal Editor, Scottish Language Dictionaries Ltd., since 2005; Editorial Director, Scottish Language Dictionaries Ltd., 2002-05; Senior Editor, Scottish National Dictionary Association, 2001-2002; Senior Editor and Editorial Director, Dictionary of the Older Scottish Tongue, 1984-2001; b. 11.3.44, Dumfries; m., Michel Dareau; 1 s.; 2 d. Educ. Annan Academy; Edinburgh University. Research Assistant on Linguistic Atlas of Late Middle English, 1967; Kennedy Scholarship to study linguistics, MIT, 1967; began work at Dictionary of Older Scottish Tongue, 1968; Editor, Concise Scots Dictionary, 1976-77, 1980-84; Glossary Editor, Edinburgh Encyclopedia of Language and Linguistics. Recreations: painting; horse riding. Address: Picoyne, 32320 Bazian, France; T.-0033562644772; e-mail: information@gasconyholidays.info
web: www.gasconyholidays.info

Darling, Alistair Maclean, LLB. MP (Labour), Edinburgh South West, since 2005, Edinburgh Central, 1987-2005; Chancellor of the Exchequer, since 2007; Secretary of State for Trade and Industry, 2006-07; Secretary of State for Transport, 2002-06; Secretary of State for Scotland, 2003-06; Secretary of State for Work and Pensions, 2001-02; Member, Faculty of Advocates, since 1984; b. 28.11.53, London; m., Margaret Vaughan; 1 s.; 1 d. Educ. Loretto School; Aberdeen University. Solicitor, 1978-83; Advocate, since 1984; Member: Lothian Regional Council, 1982-87, Lothian and Borders Police Board, 1982-87; Governor, Napier College, 1985-87; Chief Secretary to the Treasury, 1997-98; Secretary of State for Social Security, 1998-2001. Address: (b.) 22A Rutland Square, Edinburgh EH1 2BB.

Darling, Ian Marshall, FRICS. Member, Lands Tribunal for Scotland; Board Member, British Waterways, 2000-06; b. 16.4.45, Perth; m., Kate; 1 s.; 1 d. Educ. Perth Academy; London University (College of Estate Management and Wye College). Partner, Bell Ingram, 1974; Managing

Partner, 1987-96; Director, Chesterton Scotland, 1996-2001. Chairman, Royal Institution of Chartered Surveyors in Scotland, 1997-98; Master, Company of Merchants of the City of Edinburgh, 2000-01; Member, Council, RSPB and Chair of Conservation Committee; Member, Court of University of Edinburgh. Recreations: nature conservation; ornithology. Address: (b.) 126 George Street, Edinburgh EH2 4HH, T.-07766 373059.

Darwent, Rt. Rev. Frederick Charles, LTh (Hon), JP. Bishop of Aberdeen and Orkney, 1978-92; b. 20.4.27, Liverpool; m., 1, Edna Lilian Waugh (deceased); 2 d.; 2, Roma Evelyn Fraser. Educ. Warbreck School, Liverpool; Ormskirk Grammar School; Wells Theological College, Somerset. Followed a banking career, 1943-61; War Service, Far East, 1945-48; ordained Deacon, 1963, Priest, 1964, Diocese of Liverpool; Curate, Pemberton, Wigan, 1963-65; Rector: Strichen, 1965-71, New Pitsligo, 1965-78, Fraserburgh, 1971-78; Canon, St. Andrew's Cathedral, Aberdeen, 1971; Dean of Aberdeen and Orkney, 1973-78. Recreations: amateur stage (acting and production); calligraphy; music. Address: (h.) 107 Osborne Place, Aberdeen AB25 2DD; T.-01224 646497.

Das, Sachinandan, MB, BS, FRCR, DMRT. Head, Department of Radiotherapy and Oncology, Dundee University, 1987-2000; Chairman, Tayside Oncology Research Committee, since 1987; b. 1.8.44, Cuttack, India; m., Dr. Subhalaxmi; 1 s.; 1 d. Educ. Ravenshaw Collegiate School; SCB Medical College, Cuttack, India; Utkal University. Senior House Officer in Radiotherapy, Plymouth General Hospital, 1969-70; Registrar in Radiotherapy and Oncology, then Senior Registrar, Mersey Regional Centre for Radiotherapy, Liverpool, 1970-77; Consultant in administrative charge, Ninewells Hospital, Dundee, 1987-91, Clinical Director, 1991-98; Regional Postgraduate Education Advisor in Radiotherapy and Oncology, 1987-2002. Member: Standing Scottish Committee, National Medical Consultative Committee, Scottish Paediatric Oncology Group, Joint Radiological Safety Committee, Radiation Hazards Sub-Committee, Unit Medical and Dental Advisory Committee; Council Member, Scottish Radiological Society, 1987-93. Recreations: hill-walking; table tennis; reading. Address: (h.) Grapevine, 42 Menzieshill Road, Dundee DD2 1PU; T.-Dundee 642915.

Datta, Dipankar, MBBS, FRCPGlas, FRCPLond. Consultant Physician (with special interest in gastroenterology), 1975-97; former Honorary Senior Clinical Lecturer and Clinical Sub-Dean, Glasgow University; Founder Director, Scottish Overseas Aid; b. 30.1.33, Chittagong, India; m., Dr. J.B. Datta; 1 s.; 1 d. Educ. Calcutta University. Former Vice Chairman, UN Association, Glasgow; former Chairman, Overseas Doctors' Association, Scottish Division; former Chairman, British Medical Association, Lanarkshire; former Member, Central Executive Committee, Scottish Council, United Nations Association; former Member, Lanarkshire Health Board; former Member, Scottish Council, British Medical Association; former Member, Executive Committee, Scottish Council, Royal Commonwealth Society for the Blind; former Member, Senate, Glasgow University; former Member, General Medical Council; Chairman, South Asia Voluntary Enterprise; former Chairman, Scottish India Forum. Recreations: reading - history, economics and international politics. Address: (h.) 9 Kirkvale Crescent, Newton Mearns, Glasgow G77 5HB; T.-0141-639 1515; e-mail: dipankardatta@hotmail.com

Datta, Pradip Kumar, MS, FRCS(Edin), FRCS(Eng), FRCS(Ire), FRCS(Glas). Honorary Consultant Surgeon, Caithness General Hospital; b. 14.5.40, Calcutta, India; m.,

Swati; 1 s. Educ. St. Aloysius High School, Visakhapatnam, India; Andhra University, Visakhapatnam, India. Surgical Registrar: Hope Hospital, Salford, Poole General Hospital, Plymouth General Hospital, Royal Cornwall Hospital, Truro; Senior Surgical Registrar, Whittington Hospital, London; Member, Council, and Surgical Tutor, Royal College of Surgeons of Edinburgh. Visiting Lecturer: University Sains Malaysia, National University of Singapore. Recreations: playing squash; tennis; fly-fishing. Address: (h.) Garvyk, 17 Newton Avenue, Wick KW1 5LJ; T.-01955 605050.

Davenport, Dr Richard John, DM, FRCP (Edin), BMBS (Hons), BMedSci. Consultant Neurologist, Western General Hospital, Edinburgh, since 1999, Royal Infirmary, Edinburgh, since 1999; b. 22.9.63, Chester; m., Meryl Peat. Educ. King's College, Wimbledon; Nottingham University Medical School. Nottingham University Medical School, 1982-87; House Officer, Queen's Medical Centre, Nottingham, 1987-88; Senior House Officer and Registrar, Stoke-on-Trent, 1988-91; Registrar, then Research Registrar, Edinburgh, 1992-96; Advanced Neurological Trainee, Perth, Australia, 1997-98; Senior Registrar, Edinburgh, 1998. Recreations: cooking; travel; walking the dog. Address: (b.) Department of Clinical Neurosciences, Western General Hospital, Edinburgh EH4 2XU; T.-0131-537 2072.

Davey, Andrew John, BSc (Hons), DipArch, RIBA, RIAS. Partner, Simpson & Brown Architects of Edinburgh; b. 6.6.52, Exmouth, Devon; m., Christina; 2 s.; 1 d. Educ. Queen Elizabeth's School, Devon; Bartlett School of Architecture; University College London. Publication: joint author, The Care and Conservation of Georgian Houses', 1978 (now in its 4th Edition). Address: (b.) Simpson and Brown Architects, St. Ninian's Manse, Quayside Street, Edinburgh EH6 6EJ; T.-0131 555 4678; e-mail: admin@simpsonandbrown.co.uk

Davidson, Hon. Lord (Charles Kemp Davidson), MA, LLB, FRSE. Chairman, Scottish Law Commission, 1988-96; Senator of the College of Justice, 1983-96; Deputy Chairman, Boundaries Commission for Scotland, 1985-96; b. 13.4.29, Edinburgh; m., Mary Mactaggart; 1 s.; 2 d. Educ. Fettes College, Edinburgh; Oxford University; Edinburgh University. Advocate, 1956; QC (Scot), 1969; Keeper, The Advocates Library, 1972-77; Vice Dean, Faculty of Advocates, 1977-79; Dean, 1979-83; Procurator to the General Assembly of the Church of Scotland, 1972-83; Chairman, National Health Service Tribunal for Scotland, 1970-83. Address: (h.) 22 Dublin Street, Edinburgh EH1 3PP; T.-0131-556 2168.

Davidson, Professor Colin William, BSc, DipER, PhD, CEng, HonFIEE. Retired chartered engineer; b. 18.9.34, Edinburgh; m., Ranee M.N. Cleland; 2 d. Educ. George Heriot's School; Edinburgh University. Lecturer, Edinburgh University, 1956-61; Electronics Engineer, Nuclear Enterprises (GB) Ltd., 1961-64; Lecturer, Heriot-Watt College/University, 1964-67; Associate Professor, Chulalongkorn University, Bangkok, 1967-68; Heriot-Watt University: Senior Lecturer, 1968-85, Professor of Electrical Engineering, 1985-88, Dean of Engineering, 1976-79 and 1984-87, Head of Department, 1979-87. Member, Lothian Regional Council, 1990-94; Vice-President, Institution of Electrical Engineers, 1990-93, 1995-98, Honorary Treasurer, 1999-2001; Member, Engineering Council Senate and Board for Engineers' Regulation, 1996-98; Secretary, West Highland Anchorages and Moorings Association, 2001-05; Secretary, Argyll Community Housing Association, 2005-07; Member, Council, Institution of Engineering and Technology, since

2007; Freeman, City of London; Liveryman, Worshipful Company of Engineers. Recreations: sailing; CLYC. Address: (h.) Tigh-nan-Eilean, Ardfern PA31 8QN; T.-01852 500532.

Davidson, Professor Donald Allen, BSc, PhD, FRSE. Professor of Environmental Science, Stirling University, since 1991; b. 27.4.45, Lumphanan; m., Caroline E. Brown; 1 s.; 2 d. Educ. Robert Gordon's College, Aberdeen; Aberdeen University; Sheffield University. Lecturer, St. David's University College, Wales, 1971-76; Lecturer, Senior Lecturer, Reader, Strathclyde University, 1976-86; Reader, Stirling University, 1986-91. College Member, Natural Environmental Research Council; Editor of journal Soil Use and Management. Publications include: The Evaluation of Land Resources, 1992; many papers. Recreations: exploring the countryside; maintaining an old house and garden. Address: (b.) Biological and Environmental Science, Stirling University, Stirling FK9 4LA; T.-01786 467840.

Davidson, Duncan Lewis Watt, BSc (Hons), MB, ChB, FRCPEdin. Consultant in Medical Education; Consultant Neurologist, Tayside; Honorary Senior Lecturer in Medicine, Dundee University, 1976-2002; b. 16.5.40, Kingston, Jamaica; m., Dr. Anne V.M. Maiden; 4 s.; 1 d. Educ. Knox College, Jamaica; Edinburgh University. House Officer, Senior House Officer, Registrar and Senior Registrar posts in medicine and neurology, Edinburgh, 1966-75; Peel Travelling Fellowship, Montreal, 1973-74; MRC clinical scientific staff, MRC Brain Metabolism Unit, Edinburgh, 1975-76. Recreations: gardening; photography. Address: (h.) Oliver, Tweedsmuir, Biggar ML12 6QN; T.-01334 76108.

Davidson, Ian Graham, MA (Hons). MP (Labour and Co-op), Glasgow South West, since 2005 (Glasgow Pollok, 1997-2005, Glasgow Govan 1992-97); Chair, Labour Against the Euro; b. 8.9.50, Jedburgh; m., Morag Mackinnon; 1 s.; 1 d. Educ. Jedburgh Grammar School; Galashiels Academy; Edinburgh University; Jordanhill College of Education. Project Manager, Community Service Volunteers, 1985-92; Councillor, Strathclyde Regional Council, 1978-92 (Chair, Education Committee, 1986-92); Member, Public Accounts Select Committee, since 1997, Member, Committee of Selection, 1997-99; Secretary, Trade Union Group of Labour MPs, 1998-2002; Secretary, Tribune Group of MPs; Secretary, New Europe Parliamentary Group; Secretary, British Japan Parliamentary Group; Secretary, Shipbuilding Group; Chair, Namibia Group; Chair, Labour Against a European Superstate; Scottish Affairs Select Committee, since 2005. Address: House of Commons, London SW1A 0AA.

Davidson, Rev. Ian Murray Pollock, MBE, MA, BD. Minister, Allan Park South Church and Church of the Holy Rude, Stirling, 1985-94; Chairman, General Trustees, Church of Scotland, 1994-99; b. 14.3.28, Kirriemuir; m., Isla; 2 s. Educ. Montrose Academy; St. Andrews University. National Service, 1949-51; Minister: Crieff North and West Church (St. Andrew's), 1955-61, Grange Church, Kilmarnock, 1961-67, Cambuslang Old Church, 1967-85; Convener, Maintenance of the Ministry Committee and Board, Church and Ministry Department, 1981-84; General Trustee, 1975-2003. Publications: At the Sign of the Fish (history of Cambuslang Old Parish Church), 1975; A Guide to the Church of the Holy Rude. Recreations: travel; photography; reading; writing. Address: (h.) 13/8 Craigend Park, Edinburgh EH16 5XX; T.-0131-664 0074.

Davidson, John F., MB, ChB, FRCPEdin, FRCPGlas, FRCPath. Consultant Haematologist, Glasgow Royal Infirmary, 1969-98; b. 11.1.34, Lumphanan; m., Laura G. Middleton; 1 s.; 1 d. Educ. Robert Gordon's College, Aberdeen; Aberdeen University. Surgeon Lt., RN; Registrar

in Medicine, Aberdeen Royal Infirmary; Research Registrar in Medicine, then Senior Registrar in Haematology, Glasgow Royal Infirmary; Honorary Clinical Senior Lecturer, Glasgow University; Honorary Consultant Haematologist, Strathclyde University. Secretary, British Society for Haematalogy, 1983-86; President, British Society for Haematology, 1990-91; Chairman: BCSH Haemostasis and Thrombosis Task Force, 1986-91, Steering Committee NEQAS in blood coagulation, 1986-91; Member, Council, Royal College of Pathologists, two terms; Secretary, Joint Committee on Haematology, Royal College of Pathologists and Royal College of Physicians; Chairman, UK Joint Working Group on Quality Assurance. Editor, Progress in Fibrinolysis, Volumes I to VII; Chairman, International Committee on Fibrinolysis, 1976-84; Co-Editor in Chief, Fibrinolysis, 1986-96. Recreation: gardening. Address: (h.) Craigiebank, 20 Roman Road, Bearsden, Glasgow G61 2SL; T.-0141-942 3356.

Davidson, John Knight, OBE, MD, FRCP (Edin), FRCP (Glas), FRCR, (Hon) FACR, (Hon) FRACR. Consultant Radiologist; expert adviser on bone disease in compressed air and diving medicine; b. 17.8.25, Edinburgh; m., Edith E. McKelvie; 2 s.; 1 d. Educ. George Watson's Boys College, Edinburgh; Edinburgh University. Adviser in Bone Disease in Divers MRC, Aberdeen, US Navy, 1970-92; Non Executive Director, Yorkhill NHS Trust, 1993-95; Member, Council, Medical and Dental Defence Union, 1971-95; Chairman, Health Policy, Council, Scottish Conservative and Unionist Association, 1991-95; Member, BBC Medical Advisory Group, 1988-95; Consultant Radiologist in Administrative Charge, Western Infirmary and Gartnavel General, Glasgow, 1967-90; Royal College of Radiologists: Member, Council, 1974-77, 1984-87, Chairman, Examining Board, 1976-79, Scottish Committee, 1985-89; Member, Council, Royal Glasgow Institute of Fine Arts, 1978-88; Deputy President, Glasgow and Renfrewshire, British Red Cross Society, 1988-93; Honorary Fellow: Royal Australian and New Zealand College of Radiology, 1981, Scottish Radiological Society, 1990, American College of Radiology, 1992, Medical and Dental Defence Union, Scotland, 1995; Honorary Fellow and Medallist, International Skeletal Society, 1995; Rohan Williams Professor, Australasia, 1977; Aggarwal Memorial Oration, India, 1988. Editor, Aseptic Necrosis of Bone and numerous publications. Recreations: golf; water colours; golf memorabilia; Robert Louis Stevenson; bridge; meeting people. Address: (h.) 1/1, 15 Beechlands Avenue, Netherlee, Glasgow G44 3YT; T.-0141-637 0290.

Davidson, Julie Wilson. Writer; freelance contributor to radio, television, books, newspapers and magazines, since 1981; b. 11.5.43, Motherwell; m., Harry Reid (qv); 1 d. Educ. Aberdeen High School for Girls. Trainee Journalist, D.C. Thomson Ltd., Dundee, 1961-64; Feature Writer and Sub-Editor, Aberdeen Press & Journal, 1964-67; The Scotsman: Feature Writer, 1967-77, Columnist, 1977-81; Columnist, The Herald, 1995-97; Television Critic, The Herald, 1981-95. Columnist/Critic of the Year, Scottish Press Awards, 1985; Critic of the Year, Scottish Press Awards, 1988-89-92-94-95; Canada Travel Award, 1992; Travelex Travel Writers Award, 1999; Scottish Thistle Travel Media Award, 1999. Publication: Scots We Ken, 2007. Recreations: reading; cinema; walking; travelling; wildlife; lunching; e-mail: julie.davdison3@virgin.net

Davidson of Glen Clova, Lord (Neil Forbes Davidson), QC, BA, MSc, LLB, LLM. Advocate General for Scotland, since 2006; Solicitor General for Scotland, 2000-01; b. 13.9.50; m. Educ. Stirling University; Bradford University; Edinburgh University. Admitted, Faculty of Advocates, 1979; Standing Junior Counsel to Registrar General, 1982, to Department of Health and Social Security, 1988; called to the Bar, Inner Temple, 1990. Address: Faculty of Advocates, Parliament House, Edinburgh EH1 1RF; T.-0131- 226 5071.

Davidson, Professor Peter Robert Keith Andrew, BA, MA, PhD (Cantab), MA, FSAS. Professor of Renaissance Studies, Scholar-Keeper of the University's Collections, Aberdeen University, since 2000, b. 14.5.57, Glasgow; m., Jane Barbara Stevenson. Educ. Clare College, Cambridge; York University. Lecturer, St Andrews University, 1989-90; Universiteit Leiden, 1990-92; Lecturer, Warwick University, 1992-2000 (Senior Lecturer, 1995, Reader, 1998). Publications; Poems and Translations of Sir Richard Fanshawe; Poetry and Revolution; Early Modern Women's Poetry; The Idea of North; The Collected Poems of S. Robert Southwell S. J.; The Universal Baroque. Recreation: casuistry. Address: (b.) History of Art, King's College, Aberdeen AB24 3FX.

Davidson, Sheriff Richard Alexander, LLB, NP. Sheriff of Tayside Central and Fife at Dundee, since 1994; b. 3.11.47, Lennoxtown; m., Shirley Margaret Thomson; 1 s.; 1 d. Educ. Oban High School; Glasgow University. Apprentice Solicitor, 1969-72; Assistant Solicitor, 1972-76; Partner, Tindal Oatts, 1976-94. Member, Glasgow and North Argyll Legal Aid Committee, 1984-89. Address: (b.) Sheriff Courthouse, West Bell Street, Dundee.

Davidson, Professor Robert, MA, BD, DD, FRSE. Moderator, General Assembly of the Church of Scotland, 1990-91; Professor of Old Testament Language and Literature, Glasgow University, 1972-91; Principal, Trinity College, Glasgow, 1981-91; b. 30.3.27, Markinch, Fife; m., Elizabeth May Robertson; 4 s.; 4 d. Educ. Bell-Baxter School, Cupar; St. Andrews University. Lecturer in Biblical Studies, Aberdeen University, 1953-60; Lecturer in Hebrew and Old Testament Studies, St. Andrews University, 1960-66; Lecturer/Senior Lecturer in Old Testament, Edinburgh University, 1966-72. Publications: The Bible Speaks, 1959; The Old Testament, 1964; Geneses 1 - 11, 1973; Genesis 12 - 50, 1979; The Bible in Religious Education, 1979; The Courage to Doubt, 1983; Jeremiah Volume 1, 1983; Jeremiah Volume 2, Lamentations, 1985; Ecclesiastes, Song of Songs, 1986; Wisdom and Worship, 1990; A Beginner's Guide to the Old Testament, 1992; Go by the Book, 1996; The Vitality of Worship, 1998. Recreations: music; gardening. Address: (h.) 30 Dumgoyne Drive, Bearsden, Glasgow G61 3AP; T.-0141-942 1810.

Davidson, Professor Roger, MA, CertEd, PhD, FRHistS. Emeritus Professor of Social History and Leverhulme Emeritus Fellow; b. 19.7.42, Guildford; m., Mo Townson; 1 s.; 1 d. Educ. King Edward VI School, Chelmsford; St Catharine's College, Cambridge. Teacher in History and Economics, Watford Boys Grammar School, 1965-67; Research Graduate, St Catharine's College, Cambridge, 1967-70; Lecturer, 1970, Senior Lecturer, 1984, Reader, 1996, in Economic and Social History, Edinburgh University. Member, Scottish Records Advisory Council. Publications: Whitehall and the Labour Problem in Late-Victorian and Edwardian Britain, 1985; Dangerous Liaisons; A Social History of VD in 20th Century Scotland, 2000. Recreations: birdwatching; reading; guitar. Address: (b.) Economic and Social History, School of History and Classics, William Robertson Building, 50 George Square, Edinburgh EH8 9JY; T.-0131 650 3841.
E-mail: Roger.Davidson@ed.ac.uk

Davie, Ivor Turnbull, MB, ChB, FRCA, FRCPE, HonFCPS (Bd). Consultant Anaesthetist, Western General Hospital, Edinburgh, 1971-98; Honorary Senior Lecturer, Edinburgh University, 1979-97; Lecturer, Central Midwives Board (Scotland), 1974-97; b. 23.2.35, Edinburgh; m., Dr. Jane Elizabeth Fleischmann; 1 s.; 1 d. Educ. Royal High School, Edinburgh; Edinburgh University. Member, Board of Examiners, Faculty of Anaesthetists, Royal College of Surgeons of England and Royal College of Anaesthetists, 1978-91; President, Edinburgh and East of Scotland Society of Anaesthetists, 1990-91; Tutor, Faculty of Anaesthetists, 1979-87; Regional Educational Adviser, Royal College of Anaesthetists, 1988-95; Member, Editorial Board, British Journal of Obstetrics and Gynaecology, 1980-84; Visiting Medical Officer, Westmead Centre, Sydney, NSW, 1983. Address: (h.) 26 Kingsburgh Road, Edinburgh EH12 6DZ; T.-0131-337 1117.

Davies, Alan Graham, LLB(Hons), Dip. Legal Practice. Solicitor in private practice since 1983, Partner, since 1987; b. 4.2.59, Perth; m., Fiona; 2 s.; 1 d. Educ. Perth Grammar School; University of Edinburgh. Clerk to Income Tax Commissioners. Recreations: squash; golf; football; skiing. Address: (b.) 25 South Methven Street, Perth; T.-01738 620451.

Davies, Professor Sir Graeme John, Kt, BE, MA, PhD, ScD, FREng, FRSE. Vice-Chancellor, University of London, since 2003; b. 7.4.37, New Zealand; m., Florence; 1 s.; 1 d. Educ. Mt. Albert Grammar School, Auckland; University of Auckland; Cambridge University. Junior Lecturer, University of Auckland, 1960-62; Lecturer, Cambridge University, 1962-77; Professor of Metallurgy, Sheffield University, 1978-86; Vice-Chancellor, Liverpool University, 1986-91; Chief Executive: Universities Funding Council, 1991-93, Higher Education Funding Council for England, 1992-95; Principal and Vice Chancellor, Glasgow University, 1995-2003. Chairman, USS Ltd., 1996-2006; Chairman, CCLRC, 2002-07; Governor, Glasgow School of Art, since 2003; Chairman, Glasgow Science Centre, 2001-06. Hon. LLD, Liverpool, 1991; Hon. FRSNZ, 1993; Hon. DMet, Sheffield, 1995; Hon. DSc, Nottingham, 1995; Hon. FTCL, 1995; Hon. DEng, Manchester Metropolitan, 1996, Hon. FRCPSGlas, 1999; Hon. LLD, Strathclyde, 2000; Hon. DEng, Auckland, 2002; D.hon.c, Edinburgh, 2003; Hon. DUniv, Glasgow; Hon. DSc, Ulster; Hon. DUniv, Paisley, 2004; FIMechE; FIM; FRSA; CBIM; DL, Merseyside, 1989-93; Hon. DUniv, Glasgow, 2004; Hon. DSc, Ulster, 2004; Hon. DSc, London South Bank, 2006; Hon. FIPENZ, 2007. Recreations: bird-watching; golf; The Times crossword. Address: (h.) Coulter Mains, Coulter, near Biggar ML12 6PR; T.-01899 221740.

Davies, Lt-Col Hywel William, MA, ARAgS, OStJ, JP. Chairman, Peatland Group, since 2000; Managing Director, Peatland Smokehouse Ltd., 2002-06; b. 28.6.45, Pantyderi, Boncath, Pembs; m., Patricia, 1 s.; 1 d. Educ. Harrow; Magdalene College, Cambridge. Commissioned RHG (The Blues, later Blues & Royals), 1965; Staff College, 1977; Operational Requirements, MoD, 1978-80; Defence Intelligence, MoD, 1982-84; CO, Blues and Royals, 1985-87; with Pilkington Optronics, 1988-89; Chief Executive: RHASS, 1991-98; BHS, 1998-2000. Director: G. D. Golding & Son Ltd., since 1988, Challenger Consultancy Ltd., 1987-91, Ingliston Hotels Ltd., 1997-98, Scottish Farming and Educational Trust, 1991-98, Scottish Agricultural and Rural Development Centre Ltd., 1992-98; The Countryside Movement, 1995-97; Ingliston Development Trust, 1996-98; British Horse Society Trading Co. Ltd., 1998-2000. Member, Countryside Committee, Countryside Alliance, 1997-99. Chairman, Association of Show and Agricultural Organisations, 1998-99 (Hon. Life Member, 2000); Draught Horse Training Committee, 1998-2000; Royal International Horse Show, 1998-2000; Member (C), South Ayrshire Council, since 2003; Convener, Rural Communities Committee Human Resources Committee, 2004-07, Leadership Panel, 2007; Chairman: Central Region, 1998, Ayr and Arran, since 2004, Association of Order of St. John; W Lowland Cadet

Force League, 2001-07; Vice President, Ayrshire and Arran Red Cross, 2002-04. Recreations: equestrian pursuits (Member, Coaching Club; represented UK at Four-in-Hand Carriage Driving, 1984-87); shooting; fishing; gardening. Club: Farmers'. Address: (b.) Peatland, Gatehead, Ayrshire KA2 9AN; T.-01563 851020.

Davies (a.k.a. Glasse-Davies), Professor R. Wayne, MA, PhD, ScD. Robertson Professor of Biotechnology, Glasgow University, since 1989; b. 10.6.44, Cardiff; m., Victoria Glasse; 3 s.; 2 d. Educ. Queen Elizabeth's Hospital, Bristol; St. John's College, Cambridge. Research Fellow, University of Wisconsin, 1968-71; H3 Professor, Universität zu Köln, FRG, 1971-77; Lecturer, University of Essex, 1977-81; Senior Lecturer, UMIST, 1981-83; Vice-President, Scientific and Research Director, Allelix Biopharmaceuticals, Toronto, 1983-89; Neuropa Ltd.: Founding Director, 1996, CEO, 1997-2000; CEO Uman Genomics AB, Sweden, 2001-03; Director, Brainwave-Discovery Ltd., since 2007. Recreations: poetry and literature; cello; skiing. Address: (b.) Division of Molecular Genetics, Institute of Biomedical and Life Sciences, Glasgow University, University Avenue, Glasgow G12 8QQ.

Davila, James R., BA, MA, PhD. Head of the School of Divinity, University of St. Andrews, since 2006, Reader in Early Jewish Studies, since 2006; b. 08.08.60, San Diego, Ca., USA. Educ. Crawford High School; UCLA; Harvard University. Visiting Assistant Professor of Jewish Studies, Tulane University, 1988-89, Visiting Assistant Professor of Classics, 1989-91; Assistant Professor of Religion, Central College, 1991-95; Lecturer in Early Jewish Studies, University of St. Andrews, 1995-2006. Member of the editorial team that published Dead Sea Scrolls. Publications: numerous articles and books on ancient judaism and related matters. Blog: PaleoJudaica (paleojudaica blogspot.com). Address: (b.) St. Mary's College, University of St. Andrews, St. Andrews, Fife KY16 9JU; T.-01334 462834; e-mail: jrd4@st-andrews.ac.uk

Davis, Christine A.M., CBE, MA, DipEd. Chairman, Scottish Agricultural Wages Board, 1995-2004 (Member, since 1990); Member, Rail Passenger Committee for Scotland, since 1997; Member, Court, University of St. Andrews, since 2000; Trustee, Falkland Heritage Trust, since 2001; b. 5.3.44, Salisbury; m., Robin John Davis; 2 d. Educ. Perth Academy; Ayr Academy; St. Andrews University; Aberdeen University; Aberdeen College of Education. Teacher of History and Modern Studies, Cumbernauld High School and High School of Stirling, 1967-69; joined Dunblane Town Council and Perth and Kinross Joint County Council, 1972; undertook research in Canada on Ontario Hydro and small claims in Ontario courts, 1977-78; Chairman, Electricity Consultative Council for North of Scotland, 1980-90; Member: North of Scotland Hydro Electric Board, 1980-90, Scottish Economic Council, 1987-95, Scottish Committee of the Council on Tribunals, 1989-95; Clerk, Britain Yearly Meeting, Society of Friends (Quakers), 1991-95; Chairman, Scottish Legal Aid Board, 1991-98; a President, Council of Churches for Britain and Ireland, 1990-92; Trustee, Joseph Rowntree Charitable Trust. Recreations: embroidery; bird-watching; walking. Address: (h.) 24 Newton Crescent, Dunblane, Perthshire FK15 ODZ; T.-Dunblane 823226.
E-mail: christine.amd@btinternet.com

Davis, Eileen Mary, BA (Hons), PGCE. Principal, St. Margaret's School, Edinburgh, since 2001; b. 7.10.49, St. Annes on the Sea. Educ. Queen Mary School, Lytham; University of Hull. Teacher, Sheredes School,

Hoddesdon, 1972-76; The Cedars Upper School, Leighton Buzzard, 1976-78; Teacher, Head of Geography, Head of Upper 6, Bolton School Girls' Division, 1978-88; Teacher of Geography, Dollar Academy, 1988-91; Deputy Head, St. George's School, Edinburgh, 1991-2001. Council Member of Headteachers' Association of Scotland; Member of ISCO Council; Past President of the Rotary Club of Edinburgh Breakfast. Recreation: piano; travel; geology. Address: (b.) East Suffolk Road, Edinburgh EH16 5PJ; T.-0131 668 1986.

Davis, Gerry. Journalist/Public Relations Consultant, since 1970; TV Producer and Presenter, since 1989; Media Training Provider, since 1991; b. 7.10.35, Glasgow; m., June Imray; 1 s.; 1 d. Educ. Shawlands Academy, Glasgow; Strathclyde University. Trainee analytical chemist, ICI; pharmaceutical chemist; actor; television continuity announcer/programme presenter/reporter, BBC Radio Scotland. Former Radio Reporter of the Year/Presenter of the Year. Recreation: holidaying. Address: (b.) Davis Media, 10 Wellwood Terrace, Cults, Aberdeen AB15 9JA; T.-01224 862330; e-mail: gd@davismedia.co.uk

Davis, Margaret Thomson. Novelist; b. Bathgate; 2 s. Educ. Albert Secondary School. Worked as children's nurse; Red Cross nurse; short story writer; novelist; author of autobiography, The Making of a Novelist; novels include The Breadmakers, A Baby Might Be Crying, A Sort of Peace, The Prisoner, The Prince and the Tobacco Lords, Roots of Bondage, Scorpion in the Fire, The Dark Side of Pleasure, A Very Civilised Man, Light and Dark, Rag Woman Rich Woman, Daughters and Mothers, Wounds of War, A Woman of Property, A Sense of Belonging, Hold Me Forever, Kiss Me No More, A Kind of Immortality, Burning Ambition, A Darkening of The Heart, A Deadly Deception, Goodmans of Glassford Street. Committee Member: International PEN (Scottish Branch); Society of Authors; Lecturer in Creative Writing; Honorary President, Strathkelvin Writers Club. Recreations: reading; travelling; being with friends.

Davis, Ray, DipArch, MSc, DipUD, RIBA, FRIAS. Managing Director, Davis Duncan Architects, since 1981; b. 11.2.48, Glasgow; m., Ruth; 3 d. Educ. Aberdeen Grammar School; Robert Gordon University; Heriot Watt University. Alison and Hutcheson and Partners: Architect, Edinburgh Office, 1973-79, Senior Architect and Office Manager, Glasgow, 1979-81; Visiting Lecturer, Planning Department, Mackintosh School, 1979-81; formed Ray Davis Architects and Urban Design Consultants, 1981; part-time Design Tutor, Department of Architecture, Strathclyde University, 1981-86; formed current practice, 1982. Convenor, Baptist Union Property Group, 1997. Recreations: golf; sketching; skiing; church. Address: North Elgin, 6 Balfleurs Street, Milngavie, Glasgow; T.-0141-956 1458; e-mail: rdavis@davisduncan.co.uk

Davison, Timothy Paul, BA (Hons), MHSM, DipHSM, MBA, MPH. Chief Executive, NHS Lanarkshire, since 2005; b. 4.6.61, Newcastle upon Tyne; 1 s. Educ. Kenton School, Newcastle upon Tyne; Stirling University; Glasgow University. Appointments in Stirling Royal Infirmary, Royal Edinburgh Hospital, Glasgow Royal Infirmary, 1984-90; Sector General Manager, Gartnavel Royal Hospital, 1990-91; Unit General Manager, Mental Health Unit, Glasgow, 1991-92; Community and Mental Health Unit, Glasgow, 1992-94; Chief Executive, Greater Glasgow Community and Mental Health Services NHS Trust, 1994-99; Chief Executive, Greater Glasgow Primary Care NHS Trust, 1999-2002; Chief Executive, North Glasgow University Hospitals NHS Trust, 2002-05. Recreations:

tennis; military and political history. Address: (b.) NHS Lanarkshire, 14 Beckford Street, Hamilton ML3 0TA.

Dawe, Jennifer Ann (Jenny), MA, PhD. Leader, City of Edinburgh Council, since 2007; Leader, Liberal Democrat Group, City of Edinburgh Council, since 1999; b. 27.4.45, Edinburgh; 4 s. Educ. Trinity Academy; Aberdeen University; Edinburgh University. Former Librarian, Tanzania and Malawi, 1966-80; Tutor, American and Commonwealth History Department, Edinburgh University, 1985-87; Admin and Information Officer, Lothian Community Relations Council, 1988-90; Welfare Rights Officer, Lothian Regional Council, 1990-96; Senior Welfare Rights Officer, East Lothian Council, 1996-2007. Elected to City of Edinburgh Council, 1997. Recreations: travel; reading; rediscovering gardening; Hearts supporter. Address: (b.) City Chambers, High Street, Edinburgh; T.-0131-529 4987.

Dawnay, (Charles) James Payan, MA; b. 7.11.46; m., Sarah; 3 d; 1 s. Educ. Eton; Trinity Hall, Cambridge. Director: SG Warburg, 1984-85, Mercury Asset Management Group plc, 1985-91; Chairman, Mercury Fund Managers Ltd, 1987-91; Director, Martin Currie Ltd, 1992-2000, Deputy Chairman, 1999-2000; Chairman: Northern AIM VCT plc, since 2000, Investec High Income Trust plc, since 2001, Gurr Johns Ltd, since 2001, Penicuik House Preservation Trust, since 2003, CCLA Investment Management Ltd, since 2004, Resources Investment Trust, since 2001, Biggar Museum Trust, since 2005, Taiwan Opportunities Trust plc; Trustee, National Galleries of Scotland, since 2004. Recreations: fishing; collecting. Address: Symington House, by Biggar, Lanarkshire ML12 6LW; T.-01899 308211; e-mail: jdawnay@yahoo.co.uk

Dawson, Professor John Alan, BSc, MPhil, PhD, FILT, FRSE. Professor of Marketing, Edinburgh University, since 1990; Visiting Professor: Escuela Superior de Administración y Dirección de Empresas (ESADE), Barcelona; University of Marketing and Distribution Sciences, Kobe, Japan; b. 19.8.44, Hyde; m., Jocelyn Barker; 1 s.; 1 d. Educ. Lady Manners School, Bakewell; University College, London; Nottingham University. Lecturer, Nottingham University; Lecturer, Senior Lecturer, Reader, St. David's University College, Wales; Fraser of Allander Professor of Distributive Studies, Stirling University; Visiting Lecturer, University of Western Australia; Visiting Research Fellow, Australian National University; Visiting Professor: Florida State University, Chuo University, University of South Africa, University of Marketing and Distribution Sciences, Kobe, Boconni University, Milan, Saitama University, Japan. Chairman, National Museums of Scotland Retailing Ltd. Publications: Evaluating the Human Environment, 1973; Man and His World, 1975; Computing for Geographers, 1976; Small-Scale Retailing in the UK, 1979; Marketing Environment, 1979; Retail Geography, 1980; Commercial Distribution in Europe, 1982; Teach Yourself Geography, 1983; Shopping Centre Development, 1983; Computer Methods for Geographers, 1985; Retailing in Scoland 2005, 1988; Evolution of European Retailing, 1988, Retailing Environments in Developing Countries, 1990; Competition and Markets, 1992; European Cases in Retailing, 1999; The Inernationalisation of Retailing in Asia, 2003; International Retailing Plans and Strategies in Asia, 2005; Strategic Issues in International Retailing, 2006. Recreations: sport; writing. Address:(b.) Edinburgh University, 50 George Square, Edinburgh; T.-0131-650 3827.

Dawson, Rev. Morag Ann, BD, MTh. Church of Scotland Minister, Galashiels, since 2003; b. 1.11.52, Gorebridge; 1

s.; 1 d. (twins). Educ. Greenhall High School; New College, School of Divinity, University of Edinburgh. Civil Servant (CO), Register House, Edinburgh, 1970-74; Strathclyde Police (HCO), Glasgow, 1974-79; Church of Scotland Minister, since 1999. Young Offenders Institution, Falkirk; P/T Chaplain, Kilmarnock Prison. Recreations: rugby; music; reading; walking. Address: (h.) 8 Mossilee Road, Galashiels, Scottish Borders TD1 1NF; T.-01896 752420; e-mail: moragdawson@yahoo.co.uk

Dawson, Peter, MA. Secretary, Royal and Ancient Golf Club of St Andrews, since 1999; b. 28.5.48, Aberdeen. Educ. Corpus Christi College, Cambridge. Address: (b.) Royal and Ancient Golf Club of St Andrews, Fife KY16 9JD.

Dawson Scott, Robert, MA, MLitt. Theatre critic, The Times; Freelance writer on cultural affairs; Producer and Director, Lion Television; b. 24.7.56, London; 3 d. Educ. Oxford University; Strathclyde University. Formerly Head of Content, scotsman.com. Founder of Critics Awards for Theatre in Scotland (CATS). Recreations: skiing; hill-walking. Address: (b.) 6 Westercraigs, Glasgow G31 2HZ; T.-0141-554 7106.

Deakins, Professor David Arthur, BSc(Econ.), BA(Bus. Studs.), MA(Bus. Econ.), FRSA. Professor of Enterprise Development, University of the West of Scotland, since 1994, Campus Director, Dumfries; b. 5.1.50, Cheshire; m., June Patricia Eglen; 1 s.; 2 d. Educ. Sutton Secondary Modern Boys' School; University of London (External Degree); University of Essex. Lecturer: Rothenham College of Technology, 1975-81, Chelmsford College of Further Education, 1981-88, University of Central England, Birmingham, 1988-94. President, Institute for Small Business Affairs, 1999-2002. Publications: Entrepreneurship and Small Firms (4th edition), 2005; Entrepreneurship in the Nineties, 1997. Recreations: cycling; walking; mountain biking. Address: (b.) University of the West of Scotland, Dumfries Campus, Maxwell House, Dumfries DG1 4UQ; T.-01387-702-075.

Dean, (Catherine) Margaret, MA, JP. Lord Lieutenant of Fife, since 1999; b. 16.11.39, Edinburgh; m., Brian Dean; 3 d. Educ. George Watson's Ladies' College; Edinburgh University. Teacher of English; Past Chairman, Dunfermline Heritage Trust. Recreations: bridge; theatre; family (grandchildren); walking. Address: (h.) Viewforth, 121 Rose Street, Dunfermline KY12 0QT; T.-01383 722488.

Deans, Rev. Dr. Graham Douglas Sutherland, MA, BD(Hons), MTh (Oxon), DMin. Minister at Aberdeen: Queen Street, since 2008; Parish Minister, South Ronaldsay and Burray, 2002-08; b. 15.8.53, Aberdeen; m., Marina Punler. Educ. Mackie Academy, Stonehaven; University of Aberdeen; Westminster College, Oxford; Pittsburgh Theological Seminary Winner of Richard J Rapp Memorial Prize, 2006. Assistant Minister, Craigsbank Parish Church, Corstorphine, 1977-78; Parish Minister: Denbeath with Methilhill, 1978-87, St. Mary's Parish Church, Dumfries, 1987-2002. Depute Clerk and Treasurer, Presbytery of Kirkcaldy, 1981-87; Chaplain, Randolph Wemyss Memorial Hospital, 1980-87; Moderator, Presbytery of Dumfries and Kirkcudbright, 1994-95; Convener: Committee on Glebes, 1991-92, Committee on Music and Worship, 1993-96, Committee on the Maintenance of the Ministry, 1997-2000 (Vice-Convener, 1991-96), Committee on Ministry, 2000-02; Member: Assembly Committee on Probationers, 1991-97, Maintenance of the Ministry Committee, 1991-98, Board of Ministry, 1998-2002,

Ministry Support Committee, 1998-2001, Ministry Development Committee, 2001-02; Trustee, Housing and Loan Fund, 1999-2004; Member, Executive Committee, Hymn Society of Great Britain and Ireland, 1998-2001, and 2002-08. Publications: A History of Denbeath Church, 1980; Children's Addresses in the Expository Times, 1983, 1987 and 1988; Presbyterian Praise, 1999; contributions to Bulletin of the Hymn Society; contributor to Christian Hymns (new edition), 2004. Recreation: music. Address: 51 Osborne Place, Aberdeen AB25 2BX; T.-01224 646429.

Deans, Joyce Blair, CBE, DUniv, BArch, PPRIAS, RIBA, ACIArb, FRSA. Architect; President, Royal Incorporation of Architects in Scotland, 1991-93 (first woman President); b. 29.1.27, Glasgow; m., John Albert Gibson Deans; 2 s.; 2 d. Educ. Laurel Bank School for Girls; University of Strathclyde. Re-entered profession as Assistant, private practice, 1968; appointed Associate, 1972; established own practice, 1981. Elected Member, Council: Glasgow Institute of Architects, 1975-90 (first woman President, 1986-88); Royal Incorporation of Architects, 1979-95; first female Vice President, Royal Incorporation of Architects in Scotland, 1986-88; Member, Building Standards Advisory Committee, 1987-96; Chairman, BSAC (Research), 1988-96 (first woman); Chairman (first woman), Scottish Construction Industry Group, 1996-2001 (Member, since 1991); Director, Cairn Housing Association, 1988-99; Founder Member, Glasgow West Conservation Trust, 1987-2000; Governor: Laurel Bank School for Girls 1981-99, Board Member, Glasgow School of Art, 1986-98, (Vice Chairman (Estates) 1992-98); Vice Chairman of Court, Strathclyde University, 2000-03 (Member of Court, 1993-2003); elected to Management Council for Learning in Later Life Students' Association, Strathclyde University, 2003; elected President, Learning in Later Life Students' Association, 2004-06; elected Vice President, Royal Institute of British Architects, 1993-95, and 1999-2001; Member: RIBA Council, 1991-2001, Patrick Geddes Award Panel, since 1993; Industrial Assessor (Architecture) SHEFC, 1994-95; External Examiner, Part 3, since 1994; Member, Professors' Advisory Team, University of Strathclyde, since 1993; Member, MSc Management Advisory Board, University of Northumbria at Newcastle, 1997-2003. Founder Member and Chairman, Brookwood Computer Group, 2006; Member, Executive Council of Friends of Loch Lomond and the Trossachs, since 2007. Hon. DUniv (University of Strathclyde), 1996; MBE, 1989; CBE, 1999. Recreations: gardening; golf; walking; reading; theatre. Address: 11 South Erskine Park, Bearsden, Glasgow G61 4NA; T.-0141-942 6795.

Deans, Mungo Effingham, BSc(Econ), LLB. Resident Senior Immigration Judge, Asylum and Immigration Tribunal, since 2005; Regional Adjudicator, Immigration Appellate Authority, 1996-2005; part-time Legal Member, Immigration Appeal Tribunal, 2000-05; b. 25.5.56, Lytham St. Annes; m., Kathryn Atkinson; 3 s. Educ. Fettes College, Edinburgh; London School of Economics; University of Edinburgh. Admitted as Solicitor, 1981; Lecturer, Department of Law: Napier University, 1981-82, Dundee University, 1983-96; Chairman: Social Security Appeal Tribunals, 1989-99, Disability Appeal Tribunals, 1992-99; Immigration Adjudicator, 1994. Publication: Scots Public Law, 1995. Recreations: Scottish history; fine art. Address: (b.) Asylum and Immigration Tribunal, 5th Floor, Eagle Building, 215 Bothwell Street, Glasgow G2 7EZ; T.-0845 6000 877.

Dear, Graeme, PhD, BSc(Hons), HND. Managing Director, Marine Harvest (Scotland), 2000-04; Managing Director, Skretting UK & I, since 2004; b. 13.8.56, Forfar; m., Fiona; 2 s.; 1 d. Educ. Forfar Academy; Heriot Watt University. Fish Pathologist, Anglian Water, 1983-87; Fish Health Inspector, Department of Agriculture and Fisheries, Scotland, 1987-89; McConnell Salmon: Technical Director, 1989-90, Farms Director, 1991-94; Production Director, Marine Harvest, 1994-2000. Director: Scottish Quality Salmon, Scottish Salmon Producers Organisation. Recreations: golf; skiing; motorcycling; fishing. Address: (h.) 16 William Place, Scone, Perth; (b.) Skretting UK, Wincham, Northwich, Cheshire CW9 6DF; T.-01738 553898; e-mail: graeme.dear@skretting.com

Deary, Professor Ian John, BSc, PhD, MBChB, FRCPE, AFBPsS, MRCPsych, FBA, FRSE, FMedSci. Professor of Differential Psychology, University of Edinburgh, since 1995; b. 15.5.54, Carluke; m., Ann Marie Barclay; 1 s.; 2 d. Educ. Hamilton Academy; University of Edinburgh. House Officer, Royal Infirmary of Edinburgh, 1983-84; Senior House Officer in Psychiatry, Maudsley Hospital, London, 1984-85; Department of Psychology, University of Edinburgh: Lecturer, 1985-90, Senior Lecturer, 1990-92, Reader, 1992-95. Royal Society-Wolfson Research Merit Award, 2002-07. Publications: Looking Down on Human Intelligence; Intelligence – A Very Short Introduction; Personality Traits (Co-author); editor of two books on personality; over 300 refereed scientific papers, principally on human cognitive ability and cognitive ageing, and personality. Recreations: saxophone; lyric-writing; late Victorian novels; English Romantic composers; cycling; Motherwell F.C. Address: (b.) Department of Psychology, University of Edinburgh, 7 George Square, Edinburgh EH8 9JZ; T.-0131-650 3452; e-mail: I.Deary@ed.ac.uk

Delahunt, Jim, BA. Presenter, Setanta Sports, since 2006; Columnist, Sunday Herald, since 1999; b. 10.5.62, Irvine. Educ. St. Andrews Academy, Saltcoats; Glasgow Caledonian University. Reporter, Kilmarnock Free Press; Reporter, West Sound; Editor, Daily Winner; Night News Editor, Radio Clyde; Sub-Editor, The Sunday Times; Sub-Editor, Reporter then Presenter, Scottish Television, 1990-2006. Recreations: horse-racing; ex-amateur jockey; golf. Address: Setanta Sports, Pacific Quay, Glasgow G51 1PQ; T.-0141-300 3734.

Della Sala, Professor Sergio F., MD, PhD, FRSE. Professor of Human Cognitive Neuroscience; Hon. Consultant in Neurology, Edinburgh; b. 23.9.55. Chair of Neuropsychology, Aberdeen; Milan. Senior Neurologist, Milan teaching hospital; Head, Neuropsychology Unit, Veruno, Italy. Address: (b.) University of Edinburgh, 7 George Square, Edinburgh.

del Valle, José Luis. Chief Executive, ScottishPower, since 2007; m.; 4 c. Educ. Universidad Politécnica de Madrid; Massachusetts Institute of Technology (MIT); Harvard University. Joined Iberdrola in 2002. Prior to this, General Manager of Andaluza de Piritas, Senior Vice President of Banco Central, Executive Vice President of Banco Central Hispanoamericano, and at Santander Central Hispano, Executive Vice President and member of the Management Committee and Finance Director. Address: (b.) 1 Atlantic Quay, Glasgow G2 8SP; T.-0141 248 8200.

Demarco, Professor Richard, CBE, RSW, SSA, Hon. FRIAS, FRSA, DA, Hon. DFA, ACA, Hon. LLD (Dundee). Artist and Writer; Director, Richard Demarco Gallery, since 1966; b. 9.7.30, Edinburgh; m., Anne Muckle. Educ. Holy Cross Academy, Edinburgh; Edinburgh College of Art. National Service, KOSB, 1954-56; Art Master, Duns Scotus Academy, Edinburgh, 1957-67; Vice-Chairman, Board, Traverse Theatre Club, 1963-67; Director, Sean Connery's Scottish International Education Trust, 1972-73; Member:

Board of Governors, Carlisle School of Art, 1970-74; Edinburgh Festival Society, 1971-86; Contributing Editor, Studio International, 1982-84; External Assessor, Stourbridge College of Art, 1988-90; Artistic Director, European Youth Parliament, since 1993; Professor of European Cultural Studies, Kingston University, since 1993; Director, Demarco European Art Foundation, since 1993; Trustee, Kingston-Demarco European Cultural Foundation, since 1993; Honorary Member, Scottish Arts Club; Elected Member, L'Association International des Critiques D'Art (AICA), 1994. Awards: Gold Order of Merit, Polish People's Republic; Chevalier de L'Ordre Des Arts Et Des Lettres; Order of Cavaliere Della Republica d'Italia; Scottish Arts Council Award for services to Scotland's visual arts, 1975; Medal, International Theatre Institutes of Great Britain and Poland, 1992; Honorary Doctorate, Atlanta College of Art, 1993; Arts Medal, Royal Philosophical Society of Glasgow, 1995; appointed Commander, Military and Hospitaller Order of St. Lazarus of Jerusalem, 1996. Publications: The Road to Meikle Seggie; The Artist as Explorer; A Life in Pictures; Kunst=Kapital: The Adam Smith Lecture, 1995; Honouring Colmcille, 1997. Recreation: walking "The Road to Meikle Seggie".

Dempsey, Steve BSc, MSc. Headteacher, Brechin High School, since 2004; b. 2.2.54, Dungannon, Co. Tyrone. Educ. Royal School, Dungannon; Edinburgh University; Sheffield University; Moray House College of Education. Teacher of Physics, Wallace High School, Stirling, 1978-82; Auchmuty High School, Glenrothes: APT Science, 1982-86, PT Physics, 1986-95; Assistant Headteacher, Banff Academy, 1995-2001; Deputy Headteacher, Wick High School, 2001-03. Recreations: football; reading. Address: (b.) Duke Street, Brechin DD9 6LB; T.-01356 622135; e-mail: BREDempseyS@brechinhigh.angus.sch.uk

Dempster, Alastair Cox, CBE, FCIBS. Chairman, Scottish Community Foundation, 1996-2005; Chairman, sportscotland, 1999-2005; b. 22.6.40, Glasgow; m., Kathryn; 2 s. Educ. Paisley Grammar School. Royal Bank of Scotland, 1955-62; various managerial appointments, Scotland, Hong Kong, New York, 1962-81; AGM, International Division, Royal Bank of Scotland, 1981-86; Director of Commercial Banking and International/Executive Director, TSB Scotland plc, 1986-91; TSB Bank Channel Islands Ltd.: Chief Executive, 1991-92; Deputy Chairman, 1992-96; Chief Executive, Lloyds TSB Bank Scotland, 1992-98. Chairman, Committee of Scottish Clearing Bankers, 1993-95; President, Chartered Institute of Bankers in Scotland, 1995-97; Member, Scottish Council Development and Industry and Executive Committee, 1992-98; Convener, Heriot Watt Audit Committee; Member, Heriot Watt University Court, 1993-99; Director, Scottish Homes, 1994-98; Director, Office of the Banking Ombudsman; Director, Scottish Financial Enterprise, 1994-98; Chairman, St Andrews Links Trust Glasgow Housing Association (Funding) Ltd.; Director, Scottish Equity Partnership; Chairman, Aberforth Geared Income Capital Trust plc, since 2001; Chairman, Deanway Developments plc; Director, South Facing Furnishings Ltd.; Member, Glasgow Housing Association; Member, UK Sports Council, 1999-2005. Recreations: golf; tennis; bridge. Address: (h.) Dalshian, 8 Harelaw Road, Edinburgh EH13 0DR; T.-0131-441 5202.

Dempster, Harriet, MA (Hons), MSc, Dip. Social Work. Director of Social Work, Highland Council, since 1999; b. 31.3.52, Sheffield; m., Ian Dempster; 1 s.; 1 d. Educ. McLaren High, Callander; Edinburgh University; Dundee University; Stirling University. Researcher, Tayside Health Board, 1987-90; Principal Officer, Tayside Region, 1990-92; Assistant Chief Inspector,

Scottish Office Social Work Services Inspectorate, 1992-96; Head of Children's Services, Dundee City Council, 1996-99. Associate Editor, Child Abuse Review, 1990-99; Honorary Professor, Social Work Research Centre, Stirling University; Executive Member, Association of Directors of Social Work Children and Families Committee; Member, Board, Dundee Contemporary Arts. Recreations: keep-fit; films; art. Address: (b.) The Highland Council, Glenurquhart Road, Inverness IV3 5NX; e-mail: harriet.dempster@highland.gov.uk

Denholm, Alastair Kennedy, DUniv (Glasgow), FUniv (Caledonian), FCIBS, FEI, MStJ; b. 27.9.36, Glasgow; m., Rosalind Murray Hamilton. Educ. Hutchesons' (Boys) Grammar School. Clydesdale Bank PLC, 1953-91; Managing Director, Quality Management Advisers (Scotland), 1992-98; Director, The Prince's Scottish Youth Business Trust, since 1985; Member, Board, Central College of Commerce, 1991-2003; Governor, Hutchesons' Grammar School, since 1996, Chairman of Governors, since 2003; Director, Hutchesons' School, Trust and Club 1995 Ltd.; Director, Laurel Park School Co. Ltd., since 2001; Lord Dean of Guild, Merchants House of Glasgow, 2001-03; Director, Ship Venture Ltd., since 2001; Hon. President, Chartered Institute of Marketing, since 2003; Lay Member, Audit Registration Committee, Institute of Chartered Accountants of Scotland, since 1995; Director, Glasgow Bute Benevolent Society, since 1980; Director, Glasgow Native Benevolent Society, since 1991; Governor, Glasgow Caledonian University (including its founding organisation), 1978-95; Deacon, Incorporation of Hammermen, 1988-89; Chairman, Glasgow Junior Chamber of Commerce, 1976-77; President, Association of Deacons of the Fourteen Incorporated Trades of Glasgow, 2003-04; Treasurer, Action for Disaster, 1973-95; Chairman, Chartered Institute of Bankers in Scotland, Glasgow, 1987-88; Director, Glasgow Chamber of Commerce, 1994-97; Treasurer and Elder, Williamwood Parish Church of Scotland, since 1962; District Governor, Rotary International District 1230, 1999-2000; HOEC Treasurer, Rotary International World Conference 1997, 1996-98. Recreations: golf; curling; Rotary. Address: (h.) Whitley, 28 Milverton Road, Whitecraigs, Glasgow G46 7JN; T.-0141-638 2939.

Denholm, James Allan, CBE, CA, FRSA. Chairman, Scottish Provident Institution Supervisory Committee, 2001-04; Director, William Grant & Sons Ltd., 1975-96; Director, Scottish Mutual Assurance Society, 1987-2003 (Deputy Chairman, 1992-2003); Director, Scottish Cremation Society Limited, since 1980; Director, Abbey National plc, 1992-97; Director, Abbey National Life plc, 1994-2003, Member, 2001-04; Chairman of Trustees, Scottish Mutual Assurance Staff Pension Fund, 2003-06; Chairman of Trustees, Scottish Provident Institution Staff Pension Fund, 2001-06; Trustee, Institute of Chartered Accountants of Scotland Staff Pension Fund, until 2006; b. 27.9.36, Glasgow; m., Elizabeth Avril McLachlan, CA; 1 s.; 1 d. Educ. Hutchesons' Boys Grammar School, Glasgow; Institute of Chartered Accountants of Scotland. Apprenticed, McFarlane Hutton & Patrick, CA, Glasgow (Sir William McLintock prizeman); Chief Accountant, A. & W. Smith & Co. Ltd., Glasgow, 1960-66; Secretary, William Grant & Sons Ltd., 1968-96; Chairman, East Kilbride Development Corporation, 1983-94 (Member, since 1979). Council Member, Institute of Chartered Accountants of Scotland, 1978-83, 1989-93 (President, 1992-93); Director and Treasurer, Glasgow YMCA, 1966-79; Chairman, Glasgow Junior Chamber of Commerce, 1972-73; Elder, New Kilpatrick Parish Church, since 1971; Visitor of the Incorporation of Maltmen in Glasgow, 1980-81; President, The Deacons' Association of Glasgow, 1994-95; Preses, The Weavers' Society of Anderston, 1994-95; Deacon, Society of Deacons and Free Preses of Glasgow,

1999-00; Patron, Royal Incorporation of Hutchesons Hospital, 1998-2006; President, 49 Wine and Spirit Club of Scotland, 1983-84; Director, Association for the Relief of Incurables, West of Scotland, since 1999; President, The Nomads Club, 1998-99; Fellow, Society of Antiquaries of Scotland, since 1987; Deacon Convener, The Trades House of Glasgow, 1998-99; Chairman, The Western Club of Glasgow, 2004-05. Recreations: shooting; golf. Address: (h.) Greencroft, 19 Colquhoun Drive, Bearsden, Glasgow G61 4NQ; T.-0141-942 1773.

Denney, Alan Alexander, National Secretary, Scotland, Prospect (formerly IPMS), since 1990; b. 25.1.57, Stirling; m., Jacqueline May; 2 s.; 1 d. Educ. Plaistow Grammar School; East Ham College of Technology. Civil Service (Department of Trade), 1975-78; Prospect (formerly IPMS) since 1979. Address: (b.) Suite 4, Glenorchy House, 20 Union Street, Edinburgh GH1 3LR; T.-0131 558 5288; e-mail: alan.denney@prospect.org.uk

Dennis, Roy, MBE. Wildlife Consultant/Ornithologist; Specialist, species recovery projects, UK and overseas; Director, Highland Foundation for Wildlife, since 1996; b. 4.5.40. Educ. Price's School. Migration Research Assistant, UK Bird Observatories, 1958-59; Warden, Lochgarten Osprey Reserve, 1960-63; Warden, Fair Isle Bird Observatory, 1963-70; Highland Officer, RSPB, 1971-87, Regional Officer (North Scotland), 1987-91; Main Board Member, Scottish Natural Heritage, 1992-97; Director, Cairngorms Partnership, 1995-97; Member, Deer Commission for Scotland, 1999-2002. Publications: Ospreys and Speyside Wildlife; Birds of Badenoch and Strathspey; Puffins; Ospreys; Peregrine Falcons; Divers; The Loch; Golden Eagles. Recreations: travel; photography; cross-country skiing; bird-watching. Address: The Glebe, Dunphail, Forres, Moray IV36 2QH; e-mail: roydennis@aol.com; website: www.roydennis.org

Denniston, Rev. David William, BD, DipMin. Minister, North Church, Perth, since 1996; b. 23.4.56, Glasgow; m., Jane Ross; 2 s.; 1 d. Educ. Hutchesons' Boys Grammar School, Glasgow; University of Glasgow. Minister: Ruchazie Parish Church, Glasgow, 1981-86, Kennoway, Fife, 1986-96. Recreations: hill-walking; fishing; music. Address: (h.) 127 Glasgow Road, Perth PH2 0LU; T.-01738 625728; e-mail: david.denniston@ blueyonder.co.uk

Dent, John Anthony, MMEd, MD, ILTM, FRCS (Edin). Reader and Honorary Consultant, Orthopaedic and Trauma Surgery, University of Dundee, since 1990; b. 4.3.53, Kendal; m., Frances Jane Wyllie; 1 s.; 1 d. Educ. Haversham Grammar School, Cumbria; University of Dundee. Hand Research Fellow, Princess Margaret Rose Orthopaedic Hospital, Edinburgh; Christine Kleinert Hand Fellow, University of Louisville, Kentucky, USA; co-established Dundee Hand Surgery Service, Ninewells Hospital, Dundee; undergraduate teaching, Clinical Skills Centre; has worked in curriculum development and implementation, University of Dundee Medical School, since 1997; External Examiner: University of Brighton, 1995-98, University of Sunderland, 1998-2001, University of East Anglia, since 2003. Member, Examinations Committee, Royal College of Surgeons of Edinburgh, since 1997; Member, National Panel of Specialists for Training in Orthopaedic and Trauma Surgery, 1993-2000; Guest Lecturer: University of Gezira, Sudan, 1996, and to Association of Surgeons of India, Bombay, 1996. Publications: papers on upper limb surgery and medical education; The Musculoskeletal System: Core Topics in the New Curriculum (Co-Author/Editor), 1997; Churchill's Mastery of Medicine: Surgery 2 (Co-Author/Editor), 2nd ed, 2002; A Practical Guide for Medical Teachers (Co-Editor), 2nd ed, 2005. Recreations: heraldry; history; gardens. Address: (b.) University Department of Orthopaedic Surgery, Ninewells Hospital and Medical School, Dundee DD1 9SY; T.-01382 633937; e-mail: j.a.dent@dundee.ac.uk

Deregowski, Professor Jan Bronislaw, BSc, BA, PhD, DSc, FBPsS, FRSE. Professor of Psychology, Aberdeen University, since 1986 (Reader, 1981-86); b. 1.3.33, Pinsk, Poland; m., Eva Loft Nielsen; 2 s.; 1 d. Educ. London University. Lecturer, then Senior Lecturer, Aberdeen University, 1969-81. Publications: Illusions, Patterns and Pictures: a cross-cultural perspective; Distortion in Art; Perception and Artistic Style (Co-author). Address: (b.) Department of Psychology, King's College, Old Aberdeen AB24 2UB; T.-Aberdeen 272246; e-mail: j.b.deregowski@abdn.ac.uk

Dervaird, Hon. Lord (John Murray), MA (Oxon), LLB (Edin), FCIArb. Professor Emeritus, Edinburgh University, since 1999; Dickson Minto Professor of Company Law, Edinburgh University, 1990-99 (Dean, Faculty of Law, 1994-96); b. 8.7.35, Stranraer; m., Bridget Jane Godfrey; 3 s. Educ. Stranraer schools; Edinburgh Academy; Corpus Christi College, Oxford; Edinburgh University. Advocate, 1962; QC, 1974; Law Commissioner (part-time), 1979-88; Senator of the College of Justice, 1988-89; Chairman, Scottish Council for International Arbitration, 1989-2003; Member, London Court of International Arbitration, since 1990; Trustee, David Hume Institute, since 1992; Member, ICC Committee on Business Law, Paris, since 1992; Chairman, BT Scottish Ensemble, 1988-99; Member: City Disputes Panel, since 1994, Panel of Arbitrators, International Centre for Settlement of Investment Disputes, 1998-2003, Advisory Board International Arbitration, Paris, since 2000; Hon. President, Advocates' Business Law Group, since 1988; Chairman, Edinburgh Wigtownshire Association, since 1997; Hon. Vice President, Advanced Technology Arbitration, Paris, since 2000. Publications: Stair Encyclopaedia of Scots Law (Contributor); articles on legal and ornithological subjects. Recreations: farming; gardening; bird-watching; music; curling. Address: (h.) Auchenmalg House, Auchenmalg, Glenluce, Wigtownshire.

Devereux, Alan Robert, CBE, DL, CEng, MIEE, CBIM. Chairman, Scottish Ambulance Service NHS Trust, 1995-97; Founder, Quality Scotland Foundation; International Director, Gleneagles PLC, 1990-2001; Director, Scottish Mutual Assurance Society, 1976-2003; Director, Abbey National Life, 1999-2003; Chairman, Mission Aviation Fellowship, since 2004; b. 18.4.33, Frinton-on-Sea; m., 1, Gloria Alma Hair (deceased); 1 s.; 2, Elizabeth Tormey Docherty. Educ. Colchester School; Clacton County High School; Mid Essex Technical College. Marconi's Wireless Telegraph Company: apprentice, 1950-55, Standards Engineer, 1955-56; Technical Production Manager, Halex Division, British Xylonite Company, 1956-58; Technical Sales Manager, SPA Division, Sanitas Trust, 1958-65; General Manager, Dobar Engineering, 1965-67; various managerial posts, Norcros Ltd., 1967-69; Group Managing Director, Scotcros Ltd., 1969-78; Deputy Chairman, Scotcros Ltd., 1978-80. CBI: Chairman, Scotland, 1977-79 (Deputy Chairman, 1975-77), Council Member, 1972-84, Member, President's Advisory Committee, 1979; UK Regional Chairman, 1979; Chairman, Small Industries Council for Rural Areas of Scotland, 1975-77; Member, Scottish Development Agency, 1977-83; Chairman, Scottish Tourist Board, 1980-90; Director, Children's Hospice Association for Scotland; Scottish Free Enterprise Award, 1978; Deputy Lieutenant, Renfrewshire, since 1985. Recreations: walking; charities; clock restoration. Address: (h.) South Fell, 24 Kirkhouse Road, Blanefield, Glasgow G63 9BX; T.-0360 770464.

Devine, Jim. MP (Labour), Livingston, since 2005; b. 21.5.53; m.; 2 c. Chairman, Scottish Labour Party, 1994-95. Address: (b.) House of Commons, London SW1A 0AA.

Devine, Rt. Rev. Joseph, PhD. Bishop of Motherwell, since 1983; b. 7.8.37, Glasgow. Educ. St. Mary's College, Blairs, Aberdeen; St. Peter's College, Cardross; Pontifical Scots College, Rome. Ordained Priest, Glasgow, 1960; Private Secretary to Archbishop of Glasgow, 1964-65; Assistant Priest, St. Robert Bellarmine, Glasgow, 1965-67; St. Joseph's, Helensburgh, 1967-72; on staff, St. Peter's College, Cardross, 1967-74; Assistant Chaplain, Catholic Chaplaincy, Glasgow University, 1974-77; nominated Titular Bishop of Voli, and Auxiliary Bishop to Archbishop of Glasgow, 1977. President, Catholic Education Commission. Recreations: reading; watching sport. Address: (b.) Diocesan Centre, Coursington Road, Motherwell ML1 1PP; T.-01698 269114.

Devine, Professor Thomas Martin, OBE, BA, PhD, DLitt (Strathclyde), Hon DLitt (Queen's Belfast), Hon DLitt (Abertay, Dundee), Hon DUniv (Strathclyde), FRHistS, FRSE, HonMRIA, FBA. Sir William Fraser Professor of Scottish History, University of Edinburgh, since 2006; Glucksman Research Professor in Irish and Scottish Studies and Director, Research Institute of Irish and Scottish Studies, Aberdeen University, 1998-2003; Director, Arts and Humanities Research Council, Centre for Irish and Scottish Studies, 2001-05; b. 30.07.46, Motherwell; m., Catherine Mary Lynas; 2 s. of whom 1 deceased; 3 d. Educ. Our Lady's RC High School, Motherwell; Strathclyde University. Strathclyde University: Lecturer, then Senior Lecturer and Reader, Department of History, 1969-88 (Head of Department, 1990-92), Dean, Faculty of Arts and Social Sciences, 1993-94, Deputy Principal, 1994-97, Professor of Scottish History, 1988-98, Director of Research Centre in Scottish History, 1994-98; Visiting Professor, University of Guelph, Canada, 1983 and 1988 (Adjunct Professor in History, since 1988); Adjunct Professor in History, University of North Carolina; Governor, St. Andrews College of Education, 1990-94. Joint Founding Editor, Scottish Economic and Social History, 1980-84. British Academy/Leverhulme Trust Senior Research Fellow, 1992-93; Trustee, National Museums of Scotland, 1995-2002; Member, RAE Panel in History, 1992, 1996; Member, Council, British Academy, 1999-2001; Convener, Irish-Scottish Academic Initiative, 1998-2002; Chair, Joint Working Party, NMS and NTS, Museum of Scottish Country Life, 1999-2003; Member, Advisory Group, Glasgow City of Architecture and Design, 1999; Member, Secretary of State for Scotland's Advisory Committee, Friends of Scotland Initiative, 2001-03; Member, Scottish Council on Archives, since 2002; Member, Advisory Committee on ESRC Devolution Programme; Member, Research Awards Advisory Committee, The Leverhulme Trust; Trustee, Edinburgh City of Literature, since 2005; Winner: Senior Hume Brown Prize, 1977, Agnes Mure MacKenzie Prize for Scottish Historical Research, Saltire Society, 1992, Henry Duncan Prize, Royal Society of Edinburgh, 1995; Royal Gold Medal, Royal Society of Edinburgh, 2001; Hon. Fellowship, Bell College of Higher Education, 2005; John Aitkenhead Medal, Institute of Contemporary Scotland, 2006; Member, Academy of Merit, Institute of Contemporary Scotland, 2006. Publications: The Tobacco Lords, 1975; Lairds and Improvement in Enlightenment Scotland, 1979; Ireland and Scotland 1600-1850 (Co-Editor), 1983; Farm Servants and Labour in Lowland Scotland 1770-1914, 1984; A Scottish Firm in Virginia 1767-77, 1984; People and Society in Scotland 1760-1830 (Co-Editor), 1988; The Great Highland Famine, 1988; Improvement and Enlightenment (Editor), 1989; Conflict and Stability in Scottish Sociey (Editor), 1990; Irish Immigrants and Scottish Society in the Eighteenth and Nineteenth Centuries (Editor), 1991; Scottish Emigration and Scottish Society, 1992; Scottish Elites, 1993; The Transformation of Rural Scotland, 1994; Clanship to Crofters' War, 1994; Industry, Business and Society in Scotland since 1700 (Co-Editor), 1994; Glasgow: I, Beginnings to 1830, 1995; St. Mary's, Hamilton: a social history; Exploring the Scottish Past, 1995; Scotland in the Twentieth Century (Co-Editor), 1996; Eighteenth Century Scotland: New Perspectives (Co-Editor), 1998; The Scottish Nation, 1700-2000, 1999; Celebrating Columba – Irish-Scottish Connections 597-1997 (Co-Editor), 1999; Scotland's Shame? – Bigotry and Sectarianism in Modern Scotland, 2000; Being Scottish – Personal Reflections on Scottish Identity Today, 2002; Scotland's Empire, 1600-1815, 2003; The Transformation of Scotland (Co-Editor), 2005; The Scottish Nation, 1700-2007, 2006; Clearance and Improvement: Land, Power and People in Scotland, 1600-1900, 2006; Scotland and the Union, 1707-2007 (Editor), 2007. Recreations: grandchildren; walking and exploring the Hebrides; watching skilful football; travelling in the Mediterranean. Address: (b.) Scottish History (School of History, Classics and Archaeology), University of Edinburgh, Edinburgh EH8 9LN.

de Vink, Peter Henry John, BComm. Managing Director, Edinburgh Financial and General Holdings Ltd., since 1978; b. 9.10.40, Amsterdam; m., Julia Christine (Krista) Quarles van Ufford (deceased); 1 s.; 1 d. Educ. Edinburgh University. National Service, Dutch Army, 1961-63; Edinburgh University, 1963-66; Ivory and Sime Investment Managers, 1966-78, latterly as Director. Address: (b.) 3A Charlotte Square, Edinburgh EH2 4DR; T.-0131-225 6661; (h.) Huntly Cot, Temple, Midlothian EH23 4TS; T.-01875 830345.

Dewar, Alan Robert, LLB (Hons). Queen's Counsel, since 2002; Advocate, since 1989; b. 9.12.56, Edinburgh; m., Katherine Margaret Dewar; 1 s.; 2 d. Educ. Lasswade High School, Midlothian; Dundee University. Solicitor in private practice, 1982-88 (Partner in law firm, 1986-88); Writer to the Signet, since 1986; Advocate Depute, 1996-99; Standing Junior Counsel to various Government departments, including Scotland Office, 2000-02. Recreations: golf; football; squash; jazz. Address: (h.) 6 Crawfurd Road, Edinburgh; T.-0131 667 1810; e-mail: AlanRDewar@aol.com

Dewar, Gordon, MBA (Dist), BSc (Hons) MILT. Managing Director, BAA Glasgow Airport, since 2007; b. 23.3.66, Edinburgh; 2 d. Educ. Forrester High School; Strathclyde University; London School of Economics. Associate, Halcrow, 1995-99; First Group: Business Development Manager, 1999-2001, Managing Director, 2001-02, Commercial Director, 2002-04; Commercial Director: First Scotrail, 2004-06, Arriva, 2006-07. Recreations: 5-a-side football; squash; badminton; swimming. Address: (b.) BAA Glasgow Airport, Paisley PA3 2SW; T.-0141-8484500.

Dewar-Durie, Andrew Maule, CBE, DL. Chairman, Sea Fish Industry Authority, 2002-07 (Deputy Chairman, 2000-02); b. 13.11.39, Bath; m., Marguerite Kottulinsky; 2 s.; 1 d. Educ. Wellington College. Regular soldier, Argyll and Sutherland Highlanders, 1958-68, retiring with rank of Captain; Export Representative to Senior Export Director, White Horse Distillers, 1968-83; International Sales Director, Long John International, 1983-87; James Burrough Distillers: International Sales Director, 1987-89, Managing Director, 1990; Chief Executive Officer, James Burrough Ltd., 1990-91; Allied Distillers Ltd.: Managing Director, 1991-97, Chairman, 1997-99. Deputy Lieutenant, Dunbartonshire, since 1996; CBI Scotland: Council

Member, 1993, Vice Chairman, 1996, Chairman, 1997-99; Non-Executive Director, Britannic Asset Management, 2001-04; Keeper of the Quaich, since 1989, Master, since 1992; Liveryman, Worshipful Company of Distillers, since 1986; President, Edinburgh Royal Warrant Holders Association, 1999-2000; Director, Edinburgh Military Tattoo, since 2000. Recreations: tennis; rough shooting; sailing; theatre; cinema. Address: Finnich Malise, Croftamie, West Stirlingshire G63 0HA; T.-0136 066 0257.

Dewhurst, Professor David, BSc, PhD. Professor of e-learning; Director of Learning Technology, College of Medicine and Veterinary Medicine, University of Edinburgh, since 1999, formerly Assistant Principal (e-learning and e-health); b. 27.2.50, Crewe; 2 s. Educ. Crewe County Grammar School; Sheffield University. Lecturer, University of Sheffield; Lecturer/Senior Lecturer, Sheffield Hallam University; Principal Lecturer/Professor of Health Sciences, Leeds Metropolitan University. Address: (b.) Learning Technology Section, College of Medicine and Veterinary Medicine, University of Edinburgh, 15 George Square, Edinburgh EH8 9XD; T.-0131 6511564; e-mail: d.dewhurst@ed.ac.uk

Dewing, Irene Isabel Joan, DL; b. 21.9.36, Inverness; m., William Beresford Dewing; 2 d. Educ. Heatherley, Inverness. Deputy Lieutenant. Address: (h.) The Hollies, Kildary, Ross-Shire; T.-01862 842204.

Dhir, Rani, MBE, BA, DHS, FCIOH, FCIOB, FRSA. Executive Director, Drumchapel Housing Co-operative Ltd, since 1990; concurrently pursues wider interests at National Level in Business and Voluntary Community; Non Executive Director, Greater Glasgow and Clyde Health Board, since 2004; Chair, West Dunbartonshire Community Health Partnership, since 2006; Non Executive Director, Communities Scotland, since 2001; Chair, Communities Scotland Housing Regulation Board for Scotland, since 2008; Non-Executive Director, Lloyds TSB Scotland, 2000-05; b. Dundee. Educ. Morgan Academy, Dundee. First Degree, BA Business Studies; Post Graduate Diploma, Personnel and Development; Post Graduate Diploma, Housing. Pursued career in housing in Glasgow, in Independent Social Housing Sector; Pioneer in Community Ownership Housing in Scotland. Trustee, PATH (Scotland) Ltd., since 2006; Trustee, Ankur Arts, since 2007; Trustee, Lloyds TSB Foundation for Scotland, 1999-2005. Address: (b.) Drumchapel Housing Co-operative Ltd, 4 Kinclaven Avenue, Glasgow G15 7SP; T.-0141 944 4902.
E-mail: enquiries@drumchapelhc.org.uk

Di Rollo, Simon Ronald, QC, LLB (Hons). Advocate, since 1987; b. 28.10.61, Edinburgh; m., Alison Margaret Lafferty; 1 s.; 1 d. Educ. Holy Cross Academy; Scotus Academy; Edinburgh University. Admitted to Faculty of Advocates, 1987; Advocate Depute, 1997-2000. Recreations: Italian; cooking; walking; golf. Address: (b.) Advocates' Library, Parliament House, Edinburgh EH1 1RF.

Dick, David, OBE, BA (Hons), MLitt, DIC, CEng, FIET. Managing Director, Clerkington Publishing Co. Ltd., 1997-2003; b. 20.3.29, Edinburgh; m., Muriel Elsie Margaret Buchanan; 5 d. Educ. Boroughmuir School, Edinburgh; Heriot-Watt College, Edinburgh; Imperial College, London; Open University; University of Dundee. Electrical Engineer, North of Scotland Hydro-Electric Board, 1951-54; Lecturer, Dundee College of Technology, 1954-60; Head, Department of Electrical Engineering, Coatbridge

Technical College, 1960-64; Depute Principal, Napier College of Science and Technology, Edinburgh, 1964-69; Principal, Stevenson College of Further Education, Edinburgh, 1969-87. Manpower Services Commission: Chairman, Lothian District Manpower Committee, 1981-82, Member, Lothian and Borders Area Manpower Board, 1982-85; Member and Chairman, various committees: Scottish Technical Education Council, Scottish Business Education Council, 1969-87; Member and Chairman, Fire Services Examination Board (Scotland), 1968-86; Member, Construction Industry Training Board, 1976-85; Member, Electrical Engineering Services Committee, CITB, 1976-88; Member, General Convocation, Heriot-Watt University, Edinburgh, 1970-73; Past Chairman, Scottish Committee, Institution of Electronic and Radio Engineers; former Honorary President, Edinburgh and District Spastics Association; Lay Inspector of Fire Services for Scotland, 1994-99. Publications: Capital Walks in Edinburgh – The New Town, 1994; Street Biographies of the Royal Burgh of Haddington, 1997; Who was Who in the Royal Mile, Edinburgh, 1997; Who was Who in Durban Street Names, 1998; A Scottish Electrical Enlightenment (Editor), 2000; A Millennium of Fame of East Lothian, 2000. Recreations: music (flute); gardening; writing historical biographies. Address: (h.) West Lodge, Clerkington, near Haddington, East Lothian.

Dick, Dennis J.N. Chairman, Scottish Wildlife Trust, since 2005; b. 1.10.34, Dundee; m., Mary Willis; 1 s. Educ. Gordonstoun; Stirling High School. Journalist, DC Thomson, Dundee, 1956-58; Writer, Weekly Scotsman, Edinburgh, 1958-59; Publicity, BBC Scotland, Edinburgh, 1959-60; PRO (including launch of the station), Grampian TV, Aberdeen, 1961; Journalist and TV Editor, Radio Times, BBC, London, 1961-70; PRO, BBC South and West of England, Bristol, 1970-78; TV Producer/Editor TV Features, BBC West, Bristol, 1978-84; Manager, BBC Aberdeen and Radio and Television Producer, BBC Scotland, 1984-88; Chairman/Managing Director, own TV company, Wildview Productions, Aberdeen/Little Brechin, 1988-93; produced and directed over 200 TV programmes; now retired. Burgess, City of Aberdeen; President, St. Andrews Probus Club, 2002-03; Vice-Chairman, Scottish Wildlife Trust, 2002-05; Representative Member, National Trust for Scotland Council, 2003-07. Recreations: working with wildlife; hill walking; gardening; website design; photography; travel. Address: (h.) 17 Fairmount Terrace, Perth PH2 7AS; T.-01738 783840; e-mail: ddick@wildview.info

Dick, Rev. John Hunter Addison, MA, MSc, BD. Parish Minister, Aberdeen: Ferryhill, since 1982; Master, Christ's College, Aberdeen, since 2004; b. 27.12.45, Dunfermline; 3 s. Educ. Dunfermline High School; Edinburgh University. Research Assistant, Department of Geography, Edinburgh University, 1967-70; Senior Tutor, Department of Geography, Queensland University, 1970-78; student of divinity, 1978-81; Assistant Minister, Edinburgh: Fairmilehead, 1981-82. Governor, Robert Gordon's College; Trustee, Aberdeen Endowments Trust. Recreations: music; painting; walking. Address: Ferryhill Manse, 54 Polmuir Road, Aberdeen AB11 7RT; T.-01224 586933.

Dickinson, Professor Harry Thomas, BA, DipEd, MA, PhD, DLitt, FRHistS, FRSE. Professor of British History, Edinburgh University, 1980-2006; Professor of British History, Nanjing University, since 1987; b. 9.3.39, Gateshead; m., Jennifer Elizabeth Galtry; 1 s.; 1 d. Educ. Gateshead Grammar School; Durham University; Newcastle University. Teacher of History, Washington Grammar School, 1961-64; Earl Grey Fellow, Newcastle University, 1964-66; History Department, Edinburgh University: Assistant Lecturer, 1966-68, Lecturer, 1968-73, Reader, 1973-80; Associate Dean (Postgraduate), 1992-96; Convener, Senatus PGS Committee, 1998-2001; Visiting

Professor, Nanjing University, China, 1980, 1983, 1985, 1987, 1994; Fulbright Scholar, 1973; Huntington Library Fellowship, 1973; Folger Shakespeare Library Fellowship, 1973; Winston Churchill Fellow, 1980; Leverhulme Award, 1986-87; Ahmanson Fellowship, UCLA, 1987; Anstey Lecturer, University of Kent, 1989; Douglas Southall Freeman Professor, University of Richmond, Virginia, 1987; Lewis Walpole Library Fellowship (Yale University), 2004, Chairman, Publications Committee, Historical Association, 1991-94; Vice-President, Royal Historical Society, 1991-95, 2003-05; President, Historical Association, 2002-05 (Vice President, 1995-97 and since 2005, Deputy President, 1997-98); Member, Humanities Committee, CNAA, 1991-93; National Auditor, Higher Education Quality Council, 1993-95; Team Assessor, History, TQA, SHEFC, 1995-96; Member, Marshall Aid Commonwealth Commission, 1987-96; Member, QAA History Subject Benchmarking Committee, 1998-99; Academic Auditor, QAA, 1997-2001; Academic Reviewer, QAA, 1998-2001; Chair, History Panel, Arts and Humanities Research Council, 2002-06; Member, History Panel, QCA, since 2003; Editor, History, 1993-2000. Publications: Bolingbroke; Walpole and the Whig Supremacy; Liberty and Property; British Radicals and the French Revolution; The Correspondence of Sir James Clavering; Politics and Literature in the 18th Century: The Political Works of Thomas Spence; Caricatures and the Constitution 1760-1832; Britain and the French Revolution; The Politics of the People in Eighteenth-century Britain; Britain and the American Revolution; The Challenge to Westminster (Co-Author); A Companion to Eighteenth-Century Britain; Constitutional Documents of the United Kingdom, 1782-1835; British pamphlets on the American Revolution, 4 vols.; many pamphlets, essays and reviews. Recreations: reading; films. Address: (h.) 44 Viewforth Terrace, Edinburgh EH10 4LJ; T.-0131-229 1379.

Dickson, Alan David James. Chief Executive, Capability Scotland, since 1997; b. 26.3.50, Leicester; m., Janet; 1 d. Educ. Worksop College Public School. Management training, Steetley Manufacturing; Divisional Manager, Help the Aged; Scottish Organiser, LEPRA; Assistant Director, then Depute Director, Scottish Council for Spastics, renamed Capability Scotland; President, Cerebral Palsy International Sports and Recreation Association; Member of The International Paralympic Governing Board Committees. Recreations: golf; cooking; reading. Address: (b.) Westerlea, Ellersly Road, Edinburgh EH12 6HY; T.-0131-337 9876.

Dickson, Alastair Ronald. Senior Partner, Dickson Minto WS, since 1985; b. 16.1.51, Glasgow; 2 s.; 1 d. Educ. Glenalmond College; Edinburgh University. Trained, Dundas & Wilson, 1971-73; Maclay, Murray & Spens, 1973-76; Dundas & Wilson, 1976-85 (Partner, from 1978); Founding Partner, Dickson Minto WS, 1985. Recreations: golf; squash; hill-walking; skiing. Address: (b.) 16 Charlotte Square, Edinburgh EH2 4DF; T.-0131-225 4455.

Dickson, Belinda Jane, OBE, BEd. Self-employed businesswoman; b. 15.9.59, Glasgow; 2 d. Educ. Bearsden Academy; Dunfermline College. Marketing Telephone Rentals, 1981-87; self-employed, since 1987; Entrepreneur of the Year, 2000; Scottish Businesswoman of the Year, 1999; Member, Board, UK Fashion Export Council; Honorary Degree, Napier University; Doctor of Letters. Recreations: skiing; squash; swimming; walking. Address: (b.) 13a Dundas Street, Edinburgh EH3 6QG; T.-0131 557 8118; e-mail: belinda@belindarobertson.co.uk

Dickson, Professor James Holms, BSc, MA, PhD, FLS, FRSE. Emeritus Professor, since 2002; Professor of Archaeobotany and Plant Systematics, Glasgow University, since 1998 (Reader in Botany, 1993-98); b. 29.4.37,

Glasgow; m. Camilla A. Lambert, 1 s.; 1 d. Educ. Bellahouston Academy; University of Glasgow; University of Cambridge. Fellow, Clare College, University of Cambridge, 1963-70; Lecturer then Senior Lecturer in Botany, University of Glasgow, 1970-93. Leader, Trades House of Glasgow Expedition to Papua, New Guinea, 1969; Consultant, Britoil, Glasgow Garden Festival, 1988; currently working on plant remains found with 5,300 year old Tyrolean Iceman, and with 550 year old British Columbian iceman. Neill Medallist, Royal Society of Edinburgh, 1996; twice Past President, Glasgow Natural History Society; Past President, Botanical Society of Scotland; Leverhulme Emeritus Fellow, 2006-07: "Archaeobiology of Ancient Icemen". Publications: five books, including The Changing Flora of Glasgow, and Plants and People in Ancient Scotland; many papers on Scottish flora, Ice Age plants, archaeobotany, the Tyrolean Iceman. Address: (b.) Graham Kerr Building, Glasgow University; T.-0141-330 4364.

Dickson, John (Iain) Anderson, BSc, DipArch, MaPS, RIBA, PPRIAS. Architect; Partner, George Watt & Stewart, Aberdeen, since 1980; President, Royal Incorporation of Architects in Scotland, 1999 2001, b. 28.5.51, Hamilton; m., Patricia Frances Whyte. Educ. Aberdeen Grammar School; Scott Sutherland School of Architecture, Robert Gordon's Institute of Technology, Aberdeen. Architectural Assistant: Department of Housing and Construction, Darwin, Australia, 1973-74, W.G. Crerar & Partners, Inverness, 1976-77; Architect, George Watt & Stewart, Aberdeen, 1977-80. Chairman, Kincardine and Deeside Area, British Field Sports Society, 1995-98; Senior Under Officer, Aberdeen University Officer Training Corps, 1973; Chairman, RIAS Practice Board, 1995-99; Member, RIBA Council, 1999-2001; Director, Aberdeenshire Housing Partnership, 1999-2004; Member, Scottish Construction Industry Group, 1999-2001; Member, Leadership Group, Scottish Enterprise Forestry Cluster, 2000; Member, Sounding Board, Scottish Executive Review of Scotland's Cities, 2001; Director, RIAS Insurance Services Ltd., 2002-04; Member, Advisory Board, Centre for Timber Engineering, Napier University, 2002-04; Member, Executive RIAS Insurance Services, since 2004. Recreations: field sports; fishing; shooting; good food; wine. Address: (b.) 24 North Silver Street, Aberdeen AB10 1RL; T.-01224 639232.

Dickson, Sheriff Robert Hamish, LLB, WS. Sheriff of South Strathclyde, Dumfries & Galloway at Airdrie, since 1988; b. 19.10.45, Glasgow; m., Janet Laird Campbell (deceased 2004); 1 s. Educ. Glasgow Academy; Drumtochty Castle; Glenalmond; Glasgow University. Solicitor, Edinburgh, 1969-71, and Glasgow, 1971-86; Partner, Brown Mair Gemmill & Hislop, Solicitors, Glasgow, 1973-86; appointed floating Sheriff of South Strathclyde, Dumfries & Galloway at Hamilton, 1986; President, Sheriffs' Association, 2006-08. Publication: Medical and Dental Negligence, 1997. Recreations: golf; music; reading. Address: (b.) Airdrie Sheriff Court, Airdrie; T. Airdrie 751121.

Dillon, J. Shaun H., DRSAM (Comp), FSA Scot. Professional Musician; Composer, Oboist and Teacher of Woodwind; b. 30.12.44, Sutton Coldfield. Educ. Berwickshire High School; Fettes College; Royal Scottish Academy of Music; Guildhall School of Music. Studied composition with Frank Spedding and Edmund Rubbra; awarded prize for composition for Leicestershire Schools Orchestra, 1965; commissions from various bodies, including Scottish Amateur Music Association; Instructor of Woodwind: Edinburgh Corporation, 1967-72, Aberdeen Corporation (latterly Grampian Region), 1972-81;

Freelance Musician, since 1981; sometime Director of Music, St. Mary's Cathedral, Aberdeen; two suites of Airs and Graces for strings published; Secretary, Association of Instrumental and Vocal Specialists, 1975-78; Scotland and Northern Ireland Region Council member of Musicians Union, since 2005. Recreations: reading, especially history, literature; crosswords; playing flute (badly) in ceilidh bands. Address: (b.) 34 Richmond Street, Aberdeen AB25 4TR; T.-01224 630954.

Dingwall, Thomas Stewart, BEd, FRSA. Rector, Larkhall Academy, b. 7.1.51, Hamilton; m., Maxine; 2 s. Educ. Airdrie Academy; Glasgow University; Jordanhill College of Education. Teacher of History, then Assistant Principal Teacher of Guidance, Airdrie Academy, 1973-80; Principal Teacher of Guidance, Abronhill High School, Cumbernauld, 1980-85; Assistant Headteacher, Caldervale High School, Airdrie, 1985-92; Depute Headteacher, Larkhall Academy, 1992-94. Recreations: family; gardening; now largely a passive interest in sport, notably rugby, golf, tennis. Address: (b.) Larkhall Academy, Cherryhill, Larkhall ML9 1QN; T.-01698 881570; e-mail: headteacher@larkhall.s-lanark.sch.uk

Dinning, Robert James (Fred), BSc (Eng), MBA, CEng, FEI, FIET, MCMI; b. 16.12.52; m., Elizabeth Johnstone; 2 s. Educ. Kilmarnock Academy; Glasgow University. Formerly Energy and Environment Director of the Scottish Power Group (retired at end of 2005). Board Member, Scottish Environment Protection Agency; Chair, Carbon Trust Consultant Accreditation Board; Chair, Edinburgh Research Partnership Energy JRI; Member, Sustainable Development Panel; Member, Church of Scotland Church and Society Council and convenor of Council sub group on energy and environmental issues. Member, Advisory Board, WWF Scotland. Fellow of the Energy Institute and member of its Scottish Committee. Delivered a wide range of lectures and speeches on energy and environment topics affecting the UK and Scotland. Recreations: keen cruising yachtsman, hillwalker and cyclist. Address: (h.) South Brae, Dunlop, Ayrshire KA3 4BP.

Disbury, Andrew Paul, BA (Hons), MBA. Director of Admissions, University of St. Andrews, since 2007; b. 05.03.62, Aylesbury; m., Mr. Yan Liu. Educ. Bridley Moor High School, Reditch. Educ. University of Leeds. Director of Education, British Council China; Education Promotion Manager, British Council China; Principal Lecturer in International Business, Sheffield Hallam University. Address: (b.) Admissions, University of St. Andrews, St. Katharine's West, 16 The Scores, St. Andrews, Fife KY16 9AX; T.-01334 463339; e-mail: andrew.disbury@st-andrews.ac.uk

Dixon, Dr. Richard, BSc (Hons), MSc (distinction), PhD. Director, WWF Scotland, since 2005; b. 22.3.64, Dublin, Ireland; partner: Vanessa Andrews; 2 step sons; 1 d. Educ. Exeter School; St. Andrews University; Edinburgh University; Glasgow Caledonian University. Development Officer, CSV Glasgow, 1992-94; Assistant Environmental Policy Officer, Strathclyde Regional Council, 1993-94; Head of Research, Friends of The Earth Scotland, 1994-2002; Head of Policy, WWF Scotland, 2002-05. Places on Ministerial Working Groups on Deep-Sea Fisheries and Marine Strategy. Recreations: badminton; science fiction; computing. Address: (b.) Dunkeld, Little Dunkeld PH8 0AD; T.-01350 728200.
E-mail: rdixon@wwfscotland.org.uk

Dobie, Margaret G.C., OBE, MA, DipSocStud, FFCS. Hon. Vice President, Scottish Association for the Study of Delinquency; b. Galloway; m., James T.J. Dobie; 3 s. Educ. Benedictine Convent, Dumfries; Dumfries Academy; Edinburgh University. Medical Social Worker; Chair, Dumfries and Galloway Regional Children's Panel, 1971-

77; Social Worker, Child Guidance Service, Dumfries; Secretary, Scottish Association for the Study of Delinquency, 1982-87; Member, Broadcasting Council for Scotland, 1987-91; Chair, Dumfries and Galloway Children's Panel Advisory Committee, 1982-89; Chair, Children's Panel Advisory Group, 1985-88; Member, Polmont Young Offenders' Institution Visiting Committee, 1992-99; Chair, Dumfries & Galloway Valuation Appeal Panel, 1987-2004. Recreations: travel; tennis; reading. Address: (h.) 8 New Abbey Road, Dumfries DG2 7ND; T.-01387-254 595; e-mail: mqcd@naims.co.uk

Dobie, Rev. Rachel Jean Wayland, LTh. Minister, Broughton, Glenholm, Kilbucho linked with Skirling, linked with Stobo, Drumelzier linked with Tweedsmuir; b. 17.8.42, Forres; m., Kirkpatrick H. Dobie; 1 s.; 1 d. Educ. Dumfries Academy; Jordanhill College; Edinburgh University. Primary schoolteacher, 1963-80; Auxiliary Minister, Dalbeattie with Urr, 1990-93; Church of Scotland Sunday School Adviser, 1976-86; Reader, 1982-90; Chair, Marriage Guidance, Dumfries, 1984-86; Member, General Assembly Youth Education Committee, 1985-93; Vice-Convener, General Assembly Board of Parish Education 1993-97; Hon. Secretary, Church Service Society, 1997-2003; Moderator, Presbytery of Melrose and Peebles, 2002/03; Member, Mission and Discipleship Council, 2005; Contributor to BBC religious broadcasting. Publication: Time Together, 1981. Recreations: music; fine arts. Address: (h.) The Manse, Broughton, Biggar ML12 6HQ; T.-01899 830331.

Dobie, Susan, MA (Hons), CertEd. Head Teacher, Glenwood High School, Glenrothes, since 2003; b. 31.12.51, Southport, Lancashire; 1 d. Educ. Bishop Fox's Grammar School, Taunton, Somerset; Dundee University; Dundee College of Education. Assistant Teacher, Craigie High School, Dundee, 1974-78; Assistant Principal Teacher of Guidance, Whitfield High School, Dundee, 1978-81; PT Guidance, Bell Baxter High School, Cupar, 1981-86; Glenwood High School, Glenrothes: Assistant Head, 1986-95, Depute Head, 1995-2003. Council Member, Headteachers Association of Scotland. Recreations: wining; dining; my daughter. Address: (b.) South Parks Road, Glenrothes, Fife KY6 1JX; T.-01592 583404.

Dobson, Professor Alan Peter, BA, PGCE, MSc, PhD, FRHistSoc. Professor of Politics and Director, Institute of Transatlantic, European and American Studies, Dundee University, since 1999; b. 5.1.51, Withnell, Lancs; m., Beverly Jane; 3 d. Educ. Chorley Grammar School; Durham University; Southampton University; Durham University. Lecturer, Senior Lecturer, Reader, Department of Political Theory and Government, University of Wales, Swansea, 1978-99; Senior Research Fellow, Norwegian Nobel Institute, 1997. Editor, Journal of Transatlantic Studies, since 2003. Publications: (most recent) US Economic Statecraft for Survival, 1933-99. Recreations: walking; cooking; singing; gardening. Address: (b.) Department of Politics, Dundee University, Perth Road, Dundee DD1 4HN; T.-01382 344588.

Dodd, Marion Elizabeth, MA, BD, LRAM. Minister in Charge, Kelso: Old and Sprouston Parish Church, since 1989; Musical Director, Roxburgh Singers, since 1996; b. 19.4.41, Stirling. Educ. Glasgow High School; Burgh School/Knowe Park Primary (both in Selkirk); Selkirk High School; Esdaile, Edinburgh; Edinburgh University. Foreign Office, 1962-64; Iron and Steel Institute, 1964-67; BBC Singers, 1967-84; Assistant Minister, Colinton Parish Church, 1987-89 (ordained in July 1988). Member: Board of Parish Education, 1989-94, Board of World Mission,

1994-98, Panel on Worship, 1992-2000 (Music Committee Member), Church Hymnary Revision Committee, 1995-2005; Vice Convener, Panel on Review and Reform, 2005-07; President, Church Service Society, 2004-06; Moderator, Jedburgh Presbytery, 1993-94 and 2007-08. Chairperson, Abbeyfield Kelso Society Ltd., 1995-2005; Musical Director, Kelso Amateur Operatic Society, 1990-93; Chairperson, Kelso Churches Together, 1992-93, 1996-97, 2000-01, 2005-06; Teacher of solo singers, both in Kelso Opera Society and Roxburgh Singers. Recreations: music; cooking, travel; reading. Address: The Manse, Glebe Lane, Kelso, Roxburghshire TD5 7AU; T.-01573 226254; e-mail: mariondodd@btinternet.com

Dodd, Raymond Henry, PhD, MA, BMus, ARAM. Cellist and Composer; b. 31.3.29; m., Doreen Joyce; 1 s.; 1 d. Educ. Bryanston School; Royal Academy of Music; Worcester College, Oxford. Music Master, Sedbergh School, 1951-55; Aberdeen University: Lecturer in Music, 1956, Senior Lecturer in Music, 1971-91, Head of Department, 1981-88; Visiting Professor of Music, Wilson College, USA, 1972-73. Has performed widely, particularly in Scotland where he is known as a soloist and chamber music player; was for many years a member of the Aberdeen Trio; compositions include orchestral, vocal and chamber music pieces with a number of broadcasts, awarded Szymanowski Medal, Polish Ministry of Art and Culture, 1982. Address: (h.) 14 Giffordgate, Haddington, East Lothian EH41 4AS; T.-01620 824618.

Dodds, Alistair Bruce, MA (Hons), MBA, FIPD. Chief Executive, The Highland Council, since 2007; b. 23.8.53, Kelso; 1 d. Educ. Glenrothes High School; Edinburgh University; Strathclyde University; Dundee University. Assistant Director of Personnel, Fife Regional Council, 1988; Depute Director of Manpower Services, Highland Regional Council, 1991; Director of Personnel Services, The Highland Council, 1995, Director of Corporate Services/Deputy Chief Executive, 1998. Recreations: Scottish contemporary art; watching rugby; golf; walking dogs. Address: Highland Council, Glenurquhart Road, Inverness IV3 5NX; T.-01463 702845.

Doherty, Elizabeth, MA. Head Teacher, St Columba's High School, Gourock, since 1998; b. 5.7.45, Derry; m., James Doherty; 2 s.; 2 d. Educ. St Columba's High School, Greenock; Glasgow University. Teacher, St Columba's High School, 1967-68; St Stephen's Junior Secondary School, 1968-70 (became St Stephen's High School); career break, 1973-82; Teacher of English, Sacred Heart High School, Paisley, 1982-84; Assistant Principal Teacher of Guidance, St Cuthbert's High School, 1984-87; Principal Teacher/Assistant Head Teacher, St Stephen's High School, 1987-96; Depute Head, St Columba's High School, 1996-98. Recreations: reading; travelling; eating out. Address: (b.) St Columba's High School, Burnside Road, Gourock PA19 1XX; T.-01475 715250.

Doherty, (Joseph) Raymond, QC, LLB (Edinburgh), BCL (Oxon), LLM (Harvard). Advocate, since 1984; QC, since 1997; b. 30.1.58, Stirling; m., Arlene Donaghy; 1 s.; 2 d. Educ. St. Mungo's Primary School, Alloa; St Joseph's College, Dumfries; Edinburgh University; Hertford College, Oxford; Harvard Law School. Standing Junior Counsel to Ministry of Defence (Army), 1990-91; Standing Junior Counsel to Scottish Office Industry Department, 1992-97; Advocate Depute, 1998-2001. Clerk of Faculty, Faculty of Advocates, 1990-95; Joint Editor, Valuation for Rating, since 1990; Contributor, Stair Memorial Encyclopaedia of the Laws of Scotland. Address: (b.) Advocates' Library, Parliament House, Edinburgh EH1 1RF; T.-0131-226 5071.

Doherty, Una, LLB. Advocate, since 1999; b. Stirling; m., Douglas Fairley. Educ. High School of Stirling; Edinburgh University. Solicitor, 1988-98; Litigation Partner, Balfour and Manson, 1993-98. Address: (b.) Advocates' Library, Parliament House, Edinburgh EH1 1RF; T.-0131-226 5071.

Doig, P. Michael R., MA (Hons), FRSA. Head Teacher, Bearsden Academy, since 2001; b. 2.5.48, Glasgow; m., Catherine; 2 s. Educ. High School of Glasgow; Glasgow University. Teacher/Assistant Principal Teacher/Principal Teacher of Modern Languages, 1972-81; Assistant Head Teacher, Hermitage Academy, Helensburgh, 1981-85; Depute Head Teacher, Kirkintilloch High School, 1985-92; Head Teacher, Cumbernauld High School, 1992-2000. President, Headteachers' Association of Scotland (2003); Elected Member, General Teaching Council Scotland, 2005. Recreations: music; golf; current affairs. Address: (b.) Bearsden Academy, Morven Road, Bearsden, Glasgow G61 3SU; T.-0141-942 2449.

Dominiczak, Professor Anna F., OBE, MD, FRCP, FMedSci, FRSE. British Heart Foundation Chair of Cardiovascular Medicine, University of Glasgow, since 1997; Director, BHF Glasgow Cardiovascular Research Centre, since 2001; Honorary Consultant Physician and Endocrinologist, since 1993; b. 26.8.54, Gdansk, Poland; m., Dr. Marek Dominiczak; 1 s. Educ. Copernicus High School, Gdansk; Medical School, Gdansk. Junior House Officer, Glasgow Royal Infirmary, 1982; Senior House Officer (and Registrar) in Medicine, Royal Alexandra Hospital, Paisley, 1983-86; MRC Clinical Scientist and Honorary Registrar (and Senior Registrar), Western Infirmary, Glasgow, 1986-92; British-American Research Fellow and Associate Professor, University of Michigan, Ann Arbor, USA, 1990-91; University of Glasgow: Clinical Lecturer and Honorary Senior Registrar in Medicine and Endocrinology, 1992-93, British Heart Foundation Senior Research Fellow, Senior Lecturer then Reader in Medicine, 1993-97. Member, MRC Physiological Medicine Board, 2000-04; Member, British Heart Foundation Project Grant Committee, 2000-04; Member, the Wellcome Trust Physiological Sciences Committee; Secretary, International Society of Hypertension. Recreation: modern literature. Address: (b.) BHF Glasgow Cardiovascular Research Centre, 126 University Place, Glasgow G12 8TA; T.-0141-330 9420/2738; e-mail: ad7e@clinmed.gla.ac.uk

Don, Nigel. MSP (SNP), North East Scotland, since 2007; b. 16.4.54. Address: (b.) Scottish Parliament, Edinburgh EH99 1SP; Constituency Office: 8 Old Glamis Road, Dundee DD3 8HP.

Donachie, Professor William David, BSc, PhD, MAcadEurop, FAmerAcadMicrobiol, FRSE. Professor of Bacterial Genetics, Edinburgh University, 1993-2000, now Professor Emeritus; b. 27.4.35, Edinburgh; m.,Millicent Masters, BS, MS, PhD; 1 s. Educ. Dunfermline High School; Edinburgh University. Assistant Lecturer in Genetics, Edinburgh University, 1958-62; Research Associate in Biochemical Sciences, Princeton University, 1962-63; Lecturer in Genetics, Edinburgh University, 1963-65; Scientific Staff, MRC Molecular Genetics Unit, London and Edinburgh, 1965-74; Senior Lecturer/Reader in Molecular Biology, Edinburgh University, 1974-93. Publications: 93 research papers. Recreations: drawing; natural history; T'ai Chi. Address: (b.) Institute of Cell and Molecular Biology, Edinburgh University, Darwin

Building, King's Buildings, Mayfield Road, Edinburgh EH9 3JR; T.-0131-650 5354.
E-mail: William.Donachie@ed.ac.uk

Donaghy, Marie Elizabeth, PhD, BA (Hons), FCSP, FHEA. Dean, School of Health Sciences, Queen Margaret University, since 2007, Professor in Physiotherapy, since 2005; b. 24.1.49, Glasgow; m., Michael Donaghy; 2 d. Educ. Scottish Physiotherapy Hospital; Open University; Glasgow University. Physiotherapist, Stobhill, Ruchill Royal Alexandria Hospitals, 1970-79; Senior Physiotherapist, Merchiston Hospital, 1979-86; Superintendent, Dykebar Hospital, 1986-89; Lecturer in Psysiotherapy, Queen Margaret University, 1989-94, Senior Lecturer, 1994-2001, Acting Head of Psysiotherapy, 2001-02, Associate Dean, Head of School of Health Sciences, 2002-06. Publications: Cognitive Behavioural Interventions in Psysiotherapy and Occupational Therapy (Co-Author), 2008; Interventions in Mental Health: An Evidence Based Approach for Psysiotherapy and Occupational Therapists (Co-Author), 2008. Recreations: travel to South East Asia; spending time with family and grandchildren; hill walking. Address: (b.) Queen Margaret University Drive, Musselburgh, East Lothian EH21 6UU; T.-0131 474 0000; e-mail: mdonaghy@qmu.ac.uk

Donald, Andrew Robert Mitchell, BSc, DipTEFL, IAPS. Headmaster, St. Leonards-New Park, St. Andrews, since 2005; b. 6.6.55, Aberdeen; m., Valerie Colquhoun; 1 s.; 1 d. Educ. Maidstone Grammar School; University of Aberdeen; University of Wales. Ardvreck, Perthshire, 1977-79; University of Zagazig, Egypt, 1980-82; Naval Training Centre, Qatar, 1982-87; Ardvreck, Perthshire, 1987-95; Headmaster, New Park School, St. Andrews, 1995-2005. Secretary, District 11, IAPS; Member, Rotary Club. Recreations: cycling; walking; watercolours; reading. Address: (b.) St. Leonards-New Park, St. Andrews KY16 9QU; T.-01334 460470; e-mail: a.donald@stleonards-fife.org

Donald, George Malcolm, RSA, RSW, DA, ATC, MEd. Director of Summer School, Centre for Continuing Studies, ECA; Keeper, Royal Scottish Academy; former Lecturer, Edinburgh College of Art; b. 12.9.43, Ootacamund, South India; 1 s.; 1 d. Educ. Robert Gordon's College; Aberdeen Academy; Edinburgh College of Art; Hornsey College of Art; Edinburgh University. Joined Edinburgh College of Art as Lecturer, 1969; Visiting Lecturer, five Faculties of Art in India, 1979; Visiting Professor: University of Central Florida (Art, 1981, Drawing and Anatomy, 1985 to present), Strasbourg, 1986, Belgrade, 1987, Sechuan Fine Art Institute, China, 1989, Chinese Academy of Fine Art, 1994, Osaka and Kyoto Universities, Japan, 1999, 2002 and 2007; Latimer Award, RSA, 1970; Guthrie Award, RSA, 1973; Scottish Arts Council Bursary, 1973; RSA Gillies Bequest Travel Award to India, 1978, USA, 2003; SAC Travel and Study Award, Indiana, 1981; RSA Gillies Prize, 1982; RSW Mary Marshall Brown Award, 1983; RGI Cargill Award, 1987; one man shows: Florida, 1985, Helsinki, 1985, Edinburgh Festival, 1985, Belgrade, 1987, Florida, 1987, Edinburgh, 1988, 1990, London, 1992-94, Edinburgh 1993, 1994, 1995, 1998, 1999, 2002, 2003, 2005, 2007. Address: (h.) Bankhead, by Duns, Berwickshire TD11 3QJ; T.-01361 883014; e-mail: g.donald@care4free.net

Donald, Hugh R. OBE, LLB (Hons), WS. Chairman, Shepherd and Wedderburn (Chief Executive, 1994-1999); b. 5.11.51, Edinburgh; m., M. Grace Donald; 1 s.; 1 d. Educ. Melville College, Edinburgh; Edinburgh University. Shepherd and Wedderburn: legal training, 1973-75,

Assistant Solicitor, 1975-77, Partner, since 1977. Chairman, Family Mediation Scotland, Mediator. Recreations: family; church; gardening. Address: Saltire Court, 20 Castle Terrace, Edinburgh EH1 2ET; T.-0131-228 9900.

Donald, Marion Coats (nee McClure), DipArch, MPhil, RIBA, FRIAS. Principal, John and Marion Donald, Chartered Architects, 1976-2006; Professional Studies Advisor, Scott Sutherland School of Architecture, Robert Gordon University; b. 15.5.47, Aberdeen; m., John Donald; 1 s.; 1 d. Educ. Aberdeen High School for Girls; Colchester County High School for Girls; Scott Sutherland School of Architecture, RGIT; Scott Sutherland School of Architecture, Robert Gordon University. Student architect, Sir Basil Spence Glover and Ferguson, 1972; Architectural Assistant, SSHA, 1973-74; Architect, Jenkins and Marr, 1974-76. Former Chairman, Aberdeen Soroptimist Housing Society Ltd; Elder, Queen's Cross Church. RIBA Award, 1998; Aberdeenshire Design Award: 2004 (Housing), 2000 (Conservation); Association for Preservation of Scotland Award, 1995; Aberdeen Civic Society Award, 1984; Civic Trust Commendation, 1984. Recreations: family; gardening; music; art and architecture. Address: 177b Queen's Road, Aberdeen AB15 8BS; T.-01224 313014.

Donald, Rev. Peter Harry, MA, PhD, BD. Minister, Crown Church, Inverness, since 1998; b. 3.2.62, Edinburgh; m., Brigid Mary McNeill; 1 s.; 1 d. Educ. George Watson's College; Gonville and Caius College, University of Cambridge; University of Edinburgh. Scouloudi Research Fellow, Institute of Historical Research, University of London, 1986-87; Probationer Assistant, St. Michael's Church, Edinburgh, 1990-91; Minister, Leith St. Serf's Parish Church, 1991-98. Member, Faith and Order Commission. Publication: An Uncounselled King: Charles I and the Scottish Troubles 1637-1641, 1990; God in Society (Co-editor), 2003. Recreations: golf; swimming; racquet sports; piano; singing; walking; family. Address: 39 Southside Road, Inverness IV2 4XA; T.-01463 230537.

Donaldson, Alan Ramsay, BA (Hons), CA. Managing Partner, Scott-Moncrieff Chartered Accountants, since 2002; b. 24.8.56, Edinburgh; m., Christine; 2 s. Educ. George Heriot's School; Dundee College of Technology. Thomson McClintock/KPMG, 1979-88; Scott Moncrieff, since 1988. Recreations: golf; jogging; family. Address: (b.) 17 Melville Street, Edinburgh EH3 7PH; T.-0131-473-3500; e-mail: alan.donaldson@scott-moncrieff.com

Donaldson, Graham H.C., MA, MEd. HM Senior Chief Inspector of Education, since 2002; b. 11.12.46, Glasgow; m., Dilys; 2 s.; 1 d. Educ. High School of Glasgow; Glasgow University. Teacher, Craigbank Secondary School, Glasgow; Principal Teacher, Dunbartonshire Council; Lecturer, Jordanhill College; Curriculum Evaluator, Consultative Committee on the Curriculum; HM Inspector of Schools; HM Chief Inspector of Schools; HM Depute Senior Chief Inspector of Education, 1996-2002. Publication: James IV – A Renaissance King. Recreations: golf; reading. Address: (b.) HM Inspectorate of Education, Denholm House, Almondvale Business Park, Almondvale Way, Livingston EH54 6GA; T.-01506 600366; e-mail: graham.donaldson@hmie.gsi.gov.uk

Donaldson, Professor Iain Malcolm Lane, BSc, MB, ChB, MA, FRCPE, MRCP. Professor of Neurophysiology, Edinburgh University, 1987-2003; Emeritus Professor and Hon. Fellow, Edinburgh University, since 2003; b. 22.10.37; m.; 1 s. Educ. Edinburgh University. House

Physician and Surgeon, Research Fellow, Honorary Lecturer, Honorary Senior Registrar, Departments of Medicine and Surgical Neurology, Edinburgh University, 1962-69; Anglo-French Research Scholarship, University of Paris, 1969-70; Research Officer, University Laboratory of Physiology, Oxford, 1970-79; Fellow and Tutor in Medicine, St. Edmund Hall, Oxford, 1973-79; Professor of Zoology, Hull University, 1979-87; Honorary Librarian, Royal College of Physicians of Edinburgh, since 2000; Emeritus Fellow, St. Edmund Hall, Oxford, since 1979. Recreation: studying the past. Address: (b.) Royal College of Physicians of Edinburgh, 9 Queen Street, Edinburgh EH2 1JQ.

Donaldson, James Andrew, BDS, BA, DFM. Principal in general dental practice; Secretary, Dental Practitioners Association, since 2005; President, General Dental Practitioners Association, 2002-05; b. 28.2.57, Glasgow; divorced; 1 s.; 3 d. Educ. Coatbridge High School; Dundee University; Open University; Glasgow University. Dental Adviser, British Antarctic Survey, 1986-97; Member: National Council, General Dental Practitioners Association, since 1989, Scottish Dental Services Committee, 1991-93, Aberdeen District Council, 1984-86, Grampian Regional Council, 1986-88; Director, "Open Wide" Dental Courses; contested Liberal Democrat, Aberdeen North, elections to Scottish Parliament, 1999, Westminster election, 2001. Recreations: golf; skiing; football. Address: (h.) 120 Hamilton Place, Aberdeen AB15 5BB; T.-01224 646140.

Donaldson, William, MA, PhD. Writer and teacher; b. 19.7.44, Ellon; 2 s.; 1 d. Educ. Fraserburgh Academy; Aberdeen University. Publications: Popular Literature in Victorian Scotland, 1986 (Blackwell Prize); The Jacobite Song, 1988 (SAC Book Award); The Language of the People, 1989; The Highland Pipe and Scottish Society 1750–1950, 2000 (Saltire Society Research Book Award); thirty four entries on Scottish writers and musicians in Oxford Dictionary of National Biography, 2004; Pipers: a guide to the players and music of the Highland Bagpipe, 2005; editor of Grampian Hairst, 1981; David Rorie Poems and Prose, 1983; and novels by William Alexander, 1986, 1995; editor, online variorum edition of piobaireachd, 2001 - at piperanddrummer.com; From Broadside to Broadband: Two Hundred Tunes for the Highland Bagpipe, 2006. Leverhulme Fellow, 1984-85; Wingate Scholar, 1997-98. Recreation: music. Address: (b.) Open University in Scotland, 10 Drumsheugh Gardens, Edinburgh EH3 7QJ.

Donegan, Kate, BA. Governor, HMP, Perth, since 2006; b. 21.4.53, Newport on Tay; m.; Dr Chris Donegan; 2 s. Educ. Kirkcaldy High School; Stirling University. Assistant Governor: Cornton Vale, 1977-84, Barlinnie Prison, 1984-87; Deputy Governor: Reading Prison, 1987-89; Deputy Governor, Perth Prison, 1989-91; Head, Operational Manpower, Planning Unit, 1991-93; seconded to Staffing Structure Review Team, 1993-94; Deputy Governor, Barlinnie Prison, 1994-95; Deputy Chief Inspector of Prisons, 1995-96; Governor, HM Prison and Institution, Cornton Vale, 1996-2001; Governor, HMP Glenochil, 2001-06. Recreations: gardening; reading; computing. Address: (b.) HM Prison, 3 Edinburgh Road, Perth PH2 8AT; T.-01738 622293; e-mail: kathleen.donegan@sps.gov.uk

Donnachie, Ian, MA, MLitt, PhD, FRHistS, FSA (Scot). Reader in History, since 2003, Staff Tutor, since 1970, Director, Centre for Scottish Studies, Open University in Scotland; b. 18.6.44, Lanark. Educ. Lanark Grammar School; Glasgow University; Strathclyde University. Research Assistant, Galloway Project, Strathclyde University, 1967-68; Lecturer in Social Studies: Napier Polytechnic, 1968-70, Deakin University, Victoria, 1982; Visiting Fellow: Deakin University, Victoria and Sydney University, NSW, 1985; Hon. Lecturer, Dundee University, since 1998; Vice-Chairman, Friends of New Lanark. Publications include: A History of the Brewing Industry in Scotland; Industrial Archaeology in the British Isles (jointly); Scottish History 1560-1980 (jointly); That Land of Exiles: Scots in Australia (jointly); Forward! Labour Politics in Scotland 1888-1988 (Co-Editor); A Companion to Scottish History from the Reformation to the Present (jointly); The Manufacture of Scottish History (Co-editor); Historic New Lanark: the Dale and Owen Industrial Community since 1785 (Co-author); Studying Scottish History, Literature and Culture; Modern Scottish History: 1707 to the present (Co-Editor); Robert Owen, Owen of New Lanark and New Harmony; Dictionary of Scottish History (jointly); From Enlightenment to Romanticism Anthologies I-II (Co-editor); Robert Owen, Social Visionary. Recreations: walking; cycling; countryside. Address: (b.) 10 Drumsheugh Gardens, Edinburgh EH3 7QJ; T.-0131-226 3851; e-mail: i.donnachie@open.ac.uk

Donnelly, Dougie, LLB. Presenter/commentator, Golf Channel USA and worldwide coverage of European Tour Golf; sports video writer and director; b. 7.6.53, Glasgow; m., Linda; 3 d. Educ. Hamilton Academy; Strathclyde University. Presenter, BBC Television Sport, since 1978: Grandstand, World Championship snooker, Olympic Games (summer and winter), World Cup, Commonwealth Games, Ryder Cup, golf, Sportscene, Match of the Day; Mid-Morning Show, Album Show, Radio Clyde, 1976-92. Chairman, Commonwealth Games Endowment Fund; after-dinner speaker, conference and seminar host. Recreations: sport; travel; reading; good food and wine. Address: (b.) David John Associates, 16A Winton Drive, Glasgow G12 0QA; T.-0141-357 0532.

Donnelly, Mike, BA, MSc, PhD. Dean, School of Business, Enterprise and Management, Queen Margaret University, Edinburgh, since 2007; b. 10.11.50, Glasgow; m., Frances Campbell; 2 s.; 1 d. Educ. Lourdes Secondary, Glasgow; University of Stirling. Lecturer in Management Science, University of Stirling, 1979-93; Councillor and Deputy Leader of Stirling District Council, 1988-93; Lecturer in Operations Research, Glasgow Caledonian University, 1994; Senior Lecturer in Operations Management, Strathclyde University, 1994-97; Principal Lecturer, Bristol Business School, UWE, 1997-98; Special Advisor to Dr. John Reid, 1999-2001; Dean, Paisley Business School, University of Paisley, 1999-2005; Principal Special Advisor to Jack McConnell, 2001-03. Recreations: golf; reading; walking. Address: (h.) 3 Kintillo Drive, Scotstounhill, Glasgow G13 3RT; T.-0141 435 4828; e-mail: mdonnelly@qmu.ac.uk

Donnison, Professor David. Emeritus Professor, Glasgow University, since 1990, Honorary Research Fellow; b. 19.1.26. Lecturer: Manchester University, 1950-53, Toronto University, 1953-55; London School of Economics and Political Science: Reader, 1956-61, Professor, 1961-69; Director, Centre for Environmental Studies, London, 1969-75; Chairman, Supplementary Benefits Commission, 1975-80; Professor of Town and Regional Planning, Glasgow University, 1980-90. Address: 23 Bank Street, Glasgow G12 8JQ.

Donohoe, Brian H. MP (Labour), Central Ayrshire, since 2005, Cunninghame South, 1992-2005; b. 10.9.48, Kilmarnock; m., Christine; 2 s. Educ. Irvine Royal Academy; Kilmarnock Technical College. Secretary, Irvine and District Trades Council, 1973-81; Chair: North Ayrshire and Arran LHC, 1977-79, Cunninghame Industrial Development Committee, 1975-79; former full-time trade union official (NALGO). Recreation: gardening. Address: (h.) 5 Greenfield Drive, Irvine, Ayrshire; T.-01294 274419.

Donovan, Professor Robert John, OBE (2007), BSc, PhD, CChem, FRSC, FRSE. Professor of Chemistry, Edinburgh University, since 1979; b. 13.7.41, Nantwich; m., Marion Jacubeit; 1 d. Educ. Sandbach School; University College of Wales, Aberystwyth; Cambridge University. Research Fellow, Gonville and Caius College, 1966-70; Edinburgh University: Lecturer in Physical Chemistry, 1970-74, Reader in Chemistry, 1974-79. Member: Physical Chemistry Panel, Science & Engineering Research Council, 1977-80, Management Committee, SERC Synchrotron Radiation Source, Daresbury, 1977-80, SERC Synchrotron Radiation Facility Committee, 1979-84; Chairman, SERC Laser Facility Committee, 1989-92; Member, SERC Science Board, 1989-92; Chairman, Facilities Commission, SERC, 1993-94; awarded Corday-Morgan Medal and Prize, Royal Society of Chemistry, 1975; Member: Faraday Council, Royal Society of Chemistry, 1981-83, 1991-93; Vice President, Royal Society of Edinburgh, 1998-2001 (Member, Council, 1996-2001); Member of Council, CCLRC, 2004-06; Tilden Prize, Royal Society of Chemistry, 1995. Recreations: hill-walking; skiing; sail-boarding; cross-country riding. Address: (b.) School of Chemistry, Edinburgh University, West Mains Road, Edinburgh EH9 3JJ; T.-0131-650 4722; e-mail: R.Donovan@ed.ac.uk

Doran, Frank, LLB(Hons). MP (Labour), Aberdeen North, since 2005, Aberdeen Central, 1997-2005; Chair, Administration Committee, House of Commons; b. 13.4.49; 2 s. Educ. Leith Academy; University of Dundee. Solicitor, 1977-87; MP (Labour), Aberdeen South, 1987-92; Co-ordinator, National Trade Union Political Fund Ballot Campaign, 1993-96. Secretary, Trade Union Group of Labour MPs. Address: (b.) House of Commons, London SW1A 0AA; T.-020 7219 3000.
E-mail: doranf@parliament.uk

Doran, Margaret, BA, DipEd. Executive Director of Education and Social Work, Glasgow City Council, since June 2007, previously Service Director, Education, from February 2007 and Depute Director, Education Services, from May 2006. Former Headteacher. Seconded to take forward Assessment in Central Regional Council, 1990. Part time University Tutor for 3 years. Appointed Staff Development Coordinator pre 5s, primary and secondary schools, 1992. Appointed Head of Service in Stirling Council Education Services, 1995, and then in an integrated Children's Service, 2000-05. Assistant Director responsible for early years, school improvement and a community college in Southend Borough Council, from August 2005 before taking up Depute Director post in Glasgow. Recreation: being with family and friends; playing piano; saxophone and singing; hillwalking; theatre season ticket holder. Address: (b.) Wheatley House, 25 Cochrane Street, Glasgow G1 1HL; T.-0141-287-4551.

Doris, Bob. MSP (SNP), Glasgow, since 2007; b. 11.5.73. Address: (b.) Scottish Parliament, Edinburgh EH99 1SP.

Dorman, Arthur Brian, LLB, FIMgt. Solicitor; Partner, Brian Dorman, Solicitors; Director, Rita Rusk International Ltd.; b. 21.6.45, Glasgow; 1 s.; 1 d. Educ. Hillhead High School; Glasgow University. Recreation: occasional golf. Address: Madeleine Smith House, 6/7 Blythswood Square, Glasgow G2 4AD; T.-0141-221 9933.

Dorward, David Campbell, MA, ARAM. Composer, since 1944; Music Producer, BBC, 1962-91; b. 7.8.33, Dundee; m., Janet Offord; 1 s.; 2 d. Educ. Morgan Academy, Dundee; St. Andrews University; Royal Academy of Music. Teaching, 1960-61; Freelance, 1961-62. Arts Adviser, Lamp of Lothian Collegiate Trust, 1967-98; Member, Scottish Arts Council, 1972-78; Consultant Director, Performing Right Society, 1985-90; Patron's Fund Award, 1958; Royal Philharmonic Prizewinner, 1958; compositions include four string quartets, two symphonies, four concertos, Tonight Mrs Morrison (one-act opera), A Christmas Carol (musical), and incidental music for TV, radio, film and stage. Recreations: reviving old scores; walking in the country. Address: (h.) Dovecot House, Preston Road, Prestonpans EH32 9JZ; T.-01875 810 512; e-mail: ddorward@btinternet.com

Douglas, Alan. Journalist and Broadcaster; b. 16.10.51, Dundee; m., Viv Lumsden (qv); 2 d. Educ. Forfar Academy. Local newspapers, 1970-74; BBC Local Radio Reporter and Producer, 1974-78; Reporter/Presenter, BBC TV Scotland, 1978-95; freelance broadcaster and journalist, BBC TV and Radio, corporate and Scottish TV; Director, The Broadcasting Business Ltd (media consultancy); Motoring Correspondent, Scottish Field; contributor to magazines, websites, newspapers and radio on transport and travel. Former Guild of Motoring Writers' Regional Journalist of the Year. Recreations: cars; walking; eating; drinking. Address: (b.) The Broadcasting Business Ltd, Lochinch House, 86 Dumbreck Road, Glasgow G41 4SN; e-mail: alan@broadcastingbusiness.co.uk

Douglas, Allan Fraser, BSc (Hons), PGDip. Rector, Wallace Hall Academy, since 1996; b. 9.11.46, Aberdeen; m., Isabel Gordon Pearson; 2 s.; 1 d. Educ. Aberdeen Academy; Strathclyde University. Research Chemist, 1969-71; Teacher of Chemistry, Annan Academy, 1972-73, Lockerbie Academy, 1973-79; Research Chemist, St Andrews University, 1979-82; Teacher of Chemistry, Dumfries Academy, 1982-88, Assistant Head Teacher/Depute Rector, 1988-96. Recreations: dinghy sailing; gardening; hill-walking. Address: (b.) Wallace Hall Academy, Station Road, Thornhill, Dumfries and Galloway DG3 5DS; T.-01848 330294.

Douglas, Charles Edward, BA, FCII. Management Board Member, Scottish Civic Forum; Vice Convener, Humanist Society of Scotland (Convener, Public Affairs Committee); Vice Convener, Forum on Discrimination Steering Group; retired university lecturer; b. 10.8.35; m., Cynthia Dorothy; 1 s.; 1 d. SNP candidate, General Election, 1992. Recreations: wildlife and conservation. Address: (h.) Midpark, Balmaclellan, Castle Douglas DG7 3PX; T.-01644 420605.
E-mail: charles.douglas@humanism-scotland.org.uk

Douglas, Gavin Stuart, RD, QC, MA, LLB; b. 12.6.32. Educ. South Morningside School; George Heriot's School; Edinburgh University. Qualified as Solicitor, 1955; National Service, Royal Navy; admitted to Faculty of Advocates, 1958; Sub-editor (part-time), The Scotsman, 1957-61; Member, Lord Advocate's Department in London, (as Parliamentary Draftsman) 1961-64; returned to practice at Scots Bar, 1964; Junior Counsel to Board of Trade, 1965-71; Counsel to Scottish Law Commission, 1965-96; Hon. Sheriff, 1965-71; a Chairman of Industrial Tribunals, 1966-78; QC, 1971; Counsel to Secretary of State for Scotland under Private Legislation Procedure (Scotland) Act 1936, 1969-1975, Senior Counsel under that Act 1975-2002; Member, Lothian Health Board, 1981-85; Member, Board, Leith Nautical College, 1981-84; Editor, Session Cases, seven volumes, 1976-82; Temporary Sheriff, 1990-99; President, Temporary Sheriffs' Association, 1999. Recreation: golf.

Douglas, Professor Neil James, MD, DSc, FRCP, FRCPE. Professor of Respiratory and Sleep Medicine, Edinburgh University; Director, Scottish National Sleep Centre; President, Royal College of Physicians of Edinburgh; Consultant Physician, since 1983; b. 28.5.49, Edinburgh; m., Dr. Sue Galloway; 1 s.; 1 d. Educ. Dundee High School; Trinity College, Glenalmond; St. Andrews University; Edinburgh University. Lecturer in Medicine, Edinburgh University, 1974-83; MRC Travelling Fellow, University of Colorado, 1980-81. Recreations: fishing; gardening; eating. Address: (b.) Respiratory Medicine, Royal Infirmary, 51 Little France Crescent, Edinburgh EH16 4SA; T.-0131 242 1836.

Douglas-Home, Lady (Lavinia) Caroline, DL, FSA Scot. Deputy Lieutenant, Berwickshire, since 1983; b. 11.10.37 (daughter of Baron Home of the Hirsel, KT, PC). Educ. privately. Woman of the Bedchamber (Temporary) to Queen Elizabeth the Queen Mother, 1963-65; Lady-In-Waiting (Temporary) to HRH Duchess of Kent, 1966-67; Estate Factor, Douglas and Angus Estates, 1960-95; Trustee, National Museum of Antiquities of Scotland, 1982-85; President, Borders Branch, British Red Cross, since 1998; Trustee, Scottish Episcopal Church Nominees, since 1993; Trustee, Scottish Redundant Churches Trust, since 1995; Governor, Longridge Towers School, since 1995; President, Berwick Citizens Advice Bureau, since 1996. Recreations: fishing; gardening; reading; antiquities. Address: (h.) Heaton Mill House, Cornhill-on-Tweed, Northumberland; T.-01890 882303.

Douglas-Scott, Susan, DipCOT, BSc (Hons), MSc (QMUC). Chief Executive, Epilepsy Scotland, since 2005; b. 12.9.60, Glasgow; 1 s.; 1 d. Educ. Eastwood High School; Glasgow School of Occupational Therapy; Caledonian University. Occupational therapist, NHS, 1981-82; social work, 1983-87; manager, social work, 1987-92; registration and inspection officer, 1992-98; Head of Service, Sense Scotland, 1998-2000; Director, fpa Scotland, 2000-03; Chief Executive, PHACE Scotland (Promoting Health and Challenging Exclusion), 2003-05. Recreations: yoga; sewing; singing; Reiki. Address (b.) 48 Govan Road, Glasgow G51 1JL; T.-0141 427 4911; e-mail: sdouglas-scott@epilepsyscotland.org.uk

Dove, Rev. Giles Wilfred, MA, MPhil, BD, FRSA, FSA Scot. Chaplain and Head of Divinity, Glenalmond College, since 2007; Director of Development, National Library of Scotland, 2005-2007; Non-Stipendiary Curate, St. Mary's Church, Dunblane, 2005-07; b. 25.1.62, Hendon; m., Katherine Ann MacCallum; 2 s.; 1 d. Educ. Winchester College; University of St. Andrews; University of Glasgow. Alumnus Relations Officer, University of St. Andrews, 1988-91, Development Officer, 1992-97; Director of Communications and Development, University of Stirling, 1998-2005. Scottish Episcopal Church: Ordained Priest, 2006, Ordained Deacon, 2005, Convener, Standing Committee, General Synod, 2002-05, Trustee, Pension Fund, 2002-05, Convener, Budget Review Committee, General Synod, 2002-04, Convener, Resources Committee, General Synod, 1999-2002, Member, Board for Ministry, General Synod, 1999-2002; Trustee, Council for Advancement and Support of Education, 1999-2005; Governor, Aberlour Child Care Trust, 2001-04; Vice-Chairman, Board of Management, St. Mary's Episcopal Primary School, Dunblane, 2000-02; Director, Rymonth Housing Society Ltd., 1993-95; Trustee, St. Andrews Preservation Trust Ltd., 1991-94; Freeman of The City of

London. Publications: "Alma Matters: A Guide To Alumni Relations"; "Pilgrimage Sites" (in "The Fife Book"); various articles in professional journals. Recreations: choral music; ecclesiastical history; good food and drink; Scottish islands. Address: (h.) The Chaplain's House, Glenalmond College, Perth PH1 3RY; e-mail: giles.dove@glenalmondcollege.co.uk

Dover, Sir Kenneth James, MA, DLitt, Hon.LLD (St. Andrews, Birmingham), Hon.LittD (St. Andrews, Bristol, London, Liverpool, Durham), Hon.DHL (Oglethorpe), FRSE, FBA. Chancellor, St. Andrews University, 1981-2005; b. 11.3.20, Croydon; m., Audrey Ruth Latimer; 1 s.; 1 d. Educ. St. Paul's School, London; Balliol College, Oxford; Merton College, Oxford. Fellow and Tutor, Balliol College, Oxford, 1948-55; Professor of Greek, St. Andrews, 1955-76; President, Corpus Christi College, Oxford, 1976-86. Served in Royal Artillery, 1940-45; President, Hellenic Society, 1971-74; President, Classical Association, 1975; President, British Academy, 1978-81; Foreign Honorary Member, American Academy of Arts and Sciences, since 1979; Foreign Member, Royal Netherlands Academy, since 1979; Honorary Fellow, Balliol, Corpus Christi and Merton Colleges, Oxford. Recreations: gardening; historical linguistics. Address: (h.) 49 Hepburn Gardens, St. Andrews, Fife KY16 9LS; T.-01334 473589.

Dow, Rear-Admiral Douglas Morrison, CB, DL. Director, The National Trust for Scotland, 1992-97; Deputy Lieutenant, City of Edinburgh, since 1996; b. 1.7.35; m., Felicity Margaret Mona Napier; 2 s.; Educ. George Heriot's School; BRNC Dartmouth. Joined RN, 1952; served Staff of C-in-C Plymouth, 1959-61; HMS Plymouth, 1961-63; RN Supply Sch., 1963-65; Staff of Comdr FEF, 1965-67; HMS Endurance, 1968-70; BRNC Dartmouth, 1970-72; Cdr 1972; Assistant Director, Officer Appointments (S), 1972-74; Sec to Comdr British Navy Staff, Washington, 1974-76; HMS Tiger, 1977-78; NDC Latimer, 1978-79; Captain 1979; CSO(A) to Flag Officer Portsmouth, 1979; Sec to Controller of Navy, 1981; Captain, HMS Cochrane, 1983; Commodore, HMS Centurion, 1985; RCDS, 1988; Rear Admiral, 1989; Director General, Naval Personal Services, 1989-92. Vice-Chairman, George Heriot's Trust, since 1996; President, South Queensferry Sea Cadets, since 1993; President, Royal Naval Association Edinburgh, since 1994. Recreations: rugby union; fly fishing; shooting; golf; gardening. Address: (h.) Tor Lodge, 1 Eskbank Terrace, Dalkeith, Midlothian EH22 3DE.

Dow, Professor Julian Alexander Thomas, MA PhD, ScD. Professor of Molecular and Integrative Physiology, Glasgow University, since 1999 (Head, Molecular Genetics, 2001-05); b. 1957; m., Shireen-Anne Davies; 3 s.; 2 d. Educ. King's School, Gloucester; St. Catharine's College, University of Cambridge. Glasgow University: Lecturer, 1984-94, Senior Lecturer, 1994-97, Reader, 1997-99; Nuffield Fellow, 1992-94. President's Medal, Society for Experimental Biology, 1992; Member, several committees, BBSRC. Recreations: skiing; diving. Address: (b.) Molecular Genetics, University of Glasgow, Glasgow G11 6NU; e-mail: j.a.t.dow@bio.gla.ac.uk

Dow, Professor Sheila Christine, MA (Hons), MA (Econ), PhD. Professor in Economics, Stirling University, since 1996 (Head of Department, 2002-04); b. 16.4.49, Dumfries; m., Professor Alexander Dow; 2 d. Educ. Hawick High School; St. Andrews University; University of Manitoba; McMaster University; Glasgow University. Overseas Office, Bank of England, 1970-72; Economist, then Senior Economist, Department of Finance, Government of Manitoba, 1973-77; Lecturer, then Reader, Department of Economics, Stirling University, 1979-96. Chair,

International Network for Economic Method, 2001-02; special advisor to House of Commons Treasury Select Committee, since 2001. Publications: Macroeconomic Thought, 1985; Financial Markets and Regional Economic Development, 1990; Money Matters (Co-author), 1982; Money and the Economic Process, 1993; The Methodology of Macroeconomic Thought, 1996; Economic Methodology: An Inquiry, 2002; A History of Scottish Economic Thought (Co-editor), 2006. Recreations: travel; various sports. Address: (b.) Department of Economics, Stirling University, Stirling FK9 4LA; T.-01786 467474; e-mail: s.c.dow@stir.ac.uk

Dow, Sylvia, ALAM, LRAM, FRSA. Arts Education Consultant, since 2004; Head of Education, Scottish Arts Council, 1994-2004; b. 19.7.39, Edinburgh; m., Ronald Dow; 1 s.; 1 d. Educ. James Gillespie's High School for Girls; Edinburgh College of Speech and Drama. Freelance radio actor/presenter, California, 1960-65; Tutor, Edinburgh College of Speech and Drama, 1969-70; Drama Teacher (Head of Drama), Bo'ness Academy, 1970-85; Education Officer, MacRobert Arts Centre, 1985-93; Arts Co-ordinator, Central Region Education Service, 1993-94. Board Member, Scottish Ballet; Tapestry; Arts and Communities; Licketyspit Theatre Company. Recreations: arts; directing amateur drama; swimming.

Dowds, Stephen, BSc (Hons), FEIS. Rector, Culloden Academy, since 2002; b. 2.4.53, Saltcoats; m., Myna; 2 d. Educ. Ardrossan Academy, Ayrshire; Glasgow University. Instructor, Faskally Outdoor Centre, 1976-78; Biology Teacher, Dingwall Academy, 1978-80; Culloden Academy: Biology Teacher, 1980-82, Principal Teacher, Biology, 1982-90, Assistant Rector, 1990-97; Rector, Lochaber High School, Fort William, 1997-2002. National Executive Council of Educational Institute of Scotland, since 1984. Recreations: traditional music; skiing; rugby; football; shinty; Information Technology. Address: (b.) Keppoch Road, Culloden IV2 7JZ; T.-01463 790851.

Downes, Bob, DipTP, BPhil. Director (Scotland), Open Reach, since 2005; b. 10.8.51, Belfast; m., Julie McGarvey; 2 s. Educ. Portora Royal School, Enniskillen; Dundee University; Duncan of Jordanstone College of Art, Dundee. Local government, 1976-82; Dundee Project, 1982-84; SDA, 1984-87; Director: North East, SDA, 1987-90, Conran Roche Planning, London, 1990-92; independent consultant, 1992-93; Chief Executive, Dumfries and Galloway Enterprise, 1993-94; Director, Scottish Enterprise, 1994-99; BT Scotland: Director, Economic Development, 1999-2000; Director, e-business Development, 2000-01, National Manager, 2001-02, Director, 2002-05. Advisor, Flax Trust, Belfast, 1994-2001; Director: Wise Group, Glasgow, 1997-2000, Emerging Business Trust, Belfast, 1996-2004, Businesslab, 1996-2003; Director Scotland, Openreach, since 2005; Member, President's Executive Committee, National Council for Urban Economic Development, Washington D.C., 1996-2001; Ambassador, Prince and Princess of Wales Hospice Trust, since 2007; Member, Advisory Board, The Competitiveness Institute, Barcelona, 1998-99; Director, Big Issue International, 2002-04; Director, Scottish Ensemble, 2002-07; Board Member, Scottish Arts Council, 2003-05; Advisory Board Group, DA Group, since 2002; Glasgow University Business School Advisory Board, since 2005. Recreations: running; cycling; live music; travelling; films; journalists' biographies; political biographies; Kelvin walkway. Address: (h.) 21 Cleveden Road, Kelvinside, Glasgow G12 0PQ.

Downes, Professor Charles Peter, OBE, FIBiol, PhD, FRSE. Vice Principal and Head of College of Life Sciences, Professor of Biochemistry, Dundee University, since 1989 (Dean, Faculty of Life Sciences); b. 15.10.53, Manchester; m., Dr Elizabeth Naomi; 1 s.; 1 d. Educ.

Kings School, Macclesfield; Stockport College of Technology; Birmingham University. Experimental Officer, ICI Pharmaceuticals, 1973-78; MRC Training Fellow, Cambridge, 1981-83; Research Group Leader, ICI Pharmaceuticals, 1983-85; Cellular Pharmacologist/Senior Cellular Pharmacologist, Smith Kline and French/Smith Kline Beecham, 1985-89. Chairman, The Biochemical Society, 2000-2004. Recreations: golf; previously playing, now spectating, football. Address: (b.) School of Life Sciences, WTB/MSI Complex, Dundee University, Dow Street, Dundee DD1 5EH; T.-01382 345156.

Downie, Emeritus Professor Robert S., MA, BPhil, FRSE, FRSA. Honorary Professorial Research Fellow, Glasgow University; b. 19.4.33, Glasgow; m., Eileen Dorothea Flynn; 3 d. Educ. High School of Glasgow; Glasgow University; Queen's College, Oxford. Tutor, Worcester College, Oxford, 1958; Glasgow University: Lecturer in Moral Philosophy, 1959, Senior Lecturer, 1968, Professor of Moral Philosophy, 1969 (Stevenson Lecturer in Medical Ethics, 1984-88); Visiting Professor: Syracuse University, New York, 1963-64, Dalhousie University, Nova Scotia, 1976. Publications: Government Action and Morality, 1964; Respect for Persons, 1969; Roles and Values, 1971; Education and Personal Relationships, 1974; Caring and Curing, 1980; Healthy Respect, 1987; Health Promotion: models and values, 1990; The Making of a Doctor, 1992; Francis Hutcheson, 1994; The Healing Arts: an Oxford illustrated anthology, 1994; Palliative Care Ethics, 1996; Medical Ethics, 1996; Clinical Judgement – Evidence in Practice, 2000; The Philosophy of Palliative Care: Critique and Reconstruction, 2006; Bioethics and the Humanities, 2007. Recreation: music. Address: (b.) Department of Philosophy, Glasgow University G12 8QQ; T.-0141-339 8855.
E-mail: R.Downie@philosophy.arts.gla.ac.uk

Doyle, Professor Christopher John, BA, MSc. Managing Director, Larch Research Ltd., since 2003; Emeritus Professor, Scottish Agricultural College, since 2003; Adjunct Professor of Agricultural Economics, Glasgow University, 1989-2003; b. 21.8.48, Sale, Cheshire; m., Alice; 1. d. Educ. St. Ambrose College, Cheshire; Keele University; Newcastle upon Tyne University. Departmental Demonstrator in Agricultural Economics, Oxford University, 1972-76; Research Officer, Centre for Agricultural Strategy, Reading University, 1976-79; Principal Scientific Officer, Institute for Grassland and Animal Production, 1979-86; Senior Economist, Ruakura Research Centre, MAF, New Zealand, 1987; Principal Scientific Officer, Institute for Grassland and Animal Production, 1988-89; Head, Management Division, Scottish Agricultural College, 1997-2003; Head, Applied Economics and Agricultural Systems Department, Scottish Agricultural College, 1989-97; Professor of Agricultural Economics, Scottish Agricultural College, 1996-2003. Publications: 140 scientific papers and publications. Recreations: languages; foreign travel; modern history; theatre. Address: (b.) Larch Research Ltd., 28 Craigholm Road, Ayr KA7 3LJ.

Doyle, Rev. David Wallace, MA(Hons), BD(Hons). Minister, St. Mary's Parish Church, Motherwell, since 1987; b. 12.4.48, Glasgow; m., Alison W. Britton; 1 s.; 1 d. Educ. High School of Glasgow; University of Glasgow; Corpus Christi, University of Cambridge. Assistant Minister, East Kilbride Old Parish Church, 1973-74; Minister, Tulliallan and Kincardine Parish Church, Fife, 1977-87. Recreations: music; gardening. Address: (h.) Manse of St. Mary's, 19 Orchard Street, Motherwell ML1 3JE; T.-01698 263472.

Drake, Thomas (Tom) Herbert, OBE, BSc, MSc, CEng, FIET, MIMechE. Director, Scottish Qualifications Authority, since 2003; b. 26.12.45, Edinburgh; m., Anne. Educ. Portobello High School; University of Aston; University of Aberdeen. Engineering Technician,

Agricultural Research Council, 1963-71; Undergraduate, Aston University, 1971-74; Project Engineer/Senior Project Engineer, Rolls Royce plc Bristol Engine Division, 1974-77; Wolfson Research Fellow, Aberdeen University, 1977-80; Lecturer/Senior Lecturer and Director of the Computer-Aided Manufacturing Centre, 1980-87; various posts including Assistant Director, Advanced Courses Assessment and Assistant Director, Curriculum Development, The Scottish Vocational Education Council (SCOTVEC), 1987-97; various posts including Head of Data Management and Certification, General Manager, National Qualifications, Acting Director of Qualifications, Director of Operations and Quality Assurance, and acting Chief Executive, The Scottish Qualifications Authority, from 1997. Chairman, Board of Management, Jewel & Esk Valley College; English-Speaking Union Thyne Scholar, 1987. OBE for services to education in the 2007 New Year's Honours List. Recreations: reading; cooking; theatre and music. Address: (b.) SQA, The Optima Building, 58 Robertson Street, Glasgow G2 8DQ; T.-0845 2135589; e-mail: tom.drake@sqa.org.uk

Dreyer-Larsen, Angela Mary. Director, Scottish Traditions of Dance Trust, since 2003, b. 11.02.54, Stirling; divorced; 2 d. Educ. St. Modan's High School. Business Manager, MacRobert Arts Centre, 1985-90; Theatre Manager, Theatre Royal Glasgow, 1990-91; Finance Director, Rambert Dance Company, 1991-94, Executive Director, 1994-97; Director, ADL Management and Productions, 1997-2003. Recreations: wind surfing; training; meeting new people. Address: (b.) Speirs Centre, Primrose Street, Alloa FK10 1JJ; T.-01259 218444; e-mail: angela@stdt.org

Driscoll, Morag Catherine, BA (Hons), MA, MPhil, LLB, DipLP, NP, WS. Director, Scottish Child Law Centre, since 2008; formerly Reporter to the Children's Panel; formerly Court Partner; b. Dorking, Surrey. Educ. Convent of the Sacred Heart, Winnipeg, Canada; University of Manitoba; University of Winnipeg; St. Andrews University; Edinburgh University. Varied previous career including Tutor in History, Canada. Member, Council, Law Society of Scotland, since 2000 (Convener, Family Law Committee; Convener, Law Reform Committee; Convenor, Child Representation Working Party. Recreations: horses; gardening. Address: (b.) 54 East Crosscauseway, Edinburgh EH8 9HD.

Driscoll, Professor Stephen T., BA, MSc, PhD. Professor of Archaeology, University of Glasgow, since 2005, Lecturer, Department of Archaeology, since 1992; b. 11.11.58, Monterey, California, USA; m., Katherine S. Forsythe; 3 d. Educ. St. Anselm's Abbey School, Washington, DC; University of Pennsylvania, Philadelphia. Founding Director of Glasgow Archaeological Research Division (GUARD) - full contract unit, 1989-94; Research Director of GUARD, since 1994; Lecturer in Archaeology, University of Glasgow, 1992-97, Senior Lecturer, 1997-2005. Editor of Scottish Archaeological Journal, since 1998; Vice President, Glasgow Archaeological Society, since 2007. Publications: Excavations at Edinburgh Castle (Co-Author), 1997; Excavations at Glasgow Cathedral, 2002; Alba: Gaelic Kingdom of Scotland, 2002. Recreations: cycling; gaelic language. Address: 81 Albert Road, Glasgow; e-mail: s.driscoll@archaeology.gla.ac.uk

Drummond, Rev. John Whiteford, MA, BD. Minister, Rutherglen West and Wardlawhill Parish Church, since 2007; Minister, Rutherglen West Parish Church, 1986-2007; b. 27.6.46, Glasgow; m., Barbara S. Grant; 1 s.; 3 d. Educ. Bearsden Academy; University of Glasgow.

Probationer Assistant, St. Francis-in-the-East Church, Bridgeton, 1970-71; Ordained Assistant, King's Park Parish Church, Glasgow, 1971-73; Minister, Linwood Parish Church, 1973-86. Recreations: reading; television; family. Address: (h.) 12 Albert Drive, Rutherglen G73 3RT; T.-0141-569 8547.

Drummond, Rev. Norman Walker, MA, BD. Chairman, Lloyds TSB Foundation for Scotland, since 2003; Chairman, Drummond International, since 1999; Founder and Chairman, Columba 1400, Community and International Leadership Centre, Isle of Skye, since 1997; Founder and non-executive Chairman, The Change Partnership Scotland, 1999-2003; Chairman, Community Action Network Scotland, 2001-03; Non-executive Director, J&J Denholm Ltd., since 2002; b. 1.4.52, Greenock; m., Lady Elizabeth Kennedy; 3 s.; 2 d. Educ. Merchiston Castle School; Fitzwilliam College, Cambridge; New College, Edinburgh. Chaplain to the Forces, 1976-82; Depot, The Parachute Regiment and Airborne Forces, 1977-78; 1st Bn., The Black Watch (Royal Highland Regiment), 1978-82; Chaplain, Fettes College, 1982-84; Headmaster, Loretto School, 1984-95; Minister, Kilmuir and Stenscholl, Isle of Skye, 1996-98; BBC National Governor and Chairman, Broadcasting Council for Scotland, 1994-99; former Chairman, BBC Children in Need; Member, Queen's Bodyguard for Scotland (Royal Company of Archers); Past President: Victoria League for Overseas Students in Scotland, Edinburgh Bn., Boys' Brigade; former Governor, Gordonstoun School; former Chairman, Aiglon College, Switzerland; former Member, Scottish Committee for Imperial Cancer Research; former Trustee, Foundation for Skin Research; former Member, Scottish Committee, Duke of Edinburgh's Award Scheme; former Member, Court, Heriot-Watt University; former Chairman, Musselburgh and District Council of Social Services. Publications: The First Twenty Five Years (the official history of the Black Watch Kirk Session); Mother's Hands; The Spirit of Success. Recreations: rugby football; cricket; golf; curling; traditional jazz. Address: Drummond International, 35 Drummond Place, Edinburgh EH3 6PW.

Drummond, Sheriff Thomas Anthony Kevin, LLB, QC. Sheriff, Lothian and Borders at Jedburgh, Selkirk and Duns, since 2000; b. 3.11.43, Howwood, Renfrewshire; m., Margaret Evelyn Broadley; 1 d. (1 d. deceased). Educ. St. Mirin's Academy, Paisley; Blairs College, Aberdeen; Edinburgh University. Admitted, Faculty of Advocates, 1974; Advocate Depute, 1985-90; Member, Firearms Consultative Committee, 1989-97; Member, Criminal Injuries Compensation Board, 1990-96; Home Advocate Depute, 1996-97; Sheriff, Glasgow and Strathkelvin, 1997-2000. Joint Chairman, Institute of Chartered Accountants of Scotland, 1993-2000. Hon. US Deputy Marshal, 1998. Publications (legal cartoons): The Law at Work; The Law at Play; Great Defences of Our Time. Recreations: fishing; shooting. Address: (h.) Pomathorn House, Penicuik, Midlothian; T.-01968 674064.
E-mail: kdrummondqc@aol.com

Drummond Young, Hon. Lord (James Edward Drummond Young), QC. Senator of the College of Justice in Scotland, since 2001; Chairman, Scottish Law Commission; b. 1950; m.; 1 d. Educ. Cambridge University; Harvard University; Edinburgh University. Admitted, Faculty of Advocates, 1976. Address: Parliament House, Parliament Square, Edinburgh EH1 1RQ.

Drury, John Kenneth, MBChB, PhD, FRCS. Consultant, General Surgeon, Victoria Infirmary NHS Trust, since 1986 (Clinical Director, General Surgery, 1993-99); Registrar for Surgical Examinations, Royal College of Physicians and

Surgeons of Glasgow, since 1999; Director, Surgical Examinations, RCPSG, since 2003; Member, Intercollegiate Committee for Basic Surgical Examinations, since 2003; Member, Council, RCPSG, since 2003; b. 23.1.47; m., Gillian Gilmore; 1 s.; 1 d. Educ. Paisley Grammar School; University of Glasgow. Research Fellow, Department of Physiology, University of Glasgow, 1973-76; West of Scotland Surgical Training Scheme, 1976-86. Committee Member, RNLI; Member: Vascular Society of Great Britain, European Society for Vascular and Endovascular Surgery. Recreations: sailing; golf; local art. Address: (b.) Department of Surgery, South Glasgow University Hospitals NHS Trust – Victoria Infirmary, Glasgow G42 9TY; T.-0141-201 5464; e-mail: jkdalba@aol.com

Drysdale, Professor David Douglas (Dougal), BSc, PhD, MRSC, FIFireE, FSFPE, CEng, FRSE. Professor Emeritus (Fire Safety Engineering), Edinburgh University, since 2004; Chairman, International Association for Fire Safety Science, 2002-05; b. 30.9.39, Dunfermline; m., Judith McIntyre; 3 s. Educ. Edinburgh Academy; Edinburgh University; Cambridge University. Post-doctoral Fellow, University of Toronto, 1966-67; Research Lecturer, Leeds University, 1967-74; Lecturer, Fire Engineering, Edinburgh University, 1974-92; Visiting Professor, Centre for Fire Safety Studies, Worcester Polytechnic Institute, Mass., USA, 1982; Reader, Fire Safety Engineering, Edinburgh University, 1990-98, Professor, Fire Safety Engineering, 1998-2004; SFPE Man of the Year (USA), 1983; BRE Fire Research Lecturer, 1995; SFPE Arthur B. Guise Medal for eminent achievement advancing the Science of Fire Protection Engineering, 1995; IAFSS Kawagoe Medal for lifelong career in and contribution to fire safety science, 2002; IFE Rasbash Medal, 2005; International Forum of Fire Research Directors' Sjolin Award for "outstanding career in fire science", 2005. Publications: Introduction to Fire Dynamics, 1998; Handbook of Fire Protection Engineering (co-ed.), 1995; Fire Safety Journal (ed.), since 1988. Recreations: music; hill walking; curling; coarse golf. Address: (b.) School of Engineering and Electronics, Edinburgh University, King's Buildings, Edinburgh, EH9 3JN; T.-0131-650 5724.

Drysdale, James Cunison, LLB. Partner, Anderson Strathern Solicitors, since 1986; b. 30.4.56, Edinburgh; m., Fiona Jean nee Duncan Millar; 1 s.; 3 d. Educ. Winchester College; Aberdeen University. Apprentice at Brodies, 1979-81; Assistant Solicitor: Murray Beith and Murray, 1981-83, J & F Anderson, 1983-86. Treasurer and Council Member, UKELA (UK Environmental Law Association); Clerk of the Course Fife Foxhounds Point To Point; Trainer, Fife Hunt Pony Club Games Teams. Recreations: countryside pursuits. Address: (b.) 1 Rutland Court, Edinburgh EH3 8EY; T.-0131 625 7228; e-mail: james.drysdale@andersonstrathern.co.uk

Duff, Professor (Robin) Antony, BA, FBA, FRSE. Professor, Department of Philosophy, Stirling University, since 1990; b. 9.3.45, Fareham. Educ. Sedbergh School; Christ Church, Oxford. Visiting Lecturer, University of Washington, Seattle, 1968-69; Department of Philosophy, Stirling University, since 1970. British Academy Research Readership, 1989-91; Leverhulme Major Research Fellowship, 2002-05. Publications: Trials and Punishments; Intention, Agency and Criminal Liability; Criminal Attempts; Punishment, Communication and Community; Answering for Crime; The Trial on Trial. Address: (b.) Department of Philosophy, Stirling University, Stirling FK9 4LA; T.-01786 467556.

Duffin, Stuart, DA, RE, RSA. Studio Workshop Manager, Glasgow Print Studio, 1989-2002; studio etcher; b. 13.6.59. Educ. Gray's School of Art, Aberdeen. Member of staff,

Glasgow Print Studio, 1984; SAC award to study and travel in Italy, 1987; exchange visit to Senej Print Workshop, Moscow, 1992; British Council support to study at the Jerusalem Print Workshop, 1996; solo exhibitions: Glasgow Print Studio, 1995, 2001, Gallery of Jerusalem Print Workshop, 1998; Visiting lecturer tour and exhibition, New Zealand, 2002, 2007. Address: 40 Cromarty Avenue, Glasgow G43 2HG; T.-0141-632 7432; e-mail: info@stuartduffin.com; website: www.stuartduffin.com

Duffus, Professor Carol Margaret, BSc, MS, PhD, DIC, DSc, FRSE. Emeritus Professor, Crop Science, Scottish Agricultural College, since 2000; b. Belfast; m., John Henderson Duffus; 2 d. Educ. Victoria College, Belfast; Queens's University, Belfast; University of Michigan, Ann Arbor, USA; Imperial College, London; University of Edinburgh. Lecturer in Biochemistry, School of Molecular Sciences, University of Warwick, 1966; Lecturer, University of Edinburgh and East of Scotland College of Agriculture, 1968; Scottish Agricultural College: Head, Agricultural Biochemistry Department, 1987, Head, Crop Sciences Division, 1990, Professor, Crop Science and Technology, 1997-2000. Member: Scottish Natural Heritage, South East Regional Board, Scientific Advisory Committee, 1990-97, Law Society of Scotland Complaints Committee, 1993-95, Scientific Advisory Committee, Scottish Science Trust, 1999-2002; President, Association of Applied Biologists, 1999-2000; Secretary to Meetings, Royal Society of Edinburgh, 2001-04 (Member, Council, 1998-2004); Member, SAC Applied Bioscience Consultative Committee, 2003-05; Member, Council, The Rotary Club of Edinburgh, 2005; Member, Council, Scotia Agricultural Club, since 2007. Publications: Carbohydrate Metabolism in Plants (Co-Author), 1984; Toxic Substances in Crop Plants (Co-Author), 1991. Recreations: gardening; chamber music; golf. Address: (b.) Scottish Agricultural College, King's Buildings, West Mains Road, Edinburgh EH9 3JG; T.-0131-535 4000.

Duffus, John Henderson, BSc, PhD, DSc, CSci, CBiol, MIBiol, CChem, FRSC. Director, Edinburgh Centre for Toxicology (EdinTox). Educ. Arbroath High School; Edinburgh University; Heriot-Watt University. Research Fellow: Warwick University, 1965-67, Edinburgh University, 1967-70; Lecturer, Heriot-Watt University, 1970-80; Senior Lecturer in Environmental Toxicology, Heriot-Watt University, 1980-97; Hon. Fellow in Public Health Sciences, Edinburgh University, 1997; WHO Consultant, Toxicology and Chemical Safety, since 1981; Member, UK Department of the Environment Advisory Committee on Hazardous Substances, 1991-99; Titular Member, IUPAC Commission on Toxicology, 1991-2001, Chair, 1997-2001; Titular Member, IUPAC Committee on the Teaching of Chemistry, 1999-2001; Member, RSC Committee on Environment, Health and Safety; Member, UK HSE Biocides Consultative Committee; Chair, IUPAC Sub-Committee on Toxicology and Risk Assessment; Titular Member, IUPAC Division VII, Chemistry and Human Health Committee, 2004; Adjunct Professor, Asian Institute of Technology, 2004. Publications: Environmental Toxicology, 1980; Environmental Toxicology and Ecotoxicology, 1986; Magnesium in Mitosis and the Cell Cycle (Co-Author), 1987; Yeast: A Practical Approach (Co-Editor), 1988; The Toxicology of Chemicals, Series 1, Carcinogenicity, Vol III, Vol IV (Co-Editor/Author), 1991-93; Toxic Substances in Crop Plants (Co-Editor/Author), 1991; Cancer and Workplace Chemicals, 1995; Glossaries of Terms Used in Toxicology, 1993-2007; Carcinogenicity of Inorganic Substances (Chief Editor/Author), 1997; Chemical Risk Assessment (Co-Author), 1999; Risk Assessment and Elemental Speciation, 2001, 2003, 2006; Fundamental Toxicology (Co-Editor, Author), 2006. Address: (b.) Edinburgh Centre for Toxicology, 43 Mansionhouse Road, Edinburgh EH9 2JD.

Duffy, Professor John Alastair, BSc, PhD, DSc, CChem, FRSC, FSGT. Emeritus Professor of Chemistry, Aberdeen University, since 1996; Quality Assessor for Scottish Higher Education Funding Council, 1993-94; b. 24.9.32, Birmingham; m., Muriel F.L. Ramsay; 1 s.; 1 d. Educ. Solihull School, Warwickshire; Sheffield University. Research Chemist, Albright & Wilson, Oldbury, 1958-59; Lecturer in Inorganic Chemistry, Wolverhampton Polytechnic, 1959-61; Senior Lecturer in Inorganic Chemistry, NE Wales Institute, 1961-65; Lecturer, Senior Lecturer, Reader in Chemistry, Aberdeen University, 1966-96; Assessor in Inorganic Chemistry for Ordinary and Higher National Certificates and Diplomas in Scotland, 1971-82; Consultant to Schott Glaswerke, Mainz, West Germany, 1984-86; Past Chairman, NE Scotland Section, Royal Society of Chemistry. Blackwell Prize, University of Aberdeen, 1995. Publications: General Inorganic Chemistry, 1966; Bonding Energy Levels and Bands in Inorganic Solids, 1990; 150 scientific publications. Recreations: 20th-century opera; music. Address: (h.) 35 Beechgrove Terrace, Aberdeen AB15 5DR; T.-01224 641752; e-mail: j.a.duffy@abdn.ac.uk

Duffy, Sheila Sinclair, MA. Editor, GWSFH Society, since 2001; Freelance researcher; b. 6.8.46, Cumberland; m., Paul Young; 2 d. Educ. St. Joseph's, Nicosia; Boroughmuir School, Edinburgh; Edinburgh University. Auxiliary nurse, Edinburgh Royal Infirmary, 1965-66; croupier, Edinburgh night club, 1966-67; graduate trainee, Scottish Television, 1967-68, then Reporter and Interviewer; Women's Editor, Radio Clyde, 1973-99; former Columnist, Weekly News, Scottish Field, Evening Times. Vice-Chairman, Visiting Committee, Glenochil Young Offenders Institution. Glenfiddich Food Writer Award, 1986; SAFHS journal award, 2003. Address: c/o Sinclair Ancestral Research, 9 Woodside Crescent, Glasgow G3 7UL; e-mail: editor@gwsfhs.org.uk

Dugmore, Professor Andrew J., PhD, BSc, FGS, FRSA (Scot). Professor of Geosciences, University of Edinburgh, since 2007; Adjunct Professor (Research), City University of New York, USA, since 2002; b. Lowestoft; m., Thelma (nee Williamson); 1 s.; 1 d. Educ. Denes High School, Lowestoft; University of Birmingham; University of Aberdeen. Lecturer, Senior Lecturer, University of Edinburgh, 1992-2004, Reader in Tephrochronology, 2004-07. Visiting Lecturer, University of Lund, Sweden, 1997; President's Award, Royal Scottish Geographical Society, 2002. Recreations: hill walking and mountaineering. Address: (b.) Institute of Geography, School of Geosciences, University of Edinburgh, Drummond Street, Edinburgh EH8 9XP; T.-0131 650 8156.
E-mail: andrew.dugmore@ed.ac.uk

Dukes, Professor Paul, BA (Cantab), MA, PhD, FRSE. Professor of History, Aberdeen University, 1988-99, Emeritus Professor, since 1999; b. 5.4.34, Wallington; 1 s.; 1 d. Educ. Wallington County Grammar School; Cambridge University. Advisory Editor, History Today. Publications: several books on aspects of Russian, American, European and world history. Recreations: hill-walking; travel. Address: (b.) History Department, Aberdeen University, Aberdeen; T.-01224 273886.

Dumble, Graham, FFA, FRSA. Director of Risk and Regulation, Aegon UK, since 2005; b. 27.1.59, Galashiels; m., Ailsa; 2 s.; 1 d. Educ. Galashiels Academy. Joined Scottish Equitable on leaving school, 1977, management posts, primarily in customer service, then: Marketing Director, 1992, Operations Director, 1997, Managing Director, 1999; Member, Executive Board, Aegon UK,

1999; Managing Director, Aegon UK Life and Pensions, 2003. Scottish Marketeer of the Year, 1994. Recreations: most sports (especially Rugby Union) as spectator; contemporary music (well, it was contemporary once). Address: (b.) Aegon UK, Edinburgh Park, Edinburgh EH12 9SE; T.-0131-549 3905.
E-mail: graham.dumble@aegon.co.uk

Dunbar, Sir Archibald Ranulph, MA, DipAgric (Cantab), DTA (Trin). Retired; b. 8.8.27, London; m., Amelia M.S. Davidson; 1 s.; 2 d. Educ. Wellington College; Pembroke College, Cambridge. Military Service, Cameron Highlanders (attached Gordon Highlanders), 1945-48; Imperial College of Tropical Agriculture, Trinidad, 1952-53; Agricultural Officer, Colonial Service, Uganda (later Overseas Civil Service, Uganda) 1953-70; Landowner, Duffus Estate, Elgin, since 1970. Honorary Sheriff, Sheriff Court District of Moray, since 1989; Knight of Honour and Devotion, Sovereign Military Order of Malta, 1989. Recreations: railways; model railways; military models. Address: (h.) The Old Manse, Duffus, Elgin, Moray; T.-01343 830270.

Dunbar, Sheriff Ian Duncan, LLB. Resident Sheriff, Dunfermline, since 2005; Resident Sheriff, Dundee, 2000-05; Floating Sheriff, Dundee, 1998-2000; Partner, Miller Hendry, Solicitors, 1990-98; b. 31.10.48, Dundee; m., Susan Young. Educ. Lawside Academy, Dundee; Queens College, Dundee/St. Andrews University. Law apprentice, Soutar Reid & Mill, Dundee, 1969-71; Assistant Solicitor, Sneddon Campbell & Munro, Perth, 1971-72, Partner, 1972-85; merged to form Miller Sneddon, 1985, Partner, 1985-90; merged to form Miller Hendry, 1990. President, Law Society of Scotland, 1993-94. Recreations: golf; rugby; cooking; wine. Address: (h.) Craigrownie, Forgandenny Road, Bridge of Earn, Perth PH2 9HA.

Dunbar, John Greenwell, OBE, MA, FSA, HonFSA Scot, HonFRIAS. Architectural historian; Secretary, Royal Commission on the Ancient and Historical Monuments of Scotland, 1978-90; b. 1.3.30, London; m., Elizabeth Mill Blyth. Educ. University College School, London; Balliol College, Oxford. joined staff, Royal Commission on the Ancient and Historical Monuments of Scotland, 1953. Publications: The Historic Architecture of Scotland, 1966; Accounts of the Masters of Works, Volume 2 (1616-1649), (Joint Editor), 1982; Sir William Burrell's Northern Tour, 1997; Scottish Royal Palaces, 1999; Buildings of Scotland: Borders, 2006 (Joint Author). Address: (h.) Paties Mill, Carlops, by Penicuik, Midlothian EH26 9NF; T.-01968 660250.

Dunbar, Lennox Robert, DA, RSA. Head of Printmaking, Grays School of Art, since 1987; Painter and Printmaker; b. 17.5.52, Aberdeen; m., Jan Storie; 2 s.; 1 d. Educ. Aberdeen Grammar School; Grays School of Art. Part-time Lecturer, 1975-82; Etching Technician, Peacock Printmakers, 1978-82; Education Officer, Peacock Printmakers, 1982-86; appointed Lecturer in Painting and Printmaking, Grays School of Art, 1986; Visiting Lecturer, Duncan of Jordanstone College of Art, Dundee, and Newcastle University; Visiting Artist/Tutor, Louisiana State University; College of Santa FE, New Mexico; participated in many group and one-man exhibitions; numerous awards including Latimer Award, 1978, Guthrie Award, 1984, Shell Expro Premier Award, 1991, 1993 and 2006; work in many private and public collections.

Dunbar, Morrison Alexander Rankin, CBE, KCSJ, FRSAMD, FRSA. Chairman: Royal Scottish Academy of Music and Drama Trust, 1992-2004, Westbourne Music, since 1998, Cantilena Festival, Islay, since 2002; b. 27.4.29, Glasgow; m., Sally Joan Sutherland; 2 s.; 1 d. Educ. Belmont House; Gresham House. Managing Director, Morrison Dunbar Ltd. Builders, 1957-81. President: Scottish Building Contractors Association, 1968, Scottish

Building Employers Federation, 1975, Building Employers Confederation, 1980, Builders Benevolent Institution, 1987; Lord Dean of Guild, Merchants House of Glasgow, 1991-93; Chairman: Epilepsy Association of Scotland, 1990-93, Royal Scottish Academy of Music and Drama, 1987-91, Royal Scottish National Orchestra, 1993-97; Member, Trades House of Glasgow. Recreations: music; art galleries; golf. Address: (h.) 18 Devonshire Terrace Lane, Glasgow G12 9XT; T.-0141-357 1289.

Dunbar-Nasmith, Professor Emeritus Sir James Duncan, CBE, BA, DA, RIBA, PPRIAS, FRSA, FRSE. Trustee, Scottish Mining Museum; Partner, Law and Dunbar-Nasmith, Architects, Edinburgh and Forres 1957-99; b. 15.3.27, Dartmouth. Educ. Lockers Park; Winchester College; Trinity College, Cambridge; Edinburgh College of Art. Lt., Scots Guards, 1945-48; ARIBA, 1954; President: Edinburgh Architectural Association, 1967-69, Royal Incorporation of Architects in Scotland, 1971-73; Member, RIBA Council, 1967-73 (Vice-President and Chairman, Board of Architectural Education, 1972-73); Council, ARCUK, 1976-84, Board of Education, 1976-88 (Vice Chairman, 1977); Professor and Head, Department of Architecture, Heriot-Watt University and Edinburgh College of Art, 1978-88; Chairman, Scottish Civic Trust, 1995-2003; Vice-President, Europa Nostra, 1997-2005. Member: Royal Commission on Ancient and Historical Monuments of Scotland, 1972-96, Ancient Monuments Board for Scotland, 1969-82 (interim Chairman, 1972-73), Historic Buildings Council for Scotland, 1966-93; Trustee, Architectural Heritage Fund, Theatres Trust, 1983-95; Deputy Chairman, Edinburgh Festival Society, 1981-85. Recreations: music; theatre; skiing; sailing. Address: (b.) 4 Blackie House, Lady Stair's Close, Edinburgh EH1 2NY; T.-0131-225 4236; e-mail: jd.nasmith@virgin.net

Duncan, (Alan) Michael, MA, BPhil, DipEd, FEA. Rector, High School of Dundee, 1997-2008; b. 13.8.48, Glasgow. Educ. Grove Academy; St Andrews University. Morgan Academy, Dundee: Teacher of English, 1972-74, Assistant Principal Teacher of English, 1974-78; Robert Gordon's College, Aberdeen: Head of English, 1978-85, Assistant Headmaster, 1985-93, Deputy Headmaster, 1993-97. Member, Governing Board and Chairman of the Management Committee, Scottish Council for Independent Schools; Trustee, Dundee Heritage Trust. Recreations: reading; gardening. Address: (b.) High School of Dundee, Euclid Crescent, Dundee DD1 1HU; T.-01382 202921; e-mail: amduncan@dundeehigh.dundeecity.sch.uk

Duncan, Professor Archibald Alexander McBeth, MA, DUniv, FBA, FRSE, FRHistS. Professor of Scottish History, Glasgow University, 1962-93, Emeritus Professor, since 1993, currently Honorary Research Fellow; b. 17.10.26, Pitlochry; m., Ann Hayes Sawyer; 2 s.; 1 d. Educ. George Heriot's School, Edinburgh; Edinburgh University; Balliol College, Oxford. Lecturer: Balliol College, 1950-51, Queen's University, Belfast, 1951-53, Edinburgh University, 1953-61; Leverhulme Fellow, 1961-62; Clerk of Senate, Glasgow University, 1978-83; Dean of Faculties, Glasgow University, 1998-2000. Publications: Scotland, The Making of the Kingdom, 1975; revised 3rd edition of W.C. Dickinson's Scotland from Earliest Times to 1603, 1977; Regesta Regum Scottorum, v., The Acts of Robert I 1306-29, 1988; edition of John Barbour's The Bruce, 1997; The Kingship of the Scots, 842-1292, 2002. Recreation: swimming. Address: (h.) 17 Campbell Drive, Bearsden, Glasgow G61 4NF: T.-0141-942 5023.

Duncan, Arnold Durham, MIPI. Honorary Sheriff, Sheriffdom of Grampian, Highlands and Islands at Lerwick,

Shetland, since 2003; b. 10.9.46, Lerwick, Shetland. Educ. Scalloway Junior Secondary and Lerwick Central Secondary Schools, Shetland; Scottish Police College: Junior and Senior Divisions, Kincardine, Fife; Central College of Commerce, Glasgow. Appointed Boy Clerk with former Zetland Constabulary, 1962; appointed Constable in Zetland Constabulary, 1966; appointed Detective Constable, with Northern Constabulary, 1973; promoted Detective Sergeant, 1976; appointed Force Liaison officer, with responsibilities for Economic Key Points in area viz.: Dounreay Atomic Reactor, Caithness; Flotta Oil Terminal, Orkney and Sullom Voe Oil Terminal, Shetland, 1980; awarded Police Long Service and Good Conduct Medal, 1989; promoted to Inspector and Deputy Sub Divisional Officer, Shetland Islands Area, 1990; retired from Police Service, 1996; casual contract with Crown Office and Procurator Fiscal Service, as Precognition Officer/Office Manager, 2001-02; Commission held as Procurator Fiscal Depute at Lerwick, Shetland. Chairman: Scalloway Community Council, Scalloway Waterfront Trust; Chairman, Shetland Health Board Independent Review Panel; Elder, Church of Scotland, Tingwall Parish. Recreations: coastal/hill walking; local history; reading; gardening; choir member. Address: "Springbank", Houl Road, Scalloway, Shetland ZE1 0UA; T.-01595 880419; e-mail: arnold.duncan@tiscali.co.uk

Duncan, Atholl. Head of News and Current Affairs, BBC Scotland, since 2006. Educ. George Watson's College, Edinburgh; Napier University. Joined DC Thomson in 1982 as a reporter; joined BBC Scotland in 1985 as a researcher and sub-editor; worked on a variety of news and sport programmes including Focal Point, Upfront, Newsnight and Sportscene and produced more than 1,000 editions of Reporting Scotland before becoming Managing Editor for News and Current Affairs in 1996; became Director of Corporate Affairs, Scottish Water in 2003. Non-executive Director, Sportscotland, since 2001. Address: (b.) BBC Scotland, 40 Pacific Quay, Glasgow G51 1DZ.

Duncan, David John, MA, PhD. Secretary of The University of Dundee, since 2001; b. 8.8.64, Bellshill, Lanarkshire; m., Fiona; 1 s.; 1 d. Educ. Daniel Stewart's and Melville College; University of Aberdeen; Queen's University, Canada. Lecturer, University of Natal, Durban, 1990; Visiting Research Fellow, University of The Witwatersrand, Johannesburg, 1991-92; Executive Assistant, Secretary, Director, Scottish Consultative Council on the Curriculum, 1992-2000; Assistant Chief Executive, Learning and Teaching Scotland, 2000-01. Canadian Commonwealth Scholar, 1988-90; Elder, Hope Park Parish Church, St. Andrews. Publications: author, The Mills of God, 1995; We Are Motor Men, 1997. Address: (b.) University of Dundee, Dundee DD1 4HN; T.-01382 344006; e-mail: d.j.duncan@dundee.ac.uk

Duncan, Elaine Margaret, BSc (Hons) Behavioural Sciences. Chief Executive, Scottish Bible Society, since 2006; b. 29.8.58, Whitehaven, Cumbria. Educ. Whitehaven Grammar School; Huddersfield Polytechnic. Universities and Colleges Christian Fellowship, 1981-95; Scripture Union Scotland, 1995-2006. Address: (b.) 7 Hampton Terrace, Edinburgh EH12 5XU; T.-0131-337-9701; e-mail: elaine.duncan@scottishbiblesociety.org

Duncan, Geoffrey Cheyne Calderhead, BL. Lord Dean of Guild, Merchants House of Glasgow, 1993-95; b. 6.10.29, Whitecraigs, Glasgow; m., Lorna Dowling (deceased); 1 s.; 1 d. Educ. Belmont House School; Glasgow Academy; Glasgow University. Solicitor in private practice, 1951-91; Partner, Aitken, Hamilton & Duncan, 1951-70; Partner,

Kerr, Barrie & Duncan, 1970-91; Chairman, Glasgow Junior Chamber of Commerce, 1963-64; Director, The Girls' School Company Ltd., 1964-90 (Chairman, 1977-90); Chairman, St. Columba's School, 1972-83; Director, The West of Scotland School Company Ltd., 1972-92 (Chairman, 1989-92); Member: Board of Management, Glasgow South Western Hospitals, 1964-69, Clyde River Purification Board, 1969-75; Director, Glasgow Chamber of Commerce, 1972-92; Chairman, Glasgow Post Office Advisory Committee, 1974-84; Member, Post Office Users' National Council, 1974-87; Chairman, Post Office Users' Council for Scotland, 1984-87; Chairman, Advisory Committee on Telecommunications for Scotland, 1984-87; Director, The Merchants' House of Glasgow, since 1982; Trustee, Ferguson Bequest Fund, 1987-97; Member: Executive Committee, Abbeyfield Quarrier's Society (now Abbeyfield Strathgryffe Society), 1981-97 (Chairman, 1988-96), Council of Management, Quarrier's Homes, 1985-93; Director, The Scottish Cremation Society Ltd., 1978-2004 (Chairman, 1993-2001); Member, Iona Cathedral Management Board, 1990-93; Director, Iona Abbey Ltd., 1993-96; Chairman, Renfrewshire Valuation Appeal Panel, 1993-99; General Commissioner for Income Tax, 1994-2004; Patron, Royal Incorporation of Hutcheson's Hospital, 1995-2001; Director, City of Glasgow Native Benevolent Association, 1998-2005 (Chairman, 2004-05); Director, Scottish International Piano Competition, 2005-07. Recreations: gardening; photography; listening to classical music. Address: (h.) Mid Clevans, Bridge of Weir, Renfrewshire PA11 3HP; T.-01505 612566.

Duncan, James Wann, MBE, Hon. LLD, JP, MIMFT. Rector's Assessor, University of Dundee, 1992-98; former Vice-Chairman, Tayside Health Board (Convener, General Purposes Committee); Convener, Personnel and Accommodation Sub-Committee, Management Committee, Common Services Agency for the Scottish Health Service; retired Senior Chief Maxillofacial Technician, Dundee Royal Infirmary; b. 14.7.25, Dundee; m., Hilda Mackenzie Gray; 3 d. Educ. Stobswell Secondary School; Dundee College of Technology. Former Convener, Property Equipment Supplies Committee, General Board of Management, Dundee General Hospitals; former Vice-Convener, General Purposes Committee, General Board of Management, Dundee Northern Hospitals; former Member, Dundee Town Council (Senior Magistrate); former Convener: Dundee Art Galleries and Museums Committee, Further Education Committee, Dundee Police Committee; former Member, Board of Governors, Scottish Police College; Member, Dundee District Council, 1974-77 (Convener, Planning and Development Committee); Chairman, Dundee City Labour Party, 1960-62; former Member, Scottish Council, SDP; former Scottish Representative, National Committee for Dental Technicians, USDAW; former Member, STUC Health and Social Services Committee; former Member, University of Dundee Court. Recreations: golf; gardening; DIY. Address: (h.) 13 Clive Road, Downfield, Dundee DD3 8LP; T.-01382 825488.

Duncan, John. Lord-Lieutenant, Ayrshire and Arran, since 2006; m., Jess; 1 s.; 1 d.; 1 stepdaughter. Joined Renfrew and Bute Constabulary as a Police Cadet in 1959, retiring as Deputy Chief Constable of Strathclyde Police in 2001.

Duncan, Robert Alexander, BCom, CA. Non-Executive Director, Abbott Group plc, since 2003; Non-Executive Director, Havelock Europa PLC, since 2004; Business Change Director, Firstgroup PLC, 2000-03; b. 31.5.50, Aberdeen; m., Gail; 2 d. Educ. Robert Gordon's College, Aberdeen; Edinburgh University. Qualified CA, Coopers and Lybrand, Glasgow; Audit Manager, Brussels, four

years; various finance positions; Finance Director, Grampian Transport; Managing Director GRT Bus Group; Director, UK Bus and Business Change Director, First Group PLC; Governor, Robert Gordon University, Aberdeen, since 2004. Recreations: golf; fishing; cycling; art and antique hunting. Address: (b.) Minto Drive, Altens, Aberdeen; T.-01224 299600.

Duncan, William, BSc (Hons), GradIPD, PhD. Chief Executive, Royal Society of Edinburgh, since 1985; Chief Executive, RSE Scotland Foundation, since 1996; Secretary to Trustees, Scottish Science Trust, 1997-98; b. 6.12.50, Edinburgh. Educ. Linlithgow Academy; Edinburgh University. Greater London Council, 1975-78; Lothian Regional Council, 1978-85. Recreations: contemporary music; opera. Address: (b.) 22/26 George Street, Edinburgh EH2 2PQ; T.-0131-240 5000.

Duncan Millar, James, LVO, psc. Managing Partner, A&J Duncan Millar, Remony Estate, since 1986; Commissioner, Deer Commission for Scotland, 1996-2005; b. 5.4.48, Aberfeldy; m., Susan Ferrier Marshall; 1 s.; 1 d. Educ. Loretto School; RMA Sandhurst. Commissioned, The Black Watch, 1968-86; Army Staff College, Camberley, 1982. Chair, Kenmore and District Community Council; Member, Highland Perthshire Communities Partnership; Member, Blackface Sire Reference Company, 2004-06; Member, Scottish Rural Business and Property Association; Member, Association of Deer Management Groups. Recreation: downhill skiing. Address: Remony, Aberfeldy, Perthshire PH15 2HR; e-mail: remony@btinternet.com

Dundas-Bekker, Althea Enid Philippa, DL. Deputy Lieutenant, Midlothian, since 1991; b. 4.11.39, Gorebridge; m., Aedrian Ruprecht Bekker (deceased); 2 d. Business work abroad, in London, and with the National Trust for Scotland; inherited Arniston House, 1970, and restoring ever since. Recreations: Scottish history; Scottish songs; walking dogs. Address: (h.) Arniston House, Gorebridge, Midlothian EH23 4RY; T.-01875 830238. E-mail: email@dundasbekker.fsnet.co.uk

Dundee, 12th Earl of (Alexander Henry Scrymgeour). Hereditary Royal Standard-Bearer for Scotland; b. 5.6.49; m.; 1 s.; 3 d. Educ. Eton; St. Andrews University. Address: Farm Office, Birkhill, Cupar, Fife.

Dundonald, 15th Earl of (Iain Alexander Douglas Blair); b. 17.2.61; m., Marie Beatrice Louise Russo; 2 s.; 1 d. Educ. Wellington College; Royal Agricultural College, Cirencester. Company Director; Hon. Chilean Consul to Scotland. Interests: marine and rural environment; rural housing; Scottish affairs; innovation. Address: Lochnell Castle, Ledaig, Argyll.

Dunion, Kevin Harry, OBE, MA (Hons), MSc, FRSA. Scottish Information Commissioner, since 2003; Chief Executive, Friends of the Earth Scotland, 1991-2003; Honorary Senior Research Fellow, University of Strathclyde, 1998-2004; b. 20.12.55, Bridge of Allan; m., Linda Dunion (qv); 2 s. Educ. St. Andrew's High School, Kirkcaldy; St. Andrews University; Edinburgh University. HM Inspector of Taxes, 1978-80; Administrator, Edinburgh University Students Association, 1980-84; Scottish Campaigns Manager, Oxfam, 1984-91. Editor, Radical Scotland, 1982-85; Chair: Scottish Education and Action for Development, 1990-92, Friends of the Earth International, 1996-99 (Treasurer, 1993-96); Member: Secretary of State's Advisory Group on Sustainable Development, 1996-99, Scottish Executive Ministerial

Group on Sustainable Scotland, 1999-2001, Scottish Executive Cabinet Sub-Committee on Sustainable Scotland, 2001-03, Board, Scottish Natural Heritage, 2000-03, United Nations Environment and Development International Advisory Board, 1999-2002. Publications: Living in the Real World: An International Role for Scotland's Parliament, 1993; Troublemakers: the Struggle for Environmental Justice in Scotland, 2003; The Democracy of War, 2007. Address: (b.) Kinburn Castle, Doubledykes Road, St Andrews KY16 9DS; T.-01334 464610.

Dunion, Linda M., BSc (Soc Sci). Director, See-Change Social Change Consultancy; Campaign Director, See Me Anti Stigma Campaign, 2002-07; b. 15.9.56, Perth; m., Kevin Dunion (qv); 1 d. Educ. Morrisons Academy Girls' School, Crieff; Edinburgh University. Board Member, Scottish Commission for the Regulation of Care. Formerly: Councillor, Edinburgh District Council, Director, SEAD (Scottish Education and Action for Development), Director, Scottish Down's Syndrome Association, Assistant Director, Age Concern Scotland, Head of Public Affairs, BMA Scotland. Address: 39B John Street, Cellardyke, Fife KY10 3BA.

Dunkley, Professor John, BA (Hons), MA, PhD, DipEd. Professor in French Enlightenment Studies, University of Aberdeen, since 2000; Immediate Past President of The British Society for XVIIIth Century Studies, since 2008; b. 01.11.44, Guildford; m., Eileen; 1 s.; 1 d. Educ. Royal Grammar School, Guilford; Exeter University. Lecteur in English, University of Rennes, 1965-66; Tutor in French, University of Exeter, 1966-68; Assistant Etranger in English, University of Dijon, 1968-69; Temporary Lecturer in French, University of Aberystwyth, 1969-70; Lecturer in French, University of Aberdeen, 1970-86, Senior Lecturer, 1986-96, Reader, 1996-2000. Publications: books on French 18th Century Literature; Scholarly Editions of 18th Century French Plays. Recreations: running and swimming. Address: (h.) 85 Hamilton Place, Aberdeen AB15 5BU; T.-01224 643800; e-mail: j.dunkley@abdn.ac.uk

Dunlop, Sheriff Principal Alastair, QC, LLB. Sheriff Principal, Tayside Central and Fife, since 2000; b. 30.6.51, London; m., Evelyn T. Barr; 1 s.; 2 d. Educ. Glenalmond; Dundee University. Admitted Solicitor, 1976; Advocate, 1978; QC, 1990; Advocate Depute, 1985-88; Standing Junior Counsel, Department of Transport, 1988-90; part-time Chairman, Pensions Appeal Tribunal, 1991-2000; Procurator to General Assembly, Church of Scotland, 1991-2000; part-time Chairman, Employment Tribunals, 1998-2000; Commissioner, Northern Lighthouses, since 2000. Recreations: golf; sailing; skiing; music. Address: (h.) 5 Temple Village, Gorebridge, Midlothian; T.-01875 830344.

Dunlop, Alastair Barr, OBE (1989), FRICS. Deputy Chairman, Lothians Ethics of Medical Research Committee, 1984-2004; General Commissioner for Income Tax, since 1991; Member, NHS Complaints Panel; Chairman, Paintings in Hospitals Scotland, 1991-2004; b. 27.12.33, Calcutta; m., Catriona C.L.H. MacLaurin; 1 s.; 1 d. Educ. Radley. Member, British Schools Exploring Society Expedition, Arctic Norway, 1950. National Service, 1952-54 (active service, Malaya: 2nd Lt., 1st Bn., RWK); commerce, City of London, 1954-58; agricultural student, 1959-61; Land Agent, Inverness, 1962-71 (Partner, Bingham Hughes & Macpherson); Joint Founding Director, Martin Paterson Associates Ltd., 1971; ecology studies, Edinburgh University, 1973-74. Member, Lothian Health Board, 1983-91 (Vice-Chairman, 1989-91); Scottish

Member, RICS Committee for Wilson Report on Financial Institutions, 1973-74; Chairman, Edinburgh and Borders Branch, RICS, 1977; Life Member, Institute of Directors; President and Past President, Edinburgh South Conservative Association; Chairman, South Edinburgh Conservative Association, 1980-84 and 1992-00, Central and South, Scottish Conservative and Unionist Association, 1985-88; Chairman, Edinburgh Branch, World Wildlife Fund, 1982-96; elected Member, Council, National Trust for Scotland, 1992-97. Recreations: golf; skiing; fine arts. Address: (h.) 12B Corrennie Drive, Edinburgh EH10 6EG; T.-0131 447 5209.

Dunlop, Eileen. Biographer and Children's Writer; b. 13.10.38, Alloa; m., Antony Kamm (qv). Educ. Alloa Academy; Moray House College. Publications: Robinsheugh, 1975; A Flute in Mayferry Street, 1976; Fox Farm, 1978; The Maze Stone, 1982 (SAC Book Award); Clementina, 1985 (SAC Book Award); The House on the Hill, 1987 (commended, Carnegie Medal); The Valley of Deer, 1989; Finn's Island, 1991; Tales of St. Columba, 1992; Green Willow's Secret, 1993; Finn's Roman Fort, 1994; Tales of St. Patrick, 1995; Castle Gryffe, 1995; Waters of Life, 1996; The Ghost by the Sea, 1997; Warrior's Bride, 1998; A Royal Ring of Gold, 1999; Ghoul's Den, 1999; The Haunting of Alice Fairlie, 2001; Nicholas Moonlight, 2002; Weerdwood, 2003; Queen Margaret of Scotland, 2005. Co-author, with Antony Kamm: Scottish Verse to 1800, 1985; A Book of Old Edinburgh, 1983. Recreations: reading; gardening; theatre. Address: (h.) 46 Tarmangie Drive, Dollar FK14 7BP; T.-01259 742007.

Dunlop, Ian Hunter. Area Director, VisitScotland - Aberdeen and Grampian, since 2005; formerly Chief Executive, Aberdeen and Grampian Tourist Board; b. 15.10.51, Aldershot; m., Jacqueline; 3 s. Educ. Sunderland College of Education; Durham University. Park Barn School, Guildford, 1974-82; Highland Wildlife Park, Kincraig, 1983-87; Highlands and Islands Development Board, 1987-91; Highlands and Islands Enterprise, 1991-94; Scottish Tourist Board, 1994-2001. Head Coach, Cairngorm Ski Club, 1984-2000. Recreations: British Association of Snowsport Instructors – international ski teacher diploma; Scottish history. Address: (b.) Exchange House, 26-28 Exchange Street, Aberdeen AB11 6PH.

Dunlop, Sheriff William, LLB. Sheriff of North Strathclyde, since 1995; b. 7.3.44, Glasgow; m., Janina Marthe; 1 s.; 2 d. Educ. High School of Glasgow; Glasgow University. Solicitor, 1968-84; called to Scottish Bar, 1985. Governor, The High School of Glasgow, since 1999; Member, Council, Sheriffs' Association, 2001-04; International Rugby Board Match Commissioner for European Cup and Six Nations matches, since 1999; Chairman, Scottish Rugby Union Championship Appeals Panel, since 2000. Address: (b.) Sheriff Court, Dumbarton G82 1LL.

Dunn, Professor Douglas Eaglesham, OBE, BA, FRSL, Hon.LLD (Dundee, 1987), Hon.DLitt (Hull, 1995). Professor, School of English, St. Andrews University, since 1991 (Head of School, 1994-99), and Director, St. Andrews Scottish Studies Institute, since 1993; b. 23.10.42, Inchinnan. Educ. Renfrew High School; Camphill Senior Secondary School, Paisley; Hull University. Books of poems: Terry Street, 1969, The Happier Life, 1972, Love or Nothing, 1974, Barbarians, 1979, St. Kilda's Parliament, 1981, Elegies, 1985, Selected Poems, 1986, Northlight, 1988, Dante's Drum-Kit, 1993, The Donkey's Ears, 2000, The Year's Afternoon, 2000; New Selected Poems, 2003;

Secret Villages (short stories), 1985; Boyfriends and Girlfriends (short stories), 1995; Andromache (translation), 1990; Poll Tax: The Fiscal Fake, 1990; Editor: Choice of Lord Byron's Verse, 1974, The Poetry of Scotland, 1979, A Rumoured City: New Poets from Hull, 1982; Two Decades of Irish Writing: a Critical Survey, 1975; The Essential Browning, 1990; Scotland: an anthology, 1991; Faber Book of Twentieth Century Scottish Poetry, 1992; Oxford Book of Scottish Short Stories, 1995; 20th Century Scottish Poems, 2000; author of plays, and TV films using commentaries in verse. Gregory Award, 1968; Somerset Maugham Award, 1972; Geoffrey Faber Memorial Prize, 1975; Hawthornden Prize, 1982; Whitbread Award for Poetry and Whitbread Book of the Year Award, 1985; Cholmondeley Award, 1989. Honorary Visiting Professor, Dundee University, 1987; Fellow in Creative Writing, St. Andrews University, 1989-91; Honorary Fellow, Humberside College, 1987. Address (b.) School of English, St. Andrews University, St. Andrews KY16 9AL.

Dunnett, Major Graham Thomas, TD, JP. Lord Lieutenant of Caithness, 1995-2004; b. 8.3.29, Wick; m., Catherine Elizabeth Sinclair; 3 s. Educ. Wick High School; Archbishop Holgates Grammar School, York. 1st Seaforth Highlanders, Malaya, 1948-51; 11th Seaforth Highlanders, Caithness, 1951-71; became 2nd Lieutenant, 1950, Lieut., 1952, Captain, 1956, Major and Coy. Comdr., 1964; Deputy Lieutenant of Caithness, 1975; Vice Lieutenant, 1986. Recreations: gardening; walking; country dancing. Address: Cathel Sheiling, Loch Calder, Thurso KW14 7YH; T.-01847 871220.

Dupree, Professor Marguerite Wright, BA, MA, DPhil, FRHistS. Professor of Social and Medical History, University of Glasgow, since 2007; b. 18.04.50, Boston, MA, USA; m., Richard Hughes Trainor; 1 s.; 1 d. Educ. Skyline High School, Oakland, California, USA; Mount Holyoke College; Princeton University; University of Oxford. Research Officer, Nuffield College, Oxford, 1977-78; Research Fellow, Emmanuel College, Cambridge, 1978-82; Fellow, Wolfson College, Cambridge, since 1982; University of Glasgow: Research Fellow, 1986-97, Senior Lecturer, 1997-2003, Reader, 2003-06. Publication: Medical Lives in the Age of Surgical Revolution (Co-Author), 2007. Recreation: tennis. Address: (b.) Centre for the History of Medicine, Department of Economic and Social History, University of Glasgow, Lilybank House, Bute Gardens, Glasgow G12 8RT; T.-0141-330-6072. E-mail: mdupree@arts.gla.ac.uk

Durie, Roy Ross, FRICS, MIMgt. Senior Partner, Ryden, Edinburgh; b. 11.5.48, Edinburgh; m., Dorothy; 1 s.; 3 d. Educ. Edinburgh Academy; Britannia Royal Naval College, Dartmouth. Royal Navy Officer (Lt. R.N.), 1966-72; joined Ryden, 1973. Chairman, Chamber Developments Ltd.; Director, Edinburgh Chamber of Commerce; Director, Forth Sector Ltd.; Director, Social Firm Development Trust; Elder, St. Giles, Edinburgh; Past Chairman, ISVA, Scotland. Recreations: walking; swimming; sailing; skiing; golf; rugby. Address. (b.) Ryden, 46 Castle Street, Edinburgh EH2 3BN; T.-0131-225 6612; e-mail: roy.durie@ryden.co.uk

Durnin, John. Chief Executive, Pitlochry Festival Theatre, since 2007, Artistic Director, since 2003; b. 7.1.60, Kew, Surrey. Educ. St. Paul's School, London; New College, Oxford. Stage Manager, Forum Theatre, Wythenshawe, 1982-84; Assistant Director, Library Theatre Company, Manchester, 1984-87; Associate Director, Everyman Theatre, Cheltenham, 1987-89; Freelance Director, 1989-91; Artistic Director: Northcott Theatre, Exeter, 1991-98,

Theatre Venture, London, 1999-2000, Gatton Community Theatre, Surrey, 2000-03. Recreations: photography; cycling; hill walking; music. Address: (b.) Pitlochry Festival Theatre, Port-na-Craig, Pitlochry PH16 5DR; T.-01796 484600; e-mail: john.durnin@pitlochry.org.uk

Durrani, Professor Tariq Salim, OBE, FRSE, FREng, FIEEE, FIET. Professor, Department of Electronic and Electrical Engineering, Strathclyde University, since 1982; b. 27.10.43, Amraoti, India; m., Clare Elizabeth; 1 s.; 2 d. Educ. Marie Colaco High School, Karachi; Engineering University, Dacca; Southampton University. Research Fellow, Southampton University, 1970-76; joined academic staff, Strathclyde University, 1976, Chairman, Department of Electronic and Electrical Engineering, 1986-90, Deputy Principal, 1990-91, and 2000-06; Director, Scottish Electronics Technology Group, since 1983; President, IEEE Signal Processing Society, 1993-94; Chair, IEEE Periodicals Council, 1996-98; President, IEEE Engineering Management Society, 2006-07; Vice-Chair, Technical Activities, IEEE Region 8, 2003-06; Director: Glasgow Chamber of Commerce, since 2003, Institute for System Level Integration, since 2002, Kelvin Institute, since 2004; Member, Scottish Funding Council, since 2005. Publications: six books; over 330 technical research papers. Recreation: playing occasional golf badly. Address: (b.) Department of Electronic and Electrical Engineering, Strathclyde University, Glasgow; T.-0141-548 2883.

Durward, Professor Brian Ross, PhD, MSc, MCSP. Dean of School of Health and Social Care, Glasgow Caledonian University, since 2002; b. 6.10.54, Aberdeen; m., Anne; 1 s.; 1 d. Educ. Glasgow Royal Infirmary; School of Physiotherapy; Strathclyde University. Qualified as a Physiotherapist in 1977 and after working in a number of Glasgow hospitals became Head Physiotherapist at the Institute for Neurological Sciences at the Southern General Hospital, Glasgow. Became a Lecturer in Physiotherapy at Queen Margaret College, Edinburgh in 1985, then Head of Physiotherapy in 1999. Joint editor of Functional Human Movement: Measurement and Analysis; published extensively in the area of Stroke Rehabilitation. Recreations: fishing; croquet. Address: (b.) School of Health and Social Care, Glasgow Caledonian University, City Campus, Glasgow G4 0BA; T.-0141-331 8110; e-mail: b.durward@gcal.ac.uk

Durward, William Farquharson, MB, ChB, FRCP(Edin), FRCP(Glas). Consultant Neurologist, Greater Glasgow and Lanarkshire Health Boards, since 1977; Honorary Clinical Senior Lecturer in Neurology, Glasgow University, since 1978; Director, Cloburn Quarry Co. Ltd.; b. 16.9.44, Kilmarnock; m., Ann Roy Paterson; 1 s.; 1 d. Educ. Kilmarnock Academy; Glasgow University; Boston University. Employed by NHS, since 1968; specialist training grades, 1969-77. Recreations: walking; reading; railway conservation. Address: (h.) Overdale, 20 South Erskine Park, Bearsden, Glasgow G61 4NA; T.-0141-942 3143.

Duthie, Sir Robert (Robin) Grieve, CBE (1978), CA, LLD, CBIM, FRSA, FRIAS, DTech (Napier). Chairman, RG Duthie & Co. Ltd., since 1984; b. 2.10.28, Greenock; m., Violetta Noel Maclean; 2 s.; 1 d. Educ. Greenock Academy. Apprentice Chartered Accountant, Thomson Jackson Gourlay and Taylor, CA, 1946-51; joined Blacks of Greenock, 1952; appointed Managing Director, 1962; Chairman, Black & Edgington, 1972-83. Chairman, Inverkip Society, 1966; Director, Greenock Chamber of Commerce, 1966; Member, Clyde Port Authority, 1971-83 (Chairman, 1977-80); Director, Royal Bank of Scotland plc, 1978-98; Director, British Assets Trust plc, 1977-98;

Chairman, Scottish Development Agency, 1979-88; Chairman, Britoil PLC, 1988-90; Vice Chairman, BP Advisory Board Scotland, 1990-2001; Chairman, Neill Clerk Group plc, 1993-98; Director, Greenock Provident Bank, 1969-75 (Chairman, 1975); Director, Devol Engineering Ltd., 1993-2003; Member, Scottish Telecommunications Board, 1972-77; Council Member, Institute of Chartered Accountants of Scotland, 1973-78; Member: East Kilbride Development Corporation, 1976-78, Strathclyde Region Local Valuation Appeal Panel, 1976-83; CBI Tax Liaison Officer for Scotland, 1976-79; Chairman, Made Up Textile Association of Great Britain, 1972; Member: British Institute of Management Scottish Committee, 1976, Glasgow and West of Scotland Committee, Scottish Council (Development and Industry), 1975-79; Chairman, Greenock Club, 1972; Captain, Greenock Cricket Club, 1960-61; Commissioner, Queen Victoria School, Dunblane, 1972-89; Commissioner, Scottish Congregational Ministers Pension Fund, 1973-2003; Member, Scottish Economic Council, 1980-96; Member of Council, Royal Caledonian Curling Club, 1984-88; Treasurer, Greenock West URC, since 1970. Awarded Honorary Degree of Doctor of Laws, Strathclyde University, 1984. Recreation: golf. Address: (h.) Fairhaven, 181 Finnart Street, Greenock, PA16 8JA; T.-01475 722642.

Du Vivier, Paul Eastwood, FIMgt, Captain RN (Rtd.). Chief Executive, Scottish Fisheries Protection Agency, since 1995; b. 24.5.45, Bath; m., Diana Rochsoles Robertson; 1 s.; 2 d. Educ. Malvern College; Britannia Royal Naval College, Dartmouth. Service at sea, 1965-88; in command, HMS Maxton, 1974-76, HMS Achilles, 1980-81; service in MoD Naval Secretary's Department, 1977-79, Naval Plans, 1981-84; BRNC Dartmouth, 1984-86; Commander, HMS Illustrious, 1986-88; HMS Dryad, 1989-91; Board President, Admiralty Interview Board, 1991; Director, Joint Maritime Operational Training Staff, 1991-94; Chief of Staff to Flag Officer Scotland, Northern England and Northern Ireland, 1994-95; Member, Institute of Directors; Selected Naval Member, Lowland RFCA; Trustee, Seafarers UK; Trustee, Bell's Nautical Trust. Address: (b.) Pentland House, 47 Robb's Loan, Edinburgh EH14 1TY; T.-0131-244 6059.

Duxbury, Professor Geoffrey, BSc, PhD, CPhys, FInstP, FRSE. Emeritus Professor of Physics, Strathclyde University; b. 6.11.42, Blackburn; m., Mary R.; 1 s.; 1 d. Educ. Cheadle Hulme School; Sheffield University. Junior Research Fellow, National Physical Laboratory, 1967-69; Research Assistant, Research Associate, Lecturer in Chemical Physics, Bristol University, 1970-80; Senior Lecturer/Reader, Strathclyde University, 1981-86. Marlow Medal, Faraday Division, Royal Society of Chemistry, 1975. Publication: Infrared Vibration-Rotation Spectroscopy: From Free Radicals to the Infrared Sky, 2000. Address: (b.) Department of Physics, Strathclyde University, Glasgow, G4 0NG; T.-0141-548 3271.

Dye, Jonathan, BSc (Hons), CA. Chairman, English Speaking Union Scotland, since 2003; Treasurer, Edinburgh City Youth Cafe, 1997-2003; Chartered Accountant, Pricewaterhousecoopers, 1993-2003, National Australia Bank, since 2003; Head of Sarbanes-Oxley Compliance, NAB UK, since 2007; Governor, English Speaking Union of The Commonwealth, since 2003; Member, Security Board, Association of Payment and Clearing Services (APACS), 2004-07; b. 29.5.71, Dundee. Educ. Harris Academy, Dundee; St. Andrews University. Address: ESU, 23 Atholl Crescent, Edinburgh EH3 8HQ.

E

Eadie, Helen. MSP (Labour), Dunfermline East, since 1999; Chair, Scottish Parliamentary Labour Party; Member, Health and Sport Committee and Subordinate Legislation Committee, Scottish Parliament; former Depute Convener, Public Petitions Committee; former Member, Executive Committee, European Movement (Scottish Council); b. Stenhousemuir; m.; 2 d. Educ. Larbert High School; Falkirk Technical College; London School of Economics. Former Chair, STUC Youth Advisory Committee; former full-time Organiser, GMB, Glasgow; former Equal Opportunities and Political Officer, GMB, London; former Assistant to Harry Ewing MP and Alex Eadie MP (father-in-law); served in local government, 1986-99; former Vice-President, North Sea Commission; former Vice-Chair, South East Scotland Partnership in Transport; former Vice President, UK Disabled Drivers' Club. Address: (b.) Scottish Parliament, Edinburgh EH99 1SP; T.-0131-348 5749.
E-mail: helen.eadie.msp@scottish.parliament.uk

Eagles, Henry Allan, MA (Hons). Executive Producer, Sport, Scottish TV, since 2004; b. 17.4.49, Cheltenham. Educ. High School of Glasgow; Dundee University. The Scotsman, 1975-80; Scottish Television, 1981-91; freelance television producer, 1992-99; Head of News and Current Affairs, Grampian Television, 2000-2004. Address: (b.) STV, Pacific Quay, Glasgow G51 1PQ; T.-0141 300 3000.

Eagles, Professor John Mortimer, MBChB, MPhil, FRCPsych. Professor, Mental Health, Aberdeen University, since 2007; Consultant Psychiatrist, Royal Cornhill Hospital, Aberdeen, since 1985; Honorary Reader, Mental Health, Aberdeen University, 2000-07; b. 21.10.52, Newport-on-Tay; m., Janette Isobel Rorke; 2 d. Educ. Bell-Baxter High School, Cupar; Aberdeen University; Edinburgh University. Resident House Officer posts, Aberdeen, 1977-78; Senior House Officer/Registrar in Psychiatry, Royal Edinburgh Hospital, 1978-82; Lecturer, Department of Mental Health, Aberdeen University, 1982-85; Honorary Senior Lecturer, Department of Mental Health, Aberdeen University, 1985-2000; Psychiatric Tutor for trainee psychiatrists, Aberdeen, 1987-92. Chairman, North-East Regional Postgraduate Medical Education Committee, 1990-95; Chair, Scottish Division, Royal College of Psychiatrists Undergraduate Student Teaching and Recruitment Group. Recreations: cricket; golf; travel; reading. Address: (h.) 41 Binghill Park, Milltimber, Aberdeenshire AB13 0EE; T.-01224 732434.

Eaglesham, David Hillhouse, BEd. General Secretary, Scottish Secondary Teachers' Association, since 1996; b. 7.9.50, Glasgow; m., Doreen; 1 s.; 2 d. Educ. Victoria Drive Secondary School, Glasgow; Glasgow University; Jordanhill College. Teacher, Govan High School, 1973-77; Departmental Manager, Marks and Spencer, 1977-78; Teacher/Assistant Principal Teacher, Mearns Castle High School, 1978-82; Principal Teacher of Modern Studies, Cathkin High School, 1982-84; Assistant General Secretary, SSTA, 1994-96. Recreations: golf; gardening. Address: (b.) 14 West End Place, Edinburgh EH11 2ED; T.-0131 313 7300.

Eardley, Catherine Elizabeth, MA. Executive Director, Membership and Marketing, The Institute of Chartered Accountants of Scotland, since 2005; b. 22.12.62, Colne, Lancs. Educ. Buchan School, Isle of Man; Trinity Hall, Cambridge. Morgan Stanley International, 1984-88; Paribas Capital Markets, 1988-92; Chase Manhattan (later JP Morgan), 1992-2005. Chairman, Oxton and Channelkirk Community Council. Recreations: British Dressage Pyramid trainer. Address: (b.) CA House, Haymarket Yards, Edinburgh EH12 5BH; T.-0131 347 0236; e-mail: ceardley@icas.org.uk

Eassie, Rt Hon. Lord (Ronald Mackay). Senator of the College of Justice, since 1997; formerly Chairman, the Scottish Law Commission; b. 1945; m.; 1 s. Educ. Berwickshire High School; St. Andrews University; Edinburgh University. Admitted, Faculty of Advocates, 1972; QC, 1986. Address: Parliament House, Parliament Square, Edinburgh EH1 1RQ.

Eastmond, Clifford John, BSc, MD, FRCP, FRCPE. Consultant Rheumatologist in private practice, Albyn Hospital, Aberdeen, since 1997; previous appoinments: Associate Medical Director and Consultant Rheumatologist, NHS Grampian (Clinical Director of Medicine, 1995-99); Clinical Senior Lecturer, Aberdeen University; b. 19.1.45, Ashton-under-Lyne; m., Margaret Wadsworth; 2 s.; 1 d. Educ. Audenshaw Grammar School; Edinburgh University. House Officer posts, Edinburgh, one year; moved to Liverpool for further training, subsequently to Rheumatism Unit, Leeds. Elder, Church of Scotland; Past President, Westhill and District Rotary Club. Clubs: Royal Northern and University Club, Aberdeen. Recreations: skiing; hill-walking; music; shooting. Address: (h.) The Rowans, Skene, Aberdeenshire AB32 6YP; T.-01224 790370.

Easton, Sir Robert William Simpson, CBE (1980), DUniv, CEng, FIMechE, FIMarE, FRINA. Chancellor, University of Paisley, 1993-2003; Chairman, Clydeport Pension Trust, 1993-2002; b. 30.10.22, Glasgow; m., Jean Fraser; 1 s.; 1 d. Educ. Govan High School, Glasgow; Royal Technical College, Glasgow. Apprentice, Marine Engineer, 1939-51; Manager, Yarrow & Co. Ltd., 1951-65; Yarrow Shipbuilders Ltd.: Director, 1965-70, Deputy Managing Director, 1970-77, Managing Director, 1977-91; Main Board Director, Yarrow & Co. Ltd., 1971-77; Chairman: Yarrow Shipbuilders Ltd., 1979-94, Clyde Port Authority, 1983-93, GEC Scotland, 1990-99, GEC Naval Systems, 1991-94; Director: Supermarine Consortium Ltd., 1986-94, Glasgow Development Agency, 1990-94, West of Scotland Water Board, 1993-95, Caledonian MacBrayne Ltd., 1997-2000; Vice-President, Clyde Shipbuilders Association, 1972-79; Freeman, City of London, 1982; Freeman, City of Glasgow, 1989; Honorary Vice-President, RINA; Trustee, Seagull Trust, 1984; Director, Merchant House of Glasgow, 1994-2003; Member, Incorporation of Hammermen, 1989; Past President, Institute of Welding; Past President, Institute of Engineers and Shipbuilders, Scotland. Recreations: golf; walking; family. Address: (h.) Springfield, Stuckenduff Road, Shandon, Argyllshire G84 8NW; T.-01436 820 677.

Easton, Robin Gardner, OBE, MA, DUniv, DipEd, FRSA. Rector, The High School of Glasgow, 1983-2004; b. 6.10.43, Glasgow; m., Eleanor Mary McIlroy; 1 s.; 1 d. Educ. Kelvinside Academy; Sedbergh School; Christ's College, Cambridge; Wadham College, Oxford. Teacher of French and German, Melville College, Edinburgh, 1966-72; Housemaster and Deputy Head, French Department, Daniel Stewart's and Melville College, 1972-78; Head, Modern Languages, George Watson's College, 1979-83. Elder, Church of Scotland; Member, Glasgow Children's Panel; Member, Glasgow University Court; Board Member, Scripture Union, Scotland. Recreations: watching rugby; tennis; hill-walking; visiting ancient monuments. Address: (h.) 21 Stirling Drive, Bearsden, Glasgow G61 4NU; T.-0141-943 0368.

Eastwood, Martin Anthony, MB, MSc, FRCPE. Retired Gastroenterologist and Reader in Medicine, Edinburgh University; Honorary Librarian, Royal College of Physicians of Edinburgh, 1995-2000; b. 7.8.35, Hull; m.,

Jenny; 3 s.; 1 d. Educ. Minster Grammar School, Southwell; Edinburgh University. Member, Edinburgh Sculpture Workshop. Publications: papers on physiology of the colon and nutrition; History of Western General Hospital Edinburgh (Co-Author), 1995; Principles of Human Nutrition, 2nd edition, 2003; E.B. Jamieson Anatomist and Shetlander, 1999. Address: (h.) Hill House, North Queensferry KY11 1JJ.

Eddie, Rev. Duncan Campbell, MA (Hons), BD (Hons). Minister, Holburn West, Aberdeen, since 1999; b. 17.2.63, Fraserburgh; m., Dr. Carol Buchanan; 2 s. Educ. Mackie Academy, Stonehaven; Aberdeen University; Edinburgh University. Assistant Minister, Edinburgh, 1990-91; Minister, Old Cumnock: Crichton West linked with St. Ninian's, 1992-99. Recreations: music; reading. Address: 31 Cranford Road, Aberdeen AB10 7NJ; e-mail: holburnwest@ashleypark.fsnet.co.uk

Eden, Professor Colin, BSc, PhD. Professor of Management Science and Strategic Management, University of Strathclyde, since 1987, Associate Dean and Director of The International Division, Director, Graduate School of Business, 1999-2006; b. 24.12.43, Birmingham; m., Christine. Educ. Moseley Grammar School, Birmingham; University of Leicester; University of Southampton. Operational Researcher; Operational Research Manager; Management Consultant; Lecturer, then Senior Lecturer, then Reader, University of Bath School of Management. Publications: six books, most recently Making Strategy: The Journey of Strategic Management; Visible Thinking and The Practice of Making Strategy. Recreations: sailing; skiing. Address: (b.) 199 Cathedral Street, Glasgow G4 0QU; T.-0141-553 6155; e-mail: colin@gsb.strath.ac.uk

Edgar, Anne Lillian. Keeper of Books (jointly) and Librarian, Innerpeffray Library, since 2005 (Scotland's oldest free Public Lending Library, founded 1680); b. 27.12.50, British Military Hospital, Hamburg; m., Colin Miles Edgar; 2 s.; 1 d. Educ. Lillesden School, Hawkhurst, Kent; Canterbury College of Technology. Various committees. Publications: Author, Her Master's Voice - Biography; Janet Beaton 1515-1569; Captain Sherwood's Journey to Killiecrankie 1826; Westwood to the Sugar Isles, 1798-1803. In Preparation: Chronicles of Innerpeffray; Sir Edwyn Dawes KCMG, Diaries 1868 - 1875. Recreations: swimming; croquet; genealogy. Address: (b.) The School House, Innerpeffray Library, Crieff, Perthshire PH7 3RF; T.-01764 652819.
E-mail: info@innerpeffraylibrary.co.uk

Edgar, Colin Miles, MA (Cantab), PGCE (Reading) FRICS. Keeper of Books (jointly), Innerpeffray Library, since 2005 (Scotland's oldest free Public Lending Library, founded 1680); Key Holder and Lay Provost of St. Mary's Chapel, Innerpeffray, Crieff, since 2005; b. 14.4.44, Rochford, Essex; m., Anne Lillian Dawes (Burke's Landed Gentry, 1952 & 1962); 2 s.; 1 d. Educ. Felsted, Essex; Queens' College Cambridge. VSO, Falkland Islands - Goose Green & Fox Bay, 1962-63; Chartered Surveyor, Government and Private Practice, 1966-95; 2 awards; Captain, RA ret'd, served Cyprus and Germany: 32 Heavy Regiment RA: veteran The Honourable Artillery Company, London. 2 prizes. Teacher: Humanities, St. Bart's Newbury etc, 1995-2005; Editor, The Humf Letters 1910-1915; School Governor, 1980-2000. Recreations: shooting; sheep and trees; making unnoticeable improvements. Address: (b.) The School House, Innerpeffray Library, Crieff, Perthshire PH7 3RF; T.-01764 652819.

Edington, Martin G. R., LLB, NP, WS. Sheriff at Linlithgow, since 2003; b. 28.10.55; m., Susan Jane Phillips; 2 s. Educ. Fettes College; Dundee University. Partner, Turnbull Simson and Sturrock WS, 1983-2001. Recreations: travelling; curling; rugby; cricket. Address: (b.) Sheriff Court, High Street, Linlithgow EH49 7EQ; T.-01506 842922.

Edward, Rt. Hon. Sir David Alexander Ogilvy, KCMG, QC, LLD, FRSE; b. 14.11.34, Perth; m., Elizabeth Young McSherry; 2 s.; 2 d. Educ. Sedbergh School; University College, Oxford; University of Edinburgh. National Service, RNVR, 1956-57 (Sub-Lt.); Advocate, 1962; Clerk, Faculty of Advocates, 1967-70, Treasurer, 1970-77; Queen's Counsel, 1974; President, Consultative Committee, Bars and Law Societies of the European Community, 1978-80; Salvesen Professor of European Institutions, University of Edinburgh, 1985-89; (Honorary Professor, since 1990); Judge of the Court of First Instance of EC, 1989-92; Judge of the Court of Justice of EC, 1992-2004; Temporary Judge of the Court of Session, since 2004. Member: Law Advisory Committee, British Council, 1974-88, Panel of Arbitrators, International Centre for Settlement of Investment Disputes, 1981-89, 2004-; Chairman, Continental Assets Trust plc, 1986-89; Director, Adam & Company plc, 1984-89; Director, Harris Tweed Association Ltd., 1985-89; Specialist Adviser to House of Lords Select Committee on the European Communities, 1985-88; Trustee: National Library of Scotland, 1966-95, Industry and Parliament Trust, since 1995, Carnegie Trust for the Universities of Scotland, since 1995, Hopetoun Foundation (Chairman, Hopetoun Preservation Trust, 1988-92); President, Franco-Scottish Society, since 1996; President, Johnson Society, 1995-96; President, Edinburgh Sir Walter Scott Club, 2001-02. Hon. Bencher, Gray's Inn, 1992; Hon. LLD: Edinburgh University, 1993, Aberdeen University, 1997, Napier University, 1998; Dr. h.c.: Universitat des Saarlandes, 2001, Westfalische Wilhelms-Universitat Munster, 2001; Doctor of the University (D Univ) honoris causa Surrey, 2003; Knight Commander of the Order of St Michael & St George, 2004 (CMG. 1981); Privy Counsellor, 2005; Fellow of the Royal Society of Edinburgh, 1990 (Royal Medallist, 2005). Vice-President: British Institute of International and Comparative Law, International Association of Business and Parliament; Chairman: Carnegie Trust for the Universities of Scotland, Scottish Council of Independent Schools. Address: (h.) 32 Heriot Row, Edinburgh EH3 6ES; T.-0131-225 7153; e-mail: david.edward@dileas.net

Edward, Drew, BSc, CEng, MIMechE, MIOSH, AIEMA. Agency Board Member, Scottish Environment Protection Agency (SEPA), since 2004; b. 31.1.54, Dundee; 1 s.; 1 d. Educ. Arbroath High School; Heriot-Watt University. SSEB Graduate Trainee, Maintenance Engineer, Longannet Power Station, 1977-79; Plant Engineer, Project Engineer, Safety and Environment Manager, SAI Ltd., 1979-91; Environment and Safety Manager, WL Gore (UK), 1991-99; Elected Member, Fife Council, 1999-2006; Chair, Fife Council Pension Fund, 2003-06. Chair, Queen Anne High Board, 1997-99; Dunfermline Photographic Association, 1992-99, President, 1997-99, Competition Secretary, 1992-99, Secretary, since 2007. Recreations: photography; bird watching. Address: (h.) Newton House, 8 Blackburn Avenue, Dunfermline, Fife KY12 9BQ; T.-01383 734258; e-mail: drew.edward@btinternet.com

Edward, Ian, MA, LLB. Solicitor (retired); b. 3.9.35, Aberdeen; m., 1, Marguerite Anne Leiper (deceased); m., 2, Gudrun Clapier; 2 s.; 1 d. Educ. Robert Gordon's College, Aberdeen; University of Aberdeen; Fitzwilliam College, University of Cambridge. HM Colonial Service (District Officer, Northern Rhodesia), 1959-63; C. & P. H. Chalmers, Solicitors, Aberdeen (now Ledingham Chalmers): Legal Assistant, Partner, Senior Partner, Consultant, 1963-2000. Part-time Chairman of Employment Tribunals, 1997-2004; Historian, Royal Aberdeen Golf Club. Recreations: golf; gardening; hill-walking; skiing.

Address: (h.) 23 St. Fillan's Terrace, Edinburgh EH10 5PJ; T.-0131-447 8353.

Edwards, Frederick Edward, LVO, RD, DUniv, MUniv, MA, BA, FCMI, MIEEM, CEnv; b. 9.4.31, Liverpool; 2 s.; 1 d. Educ. St. Edward's College, Liverpool; Glasgow University. Midshipman to Second Officer, Alfred Holt & Co., 1948-57; awarded Perm. Commn. RNR, 1953; Lt.-Cmdr., 1963; Reserve Decoration, 1972; Clasp, 1982; Management Trainee, Morgan Crucible Group, 1957-60; Probation Service, Liverpool, 1960-69; Director of Social Work: Joint County Council of Moray and Nairn, 1969-75, Grampian Region, 1975-76, Strathclyde Regional Council, 1976-93; Visiting Professor of Social Administration and Social Work, Glasgow University, 1988-93; Trustee, New Lanark Conservation Trust, since 1993; President, Volunteer Development Scotland, 1993-99; President, Disability Scotland, 1995-99; Chairman, Capability Scotland, 1997-2001. Member: Council, Scottish Wildlife Trust, 1994-2000, Board, Scottish Environment Agency, 1999-2006; Board Member, Friends of the Earth, 1998-2007; President, Scottish Environment LINK, 2004-07; 2007 Life Fellow, Scottish Environment LINK; Awarded Hon. Doctorate, Paisley University, 1993. Recreations: hill-walking; natural history; Scottish country dancing. Address: (h.) Gardenfield, Ninemileburn, by Penicuik EH26 9LT; T.-01968 674566.

Edwards, Gareth Huw, MA (Oxon), PGCE. Principal, George Watson's College, Edinburgh, since 2001; b. 9.4.58, Swansea; m., Jane; 1 d. Educ. Tudor Grange Grammar School; Solihull Sixth Form College; Exeter College, Oxford; Bristol University. Assistant Master, King Edward School, Birmingham, 1981-85; Head of Classics, Bolton School, Boys Division, 1985-90; Vice Principal, Newcastle under Lyme School, 1990-96; Rector, Morrison's Academy, Crieff, 1996-2001. Recreations: singing; squash; modern Greek. Address: George Watson's College, Colinton Road, Edinburgh EH10 5EG; T.-0131-446 6000.

Edwards, George Lowden, FSAScot. Director, NMS Enterprises; Governor, Royal Scottish Academy of Music and Drama; b. 6.2.39, Kirriemuir; m., Sylvia Izatt; 1 d. Educ. Webster's Seminary, Kirriemuir; Dundee Institute of Technology. Production Engineer, Burroughs Machines Ltd., Cumbernauld, 1961-64; Development Division, Scottish Council (Development and Industry), Edinburgh, 1964-67; General Manager, GR Designs Ltd., Perth, 1967-68; London Director, Scottish Council (Development and Industry), 1968-78; Manager, Public Affairs Scotland, Conoco (UK) Ltd., Aberdeen, 1978-83; Manager, Public Affairs, Conoco (UK) Ltd., London, 1983-85; Head of Corporate Affairs, Clydesdale Bank PLC, 1988-96; Chairman Scotland, GPC International, 1997-2002; Chairman, Association of Professional Political Consultants in Scotland, 1998-2002. Honorary Fellow, University of Abertay, Dundee. Recreations: music; travel; food and wine. Address: (h.) 11 Almond Court East, Braehead Park, Edinburgh EH4 6AZ.

Edwards, Kevin John, MA, PhD, FRGS, CGeog, FSA, FSAScot, FRSE. Professor in Physical Geography, University of Aberdeen, since 2000, Adjunct Chair in Archaeology, since 2007; Adjunct Professor, Graduate School in Anthropology, City University of New York, since 2002; Visiting Researcher, Department of Geography and Geology, University of Copenhagen, since 2007; b. 18.9.49, Dartford; 2 s. Educ. Northfleet Boys' School; Gravesend Grammar School; St. Andrews University; Aberdeen University. Tutorial Fellow in Geography, University of Aberdeen, 1972-75; Lecturer in

Environmental Reconstruction and Research Member, Palaeoecology Centre, Queen's University of Belfast, 1975-80; University of Birmingham: Lecturer in Biogeography, 1980-90, Senior Lecturer in Geography, 1990-92, Reader in Palaeoecology, 1992-94; Honorary Research Fellow, Limnological Research Center, University of Minnesota, 1983; Professor of Palaeoecology, Department of Archaeology and Prehistory, University of Sheffield, 1994-2000 (Head of Department, 1996-99). Member, NERC Radiocarbon Dating Laboratory Committees, 1995-2000; Chairman, Oxford University Radiocarbon Accelerator Unit Users' Committee, 1995-2000; Deputy Chairman, SCAPE Trust, 2001-04. Publications: Quaternary History of Ireland (Co-Editor), 1985; Scotland: Environment and Archaeology 8000BC-AD1000 (Co-Editor), 1997; Holocene Environments of Prehistoric Britain (Co-Editor), 1999; numerous articles in geography, archaeology, botany and quaternary science. Recreations: reading; archaeology; family history. Address: (b.) Department of Geography and Environment, University of Aberdeen, Elphinstone Road, Aberdeen AB24 3UF; T.-01224 272346; e-mail: kevin.edwards@abdn.ac.uk

Edwards, Rob (Robert Philip), MA. Environment Editor, Sunday Herald, since 1999; Consultant, New Scientist, since 1994; Freelance Journalist, since 1980; Television Producer, since 1990; b. 13.10.53, Liverpool; m., Fiona Grant Riddoch; 2 d. Educ. Watford Boys Grammar School; Jesus College, University of Cambridge. Organiser, Scottish Campaign to Resist the Atomic Menace, 1977-78; Campaigns Organiser, Shelter (Scotland), 1978-80; Research Assistant to Robin Cook, 1980-83; Freelance Journalist, writing for Social Work Today, The Scotsman, New Statesman, 1980-89; Environment Editor, Scotland on Sunday, 1989-94; Correspondent, The Guardian and Columnist, Edinburgh Evening News, 1989-94; Freelance Journalist, writing for New Scientist, The Sunday Herald, The Observer etc., since 1994; various media awards. Publications: Co-author of three books, including Still Fighting for Gemma, 1995. Recreations: music; opera; walking. Address: 53 Nile Grove, Edinburgh EH10 4RE; T.-0131-447 2796; e-mail: rob.edwards@blueyonder.co.uk; website: www.robedwards.com

Edwards Chantry, Lynne, BA (Hons), DipYESTB. Part-time Commissioner, Mental Welfare Commission for Scotland, since 2001; part-time Researcher, SCRE Centre, Glasgow University, since 1989; Service User and Carer Involvement and Development (Mental Health), Napier University, 2003-05; Edinburgh Human Resource Academy, Knowledge Transfer Project developer/co-ordinator, Napier University Business School, Edinburgh; Visiting Research Fellow, Centre for Family and Community Medicine/Migration Medicine, Karolinska Institutet, Stockholm, Sweden; Member, Human Dignity and Humiliation Studies, research and education teams; b. 6.2.53, Grantham; m., Ronald Terence Edwards (deceased); 2 s. Educ. Kestuven and Grantham Girls' School; University of East Anglia. Careers adviser; Research Assistant, then Research Associate, Aberdeen University; Research Assistant, then Research Officer, SCRE Centre. Publications: Decision-Making for Energy Futures (Co-author); Supporting Bereaved Young People – A Support Pack for Secondary Schools (Co-author); Action Against Bullying – A Support Pack for Schools (Co-author); Education for Democratic Citizenship in Europe - New Challenges for Secondary Education (ed); Whatever happened to the Planning Inquiry Commission? (Co-author), Journal of Planning and Environment Law. Address: (b.) Faculty of Health, Life and Social Sciences, Napier University, Edinburgh EH4 2LD. E-mail: l.edwards@napier.ac.uk

Eglinton and Winton, Earl of. Chairman, Edinburgh Investment Trust, 1994-2003. Grieveson Grant, 1957-72

(Partner, from 1964); Gerrard & National, 1972-92 (Managing Director, from 1972, Deputy Chairman, from 1980); Chairman, Gerrard Vivian Gray, 1989-95. Address: (h.) Balhomie, Cargill, Perth PH2 6DS; T.-01250 883222.

Eilbeck, Professor John Christopher, BA, PhD, FRSE. Professor, Department of Mathematics, Heriot-Watt University, since 1986 (Head of Department, 1984-89, Dean of Science, 1998-2001); b. 8.4.45, Whitehaven; 3 s. Educ. Whitehaven Grammar School; Queen's College, Oxford; Lancaster University. Royal Society European Fellow, ICTP, Trieste, 1969-70; Research Assistant, Department of Mathematics, UMIST, Manchester, 1970-73; Heriot-Watt University: Lecturer, Department of Mathematics, 1973-80, Senior Lecturer, 1980-85, Reader, 1985-86; Long-term Visiting Fellow, Center for Nonlinear Studies, Los Alamos National Laboratory, New Mexico, 1983-84; Visiting Fellow, Corpus Christi College, Cambridge, 2001. Publications: Rock Climbing in the Lake District (Co-author), 1975; Solitons and Nonlinear Wave Equations (Co-author), 1982. Recreation: mountaineering. Address: (b.) Department of Mathematics, Heriot-Watt University, Riccarton, Edinburgh EH14 4AS; T.-0131-451 3220.

Elder, Dorothy-Grace. MSP, Glasgow, 1999-2003 (Independent, formerly SNP MSP); newspaper columnist; television scriptwriter and producer; Hon. Professor, The Robert Gordon University, Aberdeen, since 2006; m., George Welsh; 1 s.; 2 d. D.C. Thomson newspapers; Glasgow Herald as reporter, investigation writer, news feature writer, leader writer; TV and radio news, BBC Scotland; feature writer and columnist, Scottish Daily News Co-operative; feature writer and columnist, Sunday Mail; productions for Scotland and the network, BBC and Scottish TV. Political Columnist, Scottish Daily Express, since 2002. Honorary President, Glasgow NE Multiple Sclerosis Society; Honorary Patron, No Panic; Oliver Award winning columnist, 1995-96; British Reporter of the Year, UK Press Awards, 1996-97; citation, Humanitarian Aid Work, City of Pushkin, Russia, 1998, 1999. Address: 14 Turnberry Road, Glasgow G11 5AE.

Elgin, 11th Earl of, and Kincardine, 15th Earl of, (Andrew Douglas Alexander Thomas Bruce), KT (1981), DL, JP; 37th Chief of the Name of Bruce; Captain, Queen's Bodyguard for Scotland (Royal Company of Archers); b. 17.2.24; m., Victoria Usher; 3 s.; 2 d. Educ. Eton; Balliol College, Oxford. Lord Lieutenant of Fife, 1987-99; President, Scottish Amicable Life Assurance Society, 1975-94; Chairman, National Savings Committee for Scotland, 1972-78; Member, Scottish Postal Board, 1980-96; Lord High Commissioner, General Assembly, Church of Scotland, 1980-81; Grand Master Mason of Scotland, 1961-65; President, Royal Caledonian Curling Club, 1968-69; President, Boys Brigade (UK), 1963-85; Hon. LLD, Dundee, 1977, Glasgow, 1983. Address: (h.) Broomhall, Dunfermline KY11 3DU; T.-01383 872222; e-mail: lord.elgin@virgin.net

Eliott of Redheugh, Margaret Frances Boswell. Chief of Clan Elliot; Chairman, Elliot Clan Society and Sir Arthur Eliott Memorial Trust; b. 13.11.48; m., 1, Anthony Vaughan-Arbuckle (deceased); 1 s.; 1 d.; 2, Christopher Powell Wilkins. Educ. Hatherop Castle School. Address: Redheugh, Newcastleton, Roxburghshire.

Ellington, Marc Floyd, DL. Baron of Towie Barclay; Laird of Gardenstown and Crovie; Deputy Lieutenant, Aberdeenshire, since 1984; b. 16.12.45; m., Karen Leigh; 2

d. Member: British Heritage Commission (representing Scottish Tourist Board), Heritage Lottery Fund Committee for Scotland; Non Executive Director, Historic Scotland; Trustee, National Galleries of Scotland; Vice-President, Buchan Heritage Society; Chairman: Grampian Regional Council Tourism Task Force, 1992-96, Heritage Press (Scotland), Soundcraft Audio; Director: Gardenstown Estates Ltd., Heritage Sound Recordings; Director, Grampian Enterprise Ltd., 1992-96; Member, Historic Buildings Council for Scotland, 1980-98; Communications, Tourism and Heritage Consultant. Saltire Award, 1973; Civic Trust Award, 1975; European Architectural Heritage Award, 1975; SBStJ; FSA. Recreations: sailing; historic architecture; art collecting; music. Address: Towie Barclay Castle, Auchterless, Turriff, Aberdeenshire AB53 8EP; T.-01888 511347.

Elliot, Alison Janet, OBE, MA, MSc, PhD, LLD, DD, FRCPEdin. Associate Director, Centre for Theology and Public Issues, University of Edinburgh; b. 27.11.48, Edinburgh; m., John Christian Elliot; 1 s.; 1 d. Educ. Bathgate Academy; Edinburgh University; Sussex University. Research Associate, Department of Linguistics, Edinburgh University, 1973-74; Lecturer in Psychology, Lancaster University, 1974-76, Edinburgh University, 1977-85; Convener, Church and Nation Committee, Church of Scotland, 1996-2000; Moderator of the General Assembly of the Church of Scotland, 2004-05; Honorary Fellow, New College, University of Edinburgh; Convener, Scottish Council for Voluntary Organisations (SCVO), since 2007. Publications: Child Language, 1981; The Miraculous Everyday, 2005. Recreations: music; cookery. Address: (b.) CTPI, New College, Mound Place, Edinburgh EH1 2LX; e-mail: Alison.Elliot@ed.ac.uk

Elliot, Frances Mary, MB, ChB, MBA, MRCGP. Medical Director, NHS Fife; Non-executive Member, Board, HEBS, 1996-2003; Principal in general practice, 1987-98; b. 13.4.60, Edinburgh; m., John Gordon Elliot. Educ. St. Columba's High School, Dunfermline; Glasgow University; Stirling University. Recreations: hill-walking; cycling; photography; bird watching. Address: (b.) Hayfield House, Hayfield Road, Kirkcaldy, Fife KY2 5AH; T.-01592 648077.

Elliot, Sir Gerald Henry; b. 24.12.23, Edinburgh; m., Margaret Ruth Whale; 2 s.; 1 d. Educ. Marlborough College; New College, Oxford. Indian Army, 1942-46; Christian Salvesen, 1948-88. Chairman: Christian Salvesen PLC, 1981-88, Scottish Provident Institution, 1983-89, Scottish Arts Council, 1980-86, Prince's Scottish Youth Business Trust, 1987-94; Vice Chairman, Scottish Business in the Community, 1987-89; Trustee, National Museums of Scotland, 1987-91; Member of Court, Edinburgh University, 1984-93; Chairman: Scottish Unit Managers Ltd., 1984-88, Martin Currie Unit Trusts, 1988-90; Chairman, Forth Ports Authority, 1973-79; Chairman, Scottish Opera, 1987-92; Chairman of Trustees, David Hume Institute, 1985-95; Chairman, Institute of Directors, Scottish Division, 1989-92; Trustee and Director, Edinburgh Festival Theatre, 1995-98; Member, Court of Regents, Royal College of Surgeons, 1990-99; President, UN50 Scotland, 1994-95; Fellow, Royal Society of Edinburgh, since 1977; Honorary Consul for Finland in Edinburgh and Leith, 1957-89; Hon. d.h.c., Edinburgh University, 1989; Hon. LLD, Aberdeen University, 1991. Address: (b.) 39 Inverleith Place, Edinburgh EH3 5QD; T.-0131-552 6208.

Elliot, Robert John, LLB, WS. Solicitor; Deputy Keeper of W.S. Society, since 1999; b. 18.1.47, Edinburgh; m., Christine; 1 s.; 1 d. Educ. Loretto School; Edinburgh

University. Partner, Lindsays WS, since 1973; President, Law Society of Scotland, 1997-98; Chairman, Scottish Committee Council on Tribunals, 1998-2005. Recreations: golf; Scottish country dancing; detective novels; argument. Address: (b.) Caledonian Exchange, 19A Canning Street, Edinburgh EH3 8HE; T.-0131-656 5651.

Elliott, Professor Robert F., BA (Oxon), MA, FRSE. Professor of Economics and Director, Health Economics Research Unit, Aberdeen University; b. 15.6.47, Thurlow, Suffolk; m., Susan Elliott Gutteridge; 1 s. Educ. Haverhill Secondary Modern School, Suffolk; Ruskin College and Balliol College, Oxford; Leeds University. Joined Aberdeen University, 1973, as Research Fellow, then Lecturer; Director, Scottish Doctoral Programme in Economics, 1989-99; Member, Training Board, ESRC, 1995-99; Chair of Reviews for, and Consultant to, many public and private sector organisations, including Megaw Committee of Inquiry into Civil Service Pay, the EEC Commission, HM Treasury OECD, HIDB, DETR, and McCrone Committee, Scottish Executive; President, Scottish Economic Society, 2002-05; Commissioner, Low Pay Commission, since 2007. Publications: books on Pay in the Public Sector, 1981; Incomes Policies, Inflation and Relative Pay, 1981; Incomes Policy, 1981; Unemployment and Labour Market Efficiency, 1989; Labour Market Analysis, 1990; Public Sector Pay in the EU, 1999; Advances in Health Economics, 2003; Decentralised Pay Setting, 2003. Recreations: music; reading; hill-walking; golf. Address: (h.) 11 Richmondhill Place, Aberdeen AB15 5EN; T.-01224 314901.

Elliott, Hon. Lord (Walter Archibald Elliott), QC, MC, BL. President, Lands Tribunal for Scotland, 1971-92; Chairman, Scottish Land Court, 1978-92; Ensign, Queen's Bodyguard for Scotland (Royal Company of Archers); b. 6.9.22, London; m., Susan Isobel MacKenzie Ross; 2 s. Educ. Eton College; Edinburgh University. 2nd Bn., Scots Guards, 1943-45 (Staff Captain, 1947); Advocate and at the Inner Temple, Barrister-at-Law, 1950; QC (Scotland), 1963; conducted Edinburgh ring road inquiry, 1967. Publications: Us and Them: a study of group consciousness, 1986; Esprit de Corps, 1995. Recreation: gardening. Address: (h.) Morton House, 19 Winton Loan, Edinburgh EH10 7AW; T.-0131-445 2548.

Elphinstone, 19th Lord (Alexander Mountstuart Elphinstone); b. 15.4.80. Succeeded to title, 1994.

Elvidge, Sir John William, KCB, BA. Permanent Secretary, Scottish Government, since 2003; b. 9.2.51, London; m., Maureen Margaret Ann McGinn. Educ. Sir George Monoux School; St Catherine's College, Oxford. Scottish Office, 1973-88; Director of Implementation, Scottish Homes, 1988-89; Scottish Office, 1989-98, latterly as Head of Economic Infrastructure Group, Scottish Office Development Department; Cabinet Office, 1998-99 (Deputy Head of Economic and Domestic Secretariat); Head, Scottish Executive Education Department, 1999-2002; Head, Scottish Executive Finance and Central Services Department, 2002-03. Recreations: reading; theatre; music; film; painting; food; wine; sport; walking. Address: (b.) 5th Floor, St. Andrew's House, Regent Road, Edinburgh EH1 3DG; T.-0131-244 4026.

Emberson, Eleanor Avril, BSc, PhD. Chief Executive, Scottish Court Service, since 2004; Head of New Educational Developments Division, Scottish Executive Education Department, 2001-04; b. 14.9.67, Irvine. Educ. Arran High School; St Andrews University.

Senior Assistant Statistician, Retail Prices Index, Central Statistical Office, 1993-95; Head, GES Data Unit, HM Treasury, 1995-98; Finance Co-ordinaton Team Leader, Scottish Executive Finance, 1998-99; Head of Curriculum, International and Information Technology Division, Scottish Executive Education Department, 1999-2001. Address: (b.) Hayweight House, 23 Lauriston Street, Edinburgh EH3 9DQ; T.-0131 229 9200.

Emmanuel, Professor Clive Robert, BSc (Econ), MA, PhD, ACIS. Professor of Accounting and Director of CIFA; b. 23.5.47; m.; 1 s.; 2 d. Educ. UWIST; Lancaster University; UCW, Aberystwyth. Steel Company of Wales, Port Talbot, 1964-68; Lecturer, Lancaster University, 1974-78; Senior Lecturer, then Reader, UCW, Aberystwyth, 1978-87; Associate Professor, University of Kansas, 1980-82. Address: (b.) Department of Accounting and Finance, Glasgow University, Glasgow.

Emslie, Hon. Lord; Hon. (George) Nigel (Hannington) Emslie. Senator of the College of Justice in Scotland, since 2001; b. 17.4.47. Admitted, Faculty of Advocates, 1972; QC (Scotland), 1986; Dean, Faculty of Advocates, 1997-2001. Address: (b.) Parliament House, Edinburgh EH1 1RQ; T.-0131-225 2595.

Emslie, Donald Gordon. Acting Chief Executive, SMG plc, July 2006-March 2007; Chief Executive, SMG Television, 1999-July 2006; Managing Director, Broadcasting, Scottish TV, since 1997; b. 8.5.57; m., Sarah; 2 d. Appointed to SMG plc Board, 1999; Ex Chairman: ITV Council; Chairman: The Royal Lyceum Theatre Company, Scottish Industry Skills Panel; Director: Scottish Screen, Skillset Screen Academy Scotland, joint board, Scottish Arts Council and Scottish Screen Skillset UK; Fellow, Royal Television Society. Address: (b.) Pacific Quay, Glasgow G51 1PQ; T.-0141-300 3780; 32 Drumsheugh Gardens, Edinburgh EH3 7RN.

Engeset, Jetmund, LVO, FRCSE, FRCSG, ChM. Consultant surgeon, Grampian Health Board, 1974-2004; Surgeon to the Queen in Scotland, 1985-2004; b. 22.7.38; m., Anne Robertson; 2 d. Educ. Oslo University; Aberdeen University.

Entwistle, Raymond Marvin, FCIB, FCIBS. Chairman, Adam & Company Group, since 2005; Managing Director, Adam & Company Group Plc, 1993-2004; b. 12.6.44, Croydon; m., Barbara Joan Hennessy; 2 s.; 1 d. Educ. John Ruskin Grammar School. Several managerial appointments with Lloyds Bank. Governor, Edinburgh College of Art, 1989-99; Chairman, Fruit Market Gallery, Edinburgh, 1988-2000; Non-executive Director: John Davidson (Holdings) Ltd, 1992-96, JW International Plc., 1995-96, Dunedin Smaller Companies Investment Trust PLC, since 1998, I & H Brown Ltd, since 2003; Chairman, Scottish Civic Trust, since 2003. Recreations: golf; shooting; fishing; antiques. Address: (b.) 22 Charlotte Square, Edinburgh EH2 4DF; T.-0131-225 8484.

Erdal, David Edward, MA, MBA, PhD. Director, Employee Ownership Association; Director, Baxi Partnership Ltd. (Chairman, 1994-99); b. 29.3.48, Umtali, Zimbabwe; 1 s.; 1 d. Educ. Glenalmond; Brasenose College, Oxford; Harvard Business School; University of St. Andrews. English Language Teacher, London, 1972-74; Tianjin Foreign Language Institute, People's Republic of China, 1974-76; Tullis Russell Group, 1977-2004 (Director,

1981-2004; Chairman, 1985-96). Fellow, Royal Society of Arts. Recreations: sailing; skiing; reading. Address: (h.) West Court, Hepburn Gardens, St Andrews KY16 9LN; T.- 01334 473724.

Erroll, 24th Earl of (Merlin Sereld Victor Gilbert Hay). Hereditary Lord High Constable of Scotland; b. 20.4.48; m.; 2 s.; 2 d. Educ. Eton; Trinity College, Cambridge. Succeeded to title, 1978.

Erskine, Donald Seymour, DL, FRICS; b. 28.5.25, London; m., Catharine Annandale McLelland; 1 s. 4 d. Educ. Wellington College. RA (Airborne), 1943-47 (Captain); Pupil, Drumlanrig Estate, 1947-49; Factor, Country Gentlemen's Association, Edinburgh, 1950-55; Factor to Mr A.L.P.F. Wallace, 1955-61; Factor and Director of Estates, National Trust for Scotland, 1961-89; Member, Queen's Bodyguard for Scotland (Royal Company of Archers); Deputy Lieutenant, Perth and Kinross; General Trustee, Church of Scotland, 1989-2000. Recreations: golf; shooting; singing. Address: (h.) Cleish House, Cleish, Kinrossshire KY13 0LR; T.-01577 850232.

Esler, Professor Philip Francis, BA (Hons), LLB, LLM, DPhil. Chief Executive, Arts and Humanities Research Council, since 2005; Vice-Principal for Research and Provost, St Andrews University, 1998-2001; Professor of Biblical Criticism, since 1995; b. 27.8.52, Sydney, Australia; m., Patricia Kathryn Curran; 2 s.; 1 d. Educ. Marist Bros High School, Eastwood, Sydney; Sydney University; Oxford University (Magdalen). Solicitor, NSW Supreme Court, 1979-81 and 1984-86; Barrister, NSW Supreme Court, 1986-92; Reader in New Testament, St Andrews University, 1992-95. Member, Board, Scottish Enterprise Fife, 1999-2003. Publications: Community and Gospel in Luke-Acts, 1987; The First Christians in their Social Worlds, 1994; Galatians, 1998; The Early Christian World (Editor), 2000; Conflict and Identity in Romans, 2003; Visuality and Biblical Text: Interpreting Velazquez' Christ with Martha and Mary as a Test Case (Co-Author), 2004; New Testament Theology: Communion and Community, 2005; Ancient Israel: The Old Testament in Its Social Context (Editor), 2005; Lazarus, Mary and Martha: A Social, Scientific and Theological Reading of John (Co-Author), 2006. Recreations: walking; tennis; reading. Address: Kilninian House, Kemback, Fife, KY15 5TS; T.-01334 462851; e-mail: pfe@st-andrews.ac.uk

Espley, Arthur James, MBChB, DRCOG, FRCS(Edin). Consultant Orthopaedic Surgeon, Perth Royal Infirmary, 1981-2005; Honorary Senior Lecturer, Department of Traumatic and Orthopaedic Surgery, University of Dundee, 1981-2005; b. 19.2.44, Southend; m., Erica Strang; 1 s.; 2 d. Educ. Belfast Royal Academy; Edinburgh University Medical School. Governor, Craigclowan Preparatory School, Perth, 1995-2006; Honorary President, Arthritis Care, Perth, 1996-2003. Recreations: golf; gardening. Address: (h.) Couttie Bridge Cottage, Coupar Angus, Blairgowrie PH13 9HF; T.-01828 627301; e-mail: artcouttie@hotmail.com

Evans, Alan Thomson, BMedBiol, MD, FRCPath. Consultant and Honorary Senior Lecturer in Pathology, since 1993; b. 20.9.62, Buckhaven; m., Caroline; 1 s.; 1 d. Educ. Buckhaven High School; University of Aberdeen. House Officer, Aberdeen Royal Infirmary 1986-87; Senior House Officer in Pathology, Ninewells Hospital, Dundee, 1987-88; Lecturer in Pathology, University of Dundee, 1988-90; Senior Registrar in Pathology, Ninewells Hospital, Dundee, 1990-93. Chairman, Pathology Division, Scottish Melanoma Group; Examiner in Dermatopathology, Royal College of

Pathologists. Recreations: gardening; architectural history; opera. Address: Department of Pathology, Ninewells Hospital and Medical School, Dundee DD1 9SY; T.-01382 632548; e-mail: alan.evans@nhs.net

Evans, Brian Mark, BSc, Dip URP, MSc, MRTPI, FCSD. Deputy Chair, Architecture and Design Scotland, since 2004; Partner, Gillespies LLP, since 2003; Board Member: the Academy of Urbanism, since 2005, the Nordic Urban Design Association, since 2005; Member, Sheffield Urban Design Review Panel, since 2005; Enabler, Commission for the Built Environment, London, since 2003; b. 20.5.53, St. Andrews; m., Susan Ann Jones. Educ. Linlithgow Academy; University of Edinburgh; University of Strathclyde. Graduate Trainee, Planner, Cumbernauld District, 1975; Planner: Lanark District, 1976-79, William Gillespie & Partners, 1979-84; Associate, Gillespies, 1985-89; Deputy Design Coordinator, Glasgow Garden Festival, 1985-88; Partner, Gillespies, 1989-2003; Artistic Professor, Urban Design & Planning, School of Architecture, Chalmers University, Gothenburg, Sweden, 1998-2004. Publications: Learning from Place 1 (RIBA Publications 2007 - editor); Making Cities Work (Wylie 2004 - urban design advisor); Tommorows Architectural Heritage, 1991 (joint author); publications and articles in English, Swedish, Italian, Dutch on urban design and landscape planning. Recreations: running; mountain walking; cross-country skiing; music. Address: (b.) 21 Carlton Court, Glasgow G5 5JP; T.-0141 420 8200.
E-mail: brian.evans@gillespies.co.uk

Evans, David Pugh, ARCA, RSA, RSW; paints in Edinburgh; b. 20.11.42, Gwent. Educ. Newbridge Grammar School; Newport College of Art; Royal College of Art. Lecturer, Edinburgh College of Art, 1965-68; Fine Art Fellow, York University, 1968-69; Lecturer, Edinburgh College of Art, 1969-2000; travelled and painted throughout USA, 1975; solo exhibitions: Marjorie Parr Gallery, London; Mercury Gallery, London; York University; Fruitmarket Gallery, Edinburgh; Open Eye Gallery, Edinburgh; Gilbert Parr Gallery, London. Address: (h.) 17 Inverleith Gardens, Edinburgh EH3 5PS; T.-0131-552 2329.

Evans, Leslie Elizabeth, BA (Hons) Music. Director, Europe, External Affairs and Culture, Scottish Government, DG Economy, since 2007; Head of Tourism, Culture and Sport, Scottish Executive Education Department, 2006-07; b. 11.12.58; m., Derek George McVay; 1 s. Educ. Liverpool University. Assistant to Director, Greenwich Festival, 1981; Entertainments Officer, London Borough of Greenwich, 1981-83; Arts Co-ordinator, Sheffield CC, 1983-85; Senior Arts Officer, Edinburgh DC, 1985-87; Principal Officer, Stirling CC, 1987-89; City of Edinburgh Council: Assistant Director of Recreation, 1989-99, Strategic Projects Manager, 1999-2000; Scottish Executive: Head: Local Government, Constitution and Governance, 2000-03, Public Service Reform, 2003-05. Member, Scotch Malt Whisky Society. Recreations: the arts; pilates and keeping fit; handbags. Address: (b.) Scottish Government, Victoria Quay, Edinburgh EH6 6QQ; T.-0131 244 0319; e-mail: leslie.evans@scotland.gsi.gov.uk

Everest, Anne Christine, BA (Hons). Headmistress, St. Margaret's School for Girls, Aberdeen, since 2007; b. 23.9.56, Beverley; m., Paul Everest; 2 s.; 1 d. Educ. St. Mary's School for Girls, Hull; Hull University. Lecturer in Classics: Beverley High School for Girls, Robert Gordon's College, Aberdeen; Deputy Head in Senior School, Robert Gordon's College, Aberdeen, 2002-07. Recreations: walking; reading. Address: (b.) 17 Albyn Place, Aberdeen AB10 1RU; T.-01224 584466; e-mail: info@st-margaret.aberdeen.sch.uk

Everett, Peter, BSc (Hons), SPMB; b. 24.9.31, London; m., Annette Patricia Hyde; 3 s.; 1 d. Educ. George Watson's College; Edinburgh University. Royal Engineers, 1953-55 (2nd Lt.); joined Shell International Petroleum Company, 1955; Managing Director: Brunei Shell Petroleum Co. Ltd., 1979-84, Shell UK Exploration and Production, 1985-89; retired, 1989. Honorary Professor, Heriot Watt University, 1989. Recreation: golf. Address: (h.) Cluain, Castleton Road, Auchterarder, Perthshire PH3 1JW.

Ewart, Michael (Mike), BA, DPhil. Chief Executive, Scottish Prison Service, since 2007; Head of Education Department, Scottish Executive, 2002-07; b. 9.9.52, Anthorn, Carlisle; 1 s.; 1 d. Educ. St Peter's School, Southbourne, Dorset; Jesus College, Cambridge; York University. Joined Scottish Office, 1977; worked in education, criminal justice, Secretariat of Royal Commission on Legal Services in Scotland, roads and transport; Assistant Private Secretary to Secretary of State for Scotland, 1981-82; Civil Service Fellow in Politics, Glasgow University, 1982-83; Health Service management reform; Head, Schools Division, Scottish Office Education Department; joined Scottish Courts Administration, 1991; Chief Executive, Scottish Court Service, 1993-99; joined Scottish Executive Education Department, 1999, as Head of Schools Group. Recreations: books; music; military history; running; climbing (ice and rock); ski-ing. Address: (b.) Scottish Prison Service Headquarters, Communications Branch, Room 338, Calton House, 5 Redheughs Rigg, Edinburgh EH12 9HW; T.-0131 244 8745.

Ewing, Annabelle, LLB (Hons). SNP MP, Perth, 2001-05; b. 20.8.60, Glasgow. Educ. Craigholme School; Glasgow University; Johns Hopkins University; Europa Institute, Amsterdam University. Admitted Solicitor, 1986; Legal Service, EC, 1987; worked for law firms in Brussels, 1987-96; lawyer, EC, 1997; Ewing & Co., Solicitors: Associate, 1998-99, Partner, 1999-2001; Consultant, Leslie Wolfson & Co., Glasgow, 2001-03. Honorary President, SNP Brussels Branch. Recreations: walking; swimming; travel; reading.

Ewing, Fergus. MSP (SNP), Inverness East, Nairn and Lochaber, since 1999; Minister for Community Safety, since 2007; m., Margaret Ewing (deceased). Educ. Loretto School, Edinburgh; Glasgow University. Solicitor. Recreations: piano; reading; running; hill-walking; former member of local mountain rescue team. Address: (b.) Scottish Parliament, Edinburgh EH99 1SP; T.-01463 713004.

Ewing, John Anthony, BSc. Director of Transport, Scottish Government, since 2004; Chief Executive, Scottish Court Service, 1999-2004; b. 13.6.55, Glasgow; m., Caroline Ayton; 2 d. Educ. St Mungo's Academy; Glasgow University. Joined Scottish Office, 1980; Principal, Industry Department for Scotland, 1986-91; Principal, Scottish Home and Health Department, 1992-93; Assistant Secretary (Housing), Scottish Office Development Department, 1993-97; Head of Constitutional Policy Division, Constitution Group, 1997-99. Address: (b.) Scottish Government Transport Directorate, 2G-25 Victoria Quay, Edinburgh EH6 6QQ; T.-0131 244 0629.

F

Fabiani, Linda. MSP (SNP), Central Scotland, since 1999; Minister for Europe, External Affairs and Culture, since 2007; b. 14.12.56, Glasgow. Educ. Hyndland School, Glasgow; Napier College, Edinburgh; Glasgow University. Various Housing Association posts, 1982-99. Recreations: music; literature; friends. Address: (b.) Scottish Parliament, Edinburgh EH99 1SP.

Fairbairn, The Hon. Mrs Elizabeth, MBE. Chairman: Lothian Homes, Live Music Now! Scotland; Trustee, Scottish National War Memorial; President, Clan Mackay Society; b. 21.6.38; 3 d. Address: 38 Moray Place, Edinburgh EH3 6BT; T.-0131-225 2724.

Fairbairn, Martin MacLean, BCom, CA. Director of Governance and Management, Scottish Funding and Higher Education Funding Council, since 2004; b. 20.9.63, Dunfermline; m., Anne Fairbairn (nee Marshall); 2 s.; 1 d. Educ. Queen Anne High, Dunfermline; University of Edinburgh. Auditor, Touche Ross & Co., 1984-93; Director of Finance, Stevenson College Edinburgh, 1993-2000; Deputy Director, FE Funding, Scottish Funding Councils for Further and Higher Education, 2000-04. Member, Audit Committee, Mercy Corps Scotland. Recreations: church organist; youth work; badminton; golf; cycling. Address: (b.) Scottish Funding Council, Donaldson House, 47 Haymarket Terrace, Edinburgh EH12 5HD; T.-0131 313 6500; e-mail: mfairbairn@sfc.ac.uk

Fairgrieve, Brian David, OBE, DL, MB, ChB, FRCSEd. Deputy Lieutenant, Falkirk and Stirling Districts; General Surgeon, Falkirk Royal Infirmary, 1960-87; b. 21.2.27, Glasgow. Educ. Glasgow Academy; Glasgow University. RMO, 2/6th Gurkha Rifles, 1952-54; initial medical training, Western Infirmary, Glasgow, Stobhill General Hospital, Killearn Hospital; Area Scout Commissioner, 21 years; President, Forth Valley Area Scout Council; Past President, Rotary Club of Falkirk; Lecturer and Examiner, Scotish Police College; Member, Council, St. Andrew's Ambulance Association; former Director, Incorporated Glasgow Stirlingshire & Sons of the Rock Society; Hon. Vice President, Grangemouth Rugby Club; awarded Silver Wolf, 1983, and OBE, 1986, for services to International Scouting. Recreations: photography; travel. Address: (h.) 19 Lyall Crescent, Polmont, Falkirk FK2 0PL; T.-01324 715449.

Fairgrieve, James Hanratty, DA, RSA, RSW. Painter; b. 17.6.44, Prestonpans; m., Margaret D. Ross; 2 s.; 1 d. Educ. Preston Lodge Senior Secondary School; Edinburgh College of Art. Postgraduate study, 1966-67; Travelling Scholarship, Italy, 1968; Senior Lecturer in Drawing and Painting, Edinburgh College of Art, 1968-98; President, SSA, 1978-82; exhibited in Britain and Europe, since 1966. Recreation: angling. Address: (h.) Burnbrae, Gordon, Berwickshire.

Fairlamb, Professor Alan Hutchinson, CBE, MB, ChB, PhD, FLS, FRSE, FMedSci. Wellcome Principal Research Fellow, University of Dundee, since 1996, Professor of Biochemistry, since 1996, Head of Division of Biological Chemistry & Drug Discovery, since 1996, Co-Director of Drug Discovery Unit, since 2006; b. 30.4.47, Newcastle-upon-Tyne; m., Carolyn Strobos; 1 s.; 2 d. Educ. Hymers College, Hull; Edinburgh University. Surgical and Medical House Officer, Longmore and Western General Hospitals, Edinburgh, 1971-72; Faculty of Medicine Research Scholar, University of Edinburgh, 1972-75; MRC Travelling Fellow, University of Amsterdam, 1975-76; Research Fellow: University of Edinburgh, 1976-80, London School of Hygiene and Tropical Medicine, 1980-81; Assistant Professor, The Rockefeller University, New York, 1981-87; Senior Clinical Lecturer, London School of Hygiene & Tropical Medicine, 1987-90; Professor of Molecular Parasitology and Head, Biochemistry and Chemotherapy Unit, LSHTM, 1990-96. Current committee memberships: Scientific Advisory Committee for Drugs for Neglected Diseases initiative (DNDi), Scientific and Technical Advisory committee for World Health Organization Special Programme for Research and Training in Tropical Diseases (WHO/TDR). Publications: author of more than 200 scientific articles and reviews on biochemistry and chemotherapy of neglected tropical diseases. Recreations: gardening; fishing; motorcycling; photography. Address: (b.) Division of Biological Chemistry & Drug Discovery, School of Life Sciences, Wellcome Trust Biocentre, University of Dundee, Dundee DD1 5EH; T.-01382 345155; Fax: 01382 345542.
E-mail: a.h.fairlamb@dundee.ac.uk

Fairley, Douglas, LLB. Advocate, since 1999; b. 20.2.68, Glasgow; m., Una Doherty. Educ. Hutchesons' Grammar School; University of Glasgow. Solicitor, Maclay Murray and Spens, 1992-98. Publication: Contempt of Court in Scotland (Co-Author). Recreations: music; tennis; skiing; curling. Address: (b.) Advocates' Library, Parliament House, Edinburgh EH1 1RF; T.-0131-226 5071.

Fairley, Janet Christine, PhD, MPhil, BA (Hons). Elected Fellow, Institute of Popular Music, Liverpool University, 1998; b. Birkenhead; 1 s.; 2 d. Taught, Catholic University, Temuco, Chile, 1971-73; Hon. Fellow, Institute of Latin American Studies, University of Glasgow, 1989-97; Leverhulme Research Fellow, 1992; British Council-Andes Foundation Visiting Professor in Musicology, University of Chile, 1994; Director, Edinburgh Book Festival, 1995-97; AHRB Research Grant 2000; Temporary Lecturer: Institute Popular Music, Liverpool University, 2007-08, Ethnomusicology, Music Department, University of Sheffield, September-January, 2005/06; British Academy Research Grant, 2005-06; Editorial Board, Popular Music Journal, Cambridge University Press, since 1988, and Book Reviews Editor, since 2002; Editorial team, New Grove Dictionary of Music and Musicians, 1998; writer; freelance journalist since late 1980s; freelance broadcaster, since 1989, producing arts programmes (Presenter, Earthbeat, 1989-93); world music critic, fRoots, Classic CD, Gramophone, Songlines; Member, Judging Panel, BBC Radio 3 World Music Awards, 2004, 2005, 2006; numerous academic publications; contributor, Rough Guide to World Music; UK Chair, International Vice-Chair, International Association for the Study of Popular Music, 1985-92. Recreations: taichi; yoga; salsa, tango and flamenco dancing; swimming; reading; singing; music; theatre; film; occasional club DJ. Address: (h.) 7A Cluny Gardens, Edinburgh EH10 6BE.

Fairweather, Clive Bruce, CBE. HM Chief Inspector of Prisons for Scotland, 1994-2002; b. 21.5.44, Edinburgh; m., Ann; (divorced); 1 s.; 1 d. Commanding Officer: Scottish Division Depot, 1984-87, 1st Bn., King's Own Scottish Borderers, 1987-89; Divisional Colonel, The Scottish Division, 1991-94.

Falconer, Alan David, MA, BD, DLitt. Minister, St. Machar's Cathedral, Aberdeen, since 2004; b. 12.12.45, Edinburgh; m., Marjorie Ellen Falconer (ms Walters); 2 s.;

1 d. Educ. George Heriot's School, Edinburgh; Aberdeen University. Lecturer, then Director, Irish School of Ecumenics, Dublin, 1974-95 (Director, 1990-95); Director of the Faith and Order Commission, World Council of Churches, Geneva, Switzerland, 1995-2004. Publications: (ed) Understanding Human Rights, Dublin, 1980; (ed) Reconciling Memories, Dublin, 1988; A Man Alone: Meditations in Seven Lost Words, Dublin, 1987; Reformed - Roman Catholic International Dialogue, 1984. Recreations: music; reading. Address: (h.) 18 The Chanonry, Old Aberdeen AB24 1RQ; T.-01224 483688; e-mail: minister@stmachar.com

Falconer, David. Director, Pain Association Scotland, since 1989; b. Perth; m., Rosanne; 1 s.; 1 d. Educ. Perth High School. HM Forces Royal Core of Signals, 1964-78; Scottish Agriculture Industry, 1978-88; Pain Association Scotland, since 1989. Member, Scottish Cross Party, Chronic Pain; Scottish Advisory Board, Chronic Pain. Recreation: mountaineer. Address: (b.) Pain Association Scotland, Cramond House, Cramond Glebe Road, Edinburgh EH4 6NS; T.-0131 312 7955; e-mail: dfalconer@painassociation.com

Falconer, Professor Kenneth John, MA, PhD (Cantab), FRSE. Professor in Pure Mathematics, St. Andrews University, since 1993; b. 25.1.52, Middlesex; m., Isobel Jessie Nye; 1 s.; 1 d. Educ. Kingston Grammar School; Corpus Christi College, Cambridge. Research Fellow, Corpus Christi College, Cambridge, 1977-80; Lecturer, then Reader, Bristol University, 1980-93; Visiting Professor: Oregon State University, 1985-86, Isaac Newton Institute, Cambridge, 1999, IHES, Paris, 2005-06. Publications Secretary, London Mathematical Society, since 2006. Publications: The Geometry of Fractal Sets; Fractal Geometry — Mathematical Foundations and Applications; Techniques in Fractal Geometry; Unsolved Problems in Geometry (Co-author); 85 papers. Recreations: hill-walking and long distance walking (Long Distance Walkers Association: Chair, 2000-03, Editor of its journal Strider, 1987-92 and since 2006). Address: (h.) Lumbo Farmhouse, St. Andrews, Fife; T.-01334 478507.

Falkland, 15th Viscount (Lucius Edward William Plantagenet Cary). Premier Viscount of Scotland on the Roll; b. 8.5.35, London; 2 s.; 3 d. (1 deceased). Educ. Wellington College; Alliance Francaise, Paris. Formerly journalist, theatrical agent, chief executive of international trading company; entered Parliament, 1984 (SDP), 1987 (Liberal Democrats); Deputy Chief Whip, House of Lords, for Liberal Democrats, 1987-2001; Culture, Media, Sport and Tourism Spokesman, since 1994; elected Member, House of Lords, since 1999. Recreations: racing; golf; motor-cycling; cinema. Address: (b.) House of Lords, London SW1.

Fallick, Professor Anthony Edward, BSc, PhD, FRSE, FRSA. Professor of Isotope Geosciences, University of Glasgow, since 1996, b. 21.4.50, Chatham; Educ. St. Columba's High School, Greenock; University of Glasgow. Research Fellow: McMaster University, Canada, 1975-78, University of Cambridge, 1978-80; Research Fellow, Lecturer, Reader, Professor, Scottish Universities Research and Reactor Centre, East Kilbride, since 1980; Head of Isotope Geosciences Unit, Scottish Universities Research and Reactor Centre, East Kilbride, 1986-99; Director, Scottish Universities Environmental Research Centre, 1998-2007; 1997 Schlumberger Medallist, Mineralogical Society of Great Britain and Ireland; 2001 Richard A. Glenn Award, American Chemical Society; 2004 Coke Medal of the Geological Society of London; Honorary Professor in the Universities of Edinburgh and St. Andrews.

Address: (b.) S.U.E.R.C., Rankine Avenue, East Kilbride, Glasgow G75 0QF; T.-013552 23332; e-mail: t.fallick@suerc.gla.ac.uk

Fannin, A. Lorraine, OBE, BA (Hons), DipEd. Chief Executive, Publishing Scotland; Director, BookSource; Trustee, National Library of Scotland; Board Member, Edinburgh UNESCO City of Literature Trust. Educ. Victoria College, Belfast; Queen's University, Belfast; Reading University. Previously Teacher; broadcaster; journalist; children's book supplier, 1979-89. Recreations: galleries; books and friends. Address: (b.) 137 Dundee Street, Edinburgh EH11 1BG; T.-0131-228 6866; e-mail: lorraine.fannin@scottishbooks.org

Farley-Sutton, Captain Colin David, RN, CEng, FIMechE, DL. Deputy Lieutenant, Caithness, since 1986; b. 20.12.31, Rugby; m., Sheila Wilson Baldwin; 2 s.; 2 d. Educ. Rugby College of Technology and Arts; RN Engineering College, Plymouth; RN College, Greenwich. Royal Navy, 1950-82. President, Caithness Branch, Red Cross, 1991-97. Address: (h.) Shepherd's Cottage, Lynegar, Watten, Caithness KW1 5UP; T.-01955 621697.

Farmer, Professor John Gregory, BSc, PhD, CChem, FRSC, FGS. Professor of Environmental Geochemistry, Edinburgh University, since 2004; b. 18.02.47, Market Bosworth; m., Margaret Ann McClimont; 2 s.; 1 d. Educ. Kilmarnock Academy; Glasgow University. Post-Doctoral Investigator, Woods Hole Oceanographic Institution, Mass., USA, 1972-74; Research Assistant and Fellow, Department of Forensic Medicine and Science, Glasgow University, 1974-86; Lecturer, Senior Lecturer and Reader in Environmental Chemistry, Edinburgh University, 1987-2003; Chairman, 8th International Conference on Heavy Metals in the Environment, Edinburgh, 1991; President, Society for Environmental Geochemistry and Health, 2002-05; Chairman, 6th International Symposium on Environmental Geochemistry, Edinburgh, 2003; Executive Editor, Science of the Total Environment, since 2002. Member: NERC Isotope Geosciences Facility Steering Committee, 1996-2002, NERC Freshwater Sciences Committee, 1997-2000, Swedish Research Council Natural Sciences Panel, since 2006. Recreations: cricket; Kilmarnock FC; reading; walking. Address: (b.) School of Geosciences, Edinburgh University; Crew Building, West Mains Road, Edinburgh EH9 3JN; T.-0131 650 4757; e-mail: j.g.farmer@ed.ac.uk

Farmer, Sir Tom, CBE, KCSG, DL. Former Chairman and Chief Executive, Kwik-Fit Holdings PLC (1984-2002); b. 10.7.40, Edinburgh; m., Anne Drury Scott; 1 s.; 1 d. Educ. Holy Cross Academy. Founding Chancellor of Queen Margaret University. Address: (h.) Maidencraig House, 192 Queensferry Road, Edinburgh EH4 2BN; T.-0131 315 2830; e-mail: info@maidencraig.com

Farquharson, Angus Durie Miller, OBE, OStJ, MA, FRICS. Lord Lieutenant of Aberdeenshire, since 1998; Vice Lord Lieutenant, 1987-98 (DL, 1984); b. 27.3.35, Haydon Bridge; m., Alison Mary Farquharson of Finzean; 2 s.; 1 d. Educ. Trinity College, Glenalmond; Downing College, Cambridge. Chartered Surveyor, Estate Factor, Farmer and Forester; Council Member, Scottish Landowners Federation, 1980-88; Member: Regional Advisory Committee, Forestry Commission, 1980-94; Red Deer Commission, 1986-92; Nature Conservancy Committee for Scotland, 1986-91; Director, DWP Harvesting, since 1987; NE Committee, SNH, 1991-94; Hon. President, Kincardine/Deeside Scouts; Elder and General Trustee, Church of Scotland, 1996-2006; Director,

Scottish Traditional Skills Training Centre, 2006. Recreations: gardening; shooting; walking; local history; nature conservation. Address: (h.) Glenferrick Lodge, Finzean, Banchory, Aberdeenshire, AB31 6NG; T.-01330850 229.

Farquharson, Captain Colin Andrew, JP, DL, FRICS. Lord Lieutenant of Aberdeenshire, 1987-98; Chartered Surveyor and Land Agent, since 1953; b. 9.8.23; m., 1, Jean Sybil Mary Hamilton (deceased, 1985); 2 d.; 1 d. deceased; 2, Clodagh, JP, DL, widow of Major Ian Houldsworth of Dallas, Morayshire; 3 step s.; 2 step d. Educ. Rugby. Grenadier Guards, 1942-48; ADC to Field Marshal Sir Harald Alexander (Earl Alexander of Tunis), 1945; Member, Board of Management, Royal Cornhill Hospitals, 1962-74; Director, MacRobert Farms (Douneside), 1971-87; Chairman, Gordon Local Health Council, 1975-81; Member, Grampian Health Board, 1981-89; DL, Aberdeenshire, 1966; Vice Lord Lieutenant, Aberdeenshire, 1983-87; Member, Queen's Bodyguard for Scotland (Royal Company of Archers), since 1964. Recreations: shooting; fishing. Address: Whitehouse, Alford, Aberdeenshire AB33 8DP.

Farquharson, Kenny (Kenneth James), MA (Hons), DipJour. Assistant Editor, Scotland on Sunday, since 2007; b. 8.5.62, Dundee; m., Caron Stoker; 2 s. Educ. Lawside R.C. Academy, Dundee; University of Aberdeen; University College, Cardiff. Industry Reporter, Coventry Evening Telegraph, 1985-88; Scotland on Sunday: Investigative Reporter, 1989-93, Political Editor, 1993-97; Political Editor, Daily Record, 1997-98; Scottish Political Editor, The Sunday Times, 1998-2002; Assistant Editor, The Sunday Times (Scotland), 2002-07. Director, Scottish European Aid, 1993-94; Convenor, Scottish Parliamentary Journalists' Association, 1997-2000. Political Journalist of the Year, 2001, Scottish Press Awards. Publication: Restless Nation (Co-author), 1996. Recreations: cooking; architecture; art. Address: (b.) 108 Holyrood Road, Edinburgh EH8 8AS; T.-0131 630 8453; e-mail: kenny.farquharson@scotlandonsunday.com

Farrell, Sheriff James Aloysius, MA, LLB. Sheriff of Lothian and Borders, since 1986; b. 14.5.43, Glasgow; m., 1, Jacqueline Allen (divorced); 2 d.; m., 2, Patricia McLaren. Educ. St. Aloysius College; Glasgow University; Dundee University. Admitted to Faculty of Advocates, 1974; Advocate-Depute, 1979-83; Sheriff: Glasgow and Strathkelvin, 1984-85, South Strathclyde, Dumfries and Galloway, 1985-86. Recreations: sailing; cycling; hill-walking. Address: (b.) Sheriff's Chambers, Edinburgh; T.-0131-225 2525.

Fass, Rev. Michael J., MA, MTh, FCIPD. Programme Director, Institute of Directors - Scotland Division, since 2001; b. 22.6.44, Sonning, Berks; m., Iola Mary Ashton; 1 s.; 2 d. Educ. Eton College; Trinity College, Cambridge; IMD, Lausanne. Served C Squadron (Berkshire Yeomanry) Berkshire and Westminster Dragoons (TA), 1963-68; worked in industry at Hays, Miles Druce-GKN, and DTI's Small Firms Service; Director, West Lothian Enterprise Ltd., 1983-92. Director, Prince's Scottish Youth Business Trust, 1989-97; NSM Priest in Charge, Collegiate Church of St. Matthew, Rosslyn Chapel, Roslin (Scottish Episcopal Church), 1997-2006; Bishop's Officer for Ministry, Diocese of Edinburgh, since 2005; Chairman, Industrial Christian Fellowship, 2000-04. Publication: Faith in Governance - Renewing the Role of the Director, 2004 (Co-Author). Address: 60 Braid Road, Edinburgh EH10 6AL.

Faulds, Dinah Joan, BSc (Dunelm), PGD Town Planning, Chartered MCIPD. Scottish Chief Commissioner, Girlguiding Scotland, since 2007; b. 29.12.53, Halesowen, West Midlands; m., Michael Dudley Faulds; 1 s.; 1 d. Educ. King Norton Grammar School for Girls; Durham University; Birmingham Polytechnic (now University of

Central England); Open University. Town Planner; WRNS Officer, 1979-88; Personnel Officer (N Ireland medal); Management consultant; Organisation Development Manager. Girlguiding Guide Leader, Birmingham, Rutland and Dalkeith, Scotland; Chair, Midlothian Programme and Training Committee, 1996-2001; County Commissioner, Midlothian, 2001-06; UK Council Member, since 2005. Recreations: Dalkeith Singers; riding; walking; curling; church. Address: (b.) Girlguiding Scotland HQ, 16 Coates Crescent, Edinburgh EH3 7AH.

Faulkner, Professor Douglas, WhSch, PhD, DSc, DEng(Hon), RCNC, FREng, FRINA, FIStructE, FSNAME. President, Institution of Engineers and Shipbuilders in Scotland, 1995-97; Head, Department of Naval Architecture and Ocean Engineering, Glasgow University, 1973-95, now Emeritus Professor; b. 29.12.29, Gibraltar; m., Isobel Parker Campbell; 3 d. Educ. Sutton High School, Plymouth; HM Dockyard Technical College, Devonport; Royal Naval College, Greenwich. Aircraft carrier design, 1955-57; production engineering, 1957-59; structural research, NCRE Dunfermline, 1959-63; Assistant Professor of Naval Construction, RNC, Greenwich, 1963-66; Structural Adviser to Ship Department, Bath, 1966-68; Naval Construction Officer attached to British Embassy, Washington DC, 1968-70; Member, Ship Research Committee, National Academy of Sciences, 1968-71; Research Associate and Defence Fellow, MIT, 1970-71; Structural Adviser, Ship Department, Bath, and Merrison Box Girder Bridge Committee, 1971-73; UK Representative, Standing Committee, International Ship Structures Congress, 1973-85; Member, Marine Technology Board, Defence Scientific Advisory Council; Expert Assessor: Lord Donaldson's Assessment (Derbyshire), 1995, Department of Transport (re. Derbyshire survey), 1996. Awarded: David W. Taylor Medal; William Froude Medal; Peter the Great Medal. Recreations: music; croquet. Address: (h.) 4 Murdoch Drive, Milngavie, Glasgow G62 6QZ; T.-0141-956 5071.

Fawkes, Robert, BSc, BA (Hons), Headteacher, Park Mains High School, Erskine, since 1995; b. 17.7.50; m., Margaret Ann; 2 s. Educ. Knightswood Secondary School; Glasgow University. Teacher, North Kelvinside; Principal Teacher of Guidance, Cranhill Secondary School; Principal Teacher of Mathematics, Waverley Secondary School; Assistant Headteacher, Cathkin High School; Depute Headteacher, Waverley Secondary School; Headteacher, Blantyre High School. Recreations: squash; hillwalking. Address: (b.) Park Mains High School, Barrhill Road, Erskine PA8 6EY; T.-0141-812 2801.

Fearn, Professor David Ross, BSc, PhD, CMath, FIMA, FRSE. Professor of Applied Mathematics, University of Glasgow, since 1993 (Head, Department of Mathematics, 1997-2003); Dean, Faculty of Information and Mathematical Sciences, since 2004; b. 11.2.54, Dundee; m., Elvira D'Annunzio; 1 s.; 1 d. Educ. Grove Academy, Dundee; University of St. Andrews; University of Newcastle upon Tyne. Research Associate: Florida State University, 1979-80, University of Cambridge, 1980-85; University of Glasgow: Lecturer, 1985-90, Senior Lecturer, 1990-92, Reader, 1992-93. Recreations: walking; gardening; DIY. Address: (b.) University Gardens, Glasgow G12 8QW; T.-0141-330 5417.

Fee, Kenneth, MA, FRCS. Emeritus Editor, Scots Independent; b. 14.7.31, Glasgow; m., Margery Anne Dougan; 3 s.; 1 d. Educ. Gourock High School; Hamilton Academy; Glasgow University; Strathclyde University. President, Glasgow University SRC and Scottish Union of Students; Editor, Gum, Ygorra and GU Guardian; sometime in military intelligence; Sub-Editor, Glasgow Herald; former Managing Director, Strathclyde Publishing Group; itinerant teaching; Member, Scottish Executive, NASUWT, 1983-98; various SNP branch, constituency and national offices, since 1973; Editor, Scots Independent, 1985-2004. Publication: How to Grow Fat and Free. Recreations: chess; gastronomy; campaigning. Address: (h.) 157 Urrdale Road, Dumbreck G41 5DG; T.-0141-427 0117.

Fenton, Professor Emeritus Alexander, CBE, MA, BA, DLitt, HonDLitt (Aberdeen), FRSE, FSA, FRSGS, HRSA, FSA Scot. Director, European Ethnological Research Centre, 1989-2006; Honorary Professor of Antiquities to Royal Scottish Academy, since 1996; b. 26.6.29, Shotts; m., Evelyn Elizabeth Hunter; 2 d. Educ. Turriff Academy; Aberdeen University; Cambridge University. Senior Assistant Editor, Scottish National Dictionary, 1955-59; part-time Lecturer, English as a Foreign Language, Edinburgh University, 1958-60; National Museum of Antiquities of Scotland: Assistant Keeper, 1959-75, Deputy Keeper, 1975-78, Director, 1978-85; part-time Lecturer, Department of Scottish History, Edinburgh University, 1974-80; Research Director, National Museums of Scotland, 1985-89; Chair of Scottish Ethnology and Director, School of Scottish Studies, Edinburgh University, 1990-94; Honorary Fellow, School of Scottish Studies, since 1969; Foreign Member: Royal Gustav Adolf Academy, Sweden, since 1978, Royal Danish Academy of Sciences and Letters, since 1979; Honorary Member: Volkskundliche Kommission fur Westfalen, since 1980, Hungarian Ethnographical Society, since 1983, Kungl. Humanistiska Vetenskapsfundet i Lund, Sweden, since 1998; Jury Member, Europa Prize for Folk Art, 1975-95; Honorary President, Scottish Vernacular Buildings Working Group; Honorary President, Scottish Country Life Museums Trust; Trustee, Scotland Inheritance Fund; Co-Editor, Tools and Tillage, since 1968; Editor, The Review of Scottish Culture, 1984-2004. Publications: The Various Names of Shetland, 1973, 1977; Scottish Country Life, 1976, 1999 (Scottish Arts Council Book Award); The Diary of a Parish Clerk (translation from Danish), 1976; The Island Blackhouse, A Guide to the Blackhouse at 42 Arnol, Lewis, 1978 (re-issued, 1989 and 2005); A Farming Township, A Guide to Auchindrain, the Museum of Argyll Farming Life, 1978; The Northern Isles, Orkney and Shetland, 1978, 1997 (Dag Strombäck Award); The Rural Architecture of Scotland (Co-author), 1981; The Shape of the Past 1, 1985; If All The World Were a Blackbird (translation from Hungarian), 1985; The Shape of the Past II, 1986; 'Wirds an' Wark 'e Seasons Roon on an Aberdeenshire Farm, 1987; Country Life in Scotland, Our Rural Past, 1987; Scottish Country Life, 1989; The Turra Coo, 1989; Craiters...or Twenty Buchan Tales, 1995; Buchan Words and Ways, 2005; The Food of the Scots. Recreation: languages. Address: (b.) European Ethnological Research Centre, School of Literatures, Languages and Cultures, The University of Edinburgh, 27 George Square, Edinburgh EH8 9LD.

Ferguson, Professor Allister Ian, BSc, MA, PhD, FInstP, FRSE, CPhys, FFCS. Professor of Photonics, Strathclyde University, since 1989; Technical Director, Institute of Photonics, University of Strathclyde, since 1996, Deputy Principal, since 2004; b. 10.12.51, Aberdeen; m., Kathleen Ann Challenger. Educ. Aberdeen Academy; St. Andrews University. Lindemann Fellow, Stanford University, 1977-79; SERC Research Fellow, St. Andrews, 1979-81; SERC Advanced Fellow, Oxford, 1981-83; Junior Research Fellow, Merton College, Oxford, 1981-83; Lecturer, then Senior Lecturer, Southampton University, 1983-89. Fellow: Royal Society of Edinburgh, since 1993, Institute of Physics, Optical Society of America, Institution of Electrical and Electronics Engineers. Address: (b.) McCance Building, University of Strathclyde, Glasgow G1 1XQ; T.-0141 548 3264.

Ferguson, Iain William Findlay, QC, LLB (Hons), DipLP. Queen's Counsel, since 2000; b. 31.7.61, Edinburgh; m., Valerie Laplanche; 2 s. Educ. Firrhill High School, Edinburgh; Dundee University. Advocate,

1987; Standing Junior Counsel to Ministry of Defence (Army), 1991-98, and to Scottish Development Department (Planning matters), 1998-2000. Recreations: cooking; rugby; cycling. Address: (h.) 16 McLaren Road, Edinburgh EH9 2BN; T.-0131-667 1751.

Ferguson, James Gordon Dickson. Director, Stewart Ivory & Co Ltd (formerly Stewart Fund Managers Ltd), since 1974, Chairman, 1989-2000; b. 12.11.47; m., Nicola Hilland (deceased 2007); 2 s.; 1 d. Educ. Cargilfield School, Edinburgh; Winchester; Trinity College, Dublin. Joined Stewart Ivory & Co Ltd, 1970; Chairman: Value and Income Trust plc, The Scottish Oriental Smaller Companies Trust plc, The Monks Investment Trust plc, Edinburgh US Tracker Trust plc; Director: The Independent Investment Trust plc, Northern 3 VCT plc, Lloyds TSB Scotland plc; Trustee, Lloyds TSB Foundation for Scotland; former Deputy Chairman, Association of Investment Companies; Governor, Gordonstoun School. Recreations: country pursuits. Address: 25 Heriot Row, Edinburgh EH3 6EN.

Ferguson, Joan P.S., MBE, MA, ALA, FRCPEdin. Hon. Secretary, Scottish Genealogy Society, 1960-2004; b. 15.9.29, Edinburgh. Educ. George Watson's Ladies College; Edinburgh University. Scottish Central Library, 1952-66; Librarian, Royal College of Physicians of Edinburgh, 1966-94. Member, Scottish Records Advisory Council, 1987-93; Compiler: Scottish Newspapers, Scottish Family Histories; Contributor, Companion and New Companion to Scottish Culture. Recreations: genealogy; gardening; reading. Address: (h.) 21 Howard Place, Edinburgh EH3 5JY; T.-0131-556 3844.

Ferguson, John Colin, MA, DipEd. Headteacher, Alness Academy, 1997-2004; b. 4.12.48, Galashiels; m., Doreen; 1 s.; 1 d. Educ. Galashiels Academy; Edinburgh University. Teacher of Geography, Alva Academy; Principal Teacher of Geography, Alness Academy; Assistant Headteacher, Fortrose Academy; Depute Headteacher, Alness Academy. Currently working part-time for Scottish Health Promoting Schools Unit. Voluntary work for Neil Gunn Trust. Recreations: hill-walking; photography; creative writing; tennis; golf.

Ferguson, Professor Pamela Ruth, LLB (Hons), DipLP, PhD. Professor of Scots Law, University of Dundee, since 2000; b. 7.4.63, Glasgow; m., Dr. Euan W. Macdonald; 1 s. Educ. Bearsden Academy; Glasgow University; Dundee University. Procurator Fiscal Depute/Trainee Solicitor, Crown Office, Edinburgh and Procurator Fiscal's Office, Kirkcaldy, 1986-89; Lecturer, 1989-95; Senior Lecturer, 1995-99. Winner, Dr. John McCormick Prize (jointly), Most Distinguished Law Graduate, 1985; awarded Royal Society of Edinburgh Research Fellowship, 1997. Address: (b.) Department of Law, University of Dundee, Dundee DD1 4HN; T.-01382 385189. E-mail: p.r.ferguson@dundee.ac.uk

Ferguson, Patricia. MSP (Labour), Glasgow Maryhill, since 1999; former Minister for Tourism, Culture and Sport; former Deputy Presiding Officer and Minister for Parliamentary Business; b. 1958, Glasgow; m., William G. Butler. Educ. Gartnethill Convent Secondary School, Glasgow. Address: (b.) 154 Raeberry Street, Glasgow G20 6EA.

Ferguson, Ron, MA, BD, ThM. Freelance journalist and author; Minister, St. Magnus Cathedral, Orkney, 1990-2001; Columnist, The Herald, since 1997, Press and Journal, since 2002, Life and Work, since 2003; b.

27.10.39, Dunfermline; m., Cristine Jane Walker; 2 s.; 1 d. Educ. Beath High School, Cowdenbeath; St. Andrews University; Edinburgh University; Duke University. Journalist, Fife and Edinburgh, 1956-63; University, 1963-71; ordained Minister, Church of Scotland, 1972; Minister, Easterhouse, Glasgow, 1971-79; exchange year with United Church of Canada, 1979-80; Deputy Warden, Iona Abbey, 1980-81; Leader, Iona Community, 1981-88. Publications: Geoff: A Life of Geoffrey M. Shaw, 1979; Grace and Dysentery, 1986; Chasing the Wild Goose, 1988; The Whole Earth Shall Cry Glory (Co-Editor), 1985; George MacLeod, 1990; Daily Readings by George MacLeod (Editor), 1991; Black Diamonds and the Blue Brazil, 1993; Technology at the Crossroads, 1994; Love Your Crooked Neighbour, 1998; Donald Dewar Ate My Hamster, 1999; Hitler Was A Vegetarian, 2001; The Reluctant Reformation of Clarence McGonigall, 2003; Fear and Loathing in Lochgelly, 2003; Blue Rinse Dreams and Banoffee Pie, 2005; Mole Under The Fence: Conversations with Roland Walls, 2006; Helicopter Dreams: The Quest for the Holy Grail, 2006; plays: Every Blessed Thing, 1993, Orkneyinga, 1997; Ending It All, 2006; poetry: Pushing the Boat Out (Contributor), 1997. Recreation: supporting Cowdenbeath Football Club. Address: (h.) Vinbrek, Orphir, Orkney KW17 2RE; T.-01856 811378; e-mail: ronbluebrazil@aol.com

Ferguson, Professor Ronald Gillies, MA, BPhil, CertSecEd. Professor of Italian, University of St. Andrews, since 2004, Head of The School of Modern Languages, since 2005; b. 21.7.49, Birkenhaw, Lanarkshire; m., Annie Ferguson (nee Ballouard); 1 s.; 1 d. Educ. Uddingston Grammar School; University of Glasgow; University of St. Andrews; Jordanhill College of Education. University of Lancaster: Lecturer in Italian, 1979-96, Senior Lecturer in Italian, 1996-97; University of St. Andrews: Senior Lecturer in Italian, 1997-2004, first ever Chair of Italian. Made Cavaliere della Stella della Solidarietà Italiana (one of Italy's highest honours) by the President of Italy for the 'distinction in the fields of Italian Renaissance theatre, Italian identity studies, and Venetian language linguistics and culture, and for making St. Andrews a centre for the study of Italian', 2005; made Fellow of the Ateneo Veneto di Scienze, Lettere ed Arti (one of Italy's foremost learned societies) for distinguished contributions to Venetian language and culture, 2006. Publications: Italian False Friends, 1994; The Theatre of Angelo Beolco (Ruzante): Text, Context and Performance, 2000; Italian Identities (ed.), 2002; A Linguistic History of Venice, 2007. Recreations: birdwatching; reading. Address: (h.) 3 Muir Gardens, St. Andrews, Fife KY16 9NH; T.-01334 472 383; e-mail: rgf@st-and.ac.uk

Ferguson, William James, OBE, FRAgS. Farmer, since 1954; Director, Hannah Research Institute, since 1995; Vice Lord Lieutenant, Aberdeenshire; Honorary Fellow, SAC, since 1999; b. 3.4.33, Aberdeen; m., Carroll Isobella Milne; 1 s.; 3 d. Educ. Turriff Academy; North of Scotland College of Agriculture. National Service, 1st Bn., Gordon Highlanders, 1952-54, serving in Malaya during the emergency. Former Director, Rowett Research Institute, Aberdeen; former Chairman, Aberdeen Milk Company; former Chairman, North of Scotland College of Agriculture; former Member, Scottish Country Life Museums Trust Ltd.; former Vice Chairman, SAC. Recreations: golf; field sports. Address: (h.) Nether Darley, Fyvie, Turriff, Aberdeenshire AB53 8LH.

Fergusson, Alexander Charles Onslow. MSP (Independent as Presiding Officer), Galloway and Upper Nithsdale, since 2003 (South of Scotland, 1999-2003); Presiding Officer, Scottish Parliament, since 2007; b. 8.4.49, Leswalt; m., Jane Merryn Barthold; 3 s. Educ.

Eton; West of Scotland Agricultural College. Farm management adviser, 1970-71; farmer, 1971-99; restaurateur, 1981-86. Community Councillor; JP, 1998-99; Deputy Lieutenant of Ayrshire, 1998-99. Recreations: curling; rugby (spectator); cricket. Address: (h.) Grennan, Dalry, Kirkcudbright DG7 3PL; T.-01644 430250.

Fergusson of Kilkerran, Sir Charles, 9th Bt; b. 10.5.31; m., Hon. Amanda Mary Noel-Paton; 2 s.

Fergusson, Professor David Alexander Syme. MA, BD, DPhil, FRSE. Professor of Divinity, Edinburgh University, since 2000; b. 3.8.56, Glasgow; m., Margot McIndoe; 2 s. Educ. Kelvinside Academy; Glasgow University; Edinburgh University; Oxford University. Assistant Minister, St. Nicholas Church, Lanark, 1983-84; Associate Minister, St. Mungo's Church, Cumbernauld, 1984-86; Lecturer, Edinburgh University, 1986-90; Professor of Systematic Theology, Aberdeen University, 1990-2000. Chaplain to Moderator of the General Assembly, 1989-90; President, Society for the Study of Theology, 2000-02. Publications: Bultmann, 1992; Christ, Church and Society, 1993; The Cosmos and the Creator, 1998; Community, Liberalism and Christian Ethics, 1998; John Macmurray: Critical Perspectives, 2002; Church, State and Civil Society, 2004; Scottish Philosophical Theology, 2007. Recreations: football; golf. Address: 23 Riselaw Crescent, Edinburgh EH10 6HN; T.-0131-447 4022. E-mail: David.Fergusson@ed.ac.uk

Fergusson, Donald James, BSc, MEd. Head Teacher, Coltness High School, since 2001; b. 13.4.52, Borgue; m., Fiona Spiers; 4 d. Educ. Kirkcudbright Academy; Glasgow University. Teacher of Mathematics, North Kelvinside Secondary, 1976-79; Assistant Principal Teacher of Mathematics, Govan High School, 1980-85; Principal Teacher of Mathematics, Cleveden Secondary, 1985-92; Assistant Head Teacher, Dalziel High School, 1992-97; Depute Head Teacher, Crookston Castle Secondary, 1997-99; Depute Head Teacher, Clyde Valley High School, 1999-2001. Recreations: first XI coach, Glasgow University FC; golf; reading; family. Address: (b.) Coltness High School, Mossland Drive, Wishaw ML2 8LY; T.-01698 384307; e-mail: ht@coltnesshigh.n-lanark.sch.uk

Fergusson, Dr Ronald John, BSc, MBChB, MD, FRCPE. Consultant Physician, Western General Hospital, Edinburgh, since 1998; b. 8.7.53, Edinburgh; m., Margaret; 1 s.; 2 d. Educ. Hampton Grammar School; Robert Gordon's College; Edinburgh University. Trained in respiratory and general medicine, Lothian and Borders; ICRF Clinical Research Fellow (lung cancer), Edinburgh; Senior Registrar, Respiratory Medicine, Lothian Health Board; Consultant Physician, Eastern General Hospital, Edinburgh, 1993-98. Recreations: golf; wine; family. Address: (b.) Respiratory Unit, Western General Hospital, Crewe Road, Edinburgh EH4 2XU; T.-0131-537 1779. E-mail: ron.fergusson@luht.scot.nhs.uk

Fernie, Professor John, MA, MBA, PhD. Professor of Retail Marketing, Heriot-Watt University, since 1998, Head of School of Management and Languages, 2002-07 (Head of School of Management, 1999-2002); Director of Institute of Retail Studies, University of Stirling, 1996-98; b. 4.3.48, East Wemyss, Fife; m., Suzanne Ishbel; 1 s.; 1 d. Educ. Buckhaven High School; Dundee University; Edinburgh University; Bradford University. Lecturer/Senior Lecturer, Huddersfield Polytechnic,

1973-88; Senior Lecturer, University of Abertay Dundee, 1988-96; Senior Lecturer/Professor, University of Stirling, 1996-98. Recent books include: Principles of Retailing (co-author) and Logistics and Retail Management (co-author). Recreations: golf; travelling; 5 a side football. Address: (b.) Heriot-Watt University, Edinburgh EH14 4AJ; T. 0131 451-3880; e-mail: j.fernie@hw.ac.uk

Ferrell, Professor William Russell, MB, ChB, PhD, FRCP(Glas). Professor of Clinical Physiology, University of Glasgow; b. 8.3.49, St. Louis, USA; m., Anne Mary Scobie; 3 s. Educ. St. Aloysius College; University of Glasgow. University of Glasgow: Lecturer, Senior Lecturer, Reader in Physiology; Visiting Professor, University of Paisley. Recreations: skiing; computing; tennis. Address: (b.) Centre for Rheumatic Diseases, Royal Infirmary, 10 Alexandra Parade, Glasgow G31 2ER; T.-0141-211 4677; e-mail: w.ferrell@bio.gla.ac.uk

Fiddes, James Angus Gordon, OBE, DUniv, MA, DipTP, FRICS. Consultant Surveyor; b. 1.3.41, Edinburgh; m., Valerie; 2 d. Educ. George Heriot's School, Edinburgh; Gonville and Caius College, Cambridge; Edinburgh College of Art. Richard Ellis & Son, London and Glasgow, 1964-67; Richard Stanton and Son Pty, Sydney, 1967-68; Kenneth Ryden and Partners, 1969-99 (Partner, 1973, Senior Partner, 1989). Trustee, National Museums of Scotland. Recreations: sport; arts. Address: (h.) 178 Mayfield Road, Edinburgh EH9 3AX; T.-0131 667 5534; e-mail: jimfiddes@hotmail.com

Fife, 3rd Duke of (James George Alexander Bannerman Carnegie); b. 23.9.29; m., Hon. Caroline Cecily Dewar (m. diss.); 1 s.; 1 d. Educ. Gordonstoun. National Service, Scots Guards, Malaya, 1948-50; Royal Agricultural College; Clothworkers' Company and Freeman, City of London; President, ABA, 1959-73; Vice Patron, ABA, 1973-94; Ships President, HMS Fife, 1964-87; a Vice-Patron, Braemar Royal Highland Society; formerly a Vice-President, British Olympic Association. Address: Elsick House, Stonehaven, Kincardineshire AB39 3NT.

Findlay, David J., BSc (Hons), MB, ChB, FRCPsych. Consultant Psychiatrist, Tayside Primary Care, since 1991; part-time Policy Adviser, Care of the Elderly, Scottish Executive Health Department, 1998-2001, Departmental Specialty Adviser in Psychiatry (Old Age), 2001-07; Honorary Senior Lecturer, Department of Psychiatry, Dundee University, since 1991; b. 2.6.54, Duns; m., Patricia; 1 s.; 3 d. Educ. Ayr Academy; Glasgow University. Junior House Officer, 1979-80; Gartnavel Royal Hospital Training Scheme, 1980-83; Lecturer in Psychiatry, Dundee University, 1984-87; Consultant Psychiatrist and Clinical Tutor, Gartnavel Royal Hospital, 1987-91; Royal Dundee Liff Hospital: Service Manager, Old Age Psychiatry, 1993-1996, Clinical Director, Elderly Services, 1996-99; Chair, RCPsych Philosophy Special Interest Group (Scotland), 2002-07. Recreations: chess; reading; films. Address: (b.) Gourdie House, Royal Dundee Liff Hospital, Dundee DD2 5NF; T.-01382 423105; e-mail: david.findlay@nhs.net

Findlay, Donald Russell, QC, LLB (Hons), MPhil, FRSA. Advocate, since 1975; former Lord Rector, St. Andrews University; b. 17.3.51, Cowdenbeath; m., Jennifer E. Borrowman. Educ. Harris Academy, Dundee; Dundee University; Glasgow University. Sometime Lecturer in Commercial Law, Heriot-Watt University. Recreations: Glasgow Rangers FC; Egyptology; archaeology; wine;

ethics; travelling first class. Address: (b.) Advocates Library, Parliament House, Parliament Square, Edinburgh EH1 1RF; T.-0131-226 2881; e-mail: donaldrfin@aol.com

Findlay, Johan. JP, since 1987; Honorary Sheriff, since 1995; Member, Parole Board for Scotland, since 2000; b. 30.9.52, Ayr; m., David Gibson Findlay; 2 s.; 2 d. Educ. St. Joseph's Convent, Girvan. Chairman: Nithsdale Justices Committee, 1991-98, Dumfries Branch, Scottish Association for the Study of Delinquency, 1993-2000, Training Committee of the District Courts Association, 1995-96, Dumfries and Galloway Justices Committee, 1997-98; President, Lockerbie Little Theatre, 1990-96; 2007 Chair, Scottish Justices Association. Publication: All Manner of People (history of the JP in Scotland). Recreations: books; theatre. Address: (h.) No. 3 The Steading, Smallholm Farm, Hightae, Lockerbie DG11 1JY; T.-01387 810911.

Findlay, Richard. Chairman: Scottish Media Group PLC, since 2007, Iatros Ltd; formerly Group Chief Executive, Scottish Radio Holdings PLC; Founding Chairman, National Theatre of Scotland; b. 5.11.43; m., Elspeth; 2 s.; 1 d. Educ. Royal Scottish Academy of Music and Drama. Chairman of Trustees, RSAMD; Chairman, IATROS Ltd; Broadcasting Service of Saudi Arabia; Central Office of Information; Capital Radio; Radio Forth Ltd; Scottish Radio Holdings PLC. Recreations: music; golf; theatre. Address: (b.) SMG PLC, Pacific Quay, Glasgow G51 1PQ.

Findlay, Richard Martin, LLB, NP. Head of Hospitality, Leisure Entertainment and Media Law, Tods Murray LLP, Edinburgh, since 1990; b. 18.12.51, Aberdeen. Educ. Gordon Schools, Huntly; Aberdeen University. Trained, Wilsone & Duffus, Advocates, Aberdeen; Legal Assistant, Commercial Department, Maclay Murray & Spens, Glasgow and Edinburgh, 1975-78; Partner, Ranken & Reid SSC, Edinburgh, 1979-90. Member: International Association of Entertainment Lawyers, International Entertainment and Multimedia Law and Business Network, Theatrical Management Association; Trustee, Frank Mullen Trust; former Managing Editor, i2i (The Business Journal of the International Film Industry); Company Secretary: Association of Integrated Media Highlands and Islands Ltd., Gay Men's Health Ltd., Edinburgh International Jazz and Blues Festival, Moonstone International Ltd.; Vice Chairman, Royal Lyceum Theatre Company Ltd.; Director: Audio Description Film Fund Ltd., The Hill Adamson, Luxury Edinburgh Ltd.; Member, Screen Academy Scotland Advisory Board. Recreations: music; theatre; opera; cinema; photography; Scottish history and culture. Address: (b.) Edinburgh Quay, 133 Fountainbridge, Edinburgh EH3 9AG; T.-0131 656 2000.

Finkelstein, Professor David, BA (Columbia); PhD (Edin). Research Professor of Media and Print Culture, Queen Margaret University, Edinburgh, since 2003; b. 5.4.64, Bogota, Colombia; m., Alison Sinclair; 1 s. Educ. Commonwealth High School, San Juan, Puerto Rico; Columbia College, Columbia University; University of Edinburgh. Archivist, National Library of Scotland, 1990-91; British Academy Postdoctoral Research Fellow, Department of English Literature, University of Edinburgh, 1991-94; Napier University, Edinburgh: Lecturer, Print Media, Publishing and Communication Department, 1994-98, Senior Lecturer, Print Media, Publishing and Communication Department, 1998-2000; Queen Margaret University College, Edinburgh: Head of Department, Media and Communication, 2000-03; Professor of Media and Print Culture, 2002-03, Acting Head of School (Associate Dean) of Social Sciences, Media and Communication, 2003. President, Edinburgh Bibliographical Society, since 2004;

Visiting Research Fellow, Institute for Historical and Cultural Research, Oxford Brookes University, 2006; Board of Governors, Stepfamily Scotland, since 2005; Series co-editor, Journalism Studies: Key Texts, since 2005; Co-editor, Journal of the Edinburgh Bibliographical Society, since 2005; Editorial Board: Victorian Periodicals Review, since 2006, The Bibliotheck, since 2002; Advisory Board, Dictionary of Nineteenth-Century Journalism, since 2006; Member of the British Association of Victorian Studies, the Bibliographical Society; the Edinburgh Bibliographical Society; Lifetime Honorary Member, Victorian Studies Association of Western Canada. Publications: over 45 books and articles published, including: The Edinburgh History of the Book in Scotland, 1880-2000 (Co-Editor), 2007; An Introduction to Book History (Co-Author), 2005; The House of Blackwood: Author-Publisher Relations in the Victorian Era, 2002; The Book History Reader (Co-Editor), 2001, rev.ed 2006; An Index to Blackwood's Magazine, 1901-1980, 1995. Recreations: running; watching obscure films; reading idiosyncratic novels. Address: (b.) Queen Margaret University, Edinburgh, Queen Margaret University Drive, Musselburgh, East Lothian EH21 6UU; T.-0131-474-0000.
E-mail: d.finkelstein@btopenworld.com

Finlay, Robert Derek, BA, MA, FInstD, FRSA, MCIM; b. 16.5.32, London; m., Una Ann Grant; 2 s.; 1 d. Educ. Kingston Grammar School; Emmanuel College, Cambridge. Lt., Gordon Highlanders, Malaya, 1950-52; Captain, Gordon Highlanders TA, 1952-61; Mobil Oil Co. UK, 1953-61; Associate, Principal, Director, McKinsey & Co., 1961-79; Managing Director, H.J. Heinz Co. Ltd., 1979-81; Senior Vice-President, Chief Financial Officer, 1989-92, Area Vice President, 1992-93, World HQ; H.J. Heinz Co., 1981-93; Chair, Dawson International PLC, 1995-98 (non executive Chair, 1998). Member, London Committee, Scottish Council Development and Industry, 1975-2003; Member: Board, US China Business Council, 1983-93, Board, Pittsburgh Public Theatre, 1986-93, US Korea Business Council, 1986-92, Board, Pittsburgh Symphony Society, 1989-93; Vice Chairman, World Affairs Council of Pittsburgh, 1986-93; Chairman, Board of Visitors Center for International Studies, University of Pittsburgh, 1989-93; Governor, Three Rivers Rowing Association, Pittsburgh, since 1982. Publication: 2006 Autobiograpy "Time To Take Her Home - The Life and Times of RDF". Recreations: tennis; rowing; music; theatre. Address: (h.) Mains of Grantully, by Aberfeldy, PH15 2EG.

Finlayson, Niall Diarmid Campbell, OBE, MBChB, PhD, FRCPL, PPRCPE, FRCPSG, FRCSE. Consultant Physician, Royal Infirmary of Edinburgh, 1973-2003; President, Royal College of Physicians of Edinburgh, 2001-04; Director of Communications, Royal College of Physicians of Edinburgh, since 2004; Chief Medical Officer, Bright Grey Insurance, since 2003; b. 21.4.39, Georgetown, Guyana; m., Dale Kristin Anderson; 1 s.; 1 d. Educ. Loretto School, Musselburgh; Edinburgh University. Lecturer in Therapeutics, Edinburgh University, 1966-69; Assistant Professor of Medicine, Cornell University Medical College, New York Hospital, USA, 1970-72. Recreations: history; music. Address: (b.) Royal College of Physicians of Edinburgh, 9 Queen Street, Edinburgh; T.-0131-247 3638; (h.) 10 Queens Crescent, Edinburgh EH9 2AZ; e-mail: niall.finlayson@brightgrey.com

Finn, Anthony, MA (Hons), FEIS (1997). Rector, St. Andrew's High School, Kirkcaldy, 1988-2006; Senior Manager, Fife Council Education Service, since 2006; b. 4.6.51, Irvine; m., Margaret Caldwell. Educ. St. Joseph's Academy, Kilmarnock; Glasgow University. Teacher, Principal Teacher, Assistant Head Teacher, Depute Head Teacher, Acting Head Teacher, St. Andrew's Academy,

Saltcoats, 1975-88. Member, SEED Teachers' Agreement Communication Team, since 2001; Elected Member, General Teaching Council, 1991-2001; Convener, General Teaching Council Education Committee, 1993-2001; Chair, SEED Memorandum Committee, 1991-2001; Member, Executive, Catholic Headteachers' Association Scotland, 2001-06; Member, Catholic Education Commission for Scotland; Formerly: Teachers' Representative, National Committee for the Staff Development of Teachers, Member, Advisory Committee, Scottish Qualification for Headship, Governor, Moray House Institute of Education, Assessor, Teacher Education, Scottish Higher Education Funding Council, Chair, Fife Secondary Head Teachers Association. Recreations: sport; travel; literature; current affairs. Address: (h.) 1 Blair Place, Kirkcaldy KY2 5SQ; T.-01592 640109.

Finnie, James Ross, CA. MSP (Liberal Democrat), West of Scotland, since 1999; Liberal Democrat Shadow Secretary for Health and Well being; Vice Convener, Health and Sport Committee; b. 11.2.47, Greenock; m., Phyllis Sinclair; 1 s.; 1 d. Educ. Greenock Academy. Member, Executive Committee, Scottish Council (Development and Industry), 1976-87; Chairman: Scottish Liberal Party, 1982-86; Member: Inverclyde District Council, 1977-97, Inverclyde Council, 1995-99; Minister for Environment and Rural Development, Scottish Executive, 2000-07 (Minister for Rural Affairs, 1999-2000). Address: (h.) 91 Octavia Terrace, Greenock PA16 7PY; T.-01475 631495.

Firth, Professor William James, BSc, PhD, CPhys, FInstP, FRSE. Freeland Professor of Natural Philosophy Strathclyde University (Head, Department of Physics, 2001-04); b. 23.2.45, Holm, Orkney; m., Mary MacDonald Anderson; 2 s. Educ. Perth Academy; Edinburgh University; Heriot-Watt University. Lecturer to Reader, Physics, Heriot-Watt University, 1967-85. Fellow, Optical Society of America. Recreation: sports (Edinburgh University Hockey Blue, 1967-68). Address: (b.) John Anderson Building, 107 Rottenrow, Glasgow G4 0NG.

Fisher, Archie, MBE. Folk singer, guitarist, composer, broadcaster; b. 1939, Glasgow. First solo album, 1966; formerly presenter, Travelling Folk, BBC Radio; Artistic Director, Edinburgh International Folk Festival, 1988-92.

Fisher, Gregor. Actor (television, theatre, film). Credits include (BBC TV): Rab C. Nesbitt series (leading role), Naked Video series, Scotch and Wry, Para Handy, Oliver Twist, Empty. Best Actor award, Toronto Festival, for One, Two, Three.

Fitton, Professor John Godfrey, BSc, PhD, FGS, FRSE. Professor of Igneous Petrology, Edinburgh University, since, 1999; b. 1.10.46, Rochdale; m., Dr Christine Ann Fitton; 2 s.; 1 d. Educ. Bury Grammar School; Durham University. Turner and Newall Research Fellow, Manchester University, 1971-72; Edinburgh University: Lecturer, 1972-89; Senior Lecturer, 1989-94; Reader, 1994-99; served on NERC, Research Grants and ODP Committees; Co-Chief Scientist, Ocean Drilling Programme Leg 192, 2000. Publications: Alkaline Igneous Rocks (ed.); Origin and Evolution of the Ontong Java Plateau (ed.). Recreations: house restoration; walking; wine; old maps. Address: (b.) School of GeoSciences, Edinburgh University, Grant Institute, West Mains Road, Edinburgh, EH9 3JW; T.-0131-650 8529; e-mail: Godfrey.Fitton@ed.ac.uk

Fitzgerald, Professor Alexander Grant, BSc, PhD, DSc, CPhys, FInstP, FRSE. Harris Professor of Physics, Dundee University, since 1992; b. 12.10.39, Dundee; m., June; 1 s.; 2 d. Educ. Perth Academy; Harris Academy; St. Andrews University; Cambridge University. Research Fellow, Lawrence Berkeley Laboratory, University of California; Lecturer, Senior Lecturer, Reader, Professor, Dundee

University. Publications: 209 conference and journal papers; book: Quantitative Microbeam Analysis (Co-editor). Recreations: swimming; golf. Address: (b.) Department of Electronic Engineering and Physics, Dundee University, Dundee, DD1 4HN; T.-01382 384553; e-mail: a.g.fitzgerald@dundee.ac.uk

Fitzpatrick, Joe. MSP (SNP), Dundee West, since 2007; b. 1.4.67. Address: (b.) Scottish Parliament, Edinburgh EH99 1SP; Constituency Office: 8 Old Glamis Road, Dundee DD3 8HP.

Fitzpatrick, Professor Julie Lydia, BVMS (Hons), PhD, DipECBHM, ARAgs, CBiol, FIBiol, MRCVS, FRSE. Scientific Director of The Moredun Research Institute and Chief Executive of The Moredun Group, since 2004; b. 1.3.60, Glasgow; m., Dr. Andrew Fitzpatrick; 2 s. Educ. Wellington School, Ayr; University of Glasgow; University of Bristol. Veterinary Practitioner, Northumberland, 1982-87; Research Assistant, University of Bristol, 1987-88; PhD student, University of Glasgow, 1988-92; Lecturer, University of Glasgow Veterinary School, 1993-98; Head of Division of Farm Animal Medicine and Production, 1998; Personal Chair in Farm Animal Medicine, 1999. Awarded the G. Norman Hall medal for research in animal diseases, 2003; President of the Association of Veterinary Readers and Research Workers, 2003-04; Member: Royal College of Veterinary Surgeons Research Committee, since 2002, Scottish Science Advisory Committee, since 2004, Advisory Committee on Animal Feedstuffs, 2002-07; Director: Edinburgh Centre for Rural Research, since 2004, Moredun Scientific Limited, since 2005; Member: Agricultural Strategy Group for Scotland, since 2005, Scottish Animal Health and Welfare Advisory Group, since 2005; Chairman, Veterinary Policy Group of the British Veterinary Association, 2004-07. Recreations: walking; skiing; reading. Address: (b.) Moredun Research Institute, Pentlands Science Park, Bush Loan, Penicuik, nr. Edinburgh EH26 0PZ; T.-0131 445 5111; e-mail: julie.fitzpatrick@moredun.ac.uk

Fitzpatrick, Kieran, LLB (Hons), MSI, TEP. Partner, Mowat Hall Dick Solicitors, since 2005; b. 12.10.63, Belfast. Educ. Queen's University Belfast. Bird Semple, Glasgow, 1994-96; Wright Johnston and Mackenzie, Edinburgh, 1996-2005. Address: (b.) 45 Queen Charlotte Street, Leith, Edinburgh EH6 7HT; e-mail: kieran.fitzpatrick@mhdlaw.co.uk

Fladmark, Professor Emeritus, Jan Magnus, DA(Edin), DipTP, HonFRIAS. Patron, Largs Viking Festival, since 2007; Professor Emeritus, Robert Gordon University, since 2002; b. 12.2.37, Romsdal, Norway; m., Caroline Ashton Miller; 1 s.; 3 d. Educ. Gjermundnes Agricultural College; Ulvestads Commercial College; Hamar Cathedral School; Gimlemoen Military College; Edinburgh College of Art. Press Photographer, Sunnmorsposten,1953-55; National Service, Norwegian Army, 1957-58; PSV Conductor, Scottish Omnibuses, 1959-61; Architect, Molra and Moira, 1964-66; Research Fellow, Edinburgh College of Art, 1966-67; Planning Officer, Scottish Office, 1967-70; ODA Programme Director, Edinburgh University, 1970-76; Assistant Director, Countryside Commission for Scotland, 1976-92; Director, Robert Gordon University Heritage Unit, 1992-2002, Professor in Heritage Management, 1993; CEO, The Heyerdahl Institute, Norway, 2000-03; Adviser, Lima Metropolitan Authority, Peru, 1975; Adviser, Mezzogiorno Development Agency, Italy, 1980; Chairman, Royal Town Planning Institute (Scotland), 1981-82; Governor, Edinburgh College of Art, 1982-88; Council Member, Saltire Society, 1984-88; Chairman, Scottish Interagency Liaison Group, 1987-90; Secretary, Advisory Panel on National Parks, 1989-90; Founding Chairman, Countryside Around Towns Forum, 1989-91; Convener, Scottish Forum on the Environment, 1989-92; MOD Environment Committee, 1989-92; Assessor, Loch Lomond Park Authority and Central Scotland Countryside Trust, 1990-92; Trustee, Sir Patrick Geddes Memorial Trust, since 1991; Visiting Lecturer, Chinese Society of Rural Development Planning, Taiwan, 1994, Adviser, Moscow School of Social and Economic Sciences, 1998; Contributor, Indo-UK Colloquium on Conservation and Cultural Tourism, Cochin, 2004; Hon. Fellow, Edinburgh University, since 1971; Fellow, Salzburg Seminar in American Studies, 1973; Glenfiddich Living Scotland Award, 1986; Fladmark of that ilk, since 1981. Publications: The Future of Scotland (Contributing-Author), 1977; Buildings of the Scottish Countryside (Co-Author), 1985; Landscapes under stress (Contributing-Author), 1987; Countryside Planning in Practice: The Scottish Experience (Contributing-Author), 1988; The Countryside Around Towns, 1988; The Mountain Areas of Scotland: Conservation and Management (Co-Author), 1990; Tomorrow's Architectural Heritage: Landscape and Buildings in the Countryside (Co-Author), 1991; Heritage: Conservation, Interpretation and Enterprise (Editor), 1993; The SYHA Environmental Charter: Enjoying the Great Outdoors and the Cultural Riches of Scotland (Co-Author), 1994; The Wealth of a Nation: Heritage as a Cultural and Competitive Asset, 1994; Cultural Tourism (Editor), 1994; Sharing the Earth: Local Identity in Global Culture (Editor), 1995; In Search of Heritage as Pilgrim or Tourist? (Editor), 1998; Heritage and Museums: Shaping National Identity (Editor), 2000; Heritage and Identity: Shaping the Nations of the North (Editor), 2002. Recreation: fighting own ignorance. Address: (b.) Scott Sutherland School, Robert Gordon University, Aberdeen AB10 7QB; T.-07745 221101; e-mail: mfladmark@hotmail.com

Flanagan, Caroline Jane, LLB, DipLP, NP. Partner, Ross & Connel, Solicitors, Dunfermline, since 1990; Member, Council, Law Society of Scotland, since 1998; President, Law Society of Scotland, 2005/06; b. 12.1.61, Bridge of Allan; m., Roy Flanagan; 1 s.; 1 d. Educ. Dollar Academy; Edinburgh University. Trainee, then Assistant Solicitor, Edinburgh, 1982-87; Assistant, then Partner, Ross and Connel, since 1988; accredited as specialist in family law, since 1996; Dean, local Faculty of Solicitors, 1998-2000. Address: (b.) 18 Viewfield Terrace, Dunfermline, KY12 7JH; T.-01383 721156.

Fleck, Professor James, MA, BSc, MSc. Dean, Open University Business School and Professor of Innovation Dynamics, Open University (2005); Visiting Professor, University of Edinburgh Management School; b. 18.7.51, Kano, Nigeria; m., Heather Anne Morrison; 2 s.; 3 d. Educ. Perth Academy; University of Edinburgh; Manchester University. Engineer, MK-Shand, Invergordon, 1974-75; Computer Programmer, CAP Limited, London, 1976; Research Fellow and Lecturer, Technology Policy Unit, University of Aston, 1980-85; Lecturer in Operations Management, Heriot-Watt University, 1985-86; Lecturer, then Senior Lecturer, Department of Business Studies, University of Edinburgh, 1986-96, Chair of Organisation of Industry and Commerce, 1996-2004 (Director, University of Edinburgh Management School, 1996-99). Joseph Lister Lecturer for the Social Sciences, British Association for the Advancement of Science, 1995-96. Publications: Expertise and Innovation – Information Technology Strategies in the Financial Services Sector (Joint Author), 1994; Exploring Expertise (Joint Editor), 1998. Recreations: reading; DIY; windsurfing; eating out. Address: (h.) Grange Park House, 38 Dick Place, Edinburgh EH9 2JB; T.-0131-667 3176.

Fleming, Archibald Macdonald, KSJ, MA, BCom, PhD, FRSA. Educational consultant; Director of Lifelong Learning, Strathclyde University, 1987-2001 (Director, Management Development Programmes, Strathclyde

Business School, 1984-87); Lecturer, Department of Information Science, Strathclyde University, since 1968; Consultant on Management Training and Development, since 1970; b. 19.6.36, Glasgow; m., Joan Moore; 1 s.; 1 d. Educ. Langholm Academy; Dumfries Academy; Edinburgh University. W. & T. Avery, 1961-63; IBM (UK) Ltd., 1963-64; Sumlock Comptometer Ltd., 1964-68; Consultancies: Scottish Co-operative Wholesale Society, 1969, Hotel and Catering Industry Training Board, 1971, Scottish Engineering Employers Association, 1973. Member: Strathclyde Children's Panel, Committee on Food Processing Opportunities in Scotland, Scottish Council (Development and Industry), Vice-President, Royal Philosophical Society of Glasgow, 1998-2003, International Vocational Education and Training Association, Church of Scotland Education Committee, American Association of Adult and Continuing Education; Vice-Chairman, Universities Council for Adult and Continuing Education (Scotland), 1990-98; Vice Chairman, National Trust for Scotland, Bearsden and Milngavie Members' Centre, 2006; Non-Executive Director, the State Hospitals Board for Scotland. Publication: Collins Business Dictionary (with B. McKenna). Recreation: reading, observing and talking on Scotland and the Scots. Address: (b.) 1A Elm Gardens, Bearsden, Glasgow G61 3BH.
E-mail: archibald.fleming@ntlworld.com

Fleming, Professor George, BSc, PhD, FREng, FRSE, FICE, FCIWM. Emeritus Professor, since 2004, Professor of Civil Engineering, Strathclyde University, 1985-2004, and Managing Director of Envirocentre, since 1995; Director, GF & Co Ltd, since 2004; Non-Executive Director, Port of Tyne; b. 16.8.44, Glasgow; m., Irene Fleming; 2 s.; 1 d. Educ. Knightswood Secondary School, Glasgow; Strathclyde University; Stanford University, California. Research Assistant, Strathclyde University, 1966-69, Stanford University, 1967; Senior Research Hydrologist, Hydrocomp International, California, 1969-70; Research Associate, Stanford University, 1969-70; Director and Vice President, Hydrocomp International, Palo Alto and Glasgow, 1970-79; Lecturer, then Senior Lecturer, then Reader in Civil Engineering, Strathclyde University, 1971-85; Visiting Professor, University of Padova, Italy, since 1980; Vice Dean, Engineering Faculty, Strathclyde University, 1984-87. President, Institution of Civil Engineers, 1999-00; Member, Scottish Exports Forum. Publications: Computer Simulation in Hydrology, 1975; The Sediment Problem, 1977; Deterministic Models in Hydrology, 1979. Recreations: farming; fishing; food. Address: (b.) Envirocentre, Craighall Business Park, Eagle Street, Glasgow G4 9XA; T.-0141-341-5040; e-mail: gfleming@envirocentre.co.uk

Fleming, Maurice. Editor, The Scots Magazine, 1974-91; b. Blairgowrie; m., Nanette Dalgleish; 2 s.; 1 d. Educ. Blairgowrie High School. Trained in hotel management before entering journalism; worked on various magazines; has had five full-length plays performed professionally, as well as one-act plays by amateurs; founder Member: Traditional Music and Song Association of Scotland, Scottish Poetry Library; Past Chairman, Blairgowrie, Rattray and District Civic Trust; Past Chairman, Blair in Bloom. Publications: The Scots Magazine — A Celebration of 250 Years (Co-Editor); The Ghost O' Mause and Other Tales and Traditions of East Perthshire; Old Blairgowrie and Rattray; The Real Macbeth and Other Stories from Scottish History; The Sidlaws: Tales, Traditions and Ballads; Not of This World: Creatures of the Supernatural in Scotland; More Old Blairgowrie and Rattray. Recreations: walking; reading; bird-watching; enjoying the countryside; folksong and folklore. Address: (h.) Craigard, Perth Road, Blairgowrie; T.-Blairgowrie 873633.

Fleming, Tom, CVO, OBE. Actor and Director; b. 29.6.27, Edinburgh. Professional theatre debut, 1945, in company led by Edith Evans; Co-Founder, Edinburgh Gateway Company, 1953; joined Royal Shakespeare Company at Stratford upon Avon, 1962, and played several classical roles, including Prospero, Brutus, Cymbeline, Buckingham and Kent; toured with RSC in USSR, USA and Europe, 1964; Director and Founder, Royal Lyceum Theatre Company, 1965; there played title role in Galileo; Director, Scottish Theatre Company, 1982-87; awarded Roman Szlydowski Prize for his production of The Thrie Estaites, Warsaw, 1986; TV work includes portrayals of Robert Burns, William Wallace, Jesus of Nazareth, Henry IV, Weir of Hermiston, and Sir John Reith; films include Mary, Queen of Scots, King Lear, Meetings with Remarkable Men; Radio and television commentator, including Coronation, Silver Jubilee celebrations, Cenotaph service 1965-99, VE and VJ Day 50th anniversaries, ten royal and state funerals including that of Diana, Princess of Wales, HM Queen Elizabeth The Queen Mother, Edinburgh Military Tattoo, since 1966; Hon. Member, Saltire Society, Royal Scottish Pipers' Society, Scottish Arts Club. Andrew Fletcher of Saltoun Award for Services to Scotland, 2000. Publications: So That Was Spring; Miracle at Midnight; Voices Out of the Air (Editor); It's My Belief; BBC Book of Memories; A Scottish Childhood, Volume II (Contributor). D.Univ (Heriot-Watt); D.Litt (Queen Margaret University College); D.Dra, FRSAMD.

Fletcher, Sheriff Michael John, LLB. Sheriff of Tayside Central and Fife at Perth, since 2000; b. 5.12.45, Dundee; m., Kathryn Mary; 2 s. Educ. High School of Dundee; St. Andrews University. Partner, Ross Strachan & Co., 1970-88; Partner, Miller Hendry (Hendry and Fenton), 1988-94; Part-time Lecturer in Civil and Criminal Procedure, University of Dundee, 1974-94; Legal Aid Reporter, 1978-94; Temporary Sheriff, 1991-94; Sheriff of South Strathclyde Dumfries & Galloway at Dumfries, 1994-99; Sheriff of Lothian and Borders at Edinburgh, 1999-2000; Editor, Scottish Civil Law Reports, since 1999; Member, Sheriff Court Rules Council, since 2001; Vice President, Sheriffs' Association, since 2007; Member, Judicial Studies Committee, since 2006. Publication: Delictual Damages (Co-Author). Recreations: golf; gardening.

Fletcher, Professor Roger, MA, PhD, FIMA, FRSE, FRS. Professor of Optimization, Department of Mathematics, Dundee University, 1984-2005; Professor Emeritus, since 2005; Honorary Professor, University of Edinburgh, since 2005; b. 29.1.39, Huddersfield; m., Mary Marjorie Taylor; 2 d. Educ. Huddersfield College; Cambridge University; Leeds University. Lecturer, Leeds University, 1963-69; Principal Research Fellow, then Principal Scientific Officer, AERE Harwell, 1969-73; Senior Research Fellow, then Senior Lecturer, then Reader, Dundee University, 1973-84. Publications: Practical Methods of Optimization, 2nd edition, 1987. numerous others. Recreations: hill-walking; music; bridge. Address: (h.) 43 Errol Road, Invergowrie, Dundee DD2 5BX; T.-01382 562452.

Flint, Professor David, TD, MA, BL, D.Univ, CA. Professor of Accountancy, Glasgow University, 1964-85 (Vice-Principal, 1981-85); b. 24.2.19, Glasgow; m., Dorothy Mary Maclachlan Jardine; 2 s.; 1 d. Educ. High School of Glasgow; Glasgow University. Royal Signals, 1939-46 (Major; mentioned in Despatches); Partner, Mann Judd Gordon & Company, Chartered Accountants, Glasgow, 1951-71; Lecturer (part-time), Glasgow University, 1950-60; Dean, Faculty of Law, 1971-73. Council Member, Scottish Business School, 1971-77; Institute of Chartered Accountants of Scotland: President, 1975-76, Vice-President, 1973-75, Convener, Research Advisory Committee, 1974-75 and 1977-84, Convener, Working Party on Future Policy, 1976-79, Convener, Public Sector Committee, 1987-89, Convener, Taxation Review and Research Sub-Committee, 1960-64; Trustee, Scottish

Chartered Accountants Trust for Education, 1981-87; Member: Management Training and Development Committee, Central Training Council, 1966-70, Management and Industrial Relations Committee, Social Science Research Council, 1970-72 and 1978-80, Social Sciences Panel, Scottish Universities Council on Entrance, 1968-72; Chairman, Association of University Teachers of Accounting, 1969; Member, Company Law Committee, Law Society of Scotland, 1976-85; Scottish Economic Society: Treasurer, 1954-62, Vice-President, 1977-88, Hon. Vice-President, 1988-99; Member, Commission for Local Authority Accounts in Scotland, 1978-80; President, European Accounting Association, 1983-84. British Accounting Association Lifetime Achievement Award, 2004. Publications: A true and fair view in company accounts, 1982; Philosophy and Principles of Auditing, 1988. Recreation: golf. Address: (h.) 16 Grampian Avenue, Auchterarder, Perthshire PH3 1NY; T.-01764 663978.

Flockhart, (David) Ross, OBE, BA, BD, D.Univ; b. 20.3.27, Newcastle, NSW, Australia; m., Pamela Ellison Macartney; 3 s.; 1 d.; 1 d. (deceased). Educ. Knox Grammar School, Sydney; Sydney University; Edinburgh University. Royal Australian Engineers, 1945-46; Chaplain to Overseas Students, Edinburgh, 1955-58; Parish Minister (Church of Scotland), Northfield, Aberdeen, 1958-63; Warden, Carberry Tower, Musselburgh, 1963-66; Lecturer and Senior Lecturer, School of Community Studies, Moray House College of Education, 1966-72; Director, Scottish Council for Voluntary Organisations, 1972-91. Member: Scottish Arts Council, 1976-82, Court, Stirling University, 1989-98, Council, National Trust for Scotland, 1995-2000; former Trustee and Vice-Chairman, Community Development Foundation. Recreations: gardening; sailing. Address: (h.) Longwood, Humbie, East Lothian EH36 5PN; T.-01875 833208; e-mail: rossflock@lumison.co.uk

Flowerdew, Stuart Alan, LLB(Hons), DipLP, NP. Solicitor; Partner, Flowerdew Allan, solicitors, Peterhead, since 1999; Secretary and Treasurer, Faculty of Solicitors in Peterhead and Fraserburgh, since 1993; Chairman, Victim Support, Aberdeenshire, 2000-04; b. 5.2.67, Kings Lynn; m., Natalie Anne Lamb. Educ. Forres Academy; University of Dundee. Trainee/Assistant, Miller Hendry, Perth, 1989-92; Assistant: Stewart and Watson, Peterhead, 1992-94, Masson & Glennie, Peterhead, 1994-96; Associate, John MacRitchie & Co., SSC, Peterhead, 1997-1999. Recreation: cricket. Address: (b.) 2 Kirk Street, Peterhead; T.-01779 481717; (h.) Braemount, 27 Balmoor Terrace, Peterhead; T.-01779 473117.

Flyn, Derek, LLB, NP, WS, FSAScot. Solicitor in private practice, since 1977; Consultant with Macleod and MacCallum (Partner, 1978-2006); b. 22.8.45, Edinburgh; m., Fiona Mairi Macmillan; 2 s.; 1 d. Educ. Broughton School, Edinburgh; Dundee University. Scottish Court Service, 1962-72 (Sheriff Clerk Depute at Portree, 1967-70); accredited by Law Society of Scotland as specialist in crofting law since 1993; President, Scottish Law Agents Society, 1999-2000; Vice-Chairman, Crofting Law Group, 1994-2004. Publications: Crofting Law (Co-author), 1990; Green's Annotated Crofters Act (Co-author), 1993; Countryside Law in Scotland (Contributor), 2000. Recreations: music; walking; Ross County FC. Address: (b.) 28 Queensgate, Inverness IV1 1DL; T.-01463 239393.

Follett, Professor Georgina Louise Patricia, MDes, FRSA, FCSD. Dean, Duncan of Jordanstone College (formerly Head, School of Design); b. 16.7.49, London; m., Adrian Franklin; 1 s.; 1 d. Educ. Channing School; Royal College of Art. Course Leader, Sir John Cass College,

1979-88; Acting Head, Grays School of Art, 1988-93; Jeweller (exhibitions include one woman show, Jewellery Gallery, Victoria and Albert Museum). Recreations: gardening; drawing; reading. Address: Duncan of Jordanstone College, Perth Road, Dundee DD1 4HT; T.-01382 345289.

Foot, Professor Hugh Corrie, BA, PhD, FBPsS. Emeritus Professor of Psychology, Strathclyde University, since 1992, b. 7.6.41, Northwood, Middx; m., Daryl M.; 1 s.; 1 d. Educ. Durham University; Queen's College, Dundee. Research Fellow, Dundee University, 1965-68; University of Wales Institute of Science and Technology: Lecturer, 1968-77, Senior Lecturer, 1977-88; Reader, University of Wales College of Cardiff, 1989-91. Recreations: tennis; hill walking. Address: Department of Psychology, Strathclyde University, 40 George Street, Glasgow, G1 1QE; T.-0141-552 4400, Ext. 2580; e-mail: h.foot@strath.ac.uk

Forbes, 22nd Lord (Nigel Ivan Forbes), KBE (1960), DL. Premier Lord of Scotland; b. 19.2.18; m., Hon. Rosemary Katharine Hamilton-Russell; 2 s.; 1 d. Educ. Harrow; Sandhurst. Retired Major, Grenadier Guards; served WW II France, Belgium (wounded), N. Africa, Sicily, N.W. Europe; Adjutant Grenadier Guards Staff College, 1945-46; Military Assistant High Commissioner, Palestine, 1947-48; Representative Peer for Scotland, 1955-63; Minister of State, Scottish Office, 1958-59. Member: Scottish Committee, Nature Conservancy, 1961-67, Aberdeen and District Milk Marketing Board, 1962-72, Sports Council for Scotland, 1966-71; Chairman: River Don District Board, 1962-73, Scottish Branch, National Playing Fields Association, 1965-80, Rolawn Ltd., 1975-98, Alford Car Transport Service, since 2000; President: Royal Highland and Agricultural Society of Scotland, 1958-59, Scottish Scout Association, 1970-88; Deputy Chairman, Tennant Caledonian Breweries Ltd., 1964-74; Director: Grampian Television Ltd., 1960-88, Blenheim Travel Ltd., 1981-88. Address: (h.) Balforbes, Alford, Aberdeenshire AB33 8DR; T.-019755 62516.

Forbes, Alexander Douglas, MA, LLB. Chairman, Scottish Friendly Assurance Society Ltd., 1996-2006; former Partner, Robertson Paul (Solicitors), Glasgow; b. 18.2.37, Glasgow; m., Rachel Mary; 1 s.; 2 d. Educ. High School of Glasgow; Glasgow University. Solicitor, since 1961, now retired. Recreations: curling; angling; walking. Address: (h.) 29 Tannoch Drive, Milngavie, Glasgow G62 8AR; T.-0141-956 3561; e-mail: dforbes358@aol.com

Forbes, Professor Charles Douglas, DSc, MD, MB, ChB, FRCP, FRCPGlas, FRCPEdin, FRSA, FRSE. Emeritus Professor of Medicine, Dundee University; former Honorary Consultant Physician, Dundee Teaching Hospitals NHS Trust; b. 9.10.38, Glasgow; m., Janette MacDonald Robertson; 2 s. Educ. High School of Glasgow; Glasgow University. Assistant Lecturer in Materia Medica, Glasgow University; Lecturer in Medicine, Makerere, Uganda; Registrar in Medicine, Glasgow Royal Infirmary, Reader in Medicine, Glasgow University; Fellow, American Heart Association; Fullbright Fellow; Director, Regional Haemophilia Centre, Glasgow. Recreation: gardening. Address: (h.) East Chattan, 108 Hepburn Gardens, St. Andrews KY16 9LT; T.-01334 472428.

Forbes, David Fraser, LLB (Hons). Regional Officer, Scottish Health Visitors' Association/UNISON; b. 11.4.56, Glasgow; m., Isabel Hamilton; 3 d. Educ. Greenock Academy; Edinburgh University. Porter, Royal Edinburgh Hospital, and Senior Shop Steward, NUPE, 1978-87; Diploma in Accountancy, Stirling University, 1987-88.

Address: (b.) Douglas House, 60 Belford Road, Edinburgh, EH4 3UQ.

Forbes, Very Rev. Dr. Graham John Thomson, CBE (2004). Provost, St Mary's Cathedral Edinburgh, since 1990; b. 10.6.51; m., Jane; 3 s. Educ. George Heriot's School, Edinburgh; University of Aberdeen; University of Edinburgh; Edinburgh Theological College. Curate, Old St Paul's Edinburgh, 1976-82; Provost: St. Ninian's Cathedral, Perth, 1982-90; Non-Executive Director, Radio Tay, 1986-90; Founder, Canongate Youth Project, Edinburgh; President, Lothian Association of Youth Clubs, since 1986; HM (lay) Inspector of Constabulary for Scotland, 1995-98; Chairman: Scottish Executive MMR Expert Group, 2001-02, Scottish Criminal Cases Review Commission, 2002; Director, Theological Institute of the Scottish Episcopal Church, 2002-04; Member: Scottish Community Education Council, 1981-87, Children's Panel Advisory Committee, Tayside, 1986-90, Parole Board for Scotland, 1990-95, Scottish Consumer Council, 1995-98, GMC, since 1996, Clinical Standards Board for Scotland, 1999-2005, Historic Buildings Council for Scotland, 2000-02, Scottish Council, Royal College of Anaesthetists, 2001-04; Chairman, Scottish Criminal Cases Review Commission, since 2001. Recreations: fly fishing; running. Address: St. Mary's Cathedral Edinburgh, 8 Lansdowne Crescent, Edinburgh EH12 5EQ; T.-0131 225 2978; e-mail: provost@cathedral.net

Forbes, Ronald Douglas, RSA. Artist; Leverhulme Artist in Residence, Scottish Crop Research Institute, Dundee, 2006-08; Visiting Professor, University of Abertay Dundee, since 2003; Head of Painting, Duncan of Jordanstone College of Art, 1995-2001; b. 22.3.47, Braco; m., Sheena Henderson Bell; 1 s.; 2 d. Educ. Morrison's Academy, Crieff; Edinburgh College of Art. Leverhulme Senior Art Fellow, Strathclyde University, 1973-74; Head of Painting, Crawford School of Art, Cork, Ireland, 1974-78; Artist in Residence, Livingston, 1978-80; Scottish Arts Council Studio Residence Bursary, Amsterdam, 1980; Lecturer, Glasgow School of Art, 1979-83; Director, Master Fine Art postgraduate studies, Duncan of Jordanstone College of Art, University of Dundee, 1983-95; Artist in Residence, University of Tasmania Hobart Centre for the Arts. First Prize, first Scottish Young Contemporary Exhibition, 1967; BBC Scope Film Prize, 1975; RSA Guthrie Award, 1979; Scottish Arts Council Award for Film-making, 1979; Highland Society of London Award, Royal Scottish Academy, 1996. Recreations: cinema; theatre; gardening. Address: (h.) 13 Fort Street, Dundee DD2 1BS; T.-01382 641498; website: www.ronald-forbes.com

Ford, Professor Ian, BSc, PhD, FRCP (Glas), FRSE. Professor of Biostatistics and Director, Robertson Centre for Biostatistics, Glasgow University, since 1991, Director, Glasgow Clinical Trials Unit, since 2007, Dean, Faculty of Information and Mathematical Sciences, 2000-04; b. 4.2.51, Glasgow; m., Carole Louise Ford; 1 s. Educ. Hamilton Academy; Glasgow University. Visiting Lecturer, University of Wisconsin, Madison, 1976-77; Lecturer, then Senior Lecturer, Reader, Personal Professor and Professor, Glasgow University, since 1977. Publications: 164 papers. Recreations: gardening; travel. Address: (b.) Robertson Centre for Biostatistics, Boyd Orr Building, Glasgow University, Glasgow; T.-0141-330 4744.

Ford, James Allan, CB, MC. Author; b. 10.6.20, Auchtermuchty; m., Isobel Dunnett; 1 s.; 1 d. Educ. Royal High School, Edinburgh; Edinburgh University. Employment Clerk, Ministry of Labour, 1938-39; Executive Officer, Inland Revenue, 1939-40; Captain, The Royal Scots, 1940-46 (POW, Far East, 1941-45); Executive

Officer, Inland Revenue, 1946-47; Department of Agriculture for Scotland, 1947-66 (Assistant Secretary, 1958); Registrar General for Scotland, 1966-69; Under Secretary, Scottish Office, 1969-79. Trustee, National Library of Scotland, 1981-91. Publications (novels): The Brave White Flag, 1961; Season of Escape, 1963; A Statue for a Public Place, 1965; A Judge of Men, 1968; The Mouth of Truth, 1972. Address: (h.) 6 Hillpark Court, Edinburgh EH4 7BE; T.-0131 336 5398.

Ford, John Noel Patrick, KStJ, FInstD. Chancellor, The Priory of Scotland of the Order of St. John, 2002; Trustee, New Lanark Conservation Trust, since 1994; b. 18.12.35, Surbiton; m., Roslyn Madeleine Penfold; 2 s.; 2 d. Educ. Tiffin School, Kingston on Thames. Retired, 1992, as Chairman, Scotland and Northern Ireland, and Marketing Director, OCS Group Ltd; Director/Administrator, Scottish Civic Trust, 1993-2004. Deacon, Incorporation of Masons of Glasgow, 1985-86; Deacon Convener, Trades House of Glasgow, 1991-92; Regional Chairman, Glasgow, Princes Scottish Youth Business Trust, 1993-2001; Chairman, Glasgow Committee, Order of St. John, 1993-2002; Governor, Hutchesons' Educational Trust, 1986-2001; Member, Council, Europa Nostra, 1999-2005; General Commissioner of Income Revenue, Glasgow North. Recreations: golf and sport in general; gardening. Address: (h.) South Lodge, Ballindalloch, Balfron G63 0RQ; T.-01360 440347.

Forman, Robert Crawford Banks, LLB, LLM, WS. Senior Partner, McKay Norwell WS, Solicitors, since 1977; b. 30.3.48, UK; widower; 1 s.; 1 d. Educ. Royal High School; Edinburgh University. Moderator of The Society of High Constables of Edinburgh; Honorary Secretary, The Scottish Conservative Party; Member, Client Relations Committee of Law Society of Scotland; Chairman, East Scotland Salvation Army Advisory Board; Secretary, Royal High School Club. Recreations: golf; reading. Address: (b.) 5 Rutland Square, Edinburgh EH1 2AX; T.-0131 222 8111. E-mail: rforman@mckaynorwell.co.uk

Forrest, Professor Sir (Andrew) Patrick (McEwen), Kt (1986), BSc, MD, ChM, FRCS, FRCSEdin, FRCSGlas, FRCPEd, DSc (Hon), LLD (Hon), MD (Hon), FACS (Hon), FRACS (Hon), FRCSCan (Hon), FRCR (Hon), FFPHM (Hon), FIBiol, FRSE. Professor Emeritus, Edinburgh University; b. 25.3.23, Mount Vernon, Lanarkshire; m., 1. Margaret Beryl Hall (deceased); 1s.; 1d.; 2. Margaret Anne Steward; 1 d. Educ. Dundee High School; St. Andrews University. House Surgeon, Dundee Royal Infirmary; Surgeon Lieutenant, RNVR; Mayo Foundation Fellow; Lecturer and Senior Lecturer, Glasgow University; Professor of Surgery, Welsh National School of Medicine; Regius Professor of Clinical Surgery, Edinburgh University; Visiting Scientist, National Cancer Institute, USA; Associate Dean of Clinical Studies, International Medical College, Malaysia; Chief Scientist (part-time), Scottish Home and Health Department, 1981-87; Chairman, Working Group, Breast Cancer Screening, 1985-86; President: Surgical Research Society, 1974-76, Association of Surgeons of Great Britain and Ireland, 1988-89; Lister Medal, Royal College of Surgeons of England, 1987; Member, Kirk Session, St. Giles Cathedral, 1999-2003. Publications: Prognostic Factors in Breast Cancer (Co-author), 1968; Principles and Practice of Surgery (Co-author), 1985; Breast Cancer: the decision to screen, 1990. Address: (h.) 19 St. Thomas Road, Edinburgh EH9 2LR; T.-0131-667 3203.

Forrest, Robert Jack, OBE, FRAgS, DL. Past Chairman, Royal Scottish Agricultural Benevolent Institution; b. 4.1.39, Duns; m., Jennifer McCreath; 2 s.; 1 d. Educ.

Loretto School; East of Scotland College of Agriculture. Director, Royal Highland & Agricultural Society of Scotland, 1979-95 (Hon. Treasurer, 1985-88, Chairman, 1989-90, Hon. Secretary 1991-95); President, British Simmental Cattle Society, 1983-84; President, Scottish Agricultural Arbiters Association, 1993-94; Director, Scottish Borders Enterprise, 1994-98; Director, Scottish SPCA, 1998-2003; Director, Scottish Agricultural College, 1996-2004. Elder, Bonkyl Church. Address: (h.) Scotston Park, Hardens Road, Duns, Berwickshire.

Forrester, Rev. Professor Duncan Baillie, MA (Hons), BD, DPhil, HonDTheol (Iceland), HonDD (Glasgow and St. Andrews). Dean, Faculty of Divinity, New College, Edinburgh, 1996-00 (Principal, 1986-96), Professor of Christian Ethics and Practical Theology, 1978-2001, Director, Centre for Theology and Public Issues, 1984-2000; Church of Scotland Minister; b. 10.11.33, Edinburgh; m., Rev. Margaret McDonald; 1 s.; 1 d. Educ. Madras College, St. Andrews; St. Andrews University; Chicago University; Edinburgh University. Part-time Assistant in Politics, Edinburgh University, 1957-58; Assistant Minister, Hillside Church, Edinburgh, and Leader of St. James Mission, 1960-61; as Church of Scotland Missionary, Lecturer and then Professor of Politics, Madras Christian College, Tambaram, South India, 1962-70; ordained Presbyter, Church of South India, 1962; part-time Lecturer in Politics, Edinburgh University, 1966-67; Chaplain and Lecturer in Politics, Sussex University. Member, WCC Faith and Order Commission, 1983-96; President: Society for Study of Theology, 1991-93, Society for Study of Christian Ethics, 1991-94, Church Service Society, 1999-2001; Member, Nuffield Council on Bioethics, 1995-2002; Vice-President, Council on Christian Approaches to Defence and Disarmament; Templeton UK Award, 1999. FRSE, 2007. Publications: Caste & Christianity, 1980; Encounter with God (Co-author), 1983; Studies in the History of Worship in Scotland (Co-Editor), 1984; Christianity and the Future of Welfare, 1985; Theology and Politics, 1988; Just Sharing (Co-author), 1988; Beliefs, Values and Policies, 1989; Worship Now Book II (Co-editor), 1989; Theology and Practice (Editor), 1990; The True Church and Morality, 1997; Christian Justice and Public Policy, 1997; Truthful Action: Explorations in Practical Theology, 2000; On Human Worth: A Christian Vindication of Equality, 2001; Apocalypse Now? Reflections on Faith in a Time of Terror, 2005; Theological Fragments - Explorations in Unsystematic Theology, 2005. Recreations: hill-walking; reading; listening to music. Address: (h.) 25 Kingsburgh Road, Edinburgh, EH12 6DZ; T.-0131-337 5646; e-mail: forrestd@fish.co.uk

Forrester, Frederick Lindsay, MA (Hons), DipEd, FEIS. Educational journalist and consultant; Depute General Secretary, Educational Institute of Scotland, 1992-2000; b. 10.2.35, Glasgow; 1 s.; 1 d. Educ. Victoria Drive Senior Secondary School, Glasgow; Glasgow University; Jordanhill College of Education. Teacher of English, Glasgow secondary schools, 1962-64; Teacher of English and General Studies, Coatbridge Technical College, 1964-67; Assistant Secretary, Educational Institute of Scotland, 1967-75, Organising Secretary, 1975-92; Parliamentary Labour candidate, Perth and East Perthshire, 1964, Glasgow Cathcart, 1966. Member, Scottish Executive of the Ramblers' Association. Recreations: walking; cycling; swimming; foreign travel. Address: (h.) 58 North Larches, Dunfermline KY11 4NY; T.-01383 739191; e-mail: flf@eh.quik.co.uk

Forrester, Ian Stewart, QC, MA, LLB, MCL. Honorary Visiting Professor in European Law, Glasgow University, since 1991; Member, Dean's Advisory Board, Tulane University Law School, since 2006; b. 13.1.45, Glasgow;

m., Sandra Anne Therese Keegan; 2 s. Educ. Kelvinside Academy, Glasgow; Glasgow University; Tulane University of Louisiana. Admitted to Faculty of Advocates, 1972; admitted to Bar of State of NY, 1977; Queen's Counsel (Scotland), 1988; called to Bar, Middle Temple, 1996. Maclay, Murray & Spens, 1968-69; Davis Polk & Wardwell, 1969-72; Cleary Gottlieb Steen & Hamilton, 1972-81; established independent chambers, Brussels, 1981; Co-Founder, Forrester & Norall, 1981 (Forrester Norall & Sutton, 1989; White & Case/Forrester Norall & Sutton, 1998), practising before European Commission and Courts. Chairman, British Conservative Association, Belgium, 1982-86; author of numerous papers on European law; Elder, St. Andrew's Church of Scotland, Brussels. Recreations: politics; wine; cooking; restoring old houses.

Forrester, Professor John V., MD (Hons), FRCS(Ed), FRCOphth, FRCS(G), FRCP(Ed), FMedSci, FRSE. Cockburn Professor of Ophthalmology, since 1984; b. 11.9.46, Glasgow; m., Anne Gray; 2 s.; 2 d. Educ. St. Aloysius College, Glasgow; Glasgow University. Various hospital appointments, Glasgow, 1971-78; MRC Travelling Fellow, Columbia University, New York, 1976-77; Consultant Ophthalmologist, Southern General Hospital, 1979-83. Editor, British Journal of Ophthalmology, 1992-2000; Spinoza Professor, University of Amsterdam, 1997; Master, Oxford Ophthalmological Congress, 2000-02; President, European Association for Vision and Eye Research, 2002. Awards: McKenzie Medal 2006; Doyne Medal, 2007. Address: (b.) Department of Ophthalmology, Aberdeen University, Aberdeen AB25 2ZD; T.-01224 553782.

Forrester, Rev. Margaret Rae, MA, BD. b. 23.11.37, Edinburgh; m., Duncan B. Forrester; 1 s.; 1 d. Educ. George Watson's Ladies' College; Edinburgh University and New College. Assistant Pastor, Tambaram, Madras; Minister, Telscombe Cliffs URC, Sussex; Assistant Minister, St. George's West, Edinburgh; Chaplain, Napier College, Edinburgh; Minister, St. Michael's, Edinburgh, 1980-2003; Convener, Board of World Mission and Unity, Church of Scotland, 1992-96; Moderator, Presbytery of Edinburgh, 2000-01. Publications: Touch and Go, 2002; The Cat Who Decided, 2007. Recreation: gardening. Address: 25 Kingsburgh Road, Edinburgh EH12 6DZ; T.-0131-337 5646.

Forsyth of Drumlean, Rt. Hon. Lord (Michael Bruce Forsyth), PC, Kt, MA. Life Peer; MP (Conservative), Stirling, 1983-97; Non-Executive Director: Centre for Policy Studies, 2006, Denholm Brown Brothers, Denholm Industrial Holdings; Senior Managing Director, Evercore Partners, since 2006; Deputy Chairman, J.P. Morgan UK, 2002-05; Secretary of State for Scotland, 1995-97; b. 16.10.54, Montrose; m., Susan Jane; 1 s.; 2 d. Educ. Arbroath High School; St. Andrews University. National Chairman, Federation of Conservative Students, 1976; Member, Westminster City Council, 1978-83; Member, Select Committee on Scottish Affairs; Parliamentary Private Secretary to the Foreign Secretary, 1986 87; Chairman, Scottish Conservative Party, 1989-90; Parliamentary Under Secretary of State and Minister of State, Scottish Office, 1987-92; Minister of State, Department of Employment, 1992-94; Minister of State, Home Office, 1994-95; Parliamentarian of Year, 1996; Member, Select Committee on Monetary Policy, House of Lords; Member, Joint Committee of both Houses of Parliament on future of House of Lords; Director, Robert Fleming International Ltd., 1997-2000; Vice Chairman, Investment Europe, J P Morgan Chase, 2001-2002; Member, Development Board, National Portrait Gallery, 1999-2003; Patron, Craighalbert Centre for Children with Motor Impairments; Member, Steering Committee, International EB Research Appeal.

Recreations: fly fishing; mountaineering; astronomy; gardening; art; steam engines; skiing. Address: House of Lords, London SW1A 0PW.

Forsyth of That Ilk, Alistair Charles William, JP, KHS, FSCA, FSA Scot, FInstPet, CStJ. Baron of Ethie; Chief of the Name and Clan of Forsyth; b. 7.12.29; m., Ann Hughes; 4 s. Educ. St. Paul's School; Queen Mary College, London. Company Director; CStJ, 1982; KHS, 1992; Freeman of the City of London; Liveryman of the Scriveners Company. Recreations: Scottish antiquities.

Forsyth, Alistair James Menteith, OStJ, MTheol, LLB, DipLP, ACII, FSAScot. Advocate, since 1995; b. 21.12.60, Calcutta; m., Isabelle Richer. Educ. Fettes College; St. Andrews University; Buckingham University; Edinburgh University; Inns of Court School of Law. Executive, publishing and insurance, 1983-86; called to English Bar, Inner Temple, 1990, Member, Lincolns Inn, 1991; employed Lindsays WS, 1992-94; qualified as Solicitor and Notary Public, 1993. Lt., Ayrshire (Earl of Carrick's Own) Yeomanry Sqn., Queen's Own Yeomanry, 1983-88, Inns of Court and City Yeomanry, 1988-90; Member, Committee, Heraldry Society of Scotland, 1983-86; Secretary, Angus Branch, Order of St. John, 1983-86. Recreations: heraldry; genealogy; history; wine. Address: Dundrennan, Horsemarket, Falkland, Fife KY15 7BG; T.-01337 858735.

Forsyth, Bill. Film Director and Script Writer; b. 1946, Glasgow. Films include: Gregory's Girl, 1981, Local Hero, 1983, Comfort and Joy, 1984, Housekeeping, 1988, Breaking In, 1990, Being Human, 1993; Gregory's Two Girls, 1999. BAFTA Awards: Best Screenplay, 1982, Best Director, 1983.

Forsyth, Janice, MA (Hons). Broadcaster; b. Glasgow. Educ. Glasgow High School for Girls; Glasgow University. Presenter, Janice Forsyth Show, Working Lives (Radio Scotland), Artists' Question Time (Radio 3); TV includes: Filmnight (C4), Don't Look Down, NB and Festival Cinema (all Scottish); Columnist, Scotsman/Scotland on Sunday. Board Member, Giant Productions. Recreations: cinema; travel; theatre.

Forsyth, Roderick Hugh (Roddy). Journalist; b. 22.9.53, Lennoxtown; m., Marian Charlotte Reilly; 2 d. Educ. Allan Glen's School, Glasgow. Journalist, D.C. Thomson & Co., 1972-74; Scottish Daily News, 1975; Editor, Carnoustie Times, 1976-77; Editor, What's On in Glasgow, 1978-79; Editor, Clyde Guide, 1979-80; Journalist, Glasgow Herald, 1980-81; Sunday Standard, 1982-83; freelance, since 1983; Scottish Football Correspondent: The Times, 1988-93, Daily and Sunday Telegraph, since 1993, BBC Radio Sport, since 1983, RTE Ireland, since 1988, Ireland on Sunday, since 1996. Publications: The Only Game, 1990; Fields of Green, 1996; Blue and True, 1996.

Forsythe, John L.R., MD, FRCSEd, FRCSEng, MBBS. Consultant transplant surgeon, since 1995; b. 27.2.58, Co. Antrim; m., Jo; 1 s.; 2 d. Educ. Belfast Royal Academy; University of Newcastle upon Tyne. Consultant in General Surgery, Newcastle upon Tyne, 1992-95; Consultant Transplant Surgeon and Clinical Director, Royal Infirmary of Edinburgh, since 1995; Chairman, Scottish Transplant Group; Specialist Advisor to Chief Medical Officer (Scotland); President, British Transplantation Society, 2005-07; Member, NHS Quality Improvements Scotland Board; Non-Executive Board Member, NHS Blood and Transplant. Address: (b.) Transplant Unit, Royal Infirmary of Edinburgh, 51 Little France Crescent, Old Dalkeith Road, Edinburgh EH16 4SU; T.-0131 242 1715; e-mail: john.forsythe@luht.scot.nhs.uk

Forte, Professor A.D.M., LLB, MA. Professor of Commercial Law, Aberdeen University, since 1993; b.

9.5.49, Lower Largo; m.; 1 d. Educ. St Joseph's College, Dumfries; Edinburgh University. Lecturer, Glasgow University, 1977-80, Dundee University, 1981-84; Senior Lecturer, Edinburgh University, 1985-92. Recreations: fishing; sailing; coastal walking; reading. Address: (b.) School of Law, Aberdeen University, Aberdeen AB24 3UB; T.-01224 272414.

Forteviot, 4th Baron (Sir John James Evelyn Dewar Bart). Member, Queen's Bodyguard for Scotland (Royal Company of Archers); b. 5.4.38. Educ. Eton. Black Watch (RHR), 1956-58.

Forty, Professor Arthur John, CBE, BSc, PhD, DSc, LLD, DUniv, DSc (Hon. Warwick), FRSE. Principal and Vice-Chancellor, Stirling University, 1986-94; b. 4.11.28, Shrivenham; m., Alicia Blanche Hart Gough; 1 s. Educ. Headlands School, Swindon; Bristol University. RAF, 1953-56; Senior Scientist, Tube Investments Ltd., 1956-58; Lecturer, Bristol University, 1958-64; founding Professor of Physics, Warwick University, 1964-86; Pro-Vice-Chancellor, Warwick Univ., 1970-86; Member, Physics and Materials Science Committees, SERC, 1970-74; Member: UGC, 1982-86 (Vice-Chairman, 1985-86), Computer Board, Universities and Research Councils, 1982-85 (Chairman, 1988-91); Chairman, Committee of Scottish University Principals, 1990-92; Member, British Library Board, 1987-94; Chairman, Information Systems Committee, UFC, 1991-92; Hon. Fellow and Chairman, EPCC, Edinburgh University, 1994-97; Member, Board of Trustees, National Library of Scotland, 1995-2001; Member, Academic Advisory Board, University of the Highlands and Islands, since 1999; author of "Forty Report" on future facilities for advanced research computing. Recreations: dinghy sailing; gardening. Address: (h.) Port Mor, St. Fillans, Perthshire PH6 2NF.

Foster, John, CBE, FRICS, FRTPI, RIBA, ARIAS, FRSA; b. 13.8.20, Glasgow; m., Daphne Househam; 1 s.; 1 d. Educ. Whitehill School, Glasgow; Royal Technical College, Glasgow. Surveyor with private firm in Glasgow, 1937; Air Ministry during War; Assistant Planning Officer: Kirkcudbright County Council, 1945-47, Holland Joint Planning Committee, Lincolnshire, 1947-48; Deputy County Planning Officer, Holland County Council, 1948-52; Deputy Planning Officer, Peak Park Planning Board, 1952-54; Director, Peak District National Park Board, 1954-68; Director, Countryside Commission for Scotland, 1968-85. Hon. Vice-President, Ramblers Association Scotland (President, 1994-2000); Hon. Fellow, Royal Scottish Geographical Society; Hon. Member and Past Vice Chairman, Commission on National Parks and Protected Areas, World Conservation Union; Fred Packard International Parks Award, 1992; Hon. Member, European Federation of Nature and National Parks; President, Scottish Council for National Parks; Vice-President, Association for the Protection of Rural Scotland (APRS); Vice-Chairman, Heritage Unit Advisory Board, Robert Gordon University, Aberdeen, 1992-2001; Life Member, National Trust for Scotland; George Waterston Memorial Award, 1991; Hon. Fellow, Robert Gordon University. Fellow, Royal Society of Arts; Life Member, Royal Commonwealth Society. Recreations: walking; swimming; photography; philately; reading; travel. Address: (h.) Birchover, Ferntower Road, Crieff PH7 3DH; T.-01764 652336.

Foster, Professor John Odell, MA, PhD. Emeritus Professor of Social Sciences, Paisley University; b. 21.10.40, Hertford; m., Renee Prendergast; 1 d. Educ. Guildford Grammar School; St. Catherine's College, Cambridge. Postdoctoral Research Fellow, St. Catherine's College, Cambridge, 1965-68; Lecturer in Politics,

Strathclyde University, 1966-81. Vice Chair, Scottish Committee, Communist Party of Britain, (Secretary, 1988-2000). Publications: Class Struggle and the Industrial Revolution, 1974; Politics of the UCS Work-In, 1986; Track Record: the Caterpillar Occupation, 1988; Paying for the Piper (Co-author), 1996. Recreation: hill-walking. Address: (h.) 845 Govan Road, Glasgow G51.

Foulds, Emeritus Professor Wallace Stewart, CBE, MD, ChM, FRCS, FRCSGlas, DO, Hon. FRCOphth, Hon. DSc (Strathclyde), Hon. FRACO, Hon. FCMSA. Emeritus Professor of Ophthalmology, Glasgow University; Consultant in Medico-Legal Practice; Visiting Professor, National University of Singapore and Singapore National Eye Centre; Senior Consultant, Singapore Eye Research Institute; b. 26.4.24, London; m., Margaret Holmes Walls; 1 s.; 2 d. Educ. George Watson's Boys College, Edinburgh; Paisley Grammar School; Glasgow University. RAF Medical Branch, 1946-49; training posts, Moorfields Eye Hospital, London, 1952-54; Research Fellow, Institute of Ophthalmology, London University, and Senior Registrar, University College Hospital, London, 1954-58; Consultant Ophthalmologist, Addenbrookes Hospital, Cambridge, 1958-64; Tennent Professor, Glasgow University, 1964-89; Honorary Lecturer, Cambridge University and Research Fellow, London University, 1958-64; Past President: Ophthalmological Society of UK, Faculty of Ophthalmologists; Past Chairman, Association for Eye Research; Founder President, Royal College of Ophthalmologists; Hon. Fellow, Royal Society of Medicine; Hon. Fellow, Medical and Dental Defence Union of Scotland. Recreations: sailing; DIY; natural history. Address: Kinnoul Place, 68 Dowanside Road, Glasgow G12 9DL; T.-0141-334 2463.
E-mail: wallace@wsfoulds.demon.co.uk

Foulis, Alan Keith, BSc, MD, MRCPath, FRCP(Ed). Consultant Pathologist, Royal Infirmary, Glasgow, since 1983; b. 25.5.50, Glasgow; m., (1) Anne Don Martin (deceased); 1 s.; 1 d.; m., (2) Doreen P. Dobson. Educ. Glasgow Academy; Glasgow University. Trained in pathology, Western Infirmary, Glasgow, following brief flirtation with surgery at Aberdeen Royal Infirmary; C.L. Oakley Lecturer, Pathological Society, Oxford, 1987; Bellahouston Medal, Glasgow University, 1987; R.D. Lawrence Lecturer, British Diabetic Association, Manchester, 1989. Publications: research papers on diseases of the pancreas. Recreations: choral singing; walking; cycling; natural history. Address: (h.) Heathfield Drive, Milngavie, Glasgow; T.-0141-956 3092.

Foulis, Sheriff Lindsay David Robertson, LLB (Hons). Sheriff at Perth, since 2001; Honorary Professor in Scots Law, Dundee University, since 2001; b. 20.4.56, Dundee; m., Ellenore; 2 s.; 1 d. Educ. High School of Dundee; Edinburgh University. Legal apprenticeship, Balfour and Manson, Edinburgh, 1978-80; Legal Assistant, Fred Tyler; Assistant, Reid Johnston Bell and Henderson, 1981; became Partner, 1984; appointed an all-Scotland Floating Sheriff, 2000. Part-time Lecturer, Dundee University, 1994-2000; Member, Sheriff Court Rules Council, 1996-2000; Temporary Sheriff, 1998-99. Publication: Civil Court Practice materials (Co-author). Recreations: sport; now mainly golf (badly); music. Address: Sheriff's Chambers, Sheriff Court House, Tay Street, Perth PH2 8NL; T.-01738 620546; e-mail: Sheriff.LDRFoulis@scotcourts.gov.uk

Foulis, Michael Bruce, BSc (Hons). Director for Housing and Regeneration, Scottish Government, since 2007; b. 23.8.56, Kilmarnock; m., Gillian Tyson; 1 s.; 1 d. Educ. Kilmarnock Academy; Edinburgh University.

Joined Scottish Office, 1978; Private Secretary to Parliamentary Under Secretary of State, 1987-89; seconded to Scottish Financial Enterprise as Assistant Director, 1989-91; Principal Private Secretary to Secretary of State for Scotland, 1993-95; seconded to Cabinet Office as Deputy Head, Devolution Team, Constitution Secretariat, 1997-98. Trustee: New Deal and Childcare, Children 1st; Head of Group, Scottish Education and Industry Department, 1998-99; Head of Economic Development, Advice and Employment Issues Group, Enterprise and Lifelong Learning Department, Scottish Executive, 1999-2001; On secondment to Mining (Scotland) Ltd., 2006-07, working on Corporate Strategy; Head of Environment Group, Environment and Rural Affairs Department, Scottish Executive, 2001-05. Recreations: playing cello; appreciating lithographs; moderate exercise. Address: (b.) Scottish Government, Victoria Quay, Edinburgh EH6 6QQ; T.-0131 244 8400; e-mail: mike.foulis@scotland.gsi.gov.uk

Foulkes of Cumnock, Rt. Hon. Lord (George Foulkes), PC, JP, BSc. MSP (Labour), Lothians, since 2007; MP (Labour and Co-operative), Carrick, Cumnock and Doon Valley, 1979-2005; b. 21.1.42, Oswestry; m., Elizabeth Anna, 2 s., 1 d. Educ. Keith Grammar School; Haberdashers' Aske's School; Edinburgh University. Opposition Spokesman on Foreign Affairs, 1984-92, Defence, 1992-93, Overseas Development, 1994-97; Parliamentary Under-Secretary of State, Department for International Development; 1997-2001; Minister of State for Scotland, 2001-02. President, Scottish Union of Students, 1964-66; Director: European League for Economic Co-operation, 1967-68, Enterprise Youth, 1968-73, Age Concern Scotland, 1973-79; Chairman: Lothian Region Education Committee, 1974-79, Education Committee, COSLA, 1975-79; Rector's Assessor, Edinburgh University, 1968-71; Treasurer, Parliamentarians for Global Action; Chair, Labour Movement for Europe in Scotland; Member, Intelligence and Security Committee; Member, Board of Directors of Westminster Foundation for Democracy; President, Caribbean Britain Business Council. Recreations: boating; watching football (Heart of Midlothian and Ayr United). Address: (h.) 10/3 Leamington Terrace, Edinburgh EH10 4JN; The Cottage, Barclay Farm, Maybole KA19 7PE; T.-01655 740536.

Fourman, Professor Michael Paul, BSc, MSc, DPhil, FBCS, CITP. Professor, Computer Systems, The University of Edinburgh, since 1988; b. 12.09.50, Oxford; divorced; 2 s.; 1 d. Educ. Allerton Grange, Leeds; Bristol University; Linacre, Oxford. Assistant Professor, Clark University, Worcester, Mass., 1976-77; J.F. Ritt Assistant Professor, Columbia University, NYC, 1977-82; Fellow, University of Cambridge, 1979-80; Reader, Brunel University, London, 1986-87, Professor, Formal Systems, 1987-88; Technical Director, Abstract Hardware Ltd., Uxbridge, 1986-96. Recreations: cooking; sailing. Address: (b.) University of Edinburgh, School of Informatics, Appleton Tower, Crichton Street, Edinburgh EH8 9LE; T.-0131 650 2690.
E-mail: michael.fourman@ed.ac.uk

Fowkes, Professor Francis Gerald Reid, MB, ChB, PhD, FRCPE, FFPHM. Professor of Epidemiology, Edinburgh University, since 1994; Director, Wolfson Unit for Prevention of Peripheral Vascular Diseases, since 1989; Hon. Consultant Public Health Medicine, since 1985; b. 9.5.46, Falkirk; 1 s.; 1 d. Educ. George Watson's College, Edinburgh; Edinburgh University. Senior Lecturer, University of Wales, 1980-85; Reader/Professor, Edinburgh University, since 1985. Address: (b.) Department of Public Health Sciences, Edinburgh University, Teviot Place, Edinburgh EH8 9AG; T.-0131-650 3220.

Fowler, Agnes Isobel, BSc, FRSAMD, FRSA, FFCS. Former Director of Finance and Administration, Royal Scottish Academy of Music and Drama (1981-2005); b. 13.2.42, Glasgow; m., William M. Fowler; 2 s.; 1 d. Educ. Jordanhill College School; Glasgow University. Member, Merchants House of Glasgow; Trustee, Royal Scottish Academy of Music and Drama Trust; Director, Drymen Community Development Trust; Board Member, Hanover (Scotland) Housing Association. Recreations: hill-walking; swimming; gardening; Church. Address: (h.) Hillside, 7 Main Street, Drymen, Glasgow; T.-01360 660009; e-mail: fowlersat7@aol.com

Fowler, William, LLB (Hons), DipLP, NP. Partner, Semple Fraser LLP, since 2005; Director, New Horizons Edinburgh Ltd., since 2002; b. 29.1.68, Edinburgh. Educ. George Heriot's School, Edinburgh; Glasgow University. Trainee, McClure Naismith, Glasgow, 1991-93; Solicitor, MacRoberts, Edinburgh and Glasgow, 1993-2000; Legal Counsel, Kymata Limited, 2000-01; Partner, Archibald Campbell & Harley WS, 2001-05. Recreations: sailing; swimming; fell running; triathlon. Address: (b.) 80 George Street, Edinburgh EH2 3BU; T.-0131 273 3736.

Fowlie, Hector Chalmers, OBE, MB, ChB, FRCPEd, DPM. Retired Consultant Psychiatrist; b. 21.6.29, Dundee; m., Christina N.M. Walker; 2 s.; 1 d. Educ. Harris Academy, Dundee; St. Andrews University. House Officer, Maryfield Hospital, Dundee, and Perth Royal Infirmary; Registrar, Dundee Royal Mental Hospital; Lecturer, Department of Psychiatry, Medical School, Dundee University; Consultant Psychiatrist and Deputy Physician Superintendent, Gartnavel Royal Hospital, Glasgow; Physician Superintendent, Royal Dundee Liff and Strathmartine Hospitals; Consultant Psychiatrist, Tayside Health Board. Vice-Chairman, Mental Welfare Commission for Scotland, 1984-89; sometime Vice-Chairman, Parole Board for Scotland; Member, Tayside Health Board; Council of Europe Scholar; Consultant, WHO; Past Chairman: Dundee Association for Mental Health, Dundee Healthcare NHS Trust; President, Rotary Club of Claverhouse, 1999-00; Fellow, University of Abertay Dundee, formerly Member of Court. Recreations: reading; bowling. Address: (h.) 21 Clepington Road, Dundee; T.-01382 456926.

Fowlis, Angela, DCE. Director, Scottish Pre-Retirement Council, since 2000; b. 1.1.48, Dunfermline. Educ. Kings Park Secondary, Glasgow; Jordanhill College of Education. Primary/nursery Teacher, 1968-76; Lecturer, Langside College, 1976-95; Head of Department, Langside College, 1995-98. Recreations: singing; gardening; golf; badminton. Address: (b.) 260 Bath Street, Glasgow G2 4JP; T.-0141 332 9427; e-mail: info@sprc.org.uk

Fox, Colin Anthony. MSP (Scottish Socialist Party), Lothians, 2003-07; National Convener, Scottish Socialist Party, since 2005; b. 17.6.59, Motherwell; 1 s.; 1 d. Educ. Our Lady's High School, Motherwell; Bell College, Hamilton. Spent 20 years as a (socialist) political organiser; SSP Lothians Convenor, 1998-2003. Publication: Motherwell is Won for Moscow. Recreations: reading; walking; golf; sports. Address: 24/3 Ivanhoe Crescent, Edinburgh EH16 6AN; T.-0131-348 6389.

Fox, Professor Keith Alexander Arthur, BSc (Hons), MB, ChB, FRCP, FESC, FMedSci. Duke of Edinburgh Professor of Cardiology, Edinburgh University, since 1989; Honorary Consultant Cardiologist, Royal Infirmary of Edinburgh; Head, Division of Medical and Radiological

Sciences, Edinburgh University; b. 27.8.49, Salisbury, Rhodesia; m., Aileen E.M.; 1 s.; 1 d. Educ. Falcon College; Edinburgh University. Assistant Professor of Medicine, Washington University School of Medicine, 1980-85; Senior Lecturer in Cardiology and Consultant Cardiologist, University Hospital of Wales College of Medicine, 1985-89. Address: (b.) New Royal Infirmary of Edinburgh, 49 Little France Crescent, Edinburgh EH16 4SB; T.-0131 242 6378.

Fraile, Emeritus Professor Medardo, PhD. Writer; Emeritus Professor in Spanish, Strathclyde University, since 1985; b. 21.3.25, Madrid; m., Janet H. Gallagher; 1 d. Educ. Madrid University. Teacher of Spanish language and literature, Ramiro de Maeztu Secondary School, Madrid, 1956-64; Assistant in Spanish, Southampton University, 1964-67; Strathclyde University: Assistant Lecturer in Spanish, 1967-68, Lecturer, 1968-79, Reader, 1979-83, Personal Professor, 1983-85. Travelling Scholarship for authors, 1954; Premio Sesamo for short story writing, 1956; literary grant, Juan March Foundation, 1960; Book of the Year award, 1965; La Estafeta Literaria Prize for short stories, 1970; Hucha de Oro Prize for short stories, 1971; research grant, Carnegie Trust, 1975; Ibanez Fantoni Prize for journalism, 1988; Encomienda con Placa de la Orden Civil de Alfonso X El Sabio, 1999; Venezuelan Order of Don Balthasar de León, 2002. Publications: El Weir de Hermiston by R.L. Stevenson (Translator), 1995; short stories translated into eight languages (Complete Short Stories, Madrid, 1991 and 2004); Palabra en el tiempo, 2005; five books for children; a novel; books of essays and literary criticism; contributor to periodicals in many countries. Recreations: swimming; walking. Address: (h.) 24 Etive Crescent, Bishopbriggs, Glasgow G64 1ES; T.-0141-772 4421.

France, Anthony James, MA, MB, BChir, FRCP. Consultant Physician, Dundee Teaching Hospitals, since 1989; Honorary Senior Lecturer, Dundee University, since 1989; b. 5.4.54, London; m., Rosemary; 1 s.; 2 d. Educ. Perse School, Cambridge; Magdalene College, Cambridge; St. Thomas' Hospital, London. Qualified 1978; specialises in management of HIV infection, communicable diseases and respiratory medicine. Recreations: photography; gardening; woodwork. Address: (b.) Ninewells Hospital, Dundee DD1 9SY; T.-01382 660111.

France, Professor (Emeritus) Peter, MA, PhD, FBA, FRSE. Professor of French, Edinburgh University, 1980-90, Endowment Fellow, 1990-2000; b. 19.10.35, Londonderry; m., Siân Reynolds; 3 d. Educ. Bradford Grammar School; Magdalen College, Oxford. Fellow, Magdalen College, Oxford, 1960-63; Lecturer, then Reader in French, Sussex University, 1963-80; French Editor, Modern Language Review, 1979-85; President: British Comparative Literature Association, 1992-98, International Society for the History of Rhetoric, 1993-95. Chevalier de la Légion d' Honneur, 2001. Publications: Racine's Rhetoric, 1965; Rhetoric and Truth in France, 1972; Poets of Modern Russia, 1982; Diderot, 1982; Rousseau: Confessions, 1987; Politeness and its Discontents, 1992; New Oxford Companion to Literature in French, 1995; Translator: An Anthology of Chuvash Poetry, 1991, Gennady Aygi: Selected Poems, 1997; Oxford Guide to Literature in English Translation, 2000; Mapping Lives: the uses of biography, 2002; General Editor, Oxford History of Literary Translation in English, since 2005. Address: (b.) 10 Dryden Place, Edinburgh EH9 1RP; T.-0131-667 1177.

Franceschild, Donna, BA. TV Scriptwriter, since 1990; playwright, since 1979; b. 22.11.53, Illinois; partner, Richard Golding; 1 s. Educ. University of California,

Los Angeles. TV credits include: The Key, Eureka Street, A Mug's Game, Takin' Over the Asylum, And the Cow Jumped Over the Moon, Bobbin' and Weavin', The Necklace; theatre credits include: And the Cow Jumped Over the Moon, The Sunshine Cafe, Rebel!,, Songs for Stray Cats and Other Living Creatures; Tap Dance on a Telephone Line; Mutiny on the M1, Diaries, The Soap Opera, The Cleaning Lady; film credit: Donovan Quick. Creative Writing Fellow, Universities of Glasgow and Strathclyde. Recreation: hill-walking.

Franchi, (Sarah) Jane. Reporter/Presenter, BBC Scotland, 1979-2003; b. 15.10.50, Calcutta; m., Alan Franchi. Educ. Benenden School; Edinburgh College of Commerce. Reporter, Aberdeen Journals, 1970; Press and Publicity Officer, Grampian TV, 1971-79. Patron, Aberdeen Football Club Supporters Trust. Recreations: swimming; football (spectating!); embroidery; theatre. Address: (h.) 9 Osborne Place, Aberdeen AB25 2BX; T.-01224 645883.

Francis, Eileen, MPhil, MRCSLT. Chair, Scottish Institute of Human Relations; Director, Education SCF; Vice President, Values Education Council UK; b. 2.3.40, Tynemouth; m., John Francis; 2 d. Educ. Church High School, Newcastle upon Tyne; Kingdon Ward School of Speech Therapy, London. Speech and language therapist, Cardiff Hospitals, 1962; Lecturer, Moray House Institute of Education, 1971; Senior Lecturer, 1988; Vector, consultancy and training, 1992. Recreations: network building; Virginia Woolf Society. Address: (h.) 49 Gilmour Road, Edinburgh EH16 5HU; T.-0131 667 3996.

Francis, John Michael, BSc, ARCS, PhD, DIC, FRSGS, FRSE, FRZSS. Deputy Chair, UNESCO Scotland; Convener, United Nations Association - Edinburgh; Trustee, The RSE Scotland Foundation, 2006-07; Steering Group Scottish Sustainable Development Forum, since 2004; Consultant to UNESCO, since 2003; Chair, UK National Commission for UNESCO, 2000-03; Honorary Fellow, University of Edinburgh, since 2000; b. 1.5.39, London; m., Eileen; 2 d. Educ. Gowerton Grammar School, near Swansea; Imperial College of Science and Technology, London University. CEGB Berkeley Nuclear Laboratories, 1963-70; Director, Society, Religion and Technology Project, Church of Scotland, 1970-74; Senior Research Fellow, Heriot-Watt University, 1974-76; Principal, Scottish Development Department, 1976-81; Assistant Secretary, Scottish Office, 1981-84, and 1992-95; Director – Scotland, Nature Conservancy Council, 1984-92, then Chief Executive, Nature Conservancy Council for Scotland; Senior Policy Adviser, Home Department, Scottish Office, 1995-99. Consultant, World Council of Churches, 1971-83; Chairman, SRT Project, Church of Scotland, 1979-94; Member: Oil Development Council for Scotland, 1973-76, Advisory Committee for Scotland, Nature Conservancy Council, 1973-76, Council, National Trust for Scotland, 1984-92; Chairman, Edinburgh Forum, 1986-92; Professional Member, World Future Society, Washington DC, 1992-2002; Member: John Muir Trust, since 1994, British Association for the Advancement of Science; UK Representative, Millennium Project, United Nations University; Trustee, Society, Religion and Technology Project Trust, 1998-2007; Member, SUPRA, since 1999; Chairman, Sector Committee, Sustainable Development, Peace and Human Rights, UK Commission for UNESCO, 1999-2003; Member, Church and Society Council, Church of Scotland, since 2005. Publications: Scotland in Turmoil, 1972; Changing Directions, 1973; Facing Up to Nuclear Power, 1976; The Future as an Academic Discipline, 1975; The Future of Scotland, 1977; North Sea Oil and the Environment (Jointly), 1992; 'Conserving Nature: Scotland

and the Wider World' (jointly), 2005; contributions to scientific journals. Recreations: theatre; hill-walking; ecumenical travels. Address: (h.) 49 Gilmour Road, Newington, Edinburgh EH16 5NU; T.-0131-667 3996.

Francis, Michelle Ruth, BSc (Hons), MSc. Main Board Member, Scottish Natural Heritage, since 2005; Freelance Sustainability and Environmental Consultant, since 2005; b. 19.1.71, Braintree; m., James Francis; 2 s. Educ. Wallace Hall Academy, Thornhill; Marr College, Troon; University of Aberdeen; Napier University. Environmental Scientist, RSK Environment, Aberdeen, 1993-95; Environment Manager, Railtrack Scotland, Glasgow, 1995-98; Head of Environment, Railtrack/Network Rail, London, 1998-2004. Member, Royal Zoological Society of Scotland Council, then Executive Board, since 2006. Address: (h./b.) Powfoulis Stables, Bothkennar, Falkirk FK2 8PP; T.-01324 832878; e-mail: michelle@francis-hq.co.uk

Franklin, Ian Maxwell, BSc, MB, ChB, FRCP (Lond, Glasg, Edin), FRCPath, PhD. Professor of Transfusion Medicine, Glasgow University, since 1996; National Medical and Scientific Director, Scottish National Blood Transfusion Service, since 1997; Honorary Consultant, Bone Marrow Transplant Unit, Glasgow Royal Infirmary; b. 6.9.49, London; m., Dr. Anne Christine Bush; 1 s.; 1 d. Educ. Owen's Boys School, Islington; Leeds University; University College London Medical School. MRC Research Training Fellow, University College London Medical School, 1977-80; Consultant Haematologist, Queen Elizabeth Hospital, Birmingham, 1982-92; Director of Haematology, Central Birmingham Health Authority, 1989-91; Director, Glasgow and West of Scotland Blood Transfusion Service, 1996-97; Consultant-in-Administrative Charge, Bone Marrow Transplant Unit, Glasgow Royal Infirmary, 1992-97. Scientific Secretary, British Society for Haematology, 1995-98; Chairman, Working Party on Relationship Between Blood Banks and Bone Marrow Transplant Units, Council of Europe, 1995-96; Member of Council, Royal College of Pathologists, since 2002; author of various papers. Recreations: sailing; cycling; eating and drinking; music. Address: (b.) Department of Medicine, Glasgow University, Royal Infirmary, 10 Alexandra Parade, Glasgow; T.-0141-211 1202.

Franks, Peter, AGSM. Principal Trumpet, Scottish Chamber Orchestra, since 1984; Trumpet Teacher, Royal Scottish Academy of Music and Drama, since 1989; b. 22.4.58, Aylesbury; m., Maureen Hilary Rutter; 1 s.; 1 d. Educ. Aylesbury Grammar School; Guildhall School of Music and Drama. Sub-principal Trumpet, Scottish Chamber Orchestra, 1981-84. Address: 29 West Bankton Place, Murieston West, Livingston EH54 9ED; T.-01506 415514.

Fransman, Professor Martin, BA, MA, PhD. Professor of Economics, University of Edinburgh, since 1996; Director, Institute for Japanese-European Technology Studies, since 1988; b. 17.4.48, Johannesburg; m., Tamar Ludwin; 1 s.; 2 d. Educ. University of the Witwatersrand; University of Sussex. Lecturer: University of Swaziland, 1971-77, University of London, 1977-78; University of Edinburgh: Lecturer, 1978-86, Reader, 1987-96. Publications: The Market and Beyond, 1990 (Masayoshi Ohira Prize, 1991); Japan's Computer and Communications Industry, 1995; Visions of Innovation, 1999; Telecoms in the Internet Age, 2002 (Wadsworth Prize, 2003). Recreations: hill-walking; foreign travel; music; cinema. Address: (b.) Institute for Japanese-European Technology Studies, University of Edinburgh, Old Surgeons' Hall, High School Yards, Edinburgh EH1 1LZ; T.-0131-650 2450; e-mail: M.Fransman@ed.ac.uk

Fraser of Carmyllie, Lord (Peter Fraser), PC, QC. Minister of State, Department of Trade and Industry, 1995-97; Director; various companies; b. 29.5.45; m., 1 s.; 2 d. MP (Conservative), Angus South, 1979-83, Angus East, 1983-87; Solicitor-General for Scotland, 1982-89; Lord Advocate, 1989-92; Minister of State, Scottish Office, 1992-95.

Fraser, Alan Alexander, BSc (Hons), MBChB, MRCPsych. Consultant Psychiatrist, Southern General Hospital, Glasgow, since 1987; Honorary Clinical Senior Lecturer in Psychiatry, Glasgow University, since 1988; b. 17.10.55, Kilbirnie. Educ. Spier's School, Beith; Glasgow University. Address: (h.) 65 Dowanside Road, Glasgow G12 9DL; T.-0141-357 2283.

Fraser, Alan William, MA (Hons). Business Adviser; b. 17.12.51, Lennoxtown; m., Joan; 2 s.; 1 d. Educ. Daniel Stewart's College; Banff Academy; Aberdeen University. Entered Scottish Office, 1973; Assistant Secretary to Inquiry into UK Prison Services, 1978-79; Private Secretary to Minister of State, 1979-81; Manager, Scottish Office Efficiency Unit, 1985-88; Head, Industrial Policy and Technology Division, SOID, 1988-91; Principal Private Secretary to Secretary of State for Scotland, 1991-93; Head, Enterprise and Tourism Division, Scottish Office Education and Industry Department, 1993-99; Director of Personnel, Scottish Executive, 1999-2000; Director for Civil Service Reform, 2000-01; Head of 21st Century Government Unit, Scottish Executive, 2001-05. Business Adviser, since 2005; Board Member, Cruse Bereavement Care Scotland, since 2006. Recreations: hill-walking; skiing; sea kayaking; wind-surfing. Address: (h.) 10, Laverockbank Terrace, Edinburgh EH5 3BJ; T.-0131-552-1994.
E-mail: alanwilliamfraser@blueyonder.co.uk

Fraser, Andrew Kerr, MB, ChB, MPH, FRCP, FFPHM. Director of Health and Care, Scottish Prison Service, since 2006; b. 10.12.58, Edinburgh; m., Geraldine M.; 3 s.; 1 d. Educ. George Watson's College; Aberdeen University; Glasgow University. Medical Director, National Services Division, NHS in Scotland; Director of Public Health, Highland Health Board; Deputy Chief Medical Officer, Scottish Executive. Recreations: music; mountain walking. Address: (b.) Calton House, Edinburgh EH12 8HW; e-mail: andrew.fraser@sps.gov.uk

Fraser, Sir Charles Annand, KCVO, WS, DL. Partner, W. & J. Burness, 1956-92 (retired); former Chairman, Adam and Company PLC; former Director: British Assets Trust PLC, Scottish Television PLC, Scottish Business in the Community, Stakis PLC; b. 16.10.28, Humbie, East Lothian; m., Ann Scott-Kerr; 4 s. Educ. Hamilton Academy; Edinburgh University. Purse Bearer to Lord High Commissioner to General Assembly of Church of Scotland, 1969-88; served on Court, Heriot-Watt University, 1972-78; Council Member, Law Society of Scotland, 1966-72; Chairman, Lothian & Edinburgh Enterprise, 1991-94. Recreations: gardening; skiing; piping. Address: (h.) Shepherd House, Inveresk, Midlothian; T.-0131-665 2570.

Fraser, Hugh A., MA, MEd. Director of Education, Culture and Sport, The Highland Council, since 2007; b. 7.7.54, Forres; m., Mairi; 2 d. Educ. Inverness Royal Academy; Edinburgh University. Teaching posts in East Lothian, Midlothian and Edinburgh; Assistant Divisional Officer, Highland Regional Council, 1990-96, Community and Extended Education Manager, Area Education Manager, Head of Support Services, 1996-2007. Address: The Highland Council, Glenurquhart Road, Inverness IV3 5NX; T.-01463 702802.

Fraser, Ian, MSc, BEd. Director of Education and Social Care, Inverclyde Council, since 2006; b. 4.6.50; m., Sandra; 2 d. Educ. Milne's High School, Fochabers; Aberdeen University. Teacher; Headteacher; Quality Assurance Inspector in Strathclyde Region; Head of Education Services (Children & Young People), East Renfrewshire Council, 1996-2006. Recreations: sport; golf; travel. Address: (b.) Inverclyde Council, Municipal Buildings, Greenock PA15 1LY.

Fraser, James Edward, CB, MA (Aberdeen), BA (Cantab), FSA Scot. Assistant Local Government Boundary Commissioner for Scotland, since 1997; Secretary of Commissions for Scotland, 1992-94; b. 16.12.31, Aberdeen; m., Patricia Louise Stewart; 2 s. Educ. Aberdeen Grammar School; Aberdeen University; Christ's College, Cambridge. Royal Artillery, 1953-55 (Staff Captain, "Q", Tel-El-Kebir, 1954-55); Assistant Principal, Scottish Home Department, 1957-60; Private Secretary to Permanent Under-Secretary of State, Scottish Office, 1960-62; Private Secretary to Parliamentary Under-Secretary of State, Scottish Office, 1962; Principal, 1962-69: SHHD, 1962-64, Cabinet Office, 1964-66, HM Treasury, 1966-68, SHHD, 1968-69; Assistant Secretary: SHHD, 1970-76, Scottish Office Finance Division, 1976; Under Secretary, Local Government Finance Group, Scottish Office, 1976-81, Scottish Home and Health Department, 1981-91. President: Scottish Hellenic Society, Edinburgh and Eastern Scotland, 1987-93, Aberdeen Grammar School Former Pupils' Club, 1997-98 (Hon. Vice-President, since 1998). Recreations: reading; music; walking; Greece, ancient and modern; DIY. Address: (h.) 59 Murrayfield Gardens, Edinburgh EH12 6DH; T.-0131-337 2274.

Fraser, James Mackenzie, MA, MEd. Deputy Principal and Secretary to UHI Millennium Institute (UHI), since 2007, Secretary, since 2002; b. 29.07.48, Poolewe; m., Janet Sinclair (deceased). Educ. Plockton High School; University of Edinburgh; University of Stirling. Lecturer, Inverness Technical College, 1971-77; Assistant Registrar, University of Stirling, 1977-87; College Secretary, Queen Margaret College, Edinburgh, 1987-89; Secretary, University of Paisley, 1989-2002. Chair, Board of Trustees, Free Church of Scotland; Director: Free Church Nominees Company, Centre for Health Science, Inverness. Recreations: music; genealogy; cinema. Address: (b.) UHI Millennium Institute (UHI), Executive Office, Ness Walk, Inverness IV3 5SQ; T.-01463 279215; e-mail: james.fraser@uhi.ac.uk

Fraser, Jeremy William, LLB (Hons), DipLP, NP, WS. Solicitor; Partner, Brodies LLP Solicitors; b. 2.5.62, Inverness; m. Educ. Alloa Academy; Edinburgh University. Lloyds TSB Scotland (Company Secretary); Lindsay Duncan & Black WS; Lloyds Bowmaker Ltd; Morton Fraser LLP. Recreations: cycling; squash; hockey; golf; hill-walking. Address: (b.) 15 Atholl Crescent, Edinburgh EH3 8HA; T.-0131-247 1290.
E-mail: Jeremy.Fraser@brodies.co.uk

Fraser, John A.W., MA, FEIS, JP, DL. Deputy Lieutenant for Shetland, since 1985; b. 9.11.28, Lerwick; m., Jane Ann Jamieson; 2 s. Educ. Anderson Educational Institute; Edinburgh University; Moray House College of Education. Education Officer, RAF, 1950-52; Teacher, Baltasound Junior Secondary School, 1952-54; Head Teacher: Haroldswick Primary School, 1954-59, Aith Junior High School, 1959-66, Scalloway Junior High School, 1966-88. Former Member, National Council, EIS; Member: Scalloway Waterfront Trust, Shetland/Norwegian Friendship Society, Scalloway School Board; former General Commissioner of Income Tax; former Honorary

Librarian, Shetland Family History Society; Honorary Researcher, Shetland Bus Friendship Society. Recreations: genealogy; travel; gardening. Address: (h.) Broadwinds, Castle Street, Scalloway, Shetland; T.-01595 880644.

Fraser, John Kenneth, FRICS, MCMI. Chairman, Royal Institution of Chartered Surveyors in Scotland, 2002-03; Partner, Baxter Dunn & Gray, Chartered Surveyors, since 1977; b. 1.7.43, Glasgow; m., Julie; 2 s.; 1 d. Educ. St Aloysius' College, Glasgow; Glasgow College of Building. Joined Baxter Dunn & Gray, 1961; Senior Partner, Aberdeen/Glasgow and Wick, since 1992. Member, Aberdeenshire Design Forum, since 2004. Recreations: rugby; hill-walking; reading. Address: (b.) Baxter Dunn & Gray, 32 Albert Street, Aberdeen AB25 1XR; T.-01224 637667.

Fraser, Kit, BA. BBC Scotland Political Correspondent; b. 3.12.51, Giffnock; m., Fiona Morrison; 2 s. Educ. Kingussie High School; University of Stirling. Entered journalism with D.C. Thomson (worked on The People's Journal, Sunday Post, Dundee Courier); joined BBC on setting up of BBC Highland, Inverness; Radio Scotland: Producer, 1978-88, Reporter, 1988-97, Presenter, Newsdrive, Good Morning Scotland, Politics Tonight. Publications: Christie Boy, father's autobiography (Editor). Recreations: five-a-side football; golf; real ale. Address: c/o BBC Parliamentary Unit, Media Tower, Scottish Parliament, Holyrood, Edinburgh EH99 1JP.

Fraser, Lindsey M., BA (Hons), PGCE. Partner, Fraser Ross Associates, literary agency; Executive Director, Scottish Book Trust, 1991-2002; b. 15.8.61, Edinburgh. Educ. George Watson's College; York University; Froebel Institute, London. Manager, Heffers Children's Bookshop, Cambridge, 1986-91. Sir Stanley Unwin Travelling Fellowship, 1989. Address: (b.) 6 Wellington Place, Edinburgh EH6 7EQ; T.-0131-553 2759; e-mail: lindsey.fraser@tiscali.co.uk; web: www.fraserross.co.uk

Fraser, Lady Marion Anne, LT, MA, LRAM, ARCM, LLD, DUniv (Stirling). Chair: Board, Christian Aid, 1990-97; Honorary President, Scottish International Piano Competition, 1999-2007 (Chairman, 1995-99); Chair, Scottish Association of Mental Health, 1995-99; b. 17.10.32, Glasgow; m., Sir William Kerr Fraser; 3 s.; 1 d. Educ. Hutchesons' Girls' Grammar School; University of Glasgow; RSAMD. Lord High Commissioner to General Assembly of the Church of Scotland, 1994; Her Majesty's High Commissioner to the General Assembly of the Church of Scotland, 1995. Formerly Director: RGI, Scottish Opera, Laurel Bank School; Founder Chairman, Friends of the RSA; Chairman, Palcrafts Hadeel, 2003-07; Director, St. Mary's Music School; Trustee, Scottish Churches Architectural Heritage Trust; President, Scotland's Churches' Scheme, 1997; Member, Sponsoring Group, Churches' Enquiry into Unemployment and the Future of Work, 1995-2005. Recreations: family and friends; people and places. Address: (h.) Broadwood, Edinburgh Road, Gifford, East Lothian EH41 4JE; T.-01620 810 319.

Fraser, Murdo Mackenzie, LLB, DipLP. MSP (Conservative), Mid-Scotland and Fife, since 2001; Spokesman on Education and Lifelong Learning, since 2007; Deputy Leader, Scottish Conservatives, since 2005; b. 5.9.65, Inverness; m., Emma Jarvis. Educ. Inverness Royal Academy; University of Aberdeen. Solicitor, Ross Harper and Murphy and Ketchen and Stevens, WS, Edinburgh, 1989-2001. Chairman, Scottish Young Conservatives, 1989-91, National Young Conservatives, 1991-92; Parliamentary Candidate: East Lothian, 1997, North Tayside, 1999, 2001, 2003; Deputy Conservative Spokesman on Education, Culture and Sport, 2001-03; Conservative Spokesman on Enterprise and Lifelong Learning, 2003-07. Recreations: climbing; classic cars;

travel; Scottish history; Rangers FC. Address: Scottish Parliament, Edinburgh EH99 1SP; T.-0131-348 5646; e-mail: murdo.fraser.msp@scottish.parliament.uk

Fraser, Professor Patricia, MA, PhD. Aberdeen Asset Management Professor of Finance and Investment Management, University of Aberdeen, since 1995; b. 30.6.43, Arbroath; m., Finlay McRae Fraser; 3 s. Educ. Arbroath High School; University of Dundee. Lecturer in Financial Economics, Dundee University, 1989-94; Senior Lecturer in Finance, University of Stirling, 1994-95; Houblon-Norman Fellow, Bank of England, 1992. Visiting Professor: University of Tasmania, University of Western Australia, Curtin University. Recreations: reading; travel; walking; conversation with friends. Address: (b.) Accountancy and Finance, University of Aberdeen Business School, Dunbar Street, Aberdeen AB24 3QY; T.-01224 272210.

Fraser, Simon Andrew, OBE, DL, MA, FRSA (Scot). Solicitor, since 1981; b. 28.4.55, Glasgow; m., Ann Campbell; 2 s.; 2 d. Educ. Nicolson Institute, Stornoway; Aberdeen University. Solicitor, Anderson MacArthur & Co., Stornoway, 1981, Partner, 1986, now Senior Partner; Deputy Lord Lieutenant, Western Isles. Recreations: crofting agriculture; hill walking. Address: (h.) 11 Callanish, Isle of Lewis, Western Isles; T.-01851 621258; e-mail: safraser@anderson-macarthur.com

Fraser, Sheriff Simon William Hetherington, LLB, NP. Sheriff of North Strathclyde at Dumbarton, since 1989; b. 2.4.51, Carlisle; m., Sheena Janet; 1 d. Educ. Glasgow Academy; Glasgow University. Solicitor, 1973; Partner, Flowers & Co., Solicitors, Glasgow, 1976-89; Temporary Sheriff, 1987-89. Glasgow Bar Association: Secretary, 1977-79, President, 1981-82; Council member, Sheriffs' Association, since 2007. Recreations: watching cricket, and Partick Thistle. Address: (b.) Sheriff Court, Church Street, Dumbarton; T.-01389 763266.

Fraser, Professor William Hamish, MA, DPhil, FRHistS. Professor Emeritus, Strathclyde University; b. 30.6.41, Keith; m., Helen Tuach; 1 d. Educ. Keith Grammar School; Aberdeen University; Sussex University. Formerly Professor of History, Strathclyde University. Chair, Scottish Working People's History Trust. Publications: Trade Unions and Society 1850-1880, 1973; Workers and Employers, 1981; The Coming of the Mass Market, 1982; Conflict and Class: Scottish Workers 1700–1838, 1988; People and Society in Scotland 1830–1914, 1990; Glasgow 1830–1914 (Co-editor), 1996; Alexander Campbell and the Search for Socialism, 1996; A History of British Trade Unionism, 1700-1998, 1999; Scottish Popular Politics, 2000; Aberdeen: A New History (Co-Editor), 2000; Dr John Taylor, Chartist, 2006; British Trade Unions 1707-1918, 2007. Recreations: travel; golf. Address: (h.) 112 High Station Road, Falkirk FK1 5LN; T.-01324 622868.

Fraser, Sir William Kerr, GCB (1984), LLD, FRSE. Chancellor, Glasgow University, 1996-2006; b. 18.3.29; m., Lady Marion Fraser, LT (qv); 3 s.; 1 d. Educ. Eastwood Secondary School; Glasgow University. RAF, 1952-55; various posts in Scottish Office, 1955-88, including Permanent Under Secretary of State, Scottish Office, 1978-88; Principal and Vice Chancellor, Glasgow University, 1988-95. Chairman, Royal Commission on the Ancient and Historical Monuments of Scotland, 1995-2000. Address: (h.) Broadwood, Edinburgh Road, Gifford, East Lothian EH41 4JE; T.-01620 810 319.

Frater, John W.B., MA. Secretary, Environmental Campaigns (Scotland), since 2005; b. 12.5.58, Irvine; m., Caroline E. Mackenzie. Educ. Loudoun Academy; Dundee University. Recreations: reading; wine; pottering around locomotive sheds. Address: (b.) Islay House, Livilands Lane, Stirling SK8 2BG; T.-01786 471333.

Frazer, Alison Mary, MA (Hons), CertSecEd. Chief Executive (Scotland), Council for Music in Hospitals, since 1996. Address: (b.) 10 Forth Street, Edinburgh EH1 3LD; T.-0131 556 5848.

Frazer, Rev. Richard Ernest, BA, BD, DMin(Prin), SubChStJ. Minister, Greyfriars Tolbooth and Highland Kirk, Edinburgh, since 2003; Minister, St. Machar's Cathedral, Old Aberdeen, 1993-2003; b. 20.11.57, Stirling; m., Katherine Tullis Sinclair; 2 s.; 1 d. Educ. Doncaster Grammar School; University of Newcastle upon Tyne; University of Edinburgh; Princeton Theological Seminary. Assistant Minister, St. Giles Cathedral, Edinburgh, 1985-87; Minister, Schoharie, Breakabeen, N. Bleheim, New York, USA, 1987-88; Minister, Cargill-Burrelton with Collace, 1988-93. Publication: A Collace Miscellany: a History of the Parish of Collace (Co-Editor and Contributor), 1992. Recreations: family; walking; squash; slow food. Address: (b.) Greyfriars Kirk, Greyfriars Place, Edinburgh EH1 2QQ; T.-0131 225 1900.

French, William Allan, DL, BSc, MSc, CEng, FIMMM, FIET. Depute Lieutenant, Stirling and Falkirk Districts, since 1994; b. 30.12.41, Falkirk; m., Joyce; 2 d. Educ. George Watson's College, Edinburgh; Strathclyde University. Scientific Officer, UKAEA, Dounreay; Production Manager, British Aluminium Co. Ltd., Falkirk; Lecturer, Napier College, Edinburgh; Head, Department of Industrial Engineering, Falkirk College of Technology; Associate Principal, Falkirk College of Further and Higher Education, 1986-99. Director, Careers Central Ltd., 1995-99; Secretary, Forth Valley Area Scout Association; District Scout Commissioner; founder Area Chairman, Central Scotland Round Table; Past President, Larbert Rotary Club. Recreations: golf; bridge; scouting; rotary; music. Address: (h.) 26 Broomhill Avenue, Larbert FK5 3EH; T.-01324 556850; e-mail: wafrench@aol.com

Frew, Rosemary, MA, BD (Hons). Minister, Abbotshall Parish Church, Kirkcaldy, since 2005; b. 2.10.61, Glasgow; m., David J A Frew; 1 s.; 1 d. Educ. Linlithgow Academy; Edinburgh University. Assistant Minister, Markinch Parish Church, 1986-87; Minister, Largo and Newburn Parish Church linked with Largo, St. David's Parish Church, 1988-2005. Vice-Convener, Mission and Discipleship Council, Church of Scotland, 2005-07; Clerk to the Presbytery of Kirkcaldy. Recreations: ski-ing; reading; running 'mum's taxi service'. Address: (work and home) The Abbotshall Manse, 83 Milton Road, Kirkcaldy, Fife KY1 1TP; T.-01592 260315; e-mail: rosiefrew@blueyonder.co.uk

Friedrich, Karin, MA, PhD, FRHistS. Senior Lecturer in History, School of Divinity, History and Philosophy, University of Aberdeen, since 2004; School of Slavonic and East European Studies, University College London, 1995-2004; b. 12.06.63, Munich, Germany; m., Prof. Robert I. Frost; 1 s.; 1 d. Educ. Gymnasium Olching (Germany); University of Munich; Georgetown University, Washington DC. Member, Royal Historical Society. Publications: The Other Prussia. Poland, Prussia and Liberty, 1569-1772 (Cambridge 2000), Polish trans. 2006 (Orbis Prize in 2001 by American Association for the Advancement of Slavic Studies). Recreations: flute; skiing; tennis; reading; mountaineering. Address: (c) Crombie Annexe, Meston Walk, Aberdeen AB24 3FX; T.-01224 272451. E-mail: k.friedrich@abdn.ac.uk

Frier, Professor Brian Murray, BSc (Hons), MD, FRCP (Edin), FRCP (Glas). Consultant Physician, Royal Infirmary, Edinburgh, since 1987; Honorary Professor of Diabetes, Edinburgh University, since 2001; b. Edinburgh; m., Dr. Isobel M. Wilson; 1 d. Educ. George Heriot's School, Edinburgh; Edinburgh University. Research Fellow in Diabetes and Metabolism, Cornell University Medical Centre, The New York Hospital, 1976-77; Senior Medical Registrar, Royal Infirmary, Edinburgh, 1978-82; Consultant Physician, Western Infirmary and Gartnavel General Hospital, Glasgow, 1982-87. Chairman, Honorary Advisory Panel for Driving and Diabetes to Secretary of State for Transport, since 2001; Chairman, Chief Scientist Office Committee for Diabetes Research in Scotland, 2003-06; R.D. Lawrence Lecturer, British Diabetic Association, 1986; Somogyi Award, Hungarian Diabetes Association, 2004; Governor, George Heriot's Trust, Edinburgh, 1987-94. Publications: Books - Hypoglycaemia and Diabetes: clinical and physiological aspects, 1993; Hypoglycaemia in Clinical Diabetes, 1999, 2nd Edition, 2007; papers and reviews on diabetes and hypoglycaemia. Recreations: appreciation of the arts; ancient and modern history. Address: (h.) 100 Morningside Drive, Edinburgh EH10 5NT; T.-0131-447 1653.
E-mail: brian.frier@luht.scot.nhs.uk

Frith, Professor Simon, BA, MA, PhD. Tovey Professor of Music, Edinburgh University, since 2006; Professor of Film and Media, Stirling University, 1999-2005; Director, ESRC Media Economics and Media Culture Programme, 1995-2000; b. 25.6.46, England. Educ. Leys School, Cambridge; Balliol College, University of Oxford; University of California, Berkeley. Lecturer, then Senior Lecturer in Sociology, University of Warwick, 1972-87; Director, John Logie Baird Centre, 1987-99, and Professor of English Studies, 1988-99, University of Strathclyde; Rock Critic, Sunday Times, 1982-86; Pop Critic, Observer, 1987-91; Chair of Judges, Mercury Music Prize. Publications: Sound Effects, 1981; Art into Pop, 1987; Music for Pleasure, 1988; Performing Rites, 1996; Music and Copyright, 2004. Recreations: music; reading; walking. Address: (b.) Department of Music, University of Edinburgh, Alison House, 12 Nicolson Square, Edinburgh EH8 9DF; T.-0131-650-2426.

Frost, Professor Robert Ian, MA (Hons) St. Andrews, PhD (London), FRHistS. Professor of Early Modern History, University of Aberdeen, since 2004, Head of The School of Divinity, History and Philosophy, since 2004; b. 20.06.58, Edinburgh; m., Dr. Karlin Friedrich; 1 s.; 1 d. Educ. George Watson's College, Edinburgh; St. Andrews; School of Slavonic and East European Studies, University of London; Jagiellonian University, Cracow, Poland. Senior Teacher, Charterhouse, 1984-87; University Teacher, King's College London, 1987-2004, Reader in Early Modern History, History Department, 2001-04. Council of the Royal Historical Society, since 2004. Publications: Author of: After The Deluge: Poland-Lithuania and the Second Northern War, 1655-1660 (1993); The Northern Wars: War, State and Society in North Eastern Europe, 1558-1721, 2000. Address: (h.) 50 Forest Road, Aberdeen AB15 4BP; T.-01224 273903.
E-mail: robert.frost@abdn.ac.uk

Frutin, Bernard Derek, MBE, FRSA, MInstPkg. Inventor; Executive Chairman, Rocep Group of Companies; Director, Gizmo Packaging Ltd; b. 7.2.44, Glasgow; m., 1, Victoria Dykes (divorced); m., 2, Karen Smith; 1 s.; 4 d. Educ. Kelvinside Academy, Glasgow. Winner of nine international innovator awards since 1989, including John Logie Baird and British Institute of Packaging Environmental Awards; Innovator of the Year, 1989 (Institute of Packaging); Finalist, 1992 Prince of Wales Award; Institute of Packaging Starpack Award for TEC Innovation, 2001. Recreations: sailing; skiing; fine food; listening to music. Address: (b.) Rocep Lusol Holdings Ltd., Rocep Business Park, Rocep Drive, Renfrew PA4 8XY; T.-0141-885 2222.

Fry, Professor Stephen C., BSc, PhD, FRSE. Professor of Plant Biochemistry, Edinburgh University, since 1995; b. 26.11.53, Sheffield; m., Verena Ryffel; 3 d. Educ. Thornbridge School, Sheffield; Leicester University. Postdoctoral Research Fellow, Cambridge University, 1978-79; Royal Society Rosenheim Research Fellow,

Cambridge University, 1979-82; Senior Research Associate, University of Colorado, 1982-83; Lecturer in Botany, then Reader in Plant Biochemistry, Edinburgh University, 1983-95. President's Medal, Society for Experimental Biology, 1988. Publications: The Growing Plant Cell Wall: Chemical and Metabolic Analysis, 1988; 56 review articles; 159 research papers. Recreations: hill-walking; paper chromatography. Address: (b.) The Edinburgh Cell Wall Group, Institute of Molecular Plant Sciences, School of Biological Sciences, Edinburgh University, King's Buildings, Mayfield Road, Edinburgh EH9 3JH; T.-0131-650 5320; e-mail: S.Fry@ed.ac.uk

Fullerton, Manus J., MBA. Director, Wholesale Banking in Scotland, Lloyds TSB Scotland plc, since 1999; b. 11.4.49, Glasgow; m., Linda; 1 s.; 1 d. Educ. Strathclyde University. Bank of Scotland, 1966-87; Assistant General Manager, Treasury, LTSB Scotland, 1987-99. Fellow, CIOBS. BBC Scotland Children in Need Appeal Committee; SIS Board Member; Executive Member, SCDI. Recreations: painting; reading; football. Address: (b.) Henry Duncan House, 120 George Street, Edinburgh EH2 4LH; T.-0131-260-0520. E-mail: manus.fullerton@lloydstsb.co.uk

Fulton, Elaine, BA, MCLIP. Director, Scottish Library and Information Council and CILIPS (Chartered Institute of Library and Information Professionals in Scotland), since 2003; b. 1.5.60, Hamilton; 1 d. Educ. Claremont High School; Strathclyde University. Branch Librarian and Audio Librarian, East Kilbride DC, 1981-86; Librarian, Falkirk DC, 1986-94; Support Services Librarian, Strathkelvin DC, 1994-96; Operations Librarian, East Dunbartonshire DC, 1996-98; Library Systems Sales and Support, Libris Computing, 1998-99; Assistant Director, Scottish Library and Information Council and CILIPS, 1999-2002. Recreations: reading; music; sport; gardening; cooking. Address: (b.) First Floor, Building C, Brandon Gate, Leechlee Road, Hamilton ML3 6AU; T.-01698 458888.

Fulton, Rev. John Oswald, BSc, BD. General Secretary, United Free Church of Scotland, since 1994; Moderator, General Assembly, United Free Church, 2000-01; b. 9.7.53, Glasgow; m., Margaret P.; 1 d. Educ. Clydebank High School; Glasgow University. Ordained as minister, 1977; Minister, Croftfoot U.F. Church, Glasgow, 1977-94. Recreations: reading; gardening; photography. Address: (b.) 11 Newton Place, Glasgow G3 7PR; T.-0141-332 3435; e-mail: office@ufcos.org.uk

Furley, Professor Peter Anthony, MA, DPhil. Professor Emeritus and Hon. Fellow, Tropical Biogeography, since 2001; b. 5.8.35, Gravesend; m., Margaret Brenda Dunlop; 1 s.; 3 d. Educ. Gravesend Grammar School; Brasenose College, Oxford University. Tutor, Oxford; University of Edinburgh: Lecturer, 1962, Senior Lecturer, 1975; Professor of Ecology, University of Brasilia, Brazil, 1976; Reader in Tropical Biogeography and Soils, 1989; Professor of Biogeography, 1997-2001. Publications: Geography of the Biosphere, 1983; Nature and Dynamics of Forest–Savanna Boundaries, 1992; The Forest Frontier – Brazilian Roraima, 1994; Ecological and Environmental Research in Belize (three volumes), 2001-02; Fragility and Resilience of Amazonian Soils; Human impact on Amazonia: the role of traditional ecological knowledge in conservation and development, 2006; Tropical Savannas and seasonally dry forests: vegetation and environment (2007) ed. Recreations: travel; hillwalking. Address: Institute of Geography, School of Geoscience, University of Edinburgh, Drummond Street, Edinburgh EH8 9XP; T.-0131-650 2517/2523; e-mail: paf@geo.ed.ac.uk

Furlong, Professor Andy, BSc, PhD. Professor of Sociology, Glasgow University, since 2000; b. 12.5.56, Liverpool; 2 s. Educ. University of Leicester. Research Fellow, University of Edinburgh; Lecturer then Senior Lecturer, University of Strathclyde; Senior Lecturer then Reader, University of Glasgow. Editor, Journal of Youth Studies. Address: (b.) School of Business and Management, University of Glasgow, Glasgow G12 8RT, T.-0141 330 4667; e-mail: a.furlong@lbss.gla.ac.uk

Furnell, Professor James R.G., MA (Hons), DCP, PhD, LLB, FBPsS, DipLP. Advocate (called to Scottish Bar, 1993); Chartered Clinical and Forensic Psychologist; Honorary Fellow, Edinburgh University, since 1987; b. 20.2.46, London; m., Lesley Anne Ross; 1 s.; 1 d. Educ. Leighton Park Society of Friends School, Reading; Aberdeen University; Glasgow University; Stirling University; Dundee University. Clinical Psychologist, Royal Hospital for Sick Children, Glasgow, 1970-72; Forth Valley Health Board: Senior Clinical Psychologist, 1972-80, Consultant Clinical Psychologist (Child Health), 1980-98. Member: National Consultative Committee of Scientists in Professions Allied to Medicine, 1984-87 (Secretary, Clinical Psychology Sub-Committee), Forth Valley Health Board, 1984-87; Chairman, Division of Clinical Psychology, British Psychological Society, 1988-89; Visiting Professor, Caledonian University, since 1996. Recreations: flying; cross-country skiing. Address: (h.) Glensherup House, Glendevon, by Dollar, Perthshire FK14 7JY.

Furness, Professor Raymond Stephen, BA, MA, PhD. Formerly Professor of German, St. Andrews University, now Emeritus Professor; b. 25.10.33, Builth Wells; m., Janice Fairey; 1 s.; 2 d. Educ. Welwyn Garden City Grammar School; University College, Swansea. Royal Artillery and Intelligence Corps; Modern Languages Department, University of Manchester Institute of Science and Technology; Department of German, Manchester University. Publications: Expressionism; Literary History of Germany 1890-1945; Wagner and Literature; A Companion to Twentieth Century German Literature; An Introduction to German Literature 1871-1990 (Co-Author); The Dedalus Book of German Decadence; Zarathustra's Children. Recreation: claret. Address: (h.) The Dirdale, Boarhills, St. Andrews KY16 8PP; T.-01334 880469.

Furness, Col. Simon John, DL, SBOstJ. Landowner; Vice Lord Lieutenant, Berwickshire, since 1990; b. 18.8.36, Ayton. Educ. Charterhouse; RMA, Sandhurst. Commissioned Durham Light Infantry, 1956, 2nd Lt.; served Far East, UK, Germany; active service, Borneo, Northern Ireland; retired, 1978; Deputy Colonel (Durham) The Light Infantry, 1989-93. Member, Executive, National Trust for Scotland, 1986-96; Chairman: Berwickshire Civic Society, 1996-2005 (President, since 2005), Eyemouth Museum Trust, 1981-2005 (President, since 2005), Eyemouth Harbour Trust, 2003-06; Trustee, Gunscreen House Trust, since 2003. Recreations: field sports; gardening. Address: The Garden House, Netherbyres, Eyemouth, Berwickshire TD14 5SE; T.-01890 750337.

Fyfe, Maria, BA (Hons). MP, Glasgow Maryhill, 1987-2001; Vice Chair, Glasgow Housing Association, 2002-06; b. 25.11.38, Glasgow; m., James (deceased); 2 s. Educ. Notre Dame High School, Glasgow; Strathclyde University. Glasgow District Councillor, 1980-87; Senior Lecturer, Central College of Commerce, 1977-87; Member, Scottish Executive Committee, Labour Party, 1981-87; Opposition Spokesperson on Women, 1988-91; Scottish Affairs Spokesperson, 1992-95; Chair, Scottish All-Party Parliamentary Group on Children, 1996-99; Chair, Labour

Departmental Committee on International Development, 1997-2001; Member, Council of Europe, 1997-2001; Member, British-Irish Parliamentary Body, 1997-2001. Honorary Doctorate, University of Glasgow, 2002. Address: 10 Ascot Avenue, Glasgow G12 0AX.

G

Gaffney, James, DipSM, DipEM. Head of Corporate Responsibility, Laing O'Rourke Scotland, since 2001; Head of Corporate Responsibility, New City Vision Ltd., since 2003; b. 16.8.58, Glasgow. Educ. St. Mungo's Academy, Glasgow. Glasgow City Council Apprenticeship (Electrical); 15 years overseas, working in Australia, the Indian sub-continent and Europe in the petrochemical industry; 13 years in UK construction sector (last 10 years with Laing O' Rourke Scotland) in numerous posts - Health and Safety Manager, Environmental Manager and Sustainabilty Manager. Chair: The Bridges Programmes, New Roots Scotland, PEPE (Pathways to Employment for Professional Engineers), OTAR (Overseas Tradesperson Accreditation and Re-skilling), Closing the Gap (Positive Destinations for Schoolchildren), Edinburgh Construction Academy; Director, Scottish Business in the Community; Member: Bridging the Gap (Scottish Prison Service), National Employment Panel Regeneration Group, Glasgow Employer Coalition, Scottish Advisory Board for Naturalisation and Immigration. Recreation: spending quality time with my family. Address: (b.) Laing O'Rourke Scotland, 21 Woodhall, Eurocentral, Holytown, Motherwell ML1 4YT; T.-01698 731000.

Galbraith, Professor Colin A., BSc, PhD. Director of Policy and Advice, previously, Director of Scientific and Advisory Services, Scottish Natural Heritage, 2001-07, Head of Advisory Services, since 1997; b. 4.2.59, Nairobi, Kenya; m., Maria; 1 s.; 1 d. Educ. Minard; Lochgilphead; Oban High; Paisley University; Aberdeen University. Employed with The Nature Conservancy Council, 1987, then JNCC, 1991-97. Honorary Professor, Stirling University; Chair, Scientific Council to the Convention on Migratory Species (A UN Convention with 107 member countries), 1999-2005, currently Deputy Chair. Recreations: hill walking; bird watching. Address: (b.) Scottish Natural Heritage, Silvan House, 3rd Floor East, 231 Corstorphine Road, Edinburgh EH12 7AT; T.-0131 316 2601; e-mail: colin.galbraith@snh.gov.uk

Galbraith, Professor Roderick Allister McDonald, BSc, PhD (Cantab), CEng, MRAeS, FRSE. Shoda Professor of Aerospace Engineering, Glasgow University; b. 4.8.47, Lowmoor, England; m., Lynn Margaret Fraser. Educ. Greenock High School; James Watt Memorial College; Paisley College of Technology; Cambridge University. Apprentice Draughtsman/Engineer, Scott's Shipbuilding & Engineering Co. Ltd., 1964-72; Department of Aerospace Engineering, Glasgow University: joined 1975; Reader, 1989, Professor, 1992. Publications: over 100 reports and publications on aerodynamics. Recreations: sailing; walking. Address: (b.) Department of Aerospace Engineering, Glasgow University, Glasgow G12 8QQ; T.-0141-330 5295.

Galea, Paul, MD (Malta), DCH, FRCP(Glas), FRCPCH. Consultant Paediatrician, Royal Hospital for Sick Children, Yorkhill, Glasgow; previously Consultant Neonatologist, Royal Maternity Hospital, Glasgow; b. 8.10.50, Rabat, Malta; m., Irene. Educ. Royal University of Malta. Recreations: gardening; DIY, classical music. Address: (h.) 30 Garngaber Avenue, Lenzie, Glasgow G66 4LL; T.-0141-776 6031; e-mail: paul.galea@ggc.scot.nhs.uk

Gallacher, Professor James W. (Jim), MA (Hons), MSc. Professor of Lifelong Learning and Co-Director, Centre for Research in Lifelong Learning, Glasgow Caledonian University, since 1999; Council Member, Scottish Further and Higher Education Funding Council, since 2005; b. 23.12.46, Glasgow; m., Pauline; 2 s. Educ. St. Ninians School, Kirkintilloch, Glasgow; Glasgow University; London School of Economics; London University. Research Associate, Edinburgh University, 1971-73; Lecturer, Senior Lecturer, Reader, then Professor, Glasgow Caledonian University (and its predecessor institutions), since 1973. In addition to teaching on a range of full-time and part-time degrees, has worked closely with further education colleges in developing links between further and higher education in Scotland. Established the Centre for Research in Lifelong Learning (jointly with Professor Michael Osborne, University of Stirling) in 1999. This was the first research centre in Scotland to undertake policy orientated work in the field of lifelong learning. Recent and current research includes: further education and social inclusion; further education/higher education links; widening access to further and higher education; work based learning; Modern Apprenticeships; credit and qualification frameworks; the student experience in mass higher education. Member of Scottish Funding Council for Further and Higher Education (SFC); Chair of SFC Learning and Teaching Forum; Member, National Forum for Lifelong Learning; Vice Chair, Universities Association for Lifelong Learning (UALL); Adviser to Scottish Parliament's Enterprise and Lifelong Learning Committee for their inquiry into lifelong learning. Publications: numerous articles, reports and books on basis of research, including: 'Researching Widening Access to Lifelong Learning: Issues and Approaches in International Research', 2004; A Contested Landscape: International Perspectives on Diversity in Mass Higher Education, 2005; 'Learning Outside the Academy', 2006. Recreations: reading; hillwalking. Address: (b.) Centre for Research in Lifelong Learning, Glasgow Caledonian University, 6 Rose Street, Glasgow G3 6RB; T.-0141 273 1339/47; e-mail: jwga@gcal.ac.uk

Gallacher, Yvonne Jean, OBE, DPA, DCA, DTM. Chief Executive, Money Advice Scotland, since 1997; b. 11.3.58, Glasgow. Educ. Woodside Senior Secondary School; Glasgow Caledonian University; Stow College; Central College of Commerce. Local government service, 1975-87; police and trading standards, 1987-97. Member, National Consumer Council Advisory Group; Member, Personal Finance Education Group; Convenor, Money Advice Scotland, 1994-97; Member, Glasgow City Council Strategic Planning Group; former Member, Scottish Consumer Council; Recent past Member, Financial Services Authority Independent Consumer Panel; Member, UK Money Advice Trust; Member, Cross Party Working Group on Poinding and Warrant Sales; Partner, Money Advice Trust. Publications: A Guide to Money Advice in Scotland (Co-Author), 2nd and 3rd editions; Managing Debt. Regular contributor/broadcaster in respect of consumer issues relating to credit and debt. Recreations: opera; swimming; entertaining; gardening; reading. Address: (b.) Suite 306, The Pentagon Centre, 36 Washington Street, Glasgow G3 8AZ; T.-0141-572 0238; e-mail: y.gallacher@moneyadvicescotland.org.uk

Gallagher, James D. (Jim), CB, FRSE. Director General, Devolution, Ministry of Justice/Cabinet Office, since 2007; Visiting Professor of Government, University of Glasgow, since 2005; b. Glasgow; m., Una Gallagher (nee Green); 1 s.; 2 d. Educ. St. Aloysius College, Glasgow; Glasgow University; Edinburgh University. Scottish Office, Admin Trainee, 1976; Private Secretary to Minister for Home Affairs etc., 1979; various policy posts, 1981-86; Secretary, Scottish Office Management Group, 1986; Head, Urban Policy, 1988; Private Secretary to successive Secretaries of State, 1989-91; Director, HR, Scottish Prison Service,

1991-95; Head, Local Government and Europe Group, Scottish Office, 1996-99; Economic and Domestic Secretariat, Cabinet Office, 1999; Policy Advisor, No 10 Policy Unit, 2000; Head, Scottish Executive Justice Department, 2001-05; Director, Scottish Mutual, Abbey National, Life Assurance, 1996-2006; Chair, Scottish Provident Supervisory Committee, since 2001; Non Executive Director, Lothian and Borders Police Force. Address: (b.) Ministry of Justice, Selborne House, London SW1P.

Gallagher, Sister Maire T., CBE, MA (Hons), MEd, FScotVec, DCE, FSQA. Retired Headteacher; Sister of Notre Dame Religious Congregation, since 1959; b. 27.5.33, Glasgow. Educ. Notre Dame High School, Glasgow; Glasgow University; Notre Dame College of Education. Principal Teacher of History, Notre Dame High School, Glasgow; Lecturer in Secondary Education, Notre Dame College of Education; Headteacher, Notre Dame High School, Dumbarton, 1974-87; Chairman, Scottish Consultative Council on the Curriculum, 1987-91 (Member, Consultative Committee on the Curriculum, since 1976). Member, Executive, Secondary Heads Association (Scottish Branch), 1976-83; Coordinator, Christian Life Movement Groups, West of Scotland; Convener, Action of Churches Together in Scotland, 1999-2002 (Member, Central Council, 1990-99); Fellow, Scottish Qualifications Authority, 1997; Member, Glasgow Churches Together, since 2004. Recreations: reading; dress-making; bird-watching. Address: (h.) Sisters of Notre Dame, 65-67 Moorpark Avenue, Penilee, Glasgow G52 4ET; T.-0141 810 4214.

Gallhofer, Profesor Sonja, MagPhil, MA (Econ), MSc(Econ), DrPhil. Professor of Accounting and Management Control, University of Dundee, since 2006; b. Graz, Austria. Educ. Karl-Franzens Universitat; Manchester University; London School of Economics. Lecturer in Accounting, UMIST, 1988-89, Essex University, 1989-94; Associate Professor of Accounting, University of Waikato, New Zealand, 1995-98; Senior Research Fellow, Glasgow Caledonian University, 1998-99; Professor of Critical Accountancy, Glasgow Caledonian University, 1999-2004; University of Aberdeen, 2004-05. Recreations: music; theatre; walking. Address: (b.) Department of Accountancy and Business Finance, University of Dundee, Dundee DD1 4HT; T.-01382 344000.

Gallie, Philip Roy, TEng, MIPlantE. MSP (Conservative), South of Scotland, 1999-2007; formerly Conservative Spokesman on European, External and Constitutional Affairs (previously on Justice and Home Affairs); b. 3.6.39, Portsmouth; m., Marion Wands (deceased). Educ. Dunfermline High School; Kirkcaldy Technical College. Apprenticeship, H.M. Dockyard, Rosyth, 1955-60; Merchant Navy, 1960-64; electricity industry, 1964-92; MP (Conservative), Ayr, 1992-97; Business Consultant, PG Business Advice, 1998-2000. Vice-Chairman, Scottish Conservative and Unionist Party, 1995-97. Board Member, Ayr College, since 2007; Prospective Candidate, Central Ayrshire Westminster Constituency (Scottish Conservative and Unionist). Recreations: sports; politics.

Galloway, Janice. Writer; b. 2.12.56, Saltcoats. Educ. Ardrossan Academy; Glasgow University. Variety of paid and unpaid work, including 10 years' teaching English in Ayrshire; music criticism for Glasgow Herald, The Observer, Scotland on Sunday; fiction writing, including collections of short stories and novels; Co-Editor, New Writing Scotland, 1990-92; Editor, The Scotsman and Orange Short Story Collection, 2005; Times Literary Supplement Research Fellow to the British Library, 1999. Publications: The Trick Is To Keep Breathing, 1990; Blood, 1991; Foreign Parts, 1994; Where You Find It, 1996; Pipelines, 2000; Clara, 2002; This is not about me, 2008; boy, book, see, 2002; Rosengarten, 2004. Staged work: The Trick is to Keep Breathing; Fall. Song cycle: Clara; Monster, for orchestra and voices. Opera: Monster (Co-Writer).

Galloway, Rev. Kathy, BD, DPS. Leader, The Iona Community, since 2002; b. 6.8.52, Dumfries. Educ. Boroughmuir High School, Edinburgh; Glasgow University. Assistant Minister, Muirhouse Parish Church, Edinburgh, 1976-79; Co-ordinator, Edinburgh Peace and Justice Centre, 1980-83; Warden, Iona Abbey, 1983-88; freelance theological consultant, editor and writer, 1989-99; Linkworker for Scotland, Church Action on Poverty, 2000-02; Patron, Student Christian Movement. Publications include: Talking to the Bones; A Story to Live By; Walking in Darkness and Light; Sharing the Blessing. Address: (b.) The Iona Community, The Savoy Centre, 140 Sauchiehall Street, Glasgow G2 3DH; T.-0141 332 6343; e-mail: kathy.galloway@iona.org.uk

Galloway, 13th Earl of (Randolph Keith Reginald Stewart); b. 14.10.28; m.; succeeded to title, 1978. Educ. Harrow. Address: Senwick House, Brighouse Bay, Borgue, Kirkcudbrightshire, DG6 4TP.

Gamble, Alan James, LLB(Hons), LLM, Advocate. District Chairman, Tribunals Service, Glasgow, since 1993; Deputy Social Security and Child Support Commissioner, Edinburgh, since 1994; Convenor, Mental Health Tribunal for Scotland, since 2005; b. 29.4.51, Glasgow; m., Elizabeth Waugh; 2 s.; 1 d. Educ. High School of Glasgow; University of Glasgow; Harvard Law School, USA. Law Apprentice, 1974-76; admitted to Faculty of Advocates, 1978; Lecturer, then Senior Lecturer in Law, University of Glasgow, 1976-93. Bible Teacher, Christian Brethren Assemblies; Trustee, Interlink, and other charitable trusts; Dr J. McCormick Prize, 1972; Harkness Fellow, 1972-74. Publications: Contributor, Stair Memorial Encyclopedia; articles in legal journals and Christian periodicals. Recreations: reading; hill-walking. Address: (b.) Wellington House, 134-136 Wellington Street, Glasgow G2 2XL; T.-0141-354 8443.

Gammell, Geraldine, MA, CA. Director, The Prince's Trust - Scotland. Educ. Stirling University; Glasgow University. Co-founder and Director, Dundas Commercial Property Funds I and II, 2002-2006; Company Secretary, Isla Mines Ltd., since 1998; Partner, Springfords Chartered Accountants, 1993-2002; Manager, Business Services, KPMG, 1990-93; Lecturer in Business Finance and Accounting, Napier University and Edinburgh University, 1986-90; Financial Controller/Company Secretary, Ash Gupta Advertising, 1984-86; CA Apprentice, Audit Senior, Management Consultant, Thomson McLintock, 1978-83. Other non-executive Director Appointments: Lothian University Hospitals NHS Trust, 1999-2004; Sick Children's NHS Trust, 1995-99; Traverse Theatre Ltd., 1997-2001. Institute of Chartered Accountants, 1978-81; Chartered Accountant, 1981. Address: (b.) 57 Queen Street, Glasgow G1 3EN; T.-0141 204 4409.

Gammie, Professor Elizabeth, DipM, BA, CA, PhD. Professor of Accountancy, Robert Gordon University, since 2000; b. 20.12.61, Dundee; m., Robert Peter; 1 s.;

1 d. Educ. High School of Dundee; Robert Gordon University. Qualified as CA, 1986, with Ernst and Whinney; became a Lecturer, 1989. Member, Qualification Board, Institute of Chartered Accountants of Scotland. Recreation: equestrianism. Address: (h.) Bogfon Cottage, Maryculter, Aberdeen AB12 5GR; T.-01224 735403.

Garden, Malcolm, LLB, NP. Sheriff of Grampian, Highlands and Islands at Peterhead, since 2001; b. 7.8.52, Aberdeen; m., Sandra Moles; 2 s.; 1 d. Educ. Robert Gordon's College, Aberdeen; University of Aberdeen. Apprentice, then Assistant Solicitor, Watt and Cumine, Aberdeen, 1973-76; Clark and Wallace, Aberdeen: Assistant Solicitor, 1976-79, Partner, 1979-2001; Temporary Sheriff, 1994-98; Part Time Sheriff, 2000-01. Part Time Tutor, University of Aberdeen, 1980-85; Member, Aberdeen and North East Legal Aid Committee, 1980-85; Reporter to Scottish Legal Aid Board, 1984-86; Member: Law Society of Scotland, since 1976, Society of Advocates in Aberdeen, since 1978. Recreations: family; golf; football; tennis. Address: (b.) Sheriff Court House, Queen Street, Peterhead, Aberdeenshire; e-mail: sheriffm.garden@scotcourts.gov.uk

Garden, Professor Olivier James, BSc, MBChB, MD, FRCS (RCPSG), FRCS(Ed), FRCP(Ed), FRACS (Hon), FRCPSCan (Hon). Regius Professor of Clinical Surgery, Edinburgh University, since 2000; Head, School of Clinical Sciences and Community Health, 2002-06; b. 13.11.53, Carluke; m., Amanda; 1 s.; 1 d. Educ. Lanark Grammar School; Edinburgh University. Lecturer, Glasgow University, 1985-88; Chef de Clinique, Unite de Chirurgie Hepatobiliare et Digestif, Villejuif, France, 1986-87; Senior Lecturer, Edinburgh University, 1988-97; Professor of Hepatobiliary Surgery, Edinburgh University, 1997-2000; Honorary Consultant Surgeon, Royal Infirmary of Edinburgh, since 1988; Director, Scottish Liver Transplant Unit, 1992-2005; President, Association of Upper G1 Surgeons of Great Britain and Ireland, 2002-04; Honorary Company Secretary, British Journal of Surgery Society Ltd., since 2003; Surgeon to the Queen in Scotland. Recreations: golf; ski-ing. Address: (b.) Clinical and Surgical Sciences (Surgery), Royal Infirmary of Edinburgh, 51 Little France Crescent, Edinburgh; T.-0131 242 3614.
E-mail: ojgarden@ed.ac.uk

Gardiner, Iain Derek, FRICS. Chartered Surveyor, since 1957; Senior Partner, Souter & Jaffrey, Chartered Surveyors, 1986-95; b. 22.12.33, Glasgow; m., Kathleen Elizabeth Johnson; 2 s.; 1 d. Educ. Hutcheson's Grammar School, Glasgow; Royal Technical College, Glasgow. Trainee and Assistant Quantity Surveyor, John H. Allan & Sons, Glasgow, 1950-57; National Service, Royal Engineers, 1957-59; Souter & Jaffrey, Inverness: Quantity Surveyor, 1959-63, Partner, 1963-86. Past Chairman, Royal Institution of Chartered Surveyors in Scotland; Chairman: Inverness Area, RICS in Scotland, 1969-70, Quantity Surveyors Committee, RICS in Scotland, 1989-90, Friends of Eden Court Theatre, 1981-82, Inverness Area Scout Council. Recreations: swimming; travel; cookery; Scouting. Address: (h.) 77 Stratherrick Road, Inverness IV2 4LL; T.-01463 235607.

Gardiner, John Ronald, BL, WS. Consultant, Brodies WS, Solicitors, 2001-04 (Senior Partner, 1992-2001, Partner, 1964-2001); b. 25.10.38, Rangoon; m., Aileen Mary Montgomery; 1 s.; 1 s. (deceased); 1 d. Educ. Fettes College; University of Edinburgh. Admitted Solicitor, 1963; admitted Writer to the Signet, 1964; Partner, Brodie Cuthbertson & Watson W.S. (thereafter Brodies W.S.),

1964; Notary Public, 1966-2007. Governor, Fettes Trust, 1986-96; Member, Rent Assessment Panel for Scotland, 1973-97; Hon. Secretary: Standing Council of Scottish Chiefs, 1970-72, Salmon and Trout Association (Scottish Branch), 1971-84. Recreations: fishing; shooting; golf; gardening. Address: (h.) 55 Fountainhall Road, Edinburgh EH9 2LH; T.-0131-667 5604.

Gardner, Angela Joy, BSc (Hons). Independent Public Affairs Consultant, AJ Enterprises, since 1994; b. 16.9.62, Wolverhampton; m., Andrew Ronald Gardner; 2 d. Educ. Codsall High School; UMIST. BP Chemicals Ltd., South Wales and Grangemouth, 1984-90; BP Schools Link Officer, 1985-90; Senior Public Affairs Officer, BP, 1990-94. Member, General Teaching Council for Scotland, 1990-98; Member, Scottish Examination Board, 1991-94; Honorary Member, The IDES Network; Member, Scottish Qualifications Authority Engineering Advisory Group, 1999-2003; Associate, Centre for Studies in Enterprise, Career Development and Work, Strathclyde University. Address: (h.) 72 Craigcrook Road, Edinburgh EH4 3PN; T.-0131-336 5164.

Gardner, Caroline Jane, MBA, CPFA. Deputy Auditor General, Audit Scotland, since 2000, Controller of Audit, since 2004; b. 1.5.63, London; m., Paul. Educ. University of Aston. Wolverhampton MBC, 1985-88; District Audit, 1988-92; Audit Commission, 1992-95; Accounts Commission, 1995-2000. Address: (b.) 110 George Street, Edinburgh EH2 4LH; T.-0131 625 1604.

Garland, Harry Mitchell, MBE, CQSW, FBIM. Chairman, Secretary of State's Advisory Committee on Scotland's Travelling People, since 1987; b. 7.7.28, Aberdeen; m., Phyllis Sandison; 1 s.; 1 d. Educ. Rockwell Academy, Dundee; Robert Gordon's College, Aberdeen; Moray House College, Edinburgh; Edinburgh University. Probation Officer/Senior Probation Officer/Principal Probation Officer, 1958-69; Depute Director of Social Work, Aberdeen and Kincardine Counties, 1969-73; Director of Social Work: Paisley Burgh, 1973-74, Western Isles, 1974-78, Central Region, 1978-86. Chairman, National Association of Probation Officers in Scotland, 1968-69; President, Association of Directors of Social Work, 1983; Member, Forth Valley Health Board, 1986-90. Recreations: voluntary work; church; golf; walking. Address: (h.) 7 Cromarty View, Nairn IV12 4HX; T.-01667 453684.

Garner, John Angus McVicar, MB, ChB, DRCOG, DCH, FRCGP. Principal in general practice, since 1980; British Medical Association: former Chairman, Scottish Council; Vice Chairman, Medical and Dental Defence Union of Scotland; BMA Pension Fund Trustee; Lead Assessor, General Medical Council; b. 4.9.50, London; m., Catherine Lizbeth; 1 s.; 1 d. Educ. Eltham College; Edinburgh University. Lothian Local Medical Committee: Secretary, 1986-89, Chairman, 1991-92; Member: General Medical Services Committee, since 1989, National Medical Advisory Committee, 1989-95; Past Chairman, Scottish General Medical Services Committee; former Treasurer, General Medical Services Defence Fund Ltd. Recreations: amphibians and photographing fungi. Address: (h.) Idabank, Pomathorn, Penicuik EH26 8PJ; T.-01968 677870; e-mail: johngarne@aol.com

Garrick, Sir Ronald, FEng, FRSE, DL. Deputy Chairman, HBOS, since 2003; Chairman, Weir Group, 1999-2002; b. 21.8.40; m.; 2 s.; 1 d. Managing Director and Chief Executive, Weir Group, 1982-99. Non-Executive Director: Bank of Scotland, 2000-01, HBOS, since 2001.

Garrod, Professor Simon Christopher, MA, PhD, FRSE. Professor of Cognitive Psychology, Glasgow University, since 1990; b. 19.11.47, London; 1 s.; 1 d. Educ. Bradfield College, Berks; Oxford University; Princeton University. Lecturer, Senior Lecturer, Reader in Psychology, Glasgow University, 1975-90; Visiting Research Fellow, Max Plank Institute, 1980; Residential Fellow, Netherlands Institute for Advanced Study, 1988. Publications: Understanding Written Language; Language Processing; Saying, Seeing and Acting. Recreations: fishing; hill-walking; sailing. Address: (b.) Department of Psychology, Glasgow University, 58 Hillhead Street, Glasgow G12 8QT; T.-0141-330 5033.

Gartland, Professor Kevan Michael Andrew, BSc (Hons), PhD. Dean of Life Sciences, Glasgow Caledonian University, since 2005; b. 15.10.60, Birmingham; m., Jill Susan Gartland; 1 d. Educ. St Philip's Grammar School, Edgbaston; Leeds University; Nottingham University. Research Assistant, Plant Genetic Manipulation Group, Nottingham University, 1982-85; British Technology Group Research Fellow, Plant Genetic Manipulation Group, 1985-86; Lecturer, Plant Molecular Biology, De Montfort University, Leicester, 1986-92; Special Lecturer, Biotechnology, Open Learning, Greenwich University, 1992-96; University of Abertay Dundee: Senior Lecturer, Plant Biotechnology, 1992-95; Leader, Biological Sciences Division, 1995 - 98; Associate Head, Molecular and Life Sciences, 1996-98; Division Leader, Molecular and Life Sciences, School of Science and Engineering, 1998-2005; Personal Chair, Biological Sciences, 1999. Founding Director, Abertay Centre for the Environment (ACE), 2002-05; Chair, Higher Education Academy, Biosciences Subject Centre Advisory Board; Member, Heads of University Biological Sciences Executive Committee, 1997-2004; Chair: Biochemical Society Education Committee, Composting Association Scotland; Member: Biochemical Society Executive Committee and Trustees, Board of Directors of Institute of Forest Biotechnology, North Carolina, USA; Director and Chief Executive, Glasgow Caledonian University Company Ltd. Recreations: country living; gentle walking; visiting interesting places. Address: (b.) School of Life Sciences, Glasgow Caledonian University, Glasgow G4 0BA; T.-0141-331-3120; e-mail: Kevan.Gartland@gcal.ac.uk

Garvie, John Henry, BSc (Hons), AdvDipEd. Rector, Dornoch Academy, since 1994; b. 9.3.48, Aberdeen; m., Fiona Margaret Clark; 2 s.; 1 d. Educ. Aberdeen Grammar School; Aberdeen University. Teacher, Nicolson Institute, Stornoway, 1971-74; Principal Teacher of Physics, Balfron High School, 1974-85; Depute Rector, Gairloch High School, 1985-94. Recreations: hill-walking; photography; crosswords. Address: (b.) Dornoch Academy, Evelix Road, Dornoch IV25 3HR; T.-01862 810246. E-mail: john.garvie@highland.gov.uk

Gass, David Thomas, MA, LLB, DipM, DipBA. Senior Director Operations, Scottish Enterprise Borders, since 2001; b. 5.11.65, Edinburgh; m., Jacque; 2 d. Educ. Kelvinside Academy; Edinburgh University. Brand Manager, Allied Breweries (Carlsberg Tetley), 1988-91; Development Officer, University of Aberdeen, 1991-93; Manager, Scottish Management Projects, 1993-96; Export Manager, Scottish Enterprise Edinburgh and Lothian, 1996-2000; Director, Enterprise Development, Scottish Enterprise Borders, 2000-01. Past Board Member, West Lothian and Borders College; responsibility nationally for Scottish Enterprise work in rural economic development, sustainable development and inclusion; Member, Forward Strategy for Scottish Agriculture Steering Group; Member, Scottish Textiles Forum. Recreations: all sports; travelling; history; reading; parenthood. Address: (b.) Bridge Street, Galashiels TD1 1SW; T.-01896 662008; e-mail: david.gass@scotent.co.uk

Gaston, Rev. Arthur Raymond Charles, MA, BD. Minister, St. Athernase Parish, Leuchars, 1998-2002; retired, 2002; b. 25.5.36, Atherstone; m., Evelyn Wilson Mather; 1 s.; 2 d. Educ. The Gordon Schools, Huntly; Aberdeen University. Teacher of Mathematics, 1961-62; Principal of theological college in Madagascar, 1962-67; Missionary with London Missionary Society, 1967-69; Minister, Sauchie Parish Church, 1969-75, Dollar with Muckhart with Glendevon, 1975-89, Scottish Church, Knox's Chapel, Geneva, 1989-93; Secretary for Staffing, Board of World Mission, Church of Scotland, 1993-98; Secretary, Presbytery of Europe, since 1997. Recreations: water colour painting; walking; choral singing; wildlife. Address: (h.) 13 Manse Road, Dollar FK14 7AL; T.-01259 743202.

Gavin, Anthony John, CBE, KHS, Dr he, BSc, DipEd, FRSA. Head Teacher, St. Margaret's Academy, Livingston, 1993-2002; b. 11.10.41, Perth; m., Charlotte Duffy; 2 d. Educ. Perth Academy; St. Andrews University. Teacher, St. Andrew's High School, Kirkcaldy, 1964-71; Principal Teacher/Assistant Headteacher, St. David's High School, Dalkeith, 1971-77; Depute Headteacher, St. Augustine's High School, Edinburgh, 1977-79; Headteacher, St. Saviour's High School, Dundee, 1979-93; TVEI Adviser Scotland, 1986-90. Member, Scottish Community Education Council, 1993-96; Chair, Catholic Headteachers' Association of Scotland, 1994-96; Member, Strategy Group, Higher Still Development Programme Scotland, 1996-2000; former Vice-Chairman of Court and Finance Convener, University of Edinburgh; Member, Board of Catholic Education, Glasgow University, 1999; Director, St. Mary's Music School, Edinburgh; Member, Children's Services Committee, Fife Council. Recreations: music; golf. Address: (h.) 5 Colinton Court, Glenrothes KY6 3PE; T.-01592 743462.

Gavin, Derek, FRICS, DipLED. Chartered Surveyor, since 1971; Executive Director, Stirling Enterprise Park and Stirling Enterprise, since 1984; b. 12.12.46, Perth; m., Terry; 1 s. Educ. Perth Academy; College of Estate Management. Trainee Surveyor, Bell Ingram, Perth, 1964-69; Management Surveyor, Scottish Industrial Estates Corporation, Glasgow, 1969-72; Valuation Surveyor, Bell Ingram, Perth, 1972-77; Estates Property Manager, Central Regional Council, 1977-84. Recreations: golf; reading. Address: (b.) John Player Building, Players Road, Stirling; T.-01786 463416; e-mail: dgavin@stirling-enterprise.co.uk; derekgavin@aol.com

Geates, John, BSc (Hons). Director, Scottish Police College, since 2007; b. 15.08.62; m., Gillian. Joined Strathclyde Police in 1981; promoted Assistant Chief Constable, then Deputy Director of the Scottish Police College in 2006. Address: (b.) Tulliallan Castle, Kincardine FK10 4BE; T.-01259 732000.

Gebbie, George C., LLB (Hons). Advocate, since 1987; b. 27.1.58, Motherwell; m., Anne Gebbie-Oiben; 1 s.; 1 d. Educ. Dalziel High School, Motherwell; Aberdeen University. Legal apprentice to Crown Agent, 1979-81; Procurator Fiscal Depute, Glasgow, 1981-83; Solicitor in private practice, Glasgow, 1983-87. SNP candidate, East Kilbride, 1997 General Election. Recreation: socialising with friends. Address: (b.) Advocates' Library, Edinburgh, EH1 1RF; T.-0131-226 5071.

Geddes, Keith, CBE. Policy Director, Pagoda Public Relations, since 1999; b. 8.8.52, Selkirk. Educ. Galashiels Academy; Edinburgh University; Heriot Watt

University. Housing Rights Worker, Shelter, 1977-84; Chair, Lothian Region Education Committee, 1987-90; Leader, Lothian Regional Council, 1990-96; Past President, Convention of Scottish Local Authorities; Leader, City of Edinburgh Council, 1996-99. Deputy Chair, Scottish Natural Heritage; Board Member, Accounts Commission, Chair, Greenspace Scotland. Recreations: golf; cricket; hill-walking. Address: (h.) 7 Howard Street, Edinburgh EH3 5JP; T.-0131-624 2365.

Gemmell, Professor Curtis Glen, BSc, PhD, MIBiol, FRCPath. Professor of Microbial Infection, Medical School, University of St. Andrews; Honorary Senior Research Fellow, Division of Immunology, Infection and Inflammation, Glasgow University; Visiting Professor, University of Strathclyde; Honorary Bacteriologist, Greater Glasgow Health Board; Director, In Vivo Simulations Ltd; b. 26.8.41, Beith, Ayrshire; m., Anne Margaret; 2 d. Educ. Speir's School, Beith; Glasgow University. Glasgow University: Assistant Lecturer, 1966-68, Lecturer, 1968-69; Paisley College of Technology: Lecturer, 1969-71, Senior Lecturer, 1971-76; Glasgow University: Senior Lecturer, 1976-90, Reader, 1990-2000; Visiting Associate Professor, University of Minnesota, Minneapolis, 1979-80. Recreations: gardening; golf. Address: (h.) Sunninghill, 19 Lawmarnock Crescent, Bridge of Weir PA11 3AS; T.-Bridge of Weir 613350.

Gemmell, Rev. David Rankin, MA, BD. Minister, Ayr Auld Kirk, since 1999; b. 27.2.63, Girvan; m., Helen; 1 s.; 1 d. Educ. Carrick Academy; University of Glasgow. Assistant Minister, Girvan North Church, 1990-91; Minister, Fenwick Parish Church, 1991-99. Chaplain to Ayr Academy, Kyle Academy, Holmston Primary; Convener, South Ayrshire Council Standards and Ethics Committee; School Board, Ayr Academy; Trustee, McLaurin Gallery. Recreations: ex SRU rugby referee; single figure handicap golfer. Address: (h.) 58 Monument Road, Ayr KA7 2UB; T.-01292 262580; e-mail: drgemmell@hotmail.com

Gemmell, Gavin John Norman, CBE, CA. Chairman: Archangel Informal Investments, Gyneideas Ltd.; Director, Scottish Widows Group; b. 7.9.41, Edinburgh; m., Kathleen Fiona Drysdale; 1 s.; 2 d. Educ. George Watson's College. Qualified CA, 1964; joined Baillie, Gifford & Co., 1964; retired as Senior Partner, 2001; Chairman, Standing Committee, Scottish Episcopal Church, 1997-2002; Trustee, National Galleries of Scotland, 1999-2007; Chairman, Court, Heriot Watt University, since 2002. Recreations: golf; foreign travel. Address: (h.) 14 Midmar Gardens, Edinburgh EH10 6DZ; T.-0131-466 6367.
E-mail: gavingemmell@blueyonder.co.uk

Gemmell, Dr. (James) Campbell, BSc (Hons), PhD. Chief Executive, Scottish Environment Protection Agency, since 2003; b. 24.1.59, Stirling; m., Avril Gold. Educ. Stirling High School; Aberdeen University. Resident Lecturer in Glaciology, Christ Church, Oxford, 1985-89; Executive, Scottish Development Agency, 1988-90; Senior Consultant, Ecotec Research and Consulting Ltd., 1990-91; Policy Manager, then Strategist, Scottish Enterprise, 1991-94; Chief Executive, Central Scotland Countryside Trust, 1994-2001; Director of Strategic Planning, SEPA, 2001-03. Chairman, Dounreay Particles Advisory Group, 2001-03; Member, Minister's Rural Focus Group, Scottish Office, 2001-03; Member, Minister's Rural Focus Group, Scottish Office, 1992-96; Chairman, Landwise and Board Member, Wise Group. Honorary Professor, Glasgow University. Recreations: walks with our collie; eating fine seafood and drinking fine wine. Address: (b.) SEPA, Erskine Court, Castle Business Park, Stirling FK9 4TR; T.-01786-457700; e-mail: campbell.gemmell@sepa.org.uk

Gemmell, William Ruthven, LLB, WS. Partner, Murray Beith Murray WS; Chief Executive, Murray Asset

Management Limited; b. 4.4.57; m., Fiona Elizabeth Watson; 1 s.; 1 d. Educ. Loretto; Edinburgh University (Law); Aberdeen University (Accountancy). Murray Beith Murray WS, since 1985; Law Society of Scotland: President, 2006-07, Vice President, 2005-06; Financial Services Tribunal, 1993-2002, Financial Services Authority Small Business Practitioner Panel, 1999-2007 (Chairman, 2004-06); Financial Services Practitioner Panel, 2004-06; Financial Services and Markets Tribunal, since 2001; VAT and Duties Tribunal, since 2002; Pensions Review Tribunal, since 2005; Claims Management Services Tribunal, since 2006. Address: (b.) 39 Castle Street, Edinburgh EH2 3BH; T.-0131 225 1200.
E-mail: ruthven.gemmell@murraybeith.co.uk

Gemmill, Robert, MA, DUniv(Glas); b. 20.2.30; m., 1, Anne MacMurchy Gow (deceased); 2, Elisabeth Mary MacLennan; 2 s.; 1 d. Educ. High School of Glasgow; Glasgow University. Manufacturing management, Procter & Gamble Ltd., 1953-56; Management Consultant, PA Management Consultants Ltd., 1956-85. Member, Business Committee, General Council, Glasgow University, 1987-98, Assessor of the General Council on the University Court, 1990-98, and Co-opted Court Member, 1998-2001. Played rugby football for Glasgow High School FP, Northumberland, Cheshire, Barbarians and Scotland (1950 and 1951). Recreations: golf; travel; music. Address: (h.) 123 Fotheringay Road, Glasgow G41 4LG; T.-0141-423 1860.

George, Professor William David, MB, BS, FRCS, MS. Regius Professor of Surgery, Glasgow University, since 1981; b. 22.3.43, Reading; 1 s.; 3 d. Educ. Henley Grammar School; London University. Lecturer in Surgery, Manchester University, 1973-77; Senior Lecturer in Surgery, Liverpool University, 1977-81. Member, National Committees, British Association of Surgical Oncology and Surgical Research Society. Recreations: veteran rowing; golf. Address: (b.) University Department of Surgery, Western Infirmary, Glasgow G11 6NT; T.-0141-211 2166.

Geraghty, Professor Christine, BA (History and American Studies), MA (American Literature). Professor of Film and Television, University of Glasgow, since 2002; b. 27.5.48, London; m., Paul Marks, OBE. Educ. Convent of Sacred Heart, Hammersmith; University of Hull; Keele University. Administrative Officer, Local Government, 1972-78; full time administrator and national negotiator for NALGO in local government and health service, 1978-93; Senior Lecturer and Head of Department, Goldsmiths College, University of London, 1993-2002; University of Glasgow: Chair in Film and Television, since 2002, Director, Centre for Screen Studies, since 2003. Chairperson of Media, Communications and Cultural Studies Association. Publications include: Women and Soap Opera, 1991, 1992 and 1999; The Television Studies Book, 1998 (Co-Editor); British Cinema in the Fifties: Gender, Genre and the 'New Look', 2000; My Beautiful Laundrette, 2004 (now a major motion picture, 2008); Editor, Journal of British Cinema and Television; International Journal Media and Cultural Politics. Member of Editorial Advisory Board of Screen. Address: (b.) Department of Theatre, Film and Television Studies, University of Glasgow, 9 University Avenue, Glasgow G12 8QQ; T.-0141 330 3809; e-mail: c.geraghty@tfts.arts.gla.ac.uk

Gerstenberg, Frank Eric, MA (Cantab), PGCE. Principal, George Watson's College, Edinburgh, 1985-2001; b. 23.2.41, Balfron; m., Valerie MacLellan; 1 s.; 2 d. Educ. Trinity College, Glenalmond; Clare College, Cambridge;

London University. Assistant Master, Kelly College, Tavistock, 1963-67; Housemaster and Head of History, Millfield School, 1967-74; Headmaster, Oswestry School, 1974-85. Chairman of Governing Council, Glenalmond College. Recreations: skiing; sailing; travelling; music; journalism. Address: (h.) Craigmore, Whim Road, Gullane EH31 2BD; T.-01620 842805; e-mail: f.e.g@btinternet.com

Gibb, George Frederick Cullen, MA, LLB. Consultant to Messrs Marshall Wilson, Solicitors, Falkirk, since 1997; Honorary Sheriff at Falkirk, since 1987; b. 19.3.33, Edinburgh; m., Inga Mary Grieve; 1 s.; 2 d. Educ. George Heriot's School, Edinburgh; Edinburgh University. Messrs Marshall Wilson, Solicitors: Partner, 1964, Senior Partner, 1990. Recreations: golf; music; bowls; reading. Address: (h.) 17 Shirra's Brae Road, Stirling FK7 0AY; T.-01786 463235; e-mail: george@gibb43.freeserve.co.uk

Gibbs, Professor Robert, BA. Professor of Pre-Humanist Art History, University of Glasgow, since 2006; b. 02.07.46, London. Educ. Ealing Grammar School for Boys; Courtauld Institute, University of London. Research Assistant to Sir Nicolas Pevsner for The Buildings of England: Dorset, Birkbeck College, University of London, 1968-69; University of Glasgow: Lecturer, then Senior Lecturer, from 1991, then Reader, 2001-06, Department of History of Art. Publications: Iluminating the Law: Medieval Legal Manuscripts in Cambridge Collections (Co-Author), 2001; The Development of the Illustration of Legal Manuscripts by Bolognese Illuminators between 1250 and 1298, Juristische Buchproduktion im Mittelalter, 1998; Landscape as Property: Bolognese Law Manuscripts and the Development of Landscape Painting, Atti del Congresso della Societa di Storia della Miniatura, 1992; Rivista di Storia della Miniatura, 1998; L'Occhio di Tomaso, Treviso, 1981; Tomaso da Modena: Painting in Emilia and the March of Treviso, 1340-80, 1989; In search of Ambrogio Lorenzetti's Allegory of Justice in the Good Commune, 1999; also written on 19th century design. Recreations: music of all genres except 'Light Music'; popular science and evolution. Address: (b.) Department of History of Art, University of Glasgow, Glasgow G12 8QQ; T.-0141 330 5677; e-mail: r.gibbs@art.hist.arts.gla.ac.uk

Gibbs, Stephen Cokayne, OBE; b. 18.7.29, Hertingfordbury, England; m., Lavinia Bacon; 2 s.; 1 d. Educ. Eton College. Served with KRRC (60th Rifles), 1947-49; TA, service with QVR (TA), 1951-63: Lt., 1951, Captain, 1956, Major, 1958; Port Line Ltd., 1949-62: Assistant Manager, 1957, London Manager, 1959; Charles Barker PLC, 1962-87: Director, 1962, Deputy Chairman, 1982-87. Director, Swallow Group PLC, 1970-99; National Trust for Scotland: Member, Executive, 1986-2000 and Council, 1991-96; Member: TUCC for Scotland, 1992-97, Deer Commission for Scotland, 1993-2000; Chairman: Association of Deer Management Groups, 1994-2005, Isle of Arran District Salmon Fishery Board, since 1990. Recreations: shooting; fishing. Address: The Estate Office, Dougarie, Isle of Arran KA27 8EB; T.-01770 840259.

Gibby, Mary, BSc, PhD, FRSE. Director of Science, Royal Botanic Garden Edinburgh, since 2000; Member, Scientific Advisory Committee, Scottish Natural Heritage, since 2001; Honorary Professor, University of Edinburgh; b. Doncaster; 1 d. Educ. Leeds University; Liverpool University. British Museum (Natural History), 1974-2000; research scientist specialising in plant cytogenetics, molecular biology research, cryptogamic plant research; Deputy Keeper of Botany. Member, Advisory Committee, Chelsea Physic Garden. Recreations: hill-walking; canals; narrow boats. Address: (b.) Royal Botanic Garden Edinburgh, 20A Inverleith Row, Edinburgh EH3 5LR; T.-0131 248 2973; e-mail: m.gibby@rbge.org.uk

Gibson, Alexander John Michael, CBE. Chairman, Macaulay Land Use Research Institute, since 2006; Chairman, Scottish Salmon Producers Organisation, since 2006; b. 6.6.52, Glasgow; m., Susan Clare Bowser; 1 s.; 1 d. Educ. Gordonstoun. President, Highland Cattle Society, 1986-88; Scottish Landowners Federation, 1996-2002; Chair: Highland Region, 1996-99, Agricultural Committee, 1995-2000 (Vice Convenor, 2000-02); Founder Board Member, Food Standards Agency, 2000-06; Member, Meat Hygiene Advisory Committee, 2001-04; Chair, Scottish Food Advisory Committee, 2002-06. Fieldsman, Highland Cattle Society, since 1978; Scottish Food Champion, 2001-04; Member, Scottish Food & Health Council, since 2005. Recreations: field sports; skiing; walking; sailing; cattle breeding. Address: Edinvale, Dallas, Moray IV36 2RW; T.-01343 890 265; e-mail: edinvale@lineone.net

Gibson, Edgar Matheson, MBE, TD, DL, DA. Vice Lord Lieutenant, Orkney, since 2007; Deputy Lieutenant, Orkney, 1976-2007; Honorary Sheriff, Grampian, Highlands and Islands, since 1992; full-time professional artist since 1990; b. 1.11.34, Kirkwall; m., Jean McCarrick; 2 s.; 2 d. Educ. Kirkwall Grammar School; Gray's College of Art, Aberdeen. National Service, 1958-60; TA and TAVR service to 1985 with Lovat Scouts, reaching Lt. Col.; Battalion Second in Command, 2/51 Highland Volunteers, 1973-76; Joint Services Liaison Officer for Orkney, 1980-85; Cadet Commandant, Orkney Lovat Scouts ACF, 1979-86, Honorary Colonel, 1986-2004; Member, Orkney Health Board, 1991-99; Chairman, Italian Chapel Preservation Committee, since 2006; Hon. President: Society of Friends of St. Magnus Cathedral, since 1994, Orkney Craftsmen's Guild, 1997-2002 (Chairman, 1962-82); President, Orkney Branch, SSFA and FHS, since 1997 (Chairman, 1990-97); Chairman: St. Magnus Cathedral Fair Committee, 1982-2004, Northern Area, Highland TA&VR Association, 1987-93. Recreation: whisky tasting. Address: (h.) Transcona, New Scapa Road, Kirkwall, Orkney; T.-0185687 2849.

Gibson, J.N. Alastair, MD, FRCS(Edin), FRCS(Orth). Consultant Spinal Surgeon, Lothian University Hospitals, since 1993; Senior Lecturer (part-time), University of Edinburgh, since 1993; b. 21.10.54, Bellshill; m., Laurie-Ann; 2 s.; 1 d. Educ. King Edward VII Grammar School, Sheffield; Royal London Hospital Medical College, London. House Surgeon, London Hospital, 1978-79; Surgical Registrar, Ninewells Hospital, Dundee, 1981-83; Clinical Research Fellow, University of Dundee, 1984-86; University of Edinburgh: Lecturer, 1986-91, Senior Lecturer, 1993-97; Spinal Fellow, Royal North Shore Hospital, Sydney, 1992; Visiting Scholar, University of Sydney, 1992; Visiting Surgeon, Spire Murrayfield Hospital, Edinburgh, since 1998. Publications: contributor to books and professional journals; Patent: cervical disc replacement prosthesis. Recreations: golf; Vice President, Thistle LTC. Address: Department of Orthopaedic Surgery, The New Royal Infirmary of Edinburgh, Little France, Edinburgh EH16 4SU; T.-0131-242-3471; e-mail: alistair.gibson@luht.nhs.scot.uk

Gibson, Rev. James McAlpine, TD, LTh. Minister, Bothwell Parish Church, since 1989; Minister of Religion (Church of Scotland), since 1977; b. 31.3.48, Edinburgh; m., Doreen Margaret (McCracken); 1 s.; 1 d. Educ. Daniel Stewart's College, Edinburgh; University of Glasgow. Assistant Minister, Paisley Abbey, 1977-78; Minister, Grangemouth Old Parish Church, 1978-89; Territorial Army Chaplain (Royal Army Chaplains Dept.) mobilised for Gulf War (1991) and Operational Tour in

Bosnia/Croatia (1999-2000), 1986-2004; Moderator of The Presbytery of Hamilton, 2004-05; appointed Chaplain in Ordinary to HM The Queen in Scotland and installed as Member of The Chapel Royal in Scotland, 2004. Awarded The Territorial Decoration, 2001; Convener of The Board of National Mission of The General Assembly of The Church of Scotland, 2000-04; Convener of Committee on Chaplains to HM Forces for Church of Scotland, since 2006. Recreations: family; travel; theatre; music. Address: (h.) 4 Manse Avenue, Bothwell, Glasgow G71 8PQ; T.- 01698 853189; e-mail: jamesmgibson@msn.com

Gibson, Joan, LTCL (FL), LTCL (Tchr), CertEd, AdvDipEd, CAPSE. Chief Executive, National Youth Choir of Scotland, since 2007; b. Liverpool; m., Martin Gibson; 2 d. Educ. Trinity College of Music, London; University of Central England; Bristol University. Music Teacher and Flute Teacher in variety of schools leading to Head of St. Katharines, Fife and then Headmistress of Cranford House School, Oxfordshire; latterly a Business Advisor in Lanarkshire. School Inspector for ISI, 2001-05. Recreations: choral singing; travelling. Address: (b.) The Mitchell, North Street, Glasgow G3 7DN; T.-0141 287 2856; e-mail: joan.gibson@nycos.co.uk

Gibson, John Alan, MB, ChB, MD, FRCGP, FRSMed, DRCOG, FRPSEd, CBiol, PhD, MIBiol, FLS, FZS, FRGS, FRMS, FGS, FSA (Scot). President, Royal Physical Society of Edinburgh, since 2002; Senior Honorary Secretary, British Medical Association, since 1977; Chairman, Scottish Natural History Library and Editor, the Scottish Naturalist, since 1972; b. 15.5.26, Kilbarchan; m., Dr. Mary M. Baxter; 1 d. Educ. Lindisfarne School; Paisley Grammar School; Glasgow University. Family Doctor, village of Kilbarchan; Hon. Secretary, Renfrewshire Division, BMA, 1957-2006; last Secretary, Renfrewshire Local Medical Committee; first Secretary, Argyll and Clyde Area Medical Committee; Member, Central Council, Central Ethical Committee, Scottish Council and Scottish GMS Committee, BMA; Past President, West of Scotland Branch, BMA; Hon. President, Renfrewshire Division, BMA; Fellow, Royal Society of Medicine; Life Fellow, Royal College of General Practitioners; Life Fellow, BMA; formerly Senior Demonstrator of Comparative Anatomy, University of Glasgow; Scottish Representative and Vice-President, Society for the Bibliography of Natural History; Scientific Meetings Secretary, Vice-President and Hon. Member, Society for the History of Natural History; Hon. President, Friends of Glasgow University Library; Chairman, Scottish Natural History Trust; Past Chairman, Clyde Area Branch, Scottish Wildlife Trust; Chairman, Clyde Area Biological Records Centre; President, Renfrewshire Natural History Society; Vice-Chairman, Clyde Estuary Amenity Council; Consultant, Scottish Tourist Board; Secretary and Honorary Life Member, Scottish Society for the Protection of Birds; Scientific Fellow, Zoological Society of London; Life Fellow: RSPB, Royal Zoological Society of Scotland, Royal Geographical Society, Institute of Biology, British Association; Chairman: Clyde Bird Club, Clyde Mammal Group, Clyde Reptile and Amphibian Group; Honorary President, Kintyre Bird Club; Past Secretary and Life Fellow, Royal Physical Society of Edinburgh; Life Member, British Ornithologists' Union; Gold Medal, Scottish Society for the Protection of Birds, 1967; Queen's Silver Jubilee Medal, 1977; Fellowship, BMA, 1982; Gold Medal, Royal Physical Society, 2002. Publications: Mammals of West of Scotland; Birds of Clyde Area; Reptiles and Amphibians of Clyde Area, Atlas of Clyde Vertebrates; Regional Bibliography of West of Scotland Vertebrates; Bibliography of Scottish Vertebrate Zoology; 400 scientific papers, books and reports on Scottish natural history, 1939-2007. Recreations: natural history; golf (Royal Troon). Address: (h.) Foremount House, Kilbarchan, Renfrewshire PA10 2EZ; T.-01505 702419.

Gibson, Kenneth. MSP (SNP), Cunninghame North, since 2007; b. 8.9.61, Paisley. Address: (b.) Scottish Parliament, Edinburgh EH99 1SP.

Gibson, Martin Francis, OBE, DL. Chief Executive, Erskine, since 1995; b. 21.10.46, Edinburgh; m., Lesley; 1 s.; 1 d. Educ. Fettes College; Royal Military Academy, Sandhurst. Address: (b.) Erskine, Bishopton PA7 5PU; T.-0141-814 4508; Fax: 0141 812 3733; e-mail: martin.gibson@erskine.org.uk

Gibson, Robert McKay, MA (Hons). MSP (SNP), Highland and Islands, since 2003; b. 16.10.45, Glasgow; divorced. Educ. High School of Glasgow; University of Dundee. Executive Officer, Civil Service, 1965-68; Teacher (geography and modern studies), 1973-74; Assistant Principal Teacher, Guidance, 1974-77; Principal Teacher, Guidance, 1977-95; writer and musician, since 1995. Recreations: organic gardening; hill-walking; traditional music. Address: (h.) Tir nan Oran, 8 Culcairn Road, Evanton, Ross-shire IV16 9YT; T.-01349 830388; e-mail:rob.gibson.msp@scottish.parliament.uk

Gibson, Sheriff William Erle, BA, LLB. Sheriff at Hamilton, 1989-2007; b. 30.8.34, Glasgow; m., Anne; 1 s.; 2 d. Educ. Dollar Academy; Trinity Hall, Cambridge; Glasgow University. Solicitor in Glasgow, 1961-89; Clerk to General Commissioners of Taxes, City of Glasgow, 1968-89; Clerk to General Council, Glasgow University, 1976-86. Recreations: golf; fly fishing; piping; hill-walking; the family.

Gifford, Professor Paul Peerless Dennis, MA, DesL. Buchanan Professor of French, St Andrews University, since 1987; b. 23.4.44; m., Irma Cynthia Mary Warwick; 1 s.; 2 d. Educ. Wolverhampton Grammar School; King Edward VI School, Norwich; Trinity Hall, Cambridge. University of Toulouse, 1968-72 and 1983-85; University of Ulster, 1972-83 and 1985-87. Publications: Paul Valery: Le Dialogue des Choses Divines, 1989; Reading Paul Valery: Universe in Mind, 1999; Faith, Identity and the Common Era, 2001; Love, Desire and Transcendence in French Literature: Deciphering Eros, 2006; La Creation en acte, 2006. Recreations: skiing; sailing; wine-tasting. Address: (h.) 51 Radernie Place, St Andrews KY16 8QR; T.-01334 477243.

Gifford, Professor Thomas Douglas MacPharlain, MA, PhD, FRSE. Emeritus Professor and Senior Research Fellow, University of Glasgow; Honorary Librarian of Abbotsford (Walter Scott's Library), since 1993; b. 14.7.40; m., Anne Tait Gifford; 3 d. Educ. Hillhead High School; University of Glasgow; Baliol College, University of Oxford. Lecturer then Senior Lecturer, University of Strathclyde, 1967-86; University of Glasgow: Senior Lecturer, 1986, Reader, 1990, Professor and Chair of Scottish Literature, 1995. Publications: James Hogg; Neil Gunn and Lewis Grassic Gibbon; History of Scottish Literature – The Nineteenth Century (Editor), 1988; History of Scottish Women's Writing (Co-editor) 1998; Scottish Literature in English and Scots (Co-editor), 2002. Address: (h.) 9 Shielhill, Ayr KA7 4SY; T.-01292 443360.

Gilbert, Colin. Joint Managing Director, The Comedy Unit, since 1996; b. 3.4.52, Glasgow; m., Joanna; 1 s.; 1 d. Educ. St. Paul's School, Barnes; University of York. BBC Scotland: Assistant Floor Manager, 1975-79, Production Manager, 1979-80; Script Editor, Not The Nine O'Clock News, 1980-82; Head of Comedy, BBC Scotland, 1983-95; Production credits include: Naked Video, Rab C. Nesbitt,

Chewin' the Fat, City Lights, Still Game. RTS Reith Award for Services to Broadcasting; BAFTA Scotland Award for Outstanding Contribution to Film and TV Production; RTS Best Sit-Com Award (Rab C. Nesbitt). Address: The Comedy Unit, 6th Floor, 53 Bothwell Street, Glasgow G2 6TS; T.-0141-220 6400.
E-mail: colingilbert@comedyunit.co.uk

Gilbert, George, DA, RSW. Painter; Partner, Courtyard Gallery, 1994-2001; b. 12.9.39, Glasgow; m., Lesley Johnston; 3 s. Educ. Victoria Drive Secondary School, Glasgow; Glasgow School of Art. Teacher of Art, Aberdeenshire, Glasgow, Fife, 1963-89; painter (exhibited widely), since 1963. Elected: RSW, 1973 (Council Member, 1994-98); SAAC, 1991, PAI, 1992. Artstore Award, 1992; Gillies Award (RSW), 1993; RSPSG Award (RGI), 2006; Strathearn Award (RGI), 2007; RSW Council Award, 2007. Recreations: walking; reading; music; the arts. Address: 3 Osborne Terrace, Crail, Fife KY10 3RR.

Giles, Cecilia Elspeth, CBE, MA. Member, Rail Users Consultative Committee for Scotland, 1989-97; b. Dumfries. Educ. Queen Margaret's School, Yorkshire; Edinburgh University. Administrative staff, Khartoum University, 1956-57; joined Administrative staff, Edinburgh University, 1957; Assistant Secretary, Edinburgh University, 1972-87; Committee of Vice-Chancellors and Principals' Administrative Training Officer (seconded part-time), 1983-85. President, Edinburgh University Graduates' Association, 1989-91, Member, Executive Committee and Editorial Committee, since 1987, Hon. President, since 2004; Member, Business Committee, General Council, Edinburgh University, 1988-93, Convener, Constitutional Sub-Committee, 1991-93; Member, Church of Scotland Board of Stewardship and Finance, 1986-93, Vice Convener 1990-93; Member, Church of Scotland Assembly Council, 1993-96. Publication: Scotland for the Tourist (Co-author). Recreations: entertaining friends, family and godchildren; theatre. Address: (b.) Graduates' Association, 24 Buccleuch Place, Edinburgh EH8 9LN.

Gill, Rt. Hon. Lord (Brian Gill), MA, LLB, PhD, Hon. LLD (Glas), Hon.LLD (Strathclyde), Hon.LLD (St. Andrews), Hon.LLD (Edinburgh), Hon D.Acad. (RSAMD), FRSE, FRSAMD. Senator of the College of Justice in Scotland, since 1994; Lord Justice Clerk, since 2001; Chairman, Scottish Civil Courts Review, since 2007; Vice President and former Chairman, Royal Scottish Academy of Music and Drama; b. 25.2.42; m.; 5 s.; 1 d. Educ. St. Aloysius College; Glasgow University; Edinburgh University. Advocate, 1967; Advocate-Depute, 1977-79; Standing Junior Counsel: Foreign and Commonwealth Office (Scotland), 1974-77, Home Office (Scotland), 1979-81, Scottish Education Department, 1979-81; QC, 1981; called to the Bar, Lincoln's Inn, 1991; Bencher, 2002. Keeper, Advocates' Library, 1987-94; Chairman, Scottish Law Commission, 1996-2001. Address: (b.) Court of Session, Parliament House, Parliament Square, Edinburgh, EH1 1RQ.

Gill, Professor Evelyn Margaret, FRSE, BSc, PhD, BA. Chief Scientific Adviser, Scottish Executive Environment and Rural Affairs Department and Professor of Integrated Land Use, University of Aberdeen, since 2006; b. 10.1.51, Edinburgh. Educ. Mary Erskine School for Girls; Edinburgh University; Massey University, New Zealand; Open University. Researcher, Forage Intake, AFRC Grassland Research Institute, 1976-89; Overseas Development Administration, 1979-81; Natural Resources Institute, Kent, 1989-96; Chief Executive, Natural Resources International Ltd., 1996-2000; Chief Executive and

Director of Research, Macaulay Land Use Research Institute, Aberdeen, 2000-06. Recreations: hill walking; skiing; reading. Address: (b.) Pentland House, 47 Robb's Loan, Edinburgh; T.-0131 244 6042; e-mail: m.gill@abdn.ac.uk

Gill, Kerry James Graham. Journalist; b. 29.4.47, Newcastle; m., Andrea Kevan; 2 d. Educ. Durham School; Warwick University. Westminster Press, 1969-71; Evening Post, 1971-72; The Journal, 1972-77; The Scotsman, 1977-87 (Reporter and Glasgow Editor); The Observer, 1979-87; The Times, 1987-93; Daily Record, 1994; Scottish Daily Express, since 1996 (Assistant Editor, Executive Editor, Editor, Editor Politics Policy and Comment). Recreations: modern French history; gardening; reading. Address: (h.) Spout Burn, Main Street, Fintry, Stirlingshire; T.-01360 860427.

Gill, Professor Roger William Thomas, BA (Hons), BPhil, MA, PhD, AFBPsS, FCIPD, FCIM, FRSA, CPsychol. Visiting Professor, Leadership Studies, University of Strathclyde Business School, since 1997; Director, Research Centre for Leadership Studies, The Leadership Trust, 1997-2005; b. 3.10.45, Cumbria; 1 s.; 1 d. Educ. Merchant Taylors' School, Crosby; St. Peter's College, Oxford; Liverpool University; Bradford University. English Electric, 1967-68; Inbucon/AIC Management Consultants, 1969-71; Personnel Manager, De La Rue, 1971-72; Manpower Manager, Associated Weavers, 1972-74; Lecturer, Bradford University Management Centre, 1974-78; Assistant Professor, State University of New York at Binghamton, 1979-82; Managing Director, Roger Gill & Associates, Singapore, 1982-90; Regional Manager (Asia), PA Consulting Group, Singapore, 1990-91; Professor of Business Administration (HRM/OB) and Director, Executive Development Programmes, University of Strathclyde Business School, 1992-96. Publications: three books, numerous articles and research reports. Recreations: music; theatre; food and wine; reading; doing nothing. Address: (h.) Craigmarloch Cottage, Kilmacolm PA13 4SG; T.-01505 874386; e-mail: RWTGill@aol.com

Gillan, David Stewart, BSc, MDiv, PhD. Minister, St. Michael's Parish Church, Linlithgow, since 2004; b. 1.10.58, Newfoundland, Canada; m., Sarah Ormerod; 1 d. Educ. Sydney Mines High School, Nova, Scotia; Universities of Edinburgh, Toronto and Mount Allison. Interim Minister, Morija Parish, Lesotho Evangelical Church, 1986-87; Minister, Village Main Parish, Johannesburg, South Africa, 1987-98 (including Alexandra, Tembisa, Katlehong and Atteridgeville); Researcher, Commission on the Restitution of Land Rights, Mpumalanga and Northern Province, South Africa, 1997-98; Executive Director, Churches Council on Theological Education in Canada, 1999-2004. Publication: Book edited, "Church, Land and Poverty", Johannesburg, 1998. Chairperson, Commission on Faith and Witness, Canadian Council of Churches; Lieutenant Governor's Medal, NS, 75. Recreations: writing; Celtic music; guitar (with Sarah, fiddle). Address: (h.) St. Michael's Manse, Kirkgate, Linlithgow, West Lothian EH49 7AL; T.-01506 842195; e-mail: stewart@stmichaels-parish.org.uk

Gillen, Cornelius, BSc, BA, MEd, PhD, FGS, CGeol. Director of Lifelong Learning, Edinburgh University, since 2000; b. 21.5.47, Greenock; m., Patricia Maureen Lynch; 2 d. Educ. St. Columba's High School, Greenock; Glasgow University. High School Teacher, Greenock, 1971-74; Civil Engineering Lecturer, Paisley College, 1974-77; Geology Lecturer, University College Dublin, 1977-80; Adult Education Lecturer, Aberdeen University, 1980-90;

Senior Lecturer, Continuing Education, Edinburgh University, 1990-2000. Publications: Geology and Landscapes of Scotland, 2003. Recreations: athletics; classical music; learning languages; guitar. Address: (b.) Office of Lifelong Learning, Edinburgh University, 11 Buccleuch Place, Edinburgh EH8 9LW; T.-0131-651-1177; e-mail: c.gillen@ed.ac.uk

Gillespie, Professor Thomas Alastair, BA, PhD, FRSE. Professor of Mathematical Analysis, University of Edinburgh, since 1997; b. 15.2.45, Torrance; m., Judith Anne Nelmes; 2 s.; 1 d. Educ. Glasgow Academy; University of Cambridge; University of Edinburgh. Lecturer, 1968-87, Senior Lecturer, 1987-92, Reader in Mathematics, 1992-97, University of Edinburgh; Visiting Professor, Indiana University, 1973-74, 1983-84. Recreations: gardening; making music; jogging. Address: (b.) School of Mathematics, James Clerk Maxwell Building, Edinburgh EH9 3JZ; T.-0131-650 5081.

Gillies, Anne Lorne, MA, PhD, PGCE, LRAM, Drhc. Singer and Writer, since 1962; Partner, Brigh Productions; b. 21.10.44, Stirling; 1 s.; 2 d. Educ. Oban High School; Edinburgh University; London University; Jordanhill College of Education; Glasgow University. Singer: TV, radio, concert, recital, theatre, recording; writer: scripts, children's books, novels, articles, autobiography, songs; education/community development: teacher, resource development; National Education Officer, Comunn na Gaidhlig, 1988-90, Arts Development Officer, Govan Initiative Ltd., 1991-93; Producer and Writer, Scottish Television 1993-95; Lecturer in Gaelic, University of Strathclyde, 1995-98; Partner, Brigh Productions, since 2000. Awarded Rotary's Paul Harris Fellowship, 2003; Elected Speaker of Year 2005 by Association Speakers' Clubs of Great Britain. Recreation: married bliss. Address: (h.) 33 Stewarton Road, Dunlop, Ayrshire KA3 4DQ; e-mail: anne@brigh.co.uk

Gillies, Crawford Scott, LLB, ACA, MBA. Chairman, Control Risks Group Ltd., since 2006; Director, Standard Life PLC, since 2007; b. 05.56, Scotland; m., Alison; 3 s. Educ. Perth Academy; Edinburgh University. Bain and Company, since 1983; Touch Emas Ltd., since 2006; Hammonds, since 2005. Trustee of Saltire Foundation. Recreation: trees. Address: 101 George Street, Edinburgh EH2 3ES; T.-0131 226 6997. E-mail: cg@crawfordgillies.co.uk

Gillies, Norman Neil Nicolson, OBE, BA, Dr.hc (Aberdeen), MIMgt, FRSA. Director, Sabhal Mor Ostaig, since 1988; b. 1.3.47, Flodigarry, Isle of Skye; m., Jean Brown Nixon; 1 s.; 2 d. Educ. Portree High School; Strathclyde University; Open University. College Secretary, Sabhal Mor Ostaig, 1983-88; Director: Skye and Lochalsh Enterprise Ltd., 1990-99, Sabhal Mor Ostaig (Developments) Ltd., Canan Ltd., Ionad Chaluim Chille, Ile; Member: Leirsinn Research Centre; Ionad Naiseanta na h-Imrich; UHI Millennium Institute Executive Board, Academic Council, Academic Standards and Quality Committee (Chair); Sorley MacLean Trust; Gaelic Television Training Trust; The Open University in Scotland Curriculum Development Working Group; Chief, Gaelic Society of Inverness, 2000; Honorary Professor in Contemporary Highland Studies, Aberdeen University, 2002. Recreations: reading; broadcasting; family. Address: (h.) Innis Ard, Ardvasar, Isle of Skye IV45 8RU; T.-01471 844 281.

Gillies, Rt. Rev. Robert Arthur, BD, PhD. Bishop of Aberdeen and Orkney, since 2007; b. 21.10.51, Cleethorpes; m., Elizabeth; 3 s. Educ. Barton-upon-Humber Grammar School; Edinburgh University; St. Andrews University. Medical Laboratory Technician, 1968-72; Curate: Christ Church, Falkirk, 1977-80, Christ Church Morningside, and Chaplain, Napier College, 1980-84; Chaplain, Dundee University, 1984-90. Hon. Lecturer, Department of Philosophy, Dundee University, 1985-95; Rector, St. Andrew's Episcopal Church, St. Andrews, 1991-2007. Publications: A Way for Healing, 1995; Informing Faith, 1996; Healing: Broader and Deeper, 1998; New Language of Faith, 2001; Where Earth and Heaven Meet, 2005; Sounds Before The Cross, 2007. Recreations: Scotland's mountains and England's canals. Address: Diocesan Office, 39 Kings Crescent, Aberdeen AB24 3HP; T.-01224 636653.

Gillies, Valerie, MA, MLitt, FSAScot. Poet; b. 4.6.48, Edmonton, Canada; m., William Gillies; 1 s.; 2 d. Educ. Edinburgh University; University of Mysore, S. India. Writer in Residence, Duncan of Jordanstone College of Art and Dundee District Libraries; Writer in Residence, East Lothian and Midlothian District Libraries; Writer in Residence, Edinburgh University; Senior Arts Worker (Hospital Arts), Artlink; Creative Scotland Award, 2005; The Edinburgh Makar. Publications: Each Bright Eye; Bed of Stone; Tweed Journey; The Chanter's Tune; The Ringing Rock; St. Kilda Song; Men and Beasts; The Lightning Tree. Recreations: whippet-racing; field-walking; tai chi; swimming. Address: (h.) 67 Braid Avenue, Edinburgh EH10 6ED; T.-0131-447 2876.

Gillies, Professor William, MA (Edin), MA (Oxon), Hon. D.Litt. (Ulster). Professor of Celtic, Edinburgh University, since 1979; b. 15.9.42, Stirling; m., Valerie; 1 s.; 2 d. Educ. Oban High School; Edinburgh University; Corpus Christi College, Oxford; Dublin University. Dublin Institute for Advanced Studies, 1969-70; Lecturer, Edinburgh University, 1970-79; Director, SLD Ltd.; Fellow, Royal Society of Edinburgh, 1990; Fellow, Royal Historical Society, 2002. Recreations: walking; gardening; music; Taoist tai chi. Address: (h.) 67 Braid Avenue, Edinburgh EH10 6ED.

Gillingham, Professor John, CBE, MBE(Mil), FRSE, FRCSEng, FRCSEdin, FRCPEdin, MD(Hon), Thessaloniki, FRACS(Hon), FRCSI(Hon), FCMSA(Hon), FRCPGlas (Hon), FRSA. Member, Court of Regents, Royal College of Surgeons of Edinburgh; Professor Emeritus, Department of Surgical Neurology University of Edinburgh; Foundation Professor of Surgical Neurology, Kind Saud University, Saudi Arabia, 1983-85; Honorary Consultant Neurosurgeon, St. Bartholomew's Hospital, since 1980; b. 15.3.16, Dorchester, Dorset; m., Judy; 4 s. Educ. Hardy's School, Dorset; St. Bartholomew's Hospital Medical College, London University. House Officer posts, St. Bartholomew's; Lieutenant, RAMC, Military Hospital for Head Injuries, Oxford, 1940-41; Surgeon (later o/c Major), No. 4 Mobile Neurosurgery Unit, North African Desert and Italy, 1942-45; St. Bartholomew's Hospital: Senior Registrar, 1946-47, Senior Registrar, Neurosurgery Unit, 1957; Senior Lecturer, then Reader, then Professor of Surgical Neurology, Edinburgh University, 1950-79; Consultant Neurosurgeon, Royal Infirmary of Edinburgh and Western General Hospital, Edinburgh; Consultant Neurosurgeon to the Army in Scotland, 1970-83, and to the Armed Forces of Saudi Arabia, 1979-83; Hon. President, World Federation of Neurosurgical Societies, 1979; President, Royal College of Surgeons of Edinburgh, 1979-82; Honorary Member, Royal Academy of Medicine, Valencia, Spain, 1971. Clark Award for Services to Motoring (Seat Belt Legislation), 1979. Publications: Head Injuries (Editor); Stereotactic Surgery; 84 papers on stereotactic surgery, head and spinal injuries, epilepsy, cerebro-vascular surgery, postgraduate training and education. Recreations: sailing; landscape gardening (cactus).

Gillis, Richard, OStJ, FRSA. Solicitor, since 1975; Managing Director, family investment companies, since 2001; b. 22.4.50, Dundee; m., Ruth J. P. Garden. Educ. High School of Dundee. Solicitor, Greater London Council, 1975-77; Archer & Wilcock, Nairobi, Kenya, 1977-80; Shoosmiths, 1980-81; Assistant to the Secretary, TI Group plc, 1981-85; Secretary, ABB Transportation Holdings Ltd (British Rail Engineering Ltd until privatisation) & Trustee, Company Pension Scheme, 1985-95; Clerk to the Council and Company Secretary, University of Derby, 1995-2002. Secretary, Justice report on perjury; Director, then Vice-Chairman, Crewe Development Agency, 1992-95; CBI East Midlands Regional Council, 1993-95; Stakeholders' Forum Derby City Challenge, 1993-98; Chairman, Property Committee, Derbyshire Council of the Order of St. John, 1994-2003; Trustee, Priory of England and the Islands of the Order of St. John and Trustee, St. John Ambulance, 1999-2003; Chairman, Audit Committee and Priory Regulations Committee, Regional Member of Priory Chapter, 1999-2005; Honorary Life Member, Court of the University of Derby, 2003; Court of Assistants, Worshipful Company of Basketmakers, since 2004; Court, City University, since 2007. Recreations: Freemasonry; historical films; music; Clubs: Athenaeum, New (Edinburgh), City Livery, New Golf (St. Andrews). Address: (h.) Nether Kinfauns, Church Road, Kinfauns, Perth PH2 7LD; T.-01738-860886.

Gillon, Karen Macdonald. MSP (Labour), Clydesdale, since 1999; Shadow Minister for Rural Development; b. 18.8.67, Edinburgh; m., James Gillon; 2 s. Educ. Jedburgh Grammar School; Birmingham University. Youth Worker, Terminal One Youth Centre, Blantyre, 1991-94; Community Education Worker, North Lanarkshire Council, 1994-97; PA to Rt. Hon. Helen Liddell, MP, 1997-99. Recreations: sport; music; flower arranging; reading; cooking. Address: (b.) 7 Wellgate, Lanark ML11 9DS; T.-01555 660526; e-mail: karen.gillon.msp@scottish.parliament.uk

Gilloran, Professor Alan James, MA PhD. Vice Principal (Research Development), Queen Margaret University, Edinburgh, since 1996; Sociologist; b. 7.6.56, Edinburgh; m., Barbara; 1 s.; 1 d. Educ. Daniel Stewart's College, Edinburgh; University of Edinburgh. Researcher, Wester Hailes Representative Council; Research Assistant, Moray House; Research Fellow, University of Edinburgh; Lecturer in Sociology and Social Policy, University of Stirling. Member, Care Development Group on Free Personal Care for Elderly People. Publications: academic articles; book chapters; five funded research reports into dementia and mental health. Recreations: badminton; wine; travel. Address: (b.) Queen Margaret University, Craighall, Edinburgh EH21 6UU; T.-0131-474 0000; e-mail: agilloran@qmu.ac.uk

Gilmore, Professor William C., LLB, LLM, MA, PhD. Professor, International Criminal Law, Edinburgh University, since 1996, Dean and Head of the School of Law, 2004-07; b. 31.3.51, Nassau, Bahamas; m., Dr Patricia Shepherd; 1 s.; 1 d. Educ. St Joseph's College, Dumfries; Edinburgh University; University of London; Carlton University. Lecturer, Law, University of West Indies, Barbados, 1973-75; Commonwealth Projects Officer, IILED, Washington D.C., 1977-79; Lecturer/Senior Lecturer/Reader, Faculty of Law, Edinburgh University, 1979-96; Assistant Director, Legal Division/Head, Commercial Crime Unit,

Commonwealth Secretariat, Marlborough House, London, 1991-93. Publications include: Dirty Money, 3rd ed. 2004; Newfoundland and Dominion Status, 1988; The Grenada Intervention, 1984. Recreations: travel; fishing. Address: (b.) Old College, South Bridge, Edinburgh, EH8 9YL.

Gilmour, Sir John, Bt, DL. Farmer; b. 15.7.44, Edinburgh; m., Valerie Jardine Russell; 2 s.; 2 d. Educ. Eton; Aberdeen College. Captain, FFY/SH (TA); Member, Queen's Bodyguard for Scotland (Royal Company of Archers); Hon. Col. FFY/SH (CSQD/QOY); Director: The Moredun Foundation, Perth Race Course, Pentland Science Parks. Recreations: fishing; reading. Address: Balcormo Mains, Leven, Fife; T.-01333 360229.

Gilmour, John Andrew George, MA, LLB, NP. Solicitor; Marketing Consultant; Honorary Sheriff at Dumbarton, since 1991; b. 17.11.37, Balloch; m., Roma Aileen; 3 d. Educ. Morrison's Academy, Crieff; Edinburgh University. Consultant, McArthur Stanton; President, Strathclyde Junior Chamber of Commerce, 1973; Director, Dumbarton Enterprise Trust, 1985-2000; Dean, Faculty of Dunbartonshire Solicitors, 1988-90; Law Society accredited Liquor Licensing Specialist, 1993; President, Helensburgh and Lomond Chamber of Commerce, 2003-2007. Recreations: sport; music; gastronomy. Address: (h.) Cramond Cottage, 19 East Lennox Drive, Helensburgh; T.-01436 672212.

Gilmour, Simon, MA (Hons), PhD, FSA Scot. Director of The Society of Antiquaries of Scotland, since 2007; b. 12.06.70, Dundee. Educ. Alford Academy; University of Edinburgh. Department of Archaeology Tutor, University of Edinburgh, 1999-2001; numerous excavations and other archaeological projects in Scotland and abroad, 1996-2004; Aerial Survey Liaison Officer, Royal Commission on The Ancient and Historical Monuments of Scotland, 2001-05; Project Manager in the construction industry, 2005-07. Elected Vice President of The Council for Scottish Archaeology, since 2004; elected Hon. Secretary of The Council for Scottish Archaeology, 2001-04; Honorary Fellow of The University of Edinburgh, 2001-04. Recreations: skiing; eating out; cinema; archaeology. Address: (b.) Society of Antiquaries of Scotland, c/o National Museums Scotland, Chambers Street, Edinburgh EH1 1JF; T.-0131 247 4115. E-mail: director@socantscot.org

Gilson, Mike. Editor, The Scotsman. Formerly Editor, The News in Portsmouth and the Peterborough Evening Telegraph. Member of the Press Complaints Commission's code committee; Chairman, Johnston Press' Editorial Review Group and the company's working party on future digital age newsrooms. Address: (b.) 108 Holyrood Road, Edinburgh EH8 8AS.

Gimblett, Sheriff Margaret, MA, FRSA. Sheriff at Dunoon, 1999-2005, part-time Sheriff, since 2005; b. 24.9.39, Perth; m., Iain; 1 s.; 1 d. Educ. St. Leonards, St. Andrews; University of Edinburgh; University of Glasgow. Retail Management, John Lewis Partnership, London, until 1970; Partner, Russel and Aitken, Solicitors, 1972-95; Temporary Sheriff, 1994-95; Sheriff, Glasgow and Strathkelvin, 1995-99; Churchill Fellow. Recreations: gardening; tourism. Address: (h.) Croftcat Lodge, Grandtully PH15 2QS.

Gimingham, Professor Charles Henry, OBE, BA, PhD, ScD, FRSE, FIBiol. Regius Professor of Botany, Aberdeen

University, 1981-88; b. 28.4.23, Leamington; m., Elizabeth Caroline Baird; 3 d. Educ. Gresham's School, Holt, Norfolk; Emmanuel College, Cambridge. Research Assistant, Imperial College, London, 1944-45; Department of Botany, Aberdeen University: Assistant, 1946-48, Lecturer, 1948-61, Senior Lecturer, 1961-64, Reader, 1964-69, Professor, since 1969, Head of Department, 1981-88; Member: Scottish Committee of Nature Conservancy, 1966-69, Scottish Advisory Committee, Nature Conservancy Council, 1970-80, Countryside Commission for Scotland, 1980-92; President, Botanical Society of Edinburgh, 1982-84; Vice-Chairman, NE Regional Board, Nature Conservancy Council for Scotland, 1991-92; Member: NE Regional Board, SNH, 1992-96, Science Advisory Committee, SNH, 1996-99, Board of Management, Hill Farming Research Organisation, 1981-87, Governing Body, Aberdeen College of Education, 1979-87, Council of Management, Macaulay Institute for Soil Research, 1983-87, Board of Management, Macaulay Land Use Research Institute, 1987- 90; British Ecological Society: Joint Secretary, 1956-61, Vice-President, 1962-64, Joint Editor, Journal of Ecology, 1975-78, President, 1986-87; Patron, Institute of Ecology and Environmental Management, 2000; Founding Fellow, Institute of Contemporary Scotland, 2000; President, The Heather Trust, 2004-07. Publications: Ecology of Heathlands, 1972; Introduction to Heathland Ecology, 1975; Lowland Heathland Management Handbook, 1992; The Ecology, Land Use and Conservation of the Cairngorms, 2002. Recreations: hill-walking; photography; history and culture of Japan. Address: (h.) 4 Gowanbrae Road, Bieldside, Aberdeen.

Ginger, Andrew, Professor MA, DPhil (Oxon). Professor of Hispanic Studies, University of Stirling, since 2005; b. 12.04.70, Leeds; m. Dr Maria-Concepción Castrillo-Llamas. Educ. Trinity College, Oxford; Exeter College, Oxford. Queen Sofia Junior Research Fellow, Exeter College, Oxford, 1994-95; Lecturer, then Senior Lecturer, University of Edinburgh, 1996-2005. Publications: Books: Political Revolution and Literary Experiment, 1999; Antonio Ros de Olano's Experiments in Post-Romantic Prose, 2000; Painting and The Turn to Cultural Modernity in Spain, 2007. Address: (b.) School of Languages, Cultures and Religions, University of Stirling, Stirling FK9 4LA; T.-01786 467531; e-mail: a.j.ginger@stir.ac.uk

Girdwood, David Greenshields, BSc, MEd, SQH. Rector, St. Columba's School, Kilmacolm, since 2002; b. 14.10.57, Tillicoultry; m., Lisa; 2 d. Educ. Alva Academy; St. Andrews University; Jordanhill College; Stirling University; Edinburgh University. Lornshill Academy: Teacher of Chemistry, 1979-85, Assistant Principal of Science, 1985-87; Daniel Stewart's and Melville College: Principal Teacher of Chemistry and Head of Science, 1987-96, Head of Upper School, 1996-2002. Associate Assessor, HMI, 1999-2002. Recreations: rugby; refereeing; walking. Address: (b.) Duchal Road, Kilmacolm, Renfrewshire PA13 4AU; T.-01505 872238; e-mail: secretary@st-columbas.org

Girvin, Professor Brian, BA, MA, PhD. Professor of Comparative Politics, University of Glasgow, since 2000; b. 16.7.50, Cork; partner, Rona Fitzgerald; 1 s. Educ. Sullivan's Quay CBS, Cork; University College, Cork. Temporary Lecturer, National Institute for Higher Education, Limerick, 1978-82; University College, Cork: Temporary Teaching Assistant, 1983-86, Director of European Studies, 1986-88, Lecturer in Modern History, 1986-95; Senior Lecturer in Politics, University of Glasgow, 1995-2000. Publications: Politics and Society in Contemporary Ireland (Co-Editor), 1986; The Transformation of Contemporary Conservatism (Editor), 1988; Between Two Worlds: Politics and Economy in Independent Ireland, 1989; The Right in the Twentieth Century: Conservatism and Democracy, 1994; The Green Pool Negotiations and the Origins of the Common Agricultural Policy (Co-Editor), 1995; Ireland and the Second World War: Politics, Society and Remembrance (Co-Editor), 2000; From Union to Union: Nationalism, Democracy and Religion in Ireland since 1800, 2002; The Lemass Era (Co-Editor), 2005; The Emergency: Neutral Ireland, 1939-45, 2006. Recreation: mountaineering; cooking; arguing; film; music; books. Address: Department of Politics, University of Glasgow G12 8RT; T.-0141-330 5353; e-mail: b.girvin@socsci.gla.ac.uk

Glasby, Michael Arthur, BM, BCh, MA, MSc (Oxon), MA (Cantab), MD, DSc (Edin), FRCP (Edin), FRCS (Edin), FRCS (Eng). Honorary Fellow, University of Edinburgh; Consultant Neurophysiologist, Scottish National Spinal Deformity Centre, Royal Hospital for Sick Children, Edinburgh; b. 29.10.48, Nottingham; m., Celia M.E. Robinson. Educ. High Pavement Grammar School, Nottingham; Christ Church, Oxford; Oxford Medical School. Senior Scholar and Assistant Tutor in Physiology, Christ Church, Oxford, 1971-76; Surgeon, Harefield Hospital Transplant Trust, 1981-83; Fellow and Lecturer in Anatomy, New Hall, Cambridge, 1983-87; Lecturer in Anatomy, Royal College of Surgeons of England, 1984-87; joined Edinburgh University as Lecturer, 1987; Reader in Anatomy, 1992-97; Reader in Experimental Neurology, 1997-2004. Editor, anatomy textbook for surgeons and physiology textbook for surgeons; numerous articles. Recreations: golf; Latin and Greek literature; music; beekeeping; wine. Address: (h.) 3 Cluny Drive, Morningside, Edinburgh EH10 6DN; T.-0131 447 3836; e-mail: michael.glasby@ed.ac.uk

Glasgow, 10th Earl of (Patrick Robin Archibald Boyle), DL. Television Director/Producer; b. 30.7.39; m., Isabel Mary James; 1 s.; 1 d. Educ. Eton; Paris University. Sub.-Lt., RNR, 1959-60; Producer/Director, Yorkshire TV, 1968-70; freelance Film Producer, since 1971; created Kelburn Country Centre (leisure park), 1977, and now manages this and Kelburn Estate; Deputy Lieutenant, Ayrshire; Lib Dem Peer, House of Lords. Address (b.) Kelburn Castle, Fairlie, Ayrshire KA29 0BE; T.-01475 568685.

Glasier, Anna, MB, ChB, BSc, FRCOG, MD, DSc, FFPRHC, OBE. Director, Lothian Primary Care NHS Trust Family Planning and Well Woman Services, since 1990; Honorary Professor: Edinburgh University, University of London; Consultant Gynaecologist, Lothian Health Board, since 1989; Lead Clinician for Sexual Health in NHS Lothian; b. 16.4.50, Salisbury; m., Dr. David T. Baird. Educ. Lord Digby's School, Sherborne. Clinical Research Scientist, Medical Research Council Centre for Reproductive Biology, Edinburgh, 1989-90. Recreations: ski mountaineering; sailing. Address: (b.) 18 Dean Terrace, Edinburgh EH4 1NL; T.-0131-332 7941.

Glass, Rev. Alexander, OBE, MA, DipEd. Rector, Dingwall Academy, 1977-97; b. 1.6.32, Dunbar; m., Edith Margaret Duncan Baxter; 3 d. Educ. Dunbar Grammar School; Edinburgh University; Heidelberg University; University of Aix-en-Provence. Teacher of Modern Languages, Montrose Academy, 1958-60; Special Assistant Teacher of Modern Languages, Oban High School, 1960-62; Principal Teacher of Modern Languages, Nairn Academy, 1962-65; Principal Teacher of French and Assistant Rector, Perth Academy, 1965-72; Rector, Milne's High School, Fochabers, 1972-77. Former Chairman, COSPEN; former President, Highland Secondary Headteachers' Association; former Chairman, Highland Region Working Party for Modern Languages; former Chairman, Children's Panel Chairmen's Group; former Chairman, Highland Children's Panel; Chairman, Highland Children's Panel Advisory Committee's Monitoring Sub-

Committee; Reader, Church of Scotland; Auxiliary Minister, Presbytery of Ross; Moderator, Presbytery of Ross, 2006/07; Scottish Community Drama Association: Divisional Secretary/Festival Organiser, Highland Division, Member, General Council; former Chairman and Secretary, Scottish Secondary Schools' Travel Trust; Member, Highland Health Voices; Church of Scotland Representative, Highland Education Committee. Churchill Fellow, 1991. Recreations: amateur drama; foreign travel; Rotary. Address: (h.) Craigton, Tulloch Avenue, Dingwall IV15 9TU; T.-01349 863258.

Glass, Douglas James Allan, LVO, MB, ChB. General Practitioner, Ballater, since 1987; Apothecary to HM Household, Balmoral, since 1988; Partner in farm (D.L. Glass), since 1982; b. 8.10.53, Dinnet, Aboyne; divorced; 1 s.; 4 d. Educ. Aboyne Academy; Banchory Academy; Aberdeen University. Junior House Officer, 1977-78; Senior House Officer, 1978-79; General Practitioner Trainee, 1979-80; General Practice, Australia and New Zealand, 1980-81; General Practice Principal, Peterhead, 1981-87. Elder, Glenmuick Church, Ballater, since 1988. Recreations: dry stane dyking; golf; snooker; football. Address: (h.) Deecastle, Dinnet, Aboyne, Aberdeenshire; T.-013397 55686.

Glen, Duncan Munro. Writer and Lecturer; Sole Owner, Akros Publications, since 1960; b. 11.1.33, Cambuslang; m., Margaret Eadie; 1 s.; 1 d. Educ. West Coats, Cambuslang; Rutherglen Academy; Edinburgh College of Art. Book Designer, London; Lecturer in Typography; Editor, Robert Gibson & Co. Ltd.; Lecturer, then Senior Lecturer, then Head of Graphic Design, Lancashire Polytechnic; Professor and Head, Department of Visual Communication, Nottingham Trent University (Emeritus Professor); Member, Council for Academic Awards, 1979-89; Editor: Akros, poetry magazine, 1-51, ZED 2 0, 1-20, Scottish Poetry Library Newsletter; special personal award, Scottish Arts Council (for services to literature), 1975; Howard Sergeant Memorial Award, 1991; honorary doctorate, Paisley University, 2000. Author and editor of many books including Hugh MacDiarmid and The Scottish Renaissance, Selected Essays of Hugh MacDiarmid, In Appearances: Poems, The Autobiography of a Poet, Makars' Walk, The Poetry of the Scots, Selected Poems 1965-1990, Hugh MacDiarmid: Out of Langholm and Into the World; A Nation in a Parish; Four Scottish Poets; Splendid Lanarkshire; New Selected Poems, 1987-96; Illustrious Fife: literary, historical and architectural pathways and walks; A New History of Cambuslang; Scottish Literature: a new history from 1299 to 1999; Selected Scottish and Other Essays; Printing Type Designs: a new history from Gutenberg to 2000; John Atman and Other Poems, 2001; Three/tritto translators of poems by Duncan Glen – Nat Scammacca, Enzo Bonventre, Marco Scalabrino, 2001; Historic Fife Murders at Falkland, St. Andrews and Magus Muir, 2002; Ruined Rural Fife Churches, 2002; The Ruins of Newark Castle, St Monans, 2003; Kirkcaldy: a new illustrated history, 2004; Stevenson's Scotland (editor) 2005; Long Calderwood, old East Kilbride and its associations with John and William Hunter, 2005; of Marks & Memories, 2005; In Search of Serif Books, 2006; Collected Poems, 1965-2005, 2006; Small Press Publishers of Scotland, 2006. Recreation: walking. Address: (h.) 33 Lady Nairn Avenue, Kirkcaldy, Fife KY1 2AW; T.-01592 651522.

Glen, Eric Stanger, MB, ChB, FRCSGlas, FRCSEdin. Consultant Urological Surgeon, Walton Urological Teaching and Research Centre, Southern General Hospital, Glasgow, 1972-99; b. 20.10.34, Glasgow; m., Dr. Patricia. Educ. Airdrie Academy; Glasgow University. Pre-Consultant posts, Western and Victoria Infirmaries, Glasgow; Ship Surgeon, Royal Fleet Auxiliary. Formerly Medical Director, Continence Resource Centre and Helpline for Scotland; Past Chairman, Area Medical Committee; Founder and Honorary Member, International Continence Society; former Honorary Clinical Senior Lecturer, Glasgow University; former Member, Surgical Examination Panel, Royal College of Physicians and Surgeons of Glasgow; Founder, Urological Computing Society. Publications: chapters in books; papers on urodynamics, urology and computing. Recreations: travel; writing; computer applications. Address: (h.) 9 St. John's Road, Pollokshields, Glasgow G41 5RJ; T.-0141-423 0759; e-mail: eric@pollokshields.fsnet.co.uk

Glen, Marlyn. MSP (Lab), North East Scotland, since 2003; b. 30.9.51, Dundee; widowed; 1 s.; 1 d. Educ. Kirkton High School, Dundee; St. Andrews University; Dundee University; Open University. Former teacher. Address: (b.) Scottish Parliament, Edinburgh EH99 1SP; T.-0131 348 5000.

Glenarthur, 4th Baron (Simon Mark Arthur), Bt, DL, FCILT, FRAeS. DL, Aberdeenshire, since 1997; Director: Millennium Chemicals Inc., 1996-2004, Medical Defence Union, 2002-06, Audax Global Sàrl, since 2003; a Governor, Nuffield Hospitals, since 2000; b. 7.10.44; m.; 1 s.; 1 d. Educ. Eton. Retired Major, 10th Royal Hussars (PWO); Helicopter Captain, British Airways, 1976-82; a Lord in Waiting, 1982-83; Parliamentary Under Secretary of State: Department of Health and Social Security, 1983-85, Home Office, 1985-86; Minister of State: Scottish Office, 1986-87, Foreign and Commonwealth Office, 1987-89; Consultant: British Aerospace PLC, 1989-99, Hanson PLC, 1989-99, Imperial Tobacco Ltd., 1996-98; Deputy Chairman, Hanson Pacific Ltd., 1994-97; Chairman, St. Mary's Hospital, Paddington, NHS Trust, 1991-98, British Helicopter Advisory Board, 1992-2004, European Helicopter Association, 1996-2003; President: National Council for Civil Protection, 1991-2003, British Helicopter Advisory Board, since 2004; Member (Lieutenant), Queen's Bodyguard for Scotland (Royal Company of Archers); Scottish Patron, The Butler Trust, since 1994; a Commissioner, Royal Hospital Chelsea, 2001-07; Honorary Colonel, 306 Field Hospital (Volunteers), since 2001; Honorary Air Commodore, 612 (County of Aberdeen) Squadron, Royal Auxiliary Air Force, since 2004. Address: (b.) PO Box 11012, Banchory AB31 6ZJ; T.-01330 844467.

Glennie, John Ellis, FCCA, CIPFA, IHEEM. Chief Executive, NHS Borders, since 2003; Chairman: Delivering for Health, National Neurosciences Implementation Group, NHS Scotland Benchmarking Project, Sterile Services Provision Review Group, NAG Cervical and Breast Screening Group; Co-Chair, Joint Premises Project Board; b. 28.9.48, Keith; 2 s; 1 d. Educ. Keith Grammar School. Joined NHS as a trainee accountant, Aberdeen, 1966, and progressed through a number of posts to become Director of Finance, Darlington Health Authority, 1982; Director of Finance, Information and Computing, Central Manchester Health Authority, 1985-91; Director of Finance, then Deputy Chief Executive/Director of Operations, Central Manchester Healthcare NHS Trust, 1992-95; Chief Executive, Borders General Hospital NHS Trust, 1995-2003. National Treasurer, Healthcare Financial Management Association. Address: (b.) NHS Borders, Newstead, Melrose TD6 9DB; T.-01896 825515.

Gloag, Ann, OBE. Non-Executive Director, Stagecoach Group plc (Managing Director, 1986-94, Executive Director, 1986-2000); b. 10.12.42. Educ. Perth High School. Nursing, 1960-80; Founding Partner, Stagecoach, 1980. Address: (b.) Stagecoach Group, 10 Dunkeld Road, Perth PH1 5TW.

Glover, Professor Lesley Anne, BSc (Hons) Edin, PhD (Cantab), FRSE, FAAM. Chief Scientific Adviser for Scotland, since 2006; Professor of Molecular and Cell Biology, University of Aberdeen, since 2001; b. 19.04.56, Arbroath; m., Ian George. Educ. Dundee High School;

Morpeth Grammar School; Edinburgh University; Cambridge University (Kings College). Lectureship in Biochemistry, University of Aberdeen, 1983; Honorary Research Fellow, Rowett Research Institute, Aberdeen, 1992; Technical Director, Remedios Ltd., 1999-2003; Personal Chair in Molecular and Cell Biology, University of Aberdeen, since 2001; Research Associate, Macaulay Land Use Research Institute, Aberdeen, since 2002. Trustee of CL: AIRE, since 2003; Council Member of Natural Environment Research Council, since 2001; Board Member, Edinburgh International Science Festival, since 2007; Member, Development Council, Plymouth Marine Laboratory, since 2007. Recreations: sailing; cycling; reading. Address: (b.) St. Andrews House, Regent Road, Edinburgh EH1 3DG; T.-0131 244 2663; e-mail: anne.glover@scotland.gsi.gov.uk

Glover, Rev. Robert Lindsay, BMus, BD, MTh, ARCO. Minister, Chalmers Memorial, Cockenzie and Port Seton, since 1997; b. 21.7.45, Watford; m., Elizabeth Mary Brown; 2 s.; 2 d. Educ. Langholm Academy; Dumfries Academy; Glasgow University. Minister: Newton Parish, near Dalkeith, 1971-76, St. Vigeans Parish, Arbroath, 1976-85, Knox's, Arbroath, 1982-85, St. George's West, Edinburgh, 1985-97. Recreations: music; reading; travel. Address: Braemar Villa, 2 Links Road, Port Seton, Prestonpans, East Lothian EH32 0HA; e-mail: rlglover@btinternet.com

Glover, Sue, MA. Writer; b. 1.3.43, Edinburgh; divorced; 2 s. Educ. St. George's School, Edinburgh; Montpellier University; Edinburgh University. Original drama and other scriptwriting for radio, television and theatre; theatre productions include: The Seal Wife, Edinburgh Festival, 1980; An Island in Largo, Byre Theatre, 1981; The Bubble Boy, Glasgow Tron, 1981; The Straw Chair, Traverse Theatre, 1988; Bondagers, Traverse Theatre, 1991 (winner, 1990 LWT Plays on Stage Award); Sacred Hearts, 1994; Artist Unknown, 1996; Shetland Saga, Traverse Theatre, 2000; Blow-outs, Wrecks and Almanacs, 2002; television work includes: The Spaver Connection; Mme Montand and Mrs Miller; Dear Life; televised version of The Bubble Boy won a silver medal, New York Film and Television Festival, and a merit, Chicago International Film Festival, 1983. Publications: The Bubble Boy: You Don't Know You're Born, 1991; Bondagers (Made in Scotland), 1995; Bondagers and The Straw Chair, 1997; Shetland Saga, 2000. Recreations: house and garden. Address: Gloxinia, The Loan, Anstruther, Fife KY10 3HG.

Godden, Tony Richard Hillier, CB, BSc (Econ); b. 13.11.27, Barnstaple; m., Marjorie Florence Snell; 1 s.; 2 d. Educ. Barnstaple Grammar School; London School of Economics. Commissioned, RAF Education Branch, 1950; entered Civil Service, 1951; first appointed to Colonial Office; Private Secretary to Parliamentary Under Secretary of State, 1954-55; seconded to Cabinet Office, 1957-59; joined Scottish Home Department, 1961; Assistant Secretary, Scottish Development Department, 1964; Under Secretary, 1969; Secretary, Scottish Economic Planning Development, 1973-80; Secretary, Scottish Development Department, 1980-87. Member: The Council on Tribunals and its Scottish Committee, 1988-94, Advisory Board on Ancient Monuments, 1990-95; Secretary, Friends of the Royal Scottish Academy, 1988-2000. Address: 9 Ross Road, Edinburgh EH16 5QN.

Godfrey, Andrew Paul, CA. Regional Managing Partner, Scottish Region, Grant Thornton, since 1998; b. 12.8.53, Edinburgh; m., Irene; 2 s. Educ. Morrison's Academy; Edinburgh University. Joined Grant Thornton Glasgow Office, 1982; Scottish Managing Partner, 1998. Recreation: keen member of Dunblane and Gleneagles Golf Clubs.

Address: (b.) 95 Bothwell Street, Glasgow G2 7JZ; e-mail: andrew.p.godfrey@gtuk.com

Godman, Trish. MSP (Labour), West Renfrewshire, since 1999; Deputy Presiding Officer, since 2003; Convener, Local Government Committee; b. 1939; m.; 3 s. Educ. St Gerard's Senior Secondary School; Jordanhill College. Former Regional Councillor; former Member, Glasgow City Council. Recreations: allotment holder; music; dancing; reading; cinema; learning to be a grandmother. Address: (b.) Scottish Parliament, Edinburgh EH99 1SP; T.-0131-348 5837.

Gold, Lex, CBE. Chairman, Scottish Premier League; b. 14.12.40, Rigside; m., Eleanor; 1 d. Educ. Lanark Grammar School. Sub-Editor, Daily Record; professional footballer; joined Civil Service, Glasgow, 1960; Inland Revenue, two years, Civil Service Department, four years, Home Office, 21 years, Training Agency, three years; former Managing Director, Scottish Enterprise; former Director, CBI Scotland; former Director, Scottish Chambers of Commerce; former Chairman, Hibernian Football Club Ltd.; former Chairman, Lanarkshire NHS Board. Address: (b.) Scottish Premier League, Hampden Park, Glasgow G42 9DE.

Goldie, Annabel MacNicoll, DL, LLB, NP. MSP (Conservative), West of Scotland, since 1999; Leader, Scottish Conservative Party, since 2005; former Convener, Justice 2 Committee; Deputy Lord Lieutenant, Renfrewshire, since 1993; Director, Prince's Scottish Youth Business Trust, since 1994; Partner, Donaldson, Alexander, Russell and Haddow (formerly Dickson Haddow and Co.), 1978-2006; b. 27.2.50, Glasgow. Educ. Greenock Academy; Strathclyde University. Admitted Solicitor, 1974; Scottish Conservative Party: Deputy Chairman, 1995-97, Chairman, March-July 1997, Deputy Chairman, 1997-98, Deputy Leader, 1998-2005. Elder, Church of Scotland; Member, West of Scotland Advisory Board, Salvation Army; Honorary Fellow, Strathclyde University. Recreations: bird watching; cycling; listening to music. Address: (b.) Scottish Parliament, Edinburgh EH1 1SP; T.-0131-348 5663.

Gomatam, Professor Jagannathan, BSc, MSc, PhD. Emeritus Professor of Applied Mathematics, Glasgow Caledonian University, Professor, since 1990; b. 20.8.40, India; m., Jean McGregor. Educ. University of Madras; Syracuse University. Research Assistant, Physics Department, then Instructor, Mathematics Department, Syracuse University, 1966-70; Post-Doctoral Research Fellow, Physics Department, Syracuse University, 1970-71; Research Scholar, School of Theoretical Physics, Dublin Institute for Advanced Studies, 1971-73; Lecturer/Reader, Glasgow Caledonian University, 1973-90. Senior Visitor, Mathematical Institute, Oxford University, 1986-87; re-elected to Peer Review Collge, EPSRC, 2003; Visiting Professor, Strathclyde University, since 2007. Address: (b.) School of Engineering and Computing, Glasgow Caledonian University, 70 Cowcaddens Road, Glasgow G4 0BA.

Gondzio, Professor Jacek. Professor of Optimization, Edinburgh University, since 2005; b. 01.01.60, Skrzynki, Poland; m., Joanna Karpinska-Gondzio; 1 s. Educ. Warsaw University of Technology. Polish Academy of Sciences, Poland: Research Assistant, 1983-89, Assistant Professor, 1989-98; Research Fellow: Universite Paris Dauphine, France, 1990-91, University of Geneva, Switzerland, 1993-98; Lecturer, Edinburgh University, 1998-2000, Reader, 2000-05. Address: (b.) School of Mathematics, Edinburgh University, King's Buildings, Edinburgh EH9 3JZ; T.-0131 650 8574; e-mail: j.gondzio@ed.ac.uk

Good, Professor Anthony, BSc, PhD (Edin), PhD (Dunelm). Head, School of Social and Political Studies,

University of Edinburgh, since 2006, Professor of Social Anthropology in Practice, since 2004; b. 15.12.41, Congleton, Cheshire; m., Alison; 2 d. Educ. Kings School, Macclesfield; University of Edinburgh; University of Durham. Postdoctoral Research Fellow in Chemistry, University of Alberta, Canada, 1967-69; SRC Postdoctoral Fellow in Chemistry, University of Cambridge, 1969-70; Commonwealth Educational Co-operation Scheme Senior Lecturer in Chemistry, University of Peradeniya, Sri Lanka, 1970-72; Research Fellow in Chemistry, City University, London, 1973-74; SSRC Conversion Fellow in Anthropology, University of Durham, 1974-77; Lecturer in Sociology, University of East Anglia, 1978-79; Lecturer in Social Anthropology: University of Manchester, 1979-80, University of Edinburgh, 1980-91, Senior Lecturer, 1991-2004; Senior Social Development Adviser to the Joint Funding Scheme, Department for International Development, 1987-99. Member, Scottish Advisory Council, Immigration Advisory Service, since 2002. Publications: Research Practices in the Study of Kinship (Co-Author), 1984; The Femail Bridegroom: A Comparative Study of Life-Crisis Rituals in South India and Sri Lanka, 1991; Worship and the Ceremonial Economy of a Royal South Indian Temple, 2004; Anthropology and Expertise in the Asylum Courts, 2007. Address: (b.) School of Social and Political Studies, University of Edinburgh, Edinburgh EH8 9LL; T.-0131-650-3941; e-mail: a.good@ed.ac.uk

Goodman, Professor Anthony Eric, MA (Oxon), BLitt (Oxon), FRHistS. Professor of Medieval and Renaissance History, Edinburgh University, 1993-2001, Professor Emeritus, since 2001; b. 21.7.36, London; m., Jacqueline; 1 d. Educ. Selhurst Grammar School, Croydon; Magdalen College, Oxford. Joined staff, Edinburgh University, 1961. Secretary, Edinburgh Branch, Historical Association, since 1975. Publications: The Loyal Conspiracy, 1971; A History of England from Edward II to James I, 1977; The Wars of the Roses, 1981; A Traveller's Guide to Medieval Britain (Co-author), 1986; The New Monarchy, 1471-1534, 1988; John of Gaunt, 1992; Margery Kempe and Her World, 2002; The Wars of the Roses. The Soldiers' Experience (2005). Address: (h.) 23 Kirkhill Gardens, Edinburgh EH16 5DF; T.-0131-667 5988.

Goodman, Professor Timothy Nicholas Trewin, BA, MSc, DPhil, FRSE. Professor of Applied Analysis, Dundee University, since 1994; b. 29.4.47; m., Chootin; 3 d. Educ. Judd School, Tonbridge; St John's College, Cambridge; Warwick University; Sussex University. Teacher in Malaysia under VSO scheme, 1973; Teacher in Singapore, 1974-75; Lecturer in Malaysia, 1975-79; Lecturer, Dundee University, 1979-90; Professor in Texas, USA, 1990-91; Reader, Dundee University, 1992-94. Recreations: hill-walking; Scottish country dancing. Address: (b.) Department of Mathematics, Dundee University, Dundee DD1 4HN; T.-01382 344488.

Goodwin, Sir Frederick Anderson, Kt (2004), DUniv, LLB, CA, FCIBS, FCIB, LLD. Group Chief Executive, Royal Bank of Scotland Group plc, since 2000; Board Member, Bank of China, since 2006; Director, ABN AMRO, since 2007; b. 17.8.58, Paisley; m. Educ. Glasgow University. Touche Ross: joined, 1979; Partner, 1988; Chief Operating Officer, BCCI Worldwide Liquidation, 1992-95; Deputy Chief Executive, Clydesdale Bank Plc, 1995; Chief Executive/Director, Clydesdale Bank, 1996; Chief Executive/Director, Clydesdale Bank and Yorkshire Bank Plc, 1997-98; Deputy Chief Executive, Royal Bank of Scotland, Plc, 1998-2000. Chairman, The Prince's Trust. Recreations:

golf; cars. Address: (b.) Gogarburn, Edinburgh EH12 1HQ; T.-0131 523 2033.

Gordon of Strathblane, Lord (James Stuart Gordon), CBE, DLitt., DUniv, MA (Hons). Chairman, Scottish Radio Holdings, 1996-2005; Director, Johnston Press plc, since 1996, The AIM Trust plc, 1996-2003, Active Capital Trust plc, since 2003; Chairman, RAJAR, since 2003; Member, BP Scottish Advisory Board, 1990-2003; b. 17.5.36, Glasgow; m., Anne Stevenson; 2 s.; 1 d. Educ. St. Aloysius College, Glasgow; Glasgow University (President of the Union, 1958-59). Political Editor, STV, 1965-73; Managing Director, Radio Clyde, 1973-96; Chief Executive, Scottish Radio Holdings, 1991-96. Member, Court, Glasgow University, 1984-97; Chairman, Advisory Group on Listed Sports Events on Television, 1997-98; Chairman, Scottish Tourist Board, 1998-2001; Trustee, National Galleries of Scotland, 1998-2001; Member, Review Panel on the Future Funding of the BBC; Winner, Observer Mace Debating Tournament, 1957; Sony Special Award for Services to Radio, 1984. Chairman, Scottish Exhibition Centre, 1983-89; Member, Scottish Development Agency, 1981-90. Recreations: his children; genealogy; golf. Address: (b.) House of Lords, London SW1A 0PW.

Gordon, Charlie. MSP (Labour), Glasgow Cathcart, since 2005; 3 s. Councillor, Strathclyde Regional Council, 1987-96; Vice Convenor, Roads and Transport (SRC), 1990-94; Convenor, Roads and Transport (SRC), 1994-96; Councillor, Glasgow City Council, 1995-2005; Convenor, Roads (GCC), 1995-96; Chair, Strathclyde Passenger Transport, 1996-99; Deputy Leader, Glasgow City Council, 1997-99, Leader, 1999-2005. Address: (b.) Scottish Parliament, Edinburgh EH99 1SP; Constituency Office: Somerville Drive, Mount Florida, Glasgow G42 9BA.

Gordon, Donald Neil, MA, LLB, WS, NP, TEP. Partner, Blackadders (formerly Carltons) Solicitors, since 1979; Senior Tutor, Diploma in Legal Practice, University of Dundee, since 1994; Law Society accredited specialist: incapacity Law; Dean, Faculty of Procurators and Solicitors in Dundee, 1999-2001; b. 30.3.51, Aberdeen; m., Alison Mary Whyte; 1 s.; 1 d. Educ. Robert Gordon's College, Aberdeen; University of Aberdeen; University of Edinburgh. Law Apprenticeship, Edinburgh, 1973-75; Assistant Solicitor, Carlton & Reid, Dundee, 1975-79. WS, 1975; Notary Public, 1975; Chairman, Dundee Citizens Advice Bureau, 1996-2001; Honorary French Consul, Dundee, since 1996; President, Abertay Rotary Club, 2001-02; President, Dundee Orchestral Society, since 2003; Past Chairman, High School of Dundee Parents Association; Editor, Green's Practical Styles (Wills), 2005. Recreations: music; gardening; Rotary. Address: (b.) 34 Reform Street, Dundee DD1 1RJ; T.-01382 229222.

Gordon, Emeritus Professor George, MA (Hons), PhD, FRSGS, FBAASc, FRSA, FFCS. Director of Academic Practice, Strathclyde University, 1987-2005, Professor of Academic Practice, 2003-05; b. 14.11.39, Edinburgh; m., Jane Taylor Collins; 2 d. Educ. George Heriot's School; Edinburgh University. Edinburgh University: Vans Dunlop Scholar, 1962-64, Demonstrator, 1964-65; Strathclyde University: Assistant Lecturer, 1965-66, Lecturer, 1966-80, Dean, Faculty of Arts and Social Studies, 1984-87; served on SUCE and SCE Geography Panels, SCOVACT, and General Teaching Council for Scotland; Chairman, Council, Royal Scottish Geographical Society, 1999-2005; Hon. Treasurer, Society for Research into Higher Education, 2002-06, Chair of Council, since 2007; Board of Directors, The Higher Education Academy, 2004-05; Honorary Auditor, Australian Universities Quality Agency, 2002-05; Vice President, British Association for the Advancement of Science, 1991-97; former Member, General Assembly of Open University; Strathclyde University: Member, Senate 1984-2002, Member, Court, 1984-87, 2000-02; Governor, Jordanhill College of Education, 1982-93 (Chairman, 1987-

93). Publications: Regional Cities of the UK 1890-1980 (Editor), 1986; Perspectives of the Scottish City (Editor), 1985; The Making of Scottish Geography (Co-Author), 1984; Settlement Geography, 1983; Urban Geography (Co-Author), 1981; Scottish Urban History (Co-Editor), 1983; Settlement Geography (Co-Author), 1983. Recreations: theatre-going; watching sport. Address: (b.) Centre for Academic Practice and Learning Enhancement, Strathclyde University, 50 George Street, Glasgow; T.-0141-548 2637.

Gordon, Sir Gerald Henry, CBE, QC, MA, LLB, PhD, LLD, HonFRSE. Sheriff of Glasgow and Strathkelvin, 1978-99; Temporary Judge, Court of Session and High Court of Justiciary, 1992-2004; b. 17.6.29, Glasgow; m., Marjorie Joseph; 1 s.; 2 d. Educ. Queen's Park Senior Secondary School; Glasgow University. Advocate, 1953; Procurator Fiscal Depute, Edinburgh, 1960-65; Edinburgh University: Head, Department of Criminal Law and Criminology, 1965-72, Personal Professor of Criminal Law, 1969-72, Dean, Faculty of Law, 1970-73, Professor of Scots Law, 1972-76; Sheriff of South Strathclyde, Dumfries and Galloway, at Hamilton, 1976-77; Member: Interdepartmental Committee on Scottish Criminal Procedure, 1970-77, Committee on Criminal Appeals and Miscarriages of Justice, 1995-96, Scottish Criminal Cases Review Commission, since 1999. Publications: Criminal Law of Scotland, 1967, 1978; Renton & Brown's Criminal Procedure (Editor), 1972, 1983, 1996. Recreations: Jewish studies; coffee conversation; crosswords.

Gordon, Robert Smith Benzie, CB, MA. Director General, Justice and Communities, Scottish Government, since 2007, Head of Justice Department, 2004-07, Head of Legal and Parliamentary Services, since 2002; b. 7.11.50, Aberdeen; m., Joyce Cordiner; 2 s.; 2 d. Educ. Gordon Schools, Huntly; Aberdeen University. Joined Scottish Office, 1973; Principal, Scottish Development Department, 1979-85; Principal Private Secretary to Secretary of State for Scotland, 1985-87; Assistant Secretary: Department of Agriculture and Fisheries, 1988-90, Management, Organisation and Industrial Relations Division, Scottish Office, 1990-91; Director, Administrative Services, 1991-97; Head, Constitution Group, 1997-99; Head, Executive Secretariat, Scottish Executive, 1999-2001; Head, Finance and Central Services Department, Scottish Executive, 2001-02; Chief Executive, The Crown Office, 2002-04. Address: (b.) St. Andrew's House, Regent Road, Edinburgh; T.-0131-244-2120.

Gordon, Professor William Morrison, MA, LLB, PhD, LLD, FRSE. Douglas Professor of Civil Law, Glasgow University, 1969-99; Professorial Research Fellow, 1999-2001; Solicitor (non-practising), since 1956; b. 3.3.33, Inverurie; m., Isabella Evelyn Melitta Robertson; 2 s.; 2 d. Educ. Inverurie Academy; Robert Gordon's College, Aberdeen; Aberdeen University. National Service, Royal Navy, 1955-57; Assistant in Jurisprudence, Aberdeen University, 1957-60; Glasgow University: Lecturer in Civil Law, 1960-65, Senior Lecturer in Law, 1965-69 (and Sub-Dean of Faculty); Dean of Faculty, 1974-76. Elder and, until 1998, Session Clerk, Jordanhill Parish Church; Literary Director, The Stair Society, 1985-98. Publications: Studies in Transfer of Property by Traditio, 1970; Scottish Land Law, (2nd Ed.), 1999; Stair Society Miscellany III, 1992; European Legal History (3rd Ed.), (with others), 2000; Roman Law, Scots Law and Legal History: Selected Essays, 2007. Recreation: golf. Address: 26 Southbrae Drive, Glasgow G13 1PY; T.-0141-954 9037.

Gorman, Brian, MA. Vice President, Commonwealth Youth Exchange Council, since 1999; Board Member, Suspect Culture Theatre Co., 1998-2002; Chair, EK Performance, 2003-06; b. 31.10.51, Wishaw. Educ. Our Lady's High School, Motherwell; University of Glasgow; Jordanhill College. Teacher, Columba High School, Coatbridge, 1974-76; Principal Teacher of Modern Studies,

St. John's High, Dundee, 1976-78; Group Travel Manager, Cotter Tours, Glasgow, 1978-84; Director, English-Speaking Union (Scotland), 1984-93; Chairman, Suspect Culture Theatre Co., 1994-98; Member, Review of Cardio-Thoracic Transplant Services in Scotland, 2003-04. Recreations: theatre; debating. Address: (h.) 15/3 Easter Dalry Road, Edinburgh EH11 2TR; T.-0131-346 1327; e-mail: briangorman31@yahoo.co.uk

Gorrie, Donald Cameron Easterbrook, OBE, DL, MA, JP. MSP (Liberal Democrat), Central Scotland, 1999-2007; b. 2.4.33, India; m., Astrid Salvesen; 2 s. Educ. Hurst Grange, Stirling; Oundle School; Corpus Christi College, Oxford. Schoolmaster: Gordonstoun School, 1957-60, Marlborough College, 1960-66; Scottish Liberal Party: Director of Research, 1969-71, Director of Administration, 1971-75; Member, Edinburgh Town Council, 1971-75; Leader, Liberal Democrat Group: Lothian Regional Council, 1974-96, City of Edinburgh District Council, 1980-96, City of Edinburgh Council, 1995-97; MP (Liberal Democrat), Edinburgh West, 1997-2001. Director, 'Edinburgh Translations'; former Chairman, Edinburgh Youth Orchestra; Member, Board, Queens Hall; President: City of Edinburgh AC and Corstorphine AAC, Lothian Association of Youth Clubs, Edinburgh Youth Cafe; Trustee, Nancy Ovens Trust, Chairman, Corstorphine Dementia Project; Secretary, Friends of Corstorphine Hill; former Member, Board: Diverse Attractions, Castle Rock and Lothian Housing Associations, Edinburgh Festival, Scottish Chamber Orchestra, Royal Lyceum Theatre Company; Backbencher of the Year, 1999; Free Spirit of the Year, 2001; former Scottish native record holder, 880 yards. Recreations: reading; music; opera; drama; visiting ruins. Address: (h.) 9 Garscube Terrace, Edinburgh EH12 6BW; T.-0131-337 2077.

Goudie, Andrew William, FRSE, PhD, MA, BA (Econ), BA. Director-General Economy and Chief Economic Adviser, Scottish Government, since 2007, Chief Economic Adviser, since 1999, and Head of Finance and Central Services Department, 2003-07; b. 3.3.55, London; m., Christine Goudie; 2 s.; 2 d. Educ. Haberdashers' Aske's School, Elstree; Queens' College, University of Cambridge. University of Cambridge, 1978-85: Research Officer, Department of Applied Economics, Research Fellow, Queens' College, Fellow and Director of Studies, Robinson College; Senior Economist, The World Bank, Washington DC, 1985-90; Senior Economic Adviser, Scottish Office, 1990-95; Principal Economist, OECD, Paris, 1995-96; Chief Economist, DFID (formerly ODA), London, 1996-99; Doctor of Letters, University of Strathclyde, 2003. Publications: articles in learned journals. Address: (b.) Victoria Quay, Edinburgh EH6 6QQ; T.-0131-244-7937. E-mail: andrew.goudie@scotland.gsi.gov.uk

Gourlay, James, MMus, FRCM, FLCM. Deputy Principal (Music), Royal Scottish Academy of Music and Drama (RSAMD), since 2006; b. 21.05.56, Buckhaven; m., Léa Havas. Educ. Buckhaven High School; Royal College of Music; Leeds University. Principal Tuba: CBSO, 1976-79, BBCSO, 1979-89; Solo-Tuba Orchester Deroper Zürich, 1989-98; Head of Wind and Percussion, Royal Northern College of Music, 1998-2006; Director of The School of Music, Royal Scottish Academy of Music and Drama, 2006-07. Philip Jones Brass Ensemble, 1980-84. International tuba soloist; CDs: British Tuba Concertos, East Meets West, Gourlay plays tuba. Conductor of Brass Ensemble of World class. Recreation: enjoying the East Neuk of Fife. Address: (b.) 100 Renfrew Street, Glasgow G2 3DB; e-mail: j.gourlay@rsamd.ac.uk

Gow, Sir (James) Michael, GCB, DL (Edinburgh). President, Royal British Legion Scotland, 1986-96; President, Earl Haig Fund (Scotland), 1986-96, Vice-President, since 1996; Vice-President, Officers' Association Scotland, since 1996 (President, 1995-96); b. 3.6.24; m.,

Jane Emily Scott; 1 s.; 4 d. Educ. Winchester College. Enlisted, Scots Guards, 1942; commissioned, 1943; served NW Europe 1944-45, Malayan Emergency, 1949; Equerry to the late HRH Duke of Gloucester, 1952-53; Brigade Major, 1955-57; Regimental Adjutant, Scots Guards, 1957-60; Instructor, Army Staff College, 1962-64; Command, 2nd Bn Scots Guards, Kenya and England, 1964-66; GSO1, HQ London District, 1966-67; Command, 4th Guards Brigade, 1968-69; Imperial Defence College, 1970; Brigadier General Staff (Int.) HQ, BAOR and Assistant Chief of Staff, G2 HQ, Northag, 1971-73; GOC 4th Div., BAOR, 1973-75; Director of Army Training, 1975-78; General Officer Commanding, Scotland, Governor of Edinburgh Castle, 1979-80; Commander-in-Chief, BAOR and Commander, Northern Army Group, 1980-83 (awarded die Plakette des deutschen Heeres); ADC Gen. to the Queen, 1981-84; Commandant, Royal College of Defence Studies, 1984-86. Colonel Commandant: Intelligence Corps, 1973-86, Scottish Division, 1979-80. Chairman: Scottish Ex-Services Charitable Organisation, 1989-96, Scots at War Trust, since 1992, Ludus Baroque, since 1999; Patron, Disabled Income Group Scotland, since 1993; Vice-President: Scottish National Institution for the War Blinded, 1995, Royal Caledonian Schools Education Trust, 1996-2000; Captain, Queen's Body Guard for Scotland, (Royal Company of Archers), transferred to non active list, 2005; UK Member, Eurogroup US Tour, 1983; UK Kermit Roosevelt Lecturer, USA, 1984; Vice President: Queen Victoria School, Dunblane, 1979-80, Royal Caledonian Schools, Bushey, 1980-99; County Commissioner, British Scouts, W. Europe, 1980-83 (Silver Acorn); Elder, Canongate Kirk, since 1988; President, National Association of Sheltered Employment, 1993-2000; Member, The Thistle Foundation, since 2000; Freeman: City of London, 1980, State of Kansas, USA, 1984; Freeman and Liveryman, Painters' and Stainers' Company, 1980. Publications: Trooping the Colour: A History of the Sovereign's Birthday Parade by the Household Troops, 1989; Jottings in a General's Notebook, 1989; General Reflections, 1991. Recreations: sailing; music; travel; reading. Address: (h.) 18 Ann Street, Edinburgh EH4 1PJ; T.-0131-332 4752.

Grace, Professor John, BSc, PhD, FIBiol, FRSE. Professor of Environmental Biology, Edinburgh University, since 1992; Head, School of Geosciences, 2002-03; Head, Institute of Ecology and Resource Management, 2000-02; Head, Institute of Atmospheric and Environmental Sciences, since 2003; b. 19.9.45, Northampton; m., Elizabeth Ashworth; 2 s.; 1 d. Educ. Bletchley Grammar School; Sheffield University. Lecturer, then Reader in Ecology, Edinburgh University, 1970-92. Co-Editor, Functional Ecology, 1986-99; Technical Editor, International Society for Biometeorology, 1983-98; Member, Terrestrial Life Sciences Committee, Natural Environment Research Council, 1986-89; President, British Ecological Society, 2002-03. Publications: Plant Response to Wind, 1977; Plants and their Atmospheric Environment (Co-Editor), 1981; Plant-atmosphere Relationships, 1983. Recreations: hill-walking; cycling; fishing; bridge. Address: (h.) 25 Craiglea Drive, Edinburgh EH10 5PB; T.-0131-447 3030; e-mail: jgrace@ed.ac.uk

Grace, Paul Henry, BSc, FFA. Director, Scottish Equitable Policyholders Trust Ltd., since 1998; Director and Honorary Treasurer, Victim Support Scotland Ltd., 1998-2004; Chairman, National Provident Life Fund Supervisory Board, since 2000; Member, Scottish Life Fund Supervisory Committee, since 2001; b. 25.9.38, Bletchley; m., Aileen Anderson; 1 d. Educ. Bedford Modern School; St. Andrews University. Joined Scottish Equitable as Actuarial Trainee, 1960; joined Zurich Life Assurance Co. as Actuary and Life Manager, 1965; rejoined Scottish Equitable as Actuary, 1980-93; Deputy Chief Executive,

1985-93, Director, 1987-93; Managing Director and Actuary, Scottish Equitable Policyholders Trust Ltd., 1994-98. President, Faculty of Actuaries, 1996-98; Director, Student Loans Company Ltd., 1999-2002; Chairman, Groupe Consultatif Actuariel Europeen, 2004-05. Publication: Introduction to Life Assurance, 1988. Recreations: golf; gardening. Address: 16 Succoth Avenue, Edinburgh EH12 6BU; T.-0131-337 5079.

Graham, Rev. A. David M., BA, BD. Minister, Rosemount Parish Church, Aberdeen, 1990-2005; b. 17.7.40, Tralee; m., Mary A. Taylor; 2 s.; 1 d. Educ. Wesley College, Dublin; Methodist College, Belfast; Queen's University, Belfast; Glasgow University. Assistant, South Leith Parish; Secretary for Christian Education, Scottish National Council of YMCAs; Minister, Anderston Parish, Glasgow; Warden, Iona Abbey; Minister, Rosemount Parish, Aberdeen. Recreations: cycling; walking; writing.

Graham, Rev. Alasdair Giffen, BD, Dip. Ministry. Minister, Arbroath West Kirk, since 1990; Part-time Chaplain, Arbroath Infirmary; b. 20.4.54, Lanark; m., Joan Janet Forsyth; 1 d. Educ. Gordon Schools, Huntly; Kirkcaldy High School; University of Glasgow. Probationary Assistant, Mastrick Church, Aberdeen, 1980-81; Minister, Redgorton and Stanley Churches, Perthshire, 1981-86; Chaplain, HM Prison, Perth, 1982-86; Minister, St Margaret's Church, Arbroath, 1986-90. District Scout Chaplain; Chaplain, Angus Training Group. Recreations: time with family; badminton; swimming. Address: (h.) 1 Charles Avenue, Arbroath DD11 2EY; T.-01241 872244.

Graham, Professor David I., MB, ChB, PhD, FRCPath, FRCPS, FMedSci, FRSE. Emeritus Professor; b. 20.7.39, Glasgow; m., Joyce; 1 s.; 1 d. Educ. Penarth County Grammar School; Welsh National School of Medicine; Cardiff. Registrar, Western Infirmary, Glasgow, 1965-68; Lecturer, Department of Neuropathology, Glasgow, 1968-72; Fogarty Fellow, Laboratory of Neuropathology, Philadelphia, 1972-74; Senior Lecturer, Glasgow, 1974-83; Professor of Neuropathology, Glasgow University, 1983-2005; retired. Publications: several books; 300 papers. Recreations: hill-walking; music. Address: (b.) c/o Department of Neuropathology, Institute of Neurological Sciences, Southern General Hospital, Govan Road, Glasgow G51 4TF.

Graham, Elspeth Forbes, MA, PhD. Reader in Geography, St. Andrews University, since 2003, Head of School of Geography and Geosciences, since 2003; Member, Local Government Boundary Commission for Scotland, 1994-2004; Member, Parliamentary Boundary Commission for Scotland, since 1999; b. 7.2.50, Edinburgh; 1 s.; 1 d. Educ. George Watson's Ladies College, Edinburgh; St. Andrews University; Durham University. Visiting Lecturer, University of Minnesota, 1979-80; Visiting Senior Research Fellow, National University of Singapore, 2004. Publications: Postmodernism and the Social Sciences (Co-editor), 1992; The Geography of Health Inequalities in the Developed World (Co-editor), 2004; research papers on population policies and issues, including low fertility in Scotland and Singapore. Recreations: Celtic music and literature; local history. Address: (b.) School of Geography and Geosciences, University of St. Andrews, St. Andrews KY16 9AL; T.-01334 463908.

Graham, Ian, OBE, BSc (Econ) (Hons), DipEdTech (CNAA), FRSA. Principal, John Wheatley College, Glasgow, since 1992; b. 26.6.51, Devizes. Educ. Queen Victoria School, Dunblane. Lecturer/Senior Lecturer, Reid

Kerr College, Paisley, 1975-86; Head of Department, Clydebank College, 1986-88; Further Education Officer, Strathclyde Regional Council, 1988-89; HM Inspector of Schools, 1989-90; Assistant Director of Education (FE), Strathclyde Region, 1990-92. Fellow, Chartered Institute of Personnel and Development; Vice Chair, Board: Association of Scottish Colleges, Greater Easterhouse Arts Company; Member of Board: Greater Easterhouse Community Planning Partnership, East Centre and Calton Community Planning Partnership, Glasgow East Regeneration Agency, Routes Out Social Inclusion Partnership, Bridgeton Community Learning Campus. Recreations: reading; cinema; foreign travel; admiring Burmese cats. Address: (b.) John Wheatley College, 2 Haghill Road, Glasgow G31 3SR; T.-0141-588-1500.

Graham, John Michael Denning, LLB (Hons), NP, FRSA. Solicitor and Notary Public, since 1970; Director, Business Law, MacRoberts, Solicitors, Glasgow and Edinburgh; Lecturer in Law, Glasgow Graduate Law School; Honorary Fellow, Glasgow Caledonian University; Chairman, National Health Service Tribunal for Scotland; Chairman, Institute of Directors, Glasgow and West of Scotland Branch; Part-time Chairman, Appeals Service; Vice Chairman, Pharmaceutical Lists National Appeal Panel; Chairman, Scottish Society of Epicureans; Vice-Chairman, Queen's University Association, Scotland; Director, OCHRE - a national cancer charity; b. 7.9.44, Kirkintilloch; m., Christina Jeanne Sinclair; 2 s. Educ. Royal Belfast Academical Institution; Queen's University, Belfast. Founding Partner, Messrs. Paterson Robertson & Graham, Solicitors. Former Member, Court, Glasgow Caledonian University; former (founding) Director, Glasgow Solicitors Property Centre; former Director, West Glasgow NHS Trust; former Director, John Smith & Son (Glasgow) Ltd. Recreations: tennis; golf; hand-gliding. Address: (b.) 152 Bath Street, Glasgow; T.-0141 332 9988; (h.) 11, Winton Drive, Glasgow G12 0PZ.

Graham, John Murdo, DipCom, FEIS. Retired Schoolmaster; Honorary Sheriff of Grampian, Highland and Islands at Stornoway; b. 1.5.36, Coll, near Stornoway; m., Murdina Macdonald; 3 s.; 1 d. Educ. Nicolson Institute, Stornoway; Scottish College of Commerce; Jordanhill College of Education. Nicolson Institute, Stornoway: Assistant Teacher, 1959-68, Principal Teacher of Business Studies and Economics, 1968-72, Assistant Rector, 1972-88. Member, North of Scotland Electricity Consumers' Committee, 1992-2000; Panel Member, The Tribunal Service, since 1984; Member, Council, Educational Institute of Scotland, 1975-85; Elder, Stornoway Free Church; General Trustee, Free Church of Scotland, 1998-2006. Recreations: current affairs; world stock markets; walking; gardening. Address: (h.) 25 Goathill Road, Stornoway, Isle of Lewis HS1 2NL; T.-01851 703469.

Graham, John Strathie, BA. Chief Executive, Historic Scotland, since 2004; b. 27.5.50, Edinburgh; m., Anne Graham; 2 s.; 1 d. Educ. Edinburgh Academy; Corpus Christi College, Oxford. Joined Scottish Office, 1972; Principal, Scottish Economic Planning Department, 1976; Assistant Secretary, Industry Department for Scotland, 1982; Private Secretary to Secretary of State, 1983; Assistant Secretary: Planning Division, Scottish Development Department, 1985, Finance Division 1, 1990; Under Secretary, Local Government Group, 1991; Principal Finance Officer, 1996; Head of Environment and Rural Affairs Department, Scottish Executive, 1998. Recreations: exploring Scotland; listening to music. Address: (b.) Longmore House, Salisbury Place, Edinburgh EH9 1SH.

Graham, Keith H.R., LLB, WS. Principal Clerk, Scottish Land Court, since 1982; b. 29.5.47, Edinburgh; m., Patricia; 2 d. Educ. George Watson's College; Edinburgh University. Apprenticeship, Davidson & Syme, WS, 1968-70; private practice, 1970-72; Legal Assessor, Scottish Land Court,

1972-82. Publication: The Scottish Land Court: Practice and Procedure. Address: (b.) George House, 126 George Street, Edinburgh EH2 4HH; T.-0131 271 4360.

Graham, (Lord) Donald, FCIBS, BSc, MBA. Director, Adam & Company plc, since 1991; Director: KDCL Ltd., Property Developers, since 1992, Children's Music Foundation, since 1995; b. 28.10.56, Salisbury, Southern Rhodesia; m., Bridie; 1 s.; 3 d. Educ. St. Andrews College, South Africa; St. Andrews University; INSEAD. Recreations: piping; music; golf. Address: (b.) Adam & Company plc, 22 Charlotte Square, Edinburgh EH2 4DF; T.-0131-225 8484.

Graham, Professor Neil Bonnette, BSc, PhD, CChem, FRSC, FIM, FRSE. Professor in Chemical Technology, Strathclyde University, 1973-97; Emeritus Professor in Chemistry, since 1997; b. 23.5.33, Liverpool; 1 s.; 3 d. Educ. Alsop High School, Liverpool; Liverpool University. Research Chemist, Research Scientist, Canadian Industries Ltd., MacMasterville PQ, Canada, 1956-67; Assistant Group Head, then Group Head, Polymer Chemistry, ICI, Runcorn, Cheshire. Member: Advisory Committee on Dental and Surgical Materials, 1980-86, Expert Advisor to the Secretary of State on Active Medical Implants, since 1993; sometime member of various committees, Society of Chemical Industry, Royal Society of Chemistry and Plastics and Rubber Institute; Founder and Technical Director, Polysystems Ltd., 1980-90; Founder and Chairman: Smart Tech Ltd., since 2000, Ocutec Ltd., since 2001; Trustee, James Clerk Maxwell Trust; Director, Mission Aviation Fellowship (Scotland), 1999; Trustee, MacKinnon McNeill Trust. Recreations: music; walking; sailing. Address: (b.) Smart Tech Ltd., Smith Building, Jordanhill Campus, 76 Southbrae Drive, Glasgow G13 1PP; T.-0141 942 0484; e-mail: 100721.314@compuserve.com

Graham, Sir Norman William, Kt (1971), CB (1961), MA, DLitt (Heriot-Watt), DUniv (Stirling), FRSE; b. 11.10.13, Dundee; m., Catherine Mary Strathie; 2 s.; 1 d. Educ. High School of Glasgow; Glasgow University. Assistant Principal, Department of Health for Scotland, 1936; Principal, Ministry of Aircraft Production, 1941; Principal Private Secretary to Minister, 1944; Assistant Secretary, Department of Health for Scotland, 1945; Under Secretary, 1956; Secretary, Scottish Education Department, 1964-73.

Graham, Lieutenant General Sir Peter, KCB, CBE, HonDLitt. Vice Patron, Gordon Highlanders Museum; Chairman, Regimental Trust Fund, The Gordon Highlanders, 1986-2004; Chairman, The Gordon Highlanders Museum Management Committee, 1994-2003; Chairman, Gordon Highlanders Museum Appeal, 2002-06; b. 14.3.37; m., Dr Alison Mary Morren, MB, ChB, MRCGP; 3 s. Educ. Fyvie Village School, Aberdeenshire; Hall School, Hampstead; St. Paul's School, London; RMA Sandhurst. Commissioned The Gordon Highlanders, 1956; regimental appointments, Dover, Germany, Scotland, Kenya, 1957-62; HQ Highland Brigade, 1962-63; Adjutant 1 Gordons, Kenya, Edinburgh, Borneo (Despatches), 1963-66; Staff Captain, HQ 1 Br Corps, 1966-67; Australian Staff College, 1968; Company Commander, 1 Gordons, Germany, 1969-70; Brigade Maj., HQ 39 Brigade, Northern Ireland, 1970-72 (MBE); 2nd i/c, 1 Gordons, Ulster, Singapore, 1972-74; Military Assistant to Adjutant General MoD, 1974-75; CO, 1 Gordons, Scotland, Ulster, 1976-78 (OBE); COS, HQ 3 Armoured Division, Germany, 1978-82; Comd UDR, Ulster (Despatches), 1982-84; Canadian National Defence College, Ontario, 1984-85; Deputy Military Secretary, MoD, 1985-87; GOC Eastern District, 1987-89; Commandant RMA, Sandhurst, 1989-91; GOC

Army in Scotland and Governor, Edinburgh Castle, 1991-93. Colonel, The Gordon Highlanders, 1986-94; Chairman, Gordon Highlanders Museum, 1994-2003; Member, Royal Company of Archers, since 1985. Burgess of Guild, City of Aberdeen, 1994; HonDLitt, Robert Gordon University, 1996. Publication: The Gordon Highlanders Pipe Music Collection (Co-author), 1983 and 1985. Recreations: stalking; hill-walking; shooting; reading; pipe music; gardening under my wife's directions; military history. Address: (b.) c/o Home HQ, The Highlanders, Viewfield Road, Aberdeen AB15 7XH; T.-01224 318174.

Graham, Riddell, BSc, FTS. Director of Strategy, Partnerships and Communications, VisitScotland; Chief Executive, Scottish Borders Tourist Board, 1996-2005, Director, 1990-96; b. 13.2.54, Galashiels; m., Sandra; 1 s. Educ. Galashiels Academy; Edinburgh University. Borders Regional Council, 1976-83, latterly as Assistant Tourist Officer; joined Scottish Borders Tourist Board, 1983, as Assistant Director of Tourism. Recreations: cycling; watching rugby. Address: (b.) Visit Scotland, Ocean Point One, 94 Ocean Drive, Edinburgh EH6 6JH; T.-0131 472 2208; e-mail: riddell.graham@visitscotland.com

Graham, Rev. William Peter, MA, BD. Clerk, Edinburgh Presbytery, since 1993; b. 24.11.43, Edinburgh; m., Isabel Arnot Brown; 2 s. Educ. George Watson's College, Edinburgh; Edinburgh University. Assistant Minister, Dundee (St. Mary's) Parish Church, 1966-68; Minister, Chirnside Parish Church, 1968-93, Bonkyl & Preston, 1973-93, Edrom-Allanton, 1978-93; Clerk, Duns Presbytery, 1982-93; Convener, General Assembly's Nomination Committee, 1990-93, Board of Communication, 2003-05; Vice-Convener: Committee on Education for Ministry, 1996-98, Board of Ministry, 1998-99, Board of Communication, 1999-2002; Governor, George Watson's College, since 1998. Recreations: golf; theatre; reading. Address: (b.) 10 Palmerston Place, Edinburgh EH12 5AA; T.-0131-225 9137.

Graham-Bryce, Ian James, CBE, DPhil, BA, MA, BSc, HonLLD, FRSC, CChem, FRSE, FRSA. Principal and Vice-Chancellor, Dundee University, 1994-2000, now Principal Emeritus; President, Scottish Association for Marine Science, 2000-04, Vice President, since 2004; Chairman, East Malling Trust for Horticultural Research, since 2002; Member, Board of Directors, Rothamsted Experimental Station, 2000-04; Member, Royal Commission on Environmental Pollution, since 2000; b. 20.3.37; m., Anne Elisabeth Metcalf; 1 s.; 3 d. Educ. William Hulme's Grammar School, Manchester; University College, Oxford. Lecturer, UCNW; Bangor, 1961-64; Senior Scientific Officer, Rothamsted Experimental Station, 1964-70; Senior Research Officer, ICI Plant Protection Division, Berks, 1970-72; Imperial College of Science and Technology: Special Lecturer in Pesticide Chemistry, Department of Zoology and Applied Entomology, 1970-72, Visiting Professor, 1976-79, Governor, 1985-2000; Rothamsted Experimental Station: Head, Department of Insecticides and Fungicides, 1972-79, Deputy Director, 1975-79; Director, East Malling Research Station, 1979-86; Cons. Director, Commonwealth Bureau of Horticulture and Plantation Crops, 1979-86; Head, Environmental Affairs Division, Shell Internationale Petroleum Maatschappij BV, 1986-94. Society of Chemical Industry, London: President, 1982-84, Member, Council, 1969-72, 1974-89, Honorary Secretary, Home Affairs, 1977-80; President: Association of Applied Biologists, 1988, British Crop Protection Council, 1996-2000; Member, NERC, 1989-96 (Chairman, Polar Sciences Committee, 1995-96); Convener, Committee of Scottish Higher Education Principals, 1998-99; Member, Board of Directors, Educational Counselling Service, British Council, 1996-98; Member, Board of Directors,

Quality Assurance Agency for Higher Education (Chairman, Scottish Advisory Committee), 1997-98. Publications: Physical Principles of Pesticide Behaviour, 1980; papers on soil science, plant nutrition, crop protection and environmental matters. Recreations: music (especially opera); sport. Address: (b.) Scottish Association for Marine Science, Dunstaffnage Marine Laboratory, Dunbeg, Oban PA37 1QA.

Grahame, Christine, MA, LLB, DipEd, DipLLP. MSP (SNP), South of Scotland, since 1999 (Convener, Health and Sport Committee); b. 9.9.44, Burton-on-Trent; 2 s. Educ. Boroughmuir School; Edinburgh University. Secondary teacher, 1966-82; solicitor, 1987-99. Recreations: gardening; drinking malt whisky; cats. Address: Scottish Parliament, Edinburgh EH99 1SP; T.-0131-348 5000.
E-mail: christine.grahame.msp@scottish.parliament.uk

Grahame, David Currie, OBE, MA (Hons). Executive Director, LINC Scotland, since 1993; b. 10.12.53, Hawick. Educ. Langholm Academy; Lockerbie Academy; St. Andrews University. Founding Director, LINC Scotland; Member, Rating Valuation Appeals Panel; Board Member, European Business Angels Network, Brussels. Recreations: music; classic cinema; food and wine. Address: (b.) Queens House, 19 St. Vincent Place, Glasgow G1 2DT; e-mail: david_grahame@ lincscot.co.uk

Grains, Florence Barbara, OBE, JP, FFCS. Former Vice-Convener, Shetland Islands Council; Chairman, Audit and Scrutiny Committee; b. 2.11.32, Shetland; m., Alistair M. Graines (deceased); 4 s. Educ. Whiteness School; Lerwick FE Centre. Retired Subpostmaster. Former Chairman: Shetland Health Board, and Shetland Council of Social Services; Trustee, National War Memorial; Member, Scottish Museums Council; Chairman, Shetland Amenity Trust; Area Chairman, Shetland Scout Council; Chairman, Foula Electricity Trust; Member, Aith RNLI Station; Member, CPAC; Member, NCJA; Chair, Visiting Committee, Legalised Police Cells; Foundation Member, UHI; Trustee, Walls and District Agricultural Society. Address: (h.) Hoove, Whiteness, Shetland ZE1 9LL; T.-01595 840243.

Grant, Dr. Douglas, TD, FRSE, FSA Scot; b. 6.1.18; m., Enid Whitsey; 3 s. Educ. George Watson's College. Lt.-Col., RA (served W. Africa and staff), 1939-46; Scottish Widows Fund, 1936-39; Director: Oliver and Boyd Ltd., 1947-67, Edinburgh C. of C., 1952-56, New Education Ltd., 1962-66, Bracken House Publications Ltd., 1963-67, Sprint Productions Ltd., 1963-80, E. & S. Livingston Ltd., 1963-67, Darien Press Ltd., 1963-68, R. & R. Clark Ltd., 1963-80, Port Seton Offset Printers Ltd., 1965-75, T. & A. Constable Ltd., 1965-75, British Journal of Educational Psychology, 1970-91, Pindar (Scot) Ltd., 1986-89, Macdonald Lindsay (Printers) Ltd., 1978-89; Chairman: Scottish Journal of Theology Ltd., 1948-91, Robert Cunningham & Sons Ltd., 1952-76, Hunter and Foulis Ltd., 1963-75, Port Seton Offset Printers Ltd., 1965-75, Multi Media (AU) Services Ltd., 1967-75, Church of Scotland Publications Committee, 1971-76, Scottish Academic Press Ltd., 1969-91, Scottish International Review Ltd., 1970-75, Handsel Press Ltd., 1975-91, Scottish Academic Press (Journals) Ltd., 1976-91, Clark Constable Printers Ltd., 1978-89; Consultant Editor: Scottish Academic Press, 1991-99, Dunedin Academic Press, since 2000. Trustee: The Lodge Trust (Natural History), 1949-85, Darling (Ogilby) Investment Trust, 1955-78, Kilwarlin Trust, since 1964, Esdaile Trust, since 1975 (Chairman), Society for the Benefit of Sons and Daughters of the Clergy of the Church of Scotland, since 1990 (Chairman); Committee Member:

Scottish Council of Law Reporting, 1947-93, 2002-05 (Consultant, 1993-2002), The Charles Smith Trust, since 1972 (Chairman), Police Dependents' Trust (Lothian and Borders Police), 1956-79, NEDO, 1968-75, New College University of Edinburgh Finance Board, since 1970, University of Edinburgh Court, 1972-84, Scottish Arts Council, 1975-79; President: Edinburgh Master Printers' Association, 1962-64, St. Cuthbert's Parish Church, Society of Change Ringers, since 1963, Edinburgh Booksellers' Society, 1977-80, Edinburgh Amateur Angling Club, 1978-80; Honorary Fellow, Edinburgh Geological Society, 1992; Hon. DLitt, University of St. Andrews, 1986. Address: 2G East Road, North Berwick, East Lothian EH39 4HN; T.-01620 894972.

Grant, Ian David, CBE, FRAgS. Chairman and 1st Commissioner, Crown Estate, since 2002; Chairman, Scottish Exhibition Centre, since 2002; b. 28.7.43, Dundee; m., Eileen May Louisa Yule; 3 d. Educ. Strathallan School; East of Scotland College of Agriculture. Chairman, EEC Cereals Working Party, 1982-88 and International Federation of Agricultural Producers, Grains Committee, 1984-90; Board Member, Scottish Hydro-Electric, 1992-98, Scottish and Southern Energy PLC, 1998-2003 (Deputy Chairman, 2000-03); President, NFU of Scotland, 1984-90; Director: East of Scotland Farmers Ltd., 1978-2002, NFU Mutual Insurance Society Ltd. (Deputy Chairman, since 2003), Clydesdale Bank PLC, 1989-97; Member: Scottish Council, CBI, 1984-96, Board, British Tourist Authority, 1990-98, Scottish Economic Council, 1993-97; Chairman: Scottish Tourist Board, 1990-98 (Member, 1988-90), Cairngorms Partnership, 1998-2003; Vice President, Royal Smithfield Club; Honorary Doctorate, Business Administration, Napier University. Recreations: travel; swimming; music. Address: (h.) Leal House, Alyth PH11 8JQ. Tel.: 01828 632695.

Grant, Major James MacAlpine Gregor, TD, NDA, MRAC. Landowner and Farmer, since 1961; b. 18.2.38, Nakuru, Kenya; m., Sara Marjory, DL; 3 d. Educ. Eton; Royal Agricultural College, Cirencester. National Service, Queen's Own Cameron Highlanders, 1957-58; TA with 4/5th Queen's Own Cameron Highlanders; Volunteers with 51st Highland Volunteers. Member, Royal Company of Archers, Queen's Bodyguard for Scotland. Address: Roskill House, Munlochy, Ross-shire IV8 8PA; T.-01463 811207.

Grant, Professor Peter Mitchell, PhD, FIEE, FIEEE, FRSE, FREng. Regius Professor of Engineering, Edinburgh University, since 2007 (Professor of Electronic Signal Processing, 1987-2007, Head, School of Engineering and Electronics, since 2002, Head, Department of Electronics and Electrical Engineering, 1999-2002); b. 20.6.44, St. Andrews; m., Marjory Renz; 2 d. Educ. Strathallan School; Heriot-Watt University; Edinburgh University. Two Honorary DEng degrees from Heriot-Watt and Napier Universities, 2007. Publications: Digital Communications (Co-author, 2nd edition) 2003; Digital Signal Processing (Co-author, 2nd edition), 2002. Winner, the Institution of Electrical Engineers Faraday Medal, 2004. Address: (b.) School of Engineering and Electronics, Edinburgh University, Edinburgh EH9 3JL; T.-0131-650 5569.

Grant, Rhoda. MSP (Labour), Highlands and Islands, since 2007; b. 26.6.63, Stornoway. Address: (b.) Scottish Parliament, Edinburgh EH99 1SP; Constituency Office: Queensgate Business Centre, 1-3 Fraser Street, Inverness IV1 1DW.

Grant, Richard Anthony, BSocSc, MSc. Head of Waste and Pollution Reduction Division, Environment and Rural

Affairs Department, Scottish Government, since 2004; Head of Housing Division 2, Scottish Executive Development Department, 1997-2004; b. 12.6.48, Leicester; m., Jacqueline Claire; 1 s.; 1 d. Educ. Loughborough College School; Birmingham University; Strathclyde University. Research Officer/Senior Research Officer, Scottish Education Department and Scottish Development Department, 1969-75; Principal Research Officer, Housing Research Unit, Scottish Development Department, 1975-77; Principal, Sports Policy Branch, Scottish Education Department, 1977-79; Principal Research Officer, Housing and Urban Renewal Research Unit, Scottish Development Department, 1979-85; Principal: Land Use and Conservation Branch, Department of Agriculture and Fisheries, 1986-89, NHS Management Executive, 1989-91; Head of Division, Land Use and Crofting, Scottish Office Agriculture and Fisheries Department, 1991-97. Recreations: cycling; hill-walking; cross-country skiing. Address: (b.) R1J/23, Victoria Quay, Leith, Edinburgh; T.-0131-224 0235.

Grant, Dr Robert, MBChB, MD, FRCP(Glas), FRCP(Edin). Consultant Neurologist, since 1991; Clinical Director, Department of Clinical Neurosciences, Western General Hospital, Edinburgh; b. 19.4.57, Greenock; m., L. Joy C. Grant; 2 s.; 3 d. Educ. Greenock Academy; Glasgow University. Lead Clinician, Scottish Adult Neuro-Oncology Network; President Elect, European Association for Neuro-Oncology. Recreations: rugby; volleyball; golf. Address: Western General Hospital, Crewe Road South, Edinburgh EH4 2XU.

Grant, Professor Robert Alexander Dickson, MA, PhD (Cantab), FRSA. Professor of the History of Ideas, Glasgow University, since 2004; b. 21.08.45, New Malden, Surrey; m., Elizabeth; 2 d. Educ. King's College School, Wimbledon, London; Trinity College, Cambridge. Senior Rouse Ball Student and Lector in English, 1969; Research Fellow, Trinity Hall, Cambridge, 1970; Lecturer in English, Sussex, 1973; Lecturer in English, Glasgow University, 1974, Senior Lecturer, 1992, Reader, 1995; Resident Scholar Fellow, Social Philosophy and Policy Centre, Bowling Green, State University, Ohio, 1999; British Council Distinguished Guest Professor, Political Studies Institute, Lisbon, 2006. Declared undesirable person by Czechoslovak Security Bureau (St. B) 1986; Council Member, Academy of Przemysl, Poland, 1996. Publications: Oakeshott, 1990; The Politics of Sex and Other Essays, 2000; Imagining The Real: Essays on Politics, Ideology and Literature, 2003. Recreations: (b.) c/o English Department, Glasgow University, Glasgow G12 8QQ; T.-0140 330 5296.

Grant Peterkin, Major General Anthony Peter, CB, OBE, BA. Army Officer, 1967-2004; Serjeant at Arms, House of Commons, 2004-07; Landowner; b. 6.7.47, London; m., Joanna Young; 1 s.; 1 d. Educ. Ampleforth College; University of Durham; University of Madras. Commissioned into Queen's Own Highlanders, 1967: service in Middle East, Germany, Northern Ireland, Belize, Hong Kong and India; ADC to CGS; Command of 1st Bn. Queen's Own Highlanders, Belize and Germany, 1987-89; Higher Command and Staff Course, Camberley, 1991; Military Adviser to UN Mission, Iraq and Kuwait, 1991; Commander, 24 Airmobile Brigade, 1993-94; Royal College of Defence Studies, 1995; Army Director of Manning and Career Management, 1996-98; Military Secretary and Chief Executive, Army Personnel Centre, Glasgow, 2000-04; Managing Director, OSCE Mission in Kosovo, 1999; GOC, 5 Division, 2000. Recreation: travelling off the beaten track in Indochina. Address: (h.) Grange Hall, Forres, Morayshire. T.-01309 672742.

Gray, Alasdair. Artist and Writer; b. 28.12.34, Glasgow; m., Morag McAlpine; 1 s. Educ. Whitehill Senior Secondary School; Glasgow Art School. Part-time Art

Teacher, 1958-62; Scene Painter, 1963-64; has since lived by drawing, painting, writing; Associate Professor of Creative Writing: Glasgow University, Strathclyde University, 2001-03; mural painter in Oran Mor Arts and Leisure Centre, Glasgow, since 2003; Glasgow People's Palace and The Collins Gallery, Strathclyde University have collections of his paintings; extant murals: Palacerigg nature reserve, Cumbernauld; Ubiquitous Chip restaurant, Glasgow; Abbots House local history museum, Dunfermline. Publications: novels: Lanark; 1982 Janine; The Fall of Kelvin Walker; Something Leather; McGrotty and Ludmilla; A History Maker; Poor Things; Mavis Belfrage; Old Men in Love, 2007; other books: Old Negatives (a life in four verse sequences); short story collections: Unlikely Stories, Mostly; Lean Tales (this last also containing work by Jim Kelman and Agnes Owens); Ten Tales Tall and True; Five Glasgow Artists (an exhibition catalogue); Saltire Self-Portrait No. 4; Why Scots Should Rule Scotland (1992 and 1997), Working Legs, a play for people without them; The Book of Prefaces, 2000; Sixteen Occasional Poems; The Ends of Our Tethers: 13 sorry stories, 2003; A Life in Pictures (pictorial autobiography), 2008. Recreations: reading; talking to friends; drinking; walking.

Gray, Alistair B., BA, CA. Managing Director, Ortak Jewellery Limited, since 1990; Board Member, Highlands and Islands Enterprise, 1997-2004; b. 14.6.58, Kirkwall, Orkney; m., Linda; 3 s.; 1 d. Educ. Kirkwall Grammar School; Heriot-Watt University. Chartered Accountant, Arthur Young, Edinburgh, 1979-84. Address: Hatston, Kirkwall, Orkney KW15 1RW; T.-01856 872224.

Gray, Lord (Andrew Godfrey Diarmid Stuart Campbell-Gray); b. 3.9.64. Address: (h.) Airds Bay, Taynuilt, Argyll.

Gray, Sir Charles Ireland, FRSA, JP, FEIS. Formerly Chair, Education, North Lanark Council; b. 25.1.29, Gartcosh; m., Catherine; 3 s.; 2 d. Educ. Coatbridge High School. Local government, since 1958; Leader, Strathclyde Regional Council, 1986-92 (Depute Leader, 1978-86); former Director, Scottish Exhibition and Conference Centre; former Member: Scottish Enterprise Board, East Kilbride Development Corporation, Scottish Development Agency, Clyde Port Authority; former Vice-Chairman, Planning Exchange; former UK Vice-President, European Committee of Regions. Recreations: music; reading; local government.

Gray, Ethel Marian, CBE, JP, MA, LLD, DUniv, FEIS. Patron, LEAD (Scotland), since 1997 (Board Member, and Chairman, Advisory Committee, 1987-95); b. 19.4.23, Glasgow; m., George Deans Gray (deceased). Educ. Hutchesons' Girls Grammar School; Paisley Grammar School; Glasgow University. Teacher of English, 1946-52; Lecturer in English and Drama, Jordanhill College, 1952-63; Founding Principal, Craigie College of Education, Ayr, 1963-75; Director, Scottish Adult Literacy Agency, 1976-79; Chairman, National Book League Scotland, 1977-81; Convener, Adult Access to Education, Scottish Institute of Adult and Continuing Education, 1988-89 (President of Institute, 1984-87); Vice-Chairman, Board of Governors, The Queen's College, Glasgow, 1980-88; Chairman, Education Project for Older People, Age Concern Scotland, 1982-85; Member of Court, Chairman of Staffing Committee and Joint Faculty Staff Review Board, Heriot-Watt University, 1979-84; Adviser in Adult Education, IBA, 1983-88; Member: Scottish Tertiary Education Advisory Council, 1984-87, Scottish Advisory Committee, British Council, 1968-89, STV Education Advisory Committee, 1981-92, Scottish Community Education Council, 1979-85 (Chairman, Communications and Technology Group and Chairman, Management Committee, Micro-Electronics Project), Crawford Commission on Radio and Television Coverage, 1973-75, Committee of Enquiry on the Police, 1977-79, Consultative Committee on the Curriculum, 1965-71. Honorary Fellow, Institute of Contemporary Scotland, since 2001. Recreations: reading; travelling; theatre. Address: (h.) Flat 5, Varrich House, 7 Church Hill, Edinburgh EH10 4BG; T.-0131-447 5403.

Gray, Henry Withers, MD, FRCP (Lond), FRCP (Glas), FRCR. Retired Consultant Physician in Medicine and Nuclear Medicine; b. 25.3.43, Glasgow; m., Mary Elizabeth Shaw; 1 s.; 2 d. Educ. Rutherglen Academy; University of Glasgow. Lecturer in Medicine, Glasgow Royal Infirmary, 1969-77; Research Fellow, Johns Hopkins Medical Institutions, USA, 1974-76; Medical Adviser to University of Strathclyde, since 2000. Publications: chapters in 10 books; 103 articles. Recreations: swimming; guitar; photography; garden; model making. Address: (h.) 4 Winton Park, East Kilbride, Glasgow G75 8QW; T.-01355 229525; e-mail: harry.gray@blueyonder.co.uk

Gray, Iain. MSP (Labour), East Lothian, since 2007; b. 7.6.57, Edinburgh. Address: (b.) Scottish Parliament, Edinburgh EH99 1SP; Constituency Office: c/o East Lothian Labour Party, 66 High Street, Tranent EH33 1LN.

Gray, J.N. David, BA. Principal, Stewart's Melville College and Mary Erskine School, Edinburgh, since 2000; b. 30.4.55, Inverness; m., Lynda; 1 s.; 2 d. Educ. Fettes College; Bristol University. Teacher of English, Henbury School, Bristol, 1978-80; Partner, Key Language School, Athens, 1980-85; Teacher, English and Modern Greek, Dulwich College, London, 1985-88; Head of English, Leeds Grammar School, 1988-92; Headmaster, Pocklington School, East Yorks, 1992-2000. Recreations: running; swimming; golf; cricket; music. Address: (b.) Queensferry Road, Edinburgh EH4 3EZ; T.-0131 311 1000; e-mail: principal@esmgc.com

Gray, James Allan, MB, ChB, FRCPEdin. Principal Medical Officer, Scottish Widows' Fund, Edinburgh, 1990-97; b. 24.3.35, Bristol; m., Jennifer Margaret Newton Hunter; 1 s. (deceased); 2 d. Educ. St. Paul's School, London; Edinburgh University. House Surgeon and Physician posts, Edinburgh and Middlesbrough; Short Service Commission, RAF Medical Branch, 1960-63; Senior House Officer, Research Fellow and Registrar posts, Edinburgh, 1965-67; Registrar, Bristol Royal Infirmary, 1967-68; Senior Registrar, Royal Free Hospital (Department of Infectious Diseases), London, 1968-69; Consultant in Communicable Diseases, City Hospital, Edinburgh, 1969-95; Assistant Director of Studies (Medicine), Edinburgh Post-Graduate Board, 1976-84; Honorary Senior Lecturer, Department of Medicine, Edinburgh University, 1992-95; Fellow, Royal Medical Society (Senior President, 1958-59); President, British Society for the Study of Infection, 1989-91; Founder Editor, Res Medica, 1957-58; Assistant Editor, Journal of Infection, 1979-86. Publications: Antibacterial Drugs Today (Co-author), 1983; Infectious Diseases (Co-author), 1984, 1992, new edition 1998; Edinburgh City Hospital, 1999. Recreations: hill-walking; pottery collecting; photography. Address: (h.) St. Andrews Cottage, 15 Lauder Road, Edinburgh EH9 2EN; T.-0131-667 4124.

Gray, Professor James Robertson, OBE, BSc, FRSGS, DipActMaths, FFA, FIMA, CMath, FSS, FFCS. Professor and Head, Department of Actuarial Mathematics and Statistics, Heriot-Watt University, 1971-89 (now Emeritus);

b. 21.2.26, Dundee; m., Catherine McAulay Towner. Educ. High School of Dundee; Edinburgh University. Actuarial Trainee, Scottish Life Assurance Company, 1947-49; St. Andrews University: Lecturer in Mathematics, 1949-50, Lecturer in Statistics, 1950-62, Senior Lecturer in Statistics (also Head of Department), 1962-71; Heriot-Watt University: established first Department of Actuarial Science in UK; Dean, Faculty of Science, 1978-81; Council Member, Faculty of Actuaries, 1969-87 (Vice President, 1983-87); Vice-Chairman, Scottish Examination Board, 1984-90 (Convener of Examinations Committee, 1982-90); former Council Member, Royal Scottish Geographical Society and former Convener, Lecture Committee; former Vice-Chairman, Scottish Universities Council on Entrance; Past Chairman: Scottish Branch, Institute of Mathematics and Its Applications, Edinburgh Branch, Royal Statistical Society; Past President, Murrayfield-Cramond Rotary Club; Past President, Murrayfield-Cramond Probus Club; Past Captain, Senior Section of Royal Burgess Golfing Society; Statistical Consultant to Law Society of Scotland, 1978-89; Member: Royal Burgess Golfing Society, Melville Bridge Club. Recreations: golf; hill-walking; bridge; music; Probus. Address: (h.) Green Gables, 9 Cammo Gardens, Edinburgh EH4 8EI; T.-0131-339 3330.

Gray, Muriel, BA (Hons). Broadcaster; b. Glasgow. Educ. Glasgow School of Art. Worked as an illustrator; then as a designer with National Museum of Antiquities; was member of rock band, The Family Von Trapp; had own show with Radio Forth; was frequent presenter on Radio 1; co-presented The Tube, Channel 4; had own arts programme, The Works, Tyne Tees; own music programme, Studio 1, Border TV; presented Casebook Scotland, BBC Scotland; Frocks on the Box, Thames TV; Acropolis Now, ITV; presented The Media Show, Channel 4; Co-Producer and Presenter, Walkie Talkie, Channel 4; first woman Rector, Edinburgh University; Producer/ Presenter/Director, The Munro Show, Scottish TV; Producer/Presenter, Art is Dead...Long Live TV!, Channel Four; The Golden Cagoule, BBC; Ride On. Publications: The First Fifty, 1991; The Trickster (novel), 1994; Furnace (novel), 1997; The Ancient, 2001; Kelvingrove: portal to the world, 2006. Recreation: being in the Scottish Highlands — gets grumpy and miserable if can't be up a mountain every few weeks. Address: (b.) St. Georges Studios, 93-97 St. Georges Road, Glasgow G3 6JA.

Gray, Peter, LLB (Hons). Queen's Counsel, since 2002; b. 7.11.59, Inverness; m., Bridget; 1 s.; 2 d. Educ. Fettes College, Edinburgh; Southampton University. Called to Bar of England and Wales, 1983; Admitted to Faculty of Advocates, 1992; Advocate Depute, 1998-2000. Address: (b.) Compass Chambers, Advocates Library, Parliament House, Edinburgh EH1 1RF; T.-0131-2265071.
E-mail: peter@plgray.freeserve.co.uk

Gray, Professor Peter Michael David, MA, DPhil, FBCS. Professor Emeritus (formerly Professor, Department of Computing Science, Aberdeen University, 1989-2005); b. 11.2.40, Abingdon; m., Doreen F. Ross; 1 s.; 1 d. Educ. Abingdon School; Queens' College, Cambridge; Jesus College, Oxford. Systems Analyst, Plessey Co., Poole, 1966-68; Research Fellow, Computer Research Group, Aberdeen University, 1968-72; Lecturer in Computing Science, Aberdeen University, 1972-84; Visiting Associate Professor, University of Western Ontario, 1985; Senior Lecturer, 1985-89. Reader, Church of Scotland. Publication: Logic, Algebra and Databases. Recreation: croquet. Address: (b.) Department of Computing Science, King's College, Aberdeen AB24 3UE; T.-01224 272292.

Gray, Robert, CBE, OStJ, JP, DL, LLD. Chair, Education Services, Glasgow City Council, 1999-2003; Vice Lord Lieutenant, City of Glasgow, 1992-96; b. 3.3.28; m., Mary McCartney; 1 d. Educ. St Mungo's Academy, Glasgow. Lecturer, Glasgow College of

Building, 1964-65; Anniesland College, 1965-70; Senior Lecturer, Cardonald College, 1970-84; Labour Member, City of Glasgow Council, from 1974; Lord Provost and Lord Lieutenant of Glasgow, 1984-88; Deacon, Incorporation of Wrights of Glasgow, 1966. OStJ; Fellow, Glasgow College of Technology, 1987; Hon. LLD, Strathclyde, 1987 Recreations: walking; music. Address; (h.) 106 Churchill Drive, Glasgow G11 7EZ, T.-0141-357 3328.

Gray, Professor Robert Hugh, BSc (Econ), MA (Econ), PhD, FCA, FCCA. Professor of Social and Environmental Accounting, St. Andrews University, since 2004; b. 1.4.52, Manchester; 2 s. Educ. De La Salle College, Salford; Hull University; Manchester University. Qualified as accountant with KPMG Peat Marwick, 1976; Lecturer, Lancashire Polytechnic, UCNW Bangor, University of East Anglia; Mathew Professor of Accounting and Information Systems, Dundee University, 1990-2000; Professor of Accounting, Glasgow University, 2000-04; Editor, Social and Environmental Accounting; Director, Centre for Social and Environmental Accounting Research. Publications: over 200 articles; various books including Accounting for the Environment; The Greening of Accountancy; Accounting and Accountability. Recreations: sailing; rock music. Address: (b.) School of Management, University of St. Andrews, The Gateway Building, North Haugh, St. Andrews, Fife KY16 9ST; T.-01334 462799.

Green, Alexander M. S., MTheol (Hons), LLB, LLM. Director, The Law Agency (Scotland) Ltd., since 2006; Solicitor; b. 31.12.63, Worcester; divorced; 1 d. Educ. Dyson Perrins CE High School; St. Andrews University; University of Aberdeen. Article Clerk, Cameron Markby Hewitt, 1991-93; CMS Cameron McKenna LLP: Assistant Solicitor, 1993-2000, Partner, 2000-06. Board of Management, The Instant Neighbour Charity; Free Burgess and Guild Member, The Burgh of Aberdeen. Recreations: history; literature; heraldry; fly fishing. Address: (b.) 44 Fountainhall Road, Aberdeen AB15 4DT; T.-01224 639712; e-mail: alex@the-lawagency.com

Green, David Russell, OBE, MA (Hons). Convenor, Cairngorms National Park Authority; Member, Scottish Committee Big Lottery Fund, since 2007; Board Member, Scottish Agricultural College, since 2008; formerly Chairman, Crofters Commission, 2002-06 and Convenor, Highland Council, 1999-2003; b. 13.6.51, Aberdeen; m., Sheila; 1 s.; 3 d. Educ. Glasgow University. Marketing consultant; trainee chartered accountant; hotelier; snowplough driver; fully diversified crofter. Address: (h & b.) Stac Pollaidh Self Catering, Achnahaird, Achiltibuie, Ullapool IV26 2YT; T.-01854 622340; (b.) 01479 870502.
E-mail: davidgreen@cairngorms.co.uk

Green, Professor Roger Philip Hywel, MA, BLitt. Professor of Humanity (Latin), University of Glasgow, since 1995; b. 14.6.43, High Wycombe; m., Anne Mary Perry; 1 s.; 1 d. Educ. Royal Grammar School, High Wycombe; Balliol College, University of Oxford. University of St. Andrews: Assistant Lecturer, 1967-70, Lecturer, 1970-92, Senior Lecturer, 1992-94, Reader, 1994-95. Former Secretary, International Association of Neo-Latin Studies. Publications include: The Works of Ausonius, 1991; Augustine on Christian Teaching, 1997; Latin Epics of the New Testament, 2006. Recreations: walking; cycling; rail travel; birdwatching; gardening; music; architecture. Address: (b.) Department of Classics, University of Glasgow, Glasgow G12 8QQ; T.-0141-330 4276.

Greene, John Gerald, MA, PhD, FBPsS. Clinical Lecturer, Glasgow University; b. 10.3.38, Glasgow; m., Dr. Elisabeth Rose Hamil; 2 s.; 2 d. Educ. St. Aloysius College, Glasgow; Glasgow University. Clinical Tutor, Glasgow

University Master of Applied Science degree in Clinical Psychology, 1976-95; Chairman, National (Scotland) Scientific Consultative Committee on Clinical Psychological Services, 1985-87; Treasurer, International Menopause Society, 1996-99; Registrar, Board of Examiners in Clinical Psychology, British Psychological Society, 1990-2002. Publications: The Social and Psychological Origins of the Climacteric Syndrome, 1984; Clinical Psychology in the Scottish Health Service (Co-author), 1984. Recreations: music; tennis; skiing. Address: (h.) 20 Mansionhouse Gardens, Langside, Glasgow G41 3DP.

Greene, John Henderson, MA, LLB. Former Partner, MacRoberts, Solicitors, Glasgow and Edinburgh; b. 2.6.32, Kilmarnock; m., Catriona McGillivray Scott; 1 s. Educ. Merchiston Castle School, Edinburgh; Edinburgh University. Assistant: Joseph Kirkland & Son, Solicitors, Saltcoats, 1958-60, MacRoberts, Solicitors, 1960 (appointed Partner, 1961); Law Society of Scotland: former Vice-Convener, Company Law Committee, former Member, Bankruptcy and Liquidation Committee; former Council Member, Royal Faculty of Procurators, Glasgow; founder Chairman, Troon Round Table, 1964; Captain, Royal Troon Golf Club, 1989-90; Elder, Portland Church, Troon; President, Glasgow Ayrshire Society, 1985-86, 1993-94, 1998-99; Vice-Chairman, Ayrshire and Arran Health Board, 1993-2001. Publication: Law and Practice of Receivership in Scotland (Co-Author). Recreations: golf; gardening. Address: (h.) Silvertrees, 7 Lady Margaret Drive, Troon KA10 7AL; T.-Troon 312482.

Greening, Professor Andrew Peter, BSc, MBChB, FRCPE. Consultant Physician, Western General Hospital, Edinburgh, since 1984; Professor of Pulmonary Disease, University of Edinburgh; b. 10.10.48, London; m., Rosemary Jean Renwick; 2 s. Educ. George Watson's College, Edinburgh; University of Edinburgh. House Officer and Senior House Officer posts, Edinburgh, 1973-75; Registrar, Senior Registrar, MRC Training Fellow posts, St. Bartholomew's and Hammersmith Hospitals and Royal Postgraduate Medical School, London, 1975-82. Director, Scottish Adult Cystic Fibrosis Service, Western General Hospital, Edinburgh, 1992-2005; Lead Clinician, Respiratory Medicine, Lothian Health, since 2005; Associate Editor, Thorax and Respiratory Medicine; Member, Grants Committees: Chest, Heart and Stroke Association, British Lung Foundation (Chair), Cystic Fibrosis Trust. International Lecturer on asthma and cystic fibrosis; Member, Scottish, British, European and American Thoracic Societies. Address: (b.) Western General Hospital, Edinburgh EH4 2XU.

Greenman, Professor Jonathan Vaughan, BA, MA, PhD. Emeritus Professor, Department of Computing Science and Mathematics, Stirling University, since 2002, Professor of Mathematics and Its Applications, 1990-2002; b. 3.3.39, Cardiff; m., Barbara Phyllis; 2 s. Educ. Kingston Grammar School; Cambridge University. Harkness Scholar, University of California, Berkeley; Department of Physics, MIT; Stanford Research Institute, California; Department of Mathematics, Essex University; Tutor, Open University; Senior Analyst, Corporate Planning, British Petroleum plc; Industry Analyst, Centre for Global Energy Studies. Recreations: cinema; walking; travel. Address: (b.) Department of Computing Science and Mathematics, Stirling University, Stirling, FK9 4LA; T.-01786 467460.

Greenshields, David, MA, DipEd. Headteacher, Uddingston Grammar School, since 1997; b. 24.7.49, Thankerton; m., Megan Bond; 2 d. Educ. Biggar High School; University of Edinburgh; Moray House College.

History Teacher, Lanark Grammar, 1971; Assistant Principal Teacher, Social Subjects, Auchmuty High, Fife, 1973; Assistant Principal Teacher, Guidance, Lanark Grammar, 1974; various posts, Uddingston Grammar School, since 1978. Recreation: supporter of Heart of Midlothian F.C. Address: (b.) Uddingston Grammar School, Station Road, Uddingston G71 7BS; T.-01698 327400; (h.) Stonebyres, Lanark.

Greenwood, Professor Justin, BA (Hons), PhD. Professor of European Public Policy, Robert Gordon University, Aberdeen, since 1996; Visiting Professor, College of Europe (Bruges and Warsaw); b. 17.5.60, Windlesham. Educ. Newton Abbot Grammar School; Nottingham University. Editorial Advisory Board, Business and Politics, Journal of Public Affairs. Publications: Interest Representation in the EU, 2007; The Challenge of Change in EU Business Associations (Editor), 2003; Inside the EU Business Associations, 2002; The Effectiveness of EU Business Associations (Editor), 2001; Social Partnership in the European Union (Co-Editor), 2001; Representing Interests in the European Union, 1997; Organised Interests in the New Global Order (Co-Editor) 1999; Collective Action in the European Union: Interest and the New Politics of Associability (Co-Editor) 1997; European Casebook on Business Alliances (Editor) 1995; Organised Interests and the European Community, (jointly), 1992. Address: (b.) Robert Gordon University, Garthdee Road, Aberdeen, AB10 7QE; T.-01224 263406.

Greig, Rev. Alan, BSc, BD. Minister, Kintore Parish Church, since 1992; b. 19.11.51, Helensburgh; m., Ruth D. Evans; 2 s. Educ. Coatbridge High School; University of Strathclyde; University of Edinburgh. Probationer Minister, Northfield Parish, Aberdeen, 1976-77; Minister, Hurlford Reid Memorial Church, Ayrshire, 1977-83; Church of Scotland Missionary working with United Church of Zambia, 1983-92. Recreations: swimming; cycling; walking. Address: 28 Oakhill Road, Kintore, Inverurie AB51 0FH; T.-01467 632219; e-mail: greig@kincarr.free-online.co.uk

Greig, Alastair, BVM&S, FRCVS, FRAgS. Emeritus Fellow, SAC; b. 18.5.44, Aberdeen; m., Margaret; 1 s.; 1 d. Educ. Robert Gordon's College, Aberdeen; Royal (Dick) School of Veterinary Studies, Edinburgh University. Assistant in veterinary practice, Kippen, 1967-68; Veterinary Research Officer, Animal Virus Research Institute, Pirbright, 1968-73; Assistant Veterinary Investigation Officer, Dumfries Veterinary Investigation Centre, 1973-78; Assistant Veterinary Investigation Officer, St Boswells, 1978-83; Veterinary Investigation Officer, Edinburgh, 1983-91; Assistant Director, SAC Veterinary Science Division, 1991-99; Group Manager, Veterinary Services, SAC, 1999-2004. Past President, BVA Scottish Branch, and BVA Scottish Metropolitan Division; Founder Member, VetCPD and Tayside Clinical Club; Chair, Giffordtown and District Community Council, since 2004. Recreations: small-holding; gardening; walking. Address: (h.) Jacobscroft, Innerleith, Cupar, Fife KY15 7UP; T.-01337 830638.

Greig, G. Andrew, MA. Author; b. 23.9.51, Bannockburn; m., Lesley Glaister. Educ. Waid Academy, Anstruther; Edinburgh University. Full-time writer, since 1979; Writer-in-Residence, Glasgow University, 1979-81; Scottish-Canadian Exchange Fellow, 1981-82; Writer-in-Residence, Edinburgh University, 1993-94; climbed on Himalayan expeditions. Publications: six volumes of poetry including Men on Ice, Surviving Passages, The Order of the Day, Western Swing, Into You; two mountaineering books;

novels: Electric Brae, Return of John Macnab; When They Lay Bare; That Summer; In Another Light; non-fiction: Preferred Lies. Recreations: music; hills; golf. Address: 1 Melvin Place, Stromness, Orkney KY16 3DD.

Greig, Kenneth Muir, MA, PhD. Rector, Hutchesons' Grammar School, Glasgow, since 2005; b. 30.3.60, Edinburgh; m., Josephine; 1 s.; 1 d. Educ. George Heriot's School, Edinburgh; Worcester College, Oxford; University of Edinburgh. Exploration Geologist, British Petroleum, 1984-87; Mathematics Teacher and Housemaster, Christ's Hospital, 1987-93; Head of Mathematics and Director of Studies, Dollar Academy, 1993-2000; Headmaster, Pangbourne College, 2000-05. Recreations: watching rugby; rowing; beachcombing; bagpipes. Address: (b.) Beaton Road, Glasgow G41 4NW; T.-0141 423 2933; e-mail: rector@hutchesons.org

Grice, Paul Edward, BSc. Clerk and Chief Executive, Scottish Parliament, since 1999; b. 13.10.61; m.; 2 d. Department of Transport, 1985-87; Department of Environment, 1987-92; joined Scottish Office, 1992 (latterly Head of Division, Constitution Group: Referendum, Scotland Bill, then Director of Implementation); Member, Stirling University Court, since 2005; Secretary, Scotland's Futures Forum, since 2005; Hon. Fellow, Royal Incorporation of Architects in Scotland, 2006. Address: Scottish Parliament, Edinburgh EH99 1SP.

Grier, Arnold Macfarlane, MB, ChB, FRCSEdin. Consultant Ear, Nose and Throat Surgeon, Highland Health Board, since 1962; National Vice-President, Scottish Council on Deafness; b. 5.9.21, Musselburgh; m., Elisabeth J. Kluten; 2 s.; 1 d. Educ. Musselburgh Grammar School; Edinburgh University. Recreations: gardening; aviculture; painting. Address: (h.) Elmbank, 68 Culduthel Road, Inverness; T.-Inverness 234682.

Grier, Scott, OBE, MA, CA, FCIT. Chairman, Loganair Limited; b. 7.3.41, Kilmacolm; m., Frieda Gardiner; 2 s. Educ. Greenock High School; Glasgow University. Apprenticed, Grahams Rintoul & Co., 1962-66; Accountant, Ardrossan Harbour Company Ltd./Clydeport, from 1967; various posts, Loganair, since 1976; Director: Glasgow Chamber of Commerce, 1990-98, Caledonian MacBrayne Limited, 1996-2006; Chairman, Scottish Tanning Industries Ltd., 1997-2003; Governor, Scottish Sports Aid, 1993-2004; Member, Scottish Tourist Board, 1992-98; Recreations: golf; philately. Address: (h.) Lagavulin, 15 Corsehill Drive, West Kilbride, KA23 9HU; T.-01294 823138.

Grieve, Professor Andrew Robert, OBE, DDS, BDS, FDS RCSEd. Professor of Conservative Dentistry, 1980-99, Dean of Dentistry, 1993-97, Dundee University; Consultant in Restorative Dentistry, 1980-99; b. 23.5.39, Stirling; m., Frances M. Ritchie; 2 d. Educ. Perth Academy, St. Andrews University. Junior hospital appointments and general dental practice, 1961-63; Lecturer in Operative Dental Surgery and Dental Therapeutics, St. Andrews University, 1963-65; Lecturer in Conservative Dentistry, Birmingham University, 1965; appointed Senior Lecturer and Consultant in Restorative Dentistry, Birmingham Area Health Authority (Teaching), 1975. Member, Dental Council, Royal College of Surgeons of Edinburgh, 1983-88; President: British Society for Restorative Dentistry, 1986-87 (Honorary Fellow, 2000); President: Royal Odonto-Chirurgical Society of Scotland, 1994-95 (Council Member, 1985-88); Chairman, Tayside Area Dental Advisory Committee, 1987-90; Member, General Dental Council, 1989-99 (Chairman, Legislation Committee, 1994-99);

Trustee, Armitstead Lecture Trust, since 2003; Director of Training, Tayside Pre-Retirement Council, 2005. Recreations: furniture making; hill-walking; travel, especially in France, and study of French language and culture. Address: (h.) Ravensfield, 20 Albany Road, West Ferry, Dundee.

Griffin, Douglas, MA (Hons), CA. Director of Finance, Greater Glasgow and Clyde NHS Board; b. 25.4.56, Glasgow; m., Barbara; 1 s.; 1 d. Educ. High School of Glasgow; Glasgow University. Peat Marwick Mitchell & Co., 1979-84; Barr and Stroud Ltd/Pilkington Optronics, 1984-93; Director of Finance and Information, Monklands and Bellshill Hospitals NHS Trust, 1993-99; Director of Finance, Greater Glasgow Primary Care Trust, 1999-2005. Recreations: golf; hill-walking. Address: (b.) NHSGG & C, Dalian House, 350 St. Vincent Street, Glasgow G3 8YZ.

Griffiths, Nigel. MP (Labour), Edinburgh South, since 1987; Deputy Leader of the House of Commons, 2005-07; Parliamentary Under-Secretary of State (Minister for Small Business), Department of Trade and Industry, 2001-05; Minister for Competition and Consumer Affairs, 1997-98; Vice President, Institute of Trading Standards Administration, since 1994; Chair, HEAT (Home Energy Action Team), since 1999; Chair, Scottish Charities Kosovo Appeal, since 1999; b. 20.5.55; m., Sally McLaughlin. Educ. Hawick High School; Edinburgh University; Moray House College of Education. Secretary, Lothian Devolution Campaign, 1978; Rights Adviser, Mental Handicap Pressure Group, 1979-87; City of Edinburgh District Councillor, 1980-87 (Chairperson, Housing Committee); Member: Edinburgh Festival Council, 1984-87, Edinburgh Health Council, 1982-87; Executive Member, Edinburgh Council of Social Service, 1984-87; Member, Wester Hailes School Council, 1981; Executive Member, Scottish Constitutional Convention (Chair, Finance Committee); Opposition Spokesman on Consumer Affairs, 1989-97. Recreations: travel; scuba diving; live entertainment; badminton; hill-walking; rock-climbing; architecture; reading; politics. Address: 31 Minto Street, Edinburgh EH9 2BT; T.-0131-662 4520.

Griffiths, Professor Peter Denham, CBE, BSc, MD, LRCP, MRCS, FRCPath, FRCP(Edin), FCMI, FRSA. Emeritus Professor of Biochemical Medicine, Dundee University (Vice-Principal, 1979-85, Dean of Medicine and Dentistry, 1985-89); Director and Trustee, Scottish Hospitals Endowment Research Trust, 1994-98; b. 16.6.27, Southampton; m., Joy Burgess; 3 s.; 1 d. Educ. King Edward VI School, Southampton; Guy's Hospital, London University. House appointments, Guy's Hospital, 1956-57; Junior Lecturer in Physiology, Guy's Hospital, 1957-58; Registrar and Senior Registrar, Guy's and Lewisham Hospitals, 1958-64; Consultant Pathologist, Harlow Hospitals Group, 1964-66; Senior Lecturer in Clinical Chemistry/Honorary Consultant, St. Andrews University, then Dundee University, 1966-68. Member, General Medical Council, 1986-93; President, 1987-89, and sometime Chairman of Council, Association of Clinical Biochemists; Tayside Health Board: Honorary Consultant, 1966-89, Member, 1977-85; former Director, Dundee Repertory Theatre. Recreations: music; domestic activities. Address: (h.) 52 Albany Road, West Ferry, Dundee DD5 1NW; T.-01382 776772.

Grimmond, Iain William, BAcc (Hons), CA. General Treasurer, Church of Scotland, since 2005; Director of Finance, Erskine Hospital for Disabled Ex-Servicemen and Women, 1981-2004; b. 8.8.55, Girvan; m., Marjory Anne Gordon Chisholm; 1 s.; 2 d. Educ. Hutchesons' Boys

Grammar School; Glasgow University. Trainee CA, Ernst & Whinney, Glasgow, 1976-79; Assistant Treasurer, Erskine Hospital, 1979-81. Elder, Giffnock South Parish Church. Recreations: golf; football; reading. Address: (h.) 9 Wemyss Avenue, Crookfur, Newton Mearns, Glasgow G77 6AR; T.-0141-639 4894.

Grimmond, Steve, MA, MBA, FRSA. Head of Community Services, Fife Council, since 2005; b. 12.6.63, Dundee; m., Audrey Krawec; 1 s.; 1 d. Educ. Craigie High School, Dundee; Dundee University. Dundee District Council: Special Projects Officer, Principal Officer, Area Renewal; Corporate Planning Officer; Policy Planning Manager, Chief Executive's Department, Dundee City Council; Area Manager, Aberdeenshire Council; Director, Arts and Heritage, Dundee City Council; Director, Leisure and Arts, Dundee City Council; Director: Scottish Screen, Scottish Arts Council, Sportscotland, Abertay Student Centre, Collective Gallery, Byre Theatre. Recreations: football; contemporary cinema; artist; shopping at Sainsbury. Address: (b.) Rothesay House, Rothesay Place, Glenrothes KY7 5PQ; T.-08451 555555 ext. 444143; e-mail: steven.grimmond@fife.gov.uk

Grimstone, Gerry, MA, MSc. Chairman: Standard Life plc, since 2007, Candover Investments plc, since 2006; b. 27.8.49, London; 1 s.; 2 d. Educ. Whitgift School; Merton College, Oxford University. UK Civil Service, latterly HM Treasury, 1972-86; Schroders Investment Banking (London, Hong Kong, New York), 1986-2000; various public and private boards, since 2000. Address: (b.) Standard Life plc, 30 Lothian Road, Edinburgh EH1 2DH; T.-0131 245 2151.

Grinyer, Professor John Raymond, MSc, FCA. Emeritus Professor of Accountancy and Business Finance, Dundee University (Deputy Principal, 1997-2000, Dean, Faculty of Law, 1984-85, 1991-1993, Head, Department of Accountancy and Business Finance, 1976-90); b. 3.3.35, London; m., Shirley Florence Marshall; 1 s.; 2 d. Educ. Central Park Secondary Modern School, London; London School of Economics. London Electricity Board, 1950-53; National Service, RAMC, 1953-55; Halifax Building Society, 1955-56; Martin Redhead & Co., Accountants, 1956-60; Hope Agar & Co., Chartered Accountants, 1960-62; Kemp Chatteris & Co., Chartered Accountants, 1962-63; Lecturer, Harlow Technical College, 1963-66; City of London Polytechnic, 1966-71; Cranfield School of Management, 1971-76; Chairman, British Accounting Association, 1980-81 and 1990, and Scottish Representative, 1984-93. Elder, St. Stephens and West Church, Broughty Ferry. Recreations: golf; dinghy sailing; Member: Royal Tay Yacht Club, Broughty Golf Club. Address: (h.) 81 Dundee Road, Broughty Ferry, Dundee DD5 1LZ; T.-Dundee 775743.
E-mail: johngrinyer@talktalk.net

Grinyer, Professor Peter Hugh, MA (Oxon), PhD. Emeritus Professor, St. Andrews University, since 1993; b. 3.3.35, London; m., Sylvia Joyce Boraston; 2 s. Educ. Balliol College, Oxford; London School of Economics. Senior Managerial Trainee, Unilever Ltd., 1957-59; Personal Assistant to Managing Director, E.R. Holloway Ltd., 1959-61; Lecturer and Senior Lecturer, Hendon College of Technology, 1961-64; Lecturer, The City University, London, 1965-69; The City University Business School: Senior Lecturer and Co-ordinator of Research, 1969-72, Reader, 1972-74, Professor of Business Strategy, 1974-79; Esmee Fairbairn Professor of Economics (Finance and Investment), St. Andrews University, 1979-93; Chairman, Department of Economics, 1979-85; Vice-

Principal, 1985-87 (Acting Principal, 1986); Chairman, Department of Management, 1987-89; Chairman: St. Andrews Management Institute, 1989-96, St. Andrews Strategic Management Ltd.; Member, Sub-Committee on Management and Business Studies, University Grants Committee, 1979-85; Consultant to NEDO on Sharpbenders Project, 1984-86; Visiting Professor, New York University, 1992, 1996-98; Visiting Professor, Imperial College, London, since 2002; Non-Executive Director: Glenrothes Enterprise Trust, 1983-86, John Brown plc, 1984-86, Don Bros. Buist plc (now Don and Low (Holdings) Ltd.) 1985-91, Ellis and Goldstein plc, 1987-88; Chairman (non-executive), McIlroy Coates, 1991-95; Member, Scottish Legal Aid Board, 1992-2000; Member, Appeal Panel, Competition Commission, 2000-03; Member, Competition Appeals Tribunal, since 2003; Erskine Fellow, University of Canterbury, New Zealand, 1994. Recreations: mountain walking; golf; listening to music. Address: (b.) 60 Buchanan Gardens, St. Andrews KY16 9LY; T.-01334 472966.

Gronn, Professor Peter Christian, BA (Hons), BEd, PhD, FRSA, FACEL. Professor, Chair in Public Service, Edicational Leadership and Management, University of Glasgow, since 2007; b. 15.11.46, Melbourne, Australia; m., Barbara; 1 d. Educ. Canterbury State School; Camberwell Central School; Camberwell High School; University of Melbourne; Monash University. Teacher: Education Department of Victoria, 1970-73; Lecturer, Barnard State College, 1974-79; Lecturer, then Professor, Education Faculty, Monash University, 1980-2007. Publications: The Making of Educational Leaders, 1999; The New Work of Educational Leaders, 2003. Recreations: reading; music; walking; sport; travel. Address: (h.) 01/48 Cecil Street, Hillhead, Glasgow G12 8RJ; e-mail: pandbgronn@talktalk.net

Grossart, Sir Angus McFarlane McLeod, CBE, LLD, DBA, DLitt, FRSE, DL, MA, CA. Advocate; Merchant Banker; Chairman and Managing Director, Noble Grossart; Chairman, Scottish Daily Record and Sunday Mail, 1998-2007; Director: Edinburgh US Tracker Trust (Chairman), Trinity Mirror Group PLC, 1999-2007, Scottish and Newcastle PLC, since 1998; Royal Bank of Scotland (Vice Chairman, 1996-2005); The Scottish Investment Trust PLC, 1973-2003 (Chairman); The Fine Art Society (Chairman); Scotland International (Chairman); Lyon & Turnbull (Chairman); Edinburgh Partners (Chairman); b. 6.4.37, Glasgow; m., Gay Kerr Dodd; 1 d. Educ. Glasgow Academy; Glasgow University. CA, 1962; Advocate, Scottish Bar, 1963-69; Managing Director, Noble Grossart Ltd., since 1969; Chairman of Trustees, National Galleries of Scotland, 1988-97; Trustee and Deputy Chairman, National Heritage Memorial Fund, 1999-2005; Chairman of Trustees, National Museums of Scotland, since 2006; Trustee, The High Steward of Scotland's Dumfries House Trust; Chairman, Restoration of St Giles High Kirk, Edinburgh. Recreations: golf; decorative arts; historic architecture. Address: (b.) 48 Queen Street, Edinburgh EH2 3NR; T.-0131-226 7011.

Grosset, Alan George, MA, LLB, WS, NP. Retired Solicitor; formerly Partner, Alex Morison & Co., W.S.; b. 18.1.42, Edinburgh; 1 s.; 1 d. Educ. Royal High School, Edinburgh; Edinburgh University. Law Society of Scotland "Troubleshooter" from inception of scheme, until 1987; Council Member, W.S. Society, 1998-2000; President, Scottish Lawn Tennis Association, 1983-84; Council Member, Lawn Tennis Association, 1980-89; first Chairman, Scottish Sports Association, 1984-90; Vice-Chairman, Scottish Sports Council, 1994-2002 (Member since 1984); Captain, Duddingston Golf Club, 1992-94;

Depute Clerk, NHS Scotland Tribunal, since 2005; Public Interest Member, ICAS Insolvency Permit Committee, since 2005; Chairman, Confederation of British Sport, 2002-04; Director, Sports Dispute Resolution Panel Ltd. Recreations: golf; tennis.

Grosz, David Peter, BA (Hons). Vice President, Ramblers' Association Scotland, since 2000; b. 2.4.39, London. Educ. Wyggeston Boys' Grammar School, Leicester; Nottingham University; School of Education, Leicester University. School Teacher, Leicester, 1962-78, West Lothian, 1978-84. Member: Ramblers' Association Executive Committee 1983-99 (Vice Chairman, 1995-98, Chairman, 1998-99), Board of Directors, Scottish Rights of Way Society, 1984-92, Council, National Trust for Scotland, 1989-94, Board of Directors, Paths for All Partnership, 2000-04; Chairman: Friends of New Lanark, 1985-89, Ramblers' Association Scottish Council, 1985-96; Founding Member and Committee Member, Scottish Council for National Parks, 1991-95, and 2000-04. Recreations: walking; reading; campaigning with passion for public access and countryside conservation. Address: (h.) 57 Harburn Avenue, Deans, Livingston EH54 8NH; T.-01506 410493.

Groundwater, William, MB, ChB, FRCSEd; b. 20.8.36, Kirkwall, Orkney; m., Sheila M. Williamson; 1 s. Educ. Kirkwall Grammar School; Stromness Academy; Edinburgh University. MB, ChB, Edinburgh University, 1960; FRSCEd, 1966; General Surgical Practice, Thunder Bay, Ontario, 1971-73; Consultant General Surgeon, Balfour Hospital, Kirkwall, Orkney, 1973-99 (retired). Past President, Rotary Club of Orkney; Honorary Sheriff, Sheriffdom of Grampian, Highlands and Islands. Recreations: reading; book-binding. Address: (h.) Clowigar, Scapa, St. Ola, Orkney KW15 1SD; T.-01856-872965.
E-mail: clowigar@aol.com

Grubb, Rt. Hon. George, BA, BD, BPhil, DMin. Lord Lieutenant and Lord Provost, City of Edinburgh, since 2007; b. 1935; m., Liz; 1 s.; 1 d. Educ. James Gillespie's Boys School and Royal High School; University of Edinburgh; Open University. Scottish Schools Junior half mile Champion 1954; Royal High School half mile record holder. National Service in Royal Army Ordinance Corps for two years; Ordained Minister in 1962 in Stoke-on-Trent; Squadron Leader Chaplain in Royal Air Force 1962-70; served in Cosford then three years in Nicosia, Cyprus (during that time touring Tehran, Aidan, Malta and Tripoli); Parish Minister at Craigsbank Parish Church 1971-2001. Served on various Committees of the Edinburgh Presbytery and was Moderator; served as Minister in residence at Eden Seminary in St Louis, USA. During one sabbatical leave went to the United Theological College in Zambia. Elected as Councillor for Queensferry in 1999. Chairperson of the Liberal Democrat Group, 2000-07. Recreations: jogging, running, reading and family. Address: (b.) City Chambers, High Street, Edinburgh EH1 1YJ; T.-0131 529 4000.

Guild, Ivor Reginald, CBE, FRSE, MA, LLB, WS; b. 2.4.24, Dundee. Educ. Cargilfield; Rugby; New College, Oxford; Edinburgh University. Formerly Director: Fulcrum Investment Trust, Scottish Oriental Smaller Companies Trust PLC; former Partner, Shepherd & Wedderburn, WS; former Procurator Fiscal to the Lyon Court. Recreations: golf; genealogy. Address: New Club, 86 Princes Street, Edinburgh EH2 2BB; T.-0131-220 1085.

Gunn, Alexander MacLean, MA, BD. Minister, Aberfeldy with Amulree and Strathbraan with Dull and Weem, 1986-2006; b. 26.2.43, Inverness; m., Ruth T.S.; 1 s.; 1 d. Educ. Edinburgh Academy; Beauly; Dingwall Academy; Edinburgh University and New College. Parish Minister: Wick St. Andrews and Thrumster, 1967-73; Member,

Caithness Education Committee, 1968-73; Parish Minister, Glasgow St. David's Knightswood, 1973-86; Convener: Church of Scotland Rural Working Group, 1988-90, General Assembly's Presbytery Development Committee, 1990-92, General Assembly's Mission and Evangelism Resource Committee, 1992-95; Interim Convener, Board of National Mission, 1996; Convener, Regional Committee, Scripture Union Scotland, 1998-2005. Chairman, Breadalbane Academy School Board, 1989-92 and 1996-2002. Address: "Navarone", 12 Cornhill Road, Perth PH1 1LR; T.-01738-443216; e-mail: sandygunn@btinternet.com

Gusterson, Professor Barry Austin, PhD, FRCPath. Professor of Pathology, Glasgow University, since 2000, Head, Division of Cancer Sciences and Molecular Pathology, since 2002; b. 24.10.46, Colchester; m., Ann Josephine Davies; 1 s.; 2 d. Educ. St Bartholomew's Hospital, London. Senior Clinical Scientist and Consultant, Ludwig Institute of Cancer Research, London, 1983-86; Consultant in Histopathology, Royal Marsden Hospital, 1984; Professor of Histopathology and Chairman, Section on Cell Biology and Experimental Pathology, Institute of Cancer Research, London University, 1986-2000; Founding Director, Toby Robins Breast Cancer Research Centre, London, 1998. Director, Pathology, International Breast Cancer Study Group, Berne, 1995; Oakley Lecturer, Pathological Society of Great Britain and Ireland, 1986; Chairman, Pathology Group, Organisation of European Cancer Institutes, Geneva, 1992-96. Recreations: antique English glass and furniture; gardening; walking; reading. Address: (b.) Department of Pathology, Western Infirmary, Glasgow, G11 6NT; T.-0141-211 2233.

Gwilt, George David, MA, FFA, FBCS, CITP; b. 11.11.27, Edinburgh; m., Ann Sylvester; 3 s. Educ. Sedbergh; St. John's College, Cambridge. Standard Life, 1949-88, latterly as Managing Director; Director: European Assets Trust NV, 1979-2000, Scottish Mortgage & Trust plc, 1983-98, Hodgson Martin Ltd., 1989-2000, Edinburgh Festival Society Ltd., 1989-95; President, Faculty of Actuaries, 1981-83; Trustee, South of Scotland TSB, 1966-83; Member: Younger Committee on Privacy, 1970-72, Monopolies and Mergers Commission, 1983-87; Convener, Scottish Poetry Library, 1988-2000. Recreations: flute playing; squash. Address: (h.) 39 Oxgangs Road, Edinburgh EH10 7BE; T.-0131-445 1266.

H

Habib, Fouad Kamal, BA, PhD, CChem, FRSC, DSc. Reader in Biochemistry and Cell Biology, Cancer Research Centre, Edinburgh University, since 1992; Head, Prostate Research Group, School of Molecular and Clinical Medicine, Western General Hospital, Edinburgh, since 1999; b. 17.11.42, Leeds; m., Vanessa Elizabeth; 1 s. Educ. University of Utah; Leeds University. Lecturer in Steroid Biochemistry, Department of Surgery, Edinburgh University Medical School, 1978-87; Senior Lecturer in Biochemistry, Western General Hospital, Edinburgh, 1987-92. Chairman, British Prostate Group, 1994-98; Chairman, European Society for Urological Research, 1995-98; Member, WHO Advisory Board on BPH and prostate cancer, since 2000. Recreations: reading; tennis. Address: (b.) Prostate Research Group, University of Edinburgh, Cancer Research Centre, MRC Building Level 4, Western General Hospital, Crewe Road South, Edinburgh EH4 2XU; T.-0131 467 8449; e-mail: f.k.habib@ed.ac.uk

Hadden, William A., BSc, BAO, BCh, MB, FRCSEd and Orth. Consultant Orthopaedic Surgeon, since 1984; b. 23.5.46, Northern Ireland; 3 s. Educ. Methodist College, Belfast; Portadown College, Co. Armagh; Queen's University, Belfast. Surgical training, Northern Ireland, Edinburgh, Dundee, Christchurch (New Zealand). Recreations: golf; squash. Address: (b.) Perth Royal Infirmary, Perth PH1 1NX; T.-01738 473698.

Haddington, 13th Earl of (John George Baillie-Hamilton); b. 21.12.41; m.; 1 s.; 2 d. Succeeded to title, 1986. Educ. Ampleforth. Address: Mellerstain, Gordon, Berwickshire, TD3 6LG.

Haddock, Graham, MBChB, MD, FRCS (Glas), FRCS (Edin), FRCS(Paed). Consultant Paediatric Surgeon, since 1995; Clinical Director of Surgery, 2000-03; b. 7.8.60, Greenock. Educ. Notre Dame High School, Greenock; Glasgow University. Trained in adult general surgery, Glasgow and Edinburgh, in paediatric surgery, Royal Hospital for Sick Children, Yorkhill, Royal Hospital for Sick Children, Edinburgh, and Hospital for Sick Children, Toronto. Honorary Clinical Senior Lecturer, Glasgow University; formerly Secretary, Scottish Colleges Committee, Children's Surgical Services. Formerly National (UK) Commissioner for Explorer Scouts (The Scout Association), 2001-06; Depute Chief Commissioner for Scotland (Programme) and UK Trustee (The Scout Association). Address: (b.) Department of Paediatric Surgery, Royal Hospital for Sick Children, Yorkhill, Glasgow G3 8SJ; T.-0141-201 0289.

Haddow, Christopher, QC, LLB (Hons); b. 15.5.47, Edinburgh; m., Kathleen; 3 s. Educ. George Watson's College; Edinburgh University. Admitted to Faculty of Advocates, 1971; Queen's Counsel, 1985. Former Member, Secretary of State's Valuation Advisory Council and of Scottish Valuation and Rating Council; Joint Editor, Armour on Valuation for Rating, since 1990. Recreations: hockey; walking; classic cars. Address: (h.) Abbot's Croft House, North Berwick EH39 5NG.

Hadley, Geoffrey, MBE, BSc (Hons), PhD. Honorary Senior Lecturer, Aberdeen University, since 1985; Consultant Microbiologist, since 1985; b. 7.2.32, Stoke-on-Trent; m., Margaret Murison; 3 d. by pr. m. Educ. Longton High School; Birmingham University. Research Fellow, Nottingham University, 1956-58; Lecturer, Glasgow

University, 1958-60; Lecturer, then Senior Lecturer, Aberdeen University, 1960-85; seconded to University of Malaya, 1967-68; Member, Aberdeen County Council, 1973-75, Grampian Regional Council, 1974-94; Convener, Grampian Regional Council, 1986-90; British Mycological Society: Chairman of Publications, 1985-2004, Editor, Mycologist, Vice-President, 1987; Chairman, Aberdeen Civic Society, 1994-2000; Chairman, Grampian Heart Campaign, 1991-96; Member, Management Committee, Hanover (Scotland) Housing Association. Recreations: classical music; home brewing and wine-making; cricket; DIY. Address: (h.) 5, Kirk Crescent North, Cults, Aberdeen AB15 9RP; T.-01224 865855.

Haggart, Mary Elizabeth, OBE; b. 8.4.24, Leicester; m., Rt. Rev. A.I.M. Haggart (deceased). Educ. Wyggeston Grammar School for Girls, Leicester; Leicester Royal Infirmary and Children's Hospital. Leicester Royal Infirmary: Staff Nurse, 1947-48, Night Sister, 1948-50, Ward Sister, 1950-56, Night Superintendent, 1956-58, Assistant Matron, 1958-61; Assistant Matron, Brook General Hospital, London, 1962-64; Matron, Dundee Royal Infirmary and Matron Designate, Ninewells Hospital, Dundee, 1964-68; Chief Nursing Officer, Board of Managements, Dundee General Hospitals and Ninewells Hospital, 1968-73; Chief Area Nursing Officer, Tayside Health Board, 1974-82; President, Scottish Association of Nurse Administrators, 1972-77; Member: Scottish Board, Royal College of Nursing, 1965-70, General Nursing Council for Scotland, 1965-70 and 1978-82; Chairman, Scottish Board of Nursing Midwifery and Health Visiting, 1980-83; Member: Standing Nursing and Midwifery Committee, 1971-74 (Vice Chairman, 1973-74), Action on Smoking and Health Scotland, 1978-82 (Chairman, Working Party, Smoking and Nurses); Governor, Dundee College of Technology, 1978-82; Honorary Lecturer, Department of Community Medicine, Dundee University and Medical School, 1980-82; Member: Management Committee, Carstairs State Hospital, 1982-92, United Kingdom Central Council for Nursing Midwifery and Health Visiting, 1980-82, Scottish Hospital Endowments Research Trust, 1986-96. Recreations: walking; music; travel. Address: (h.) 14/2 St. Margaret's Place, Edinburgh EH9 1AY.

Haig of Bemersyde, The Earl (George Alexander Eugene Douglas), OBE, DL, MA, RSA, KStJ. Painter; b. 15.3.18, London; 1 s.; 2 d. Educ. Cargilfield; Stowe School; Christ Church, Oxford. 2nd Lt., Royal Scots Greys, 1938; retired on account of disability, 1951 (rank of Captain); attended Camberwell School of Arts and Crafts; paintings in many public and private collections; served Second World War; taken prisoner, 1942; Member, Royal Fine Art Commission for Scotland, 1958-61; Chairman, SE South East Scotland Disablement Advisory Committee, 1960-73; Trustee, Scottish National War Memorial, 1961-96; Trustee, National Galleries of Scotland, 1962-72; Member, Scottish Arts Council, 1968-74; Past Chairman, Royal British Legion Scotland; President: Earl Haig Fund Scotland/Royal British Legion Scotland, 1980-86, Scottish Branch, Officers Association, 1978-95, Scottish Craft Centre, 1952-73; Vice President, Scottish National Institution for War Blinded and of Royal Blind Asylum, since 1960; Past President, National Ex-Prisoners of War Association (1999-2005). Recreations: fishing; shooting. Address: (h.) Bemersyde, Melrose TD6 9DP; T.-01835 822762.

Hair, Professor Graham Barry, MMus, PhD. Composer; Professor of Music, Glasgow University, since 1990; b. 27.2.43, Geelong, Australia; m., Dr Greta Mary Hair. Educ. Geelong College, Australia; Melbourne University; Sheffield University. Senior Lecturer, Latrobe University,

1975-80; Head, School of Composition, Sydney Conservatorium of Music, 1980-90; has had many commissions, performances, CD recordings, broadcasts and musical works published. Address: (h.) 45 St. Vincent Crescent, Glasgow G3 8NG; T.-0141-221 4933; e-mail: graham.hair@virgin.net

Haites, Professor Neva, OBE, MB, ChB, PhD, FRCP, FRCPath, FMedSci. Professor in Medical Genetics, University of Aberdeen; Head of College of Life Science and Medicine, Vice Principal, University of Aberdeen; Honorary Consultant in Clinical Genetics; b. 4.6.47, Brisbane, Australia; m., Roy; 2 d. Educ. Somerville House, Brisbane; Queensland University; University of Aberdeen. Member, HFEA; Formerly: Lead Clinician, North of Scotland Cancer Network, Member, National Screening Committee, Head of Service in Medical Genetics. Address: College Office, Medical School, University of Aberdeen, Foresterhill, Aberdeen; T.-01224 559241; e-mail: n.haites@abdn.ac.uk

Hajivassiliou, Constantinos, BSc (Hons), MBChB, FRCS(Edin), FRCS(Glas), FRCS(Paed), MD, Consultant Paediatric/Neonatal Surgeon, Royal Hospital for Sick Children, Glasgow, since 1998; Wellcome Trust Senior Lecturer, Glasgow University, since 1999; b. 27.4.61, Nicosia; m., Eva; 2 d. Educ. Edinburgh University. House Officer, then Senior House Officer, 1986-89; Registrar, West of Scotland Rotation, 1989-92; Senior Registrar/Lecturer, Yorkhill and Glasgow University, 1992-98. Lord Moynihan Prize, Association of Surgeons of Great Britain and Ireland, 1995; many other prizes. Recreations: radio amateur; diving; flying; fishing; cooking. Address: (b.) Department of Paediatric Surgery, Royal Hospital for Sick Children, Yorkhill, Glasgow G3 8SJ; T.-0141-201 0170.

Haldane of Gleneagles, James Martin, MA, DUniv (Stirling), CA, FRSA. 28th Laird of Gleneagles; Director: Investors Capital Trust PLC, since 1995 (Chairman, since 2004); (Stace Barr Angerstein PLC, 1997-2004), Shires Income plc, since 1996 (Chairman, since 2003); former Chairman, Chiene & Tait, CA (Partner, 1989-2001); former Deputy Chairman, Scottish Life Assurance Co. (Director, 1990-2001); Chairman, Queen's Hall (Edinburgh) Ltd., 1987-2001; b. 18.9.41, Edinburgh; m., Petronella Victoria Scarlett; 1 s.; 2 d. Educ. Winchester College; Magdalen College, Oxford. Partner, Arthur Young, 1970-89. Chairman, Scottish Chamber Orchestra, 1978-85; Chairman, Craighead Investments PLC, 1982-90; Trustee, D'Oyly Carte Opera Trust, 1985-92; Treasurer, Queen's Bodyguard for Scotland (Royal Company of Archers), 1992-2001; Member: Council, Edinburgh Festival Society, 1985-89, Northern and Scottish Board, Legal and General Assurance Co., 1984-87, Council, National Trust for Scotland, 1992-97, Court, Stirling University, 1997-2005; Chairman of Governors, Innerpeffray Library, 1994-2006. Recreations: music; golf. Address: (h.) Gleneagles, Auchterarder PH3 1PJ; T.-01764 682 388; (h.) 01764 682535; e-mail: haldane@gleneagles.org

Haldane, Professor John Joseph, BA, PGCE, BA, PhD, Hon LLD, FRSA, FRSE, KHS. Professor of Philosophy, St. Andrews University, since 1994; Director, Centre for Ethics, Philosophy and Public Affairs; b. 19.2.54, London; m., Hilda Marie Budas; 2 s.; 2 d. Educ. St. Aloysius College, Glasgow; Wimbledon School of Art; London University. Art Master, St. Joseph's Grammar School, Abbey Wood, 1976-79; Lecturer in Moral Philosophy, St. Andrews University, 1983-90, Reader, 1990-94; Stanton Lecturer, University of Cambridge, 1999-2002; Royden Davis Professor of Humanities, Georgetown University,

2001-02; Gifford Lecturer, University of Aberdeen, 2004; Joseph Lecturer, Gregorian University, Rome, 2004; Visiting Professor, Institute for the Psychological Sciences, Virginia, USA, since 2005; Consultor to Pontifical Council for Culture, Vatican, since 2005. Vice President (Scotland), Catholic Union; Member, Editorial Board: American Journal of Jurisprudence, Cambridge Studies in Philosophy, Ethical Perspectives, Journal of Philosophy of Education, Philosophical Explorations, Philosophical Quarterly; Contributor: The Scotsman, The Tablet, Modern Painters etc; and to BBC radio and television. Address: (b.) Department of Moral Philosophy, St. Andrews University, St. Andrews KY16 9AL; T.-01334 462488; e-mail: jjh1@st-and.ac.uk

Halden, Derek, BSc (Hons), MEng, CEng, FCILT, MICE. Director, DHC Ltd., Transport Planning Consultancy, since 1996; Editor, Scottish Transport Review, since 2004; b. 3.10.60, Irvine; m., Deborah; 1 s.; 1 d. Educ. Glasgow High School; Merchiston Castle School; University of Aberdeen; University of Glasgow. Jamieson, Mackay and Partners, Transport Planning Consultants, Glasgow and Sir William Halcrow and Partners, 1982-86; Civil Service - Scottish Office Road and Bridge Projects, Transport Policy, Research, and Transport Research Laboratory, 1987-96. Honorary Research Fellow, University of Aberdeen, since 2003; Committee Member: European Transport Conference, since 2003, Scottish Transport Studies Group, since 1995 (Chair, since 2007). Recreations: tennis; squash; hill walking; guitar. Address: 10 St. Magdalenes, Linlithgow EH49 6AQ; T.-0870 350 4200; e-mail: derek@dhc1.co.uk

Haley, Christopher Simon, BSc, PhD. Formerly Head, Division of Genetics and Biometry, Roslin Institute; b. 3.5.55, Rickmansworth; m., Sara Knott; 2 s.; 2 d. Educ. Royal Grammar School, Guildford; University of Birmingham. Post-doctoral Scientist, University of Birmingham, 1980-84; Senior Scientific Officer, Animal Breeding Research Organisation, then Institute of Animal Physiology and Genetics Research, Edinburgh, 1984-91; Principal Scientific Officer, Institute of Animal Physiology and Genetics Research, then Roslin Institute, 1991-95. Recreations: children; cooking; eating; gardening; walking; Morgan sports cars. Address: (b.) Roslin Institute, Roslin, Midlothian EH25 9PS; T.-0131-527 4200.

Halfhide, Nicholas Robert, BA Hons (English Lit). Chief Executive, Deer Commission for Scotland, since 2006; b. 3.11.69, Kent; m., Elspeth Jean Mackenzie; 1 s.; 2 d. Educ. Tonbridge School; Christ Church, Oxford. Scottish Office, 1992-95; Company Secretary, Cairngorms Partnership, 1996-2003; Head of Strategic Policy and Programme Management, Cairngorms National Park Authority, 2003-06. Recreations: gardening; swimming; walking; reading. Address: (b.) Great Glen House, Leachkin Road, Inverness IV3 8NW; T.-01463 725377; e-mail: nick.halfhide@dcs.gov.uk

Halford-MacLeod, Col. Ret. Aubrey Philip Lydiat, MA (Hons). Army careers advisor; late Black Watch (RHR); retired Army Officer, University Liaison Officer (Scotland), Recruiting and Liaison, Scotland; Vice President of the Queich Curling Club; b. 28.4.42, Bagdad; m., Alison Halford-MacLeod (nee Brown) DL; 2 s.; 1 d. Educ. Winchester College; RMA Sandhurst; Magdalen College, Oxford. Commissioned into Black Watch, 1962; Lt., 1964; Capt., 1968; Maj., 1975; Lt. Col., 1985; appointed Commanding Officer, Glasgow and Strathclyde Universities OTC, 1985; Chief of Staff, The Scottish Division, 1988; UK Liaison Officer (as Colonel), US European Command Stuttgart, 1991; SO1 G1 Action and

Support Team (Demob Cell), Army HQ Scotland, 1992; Commandant, The Black Watch ACF Battalion, 1993, as a Colonel, 2000; reverted to Lieutenant to carry out other duties; retired completely, 2002. Recreations: walking the dogs; shooting; fishing; opera; model soldiers; curling; country dancing. Address: (b.) ACA (O) Scottish Schools, Recruiting Group Scotland, Building 105, Forthside, Stirling FK7 7RR; T.-0131 310 3757; (h.) The Old Manse, 28 Skene Street, Strathmiglo KY14 7QL; T.-01337 860715/868930; e-mail: philip_h@madasafish.com

Halfpenny, Lynne J., BA, DRLP, MILAM, FFCS. Head of Culture and Sport, City of Edinburgh Council, since 2007; Head of Museums and Arts, City of Edinburgh Council, Culture and Leisure Department, 2002-06; Board Member, Scottish Museums Council, 2006; with Edinburgh Arts Development team, since 1989; b. 18.12.63, Aberdeen; m., Bob; 1 s.; 1 d. Educ. Waid Academy; Queen Margaret University College; Dunfermline College of Physical Education. Arts Promotion Officer, Renfrew District Council, 1987-89; freelance arts and events manager, 1985-89. Address: (b.) The City of Edinburgh Council, Waverley Court, 4 East Market Street, Edinburgh EH8 8BG; e-mail: lynne.halfpenny@edinburgh.gov.uk

Hall, Professor Christopher, MA, DPhil, DSc, CEng, FRSC, FIM. Professor of Materials, Edinburgh University, since 1999; Director, Centre for Materials Science and Engineering, Edinburgh University, since 1999; Director of Research, School of Engineering and Electronics, Edinburgh University, since 2002; b. 31.12.44, Henley-on-Thames; m., Sheila McKelvey (deceased); 1s.; 1d. Educ. Royal Belfast Academical Institution; Trinity College, Oxford. Lecturer, Building Engineering, UMIST, 1972-83; Head, Rock and Fluid Physics, Schlumberger Cambridge Research, 1983-88; Head, Chemical Technology, Dowell Schlumberger, St Etienne, France, 1988-89; Scientific Advisor, Schlumberger Cambridge Research, 1990-99; Visiting Fellow, Princeton Materials Institute, Princeton University, USA, 1998; Visiting Professor, University of Manchester; Visiting Scientific Advisor, Schlumberger Cambridge Research, Senior Member, Robinson College, Cambridge; Royal Society Mercer Senior Award for Innovation, 2001. Address: (h.) 36 Mayfield Terrace, Edinburgh, EH9 1RZ; T.-0131-662 9285; e-mail: Christopher.Hall@ed.ac.uk

Hall, Professor Denis, BSc, MPhil, PhD, MBA, FInstP, FIEE, FIEEE, FOSA, FRSE, CEng. Professor of Photonics, Department of Physics, Heriot-Watt University, since 1987, and Deputy Principal (Research), since 1998; b. 1.8.42, Cardiff; m., Pauline; 2 c. Educ. Manchester University; St Bartholomew's Hospital Medical College; Case Western Research University, Cleveland, Ohio, USA. Senior Research Scientist, Avco Everett Research Laboratory, Boston, 1972-74; Principal Scientific Officer, Royal Signals and Radar Establishment, 1974-79; Senior Lecturer/Reader in Applied Laser Physics, Hull University, 1979-87. Chairman, Quantum Electronics Group Committee, Institute of Physics, 1991-94; Chairman, Quantum Electronics and Optics Division, European Physical Society, 1998-2000. Publications: 150 in journals; 200 papers at conferences. Address: (b.) Department of Physics, Heriot-Watt University, Edinburgh EH14 4AS; T.-0131-451 3081.

Hall, Professor Graham Stanley, BSc, PhD, FRSE, FRAS. Professor of Mathematics, University of Aberdeen, since 1996; b. 5.9.46, Warrington; 1 s.; 1 d. Educ. Boteler

Grammar School, Warrington; University of Newcastle upon Tyne (Earl Grey Memorial Fellow, 1971-73); Lecturer in Mathematics, University of Aberdeen, since 1973 (Senior Lecturer, 1982, Reader, 1990, Head of Department, 1992-95). Over 150 invited lectures worldwide. Publications: over 140 articles in research journals; General Relativity (Co-Editor), 1996; book: Symmetries and Curvature; Structure in General Relativity (Author), 2004. Recreations: music (piano); reading; astronomy; sport. Address: (b.) Department of Mathematical Sciences, University of Aberdeen, Aberdeen AB24 3UE; T.-01224 272748; e-mail: g.hall@maths.abdn.ac.uk

Hall, Rev. Keith Ferrier, BD, MTh. Minister, Dundee Parish Church (St. Mary's), since 1994; Chaplain, Dundee High School, since 1994; b. 20.10.55, Arbroath; m., Amilia Elaine Donaldson; 2 s.; 1 d. Educ. Arbroath High School; University of St. Andrews. Minister: Blairgowrie, St. Mary's South, 1981-87, Alloa Parish, St. Mungo's, 1987-94. Recreations: family; fitness; theatre. Address: (b.) Dundee Parish Church (St. Mary's), Nethergate, Dundee DD1 4DG; T.-01382 226271; e-mail: office@dundeestmarys.co.uk

Hall, William, CBE, DFC, FRICS. Honorary Sheriff, Paisley, since 1974; b. 25.7.19, Paisley; m., Margaret Semple Gibson; 1 s.; 3 d. Educ. Paisley Grammar School. Pilot, RAFVR, 1939-45 (Despatches); Senior Partner, R. & W. Hall, Chartered Surveyors, Paisley, 1949-79; Chairman, Royal Institution of Chartered Surveyors in Scotland, 1971; Member: Valuation Advisory Council, 1970-80, Lands Tribunal for Scotland, 1971-91, Lands Tribunal for England and Wales, 1979-91; Executive Member, Erskine Hospital, 1976-99. Recreation: golf. Address: (h.) Windyridge, Brediland Road, Paisley PA2 9HF.

Hall, (William) Douglas, OBE (1985), BA, FMA; b. 9.10.26, London; m., 1, Helen Elizabeth Ellis (m. diss.); 1 s.; 1 d.; 2, Matilda Mary Mitchell. Educ. University College School, Hampstead; University College and Courtauld Institute of Art, London University, 1948-52. Intelligence Corps, 1945-48 (Middle East); Manchester City Art Galleries: Keeper, Rutherston Collection, 1953-58, Keeper, City Art Gallery, 1958-59, Deputy Director, 1959-61; Keeper, Scottish National Gallery of Modern Art, 1961-86. Recreations: music; enjoying old age. Address: (h.) Wellgate, Morebattle, Roxburghshire TD5 8QN; T.-01573 440687.

Hallett, Professor Christine, MA (Cantab), PhD, FRSE. Principal and Vice-Chancellor, Stirling University, since 2003, and Professor of Social Policy, since 1995; b. 4.5.49, Barnet. Educ. Queen Elizabeth's Grammar School for Girls, Barnet; Newnham College, Cambridge. Civil Servant, Department of Health and Social Security; Research Officer, Oxford University, Keele University; Lecturer in Social Policy, Keele University; Senior Lecturer in Social Policy, University of West Australia; Lecturer, University of Leicester. Recreations: golf; tennis. Address: (b.) Stirling University, Stirling, FK9 4LA.

Halliday, David James Finlay, LLB (Hons), DipLP, NP, WS. Partner and Head of Litigation, Boyds Solicitors LLP, since 1999; b. 25.7.62, Dunfermline; m., Rona Dougall; 2 d. Educ. High School of Dundee; University of Edinburgh. Qualified as Solicitor, 1988; Assistant Solicitor, Edinburgh, 1989-92; Partner, ORR MacQueen, Solicitors, 1992-99. Recreations: music; current affairs; golf; cycling; family. Address: (b.) 86 George Street, Edinburgh EH2 3BU; T.-0131-226 9130; e-mail: david.halliday@boydslaw.com

Halliday, James, MA, MLitt, JP. Chairman, Scots Independent Newspapers; b. 27.2.27, Wemyss Bay; m., Olive Campbell; 2 s. Educ. Greenock High School; Glasgow University. Teacher: Ardeer FE Centre, 1953, Kildonan Secondary School, Coatbridge, 1954-56,

Uddingston Grammar School, 1956-58, Dunfermline High School, 1958-67; Lecturer in History, Dundee College of Education, 1967-79; Principal Lecturer in History, 1979-87. Chairman, Scottish National Party, 1956-60, Vice President in most years, 1960-80; Parliamentary candidate: Stirling and Falkirk Burghs, 1955 and 1959, West Fife, 1970. Publications; World in Transformation — America; Scotland The Separate; A Concise History of Scotland; 1820: The Radical War; Story of Scotland (Co-author). Recreations: reading; folk music; football spectating; American history and politics. Address: (h.) 72 Fintry Place, Broughty Ferry, Dundee DD5 3BH.

Halliday, Dr John Dixon, BA (Hons), PhD. Rector, High School of Dundee, since 2008; Headmaster, Albyn School, 2002-08; b. 24.6.55, Wantage, Berkshire; m., Anna Salvesen; 2 s.; 1 d. Educ. Abingdon School; Exeter University; Robinson College, Cambridge. Lecturer in English, Universitat Passau, Germany; freelance translator; Head of German, Merchiston Castle School; Head of Modern Languages, Housemaster and Director of Middle School, Sedbergh School; Headmaster, Rannoch School; Teacher of Modern Languages, Dollar Academy. Member, Board, SCIS. Recreations: music – singing, viola; sport; coaching and refereeing; reading. Address: (b.) High School of Dundee, Euclid Crescent, Dundee DD1 1HU; T.-01382 202921.

Halliday, Rt. Rev. Robert Taylor, MA, BD. Bishop of Brechin, 1990-96; b. 7.5.32, Glasgow; m., Dr. Gena M. Chadwin; 1 d. Educ. High School of Glasgow; Glasgow University; Trinity College, Glasgow; Episcopal Theological College, Edinburgh. Deacon, 1957; Priest, 1958; Assistant Curate, St. Andrew's, St. Andrews, 1957-60, St. Margaret's, Newlands, Glasgow, 1960-63; Rector, Holy Cross, Davidson's Mains, Edinburgh, 1963-83; External Lecturer in New Testament, Episcopal Theological College, Edinburgh, 1963-74; Canon, St. Mary's Cathedral, Edinburgh, 1973-83; Rector, St. Andrew's, St. Andrews, 1983-90; Tutor in Biblical Studies, St. Andrews University, 1984-90. Recreations: walking; reading; visiting gardens and art exhibitions. Address: 28 Forbes Road, Edinburgh EH10 4ED; T.-0131-221 1490.

Halling, Professor Peter James, BA, PhD, FRSE. Robertson Professor of Bioprocess Technology, Strathclyde University, since 1996; b. 30.3.51, London. Educ. Calday Grammar School; Churchill College, Cambridge; Bristol University. Postdoctoral Fellow, University College, London, 1975-78; Research Scientist, Unilever Research, Bedford, 1978-83; Professor of Biocatalyst Science, Strathclyde University, 1990-96. Recreation: orienteering. Address: (h.) 34 Montague Street, Glasgow G4 9HX; T.-0141-552 4400.

Halliwell, Professor Francis Stephen, MA, DPhil(Oxon). Professor of Greek, University of St. Andrews, since 1995; b. 18.10.53, Wigan; m., Helen Ruth Gainford; 2 s. Educ. St. Francis Xavier's, Liverpool, Worcester College, University of Oxford. Lecturer in Classics and Drama, Westfield College, London, 1980-82; Fellow in Classics, Corpus Christi College, University of Cambridge, 1982-84; Lecturer, Senior Lecturer, Reader in Classics, University of Birmingham, 1984-95; Visiting Professor in Classics, University of Chicago, 1990; Visiting Faculty Fellow, University of California at Riverside, 1993; Visiting Professor, University of Rome, 1998. Publications: eight books and 70 articles on Greek literature and philosophy, including Aristophanes, Plato and Aristotle. Recreation: music. Address: (b.) School of Classics, Swallowgate, University of St. Andrews, St. Andrews KY16 9AL; T.-01334 462617; e-mail: fsh@st-and.ac.uk

Hally, Paul William. Partner, Shepherd and Wedderburn LLP, since 1987. Address: (b.) Saltire Court, 20 Castle Terrace, Edinburgh EH1 2ET; T.-0131 473 5183; e-mail: paul.hally@shepwedd.co.uk

Hamblen, Professor David Lawrence, CBE, MB, BS, PhD, DSc (Hon), FRCS, FRCSEdin, FRCSGlas. Chairman, Greater Glasgow NHS Board, 1997-2002; Emeritus Professor of Orthopaedic Surgery, Glasgow University; Hon. Consultant Orthopaedic Surgeon to Army in Scotland, 1976-99; b. 31.8.34, London; m., Gillian; 1 s.; 2 d. Educ. Roan School, Greenwich; London University. The London Hospital, 1963-66; Teaching Fellow in Orthopaedics, Harvard Medical School/Massachusetts General Hospital, 1966-67; Lecturer in Orthopaedics, Nuffield Orthopaedic Centre, Oxford, 1967-68; Senior Lecturer in Orthopaedics/ Honorary Consultant, Edinburgh University/South East Regional Hospital Board, 1968-72; Professor of Orthopaedic Surgery, Glasgow University; 1972-99. Honorary Consultant in Orthopaedic Surgery, Greater Glasgow Health Board, 1972-99; Visiting Professor to National Centre for Training and Education in Prosthetics and Orthotics, Strathclyde University, 1981-2008; Member, Chief Scientist Committee and Chairman, Committee for Research on Equipment for Disabled, 1983-90; Chairman, Journal of Bone and Joint Surgery, 1995-2002 (Member, Editorial Board, 1978-82 and 1985-89); Secretary and Treasurer, JBJS Council of Management, 1992-95; Member, Physiological Systems Board, Medical Research Council, 1983-88; President, British Orthopaedic Association, 1990-91 (Chairman, Education Sub-Committee, 1986-89); Non-Executive Director, West Glasgow Hospitals University NHS Trust, 1994-97; Interim Board Member, Medical Devices in Scotland, 2001-02; Consulting Medical Editor, Orthopaedics Today International, since 2002. Publications: Outline of Fractures (Co-Author), (12th edition, 2007); Outline of Orthopaedics (Co-Author), (13th edition, 2001). Recreations: golf; curling. Address: (h.) 3 Russell Drive, Bearsden, Glasgow G61 3BB.

Hamilton, 15th Duke of, (Angus Alan Douglas Douglas-Hamilton), MA, CEng, MIMechE. Premier Peer of Scotland; Hereditary Keeper of Palace of Holyroodhouse; b. 13.9.38; m., 1972, Sarah Scott (deceased); 2 s.; 2 d.; m., Kay Carmichael, 1998. Educ. Eton; Balliol College, Oxford. Joined RAF, 1956; Flt.-Lt., 1963; flying instructor, 1965; Instrument Rating Examiner, 1966; invalided, 1967; Senior Commercial Pilot, 1968; Test Pilot, Scottish Aviation, 1971-72; Knight of St. John, 1974, Prior for Scotland, 1975-82; Patron, British Airways Pipe Band, 1977; Member: European Community Sub-Committee on Energy and Transport, 1975-77, Piobaireachd Society, since 1976, Royal Scottish Pipers Society, 1977, Queen's Bodyguard for Scotland (Royal Company of Archers), since 1976, Royal Scottish Pipers Society, 1977, Piobaireachd Society, 1979, Honorary Air Commodore, No. 2 (City of Edinburgh) Maritime Headquarters Unit, R.Aux.AF, 1982-93; led team which broke more than 150 British and international land speed records, mostly in diesel vehicles, 1992-2001; authorised aerobatic display pilot, since 1998. Publication: MARIA R, 1991. Address: (b.) Lennoxlove, Haddington, East Lothian, EH41 4NZ, T.-0162 082 3770; (h.) Archerfield, by Dirleton, East Lothian EH39 5HQ; T.-0162 085 0298.

Hamilton, Rt. Hon. Lord (Arthur Campbell Hamilton), BA (Oxon), LLB (Edin). Lord Justice General of Scotland and Lord President of the Court of Session, since 2005; b. 10.6.42, Glasgow; m., Christine Ann; 1 d. Educ. High School of Glasgow; Glasgow University; Worcester College, Oxford; Edinburgh University. Advocate, 1968; Standing Junior Counsel to Scottish Development Department, 1975-78, Inland Revenue (Scotland), 1978-82;

Queen's Counsel, 1982; Advocate Depute, 1982-85; Judge of the Courts of Appeal of Jersey and of Guernsey, 1988-95; President, Pensions Appeal Tribunals for Scotland, 1992-95; Senator of the College of Justice, 1995-2005. Hon. Fellow, Worcester College, Oxford, 2003. Recreations: hill-walking; music; history. Address: (b.) Parliament House, Edinburgh EH1 1RQ; T.-0131-225 2595.

Hamilton, Rev. Alan James, LLB, BD, DipLP. Minister, Killermont Parish Church, Bearsden, since 2003; b. 14.8.63, Glasgow; m., Hazel; 3 s. Educ. Williamwood High School; Eastwood High School; Glasgow University; Edinburgh University. Solicitor, 1987; Advocate, 1990. Address: 8 Clathic Avenue, Bearsden, Glasgow G61 2HF; T.-0141 942 0021; e-mail: alanj@hamilton63.freeserve.co.uk

Hamilton, Alex. Writer of fiction; b. 14.4.49, Glasgow. Publications: Three Glasgow Writers, 1976; Gallus, Did You Say?, 1982; Abdul the Tobacco Curer, forthcoming; The Formulae, forthcoming; many articles, songs, stories, reviews, broadcasts, audio and videotapes. Recreations: language; literature; music; theatre. Address: (h.) 12 Woodlands Drive, Glasgow G4 9EH; T.-0141-339 2258.

Hamilton, Alexander Macdonald, CBE, JP, MA, LLB. Former Vice Chairman: Royal Bank of Scotland Group plc, Royal Bank of Scotland plc; b. 11.5.25, Motherwell; m., Catherine; 2 s.; 1 d. Educ. Hamilton Academy; Glasgow University. Former Senior Partner, subsequently Consultant, McGrigor Donald, Solicitors, Glasgow; former Member, Council, Law Society of Scotland; President of the Society, 1977-78; former Member, Court House Committee, Royal Faculty of Procurators of Glasgow; Past President, Glasgow Juridical Society; former Chairman, Scottish Committee, The Scout Association; President, Greater Glasgow Scout Association; Secretary, Cambuslang Old Parish Church; former Vice-Chairman and Legal Adviser, Cambuslang Community Council. Recreations: sailing; golf. Address: (h.) 30 Wellshot Drive, Cambuslang; T.-0141-641 1445.

Hamilton, Andrew Drummond, MA, DipLE, MRICS, FAAV. Partner, Strutt and Parker (rural practice Chartered Surveyors), since 1989; Deer Commissioner, Deer Commission for Scotland, Inverness, since 2005; b. 18.10.57, Edinburgh; m., Annie; 1 s.; 1 d. Educ. George Watson's Boys College, Edinburgh; University of St. Andrews; University of Aberdeen. Land Management Adviser, MAFF, Northumberland and Durham, 1985-87; Regional Land Agent, Nature Conservancy Council, Edinburgh and Aberdeen, 1987-89. Qualified Rural Practice Chartered Surveyor (MRICS) and Fellow, The Central Association of Agricultural Valuers, 1987; Chairman, RICS Rural Practice Division in Scotland, 1998-99; Chairman, RICS Working Parties on Land Reform and Agricultural Holdings Legislation, since 1998; Member, National Trust for Scotland Countryside and Nature Conservation Advisory Panel; Member, Scottish Ministers' Panel of Arbiters; Member, Scottish Executive's Expert Working Group on Nature Conservation Act/Bill; Chairman, St. Cyrus Community Council, 2003-07. Recreations: fishing; sailing; shooting; cooking and cricket. Address: (h.) Rock Hall, St. Cyrus, Montrose, Angus DD10 0DQ; T.-01330 824888; e-mail: ah@andyhamilton.com

Hamilton, David, MP. Labour MP, Midlothian, since 2001; b. 24.10.50, Dalkeith; m., Jean; 2 d. Educ. Dalkeith High School. Former coal miner, landscape gardener, training officer, training manager, chief executive, and local councillor. Recreations: films; five grandchildren. Constituency Address: (b.) 95 High Street, Dalkeith, Midlothian EH22 1AX; T.-0131-654 1585; e-mail: hamiltonda@parliament.uk

Hamilton, Gordon MacMillan, MB, ChB, DFM, MPhil, CLEM, FFCS. Medical Director, Glasgow University Health Service, since 1989; Hon. Senior Lecturer, Glasgow University, since 1989; Branch Medical Officer, Glasgow and Renfrewshire Branch, British Red Cross, since 1992; b. 6.2.54, Motherwell. Educ. Glasgow University. Various hospital appointments, 1977-89. Past Chairman, Friends of the S.N.O.; Member: Glasgow Art Club, The Hallion Club, Glasgow. Recreations: tennis; squash; keep-fit; art; antiques; music. Address: (b.) University Health Service, Glasgow University, 63 Oakfield Avenue, Glasgow G12 8LP; T.-0141-330 4538.
E-mail: G.Hamilton@admin.gla.ac.uk

Hamilton, Ian Robertson, QC (Scot), BL, LLD (Hon); b. 13.9.25, Paisley; m., Jeannette Patricia Mairi Stewart; 1 s.; 1 s., 2 d. by pr. m. Educ. John Neilson School, Paisley; Allan Glen's School, Glasgow; Glasgow University; Edinburgh University. RAFVR, 1944-48; called to Scottish Bar, 1954, and to Albertan Bar, 1982; Founder, Castle Wynd Printers, Edinburgh, 1955; Advocate Depute, 1962; Director of Civil Litigation, Republic of Zambia, 1964-66; Hon. Sheriff of Lanarkshire, 1967; retired from practice to work for National Trust for Scotland and later to farm in Argyll, 1969; returned to practice, 1974; Sheriff of Glasgow and Strathkelvin, May-December, 1984; returned to practice. Chief Pilot, Scottish Parachute Club, 1979-90; Student President, Heriot-Watt University, 1990-96; Rector, Aberdeen University, 1994-96; Honorary Member, Sir William Wallace Free Colliers of Scotland, 1997. University of Aberdeen, 1997: LLD (Hon), Hon Research Fellow. Publications: No Stone Unturned, 1952; The Tinkers of the World, 1957 (Foyle award-winning play); A Touch of Treason, 1990; The Taking of the Stone of Destiny, 1991; A Touch More Treason, 1993. Recreation: motor-biking. Address: (h.) Lochnaheithe, North Connel, Argyll PA37 1QX; T.-01631 710 427.

Hamilton, Rev. Ian William Finlay, BD, LTH, ALCM, AVCM. Minister, Nairn Old Parish Church, since 1986; b. 29.11.46, Glasgow; m., Margaret McLaren Moss; 1 s.; 2 d. Educ. Victoria Drive Senior Secondary School, Glasgow; University of Glasgow and Trinity College. Employed in banking, then music publishing; ordained, Alloa North Parish Church, 1978. Moderator, Presbytery of Inverness, 1990-91; Member: General Assembly Parish Re-appraisal Committee, 1994-97; former Member, General Assembly Maintenance of the Ministry Committee; Chaplain to the Moderator of the General Assembly of the Church of Scotland, 2005/06; has participated in seven pulpit exchanges, Reformed Church, New Jersey, USA; Presenter, Reflections (Grampian TV), Crossfire (Moray Firth Radio). Publications: Reflections from the Manse Window; Second Thoughts; They're Playing My Song; Take Four!; I'm Trying to Connect You!; A Century of Christian Witness; several children's talks published in The Expository Times; regular contributor to Manse Window page in People's Friend. Recreations: music (piano and organ); writing; broadcasting on radio and television. Address: (h.) Nairn Old Parish Manse, 3 Manse Road, Nairn IV12 4RN; T.-01667 452203; e-mail: reviwfh@btinternet.com

Hamilton, John, MA, BSc. Head Teacher, Boroughmuir High School, Edinburgh, since 2000; b. 10.1.51, Edinburgh. Educ. Trinity Academy, Edinburgh; Edinburgh University. Tynecastle High School: Teacher, History/Geography/Modern Studies, 1975-77; Teacher, Social Subjects, 1977-82; Principal Teacher Guidance, 1982-89; Assistant Head Teacher, 1989-92; Depute

Head Teacher, James Gillespie's High School, 1992-99. Recreations: rugby; cricket; golf; music; travel. Address: (b.) Boroughmuir High School, Viewforth, Edinburgh; T.-0131-229 9703.

Hamilton, John Fleming, LLB, NP. Senior Partner, Maclean and Lowson, Solicitors, since 1992; b. 4.3.57, Forfar; m., Lindsey; 1 s.; 2 d. Educ. Websters High School, Kirriemuir; University of Dundee. Legal Assistant, Clark and Wallace, Solicitors, Aberdeen; Legal Assistant then Partner, Maclean and Lowson , Solicitors, Forfar and Kirriemuir. Member, Council, Law Society of Scotland (Member, Client Care, Client Relations Committee C, Competence, Guarantee Fund, and Professional Practice committees). Recreations: walking; travel; Rotary Club. Address: (b.) 94 East High Street, Forfar, Angus DD8 2ET; T.-01307 462103.

Hamilton, Dr Mark Patrick Rogers, MBChB, MD, FRCOG. Consultant Gynaecologist, Aberdeen Maternity Hospital; Honorary Senior Lecturer, Aberdeen University; b. 24.4.55, Glasgow; m., Susan Elizabeth Duckworth; 1 s.; 1 d. Educ. High School of Glasgow; Glasgow University Lecturer, National University of Singapore, 1985-87; Senior Registrar, Glasgow Royal Infirmary, 1987-90. Member, British Fertility Society Committee, since 1995 (Treasurer, 2001-05, Chair, since 2006). Address: (b.) Aberdeen Maternity Hospital, Foresterhill, Aberdeen AB25 2ZD; T.-01224 553504.

Hamilton, Steven, MBA, FRCP, MBChB. Consultant Physician, Honorary Senior Lecturer, Aberdeen University, since 1986; Associate Medical Director, NHS Grampian, since 2000; b. 22.6.55, Broughty Ferry; m., Anita Anne. Educ. Edinburgh Academy; Aberdeen University; Stirling University. British Foundation for Age Research Fellow, Oxford; Senior Registrar, Oxford NHS; developed Stroke Rehabilitation Centre, Woodend Hospital. Life Member, Ocean Youth Trust Scotland. Recreations: sailing; walking. Address: (b.) Woodend Hospital, Eday Road, Aberdeen AB15 6XS; T.-01224 556513.

Hamilton, Thomas Hunter, BEd, BA (Hons), MEd. Director, Educational Policy, The General Teaching Council Scotland, since 2006; b. 6.8.55, Ayr; m., Margaret. Educ. Ayr Academy; Craigie College of Education; University of Strathclyde. Teacher of English, Belmont Academy, Ayr, then Cumnock Academy; Principal Teacher of English, Doon Academy, Dalmellington; Lecturer, Senior Lecturer, Associate Head of School, Associate Dean, School of Education, Craigie College/University of Paisley; Professional Officer, General Teaching Council Scotland. Recreation: golf. Address: (b.) General Teaching Council Scotland, Clerwood House, 96 Clermiston Road, Edinburgh EH12 6UT; T.-0131 314 6051; e-mail: tom.hamilton@gtcs.org.uk

Hamilton, William Francis Forbes, BCom, CA. Chairman, Macrae & Dick Ltd., since 1994; b. 19.4.40; m., Anne Davison; 1 s. Educ. Inverness Royal Academy; Edinburgh University. Macrae & Dick Ltd.: Company Secretary, 1968-80, Finance Director, 1971-80, Managing Director, 1980-94; Chairman, Menzies BMW, since 1988; Member, BL Cars Distributor Council, 1977-78; Member, Highland Committee, Scottish Council Development and Industry, since 1971; Director, Highlands and Islands Airports Ltd., 1995-2001; Member, Highland Committee, Police Dependants' Trust, since 1998; Director: Highland Hospice, 1992-95, Highland Hospice Trading Co., since

1995, Fresson Trust; DL, since 2000, Vice Lord Lieutenant, since 2002. Recreations: sailing; travel. Address: Craigrory, North Kessock, Inverness IV1 3XH; T.-01463 230430; e-mail: wfhamilton@macraeanddick.co.uk

Hamilton-Grierson, Philip John, OBE, MA. Chairman, A1 Welders Ltd.; Director: University of Highlands and Islands, Millennium Institute, Made In Scotland Ltd.; b. 10.10.32, Inveresk; m., Pleasaunce Jill Cardew; 1 s.; 2 d. Educ. Rugby School; Corpus Christi College, Oxford. Contracts Manager, Bristol Aircraft Ltd.; Economic Adviser, Joseph Lucas Industries Ltd.; Secretary to Liberal Parliamentary Party; Director, Gallaher Ltd.; former Deputy Chairman, Highlands and Islands Development Board; former Chairman: State Hospital, Raigmore NHS Trust, Northern College, Inverness College. Fellow, Royal Society of Arts. Recreations: hill-walking; tennis; music. Address: Pitlundie, North Kessock, Rossshire IV1 3XG; T.-01463 731392.

Hamnett, Professor Andrew, DL, MA, DPhil, HonDSc, CChem, FRSC, FRSE. Principal and Vice-Chancellor, Strathclyde University, since 2001. Educ. Oxford University. Research and academic posts, University of British Columbia, Oxford University, Newcastle University; Pro Vice-Chancellor, 1993-97, Deputy Vice-Chancellor, 1997-2000, Professor of Physical Chemistry, Newcastle University; physical chemist; 200 publications in books and scientific journals, covering spectroscopy, quantum theory and electrochemistry; former Chairman, Physical Chemistry sub-committee, UK Engineering and Physical Sciences Research Council. Address: (b.) 16 Richmond Street, Glasgow, G1 1XQ; T.-0141-548 2099; e-mail: principal@strath.ac.uk

Hancock, Professor Peter J. B., PhD, MSc, MA. Professor of Psychology, University of Stirling, since 2007; b. 1958, UK; m., Clare Allan; 2 s. Educ. Leighton Park School, Reading; Trinity College, Oxford. Synthetic chemist, computer programmer, systems manager, Amersham International plc, 1980-87; University of Stirling: Research Fellow, 1987-95, Lecturer, Psychology, 1995, Senior Lecturer, 2002. Recreation: photography. Address: (b.) Department of Psychology, University of Stirling, Stirling FK9 4LA; T.-01786 467675; e-mail: p.j.b.hancock@stir.ac.uk

Hankey, Maurice S., BSc, PhD. Chief Executive, RSABI, since 2006; formerly Director General, Scottish Rural Property and Business Association (previously Scottish Landowners Federation); b. 3.7.54, Newcastle upon Tyne; m., Catherine; 1 s.; 1 d. Educ. Royal Grammar School, Newcastle upon Tyne; Wye College, London; Newcastle upon Tyne University. Specialist Adviser, East of Scotland College of Agriculture, 1978-80; Lecturer, Newcastle upon Tyne University, 1980-83; farming, 1983-90; Land Use Specialist, Scottish Landowners Federation, 1992-96. Past Member: Scottish Agricultural Wages Board, Board of Governors, Macaulay Land Use Research Institute. Recreations: landscape gardening; computing; rural interests. Address: (b.) Rural Centre, Ingliston, Newbridge, Edinburgh EH28 8LT; T.-0131-472-4166; e-mail: rsabi@rsabi.org.uk

Hanlon, Professor Philip, BSc, MD, MRCGP, FRCP, FFPHM, MPH. Professor of Public Health, Glasgow University, since 1999; b. 24.6.54, British North Borneo; m., Lesley; 1 s.; 1 d. Educ. Uddingston Grammar School; Glasgow University. Research Scientist, Medical Research Council, The Gamba, 1984-87;

Consultant in Public Health Medicine and Director of Health Promotion, Greater Glasgow Health Board, 1988-93; Medical Director, Royal Alexandra Hospital, Paisley, 1993-94; Senior Lecturer in Public Health, Glasgow University, since 1999; Director, Public Health Institute of Scotland, 2001-03. Recreations: cycling; walking; reading; spending time with family. Address: (b.) Dept. of Public Health, University of Glasgow, 1 Lilybank Garden G12 8RZ. T.-0141 330 5641.

Hannaford, Professor Philip Christopher, MD, MBChB, FRCGP, FFPH, FFFP, DRCOG, DCH. NHS Grampian Professor of Primary Care, since 1997; Guardian, RCGP National Epidemiological Databases, since 2001; Director, Institute of Applied Health Sciences, University of Aberdeen, since 2002; Research Director, College of Life Sciences and Medicine, University of Aberdeen, since 2004; b. 1.7.58, London; m., Dr. Anne Carol Gilchrist; 1 s.; 1 d. Educ. Aberdeen Grammar School; Aberdeen University. GP training, Sheffield, 1982-85; research training posts, RCGP Manchester Research Unit, 1986-94; Principal, general practice, Manchester, 1986-92; Director, RCGP Manchester Research Unit, 1994-97. Publications: Evidence Guided Prescribing on the Pill (Co-editor); over 160 contributions on contraception, cardiovascular disease, HRT in scientific journals. Recreations: family; walking; music. Address: (b.) Department of General Practice and Primary Care, Foresterhill Health Centre, Westburn Road, Aberdeen AB25 2AY; T.-01224 551278.

Hanson, Professor William Stewart, BA, PhD, FSA, FSA Scot. Professor of Roman Archaeology, Glasgow University, since 2000 (Head, Department of Archaeology, 1999-2005); b. 22.1.50, Doncaster; m., Lesley Macinnes; 1 d. Educ. Gravesend Grammar School; Manchester University. Glasgow University: Lecturer in Archaeology, 1975; Senior Lecturer in Archaeology, 1990-2000. Chairman: Scottish Field School of Archaeology, 1982-89, Scottish Archaeological Link, 1990-96; Council for British Archaeology: Member, Executive Committee, 1989-98, Vice-President, 1995-98; President, Council for Scottish Archaeology, 1989-96; Director, large-scale archaeological excavations at several sites in Scotland and northern England, including complete excavation of the Roman Fort at Elginhaugh, Dalkeith; recipient, Glenfiddich Living Scotland Award, 1987. Publications include: Agricola and the conquest of the north; A Roman frontier fort in Scotland: Elginhaugh; Rome's north-west frontier: the Antonine Wall (Co-Author); Scottish archaeology: new perceptions; Roman Dacia: the making of a provincial society (Co-Editor); papers and articles. Recreations: tennis; film; karate. Address: (h.) 10 Royal Gardens, Stirling FK8 2RJ; T.-01786 465506.

Hardcastle, Professor William John, BA, MA, PhD, FRSA, FBA, FRSE. Director, Speech Science Research Centre, since 2004; Dean of Research, Queen Margaret University College, 1999-2004; Professor of Speech Sciences, since 1993; Dean of Health Sciences, 1999-2002; b. 28.9.43, Brisbane; m., Francesca; 2 s.; 1 d. Educ. Brisbane Grammar School; University of Queensland; Edinburgh University. Lecturer, Institut für Phonetik, Universität Kiel, 1973-74; Lecturer, then Reader, then Professor, Department of Linguistic Science, Reading University, 1974-93; Director, Scottish Centre for Research into Speech Disability, 1997-2003. President, International Clinical Phonetics and Linguistics Association, 1991-2000; Convenor, Scottish Universities Research Policy Consortium, since 2001. Publications include: Physiology of Speech Production; Disorders of Fluency and their Effects on Communication (Co-Author); Speech Production and Speech Modelling (Co-Editor); Handbook of Phonetic Sciences (Co-Editor); Co-articulation: Theory, Data and Techniques (Co-Editor). Recreations: hill-walking; badminton; gardening; golf. Address: (b.) Queen Margaret University, Queen Margaret University Drive, Musselburgh, East Lothian EH21 6UU; T.-0131-4740000.

Harden, Alan Jerry. Chief Executive, Alliance PLC, since 2004; b. 30.1.58, Burtonwood; m. Fiona; 1 s. Senior Investment Manager, HSBC Investment Management, Middle East, Hong Kong, 1984-90; Managing Director for South East Asia for Asset Management, Standard Chartered Bank, 1990-94; Global Head of Investment Services, Standard Chartered Bank, 1994-2000; Managing Director and Regional Head of Asia Pacific and Japan - Citigroup, 2003-04. 2001 Global Fund Leader, Global Fund News. Recreations: golf; skiing; triathlon; endurance sports. Address: (b.) Meadow House, 64 Reform Street, Dundee DD1 1TJ; T.-01382 306041.

Hardie, Rt. Hon The Lord (Andrew Rutherford Hardie), PC, QC (Scot). Senator of the College of Justice, since 2000; b. 8.1.46, Alloa; m., Catherine Storrar Elgin; 2 s.; 1 d. Educ. St. Modan's High School, Stirling; Edinburgh University. Enrolled Solicitor, 1971; Member, Faculty of Advocates, 1973; Advocate Depute, 1979-83; Dean, Faculty of Advocates, 1994-97; Lord Advocate, 1997-2000; created Life Peer and Privy Counsellor, 1997. Address: (b.) Court of Session, Parliament House, Parliament Square, Edinburgh EH1 1RF.

Hardie, David, LLB Hons, WS NP. Partner, Dundas & Wilson, since 1983, Senior Corporate Partner, since 2003; b. 17.9.54, Glasgow; m., Fiona Mairi Willox; 3 s. Greenock High School; University of Dundee. Apprentice Solicitor, Dundas & Wilson, 1976-78, Solicitor, 1978-83, Head of former Corporate Department and latterly Head of Corporate Finance, 1987-97, Interim Managing Partner and Head of Corporate Finance, 1997-98, Head of Corporate, 1998-2004. Office Bearer (Fiscal), The Society of Writers to Her Majesty's Signet. Address: (b.) Saltire Court, 20 Castle Terrace, Edinburgh EH1 2EN; e-mail: david.hardie@dundas-wilson.com

Hardie, Donald Graeme, KStJ, TD, JP, FIM. Director, Hardie Polymers Ltd., 1976-2001; b. 23.1.36, Glasgow; m. 1, Rosalind Allan Ker (divorced); 2 s.; m. 2, Sheena. Educ. Blairmore and Merchiston Castle. Commissioned 41st Field Regiment RA, 1955; Battery Commander 277 (Argyll & Sutherland Highlanders) Regiment RA (TA), 1966; Commanding Officer GSVOTC, 1973; TA Col. Lowlands, 1976; TA Col. DES, 1980; TA Col. Scotland, 1985; ACF Brigadier Scotland, 1987; Hon. Colonel Commandant, Royal Regiment of Artillery, since 2003; Vice President, NAA, since 2003. UTR Management Trainee, 1956-59; F.W. Allan & Ker, Shipbrokers, 1960-61; J. & G. Hardie & Co. Ltd., 1961-2001 (former Chairman); Director, Gilbert Plastics Ltd., 1973-76; Director, Ronaash Ltd., 1988-99; Director, Preston Associates (Europe) Ltd., 2002-04; Managing Director, Preston Stretchform Ltd., since 2004. Lord Lieutenant, Dunbartonshire, 1990-2007; Hon. Col. 105 Regiment RA(V), 1992-99; Hon. Col. Glasgow & Lanarkshire ACF, 1991-2000; Keeper, Dumbarton Castle, since 1996; Chairman, RA Council of Scotland, 1993-2000; Chieftain, Loch Lomond Games; Trustee, Tullochan Trust; Patron, Cornerstone; Patron, Craigalbert Centre. Recreations: skiing; sailing; shooting; fishing. Address: (h.) Boturich Castle, Alexandria, Dunbartonshire G83 8LX.

Hardie, Fraser. Partner, Harper Macleod LLP, since 2005; b. 4.4.59. Educ. Aberdeen University. Address: (b.) 8 Melville Street, Edinburgh EH3 7NS; T.-0131-247-2528; e-mail: fraser.hardie@harpermacleod.co.uk

Hardie, William Dunbar, MBE, MA, BA, MUniv. Writer and Entertainer; b. 4.1.31, Aberdeen; m., Margaret Elizabeth Simpson; 1 s.; 1 d. Educ. Robert Gordon's

College, Aberdeen; Aberdeen University; Sidney Sussex College, Cambridge. Administrative Assistant, then Assistant Secretary, NE Regional Hospital Board; District Administrator, North District, Grampian Health Board; Secretary, Grampian Health Board, 1976-83. Co-Writer and performer, Scotland The What? (comedy revue); Writer, Dod'n'Bunty column, Aberdeen Evening Express, 1983-2003; Director, Aberdeen Performing Arts, since 2002. Recreations: reading; TV-watching; film and theatre-going; sport; avid and totally biased follower of Aberdeen's football team, Scotland's rugby team, and England's cricket team. Address: (h.) 50 Gray Street, Aberdeen AB10 6JE; T.-01224 310591.

Harding, Professor Dennis William, MA, DPhil, FRSE. Abercromby Professor of Archaeology, University of Edinburgh, 1977-2007; b. 11.4.40. Educ. Keble College, University of Oxford. Assistant Keeper, Department of Antiquities, Ashmolean Museum, University of Oxford, 1965; Lecturer in Celtic Archaeology, University of Durham, 1966 (Senior Lecturer, 1975); Dean, Faculty of Arts, 1983-86, Vice-Principal, 1988-91, University of Edinburgh. Member, S.A.A.S. Studentships Committee, 1982-2001 (Chairman, 1997-2001). Address: (b.) Department of Archaeology, The Old High School, Infirmary Street, Edinburgh EH1 1LT; T.-0131-650 2364.

Harding-Edgar, John George Keith, LLB, ACIB, WS. Partner, Maclay Murray & Spens, since 1996; b. 13.5.49, Edinburgh; 3 d. Educ. Trinity College, Glenalmond; University of Aberdeen. James Finlay Group - UK, Australia, New Zealand and Canada, 1974-82; Hong Kong and Shanghai Banking Corporation, Edinburgh, 1982-84; Dundas & Wilson CS, 1984-86; Maclay Murray and Spens, since 1987. Recreations: golf; squash; tennis; photography. Address: (b.) 3 Glenfinlas Street, Edinburgh EH3 6AQ; T.-0131-226-5196; e-mail: john.harding-edgar@mms.co.uk

Hare Duke, Rt. Rev. Michael Geoffrey, BA, MA, DD. Bishop of St. Andrews, Dunkeld and Dunblane, 1969-94 (retired); Chair, RSVP Scottish Forum on Older Volunteering, since 2001; b. 28.11.25, Calcutta; m., Grace Lydia Frances Dodd; 1 s.; 1 d. Educ. Bradfield College; Trinity College, Oxford; Westcott House, Cambridge. Sub-Lt., RNVR, 1944-46; Deacon, 1952; Priest, 1953; Curate, St. Johnswood, London, 1952-56; Vicar, Bury, 1956-62; part-time Chaplain, Bury General Hospital, 1956-62; Pastoral Director, Clinical Theology Association, 1962-64; Vicar, St. Paul's Daybrook and Officiating Chaplain, E. Midlands District HQ, 1964-69. Chairman, Scottish Association for Mental Health; Member, Anglican Communion Peace and Justice Network, Convener, 1992-94; Chairman, Age Concern Scotland, 1994-00; Chairman, RSVP National Forum on Older Volunteering, 2000-03; Episcopalian Chaplain, Perth Royal Infirmary, since 2002. Publications: The Caring Church (Co-author); First Aid in Counselling (Co-author); Understanding the Adolescent; The Break of Glory; Freud; Good News; Stories Signs and Sacraments of the Emerging Church; Praying for Peace, reflections on the Gulf crisis; Hearing the Stranger; One Foot in Heaven, growing older and living to the full. Recreations: walking; writing; broadcasting. Address: (h.) 2 Balhousie Avenue, Perth PH1 5HN; T.-01738 622642. E-mail: BishMick@blueyonder.co.uk

Hargreave, Timothy Bruce, MB, MS, FRCSEdin, FRCS, FEB (Urol), FRCP(Ed). Senior Fellow, Department of Oncology, University of Edinburgh, Western General Hospital; b. 23.3.44, Lytham; m., Molly; 2 d. Educ. Harrow; University College Hospital, London University. Senior Registrar: Western Infirmary, Glasgow, University College Hospital, London; Medical Officer, Paray Mission

Hospital, Lesotho. Chair, Scientific and Ethical Review Group, Human Reproduction Programme, World Health Organisation, Geneva. Publications: Diagnosis and Management of Renal and Urinary Disease; Male Infertility (Editor); Practical Urological Endoscopy; The Management of Male Infertility. Recreation: skiing. Address: (h.) 20 Cumin Place, Edinburgh.

Hargreaves, Jonathan, BSc, PhD, FICE, CBiol. Chief Executive, Scottish Water, since 2002; Chief Executive, East of Scotland Water, 2000-2002; b. 10.3.50; m., Hilary; 2 d. Educ. St Bees, Cumbria; Hatfield Polytechnic; Durham University. Business Development Manager, Northumbrian Water Group, 1990-91; Managing Director, Entec Europe Ltd., 1991-92; Managing Director, Northumbrian Water Ltd, 1993; Managing Director, Northumbrian Lyonnaise International, 1996. Recreations: gardening; skiing; DIY. Address: (b.) Castle House, 6 Castle Drive, Dunfermline KY11 8GG; T.-01383 848475.

Harkess, Ronald Dobson, OBE, BSc, MS, PhD, NDA, CBiol, MIBiol, FRAgS, FRSA, FFCS. Emeritus Fellow, Scottish Agricultural College; Agricultural Scientist and Consultant; b. 11.7.33, Edinburgh; m., Jean Cuthbert Drennan (deceased); 2 d. Educ. Royal High School, Edinburgh; Edinburgh University; Cornell University. Senior Fison Research Fellow, Nottingham University, 1959-62; Assistant Grassland Adviser, West of Scotland Agricultural College, Ayr, 1962-72; Senior Agronomist, 1972-86; Technical Secretary, Council, Scottish Agricultural Colleges, 1986-90, Company Secretary, 1987-90; Company Secretary, Scottish Agricultural College, 1990-91; Assistant Principal, Scottish Agricultural College, 1991-93. Chairman, Friends of Perth Festival of the Arts, since 1997; Delegate, Association of Scottish Philatelic Societies, since 2003; Vice-President, Scotia Agricultural Club, since 2007; Chairman, Perth Camcorder Club, since 2003; Secretary, Perth Amateur Radio Group, since 1993; Past President, Tay Probus. Recreations: amateur radio; philately; gardening. Address: (h.) Friarton Bank, Rhynd Road, Perth PH2 8PT; T.-01738 643435.

Harkiss, Professor Gordon David, BSc, PhD. Professor of Veterinary Immunopathology, Edinburgh University, since 2000; Director, Wellcome Trust Laboratory for Research in Comparative Respiratory Medicine, 1998-2007; b. 3.8.47, Glasgow; m., Helen Diana Jane Harkiss; 1 s.; 1 d. Educ. Vale of Leven Academy; Edinburgh University. Research Officer, Tissue Physiology Department, Strangeways Research Laboratory, Cambridge, 1974-76; Scientific Officer/Senior Scientific Officer/Principal Scientific Officer, Department of Clinical Immunology, Addenbrooke's Hospital, Cambridge, 1976-83; New Blood Lecturer/Senior Lecturer/Reader, Department of Veterinary Pathology, Edinburgh University, 1998-2000. Recreations: music; reading; hill walking. Address: (b.) Division of Veterinary Biomedical Sciences, Edinburgh University, Summerhall, Edinburgh EH9 1QH; T.-0131-650-6177; e-mail: Gordon.Harkiss@ed.ac.uk

Harkness, Very Rev. James, KCVO, CB, OBE, MA, DD, FRSA, ChStJ. Extra Chaplain to the Queen, since 2006; Dean of the Chapel Royal in Scotland, 1996-2006; Moderator, General Assembly of the Church of Scotland, 1995-96; Dean of the Order of St. John in Scotland, since 2005; President: Royal British Legion, Scotland, 2001-06, Earl Haig Fund Scotland, 2001-06, The Officers' Association, Scotland, 2001-06; Member, Board, Mercy Corps Scotland, since 2001; b. 20.10.35, Thornhill; m., Elizabeth Anne; 1 s.; 1 d. Educ. Dumfries Academy;

Edinburgh University. Assistant Minister, North Morningside Parish Church, 1959-61; Chaplain: KOSB, 1961-65, Queen's Own Highlanders, 1965-69; Singapore, 1969-70; Deputy Warden, RAChD, 1970-74; Senior Chaplain, Northern Ireland, 1974-75; 4th Division, 1975-78; Staff Chaplain, HQ BAOR, 1978-80; Assistant Chaplain, Scotland, 1980-81; Senior Chaplain, 1st British Corps, 1981-82; BAOR, 1982-84; Deputy Chaplain General, 1985-86; Chaplain General to the Forces, 1987-95. QHC, 1982-95; General Trustee, Church of Scotland, since 1996; Chairman, Carberry Board, 1997-2000; Member, Committee on Chaplains to HM Forces, 1997-2005; Member, Board of World Mission, 1997-2000; President, Army Cadet Force Association Scotland, 1996-2004; President, Society of Friends of St. Andrew's, Jerusalem, 1998-2005. Hon. Chaplain to BLESMA, 1995-2002, Royal British Legion Scotland, 1996-2001; Governor, Fettes College; Trustee, Scottish National War Memorial, since 2003. Recreations: walking; reading; watching sport. Address: (h.) 13 Saxe-Coburg Place, Edinburgh EH3 5BR; T.-0131-343 1297.

Harlen, Professor Wynne, OBE, MA (Oxon), MA (Bristol), PhD. Director, Scottish Council for Research in Education, 1990-99; Visiting Professor: Liverpool University, 1990-99, University of Bristol, since 1999; Visiting Scholar, Exploratorium, San Francisco, since 1999; Project Director, University of Cambridge, 2003-06; b. 12.1.37, Swindon; 1 s.; 1 d. Educ. Pate's Grammar School for Girls, Cheltenham; St. Hilda's College, Oxford; Bristol University. Teacher/Lecturer, 1958-66; Research Associate, Bristol University School of Education, 1966-73; Research Fellow, Project Director, Reading University, 1973-77; Research Fellow, Centre for Science Education, King's College, London, 1977-84; Sidney Jones Professor of Science Education, Liverpool University, 1985-90. Chair, Children in Scotland Early Years Forum, 1991-95; Member, Secretary of State's Working Party on the Development of the National Curriculum in Science, 1987-88; President, British Educational Research Association, 1993-94; Chair, OECD Science Expert Group, 1997-2003; Fellow, Educational Institute of Scotland, 2000; Fellow, Scottish Council for Research in Education, 2002; Member, Interacademies Working Group on IBSE, since 2005. Publications: 34 books, and contributions to 44 others; 156 papers. Recreations: concerts; opera; hill-walking. Address: Haymount Coach House, Bridgend, Duns, Berwickshire TD11 3DJ; T.-01361 884710.
E-mail: wynne@torphin.freeserve.co.uk

Harley, Professor Simon Leigh, BSc (Hons), MA (Oxon) PhD, FRSE. Professor of Lower Crustal Processes, Edinburgh University, since 1997; b. 2.7.56, Sydney, Australia; m., Anne Elizabeth; 3 s.; 1 d. Educ. Punchbowl Boys' High School; University of New South Wales; University of Tasmania. Post-doctoral Research Assistant, ETH-Zentrum, Zurich, 1981-83; Lecturer: Oxford University/Fellow St Edmund Hall, 1983-88; Edinburgh University, 1988-92; Reader, Edinburgh University, 1992-97. Member: Sciennes School Board, 1992-96, Australian National Antarctic Research Expeditions (ANARE), 1979-80, 1982-83, 1987-88, 1992-93 and 2006-07; Polar Medal, 2002; Member, CoRWM, 2007-2010. Recreations: hill walking; skiing; hockey; various racquet sports; Antarctic Society. Address: (h.) 15 Moston Terrace, Newington, Edinburgh EH9 2DE; T.-0131-622 0511; e-mail: Simon.Harley@ed.ac.uk

Harper, Anne Courage. Business Consultant, since 1992; Director, SIS Seafarms Ltd., 2006; Director, Mid-Deeside Ltd., 2001-03; b. 17.9.50, Kumasi, Ghana; m. 1, H.W. (Harry) Bawden (deceased); 2 step-s.; 1 step-d. Educ. Aberdeen High School for Girls; University of Aberdeen; University College London. Manager, British Petroleum, 1974-92; Manager, External Affairs, BP in Scotland, 1991-

92. Director, Art in Partnership, 1991-2001; Lay Member, H.M. Inspectorate of Schools, since 1993; Member, Scottish Churches Industrial Mission, 1993-2003; Member, General Teaching Council for Scotland, 1995-2000; President, Scottish Oil Club, 1996-98; Vice Chairman, Conservative Group for Europe, 1998-2000; Member, Court, University of Aberdeen, since 2000; Trustee, Gordon Cook Foundation, 2007. Recreations: gardening; hillwalking. Address: (h.) Bridgend Cottage, Aboyne, Aberdeenshire AB34 5HB; T.-013398 86919.

Harper, Rev. Anne J. McInroy, BD, STM, MTh, Cert.Soc.Psych. Lead Chaplain, North Glasgow, NHS Greater Glasgow and Clyde, since 1990; b. 31.10.49, Glasgow. Educ. Camphill Senior Secondary School, Paisley; Glasgow University; Union Theological Seminary, New York. Graduate Fellow, Union Theological Seminary, and Assistant Minister, 2nd Presbyterian Church, New York City, 1974-75; research, Church history and liturgics, Glasgow University, 1975-78; Assistant Minister, Abronhill Church, Cumbernauld, 1978-79; Christian Education Field Officer, Church of Scotland Department of Education, 1979-84; Minister, Linthouse St. Kenneth's Parish Church, 1984-90. Holder (first woman), The Scots Fellowship awarded by Union Theological Seminary, New York, 1974. President, Scottish Association of Chaplains in Health Care, 1999-2002. Address: The Chaplain's Office, Glasgow Royal Infirmary, Glasgow G4 0SF; T.-0141-211 4000.

Harper, Rev. David Little, BSc, BD (Hons). Minister, St. Meddan's Church, Troon, since 1979; b. 31.10.47, Moffat; m., Janis Mary Clark; 2 s. Educ. Morton Academy, Thornhill; Dumfries Academy; Edinburgh University. Assistant Minister, Cumbernauld St. Mungo's, 1971-72; first Minister, New Erskine Parish Church, 1972-79. Moderator, Presbytery of Ayr, 1991-92; Member, Scottish Advisory Committee, Independent Broadcasting Authority, 1974-79; Scottish Member, Religious Advisory Panel, IBA, 1978-79; Director, Church of Scotland's Assessment Scheme for Ministry, 2000-06. Recreations: golf; hillwalking; jogging. Address: St. Meddan's Manse, 27 Bentinck Drive, Troon, Ayrshire KA10 6HX; T.-01292 311784; e-mail: d.l.harper@btinternet.com

Harper, George, MA, DipTP, MRTPI. Strategic Director of Development Services, Argyll and Bute Council, since 1996; b. 21.3.51, Perth; m., Katherine; 1 s.; 1 d. Educ. Perth Academy; Aberdeen University; Heriot-Watt University (Diploma, Town and Country Planning). Planner, Dundee Corporation, 1972-75; Planner/Senior Planner, Tayside Regional Council, 1975-88; Depute Director of Planning, Argyll and Bute District Council, 1988-90; Director of Planning, Development and Tourism, Argyll and Bute District Council, 1990-96. Director, Strathclyde Building Preservation Trust. Recreations: hill-walking; football; golf; gardening; family. Address: (b.) Kilmory Castle, Lochgilphead, Argyll; T.-01546 604225; e-mail: george.harper@argyll-bute.gov.uk

Harper, John Ross, CBE, MA, LLB, DUniv (Glasgow). Consultant and Founder, Ross Harper and Murphy and Harper Macleod, Solicitors; b. Glasgow; m., Ursula; 2 s.; 1 d. Educ. Hutchesons' Boys' Grammar School; Glasgow University. Parliamentary Commissioner; Emeritus Professor of Law, Strathclyde University; Past President: Law Society of Scotland, Scottish Conservative & Unionist Association, International Bar Association; former Chairman, Society of Scottish Conservative Lawyers; former Parliamentary candidate (Conservative), Hamilton and West Renfrewshire; Chairman, Admiralty Resources NL. Publications: Glasgow Rape Case; My Client My Lord; A Practitioner's Guide to the Criminal Courts; Fingertip

Criminal Law; Rates Revaluation; Devolution; New Unionism; Scotland '97; Referendums are Dangerous; Global Law in Practice. Recreations: angling; bridge. Address: (b.) The Ca'd'oro, 45 Gordon Street, Glasgow, G1 3PE; T.-0141-221 8888; (h.) Flat 1, 67 Cadogan Square, London SW1X 0DY.

Harper, Robin C. M., MA, DipGC, FRSA, FEIS, FRSSA. MSP (Green), Lothians, since 1999; Co-Convener, Scottish Green Party; b. 4.8.40, Thurso; m., Jenny Helen Carter Brown. Educ. St. Marylebone Grammar School; Elgin Academy; Aberdeen University. Teacher Braehead School, Fife, 1964-68; Education Officer, Kenya, 1968-70; Assistant Principal Teacher, Boroughmuir High School, 1972-99; Musical Director, Theatre Workshop, Edinburgh, 1972-75; President, Edinburgh Classical Guitar Society, 1980-90; Member, Lothian Children's Panel, 1985-88; Member, Lothian Health Council, 1993-97; President, EIS Edinburgh Local Association, 1990-91; elected Rector: University of Edinburgh, 2000-03, Aberdeen University, 2005-08; Board Member, Whale Arts and Theatre Workshop, Edinburgh; Patron, FTC Theatre, SOS Theatre, 2001; Convener, CPG (Cross Party Group): Children and Young People, Architecture and the Built Environment, Renewable Energy and Energy Efficiency; Member, Petitions Committee. Recreations: music; walking; travel; theatre; growing trees. Address: 11 Greenbank Terrace, Edinburgh EH10 6ER; T.-0131-447 1843.

Harries, Professor Jill Diana, MA, DPhil, FRHistS. Professor of Ancient History, St Andrews University, since 1997 (Head of School, Greek, Latin and Ancient History, 2000-03); b. 20.5.50, London. Educ. Bromley High School GPDST; Somerville College, Oxford. Kennedy Scholar, 1973-74; Lecturer in Ancient History, St Andrews University, 1976-95; Senior Lecturer, 1995-97; Visiting Fellow, All Souls College, Oxford, 1996-97; Leverhulme Fellow, 1996-97; Bird Exchange Fellow, Emory, Atlanta, 2003; Member of Council, St Leonard's School, St Andrews, 1998-2000. Publications: Religious Conflict in Fourth Century Rome, 1983; The Theodusian Code (Editor), 1993; Sidonius Apollinaris and the Fall of Rome, 1994; Law and Empire in Late Antiquity, 1998; Cicero and the Jurists, 2006; Law and Crime in the Roman World, 2007. Recreations: travel; hill-walking. Address: (b.) School of Classics, St Salvator's College, St Andrews KY16 9AL; T.-01334 462600.

Harris, Rev. John William Forsyth, MA. Minister, Bearsden Cross Church, since 2006; b. 10.3.42, Hampshire; m., Ellen Lesley Kirkpatrick Lamont; 1 s.; 2 d. Educ. Merchant Taylors' School, London; St. Andrews University; New College, Edinburgh. Ordained Assistant, St. Mary's, Haddington, 1967-70; Minister: St. Andrew's, Irvine, 1970-77, St. Mary's, Motherwell, 1977-87, Bearsden South, 1987-2006. Convener: Scottish Churches' Christian Aid Committee, 1986-90, Scottish Christian Aid Committee, 1990-98, Scottish Television's Religious Advisory Committee, 1990-98, Jubilee Scotland, 2001-06; Scottish Palestinian Forum West of Scotland Committee, 2005-07; Vice-Convener, Board of World Mission, 1996-99; Member: Jubilee 2000 Scottish Coalition Steering Group, 1997-2000, Board of Christian Aid, 1990-98, Executive, Church and Nation Committee, 1985-91, Executive, Scottish Churches Council, 1986-90, Make Poverty History Scottish Coalition Steering Group, 2005. Moderator, Dumbarton Presbytery, 1994-95. Fencing Blue, St. Andrews and Edinburgh; Scottish Fencing Team, 1963-66; Scottish Sabre Champion, 1965. Recreations: enjoying grandchildren; Beardie walking and holiday home in Kintyre. Address: 61 Drymen Road, Bearsden, Glasgow G61 2SU; T.-0141-942 0507.
E-mail: jwfh@bearsdencross.org

Harris, Julie Elizabeth, LLB (Hons), DipLP, NP. Solicitor Advocate; b. 10.12.71, Farnborough, Kent. Educ. John Paul Academy, Glasgow; Strathclyde University. Joined Allan McDougall & Co, SSC, as trainee Solicitor, 1994; Qualified Solicitor, since 1996. Address: (b.) 3 Coates Crescent, Edinburgh EH3 7AL; T.-0131-225 2121.

Harris, Marshall James, DPA. Former Director, Scottish Educational Trust for United Nations and International Affairs; Consultant, North Lanarkshire Education; b. 14.3.28, Edinburgh; m., Matilda Currie Main; 2 s.; 1 d. Educ. Armadale Secondary; Glasgow University. Accountancy, pre-1958; Scottish National Officer, UN Association, 1958-86; Secretary, Scottish Standing Committee for Voluntary International Aid. Former Liberal and Alliance candidate. Recreations: reading; member of Probus. Address: (h.) Hopetoun, Charlotte Street, Brightons, Falkirk; T.-01324 715203.

Harris, Ray Richard, BSc (Hons), PhD, ARCS, FSS, CStat. Principal and Chief Executive, Edinburgh's Telford College, since 2002; b. 9.5.48, Carshalton, Surrey. Educ. Imperial College, London; Fitzwilliam College, Cambridge. Lecturer, Mathematical Statistics, Exeter University; Principal Lecturer, Applied Statistics, Sheffield City Polytechnic; Professor of Applied Statistics, Lancashire Polytechnic/University of Central Lancashire; Assistant Principal Academic Development, University of Abertay Dundee; Depute Principal, Perth College; Principal, Stevenson College, Edinburgh. Board Member, Association of Scotland's Colleges. Recreations: Scotch whisky; playing guitar badly. Address: (b.) 350 West Granton Road, Edinburgh EH5 1QE.

Harris, Tom. Labour MP, Glasgow South, since 2005; Glasgow Cathcart, 2001-05; b. 20.2.64, Irvine; m.; 3 s. Educ. Garnock Academy; Napier College. Reporter, East Kilbride News/Paisley Daily Express, 1986-90; Press Officer, Labour Party in Scotland, 1990-92; Press Officer, Strathclyde Regional Council, 1993-96; Senior Media Officer, Glasgow City Council, 1996; Public Relations Manager, East Ayrshire Council, 1996-98; Chief Public Relations Officer, SPTE, 1998-2001; Parliamentary Private Secretary to Rt. Hon. Patricia Hewitt MP, 2005-06; Parliamentary Under Secretary of State for Transport, since 2006. Recreations: tennis; astronomy; cinema; hill-walking. Address: (b.) House of Commons, Westminster, London SW1A 0AA; T.-020 7219 8237.

Harris, Emeritus Professor William Joseph, BSc, PhD. Professor of Genetics, University of Aberdeen, 1987-2005; Biotechnology Consultant, since 1995; b. 17.11.44, Dundee; m., Linda McPherson; 2 s.; 1 d. Educ. Lawside Academy, Dundee; St. Andrews University. Lecturer in Biochemistry, University of Aberdeen, 1969-78; Head, In Vitro Toxicology/Biotechnology, Inveresk Research International, Musselburgh, 1978-87; Research Director, Bioscot, 1986-88; Manager, Biotechnology Investments, Cogent Ltd., 1984-87; Managing Director, Scotgen Ltd., 1987-92; Chief Scientific Officer, Scotgen Biopharmaceuticals Inc., 1992-94; Director, NCIMB Ltd., 1995-99. Co-Inventor, 18 patent applications; four DTI Smart Awards, 1987-92. Publications: over 70 scientific papers; 15 book chapters; Therapeutic Antibodies (Co-author), 1995; Antibody Therapeutics (Co-editor), 1997. Recreations: golf; football; folk music; pubs. Address: (h.) 18 Queen Street, Carnoustie DD7 7AB; T.-01241 853900; e-mail: billharris@golfershome.co.uk

Harrison, Professor Andrew, BA, MA, DPhil (Oxon), CChem, MRSC, FRSE. Professor of Solid State Chemistry, Edinburgh University, since 1999; b. 3.10.59, Oxford; m., Alison Ironside-Smith; 3 d. Educ. Newcastle-under-Lyme High School; St John's College,

Oxford. Fereday Fellow, St John's College, Oxford, 1985-88; Research Fellow, McMaster University, Canada, 1988-89; Royal Society University Research Fellow, 1990-92; Reader, Department of Chemistry, Edinburgh University, 1996; Nuffield Research Fellow, 1997-98; Eminent Visiting Professor, Riken, Japan, since 2000; British Director, Institut Laue-Langevin, Grenoble, Seconded from Edinburgh University, since 2006. Recreations: hill walking; running; cycling; eating and drinking. Address: (b.) Institut Laue-Langevin 6, Rue Jules Horowitz, BP-156-38042, Grenoble Cedex 9, France; T.-0033 47620 7100; e-mail: harrison@ill.fr

Harrison, Professor Bryan Desmond, CBE, BSc, PhD, Hon. DAgricFor, FRS, FRSE. Emeritus Professor of Plant Virology, Dundee University, since 1997 (Professor of Plant Virology, 1991-96); b. 16.6.31, Purley, Surrey; m., Elizabeth Ann Latham-Warde; 2 s.; 1 d. Educ. Whitgift School, Croydon; Reading University. Agricultural Research Council Postgraduate Research Student, 1952-54; Scientific Officer, Scottish Horticultural Research Institute, 1954-57; Senior and Principal Scientific Officer, Rothamsted Experimental Station, 1957-66; Scottish Horticultural Research Institute/Scottish Crop Research Institute: Principal Scientific Officer, 1966, Senior Principal Scientific Officer (Individual Merit), 1969, Deputy Chief Scientific Officer (Individual Merit), 1981; Head, Virology Department, 1966-91; Foreign Associate, US National Academy of Sciences; Honorary Professor, Department of Biochemistry and Microbiology, St. Andrews University, 1987-99; Honorary Research Professor, Scottish Crop Research Institute, since 1991; Honorary Visiting Professor, Dundee University, 1987-91; Honorary Visiting Professor, Zhejiang University, China, since 2001; Past President, Association of Applied Biologists; Honorary Member: Association of Applied Biologists, Phytopathological Society of Japan, Society for General Microbiology. Recreation: gardening. Address: (b.) Scottish Crop Research Institute, Invergowrie, Dundee DD2 5DA; e-mail: bharri@scri.sari.ac.uk

Harrison, Professor David James, BSc, MBChB, MD, FRCPath, FRCPE, FRCSE. Professor and Head, Division of Pathology, University of Edinburgh, since 1998; Director, University of Edinburgh Cancer Research Centre and Cancer Research UK Clinical Cancer Centre, since 2005; Adjunct Professor of Medicinal Chemistry, University of Florida, Gainesville, 2003; Adjunct Professor of Pathology and Forensic Education, University of Canberra, 2004; b. 24.3.59, Belfast; m., Jane; 2 d. Educ. Campbell College, Belfast; Edinburgh University. House Surgeon to Professor Sir Patrick Forrest, Royal Infirmary of Edinburgh, 1983-84, and House Physician to Professor J S Robson, 1984; University Department of Pathology, Edinburgh: Registrar and Senior House Officer, 1984-86, Lecturer, Honorary Registrar, 1986-87; Lecturer, Honorary Senior Lecturer, 1987-91, Senior Lecturer, 1991-97 (and Honorary Consultant, Lothian University Hospitals Division). Chairman of two healthcare charities. Address: (b.) Division of Pathology, Cancer Research Centre, University of Edinburgh, Crewe Road South, Edinburgh EH4 2XR; e-mail: david.harrison@ed.ac.uk

Hart, Rt. Rev. Monsignor Daniel J., PhL, STL, MA(Hons), Dip Ed. Retired Parish Priest, St. Helen's Langside, Glasgow (1984-2007); Domestic Prelate to His Holiness The Pope; b. 29.5.32, Shenfield. Educ. St. Patrick's High School, Dumbarton; Blairs College, Aberdeen; Pontifical Gregorian University, Rome; University of Glasgow. Principal Teacher of History, Blairs College, Aberdeen, 1961-69; Notre Dame College of Education, 1969-81: Lecturer in Religious Education,

Lecturer, In-Service Department, Director, Postgraduate Secondary Course; Director, Papal Visit to Scotland, 1981-82; Director, Religious Education Centre, Archdiocese of Glasgow, 1981-83; Catholic Church Representative, Strathclyde Regional Education Committee, 1983-84; Chairman, Children's Panel Advisory Committee for Strathclyde, 1977-84 (Vice-Chairman, National Advisory Committee, 1977-84); Judge, Collegiate Court, Scottish Catholic National Marriage Tribunal, since 1989; Member, Archdiocese of Glasgow Finance Council, 1986-90; Vice-Chairman, Archdiocesan Council of Priests, 1982-84 and 1998-2005; Member, Board of Governors, St. Andrew's College of Education, 1991-99; Member, Merger Committee, St. Andrew's College of Education and University of Glasgow, 1997-99. Recreations: golf; photography; swimming; travel. Address: 33 Sanderling View, 1 Barassie Street, Troon KA10 6LU.

Hart, John Francis, MA, LLB. Solicitor; b. 18.10.38, Clydebank; m., Winefride; 3 s. Educ. St Aloysius College; Glasgow University. Solicitor, since 1962; former Lecturer, Glasgow University. Board Member, Mainstay Trust Ltd., St Aloysius Children's Fund. Recreations: golf; reading; opera. Address: (h.) 9A Crosbie Road, Troon KA10 6HE; T.-01292 311987.

Hart, Lesley Ann, MBE, MA, MSc, FRSA. Director of Lifelong Learning, Strathclyde University, since 2002; Trustee, National Museums of Scotland, since 2003; b. Glasgow; m., Campbell; 1 s.; 1 d. Educ. Hutchesons' Grammar School; Glasgow University; Strathclyde University. Local education authority careers officer, senior careers officer, senior administrative officer, 1982-87; Strathclyde University: Deputy Director of Continuing Education, 1982-87, Co-ordinator of Extension Programme, 1987-91, Head of Senior Studies Institute, 1991-2001. Publications: Strategic Women (Co-author); many articles on women's issues and on ageing. Recreations: reading; music; travel; sports. Address: (b.) Centre for Lifelong Learning, Graham Hills Building, 40 George Street, Glasgow G1 1QE; T.-0141-553 4183; e-mail: l.hart@strath.ac.uk

Hart, Morag Mary, JP, DL, RGN, RSCN. Deputy Lieutenant, Dunbartonshire, since 1989; Director, Scotsell Ltd., 1982-2007; b. 19.4.39, Glasgow; m., Tom Hart; 1 s.; 1 d. Educ. Westbourne School for Girls, Glasgow. Sick Children's Hospital, Glasgow, 1956-59; Western General Hospital, Edinburgh, 1960-62. County Commissioner, Girlguiding Dunbartonshire, 1982-90; Chairman, Dunbartonshire Area Scout Council, 1994-2004; Member, The Guide Association Council for Scotland, 1982-2000. Justice of the Peace for East Dunbartonshire Commission Area, since 1992. Recreations: reading; gardening; walking. Address: (h.) 18 Campbell Drive, Bearsden, Glasgow G61 4NE; T.-0141-942 1216.

Hart, Professor Robert Albert, BA (Hons), MA, FRSE. Professor of Economics, Stirling University, since 1986; b. 7.1.46, Hartlepool; m., Shirley; 3 d. Educ. Hartlepool Grammar School; Liverpool University. Economics Lecturer, Aberdeen University, 1969-73, Leeds University, 1974-75; Senior Lecturer, Strathclyde University, 1976-80; Senior Research Fellow, Science Centre, Berlin, 1980-86; Head, School of Management, Stirling University, 1991-94. Recreations: walking; reading; drinking beer. Address: (b.) Department of Economics, Stirling University, Stirling FK9 4LA; T.-01786 467471; e-mail: r.a.hart@stir.ac.uk

Hart, Professor Susan Jane Ritchie, BA (Hons), PhD, DipMRS. Professor of Marketing, Strathclyde University, since 1998; Vice Dean, Strathclyde Business School, since 2005; b. 18.7.60, Edinburgh; 1 s.; 1 d. Educ. Bearsden Academy; Strathclyde University. Lecturer, Department of Marketing, Strathclyde University, 1987-92; Professor of Marketing, Heriot-Watt University, 1993-95; Professor of Marketing, Stirling University, 1995-98. Editor, Journal of Marketing Management. Publications: Marketing Changes, 2003; New Product Development, 1996; Product Strategy and Management, 2007. Recreations: cycling; skiing. Address: (b.) Department of Marketing, University of Strathclyde, Stenhouse Building, 173 Cathedral Street, Glasgow G4 0RQ.

Hart, Thomas, MA, LLB. Editor, Scottish Transport Review, 1998-2004; Vice President, Scottish Association for Public Transport, since 1976; Lecturer, Department of Economic and Social History, Glasgow University, 1965-98, Honorary Research Fellow, since 1998; b. 15.11.39, Kilmarnock; m., Ellen Elizabeth Jones; 2 s. Educ. Spiers School, Beith; Glasgow University. Consultant on transport and environmental issues; Founder Member of Scottish Transport Studies Group (Secretary, 1984-94, Chair, 1994-2004), Founder Member, Scottish Railway Development Association (Secretary, 1962-67, Vice Chairman, 1967-72); Chairman, Scottish Association for Public Transport, 1972-76; Member, Board, TRANS*form* Scotland, since 1997; External Member, SPT (Strathclyde Partnership for Transport), since 2006. Recreations: walking; travel; gardening. Address: (h.) Birchfield, Kings Road, Beith, Ayrshire KA15 2BN; T.-01505 502164; e-mail: thstsg@aol.com

Harte, Professor Ben, BA, MA, PhD(Cantab), FRSE. Professor of Metamorphism, Edinburgh University, since 1991, and P.I. for Edinburgh Materials and Microanalysis Centre; b. 30.5.41, Blackpool; m., Angela Elizabeth; 1 s.; 2 d. Educ. Salford Grammar School; Trinity College, Cambridge University. Lecturer/Reader, Edinburgh University, 1965-91; Guest Research Investigator, Carnegie Institution of Washington, 1974-75; Visiting Associate Professor, Yale University, 1982; Visiting Research Fellow, University of Cape Town, 1990; JSPS Research Fellow, Ehime University, Japan, 1999. Address: (b.) School of GeoSciences, Grant Institute, King's Buildings, Edinburgh EH9 3JW; T.-0131-651 7220; e-mail: ben.harte@ed.ac.uk

Hartley, Graeme Edward, BA, MCIArb. Director, RICS Scotland, since 2004; b. 9.4.61, Edinburgh; m., Lee Adams Rankine; 1 s. Educ. Perth High School; Napier University. Dundee Chamber of Commerce, 1983-85; Electrical Contractors' Association of Scotland, 1985-90. Director, Scottish Building Contract Committee Ltd; Member: Scottish Construction Industry Group, Council, National Trust for Scotland, Asset Skills Scotland Board. Recreations: golf; running. Address: (b.) 9 Manor Place, Edinburgh EH3 7DN; T.-0131-225 7078; e-mail: ghartley@rics.org.uk

Hartley, Keith Scott, BA, MA. Deputy Director, Scottish National Gallery of Modern Art; b. 27.1.49, Evesham. Educ. Prince Henry's Grammar School, Evesham; St. Catherine's College, University of Oxford; Courtauld Institute, University of London; Freie Universität, W. Berlin. Curator of numerous exhibitions, and author of corresponding catalogues, including: Scottish Art Since 1900, 1989, Otto Dix, Tate Gallery, 1992, The Romantic Spirit in German Art 1790-1990, 1994. A Director, Art in Partnership (Scotland). Recreations: travel; reading. Address: (b.) Scottish National Gallery of Modern Art, Belford Road, Edinburgh EH4 3DR; T.-0131-624 6251.

Hartley, Mike, BSc, MBA. Chairman, Dawson International PLC, since 2003; Non Executive Chairman, Servocell plc, since 2006; Non Executive Director, ITE Group PLC, since 2003; b. 26.1.49, Watford; m., Valerie; 1 s.; 1 d. Educ. Goole Grammar School; City University;

Manchester Business School. Marks and Spencer plc, 1971-76; Liverpool Daily Post and Echo plc, 1977-79; Barker and Dobson plc, 1979-85; Coats Viyella plc, 1985-2001; Private Equity and Consultancy, since 2002. Recreations: walking; windsurfing; travel. Address: Dawson International PLC, Lochleven Mills, Kinross KY13 8GL.

Harvey, Professor Alan L., BSc, PhD, MBA, CBiol, FIBiol. Director, Strathclyde Institute for Drug Research, since 1988; Professor in Pharmacology, Strathclyde University, since 1986; b. 23.6.50, Glasgow. Educ. Hutchesons', Glasgow; Strathclyde University. Lecturer in Physiology and Pharmacology, Strathclyde University, 1974-83; Senior Lecturer, 1983-86. British Pharmacological Society Sandoz Prize, 1983; Redi Award, International Society on Toxicology, 2000; British Pharmaceutical Conference Science Award, 1983. Publications: Toxicon (Editor); Advances in Drug Discovery Techniques, 1998; Natural Product Pharmaceuticals, 2001. Address: (b.) Institute of Pharmacy and Biomedical Sciences, Strathclyde University, Glasgow, G4 0NR; T.-0141-553 4155.

Harvey, Rev. William John, BA (Hons), BD (Hons). Moderator, Glasgow Presbytery, 1998-99; b. 17.5.37, Glasgow; m., Isabel Mary Douglas; 2 s.; 2 d. Educ. Fettes College, Edinburgh; Oxford University; Glasgow University. National Service, Argyll & Sutherland Highlanders, 1956-58; Ordained Assistant, Govan Old Parish Church, 1964-66; Member, Gorbals Group Ministry, 1963-71; Minister, Laurieston-Renwick Parish Church, Glasgow, 1968-71; Warden, Iona Abbey, 1971-76; Minister: Raploch Parish Church, Stirling, 1976-81, Govan Old Parish Church, 1981-88; Leader, The Iona Community, 1988-95. Member, Church of Scotland Committee on Church and Nation, 1978-86; Kerr Lecturer, Glasgow University, 1987; Team Member, The Craighead Institute of Life and Faith, Glasgow, 1995-2000; Interim Minister, Board of Ministry, The Church of Scotland, 2000-03. Recreations: reading; history; bread and wine-making; seabird watching. Address: (h.) 501 Shields Road, Glasgow G41 2RF; T.-0141-429 3774.
E-mail: jonmol@phonecoop.coop

Harvey-Miller, Nicholas Thomas. Chairman, Harvey-Miller Wine and Spirit Agencies, since 2004; Chairman, The Scotch Embassy Ltd., since 2002; Director, Recycled Energy Solutions Ltd.; b. 4.2.54, Reading. Educ. Milton Abbey. Sales Director, Wm Grant and Sons, 1981-87; Managing Director: Grants of St. James (Samuel Dow), 1987-90, Forth Wines Ltd., 1990-2002; Director, Mathew Clarke Ltd., 2000-02; Chief Executive, Wm Morton Ltd, 2002-04; Director: The Duckworth Group, 1992-2003, McKinley Vintners Ltd., since 2006. Formerly Chairman, Scottish Association for Country Sports. Recreations: managing local heather uplands; shooting; fishing. Address: (h.) Craigton House, Fintry, Stirlingshire G63 0XQ; T.-01360 860377; e-mail: nick@hmwsa.com

Harvie, Professor Christopher Thomas, MA Hons (Edin), PhD (Edin). MSP (SNP), Mid Scotland and Fife, since 2007; Professor of British and Irish Studies, University of Tubingen, since 1980; Professor (Hon.) of History, Strathclyde, since 1995; b. 21.9.44, Motherwell; m., Virginia Roundell (deceased); 1 d. Educ. St. Boswells Primary School; Kelso High School; Royal High School, Edinburgh; Edinburgh University. Tutor, Edinburgh University, 1966-69; Lecturer/Senior Lecturer in History, Open University, 1969-80; Professor of British Studies, Eberhard-Karls Universitat, Tubingen, since 1980; Visiting Fellow, Merton and Nuffield Colleges, Oxford, Strathclyde and Edinburgh; Hon. Professor: Strathclyde University, since 1999,

Aberystwyth, since 1996. Founder, Freudenstadt Colloquium, 1991; Co-Chair, Baden-Wurttemberg Colloquium, 1996; Hon. President, Scottish Association for Public Transport, since 2002. Candidate (SNP) for Kirkcaldy (Scottish Parliament), 2007. Publications: The Lights of Liberalism, 1860-86, 1976; Scotland and Nationalism, 1976, 4 eds by 2004; No Gods and Precious Few Heroes, 4 eds by 2000; The Centre of Things: British Political Fiction, 1991; Cultural Weapons: Scotland and Europe, 1992; The Rise of Regional Europe, 1993, 2nd ed. 2006; The Road to Home Rule (Co-Author), 1999; Travelling Scot, 1999; Scotland: a Short History, 2002; Scotland's Transport, 2001; Mending Scotland, 2004; A Floating Commonwealth: Politics, Technology and Culture on the West Coast, 1860-1930, 2008; International Men: Liberals in European Politics, 2008; Scotland the Brief, 2008; essays; articles; reviews. Recreations: any human activity except sport (but principally painting, music, travel). Address: (b.) Scottish Parliament, Edinburgh EH99 1SP.
E-mail: christopher.harvie.msp@scottish.parliament.uk; website: www.intelligent-mr-toad.de

Harvie, Patrick. MSP (Green), Glasgow, since 2003; b. 18.3.73. Educ. Dumbarton Academy; Manchester Metropolitan University. Address: (b.) Scottish Parliament, Edinburgh EH99 1SP; T.-0131 348 6363.

Haslam, Shona, MA (PolStud). National Director, Asthma UK Scotland, since 2007; b. 6.9.74, Kirkcaldy, Fife; m., Marc Haslam; 1 s. Educ. Peebles High School; Aberdeen University. Parliamentary Officer, Evangelical Alliance, 1996-2003; Public Affairs Manager, Asthma UK Scotland, 2003-07. Recreations: walking; family; church; cooking. Address: (b.) Asthma UK Scotland, 4 Queen Street, Edinburgh EH2 1JE; T.-0131 226 2544; e-mail: shaslam@asthma.org.uk

Hastings, Gavin, OBE, DUniv (Paisley). Former rugby player; Chairman, Platinum One Scotland; b. 1962, Edinburgh. Educ. George Watson's College, Edinburgh; Paisley University; Cambridge University. 61 Scotland Caps, 1986-95 (20 as Captain); 3 World Cups, 1987, 1991, 1995; 2 British Lions Tours: 1989, Australia, 3 Tests, 1993, New Zealand (Captain), 3 Tests; e-mail: info@platinum-one.co.uk

Hatwell, Anthony, DFA(Lond). Sculptor; Head, School of Sculpture, Edinburgh College of Art, 1969-90; b. 21.6.31, London; m., Elizabeth; 2 d. Educ. Dartford Grammar School; Slade School of Fine Art; Borough Polytechnic; Bromley College of Art. Some exhibitions: Scottish Arts Council Edinburgh Festival Exhibition, 1978; British Sculpture in the 20th Century, Whitechapel Gallery, 1981; Built in Scotland exhibition in Edinburgh, Glasgow, and London, 1983; Slade Postgraduate Scholarship, 1956; Boise Travelling Scholarship, 1957; Assistant to Henry Moore, 1958; Member, London Group, 1959-69 (Vice-President, 1961-63); works in collections of Scottish National Gallery of Modern Art, Arts Council of GB, Scottish Arts Council, Edinburgh City Art Centre, Dundee University and private collections. Address: (h.) 4 North Street, Belhaven, Dunbar, East Lothian.

Haughey, William, OBE (2003). Chairman, Scottish Enterprise Glasgow; Joint Owner and Executive Chairman, City Refrigeration Holdings (UK) Ltd, since 1985; Non-Executive Director, Dunedin Enterprise Trust; b. 2.7.56, Glasgow; m., Susan nee Moore; 1 s. Educ. Holyrood Senior Secondary School, Glasgow; Springburn College,

Glasgow. Energy Supervisor, Turner Refrigeration Ltd, 1973-83; Head of Engineering, UAE UTS Carrier, 1983-85; Charter Member, Duke of Edinburgh Awards Scheme; Member, Growth Fund Panel, Prince's Scottish Youth Business Trust; Patron, CSV; Entrepreneur of the Year, Entrepreneurial Exchange, 2000 (finalist 1999); Business to Business section and Masterclass winner, Ernst & Young Awards, 2000; Refrigeration Industry Business of the Year, 2000; Lanarkshire Business of the Year, 2002; Business Man of the Year, Award Insider Publications, 2003; Bighearted Business Person of the Year, 2004; Excellence in Public Service Award, 2004; Business Award, Great Scot 2005 Awards, Sunday Mail, 2005; Loving Cup from Lord Provost of Glasgow for charity work, 2001; Hon DTech, Glasgow Caledonian University. 2005; St Mungo Medal (awarded to the citizen of Glasgow who has worked tirelessly to promote and enhance the wellbeing of its less fortunate citizens, and at the same time adding to the reputation of Glasgow the Caring City), December 2006. Recreations: golf; reading; football. Address: (b.) City Refrigeration Holdings (UK) Ltd, 17 Lawmoor Street, Glasgow G5 0US; T.-0141 613 6107; e-mail: willie.haughey@city-holdings.co.uk

Hawkins, Anthony Donald, CBE, BSc, PhD, FSA Scot, FRSE. Director, Loughine Ltd; Director of Fisheries Research for Scotland, 1987-2002; Honorary Professor, Aberdeen University; b. 25.3.42, Dorset; m., Susan Mary; 1 s. Educ. Poole Grammar School; Bristol University. Entered Scottish Office as Scientific Officer, Marine Laboratory, Aberdeen, 1965; Senior Scientific Officer, 1969, Principal Scientific Officer, 1972, Senior Principal Scientific Officer, 1978, Deputy Chief Scientific Officer, 1983; Deputy Director of Fisheries Research for Scotland, 1983; conducts research into behaviour and physiology of fish; awarded A.B. Wood Medal, Institute of Acoustics, 1978; Chairman, The Green Wedge; Chairman, North Sea Commission Fisheries Partnership. Publications: books on fish physiology and aquarium systems. Recreations: reading; angling; soccer; breeding whippets. Address: Kincraig, Blairs, Aberdeen; T.-01224 868984; e-mail: a.hawkins@btconnect.com

Hawkins, Nigel, FRSA. Director and Chief Executive, John Muir Trust, since 1996; b. 12.9.46, Dundee. Educ. Madras College, St Andrews. Principal Founder, John Muir Trust, 1982 (Trustee, 1982-96, Director, since 1996); Creator, Dundee City of Discovery Campaign, 1985; Chairman, Prospect PR Ltd., 1985-2006; Co-Founder, The Knoydart Foundation, 1983 (Director, 1998-2003); Director, North Harris Trust, since 2003; Director, Assynt Foundation, since 2005; Deputy Chairman and Director, Dundee Science Centre Trust, 1998-2004; Director, Sensation Ltd., 1999-2004; University of Abertay Dundee: Fellow, 1998, Member, Court, since 1999 and Deputy Chairman, Court, since 2006; President, Dundee and Tayside Chamber of Commerce and Industry, 1997-98; Board Member, North of Scotland Water Authority, 1998-2002. Recreations: mountaineering; cycling; running; good food. Address: (b.) 1 Auchterhouse Park, Auchterhouse, by Dundee DD3 0QU; T.-01382 320252; e-mail: nigel@jmt.org

Hay, Alison. Member, Argyll and Bute Council (Leader, 1999-2001); COSLA Spokesperson on Environment, Sustainability and Community Safety; b. 5.3.52; m., John Hay; 2s. Educ. Invergordon Academy. Liberal Democrat Councillor, Argyll and Bute District Council, 1988-94; elected Strathclyde Regional Council, 1994; elected, Argyll and Bute Council, 1995; Leader of the Opposition, 1995-99 and 2001-06; Chair, Auchedrain Museum Trust; Member: Mid Argyll Partnership, Mid Argyll Locality Planning Group, Main Board of Scottish

Environmental Protection Agency, Group for Recycling in Argyll and Bute. Recreations: walking; reading. Address: (b.) Argyll and Bute Council, Kilmory, Lochgilphead, Argyll, PA31 8RT; T.-01546 604305.

Hay, Ian, OBE, FCIBS, FFCS, FRSA, ГІАМ, FHS. Chairman: Food Trade Association Management, Xtra-Mile.com Ltd., Flight Bureau Ltd, Charterhall Finance Ltd; Vice Chairman, Bakery Training Council; Finance Director: Scottish Association of Master Bakers, Scottish Bakery Training Council; b. 31.8.39, Aberdeen; m., Amelia Robertson; 3 s.; 1 d. Educ. Ellon Academy. Member: Low Pay Commission, Employment Tribunal Panel. Recreations: golf; football; reading; complementary medicine. Address: (b.) 4 Torphichen Street, Edinburgh EH3 8JQ; T.-0131-466-0109.
E-mail: charterhall@blueyonder.co.uk

Hay, James Taylor Cantlay, MBE, BSc (Hons), DTech, FInstPet, SPE, AAPG. Oil and Gas Consultant; Director, Melrose Resources plc, since 1999; b. 13.6.35, Huntly; m., Mary Gordon Davidson; 1 s.; 2 d. Educ. Banchory Academy, Aberdeen University. Geologist, Iraq Petroleum Co. Ltd., Iraq, 1958-66; Head of Geology, Abu Dhabi Petroleum Co. Ltd., Abu Dhabi, 1967-71; Lecturer in Geology, Aberdeen University, 1971-74; Senior Production Geologist, Burmah Oil, London, 1974-76; various management roles, BNOC, Aberdeen and Glasgow, 1977-80; General Manager: BNOC/Britoil, Aberdeen, 1980-87, BP Exploration, Aberdeen, 1988-91. Recreations: golf; shooting. Address: (h.) 67 Fountainhall Road, Aberdeen; T.-01224 645955.

Hay, Sheriff Robert Colquhoun, CBE, MA, LLB, WS. Sheriff Principal of North Strathclyde, 1989-98; b. 22.9.33, Glasgow; m., Olive Black; 2 s.; 2 d. Educ. Edinburgh University. Chairman, Industrial Tribunals (Scotland), 1976-81, President, 1981-89; Commissioner of Northern Lights, 1989-98, Chairman, 1992-93; Member, Sheriff Court Rules Council, 1990-95, Chairman, 1993-95; Commissioner for Clan Hay, 1995-2002. Address: (h.) Rocklee, Cove, Argyll G84 0NN.

Hay, Robert King Miller, BSc, MSc, PhD, FIBiol. Writer and Editor; Visiting Professor, Swedish University of Agricultural Sciences, Uppsala, 2005-07; Director, Scottish Agricultural Science Agency, 1990-2004; Honorary Fellow of SAC (Scottish Agricultural College), since 2004; b. 19.8.46, Edinburgh; m., Dorothea Harden Vinycomb; 2 s.; 1 d. Educ. Forres Academy, Moray; Aberdeen University; University of East Anglia. AFRC Research Fellow, Edinburgh University, 1971-74; Lecturer in Crop Production: University of Malawi, 1974-76, Edinburgh University, 1976-77; Lecturer in Environmental Sciences, Lancaster University, 1977-82; Leverhulme European Fellow, Agricultural University of Norway, 1981; Head of Plant Sciences, Scottish Agricultural College, Ayr, 1982-90; British Council Research Fellow, University of Western Australia, 1989; Visiting Scientist, McGill University, Montreal, 1997. Publications: Environmental Physiology of Plants, 1981, 1987, 2002; Chemistry for Agriculture and Ecology; The Physiology of Crop Yield, 1989, 2006; Volatile Oil Crops (Ed); Science Policies in Europe: Unity and Diversity (Ed); Lochnavando No More: The Life and Death of a Moray Farming Community, 1750-1850; Annals of Botany (Editor), 1995-2006; 60 scientific papers. Recreations: walking; working with stone; history; music. Address: (h.) Park Steading, Isle of Lismore, Oban PA34 5UN; T.-01631 760 393.
E-mail: dot.bob@btopenworld.com

Haydon, Professor Daniel Thomas, BSc, PhD. Professor of Population Ecology and Epidemiology, University of Glasgow, since 2007; b. 10.06.65, Cambridge; m., Dr. Barbara Mable (common-law). Educ. Perse School, Cambridge; University of Southampton; University of Texas at Austin. Post-doctoral research assistant at University of Oxford, 1992-96, University of British Columbia, 1996-98, University of Edinburgh, 1998-2001, University of Guelph, 2001-04; Lecturer, University of Glasgow, 2004-07. Scientific Medal (Zoological Society of London, 2005); British Lichen Society. Recreations: mountaineering; hill-walking; photography. Address: (b.) Graham Kerr Building, University of Glasgow, Glasgow G12 8QQ; T.-0141 330 6637; e-mail: d.haydon@bio.gla.ac.uk

Hayes, Professor Peter Clive, BMSc, MBChB, MD, PhD, FRCPE. Professor of Hepatology, Edinburgh Royal Infirmary, since 1998; Lead Clinician for Clinical Research Facilities in Edinburgh; b. 19.1.57, Cheshire; m., Sharon; 2 s.; 1 d. Educ. Royal High School, Edinburgh; Dundee University. Research Fellow and Honorary Lecturer, Liver Unit, King's College Hospital, London; Lecturer in Gastroenterology and Medicine, then Senior Lecturer in Hepatology, Edinburgh Royal Infirmary. Recreations: cricket; salmon fishing. Address: (b.) Department of Internal Medicine, Royal Infirmary, Edinburgh; T.-0131 242 1628.

Haywood, Brent William, LLB, BA, Dip Forensic Medicine. Solicitor Advocate; Partner, Biggart Baillie, since 2002; b. 14.8.65, Riverton, New Zealand; m., Heather; 2 s. Educ. Southland Boys' High School, New Zealand; Otago University, Dunedin, New Zealand. Writer to Her Majesty's Signet (W.S.); Company Secretary, The Raven Trust; Trustee, Business Matters; Director, The Signet Accreditation Limited; Elder of Brightons Parish Church. Recreations: ultra distance running and cycling. Address: (b.) 7 Castle Street, Edinburgh EH2 3AP; T.-0131 226 5541; e-mail: bhaywood@biggartbaillie.co.uk

Hazel, Professor George McLean, OBE, BSc, MSc, PhD, CEng, MICE, FCIT, FIHT. Managing Director, MRC McLean Hazel, since 2005; McLean Hazel Ltd., 2001-05; Professor of Transport Policy, Robert Gordon University, 1999-2001; b. 27.1.49, Dunfermline; m., Fiona Isabella Gault; 1 s.; 2 d. Educ. Dunfermline High School; Heriot-Watt University; Cranfield Institute of Technology. Transportation Engineer: City of Edinburgh Corporation, 5 years, Lothian Regional Council, 4 years; Lecturer, Senior Lecturer, Head of Dept., and first Professor of Transport in Scotland, Napier College/Polytechnic/University, 11 years; Director, Oscar Faber TPA, three years; Director of Transportation, Lothian Regional Council, three years; Director of City Development, City of Edinburgh Council, 1996-99. Member, Secretary of State for Scotland's Advisory Group on Sustainable Development; Chair, Urban Design Alliance, 2004/06; Member, Secretary of State's Steering (2004) Group on National Road User Charging; Advisor to the Commission for Integrated Transport, Lorry Road User Charging Committee of Transport, 2000; Chairman, Edinburgh and East of Scotland Association, Institution of Civil Engineers; President, Institution of Highways and Transportation, 2003-04. Recreations: golf; gardening; travel; music; vintage cars. Address: (h.) 7 Glenlockhart Valley, Edinburgh EH14 1DE; e-mail: george.hazel@mrcmcleanhazel.com

Healy, Brendan John Patrick. Chief Executive Officer, St. Andrew's Ambulance Association, since 1995; b. 25.3.46, Dublin; m., Catherine; 1 s.; 2 d. Educ. Britania Royal Naval College. Specialised in naval aviation; Joint Service Defence College, 1987; Commanding Officer, Royal Naval Air Station, Prestwick, 1990-93. Recreations: golf; philately; travel. Address: (b.) St. Andrew's House, 48 Milton Street, Glasgow G4 0HR.

Hearne, John Michael, BMus, MMus, DMus. Publisher (Longship Music); Freelance Composer and Professional Singer; Conductor and Copyist; b. 19.9.37, Reading; m., Margaret Gillespie Jarvie. Educ. Torquay Grammar School; St. Luke's College, Exeter; University College of Wales, Aberystwyth. Teaching, Rugeley, Staffordshire, 1959-60; Warehouseman/ Driver, Torquay, 1961-64; Teaching: Tonlistarskoli Borgarfjardar, Iceland, 1968-69, UCW Aberystwyth, 1969-70; Lecturer, Aberdeen College of Education, 1970-87. Composer, vocal, instrumental and incidental music: BBC commission for BBCSSO, 1990 (trumpet concerto); McEwen Commission, Glasgow University, 1979; A Legend of Margaret, commissioned to celebrate 150th anniversary of St. Margaret's School, Aberdeen, 1996; Into Uncharted Seas, commissioned to commemorate centenary of launch of Discovery on Antarctic expedition; The Ben – a Cantata for Bennachie, commissioned by Gordon Forum for the Arts, 2001; Member, John Currie Singers, 1973-2003; Awarded Radio Forth Trophy, 1985, for most outstanding work on Edinburgh Festival Fringe; joint winner, Gregynog Composers' Award for Wales, 1992. Chorus Manager, Aberdeen International Youth Festival, since 1978; Chairman: Scottish Music Advisory Committee, BBC, 1986-90, Gordon Forum for the Arts, 1991-94; Conductor, Stonehaven and District Choral Society; Past Chairman, Scottish Society of Composers; former Member, Board, National Youth Choir of Scotland; Winner, Gregynog Composers' Award for Wales, 1998; Conductor, Inverurie Choral Society, 1998-2003; Warden, Performers and Composers Section, Incorporated Society of Musicians, 1999; Member, Board, Enterprise Music Scotland. Recreations: motoring and travel (1954 Daimler Roadster, 1991 SAAB 900 Aero). Address: (h.) Smidskot, Fawells, Keith-Hall, Inverurie AB51 OLN; T.-01651 882 274.

Heatly, Sir Peter, CBE, DL, BSc, CEng, FICE. Chairman, Peter Heatly & Co. Ltd., 1958-96; b. 9.6.24, Edinburgh; m., Mae Calder Cochrane (deceased 2003). Educ. Leith Academy; Edinburgh University. Structural Designer, Redpath Brown & Co. Ltd., 1946; Lecturer in Civil Engineering, Edinburgh University, 1948. Chairman: Scottish Sports Council, 1975-87, Commonwealth Games Federation, 1982-90, International Diving Committee, 1984-88; Master, Edinburgh Merchant Company, 1988-90; awarded Honorary Doctorate, Edinburgh University, 1992, Queen Margaret College, 1994; Honorary Doctorate, Stirling University, 1998. Recreations: swimming; gardening; travel. Address: (h.) Lanrig, Balerno, Edinburgh EH14 7AJ; T.-0131-449 3998.

Heavens, Professor Alan Francis, MA, PhD, FRAS. Professor of Theoretical Astrophysics, since 2002; b. 24.3.59, Reading; m., Ann; 1 s.; 1 d. Educ. St Peter's School, York; Cambridge University (Churchill College). SERC Research Fellow, Edinburgh University, 1983-84; Demonstrator, Lecturer, Reader, Edinburgh University, 1984-2002. Recreations: chess; cricket; choral singing. Address: (b.) Royal Observatory, Blackford Hill, Edinburgh EH9 3HJ; e-mail: afh@roe.ac.uk

Hedderwick, Mairi Crawford, DA (Edin). Illustrator, Writer and Public Speaker; b. 2.5.39, Gourock; 1 s.; 1 d. Educ. St. Columba's School, Kilmacolm; Edinburgh College of Art; Jordanhill College of Education. Publications: for children: Katie Morag series, A Walk with Grannie; The Utterly Otterleys; for adults: An Eye on the Hebrides, Highland Journey; Sea Change. Hon. Doctorate, Stirling University. Recreations: a day outside ending round a table with friends, food and wine.

Heggie, Professor Douglas Cameron, MA, PhD, FRAS, FRSE. Professor of Mathematical Astronomy, Edinburgh University, since 1994; b. 7.2.47, Edinburgh; m., Linda Jane Tennent; 2 d. Educ. George Heriot's School,

Edinburgh; Trinity College, Cambridge. Research Fellow, Trinity College, Cambridge, 1972-76; Lecturer in Mathematics, Edinburgh University, 1975-85, Reader, 1985-94; Council Member, Royal Astronomical Society, 1982-85; President, Commission 37, International Astronomical Union, 1985-88; Member, Board of Editors, Monthly Notices of the RAS, since 1994. Publications: Megalithic Science; The Gravitational Million-Body Problem; scientific papers on dynamical astronomy. Recreations: family life; walking; music. Address: (b.) Edinburgh University, School of Mathematics, King's Buildings, Edinburgh EH9 3JZ; T.-0131-650 5035; e-mail: d.c.heggie@ed.ac.uk

Heller, Martin Fuller Vernon, FRSAMD. Actor, since 1947; Artistic Director, Prime Productions; b. 20.2.27, Manchester; m., Joyce Allan; 2 s.; 4 d. Educ. Rondebosch Boys High School, Cape Town; Central School of Speech Training and Dramatic Art, London. Compass Players, 1948-52; repertory seasons and/or individual productions at following Scottish theatres: St. Andrews Byre, Edinburgh Gateway, Glasgow Citizens' (eight seasons), Edinburgh Royal Lyceum, Edinburgh Traverse, Dundee Repertory, Perth Repertory, Pitlochry Festival; Founder/Artistic Director, Prime Productions; extensive television and radio work; Member: Scottish Arts Council, 1975-82 (latterly Chairman, Drama Committee); Governor, Pitlochry Festival Theatre (retired 2005); Governor, Royal Scottish Academy of Music and Drama, 1982-94. Recreations: politics; history; listening to music. Address: (h.) 54 Hermiston, Currie, Midlothian EH14 4AQ; T.-0131-449 4055.

Helms, Professor Peter Joseph, MB, BS, PhD, FRCP, FRCPCH. Professor of Child Health, Aberdeen University, since 1991; Consultant Paediatrician, since 1982; b. 26.6.47, Melbourne; m., Kathleen Mary; 1 s.; 3 d. Educ. Wimbledon College; Royal Free Hospital School of Medicine; London University. SHO, Hospital for Sick Children, Great Ormond Street, 1976; Lecturer in Paediatrics, Charing Cross Hospital Medical School, 1977-78; Research Fellow, Institute of Child Health, London, 1978-81, National Heart and Lung Institute, London, 1981-82; Senior Lecturer, Institute of Child Health, 1982-91; Honorary Consultant Paediatrician, Hospital for Sick Children, Great Ormond Street, 1982-91. Recreations: music; hill-walking; European history. Address: (b.) Department of Child Health, Royal Aberdeen Children's Hospital, Foresterhill, Aberdeen, AB25 2ZG; T.-01224 552471.

Henderson, Andrew Kerr, MBE, MB, ChB, FRCP (Glas and Edin). Consultant Physician (retired), Lorn and the Islands District General Hospital, Oban; Honorary Clinical Senior Lecturer, Glasgow University; b. 1.3.46, Hawick; m., Doreen Innes Wilkinson; 1 s.; 2 d. Educ. Glasgow Academy; Glasgow University. Medical Registrar, Western Infirmary, Glasgow; Medical Registrar/Senior Registrar, Glasgow Royal Infirmary. Recreations: gardening; hill-walking. Address: (h.) Birkmoss, North Connel, Argyll; T.-01631 710379; e-mail: akh379@hotmail.com

Henderson, Fiona, BA. Presenter/Reporter, BBC Reporting Scotland, since 1992; b. 26.6.63, Londonderry; m., David Nisbet; 1 s.; 1 d. Educ. Foyle College, N. Ireland; Stirling University. Radio Reporter/Producer, BBC N. Ireland, 1986-87; Researcher, TV News and Current Affairs, BBC Scotland, 1987-88; Presenter, BBC TV News, BBC Scotland, 1988-90; Presenter/Reporter, Inside Ulster, BBC N. Ireland, 1988-90; News and Current Affairs, BBC Scotland since 1991. Recreations: her family; architecture; Edinburgh; riding; reading; making sticky buns. Address: Newsroom, BBC Scotland, 40 Pacific Quay, Glasgow G51 1DZ; e-mail: fiona.henderson.01@bbc.co.uk

Henderson, John Gunn, BA, FRSA. Deputy Director, Scotland Office, since 2007; Head, International Division,

Scottish Executive, 2003-07; Euro 2008 Bid Director, Scottish Football Association (on secondment from the Scottish Executive), 2001-03; b. 29.5.53, Edinburgh; m., Caroline; 1 s.; 2 d. Educ. Broughton Secondary, Edinburgh; Open University. Scottish Development Department, 1970-78; Department of Agriculture and Fisheries for Scotland, 1978-85; Scottish Development Department, Trunk Roads Division, 1985-88; Scottish Office Education and Industry Department, 1988-97 (Head, Further Education Funding Unit, 1992-97); Assistant Director of Finance and Head, Private Finance Unit, 1997-2001. Recreations: reading; gardening; beachcombing. Address: (b.) Scotland Office, 1 Melville Crescent, Edinburgh EH3 7HW; T.-0131 244 9010.

Henderson, Meg. Author, Journalist and Scriptwriter; b. 1948, Glasgow; m., Rab; 1 s.; 2 d. Educ. Garnethill Convent Secondary School (reluctantly). Chief Cardiology Technician, Western Infirmary and Royal Infirmary, Glasgow; VSO, India; spent years fostering children; has worked for the broadsheets, Daily Mail, BBC, Channel 4. Publications: Finding Peggy, 1994; The Holy City, 1997; Bloody Mary, 1998; Chasing Angels, 2000; The Last Wanderer, 2002; Second Sight, 2004; Daisy's Wars, 2005; A Scent of Bluebells, 2006. Recreations: reading, history, walking, radio, peace and quiet, golf, tennis, F1 racing (without having the slightest aptitude for any of them); shouting at politicians on television (or wherever encountered). Address: c/o Karen Duffy, Flamingo Publicity, HarperCollins Publishers, 77-85 Fulham Palace Road, London W6 8JB.

Henderson, Major Sir Richard Yates, KCVO, TD, JP, BA (Oxon), LLB. Lord Lieutenant, Ayrshire and Arran, 1991-2006; b. 7.7.31, Nitshill; m., Frances Elizabeth Chrystal; 3 s. (inc. 1 s. dec.); 1 d. Educ. Rugby; Hertford College, Oxford; Glasgow University. Royal Scots Greys, 1950-52; TA Ayrshire (ECO) Yeomanry, 1953-69 (Major); Deputy Lieutenant, Ayrshire and Arran, 1970-90; Partner, Mitchells Roberton, Solicitors, 1958-90, Consultant, 1991-92. Ensign, Queen's Bodyguard for Scotland (Royal Company of Archers); President, Lowland TAVRA, 1996-2000; Hon. Colonel, Ayrshire Yeomanry Sqn., Scottish Yeomanry, 1992-97; Honorary Sheriff, South Strathclyde Dumfries and Galloway at Ayr, since 1997. Recreations: shooting; tennis; golf. Address: (h.) Blairston, by Ayr, KA7 4EF; T.-01292 441601.

Henderson-Howat, David Barclay, BSc, MA, MBA. Head of Agriculture Division, Rural Directorate, Scottish Government, since 2005; b. 23.1.54, Trinidad; m., Jean Buchanan-Smith; 1 s.; 3 d. Educ. Abingdon School; University of Edinburgh; Magdalene College, University of Cambridge; University of Strathclyde. Scottish Office, 1976-79; Personal Assistant to Chief Executive, Scottish Development Agency, 1979-80; Harvesting and Marketing Manager, Thetford Forest, 1980-84; Forest Manager, Shiselweni Forest, Swaziland, 1984-86; Forest District Manager, Aberfoyle, Perthshire, 1986-90; Forestry Commission Headquarters, 1990-96; Chief Conservator, Forestry Commission Scotland, 1996-2003; United Nations Forum on Forests, 2003-05; Elder, Kirkurd and Newlands Church. Recreations: walking; sailing. Address: (h.) Stoneyknowe, West Linton, Peeblesshire EH46 7BY; T.-01968 660677.

Hendry, Dr. Joy McLaggan, MA (Hons), DipEd, DLitt (Hon) (Edin). Editor, Chapman Magazine, since 1972; Writer; b. 3.2.53, Perth; m., Ian Montgomery. Educ. Perth Academy; Edinburgh University. Former teacher; Co-Editor, Chapman, 1972-76, Sole Editor, since 1976; Deputy Convener, Scottish Poetry Library Association, 1983-88;

Convener, Committee for the Advancement of Scottish Literature in Schools; Member AdCas; Scottish National Theatre Steering Committee; Campaign for a Scottish Assembly; Member, Drama Committee, Scottish Arts Council; Chair, Scottish Actors Studio, 1993-2000; Member, Literature Forum for Scotland; Member, Scottish Parliament Scots Language Cross-Party Group; Lecturer in drama, Queen Margaret University College, 2000-04; Lecturer in periodical journalism, Napier University, 2000-04; poet and playwright; gives lectures and talks and performances of poetry and song; radio critic, The Scotsman, 1988-97; theatre reviewer; Writer-in-Residence, Stirling District Council, 1991-93. HonDL, University of Edinburgh, 2005. Publications: Scots: The Way Forward; Poems and Pictures by Wendy Wood (Editor); The Land for the People (Co-Editor); Critical Essays on Sorley MacLean (Co-Editor); Critical Essays on Norman MacCaig (Co-Editor); Autobiographical Essay in 'Spirit of the Age' (Saltire Society); Gang Doun wi a Sang (play); radio: The Wa' at the Warld's End, Radio 3 (play); A Many-Faceted Thing (Memory), Radio 4 (major 4-part series). Recreations: going to theatre; cinema; reading. Address: 4 Broughton Place, Edinburgh EH1 3RX; T.-0131-557 2207.

Hendry, Stephen, MBE, Professional snooker player; b. 13.1.69; m., Mandy. Youngest-ever Scottish Amateur Champion (aged 15); has won 72 major titles worldwide; youngest player to attain No. 1 ranking; youngest player to win World Championship, 1990; World Champion seven times; UK Champion, five times; Masters Champion, six times. Address: (b.) 110 Sport Management Ltd.; 1st Floor, Pavilion 1, Castlecraig Business Park, Players Road, Stirling FK7 7SH; T.-01786 462634.

Hendry, Stuart, LLB (Hons), LLM, NP. Partner, MBM Commercial LLP, since 2005; b. 12.1.73, Aberdeen. Murray Beith Murray WS: Solicitor, 1999-2003, Associate Partner, 2003-05. Address: (b.) 107 George Street, Edinburgh EH2 3EJ; T.-0845 408 5453; e-mail: stuart.hendry@mbmcommercial.co.uk

Henley, Professor John Sebastian, BSc (Eng), PhD. Head, Strategy and International Business Group and Professor of International Management, University of Edinburgh Management School; b. 5.4.43, Malvern; m., Sarah J. Sieley; 2 d. Educ. King Edward's School, Birmingham; University College, London; London School of Economics. Personnel Officer, Glaxo Laboratories, 1966-68; Lecturer, Industrial Relations Department, London School of Economics, 1968-72; Lecturer, Faculty of Commerce, University of Nairobi, 1972-75; joined Department of Business Studies, University of Edinburgh, 1975. Publications: co-author of three books; editor of two books; author of over 50 academic papers. Recreations: gardening; theatre; opera; sailing. Address: (b.) University of Edinburgh Management School, 50 George Square, Edinburgh EH8 9JY; T.-0131-650 3814; e-mail: J.Henley@ed.ac.uk

Henry, Hugh. MSP (Labour), Paisley South, since 1999. Former Deputy Minister for: Justice, Social Justice, Health and Community Care; former Convener, European Committee; b. 1952, Glasgow; m.; 1 s.; 2 d. Leader, Renfrewshire Council, 1995-99. Address: (b.) Scottish Parliament, Edinburgh EH99 1SP; T.-0131-348 5928.

Henry, Captain Michael Charles, RN (Rtd.), DL. Deputy Lieutenant, Dunbartonshire, since 1989; Director, Merchants House of Glasgow, 1990-96, and 2000-03; b. 4.6.28, London; m., Nancie Elma Nicol; 2 s.; 3 d. Educ. Royal Naval College, Dartmouth. Naval career, Cadet to

Captain, 1942-78; submarine specialist; commanded HM Submarines Seraph, Trump and Resolution, Britain's first Polaris submarine; fired first British missile, Cape Canaveral, and conducted first deterrent patrol, 1968; commanded 10th (Polaris) Submarine Squadron, Faslane, and Queen's Harbour Master, Clyde, 1972-74; commanded HMS Hampshire, 1975-76; Director of Naval Operations and Trade, 1976-78; Marine Manager, British National Oil Corporation, Aberdeen, 1978-80; Naval Regional Officer Scotland and Northern Ireland, Glasgow, 1980-90. Recreation: sailing. Address: (h.) Aldavhu, Garelochhead, Helensburgh G84 0EL; T.-01436 810533.

Hepburn, James Douglas, MSP (SNP), Central Scotland, since 2007; b. 21.5.79, Glasgow; m., Julie Shackleton. Educ. Hyndland Secondary, Glasgow; University of Glasgow. Recreations: football; reading; cinema. Address: (b.) Scottish Parliament, Edinburgh EH99 1SP; T.-0131 3486573.
E-mail: jamie.hepburn.msp@scottish.parliament.uk

Herald, Sheriff John Pearson, LLB, NP, SSC. Sheriff of North Strathclyde at Greenock and Rothesay, since 1992; b. 12.7.46, Glasgow; m., Catriona; 1 d. Educ. Hillhead High School, Glasgow; Glasgow University. Partner, Carlton Gilruth, Solicitors, Dundee, 1970-91; Depute Town Clerk, Newport-on-Tay, 1970-75; Member, Angus Legal Aid Committee, 1970-79, Secretary, 1979-87; Member, Legal Aid Central Committee, 1981-87; Temporary Sheriff, 1984-91; part-time Chairman, Industrial Tribunals, 1984-91. Chairman, Dundee Citizens Advice Bureau, 1972-79 and 1982-91; President, Rotary Club of North Fife, 1989. Recreations: football; golf; reading. Address: (b.) Sheriff Court House, Nelson Street, Greenock; T.-01475 787073.

Herbert, Professor Rodney Andrew, BSc, PhD, CBiol, FIBiol, FRSE, FRSA. Emeritus Professor, Environmental and Applied Biology Department, Dundee University, formerly Professor of Microbiology; b. 27.6.44, York; m., Helen Joyce Macpherson Millard; 2 s. Educ. Archbishop Holgate's Grammar School, York; Bradford University; Aberdeen University. Research Fellow, Edinburgh University, 1970-71; Lecturer/Reader in Microbiology, Dundee University, 1971-92. General Secretary, Society for General Microbiology, 1989-94; President, Society for Applied Microbiology, 1997-99; Senior Visiting Scientist: British Antarctic Survey, 1976-77, Ross Sea, Antarctica, 1982-83. Recreations: music; walking; gardening. Address: (b.) Division of Environmental and Applied Biology, Biological Sciences Institue, Dundee University, Dundee DD1 4HN; T.-Dundee 23181, Ext. 4262.

Herdman, John Macmillan, MA (Hons), PhD (Cantab), DipTh. Writer, since 1963; b. 20.7.41, Edinburgh; m., Mary Ellen Watson. Educ. Merchiston Castle School, Edinburgh; Magdalene College, Cambridge. Creative Writing Fellow, Edinburgh University, 1977-79; Scottish Arts Council bursaries, 1976, 1982, 1998, 2004; Scottish Arts Council Book Awards, 1978 and 1993; Hawthornden Writer's Fellowship, 1989 and 1995; William Soutar Fellowship, 1990-91. Publications: Descent, 1968; A Truth Lover, 1973; Memoirs of My Aunt Minnie/ Clapperton, 1974; Pagan's Pilgrimage, 1978; Stories Short and Tall, 1979; Voice Without Restraint: Bob Dylan's Lyrics and Their Background, 1982; Three Novellas, 1987; The Double in Nineteenth Century Fiction, 1990; Imelda and Other Stories, 1993; Ghostwriting, 1996; Cruising (play), 1997; Poets, Pubs, Polls and Pillar Boxes, 1999; Four Tales, 2000; The Sinister Cabaret, 2001; Triptych, 2004; My Wife's Lovers, 2007. Recreations: reading; walking; listening to music. Address: (h.) Roselea, Bridge of Tilt, Blair Atholl, Perthshire; T.-01796 481437.

Hewitt, Professor David S., MA, PhD, FEA, FRSE. Regius Chalmers Professor of English Literature, Aberdeen University; b. 22.4.42, Hawick; m., Angela Catherine Williams; 1 s.; 1 d. Educ. Melrose Grammar School; George Watson's College, Edinburgh; Edinburgh University; Aberdeen University. Aberdeen University: Assistant Lecturer in English, 1964, Lecturer, 1968, Senior Lecturer, 1982; Treasurer, Association for Scottish Literary Studies, 1973-96; Editor-in-Chief, Edinburgh Edition of the Waverley Novels, 1984; President, Edinburgh Sir Walter Scott Club, 1988-89; Honorary Member, Association for Scottish Literary Studies, 1996; Session Clerk, Cathedral Church of St. Machar, Old Aberdeen; Managing Editor, New Writing Scotland, 1983-86. Publications: Scott on Himself (Editor), 1982; Literature of the North, 1983; Scott and His Influence, 1984; Longer Scottish Poems, Vol. 2 1650-1830, 1987; Scott in Carnival, 1993; The Antiquary, 1995; Northern Visions, 1996; The Edinburgh Edition of the Waverley Novels: A Guide for Editors, 1996; Redgauntlet, 1997; The Heart of Mid-Lothian, 2003; Rob Roy, 2008. Address: (b.) School of Language and Literature, Aberdeen University, Aberdeen AB24 3UB; T.-01224 273777; e-mail: david.hewitt@abdn.ac.uk

Hewitt, Gavin Wallace, CMG, MA. Chief Executive, The Scotch Whisky Association, since 2003; b. 19.10.44, Hawick; 2 s.; 2 d. Educ. George Watson's College, Edinburgh; University of Edinburgh. Ministry of Transport, 1967; seconded to HM Diplomatic Service, and posted to serve overseas at Brussels for negotiation of EC entry, 1970; HM Diplomatic Service with service at home and overseas, 1972, culminating in HM Ambassador to Croatia, 1994-97; HM Ambassador to Finland, 1997-2000; HM Ambassador to Belgium, 2001-2003. Address: (b.) 20 Atholl Crescent, Edinburgh EH3 8HF; T.-0131 222 9200; e-mail: ghewitt@swa.org.uk

Heycock, Professor Caroline Bridget, MA, PhD. Professor of Syntax, University of Edinburgh, since 2007; b. 22.11.60, Folkestone; m., Robert Sandler. Educ. St. Columba's School; King's College, Cambridge University; University of Pennsylvania. Assistant Professor: Oakland University, USA, 1991-92, Yale University, USA, 1992-94; University of Edinburgh: Lecturer, 1994-99, Reader, 1999-2007. Editor, Journal of Linguistics. Recreations: walking; cycling. Address: (b.) Linguistics and English Language, University of Edinburgh, Edinburgh; T.-0131 650 3961.

Heys, Professor Steven Darryll, BMedBiol, MB, ChB, MD, PhD, FRCS(Glas), FRCS(Ed), FRCS(Eng). Professor of Surgical Oncology, University of Aberdeen, since 1999; Director, Surgical Nutrition and Metabolism Unit, University of Aberdeen, since 1995; Consultant Surgeon, Aberdeen Royal Infirmary, since 1992; Honorary Research Fellow, Rowett Research Institute, since 1992; b. 5.7.56, Accrington; m., Margaret Susan Proctor; 2 s.; 1 d. Educ. St. Mary's College, Blackburn; Aberdeen University Medical School. House Officer/SHO, Surgery, Aberdeen Royal Infirmary, 1981-84; Registrar, Grampian Health Board, 1984-87; Wellcome Research Training Fellow, Rowett Research Institute, 1987-89; Lecturer in Surgery, Aberdeen University, 1989-92; Senior Lecturer, 1992-96, Reader, 1996-99. Examiner in Surgery, Royal College of Surgeons of Glasgow; External Examiner in Surgery, Royal College of Surgeons of England. Publications: numerous scientific papers on aspects of breast cancer, oncology, nutrition and metabolism; book chapters on nutrition, metabolism, oncology. Recreations: karate; hill-walking; flying. Address: (b.) University Medical Buildings, Foresterhill, Aberdeen AB9 2ZD.

Heywood, Peter. Director, The Living Tradition Ltd., publisher, since 1993; b. 4.10.49, Manchester; m., Heather; 3 d. Educ. Heywood Grammar School. Long involvement with traditional music; founded The

Tradition Bearers, recording traditional musicians, 1999; founded Common Ground on the Hill, Scotland, 2001. Recreations: traditional music; hill-walking. Address: (b.) The Living Tradition, PO Box 1026, Kilmarnock KA2 0LG; T.-01563 571220; e-mail: pctc@thetraditionbearers.com

Higgins, Professor James, MA (Glasgow), L-ès-L (Lyon). PhD (Liverpool), FBA. Emeritus Professor, Latin American Literature, University of Liverpool, since 2004; Honorary Research Fellow in Hispanic Studies, University of Stirling, since 2006; b. 28.05.39, Bellshill; m., Kirstine Anne Atwell; 2 s. Educ. Our Lady's High School, Motherwell; University of Glasgow; University of Lyons. University of Liverpool: Assistant Lecturer in Latin American Studies, 1964-67, Lecturer, 1967-73, Senior Lecturer, 1973-83, Reader, 1983-88, Professor of Latin American Literature, 1988-2004, Head of Department of Hispanic Studies, 1980-82, 1988-97. Visiting Professor: University of Pittsburgh, 1968, University of Waterloo, 1974, University of West Indies, 1979, University of Wisconsin, 1990. Publications include: César Vallejo en su poesia, 1990; Cambio social y constantes humanas, La narrativa corta de Ribeyro, 1991; Hitos de la poesia peruana, 1993, Myths of the Emergent. Social Mobility in Contemporary Peruvian Fiction, 1994; The Literary Representation of Peru, 2002; ed., Heterogeneidad y Literatura en el Peru, 2003; Lima. A Cultural and Literary History, 2005; Historia de la literatura peruana, 2006. Recreations: reading; walking; gardening; classical music; travel; whisky. Address: (h.) 6 Carlton House, 15 Snowdon Place, Stirling FK8 2NR; T.-01786 470 641; e-mail: jameshig0@googlemail.com

Higgins, John, MBE. Professional snooker player; b. 18.5.75, Wishaw, North Lanarkshire. Two time World Champion winning in 1998 and 2007. Has won 27 major titles worldwide. Lives in Wishaw, Lanarkshire.

Higgs, Professor Peter Ware, BSc, MSc, PhD, FRS, FRSE, HonFInstP, DSc (Hon). Professor of Theoretical Physics, Edinburgh University, 1980-96; b. 29.5.29, Newcastle-upon-Tyne; m., Jo Ann Williamson; 2 s. Educ. Cotham Grammar School, Bristol; King's College, London. Postdoctoral Fellow, Edinburgh University, 1954-56, and London University, 1956-58; Lecturer in Mathematics, University College, London, 1958-60; Lecturer in Mathematical Physics, then Reader, Edinburgh University, 1960-80. Hughes Medal, Royal Society, 1981; Rutherford Medal, Institute of Physics, 1984; James Scott Prize, Royal Society of Edinburgh, 1993; Paul Dirac Medal and Prize, Institute of Physics, 1997; High Energy and Particle Physics Prize, European Physical Society, 1997; Royal Medal, Royal Society of Edinburgh, 2000; Wolf Prize, 2004. Recreations: music; walking; swimming. Address: (h.) 2 Darnaway Street, Edinburgh EH3 6BG; T.-0131-225 7060.

Hill, Dominic, BA (Hons). Artistic Director, Traverse Theatre, since 2008; Artistic Director, Dundee Rep Theatre, 2003-07; b. 22.4.69, London. Educ. Douai School; Lincoln College, Oxford University. Assistant Director, Perth Theatre, 1994-96; Associate Director: Orange Tree Theatre, Richmond, 1998, Dundee Rep Theatre, 2002; freelance director at other times. Address: (b.) 10 Cambridge Street, Edinburgh EH1 2ED; T.-0131 228 3223; e-mail: dominic.hill@traverse.co.uk

Hill, Professor Malcolm, PhD. Research Professor, University of Strathclyde; formerly Professor for the Child and Society and Professor of Social Work, University of Glasgow; b. 18.9.46, London; m., Dr. Wan Ying Hill; 1 s.; 1 d. Educ. Latymer Upper School, Hammersmith; St. Edmund Hall, Oxford; University of London; University of Edinburgh. Social Worker, 1968-79; Researcher, 1979-84; Lecturer, 1985-93; Senior Lecturer, 1993-96. Publications: books on adoption, child care, youth crime, foster care, middle childhood, children and society. Recreations: bridge; gardening; swimming. Address: 66 Oakfield Avenue, Glasgow G12 8LS.

Hill, Professor William George, OBE, BSc, MS, PhD, DSc, DSc (hc), Dhc, FRSE, FRS. Emeritus Professor of Animal Genetics, Edinburgh University, since 2003; Professor of Animal Genetics, 1983-2003; b. 7.8.40, Hemel Hempstead; m., C. Rosemary Austin; 1 s.; 2 d. Educ. St. Albans School; London University; University of California; Iowa State University; Edinburgh University. Edinburgh University: Assistant Lecturer, 1965-67, Lecturer, 1967-74, Reader, 1974-83, Head, Department of Genetics, 1989-90, Institute of Cell, Animal and Population Biology, 1990-93, and Division of Biological Sciences, 1993-98, Dean and Provost, Faculty of Science and Engineering, 1999-2002. Visiting Research Associate, Iowa State University, 1967-68-69-72; Visiting Professor: University of Minnesota, 1966, Iowa State University, 1978, North Carolina State University, 1979, since 1985; Consultant Geneticist: Cotswold Pig Development Co., 1965-99, Holstein Friesian Society, 1978-98; Editor, Genetical Research, since 1996; Editor-in-Chief, Proceedings Royal Society B, since 2005; Member: AFRC Animals Research Grant Board, 1986-92, Director's Advisory Group, AFRC Animal Breeding Research Organisation, 1982-86, AFRC Institute of Animal Physiology and Genetics Research, 1986-93, Governing Council, Roslin Institute, 1994-2002, Council, Royal Society, 1993-94, Commonwealth Scholarships Commission, 1998-2004 (Deputy Chair, 2002-04), RAE Panel, 1996, 2001 (Chairman); British Society of Animal Science: Vice-President, 1997-99, President, 1999-00; Genetics Society: Vice President, since 2004. Recreations: farming; bridge. Address: (h.) 4 Gordon Terrace, Edinburgh EH16 5QH; T.-0131-667 3680; e-mail: w.g.hill@ed.ac.uk

Hillhouse, Sir (Robert) Russell, KCB, FRSE. Governor, Royal Scottish Academy of Music and Drama, since 2000; b. 23.4.38, Glasgow; m., Alison Fraser; 2 d. Educ. Hutchesons' Grammar School, Glasgow; Glasgow University. Entered Home Civil Service as Assistant Principal, Scottish Education Department, 1962; Principal, 1966; HM Treasury, 1971; Assistant Secretary, Scottish Office, 1974; Scottish Home and Health Department, 1977; Principal Finance Officer, Scottish Office, 1980; Under-Secretary, Scottish Education Department, 1985; Secretary, 1987; Permanent Under-Secretary of State, Scottish Office, 1988-98. Director: Bank of Scotland, 1998-2001, Scottish Provident Institution, 1999-2001. Recreation: making music. Address: 12 Russell Place, Edinburgh EH5 3HH; e-mail: rhillhouse@blueyonder.co.uk

Hillier, Professor Stephen Gilbert, BSc, MSc, PhD, DSc, FRCPath. Professor, Centre for Reproductive Biology, Edinburgh University, since 1994, Director, Reproductive Medicine Laboratory, since 1985, Director, Postgraduate and International Relations, College of Medicine and Veterinary Medicine, since 2002; Editor-in-Chief, Journal of Endocrinology, 2000-05; Editor-in-Chief, Molecular Human Reproduction, since 2007; b. 16.1.49, Hillingdon; m., Haideh; 2 d. Educ. Hayes County Grammar School; Leeds University; Welsh National School of Medicine. Postdoctoral Research Fellow, National Institutes of Health, USA, 1976-78; Research Scientist, University of Leiden, 1978-82; Senior Lecturer: Reproductive Biochemistry, RPMS, London University, 1982-85, Department of

Obstetrics and Gynaecology, Edinburgh University, 1985-94. Member: Interim Licensing Authority for Human Fertilisation and Embryology, 1987-91, Human Fertilisation and Embryology Authority, 1990-96; 1991 Society for Endocrinology Medal; 2004 British Fertility Society Patrick Steptoe Medal; 2006 Society for Endocrinology Jubilee Medal. Publications: Ovarian Endocrinology, 1991; Scientific Essentials of Reproductive Medicine, 1996. Recreation: fly-fishing. Address: (b.) Edinburgh University Centre for Reproductive Biology, Queen's Medical Research Institute, 47 Little France Crescent, Edinburgh EH16 4TJ; T.-0131-242 2697; e-mail: s.hillier@ed.ac.uk

Hillman, John Richard, BSc, PhD, HonDSc, CBiol, FIBiol, FLS, FCMI, FIHort, FRSA, FRSE. Consultant in agriculture and industrial biotechnology; Director, Scottish Crop Research Institute, 1986-2005; Visiting Professor, Dundee University, Edinburgh University and Glasgow University; Founder and Deputy Chairman, Mylnefield Research Services Ltd., 1989-2005; Director, Mylnefield Trust and Mylnefield Holdings Ltd., 2000-05; b. 21.7.44, Farnborough, Kent; m., Sandra Kathleen Palmer; 2 s. Educ. Chislehurst and Sidcup Grammar School; University of Wales. Assistant Lecturer, 1968, and Lecturer, 1969, Physiology and Environmental Studies, Nottingham University; Lecturer, 1971, Senior Lecturer, 1977, Reader, 1980, Professor and Head of Botany, 1982, Glasgow University; Chairman, Agriculture, Natural Resources and Environment Sector Panel, UK Technology Foresight Programme, 1994-95, Agriculture, Horticulture and Forestry Sector Panel, 1995-97; Member, Court, University of Abertay, Dundee, 1997-2005; Member, Board, BioIndustry Association; Chair, Industrial Biotechnology Group, 1996-2005; Member, Scottish Higher Education Funding Council Research and Knowledge Transfer Committee; Honorary Research Fellow of Scottish Crop Research Institute; Angus, Dundee and Perth Employer Support Committee for Reservists; Regulation Working Group NFU Scotland; Bawden Jubilee Lecturer, 1993; British Potato Industry Award, 1999; World Potato Congress 2000 Industry Award; Dr Hardie Memorial Prize; Scottish Horticultural Medal, 2003. Recreations: landscaping; building renovations; horology; reading. Address: (b.) Scottish Crop Research Institute, Invergowrie, Dundee DD2 5DA; T.-01382 562731.

Hills, Professor Sir Graham (John), PhD, DSc, FRSE, Hon DSc (Lodz, Southampton, Lisbon), Hon. LLD (Glasgow, Waterloo and Strathclyde), DUniv (Paisley). Principal and Vice-Chancellor, Strathclyde University, 1980-91; b. 9.4.26, Leigh-on-Sea; m., 1, Brenda Stubbington; 2, Mary Jane McNaughton; 1 s.; 3 d. Educ. Westcliff High School for Boys; Birkbeck College and Imperial College, London University. Lecturer in Physical Chemistry, Imperial College, 1949-62; Professor of Physical Chemistry, Southampton University, 1962-80. Visiting Professor, University of Western Ontario, 1968; Visiting Professor and National Science Foundation Fellow, Case-Western Reserve University, Ohio, 1968-69; Visiting Professor, Buenos Aires University, 1976; Member, Advisory Council on Science and Technology, 1987-93; (Non-Executive) Member, Scottish Post Office Board, 1986-2000; Non-Executive Director, Scottish Enterprise, 1988-94; National Governor for Scotland, BBC, 1989-94; Fellow, Birkbeck College; Fellow, Royal Scottish Academy of Music and Drama; Fellow, Royal College of Physicians and Surgeons of Glasgow; Honorary Fellow, Chartered Society of Designers, 1996; Fellow, University of East London; Fellow, University of the Highlands and Islands Millennium Institute, 2002; Honorary Doctorate from the universities of Glasgow, Strathclyde, Southampton, Paisley, Lodz (Poland), Waterloo (Canada), Abertay; Director, Glasgow Chamber of Commerce, since 1981; President: Friends of Glasgow Cathedral, 1987-95, Society of

Chemical Industry, 1991-93; Chairman, Quarriers Homes, 1992-97; Commander Insignia: Order of Merit of Polish People's Republic, Royal Norwegian Order of Merit. Publications: Reference Electrodes, 1961; Polarography, 1964. Recreations: music; literature. Address: (h.) The Coach House, 2B Strathearn Road, Edinburgh EH9 2AH.

Hinds, Lesley. Lord Lieutenant and Lord Provost, City of Edinburgh, 2003-07; b. 3.8.56, Dundee; m., Martin; 1s.; 2d. Educ. Kirkton High School, Dundee; Dundee College of Education. Teacher, Deans Primary School, 1977-80; Chair, Health Scotland, 2001-07; Labour Councillor, Edinburgh DC, 1984-96 (Leader, 1993-96); City of Edinburgh Council, since 1996; Past Chair: Edinburgh International Festival Society; Edinburgh Military Tattoo Ltd; N Edinburgh Area Renewal (NEAR); Director: N Edinburgh Arts; former Chair, Edinburgh International Conference Centre. Recreations: theatre; dance; swimming; travel. Address: (b.) City Chambers, High Street, Edinburgh EH1 1YJ; T.-0131 529 3235.
E-mail: lesley.hinds@edinburgh.gov.uk

Hine, Professor Harry Morrison, MA, DPhil (Oxon). Scotstarvit Professor of Humanity, St. Andrews University, since 1985; b. 19.6.48, Portsmouth; m., Rosalind Mary Ford; 1 s.; 1 d. Educ. King Edward's School, Birmingham; Corpus Christi College, Oxford. P.S. Allen Junior Research Fellow, Corpus Christi College, 1972-75; Lecturer in Humanity, Edinburgh University, 1975-85. Editor (Joint), The Classical Review, 1987-93. Publications: An Edition with Commentary of Seneca, Natural Questions, Book Two, 1981; Studies in the Text of Seneca's Naturales Quaestiones, 1996; L. Annaei Senecae Naturales Quaestiones (Editor), 1996; Seneca, Medea, Translation and commentary, 2000. Recreations: walking; reading. Address: (h.) 33 Drumcarrow Road, St. Andrews, Fife KY16 8SE; T.-01334 474459; e-mail: hmh@st-and.ac.uk

Hirst, Sir Michael William, LLB, CA, FRSA, MCIPR, DLitt (2004). Chairman, Scottish Conservative and Unionist Party, 1993-97; b. 2.1.46, Glasgow; m., Naomi Ferguson Wilson; 1 s.; 2 d. Educ. Glasgow Academy; Glasgow University. Partner, Peat Marwick Mitchell & Co., Chartered Accountants, until 1983; Director of and Consultant to various companies; contested: Central Dunbartonshire, February and October, 1974, East Dunbartonshire, 1979; MP (Conservative), Strathkelvin and Bearsden, 1983-87; Member, Select Committee on Scottish Affairs, 1983-87; Parliamentary Private Secretary, Department of Energy, 1985-87; Vice-Chairman, Scottish Conservative Party, 1987-89; Chairman, Scottish Conservative Candidates Association, 1978-81; Member, Court, Glasgow Caledonian University, 1992-98; Member, Council of the Imperial Society of Knights Bachelor and Chairman, Scottish Division, since 2002; President, Scottish Conservative and Unionist Association, 1989-1992; Chairman, Diabetes UK, 2001-06, Vice President, since 2006; Vice-President, International Diabetic Federation, since 2006; Chairman, The Park School Educational Trust, since 1993; Chairman, Friends of Kippen Kirk Trust, since 2003; Director, Children's Hospice Association Scotland, 1995-2005; Director, Erskine Hospital, Erskine; Elder, Kippen Parish Church. Recreations: golf; hill-walking; skiing. Address: (h.) Glentirran, Kippen, Stirlingshire FK8 3JA; e-mail: michael.hirst@pagodapr.com; smh@glentirran.co.uk

Hislop, William Stuart, BSc, MBChB, FRCP, FACG. Consultant Physician, Royal Alexandra Hospital, Paisley, since 1982; b. 27.2.48, Edinburgh; m., Dr. Linda J. Hislop; 1 s.; 3 d. Educ. Dundee High School; Kilmarnock Academy; Glasgow University. Junior House Officer, Stobhill Hospital and Southern General Hospital, 1973-74; Western Infirmary, Glasgow: Senior House Officer, 1974-76, Medical Registrar, 1976-77; Senior Registrar, Ninewells

Hospital, Dundee, 1977-82. Recreations: walking; cycling; gardening; cricket; music (country and western). Address: (b.) Ross Hall Hospital, 221 Crookston Road, Glasgow G52 3NQ; T.-0141-810 3151.

Hitchman, Professor Michael L., BSc, DPhil, CChem, FRSC, FRSA, FRSE. Young Professor of Chemistry, Strathclyde University, 1984-2004; b. 17.8.41, Woburn, Bedfordshire; 1 s.; 2 d. Educ. Stratton Grammar School, Biggleswade; Queen Mary College and King's College, London University; University College, Oxford. Assistant Lecturer in Chemistry, Leicester Regional College of Technology, 1963-65; Junior Research Fellow, Wolfson College, Oxford, 1968-70; ICI Postdoctoral Research Fellow, Physical Chemistry Laboratory, Oxford University, 1968-70; Chief Scientist, Orbisphere Corporation, Geneva, 1970-73; Staff Scientist, Laboratories RCA Ltd., Zurich, 1973-79; Lecturer, then Senior Lecturer, Salford University, 1979-84; Strathclyde University: Chairman, Department of Pure and Applied Chemistry, 1986-89, Vice-Dean, Faculty of Science, 1989-92; Honorary Professor, Taiyuan University of Technology, China, since 1994; Visiting Professor, University of West of Scotland, since 2006; Editor, Advanced Materials CVD, since 1995. Royal Society of Chemistry: Chairman, Electro-analytical Group, 1985-88, Treasurer, Electrochemistry Group, 1984-90; Member, Chemistry and Semiconductor Committees, Science and Engineering Research Council; Member, since 1985, Chairman, 1989-92, International Advisory Board, EUROCVD; Director, Thin Film Innovations Ltd.; Director, Jinju Consultancies Ltd.; Medal and Prize, British Vacuum Council, 1993. Editor, Advanced Materials Chemical Vapor Deposition, since 1995. Publications: Ring-disk Electrodes (Co-Author), 1971; Measurement of Dissolved Oxygen, 1978; Chemical Vapor Deposition (Co-Editor), 1993. Recreations: humour; cooking; eating; rambling; losing weight. Address: (b.) Thin Film Innovations Ltd., Block 7, Kelvin Campus, West of Scotland Science Park, Glasgow G20 0TH; T.-0141 579 3028.

Hodge, Hon. Lord (Patrick Stewart Hodge), BA, LLB, QC. Advocate; Senator of the College of Justice in Scotland, since 2005; Judge of the Courts of Appeal of Jersey and Guernsey, 2000-05; Procurator to General Assembly of Church of Scotland, 2000-05; b. 19.5.53, Dundee; m., Penelope Jane Wigin; 2 s.; 1 d. Educ. Trinity College, Glenalmond; Corpus Christi College, Cambridge; Edinburgh University. Scottish Office, 1975-78; admitted Faculty of Advocates, 1983; Standing Junior Counsel: to Department of Energy, 1989-91; Inland Revenue in Scotland, 1991-96; Commissioner (part-time), Scottish Law Commission, 1997-2003. Governor, Merchiston Castle School, Edinburgh, since 1998. Publication: Scotland and the Union, 1994. Recreations: opera; ski-ing. Address: Parliament House, Edinburgh EH1 1RQ; T.-0131 225 2595.

Hodge, Robin Mackenzie, BA (Hons). Publisher, The List magazine, since 1985; b. Edinburgh. Educ. Edinburgh Academy; Clifton College, Bristol; Durham University. Certificat Europeen en Administration de Projects Culturels (Bruxelles). Production Director, Canongate Publishing Ltd., 1981-84; restoration of 16th-century buildings around Tweeddale Court, Edinburgh Old Town, 1981-88; founded The List, 1985; Chairman, PPA Scotland, 2002-04. Address: (b.) 14 High Street, Edinburgh EH1 1TE; T.-0131-550 3050.

Hogg of Cumbernauld, Lord (Norman), FSA Scot. MP, Cumbernauld and Kilsyth, 1983-97 (MP, East Dunbartonshire, 1979-83); Member, House of Lords Delegated Powers and Regulatory Reform Committee, 1999-2002; Chairman, Scottish Peers Association, 2002-04; Deputy Speaker, House of Lords, 2002-04; b. 12.3.38, Aberdeen; m., Elizabeth M. Christie. Educ. Ruthrieston

Secondary School, Aberdeen. Local Government Officer, Aberdeen Town Council, 1953-67; District Officer, NALGO, 1967-79; Member: Transport Users Consultative Committee for Scotland, 1977-79, Select Committee on Scottish Affairs, 1979-82; Scottish Labour Whip, 1982-83; Chairman, Scottish Parliamentary Labour Group, 1981-82; Deputy Chief Opposition Whip, 1983-87; Scottish Affairs Spokesman, 1987-88; Member, Public Accounts Committee, 1991-92. Lord High Commissioner, General Assembly of the Church of Scotland, 1998, 1999; Hon. President, YMCA Scotland, 1998-2005; Chairman, Bus Appeals Body, since 2000; Patron, Scottish Centre for Children with Motor Impairments, since 1997; Hon.LLD, University of Aberdeen, 1999. Recreation: music. Address: House of Lords, Westminster, London SW1A 0PW; T.020 7219 4214.

Hogg, Lt. Col. Colin Grant Ogilvie, OBE, DL. King's Own Scottish Borderers (KOSB), since 1962; Regimental Secretary, since 1991; b. 6.12.43, Glasgow; m., Cynthia Rose Mackenzie; 2 d. Educ. St. Mary's Preparatory School; Merchiston Castle School. Commissioned into KOSB, 1965; service with 1st Battalion in Aden, Hong Kong, Borneo, BAOR, Berlin, Northern Ireland; Deputy Adjutant General, HQ of 1st Armoured Division, Germany, 1981-83; on directing staff, Royal Military Academy, Sandhurst, 1983-84; Commanding Officer, 2nd Battalion, 52 Lowland Volunteers, 1985-88; SOI, Foot Guards and Infantry Manning and Records Office, 1988-91; retired from active list, 1991; Honorary Colonel of the Lothian and Border Army Cadet Force, 1997-2006. Member, Queen's Bodyguard for Scotland, since 1986; Member, Ancient Order of Mosstroopers; Chairman, Borders Branch, SSAFA Forces Help, since 1993, Member, National Council, 2000-06; Member, Board, South of Scotland Youth Awards Trust, since 1994; Chairman, Roxburgh and Berwickshire Conservative and Unionist Association, 1995-98; Governor: Oxenfoord Castle School, 1986-93, St. Mary's School, Melrose, 1994-98; President, Jedburgh Branch, Royal British Legion Scotland, 2005; Member, National Council, Royal British Legion Scotland, 1998-2004; Board Member, Earl Haig Fund, since 2000; Honorary Director, Lord Roberts Workshops; Deputy Lieutenant, Roxburgh, Ettrick and Lauderdale, since 1995. Recreations: field sports and equestrian events. Address: (h.) Mounthooly, Jedburgh TD8 6TJ; T.-01835 863368.

Hogg, Ian Alisdair Lawrence, MA, CA, OBE; Retired; b. 13.6.40, Edinburgh; m., Louise; 1 s.; 1 d. Educ. George Watson's College; Edinburgh University; Institute of Chartered Accountants of Scotland. Accountant, 1961-78; Treasurer, Scottish Rugby Union, 1978-83; Secretary, Scottish Rugby Union, 1983-2005. Appointed OBE, June 2006. Recreations: rugby; cricket. Address: (c/o.) Scottish Rugby Union, Murrayfield, Edinburgh EH12 5PJ; T.-0131-346 5000.

Holden, Catherine Ann, BA. Director of Marketing and Development, National Museums Scotland, since 2004; b. 26.9.64, Blackburn. Educ. Droitwich High School; Oxford University. Brand Manager, Rank Hovis McDougall, 1987-90; Marketing Manager, National Theatre, 1990-94; Head of Marketing, Tate, 1994-2001; Head of Communications, National History Museum, 2001-04. Arts Marketing Association Board Member, 1998-2001; Edinburgh Art Festival Board Member, since 2004. Recreations: reading; theatre; visual art and crafts; horse riding. Address: (b.) National Museums Scotland, Chambers Street, Edinburgh EH1 1JF; T.-0131 247 4332.

Holloway, James Essex, BA (Hons), FSA Scot. Director, Scottish National Portrait Gallery, since 1997; b. 24.11.48, London. Educ. Marlborough College; Courtauld Institute, London University. Assistant Keeper, National Gallery of Scotland; Assistant Keeper,

National Museum of Wales; Deputy Keeper, Scottish National Portrait Gallery. Trustee, Hopetoun House, Paxton House; Member, Curatorial Panel, National Trust for Scotland. Recreations: India; motorbikes. Address: (b.) 1 Queen Street, Edinburgh EH2 1JD; T.-0131-624 6401.

Holloway, Rt. Rev. Richard Frederick, BD, STM, DUniv (Strathclyde), DD (Aberdeen), DLitt (Napier), DD (Glasgow), FRSE, DUniv (OU). Gresham Professor of Divinity, 1997-2001; Bishop of Edinburgh, 1986-2000; Primus of the Scottish Episcopal Church, 1992-2000; Chair, SAC, since 2005; Chair, Scottish Screen, since 2007; Chair, Creative Scotland Joint Board, since 2007; b. 26.11.33; m., Jean Elizabeth Kennedy; 1 s.; 2 d. Educ. Kelham Theological College; Edinburgh Theological College; Union Theological Seminary, New York. Curate, St. Ninian's, Glasgow, 1959-63; Priest-in-charge, St. Margaret and St. Mungo's, Glasgow, 1963-68; Rector, Old St. Paul's, Edinburgh, 1968-80; Rector, Church of the Advent, Boston, Mass, 1980-84; Vicar, St. Mary Magdalen's, Oxford, 1984-86. Recreations: long-distance walking; reading; going to the cinema; listening to music. Address: (h.) 6 Blantyre Terrace, Edinburgh EH10 5AE.

Holmes, George Dennis, CB (1979), FRSE, FICfor. Forestry Consultant, since 1987; b. 9.11.26, Conwy; m., Sheila Rosemary; 3 d. Educ. John Bright's School, Llandudno; University of Wales, Bangor. Forestry Commission, 1948-86 (Director General, 1976-86). Recreations: fishing; golf. Address: (h.) 7 Cammo Road, Barnton, Edinburgh EH4 8EF; T.-0131-339 7474.

Holmes, Dr Megan Christine, BSc, PhD. Reader, Department of Clinical Neurosciences, Edinburgh University, since 1998; m., Dr Ferenc A. Antoni; 3 s. Educ. Stourbridge Girls' High School; London University. Exchange Fellow, Royal Society, London, and Hungarian Academy of Sciences, Budapest, at Institute of Experimental Medicine, Budapest, 1982-83; Fogarty Visiting Fellow, Endocrinology and Reproduction Research Branch, National Institute of Child Health, Bethesda, 1983-85; Department of Medicine, Western General Hospital, Edinburgh: Wellcome Postdoctoral Fellowship, 1992-94, Wellcome Career Development Fellowship, 1995-98. Recreation: hill-walking. Address: (b.) Endocrine Unit, Centre for Cardiovascular Sciences, Queen's Medical Research Institute, Little France, Edinburgh EH16 4TJ; T.-0131 242 6737.

Holmes, Professor Peter Henry, OBE, BVMS, PhD, DrHC, FRCVS, FRSE. Professor of Veterinary Physiology, University of Glasgow, since 1982; currently Pro Vice-Principal; Vice-Principal, 1997-2005; b. 6.6.42, Cottingham, Yorkshire; m., Ruth Helen; 2 d. Educ. Beverley Grammar School, Yorkshire; University of Glasgow. Joined staff of University of Glasgow Veterinary School, Department of Veterinary Physiology, 1966. Member, Court, University of Glasgow, 1991-95; served on committees of ODA (DfID), BVA, UFAW; Chairman, International Programme Against African Trypanosomiasis. Recreations: hillwalking; tennis; cycling. Address: (b.) Research and Enterprise, No. 11 The Square, University of Glasgow, Glasgow G12 8QQ; T.-0141-330 3836.

Holroyd, Nicholas Weddall, BCL (Oxon), LLB, TEP, FSA Scot. Advocate, since 1992; b. 11.3.64, Edinburgh. Educ. Christ Church, Oxford University; University of Edinburgh. Thow Scholarship in Jurisprudence. Trainee, Dundas and Wilson, CS, 1989-91; "devilling" for the Bar, 1991-92;

part-time Tutor, Edinburgh University, 1993-2001; Clerk to Faculty of Advocates Law Reform Committee, 1996; Member of Faculty Council, 2004-07; Contributor, Greens' Litigation Styles, since 1996; Contributor, Tolley's Pension Dispute Procedures and Remedies; Chairman, New Town Branch, Edinburgh North and Leith Conservative Association, 2000-04; Committee Member, Society of Trust and Estate Practitioners (Scotland), since 2007. Recreation: golf. Address: Advocates Library, Old Parliament House, Edinburgh EH1 1RF; T.-0131-226 5071.

Holton, Yvonne, BA (Hons), FGA, DGA, FRSA. Herald Painter in Scotland, since 2004; b. 2.7.59, Aberdeen; m., Derek Holton. Educ. St. Margaret's School for Girls, Aberdeen; Edinburgh College of Art. Book Iustrator and Silversmith. Heraldic Artist appointed to The Court of The Lord Lyon in 1990. Recreations: gemmologist; gardening. Address: 11 Mayburn Terrace, Loanhead, Midlothian EH20 9EH; e-mail: yholton@freeuk.com

Home, Earl of (David Alexander Cospatrick Douglas-Home), CVO, CBE. Chairman, Grosvenor Group Ltd., since 2007; Chairman, Coutts & Co., since 1999; b. 20.11.43, Coldstream; m., Jane Margaret Williams-Wynne; 1 s.; 2 d. Educ. Eton; Christ Church, Oxford. Joined Morgan Grenfell & Co. Limited, 1966; appointed Director, 1974 (retired, 1999); Chairman, Morgan Grenfell (Scotland) Ltd., 1986 (resigned 1999); ECGD: Member, Export Advisory Council, 1988-93, Member, Projects Committee, 1989-93; Member, Advisory Board, National Forest, 1991-94; Chairman, CEGELEC Controls Ltd., 1991-94; Council Member, Glenalmond School, since 1995; Conservative Front-Bench Spokesman on Trade, Industry and Finance, 1997-98; appointed Director, Coutts & Co., 1999; Trustee, The Grosvenor Estate, since 1993; Chairman, MAN Ltd., since 2000. Recreations: outdoor sports. Address: (b.) Coutts & Co., 440 Strand, London WC2R 0QS; T.-020 7753 1000.

Home Robertson, John David. MSP (Labour), East Lothian, 1999-2007 (Convenor, Holyrood Progress Group, 2000-04, Scottish Executive Depute Minister for Rural Affairs, 1999-2000, former Member, Communities Committee, Scottish Parliament); MP (Labour), East Lothian, 1983-2001 (Berwick & East Lothian, 1978-83); b. 5.12.48, Edinburgh; m., Catherine Brewster; 2 s. Educ. Ampleforth College; West of Scotland Agricultural College. Farmer; Member: Berwickshire District Council, 1974-78, Borders Health Board, 1975-78; Chairman, Eastern Borders Citizens' Advice Bureau, 1976-78; Member, Select Committee on Scottish Affairs, 1979-83; Chairman, Scottish Group of Labour MPs, 1983; Scottish Labour Whip, 1983-84; Opposition Front Bench Spokesman on Agriculture, 1984-87, on Scotland, 1987-88, on Agriculture, 1988-90; Member, Select Committee on Defence, 1990-97; Member, British-Irish Parliamentary Body, 1993-99; Parliamentary Private Secretary to Dr Jack Cunningham, 1997-99; established Paxton Trust, 1988; Edinburgh Direct Aid convoys to Bosnia, 1994 and 1995 (HGV driver); Observer, elections in Sarajevo, 1996.

Honeyman, Greig, LLB (Hons), NP, WS. Partner (Managing Partner), Fyfe Ireland LLP, since 2005; b. 1.10.55, Kirkcaldy; m., Alison; 1 s.; 1 d. Educ. Dunfermline High School; University of Edinburgh. Apprenticeship, W. & J. Burness, WS, 1977-79; enrolled as a Solicitor, 1979; Solicitor, Scottish Special Housing Association, 1979-81; Admitted as Notary Public, 1983; Admitted to the WS Society, 1984; Partner: McNiven & Co., 1981-85, Honeyman & Mackie, 1985-90, Bird Semple

Fyfe Ireland - (demerger 1994), later Fyfe Ireland WS, 1990-2005. Recreations: gardening; rugby spectating. Address: (b.) 32 Charlotte Square, Edinburgh EH2 4ET. E-mail: ghoneyman@fyfeireland.com

Hood, James MP (Labour), Clydesdale, 1987-2005, Lanark and Hamilton East, since 2005; b. 16.5.48, Lesmahagow; m., Marion; 1 s.; 1 d. Educ. Lesmahagow High School; Nottingham University. Local councillor, 1973-87; official of NUM, 1973-87; Leader, Nottingham striking miners, 1984-85; Chairman, Miners' Parliamentary Group, 1991-92; former Chairman, All-Party Group on ME; former Chairman, European Legislation Select Committee (1992-98); former Chairman, European Scrutiny Committee (1998-2006); Member, Speaker's Panel of Chairmen; Member, UK Delegation to NATO Parliamentary Assembly; former Convenor, Scottish Labour Group of MPs Home Affairs Committee; sponsor of four Private Members' Bills on under-age drinking, Bill on ME, and Bill on school transport safety. Address: (b.) House of Commons, London SW1A 0AA; T.020 7219 4585; 01555 673177; e-mail: hoodj@parliament.uk; website: www.jimhoodmp.co.uk

Hook, Professor Andrew Dunnet, MA, PhD, FRSE, FBA. Bradley Professor of English Literature, Glasgow University, 1979-98; b. 21.12.32, Wick; m., Judith Ann (deceased); 2 s.; (1 deceased); 1 d. (deceased). Educ. Wick High School; Daniel Stewart's College, Edinburgh; Edinburgh University; Manchester University; Princeton University. Edinburgh University: Assistant Lecturer in English Literature, 1961-63, Lecturer in American Literature, 1963-70; Senior Lecturer in English, Aberdeen University, 1970-79; Chairman, Committee for Humanities and Member, Committee for Academic Affairs, CNAA, 1987-92; Chairman: Scottish Universities Council on Entrance English Panel, 1986-92, Universities and Colleges Admissions Service English Panel, since 1995; Member: Scottish Examination Board, 1984-92, Scottish Qualifications Authority English Panel, 1996-99; President, Eighteenth-Century Scottish Studies Society, 1990-92. Publications: Scotland and America 1750-1835, 1975; American Literature in Context 1865-1900, 1983; Scott's Waverley (Editor), 1971; Charlotte Brontë's Shirley (Editor, with Judith Hook), 1974; Dos Passos: A Collection of Critical Essays (Editor), 1974; The History of Scottish Literature II, 1660-1800 (Editor), 1987; Scott Fitzgerald, 1992; The Glasgow Enlightenment (Co-Editor), 1995; From Goosecreek to Gandercleugh, 1999; Scott's The Fair Maid of Perth (Co-Editor); F. Scott Fitzgerald: A Literary Life, 2002. Recreations: theatre; opera; catching up on reading. Address: 5 Rosslyn Terrace, Glasgow G12 9NB; e-mail: nassau@palio2.vianw.co.uk

Hooper, Ian Ross, BA. Head of Landscapes and Habitats Division, Scottish Executive, since 2003; b. 26.5.49, Edinburgh; m., Julie Ellen Vaughan; 1 s.; 1 d. Educ. Hornchurch Grammar School; University of East Anglia. Department of the Environment, 1973-89; seconded to English Heritage, 1984-85; Deputy Director (Resources) and Director, Museum of Scotland Project, National Museums of Scotland, 1989-99; Head of Economy and Industry Division, Scotland Office, 1999-2003. Recreations: historic buildings; hill-walking; golf. Address: (b.) Scottish Executive, Victoria Quay, Edinburgh EH6 6QQ; T.-0131 244 6416; e-mail: ian.hooper@scotland.gsi.gov.uk

Hooper, Professor Martin Leslie, MA, PhD, FRCPE, FRSE. Professor of Molecular Pathology, University of Edinburgh, since 1996; b. 1.3.47, Walsall. Educ. Queen Mary's School, Walsall; University of Cambridge. MRC Research Scholar, MRC Laboratory of Molecular Biology,

University of Cambridge, 1968-71; EMBO Research Fellow, Centre de Génétique Moléculaire, Gif-sur-Yvette, 1972-73; Research Fellow, Institute of Genetics, Glasgow, 1973-80; University of Edinburgh: Senior Lecturer in Experimental Pathology, 1980-90, Reader, Department of Pathology, 1990-96. Co-recipient, Margaret MacLellan Award, Tenovus Scotland, 1996. Recreations: walking; watching cricket; opera. Address: (b.) Sir Alastair Currie Cancer Research UK Laboratories, Molecular Medicine Centre, Western General Hospital, Edinburgh EH4 2XU; T.-0131-651 1071.

Hope of Craighead, Rt. Hon. Lord (James Arthur David Hope), PC, FRSE. A Lord of Appeal in Ordinary, since 1996; Chancellor, Strathclyde University, since 1998; b. 27.6.38, Edinburgh; m., Katharine Mary Kerr; 2 (twin) s.; 1 d. Educ. Edinburgh Academy; Rugby School; St. John's College, Cambridge (BA); Edinburgh University (LLB); Hon. LLD, Aberdeen (1991), Strathclyde (1993), Edinburgh (1995); Fellow, Strathclyde, 2000. National Service, Seaforth Highlanders, 1957-59; admitted Faculty of Advocates, 1965; Standing Junior Counsel to Inland Revenue, 1974-78; QC, 1978; Advocate Depute, 1978-82; Chairman, Medical Appeal Tribunal, 1985-86; Legal Chairman, Pensions Appeal Tribunal, 1985-86; Dean, Faculty of Advocates, 1986-89; A Senator of the College of Justice, Lord Justice General of Scotland, and Lord President of the Court of Session, 1989-96. President, The Stair Society, since 1993; President, Commonwealth Magistrates' and Judges' Association, 2003-06; Hon. Professor of Law, Aberdeen, 1994; David Kelbie Award, 2007; Baron (Life Peer), 1995. Publications: Gloag and Henderson's Introduction to Scots Law (Joint Editor, 7th edition, Assistant Editor, 8th and 9th editions, Contributor, 11th edition); Armour on Valuation for Rating (Joint Editor, 4th and 5th editions); (Contributor) Stair Memorial Encyclopaedia of Scots Law and Court of Session Practice. Address: (h.) 34 India Street, Edinburgh EH3 6HB; T.-0131-225 8245; e-mail: hopejad@parliament.uk

Hope, Colin John Filshill, OStJ, BA, FCII, FCIS, FCIT, FBIM, FCILT, MCIM, DipM. Director, Merchants House of Glasgow, 1981-87, 1988-94, 1995-2001, and 2002-05; former Governor, Glasgow Educational and Marshall Trust; b. 24.6.24, Dullatur; m., Jean Calder Douglas; 1 s.; 2 d. Educ. Glasgow High School; Glasgow Academy; Open University. RAF, 1942-47; joined Stenhouse & Partners, 1947; appointed Director, 1949; served in many capacities, including Managing Director, Stenhouse International; joined Norman Frizzell Scotland Ltd. as Managing Director, 1974; additionally Director, Norman Frizzell UK Ltd., 1976-81; Director, G.T. Senior, 1981-83 (Consultant, 1983-85); a Director, Glasgow Chamber of Commerce, 1979-88. Member: Scottish Consumer Council, 1979-85, Electricity Consultative Council for Scotland, 1979-87, General Convocation, Strathclyde University, 1980-90, Council, Insurance Ombudsman Bureau, 1981-94, Glasgow Airport Consultative Committee, since 1984; Governor, Keil School, 1986-91; former Chairman, Scottish Transport Users Consultative Committee; Member: Air Transport Committee, Association of British Chambers of Commerce, 1986-90, South of Scotland Electricity Consultative Committee, 1990-91; Director, Glasgow Native Benevolent Association, 1988-91, 1992-98 (Chairman, 1997-98); Member, Dumbartonshire Committee, Order of St. John, 1987-93. Address: (h.) 15 Chapelacre Grove, Helensburgh G84 7SH; T.-01436 673091.

Hopkins, Professor David James, PhD, MA (Dist), PGCE (Dist), BA (Hons). Professor of Art History, University of Glasgow; b. 29.08.55, Derby; 1 s. Formerly Lecturer at Universities of Edinburgh, St. Andrews and Edinburgh College of Art; from 2000 has been Senior Lecturer, Reader and now Professor, Glasgow University. Publications: books include: 'Marcel Duchamp and Max Ernst', 1998; After Modern Art: 1945-2000, 2000; Dada and Surrealism, 2003; Dada's Boys: Masculinity after Duchamp, 2007. Address: (b.) Department of Art History, University of Glasgow G12 8QH.

Horne, Rev. Archibald Sinclair. Secretary and Lecturer, Scottish Reformation Society, since 1964; b. 9.3.27, Port Seton; 2 s.; 1 d. Educ. Preston Lodge Secondary; London Bible College (External Student); New College, University of Edinburgh. Publications: Torchbearers of the Truth, 1966; In the Steps of the Covenanters, 1974. Recreations: golf; gardening; photography; producing video films. Address: (b.) Magdalene Chapel, 41 Cowgate, Edinburgh EH1 1EE; T.-0131-220 1450.
E-mail: ashbethany43@hotmail.com

Horner, Professor Robert Malcolm Wigglesworth, CEng, BSc, PhD, FRSE, FICE, MCMI. Professor Emeritus, Dundee University, since 2006, Professor of Engineering Management, 1986-2006, Deputy Principal, 2002-06, and Director, Enterprise Management, 2000-06 (Chair, School of Engineering and Physical Sciences, 1997-99); b. 27.7.42, Bury; m., Beverley Anne Wesley; 1 s.; 1 d. Educ. The Bolton School; University College, London. Civil Engineer, Taylor Woodrow Construction Ltd., 1966-77; Lecturer, Senior Lecturer, Head, Department of Civil Engineering, Dundee University, 1977-91; Managing Director, International Maintenance Management, 1996-97. Founder Chairman, Dundee Branch, Opening Windows on Engineering; Winner, CIOB Ian Murray Leslie Award, 1980 and 1984; Atlantic Power and Gas Ltd.: Non-executive Director, 1991-97, Director, Research and Development, 1993-97; Chairman: Winton Caledonian Ltd., 1995-97, Whole Life Consultants Ltd., since 2004; Director, Dundee Rep., since 1991; Director, Scottish Institute for Enterprise, 1999-2005; Director, Objective 3 Partnership, 2000-03 (Vice Chairman, 2002-03); Member, Council, National Conference of University Professors, 1989-93; Director, Scottish International Resource Project, 1994-95; Member: Technology Foresight Construction Sector Panel, 1994-98, British Council Advisory Committee on Science, Engineering and the Environment, 1994-2005; Member, Construction Futures Technical Reference Group, since 2005; Director, Scottish Enterprise Tayside, since 2003, Chair, since 2005; Member, Tayside and Central Scotland Transport Planning Partnership Executive, since 2006; Director, Citizens Advice Bureau, Dundee, 1993-2003; Chairman, Friends of St. Paul's Cathedral, 1993-95. Recreations: squash; gardening. Address: (h.) Westfield Cottage, 11 Westfield Place, Dundee DD1 4JU; T.-01382 225933.

Hosie, Stewart. MP (SNP) Dundee East, since 2005; Deputy Leader and Chief Whip, SNP (Westminster), since 2007; b. 1963, Dundee. Educ. Carnoustie High School; University of Abertay; m., Shona Robison; 1 d. Address: (b.) House of Commons, London SW1A 0AA.

Hossack, Dr. William Strachan, MB, ChB, DObstRCOG, Cert. Aviation Medicine; b. 10.9.29, Macduff; m., Catherine Sellar (widower); 1 s.; 1 d. Educ. Banff Academy; Aberdeen University. House Officer, Aberdeen Maternity Hospital and City Hospital, Aberdeen; Junior Specialist Obstetrics, RAF Hospital, St. Athan; GP, Banff, Visiting M.O., Chalmers Hospital and Ladysbridge Hospital, Banff; authorised Medical Examiner (PPL), Civil Aviation Authority. Hon. Medical Adviser, RNLI Macduff; Chairman, Banffshire Hospitals Board; Honorary Sheriff, Grampian Region; General Comissioner, Inland Revenue;

Chairman, Martin Trust. Recreations: music; choral singing; watercolour painting; amateur radio. Address: (h.) Kincraig, 39 Skene Street, Macduff, Aberdeenshire AB44 1RP; T.-01261 832099.

Hough, Professor James, BSc, PhD, FRS, FRSE, FAPS, FInstP, FRAS. Professor of Experimental Physics, Glasgow University, since 1986; Director, Institute for Gravitational Research, since 2000; Member, PPARC Council, 2005-07; Chair, PPARC (now STFC) Education and Training Committee, since 2006; b. 6.8.45, Glasgow; m., Anne Park McNab (deceased); 1 s.; 1 d. Educ. High School of Glasgow; Glasgow University. Glasgow University: Lecturer in Natural Philosophy, 1972, Senior Lecturer, 1983; Visiting Fellow, JILA, University of Colorado, 1983; Max Planck Research Prize, 1991; Duddell Prize, IOP, 2004; PPARC Senior Fellowship, 1997-2000. Publications: 100 refereed publications in learned journals; 60 contributions in books/conference reports. Address: (b.) Department of Physics and Astronomy, University of Glasgow, Glasgow G12 8QQ; T.-0141-330 4706; e-mail: j.hough@physics.gla.ac.uk

Hounsell, Professor Dai (David John), BA, PhD. Professor of Higher Education, University of Edinburgh, since 2000; b. 5.7.47, Southampton; m., Jenny; 2 s. Educ. City of Bath Boys' Grammar School; Poole Grammar School; Portsmouth Polytechnic; University of Lancaster. Research Assistant, Portsmouth Polytechnic and North-East London Polytechnic, 1969-72; Information and Research Officer/Senior Research Officer, Institute for Research and Development in Post-Compulsory Education, University of Lancaster, 1972-85; Visiting Research Fellow, University of Gothenburg, 1981-82; Director/Co-Director, Centre for Teaching, Learning and Assessment, University of Edinburgh, 1985-98 (Head, Department of Higher and Further Education, 1988-2001). Editor, Higher Education, since 1988. Publications: How Students Learn (Co-Author), 1976; The Experience of Learning (Joint Author), 1984; Essay Writing for Active Learning, 1996; The ASSHE Inventory: Changing Assessment Practices in Scottish Higher Education (Joint Author), 1996; Reviewing Your Teaching (Joint Author), 1998. Recreations: hillwalking; light joinery; reading contemporary fiction. Address: (b.) Moray House School of Education, University of Edinburgh, Paterson's Land, Holyrood Road, Edinburgh EH8 8AQ; T.-0131-651 6667.
E-mail: dai.hounsell@ed.ac.uk

Housden, Stuart David, OBE, BSc (Hons) (Zoology). Director, RSPB Scotland, since 1993; b. 24.6.53, Croydon; m., Catherine Juliet Wilkin; 3 d. Educ. Selhurst Grammar School; Royal Holloway College, London University. Freshwater biologist, Thames Water, 1976; RSPB: Species Investigation Officer, 1977-79, Parliamentary Officer, 1979-82, Manager — Government Unit, 1982-85, Head, Conservation Planning Department, 1985-90, Head, Conservation Planning, 1990-93. Member, Cairngorms Partnership Board, 1995-97; Member, ScottishPower Environment Forum, since 1999; Member, Scottish Executive's Agricultural Strategy Group, and Scottish Biodiversity Group; Churchill Fellow, 1992. Publications: Important Bird Areas in the UK (Co-Editor); numerous articles. Recreations: ornithology; travel; rugby football; politics; work. Address: (b.) Dunedin House, 25 Ravelston Terrace, Edinburgh EH4 3TP.

Houslay, Professor Miles Douglas, BSc, PhD, FRSE, FRSA, FIBiol, CBiol, FMedSci. Gardiner Professor of Biochemistry, Glasgow University, since 1984; b. 25.6.50, Wolverhampton; m., Rhian Mair; 2 s.; 1 d. Educ. Grammar School, Brewood, Stafford; University College, Cardiff;

King's College, Cambridge; Cambridge University. ICI Research Fellow and Fellow, Queens' College, Cambridge, 1974-76; Lecturer, then Reader in Biochemistry, UMIST, 1976-82; Selby Fellow, Australian Academy of Science, 1984; Colworth Medal, Biochemical Society of Great Britain, 1984; Honorary Research Fellow, California Metabolic Research Foundation, since 1981; Editor in Chief, Cellular Signalling; Deputy Chairman, Biochemical Journal, 1984-89; Editorial Board, Biochimica Biophysica Acta; Member: Committee, Biochemical Society, 1982-85, Research Committee, British Diabetic Association, 1986-91; Chairman, Grant Committee A, Cell and Disorders Board, Medical Research Council, 1989-92; Member: Scientific and Medical Grant Committee, Scottish Home and Health Department, 1991-94, Advisory Board for External Appointments, London University, 1990-92, HEFC RAE Basic Medical and Dental Sciences Panel, since 1996, Wellcome Trust BMB Grant Panel, 1996-2000; Chairman, British Heart Foundation Project Grant Panel; Member, British Heart Foundation Chairs and Programme Grant Panel, 1997-2000; Trustee, British Heart Foundation, 1997-2001; 1998 Founder Fellow, Academy of Medical Sciences; Burroughs-Wellcome Visiting Professor, USA, 2001; Consultant, various pharmaceutical companies in UK, Europe and USA. Publication: Dynamics of Biological Membranes; over 400 scientific papers. Address: (b.) Department of Biochemistry, Glasgow University, Glasgow G12 8QQ; T.-0141-330 4624.

Housley, Edward, MB, ChB, FRCPEdin, FRCP. Retired Medical Specialist, Armed Forces Scotland (1975-2007); Consultant Physician to the Army in Scotland, 1995-2006; retired Consultant Physician, Edinburgh Royal Infirmary; b. 10.1.34, Chester, USA; 1 d. Educ. Mundella Grammar School, Nottingham; Birmingham University. Postgraduate training, Department of Medicine, Birmingham University and McGill University, Montreal; former Honorary Senior Lecturer, Department of Medicine, Edinburgh University. Recreation: crossword puzzles. Address: (h.) 6 Kew Terrace, Edinburgh EH12 5JE.
E-mail: edhousley@btinternet.com

Houston, Alexander Stewart, BSc (Hons), PhD, FIPEM. Honorary Professor, University of Stirling, since 2007; Medical Imaging Consultant, Hermes Medical Systems, since 2004; b. 16.06.44, Glasgow; m., Roberta Ann; 1 s.; 2 d. Educ. Woodside Senior Secondary School, Glasgow; University of Glasgow; University of Edinburgh. Research Assistant, University of Dundee, 1971-75; Clinical Scientist: Royal Naval Hospital Haslar, 1975-2001, Portsmouth Hospitals NHS Trust, 2001-04; Visiting Professor, University of Portsmouth, 2004-07. Norman Veall Medal, 2001; Advisory Editor, Nuclear Medicine Communications, since 2005. Recreations: astronomy; audio-visual; bridge; photography; watching Partick Thistle. Address: (b.) Department of Psychology, University of Stirling FK9 4LA; T.-01786-467640; e-mail: alex.houston@stir.ac.uk

Houston, Anne C., CQSW. Chief Executive, Children 1st, since 2007; Director, ChildLine Scotland, 1994-2007 and Deputy Chief Executive, Childline UK, 2003-07; b. 28 8 54, Glasgow. Educ. Bishopbriggs High School; Strathclyde University. Social Worker, Intermediate Treatment Officer, Team Leader, Southampton Social Services Department, 1980-86; Project Manager/Tutor, Richmond Fellowship, Glasgow, 1986-90; Counselling Manager, Childline Scotland, 1990-94. Recreations: reading; music; swimming; gardening; animals; food and wine with friends; travel; attending rock concerts. Address: (b.) 83 Whitehouse Loan, Edinburgh EH9 1AT.

Houston, Major General David, CVO, CBE. Lord Lieutenant of Sutherland, 1991-2004; b. 24.2.29; m.; 2 s. Educ. Latymer Upper School. Military Attaché and Commander, British Army Staff, Washington, 1977-79; HQ UKLF, 1979-80; President, Regular Commissions Board, 1980-83.

Houston, Guy, BA, CA, FCILT. Director of Finance and Corporate Services, Transport Scotland, since 2006; b. 25.7.71, Irvine; m., Karen; 1 d. Educ. Crieff High School; Napier University, Edinburgh. Institute of Chartered Accountants in Scotland (ICAS) Training, French Duncan, 1992-95; Internal Audit Manager and Group Accountant, Stagecoach Group plc, 1995-97; Regional Finance Director, Stagecoach East Midlands, Cambus and Supertram, 1997-99; Divisional Finance Director, First Manchester Ltd (subsidiary of First Group plc), 1999-2001; Finance Director, UK Bus for First Group plc, 2001-06. Recreations: 5-a-side football; mountain biking; circuit training. Address: (b.) Buchanan House, 58 Port Dundas Road, Glasgow G4 0HF; T.-0141-272-7131.
E-mail: guy.houston@transportscotland.gsi.gov.uk

Houston, John, OBE, RSA, RSW, RGI. Artist; b. 1.4.30, Buckhaven; m., Elizabeth V. Blackadder. Educ. Buckhaven High School; Edinburgh College of Art. Travelling scholarship to Italy, 1953-54; started teaching, Edinburgh College of Art, 1955; elected: Associate, Royal Scottish Academy, 1964, Academician, 1977; Depute Head, School of Drawing and Painting, Edinburgh College of Art, 1982-89. Guthrie Award, RSA, 1964; Cargill Prize, Royal Glasgow Institute of Fine Arts, 1965, 1988; Lothians Award, RSA, 1982; Sir William Gillies Prize, RSW, 1990; LLD (Heriot-Watt University), 2004; DHC, Aberdeen University, 2005. Recreations: golf; fishing; travel. Address: (h.) 57 Fountainhall Road, Edinburgh EH9 2LH; T.-0131-667 3687.

Houstoun, Andrew Beatty, OBE, MC, JP, DL. Vice President, Scottish Landowners Federation, 1984-98, b. 15.10.22, Cranleigh; m., Mary Elizabeth Spencer-Nairn; 4 s. Educ. Harrow. Regular Army, 1941-56; retired as Major, 1st The Royal Dragoons; farming, Angus and Perthshire, since 1956; commanded Fife and Forfar Yeomanry/Scottish Horse (TA), 1962-65; retired Brevet Col. and Lt. Col, 1965; Angus County Councillor, 1966-75 (Vice Chairman, Education Committee); Convener, Scottish Landowners Federation, 1979-82; Chancellor's Assessor, Dundee University Court, 1981-92; Vice Lord Lieutenant, Angus, 1986-2001. Address: Kirkhill, Lintrathen, Kirriemuir, Angus DD8 5JH; T.-01575 560228.

Howard, Ashley, BSc (Hons), MBA. Chief Executive Officer, Scottish Swimming, since 2004; b. Vancouver, Canada. Educ. Queen's University; University of Victoria. Consultant, Canadian Health Care; Special Projects Manager, Technology Company; Director of Achieving Excellence, sportscotland. Recreations: sport; yoga; coaching. Address: (b.) National Swimming Academy, University of Stirling, Stirling FK9 4LA.

Howard, Dr Grahame Charles William, BSc (Hons), MBBS, MD, FRCP(Ed), FRCR. Consultant Clinical Oncologist and Honorary Senior Lecturer, Edinburgh University, since 1987; Clinical Director, Edinburgh Cancer Centre, 1999-2005; Clinical Director, Cancer Services, since 2005; b. 15.5.53, London; 3 s. Educ. King Edward VI School, Norwich; St Thomas' Hospital Medical School, London University. Registrar in Oncology, Royal Free Hospital, London; Senior Registrar, Addenbrookes Hospital, Cambridge; appointed Consultant Oncologist, Edinburgh Cancer Centre, 1987; Head of Radiotherapy then Clinical Director, 1999-2005; several commitments to Royal College of Radiologists; previously Vice-Chair, Scottish

Intercollegiate Guideline Network and Chair, Cancer subgroup, until 2007; Chair, Oncology Section, S.E. Scotland Urological Oncology Group, until 2007. Publications: Assistant Editor, Clinical Oncology; author of scientific papers. Recreations: music; sailing; reading. Address: (h.) 4 Ormelie Terrace, Joppa, Edinburgh EH15; T.-0131 537 2211.

Howard, Professor Ian, MA (Hons), RSA. Principal, Edinburgh College of Art, since 2001; b. 5.11.52, Aberdeen; m., Ruth D'Arcy; 2 d. Educ. Aberdeen Grammar School; Edinburgh College of Art; Edinburgh University. Travelling scholarship to Italy, 1976; part-time Lecturer in Painting, Gray's School of Art, Aberdeen, 1977 (appointed full-time, 1980); Dean of Faculty, Duncan of Jordanstone College of Art, University of Dundee, 1999-2001. Scottish Arts Council Award, 1979, Bursary, 1985-86; Chicago Prize, 2000; numerous one-man and group exhibitions; Faculty of Fine Art, British School at Rome, 1996-2002. Recreations: reading; music; cooking. Address: (b.) Principal's Office, Edinburgh College of Art, Lauriston Place, Edinburgh; T.-0131-221 6060.

Howard, Philip, MA (Hons) (Cantab), MLitt. Artistic Director, Traverse Theatre, Edinburgh, 1996-2007; b. 27.5.63, York. Educ. Ampleforth College, York; Girton College, Cambridge; St. Andrews University. Assistant Director, Royal Court Theatre, London, 1988-90; Director, National Gaelic Youth Theatre, Isle of Benbecula, 1989-92. Address: 3 Rutland Square, Edinburgh EH1 2AS.

Howat, Rev. Angus John, MA. Minister, Campbeltown, Tarbert and Islay Free Church, since 1996; Assistant Clerk, General Assembly, Free Church of Scotland, since 1998; b. 5.8.44, Monifieth; m., Irene Agnes Gardner Bickerton; 3 d. Educ. Daniel Stewart's College, Edinburgh; Edinburgh University; Strathclyde University; Free Church College. Assistant Librarian, Ayr Public Library, 1966-71; Depute County Librarian, Moray and Nairn, 1971-75; Principal Librarian, Moray District Council at Elgin, 1975-85; Temporary Assistant Librarian, Free Church College, 1988-90; Minister, Campbeltown Free Church, 1990-96. Publication: Churches of Moray (Joint Author). Recreations: family history; walking. Address: Free Church Manse, Kilberry Road, Tarbert PA29 6XX; T.-01880 820134.

Howat, Bill, BA (Hons), MSc. Chair, Volunteer Development Scotland; Chief Executive, Comhairle Nan Eilan Siar, 2000-05 (ret'd); Leader, SE Budget Review Group, 2006; Member, Local Government Reform Taskforce NI, 2006; b. 11.5.47, Greenock; m., Eleanor; 1 s.; 1 d. Educ. Greenock High School; Strathclyde University. Lecturer, Glasgow College of Technology, 1969-74; Principal Researcher, The Planning Exchange, 1974-79; civil servant, Scottish Office/Executive, 1979-2000. Recreations: reading; music; squash. Address: (b.) Volunteer Development Scotland, Stirling Enterprise Park, Stirling FK7 7RP.

Howatson, William, MA (Hons), JP. Freelance journalist and columnist, since 1996; b. 22.1.53, Dumfries; m., Hazel Symington Paton; 2 d. Educ. Lockerbie Academy; Edinburgh University. Press and Journal: Agricultural Editor, 1984-96, Leader Writer, 1990-96. Chairman, Guild of Agricultural Journalists, 1995; Member, Scottish Water and Sewerage Customers Council, 1995-99; Member, Angus College Board of Management, since 1996 (Chairman, 2003-06, Vice Chairman, since 2006); Member, Health Education Board for Scotland, 1997-2003; Vice Chair, NHS Health Scotland, 2003-05; Member, East Areas

Board, Scottish Natural Heritage, 1997-2003 (Deputy Chairman, 2000-03); Non Executive Director, Angus NHS Trust, 1998; Governor, Macaulay Land Use Research Institute, 1998-2003; Member, Aberdeenshire Council, since 1999; Chairman, North of Scotland Agriculture Advisory Committee, since 2003; Director, Ash Scotland, since 2006; Board Member, Scottish Environment Protection Agency, 1999-2005 (Chairman, East Regional Board, 2003-05); Member, East Regional Board, since 2006; Member, Rail Passenger Committee for Scotland, 2001-03; Member, Esk District Salmon Fishery Board, 2003-07; Provost, Aberdeenshire Council, since 2007; Chairman, North East of Scotland Fisheries Development Partnership; Member, NHS Grampian Health Board, since 2007. Columnist of the Year, Bank of Scotland Press Awards, 1992; Fellow of the Royal Agricultural Societies. Publication: Farm Servants and Labour in Lowland Scotland, 1770-1914 (Contributor). Recreations: gardening; hillwalking; reading; Scottish history. Address: (h.) Stone of Morphie, Hillside, Montrose; T.-01674 830746; e-mail: billhowatson@aol.com

Howe, Professor Christine Joyce, BA, PhD, CPsychol, AFBPS. Professor of Education, University of Cambridge, since 2006; b. 21.11.48, Birmingham; m., William Robertson; 1 s.; 1 d. Educ. King Edward VI Camp Hill School for Girls; Sussex University; Cambridge University. Career in teaching and research since 1976. Publications: Learning Language in a Conversational Context, 1983; Language Learning, 1993; Group and Interactive Learning, 1994; Conceptual Structure in Childhood and Adolescence, 1998; Gender and Classroom Interaction, 1997. Recreations: bridge; tennis; cycling; hillwalking; theatre; film; politics. Address: Dunalvis, Drumbeg Loan, Killearn G63 9LG; T.-01360 550378; e-mail: cjh82@cam.ac.uk

Howie, Andrew Law, CBE, FRAgrS. Chairman: Howie Animal Feed Ltd., 2001-04, Robert Howie & Sons, 1982-2001, Scottish Milk Ltd., 1994-95; b. 14.4.24, Dunlop; m., Joan Duncan; 2 s.; 2 d. Educ. Glasgow Academy. Joined Robert Howie & Sons, 1941; War Service, RN; became Director, 1965; President, Scottish Compound Feed Manufacturers, 1968-70 and 1983-85; President, Compound Animal Feed Manufacturers National Association, 1971-72; Director, Scottish Corn Trade, 1976-78; Vice-President/Feed, UK Agricultural Supply Trade Association, 1980-81; Chairman, Scottish Council, UKASTA, 1985-87; Director, Scottish Milk Marketing Board, 1980-94 (Chairman, 1982-94); Member, CBI Scottish Council, 1989-95. Recreations: golf; gardening; wood-turning. Address: (h.) Newmill House, Dunlop, Kilmarnock KA3 4BQ; T.-01560 484936.

Howie, Professor John Garvie Robertson, CBE, MD, PhD, Hon DSc, FRCPE, FRCGP, FMedSci. Professor of General Practice, Edinburgh University, 1980-2000; b. 23.1.37, Glasgow; m., Elizabeth Margaret Donald; 2 s.; 1 d. Educ. High School of Glasgow; Glasgow University. Registrar, Laboratory Medicine, Western Infirmary, Glasgow, 1962-66; General Practitioner, Glasgow, 1966-70; Lecturer/Senior Lecturer in General Practice, Aberdeen University, 1970-80; Member: Biomedical Research Committee, SHHD, 1977-81, Health Services Research Committee, SHHD, 1982-86, Chief Scientist Committeee, SHHD, 1987-97, Committee on the Review of Medicines, 1986-91. Publications: Research in General Practice; A Day in the Life of Academic General Practice. Recreations: golf; gardening; music. Address: (h.) 4 Ravelrig Park, Balerno, Midlothian EH14 7DL; T.-0131-449 6305; e-mail: John.Howie00@btinternet.com

Howie, Professor John Mackintosh, CBE, MA, DPhil, DSc, HonDUniv, FRSE. Regius Professor of Mathematics, St. Andrews University, 1970-97; b. 23.5.36, Chryston, Lanarkshire; m., Dorothy Joyce Miller; 2 d. Educ. Robert

Gordon's College, Aberdeen; Aberdeen University. Assistant in Mathematics, Aberdeen University, 1958-59; Assistant, then Lecturer in Mathematics, Glasgow University, 1961-67; Senior Lecturer in Mathematics, Stirling University, 1967-70; visiting appointments: Tulane University, 1964-65, State University of New York at Buffalo, 1969-70, University of Western Australia, 1968, Monash University, 1979, Northern Illinois University, 1988, University of Lisbon, 1996; Dean of Science, St. Andrews University, 1976-79. President, Edinburgh Mathematical Society, 1972-73; Vice-President, London Mathematical Society, 1984-86 and 1990-92; Convener, SCEEB Mathematics Panel, 1970-73; Chairman, Scottish Central Committee on Mathematics, 1975-81; Member, Committee to Review Examinations (Dunning Committee), 1975-77; Chairman, Governors, Dundee College of Education, 1983-87; Keith Prize, Royal Society of Edinburgh, 1979-81; Chairman, Committee to review Fifth and Sixth Years (Howie Committee), 1990-92. Publications: An Introduction to Semigroup Theory, 1976; Automata and Languages, 1991; Fundamentals of Semigroup Theory, 1995; Real Analysis, 2001; Complex Analysis, 2003; Fields and Galois Theory, 2006; papers in mathematical journals. Recreations: music; gardening. Address: (h.) 19 Strathkinness High Road, St. Andrews KY16 9UA; (b.) Mathematical Institute, St. Andrews University, North Haugh, St. Andrews, KY16 9SS; T.-01334 463746; e-mail: jmh@st-and.ac.uk

Howison, John Andrew, FRSA, BSc, MSc, CEng, MICE, MCIArb. Chief Road Engineer and Director, Trunk Roads: Infrastructure and Professional Services, Transport Scotland, since 2006; b. 12.8.46, Ruislip; m., Teresa Maria; 2 s.; 2 d. Educ. Surbiton Grammar School; Edinburgh University; Heriot Watt University. Edinburgh Corporation, 1968-70; Livingston Development Corporation, 1970-73; Department of Environment/ Department of Transport/Scottish Office, 1973-99 (Deputy Chief Engineer, Roads Directorate, Scottish Office Industry Department, 1992-99, Scottish Executive (Enterprise, Transport and Lifelong Learning Department, Chief Road Engineer, 1999-2005). Address: (b.) Buchanan House, Glasgow; T.-0141 272 7215.

Howson, Peter. Painter; b. 1958, London; m., 1 d. Moved to Glasgow, 1962; attended Glasgow School of Art, 1975-77; spent a short period in the Scottish infantry, travelling in Europe; returned to Glasgow School of Art, 1979-81, studying under Sandy Moffat; Artist in Residence, St Andrews and part-time Tutor, Glasgow School of Art, 1985; commissioned by Imperial War Museum to visit Bosnia as war artist, 1993. Address: c/o Flowers East, 82 Kingsland Road, London E2 8DP.

Hoy, Chris, MBE, BSc (Hons). Scottish track cyclist; b. 23.3.76. Educ. George Watson's College; University of St. Andrews; Moray House, University of Edinburgh. Multiple world champion and Olympic Games gold and silver medal winner. Awarded honorary doctorates from Edinburgh University and Heriot-Watt University in 2005.

Ho-Yen, Darrel Orlando, BMSc (Hons), MBChB, MD, FRCPath, FRCP, DSc. Consultant Microbiologist, Raigmore Hospital, Inverness, since 1987; Head of Microbiology; Director, Scottish Toxoplasma Reference Laboratory, since 1987; National Lyme Disease Testing; Honorary Clinical Senior Lecturer, Aberdeen University, since 1987; b. 1.5.48; 2 s. Educ. Dundee University. Ninewells Hospital and Medical School, Dundee, 1974-83; Regional Virus Laboratory, Ruchill Hospital, Glasgow, 1983-87. Publications: Better Recovery from Viral

Illnesses; Diseases of Infection (Co-Author); Unwind; Human Toxoplasmosis (Co-Author); Climbing Out; Ticks (Co-author); Scientist's Quest. Address: (b.) Microbiology Department, Raigmore Hospital, Inverness IV2 3UJ; T.-01463 704206.

Hubbuck, Professor John Reginald, BA (Cantab), MA, DPhil (Oxon), FRSE, FRSA, CMath, FIMA. Emeritus Professor of Mathematics, Aberdeen University; b. 3.5.41, Girvan; m., Anne Neilson; 1 s.; 1 d. Educ. Manchester Grammar School; Queens' College, Cambridge; Pembroke College, Oxford. Fellow: Gonville and Caius College, Cambridge, 1970-72, Magdalen College, Oxford, 1972-78; President, Edinburgh Mathematical Society, 1985-86. Recreation: hill-walking. Address: (h.) 8 Fonthill Terrace, Aberdeen AB11 7UR; T.-01224 588738.

Hudghton, Ian. Member of the European Parliament (SNP), since 1998; m., Lily; 1 s.; 1 d. Ran family home decorating business, 20 years; former Member, EU's Committee of the Regions; elected to Angus District Council, 1986 (Housing Convener, eight years); Depute SNP Group Leader and Property Convener, Tayside Regional Council, 1994-96; elected to Angus Council, 1995 (Leader, 1996-98); President, Scottish National Party, since 2005; President, European Free Alliance, since 2004. Address: (b.) 8 Old Glamis Road, Dundee DD3 8HP.

Hudson, Barbara Jean, BA (Hons). Dip. App.Soc.Studies. Director BAAF (Adoption and Fostering) Scotland, since 1998; b. Scunthorpe. Educ. King Edward VI Grammar School, Louth; Manchester University; Leeds University. VSO, Nigeria, 1972; Social Work Department, Norwich hospitals, 1973-75; Leeds Social Services Department, 1976-86; Bradford Social Services, 1986-98. Recreations: walking; opera; theatre; friends. Address: (b.) 40 Shandwick Place, Edinburgh EH2 4RT; T.-0131-220 4749; e-mail: scotland@baaf.org.uk

Hudson, Rev. Eric Vallance, LTh. Retired Minister, Westerton Fairlie Memorial Church (1990-2007); b. 22.2.42, Glasgow; 1 s.; 1 d; m. (2), Anne Morrison. Educ. Paisley Grammar School; Wollongong High School, NSW; Christ's College, Aberdeen and Aberdeen University. Sub-Editor, D.C. Thomson & Co. Ltd., Dundee, 1961-66; Student Assistant, West Kirk of St. Nicholas, Aberdeen, 1966-69; Senior Assistant Minister, New Kilpatrick Parish Church, Bearsden, 1971-73; Minister, Kintore Parish Church, 1973-78; Religious Programmes Officer, Scottish Television, 1978-89; Convener, Association of Bearsden Churches, 1997-99; Convener, Religious Advisory Committee, Radio Clyde, 2004-05; Moderator, Dumbarton Presbytery, 1998-99. Address: 2 Murrayfield Drive, Bearsden, Glasgow G61 1JE.

Hughes of Woodside, Lord (Robert Hughes). Life Peer; MP (Labour), Aberdeen North, 1970-97; b. 3.1.32; m.; 2 s.; 3 d. Educ. Powis Secondary School, Aberdeen; Robert Gordon's College, Aberdeen; Benoni High School, Transvaal; Pietermaritzburg Technical College, Natal. Engineering apprenticeship, South African Rubber Company, Natal, 1949-54; draughtsman, C.F. Wilson & Co., Aberdeen, 1954-70; Member, Aberdeen City Council, 1962-71; Chairman, Aberdeen City Labour Party, 1961-69; Member, Select Committee on Scottish Affairs, 1971; Opposition Junior Spokesman on Scottish Affairs, 1972-74; Parliamentary Under Secretary of State, Scottish Office, 1974-75; Chairman, Select Committee on Scottish Affairs, 1981; Opposition Junior Spokesman on Transport, 1981-83; Opposition Principal Spokesman on Agriculture, 1984-85, on Transport, 1985-87; Member, General Medical Council, 1976-79; Chairman: Anti Apartheid Movement, 1976-94, Action for Southern Africa (ACTSA), 1994-99 (Honorary President, since 1990); Vice-Convenor, Scottish Group, Labour MPs, 1989; Convenor, Scottish Group of Labour MPs, 1990-91; Member, Select Committee on Scottish

Affairs, 1992-97; South African National Order 'Grand Companion of OR Tambo', conferred 2004; Trustee, Canon Collins Education Trust for Southern Africa, 1997-2004. Address: (b.) House of Lords, London.

Hughes, Rev. Clifford Eryl, MA, BD, CertEd. Minister, St. Mary's Parish Church, Haddington, 1993-2001; b. 16.12.36, Newport, S. Wales; m., Kathleen Mackenzie Craig; 1 s.; 1 d. Educ. Dulwich College, London; King's College, University of Cambridge; New College, University of Edinburgh. Teacher, Hurst Grange School, Stirling; Headmaster, Beaconhurst School, Bridge of Allan; Headmaster, Loretto Junior School. Professional singer (opera, concert hall, radio and television performances). Recreations: speaking out for laryngectomees. Address: Pavilion Cottage, Briglands, Rumbling Bridge, Kinross KY13 0PS; T.-01577 840506.

Hughes, Dale William Alexander, LLB (Hons), DipLP. Advocate, since 1993; b. 21.1.67, Glasgow; m., Sally Jane Henderson (deceased); 2 s.; 1 d. Educ. Kirkcaldy High School; George Watson's College, Edinburgh; Aberdeen University; Edinburgh University. Solicitor, 1990-93. Tutor, University of Edinburgh. Recreations: travel; arts; sport. Address: (b.) Advocates Library, Edinburgh.

Hughes, Derek Walter, BSc, BD (Hons), DipEd. Parish Minister, Dalziel St. Andrew's Parish Church, Motherwell, since 1996; b. 27.4.60, Motherwell; m., Elizabeth; 1 s.; 2 d. Educ. Garrion Academy, Wishaw; Stirling University; Edinburgh University. Teacher of Chemistry, Berwickshire High School, Duns, 1981-86; Parish Minister, Townhead Parish Church, Coatbridge, 1990-96. Recreations: reading; gardening. Address: Church Manse, 4 Pollock Street, Motherwell ML1 1LP; T.-01698 263 414; e-mail: derekthecleric@btinternet.com

Hughes, Professor Derek William, MA (Oxon), PhD (Liverpool). Sixth Century Professor of English, University of Aberdeen, since 2004; b. 07.11.44, Birkenhead; m., Janet Margaret Todd; 1 d. Educ. Birkenhead School; Merton College, Oxford; University of Liverpool. Lecturer, Brock University, Ontario, 1967-70; William Noble Fellow, University of Liverpool, 1971-72; Lecturer, subsequently Professor, University of Warwick. Publications: books: Dryden's Heroic Plays, 1981; English Drama, 1660-1700, 1996; The Theatre of Aphra Behn, 2001; Versions of Blackness, 2007; Culture and Sacrifice, 2007. Recreations: music; art; theatre; cooking. Address: (b.) School of Language and Literature, Taylor Building, King's College, Aberdeen AB24 3UB; e-mail: d.w.hughes@abdn.ac.uk

Hughes, Professor John, OBE, BSc, CEng, FIMechE, Hon.FISPO. Professor and Director, National Centre for Prosthetics and Orthotics, Strathclyde University, 1972-99, Emeritus Professor, 1999; b. 20.4.34, Renfrew; m., Margaret Scoular Crichton; 2 d. Educ. Camphill School; Strathclyde University. Worked in shipbuilding and engineering, 1950-63; Strathclyde University: Lecturer in Mechanical Engineering Design, 1963-67, Senior Lecturer, Bioengineering Unit, 1967-72; Past President, International Society for Prosthetics and Orthotics. Recreations: golf; gardening. Address: (b.) 4 Oxford Road, Renfrew PA4 0SJ; T.-0141-886 3883.

Hughes, Professor Michael David. Professor of Management, Head of School, University of Aberdeen Business School, since 2005; b. 8.2.47, London; m., Ewa Maria Helinska-Hughes; 1 s.; 2 d. Educ. Farnborough Grammar School; Brunel University. Address: (b.)

University of Aberdeen Business School, Edward Wright Building, Aberdeen AB24 3QY; T.-01224 272167.

Hughes, Peter Travers, OBE, DUniv (Paisley), DSc (Strathclyde), DEng (Napier), FREng, FIMMM, FRSA, MBA, FCMI. Chief Executive, Scottish Engineering, since 1998; b. 24.12.46, Bellshill; 3 s. Educ. Wishaw High School; Technical College, Coatbridge; Strathclyde University; Dundee University. Foundry Metallurgist, Clyde Alloy, 1965-68; Foundry Metallurgist/ Chief Metallurgist/Foundry Manager, North British Steel Group, Armadale and Bathgate, 1968-76; Director and General Manager, Lake and Elliot Steelfounders and Engineers, 1976-80; Managing Director, National Steel Foundry (1914) Ltd., 1980-83; Chairman and Managing Director, Glencast Ltd, 1983-98. UK President, Institute of British Foundrymen, 1994-95; former President, Scottish Engineering; former Governor and Member, Court, University of Abertay. Address: (b.) 105 West George Street, Glasgow, G2 1QL; T.-0141-221 3181; e-mail: peterhughes@ scottishengineering.org.uk

Hughes, Rhona Grace, MD, FRCOG. Consultant Obstetrician, since 1996; Honorary Senior Lecturer, since 1996; b. 29.1.58, Portsmouth; m., Tommy Hepburn; 2 s.; 1 d. Educ. Craigmount High School, Edinburgh University. House Officer in Medicine and Surgery, 1983-84; Senior House Officer in Obstetrics and Gynaecology, 1984-85; Research Fellow in Virology and Gynaecology, 1985-87; Registrar in Obstetrics and Gynaecology, 1987-90; Senior Registrar, 1990-96 (job share). Member, RCOG Guidelines and Audit Committee; Chair, NICE Antenatal Care Update Guideline Development Group; Member, Health Protection Agency Group B Streptococcus Working Group. Recreations: hill-walking; travel; literature; family. Address: (b.) New Royal Infirmary, Little France, Edinburgh; T.-0131 242 2524; e-mail: rhona.hughes@luht.scot.nhs.uk

Hughes, Roger Llewellyn, MD, FRCP (Glas), FRCA. Consultant in Anaesthesia and Intensive Care, since 1980; Honorary Senior Lecturer, since 1985; b. 2.6.47, Douglas, Isle of Man; m., Pamela Jane Finlayson; 4 d. Educ. High School of Glasgow; Glasgow University. SHO and Registrar in Anaesthesia, Glasgow Royal Infirmary; Senior Registrar then Lecturer in Anaesthesia, University of Glasgow. Chairman, Greater Glasgow Area Clinical Forum; Chairman, Area Medical Committee; Member, Greater Glasgow Unified Health Board, 2001-03; Chairman, West of Scotland Intensive Care Society, 1997-2000. Recreations: reading; walking; foreign travel. Address: 7 Ballaig Avenue, Bearsden, Glasgow G61 4HA; T.-0141-942 5626.

Hughes, Thomas George, LLB. Sheriff, since 2004; b. 2.1.55, Glasgow; m., Janice; 1 s.; 1 d. Educ. St. Mirin's Academy, Paisley; Strathclyde University. Solicitor, 1979-2004. Recreations: sport; reading. Address: (b.) Sheriff Court House, 6 West Bell Street, Dundee; T.-01382 229961; e-mail: sheriffthughes@scotcourts.gov.uk

Hughes Hallett, Professor Andrew Jonathan, BA (Hons), MSc (Econ), DPhil, FRSA, FRSE. Professor of Economics, George Mason University (USA) and St. Andrews University; council of economic advisers to the Scottish Government; formerly Professor of Economics, Strathclyde University; Fellow, Royal Society of Edinburgh, since 2000; Research Fellow, Centre for Economic Policy Research, since 1985; Consultant to World Bank, European Commission, UN, IMF, since 1986; Professor and Fulbright

Fellow, Princeton University, 1992-94; Jean Monet Professor, since 1996; b. 1.11.47, London; m., Claudia; 2 s.; 1 d. Educ. Radley College; Warwick University; LSE; Oxford University. Lecturer in Economics, Bristol University, 1973-77; Associate Professor, Erasmus University, Rotterdam, 1977-85; David Dale Professor, Newcastle University, 1985-89. Publications: six books; 250 papers. Address: (b.) 41 Clerk Street, Edinburgh EH8 9JQ; T.-0131-662-4819.

E-mail: ahugheshallett@yahoo.com

Hughes Hallett, David John, FRICS. Consultant; Director, Scottish Wildlife Trust, 1989-98; Main Board Member, Scottish Environment Protection Agency, 1995-2002; Board Member, Loch Lomond and the Trossachs National Park Authority, since 2002 (Deputy Convener, since 2006); Member, East Areas Board of Scottish Natural Heritage and Local Advisory Forum, since 2005; Panel Member, Waterwatch Scotland, since 2006; b. 19.6.47, Dunfermline; m., Anne Mary Wright; 2 s.; 1 d. Educ. Fettes College; Reading University. Chartered Surveyor, rural practice, 1966-76; Land Use Adviser, then Director, Scottish Landowners' Federation, 1976-89. Chairman, Royal Institution of Chartered Surveyors in Scotland, 1988-89; Member, Policy Committee, Scottish Council for Voluntary Organisations, 1997-2002. Recreations: sailing; sea kayaking; cycling; singing. Address: (h.) The Old School, Back Latch, Ceres, Fife KY15 5NT; e-mail: david@hugheshallett.co.uk

Hughson, A.V. Mark, MD, MB, ChB, FRCPsych, DPM. Consultant Psychiatrist, Leverndale Hospital, Glasgow, since 1990; Honorary Clinical Senior Lecturer, Glasgow University, since 1991; b. 12.3.47, Edinburgh; m., Joan Scally; 2 s. Educ. George Watson's College, Edinburgh; Glasgow University. Publication: papers on psycho-oncology and other topics. Recreations: playing the organ (not too badly); skiing (badly). Address: (h.) 1 Cleveden Gardens, Glasgow G12 0PU; T.-0141-334 2473.

Hume, David, BSc, MSc, MBA, ARSGS. Chief Executive, Scottish Borders Council, since 2002; b. Edinburgh; m., Ann Crawford; 3 d. Educ. George Heriot's School, Edinburgh; St Andrews University; University of Wales; Edinburgh University. Researcher, University of Wales Institute of Science and Technology, 1978-80; Senior Research Officer, Strathclyde Regional Council, 1980-86; Lothian Regional Council: Senior Principal Officer, Management and Information Services, 1986-90, Depute Director Corporate Services, 1990-96; City of Edinburgh Council: Director Strategic Policy, 1996-98, Director of Corporate Services, 1998-2002. Board Member, Scottish Institute for Excellence in Social Work Education. Recreations: cycling; motor-cycling; jazz. Address: (b.) Council HQ, Newtown St. Boswells, Melrose TD6 0SA.

Hume, Jim. MSP (Liberal Democrat), South of Scotland, since 2007; b. 4.11.62. Address: (b.) Scottish Parliament, Edinburgh EH99 1SP.

Hume, John Robert, OBE, BSc, ARCST, FSA Scot, Hon FRIAS. Honorary President: Faculty of Arts, University of Glasgow, since 1998, School of History, University of St. Andrews, since 1999; Honorary Life President, Seagull Trust, since 1994 (Chairman, 1978-93); Honorary Vice-President, Association for Industrial Archaeology; Honorary Vice-President, Scottish Railway Preservation Society, since 2000 (Chairman, 1967-76); b. 26.2.39, Glasgow; m., Catherine Hope Macnab; 4 s. Educ. Hutchesons' Boys' Grammar School; Glasgow University;

Royal College of Science and Technology. Assistant Lecturer, Lecturer, Senior Lecturer in Economic History, Strathclyde University, 1964-91; Chief Inspector of Historic Buildings, Historic Scotland, 1993-99. Member, Inland Waterways Amenity Advisory Council, 1974-2001; Director, Scottish Industrial Archaeology Survey, 1978-84; Member, Ancient Monuments Board for Scotland, 1981-84; Member, Committee on Artistic Matters, Church of Scotland (Convener, since 2003); Member, Mission and Discipleship Council, Church of Scotland; Member, Emerging Ministries Task Group, Church of Scotland; Advisory Member, General Trustees, Church of Scotland; Chairman, Scottish Stained Glass Symposium; Trustee: Scottish Maritime Museum, 1983-98, The Waterways Trust, since 2000, Scotland's Churches Scheme, since 2000; Member, Industrial Archaeology Sub-Committee, English Heritage, 1985-2002; Chair, Royal Commission on the Ancient and Historical Monuments of Scotland, since 2005. Publications: The Industrial Archaeology of Glasgow; The Industrial Archaeology of Scotland; Dumfries and Galloway, an illustrated architectural guide; Vernacular Buildings of Ayrshire, Scotland's Best Churches; as Co-Author: Workshop of the British Empire: Engineering and Shipbuilding in the West of Scotland; Beardmore: the History of a Scottish Industrial Giant; The Making of Scotch Whisky; A Bed of Nails: a History of P. MacCallum & Sons Ltd.; Shipbuilders to the World: a History of Harland and Wolff; Steam Entertainment; Historic Industrial Scenes: Scotland; Industrial History in Pictures: Scotland; Glasgow's Railway Stations. Recreations: photography; reading. Address: (h.) 28 Partickhill Road, Glasgow G11 5BP.

Hume, Professor Robert, BSc, MBChB, PhD, FRCP(Edin), FRCPCH. Professor of Developmental Medicine, Dundee University; Consultant Paediatrician, Tayside Universities NHS Trust; b. 5.4.47, Edinburgh; m., Shaena Finlayson Blair; 2 d. Educ. Dalkeith High School; Edinburgh University. MRC Fellow, Department of Biochemistry, Edinburgh University, 1975-78; Lecturer, Department of Child Life and Health, Edinburgh University, 1978-80; Senior Lecturer, Department of Child Life and Health, Edinburgh University. Address: (b.) Maternal and Child Health Sciences, Ninewells Hospital and Medical School, Dundee DD1 9SY; T.-01382 660111.

Humes, Professor Walter Malcolm, MA, MEd, PhD, FCS. Research Professor in Education, University of Paisley, since 2006; b. 10.12.45, Newton Mearns. Educ. Eastwood Senior Secondary School; University of Aberdeen; University of Dundee; University of Glasgow. Teacher of English, London and Renfrewshire, 1968-74; Lecturer in English, Notre Dame College, Glasgow, 1974-76; Lecturer in Education, University of Glasgow, 1976-94; Director of Professional Studies, St. Andrew's College, 1994-99; Head of Educational Studies: University of Glasgow, 1999-2000, University of Strathclyde, 2001-04; Professor of Education, University of Aberdeen, 2004-06. Editor, Scottish Educational Review, 1990-94. Publications: Scottish Culture and Scottish Education 1800-1980 (Co-editor), 1983; The Leadership Class in Scottish Education, 1986; The Management of Educational Policy: Scottish Perspectives (Co-editor), 1994; Scottish Education (Co-editor), 1999 (2nd edition, 2003); chapters in books and articles in journals on a wide range of educational topics. Recreations: literature; music; swimming. Address: (b.) University of Paisley, Beech Grove, Ayr KA8 0SR; T.-01292 886334; e-mail: walter.humes@paisley.ac.uk

Humfrey, Professor Peter Brian, BA, MA, PhD, FRSE. Professor of Art History, University of St. Andrews, since 1995; b. 9.4.47, Cyprus; m., Margaret Zarina; 2 s. Educ. Cranleigh School, Surrey; Trinity College, Dublin;

Courtauld Institute of Art, London. Lecturer in Art History, University of St. Andrews, 1977; Senior Visiting Fellow, Center for Advanced Studies in the Visual Arts, National Gallery of Art, Washington D.C., 1986; Fellow, Harvard Center for Italian Renaissance Studies, Villa I Tatti, Florence, 1987, 1991; Member, Institute for Advanced Study, Princeton, 1988; Guest Curator, The Age of Titian exhibition, National Galleries of Scotland, 2004; Cavaliere dell'Ordine della Stella della Solidarietà Italiana, 2005. Publications: Cima da Conegliano, 1983; The Altarpiece in Renaissance Venice, 1993; Painting in Renaissance Venice, 1995; Lorenzo Lotto, 1997; Dosso Dossi (Co-Author), 1998. Address: (b.) School of Art History, University of St. Andrews, St. Andrews KY16 9AR; T.-01334 462400.

Humphrey, James Malcolm Marcus, CBE, DL, OStJ, MA, FRICS. Member, Aberdeenshire Council, since 1995 (Member, Grampian Regional Council, 1974-94); Leader, Conservative Group, since 1999; Deputy Lieutenant, Aberdeenshire, since 1989; b. 1.5.38, Montreal, Canada; m., Sabrina Margaret Pooley; 2 s.; 2 d. Educ. Eton College; Oxford University. Conservative Parliamentary candidate, North Aberdeen, 1966, Kincardine and Deeside, 1991; Council Member, National Farmers Union of Scotland, 1968-73; Member, Aberdeen County Council, 1970-75 (Chairman of Finance, 1973-75); Grampian Regional Council, 1974-94 (Chairman of Finance, 1974-78, Leader, Conservative Group); Member, Aberdeenshire Council, since 1995; Deputy Provost, 2007; Member, Cairngorms National Park Authority Board, since 2004; Grand Master Mason of Scotland, 1983-88; former Chairman, Clinterty Agricultural College Council; Member, Queen's Bodyguard for Scotland (Royal Company of Archers); Chairman, North of Scotland Board, Eagle Star Group, 1973-91; Non-Executive Director, Grampian Healthcare NHS Trust, 1993-99; Alternate Member, European Committee of the Regions, 1994-2002. Recreations: shooting; fishing; photography. Address: (h.) Dinnet, Aboyne, Aberdeenshire.

Hunt, Gordon Lansallas, BA (Hons), MA, MCLIP. Director, Customer Services, National Library of Scotland, since 2003; b. 25.7.68, Plymouth; m., Susan. Educ. Saltash School; Durham University; Sheffield University. Reader Services Librarian, Leeds University, 1991-94; Sub-Librarian, Gonville and Caius College, Cambridge, 1995-98; Head of Learning and Information Services, Westminster College, 1998-99; Head of Information Services, Royal Scottish Academy of Music and Drama, 1999-2003. Board Member, Wee Stories Theatre Company; Director, Gadabout Theatre Company; Secretary, Scottish Confederation of University and Research Libraries. Recreations: acting; writing; directing; poetry. Address: (b.) National Library of Scotland, George IV Bridge, Edinburgh EH1 1EW; T.-0131 623 3850; e-mail: g.hunt@nls.uk

Hunter, Andrew Reid, BA (Hons), PGCE. Headmaster, Merchiston Castle School, Edinburgh, since 1998; b. 28.9.58, Nairobi, Kenya; m., Barbara G.; 2 s.; 1 d. Educ. Kenton College, Nairobi; Aldenham School, Elstree; University of Manchester; St. Luke's College, Exeter. Westbrook Hay Preparatory School, 1978-79; Worksop College, 1983-91 (Housemaster, 1987-91); Bradfield College, 1991-98 (Housemaster, 1992-98). Former Chairman, Public Schools Hockey Festival, Oxford; Committee Member, Public Schools Lawn Tennis Association. Recreations: reading; attending theatre; former men's county player, tennis, squash and hockey. Address: Castle Gates, Merchiston Castle School, Colinton, Edinburgh EH13 0PU; T.-0131-312 2202.

Hunter, Archibald Sinclair, DL, CA. Chairman, Macfarlane Group PLC; Non Executive Director, The Royal Bank of Scotland Group; Non Executive Director, Edinburgh US Tracker Trust; Governor, The Beatson Institute; Chair, Strathclyde University Court, 2002-07;

Senior Partner, Scotland, KPMG, 1992-99; b. 20.8.43, Glasgow; m., Pat; 2 s.; 1 d. Educ. Queen's Park School, Glasgow. Trained with Mackie & Clark, CA, Glasgow; qualified as CA, 1966; joined Thomson McLintock, 1966; Partner, 1974; UK Board, 1992-96; Latin American Board, 1995-99; President, Institute of Chartered Accountants of Scotland, 1997-98. DUniv (Strathclyde), 2006. Recreations: golf; swimming; walking. Address: (b.) ASH Business Services, 2nd Floor, The Regus Building, 69 Buchanan Street, Glasgow G1 3HL; T.-0141 314 3979.

Hunter, Colin M., OBE, MB, ChB, FRCP(Ed), FRCGP, FIHM(Hon). Hon. Treasurer, Royal College of General Practitioners, since 2003; Hon. Fellow, Institute of Healthcare Management, since 1996; b. 28.4.58, Stirling. Educ. High School of Stirling; Aberdeen University. Principal in general practice, Skene Medical Group, 1986; Honorary Senior Lecturer, Aberdeen University, 1988; Hon. Secretary, N.E. Scotland Faculty, RCGP, 1989-96; first member, RCGP in Scotland, to attain Fellowship of Royal College by Assessment, 1993; Sally Irvine Lecture, Glasgow, 1996; Ian Murray - Scott Lecture, 2003; Chairman, Scottish Council, Royal College of General Practitioners, 1996-2000; National Co-ordinator Primary Care, NHS Education for Scotland, 1999-2005. Recreations: hill-walking; singing. Address: The Langdales, 1 Craigston Gardens, Westhill, Aberdeen AB32 6NL; T.-01224 742594.
E-mail: colin.hunter@skene.grampian.scot.nhs.uk

Hunter, George Alexander, OBE (1980), KStJ, KLJ. Founder Governor, Scottish Sports Aid Foundation, since 1980; Member, Edinburgh City Council, since 1992; b. 24.2.26, Edinburgh; m., Eileen Elizabeth. Educ. George Watson's College, Edinburgh. Served with Cameronians, seconded to 17th Dogara Regiment, Indian Army, 1944-47 (Captain); Lawson Donaldson Seeds Ltd., 1942-82 (Director, 15 years); Honorary Consul for Malta; Secretary, Scottish Amateur Rowing Association, 1948-78 (President, 1978-84); Commonwealth Games Council for Scotland: Treasurer, 1962-78, Secretary, 1978-99; Adviser, Sports Aid Foundation, since 1979; Member, Scottish Sports Council, 1976-84 (Chairman, Games and Sports Committee, 1976-84); Chairman, Scottish Standing Conference for Sport, 1977-84; Secretary, Order of St. John Edinburgh and South East Branch, since 1987. Address: (h.) 1 Craiglockhart Crescent, Edinburgh EH14 1EZ; T.-0131-443 2533.

Hunter, Hugh. Leader, South Ayrshire Council, since 2007. Address: (b.) County Buildings, Wellington Square, Ayr KA7 1DR; T.-01292 612000.

Hunter, James, CBE, MA (Hons), PhD. Writer and Historian; Director, UHI Centre for History; Member, Board of Scottish Natural Heritage; former Chairman, Highlands and Islands Enterprise; b. 22.5.48, Duror, Argyll; m., Evelyn; 1 s.; 1 d. Educ. Oban High School; Aberdeen University; Edinburgh University. Former Director, Scottish Crofters Union; former Chairman, Skye and Lochalsh Enterprise; former Member, Broadcasting Council for Scotland. Publications: The Making of the Crofting Community, 1976; Skye: The Island, 1986; The Claim of Crofting, 1991; Scottish Highlanders: A People and their Place, 1992; A Dance Called America: The Scottish Highlands, the United States and Canada, 1994; On the Other Side of Sorrow: Nature and People in the Scottish Highlands, 1995; Glencoe and the Indians, 1996; Last of the Free: A Millennial History of the Highlands and Islands of Scotland, 1999; Culloden and the Last Clansman, 2001; Scottish Exodus: Travels Among a Worldwide Clan, 2005. Address: (b.) Rowanbrae, Kiltarlity, Beauly IV4 7HT; T.-01463 741644.

Hunter, Professor John Angus Alexander, OBE, BA, MD, FRCPEdin. Professor Emeritus of Dermatology,

University of Edinburgh, since 2000; Grant Professor of Dermatology, Edinburgh University, 1981-99; b. 16.6.39, Edinburgh; m., Ruth Mary Farrow; 1 s.; 2 d. Educ. Loretto School; Pembroke College, Cambridge; Edinburgh University. Research Fellow, Institute of Dermatology, London, 1967; Registrar, Department of Dermatology, Edinburgh Royal Infirmary, 1968-70; Exchange Research Fellow, Department of Dermatology, Minnesota University, 1968; Lecturer, Department of Dermatology, Edinburgh University, 1970-74; Consultant Dermatologist, Lothian Health Board, 1974-80; Member: Executive Committee of Investigative Group, British Association of Dermatologists, 1974-76; Executive Committee, British Association of Dermatologists, 1977-79; SEC, Scottish Dermatological Society, 1980-82; Specialist Advisory Committee, (Dermatology), Joint Committee on Higher Medical Training, 1980-87 (Chairman, 1986-90); Medical Appeal Tribunal, 1981-99; Scottish Committee for Hospital Medical Services, 1983-85; President: Section of Dermatology, Royal Society of Medicine, 1993-94, Scottish Dermatological Society, 1994-97, British Association of Detmatologists, 1998-99. Publications: Common Diseases of the Skin (Co-author); Clinical Dermatology, 1st, 2nd, 3rd and 4th edition (Co-author); Skin Signs in Clinical Medicine (Co-author); Davidson's Principles and Practice of Medicine, 18th, 19th and 20th edition (Co-editor); Davidson's International Clinical Cases (Co-editor). Recreations: music; gardening; golf. Address: (h.) Sandy Lodge, Nisbet Road, Gullane EH31 2BQ; T.-01620-842-220.

Hunter, Kirk John, MA (Hons), ACIS. Chief Executive, Scottish Association of Master Bakers, since 2001; Scotland Director, Dairy UK, since 2005; b. 1.12.54, Glasgow; m., June Wilson. Educ. George Heriots School; Dundee University. Graduate Trainee, SSEB, 1977-79; Trade Association Executive, Thomson McLintock, Glasgow, 1980-83; Commercial Officer, Metal Trades Confederation, London and Glasgow, 1983-86; Peat Marwick McLintock, Glasgow, 1986-89. Recreations: sailing; cycling. Address: (h.) 18 Ravelston Road, Bearsden, Glasgow G61 1AW; T.-0141-942 3799.

Hunter, Sir Laurence Colvin, Kt, MA, DPhil, FRSE, DUniv (Paisley). Professor of Applied Economics, Glasgow University, 1970-2003, Emeritus Professor, since 2003; b. 8.8.34, Glasgow; m., Evelyn Margaret Green; 3 s.; 1 d. Educ. Hillhead High School, Glasgow; Glasgow University; University College, Oxford. Assistant Lecturer, Manchester University, 1958-59; 2nd Lt., RAEC, 1959-61; Walgreen Postdoctoral Fellow, University of Chicago, 1961-62; joined Glasgow University as Lecturer, 1962; Vice-Principal, 1982-86; Director: External Relations, 1987-90, Business School 1996-99. Council Member, ACAS, 1974-86; Chairman, Police Negotiating Board, 1986-2000; Council Member, Economic and Social Research Council, 1989-92; Editor, Scottish Journal of Political Economy, 1966-97; President, Scottish Economic Society, 1993-96; Treasurer, Royal Society of Edinburgh, 1999-2004. Recreations; golf; painting; curling. Address: (h.) 7 Boclair Crescent, Bearsden, Glasgow G61 2AG; T.-0141-563 7135.

Hunter, Mollie. Writer; b. 30.6.22, Longniddry; m., Thomas McIlwraith; 2 s. Educ. Preston Lodge School. Freelance Journalist, until 1960; Past Chairman, Society of Authors in Scotland; writer of various types of fiction (fantasy, historical novels, "realism") for children of varying age groups; 30 titles published, including Talent Is Not Enough, on the craft of writing for children; travelled extensively (Australia, New Zealand, Canada, USA); Lecturer on writing for children; Writer-in-Residence, Dalhousie University, Halifax, Canada, on two occasions; awarded Arbuthnot Lectureship, 1975, and Carnegie Medal,

1975; Phoenix Award, 1992. Recreations: reading; gardening; music. Address: Rose Cottage, 7 Mary Ann Court, Inverness IV3 5BZ; T.-01463 713914.

Hunter, Peter Matheson, BSc, MPhil, LLB. Legal Officer, UNISON Scotland; Member, Equal Opportunities Commission Equal Pay Advisory Panel, 2000-03; Lay Member, Employment Appeal Tribunal, since 2000; Member, Scottish Consumer Council, 2003-06; b. 11.12.65, Aberdeen. Educ. Cults Academy; Edinburgh University; Glasgow University; Strathclyde University. Hotel worker and shop steward, 1987-90; Edinburgh Employment Rights Campaign, 1990-91; Citizens' Rights Office, 1989-92; joined Scottish Low Pay Unit, 1992, Director, 1999-2001. Lay Member, Employment Tribunal, 1995-2000; founder Member and Parliamentary Candidate for Cairdeas, The Highland and Islands Alliance. Recreation: Aberdeen FC. Address: (b.) 14 West Campbell Street, Glasgow G2 6RX; T.-0870 7777 006.

Hunter, R. Douglas, LLB (Hons). Partner, Real Estate/Commercial Property, Dundas & Wilson CS LLP, since 1998; b. 8.5.65, Glasgow; m., Lesley; 2 s. Educ. Kelvinside Academy, Glasgow; University of Glasgow. Joined Dundas & Wilson CS as Trainee, 1988. Member, British Council of Offices; British Property Federation; Scottish Property Federation; Founder Member, The Property Standardisation Group. Recreations: golf; rugby (watching); hill walking. Address: (b.) Saltire Court, 20 Castle Terrace, Edinburgh EH1 2EN; T.-0131-200 7437; e-mail: douglas.hunter@dundas-wilson.com

Hunter, Richard J. A., BA, CA. Group Finance Director, The Edrington Group Ltd., since 1994; Finance Director, Robertson and Baxter, since 1985; b. 11.5.55, Glasgow; m., Christine; 1 s.; 2d. Educ. Kelvinside Academy; Glenalmond College; Strathclyde University. Qualified CA, Arthur Young McClelland Moores, 1978; joined Edrington Group, 1981. Member, Council, CBI Scotland; Member, Group of Scottish Finance Directors. Recreations: sailing; fishing; golf. Address: (b.) 2500 Great Western Road, Glasgow G15 6RW.

Hunter, Sir Thomas Blane, Kt (2005), BA. Entrepreneur; Chairman: West Coast Capital, since 1998, Hunter Foundation, since 1998; Chief Executive Officer, Sports Division, 1984-98. b. 6.5.61, Irvine; m., Marion McKillop; 2 s.; 1 d. Educ. Cumnock Academy; University of Strathclyde. Address: Marathon House, Olympic Business Park, Drybridge Road, Dundonald KA2 9AE; T.-01563 852226.

Hunter, William Hill, CBE, CA, JP, DL. Partner, McLay, McAlister & McGibbon, CA, 1946-91, Consultant, since 1991; Director, J. & G. Grant, Glenfarclas Distillery, 1966-92; b. 5.11.16, Cumnock; m., Kathleen Cole; 2 s. (1 s. deceased). Educ. Cumnock Academy. Enlisted as private, RASC, 1940; commissioned Royal Artillery, 1941, Staff Captain, Middle East, 1944-46; Director: Abbey National Building Society (Scottish Advisory Board), 1966-86, City of Glasgow Friendly Society, 1966-88 (President, 1980-88); Member: CBI Scottish Council, 1978-84, Institute of Directors West of Scotland Committee, 1980-91; President: Renfrew West and Inverclyde Conservative and Unionist Association, 1972-99, Scottish Young Unionist Association, 1958-60, Scottish Unionist Association, 1964-65; contested (Unionist), South Ayrshire, 1959 and 1964; Hon. Treasurer, Quarrier's Homes, 1972-94 (Chairman, 1991-94); Member, Council of Management, Erskine Hospital, since 1998 (Hon. Financial Advisor, 1981-98); Session Clerk,

Kilmacolm Old Kirk, 1972-77; Chairman: Salvation Army Advisory Board in Strathclyde, 1982-93, Salvation Army Housing Association Scotland Ltd., 1986-91; admitted to Distinguished Order of Auxiliary Service of Salvation Army, 1981; Deacon Convener, Trades House of Glasgow, 1986-87; Honorary Vice President, Royal Scottish Agricultural Benevolent Institution, since 1994; Honorary President, Friends of Glasgow Botanic Gardens, 1994-2004. Recreations: gardening; golf; swimming; music. Address: (h.) Armitage, Kilmacolm PA13 4PH; T.-0150587 2444.

Huntingtower, Lord (John Peter Grant of Rothiemurchus), DL. Landowner; b. 22.10.46, Rothiemurchus; m., Philippa; 1 s.; 2 d. Educ. Gordonstoun. Chairman and Director, Scot Trout Limited, 1989-95; Past Chairman, Highland Region, Forestry, Farming and Wildlife Advisory Group; Patron, Highland Hospice; Vice-President, Scottish Landowners' Federation, 1991-2004; Deputy Lieutenant, Districts of Lochaber, Inverness, Badenoch and Strathspey, 1986-2001; Member: Council, National Trust for Scotland, 1990-95, Native Woodlands Advisory Panel to the Forestry Commission, 1993-97, National Access Forum, 1993-99, Cairngorm Partnership, 1995-2003; Chairman, Tourism and Enivronment Task Force, 1995-98; President, Royal Zoological Society of Scotland, 1996-2006. Recreations: skiing; shooting. Address: (b.) Doune of Rothiemurchus, by Aviemore, Inverness-shire PH22 1QP; T.-01479 810647; e-mail: rothie@enterprise.net

Huntly, Marquess of (Granville Charles Gomer). Chief, House of Gordon, since 1988; b. 4.2.44, Aberdeen; m., 1, Jane Gibb; m., 2, Catheryn Kindersley; 1 s.; 3 d. Educ. Gordonstoun School; Institute of Commercial Management. Chairman: Hintlesham Holdings Ltd., Cock O' The North Liqueur Co. Ltd.; Director, Ampton Investments Ltd.; Chairman, Leadx.com; President, Institute of Financial Accountants, 1989-2000; Chief, Aboyne Highland Games. Recreations: country sports. Address: Aboyne Castle, Aberdeenshire AB34 5JP; T.-01339 887 778.

Hurford, Professor James Raymond, BA, PhD. Professor of General Linguistics, Edinburgh University, since 1979; b. 16.7.41, Reading; m., Sue Ann Davis; 2 d. Educ. Exeter School; St. John's College, Cambridge; University College, London. Assistant Professor, Department of English, University of California, Davis, 1968-71; Lecturer, then Senior Lecturer, Department of Linguistics, Lancaster University, 1972-79. Publications: Language and Number: the emergence of a cognitive system; Semantics: a coursebook (Co-author); The Linguistic Theory of Numerals; Grammar: a student's guide; The Origins of Meaning. Address: (b.) Edinburgh University, Edinburgh EH8 9YL.

Hurtado, Professor Larry Weir, BA, MA, PhD. Professor of New Testament Language, Literature and Theology, School of Divinity, Edinburgh University, since 1996; b. 29.12.43, Kansas City; m., Shannon Hunter; 1 s.; 2 d. Educ. Case Western Reserve University. Pastor, North Shore Assembly of God, Illinois, 1971-75; Assistant Professor of New Testament, Regent College, Vancouver BC, 1975-78; Professor of Religion, University of Manitoba, Winnipeg, 1978-96. Address: (b.) New College, Mound Place, Edinburgh EH1 2LX; T.-0131-650 8920.

Hutcheon, William Robbie. Editor, Courier and Advertiser, Dundee, since 2002; b. 19.1.52, Aberdeen; m., Margo; 1 s.; 2 d. Educ. Aberdeen Academy. Reporter (D.C. Thomson Office in Aberdeen), 1969-70; Sports Sub-Editor, Sports Editor, Chief Sub-Editor, Night News Editor, Deputy Editor, Editor, since 1970, with Courier and Advertiser. Chairman, Editors' Committee, Scottish Daily Newspaper Society. Recreations: sport; travel; music; computing. Address: (h.) 42 Ferndale Drive, Broughty Ferry, Dundee DD5 3DF; T.-01382 774552; e-mail: Billhutcheon@aol.com

Hutcheson, Rev. Norman McKenzie, MA, BD, BA. Minister, Dalbeattie and Urr Parish Churches; Vice Convenor, ACTS, since 2007; b. 11.10.48, Leven; m., Elizabeth; 2 d. Educ. Hillhead High School, Glasgow; Glasgow University; Edinburgh University; Open University. Minister, St. Andrews, Kirkcaldy, 1973-88. Recreations: photography; travel; reading. Address: (h.) 36 Mill Street, Dalbeattie DG5 4HE; T.-01556 610029; e-mail: norman.hutcheson@virgin.net

Hutchinson, Peter, PhD, FIFM. Assistant Secretary, North Atlantic Salmon Conservation Organization, since 1986 (Chairman, Scientific Committee, since 1992); b. 26.5.56, Glasgow; m., Jane MacKellaig; 1 s.; 1 d. Educ. Queen Elizabeth's Grammar School, Blackburn; Edinburgh University. Project Co-ordinator, Surface Water Acidification; Research Biologist: Institute of Terrestrial Ecology, Edinburgh University; Member, Consular Corps in Edinburgh and Leith, since 1991. Recreations: golf; squash; rugby union; angling. Address: (h.) 3 St. Ronan's Terrace, Morningside, Edinburgh.

Hutchison, David, MA, MLitt. Research Fellow in Media Policy, Glasgow Caledonian University; Acting Director, Scottish Centre of Journalism Studies, 2003-04; Visiting Professor, Brock University, Canada, 2004; b. 24.9.44, West Kilbride; m., Pauleen Frew; 2 d. Educ. Ardrossan Academy; Glasgow University. Tutor/Organiser, WEA (West of Scotland), 1966-69; Teacher, Reid Kerr College, Paisley, 1969-71; Lecturer in Communication Studies, Glasgow College of Technology (now Glasgow Caledonian University), 1971-75, Senior Lecturer, 1975-2004; Member, West Kilbride District Council, 1970-75 (Chairman, 1972-75); Governor, Scottish Film Council, 1987-95; Member, General Advisory Council, BBC, 1988-96; author of play, Deadline, Pitlochry Festival Theatre, 1980. Publications: The Modern Scottish Theatre, 1977; Headlines (Editor), 1978; Media Policy, 1998; The Media in Scotland (Co-Editor), 2008; various articles/chapters. Recreations: walking; sitting in cafés dreaming; the arts; golf. Address: (b.) Caledonian University, Cowcaddens Road, Glasgow G4 OBA; T.-0141-331 8852; e-mail: dhu@gcal.ac.uk

Hutchison, Professor James Douglas, MBChB, PhD, FRCS(Edin), FRCSE, FRCS(Glas). Regius Professor of Surgery, University of Aberdeen, since 2000; Sir Harry Platt Professor of Orthopaedics, University of Aberdeen, since 1995; b. 8.10.55, Dundee; m., Kate Douglas; 2 s.; 1 d. Educ. High School of Dundee; University of Dundee. Lecturer in Orthopaedics, Edinburgh and Aberdeen, 1986-91; Senior Lecturer, Aberdeen, 1991-95; Honorary Consultant Orthopaedic Surgeon, Aberdeen, since 1991. Past Chairman, Scottish Committee for Orthopaedics and Trauma; Specialty Advisor in Orthopaedics to CMO and SEHD. Recreations:family; dogs; shooting; golf; art. Address: (b.) Department of Surgery, Medical School, Polwarth Building, Foresterhill, Aberdeen AB25 2ZD; T.-01224 553004; e-mail: j.d.hutchison@abdn.ac.uk

Hutchison, John Charles, JP, BSc (Hons), CEng, FICE, FIHT, FIES. Lochaber Area Manager, The Highland Council, 1995-2007; b. 23.7.47, Edinburgh; m., Christine Laidlaw; 1 s.; 2 d. Educ. Leith Academy; Heriot-Watt

University. Student Apprentice, Redpath Brown and Co., Edinburgh, 1965-69; Graduate Engineer, Redpath Dorman Long, Bedford, 1969-71; Inverness County Council, Skye: Assistant Engineer, 1971-72, Senior Resident Engineer, 1972-75; Highland Regional Council, Lochaber: Sub-Divisional Engineer, 1975-78, Divisional Engineer, 1978-96. Honorary Sheriff and Justice of the Peace; Chair, Isle of Eigg Heritage Trust; Vice Convener, Mòd Lochabair, 2007. Recreations: singing; walking; reading; Scottish culture; community development; Gaelic; Europe; land. Address: (b.) Taigh na Coille, Badabrie, Fort William PH33 7LX; T.-01397 772252.

Hutchison, Sir Peter Craft, Bt, CBE, FRSE. Board Member, Loch Lomond and the Trossachs National Park Authority, since 2002; formerly Chairman, Hutchison & Craft Ltd., Insurance Brokers; b. 5.6.35, London; m., Virginia Colville; 1 s. Educ. Eton; Magdalene College, Cambridge. National Service, Royal Scots Greys (2nd Lt.); Northern Assurance Co. (London); Director of various companies; Past Chairman, Ailsa Shipbuilding Co. Ltd.; Director, Stakis plc, 1979-91; Board Member, Scottish Tourist Board, 1981-87; Vice Chairman, British Waterways Board, 1988-97; Chairman, Board of Trustees, Royal Botanic Garden, Edinburgh, 1985-94; Chairman, Loch Lomond and Trossachs Working Party, 1991-93, Chairman, Forestry Commission, 1994-2001; Deacon, Incorporation of Hammermen of Glasgow, 1984-85. Recreations: plant hunting; gardening; calligraphy. Address: (h.) Broich, Kippen, Stirlingshire FK8 3EN; T.-01786 870317.

Hutton, Alan, BCom, MA. Senior Lecturer in Economics, Glasgow Caledonian University, since 1976; Member, Scottish Consumer Council, since 2003; b. 26.8.45, Sunderland; m., Alma; 2 s. Educ. Easingwold School; Universities of Leeds and Strathclyde. Lecturer in Economics, Glasgow College of Technology, 1971-76; Fellow, Salzburg Seminar in American Studies, 1976; Visiting Scholar, Department of Applied Economics, University of Cambridge, 1983; Senior Research Fellow, Stirling Centre for Economic Methodology, University of Stirling, since 2006. Member: Energywatch Scottish Committee, 2002-08, Advisory Group of The National Consumer Council, since 2003, Scottish Consumer Council, since 2003. Recreations: cycling; walking; history; music and other arts (as consumer). Address: (b.) Division of Public Policy, CBS, Glasgow Caledonian University, Cowcaddens Road, Glasgow G4 0BA; T.-0141 331 3313; e-mail: a.hutton@gcal.ac.uk

Hutton, Alasdair Henry, OBE, TD. Writer and Narrator, Edinburgh Military Tattoo and other public events, videos and audio guides; Convener, Scottish Borders Council (Councillor, Kelso Central, since 2002); Scottish Trustee and Scottish Chairman, Community Service Volunteers; Chairman, Disease Prevention Organisation; 2006 Honorary Colonel, Lothian and Borders Battalion ACF; b. 19.5.40, London; m. Educ. Dollar Academy; Brisbane State High School. Journalist, The Age, Melbourne, 1959-61; Aberdeen Journals, 1962-64; Broadcaster, BBC, 1964-79; Member, European Parliament, 1979-89. Member, Queen's Bodyguard for Scotland (Royal Company of Archers); Former 2ic, 15th (Scottish Volunteer) Bn., The Parachute Regiment; President, Kelso Branch, Royal British Legion; Elder, Kelso North Church of Scotland; Patron ROKPA; Vice President, John Buchan Society; Life Member, Edinburgh Sir Walter Scott Club; Fellow, Industry and Parliament Trust; Patron, Kelso Laddies' Association; River Tweed Commissioner, since 2004; Reader, Borders Talking Newspaper, since 1997. Address: 4 Broomlands Court, Kelso TD5 7SR; T.-01573 224369; e-mail: AlasdairHutton@yahoo.co.uk

Hutton, Graeme, BSc (Hons), DipArch. Dean of Architecture, University of Dundee, since 2002; Practising Architect, since 1990; b. 2.6.64, Shrewsbury;

m., Julie; 1 s.; 2 d. Educ. Carnoustie High School; Robert Gordon University. Assistant Architect, RMJM Scotland Ltd., 1990-92; Partner, Hutton Rattray Architects, 1992-96; Part-Time Tutor, Robert Gordon University, 1992-96; Design Architect, RMJM Scotland Ltd., 1996-99; University of Dundee, since 1999; Design Consultant, LJRH Architects Dundee, since 2000. RIAS Education Committee; RIAS Research and Development Committee. Recreations: photography; painting; music. Address: (h.) 50 Forfar Road, Dundee DD4 7BA; T.-01382 520316; e-mail: the.huttons@blueyonder.co.uk

Hutton, Professor Neil, MA, PhD. Dean, Faculty of Law, Arts and Social Sciences, University of Strathclyde, since 2005, Professor of Criminal Justice, since 2001; b. 20.12.53, Dundee; m., Michele Burman; 2 d. Educ. High School of Dundee; Edinburgh University. Research Fellow: University of Dundee, 1981-83, University of Edinburgh, 1984-87, Victoria University of Wellington, NZ, 1987-90; joined University of Strathclyde in 1990 as Lecturer, then became Senior Lecturer. Member: Sentencing Commission for Scotland, 2003-06, National Advisory Body on Offender Management, since 2006. Recreations: cooking; golf. Address: (b.) McCance Building, Richmond Street, Glasgow G1 1XQ; T.-0141-548-3878; e-mail: n.hutton@strath.ac.uk

Hutton, William Riddell, BDS. Dentist, since 1961; Honorary Sheriff, since 1996; b. 22.10.38, Glasgow; m., Patricia Margaret Burns; 1 s.; 1 d. Educ. Hamilton Academy; Glasgow University Dental School. International Grenfell Association, Newfoundland and Labrador, 1961-64; General Practice, Lanark, 1967-2001; Member, Secretary and Chairman, Lanarkshire Local Dental Committee, 1964-94; Member and Chairman, Lanarkshire Area Dental Committee, 1975-94. Recreations: music; golf; hillwalking; travel. Address: (h.) St. Anthony, 9 Braedale Road, Lanark ML11 7AW; T.-01555 662927; e-mail: william.hutton@homecall.co.uk

Huxham, Professor Chris, DPhil, MSc, BSc. Head of Department and Professor of Management, Department of Management, University of Strathclyde Business School, since 1997; Senior Fellow, Advanced Institute of Management Research, since 2003; b. 18.3.54, Felixstowe. Educ. South Wilts Grammar School; Sussex University. Lecturer, University of Aston Management Centre, 1979-84; Lecturer/Senior Lecturer in Management Science, University of Strathclyde, 1984-97. Member, Scottish Executive Task Force on Community Planning, 2001-03; Academy of Management Awards (USA), 1997, 2001, 2005. Publications: Managing to Collaborate, 2005; Creating Collaborative Advantage (Editor), 1996. Address: (b.) University of Strathclyde Business School, Department of Management, 199 Cathedral Street, Glasgow G4 0QU; T.-0141-553 6113; e-mail: chris@gsb.strath.ac.uk

Hyslop, A. Graeme, BA (Hons), MSc, TQ(FE), FRSA. Principal, Langside College, Glasgow, since 1999; b. 23.3.53, Glasgow; m., Aileen; 1 d. Educ. High School of Glasgow; Glasgow Caledonian University; Glasgow University; Strathclyde University. Car Park Attendant, 1979-80; College Lecturer, 1980-88; Further Education Officer, Strathclyde Regional Council, 1988-91; Depute Principal, Langside College, Glasgow, 1991-98. Board Member: Association of Scotland's Colleges Board, Glasgow South East Regeneration Agency, Castlemilk Economic Development Agency, Continuing Education Gateway; Chair, West of Scotland Colleges Partnership. Recreations: sport (football, squash, golf); reading; cinema. Address: (b.) 50 Prospecthill Road, Glasgow G42 9LB; T.-0141-272 3620.

Hyslop, Fiona J., MA (Hons). MSP (SNP), Lothians, since 1999; Cabinet Secretary for Education and Lifelong Learning, since 2007; b. 1.8.64, Irvine; m.; 1 s.; 1 d. Educ. Ayr Academy; Glasgow University. Standard Life, 1986-99, various sales and marketing positions, latterly Marketing Manager. Recreations: swimming; cinema. Address: (b.) Scottish Parliament, Edinburgh EH99 1SP; T.-0131-348 5000.

I

Ibbotson, Sally Helen, BSc (Hons), MD, MBChB (Hons), FRCP (Edin), Clinical Senior Lecturer in Photobiology, Honorary Consultant Dermatologist, University of Dundee, Ninewells Hospital and Medical School, since 1998; b. 18.2.62, Newcastle upon Tyne. Educ. Central Newcastle High School for Girls; University of Leeds. House Physician and House Surgeon, Leeds General Infirmary and St. James' University Hospital, 1986-87; Teaching Fellow in Medicine, Leeds General Infirmary, 1987-89; Research Fellow, University of Leeds, 1989-92; Royal Victoria Infirmary, Newcastle upon Tyne: Registrar in Dermatology, 1992-94, Senior Registrar in Dermatology, 1994-98; Research Fellow, Harvard University, Boston, USA, 1996-97. Address: (b.) Photobiology Unit, Dermatology Department, University of Dundee, Ninewells Hospital and Medical School, Dundee DD1 9SY; T.-01382 425717; e-mail: s.h.ibbotson@dundee.ac.uk

Illius, Professor Andrew Warwick, BSc (Hons), PhD, FRSE. Professor of Animal Ecology, since 2001; Head, School of Biological Sciences, since 2003; b. 3.8.50, Durban; m., Dinah Dawson; 2 s. Educ. St Edward's, Oxford; Edinburgh University; Nottingham University. Lecturer in Animal Physiology, Nottingham University, 1975; Visiting Researcher, Mammal Research Institute, University of Pretoria, 1976; Lecturer in Agriculture, Barony College, 1977; Lecturer in Animal Production, East of Scotland College of Agriculture, 1978; Lecturer in Animal Production, Edinburgh University, 1979; Reader in Animal Ecology, 1998. Honorary Research Fellow, Macaulay Institute. Recreations: horses, hounds and gardens. Address: (b.) School of Biological Sciences, Edinburgh University, Edinburgh EH9 3JT; T.-0131 650 5525; e-mail: a.illius@ed.ac.uk

Ingle, Professor Stephen James, BA, MA (Econ), DipEd, PhD. Emeritus Professor of Politics, Stirling University; b. 6.11.40, Ripon; m., Margaret Anne; 2 s.; 1 d. Educ. The Roan School, London; Sheffield University; Wellington University, NZ. Commonwealth Scholar, 1964-67; Lecturer in Politics, Hull University, 1967-80; Senior Lecturer, 1980-91; Head of Department, 1985-90. Secretary, Political Studies Association, 1988-89; Member, East Yorkshire Health Authority, 1985-90; Visiting Research Fellow, Victoria University of Wellington, 1993; Academic Fellow of the Open Society Institute, 2006. Publications: Socialist Thought in Imaginative Literature, 1979; Parliament and Health Policy, 1981; British Party System, 1987, 1989, 1999; George Orwell: a political life, 1993; Narratives of British Socialism, 2002; The Social and Political Thought of George Orwell: A Reappraisal, 2006. Recreations: reading; music; hill-walking. Address: (b.) Department of Politics, Stirling University, Stirling FK9 4LA; T.-01786 467568.

Inglis, Professor David, MA, PhD, ACSS. Professor of Sociology, University of Aberdeen, since 2006; b. 04.03.73, Bellshill. Educ. Eastbank Academy, Glasgow; University of Cambridge; University of York. Senior Lecturer in Sociology, University of Aberdeen, 2003-06. Academician of Learned Societies in the Social Sciences (ACSS). Recreations: fine and antique wines; poetry; classical music. Address: (b.) School of Social Sciences, University of Aberdeen, Aberdeen AB24 3QY; T.-01224 272760; e-mail: d.inglis@abdn.ac.uk

Inglis, Professor Emeritus James Alistair Macfarlane, CBE (1984), MA, LLB. Emeritus Professor, Glasgow University; Professor of Conveyancing, Glasgow University, 1979-93; Professor of Professional Legal Practice, Glasgow University, 1984-93; Partner, McClure,

Naismith, Solicitors, Glasgow, 1956-93; Honorary Member, Court of Patrons, Royal College of Physicians and Surgeons of Glasgow, since 1995; b. 24.12.28, Kilmarnock; m., Mary Elizabeth Howie (deceased); 2 s.; 3 d. Educ. Kilmarnock Academy; Fettes College; St. Andrews University; Glasgow University. Qualified as Solicitor, 1952; Member: Board of Management, Victoria and Leverndale Hospitals, 1964-74, Greater Glasgow Health Board, 1975-83; President, Rent Assessment Panel for Scotland, 1976-87; Chairman, Glasgow Hospitals Auxiliary Association, 1985-2001; Dean, Royal Faculty of Procurators in Glasgow, 1989-92; Convener, Ad Hoc Committee, Church of Scotland, into Legal Services of Church, 1978-79; Session Clerk, Caldwell Parish Church, since 1963; General Trustee, Church of Scotland, 1994-2004. Address: (h.) Crioch, Uplawmoor, Glasgow; T.-01505 850315.

Inglis, John, PRSW, FSA Scot, DA. Painter and Lecturer; b. 27.7.53, Glasgow; m., Heather; 2 s.; 2 d. Educ. Hillhead High School; Gray's School of Art. Travelling scholarships to Italy, 1976; Member, Dundee Group, 1979-84; one-man exhibitions: Aberdeen, 1976 and 1977; Glasgow, 1980; Skipton, 1981; Aberdeen Hospitals, 1989; Alloa Museum, 1989; Smith Art Gallery, Stirling, 1993; Illinois, USA, 1997. Scottish Arts Council Award, 1981; RSA Keith Prize, 1975; SAC Bursary, 1982; RSA Meyer Oppenheim Prize, 1982; RSW EIS Award, 1987; SAC Grant, 1988; May Marshall Brown Award, 1994, 2000; Paisley Art Institute Bessie Scott Award, 2007. Address: (h.) 84 Burnhead Road, Larbert.

Ingold, Professor Timothy, PhD, FBA, FRSE. Professor of Social Anthropology, University of Aberdeen, since 1999; b. 1.11.48, Sevenoaks; m., Anna Kaarina; 3 s.; 1 d. Educ. Leighton Park School; Churchill College, Cambridge University. University of Manchester: Lecturer, Department of Social Anthropology, 1974-85, Senior Lecturer, 1985-90, Professor, 1990-95, Max Gluckman Professor of Social Anthropology, 1995-99; Visiting Professor: University of Helsinki, 1986, University of Tromsø, 1996-2000. Royal Anthropological Institute Rivers Memorial Medal, 1989; Award of Jean-Marie Delwart Foundation, Belgian Academy of Sciences, 1994; Retzius Medal, Swedish Society for Anthropology and Geography, 2000. Publications: The Skolt Lapps Today, 1976; Hunters, Pastoralists and Ranchers, 1980; Evolution and Social Life, 1986; What Is An Animal? (Editor), 1988; Tools, Language and Cognition in Human Evolution (Co-Editor), 1993; Companion Encyclopedia of Anthropology: humanity, culture and social life (Editor), 1994; Key Debates in Anthropology (Editor), 1988-93, 1996; The Perception of the Environment, 2000; Creativity and Cultural Improvisation (Co-Editor), 2007; Lives: a brief history, 2007. Recreation: music. Address: (b.) Department of Anthropology, University of Aberdeen, Aberdeen AB24 3QY; T.-01224 274350; e-mail: tim.ingold@abdn.ac.uk

Ingram, Rt. Hon. Adam. MP (Labour), East Kilbride, since 1987; Minister of State for the Armed Forces, 2001-07; b. 1.2.47, Glasgow; m., Maureen McMahon. Educ. Cranhill Senior Secondary School. Programmer/analyst, 1965-1970; systems analyst, 1970-77; trade union official, 1977-87; Councillor, East Kilbride District Council, 1980-87 (Leader of the Council, 1984-87); PPS to Neil Kinnock, Leader of the Opposition, 1988-92; Labour Opposition Spokesperson on Social Security, 1993-95, Science and Technology, 1995-97; Minister of State for Northern Ireland, 1997-2001; JP. Recreations: fishing; cooking; reading. Address: (b.) House of Commons, London SW1A 0AA; T.-020 7219 4093.

Ingram, Professor Emeritus Adam Hamilton, BA (Hons). MSP (SNP), South of Scotland, since 1999; Minister for Children and Early Years, since 2007; b. 1.5.51, Kilmarnock; m., Gerry; 3 s.; 1 d. Educ. Kilmarnock Academy; Paisley College. Manager, A.H. Ingram & Son, Bakers, 1971-

76; Senior Economic Assistant, Manpower Services Commission, 1985-86; Researcher and Lecturer, Paisley College, 1987-88; economic development consultant, 1989-99. Recreation: golf. Address: (b.) Scottish Parliament, Edinburgh EH99 1SP; T.-0131-348 5720.

Ingram, Professor David Stanley, OBE, VMH, BSc, PhD, MA, ScD, HonDUniv (Open), FLS, FIBiol, FIHort, FRSGS (Hon), FRCPEd, FRSE. Honorary Professor and Adviser on Public Engagement with Science, University of Edinburgh, since 1991; Honorary Professor in Botany, Glasgow University, since 1991; Programme Convenor and Chair, Science and Society Steering Group, Royal Society of Edinburgh, since 2005; Senior Visiting Fellow, ESRC Genomics Forum, University of Edinburgh, since 2006; Independent Member and Deputy Chairman, Joint Nature Conservation Committee, 2001-08; Master, St. Catherine's College, Cambridge, 2000-06; Fellow: Institute of Biology, Institute of Horticulture and Royal College of Physicians, Edinburgh; Honorary Fellow: Royal Botanic Garden, Edinburgh, since 1998, Royal Scottish Geographical Society, since 1998, Downing College, Cambridge, since 2001, Myerscough College, since 2001, Worcester College, Oxford, since 2003, St. Catherine's College, Cambridge, since 2006; b. 10.10.41, Birmingham; m., Alison; 2 s. Educ. Yardley Grammar School, Birmingham; Hull University; Cambridge University. Research Fellow, Glasgow University, 1966-68, Cambridge University, 1968-69; Senior Scientific Officer, Unit of Development Botany, Cambridge, 1969-74; Lecturer, then Reader in Plant Pathology, Botany Department, Cambridge University, 1974-90; Fellow (also Tutor, Dean and Director of Studies in Biology), Downing College, Cambridge, 1974-90; Regius Keeper (Director), Royal Botanic Garden, Edinburgh, 1990-98; Honorary Professor of Horticulture, Royal Horticultural Society, 1995-2000; President, International Congress of Plant Pathology, 1998; President, British Society for Plant Pathology, 1998; Chairman, Advisory Committee to the Darwin Initiative for the Survival of the Species, 1999-2005; Awarded Victoria Medal of Honour, Royal Horticultural Society, 2004; Member, Board, Scottish Natural Heritage, 1999-2000; author of several books and many papers in learned journals on botany, plant pathology, horticulture and conservation. Recreations: gardening; entertaining grandchildren; music; ceramics. Address: Royal Society of Edinburgh, 22-26 George Street, Edinburgh EH2 2PQ.

Ingram, Greig Webster, MA. Rector, High School of Stirling, since 1994; b. 20.11.47, Burnhervie; m., Patricia Annette Miller. Educ. Mackie Academy, Stonehaven; Aberdeen University; Aberdeen College of Education. Teacher of Modern Studies and History, 1970-74; Principal Teacher of Modern Studies, St. Margaret Mary's Secondary, Glasgow, 1974-84; Assistant Head Teacher, Eastbank Academy, Glasgow, 1984-89, Depute Head Teacher, 1989-94. Founding Fellow, Institute of Contemporary Scotland; Her Majesty's Commissioner, Queen Victoria School. Recreations: reading; music; travel; running; soccer. Address: (b.) Ogilvie Road, Stirling FK8 2PA; T.-01786 472451; e-mail: ingram06s@stirling.gov.uk

Ingram, Hugh Albert Pugh, BA (Cantab), PhD (Dunelm); b. 29.4.37, Rugby; m., Dr. Ruth Hunter; 1 s.; 1 d. Educ. Lawrence Sheriff School, Rugby; Rugby School; Emmanuel College, Cambridge; Hatfield College, Durham. Demonstrator in Botany, University College of North Wales, Bangor, 1963-64; Staff Tutor in Natural Science, Department of Extra-Mural Studies, Bristol University, 1964-65; Lecturer, then Senior Lecturer in Botany (Ecology), Dundee University, 1966-97; Editor, Journal of Applied Ecology, 1991-97; Member: Executive Committee, Scottish Field Studies Association, 1989-99, Museums and

Galleries Commission Working Party on the non-national museums of Scotland, 1984-86; Trustee, National Museums of Scotland, 1987-94; Chairman, Council, Scottish Wildlife Trust, 1996-99 (Vice-Chairman, Conservation and Science, 1982-87); Royal Society for Nature Conservation: Scottish Trustee, 2000-01, Trustee, 2003, Christopher Cadbury Medal, 2001. Publications: numerous scientific research papers on hydrological aspects of the ecology of peat bogs and other mires. Recreations: music (clarinet, piano); literature; rural history; hill-walking. Address: Johnstonfield, Dunbog, Cupar, Fife KY14 6JG; e-mail: h.a.p.ingram@dundee.ac.uk

Ingram, Professor Malcolm David, BSc, PhD, DSc, CChem, FRSC, FRSA. Emeritus Professor of Chemistry, Aberdeen University; b. 18.1.39, Wallasey; m., Lorna Hardman; 1 s.; 1 d. Educ. Oldershaw Grammar School; Liverpool University. Career at Aberdeen University. Chairman, Aberdeen and North of Scotland Section, Royal Society of Chemistry, 1990-93; Humboldt Research Award Winner, 2002; Editor, Physics and Chemistry of Glasses, 1998-2008. Publications: 200 in scientific journals. Recreations: gardening; foreign travel. Address: (b.) Department of Chemistry, Aberdeen University, Aberdeen AB24 2UE; T.-01224 272943.

Innes, Andrew, MBChB, MD, MRCP, FRCP(Glas), FRCP(Edin). Consultant Physician/Nephrologist, Crosshouse Hospital, Kilmarnock, since 1994; b. 29.7.56, Inverness; m., Nora; 1 s.; 2 d. Educ. Dingwall Academy; University of Aberdeen. Medical Registrar, Aberdeen teaching hospitals; Senior Medical Registrar, City Hospital, Nottingham; Clinical Research Fellow, Centre de Rein Artificiel, Tassin, France. Address: (b.) Crosshouse Hospital, Kilmarnock KA2 0BE; T.-01563 577358.

Innes, Emeritus Professor John, BCom, PhD, CA, FCMA. Professor of Accountancy, University of Dundee, 1991-01, now Professor Emeritus; b. 11.7.50, Edinburgh; m., Ina. Educ. George Watson's College; University of Edinburgh. Student Accountant and Staff Auditor, KPMG, 1972-75; International Operational Auditor, Uniroyal Inc., 1975-78; Lecturer and Senior Lecturer in Accounting, University of Edinburgh, 1978-91; Canon Foundation Visiting Research Fellow, 1992-93; Visiting Professor, University of Nantes, 1997-99. Publication: various books including Handbook of Management Accounting, 2004. Recreation: tennis. Address: School of Accounting and Finance, University of Dundee, Dundee DD1 4HN; T.-01382 344193; e-mail: j.innes@dundee.ac.uk

Innes of Edingight, Sir Malcolm Rognvald, KCVO, MA, LLB, WS, KStJ. Lord Lyon King of Arms and Secretary to Order of the Thistle, 1981-2001; b. 25.5.38, Edinburgh; m., Joan Hay; 3 s. Educ. Edinburgh Academy; Edinburgh University. Carrick Pursuivant, 1958; Marchmont Herald, 1971; Lyon Clerk and Keeper of the Record, 1966; Member, Queen's Bodyguard for Scotland (Royal Company of Archers). Recreation: shooting. Address: Castleton of Kinnairdy, Bridge of Marnoch, Huntly, Aberdeenshire AB54 7RT; T.-01466 780866.

Innes, Norman Lindsay, OBE, BSc, PhD, DSc, FRSE. Agricultural Research Consultant; b. 3.5.34, Kirriemuir; m., Marjory Niven Farquhar, MA; 1 s.; 1 d. Educ. Webster High School, Kirriemuir; Aberdeen University; Cambridge University. Senior Cotton Breeder: Sudan, 1958-66, Uganda, 1966-71; Head, Cotton Research Unit, Uganda, 1972; National Vegetable Research Station, Wellesbourne: Head, Plant Breeding Section, 1973-84, Deputy Director, 1977-84; Scottish Crop Research Institute: Deputy Director,

1986-94, Head, Plant Breeding Division, 1984-89; Honorary Lecturer, then Honorary Professor, Birmingham University, 1973-84; Governing Board Member, International Crops Research Institute for Semi-Arid Tropics, India, 1982-88; Honorary Professor, Dundee University, 1988-95; Honorary Research Professor, Scottish Crop Research Institute, since 1994; Governing Board Member, International Potato Centre, Peru, 1988-95, Chairman, 1991-95; Vice-President, Association of Applied Biologists, 1990-92, President, 1993-94; Governing Council Member, 1996-2001, Chairman, 1997-2000, International Centre of Insect Physiology and Ecology, Kenya; Member, Board of Trustees, West Africa Rice Development Association, Côte d' Ivoire, 1998-2004, Chairman, 2000-03; Member, Oxfam Council of Trustees, 1982-85. Recreations: photography; travel. Address: (b.) Scottish Crop Research Institute, Invergowrie, Dundee DD2 5DA; T.-01382 562731; e-mail: minnes1960@aol.com

Inverarity, James Alexander (Sandy), CBE, FRSA, FRAgS, CA. Farmer and Landowner; Chairman: Scottish Agricultural College, 1990-98, Scottish Agricultural Securities Corporation, plc, since 1987; President, Scottish Farm and Countryside Educational Trust, 1990-98; b. 17.9.35; m., Jean (deceased); 1 s.; 2 d. Educ. Loretto School. President, National Farmers Union of Scotland, 1970-71; Member: Eggs Authority, 1971-74, Farm Animal Welfare Council, 1978-88, Panel of Agricultural Arbiters, 1983-2007, Governing Body, Scottish Crop Research Institute, 1984-97, Dairy Produce Quota Tribunal for Scotland, 1984-85; Director, United Oilseed Producers Ltd., 1985-97 (Chairman, 1987-97). Recreations: shooting; curling. Address: Cransley, Fowlis, Dundee DD2 5NP; T.-01382 580327.

Ireland, Sheriff Ronald David, QC, HonLLD. Sheriff Principal, Grampian, Highland and Islands, 1988-93; b. 13.3.25, Edinburgh. Educ. George Watson's College, Edinburgh; Balliol College, Oxford (Scholar); Edinburgh University. Advocate, 1952; Clerk, Faculty of Advocates, 1957-58; Professor of Scots Law, Aberdeen University, 1958-71; QC, 1964; Dean, Faculty of Law, Aberdeen University, 1964-67; Chairman, Board of Management, Aberdeen General Hospitals, 1964-71; Sheriff, Lothian and Borders at Edinburgh, 1972-88; Director, Scottish Courts Administration, 1975-78. Address: (h.) 6A Greenhill Gardens, Edinburgh EH10 4BW.

Ireland, W. Seith S., LLB (Hons). Sheriff, Kilmarnock Sheriff Court, since 2003; b. 5.4.56, Glasgow; m., Elizabeth. Educ. The High School of Glasgow; University of Glasgow. President: Student Representative Council, University of Glasgow, 1977-78, Glasgow Bar Association, 1993-94; Member, Council of Law Society, 1995-98; Convener, Law Society Devolution Committee, 1997-98; Member, Business Committee, General Council of University of Glasgow, since 2005; Admitted Solicitor, 1982 - Assistant: Ross Harper and Murphy, 1982-85, Jim Friel & Co, 1985-86; Principal, Ireland & Co Solicitors, Glasgow, 1986-2003. Recreations: golf; theatre; cooking. Address: (b.) Sheriffs' Chambers, Sheriff Court House, Kilmarnock, Ayrshire KA1 1BD; T.-01563 550024; e-mail: sheriff.wsireland@scotcourts.gov.uk

Irons, Norman MacFarlane, CBE, DL, DLitt, DUniv, Hon. FRCS Ed, CEng, MIMechE, MCIBSE, JP. Lord Provost and Lord Lieutenant of the City of Edinburgh, 1992-96; Partner, Building Services Consulting Engineers, since 1993; Royal Danish Consul, Edinburgh and Leith, since 2000; b. 4.1.41, Glasgow; m., Anne Buckley; 1 s.; 1 d. Held various posts as Consulting Engineer; founded own practice, 1983. SNP Member, City of Edinburgh District Council, 1976-96; President, Edinburgh Leith and District Battalion, Boys' Brigade, 1998-2003. Recreation: rugby football. Address: (h.) 141 Saughtonhall Drive, Edinburgh EH12 5TS; T.-0131-337 6154.
E-mail: n.irons@ironsfoulner.co.uk

Ironside, Leonard, CBE, JP, FR3A. Member, Aberdeen City Council, since 1995 (Council Leader, 1999-2003; Convener, Social Work Committee); Chairman, Horizon Rehabilitation Centre, 1997-2004; former Director, Grampian Food Resource Centre Ltd; North of Scotland Area Manager, Parkinsons Disease Society, since 2003; Patron, Grampian Special Olympics for Handicapped; Commonwealth Professional Wrestling Champion, since 1981; Athletics Coach, Bon Accord (Special Needs); Member, Board, Robert Gordon University; Feature Writer - Freelance, Aberdeen Independent Newspapers; Member, Board, NHS Grampian, 2001-03; b. Aberdeen; m., Wendy; 2 d. Educ. Hilton Academy, Aberdeen. Member, Grampian Regional Council, 1982-96; Inspector, contributions agency, DHSS, since 1990; formerly Chairman and Founder Member, Grampian Initiative; won Commonwealth Professional Wrestling Championship at Middleweight, 1979; lost Championship, 1981; regained title, 1981; gained European Lightweight title, 1985, relinquished title, 1989; Grampian Ambassador for services to industry, 1996; awarded Scottish Sports Council Rosebowl for services to disabled sports; former Director: Grampian Enterprise Ltd., Scottish Sub-Sea Technology Group; former Chair, Aberdeen International Youth Festival; Member: Grampian Racial Equality Commission, Aberdeen Sports Council; former Director, Voluntary Service, Aberdeen; Area Manager, Parkinson's Disease Society. Recreations: yoga teacher; also plays tennis, squash, badminton; cycling; after-dinner speaking. Address: (h.) 42 Hillside Terrace, Portlethen, Kincardineshire; T.-01224 780929; e-mail: ironside@ifb.co.uk

Irvine of Drum, (David Charles Irvine), ACIB. 26th Laird of Drum and Chief of the name Irvine of Drum, since 1992; b. 20.1.39, Birkenhead, Merseyside; m., Carolyn Colbeck; 2 s.; 1 d. Educ. Radley College. Hon. Treasurer, Standing Council of Scottish Chiefs. Recreations: family history; golf; gardening. Address: (h.) Holly Leaf Cottage, Inchmarlo, Banchory, Kincardineshire; T.-01330-823702; e-mail: drum26@btinternet.com

Irvine of Lairg, Baron (Alexander Andrew Mackay Irvine), PC. Lord High Chancellor of Great Britain, 1997-2003; b. 23.6.40; m. Alison Mary; 2 s. Educ. Inverness Academy; Hutchesons' Boys' Grammar School, Glasgow; Glasgow University; Christ's College, Cambridge. Called to the Bar, Inner Temple, 1967; Bencher, 1985; QC, 1978; a Recorder, 1985-88; Deputy High Court Judge, 1987-97; Lecturer, LSE, 1965-69; Contested (Labour), Hendon North, 1970; elevated to the Peerage, 1987; Opposition Spokesman on Legal and Home Affairs, 1987-92; Shadow Lord Chancellor, House of Lords, 1992-97; Joint President: Industry and Parliamentary Trust, since 1997, British American Parliamentary Group, since 1997, IPU, since 1997, CPA, since 1997; President, Magistrates' Association; Church Commissioner; Trustee: John Smith Memorial Trust, 1992-97, and since 2003, Whitechapel Art Gallery, since 1990, Hunterian Collection, since 1997; Member, Committee, Friends of the Slade, since 1990; Honorary Bencher, Inn of Court of NI, 1998; Fellow, US College of Trial Lawyers, 1998; Honorary Fellow, Society for Advanced Legal Studies, 1997; Honorary Member, Polish Bar, 2000; Commander's Cross, with a star of the Order of Merit of the Republic of Poland, 2004; Hon. LLD, Glasgow, 1997; Honorary Fellow, London School of Economics, 2001; Dr hc, Siena, 2000; Honorary Fellow, Christ's College, Cambridge, 1996; Visiting Professor,

University College London, 2004. Recreations: cinema; theatre; collecting paintings; travel. Address: House of Lords SW1A 0PW.

Irvine, Fiona, BA (BusEcon). HR Director, First ScotRail, since 2006; b. 24.9.69, Johnstone; m., Brian; 2 d. Educ. Paisley Grammar School; Paisley University. Training and Development Assistant, Keyline Business Merchants, 1989-92; Staff Manager, Sainsbury Homebase, 1992; HR Business Partner, Royal Bank of Scotland, 1993-2002; Senior Human Capital Consultant, PWC, 2002; Lloyds TSB: Head of HR, 2003-04, Head of Reward, 2004-05. HR Director of the Year, HR Network Scotland. Address: Atrium Court, 50 Waterloo Street, Glasgow G2 5SH; T.-07739 447369; e-mail: fiona.irvine@firstgroup.com

Irvine, Jane. Scottish Legal Services Ombudsman, since 2006. Member, Mediation Panel for Edinburgh Sheriff Court. Address: (b.) 17 Waterloo Place, Edinburgh EH1 3DL.

Irving, Gordon, MA (Hons). Writer, Journalist and Broadcaster; b. 4.12.18, Annan; m., Elizabeth Dickie (deceased). Educ. Dumfries Academy; Edinburgh University. Staff Journalist, Daily Record, Edinburgh and Glasgow; Reuters' News Agency, London; TV Guide, Scotland; The Viewer, Scotland; Freelance Writer/Journalist, since 1964; Travel Correspondent, UK and overseas media; Scotland Correspondent, Variety, New York. Publications: Great Scot! (biography of Sir Harry Lauder); The Good Auld Days; The Solway Smugglers; The Wit of the Scots; The Wit of Robert Burns; The Devil on Wheels; Brush Up Your Scotland; Annie Laurie; Take No Notice and Take No More Notice! (World's Funniest Signs); The First 200 Years (Story of Dumfries and Galloway Royal Infirmary); 90 Glorious Years (Story of the King's Theatre, Glasgow); television script: Standing Room Only (The Scottish Music Hall). Recreations: making video films of personal travels; collecting trivia; researching Scottish music-hall history; fighting snobs and bumbling bureaucrats; reading all the Sunday broadsheets; surfing the World Wide Web on Internet. Address: (h.) 36 Whittingehame Court, Glasgow G12 OBG; T.-0141-357 2265; e-mail: gordirving@aol.com

Irwin, Professor David George, MA, PhD, FSA, FRSA. Professor Emeritus, History of Art, Aberdeen University (Professor and Head of Department, 1970-96); b. 24.6.33, London; m., Francina Sorabji; 1 s.; 1 d. Educ. Holgate Grammar School, Barnsley; Queen's College, Oxford (Exhibitioner); Courtauld Institute of Art, London University. Lecturer in History of Fine Art, Glasgow University, 1959-70; Past President, British Society for 18th Century Studies; former Council Member, Walpole Society; former Member, Art Panel, Scottish Arts Council; Member, Editorial Board, British Journal of 18th Century Studies; Committee Member: Aberdeen Art Gallery, Architectural Heritage Society of Scotland; elected Member, International Association of Art Critics; Vice-Chairman, Arran Civic Trust; won Laurence Binyon Prize, Oxford, 1956. Exhibition: Pastel Society, London. Publications: English Neoclassical Art; Paul Klee; Visual Arts, Taste and Criticism; Designs and Ornaments of Empire Style; Winckelmann, Writings on Art; John Flaxman, Sculptor, Illustrator, Designer; Neoclassicism; Scottish Painters, At Home and Abroad, 1700 to 1900 (with Francina Irwin). Recreations: painting; travel. Address: Balmichel Bridge Cottage, Shiskine, Isle of Arran KA27 8DT; T./fax-01770 860408.

Isaacs, Professor Neil William, BSc, PhD, FRSE. Joseph Black Professor of Protein Crystallography, University of Glasgow, since 1989; b. 11.6.45, Brisbane, Australia; m., Margaret; 3 d. Educ. St. Patrick's College, Brisbane; University of Queensland. Research Assistant, University Chemical Laboratories, Cambridge, 1969-72; IBM

Research Fellow, University of Oxford, 1972-75; IBM World Trade Research Fellow, IBM T.J. Watson Research Center, New York, 1976; Research Fellow, University of York, 1977-78; NH and MRC Senior Research Fellow, St. Vincent's Institute of Medical Research, Melbourne, 1978-88. Publications: over 100 in scientific literature on molecular structures. Recreations: walking; gardening; reading. Address: (h.) Eastwood, Shore Road, Cove, Helensburgh G84 0NA; T.-01436 842660.

Ivory, Sir Brian Gammell, CBE, MA (Cantab), CA, FRSA, FRSE. Chairman, The National Galleries of Scotland, since 2000; Chairman, The Scottish American Investment Company PLC, since 2001 (Director, since 2000); Director, Bank of Scotland, 1998-2007; Director, HBOS plc, 2001-07; b. 10.4.49, Edinburgh; m., Oona Mairi MacPhie Bell-Macdonald (see Oona Mairi MacPhie Ivory); 1 s.; 1 d. Educ. Eton College; Magdalene College, Cambridge. CA apprentice, Thomson McLintock, 1971-75; joined Highland Distillers, 1976, became Director, 1978, Managing Director, 1988, Group Chief Executive, 1994-97, Chairman, 1997-99; Chairman, Macallan Distillers Ltd., 1997-99; Director, Orpar SA, since 2003; Director, Remy Cointreau SA, since 1991; Chairman, Retec Digital plc, since 2006; Director: Insight Investment Management Ltd., since 2003, Synesis Life Ltd., since 2007, Marathon Asset Management, since 2007; Member, Scottish Arts Council, 1983-92 (Vice-Chairman, 1988-92); Member, Arts Council of GB, 1988-92; Chairman, The National Piping Centre, since 1996; CIMgt, 1997; Member, Queen's Bodyguard for Scotland (Royal Company of Archers). Recreations: the arts; farming; hill-walking. Address: (h.) 12 Ann Street, Edinburgh, EH4 1PJ.

Ivory, Lady Oona Mairi MacPhie, DL, MA (Cantab), ARCM, FRSA. Professional Musician; former Chairman, Scottish Ballet; Governor, Royal Scottish Academy of Music and Drama; Trustee, The Piping Trust; Founder Director, The National Piping Centre; Deputy Lieutenant, City of Edinburgh; b. 21.7.54, Ayr; m., Brian Gammell Ivory (qv); 1 s.; 1 d. Educ. King's College, Cambridge; Royal Scottish Academy of Music and Drama; Royal Academy of Music. Recreations: visual and performing arts; wild places; sailing. Address: (h.) 12 Ann Street, Edinburgh EH4 1PJ.

Izod, Professor (Kenneth) John, BA (Hons), PhD, FRSA, FFCS. Professor of Screen Analysis, Stirling University, since 1998 (Dean, Faculty of Arts, 1995-98; Senior Lecturer, Department of Film and Media Studies, 1978-98); Head, Department of Film and Media Studies, 2005-07; b. 4.3.40, Shepperton; m., Irene Chew Geok Keng (divorced 1994); 1 s.; 1 d. Educ. Prince Edward School, Harare City, Zimbabwe; Leeds University. Clerk articled to Chartered Accountant, 1958-63; Projectionist, mobile cinema unit, 1963; Lecturer in English, New University of Ulster, 1969-78; former Governor, Scottish Film Council; Chairman, Stirling Film Theatre, 1982-89 and 1991-92; Principal Investigator, Arts and Humanities Research Council funded project 'The Cinema Authorship of Lindsay Anderson', 2007-10. Publications: Reading the Screen, 1984; Hollywood and the Box Office 1895-1986, 1988; The Films of Nicolas Roeg, 1991; Introduction to Television Documentary (Co-Author); Myth, Mind and the Screen, 2001; Screen, Culture, Psyche, 2006. Address: (b.) Film and Media Studies, University, Stirling FK9 4LA; T.-01786 467520; e-mail: k.j.izod@stir.ac.uk

J

Jack, Alister William. Chairman, Alligator Self Storage Ltd., since 2001; Managing Director, Armadillo Self Storage Ltd., 2003-07; Director (Non-executive), James Gordon (Engineers) Ltd., since 2003; b. 7.7.63, Dumfries; m., Ann Hodgson; 1 s.; 2 d. Educ. Trinity College, Glenalmond. Knight Frank, 1983-86; Managing Director, Aardvark Self Storage Limited, 1995-2002; Director, Field and Lawn (Marquees) Ltd., since 1986. Member, Executive Board, Scottish Conservative Party, 1997-2001; Parliamentary Candidate, Tweeddale, Ettrick and Lauderdale, 1997 General Election; Vice Chairman, Scottish Conservative and Unionist Party, 1997-2001 (Scottish Conservative Party Spokesman on Industry and Economic Affairs, 1996-99); Member, High Constabulary, Port of Leith; Winner, Leith Enterprise Award, 1989; Finalist, The New Venturers 1990. Recreations: field sports; golf; sailing; skiing. Address: 19 Moray Place, Edinburgh EH3 6DA; T.-0131 226 0862.

Jack, James Alexander Penrice, BSc (Hons), BArch, BD, DMin, RIBA, ARIAS. Minister of Duddingston, since 2001; b. 10.12.60, Bellshill. Educ. Dalziel High School; University of Strathclyde; University of Glasgow; Princeton Theological Seminary. Pentland & Baker (Architects) Toronto, Canada, 1981-82; Estates & Buildings Division, University of Strathclyde, 1983-85; Student Placement at parish of Rogart, Sutherland, 1986-87; Probationary Assistant, Dundee Parish (St. Mary's), 1988-89; Minister of Abernyte *linked with* Inchture & Kinnaird *linked with* Longforgan, 1989-2001. Senior Chaplain at HM Prison Castle, Huntly, 1989-2001; Chaplaincies work at three primary schools and one secondary school, 1989-2001; Chaplaincy at Duddingston Primary, since 2001. General Trustee of the Church of Scotland, since 1995 (appointed Convener of Fabric Committee of the General Trustees, 2005 and Vice Chairman, 2007); Member of Board of Practice and Procedure, 1999-2006. Publications: author of "Summer in a Highland Parish", article, 1986; co-author, "And You Visited Me", 1993; "Understanding a ministry to Prison Officers" in "Theology Scotland", 2003. Recreations: genealogy; painting and visiting Edinburgh. Address: (b.) The Manse of Duddingston, 5 Old Church Lane, Edinburgh EH15 3PX; T.-0131 661 4240.

Jack, Professor Robert Barr, CBE, MA, LLB, HonDUniv (Glasgow). Senior Partner, McGrigor Donald, Solicitors, Glasgow, Edinburgh and London, 1990-93 (Partner, 1957-93); Professor of Mercantile Law, Glasgow University, 1978-93; b. 18.3.28; m., Anna Thorburn Thomson; 2 s. Educ. Kilsyth Academy; High School of Glasgow; Glasgow University. Admitted a Solicitor in Scotland, 1951; Member, Scottish Law Commission, 1974-77; Observer, Department of Trade's Insolvency Law Review Committee, 1977-82; Member, Council for the Securities Industry, 1983-85; Lay Member, Council of the Stock Exchange, 1984-86; Independent Member, Board, Securities and Futures Authority (formerly Securities Association), 1986-94; Board Member, Securities and Investments Board, 1994-97; Chairman, Review Committee on Banking Services Law, 1987-89; Member: Panel on Takeovers and Mergers, 1992-2001, Financial Law Panel, 1993-2002; Chairman: Brownlee plc, Timber Merchants, Glasgow, 1984-86 (Director, 1974-86); Joseph Dunn (Bottlers) Ltd., Soft Drink Manufacturers, Glasgow, 1983-2003; Director: Bank of Scotland, 1985-96, Scottish Metropolitan Property plc, 1980-98 (Deputy Chairman, 1991-98), Scottish Mutual Assurance plc, 1987-98 (Chairman, 1992-98), Clyde Football Club Ltd., 1980-96,

Gartmore Scotland Investment Trust PLC, 1991-2001, Glasgow Development Agency, 1992-97; Chairman, Audit Committee, Glasgow University, 1996-2003; President, Scottish National Council of YMCAs, 1983-98 (Chairman, 1966-73); Governor, Hutchesons' Educational Trust, Glasgow, 1978-87 (Chairman, 1980-87); Chairman, The Turnberry Trust, since 1983; Member, Scottish Higher Education Funding Council, 1992-96; Governor, Beatson Institute for Cancer Research, 1989-2004; Trustee, Football Trust, 1998-2000; Member, West of Scotland Advisory Board, The Salvation Army, since 1995; Member, Committee of Management, Malin Housing Association, Turnberry, since 1973. Publications: lectures and articles on various aspects of company law, the statutory regulation and self-regulation of the City, and banking and insolvency law. Recreations: golf; music; hopeful supporter of one of Scotland's less fashionable football teams; an erstwhile dedicated lover of the Isle of Arran. Address: (h.) 50 Lanton Road, Lanton Park, Newlands, Glasgow G43 2SR; T.-0141-637 7302; e-mail: robertjack75@aol.com

Jack, Professor Ronald Dyce Sadler, MA, PhD, DLitt, FEA, FRSE, FFCS. Emeritus Professor of Scottish and Medieval Literature, Edinburgh University; b. 3.4.41, Ayr; m., Kirsty Nicolson; 2 d. Educ. Ayr Academy; Glasgow University; Edinburgh University. Department of English Literature: Assistant Lecturer, 1965, Lecturer, 1968, Reader, 1978, Professor, 1987, Associate Dean, Faculty of Arts, 1971-73; Visiting Professor, Virginia University, 1973-74; Director, Universities Central Council on Admissions, 1988-94 (Member, 1973-76); Pierpont Morgan Scholar, British Academy, 1976; Advising Editor: Scotia, 1980-96, Scottish Literary Journal, 1996-2000, Scottish Studies Review, since 2000; Member, Scottish Universities Council on Entrance, since 1981; Governor, Newbattle Abbey College, 1984-89; Beinecke Fellow, Yale, 1992; Visiting Professor, Strathclyde University, 1993; Lynn Woods Neag Distinguished Visiting Professor of British Literature, University of Connecticut, 1998; Joint Director, Bibliography of Scottish Literature in Translation, since 2000; W. Ormiston Rey Fellow, University of South Carolina, 2003. Publications: Robert MacLellan's Jamie the Saxt (Co-Editor), 1970; Scottish Prose 1550-1700, 1972; The Italian Influence on Scottish Literature, 1972; A Choice of Scottish Verse 1560-1660, 1978; The Art of Robert Burns (Co-Author), 1982; Sir Thomas Urquhart, The Jewel (Co-Author), 1984; Alexander Montgomerie, 1985; Scottish Literature's Debt to Italy, 1986; The History of Scottish Literature, Volume 1, 1988; Patterns of Divine Comedy, 1989; The Road to the Never Land, 1991; Of Lion and of Unicorn, 1993; The Poems of William Dunbar, 1997; The Mercat Anthology of Early Scottish Literature (Co-Editor), 1997 (revised edition, 2000); New Oxford Dictionary of National Biography (Assoc. Ed.) 2004; Scotland in Europe (Co-Editor), 2006. Address: (b.) Department of English Literature, Edinburgh University, David Hume Tower, George Square, Edinburgh EH8 9JX.

Jackson, Alice-Ann, BA Hons (Politics). Freelance Consultant/Researcher, since 1996; b. 6.8.53, Dingwall; 1 s. Educ. Dingwall Academy; Strathclyde University. Housing Aid Worker, Shelter Scotland, 1977-83; Researcher, Law School, Strathclyde University, 1983-86; Development Worker, GIUSH, 1987-88; Project Officer, Young Persons Development Worker, Glasgow Council for Single Homeless, 1988-96. Convener: Say Women, Steering Group of Scottish Youth Housing Network and SHASC. Address: (h. and b.) 47 Apsley Street, Glasgow G11 7SN; T.-0141 357 4371; e-mail: aliceann@tiscali.co.uk

Jackson, Jack, OBE, BSc (Hons), PhD, FIBiol, CIBiol; b. 31.5.44, Ayr; m., Sheilah Margaret Fulton; 1 s.; 3 d. Educ. Ayr Academy; Glasgow University; Jordanhill College of

Education. Demonstrator, Zoology Department, Glasgow University, 1966-69; Lecturer in Zoology, West of Scotland Agricultural College, 1969-72; Assistant Teacher of Biology, Cathkin High School, 1972-73; Principal Teacher of Biology, Ayr Academy, 1973-83. Senior Examiner and Setter, Scottish Examination Board, 1978-83; Director, Board, Scottish Youth Theatre, 1979-82; Member: Scottish Council, Institute of Biology, 1980-83, School Board, Balerno High School, 1989-99; former Assistant Chief Inspector of Schools with responsibility for science subjects, currently working on a part-time basis. Visiting Professor, Department of Curricular Studies, University of Strathclyde, since 2007. Recreations: family life; gardening; hill-walking; conservation. Address: (b.) HM Inspectorate of Education, Denholm House, Almondvale Business Park, Almondvale Way, Livingston EH54 6GA; T.-01506 600346; e-mail: jack.jackson@hmie.gsi.gov.uk

Jackson, Jim, OBE, BA. Chief Executive, Alzheimer Scotland, since 1994; b. 10.2.47, Bradford; m., Jennifer; 1 s.; 1 d. Educ. Stand Grammar School; West Ham College of Technology; Open University. Playleader, 1969-72; Community Development Worker, 1972-77; Principal Assistant, Community Services and Development, Wirral, 1977-81; Consultant, Home Office Voluntary Services Unit, 1981-84; Assistant Director, Scottish Council for Voluntary Organisations, 1984-93; Director, Alzheimer's Scotland, 1993-94. Recreations: the allotment; hill-walking; modern jazz. Address: (b.) 22 Drumsheugh Gardens, Edinburgh, EH3 7RN; T.-0131-243 1453; e-mail: jjackson@alzscot.org

Jackson, Dr Sylvia, BPhil, PhD (Ed). MSP (Labour), Stirling, 1999-2007; b. 3.12.46; m., Michael Peart Jackson (deceased); 1 s.; 1 d. Educ. Brigg Girls High School; University of Hull; University of Stirling. Teacher of Chemistry and Physics: taught in schools in Hull, Alva, Stirling, Cumbernauld and Kirkintilloch; Assistant Science Adviser for Edinburgh Council and Lothian Regional Council; Research Fellow, University of Stirling; and Lecturer, Moray House Institute of Education, University of Edinburgh, until 1999. Scottish Parliament Appointments (1999-2007): Ministerial Aide to Scottish Health Minister; Convenor, Subordinate Legislation Committee; Vice Convener, Local Government Committee; Member, Local Government and Transport Committee; Convener of Cross Party Group (CPG), Animal Welfare; Co-Convener of Cross Party Group on Affordable Housing; Vice Convener of Cross Party Group on Drugs and Alcohol; Co-Convener of Cross Party Group on Renewables. Publications: Introducing Science (series of 12 pupil books and 6 teacher guides); contributed to journals and publications mainly dealing with the professional development of teachers. Recreations: walking; reading.

Jaconelli, Rt. Rev. Dom Raymond. Abbot of Nunraw, since 2003; b. 1933. Educ. Marist School, St Mungo's Academy, Glasgow. Entered Nunraw, 1951; solemn profession, 1956; received priesthood, 1958; guest master for 20 years; organist. Address: (b.) Nunraw, Garvald, Haddington EH41 4LW.

Jakimciw, Tony, MA, PGCE. Principal, Dumfries and Galloway College, since 1999; b. 28.6.51, Consett; m., Alice; 1 s.; 1 d. Educ. Hookergate Grammar School; Edinburgh University; Leicester University. Lecturer in Communications, Gateshead College, 1975-84; Senior Lecturer/Director of Development, Hartlepool College, 1984-88; Vice Principal, Carlisle College, 1989-99. Member, Dumfries and Galloway Local Economic Forum; Chair: Dumfries and Galloway Lifelong Learning Partnership, JISC RSC Board; Member, JISC. Recreations: family life; cooking; reading; walking. Address: (b.)

Heathhall, Dumfries DG1 3QZ; T.-01387 243808; e-mail: principal@dumgal.ac.uk

James, Mary Charlotte, BA (Hons), FFCS; b. 2.4.44; m., Lawrence Edwin James; 2 s. Educ. St. Leonards School; York University; St. Anne's College, Oxford. Headmistress, Queen Ethelburga's School, Harrogate, 1984-88; Headmistress, St. Leonards School, St. Andrews, 1988-2000. Member: Scottish Council, ISCO, 1988-99, Scottish ISIS, 1988-2000, Board, SCIS Council, 1996-99; Chairman, Demarco European Cultural Initiative, 1997-2005; Governor, King William's College, Isle of Man; Trustee, Bishop Barrow's Charity, 2000-06. Recreations: reading; cooking; walking; sleeping. Address: Priorwell, Balmerino, Fife DD6 8SE; T.-01382 330 888.

Jameson, Brigadier Melville Stewart, CBE. Lord Lieutenant for Perth and Kinross; b. 17.7.44, Clunie; m., Sarah Amy Walker Munro; 2 s. Educ. Glenalmond; RMA, Sandhurst. Commissioned into Royal Scots Greys, 1965; served with regiment in Germany, Northern Ireland, Cyprus, Middle East and Edinburgh (where, in 1971, regiment amalgamated with 3rd Carabiniers to form Royal Scots Dragoon Guards); following tour as Chief of Staff 52 Lowland Brigade, commanded Royal Scots Dragoon Guards, 1986-88, at Tidworth; posted as Instructor to Joint Service Defence College Greenwich; Colonel PB17 on Military Secretary's staff, Ministry of Defence; Command, 51 Highland Brigade, 1994-96 based in Perth; Producer and Chief Executive, Edinburgh Military Tattoo, 1995-2007. Officer, Royal Company of Archers; Colonel, The Royal Scots Dragoon Guards. Recreations: shooting; gardening; polo; music (Highland bagpipes). Address: (b.) Home HQ, Royal Scots Dragoon Guards, The Castle, Edinburgh EH1 2YT.

Jamie, Kathleen, MA. Writer; part-time Lecturer in Creative Writing, School of English, University of St. Andrews; b. 13.5.62, Johnstone. Educ. Currie High School; Edinburgh University. Publications: The Way We Live; The Autonomous Region; The Queen of Sheba; The Golden Peak; The Tree House (won the 2004 Forward Poetry Prize and Scottish Arts Council Book of Year award, 2005); Findings, 2005; Waterlight: selected poems, 2007.

Jamieson, Cathy, BA (Hons), CQSW. MSP (Labour and Co-operative), Carrick, Cumnock and Doon Valley, since 1999; former Minister for Justice; Minister for Education and Young People, Scottish Executive, 2001-03; b. 3.11.56, Kilmarnock; m., Ian Sharpe; 1 s. Educ. James Hamilton Academy, Kilmarnock; Glasgow Art School; Glasgow University; Goldsmiths College, London; Caledonian University. Professional qualification in art therapy; later trained in social work; Senior IT Worker, Strathclyde Region; Principal Officer, Who Cares? Scotland, developing policy and legislation for young people in care; Member, inquiry team which investigated child abuse in Edinburgh children's homes. Recreation: football (Kilmarnock supporter). Address: (b.) Constituency Office, Ayr College East, Block 1, Caponacre Industrial Estate, Cumnock KA18 1SH; T.-0845 458 1800.

Jamieson, George, LLB (Hons), DipLP. Solicitor (Scotland, since 1985, England and Wales, since 2002); b. 21.8.61, Paisley. Educ. Paisley Grammar School; Strathclyde University. Trainee Solicitor, Hart, Abercrombie, Caldwell and Co., Paisley, 1984-86; Walker Laird, Paisley: Assistant Solicitor, 1986-89, Partner, 1990-2001; Consultant, Pattison and Sim, Paisley, since 2001. Part-time Immigration Adjudicator, 2002-05; Immigration

Judge, since 2005; Part Time Sheriff, since 2006; Council Member, Paisley Sheriff Court District, Law Society of Scotland, 1997-2005. Publications: Parental Responsibilities and Rights, 1995; Summary Applications and Suspensions, 2000; Scottish Family Law Legislation (Editor), 2002; Family Law Agreements, 2005. Address: (b.) 19 Glasgow Road, Paisley PA1 3QX; T.-0141-889 3296; e-mail: georgegjst@aol.com

Jamieson, Rev. Gordon David, MA, BD. Head of Stewardship, Church of Scotland, since 2000; b. 1.3.49, Glasgow; m., Annette; 1 s.; 1 d. Educ. Hamilton Academy; Edinburgh University. Assistant Minister, Tron Moredun, Edinburgh, 1973-74; Minister: Schaw Kirk, Drongan, 1974-79, Elie Parish Church, linked with Kilconquhar and Colinsburgh Parish Church, 1979-86, Barnhill St. Margaret's Parish Church, Dundee, 1986-2000. Address: (b.) 121 George Street, Edinburgh EH2 4YN; T.-0131-225 5722; (h.) 41 Goldpark Place, Livingston EH54 6LW; T.-01506 412020.

Jamieson, William, BA (Econ), FRSA. Executive Editor, The Scotsman, since 2000; Director, Policy Institute, since 2000; b. 9.6.45, Newmilns; m., Elaine Margaret Muller; 1 s. Educ. Hurst Grange School, Stirling; Sedbergh School, Yorkshire; Manchester University. Economics Correspondent, Thomson Regionals, 1973-77; City Reporter, Daily Express, 1978; City Editor, Thomson Regionals, 1979-86; Deputy City Editor, Today, 1986; Sunday Telegraph: Deputy City Editor, 1986-95, Economics Editor, 1995-2000. Publications: Goldstrike, 1989; Britain Beyond Europe, 1994; UBS Guide to Emerging Markets (Editor), 1996; Illustrated Guide to the British Economy, 1998; Illustrated Guide to the Scottish Economy (Editor), 1999; Editor, Practical Investors Journal, since 2004. Recreation: reading other people's newspapers. Address: (b.) The Scotsman, 108 Holyrood Road, Edinburgh EH8 8AS; T.-0131-620 8361; e-mail: bjamieson@scotsman.com; (h.) Inverogle, Lochearnhead FK19 8PR.

Jardine, Professor Alan George. Professor of Renal Medicine, University of Glasgow, since 2006; Consultant Physician, Western Infirmary, Glasgow, since 1996; b. 27.08.60, Thurso; m., Catherine Pickering; 1 s.; 2 d. Educ. Bearsden Academy; University of Glasgow. MRC Clinical Scientist, 1987-90; MRC Blood Pressure Unit, Registrar in Nephrology, 1990-92, then Lecturer in Medicine and Senior Registrar in Medicine, Inverness and Aberdeen, 1992-93, joined University of Glasgow in 1994 as Lecturer, became Senior Lecturer, then Reader of Renal Medicine. Articles on renal, transplant and cardiovascular medicine. Recreation: golf. Address: 7 Clevedon Crescent, Glasgow G12 0PD; T.-0141 357 4062. E-mail: a.g.jardine@clinmed.gla.ac.uk

Jardine, Ian William, BSc, PhD, FRSA. Chief Executive, Scottish Natural Heritage; b. 22.5.59, Edinburgh; m., Anne Daniel; 3 s. Educ. Royal High School, Edinburgh; Durham University; Leeds University. Joined Scottish Office, 1984; worked in various departments, including Scottish Development and Industry Departments, Private Secretary to Ian Lang MP; involved in setting-up of urban partnership initiatives and management of Castlemilk Partnership; Scottish Natural Heritage: joined 1992, former Director of Strategy and Operations (East); President, Eurosite, since 2007. Recreations: acting; gardening; natural history. Address: (b.) Great Glen House, Westercraigs, Leachkin Road, Inverness IV3 8NW; T.-01463 725001.

Jardine, Leslie Thomas, LLB. Director for Corporate Services, Dumfries and Galloway Council; b. 4.6.49, Dumfries; m., Angela; 1 s. Educ. Dumfries Academy; Glasgow University. Law apprentice, then Legal Assistant, Dumfries County Council, 1972-75; Dumfries and Galloway Regional Council: Policy Planning Assistant, then Regional Public Relations Officer, then Director of Economic Development, then Director for Community Resources. Solicitor. Recreation: riding. Address: (b.) Council Offices, English Street, Dumfries; T.-01387 260015; e-mail: LeslieJ@dumgal.gov.uk

Jarrett, Professor James Oswald, PhD, BVMS, MRCVS, FRSE. Honorary Senior Research Fellow, University of Glasgow, since 2002; b. 19.3.40, Glasgow; m., Angela Marie Pacitti; 3 s. Educ. Lenzie Academy; University of Glasgow. Glasgow University: Research Fellow, Department of Experimental Veterinary Medicine, 1965-73, Lecturer/Senior Lecturer, Department of Veterinary Pathology, 1973-79, Professor, since 1980. Visiting Scientist, Scripps Institute, San Diego, 1980; Honorary President, Feline Advisory Bureau; Chairman, The Cat Group; John Henry Steele Memorial Medal, Royal College of Veterinary Surgeons, 2000. Publications: over 200 scientific publications. Recreations: sailing; skiing. Address: (b.) University of Glasgow, Institute of Comparative Medicine, Faculty of Veterinary Medicine, Bearsden G61 1QH; T.-0141-956 2111; e-mail: o.jarrett@btinternet.com

Jarvie, Professor Grant, BEd, MA, PhD. Deputy Principal, University of Stirling, since 2006; Chair, Sports Studies, University of Stirling, since 1997; b. 7.11.55, Motherwell. Educ. School, Edinburgh; University of Exeter; Queen's University; University of Leicester. Secondary School Teacher, 1979-81; Lecturer/Senior Lecturer, Leeds, 1982-86; Lecturer/Senior Lecturer, University of Warwick (Director, Warwick Centre for the Study of Sport, Chairman, Physical Education Department), 1986-95; Chair/Head of Sport and Leisure, Moray House Institute, Heriot-Watt University, 1995-97. President, British Society of Sports History, 1996-2001; Panel Member, Scottish Sports Hall of Fame, since 2003; Chair, Central Area Institute of Sport, 2004-05. Publications: Class, Race and Sport in South Africa's Political Economy, 1985; Highland Games: The Making of the Myth, 1991; Sport, Racism and Ethnicity (Editor), 1991; Scottish Sport in the Making of the Nation: Ninety-Minute Patriots? (Co-editor), 1994; Sport and Leisure in Social Thought, Revised 1st Ed., 1995 and Revised 2nd Ed., 1999 (Co-author); Sporting Worlds: A Critical Perspective (Co-author), 1999; Sport, Scotland and the Scots (Co-editor), 2000; Sport in the Making of Celtic Cultures (Editor), 1999; The Encyclopedia of British Sport (Co-Editor), 2000; Sport Worlds, A Sociological Perspective, 2002; Sport, Revolution and the Beijing Olympics (Co-author), 2008; Sport, Culture and Society: Can Sport Change the World?, 2006; numerous book chapters and journal articles. Recreations: squash; hillwalking. Address: Deputy Principal's Office, University of Stirling, Stirling FK9 4LA; T.-01786 467013.

Jarvie, Sheriff (Marie-Lesley) Elizabeth, QC, MA (Hons), LLB. Sheriff of Lothian and Borders at Edinburgh, since 1997; b. 22.1.52, Falkirk; m., John Jarvie; 1 s.; 4 d. Educ. Larbert High School; Edinburgh University. Admitted, Scottish Bar, 1981; Crown Counsel, 1989-92; QC, 1994. Recreations: skiing; current affairs.

Jarvis, Professor Paul Gordon, PhD, Fil dr, FRS (London), FRSE, FRS (Uppsala), FIBiol, FIChFor. Professor of Forestry and Natural Resources, Edinburgh University, 1975-2001, Emeritus Professor, since 2001; b. 23.5.35, Tunbridge Wells; m., Margaret Susan Gostelow; 1 s.; 2 d. Educ. Sir Anthony Brown's School, Brentwood; Oriel College, Oxford. PhD study, Sheffield University, 1957-60; Postdoctoral Fellow, NATO, Institute of Plant

Physiology, Uppsala University, 1960-62; Fil dr, Uppsala University, 1963; Senior Lecturer in Plant Physiology, Royal College of Agriculture, Uppsala; Aberdeen University: Lecturer in Botany, 1966-72, Senior Lecturer, 1972-75. Council Member, Society for Experimental Biology, 1977-80, President, 1993-95; Commissioner, Countryside Commission for Scotland, 1976-78; Member, Governing Body, Scottish Crops Research Institute, 1977-86; Council Member, National Trust for Scotland, 1987-2005; Trustee, John Muir Trust, 1989-2007; Trustee, Highland Perthshire Communities Land Trust; Member, Forest Research Advisory Committee, since 2002; Honorary Dr. Forestry, Swedish University of Agriculture and Forestry, 2007; Co-Founder, Plant, Cell and Environment; present interests: environmental change, biodiversity, forest ecology and carbon sequestration; serves on various editorial and review boards. Recreations: hill-walking; gardening; growing trees. Address: (h.) Duireaskin, by Aberfeldy, Perthshire PH15 2ED; T.-01887 820988; e-mail: margaretsjarvis@aol.com

Jasper, Professor David, MA (Cantab), MA (Oxon), BD, PhD, DD (Oxon), DTh (Uppsala hc), FRSE, FRSA. Professor of Literature and Theology, University of Glasgow, since 1998; b. 1.8.51, Stockton; m., Alison Elizabeth Collins; 3 d. Educ. Dulwich College; Jesus College, Cambridge; St. Stephen's House, Oxford; Durham University. Curate of Buckingham (Anglican), 1976-79; Chaplain and Fellow, Hatfield College, Durham, 1979-87; Principal, St. Chad's College, Durham, 1988-91; Senior Lecturer then Reader, University of Glasgow, 1991-98; Director, Centre for Literature and Theology, University of Glasgow, 1991-99. Publications: seven books, most recently The Sacred Desert, 2004. Recreations: reading; photography; walking. Address: Department of Theology and Religious Studies, University of Glasgow, Glasgow G12 8QQ; T.-0141-330 4405.

Jauhar, Pramod, MBBS, DPM, FRCPsych. Consultant Psychiatrist, since 1981; HM Medical Commissioner (part-time), since 1998; b. 15.3.48, Agra, India; m., Pamela; 2 s.; 1 d. Educ. St. Xavier School, Jaipur, India; Armed Forces Medical College, Pune, India. General professional training in psychiatry, St. Bernard's Hospital and Charing Cross Hospital, London, 1974-77; higher professional training, St. Thomas' Hospital, 1977-80; Consultant Psychiatrist, St. Brendan's Hospital, Bermuda, 1979-81; Consultant Psychiatrist and Honorary Clinical Senior Lecturer, 1981; Clinical Director, Medicines Resource Management Group - Mental Health, 10 year period; Member, Executive Committee, Medical Council for Alcohol, 1999; HM Medical Commissioner (part-time), Mental Welfare Commission for Scotland, 8 year period; Clinical Director, Medicines Resource Management, Greater Glasgow and Clyde NHS (sessional); Consultant Psychiatrist, University Health Service, University of Glasgow (sessional); Member, Interim Orders Panel, General Medical Council; Past Member, Fitness to Practice Panels, General Medical Council; Past Regional Adviser in Addictions, Royal College of Psychiatrists; Past Regional Adviser, Medical Council of Alcohol; Member, Executive Faculty of Substance Misuse, Royal College of Psychiatrists, 2002; President, Rotary Club, Queen's Park, Glasgow, 2000; Governor to the University Court, Glasgow Caledonian University; sessional work in relation to Mood Disorders and Addiction Disorders, Priory Hospital Glasgow, since 2006. Recreations: golf; travel. Address: (b.) Priory Hospital, 38 Mansionhouse Road, Glasgow G41 3DW.

Jeeves, Professor Malcolm Alexander, CBE, MA, PhD (Cantab), Hon. DSc (Edin), Hon. DSc (St. And.), Hon. DUniv (Stir.), FBPsS, FMedSci, FRSE, PPRSE. Professor of Psychology, St. Andrews University, 1969-93, Emeritus Professor, since 1993; President, Royal Society of Edinburgh, 1996-99 (Vice-President, 1990-93); b. 16.11.26, Stamford, England; m., Ruth Elisabeth Hartridge; 2 d. Educ. Stamford School; St. John's College, Cambridge University. Lt., 1st Bn., Sherwood Foresters, BAOR, 1945-48; Exhibitioner, St. John's College, Cambridge, 1948-52; research and teaching, Cambridge and Harvard Universities, 1952-56; Lecturer, Leeds University, 1956-59; Professor and Head, Department of Psychology, Adelaide University, 1959-69 (Dean, Faculty of Arts, 1963-64); Member: Council, SERC, 1985-89, Neuroscience and Mental Health Board, MRC, 1985-89, Council, Royal Society of Edinburgh, 1985-88 (Vice President, 1990-93); Director, Medical Research Council Cognitive Neuroscience Research Group, 1983-88; Vice-Principal, St. Andrews University, 1981-85; Chairman, Executive Committee, International Neuropsychological Symposium, 1986-91; Editor-in-Chief, Neuropsychologia, 1990-93; Cairns Memorial Lecturer, Australia, 1986; New College Lecturer, University of NSW, 1987; Drummond Lectures, Stirling University, 2001. Honorary Sheriff, Fife, since 1986. Publications: Analysis of Structural Learning (Co-Author); Psychology Survey No. 3 (Editor); Experimental Psychology: An introduction for biologists; The Effects of Structural Relations upon Transfer (Co-Author); Thinking in Structures (Co-Author); Behavioural Science and Christianity (Editor); Free to be Different (Co-Author); Psychology and Christianity: The View Both Ways; The Scientific Enterprise and Christian Faith; Psychology: Through the eyes of faith (Co-Author); Mind Fields; Human Nature at the Millennium; Science, Life and Christian Belief (Co-Author); From Cells to Souls – and Beyond (Editor and Contributor); Human Nature (Editor and Contributor). Recreations: walking; music; fishing. Address: (b.) School of Psychology, St. Andrews University, St. Andrews KY16 9JU; T.-01334 462072.

Jeffcoat, Marilyn Annette, BCom, FCCA. Finance Director, Spanoptic Ltd., and Bandrum Nursing Home Ltd.; Director, Countability Ltd.; b. 7.4.47, Birmingham; m., 1, David Jeffcoat (marriage dissolved); 5 s.; 1 d.; m., 2, Donald Leach (qv). Educ. Erdington Grammar School, Birmingham; Edinburgh University. Worked in investment management, tax accountancy and audit with Baillie Gifford, Ivory & Sime, and Coopers & Lybrand until 1978, qualifying as a certified accountant in 1976; public practice since 1979. Member of Court, Napier University, 1990-2001 (Chairman, Audit Committee, 1994-2001); Commissioner, Mental Welfare Commission, 1992-98; Convener, One Parent Families, Scotland, 1994-99; Director, St. Mary's Cathedral Workshop Ltd.; Treasurer: Society of Scottish Artists, 1978-93, St. Mary's Episcopal Cathedral, Edinburgh, since 1979; Treasurer and Organiser, Royal Scottish Country Dance Society, 1982-2004; Trustee, Mendelssohn on Mull Trust; Trustee, Strachey Trust. Recreations: music; Scrabble; seeing the world. Address: (b.) 146 Rose Street Lane South, Edinburgh EH3 4BB.

Jeffrey, John, BSc (Hons) Ag, FRAgS, JP. Chairman, Moredun Research Institute, since 2004; Manager, Scotland U21 Rugby Team, since 2003; b. 25.3.59, Kelso; m., Anne Turnbull; 1 d. Educ. St. Mary's School, Melrose of Merchiston Castle; Newcastle University. Moredun Foundation, 15 years - Executive Board, 5 years; Chairman, Regional Board Members, 8 years; former European Rugby Cup Director. Executive Committee, Border Union Agricultural Society; Tenants Working Panel, SNFU. Rugby: Scotland 40 Caps, 2 World Cups, 2 British Lions Tours; Barbarians Committee. Recreations: golf; ski-ing and spoofing. Address: (h./b.) Kersknowe, Kelso TD5 8AA; e-mail: jj@kersknowe.co.uk

Jeffrey, Rev. Kenneth Samuel, BA, BD, PhD. Minister, The Parish Church of Cupar Old and St Michael of Tarvit, since 2002; b. 30.09.69, Dundonald, Northern Ireland; m., Linda; 2 s.; 1 d. Educ. Sullivan Upper School, Holywood,

Co. Down; Stirling University; Aberdeen University. Teacher, Livingstonia Secondary School, Malawi, 1992-94; Assistant Minister, Rubislaw Parish Church, Aberdeen, 2000-02. Publications: 'When The Lord Walks The Land - The 1858-62 Revival in the North East of Scotland', 2002; contributed to several other books. Recreations: walking; reading; supporting Manchester United. Address: (h.) 76 Hogarth Drive, Cupar, Fife KY15 5YU; T.-01334 653196; e-mail: ksjeffrey@btopenworld.com

Jeffrey, Richard, BSc (Eng), MICE. Managing Director, Babcock & Brown; President, Edinburgh Chamber of Commerce, since 2006; b. 17.2.66, Staffordshire; m., Liz; 2 d. Educ. St. Thomas More High School, Stoke-on-Trent; Imperial College London. Member, Institution of Civil Engineers, since 1994; Director, Europe and Africa, BAA International; Managing Director, Aberdeen Airport, 1999-2001; Managing Director, Edinburgh Airport, 2001-07. Chair, Edinburgh Tourism Action Group, 2004-07. Recreations: sailing; riding; walking; family. Address: The Paphle, Cleish, Kinross KY13 0LR; T.-07785 220565; e-mail: richard@cleish.com

Jeffreys-Jones, Professor Rhodri, BA (Wales), PhD (Cantab), FRHistS. Professor of American History, Edinburgh University, since 1997 (Chair of History 2001-03); b. 28.7.42, Carmarthen; m., Mary Fenton; 2 d. by pr. m. Educ. Ysgol Ardudwy; University of Wales; Cambridge University; Michigan University; Harvard University. Tutor: Harvard, 1965-66, Fitzwilliam College, Cambridge, 1966-67; Assistant Lecturer, Lecturer, Senior Lecturer, Reader, Edinburgh University, 1967-97; Fellow, Charles Warren Center for the Study of American History, Harvard, 1971-72; Canadian Commonwealth Visiting Fellow and Visiting Professor, University of Toronto, 1993; Chair, Scottish Association for the Study of America, 1998-2001. Publications: Violence and Reform in American History; American Espionage: From Secret Service to CIA; Eagle Against Empire: American Opposition to European Imperialism 1914-82 (Editor); The Growth of Federal Power in American History (Joint Editor); The CIA and American Democracy; North American Spies (Joint Editor); Changing Differences: Women and the Shaping of American Foreign Policy, 1917-1994; Eternal Vigilance? – 50 years of the CIA (Joint Editor); Peace Now! American Society and the Ending of the Vietnam War; American-British-Canadian Intelligence Relations 1939-2000 (Joint Editor); Cloak and Dollar – A History of American Secret Intelligence; The FBI: A History. Recreations: snooker; vegetable gardening. Address: (b.) History/School of History and Classics, Edinburgh University, William Robertson Building, George Square, Edinburgh EH8 9JY; T.-0131-650 3773/3780; e-mail: R. Jeffreys-Jones@ed.ac.uk

Jenkins, Blair, MA (Hons). Chairman, Scottish Broadcasting Commission, since 2007; former Head of News and Current Affairs, BBC Scotland (2000-06); b. 8.1.57, Elgin; m., Carol Sinclair; 3 d. Educ. Elgin Academy; Edinburgh University. Reporter, Aberdeen Evening Express, 1974-76; student, 1976-80; Producer, BBC Television News, London, 1981-84; Producer, Reporting Scotland, BBC Scotland, 1984-86; Scottish Television; Producer, Scotland Today, 1986-90, Head of News, 1990-93, Head of Regional Broadcasting, 1993-94, Director of Broadcasting, 1994-97; Media Consultant, 1998-2000. Young Journalist of the Year, Scottish Press Awards, 1977; Chairman, BAFTA Scotland, 1998-2004. Address: (h.) 7 Fotheringay Road, Glasgow G41 4LZ; T.-0141 424 3118; e-mail: blair.jenkins@btinternet.com

Jennings, James, OBE, JP. Member, North Ayrshire Council, 1996-2003 (Chair, Social Work Committee);

Former Convener, Strathclyde Regional Council; Honorary Sheriff, Kilmarnock, since 1991; Chairman, Police Negotiating Board, 1990-92; b. 18.2.25; m., 1, Margaret Cook Barclay (deceased); 3 s.; 2 d.; 2, Margaret Mary Hughes, JP; 2 d. Educ. St. Palladius School, Dalry; St. Michael's College, Irvine. Steel industry, 1946-79. Member: Ayr County Council, 1958, Strathclyde Regional Council, 1974 (Vice-Convener, 1982-86); Chairman: Ayr CC Police and Law Committee, 1964-70, Ayrshire Joint Police Committee, 1970-75, North Ayrshire Crime Prevention Panel, 1970-82, Police and Fire Committee, Strathclyde Regional Council, 1978-82; contested Perth and East Perthshire, 1966; Honorary Vice-President, Royal British Legion Scotland (Dalry and District Branch); JP, Cunninghame, 1969 (Chairman, Cunninghame Justices Committee, 1974-95); Vice-Chairman, Official Side, Police Negotiating Board, 1984-86, Chairman, 1986-88; Chairman, Garnock Valley Development Executive, 1988-91; Freeman of North Ayrshire, since 1997. Recreation: local community involvement. Address: (h.) 4 Place View, Kilbirnie KA25 6BG; T.-Kilbirnie 3339.

Jennings, Kevin, MB, FRCP. Consultant Cardiologist, Aberdeen Royal Infirmary, since 1983; b. 9.3.47, Charleville, Eire; m., Heather; 2 s.; 1 d. Educ. Downside; St. Bartholomew's Hospital, London. Registrar: King's College Hospital, London, London Chest Hospital; Senior Registrar, Freeman Hospital, Newcastle-upon-Tyne. Vice-President, British Cardiac Society, since 2006. Recreations: theatre; ballet; golf; windsurfing. Publication: Acute Cardiac Care. Address: 58 Rubislaw Den South, Aberdeen AB15 4AY; T.-Aberdeen 311466.

Jessamine, Rev. Alistair Lindsay, MA, BD. Minister of Dunfermline Abbey, since 1991; b. 17.6.49, Hill of Beath; m., Eleanor Moore. Educ. Beath High School, Cowdenbeath; University of Edinburgh. Assistant Minister, Newlands South Parish Church, Glasgow, 1978-79; Minister, Rankin Parish Church, Strathaven linked with Chapelton, 1979-91; Chaplain: HM Prison, Dungavel, 1979-91, RAF Pitreavie Castle, 1991-95; Moderator, Presbytery of Dunfermline, 1993-94. Recreations: travel; cooking; golf. Address: Abbey Manse, 12 Garvock Hill, Dunfermline, Fife KY12 7UU; T.-01383 721022.

Jessop, Sheriff Alexander Smethurst, MA, LLB. Sheriff at Aberdeen, since 1990; b. 17.5.43, Montrose; m., Joyce Isobel Duncan; 2 s.; 1 d. Educ. Montrose Academy; Fettes College; Aberdeen University. Partner, Campbell, Middleton, Burness and Dickson, Montrose; Procurator Fiscal Depute, Perth, 1976-78; Assistant Solicitor, Crown Office, 1978-80; Senior Assistant Procurator Fiscal, Glasgow, 1980-84; Regional Procurator Fiscal, Aberdeen, 1984-87, Glasgow, 1987-90. Member, Scottish Legal Aid Board; External Examiner, Aberdeen University. Recreation: golf (Captain, Royal Montrose Golf Club). Address: (b.) Sheriff Court House, Aberdeen AB10 1WP; T.-01224 657200.

Jiwa, Shainool, PhD. Head, Department of Community Relations at The Institute of Ismaili Studies, London; Commissioner, Mental Welfare Commission for Scotland, 1998-2002; Chief Examiner, International Baccalaureate Organization, since 2002; Associate Assessor with Her Majesty's Inspectorate for Education, Scotland, since 2003; b. 29.3.58, Shahnavaz Jiwa; 1 s.; 1 d. Educ. McGill University, Montreal (MA); Edinburgh University (PhD). Began career as part-time Lecturer in Islamic History, Edinburgh University, 1989-91; embarked on career in community development, training and practising as a counsellor; leading role in setting up a range of community-based services for minority ethnic women in Edinburgh,

1991-99; volunteer counsellor, Edinburgh Association for Mental Health, 1996-98; voluntary involvement with Ismaili Muslim community in UK. Recreations: swimming; reading; walks.

Jodrell, Duncan Ian, DM, MSc, FRCPE. Professor of Cancer Therapeutics, Edinburgh University, since 2006; Consultant in Medical Oncology, Edinburgh Cancer Centre, since 1994; b. 8.10.58, Warrington. Educ. Sir Thomas Rich's, Gloucester; Southampton University. House Physician, Southampton University; House Surgeon, Winchester; Senior House Officer, Southampton University; Registrar, St George's Hospital, London; Research Fellow, Institute of Cancer Research and Visiting Professor, University of Maryland; Senior Registrar, Beatson Oncology Centre, Glasgow. Recreations: golf; hill-walking. Address: (b.) Edinburgh Cancer Centre, Western General Hospital, Edinburgh EH4 2XU; T.-0131 777 3516; e-mail: duncan.jodrell@ed.ac.uk

Johnson, Professor Christopher William, MA, MSc, DPhil, CEng, FBCS. Professor, Computing Science, Glasgow University; b. 15.4.65, Edinburgh; m., Fionnuala Muireann; 4 s. Educ. Verulam School, St. Albans; Trinity College, Cambridge. Lecturer in Computing Science, University of York, 1991-94; Senior Lecturer in Computing Science, University of Glasgow, 1994-97. Secretary, IFIP Working Group 13.5 (Human Error and Systems Development). Winner, 2002 NASA/ICASE Fellowship; 2003 award, International Systems Safety Society. Publications: over 200 papers and articles. Recreation: running. Address: (b.) Department of Computing Science, University of Glasgow, Glasgow G12 8QQ; T.-0141-330 6053.

Johnson, David (Charles), MA, BA, PhD. Composer; Musicologist; Publisher; 27.10.42, Edinburgh; 1 s. Educ. Aberdeen University; St. John's College, Cambridge. Cellist, McGibbon Ensemble, 1980-96; Tutor, Edinburgh University Music Faculty, 1988-94; compositions include five operas, an orchestral suite, chamber music, songs, a piano concerto, church music, three cello suites. Publications: Music and Society in Lowland Scotland, 1972; Scottish Fiddle Music in the 18th Century, 1984; The Scots Cello Book, 1990; Stepping Northward, 1990; 12 Preludes and Fugues, 1996; Chamber Music of 18th Century Scotland, 2000; contributions to New Grove Dictionary of Music, 2001; The Art of Robert Burns CD series, since 2003; Thistle & Minnet, 2005; Enlightenment Edinburgh Series of music editions, since 2006. Address: (h.) 8 Shandon Crescent, Edinburgh EH11 1QE. T.-0131-337 4621.

Johnson, Ian Edward, MSc, DipTP (Dist), MRTPI, FSA (Scot). Manager, Ayrshire Joint Structure Plan and Transportation Committee, since 1996; Member, Historic Environment Advisory Council for Scotland, since 2003; b. 7.6.45, Lincoln; m., Dr. Carol Swanson. Educ. Lincoln School; Nottingham College of Art and Design; University of Edinburgh. Team Leader, City Centre Planning Team, Glasgow Corporation, 1970-75; Strathclyde Regional Council: Principal Planner, Strategy, 1975-84, Principal Planner, Heritage, 1984-96. Member: Forestry Commission Regional Advisory Committee, Forestry Commission South of Scotland Regional Forestry Forum, Scottish Gardens Advisory Group, Forestry Commission Scotland: National Forest Land Scheme Examination Panel. Recreations: collecting art deco; industrial archaeology; travelling in Central Europe; landscape gardens. Address: (b.) 15 Links Road, Prestwick, Ayrshire KA14 3AE; T.-01292 476716; e-mail: ian.johnson@south-ayrshire.gov.uk

Johnson, Professor Ian M., BA, FCILIP, FCMI. Professor, Aberdeen Business School, Robert Gordon University, Aberdeen, since 1989, Associate Dean, 2002-07; b. 17.3.45, Sheffield; m., Jean Trevena. Educ. King Edward VII School, Sheffield; Liverpool College of Commerce; Leeds Polytechnic. Sheffield City Libraries, 1962-74; Department of Education and Science (Office of Arts and Libraries), 1970-72 (on secondment); Rotherham M.B. Council, 1974-78; College of Librarianship Wales, 1978-89. Chairman, Professional Board, International Federation of Library Associations and Institutions, 1993-95; Chairman, Library Association Personnel Training and Education Group, 1994-95; Member, Library Association Council, 1996-2000; Chairman: Heads of Schools and Departments Committee, British Association for Information and Library Education and Research, 1997-2000; Chairman: EUCLID, 1998-2002, European Association for Library and Information Research. Recreations: theatre; cinema; travel. Address: (b.) Garthdee Road, Aberdeen AB10 7QE.

Johnson, Dr Peter R.E., MD, FRCP, FRCPath. Consultant Haematologist, since 1996; b. 21.6.61, Altrincham; m., Fiona. Educ. Daniel Stewart's and Melville College, Edinburgh; Aberdeen University. Senior House Officer/Registrar, Aberdeen Teaching Hospitals, 1985-88; Research Fellow, Manchester Royal Infirmary, 1988-90; Registrar/Senior Registrar, North Western Region Haematology Rotation, 1990-96. Founder, Scotland Leukaemia Registry; Member, Executive Committee, Scottish Haematology Society. Recreations: walking; fishing. Address: (b.) Department of Haematology, Western General Hospital, Crewe Road, Edinburgh EH4 2XU; T.-0131 537 2595; e-mail: peter.johnson@luht.scot.nhs.uk

Johnston, Rt. Hon. Lord (Alan Charles Macpherson), BA (Hons) (Cantab), LLB, DUniv (Heriot Watt), QC. Senator of the College of Justice, since 1994; Privy Councillor (2005); Queen's Counsel (1980); b. 13.1.42, Stirling; m., Anthea Jean Blackburn; 3 s. Educ. Edinburgh Academy; Loretto School; Jesus College, Cambridge; Edinburgh University. Advocate, 1967; Standing Junior Counsel, Scottish Home and Health Department, 1972; Advocate Depute, 1978-82; Chairman: Industrial Tribunal, 1982-85, Medical Appeal Tribunal, 1985-89; Treasurer, Faculty of Advocates, 1977-89, Dean, Faculty of Advocates, 1989-93. Publication: Introduction to Law of Scotland 7th Edition (Joint Editor). Address: (h.) 3 Circus Gardens, Edinburgh; T.-0131-225 1862.

Johnston, Frederick Patrick Mair, CBE, FRSA, MA. Chairman, Johnston Press plc (formerly F. Johnston & Co. Ltd.), 1973-2001, Non-Executive Director, since 2001; Director, Lloyds TSB Scotland plc, 1996-2003; Director, Scottish Mortgage & Trust plc, 1991-2002; b. 15.9.35, Edinburgh; m., Elizabeth Ann Jones; 2 s. Educ. Morrison's Academy, Crieff; Lancing College, Sussex; New College, Oxford. Editorial Department, Liverpool Daily Post and Echo, 1959; Assistant Secretary, The Times Publishing Co. Ltd., 1960; Company Secretary, F. Johnston & Co. Ltd., 1969. Chairman, Central Scotland Manpower Committee, 1976-83; Member, Press Council, 1974-88; President, Scottish Newspaper Proprietors' Association, 1976-78; Treasurer, Society of Master Printers of Scotland, 1981-86; President, The Newspaper Society, 1989-90; Chairman, Edinburgh International Book Festival, 1996-2001; Director, Press Association Ltd., 1997-2001. Recreations: reading; travelling. Address: (b.) 53 Manor Place, Edinburgh EH3 7EG; T.-0131-225 3361.

Johnston, Geoffrey Edward Forshaw, LLB, CA. Vice Chairman, Scottish Friendly Assurance Society Ltd.;

Managing Director, Arbuckle, Smith and Company, 1972-99; Chairman, Scottish Chambers of Commerce, 1996-2000; b. 20.6.40, Burton-Wirral, England; m., Elizabeth Anne Lockhart; 2 d. Educ. Loretto School, Musselburgh; University of St. Andrews. Wilson Stirling & Co. CA, 1959-65; Arbuckle Smith Group, since 1965: Director, 1968, management buy-out, 1984. Honorary Consul for Belgium, Scotland West and Northern Islands, 1989-95; National Chairman, British International Freight Association, 1990-91; President, Glasgow Chamber of Commerce, 1994-95; Member, Scottish Valuation and Rating Council, 1981-2001; Chairman, Central College of Commerce, 1999-2005; Chairman, Roses Charitable Trust. Recreations: sailing; skiing; hillwalking; golf. Address: (h.) Upper Dunard, Station Road, Rhu, Dunbartonshire G84 8LW; T.-01436 820563.

Johnston, George Bonar, DA, RSW. Artist; b. 14.6.33, Edinburgh; m., Margaret (deceased); 1 s.; 1 d. Educ. Bathgate Academy; Edinburgh College of Art. Teacher, 1955-56; Army Officer, 1956-58; Teacher, 1958-59; Lecturer, 1959-66; Art Adviser, Tayside Region, 1966-91. Paintings in private and public collections in Scotland, England, France, North America, Canada. Recreations: fly fishing; reading. Address: 10 Collingwood Crescent, Barnhill, Dundee DD5 2SX; T.-01382 779857.

Johnston, Grenville Shaw, OBE, TD, KCSG, JP, CA. Chartered Accountant, since 1968; President, Institute of Chartered Accountants of Scotland, 2000-01; Vice Lord Lieutenant of Moray, 1996-2005, Lord Lieutenant, since 2005; Territorial Army Officer, 1964-89 (Lt. Col.); b. 28.1.45, Nairn; m., Marylyn Jean Picken; 2 d. Educ. Blairmore School; Fettes College. Qualified in Edinburgh with Scott Moncrieff Thomson & Sheills; Thomson McLintock & Co., Glasgow, 1968-70; joined family firm, W.D. Johnston & Carmichael, Elgin, 1970, Senior Partner, 1975-2001, Consultant, 2001-05 (retired). Commanding Officer, 2nd 51st Highland Volunteers, 1983-86; Hon. Col., 3rd Highland Volunteers, 1997-99; Knight Commander, Order of St. Gregory, 1982, for work for Pluscarden Abbey; OBE for services to Territorial Army; Chairman, Grampian Committee, Royal Jubilee Trusts, 1982-91; Member, Cairngorm Mountain Trust Ltd.; Trustee and Council Member: Queens Own Highlanders, The Highlanders; Trustee, National Museums of Scotland, 1998-2006; Director: Cairngorm Mountain Ltd., since 1999, Highlands and Islands Airports Ltd, since 2001; Chairman, Caledonian Maritime Assets Ltd, since 2006. Recreations: shooting; fishing; hockey; golf; skiing; singing (tenor); curling. Address: (h.) Spynie Kirk House, Spynie, By Elgin, Moray IV30 8XJ.

Johnston, Professor Ian Alistair, BSc, PhD, FRSE. Chandos Professor of Physiology, since 1997 and Director, Gatty Marine Laboratory, since 1985; b. 13.4.49, Barking, Essex. Educ. Addey and Stanhope Grammar School, London; Hull University. NERC Postdoctoral Research Fellow, Bristol University, 1973-75; Lecturer in Physiology, St. Andrews University, 1976-84; Reader, 1984-85; Visiting Senior Lecturer, Department of Veterinary Physiology, Nairobi University, 1981; Visiting Scientist, British Antarctic Survey base, Signy Island, South Orkneys, 1983-84; Council Member, NERC, 1995-2000; Chairman, NERC Marine Science and Technology Board; awarded Scientific Medal, Zoological Society of London; President, Society for Experimental Biology, since 2007. Recreations: photography; walking; reading. Address: (b.) School of Biology, St. Andrews University, St. Andrews KY16 8LB; T.-01334 463440.

Johnston, James George, BSc (Hons), AdvDip Ed, FRSA, MIM. Head Teacher, Whalsay School, Shetland, since 1996; b. 1.5.54, Glasgow; m., Marilyn; 1 s. Educ. Cumbernauld High School; Glasgow University. Teacher, Greenfaulds High, 1977-80; Head of Department, Oxenford, 1980-83; Assistant Head Teacher, Oxenford, 1983-84; Head Teacher, Leverhulme Memorial School, 1984-96. Recreations: DIY. art; golf; cooking. Address: (h.) Laarsund, Hillswick, Shetland, ZE2 9RW; T.-01806 503342.

Johnston, Jim A., MA. Headteacher, Farr High School, since 1991; b. 11.9.50, Lerwick; m., Jenny Mackay; 1 d. Educ. Anderson Educational Institute; Aberdeen University; Aberdeen College of Education. Farr High School: Assistant Teacher of English, 1973-75, Principal Teacher of English, 1975-77, Depute Head, 1977-91. Chairman, Bettyhill, Strathnaver and Altnaharra Community Council, 1977-88; Company Secretary, Tongue and Farr Sports Association Ltd., since 1991; founding Chairman, Scottish Peat and Land Development Association (Caithness Branch); Chairman, Project Area Advisory Group, Duthchas Community Regeneration Project. Publications: A Future for Peat, 1981; Tongue and Farr, 1984, Gleannan am Fraoch, 1988; The Best of the Bard (Editor), 1987; Strathnaver – An Introduction and Guide, 2002. Recreations: journalism, including "Skywatching", a monthly column on astronomy; photography; crofting; reading; hillwalking. Address: (h.) Vaila, Bettyhill, by Thurso, Caithness KW14 7SS; T.-01641 521302; e-mail: jim.a.johnston@highland.gov.uk

Johnston, Professor Marie, BSc, PhD, DipClinPsych, FBPsS, CPsychol, FRSE, FMedSci, ACSS. Professor in Psychology, Aberdeen University, since 2003; b. 6.7.44, Aberdeen; m., Derek Johnston. Educ. High School for Girls, Aberdeen; Aberdeen University; Hull University. Research Officer, Oxford University, 1971-77; Lecturer, Senior Lecturer, Reader, Royal Free Hospital School of Medicine, 1977-90; Reader, Professor of Psychology, St. Andrews University, 1990-2003; Honorary Clinical Psychologist, Tayside and Fife Health Boards, since 1991; first Chair, Section of Health Psychology, British Psychological Society; Past President, European Health Psychology Society. Recreation: gardening. Address: (b.) School of Psychology, Aberdeen University, King's College, Aberdeen AB24 2UB.

Johnston, Robin Alexander, BSc, MB, BCh, BAO, MD, FRCSEd, FRCSGlas. Consultant Neurosurgeon, since 1985 (of Queen Elizabeth National Spinal Injury Unit, since 1992); b. 30.3.49, Belfast; m., Ann. Educ. Belfast Royal Academy; Queens University, Belfast. Various surgical posts, UK, 1974-77; neurosurgical training, Belfast, Dallas, Glasgow, 1977-85. Address: (b.) Institute of Neurological Sciences, Southern General Hospital, Glasgow; T.-0141-201 2021.

Johnston, Thomas Lothian, DL, MA, PhD, FRSA, FRSE, CIMgt, FIPD, DrHC, DEd, LLD, DUniv, DLitt, FEIS. President, Royal Society of Edinburgh, 1993-96; Chairman, Scottish Committee, Royal Society of Arts, 1991-95; b. 9.3.27, Whitburn; m., Joan Fahmy; 2 s.; 3 d. Educ. Hawick High School, Edinburgh University; Stockholm University. Served RNVR (Sub. Lieut.), 1944-47; Lecturer in Political Economy, Edinburgh University, 1953-65; Professor of Economics, Heriot-Watt University, 1966-76; Vice-Chancellor, Heriot-Watt University, 1981-88; industrial relations arbitrator and mediator; Member, National Industrial Relations Court, 1971-74; Chairman, Manpower Services Committee for Scotland, 1977-80; Member, Scottish Economic Council, 1977-91; Chairman, Enquiry into Staff Representation, London Clearing Banks, 1978-79; Member, Review Committee, New Zealand Universities, 1987; Scottish Chairman, Industry Year, 1986, and Industry Matters, 1987-89; Trustee, National Galleries of Scotland, 1989-95; academic appointments in other countries:

University of Illinois, 1957, 1962-63, Queen's University, Canada, 1965, Western Australian Institute of Technology, 1979, Visiting Professor, International Institute for Labour Studies, Geneva, 1973. Publications: Collective Bargaining in Sweden, 1962; Economic Expansion and Structural Change, 1963; The Structure and Growth of the Scottish Economy (Co-Author), 1971; Introduction to Industrial Relations, 1981; translations from Swedish. Recreations: gardening; walking. Address: (h.) 14 Mansionhouse Road, Edinburgh EH9 1TZ; T.-031-667 1439.

Johnstone, Alex. MSP (Conservative), North East Scotland, since 1999; Party Spokesman on Transport, Infrastructure and Climate Change; m.; 2 c. Dairy and arable farmer. Address: (b.) Scottish Parliament, Edinburgh EH99 1SP; T.-0131-348 5649.

Johnstone, Professor Eve Cordelia, CBE, MB, ChB, MD, FRCP, FRCPsych, FMedSci, FRSE, DPM. Professor of Psychiatry and Head, Department of Psychiatry, University of Edinburgh, since 1989; b. 1.9.44, Glasgow. Educ. Park School, Glasgow; University of Glasgow. Junior posts in Glasgow hospitals; Lecturer in Psychological Medicine, University of Glasgow, 1972-74; Member of Scientific Staff, Medical Research Council, Clinical Research Centre, Northwick Park, 1974-89. Member of Council, Medical Research Council, 1997-2002; Chairman, MRC Neurosciences Board, 1999-2002. Publications: seven books on psychiatric illness; over 200 papers on biological psychiatry. Address: (b.) Royal Edinburgh Hospital, Morningside Park, Edinburgh.

Johnstone, Rev. Mark Edward, MA, BD. Minister of Religion, St. Mary's Manse, Kirkintilloch, since 2000; b. 28.5.68, Glasgow; m., Audrey Gail Cameron; 2 s.; 1 d. Educ. Kingsridge Secondary, Drumchapel; University of Glasgow; Trinity College. Parish Minister, Denny, Falkirk; Chaplain to Strathcarron Hospice, Bellsdyke Psychiatric Hospital; Minister In Charge, Northminster United Church, Toronto, Canada; Parish Minister, St. Mary's, Kirkintilloch; Convener, Eldership Working Party/Membership. Provincial Grand Junior Chaplain of Dunbartonshire. Recreations: gym; conjouring; dog walking; fishing. Address: (h.) The Manse, 60 Union Street, Kirkintilloch G66 1DH; T.-0141-776-1252.
E-mail: mark.johnstone2@ntlworld.com

Johnstone, Sir Raymond, CBE, BA, CA. Director, The Nuclear Trust, since 1996; Director, The Nuclear Liabilities Fund Ltd., 1996-2007; Director, RJ KILN PLC, 1995-2002; Chairman, Atrium Underwriting PLC (formerly Lomond Underwriting plc), 1993-2003; b. 27.10.29, London; m., Susan Sara; 5 step s.; 2 step d. Educ. Eton; Trinity College, Cambridge. Investment Analyst, Robert Fleming & Co. Ltd., London, 1955-60; Partner (CA), Brown, Fleming & Murray (later Whinney Murray & Co.), 1960-68; Director: Scottish Amicable Life Assurance Society, 1971-97 (Chairman, 1983-85); Dominion Insurance Co. Ltd., 1973-95 (Chairman, 1978-95); Scottish Financial Enterprise, 1986-91 (Chairman, 1989-91); Summit Group PLC (Chairman, 1989-98); Murray Income PLC, 1989-99; Murray International PLC, 1989-2005; Murray Global Markets PLC, 1989-2000; Murray Ventures PLC, 1984-99; Murray Enterprise PLC, 1989-00; Chairman, Murray Johnstone Ltd., 1984-91 (Managing Director, 1968-88); Chairman, Forestry Commission, 1989-94; Chairman, Murray Split Capital Trust PLC, 1991-98; Chairman, 1982-86, Hon. President, 1986-97, Scottish Opera; Governor, Patrons of the National Galleries of Scotland, 1995-2003, Chairman, 1995-99; Chairman, Historic Buildings Council for Scotland, 1995-2002; Chairman, The Nuclear Trust, 1996-2003. Recreations: fishing; shooting; opera; farming. Address: (h.) 20 Ann Street, Edinburgh EH4 1PJ.

Johnstone, Professor William, BD, MA (Hons), DLitt. Professor of Hebrew and Semitic Languages, Aberdeen

University, 1980-2001, Emeritus Professor, since 2001; Minister, Church of Scotland, since 1963; b. 6.5.36, Glasgow; m., Elizabeth M. Ward; 1 s.; 1 d. Educ. Hamilton Academy; Glasgow University; Marburg University. Lecturer in Hebrew and Semitic Languages, Aberdeen University, 1962-72, Senior Lecturer, 1972-80, Dean, Faculty of Divinity, 1983-87; President, Society for Old Testament Study, 1990. Recreation: alternative work. Address: (h.) 9/5 Mount Alvernia, Edinburgh EH16 6AW.

Jones, Alan, BEd, MEd. Leisure consultant, since 2002; Director of Cultural and Leisure Services, Highland Council, 1987-2002; Member, Board, Sportscotland; b. 14.7.56, Bathgate; m., Joyce; 2 d. Educ. St Mary's Academy, Bathgate; Jordanhill College, Glasgow; Glasgow University; Stirling University. Lecturer, Physical Recreation, Stirling University, 1978-81; Sports Officer, Stirling District Council, 1981-86; Community and Leisure Manager, Clackmannan District Council, 1986-87; Director of Leisure and Recreation, Inverness District Council, 1987-95. Set up project to "Green" Inverness; winner, Queen Mother's Birthday Award. Recreations: Member, Physical Activity Task Force; golf; ski-ing. Address: 62 Boswell Road, Inverness IV2 3EJ; T.-01463 718715; e-mail: alanjonesassociates@btopenworld.com

Jones, Bernadette. Rector, St. Joseph's College, Dumfries, since 2008. Address: (b.) Craigs Road, Dumfries DG1 4UU.

Jones, Professor Colin Anthony, BA (Hons). MA. Professor of Estate Management, Heriot-Watt University, since 1998; b. 13.1.49, Wallasey; m., Fiona Jones; 2 d. Educ. Price's School, Fareham, Hants; Wallasey Grammar School; York University; Manchester University. Research associate, Manchester University; Lecturer, Applied Economics, Glasgow University, 1975-80; Department of Land Economics, Paisley University, 1980-98; Member, UK Board, Shelter, 1978-84, and 1990-2007. Publication: The Right to Buy. Address: (b.) School of the Built Environment, Heriot-Watt University, Riccarton, Edinburgh, EH14 4AS; T.-0131-451 4628; e-mail: c.a.jones@hw.ac.uk

Jones, David, BA, CertEd. Chief Executive, Clackmannanshire Council, since 2001; b. 18.10.49, South Shields; m., Lesley; 2 d. Educ. Didsbury College; Open University. Mathematics Teacher: Hylton Red House School, Sunderland, 1971-75, West Southwick School, Sunderland, 1975-76, Houghton School, Sunderland, 1976-80, Biddick School, Sunderland, 1980-87; Deputy Head, Bede School, Sunderland, 1987-90; Headteacher, Washington School, Sunderland, 1991-99; Assistant Director of Education, Sunderland, 2000-01. Recreations: MENSA; bird watching; caravaning; motoring. Address: Greenfield, Alloa FK10 2AD; T.-01259 452002.

Jones, Emeritus Professor Douglas Samuel, MBE, MA, DSc, FIMA, CMath, FRSE, CEng, CSci, FIEE, FRS. Ivory Professor of Mathematics, University of Dundee, 1965-92, now Emeritus Professor; b. 10.1.22; m., Ivy Styles; 1 s.; 1 d. Educ. Wolverhampton Grammar School; Corpus Christi College, Oxford. University of Manchester: Assistant Lecturer in Mathematics, 1948-51, Lecturer, 1951-54; Research Professor, New York University, 1955; Senior Lecturer in Mathematics, University of Manchester, 1955-57; Professor of Mathematics, University of Keele, 1957-64. Visiting Professor, Courant Institute, 1962-63. Hon.DSc, Strathclyde, 1975; Keith Prize, RSE, 1974; IEE Marconi Prize, 1974; van der Pol Gold Medal, International

Union of Radio Science, 1981; Naylor Prize, London Mathematical Society, 1987. Trustee, Quarterly Journal of Mechanics and Applied Mathematics, 1980-92; Associate Editor: IMA Journal, 1964-2003, Mathematical Methods in the Applied Sciences, 1977-2002, Methods and Applications of Analysis, since 1992, Journal of Engineering Mathematics, since 1992; Communications in Applied Analysis, since 1997. Publications; Electrical and Mechanical Oscillations, 1961; Theory of Electromagnetism, 1964; Generalised Functions, 1966; Introductory Analysis, Vol. I, 1969, Vol. II, 1970; Methods in Electromagnetic Wave Propagation, 1979, 2nd ed., 1994; Elementary Information Theory, 1979; The Theory of Generalised Functions, 1982; Differential Equations and Mathematical Biology, 1983, 2nd ed., 2003; Acoustic and Electromagnetic Waves, 1986; Assembly Programming and the 8086 Microprocessor, 1988; 80X86 Assembly Programming, 1991; Introduction to Asymptotics, 1997. Recreations: golf; walking; photography. Address: 1 The Nurseries, St. Madoes, Glencarse, Perth PH2 7NX.

Jones, Professor Hamlyn Gordon, MA (Cantab), PhD, FIHort. Professor of Plant Ecology, University of Dundee, since 1997; Honorary Research Professor, Scottish Crop Research Institute, Dundee, since 1998; b. 7.12.47, Kuala Lumpur, Malaysia; m., Amanda Jane Corry; 2 d. Educ. St. Lawrence College, Ramsgate; St. John's College, University of Cambridge; Australian National University, Canberra. Research Fellow, St. John's College, Cambridge, 1973-76; Researcher, Plant Breeding Institute, Cambridge, 1972-76; Lecturer in Ecology, University of Glasgow, 1977-78; Leader of Stress Physiology Group, East Malling Research Station, Kent, 1978-88; Director, Crop Science Research and Head of Station, Horticulture Research International, Wellesbourne, Warwick, 1988-97; Special Professor, University of Nottingham, 1991-97; Honorary Professor, University of Birmingham, 1995-98. Member, Scientific Advisory Committee, Scottish Natural Heritage, since 2005. Publications: Plants and Microclimate, 1983/1992; joint editor of five other books; on editorial board of six scientific journals. Recreations: squash; tennis; mountains; lounging. Address: (b.) Plant Research Unit, School of Life Sciences, University of Dundee at SCRI, Invergowrie, Dundee DD2 5DA; T.-01382 562731.

Jones, Emeritus Professor Huw, BA, MA. Emeritus Professor of Geography, Dundee University; b. Llanidloes; 2 s. Educ. Newtown Boys Grammar School, Powys; University College of Wales, Aberystwyth. Address: (b.) 43 Albert Road, Broughty Ferry, Dundee DD5 1AY; T.-01382-738513; e-mail: huwrjones@yahoo.co.uk

Jones, Ian Stewart, BSc, MStJ. Rector, Madras College, St. Andrews, since 2007; b. 17.9.53, Edinburgh; m., Elizabeth; 1 s.; 1 d.; 2 step d. Educ. George Heriot's School; Edinburgh University; Moray House College of Education. Teacher of Mathematics, Assistant Principal Teacher, Principal Teacher, Liberton High School, Edinburgh, 1976-90; 5-14 Development Officer, Lothian Regional Council, 1990-91; Assistant Head Teacher, Depute Head Teacher, Gracemount High School, Edinburgh, 1991-97; Depute Head Teacher, Lasswade High School Centre, 1997-2001; Headteacher, Menzieshill High School, Dundee, 2001-07. Member, Scottish Secondary Mathematics Group; Chair, Tayside Board, The Prince's Trust Scotland. Recreations: ski-ing; mountaineering; sailing; curling; travel. Address: (b.) Madras College, South Street, St. Andrews KY16 9EJ; T.-01334 659402; e-mail: ian.jones-mo@fife.gov.uk

Jones, Most Revd. Idris, BA, DMin. Episcopal Bishop of Glasgow and Galloway, since 1998; Primus, Scottish Episcopal Church, 2006; b. 1943. Educ. University College St. David, Lampeter; New College, Edinburgh; Edinburgh Theological College. Deacon, 1967; Priest, 1968; Curate, St. Mary's, Stafford, 1967-70; Precentor, St. Paul's Cathedral, Dundee, 1970-73; Priest-in-Charge, St. Hugh's, Gosforth, Newcastle, 1973-80; Chaplain, St. Nicholas Hospital, 1975-80; Rector, St. Mary's and St. Peter's, Montrose with St. David's, Inverbervie, 1980-89; Anglican Chaplain, Dundee University and Priest-in-Charge, All Souls, Invergowrie, 1989-92; Canon, St. Paul's Cathedral, Dundee, 1984-92; Rector, Holy Trinity, Ayr, 1992-98; Director, Pastoral Studies, TISEC, 1995-99; Patron, Hutcheson's Hospital, 2002; Governor, Hutcheson Educational Trust, since 2002; President, Rotary Club of Queens Park, 2003; Deacon, Incorporation of Skinners and Glovers, 2007; Hon. Fellow, University of Wales, 2007; President, Glasgow XIII, 2005, Member. Address: Diocesan Centre, 5 St. Vincent Place, Glasgow G1 2DH.

Jones, Keith Greig, LLB. Head of Law and Administration (North Division), Aberdeenshire Council, 1996-2007 (retired); b. 10.9.48, Edinburgh; m., Margaret. Educ. Aberdeen Grammar School; Aberdeen University. Various appointments in private legal practice, 1969-75; joined Law and Administration Department, Kincardine and Deeside District Council, 1975; Director of Legal Services and Depute Chief Executive, 1985-96. Trustee: Grampian Transport Museum Trust, Kinneff Old Church Preservation Trust; Board Member, Grampian Housing Association; Member, Scottish Charity Law Review Commission, 2000-01; President, Society of Local Authority Lawyers and Administrators, 2002-03; Chairman, Great North of Scotland Railway Association, 2001-07. Address: (h.) 78 Louisville Avenue, Aberdeen AB15 4TX.

Jones, Mervyn David, BSc, MPhil. Partner, Maple Jones and various Public and Private Sector Boards, since 2003; Council Member, Scottish Funding Council, since 2005; b. 28.11.56, Poole; m., Pauline; 2 s.; 1 d. Educ. Poole Grammar School; Wales and Reading Universities. Research Demonstratorship, University of Reading, 1978-81; Trading, BP Oil International, London and New York, 1981-91; commercial and restructuring management roles, BP Brussels and BP Grangemouth. Chairman, Aquamarine Power Limited; various CSR Projects (MFIF, ACE); Chairman, Falkirk Community Stadium; Member: SFC Research and Knowledge Transfer Committee, SFC Capital Committee; Chair, SFC Knowledge Transfer Group. Recreations: fishing; golf; skiing; rugby; baroque music; opera; gardening. Address: (h.) 6 Blackford Road, Edinburgh EH9 2DS; T.-0131-446-0368 (business). E-mail: mervyn@maplejones.co.uk

Jones, Professor Peter (Howard), MA, FRSE, FRSA, FSA Scot. Director, Foundation for Advanced Studies in the Humanities, 1997-2002; Member, Spoliation Advisory Panel, since 2000; Professor of Philosophy, University of Edinburgh, 1984-98, Professor Emeritus, since 1998; Director, Institute for Advanced Studies in the Humanities, 1986-2000, b. 18.12.35, London; m., Elizabeth Jean Roberton; 2 d. Educ. Highgate School; Queens' College, Cambridge. Regional Officer, The British Council, London, 1960-61; Research Scholar, University of Cambridge, 1961-63; Assistant Lecturer in Philosophy, Nottingham University, 1963-64; University of Edinburgh: Lecturer in Philosophy, 1964-77, Reader, 1977-84; Visiting Professor of Philosophy: University of Rochester, New York, 1969-70, Dartmouth College, New Hampshire, 1973, 1983, Carleton College, Minnesota, 1974, Oklahoma University, 1978, Baylor University, 1978, University of Malta, 1993, Belarusian State University, 1997, Jagiellonian University, Cracow, since 2001; Distinguished Foreign Scholar, Mid-America State Universities, 1978; Visiting Fellow,

Humanities Research Centre, Australian National University, 1984, 2002; Calgary Institute for the Humanities, 1992; Lothian Lecturer, 1993; Gifford Lecturer, University of Aberdeen, 1994-95; Loemker Lecturer, Emory University, 1996; Trustee: National Museums of Scotland, 1987-99 (Chairman, Museum of Scotland Client Committee, 1991-99), University of Edinburgh Development Trust, 1990-98, Morrison's Academy, Crieff, 1984-98, Fettes College, 1995-2005, Scots at War Trust, Policy Institute, 1999-2008, MBI; Member: Court, University of Edinburgh, 1987-90, Council, Royal Society of Edinburgh, 1992-95, UNESCO forum on Tolerance, Tblisi, 1995, UNESCO dialogue on Europe and Islam, since 1997; Founder Member, The Hume Society, 1974. Publications: Philosophy and the Novel, 1975; Hume's Sentiments, 1982; A Hotbed of Genius, 1986; Philosophy and Science in the Scottish Enlightenment, 1988; The Science of Man in the Scottish Enlightenment, 1989; Adam Smith Reviewed, 1992; James Hutton, Investigation of the Principles of Knowledge, 1999; The Enlightenment World, 2004; Lord Kames: Elements of Criticism, 2005; The Reception of David Hume in Europe, 2005; Ove Arup - Masterbuilder of the Twentieth Century, 2006. Recreations: opera; chamber music; the arts; architecture. Address: 6 Greenhill Terrace, Edinburgh EH10 4BS; T.-0131-447 6344.

Jones, Philip Neville, MSc, MCMI, CMgr. Chief Executive, Dumfries and Galloway Council, since 1998; b. 8.6.51; m., Jacqueline Fiona; 3 s. Educ. Kelsterton College, Deeside; University of Strathclyde. Productivity Services Officer, Unilever, Port Sunlight, 1976-80; Dumfries and Galloway Regional Council: Assistant Regional Management Services Officer, 1980-86, Assistant Director Information Technology, 1986-89, Corporate Business Manager, 1989-96; Dumfries and Galloway Council: Head of Corporate Business, 1995-99, Council Monitoring Officer, 1997-99, Depute Chief Executive, 1995-98. Recreations: golf; gardening; walking. Address: Council Offices, English Street, Dumfries DG1 2DD; e-mail: chief.executive@dumgal.gov.uk

Jones, Raymond J. Chief Executive, Royal Highland and Agricultural Society of Scotland, since 1998; b. 30.9.47, Birmingham; 2 s.; 1 d. Educ. Lordswood; Harper Adams Agricultural College. Alfa-Laval; Unilever; Managing Director, LI Ireland, 1990-92; Regional Managing Director, Diverseylever, 1992-98. Recreations: walking; sailing. Address: (b.) Royal Highland Centre, Ingliston, Edinburgh EH28 8NF; T.-0131-335 6200.

Jones, Rev. William Gerald, MA, BD, ThM. Minister, Kirkmichael with Straiton St. Cuthbert's, since 1985; b. 2.11.56, Irvine; m., Janet Blackstock. Educ. Dalry High School; Garnock Academy, Kilbirnie; Glasgow University; St. Andrews University; Princeton Theological Seminary, Princeton, New Jersey. Assistant Minister, Glasgow Cathedral, 1983-85. Freeman Citizen of Glasgow, 1984; Member, Incorporation of Gardeners of Glasgow, 1984; Moderator, Presbytery of Ayr, 1997-98; Member: General Assembly Panel on Worship, 1987-91, Council, Church Service Society, 1986-98, Committee to Nominate the Moderator of the General Assembly, 1988-92 and 1998-2003, Committee on Artistic Matters, 2000-01; Societas Liturgica, since 1989; Officer and Assistant Chaplain, Order of St. Lazarus of Jerusalem, 1995; Ayr Presbytery Representative, Ayrshire Regional Council of the Scottish Episcopal Church, since 2002; Convener, Administration Committee, Presbytery of Ayr, 1988-91 and 2005-08; Member: Society for Liturgical Study, since 1995; Society for the Study of Theology, since 2000; Council, Scottish Church Society, 2000-06, Secretary, since 2004, and Editorial Committee member, since 2006; Society for the Study of Christian Ethics, since 2003; Honorary Chaplain, York Minster, since 2001; Member, The Priory of Scotland of The Order of St. John of Jerusalem, 2006; Life Member, Ayrshire Archaeological and Natural History Society; broadcaster, West Sound Radio, since 1998. Publications: Prayers for the Chapel Royal in Scotland, 1989; Worshipping Together (Contributor), 1991; Common Order (Contributor), 1994; The Times Book of Prayers (Contributor), 1997; A Lenten Meditation (Scottish Church Society), 2005; Sharing the Past: Shaping the Future (Co-editor), 2008. Recreations: music; books; writing; country life. Address: The Manse, Kirkmichael, Maybole, Ayrshire KA19 7PJ; T.-01655 750286.

Jowitt, Professor Paul William, PhD, DIC, BSc(Eng), FCGI, CEng, FICE, FRSA, FRSE. Professor of Civil Engineering Systems, Heriot-Watt University, since 1987; Editor, Civil Engineering and Environmental Systems, since 1985; b. 3.8.50, Doncaster. Educ. Maltby Grammar School; Imperial College. Lecturer in Civil Engineering, Imperial College 1974-86 (Warden, Falmouth Hall, 1980-86); Director, Tynemarch Systems Engineering Ltd., 1984-91 (Chairman, 1984-86); Head, Civil Engineering Department, Heriot-Watt University, 1989-91, Head, Civil and Offshore Engineering, 1991-99. Director, Scottish Institute of Sustainable Technology, since 1999; Member, East of Scotland Water Authority, 1999-2002; Member, Scottish Water, since 2002. Recreations: painting; Morgan 3-wheelers; restoring old houses. Address: (h.) 14 Belford Mews, Edinburgh EH4 3BT; T.-0131-225 7583; e-mail: p.w.jowitt@hw.ac.uk

Joyce, Eric. BA, MA, MBA, PGCE. MP (Labour), Falkirk, since 2005, Falkirk West, 2000-05; b. 13.10.60, Perth; m., Rosemary Jones. Soldier, Black Watch, 1978-81; Officer, Adjutant General's Corps, 1987-99; Public Affairs Officer, Commission for Racial Equality, 1999-2000. Executive Member, Fabian Society, 1998-2006; Chair, 2004-05; Member, Camelon Labour Club; former Scottish judo champion. Address: (b.) House of Commons, London, SW1A 0AA. Constituency Address: The Studio, Burnfoot Lane, Falkirk FK1 5BH.

Judge, Professor David, BA, PhD, FRSA. Professor of Politics, University of Strathclyde, since 1994; b. 22.5.50, Sheffield; m., Lorraine; 1 s.; 1 d. Educ. Westfield School; Exeter University; Sheffield University. Lecturer, Paisley College, 1974-88; University of Strathclyde: Lecturer, 1988-90, Senior Lecturer, 1990-91, Reader, 1991-94; Fulbright Fellow and Visiting Professor, University of Houston, USA, 1993-94; Visiting Professor, College of Europe, Bruges, since 2004. Publications: Backbench Specialisation in the House of Commons, 1981; The Politics of Parliamentary Reform (Editor), 1983; The Politics of Industrial Closure (Joint Editor), 1987; Parliament and Industry, 1990; A Green Dimension for the European Community (Editor), 1993; The Parliamentary State, 1993; Theories of Urban Politics (Co-Editor), 1995; Representation: Theory and Practice in Britain, 1999; The European Parliament (Co-Author), 2003; Political Institutions in the UK, 2005. Recreation: breathing. Address: (b.) Department of Government, University of Strathclyde, Glasgow G1 1XQ; T.-0141-548 2365; e-mail: d.judge@strath.ac.uk

Jung, Roland Tadeusz, BA, MA, MB, BChir, MD, MRCS, LRCP, MRCP, FRCPEdin, FRCPLond. Consultant Physician (Specialist in Endocrinology and Diabetes), since 1982; Chief Scientist, Scottish Executive Health Department, 2001-06; Honorary Professor, Dundee University; Chairman, Scottish Hospital Endowments Research Trust, 2000-01; Senior Distinction Advisor

(Eastern Region) for Scottish Advisory Committee on Distinction Awards, since 2003; b. 8.2.48, Glasgow; m., Felicity King; 1 d. Educ. St. Anselm's College, Wirral; Pembroke College, Cambridge; St. Thomas Hospital and Medical School, London. MRC Clinical Scientific Officer, Dunn Nutrition Unit, Cambridge, and Honorary Senior Registrar, Addenbrooke's Hospital, Cambridge, 1977-79; Senior Registrar in Endocrinology and Diabetes, Royal Postgraduate Medical School, Hammersmith Hospital, London, 1980-82; Clinical Director of General Medicine, Dundee Teaching Hospitals Trust, 1991-94; Director of R and D, Tayside NHS Consortium, 1997-2001. Publication: Endocrine Problems in Oncology (Co-Editor), 1984; Colour Atlas of Obesity, 1990. Recreations: gardening; visiting gardens of distinction; 'paved' walking. Address: (b.) Diabetes Centre, Ninewells Hospital and Medical School, Dundee; T.-Dundee 660111.

Junor, Gordon James, LLB (Hons). Advocate, since 1993; b. 18.1.56, Stannington, Northumberland. Educ. King Edward VI Grammar School, Morpeth; Edinburgh University. Solicitor, local government, 1982-92. Consulting Editor, Reparation Bulletin. Publication: Scottish Older Client Law Service (Housing). Recreation; hillwalking. Address: Freelands, 9 Taits Hill, Selkirk TD7 4LZ; T.-01750 22121.

Juster, Professor Neal Peter, BSc, PhD, CEng, FIMechE, FRSA. Vice-Principal (Strategy and Resources), University of Glasgow, since 2007; b. 10.9.61, Carshalton; m., Sandra; 1 s.; 1 d. Educ. Emanuel School; University of Leeds. Royal Navy Engineering Officer (Under Training), 1980-84; University of Leeds: Lecturer in Computer Aided Engineering, Department of Mechanical Engineering, 1988-94, Senior Lecturer, Department of Mechanical Engineering, 1994-97; University of Strathclyde: Head of The Department of Design, Manufacturing and Engineering Management, 1997-2002, Dean of The Faculty of Engineering, 2002-06, Pro Vice-Principal, 2006-07, Professor, Computer Aided Engineering, 1997-2007. Chair, Academic Standards Committee, Institution of Mechanical Engineers; Member, Qualifications and Membership Board, Institution of Mechanical Engineers. Recreations: coaching youth football. Address: (b.) Room 243, The Cloisters, Gilbert Scott Building, University of Glasgow, University Avenue, Glasgow G12 8QQ; T.-0141 330 6363; e-mail: n.juster@admin.gla.ac.uk

K

Kabir, Professor Rezaul, PhD, MA, MBA. Professor of Finance, University of Stirling, since 2005. University of Tilburg, The Netherlands, 1990-2005; University of Antwerp, Belgium, 1996-2004. Address: Department of Accounting and Finance, University of Stirling, Stirling FK9 4LA.

Kamm, Antony, MA. Author; b. 2.3.31, London; m., Eileen Dunlop (qv). Educ. Charterhouse; Worcester College, Oxford. Editorial Director, Brockhampton Press, 1960-72; Senior Education Officer, Commonwealth Secretariat, 1972-74; Managing Editor (Children's Books), Oxford University Press, 1977-79; Consultant to UNESCO and other international organisations, 1963-76; part-time Lecturer in Publishing Studies, Stirling University, 1988-95; Chairman, Children's Book Group, The Publishers Association, 1963-67, and of Children's Book Circle, 1963-64; played cricket for Middlesex, 1952. Publications include: Collins Biographical Dictionary of English Literature, 1993; The Romans, 1995 (web site version, 2006); The Israelites, 1999; John Logie Baird: a Life, (Co-author), 2002; The Last Frontier, 2004; Julius Caesar: a Life, 2006; children's information books and several anthologies. Address: (h.) 46 Tarmangie Drive, Dollar FK14 7BP; T.-01259 742007.

Kane, Archie Gerard, BACC, CA, MBA, IOCAS. Group Executive Director, Insurance and Investments, Lloyds TSB Group plc, and Chief Executive, Scottish Widows plc, since 2003; b. 16.6.52, Bellshill; m., Diana Muirhead; 2 d. Educ. Glasgow University; City University; Harvard Business School. Student Chartered Accountant, Mann Judd, Chartered Accountants, 1974-77; Assistant Manager, Price Waterhouse, 1978-80; Senior Management Auditor, General Telephone and Electronics Corporation (SYLVANIA), 1980-82; General Telephone and Electronic Corporation (Directories Corp): Assistant Financial Controller, 1982-83, Finance Director, 1983-85; Finance Director, British Telecom Yellow Pages Sales Ltd., 1986; Group Finance Controller, TSB Commercial Holdings Ltd., 1986-89; TSB Bank PLC: Financial Controller, Retail Banking Division, 1989, Director of Financial Control, Retail Banking Division, 1989-91, Director of Financial Control, Retail Banking and Insurance, 1991-92, Operations Director, Retail Banking and Insurance, 1992-94, Group Strategic Development Director, 1994-96; Lloyds TSB Group PLC: Project Director, Post Merger Integration, 1996, Retail Financial Services Director, 1996, Director of Group IT and Operations, 1997-99, Group Executive Director, IT and Operations, 2000-03. Chairman, Association of British Insurers, since 2007. Recreations: golf; tennis; skiing. Address: (b.) Lloyds TSB Group plc, 25 Gresham Street, London EC2V 7HN; T.-0207 356 1409; e-mail: archie.kane@lloydstsb.co.uk

Kane, Michael A., LLB (Hons), DipLP. Partner and Head of Corporate Department, Bell & Scott LLP, since 2004; b. 11.11.70, London; m., Susan F. J. Faithfull; 3 s.; 1 d. Educ. Sea Point Boys' School, Cape Town, South Africa; Buckhaven High School, Fife; Dundee University. Trainee Solicitor, Aberdeen, 1993-95, Assistant Solicitor, 1995-2000; Partner, Davidson Chalmers, Edinburgh, 2000-04. ICAS Technical Bulletin Committee. Recreations: golf; family. Address: (b.) 16 Hill Street, Edinburgh EH2 3LD; T.-0131 2266703; e-mail: m.kane@bellscott.co.uk

Kane, Patrick Mark, MA (Hons). Writer and Broadcaster; Co-Director, New Integrity (human potential consultancy); b. 10.3.64, Glasgow; m., Joan McAlpine; 1 d. Educ. St. Ambrose RC Secondary, Coatbridge; Glasgow University. Worked in London as a freelance writer; returned to Scotland to start professional music career with brother Gregory; achieved Top 10 and Top 20 singles and albums successes with Hue and Cry, 1987-89; TV arts presenter; former Rector, Glasgow University. Publication: The Play Ethic: A Manifesto for a Different Way of Living, 2004.

Kavanagh, George Collins, KCHS. Sheriff, North Strathclyde at Paisley, since 1999; b. Cumnor, Ayrshire; m., Rosaleen. Educ. St. Joseph's Academy; Glasgow University. HM Civil Service, 1961-70; Hughes Dowdall: Solicitor, 1970-90, Senior Partner, 1990-99. Address: (b.) Sheriff's Chambers, Sheriff Court House, St. James Street, Paisley PA3 2HW.

Kay, Professor Christian Janet, MA, AM, DipGenLing. Professor of English Language, Glasgow University, 1996-2005 (retired); Honorary Professorial Research Fellow; b. 4.4.40, Edinburgh. Educ. Mary Erskine School; Edinburgh University; Mount Holyoke College. Lecturer, Glasgow University, 1979-89; Senior Lecturer, Glasgow University, 1989-96. Publications: A Thesaurus of Old English (Co-editor), 1995; Lexicology, Semantics and Lexicography (Co-editor), 2000; Lexis and Texts in Early English (Co-editor), 2001; Proceedings of the 12th International Conference on English Historical Linguistics, 2 vols (Co-editor), 2004; Categorization in the History of English (Co-editor), 2004; Perspectives on the Older Scottish Tongue (Co-editor), 2005; Progress in Colour Studies: Language and Culture (Co-editor), 2006. Recreation: music. Address: (b.) Glasgow University, Glasgow, G12 8QQ; e-mail: c.kay@englang.arts.gla.ac.uk

Kay, Stefan George, OBE, BSc, CEng, FIMechE, CCMI, FRSA. Group Managing Director, Inveresk PLC, 1989-2001; Non-Executive Director: Dunedin Enterprise Investment Trust PLC, 1995-2004, Bio-Regional Minimills Ltd., since 2001, Georgia Pacific Britain Corp., 1996-2006, Servisan Ltd., since 2002; b. 25.7.44, Peebles; m., Helen Eugenia; 2 d. Educ. Holy Cross Academy; Heriot-Watt University. Graduate Trainee, Production Superintendent, Chief Chemist, Thames Board Ltd., 1967-73; Production Manager, Dexter Ltd., Berwickshire, 1973-78; Mill MD, St. Regis Paper Co. Ltd., Berkshire and Devon, 1979-88. Past President, Paper Federation of Great Britain; awarded paper industry Gold Medal, 1996; Chairman, Environment Committee, Confederation of European Paper Industries, 1998-2000; Director of Campus Services, Scottish Borders Campus, Heriot Watt University, since 2003; Chair, Leadership Committee, Scottish Forest Industries Cluster, since 2002; Chair, Scottish Railway Preservation Society, 2001-05; Member, Local Advisory Board, Careers Scotland Borders, since 2003; Liveryman, Worshipful Company of Stationers and Newspaper Makers. Recreations: steam railways; classical music; science fiction and historical literature. Address: (h.) 7 King's Cramond, Edinburgh EH4 6RL; T.-0131-336 5506.
E-mail: sgk@stefankay.abelgratis.co.uk

Kay, William (Billy), MA. Freelance Broadcaster/Writer/Producer; Director, Odyssey Productions; b. 24.9.51, Galston, Ayrshire; m., Maria João de Almeida da Cruz Dinis; 1 s.; 2 d. Educ. Galston High School; Kilmarnock Academy; Edinburgh University. Producer, Odyssey series, Radio Scotland; produced about 240 documentaries on diverse aspects of working-class oral history; Writer/Presenter, TV documentaries, including Miners, BBC Scotland; Presenter, Kay's Originals, Scottish TV. Commandeur d'Honneur, Commanderie du Bontemps de Médoc et des Graves; won Australasian Academy of Broadcast Arts and Sciences Pater award, 1987, 1988; Medallist, International Radio Festival of New York, 1990-

92; Sloan Prize for writing in Scots, 1992; Wine Guild of UK 1994 Houghton Award, for Fresche Fragrant Clairettis; Winner: Heritage Society Award, 1995, Wines of France Award, 1996. Publications: Odyssey: Voices from Scotland's Recent Past (Editor); Odyssey: The Second Collection (Editor); Knee Deep in Claret: A Celebration of Wine and Scotland (Co-author); Made in Scotland (poetry); Jute (play for radio); Scots — The Mither Tongue; They Fairly Mak Ye Work (for Dundee Repertory Theatre); Lucky's Strike (play for radio); The Dundee Book; The Scottish World. Recreations: the weans; languages; films; Dundee United. Address: (h.) 72 Tay Street, Newport on Tay, Fife DD6 8AP; e-mail: billykay@sol.co.uk

Kayne, Steven Barry, BSc, PhD, MBA, LLM, MSc (Med Sci), FRPharmS, FCPP, FIPMI, DAgVetPharm, FFHom, MPS(NZ), FNZCP. Consultant Homoeopathic and Veterinary Pharmacist; medical journalist; b. 8.6.44, Cheltenham Spa; m., Sorelle; 2 s. Educ. Westcliff High School; Aston University; Strathclyde University; Glasgow University; University of Wales. Lecturer; Visiting Lecturer, University of Strathclyde School of Pharmacy; Honorary Consultant Pharmacist, Glasgow Homeopathic Hospital; Pharmacy Dean to UK Faculty of Homoeopathy, 1998-2003; Member: Scottish Executive, Royal Pharmaceutical Society of Great Britain, 2000-07, Academic Board, UK Faculty of Homoeopathy, 1999-2003, Government Advisory Board on Homoeopathic Registration, Herbal Medicines Advisory Committee, Veterinary Products Committee of Veterinary Medicines Directorate; Governor and Hon. Treasurer, College of Pharmacy Practice; Chairman, College of Pharmacy Practice in Scotland. Publication: Homoeopathic Pharmacy, 1997 (2nd edn 2005); People are Pets (Co-author), 1998; Complementary Therapies for Pharmacists, 2001; Veterinary Pharmacy (Co-editor), 2003; Pharmacy Business Management (Editor), 2004; Sports Medicine for Pharmacists (Editor), 2005; Pocket Companion Homeopathic Prescribing (Joint Author), 2007; Homeopathic Prescribing (Joint Author), 2007; Homeopathic Practice (Editor), 2008; 300 papers and articles. Recreations: walking in Spey Valley; watching rugby; photography. Address: (b.) 20 Main Street, Busby, Glasgow G76 8DU; T.-07788 150345.
E-mail: steven.kayne@strath.ac.uk

Keane, Sheriff Francis Joseph, PhL, LLB. Sheriff of Tayside, Central and Fife, at Kirkcaldy, 1998-2004; b. 5.1.36, Broxburn; m., Lucia Corio Morrison; 2 s.; 1 d. Educ. Blairs College, Aberdeen; Gregorian University, Rome; Edinburgh University. Partner, McCluskey, Keane & Co., 1959; Procurator Fiscal Depute, Perth, 1961, Edinburgh, 1963; Senior PF Depute, Edinburgh, 1971; Senior Legal Assistant, Crown Office, Edinburgh, 1972; Procurator Fiscal, Airdrie, 1976; Regional Procurator Fiscal, South Strathclyde, Dumfries and Galloway, 1980; Sheriff of Glasgow and Strathkelvin, 1984-93; Sheriff of Lothians and Borders, 1993-98; President, Procurators Fiscal Society, 1982-84. Recreations: music; tennis; walking; painting. Address: (h.) 1/1 West Cherrybank, Stanley Road, Edinburgh EH6 4SW.

Kearney, Nora, RGN, MSc. Professor of Cancer Care, University of Stirling, since 2003; Director, Cancer Care Research Centre, since 2003; b. 10.09.59, Glasgow; 1 s. Educ. St. Ninian's High School, Kirkintilloch; University of Glasgow. Staff Nurse, 1981-83; Ward Sister, 1983-86; Oncology, Gartnavel Hospital Glasgow, 1986-92; Clinical Nurse Specialist, Beatson Oncology Centre, Glasgow, 1992-95; Lecturer in Cancer Nursing: University of Glasgow, 1995-98, University of Edinburgh, 1999-2001; Senior Lecturer in Cancer Nursing, University of Glasgow, 2001-03, Head of School of Nursing and Midwifery, 2001-

03. President, European Oncology Nursing Society, 1997-99; Member, Board of the Federation of European Cancer Societies, 1997-2001; numerous Scottish Executive/Government committees, since 1998. Publications: edited books: Nursing Patients with Cancer: Principals and Practice, 2006; Cancer Nursing Practice: A Textbook for the Specialist Nurse, 2000; WISECARE: Workflow Information Systems for European Nursing Care, 2000; contributed to multiple papers in the area of cancer care. Recreations: contemporary and classical literature; opera; hill walking; watching football. Address: (b.) Cancer Care Research Centre, University of Stirling, Unit 1, Scion Park, Stirling University Innovation Park, Stirling FK9 4NF; T.-01786 460062; e-mail: cancercare@stir.ac.uk

Kearns, Professor Ade J., BA (Hons). Professor of Urban Studies, University of Glasgow, since 2000; b. 11.10.59, Luton; m., Susan Joan; 1 s.; 1 d. Educ. Cardinal Newman RC Secondary, Luton; Sidney Sussex College, Cambridge University. Research, Shelter; Senior Housing Investment Analyst, Housing Corporation; University of Glasgow: Research Fellow, Lecturer, Senior Lecturer; Deputy Director, ESRC Centre for Housing Research and Urban Studies; Acting Director, ESRC Cities Research Programme; Co-Director, ESRC Centre for Neighbourhood Research, 2001-05; Director, ESRC/ODPM Postgraduate Research Programme, 2003-06. Editor, two special issues, Urban Studies journal. Recreations: reading contemporary fiction; listening to music, especially pop and jazz; collecting antique furniture, metalwork and art of the Arts and Crafts movement; city and country walking. Address: Department of Urban Studies, 25-29 Bute Gardens, University of Glasgow, Glasgow G12 8RS; T.-0141-330 5049; e-mail: a.j.kearns@socsci.gla.ac.uk

Keating, Professor Michael James, MA, PhD, FRSE. Professor of Scottish Politics, Aberdeen University, since 1999; Professor of Regional Studies, European University Institute, since 2000; b. 2.2.50, Hartlepool; m., Patricia Ann; 1 s. Educ. St Aidan's Grammar School, Sunderland; Oxford University; Glasgow College of Technology. Part-time Lecturer, Glasgow College of Technology, 1972-75; Senior Research Officer, Essex University, 1975-76; Lecturer, North Staffs Polytechnic, 1976-79; Lecturer/Senior Lecturer, Strathclyde University, 1979-88; Professor of Political Science, University of Western Ontario, 1988-99. Publications include: The Politics of Modern Europe; Nations against the State, the new politics of nationalism in Quebec, Catalonia and Scotland; The Government of Scotland. Recreations: sailing; hill-walking; traditional music; reading. Address: (h.) Middleton of Dudwick, Ellon, Aberdeenshire AB41 8EG.

Keatings, Richard Henry, BSc, DipEd, SQH. Headteacher, Kinross High School, since 2006; b. 21.12.55, Dunfermline; m., Fiona; 1 s.; 2 d. Educ. Beath High School, Cowdenbeath, Fife; Heriot Watt University, Edinburgh. Teacher of Mathematics, Dalwearie HS, Kirkcaldy; APT Maths, Glenrothes HS; PT Maths, Viewforth HS, Kirkcaldy; AHT, Kinross HS; Deputy Rector, Perth Academy. Address: (b.) Kinross High School, 8 High Street, Kinross KY13 8AW; T.-01577 862430.
E-mail: headteacher@kinrosshigh.pkc.sch.uk

Kee, Professor A. Alistair, MA, BD, STM, PhD, DLitt. Professor of Religious Studies, Edinburgh University; b. 17.4.37, Alexandria; m., Anne Paterson; 1 s.; 1 d. Educ. Clydebank High School; Glasgow University; Union Theological Seminary, New York. Lecturer: University College of Rhodesia, 1964-67, Hull University, 1967-76;

Glasgow University: Senior Lecturer, then Reader (Head, Department of Religious Studies, 1976-88); Visiting Professor: Augusta College, Georgia, 1982-83, Dartmouth College, New Hampshire, 1990,1995; delivered Jaspers Lectures, Ripon Hall, Oxford, 1975; Ferguson Lectures, Manchester University, 1986. Publications: The Way of Transcendence; A Reader in Political Theology; Constantine Versus Christ; Being and Truth; Domination or Liberation; The Roots of Christian Freedom; Marx and the Failure of Liberation Theology; From Bad Faith to Good News; Nietzsche against the Crucified; The Rise and Demise of Black Theology. Clubs: The New Club, Edinburgh, Bruntsfield Links Golfing Society. Address: (b.) Department of Religious Studies, Edinburgh University, New College, Mound Place, Edinburgh EH1 2LX; T.-0131-650 8921; e-mail: Alistair.Kee@ed.ac.uk

Keeble, Professor Neil Howard, BA, DPhil, DLitt, FRSE, FRHistS, FEA, FRSA. Professor of English, Stirling University, since 1995; Senior Deputy Principal, since 2003; Deputy Principal, since 2001; Head, Department of English Studies, 1997-2000; b. 7.8.44, London; m., Jenny Bowers; 2 s.; 1 d. Educ. Bancroft's School, Woodford Green; St. David's College, Lampeter; Pembroke College, Oxford. Foreign Lektor, Department of English, University of Aarhus, Denmark, 1969-72; Lecturer in English, Aarhus, 1972-74; Lecturer in English, Stirling University, 1974-88; Reader in English, Stirling University, 1988-95. Honorary Fellow, University of Wales, Lampeter, 2000. Publications: Richard Baxter: Puritan Man of Letters, 1982; The Literary Culture of Nonconformity in later seventeenth-century England, 1987; The Autobiography of Richard Baxter (Editor), 1974; The Pilgrim's Progress (Editor), 1984; John Bunyan: Conventicle and Parnassus (Editor), 1988; A Handbook of English and Celtic Studies in the United Kingdom and the Republic of Ireland (Editor), 1988; The Cultural Identity of Seventeenth-Century Woman (Editor), 1994; Lucy Hutchinson, Memoirs of the Life of Colonel Hutchinson (Editor), 1995; Cambridge Companion to Writing of the English Revolution (Editor), 2001; John Bunyan: Reading Dissenting Writing (Editor), 2002; Calendar of the Correspondence of Richard Baxter (Co-Compiler), 1991; Daniel Defoe, Memoirs of the Church of Scotland (Editor), 2002; The Restoration: England in the 1660s, 2002; Andrew Marvell, Remarks upon a Late Disingenuous Discourse (Editor), 2003; Daniel Defoe, Memoirs of a Cavalier (Editor), 2008. Recreations: books and book-collecting; films; the Midi. Address: (b.) Deputy Principals' Office, University of Stirling, Stirling FK9 4LA; e-mail: n.h.keeble@stir.ac.uk

Keel, Aileen, MB, ChB, FRCP(G), FRCP(E), FRCPath, MFPH. Deputy Chief Medical Officer, Scottish Government Health Directorate; Honorary Consultant Haematologist, Edinburgh Royal Infirmary; b. 23.8.52, Glasgow; m., Paul Dwyer; 1 s. Educ. Glasgow University. Postgraduate training in general medicine and haematology, 1976-87; practised haematology at consultant level in both NHS and private sector in London, 1987-92, including period as Director of Pathology, Cromwell Hospital; Senior Medical Officer, Scottish Office Department of Health, 1992-98; Principal Medical Officer, 1999. Member of a number of medical advisory committees in Scotland and UK. Recreations: arts in general; music in particular, especially opera; keeping fit; current affairs; Member of Art in Healthcare. Address: (b.) St. Andrew's House, Edinburgh EH1 3DG.

Keeling, Dr Jean Winifred, FRCPath, FRCPEd, FRCPCH. Retired; formerly Consultant Paediatric Pathologist, Royal Hospital for Sick Children, Edinburgh (1989-2005); Honorary Senior Lecturer, Pathology,

Edinburgh University, since 1990; b. 13.3.40, Doncaster; m., 1, Anthony Millier; 1 s.; 1 d.; 2, Frederick Walker. Educ. Pontefract and District Girls' School; Royal Free Hospital School, London University. Lecturer in Morbid Anatomy, Institute of Child Health, London University; Consultant Paediatric Pathologist, John Radcliffe Hospital, Oxford; Hon. Clinical Lecturer, Oxford University; Member, Royal Liverpool Children's Inquiry; Past President, Paediatric Pathology Society; Past President, International Paediatric Pathology Association. Publications: Fetal Pathology; Fetal and Neonatal Pathology (Editor); papers on fetal and paediatric pathology. Recreations: walking; cooking. Address: (h.) 9 Forres Street, Edinburgh EH3 6BJ; T.-0131 225 9673; e-mail: jeanwkeeling@aol.com

Keen, Richard Sanderson, LLB (Hons). Queen's Counsel, 1993; Dean of The Faculty of Advocates, since 2007; b. 29.03.54, Rustington, Sussex; m., Jane; 1 s.; 1 d. Educ. Dollar Academy; University of Edinburgh. Admitted to the Faculty of Advocates, 1980; Standing Counsel to the DTI, 1986-93; Elected Treasurer of the Faculty of Advocates, 2006. Trustee, The National Library of Scotland. Recreations: golf; skiing; shooting. Address: (b.) Parliament House, Parliament Square, Edinburgh EH1 1RF; e-mail: rsk@rskeenqc.com

Keighley, Brian Douglas, MB, ChB, FRCGP. General Practitioner Principal, Balfron, since 1975; Chairman, Scottish General Medical Services Committee (BMA), 1995-98; Chairman, Joint Committee on Postgraduate Training for General Practice, 1997-2000; b. 21.5.48, Glasgow; m., Ruth Patricia Maguire (divorced); 2 s. Educ. Glasgow Academy; Glasgow University. House Officer, Law Hospital, Stobhill Hospital, 1972-73; SHO, Robroyston Hospital, 1973; SHO, Falkirk Royal Infirmary, 1974; Trainee GP, Balfron, 1974. Member: GMSC (UK) since 1992, General Medical Council, since 1994 (Deputy Treasurer, since 2003, Chairman, GMC Staff Pension Fund Trustees), BMA Scottish Council, BMA Council, 1998-2002 and since 2006, TSMA Audit Committee, since 1998, Clinical Standards Board for Scotland, 1999-2002; Vice Chairman, Scottish Council for Postgraduate Medical and Dental Education (Chairman, Audit Committee, 1991-2002); Director, BMJ Publications Group Ltd., since 2002 and Board Vice Chairman, 2006; Treasurer, GPDF Ltd., since 2002. Publication: Guide to Postgraduate Medical Education, 1996. Recreations: reading; politics; angling; jogging; squash. Address: (h.) Hector Cottage, Banker's Brae, Balfron G63 0PY; T.-01360 440520; e-mail: Bkeighley@aol.com

Keiller, Mike, CA. Chief Executive, Morrison Bowmore Distillers, since 2000; b. 14.8.54, Perth; m., Helen; 1 s.; 1 d. Educ. Perth Academy; Dundee University. Guinness/UD, 1987-95; Director of Financial Planning and Control, British Telecom, 1998-2000. Recreations: hockey; golf; gardening. Address: (b.) Springburn Bond, Carlisle Street, Glasgow G21 1EQ; T.-0141-558 9011.

Keir, Professor Hamish Macdonald, BSc, PhD, DSc, CBiol, FIBiol, CChem, FRSC, FRSE. Professor of Biochemistry, Aberdeen University, 1968-96 (Vice-Principal, 1982-84); b. 5.9.31, Moffat; m., 1, Eleanor Campbell; 1 s.; 2 d.; 2, Linda Gerrie; 2 d. Educ. Ayr Academy; Glasgow University; Yale University. Hon. Secretary, The Biochemical Society, 1970-77, Chairman, 1986-89; Member, Cell Board, Medical Research Council, 1970-74; Scottish Home and Health Department, BRC, 1974-78; Ethical and Research Committees, Grampian Health Board; Science and Engineering Research Council (Biology), 1980-84; University Grants Committee

(Biology), 1984-90; Royal Society — British National Committee for Biochemistry, 1986-90; Board of Governors: North of Scotland College of Agriculture, 1976-91, Longridge Towers School, since 1988; Tenovus — Scotland, Grampian Region, 1980-86; Committees of the International Union of Biochemistry, 1974-82; Chairman: Natural Environment Research Council, Institute of Marine Biochemistry, 1969-84, Universities of Scotland Purchasing Consortium, 1988-96, Board of Governors, Rowett Research Institute, 1989-93; Vice-Chairman, Governors, Macaulay Land Use Research Institute, 1987-98; President, European Union of Societies for Experimental Biology, 1989-96; European Science Foundation, 1989-99; President, Council, Federation of European Biochemical Societies, 1980-83; Member, Executive, Ross, Skye and Lochaber, Scottish Conservative and Unionist Association, since 1996; Director, Groam House Museum, since 2003; Elder, Church of Scotland, since 1964. Recreations: piano; politics; travel. Address: (h.) Dundalachie, Fortrose, The Black Isle, Ross and Cromarty IV10 8TB; T.-01381 621239; e-mail: harrkeir@btinternet.com

Kellas, Professor James Grant, MA, PhD, FRHistS. Professor of Politics, Glasgow University, 1984-2001; b. 16.3.36, Aberdeen; m., Norma Rennie Craig; 2 s.; 1 d. Educ. Aberdeen Grammar School; Aberdeen University; London University. Tutorial Fellow in History, Bedford College, London University, 1961-62; Assistant in History, Aberdeen University, 1962-64; Glasgow University: Lecturer in Politics, 1964-73; Senior Lecturer, 1973-77, Reader, 1977-84. Member, Study of Parliament Group. Publications: Modern Scotland, 1968, 1980; The Scottish Political System, 1973, 1975, 1984, 1989; The Politics of Nationalism and Ethnicity, 1991, 1998; Nationalist Politics in Europe, 2004. Recreations: mountaineering; music. Address: (h.) 178 Southbrae Drive, Glasgow G13 1TX; T.-0141-959 5566.

Kelly, Dame Barbara Mary, CBE, DL, LLD, DipEd. Convener, Millennium Forest for Scotland Trust; Trustee: Robertson Trust, Royal Botanic Garden Edinburgh; Convenor, Crichton Foundation; Partner in farming enterprise; Chairman, Dumfries and Galloway Arts Festival; b. 27.2.40, Dalbeattie; m., Kenneth A. Kelly; 1 s.; 2 d. Educ. Dalbeattie High School; Kirkcudbright Academy; Moray House College. Past Member, Scottish Board BP plc; Past Director, Scottish Post Office Board; Past Chairman, Scottish Consumer Council; former Member: Scottish Economic Council, National Consumer Council, Scottish Enterprise Board, Scottish Tourist Board, Priorities Board, MAFF, Board, Scottish Natural Heritage (and former Chair, West Areas Board), Broadcasting Council for Scotland; former Vice-Chairman, SWRI; Duke of Edinburgh's Award; former Chairman, Scottish Advisory Committee and former Member, UK Advisory Panel; former EOC Commissioner for Scotland; Past Chairman, Dumfries and Galloway Area Manpower Board, Manpower Services Commission; former Director, Clydesdale Bank plc; Past President, Rural Forum; former Chairwoman, Architects' Registration Board. Recreations: painting; music. Address: (h.) Barncleugh, Irongray, Dumfries DG2 9SE; T.-01387 730210.

Kelly, Daniel, QC, LLB (Hons), CertAdvEurStud. Advocate, since 1991; b. 22.1.58, Dunfermline; m., Christine Marie MacLeod; 3 s.; 1 d. Educ. Edinburgh University; College of Europe, Bruges. Apprenticeship, Dundas and Wilson CS, 1979-81; Solicitor, Brodies WS, and Tutor in European Institutions, Edinburgh University, 1982-83; Solicitor, Community Law Office, Brussels, 1983-84; Procurator Fiscal Depute, 1984-90; Temporary Sheriff, 1997-99; Part-time Sheriff, since 2005. Editor: Scots Law Times, Sheriff Court Reports,

since 1992. Queen's Counsel, since 2007. Publication: Criminal Sentences, 1993. Recreations: swimming; cycling; golf. Address: (b.) Advocates Library, Parliament House, Edinburgh EH1 1RF.

Kelly, James. MSP (Labour), Glasgow Rutherglen, since 2007; b. 23.10.63. Address: (b.) Scottish Parliament, Edinburgh EH99 1SP; Constituency Office: 51 Stonelaw Road, Rutherglen, South Lanarkshire G73 3TN.

Kelly, Professor John Shearer, BSc, MB ChB, PhD, MA, FRSE, FRCPE, FMedSci, FBPS (Hon). Emeritus Professor of Pharmacology, University of Edinburgh, since 2002; Director, Fujisawa Institute of Neuroscience, since 1992; Deputy Editor, Journal of the Royal College of Physicians, Edinburgh, since 2002; b. 3.3.37, Edinburgh; m., E. Anne Wilkin; 1 s.; 1 d. Educ. George Heriot's School, Edinburgh; University of Edinburgh. House Physician, Western General Hospital, Edinburgh, 1962; House Surgeon, Royal Hospital for Sick Children, Edinburgh, 1963; University of Edinburgh, Department of Pharmacology: Assistant Lecturer, 1963-65, Lecturer, 1965-68; McGill University, Canada: Wellcome Post-doctoral Fellow, Department of Research in Anaesthesia, 1967-68, Canadian Medical Research Council Scholar and Assistant Professor, Departments of Research in Anaesthesia and Physiology, 1968-71; IBRO Research Fellow, University of Geneva, 1970; MRC Scientific Staff, Department of Pharmacology, Cambridge, 1971-79; Fellow of King's College, Cambridge and Lecturer in Pharmacology and Neurobiology, 1976-79; Professor and Chairman, Pharmacology, St. George's Hospital Medical School, London, 1979-85; Professor of Pharmacology, Edinburgh University, 1985-2002. Publications: 132 papers on neuroscience; 59 book chapters; 216 abstracts. Recreations: Japan; classical music; Scottish Malt Whisky Society; Scottish restaurants; sailing; Scottish outdoors. Address: (b.) Division of Neuroscience, University of Edinburgh, 1 George Square, Edinburgh EH8 9JZ; e-mail: j.s.kelly@ed.ac.uk

Kelly, Michael, CBE (1983), OStJ, JP, BSc(Econ), PhD, LLD, DL, FCIM. Public Relations Consultant, since 1984; Honorary Vice-President, Children 1st, since 1996 (Chairman, Royal Scottish Society for the Prevention of Cruelty to Children, 1987-96); Columnist: Scotsman, Evening Times; Broadcaster, Radio Clyde; Member, Economic and Social Research Council's Advisory Committee, since 2000; b. 1.11.40, Glasgow; m., Zita Harkins; 1 s.; 2 d. Educ. St. Joseph's College, Dumfries. Assistant Lecturer in Economics, Aberdeen University, 1965-67; Lecturer in Economics, Strathclyde University, 1967-80; Lord Provost of Glasgow, 1980-84; Rector, Glasgow University, 1984-87; Member, National Arts Collection Fund, 1990-96; Secretary, Scottish Industry Forum, 1995-2000; Scottish Convener, Socialist Civil Liberties Association, since 2002; British Tourist Authority Medal for services to tourism, 1984; Robert Burns Award from University of Old Dominion, Virginia, for services to Scottish culture, 1984; Scot of the Year, 1983; Radio Scotland News Quiz Champion, 1986, 1987; Radio Scotland Christmas Quiz Champion, 1987; Honorary Mayor of Tombstone, Arizona; Kentucky Colonel, 1983. Publications: Paradise Lost: the struggle for Celtic's soul, 1994; London Lines: the capital by underground, 1996. Recreations: golf; skiing. Address: (b.) 50 Aytoun Road, Pollokshields, Glasgow G41 5HE.

Kelly, Neil Joseph, LLB (Distinction), DipLP, NP, WS, HonRICS, ACIArb. Solicitor, since 1984; Partner, MacRoberts, Solicitors, since 1991, Head of Construction, since 2003; b. 28.6.61, Bellshill; m., Alison Jane (Whyte); 2 s.; 1 d. Educ. St. Patrick's High

School; Aberdeen University. Qualified in all forms of dispute resolution mechanisms with particular focus on construction industry. Editor, Scottish Construction Law Review; Contributor, MacRoberts on Scottish Building Contracts; Commissioner, Scottish Council for International Arbitration; Convener, Adjudication Society (Scottish Region). Recreations: travel; opera; classical music. Address: (b.) 30 Semple Street, Edinburgh EH3 8BL; T.-0131-229-5046.
E-mail: neil.kelly@macroberts.com

Kelly, Patrick Joseph, BSc. Non-Executive Director, Scottish Water, since 2003; Non-Executive Director, NHS 24, since 2001; b. 26.10.50, Glasgow; married to Rhona; 1 s.; 3 d. Educ. St. Mungo's Academy, Glasgow; Glasgow University. Civil Engineer, Central Regional Council, 1973-86; became active in local government union Nalgo and was elected to National Executive, 1979-86; Scottish Secretary, Society of Civil and Public Servants, 1986-99; former Member and President (1998), General Council, STUC; since 1999, working on various Boards in the public sector, including Civil Service Appeal Board; Board Member, Scottish Enterprise, Edinburgh and Lothian, 1991-2000; Management Committee, War on Want (charity); Anti-apartheid Scottish Committee. Recreations: golf; watching football; reading; walking. Address: (h.) 47 Fraser Crescent, Edinburgh EH5 2AJ; T.-0131 552 3540; e-mail: pat@pkelly.plus.com

Kelly, Robert Fraser, MA (Hons). Rector, Berwickshire High School, since 1998; b. 8.11.47, Glasgow; m., Norma; 2 d. Educ. Knightswood Secondary School, Glasgow; Glasgow University. Teacher of Modern Languages, Allan Glen's School, 1971-76; Assistant Principal, Hamilton Grammar School, 1976-78; Ballerup High School: Principal Teacher, 1978-88, Assistant Head, 1988-94, Depute Head, 1994-98. Recreations: reading; gardening; hill-walking. Address: (h.) Norwood, Bowmont Street, Kelso TD5 7EE; T.-01573 224386.

Kelman, James. Novelist; b. 1946, Glasgow. Works include: The Busconductor Hines; A Chancer; Greyhound for Breakfast; A Disaffection; How Late It Was How Late (Booker Prize, 1994); The Good Times (Scotland on Sunday/Glenfiddich Spirit of Scotland Award and the Stakis Prize for Scottish Writer of the Year, 1998); Translated Accounts, 2001; And the Judges Said... (essays), 2002; You have to be careful in the Land of the Free, 2004; Kieron Smith, Boy, 2008. Address: c/o Rogers, Coleridge and White, 20 Powis Mews, W11 1JN.

Kelnar, Professor Christopher J.H., MA, MD, FRCP, FRCPCH, DCH. Consultant Paediatric Endocrinologist, Royal Hospital for Sick Children, Edinburgh, since 1983; Honorary Professor of Paediatric Endocrinology, Department of Child Life and Health, Edinburgh University; b. 22.12.47, London; m., Alison; 1 s.; 2 d. Educ. Highgate School, London; Trinity College, Cambridge; St. Bartholomew's Hospital, London. Research Fellow, Paediatric Endocrinology, Middlesex Hospital, London, 1979-81; Senior Registrar, Hospital for Sick Children, Great Ormond Street, London, and Tutor, Institute of Child Health, London, 1981-83. Publications: The Sick Newborn Baby, 1981 (3rd edition, 1995); Childhood and Adolescent Diabetes, 1995; Growth Disorders, 1998 (2nd edition, 2007); chapters and papers on paediatric endocrinology. Recreations: music; gardening. Address: (b.) Royal Hospital for Sick Children, Sciennes Road, Edinburgh EH9 1LF; T.-0131-536 0611.

Kelsey, Rachael Joy Christina, LLB, DipLP, NP. Partner, Family Law Team, Pagan Osborne; b. 12.8.71, Belper; m., Michael James Stewart; 1 s.; 1 d. Educ. Culloden Academy, Inverness; Edinburgh University. Accredited as Specialist in Family Law by Law Society of Scotland, 2004; Treasurer, Family Law Association, 2003-05; Chair, Family Law Association, 2005-06; appointed as Curator Ad Litem and Court Reporter. Recreations: wine; gardening; children. Address: (b.) 55-56 Queen Street, Edinburgh EH2 3PA; T.-0131 226 4081; e-mail: rkelsey@pagan.co.uk

Kemp, Peter, MA, PhD. Director of Information Services, University of Stirling, since 1997; b. 22.4.44, Maidstone; m., Joan; 2 s.; 1 d. Educ. Maidstone Grammar School; Gonville and Caius College, Cambridge. Lecturer, University of Lancaster, 1970-71; Computer Officer, University of Cambridge, 1971-76, and Fellow, Gonville and Caius College, 1972-76; Head of User Services, University of Newcastle-upon-Tyne, 1976-82; Associate Professor, University of Delaware (USA), 1982-83; Director of The Computing Service: University of Reading, 1983-87, University of Glasgow, 1987-97. Trustee, National Library of Scotland, since 2002. Recreations: sailing; walking; travel. Address: (b.) The Library, University of Stirling, Stirling FK9 4LA; T.-01786 467227; e-mail: peter.kemp@stir.ac.uk

Kemp, Robert Andrew, BA, FCMA. Director of Finance and Deputy Chief Executive, NHS Borders Board, since 2002; b. 7.5.55, Liverpool; m., Anne Kemp. Educ. Waterloo Grammar School; Liverpool Polytechnic. Liverpool Health Authority: Financial Assistant, 1975-80, Unit Accountant, 1980-86; Borders Health Board: Unit Accountant, 1986-88, Deputy Director of Finance, 1986-94; Director of Finance and Deputy Chief Executive: Borders Community Health Services NHS Trust, 1994-99, Borders Primary Care Trust, 1999-2002. Recreations: music of Yes; cricket; photography; National Trust for Scotland; Royal Zoological Society for Scotland. Address: (b.) Borders Health Board, Newstead, Melrose TD6 9DB; T.-01896 828282.

Kennedy, Alison Louise, BA (Hons). Writer; b. 22.10.65, Dundee. Educ. High School of Dundee; Warwick University. Community Arts Worker, 1988-89; Writer in Residence, Project Ability, 1989-94; Writer in Residence, Hamilton/East Kilbride Social Work Department, 1990-92; fiction critic for Scotsman, etc.; Booker Prize Judge, 1996; five S.A.C. book awards; Saltire Best First Book Award; Saltire Best Book Award; John Llewellyn Rees/Mail on Sunday Prize; listed, Granta/Sunday Times Best of Young British Novelists; Encore Award; Festival Fringe First; Social Work Today Award; Premio Napoli Lannan Award for Literature; Austrian State Prize for European Literature. Publications: Night Geometry and the Garscadden Trains; Looking for the Possible Dance; Now That You're Back; So I Am Glad; Original Bliss; The Life and Death of Colonel Blimp (essay); Everything You Need; On Bull Fighting (non-fiction); Indelible Acts; Paradise; Day; The Audition (play); Stella Does Tricks (film); Delicate (performance piece); True (performance piece). Recreations: cinema; banjo; Tai Chi.

Kennedy, (Alistair James) Spencer, MA, LLB, SSC, NP. Partner, Balfour & Manson, since 1991; b. 3.5.45, Dumfries; m., Joan Margaret Whitelaw. Educ. Royal High School of Edinburgh; Edinburgh University. Estate Duty Office, 1965-68; Connell & Connell, 1968-70; Nightingale & Bell, SSC, 1970-90; Past President, Society of Solicitors in the Supreme Courts of Scotland. Recreations: hill-walking; horticulture. Address: (b.) 58 Frederick Street, Edinburgh EH2 1LS; T.-0131-200 1240.

Kennedy, Professor Angus Johnston, MA, PhD. Commandeur dans l'Ordre des Palmes Academiques.

Stevenson Professor of French Language and Literature, Glasgow University; b. 9.8.40, Port Charlotte; m., Marjory McCulloch Shearer; 2 d. Educ. Bearsden Academy; Glasgow University. Glasgow University: Assistant Lecturer in French, 1965, then Lecturer, Senior Lecturer, Reader; former Secretary, British Branch, International Arthurian Society. Publications: books on Christine de Pizan. Address: (b.) French Department, Glasgow University, Glasgow.
E-mail: A.Kennedy@french.arts.gla.ac.uk

Kennedy, Professor Arthur Colville, CBE, MD, FRCP(Lond), FRCPE, FRCP(Glas), FRCPI, FRSE, FACP(Hon.), FRACP (Hon.). Consultant Physician, Royal Infirmary, Glasgow, 1959-88; Muirhead Professor of Medicine, Glasgow University, 1978-88; President, Royal College of Physicians and Surgeons of Glasgow, 1986-88; b. 22.10.22, Edinburgh; m., Agnes White Taylor; 1 s. (deceased); 2 d. Educ. Whitehill School, Glasgow; Glasgow University. Medical Officer, RAFVR, 1946-48; junior NHS posts, 1948-57; Lecturer in Medicine, Glasgow University, 1957; Senior Lecturer, 1961; Reader, 1966; Titular Professor, 1969; responsible for establishment of Kidney Unit, Glasgow Royal Infirmary, 1959; Chairman, MRC Working Party in Glomerulonephritis, 1976-88; Member, Executive Committee, National Kidney Research Fund, 1976-83; Expert Adviser to WHO on Renal Disease; Adviser to EEC on Nephrology in Developing Countries; Chairman, Professional and Linguistic Assessments Board (PLAB), GMC, 1987-89; President: Royal Medico-Chirurgical Society of Glasgow, 1971-72, European Dialysis and Transplant Association, 1972-75, Scottish Society of Physicians, 1983-84, Harveian Society of Edinburgh, 1985; Member: Greater Glasgow Health Board, 1985-89, General Medical Council, 1989-92; President, British Medical Association, 1991-92. Recreations: gardening; walking; reading; photography. Address: (h.) 16 Boclair Crescent, Bearsden, Glasgow G61 2AG; T.-0141-942 5326.

Kennedy, Rt. Hon. Charles Peter, MA (Hons). MP (Liberal Democrat, formerly SDP), Ross, Cromarty and Skye, since 1983, Ross, Skye and Inverness West, since 1997; Leader, Liberal Democrats, 1999-2006; b. 25.11.59, Inverness; m., Sarah Gurling; 1 s. Educ. Lochaber High School, Fort William; Glasgow University; Indiana University. President, Glasgow University Union, 1980-81; Winner, British Observer Mace for Student Debating, 1982; Journalist, BBC Highland, Inverness, 1982; Fulbright Scholar, Indiana University (Bloomington Campus), 1982-83. Chairman, SDP Council for Scotland, 1986-88; SDP Spokesman on Health and Social Services, and Scotland, 1983-87; Alliance Election Spokesman, Social Security, Jan.-June, 1987; Member, Select Committee on Social Services, 1985-87; SLD Interim Joint Spokesman, Social Security, 1988; SLD Spokesman, Trade and Industry, 1988-89; President, Liberal Democrats, 1989-94; Liberal Democrat Spokesman: Health, 1989-92, Europe, 1992-97, Agriculture and Rural Affairs, 1997-99; Member: Select Committee on Health (circa 1984-85), House of Commons Television, 1988, Standards and Privileges Committee, 1997-99. Honorary doctorate, University of Glasgow, 2001; Fellow of the Royal Society of Arts, since 2005; "The Spectator" Politician of the Year Award, 2005; Visiting Parliamentary Fellow, St. Antony's College, Oxford, 2007; President, European Movement, since 2007. Recreations: reading; writing. Address: (b.) House of Commons, London SW1A 0AA; T.-020 7219 0356.

Kennedy, Professor Gavin, BA, MSc, PhD. Professor Emeritus, Heriot-Watt University; Director, Negotiate Ltd., Edinburgh; Trustee, David Hume Institute; b. 20.2.40, Collingham, Yorkshire; m., Patricia Anne; 1 s.; 2 d. Educ.

London Nautical School; Strathclyde University. Lecturer: Danbury Management Centre, 1969-71, Brunel University, 1971-73. Lecturer, National Defence College, Latimer, 1972-74; Senior Lecturer in Economics, Strathclyde University, 1973-83; Professor: Defence Finance, Heriot-Watt University, 1983-86, Edinburgh Business School, 1987-2005. Publications: Military in the Third World, 1974; Economics of Defence, 1975; Bligh, 1978 (Yorkshire Post Book of the Year, 1979); Death of Captain Cook, 1978; Burden Sharing in NATO, 1979; Mathematics for Innumerate Economists, 1982; Defence Economics, 1983; Invitation to Statistics, 1983; Everything is Negotiable, 1984; Negotiate Anywhere, 1985; Macro Economics, 1985; Superdeal, 1985; The Economist Pocket Negotiator, 1987; Captain Bligh: the man and his mutinies, 1988; Do We Have A Deal?, 1991; Simulations for Training Negotiators, 1993; The Perfect Negotiation, 1993; Negotiation, 1994; Local Pay Bargaining, 1995; The Negotiate Trainer's Manual, 1996; Kennedy on Negotiation, 1997; The New Negotiating Edge, 1998; Profitable Negotiation, 1999; Influencing, 1999; Adam Smith's Lost Legacy, 2004; Strategic Negotiation, 2005; Adam Smith, 2007. Recreation: reading. Address: (h.) 99 Caiyside, Edinburgh; T.-0131-445 7778; e-mail: gavin@negweb.com

Kennedy, Rev. Gordon, BSc, BD, MTh. Church of Scotland Minister, Portpatrick linked with Stranraer St. Ninian's, since 2000; b. 15.9.63, England. Educ. Crookston Castle Secondary; University of Strathclyde; University of Glasgow. Graduate Civil Engineer, Strathclyde Regional Council, 1985-89; Probationer Assistant, Bearsden North Parish Church, 1992-93; Minister, New Cumnock Parish Church, Ayrshire, 1993-2000. 2005 Master of Theology, University of Glasgow. Address: 2 Albert Terrace, London Road, Stranraer DG9 8AB; T.-01776 702443; e-mail: gordon.k@tiscali.co.uk

Kennedy, Gordon Philip, MA (Hons), MPhil, MBA, MRTPI, MIED. Deputy Chief Executive, Scottish Enterprise Glasgow, since 2001; b. 30.5.57, Glasgow. Educ. St. Mungo's Academy; Glasgow University; Strathclyde University. Planning Assistant, Clydebank District Council, 1982-85; Industrial Economist, Scottish Development Agency, 1985-91; Glasgow Development Agency: Head of Strategic Projects, 1991, Head of Corporate Strategy, 1991-93; Director, Corporate Development, Glasgow Development Agency, 1993-99; Deputy Chief Executive, Scottish Enterprise Glasgow, 1999-2001. Member, Board, The Lighthouse. Recreations: cinema; theatre; eating out. Address: (b.) Atrium Court, 50 Waterloo Street, Glasgow G2; T.-0141-204 1111.

Kennedy, Professor Hugh Nigel, PhD, FRSE. Professor of Middle Eastern History, St Andrews University, since 1998; b. 22.10.47, Hythe, Kent; m., Hilary Ann Kennedy; 1 s.; 3 d. Educ. Marlborough College; Pembroke College, Cambridge. Lecturer in Mediaeval History, St Andrews University, 1972-90, Reader in Mediaeval History, 1990-98. Publications include: The Early Abbasid Caliphate, 1981; The Prophet and the Age of the Caliphates, 1986; Crusader Castles, 1994; Muslim Spain and Portugal, 1996; The Armies of the Caliphs, 2001. Recreations: archaeology; architectural history. Address: (b.) Department of Mediaeval History, St Andrews University, St Andrews KY16 9AL; T.-01334 463316; e-mail: hnk@st-and.ac.uk

Kennedy, Norman Stewart Joseph, BSc, PhD, CSci, FIPEM. Head of Nuclear Medicine, Ninewells Hospital, Dundee, since 1989; b. 5.3.51, Edinburgh; m., Patricia Meadowcroft; 4 s. Educ. Broxburn Academy; Edinburgh University. Research Medical Physicist, Western

General Hospital, Edinburgh, 1978-82; Senior Medical Physicist, Ninewells Hospital, Dundee 1982-89. Member, ARSAC. Publications: 52 papers. Recreations: badminton; bridge. Address: (h.) St. Mary's Drive, Kinnoull Hill, Perth PH2 7BY; T.-01738 632282.
E-mail: nsjkennedy@tuht.scot.nhs.uk

Kennedy, Professor Peter Graham Edward, MB, BS, MPhil, MLitt, PhD, MD, DSc, FRCPath, FRCPLond, FRCPGlas, FRSE, FMedSci. Burton Professor of Neurology and Head of Department, Glasgow University, since 1987; Consultant Neurologist, Institute of Neurological Sciences, Southern General Hospital, Glasgow, since 1986; b. 28.3.51, London; m., Catherine Ann; 1 s.; 1 d. Educ. University College School, London; University College, London; University College Medical School. Medical Registrar, University College Hospital, 1977-78; Hon. Research Assistant, MRC Neuroimmunology Project, University College, London, 1978-80; Research Fellow, Institute of Virology, Glasgow University, 1981; Registrar and Senior Registrar, National Hospital for Nervous Diseases, London, 1981-84; Assistant Professor of Neurology, Johns Hopkins University School of Medicine, 1985; "New Blood" Senior Lecturer in Neurology and Virology, Glasgow University, 1986-87. BUPA Medical Foundation "Doctor of the Year" Research Award, 1990; Linacre Medal and Lectureship, Royal College of Physicians of London, 1991; T.S. Srinivasan Endowment Lecturer and Gold Medal, 1993; Fogarty International Scholar, NIH, USA, 1993-94; Senior Associate Editor, Journal of Neurovirology; Member: Medical Research Advisory Committee, Multiple Sclerosis Society, 1987-98, Association of Physicians Great Britain and Ireland, Association of British Neurologists; Fellow of the Academy of Medical Sciences; President, International Society for Neurovirology, since 2004. Publications: Infectious Diseases of the Nervous System (Co-Editor), 2000; numerous papers on neurology, neurovirology and neurobiology; The Fatal Sleep, 2007. Recreations: reading and writing; music; astronomy; tennis; walking in the country; philosophy. Address: (b.) Institute of Neurological Sciences, Southern General Hospital, Glasgow G51; T.-0141-201 2474.

Kennedy, Professor Robert Alan, BA, PhD, FBPsS, FRSE. Professor of Psychology, University of Dundee, since 1972; b. 1.10.39, Stourbridge; m., Elizabeth Wanda; 1 d. Educ. King Edward VI Grammar School, Stourbridge. Senior Tutor then Lecturer in Psychology, University of Melbourne, 1963-65; Lecturer in Psychology: Queen's College, University of St. Andrews, University of Dundee, 1965-72; Senior Lecturer in Psychology, University of Dundee, 1972. Member, Psychology Committee, Social Science Research Council (UK), 1980-82; Committee Member, Experimental Psychology Society, 1984-88; Member, Scientific Affairs Board, British Psychological Society, 1986-88; Member, MRC Neuropsychology Subcommittee, 1982-89; Editorial Board: Acta Psychologica, 1980-88, Psychological Research, 1978-88; Founder Member, European Conference on Eye Movements, since 1980; Convener, Scottish Group of Professors of Psychology, 1985-91; Governor, Dundee College of Education, 1974-78; Member of Court, University of Dundee, 1976-80 and 1990-99; Convener, University Research Committee, 1994-97; Member, Council, Royal Society of Edinburgh, 1999-2001. Publications: Studies in Long-Term Memory (Co-author); The Psychology of Reading; Reading as a Perceptual Process (Editor); Eye Movements and Information Processing During Reading (Co-editor). Recreations: hill-walking; playing the piano. Address: (b.) Psychology Department, University of Dundee, Dundee DD1 4HN; T.-01382 344622.

Kenway, Professor Richard Donovan, FRSE, BSc, DPhil, CPhys, FInstP. Tait Professor of Mathematical Physics, Edinburgh University, since 1994; b. 8.5.54,

Cardiff; m., Anna Kenway; 1 s.; 2 d. Educ. Stanwell School, Penarth; Exeter University; Oxford University. Research Associate, Brown University, 1978-80; Post-doctoral Fellow, Los Alamos National Laboratory, 1980-82; Edinburgh University: Post-doctoral Fellow, 1982-83; Lecturer, 1983-90; Reader, 1990-94; Director of Edinburgh Parallel Computing Centre, 1993-97; Head, Department of Physics and Astronomy, 1997-2000; Chairman, Edinburgh Parallel Computing Centre, since 1997; Chairman, UK National e-Science Centre, since 2001; PPARC Senior Research Fellow, 2001-04; Assistant Principal, 2002-05; Vice Principal, since 2005; Member, National and International Peer Review and Research Strategy Committees. Publications: co-authored one book; co-edited two books; 120 papers on theoretical particle physics and high performance computing. Recreations: munroing; running. Address: (b.) School of Physics, Edinburgh University, The King's Buildings, Edinburgh, EH9 3JZ; T.-0131-650 5245; e-mail: r.d.kenway@ed.ac.uk

Kerby, Nigel Wells, BSc, PhD, CBiol, FIBiol. Managing Director, Mylnefield Research Services Ltd., since 1993; Director, Scottish Potato Technology Ltd.; Director of Mylnefield Holdings Ltd.; Trustee of Mylnefield Trust; b. 5.4.53, Anglesey; m., Marigold; 1 s. Educ. Sedbargh School; United World College of the Atlantic; Leeds University, 1979-82. AFRC Fellowship, Dundee University, 1982-90; Lecturer in Microbiology, Dundee University, 1990-93; Chairman, Institute of Directors, Tayside Branch, 2004-07; China-Britain Business Council Board Member, 2003, Institute of Advanced Motorists. Recreations: gardening; travel; golf. Address: (b.) Mylnefield Research Services Ltd., Invergowrie, Dundee, DD2 5DA; T.-01382 568568; e-mail: n.kerby@mrsltd.com

Kerevan, George, MA (Hons). Associate Editor, The Scotsman, since 2000; Chief Executive, What If Productions (Television) Ltd., since 2000; b. 28.9.49, Glasgow. Educ. Kingsridge Secondary School, Drumchapel; Glasgow University. Academic posts, Napier University, 1975-2000; freelance journalist and broadcaster, since 1980; Creative Director, Alba Communications Ltd., 2005-06; TV director, producer and script writer, Lamancha Productions Ltd., 1989-2000; Chair, Edinburgh Technology Transfer Centre, 1985-92; Board, Edinburgh Co-operative Development Agency, 1987-92; Chair, EDI Ltd., 1988-95; Board, Edinburgh Venture Trust, 1988-93; Board, Capital Enterprise Trust, 1993-94; Chairman, New Edinburgh Ltd., 1989-95; Board, Lothian and Edinburgh Enterprise Trust, 1989-96; Chair, Edinburgh and Lothians Tourist Board, 1992-95; Board, Traverse Theatre, 1980-84; Council, Edinburgh International Festival, 1984-92; Board, Assembly Productions, 1984-88; Board, Royal Lyceum Theatre, 1984-88; Board, Edinburgh Old Town Trust, 1984-90; Board, 7:84 Theatre Company, 1986-88; Board, Edinburgh International Film Festival, 1988-94; Chair, Edinburgh International Science Festival, 1989-95; Chair, Edinburgh Film House, 1989-94; Board, Boxcar Films, 1993; Chair, Manifesto International Festival of Architecture, 1995; elected Member, Edinburgh District Council, 1984-96 (Convenor, Economic Development Committee, 1986-95); Vice-Convenor, Economic Affairs Committee, COSLA, 1988-90; Board, John Wheatley Centre for Public Policy Research, 1988-93; SNP National Council, 1996-98; SNP environment spokesperson, 1996-98; SNP Prospective Parliamentary Candidate for Edinburgh East, since 2008. Recreations: cooking; cats; cinema. Address: (h.) Brunstane House (South Wing), Brunstane Road South, Edinburgh EH15 2NQ; T.-0131-669 8234; e-mail: gkerevan@scotsman.com

Kernahan, Robbie, BSc (Ecological Science). Director of Deer Management, Deer Commission for Scotland, since

2002; b. 25.09.75, St. Andrews; m., Jacquiline Phillips; 1 s. Educ. Bell Baxter High School, Cupar, Fife; Edinburgh University. Deer Commission for Scotland, 1997; Ecological Contractor (Self Employed), 1998-2001; Head Ranger, Scottish Deer Centre, 2001-02; Deer Commission for Scotland, since 2002. Recreations: sea kayaking; walking; playing football. Address: (b.) DCS, Great Glen House, Leachkin Road, Inverness IV3 8NW; T. 01463 725353; e-mail: robbie.kernahan@dcs.gov.uk

Kernohan, Robert Deans, OBE, MA, FFCS. Journalist, Writer and occasional Broadcaster; b. 9.1.31, Mount Vernon, Lanarkshire; m., Margaret Buchanan Bannerman; 4 s. Educ. Whitehill School, Glasgow; Glasgow University; Balliol College, Oxford. RAF, 1955-57; Editorial Staff, Glasgow Herald, 1957-67 (Assistant Editor, 1965-66, London Editor, 1966-67); Director-General, Scottish Conservative Central Office, 1967-71; Freelance Journalist and Broadcaster, 1972; Editor, Life and Work, The Record of the Church of Scotland, 1972-90. Chairman, Federation of Conservative Students, 1954-55; Conservative Parliamentary candidate, 1955, 1959, 1964; Member: Newspaper Panel, Monopolies and Mergers Commission (subsequently Competition Commission), 1987-99, Ancient Monuments Board for Scotland, 1990-97, Broadcasting Standards Council, 1994-97, Broadcasting Standards Commission, 1997-99; Chairman, Scottish Christian Conservative Forum, 1991-97; HM Inspector of Constabulary for Scotland (Lay Inspector), 1992-95; Director, Handsel Press Ltd, 1996-2003; Elder, Cramond Kirk, Edinburgh; Honorary President, Scottish Church Theology Society, 1994. Publications: Scotland's Life and Work, 1979; William Barclay, The Plain Uncommon Man, 1980; Thoughts through the Year, 1985; Our Church, 1985; The Protestant Future, 1991; The Road to Zion, 1995; The Realm of Reform (Editor), 1999; John Buchan in a Nutshell, 2000; An Alliance across the Alps, 2005; various contributions to collective works and reference books, including New Dictionary of National Biography. Recreations: rugby-watching; travel; pontification; patriarchy. Address: (h.) 5/1 Rocheid Park, Edinburgh EH4 1RP; T.-0131-332 7851.

Kerr, Andrew Palmer. MSP (Labour), East Kilbride, since 1999; Minister for Health and Community Care, 2004-07; Minister for Finance and Public Services, Scottish Executive, 2001-04; b. 17.3.62, East Kilbride; m., Susan; 3 d. Educ. Claremont High School; Glasgow College. Research Officer, Strathkelvin District Council, 1987-90; Achieving Quality Consultancy, 1990-93; Glasgow City Council, 1993-99. Address: (b.) Civic Centre, East Kilbride; T.-01355 806223.

Kerr, Sheriff Principal Bruce Alexander, QC. Sheriff Principal of North Strathclyde, since 1999; b. 28.4.46. Admitted, Faculty of Advocates, 1973; QC, 1986; Standing Junior Counsel to Home Office, 1982-85; Advocate Depute, 1986-89; Temporary Sheriff, 1991; Permanent Sheriff, since 1994. Address: (b.) Sheriff Court House, St James Street, Paisley PA3 2HW; T.-0141-887 5291.

Kerr, Norman. Director and Company Secretary, Energy Action Scotland, since 2005. Car Industry, Engineer, 1971-81; Heatwise Glasgow (now The Wise Group), Insulation Supervisor then Production Unit Manager, 1984-96; Development Manager and Deputy Director, Energy Action Scotland, 1996-2005. Trustee: National Energy Action, Scottish Power's Energy People Trust. Address: (b.) Energy Action Scotland, Suite 4A, Ingram House, 227 Ingram Street, Glasgow G1 1DA; T.-0141 226 3064. E-mail: norman.kerr@eas.org.uk

Kerr, Rev. Mgr. Philip John, PhB, STL. Parish Priest, St. Francis Xavier, Falkirk and Vicar General, Archdiocese of St. Andrews and Edinburgh, since 1999; b. 23.4.56, Edinburgh. Educ. Holy Cross Academy; St. Augustine's High School, Edinburgh; Scots College and Gregorian University, Rome. Assistant Priest, St. Francis Xavier's, Falkirk, 1980-82; Lecturer in Systematic Theology, St. Andrew's College, Drygrange, 1982-86; Vice-Rector and Lecturer in Systematic Theology, Gillis College, Edinburgh, 1986-93; Lecturer in Systematic Theology, Scotus College, Bearsden, 1993-96; R.C. Chaplain, Stirling University, 1993-99; Parish Priest: Sacred Heart, Cowie, 1993-99, Our Lady and St. Ninian, Bannockburn, 1996-99. Recreations: classical music; walking. Address: St. Francis Xavier, Hope Street, Falkirk FK1 5AT; T.-01324 623567.

Kerr, William Revill, PhD, FCIS, FCIM, FIH, MBA, MSc. General Manager, The Glasgow Academy, since 2003; b. 26.4.48, East Kilbride; m., Maria. Educ. Duncanrig Senior Secondary School, East Kilbride; Glasgow University; Strathclyde University; Glasgow Caledonian University. Former Secretary, Malin Housing Association, 1988-2003; Chair, Scottish Enterprise Ayrshire, 2000-03; Advisory Board Member, Scottish Enterprise, 2001-02; Ambassador, Princes Scottish Youth Business Trust, 2000. Local Enterprise Company Chairs Group, 2000-03; Director, Scottish Enterprise Ayrshire, 1998-2003; Director, Investors in People, Scotland, 2000-02; Director, Ayrshire Development Loan Fund, 2000-02; Director, Business Excellence Ayrshire, 1998-2000; Director, Springboard, 1998-2000; Member, Scottish Disability Consulting Group, 1999-2000; Member, Scottish Qualifications Authority SVQ Advisory Board, 1998-2000; Chairman, Ayrshire and Arran Tourism Industries Forum, 1993-2000; Vice-Chairman, Scotland Committee, British Hospitality Association, 2001; Panel Member, Investors in People, since 1997. Publication: Tourism, Public Policy and the Strategic Management of Failure, 2003. Recreations: sport; writing; cycling; old books. Address: (h.) 20 Burness Avenue, Alloway, Ayrshire KA7 4QB; (b.) The Glasgow Academy, Colebrook Street, Glasgow G12 8HE; T.-0141 334 8558; e-mail: bill.kerr@tga.org.uk

Kerrigan, Professor Herbert Aird, QC, MA, LLB (Hons), PGDipTh (Oxon); b. 2.8.45, Glasgow; 1 s. Educ. Whitehill School, Glasgow; Aberdeen University; Keele University; Hague Academy; University of Oxford. Admitted to Faculty of Advocates, 1970; Lecturer in Criminal Law and Criminology, Edinburgh University, 1969-73; Lecturer in Scots Law, Edinburgh University, 1973-74; Member, Longford Commission, 1972; Church of Scotland: Elder, 1967 (now at Greyfriars Tolbooth and Highland Kirk), Reader, 1969, elected Member, Assembly Council, 1981-85, Senior Chaplain to Rt. Rev. John Cairns, Moderator of the General Assembly of the Church of Scotland, 1999-00; called to the English Bar (Middle Temple), 1990; joined Chambers of Lord Carlisle QC, 1991; appointed QC in Scotland, 1992; President, Edinburgh Royal Infirmary Samaritan Society, since 1992; Convener, General Assembly of the Church of Scotland's Committee on Chaplains to Her Majesty's Forces, 2002-06; Trustee, The Thistle Trust, Edinburgh. Publications: An Introduction to Criminal Procedure in Scotland, 1970; Ministers for the 1980s (Contributor), 1979; The Law of Contempt (Contributing Editor), 1982; The Law of Sport (2nd edition) (Contributor), 1995. Recreation: travel. Address: (h.) 20 Edinburgh Road, Dalkeith, Midlothian EH22 1JY; T.-0131-660 3007.

Kesting, Rt. Rev. Sheilagh Margaret. Moderator of The General Assembly of The Church of Scotland, 2007-08; Secretary, Ecumenical Relations, Church of Scotland, since 1993; b. 10.6.53, Stornoway. Educ. Nicolson Institute;

Edinburgh University. Parish Minister: Overtown, Lanarkshire, 1980-86, St. Andrews High, Musselburgh, 1986-93. Recreations: gardening; photography; embroidery. Address: (b.) Church of Scotland Offices, 121 George Street, Edinburgh EH2 4YN; T.-0131 225 5722; e-mail: moderator@cofscotland.org.uk

Kettle, Ann Julia, OBE, MA, FSA, FRHistS, FRSA, FICS. Honorary Lecturer, Mediaeval History, University of St. Andrews; b. 2.8.39, Orpington. Educ. Lewes Grammar School; St. Hugh's College, Oxford. University of St. Andrews: Hebdomadar, 1991-94, Dean of Arts, 1998-2002; President, Association of University Teachers (Scotland), 1994-96; Member, Scottish (Garrick) Committee of National (Dearing) Committee of Inquiry into Higher Education, 1996-97; Member, Scottish Higher Education Funding Council, 1997-2000; Trustee, Arts and Humanities Research Board, 2001-05; Chair, Board of Governors, Newbattle Abbey College, since 2004. Address: (b.) Department of Mediaeval History, University of St. Andrews, St. Andrews KY16 9AL; T.-01334 473057; e-mail: ajk@st-and.ac.uk

Kidd, Bill. MSP (SNP), Glasgow, since 2007; b. 24.7.56. Address: (b.) Scottish Parliament, Edinburgh EH99 1SP.

Kidd, Emeritus Professor Cecil, BSc, PhD, FIBiol, FRSA. Regius Professor of Physiology, Aberdeen University, 1984-97, Professor of Physiology (part-time), 1997-2000, Professor Emeritus, since 2000; b. 28.4.33, Shotley Bridge, Co. Durham; m., Margaret Winifred; 3 s. Educ. Queen Elizabeth Grammar School, Darlington; King's College, Newcastle-upon-Tyne; Durham University. Demonstrator in Physiology, King's College, Newcastle-upon-Tyne; Lecturer/Senior Lecturer/Reader in Physiology, Senior Research Associate in Cardiovascular Studies, Leeds University. Recreations: opera; gardening. Address: (b.) School of Medical Sciences, College of Life Sciences and Medicine, Foresterhill Campus, Aberdeen University, Aberdeen AB25 2ZD; T.-01224 273004; e-mail: c.kidd@abdn.ac.uk

Kidd, Professor Colin Craig, MA, DPhil, FRSE, FRHistS, FSA Scot. Professor of Modern History, University of Glasgow, since 2003; b. 5.5.64, Ayr; m., Lucy Armstrong; 1 s.; 1 d. Educ. Glasgow Academy; Gonville and Caius College, Cambridge University. Choate Fellow, Harvard University, 1985-86; Fellow, All Souls College, Oxford University, 1987-94, 2005-; Lecturer then Reader, University of Glasgow, 1994-2003. Governor, Glasgow Academicals' War Memorial Trust, since 2002. Publications: Subverting Scotland's Past, 1993; British Identities Before Nationalism, 1999; The Forging of Races, 2006. Recreations: Watergate; Galloway. Address: (b.) Department of History (Scottish), University of Glasgow, 9 University Gardens, Glasgow G12 8QH; T.-0141-330 4576; e-mail: c.kidd@history.arts.gla.ac.uk

Kidd, David Hamilton, LLB, LLM, WS, NP. Partner, Biggart Baillie, since 1978; Solicitor Advocate, since 1994; b. 21.9.49, Edinburgh. Educ. Edinburgh Academy; Edinburgh University. Recreations: cycling; skiing; hill-walking. Address: (b.) 7 Castle Street, Edinburgh EH2 3AP; T.-0131-226 5541; e-mail: dkidd@biggartbaillie.co.uk

Kidd, James Cameron, LLB (Hons). District Chairman, The Appeals Service, since 1995; b. 17.4.48, Glasgow; m., Eileen Theresa McGinlay; 1 s.; 1 d. Educ. Hillhead High School, Glasgow; University of Glasgow. Apprentice, Bishop Milne Boyd and Co., Solicitors, Glasgow, 1971-73;

Partner: Macdonalds, Solicitors, Glasgow, 1973-90, Macpherson Gibb Maguire Cook, Solicitors, Glasgow, 1990-95. Recreations: golf; opera; crosswords. Address: (h.) Flat 3, 10 Kirklee Mansions, Kirklee Gate, Glasgow G12 0SZ; T.-0141-959 2592.
E-mail: jimkidd17@hotmail.com

Kidd, Mary Helen (May), JP, MA. Deputy World President, Associated Country Women of The World, 2007-2010; Area President (Europe and the Mediterranean), Associated Country Women of the World, 2001-07; former Member, Advisory Board and Council, Scottish Agricultural College; m., Neil M.L. Kidd; 2 s. Educ. Brechin High School; Edinburgh University. Partner in family farming business; former Member: MAFF Consumer Panel, Scottish Consumer Council, Women's National Commission; National Chairman, Scottish Women's Rural Institutes, 1993-96. Recreations: playing piano and organ; creative writing. Address: (h.) Holemill of Kirkbuddo, Forfar, Angus DD8 2NQ; T.-01307 820 318.

Killham, Professor Kenneth Stuart, BSc, PhD, FRSE, FAAM. Established Chair of Soil Science, Aberdeen University, since 1995 (Head, Department of Plant and Soil Science, 1996-2000); President, British Society of Soil Science, since 2000; Director of Research, School of Biological Science, since 2002; Scientific Director, Remedios Ltd., since 1999; b. 1.3.57, Formby; m., Pauline. Educ. Merchant Taylors School, Crosby; Sheffield University. Visiting Scientist, University of California, Berkeley, 1981-83; Lecturer in Soil Microbiology, Aberdeen University, 1983-90; Reader in Soil Microbiology, Aberdeen University, 1990-93. Chairman, UK Soil Science Advisory Committee, 1997-2000. Publications: Soil Ecology; Soil Chemistry – Theory and Applications. Recreation: sailing. Address: (b.) Cruickshank Building, University of Aberdeen, St. Machar Drive, Aberdeen AB24 3UU; T.-01224 272260.

Kilpatrick, Iain W., BA, MEd, FRSA. Headmaster, Beaconhurst School, Bridge of Allan, Stirling, since 2005; b. 8.11.67, Glasgow; m., Katrina; 1 s.; 1 d. Educ. High School of Stirling; University of Stirling; University of Edinburgh. Assistant Master, Strathallan School, 1995-2000, Housemaster and Head of Expressive Arts, 2000-05. Fellow, Royal Society for the Encouragement of Arts, Manufactures and Commerce; Member, Scottish Guidance Association. Recreations: theatre; sailing; reading. Address: (b.) 52 Kenilworth Road, Bridge of Allan, Stirling FK9 4RR; T.-01786 832146.
E-mail: headmaster@beaconhurst.com

Kilpatrick, Lord (Robert Kilpatrick), MD, FRCP(Edin), FRCP, FRCPS(Glas), HonFRCS, HonFRCP(Dub), HonFRCS(Edin), FRSE. Chairman, Scottish Hospital Endowment Research Trust, 1996-2000; b. 29.7.26, Wemyss; m., Elizabeth Forbes; 2 s.; 1 d. Educ. Buckhaven High School; Edinburgh University. House Officer, Senior House Officer, Registrar, Edinburgh, 1949-54; Lecturer and Senior Lecturer, Sheffield University, 1955-66; Professor of Clinical Pharmacology, Sheffield University, 1966-75; Professor of Clinical Pharmacology and Medicine, Leicester University, 1975-89; President, General Medical Council, 1989-95; President, British Medical Association, 1997-98; Hon. Degrees: DrHc (Edin), LLD (Dundee), DSc (Hull), DSc (Leics), LLD (Sheff). Recreation: golf. Address: (h.) 12 Wester Coates Gardens, Edinburgh EH12 5LT; T.-0131-337 7304.

Kilshaw, David Andrew George, OBE. Solicitor, since 1979; Chairman, Borders Health Board, 1993-2001; b.

18.3.53, Glencoe; 3 s. Educ. Keil School, Dumbarton. Traineeship, Brunton Miller, Solicitors, Glasgow, 1975-80; Solicitor, Borders Regional Council, 1980-83; Partner, Cullen Kilshaw Solicitors, Galashiels, Melrose and Peebles, since 1983; Chair: Borders Solicitors Property Centre, since 2000, Border Reivers Professional Rugby Team Board, 2006. Recreations: golf; fishing. Address: (b.) 23 Northgate, Peebles; T.-01721 723999.

Kinclaven, Lord (Alexander Featherstonhaugh Wylie), QC, LLB, FCIArb. Lawyer; Member of the Scottish Bar, since 1978; b. 2.6.51, Perth; m., Gail Elizabeth Watson Duncan; 2 d. Educ. Edinburgh University. Qualified Solicitor in Scotland, 1976; called to Scottish Bar, 1978; Standing Junior Counsel to Accountant of Court, 1986-89; Advocate Depute, 1989-92; called to English Bar, 1990; QC (Scot), 1991. Part-time Joint Chairman, Discipline Committee, Institute of Chartered Accountants of Scotland, 1994-2005; Member, Scottish Legal Aid Board, 1994-2002; part-time Sheriff, 2000-05; part-time Chairman, Police Appeals Tribunal, 2001-05; Member, Scottish Criminal Cases Review Commission, 2004-05. Address: (b.) Parliament House, Edinburgh EH1 1RQ.

Kindley, Dr Angus David, MBChB, DCH, FRCP(Lond), FRCPEdin, FRCPH. Director, Raeden Regional Child Development Centre, Aberdeen, since 1991; Consultant, Royal Aberdeen Children's Hospital, since 1991; b. 26.4.49, Newcastle upon Tyne; m., Ceri; 1 s.; 1 d. Educ. Royal Grammar School, Newcastle upon Tyne; Leeds University. Senior Registrar, Paediatric Neurology, Alder Hey Children's Hospital; Consultant Paediatrician, Bury; Hon. Clinical Senior Lecturer, Aberdeen University. Trustee, Aberdeen Gomel Trust; Past President, Aberdeen Philatelic Society. Recreations: philately; postal history; fishing; falconry. Address: (b.) Raeden Centre, Midstocket Road, Aberdeen AB15 5TD; T.-01224 321381.

King, Professor Bernard, CBE, MSc, PhD, CCMI, FIWSc, CBiol, FIBiol. Principal and Vice-Chancellor, University of Abertay, Dundee, since 1992; b. 4.5.46, Dublin; m., Maura Antoinette Collinge; 2 d. Educ. Synge St. Christian Brothers School, Dublin; College of Technology, Dublin; University of Aston in Birmingham. Research Fellow, University of Aston, 1972-76; Dundee Institute of Technology, 1976-91: Lecturer, Senior Lecturer, Head, Department of Molecular and Life Sciences, Dean, Faculty of Science; Assistant Principal, Robert Gordon Institute of Technology/Robert Gordon University, 1991-92. Member, Board of Scottish Leadership Foundation; Chairman, Scottish Crop Research Institute; Governor, Board, Unicorn Preservation Society; Board of Higher Education Academy; Vice-Chair, Universities Scotland. Recreations: reading; music; sailing. Address: (h.) 11 Dalhousie Place, Arbroath, DD11 2BT; T.-01382 308012.

King, Professor David Neden, MA, DPhil, CertEd. Professor of Public Economics, Stirling University, since 2002, b. 10.04.45, Birmingham; m., Victoria Susan Robinson; 2 s. Educ. Gresham's School, Norfolk; Magdalen College, Oxford; York University. Consultant Economist, Royal Commission on the Constitution, 1971-72; Economics Master and Head of Economics, Winchester College, 1972-78; Lecturer, Stirling University, 1972-78; Economics Adviser, Department of the Environment, 1987-88; Senior Lecturer, Stirling University, 1987-2002. Conductor, Stirling University Choir, since 1990. Consultant to OECD and the World Bank. Publications: Financial and Economic Aspects of Regionalism and Separatism, 1973; Taxes on Immovable Property, 1983; Fiscal Tiers: the Economics of Multi-level Government,

1984; An Introduction to National Income Accounting, 1984; Banking and Money, 1987; The Complete Works of Robert and James Adam, 1991; Financial Claims and Derivatives, 1999; Unbuilt Adam, 2001. Recreations: architecture; music. Address: (b.) Department of Economics, Stirling University, Stirling FK9 4LA; T.-01786 467475; e-mail: d.n.king@stir.ac.uk

King, Elspeth Russell, MA, FMA, DUniv. Director, Smith Art Gallery and Museum, Stirling, since 1994; b. 29.3.49, Lochore, Fife. Educ. Beath High School; St. Andrews University; Leicester University. Curator, People's Palace, Glasgow, 1974-91, with responsibility for building up the social history collections for the city of Glasgow; Director, Dunfermline Heritage Trust, 1991-94; responsible for restoration of, and new displays in, Abbot House. Honorary Doctorate, Stirling University, 2005; Fletcher Award, Saltire Society, 2006. Publications include: The Thenew Factor: the hidden history of women in Glasgow, 1993; Blind Harry's Wallace by Hamilton of Gilbertfield (Editor), 1998; Stirling Girls, 2003; The Face of Wallace, 2005. Address: (b.) Stirling Smith Art Gallery and Museum, Dumbarton Road, Stirling FK8 2RQ; T.-01786 471917; e-mail: museum@smithartgallery.demon.co.uk

King, Steve, MBE. Composer/Music Educationalist; Musician in Residence, Heriot-Watt University, since 1998; Viola Player, Scottish Chamber Orchestra, since 1984; b. 4.12.56, Waltham Cross; 2 s. Educ. Queen Eleanor Grammar School; Royal Northern College of Music. Address: (h.) 8 Hopeward Mews, Dalgety Bay KY11 9TB; T.-01383 821187.

Kingarth, Rt. Hon. Lord (Hon. Derek Emslie). Senator of the College of Justice, since 1997; b. 21.6.49. Educ. Cambridge University; Edinburgh University. Advocate, 1974; Advocate Depute 1985-1988. Address: Parliament Square, Edinburgh EH1 1RQ.

Kinghorn, Carol. Lord Lieutenant of Kincardineshire, since 2007; b. Aberdeen; m., Roderick; 4 c. Educ. Aberdeen; St Andrews. Qualified physiotherapist, spent a number of years working for Westminster Healthcare; worked for the area Red Cross, formerly trustee of the Crombie Trust (a charitable trust for elderly ladies); regional committee member of the Soldiers, Sailors, Airmen and Families Association; active member of a number of local and regional sports clubs and arts societies.

Kinnaird, Alison, MBE, MA, FGE. Glass Engraver and Artist; Clarsach Player; b. 30.4.49, Edinburgh; m., Robin Morton; 1 s.; 1 d. Educ. George Watson's Ladies College; Edinburgh University. Freelance glass artist, since 1971; exhibitions in Edinburgh, 1978, 1981, 1985, in London, 1988, 1995; work in many public and private collections; professional musician, since 1970; has produced three LPs as well as film and TV music; served on Council, Scottish Craft Centre, 1974-76; Council, SSWA, 1975-76; Member: BBC Scottish Music Advisory Committee, 1981-84, BBC Broadcasting Council for Scotland, 1984-88, SAC Crafts Commitee, 1993-96; awarded: SDA/CCC Craft Fellowship, 1980, Glass-Sellers of London Award, 1987, Creative Scotland Award, 2002. Recreations: children; cooking; garden. Address: (h.) Shillinghill, Temple, Midlothian EH23 4SH; T.-01875 830328.

Kinnis, William Kay Brewster, PhD, FRSA. Retired Solicitor and Notary Public; b. 5.1.33, St. Andrews; m., Agnes Inglis Erskine, MA; 2 d. Educ. Hamilton Academy; Glasgow University; London University (External). Partner:

MacArthur Stewart & Orr, Solicitors, Oban and Lochgilphead, 1959-62; Town Clerk and Burgh Chamberlain, Lochgilphead, 1960-62; Partner, Murdoch Jackson, Solicitors, Glasgow, 1963-92; Senior Partner: Miller Jackson, Solicitors, Lenzie, 1982-92, Cannon, Orpin & Murdochs, 1992-95; Consultant Lawyer, Stewarts & Murdochs, Solicitors, Glasgow, 1995-2000. Council Member, Member, Royal Faculty of Procurators, 1980-83; Governor, Baillie's Institution, 1983-94. Choral Scholar, Glasgow University, 1954-58; Choirmaster, Lochgilphead Parish Church, 1959-62; Reader, Church of Scotland, since 1960; Reader Emeritus, since 2006; Member, Church of Scotland Board of Practice and Procedure (Vice-Convener) and Law Committee (Convener), 1990-99; Lay Member, school inspection teams, 1995-2002. Recreations: choral singing; swimming; reading; travel. Address: (h.) 4 Dempster Court, St. Andrews KY16 9EU; T.-01334 476959; e-mail: drwilliamkinnis@btinternet.com

Kinnoull, 15th Earl of (Arthur William George Patrick Hay); b. 26.3.35; m.; 1 s.; 3 d. Educ. Eton. Chartered Land Agent; succeeded to title, 1938; former Conservative Spokesman on Aviation, House of Lords; Past President, National Council on Inland Transport.

Kinross, Lord (Christopher Patrick Balfour), LLB, WS. Solicitor, since 1975; b. 1.10.49, Edinburgh; m., Susan Jane Pitman (divorced); m. (2), Catherine Taylor; 2 s. Educ. Eton College; Edinburgh University. Member, Royal Company of Archers, Queen's Bodyguard for Scotland; James IV Association of Surgeons; Grand Baili to The Military and Hospitaller Order of St. Lazarus of Jerusalem. Recreations: off-road motorsport; shooting. Address: (b.) HBJ Gateley Wareing, Exchange Tower, 19 Canning Street, Edinburgh; T.-0131-228 2400.

Kinsman, Stewart Hayes, OBE, BSc, FRICS. Chief Executive, Hanover (Scotland) Housing Association Ltd., 1979-2007; Chairman, Edinburgh Flood Prevention Group, 2000-06; b. 18.9.43, Burntisland, Fife; 1 s.; 1 d. Educ. Kirkcaldy High School; Heriot-Watt University. Chartered Surveyor, 1966-71; Estates and Buildings Officer, Stirling University, 1971-76; Regional Manager, Hanover Housing Association (GB), 1976-79. Chairman, Scottish Federation of Housing Associations, 1998-2001. Recreations: sailing; wines; digital photography; natural history. Address: (h.) 14 Dryburn Brae, West Linton EH46 7JG; T.-01968 660 198; e-mail: stewart@kinsmans.demon.co.uk

Kintore, 14th Earl of (James William Falconer Keith); b. 1976. Succeeded to title, 2004.

Kirk, Carol, DCE, BA, MEd. Corporate Director (Educational Services), North Ayrshire Council; b. 30.5.57, Glasgow; m., Drew Grieve. Educ. Hillhead High School, Glasgow; Jordanhill College; Open University; Stirling University. Teaching: Glasgow, Elgin, Balfron, 1978-94; Education Development Officer, Strathclyde Region, 1994-96; Principal Officer, North Lanarkshire Council, 1996; Service Manager, Stirling Council, 1996-2005; Head of Service, North Ayrshire Council, 2005-07. Address: (b.) Cunninghame House, Irvine KA12 8EE; T.-01294 324411.

Kirk, David, MA, BM, BCh, DM, FRCS (Eng), FRCS-RCPS (Glas), FRCS Edin); b. 26.5.43, Bradford; m., Gillian Mary Wroot; 1 s.; 2 d. Educ. King Edwards School, Birmingham; Balliol College, Oxford; Oxford University Clinical Medical School. Resident House Physician and House Surgeon, Radcliffe Infirmary, Oxford; University Demonstrator, Oxford; clinical surgical posts, Oxford and Bristol; Arris and Gale Lecturer, Royal College of Surgeons (England), 1980-81; rotating surgical Registrar appointment, Sheffield; academic surgical research, Sheffield University; Senior Registrar in General Surgery, then in Urology, Bristol; Honorary Clinical Lecturer, Glasgow University, 1984-95; Consultant Urological Surgeon, NHS Greater Glasgow, 1982-2005; Honorary Professor, Glasgow University, 1995-2005. Secretary/Treasurer, 1983-85, Chairman, 1985-88, Scottish Urological Oncology Group; Council Member: Urology Section, Royal Society of Medicine, 1984-87, British Association of Urological Surgeons, 1988-91; Chairman: Prostate Forum, 1991-94, Intercollegiate Board in Urology, 1994-97; Specialist Adviser in Urology, National Medical Advisory Committee (Scottish Executive), 1996-2004; Member, Specialist Adviser in Urology, Joint Committee on Higher Surgical Training, 1999-2004; President, Scottish Urology Society, 2004-06; Chair, Forth Valley Branch, Cruse Bereavement Care Scotland, 2004-07; Performance Assessor, General Medical Council, 2006; Clinical Adviser, Healthcare Commission, 2007. Publications: Understanding Prostate Disorders (author); Managing Prostate Disease (author); International Handbook of Prostate Cancer (editor); book chapters and original papers on urological cancer and other topics. Recreations: skiing; hill-walking; classical music. Address: (h.) The Biggins, Keir, Dunblane FK15 9NX; T.-01786 820291.
E-mail: david_kirk@tiscali.co.uk

Kirk, Professor David, BSc (Hons), MPhil, FIFST, FIH. Vice Principal (Learning and Teaching), Queen Margaret University, since 2004; b. 30.7.45, Stockport; m., Helen Kathleen; 2 s. Educ. New Mills Grammar School; University of Reading; University of Surrey. Food Technologist, International Stores; Research Fellow, University of Surrey; Lecturer, Polytechnic of the South Bank; Senior/Principal Lecturer, Sheffield City Polytechnic; Dean of Faculty, Queen Margaret University College. Publications: Hospitality Operations, a systems approach; Environmental Management for Hotels; Kitchen Planning and Management; The Design and Operation of Catering Equipment. Recreations: music; gardening. Address: (b.) Queen Margaret University, Edinburgh EH21 6UU; T.-0131 474000; e-mail: dkirk@qmu.ac.uk

Kirk, Professor Gordon, OBE, MA, MEd, PhD, DUniv, FRSA. Vice-Principal, University of Edinburgh, 2002-03 (Dean, Faculty of Education, 1998-2002); Vice-Convener, General Teaching Council, 1992-2001; b. 8.5.38, Dunfermline; m., Jane D. Murdoch; 1 s.; 1 d. Educ. Camphill Secondary School, Paisley; Glasgow University. Lecturer in Education, Aberdeen University, 1965-74; Head, Education Department, Jordanhill College of Education, 1974-81; Principal, Moray House Institute of Education, 1981-98. Member, Munn Committee on the Curriculum of the Secondary School, 1974-77; Chairman: Educational Broadcasting Council, Scotland, 1985-91, Scottish Council for Research in Education, 1984-92; Member: General Teaching Council for Scotland, 1984-2002, Consultative Committee on the Curriculum, 1984-91, Council for National Academic Awards, 1979-93; Vice-Convener, Committee of Scottish Higher Principals, 1993-94. Publications: Scottish Education Looks Ahead (Assistant Editor), 1969; Curriculum and Assessment in the Scottish Secondary School, 1982; Moray House and Professional Education (Editor), 1985; The Core Curriculum, 1986; Teacher Education and Professional Development, 1988; Handbook of Educational Ideas and Practices (Associate Editor), 1990; Scottish Education and the European Community (Editor), 1992; 5-14: Scotland's National Curriculum (Editor), 1994; Moray House and Change in Higher Education (Editor), 1995; Professional Issues in Education series (Co-Editor); Enhancing Quality in Teacher Education, 2000; Moray House and the Road to Merger, 2002; The Chartered Teacher (Co-author), 2004. Recreations: baseball; walking; bridge. Address: (h.)

Craigroyston, Broadgait, Gullane, East Lothian; T.-01620 843299.

Kirk, Professor James, MA, PhD, DLitt, FRHistS, FRSE. Professor of Scottish History, Glasgow University, 1999-2005; currently Hon. Professorial Research Fellow in Ecclesiastical History, School of Divinity, University of Glasgow; b. 18.10.44, Falkirk; m., Dr. Daphne Waters. Educ. Stirling High School; Edinburgh University. Lecturer in Scottish History, Glasgow University, 1972-89, Senior Lecturer, 1989-90, Reader, 1990-99. David Berry Prize, Royal Historical Society, 1973; Wolfson Award, 1977; Hume Brown Senior Prize in Scottish History, 1977; British Academy Major Research Awards, 1989-96; ESRC Research Award, 1993-95. President, Scottish Church History Society, 1992-93; Hon. Secretary: Scottish Record Society, since 1973, Scottish Society for Reformation History, 1980-90; Scottish Section Editor, Royal Historical Society, Annual Bibliography of British and Irish History; an Associate Editor, The New Dictionary of National Biography, 1998. Publications: The University of Glasgow 1451-1577, 1977; Records of the Synod of Lothian and Tweeddale, 1977; The Second Book of Discipline, 1980; Stirling Presbytery Records, 1981; Visitation of the Diocese of Dunblane, 1984; Patterns of Reform, 1989; Humanism and Reform, 1991; The Books of Assumption of the Thirds of Benefices: Scottish Ecclesiastical Rentals at the Reformation, 1995; Scotland's History (Editor), 1995; The Medieval Church in Scotland (Editor), 1995; Her Majesty's Historiographer, 1996; Calendar of Scottish Supplications to Rome 1447-1471, vol. 5 (Editor), 1997; The Church in the Highlands (Editor), 1998; The Scottish Churches, Politics and the Union Parliament (Editor), 2001; Contributor to: The Renaissance and Reformation in Scotland, 1983; Voluntary Religion, 1986; The Seventeenth Century in the Highlands, 1986; Scotland Revisited, 1991; Encyclopedia of the Reformed Faith, 1992, Dictionary of Scottish Church History and Theology, 1993, The Oxford Encyclopedia of the Reformation, 1996; John Knox and the British Reformations, 1999; The New Dictionary of National Biography, 2004. Recreations: living in Wester Ross; viticulture. Address: (h.) Woodlea, Dunmore, Stirlingshire FK2 8LY; T.-01324 831240; e-mail: james@kirk11.fsnet.co.uk

Kirkhill, Lord (John Farquharson Smith); b. 7.5.30; m.; 1 step d. Lord Provost of Aberdeen, 1971-75; Minister of State, Scottish Office, 1975-78; Chairman, North of Scotland Hydro-Electric Board, 1979-82; Delegate, Parliamentary Assembly, Council of Europe, and W.E.U., 1987-2000 (Chairman, Committee on Legal Affairs and Human Rights, 1991-95); Hon LLD, Aberdeen University, 1974.

Kirkwood of Kirkhope, Lord (Archy Kirkwood), Kt, BSc; b. 22.4.46, Glasgow; m., Rosemary Chester; 1 s.; 1 d. Educ. Cranhill School; Heriot-Watt University. Solicitor, Notary Public; Aide to Sir David Steel, 1971-75, 1977-78; MP (Liberal Democrat), Roxburgh and Berwickshire, 1983-2005; Liberal Spokesman on Health and Social Services, and on Social Security, 1985-87; Alliance Spokesman on Overseas Development, 1987; Liberal Scottish Whip, 1987-88; Social and Liberal Democrat Convener on Welfare, Health and Education, 1988-89; Liberal Democrat Deputy Chief Whip, and Spokesman on Welfare and Social Security, 1989-92, Community Care, 1994-97; Chief Whip, 1993-97; Chairman, Work and Pensions Select Committee (formerly Social Security Select Committee), 1997-2005. Former Trustee, Joseph Rowntree Reform Trust; former Governor, Westminster Foundation for Democracy. Recreations: music; photography. Address: (b.) House of Lords, London SW1A 0PW.

Kirkwood, Susan, BSc, MSc, MBA. Chairman, Scottish Culture and Traditions Association; b. 18.5.50, Edinburgh. Educ. James Gillespie's High School,

Edinburgh; Edinburgh University; Durham University; INSEAD. Exploration Geophysicist, 1973-83; Business Analyst, 1985-94; Company Director, since 1994. JP. Address: (h.) 78 Cairnfield Place, Aberdeen; T.-01224 630979.

Kirwan, Frank, BA, MA. Chairman, KAL Ltd.; Vice-Chair, OSCR; Visiting Professor, University of Edinburgh Management School; Director: Graham Technology, Standard Life Assurance Ltd.; Member, East Lothian Children's Panel, 1999-2007; Trustee: Actionaid Int., Oxfam GB, 2001-07; Member, Accounts Commission, 1994-2002; b. 16.7.52, Dublin; 1 s.; 1 d. Educ. Colaiste Mhuire, Dublin; Trinity College, University College, Dublin. Economic and Social Research Institute, 1974-76; Strathclyde University, 1976-81; Lund University, 1981-82; Fraser of Allander Institute, 1983-84; Scottish Development Agency, 1984-88; Royal Bank of Scotland, 1988-97. Recreation: gardening; hill-walking; moountain biking. Address: (h.) 30 Erskine Road, Gullane EH31 2DQ.

Kirwan, Michael Ralph, FCA. Trustee, National Museums Scotland, since 2005; Trustee, Roslin Foundation, since 2006; b. 17.5.41, Blackpool; m., Elizabeth Valerie (nee Hartley); 2 stepsons; 2 stepdaughters; 1 d. Educ. Cheltenham College. Accountancy Training, Peat Marwick Mitchell (now KPMG), 1959-64; Area Accountant, Cameroon Development Corporation, Cameroon, 1965-66; Chief Accountant, GA Harvey & Co. (London) Ltd., 1967-71; Deloitte Haskins & Sells, Management Consultants, 1971-90 (Partner, from 1975); Executive Director, Finance, Nuclear Electric plc, 1990-96; Group Finance Director, British Energy plc, 1996-2002; Member, Corporate Finance Advisory Board, Pricewaterhouse Coopers (PWC), 2002-05. Recreations: philately; bird-watching; architecture; watching sport. Address: (h.) 18 Greenhill Gardens, Edinburgh EH10 4BW; T.-0131-447-3420; e-mail: michael@kirwans.net

Kitchen, John Philip, MA, BMus, PhD (Cantab), FRCO, LRAM. Senior Lecturer in Music, Edinburgh University, since 1987; Concert Organist, Harpsichordist, Pianist; Edinburgh City Organist, since 2002; b. 27.10.50, Airdrie. Educ. Coatbridge High School; Glasgow University; Cambridge University. Lecturer in Music, St. Andrews University, 1976-87; Harpsichordist/Organist, Scottish Early Music Consort, 1977-98; BBC and commercial recordings; music reviewer; Director of Music, Old St. Paul's Episcopal Church, Edinburgh. Recreations: more music; entertaining. Address: (b.) Faculty of Music, Alison House, 12 Nicolson Square, Edinburgh EH8 9DF; T.-0131-650 2432; e-mail: J.Kitchen@ed.ac.uk

Kitson, Professor Peter John, BA, PhD. Professor of English, University of Dundee, since 2000; b. 26.4.58, Bradford. Educ. Hanson School, Bradford; University of Hull. Lecturer, School of English, University of Exeter, 1986-89; Lecturer/Senior Lecturer, University of Wales, Bangor, 1989-2000. President of the English Association, since 2007; President of the British Association for Romantic Studies, since 2007. Panel Judge, Keats Shelley Essay and Poetry Prize, 2002-07. Publications: Romantic Literature, Race and Colonial Encounter, 2007; Literature, Science and Exploration in the Romantic Period, 2004; Travels, Explorations and Empires (editor), 2001-02; Slavery, Abolition and Emancipation (editor), 1999; numerous other books and articles on Romantic Period Writing. Recreations: cinema; travel; swimming. Address: (h.) 2 Burnside Road, Letham, Forfar, Angus DD8 2PH; T.-01307 818020; e-mail: peterjkitson@aol.com

Klein, Bernat, CBE, FCSD, Hon. FRIAS, HonDLitt (Heriot Watt University); b. 6.11.22, Senta, Yugoslavia; m., Margaret Soper; 1 s.; 2 d. Educ. Senta, Yugoslavia; Bezalel School of Arts and Crafts, Jerusalem; Leeds University. Designer: Tootal, Broadhurst, Lee, 1948-49, Munrospun,

Edinburgh, 1949-51; Chairman and Managing Director, Colourcraft, 1952-62; Managing Director, Bernat Klein Ltd., 1962-66; Chairman and Managing Director: Bernat Klein Design Ltd., 1966-81, Bernat Klein Ltd., 1982-92. Member: Design Council, 1962-68, Royal Fine Art Commission for Scotland, 1981-87. Publications: Eye for Colour, 1965; Design Matters, 1975. Recreations: tennis; reading. Address: High Sunderland, Galashiels; T.-01750 20730.

Knight, Alanna, FSA Scot. Novelist; b. Co. Durham; m., Alistair Knight; 2 s. Educ. Jesmond High School. Writing career began, 1965; novels: Legend of the Loch, 1969 (RNA First Novel Award), The October Witch, 1971, This Outward Angel, 1971, Castle Clodha, 1972, Lament for Lost Lovers, 1972, The White Rose, 1974, A Stranger Came By, 1974, The Wicked Wynsleys, 1977; historical novels: The Passionate Kindness, 1974, A Drink for the Bridge, 1976, The Black Duchess, 1980, Castle of Foxes, 1981, Colla's Children, 1982, The Clan, 1985; Estella, 1986; detective novels: Enter Second Murderer, 1988, Blood Line, 1989, Deadly Beloved, 1989, Killing Cousins, 1990, A Quiet Death, 1991, To Kill A Queen, 1992; The Evil that Men Do, 1993, The Missing Duchess, 1994, Inspector Faro and the Edinburgh Mysteries, 1994, The Bull Slayers, 1995; Murder by Appointment, 1996; Inspector Faro's Second Casebook, 1996; The Coffin Lane Murders, 1998; The Final Enemy, 2002; Unholy Trinity, 2004; crime novels: the Sweet Cheat Gone, 1992, This Outward Angel, 1994; Angel Eyes, 1997; The Royal Park Murder, 1998; The Monster in the Loch, 1998; Dead Beckoning, 1999; The Inspector's Daughter, 2000; The Dagger in the Crown, 2001; Dangerous Pursuits, 2002; An Orkney Murder, 2003; Ghost Walk, 2004; The Gowrie Conspiracy, 2003; Faro and the Royals, 2004; The Stuart Sapphire, 2005; Destroying Angel, 2007; plays: The Private Life of R.L.S., 1973, Girl on an Empty Swing, 1977; Inspector Faro Investigates, 2001; non-fiction: The Robert Louis Stevenson Treasury, 1985; RLS in the South Seas, 1986, Bright Ring of Words (Co-Editor), 1994; true crime: Close and Deadly, 2002; Burke & Hare, 2007; radio short stories, plays and documentaries. Recreations: walking; reading; painting. Address: (h.) 24 March Hall Crescent, Edinburgh EH16 5HL; T.-0131-667 5230; website: www.alannaknight.com

Knight, David James, MBChB, FRCPS(Glas), FRCS Edin (Orth). Consultant Orthopaedic Surgeon, Aberdeen Royal Infirmary and Woodend Hospital, since 1995; b. 13.10.55, Inverness. Educ. Elgin Academy; University of Aberdeen. Orthopaedic Registrar, Glasgow, 1983-90; Orthopaedic Senior Registrar, Aberdeen, 1990-93; Visiting Orthopaedic Surgeon, The Third Teaching Hospital, Beijing, China, 1991-92; Consultant Orthopaedic Surgeon, Dr. Gray's Hospital, Elgin, 1993-95. Recreations: hill-walking; reading. Address: (h.) 47 Braemar Place, Aberdeen AB10 6EN; e-mail: davidknight20@aol.com

Knipe, David, DPE. Headteacher, The Community School of Auchterarder (Secondary), since 1993; b. 22.2.47, Dunoon, Argyll; m., Annie; 1 s., 1 d. Educ. Dunoon Grammar School; Jordanhill College of Education (Scottish School of Physical Education). West Calder High School: Assistant Teacher of PE, 1968-73; APT Guidance, 1973; Penicuik High School: PT Physical Education, 1973-82; AHT, 1982-87; Deputy Headteacher, Morgan Academy, 1987-93. Recreations: travel; music; running. Address: (b.) Auchterarder, Perthshire PH3 1BL; T.-01764 662182.

Knops, Professor Robin John, BSc, PhD, Hon.DSc, FRSE. Emeritus Professor of Mathematics, Heriot-Watt University; b. 30.12.32, London; m., Margaret; 4 s.; 2 d. Educ. Nottingham University. Nottingham University:

Assistant Lecturer in Mathematics, 1956-59, Lecturer in Mathematics, 1959-62; Newcastle-upon-Tyne University: Lecturer in Applied Mathematics, 1962-68, Reader in Continuum Mechanics, 1968-71; Professor of Mathematics, Heriot-Watt University, Edinburgh, 1971-98 (Head, Department of Mathematics, 1971-83; Dean of Science, 1984-87, Vice Principal, 1988-95; Special Adviser to the Principal, 1995-97). Visiting Professor: Cornell University, 1967 and 1968; University of California, Berkeley, 1968; Pisa University, 1974; Ecole Polytechnique Federale Lausanne, Switzerland, 1980; Royal Society of Edinburgh: Council Member, 1982-92, Executive Committee Member, 1982-92, Meetings Secretary, 1982-87, Chief Executive Editor, Proceedings A, 1982-87, Curator, 1987-92; President: Edinburgh Mathematical Society, 1974-75, International Society for the Interaction of Mechanics and Mathematics, President, 1991-95 (Vice-President, 1995-99); Editor, Applied Mathematics and Mathematical Computation, 1990-2002; Convener, Executive Committee, International Centre for Mathematical Sciences, Edinburgh, 1996-99; Leverhulme Emeritus Fellowship, 2000-02. Publications: Uniqueness Theories in Linear Elasticity (Co-author), 1971; Theory of Elastic Stability (Co-author), 1973. Recreations: walking; reading. Address: (b.) School of Mathematical and Computer Sciences, Colin Maclaurin Building, Heriot-Watt University, Edinburgh EH14 4AS; T.-0131-451 3363; e-mail: r.j.knops@ma.hw.ac.uk

Knowles, Professor Dudley Ross, BA, MLitt. Professor of Political Philosophy, University of Glasgow, since 2005; b. 20.07.47, Preston, Lancs; m., Anne; 2 d. Educ. Kirkham Grammar School; University of London. Manager, Clachaig Inn, Glencoe, 1970-71; Lecturer in Philosophy, University of Glasgow, 1973-92; Warden, Queen Margaret Hall, 1974-89; Senior Lecturer in Philosophy, University of Glasgow, 1992-2005. Publications: Political Philosophy 2001; Hegel and the Philosophy of Right, 2002. Recreations: birdwatching; walking; bridge. Address: (b.) Department of Philosophy, University of Glasgow G12 8QQ; T.-0141-357-3239.
E-mail: dudley.anne@btopenworld

Knox, Jack, RSA, RGI, RSW, HonFRIAS, DLitt. Painter; b. 16.12.36, Kirkintilloch; m., Margaret K. Sutherland; 1 s.; 1 d. Educ. Lenzie Academy; Glasgow School of Art; André Lhôte Atelier, Paris. Lecturer in Drawing and Painting, Duncan of Jordanstone College of Art, 1965-81; Head of Painting Studios, Glasgow School of Art, 1981-92. Solo exhibitions: Scottish Gallery, Edinburgh; Richard Demarco Gallery, Edinburgh; Serpentine Gallery, London; Buckingham Gallery, London; Civic Arts Centre, Aberdeen; retrospective – Fruit Market Gallery, Edinburgh, Third Eye Centre, Glasgow, touring to Aberdeen, Inverness Dundee; Kelvingrove Art Gallery and Museum, Glasgow; Open Eye Gallery, Edinburgh; many mixed exhibitions internationally; work in numerous private and public collections. Member, Scottish Arts Council, 1974-79; Member, Trustees Committee, Scottish National Gallery of Modern Art, 1975-82; Trustee, National Galleries of Scotland, 1982-87; Secretary, Royal Scottish Academy, 1990-91; Many awards, most recently, Maude Gemmell Hutchison Prize, RSA, 1998; Maude Gemmell Hutchison Prize for animal drawing, RSA, 2004; Alexander Graham Monro Award, RSW, 2004. Books illustrated: The Scottish Bestiary, by George Mackay Brown, 1986; La Pontinière, by David and Hilary Brown. Address: 66 Seafield Road, Broughty Ferry, Dundee DD5 3AQ; T.-01382 770 411.

Knox, Lesley Mary, MA (Cantab). Chairman, Alliance Trusts PLC, since 2004; Hays PLC, SID and Chair, Remuneration Committee, since 2002; b. 19.9.53, Johannesburg, South Africa; m., Brian Knox; 1 d. Educ. St. Denis, Edinburgh; Cheltenham Ladies College; Cambridge

University. Slaughter and May (qualified as Solicitor), 1976-79; Shearman and Sterling New York (qualified as Attorney), 1979-80; Kleinwort Benson, Corporate Finance Division, 1981-91 (became Director in 1986); Head of Institutional Asset Management, Kleinwort Investment, 1991-96; NED, Bank of Scotland, 1993-2001; NED, Scottish Provident, 1995-2001; British Linen Bank, 1997-99 (became Governor in 1998); wholly Non Executive of a number of companies, 2002; Chairman, Alliance Trust plc; Governor, Museum of London. Recreations: family; contemporary arts and crafts; opera. Address: (h.) 10A Circus Lane, Edinburgh EH3 6SU; T.-07768 046 422.

Knox, Liz, DA (Edin), PAI, PPAI. Artist, since 1971; President, Paisley Art Institute, since 2007; b. 20.01.45, Glasgow; m., Peter Whittle; 2 s. Educ. Hillhead High School; Glasgow and John Neilson, Paisley; Edinburgh College of Art. Art Teacher, Secondary Education, 1971-73; bringing up sons and lecturing part time, 1973-83; Lecturer in Fine Art for Further Education, 1983-2003; painting part time, from 1971; full time artist, since 2003 (exhibiting throughout Britain including London, Edinburgh and Glasgow, since 2003). Member, committee of Paisley Art Institute, since 2003, Member of council. The Glasgow Art Club, since 2006; Vice President, Paisley Art Institute, 2004-07; Awards: Winner of the Aspect Prize, 2003, The Bessie Scott Award at PAI, 2004, The Diploma of Paisley Art Institute, "PAI", 2005, The University of Paisley (now University of the West of Scotland) Award, 2006, The Blythswood Square Quaich at Glasgow Society of Women Artists, 2007. Recreation: photography. Address: (h.) Jesmond High Street, Neilston, Glasgow G78 3HJ; T.-0141 587 5559; e-mail: lizknox1@ntlworld.com; web: www.lizknox.com

Kocovsky, Professor Pavel, PhD, DSc, FRSC. Sir William Ramsay Professor of Chemistry, University of Glasgow, since 1999; b. 7.1.51, Rychnov, Czech Republic; m., Eva Sramkova; 2 d. Educ. Technical University, Prague; Czech Academy of Sciences, Prague. Lecturer, Chemistry, Institute of Organic Chemistry and Biochemistry, Czechoslovak Academy of Sciences, Prague, 1977-91; Research Associate, Cornell University, Ithaca, NY, USA, 1983-84; Visiting Professor, University of Uppsala, Sweden, 1989-90; Reader, Organic Chemistry, University of Leicester, 1991-99. Publications: over 180 research papers in chemistry journals; Synthesis of Natural Products, 1986. Recreations: photography; travel; classical music. Address: (b.) Department of Chemistry, University of Glasgow, Glasgow, G12 8QQ; T.-0141-330 4199; e-mail: P.Kocovsky@chem.gla.ac.uk

Kubie, Professor Jorge, BSc (Eng), PhD, DSc(Eng), CEng, FIMechE. Professor of Mechanical Engineering, Napier University, Edinburgh, since 1997; Head, School of Engineering, Napier University, since 1998; b. 13.6.47, Prague; m., Amanda Jane Kubie; 1s.; 4d. Educ. Czech Technical University; University College London; Aston University. Research and technical posts in the electricity supply industry, 1974-90; Professor, Mechanical Engineering, Middlesex University, London, 1990-97; Member, Board of Management, Borders College, 2000-02. Address: (b.) School of Engineering, Napier University, Edinburgh, EH10 5DT; T.-0131-455 2595.

Kuenssberg, Nicholas Christopher, OBE, BA (Hons) (Oxon), FCIS, FIoD, CCMI, FRSA. Chairman: eTourism Ltd., since 2007; Keronite plc, since 2006, iomart Group plc, since 2000, Canmore Partnership Ltd., since 1999, Scottish Networks International, since 2000; Member,

Scottish Environment Protection Agency, since 1999 (Deputy Chairman, since 2003); b. 28.10.42, Edinburgh; m., Sally Robertson; 1 s.; 2 d. Educ. Edinburgh Academy; Wadham College, Oxford. Director, J. & P. Coats Ltd., 1978-91; Chairman, Dynacast International Ltd, 1978-91; Director, Coats Patons plc, 1985-91; Director, Coats Viyella plc, 1986-91; Managing Director, Dawson International plc, 1994-95 (Managing Director, Premier Brands, 1991-94); Non-executive Director: Bank of Scotland West of Scotland Board, 1984-88, ScottishPower plc, 1984-97, Standard Life Assurance Company, 1988-99, Baxi Partnership Ltd., 1996-99; Non-executive Director: Chamberlin and Hill plc, 1999-2006, Armino Technologies plc, 2004-07; Chairman: GAP Group Ltd., 1996-2005, Stoddard International PLC, 1997-2000, David A. Hall Ltd., 1996-98, Scotland the Brand, 2002-04, ScotlandIS, 2001-03, Institute of Directors, Scotland, 1997-99, Association for Management Education and Training in Scotland, 1996-98; Governor, Queen's College, 1988-91; Visiting Director, Strathclyde Business School, 1988-91; Member, Advisory Group to Secretary of State on Sustainable Development, 1996-99; Member, Scottish Legal Aid Board, 1996-2004; Member, British Council, Scottish Committee, since 1999; Board Member, Citizens Theatre, Glasgow, 2000-03; Chairman, Glasgow School of Art, since 2003. Recreations: languages; opera; travel; sport. Address: (b.) 6 Cleveden Drive, Glasgow, G12 0SE; e-mail: horizon@sol.co.uk

Kuenssberg, Sally, CBE, BA, DipAdEd, FRSA. Chair, Scottish Council, Save The Children; b. 30.7.43, Edinburgh; m., Nicholas; 1 s.; 2 d. Educ. St Leonard's School; University of Oxford. Language Teaching, Europe and South America, 1966-78; Partner, Heatherbank Press, Milngavie, 1981-90; Children's Panel Training Organiser, Department of Adult and Continuing Education, University of Glasgow, 1990-95; Chairman, Scottish Children's Reporter Administration, 1995-2002; Chair, Yorkhill NHS Trust, 2001-04; Member, NHS Greater Glasgow and Clyde Health Board, 2001-07; Adult Literacy Tutor, 1979-83; Member, Children's Panel, Glasgow, 1984-90.

Kunkler, Professor Ian Hubert, MA, MB, BChir, DMRT, FRCR, FRCPE, FRSA. Consultant and Honorary Professor in Clinical Oncology, Western General Hospital, University of Edinburgh; b. Wilmslow; m., Alison Jane; 1 s. Educ. Clifton College, Bristol; Magdalene College, Cambridge; St Bartholomew's Hospital, London. President, London Medical Group, 1976-77; House Officer, 1978-79; Senior House Officer, Nottingham City Hospital, 1979-81; Registrar and Senior Registrar, Clinical Oncology, Western General Hospital, Edinburgh; French Government and EEC Research Fellow, Institut Gustave Roussy, Paris, 1986-87; Consultant and Hon. Lecturer in Clinical Oncology, Weston Park Hospital, Sheffield, 1988-92; Honorary Reader, University of Edinburgh, 2006. President, British Oncological Association, 2000-02; Founder and Trustee, Clerk Maxwell Cancer Research Fund, 1998-2004; Member, IAEA international quality assurance group for radiotherapy, since 2005; International adviser in radiotherapy, Institut National du Cancer, France; 2006 British Oncological Association, Excellence in Oncology Team of The Year; Chief Investigator, MRC Supremo, Breast Cancer Trial. Publications: Walter and Miller's Textbook of Radiotherapy, 1993, 2002; various papers on breast cancer, radiotherapy and telemedicine. Address: (b.) Department of Clinical Oncology, Western General Hospital, Edinburgh EH4 2XU; T.-0131-537-2214; Fax: 0131-537-2216; e-mail: i.kunkler@ed.ac.uk

Kyle, James, CBE, DSc, MCh, FRCS. Chairman, Raigmore Hospital NHS Trust, Inverness, 1993-97; b.

26.3.25, Ballymena, Northern Ireland; m., Dorothy
Elizabeth Galbraith; 2 d. Educ. Ballymena Academy;
Queen's University, Belfast. Scholarship to Mayo Clinic,
USA, 1950; Tutor in Surgery, Royal Victoria Hospital,
Belfast, 1952; Lecturer in Surgery, Liverpool University,
1957; Senior Lecturer in Surgery, Aberdeen University,
1959-60, and Surgeon, Aberdeen Royal Infirmary, 1959-89.
Member, Grampian Health Board, 1973-77, Chairman,
1989-93; Chairman, Scottish Committee for Hospital
Medical Services, 1976-79; elected Member, General
Medical Council, 1979-94; Chairman: Scottish Joint
Consultants Committee, 1984-89, Representative Body,
British Medical Association, 1984-87; President, Aberdeen
Medico-Chirurgical Society, 1989-90; British Council
Lecturer, SE Asia and South America, 1963-85; Examiner:
Belfast, Dublin, Dundee, Edinburgh, Sydney, University of
West Indies; Burgess of Aberdeen. Patron: Royal Scottish
National Orchestra, Scottish Opera. Publications: Peptic
Ulcer; Pye's Surgical Handicraft; Crohn's Disease;
Scientific Foundations of Surgery. Recreations: Fellow,
Royal Philatelic Society, London; Fellow, Royal
Astronomical Society, London; licensed radio amateur,
GM4 CHX. Address: (h.) 7 Fasaich, Strath, Gairloch IV21
2DH; T.-01445 712398.

Kyle, Peter McLeod, MBChB, FRCS(Edin), FRCS(Glas),
FRCOphth. Consultant Ophthalmologist, Southern General
Hospital NHS Trust, since 1982 (Clinical Director of
Ophthalmology, 1995-2000); Honorary Clinical Senior
Lecturer, Glasgow University, since 1985; Member,
Medical Appeal Tribunals, Scotland, since 1986; Member,
General Optical Council; b. 19.8.51, Rutherglen; m.,
Valerie Anne Steele; 1 s.; 2 d. Educ. High School of
Glasgow; Glasgow University. Lecturer in Ophthalmology,
Glasgow University, 1980-84. Convener, Ophthalmology
Sub-committee, Royal College of Physicians and Surgeons
of Glasgow; Member, Opthalmology Specialist Advisory
Board, Royal College of Surgeons of Edinburgh; Deacon,
Incorporation of Barbers of Glasgow, 1998-99.
Recreations: walking; skiing. Address: (h.) 36 Sutherland
Avenue, Glasgow; T.-0141-427 4400; The Stables,
Earlsferry, Fife; T.-01333 330647.

Kynoch, George Alexander Bryson, BSc. Non-Executive
Chairman: Muir Matheson Ltd., London Marine Group
Ltd., 1997-2004, Benson Group Ltd., 1998-2005, The TEP
Exchange Group PLC, RDF Group PLC, 2003-06,
TOLUNA PLC; Non-Executive Director: Talent Group
PLC, TECC-IS PLC, 2003-05; Non Executive Chairman:
OCZ Technology Group Inc. Madwaves (UK) Ltd.,
Mercury Group PLC, since 2007; MP (Conservative),
Kincardine and Deeside, 1992-97; b. 7.10.46, Keith; m., Dr.
Rosslyn Margaret McDevitt (deceased); 1 s.; 1 d. Educ.
Cargilfield School, Edinburgh; Glenalmond College, Perth;
Bristol University. Plant Engineer, ICI Ltd., Nobel
Division, 1968-71; G. and G. Kynoch PLC, 1971-92,
latterly as Group Executive Director; Parliamentary Under
Secretary of State for Scotland – Minister for Industry and
Local Government, 1995-97; Non-Executive Director:
Kynoch Group PLC, Aardvark Clear Mine Ltd., 1992-95,
PSL Holdings Ltd., 1998, Silvertech International plc,
1997-2000, Midmar Energy Ltd., 1998-99, Premisys
Technologies PLC, 1998-2001, Jetcam International
Holdings Ltd., 1998-2003; Member, Aberdeen and District
Milk Marketing Board, 1988-92; Director, Moray Badenoch
and Strathspey Local Enterprise Co. Ltd., 1991-92;
Chairman, Scottish Woollen Publicity Council, 1983-90;
President, Scottish Woollen Industry, 1990-91; Vice
Chairman, Northern Area, Scottish Conservative and
Unionist Association, 1991-92. Recreations: golf; skiing;
travel. Address: (h.) Newton of Drumduan, Dess, Aboyne,
Aberdeenshire AB34 5BD.

L

Lacy, Very Rev. Dr. David William, BA, BD, DLitt. Minister, Henderson Parish Church, Kilmarnock, since 1989; Moderator of the General Assembly of the Church of Scotland, 2005-06; b. 26.4.52, Inverness; m., Joan Stewart Roberston; 1 s.; 1 d. Educ. Aberdeen Grammar School; High School of Glasgow; University of Strathclyde; University of Glasgow and Trinity College. Assistant Minister, St. George's West, Edinburgh, 1975-77; Minister, Knightswood: St. Margaret's, Glasgow, 1977-89. Recreations: sailing; snooker; choral singing. Address: 52 London Road, Kilmarnock, Ayrshire KA3 7AJ; T.-01563 523113.

Laidlaw, Bruce, ACIS. Administrative Secretary, Royal Scottish Academy, since 1995; b. 11.7.45, Edinburgh; m., Sandra; 1 s.; 1 d. Educ. Royal High School; Napier College, Edinburgh. Assistant Secretary, Cranston London Hotels Co. Ltd., 1963-65; public service, Edinburgh City, 1966-74; Elections Officer, Lothian Regional Council, 1975-79; public service, Lothian Regional Council, 1980-95. Recreations: fishing; skiing. Address: (b.) Royal Scottish Academy, The Mound, Edinburgh EH2 2EL; e-mail: info@royalscottishacademy.org

Laing, Alasdair North Grant, OBE, MRICS. Director, PDG Helicopters Ltd, since 1975; President, Royal Highland and Agricultural Society of Scotland, 2004/05; Director, Scottish Agricultural College, 1995-2003; Vice Convenor, Scottish Landowners Federation, 2000-04; b. 30.12.49, Forres; m., Lucy Ann Anthea Low; 2 s.; 1 d. Educ. Belhaven Hill; Eton College; Royal Agricultural Collge, Cirencester. Recreations: skiing; fishing; stalking. Address: (b.) Logie Estate Office, Forres, Moray IV36 2QN; T.-01667 458900.

Laing, Anne Katherine, LLB, NP. Solicitor (sole practitioner, since 1999); b. 18.1.54, Galashiels. Educ. Grangemouth High School; University of Dundee. Peter Young, Bo'ness: Apprenticeship, Partner, 1980, took over business in 1983, sole practitioner until 1990; Senior Partner, P.H. Young & Co., Solicitors, 1990-99; Honorary Sheriff, Tayside Central and Fife; former Director (Past President), Central Scotland Chamber of Commerce; Board Member, Scottish Enterprise Forth Valley, 1993-2000; Director, Careers Central Limited, 1995-2002 (Chair, 1997-2002). Recreations: gym; gardening; travel; food and wine. Address: (b.) 54 South Street, Bo'ness EH51 826166; e-mail: anne@phyoung.co.uk

Laing, David Kemlo, LLB. Chairman, Ledingham Chalmers LLP; b. 17.6.53, Aberdeen; m., Marina Maclean; 2 d. Educ. Robert Gordon's College, Aberdeen; University of Edinburgh. Clark and Wallace, Aberdeen, 1974-76; C. & P. H. Chalmers, Aberdeen, 1976-78, Partner, 1978-90; Partner, Ledingham Chalmers, 1991. Chairman, Scottish Bible Society; Elder, Bristo Memorial Church, Craigmillar. Recreations: music; outdoors. Address: (b.) Johnstone House, 52-54 Rose Street, Aberdeen AB10 1HA; T.-01224 408501.

Laing, Gerald (Ogilvie-Laing of Kinkell, Gerald), NDD, FRBS. Sculptor; b. 11.2.36; 4 s.; 1 d. Educ. Berkhamsted School; RMA, Sandhurst. Commissioned Fifth Fusiliers, 1955-60; resigned commission and attended St. Martin's School of Art, 1960-64; lived in New York, 1964-69; Artist in Residence, Aspen Institute for Humanistic Studies, Colorado, 1966; moved to north of Scotland, 1969, and restored ruins of Kinkell Castle; Civic Trust Award, 1971; established a tapestry workshop in north of Scotland; Visiting Professor, University of New Mexico, 1976-77; set up bronze foundry, Kinkell Castle, to produce own work; Member, Art Committee, Scottish Arts Council, 1978-80; Professor of Sculpture, Columbia University, New York, 1986-87; Commissioner, Royal Fine Art Commission for Scotland, 1987-95; public sculpture includes Callanish, Strathclyde University, 1971; Frieze of the Wise and Foolish Virgins, Edinburgh, 1980; Fountain of Sabrina, Bristol, 1982; Conan Doyle Memorial, 1991, Edinburgh; Axis Mundi, 1991; Bank Underground Station Dragons, London, 1995; St. George and Dragon Series, Harrow, 1996; Four Rugby Players, Twickenham, 1996; portrait bust, Sir Paul Getty, National Gallery, London, 1997; Cricketer, Wormsley Cricket Ground, Bucks, 1999; Glass Wise and Foolish Virgins, Edinburgh, 1999; The Batsman, MCC, Lord's Ground, London; Glengarry Memorial, Skye (with Emma Lavender), 2000; Falcon Square, Inverness, 2003; a series of anti-Iraq War paintings which have been exhibited in Edinburgh, New York, Paris, King's College Cambridge and London, 2004-07. Address: (h.) Kinkell Castle, Dingwall IV7 8AT; T.-01349 861485; e-mail: kinkell@btinternet.com

Laing, Malcolm Donald, MA, LLB, NP. Partner, Ledingham Chalmers LLP, Solicitors; b. 28.11.55, Aberdeen. Educ. Robert Gordon's College; Aberdeen University. Morton Fraser & Milligan, Edinburgh, 1978-82; C. & P.H. Chalmers, 1982-90 (Partner, 1985). Director, Cornerstone Community Care. Recreations: travel; mountaineering; music. Address: (b.) Johnstone House, 52-54 Rose Street, Aberdeen AB15 8JL; T.-01224 408511.

Laing, The Hon. Mark Hector, MA. Managing Director, Nairn's Oatcakes Ltd., since 1996; Director, Scottish Business in the Community; Director, Tomorrow's Company in Scotland; Chairman, Friends of Craigmillar; b. 22.2.51, London; m., Susanna Crawford; 1 s.; 2 d. Educ. Eton College; Cambridge University. United Biscuits p.l.c., 1972-96: Factory Director, Glasgow, 1985; Production Director, McVities, 1988; Managing Director, Simmers Biscuits, 1990. Recreations: walking; gardening; fishing; shooting. Address: (b.) Nairn's Oatcakes Ltd., 90 Peffermill Road, Edinburgh EH16 5UU; T.-0131-620 7000.

Lall, Vikram, CBE (2005), BA (Hons) Econs, CA. Director, Heriot Services Ltd., since 1996; b. 5.12.46; m., Carol Anne Ask; 1 s.; 1 d. Educ. Doon School, Dehra Dun; St Stephen's College, Delhi. Executive Director: Noble Grossart Ltd., 1975-77, Vikram Lall & Co. Ltd., 1977-82, McNeill Pearson Ltd., 1982-85, Heriot & Co. Ltd., 1985-87, Bell Lawrie White & Co., 1987-2003, Brewin Dolphin Holdings plc, 1989-2003 (now non-executive Director). Non-executive Director: Isis Property Trust, since 2003; Crown Place VCT, Ramco Holdings Ltd., since 2005; non-executive Chairman, Ryden LLP, since 2005. Chairman, Scottish Industrial Development Advisory Board, since 2002 (Member, since 2000); Member, Board, Royal Lyceum Theatre Co., since 2002, Governing Body, Queen Margaret UC, Edinburgh, since 2003, Finance and Investments Committee, RCSE, since 2005. Recreations: golf; travel; mind exercise. Address: Newmains House, Drem, East Lothian EH39 5BL; T.-01620 825130; e-mail: vikramlall@macace.net

Lally, Patrick James, JP, DL, LLD, KLJ, HRGI, FRSA. Rt. Hon. Lord Provost of the City of Glasgow and Lord Lieutenant, City of Glasgow, 1996-1999; Deputy Lieutenant, Glasgow; Commandeur, Ordre National du

Merite (France); Chairman, Greater Glasgow and Clyde Valley Tourist Board, 1996-99; Director, Glasgow Cultural Enterprises, 1988-99; b. Glasgow; m., Margaret Beckett McGuire (deceased); 2 s. Elected, Corporation of Glasgow, 1966-75 (Deputy Leader, 1972-75); elected City of Glasgow Council, 1975-77, and 1980-96; City Treasurer, 1984-86; Leader, City of Glasgow District Council, 1986-92 and 1994-96; Chairman, Greater Glasgow Tourist Board, 1989-96; President, Glasgow International Jazz Festival; Hon. Director, Chinese Peoples Association for Friendship with Foreign Countries; Hon. Member, Royal Glasgow Institute of Fine Arts; Hon. Member, Rotary International; Hon. Citizen, Dalian, China; Hon. Member, Royal Faculty of Procurators in Glasgow; Knight, Order of St. Lazarus; Member, Merchants House of Glasgow; Member, Incorporation of Tailors, Glasgow; Member, Incorporation of Gardeners, Glasgow; Chairman, Scottish Senior Citizens Unity Party; President, Glasgow South East Health Forum; awarded Scottish Tourist Board Silver Thistle Award, 1999. Recreations: enjoying the arts; reading; watching TV; football. Address: 2 Tamera Avenue, Glasgow G44 5BU.

Lamb, Professor Joseph Fairweather, MB, ChB, BSc, PhD, FRCPEdin, FRSE. Emeritus Professor; Chandos Professor of Physiology, St. Andrews University, 1969-93; b. 18.7.28, Brechin; m., 1, Olivia Jane Horne; 3 s.; 1 d.; 2, Bridget Cecilia Cook; 2 s. Educ. Brechin High School; Edinburgh University. National Service, 1947-49; House Surgeon, Dumfries Royal Infirmary, 1955-56; House Physician, Eastern General Hospital, Edinburgh, 1956; Research Scholar, then Lecturer, Edinburgh University, 1957-61; Lecturer, then Senior Lecturer, Glasgow University, 1961-69; Editor, Journal of Physiology, 1968-74; Senior Secretary, Physiological Society, 1982-85; Chairman, Gas Greed campaign, 1994-95; Governor, Rowett Research Institute, 1998-2004; Chairman and Founder, Save British Science, 1986-97; Member, Appeals Panels, DHSS, 1995-2001. Publications: Essentials of Physiology, 1980; research papers on physiology, medicine and sailing. Recreations: boat-building; sailing; amateur radio. Address: (h.) 53 Darnell Road, Edinburgh EH5 3PH.

Lambert, Roderick Stewart, LLB (Hons), LLM (Cantab), DipLP. Partner and Head of EU/Competition, McGrigors, London and Edinburgh; Advocate, Scottish Bar, since 1991; b. 17.8.65, St. Andrews; m., Elaine; 1 d.; 1 s. Educ. Madras College, St. Andrews; University of Edinburgh; Trinity Hall, Cambridge. Called to Bar, 1991; admitted as Barrister and Solicitor, High Court of New Zealand, 1995; admitted as Solicitor, England and Wales, 2000; Legal 500, Chambers and Legal Experts listed expert in competition law; occasional lecturer; published in the UK and US on antitrust law. Recreations: climbing; snowboarding; cricket. Address: (h.) 3C Gillisland Road, Merchiston, Edinburgh EH10 5BW; T.-0131-337 4130.

Lambie, David, BSc (Hons), DipEd, FEIS. Chairman, Development Committee and Member, Management Committee, Cunninghame Housing Association, since 1992; Member, Board, Galloway Training Association Ltd., since 1997; MP (Labour), Cunninghame South, 1970-92; b. 13.7.25, Saltcoats; m., Netta Merrie; 1 s.; 4 d. Educ. Ardrossan Academy; Glasgow University; Geneva University. Teacher, Glasgow Corporation, 1950-70. Secretary, All Party Committee for Energy Studies, 1980-92; chaired Select Committee on Scottish Affairs, 1981-87; UK Member, Council of Europe and Western European Union, 1987-92; Chairman, PLP Aviation Committee, 1988-92; Chairman, Saltcoats Labour Party, 1992-96. Recreation: watching junior football. Address: (h.) 11 Ivanhoe Drive, Saltcoats, Ayrshire KA21 6LS; T.-01294 464843.

Lamond, June Rose; b. 6.12.33, Aberdeen; m., James Alexander Lamond; 3 d. Educ. Demonstration School; Commercial College. Regional and City Councillor,

since 1974; Chairperson Aberdeen Women's Aid, 1976-86; Member, Grampian Health Board, 1975-87; Committee Member, Grampian Society for the Blind, since 1998. Recreations: walking; travelling; reading. Address: 15 Belvidere Street, Aberdeen AB25 2QS.

Lamont, D. Murray, BA, MHCIMA (Dip), MSIM, ACIM. Honorary Sheriff, Wick; Hotelier; Company Director; Proprietor: Mackays Hotel Wick, Bin Ends, The Fine Wine Shops, since 1995; b. 1.9.57, Wick, Caithness; 1 d. Educ. Wick High School; Abertay University. Purchased and developed Mackays Hotel; started and developed Bin Ends, The Fine Wine Shops; started and developing, Ebenezer Leisure Ltd. Chairman, Wick Branch RNLI; Director: The Highland Tourism Operators Group, The Scottish Licensed Trade Benevolent Society. T.-01955 602678; e-mail: murray@mackayshotel.co.uk

Lamont, Johann, MA (Hons). MSP (Labour), Glasgow Pollok, since 1999; Deputy Minister for Justice, 2006-07; Deputy Minister for Communities, 2004-06; Convener, Communities Committee, 2001-04 (former Deputy Convener, Local Government Committee); b. 1957, Glasgow; m.; 1 s.; 1 d. Educ. Woodside Secondary School; Glasgow University; Jordanhill College of Education; Strathclyde University. Former teacher. Address: (b.) Scottish Parliament, Edinburgh EH99 1SP; T.-0131-348 5846.

Lamont, John. MSP (Conservative), Roxburgh and Berwickshire, since 2007; b. 15.4.76, Irvine. Educ. Kilwinning Academy, Ayrshire; Glasgow University. Solicitor: Brodies, 2005-07, Freshfields, London, 2000-06, Bristows, London, 2006-07. Recreations: cycling; swimming; cooking. Address: (h.) 63 High Street, Coldstream TD12 4DL; (b.) 25 High Street, Hawick; Scottish Parliament, Edinburgh EH99 1SP; T.-0131 348 6533; e-mail: john.lamont.msp@scottishparliament.uk

Lamont-Brown, Raymond, JP, MA, AMIET, MJS, FSA (Scot). Author and Broadcaster; Lecturer, Centre for External Services, St. Andrews University, 1978-98, Centre for Continuing Education, Dundee University, 1988-98; Founder, Japan Research Projects, since 1965; b. 20.9.39, Horsforth, Leeds; m., Dr. Elizabeth Moira McGregor. Educ. Wheelwright Grammar School, Dewsbury; Bradford Technical College; SOAS; Nihon Daigaku, Japan. Honorary Secretary/Treasurer, Society of Authors in Scotland, 1982-89; Past President, St. Andrews Rotary Club; Vice-Chairman, St. Andrews Community Council, 1988-91; Chairman, Arthritis Care Liaison Committee (Central, Fife and Tayside), 1991-97; Member, Council, Arthritis Care, 1991-97. Publications: 58 published books, including Discovering Fife; Phantoms of the Sea; The Life and Times of Berwick-upon-Tweed; The Life and Times of St. Andrews; Royal Murder Mysteries; Scottish Epitaphs; Scottish Superstitions; Scottish Traditions and Festivals; Famous Scots; Scottish Witchcraft; Around St. Andrews; Scottish Folklore; Kamikaze: Japan's Suicide Samurai; Scotland of 100 Years Ago; Kempeitai: Japan's Dreaded Military Police; Edward VII's Last Loves; Tutor to the Dragon Emperor; John Brown; Royal Poxes and Potions; Ships from Hell; Fife in History and Legend; Villages of Fife; Humphry Davy; Andrew Carnegie; St Andrews: City by the Northern Sea. Address: (h.) 11 Seabourne Gardens, Broughty Ferry, Dundee DD5 2RT; T.-01382 732032.

Landale, Sir David William Neil, KCVO, DL, MA, FRSA; b. 27.5.34, London; m., (Norah) Melanie Roper; 3 s. Educ. Eton College; Balliol College, Oxford. Black Watch,

Royal Highland Regiment, 1952-58; Jardine Matheson & Co. Ltd., 1958-75, served in Hong Kong, Thailand, Taiwan and Japan (Director, 1967-75); Director, Matheson & Co. Ltd., 1975-86; Director, Pinneys Holdings, 1976-93; Secretary and Keeper of the Records, Duchy of Cornwall, 1987-93; Director, Duchy Originals, 1989 94. Member, Executive Committee, National Trust for Scotland, 1978-84; Member, Executive Committee, Scottish Landowners Federation, 1980-87; Chairman, Timber Growers Association, 1983-86; Director, Dumfries and Galloway Enterprise, 1993; President, Royal Highland and Agricultural Society, 1994; Chairman, Scottish Forestry Trust, 1994-2001; Chairman and Founding Trustee, Maggie Keswick Cancer Caring Trust, 1995-98 and Chairman, 2003-05; Chairman for Scotland, Malcolm Sargent Fund, 1996-99; Deputy Chairman and Trustee, Crichton Endowment Trust, 1995-99; Chairman, Royal Scottish Forestry Trust Co. (Cashell), since 1998; Convener, Crichton Foundation, since 2000 (Chairman, 1998-2000); DUniv (Glasgow), DUniv (Paisley). Recreations: all countryside pursuits; theatre; reading (history). Address: (h.) Dalswinton, Dumfries; T.-01387 740 208/279.

Lander, Ronald, OBE, BSc, FIEE, FScotvec, FSQA. Chairman and Managing Director: Scotlander plc, since 1985, Scotlander Ltd., since 1986; Director: Logical Innovations Ltd., since 2001, Pyramid Research and Development Ltd., 2000-06, Young Enterprise Scotland, 1998-2001; Director and Chairman, Armadale Tech. Ltd., since 2007; b. 5.8.42, Glasgow; m., Elizabeth Stirling; 2 s. Educ. Allan Glen's School; Glasgow University. Chairman and Managing Director, Lander Grayburn & Co. Limited, 1970-83; Deputy Managing Director, Lander Alarm Company (Scotland) Limited, 1975-79; Managing Director, Lander Alarms Limited and Lander Alarms (Scotland) Limited, 1979-85; Chairman, Lander & Jess Limited, 1983-87; Director, Centre for Entrepreneurial Development, Glasgow University, 1985-88; Chairman, Newstel Information Ltd., 1998-99; Member, CBI Scottish Council, 1977-83, 1984-90 and since 1992; (founding) Chairman, CBI Scotland's Smaller Firms' Working Group, 1977-80; founding Chairman, Entrepreneurial Exchange, 1995-96; founder Member, CBI Industrial Policy Committee, London, 1978-86; Chairman, CBI Scotland Smaller Firms' Committee, 1993-95; Chairman, Scottish Fire Prevention Council, 1979-80; Member, Glasgow University Appointments Committee, since 1979; CBI Representative, Home Office/CBI/TUC Joint Committee on Prison Industries, 1980-87; Industrial Member, Understanding British Industry, Scotland, 1981-89; Member, Council, Scottish Business School, 1982-87; Director, British Security Industry Association Council, 1984-85; Governor, Scottish Sports Aid Foundation, 1985-88; Member: Kincraig Committee (review of parole system and related matters), 1987-89, Manpower Services Committee for Scotland (later the Training Agency), 1987-88; founder Chairman, Local Employer Network (LENS) Scottish Co-ordinating Committee, 1987; Chairman, CBI Scotland Education and Training Committee, 1987-89; Director, SCOTVEC, 1987-93; Member, CBI Business/Education Task Force (the Cadbury Report), 1988; Member, Scottish Consultative Council on the Curriculum, 1988-91; Vice Convener, Scottish Education/Industry Committee, 1988-91; Founder Member, Glasgow Action, 1985; Member, Secretary of State for Scotland's Crime Prevention Committee, 1984-87; Companion IEE, 1986; Board Member, Glasgow Development Agency, 1991-99; Visiting/Honorary Professor, Glasgow University, since 1991; National Judge, National Training Awards, 1989-92; Board Member, Glasgow Science Centre, 1999-2007; Director, Picardy Media Group Plc, 1998-2001. Address: (b.) Scotlander Ltd., PO Box 9219, Kilmacolm PA13 4YL.

Lane, Professor Sir David Philip, Kt 2000, PhD, FRCPath, FMedSci, FRS 1996, FRSE. Professor of Molecular Oncology, University of Dundee, since 1990;

Executive Director, Institute of Molecular and Cell Biology, Proteos, Singapore, 2004-07 (on sabbatical); Chairman, Biomedical Research Council, Agency for Science, Technology and Research (A*STAR), Singapore, since 2007; Chief Executive Officer, Experimental Therapeutic Centre, since 2007; Chief Scientist, Cancer Research-UK (CR-UK), London, since 2008; b. 1.7.52; m., Ellen Birgitte Muldal; 1 s.; 1 d. Educ. John Fisher School, Purley; University College, London (BSc 1973, PhD 1976; Fellow). FRCPath 1996. FRSE 1992. Res. Fellow, ICRF, 1976-77; Lectr. Imperial Coll., 1977-85; Staff Scientist, ICRF, 1985-90. Vis. Fellow, Cold Spring Harbor Labs, NY, 1978-80: Gibb Fellow, Cancer Res. UK (formerly CRC), 1990-. Mem., EMBO, 1990. Founder FMedSci 1998, Hon. DSc: Abertay Dundee, 1999; Stirling, 2000; Aberdeen, 2002; Birmingham, 2002. Prize, Charles Rodolphe Brupbacher Foundation, 1993; Prize, Joseph Steiner Foundation, 1993; Howard Hughes International Scholar, Howard Hughes Med. Inst., 1993; Yvette Mayent Prize, Inst. Curie, 1994; Medal, Swedish Soc. of Oncology, 1994; Prize, Meyenberg Foundation, 1995; Black Prize, Jefferson Hosp., 1995; Silvanus Thompson Medal, British Inst. of Radiol., 1996; Henry Dryerre Prize, 1996; Paul Ehrlich Prize, 1998; Tom Connors Prize, 1998; Bruce-Peller Prize, 1998; SCI Medal, 2003; Anthony Dipple Carcinogenesis Award, 2004; Buchanan Medal, Royal Soc., 2004; Biochem. Soc. Award, 2004; Internat. Agency for Res. on Cancer Medal, 2005; Sergio Lombroso Award for Cancer Research Work, 2005; INSERM Medal D'Estranger, 2006; Honorary Degree of Doctor of Medicine, The University of Nottingham, 2006; Gregor Mendel Memorial Medal, Masaryk Memorial Cancer Institute, Czech Republic, 2006; AICR (Association for International Cancer Research) Colin Thomson Memorial Medal Lecture, Beatson Institute for Cancer Research, Glasgow, UK, 2007; David Hungerford Lecture Medal, Bangalore, 2007; Doctor Honoris causa, University Paul Sabatier, Toulouse, 2007. Publications: Antibodies, a laboratory manual, 1988; numerous papers in learned journals. Recreations: walking; tennis; motor cycles. Address: (b.) Cancer Research UK Laboratories, Department of Surgery and Molecular Oncology, University of Dundee, Dundee DD1 9SY; T.-01382 496362.

Lang of Monkton, Baron (Ian Bruce Lang), DL, PC, OStJ, BA. Life Peer; Deputy Lieutenant, Ayrshire and Arran, since 1998; President of the Board of Trade, 1995-97; Company Directorships including: Marsh & McLennan Inc., Thistle Mining Inc., US Special Opportunities Trust plc, Lithgows Ltd.; Chairman, Patrons of the National Galleries of Scotland, 1999-2006; b. 27.6.40, Glasgow; m., Sandra Caroline Montgomerie; 2 d. Educ. Lathallan School; Rugby School; Sidney Sussex College, Cambridge. MP (Conservative) Galloway and Upper Nithsdale, 1983-97 (Galloway, 1979-83); Member, Select Committee on Scottish Affairs, 1979-81; Trustee, Glasgow Savings Bank and West of Scotland TSB, 1969-82; Lord Commissioner of HM Treasury, 1983-86; Scottish Whip, 1981-83; Vice-Chairman, Scottish Conservative Party, 1983-87; Parliamentary Under Secretary of State, Scottish Office, 1986-87, and at Department of Employment, 1986; Minister of State, Scottish Office, 1987-90; Secretary of State for Scotland, 1990-95. Member, Queen's Bodyguard for Scotland (Royal Company of Archers), since 1974; Governor, Rugby School, since 1997; President, Association for the Protection of Rural Scotland, 1998-2001; Hon. President, St. Columba's School, Kilmacolm, since 1999. Publication: Blue Remembered Years, 2002. Address (b.) House of Lords, Westminster, London SW1A OPW.

Lang, Dr Brian Andrew, MA. PhD. Principal and Vice-Chancellor, St Andrews University, since 2001; b. 2.12.45; 2 s.; 1 d. Educ. Royal High School, Edinburgh;

Edinburgh University. Social anthropology research, Kenya, 1969-70; Lecturer, Social Anthropology, Aarhus University, 1971-75; Scientific Staff, SSRC, 1976-79; Secretary, Historic Buildings Council for Scotland, 1979-80; Secretary, National Heritage Memorial Fund, 1980-87; Director, Public Affairs, National Trust, 1987-91; Chief Executive and Deputy Chairman, British Library, 1991-2000; Chairman, European National Libraries Forum, 1993-2000; Chair, Heritage Image Partnership, 2000-02; Board Member, Scottish Enterprise Fife, since 2003; Member: Library and Information Services Council (England), 1991-94, Library and Information Commission, 1995-2000, Council, St. Leonards School, St Andrews, since 2001; FRSE, 2006; Visiting Professor, Napier University, Edinburgh, since 1999; Visiting Scholar, Getty Institute, Los Angeles, California, 2000; Pforzheimer Lecture, University of Texas, 1998; Trustee: 21st Century Learning Initiative, 1995-99, Hopetoun House Preservation Trust, 2001-05; Deputy Chair, National Heritage Memorial Fund, since 2005; Member, Council, National Trust for Scotland, 2001-04; President, Institute of Information Scientists, 1993-94 (Hon. Fellow, 1994); Hon. FLA, 1997; Chairman of Trustees, Newbattle Abbey College, since 2004; Member: Committee for Scotland, Heritage Lottery Fund, since 2004 (Chair, since 2005), Cultural Commission, 2004-05. Publications: numerous articles and contributions to professional journals. Recreations: music; museums and galleries; pottering. Address: (b.) Office of the Principal, College Gate, St Andrews University, North Street, St Andrews, Fife, KY16 9AJ; T.-01334 462545; e-mail: principal@st-and.ac.uk

Lang, Stephen, MBChB, FRCPath. Consultant Histopathologist, Ninewells Hospital, Dundee, since 1990; Honorary Senior Lecturer in Histopathology, University of Dundee, since 1990; b. 19.9.58, Glasgow; separated; 2 s.; 1 d. Educ. Holy Cross High School, Hamilton; Glasgow University. RAF Medical Officer, 1982-87 (RAF Leuchars, 1982-83, RAF Halton, 1983-87); Lecturer/Honorary Senior Registrar in Histopathology, St. Bartholomew's Hospital and The Hospital for Sick Children, Great Ormond Street, London, 1987-90. Recreations: football; golf; cinema; theatre. Address: 56 Wyvis Road, Broughty Ferry, Dundee DD5 3SU; T.-01382 800886; e-mail: stephen.lang@nhs.net

Langford, Professor David Anthony, FCIOB, MSc, MPhil. Professor of Construction Management, Glasgow Caledonian University; b. 6.5.50, Notingham; m., Victoria; 1 d. Educ. Barstable School, Basildon; Bristol Polytechnic; Aston University; Cranfield School of Management. MSc Course Director, Department of Building Technology, Brunel University, 1975; Director of Postgraduate Studies, Bath University, 1987; Barr Chair of Construction, Strathclyde University, 1991. Address: (b.) School of Built and Natural Environment, Glasgow Caledonian University, Glasgow G4 0BA; T.-0141-331-3092.

Langlands, Sir (Robert) Alan, KT, BSc, DUniv(Glas), Hon.FRCP, FRCS(Edin), FRCPS(Glas), FRCGP, FFPHM, FIA, FCGI, CIMgt, FRSE. Principal and Vice-Chancellor, Dundee University, since 2000; b. 29.5.52; m., Elizabeth McDonald; 1s.; 1d. Educ. Allan Glen's School; Glasgow University. Graduate Trainee, NHS Scotland, 1974- 76; Argyll and Clyde Health Board, 1976-78; Simpson Memorial Maternity Pavilion, Elsie Inglis Hospital, 1978-81; Unit Administrator, Middlesex and University College Hospitals and Hospital for Women, Soho, 1981-85; District General Manager, Harrow Health Authority, 1985-89; Practice Leader, Health Care, Towers Perrin, 1989-91; General Manager, NW Thames Regional Health Authority, 1991-92; Deputy Chief Executive, 1993-94, Chief Executive, 1994-2000, NHS Executive; Member: Central R&D Committee, NHS, 1991-92, National Forum R&D, 1994-99, Health Sector Group BTI, 1998-2000, Council and Court York University, 1998-2000, External Advisory Board, RCP; Member, International Council of the Johns Hopkins Bioethics Institute; Hon. Professor, since 1996; Board Member, Warwick University Business School, 1999-2000; Chairman, Scottish Institute for Enterprise, 2001-04; Development Board Member, International Virtual Medical School, since 2002; Chairman, UK Biobank, since 2004. Recreations: living and walking in Scotland and Yorkshire. Address: (b.) Dundee University, DD1 4HN.

Langley, Crawford James, LLB (Hons), BD, DPA, ACIS, NP. Senior Depute Returning Officer, Aberdeen Constituencies, since 1996; Corporate Director for Legal and Democratic Services, Aberdeen City Council, 2002-06 (Director of Legal and Corporate Services, 1995-2002); Advocate in Aberdeen; b. 21.11.51, Glasgow; m., Janette Law Hamilton (deceased); m. (2), Judith Cripps. Educ. Bellahouston Academy, Glasgow; Glasgow University. Legal apprentice, Corporation of Glasgow, 1973-75; various legal posts, Strathclyde Regional Council, 1975-89, Principal Solicitor, 1984-89; Depute Director of Law and Administration, Tayside Regional Council, 1989-91; Director of Law and Administration, Tayside Regional Council, 1991-95. Recreation: travel. Address: (h.) "Canouan", Eassie, Angus DD8 1SG.

Last, Professor Frederick Thomas, OBE, DSc, ARCS, SHM, VMM, FRSE. Applied Biologist; Honorary Professor, Institute of Ecology and Resource Management, Edinburgh University, since 1972; b. 5.2.28, Wembley; m., 1, Pauline Mary Cope (deceased); 2 s.; 2, Pauline Mary Smith. Educ. Haberdashers' Aske's Hampstead School; Imperial College of Science and Technology, London. Rothamsted Experimental Station, Herts, 1950-61; Chief Plant Pathologist to Government of Sudan, 1956-58; Head, Mycology and Bacteriology, Glasshouse Crops Research Institute, Sussex, 1961-69; Visiting Professor, Pennsylvania State University, 1969-70; Member of Directorate, Institute of Terrestrial Ecology, Midlothian, 1970-86; President, Association of Applied Biologists, 1977-78; Commissioner, Red Deer Commission, 1981-86; Visiting Professor, Agriculture and Environmental Science, Newcastle upon Tyne University, 1986-94; Chairman, Advisory Committee on Sites of Special Scientific Interest, 1992-96; Trustee, Tree Advice Trust, since 1993 (Founder Chairman, 1993-98); Advisor, Chongqing Institute of Environmental Science, since 1993; Founder President, Dunbar's John Muir Association, 1994-97 (Patron, since 1999); Board Member, Scottish Natural Heritage, 1996-99 (Member, Scientific Advisory Committee, 1999-2001); Member, Joint Nature Conservation Committee, 1996-99; Founder Chairman, Gardening Scotland (1999-2005). Publications: Tree Physiology and Yield Improvement (Joint Editor), 1976; Land and its Uses, Actual and Potential: An Environmental Appraisal (Joint Editor), 1986; Acidic Deposition, Its Nature and Impacts (Joint Editor), 1991; Tree Crop Ecosystems, 2001. Recreations: gardening; philately; travelling. Address: (h.) Furuly, Seton Mains, Longniddry, East Lothian EH32 0PG; T.-01875 852102.

Latimer, Ian James, MA. Chief Constable, Northern Constabulary, since 2001; b. 19.3.56, Carlisle; m., Margaret; 3 c. Educ. Carlisle Grammar School; Manchester University; Fitzwilliam College, Cambridge University. Joined Merseyside Police, 1981; appointed Assistant Chief Constable, Devon and Cornwall Constabulary, 1999. Address: (b.) Police Headquarters, Inverness IV2 3SY; T.-01463 715555.

Lauderdale, 17th Earl of (Patrick Francis Maitland), BA (Hons) (Oxon). Former Elf oil company Director; b. 17.3.11, Walsall; m., Stanka Lozanitch (deceased); 2 s.; 2 d. Educ, Lancing College; Brasenose College, Oxford. Journalist, Fleet Street, 1934-39; War Correspondent, Poland, 1939; Balkans/Danubian Correspondent, The Times, 1939-41; War Correspondent, with US Forces in the Pacific, News Chronicle, 1941-43; Foreign Office, 1943-45; Editor, The Fleet Street Letter Service, 1939-51; MP (Conservative), Lanark, 1951-59; Member, House of Lords, 1968-99; Chairman, Sub Committee B, Lords EEC Scrutiny Committee, 1974-79; Founder, Parliamentary Group for Energy Studies, 1983; Guardian, Shrine of Our Lady of Walsingham, since 1955; Hereditary Bearer of the National Flag of Scotland. Recreations: reading; pilgrimages to St. Mary's, Haddington.

Lauder-Frost, Gregory MacLennan Scholey, BA Hons (Oxon). Director, Focus Inc Ltd., since 2006; Company Secretary, Focus Inc Ltd., 1996-2005; Editor, The Scottish Genealogist, 2004-07; Clerk to Foulden Mordington & Lamberton Community Council, since 2002; b. 8.8.51; m. (1); Joanna Margaret nee Pecka (div. 1987); 1d.; m. (2); Sarah-Jane nee Gladstone; 2 d. Educ. Oxford; Sydney, London (Birkbeck) University. Certified Public Accountant, 1975, Certificate in Business Management, Oxford Centre for Management Studies, Oxon, 1976. Manager/auditor for EMI Ltd., 1975-76; administration, Westminster Hospital, 1977; Executive Officer, Medical Research Council (fixed term), 1978; senior administrator (finance), NHS, 1979-92; Company Director, Korostovetz (Russia) Ltd., 1991-93; Company Director, UK Books (Export) Ltd., 1992-95; Company Secretary, Mediterranean Entertainments Ltd., 1994-96. Fellow, Royal Commonwealth Society, since 1971; Fellow, Society of Antiquaries (Scotland), since 1989; Member, Society of Genealogists, London, since 1977; Life Member (2003), Order of the Crown of Charlemagne; Member: The Freedom Association, 1976-80, The Primrose League, 1977-93; Life Member (Jan. 1977), The International Monarchist League, and subsequently its Publications Officer, 1987-92 and Secretary-General, 1990-91; Member, 1977-92, Conservative Monday Club, and subsequently Secretary (1987) & Chairman (1988-92) of its Foreign Affairs Committee, & Club Political Secretary (1989-92); Ward Secretary & Executive Council Member of the Chelsea Conservative Association, 1977-84; Member (1986-88) and Patron & Executive Council Member (1988-92) Roxburgh & Berwickshire Conservative Association; Member (1981-) & of the Governing Council (since Feb. 2002), Scottish Genealogy Society, Edinburgh; Governor (1985-92) RNLI's Shoreline group; Member, Travellers Club, London, 1988-92; Vice-President, The Western Goals Institute, 1989-2000; Vice President, The Traditional Britain Group, since 2001; Member: Borders Family History Society, since 1994 (its Council since 2004, Acting Editor, 2005-06), Council, Berwickshire Civic Society, since 2001, The Architectural Heritage Society of Scotland, The Scottish Record Society, The Scottish Heraldry Society, The Royal Stuart Society, The Foundation for Medieval Genealogy, The Harleian Society, The Swinton Circle, The Conservative Democratic Alliance (Founder Member). Publications: Editor, Harry Lauder in the Limelight by William Wallace, 1988; major articles in numerous journals and magazines including European Dawn, The Monarchist League Newsletter, The Scottish Genealogist, The Borders Family History Society Magazine, East Lothian Life, and The Double Tressure; several genealogical articles on the famous Electric Scotland website. Recreations: riding; walking; reading; classical music; travel; historical and political writing. Clubs: The Lansdowne, Mayfair, W1. The Royal Commonwealth, London, WC2. Address: The Old School House, Mordington, Berwickshire TD15 1XA; T.-01289 386779; e-mail: lauderfrost@btinternet.com

Laurie, Thomas, OBE, FRICS. Proprietor, Laurie Consultancy Group; Chairman, St. Andrews in the Square Trust; Trustee, Scottish Civic Trust; Trustee, Glasgow City Heritage Trust; b. 11.11.38, Wishaw; m., Jennifer Rose Dunthorne; 1 s.; 2 d. Educ. Hamilton Academy; Glasgow Technical College. Partner, Robert H. Soper & Co., Cumbernauld, 1964-77; Sole Principal, Thomas Laurie Associates, Cumbernauld and Glasgow, 1977-90; Senior Partner, Keillor Laurie Martin Partnership, 1990-2000. Founder Member, Cumbernauld Theatre Group, 1961; Board Member: Cottage Theatre, Cumbernauld, 1964-72, Traverse Theatre, 1972-76 (Chairman); Chairman, WASPS; Chairman, St. Andrews In The Square Trust (Glasgow Centre for Scottish Culture), since 2000; Member: Drama Panel, Scottish Arts Council, 1973-82, SAC, 1976-82. Recreations: traditional singing; all forms of art appreciation; hill-walking. Address: (h.) 21 Dunglass Avenue, Glasgow G14 9ED; T.-0141-959 4025.

Law, Professor Derek, MA, DUniv, FLA, FIInfSc, FKC, FRSE, FCLIP. Librarian and Head of Information Resource Directorate, University of Strathclyde, since 1998; b. 19.6.47, Arbroath; m., Jacqueline Anne; 2 d. Educ. Arbroath High School, George Watson's College, Edinburgh; University of Glasgow. Assistant Librarian, St. Andrews University, 1970-77; Sub Librarian, Edinburgh University, 1977-81; Librarian, Erskine Medical Library, 1981-83; Director of Automation, Edinburgh University Library, 1983-84; King's College, London: Librarian, 1984-93, Director of Information Services, 1993-98. Barnard Prize for Informatics, 1993; IFLA Medal, 2003. Hon. Doctorate, University of Paris. Publications: Royal Navy in World War Two; The Battle of the Atlantic; Networking and the Future of Libraries; Digital Libraries. Address: (b.) Alexander Turnbull Building, 155 George Street, Glasgow G1 1RD; T.-0141-548 4997; e-mail: d.law@strath.ac.uk

Law, Professor Robin C. C., BA, PhD, FRHS, FBA, FRSE. Professor of African History, University of Stirling, since 1993; b. 7.8.44, Chester. Educ. Southend-on-Sea High School; Balliol College, University of Oxford; Centre of West African Studies, Birmingham. Research Assistant in African History, University of Lagos, Nigeria, 1966-69; Research Fellow in West African History, University of Birmingham, 1970-72; University of Stirling: Lecturer in History, 1972-78, Senior Lecturer, 1978-83, Reader, 1983-93. Editor, Journal of African History, 1974-82, 1991-95; Series Editor, Hakluyt Society, 1998-2003. Publications: The Oyo Empire c.1600-c.1836, 1977; The Horse in West African History, 1980; The Slave Coast of West Africa, 1550-1750, 1991; The Kingdom of Allada, 1997; The Biography of Mahommah Gardo Baquaqua (Co-author), 2001; Ouidah: The social history of a West African slaving 'port', 1727-1892, 2004. Address: (b.) Department of History, University of Stirling, Stirling FK9 4LA; T.-01786 467583; e-mail: r.c.c.law@stir.ac.uk

Lawrence, Professor Andrew, BSc, PhD, FRAS, FRSE. Regius Professor of Astronomy, Edinburgh University, since 1994; Head of Physics, since 2004; b. 23.4.54, Margate; partner, Debbie Ann Capel, 3 s.; 1 d. Educ. Chatham House Grammar School, Ramsgate; Edinburgh University; Leicester University. Exchange Scientist, Massachusetts Institute of Technology, 1980-81; Senior Research Fellow, Royal Greenwich Observatory, 1981-84; Research Assistant, then SERC Advanced Fellow, School of Mathematical Sciences, Queen Mary College, London, 1984-89; Lecturer, Physics Department, Queen Mary and Westfield College, London, 1989-94. Publications: over 100 in learned journals. Recreations: painting electrons and teasing publishers; acting. Address: (b.) Institute for Astronomy, Edinburgh University, Royal Observatory, Blackford Hill, Edinburgh.

Lawrie, Nigel Gilbert, OBE, BSc, PhD. Formerly Head of Service, Department of Education Services, Inverclyde Council (retired); b. 2.6.47, Edinburgh; m., Janet Clark Warnock; 1 d. Educ. Bearsden Academy; Strathclyde University. Chemistry Teacher, Hermitage Academy, Helensburgh, 1972-75; Principal Teacher of Chemistry, Dunoon Grammar School, 1975-81; Assistant Head Teacher, Garnock Academy, 1981-84; Depute Head Teacher, Castlehead High School, Paisley, 1984-85; Head Teacher, Port Glasgow High School, 1985-2004. President, Headteachers' Association of Scotland, 1998-99; Member: Scottish Examination Board, 1994-97, Board, SCOTVEC, 1995-97, Board, SQA, 1997-99. Recreations: reading; gardening; football; golf. Address: (h.) 6 Cunningham Drive, Largs, Ayrshire.

Lawrie, Paul, MBE. Professional golfer; b.1.1.69, Aberdeen; m., Marian; 2 s. Assistant, Banchory; turned professional, 1986; Winner, UAP Under 25s Championship, 1992; Winner, Open Golf Championship, 1999. Honorary law doctorate, Robert Gordon University; Honorary Life Member, European Tour. Recreations: snooker; Aberdeen Football Club; cars. Attached to Meldrum House Golf Club.

Lawson, Isobel, FFCS. Director/Company Secretary, Stepping Stones for Families, since 1988; Board Member, Childcare First Paisley Partnership; Chair, South Ayrshire Local Childcare Partnership; b. Paisley; 2 d. Training and consultancy, voluntary sector childcare/education development. Vice Convenor, Scottish Council for Voluntary Organisations. Address: (b.) Studio 3003A, Mill Hill, Paisley PA1 3LY.

Lawson, John Philip, MBE, BSc, FEIS. Honorary President, Scottish Youth Hostels Association, since 2001 (Chairman, 1980-2001); Headteacher, St. Joseph's School, Linlithgow, 1974-94; b. 19.8.37, Bathgate; m., Diana Mary Neal. Educ. St. Mary's Academy, Bathgate; Edinburgh University; Moray House College of Education. Teacher, West Lothian, 1962-94; held various offices in the Educational Institute of Scotland, including President, West Lothian Local Association and Chairman, Lothian Regional Executive; Member, West Lothian Children's Panel, 1972-81; Member, SYHA National Executive, since 1966; Vice-Chairman, SYHA, 1975-80; awarded: Richard Schirrmann Medal by German Youth Hostels Association, 1988, Gezel van de Rugzak, Flemish Youth Hostels Association, 1993; a Director, Scottish Rights of Way Society Ltd., since 1979; a Director, Gatliff Hebridean Hostels Trust, since 1988; President, West Lothian Headteachers' Association, 1986-88; President, Federation of Youth Hostels Associations in the European Community, 1990-2001; Vice-President and Board Member, International Youth Hostel Federation, 1994-2002; Member, The Gatliff Trust, since 2003. Recreations: hill-walking; travel; music; reading. Address: (h.) Ledmore, Carnbee, Anstruther KY10 2RU; T.-01333 720312.

Lawson, Lilian Keddie, OBE, BSc (Hons), MBA. Director, Scottish Council on Deafness, since 2000; b. 23.2.49, Pittenweem; m., John McDonald Young (deceased); 2 d. Educ. Donaldson's School, Edinburgh; Mary Hare Grammar School, Newbury; Edinburgh University; Strathclyde University. Administrative Assistant, progressing to Head of Administration, British Deaf Association, 1981-92; Manager, Sign Language Interpreting Services, Strathclyde Regional Council, 1992-93; Director, RNID Scotland, 1993-2000. Publication: Words in Hand (Co-Author), 1984. Recreations: gardening; her children. Address: (b.) Central Chambers, Suite 62, 93 Hope Street, Glasgow G2 6LD; T.-0141 248 2474.

Lawson, Peter A., LLB (Hons), DipLP. Partner, Burness LLP, since 2001; b. 20.7.70, Edinburgh; m., Andrea. Educ. Dunfermline High School; Edinburgh University. Trainee, Burness LLP, 1994-96, Assistant, 1996-98; Associate, Freshfields Bruckhaus Deringer, 1998-2001. Recreation: sport. Address: (b.) 50 Lothian Road, Edinburgh EH3 9WJ; T.-0131 473 6108; e-mail: peter.lawson@burness.co.uk

Lawson, Peter John, LLB, NP. Solicitor; Partner, Hill Brown, Glasgow, since 1990; b. 25.3.58, Visakapatnam, India. Educ. Glasgow University. Chairman, Tron Theatre, Glasgow; Director, Raindog TV Ltd; Committee Member, BAFTA Scotland. Recreations: theatre; travel. Address: (b.) 3 Newton Place, Glasgow G3 7PU; T.-0141-332 3265; e-mail: plawson@hillbrown.co.uk

Laybourn, Professor Peter John Robert, MA (Cantab), PhD, FIEE, FRSE. Professor of Electronic Engineering, Glasgow University, since 1985, now Emeritus; b. 30.7.42, London; m., Ann Elizabeth Chandler; 2 d. Educ. William Hulme's Grammar School; Bristol Grammar School; Clare College, Cambridge. Research Assistant, Leeds University, 1963-66; Research Fellow, Southampton University, 1966-71; Lecturer, then Senior Lecturer, then Reader, Glasgow University, 1971-85. Recreations: sailing; boat-building; tree collecting. Address: (h.) Ashgrove, Waterfoot Row, Thorntonhall, Glasgow; T.-0141-644 3992.

Layden, Patrick John, QC, TD, LLB (Hons). Deputy Solicitor, Scottish Government Legal Directorate, since 2003; Legal Secretary to the Lord Advocate, 1999-2003; b. 27.6.49, Edinburgh; m., Patricia Mary Bonnar; 3 s.; 1 d. Educ. Holy Cross Academy, Edinburgh; University of Edinburgh. Scottish Bar, 1973-77; Junior Legal Secretary/Assistant Parliamentary Counsel, Lord Advocate's Department, 1977-83; Assistant Legal Secretary and Scottish Parliamentary Counsel, 1983-99. University of Edinburgh OTC, 1967-71; 2/52 Lowland Vol., 1971-77; 1/51 Highland Vol., 1977-81 (O.C., London Scottish, 1978-81); O.C., 73 Ord. Co. (V), 1981-84. Recreations: walking; reading. Address: (b.) Scottish Government Legal Directorate, Victoria Quay, Edinburgh EH6 6QQ; T.-0131 244 0959; e-mail: patrick.layden@scotland.gsi.gov.uk

Lazarev, Alexander Nikolaevich. Principal Conductor, Royal Scottish National Orchestra, 1997-2005; b. 5.7.45, Moscow; m., Tamara; 1 d. Educ. Moscow Conservatory. Won first prize in Soviet Union's national competition for conductors, 1971; Chief Conductor and Artistic Director, Bolshoi Theatre, 1987-95; has worked as a regular guest with St Petersburg Philharmonic; Principal Guest Conductor, BBC Symphony Orchestra, 1992-95; Conductor Emeritus, Royal Scottish National Orchestra, since 2005; Principal Conductor, Japan Philarmonic Orchestra, 2008-2011; founded Ensemble of Soloists of Bolshoi Theatre, 1978; prolific recording artist; work with RSNO has included a complete cycles of the Shostakovich and Prokofiov symphonies, appearances at the Proms and tours of Spain, Norway, Greece and Sweden. Hon. Professorship, Department of Slavonic Studies, Glasgow University, since 2005. Address: (b.) Tennant Artists, Unit 2, 39 Tadema Road, London SW10 0PZ; e-mail: info@tennantartists.com

Lazarowicz, Mark, MA, LLB, DipLP. MP, Edinburgh North and Leith, since 2001 (Member, Select Committee on Scottish Affairs, 2001-02; Member, Select Committee on Environment, Food and Rural Affairs, since 2002; Member, Select Committee on Regulatory Reform, since 2001); Advocate; b. 8.8.53. Educ. St. Andrews University; Edinburgh University. Member, Edinburgh District Council, 1980-96: Leader of the Council, 1986-93, Chairperson, Labour Group, 1993-94; Member, City of Edinburgh Council, 1999-2001 (Executive Member for Transport, 2000-01, Convenor, Transportation Committee,

1999-2000); Deputy Leader, COSLA Labour Group, 1990-93; Vice-Chairperson, 1988-89, Chairperson, 1989-90, Scottish Labour Party; Founder Member and Board Member, Centre for Scottish Public Policy, since 1990; Chairperson, Edinburgh International Conference Centre Ltd., 1992-93; Chairperson, Edinburgh Tourist Board, 1993-94. Address: (b.) 86-88 Brunswick Street, Edinburgh EH7 5HU; T.-0131-557 0577.

Lea, Judith Verna, LLB, DipL, MBA, MSc. Clerk to the Scottish Solicitors Discipline Tribunal, since 2001; Immigration Judge, since 2001; b. 7.1.60, Exeter; m., Alan Finnie; 2 s.; 1 d. Educ. Bridge of Don Academy, Aberdeen; Aberdeen University; Dundee University; Napier University. Trainee Solicitor and Solicitor in Private Practice; Senior Legal Assistant with North East Fife District Council; District Court Manager and Legal Adviser with Dundee City Council. Address: (b.) Unit 3.5, The Granary Business Centre, Cupar, Fife KY15 5YQ; T.-01334 659088; e-mail: ssdt@judithvlea.plus.com

Leach, Professor Donald, CBE, BSc, CMath, FIMA, CPhys, MInstP, CEng, MBCS, FRSA, Hon DEd (QMU) Principal, Queen Margaret College, Edinburgh, 1985-96; Chairman, D.M. Vaughan and Co. Ltd., 1999-2004; b. 24.6.31, Croydon; m., 1, June Valentine Reid (deceased); 2 s.; 1 d.; m., 2, Marilyn Annette Jeffcoat (qv). Educ. John Ruskin Grammar School, Croydon; London University (External). Pilot Officer, Navigator, RAF, 1951-53; Physicist, British Jute Trade Research Association, Dundee, 1955-65; Technical Director, A.R. Bolton & Co. Ltd., Edinburgh, 1965-66; Napier College: Lecturer and Senior Lecturer in Mathematics, 1966-68, Head, Department of Mathematics and Computing, 1968-74, Assistant Principal/Dean, Faculty of Science, 1974-85. Member, South-Eastern Regional Hospital Board, 1969-74, and Lothian Health Board, 1977-81; Member: Scottish Health Service Information Processing and Computer Systems Advisory Group, 1979-86, Computer Steering Committee (Chairman), 1981-86; Institute of Mathematics: Council Member, 1978-81, Chairman, Scottish Branch, 1980-83, Member, Joint IMA-Royal Society of London Mathematical Education Committee, 1981-84; Council for National Academic Awards: Member, various boards, 1975-79, Science Technology and Society Board, 1979-82 (Chairman, 1981-82), Committee for Scotland, 1987-92; Chairman: Science Technology and Society Association, 1982-85, Hon. Secretary, Committee of Principals and Directors of Scottish Central Institutions (COPADOCI), 1985-88, Chairman, 1988-92; Member: Council for Professions Supplementary to Medicine, 1985-97, Council, World Association for Cooperative Education, 1991-97, Board of Directors, Higher Education Quality Council, 1992-96; President, Leith Chamber of Commerce, 1994-96; President, Edinburgh Chamber of Commerce, 1996-98; Interim Chief Executive, Edinburgh's Lifelong Learning Partnership, 1998; Director, Mull Theatre Ltd., since 2004; Trustee, Mendelssohn on Mull Trust, since 2005; Honorary Fellow, Society of Chiropodists and Podiatrists, 1991; Liberal candidate, West Edinburgh, 1959, East Fife, 1961; Labour candidate, West Perthshire, 1970. Recreations: cooking; music; Scrabble. Address: (h.) 18 Rothesay Terrace, Edinburgh EH3 7RY; T.-0131-226 7166; e-mail: d.f.leach@blueyonder.co.uk

Leake, Professor Robin, MA, DPhil. Pro Vice-Principal (Physical Sciences and Engineering), Glasgow University; Professor of Endocrine Oncology, since 1998; b. 16.8.43, Tettenhall. Educ. Lancaster Royal Grammar School; St Peter's and Wolfson Colleges, Oxford. Population Council Fellow, University of Illinois; Lecturer/Senior Lecturer/Reader, Glasgow University; Past President, British Gynaecological

Cancer Society; Past Secretary, British Breast Group. Chair, Kelvinside Community Council. Recreations: cricket; golf; tennis; hill-walking. Address: (b.) No.11, The Square, Glasgow University, Glasgow; T.-0141-330 5206.

Learmont, Alastair Murray, BA (Hons), DipLP. Advocate, since 1993, b. 25.10.64, Bearsted. Educ. Edinburgh Academy; Bristol University; City University; Edinburgh University. Trainee Solicitor, Anderson Strathern WS, 1991-93; Commissioning Editor, Butterworths (Scotland), 1998-99. President, Bristol University Classical Society, 1984-85; part-time Tutor, Edinburgh University, 1994-95; Tour Leader, Alternative Travel Group, Oxford, since 2000. Recreations: playing the flute; chamber music; the outdoors; exploring Italy on foot. Address: (h.) 48/2 Candlemaker Row, Edinburgh EH1 2QE; T.-0131-225 9018; e-mail: alastairlearmont@hotmail.com

Lederer, Peter J., CBE. Chairman, Gleneagles Hotels Limited, since 2007, Managing Director and General Manager, since 1984; Director, Guinness Enterprises, since 1987; Chairman, VisitScotland; b. 30.11.50; m., Marilyn Ruth MacPhail. Four Seasons Hotels, Canada, 1972-79; Vice President, Westin Hotels Ltd., Toronto, 1979-81; General Manager, Plaza Group of Hotels, Toronto, 1981-83. Patron, Hospitality Industry Trust Scotland; Trustee, Springboard Educational Trust; Board Member: Leading Hotels of the World, VisitBritain; Freeman, City of London; FHCIMA; Master Innholder; Liveryman, Worshipful Company of Innholders. Address: (b.) The Gleneagles Hotel, Auchterarder, Perthshire PH3 1NF; T.-01764 662231.

Ledingham, Professor Iain McAllan, MD(Hons), FRCS(Ed), FRCP(Ed, Glas), FInstBiol, FCCM, DMI (RCSEd), FRSE. Professor Emeritus of Medical Education, University of Dundee; formerly Consultant, Middle East Affairs, Royal College of Surgeons of Edinburgh; Special Adviser, University of Durham; b. 26.2.35, Glasgow; m., Eileen; 3 s. Educ. King's Park Senior Secondary, Glasgow; Central School, Aberdeen; University of Glasgow. Early training in surgery/trauma/intensive care; MRC Senior Research Fellow in hyperbaric medicine; first UK Professor of Intensive Care Medicine, University of Glasgow, 1980; Chair, Intensive Care Therapy Unit, Western Infirmary, Glasgow, 1985; Foundation Chair, Department of Emergency and Critical Care Medicine, Faculty of Medicine and Health Sciences, United Arab Emirates University, 1988 (Dean, FMHS, 1989). First Chair, Intensive Care Society, UK; President: European Shock Society, European Society of Intensive Care Medicine; Bellahouston Medal, University of Glasgow; La Médaille de la Ville de Paris; The College Medal (RCSEd). Recreations: jogging; hill-walking; music; reading; tree propagation; woodworking; occasional bad golf. Address: Kir Royale, Westown, by Errol, Perthshire PH2 7SU; T.-01821 670210; e-mail: iml@scotpad.co.uk

Lee, Laura Elizabeth, RGN, MSC, DipN. Chief Executive, Maggie's Cancer Caring Centres, since 1996; b. 15.10.66, Whithank, South Africa; m., Hani Gabra; 2 s.; 1 d. Educ. Peterhead Academy; Birmingham University. Qualified RGN, 1987; various posts in nursing in cancer care in Edinburgh and London, 1987-91; clinical nurse specialist, Edinburgh Breast Unit, 1991-96. Recreations: reading; swimming. Address: (b.) The Stables, Western General Hospital, Crewe Road, Edinburgh, EH4 2XG; T.-0131-537 2456.

Lees, James George Grahame, MA, LLB, NP. Partner, McLean & Stewart, Solicitors, Dunblane, since 1974; b. 22.6.46, Perth; m., Hazel Margaret Raffan; 1 s.; 2 d. Educ. Dundee High School; St. Andrews University; Edinburgh University. Solicitor, J. & F. Anderson, WS, Edinburgh,

1969-72; Solicitor, McLean & Stewart, Solicitors, Dunblane, since 1972; Accredited Specialist in Agricultural Law; Member, Accreditation Panel, Law Society of Scotland; Deputy Chairman, Church of Scotland Housing and Loan Fund; Elder, Dunblane Cathedral Church of Scotland. Recreations: walking; photography; fishing. Address: (h.) Northbank, St. Margaret's Drive, Dunblane, FK15 ODP; T.-Dunblane 822928.

Lees, Martin McArthur, MD, FRCP(Edin), FRCS(Ed), FRCOG. Consultant Obstetrician and Gynaecologist, Royal Infirmary of Edinburgh, and Senior Lecturer and Director of Studies, Edinburgh University (retired); b. 24.4.35; m., Maureen Yetton. Educ. Aberdeen Grammar School; Aberdeen University. Formerly Director, Board of Management, Medical and Dental Defence Union of Scotland; Inspector, Human Fertilisation and Embryology Authority; Social Convenor and Member of Council, Royal College of Physicians of Edinburgh; National Advisor, National Counselling Service for Sick Doctors; Harveian Orator. Recreations: music; ornithology; reading. Address: (b.) Royal College of Physicians of Edinburgh, 9 Queen Street, Edinburgh EH2 1JQ; T.-0131 225 7324.

Legge, Graham, BEd, MEd. Rector, Aberdeen Grammar School, since 2004; b. 9.4.56, Buckie. Educ. Buckie High School; Aberdeen University. Teacher of Modern Studies, Speyside High School; Teacher of Geography, Northfield Academy; Assistant Principal Teacher, Hilton Academy; Principal Teacher, Geography, The Gordon Schools, Huntly; Assistant Rector, Aboyne Academy; Depute Rector, Banchory Academy; Rector, Kemnay Academy, 1998-2004. Recreations: hill-walking; travel; gardening. Address: (b.) Aberdeen Grammar School, Skene Street, Aberdeen AB10 1HT; T.-01224 642299.

Leighton, John, MA (Hons) Edin, MA. Director-General, National Galleries of Scotland, since 2006; b. 22.2.59, Belfast; m., Gillian Keay; 1 s.; 1 d. Educ. Portora Royal School, Enniskillen; University of Edinburgh; Edinburgh College of Art; Courtauld Institute. Lecturer and Tutor, Department of Humanities, Edinburgh College of Art, 1983-86; Curator, 19th-Century Paintings, National Gallery, London, 1986-96; Director, Van Gogh Museum, Amsterdam, 1997-2006. Board Member, De Pont Museum for Contemporary Art, Tilburg, since 1998; Advisory Board Member, Vereniging Rembrandt (Dutch Association for funding Museum acquisitions), since 1999. Appointed Chevalier in the French Ordre des Arts et des Lettres; numerous exhibitions organised. Recent publications include (Books and Exhibition Catalogues): Co-Author, Signac 1863-1935, 2001; The Van Gogh Museum: A portrait, 2003; Co-Author, Manet and the Sea, 2003. Address: (b.) The Dean Gallery, 73 Belford Road, Edinburgh EH4 3DR.

Leighton-Beck, Dr Linda Bryce, PhD, DRM, MSc, BEd (Hons). Social Inclusion Programme Manager, NHS Grampian, since 2003; Honorary Senior Lecturer, Department of General Practice and Primary Care, Aberdeen University, since 2001; b. 23.5.53, Greenock; m., David; 2 d. Educ. Greenock Academy; Aberdeen University; Purdue University; Dunfermline College of Physical Education (now University of Edinburgh). Teacher of P.E., Strathclyde Regional Council, 1975; Lecturer, Dunfermline College of Physical Education; Assistant Director of Leisure Services, East Lothian District Council; Researcher, Scottish Council for Research in Education; Executive Manager, North of Scotland Health Services Research Network, Aberdeen University; Education Manager (North-North East), Scottish Council for Postgraduate Medical and Dental Education (now NHS Education Scotland); Health Improvement Programme Manager, NHS Grampian. Board Member, Sportscotland; Member, Board of Directors, Aberdeen Foyer. Recreations: running; badminton; tennis; cycling; music; cooking. Address: (b.) NHS Grampian, Summerfield House, 2 Eday Road, Aberdeen; T.-01224 558743.

Leiper, Joseph, OBE, DL, MA, DipEd, ACII. Rector, Oldmachar Academy, 1984-2004; b. 13.8.41, Aberdeen; m., Moira Taylor; 2d. Educ. Aberdeen Grammar School; Aberdeen University. English Teacher: Robert Gordon's College, 1972-73; Bankhead Academy, 1973-75; Principal Teacher, English, Bankhead Academy, 1975-80; Assistant Rector, 1980-82; Depute Rector, Ellon Academy, 1982-84; Chairman, Aberdeen University Business Committee, General Council, 2000-06; appointed to Court, Aberdeen University, General Council Court Assessor, 2000; appointed as Deputy Lieutenant of Aberdeen City, 2005; appointed as part-time Associate Teaching Fellow in the School of Education, University of Aberdeen, 2005-07; appointed Burgess of Guild of Aberdeen City, 2005. Recreations: sailing; reading; walking. Address: (h.) 5 Fairview Place, Bridge of Don, Aberdeen AB22 8ZJ.

Leishman, Brian Archibald Scott, MBE. Event Consultancy and Organisation; Editor, Regimental Journal, The Cameronians (Scottish Rifles); b. 16.9.36; 1 s.; 1 d. Educ. Fettes College. Retired Regular Army Officer; commissioned The Cameronians (Scottish Rifles), 1956; re-badged The King's Own Scottish Borderers, 1968; service in the Arabian Gulf, East Africa and Europe; Italian Staff College, 1971-73; Assistant Defence Attache, British Embassy, Rome, 1974-76; Business Manager, Edinburgh Military Tattoo, 1978-97. Scottish Tourist Board Silver Thistle Award, 1996; Box Office Management International (New York) Lifetime Achievement Award, 1997; variously European Co-ordinator, International Ticketing Association (New York), 1998-2003; Board Member, Edinburgh Military Tattoo Ltd; Founder Member, Edinburgh Capital Group (Edinburgh Entertains), Ticketing Consultant XIII Commonwealth Games Edinburgh, 1986; Chairman, Edinburgh International Jazz and Blues Festival; Board Member, Edinburgh Tourist Board and Edinburgh and Lothians Tourist Board; Member, Advisory Board, International Festival and Events Association (Europe). Recreations: music; photography. Address: (h.) 61 Northumberland Street, Edinburgh EH3 6JQ; T.-0131 557 0187.

Leishman, Marista Muriel, MA. Former Senior Partner, The Insite Consultancy for Management and Training; b. 10.4.32, Beaconsfield; m., Murray Leishman; 1 s.; 3 d. Educ. St. George's School, Ascot; St. Andrews University. First Head of Education, National Trust for Scotland, 1979-86; writer: occasional pieces published; memoir of Sir Jamie Stormonth Darling; (2006); memoir: 'My Father: Reith of the BBC'. Recreations: music; painting; writing; hill-walking. Address: (h.) Donavourd Cottage, Donavourd, by Pitlochry PH16 5JS; T.-01796 473 120.

Leishman, Struan, LLB, WS, NP. Partner, HBJ Gateley Wareing (Scotland) LLP, since 2006; Solicitor, since 1971; b. 26.7.47, Nottingham; m., Fiona K. A. Robertson; 1 s.; 1 d. Educ. Merchiston Castle School, Edinburgh; Edinburgh University. Partner: Allan, Dawson, Simpson & Hampton WS, 1973-90, Henderson & Jackson WS, 1990-93, Henderson Boyd Jackson WS, 1993-2005. Recreations: golf; swimming; hill walking. Address: (b.) Exchange

Tower, 19 Canning Street, Edinburgh EH3 8EH; T.-0131-228-2400; e-mail: sleishman@hbj-gw.com

Leitch, Donald H., DMS, FHCIMA, FCFA. Vice Principal (Corporate Development), Glasgow Metropolitan College; formerly Vice Principal, Glasgow College of Food Technology (Depute Principal, 1991-98); b. 2.4.48, Glasgow; m., Mary B.; 2 s. Educ. Hyndland Senior Secondary School; Langside College, Glasgow; Glasgow College of Technology. Catering management, Health Service, 1967-70; Depute Catering Officer, Glasgow University, 1970-74; Lecturer then Senior Lecturer, Glasgow College of Food Technology, 1974-85; Head of Department, Cambuslang College, Glasgow, 1985-91. Past Chairman, Scottish Division, Cookery and Food Association. Recreations: hill-walking; gardening. Address: (b.) 60 North Hanover Street, Glasgow G1 2BP; T.-0141 566 6222.

Lenman, Professor Bruce Philip, MA (Aberdeen), MLitt, LittD (Cantab), FRHistSoc, FRSE. Emeritus Professor of Modern History, St. Andrews University, since 2003 (formerly Professor of Modern History); b. 9.4.38, Aberdeen. Educ. Aberdeen Grammar School, Aberdeen University; St. John's College, Cambridge. Assistant Professor, Victoria University, Canada, 1963; Lecturer in Imperial and Commonwealth History, Queen's College, Dundee (St. Andrews University), 1963-67; Lecturer, Dundee University, 1967-72; United College, St. Andrews: Lecturer, Department of Modern History, 1972-78, Senior Lecturer, 1978-83; British Academy Fellow, Newberry Library, Chicago, 1982; John Carter Brown Library Fellow, Brown University, Providence, RI, 1984; Harrison Professor, College of William & Mary, VA, 1988-89; Mayers Fellow, Huntington Library, CA, 1997; Hill Fellow, 2004; Bird Professor, Emory University, Atlanta, GA, 1998. Publications: Esk to Tweed, 1975; An Economic History of Modern Scotland 1660-1976, 1977 (Scottish Arts Council Award); The Jacobite Risings in Britain 1689-1746, 1980 (Scottish Arts Council Award); Scotland 1746-1832, 1981; The Jacobite Clans of the Great Glen 1650-1784, 1984; The Jacobite Cause, 1986; The Jacobite Threat (Co-Author), 1990; The Eclipse of Parliament, 1992; England's Colonial Wars, 2000; Britain's Colonial Wars, 2001; Editor, Chambers Dictionary of World History, 1993, 3rd ed., 2005. Recreations: golf; curling; swimming. Address: (h.) Flat 4, 55 Victoria Place, Stirling FK8 2QT; T.-01786-446090.

Lennon, Francis P, OBE, MA (Hons), MPhil. Head Teacher, St. Modan's High School, Stirling, since 1996; b. 18.6.52, Glasgow; m., Marie Lennon; 1 s.; 4 d. Educ. Salesian College, Cheshire; Holy Cross High, Hamilton; Glasgow University. Teaching career: St Gerard's Secondary, Govan, 1975-78; Columba of Iona Secondary, Glasgow, 1978-81; Holyrood Secondary, Glasgow, 1981-84; Holy Cross High School, Hamilton, 1984-90; St Patrick's High School, Coatbridge, 1990-93; St Andrew's Secondary, Glasgow, 1993-96. Recreations: football; American football; theatre. Address: (b.) Barnsdale Road, Stirling; T.-01786 470962; e-mail: lennonf@stirling.gov.uk

Leonard, Professor Tom. Poet; Professor, Creative Writing, Glasgow University, since 2001; b. 22.8.44, Glasgow; m., Sonya; 2 s. Educ. Lourdes Secondary, Glasgow; Glasgow University. Writer in Residence, Paisley Library, 1986-89; Glasgow University, 1991; Bell College, Hamilton, 1993-95. Publications: Intimate Voices: Poems 1965-93; access to the silence: Poems 1984-2004; Reports from the Present; Places of the Mind: The Life of James Thomson ("B.V."); (ed.)

Radical Renfrew: Poetry from the French Revolution to the First World War. Address: 56 Eldon Street, Glasgow G3 6NJ; e-mail: mail@tomleonard.co.uk; web: www.tomleonard.co.uk

Leslie, Martin Rowley Melville, CVO, FRICS. Chartered Surveyor (retired); Factor to Her Majesty Queen Elizabeth the Queen Mother, 1975-2002; Honorary Secretary and Factor to Queen Elizabeth Castle of Mey Trust, 1996-2002; President, Aberdeen Angus Cattle Society of Great Britain and Ireland, 1999-2000; b. 12.8.32, Malawi, Central Africa; m., Catriona Bridget Macdonald; 1 s.; 2 d. Educ. King's School, Canterbury; Royal Dick Veterinary College, Edinburgh University; College of Estate Management (correspondence course). National Service, Seaforth Highlanders and Argyll and Sutherland Highlanders (2nd Lt.), 1951-53; TA, 11th Bn., Seaforth Highlanders (retired as Captain), 1953-67; Seaforth Highlander's Regimental Association Executive Committee, since 2003, Trustee, since 2007; Pupil Factor, Moray Estates Development Company, Forres, 1959-60; Assistant Factor, Fairburn Estates, Conan and Gairloch Estates, Ross-shire, 1960-62; 1962-79: Factor to Welbeck Estates Company, Caithness and Ross-shire, Factor to Achentoul Estate Company, Sutherland and Ross-shire; Factor to Her Majesty the Queen, Balmoral Estates, Aberdeenshire, 1979-95. Skye District Salmon Fisheries Board Representative on Association of Scottish District Salmon Fisheries Board, 1997-2002; Chairman, Skye District Salmon Fishery Board, 1998-2007; Vice Chairman, Skye Deer Management Group, 2001-06, Chairman, since 2006. Recreations: country sports; German shorthaired pointers; reading. Address: Redcliff, Portree, Isle of Skye IV51 9DH; T.-01478 612014.

Lessels, Norman, CBE, CA; b. 2.9.38, Edinburgh; m., Christine Stevenson Hitchman; 1 s. Educ. Edinburgh Academy. Partner, Ernst & Whinney, until 1980; Partner, Chiene & Tait, CA, until 1998. President, Institute of Chartered Accountants of Scotland, 1987-88; former Director: Standard Life Assurance Company (Chairman, 1988-98), Bank of Scotland, Cairn Energy, Robert Wiseman Dairies PLC. Recreations: golf; music; bridge. Address: (h.) 17 India Street, Edinburgh EH3 6HE; T.-0131-225 5596.

Leven and Melville, Earl of (Alexander Robert Leslie Melville). Lord Lieutenant of Nairn, 1969-99; b. 13.5.24, London; m., Susan Steuart-Menzies; 2 s.; 1 d. Educ. Eton. Coldstream Guards, 1942-52 (retired as Captain); ADC to Governor General of New Zealand, 1951-52; Convener, Nairn County Council, 1970-74. Chairman of Governors, Gordonstoun School, 1971-89; President, British Ski Federation, 1981-85. Address: (h.) Raith, Old Spey Bridge, Grantown-on-Spey, Morayshire PH26 3NQ; T.-01479 872908.

Leven, Marian Forbes, DA, RSA(elect), RSW. Artist; b. 25.3.44, Edinburgh; m., Will Maclean; 2 s.; 1 d. Educ. Bell-Baxter School, Cupar; Gray's School of Art, Aberdeen. Exhibited RSA, RSW, RGI, SSA, AAS; work in private and public collections; Winner, Noble Grossart Painting Prize, 1997. Address: (h.) Bellevue, 18 Dougall Street, Tayport, Fife DD6 9JD.

Levinthal, Terrence Scott, BES, DipUD, FSAScot. Director, Scottish Civic Trust, since 2002 (Technical Director, 1999-2002); Board Member, Loch Lomond and the Trossachs National Park Authority; b. 9.12.61, Winnipeg. Educ. University of Waterloo; Heriot-Watt/Edinburgh College of Art. Investigator, Royal Fine Art Commission for Scotland, 1988-92; Secretary, The

Cockburn Association (Edinburgh Civic Trust), 1992-99. Recreations: hill-walking, skiing, cycling and other outdoor pursuits; the arts; woodworking. Address: (b.) Scottish Civic Trust, The Tobacco Merchant's House, 42 Miller Street, Glasgow G1 1DT; T.-0141-221 1466.

Levison, Rev. Mary Irene, BA, BD, DD. Minister of the Church of Scotland (retired); (Extra) Chaplain to the Queen in Scotland, since 1991; Vice-President, St. Leonard's School, since 1996; b. 8.1.23, Oxford; m., Rev. Frederick Levison. Educ. St. Leonard's School, St. Andrews; Oxford University; Edinburgh University. Administrative Assistant, Scottish Home Department, 1943-46; Deaconess, Church of Scotland, Musselburgh, 1954-58; Tutor, St. Colm's College, 1958-61; Assistant Chaplain, Edinburgh University, 1961-64; Assistant Minister, St. Andrew's and St. George's Church and Chaplain to the retail trade, Edinburgh, 1978-83; Moderator, Edinburgh Presbytery, 1988. Publication: Wrestling with the Church, 1992. Recreations: music; travel. Address: (h.) 2 Gillsland Road, Edinburgh EH10 5BW; T.-0131-228 3118.

Liddell, Colin. Director, Liddell Thomson Consultancy; b. 28.8.47, Falkirk; m., Sheena Wood Mackay. Educ. Denny High School. Journalist, Johnston Newspaper Group, 1964-69; Editor, Linlithgow Journal & Gazette, 1968-69; Journalist, Scotsman Publications, 1969-77; Senior Press Officer, Scottish Development Agency, 1977-82; PR Director, then Chief Executive, Charles Barker Scotland, 1982-86; Public Affairs Director, United Distillers, 1986-93; Corporate Communications Director, Scottish Power plc, 1993-95. Non-Executive Director, Billcliffe Gallery, 1998; Member, Council, CBI Scotland. Recreations: golf; gardening; football. Address: (b.) 225 West George Street, Glasgow G2 2ND.

Liddell, David, BSc (Hons), CQSW. Director, Scottish Drugs Forum, since 1993; b. 1957; 3 s.; 1 d. Educ. Riddlesdown High School; Sheffield University; Edinburgh University. Bristol Cyrenians, 1978; Dublin Simon Community, 1979; Biochemist: Queen Charlotte's Hospital, London, 1980, Temple Street Children's Hospital, Dublin, 1980; Dublin Committee for Travelling People, 1981-82; Fieldworker, Standing Conference on Drug Abuse, 1985-86; Co-ordinator, Scottish Drugs Forum, 1986-93. Member, Ministerial Drug Task Force, 1994; currently Member: Scottish Advisory Committee on Drug Misuse. Publications: Drug Problems in Edinburgh (Co-author), 1987; Understanding Drug Problems in Scotland (Co-author), 1998; Understanding Drug Issues in Scotland (Co-author), 2000. Recreations: landscape gardening; camping; hostelling; allotment; chauffeur. Address: (b.) 5 Waterloo Street, Glasgow G2 6AY; T.-0141-221 1175; e-mail: dave@sdf.org.uk

Light, John Vernon, MA (Cantab). Rector, Edinburgh Academy, since 1995; b. 25.4.48, Otley, West Yorkshire; m., Katy; 1 s.; 3 d. Educ. Sedbergh School; Clare College, Cambridge. Industrial Experience, 1969-75; Glenalmond College, 1975-78; Uppingham School, 1978-83; Housemaster, Sedbergh School, 1983-92; Head, Oswestry School, 1992-95. Recreations: music; squash; golf; mountaineering. Address: (b.) 42 Henderson Row, Edinburgh EH3 5BL; T.-0131 5564603.

Lilley, Professor David Malcolm James, FRS, FRSE, FRSC. Professor of Molecular Biology, Dundee University, since 1989; b. 28.5.48, Colchester; m., Patricia Mary; 2 d. Educ. Gilberd School, Colchester; Durham University. Joined Biochemistry Department, Dundee University, 1981; awarded: Colworth Medal by Biochemical Society, 1982,

Gold Medal of G. Mendel, Czech Academy of Sciences, 1994, Gold Medal of V. Prelog in Stereochemistry, ETH, Zurich; Royal Society of Chemistry Award in RNA and Ribozyme Chemistry. Publications: 290 scientific papers. Recreations: foreign languages; running; skiing. Address: (b.) School of Life Sciences, Dundee University, Dundee DD1 5EH; T.-01382 344243.

Lindhorst, Gordon John S., LLB (Hons), DipLP, LLM. Advocate, since 1995. Educ. University of Edinburgh; University of Glasgow; Universität Heidelberg. Admitted as Solicitor, 1991; Notary Public, 1992. Scottish Parliamentary Candidate, Linlithgow, 1999 and 2003; Westminster Parliamentary Candidate, Linlithgow, 2001; Legal Reporter: Scots Law Times, 1995-2000, Session Cases, since 2000. Recreations: hillwalking; cabinet making; music. Address: (b.) Parliament House, Edinburgh; EH1; T.-0131-226 5071.

Lindsay, 16th Earl of (James Randolph Lindsay-Bethune). Chairman, Scottish Quality Salmon, 1998-2006; Chairman, United Kingdom Accreditation Service, since 2002; Managing Director, Marine Stewardship Council International, 2001-05; Chairman, RSPB Scotland, 1998 - 2003, Vice President, since 2004 (Council Member, RSPB UK); Board Member, Cairngorms Partnership, 1998-2002; Non-Executive Director, UA (Scotland) plc, 1998-2005; Member, Scottish Power Environment Forum, 1998-2002; President, International Tree Foundation, 1995-2005, Vice President, since 2005; Chairman, Genesis Quality Assurance, 2001-02; Chairman, Elmwood College, since 2001; Non-Executive Director, Scottish Resources Group Ltd., since 2001; Non-Executive Director, SAC Ltd., since 2005, Chairman, since 2007; Non-Executive Director, BPI plc, since 2006; Member, Better Regulation Commission, since 2006, Deputy Chairman, since 2007; President, Royal Scottish Geographical Society, since 2005; Chairman, Moorland Forum, since 2007; Associate Director, National Non-Food Crops Centre, since 2007; b. 19.11.55; m., Diana Mary Chamberlayne-Macdonald. Educ. Eton; Edinburgh University; University of California, Davis. Lord in Waiting (Government Whip), 1995; Parliamentary Under Secretary of State, Scottish Office, 1995-97; Member, Secretary of State's Advisory Group on Sustainable Development, 1998-99; Member, Select Committee on European Community Affairs: Environment, Public Health and Consumer Protection Sub-Committee, 1997-99; Member, UK Round Table on Sustainable Development Sub-Group, 1998-2000; Chairman, Assured British Meat Ltd., 1997-2001; President, Royal Highland Agricultural Society of Scotland (RHASS), 2005-06; Green Ribbon political award, 1995. Address: (h.) Lahill, Upper Largo, Fife KY8 6JE.

Lindsay, Frederic, MA (Hons). Writer; b. 12.8.33, Glasgow; m., Shirley; 1 s.; 3 d. Educ. North Kelvinside Senior Secondary School; Glasgow University; Jordanhill College; Edinburgh University. Worked as library assistant, teacher, lecturer; since becoming full-time writer in 1979, has published nine novels: Brond, 1984, Jill Rips, 1987, A Charm Against Drowning, 1988, After the Stranger Came, 1992, Kissing Judas, 1997, A Kind of Dying, 1998, Idle Hands, 1999, Death Knock, 2000, Darkness in My Hand, 2001; The Endings Man, 2005; My Life As A Man, 2006; Tremor of Demons, 2007; The Stranger From Home, 2008; has written plays for Scottish Youth Theatre; radio plays for children; adapted Brond as serial for Channel 4. Former Chair, Society of Authors in Scotland; former Vice-President, PEN Scotland; former Member, Scottish Arts Council, Literature Committee. Recreations: cinema; theatre; television; reading. Address: (h.) 28 The Green, Pencaitland EH34 5HE; T.-01875 340955; e-mail: fredericlindsay@hotmail.com

Lindsay, John Maurice, CBE, TD, DLitt, HonFRIAS. Director/Consultant, Scottish Civic Trust, 1983-2002 (Director, 1967-83), Honorary Trustee, since 2002;

Hon.Governor, The Glasgow Academy, since 2003; b. 21.7.18; m., Aileen Joyce Gordon; 1 s.; 3 d. Educ. Glasgow Academy; Scottish National Academy of Music. Drama Critic, Scottish Daily Mail, 1946-47; Music Critic, The Bulletin, 1946-60; Border Television: Programme Controller, 1961-62, Production Controller, 1962-64, Features Executive and Chief Interviewer, 1964-67. Atlantic-Rockefeller Award, 1946; Editor: Scots Review, 1949-50, The Scottish Review, 1975-85; Member, Historic Buildings Council for Scotland, 1976-87; Secretary-General, Europa Nostra, 1983-91; Council Member, Association of Scottish Literary Studies, 1983-94, President, 1988-90; Trustee: New Lanark Conservation Trust, 1985-94, National Heritage Memorial Fund, 1980-84; HonDLitt, Glasgow, 1982. Publications: poetry: The Advancing Day, 1940; Perhaps To-morrow, 1941; Predicament, 1942; No Crown for Laughter: Poems, 1943; The Enemies of Love: Poems 1941-45, 1946; Selected Poems, 1947; Hurlygush: Poems in Scots, 1948; At the Wood's Edge, 1950; Ode for St. Andrew's Night and Other Poems, 1951; The Exiled Heart: Poems 1941-56, 1957; Snow Warning and Other Poems, 1962; One Later Day and Other Poems, 1964; This Business of Living, 1969; Comings and Goings: Poems, 1971; Selected Poems 1942-72, 1973; The Run from Life, 1975; Walking Without an Overcoat, Poems 1972-76, 1977; Collected Poems, 1979; A Net to Catch the Winds and Other Poems, 1981; The French Mosquitoes' Woman and other diversions and poems; Requiem for a Sexual Athlete; Collected Poems 1940-90; On the Face Of It: Collected Poems, Vol. 2; News of the World: Last Poems; Speaking Likenesses: A Postscript; Looking Up Where Heaven Isn't, 2004; prose: Worlds Apart; Pocket Guide to Scottish Culture; The Scottish Renaissance; The Lowlands of Scotland: Glasgow and the North; Robert Burns: The Man, His Work, The Legend; Dunoon: The Gem of the Clyde Coast; The Lowlands of Scotland: Edinburgh and the South; Clyde Waters: Variations and Diversions on a Theme of Pleasure; The Burns Encyclopedia; Killochan Castle; By Yon Bonnie Banks: A Gallimaufry; Environment: A Basic Human Right; Portrait of Glasgow; Robin Philipson; History of Scottish Literature; Lowland Scottish Villages; Francis George Scott and the Scottish Renaissance; The Buildings of Edinburgh (Co-Author); Thank You For Having Me: A Personal Memoir; Unknown Scotland (Co-Author); Castles of Scotland: A Constable Guide; Count All Men Mortal: The Story of the Scottish Provident Institution; Victorian and Edwardian Glasgow; An Illustrated Guide to Glasgow; The Comic Poems of William Tennant (Co-Editor); Edinburgh Past and Present (Co-Author); The Youth and Manhood of Cyril Thornton (Editor); The Scottish Dog (Co-Author); A Pleasure of Gardens (Co-Author); The Scottish Quotation Book (Co-Author); The Music Quotation Book (Co-Author); The Theatre and Opera Lover's Quotation Book (Co-Author); The Burns Quotation Book (Co-Author); The Chambers Guide to Good Scottish Gardens (Co-Author); Glasgow: Fabric of a City, 2003; A Book of Scottish Verse; The Edinburgh Book of Twentieth Century Scottish Poetry, 2005 (Co-Editor). Recreations: music; cooking. Address: (h.) Park House, 104 Dumbarton Road, Bowling, Dunbartonshire G60 5BB.

Lindsay, Mark Stanley Hunter, LLB (Hons), DipLP. Advocate, since 1995; Standing Counsel to Home Secretary, since 2000; b. 17.5.69, Maybole; m., Rosemary; 2 s.; 1 d. Educ. Carrick Academy, Maybole; University of Glasgow. Energy Consultant, Jacek Mawkowski Associates, Boston, Mass., USA; Congressional Intern, Capitol Hill, Washington DC; Articled Clerk, Macallister Mazengarb, Wellington, NZ; Trainee Solicitor, Tods Murray, WS, Edinburgh; Solicitor, Scottish Office. Recreations: hillwalking; squash; classic cars; American history. Address: Advocates' Library, Parliament House, Edinburgh EH1 1RF; T.-0131-226 5071; (h.) 0131-467 1451; e-mail: MshLindsay@aol.com

Lindsay, Ranald Bruce, LLB(Hons), DipLP, NP. Solicitor-Advocate, since 1993; Solicitor, since 1986; b. 18.3.62, Bellshill; 2 s.; 1 d. Educ. Wishaw High; University of Glasgow. Trained with Bishop & Co., Glasgow, 1984-86; qualified as first Solicitor Advocate in both civil and criminal law, 1993; established own practice, 1994; elected Law Society of Scotland Council Member for Dumfries, 2005; Convenor, Law Society of Scotland Access to Justice Committee. Recreations: reading; films; history; model aircraft; getting away from it all. Address: (b.) Lindsay Solicitors, 33 Buccleuch Street, Dumfries DG1 2AB; T.-01387 259236.

Lingard, Joan Amelia, MBE. Author; b. Edinburgh; 3 d. Educ. Bloomfield Collegiate School, Belfast; Moray House College of Education, Edinburgh. Member, Scottish Arts Council, 1980-85; Chair, Society of Authors in Scotland, 1980-84; a Director, Edinburgh Book Festival, 1994-98; Hon. Vice-President, Scottish PEN, since 2001; first novel published, 1963; has also written plays for TV, including 18-part series, Maggie, adapted from quartet of teenage books; novels: Liam's Daughter, 1963; The Prevailing Wind, 1964; The Tide Comes In, 1966; The Headmaster, 1967; A Sort of Freedom, 1968; The Lord on our Side, 1970; The Second Flowering of Emily Mountjoy, 1979; Greenyards, 1981; Sisters By Rite, 1984; Reasonable Doubts, 1986; The Women's House, 1989; After Colette, 1993; Dreams of Love and Modest Glory, 1995; The Kiss, 2002; Encarnita's Journey, 2005; After You've Gone, 2007; 40 children's books; Awards: ZDF Preis der Leseratten, W. Germany, for The Twelfth Day of July, 1986; Buxtehuder Bulle, W. Germany for Across the Barricades, 1987; Scottish Arts Council awards for After Colette, 1994, Tom and the Tree House, 1998; Tug of War shortlisted for 1989 Carnegie Medal, 1989 Federation of Children's Book Groups Award, 1989 Sheffield Book Award, runner-up for 1990 Lancashire Children's Book Club of the Year; MBE for Services to Children's Literature, 1999; shortlisted, Scottish Royal Mail Awards for The Sign of The Black Dagger, 2006; nominated for the Astrid Lingren Award, 2006. Recreations: reading; walking; travelling. Address: (b.) David Higham Associates, 5-8 Lower John Street, Golden Square, London W1R 4HA.

Lingard, Robin Anthony, MA, FTS. Independent Consultant; b. 19.7.41, Enfield; m., Margaret; 2 d. Educ. Felsted School; Emmanuel College, Cambridge. Joined Ministry of Aviation, 1963; Private Secretary to Joint Parliamentary Secretary, Ministry of Technology, 1966-68; appointments, Department of Industry, DTI, etc., to 1984; Head, Enterprise Unit, Cabinet Office, 1984-85; Head, Small Firms and Tourism Division, Department of Employment, 1985-87; full-time Board Member, Highlands and Islands Development Board, 1988-91; Director of Training and Social Development, Highlands and Islands Enterprise, 1991-93; Project Director, University of the Highlands and Islands Project, 1993-97. Member, Scottish Tourist Board, 1988-92; Chairman, Prince's Trust Committee for Highlands, Western Isles and Orkney; Member, Management Board, Prince's Trust and Royal Jubilee Trusts, 1989-95; Chairman, Youth Link Scotland, 1997-2000; Chairman, BBC Scotland Children in Need and Appeals Advisory Committee, 1999-2004; Chairman, Fusion Scotland, 2002-05; Chairman, Sustainable Development Research Centre, since 2004; Chairman, Highland Community Care Forum, since 2007; DUniv (Open), 1999; Hon. Fellow, UHI Millennium Institute, 2006. Recreations: watching birds; walking; reading; aviation history; dinghy sailing. Address: (h.) Kinnairdie House, Dingwall IV15 9LL; T.-01349 861044.

Linklater of Butterstone, Baroness (Veronica Linklater). Life Peer, since 1997; Founder and President, The New

School, Butterstone, since 1991; President, Society of Friends of Dunkeld Cathedral, since 1989; Trustee, Esmée Fairbairn Foundation, since 1991; b. 15.4.43, Meikleour, Perthshire; m., Magnus Duncan Linklater (qv); 2 s.; 1 d. Educ. Cranborne Chase; Sorbonne; University of Sussex; University of London. Child Care Officer, London Borough of Tower Hamlets, 1967-68; Co-Founder, Visitors Centre, Pentonville Prison, 1971-77; Governor, three Islington schools, 1970-85; Prison Reform Trust Winchester Prison Project, 1981-82; Butler Trust: Founder, Administrator, Consultant, 1983-87, Trustee, 1987-2001, Vice President, since 2001; JP, Inner London, 1985-88; Co-ordinator, Trustee, Vice Chairman, Pushkin Prizes (Scotland), since 1989; Member, Children's Panel, Edinburgh South, 1989-97; Committee Member, Gulliver Award for the Performing Arts in Scotland, 1990-96; Patron, Sutherland Trust, 1993-2003; Trustee, Young Musicians Trust, 1993-97; Candidate (Liberal Democrat), Perth & Kinross By-Election, 1995; Director, Maggie Keswick Jencks Cancer Caring Centres Trust, 1997-2004; Foundation Patron, Queen Margaret University College, since 1998; Member, Beattie Committee on Post School Provision for Young People with Special Needs, 1998-99; Trustee, Development Trust, University of the Highlands and Islands, 1999-2001; Secretary, Scottish Peers Association, 2000-07; Chancellor's Assessor, Napier University Court, 2001-04; Patron, Family and Parenting Institute, since 2002; Patron, National Schizophrenia Fellowship, Scotland, since 2000; Patron, The Probation Boards Association; Appeal Patron, Hopetoun House Preservation Trust, 2001; Member, Advisory Board, The Beacon Fellowship Charitable Trust, since 2003; Member, Scottish Committee, Barnardo's, 2001-04; Patron, Research Autism, since 2004; Council Member, The Winston Churchill Memorial Trust; Patron, Home Start Perth, since 2006; Patron, Push, since 2007; President, Crime Reduction Initiative, since 2007. Hon. Degree, Queen Margaret University College, Edinburgh. Recreations: music; theatre; gardening. Address: (h.) 5 Drummond Place, Edinburgh EH3 6PH; T.-0131-557 5705; e-mail: v.linklater@blueyonder.co.uk

Linklater, Emeritus Professor Karl Alexander, BVM&S, PhD, CBiol, FIBiol, FRAgS, FRCVS, FRSE. Principal, Scottish Agricultural College, 1999-2002, Emeritus Professor, since 2002; Professor of Agriculture, University of Glasgow, 1999-2002; a Director, The Moredun Foundation, since 1991; Director, Vet CPD, 1992-98; Director, the British Veterinary Association, 2003-06; Honorary Fellow, University of Edinburgh, since 1998; b. 1.9.39, Stromness, Orkney; m., Margaret; 1 s.; 1 d. Educ. Robert Gordon's College, Aberdeen; Edinburgh University. General veterinary practice, Tarland, Aberdeenshire, 1962-66; North of Scotland College of Agriculture, Aberdeen, 1966-67; Royal (Dick) School of Veterinary Studies, Edinburgh University, 1967-73; East of Scotland College of Agriculture, St. Boswells, 1973-86; Director, SAC Veterinary Services, 1986-97; Vice Principal, SAC, 1997-99; Member, Veterinary Products Committee, 1990-2001; President: Sheep Veterinary Society, 1983-85, British Veterinary Association, 1996-97, Association of Veterinary Teachers and Research Workers (Scotland), 1988-90, Scottish Branch, British Veterinary Association, 1992-94, Scottish Metropolitan Division, BVA, 1979-80; Alan Baldry Award, 1982. Recreations: sport; gardening; sheep breeding. Address: (h.) Bridge Park, Old Bridge Road, Selkirk TD7 4LG; T.-01750 20571; e-mail: k.linklater@btopenworld.com

Linklater, Magnus Duncan. Journalist; Scotland Editor and Columnist for The Times; Chairman, The Little Sparta Trust, since 2000; b. 21.2.42, Harray, Orkney; m., Veronica Lyle; 2 s.; 1 d. Educ. Eton College; Cambridge University. Reporter, Daily Express, Manchester, 1965-66; London Evening Standard: Diary Reporter, 1966-67, Editor, Londoner's Diary, 1967-69; Sunday Times: Editor, Spectrum, 1969-72, Editor, Colour Magazine, 1972-75, News Editor/Features Editor, 1975-83; Managing Editor, The Observer, 1983-86; Editor, London Daily News, 1986-87; Editor, The Scotsman, 1988-94; Chairman, Edinburgh Book Festival, 1994-96; Chairman, Scottish Arts Council, 1996-2001; Presenter, Eye to Eye, Radio Scotland, 1994-97; Columnist, The Times and Scotland on Sunday; Member, National Cultural Strategy Review Group, 1999-2000. Publications: Hoax: the Howard Hughes-Clifford Irving Affair (Co-Author); Jeremy Thorpe: A Secret Life (Co-Author); The Falklands War (with Sunday Times Insight team); Massacre — the story of Glencoe; The Fourth Reich — Klaus Barbie and the Neo-Fascist Connection (Co-Author); Not With Honour — the inside story of the Westland Affair (Co-Author); For King and Conscience — John Graham of Claverhouse, Viscount Dundee (Co-Author); Anatomy of Scotland (Co-Editor); Highland Wilderness; People in a Landscape. Fellow, Royal Society of Edinburgh; Honorary Doctor of Arts, Napier University; Honorary Doctor of Law, Aberdeen University; Honorary Doctor of Letters: Glasgow University, Queen Margaret University. Recreations: book-collecting; fishing. Address: (h.) 5 Drummond Place, Edinburgh EH3 6PH; T.-0131-557 5705.

Linkston, Alex Millar, IPFA. Chief Executive Officer, West Lothian Council, since 1996; b. 13.12.49, Bathgate; m., Margaret Cuddihy; 2 d. Educ. Lindsay High School, Bathgate; Glasgow College of Commerce. Joined West Lothian County Council as trainee accountant, 1965. Recreations: horse riding; swimming; Rotary. Address: (b.) West Lothian Council, West Lothian House, Livingston EH54 6QG; T.-01506 777141; e-mail: alex.linkston@westlothian.gov.uk

Linlithgow, 4th Marquess of (Adrian John Charles Hope); b. 1.7.46; m.; 1 s.; 1 d.; 2 s. by pr. m.; succeeded to title, 1987. Educ. Eton. Stockbroker. Address: Philpstoun House, Linlithgow, West Lothian EH49 7NB.

Lishman, Professor Joyce, MA (Oxon), PhD, DipSW, FFCS. Head, School of Applied Social Studies, Robert Gordon University, since 1993; m., Dr. J.R. Lishman; 1 s.; 1 d. Educ. Normanton Girls High School; St. Hilda's College, Oxford University; Edinburgh University; Aberdeen University. Social Worker/Senior Social Worker, Departments of Child and Family Psychiatry, Edinburgh; Research Assistant/Research Fellow, Aberdeen University; Editor, Research Highlights Series; Malcolm Sargent Social Worker, Royal Aberdeen Children's Hospital; Lecturer/Senior Lecturer, RGIT; Lead Assessor, Quality Assessment of Social Work, 1995-96; Trustee, Lloyds TSB (Scotland), since 2003. Publications: Handbook of Theory for Practice Teachers in Social Work (Editor); Communication in Social Work; The Role of Volunteer Coordinators in the Provision of Care (Co-Author); Evaluation and Social Work Practice (Co-Author); Research Highlights in Social Work series (General Editor). Recreations: family and friends; music; theatre; reading; travel. Address: (b.) School of Applied Social Studies, The Robert Gordon University, Kepplestone Annexe, Queen's Road, Aberdeen AB9 2PG; T.-01224 263201; e-mail: j.lishman@rgu.ac.uk

Lister, Brian. Chief Executive, Scottish Further Education Unit. Address: (b.) Argyll Court, Castle Business Park, Stirling FK9 4TY; T.-01786 892000.

Lister-Kaye, Sir John, 8th Bt. of Grange, OBE, DUniv, DSc. Naturalist, Author, Lecturer; Member, International

Committee, World Wilderness Foundation, since 1984; Vice President, Association for the Preservation of Rural Scotland, since 1998; President, Scottish Wildlife Trust, 1996-2001; Vice President, RSPB, 2006; b. 8.5.46; m., 1, Lady Sorrel Deirdre Bentinck; 1 s.; 2 d.; 2, Lucinda Anne Law; 1 d. Educ, Allhallows School. Founded Field Studies Centre, Highlands, 1970; founder Director, Aigas Trust, 1979; Director, AigasQuest Ltd., 1997; Director, Ninovus Estates Ltd., 1999; Director, Naturedays Ltd., 2006; Chairman, Scottish Committee, RSPB, 1985-92; Member, Committee for Scotland, NCC, 1989-90; NW Regional Chairman, Scottish Natural Heritage, 1992-96; Honorary Doctorate, University of Stirling, 1995; Honorary Doctorate, St. Andrews University, 2005. Publications: The White Island, 1972; Seal Cull, 1979; The Seeing Eye, 1980; One for Sorrow, 1994; Ill Fares the Land, 1995; Song of the Rolling Earth, 2003; Nature's Child, 2004. Address: (h.) House of Aigas, Beauly, Inverness-shire IV4 7AD; e-mail: jlk@aigas.co.uk

Lithgow, Sir William (James), 2nd Bt. of Ormsary, DL, LLD, CEng, FRINA, CCMI. Industrialist; Farmer; Vice Chairman, Lithgows Limited (Director, since 1956, Chairman, 1959-68, 1988-99); b. 10.5.34; m., 1, Valerie Helen Scott (deceased); 2, Mary Claire Hill; 2 s.; 1 d. Educ. Winchester College. Chairman, Hunterston Development Company Limited, 1987 (Director, since 1971); Director: Lithgows Limited, Lithgows Pty Limited; Chairman, Scott Lithgow Drydocks Ltd., 1967-78; Vice-Chairman, Scott Lithgow Ltd., 1968-78; Chairman, Western Ferries (Argyll) Ltd., 1972-85; Director, Bank of Scotland, 1962-86; Founder, Landcatch Ltd., 1979. Member: British Committee, Det Norske Veritas, 1966-92, Greenock District Hospital Board, 1961-66, General Board (Royal Society Nominee), Nat. Physical Lab., 1963-66; Honorary President, Students Association, and Member, Court, Strathclyde University, 1964-69; Member: Executive Committee, Scottish Council Development and Industry, 1969-85, Scottish Regional Council, CBI, 1969-76, Clyde Port Authority, 1969-71, West Central Scotland Plan Steering Committee, 1970-74, Board, National Ports Council, 1971-78, Scottish Milk Marketing Board, 1979-83; Chairman, Iona Cathedral Trustees Management Board, 1979-83; Council Member, Winston Churchill Memorial Trust, 1979-83; Member, Queen's Body Guard for Scotland (Royal Company of Archers), 1964; Fellow, Scottish Council Development and Industry; Honorary Vice President: Inverclyde Battalion Boys' Brigade, Mid-Argyll Agricultural Society. Recreations: rural life; invention; photography. Address: (b.) PO Box 7, Lochgilphead, Argyll PA31 8JH; T.-01880 770252.

Little, Professor Gavin Forbes Macleod, LLB (Hons), PhD (Edin), DipLP, Solicitor. Professor of Public Law, University of Stirling, since 2004; b. 21.01.64, Glasgow; m., Tikus Amanda; 2 s. Educ. The High School of Glasgow; The University of Edinburgh. Lecturer in Law, University of Dundee, 1988-93; Trainee Solicitor, 1994-96; Lecturer in Law, University of Stirling, 1996-2001; Senior Lecturer in Law, 2001-04. Head of the Department of Accounting, Finance and Law, 2002-05, Head of The School of Law, 2005-07. Recreations: writing historical fiction; cycling; hillwalking. Address: (b.) The School of Law, University of Stirling, Stirling FK9 4LA; T.-01786 467301.
E-mail: g.f.m.little@stir.ac.uk

Little, Graham Edgar, FRSGS. Head of Field Production, Ordnance Survey, since 2003; b. 6.3.49, Leeds; m., Dr Christina Woodrow; 1 s.; 1 d. Educ. Ayr Academy. Worked for Ordnance Survey since leaving school; resurvey of the Highlands and Islands of Scotland, 1970s; managing mapping activity in Southern

and Central Scotland, 1980s; Account Manager (Sales and Marketing), 1988-98; Operations Manager for Scotland, 1998-2003. Member, Executive Board Scotland, Association of Geographic Information, 1999-2002; President, Mountaineering Council of Scotland, 1986-89; Chairman, Scottish Mountain Safety Group, 1990-92. Recreations: mountaineering; lecturing; writing; travel; bridge. Address: (b.) Ordnance Survey, Grayfield House, 5 Bankhead Avenue, Edinburgh EH11 4AA; T.-0131-458 8303.

Littlejohn, Professor David, BSc, PhD, CChem, FRSC, FRSE. Professor of Analytical Chemistry, Strathclyde University, since 1988; b. 1.5.53, Glasgow; m., Lesley Shaw MacDonald; 1 d. Educ. Duncanrig Secondary School, East Kilbride; Strathclyde University. Technical Officer, ICI Petrochemicals Division, Wilton, Middlesborough, 1978-80; Lecturer/Senior Lecturer in Chemistry, Strathclyde University, 1981-88; Head of Department, since 2005. Awarded 15th SAC Silver Medal by Royal Society of Chemistry, 1987; Theophilus Redwood Lectureship, 2001; Royal Society of Chemistry Award in Chemical Analysis and Instrumentation, 2005; joint Editor in Chief, Talanta, International Journal of Pure and Applied Analytical Chemistry, 1989-91. Publications: 178 research papers, 10 reviews, 1 book; 6 book chapters. Address: (b.) Department of Pure and Applied Chemistry, Strathclyde University, 295 Cathedral Street, Glasgow G1 1XL; T.-0141-548 2067; e-mail: d.littlejohn@strath.ac.uk

Littlejohn, Doris, JP, BL, DUniv, CBE. Former President, Employment Tribunals (Scotland); b. 19.3.35, Glasgow; m., Robert; 3 d. Educ. Queen's Park School, Glasgow; University of Glasgow. Solicitor in private practice in Stirling until 1977. Chairman of Court, University of Stirling; former Member: Lord Chancellor's Panel on Review of Tribunals, Review Panel on Retention of Organs after Post Mortems, Human Genetics Advisory Commission, Broadcasting Council for Scotland, General Advisory Committee, BBC. Address: Suilven, 125 Henderson Street, Bridge of Allan FK9 4RQ; T.-01786 832032.

Littlejohn, Robert King, MA (Aberdeen), MA (Sussex), MCIPD, FFCS. Regional SaBRE Campaign Director, Lowland Reserve Forces' and Cadets' Association, since 2006; b. 17.3.46, Aberdeen; m., Anna; 1 s.; 2 d. Educ. Morrison's Academy, Crieff; Aberdeen University; Moray House College; Sussex University. Administrative (Education) Officer, RAF, 1969-96 including: Directorate of Air Staff Briefing and Co-ordination, 1987-90; Officer Commanding Administration Wing, RAF Leeming, 1990-93; Head of RAF Resettlement Service, 1993-96; retired in rank of Wing Commander; Registrar, Royal College of Physicians and Surgeons of Glasgow, 1996-2005. Recreations: golf; hill-walking; opera; Aberdeen FC. Address: (b.) Lowland House, 60 Avenuepark Street, Glasgow G20 8LW; T.-0141 945 4951; e-mail: lo-employer@lo.rfca.mod.uk

Livingston, Professor Kay, BEd, MEd, PhD, FRSA. Professor of Educational Research, Policy and Practice, Glasgow University, since 2007, Director of The International Educational Consultancy, since 2007; Head of International Education, Learning and Teaching Scotland (LTS), since 2007; b. Girvan; m.; 1 s. Educ. Glasgow University. Teacher, 1978-87; Lecturer, Craigie College of Education, Ayr, 1987-92; Secondment to Socrates Technical Assistance in European Commission, Brussels Special Project Officer, Open and Distance Learning, 1997; Senior Lecturer, Coordinator of International Education, University of Paisley, 1993-2001; Director of Quality in

Education Centre (QIE), University of Strathclyde, Reader in Education, 2001-05; Professor of Education, University of Aberdeen, Director of Scottish Teachers For A New Era, 2005-07. Editor, European Journal of Teacher Education; Member, UNESCO Scotland Committee. Recreations: running; skiing; hillwalking; reading.

Livingstone, Andrew Hugh, BSc (Hons), DipEd. Director, Colm Consultants; Education Officer, The Defence Academy of the United Kingdom and The Stewart Ivory Foundation; Rector, St. Columba's School, Kilmacolm, 1987-2002; b. 7.12.44, Campbeltown; m., 1, Christine Margaret Henderson (deceased), 2, Alison Brown Reid; 1 s.; 1 d. Educ. Campbeltown Grammar School; University of Aberdeen; University of Glasgow; Jordanhill College of Education. High School of Glasgow, 1968-70; Principal Teacher, Mathematics, Paisley Grammar School, 1970-79; Assistant Rector, Williamwood High School, 1979-83; Depute Rector, Paisley Grammar School, 1987. Recreations: golf; bridge; walking; skiing. Address: (h.) Nithsdale, Lyle Road, Kilmacolm; T.-01505 872404; e-mail: livingstoneah@btinternet.com

Livingstone, Bill (William). Editorial Director, Dunfermline Press Group, since 1997; Life Trustee, Carnegie Dunfermline and Hero Fund Trusts, since 1991; Trustee, Carnegie United Kingdom Trust, since 2002; b. 23.7.44, Dunfermline; m., Margaret Stark; 2 s.; 2 d. Educ. Dunfermline High School. Entire career with Dunfermline Press Group: Editor, Dunfermline Press, 1984-96. Chairman, Guild of Editors (Scotland), 1994-96; Hon. Vice-President, Dunfermline and District Bn., Boys' Brigade. Address: (b.) Pitreavie Business Park, Dunfermline, Fife KY11 8QS; T.-01383 728201.

Livingstone, George, MA, DipEd, MEd, FEIS. Consultant and Adviser, Ministry of Education, Ethiopia, 2000-03; Consultant on teacher education, the Education Ministries of The Gambia, Rwanda (2005) and Lesotho (2006); b. 19.5.38, Tranent; m., Jean Laidlaw Ritchie; 2 s. Educ. Preston Lodge; Edinburgh University; Glasgow University. Teacher/Head of Department, primary and secondary schools, East Lothian and Tanzania, 1960-67; Head Teacher, Glendinning School, Galashiels, 1967-70; Hamilton College of Education: Lecturer/Research Officer, 1970-78, Head of Department, 1978-83; Jordanhill College of Education: Senior Lecturer, 1983-90, Course Director, 1990-94; Vice Dean, Faculty of Education, 1994-98, then Senior Lecturer, University of Strathclyde. President, Association of Lecturers in Colleges of Education in Scotland, 1982-86; Member, General Teaching Council for Scotland, 1986-98 (Convener, Supply Committee, Vice-Convener, Exceptional Admissions Committee); Chairman, S.J.N.C. (F.E.), 1988-92; Selector, Glasgow District Rugby Union, 1988-94. Publications: Co-author three series of books for children; Scotland – Still a Half-educated Nation (Co-author), 1986; Scottish Education (Contributor), 1999; academic journal papers. Recreations: rugby union; walking; literature. Address: (h.) 1 Scott Grove, Hamilton; T.-01698 429756; e-mail: geoliving@hotmail.com

Livingstone, Ian Lang, CBE, BL, NP. Chairman: Lanarkshire Health Board, 1993-2002, Lanarkshire Development Agency, 1991-2000, New Lanarkshire Ltd.; Consultant Solicitor, since 1989; Director, Kingdom FM Ltd.; Chairman, Scottish Local Authorities Remuneration Committee; b. 23.2.38, Hamilton; m., Diane; 2 s. Educ. Hamilton Academy; Glasgow University. Qualified as Solicitor, 1960; Partner, Senior Partner, Ballantyne & Copland, Solicitors, Motherwell, 1962-86, now a Consultant; Chairman and Director, family property investment and development company, since 1987. Former Chairman, Motherwell Football Club; Chairman, Board, Motherwell College, 1989-97; Member, Dalziel High School Board; Governor, David Livingstone Memorial Trust; Elder, St. Mary's Parish Church, Motherwell; Honorary President, Lanarkshire Chamber of Commerce, since 2006. Recreations: walking; football; music. Address: (h.) 223 Manse Road, Motherwell ML1 2PY; T.-01698 253750.

Livingstone, Marilyn. MSP (Labour), Kirkcaldy, since 1999; b. 1952, Kirkcaldy. Educ. Viewforth Secondary School; Fife College. Fife College of Further and Higher Education: Head of Section – Administration and Consumer Studies, Youth Training Manager, Head of Business School. Member, Kirkcaldy District Council, four years; Member, Fife Council, five years (Chair, Vocational Education and Training Committee, Chair, Fife Vocational and Training Strategy, Member, New Deal Steering Group, Member, Kerley Committee). Convenor, CPWG Survivors of Childhood Sexual Abuse; Member, Equal Opportunities Committee; Ministerial Parliamentary Assistant to First Minister. Address: (b.) Wing A, Suite D, Carlyle House, Carlyle Road, Kirkcaldy KY1 1DB; T.-01592 564114.

Lloyd, Ivor Graham, BA, MLib, MCLIP. Depute Principal, University of Abertay Dundee, since 2005; b. 28.10.50, Edinburgh; m., Rosemary; 1 s.; 1 d. Educ. Ainslie Park Secondary School, Edinburgh; University of Strathclyde; University of Wales. Assistant Librarian, Kirkcaldy Technical College, 1975-76; Subject Librarian, Duncan of Jordanstone College of Art, 1976-84; Depute Chief Librarian, Dundee College of Technology, 1984-89; Chief Librarian, University of Abertay Dundee, 1989-96, Head of Information Services, 1996-2005. President, CILIPS. Recreations: golf; gardening. Address: (b.) University of Abertay Dundee, Bell Street, Dundee; T.-01382 308866.

Lloyd-Jones, Glyn Robin, MA, BA. Author and Novelist; President, Scottish PEN International, 1997-2000; b. 5.10.34, London; m., Sallie Hollocombe; 1 s.; 2 d. Educ. Blundell's School, Tiverton; Selwyn College, Cambridge University; Jordanhill College of Education. Teaching in Scottish secondary schools; Director, Curriculum Development Centre, Clydebank; English-Speaking Union Thyne Travel Scholarship to America, 1974; President, Scottish Association of Writers, 1981-86; Adviser, Education Department, Dunbartonshire, 1972-89; Co-ordinator, Scottish Forum for Development Education in Schools, 1996-99; radio drama: Ice in Wonderland, 1992 (winner, Radio Times new drama script award); Rainmaker, 1995. Publications: children's: Where the Forest and the Garden Meet, 1980; Red Fox Running, 2007; novels: Lord of the Dance (Winner, BBC/Arrow First Novel Competition, 1983); The Dreamhouse, 1985; Fallen Angels, 1992; education books: Assessment: From Principles to Action, 1985; How to Produce Better Worksheets, 1985; non-fiction: Argonauts of the Western Isles, 1989; Fallen Pieces of the Moon, 2006. Recreations: mountaineering; sea-kayaking; photography; chess. Address: (h.) 26 East Clyde Street, Helensburgh G84 7PG; T.-01436 672010.

Loasby, Professor Brian John, MA, MLitt, DUniv, FBA, FRSE. Emeritus and Honorary Professor of Economics, University of Stirling, since 1984; b. 02.08.30, Kettering; m., Judith Ann (Robinson); 2 d. Educ. Kettering Grammar School; Emmanuel College, Cambridge. Assistant in Political Economy, University of Aberdeen, 1955-58; Bournville Research Fellow, University of Birmingham, 1958-61; Tutor in Management Studies, University of Bristol, 1961-67; Lecturer in Economics, University of Stirling, 1967-68, Senior Lecturer in Economics, 1968-71,

Professor of Management Economics, 1971-84. Publications: The Swindon Project, 1973; Choice, Complexity and Ignorance, 1976; The Mind and Method of The Economist, 1989; Equilibrium and Evolution, 1991; Knowledge, Institutions and Evolution in Economics, 1999 Schumpeter Prize, 2000; articles and book chapters. Address: (b.) Department of Economics, University of Stirling, Stirling FK9 4LA; T.-01786 472124; e-mail: b.j.loasby@stir.ac.uk

Lochhead, Liz. Poet and Playwright; b. 1947, Motherwell. Educ. Glasgow School of Art. Combined teaching art and writing for eight years; became full-time writer after selection as first holder, Scottish/Canadian Writers' Exchange Fellowship, 1978; former Writer in Residence, Tattenhall Centre, Chester. Publications include: Memo for Spring, Islands, Grimm Sisters, Dreaming of Frankenstein, True Confessions; plays include: Blood and Ice, Dracula, Same Difference, Sweet Nothings, Now and Then, True Confessions, Mary Queen of Scots Got Her Head Chopped Off, The Big Picture; Perfect Days; poetry includes: The Colour of Black and White: Poems 1984-2003, 2003.

Lochhead, Richard Neilson, BA (Hons). MSP (SNP), Moray, since 2006, North East of Scotland, 1999-2006; Cabinet Secretary for Rural Affairs and the Environment, since 2007; b. 24.5.69, Paisley. Educ. Williamwood High School, Clarkston; Stirling University. Financial trainee, South of Scotland Electricity Board, 1987-89; Economic Development Officer, Dundee City Council, 1998-99; Office Manager for Alex Salmond, 1994-98. Recreations: cinema; reading; travel; five-a-side football; road and off-road cycling. Address: (b.) 9 Wards Road, Elgin, Moray IV30 1NL; T.-01343 551111.

Locke, Alasdair James Dougall, MA. Executive Chairman, Abbot Group PLC; Chairman, First Property Online plc, since 2000; Chairman, Moyle Interconnector plc, since 2003; b. 29.8.53, Aldershot; m., Kathleen Anne; 2 s. Educ. Uppingham School, Rutland; Wadham College, Oxford University. Assistant Vice President: Citibank N. A., 1974-78, Oceanic Finance Corporation, 1978-81; Vice President, American Express Leasing Corporation, 1981-83; Director, Henry Ansbacher and Co., Ltd., 1983-87; Deputy Chairman, Kelt Energy PLC, 1987-91. Former Member, OSO Advisory Board. Recreations: shooting; golf; skiing. Address: (b.) Minto Drive, Altens, Aberdeen AB12 3LW; T.-01224 299600.

Lockerbie, Catherine, MA (Hons). Director, Edinburgh International Book Festival, since 2000; b. 4.9.58; 1 s. Educ. High School of Stirling; Edinburgh University. Freelance writer, teacher and broadcaster; The Scotsman: Deputy Arts Editor, Chief Leader Writer, Literary Editor. Hon. LLD (Dundee), 2005; Hon. DLitt: (Queen Margaret UC), 2006, Edinburgh, 2007; DUniv (Open), 2007. Recreation: reading. Address: (b.) Edinburgh International Book Festival, 5a Charlotte Square, Edinburgh EH2 4DR; T.-0131 718 5666.

Lockhart of the Lee, Angus Hew, b. 17.8.46, Dunsyre; m., Susan Elizabeth Normand; 1 s.; 1 d. Educ. Rannoch School, Perthshire; North of Scotland College of Agriculture. Recognised as Chief of the Name Lockhart, 1957; Owner and Manager, Lee and Carnwath Estates; Member, Standing Council of Scottish Chiefs. Recreations: shooting; skiing. Address: (h.) Newholm, Dunsyre, Lanark ML11 8NQ; T.-01968 682254.

Lockhart, Sheriff Principal Brian Alexander, BL. Sheriff Principal, South Strathclyde, Dumfries and Galloway, since 2005; b. 1.10.42, Ayr; m., Christine Ross Clark; 2 s.; 2 d. Educ. Glasgow Academy; Glasgow University. Partner, Robertson Chalmers and Auld, Solicitors, 1967-79; Sheriff, North Strathclyde, at Paisley, 1979-81; Sheriff, Glasgow

and Strathkelvin, 1981-2005; President, Sheriffs' Association, 2003-05; Member, Parole Board for Scotland, 1997-2003. Recreations: fishing; golf; family. Address: (h.) 18 Hamilton Avenue, Glasgow G41; T.-0141-427 1921.

Lockhart, Brian Robert Watson. MA (Hons), DipEd. Headmaster, Robert Gordon's College, Aberdeen, 1996-2004; b. 19.7.44, Edinburgh; m., Fiona Anne Sheddon; 1 s.; 2 d. Educ. George Heriot's School, Edinburgh; Aberdeen University. Teacher of History and Economic History, George Heriot's School, 1968-72; Principal Teacher of History, 1972-81; Deputy Rector, High School of Glasgow, 1981-96. Headteachers' Association of Scotland: Member, Council, 1988-2003, Member, Executive, 1989-94; Chair, Universities and Colleges Admissions Service Scottish Standing Committee, 1998-2000 and 2002-03; Member, Higher Still Implementation Group, 1998-2001; Member, Headmasters Conference Universities Committee, 1998-2003; Secretary, HMC (Scottish Division), 2003; Chairman, HMC (Scottish Division), 2004; Member, Business Committee, Aberdeen University, since 1999, Vice-Convener, since 2006; Member, Council, St. Margaret's School for Girls, Aberdeen, since 2004; Member, Board of Voluntary Service Aberdeen (VSA), since 2004; Member, Board of Hutchesons' Educational Trust, Glasgow, since 2005; Member, Audit Committee, Aberdeen University, since 2007. Publications: Jinglin' Geordie's Legacy, 2003; Robert Gordon's Legacy, 2007. Recreations: reading biographies; sport; films; politics. Address: (h.) 80 Gray Street, Aberdeen AB10 6JE; T.-01224 315776.

Lockhead, Moir, OBE, IEng, MCIT, MIRTE. Deputy Chairman and Chief Executive, FirstGroup plc; b. 25.4.45, Sedgefield; m., Audrey; 3 s.; 1 d. Joined Grampian Regional Transport as General Manager, 1985; Executive Chairman, GRT Bus Group PLC, 1989 (employee/ management buy-out, 1989, becoming FirstGroup, 1995). Address: (b.) 395 King Street, Aberdeen AB24 5RP; T.-01224 650102; e-mail: moir.lockhead@firstgroup.com

Lockley, Stephen Randolph, BSc, CEng, MICE, FILT, MIHT, DipTE. Transport Consultant, since 1997; b. 19.6.43, Manchester; m., Angela; 2 d. Educ. Morecambe Grammar School; Manchester University. Highway and Planning Engineer, Lancashire County Council, 1964-72; Transportation and Planning Engineer, Lanarkshire County Council, 1972-75; Strathclyde Regional Council: Principal Engineer (Transportation), 1975-77, Depute Director of Policy Planning, 1977-80, Principal Executive Officer, 1980-86; Director General, Strathclyde Passenger Transport Executive, 1986-97. Address: 64 Townhead Street, Strathaven, Lanarkshire ML10 6DJ; T.-01357 529395.

Lockwood, Roger Graham, CB, BA, FCIPD. Chief Executive, Northern Lighthouse Board, since 2006; b. 26.6.50, Hitchin; m., Susan Jane (nee Cant); 3 s.; 2 d. Educ. Kimbolton School, Cambridgeshire; University of Warwick. Royal Navy, 1971-2005; Private Secretary to Second Sea Lord, 1995-96; Private Secretary to First Sea Lord, 1996-98; Commodore, HMS Raleigh, 1998-2000; Rear Admiral, 2000; Chief of Staff to Second Sea Lord, 2000-02; Senior Directing Staff (Navy), Royal College of Defence Studies, 2002-05. Commissioner, Queen Victoria School, Dunblane; Chairman, Perth Sea Cadets; Area Vice Patron (Scotland), War Memorials Trust. Recreations: family; learning to play the clarinet. Address: (b.) 84 George Street, Edinburgh EH2 3DA; T.-0131-473-3112; e-mail: rogerl@nlb.org.uk

Lodder, Professor Christina Anne, BA, DPhil, FRSE, FRSA. Professor, School of Art History, St Andrews

University, since 1995; b. 21.2.48, Colchester; 1 d. Educ. York University; University of Sussex. St Andrews University: Lecturer in Art History, 1979, Reader in Art History, 1990-95, Professor in Art History, since 1995; Trustee, National Galleries of Scotland, 1996-2003; Member, Council, Royal Society of Edinburgh, 1999-2001. Publications: Russian Constructivism, 1983; Constructing Modernity: The Art and Career of Naum Gabo (Co-author), 2000; Gabo on Gabo: Texts and Interviews (Co-author), 2000; Constructive Strands in Russian Art, 2005; Rethinking Malevich (Co-editor), 2007. Recreations: music; opera; gardening; theatre; novels. Address: (b.) School of Art History, St Andrews University, St Andrews KY16 9AR; T.:-01334 462400.

Logan, Rev. Robert James Victor, MA, BD. Minister, Abdie and Dunbog linked with Newburgh, 1998-2001; Minister, Crown Church, Inverness, 1970-98; b. 8.6.38, Kilmarnock; m., Catherine Steel Young. Educ. Dundee High School; St. Andrews University; Edinburgh University. Assistant Minister, Auld Kirk of Ayr, 1962-64; Minister, Newton Parish Church, Dalkeith, 1964-70; Member, Church Boundaries' Commission, 1974-75; Clerk: Synod of Moray, 1972-75, Synod of the Southern Highlands, 1976-92, Inverness Presbytery, 1980-96; Convener, Nomination Committee, General Assembly, 1979-82; Chairman, successful group applying for franchise to operate Moray Firth Radio, 1979-81. Publication: The Lion, The Pit and the Snowy Day. Recreations: classical music; opera; reading history. Address: (h.) Lindores, 1 Murray Place, Smithton, Inverness IV2 7PX; T.-01463 790226; e-mail: rjvlogan@btinternet.com

Logan, Stephen Douglas, BSc, PhD. Senior Vice-Principal, University of Aberdeen, since 2004; b. 16.10.50, Glasgow; m., Anne; 2 s. Educ. Annan Academy, Dumfriesshire; University of St. Andrews. Medical Research Council Fellow, Senior Lecturer and Professor of Neuroscience, University of Birmingham; Professor of Neuroscience, University of Aberdeen, 1994-96, Head of Department of Biomedical Sciences, 1996-98, became Vice-Principal and Dean of The Faculty of Medicine and Medical Sciences in 1998. Chairman, Grampian University Hospitals NHS Trust, 2002-04, Vice-Chairman, 1998-2002; Member, NHS Grampian Board, 2002-04; Member, SHEFC, 2003; Head of College of Life Sciences and Medicine, 2003. Over 100 research publications. Recreations: rugby; golf; reading. Address: (b.) University of Aberdeen, University Office, King's College, Aberdeen AB24 3FX; T.-+44 (0)1224 272017; e-mail: s.d.logan@abdn.ac.uk

Logan, Rt. Rev. Vincent, DipRE. Roman Catholic Bishop of Dunkeld, since 1981; b. 30.6.41, Bathgate. Educ. Blairs College, Aberdeen; St. Andrew's College, Drygrange. Ordained Priest, 1964; Assistant Priest, St. Margaret's, Edinburgh, 1964-66; Corpus Christi College, London, 1966-67; Chaplain, St. Joseph's Hospital, Rosewell, Midlothian, 1966-67; Adviser in Religious Education, Archdiocese of St. Andrews and Edinburgh, 1967; Parish Priest, St. Mary's, Ratho, 1977-81; Vicar Episcopal for Education, Edinburgh, 1978. Address: Bishop's House, 29 Roseangle, Dundee DD1 4LS; T.-01382 224327.

Logie, Professor Robert Howie, BSc, PhD, CPyschol, FBPsS, FRSA, FRSE. Professor of Human Cognitive Neuroscience, Edinburgh University, since 2004; Anderson Professor of Psychology, Aberdeen University, 1998-2003 (Head, Department of Psychology, 1997-2002); b. 23.3.54, Ajmer, India; m., Elizabeth; 2 s. Educ. Aberdeen Academy; Aberdeen University; University College, London. Researcher, MRC Applied Psychology Unit, Cambridge,

1980-86; Aberdeen University: Lecturer in Psychology, 1987, Senior Lecturer, 1992, Personal Professor, 1995. Publications: over 150 including 12 authored or edited books, notably Visuo Spatial Working Memory, 1995. Dorothy Hodgkin Lecturer, British Association for the Advancement of Science, 1995.

Long, Philip Reginald, BA (Hons), MA. Senior Curator, Scottish National Gallery of Modern Art; b. 5.1.66, Edinburgh; m., Anne Violet Clark Campbell; 2 s. Educ. Daniel Stewart's and Melville College; Lancaster University; Essex University. Research Assistant, then Assistant Curator, then Senior Curator, Scottish National Gallery of Modern Art, from 1993; Project Advisor, National Gallery of Scottish Art and Design, 1997-98. Scottish Arts Council committee memberships, since 1998; Exhibitions and Projects Panel (Chair, 2001-02); Visual Arts Committee (Acting Chair, 2003); Creative Arts Committee; Lottery Committee; Appeals Committee; Edinburgh Art Festival Committee. Publications: Encyclopedia of Scotland, 1994 (co-author, visual art entries); William Gillies, 1994; Anne Redpath, 1996; John Maxwell, 1998; The Scottish Colourists, 2000 (co-author); Illustrated Encyclopedia of Scotland, 2004 (visual art entries); John Houston, 2005; Charles Rennie Mackintosh in France, 2005 (co-author); Basil Spence (co-editor). Recreations: visiting exhibitions; foreign travel; running. Address: (h.) 6 Hillside Crescent, Edinburgh EH7 5DY; T.-0131-556 1637; e-mail: plong@nationalgalleries.org

Longmuir, Rev. T Graeme, KJSJ, MA (Oxon), BEd, Cert Theol. Minister, St. Andrew's Parish Church, Inverurie, since 2001; Prelate and Chaplain, The Priory of St Margaret of Scotland (Order of St John of Jerusalem - Knights Hospitaller); b. 26.7.49, Greenock, Renfrewshire. Educ. The Friends' School, Lancaster; Lancaster & Mansfield College, Oxford. Christ Church, Morecambe, 1976-83 (Assistant Minister, 1976-80, Collegiate Minister, 1980-83); Chaplain and Head of Department, Strathallan School, 1983-2000. Governor, Morecambe High School; Chairman, Christian Aid Committee; Chaplain, Sea Cadets Company; Chairman, Cumbria and North Lancs RSPCA; Examiner, Oxford and Cambridge Examinations Board, NEA; Vice-Convener, Church of Scotland Panel on Worship, 1985-95; (Songs of God's People, Common Order) Convener, Liturgical Committee, 1985-95. Publications: contributor to: Expository Times, Liturgical Review, Reform, Trout and Salmon, Salmon, Trout and Sea Trout; Editor: The Art of Sea Trout Fishing, The Record, Journal of The Scottish Church Service Society, 1986-99; Editorial Board, Songs of God's People and Common Order, 1994. Recreations: Scottish deerhounds; salmon and sea trout fishing; skiing & snowboarding; tree planting (in the Hebrides); music (classical and ecclesiastical); writing; bagpipe music; Taizé community. Address: (b.) St Andrew's Manse, 1 Ury Dale, Inverurie, Aberdeenshire AB51 3XW; (h.) Dusary Millhouse, Dusary, Claddach Kyles, Isle of North Uist, HS6 5EW; T. (b.) -01467-620468; e-mail: standrew@ukonline.co.uk

Lord, Geoffrey, OBE, MA, AIB, FRSA. Founder The ADAPT Trust, 1989; Council Member, National Youth Orchestras of Scotland, since 1998; Trustee and Secretary, Edinburgh Voluntary Organisations Trusts, since 1997; Trustee, PlayRight Scotland Trust, 1998-2005; b. 24.2.28, Rochdale; m., Jean; 1 d. Educ. Rochdale Grammar School; Bradford University. Midland Bank Ltd., 1946-58; Greater Manchester Probation and After-Care Service, 1958-76 (Deputy Chief Probation Officer, 1974-76); Secretary and Treasurer, Carnegie UK Trust, 1977-93; Vice-President, Selcare Trust; former Chairman, Pollock Memorial Missionary Trust; Honorary Fellow, Manchester Metropolitan University, 1987; Former Trustee and

Chairman, HomeStart UK; Chairman, The Unemployed Voluntary Action Fund, 1990-95; Past President, Centre for Environmental Interpretation; Trustee, Faith in Older People Trust (FIOP Trust), 2007. Publications: The Arts and Disabilities, 1981; Interpretation of the Environment, 1984; Access for Disabled People to Arts Premises - The Journey Sequence (Co-author), 2004. Recreations: the arts; philately; walking; enjoying life. Address: (h.) 9 Craigleith View, Edinburgh.

Lord, Jonathan Christopher, MA. Director, RSAC Motorsport Ltd and independent motor sport consultant; b. 29.4.53, Alverstoke; 1 s. Educ. Dollar Academy; St. Andrews University. Ministry of Defence (Naval), 1975-76; Royal Scottish Automobile Club, 1976-2006; Member, British Motor Sports Council, 1991-2003; MSA Rallies Committee, 1982-2003; FIA Observer for International Rallies; MSA Steward; Clerk of the Course, RSAC International Scottish Rally, since 1982 and other international rallies; Secretary to the Vestry, St. Bride's Episcopal Church, Glasgow, since 1991. Recreations: music (especially choral singing); cricket; motor sport; following Dunfermline Athletic FC. Address: (h.) 11 Melrose Gardens, Glasgow G20 6RB; T.-0141-946 5045.

Lorimer, A. Ross, CBE, MD, DUniv (Glasgow), FMedSci, FRCP. Retired. Previously President, Royal College of Physicians and Surgeons of Glasgow (2000-03); Honorary Professor, Glasgow University; Consultant Physician and Cardiologist, Glasgow Royal Infirmary; b. 5.5.37, Bellshill; m., Fiona Marshall; 3 s. Educ. Uddingston Grammar School; High School of Glasgow; Glasgow University. Recreations: reading; walking. Address: 12, Uddingston Road, Bothwell G71 8PH.

Lorimer, Thomas Aitken (Ken), BEd, MInstAM, FCMI, FFCS. Director and Chief Executive, Hansel Foundation, since 1998; Director and Chief Executive, Hansel Alliance, since 1998; b. 17.5.54, Mauchline; 2 d. Educ. Belmont Academy, Ayr; Ayr Academy; Ayr College; Craigie College of Education; Strathclyde University. Joined Ayr County Council, 1971, transferred to Strathclyde Regional Council, 1975, held administrative and public relations appointments with both; Hansel Village: General Administrator, 1985; General Manager, 1992. Member, Scottish Committee, Association for Residential Care; Founding Fellow of the Institute of Contemporary Scotland. Recreations: music; theatre/cinema; literature. Address: (b.) Hansel Foundation/Alliance, Broad Meadows, Symington, Ayrshire KA1 5PU; T.-01563 830340.

Lothian, Marquis of (Rt. Hon. Michael Andrew Foster Jude Kerr Ancram), PC, DL, QC. Advocate; MP (Conservative), Devizes, since 1992; Deputy Leader of the Opposition and Shadow Foreign Seretary, 2001-05; Shadow Defence Secretary, 2005; former Chairman, Conservative Party; Member, Intelligence and Security Committee, since 2006; b. 7.7.45; m.; 2 d. Educ. Ampleforth; Christ Church, Oxford; Edinburgh University. MP: Berwickshire and East Lothian, 1974, Edinburgh South, 1979-87; Parliamentary Under Secretary of State, Scottish Office, 1993-94; Minister of State, Northern Ireland Office, 1994-97; Chairman, Conservative Party in Scotland, 1980-83. DL, Roxburgh District. Address (b.): House of Commons, London SW1A 0AA.

Loudon, Alasdair John, LLB, NP, WS. Partner, Turcan Connell WS, Edinburgh, since 2001; b. 7.4.56, Edinburgh; 2 s.; 1 d. Educ. Edinburgh Academy; Dundee University. Apprentice, Tods, Murray and Jamieson, WS, 1978-80; Qualified Assistant, Warner & Co., 1980-82, Partner, 1982-

92; founded Loudons WS, 1992, Senior Partner, until 2001; accredited as specialist in family law; formerly Member, Sheriff Court Rules Council for Scotland; President, Edinburgh Bar Association, 1996-98; Director, Couple Counselling Lothian. Recreations: golf (Bruntsfield Links and Luffness New); football (Heart of Midlothian supporter). Address: (b.) Princes Exchange, 1 Earl Grey Street, Edinburgh EH3 9EE; e-mail: ajl@turcanconnell.com

Loudon, John Alexander, LLB, NP, SSC. Consultant, Loudons Liquor Licensing and Gambling Consultancy; Consultant to Lindsay WS; Consultant, Dundas & Wilson CS LLP; accredited specialist in Liquor Licensing (Betting and Gaming) Law; b. 5.12.49, Edinburgh; m., Alison Jane Bruce Laird; 2 s. Educ. Edinburgh Academy; Dundee University. Apprenticeship, Tindal, Oatts and Roger, Solicitors, Glasgow. Former Member, Council, Law Society of Scotland; Legal advisor, Scotland Committee, British Hospitality Association; Past President, SSC Society; High Constable, City of Edinburgh Ward XV. Recreations: children; shooting; stalking; skiing. Address: (b.) c/o Lindsays WS, Caledonian Exchange, 19A Canning Street, Edinburgh EH3 8HE.

Loudon, William Euan Buchanan (Euan), CBE, FCMI. Chief Executive and Producer, Edinburgh Military Tattoo, since 2007; b. 12.3.56, Lanarkshire; m., Penny. Educ. Uddingston Grammar School and RMA Sandhurst. Commissioned into The Royal Highland Fusiliers, 1975; served at regimental duty and with the Commando Training Centre in Devon, before attending the Army Staff College in 1988; Chief of Staff 7 Armoured Brigade, 1988-91; appointed OBE after Operation GRANBY, 1991; Military Assistant to Chief of the General Staff, 1993-94; Chief Operations Officer of the UN Military Observer Mission to Croatia, Bosnia, Montenegro, Macedonia and the remainder of the former Yugoslavia; Commanding Officer, 1st Battalion, The Royal Highland Fusiliers, 1995-97; Colonel, Army Personnel Centre, Glasgow, 1997-99; commanded 39 Infantry Brigade, 1999-2001; Chief of Staff and Commander Force Troops, HQNI, 2001-03; General Officer Commanding 2nd Division and Governor of Edinburgh Castle, 2004-07. Appointed CBE, 2004; Graduate of Higher Command and Staff Course and attended the Royal College of Defence Studies, January-March 2004. Recreations: golf; shooting and conservation; hobby farming; fishing; Scottish Contemporary Art.

Loughborough, Natalie R., BA (Hons), PGCE (FE). Customer Service Director, First Scotrail, since 2006; Service Quality Director, since 2005; b. 29.3.73, Hartlepool. Institute of Directors Committee Member, West of Scotland. Address: (b.) First Scotrail, 1st Floor, Atrium Court, 50 Waterloo Street, Glasgow G2 6HQ; T.-0141 335 5050.
E-mail: natalie.loughborough@firstgroup.com

Lovat, 16th Lord (Simon Fraser); b. 13.2.77. Educ. Harrow; Edinburgh University. Succeeded to title, 1995.

Love, Frances Mary. Tutor and Lecturer, Scottish Human Relations and Counselling Course, since 1986; Organisational Consultant, SIHR, since 1986; former Chief Executive, Couple Counselling Scotland (retired); b. 2.7.38, Edinburgh; m., James Love; 1 d. Educ. Broughton Secondary School. Edinburgh Public Library Service; voluntary playleader, Edinburgh Toddlers Playcentres; Pre-School Playgroup Association: playgroup supervisor, fieldworker, Scottish Adviser; General Secretary, Pre-School Playgroups Association; Executive Officer/Company Secretary, Scottish Council for Opportunities in Play Experience (SCOPE). Company Secretary, Scottish Institute of Human Relations; Member, Council, Stepfamily Scotland; Convenor, Edinburgh and Lothian Council on Alcohol. Recreations: gardening;

reading; theatre; dress-making; grandson. Address: (b.) 142 West Savile Terrace, Edinburgh EH9 3EJ.

Love, Hugh Martin, MICM. Chairman, HM Love and Co LLP; Messenger-At-Arms, since 1976; Sheriff Officer, since 1966; b. 30.6.45; m., Moira; 1 s.; 1 d. Educ. Tynecastle Senior Secondary School. Qualified as Officer of Court, 1966; Started own Practice, 1975; President, Society of Messengers-At-Arms and Sheriff Officers, 1983-85; Chairman, Examination Committee of Society of MA and SO, 1997-99; currently Member, Advisory Council on Messengers-At-Arms and Sheriff Officers; Macer to the Lyon Court. Recreations: golf; soccer. Address: (b.) 19 Heriot Row, Edinburgh EH3 6JR; T.-0131 557 0100; e-mail: hugh.love@hmlove.co.uk

Love, Professor James, BA, MSc, PhD. Vice Principal, Strathclyde University, since 2006, Pro Vice-Principal, 2004-06, Professor of Economics, since 1995; b. 31.7.48, Dunfermline; m., Jane Lindores Scott; 2 d. Educ. Beath High School; Strathclyde University. Lecturer, Haile Sellassie 1 University, 1971-74; Lecturer, Strathclyde University, 1974-79; Lecturer, Ghana University, 1979-80; Senior Lecturer, University of Lund, 1980-81; Senior Research Fellow, Fraser of Allander Institute, 1984-86; Lecturer, Senior Lecturer, Reader, Strathclyde University, 1986-95; Head, Department of Economics, and Vice-Dean (Research), Strathclyde Business School, 1994-99, Dean, 1999-2004. Chairman, Board of Trustees, SOLAS. Recreations: sport; particularly the (mis)fortunes of Aberdeen FC and Cowdenbeath FC. Address: (b.) Strathclyde University, Glasgow G1 1XQ; T.-0141-548 5859.

Love, Robert Malcolm, MA (Hons), FRSAMD. Independent Producer; Former Controller of Drama, Scottish Television; b. 9.1.37, Paisley. Educ. Paisley Grammar School; Glasgow University; Washington University, St. Louis. Actor and Director, various repertory companies, including Nottingham Playhouse, 1962-65; Producer, Thames TV, 1966-75, including Public Eye, Van Der Valk; freelance Producer, 1976-79, including Thames TV, LWT, Seacastle Film Productions, Scottish TV. Awards including: Commonwealth Festival, New York TV and Film Festival, Chicago Film Festival, BAFTA Scotland, nominated for International Emmy, New York, 1982; productions for Scottish include Taggart, High Road, Doctor Finlay, McCallum. Governor, RSAMD, 1994-2002; Member, Scottish Arts Council, 1994-99; Chair, Beckett Time Festival, 2000; opera productions include Tosca, Susanna's Secret, Scott at the Opera. Recreations: literature; music; theatre; travel.

Love, Professor Sandy, BVMS, PhD. Chair, Equine Clinical Studies, University of Glasgow, since 1997; b. 14.3.60, Paisley. Educ. Kelvinside Academy; University of Glasgow. Private practice, Wetherby, Yorkshire 1982-84; Junior Fellow in Veterinary Surgery, University of Bristol, 1984-86; Horserace Betting Levy Board Research Scholar, 1986-87; Lecturer, Equine Medicine, University of Glasgow, 1987-97. Trustee, Home of Rest for Horses; Past President, British Equine Veterinary Association; Chairman, BEVA Trust. Recreations: racehorse owner; Aberdeen Angus cattle breeder. Address: Meikle Burntshields, Kilbarchan PA10 2PD; T.-01505 702642; e-mail: s.love@vet.udcf.gla.ac.uk

Lovelace, 5th Earl of (Peter Axel William Locke King); b. 26.11.51; m.; succeeded to title, 1964. Address: Torridon House, Torridon, IV22 2HA.

Lovell, Deborah Anne, LLB (Hons), DipLP. Partner, Anderson Strathern, Solicitors, since 2004; b. 28.12.72, Kirkcaldy. Educ. Balwearie High School, Kirkcaldy; Aberdeen University; Edinburgh University. Trainee, Campbell Smith WS, 1995-97; Assistant, McKay &

Norwell, Solicitors, 1997-98; Assistant Solictor, Shepherd and Wedderburn, Solicitors, 1998-2002; Anderson Strathern, Solicitors, since 2002. Notary Public; Member, The WS Society Education Committee; Tutor in Property on The University of Edinburgh Diploma in Legal Practice; Tutor on WS Society/Glasgow School of Law Professional Competence Course; Member, Women in Property; voted a "Rising Star" in the World of Commercial Real Estate by Property Executive Magazine; Member, The Anderson Strathern Team which won The Scott & Co. Specialist Client Team of The Year Award at The Scottish Legal Awards, 2006 for Property Work on The Stirling-Alloa Kincardine Railway Act. Recreations: horse riding; reading; ski-ing. Address: Anderson Strathern, 1 Rutland Court, Edinburgh EH3 8EY; T.-0131 270 7700; e-mail: deborah.lovell@andersonstrathern.co.uk

Low, Alistair James, BSc, FFA. Director: Scottish Golf Union, Cruden Investments; b. 2.8.42, Dundee; m., Shona Wallace; 2 s.; 1 d. Educ. Dundee High School; St. Andrews University. Recreations: golf; skiing; bridge. Address: (h.) Thornfield, Erskine Loan, Gullane, East Lothian.

Low, Eur Ing. Sir James (Richard) Morrison-, 3rd Bt, DL, DFH, CEng, MIEE. Director, Osborne & Hunter Ltd., Glasgow, 1956-89; b. 3.8.25; m., Ann Rawson Gordon; 1 s.; 3 d. Educ. Ardvreck; Harrow; Merchiston; Faraday House, London. Royal Corps of Signals, 1943-47 (Captain). President, Electrical Contractors Association of Scotland, 1982-84; Director, National Inspection Council of Electrical Installation Contractors, 1982-88 (Chairman, Scottish Committee, 1982-88); Chairman, Electrical Industry Liaison Committee, 1986-88; Chairman, Fife Area Scout Council, 1966-84; Chairman, Cupar Branch, East Fife Conservative Association, 1965-78; Trustee, TSB, 1960-80; President, Elecrical Contractors Association of Scotland, 1982-84; DL, Fife, 1978.

Lowden, Professor Gordon Stuart, MA, LLB, CA; b. 22.5.27, Bangkok; m., Kathleen; 2 s.; 1 d. Educ. Dundee High School; Strathallan School; St. John's College, Cambridge; St. Andrews University. Trained with Moody Stuart & Robertson, CA, Dundee; became Partner, 1959; part-time Lecturer/Senior Lecturer, Dundee University, 1955-83; Honorary Professor, Department of Accountancy and Business Finance, Dundee University, since 1987; Honorary Sheriff, since 1991; former Chairman, Dundee Port Authority; Past President, Institute of Chartered Accountants of Scotland. Recreations: golf; watching rugby; bridge. Address: (h.) 169 Hamilton Street, Barnhill, Dundee DD5 2RE; T.-01382 778360.

Lowe, Professor Gordon Douglas Ogilvie, DSc, MB, ChB, MD, FRCPEdin, FRCPGlas, FRCPLond, FFPH. Professor of Vascular Medicine, Glasgow University, since 1993; Consultant Physician, Glasgow Royal Infirmary, since 1985; Co-Director, West of Scotland Haemophilia and Thrombosis Centre, since 1987; b. 2.1.49, London; m., Ann Harvie; 1 s.; 1 d. Educ. Dundee High School; St. Andrews University. House Officer, Royal Infirmary and Maryfield Hospital, Dundee, 1972-73; Senior House Officer, City Hospital, Nottingham, 1973-74; Registrar, Royal Infirmary, Glasgow, 1974-77; Lecturer, Glasgow University, 1978-85, Senior Lecturer, 1985-92, Reader, 1992-93. Former Assessor, RCPEdin.; Chairman, SIGN, 2002-07; Past President, British Society for Haemostasis and Thrombosis. Publications: editor of books and author of publications on thrombosis and bleeding disorders. Recreations: travel; railways; gardening. Address: (b.) Department of Medicine, Royal Infirmary, Glasgow G31 2ER; T.-0141-211 5412.

Lowe, Dr. Janet, CBE, BA (Hons), MBA, EdD. Member, Scottish Further and Higher Education Funding Council, since 2005; b. 27.9.50, South Normanton; m., Donald Thomas Stewart. Educ. Swanwick Hall Grammar School; Hull University; Dundee University; Stirling University.

Immigration Officer, Home Office, 1973-76; Personnel Assistant, Hull University, 1976-80; Administrator, Lothian Region Social Work Department, 1980-82; Napier University: Examinations Officer, Personnel Officer, Assistant Academic Registrar, 1982-88; Secretary and Registrar, Duncan of Jordanstone College of Art, 1988-93; Lauder College: Depute Principal, 1993-96, Principal, 1996-2005. Member: Local Government Finance Review Committee, 2004-06, Board of Management, Scottish Further Education Unit, 1993-2001, Court, Heriot-Watt University, 1999-2005, Court, Dundee University, since 2005, Board, Scottish Enterprise, 1998-2004. Recreations: travel; literature; gardening. Address: 42 Gamekeepers Road, Kinnesswood, Kinross KY13 9JR; T.-01592 840277; e-mail: janetlowe@aol.com

Lowe, Martin John Brodie, OBE, BSc, PhD. Secretary to Edinburgh University, 1990-2002; b. 10.4.40, Dorking; m., Janet MacNaughtan; 3 s.; 1 d. Educ. Dunfermline High School; St. Andrews University. British Council Officer, with service in Tanzania and South India, 1965-69; Strathclyde University: Administrative Assistant, 1969-71, Assistant Registrar, 1971-73, Secretary to Senate, 1973-81; Secretary and Registrar, St. Andrews University, 1981-89. National Council, Voluntary Service Overseas, 1976-83; Honorary Secretary, then Chairman, Glasgow and West of Scotland VSO Committee, 1973-81; Hon. Secretary, Royal Scottish Pipers' Society, 1997-2001 and since 2003; Hon. Pipe Major, 2001-03; Board Member: National Piping Centre, Glasgow, since 1999, Student Awards Agency Scotland, since 2004; Chairman, Victoria League in Scotland, since 2003. Recreations: piping; hill-walking; golf; family interests. Address: (h.) Ingleton, Whim Road, Gullane, East Lothian EH31 2BD.

Lowth, Simon Jonathan, MA, MBA. Executive Director (Corporate Strategy and Development), Scottish Power plc, since 2003; b. 8.9.61; m., Helene, nee Theodoly; 4 c. Educ. Gonville & Caius College, Cambridge; London Business School. Design Engineer, Ove Arup & Partners, 1983-85; Director, McKinsey and Co, 1987-2003. Address: (b.) Scottish Power plc, 1 Atlantic Quay, Glasgow G2 8SP; T.-0141 248 8200.
E-mail: simon.lowth@scottishpower.com

Lowther, Gordon William, BSc, DipRCPath. Head of Cytogenetics, Institute of Medical Genetics, Glasgow, since 1997; b. 5.12.55, Newcastle upon Tyne. Educ. Dame Allans Boys School; Sheffield University. Clinical Cytogeneticist, Centre for Human Genetics, Sheffield, 1979-87; Principal Cytogeneticist, then Consultant Clinical Cytogeneticist, Medical Genetics Glasgow. Member, Association of Clinical Cytogeneticists Council. Address: (b.) Institute of Medical Genetics, NHS GG, Yorkhill Division, Glasgow G3 8SJ; T.-0141-201 0365.

Ludlam, Professor Christopher A., BSc (Hons), MB, ChB, PhD, FRCP, FRCPath. Professor of Haematology and Coagulation Medicine, University of Edinburgh; Consultant Haematologist, Edinburgh Royal Infirmary, since 1980; Director, Edinburgh Haemophilia and Thrombosis Centre, since 1980; b. 6.6.46, Edinburgh. Educ. Edinburgh University. MRC Research Fellow, 1972-75; Senior Registrar in Haematology, University Hospital of Wales, Cardiff, 1975-78; Lecturer in Haematology, University of Wales, 1979. Address: (b.) Department of Haematology, Royal Infirmary, Edinburgh; T.-0131 242 6811; e-mail: Christopher.Ludlam@ed.ac.uk

Lugton, Charles Michael Arber, MA. Chief Executive, Scottish Law Commission, 2005-08; b. 5.4.51, South Africa; m. Joyce Graham; 2 s. Educ. St. John's College, Johannesburg; the Edinburgh Academy; University of Edinburgh. Joined Scottish Office in 1973; Private Secretary to Permanent Under Secretary of State, 1976-78;

Principal Private Secretary to successive Secretaries of State, 1995-97; Head of Constitution and Legal Services Group, Scottish Executive, 2004-05. Address: (b.) 140 Causewayside, Edinburgh EH9 1PR; T.-0131 668 2131; e-mail: michael.lugton@scotlawcom.gov.uk

Lumsden of Cushnie, David Gordon Allen d'Aldecamb, MA (Cantab), FSA (Scot). Garioch Pursuivant of Arms, since 1986; Chairman, Castles of Scotland Preservation Trust, since 1985; President, 1745 Association, since 1991; b. 25.5.33, Quetta, Baluchistan, Empire of India. Educ. Allhallows, Devon; Bedford School; Jesus College, Cambridge. London Scottish TA; Executive, British American Tobacco, 1959-82; Director: Heritage Porcelain Ltd., Heritage Recordings Ltd.; Member of Lloyds, 1985-2001; Co-Founder, Scottish Historic Organs Trust, 1991; Member, Council, Royal Stuart Society; Convenor, Monarchist League of Scotland, 1993; Knight of Malta Honour and Devotion, 1980; Chancellor, Order of the Crown of Stuart, 1986; Knight of Justice Sacred Military Constantinian Order of St George, 1978; Knight Order of St. Maurice and St. Lazarus, 1999; Patron, Aboyne Highland Games, since 1999; Freedom of the City of London, 2006; Liverymen of The Worshipful Company of Spectacle Makers, 2006. Recreations: polo; rowing; sailing; architectural history; Scottish history; heraldry. Address: Hamilton House, West Loan, Prestonpans EH32 9JY; T.-01875 813681; e-mail: lumcush@hotmail.com

Lumsden, James Alexander, MBE, TD, MA, LLB, DL. Director, Bank of Scotland, 1958-85; Director, Scottish Provident Institution, 1968-85; b. 24.1.15, Arden, Dunbartonshire; m., Sheila Cross; 3 s. Educ. Cargilfield School, Edinburgh; Rugby School; Corpus Christi College, Cambridge; Glasgow University. Territorial Army, 1937-46; Partner, Maclay Murray & Spens, Solicitors, Glasgow and Edinburgh, 1947-82; Director of certain Investment Trust companies managed by Murray Johnstone Ltd., 1967-85; Director, Burmah Oil, 1957-76; Member, Queen's Body Guard for Scotland (Royal Company of Archers), 1963; Commissioner of Income Tax, County of Dumbarton, 1964-90; Member, Committee on Company Law, 1960-62; Fellow, Law Society of Scotland. Address: (h.) Arden-Beag, 7 Station Road, Craigendoran, Helensburgh G84 7BG; T.-01436 676204.

Lumsden, Professor Keith Grant, MA, PhD, FRSE. Professor and Director, Edinburgh Business School, Heriot-Watt University; b. 7.1.35, Bathgate; m., Jean Baillie MacDonald; 1 s. Educ. Bathgate Academy; Edinburgh University; Stanford University, California. Instructor, Department of Economics, then Assistant Professor, Graduate School of Business, Stanford University, 1960-67; Research Associate, Stanford Research Institute, 1965-71; Director, Stanford University Conference: NDTE, 1966, RREE, 1968; Associate Professor, Graduate School of Business, Stanford University, 1968-75; Visiting Professor of Economics, Heriot-Watt University, 1969-70; Director: Economics Education Project, 1969-74, Behavioral Research Laboratories, 1970-72, Capital Preservation Fund Inc., 1971-75, Nielsen Engineering Research Inc., 1972-75; Member, American Economic Association Committee on Economic Education, 1978-81; Academic Director, Sea Transport Executive Programme (STEP), since 1979; Professor of Economics, Advanced Management College, Stanford University, since 1971; Affiliate Professor of Economics, INSEAD, France; Member: Economics Education 14-16 Project, Manchester University, Advisory Council, David Hume Institute, 1984-99, Board of Directors, Hewlett Packard Ltd., 1982-92; Henry Villard Award, Economics America, 1994. Publications: The Free Enterprise System, 1963; The Gross National Product, 1964; International Trade, 1965; Microeconomics: A

Programmed Book, 1966; Macroeconomics: A Programmed Book, 1966; New Developments in the Teaching of Economics (Editor), 1967; Excess Demand and Excess Supply in World Tramp Shipping Markets, 1968; Recent Research in Economics Education (Editor), 1970; Basic Economics: Theory and Cases, 1973; Efficiency in Universities: The La Paz Papers (Editor), 1974; Economics Education in the United Kingdom, 1980; Economics: a distance learning study programme, 1991. Recreations: tennis; deep sea sports fishing. Address: (h.) 40 Lauder Road, Edinburgh EH9 1UE.

Lumsden, Vivien Dale Victoria, DSD, CDS. Journalist and Television and Radio Presenter, since 1984; Director, Prince and Princess of Wales Hospice, Glasgow; Restaurant Critic, Scottish Field; b. 22.11.52, Edinburgh; m., Alan Douglas (qv); 1 s.; 1 d. Educ. James Gillespie's High School for Girls, Edinburgh; RSAMD. Full-time mother, 1975-82; AA Traffic News Reporter, 1982-84; BBC Scotland: Breakfast Newsreader, 1984-85, Reporting Scotland Presenter, 1985-89, Garden Party, 1988; joined Scottish TV as Presenter, Scotland Today, 1989; also presented chat show, Telethon, BAFTA Awards, Business Game, Home Show. Recreations: acting; cooking; writing; wine; food; travel. Address: (b.) Broadcasting Business Ltd, Lochinch House, Dumbreck Road, Glasgow G41 4SN; e-mail: viv.lumsden@ntlworld.com

Lunan, Charles Burnett, MD, FRCOG, FRCS. Consultant Obstetrician, Princess Royal Maternity, Glasgow, 1977-2005; Consultant Gynaecologist, Royal Infirmary, Glasgow, 1977-2005; b. London; m., Helen Russell Ferrie; 2 s.; 1 d. Educ. High School of Glasgow; Glasgow University. Lecturer, Obstetrics and Gynaecology, Aberdeen University, 1973-75; Senior Lecturer, University of Nairobi, 1975-77; WHO Consultant, Family Planning Programme, Bangladesh, 1984-85. Treasurer, 1982-90, Vice-President, 1990-91, President, Royal Medico-Chirurgical Society of Glasgow, 1991-92; Secretary, Glasgow Obstetrical and Gynaecological Society, 1978-82, Vice President, 1998-2002, President, 2002-04. Recreations: gardening; photography; hill-walking. Address: (h.) Newhall Cottage, Kinrossie, Perthshire PH2 6HP.

Lunn, John Alexander, LLB (Hons), DipLP, NP. Partner, Morton Fraser LLP, since 2002, Solicitor, since 1988; b. 23.2.64, Haddington; m., Joan; 2 s. Educ. Knox Academy, Haddington; Edinburgh University. Traineeship with East Lothian District Council, 1986-88. SRU Accredited Rugby Coach; coaching North Berwick Mini RFC. Recreations: karate; skiing. Address: (b.) 30-31 Queen Street, Edinburgh EH2 1JX; T.-0131 247 1066.
E-mail: john.lunn@morton-fraser.com

Lunney, James Thomas, LLB, NP. District Chairman, The Appeals Service, since 1999; Full-time Chairman, Independent Tribunal Service, 1995-99; b. 24.7.54, Glasgow; m., Patricia Anne Lunney, BDS, BA; 2 d. Educ. St. Mirin's Academy, Paisley; Strathclyde University. Apprentice to Pattison & Sim, Solicitors, Paisley, 1979-81; Assistant, 1981-83, Partner, 1983-95; part-time Chairman, Independent Tribunal Service, 1992-95. Recreations: golf; reading; architecture; skiing; motor-cycling. Address: (b.) Wellington House, 134-136 Wellington Street, Glasgow G2 2XL.

Luscombe, Rt. Rev. Lawrence Edward, ChStJ, MA, MPhil, PhD, LLD, DLitt, CA, FRSA, FSA Scot. Primus of the Scottish Episcopal Church, 1985-90, and Bishop of Brechin, 1975-90; a Trustee of the Scottish Episcopal Church, since 1985; b. 10.11.24; m., Dr. Doris Morgan (deceased); 1 d. Educ. Kelham College; King's College, London; Dundee University. Indian Army, 1942-47; Major; Chartered Accountant, 1952; Partner, Galbraith Dunlop & Co. (later Watson and Galbraith), CA, 1953-63; Curate, St. Margaret's, Glasgow, 1963-66; Rector, St. Barnabas', Paisley, 1966-71; Provost, St. Paul's Cathedral, Dundee, 1971-75. Honorary Canon, Trinity Cathedral, Davenport, Iowa, since 1983; Member, Education Committee, Renfrew County Council, 1967-71; Chairman, Governing Body: Glenalmond College, 1986-94; President, Old Glenalmond Club, 1998-2007; Chairman, Governing Body, Edinburgh Theological College, 1985-90; Governor: Lathallan School, 1982-2000, Dundee College of Education, 1982-87; Chairman, Inter-Anglican Finance Committee, 1989-93; Member, Tayside Health Board, 1989-93; Honorary Research Fellow, Dundee University, since 1993; Member, Court of Corporation of the Sons of the Clergy, 1985-99. Address: (h.) Woodville, Kirkton of Tealing, by Dundee DD4 0RD; T.-01382 380331.

Lusk, Christine (Chris), BSc (Edin), CQSW, DipSW, PTA. Director of Student Services, University of St. Andrews, since 2006; b. 04.06.59, Glasgow; m., Andy Neil; 2 s.; 2 d. Educ. Madras College; Universities of Edinburgh and Dundee. Social Worker in Childcare, NAI Investigations and Homefinding work, 1981-92; University of St. Andrews: Welfare Adviser, Students' Association, 1992-97, Assistant Hebdomadar, 1997-2001, Director of Student Support, 2001-06. Currently completing a PhD (2008) on the cultural interaction between the diverse student and ancient higher education. Recreations: hill-walking; music; cinema; running; family. Address: (b.) Student Experience Office, 101A North Street, St. Andrews; T.-01334-462020; e-mail: clusk@st-ands.ac.uk

Lyall, Professor Fiona, BSc, PhD, MBA, MRCPath. Professor of Maternal and Fetal Health, Yorkhill Hospital, Glasgow, since 2003; b. Johnstone. Educ. Uddingston Grammar Secondary School; University of Glasgow. British Heart Foundation Fellow, MRC Blood Pressure Unit, Glasgow, 1990-92; Obstetrics and Gynaecology, University of Glasgow: Lecturer, 1992-97, Senior Lecturer, 1997-2001, Reader, 2001-02. Member of Medical Advisory Committee for "Tommys The Baby Charity". Publicaton: Pre-Eclampsia: Etiology and Clinical Practice, 2007. Recreations: aerobics instructor; ski instructor; own horse and dogs. Address: (b.) Institute of Medical Genetics, Yorkhill, Glasgow G3 8SJ; T.-0141 201 0657; e-mail: f.lyall@udcf.gla.ac.uk

Lyall, Fiona Jane, MBE, DL, MB, ChB, DPH. Family Doctor, Laurencekirk, since 1959; Director, Grampian Television PLC, since 1980; Non-Executive Director: Aberdeen Royal Hospitals NHS Trust, since 1992, Templehill Community Council, since 1990; Deputy Lieutenant, Kincardineshire, since 1985; b. 13.4.31, Inverness; m., Dr. Alan Richards Lyall; 1 s.; 1 d. Educ. Inverness Royal Academy; Aberdeen University. Former Member, Laurencekirk Burgh Council; former Kincardine County and Grampian Regional Councillor; Member: Grampian Health Board, 1974, and Kincardine & Deeside Health Council, 1974, Children's Panel Advisory Committee, 1974, Grampian Valuation Appeals Committee, Prince's and Royal Jubilee Trust for Grampian; Treasurer, Action Research for Crippled Child; Trustee, Kincardineshire Silver Jubilee Trust, since 1985. Recreations: skiing; riding; golf. Address: Melrose Bank, Laurencekirk AB30 1FJ; T.-01561 377220; e-mail: alanlyall@aol.com

Lyall, Ian James Graeme, MA, LLB, NP. Partner (Property Finance), McGrigors, Solicitors, Edinburgh, since 1987; b. 25.4.55, Glasgow; m., Pamela Lyall (nee Coats); 2 s.; 2 d. Educ. Greenock Academy; Aberdeen University. McGrigors, Glasgow Office, Trainee/Apprentice, 1978-80;

Assistant Solicitor: McGrigors, Glasgow Office, 1980-84, Baker & McKenzie, London, 1984-86; Head of Real Estate, McGrigors, 1997-2000. Deputy Chairman, EMMS Nazareth (Scottish Charity owning and operating a hospital and school of nursing in Nazareth, Israel). Recreations: skiing; church; motorcycling; family. Address: (h.) 16 Nile Grove, Morningside, Edinburgh EH10 4RF, T.-0131 777 7033; e-mail: ian.lyall@mcgrigors.com

Lyall, Michael Hodge, MB, ChB, ChM, FRCSEdin. Consultant Surgeon, Tayside University Hospitals NHS Trust, 1975-2006, Medical Director, 2001-06; Honorary Senior Lecturer, Dundee University, since 1975; b. 5.12.41, Methilhill, Fife; m., Catherine B. Jarvie; 3 s. Educ. Buckhaven High School; St. Andrews University. Past President, North Fife Rotary Club; Paul Harris Fellow. Recreation: digital photography. Address: 1 Vernonholme, Riverside Drive, Dundee DD2 1QJ.

Lyddon, William Derek Collier, CB, DLitt, BA (Arch), DipTP, FRSGS, FRTPI (Rtd). B. 17.11.25, Loughton, Essex; m., Marian Louise Kaye Charlesworth; 2 d. Educ. Wrekin College; University College, London. Depute Chief Architect Planner, Cumbernauld Development Corporation; Chief Architect Planner, Skelmersdale Development Corporation; Chief Planner, Scottish Development Department, 1967-85. President, International Society of City and Regional Planners, 1981-84; Chairman, The Planning Exchange, 1992-95; Acting Chairman, Edinburgh Old Town Renewal Trust, 1997-99; Vice Chairman, Edinburgh World Heritage Trust, 1999-2004. Address: (h.) 31 Blackford Road, Edinburgh EH9 2DT; T.-0131-667 2266.

Lyell, 3rd Baron (Charles Lyell), Bt. Elected Member, House of Lords, since 1999; Parliamentary Under-Secretary of State, Northern Ireland Office, 1984-89; b. 27.3.39. Educ. Eton; Christ Church, Oxford. Scots Guards, 1957-59; CA; Opposition Whip, 1974-79; Government Whip, 1979-84; Member, Queen's Bodyguard for Scotland (Royal Company of Archers); DL, Angus, 1988. Address: (h.) Kinnordy House, Kirriemuir, Angus.

Lyle, David Angus, MA, LLB, NP, SSC, FCIS. Consultant, Solicitor, and Chartered Company Secretary, in private practice, since 1993; b. 7.9.40; m. (1) (1969), Dorothy Ann Clark (marr. diss. 2004); 1 s.; 3 d.; m. (2) (2007), Joyce Simpson (nee Walton). Educ. George Watson's College, Edinburgh; Edinburgh University. Account Executive, Advertising Agencies, London; Indentured, Edinburgh Corporation; Solicitor, Lloyds and Scottish Finance Ltd., Edinburgh; Depute County Clerk, East Lothian County Council; Director of Administration and Law, Dumfries and Galloway Regional Council; Agency Secretary, Scottish Development Agency; Director/Company Secretary, Scottish Enterprise. Recreations: shooting; golf; bridge. Address: (h.) 56 Strathspey Drive, Grantown-on-Spey, Morayshire PH26 3EY; T.-01479 873814.

Lynch, Professor Michael, MA, PhD, FRHistS, FSAScot. Sir William Fraser Professor of Scottish History, University of Edinburgh, 1992-2005; Chairman, Ancient Monuments Board for Scotland, 1996-2002; President, Society of Antiquaries of Scotland, 1996-99; Trustee, National Museums of Scotland, since 2002; b. 15.6.46, Aberdeen. Educ. Aberdeen Grammar School; University of Aberdeen; University of London. Lecturer, Department of History, University College, Bangor, 1971-79; Department of Scottish History, University of Edinburgh: Lecturer, 1979-88, Senior Lecturer, 1988-92. Chairman, Historical

Association Committee for Scotland, since 1992; Editor, The Innes Review, 1984-92. Publications: Edinburgh and the Reformation, 1981 (SAC Literary Award); The Early Modern Town in Scotland, 1986; The Scottish Medieval Town, 1987; Mary Stewart: Queen in Three Kingdoms, 1988; Scotland: A New History, 1991 (SAC Literary Award); The Reign of James VI, 2000; The Oxford Companion to Scottish History, 2001; Aberdeen before 1800: A New History, 2002; The University of Edinburgh: An Illustrated History, 2003. Address: (b.) Scottish History, University of Edinburgh, 17 Buccleuch Place, Edinburgh EH8 9LN; T.-0131-650 4032.

Lyon, Catherine E., MA, BA, FCS. Bailie, City of Glasgow, 1999-2003; Member, Glasgow City Council, 1995-2003, Conservative Group Leader, 1997-1999; b. Scotland; m., Andrew. Educ. International Christian University. Japan International Cultural Institute; Teacher of English as a Foreign Language; freelance interpreter. Constituency Chairman: Pollok Conservative Association, 1982-86, Govan Conservative Association, 1995-2002; former Strathclyde Regional Councillor and Chairman, Scottish Conservative Councillors Association; Depute Chairman, Tory Reform Group (Scotland), 1996-2004; Member, Strathclyde Fire Board, 1996-2003; Patron, Hutchesons' Hospital, 1996-2003; Trustee, Hutchesons' Educational Trust and Member, Board of Governors, Hutchesons' Grammar School, 1997-2007; Member, Institute of Linguists (Scotland); Ambassador for Girl Guiding (Scotland). Recreations: art; history; music; theatre; literature; antiques; food and wine; gardens; architecture; my animals. Address: (h.) 26A Woodrow Road, Glasgow G41 5PN; T.-0141 427 0040.

Mac/Mc

Recreations: fishing; shooting. Address: (h.) Kilcoy Castle, Muir of Ord, Ross-shire IV6 7RX; T.-01463 871 393.

McAdam, Douglas, BSc. Chief Executive, Scottish Rural Property and Business Association, since 2006; b. 13.10.66, Haddington, East Lothian; m., Diah; 1 d. Educ. George Watsons College; Dollar Academy; St. Andrews University. General Management Career with John Swire & Sons based in the Far East, 1988-98; General Management with Thames Water (running their Scottish based operations), 1998-2006. Recreations: classic cars; mountain biking; field sports. Address: (b.) Stuart House, Eskmills Business Park, Musselburgh.

McAllion, John, MA (Hons). MSP (Labour), Dundee East, 1999-2003; b. 13.2.48, Glasgow; m., Susan Jean; 2 s. Educ. St. Augustine's Secondary, Glasgow; St. Andrews University. Secondary, Dundee, 1973-78, Social Studies, Balgowan List D School, Dundee, 1978-82; Research Assistant to Bob McTaggart, MP, 1982-86; Regional Councillor, 1984-87; Convener, Tayside Regional Council, 1986-87; Member, Scottish Executive, Labour Party, 1986-88; Senior Vice Chairperson, Dundee Labour Party, 1986, 1987; MP (Labour), Dundee East, 1987-2001. Member, Scottish Socialist Party. Recreations: football; reading; music. Address: (h.) 3 Haldane Street, Dundee DD3 0HP; T.-01382 466700.

McAloon, Jim. Operations Director, Scottish Enterprise Dunbartonshire, since 2006. Board Member: West Dunbartonshire Social Inclusion Partnership, East Dunbartonshire Community Planning Forum, East Dunbartonshire Enterprise Trust, Princes Trust, Dunbartonshire. Address: (b.) Spectrum House, Clydebank Business Park, Clydebank, Glasgow G81 2DR.

McAlpine, Joan, MA (Hons). Features Editor and Columnist, Sunday Times Scotland, formerly Assistant Editor; Deputy Editor, The Herald, 2001-06; Editor, Sunday Times Scotland, 2000-01; b. 28.1.64, Gourock; m., Pat Kane (qv) (separated); 2 d. Educ. St. Columba's RC Comprehensive, Greenock; James Watt Further Education College, Greenock; Glasgow University; City University, London. Reporter, Greenock Telegraph, The Scotsman; Reporter, Feature Writer, Columnist, The Scotsman, 1992-95; Feature Writer and Columnist, Daily Record, 1995; Columnist and Feature Writer, then Deputy Editor (News), Sunday Times, 1996-2000. Journalist of the Year, Scottish Press Awards, 1999; Feature Writer of the Year, Scottish Press Awards, 1999. Publication: A Time to Rage (Co-author), 1994. Recreations: family; listening to R&B; visiting Islay; Scotland. Address: (b.) Sunday Times Scotland, 142 Portman Street, Kinning Park, Glasgow G41 1EJ.

McAndrew, Nicolas, CA. Chairman: Martin Currie Enhanced Income Investment Trust PLC, 1998-2005, Beauly District Fishery Board, since 2003; Director, Liverpool Victoria Friendly Society, 1996-2005; b. 9.12.34, London; 2 s.; 1 d. Educ. Winchester College. National Service (The Black Watch) commission, 1953-55; articled clerk, Peat Marwick Mitchell, 1955-61; qualified CA, 1961; S.G. Warburg & Co. Ltd., Merchant Bankers, 1962-78; became Chairman, Warburg Investment Management Ltd., and Director, Mercury Securities Ltd.; Managing Director, N.M. Rothschild & Sons Ltd., Merchant Bankers, 1979-88; Chairman: Murray Johnstone Ltd., 1992-99, Derby Trust PLC, 1999-2003. Master, Worshipful Company of Grocers, 1978-79; Board Member: Highlands and Islands Enterprise, 1993-97, North of Scotland Water Authority, 1995-2002.

McAra-McWilliam, Professor Irene, MA, FRSA. Professor of Design, Head of School of Design, The Glasgow School of Art, since 2005; Consultant to industry and government, since 2001; b. 4.2.54, Dufftown; m., Angus McAra. Educ. Mortlach Senior Secondary School; University of Aberdeen. Director of Design Research, Philips Electronics, The Netherlands, 1992-2001; Advisor to European Commission, 1995-2001; Professor of Design Research, University of Technology, Eindhoven, The Netherlands, 2003-05; Professor of Interaction Design and Head of Department, Royal College of Art, London, 2001-04. FRSA; FRCA. Address: (b.) The Glasgow School of Art, 167 Renfrew Street, Glasgow G3 6RQ; T.-0141-353-4589; e-mail: i.mcara-mcwilliam@gsa.ac.uk

McArdle, David Anthony, LLB, PhD. Senior Lecturer, School of Law, Stirling University, since 2005; b. 03.09.67, Chesterfield; partner, Charity Smith; 2 s.; 1 d. Educ. Chesterfield School; University of Wales Aberystwyth; Manchester Metropolitan University. Research Assistant, Manchester Metropolitant University, 1993-97; Research Fellow, De Montfort, Middlesex University, 1997-2001; Lecturer, Robert Gordon University, 2002-05. Several books and numerous articles on legal issues in sport; advice work for various sports bodies and local authorities. Recreations: running; cycling; hillwalking. Address: (b.) School of Law, University of Stirling, Stirling FK9 4LA; T.-01786 467285; e-mail: d.a.mcardle@stir.ac.uk

McArdle, Harry John, BSc (Hons), PhD, MIBiol, CBiol, FFCS. Deputy Director (Science), Rowett Research Institute, since 1997; Honorary Professor, in Biomedical Sciences, University of Aberdeen, since 2000; b. 4.1.53, Glasgow; m., Karen Ann. Educ. St. Augustine School, Edinburgh; St. Andrews University. Raines Research Fellow, University of Western Australia; Senior Scientist, Murdoch Institute for Research into Birth Defects, Melbourne, Australia, 1985-90; Lecturer/Senior Lecturer, Department of Child Health, University of Dundee, 1990-96. Recreations: hillwalking; horse riding; skiing. Address: (b.) Rowett Research Institute, Bucksburn, Aberdeen AB21 9SB; T.-01224 716628; e-mail: hjm@rowett.ac.uk

McArdle, Karen Ann, MA (Hons), MEd. Senior Lecturer, University of Aberdeen, since 2003; b. 16.03.58, Leeds; m., Harry John McArdle. Educ. Harrogate Grammar School; St. Andrews University; La Trobe University. Training and Development Officer, RYMC Training and Development Service, 1981-84; University of Western Australia: Graduate Research Assistant, 1984-85, Extension Officer, 1985-86; Manager, Special Projects, Melbourne College of Textiles, 1986-89; Senior Research Consultant, State Training Board, Australia, 1989-90; Executive Officer, Fife Regional Council, 1990-94; Northern College of Education: Lecturer, 1994-96, Programme Director, 1996-2003. Recreations: horse riding; hillwalking; reading. Address: (b.) University of Aberdeen, King's College Campus, Aberdeen AB24 5UA; T.-01224 274654; e-mail: k.a.mcardle@abdn.ac.uk

Macarthur, Edith, MBE. Actress; b. Ardrossan, Ayrshire. Educ. Ardrossan Academy. Began career, 1948, with Wilson Barrett Company, then Perth Repertory, Gateway Theatre Company, Citizens' Theatre, Glasgow, Bristol Old Vic, Royal Shakespeare Company, Ochtertyre Theatre, Royal Lyceum Theatre Company, West End; television work includes The Borderers, Sunset Song, Weir of Hermiston, Sutherland's Law, Take the High Road, Dr.

Finlay, Hamish Macbeth; Taggart; Golden Wedding; nominated for Scottish BAFTA award in The Long Roads, 1993; recent stage appearances: solo-performance play, Marie of Scotland, Jamie the Saxt and The Thrie Estates for the Scottish Theatre Company at Edinburgh Festivals and Warsaw International Festival, 1986, Judith Bliss in Hay Fever, Royal Lyceum Theatre, 1987, Charley's Aunt, Death of a Salesman, Royal Lyceum, 1988, Daphne Laureola, Pygmalion, Pride and Prejudice, Pitlochry Festival Theatre, 1988; The Cherry Orchard, Royal Lyceum, 1989; The Cherry Orchard, The Circle, Arsenic and Old Lace, Pitlochry, 1990; Driving Miss Daisy, Perth, 1991; Cinderella, Glasgow and Edinburgh, 1990, 1991; Good, Glasgow and Edinburgh, 1992; Long Day's Journey into Night, Dundee, 1994 (TMA/Martini Best Actress nomination); The Prime of Miss Jean Brodie, London, 1994-95; The Flou'ers o' Edinburgh; On Golden Pond; Long Day's Journey into Night, Pitlochry Festival Theatre, and tour, 1996; Widows, Traverse Theatre, and tour, 1997. Recreations: music; books.

McArthur, George, OBE. Convener, Edinburgh Peace and Justice Resource Centre, 1992-2002; Chairman, Scottish Churches Housing Agency, 1993-2000; b. 22.7.30, Edinburgh; m., Margaret Moffat Wilson; 1 s.; 1 d. Educ. Leith Academy. Missionary (youth worker), Church of Scotland, South Africa, 1956-71; Official Correspondent for Church of Scotland's List D schools, 1972-77; involved in formation of Kirk Care Housing Association Ltd., 1973, becoming its first Director, 1978, retired, 1992. Chairman, Council, Scottish Federation of Housing Associations, 1984-86; a Vice-President, Churches National Housing Coalition, 1995. Recreations: golf; supporting Hibernian F.C.; walking; reading. Address: (h.) 3 Craigcrook Road, Edinburgh EH4 3NQ; T.-0131-477 0312.

McArthur, Liam, MA (Hons). MSP (Liberal Democrat), Orkney, since 2007; b. 8.8.67; m.; 2 s. Educ. Kirkwall Grammar School, Orkney; Edinburgh University. Researcher, Jim Wallace MP, House of Commons, 1990-92; Trainee, European Commission (External Affairs directorate), 1992-93; Account Executive, various EU public affairs consultancies, 1993-96; Associate Director, APCO and APCO Europe, 1996-2002; Special Adviser to Deputy First Minister, Jim Wallace MSP, 2002-05; Director, Greenhaus communications, 2005-06; self employed political consultant, 2006-07. Address: (b.) Scottish Parliament, Edinburgh EH99 1SP; T.-0131 348 5815; Constituency Office: 31 Broad Street, Kirkwall, Orkney KW15 1DH; T.-01595 690044; e-mail: liam.mcarthur.msp@scottish.parliament.uk

MacAskill, Kenny, LLB (Hons). MSP (SNP), Lothians, since 1999; Cabinet Secretary for Justice, since 2007; Shadow Justice Minister, 2004-07; b. 1958, Edinburgh; m.; 2 s. Educ. Linlithgow Academy; Edinburgh University. Solicitor. Address: (b.) Scottish Parliament, Edinburgh EH99 1SP; T.-0131-348 5012.
E-mail: kenny.macaskill.msp@scottish.parliament.uk

McAteer, Charles, MA, BA (Hons). Rector, Dumfries Academy, since 1995; Director, Scottish Parent Teacher Council; Member, UCAS Standing Committee; Immediate Past President, Headteachers' Association of Scotland; b. 5.5.50, Glasgow; m., Anne Neil; 1 s.; 3 d. Educ. Our Lady's High School, Motherwell; Edinburgh University; Moray House College; Strathclyde University. Teacher of English, St. Augustine's High School, Edinburgh, 1972-74; Principal Teacher of English, St. Kentigern's Academy, W. Lothian, 1974-83; Depute Rector, Moffat Academy, 1983-88; Rector, Dalbeattie High School, 1988-95. Recreations:

indoor football; reading; walking; film; family; travel; cooking; good food and wine. Address: (b.) Dumfries Academy, Academy Street, Dumfries, DG1 1DD; T.-01387 252846; e-mail: mcateerc@alg.dumgal.org.uk

McAteer, Dympna, MB, BCh, BAO, FRCP, MRad, FRCR. Consultant Radiologist, since 1999; b. 7.11.65, Letterkenny. Educ. Loreto College, Milford; Trinity College Dublin. Junior House Officer, Altnagelvin Hospital, Derry, 1989-90; Medical Senior House Officer, Royal Victoria Hospital, Belfast, 1990-92; Medical Registrar, Belfast City and Whiteabbey Hospitals, 1992-94; Radiology Registrar, Aberdeen Royal Infirmary, 1994-99. Recreations: squash; running; skiing. Address: Department of Radiology, Aberdeen Royal Infirmary, Foresterhill, Aberdeen AB25 2ZN; T.-01224 681818, Ext. 52178; e-mail: d.mcateer@abdn.ac.uk

Macaulay of Bragar, Rt. Hon. Lord (Donald Macaulay), QC; b. 1933. Advocate, 1963; QC (Scot), 1975; Life Peer, since 1989. Address: (b.) House of Lords, London SW1A 0PW.

MacAulay, Professor Emeritus Donald, MA, BA, DipGenLing. Professor of Celtic, Glasgow University, 1991-96; b. 21.5.30, Isle of Lewis; m., Ella Murray Sangster; 1 s.; 1 d. Educ. Nicolson Institute, Stornoway; Aberdeen University; Cambridge University. Lecturer in English Language, Edinburgh University, 1957-60; Lecturer in Irish and Scottish Gaelic, Trinity College, Dublin, 1960-63; Lecturer in Applied Linguistics, Edinburgh University, 1963-67; Senior Lecturer in Celtic, then Reader in Celtic, Aberdeen University, 1967-91. Publications: Seobhrach as a' Chlaich; Nua-bhardachd Ghaidhlig; The Celtic Languages. Recreations: poetry; living. Address: (b.) 5 Meggetland Terrace, Edinburgh EH14 1AN; T.-0131-443 1823.

MacAulay, Fred. Comedian; Television and Radio Presenter. Presenter, The Fred MacAulay Show, BBC Radio Scotland; television includes: Presenter, Life According to Fred; Co-host, New Year Live; Co-host, series and World Cup special, McCoist and MacAulay; Co-host, The 11 O'Clock Show; Team Captain, The Best Show in the World...Probably; Team Captain, Bring Me the Head of Light Entertainment; Team Captain, A Game of Two Halves; Presenter, Comedy Rules; Presenter, Now You See It; theatre: Bad and Crazy in a Jam.

Macaulay, Rev. Glen Donald, BD. Parish Minister, Falkirk: Erskine Parish Church, since 1999; b. 9.1.52, Musselburgh; m., Janet D. McDougall; 1 s.; 1 d. Educ. Preston Lodge High School, Prestonpans; Edinburgh University. Scottish Office, 1965-94: various posts held in Scottish Education Department and Scottish Courts Administration; Secretary, Scottish Fire Services Training School, Industry Department for Scotland and Staff Training and Development Manager for General Registrar Office. Member, Church of Scotland Panel on Worship. Recreations: music and choirs. Address: Erskine Manse, Burnbrae Road, Falkirk FK1 5SD; T.-01324 623701.

McAveety, Frank (Francis), BA (Hons). MSP (Labour and Co-Op.), Glasgow Shettleston, since 1999; Minister of Tourism, Culture and Sport, 2003-04; Deputy Minister of Health and Community Care, 2002-03; Deputy Minister for Local Government, 1999-2000; b. 27.7.62, Glasgow; m., Anita Mitchell; 1 s.; 1 d. Educ. All Saints Secondary School, Glasgow; Strathclyde University; St. Andrew's College, Bearsden. Councillor, Glasgow District Council,

1988-96; Leader, Glasgow City Council, 1997-99, Councillor, 1995-99. Member, Board, Arches Theatre Company; Chairperson, Glasgow North Co-operative Party. Recreations: labour history; record collecting; football. Address: (h.) 156 Glenbuck Avenue, Robroyston, Glasgow G33 1LW; T.-0141-558 1341.

McAvoy, Rt. Hon. Thomas McLaughlin, PC. Government Whip, Comptroller of Her Majesty's Household, since 1997; MP (Labour and Co-operative), Glasgow Rutherglen, since 1987; b. 14.12.43, Rutherglen; m., Eleanor Kerr; 4 s. Member, Strathclyde Regional Council, 1982-87; Opposition Whip, 1990-93. Address: (b.) House of Commons, London SW1A 0AA.

McBryde, Professor William Wilson, LLB, PhD, LLD, FRSE. Professor of Commercial Law, Edinburgh University, 1999-2005; b. 6.7.45, Perth; 1 s; 2 d. Educ. Perth Academy; Edinburgh University. Apprentice and Assistant, Morton, Smart, Macdonald & Milligan, WS, Edinburgh, 1967-70; Court Procurator, Biggart, Lumsden & Co., Glasgow, 1970-72; Lecturer in Private Law, Glasgow University, 1972-76; Member, Scottish Law Commission Working Party on Contract Law, 1975-2000; Senior Lecturer in Private Law, Aberdeen University, 1976-87; Professor of Scots Law, Dundee University, 1987-99 (Deputy and Vice Principal, 1991-94); Visiting Professor, L'Université de Paris V, 2000-05; Van der Grinten Professor of Commercial Law, University of Nijmegen, 2002-07. Specialist Parliamentary Adviser to House of Lords Select Committee on the European Communities, 1980-83; Member: Scottish Consumer Council, 1984-87, Scottish Advisory Committee on Arbitration, since 1986, Member, DTI Working Party on Rights in Security over Moveables, since 1994, Member, International Working Group on Principles of Insolvency Law, since 2000; Director, Scottish Universities' Law Institute, 1989-95; Honorary Sheriff, Tayside, Central and Fife, at Dundee, since 1991. Recreations: walking; photography. Address: (b.) Faculty of Law, University of Edinburgh, Old College, South Bridge, Edinburgh EH8 9YL.

McCabe, Thomas. MSP (Labour), Hamilton South, since 1999; former Minister for Finance and Public Service Reform, Scottish Executive; former Deputy Health Minister and Minister for Parliament; b. 28.4.54, Hamilton. Educ. St. Martin's Secondary; Bell College of Technology. Senior Shop Steward, Hoover Ltd., 1974-93; Welfare Rights Officer, 1993-98; Leader, Hamilton District Council, 1992-96; Leader, South Lanarkshire Council, 1995-99; Vice-Convener, Strathclyde Joint Police Board, 1995-99; Member: Lanarkshire Development Agency Board, 1995-99, Executive, Scottish Labour Party, 1991-2001. Recreations: walking; reading; cinema; golf. Address: (b.) Scottish Parliament, Edinburgh EH99 1SP; T.-0131-348 5830.

McCafferty, Rev. Allan, BSc, BD (Hons). Minister, Kirkwall East Church, since 1993; b. 19.1.67, Motherwell. Educ. Garrion Academy, Wishaw; Glasgow University; Edinburgh University. Probationer Minister, Holy Trinity Church, Bridge of Allan, 1991-93. Recreations: choral singing; hill-walking; bowling. Address: East Church Manse, Thoms Street, Kirkwall KW15 1PF; T.-01856 875469.

McCafferty, James Patrick, BSc, CEng, FICE, FIStructE, FIHT, FHKIE, MCIArb, FConsE. Director, Scott Wilson Scotland, 1987-2007, Managing Director Scotland and Main Board Director, Scott Wilson Holdings, 1995-2005, Chairman, SW Scotland and Ireland, 2005-07, now retired; Chairman, Institution of Civil Engineers, Glasgow and West of Scotland Association, 1998/1999; b. 16.8.45, Kirkintilloch; m., Yvonne Muriel Landles; 3 d. Educ. St Ninian's High School, Kirkintilloch; Strathclyde University. Scott Wilson, since 1967; worked on design and construction of Glasgow's urban motorways, then on major projects in Hong Kong, 1976-82; since mid-1980s has been involved in a broad range of major infrastructure projects at home and abroad; Institution of Civil Engineers: Committee Member, 1993-2003, Member of Council, 1999-2003, Representative on Scottish Council Development and Industry Executive, 2001-03; Association of Consulting Engineers: Committee Member, 1994-2003, Hon. Secretary, 1994-98; ACE Representative, Scottish Construction Industry Group, 2001-03; Member, Adjudication Panel, Saltire Society Awards for Civil Engineering, 1993-96; Chairman, ICE Organising Committee, Glasgow City of Architecture and Design '99; Member, Advisory Group for Civil Engineering Degrees, University of Glasgow, 1999-2006; winner of several awards; author of many technical papers. Recreations: historical engineering works; architecture; travel; gardening; flying kites. Address: (b.) Scott Wilson, Citypoint 2, 25 Tyndrum Street, Glasgow G4 0JY.
E-mail: jp.mccafferty@btinternet.com

McCaig, Professor Colin Darnley, BSc, PhD, FRSE. Regius Professor of Physiology, University of Aberdeen, since 2002, Head of School of Medical Sciences, since 2003; b. 26.6.53, Galashiels; 1 s.; 2 d. Educ. The High School of Glasgow; University of Edinburgh; Glasgow University. Beit Memorial Fellow, University of Edinburgh, 1983-86; Wellcome University Award Lecturer, University of Aberdeen, 1988-2002. Address: (b.) Institute of Medical Sciences, University of Aberdeen, Aberdeen AB25 2ZD; e-mail: c.mccaig@abdn.ac.uk

McCall, Professor James, BSc, MEd, PhD, CPsychol, AFBPsS, FRSA. Emeritus Professor, Department of Educational Studies, Strathclyde University; b. 14.7.41, Kilmarnock; m., Mary Elizabeth Stuart Maclean; 3 s. Educ. Kilmarnock Academy; Glasgow University; Aberdeen University; Jordanhill College of Education. Teacher of Science, Hillhead High School, Glasgow; Principal Teacher of Physics, Queen's Park Secondary School, Glasgow; Lecturer in Educational Psychology, Aberdeen College of Education; Jordanhill College of Education: Head, Psychology Department, Vice Principal, 1983-92, Acting Principal, 1992-93, Dean, Faculty of Education, 1993-97; Member: Board of Governors, Glasgow School of Art, 1986-98, CNAA Committee on Teacher Education, 1989-92, General Teaching Council for Scotland, 1992-97; Editor, European Journal of Teacher Education, 2002-06. Publications: Techniques for the Assessment of Practical Skills in Foundation Science, 1983; Techniques for Assessing Process Skills in Practical Science, 1988; Teacher Education in Europe, 1990; How to assess open-ended practical investigations in Biology, Chemistry and Physics, 1991; Partnership and Co-operation in Teacher Education, 1997. Recreations: bridge; golf. Address: (b.) Jordanhill Campus, Strathclyde University, Southbrae Drive, Glasgow G13 1PP; T.-0141-950 3366.

McCall, Kathleen Mary, DL, LRAM. Deputy Lieutenant for Borders Region, District of Tweeddale, since 1988; Patron, Borders Branch, British Red Cross Society, since 1998; b. 20.2.33, Karachi; m., J.A.G. McCall, CMG. Educ. Calder Girls' School, Seascale; Royal Scottish Academy of Music and Drama. Held various teaching posts; voluntary offices with Red Cross in Nigeria. West Linton Citizen of the Year, 2001. Recreations: music; walking; the arts.

Address: (h.) Burnside, West Linton EH46 7EW; T.-01968 660488.

McCall Smith, Professor Alexander, CBE, LLB, PhD, FRSE, FRCP(E)(Hon), DIuris (hc), DLitt (hc), LLD (hc), DSc (hc), LittD (hc). Professor Emeritus, Faculty of Law, Edinburgh University; Author; Member, International Bioethics Commission, UNESCO, 1998-2004; Vice Chairman, Human Genetics Commission, 2000-04; b. 24.8.48, Zimbabwe; m., Dr. Elizabeth Parry; 2 d. Publications: (non-fiction): Law and Medical Ethics (Co-Author); Butterworth's Medico-Legal Encyclopaedia (Co-Author); Scots Criminal Law (Co-Author); The Duty to Rescue (Co-Author); The Criminal Law of Botswana; Forensic Aspects of Sleep (Co-Author); Errors, Medicine and the Law (Co-Author); Justice and the Prosecution of Old Crimes (Co-Author); fiction: Children of Wax; Heavenly Date; The No. 1 Ladies' Detective Agency; Tears of the Giraffe; Morality for Beautiful Girls; The Kalahari Typing School for Men; The Full Cupboard of Life; In The Company of Cheerful Ladies (Saga Prize for wit, 2003); (Portuguese Irregular Verbs; The Finer Points of Sausage Dogs; At the Villa of Reduced Circumstances; The Sunday Philosophy Club; The Girl who Married a Lion; 44, Scotland Street; Friends, Lovers, Chocolate; Espresso Tales; The Right Attitude to Rain; Dream Angus; The Good Husband of Zebra Drive; The Careful Use of Compliments; The World According to Bertie; numerous books for children. Author of The Year, 2004, British Book Awards Booksellers' Association Waterstones; Walpole Award for Excellence, 2005. Recreation: wind instruments. Address: (b.) c/o David Higham Associates Ltd, 5-8 Lower John Street, Golden Square, London W1F 9HA.

MacCallum, Emeritus Professor James Richard, BSc, PhD, DSc, CChem, FRSC, FRSE. Professor of Polymer Chemistry, St. Andrews University, now Emeritus Professor (Vice-Principal, 1992-96; Pro-Principal, 1997); b. 3.5.36, Kilmartin; m., Eleanor Margaret Thomson; 2 s.; 1 d. Educ. Dumfries Academy; Glasgow University. Technical Officer, ICI Fibres Division, 1961-62; ICI Research Fellow, Aberdeen University, 1962-63; Lecturer, St. Andrews University, 1964; Dean of Science, 1987; Master, United College, 1988-92; Vice-Principal, 1992-96; Pro-Principal, 1996-97. Recreation: golf. Address: (h.) 9 Cairnsden Gardens, St. Andrews, Fife; T.-01334 473152.

McCann, James Aloysius, MA, LLB. Solicitor and Notary Public; a founding Director, Legal Defence Union in Scotland, 1987, Chairman, since 1990; b. 14.8.39, Glasgow; m., Jane Marlow; 3 s.; 1 d. Educ. St. Mungo's Academy, Glasgow; Glasgow University. Former Member, Legal Aid Central Committee; Dean, Faculty of Dunbartonshire Solicitors, 1986-88; Convenor for Law Society PQLE Advocacy Training Courses, 1983-91; Senior Tutor (Professional Legal Practice), Glasgow University, 1981-91; Member, Law Society of Scotland Legal Aid Committee, 1987-97; Reporter, Scottish Legal Aid Board (Co-opted Member, Criminal Applications Committee, 1987-93); appointed Honorary Sheriff at Dumbarton, 1990; Temporary Sheriff, 1991-99. Recreations: sailing; chess; music; windsurfing; golf. Address: (b.) 499 Kilbowie Road, Clydebank G81 2AX.

McCarter, Ann Iestyn, SRN. Chair, Scottish Redundant Churches Trust, since 2000; Past Convener: Board of Practice and Procedure, and Business Committee, General Assembly of the Church of Scotland; Session Clerk, Newbattle Church, Dalkeith, 1994-2005; b. 9.5.41, Glamorgan, S. Wales; m., Iain McCarter; 1 s.; 3 d. Educ. Cheltenham Ladies' College; Western General Hospital, Edinburgh; Guy's Hospital, London. Staff Nurse/Sister, Roodlands Hospital, Haddington. Church of Scotland: Past Member: Board of Social Responsibility, Assembly Council, Board of National Mission; Member, Special Commission looking at Livingston ecumenical experiment; Past President, Dalkeith Branch, British Red Cross Society (awarded Badge of Honour). Recreations: choral singing; dress-making, sailing; gardening. Address: (h.) 5 Westfield Grove, Eskbank, Dalkeith EH22 3JH; T.-0131-663 3896.

McCarter, Keith Ian. Sculptor; b. 15.3.36; m., Brenda Maude Edith; 1 s.; 1 d. Educ. The Royal High School of Edinburgh; Edinburgh College of Art. National Service, RA, 1954-56; sculptor: primarily involved in architectural and landscaped situations; numerous commissions including: Ordnance Survey HQ Southampton, 1967, Lagos Nigeria, 1974, Wingate Centre City of London, 1980, Goodmans Yard City of London, 1982, 1020 19th Street Washington DC, 1983, American Express Bank City of London, 1984, Guy's Hospital NCC London, 1986, Royal Executive Park NY, 1986, Evelyn Gardens London, 1987, London Docklands 1988, Midland Bank London, 1989, Vogans Mill London, 1989, Moody Gardens Galveston Texas USA (with Sir Geoffrey Jellicoe), Abbey Road London 1991, Monks Cross York, 1992, John Menzies HQ Edinburgh, 1995, Aldermanbury Bradford, 1998, F I Group Edinburgh, 1999; Monks Cross Technology Park, York, 2001; Norfolk & Norwich University Hospital, 2002; works in private collections world-wide. Sir Otto Beit medal RBS, 1993; FRSA 1970; ARBS 1991. Appointed Art Strategy Consultant by NGP for their Edinburgh waterfront development masterplanned by Foster and Partners; exhibits at Cyril Gerber Fine Art Gallery, Glasgow and Open Eye Gallery, Edinburgh. Recreations: music; literature; beachcombing. Clubs: Farmers', Melrose RFC. Address: (h.) 10 Coopersknowe Crescent, Galashiels TD1 2DS; T.-01896 751112; Fax: 01896 759010; e-mail: keith@keith-mccarter.com; web: keith-mccarter.com

McCarthy, James, BSc, FRZSS (Hon). Lecturer and writer; b. 6.5.36, Dundee; m.; 2 s.; 1 d. Educ. Harris Academy, Dundee; Aberdeen University; University of East Africa, Kampala. Military Service, 1954-56 (Royal Marines, commissioned Black Watch, seconded King's African Rifles); Leverhulme Scholar, Makerere College, Kampala, 1959-61; Assistant Conservator of Forests, Tanzania, and Lecturer in Forest Ecology, Forest Training School, 1961-63; Deputy Regional Officer (North England), Nature Conservancy, 1963-69; Deputy Director (Scotland), Nature Conservancy Council, 1975-91; Churchill Fellow, USA, 1976; Nuffield/ Leverhulme Fellow, 1988. Recreation: cross-country skiing. Address: (h.) 6a Ettrick Road, Edinburgh; T.-0131-229 1916; e-mail: jmc36@ukonline.co.uk

McCausland, W. David, BSc (Econ), MSc (Econ), PhD. Senior Lecturer in Economics, University of Aberdeen, since 1995; b. 02.05.69, Sheffield. Educ. University of Hull. Co-Author, Interactyx Live Econ (innovative e-learning software developed in Aboyne); Associate of Higher Education Academy's Economics Network; Member, QAA for Scotland Enhancement Themes Steering Committee for the First Year Experience Theme. Address: (b.) University of Aberdeen Business School, Old Aberdeen AB24 3QY; T.-01224 272180.
E-mail: d.mccausland@abdn.ac.uk

McClatchie, Colin James Stewart, BSc (Econ) (Hons). Chairman, Scottish Opera, since 2008 (Vice-Chairman, 2004-07, Director, since 2003); Chairman, Prescient, since 2007; Non-executive Director: Dunfermline Press Ltd, since 2007, Beattie Communications, since 2007, Scottish

Enterprise, since 2004 (Chairman, Nominations and Remuneration Committees); Governor, St Columbas School, Kilmacolm, since 2007; b. 1.1.49, Belfast; m., Claire McConaghy; 2 d. Educ. Coleraine Academical Institution; Queen's University, Belfast. Senior management positions, Thomson Regional Newspapers, Belfast, Newcastle, Reading, Edinburgh, 1971-84; Circulation/Marketing Director, Scottish Daily Record and Sunday Mail Ltd., 1984-94 (and Managing Director, Maxwell Free Newspapers Ltd., 1990-93); Marketing Consultant, 1995. General Manager, News International Newspapers (Scotland) Ltd., 1995-2004; Managing Director, Scotland & Ireland, News International Newspapers, 2004-07. Life Vice President, Newspaper Press Fund (Chairman, West of Scotland District, 1998-2000); Chairman, Institute of Directors, Scotland, 2002-04 (Chairman, West of Scotland Branch, 2001-02); Director, Scottish Networks International, 2001-03; Director, Scottish Enterprise Glasgow, 2002-04; Chairman, Scottish Society of Epicureans, 2002-04; President, Queens University Association Scotland, 2003-05. Clubs: Saints & Sinners, since 2001, Edinburgh Oyster, since 2003. Recreations: family; golf; opera; theatre.
E-mail: colin@mcclatchie.co.uk

McCleery, Professor Alison, MA, PhD, FRGS. Professor of Social and Cultural Geography, Napier University, Edinburgh, since 1999, Associate Dean (Research Development), since 2006; b. 13.10.53, Edinburgh; m., Professor Alistair McCleery (qv); 3s.; 1d. Educ. George Watson's Ladies College; Mary Erskine School; St Andrews University; Glasgow University. Research Officer/Senior Research Officer, Central Research Unit, Scottish Office, 1978-81; Senior Lecturer, Social Science, Napier University, 1981-97; Reader in Geography, 1997-99; Director of Research for the Faculty of Arts and Social Science, 2004-06; lately Demographic Consultant, Council of Europe and Visiting Research Fellow, Institut National d'Etudes Demographiques, Paris; Sectional Vice-Chair, Royal Scottish Geographical Society; Secretary, International Society for Marginal Regions; Winner, Royal Scottish Geographical Society President's Award, 1996; Editor, Scottish Geographical Journal, 1998-2005; Member, Universities Scotland, Research and Commercialisation Committee and Convenor, Research Training Sub-Committee; Member, International Geographical Union, Commission on Marginality and Globalisation; Public Interest Member, Final (TPE) Examination Board of the Institute of Chartered Accountants of Scotland. Recreations: French language, culture and society; Member, Scottish Chamber Choir, and Treasurer, Friends of the Music, St. Mary's Episcopal Cathedral. Address: (b.) Social Sciences, Craighouse Campus, Napier University, Edinburgh EH10 5LG; T.-0131-455 6002; e-mail: am.mccleery@napier.ac.uk

McClellan, John Forrest, MA, Hon. FDIT; b. 15.8.32, Glasgow; m., Eva Maria Pressel; 3 s.; 1 d. Educ. Aberdeen Grammar School; Aberdeen University. 2nd Lt., Gordon Highlanders and Nigeria Regiment, Royal West African Frontier Force, 1954-56; entered Civil Service, 1956; Assistant Principal, Scottish Office, 1956-59; Private Secretary to Permanent Under Secretary of State, Scottish Office, 1959-60; Principal, Scottish Office, 1960-68; Civil Service Fellow, Glasgow University, 1968-69; Assistant Secretary, Scottish Office, 1969-77; Under Secretary, Scottish Office, 1977-85; Director, Scottish International Education Trust, 1986-2001. Member, Management Committee, Hanover (Scotland) Housing Association, 1986-2007. Publication: Then A Soldier (novel), 1991. Recreations: gardening; walking. Address: (h.) 7 Cumin Place, Edinburgh EH9 2JX; T.-0131 667 8446.

McClelland, John Ferguson, CBE, CIMgt, FRSA, FRSE. Chairman, Scottish Further and Higher Education Council;

Director, Rangers FC PLC; Chairman, Technology Ventures Scotland; Chairman, Public Procurement Reform Board; Chairman, NQ Consulting Ltd.; Vice Chairman, UEFA Club Board and Member, UEFA Club Competitions Committee; b. 27.3.45, Glasgow; m., Alice; 1 d. Educ. North Kelvinside School; Glasgow College. South of Scotland Electricity Board, 1963-68; IBM Corporation, 1968-95: Controller, Greenock Manufacturing, 1977, European Director of Operations, 1980, European Manufacturing Controller, 1983, Director of Manufacturing, Greenock, 1987, Director of UK Manufacturing, 1992, Vice President, Worldwide Manufacturing, 1994; Digital Corporation, 1995-98, V.P. Worldwide Manufacturing; Global Chief Industrial Officer, Philips B.V., 1998-99; 3 Com Corporation, 1999-2003: Senior Vice President, Worldwide Operations, 1999-2001, President, Business Networks Company, 2001-03; former Chairman: Judging Panel, Quality Scotland Excellence Award, Renfrewshire Enterprise Company, Higher Education Funding Council's Quality Assessment Committee, CBI UK Technology and Innovation Committee, Rangers FC PLC. Conducted Review of Public Procurement in Scotland, 2005. Recreations: golf; football.

McClements, David Elliott, LLB (Hons), DipLP. Partner, Russel and Aitken, Solicitors, Denny, since 1998; b. 25.6.67, Kilmarnock; m., Louise; 2 d. Educ. Falkirk High School, University of Edinburgh. Russel and Aitken, Denny, 1990-92, and since 1995; Sandeman and Co., Falkirk, 1992-93; John G. Gray and Co., Edinburgh, 1993-95. Member, Council, Law Society of Scotland; Member, Council, Alzheimer Scotland – Action on Dementia. Publication: Butterworth's Scottish Older Client Law Service (Contributor). Recreations: Round Table; golf; Boys' Brigade. Address: (h.) 10 Fordyce Gardens, Falkirk FK1 5BA.

McClure, J. Derrick, MBE, MA, MLitt. Senior Lecturer (Part-Time), Aberdeen University, since 2007; b. 20.7.44, Ayr; m., Ann Celeste nee Bolinger; 3 s. Educ. Ayr Academy; Glasgow University; Edinburgh University. Lektur in Englische Phonetik, University of Tübingen, Germany, 1968-69; Chargé de Cours in Linguistique, University of Ottawa, Canada, 1970-72; English Department, Aberdeen University: Lecturer, 1972-90, Senior Lecturer, 1990-2006. Chairman, Forum for Research in the Languages of Scotland and Ulster; Member: Scottish Dictionaries Joint Council, Association for Scottish Literary Studies, Language and International Committees, Bibliography of Scottish Literature in Translation Committee. Publications: Why Scots Matters, Language, Poetry and Nationhood (author); Doric. The Dialect of North-East Scotland; numerous articles on Scottish language and literature; translations of gaelic and other poetry. Recreations: native American history; Japanese language and literature; amateur musical theatre. Address: (b.) School of Language and Literature, University of Aberdeen, Old Aberdeen AB24 2UB; T.-01224-272625; e-mail: j.d.mcclure@abdn.ac.uk

McClure, Judith, CBE, MA (Oxon), DPhil, FRSA, FSAScot. Head, St. George's School, Edinburgh, since 1994; Chairman, Scottish Region, 1995-98, and Member, Council, Girls' Schools Association; b. 22.12.45, Stockton; m., Dr. Roger Collins. Educ. Newlands Grammar School, Middlesbrough; Somerville College, Oxford. Sir Maurice Powicke Research Fellow, Lady Margaret Hall, Oxford, 1976-77; Lecturer in Medieval Latin and Medieval History, Liverpool University, 1977-79; Lecturer in History, Oxford University (Jesus, Somerville and Worcester Colleges), 1979-81; Teacher and Head of Department in History and Politics, School of St. Helen & St. Katherine, Abingdon, 1981-84; Assistant Head, Kingswood School, Bath, 1984-

87; Head, Royal School, Bath, 1987-93. Member: Court, University of Bath, 1989-92, General Convocation, Heriot Watt University, since 1994, Court, Heriot Watt University, since 2003, Board of Governors, Clifton Hall School, 1994-99, Governing Body, Scottish Council of Independent Schools, 1995-2007, Management Committee, 1998-2007 (Chairman, Management Committee, 2001-07), Board, Scottish Qualifications Authority, 1999-2000, Board, Merchiston Castle School, 1999-2005, Ministerial Strategy Committee on Continuing Professional Development, 2000-03 (Chairman, Leadership and Management Sub-group, 2001-03); Member, Open University Scottish Advisory Committee (Education), since 2002; Member, Advisory Group for Edinburgh Youth Crime Transitions Study, since 2002; Member, Scottish Executive Education Department Advisory Committee on Continuing Professional Development and of its Leadership sub-group; Trustee, Hopetoun House, 1997-2002; Member, Board, Institute of Science Education Scotland, since 2003; Convener, Scottish Educational Leadership Management and Administration Society, since 2003; Member, Scottish Executive Education Department Advisory Committee on Continuing Potential Development, since 2004; Member, Judicial Studies Committee, since 2006; Member, China Planning Group, Scottish Government, since 2006; Convener, Scotland-China Educational Network, since 2006; Member, Advisory Board, Confucius Institute for Scotland, University of Edinburgh, since 2007. Publication: Bede: The Ecclesiastical History (Co-author), 1994. Recreations: reading; using a computer; travelling. Address: (b.) St. George's School for Girls, Garscube Terrace, Edinburgh EH12 6BG; T.-0131 311 8000.

McClure, Roger Niall, MA, CIPFA, CCMI. Chief Executive, Scottish Further and Higher Education Funding Council, since 2002; b. 28.12.50, Belfast; m., Catherine Lynne Thomas; 4 d. Educ. King Edward VI School, Norwich; Corpus Christi College, Cambridge; Corpus Christi College, Oxford. Auditor, National Audit Office, 1978-84; Senior Consultant, Manager, Deloitte, Haskins & Sells Management Consultancy, 1984-88; seconded as Financial Adviser to the University Grants Committee, 1985-87; Director of Finance: Polytechnics and Colleges Funding Council, 1988-92, Further Education Funding Council, 1992-96; Pro-Rector, The London Institute, 1996-2002. Member of Council: King's College London, 1988-97, Business and Technology Council, 1995-98, City Literary Institute, 1998-2002. Harkness Fellow, Center for Higher Education Studies, University of California, Berkeley, 1990-91; Special Adviser to H of C Education Sub-committee, 1997-98. Recreations: music; sport; current affairs; reading; cinema. Address: (b.) Scottish Funding Council, Donaldson House, 97 Haymarket Terrace, Edinburgh EH12 5HD; T.-0131-313-6505; e-mail: rmcclure@sfc.ac.uk

McCluskey, Baron (John Herbert McCluskey), LLD (Dundee). Former Senator of the College of Justice in Scotland; Life Peer, since 1976; Chair, John Smith Memorial Trust, 1997-2004; b. 12.6.29, Glasgow; m., Ruth Friedland; 2 s.; 1 d. Educ. St. Bede's Grammar School, Manchester; Holy Cross Academy, Edinburgh; Edinburgh University; MA, LLB. Admitted Faculty of Advocates, 1955; Standing Junior Counsel to Ministry of Power (Scotland), 1963; Advocate-Depute, 1964-71; QC (Scot), 1967; Chairman, Medical Appeal Tribunals for Scotland, 1972-74; Sheriff Principal of Dumfries and Galloway, 1973-74; Solicitor General for Scotland, 1974-79; Chairman, Scottish Association for Mental Health, 1985-94; Independent Chairman: Scottish Football League Compensation Tribunal, SFA Appeals Tribunal; Chair, Age Concern (Scotland), 2000-01; Reith Lecturer, BBC, 1986; LLD (Dundee), 1989; Chairman, John Smith Memorial Trust, 1997-2004; Editor, Butterworth's Scottish Criminal

Law and Practice series. Publications: Law, Justice and Democracy, 1987; Criminal Appeals, 1992. Recreations: tennis; pianoforte. Address: (b.) House of Lords, Westminster, London SW1A 0PW.

McCluskey, Mary, DCE. Artistic Director (Chief Executive), Scottish Youth Theatre, since 1992; freelance Theatre Director/Drama Tutor, since 1985; b. 16.9.54, Glasgow. Educ. West Senior High School, Garden City, Michigan, USA; Hamilton College of Education; Royal Scottish Academy of Music and Drama. President, Hamilton College of Education SRC, 1975-76; Teacher, Glenlee Primary, Hamilton, 1976-79; Assistant Stage Manager, Dundee Repertory Theatre, 1980-81; YOP Supervisor, Community Projects Agency (East End), 1981-83; YTS Training Officer, Community Projects Agency (South East), 1983-85; Associate Director, Scottish Youth Theatre, 1989-91; Education Officer, Royal Shakespeare Company, 1991-92. Member, BAFTA. Adapted: Wee MacGreegor, Wee MacGreegor Enlists, Medea, Hamlet, Macbeth, The Glory; Jury's Prize for Direction and Pedagogy, Rainbow Festival, St. Petersburg (for Born Bad). Recreations: theatre; films; books; visiting historic sites. Address: (b.) Scottish Youth Theatre, The Old Sheriff Court, 105 Brunswick Street, Glasgow G1 1TF; T.-0141 552 3988.
E-mail: marymccluskey@scottishyouththeatre.org

McCluskie, John Cameron, LLB, CB, QC. Consultant Parliamentary Counsel to Government of Ireland, since 2006; b. 1.2.46, Glasgow; m., Janis Mary Helen McArthur; 1 s.; 1 d. Educ. Hyndland School, Glasgow; Glasgow University. Apprentice Solicitor, Boyds Glasgow, 1967-69; Assistant Town Clerk, Cumbernauld, 1969-70; Assistant Solicitor, Macdonald Jameson & Morris, Glasgow, 1970-71; Assistant Solicitor, SSEB, 1971-72; Assistant, Deputy, Scottish Parliamentary Counsel and Assistant Legal Secretary to Lord Advocate, 1972-89; First Scottish Parliamentary Counsel and Legal Secretary to Lord Advocate, 1989-99; First Scottish Parliamentary Counsel, Edinburgh, 1999-2006. Recreations: walking dogs; watching mogs; cutting logs. Address: (h.) Law View, Redside Farm Steading, North Berwick; T.-01620 890296.

McCoist, Alistair (Ally) Murdoch, MBE. Assistant Manager, Glasgow Rangers; former footballer: Glasgow Rangers F.C., Kilmarnock F.C.; b. 24.9.62, Bellshill; divorced; 4 s. Educ. Hunter High School. Debut for St. Johnstone aged 16; signed for Sunderland, 1981; joined Rangers, 1983; became club's leading goal-scorer, August 1997 (421 goals); 61 caps for Scotland, since 1986; Member, Scotland squad, 1990 World Cup Finals, 1992 and 1996 European Championships; former contributor to Question of Sport, BBC TV; ITV football pundit. Scottish Sports Personality of the Year, 1992; Scottish Sports Writers' Player of the Year, 1992. Recreations: reading autobiographies; listening to music. Address: (b.) 16 Royal Terrace, Glasgow G3 7NY.

McColgan, Elizabeth. Athlete; b. 24.5.64, Dundee; m., Peter Conor McColgan; 2 s.; 1 d. Educ. University of Alabama. Commonwealth Games Gold medallist (10,000 metres), 1986; Silver medallist, World Cross Country Championships, 1987; Olympic Games Silver medallist (10,000 metres), 1988; Silver medallist, World Indoor Championships, 1989; Gold medallist (10,000 metres) and Bronze medallist (3,000 metres), Commonwealth Games, 1990; World 10,000 Meters Champion (Track), 1991; New York Marathon Winner, 1991; Tokyo Marathon Winner, 1992; London Marathon Winner, 1996; world records: 5,000, 10,000, half marathon on roads; coaches young athletes in Dundee.

McColl, Sheriff Isabella Garden, LLB. Sheriff of Lothian and Borders at Edinburgh, since 2005; b.

7.11.52, Edinburgh; m., Alexander James; 1 s.; 2 d. Educ. James Gillespie's High School, Edinburgh; Edinburgh University. Solicitor, 1975-92; Advocate, 1993-2000; Temporary Sheriff, 1999; Sheriff of Tayside Central and Fife at Dunfermline, 2000-05. Address: (b.) Sheriff's Chambers, Sheriff Court House, 27 Chambers Street, Edinburgh EH1 1LB.

McColl, James Hamilton, MBE, NDH, SDH, SHM, FRAgS, (Hon) FSAC. Freelance Horticulturalist; b. 19.9.35, Kilmarnock; m., Billie; 1 s.; 1 d. Educ. Kilmarnock Academy; West of Scotland Agricultural College. Staff Member, WSAC, Auchincruive, Ayr, 1956-59; Assistant Head Gardener, Reading University Botanic Garden, 1959-61; Horticultural Adviser/Lecturer, Shropshire Education Authority, 1961-67; Horticultural Adviser: MAFF, Leicestershire, Northants and Rutland, 1967-73; North of Scotland College of Agriculture, 1973-78; former PRO, Morrison Bowmore Distillers Ltd.; Co-Presenter, The Beechgrove Garden, BBC TV Scotland, 1978-89, since 1994; Chairman, Gardening Scotland, since 2005; Board Member, The Calyx. Recreations: golf; music; rugby. Address: (h.) Ayrshire House, Oldmeldrum, Aberdeenshire; T.-01651 873955.

McComb, Professor (William) David, BSc, MSc, PhD. Emeritus Professor of Physics, Edinburgh University, since 2006; awarded Leverhulme Emeritus Fellowship, 2006; b. 31.10.40, Belfast; m., Doyleen M. McLeod; 3 d. Educ. Methodist College, Belfast; Queens University, Belfast; Manchester University. Senior Scientific Officer, Theoretical Physics Division, AERE, Harwell; Edinburgh University: Lecturer in Engineering Science, Lecturer in Physics, Reader in Physics, Professor of Statistical Physics. Guest Professor, The Technical University of Delft, 1997; Visiting Fellow, Wolfson College, Cambridge, 1999. Publications: The Physics of Fluid Turbulence, 1990; Dynamics and Relativity, 1999; Renormalization Methods: a guide for beginners, 2003. Recreations: reading; gardening; listening to music. Address: (b.) School of Physics, King's Buildings, Edinburgh University, Edinburgh.

McConnachie, Brian, LLB, DipLP. QC, since 2005; Principal Advocate Depute, since 2006; b. 20.4.59, Dundee; m., Sharon Steedman; 3 s.; 1 d. Educ. Lawside Academy; Alva Academy; University of Glasgow. A.C. Bennett and Fairweather, Edinburgh: Legal Trainee, 1981-83, Solicitor, 1983-84; Solicitor, A.C. Miller and Mackay, Perth, 1984-93; devilling, 1993-94; Advocate. Recreations: family; football; Guinness. Address: Parliament House, Parliament Square, Edinburgh; T.-07739 158234; e-mail: bas@sidlawview.freeserve.co.uk

McConnell, Bridget Mary, MA (Hons), DIA, MEd, FRSA, FFCS. Chief Executive, Culture and Sport Glasgow, since 2007; Executive Director, Culture and Sport, Glasgow City Council, 2005-07, Director, Cultural and Leisure Services, 1998-2005; b. 28.5.58, Lennoxtown; m., Jack Wilson McConnell (qv); 1 s.; 1 d. Educ. St. Patrick's High School, Kilsyth; Our Lady's High School, Cumbernauld; St. Andrews University; Dundee College of Commerce; Stirling University. Curator, Doorstep Gallery, Fife Regional Council, 1983-84; Arts Officer, Stirling District Council, 1984-88; Principal Arts Officer, The Arts in Fife, Fife Regional Council, 1988-96; Service Manager, Community Services, Fife Council, 1996-98. Conference Co-ordinator, Fourth International Conference in Adult Education and the Arts, St. Andrews, 1995; External Verifier, SCOTVEC Arts and Leisure Management Courses, 1990-97; Member, Board, Workshop and Artists Studio Provision Scotland (WASPS) Ltd, 1985-90; Chair,

Scottish Youth Dance Festival, 1993-96 (Founder Member, 1988); Chair, Scottish Local Authority Arts Officers Group, 1993-96 (Founder Member, 1991); Vice Chair, Scottish Arts Lobby (SALVO), 1995-97; Member, Scottish Arts Council Combined Arts Committee, 1988-94; Arts Adviser to COSLA, 1997-2001; Member, Scottish Executive, National Culture Strategy Focus Group, 1999-2000; Member, Scottish Executive, Social Inclusion Task Group, 1999-2000; Board Member, RSAMD, since 2001, Vice Chair, since 2007; Member, Heritage Lottery Fund Committee, since 2004; Awards: British/American Arts Association/University of Minnesota Fellowship, 1987. Publications: Modernising Britain: Creative Futures (Co-Author), 1997; conference papers on arts and adult education. Recreations: walking; playing piano; swimming; reading. Address: (b.) 20 Trongate, Glasgow G1 5FS; T.-0141-287 5058.

McConnell, Charles Stephen, BA (Hons), MPhil, FRSA. Chief Executive, Carnegie UK Trust; former Head of Community Learning and Development, Scottish Executive; b. 20.6.51, Harrogate; m., Natasha; 1 s.; 1 d. Public and European Affairs Director, Community Development Foundation; Chief Executive, Scottish Community Education Council; Chief Executive, Community Learning Scotland; former Labour Party Parliamentary candidate; former National Secretary, UK Consumers Congress; former Vice President, European Social Action Movement; former Chairman, UK National Training Standards Organisation for Community Learning and Development; former Secretary General, International Association for Community Development. Publications: Community Worker as Politiciser of the Deprived; Deprivation, Participation and Community Action; Community Education and Community Development; Post 16 — Developments in Continuing Education in Scotland; Classroom Commercials — business sponsorship of education; Consumer Action and Community Development; Community Development — the European dimension; A Citizen's Europe; Promoting Community Development in Europe; Community Development and Urban Regeneration; Community Learning and Development: The Making of an Empowering Profession. Recreation: fell-walking. Address: (b.) Garden Cottage, Back Dykes, Kinnesswood, Perthshire KY13 9HJ.

McConnell, Rt. Hon. Jack Wilson, BSc, DipEd. MSP (Labour), Motherwell and Wishaw, since 1999; First Minister of Scotland, 2001-07 (Minister for Education, Europe and External Affairs, 2000-2001, Minister for Finance, 1999-2000); b. 30.6.60, Irvine; m., Bridget (qv); 1 s.; 1 d. Educ. Arran High School; Stirling University. Mathematics Teacher, Lornshill Academy, 1983-92; General Secretary, Scottish Labour Party, 1992-98; Chief Executive, Public Affairs Europe Limited, 1998. Member, Stirling District Council, 1984-93, Council Leader, 1990-92, Treasurer, 1988-92, Chair, Leisure and Recreation Committee, 1986-87, Equal Opportunities Committee, 1986-90; Member, European Committee of the Regions, 2001-07; President, 1980-82, Hon. President, 1984-85 and 1991-93, Stirling University Students Association; Executive Member, Scottish Constitutional Convention, 1990-98; Deputy President, NUS Scotland, 1982-83; Chair, Board of Directors, Stirling Windows Ltd., 1988-92; Member, Labour Party Scottish Executive Committee, 1989-92; Parliamentary candidate, Perth and Kinross, 1987. Publication: Proposals for Scottish Democracy, 1989. Recreations: golf; gardening; cinema; music. Address: (b.) 265 Main Street, Wishaw ML2 7NE; T.-01698 303040; Scottish Parliament, Edinburgh EH99 1SP; T.-0131-348 5831; e-mail: jack.mcconnell.msp@scottish.parliament.uk

McConnell, Walter Scott, OBE, FRPharmS, PhC. Community Pharmacist, since 1962; former Vice Chairman, Ayrshire and Arran Community Health Care Trust; b. 7.4.36, Kilmarnock; m.; 3 d. Educ. Kilmarnock

Academy; Royal Technical College, Glasgow. Former Chairman, Pharmaceutical General Council (Scotland). Recreations: curling; golf. Address: (h.) 27 Mauchline Road, Hurlford, Kilmarnock KA1 5AB; T.-01563 525393.

McCorkindale, Rev. Donald George Bruce, BD, DipMin. Church of Scotland Minister at Dalgety, since 2000; b. 21.12.63, Glasgow; m., Lesley Rona (Page); 1 s. Educ. Kelvinside Academy, Glasgow; St. Andrews University. Minister, Bonnybridge St. Helens Church, 1992-2000. Publication: The Millennium Challenge, 2000. Address: (h.) The Manse, 9 St. Colme Drive, Dalgety Bay KY11 9LQ; T.-01383 822316; e-mail: donald@dalgety-church.co.uk

MacCormick, Professor Sir (Donald) Neil, Kt., QC (Hon), MA, LLD, Hon. LLD (Uppsala), Hon. LLD (Saarland), Hon. LLD (Queen's University, Ontario), Hon. LLD (Macerata), Hon. LLD (Glasgow), HonDLitt QMUC Edinburgh, FRSE, FBA. Special Advisor to First Minister on European and External Affairs, since 2007; President, International Association for Philosophy of Law and Social Philosophy, 2007-11; Vice-Principal, 1997-1999, and Regius Professor of Public Law, Edinburgh University, 1972-97; Leverhulme Personal Research Professorship, 1997-99, 2004-07; Member (SNP) of European Parliament for Scotland, 1999-2004; Vice-President, Scottish National Party, 1999-2004; b. 27.5.41, Glasgow; m., 1, Karen (Caroline) Rona Barr (m. diss.); 3 d.; 2, Flora Margaret Britain. Educ. High School of Glasgow; Glasgow University; Balliol College, Oxford. Lecturer in Jurisprudence, Queen's College, Dundee, 1965-67; Fellow, Balliol College, Oxford, 1967-72; Oxford University: CUF Lecturer, 1968-72, Pro-Proctor, 1970-71; Dean, Faculty of Law, Edinburgh University, 1973-76 and 1985-88; Senate Assessor, University Court, 1982-85; Provost, Faculty Group of Law and Social Sciences, 1993-97; Member, Broadcasting Council for Scotland, 1985-89; Vice President: International Association for Legal and Social Philosophy, 1991-95, Royal Society of Edinburgh, 1991-94; Member, Economic and Social Research Council, 1995-99; Member, Scottish Examination Board, 1994-97. President, Oxford Union, 1965; Scottish National Party: Executive Member, 1978-81, Council Member, 1978-84 and 1989-97; Foreign Member, Finnish Academy of Science. Publications: as author or editor, books on philosophy of law, political philosophy, etc, including Questioning Sovereignty, 1999; Rhetoric and the Rule of Law, 2005; Who's afraid of a European Constitution? (1999). Address: (h.) 19 Pentland Terrace, Edinburgh EH10 6AA; T.-0131-447 7945.

McCormick, John, FRSE, MA, MEd. Chairman, Scottish Qualifications Authority, since 2004; m., Jean Frances Gibbons; 1 s.; 1 d. Educ. St. Michael's Academy, Irvine; University of Glasgow. Teacher, St. Gregory's Secondary School, Glasgow, 1968-70; Education Officer, BBC School Broadcasting Council, 1970-75; Senior Education Officer, Scotland, 1975-82; Sec., and Head of Information, BBC Scotland, 1982-87; The Sec. of the BBC, 1987-92; Controller of BBC Scotland, 1992-2004. Chairman, Edinburgh International Film Festival, since 1996; Member, Board, Scottish Screen, 1997-2005 (Vice-Chairman, 2004-05); Member, Board, Skillset, 2002-04; Member, Glasgow Science Centre Charitable Trust, 1999-2005; Member, Board, Scottish Opera, since 2005; Member, Board, Glasgow School of Art, 2004-07; Electoral Commissioner, since 2008; Member, Board, Royal Scottish Academy of Music and Dance, since 2003; Non-executive Director, Lloyds TSB Scotland, since 2005; appointed Electoral Commissioner, from January 2008; Member, Court, University of Strathclyde, 1996-2002. FRTS 1998; FRSE 2003. Hon. DLitt (Robert Gordon University, Aberdeen),

1997; Hon. LLD (Strathclyde), 1999; DUniv: Glasgow, 1999; Paisley, 2003. Recreation: newspapers. Address: (b.) Scottish Qualifications Authority, The Optima Building, 58 Robertson Street, Glasgow G2 8DQ.

McCormick, John William Penfold, BSc, PhD. Chairman, Scottish Association for Public Transport, since 1988; Information Technology Manager, Weir Pumps Ltd., 1979-2003; I.T. and transport consultant; b. 9.6.46, Renfrew; m., Linda M.L.; 1 d. Educ. Paisley Grammar School; Glasgow University. Research Fellow, Glasgow University, 1971-74; computer management, since 1975. Recreations: hill-walking; transport; music. Address: (b.) 11 Queens Crescent, Glasgow G4 9BL; T.-07760 381 729; e-mail: mail@sapt.org.uk

McCourt, Arthur David, CBE, BSc (Hons). Chief Executive, Highland Council, 1995-2007; b. 11.7.47, Newburgh, Fife; m., Jan; 1 d. Educ. Bell-Baxter High School, Cupar; Edinburgh College of Art; Heriot-Watt University. Various posts with Northumberland County Council, Central Regional Council, Stirling District Council; Assistant Chief Executive, Tayside Regional Council, 1990-93. Recreation: mountaineering. Address: (b.) Westcroft, Lentran, Inverness IV3 8RN; T.-01463 702838.

McCreadie, Robert Anderson, QC, LLB, PhD, Advocate; b. 17.8.48, St. Andrews. Educ. Madras College, St. Andrews; Edinburgh University; Christ's College, Cambridge. Lecturer, Dundee University, 1974-78; Edinburgh University, 1978-93; called to Scottish Bar, 1992; Standing Junior Counsel, Department of Transport, 1994-95, Scottish Home and Health Department, 1995-99, Home Affairs and Justice Department, 1999-2000, Advocate Depute, 2000-02; Standing Junior Counsel to Advocate General for Scotland, 2002-03; Queen's Counsel, 2003; part-time Sheriff, 2003-04; Sheriff of Tayside Central and Fife at Perth, since 2004. Recreations: music; Scottish history; walking. Address: (h.) 40 Marchmont Crescent, Edinburgh EH9 1HG; T.-0131-667 1383.

McCrone, Iain Alistair, CBE (1987), SDA, ARAgS. Farmer and Company Director; b. 29.3.34, Glasgow; m., Yvonne Findlay (div.); 4 d. Educ. Glasgow Academy; Trinity College, Glenalmond; West of Scotland Agricultural College. Farming on own account, since 1956; Managing Director, McCrone Farmers Ltd., since 1958; began fish farming, 1968; Director: Highland Trout Co. (now Marine Harvest McConnell), 1968-97, Otter Ferry Salmon Ltd., since 1974; Member: Fife Regional Council, 1978-82; Parliamentary candidate (Conservative), Central Fife, 1979, Council, National Farmers Union of Scotland, 1977-82, Board, Glenrothes Development Corporation, 1980-96, Fife Health Board, 1983-91; Chairman, Oxford Farming Conference, 1988; Chairman, The Farmers Club, 2001; Nuffield Farming Scholar, 1966; President, Scottish Conservative and Unionist Association, 1985-87. Recreations: golf; rugby (spectator). Address: (h.) Cardsknolls, Markinch, Fife KY7 6LP; T.-01337 830267; e-mail: iain-mccrone@talk21.com

McCrone, Professor Robert Gavin Loudon, CB, MA, MSc, PhD, Hon.LLD, FRSE, Hon FRSGS. General Secretary, Royal Society of Edinburgh, 2005-07 (Vice President, 2002-05); Hon. Fellow of the Europa Institute, since 1992, Edinburgh University; Commissioner, Parliamentary Boundary Commission for Scotland, since 1999; Trustee, Scottish Opera Endowment Trust, since 1998; b. 2.2.33, Ayr; m., 1, Alexandra Bruce Waddell (deceased); 2 s.; 1 d.; m., 2, Olive Pettigrew Moon (née

McNaught); 2 step-d. Educ. St. Catharine's College, Cambridge; University of Wales; Glasgow University. National Service with RASC, 1952-54; Fisons Ltd., 1959-60; Lecturer in Economics, Glasgow University, 1960-65; Fellow, Brasenose College, Oxford, 1965-70; Consultant, UNESCO, 1964; Member, NEDC Working Party on Agricultural Policy, 1967-68; Adviser, House of Commons Select Committee on Scottish Affairs, 1969-70; Chief Economic Adviser, Scottish Office, 1970-92; Under Secretary, 1972-80; Secretary, Industry Department for Scotland, 1980-87; Secretary, Scottish Office Environment Department, 1987-92; Professor, Centre for Housing Research, University of Glasgow, 1992-94; Visiting Professor, Edinburgh University Management School, 1994-2005. Member: Economic and Social Research Council, 1986-89; Council, Royal Economic Society, 1977-82, Council, Scottish Economic Society, 1982-91, Board, Scottish Opera, 1992-98, Advisory Committee, Inquiry into Implementation of Constitutional Reform, 1995-97, National Review of Resources Allocation in the NHS in Scotland, 1998-2000, Board, Queen's Hall, 1998-2002; Deputy Chairman: Royal Infirmary of Edinburgh NHS Trust, 1994-99, Lothian University Hospitals' Trust, 1999-2001; Vice Chairman: Royal Society of Edinburgh Inquiry into Foot and Mouth Disease in Scotland, 2001-02, Royal Society of Edinburgh inquiry into the crisis in the Scottish fishing industry, 2003; Chairman, Committee of Inquiry into Professional Conditions of Service for Teachers, 1999-2000; Chairman, Royal Society of Edinburgh's Inquiry into the Future of Scotland's Hill & Island Areas, 2007-08. Publications: The Economics of Subsidising Agriculture, 1962; Scotland's Economic Progress 1951-60, 1963; Regional Policy in Britain, 1969; Scotland's Future, 1969; Housing Policy in Britain and Europe (Co-Author), 1995; European Monetary Union and Regional Development, 1997. Recreations: music; walking. Address: (b.) 11A Lauder Road, Edinburgh EH9 2EN; T.-0131 667 4766.

McCulloch, Andrew Grant, LLB, BSc(Soc Sci). Sheriff at Dundee; b. 10.2.52, Edinburgh; m.; 1 s.; 1 d. Educ. Glasgow Academy; Edinburgh University. Trained, then Assistant, Drummond & Co., 1974-79; Partner, 1979-2004; Member, Council, Law Society of Scotland, 1987-98, President, 1996-97; Solicitor Advocate, since 1992; Temporary Sheriff, 1992-99; part-time Sheriff, 2003-04. President, Grange Sports Club, 1990-92. Recreations: golf; cricket; wine. Address: (b.) Sheriff Court House, Dundee.

McCulloch, Ian, DA, RSA. Painter and Printmaker; b. 4.3.35, Glasgow; m., Margery Palmer; 2 s. Educ. Eastbank Academy; Glasgow School of Art. Elected Member, Society of Scottish Artists, 1964; elected Associate, Royal Scottish Academy, 1989; elected Academician, Royal Scottish Academy, 2005; paintings in many private and public collections; numerous one-man and group exhibitions; 1st prize, Stirling Smith Biennial, 1985; winner, Glasgow International Concert Hall Mural Competition, 1989-90; Fine Art Fellow, Strathclyde University, since 1994. Address: (h.) 51 Victoria Road, Lenzie, Glasgow G66 5AP; T.-0141-776 1053; e-mail: imccstudio@waitrose.com

McCulloch, Professor James, BSc, PhD. Professor of Neuropharmacology, Edinburgh University, since 2002; b. 7.4.51; m., Mailis Christina; 2 s. Educ. Spiers School, Beith; Glasgow University. Glasgow University: Lecturer, 1978-86, Reader, 1986-88, Professor, 1988-2002. Editor, Journal of Cerebral Blood Flow and Metabolism, 1997-2003; President, International Society of Cerebral Blood Flow and Metabolism. Publications: four books; 240 scientific papers. Recreations: squash; golf; skiing. Address: (b.) Edinburgh University, 1 George Square, Edinburgh EH8 9JZ; T.-0131 651 1906.

McCulloch, James Donald, BD, MIOP, MIP3. Minister of Hurlford Church, since 1996; b. 11.4.51, Coatbridge; m., Ann; 2 d. Educ. Coatbridge High School (Senior Secondary); University of Glasgow, Trinity College. Winner, Marcus Dodds Prize in Advanced Ordinary New Testament Studies, 1995. Newspaper and Commercial Hot Metal Compositor, Baird & Hamilton, then Scottish & Universal Newspapers Hamilton, 1969-91; Glasgow College of Building and Printing: Printing Technician's Certificate, 1974, Winner of Andrew Holmes Memorial Scholarship, 1975; Probationary Minister, Bothwell Parish Church; Past Moderator, Presbytery of Irvine and Kilmarnock (2004-05). Recreations: university gymnasium; reading (non-fiction). Address: (h.) Hurlford Church Manse, 12 Main Road, Crookedholm, Kilmarnock, East Ayrshire KA3 6JT; T.-01563 535673.

McCulloch, James Macdonald, BA, MRTPI. Chief Reporter, Scottish Government, since 2002; b. 3.12.48, Dorchester; m., Jennifer Anne Hay; 3 s. Educ. Hardye's School, Dorchester; Lanchester Polytechnic, Coventry. Planning Assistant, Coventry Corporation, 1971-73; Senior Planner and Principal Planner, Scottish Development Department, 1973-84; Reporter then Principal Reporter then Deputy Chief Reporter, 1984-2002. Recreations: walking; eating; the people, landscapes and language of Spain. Address: (b.) Directorate for Planning and Environmental Appeals (DPEA), 4 The Courtyard, Callendar Business Park, Callendar Road, Falkirk FK1 1XR; T.-01324 696471.

McCulloch, John David, DL. Deputy Lieutenant, Midlothian, since 1992; Clerk to Church of Scotland Presbytery of Lothian, since 1994; b. 5.4.37, Edinburgh; m., Cicely Blackett; 2 s.; 2 d. Educ. Belhaven Hill, Dunbar; Marlborough College. Address: (h.) Auchindinny House, Penicuik EH26 8PE; T.-01968 672943.

McCulloch, Margery Palmer, BA, MLitt, PhD, LRAM. Literary scholar; m., Ian McCulloch; 2 s. Educ. Hamilton Academy; London University; Glasgow University. Publications include: The Novels of Neil M. Gunn: a critical study, 1987; Edwin Muir: poet, critic and novelist, 1993; Lewis Grassic Gibbon: A Centenary Celebration, 2003; Literature and Society in Scotland, 1918-1939, 2004. Recreation: music. Address: (h.) 51 Victoria Road, Lenzie, Glasgow G66 5AP; T.-0141-776 1053; e-mail: mpm@waitrose.com

McCulloch, Stuart J., BSc, MEd, DipEd. Former Headmaster, Belmont House School (1999-2005); Secretary, Stewartry Agricultural Society; b. 26.12.50, Melfort; m., Anne Elizabeth (deceased); 2 s.; 1 d. Educ. Queen Mary College, London; Stirling University. Head of Geography, Stewarts Melville, Edinburgh, 1973-92; Deputy Head, Beaconhurst School, 1992-98. Recreations: most things, especially bagpipes and books. Address: (h.) Montego, Colvend, Kirkcudbrightshire DG5 4QE; T.-01556 630324; e-mail: maculafailte@yahoo.co.uk

McCunn, Archibald Eddington, OBE, BSc (Hons), CEng, MIMechE, FCMI; b. 27.5.27, Motherwell; m., Olive Isobel Johnston; 1 s.; 1 d. Educ. Dalziel High School; Strathclyde University. Engineering Management, Colvilles Ltd. BSC, 1952-64; Senior Consultant, Inbucon/AIC, 1964-67; Divisional Chairman, Stenhouse Industries, 1967-71; Divisional Chairman/Consultant, Grampian Holdings plc, 1971-89; Board Member, Highlands and Islands Development Board, 1985-89; Director: A.E. McCunn Consultants Ltd., 1985-95; Chairman, Craftpoint Ltd., 1986-91; Director, McConnell Salmon Ltd., 1990-94; Vice Chairman and Trustee, Argyll and Bute Countryside Trust,

1990-95; Hon. Vice-President, Scottish Salmon Growers Association, 1990-95; Board Member: State Hospital, 1992-96, Scottish Natural Heritage (South West), 1992-97; Board Member, Scottish Greenbelt Foundation, 1992-99; Elder, Church of Scotland, since 1949. Recreations: painting; music; writing; cycling; gardening. Address: (h.) 2 McIntosh Way, Motherwell ML1 3DD; T. 01698 253500; e-mail: archiemccunn@blueyonder.co.uk

McDaid, Professor Seamus, CA, MBA. Principal and Vice-Chancellor, University of the West of Scotland (formerly Paisley University), since 2005; b. 23.7.52, Glasgow; m., Alice; 2 d. Educ. St. Mungo's Academy; Glasgow University; Strathclyde University. Qualified as CA, 1974; trained with Wylie & Bisset, CA; worked for Coopers & Lybrand; joined Glasgow College as Lecturer, 1976; Senior Lecturer, 1980, Head, Department of Finance and Accounting, 1987; Dean, Faculty of Business, Glasgow Caledonian University, 1992; Vice Principal, University of Paisley, 1997-2005. Recreations: football; badminton. Address: (b.) University of the West of Scotland, Paisley PA1 2BE; T.-0141 848 3000.

McDevitt, Emeritus Professor Denis Gordon, DSc, MD, FRCP, FRCPI, FRCPEd, FFPM, FRSE. Professor of Clinical Pharmacology, Dundee University Medical School, 1984-2002, now Emeritus Professor (Dean, Faculty of Medicine, Dentistry and Nursing, 1994-97); Honorary Consultant Physician, Tayside Universities Hospitals Trust, 1984-2002; Civil Consultant in Clinical Pharmacology, RAF, 1987-2002; Member, General Medical Council, 1996-2003 (Treasurer, 2001-03); b. 17.11.37, Belfast; m., Anne McKee; 2 s.; 1 d. Educ. Campbell College, Belfast; Queen's University, Belfast. Assistant Professor of Medicine and Consultant Physician, Christian Medical College, Ludhiana, North India, 1968-71; Senior Lecturer in Clinical Pharmacology and Consultant Physician, Queen's University Medical School, 1971-76; Merck International Fellow in Clinical Pharmacology, Vanderbilt University, Nashville, Tennessee, 1974-75; Reader in Clinical Pharmacology, Queen's University Medical School, 1976-78; Professor of Clinical Pharmacology, Queen's University of Belfast and Consultant Physician, Belfast Teaching Hospitals, 1978-83. Chairman, Clinical Section, British Pharmacological Society, 1985-88 (Secretary, 1978-82); Member, Medicines Commission, 1986-95; President, Association of Physicians of Great Britain and Ireland, 1987-88; Member, Council, Royal College of Physicians of Edinburgh, since 2003; Member, Board, Faculty of Pharmaceutical Physicians, since 2003. Recreations: golf; classical music. Address: (h.) 10 Ogilvie Road, Broughty Ferry, Dundee DD5 1LU.

Macdonald, 8th Baron, (Godfrey James Macdonald of Macdonald). Chief of the Name and Arms of Macdonald; b. 28.11.47; m., Claire Catlow; 1 s.; 3 d. Address: (h.) Kinloch Lodge, Isle of Skye.

Macdonald of Tradeston, Rt. Hon. Lord (Gus Macdonald), CBE. House of Lords Select Committee on Economic Affairs, since 2004; Chairman, All Party Parliamentary Humanist Group, since 2005; Council Member, Sussex University, since 2006; Chancellor, Glasgow Caledonian University, since 2007; Senior Advisor, Macquarie Bank Ltd., since 2004; Patron, Dystonia Society, since 2006; Minister for the Cabinet Office and Chancellor of Duchy of Lancaster, 2001-03; Minister for Transport, Department of Environment, Transport and the Regions, 1999-2001; Minister for Business and Industry, Scottish Office, 1998-99; b. 20.8.40, Larkhall; m., Teen; 2 d. Educ. Allan Glen's School, Glasgow. Marine engineer, Stephens, Linthouse, 1955-62;

Circulation Manager, Tribune, 1963-65; Journalist, The Scotsman, 1965-67; Television producer/presenter, Granada, 1967-85; C4 Viewers Ombudsman, Right to Reply, 1982-88; Scottish Television: Director of Programmes, 1986-90, Managing Director, 1990-96; Chairman, Scottish Television, subsequently Scottish Media Group plc, 1996-98; Scottish Business Elite Awards: Business Leader of the Year, Chairman of the Year, 1997; founder Chairman, Edinburgh International Telvision Festival, 1976; Chairman, Edinburgh International Film Festival, 1993-96; Governor, National Film and Television School, 1986-97; Visiting Professor, Film and Media, Stirling University, 1986-98; Member, Boards: Scottish Enterprise, 1998, Bank of Scotland, 1998, Scottish Screen, 1997, British Film Institute, 1997-98; Chairman, Cairngorms Partnership, 1997-98; Chairman, Taylor and Francis Group plc, 1997-98. Recreations: words; music; pictures; sports. Address: (b.) House of Lords, London SW1A 0PW.

Macdonald, Aileen. Deputy Director of Operations (Acting), Apex Scotland, since 2007; b. 03.07.55, Dundee; m., Gordon Macdonald; 2 s. Educ. Kirkton High School, Dundee; Dundee College of Education. Adult Basic Education Unit, Aberdeen, 1986-96; Apex Scotland, since 1996. Recreations: cooking; golf; family; watching football; keeping fit. Address: (b.) Apex Scotland, 9 Great Stuart Street, Edinburgh EH3 7TP; T.-0131 220 0130; e-mail: aileen@apexscotland.org.uk

McDonald, The Very Reverend Alan Douglas, LLB, BD, MTH, DLitt (honoris causa), DD (honoris causa). Parish Minister, St, Leonard's and Cameron, St. Andrews, since 1998; b. 06.03.51, Glasgow; m., Dr Judith McDonald (nee Allen); 1 s.; 1 d. Educ. Glasgow Academy; Strathclyde University; Edinburgh University; St. Andrews University. Legal Apprentice, Biggart Baillie & Gifford, 1972-74; Solicitor, Farquharson Craig, 1974-75; Community Minister, Pilton, Edinburgh, 1979-83; Minister, Holburn Central, Aberdeen, 1983-98; Convener, Church and Nation Committee, 2000-04; Moderator of the General Assembly of the Church of Scotland, 2006-07. Presenter of Thought for the Day, BBC Radio Scotland. Recreations: running; walking; golf; music; poetry; travel; football. Address: (h.) 1 Cairnhill Gardens, St. Andrews KY16 8QY; T.-01334 472793; e-mail: alan.d.mcdonald@talk21.com

McDonald, Very Rev. Dr. Alexander, BA, DUniv (Open), CMIWS. Moderator of the General Assembly, Church of Scotland, 1997-98; b. 5.11.37, Bishopbriggs; m., Essdale Helen McLeod; 2 s.; 1 d. Educ. Bishopbriggs Higher Grade School; Whitehill Senior Secondary School, Glasgow; Glasgow University and Trinity College. RAF, 1954-56; Management in timber trade: 1952-54, 1956-58; motor trade, 1958-62; student, 1962-68; Minister: St. David's Bathgate, 1968-74, St. Mark's, Old Hall, Paisley, 1974-88; General Secretary, Church of Scotland, Board of Ministry, 1988-2002; Honorary President, Boys' Brigade, Glasgow Battalion, 2004; wide range of involvement with Boys' Brigade in Scotland, ACCORD, Christian Aid and many others; regular broadcaster. Recreations: reading; walking; fishing. Address: 36 Alloway Grove, Paisley PA2 7DQ; T.-0141-560 1937.

MacDonald, Allan, MA. Managing Director, MNE Media, since 1989; Chairman, Producers Alliance for Cinema and Television (PACT), Scotland, since 2002; Member of Nations and Regions Committee, PACT, and Director, PACT Council, London; b. 11.6.53, Eriskay; m., Marion Margaret; 1 d. Educ. St. Vincent's College, Langbank; Blairs College, Aberdeen; Glasgow University. Senior Producer, BBC Highland, Inverness; Senior

Producer/Manager, BBC Radio Nan Eilean, Stornoway; Manager, BBC Highland, Inverness; Television Producer, BBC Scotland, Glasgow; Head of Gaelic Television, Grampian TV, 1992-94. Member, Board of Management, Lews Castle College, 1992-95. Address: (h.) 39 Hughenden Gardens, Hyndland, Glasgow G12 9YH; e-mail: allan@mnemedia.tv

Macdonald, Angus David, MA (Hons) (Cantab), DipEd. Headmaster, Lomond School, Helensburgh, since 1986; Chairman, Clan Donald Lands Trust; b. 9.10.50, Edinburgh; m., Isabelle Marjory Ross; 2 d. Educ. Portsmouth Grammar School; Cambridge University; Edinburgh University. Assistant Teacher, Alloa Academy, 1972-73; Assistant Teacher, Edinburgh Academy, 1973-82 (Exchange Teacher, King's School, Parramatta, NSW, 1978-79); George Watson's College, Edinburgh: Principal Teacher of Geography, 1982, Deputy Principal, 1982-86. Recreations: outdoor recreation; sport; piping; gardening. Address: 8 Millig Street, Helensburgh, Argyll; T.-01436 679204.

Macdonald, Professor Angus John, BSc (Hons), PhD, FSA (Scot), HonFRSGS. Writer on architecture; School of Arts, Culture and Environment, University of Edinburgh, since 2002 (Senior Lecturer, Department of Architecture, 1988-2002, Head of Enivronmental Studies Planning Unit, 1998-2002); b. 17.1.45, Edinburgh; m., Patricia Clare Mazoura Morrow Scott. Educ. George Heriot's School, Edinburgh; University of Edinburgh. Partner, Aerographica, since 1986; Commissioner, Royal Commission on the Ancient and Historical Monuments of Scotland, since 1999; Member, Board of Governors, Edinburgh College of Art, since 2003. Publications: Wind Loading on Buildings, 1975; Above Edinburgh, 1989; The Highlands and Islands of Scotland, 1989; Granite and Green, 1992; Structure and Architecture, 1994; Structural Design for Architecture, 1997; Anthony Hunt, 2000. Recreations: hillwalking; music. Address: Department of Architecture, University of Edinburgh, 20 Chambers Street, Edinburgh EH1 1JZ; T.-0131-650 2323; e-mail: Angus.Macdonald@ed.ac.uk

Macdonald, Calum Sutherland, MREHIS. Director of Environmental and Organisational Strategy, Scottish Environment Protection Agency, since 2004; b. 18.7.54, Glasgow; m., Nancy; 1 s.; 2 d. Educ. Allan Glen's School, Glasgow; Glasgow College of Food Technology. Glasgow City Council; Environmental Health Department Student Sanitary Inspector; Environmental Health Officer; Senior Environmental Health Officer; Pollution Control Manager; Principal Environmental Health Officer, 1973-96; Scottish Environment Protection Agency, Divisional Manager West; Environmental Regulation and Improvement Manager, Highlands, Islands and Grampian; Environmental Development Manager; Acting Director of Strategic Planning, 1996-2004. Vice President, Environmental Protection UK; Member, Board of Trustees of Contaminated Land Applications in Real Environments (CLAIRE); Member, Board of The Scottish and Northern Ireland Forum for Environmental Research (SNIFFER). Recreations: 2nd XV Team Manager, West of Scotland (Rugby) Football Club. Address: (b.) Scottish Environment Protection Agency, Corporate Office, Erskine Court, Castle Business Park, Stirling FK9 4TR; T.-01786 452 438; e-mail: calum.macdonald@sepa.org.uk

Macdonald, Professor Caroline Mary, BSc, PhD, CBiol, FIBiol, FHEA. Pro Vice-Chancellor, Glasgow Caledonian University, since 2004. Previously Assistant Principal, Paisley University, 1997-2004, and Professor and Head, Department of Biological Sciences, 1992-97; b. 4.9.51, Edinburgh; m., Alastair MacDonald; 2 d. Educ. Glasgow High School for Girls; Glasgow University. Lecturer/Senior Lecturer, Strathclyde University, 1983-92; Chairman, European Society for Animal Cell Technology, 1994-97 (Secretary and Treasurer, 1991-94); Chief Editor, Genetic Engineer and Biotechnologist, 1994-97; Member, Executive Committee, Heads of University Biological Sciences, 1992-2000 (Secretary, 1997-2000); Member, Executive Committee, Modern Universities Research Group (Treasurer, 1998-2003, Chair, 2003-05). Recreations: family; gardening; travel. Address: (b.) Glasgow Caledonian University, Cowcaddens Road, Glasgow G4 0BA; T.-0141 331 3624.
E-mail: caroline.macdonald@gcal.ac.uk

Macdonald, Professor David Iain Macpherson, BSc, PhD, CGeol, FGS, FRGS, Polar Medal. Professor of Petroleum Geology, University of Aberdeen, since 1999; Head of School of Geosciences, since 2005; b. 31.5.53, Bridge of Allan; m., Dr. Christine Mousley; 2 d. Educ. High School of Stirling; University of Glasgow; University of Cambridge. Geologist, British Antarctic Survey, Cambridge, 1975-80; Post Doctoral Demonstrator, University of Keele, 1980-82; Geologist, BP Petroleum Development, London, 1982-84; Senior Sedimentologist, British Antarctic Survey, 1984-93; Director, Cambridge Arctic Shelf Programme, 1993-99. Publications: Sedimentation, Tectonics and Eustasy, 1991; more than 50 scientific papers. Recreations: hillwalking; reading. Address: (b.) University of Aberdeen, School of Geosciences, St. Mary's, Elphinstone Road, Aberdeen AB24 3UF; T.-01224 272672.
E-mail: d.macdonald@abdn.ac.uk

Macdonald, Professor Donald Murray, MB, ChB, FRCS(Edin), Dip.Theol. Moderator, Free Church of Scotland, 1997; Professor of Apologetics and Practical Theology, Free Church College, Edinburgh, since 1997; b. 16.1.44, Kildonan, Sutherland; m., Joan; 1 s.; 3 d. Educ. Golspie Senior Secondary School; Edinburgh University. Medical and surgical training posts, Edinburgh area, 1967-73; Medical Superintendent, Lakhnadon Christian Hospital, Seoni District, India, 1973-88; divinity training, Free Church College, 1988-90; Minister Bishopbriggs Free Church of Scotland, 1990-97. Address: (b.) Free Church College, The Mound, Edinburgh EH1 2LS; T.-0131-226 5286; e-mail: dmmacdonald@freescotcoll.ac.uk

Macdonald, Very Rev. Finlay Angus John, MA, BD, PhD, DD. Principal Clerk, General Assembly of the Church of Scotland; Moderator, General Assembly, Church of Scotland, 2002-03; Chaplain in Ordinary to HM the Queen; b. 1.7.45, Watford; m., Elizabeth Mary Stuart; 2 s. Educ. Dundee High School; St. Andrews University. Assistant Minister, Bo'ness Old Kirk, 1970-71; Minister, Menstrie Parish Church, 1971-77; Junior Clerk and Treasurer, Stirling and Dunblane Presbytery, 1973-77; Minister, Jordanhill Parish Church, Glasgow, 1977-96; Convener, General Assembly Board of Practice and Procedure, 1988-92; Convener, General Assembly Business Committee, 1989-92; Depute Clerk, General Assembly, 1993-96. Fellow of University of Strathclyde; Member, Scottish Inter Faith Council, since 2005. Recreations: music; hill-walking; reading; gardening. Address: (b.) 121 George Street, Edinburgh EH2 4YN; T.-0131-225 5722.

Macdonald, Fiona Margaret Taylor, LLB, NP. Solicitor, since 1981; Honorary Depute Procurator Fiscal, Stornoway, since 1999; b. 14.4.56, Glasgow; m., Norman Lewis Macdonald; 1 s. Educ. Hillpark Secondary School; Dundee University. Solicitor, Inverclyde District Council, 1981-83; Solicitor, Bird Semple & Crawford Heron, Stornoway, 1983-89; Solicitor, Western Isles Islands Council, 1989-98. Member, Council, Law Society of Scotland, 1992-96;

Member, Western Isles Health Board, 1993-99. Address: (h.) Valasay, Goathill Crescent, Stornoway HS1 2TA; T.-01851 70 6364; e-mail: fionastornoway@aol.com

McDonald, Sheriff Iona Sara, MA, LLB, NP. Solicitor, since 1980; Sheriff of North Strathclyde at Kilmarnock and Paisley, since 2002, All Scotland Sheriff (floating), 2000-02; former Partner, Mathie Morton Black and Buchanan, Ayr; former Temporary Sheriff (all Scotland jurisdiction); b. 18.11.54; m., Colin Neale McDonald; 1 s.; 1 d. Educ. Cumnock Academy; Glasgow University. Apprentice Solicitor, Cannon Orpin and Co., Glasgow, 1978-80; joined Mathie Morton Black and Buchanan, Ayr, 1980. Safeguarder; Reporter to the Court and Curator Ad Litem in adoption hearings.

McDonald, Emeritus Professor Janet B.I., MA, FRSE, FRSAMD. Professor of Drama, Glasgow University, 1979-2005 (Head, Department of Theatre, Film and Television Studies, 2001-04; b. 28.7.41, Netherlee, Renfrewshire; m., Ian James McDonald; 1 d. Educ. Hutchesons' Girls' Grammar School; Glasgow University. Member: Governing Body, Royal Scottish Academy of Music and Drama, 1979-94, Academic Council, 1994-2002, Board, Citizens' Theatre, 1979-82 and since 1989 (Chair, 1991-2005); Member, Glasgow University Court, 1991-94; Council Member, Royal Society of Edinburgh, 1994-97, Vice-President, since 2005; Chairman: Drama and Theatre Board, Council for National Academic Awards, 1981-85, Standing Committee of University Departments of Drama, 1982-85, Drama Committee, Scottish Arts Council, 1985-88; Chair, Creative and Performing Arts Committee, CNAA, 1989-91; Member, RAE Drama Panel, 1988, 1992; Member, Performing Arts Advisory Group, Scottish Qualifications Authority, 1999-2002; Member, Music and Performing Arts Research Committee, Arts and Humanities Research Board, 2000 (Chair, 2001-04), Board Member, 2002-04; Director, Merchants House, Glasgow, since 2002; Dean of Faculties, Glasgow University, since 2007. Address: (h.) 61 Hamilton Drive, Glasgow G12 8DP; T.-0141 339 0013.

MacDonald, John Neil, BA. Director for Scotland, Community Transport Association, since 2006; Chief Executive, Royal Scottish Agricultural Benevolent Institution, 2002-06; b. 8.1.60, Daliburgh, South Uist. Educ. St. Vincent's College, Langbank; Blairs College, Aberdeen; Nicolson Institute, Stornoway, Napier College; Strathclyde University. Contracts Supervisor, SGB plc, 1984-86; Sales Executive: Mannesmann Kienzle, 1986-88; Decision Data Computer (GB) Ltd., 1988-89; Sales and Marketing Consultant, Sequel UK Ltd., 1989-91; Development Officer, Scottish Council for Voluntary Organisations, 1991-2002. Recreations: football; literature; cinema. Address (b.) Community Transport Association, 46A Channel Street, Galashiels TD1 1BA.

MacDonald, Margo. MSP (Independent), Lothians, since 2003 (SNP Member, 1999-2003); freelance journalist and broadcaster; b. Hamilton; m., Jim Sillars; 1 step s.; 2 d.; 1 step-d. Educ. Hamilton Academy; Dunfermline College. Teacher, 1963-65; barmaid and mother, 1965-73; Member of Parliament, 1973-74; Broadcaster/Writer, 1974-78, Director, Shelter, Scotland, 1978-81; Radio Forth: Broadcaster, 1981-83, Editor, Topical Programmes, 1983-85; political and current affairs broadcasting as reporter/presenter, 1985-91; former Chief Executive, Network Scotland (1992-94); Broadcasting and print journalism, 1994-99.

Macdonald, Mhorag, MA (Hons), BD (Hons). Minister of Cambusnethan Parish Church, since 1989; Moderator, Hamilton Presbytery, 2006-07; b. 6.4.53, Lagos, Nigeria. Educ. Dumbarton Academy; Glasgow University. Secondary Teacher (Modern Languages), Boclair Academy, Bearsden, 1978-83 (Exchange Teacher, Soultz, Haut Rhin,

France, 1981-82); Principal Teacher (Modern Languages), Grovepark, Greenock, 1983-85; Probationer Minister, Bishopton Erskine Church, 1988-89; Ordained and Inducted to Cambusnethan North Parish Church as Parish Minister in 1989. Part-Time Chaplain, Wishaw General; Chaplain, Cambusnethan Primary and Coltness High; Advisor to Board of MADE4U in ML2. Recreations: gardening; walking dog; sudoku, music; photography. Address: (h. and b.) 350 Kirk Road, Wishaw ML2 8LH; T.-01698 381305; e-mail: mhoragmacdonald@btinternet.com

McDonald, Moira, MA, BD. Minister of Corstorphine Old Parish Church, Edinburgh, since 2005; b. 6.1.69, Elderslie; m., Ian Gates; 1 s. Educ. Renfrew High School; University of Dundee; University of Edinburgh. Minister of Musselburgh: St. Clement's and St. Ninian's Parish Church, 1997-2005. Recreations: gardening; cycling; reading. Address: (h.) 23 Manse Road, Edinburgh EH12 7SW; e-mail: moira.mc@tesco.net

Macdonald, Professor Murdo, MA, PhD, LCAD, FRSA, FSA (Scot). Professor of History of Scottish Art, University of Dundee, since 1997; b. 25.1.55, Edinburgh. Educ. Hammersmith College of Art; University of Edinburgh. Commissioning Editor, Polygon Books, 1982-94; freelance art school and university lecturing, 1986-90; freelance Art Critic (mainly for The Scotsman), 1987-92; Editor, Edinburgh Review, 1990-94; Lecturer and Adviser in Scottish Studies, Centre for Continuing Education, University of Edinburgh, 1990-97. Trustee, Sir Patrick Geddes Memorial Trust. Publications: papers on Sir Patrick Geddes; Scottish Art, 2000. Recreation: hill-walking. Address: Department of History, University of Dundee, Dundee DD1 4HN; T.-01382 344516.

MacDonald, Neil, FInstP, FEI, MIWM, MIIM. Chairman: Martin Aerospace Ltd., since 2005, Barr and Wray (Group) Ltd., since 1997; Proprietor, Leaders Management and Investment, since 1995; Board Member, Scottish Industrial Development Advisory Board (SIDAB); Member, Scottish Enterprise Investment Advisory Board; b. 13.12.45, Bracadale, Isle of Skye; m., Marion Storrie Ruthven Wilson; 1 s.; 1 d. Educ. Biggar High School; Coatbridge Technical College; Hartford Graduate Centre. Design Engineer, Marshall and Anderson Ltd., 1961-69; Manufacturing Director: Gray Tool (UK) Ltd., 1969-79, Gray Tool (Europe) Ltd., 1979-83; General Manager, North America, Gray Tool Co. Inc., 1983-85; Managing Director: Sealand Industries PLC, 1985-91, Vickers Shipbuilding (USEL) Offshore, 1991-96; Chairman: Seaboard Lloyd Ltd., 1994-96, Edinburgh Petroleum Services, 1995-2004. Past Chairman: Scottish Enterprise Lanarkshire, Cumbernauld Area Enterprise Trust, East Kilbride Enterprise Trust, Hamilton Group Engineering Centre; Past Member: Lloyds Register of Shipping Scottish Committee, Offshore Engineering Technology Board, Scottish Oil and Gas Innovation Forum, Scottish Enterprise Energy Advisory Board; Founder Member, Institute of Petroleum West of Scotland Branch. Recreations: family; motor sport; the countryside. Address: (b.) Parkboro, 133 Hyndford Road, Lanark ML11 9BB; T.-01555 666908; e-mail. leadlan@aol.com

McDonald, Norman Hamilton, FRSA, FSAScot. Historian and Archivist, Clan Donald Society of Edinburgh (President, 1993-2002 and since 2007); Historian to the High Council of Clan Donald, since 2000; b. 4.3.33, Edinburgh; m., Morag Young McKenzie. Educ. Royal High School, Edinburgh. RAF, 1953-55; accountancy, 1955-63; S.E. Regional Hospital Board, 1963-67; Edinburgh Corporation, later Edinburgh District Council, 1967-91 (retired); Chairman, The 1745 Association, 1991-97;

President, Edinburgh Gaelic Choir, 1995-97. Editor, Clan Donald Magazine. Publications: histories of MacDonalds of Glengarry and Keppoch; two cassette recordings of Gaelic and Scots songs. Address: (h.) Ceapach, 8 Ethel Terrace, Edinburgh EH10 5NB: T.-0131-447 3970.

Macdonald, Peter Cameron, DL, SDA. Farmer, 1961-96; Director, J. Dickson & Son, Gunmakers, 1968-99, Chairman, 1997-99; b. 14.12.37, Edinburgh; m., Barbara Helen Drimmie Ballantyne (deceased); 2 step-s. Educ. Loretto; East of Scotland College of Agriculture. Vice-President, Scottish Landowners' Federation, 1990-2001 (Convener, 1985-88, Council Member, 1976-2001); Council Member, Blackface Sheepbreeders Association, 1970-74; Member, Forth River Purification Board, 1979-87; Director, Royal Highland and Agricultural Society of Scotland, 1985; Deputy Lieutenant, West Lothian, since 1987. Recreations: fishing; shooting; golf. Address: Waterheads, Eddleston, Peeblesshire EH45 8QX; T.-01721 730229; e-mail: pmacdonald63@ hotmail.com

Macdonald, Roderick, BSc (Agri), MSc. Member, Scottish Land Court, 1986-92; b. 6.2.27, Benbecula; m., Elizabeth MacLeod; 3 d. Educ. Portree High School; Aberdeen University; Michigan State University, USA. Bayer Agriculture, 1952-54; Lands Division, Department of Agriculture and Fisheries for Scotland, 1954-67 and 1972-86, latterly as Assistant Chief; Head, Land Development Division, Highlands and Islands Development Board, 1967-72; appointed Gaelic Speaking Member, Scottish Land Court, 1986; Trustee and Surveyor, Glebes Committee, Church of Scotland, since 1994; Secretary, Highland Fund, since 1993. Recreations: golf; fiddle playing; fishing. Address: 19 Cherrytree Loan, Balerno, Edinburgh; T.-0131-449 3600.

Macdonald, (Roderick) Lewis, MA, PhD. MSP (Labour), Aberdeen Central, since 1999; Deputy Minister for Health and Community Care, 2005-07; for Environment and Rural Development, 2004-05; Deputy Minister for Enterprise and Lifelong Learning, 2003-04; for Enterprise, Transport and Lifelong Learning, 2001-03; for Transport and Planning, 2001; Convener, Holyrood Progress Group, 2000-01; b. 1.1.57, Stornoway; m., Sandra Inkster; 2 d. Educ. Inverurie Academy; Aberdeen University. Research and teaching posts outwith politics, 1983-87, 1992-93; Parliamentary Researcher, office of Frank Doran MP, 1987-92; Shadow Cabinet Adviser to Tom Clarke MP, 1993-97; Member, Labour Party Scottish Executive Committee, 1997-99; Parliamentary candidate, Moray, 1997; Parliamentary Researcher, office of Frank Doran MP, 1997-99. Member, Management Committee, Aberdeen Citizens' Advice Bureau, 1997-99; Member, Grampian Racial Equality Council. Recreations: history; sports and games; the countryside. Address: (b.) 70 Rosemount Place, Aberdeen AB25 2TJ; T.-01224-646333; Fax: 01224 645450.
E-mail: Lewis.Macdonald.msp@scottish.parliament.uk
website: www.lewismacdonaldmsp.com

MacDonald, Professor Ronald, BA, MA, PhD, FRSE. Adam Smith Professor of Political Economy, Glasgow University, since 2006; b. 23.4.55, Glasgow; m., Catriona Smith. Educ. Falkirk High School; Heriot Watt University; Manchester University. Midland Bank Fellow in Monetary Economics, Loughborough University, 1982-84; Lecturer in Economics, Aberdeen University, 1984-88; Senior Lecturer, 1988-89; Robert Fleming Professor of Finance and Investment, Dundee University, 1989-93; Professor of International Finance, Strathclyde University, 1993-2004; Bonar MacFie Professor of Economics, Glasgow

University, 2005-06. Visiting Professor: Queen's University, Canada, 1988, University of New South Wales, Australia, 1989, European University Institute, Florence, 1998 and 2000, University Cergy-Pontoise, 1999, Centre for Economic Studies, 1999, Reserve Bank of New Zealand, 2000; Visiting Scholar, Monetary Authority of Singapore, 2003; Visiting Economist, African Department, International Monetary Fund, Washington DC, 2003; Visiting Scholar, Central Bank of Norway, 2003; Member, European Monetary Forum, since 1994; Visiting Scholar, International Monetary Fund, Washington DC, since 1991; Research Fellow, CESIFO, Munich, since 2000; International Fellow of Kiel Institute for World Economics; Consultant to the European Commission and European Central Bank. Publications: Floating Exchange Rates; Exchange Rate Economics: Theories and Evidence; International Money: theory evidence and institutions (Co-Author); five co-edited books; over 100 refereed journal articles. Recreations: music; windsurfing; boating; cycling. Address: (b.) Department of Economics, Adam Smith Building, Glasgow University, Glasgow G12 8RT; T.-0141-330-1988; e-mail: r.macdonald@socsci.gla.ac.uk

McDonald, Sheena Elizabeth, MA, HC, DLitt. Journalist and broadcaster; currently presents an education-focused news programme for cable channel Teachers' TV. Address: (b.) Curtis Brown, 28/9 Haymarket, London SW1Y 4SP.

MacDonald, Professor Simon Gavin George, MA, PhD, FInstP, FRSE; b. 5.9.23, Beauly, Inverness-shire; m., Eva Leonie Austerlitz; 1 s.; 1 d. Educ. George Heriot's, Edinburgh; Edinburgh University. Junior Scientific Officer, Royal Aircraft Establishment, Farnborough, 1943-46; Lecturer in Physics, St. Andrews University, 1948-57; Senior Lecturer in Physics: University College of the West Indies, 1957-62, St. Andrews University, 1962-67; Dundee University: Senior Lecturer in Physics, 1967-73, Professor of Physics, 1973-88, Dean of Science, 1970-73, Vice-Principal, 1974-79, Head, Department of Physics, 1979-85; Chairman, Statistics Committee, Universities Central Council on Admissions, 1989-93; Member, Scottish Universities Council on Entrance, 1969-82 (Vice-Convener, 1973-77, Convener, 1977-82); Chairman, Technical Committee, UCCA, 1979-83; Deputy Chairman, UCCA, 1983-89; Chairman, Board of Directors, Dundee Repertory Theatre, 1975-89. Publications: Problems and Solutions in General Physics; Physics for Biology and Premedical Students; Physics for the Life and Health Sciences. Recreations: bridge; golf; fiction writing. Address: (h.) 7A Windmill Road, St Andrews KY16 9JJ; T.-01334 478014.

McDonald, Thomas, MA. Headteacher, Holyrood R.C. Secondary School, Glasgow, since 2005; b. 28.7.53, Helensburgh; m., Carol; 2 s. Educ. St. Patrick's High School, Dumbarton; University of Glasgow; Jordanhill College. Teacher of Modern Languages, St. Patrick's High School, Dumbarton, 1976-82; Principal Teacher of Modern Languages, St. Andrew's High School, Clydebank, 1982-89; Assistant Head Teacher, St. Mungo's Academy, Glasgow, 1989-96; Depute Head Teacher, Bellarmine R.C. Secondary School, Glasgow 1996-98; Headteacher, All Saints R.C. Secondary School, Glasgow, 1998-2005. Address: (b.) 100 Dixon Road, Glasgow G42 8AU; T.-0141 582 0120.
E-mail: tmcdonald@holyrood-sec.glasgow.sch.uk

McDonald, Very Rev. William James Gilmour, MA, BD, Hon. DD (Edinburgh); b. 3.6.24, Edinburgh; m., Patricia Watson; 1 s.; 2 d. Educ. Daniel Stewart's College; Edinburgh University; Gottingen University. Royal Artillery and Indian Artillery, 1943-46; Parish Minister, Limekilns, 1953-59; Minister, Mayfield Parish Church,

Edinburgh, 1959-92; Convener, Assembly Council, 1984-87; Moderator, General Assembly of Church of Scotland, 1989-90. Warrack Lecturer, 1993-95; Turnbull Trust Preacher, Melbourne, 1993-94. Address: (h.) 7 Blacket Place, Edinburgh EH9 1RN; T.-0131-667 2100.

Macdonell, Hamish Alasdair, BA (Hons). Scottish Political Editor, The Scotsman, since 2001; b. 5.1.68, Inverness; m., Louisa Mary Buller; 2 s. Educ. Fettes College, Edinburgh; University of York. Reporter, Yorkshire Evening Press, 1990-94; freelance journalist, Africa and Australia, 1994-95; Press Association: Parliamentary Reporter, 1995-97, Scottish Political Editor, 1997-98; Political Editor, Scottish Daily Mail, 1998-2001. Recreations: golf; rugby; jazz. Address: 11, East Hermitage Place, Edinburgh EH6 8AA; T.-0131-466 6100; e-mail: hmacdonell@scotsman.com

McDonnell, Michael Anthony, BD, DipTheol, DipCE, FIRSO. Director, Road Safety Scotland (formerly Scottish Road Safety Campaign), since 2004; b. 13.5.55, Bellshill; m., Rosemary Boyle; 1 s. Educ. St. Patrick's High School, Coatbridge; Hamilton College of Education; St. Andrew's College Drygrange; Chesters College, Glasgow. Strathclyde Regional Council, 1976-81, 1982-83, 1988-90, latterly as Road Safety Training Officer. Recreations: football; golf; cinema. Address: (b.) Heriot Watt Research Park (North), Riccarton, Currie, Edinburgh EH14 4AP.

MacDougall, James Taylor, CBE; b. 14.5.30, Perth; m., Fiona; 1 d. Educ. Perth Academy; St. Andrews University (University College, Dundee). Admitted as a Solicitor, 1953; National Service, commissioned Royal Armoured Corps (3 Royal Tank Regiment), 1953-55; private practice/local government, 1955-59; Procurator Fiscal Depute at Dumfries, 1959-69; Procurator Fiscal: at Elgin, 1969-76, at Dumfries, 1976-93 (including Kirkcudbright, 1987-93); Honorary Sheriff at Dumfries, since 1995. Recreations: fishing; shooting; colour photography. Address: (h.) Wheatyards, Torthorwald, Dumfries DG1 3QE; T.-01387 750683.

MacDougall, John William, MP. Labour MP, Glenrothes, since 2005, Fife Central, 2001-05; Chair, All Party British-Netherlands Parliamentary Group; Secretary, All Party Singapore Parliamentary Group; Member: Scottish Affairs Select Committee, Select Committee on Statutory Instruments; b. 8.12.47; m., Catherine; 1 s.; 1 d. Educ. Rosyth Dockyard College; Fife College; Glenrothes College. Leader of the Administration, Fife Council, 1987-96, Convener of the Council, 1996-2001; former Vice-Chairman, St Andrews Links Trust; former Chairman, Community Business Fife Ltd. Address: (b.) House of Commons, London SW1A 0AA.

Macdougall, Rev. Malcolm McAllister (Calum), BD, DChrEd, MTh. Minister, Eddleston linked with Peebles Old Parish Church, since 2001; b. 20.3.52, Greenock; m., Janet MacVicar; 1 s.; 1 d. Educ. Greenock Academy; Kelvinside Academy; University of Edinburgh. Worked in Rope and Canvas Industry and in Banking before entering The Church of Scotland Ministry; served as Probationary Assistant Minister, Greenbank Parish Church, Edinburgh, 1980-81; Minister, St James' Parish Church, Portobello, 1981-2001. Former member: General Assembly's Committee on Church and Nation, General Assembly's Committee on Education; former Chairman, Edinburgh Hospital Broadcasting Service; Chairman, Edinburgh and District Churches Council on Local Broadcasting. Recreations: walking; music; broadcasting. Address: (h.)

Old Parish Manse, Innerleithen Road, Peebles EH45 8BD; T.-01721 720568. E-mail: calum.macdougall@btopenworld.com

McDougall, Peter. Screenwriter; b. 1947, Greenock. Television and film work includes: Just Another Saturday, 1974 (Prix Italia); Elephant's Graveyard, 1976; Just A Boy's Game, 1979; Shoot for the Sun, 1985; Down Where The Buffalo Go, 1988; Down Among The Big Boys, 1993.

MacDougall, Robert Hugh, MB, ChB, DMRT, FRCS, FRCR, FRCPEdin. Bute Professor and Dean of Medicine, Bute Medical School, University of St. Andrews, since 2002; Honorary Consultant Clinical Oncologist, Edinburgh Cancer Centre, Western General Hospital, Edinburgh; b. 9.8.49, Dundee; m., Moira Jean Gray; 1 s.; 2 d. Educ. High School of Dundee; St. Andrews University; Edinburgh University. Demonstrator in Anatomy, St. Andrews University; Registrar in Surgery, Aberdeen Royal Infirmary; Lecturer in Clinical Oncology, Edinburgh University; Consultant Radiotherapist and Oncologist, Tayside Health Board; Clinical Director, Department of Clinical Oncology, Western General Hospitals, Edinburgh. Recreation: reading. Address: (b.) Bute Medical School, University of St. Andrews, St. Andrews KY16 9TS.

McDowall, David, MBE, FIET, FBCS, CITP. General Officer Commanding 2nd Division, Governor, Edinburgh Castle, since 2007; Signal Officer in Chief (Army), 2002-05; b. 16.08.54, Stranraer; m., Valerie; 2 s.; 1 d. Educ. Rephard Academy; Stranraer Academy. Joined Army as a Private Soldier; served 6 years in ranks, commissioned at RMA Sandhurst, 1978; commanded at Troup, Squadron, Regiment and Brigade Level, and most recently at Division Level; now Head of Army in Scotland and North of England; operational service in Northern Ireland and Balkans. Chairman, Army Football; President, Army Bagpipes and Highland Drumming; Patron, FEBA; Colonel Commandant, Royal Corps of Signals. Recreations: all sports. Address: (b.) Annandale Block, Craigiehall, South Queensferry EH30 9TN; T.-07766441814. E-mail: dmd1@btopenworld.com

McDowall, Stuart, CBE, MA. Local Government Boundary Commissioner for Scotland, 1982-99; b. 19.4.26, Liverpool; m., Margaret B.W. Gyle (deceased); 3 s. Educ. Liverpool Institute; St. Andrews University. Royal Air Force, 1944-47; Lecturer then Senior Lecturer in Economics, St. Andrews University, 1961-91; Deputy Chairman, Central Arbitration Committee, 1976-96; Master, United College of St. Salvator and St. Leonard, St. Andrews University, 1976-80; Member: Monopolies and Mergers Commission, 1985-90, Restrictive Practices Court, 1993-96; Chairman, Fife Healthcare NHS Trust, 1994-96; Secretary, Scottish Economic Society, 1970-76. Recreations: golf; gardening; music. Address: (h.) 10 Woodburn Terrace, St. Andrews, Fife KY16 8BA; T.-01334 473247.

MacDowell, Professor Douglas Maurice, MA, DLitt, FRSE, FBA. Professor of Greek, Glasgow University, 1971-2001, now Emeritus Professor; b. 8.3.31, London. Educ. Highgate School; Balliol College, Oxford. Schoolmaster, 1954-58; Manchester University: Assistant Lecturer, 1958-61, Lecturer, 1961-68, Senior Lecturer, 1968-70, Reader, 1970-71; Visiting Fellow, Merton College, Oxford, 1969; President, Glasgow Centre, Classical Association of Scotland, 1973-75, 1977-79, 1982-84, 1988-90; Chairman, 1973-76, and Vice President, since 1976, Scottish Hellenic Society; Chairman, Council, Classical Association of Scotland, 1976-82. Publications:

Andokides: On the Mysteries, 1962; Athenian Homicide Law, 1963; Aristophanes: Wasps, 1971; The Law in Classical Athens, 1978; Spartan Law, 1986; Demosthenes: Against Meidias, 1990; Aristophanes and Athens, 1995; Antiphon and Andocides (Co-author), 1998; Demosthenes: On the False Embassy, 2000; Demosthenes: Speeches 27-38, 2004. Address: 2 Grosvenor Court, 365 Byres Road, Glasgow G12 8AU.

McEachran, Colin Neil, QC, MA, LLB, JD. QC, since 1981; b. 14.1.40, Glasgow; m., Kathrine Charlotte; 2 d. Educ. Glenalmond College; Merton College, Oxford; Glasgow University; University of Chicago. Advocate, since 1968; Advocate Depute, 1974-77; QC, 1981; Member, Scottish Legal Aid Board, 1990-98; President, Pension Appeal Tribunal Scotland, since 1995; Chairman, Commonwealth Games Council for Scotland, 1995-99. Recreations: target shooting; golf; hill-walking. Address: 13 Saxe Coburg Place, Edinburgh; T.-0131-332 6820.

McEwan, Hon. Lord (Robin Gilmour McEwan), QC, LLB, PhD. Senator of the College of Justice, since 2000; b. 12.12.43, Glasgow; m., Sheena McIntyre; 2 d. Educ. Paisley Grammar School; Glasgow University. Faulds Fellow in Law, Glasgow University, 1965-68; admitted to Faculty of Advocates, 1967; Standing Junior Counsel, Department of Energy, 1974-76; Advocate Depute, 1976-79; Chairman, Industrial Tribunals, 1981; Sheriff of Lanark, 1982-88, of Ayr, 1988-2000; Member, Scottish Legal Aid Board, 1989-96; Temporary Judge, Court of Session and High Court of Justiciary, 1991-99; Member, Gill Committee on Scottish Civil Courts Review, 2007; Deputy Chairman, Boundaries Commission for Scotland, 2007. Publications: Pleading in Court, 1980; A Casebook on Damages (Co-author), 1983; Contributor to Stair Memorial Encyclopaedia of the Laws of Scotland, 1986.

McEwan, Angus Maywood, BA (Hons), RSW, VAS. Artist; Lecturer (part-time) in Art and Design, Dundee College, since 1997; b. 19.7.63, Dundee; m., Wendy Ann Bell McEwan; 3 s. Educ. Carnoustie High School; Duncan of Jordanstone College of Art. Elizabeth Greenshields Foundation Award, Canada, 1987, 1990; RSA Latimer Award, 1995; scholarship to China, 1996; RSW Prize 1999, Alexander Graham Munro Award; RSW Prize 2001, Glasgow Arts Club Fellowship; RSA Diana King /Scottish Gallery Prize, 2002; John Gray Award, RSW Prize, 2004; John Blockley Prize, Royal Institute of Painters in Watercolours (RI), 2005; 2nd Prize, Kaupthing Singer and Friedlander Watercolour Competition; elected Member of International Guild of Realism, USA; solo exhibitions: Riverside Gallery, Stonehaven, 1990, Tolquhon Gallery, Aberdeenshire, 1992, Gallery 41, Edinburgh, 1994, Royal Scottish Academy, 1996, Leith Gallery, 1997, Le Mur Vivant Fine Art, London, 1997, Leith Gallery, 2000, Open Eye Gallery, Edinburgh, 2002; Glasgow Arts Club, 2002; solo shows: Open Eye Gallery, 2004, Queens Gallery, 2005, Open Eye Gallery, 2006; many mixed and group exhibitions; work in public and private collections; Treasurer of Hospitalfield Alumni Association. Recreations: art; photography; reading; playing with children; enjoying life. Address: (h.) 7 Glenleven Drive, Wormit, Newport on Tay, Fife DD6 8NA; T.-01382 542314; e-mail: art@angusmcewan.com
Blogsite: www.artmcewan.blogspot.com

McEwan, Leslie J., JP, MA, DipSA, DipSW. Director of Social Work, City of Edinburgh Council, 1996-2003 (retired); b. 26.2.46; m., Catherine; 2 s. Educ. St. Andrews University; Dundee University; Edinburgh University. Midlothian, East Lothian and Peebles: Child Care Officer, Children's Department, 1967-69, Social Worker, 1969-71,

Senior Social Worker, 1971-74, Social Work Advisor, 1974-75; Lothian Regional Council: Divisional Director of Social Work, Midlothian, 1975-80, West Lothian, 1980-85, Depute Director of Social Work, 1985-90, Senior Depute Director of Social Work, 1990-95; Director of Social Work, 1995-96. Associate Consultant, Care and Health. Recreations: fly-fishing; golf; woodturning.

McEwan, Roy James, BSc (Econ), DAARL, FRSA. Managing Director, Scottish Chamber Orchestra, since 1993; Member, Scottish Arts Council, 2003-07; Chairman, Glasgow Grows Audiences, since 2004; b. 12.5.51, Dumfries. Educ. Dumfries High School; Carlisle Grammar School; London School of Economics; Polytechnic of Central London. House Manager, St. George's Theatre, London, 1977-78; Manager, Whitechapel Art Gallery, 1978-79; Administrator, then Director, MacRobert Arts Centre, Stirling, 1979-91; Director of Arts Development, North West Arts Board, Manchester, 1991-93. Chairman, Federation of Scottish Theatres, 1988-91; Scottish Arts Council: Member, Drama Committee, 1991, Member, Combined Arts Committee, 1993-99; Member, Board, Association of British Orchestras, 1993-2003; Member, Board, Scottish Music Information Centre, 1994-2000. Address: (b.) 4 Royal Terrace, Edinburgh EH7 5AB.

McEwen, Professor James, MB, ChB, FRCP (Glasgow, Edinburgh, London), FFPH, FFOM, FDSRCS, DIH, FMedSci. Emeritus Professor and Honorary Senior Research Fellow, Glasgow University, since 2001; Chair, UK Voluntary Register for Public Health Specialists, since 2003; Chair, Pharmacy Health Link, since 2004; Chair, Advisory Group, Health Protection Scotland, since 2005; Professor of Public Health, Glasgow University, 1999-2001; Henry Mechan Professor of Public Health, 1989-99; Consultant in Public Health Medicine, Greater Glasgow Health Board; b. 6.2.40, Stirling; m., Elizabeth May Archibald; 1 s.; 1 d. Educ. Dollar Academy; St. Andrews University. Lecturer in Industrial Medicine, Dundee University; Senior Lecturer in Community Medicine, Nottingham University; Chief Medical Officer, The Health Education Council; Professor of Community Medicine, King's College, University of London. President, Faculty of Public Health Medicine, Royal Colleges of Physicians UK, 1998-2001. Recreations: church; gardening. Address: (b.) Auchanachie, Ruthven, Huntly, Aberdeenshire AB54 4SS; T.-01466 760742; e-mail: j.mcewen@tiscali.co.uk

McFadden, Jean Alexandra, CBE, JP, DL, MA, LLB. Member, Garscadden/Scotstounhill Ward, Glasgow City Council, since 2007, Chair, Finance, Policy Development and Scrutiny Committee, since 2007, Convener, Labour Group, since 1995, Convener, Strathclyde Joint Police Board, 2003-07; Senior Lecturer in Law, Strathclyde University; b. 26.11.41, Glasgow; m., John (deceased). Educ. Hyndland Secondary School; Glasgow University; Strathclyde University. Principal Teacher of Classics, Strathclyde schools, 1967-86; entered local government as Member, Cowcaddens Ward, Glasgow Corporation, 1971; Glasgow District Council: Member, Scotstoun Ward, 1984, Chairman, Manpower Committee, 1974-77, Leader, Labour Group, 1977-86, and 1992-94, Leader, Council, 1980-86, and 1992-94, Treasurer, 1986-92, Convener, 1995-96, Convener, Social Strategy Committee, 1996-99; Vice Lord Lieutenant, City of Glasgow, 1980-92; President, COSLA, 1990-92; Convener, Scottish Local Government Information Unit, since 1984; Member, Board, Scottish Development Agency, 1989-91, GDA, 1992-2000; Chairman, Mayfest, 1983-97; Member, Secretary of State's Health Appointments Advisory Committee, 1994-2000; Convener, West of Scotland Archaeological Joint Committee, since 1996; Chair, Charity Law Review Commission in Scotland, 2000-01; Member, Ancient

Monuments Board for Scotland, 2000-03. Recreations: cycling; theatre; walking; golf; West Highland terriers. Address: (h.) 16 Lansdowne Crescent, Glasgow G20 6NG; T.-0141-334 3522.

McFadden, John Alexander Crawford, MA, LLB. Solicitor (retired); b. 11,9,36, Dunoon; m., Patricia Mary Thompson; 1 s. 2 d. Educ. Robert Gordon's College, Aberdeen; Aberdeen University. Solicitor in private practice, 1962-99; Honorary Sheriff Substitute at Dumfries, since 1995. Recreation: reading. Address: (h.) Braeside, 54 Moffat Road, Dumfries DG1 1NY; T.-01387 253077.

MacFadyen, Alasdair Lorne, LLB. Sheriff, Grampian Highland and Islands at Dingwall, Inverness and Portree, since 2002; b. 18.9.55, Glasgow; m., Lynne Ballantyne; 2 d. Educ. High School of Glasgow; Glasgow University. Qualified as Scottish Solicitor, 1978; practised as Solicitor in Private Practice, Edinburgh, Glasgow and Inverness, 1978-2001; Temporary Sheriff, 1995-2000; Part-Time Chairman, Employment Tribunals (Scotland), 2000-01; Part-Time Sheriff, 2000-01; All Scotland Floating Sheriff, based in Aberdeen, 2001-02. Recreations: sailing in Tall Ships; music; cycling. Address: (b.) Sheriff Court, Ferry Road, Dingwall, Ross-shire IV15 9QX; T.-01349 863153.

McFall, John, BSc (Hons), BA, MBA. MP (Labour), Dumbarton, since 1987; Chairman, Treasury Committee, since 2001; Parliamentary Under Secretary of State, Northern Ireland Office, 1998-99; serves on: Information Committee, Parliamentary and Scientific Committee, Executive Committee – Parliamentary Group for Energy Studies, British/Italian Group, British/Peru Group, Retail Industry Group, Roads Study Group, Scotch Whisky Group, Parliamentary and Scientific Committee; formerly Opposition Whip with responsibility for Foreign Affairs, Defence and Trade and Industry (resigned post at time of Gulf War); former Deputy Shadow Secretary of State for Scotland; Scottish Whip, 1997-98. Recreations: jogging; reading; golf. Address: (b.) House of Commons, Westminster, London.

Macfarlane of Bearsden, Lord, (Norman Somerville Macfarlane), KT (1996), Kt (1983), DL, FRSE. Life Peer; Honorary Life President, Macfarlane Group PLC (Chairman, 1973-98, Managing Director, 1973-90, Honorary Life President, 1999, Macfarlane Group (Clansman PLC); Honorary Life President, United Distillers (Chairman, 1987-96); Lord High Commissioner, General Assembly of Church of Scotland, 1992, 1993, 1997; b. 5.3.26; m., Marguerite Mary Campbell; 1 s.; 4 d. Educ. High School of Glasgow. Commissioned, Royal Artillery, 1945, served Palestine, 1945-47; founded N.S. Macfarlane & Co. Ltd., 1949 (became Macfarlane Group (Clansman) PLC, 1973); Underwriting Member of Lloyd's, 1978-97; Chairman: The Fine Art Society PLC, 1976-98 (Honorary Life President, 1998), American Trust PLC, 1984-97 (Director, since 1980), Guinness PLC, 1987-89 (Joint Deputy Chairman, 1989-92); Director: Clydesdale Bank PLC, 1980-96 (Deputy Chairman, 1993-96), General Accident Fire and Life Assurance Corporation plc, 1984-96, Edinburgh Fund Managers plc, 1980-98, Glasgow Chamber of Commerce, 1976-79; Member: Council, CBI Scotland, 1975-81, Board, Scottish Development Agency, 1979-87; Chairman, Glasgow Development Agency, 1985-92; Vice Chairman, Scottish Ballet, 1983-87 (Director, 1975-87), Hon. President, since 2001; Director, Scottish National Orchestra, 1977-82; President, Royal Glasgow Institute of the Fine Arts, 1976-87; Member, Royal Fine Art Commission for Scotland, 1980-82; Scottish Patron, National Art Collection Fund, since 1978; Governor, Glasgow School of Art, 1976-87, Hon. President, since 2001; Trustee: National Heritage Memorial Fund, 1984-97, National Galleries of Scotland, 1986-97; Director, Third Eye Centre, 1978-81; Hon. President, Charles Rennie Mackintosh Society, since 1988; Hon. President, High School of Glasgow, since 1992 (Chairman of Governors, 1979-92); Member, Court, Glasgow University, 1979-87; Regent, RCSE, since 1997; President: Stationers' Association of GB and Ireland, 1965, Company of Stationers of Glasgow, 1968-70, Glasgow High School Club, 1970-72; Patron, Scottish Licensed Trade Association, since 1992; Honorary Patron, Queen's Park FC; Vice President, Professional Golfers Association; KT, 1996; DL, Dunbartonshire, 1993, CIMgt, 1996, HRSA, 1987, HRGI, 1987, Hon. FRIAS, 1984, FRSE, 1991, Hon.FScotvec, 1991, Hon. FRCPS Glas., 1992, Hon. Fellow, Glasgow School of Art, 1993; Hon. LLD: Strathclyde, 1986, Glasgow, 1988, Glasgow Caledonian, 1993, Aberdeen, 1995; DUniv., Stirling, 1992; Dr (hc), Edinburgh, 1992; Glasgow St. Mungo Award, 2005; Hon. President, Tenovus Scotland, 2006; Hon. Life Member, Scottish Football League, 2006; Freeman of Dumfries and Galloway, 2006; Freeman of the City of Glasgow, 2007. Recreations: golf; cricket; theatre; art. Address: (b.) Macfarlane Group PLC, Clansman House, 21 Newton Place, Glasgow G3 7PY; (h.) 50 Manse Road, Bearsden, Glasgow G61 3PN.

MacFarlane, Professor Sir Alistair George James, Kt, CBE, PhD, DSc, MA, ScD, FIEE, FEng, FRS, FRSE. Principal and Vice Chancellor, Heriot-Watt University, 1989-96; Chairman, Advisory Group for Scottish University for Industry, 1998-2000; Chairman, Academic Advisory Board, University of Highlands and Islands Project, 1999-2002 (Acting Chief Executive Officer, 2000-01); Rector, UHI Millennium Institute, 2001-04; b. 1931, Edinburgh; m., Nora (deceased, 2005); 1 s. Educ. Hamilton Academy; Glasgow University. Metropolitan-Vickers Electrical Company Ltd.: Electronic Engineer, Radar and Servo Division, Group Leader, Moving Target Indication and Receiver Laboratories; Lecturer, Electrical Engineering, Queen Mary College, London University, 1959 (Reader, 1965); UMIST: Reader in Control Engineering, 1966, Professor, 1969; Cambridge University: Chair, Engineering, 1974, Head, Information Engineering Division, Fellow, Selwyn College, 1974-78 (Vice-Master, 1980-88, Honorary Fellow, since 1978); Chairman, Scottish Council for Research in Education, 1993-98; Chairman, Scottish Library and Information Council, 1994-98; Non-Executive Director, BNFL plc, 1994-2000; Member, BT Advisory Forum in Scotland, 1996-98; former Consultant Editor, International Journal of Control. Past Member: SERC Computer Board, Joint Policy Committee for National Facilities for Advanced Research Computing, Advisory Committee on Safety of Nuclear Installations; Vice-President, Royal Society, 1997-99. American Society of Mechanical Engineers Centennial Medal, 1980; Sir Harold Hartley Medal, Institute of Measurement and Control,1982; IEE Achievement Medal, 1992; IEE Faraday Medal, 1993; American Society of Mechanical Engineers Oldenburger Medal, 2004.

Macfarlane, Rev. Alwyn James Cecil, BA, MA; b. 14.6.22, Edinburgh; m., Joan Cowell Harris; 1 s.; 1 d. Educ. Cargilfield School, Edinburgh; Rugby School; New College, Oxford; New College, Edinburgh. Captain, 6th Black Watch, North Africa, Italy and Greece, 1940-45; entered Ministry, Church of Scotland, 1951; Minister: Foddferty and Strathpeffer, 1952-59, St. Cuthbert's Church, Edinburgh (Associate), 1959-63, Portobello Old, Edinburgh, 1963-68, Newlands (South), Glasgow, 1968-85; Associate Minister, The Scots' Church, Melbourne, 1985-88. Chaplain to The Queen in Scotland; Member, The Queen's Household in Scotland. Recreations: photography; travel. Address: Flat 12, 177 Fenwick Road, Giffnock, Glasgow G46 6JD.

McFarlane, Jim. Managing Director, Regional Operations, Scottish Enterprise, since 2005; b. 14.5.53, Glasgow; m., Carol; 2 d. Educ. Glasgow School of Art (DipTP). Leith Project Manager, SDA, Edinburgh, 1981-86;

Director of Operations, Glasgow Garden Festival Ltd., 1986-88; Regional Head of Projects/Property, SDA, Edinburgh, 1988-91; Director of Property and Environment, Lothian and Edinburgh Enterprise Ltd., 1991-98; Director of Projects, LEEL, 1998-99; Chief Executive, Scottish Enterprise Borders, Galashiels, 1999-2001; Senior Director Business Transformation, Scottish Enterprise, Glasgow, 2001-03; Chief Executive, Scottish Enterprise Edinburgh and Lothian, 2003-05. Address: (b.) Apex House, 99 Haymarket Terrace, Edinburgh EH12 5HD; T.-0131 313 4000.

Macfarlane, Professor Peter Wilson, DSc, FBCS, FRCP(Glasg), FESC, FRSE. Professor of Electrocardiology, Glasgow University, since 1995; b. 8.11.42, Glasgow; m., Irene Grace Muir; 2 s. Educ. Hyndland Senior Secondary School, Glasgow; Glasgow University. Glasgow University: Assistant Lecturer in Medical Cardiology, 1967, Lecturer, 1970, Senior Lecturer, 1974, Reader, 1980, Professor, 1991; President, 5th International Congress on Electrocardiology, Glasgow, 1978; Chairman, 15th and 18th Annual Conferences, International Society of Computerized Electrocardiology, 1990, 1993; President, International Society of Electrocardiology, since 2007. Author/Editor, 14 books. Recreations: watching football; running half-marathons; playing violin. Address: (h.) 12 Barrcraig Road, Bridge of Weir PA11 3HG; T.-01505 614443.

MacFarlane, Emeritus Professor Thomas Wallace, DDS, DSc, FRSE, FDS RCSEdin. Professor of Oral Microbiology, Glasgow University, 1991-2001; Honorary Consultant in Oral Microbiology; Dean of the Dental School, 1995-2000; b. 12.12.42, Glasgow; m., Nancy McEwan Fyfe; 1 s. Educ. Hyndland Senior Secondary School; Glasgow University. Assistant Lecturer, Dental Histology and Pathology, 1966-69; trained in Medical Microbiology and Histopathology, Glasgow Royal Infirmary; Lecturer in Oral Medicine and Pathology, 1969-77; organised and ran the diagnostic service in Oral Microbiology, Glasgow Dental Hospital and School; Senior Lecturer in Oral Medicine and Pathology and Consultant in Oral Microbiology, 1977; Reader in Oral Medicine and Pathology, 1984-91; Head, Department of Oral Sciences, 1992-95. Recreations: music; reading; painting; walking. Address: 5 St. Baldred's Crescent, North Berwick, East Lothian EH39 4PZ; T.-01620-892096.

McFarlane, William Stewart, CA; b. 26.3.33, Glasgow; m., Sandra; 1 d. Educ. High School of Glasgow. Trained as Chartered Accountant, Wilson Stirling (now Deloittes Touche), Glasgow; Parlane McFarlane CA, 1957-58; National Service (Second Lieutenant, Royal Corps of Signals), 1959-60; Partner, McFarlane, Son & Co., CA, 1961-62, merged with Dickson, McFarlane & Robinson, CA, 1963-84, merged with Wylie & Bisset, CA, 1985-98. Member, Council, Institute of Chartered Accountants of Scotland, 1971-76, Institute's representative, directorate of Glasgow Chamber of Commerce, 1970-88; President, Glasgow Chamber of Commerce, 1990-92; Past Finance Convener, Scottish Golf Union; Past Treasurer, Scottish Squash Rackets Association; Captain, Association of Golf Club Secretaries, 1980; Past Deacon, Incorporation of Masons of Glasgow; Past President, Rotary Club of Charing Cross. Recreations: golf; curling; swimming. Address: (h.) 2d Southwood Crescent, Rosemount Avenue, Newton Mearns, Glasgow G77 5TN; T.-0141 639 6605.

Macfarlane Smith, William Holmes, BSc, PhD, CBiol, MIBiol. Honorary Research Fellow, Scottish Crop Research Institute, since 2002; Managing Director, Biomac Consultancy Ltd., since 2003; Honorary Secretary, Scottish Society for Crop Research, since 2004; b. 23.4.42, Newcastle upon Tyne; m., Daphne Henderson; 3 s. Educ. Aberdeen Grammar School; Dundee High School; Aberdeen University; Reading University. Post-doctoral

research, University of Dundee, 1971-72; Rothwell Plant Breeders (Shell Nickerson): Barley Breeder, Senior Barley Breeder, Head of Barley Breeding Team, Technical Manager, 1972-78; Scottish Plant Breeding Station, subsequently Scottish Crop Research Institute: Rape and Swede Breeder, Head of Brassica Department, Leader, Commercial Brassica Breeding, 1978-95; Head of Scientific Liaison and Information Services, 1995-2002. Vice-Chairman of Board, Dundee High School, 2000-07; Past President, Dundee High School Old Boys Club; Past President, Dundee Rotary Club; Assistant Governor, Rotary District 1010, 2006-08; District Governor Nominee, Rotary District 1010, 2007-08. Recreations: golf; hillwalking; photography. Address: (h.) 42 Holly Road, Broughty Ferry, Dundee DD5 2LZ; T.-01382 739148; e-mail: bill@biomac.co.uk

McGarry, Gerald William. MBChB, MD, FRCS(Glas), FRCS(Ed), FRCS(ORLHNS). Consultant Otolaryngologist, Head and Neck Surgeon, since 1995; Honorary Senior Lecturer, University of Glasgow, since 1995; b. 30.1.62, Glasgow; m., Carol; 3 s. Educ. St. Augustine Secondary School, Glasgow; Glasgow University. Senior Registrar in Otolaryngology: Glasgow Rotational Scheme, 1992, Royal Brisbane Hospital, Australia, 1993; Locum Consultant Otolaryngologist, Glasgow Royal Infirmary, 1994. Former MATTUS Tutor; former Council Member, Otorhinolaryngological Society; former Member, Medical Appeals Tribunal; Founder, Scottish Sinus Surgery Group. Publications: Picture Tests in ENT, 1999; Endoscopic Dissection of the Nose and Paranasal Sinuses; papers on rhinology and head and neck cancer; textbook contributor. Recreations: mountaineering; aviation. Address: Department of Otolaryngology, Royal Infirmary, Glasgow G31 2ER; T.-0141-211 1660.

McGeoch, Duncan J., BSc, PhD, FRSE. Director, Medical Research Council Virology Unit, Glasgow, since 1995; Honorary Professor, Glasgow University, since 1996. Educ. Hutchesons' Grammar School; Glasgow University. Jane Coffin Childs Memorial Fund Fellow, Department of Microbiology and Molecular Genetics, Harvard Medical School, 1971-73; Researcher, Division of Virology, Department of Pathology, University of Cambridge, 1973-76; Staff Member, MRC Virology Unit, Glasgow, since 1976. Fleming Award, Society for General Microbiology, 1980; Editor, Journal of General Virology, 1984-87, Editor-in-Chief, 1988-92. Address: (b.) MRC Virology Unit, Church Street, Glasgow G11 5JR.

McGeough, Professor Joseph Anthony, FRSE, BSc, PhD, DSc, CEng, FIMechE, FIET. Regius Professor of Engineering, Edinburgh University, 1983-2005; Emeritus Professor, since 2005; Senior Honorary Professorial Fellow, 2007-08; Honorary Professor, Nanjing Aeronautical and Astronautical University, China, since 1991; Visiting Professor: University Federico II of Naples, 1994, Glasgow Caledonian University, 1997-2003, Tokyo University of Agriculture and Technology, 2004, Monash University, 2005; b. 29.5.40, Kilwinning; m., Brenda Nicholson; 2 s.; 1 d. Educ. St. Michael's College; Glasgow University; Aberdeen University. Research Demonstrator, Leicester University, 1966; Senior Research Fellow, Queensland University, Australia, 1967; Research Metallurgist, International Research and Development Co. Ltd., Newcastle-upon-Tyne, 1968-69; Senior Research Fellow, Strathclyde University, 1969-72; Lecturer in Engineering, Aberdeen University, 1972-77 (Senior Lecturer, 1977-80, Reader, 1980-83). Member, Council, IMechE, 2000-03, Trustee, Board, 2004-08, Vice-President, 2006-2010; Member of Council, CIRP, 2006-08, Fellow, since 2006; Chairman, CIRP UK, 2000-03; Editor, Journal of Processing of Advanced Materials, 1991-94; CIRP Editor, Journal of Materials Processing Technology, since 1991; Editor, Proceedings of International Conference on Computer-Aided Production Engineering, since 1986.

Publications: Principles of Electrochemical Machining, 1974; Advanced Methods of Machining, 1988; Micromachining of Engineering Materials (Editor), 2001. Recreations: gardening; golf. Address: (h.) 39 Dreghorn Loan, Colinton, Edinburgh EH13 ODF; T.-0131-441 1302.

McGettrick, Professor Andrew David, BSc, PhD, FRSE, FIEE, FBCS, CEng. Professor of Computer Science, Strathclyde University, since 1984; Head, Computer and Information Sciences Department, since 2001 (Head, Computer Science Department, 1996-2001); b. 15.5.44, Glasgow; m., Sheila Margaret Girot; 5 s.; 1 d. Educ. St. Aloysius College, Glasgow; Glasgow University; Cambridge University. Lecturer, then Reader, then Professor, Strathclyde University, since 1969; Editor, Addison Wesley's International Computer Science series; Chairman, IEE Safety Critical Systems Committee; Chairman, UK Computer Science Professors Conference, 1991-93; Vice-President, British Computer Society, since 2004; Joint Chair, Education Board of US Association for Computing Machinery (ACM). Publications: four books as author, three books edited. Recreations: running; golf; squash. Address: (b.) Strathclyde University, Glasgow G1 1XH; T.-0141-548 3589.

McGettrick, Professor Bartholomew John, OBE, FRSAMD, KC*HS, DLitt, DHLitt, FRSA, BSc (Hons), MEd (Hons), Silver Palm of Jerusalem (1996). Professor, Glasgow University; former Dean, Faculty of Education; Member, General Teaching Council for Scotland, 1986-2001; Member, various CNAA committees; Chairman, Committee on Assessment 5-14; Chairman, Schools Commission for the Holy Land, 1999; Member, Council, International Federation of Catholic Universities; b. 16.8.45, Glasgow; m., Elizabeth Maria McLaughlin; 2 s.; 2 d. Educ. St. Aloysius' College, Glasgow; Glasgow University. Teacher and Head, Department of Geography, St. Aloysius' College, Glasgow, 1968-72; Educational Psychologist, Scottish Centre for Social Subjects, 1972-75; Assistant Principal, then Vice-Principal, Notre Dame College of Education (latterly St. Andrew's College of Education), 1975-85; Principal, St. Andrew's College of Education, 1985-99. Chairman, Catholic Education Commission for Scotland, 1981-87; Chair, "Higher Still" Task Group – Staff Development; Member, Council for Educational Technology, 1982-86; Chairman, Committee of Principals of Colleges of Education, 1990-92; Honorary President, Association Catholique Internationale des Institutions de Sciences de L'Education; Board of Governors, St. Aloysius' College, Glasgow; Chairman of Governors, Clifton Hall School, Edinburgh; Trustee: Kilgraston School, Craighalbert Centre, The New School, Butterstone; Chairman, Governors, Craighead Institute; Member, International Committee for the Education of Teachers; Vice Chair: Educational Broadcasting Council for Scotland, 1995-99, Advisory Group on Sustainable Development; Chairman, Education for Sustainable Development Group; Chairman, Scottish Council for Independent Schools, 1997-2005; Trustee, Gordon Cook Foundation; Chairman, Schools Commission for the Holy Land; Member, International Board, Regents of Bethlehem University, Palestine; HM Commissioner, Queen Victoria School, Dunblane; Member, Scottish Social Services Council. Recreation: sports. Address: (h.) 174 Carmunnock Road, Glasgow G44 5AJ; T.-0141-637 8112; e-mail: bjm@educ.gla.ac.uk

McGhee, Charles. Editor, The Herald, since 2006. Formerly Editor, Evening Times. Address: (b.) 200 Renfield Street, Glasgow G2 3QB; T.-0141-302 7005.

McGhie, Hon. Lord (James Marshall), QC, LLB (Hons). Chairman, Scottish Land Court; President, Lands Tribunal for Scotland, since 1996; b. 15.10.44, Perth; m., Ann M. Cockburn; 1 s.; 1 d. Educ. Perth Academy; Edinburgh University. Scots Bar, 1969; QC, 1983; Advocate-Depute,

1983-86; part-time Chairman, Medical Appeal Tribunals, 1987-92; Member, Criminal Injuries Compensation Board, 1992-96. Address: (b.) George House, 126 George Street, Edinburgh; T.-0131 271 4360.

McGhie, Duncan Clark, CA. Chairman, Scottish Ballet and Scottish Opera, 1999-2004; b. 6.12.44, Newton Mearns, Renfrewshire; m., Una G. Carmichael; 1 s.; 1 d. Educ. George Watson's College; Institute of Chartered Accountants. CA apprenticeship, 1962-67; Financial Controller, Scottish Division, British Steel Corporation, 1967-78; Group Finance Director, Wm. Collins Publishers, 1978-84; Partner, Coopers and Lybrand (latterly Pricewaterhouse Coopers), 1984-2000. Elder, Church of Scotland. Recreations: golf; music; walking. Address: (b.) 65 Corrour Road, Newlands, Glasgow, G43 2ED; T.-0141-632 4502.

McGiffen, Diane, MA, MSc. Director of Corporate Services, Audit Scotland, since 2000; b. 24.8.63, Cumbernauld; m., Ross Thomson; 1 s. Educ. Greenfaulds High School, Cumbernauld; Glasgow University; Edinburgh University. Hansard, House of Commons, 1986-89; Edinburgh District Council, 1989-91; COSLA, 1991-92; Wester Hailes Partnership, 1992-96; Accounts Commission, 1996-2000. Address: (b.) 110 George Street, Edinburgh EH2 4LH; T.-0131 625 1608; e-mail: dmcgiffen@audit-scotland.gov.uk

MacGillivray, Alan, MA, DipEd. Educational writer, since 1987; President, Association for Scottish Literary Studies, 2002-06; b. 5.6.35, Kirkcaldy; m., Isobel McCorkindale; 2 s.; 1 d. (deceased). Educ. Dumfries Academy; Edinburgh University. Teacher of English, 1958-67: Ardrossan Academy, Annan Academy, Inverness Royal Academy; Principal Teacher of English, Anderson High School, Lerwick, 1967-72; Lecturer/Senior Lecturer in English, Jordanhill College of Education, Glasgow, 1973-87; Honorary Lecturer in Scottish Literature, University of Strathclyde, 1987-2003. Director, Jordanhill Scottish Literature and Language Project, 1980-82. Publications: The Ring of Words (Joint Editor), 1970; Teaching Scottish Literature (Editor), 1997; Scottish Literature in English and Scots (Joint Editor), 2002; study guides on George Mackay Brown and Iain Banks; Kindly Clouds (Poems), 2005; The Bountiful Loch (Poems), 2007; articles, teaching materials, short stories, etc. Recreations: reading; verse writing; walking. Address: (h.) 482 Clarkston Road, Glasgow G44 3QE; T.-0141-571 7562.

McGillivray, Rev. (Alexander) Gordon, MA, BD, STM; b. 22.9.23, Edinburgh; m., Winifred Jean Porter; 2 s.; 2 d. Educ. George Watson's Boys' College, Edinburgh; Edinburgh University; Union Theological Seminary, New York. Royal Artillery, 1942-45; Assistant Minister, St. Cuthbert's Parish Church, Edinburgh; Minister: Waterbeck Church, 1951-58, Nairn High Church, 1958-73; Clerk, Presbytery of Edinburgh, 1973-93; Clerk, General Assembly of Church of Scotland, 1971-94, retired. Editor, Church of Scotland Yearbook, 1996-99. Recreations: golf; theatre. Address: 7 Greenfield Crescent, Balerno, Midlothian EH14 7HD; T.-0131-449 4747.

McGillivray, Professor Mark, BEc, BA (Hons), PhD. Professor of Development Economics, University of Glasgow, since 2005; Deputy Director, World Institute for Development Economics Research, United Nations University, Helsinki, Finland, since 2006; b. 10.09.60, Koroit, Australia; 2 s. Educ. Hawkesdale High School; La Trobe University. Tutor and Senior Tutor in Economics, La Trobe University, Melbourne, Australia, 1984-88; Lecturer in Economics, Deakin University, Geelong, Australia, 1988-90, Senior Lecturer in Development Studies, 1991-98; Visiting Research Fellow: Centre for Research in International Trade and Economic Development, Department of Economics, University of Nottingham, 1994,

Institute for Social Studies, The Hague, The Netherlands, 1994; Director, Centre for the Study of Asian and the Middle East, Deakin University, Melbourne, Australia, 1994-97, Director, International Development Studies Program, 1997-98; Associate Professor and Discipline Leader, International Development Program, Royal Melbourne Institute of Technology, Melbourne, Australia, 1998-2002; Senior Research Fellow, World Institute for Development Economics Research, United Nations University, Helsinki, Finland, 2002-07. Inaugural Fellow, Human Development and Capability Association Fellow, Centre for Research in Economic Development and International Trade, University of Nottingham. Recreations: cycling; food and wine; travel. Address: (b.) Wider, Katajanokanlaituri 6B, 00160 Helsinki, Finland; T.-4358 961599213; e-mail: mark@wider.unu.edu

McGlinchey, Scott, BA, DipM, FRSA. Chief Operating Officer, Exception Ltd., since 2005; b. 16.8.61, Edinburgh; m.; 3 s. Educ. Royal High School; Napier University. Marketing Analyst, ISTEL, 1985-87; ICL, customer and sales management, 1987-94; Client Manager, NHS, 1994-95; UK Sales and Marketing Director, IT consultancy; 1995-98; Director, ICL Scotland, 1998-2002; Chief Operating Officer, Newell and Budge, 2002-04. Director, Young Scot; Founding Member, Generation Science; Director, Edinburgh Chamber of Commerce, 2000-02; Member, Scottish Executive Digital Task Force, 1999; Member, Scottish Executive Modernising Government Reference Group. Recreations: rugby; music. E-mail: scott.mcglinchey@blueyonder.co.uk

McGlynn, Rt. Rev. Abbot Emeritus (James Aloysius) Donald, OCSO, STL, SLJ. Monk, Order of Cistercians of Strict Observance, since 1952; Abbot of Nunraw, 1952-2003 (Emeritus); b. 13.8.34, Glasgow. Educ. Holyrood School, Glasgow; St. Bernardine's School, Buckinghamshire; Gregorian University, Rome. President: Scottish Council of Major Religious Superiors, 1974-77, British Isles Regional Council of Cistercian Abbeys, 1980-84; Chairman, Union of Monastic Superiors, 1985-89; Official Roman Catholic Visitor to the General Assembly, Church of Scotland, 1976 and 1985; Commandeur Ecclesiastique, Military & Hospitaller Order of St. Lazarus of Jerusalem, 1985; Chief Akaoluchukwu Nsugbe, Anambra State, Nigeria; Patron, Haddington Pilgrimage of St. Mary & the Three Kings. Address: Sancta Maria Abbey, Nunraw, Garvald, Haddington EH41 4LW; T.-0162 083 0223; e-mail: domdonald@yahoo.co.uk; web: www.nunraw.org.uk

McGorum, Professor Bruce Campbell, BSc, BVMS, PhD, CEIM, DECEIM, MRCVS. Professor of Equine Medicine, University of Edinburgh since 2002; b. 9.3.61, Dunfermline; m., Isabel Maria McGorum; 3 d. Educ. Queen Anne High School; University of Edinburgh. Veterinary Practitioner, Buckinghamshire, 1985-87; University of Edinburgh: Horserace Betting Levy Board Resident in Equine Studies, 1987-90, Lecturer, then Senior Lecturer, Easter Bush Veterinary Centre, 1990-98, RSE/SOEID Support Research Fellow, 1998-99, Senior Lecturer, 1999-2002. 2004 Animal Health Trust Veterinary Achievement Award. Recreations: outdoor sports. Address: (b.) Easter Bush Veterinary Centre, Easter Bush, Roslin, Midlothian EH25 9RG; T.-0131-650-6230.
E-mail: bruce.mcgorum@ed.ac.uk

McGougan, Donald, CPFA. Director of Finance, City of Edinburgh Council, since 1995; Director, Edinburgh Military Tattoo, since 1995; b. 26.12.50; Glasgow; m., Mandy; 1 s.; 1 d. Educ. Hermitage Academy, Helensburgh. Trainee Accountant, Midlothian County Council, 1971; Professional Assistant, City of Edinburgh District Council, 1975; Falkirk District Council: Principal Assistant, 1979, Depute Director of Finance, 1981; Depute Director of Finance, City of Edinburgh District Council, 1987.

Recreations: family; golf; rugby. Address: (b.) Waverley Court, 4 East Market Street, Edinburgh EH8 8BG; T.-0131-469 3005.

McGovern, James. MP (Labour), Dundee West, since 2005; b. 17.11.56. Address: (b.) House of Commons, London SW1A 0AA.

McGowan, Professor David Alexander, MDS, PhD, FDSRCS, FFDRCSI, FDSRCPSG, FDSRCS (Edin). Professor of Oral Surgery, Glasgow University, 1977-99, Emeritus Professor, since 1999 (Dean of Dental Education, 1990-95); Consultant Oral Surgeon, Greater Glasgow Health Board, 1977-99; b. 18.6.39, Portadown, Co. Armagh; m., Margaret Vera Macaulay; 1 s.; 2 d. Educ. Portadown College; Queen's University, Belfast. Oral surgery training, Belfast and Aberdeen, 1961-67; Lecturer in Dental Surgery, Queen's University, Belfast, 1968; Lecturer, then Senior Lecturer and Deputy Head, Oral and Maxillofacial Surgery, London Hospital Medical College, 1968-77. Postgraduate Adviser in Dentistry, Glasgow University, 1977-90; Chairman, Dental Committee, Scottish Council for Postgraduate Medical Education, 1980-90; Dean, Dental Faculty, and Member of College Council, Royal College of Physicians and Surgeons of Glasgow, 1989-92; Member and Vice-Chairman of Executive, General Dental Council, 1989-99; Member, Court, Glasgow University, 1995-99; Chairman, National Dental Advisory Committee, 1996-99; Member, EC Advisory Committee on Training of Dental Practitioners, 1993-2001; former Council Member, British Association of Oral and Maxillofacial Surgeons. Recreations: sailing; music. Address: Rhu Lodge, Rhu, Helensburgh G84 8NF.

McGowan, Sheriff John, LLB. Sheriff of South Strathclyde Dumfries and Galloway at Ayr; b. 15.1.44, Kilmarnock; m., Elise Smith; 2 s. Educ. St. Joseph's Academy, Kilmarnock; Glasgow University. Admitted Solicitor, 1967; Temporary Sheriff, 1986-93; Sheriff of Glasgow and Strathkelvin, 1993-2000. Council Member, Law Society of Scotland, 1982-85. Recreations: golf; tennis; listening to music. Address: (h.) 20 Auchendoon Crescent, Ayr KA7 4AS; T.-01292 260139; (b.) Sheriff Court House, Wellington Square, Ayr; T.-01292 268474; e-mail: Sheriff.J.McGowan@scotcourts.gov.uk

McGrath, Professor John Christie (Ian), BSc, PhD. Regius Professor of Physiology, Glasgow University, since 1991; Chairman, The Physiological Society, 2006-08; b. 8.3.49, Johnstone; m., Wilma Nicol (deceased); 1 s.; 1 d. Educ. John Neilson Institution, Paisley; Glasgow University. Glasgow University: Research Fellow in Pharmacology and Anaesthesia, 1973-75, Lecturer, 1975-83, Senior Lecturer, 1983-88, Reader, 1988-89, Titular Professor, 1987-91; Co-Director, Clinical Research Initiative in Heart Failure, 1994-2000; Head of Division, Department of Neuroscience and Biomedical Systems, Institute of Biomedical and Life Sciences, 1991-93, 1997-2004. Sandoz Prizewinner, British Pharmacological Society, 1980; Pfizer Award for Biology, 1983; Senior Editor, British Journal of Pharmacology, 2001-07. Recreations: running; politics; travel. Address: (b.) West Medical Building, Glasgow University, Glasgow; T.-0141-330 4483.

McGrath, Tom. Playwright and Poet; b. 1940, Rutherglen. Educ. Glasgow University. Founder Editor, International Times, 1966-67; Musical Director, Great Northern Welly Boot Show; Director, Third Eye Centre, Glasgow, 1974-77; plays include: Laurel and Hardy, 1976, The Hardman, 1977.

McGregor, Rev. Alistair Gerald Crichton, QC, BD, BA, LLB, WS. Former Minister, North Leith Parish Church, Edinburgh (1987-2002); Temporary Sheriff, 1984-87; b. 15.10.37, Sevenoaks, Kent; m., Margaret Dick Lees or

McGregor; 2 s.; 1 d. Educ. Charterhouse; Pembroke College, Oxford; Edinburgh University. Solicitor; Advocate; QC; former Standing Junior Counsel to Queen's and Lord Treasurer's Remembrancer, to Scottish Home and Health Department and to Scottish Development Department; Past Chairman, Discipline Committee, Potato Marketing Board; former Clerk, Rules Council, Court of Session; former Tutor in Scots Law, Edinburgh University; former Chairman, Family Care; former Director, Apex (Scotland) Ltd; former Governor, Loretto School; Governor, Palcrafts (UK) Ltd and Dean Orphanage Trust; former Chairman, Drug Prevention Group; General Trustee of Church of Scotland. Publication: Obscenity (Co-Author). Recreations: squash; tennis; swimming; travel; cinema. Address: (h.) 22 Primrose Bank Road, Edinburgh EH5; T.-0131-551 2802.

McGregor, Bill, MA, MEd. General Secretary, Headteachers' Association of Scotland, since 2004; b. 14.2.44, Kilmarnock; m., Elspeth Barbara Greene; 1 s.; 1 d. Educ. Kilmarnock Academy; Glasgow University. Teacher, Assistant Rector, Depute Rector, Mainholm Academy, Ayr, 1968-89; Rector, James Hamilton Academy, Kilmarnock, 1989-2004. Member, National Executive, Headteachers' Association of Scotland (Convener, Public and Parliamentary Committee). Publications: bus histories. Recreations: photography (transport); writing. Address: (h.) 25 Blackburn Drive, Ayr KA7 2XW; T.-01292 282043; e-mail: valayrmac@btinternet.com

MacGregor, Professor Bryan Duncan, BSc, MSc, PhD, DipSurv, CertHE, MRTPI, MRICS. MacRobert Professor of Land Economy, Aberdeen University, since 1990, Dean of Social Science and Law, 2002-03; Vice Principal and Head, College of Arts and Social Sciences, since 2003; b. 16.10.53, Inverness; m., Nicola; 2 twin d. Educ. Inverness Royal Academy; Edinburgh University; Heriot Watt University; Cambridge University; College of Estate Management; Sabhal Mor Ostaig (Gaelic College). Lecturer, Department of Land Management, Reading University, 1981-84; Lecturer, Department of Town and Regional Planning, Glasgow University, 1984-87; Deputy, then Property Research Manager, Prudential Portfolio Managers, 1987-90. Recreations: Gaelic; hill-walking; football; literature; music; thinking. Address: (b.) College Office, Powis Gate, College Bounds, University of Aberdeen, King's College, Aberdeen AB24 3UG; T.-01224 272080.

Macgregor, Dr Donald Finlay, BSc, MBChB, FRCP(Edin), FRCPCH. Consultant Paediatrician (Hon. Senior Lecturer), Tayside University Hospitals, Dundee, since 1996; b. 22.9.56, Bridge of Allan; m., Elspeth Mary McLeod; 1 s.; 3 d. Educ. Falkirk High School; St Andrews University; Manchester University. Senior House Officer, 1984; Registrar, 1984-88; Provincial Paediatrician, Eastern Highlands, Papua New Guinea, 1986-88; Fellow, University of British Columbia, Vancouver, 1988-90; Clinical Fellow, BC Children's Hospital, Vancouver, 1988-90; Senior Registrar, Royal Hospital for Sick Children, Edinburgh, 1990-92; Consultant Paediatrician, Lancaster and Kendal Hospitals, 1992-96. Secretary, Scottish Paediatric Society; Regional Advisor, Royal College of Paediatrics and Child Health. Recreations: family; outdoor pursuits; Third World issues. Address: (h.) Bon Accord, 2 Viewlands Road, Perth PH1 1BH; T.-01738 625796.

MacGregor of MacGregor, Major Sir Malcolm. Chief of Clan Gregor, since 2003.

McGregor, Iain. Honorary Secretary, SABRE (Scotland Against Being Ruled By Europe); b. 19.3.37, Stirling. Educ. Selkirk High School; Kelso High School. Army Service, REME; International Trade Exhibitions Publicist, London; Editor, BIPS International Photo-Feature Agency;

Journalist, Fleet Street and provinces; Writer and Lecturer in Journalism, Asia, Europe, North America; Founding Director, Institute for Christian Media (Canada); Editor, The Patriot for Scotland; Editor and Publisher, Social Credit International. Recreations: local history; travel; music; theatre; film; books. Address: (h.) 8 Baileyfield Road, Edinburgh EH15 1DL; T.-0131-669 5275.

Macgregor, Jimmie, MBE, DA, FRZSS. Radio and Television Presenter; Author; Lecturer; President, Association for the Protection of Rural Scotland. Educ. Springburn Academy; Glasgow School of Art. Forefront of British folk revival for more than 20 years; countless radio and TV appearances, tours in Britain and abroad; more than 20 albums recorded; own daily radio programme, Macgregor's Gathering, for more than 10 years; regular TV series on long-distance walks; various books on folk song and the outdoors; has written theme music for TV and radio, illustrated books; gives regular lectures and slide shows; Life Member: RSPB, Scottish Wildlife Trust, Friends of Loch Lomond, John Muir Trust; President, Friends of River Kelvin; Vice-President, Scottish Conservation Projects and Scottish Youth Hostels Association; twice Scot of the Year. Recreations: collecting paintings, pottery, glass, furniture; the outdoors; wildlife; hill-walking; theatre; art; music; antiques; old cars; anything and everything Scottish.

McGregor, Margaret Morrice, MA, JP, DL. Director, McGregor Connexions, since 1998; Board Member, Zero Tolerance Charitable Trust, since 1999; Co-ordinator, British Thyroid Foundation, since 2004; b. 22.10.42, Aberdeen; m., Michael McGregor; 2 s.; 2 step d. Educ. Aberdeen Academy; Aberdeen University. Member, Edinburgh District Council, 1987-96 (Chair, Women's Committee, 1988-96, Licensing Board, 1992-96); Chair, Equal Opportunities Committee, COSLA, 1992-96; Member, City of Edinburgh Council, 1996-99 (Chair, Women's Committee, 1996-99); Depute Lord Provost, 1996-99; Chair, Scottish Refugee Council, 1995-2000; Recreations: campaigning (human rights, prison reform, animal welfare); reading; sailing. Address: (h.) 17 Greenpark, Liberton, Edinburgh EH17 7TA; T.-0131-664 7223; e-mail: m2mcgregor@aol.com

McGrigor, Sir James Angus Roderick Neil, Bt. MSP (Conservative), Highlands and Islands, since 1999; b. 19.10.49, London; m.; 1 s.; 4 d. Educ. Eton; Neuchatel University, Switzerland. Traveller, shipping agent, stockbroker, fish farmer, hill farmer; Conservative candidate, Western Isles, 1997; Euro candidate, Scottish list, 1999; Chairman, Loch Awe Improvement Association; Member, Atlantic Salmon Trust Council. Recreations: music; films; fishing; literature. Address: (h.) Ardchonnel, by Dalmally, Argyll; T.-01546 603811.

McGuiness, David Newell, DipEM, FIET, MCMI. Managing Director, Electrical Contractors' Association of Scotland (SELECT), since 2004; The Director, Scottish Joint Industry Board, since 2004; Director: Scottish Electrical Contractors' Insurance Ltd., since 2004, Electrical Engineering Training Foundation, Electrical Safety Trust, Scottish Electrical Training Trust, since 2004; b. 25.6.59, Banbridge, Northern Ireland; m., Di Dianne Elizabeth, nee Marshall. Educ. Banbridge Academy; Ulster Polytechnic; Strathclyde University. Recreations: golf; cycling; reading; wine. Address: (b.) The Walled Garden, Bush Estate, Midlothian EH26 0SB; T.-0131 445 5577.

McGuire, Anne, MP, MA (Hons). MP (Labour), Stirling, since 1997; Parliamentary Under Secretary of State (Minister for Disabled People), Department of Work and Pensions, since 2005; b. 26.5.49, Glasgow; m., Len McGuire, JP, CA; 1 s.; 1 d. Educ. Our Lady and St. Francis School, Glasgow; University of Glasgow; Notre Dame

College of Education. Development Officer, Community Service Volunteers, 1984-88; National Officer, CSV, 1988-93; Depute Director, Scottish Council for Voluntary Organisations, 1993-97. Assistant Government Whip (Scotland), 1998-2001; Lord Commissioner, HM Treasury (Government Whip), 2001-02; Parliamentary Under Secretary of State (Scotland Office), 2002-05. Address: (b.) 22 Viewfield Street, Stirling FK8 1UA; T.-01786 446515.

McGuire, Edward, ARCM, ARAM. Composer; b. 15.2.48, Glasgow. Educ. St. Augustine's Secondary School, Glasgow; Junior Department, RSAMD; Royal Academy of Music, London; State Academy of Music, Stockholm. Won National Young Composers Competition, 1969; Rant selected as test piece for 1978 Carl Flesch International Violin Competition; Proms debut, 1982, when Source performed by BBC SSO; String Quartet chosen for 40th Anniversary Concert, SPNM, Barbican, 1983; featured composer, Park Lane Group series, Purcell Room, 1993, Bath International Guitar Festival, 1996, Proms, 1997; International Viola Congress, 1998; frequent commissions and broadcasts including Euphoria (EIF/Fires of London), Songs of New Beginnings (Paragon Ensemble), Quintet II (Lontano), Peter Pan (Scottish Ballet), A Glasgow Symphony (NYOS), The Loving of Etain (Paragon Opera), Trombone Concerto (Aix-en-Provence Festival), Violin Concerto (Perth Festival, 2000), Hall of Memories (BBC SSO, 2006), plays flute with and writes for Whistlebinkies folk group, CDs include Albanach (Greentrax), 2006. His own CD with Delphian Records was Editor's Choice, Gramophone Magazine, 2006. Recipient of British Composer Award, 2003 and Creative Scotland Award, 2004; Chair, Scottish Region Musicians' Union, since 2003; Chair, Scottish Campaign Against Euro Federalism, since 2001. Address: c/o Scottish Music Centre, City Hall, Candleriggs, Glasgow G1 1NQ.
Website: www.scottishmusiccentre.com/edward_mcguire

McIlvanney, William. Novelist and Poet; b. 1936, Kilmarnock. Educ. Kilmarnock Academy; Glasgow University. Teacher (Assistant Rector (Curriculum); Greenwood Academy, Irvine, until 1975); Creative Writing Fellow, Strathclyde University, 1972-73; author of Remedy is None, 1966 (joint winner, Geoffrey Faber Memorial Award, 1967), A Gift from Nessus, 1968 (Scottish Arts Council Publication Award, 1969), Docherty, 1975 (Whitbread Award for Fiction, 1975), Laidlaw, 1977, The Papers of Tony Veitch, 1983, The Big Man, 1985, Dreaming, 1989, Strange Loyalties, 1990, The Kiln, 1996 (Saltire Society Scottish Book of the Year Award), Weekend, 2006; three books of poetry: The Longships in Harbour, 1970, Weddings and After, 1983, In Through the Head, 1985; Surviving the Shipwreck (essays and collected journalism), 1991.

McIlwain, Alexander Edward, CBE, MA, LLB, SSC, WS, FFCS. Retired Solicitor, formerly Senior Partner, Leonards, Solicitors, Hamilton; Honorary Sheriff, South Strathclyde, Dumfries and Galloway, at Hamilton, since 1981; b. 4.7.33, Aberdeen; m., Moira Margaret Kinnaird; 3 d. Educ. Aberdeen Grammar School; Aberdeen University. President, Students Representative Council, 1956-57. Commissioned, Royal Corps of Signals, 1957-59; Depute Prosecutor then District Prosecutor, Hamilton, 1966-76; Dean, Society of Solicitors of Hamilton, 1981-83; President, Law Society of Scotland, 1983-84; Chairman, Legal Aid Central Committee, 1985-87; Member: Central Advisory Committee for Scotland on Justices of the Peace, 1986-96; Lanarkshire Health Board, 1986-96; The Scout Council (UK), 1981-96, Cameron Committee on Shrieval Training, 1995-97, Judicial Studies Committee, 1997-2000; Honorary Member, American Bar Association; Chairman, Lanarkshire Scout Area, 1981-91; Chairman, Hamilton

Sheriff Court Project, 1990-94; Temporary Sheriff, 1984-99; President, Temporary Sheriffs Association, 1994-98; Member: Criminal Injuries Compensation Appeal Panel, Criminal Injuries Compensation Board. Publications: Time Costing and Time Recording (in collaboration); Supporting Victims in the Criminal Justice System. Recreations: gardening. Address: (h.) 7 Bothwell Road, Uddingston, Glasgow; T.-01698 813368.

McInnes, Alison. MSP (Liberal Democrat), North East Scotland, since 2007; b. 17.7.57; m. Address: (b.) Scottish Parliament, Edinburgh EH99 1SP.

Macinnes, Professor Allan Iain, MA, PhD, FRHistS, FRSA, FFCS. Professor of Early Modern History, University of Strathclyde; b. 26.11.49, Inverness; m., Tine Wanning. Educ. Oban High School; University of St. Andrews; University of Glasgow. University of Glasgow: Lecturer in Scottish History, 1973-89, Senior Lecturer in Scottish History, 1989-93, Director, Postgraduate School of Scottish Studies, 1992-93; Burnett-Fletcher Professor of History, University of Aberdeen, 1993-2007; Head, Department of History, Aberdeen University, 1994-97, 1998-2001. Associate Graduate Faculty, University of Guelph, since 1998; Visiting Professor in British History, University of Chicago, 2003; Chair, Scottish Land Commission, 1996-99; Member, Advisory Panel, Scottish Parliamentary Records Project, University of St. Andrews, since 1997; Joint Founder (Chair, Steering Committee), Northern European Historical Research Network, 1997-2002. Research Fellow of the Huntington Library, San Marino, California, 1993, 2002 and 2005; Ecole des Hautes Etudes en Sciences Sociales, Paris, 2005; Frank Watson Prize in Scottish History, University of Guelph, 1997. Publications: Charles I and the Making of the Covenanting Movement, 1625-41, 1991; Clanship, Commerce and the House of Stuart, 1603-1788, 1996; The British Revolution, 1629-1660, 2004; Union & Empire: The Making of the United Kingdom in 1707, 2007; published extensively on covenants, clans and clearances. Recreations: supporting Hibernian; gardening with a touch of zen; hillwalking; listening to music – especially jazz; drinking malt whisky. Address: Department of History, University of Strathclyde, McCance Building, 16 Richmond Street, Glasgow G1 1XQ.

McInnes, Professor Colin Robert, DSc., CEng, FRAS, FInstP, FRAeS, FREng, FRSE. Professor of Engineering Science, Department of Mechanical Engineering, University of Strathclyde, since 2004; b. 12.2.68, Glasgow; m., Dr. Karen McLaughlin; 3 s. Educ. Knightswood Secondary School; University of Glasgow. Department of Aerospace Engineering, University of Glasgow: Lecturer, 1991-96, Reader, 1996-99, Professor of Space Systems Engineering, 1999-2004. Royal Society of Edinburgh Bruce Preller Prize Lecture, 1998; Royal Society of Edinburgh Makdougall-Brisbane Prize, 2006; Royal Aeronautical Society Pardoe Space Award, 2000; Philip Leverhulme Prize, 2001; Royal Aeronautical Society Ackroyd Stuart Prize, 2004; Association of Space Explorers Leonov Medal, 2007. Publications: Solar Sailing, 1999; around 100 journal and conference papers. Recreations: photography; hillwalking; history of science. Address: Department of Mechanical Engineering, University of Strathclyde, Glasgow G1 1XJ; T.-0141-548-2049; e-mail: colin.mcinnes@strath.ac.uk

MacInnes, Hamish, OBE, BEM, DUniv. Writer and Designer; b. 7.7.30, Gatehouse of Fleet. Educ. Gatehouse of Fleet. Mountaineer with numerous expeditions to Himalayas, Amazon and other parts of the world; Deputy Leader, 1975 Everest SW Face Expedition; film Producer/Advisor/safety expert, with Zinnemann, Connery,

Eastwood, Putnam, etc.; Advisor, BBC TV live outside broadcasts on climbing; author of 22 books on travel and adventure, including two autobiographies and fiction; designed the first all-metal ice axe, Terodactyl ice climbing tools, the MacInnes stretchers; Founder, Search and Rescue Dog Association; Honorary Member, Scottish Mountaineering Club; former President, Alpine Climbing Group; world authority on mountain rescue; Doctor of Laws (Hons), Glasgow University; Hon. DSc: Heriot Watt University, Aberdeen University; Doctor of the University, University of Stirling, 1997; Doctor of Laws, University of Dundee, 2004; Member, Scottish Sporting Hall of Fame; President, Guide Dogs Adventure Group; Founder and former Leader, Glencoe Mountain Rescue Team. Recreations: as above. Address: (h.) Glencoe, Argyll; T.-01855 811258.

McInnes, Sheriff Principal John Colin, QC, BA (Hons) (Oxon), LLB (Edin), HonLLD (St. Andrews), DL. Advocate; Sheriff Principal of South Strathclyde, Dumfries and Galloway, 2000-06; Deputy Lieutenant for Fife, since 1997; Member, Parole Board for Scotland, since 2005; b. 21.11.38, Cupar, Fife; m., Elisabeth Mabel Neilson; 1 s.; 1 d. Educ. New Park School, St. Andrews; Cargilfield School, Edinburgh; Merchiston Castle School, Edinburgh; Brasenose College, Oxford; Edinburgh University. 2nd Lt., 8th Royal Tank Regiment, 1956-58; Lt., Fife and Forfar Yeomanry, Scottish Horse, TA, 1958-64; Advocate, 1963; Director, R. Mackness & Co. Ltd., 1963-70; Chairman, Fios Group Ltd., 1970-72; Parliamentary candidate (Conservative), Aberdeen North, 1964; Tutor, Law Faculty, Edinburgh University, 1965-72; in practice, Scottish Bar, 1963-73; Sheriff of Lothian and Peebles, 1973-74; Sheriff, Tayside, Central and Fife, 1974-2000; Acting Sheriff Principal, Grampian, Highland and Islands, 2000-01. Member, St. Andrews University Court, 1983-91; Chairman, Fife Family Conciliation Service, 1988-90; Member and Vice-President: Security Service Tribunal, 1989-2001, Intelligence Services Tribunal, 1994-2001; President, The Sheriffs' Association, 1995-97; Member: Scottish Criminal Justice Forum, 1996-2000, Judicial Studies Committee, 1996-2000, Investigatory Powers Tribunal, since 2000; Chairman, Committee to Review Summary Justice in Scotland, 2001-04; Chairman, Youth Court Feasibility Study Project Group, 2002. Publication: Divorce Law and Practice in Scotland, 1990. Recreations: fishing; shooting; hill-walking; skiing; photography. Address: Parkneuk, Blebocraigs, Cupar, Fife KY15 5UG.

McInnes, Professor William McKenzie, MSc, PhD, CA, FRSA, ILTM. Professor of Accounting, Stirling University, since 1994; (Head, Department of Accounting, Finance and Law, 1995-98, Vice-Dean, Faculty of Management, 1996-97); b. 24.5.42, Hawick; m., Christine Mary; 1 s.; 1 d. Educ. George Watsons College, Edinburgh; Durham University; Glasgow University. Management Accountant, IBM (UK) Ltd., 1966-68; Lecturer, Kirkcaldy Technical College, 1968-70; Audit Senior, Coopers and Lybrand, Bermuda, 1970-72; Senior Lecturer, Newcastle upon Tyne Polytechnic, 1974-76; Lecturer, then Senior Lecturer, Strathclyde University, 1976-91; Director of Research, Institute of Chartered Accountants of Scotland, 1992-93; SHEFC Team Leader for Quality Assessment of Finance and Accounting, 1995-96; Elder, Cadder Parish Church. Recreations: golf; tennis; music. Address: (b.) Department of Accounting and Finance, Stirling University, Stirling FK9 4LA; T.-01786 467280.
E-mail: W.M.McInnes@stirling.ac.uk

McIntosh, Alisdair Douglas, BA (Hons), MA. Head of Regeneration Policy and Housing Support, Scottish Government, since 2005; b. 19.7.63, Addlestone, Surrey; m., Sarah Mary Burnett; 1 s.; 1 d. Educ. Strode's School,

Egham, Surrey; University of Durham; Sorbonne, Paris; University of London. HM Treasury, 1987; UK Permanent Representation to the European Union, Brussels, 1991; Cabinet of the Vice-President, European Commission, Brussels, 1997; Secretary to Committee of Inquiry into Professional Conditions of Teachers, Edinburgh, 1999; Head of Access to Justice Division, Justice Department, Scottish Executive, 2000-03; Head of Anti Social Behaviour Unit, Scottish Executive, 2003-05. Recreations: books; food; wine; fresh air; his children. Address: (h.) 81 St. John's Road, Edinburgh EH12 6NN; (b.) Victoria Quay, Edinburgh EH6 6QQ.
E-mail: alisdair.mcintosh@scotland.gsi.gov.uk

McIntosh, Gordon, BSc, CAS. Corporate Director, Neighbourhood Services (South), Aberdeen City Council; b. 10.8.56; 2 s.; 1 d. Educ. Keith Grammar School; Glasgow University; Aberdeen University. KPMG (Thomson McLintock), Chartered Accountants, 1979-84; Grampian Regional Council, 1984-96; Director of Economic Development, Aberdeen City Council. Past Chairman, Scottish Local Authorities Economic Development Officers; Past Chairman, Aberdeen and St. John Mountain Rescue Association; Past President, Junior Chamber; Director, Transition Extreme Sports Ltd.; Director, Aberdeen Exhibition and Conference Centre Ltd. Recreations: mountaineering; angling; golf. Address: (b.) Aberdeen City Council, St Nicholas House, Broad Street, Aberdeen AB10 1BY; T.-01224 522000.

Macintosh, Kenneth Donald, MA, MSP (Labour), Eastwood, since 1999; b. 15.1.62, Inverness; m., Claire Kinloch Anderson; 2 s.; 3 d. Educ. Royal High School, Edinburgh; Edinburgh University. Joined BBC, 1987; worked in News and Current Affairs, including Breakfast News, Breakfast with Frost, Nine O'Clock News; left as Senior Broadcast Journalist, 1999. Recreations: reading; music; sport – football, golf, tennis. Address: (b.) 238 Ayr Road, Newton Mearns G77 6AA; T.-0141-577 0100.

McIntosh, Sir Neil, CBE, JP, DL, FIPM, ACIS, FRSA. Member, UK Electoral Commission, since 2001; Chairman, Judicial Appointments Board for Scotland, since 2002; Independent Expert Adviser to N. Ireland Executive Review of Public Administration, 2002-06; Trustee, National Museums of Scotland, since 2000; Member, BBC Audience Council for Scotland, since 2007; b. 30.1.40, Glasgow; m., Marie; 1 s.; 2 d. Educ. King's Park School, Glasgow. Industry and local government, 1957-69; Director of Personnel, Inverness County/Highland Region, 1969-85; Chief Executive: Dumfries and Galloway Region, 1985-92, Strathclyde Region, 1992-96; various public service duties, since 1996, including: Counting Officer, Scottish Parliament Referendum, Chairman, Commission on Local Government and the Scottish Parliament, Crown Agent's Adviser, Shanghai Municipal Government; Convener, Scottish Council for Voluntary Organisations, 1995-2001. Hon. Doctorate, Syracuse University, and Hon. Doctorate, Glasgow Caledonian University. Recreations: bottle collecting; dry stane dyking.

McIntosh, Robert, BSc, PhD, FICF. Director Scotland, Forestry Commission, since 2003; Chief Executive, Forest Enterprise, 1997-2003; b. 6.10.51, Edinburgh; m., Elizabeth Ann (div.). Educ. Linlithgow Academy; Edinburgh University. Joined Forestry Commission, 1973: District Manager, Research Scientist, Operations Director. Recreations: shooting; farming; fishing. Address: (b.) 231 Corstorphine Road, Edinburgh EH12 7AT; T.-0131-314 6456; e-mail: carol.finlayson@forestry.gsi.gov.uk

McIntosh, Stewart, BA (Hons). Journalist; b. 7.5.48, Glasgow; m., Marion; 2 d. Educ. Rutherglen Academy;

Strathclyde University. Assistant Secretary, STUC, 1976-79; Education Officer, GMB, 1979-83; Freelance Researcher/Reporter, BBC Scotland, 1983-87; Freelance Journalist and Writer, since 1987. UK Property Writer of the Year, 1997. Recreations: athletics; mountain biking; Rioja; Tennent's Bar; Spain. Address: (b.) 29 Cleveden Road, Glasgow G12 0PQ; T.-0141-334 8475.

McIntyre, Alasdair Duncan, CBE, BSc, DSc, FRSE, FIBiol, FRSA. Chairman, Atlantic Frontier Environmental Forum, since 1996; Chairman, Falkland Islands Exploration and Production Environmental Forum, since 1997; Emeritus Professor of Fisheries and Oceanography, Aberdeen University, since 1986; b. 17.11.26, Helensburgh; m., Catherine Helen; 1 d. Educ. Hermitage School, Helensburgh; Glasgow University. Senior Principal Scientific Officer in charge of environmental team, Marine Laboratory, Aberdeen, 1973-79; Deputy Director, Department of Agriculture and Fisheries for Scotland, Marine Laboratory, Aberdeen, 1979-83; Director of Fisheries Research for Scotland, 1983-86; Co-ordinator, UK Fisheries Research and Development, 1986; President: Estuarine and Coastal Sciences Association, 1992-95, Sir Alister Hardy Foundation for Ocean Science, 1992-99; Member, Research Board, Scottish Natural Heritage, 1992-96; Chairman: Marine Forum for Environmental Issues, 1990-98, Buckland Foundation, 1994-99; Editor, Fisheries Research. Hon. doctorate, Stirling University, 1997; Hon. doctorate, Napier University, Edinburgh, 2005. Recreations: reading; food and wine; walking. Address: (h.) 63 Hamilton Place, Aberdeen AB15 5BW; T.-01224 645633; e-mail: a.d.mcintyre@abdn.ac.uk

McIntyre, Archibald Dewar, CBE, MB, ChB, DPH, FFCM, FRCPE, DIH, DTM&H; b. 18.2.28, Dunipace; m., Euphemia Hope Houston; 2 s.; 2 d. Educ. Falkirk High School; Edinburgh University. Senior Medical Officer, Overseas Civil Service, Sierra Leone; Depute Medical Officer of Health, Stirling County Council; Depute Secretary, Scottish Council for Postgraduate Medical Education; Senior Medical Officer, Scottish Home and Health Department; Principal Medical Officer, Scottish Home and Health Department, 1977-93. Recreations: gardening; photography. Address: (h.) Birchlea, 43 Falkirk Road, Linlithgow EH49 7PH; T.-01506 842063.

McIntyre, Derrick William McEwen, LLB. Sheriff; b. 16.6.44, S. India; m., Janet Anna Fraser; 1 s. (deceased); 2 d. (1 deceased). Educ. Wellington College, Berkshire; St. Andrews University. Lt-6th Gurkha Rifles - FARELF, 1966-68; Shipping and Banking, 1968-70; Lawyer, Private Practice, 1970-2000; Temporary Sheriff, 1982-98; Permanent Sheriff, since 2000. Deputy Chairman, Gurkha Welfare Trust (Scotland). Address: (b.) Edinburgh Sheriff Court, 27 Chambers Street, Edinburgh; T.-0131 225 2525; e-mail: sheriff.DMcIntyre@scotcourts.gov.uk

Macintyre, Iain Melfort Campbell, MB, ChB, MD, FRCSE, FRCPE, FSA (Scot). Formerly Consultant Surgeon, Edinburgh; Surgeon to the Queen in Scotland, 1997-2004; Vice President, Royal College of Surgeons of Edinburgh; Chairman, Edinburgh Postgraduate Board for Medicine, 1995-2000; b. 23.6.44, Glasgow; m., Tessa Lorna Mary Millar; 3 d. Educ. Daniel Stewart's College, Edinburgh; Edinburgh University. Lecturer in Surgery, Edinburgh University, 1974-78; Visiting Professor, University of Natal, 1978-79; Council of Europe Travelling Fellow, 1986; Honorary Secretary, Royal College of Surgeons of Edinburgh, 2001-03; Member, Council, National Medical Advisory Committee, 1992-95. Recreations: Scottish history; photography; skiing; sailing.

McIntyre, Rev. Mgr. John, MA (Hons), STL, PhL, DipEd. Parish Priest, St. Bridget's, Baillieston, since 1995; Member, Scottish Catholic Heritage Commission, since 1981; b. 12.11.37, Airdrie. Educ. St. Aloysius College,

Glasgow; Gregorian University, Rome; Glasgow University; Jordanhill College of Education. Ordained to priesthood, Rome, 1961; Assistant, St. Monica's, Coatbridge, 1962-63; student, 1963-68; staff, St. Vincent's College, Langbank, 1968-69, St. Mary's College, Blairs, Aberdeen, 1969-86 (Rector, 1985-86); Parish Priest, St. Bride's, East Kilbride, 1986-89; Rector, Scots College, Rome, 1989-95. Bradley Medal, Glasgow University, 1967. Publications: Scotland and the Holy See (Editor), 1982; The Scots College, Rome 1600–2000 (Co-Author), 2000. Recreations: English literature; bird-watching; history. Address: 15 Swinton Road, Baillieston, Glasgow G69 6DT; T.-0141-771 1058; e-mail: johnmcintyre@stbridgetsparish.fsnet.co.uk

Macintyre, Lorn, BA (Hons), PhD. Freelance Writer; b. 7.9.42, Taynuilt, Argyll; m., Mary. Educ. Stirling University; Glasgow University. Novelist and Short Story Writer; publications include Cruel in the Shadow, The Blind Bend, Empty Footsteps and The Broken Lyre in Chronicles of Invernevis Series; Tobermory Days and Tobermory Tales (short stories). Recreations: Scottish country dancing; nightjars; the paranormal. Address: (h.) Priormuir, by St. Andrews, Fife; T.-01334 476428.

McIntyre, Major Robert George. Salvation Army Officer, since 1967 (Divisional Commander for East Scotland Division and Scotland Secretary); b. 15.10.44, Glasgow; m., Isobel Laird. Educ. Woodside Senior Secondary School; Stow College of Engineering. Commanded Salvation Army churches in Scotland, 21 years; Divisional Youth Secretary, 1984-87; Church Growth Consultant, 1991-98. Recreations: piano; brass banding; reading; hill-walking; computing; watching all sports. Address: 12A Dryden Road, Loanhead, Midlothian EH20 9LZ; T.-0131 440 9100; e-mail: robert.mcintyre@salvationarmy.org.uk

Macintyre, Professor Sally, CBE, FRSE, BA, MSc, PhD, HonDSc. Director, Medical Research Council Social and Public Health Sciences Unit, since 1998; Honorary Professor, Glasgow University, since 1991; b. 27.2.49, Edinburgh; m., Dr. Guy Muhlemann. Educ. Durham, London and Aberdeen Universities. Research Fellow, Aberdeen University, 1971-75; Researcher, MRC Medical Sociology Unit, Aberdeen, 1975-83; Director, MRC Medical Sociology Unit, University of Glasgow, 1983-98. Fellow, Royal Society of Medicine; Foundation Fellow, Academy of Medical Sciences. Recreations: skiing; hill-walking; climbing. Address: (b.) MRC Social and Public Health Sciences Unit, 4 Lilybank Gardens, Glasgow G12 8RZ; T.-0141-357 3949.

MacIver, Donald John Morrison, MA (Hons). Consultant, Translator, Adviser on Gaelic educational matters. Education Adviser and Quality Improvement Officer, Comhairle nan Eilean Siar, 1989-2007; b. 12.11.42, Stornoway; m., Alice Macleod; 1 s. Educ. Nicolson Institute; Aberdeen University. Teacher of Gaelic, 1968-73; Principal Teacher of Gaelic, Nicolson Institute, 1973-89. President, An Comunn Gaidhealach, 1985-90; winner of Bardic Crown at Royal National Mod, 2000; former Director, National Gaelic Arts Project; former Member, Gaelic Books Council; former Director, Acair Publishing Co.; former Editor, Sruth (newspaper of An Comunn Gaidhealach); Gaelic columnist, Stornoway Gazette, 2002-07. Publications: Camhanaich; Eadar Peann Is Paipear; Coinneach Odhar; Grian is Uisge; Co Rinn E?; A'Chlach; numerous educational books and materials. Recreations: writing (prose and poetry); computing; reading poetry; gardening. Address: (h.) 32 Goathill Road, Stornoway, Isle of Lewis HS1 2NL; T.-01851 702582.

Maciver, Rev. James, MA, BD, DipTheol. Principal Clerk of Assembly, Free Church of Scotland, since 2000; Minister, Knock Free Church, Isle of Lewis, since 1997; b. 9.4.54, Stornoway; m., Donna Mary; 2 s.; 1 d. Educ.

Nicolson Institute, Stornoway; Glagsow University; Free Church College, Edinburgh; London University. Minister, East Kilbride Free Church, 1987-97; Clerk to Southern Synod, 1990-95; Visiting Lecturer, Glasgow Bible College, 1989-95. Chairman, Bethesda Nursing Home and Hospice, 1998-2002; Chairman, BBC Gaelic Advisory Committee, since 2003. Recreations: reading; classical music; Gaelic music; golf. Address: (b.) Free Church Manse, Garrabost, Isle of Lewis; T.-01851 870207.

Maciver, John Angus, LLB (Hons) (First Class), DipLP. Partner, DLA Piper, since 2004; b. 17.1.73, Inverness. Educ. Currie High School, Edinburgh; University of Edinburgh. McGrigor Donald, Glasgow and Edinburgh, 1997-2002; Clifford Chance, London, 2002-04. Recreations: golf; skiing; travel. Address: (b.) Collins House, Rutland Square, Edinburgh EH1 2AA; e-mail: john.maciver@dlapiper.com

MacIver, Kenneth, BSc (Econ) (Hons), MA (Ed). Headteacher, Alness Academy, since 2004; b. 23.6.54, Glasgow; m., Sheila; 1 s.; 1 d. Educ. Shawlands Academy, Glasgow; London University; Open University. Teacher of Modern Studies and Economics: Cranhill Secondary, Smithycroft Secondary; Assistant Principal Teacher of Modern Studies, Mearns Castle High; Principal Teacher of Modern Studies and Economics, Smithycroft Secondary; Assistant Headteacher, Inverness Royal Academy; Depute Headteacher, Culloden Academy. Recreations: hillwalking; ski-mountaineering; travel; reading. Address: (b.) Alness Academy, Alness, Ross-shire IV17 0UY; T.-01349 883341; e-mail: kenneth.maciver@highland.gov.uk

MacIver, Matthew M., MA, MEd, FEIS, FRSA. Chief Executive/Registrar, General Teaching Council for Scotland, since 2001; Chair, Bòrd na Gàidhlig, since 2006; Chairman, Highlands and Islands Educational Trust, since 1994; b. 5.7.46, Isle of Lewis; m., Katrina; 1 s.; 1 d. Educ. Nicolson Institute, Stornoway; Edinburgh University; Moray House College. History Teacher, 1969-72; Principal Teacher of History, Craigmount High School, 1972-80; Assistant Rector, Royal High School, 1980-83; Depute Head Teacher, Balerno High School, 1983-86; Rector, Fortrose Academy, 1986-89; Rector, Royal High School, Edinburgh, 1989-98; Depute Registrar (Education), General Teaching Council for Scotland, 1998-2001. Chairman, Comataidh Craolaidh Gaidhlig (Gaelic Broadcasting Committee), 1996-2001; Member for Scotland on the Ofcom Content Board, 2003-06; Winston Churchill Travelling Fellowship, 1998. Address: (h.) 21 Durham Road, Edinburgh EH15 1NY; T.-0131-669 5029.

McKain, Bruce, LLB (Hons). Director of Public Affairs, Faculty of Advocates, since 2003; Law Correspondent, The Herald, 1978-2003; b. 23.6.48, Dundee; m., Helen Murray Lennox, 2 s. Educ. Madras College, St. Andrews; Edinburgh University. Joined D.C. Thomson, 1970; Weekly News, Manchester and London; Peterborough Evening Telegraph; Radio Clyde; Aberdeen Evening Express. Publication: Scots Law for Journalists (Co-author). Recreations: golf; reading; cinema. Address: (b.) Mackenzie Building, Old Assembly Close, 172 High Streeet, Edinburgh; T.-0131 260 5615.

Mackay of Clashfern, Lord (James Peter Hymers), Baron (1979), PC (1979), KT (1999), FRSE, Hon. FRICE, FRCOG, FRCP, FRCS. Lord Clerk Register, since 2007; Lord High Commissioner to the General Assembly of the Church of Scotland, 2005 and 2006; Lord High Chancellor of Great Britain, 1987-97; Chancellor, Heriot Watt University, 1991-2005; b. 2.7.27, Edinburgh; m., Elizabeth

Gunn Hymers; 1 s.; 2 d. Educ. George Heriot's School, Edinburgh; Edinburgh University. Lecturer in Mathematics, St. Andrews University, 1948-50; Major Scholar, Trinity College, Cambridge, in Mathematics, 1947, taken up, 1950; Senior Scholar, 1951; BA (Cantab), 1952; LLB Edinburgh (with distinction), 1955; admitted, Faculty of Advocates, 1955; QC (Scot), 1965; Standing Junior Counsel to: Queen's and Lord Treasurer's Remembrancer, Scottish Home and Health Department, Commissioners of Inland Revenue in Scotland; Sheriff Principal, Renfrew and Argyll, 1972-74; Vice-Dean, Faculty of Advocates, 1973-76; Dean, 1976-79; Lord Advocate of Scotland, 1979-84; a Senator of the College of Justice in Scotland, 1984-85; a Lord of Appeal in Ordinary, 1985-87. Part-time Member, Scottish Law Commission, 1976-79; Hon. Master of the Bench, Inner Temple, 1979; Fellow, International Academy of Trial Lawyers, 1979; Fellow, Institute of Taxation, 1981; Director, Stenhouse Holdings Ltd., 1976-77; Member, Insurance Brokers' Registration Council, 1977-79; a Commissioner of Northern Lighthouses, 1975-84; Hon. LLD: Edinburgh, 1983, Dundee, 1983, Strathclyde, 1985, Aberdeen, 1987, Cambridge, 1989, Birmingham, 1990, University of India Law School, 1994, Glasgow 1994, Bath, 1996, Leicester University, 1996, De Montfort, 1999; Hon. DCL: Newcastle, 1990, Oxford, 1998, Robert Gordon, 2000; Hon. Doctor of Laws, College of William and Mary, 1989; Hon. Fellow, Institution of Civil Engineers, 1988; Hon. Fellow, Trinity College, Cambridge, 1989; Hon. Fellow, Girton College, Cambridge, 1989; Hon. Fellow, Royal College of Surgeons, Edinburgh, 1989; Hon. Fellow, Royal College of Physicians of Edinburgh, 1990; Hon. Fellow, Royal College of Obstetricians and Gynaecologists, 1996; Fellow, American College of Trial Lawyers, 1990. Recreation: walking. Address: House of Lords, London, SW1A 0PW.

Mackay of Drumadoon, Rt. Hon. Lord (Donald Sage Mackay), PC, LLB, LLM, LLM (University of Virginia); Senator of the College of Justice in Scotland since 2000; b. 30.1.46, Aberdeen; m., Lesley; 1 s.; 2 d. Educ. George Watson's Boys' College, Edinburgh; Edinburgh University; University of Virginia. Solicitor, 1971-76; called to Scottish Bar, 1976; QC, 1987; Advocate Depute, 1982-85; Member, Criminal Injuries Compensation Board, 1989-95; Solicitor-General for Scotland, 1995; Lord Advocate, 1995-97; Opposition Spokesman on Scotland and Constitutional Affairs, House of Lords, 1997-2000. Recreation: Isle of Arran. Address: (h.) 39 Hermitage Gardens, Edinburgh EH10 6AZ; T.-0131-447 1412.

Mackay, Alexander Douglas, CA. Partner, CA Firm, Gibson McKerrell Brown, since 1972; Secretary, Royal Society for the Relief of Indigent Gentlewomen of Scotland, since 2002; b. 9.3.47, Birmingham; m., Laura; 3 d. Educ. George Heriot's, Edinburgh. Qualified CA, 1970; Whinney Murray, CA, London, 1970-72; Secretary, Edinburgh Housing Trust Ltd., since 1981. Recreations: bowling; angling. Address: (h.) 70 East Craigs Rigg, Edinburgh EH12 8JA; T.-0131 317 7014; e-mail: sandy@g-m-b.co.uk

Mackay, Angus Victor Peck, OBE, MA, BSc (Pharm), PhD (Cantab), MB, ChB, FRCPsych, FRCP (Ed), TPsych. Board Member, Medicines and Healthcare Products Regulatory Agency (UK); Chairman, Scottish Government's Independent Scrutiny Panel for health services along the Clyde; Member, Mental Health Tribunal for Scotland; past Chairman, Health Technology Board for Scotland; Physician Superintendent and Clinical Director, Lomond and Argyll Mental Health Service; Honorary Professor in Psychological Medicine, Glasgow University, since 1980; Member, Faculty of Neuroscience, University of Edinburgh; Chairman, Working Group on the Scottish Health Technology Assessment Centre; Member, Panel of Experts for the European Medicines Evaluation Agency; Psychiatric Representative, Committee on Safety of Medicines, DHSS, since 1983; b. 4.3.43, Edinburgh; m., Elspeth M.W. Norris; 2 s.; 2 d. Educ. George Heriot's School, Edinburgh; Edinburgh University; Churchill and Trinity Colleges, Cambridge. MRC Research Fellow, Cambridge; Member, senior clinical staff, MRC Neurochemical Pharmacology Unit, Cambridge, with appointment as Lector in Pharmacology, Trinity College (latterly, Deputy Director of Unit). Deputy Chairman, Health Services Research Committee of the Chief Scientist for Scotland; Chairman: Scottish Working Group on Mental Illness, Research and Clinical Section of Royal College of Psychiatrists (Scotland), National Mental Health Reference Group; Member: Research Committee, Mental Health Foundation, Scottish Executive, Royal College of Psychiatrists, NHS Policy Board for Scotland; Honorary Senior Lecturer, Department of Psychology, University of St. Andrews; Medical Director, Argyll and Bute NHS Trust. Recreations: rowing; sailing; rhododendrons. Address: (h.) Tigh an Rudha, Ardrishaig, Argyll; T.-01546 603272.

MacKay, Colin, CBE, BSc, MB, ChB, FRCSEng, FRCSEd, FRCSGlas. Chairman, Board of Governors, UHI Millennium Institute, since 2001; b. 8.11.36, Glasgow; m., Dr Helen MacKay; 1 s.; 2 d. Educ. Hillhead High School; Glasgow University. Surgical training, Western Infirmary, Glasgow, 1961-69; MRC Travelling Fellowship, Boston University, 1969-70; Senior Lecturer in Surgery, Glasgow University, 1970-82; Consultant Surgeon, Western Infirmary/ Gartnavel General Hospital, Glasgow, 1982-96; Royal College of Physicians and Surgeons of Glasgow: Hon. Treasurer, 1976-86, Vice-President Surgical, 1992-94, Visitor, 1996-97, President, 1997-2000; President, Moynihan Chirurgical Club, 1995-96. Publications: Textbook of Surgical Physiology, 1978, 1988; various publications in medical journals. Recreations: travel; walking. Address: (h.) 73 Buchanan Drive, Bearsden, Glasgow G61 2EP; T.-0141-942 8759; and 4 Lawers Place, Aberfeldy.

McKay, Sheriff Colin Graham, MA, LLB. Retired Sheriff of North Strathclyde at Kilmarnock (2001-07); b. 20.1.42, Bearsden; m., Sandra Anne Coli; 1 s.; 1 d. Educ. St Aloysius College; Clongowes Wood College; Glasgow University. Solicitor, 1966-90; Temporary Sheriff, 1986-90; Sheriff, since 1990; part-time Sheriff, since 2007.

MacKay, Colin Hinshelwood, MA (Hons), FSA Scot. Partner, Colin MacKay Associates; Broadcaster and Writer; b. 27.8.44, Glasgow; m., Olive E.B. Brownlie; 2 s. Educ. Kelvinside Academy, Glasgow; Glasgow University; Jordanhill College of Education. Reporter/Presenter: Border Television Ltd., 1967-70, Grampian Television Ltd., 1970-73; Political Editor, Scottish Television PLC, 1973-92 (Presenter, Ways and Means, 1973-86), Parliamentary Lobby Correspondent, 1985-95; recent programmes include: A Life in Question, People and Power, Politics Tonight, Scotland at Ten, and Sunday Morning with Colin MacKay (BBC Radio Scotland); Talk-In Sunday (Radio Clyde); Westminster File (Border TV); Eikon (Scottish TV); General Assembly (BBC TV/Radio); contributions to BBC World Service, Radio 4, Radio 5 Live; ITV Commentator: Papal Visit to Scotland, 1982, CBI Conference, Glasgow, 1983. Winner, Observer Mace, 1967 (British Universities Debating Championship); Member, two-man British Universities Canadian Debating Tour, 1967; Commonwealth Relations Trust Bursary to Canada, 1981; Member, Scottish Arts Council, 1988-94; BT Scottish Radio News Broadcaster of the Year, 1997. Publications:

Kelvinside Academy: 1878-1978, 1978; The Scottish Dimension in Central and Eastern Canada, 1981. Recreations: music (especially opera); reading; writing. E-mail: colin.mackay@hotmail.co.uk

McKay, Colin Ian, LLB (Hons), DipLP, MPhil. Head of Access to Justice, Scottish Government, since 2007; b. Scotland; m., Allison Brisbane; 1 s.; 1 d. Educ. North Berwick High School; Edinburgh University; Glasgow University. Solicitor in Private Practice, 1984-86; Solicitor, Lothian Regional Council, 1986-88; Legal and Policy Adviser, Enable (Scottish Society for the Mentally Handicapped), 1989-98; Civil Servant, since 1999 (Secretary, Millan Committee on Mental Health Law and Maclean Committee on Violent and Sexual Offenders, 2001-03, Head of Mental Health Bill Team, 2003-04, Member, latterly Acting Head, Strategy and Delivery Unit, 2004, Head, Efficient Government Unit); Head of Public Service Reform Development Division, Scottish Executive, 2005-07. Commissioner, Mental Welfare Commission for Scotland, 1996-98. Address: (b.) Scottish Government, St. Andrew's House, Edinburgh EH1 3DG; e-mail: colin.mckay@scotland.gsi.gov.uk

Mackay, David James, FCILT. Deputy Chairman, Portland Media Group UK Ltd., since 2007; Director, TEL Ltd. (Transport Edinburgh), since 2005; Chairman, TEL Ltd., since 2006; Chairman, Malcolm Group, 2003-05; Chairman, Executive Board, Scottish Rugby Union, 2003-05; Hon. Colonel, Scottish Transport Regiment, since 2004; Chief Executive, John Menzies PLC, 1997-2003; b. 20.5.43, St. Andrews; m., Jane; 1 s.; 1 d. Educ. Kirkcaldy High School; Bradford University; Edinburgh University; Companion, Institute of Management, 1998; FCIT, 1993. Recreations: golf; walking. Address: (h.) 4 East Harbour Road, Charlestown, Fife KY11 3EA.

McKay, David Sutherland, OBE; b. 28.8.38, Wick; m., Catherine Margaret; 2 d. Educ. Wick High School; Robert Gordon's College. Apprenticeship in control engineering; Design Engineer, British Oxygen Co.; joined Honeywell Control Systems as Design Engineer; appointed Technical Director, 1983; Director and General Manager, JVC Manufacturing UK Ltd., 1988-98, now retired. Director, SETG Ltd., since 1984; Honorary Fellow, Bell College; Visiting Professor, Strathclyde University; Honorary Fellow, Glasgow University, since 2001. Recreation: gardening; DIY. Address: (h.) Green Garth, Nethan Glen, Crossford ML8 5QU.

Mackay, Derek. Leader of Renfrewshire Council, since 2007. Address: (b.) North Building, Cotton Street, Paisley PA1 1UJ; T.-0141-840 3491.

Mackay, Donald George, MA PhD. Honorary Research Fellow, Aberdeen University, since 1990; b. 25.11.29; m. (1), Elizabeth Ailsa Barr (deceased); 2 s.; 1 d.; m. (2), Catherine Anne McDonald. Educ. Morgan Academy, Dundee; St. Andrews University; Aberdeen University. Assistant Principal, Scottish Home Department, 1953; Secretary, Royal Commission on Local Government in Scotland, 1966-69; Assistant Secretary, Scottish Development and Agriculture Departments, 1969-83; Under Secretary, Scottish Agriculture and Environment Departments, 1983-88. Member, Scottish Agricultural Wages Board, 1991-97. Publication: Scotland's Rural Land Use Agencies, 1995. Recreation: hill walking; photography; music. Address: (h.) 20 Ben Bhraggie Drive, Golspie, Sutherland KW10 6SX; T.-01408 633975.

MacKay, Professor Sir Donald Iain, MA, FRSE, FRSGS. Chairman, Scottish Mortgage Investment Trust, since 2003; Director, Edinburgh New Income Trust; Honorary Professor, Heriot-Watt University, since 1982; b. 27.2.37, Kobe, Japan; m., Diana Marjory Raffan; 1 s.; 2 d. Educ. Dollar Academy; Aberdeen University. Professor of

Political Economy, Aberdeen University, 1971-76; Professor of Economics, Heriot-Watt University, 1976-82; Chairman, Scottish Enterprise, 1993-97; Chairman, Picola plc, 1985-2001; Chairman, Grampian Holdings and Malcolm Group, 1998-2003; Vice President, Scottish Association of Public Transport; Governor, National Institute of Economic and Social Research. Recreations: tennis; bridge. Address: (h.) Newfield, 14 Gamekeepers Road, Edinburgh; T.-0131-336 1936.

MacKay, Donald Stewart, BA, DipPE, AUPE. Director of Education and Communities, Midlothian Council, since 1996; b. 18.4.50, Edinburgh; 2 s. Educ. Firrhill Secondary, Boroughmuir Secondary, Edinburgh; Moray House College of Education; Open University. Teacher/Assistant Head Teacher/Headteacher, Fife; Curriculum Development Officer, Fife; Advisor in Primary Education, Lothian; Assistant Director of Education, Lothian. Recreations: skiing; football. Address: (b.) Fairfield House, 8 Lothian Road, Dalkeith EH22 3ZG; T.-0131-270 7500.

Mackay, Rev. Canon Douglas Brysson, FFCS. Rector, Church of the Holy Rood, Carnoustie, 1972-97; Synod Clerk, Diocese of Brechin, since 1981; Honorary Chaplain, St. Paul's Cathedral, Dundee, since 1999; Tutor and Examiner, Communication Skills, Primary Care Medicine, University of Dundee; Chaplain, British Legion, since 2001; b. 20.3.27, Glasgow; m., Catherine Elizabeth; 2 d. Educ. Possil Senior Secondary School; Edinburgh Theological College; DipNAG, 1954. Precentor, St. Andrew's Cathedral, Inverness, 1958; Rector, Gordon Chapel, Fochabers, 1961 (also Priest-in-Charge, St. Margaret's Church, Aberlour, 1964); Canon, St. Andrew's Cathedral, Inverness, 1965; Synod Clerk, Diocese of Moray, Ross, Caithness, 1965; Honorary Canon, St. Andrew's Cathedral, Inverness, 1972; Convenor of Youth, Moray Diocese, 1965; Brechin Diocese: Convenor, Social Service Board, 1974, Convenor, Joint Board, 1974, Convenor, Administration Board, 1982, Synod Clerk, 1981; Honorary Canon, St Paul's Cathedral, Dundee, 1998; Chairman, Truth and Unity Movement, 1980-87. President: British Red Cross, Carnoustie, 1974-82, British Legion, Carnoustie, 1981; Vice-Chairman, Carnoustie Community Care, 1981; Chairman, Carnoustie Community Council, 1979-81; President, Carnoustie Rotary Club, 1976; Joint Founder and Vice Chairman, Carnoustie Community Care; Carnoustie Citizen of the Year, 1998; Special Deputy Sheriff, Jasper County, Iowa, USA, 1987; Vice Provost, St. Paul's Cathedral Dundee, 2006. Recreations: golf; snooker; reading; music. Address: Balmore House, 24 Philip Street, Carnoustie DD7 6EB.

McKay, Ian, BA (Hons), DipEd. Director of Scottish Affairs, Royal Mail Group, since 2003; b. 2.2.55, Longridge; m., Yvonne Strachan; 1 s.; 1 d. Educ. Whitburn Academy; Stirling University. Senior Lecturer, Stevenson College of Further Education, 1983-88; Assistant General Secretary, Educational Institute of Scotland, 1988-2003. Member, Scottish Council, CBI; Member, Executive, Scottish Council Development and Industry; Board Member, Scottish Business Crime Centre; Trustee, Edinburgh UNESCO City of Literature Trust; Member, UK NHS Pay Review Body. Recreations: films; hill-walking. Address: (b.) 10 Brunswick Road, Edinburgh EH7 5XX; T.-0131-550 8220.

Mackay, Ian Munro, BCom, CA, FFCS. Principal, Mackay & Co. Chartered Accountants; Honorary Sheriff, Dornoch Sheriff Court, since 1985; b. 14.9.47, Brora; m., Maureen; 2 s.; 2 d. (1 d. deceased). Educ. Golspie High School; Edinburgh University. Trained as CA in Edinburgh, qualifying in 1973; has worked in the profession since,

spending three years in United Arab Emirates, returning to UK in 1979 to set up own practice. Secretary, Dornoch Curling Club, since 1984; Past President, Sutherland Curling Province; Member, Scots centenary curling tour to Canada, 2003, winning back Strathcona Cup. Recreations: curling; local history; holidays in Scotland, France or USA; garden; golf; following most sports. Address: (h.) 4 Sutherland Road, Dornoch, Sutherland; T.-01862 810333.

Mackay, John, TD, MA, FRSGS, FInstD; b. 14.9.36, St. Andrews; m., Barbara Wallace; 1 s.; 2 d. Educ. Madras College; Dunfermline High School; Kirkcaldy High School; Edinburgh University. Lieutenant, 1st East Anglian Regiment, 1959-63; Territorial Army, 1964-86: Colonel, Royal Engineers (Postal and Courier); Royal Mail, 1963-96: Director, Philately, 1979-84, Chairman, Scottish Post Office Board, 1988, Operations Director, UK, 1991-92, Director and General Manager, Scotland and Northern Ireland, 1986-96; Chairman, Earl Haig Fund Scotland, 1999-2004. President, Lord's Taverners Scotland, 1994-98; Chairman: Scottish Premier Rugby Limited, 1996-97, Scottish Business in the Community Executive Council, 1995-98, Scotland the Brand Judging Panel, 1998-2002, Edinburgh Common Purpose, 1995-96; Member: Committee, Army Benevolent Fund Scotland, 1988-98, Board, Quality Scotland, 1991-98, Board, Scottish Business in the Community, 1993-98, Quality Assessment Committee, Scottish Higher Education Funding Council, 1994-96; Chairman, Lowland Employers Liaison Committee, 2001-03; Founder Member, The Breakaways Golf Club. Recreations: golf; watching cricket and rugby; military and European history; Battlefields 19th Century German Art. Address: (h.) Kinrymont, 8 Damside, Dean Village, Edinburgh EH4 3BB; T.-0131-226 2512.

MacKay, John, OBE, MB, ChB, FRCGP. Retired General Medical Practitioner; Member, General Medical Council; Member, Scottish National Board for Nursing, Midwifery and Health Visiting; b. 24.7.26, Glasgow; m., Matilda MacLennan Bain; 2 s.; 2 d. Educ. Govan High School; Glasgow University. Junior House Doctor, Victoria Infirmary and Southern General Hospital, Glasgow, 1949; Ship's Surgeon, 1950; Assistant in General Practice, Govan, 1951-52 (Principal, since 1953); Member, Board of Management, Glasgow South West Hospitals, prior to 1973; Tutor, University Department of General Practice, Glasgow; part-time Medical Referee, Scottish Home and Health Department; Honorary Life Manager, Govan Weavers Society; Member, Scottish General Medical Services Committee. Recreations: angling; golf; gardening. Address: (h.) Moorholm, Barr's Brae, Kilmacolm, Renfrewshire PA13 4DE; T.-Kilmacolm 3234.

Mackay, John Angus, OBE, MA, MSc, FRSA. Former Director, Gaelic Media Service; Member, Bord Na Gaidhlig; Member, An Lanntair; Chair, NHS Western Isles Board; b. 24.6.48, Shader, Isle of Lewis; m., Maria. Educ. Nicolson Institute; University of Aberdeen; Jordanhill College. Sales Rep, D.C. Thomson, Aberdeen, 1971-72; English teacher, Glasgow, 1973-77; Co-operative Development Officer, Highlands and Islands Development Board, 1977-80; Investigating Officer and Senior Development Manager, Highland and Islands Development Board, 1980-84; Chief Executive, Communn na Gaidhlig, 1985-91. Recreations: books; skiing; swimming. Address: (h.) Druimard Arnol, Isle of Lewis, H52 98DB; T.-01851 710479.

McKay, John Henderson, CBE (1987), DL, JP, BA (Hons), PhD, Dr h.c. (Edinburgh). Chairman: Scottish Working Peoples' History Trust, 1992-2000, Edinburgh Quartet Trust, 1996-2000; Hon. Vice-President, St. Andrew

Society, 1989-2003; Hon. President, Scottish Craftsmanship Association, 1987-2001; Patron, Scotland Yard Adventure Centre, 1988-2002; b. 12.5.29, Kirknewton; m., Catherine Watson Taylor; 1 s.; 1 d. Educ. West Calder High School; Open University. Labourer and Clerk, Pumpherston Oil Co. Ltd., 1948-50; National Service, Royal Artillery, 1950-52; Customs and Excise, 1952-85; Lord Provost of Edinburgh, 1984-88. Vice President, Royal Caledonian Horticultural Society, 1984-88 and 1993-96, Secretary and Treasurer, 1988-93; Convener, Business Committee, General Council, Edinburgh University, 1992-96; General Council Assessor, Edinburgh University Court, 1996-99; Honorary Vice President, Royal Caledonian Horticultural Society, since 1997. Publications: contributed to: A Sense of Place, 1988; Local Population Studies, 1998; Pumpherston, the story of a shale oil village, 2002; Participating in the knowledge society, 2005; contributed to Nigel Goose (ed) 2007, Women's Work in Industrial England. Recreations: gardening; reading; listening to music. Address: (h.) 2 Buckstone Way, Edinburgh EH10 6PN; T.-0131-445 2865.

McKay, Rev. Johnston Reid, MA (Glasgow), BA (Cantab), PhD (Edin). Clerk to the Presbytery of Ardrossan, since 2003; Barony St. John's Church, Ardrossan, since 2002; b. 2.5.42, Glasgow. Educ. High School of Glasgow; Glasgow University; Cambridge University. Assistant Minister, St. Giles' Cathedral, 1967-71; Church Correspondent, Glasgow Herald, 1968-70; Minister, Bellahouston Steven Parish Church, 1971-78; Governor, Paisley College; Minister, Paisley Abbey, 1978-87; Senior Producer, Religious Programmes, BBC Scotland, 1987-99; Editor, Religious Programmes, BBC Scotland, 1999-2002. Editor, The Bush (newspaper of Glasgow Presbytery), 1975-78; Chairman, Scottish Religious Advisory Committee, BBC, 1981-86; Stanley Mair Lecturer on Preaching, Glasgow University, 1995; Trustee, Baird Trust, since 1999; Wallace Lecturer, 2000. Publications: From Sleep and From Damnation (with James Miller), 1970; Essays in Honour of William Barclay (Joint Editor), 1976; Through Wood and Nails, 1982; This Small Pool, 1996; The Very Thing, 2001; Glimpses of Hope – God Beyond Ground Zero, 2002; Netting Citizens (ed), 2004; A Touch Personal, 2005. Recreations: walking; gardening. Address: 17 Montgomerie Avenue, Fairlie KA29 0EE; T.-01475 568802; e-mail: johnston.mckay@btopenworld.com

Mackay, Kenneth James, MA, BD. Minister of St Nicholas Sighthill Church, 1976-2007; b. 14.9.41, Inverness; m., Janet; 1 s.; 1 d. Educ. Fortrose Academy; Aberdeen University. Minister of Church of Scotland, Maryfield - Victoria St., Dundee, 1971-76. Member: Botanical Society of Scotland, Scottish Wildlife Trust. Recreations: hill-walking; golf. Address: (h.) 46 Chuckethall Road, Livingston EH54 8FB; T.-01506 410 884.

McKay, Linda, MA (Hons). Principal and Chief Executive, Forth Valley College of Further and Higher Education, since 2005; b. 27.5.51, Dunfermline. Educ. Aberdeen High School for Girls; Aberdeen University; Universite de Haute-Bretagne; Scottish School of Further Education, Jordanhill. Assistant Principal, Dundee College of Further Education, 1990-93; Depute Principal, Glenrothes College, 1993-99; Principal and Chief Executive, Falkirk College of Further and Higher Education, 1999-2005. Board Member, Scottish Qualifications Authority and Chair, Scottish Qualifications Authority Advisory Council; Board Member, Scottish Enterprise Forth Valley; Board Member, Scotland's Colleges International; Member, Goodison Group in Scotland; Member, Scottish Funding Council Skills Committee. Address: (b.) Grangemouth Road, Falkirk FK2 9AD; T.-01324 403203.

MacKay, Neville Patrick, BA (Hons) Geog. Chief Executive, Scottish Public Pensions Agency, since 2004; b. 22.6.58; m., Gillian Anne Prole; 2 d. Educ. Brentwood School; Lancaster University; University College London. Researcher, DoE, 1983-90; DFE, 1990-92; Department for National Heritage, later Department for Culture, Media and Sport, 1992-99; Deputy Head, Heritage Division, 1995-97; Head, Libraries and Information Division, 1997-99; Chief Executive, Resource, Council for Museums, Archives and Libraries, 2000-02; Head, Voluntary Issues Unit, Scottish Executive, 2002-04. Recreations: motor sports; walking; camping; being with my family. Address: (b.) Scottish Public Pensions Agency, 7 Tweedside Park, Galashiels TD1 3TE.

MacKay, Professor Norman, CBE, MD, FRCP(Glas), FRCP(Edin), FRCS(Edin), FRCGP, FCPSP, FACP(Hon), FRACP(Hon), FAMS, FAMM, FRCS(Eng), FRCS(I), FRCP(I), FCPSBangl., FCCP(Hon). Dean of Postgraduate Medicine and Professor of Postgraduate Medical Education, Glasgow University, 1989-2001; Consultant Physician, Victoria Infirmary, Glasgow, 1974-89; Member, General Medical Council, 1999-2003; b. 15.9.36, Glasgow; m., Grace Violet McCaffer; 2 s.; 2 d. Educ. Govan High School; Glasgow University. Honorary Secretary: Royal College of Physicians and Surgeons of Glasgow, 1973-83, Standing Joint Committee, Scottish Royal Colleges, 1978-82, Conference of Royal Colleges and Faculties in Scotland, 1982-91; Speciality Adviser in Medicine, West of Scotland Committee of Postgraduate Medical Education, 1982-89; President, Royal Medico-Chirurgical Society of Glasgow, 1982-83; Member, Area Medical Committee, Greater Glasgow Health Board, 1987-89; President, Southern Medical Society, 1989-90; President, Royal College of Physicians and Surgeons of Glasgow, 1994-97; Member, Specialist Training Authority, 1999-2001. Address: (h.) 5 Edenhall Grove, Glasgow G77 5TS; T.-0141-616 2831.

Mackay, Peter, CB. Chairman, Local Government Boundary Commission for Scotland, since 2007; Commissioner, Northern Lighthouse Board, since 1999; Chairman, 2005-07; Chairman, Pacific Horizon Investment Trust, since 2004; b. 6.7.40, Arbroath; m., Sarah Holdich; 1 s.; 2 d. Educ. Glasgow High School; St. Andrews University. Teacher, New South Wales, Australia, 1962-63; Private Secretary to Secretaries of State for Scotland, 1973-75; Director for Scotland, Manpower Services Commission, 1983-85; on secondment from Scottish Office to Department of Employment, London, 1985; Under Secretary, Scottish Education Department (Further and Higher Education, Arts and Sport), 1987-89; Secretary and Chief Executive, Scottish Office Industry Department, 1990-95; Executive Director, Advanced Management Programme in Scotland, 1995-97; former Member, Board, Business Banking Division, Bank of Scotland; Member, Competition Commission (formerly Monopolies and Mergers Commission), 1996-2002; Member, Board, Scottish Natural Heritage, 1997-2003; Member, Court, Napier University, 1995-2004. Recreations: Scotland; high altitudes and latitudes; dinghy sailing; sea canoeing. Address: (h.) 6 Henderland Road, Edinburgh EH12 6BB; T.-0131-337 2830.

Mackay, Rev. William Morton, MA(Hons), DipEd, FCS, ARSGS, AFAPC, MACE. Moderator, General Assembly of Free Church of Scotland, 2001; Part-time Lecturer in Church History, Free Church of Scotland College, Edinburgh, 1998-2005; Free Church of Scotland: Clerk of Public Questions, Religion and Morals Committee, 1999-2002, Chairman, International Missions Board, 2002-07; b. 26.3.34, Dundee; m., Catherine; 2 s.; 1 d. Educ. Morgan Academy, Dundee; Queen's College, Dundee; University of St. Andrews; Dundee College of Education; Free Church of

Scotland College, Edinburgh. Teacher, Buckhaven High School, Fife, 1959-61; ordained, 1961; Teacher, Colegio San Andres, Lima, Peru, 1961-65, Headmaster, 1966-78; Teacher, Lothian Regional Council, 1978-85; Principal, Presbyterian Ladies' College, Burwood, Victoria, Australia, 1986-97. Diploma of Honour, Government of Peru, for services to education. Treasurer, Edinburgh Centre, Member of Council, Royal Scottish Geographical Society, 2003-06. Publication: Thomas Chalmers: A Short Appreciation, 1980. Recreations: music; photography; cricket; rugby; reading; walking. Address: 53 Lauderdale Street, Edinburgh EH9 1DE.

McKean, Professor Charles Alexander, BA, FRSE, FRSA, FSA Scot, HonFRIBA, Hon FRIAS, HonFRSGS. Professor of Scottish Architectural History, Dundee University; b. 16.7.46, Glasgow; m., Margaret Yeo; 2 s. Educ. Fettes College; Bristol University. RIBA: Secretary, London Region, 1968-76, Secretary, Eastern Region, 1972-79, Secretary, Community Architecture, 1976-79; Secretary, Royal Incorporation of Architects in Scotland, 1979-94; Architectural Correspondent, The Times, 1977-83; Trustee, Thirlestane Castle, 1982-92; Member, Historic Environment Advisory Committee for Scotland; Member, Scottish Committee, Heritage Lottery Fund; Hon. President, St. Andrews Preservation Trust; Chairman, Edinburgh World Heritage; author of architectural guides to Edinburgh, Dundee, Stirling, London, Cambridge, Moray, Central Glasgow, Banff and Buchan; General Editor, RIAS/Landmark Trust Guides to Scotland. Publications: The Scottish Thirties; Edinburgh: Portrait of a City; Claim!; The Making of the Museum of Scotland; The Scottish Château; Battle for the North. Recreations: books; glasses; gardens; stately homes. Address: (b.) Department of History, Dundee University, Perth Road, Dundee DD1 4HN; T.-01382 345738.

McKechin, Ann, LLB, DipLP. Labour MP, Glasgow North, since 2005, Glasgow Maryhill, 2001-05; Solicitor; b. 22.4.61, Johnstone. Educ. Paisley Grammar School; Strathclyde University. Partner, Pacitti Jones, Solicitors, 1990-2000. Director, World Development Trust and Mercycorps Scotland. Recreations: films; art history; dancing. Address: (b.) 154 Raeberry Street, Glasgow G20 6EA; T.-0141-946 1300.

McKechnie, Alasdair A., MD, FRCPE, FRC (Psych), DPM. Honorary Sheriff, West Lothian, since 1995; b. 17.10.36, Inverness (shire); m., Sheila; 1 s.; 1 d. Educ. Inverness Royal Academy; Aberdeen University. Physician Superintendent, Bangour Village Hospital, 1970-89; Medical Director, Mental Welfare Commission, 1989-93; Consultant Psycho, Geriatric Services, Midlothian, 1993-95. Member, Royal Scottish Forestry Society. Publications: various papers on rehabilitation in Psychiatry, outcome of detention under Mental Health Act Scotland. Recreations: forestry; gardening; fishing; bridge; walking the dog. Address: (h.) 13 Jocks Hill Crescent, Linlithgow EH49 7BJ; T.-01506 842293.

McKee, Graham Hamilton, BSc, BPhil. Director of Strategic Planning, University of Dundee; b. 11.9.51; m., Pilar; 1 s.; 2 d. Educ. Hutchesons' Grammar School, Glasgow; Glasgow University; Newcastle-upon-Tyne University. Assistant Planner, Burnley Borough Council, 1975-77; Scottish Development Agency, 1977-91, latterly as Regional Manager; Scottish Enterprise Tayside: Director Economic Development, 1991-93, Chief Executive, 1994-2001; Senior Director, Scottish Enterprise, 2001-05. Recreation: family. Address: (b.) University of Dundee, Dundee DD1 4HN; T.-01382 385557; e-mail: g.h.mckee@dundee.ac.uk

McKee, Ian, MBE, MBChB, DObst, RCOG, FSOMW. MSP (SNP), Lothians, since 2007; b. 2.4.40, South Shields; m., Penelope Ann; 1 s. and 1 stepson; 2 d. and 1 stepdaughter. Educ. Fettes College; Edinburgh University. House Officer: Ingham Infirmary, South Shields, 1965-66, Royal Infirmary Edinburgh, 1966; Medical Officer, Royal Air Force, 1966-71; General Practitioner, Sighthill and Wester Hailes Health Centres, Edinburgh, 1971-2006; Managing Director, Hermiston Publications, 1980-2000. Member, Company of Merchants, City of Edinburgh, since 1982; Burgess of Edinburgh, since 2007; Deputy Convener, Cross Party Group on Culture and Media, since 2007; Member, Scottish Parliament Art Advisory Group, since 2007. Recreations: hill walking; music. Address: (b.) Scottish Parliament, Edinburgh EH99 1SP; T.-0131 348 6815; e-mail: ian.mckee.msp@scottish.parliament.uk

McKee, Professor (James Clark St. Clair) Sean, BSc, MA, PhD, DSc, FIMA, CMath, FRSE. Professor of Mathematics, Strathclyde University, since 1988; b. 1.7.45, Belfast. Educ. George Watson's College, Edinburgh; St. Andrews University; Dundee University; Oxford University. NCR Research Fellow, 1970-72; Lecturer in Numerical Analysis, Southampton University, 1972-75; Fellow, Hertford College, Oxford, 1975-86; Professor of Industrial Mathematics, Strathclyde University, and Consultant Mathematician, Unilever Research, 1986-88. Member, Council, ECMI; Member, IMA Programmes Committee; Founding Fellow, Institute of Contemporary Scotland. Publications: 170 papers; Industrial Numerical Analysis (Co-Editor), 1986; Vector and Parallel Computing (Co-Editor), 1989; Artificial Intelligence in Mathematics (Co-Editor), 1994; homenagem, 2003. Recreations: climbing Munros; golf; theatre; gardening. Address: (b.) Department of Mathematics, Strathclyde University, Glasgow G1 1XH; T.-0141-552 4400.

McKellar, Kenneth, BSc. Singer, Composer, Writer; b. 23.6.27, Paisley. Gave first concert in local hall, aged 13; continued singing while at school, university and during his first two years working in forestry; has made numerous records of classical and popular music; numerous tours, especially in Australia and New Zealand; has appeared a number of times at the London Palladium.

McKellar, Peter Archibald, LLB (Hons). Chief Investment Officer, Standard Life Investments, since 1999; b. 28.5.65, Glasgow; m., Kathleen Scarlett; 2 s. Educ. Daniel Stewart's and Melville College, Edinburgh; Edinburgh University. J.P. Morgan, Investment Bank, New York and London, 1986-88; EFT Group PLC, Corporate Finance Division, 1988-89; London and Edinburgh Trust plc, 1989-90; Co-Founder, Barry McKellar Ltd., 1990-95; Finance Director, Clydeport plc, 1995-98; Group Finance Director, Donside Paper Company Limited, 1998-99; Non-Executive Director, Red Lemon Studios Ltd, 1998-99; Governor, Cargilfield School, since 2002. Recreations: golf; shooting; swimming. Address: (b.) 1 George Street, Edinburgh EH2 2LL; T.-0131-245 8368.

McKelvey, William Alexander Campbell, BVMS, PhD, MRCVS, CBiol, FIBiol, FRAgS. Chief Executive and Principal, Scottish Agricultural College, since 2002; b. 10.1.53, Belfast; m., Anne; 1 s.; 2 d. Educ. Regent House School; Glasgow University; Aberdeen University. Ontario Veterinary College, Canada, 1975-76; general veterinary practice, Gloucester and Peebles, 1976-83; Senior Veterinary Officer, Rowett Institute, Aberdeen, 1983-87; Senior Veterinary Officer, Macaulay Institute, Edinburgh, 1987-89; General Manager, Edinburgh Genetics, 1989-95; Assistant Director, SAC Veterinary Services, 1995-97; Director,

SAC Veterinary Science Division, 1997-99; Director of Operations, SAC, 1999-2002. Recreations: fishing; hill-walking; conservation. Address: (b.) SAC, Central Office, Kings Buildings, West Mains Road, Edinburgh EH9 3JG; T.-0131-535 4001.

McKelvie, Christina. MSP (SNP), Central Scotland, since 2007; b. 4.3.68. Address: (b.) Scottish Parliament, Edinburgh EH99 1SP.

McKenna, David. Chief Executive, Victim Support Scotland, since 2001; b. 24.1.58, Glasgow. Educ. Queens Park Secondary School, Glasgow; Glasgow College of Technology. Principal Officer, Victim Support Strathclyde, 1986-93; Director of Operations, Victim Support Scotland, 1993-2000. Member: Scottish Association for the Study of Delinquency, Summary Justice Group, Victims Steering Group, Community Safety Forum, European Forum of Victim Services, Youth Justice Implementation Steering Group, Sentencing Commission (November 2003), National Advisory Body on Offender Management; Secretary and Member, Victim Support Europe; Member, World Society for Victimology. Recreations: travel; history. Address: (b.) 23 Hardwell Close, Edinburgh EH8 9RX; T.-0131-662 5402.

McKenna, Rosemary, CBE, DCE. MP (Labour), Cumbernauld and Kilsyth; Member: Select Committee on Culture, Media and Sport, since 2001, Select Committee on Procedure, since 2001; Chair of Committee of Selection Select Committee; b. 8.5.41, Kilmacolm; m., James Stephen McKenna; 3 s.; 1 d. Educ. St. Augustine's Secondary School, Glasgow; St. Andrew's College, Bearsden. Taught in various primary schools, 1974-93; Leader of Council, Cumbernauld and Kilsyth, 1984-88, Provost 1988-92, Leader of Council, 1992-94; former Member, North Lanarkshire Council; former Police Board Member: Local Government Management Board, Local Government International Bureau; former Member, Board, Scottish Enterprise; former Member, Executive, Scottish Constitutional Convention; Chair, Scottish Libraries and Information Council, 1999-2002; PPS to John Battle, MP, 1998-2000, to Brian Wilson, MP, 2000-01; President, Convention of Scottish Local Authorities, 1994-96. Recreations: reading; cooking. Address: (b.) House of Commons, London SW1A 0AA; e-mail: mckennar@parliament.uk

McKenna, Revd. Scott S., BA, BD (Hons), MTh. Minister, Edinburgh: Mayfield Salisbury Church, since 2000; b. 3.2.66, Dunfermline; m., Shelagh M. Laird; 1 s. Educ. Kirkton High School, Dundee; St. Mary's College, University of St. Andrews. Accountant; Probationer Minister, Wellington Church, Glasgow, 1992-93; Minister, Viewpark Parish Church, Uddingston, 1994-2000. Member, Panel on Worship, General Assembly, 1994-98; Member, World Mission Council, General Assembly, since 2005. Address: (b.) 26 Seton Place, Edinburgh EH9 2JT; T.-0131-667 1286; e-mail: scottsmckenna@aol.com

MacKenzie, Angus Alexander, OBE, CA. Chartered Accountant, since 1955; b. 1.3.31, Nairn; m., Catherine; 1 d. Educ. Inverness Royal Academy; Edinburgh University. National Service, RAF, 1955-57; in private practice as CA Assistant in Edinburgh, 1957-59; in private practice in Inverness, since 1959. Recreations: shooting; stalking; hill-walking; gardening. Address: (h.) Tigh an Allt, Tomatin, Inverness-shire; T.-01808 511270.

Mackenzie, Professor Ann Logan, MA. E. Allison Peers Professorial Research Fellow, Glasgow University, since 2006; Ivy McClelland Research Professor of Spanish, Glasgow University, since 1995; General Editor, Bulletin of Spanish Studies (1923-), since 1992; b. Greenock. Educ. Greenock Academy; Glasgow University. Lecturer, Senior Lecturer, Reader, Liverpool University, 1968-95. Publications: books and articles on the theatre and literature of 17th-century Spain and on the history of British Hispanism. Recreations: theatre; walking the dogs; house improvements. Address: (b.) 68 Oakfield Avenue, Glasgow University, Glasgow, G12 8LS; T.-0141-330 5665; e-mail: A.Mackenzie@hispanic.arts.gla.ac.uk

MacKenzie, Archibald MacIntosh, DL. Vice Lord Lieutenant, Dunbartonshire, since 1990; b. 3.6.33, Inveraray; m., Margaret Young Ritchie; 1 s.; 1 d. Educ. Hermitage School, Helensburgh. Assistant Chief Constable, British Transport Police, 1982-92; Vice-President, Royal National Lifeboat Institution (Chairman, Dumbarton Branch); Convenor, Scottish Lifeboat Council, 1996-2003; Chairman, Scottish Lifeboat Executive Committee, 1990-96; Member, Committee of Management, Royal National Lifeboat Institution; Honorary Life Governor, Royal National Lifeboat Institution, 2007; Director, Dunbartonshire Branch, British Red Cross, 1992-95; Non-Executive Director, Lomond Health Trust, 1995-99; Chairman, 2319 Sqd. ATC Committee, 1994-2005; Elder, Church of Scotland. Recreations: sailing; golf; reading; classical music. Address: (h.) Millerston, 10 Boghead Road, Dumbarton; T.-Dumbarton 763654.

Mackenzie, Sheriff Colin Scott, DL, BL, FSA Scot. Sheriff of Grampian Highland and Islands, at Lerwick and Kirkwall, 1992-2003; part-time Sheriff, since 2004; b. 7.7.38, Stornoway; m., Christeen E.D. MacLauchlan. Educ. Nicolson Institute; Fettes College; Edinburgh University. Procurator Fiscal, Stornoway, 1969-92; Burgh Prosecutor, Stornoway, 1971-75; JP Fiscal, 1971-75; Deputy Lieutenant and Clerk to Lieutenancy of the Western Isles, 1975-92; Vice Lord Lieutenant of Islands Area, Western Isles, 1984-92; Founder President, Stornoway Flying Club, 1970; Founding Dean, Western Isles Faculty of Solicitors; elected Council Member, Law Society of Scotland, 1985-92; Convener, Criminal Law Committee, 1991-92; Council Member, Sheriffs' Association, 2002-03; Elder, Church of Scotland, since 1985; Member, Board of Social Responsibility, Church of Scotland, 1990-96; Convener, Assembly Study Group on Young People and the Media, 1991-93; President, Stornoway Rotary Club, 1977; President, Lewis Pipe Band. Publications: author of article on Lieutenancy, Stair Memorial Encyclopaedia of Law of Scotland, 1987; The Last Warrior Band, 2000. Recreation: fishing. Address: (h.) Park House, Matheson Road, Stornoway, Lewis.

MacKenzie, Professor Donald, BSc, PhD, FRSE, FBA. Professor of Sociology, University of Edinburgh, since 1992; b. 3.5.50, Inverness; m., Caroline Bamford; 1s.; 1 d. Educ. Golspie High School; University of Edinburgh. University of Edinburgh: Lecturer in Sociology, 1975-88, Reader in Sociology, 1988-92. Visiting Professor of the History of Science, Harvard University, 1997. Co-winner, U.S. Navy Prize in Naval History, 1989; American Sociological Association Merton Award, 1993 and 2003, and Zelizer Prize, 2005; Society for Social Studies of Science Fleck Prize, 1993 and 2003. Publication: Mechanizing Proof, 2001. Recreations: cycling; walking; chess. Address: (b.) School of Social and Political Studies, George Square, Edinburgh EH8 9LL; T.-0131-650 3980.

Mackenzie, Elizabeth Alice, MA (Post-Grad), CertEd., AMBDA. Educational Consultant (Dyslexia); Member of Management Team, Transition Dyslexia; b. 10.9.41, Glasgow; m., Ian Mackenzie (deceased); 1 s.; 1 d. Educ. St Columba's, Kilmacolm; Laurel Bank, Glasgow; St George's, Edinburgh; Froebel Educational Institute,

Roehampton; Kingston University. Primary teacher in London and Scottish schools, 1963-68; Adviser on Children's Religious Programmes, ABC TV, 1965-68; research into children's books for ABC TV, 1968-70; Senior Teacher, Dyslexia Institute, Glasgow, 1989-92; Principal, Dyslexia Institute Scotland, 1992-2004. Management Team, "Dyslexia At Transition", Parents Transition Support Materials and DVD-Rom for Secondary Schools, 2004-07; Member, Scottish Dyslexia Forum, 1996-2004; Project Team, "Count Me In: Responding to Dyslexia", pack of materials for Scottish Primary Schools, 2002-04; Course Director, Dyslexia Institute Teacher Training Course, 1994-98; Course Tutor, Post Graduate Course in Dyslexia and Literacy, York University, 2003-04; Self Esteem Research Project (Glasgow/Paisley Universities), 2003-04. Publications: Dimensions of Dyslexia, Volume I (Contributor); Dyslexia and the Young Offender (paper). Recreations: cooking; design; watching seals. Address: (h.) 1 Glenan Gardens, Helensburgh, Argyll and Bute G84 8XT; T.-01436 673429.

Mackenzie, Fiona I., MA (Hons), MBA, MIHM (Dip). Chief Executive, NHS Board Forth Valley, since 2001; b. 19.7.58, Edinburgh. Educ. Eastwood High School, Glasgow; University of St. Andrews; Hull University. NHS Graduate Trainee, 1980-82; Hospital Administrator, West Lothian, 1982-84; Operational Manager, Royal Edinburgh Hospital, 1986-89; Assistant Unit General Manager, Mental Health Unit, Lothian Health Board, 1989-91; Acute Services Manager, Monklands Hospital, Lanarkshire Health Board; Director of Planning, Monklands and Bellshill NHS Trust, 1993-96; Chief Executive, Highland Communities NHS Trust, 1996-99; Chief Executive, Highland Primary Care NHS Trust, 1999-2001. Board Member, NHS Education, Scotland. Recreations: sport; outdoor activities; cooking. Address: 6 Learmonth Avenue South, Edinburgh EH4 1PE; T.-0131-332 5211; e-mail: fmackenzie@nhs.net

MacKenzie, George P., BA, MLitt. Keeper of the Records of Scotland, since 2001; b. 22.9.50, Lenzie. Educ. George Watson's College; Leeds Grammar School; University of Stirling. Archivist, Scottish Record Office, 1975-84; Departmental Records Officer, General Register Office for Scotland, 1985-86; Head of Liaison Branch, Head of Preservation Services, Scottish Record Office, 1987-94; Deputy Secretary General, International Council on Archives, Paris, 1995-96; Head of External Relations, National Archives of Scotland, 1997-2000. Recreations: travel; reading. Address: (b.) National Archives of Scotland, HM General Register House, Edinburgh EH1 3YY; T.-0131-535 1312; e-mail: george.mackenzie@nas.gov.uk

McKenzie, Howard John Malcolm, MBA, FCMI, MCGI, CertEd. Principal and Chief Executive, Jewel and Esk Valley College, since 2001; b. 26.7.55, Hammersmith; m., Rachel Jane Chaffey; 2 d. Educ. Ardingly College; Wolverhampton Polytechnic; University of Hertfordshire. Farm student, 1972-77; dairy farm manager, 1977-79; tenant farmer, 1979-85; Lecturer in Agriculture, 1985-88; Business Development Manager, Hertfordshire College of Agriculture, 1988-91; Director of Business Development, Oaklands College, St Albans, 1991-95; Director of Corporate Development, Motherwell College, and Managing Director, AMCOL Scotland Ltd., 1995-2001. Director, Midlothian Enterprise Trust Ltd; Director, Scottish Parliament Business Exchange Ltd.; Member, Local Economic Forum for Edinburgh and Lothians; Vice Chair of the Association of Scottish Colleges. Recreations: rugby; gardening; comedy; painting. Address: (b.) 24 Milton Road East, Edinburgh EH15 2PP; T.-0131 660 1010.

MacKenzie, Hugh D., MA (Hons), FEIS, JP, FRSA. Headteacher, Craigroyston Community High School, 1972-93; Director, Craigroyston Curriculum Project, since 1980;

b. 29.5.33, Edinburgh; m., Helen Joyce; 1 s.; 1 d. Educ. Royal High School; Edinburgh University; Moray House College of Education, Edinburgh. Education Officer, RAF, 1956-58; Assistant Teacher, Niddrie Marischal Junior Secondary School and Falkirk High School, 1958-62; Principal Teacher: Broxburn Academy, 1962-64, Liberton High School, 1964-70; Deputy Headteacher, Craigmount High School, 1970-72; Scottish Representative, Northern Regional Examination Board, 1973-88; Vice-Chairman, Lothian Regional Consultative Committee, 1984-87; a Director, Royal Lyceum Theatre, Edinburgh, since 1985, Scottish Community Education Council, 1985-88; President, Royal High School Rugby Club; President and Founder Member, Edinburgh Golden Oldies Rugby Club. Publication: Craigroyston Days, 1995. Recreations: rugby; squash; golf; ornithology; philately; jazz. Address: (h.) 3 Beechwood Mains, Edinburgh.

McKenzie, John Murchison, LLB, MCLIP. Chief Executive and Faculty Librarian, Royal Faculty of Procurators in Glasgow, since 2002; b. 7.8.71, Lakhnadon, M. P., India; m., Eleanor; 1 s.; 1 d. Educ. Hebron School, TN, India; High School of Glasgow; Dundee University; Strathclyde University. Legal Librarian, Glasgow City Council, 2000-02. Recreations: football; reading; crafts. Address: (b.) Royal Faculty of Procurators in Glasgow, 12 Nelson Mandela Place, Glasgow G2 1BT; T.-0141 332 3593; e-mail: jmckenzie@rfpg.org

MacKenzie, Ken. Chairman, Scottish Retail Consortium, since 2006; Chief Officer, Scottish Co-op. Member of the Executive of the Scottish Grocers' Federation; Vice-Chair of Skillsmart, the UK retail sector skills council. Chairman of Caravan Scotland, formerly the National Grocers' Benevolent Fund. Address: (b.) The Scottish Retail Consortium, PO Box 13737, Gullane EH31 2WX; T.-0870 609 3631.

MacKenzie, Kenneth John, CB, MA, AM. Chairman, Historic Scotland Foundation, since 2001; Honorary Professor, Department of Politics and International Relations, University of Aberdeen, 2001-04; Member, National Board of Christian Aid, since 2005; Member, British Waterways Scotland Group, 2002-07; Associate Consultant, Public Administration International, since 2002; b. 1.5.43, Glasgow; m., Irene Mary Hogarth; 1 s.; 1 d. Educ. Birkenhead School, Cheshire; Pembroke College, Oxford; Stanford University, California. Assistant Principal, Scottish Home and Health Department, 1965-70; Private Secretary to Joint Parliamentary Under Secretary of State, Scottish Office, 1969-70; Principal: General Register Office, 1970, Regional Development Division, Scottish Office, 1970-73; Scottish Education Department, 1973-77; Civil Service Fellow: Downing College, Cambridge, 1972, Department of Politics, University of Glasgow, 1974-75; Principal Private Secretary to Secretary of State for Scotland, 1977-79; Assistant Secretary: Scottish Economic Planning Department, 1979-83, Scottish Office Finance Division, 1983-85; Principal Finance Officer, Scottish Office, 1985-88; Under Secretary, Scottish Home and Health Department, 1988-91; Scottish Office, Agriculture and Fisheries Department: Under Secretary, 1991-92, Secretary, 1992-95; Head Economic and Domestic Secretariat, Cabinet Office, 1995-97; Head, Constitution Secretariat, Cabinet Office, 1997-98; Secretary and Head of Department, Scottish Executive Development Department, 1998-2001. Member, Agriculture and Food Research Council, 1992-94; Member, Biotechnology and Biological Sciences Research Council, 1994-95; Quinquennial Reviewer for Court Service, Lord Chancellor's Department, 2001-02. Recreations: amateur dramatics (Member, Edinburgh Makars); church activities (Elder, St Cuthbert's Parish Church, Edinburgh). Address: (h.) 30 Regent

Terrace, Edinburgh EH7 5BS; T.-0131-557 4530; e-mail: kjmackenzie@freeuk.com

MacKenzie, Madeleine, LLB (Hons), DipLP. Scottish Parliamentary Counsel, since 2002; b. 27.8.63, Inverness; d. of William Gordon MacKenzie and Veronica Dorothy Rachel MacKenzie. Educ. Inverness High School; Aberdeen University. Solicitor in private practice, 1986-90; Assistant, then Depute Scottish Parliamentary Counsel, 1990-2002. Recreations: reading; bridge; music. Clubs: Athenaeum, New. Address: (b.) Office of the Scottish Parliamentary Counsel, Victoria Quay, Edinburgh EH6 6QQ; T.-0131-244 1667.
E-mail: madeleine.mackenzie@ scotland.gsi.gov.uk

Mackenzie, Professor Robin Kenneth; BSc, MSc, PhD, CEng, FIOA, FRSA. Vice Principal (Research and Knowledge Transfer), Napier University; b. 28.8.44, Edinburgh; m., Georgina Fiona; 3 s. Educ. Trinity Academy; Heriot-Watt University, Edinburgh University; MIT (USA). Research Fellow, Massachusetts Institute of Technology, 1970-72; Lecturer/Senior Lecturer, Heriot-Watt University, 1973-85; Reader in Acoustics, Heriot-Watt University, 1985-90; Royal Society Industrial Fellow, 1990-93; Head, Department of Building, Sheffield Hallam University, 1993-95; Cruden Fellowship, National Science Foundation Fellowship (USA); Tyndall Medal, Institute of Acoustics, 1980; Chairman of various ISO and BSI committees on sound insulation. Publications: Auditorium Acoustics, 1974. Recreations: tennis; golf; chess; skiing. Address: (b.) Napier University, Craighouse Campus, Edinburgh, EH10 5LG; T.-0131-455 2645; e-mail: r.mackenzie@napier.ac.uk

Mackenzie, Simon James, MB, ChB, FRCA. Consultant, Intensive Care and Anaesthetics, Royal Infirmary of Edinburgh, since 1995; Honorary Senior Clinical Lecturer, University of Edinburgh; b. 29.12.60, Edinburgh; m., Nesta; 2 s.; 1 d. Educ. Daniel Stewarts and Melville College; University of Edinburgh. Former Consultant, Western General Hospital, Edinburgh. Associate Medical Director, NHS Lothian; President, Scottish Intensive Care Society. Publications: papers on intensive care medicine. Recreations: sailing; reading. Address: (b.) Lauriston Rooms, Royal Infirmary, Little France, Edinburgh; T.-0131 242 3200.

McKenzie Smith, Ian, OBE, PPRSA, PPRSW, RGI, LLD, DArt, FSA (Scot), FMA. Artist (painter); b. 3.8.35; m., Mary Rodger Fotheringham; 2 s.; 1 d. Educ. Robert Gordon's College, Aberdeen; Gray's School of Art, Aberdeen; Hospitalfield College of Art, Arbroath; Aberdeen College of Education. Teacher of Art, 1960-63; Education Officer, Council of Industrial Design, Scottish Committee, 1963-68; Director, Aberdeen Art Gallery and Museums, 1968-89; City Arts and Recreation Officer, City of Aberdeen, 1989-96. Institute of Contemporary Prints Award, 1969; RSA Guthrie Award, 1971; RSA Gillies Award, 1980; EUS Thyne Scholarship, 1980; RSW May Marshall Brown Award, 1980. Work in permanent collections: Scottish National Gallery of Modern Art, Scottish Arts Council, Arts Council of Northern Ireland, Contemporary Art Society, Aberdeen Art Gallery and Museums, Glasgow Art Gallery and Museums, Abbot Hall Art Gallery, Kendal, Hunterian Museum, Glasgow, Nuffield Foundation, Carnegie Trust, Strathclyde Education Authority, Lothian Education Authority, Royal Scottish Academy, Department of the Environment, City Art Centre, Edinburgh, Perth Art Gallery, IBM, Robert Fleming Holdings, Deutsche Bank, Grampian Hospital Art Trust;

Member, Scottish Arts Council, 1970-77; Member, Scottish Museums Council, 1980-87; Member, Committee of Enquiry into the Economic Situation of the Visual Artist, Gulbenkian Foundation, 1978; Arts Advisor, COSLA, 1977-84; Member, Aberdeen University Museums Committee, 1970-96, and Music Committee, 1970-96; Honorary Member: Friends of Aberdeen Art Gallery and Museums, 2000-07, Peacock Printmakers, 1993; Trustee: Third Eye Centre, 1966-70, Glasgow Arts Centre, 1966-68, Alba Magazine, 1977-80, WASPS (Scotland), 1973-77, Painters Workshop (Scotland), 1975-89, John Kinross Fund, 1990-2007, Alexander Naysmith Fund, 1990-2007, Spalding Fund, 1990-2007, Sir William Gillies Fund, 1990-2007, Hospitalfield Trust, 1990-2007 (Chair, since 2003), RSA Enterprise, 1972-2007; Member, ICOM International Exhibitions Committee, 1986-96; Member, Advisory Council on the Export of Works of Art, 1991-2007; Member, Re:Source AIL Panel, 2000-01; External Assessor, Glasgow School of Art, 1982-86, Duncan of Jordanstone College of Art, Dundee, 1986-90, SAC Gifting Scheme, 1997; Assessor: Ruth Davidson Memorial Trust, Morrison Portrait Award, Salvesen Art Trust, Noble Grossart Award; President, RSW, 1988-98; President, Royal Scottish Academy, 1998-2007; Deputy President, RSA, 1990-91, Treasurer, 1990, Secretary, 1991-98; Governor: Edinburgh College of Art, 1976-88 (Chair, Andrew Grant Committee, 1977-88), The Robert Gordon University, 1989-95; Member, Advisory Board, Robert Gordon University Heritage Unit, 1993-95; Member, Board, Scottish Sculpture Workshop, 1976-2000; Member, National Heritage Scottish Group, 1977-99; National Trust for Scotland: Member, Curatorial Committee, 1991-2001, Member of Council, 1995-99, Member, Buildings Committee, 1998-2000; Commissioner, Museums and Galleries Commission, 1997-2000; Trustee, National Galleries of Scotland, 1999-2007; Vice President, NADFAS, 2000-07; Fellow, Salzburg Seminar, 1981, 1984, FRSA; FRSE; Hon. RA, Hon. RHA, Hon. RUA; Hon. RWA. Address: (h.) Heron House, Angus DD10 9TJ; T.-01674 675898; e-mail: i.mckenziesmith@btinternet.com

McKeown, James Patrick, LLB, DipLP, NP. Solicitor; b. 17.3.59, Coatbridge; m., Pamela Mary; 2 s.; 1 d. Educ. Aberdeen University. Assistant, Esslemont & Cameron, Aberdeen, 1983-85; Company Secretary, Sysdrill Ltd., 1985-86; Assistant, C. & D. Mactaggart, 1986, appointed Partner, 1987. Chairman, Appeals Service; Vice-Chairman, Scottish Liberal Democrats, Argyll and Bute, 1990-97; former Vice President, Scottish Young Lawyers Association. Recreations: politics; travel. Address: (b.) Castlehill, Campbeltown, Argyll PA28 6AR; T.-01586 552317.

McKerracher, Colin William, QPM, LLB. Chief Constable, Grampian Police, since 2004; b. 16.12.54, Glasgow; m., Christine; 1 s.; 1 d. Educ. Strathclyde University. Strathclyde Police: Chief Superintendent, 1998-99, Assistant Chief Constable, 1999-2001, Deputy Chief Constable, 2001-04. Member, Association of Chief Police Officers in Scotland (ACPOS). Address: (b.) Grampian Police, Police Headquarters, Queen Street, Aberdeen AB10 1ZA; T.-01224-306054.
E-mail: executive@grampian.pnn.police.uk

McKerrell of Hillhouse, Charles James Mure, OStJ, FSA Scot. Matriculated Arms 1973, Court of the Lord Lyon, and recognised by interlocutor of the Lord Lyon as Head of the Name and Family. Tartans:- McKerrell of Hillhouse recorded Court of the Lord Lyon, 25 June 1982; McKerrell of Hillhouse (Dress) recorded Court of the Lord Lyon, 2002. Recognised by the Chief Herald of Ireland as 15th Head of the Name, 1975; b. 23.1.51; m., May dau of the late Matthew Cochrane White, BSc, MICE. Educ. Cranleigh.

Honorary Captain, Canadian Bush Pilots; Freeman, City of London; Member: Royal Celtic Society, Saltire Society; Director of The Border Gathering. Guardian of the Nobiliary Fraternity of the Nia Naisc, Knight of St Micheil of the Wing (Granted by HRH The Duke of Braganza), Hereditary Companion of the Royal House of O'Conor, GCLJ, Knight Grand Cross of St Antioche. Address: (h.) Magdalene House, Lochmaben, Dumfries DG11 1PD; T.-01387 810439.
E-mail: mckerrellofhillhouse@ukonline.co.uk

McKerrow, Maureen Grant. President, Scottish Licensed Trade Association, 2001-03; b. 7.12.54, Dumfries; m., Gordon McKerrow; 2 s. Educ. Dumfries Academy. Technician, 1972-78; Director, Globe Inn Ltd., 1977-79; Managing Director, Globe Inn Ltd., since 1999; Chairman, Scottish Ladies Golf Association, 1992; Member, Nicholson Committee on Licensing Reform, 2001. Recreations: curling; golf; art; Robert Burns. Address: (b.) Globe Inn Ltd., 56 High Street, Dumfries DG1 2JA; T.-01387 252335.

MacKessack-Leitch, Hilda Jane Marshall. Deputy Lieutenant, Moray, since 1993; b. 4.9.40, Rothes; m., 1, Dr. Ernest V. C. Dawson (deceased); 2, David C. MacKessack-Leitch (deceased); 2 s. Educ. Elgin Academy. Past County Commissioner, The Guide Association, Moray; Past Chairman, Cancer Research Campaign Committee, Elgin and District; Elgin Local Organiser, WRVS, 1976-2000. Recreations: cooking; walking; reading; music. Address: (h.) Sillerton, 61 Mayne Road, Elgin, Moray IV30 1PD; T.-01343 544711.

McKie, Alastair John. Partner, Head of Planning and Environment, Anderson Strathern, since 1998; b. 15.6.62, Ipswich, Suffolk; m., Dr. Margaret Mitchell; 1 d. Educ. Lornshill Academy, Alloa; Dundee University. Qualified as a Solicitor, 1987; elected Legal Associate, Royal Town Planning Institute; Accredited as Specialist in Planning Law, Law Society of Scotland; Writer to Her Majesty's Signet. Recreations: hill walking; fishing; tennis; dogs. Address: (b.) 1 Rutland Court, Edinburgh EH3 8EY; T.-0131 625 7257.
E-mail: alastair.mckie@andersonstrathern.co.uk

McKie, Professor Linda, BA (Hons), MSc, PhD. Research Professor in Sociology, Glasgow Caledonian University, since 1999; Associate Director, Centre for Research on Families and Relationships, since 2001; b. 29.9.56, Belfast; 1 d. Educ. Richmond Lodge; University of Ulster; University of Bath; University of Durham. Lecturer: University of Teesside, 1986-88, University of Glasgow, 1989; Head of Intelligence Unit, Equal Opportunities Commission, Manchester, 1990; Head of Sociology and Social Policy, Queen Margaret University College, 1991-93; Senior Lecturer, Department of General Practice and Primary Care, University of Aberdeen, 1993-99. Trustee, Evaluation Support Scotland; Trustee, Institute of Rural Health. Publications: ten books and over 80 papers on organisations, work and care, health and evaluation, and gender and violence. Recreations: gym training; travel; food and wine. Address: (b.) School of Law and Social Sciences, Glasgow Caledonian University, Glasgow G4 0BA; T.-0141-331 8627; e-mail: l.mckie@gcal.ac.uk

McKiernan, Professor Peter, BA, MA, PhD, CMI, FBAM, FRSA, ALSS. Professor of Strategic Management St. Andrews University, since 1992, Dean, School of Management; b. 28.12.53, Accrington; m., Morna; 1 s.; 1 d. Educ. Preston Catholic College; Lancaster University; Surrey University. Former M.D. of mechanical engineering

company; Lecturer in Management, St. Andrews University; Senior Lecturer in Strategic Management, Warwick University; Head of School of Management, University of St. Andrews; Chairman and President, British Academy of Management, 2001-06; Vice President and President, European Academy of Management, since 2001; Companion, Association of Business Schools. Publications: Sharpbenders; Strategies of Growth, Inside Fortress Europe; Historical Evolution of Strategic Management; Scenarios for Scotland. Recreations: soccer; sailing; cricket; poetry. Address: (b.) School of Management, St. Andrews University KY16 9AL; T.-01334 462800.

McKillop, Professor James Hugh, BSc, MB, ChB, PhD, FRCP, FRCR, FMedSci. Muirhead Professor of Medicine, Glasgow University, since 1989 (Associate Dean for Medical Education, 2000-03 and Head of Medical School, 2003-06, Deputy Dean of Medicine, since 2007); Honorary Consultant Physician, NHS Greater Glasgow, since 1982; b. 20.6.48, Glasgow; m., Caroline A. Oakley; 2 d. Educ. St. Aloysius' College, Glasgow; Glasgow University. Hall Fellow in Medicine, then Lecturer in Medicine, Glasgow University, 1974-82; Postdoctoral Fellow, Stanford University Medical Center, California, 1979 and 1980; Senior Lecturer in Medicine, Glasgow University, 1982-89. Harkness Fellowship, Commonwealth Fund of New York, 1979-80; Robert Reid Newall Award, Stanford University, 1980; Honorary Treasurer, Scottish Society of Experimental Medicine, 1982-87; Honorary Secretary, British Nuclear Cardiology Group, 1982-87; Symposium Editor, Scottish Medical Journal, 1984-93; Council Member, British Nuclear Medicine Society, 1985-94 (Hon. Secretary, 1988-90, President, 1990-92); Editor, Nuclear Medicine Communications, 1989-98; Congress President, European Association of Nuclear Medicine, 1997, Member, Executive Committee, 1995-98, Chairman, Education Committee, 1998-2001, Member, Strategy Committee, since 1999; Chairman, Administration of Radioactive Substances Advisory Committee, Department of Health, 1996-2004 (Vice Chairman, 1989-95); Member, National Radiation Advisory Committee, 1995-98; Specialty Adviser on Nuclear Medicine, SODOH, 1998-2007; Vice-President, Nuclear Medicine Section, Union Europeene Medecines Specialistes; Member, Scottish Medical and Scientific Advisory Committee, 1999-2001, Chairman, 2001-07; Member, Executive Committee, Association of Physicians of Great Britain and Ireland, 2000-03; Team Leader for GMC Quality Assurance of Basic Medical Education, since 2003; Chairman, Medical Advisory Group, NHS Education for Scotland, since 2004; Chairman, Scottish Deans' Medical Curriculum Group, since 2005. Recreations: music (especially opera); history; football. Address: (b.) Wolfson Medical School Building, Glasgow University, Glasgow G12 8QQ; T.-0141 330 8041.

McKillop, Stewart, MA (Hons), DipAcc, DipEd. Principal, South Lanarkshire College, East Kilbride, since 2001; b. 16.10.55, Glasgow. Educ. Glasgow University. Associate Principal, James Watt College of Further and Higher Education, 1991-2001. Address: (b.) 1 College Way, East Kilbride G75 0NE, T.-0141-641-6600.
E-mail: angelamartin@slc.ac.uk

McKillop, Sir Thomas Fulton Wilson, Kt (2002), PhD, FRS (2005), FRSE. Chairman, Royal Bank of Scotland Group, since 2006 (Deputy Chairman, 2005-06); b. 19.3.43, Dreghorn; m., Elizabeth Kettle; 1 s.; 2 d. Educ. Irvine Royal Academy; University of Glasgow; Centre de Mécanique Ondulatoire Appliquée, Paris. Research Scientist, ICI Corporate Lab., 1969-75; ICI Pharmaceuticals: Head, Natural Products Research, 1975-78, Research Director, France, 1978-80, Chemistry Manager, 1980-84, General Manager, Research, 1984-85,

Development, 1985-89, Technical Director, 1989-94; Zeneca Group, then AstraZeneca: CEO, Zeneca Pharmaceuticals, 1994-99, Director, 1996-2006, Chief Executive, 1999-2006. Non-executive Director: Lloyds TSB Group PLC, 1999-2004, BP plc, 2004. President: European Federation of Pharmaceutical Industries and Associations, 2002-04, The Science Council, 2007. Trustee, Council for Industry and Higher Education, since 2002. NE Director, Almirall, 2007. MRI; FRSC; MACS. Trustee, Darwin Trust of Edinburgh, since 1995. FMedSci 2002; Hon. LLD Manchester, 1999; Hon. DSc: Glasgow, 2000, Leicester, 2000, Huddersfield, 2000, Nottingham, 2001. Recreations: music; sport; reading. Address: (b.) Royal Bank of Scotland Group, Gogarburn, Edinburgh EH12 1HQ.

McKinnon, Professor Alan Campbell, MA, PhD, FILT. Professor of Logistics, School of Management and Languages, Heriot-Watt University, since 1995; b. 19.9.53, Motherwell; m., Sabine Rohde; 2 s. Educ. Perth Academy; Aberdeen University; University of British Columbia; University College, London. Lecturer, University of Leicester, 1979-87; joined staff Heriot-Watt University, 1987 as Lecturer/Senior Lecturer/Reader/Professor; Chairman, Scottish Transport Studies Group, 1989-92; Chairman, Retail Logistics Task Force (UK Government Foresight Programme), 2000-01; Chairman, Institute of Logistics and Transport Professional Development Policy Committee, 2003-07; Specialist Advisor, House of Commons Scottish Affairs Committee in its study of the future of Scotland's transport links with Europe, 1992-93; European Editor, International Journal of Physical Distribution and Logistics Management, 1990-95; Member: Scottish Office's National Transport Forum, 1998-2000, UK Government Foresight Panel on the Built Environment and Transport, 1999-2001; Member, Department of Transport's Freight and Logistics Research Group, since 2003; Specialist adviser to Local Government and Transport Committee of the Scottish Parliament on its Inquiry into Freight Transport in Scotland, 2006; received Herbert Crow Memorial Award, Worshipful Company of Carmen of London; Sir Robert Lawrence Award, Institute of Logistics and Transport, 2003. Publications: Physical Distribution Systems, 1989; Transport Logistics, (Editor), 2002. Recreations: piano playing; hill walking. Address: (b.) Heriot-Watt University, Edinburgh, EH14 4AS; T.-0131-451 3850; e-mail: a.c.mckinnon@hw.ac.uk

MacKinnon, Donalda. Joint Head of Programmes and Services for BBC Scotland, since 2005; formerly Head of CBBC Scotland and Gaelic; responsible for all of BBC Scotland's output in and from Scotland on TV, Radio and Online across every genre. Address: (b.) BBC Scotland, 40 Pacific Quay, Glasgow G51 1DZ.

Mackinnon, James Gordon, MA (Hons), DipTP, MRTPI. Director and Chief Planner, Scottish Government, since 2000; b. 17.6.52, Forres; m., Gwen Moggach; 2 s. Educ. Forres Academy; Edinburgh University; Strathclyde University. Graduate planner, Burgh of Motherwell and Wishaw, 1975-79; Scottish Office: Senior Planner, 1979-86, Principal Planner, 1986-96, Assistant Chief Planner, 1996-99, Head of Planning Division, 1999-2000. Recreations: family and friends; blues; jazz; golf; squash. Address: (b.) Victoria Quay, Edinburgh EH6 6QQ; T.-0131-244 0770.

Mackintosh, Hugh Robertson, CBE, MSocSc. Director, Barnardo's Scotland, 1991-2007; b. 10.12.47, Blair Atholl. Educ. Pitlochry High School; University of Bristol;

University of Birmingham. Caldecott Community Kent (latterly as a Director), 1970-76; Assistant Director: Barnardo's, London, 1976-81, Barnardo's Scotland, 1981-91. Elder, Church of Scotland. Recreations: golf; fly-fishing; curling; bowling; wine appreciation.

Mackintosh, Simon, MA, LLB, WS. Partner, Turcan Connell, WS, since 1997; Director, MacPhie of Glenbervie Ltd., since 1993; b.2.2.57, Wisbech; m., Catriona; 2 s.; 1 d. Educ. Edinburgh Academy; Glenalmond; Magdalene College, Cambridge University; Edinburgh University. W. & J. Burness: Apprentice, 1980-82, Assistant Solicitor, 1982-85; secondment, Boodle Hatfield, 1983; Partner, W. & J. Burness, 1985-97. Former Convener, Tax Law Committee, Law Society of Scotland; Member, International Academy of Estate and Trust Law; Chairman, Scottish Episcopal Church Pension Trustees; Board Member, Edinburgh Book Festival, 1996-2001; Chairman, Court of Directors of The Edinburgh Academy. Recreations: gardening; golf; rugby. Address: (b.) Princes Exchange, 1 Earl Grey Street, Edinburgh EH3 9EE; T.-0131-228 8111.

McLaren, Bill, b. 16.10.23. Former Rugby Union Commentator, BBC. Played wing forward for Hawick; had trial for Scotland but forced to withdraw because of illness; became reporter on local newspaper; first live radio broadcast, Glasgow v. Edinburgh, 1953; former teacher of physical education.

McLaren, Duncan Bruce, MB, BS, BSc, FRCR, FRCP (Edin). Consultant Clinical Oncologist, Western General Hospital, Edinburgh, since 1998; b. 20.3.65, Redditch; m., Dr. Pamela McLaren; 2 d. Educ. Finham Park School; St. Mary's Hospital Medical School, London. Specialist in urological cancer; Member, National Cancer Studies Groups in Prostate and Bladder Cancer; Lead, Scottish Cancer Trials Network, SE Scotland GU Trials Group. Recreations: avid sportsman – former rugby player, now keen squash player and golfer. Address: (b.) Edinburgh Cancer Centre, Western General Hospital, Edinburgh EH4 2XU; T.-0131-537 2215. E-mail: duncan.mclaren@luht.scot.nhs.uk

McLaren, Iain Archibald, BA, CA. Senior Partner, KPMG Scotland, since 1999; b. 21.2.51, Edinburgh; m., Fiona; 2 s.; 2 d. Educ. Daniel Stewart's College, Edinburgh; Heriot-Watt University. CA apprentice and qualified CA, Peat Marwick Mitchell, 1971-76; Internal Audit Manager, Miller Group, 1976-78; Audit Manager, Edward Moore & Sons, 1979-81. Recreations: golf; tennis; hill-walking. Address: (b.) Saltire Court, 20 Castle Terrace, Edinburgh EH1 2EG; T.-0131-222 2000.

MacLaren, Iain Ferguson, MB, ChB, FRCSEdin, FRCS, FRCP Edin. Consultant Surgeon, Royal Infirmary, Edinburgh, 1974-92; b. 28.9.27, Edinburgh; m., Dr. Fiona Barbara Heptonstall; 1 s.; 1 d. Educ. Edinburgh Academy; Fettes College; Edinburgh University. Captain, RAMC, Egypt, 1950-52; Surgical Registrar, Royal Hospital for Sick Children, Edinburgh, 1956-58; Senior Surgical Registrar, Royal Infirmary, 1959-63 and 1964-67; Fellow in Surgical Research, Hahnemann Medical College and Hospital, Philadelphia, 1963-64; Consultant Surgeon, Deaconess Hospital, Edinburgh, 1967-85; Vice-President, Royal College of Surgeons of Edinburgh, 1983-86 (Council Member, 1977-83 and 1987-94); Fellow, Royal Medical Society (Honorary Treasurer, 1979-85); Chairman, Royal Medical Society Trust, 1985-2003; Honorary Pipe-Major, Royal Scottish Pipers' Society, 1959-62; Honorary Secretary: Harveian Society of Edinburgh, 1968-87,

Aesculapian Club, 1978-2004; Hon. Secretary, Royal College of Surgeons of Edinburgh, 1972-77; Secretary, Edinburgh University General Council, 1993-97; Chairman: Professional and Linguistic Assessments Board, General Medical Council, 1996-99, Clan MacLaren Society, 1968-91; Chieftain, Clan Labhran, 1991; President, Edinburgh University Graduates' Association, 1999-2002, Recreations: music; the study of military history; all aspects of Scottish culture. Address: (h.) 3 Minto Street, Edinburgh EH9 1RG; T.-0131-667 3487.

McLatchie, Cameron, CBE, LLB. Chairman, British Polythene Industries, since 2003, formerly Scott & Robertson PLC, 1988-2003; b. 18.2.47, Paisley; m., Helen Leslie Mackie; 2 s.; 1 d. Educ. Boroughmuir School, Edinburgh; Largs High School; Ardrossan Academy; Glasgow University. Whinney Murray & Co., Glasgow, 1968-70; Thomas Boag & Co. Ltd., Greenock, 1970-75; Chairman and Managing Director, Anaplast Ltd., Irvine, 1975-83; this company purchased by Scott & Robertson. Deputy Chairman, Scottish Enterprise, 1997-2000; Non-Executive Director, Royal Bank of Scotland Group PLC, 1998-2002. Recreations: bridge; golf. Address: (b.) 96 Port Glasgow Road, Greenock; T.-01475 501000.

McLaughlan, Ian, FCMI, BA, DipVAMP, DipHE. Chief Executive, Scottish Pre-school Play Association, since 2001; b. 31.8.54, Motherwell; m., Ann; 2 s. Educ. Canterbury of Kent University; City of London University Business School. Boys' Brigade Scotland: Training Development Officer, 1988-96, National Director, 1996-2001. Recreations: cycling; walking; reading. Address: (b.) 45 Finnieston Street, Glasgow G3 8JU; T.-0141-221 4148.

MacLaverty, Bernard. Writer; b. 14.9.42, Belfast; m., Madeline McGuckin; 1 s.; 3 d. Educ. St Malachy's College, Belfast; Queen's University, Belfast. Moved from Belfast to Scotland, 1975; has been a medical laboratory technician, a mature student, a teacher of English and, for two years in the mid-1980s, Writer-in-Residence at Aberdeen University; has been a Guest Writer for short periods at University of Augsburg and Iowa State University; Member, Aosdana in Ireland; has published five collections of short stories and four novels; has written versions of his fiction for other media, including radio plays, television plays and screenplays. Publications: Secrets and Other Stories, 1977; Lamb, 1980; A Time to Dance and other Stories, 1982; Cal, 1983; The Great Profundo and Other Stories, 1987; Walking the Dog and Other Stories, 1994; Grace Notes, 1997; The Anatomy School, 2001; Matters of Life & Death and other stories, 2006.

Maclay, Baron (Joseph Paton Maclay), 3rd Baron; Bt. Deputy Lieutenant, Renfrewshire, since 1986; Director, Altnamara Shipping Plc, 1994-2002; Chairman, Renfrew Lighthouse Board, 2001-03 (Commissioner, 1996-2003, Vice Chairman, 2000-01); Chairman, Scottish Maritime Museum, 1998-2005; Chairman, Scottish Nautical Welfare Society, 2002-04; b. 11.4.42; m., Elizabeth Anne Buchanan; 2 s.; 1 d. Educ. Winchester; Sorbonne. Managing Director: Denholm Maclay Co. Ltd., 1970-83, Denholm Maclay (Offshore) Ltd., Triport Ferries (Management) Ltd., 1975-83; Deputy Managing Director, Denholm Ship Management Ltd., 1982-83; Director: Milton Shipping Co. Ltd., 1970-83, Marine Shipping Mutual Insurance Company, 1982-83; President, Hanover Shipping Inc., 1982-83; Director: British Steamship Short Trades Association, 1978-83, North of England Protection and Indemnity Association, 1976-83; Chairman, Scottish Branch, British Sailors' Society, 1979-81; Vice-President, Glasgow Shipowners & Shipbrokers Benevolent Association, 1982-83 and 1997-98; President,

Glasgow Shipowners and Shipbrokers Benevolent Association, 1998-99; Director, Denholm Ship Management (Holdings) Ltd., 1991-93; Group Marketing Executive, Acomarit Group, 1993-99; Trustee: Cattanach Charitable Trust, since 1991, Western Isles Fisheries Trust, 2004-06, Western Isles Salmon Fisheries Board, 2004-06. Address: (h.) Duchal, Kilmacolm, Renfrewshire PA13 4RS.

MacLean, Rt. Hon. Lord (Ranald Norman Munro MacLean), BA, LLB, LLM, PC, LLD, FSA(Scot), FRSE. Senator of the College of Justice, 1990-2005; Queen's Counsel, since 1977; b. 18.12.38, Aberdeen; m., Pamela Ross (m. dissolved); 2 s.; 1 d. Educ. Inverness Royal Academy; Fettes College, Edinburgh; Cambridge University; Edinburgh University; Yale University. Advocate, 1964; Advocate Depute, 1972-75; Advocate Depute (Home), 1979-82; Chairman, The Cockburn Association (Edinburgh Civic Trust), 1988-96; Member, Secretary of State for Scotland's Criminal Justice Forum, 1996-2000; Member, Parole Board for Scotland, 1998-2000; Chairman, Committee on Serious Violent and Sexual Offenders, 1999-2000; Member, Scottish Judicial Appointments Board, 2002-05; Chairman, Sentencing Commission for Scotland, 2003-05; Chairman, The Billy Wright Inquiry (Belfast), since 2004; Chairman of Governors, Fettes College, 1996-2006. Recreations: hillwalking; swimming. Address: (h.) 38 Royal Terrace, Edinburgh EH7 5AH.

MacLean, A. Duncan, LLB, DipLP, NP, WS. Partner, Brodies LLP, since 2004; b. 19.2.66, Inverness; m., Esther; 2 d. Educ. Achtercairn Secondary; Dingwall Academy; Edinburgh University. Admitted as Solicitor, 1988; Trained, Guild & Guild, WS, Edinburgh; Solicitor, Brodies, WS, 1989-94; Associate, Henderson Boyd Jackson, Edinburgh, 1994, then Partner, 1996. Founding Trustee, Business Alpha Edinburgh; Vestry Member, St. Paul's and St. George's Church; Member of Council, WS Society. Recreations: family; church; the outdoors. Address: (b.) 15 Atholl Crescent, Edinburgh EH3 8HA.

Maclean, Alastair David, LLB (Hons), DipLP, IAC. Corporate Lawyer, Partner of Maclay Murray & Spens LLP, since 2006; b. 23.10.72, Edinburgh. Educ. Daniel Stewart's and Melville College; University of Edinburgh. Trainee Solicitor, Lindsays WS, 1995-96; Maclay Murray & Spens: Assistant Solicitor (Commercial Property Department), 1996-99, Associate Solicitor (Corporate Department), 1999-2006. Recreations: canoeing; hillwalking; skiing. Address: (b.) Maclay Murray & Spens LLP, Quartermile One, 15 Lauriston Place, Edinburgh EH3 9EP; T.-0131 228 7166.
E-mail: alastair.maclean@mms.co.uk

McLean, Catriona Mary, MB, BS, MRCP, FRCR. Consultant Clinical Oncologist, Western General Hospital, Edinburgh, and Honorary Senior Lecturer, University of Edinburgh, since 1996; b. 30.3.62, Kampala, Uganda; m., Cliff Culley; 1 s. Educ. Sutton High School GPDST; St. Bartholomew's Medical College, London. Address: (b.) Department of Clinical Oncology, Western General Hospital, Edinburgh; T.-0131-537 1000.

Maclean of Dunconnel, Sir Charles (Edward), Bt; b. 31.10.46; m.; 4 d. Educ. Eton; New College, Oxford. Publications: The Wolf Children; The Watcher; Island on the Edge of the World; Scottish Country; Romantic Scotland; The Silence. Address: (h.) Strachur House, Cairndow, Argyll PA27 8BX.

Maclean, Christian. Manager, Floris Books, since 1976; b. 14.2.50, Edinburgh; m., Astrid; 2 s.; 1 d. Educ. Rudolf Steiner School. Treasurer, Publishing Scotland; Director, Scottish Book Source. Address: (b.) 15 Harrison Gardens, Edinburgh; T.-0131-337 2372.

MacLean, Colin R., BSc (Hons), DipEd, MSc. Director: Children, Young People and Social Care, Scottish Government, since 2002; b. 22.5.51, Dundee; m., Ilse; 2 s.; 1 d. Educ. Forfar Academy; Edinburgh University. Teacher of Mathematics, Edinburgh, 1973-79; Education Adviser (Microelectronics/Computing), Lothian Regional Council, 1980-85; HM Inspector of Schools, 1985-96; Chief Statistician, Scottish Office, 1996-99; HM Depute Senior Chief Inspector of Schools, 1999-2000; Depute Head, Schools Group, 2000-02 (National Exam Co-ordinator, 2001). Recreations: gardening; music; travel. Address: (b.) 3D-93 Victoria Quay, Edinburgh; T.-0131-244 0859.

McLean, Colin William, MA, MBA, FFA, FSIP, FSII. Managing Director, SVM Asset Management, since 1990; b. 1.10.52. Educ. Jordanhill College School, Glasgow; Glasgow University; Deputy General Manager, FS Assurance, 1974-86; Chief Investment Officer, Scottish Provident, 1986-88; Managing Director, Templeton International, 1988-90; Vice-Chairman, Chest Heart and Stroke, Scotland; Visiting Professor, Glasgow Caledonian University, Caledonian Business School. Address: (b.) SVM Asset Management Ltd, 7 Castle Street, Edinburgh, EH2 3AH; T.-0131-226 6699.

Maclean, Sir Donald, FCOptom. Ophthalmic Optician (retired); Chairman, Ayrshire Medical Support Ltd.; b. Annan; m., Muriel Giles (deceased); 1 s.; 1 d.; m., 2, Margaret Ross. Educ. Morrison's Academy, Crieff; Heriot-Watt, Edinburgh. Ophthalmic Optician in Edinburgh, Newcastle, Perth, Ayr; Chairman, Ayrshire Local Optical Committee, 1986-88; former Member, Transport Users Local Consultative Committee; Chairman, Ayr Constituency Conservative Association, 1971-75; Chairman, West of Scotland Area Council, Scottish Conservative Association, 1977-78-79; President, Scottish Conservative and Unionist Association, 1983-85; Scottish Conservative Party: Deputy Chairman, 1985-89, Vice Chairman, 1989-91; Chairman, Carrick, Cumnock and Doon Valley Conservative Association, 1998-2000; Chairman, Bell Hollingworth Ltd., 1996-99; Dean of Guildry, Ayr Guildry, 1993-95; Elder, Church of Scotland; Past President, West Highland Steamer Club; Liveryman of the Worshipful Company of Spectacle Makers; Freeman, City of London. Recreations: photography; reading; angling.

MacLean, Eoghainn Charles McEwen, LLB (Private Law Hons), DipLP. Advocate, since 1995; b. 17.4.66, Port of Aden; 2 s. Educ. High School of Glasgow; Glasgow University. Trainee and Solicitor, McClure Naismith, 1989-93; Solicitor, McGrigor Donald, 1993-94; devil, 1994-95; called to Scots Bar, 1995. Address: (h.) 4 Athole Gardens, Glasgow G12 9AY; T.-0141 560 2003.

Maclean, Iain Farquhar, LLB (Hons), LLM, MSc, DipLP. Advocate. Educ. Portree High School; University of Aberdeen; Emmanuel College, Cambridge; University of Edinburgh. Trainee Solicitor, Brodies WS, 1990-92; Legal Assistant to the Lord President, Court of Session, 1992-93; admitted, Faculty of Advocates, 1994. Contributor, Greens Annotated Rules of the Court of Session. Address: (b.) Advocates' Library, Parliament House, Edinburgh EH1 1RF; T.-0131-226 5071.

McLean, Jack, DA, MSIAD. Freelance Writer and Broadcaster; b. 10.8.46, Irvine. Educ. Allan Glen's School; Edinburgh College of Art; Jordanhill College. Art Teacher in Glasgow for many years; The Scotsman, 1977-81;

Glasgow Herald, 1981-97; The Scotsman, 1997-98; Scotland on Sunday, 1997-99; Sports Columnist, Scottish Daily Mail, 1999-2000; Columnist, The Herald, 2000-06; Radio Clyde, 1982-85; BBC Scotland Art Critic and Adviser, 1991-95; Presenter, The Jack McLean Talk Show, Scottish Television. Columnist of the Year, British Press Awards, 1985; Recipient of several Scottish Press Awards. Publications: The Bedside Urban Voltaire; More Bedside Urban Voltaire; The Sporting Urban Voltaire; City of Glasgow; Hopeless But Not Serious; Earthquake; The Compendium of Nosh, 2006. Recreations: smoking; poverty; dressing; cooking.

McLean, James Angus, BA, LLB, WS. Partner, Burness, since 1974; b. 25.4.47, Gosforth; m., Carol Inglis; 1 s.; 2 d. Educ. Dunoon Grammar School; Fettes College; Sidney Sussex College, Cambridge; Edinburgh University. Solicitor, 1972. Member, High Constables of Edinburgh; Member, Scottish Lawyers European Group; Member, various committees, Law Society of Scotland. Recreations: swimming; cycling; theatre. Address: (b.) 50 Lothian Road, Festival Square, Edinburgh EH3 9WJ; e-mail: james.mclean@burness.co.uk

MacLean, James Gordon Bruce, MBChB, FRCS. Consultant Orthopaedic Surgeon, Perth Royal Infirmary and Ninewells Hospital, Dundee, since 1994; Honorary Lecturer, Dundee University, since 1994; b. 17.5.58, Carlisle; m., Susan Jane Roberts; 2 s.; 2 d. Educ. Merchiston Castle School, Edinburgh; Dundee University Medical School. Basic surgical training, Norfolk and Norwich Hospitals; specialist orthopaedic training, St Bartholomew's Hospital, Great Ormond Street, Stanmore; Research Fellow/Junior Consultant, University of Capetown; Regional Children's Orthopaedic Surgeon, Tayside. Recreations: hill-walking; rugby; racquet sports; boating. Address: (b.) Orthopaedic Department, Perth Royal Infirmary, Perth PH1 1NX; T.-01738 623311.

Maclean of Duart, Major The Hon. Sir Lachlan, DL. Major, Scots Guards retired; 28th Chief of Clan Maclean; b. 25.8.42.

MacLean, Rev. Marjory Anne, LLB, BD, PhD, RNR. Depute Secretary, Legal Questions Committee, and Depute Clerk, General Assembly of Church of Scotland (full-time, since 1998). Royal Naval Reserve Chaplain, since 2004. Acting Principal Clerk, 2002-03; Minister, Stromness Parish Church, 1992-98. B. 11.6.62, Forfar. Educ. Forfar Academy; Edinburgh University; Trainee Solicitor, T.P. & J.L. Low, Kirkwall, 1985-87; Probationer then Assistant Minister, Fairmilehead Parish Church, Edinburgh, 1990-92. Company Member, St. Magnus Festival, Orkney; Member of Court, St. Andrews University, 2006-10. Recreation: chamber singing. Address: (b.) 121 George Street, Edinburgh EH2 4YN; T.-0131-240 2232.

McLean, Miller Roy, MA, LLB, NP, FCIB (Scotland). General Counsel, Legal and Regulatory Affairs and Group Secretary, The Royal Bank of Scotland Group plc, since 2000; Director, Adam and Company PLC; Executive Director, Ulster Bank; Chairman, Royal Bank of Scotland Pension Trustee Ltd; Executive Director, Royal Bank of Scotland International; Chairman, Whitehall and Industry Group; Director, Scottish Parliament and Business Exchange; Trustee, Industry and Parliament Trust; b. 4.12.49, Scotland; m., Anne Charlotte Gourlay; 1 s.; 1 d. Educ. Vale of Leven Academy; Glasgow University; Edinburgh University. The Royal Bank of Scotland Group plc: Assistant Secretary, 1982-83, Secretary, 1983-88; The

Royal Bank of Scotland plc: Secretary, 1985-88, Group Secretary, 1988-90, Assistant Director, Legal and Administration, 1990-91, Director, Legal and Regulatory Affairs, 1991-94; Director, Group Legal and Regulatory Affairs and Group Secretary, 1994-2000. Recreations: golf; gardening; reading; music. Address: (b.) Gogarburn: Business House G, Edinburgh EH12 1HQ; T.-0131-523 2223.

Maclean, Rob. Presenter, Setanta Sports, since 2004; b. 26.11.58, Inverness; m., Pauline; 1 s.; 1 d. Educ. Invergordon Academy. Trainee Journalist, Highland News Group; Reporter, Aberdeen News and PR Services; Head of News and Sport, North Sound Radio; Television News Reporter, BBC Scotland; Sports Presenter/Reporter, Scottish Television; Television Presenter/Sports Commentator, BBC Scotland Sport. Recreations: playing football; golf; skiing; music; movies. Address: Setanta Sports, Pacific Quay, Glasgow G51 1PQ.

McLean, Una, MBE. Actress; b. 1930, Strathaven. Trained, Royal Scottish Academy of Music and Drama; professional debut, Byre, St. Andrews, 1955; pantomime debut, Mother Goose, 1958; joined Citizens' Theatre, Glasgow, 1959, appeared in Five Past Eight revue, 1960s; many television appearances.

Maclean, Emeritus Professor William James, MBE (2006), DA, RSA, RGI, RSW. Emeritus Professor of Visual Arts, University of Dundee, since 2002, formerly Professor of Fine Art, Duncan of Jordanstone College, University of Dundee; b. 12.10.41, Inverness; m., Marian Forbes Leven; 2 s.; 1 d. Educ. Inverness Royal Academy; HMS Conway; Grays School of Art, Aberdeen. Postgraduate and Travel Scholarship, Scottish Education Trust Award, Visual Arts Bursary, Scottish Arts Council; Benno Schotz Prize; one-man exhibitions in Rome, Glasgow, Edinburgh and London; group exhibitions in Britain, Europe and North America; represented in private and public collections including Arts Council, British Museum, Scottish National Gallery of Modern Art, Fitzwilliam Museum, Cambridge, and Scottish museum collections. Hon. DLitt, St. Andrews University. Address: (h.) Bellevue, 18 Dougall Street, Tayport, Fife.

MacLeary, Alistair Ronald, MSc, DipTP, FRICS, FRTPI, FRSA. Honorary Fellow, Commonwealth Association of Surveying and Land Economy; Honorary Professor, Heriot-Watt University; Member, Administrative Justice and Tribunals Council and Chairman of its Scottish Committee, 2007-09; Member, Council on Tribunals and Chairman of its Scottish Committee, 2005-07; Member, Lands Tribunal for Scotland, 1989-2005; MacRobert Professor of Land Economy, Aberdeen University, 1976-89 (Dean, Faculty of Law, 1982-85); b. 12.1.40, Glasgow; m., Claire Leonard; 1 s.; 1 d. Educ. Inverness Royal Academy; College of Estate Management; Heriot-Watt University; Strathclyde University. Assistant Surveyor, Gerald Eve & Co., Chartered Surveyors, 1962-65; Assistant to Director, Murrayfield Real Estate Co. Ltd., 1965-67; Assistant Surveyor and Town Planner/Partner, Wright & Partners, 1967-76; seconded to Department of the Environment, London, 1971-73; Member: Committee of Inquiry into the Acquisition and Occupancy of Agricultural Land, 1977-79, Home Grown Timber Advisory Committee, Forestry Commission, 1981-87; Chairman, Board of Education, Commonwealth Association of Surveying and Land Economy, 1981-90; President, Planning and Development Division, Royal Institution of Chartered Surveyors, 1984-85; Editor, Land Development Studies, 1986-90; Member, Natural Environment Research Council, 1988-91. Recreations: shooting; golf. Address: (h.) St. Helen's, St. Andrew's Road, Ceres, Fife KY15 5NQ; T.-01334 828862.

McLeary, Bernard, MA. Chief Executive, Learning and Teaching Scotland, since 2004; b. 29.10.51, Greenock; m.,

Julie; 1 s.; 2 d. Educ. St. Columba's High School, Greenock; Glasgow University. St. Stephen's High School, Port Glasgow: Teacher, 1973-82, Assistant Headteacher, 1982-84; Strathclyde Regional Council: Education Adviser, 1984-88, Education Officer, 1988-95; Director of Education Services, Inverclyde Council, 1995-2004. Member, various National and International Educational Organisations. Recreations: collects books on Russia; has a strong interest in the arts and is a Trustee of various music and dance organisations. Address: (b.) Learning and Teaching Scotland, The Optima, 58 Robertson Street, Glasgow G2 8DU; T.-0141 282 5001.
E-mail: b.mcleary@ltscotland.org.uk

McLeish, Rt. Hon. Henry Baird, PC. MP (Labour), Fife Central, 1987-2001; MSP (Labour), Central Fife, 1999-2003; First Minister of Scotland, 2000-01, Minister for Enterprise and Learning, 1999-2000; Consultant: Halogen Communications Ltd., J. Chandler & Co.; b. 15.6.48; m.; 1 s.; 1 step-s.; 1 d.; 1 step-d. Educ. Buckhaven High School, Methil; Heriot-Watt University. Former Research Officer and Planning Officer in local government; former Member, Kirkcaldy District Council and Fife Regional Council (Leader, 1982-87); Scottish Front Bench Spokesman for Education and Employment, 1988-89, for Employment and Training, 1989-92; Shadow Scottish Minister of State, 1992-94; Shadow Minister of Transport, 1994-95; Shadow Minister for Health, 1995-97; Minister of State, Scottish Office (Minister for Home Affairs, Local Government and Devolution), 1997-99. Visiting Professor: University of Arkansas, University of Denver; Visiting Lecturer, US Airforce Academy, Colorado. Honorary Fellow: Edinburgh University; Cambridge Land Institute at Fitzwilliam College, Cambridge. Publications: Scotland First: truth and consequences, 2004; Global Scots: Making It in the Modern World (Co-Author), 2006; Wherever the Saltire Flies (Co-Author), 2006; Scotland: The Road Divides (Co-Author), 2007. Recreations: reading; history; life and work of Robert Burns; malt whisky; Highlands and Islands. Address: 49 George Street, Cellardyke, Fife KY10 3AS.

McLellan, Very Rev. Andrew Rankin Cowie, MA, BD, STM, DD. HM Chief Inspector of Prisons for Scotland, since 2002; Minister, St. Andrew's and St. George's, Edinburgh, 1986-2002; Moderator, General Assembly, Church of Scotland, 2000; b. 16.6.44, Glasgow; m., Irene L. Meek; 2 s. Educ. Kilmarnock Academy; Madras College, St. Andrews; St. Andrews University; Glasgow University; Union Theological Seminary, New York. Assistant Minister, St. George's West, Edinburgh, 1969-71; Minister: Cartsburn Augustine, Greenock, 1971-80, Viewfield, Stirling, 1980-86; Member, Inverclyde District Council, 1977-80; Tutor, Glasgow University, 1978-82; Chaplain, HM Prison, Stirling, 1982-85; Convener, Church and Nation Committee, General Assembly, 1992-96; Chairman, Scottish Religious Advisory Committee, BBC, 1996-2001; Moderator, Church and Society Forum, Churches Together in Britain and Ireland, 1999-2002; Convener, Parish Development Fund, General Assembly, 2002-06; Director, Scottish Television, 2003-07. Warrack Lecturer on Preaching, 2000. Publications: Preaching for these People, 1997; Gentle and Passionate, 2001. Recreations: sport; travel; books; gardening. Address: (h.) 4 Liggars Place, Dunfermline KY12 7XZ; T.- (work) 0131-244-8481.

McLellan, Douglas Richard, MD, FRCPath, FRCP (Glas), DipFM. Consultant Pathologist, Victoria Infirmary/Southern General Hospital, Glasgow, since 1989; Honorary Senior Lecturer, Glasgow University, since 1989; b. 13.6.55, Glasgow; m., Caitriona; 3 s. Educ. High School of Glasgow; Glasgow University. Registrar in Pathology, Southern General Hospital, Glasgow, 1978-81; Honorary Senior Registrar in Neuropathology (MRC Head Injury

Project), Institute of Neurological Sciences, Glasgow, 1981-84; Senior Registrar in Pathology, Western Infirmary, Glasgow, 1984-89. Recreations: bibliomania; Celtology. Address: (h.) 8 Calderwood Road, Newlands, Glasgow G43 2RP.

Maclellan, Professor Euphemia (Effie), FLCM, LGSM, CertPrimEd, DipRSA, BA (Hons), PhD, CPsychol, FHEA, CSci. Professor of Education, Department of Educational and Professional Studies, University of Strathclyde, since 2005, Vice Dean (Research), since 2005, Reader, Department of Educational Studies, since 2002; b. 09.09.47, Glasgow; m., Alasdair James Graham. Educ. Strathbungo Senior Secondary. Class Teacher, Primary Education, Glasgow, 1967-68; Assistant Teacher, in Residential Education, Argyll, 1968-73; Head Teacher, in Residential Education, Argyll, 1973-77; Class Teacher and Assistant Head Teacher in Primary Education, Glasgow (taught at all stages of the school), 1977-88; Lecturer, Department of Educational Studies, University of Strathclyde, 1988-96; Associate Lecturer, Open University, 1992-99; Senior Lecturer, Department of Educational Studies, University of Strathclyde, 1996-2002. Member: British Psychological Society, General Teaching Council (Scotland); represents University of Strathclyde on the Research and Development Committee of the Universities Council for the Education of Teachers (UCET); Visiting Examiner in Psychology at the Institute of Education, London. Many publications in peer-reviewed journals. Address: (b.) Department of Educational and Professsional Studies, University of Strathclyde, Southbrae Drive, Glasgow G13 1PP; T.-0141 950 3220; e-mail: e.maclellan@strath.ac.uk

McLellan, Gavin. National Secretary, Christian Aid Scotland; Chair, Disaster Emergency Committee Scotland, GCAP Scotland; Director, Stop Climate Chaos Scotland; b. 1970. Educ. Park Mains High School (1987); University of Paisley (BSc Land Economics, 1994). Address: (b.) Pentagon Centre, 36 Washington Street, Glasgow G3 8AZ.

McLellan, James Alexander, LLB. Chief Executive, Argyll and Bute Council, since 1995 (Director of Administration, Argyll and Bute District Council, 1978-95); b. 23.12.50, Lochgilphead; m., Alexis; 2 s.; 1 d. Educ. Keil School; Glasgow University. Recreations: fishing; gardening. Address: (b.) Kilmory, Lochgilphead, Argyll PA31 8RT; T.-01546 602127.

McLellan, John Crawford, BA. Editor, Edinburgh Evening News, since 2004; b. 8.2.62, Glasgow; m., Patricia; 2 s.; 1 d. Educ. Hutchesons' Grammar School; Stirling University; Preston Polytechnic. Chester Observer, 1984-86; NW Evening Mail, 1987-90; The Journal, Newcastle, 1990-93; Edinburgh Evening News, 1993-2001 (Editor, 1997-2001) and since 2004; Editor, Scotland on Sunday, 2002-04. Recreations: rugby; football; music. Address: (b.) 108 Holyrood Road, Edinburgh, EH8 8AS; T.-0131 620 8424.

McLennan, John Alan, DipArch (Glas), RIBA, FRIAS, FASI, MCIArb, MAPS, MAPM, FCIOB. Partner, The McLennan Partnership, since 1981; Director, The McLennan Partnership Ltd.; b. 29.3.50, Rutherglen; m., Jemima; 1 d. Educ. Rutherglen Academy; Glasgow University. Past President, Glasgow Institute of Architects; Past Deacon, Incorporation of Tailors of Rutherglen; Chairman, RIAS Insurance Services. Recreations: rugby; football; squash; skiing; bowling; gardening. Address: Burnside House, Beech Avenue, High Burnside, Glasgow G73 4RJ; T.-0141-634 3322; e-mail: alan.mclennan@mclarchitects.co.uk

Maclennan of Rogart, Rt. Hon. Lord (Robert Adam Ross Maclennan), PC. Liberal Democrat Spokesman on Cabinet Office and Scotland, House of Lords, since 2005; MP (Lib. Dem.), Caithness, Sutherland and Easter Ross, 1999-2001 (MP, Caithness and Sutherland, 1966-99); Barrister-at-Law; b. 26.6.36, Glasgow; m., Helen Cutter Noyes; 2 s.; 1 d. Educ. Glasgow Academy; Balliol College, Oxford; Trinity College, Cambridge; Columbia University, New York. Parliamentary Private Secretary to Secretary of State for Commonwealth Affairs, 1967; Opposition Spokesman on Scottish Affairs and Defence, 1970; Parliamentary Under-Secretary of State, Department of Prices and Consumer Protection, 1974-79; Opposition Spokesman on Foreign Affairs, 1979; Member, Public Accounts Committee, 1979-99; Founder Member, SDP, 1981; Parliamentary Spokesman on Agriculture, 1981, Home Affairs, 1983, Economic Affairs, 1987; elected Leader, SDP, 1987; President, Liberal Democrats, 1994-98; Lib Dem Spokesman on Home Affairs and Arts, 1988-94, Constitutional Affairs and Culture, 1994-2001, and on Europe, 2001-05; Alternate Member, Convention on Future of Europe, 2002-03. Recreations: music; theatre; visual arts. Address: (b.) House of Lords, London SW1A 0PW; T.-020 7219 4133.

MacLeod, Alasdair Fraser, MA (Hons). Executive Editor, News Programmes, BBC Scotland, since 2007; b. 11.1.64, Inverness; m., Catriona Murray; 1 s.; 2 d. Educ. Millburn Academy, Inverness; Glasgow University. BBC Scotland: trainee journalist, Radio Nan Gaidheal, 1986; Researcher, Gaelic television, 1987; Producer, Radio Nan Gaidheal, 1988; Producer, Radio Scotland, 1990; Senior Producer, Radio Scotland, 1993; Editor, weekly programmes, News and Current Affairs, 1994; Editor, Scottish Parliamentary Unit, 1999-2004; Executive Editor, Political Programmes, 2004-07. Member, Scottish Parliament Advisory Committee on Broadcasting. Address: (b.) BBC Scotland, Pacific Quay, Glasgow G51 5DA.

MacLeod, Andrew Kenneth, BA. Divisional Head, Patient Quality and Support, Scottish Government Health Directorate, since 2002; b. 28.3.50, Elgin; m., Sheila Janet; 2 d. Educ. Fettes College, Edinburgh; St. John's College, Oxford. Nuffield College, Oxford, 1971-74; National Economic Development Office, 1974-78; Economic Adviser, Manpower Services Commission, Office for Scotland, 1978-83; Economic Adviser/Principal, Scottish Office, 1983-90; Head, Fisheries Division III, 1990-91; Chief Executive, Scottish Fisheries Protection Agency, 1991-95; Head, Employment and Welfare to Work Division, Scottish Executive Enterprise and Lifelong Learning Department, 1995-2002. Address: (b.) St. Andrew's House, Regent Road, Edinburgh EH1 3DG; T.-0131-244 5079.
E-mail: andrew.macleod@scotland.gsi.gov.uk

MacLeod, Calum Alexander, CBE, MA, LLB, LLD. Chairman, Albyn Ltd., since 1973; b. 25.7.35, Stornoway; m., Elizabeth M. Davidson; 2 s.; 1 d. Educ. Nicolson Institute; Glenurquhart High School; Aberdeen University. Partner, Paull & Williamsons, Advocates, Aberdeen, 1964-80; Member, White Fish Authority, 1973-80; Member: North of Scotland Hydro-Electric Board, 1976-84, Highlands and Islands Development Board, 1984-91; Chancellor's Assessor, Aberdeen University, 1979-90; Chairman of Governors, Robert Gordon's College, 1981-94; Chairman, Scottish Council of Independent Schools, 1991-97; Chairman, Grampian Health Board, 1993-2000; Chairman, Britannia Building Society, 1994-1999, North Board Member, Bank of Scotland, 1980-2000; Chairman, Aberdeen Development Capital plc, 1986-2005; Deputy Chairman, SMG plc, 1997-2005; Trustee, Carnegie Trust for the Universities of Scotland, since 1997; Vice

Chairman, UHI Millennium Institute, since 2002. Recreations: golf; fishing; Hebridean coastal walking; reading; music. Address: (b.) 6 Westfield Terrace, Aberdeen AB25 2RU; T.-01224 641614.

MacLeod, Donald Roderick, LLB, QC, DipFMS. Queen's Counsel (in Practice at The Scottish Bar), since 2005; Advocate (in Practice at The Scottish Bar), since 1978; b. 24.09.48, Inverness; m., Susan Mary (nee Fulton); 2 d. Educ. High School of Stirling; University of Glasgow. Solicitor, 1973-78; Advocate, 1978-2005; sometime Temporary Sheriff. Labour Parliamentary Candidate, Kinross and W. Perthshire, 1979; Elder, Greenbank Church of Scotland; Member of Board, Scottish Medico-Legal Society; Hon. Secretary, Faculty of Advocates Criminal Bar Association; currently writing book on Firearms Law. Recreations: angling; tying classic salmon flies; music; opera; walking. Address: Advocates Library, Parliament House, Edinburgh; T.-0131-260-5607.

MacLeod, Duncan James, CBE; b. 1.11.34, Edinburgh; m., Joanna Bibby (deceased 2007); 2 s.; 1 d. Educ. Eton College. Partner, Brown, Fleming and Murray, Glasgow (now Ernst and Young), 1960; Managing Partner, Ernst and Whinney, Glasgow, 1985-89; Director: Hunterston Development Co. Ltd., since 1983, MacLeod Hotels Ltd., since 1960, de Jersey Co. Ltd., 1991-2005, Gartmore SNT Plc, 1998-2005, Bank of Scotland, 1973-91, Scottish Provident Institution, 1976-2001, Weir Group Plc, 1976-97, Motherwell Bridge Holdings Ltd., 1990-2001. DUniv (Stirling). Recreations: golf; shooting; fishing. Address: Monkredding House, Kilwinning KA13 7QN; T.-01294 552336; e-mail: skyeman2@tiscali.co.uk

MacLeod, Professor Iain Alasdair, BSc, PhD, CEng, FICE, FIStructE, FRSA. Professor Emeritus; Professor of Structural Engineering, Strathclyde University, 1981-2004; b. 4.5.39, Glasgow; m., Barbara Jean Booth; 1 s.; 1 d. Educ. Lenzie Academy; Glasgow University. Design Engineer, Crouch and Hogg, Glasgow, 1960-62; Assistant Lecturer in Civil Engineering, Glasgow University, 1962-66; Design Engineer, H.A. Simons Ltd., Vancouver, 1966-67; Structural Engineer, Portland Cement Association, Illinois, 1968-69; Lecturer in Civil Engineering, Glasgow University, 1969-73; Professor and Head, Department of Civil Engineering, Paisley College of Technology, 1973-81; Chairman, Scottish Branch, Institution of Structural Engineers, 1985-86; Vice-President, Institution of Structural Engineers, 1989-90; Member, Standing Committee on Structural Safety, 1989-97. Recreations: climbing; sailing. Address: (b.) Department of Civil Engineering, Strathclyde University, 107 Rottenrow, Glasgow.

McLeod, Ian, DA, RSW. Artist; Tutor in Drawing and Painting (part-time), Glenrothes College, 1994-2004; retired; b. 27.6.39, Port Glasgow; m., Mary N. B. Rintoul; 1 s.; 1 d. Educ. Kirkcaldy High School; Burntisland Secondary School; Edinburgh College of Art; Regent Road Institute for Adult Education; Moray House Institute of Education. Welder, Burntisland Shipbuilding Co., Fife, 1954-61; Teacher of Art, Auchmuty High School, Fife, 1967-90; 10 one-man exhibitions; various Scottish Arts Council exhibitions including: Scottish Realism: Bellany, Crozier, Gillon, McLeod and Moffat, 1971, Facts and Fantasy, 1972, Expressionism in Scottish Painting, 1977; over 50 group exhibitions; work in private and public collections. Elected: SSA, 1968, GLA, 1978, RSW, 1996. Recreations: people; books; all kinds of music, especially popular 30s and 40s; left-wing politics; detesting New Labour; hoping for an independent Scotland in his lifetime; gentle hillwalking. Address: (h.) 33 Craigkennochie Terrace, Burntisland, Fife KY3 9EN; T.-01592 873440.

Macleod, Iseabail Campbell, MA. Editorial Consultant, Scottish Language Dictionaries Ltd., since 2002; b. 27.5.36,

Glasgow. Educ. Clydebank High School; Lenzie Academy; Glasgow University. Teacher, 1958-64; Editorial Assistant, Europa Publications, 1965-66; Editor of bilingual dictionaries, Collins, Glasgow, 1966-74; Dictionaries Editor, Editorial Director, W. & R. Chambers, Edinburgh, 1974-77; freelance editor, since 1977; Editorial Director, Scottish National Dictionary Association Ltd., 1986-2002. Publications: Pocket Guide to Scottish Words, 1986, 2nd edition, 2006; Pocket Scots Dictionary (Co-Editor), 1988, Scots Thesaurus (Co-Editor), 1990; Concise English-Scots Dictionary (Co-Editor), 1993; Scots School Dictionary (Co-Editor), 1996; Edinburgh Pocket Guide, 1996; Ilustrated Encyclopedia of Scotland (General Editor), 2004; New Supplement to Scottish National Dictionary (Co-Editor), 2005; About Scotland: People, Places, Heritage (General Editor), 2007. Recreations: hill-walking; cooking; languages; music. Address: (h.) 11 Scotland Street, Edinburgh EH3 6PU; T.-0131-556 5683.

MacLeod, Professor James Summers, LLM, CA, FTII. Director: Scottish Investment Trust PLC, British Assets Trust PLC, Invesco Perpetual AIM VCT PLC, Invesco Perpetual Recovery Trust 2011 PLC; Honorary Professor, Department of Accountancy, Edinburgh University, since 1984; b. 3.8.41, Dumfries; m., (1.) Sheila Stromier (deceased); (2.) Rosemary Hoy; 2 s.; 1 d. Educ. Dumfries Academy; Glasgow University. Lecturer, Edinburgh University, 1965-68; Lecturer, Heriot Watt University, 1968-71; joined Arthur Young (now Ernst & Young), 1971; Partner, Ernst & Young, Edinburgh, 1973-98. Publications: Taxation of Insurance Business (Co-author), 4th edition, 1998; 250 papers. Recreations: bridge; music; reading. Address: (h.) 50 New Swanston, Edinburgh; T.-0131-445 4748.

MacLeod of MacLeod, Hugh. 30th Chief of Clan MacLeod; b. 24.07.73, London; m., Frederique Feder; 1 s. Succeeded to title, 2007. Address: (h.) Dunvegan Castle, Isle of Skye IV55 8WF; T.-01470 521 206.

MacLeod, Rev. John. Moderator of General Assembly of the Free Church of Scotland (Continuing), 2006; Principal Clerk of Assembly, Free Church of Scotland (Continuing), since 2000; Minister, Tarbat Free Church, Portmahomack, since 1978; b. 14.5.48, Fearn; m., Joy Morrison; 7 s.; 2 d. Educ. Tain Royal Academy; Aberdeen University. Pensions Legal Department, Standard Life Assurance, 1969-71; Missioner to Aberdeen students, 1974-75; Highland Church, Vancouver, 1976; Supply Preacher, Toronto, Detroit and Prince Edward Island, 1976-78; Clerk to Training of Ministry Committee, Free Church of Scotland, 1985-2001. Recreations: squeezing quarts into pint pots and getting blood out of stones. Address: Free Church Manse, Portmahomack, Tain; T.-0845 1297055; e-mail: principalclerk@fccontinuing.org

Macleod, John Alasdair Johnston, MBE, DL, FRCGP, FRCP (Glas), DCH, DObsRCOG. General Practitioner, North Uist, 1973-2000; Secretary, Western Isles Local Medical Committee (GP), 1977-91; Deputy Lieutenant, Western Isles, since 1979; Director, Taigh Chearsabhagh Trust, since 2000; Chairman, Comann na Mara, since 2001; b. 20.1.35, Stornoway; m., Lorna Jean Ferguson; 2 s.; 1 d. Educ. Nicolson Institute; Keil School, Glasgow University. National Service, Royal Navy, 1957-59; hospital posts, Glasgow and London, 1963-73; Non-Executive Director, Olscot Ltd., 1969-93; trainer in general practice, 1975-95; Visiting Professor: Department of Family Medicine, University of North Carolina, 1985, University of Western Ontario, Canada, 1998; Visiting Lecturer, Middlebury College, Vermont, USA, 1998; Honorary Life Member, World Organisation of National Colleges Academique of Family Practice, since 2001 (Member, since 1989, Member, WONCA World Rural Group, 1992-2003); Member, General Practitioner Writers Association, since 1986 (Winner, GPWA Writer, 2000). Member, Committee of

North Uist Highland Gathering; Fellow, Royal Society of Medicine; Admiralty Surgeon and Agent, 1974-91; EURIPA/WONCA Lifetime Award, 2003; Visiting Lecturer, James Cook University, 2002; author of papers and articles, singly and jointly, on aspects of isolated practice. Lifetime UK National Award - Fishing News, 2007, for work in trying to get fishermen to wear a Personal Flotation Device (PFD). Recreations: boating; horticulture; photography; time-sharing. Address: (h.) Tigh-Na-Hearradh, Lochmaddy, Isle of North Uist HS6 5AE; T.-01876 500224; e-mail: johnajmacleod@debrett.net

Macleod, John Francis Matheson, MA, LLB, NP. Solicitor in Inverness, 1959-94; b. 24.1.32, Inverness; m., Alexandra Catherine (deceased); 1 s. Educ. Inverness Royal Academy; George Watson's College; Edinburgh University. Solicitor, Fife County Council, 1957-59; in private practice, 1959-94; Parliamentary candidate (Liberal): Moray and Nairn, 1964, Western Isles, 1966; Chairman, Highland Region, Scottish Liberal Party, until 1978; former Vice-Chairman, Broadcasting Council for Scotland; Dean, Faculty of Solicitors of the Highlands, 1988-91; Chairman, Crofters Commission, 1978-86; Member, Council, Law Society of Scotland, 1988-92; Chairman of Council, Gaelic Society of Inverness, 1996-97; Chief for 2005; Chairman, National Trust for Scotland's Culloden Advisory Committee. Address: (h.) Bona Lodge, Aldourie, Inverness; T.-01463 751327.

MacLeod, John Murray, MA (Hons). Crofter; Writer at large; Columnist, The Herald, 1991-2002; Columnist, Scottish Daily Mail, since 2002; b. 15.4.66, Kilmallie, Inverness-shire. Educ. Jordanhill College School, Glasgow; James Gillespie's High School, Edinburgh; Edinburgh University. Freelance journalist and broadcaster, since 1988; Scottish Journalist of the Year, 1991; Young Scottish Journalist of the Year, 1991-92; Commended, Columnist of the Year, 1992; Commended, Feature Writer of the Year, 1996; nominated Columnist of the Year, 1999, 2001 and 2003; Columnist of the Year, UK Press Gazette Regional Newspaper Awards, 1996. Publications: No Great Mischief If You Fall – The Highland Experience, 1993; Highlanders – A History of the Gaels, 1996; Dynasty – The Stuarts 1560-1807, 1999. Recreations: tennis; meeting the boat; vital religion. Address: (h.) Twin Peaks, South Shawbost, Isle of Lewis HS2 9BJ; T.-mobile 07776 236 337; 01851 710 336; e-mail: jm.macleod@btinternet.com

MacLeod, Lorne Buchanan, BA, CA. Self-employed Chartered Accountant; b. 13.4.63, Oban. Educ. Oban High School; University of Strathclyde. Ernst and Whinney, Inverness, 1983-87; Highlands and Islands Development Board, 1987-92; Chief Executive, Skye and Lochalsh Enterprise, 1992-98; Director of Strengthening Communities, Highlands and Islands Enterprise, 1998-2000. Director, Comunn na Gaidhlig, 1998-2000; Director, Highlands and Islands Screen Services Ltd., 1998-2000; Board Member, Community Fund, 2001-03. Council Member, Scottish Further Education Funding Council, 2001-05; Director: Isle of Gigha Heritage Trust, since 2002, Oban War and Peace Museum, 2003-07; Chairman, Highlands & Islands Community Energy Company, since 2004; Director: Gigha Renewable Energy Ltd., since 2004, Jansvans Limited, since 2001, Jansport Limited, since 2004, Canan Limited, since 2006, Cal Mac Ferries Limited, since 2006, David MacBrayne Limited, since 2006, South Uist Estates, since 2007. Winston Churchill Travelling Fellowship, 1997. Recreations: hillwalking; sailing. Address: Orasaig, Crannaig-a-Mhinister, Oban, Argyll PA34 4LU; e-mail: lorne.macleod@ecosse.net

McLeod, Professor Malcolm Donald, CBE, MA, BLitt (Oxon), FRSE. Vice-Principal, Advancement, University of Glasgow, 1999-2005, Pro Vice-Principal, 2005-06; Trustee, The Hunterian Collection, London, since 1998; b. 19.5.41, Edinburgh; 2 s.; 1 d. Educ. Birkenhead School; Hertford

and Exeter Colleges, Oxford. Research Assistant, Institute of Social Anthropology, Oxford, 1964-65; Lecturer, Sociology Department, University of Ghana, 1967-69; Assistant Curator, Museum of Archaeology and Ethnology, Cambridge, 1969-74; College Lecturer and Director of Studies, Magdalene and Girton Colleges, Cambridge, 1969-74; Fellow, Magdalene College, 1972-74; Keeper of Ethnography, British Museum, 1974-90; Director, Hunterian Museum and Art Gallery, Glasgow University, 1990-99; Honorary Lecturer, Department of Anthropology, UCL, 1976-81; Honorary Lecturer, Department of Archaeology, University of Glasgow, since 1992; Chairman, Scottish Museums Council, 1996-2001; Curator, The Royal Society of Edinburgh, 1999-2002; Chairman, Caledonian Foundation Inc., USA, 2003-07; Trustee, National Museum of Scotland, since 2005. Publications: The Asante, 1981; Treasures of African Art, 1981; Ethnic Sculpture (Co-author), 1985; Jacob Epstein Collector (Co-author), 1989. Address: (h.) The Schoolhouse, Oxnam, Jedburgh TD8 6NB.

Macleod, Mary Elizabeth, LLB (Hons), DipLP, NP. Depute Solicitor of the Church of Scotland, since 1995; b. 23.12.63, Stornoway. Educ. Nicolson Institute, Stornoway; Edinburgh University. Trainee Solicitor, Anderson, Shaw and Gilbert, Inverness, 1986-88; Assistant: Morton, Fraser and Milligan, WS, Edinburgh, 1988-90, Skene, Edwards and Garson, W. S., Edinburgh, 1990-92, Campbell Smith, Edinburgh, 1992-95. Recreations: travel; music; reading. Address: (b.) 121 George Street, Edinburgh EH2 4YN; T.-0131-225 5722.

Macleod, Murdoch, MBE, JP. Honorary Sheriff; b. 11.8.32, Shawbost, Isle of Lewis; m., Crisybil; 1 s.; 1 d. Educ. Nicolson Institute, Stornoway. Ross and Cromarty Council: Highways Department, 1955-57, Education Department, 1957-65; Stornoway Town Council: Town Clerk's Department, 1965-68, Town Clerk, 1968-75; General Manager, Secretary and Treasurer, Stornoway Pier and Harbour Commission, 1975-96. Former Deputy Chairman, Transport Users Consultative Committee for Scotland; Past Chairman, District Courts Association; Past Chairman, Western Isles Justices Committee; former Member, Council, British Ports Asssociation; former Chairman, Scottish Port Members, British Ports Association; former Deputy Chairman, British Ports Federation; former Director, Western Isles Development Fund Ltd.; Honorary President, Lewis Pipe Band; former Member, British Airways Consumer Council for Highlands and Islands; Trustee, Scottish Hydro Electric Community Trust; Past Chairman, League of Friends, Stornoway Hospitals and Homes; former Chairman, Stornoway Historical Society; former Member, General Advisory Council and Scottish Advisory Committee, Independent Broadcasting Authority; former Member, Western Isles Health Board. Recreations: reading; local history. Address: (h.) 46 Barony Square, Stornoway, Isle of Lewis; T.-01851 703024; e-mail: murdochmac@aol.com

MacLeod, Sheriff Principal Norman Donald, QC, MA, LLB. Sheriff Principal of Glasgow and Strathkelvin, 1986-97; b. 6.3.32, Perth; m., Ursula Jane Bromley; 2 s.; 2 d. Educ. Mill Hill School; George Watson's Boys College; Edinburgh University; Hertford College, Oxford. Called to the Bar, 1956; District Officer and Crown Counsel, Colonial Service, East Africa, 1957-63; at the Bar, 1963-67; Sheriff at Glasgow, 1967-86; Commissioner, Northern Lighthouse Board, 1986-97 (Chairman, 1990-91); Visiting Professor of Law, Strathclyde University, 1986-97; Honorary Sheriff, North Strathclyde. Recreation: rustic pursuits. Address: (h.) Calderbank, Lochwinnoch, Renfrewshire PA12 4DJ; T.-01505 843340; e-mail: mandj@normanandjane.plus.com

MacLeod, Peter, MCIBS. Retired Banker; Honorary Sheriff of North Strathclyde at Oban, since 1988; b. 9.6.33, Ruaig, Isle of Tiree; m., Jean MacDonald Buchanan; 2 s. Educ. Oban High School. Served as Captain, Royal Signals, AER; joined Royal Bank of Scotland, 1949; Bank Manager. Past Commodore and Trustee, Royal Highland Yacht Club; Trustee, RHYC Sail Training Trust; Past Chairman and Founder Treasurer, Oban Round Table; Trustee, The MacDougall Trust; Founder Chairman, West Highland Anchorages and Moorings Association. Publication: History of Royal Highland Yacht Club, 1881-1999. Recreations: sailing; island wandering; impromptu ceilidhs; beachcombing. Address: (h.) The Wheelhouse, Ganavan, Oban, Argyll; T.-01631 563577.

MacLeod, Roderick Alexander Randle, BA, MBA, BD. Minister, Parish Church of The Holy Trinity, St. Andrews, since 2004; b. 16.2.65, Edinburgh; m., Annice (nee MacDonald); 1 s.; 2 d. Educ. Fettes College; Universities of Cambridge, Edinburgh and St. Andrews. Army: Short Service Limited Commission (SSLC), Queens Own Highlanders; Teaching: Schoolmaster, Loretto School, Musselburgh; Church: Assistant Minister, Portree, Isle of Skye, Parish Minister, Bracadale, Isle of Skye, Navy Chaplain, 40 Commando; Commando Training Centre, Royal Marines, Poole, Parish Minister, Holy Trinity, St. Andrews. Chairman, St. Andrews Festival. Recreations: bagpipes; outdoor pursuits; travel. Address: (h.) 19 Priory Gardens, St. Andrews, Fife KY16 8XX; (Church) Parish Church of The Holy Trinity, South Street, St. Andrews, Fife KY16 9QX; T.-01334 461098; e-mail: rory@holyt.co.uk

MacLeod, Roderick John, BSc. Principal, The National Piping Centre, since 1996; b. 26.8.62, Johnstone; m., Margaret. Educ. Eastwood High School; University of Strathclyde. Mathematics Teacher, Cleveden Secondary School, Glasgow, 1983-93; Assistant Principal, Mathematics, Dalziel High School, Motherwell, 1993-96. Winner, Highland Society of London gold medals; winner, piping, National Mod; Editor, Piping Today. Publication: The Highland Bagpipe Tutor Book (Editor). Address: (h.) 12 Medrox Gardens, Condorrat, Cumbernauld; T.-0141 353 0220; e-mail: rmacleod@thepipingcentre.co.uk

Macleod, Rev. William, BSc, ThM. Minister, Thornwood Free Church (Continuing), since 2006; Principal, Free Church Seminary, since 2002; Editor, Free Church Witness; b. 2.11.51, Stornoway; m., Marion; 2 s.; 1 d. Educ. Aberdeen University; Free Church College; Westminster Seminary. Minister: Partick Free Church, Glasgow, 1976-93; Portree Free Church, 1993-2006. Editor, Free Church Foundations, 1997-2000; former Chairman, Portree High School Board. Recreations: gardening; fishing; reading. Address: (h.) 25 Branklyn Crescent, Academy Park, Glasgow G13 1GJ; T.-0141 959 0292.

McLernan, Sheriff Kieran Anthony, KCHS, MA, LLB. Sheriff of Grampian Highlands and Islands at Banff and Peterhead, since 1991, and Aberdeen, since 2000; b. 29.4.41, Wemyss Bay; m., Joan Doherty; 1 s.; 3 d. Educ. St. Aloysius College, Glasgow; Glasgow University. Solicitor, 1965-91; Temporary Sheriff, 1986-91; Tutor, Glasgow University, 1987-91; Chairman, Aberdeen Branch, SASO, 1993; Member, Sheriffs Association Council, 1998-2001, and 2003-06. Recreations: golf; hockey; skiing.

McLetchie, David William, LLB (Hons), WS. MSP, (Conservative), Lothians, 1999-2003, Edinburgh Pentlands, since 2003; former Leader, Scottish Conservative Parliamentary Group (1999-2005); Business Manager and Chief Whip, since 2007; b. 6.8.52, Edinburgh; m., 1,

Barbara Gemmell Baillie (deceased); 1 s.; 2, Sheila Elizabeth Foster. Educ. George Heriot's School; Edinburgh University. Solicitor; Partner, Tods Murray WS, 1980-2005. President, Scottish Conservative and Unionist Association, 1994-97. Recreations: golf; football (Heart of Midlothian); music; reading crime fiction. Address: (b.) The Scottish Parliament, Edinburgh EH99 1SP; T.-0131-348 5659.

McLusky, Donald S., BSc, PhD. Senior Lecturer in Marine Biology, Stirling University, 1977-2003; Editor, Estuarine Coastal and Shelf Science, since 2000; b. 27.6.45, Harrogate; m., Ruth Alicia Donald; 1 s.; 2 d. Educ. Latymer Upper School, London; Aberdeen University; Stirling University. Stirling University: Assistant Lecturer, 1968-70, Lecturer, 1970-77, Head of Department of Biological Sciences, 1985 and 1992-98. Member, Council, Scottish Marine Biological Association, 1976-82, and 1985-91; Member, Scientific Advisory Committee, Scottish Natural Heritage, 1999-2005; Trustee, Estuarine and Coastal Sciences Association; Member, Central Scotland Valuation Appeal Committee. Publications: Ecology of Estuaries, 1971; Physiology and Behaviour of Marine Organisms, 1977; The Estuarine Ecosystem, 2004; The Natural Environment of the Estuary and Firth of Forth, 1987; North Sea – Estuarine Interactions, 1990; The Estuaries of Central Scotland, 1997; Central Scotland, Land, Wildlife, People, 1993; The Freshwaters of Scotland, 1994. Recreations: nature; walking; swimming; travel. Address: (h.) Ardoch Cottage, Strathyre, Callander FK18 8NF; T.-01877 384309; e-mail: d.mclusky@tiscali.co.uk

McMahon, Hugh Robertson, MA (Hons), FEIS. Member (Labour), European Parliament, Strathclyde West, 1984-99; Scottish Political Editor, World-Parliamentarian Magazine, since 1999; Lecturer/Consultant, James Watt College, since 1999; Lecturer, Politics, University of Edinburgh, since 2003; Visiting Professor, Brookdale CC, New Jersey, 2001; b. 17.6.38, Saltcoats; m., Helen Paterson Grant; 1 s.; 1 d. Educ. Stevenston High School; Ardrossan Academy; Glasgow University. Schoolteacher in Ayrshire (Largs High, Stevenston High, Irvine Royal Academy, Mainholm Academy); Assistant Head, Ravenspark Academy, 1971-84. Vice-Chair, EP Social Affairs, Employment and Working Environment Committee, 1992-94; Member, Social Affairs, Fisheries and Transport Committees; Chair, EP Delegation with Norway, 1989-92; Member: Delegation with Czechoslovakia, EIS, NUJ, GMB; Delegation with Hungary, 1994-96. Recreation: golf. Address: (b.) 9 Low Road, Castlehead, Paisley PA2 6AQ.

MacMahon, Rev. Janet P.H., BD, MSc, LCST, LLCM. Minister of Kilmaronock-Gartocharn Parish Church, since 2006; Minister, Castlemilk West Parish Church, 2002-06; b. 31.5.44, Glasgow; m., Professor M.K.C. MacMahon (qv); 1 s.; 1 d. Educ. Glasgow High School for Girls; Glasgow University; Glasgow School of Speech Therapy. Senior Speech Therapist, 1965-80; Chief Speech Therapist, Greater Glasgow Health Board, 1980-82; Senior Speech Therapist, Scottish Council for Spastics, 1983-85; Assistant Minister, Cairns Church, Milngavie, and Govan Old Church, 1989-90; Research and Development Officer in special educational needs, Department of Education, Church of Scotland, 1990-92; Chaplaincy Co-ordinator, Southern General Hospital, Glasgow, 1992-2002. Publications include: Walk in God's Ways, 1993. Recreations: reading crime novels; watching TV soaps. Address: (h.) Manse of Kilmaronock, Gartocharn, Alexandria, West Dunbartonshire G83 8SB; T.-01360-660295.

McMahon, Professor Malcolm Iain, BSc, PhD, DSc, FInstP. Professor of High Pressure Physics, The University of Edinburgh, since 2007; b. 13.01.65, Dundee. Educ. Carnoustie High School; The University of Edinburgh. Postdoctoral Research Associate, University of Edinburgh, 1990-96; Royal Society University Research Fellow: University of Liverpool, 1996-98, University of Edinburgh,

1998-2003; Reader in Physics, University of Edinburgh, 2002-07. Recreations: hillwalking; whisky appreciation. Address: (b.) School of Physics, The University of Edinburgh, Mayfield Road, Edinburgh EH9 3JZ; T.-0131 650 5956; e-mail: mim@ph.ed.ac.uk

McMahon, Michael, BA (Hons). MSP (Labour), Hamilton North and Bellshill, since 1999; Convener, Public Petitions Committee, Scottish Parliament, 2003-07; Shadow Deputy Minister for Parliament and Labour Chief Whip, since 2007; m.; 1 s.; 2 d. Educ. Our Lady's High School, Motherwell. Worked as a welder before leaving to go to university; then pursued a career in social and political research. Address: (b.) Parliamentary Advice Office, 188 Main Street, Bellshill, Lanarkshire ML4 1AE; T.-01698 304501.

MacMahon, Professor Michael Kenneth Cowan, BA, PhD, DipLing, FRSA. Professor of Phonetics, Glasgow University, since 1997; b. 7.8.43, Winchester; m., Rev. Janet P.H. MacMahon (qv); 1 s.; 1 d. Educ. Hymers College, Hull; Durham University; Göttingen University; Glasgow University; Reading University. Lecturer in Phonetics and Linguistics, Jordanhill College, Glasgow, 1966-72; Lecturer in Linguistics and Phonetics, 1972-83, Lecturer in English Language, 1983-87, Senior Lecturer in English Language, 1987-97, Glasgow University. Governor, Hutchesons' Educational Trust; Treasurer, International Phonetic Association, 2003-07; Member, Executive Committee, Henry Sweet Society; Archivist and Secretary, British Association of Academic Phoneticians; Member, Council, British Flute Society. Publications: numerous. Recreations: flute-playing; singing. Address: (h.) Manse of Kilmaronock, Gartocharn, Alexandria, West Dunbartonshire G83 8SB; T.-01360-660295; e-mail: m.macmahon@englang.arts.gla.ac.uk

McManus, James John, LLB, PhD. Professor, Criminal Justice, Glasgow Caledonian University; Member, Risk Management Authority, since 2004; b. 23.6.50, Cleland; m., Catherine MacKellaig; 1 s.; 4 d. Educ. Our Lady's High School, Motherwell; University of Edinburgh; University of Dundee. Tutor, University of Edinburgh, 1972-74; Lecturer, University of Wales, 1974-76; Lecturer, then Senior Lecturer, University of Dundee, 1976-2004; Scottish Prisons Complaints Commissioner, 1994-99; Chair, Parole Board for Scotland, 2000-05. Expert Adviser, Council of Europe, since 1993. Publications: Prisons Prisoners and the Law, 1994; Mental Health and Scots Law in Practice, 2005 (co-author). Recreations: golf; cycling. Address: (b.) Centre for Criminal Justice, Glasgow Caledonian University, Cowcaddens, Glasgow G4 0BA; T.-0141 331 3597; e-mail: jmm2@gcal.ac.uk

McManus, Professor John, DSc, PhD, ARCS, DIC, FRSE, CGeol. Professor of Geology, St. Andrews University, 1993-2001, now Emeritus Professor (Reader, 1988-93); Honorary Director, Tay Estuary Research Centre, 1979-92; b. 5.6.38, Harwich; m., J. Barbara Beveridge (deceased 2007); 2 s.; 1 d. Educ. Harwich County High School; Imperial College, London University. Assistant, then Lecturer, St. Andrews University, 1964-67; Lecturer, Senior Lecturer, Reader, Dundee University, 1967-88; UNESCO Representative, International Commission on Continental Erosion, 1980-84 and 1986; Member: Scottish Natural Heritage East Areas Board and Scientific Advisory Committee, 1992-99, Secretary of State's Committee on Waste Discharges into the Marine Environment; President, Estuarine and Brackish Water Sciences Association, 1995-98; Member, Executive, European Union for Coastal Conservation, 1997-2000; Member, Scottish Environment Protection Agency East Region Board, since 2000; Member, Eden Estuary Nature Reserve Management Committee; former Treasurer, British Sedimentological Research Group; Consultant on Coastal Erosion and Protection to four Regional Councils; Honorary Fellow,

Royal Scottish Geographical Society, since 2001; Executive Editor, Transactions of the Royal Society of Edinburgh, Earth Sciences, 1988-95; Associate Editor, Continental Shelf Research. President: Cupar Choral Association, 1968-78, Cupar Amateur Opera, 1979-91. Recreations: music; East Fife Male Voice Choir; bird-watching; swimming; stamp collecting. Address: (b.) School of Geography and Geology, Purdie Building, St. Andrews University, St. Andrews, Fife KY16 9AL.

McMaster, Sir Brian, CBE. Director and Chief Executive, Edinburgh International Festival, 1991-2006. General Administrator, subsequently Managing Director, W.N.O., 1976-91. Address: (b.) 13/5 James Court, Lawnmarket, Edinburgh EH1 2VB; T.-0131 226 5520.

McMenamin, Frances Jane, QC, BA, LLB. Queen's Counsel, since 1998; b. 21.5.51, Glasgow; m., Ian McCarry. Educ. Notre Dame High School, Glasgow; Strathclyde University. Legal apprenticeship, Hughes, Dowdall & Co., Solicitors, Glasgow, 1974-76; Procurator Fiscal Depute, 1976-84; devilling at Scottish Bar, 1984-85; admitted, Faculty of Advocates, 1985; Junior Counsel practising in criminal law, 1985-98; Temporary Sheriff, 1991-97; Advocate Depute, 1997-2000; criminal defence work, since 2000; Visiting Lecturer, Scottish Police College, Tulliallan, since 1991. Member, Strathclyde University Law School Advisory Panel, since 2000; Director of Faculty Services Ltd., 2003-07; Member of Management Committee of Faculty of Advocates Free Legal Advice Unit, since 2005; Member of Court, Strathclyde University, since 2005; Vice Chairperson, Faculty of Advocates Criminal Bar Association, since 2007. Recreations: golf; exercise classes; Argentinian tango; reading; travelling with her husband. Address: (h.) 59 Hamilton Drive, Glasgow G12 8DP; T.-0141-339 0519; (b.) Advocates Library, Parliament House, Edinburgh EH1 1RF; T.-0131-226 5071.

McMicking, Major David John, LVO, MSc. Consultant, Human Resources/Sporting, since 1986; b. 29.4.39, Jerusalem; m., Janetta; 1 s.; 1 d. Educ. Eton; RMA, Sandhurst; Strathclyde University. Career soldier, Black Watch, rising to rank of Major; left Army, 1973; various positions, John Menzies Holdings Ltd., 1973-86; family farming interests, since 1996. Formerly Extra Equerry, Queen Elizabeth The Queen Mother; Chairman, Officers Association Scotland; Director, Earl Haig Fund Scotland, 1997-2000; Secretary, Friends of St. Andrew's, Jerusalem, 1994-2007. Recreation: field sports. Address: (b.) Drumknock, Kilry, Blairgowrie PH11 8HR; T.-01575 560731.

McMillan, Alan Charles, MA (Hons), LLB, DipLP, LLM, NP. Partner, Commercial Dispute Resolution, Burness LLP, since 2005; b. 5.12.64, Hamilton; m., Isla; 2 s.; 1 d. Educ. Garrion Academy; University of Edinburgh. Teacher of English as a Foreign Language, for Business Purposes in Spain, Thailand and Scotland, 1987-91; Trainee Solicitor, MacRoberts, 1995-96; Solicitor, Dundas & Wilson CS, 1996-2005. Co-Editor, "Dilapidations in Scotland" (2nd ed.); Chair, Property Litigation Association (Scotland); CEDR - accredited Mediator. Recreations: reading; cycling; music; languages. Address: (h.) 28 Inverleith Row, Edinburgh EH3 5QH; T.-0131-473-6141 (day); e-mail: alan.mcmillan@burness.co.uk

Macmillan, Angus. Area Director, Outer Hebrides, VisitScotland; b. 3.12.55, Ness, Isle of Lewis; m., Isabel; 3 d. Educ. Govan High School, Glasgow. Address: (b.) 4 South Beach, Stornoway HS1 2XY; T.-01851 701818.

MacMillan of MacMillan and Knap, George Gordon, MA (Cantab). Chief of Clan MacMillan; b. 20.6.30, London; m., (Cecilia) Jane Spurgin (deceased 2005); 2 s. Educ. Aysgarth School; Eton; Trinity College, Cambridge. Schoolmaster, Wellington College, 1953-63; Lecturer,

Trinity College, Toronto, 1963-64; Lecturer, Bede College, Durham, 1965-74. Resides in small historic house with gardens and woods open to the public. Address: (h.) Applehouse, Finlaystone, Langbank, Renfrewshire PA14 6TJ; T.-01475 540285; e-mail: chief@clanmacmillan.org

Macmillan, Very Rev. Gilleasbuig Iain, MA, BD. Minister, St. Giles', The High Kirk of Edinburgh, since 1973; Chaplain to the Queen in Scotland, since 1979; Dean of the Order of the Thistle, since 1989.

Macmillan, Gordon. Head of News and Current Affairs, STV. Address: (b.) STV, Pacific Quay, Glasgow G51 1PQ.

Macmillan, Sheriff Iain Alexander, CBE, LLD, BL. Sheriff of South Strathclyde, Dumfries and Galloway, at Hamilton, 1981-92; b. 14.11.23, Oban; m., Edith Janet McAulay; 2 s.; 1 d. Educ. Oban High School; Glasgow University; Scottish Commercial College. RAF (France, Germany, India), 1944-47; Solicitor (Sturrock & Co., Kilmarnock), 1952-81; Council Member, Law Society of Scotland, 1964-79 (President, 1976-77). Recreations: golf; music. Address: (h.) 2 Castle Drive, Kilmarnock, Ayrshire; T.-01563 525864; e-mail: mick.millan@virgin.net

McMillan, Iain Macleod, CBE, FCIB, FCIBS, FAIA, CCMI, FRSA, FSQA. Director, CBI Scotland, since 1995; Chairman, Scottish Business Education Coalition, 2002-07; Vice Chairman, Scottish Qualifications Authority (Chairman, International and Commercial Committee), 2004-06, Member, Board, 1997-2006; Non-Executive Director, Scottish Ambulance Service (Chairman, Audit Committee); Member, Board, Scottish North American Business Council; Member, Advisory Committee, Scottish Economic Policy Network (scotecon), 2002-07; Chairman, Advisory Board, University of Strathclyde Business School; Member, Advisory Board, Scottish Co-investment Fund; Trustee, The Industrial Mission Trust; Trustee, The Teaching Awards Trust; b. 25.4.51, Glasgow; m., Giuseppina; 3 s. Educ. Bearsden Academy. Trainee Banker, 1970-76; TSB Group plc: Manager, 1976-89, Senior Manager, 1989-93; Assistant Director, CBI Scotland, 1993-95. Member, Scottish Advisory Board, Equal Opportunities Commission, 1995-2001; Chairman, Higher Still Employment and Training Group, 1997-2000; Member, Scottish Executive's Committee of Review into the Careers Service, 1999-2000; Member, Board, Young Enterprise Scotland, 1999-2003. Publications: Manufacturing Matters (Co-Author), 1994; The Challenge for Government in Scotland (principal author), 1996, Scottish Manufacturing: a shared vision (Co-Author), 1997; Business and Parliaments – Partners for Prosperity (Co-Author), 1998; Towards a Prosperous Scotland (Co-Author), 1999; Scotland's Economy: an agenda for growth (Co-author), 2003; The Scottish Economy: The Priority of Priorities (Co-author), 2006. Recreations: squash; walking. Address: (b.) 16 Robertson Street, Glasgow G2 8DS; T.-0141-222 2184; e-mail: iain.mcmillan@cbi.org.uk

MacMillan, James Loy, CBE, BMus, PhD. Composer and Conductor; Composer/Conductor, BBC Philharmonic, since 2000; Affiliate Composer, Scottish Chamber Orchestra, since 1990; part-time Teacher, Royal Scottish Academy of Music and Drama, since 1989; Visiting Composer, Philharmonia, since 1991; Visiting Professor, University of Strathclyde, since 1997; b. 16.7.59, Kilwinning; Educ. Cumnock Academy; Edinburgh University; Durham University. Principal compositions: The Confession of Isobel Gowdie, London Proms, 1990; Busqueda, Edinburgh International Festival, with Diana Rigg, 1990; featured composer, Musica Nova, 1990, Huddersfield Contemporary Music Festival, 1991; Veni, Veni, Emmanuel, percussion concerto for Evelyn Glennie, London Proms, 1992; Visitatio Sepulchri, one act opera, Mayfest, 1993; Ines de Castro, for Scottish Opera, Edinburgh International

Festival, 1996; The World's Ransoming, for orchestra and cor anglaise, 1996; Cello Concerto, 1996; Symphony: Vigil, 1997; featured composer, Edinburgh International Festival, 1993; recording of Tryst and The Confession of Isobel Gowdie by BBC SSO won Gramophone Award, contemporary music category, 1993; Seven Last Words, BBC TV, 1994; Raising Sparks, 1997, for chamber ensemble; String Quartet: Why Is This Night Different?, 1988; featured composer, Raising Sparks Festival, South Bank Centre, London, 1997 (South Bank Show Award for Classical Music, 1997); Evening Standard Classical Music Award, 1997 for Outstanding Artistic Achievement for Symphony: Vigil and Raising Sparks Festival. DUniv, (Paisley); DLitt (University of Strathclyde); FRASMD; HonFRIAS.

Macmillan, Emeritus Professor (John) Duncan, MA, PhD, LID, FRSA, FRSE, HRSA. Emeritus Professor of the History of Scottish Art, Edinburgh University; Curator, Talbot Rice Gallery, Edinburgh University, 1979-2004; Hon. Keeper of Portraits, Royal College of Surgeons, Edinburgh; Art Critic, The Scotsman; b. 7.3.39, Beaconsfield; m., Vivien Rosemary Hinkley; 2 d. Educ. Gordonstoun School; St. Andrews University; London University; Edinburgh University. Lecturer, then Senior Lecturer, then Reader, Department of Fine Art, Edinburgh University. Recreation: walking. Address: (h.) 20 Nelson Street, Edinburgh; T.-0131-556 7100.

Macmillan, John Ernest Newall, LLB, NP. Employment Partner, MacRoberts Glasgow, Managing Partner, 1998-2005; b. 27.9.56, Kilmarnock; m., Caroline Elizabeth; 2 s.; 2 d. Educ. Merchiston Castle School, Edinburgh; Dundee University. Apprenticeship, Bird Semple and Crawford Herron, Glasgow, 1978-80; Solicitor, J. and J. Sturrock & Co., Kilmarnock, 1980-82; Solicitor, MacRoberts Glasgow, 1982-86, Partner (Litigation and Employment), since 1986. Former Captain, Kilmarnock (Barassie) Golf Club; Trustee, St. Aloysius College Charitable Fund. Recreations: golf; skiing; bridge; travel. Address: (b.) 152 Bath Street, Glasgow; T.-0141-332 9988.
E-mail: john.macmillan@macroberts.com

McMillan, Joyce Margaret, MA (Hons), DipEd, DLitt. h.c. (Queen Margaret Univ. College). Journalist and Arts Critic; Theatre Critic and Columnist, The Scotsman, since 1998; b. 29.8.52, Paisley. Educ. Paisley Grammar School; St. Andrews University; Edinburgh University. Theatre Reviewer, BBC Radio Scotland and The Scotsman, 1979-81; Theatre Critic, Sunday Standard, 1981-83; Radio Critic, The Herald, 1983-95; Scottish Theatre Critic, The Guardian, 1984-93; Scotland on Sunday: Social/Political Columnist, 1989-97, Theatre Critic, 1993-97; Arts/Political Columnist, The Herald, 1997-98. Chair, NUJ Freelance Branch, Edinburgh; Member, National Executive Committee, NUJ, London; Member, Consultative Steering Group on the Scottish Parliament, 1998-99; Member, Scottish National Theatre Working Group, 2000-01; Chair, Hansard Society Working Group, Scotland; Visiting Professor, Drama and Creative Industries, Queen Margaret University, Edinburgh, 2006. Publications: The Traverse Story, 1963-88, 1988; Charter for the Arts in Scotland, 1992. Recreations: food; drink; films; music; talking politics. Address: 8 East London Street, Edinburgh, EH7 / 4BH; T.-0131-557 1726.

McMillan, Lorraine Anne, BSc (Hons), MBA. Director of Operations, Scottish Enterprise Renfrewshire, since 1999; b. 12.8.61, Johnstone; m., Ian Stuart McMillan; 1 s.; 1 d. Educ. Glasgow University; Strathclyde University. Barr and Stroud, 1982-89; Scottish Development Agency, 1989-91; Dunbartonshire Enterprise, 1991-99. Address: (b.) 27 Causeyside Street, Paisley PA1 1UL; T.-0141-848 0101.

McMillan, Malcolm. Chief Executive, Scottish Law Commission, since 2008; b. 27.3.55, Ayr; m., Mary Clare

Campbell; 3 d. Educ. Royal High School, Edinburgh; University of Edinburgh. Admitted as Solicitor in 1979; Legal Assistant, Argyll and Bute District Council, 1979-80; Legal Adviser in the Office of Solicitor to the Secretary of State for Scotland, 1982-99; Deputy Legal Secretary to the Lord Advocate, 1999-2003; Divisional Solicitor for the Rural Affairs Division in the Scottish Government Legal Directorate, 2003-08. Recreations: hill walking; swimming; surfing. Address: (b.) Scottish Law Commission, 140 Causewayside, Edinburgh EH9 1PR; T.-0131 668 2131.

Macmillan, Maureen, MA (Hons). MSP (Labour), Highlands and Islands, 1999-2007; b. 1943, Oban; m.; 2 s.; 2 d. Educ. Oban High School. Co-founder, Ross-shire Women's Aid; former teacher of English.

McMillan, Michael Dale, BSc, LLB, NP, FFCS. Managing Partner, Burnett & Reid, Solicitors, Aberdeen; Senior Tutor (part-time), School of Law, University of Aberdeen, since 2000; b. 15.2.44, Edinburgh; m., Isobel Ross Mackie; 2 s.; 1 d. Educ. Edinburgh Academy; Edinburgh University. Partner, Macdonalds Sergeants, Solicitors, East Kilbride and Glasgow, 1971-92; Secretary: East Kilbride Chamber of Commerce, 1971-86, East Kilbride Chamber of Trade, 1971-92; Board Member, East Kilbride Development Corporation, 1979-84; Secretary, Pilgrim Legal Users' Group, 1985-92; Captain, East Kilbride Golf Club, 1979; Chairman, Strathaven Academy School Board, 1991-92; President, East Kilbride Burns Club, 1989-91; Captain, Inchmarlo Golf Club (Banchory), 1997-99; President, Deeside Musical Society, 1998-2000 and 2007-08; Burgess of Guild, City of Aberdeen. Recreations: golf; sailing; gardening. Address: (h.) Belnies, Strachan, Banchory, Aberdeenshire AB31 6LU; T.-01330 850249.

McMillan, Stuart, MBA, BA (Hons). MSP (SNP), West of Scotland, since 2007; b. 6.5.72, Barrow-in-Furness; m., Alexandra; 1 d. Educ. Port Glasgow High School; University of Abertay, Dundee. Supply Analyst, IBM UK Ltd., Greenock, 1998-2000; Parliamentary Researcher, SNP Whips Office, Westminster, London, 2000-03; Office Manager, Bruce McFee MSP, Scottish Parliament, 2003-07. Recreations: play bagpipes; sport; travel. Address: (b.) Scottish Parliament, Edinburgh EH99 1SP; e-mail: stuart.mcmillan.msp@scottish.parliament.uk; Constituency Office: Parliamentary Office, 14 William Street, Paisley PA1 2LZ; T.-0141 889 9519.

McMillan, Professor Thomas Murray, BSc, MAppSci, PhD, FBPsS. Professor of Clinical Neuropsychology, Glasgow University, since 1999; Adviser to Greater Glasgow Health Board, since 1999; b. 7.3.54, Prestwick; m., Sarah Louise Wilson; 1 d. Educ. Prestwick High School; Ayr Academy; Aberdeen University; London University; Glasgow University. Lecturer in Clinical Psychology, Institute of Psychiatry, London; Head of Clinical Neuropsychology, St George's Healthcare, London; Professor of Clinical Psychology, Surrey University. Publications include: Handbook of Neurological Rehabilitation; Neurobehavioural Disability and Social Handicap. Recreations: cross-country running. Address: (b.) Department of Psychological Medicine, Gartnavel Royal Hospital, Glasgow, G12 0XH; T.-0141-211 0694.

McMillan, William Alister, BL. Solicitor, since 1955; b. 19.1.34, Ayr; m., Elizabeth Anne; 3 d. Educ. Strathallan; Glasgow University. Clerk of the Peace, County of Ayr, 1974-75; Honorary Sheriff, Ayr; Hon. Governor, Strathallan School. Recreations: sailing; golf; philately. Address: (h.) Afton Lodge, Mossblown, by Ayr; T.-01292 520 710.

Macmillan Douglas, Angus William, OBE, BA. Former Director, National Support Services, NHS Scotland; National Director, Scottish Blood Transfusion Service, 1997-2004; b. 18.11.46, Edinburgh; m., Rosemary-Jane Meynell; 2 d. Educ. Blairmore School; Wellington College; Ealing Business School; INSEAD. Assistant UK Co-ordinator, British Petroleum International, 1981-84; Business Manager, BP Information Systems, 1984-85; European Developments Manager, BP Gas International, 1985-88; Managing Director, East Africa Trading, British Petroleum, 1988-91; Head of Political Affairs, British Petroleum Group, 1991-96. Representative, East African Trade Organisation, 1988-91; Member, Energy Policy Committee, CBI, 1992-96; Member, Management Committee, Industry and Parliament Trust, 1992-96; Director, European Blood Alliance, 1998-2007; Chairman, Angus Conservative Association, since 2005; Chairman, UK Forum of Blood Services, 2001-04; Member, Royal Company of Archers (Queen's Bodyguard for Scotland); Governor, Kilgraston School, 1999-2005; Trustee, Transfusion Medicine, Education and Research Foundation; Member, Scottish Conservative Policy Advisory Group; Member, Executive Board, Scottish Conservative Party, since 2007; Member, Court, Abertay University; set up own management consultancy. Recreations: family; tennis; walking. Address: (b.) Brigton, Douglastown, by Forfar DD8 1TP; T.-01307-820-215.

McMullan, Pat. Chairman, Apex Scotland. Address: (b.) 9 Great Stuart Street, Edinburgh EH3 7TP.

McMurdo, Ian David, BSc (Chem). Director, Community Learning, Scotland, since 2000; Management Consultant; former Director of Education and Cultural Services, West Dunbartonshire Council; b. 28.5.49, Irvine; m., Agnes McMurdo; 1 s.; 1 d. Educ. Cumnock Academy; Strathclyde University. Teacher/Assistant Principal Teacher, Chemistry; Principal Teacher, Chemistry; Assistant Head Teacher; PA, Chairman Education Committee, Strathclyde Regional Council; Education Officer, Dumbarton then Ayr Division, Strathclyde Regional Council; Director of Education; Member, ADES; Advisor, COSLA. Recreations: golf; hill walking; travelling; reading Burns. Address: (h.) 33 Hoyle Crescent, Cumnock, Ayrshire, KA18 1RX; T.-01290 421412; e-mail: ian.mcmurdo@west-dunbarton.gov.uk

McMurdo, Professor Marion Elizabeth Taylor, MBChB, MD, FRCPEdin, FRCPGlas, FRCPLond, CBiol, FIBiol. Professor of Ageing and Health, University of Dundee, since 1997; Honorary Consultant, Medicine for the Elderly, Tayside Primary Care Trust, since 1997; b. 16.11.55, Glasgow; m., Dr. Grant L. Hutchison. Educ. Marr College, Troon; University of Dundee. Deputy Medical Director, Drug Development (Scotland) Ltd., 1984-86; Lecturer in Geriatric Medicine, University of Dundee, 1986-88, Senior Lecturer/Reader in Ageing and Health; External Tutor to International Institute on Ageing, since 1997; British Geriatrics Society Regional Training Adviser, since 1993. Recreations: golf; swimming; hill-walking; photography. Address: Department of Medicine, Ninewells Hospital and Medical School, Dundee DD1 9SY; T.-01382 632436.

McMurray, Professor John J.V., BSc (Hons), MBChB (Hons), MD, FRCP (Edin and Glas), FESC, FACC, FAHA. Professor of Medical Cardiology, Glasgow University, since 1999; Honorary Consultant Cardiologist; Western Infirmary, Glasgow, since 1995; b. 17.12.58, Enniskillen, Co. Fermanagh; m., Christine; 5 s.; 1 d. Educ. St Patrick's College, Knock, Belfast; Manchester University. Consultant Cardiologist, Western General Hospital, Edinburgh, 1993-95.

Publications: 350 medical and scientific papers; 15 books. Recreations: reading; travelling; Celtic FC. Address: (b.) Department of Cardiology, Western Infirmary, Glasgow G11 6NT; T.-0141-211 6311 and T.-0141 330 3479; Fax: 0141 330 6955.

Macnab of Macnab, Hon. Diana Mary Anstruther-Gray, DL. Honorary Vice President, Scotland's Gardens Scheme, since 1991 (Chairman, 1983-91); Deputy Lieutenant, Fife, since 1992; b. 6.6.36, Edinburgh; m., J.C. Macnab of Macnab (qv); 2 s.; 2 d. Member, Executive Committee, National Trust for Scotland, 1991-96; Chairman, East Fife Members' Centre, National Trust for Scotland, 1995-98. Address: (h.) Leuchars Castle Farmhouse, Leuchars, St. Andrews KY16 0EY; T.-01334 838777.

Macnab of Macnab, James Charles — The Macnab. 23rd Chief, Clan Macnab; Senior Consultant, Hill Samuel Investment Services Ltd., 1982-92, now retired; b. 14.4.26, London; m., Hon. Diana Mary Anstruther-Gray (see Hon. Mrs. Macnab of Macnab); 2 s.; 2 d. Educ. Radley College; Ashbury College, Ottawa. Served, RAF and Scots Guards, 1944-45; Lt., Seaforth Highlanders, 1945-48; Assistant Superintendant and Deputy Superintendant, Federation of Malaya Police Force, 1948-57; Captain, Seaforth Highlanders (TA), 1960-64; managed family estate and farms, 1957-82; District Councillor, Perth, 1961-64; County Councillor, Perth and Kinross Joint County Council, 1964-75; JP, 1968-86; Member: Central Regional Council, 1978-82, Queen's Bodyguard for Scotland (Royal Company of Archers). Address: (h.) Leuchars Castle Farmhouse, Leuchars, St. Andrews KY16 0EY; T.-01334 838777.

McNab, Douglas Gordon, BA, BD (Hons). Minister, Girvan: North Parish Church, since 1999; b. 3.7.55, Glasgow; m., Lorraine; 2 s. Educ. The Royal High School, Edinburgh; University of Edinburgh. Senior Teacher, Craigshill High School, Livingston, 1978-92 (promoted to Principal Teacher of History); School Teacher, Inveralmond Community High School, Livingston, 1992-94 (P.T. History); Trained for the Ministry of Church of Scotland at New College, Edinburgh, 1994-97; Probationer Minister at Kirk of Calder, Midcalder, 1997-99. Recreations: sport; played football at part-time professional senior level; golf; walking; swimming. Address: 38, The Avenue, Girvan KA26 9DS; T.-01465-713203.
E-mail: dougmcnab@aol.com

Macnair, Charles Neville, QC, LLB. Queen's Counsel, since 2002; Sheriff (floating), Tayside Central and Fife at Dunfermline, since 2006; b. 18.3.55, London; m., Patricia Anne Dinning; 2 d. Educ. Bryanston School; Aberdeen University. Served, Queen's Own Highlanders, 1977-80 (2nd Lieutenant, Lieutenant, then Captain); Solicitor, 1982-87; admitted, Faculty of Advocates, 1988; Part time Sheriff, 2005-06. Recreations: sailing; reading. Address: Sheriff Court House, 1/6 Carnegie Drive, Dunfermline KY12 7HJ.

Macnair, Terence Crawford, LLB, NP. Solicitor, since 1967 (now retired); Honorary Sheriff, North Strathclyde, since 1988; b. 16.12.42, Kingston, Jamaica; m., Ishbel Ross Hunter; 1 s. Educ. High School of Glasgow; Glasgow University. Town Clerk, Lochgilphead, 1970-75; Partner, MacArthur Stewart & Orr, 1970-81; Senior Partner, MacArthur Stewart, 1981-2003, Consultant, since 2003. Past President, Rotary Club of Oban. Recreations: tennis; squash; golf; curling; bridge; music. Address: (b.) Boswell House, Oban; T.-01631 562215.

Macnaughton, Rev. (Gordon) Fraser (Hay), MA, BD, DipCPC. Minister, St. Magnus Cathedral, Kirkwall, Orkney, since 2002; b. 27.3.58, Glasgow; m., Carole; 2 d. Educ. Glasgow Academy; Glasgow University; Edinburgh University. Assistant, Newlands South Church, Glasgow, 1981-85; Minister, Fenwick Parish Church, 1985-91; Chaplain, Dundee University, 1991-97; Parish Minister, Killermont Parish Church, Bearsden, 1997-2002. Coach to Scottish Universities Rugby XV, 1995-97. Recreations: rugby; bird-watching; conservation issues; history; volleyball; cycling; seafishing. Address: (h.) Cathedral Manse, Berstane Road, Kirkwall, Orkney KW15 1NA; T.-01856 873312.

McNaughton, James Leslie, LLB. Consultant with Stewart and Watson, Solicitors, Banff, since 2000; Safeguarder with Aberdeenshire Council, since 1996; Honorary Sheriff at Banff, since 2005; b. 8.12.43, Aberdeen; m., Pauline nee Booth; 1 s.; 1 d. Educ. Robert Gordon's College, Aberdeen; Aberdeen University. Assistant, then Partner with Stewart and Watson, Solicitors, Banff, Turriff and elsewhere. Past President: Rotary Club of Banff, Society of Solicitors of Banffshire, Banff Town and County Club. Recreations: golf; reading; walking; good food and wine. Address: (h.) 1 George Street, Banff, Aberdeenshire AB45 1HS; T.-01261-812349; e-mail: j.jim@btinternet.com

McNaughton, John Ewen, OBE, JP, FRAgS. Member, Scottish Beef Council, since 1997; Chairman, Forth Valley Countryside Initiative, 1999-2003; b. 28.5.33, Edinburgh; m., Jananne Ogilvie Honeyman; 2 s.; 2 d. Educ. Cargilfield; Loretto. Born and bred a hill sheep farmer; after a short spell in America, began farming at Inverlochlarig with father; served on Council, NFU of Scotland; Chairman, Scotch Quality Beef & Lamb Association, 1981-97; Vice President, Royal Highland and Agricultural Society of Scotland, 1997-98; Member: British Wool Marketing Board, 1975-2000, Panel of Agricultural Arbiters, 1973-98, Red Deer Commission, 1975-92; Elder, Church of Scotland. Recreations: yachting; stalking. Address: Inverlochlarig, Balquhidder, Lochearnhead, Perthshire FK19 8PH; T.-01877 384 232; e-mail: braes@lochlarig.freeserve.co.uk

Macnaughton, Professor Sir Malcolm Campbell, MD, LLD, FRCPGlas, FRCOG, FFFP, FRSE, FSLCOG (Hon.), FACOG (Hon.), FRCA (Hon.), FRACOG (Hon.). Vice President, Royal College of Midwives; Professor of Obstetrics and Gynaecology, Glasgow University, 1970-90; b. 4.4.25, Glasgow; m., Margaret-Ann Galt; 2 s.; 3 d. Educ. Glasgow Academy; Glasgow University. RAMC, 1949-51; Lecturer in Obstetrics and Gynaecology, Aberdeen University, 1957-61; Senior Lecturer, St. Andrews University, 1961-66; Consultant, Eastern Regional, 1966-70. Member: Chief Scientist Committee, SHHD, Biomedical Research Committee and Health Service Research Committee, SHHD, MRC Grant Committee and Cell Systems Board, MRC, Scientific Committee, Hospital Recognition Committee, RCOG; President: RCOG, 1984-87, British Fertility Society, 1993-95; Chairman: Scottish Perinatal Mortality Advisory Group, SCOTMEG Working Party on Accident and Emergency Services in Scotland. Recreations: walking; fishing. Address: (h.) 9 Glenburn Road, Bearsden, Glasgow GL1 4PT; T.-0141-942-1909.

McNay, W. Gordon, OBE, DL, BL; b. 11.12.25, Wishaw; m., Margaret C. MacKay. Educ. Wishaw High School; Glasgow University. Depute Town Clerk, Burgh of Airdrie, 1952-53; Senior Depute Town Clerk, Burgh of Motherwell and Wishaw, 1953-63; Town Clerk, Burgh of East Kilbride, 1963-75; Chief Executive, East Kilbride District Council, 1975-88. Deputy Lieutenant, Lanarkshire (retired List); Honorary Freeman, East Kilbride District. Recreations: golf; photography; philately. Address: (h.) Solbakken, 17 Kibblestane Place, Strathaven ML10 6EL; T.-01357 520889.

MacNeacail, Aonghas. Writer (poetry, journalism, scriptwriting for TV, film and radio, librettoes); b. 7.6.42, Uig, Isle of Skye; m., Gerda Stevenson (qv); 1 s. Educ. Portree High School; Glasgow University. Writing fellowships: Sabhal Mor Ostaig, 1977-79, An Comunn

Gaidhealach, 1979-81, Ross and Cromarty District Council, 1988-90, Glasgow and Strathclyde Universities, 1993-95, Sabhal Mor Ostaig, 1995-98; tours to Ireland, Germany, North America, Japan, Israel, etc.; opera librettoes for Alasdair Nicolson and William Sweeney; songs for Capercaillie, Phil Cunningham; art with Simon Fraser, Kenny Munro, Diane MacLean; short-listed, Paul Hamlyn Foundation Award for Poets, 1997; Stakis Award, Scottish Writer of the Year, 1997. Publications: books: An Seachnadh, 1986; Rock-Water, 1990; Oideachadh Ceart, 1996; poems widely anthologised. Recreations: newsprint; red wine; thinking about walking.

McNee, Sir David Blackstock, Kt, QPM, FBIM, FRSA, KStJ. Non-Executive Director and Adviser to a number of public limited companies; b. 23.3.25; m., 1, Isabella Clayton Hopkins (deceased); 1 d.; 2, Lilian Bissland Campbell Bogie. Educ. Woodside Senior Secondary School, Glasgow. Joined City of Glasgow Police, 1946; Deputy Chief Constable, Dunbartonshire Constabulary, 1968; Chief Constable: City of Glasgow Police, 1971-75, Strathclyde Police, 1975-77; Commissioner, Metropolitan Police, 1977-82. Honorary Vice-President, Boys' Brigade, since 1980; Vice-President, London Federation of Boys Clubs, since 1982; Patron, Scottish Motor Neurone Association, 1982-97; President, National Bible Society of Scotland, 1983-96; Freeman, City of London, 1977; President, Glasgow City Committee, Cancer Relief, 1987-92. Recreations: fishing; golf; music.

MacNee, Professor William, MB, ChB, MD(Hons), FRCP(Glas), FRCP(Edin). Professor of Respiratory and Environmental Medicine, Edinburgh University; Visiting Professor, Department of Biological Sciences, Napier University; Honorary Consultant Physician, Lothian Health Board, since 1987; Clinical Director, Respiratory Medicine Unit, 1992-98; Clinical Director, Respiratory Medicine, Lothian University Hospitals NHS Trust, 1998-2005; b. 18.12.50, Glasgow; m., Edna Marina Kingsley; 1 s.; 1 d. Educ. Coatbridge High School; Glasgow University. House Physician/House Surgeon, Glasgow and Paisley, 1975-76; SHO/Registrar in Medicine, Western Infirmary/Gartnavel Hospitals, Glasgow, 1976-79; Registrar in Respiratory Medicine, City Hospital, Edinburgh, 1979-80; MRC Research Fellow/Honorary Registrar, Department of Respiratory Medicine, Royal Infirmary, Edinburgh, 1980-82; Lecturer, Department of Respiratory Medicine, City Hospital, Edinburgh, 1982-83; Senior Registrar, Respiratory Medicine/Medicine, Lothian Health Board, 1983-87; MRC Research Fellow, University of British Columbia, Vancouver, 1985-86; Senior Lecturer in Respiratory Medicine, 1987-93; Reader in Medicine, Edinburgh University, 1993-97; Head, Cardiovascular-Thoracic Service, Royal Infirmary of Edinburgh, 1998-99. Council Member, Scottish Thoracic Society, 1990-93; Hon. Secretary, British Lung Foundation (Scotland); Chairman, British Lung Foundation Scientific Committee, 1997-2000; Chairman, European Respiratory Society Scientific Programme Committee, 1999-2003; Congress Chair, European Respiratory Society, 2003-04; President, European Respiratory Society, 2006-07; Council Member, Royal College of Physicians of Edinburgh, since 2001; Vice President, British Lung Foundation, since 2005. Publications: scientific papers, reviews and books on respiratory medicine topics. Recreations: music; sport. Address: (b.) ELEGI Colt Research, MRC/uoE Centre for Inflammation Research, Level 2, The Queen's Medical Research Institute, 47 Little France Crescent, Edinburgh EH16 4TJ; T.-0131 242 6583; e-mail: w.macnee@ed.ac.uk

Macneil of Barra, Ian Roderick, BA, LLB, FSA Scot. Wigmore Professor of Law, Northwestern University, Chicago, 1980-99, Professor Emeritus, since 1999; b.

20.6.29, New York City; m., Nancy C. Wilson; 2 s.; 1 d. Educ. Scarborough School; University of Vermont; Harvard University. Lt., AUS, 1951-53; Commissioned Officer, USAR, 1950-67; practised law, 1956-59; Member, Cornell Law School Faculty, 1959-72, 1974-80; Visiting Professor, University College, Dar es Salaam, 1965-67, Duke Law School, 1971-72; Professor of Law and Member, Centre for Advanced Studies, Virginia University, 1972-74; Visiting Fellow, Centre for Socio-Legal Studies, Wolfson College, Oxford, 1979, and Edinburgh University Faculty of Law, 1979, 1987; Visiting Professor, Harvard University, 1988-89; Guggenheim Fellow, 1978-79; Fellow, American Academy of Arts and Sciences. Member, Standing Council of Scottish Chiefs; author of numerous books and articles. Recreations: walking; reading; historical studies. Seat: Kisimul Castle, Isle of Barra. Address: (h.) 95/6 Grange Loan, Edinburgh EH9 2ED; T.-0131-667 6068.

MacNeil, Angus. MP (SNP), Western Isles, since 2005. Address: (b.) House of Commons, London SW1A 0AA.

McNeil, Duncan. MSP (Labour), Greenock and Inverclyde, since 1999. Former shipyard worker and union organiser. Address: (b.) Scottish Parliament, Edinburgh EH99 1SP.

McNeil, Lynne. Editor, Life and Work, since 2002; b. 19.12.67, Dunfermline; m., Charles Craig Robin McNeil. Educ. Inverkeithing High School; Napier College, Edinburgh. East Lothian Courier, 1986-89; United News Service, Edinburgh, 1989-94; Telegraph and Argus, Bradford, 1994; Railtrack North East, 1994; Greenock Telegraph, 1994-95; The Herald, 1995-2002. Recreations: reading; swimming. Address: (b.) 121 George Street, Edinburgh EH2 4YN; T.-0131 225 5722.

McNeil, Neil, MB, ChB, DPH, DPA, FFCM, FFPHM, MREHIS. Consultant in Public Health Medicine/Director of Community Medicine/Unit Medical Officer/District Medical Officer, Lanarkshire Health Board, 1976-92; Honorary Senior Clinical Lecturer/Honorary Clinical Lecturer, Department of Public Health, Glasgow University, 1976-92; b. 4.6.31, Glasgow; m., Florence Ward Butterworth; 2 s.; 1 d. Educ. Govan High School; Glasgow University. SHO, Senior Resident, House Physician and House Surgeon, Western Infirmary, Glasgow, 1956-58; Hall Fellow, Glasgow University, 1958-60; Registrar, Western Infirmary, Glasgow, 1960-61; Divisional Medical Officer of Health, City of Glasgow, 1962-65; Principal Lecturer in Health Education and Medical Officer, Jordanhill College, Glasgow, 1965-68; Medical Officer of Health, North-East Hampshire, and Honorary Consultant, Aldershot, 1968-69; Medical Officer, Scottish Home and Health Department, 1969-73; Honorary Lecturer, Departments of Materia Medica and Community Medicine, Glasgow University, 1973-74; Consultant Epidemiologist, Communicable Diseases (Scotland) Unit, Ruchill Hospital, 1973-74; Senior Medical Officer, Scottish Home and Health Department, 1974-76. Dr. MacKinlay Prize in Public Health and Preventive Medicine, Glasgow University, 1962. Publications on community medicine, environmental medicine, public health, immunisation and infectious disease control. Recreations: tennis; photography; natural history; Gaelic language and culture; Scottish history and archaeology. Address: (h.) Claddach, 25 Waterfoot Road, Newton Mearns, Glasgow G77 5RU.

Macneill, Sheriff Deirdre, LLB, QC. Sheriff, Glasgow and Strathkelvin at Glasgow, since 1999; b. 4.6.54, Aberdeen; 1 s. Educ. St. Margaret School for Girls, Aberdeen; Aberdeen University. Solicitor, 1974-80; Faculty of Advocates, 1981-99; QC, 1994.

MacNeill, Dugald Brown, BSc, FRSC. Principal, College of Piping, 1996-2000; Hon. Secretary, Piobaireachd Society, since 1996; Hon. Secretary, College of Piping, since 1992, Chairman, since 1996; b. 17.11.30; m., Helen McKellar; 2 s.; 1 d. Educ. Ardrishaig School; Hyndland School; Glasgow University. Member/Founder Pupil, College of Piping, 1944. Recreations: bagpipe and its music; hill climbing. Address: (h.) 20 Craigleith View, Edinburgh EH4 3JZ; T.-0131-346 1155.

McNeill, James Walker, QC. Advocate, since 1978; a Judge of the Courts of Appeal of Jersey and Guernsey, since 2005; b. 16.2.52, Dunoon; m., Katherine Lawrence McDowall; 2 s.; 1 d. Educ. Dunoon Grammar School; Sidney Sussex College, Cambridge; Edinburgh University. QC, 1991; Standing Junior Counsel, Department of Transport in Scotland, 1984-88, Inland Revenue, 1988-91. Member of Council, Commonwealth Law Association, since 2005; Session Clerk, St. Andrew's and St. George's Parish Church, Edinburgh, 1999-2003; Member of Board, Scottish International Piano Competition. Recreations: music; hill-walking; golf; sailing; travel. Address: (b.) Advocates' Library, Parliament House, Edinburgh EH1 1RF; T.-0131-226 5071.

McNeill, Pauline, LLB. MSP (Lab), Glasgow Kelvin, since 1999; b. 12.9.62, Paisley; m., William Joseph Cahill. Educ. Our Lady's High School, Cumbernauld; Strathclyde University. President, National Union of Students (Scotland), 1986-88; Regional Organiser, GMB, 1988-99. Recreations: music; films; guitar; singing. Address: (b.) 1274 Argyle Street, Glasgow G3 8AA; T.-0141-589 7120; e-mail: pauline.mcneill.msp@ scottish.parliament.uk

McNeill, Sheriff Peter Grant Brass, PhD, MA (Hons), LLB, QC. Formerly Sheriff of Lothian and Borders at Edinburgh; Writer; b. 3.3.29, Glasgow; m., Matilda Farquhar Rose; 1 s.; 3 d. Educ. Hillhead High School, Glasgow; Morrison's Academy, Crieff; Glasgow University. Law apprentice, Biggart Lumsden & Co., Glasgow, 1952-55; Carnegie Fellowship, 1955; Faulds Fellowship, 1956-59; Scottish Bar, 1956; Honorary Sheriff Substitute of Lanarkshire, and of Stirling, Clackmannan and Dumbarton, 1962; Standing Junior Counsel to Scottish Development Department (Highways), 1964; Advocate Depute, 1964; Sheriff of Lanarkshire, subsequently of Glasgow and Strathkelvin, at Glasgow, 1965-82; Sheriff of Lothian and Borders at Edinburgh, 1982-98, retired; Member, Scottish Records Advisory Council, 1989-94; Temporary Sheriff, 1996-98; President, Sheriffs' Association, 1982-85; Chairman: Council, Stair Society, 1990-98, Scottish Legal History Group, 1990-97, Council, Scottish National Dictionary Association Ltd., 1987-2001, Chairman, 1997-2001; Trustee, The Scottish Medievalists: the Colloquium for Scottish and Medieval Studies, 2007; Vice President, Stair Society, 2007. Publications: Balfour's Practicks (Editor), 1962-63; An Historical Atlas of Scotland c. 400 - c. 1600 (Co-Editor), 1975; Adoption of Children in Scotland, 1982, 3rd ed., 1998; Atlas of Scottish History to 1707 (Co-Editor), 1996. Recreations: legal history; gardening; book-binding. Address: (h.) 31 Queensferry Road, Edinburgh EH4 3HB.

McNeilly, Professor Alan S., BSc, PhD, DSc, FRSE. Deputy Director, MRC Human Reproductive Sciences Unit, Edinburgh, since 1998, Acting Director, 1996-98; Honorary Professor, University of Edinburgh, since 1994; b. 10.2.47, Birmingham; m., Judy; 1 s.; 3 d. Educ. Handsworth Grammar School, Birmingham; Nottingham University; Reading University; Edinburgh University. Research

Lecturer, Department of Reproductive Medicine, St. Bartholomew's Hospital, London, 1971-75; Visiting Professor, University of Manitoba, Canada, 1975-76; Research Scientist, MRC Reproductive Biology Unit, Edinburgh, since 1976, Deputy Director, since 1986. Member, Home Office APC, 1998-2006; Chairman, Society for Reproduction and Fertility, 1999-2005. Society for Endocrinology Dale Medallist, 2008; Society for Reproduction and Fertility Marshall Medallist, 2008. Recreations: walking; golf; orienteering; bee-keeping; gardening. Address: (b.) MRC, HRSU, The Queen's Medical Research Institute, 47 Little France Crescent, Edinburgh EH16 4TJ; T.-0131-242 6162; e-mail: a.mcneilly@hrsu.mrc.ac.uk

Macnicol, Malcolm Fraser, MBChB, BSc (Hons), FRCS, MCh, FRCP, FRCSEd (Orth), DipSportsMed. Consultant Orthopaedic Surgeon, Children and Adults, since 1979; Senior Orthopaedic Lecturer, Edinburgh University, 1979-2005; b. 18.3.43; m., Anne Morag; 2 s.; 1 d. Educ. Royal High School, Edinburgh; Edinburgh University. Research Fellow, Stanford and Harvard Universities; Lecturer in Orthopaedic Surgery, Edinburgh, 1976-78; Senior Lecturer, Perth, W. Australia, 1978-79; UK European Travelling Orthopaedic Fellow, 1981; ABC Travelling Fellow, 1982; Member, Council of Management, Journal of Bone and Joint Surgery, 1998-2002; Treasurer, Royal College of Surgeons, Edinburgh, 1987-90; President, British Orthopaedic Association, 2001-2002; Chairman, BOA Medicolegal Subcommittee, 1999-2003; Honorary Medical Adviser to the Scottish Rugby Union, since 2004. Publications: six books; 156 professional papers. Recreations: painting; tennis. Address: (h.) Redhouse, 1 South Gillsland Road, Edinburgh EH10 5DE; T.-0131-447 9104; (b.) 0131 536 1000.

McNicoll, Emeritus Professor Iain Hugh, BA, PhD, FRSA. Professorial Fellow, IRD (Information Resources Directorate), Strathclyde University, since 2002; Professor of Applied Economics, Strathclyde University, 1987-2003; b. 24.6.51, Glasgow; m. Educ. St. Mungo's Academy, Glasgow; Stirling University. Leverhulme Research Fellow, Industrial Science, Stirling University, 1974-76; Lecturer, Business Studies, Edinburgh University, 1976-79; Fellow/Senior Fellow, Director of Research, Acting Director/Director, Fraser of Allander Institute, 1979-89; ONS Preferred Supplier on National Statistics Advice, since 2001. Member, numerous UK government committees and advisory groups, since 1980; past visiting professorships, Toulouse Business School and University of Wittswattersrand; international assignments for World Bank, UNDP, ODA and others. Publications: two books; 20 monographs; 60 academic journal and book articles; over 200 research reports. Recreations: hi-fi; aquaria; astronomy. Address: (b.) Information Resources Directorate, Strathclyde University, 155 George Street, Glasgow G1 1RD; T.-0141 548 3254.

Macniven, Duncan, TD, MA, MLitt. Registrar General for Scotland, since 2003; b. 1.12.50, Edinburgh; m., Valerie; 2 d. Educ. Melville College, Edinburgh; Aberdeen University. Scottish Office, 1973-99 (Deputy Director, Historic Scotland, 1991-95, Head of Police Division, 1995-97, Head of Police, Fire and Emergency Planning Group, 1997-99); Forestry Commission, 1999-2003 (Commissioner and Head of Corporate Services). Recreations: hill-walking; ski-ing; Scottish history; local church. Address: (b.) New Register House, West Register Street, Edinburgh EH1 3YT; T.-0131 314 4435.

Macniven, Valerie Margaret, MA (Hons). Director of Criminal Justice, Scottish Government, since 2005; b. 14.1.51, Perth; m., Duncan Macniven (qv); 2 d. Educ. Aberdeen High School for Girls; Edinburgh University. Scottish Office, 1973-82 and 1987-99; Head of Civil and

International Justice Group, Scottish Executive Justice Department, 2000-05. Elder, Church of Scotland. Recreations: skiing; tennis; travel. Address: (b.) St. Andrew's House, Edinburgh EH1 3DG; T.-0131-244 8491; e-mail: valerie.macniven@ scotland.gsi.gov.uk

McNulty, Des, BA. MSP (Labour), Clydebank and Milngavie, since 1999; Shadow Environment Minister; b. 28.7.52, Stockport; m.; 2 s. Educ. St. Bede's College Manchester; University of York; University of Glasgow. Senior Lecturer in Sociology, Glasgow Caledonian University; Director of Strategic Planning, Glasgow Caledonian University; Member, Strathclyde Regional Council, 1990-96; Member, Glasgow City Council, 1995-99; Member of Court, University of Glasgow, 1994-99; Assessor to Board, Scottish Opera, 1996-99; Chair, Glasgow Healthy City Partnership, 1995-99; Chair, Glasgow 1999 Festival of Architecture and Design; Non Executive Director, Greater Glasgow Health Board, 1998-99; Board Member, The Wise Group. Address: The Scottish Parliament, Edinburgh EH99 1SP; T.-0131-348 5918; Constituency Office, Clydebank Central Library, Dumbarton Road, Clydebank G81 1XH; T.-0141-952 7711.

McOwan, Rennie, DUniv, FSA Scot. Writer and Broadcaster; b. Stirling; m., Agnes Mooney; 3 s.; 1 d. Educ. Alva Academy. Reporter, Stirling Journal; Sub-Editor, Kemsley Newspapers, Daily Record; Public Relations, Roman Catholic Church; Sub-Editor, Features Writer, Scotsman Publications; Assistant Publicity Secretary, National Trust for Scotland; Scottish Book Trust Lecturer under Writers in Schools and Writers in Public schemes; former Guest Lecturer, Film and Media Studies, Stirling University; Contributor to newspapers and magazines in Britain and overseas; radio and TV scripts and research; Outdoor Writers Guild Golden Eagle award for access campaigning and writing about Scottish subjects, 1997; Provost of Stirling's Civic Award (Arts and Culture), 1998; Honorary Doctorate, University of Stirling, 1996. Publications: Light on Dumyat; The White Stag Adventure; The Day the Mountain Moved; Jewels On The Move; Robert Burns for Beginners; St. Andrew for Beginners; Magic Mountains; Walks in the Trossachs and the Rob Roy Country; The Green Hills; Kilchurn Castle: a history; Loch Lomond and The Trossachs; contributed to: Walking in Scotland; Poetry of the Scottish Hills; Speak to the Hills; Wild Walks; The Story of Scotland; Discover Scotland; Great Walks, Scotland; Classic Coastal Walks of Britain; On Foot Through History. Recreations: mountaineering; Scottish history and literature. Address: 7 Williamfield Avenue, Stirling FK7 9AH; T.-01786 461316; e-mail: mcowan@onetel.net

Macphail, The Hon Lord (Iain Duncan Macphail), FRSE. Senator of the College of Justice, since 2005; b. 24.1.38; m., Rosslyn Graham Lillias Hewitt; 1 s.; 1 d. Educ. George Watson's College; Edinburgh University (MA Hons); Glasgow University (LLB). Admitted Faculty of Advocates, 1963; practice, Scottish Bar, 1963-73; Faulds Fellow in Law, Glasgow University, 1963-65; Lecturer in Evidence and Procedure, Strathclyde University, 1968-69, Edinburgh University, 1969-72; Standing Junior Counsel to Scottish Home and Health Department and Department of Health and Social Security, 1971-73; Extra Advocate-Depute, 1973; Sheriff of Glasgow and Strathkelvin (formerly Lanarkshire), 1973-81; Sheriff of Tayside, Central and Fife at Dunfermline and Alloa, 1981-82; Sheriff of Lothian and Borders at Linlithgow, 1982-88, at Edinburgh, 1988-89, 1995-2002; Sheriff Principal of Lothian and Borders and Sheriff of Chancery, 2002-05. Member, Scottish Law Commission, 1990-94; Arthur Goodhart Professor in Legal Science, Cambridge University, 2001-02; Chairman, Scottish Association for the Study of Delinquency, 1978-81; Chairman, Sheriff Court Rules Council, 2003-05; QC, 1990; Hon. LLD, Edinburgh, 1992; FRSE, 2005. Publications: Evidence, 1987; Sheriff

Court Practice, 1988. Address: (b.) Parliament House, 11 Parliament Square, Edinburgh EH1 1RQ; T.-0131 225 2595.

McPhee, George, MBE, BMus, FRCO, DipMusEd, RSAM, Hon. FRSCM, Hon. FGCM. Visiting Professor of Organ, St. Andrews University; Chairman, Paisley International Organ Festival; Organist and Master of the Choristers, Paisley Abbey, since 1963; b. 10.11.37, Glasgow; m., Margaret Ann Scotland; 1 s.; 2 d. Educ. Woodside Senior Secondary School, Glasgow; Royal Scottish Academy of Music and Drama; Edinburgh University. Studied organ with Herrick Bunney and Fernando Germani; Assistant Organist, St. Giles' Cathedral, 1959-63; joined staff, RSAMD, 1963; Conductor, Scottish Chamber Choir, 1971-75; Conductor, Kilmarnock and District Choral Union, 1975-84; since 1971, has completed 12 recital tours of the United States and Canada; has been both Soloist and Conductor with Scottish National Orchestra; numerous recordings and broadcasts; has taken part in numerous music festivals as Soloist; Adjudicator; Examiner, Associated Board, Royal Schools of Music; Special Commissioner, Royal School of Church Music; President, Incorporated Society of Musicians, 1999-2000; Silver Medal, Worshipful Company of Musicians; Honorary Doctorate, University of Paisley; Vice President, Royal College of Organists. Recreations: golf; walking. Address: (h.) 17 Main Road, Castlehead, Paisley PA2 6AJ; T.-0141-889 3528; e-mail: profmcphee@aol.com

McPhee, Susan Anne, LLB, BA, NP. Head of Social Policy and Public Affairs of Citizens Advice Scotland, since 1998; Member of Scottish Legal Aid Board, since 2005; b. 3.3.59, Edinburgh; m., Gordon Annand; 2 s. Educ. James Gillespie's High School; Aberdeen University; Open University. Edinburgh City Council, 1979-81; Solicitor with Messrs Lindsay and Kirk, Advocates in Aberdeen, 1981-90; Legal Services Adviser, Citizens Advice Scotland, 1990-98. Member of Scottish Parliament Working Group on Replacement for Poinding and Warrant Sales; Member of Scottish Executive Debt Relief Working Group; Member of Cross Party Cross Parliamentary Group on Tackling Debt. Recreations: music; films; junk jewellery. Address: (b.) 2 Powderhall Road, Edinburgh EH7 4GB; T.-0131 550 1000; e-mail: susan.mcphee@cas.org.uk

Macpherson of Biallid, Sir (Ronald) Thomas Stewart, kt (1992), CBE (1967), MC (and 2 bars), TD, DL, Chev de La Legion d'Honneur, Croix de Guerre, FRSA, FIM; b. 4.10.20. Educ. Cargilfield, Fettes; Trinity College, Oxford; m., Jean; 2 s.; 1 d. Served in World War 2, 1939-43; current directorships: Annington Holdings plc (Chairman), since 1996, Boustead PLC (Chairman), since 1986, Deutsche Annington Immobilien GmbH, since 2001, Emerging Markets Advisory Corporation Ltd (Chairman), since 2006, Entuity Ltd., (Chairman), since 2000, Fitzwilton (UK) PLC, since 1990, Nexus Investments PCC (Chairman), since 2001; Advisory Board, Capgemini Kanbay (UK) Ltd. (Chairman), since 2006; Terra Firma Capital Partners Advisory Council, since 2001. President, Royal Scottish Corporation, since 2003; President, Friends of Scottish Rugby, since 2000; Hon. President: Association European Chambers of Commerce, Queen's Bodyguard for Scotland (Royal Company of Archers); Foundation Trustee, Academy of European Law Germany, since 1994. Recreations: fishing; shooting; outdoor sport. Address: (h.) Speyville House, Station Road, Newtonmore PH20 1AR; T.-01540 673 224.
E-mail: macphersonfamily@btinternet.com

Macpherson of Drumochter, Lord (James Gordon Macpherson), 2nd Baron, JP, FRES, FRSA, FZS.

Chairman and Managing Director, Macpherson, Train & Co. Ltd., since 1964; Chairman, A.J. Macpherson & Co. Ltd., since 1973; b. 22.1.24; m., 1, Dorothy Ruth Coulter (deceased); 2 d.; 1 s. deceased; 2, Catherine MacCarthy; 1 s.; 2 d. Educ. Loretto; Wells House, Malvern. RAF, 1939-45; Member, Council, London Chamber of Commerce, 1952-73; Chief, Scottish Clans Association of London, 1972-74; Chairman, Macpherson Clan Association, 1963-64; Life Managing Governor, Royal Scottish Corporation; Freeman, City of London. Address: (h.) Kyllachy, Tomatin, Inverness-shire IV13 7YA.

Macpherson, Archie. Sports broadcaster and journalist. Former headmaster; football commentator, BBC Scotland, until 1990; reported Olympic Games, 1984 and 1988, for BBC network; commentator, Scottish Television, since 1988; author of: Action Replays, 1991, Blue and Green, 1989, 'Jock Stein' Definitive Biography, 2004; 'Flower of Scotland?', 2005; e-mail: archie613@btinternet.com

McPherson, James Alexander Strachan, CBE, MA, BL, LLB, FSA Scot, JP. Lord Lieutenant, Banffshire, 1987-2002; Senior Partner, then Consultant, Alexander George & Co., Solicitors, Macduff, retired 2001; Honorary Sheriff, Grampian, Highland and Islands at Banff, since 1972; b. 20.11.27, Wormit, Fife; m., Helen Marjorie Perks, MA; 1 s.; 1 d. Educ. Banff Academy; Aberdeen University. Member, Macduff Town Council and Banff County Council, 1958-75; Provost of Macduff, 1972-75; Convener, Banff County Council, 1970-75; Member: Grampian Health Board, 1974-82, Post Office Users National Council for Scotland, 1976-80, Police Advisory Board for Scotland, 1974-86, Grampian Regional Council, 1974-90; Chairman, Public Protection Committee, 1974-86; Governor, Scottish Police College, 1974-86; President, Banffshire Society of Solicitors, 1977-80; Chairman, Banff and Buchan JP Advisory Committee, 1987-98; Chairman, Aberdeenshire JP Advisory Committee, 1998-2002; Member, Scottish Solicitors Discipline Tribunal, 1990-94; Vice President, Highland Territorial and Reserve Forces Association; Member, Aberdeen University Court, 1993-97; Director, Banffshire Partnership Ltd.; North East of Scotland Preservation Trust; Deveron Care Services; Chairman, Banffshire Field Club. Recreations: reading; local history; sailing; swimming. Address: (h.) Dun Alastair, 126 Gellymill Street, Macduff; T.-Macduff 832377.

Macpherson, John Hannah Forbes, CBE, OStJ, CA, DUniv; b. 23.5.26, Glasgow; m., Margaret Graham Roxburgh; 1 s. Educ. Glasgow Academy; Merchiston Castle School, Edinburgh. Royal Naval Volunteer Reserve, 1943; Apprentice CA, Wilson Stirling & Co., 1947 (qualified, 1949); Partner, Wilson Stirling & Co. (subsequently Touche Ross & Co.), 1956-86; Chairman: Glasgow Junior Chamber of Commerce, 1965, Scottish Mutual Assurance Society, 1971, Scottish Industrial Estates Corporation, 1972, Irvine Development Corporation, 1976, TSB Scotland plc, 1984, Glasgow Development Agency, 1990; President, Glasgow Chamber of Commerce, 1980; Director: Scottish Metropolitan Property plc, 1986, TSB Group plc, 1985; Deputy Chairman, Hill Samuel Bank Ltd., 1991; Director, PCT Group plc, 1992; Governor, Merchiston Castle School, 1988; Member, Charity Appeals Committee for Prince and Princess of Wales Hospice; Director, Glasgow Native Benevolent Society; former Chairman of Court, University of Glasgow; former Lord Dean of Guild, Glasgow; former Preceptor, Royal Incorporation of Hutchesons' Hospital. Recreations: travel; gardening; reading. Address: (h.) 16 Collylinn Road, Bearsden, Glasgow; T.-0141-942 0042.

McPherson, Malcolm Henry, LLB, WS. Solicitor; Senior Partner, HBJ Gateley Wareing (Scotland) LLP; b. 22.5.54, Edinburgh; m., Fiona Sutherland Hogg; 1 s.; 3 d. Educ. George Watson's College, Edinburgh; Edinburgh University. Apprentice, Henderson & Jackson, WS, 1975-

77; Partner, since 1978. Recreations: field sports; sailing; golf. Address: (b.) Exchange Tower, 19 Canning Street, Edinburgh EH3 8EH; T.-0131-228 2400; e-mail: mmcpherson@hbj-gw.com

Macpherson, Peter, FRCP, FRCR, DTCD, FLS. Emeritus Consultant Neuroradiologist, Institute of Neurological Sciences; President: British Society of Neuroradiologists, 1990-92, Botanical Society of the British Isles, 1991-93; b. 10.10.25, Inveraray; m., Agnes Cochrane Davidson; 4 d. Educ. Inveraray Grammar School; Keil School, Dumbarton; Anderson College, Glasgow. House Surgeon, Royal Infirmary, Stirling; Junior Hospital Medical Officer, Robroyston Hospital, Glasgow; Chest Physician, Argyll; Registrar/Senior Registrar, Western Infirmary, Glasgow. Commodore, Oban Sailing Club, 1958-60; President, Glasgow Natural History Society, 1979-81 and 1983-86; Honorary Secretary, Botanical Society of the British Isles, Committee for Scotland, 1977-95, Chairman, 1995-99; Plant Recorder for Lanarkshire, since 1978; Elder, Church of Scotland, since 1957. Recreations: natural history; sailing. Address: (h.) Ben Alder, 15 Lubnaig Road, Glasgow; T.-0141-632 0723.

MacPherson, Robin David, BA (Hons), MLitt. Director, Screen Academy Scotland, since 2006; Acting Head of School of Creative Industries, Napier University, since 2007; b. 24.12.59, Lennoxtown; 1 d. Educ. Garthamlock Secondary, Glasgow; Stirling University. Freelance Photographer, Writer and Bookseller, 1980-89; Producer/Director of Documentary, Current Affairs and Drama for Edinburgh Film Workshop Trust, 1989-97; Independent Television Producer/Managing Director, Asylum Pictures Ltd., Edinburgh, 1997-99; Development Executive, Scottish Screen, 1999-2002; Napier University, since 2002 (Lecturer, then Senior Lecturer). BAFTA (UK) Nomination 1996, for Channel 4 Drama 'The Butterfly Man'; Vice Chair, Producers Association for Cinema and Television, 1997-99; Trustee, Edinburgh Television Trust, 1993-99. Recreation: hillwalking. Address: (b.) Napier University, 10 Colinton Road, Edinburgh EH10 5DT; T.-01311 455 2687; e-mail: r.macpherson@napier.ac.uk

Macpherson, Shonaig, CBE, LLB (Hons), FRSE. Solicitor. Chairman, National Trust for Scotland, since 2005; Chairman, ITI Scotland Limited, since 2005; Chairman, SCDI, since 2004; Senior Partner, McGrigors, 2002-04; b. 29.9.58. Educ. University of Sheffield; College of Law, Chester. Articled Clerk, Norton Rose, London, 1982-85; qualified as Solicitor (England), 1984; Solicitor in Corporate/Commercial Department, Knapp Fisher, London, 1985-87; Assistant Company Secretary, Storehouse PLC, 1987; in-house lawyer, Harrods Ltd., and associated companies, 1987-89; Partner, Calow Easton, London 1989-91; Partner, McGrigor Donald, London and Edinburgh, 1991; qualified as Solicitor (Scotland), 1992; Managing Partner, McGrigor Donald, Edinburgh, 1996; appointed Senior Partner (Scotland), McGrigor, 2002. Non-executive Member, Scottish Executive Management Group, 2001-07; President, Edinburgh Chamber of Commerce and Enterprise, 2002-04; Visiting Professor, Department of Mechanical Engineering, Heriot Watt University; Chairman, Scottish Council for Development and Industry; Chairman, Scottish Council Foundation, since 2004; Secretary, Macpherson Coaches Ltd.; Director and Secretary, Edinburgh International Film Festival; Director, Young Enterprise Scotland, 2001-04; Deputy President, British Chambers of Commerce, 2004-06; Director, Edinburgh International Conference Centre Limited; formerly: Director, Scottish Enterprise Edinburgh and Lothian, Member, Knowledge Economy Task Force; Chairman, Princes Scottish Youth Business Trust Limited, since 2005; Director, Braveheart Investment Group plc, since 2006; Trustee, The Princes's Trust Council, 2007; Trustee, The Robertson Trust; Governor, Edinburgh College of Art. Recreations: film; music; reading. Address: (b.) Lochcote, Linlithgow EH49 6QE; e-mail: shonaigm@btconnect.com

Macpherson, Professor Stuart Gowans, OBE, MB, ChB, FRCS(Glas), FRCP(Edin), FRCS(Edin), FRCS(England), FRCGP. Postgraduate Dean and Professor of Postgraduate Medical Education, University of Edinburgh, since 1999; b. 11.7.45, Glasgow; m., Norma Elizabeth Carslaw; 2 s.; 1 d. Educ. Alan Glen's School, Glasgow; University of Glasgow. Formerly Senior Lecturer in Surgery, University of Glasgow and Consultant General Surgeon. Sits on Scottish and UK national committees on postgraduate medical education; Board Member, Postgraduate Medical Education and Training Board. Recreations: travelling; family; golf. Address: The Lister, 11 Hill Square, Edinburgh EH8 9DR; T.-0131-650 2609; e-mail: stuart.macpherson@nes.scot.nhs.uk

Macpherson of Cluny (and Blairgowrie), The Honourable Sir William, KB (1983), TD, MA. 27th Hereditary Chief of the Clan Macpherson (Cluny-Macpherson); b. 1.4.26; m., Sheila McDonald Brodie (deceased 2003); 2 s.; 1 d. Educ. Summer Fields, Oxford; Wellington College; Trinity College, Oxford (Hon. Fellow, 1991). Scots Guards, 1944-47 (Captain); 21st Special Air Service Regiment (TA), 1951-65 (Lt.-Col. Commanding, 1962-65); Honorary Colonel, 21st SAS, 1983-91. Called to the Bar, Inner Temple, 1952; Queen's Counsel, 1971-83; Recorder of the Crown Court, 1972-83; Member, Senate and Bar Council, 1979-83; Bencher, Inner Temple, 1978; Judge of the High Court of Justice (of England and Wales), Queen's Bench Division, 1983-96; Honorary Member, Northern Circuit, since 1987. Member, Queen's Bodyguard for Scotland (Royal Company of Archers), since 1976, Brigadier, 1989, Ensign, 2002, Lieutenant, 2003-06; Vice President, Royal Scottish Corporation, until 2006; President, Highland Society of London, 1991-94; Hon. LLD, Dundee University, 1999. Recreations: golf; fishing; rugby football; archery. Address: (h.) Newton Castle, Blairgowrie, Perthshire PH10 6SU.

MacQuarrie, John Kenneth (Ken), MA (Eng/Hist), DipEd. Controller, BBC Scotland, since 2004; b. 5.6.52, Tobermory; m., Angela Sparks; 1 s.; 2 d. Educ. Oban High School; Edinburgh University; Moray House College of Education. Joined BBC Scotland as Researcher, 1975; Radio Producer, BBC Highland, 1976; Producer, Television, 1979; Head of Gaelic, 1988; Head of Gaelic and Features, 1992; Head of Broadcast, 1997; Head of Programmes and Scottish Services, 2000. Board Member, Gaelic Media Service; Vice Chair, Celtic Film and Television Association, 1986-93; Founder Member, Scottish Screen Forum; Former Governor, Scottish Film Council. Recreations: sailing; reading; walking. Address: (b.) BBC Scotland, 40 Pacific Quay, Glasgow G51 1DA; T.-0141 422 6100; e-mail: ken.macquarrie@bbc.co.uk

MacQueen, Professor Hector Lewis, LLB (Hons), PhD, FRSE, FBA. Professor of Private Law, Edinburgh University, since 1994; Dean of Law, 1999-2003; Dean of Research, College of Humanities and Social Science, since 2004; b. 13.6.56, Ely; m., Frances Mary Young; 2 s.; 1 d. Educ. George Heriot's School, Edinburgh; Edinburgh University. Lecturer, Senior Lecturer, Reader, all in Law, Edinburgh University, 1979-94; Director, David Hume Institute, Edinburgh, 1991-99; Visiting Professor, Cornell University, 1991; Visiting Professor, Utrecht University, 1997; Secretary, Scottish Historical Review, 1986-99; Editor, Hume Papers on Public Policy, 1993-99; Editor,

Edinburgh Law Review, 1996-2001; Editor, Scots Law News (www.law.ed.ac.uk/sln), since 1996; Scottish Representative, European Contract Commission, since 1995; Member, Co-ordinating Committee, Study Group towards a European Civil Code, since 1999; Literary Director, Stair Society, since 1999; Chair, Scottish Records Advisory Council, since 2001; Member, DTI Intellectual Property Advisory Committee, 2003-05; Dept. of Constitutional Affairs Advisory Panel on Public Sector Information, since 2004; Director, AHRC Research Centre for Studies in Intellectual Property and Information Technology Law, Edinburgh University, 2002-07. Publications: Common Law and Feudal Society in Medieval Scotland; Studying Scots Law; Copyright, Competition and Industrial Design; Contract Law in Scotland (Co-Author); Unjustified Enrichment Law Basics; Contemporary Intellectual Property: Law and Policy (Co-Author). Recreations: Scotland; cricket; walking – sometimes with golf clubs; reading. Address: (b.) School of Law, Edinburgh University, Edinburgh EH8 9YL; T.-0131-650 2060; e-mail: hector.macqueen@ed.ac.uk

MacQueen, Professor Emeritus Jack (John), MA (Glasgow), MA (Cantab), Hon DLitt, FRAS, FRSE. Professor Emeritus, Edinburgh University, since 1988; b. 13.2.29, Springboig; m., Winifred W. MacWalter; 3 s. Educ. Hutchesons' Boys Grammar School; Glasgow University; Christ's College, Cambridge. RAF, 1954-56 (Pilot Officer, Flying Officer); Assistant Professor of English, Washington University, St. Louis, Missouri, 1956-59; Edinburgh University: Lecturer in Medieval English and Scottish Literature, 1959-63, Masson Professor of Medieval and Renaissance Literature, 1963-72; Director, School of Scottish Studies, 1969-88; Professor of Scottish Literature and Oral Tradition, 1972-88; Endowment Fellow, 1988-92. Publications: St. Nynia, 1961, 1990, 2005; Robert Henryson, 1967; Ballattis of Luve, 1970; Allegory, 1970; Progress and Poetry, 1982; Numerology, 1985; Rise of the Historical Novel, 1989; Scotichronicon III and IV (with W. MacQueen), 1989; Scotichronicon I and II (with W. MacQueen), 1993; Scotichronicon V and VI (with W. MacQueen and D.E.R. Watt), 1995; Place-Names in the Rhinns of Galloway and Luce Valley, 2002; Complete and Full with Numbers, 2006; Latin Poems of Archibald Pitcairne (with W. MacQueen), 2008; Oxford Book of Scottish Verse (with T. Scott), 1966; A Choice of Scottish Verse 1470-1570 (with W. MacQueen), 1972; Humanism in Renaissance Scotland (Co-Author), 1990. Recreations: walking; occasional archaeology; music; astronomy. Address: (h.) Slewdonan, Damnaglaur, Drummore, Stranraer DG9 9QN; e-mail: Jackmacqueen@aol.com/

McQueen, James Donaldson Wright, MA, PhD, ARSGS. Food Industry Analyst; Map Publisher; Honorary Research Fellow, Department of Geographical and Earth Sciences, University of Glasgow; Council Member, Royal Scottish Geographical Society; b. 14.2.37, Dumfries; m., Jean Evelyn Brown; 2 s.; 1 d. Educ. King's Park School, Glasgow; Glasgow University. Assistant Lecturer, Department of Geography, Glasgow University, 1960-61; Milk Marketing Board Executive, 1961-89 (England & Wales, 1961-62, Scotland, 1963-89); Deputy Managing Director, Scottish Milk Marketing Board, 1985-89; Chief Executive, Scottish Dairy Trade Federation (latterly Scottish Dairy Association), 1989-95; Adviser on Milk Industry Matters to the States of Jersey, 2003-07; Chairman, Milk Price Review Panel, States of Guernsey, 2007. Address: Ormlie, 53 Kingston Road, Bishopton, Renfrewshire PA7 5BA; T.-01505 862380; e-mail: mcqueen@agri-food.co.uk

MacQueen, Norrie, BA, MSc (Econ), DPhil. Senior Lecturer, Dundee University; Head of Department of

Politics, 1998-2005; b. 11.4.50, Glasgow; m., Betsy (nee King); 1 d. Educ. Shawlands Academy; University of Ulster; London School of Economics. Ministry of Education, Mozambique, 1977-79; Research Officer, Glasgow University, 1980-83; Senior Lecturer, University of Papua New Guinea, 1986-90; Research Fellow, Australian National University, 1990; Reader, University of Sunderland, 1990-96; joined Dundee University, 1996. Publications: The Decolonization of Portuguese Africa, 1997; United Nations Peacekeeping in Africa, 2002; Peacekeeping and the International System, 2006; Colonialism, 2007. Recreations: hillwalking; cycling; music. Address: (b.) Department of Politics, University of Dundee, Nethergate, Dundee DD1 4HN; T.-01382 344591; e-mail: n.j.d.macqueen@dundee.ac.uk

McQuillin, Robert, BSc, MSc, FGS, FRSE. Director, Hydrocarbon Management International Ltd., since 1991; Senior Consultant, R. McQuillin & Associates, since 1990; b. 28.5.35, Cumbria; m., Angela; 2 s. Educ. White House School, Brampton; Durham University; London University. British Geological Survey: Staff Geophysicist, 1957-66; set up offshore geophysical exploration of UK shelf, 1966-73; Head, Marine Geophysics Unit, 1973-85, Deputy Director, Marine Surveys, Hydrocarbons and Geothermal Energy Division, 1983-85; Britoil: Chief Geophysicist, 1985-88, Chief Scientist and Deputy Exploration Manager, 1986-88; Scientific Adviser, BP NW Europe, Exploration and Production, 1988-89; Oil Industry Consultant, 1990-2001. Former Vice-President, Geological Society of London and of Geological Society of Edinburgh. Publication: An Introduction to Seismic Interpretation (principal author), 1986. Recreations: wine and food; good hotels; golf. Address: (b.) HMI Ltd., 94 Liberton Drive, Edinburgh EH16 6NR; T.-0131-664 2193.

MacRae, Donald J. R., BSc (Hons), MBA, FCIBS, FRSE, FRAgS. Banker; Strategy and Finance Director, Lloyds TSB Scotland plc, since 2001; Board Member, Scottish Enterprise, since 2004; b. 12.8.54, Inverness; m., Anne de Diesbach; 1 s.; 1 d. Educ. Fortrose Academy; Edinburgh University. Economist/Analyst, Imperial Chemical Industries, 1979-82; Project Manager, Farmplan Computer Systems, 1982-84; Lecturer, University of Newcastle upon Tyne, 1984-86; TSB Bank Scotland plc: Manager, 1986-90, Senior Manager, 1990-98, Chief Manager, Strategy and Development, 1998-2001. Member, Advisory Board, Interface; Past Member, Scottish Government: Purchasers Information Advisory Group, Economists Advisory Group; Member: Economic Statistics Advisory Group, Economists Advisory Group, Committee of Inquiry on Crofting; Trustee, David Hume Institute. Recreations: music; film; theatre; vintage tractors. Address: (b.) Henry Duncan House, 120 George Street, Edinburgh EH2 4TS; T.-0131 260 0268.

McRoberts, Rev. Douglas, BD, CPS, FRSA. Church of Scotland Minister (Keith North Churches Team Leader), since 2002; Vice-Convener, Church of Scotland Publishing Comm., since 2005; b. 18.9.49, Glasgow; m., Lesley Irvine; 4 s.; 1 d. Educ. Hutchesons' Grammar School; University of Glasgow; Trinity College. Ordained to Church of Scotland Ministry, 1975; Minister, Pathhead Parish Church, Kirkcaldy, 1976-78; Producer/Presenter/News Editor, BBC Scotland, 1978-85; Head of Information, UKAEA, Dounreay, 1985-89; Chief Press Officer, UKAEA, London, 1989-90; Media Relations Manager, Nuclear Electric plc, 1990-95; Director, Public Relations, British Energy plc, 1995-2002; President and Chairman, NucNet International News Agency, Berne, 1999-2002. Founder Member, Spitfire Society; lead guitar, "White Light" (rock band), 1970-74; Scotland plc "Excellence in Communications" Award, 1999. Publication: Author, "Lions Rampant - The

Story of 602 Spitfire Squadron" (1985). Recreations: classic cars (Stag and Rover); rock music; writing; modelmaking. Address: North Manse, Church Road, Keith AB55 5BR; T.-01542 882559.
E-mail: doug.mcroberts@btinternet.com

McSherry, Sheriff John Craig Cunningham, LLB (Hons). Advocate; part-time Sheriff, 2000-03; All-Scotland Floating Sheriff, 2003-06; resident Sheriff at Dunfermline, since 2006; b. 21.10.49, Irvine; m., Elaine Beattie; 2 s. Educ. Ardrossan Academy; Glasgow University. Senior Partner, McSherry Halliday, Solicitors, 1983-92. Chairman, Largs and Saltcoats Citizens Advice Bureaux, 1976-83; Council Member, Law Society of Scotland, 1982-85; part-time Immigration Appeals Adjudicator, 2001-03. Recreations: country pursuits; skiing; music; bridge; golf. Address: (h.) 2 Heriot Row, Edinburgh EH3 6HU; T.-0131-556 8289; e-mail: jccmcs@hotmail.com

MacSween, Professor Sir Roddy N. M., Kt, Hon. DSc, Glas (2007), BSc, MD, FRCPGlas, FRCPEdin, Hon. FRCP Lond, Hon. FRCSEdin, Hon. FRCSLond, Hon. FCPath S. Africa, FRCPath, FRSE, FIBiol, FMedSci. Professor of Pathology, Glasgow University, 1984-99; Honorary Consultant Pathologist, Western Infirmary, Glasgow, 1970-99; President, Royal College of Pathologists, 1996-99; Chairman, Academy of Medical Royal Colleges, 1998-2000; Member, General Medical Council, 1999-2003; Chairman, Unrelated Live Transplant Regulatory Authority, 1999-2006; Chairman, Tenovus Scotland, since 2006; b. 2.2.35, Kinloch, Lewis; m., Marjory Pentland Brown; 1 s.; 1 d. Educ. Inverness Royal Academy; Glasgow University. Honorary Fellow, South African Society of Pathologists, 1982; Otago Savings Bank Visiting Professor, Otago University, 1983; Hans Popper Lecturer in Liver Pathology, Columbia University College of Physicians and Surgeons, New York, 1988; Henry Moon Lecturer, University of California, San Francisco, 1991; Basil Morson Lecturer, British Society of Gastroenterology, 1995; President, Royal Medico-Chirurgical Society of Glasgow, 1978-79; President, International Academy of Pathology, British Division, 1988-90; Editor, Histopathology (Journal), 1985-96. President, Bridgeton Burns Club, 1983-84; Past Captain, Dunaverty Golf Club (1973) and Machrihanish Golf Club (1980). Publications: Muir's Textbook of Pathology, 13th edition (Co-Editor); Pathology of the Liver, 1st to 4th edition (Senior Editor); MacSween's Pathology of the Liver, 5th edition; Recent Advances in Histopathology, Nos. 11-17 (Co-Editor); Recent Advances in Hepatology, No. 1 (Co-Editor); numerous scientific papers on various aspects of liver pathology and diseases. Recreations: golf; gardening; opera; hill-walking; more golf! Address: (h.) 32 Calderwood Road, Newlands, Glasgow G43 2RU; T.-0141 637 4355; e-mail: roddymacsween@hotmail.com

McTeague, Karina Trudy, LLB (Hons), DipLP, NP. Head of Legal and Risk, and Company Secretary, Lloyds TSB Scotland plc, since 2003; b. 9.5.62, Bearsden; partner: Ewan Malcolm. Educ. Park School, Glasgow; Strathallan School, Perthshire; Edinburgh University. Associate, Shepherd & Wedderburn, until 1992; Deputy Group Counsel, Bank of Scotland, 1999-2001; Harvard General Managers Programme, 2001; Principal Risk Adviser, Insurance and Investment Division, HBOS plc, 2002. Member, Legal Committee, Scottish Committee of Clearing Banks; CSCB representative on the Council of the Law Society of Scotland, and a member of the Audit Committee of the Law Society of Scotland. Recreations: travel; hill walking; gardening. Address: (b.) Henry Duncan House, 120 George Street, Edinburgh EH2 4LH; T.-0131 260 0953; e-mail: karina.mcteague@lloydstsb.co.uk

McTernan, Lucy, MA (Hons) Edin. Deputy Chief Executive, Scottish Council for Voluntary Organisations (SCVO), since 1993; Member, Scotland Committee, The Big Lottery Fund, since 2007; b. 18.1.69, Littleborough; m.,

Michael McTernan; 2 d. Educ. Huddersfield New College; Edinburgh University. Address: (b.) SCVO, Mansfield Traquair Centre, 15 Mansfield Place, Edinburgh EH3 6BB; e-mail: lucy.mcternan@scvo.org.uk

McVicar, William, RD*, CA. Chairman of Trustees, Church of Scotland Housing and Loan Fund for Retired Ministers and Widows and Widowers of Ministers, since 1983 (Trustee, since 1976); Retired Chartered Accountant; b. 29.6.32, Rutherglen; m., Doreen Ann; 1 s.; 1 d. Educ. George Heriot's School, Edinburgh. Royal Navy, 1950-52; RNVR/RNR, 1955-86 (retired list, Commander RNR); Admitted ICAS, 1958 (T.C. Garden & Co., CA, Edinburgh); Partner, T.C. Garden & Co., CA, Edinburgh, 1962-79; Partner, Coopers and Lybrand, 1979-91. Recreations: travel; food and wine; gardening; grandchildren. Address: (h.) The Ley, Innerleithen, Peeblesshire EH44 6NL; T.-01896 830 240.

McVitie, Alasdair Hugh, TD, MA, LLB, NP, WS. Consultant, Messrs Gillespie Macandrew LLP WS., Edinburgh; b. 4.9.38, Edinburgh; m., Margaret; 1 s.; 1 d. Educ. The Edinburgh Academy; Edinburgh University. Solicitor, since 1964; Writer to the Signet, since 1968. Hon. Director (now Chairman), Lord Roberts Workshops, Livingston; Treasurer, Scottish Association for the Study of Offending; Hon. Director, Scottish Borders Community Orchestra; Hon. Secretary, The Royal Scots Territorial Officers Association; Member, Charitable Services Committee, Poppy Scotland (formerly Earl Haig Fund). Recreations: fishing; handling gundogs; golf; gardening; choral singing. Address: (h.) Eastmount, High Road, Galashiels TD1 2BD; T.- (day) 0131 2400787; T.-(evening/weekend) 01896 758637.
E-mail: alasdair.mcvitie@gillespiemacandrew.co.uk

MacWalter, Ronald Siller, BMSc (Hons), MB, ChB (Hons), MD, MRCP(UK); FRCP(Edin); FRCP (Glas). Consultant Physician in General Medicine, Ninewells Hospital, Dundee, since 1997; Consultant Physician in Medicine for the Elderly, Royal Victoria Hospital, Dundee, 1986-97; Honorary Reader in Medicine, Dundee University, Ninewells Hospital, Dundee, since 1986; Honorary Associate Professor of Medicine, Kigezi International School of Medicine, Cambridge, 2001-04; b. 14.12.53, Broughty Ferry; m., Sheila Margaret Nicoll; 2 s. Educ. Harris Academy, Dundee; Dundee University; University of Florida. Registrar in Medicine and Haematology, Department of Clinical Pharmacology, Ninewells Hospital, Dundee; Senior Registrar in General Medicine and Geriatric Medicine, Nuffield Department of Medicine, John Radcliffe Hospital, Oxford. Publication: Secondary Prevention of Stroke; Managing Stroke and TIAs in Practice; Aids to Clinical Examination; papers on stroke.

McWilliam, Rev. Thomas Mathieson, MA, BD. Retired Minister; Clerk, Presbytery of Ross, since 2000; b. 12.11.39, Glasgow; m., Patricia Jane Godfrey; 1 s.; 1 d. Educ. Eastwood Secondary School; Glasgow University; New College, Edinburgh. Assistant Minister, Auld Kirk of Ayr, 1964-66; Minister: Dundee St. David's North, 1966-72, East Kilbride Greenhills, 1972-80, Lylesland Parish Church, Paisley, 1980-97, Contin Parish, 1997-2003. Convener, Youth Education Committee, General Assembly, 1980-84; Moderator, Paisley Presbytery, 1985-86; Convener, Board of Practice and Procedure, General Assembly, 1992-96. Recreations: walking; reading; gardening; bowling. Address: (h.) 7 Woodholme Croft, Culbokie, Ross-shire IV7 8JH; T.-01349 877014.

M

Maan, Bashir Ahmed, CBE, JP, DL, MSc. President, Scottish Council of Voluntary Organisations, 2001 06; President, National Association of British Pakistanis, 1999-2007; Chair, Scottish Police Authorities Forum, 2000-03; b. 22.10.26, Maan, Pakistan; 1 s.; 3 d. Educ. D.B. High School, Quila Didar Singh; Punjab University. Involved in the struggle for creation of Pakistan as a student, 1943-47; organised rehabilitation of refugees from India in Maan and surrounding areas, 1947-48; emigrated to UK and settled in Glasgow, 1953; Founder Secretary, Glasgow Pakistan Social and Cultural Society, 1955-65 (President, 1966-69); Member, Executive Committee, Glasgow City Labour Party, 1969-70; Vice-Chairman, Glasgow Community Relations Council, 1970-75; Member, Glasgow Corporation, 1970-75 (Magistrate, City of Glasgow, 1971-74; Vice-Chairman, then Chairman, Police Committee, 1971-75); Member, National Road Safety Committee, 1971-74 and Scottish Accident Prevention Committee, 1971-75; Member, BBC Immigrant Programmes Advisory Committee, 1972-80; Convenor, Pakistan Bill Action Committee, 1973; contested East Fife Parliamentary seat, February 1974; President, Standing Conference of Pakistani Organisations in UK and Eire, 1974-77; Police Judge, City of Glasgow, 1974-75; Member: City of Glasgow District Council, 1975-84, Glasgow City Council, 1995-2003; Bailie, City of Glasgow, 1980-84 and 1996-99; Deputy Chairman, Commission for Racial Equality, 1977-80; Member, Scottish Gas Consumers Council, 1978-81; Member, Greater Glasgow Health Board, 1981-92; Deputy Lieutenant, Glasgow, since 1982; Hon. Research Fellow, Glasgow University, 1988-91; Hon. Fellow, Glasgow Caledonian University, since 2003; Founder Chairman, Scottish Pakistani Association, 1984-91, and 1994-2000; Judge, City of Glasgow District Courts, 1968-97; Chairman, Strathclyde Community Relations Council, 1986-93 and 1994-96; Member, BBC General Advisory Council, 1992-95; a Governor, Jordanhill College of Further Education, 1987-91; Chairman, Mosque Committee, Islamic Centre, Glasgow, 1986-91; Convener, Strathclyde Joint Police Board, 1999-2003; Member, Police Advisory Board Scotland, 1999-2003; National Council of the Muslim Council of Britain, since 1998; Chair, Council of Ethnic Minority Organisations Scotland (CEMVO), since 2003; Trustee, Ethnic Minority Foundation (EMF), since 2003; Trustee, British Muslim Research Centre (BMRC), since 2002; President, Islamic Centre, Glasgow, since 2007; LLD, University of Strathclyde, 1999; DUniv, Glasgow, 2001; DLitt (Glasgow Caledonian), 2002. Publication: The New Scots; The Thistle of The Crescent, 2008. Recreations: golf; reading. Address: (h.) 8 Riverview Gardens, Glasgow G51 8EL; T.-0141-429 7689.

Mack, Professor Douglas Stuart, MA, PhD, FRSE. Professor Emeritus, Stirling University; Professor, 2000-04; General Editor, Association for Scottish Literary Studies, 1980-90; General Editor, Stirling/South Carolina Edition of James Hogg, since 1990; President, The James Hogg Society, 1982-2006; b. 30.1.43, Bellshill; m., Wilma Stewart Grant; 2 s. Educ. Uddingston Grammar School; Glasgow University; Stirling University. Research Assistant, National Library of Scotland, 1965-66; Assistant Librarian: St. Andrews University, 1966-70, Stirling University, 1970-86; Lecturer, Stirling University, 1986-94, Reader, 1994-99. Editor of various books by James Hogg and Sir Walter Scott. Recreations: watching Hamilton Accies; sailing on paddle steamers. Address: (h.) 2 Law Hill Road, Dollar FK14 7BG; T.-Dollar 742452; e-mail: d.s.mack@stir.ac.uk

Mack, William, MCIBS. Chairman, Edinburgh and South East Scotland Blood Transfusion Association, since 1999; Secretary and Treasurer, Scottish National Blood Transfusion Association, since 1995; Secretary and Treasurer, Scottish Language Dictionaries; b. 10.11.43, Douglas; m., Eileen Marion McFarlane; 1 s.; 1 d. Educ. Lanark Grammar School. Royal Bank of Scotland, 1960-95. Recreations: New Orleans jazz; DBA support; walking; gardening. Address: (h.) 2 Otterburn Park, Edinburgh EH14 1JX, T.-0131-443 7636.

Mackie of Benshie, Baron (George Yull Mackie), CBE, DSO, DFC, LLD. Farmer; former Liberal Democrat Spokesman, House of Lords, on Devolution, Agriculture, Scotland, Industry; Member, Council of Europe and Western European Union, 1986-96; b. 10.7.19, Aberdeen; m., 1, Lindsay Lyall Sharp (deceased, 1985); 1 s. (deceased); 3 d.; 2, Mrs Jacqueline Lane. Educ. Aberdeen Grammar School; Aberdeen University. Bomber Command and Air Staff, 1944. Contested South Angus, 1959; Vice-Chairman (Organisation), Scottish Liberal Party, 1959-64; MP (Liberal), Caithness and Sutherland, 1964-66; Chairman, Scottish Liberal Party, 1965-70; contested Caithness and Sutherland, 1970; contested NE Scotland, European Parliamentary Election, 1979; Member, EEC Scrutiny Committee (D), House of Lords; Executive, Inter-Parliamentary Union; Chairman: Caithness Glass, 1966-84, Industrial Appeal Committee, Pitlochry Festival Theatre, 1979, Angus Committee, Salvation Army, 1976-84; Rector, Dundee University, 1980-83; Director, Scottish Ballet, 1986-88. Address: (h.) Benshie Cottage, Oathlaw, by Forfar, Angus.

Mackie, Maitland, CBE, BSc, MA, LLD. Farmer; Owner, Mackie's; Director: Farmdata, Whatever Ltd., Ice Robotics; former Chairman, Scottish Agricultural College; former Director: Rowett Research Institute, Lloyds TSB Scotland; b. 21.9.37, Aberdeen; m., Dr. Halldis Mackie; 1 s.; 2 d. Educ. Aberdeen Grammar School; Aberdeen University. Former Chairman: Grampian Enterprise Ltd., Food and Animal Committees, Agricultural and Food Research Council, Farm Assured Scotch Livestock, Scottish Pig Industry Initiative; former Vice-President, National Farmers Union of Scotland; Court Member, University of Aberdeen; Hon. Professor, RGU. Recreations: skiing; sailing; Norway. Address: Westertown, Rothienorman, Aberdeenshire; T.-01467 671466.

Magee, Jane Deborah, MA (St Andrews), MA (London), PGCE (Dundee). Director, English Language Teaching (ELT), since 2006; b. 26.07.51, Glasgow; m., Stephen Magee; 2 s.; 1 d. Educ. Park School, Glasgow; St. Andrews; Institute of Education, University of London. Legal Executive, London, 1977-79; Librarian, University of London, 1974-75; Teacher: Scotland, 1975-77, Markopoulo, Greece, 1979-80; Management Accountant: Schlumberger, London, 1982-84, Schlumberger, China, 1985-86; Administrator, Beijing Normal University, 1987-89; Programme Director, ELT, St. Andrews, 1996-2006. Recreations: photography; (slow) walking; swimming; gardening; running; travelling. Address: (h.) Kinness Burn, Kennedy Gardens, St. Andrews, Fife KY16 9DJ; T.-01334-462255; e-mail: jane.magee@st-andrews.ac.uk

Magee, Stephen Robert, MA, PGCE, MSc. Vice Principal, University of St. Andrews, since 2003; b. 19.4.53, Glasgow; m., Jane; 2 s.; 1 d. Educ. Marr College, Troon; Universities of St. Andrews, London and Edinburgh. Management Trainee, Williams and Glyns Bank, 1976; Teacher, Frontistirion Klavas, 1979; Lecturer, Waltham Forest College, 1981; Senior Lecturer, Beijing Foreign Studies University, 1985; University of St. Andrews: Director, ELT, 1989, Director, Admissions, 1996-2003. Publications: Seventy Five Years Since Saussure: Magee et al. Editors (Beijing), 1988; Introducing Linguistics: Liu, Magee and Nang (Beijing), 1989. Recreations: spectating and travelling. Address: University of St. Andrews, St. Katharine's West, The Scores, St. Andrews, Fife KY16 9AX; T.-01334 463320; e-mail: vpext@st-andrews.ac.uk

Magnusson, Sally Anne, MA (Hons). Presenter, Reporting Scotland, BBC, since 1998; Presenter, Hard Cash, BBC, 2000-02; Reporter, 4 X 4 Reports, 2001-03; Presenter, Britain's Secret Shame, 2003-04; Presenter, Songs of Praise, BBC, since 1983; Presenter, Daily Politics, BBC; b. 11.10.55, Glasgow; m., Norman Stone; 4 s.; 1 d. Educ. Laurel Bank School; Edinburgh University. Reporter, The Scotsman, 1979-81; News/Feature Writer, Sunday Standard, 1981-83; Reporter, Current Account, BBC Scotland, 1983, Presenter, Sixty Minutes, BBC, 1983-84; Presenter, London Plus, BBC, 1984-85; Presenter, Breakfast News (formerly Breakfast Time), BBC, 1985-99. Feature Writer of the Year, Fraser Scottish Press Awards, 1982. Publications: The Flying Scotsman, 1981; Clemo-A Love Story, 1984; A Shout in the Street, 1990; Family Life, 1999; Dreaming of Iceland, 2004; Glorious Things, 2004. Address: (b.) Langshot Farm, Torrance, Glasgow G64 4DL; e-mail: sally.magnusson@bbc.co.uk

Maguire, Frank, PHB (Philosophy), LLB. Partner, Thompsons, Glasgow; b. 4.10.55, Glasgow; m., Fiona Macdonald; 4 s. Educ. St. Vincent's College, Langbank; Gregorian University, Rome; St. Mary's College, Blairs; Aberdeen University. Apprentice, McLachlan & McKenzie, Edinburgh, Robin Thompson & Partners, Edinburgh; Assistant Solicitor, Robin Thompson & Partners; Salaried Partner, Thompsons; Equity Partner, Thompsons, Solicitor Advocate, 1994; Vice President, Society of Solicitor Advocates, 2000; President, Society of Solicitor Advocates, 2001-04; Panel Member, Solicitor Advocates Personal Injury Panel and Steering Group, Law Society of Scotland; Member, Steering Committee, Piper Alpha Trade Union Group; Legal Adviser to Scottish Trade Union Congress; Clydeside Action on Asbestos, Clydebank Asbestos Group and Scottish Haemophilia Group Forum; Member of Expert Group on Hepatitis C, Scottish Parliament; Committee Member, Scottish Branch of the British Lung Foundation; Member, Royal Society of Procurators; Member, AMICUS Union. Recreations: sailing; windsurfing; running; snow boarding. Address: (b.) Berkeley House, 285 Bath Street, Glasgow G2 4HQ; T.-0141-221 8840.

Mahmood, Tahir Ahmed, MBBS, BSc, MD, FRCOG, FRCP(Ireland); MFFP, MBA (HCM). Consultant Obstetrician and Gynaecologist, Forth Park Hospital, Kirkcaldy, since 1990; Clinical Senior Lecturer, Obstetrics and Gynaecology, Aberdeen University, since 1990; Senior Lecturer, School of Biological and Medical Sciences, St. Andrews University, since 1995; Clinical Senior Lecturer, University of Edinburgh, since 1996; Teaching Sub Dean, Medical School, Dundee, since 2001; Director, Women and Children's Health Directorate, Fife Acute NHS Hospitals Trust, 1998-2006; Member, BMA Scottish Council, 1996-2003; b. 7.10.53, Pakistan; m., Aasia Bashir; 2 s. Educ. King Edward Medical College, Lahore, Punjab University. Member, Scottish Hospital Staffing Review Committee, sub-speciality of obstetrics and gynaecology, 1986-88; Member, Minimal Invasive Surgery Subgroup and Clinical Resource Management — Procurement Group for Acute Unit, Fife, 1991-92; Ethicon RCOG Travelling Fellowship, 1991; Member, Senate, Aberdeen University, 1992-2000; Hon. Secretary, Northern Obstetrical and Gynaecological Society, 1993-98, Chairman, since 1999; Member, Area Medical Committee, Fife, 1993-98, Chairman, 1995-98; Member, Council, Royal College of Obstetricians and Gynaecologists, 1994-2000, and since 2002, and of Scottish Committee, RCOG, 1994-2000, and since 2002; Honorary

Secretary, Scottish Committee, RCOG, 2004-07; Chairman, Hospital Recognition Committee of the RCOG, 2005-07; Vice President, Royal College of Obstetricians and Gynaecologists, since 2007. Recreations: reading; history; walking. Address: (b.) Forth Park Hospital, 30 Bennochy Road, Kirkcaldy, Fife; T.-01592 643355.

Main, Very Rev. Professor Alan, TD, MA, BD, STM, PhD, DD. Professor of Practical Theology, Christ's College, Aberdeen, 1980-2001; Moderator, General Assembly, Church of Scotland, 1998-99; b. 31.3.36, Aberdeen; m., Anne Louise Swanson; 2 d. Educ. Robert Gordon's College, Aberdeen; University of Aberdeen; Union Theological Seminary, New York. Minister, Chapel of Garioch Parish, Aberdeenshire, 1963-70; Chaplain, University of Aberdeen, 1970-80; Chaplain, 153(H) Artillery Support Regiment, RCT(V), 1970-92; Provost, Faculty of Divinity, Aberdeen University, 1990-93; Master, Christ's College, 1992-2001. Moderator: Garioch Presbytery, 1969-70, Aberdeen Presbytery, 1984-85; Convener, Board of World Mission, 2000-02; Adviser in Religious Broadcasting, Grampian Television, 1976-86; Chairman: Grampian Marriage Guidance, 1977-80, Cruse, 1981-84; Patron, Seven Incorporated Trades of Aberdeen, since 2000; Minister, St. Andrews Scots Kirk, Colombo, 2002-03; Convener, Israel Centres, 2003-04; President, The Boys' Brigade, 2005-07. Recreations: music; golf. Address: (h.) Kirkfield, Barthol Chapel, Inverurie AB51 8TD.

Main, Professor Brian G.M., BSc, MBA, MA, PhD, FRSE. Professor of Business Economics, Edinburgh University, since 1991; Academic Director, David Hume Institute; b. 24.8.47, St. Andrews; m., June Lambert; 2 s.; 1 d. Educ. Buckhaven High School; St. Andrews University; University of California, Berkeley. Lecturer, then Reader in Economics, Edinburgh University, 1976-87; Professor of Economics and Chairman, Department of Economics, St. Andrews University, 1987-91. Recreation: fishing. Address: (b.) Management School and Economics, Edinburgh University, George Square, Edinburgh EH8 9JY; T.-0131-650 8361.

Main, Carol B.L.D., BA. Director, Live Music Now Scotland, since 1984; Director, National Association of Youth Orchestras, 1979-2003; Classical Music Editor, The List, since 1985; b. 21.12.58, Kirkcaldy; 1 d. Educ. Kirkcaldy High School; Edinburgh University. Freelance music critic, specialist music adviser, Scottish Arts Council; radio broadcaster. Chair, Hebrides Ensemble; Vice-Chair, Voluntary Arts Scotland; Board Director, Edinburgh Festival Fringe Society, 1986-2005; Chair, Enterprise Music Scotland, 1999-2001. Address: (b.) 14 Lennox Street, Edinburgh EH4 1QA; T.-0131 332 2110.

Main, Professor Ian Graham, BSc, MSc, PhD. Professor of Seismology and Rock Physics, University of Edinburgh, since 2000; Director, Joint Research Institute in Subsurface Science and Engineering, since 2007; b. 8.9.57, Aberdeen; m., 1. Anthea Stephen (divorced); 1 d.; 2, Melanie Miller; 1 d. Educ. Ross High School, Tranent, East Lothian; University of St. Andrews; University of Durham; University of Edinburgh. Lecturer in Geophysics, University of Reading, 1985-89; Lecturer, then Reader in Seismology and Rock Physics, University of Edinburgh, 1989-2000; Visiting Professor: Ecole Normale Supérieure, Paris, 1999, University of Bologna, 2000. Member, International Seismological Centre Governing Council, 1988-89; Member, International Association of Seismology and Physics of the Earth's Interior sub-commissions on Significant Earthquake Precursors, 1990-94, and Modelling the Earthquake Source, 1991-95; Associate Member, Petroleum Science and Technology Institute, 1990-96;

Associate Editor: Geology, 1994-97, Journal of Geophysical Research, 1997-2001, Natural Hazards, 2000-04; Member, American Geophysical Union Committee on the Properties of Earth Materials, 2000-04. Recreations: writing and performing folk music; running (very slowly). Address: (h.) School of Geosciences, University of Edinburgh, West Mains Road, Edinburgh EH9 3JW; T,-0131-650 4911; e-mail: ian.main@ed.ac.uk

Main, Sir Peter (Tester), ERD, MD, LLD (Hon.), FRCPE, CIMgt; b. 21.3.25, Aberdeen; m., 1, Margaret Tweddle (deceased); 2 s.; 1 d.; 2, May Hetherington McMillan. Educ. Robert Gordon's College; Aberdeen University. House Surgeon, Aberdeen Royal Infirmary, 1948-49; Captain, RAMC, 1949-51; Medical Officer with Field Ambulance (Suez), 1956; Lt. Col., RAMC (AER), retired 1964; general practice, 1953-57; The Boots Co. PLC: joined Research Department, 1957; Director of Research, 1968; Managing Director, Industrial Division, 1979; Director, 1973-85, Vice Chairman, 1980-81, Chairman, The Boots Co. PLC, 1982-85; Director: Scottish Development Agency, 1986-91, W.A. Baxter & Sons Ltd., 1985-91. Member, National Economic Development Council, 1984-85; Chairman, Committee of Inquiry into Teachers' Pay and Conditions, Scotland, 1986; Governor, Henley Management College, 1983-86; Elder, Chirnside Parish Church. Recreations: fishing; Scottish music. Address: Ninewells House, Chirnside, Duns, Berwickshire TD11 3XF; T.-01890 818191.

Mair, Alexander, MBE (1967). Governor, Robert Gordon's College, Aberdeen, 1988-2002; b. 5.11.22, Echt; m., Margaret Isobel. Educ. Skene Central School; School of Accountancy, Glasgow. Company Secretary, Grampian TV, 1961-70; appointed Director, 1967; Director and Chief Executive, 1970-87. President, Aberdeen Chamber of Commerce, 1989-91; Chairman: Aberdeen International Football Festival, 1988-91, Oil Industry Community Fund, 1993-2001, RGIT Limited, 1989-98. Recreations: golf; skiing; gardening. Address: (h.) Ravenswood, 66 Rubislaw Den South, Aberdeen AB15 4AY; T.-01224 317619.

Mair, Alistair S.F., MBE, DL, LLD, BSc, BA, FCIM, FRSA. Managing Director, Caithness Glass Ltd., 1977-98, Chairman, 1991-98; b. 20.7.35, Drumblade; m., 1, Anne Garrow (deceased); 2, Mary Bolton; 4 s.; 1 d. Educ. Robert Gordon's College, Aberdeen; Aberdeen University; Open University. Rolls Royce, Glasgow, 1957-71: graduate apprentice, PA to General Manager, Production Control Manager, Product Centre Manager; RAF, 1960-62 (short-service commission, Technical Branch); Managing Director, Caithness Glass Ltd., 1971-75; Marketing Director, Worcester Royal Porcelain Co., 1975-76. Non-Executive Director: Grampian Television, 1986-2001, Crieff Hydro Ltd., 1994-2003 (Chairman, 1996-2003), Murray VCT 3 PLC, 1997-2005; Governor, Morrison's Academy, Crieff, 1985-2006 (Chairman, 1996-2006); Commissioner, Queen Victoria School, Dunblane, 1992-97; Member, Aberdeen University Court, since 1993, Convener, Finance and Estates Committee, 1998-2003, Chancellor's Assessor, Senior Lay Member, and Vice Chairman, since 2000; Chairman, Scottish Committee of University Chairmen, 2001-07; Chairman, CBI Scotland, 1989-91, and Member, CBI Council, 1985-97; President, British Glass Manufacturers Confederation 1997, 1998; Chairman, Crieff Auxiliary Association (Richmond House), 1993-99; Honorary President, Duke of Edinburgh Award, Perth and Kinross, since 1993; Chairman, Perth, Ochil and South Perthshire Conservative and Unionist Associations, since 1999. Recreations: reading; history; gardening; walking; current affairs. Address: (h.) Woodend, Madderty, Crieff PH7 3PA; T.-01764 683210.

Mair, Colin David Robertson, MA, CertED. Rector, The High School of Glasgow, since 2004; b. 4.8.53, Edinburgh. Educ. Kelvinside Academy; St. Andrews University; Glasgow University; Jordanhill College. The High School

of Glasgow: Teacher of Latin, 1976-79, Head of Rugby, 1977-88, Head of Latin, 1979-85, Bannerman Housemaster, 1982-85, Assistant Rector, 1985-96, Deputy Rector, 1996-2004. Commonweal Committee, Trades House of Glasgow, 2004-06; Member, Headteachers' Association of Scotland Council; received Scottish Cricket Writers Award, 1993 "for services to cricket". Recreations: cricket; golf; rugby; walking, watching Partick Thistle. Address: (h.) 17 Ladywood, Milngavie, Glasgow G62 8BE; T.-0141 956 5792; e-mail: rector@hsog.co.uk

Maitland, Peter Salisbury, BSc, PhD, FRSE. Independent Consultant in Freshwater Ecology, since 1986; Visiting Professor, Glasgow University, since 1997; Founder, Scottish Freshwater Group; b. 8.12.37, Glasgow; m., Kathleen Ramsay; 1 s.; 2 d. Educ. Bearsden Academy; Glasgow University. Lecturer in Zoology, Glasgow University, 1959-67; Senior Scientific Officer, Nature Conservancy, 1967-70; Principal Scientific Officer, Institute of Terrestrial Ecology, 1970-86; Senior Lecturer in Ecology, St. Andrews University, 1978-82. Royal Society of Edinburgh Fellowship, 1980; Neill Medal, 1993; Freshwater Biological Association Fellowship, 1996; Zoological Society of London's Marsh Wildlife Award for Conservation, 1999, Publications: ten books; 200 scientific papers. Recreations: wildlife conservation; fish-keeping; gardening; walking; music. Address: (h.) Nether Sunnyside, Gladshot, Haddington EH41 4NR; T.-01620 823691.

Maitland-Carew, The Hon. Gerald Edward Ian, DL. Lord Lieutenant, Roxburgh, Ettrick and Lauderdale, since 2007; b. 28.12.41, Dublin; m., Rosalind Averil Speke; 2 s.; 1 d. Educ. Harrow School. Army Officer, 15/19 The Kings Royal Hussars, 1960-72; looked after family estates, since 1972; Brigadier, Royal Company of Archers; Chairman, Lauderdale Hunt, 1980-2000; Chairman, Lauderdale and Galawater Branch, Royal British Legion Scotland; Deputy Lieutenant, Ettrick and Lauderdale and Roxburgh, 1989; elected Member, Jockey Club, 1987; Member, Border Area, TA Committee; Chairman, International League for the Protection of Horses, 1999; President, Border Rifle League, 1994; Chairman, Gurkha Welfare Trust of Scotland, 1996-2003; Racecourse Steward at Ayr, Kelso, Newcastle, Cheltenham and Newmarket. Recreations: racing; hunting; shooting. Address: (h.) Thirlestane Castle, Lauder, Berwickshire; T.-07971196351.
E-mail: maitlandcarew@thirlestanecastle.co.uk

Maizels, Professor Rick, BSc, PhD, FRSE. Professor of Zoology, Edinburgh University, since 1995; b. 14.5.53, London. Educ. University College London. MRC Scientific Staff, NIMR, Mill Hill, 1979-83; Lecturer, Reader and Professor, Department of Biology, Imperial College, London, 1983-95. Address: (b.) Ashworth Laboratories, Edinburgh University EH9 3JT; T.-0131-650 5511.

Majewsky, Isabell. Chief Executive, Glasgow Opportunities, since 2007. Formerly Director, Connect Midlands. Address: (b.) GO, 36 North Hanover Street, Glasgow G1 2AD; T.-0845 602 1249.
E-mail: info@thegogroup.co.uk

Malik, Councillor Hanzala, JP, BSc. Member, Glasgow City Council, since 1995; Bailie, 1999-2003; b. 26.11.56, Glasgow; m., Halema Sadia; 1 s.; 1 d. Educ. Paisley University. Manager, Dhool Farms Ltd, 1982-87; Financial Consultant, 1987-88; Director, Azad Video, 1988-92. Executive Member, International Links, Glasgow City Council; Chair: Justice and Minorities, Multicultural Media Forum, Woodlands Education Trust, Board, National Resource Centre for Ethnic Minorities, West of Scotland

Racial Equality Council; Member, Board, NHS Greater Glasgow; Chair, West Community Health & Care Partnership. Recreations: badminton; charity work; community work; cooking; overseas travel; philately; politics; swimming. Address: (b.) Glasgow City Council, George Square, Glasgow G2 1DU; T.-0141-287 2000/7041; e-mail: hanzala.malik@councillors.glasgow.gov.uk

Mallinson, Edward John Harold, LLM, MPharm, FRPharmS, FRSH, ACPP, HonMFPH. Consultant in Pharmaceutical Public Health (formerly Chief Administrative Pharmaceutical Officer), NHS Lanarkshire; b. 15.3.50, Bingley; m., Diana Gray; 2 d. Educ. Bradford Grammar School; Bradford University; Cardiff Law School. Staff Pharmacist (Ward Pharmacy Services), Bradford Royal Infirmary, 1973-78; District Pharmaceutical Officer, Perth and Kinross District, 1978-83. Secretary, Scottish Specialists in Pharmaceutical Public Health, formerly Scottish Chief Administrative Pharmaceutical Officers' Group, 1988-90, 1996, and 1999-2001 (Chairman, 1990-92, and 1997-98); Member, Scottish Executive, Royal Pharmaceutical Society of Great Britain, 2000-02 (Hon. Secretary, Bradford & District Branch, 1978, Hon. Secretary, Dundee & Eastern Scottish Branch, 1979-83, Hon. Secretary and Treasurer, Lanarkshire Branch, 1984-2004, Chairman, since 2006); Charter Silver Medallist, 2001; Member of Council, Royal Society of Health, 1992-96, and since 2004, Honorary Treasurer, 1996; Vice Chairman and Secretary, Pharmaceutical Group, Royal Society of Health, 1986-89; Chairman, Strathclyde Police/Lanarkshire Health Board Drug Liaison Committee, 1985-91; Member, General Synod, Scottish Episcopal Church, 1986-95; Honorary Treasurer, Comunn Gaidhlig na h-Eaglais Easbaigich; Honorary Treasurer, Affirming Apostolic Order, 1993-98; Secretary, Lanarkshire Branch, British Institute of Management, 1989-91, Chairman, 1991-94. Recreations: genealogy; Gaelic language and culture; heraldry photography; cooking. Address: (h.) Malden, North Dean Park Avenue, Bothwell, Glasgow G71 8HH; T.-01698 852973; e-mail: ema.bothwell54@virgin.net

Malone, Bernadette, MA, DipEd, MBA. Chief Executive, Perth and Kinross Council, since 2003; b. 2.7.58, Dundee; m., Mick Kennelly. Educ. Lawside Academy; Dundee University. Project Supervisor, Dundee University; Lecturer in Psychology, Dundee College; Soical Strategy Officer, Tayside Regional Council; Strategic Policy Manager, Clackmannanshire Council; Strategic Planning Manager, Head of Performance Planning and Management, Perth and Kinross Council; Clerk to the Lord Lieutenancy, Perth and Kinross. Recreations: fishing; reading; theatre; cinema. Address: (b.) 2 High Street, Perth PH1 5PH: T.-01738 475001.

Malone, Brandon James, LLB, DipLP, LLM, MCIArb, NP, WS. Solicitor Advocate; Partner, Head of Construction, Bell & Scott LLP, since 2001; b. 4.11.70, Aberdeen; m., Hazel Robertson; 2 s.; 1 d. Educ. Banff Academy; University of Aberdeen; University of Strathclyde. Peterkins, Aberdeen, 1992-97; Bell & Scott LLP, since 1997. Member, Board of Governors, Filmhouse, Edinburgh; Committee Member, Chartered Institute of Arbitrators (Scottish Branch). Recreations: family; film; playing rugby; screenwriting. Address: (b.) 16 Hill Street, Edinburgh; T.-0131 226 6703; e-mail: b.malone@bellscott.co.uk

Malone, Wilson, CA, MPhil. Head, Enterprise Networks, Enterprise, Energy and Tourism Directorate, Scottish Government; b. 20.6.55, Glasgow; 1 s. Educ. Hillhead High school; Glasgow Technical College; Glasgow University. CA trainee, 1975-79; Accountant, John G. Kincaid & Co.,

1980-82; Civil Servant, since 1983; Deputy Director, Locate in Scotland, 1988-94. Recreations: sailing; music. Address: (b.) Meridian Court, 5 Cadogan Street, Glasgow G2 6AT; T.-0141-242 5449.

Malygin, Vladimir. Consul General of the Russian Federation, since 2003. Address: (b.) 58 Melville Street, Edinburgh EH3 7HF; T.-0131 225 7098.

Manion, David Howard, BA (Hons), DMS (dist). Chief Executive, Age Concern Scotland, since 2005; b. 10.1.57, Huddersfield; m., Susan; 1 s.; 1 d. Educ. Ravenswood School for Boys; Hull University. Deputy Chief Executive, Mid Essex NHS Trust, until 2002; Press and Campaigns Officer, The London Labour Party, 2003; Director, Age Concern London, 2004. Address: (b.) Causewayside House, 160 Causewayside, Edinburgh EH9 1PR; T.-0845 833 0200; e-mail: david.manion@acscot.org.uk

Mann, Very Rev. Andrew Charles, STB, BA (Hons), Adv.Dip.Crim. Parish Priest of St. Columba's, Banchory and Parish of Upper Deeside, since 2004; b. 8.6.56, Keith. Educ. St. Thomas' School, Keith; St. Vincent's School, Langbank; St. Mary's College, Blairs; Royal Scots College, Spain. Curate, St. Mary's Cathedral, Aberdeen, 1980-83; Parish Priest: St. Mary's Peterhead and Our Lady and St. John the Baptist, Ellon, 1983-89, St. Duthac's, Dornie, 1989-91; Diocesan Director of Pastoral Planning, 1991-93; Parish Priest of St. Peter's, Aberdeen and Sacred Heart, Aberdeen, 1993-2004; Administrator, St. Mary's R.C. Cathedral, Aberdeen, 2000-04; Parish Priest, Banchory and Upper Deeside, since 2004; Vicar General, R.C. Diocese of Aberdeen, since 2003. Recreations: reading; cinema; computing. Address: St. Columba's, 5 High Street, Banchory AB31 5RP; T.-01330-822835.

Mann, Professor David George, BSc, BA, PhD, DSc. Senior Principal Research Scientist, Royal Botanic Garden, Edinburgh, since 1996; Hon. Professor, Glasgow University, since 1996; Faculty, University of Maine, USA; b. 25.2.53, Romford, Essex; m., Lynn Barbara; 1 s.; 1 d. Educ. Brentwood School; Bristol University; Edinburgh College of Art. Edinburgh University: Demonstrator, 1978-81, Lecturer, 1981-90, Director of Studies, 1989-90; Deputy Regius Keeper (Deputy Director), Royal Botanic Garden, Edinburgh, 1990-96. G.W. Prescott Award, 1991, 1997. Publications: editor/author of 130 papers and books. Recreations: classical piano; printmaking and painting. Address: (b.) Royal Botanic Garden, Inverleith Row, Edinburgh EH3 5LR; T.-0131-552 7171; e-mail: d.mann@rbge.org.uk

Mann, Gordon Laurence, OBE, DipTP, MRTPI. Managing Director, Crichton Development Company; b. 28.4.48, Dundee. Director of Planning, Shetland Islands Council, 1980-87; Director of Physical Planning, Dumfries and Galloway Regional Council, 1987-96; Chief Planning Officer, Dumfries and Galloway Council, 1996-97. Address: (b.) Grierson House, The Crichton, Dumfries DG1 4ZE; T.-01387 247544; e-mail: gordon.mann@crichton.co.uk

Manning, Professor Aubrey William George, OBE, BSc, DPhil, FInstBiol, Dr (h c) (Toulouse), DUniv (Open), FRZSS, FRSE, HonDSc (St. Andrews), HonMA (Worcs). Professor of Natural History, Division of Biological Sciences, Edinburgh University, 1973-97, Professor Emeritus, since 1997; President, Scottish Earth Science Education Forum; b. 24.4.30, London; m.; 3 s., inc. 2 by pr. m. Educ. Strode's School, Egham; University College, London; Merton College, Oxford. Research, 1951-54; National Service, Royal Artillery, 1954-56; Lecturer, then Reader in Zoology, Edinburgh University, 1956-73; Secretary-General, International Ethological Committee, 1971-79; President: Association for the Study of Animal Behaviour, 1981-84, Biology Section, British Association for the Advancement of Science, 1993; Member: Scottish Advisory Committee, Nature Conservancy Council, 1982-89, Advisory Committee on Science, NCC, 1985-89; Chairman of Council, Scottish Wildlife Trust, 1990-96; Trustee, National Museums of Scotland, 1997-2005; President, Royal Society of Wildlife Trusts, since 2006. Association for the Study of Animal Behaviour Medal, 1998; Member, Wellcome Trust Population Studies Panel, 1996-99; Patron, Optimum Population Trust; Dobzhansky Memorial Award, Behavioural Genetics Association, 1996; Zoological Society of London Silver Medal, 2003; Presenter: Earth Story series, BBC2, 1998, Talking Landscapes series, BBC 2, 2001, Landscape Mysteries series, BBC2, 2003, Unearthing Mysteries series, Radio 4, 1999-2006; The Sound of Life, 2004; The Rules of Life, 2005. Publication: An Introduction to Animal Behaviour, 5th edition, 1998; research papers in biological journals. Recreations: woodland conservation; walking; architecture. Address: (h.) The Old Hall, Ormiston, East Lothian EH35 5NJ; T.-01875 340536; e-mail: amanning@ed.ac.uk

Mansfield and Mansfield, 8th Earl of (William David Mungo James Murray), JP, DL; b. 7.7.30; m., Pamela Joan Foster; 2 s.; 1 d. Educ. Eton; Christ Church, Oxford. National Service, Malayan Campaign; called to Bar, Inner Temple, 1958; Barrister, 1958-71; Member, British Delegation to European Parliament, 1973-75; Minister of State, Scottish Office, 1979-83; Minister of State, Northern Ireland Office, 1983-84; Director: General Accident Fire and Life Assurance Corporation Ltd., 1972-79, and 1985-98; The American Trust Ltd., 1985-2002; Pinneys of Scotland Ltd., 1985-89; Ross Breeders Ltd., 1989-90; Hon. President, St. Andrews Society of Glasgow, 1972-92; President, Royal Scottish Country Dance Society, 1977-2007; Hon. Member, RICS; First Crown Estate Commissioner, 1985-95. Address: (h.) Scone Palace, Perthshire PH2 6BE.

Manson, Alexander Reid, CBE, SDA, FRAgS. Farmer; General Commissioner of Income Tax, 1991-2006; b. 2.9.31, Oldmeldrum; m., Ethel May Philip; 1 s.; 2 d. Educ. Robert Gordon's College; North of Scotland College of Agriculture. Member, Oldmeldrum Town Council, 1960-65; founder Chairman, Aberdeen Beef and Calf Ltd., 1962; Past President, Scottish Agricultural Organisation Society Ltd.; Chairman, Buchan Meat Producers Ltd., 1982-92; Member, Meat and Livestock Commission, 1986-95; Past President, Federation of Agricultural Cooperatives; Member, Williams Committee of Enquiry, 1989; Member, EU Beef Advisory Committee, 1986-96; Director, National Animal Data Centre, 1992-95; Chairman, Oldmeldrum Heritage Society, since 2000. Recreations: golf; bird-watching. Address: (h.) Kempswood, Oldmeldrum, Inverurie AB51 ODN; T.-01651 872226.

Manson, Frank, MA, MIOSH, MIIRSM. Managing Director; Frank Manson Consultants, since 2006, Registers of Scotland, 1996-2006; b. 18.3.50, Lerwick; m., Mary. Educ. Anderson Educational Institute, Lerwick; Edinburgh University. HM Inspector of Factories, Health and Safety Executive, 1976-80; Technical Executive, BP Detergents International, 1980-84; Production Controller, William Muir Ltd., 1984-85; Business Development Manager, Unisys Corporation, 1985-89; Management Consultant, 1989-92; Assistant Director of Property, Tayside Region, 1992-96; Head of Central Services, Angus Council, 1995-96. Recreations: reading; walking; rugby. Address: (b.) 24A Coates Gardens, Edinburgh EH12 5LE.

Manson, Shirley. Lead singer and guitarist, Garbage, since 1995; b. 26.8.66; m., Eddie Farrell; previous bands: Goodbye Mr MacKenzie, Angelfish; albums: Garbage,

1995, Version 2.0, 1998, beautifulgarbage, 2001, Bleed Like Me, 2005; performed theme song for Bond film, The World is Not Enough.

Mapstone, Sally Louise, DPhil. President, Scottish Text Society, since 2001; Fellow and Tutor in English, St. Hilda's College, Oxford, since 1989; b., Hillingdon, Middlesex; m., Martin Griffiths. Educ. Vyners Grammar School, Ickenham, Middlesex; Wadham College, Oxford University. Editor, Weidenfeld & Nicolson Publishers, London, 1978-81; Junior Research Fellow, St. Hilda's College, Oxford, 1984-86; Lecturer and Supernumerary Fellow, St. Hilda's College, Oxford, 1986-89; Junior Proctor, Oxford University, 2006-07. Publications: author and editor of 7 books on older Scots literature, and numerous articles on the same subject. Recreations: reading and running. Address: (b.) c/o 27 George Square, Edinburgh EH8 9LD; T.-01865 276 860; e-mail: sally.mapstone@st-hildas.ox.ac.uk

Mar and Kellie, Earl of (James Thorne Erskine). Estate Worker; Scottish Liberal Democrat Life Peer, sitting as Lord Erskine of Alloa Tower (Liberal Democrat Spokesman on Scotland, 2001-04, Member, House of Lords Select Committee on the Constitution, 2001-04); Liberal Democrat Assistant Whip, 2002-07; Assistant Transport Spokesman, since 2004; b. 10.3.49, Edinburgh; m., Mary Irene; 1 step s.; 3 step d.; 1 step d. deceased. Educ. Eton; Moray House College of Education; Inverness College. Community Service Volunteer, York, 1967-68; Youth and Community Worker, Craigmillar, 1971-73; Social Worker, Sheffield, 1973-76, Grampian Region, 1976-78; Social Worker, Prison Social Worker, Community Service Supervisor, Highland Region, 1979-87; Builder, Kincardine, 1990-92; Project Worker, SACRO, Falkirk, 1992-93; Royal Auxiliary Air Force Regiment, 1979-85; Royal Naval Auxiliary Service, 1985-88; Chairman, Strathclyde Tram Inquiry, 1996; Parliamentary Commissioner, Burrell Collection (Lending) Inquiry, 1997; Member, House of Lords Select Committee on Religious Offences, 2002-03; Member, House of Lords administration and works committee, since 2004; campaigning for a Dominion with UN, NATO and EU Member status, since 2004; Member, Independence Convention, since 2005. Recreations: canoeing; hill-walking; boat building; Alloa Tower. Address: Hilton Farm, Alloa FK10 3PS.

Maran, Emeritus Professor Arnold George Dominic, MB, ChB, MD, FRCS, FACS, FRCP, FRCS (Eng), FDS (Hon), DSc (Hon). Former Professor of Otolaryngology, Edinburgh University, now Emeritus Professor; Past President, Royal College of Surgeons; Consultant Surgeon, Royal Infirmary and City Hospital, Edinburgh, since 1974; b. 16.6.36, Edinburgh; m., Anna; 1 s.; 1 d. Educ. Daniel Stewart's College; Edinburgh University; University of Iowa. Fifteen Visiting Professorships to foreign universities; Honorary Fellowship, Royal College of Surgeons of South Africa, Royal College of Surgeons of Hong Kong, Royal College of Physicians of Edinburgh, Royal College of Surgeons of England, Royal College of Physicians and Surgeons of Glasgow, Royal Society of Medicine. Order of Gorka Dakshina Bahu, Nepal. Publications: six surgical textbooks and 160 scientific papers; The Voice Doctor (Book Guild 2006); The Three Mafias (Mainstream 2008). Recreations: golf; playing piano; writing; living in Italy. Address: (h.) 2 Orchard Brae, Edinburgh EH4 1NZ; T.-0131-332 0055.

Marcella, Professor Rita Christina, MA (Hons), DipLib, DipEd, PhD, FCMI, FCILIP. Dean, Aberdeen Business School, Robert Gordon University, since 2004, Professor of Corporate Communication, since 2002; b. 10.7.56,

Fraserburgh; m., Philip Marcella; 1 s.; 1 d. Educ. Peterhead Academy; Aberdeen University; Robert Gordon University. Librarian, RGIT, 1983-86; Lecturer, Robert Gordon University, 1986-94; Senior Lecturer, 1994-97; Depute Head of School, Robert Gordon University, 1998-2001; Head of School, Northumbria University, 2001-02. Committee Member: Scottish Council for Development and Industry (SCDI) North East, Grampian Racial Equality Council; Arts and Humanities Research Council Panel Member. Recreations: reading; visiting Italy. Address: (b.) Aberdeen Business School, Robert Gordon University, Garthdee Road, Aberdeen AB10 7QE; T.-01224 263904; e-mail: r.c.marcella@rgu.ac.uk

Marchant, Ian, BA, ACA. Chief Executive, Scottish and Southern Energy, since 2002; b. 9.2.61, Croydon; m., Elizabeth; 1 s.; 1 d. Educ. Trinity School of John Whitgift; Hatfield College; Durham University. Accountancy training with Pricewaterhouse Coopers, 1983-92, including two-year secondment at Department of Energy; joined Southern Electric, 1992, and appointed Finance Director, 1996. Address: (b.) 200 Dunkeld Road, Perth PH1 3AQ; T.-01738 455220.

Marchant, Russell, MBA, BSc, CertEd. Principal and Chief Executive, Barony College, since 2001; b. 15.7.58, Windsor; divorced; m., Amanda Niven; 1 s.; 1 d. Educ. Queen Victoria School, Dunblane; University of Edinburgh; Open University. Lecturer, Derbyshire College of Agriculture, 1981-86; Barony College: Senior Lecturer, 1986-89, Depute Principal, 1989-2001. Secretary, Scotland's Rural Colleges; Chairman, Scotland's Rural Colleges; Board Member, Association of Scottish Colleges. Publications: Inter College Collaboration (Co-Author); An Introduction to Red Deer Farming in Britain. Recreations: rugby; golf; photography; travel; food. Address: (b.) Barony College, Parkgate, Dumfries, DG1 3NE; T.-01387 860251; e-mail: rmarchant@barony.ac.uk

Marjoribanks, John Logan, MA (Cantab). Local Government Political Restrictions Exemptions Adjudicator for Scotland, since 2007; Chairman, Local Government Boundaries Commission for Scotland, 2000-07; Member, Committee of Management, Berwickshire Housing Association, 2001-07; Member, East Regional Board, Scottish Environment Protection Agency, 2002-05; Member, Board of Governors, Macaulay Land Use Research Institute, Aberdeen, 2004-07; b. 21.8.44, Nicosia, Cyprus; m., Andrea Ruth; 1 s.; 2 d. Educ. Merchiston Castle School, Edinburgh; St. John's College, Cambridge. Scottish Agricultural Industries Ltd., 1965-73; Overseas Development Ministry, on secondment to Government of Zambia, Department of Agriculture, 1973-78; Commonwealth Development Corporation (now CDC Group plc), 1979-2000: latterly Director, Public Affairs. Recreations: heraldry; competitive cycling. Address: (h.) Eden House, Gavinton, Duns TD11 3QS; T.-01361 884523; e-mail: john@marjoribanks.com

Markland, John A., CBE, MA, PhD, ACIS. Member of Court, University of Edinburgh, since 2001, Convener of Audit Committee, 2003-06, Vice Convener of Court, since 2006; Chairman, Scottish Leadership Foundation, since 2001; Board Member, Horsecross Arts Ltd., since 2007; President, Old Boltonians Association, 2006-07; b. 17.5.48, Bolton; m., Muriel Harris; 4 d. Educ. Bolton School; Dundee University. Demographer, Somerset County Council, 1974-76; Senior Professional Assistant, Tayside Regional Council, 1976-79; Personal Assistant to Chief Executive, then Assistant Chief Executive, then Chief Executive, Fife Regional Council, 1979-95; Chief Executive, Fife Council, 1995-99; Chairman, Scottish

Natural Heritage, 1999-2006. Vice Chairman, then Chairman, Environmental Campaigns, 2000-06; Chairman: Forward Scotland, 1996-2000, Society of Local Authority Chief Executives (Scotland), 1993-95, Secretary of State for Scotland's Advisory Group on Sustainable Development, 1998-99. Recreation: trying to keep fit. Address: 3, St. Leonard's Bank, Perth PH2 8EB; T.-01738 441798.

Marks, Frederick Charles, OBE, MA, LLB. Commissioner for Local Administration in Scotland (Local Government Ombudsman), 1994-2000; Local Government Adjudicator, 1994-2000; b. 3.12.34, Bellshill; m., Agnes M. Bruce; 3 s.; 1 d. Educ. Wishaw High School; Glasgow University. Depute Town Clerk, Dunfermline, 1963-68; Town Clerk, Hamilton, 1968-75; Chief Executive, Motherwell, 1974-83; General Manager, Scottish Special Housing Association, 1983-89; Deputy Chairman, Local Government Boundary Commission for Scotland, 1989-94; Vice Chairman, Fife Acute Hospitals NHS Trust, 1999-2001; Vice Chairman, Queen Margaret Hospital NHS Trust, 1994-1999. Address: (h.) 5 Queen Margaret Fauld, Dunfermline, Fife KY12 0UY; T.-01383 723501.

Marnoch, The Rt. Hon. Lord (Michael Stewart Rae Bruce), QC (Scot), MA, LLB, LLD (Aberdeen). Senator of the College of Justice, 1990-2005 (retired); b. 26.7.38; m., Alison Stewart; 2 d. Educ.; Loretto; Aberdeen University. Advocate, 1963; QC, 1975; Standing Counsel to Department of Agriculture and Fisheries for Scotland, 1973; to Highlands and Islands Development Board, 1973; Advocate-Depute, 1983-86; Member, Criminal Injuries Compensation Board, 1986-89. Chairman for Scotland, Salmon and Trout Association, 1989-94. Recreations: golf; fishing. Address: (b.) Parliament House, Edinburgh; T.-0131-225 2595.

Marquis, Alistair Forbes, BA, MEd, DipCE, FCollP. Chairman, Scotland Committee of The Boys' Brigade, 1991-2000, elected Representative, UK Brigade Executive for East Lowland Area, 1989-2000, Scottish Member, UK Management Committee, 1991-99, President, West Lothian Battalion, 2000-04 and 2007-08; Hon. Vice President, The Scout Association, The Scottish Council, 1996-2000; b. 13.1.50, Glasgow; m., Margaret Jarvie Greenlees; 1 d. Educ Queen's Park Secondary School; Jordanhill College, Glasgow; Open University; Edinburgh University. Assistant Teacher, Leithland Primary School, Glasgow, 1971-77; Assistant Head Teacher, Dedridge Primary School, West Lothian, 1977-79; Head Teacher, Bankton Primary School, West Lothian, 1979-89; HM Inspector of Schools, 1989-2003, HM Assistant Chief Inspector of Education, 2003; Member, Scottish Committee on Special Educational Needs, 1985-88; Chairman, Lanthorn Community Complex Management Committee, 1979-82; SFA Football Referee, 1972; Church of Scotland Elder and (2005) appointed Member, National Safeguarding Committee; elected Vice-Chair, Livingston Ecumenical Parish, 2006; Member, Rotary International. Recreations: gardening; reading; walking; football refereeing. Address: (h.) 39 Bankton Drive, Murieston, Livingston EH54 9EH. E-mail: alistair.marquis@hmie.gsi.gov.uk

Marr, Colin. Theatre Director, Eden Court Theatre, since 1997; b. 3.4.66, Glasgow; m., Nicky; 2 d. Educ. Hutcheson's Grammar School; University of Edinburgh; Open University. Hall Manager, Queen's Hall, Edinburgh, 1988-92; Theatre and Commercial Manager, Traverse Theatre, Edinburgh, 1992-97. Address: (b.) Bishop's Road, Inverness IV3 5SA; T.-01463 239841.

Marr, Douglas, CBE, MA, MEd. Her Majesty's Inspector of Education (HMIE) (part-time), since 2004; Principal Consultant, Acorn Consulting (Scotland), since 2004; School Management and Curriculum Co-ordinator, Aberdeenshire Education and Recreation, 2002-04; Senior Teaching Fellow, University of Aberdeen, School of

Education, 2004-06; b. 7.2.47, Aberdeen; m., Alison; 1 d. Educ. Aberdeen Grammar School; University of Aberdeen. Teacher of History, Hilton Academy, Aberdeen, 1970-71; Assistant Principal Teacher of History, Aberdeen Grammar School, 1971-76; Principal Teacher of History, Hilton Academy, Aberdeen, 1976-81; Assistant Rector, Kemnay Academy, 1981-84; Depute Rector, The Gordon Schools, Huntly, 1984-87; Headteacher: Hilton Academy, 1987-88, St. Machar Academy, Aberdeen, 1988-95; Rector, Banchory Academy, 1995-2002. Member, Business Management Committee, University of Aberdeen, 2001-06; Member, Aberdeen University Court, 2002-06. Publication: Leisure Education and Young People's Leisure (Co-Author), 1988. Recreations: squash; suffering at the hands (and feet) of Aberdeen F. C.; Member, Leicestershire County Cricket Club. Address: (h.) Oak Lodge, Alford, Aberdeenshire AB33 8DH; T.-019755 63062; e-mail: douglas.marr@alford.co.uk

Marrian, Ian Frederic Young, MA, CA. Accountancy Education Advisor; b. 15.11.43, Kilwinning; m., Moira Selina McSwan; 1 s.; 2 d. Educ. Royal Belfast Academical Institution; Queens University, Belfast; Edinburgh University. Qualified as CA, 1969; Deloitte Haskins & Sells: audit practice, Rome, 1969-72, London, 1972-73, Audit Partner, Edinburgh, 1973-78, Technical Partner, London, 1978-81; Chief Executive and Secretary, Institute of Chartered Accountants of Scotland, 2003-04. Visiting Chair, Edinburgh University. Recreations: gardening in the grand scale; wines. Address: (h.) Walled Garden, Bowerhouse, Dunbar EH42 1RE; T.-01368-862293; e-mail: ian@ianmarrian.co.uk

Marsack, Robyn Louise, BA, BPhil, DPhil. Director, Scottish Poetry Library, since 2000; b. 30.1.53, Wellington, New Zealand; m., Stuart Airlie; 1 d. Educ. Wellington Girls' College; Victoria University, Wellington; Oxford University. Junior Research Fellow, Wolfson College, Oxford, 1979-82; Editor, Carcanet Press, 1982-86, Editorial Manager and Member, Board of Directors, 1986-87; freelance editor, translator and writer, 1987-99. Member, Scottish Arts Council Literature Committee, 1994-99, Chair, Grants to Publishers Panel, 1996-99; Member, Society of Authors Committee of Management, 2001-04. Publications: The Cave of Making: the poetry of Louis MacNeice, 1985; Sylvia Plath, 1992; translations of several books. Recreations: reading, reading, reading. Address: (b.) Scottish Poetry Library, 5 Crichton's Close, Canongate, Edinburgh EH8 8DT; T.-0131-557 2876; e-mail: rmarsack@spl.org.uk

Marsh, Professor John Haig, BA, MEng, PhD, CEng, FREng, FIET, FInstP, FRSA, FIEEE, FRSE, FFCS. Professor of Optoelectronic Systems, University of Glasgow, since 1996; Founder and Chief Technical Officer, Intense Ltd, since 2000; b. 15.4.56, Edinburgh; m., Anabel Christine Mitchell. Educ. Glasgow Academy; Cambridge University; Liverpool University; Sheffield University. University of Sheffield. Research Fellow, 1980-83, Research Scientist, 1983-86; Department of Electronics and Electrical Engineering, University of Glasgow: Lecturer, 1986-90, Senior Lecturer, 1990-94, Reader, 1994-96. Director, NATO Advanced Study Institute, Glasgow, 1990; Member, IET Executive Committee for Photonics Network; Founding Chair, Scottish Chapter, IEEE/LEOS, 1996-98; Vice President, LEOS, 1999-2001 and 2003-05; President, 2008-09 (of IEEE LEOS); elected Member, Board of Governors, 2001-03. Awarded LEOS Engineering Achievement, 2006 (jointly with A.C. Bryce); LEOS Distinguished Service Award, 2006. Publications: Waveguide Optoelectronics (Co-editor); more than 500 papers, book chapters and patents. Recreations: walking; cooking; music; malt whisky. Address: (b.) Intense Ltd., 4 Stanley Blvd., Hamilton International Technology Park, Blantyre, Glasgow G72 0BN. E-mail: john_marsh@intenseco.com

Marshall, David. MP (Labour), Glasgow East, since 2005, Glasgow Shettleston, 1979-2005; b. 1941; m.; 2 s.; 1 d. Chairman, Select Committee on Scottish Affairs. Address: (b.) House of Commons, London, SW1A 0AA.

Marshall, Enid Ann, MA, LLB, PhD, Assoc. Hon. RICS, ACIArb, FRSA, Solicitor. Reader, Scots Law Research Unit, Stirling University, since 1994; Editor, Scottish Law Gazette, since 1983; Chairman, Social Security Appeal Tribunal, Stirling and Falkirk, since 1984; b. 10.7.32, Boyndie, Banffshire. Educ. Whitehills Junior - Secondary School; Banff Academy; Bell-Baxter School, Cupar; St. Andrews University. Apprentice Solicitor, 1956-59; Lecturer in Law, Dundee College of Technology, 1959-72; Lecturer, then Senior Lecturer, then Reader in Business Law, Stirling University, 1972-94. Departmental Editor, Arbitration Section, Journal of Business Law, since 1976. Publications: General Principles of Scots Law; Scottish Cases on Contract; Scottish Cases on Agency; Scottish Cases on Partnerships and Companies; Scots Mercantile Law; Gill on Arbitration (3rd and 4th editions); Charlesworth and Morse Company Law (Scottish Editor); Notes on the Law of Property in Scotland (Editor, 3rd edition); M.C. Oliver's Company Law (10th, 11th, 12th editions). Recreations: animal welfare; veganism. Address: (h.) 3 Ballater Drive, Stirling FK9 5JH; T.-01786 472125.

Marshall, Professor Ian Howard, MA, BD, PhD (Aberdeen), BA (Cantab), DD (Asbury). Professor of New Testament Exegesis, Aberdeen University, 1979-99, Emeritus, since 1999; b. 12.1.34, Carlisle; m., Joyce Elizabeth (deceased); 1 s.; 3 d. Educ. Aberdeen Grammar School; Aberdeen University; Cambridge University; Göttingen University. Assistant Tutor, Didsbury College, Bristol; Methodist Minister, Darlington; Lecturer, then Senior Lecturer and Reader in New Testament Exegesis, Aberdeen University. Publications: Kept by the Power of God; Luke: Historian and Theologian; The Origins of New Testament Christology; New Testament Interpretation (Editor); The Gospel of Luke; I Believe in the Historical Jesus; The Epistles of John; Acts; Last Supper and Lord's Supper; Biblical Inspiration; 1 and 2 Thessalonians; Jesus the Saviour; 1 Peter; Philippians; The Acts of the Apostles; Witness to the Gospel (Co-Editor); The Pastoral Epistles; Exploring the New Testament Vol. II (Co-Author); Moulton and Geden Concordance to the Greek New Testament (Editor); Beyond the Bible; New Testament Theology; Aspects of the Atonement. Address: (b.) School of Divinity and Religious Studies, King's College, Aberdeen AB24 3UB; T.-01224 272388.

Marshall, Leon McGregor, CA. Senior Partner, Stevenson & Kyles, CA, Glasgow, since 1995; Vice-Convener, Church of Scotland World Mission Council, since 2006; Moderator, Presbytery of Greenock, 2002-03; Session Clerk, Kilmacolm Old Kirk, since 1997; b. 10.6.50, Glasgow; m., 1, Barbara Anne McLean (deceased); 2 s.; 1 d.; 2, Judith Margaret Miller. Educ. High School of Glasgow; Glasgow University (as part of CA training). Joined Stevenson & Kyles as a student, 1967; qualified CA, 1972 (joint winner, ICAS Gold Medal); made Partner, 1974. Treasurer, St Enoch's Hogganfield Church, Glasgow, 1973-80; Treasurer, Kilmacolm Old Kirk, 1984-97; Convener, Church of Scotland Central Services Committee, 2001-05; Member, Board of Stewardship and Finance, General Assembly, Church of Scotland, 1990-2001 (Convener, 1997-2001; Convener, Budget and Allocation

Committee, 1993-97); Reader, Church of Scotland, since 1987. Recreations: reading; travel; watching football. Address: (b.) 25 Sandyford Place, Glasgow G3 7NJ; T.-0141-248 3856; e-mail: lm@stevenson-kyles.co.uk

Marshall, Professor Mary Tara, OBE, MA, DSA, DASS, FRSE. Former Director, Dementia Services Development Centre, Stirling University; b. 13.6.45, Darjeeling, India. Educ. Mary Erskine School for Girls; Edinburgh University; London School of Economics; Liverpool University. Child Care Officer, London Borough of Lambeth, 1967-69; Social Worker, Personal Service Society, Liverpool, 1970-74; Research Organiser, Age Concern, Liverpool, 1974-75; Lecturer in Social Studies, Liverpool University, 1975-83; Director, Age Concern Scotland, 1983-89. Member, Alzheimers Care Quarterly Editorial Advisory Board; former Member, Royal Commission on Long-term Care of the Elderly; Member, 21 Century Social Work Committee; Hon. DEd, Queen Margaret University College; Hon. Degree of Doctor of Science in Social Science, University of Edinburgh, 2004; Hon DUniv, University of Stirling, 2006; Fellow of the Royal Society of Arts; Fellow of the Royal Society of Edinburgh. Member, Independent Funding Review of Free Personal and Nursing Care, since 2006; Sessional Inspector with Social Work Inspection Agency, since 2007. Publications: The State of Art in Dementia Care, 1997; Food Glorious Food, perspectives on food and dementia, 2003; Perspectives on Rehabilitation and Dementia, 2005 (Ed); Walking not Wandering, 2006 (Ed) (Co-Author); Social Work and people with dementia (Co-author), 2006. Recreations: photography; bird-watching. Address: (h.) 24 Buckingham Terrace, Edinburgh EH4 3AE; T.-0131 343 1732.

Marshall, Nicholas, BSc, MSc. Environmental Consultant, and Tree Nursery Manager, since 1998; b. 18.6.57; 2 s.; 1 d. Educ. Daniel Stewarts and Melville College; University of Edinburgh; University of Wales, Bangor. Agroforestry Project Manager, VSO and Oxfam, Kenya, 1981-84; Managing Director, Lothian Trees and Timber Ltd., 1984-86; Community Forestry Project Manager, Care International, 1986-90; Forestry Consultant, 1991-92; Forestry Officer, Royal Society for the Protection of Birds, 1992-96; Regional Officer, Millennium Forest for Scotland, 1996-98; Projects Co-ordinator, Reforesting Scotland, 1998-2004. Council Member, Scottish Civic Forum; Director, Environmental Informational Service (Scotland); Editor, Native Woodlands Discussion Group newsletter, 1999-2003; Member, Forestry Commission Advisory Panel, 1999-2003. Recreations: hillwalking; gardening. Address: 64 The Causeway, Duddingston Village, Edinburgh EH15 3PZ; T.-0131-661 2019; e-mail: nick@leaf.me.uk

Marshall, Rosalyn Adela, BSc (Hons), FCCA. Vice Principal and University Secretary, Queen Margaret University, since 2007, Vice Principal (Strategic Projects), since 1997; Member, Accounts Commission for Scotland, 1997-2003; Member, Historic Scotland Audit Committee, since 2005; Member, Board, Edinburgh Academy, 2000-06; Member, Board, Loretto School, since 2007; b. 22.7.54, Dundee. Educ. High School of Dundee; Dundee University. Financial Accountant, Lothian Regional Council, 1976-79; Development Officer, Lothian Health Board, 1979-81; Edinburgh District Council: Administrative Officer, 1982-85, Principal Officer (Financial Incentives), Department of Economic Development and Estates, 1985-86; Financial Controller, Graphic Partners, Edinburgh, 1986-92; Assistant Principal, Administration and Finance, Queen Margaret College, 1992-97. Recreations: golf; theatre; art; travel. Address: (b.) Queen Margaret University, Edinburgh EH21 6UU; T.-0131 474 0000; e-mail: rmarshall@qmu.ac.uk

Marshall, Professor William James, BA, M-ès-L, DPhil, MA. Professor of Modern French Studies, Glasgow University, since 2000; b. 21.2.57, Newcastle

Upon Tyne. Educ. Gosforth High School; Westfield College, London; Université de Paris-X Nanterre; University of Oxford; Polytechnic of Central London. Lecteur, Université de Paris-X Nanterre, 1978- 79; Lecturer, Sunderland Polytechnic, 1982-83; Lecturer, University of Liverpool, 1983-84; Lecturer/Senior Lecturer/Reader, Southampton University, 1984-2000. Publications: Victor Serge the Uses of Dissent, 1992; Guy Hocquenghem, 1996; Quebec National Cinema, 2000; Musicals Hollywood and Beyond (co-ed.) 2000; France and the Americas: Culture, Politics and History (ed.), 2005. Address: (b.) Department of French, 16 University Gardens, Glasgow, G12 8QL; T.-0141-330 4590; e-mail: b.marshall@french.arts.gla.ac.uk

Martin, David McLeod, DA, RSW, RGI. Painter; b. 30.12.22, Glasgow; m., Isobel Agnes Fowlie Smith (deceased); 4 s. Educ. Govan High School; Glasgow School of Art; Jordanhill College of Education. RAF, 1942-46. Principal Teacher, Hamilton Grammar School, 1973-83; retired early to paint full-time; exhibits regularly in Scotland; exhibited RA, 1984; numerous group shows; one man shows, Glasgow, Edinburgh, Perth, Greenock, Newcastle, Stenton, London; mixed shows: New York Art Fair, 1998, 2002, Johannesburg, 1999; featured artist, Perth festival, 1999; 2004: John Martin Gallery, London, The Albany Gallery, Edgar Modern Gallery, Bath, Lemon Street Gallery, Truro, Richmondhill Gallery, London; Smithy Gallery, Dunblane, 2005; 2006/07: The Everard Reid Gallery, Johannesburg; "Lalique", Madison Avenue, New York; The Chelsea Gallery, Palo Alto, California. Former Vice President, RSW. Address: (h.) The Old Schoolhouse, 53 Gilmour Street, Eaglesham, Glasgow G76 0LG.

Martin, David Weir, BA (Econ), MA. Vice-President, European Parliament, 1989-2004, Member (Labour) for Lothians, 1984-99, Senior Member for Scotland, since 1999; b. 26.8.54, Edinburgh; 1 s.; 1 d. Educ. Liberton High School; Heriot-Watt University; Leicester University. Worked as stockbroker's assistant and animal rights campaigner; became Lothian Regional Councillor, 1982; Rapporteur; Intergovernmental Conferences. Publications: The EU's Aid for Trade; Economic Relations with Korea; Bringing Common Sense to the Common Market — A Left Agenda for Europe; European Union and the Democratic Deficit; Europe — An Ever Closer Union; Towards a Wider, Deeper, Federal Europe; Maastricht in a Minute; 1996 and all that; A Partnership Democracy for Europe. Recreations: soccer; reading. Address: (b.) PO Box 27030, Edinburgh EH10 7YP.

Martin, Graham Dunstan, MA, BLitt, GradCertEd. Writer; Senior Lecturer, Edinburgh University, 1982-2000; b. 21.10.32, Leeds; m., 1, Ryllis Daniel; 2 s.; 1 d.; 2, Anne Crombie; 2 s. Educ. Leeds Grammar School; Oriel College and Linacre College, Oxford. Schoolteacher, 1956-65; Assistant Lecturer, then Lecturer, in French, Edinburgh University, 1965-82. Publications: (philosophy) Language, Truth and Poetry, 1975; The Architecture of Experience 1981, Shadows in the Cave, 1990; Inquiry into Speculative Fiction, 2003; Does it Matter?, 2005; Living on Purpose, 2008; (novels) Giftwish, 1980; Catchfire, 1981; The Soul Master, 1984; Time-Slip, 1986; The Dream Wall, 1987; Half a Glass of Moonshine, 1988; poems and poetry translations. Recreations: music; jazz; walking; good food; the Celtic past. Address: 21 Mayfield Terrace, Edinburgh EH9 1RY; T.-0131-667 8160.

Martin, Rev. Iver, BSc, DipTheol. Minister, Stornoway Free Church of Scotland, since 2003; b. 29.6.57, Grantown on Spey; m., Mairi Isabel Macdonald; 2 s.; 4 d. Educ. Camphill High School, Paisley; Robert Gordon's Institute of Technology; Free Church College. National Semiconductor (UK) Ltd.: Graduate Process Engineer, 1980, Senior Engineer, 1983; European Process Engineer, Lam Research Corporation Ltd., 1985; European Product and Sales

Engineer, Silicon Glen Technology, 1987-90; own company, Solus (UK) Ltd., 1990-92; Assistant Minister, Stornoway Free Church, 1995-97; Minister, Bon Accord Free Church, Aberdeen, 1997-2003. Recreations: cycling; reading; music. Address: 46 Francis Street, Stornoway, Isle of Lewis; T.-0185 170 2279; e-mail: iverm@aol.com

Martin, Rev. James, MA, BD, DD. Minister, High Carntyne, Glasgow, 1954-87; b. 21.1.21, Motherwell; m., Marion Gordon Greig; 2 d. Educ. Dalziel High School, Motherwell; Glasgow University. Minister, Newmilns West Church, 1946-54; Convener, Publications Committee, General Assembly, 1978-83 and Board of Communications, 1983-87; Bruce Lecturer, Trinity College, 1960-64. Publications: Did Jesus Rise from the Dead?; The Reliability of the Gospels; Letters of Caiaphas to Annas; Suffering Man, Loving God; The Road to the Aisle; People in the Jesus Story; A Plain Man in the Holy Land; Listening to the Bible; William Barclay: A Personal Memoir; My Friend Bobby; It's You, Minister; It's My Belief; Travels in the Holy Land; God-Collared; William Barclay in a Nutshell; You Can't Be Serious; A Parish Minister's Hats; More About Bobby; Grit for the Road of Life; Seen From My Manse Window; More Grit for Life's Road; More Views from My Manse Window; Manse Memories; People, Places and Puzzles of the New Testament; More Manse Memories; Tales From My Ministry. Recreations: football; conversation. Address: 9 Magnolia Street, Wishaw; T.-01698 385825.

Martin, Rt. Hon. Michael John. Speaker of the House of Commons, since 2000 (Deputy Speaker, 1997-2000); MP (Labour, then Speaker), Glasgow Springburn, 1979-2005; Glasgow (North East), since 2005; b. 3.7.45, Glasgow; m., Mary McLay; 1 s.; 1 d. Educ. St. Patrick's Boys' School, Glasgow. Member, Glasgow Corporation, 1973-74, and of Glasgow District Council, 1974-79. Member, Speaker's Panel of Chairmen, since 1987; Chairman, Scottish Grand Committee, 1987-97. Fellow, Parliament and Industry Trust; Member, College of Piping; Union: AEEU. Recreations: hill-walking; local history; piping; Forth and Clyde Canal enthusiast. Address: (h.) Speaker's House, House of Commons, Westminster, London SW1A 0AA.

Martin, Paul. MSP (Labour), Glasgow Springburn, since 1999; b. 1967, Glasgow; m., Marie. Former Glasgow City Councillor. Recreations: golf; football (in goals), playing keyboard. Address: (b.) Scottish Parliament, Edinburgh EH99 1SP; T.-0141 564 1364.

Martin, Emeritus Professor Peter, BSc, PhD, CEng, FIEE, FInstP. Emeritus Professor, since 2005; Professor of Electronic Systems, University of Abertay Dundee, 1995-2005 (Depute Principal, 2001-05); b. 19.2.47, Richmond, Yorkshire. Educ. Wimbledon College; Newcastle University; Durham University. Lecturer, Oldham College of Technology, 1971-76; Lecturer, Luton College of Higher Education, 1976-79; Senior Lecturer, Trent Polytechnic, 1979-83; Lecturer/Senior Lecturer, Dundee Institute of Technology, 1983-94; Associate Head/Head of School, University of Abertay Dundee, 1994-2001. Member, SQA Engineering Advisory Group, 1993-2003; Convener, Universities Scotland Teaching Quality Forum, 2003-05; Member, Scottish Advisory Committee on Credit and Access, 2001-04. Recreations: travel; walking. Address: (b.) University of Abertay Dundee, Bell Street, Dundee, DD1 1HG; T.-01382 308048.
E-mail: P. Martin@abertay.ac.uk

Martin, Robert (Roy) Logan, QC, LLB. Advocate, since 1976; Barrister, since 1990; b. 31.7.50, Glasgow; m., Fiona Frances Neil; 1 s.; 2 d. Educ. Paisley Grammar School; Glasgow University. Solicitor, 1973-76; admitted to Faculty of Advocates, 1976; Member, Sheriff Courts Rules Council, 1981-84; Standing Junior Counsel, Department of

Employment (Scotland), 1983-84; Advocate-Depute, 1984-87; admitted to Bar of New South Wales, 1987; Queen's Counsel, 1988; called to the Bar, Lincoln's Inn, 1990; Chairman (part-time), Industrial Tribunals, 1990-96; Chairman, Scottish Planning, Local Government and Environmental Bar Group, 1991-96; Chairman, Police Appeals Tribunal, since 1997; Vice-Dean, Faculty of Advocates, 2001-04; Dean, Faculty of Advocates, 2004-07; Co-Chair, Forum for Barristers and Advocates, 2002-06; Co-Chair, International Council for Advocates and Barristers, since 2004; Trustee, National Library of Scotland, since 2004; Honorary Professor, University of Glasgow, since 2006; Affiliate, Royal Incorporation of Architects in Scotland, 1995; Honorary Secretary, The Wagering Club, 1982-91; Governor, Loretto School, since 2002. Recreations: shooting; skiing; modern architecture; vintage motor cars. Address: (h.) Kilduff House, Athelstaneford, East Lothian EH39 5BD; T.-01620 880202.

Martin, Professor William, BSc, PhD. Professor of Cardiovascular Pharmacology, since 1995 and Head of Division of Neuroscience and Biomedical Systems, Glasgow University, since 2004; b. 12.7.55, Glasgow; m., Anne Marie McCartney; 1 s.; 1 d. Educ. Glenwood Secondary; Glasgow University. Post-doctoral Research Fellow, Babraham, Cambridge, 1980-83; Post-doctoral Research Fellow, State University of New York, 1983-85; Lecturer, Department of Cardiology, University of Wales College of Medicine, 1985-87; External Examiner: University College, Dublin, since 2002, University of Nottingham, since 2002, King's College London, since 2006. Member, Research Assessment Exercise Panel, Unit of Assessment 5-8, 2001. Institute for Scientific Information Highly Cited Researcher Award, 2002. Recreations: hill-walking; ballroom dancing; keeping fit. Address: (b.) Division of Neuroscience and Biomedical Systems, Institute of Biomedical and Life Sciences, Glasgow University, Glasgow, G12 8QQ; T.-0141-330 4489.

Marwick, George Robert, SDA, CVO. Lord Lieutenant for Orkney, 1997-2007 (Vice Lieutenant, 1995, Deputy Lieutenant, 1976); Chairman, Swannay Farms Ltd., since 1972; Chairman, Campbeltown Creamery (Holdings) Ltd., 1974-90; Honorary Sheriff, Grampian Highlands and Islands, since 2000; b. 27.2.32, Edinburgh; m., 1, Hanne Jensen; 3 d.; 2, Norma Gerrard. Educ. Port Regis; Bryanston; Edinburgh School of Agriculture. Councillor, local government, 1968-78; Vice-Convener, Orkney County Council, 1970-74, Convener, Orkney Islands Council, 1974-78; Chairman, North of Scotland Water Board, 1970-73; Member, Scottish Agricultural Consultative Panel, 1972-98 (formerly Winter Keep Panel, 1964-72); Director, North Eastern Farmers Ltd., 1968-98;, Member: Countryside Commission for Scotland, 1978-86, Council, National Trust for Scotland, 1979-84. Recreations: shooting; tennis; motor sport. Address: (h.) Swannay House, by Evie, Orkney; T.-01856 721263.

Marwick, Tricia. MSP (SNP), Mid-Scotland and Fife, since 1999; b. 5.11.53, Cowdenbeath; m., Frank; 1 s.; 1 d. Public Affairs Office, Shelter Scotland, 1992-99; Advisory Board Member, World Development Movement (Scotland). Recreations: reading; watching sport. Address: Scottish Parliament, Edinburgh EH99 1SP; T.-0131-348 5680; e-mail: tricia.marwick.msp@scottish.parliament.uk

Mason, Christopher, MA, PhD. Member, Glasgow City Council, since 1995; Chairman, Clyde Maritime Trust, since 1991; b. 8.3.41, Hexham; m., 1, Stephanie Maycock, 2, Marie Blair Reid; 2 d. Educ. Marlborough College; Magdalene College, University of Cambridge. Lecturer in Politics, University of Glasgow, 1966-93; Temporary First Secretary, Foreign and Commonwealth Office, 1971-73; Member, Strathclyde Regional Council, 1982-96 (Liberal

Democrat Group Leader, 1986-96); Chairman, Scottish Liberal Party, 1987-88; founded Clyde Maritime Trust, 1991. Publication: The Effective Management of Resources – The International Politics of the North Sea, 1979; various articles. Recreations: sailing; gardening; holidays. Address: (b.) Clyde Maritime Centre, 100 Stobcross Road, Glasgow G3 8QQ; T.-0141-222 2513; e-mail: info@thetallship.com

Mason, Professor Sir David Kean, KB, CBE, BDS, MD, FRCS, FDS, FRCPath, FRSE, Hon. DSc, Hon. DChD, Hon. LLD, Hon. FFD, Hon. FDS, Hon. FRCS. President, General Dental Council, 1989-94; b. 5.11.28, Paisley; m., Judith Armstrong; 2 s.; 1 d. Educ. Paisley Grammar School; Glasgow Academy; St. Andrews University; Glasgow University. RAF Dental Branch, 1952-54; Registrar in Oral Surgery, Dundee, 1954-56; Senior Lecturer in Dental Surgery and Pathology, Glasgow University, 1964-67; Professor of Oral Medicine, Glasgow University, 1967-92 (Dean of Dental Education, 1980-90); Chairman, National Dental Consultative Committee, 1976-80; Member: Medicines Commission, 1976-80, Dental Committee, MRC, 1973-83, Physiological Systems Board, MRC, 1976-80, GDC, 1976-93, Dental Strategy Review Group, 1980-81, Dental Review Working Party, UGC, 1986-87, WHO Expert Committee on Oral Health, 1991-98; Convener, Dental Council, RCPSGlas, 1977-80; John Tomes Prize, RCS England, 1979; Colyer Prize RCS England, 1993; Honorary Member, British Dental Association, 1993; Honorary Member, American Dental Association, 1994. Publications: Salivary Glands in Health and Disease (Co-Author); Introduction to Oral Medicine (Co-Author); Self Assessment: Manuals I and II (Co-Editor); Oral Manifestations of Systemic Disease. Recreations: golf; tennis; gardening; enjoying the pleasure of the countryside. Address: (h.) Cherry Tree Cottage, Houston Road, Kilmacolm, Renfrewshire; T.-Kilmacolm 2001.

Mason, John Kenneth, BA (Oxon), MPhil. Director, Climate Change and Water Industry and Environmental Quality Directorates, Scottish Government; b. 26.6.56, Chichester; m., Alison Margaret Cruickshanks; 1 s.; 2 d. Educ. Chichester High School; Hertford College, Oxford; University College, London. Kent County Council; Department of Environment; Scottish Office; Registers of Scotland; Head of Enterprise and Industry, Scottish Executive; Principal Private Secretary to the First Minister, Scottish Executive, Head of Tourism, Culture and Sport Group. Director of Scottish Swimming and Edinburgh International Film Festival. Recreations: photography; gardening. Address: (b.) Victoria Quay, Edinburgh EH6 6QQ; T.-0131-244 0779.

Mason, Professor Emeritus John Kenyon French, CBE, MD, LLD, FRCPath, FRCP(Ed), DMJ, FRSE. Regius Professor of Forensic Medicine, Edinburgh University, 1973-85; Honorary Fellow, Faculty of Law, Edinburgh University, since 1985; b. 19.12.19, Lahore; m., Elizabeth Latham (deceased); 2 s. Educ. Downside School; Cambridge University; St. Bartholomew's Hospital. Regular Officer, Medical Branch, RAF, following War Service; Consultant in charge, RAF Department of Aviation and Forensic Pathology, 1957-73. President, British Association in Forensic Medicine, 1981-83; Swiney Prize in Jurisprudence, 1978. Publication: Forensic Medicine for Lawyers, 4th edition; Law and Medical Ethics, 7th edition (Co-Author); Medico-legal Aspects of Reproduction and Parenthood, 2nd edition; Legal and Ethical Aspects of Healthcare (Co-author); The Troubled Pregnancy. Address: (h.) 66 Craiglea Drive, Edinburgh EH10 5PF; T.-0131-447 2301; e-mail: Ken.Mason@ed.ac.uk

Massie, Allan Johnstone, BA, FRSL. Author and Journalist; b. 16.10.38, Singapore; m., Alison Langlands; 2 s.; 1 d. Educ. Drumtochty Castle; Trinity College, Glenalmond; Trinity College, Cambridge. Schoolmaster, Drumtochty Castle, 1960-71; taught EFL, 1972-75;

Creative Writing Fellow, Edinburgh University, 1982-84, Glasgow and Strathclyde Universities, 1985-86; Editor, New Edinburgh Review, 1982-84; Fiction Reviewer, The Scotsman, since 1975; Television Critic, Sunday Standard, 1981-83 (Fraser of Allander Award, Critic of the Year, 1982); Sports Columnist, Glasgow Herald, 1985-88; Columnist: Daily Telegraph, Daily Mail, The Scotsman, Sunday Times. Publications: (novels): Change and Decay in all around I see; The Last Peacock; The Death of Men (Scottish Arts Council Book Award); One Night in Winter; Augustus; A Question of Loyalties; The Sins of the Father; Tiberius; The Hanging Tree; Shadows of Empire; Caesar; These Enchanted Woods; The Ragged Lion; King David; Antony; Nero's Heirs; (non-fiction): Muriel Spark; Ill Met by Gaslight; The Caesars; Portrait of Scottish Rugby; Colette; 101 Great Scots; Byron's Travels; Glasgow; Edinburgh; (as Editor): Edinburgh and the Borders in Verse; (radio play): Quintet in October; (plays): The Minstrel and the Shirra; First-Class Passengers. Recreations: reading; watching rugby, cricket, racing; walking the dogs. Address: (h.) Thirladean House, Selkirk, TD7 5LU; T.-Selkirk 20393.

Masson, Alastair H.B., BA, MB, ChB, FRCSEdin, FRCA; b. 30.1.25, Bathgate; m., Marjorie Nan Paisley-Whyte; 3 s.; 1 d. Educ. Bathgate Academy; Edinburgh University. Consultant Anaesthetist, Edinburgh Royal Infirmary (retired); Visiting Professor of Anesthesiology, South Western Medical School, Dallas, Texas, 1962-63. President: Scottish Society of Anaesthetists, 1978-79, British Society of the History of Medicine, 1989-91; Honorary Archivist, Royal College of Surgeons, Edinburgh; President, Scottish Society of the History of Medicine, 1984-87. Publications: Portraits, Paintings and Busts in the Royal College of Surgeons of Edinburgh, 1995; A College Miscellany – Some Treasured Possessions of the Royal College of Surgeons of Edinburgh, 2001. Recreations: golf; hill-walking; music; travel. Address: (h.) 28 Beechmount Park, Edinburgh.

Masters, Christopher, CBE, BSc (Hons), PhD, AKC, HonD (BA), FRSE. Chairman, Sagentia Group AG, since 2006; b. 2.5.47, Northallerton; m., Gillian Mary Hodson; 2 d. Educ. Richmond School; King's College, London; Leeds University. Shell Research BV/Shell Chemicals UK Ltd., 1971-77; joined Christian Salvesen as Business Development Manager, 1979; transferred to Christian Salvesen Inc., USA, 1982, as Director of Planning; Managing Director, Christian Salvesen Seafoods, 1983-85; Managing Director, Industrial Services Division, 1985-89; a Director, Christian Salvesen PLC, 1987-97; Chief Executive, Christian Salvesen PLC, 1989-97; Executive Chairman, Aggreko plc, 1997-2002; Chairman, Babtie Group Ltd., 2002-04, Voxar Ltd., 2002-04, SMG plc, 2004-07; Chairman, Young Enterprise Scotland, 1994-97; Chairman, Quality Assessment Committee of Higher Education Funding Council, 1991-95; Vice Chairman, Scottish Opera, 1996-99; Member, Scottish Higher Education Funding Council, 1995-2005, Chairman, 1998-2005; Chairman, Festival City Theatres Trust, since 2002; Non-Executive Director: British Assets Trust, since 1989, Scottish Widows, 1991-2000, Scottish Chamber Orchestra Trust, since 1993, John Wood Group PLC, since 2002, The Alliance Trust PLC, since 2002, The Crown Agents, since 2005; Master, The Merchant Company of Edinburgh, since 2007; Honorary Degrees: Strathclyde University and St. Andrews University, 2006, University of Abertay Dundee and Edinburgh University, 2007. Recreations: wines; music. Address: (h.) 12 Braid Avenue, Edinburgh EH10 6EE; T.-0131-447 0812.

Masterton, Gordon Grier Thomson, DTech, BSc, BA, MSc, DIC, FREng, FRSE, FICE, FIStructE, FIES. Vice

President, Jacobs Babtie, since 2002; President, The Institution of Civil Engineers, 2005-06; b. 9.6.54, Charlestown, Fife; m., Lynda Christine Jeffries; 1 s.; 1 d. Educ. Dunfermline High School; University of Edinburgh; Imperial College London; Open University. Babtie Shaw & Morton, 1976; Director, Babtie Group Ltd., 1993; Director, Babtie International Ltd., 1993; Director, Babtie Malaysia, 1995 (based in Kuala Lumpur); Managing Director, Facility Business, 2002. Visiting Professor, University of Paisley, 2001-05; Member, Smeatonian Society, since 2004; Chairman, Construction Industry Council, Scotland, 2002-04; Royal Commissioner on the Ancient and Historical Monuments of Scotland, since 2003. Recreations: opera; engineering history; racquet sports; walking. Address: (b.) Jacobs Babtie, 95 Bothwell Street, Glasgow G2 7HX; T.-0141 566 8331; e-mail: gordon.masterton@jacobs.com

Mather, Jim. MSP (SNP), Argyll and Bute, since 2007, Highlands and Islands, 2003-07; Minister for Enterprise, Energy and Tourism, since 2007; b. 6.3.47; m.; 1 s.; 1 d. Educ. Paisley Grammar School; Greenock High School; Glasgow University. Chartered Accountant. Address: (b.) Scottish Parliament, Edinburgh EH99 1SP; T.-0131 348 5000.

Matheson, Alexander (Sandy), OBE, FRPharmS, JP. Lord Lieutenant, Western Isles Area, since 2001; Chairman, Highlands and Islands Airports Ltd., 2001-07; Chairman, Harris Tweed Authority; b. 16.11.41, Stornoway; m., Irene Mary Davidson, BSc, MSc; 2 s.; 2 d. Educ. Nicolson Institute, Stornoway; Robert Gordon's Institute of Technology, Aberdeen. Chairman, Stornoway Pier and Harbour Commission, 1991-2001 (Member, since 1968); Member, Stornoway Trust Estate, since 1967 (Chairman, 1971-81); Chairman: Stornoway Branch, RNLI (1974-81 and 1994-2004), Western Isles Development Fund, 1972-98, Western Isles Health Board, 1993-2001 (Member, 1973-2001); Member, Stornoway Town Council, 1967-75; Provost of Stornoway, 1971-75; Member: Ross and Cromarty County Council, 1967-75, Western Isles Islands Council, 1974-94 (Chairman, Development Services, 1974-80, Vice-Convener, 1980-82, Convener, 1982-90); President, Islands Commission of the Conference of Peripheral Maritime Regions of Europe, 1987-91 and 1993-94; Honorary Sheriff, since 1972; Chairman, Roderick Smith Ltd., Stornoway. Address: (h.) 33 Newton Street, Stornoway, Isle of Lewis; T.-01851 702082.

Matheson, Allen Short, CBE, FRIBA, PPRIAS, MRTPI (Rtd). Retired Partner, Matheson Gleave Partnership; b. 28.2.26, Egypt; m., Catherine Anne; 2 s. Educ. George Watson's College; Edinburgh College of Art. Past President, Royal Incorporation of Architects in Scotland; Past Chairman, Scottish Construction Industry Group; former Vice-Chairman, Board of Governors, Glasgow School of Art; former Director, Glasgow Chamber of Commerce; former Member, Royal Fine Art Commission for Scotland; Past Chairman, Joint Standing Committee of Architects, Surveyors and Building Contractors. Address: (h.) 11 Spence Street, Glasgow G20 0AW; T.-0141-946 5670.

Matheson, Angus Macrae, MA, LLB. Solicitor and Notary Public; Partner, Burnett & Reid, Solicitors, since 1979; b. 25.9.51, Inverness; m., Paula Louise Taylor; 4 s.; 1 d. Educ. Inverness Royal Academy; University of Aberdeen. Apprentice, 1974-76; Assistant, 1976-79. Past President, Gordonian Rugby Club; Past Chairman, Seafield Club; HIE Ambassador. Recreations: rugby; golf; music; wine; touring Scotland. Address: (b.) 15 Golden Square, Aberdeen AB10 1WF; T.-01224 644 333; e-mail: ammatheson@burnett-reid.co.uk

Matheson, Ann, OBE, MA, MLitt PhD Hon. DLitt; b. 5.7.40, Wester Ross; m., T. Russell Walker. Educ. Dingwall Academy; St Andrews University; Edinburgh University. Ferranti Ltd., 1962-64; Teaching in Finland,

1964-67; National Library of Scotland: Assistant Keeper, 1972-83, Keeper, 1983-2000. Chairman, Literature Committee, Scottish Arts Council, 1997-2003; Chairman, Consortium of European Research Libraries; Chairman, NEWSPLAN 2000; Secretary, General Council, University of Edinburgh; Saltire Society Literary Panel; Secretary General, Ligue des Bibliothèques Européennes de Recherche. Publications: Theories of Rhetoric, 1995; Gaelic Union Catalogue (Co-Editor) 1984; For the Encouragement of Learning, (Co-Editor), 1989. Recreations: literature; travel. Address: Yewbank, 52 Liberton Brae, Edinburgh, EH16 6AF; T.-0131-664 2717.
E-mail: a.matheson@tinyworld.co.uk

Matheson, Gordon, MA, MCIPD, FRSA. Member, Glasgow City Council, since 1999, currently Executive Member for Education and Social Renewal; Bailie of the City, since 2003; b. 1.11.66, Glasgow; Civil Partner: Stephen Wallace. Educ. St. Stephen's High School, Port Glasgow; University of Glasgow; University of Strathclyde. Advisor and Tribunal Representative, Citizens' Advice Bureau, 1991-92; Employment Counsellor and Trainer, Castlemilk Economic Development Agency, 1992-96; Employment Consultant/Parliamentary Manager, Royal National Institute of the Blind, Scotland, 1996-2007. Chair, Kelvin Constituency Labour Party, 1997-2001; Member, Scottish Labour Party Policy Forum, since 2000; Former Member, Board: Royal Scottish National Orchestra, Scottish Low Pay Unit; Substitute Member, Strathclyde Joint Police Board; Chair, Merchant City Festival; Chair, Local Community Planning Partnership Board; Member, Strathclyde University Court; Member, Board of Glasgow Royal Concert Hall Ltd. Publication: Standards in Vocational Guidance for People with a Visual Impairment (Co-Author), 2000. Recreations: theatre; orchestral concerts; eating out with friends; ran Great Scottish Run and New York Marathon, 2002). Address: (b.) Glasgow City Council, City Chambers, George Square, Glasgow G2 1DU; T.-0141 287 5480.
E-mail: gordon.matheson@councillors. glasgow.gov.uk

Matheson, John Alexander, BA, MBA, CPFA. Finance Director, NHS Lothian, since 2000; Past Chairman, Scottish Branch, Chartered Institute of Public Finance and Accountancy; Member, Board of Management, Edinburgh's Telford College, 1998-2007; b. 23.6.55, Dingwall; m., Judi; 1 s.; 1 d. Educ. Invergordon Academy; Heriot-Watt University; Edinburgh University. Finance Director, Edinburgh Healthcare NHS Trust, 1994-99. Finance Director of the Year, 2004 (non profit sector). Recreation: hill-walking; golf. T.-0131-536 9086.

Matheson, Michael, BSc, BA, Dip. Applied Soc Sci. MSP (SNP), Falkirk West, since 2007, Central Scotland, 1999-2007; Member, Health and Sport Committee, since 2007; Member: Justice and Home Affairs Committee, 2000-01, Enterprise and Culture Committee, since 2004; Vice Convener, Cross Party Group on Cuba; b. 8.9.70, Glasgow. Educ. John Bosco Secondary School; Queen Margaret College, Edinburgh; Open University. Community Occupational Therapist: Highland Regional Council, Social Work Department, 1991-93, Stirling Council, Social Work Department, 1993-99. Member: Ochils Mountain Rescue Team, Advisory Board, Caledonian Club House, Falkirk; Hon. Vice President, English Speaking Union, Scotland. Recreation: mountaineering. Address: (b.) 15A East Bridge Street, Falkirk FK1 1YD; T.-01324 629271.

Matheson, Susan Margaret Graham, BSc (Soc Sci). Chief Executive, Sacro, since 1996; b. 6.6.49, Tarbert,

Harris; m., Edward Smith; 1 d.; 2 step-s.; 1 step-d. Educ. St. George's School for Girls, Edinburgh; Edinburgh University. Antique dealer, 1971-73; Research Officer, then Senior Research Officer, Scottish Office Central Research Unit, 1973-88; Director, Family Mediation Scotland, 1988-96. Honorary Member, UK College of Family Mediators. Publications: several Government research reports and other publications. Address: (b.) 1 Broughton Market, Edinburgh EH3 6NU; T.-0131-624 7270.

Mathewson, David Carr, BSc, CA. Merchant Banker; Director, Noble and Company Limited, since 2003; b. 26.7.47, Broughty Ferry; m., Jan McIntyre; 1 s.; 1 d. Educ. Daniel Stewart's College, Edinburgh; St. Andrews University. Deloitte Haskins & Sells, Edinburgh, 1968-72; Williams Glyn & Co., London, 1972-75; Nedbank Group, South Africa, 1976-86; Director: Noble Grossart Limited, 1989-2000, Edinburgh UK Tracker Trust plc, since 1998, Amazing Holdings plc (Chairman, since 2004), Asian Growth Properties Limited (Chairman), Corsie Group plc (Chairman); Director: Robertson Group Limited, various private companies; Member, Board of Trustees, Royal Botanic Garden, Edinburgh. Recreations: family interests; golf; shooting; athletics. Address: Dalveen, 7 Barnton Park, Edinburgh EH4 6JF.

Mathewson, Sir George Ross, CBE, BSc, PhD, MBA, LLD (Dundee), LLD (St. Andrews), DUniv (Glasgow), Dr.hc (Edinburgh), FCIBS, CEng, MIEE, CCMI. Chairman, Royal Bank of Scotland Group plc, 2001-06; Non-Executive Director, Stagecoach Group, since 2006; Chairman, Toscafund Holdings, since 2006; Chairman, Cheviot Capital, since 2006; President, International Monetary Conference, 2005-06; Director: Scottish Investment Trust Ltd., since 1981; b. 14.5.40, Dunfermline; m., Sheila Alexandra Graham Bennett; 2 s. Educ. Perth Academy; St. Andrews University; Canisius College, Buffalo, New York. Assistant Lecturer, St. Andrews University, 1964-67; Systems Engineer (various positions), Bell Aerospace, Buffalo, New York, 1967-72; ICFC: Executive in Edinburgh Area Office, 1972-81, Area Manager, 1974-79, Director and Assistant General Manager, 1979-81; Chief Executive, Scottish Development Agency, 1981-87; Royal Bank of Scotland Group plc: joined as Director, Strategic Planning and Development, 1987, Group Chief Executive, 1992-2000, Executive Deputy Chairman, 2000-2001. Chairman: Royal Botanic Garden Edinburgh Campaign Board, Wood Mackenzie Ltd., since 2007, Council of Economic Advisers to the Scottish Government, since 2007. Recreations: tennis; skiing; gardening; rugby; golf; business; shooting.

Mathieson, Fiona McDougall, BEd, BD, PGCommEd. Minister, Carrick Knowe Parish, Edinburgh, since 2001; b. 28.12.62, Lennoxtown; m., Angus Mathieson. Educ. Mearns Castle High; Williamwood Secondary; Jordanhill College; Glasgow University; Edinburgh University; Heriot Watt University. Career History: Assistant Minister, Greenbank Edinburgh; Church of Scotland National Youth Adviser; Chaplain to The University of Glasgow. Director, Corstorphine Dementia Project. Recreations: food; wine and friends. Address: 21 Traquair Park West, Corstorphine, Edinburgh EH12 7AN; T.-0131-334-9774; e-mail: fiona.mathieson@ukgateway.net

Mathieson, Janet Smith, MA (Hons), BD (Hons), ALCM. Minister of Parishes of Cawdor linked with Croy and Dalcross; Presbytery of Inverness, since 2003; b. 6.11.57, Kilmarnock. Educ. Bentinck Primary School, Kilmarnock; James Hamilton Academy, Kilmarnock; Jordanhill College of Education; University of Glasgow; New College, University of Edinburgh. Career History: Principal Teacher

of English: James Hamilton Academy, Kilmarnock and Ardrossan Academy; Part-Time Assistant Minister, Kilmarnock: Henderson; Assistant Minister, Kilmarnock: St. Kentigern's; Chaplain to Moderator of General Assembly of Church of Scotland, 2005-06. Chairman of Trustees, Christian Education Association Scotland; Trustee, Frank Mullen Tourism Trust. Address: The Manse, Croy, Inverness IV2 5PH; T.-01667 493 217.

Mathieson, John George, CBE, TD, DL, BL. Retired Solicitor; Chairman, Thorntons, WS, Tayside, 1990-97; b. 15.6.32, Argyll; m., Shirley Bidder; 1 s.; 1 d. Educ. George Watson's College, Edinburgh; Glasgow University. Territorial Army, 1951-86: Commanding Officer The Highland Regiment RA, TA Colonel for Highlands, Honorary Colonel 105 Regiment RA(TA), Chairman, Highlands TA Association; ADC TA, the Queen, 1975-80. Scottish Director, Woolwich Building Society, 1975-96; Chairman: Independent Tribunal Service, 1992-2004, Arbroath Branch, Royal British Legion, Scotland and Earl Haig Fund, Scottish Solicitors Discipline Tribunal, 1986-92, Royal Artillery Council for Scotland, Dundee SSAFA, 2002, Lloyds TSB Foundation Scotland, 1999-2002, SSAFA Dundee, 2002-07; Deputy Lieutenant, Angus, 1977; Honorary President, Angus Bn., Boys' Brigade; Elder, Colliston Parish Church. Recreations: shooting; golf; gardening. Address: (h.) Willanyards, Colliston, Arbroath, Angus; T.-01241 890286.

Matthew, Alan Stuart, LLB. Solicitor, since 1980; b. 9.12.56, Dundee; m., Eileen; 2 d.. Educ. Morgan Academy, Dundee; University of Dundee. Apprentice Solicitor, J. R. Stevenson and Marshall, Dunfermline, 1978-80; Solicitor: Thorntons & Dickies, Dundee, 1980-82, Clark Oliver, Arbroath and Forfar, 1982-84, Messrs Burns Veal and Gillan (later Burns Veal), Dundee, 1984-85; Partner: Burns Veal, 1985-98, Partner, Miller Hendry (incorporating Burns Veal), since 1998. Director, Solicitors Financial Services Ltd., 1990-2000; Member, Council, Law Society of Scotland, since 1997; Member, Council, Faculty of Solicitors and Procurators in Dundee, since 1997. Recreations: rugby; hillwalking; after dinner speaking. Address: (b.) 13 Ward Road, Dundee DD1 1LU; T.-01382 200000.

Matthew, Colin, MBA, FIB. Executive Director, HBOS plc, since 2001; Treasurer, Bank of Scotland, since 2005; b. 9.9.50, Duns; m., Linda; 1 s. Educ. Ayr Academy; Strathclyde University. Address: (b.) The Mound, Edinburgh EH1 1YZ; T.-0131 243 5511.

Matthews, Baird, BL. Solicitor in private practice, 1950-2003; Honorary Sheriff, Kirkcudbright and Stranraer; b. 19.1.25, Newton Stewart; m., Mary Thomson Hope; 2 s.; 1 d. Educ. Douglas Ewart High School; Edinburgh University. Commissioned, Royal Scots Fusiliers, 1944; demobilised as Captain, 1st Bn., 1947; Partner, A. B. & A. Matthews, Solicitors, Newton Stewart; Clerk to General Commissioners of Income Tax, Stranraer and Newton Stewart Districts, 1952; Burgh Prosecutor, Newton Stewart, 1968; Depute Procurator Fiscal for Wigtownshire, 1970; Chairman, Board of Local Directors, General Accident Fire and Life Assurance Corporation, 1988; Director, Newcastle Building Society (Scottish Board), 1991; Dean of Faculty of Stewartry of Kirkcudbright Solicitors, 1979; Dean of Faculty of Solicitors of the District of Wigtown, 1983; Chairman, Appeals Tribunal; President, Newton Stewart Golf Club. Recreations: golf; travel; conversation. Address: (h.) Marchbank, Newton Stewart; T.-01671 403143.

Matthews, the Hon. Lord (Hugh Matthews). Senator of the College of Justice, since 2007; b. 4.12.53, Port Glasgow; m., Lindsay Mary Auld Wilson. Educ. St Joseph's Academy, Kilmarnock; Glasgow University. Admitted to Faculty of Advocates, 1979; Standing Junior Counsel, Department of Employment, 1984-88;

Advocate Depute, 1988-93; QC, 1992; Temporary Sheriff, 1992-97; Sheriff of Glasgow and Strathkelvin, 1997-2007; Temporary Judge, 2004-07. Recreations: Celtic; looking after animals; golf; science fiction; pub quizzes. E-mail: lordmatthews@scotcourts.gov.uk

Matthews, Professor John Burr Lumley, MA, DPhil, FRSE, FRSA, FFCS. Honorary Professor, University of Stirling, since 1984; Honorary Fellow, Scottish Association for Marine Science; b. 23.4.35, Isleworth; m., Jane Rosemary; 1 s.; 2 d. Educ. Warwick School; St. John's College, Oxford University. Research Scientist, Oceanographic Laboratory, Edinburgh, 1961-67; Senior Lecturer, later Professor, Department of Marine Biology, University of Bergen, Norway, 1967-84; Visiting Professor, University of British Columbia, Canada, 1977-78; Deputy Director, Dunstaffnage Marine Laboratory, 1984-88; Director, NERC Dunstaffnage Marine Laboratory and Scottish Association for Marine Science, 1988-94; Secretary, The Scottish Association for Marine Science, 1988-99. Deputy Chairman, South West Regional Board, Scottish Natural Heritage, 1994-97; Secretary, International Association for Biological Oceanography, 1994-2003; Trustee, Oban Hospice Ltd., 1999-2006; Trustee, Hebridean Whale and Dolphin Trust, since 1999 (Chairman, since 2001); Trustee, NADAIR Trust, 2003-07. Recreations: hill walking; gardening; pethau cymreig. Address: (h.) The Well, 18 Manse Road, Milnathort, Perth and Kinross KY13 7YQ; T.-01577 861066.

Matthews, Trevor John, MA, FIA, FIAA. Chief Executive, UK Financial Services, Standard Life, since 2007, joined, 2004; President and CEO, Manulife Japan, since 2001; b. 25.3.52, Sydney, Australia; m., Michele; 3 s. Educ. Punchbowl Boys' High, Sydney, Australia; Macquarie University, Sydney, Australia. Actuarial Cadet, Legal and General, 1970-72; various roles, Legal and General, Australia, 1973-89; Managing Director, Legal and General, Australia, 1989-96; General Manager, Personal Financial Services, National Australia Bank, 1996-98; Executive General Manager, Canadian Operations, Manulife Financial Corporation, 1998-2001. President, Institute of Actuaries of Australia, 1997; Inaugural Member, Life Insurance Actuarial Standards Board, 1995, Australia. Recreations: travel; reading; Australian cricket and rugby. Address: (h.) 2 Ettrick Road, Edinburgh EH10 5BJ; T.-+44 771 2485430.
E-mail: trevor_matthews@standardlife.com

Maver, Professor Thomas Watt, BSc (Hons), PhD, HonFRIAS, FRSA. Honorary Professor, Mackintosh School of Architecture, Glasgow School of Art; Emeritus Professor of Computer Aided Design, Department of Architecture and Building Science, and Director of the Graduate School, Strathclyde University, 1982-2003 (Head of Department, 1983-85, 1988-91, Vice-Dean, Faculty of Engineering, 1993-2002); b. 10.3.38, Glasgow; m., Avril Elizabeth Cuthbertson; 2 d. Educ. Eastwood Secondary School; Glasgow University. Special Research Fellow, Engineering Faculty, Glasgow University, 1961-67; Strathclyde University: Research Fellow, School of Architecture, 1967-70, Director, Architecture and Building Aids Computer Unit, Strathclyde, since 1970, Visiting Professor: Technical University Eindhoven, Universiti Sains Malaysia, University of Rome (La Sapienza); Past Chairman and first Honorary Fellow of the Design Research Society; CIBS Bronze Medal, 1966; Royal Society Esso Gold Medal, 1989; BEPAC Distinguished Service Award, 1997; Founder, CAAD Futures and ECAADE. Recreation: experiencing Europe and beyond. Address: (h.) 8 Kew Terrace, Glasgow G12 0TD; T.-0141-339 7185.

Mavor, Prof. John, BSc, MPhil, PhD, DSc (Eng), FREng, FRSE. Vice-President (Physical Science and Engineering), Royal Society of Edinburgh, 2004-Sept. 2007; Principal and Vice-Chancellor, Napier University, 1994-2002; b. 18.7.42;

m., Susan Christina Colton; 2 d. Educ. City University, London; London University. AEI Research Labs, London, 1964-65; Texas Instruments Ltd, Bedford, 1968-70; Emihus Microcomponents, Glenrothes, 1970-71; University of Edinburgh: Lecturer, 1971, Reader, 1979, Lothian Chair of Microelectronics, 1980, Head of Department of Electrical Engineering, 1984-89, Professor of Electrical Engineering, 1986-94, Dean, 1989-94, and Provost, 1992-94, Faculty of Science and Engineering. FInstP; FIEEE; FIET; Hon. DSc: Greenwich, 1998, City, 1998. Publications: MOST Integrated Circuit Engineering, 1973; Introduction to MOS LSI Design, 1983; over 150 technical papers in professional electronics journals. Recreations: gardening; walking; steam railways. Address: 8 Heriot Row, Edinburgh EH3 6HU.

Maxwell, Donald, MA, DMus(Hon), FRWCMD, FLCM. Professional Singer; b. 12.12.48, Perth; 1 d. Educ. Perth Academy; Edinburgh University. Former Teacher of Geography; since 1976, professional Singer with British opera companies and orchestras; Principal Baritone, Scottish Opera, 1978-82; Principal Baritone, Welsh National Opera, 1982-85; guest appearances, BBC Proms, Edinburgh Festival, Royal Opera House, London, Vienna, Paris, Milan, Tokyo, New York, Amsterdam, Salzburg, Buenos Aires - notably as Falstaff; Director, National Opera Studio; Head of Opera, RWCMD; comedy - The Music Box with Linda Ormiston. Recreation: railways. Address: (b.) Music International, 13 Ardilaun Road, Highbury, London N5 2QR; T.-020 7359 5183.

Maxwell, Ingval, OBE, DA (Dun), RIBA, FRIAS, AABC, FSA Scot. Director, Technical Conservation Research and Education, Historic Scotland, since 1993; b. 28.5.44, Penpont; m., Susan Isabel Maclean; 1 s.; 1 d. Educ. Dumfries Academy; Duncan of Jordanstone College of Art, Dundee. Joined Ministry of Public Buildings and Works as Architect, 1969; Area Architect, then Principal Architect, Ancient Monuments Branch, 1972-85; Assistant Director of Works, Historic Scotland, 1985-93; RIBA Research Award, 1970-71; RIAS Thomas Ross Award, 1988; Chairman, Scottish Vernacular Buildings Working Group, 1990-94; Chairman: Scottish Conservation Forum in Training and Education, since 1994, Scottish Stone Liaison Group, 1997-2007; Member, RIAS Conservation Committee; Member, European Commission COST Action C5, 1996-2000; Chairman, European Science Foundation COST Action C17, 2002-06; Member, European Construction Technology Platform - Focus Area Cultural Wastage, since 2006; Director, Architects Accredited in Building Conservation, 1999-2005; Member, ICOMOS UK Executive Committee, 1995-2006; Member, ICOMOS International Scientific Committee on Stone, since 2000; Member, UCL Centre for Historic Buildings, Collections and Sites Academic Advisory Committee, since 2001; Member, UK and Ireland Blue Shield Organisation, since 2001; Trustee: Charles Wallace India Trust, since 2003. Publications: Building Materials of the Scottish Farmstead, 1996; Conservation of Historic Graveyards Guide for Practitioners (Co-Author), 2001; Stone in Scotland (Co-Author), 2006; INFORM - Masonry Decay, 2005, Fire Safety, 2005, Repairing Scottish Slate Roofs, 2006, Repointing Rubble Stonework, 2007, Cleaning Sandstone, 2007; COST Action C17 "Fire Loss to Historic Buildings" Final Report (3 vols) (Editor), 2007; COST Action C17 "Fire Loss to Historic Buildings" Conference Proceedings (3 vols) (Editor), 2007. Recreations: photography; astronomy; aircraft; buildings. Address: (h.) 135 Mayfield Road, Edinburgh EH9 3AN.

Maxwell, Simon, BSc, MB, ChB, MD, PhD, FRCP, FRCPE, FBPharmacolSci. Consultant Physician, Western General Hospital, Edinburgh, since 1998; Senior Lecturer,

Edinburgh University, since 1998; b. 14.2.62, Edinburgh; m., 1 s. Educ. Nottingham High School; Birmingham University. Lecturer in Medicine, Birmingham Medical School, 1990-96; Senior Lecturer in Medicine, Leicester Medical School. Chairman, Scottish Medical Academic Staff Committee, BMA; Vice-President, British Pharmacological Society; Chairman, Lothian University Hospitals Drug and Therapeutics Committee. Address: (b.) Clinical Pharmacology Unit, University of Edinburgh, Queens Medical Research Institute, Royal Infirmary of Edinburgh, Edinburgh EH16 4TJ; T.-0131 242 9332; e-mail: s.maxwell@ed.ac.uk

Maxwell, Stewart, MSP, BA (Hons). MSP (SNP), West of Scotland, since 2003; Minister for Communities and Sport, since 2007; SNP Parliamentary Group Secretary, 2003-07; b. 24.12.63, Glasgow; m., Mary; 1 d. Educ. King's Park Secondary School; Glasgow College of Technology. Strathclyde Fire Brigade: Industrial Training Manager, 1993-94; Senior Admin Officer, 1994-2000; Management Information System Project Manager, 2000-03. SNP Deputy Health Spokesperson, 2004-06; SNP Spokesperson on Sport, Culture and Media, 2006-07; Honorary Vice President, Royal Environmental Health Institute of Scotland, since 2006. Recreations: reading; swimming; watching rugby; eating out. Address: (b.) Scottish Parliament, Edinburgh EH99 1SP; T.-0131 348 5669.
E-mail: Stewart.Maxwell.msp@scottish.parliament.uk; Ministerforcommunitiesandsport@scotland.gsi.gov.uk

Maxwell-Irving, Alastair Michael Tivey, BSc, CEng, MIEE, MIMgt, FSA, FSAScot, industrial Archaeologist; b. 1.10.35, Witham, Essex; m., Esther Mary Hamilton, MA, LLB. Educ. Lancing College; London University; Oxford University (1975); Stirling University. General Electric Company, 1957; English Electric Company, 1960; Assistant Factor, Annandale Estates, 1966; Weir Pumps Ltd., 1970-91; founder Member and Secretary, 1975-78, Central Scotland Branch, British Institute of Management. Contributor, Burke's Landed Gentry, 1963-2001; Nigel Tranter Memorial Award, 2003; Trustee, Bonshaw Preservation Trust, 2007. Publications: Genealogy of the Irvings of Dumfries, 1965; The Irvings of Bonshaw, 1968; The Irvings of Dumfries, 1968; Lochwood Castle, 1968; Early Firearms and their Influence on the Military and Domestic Architecture of the Borders, 1974; Cramalt Tower: Historical Survey and Excavations, 1977-79, 1982; Borthwick Castle: Excavations 1979, 1982; Andrew Dunlop (Clockmakers' Company 1701-32), 1984; Hoddom Castle: A Reappraisal of its Architecture and Place in History, 1989; Lochwood Castle, 1990; The Castles of Buittle, 1991; Lockerbie Tower, 1992; Torthorwald Castle, 1993; Scottish Yetts and Window Grilles, 1994; The Tower-Houses of Kirtleside, 1997; Kenmure Castle, 1997; The Border Towers of Scotland: their history and architecture – The West March, 2000; The Maxwells of Caerlaverock (in Lordship and Architecture in Medieval and Renaissance Scotland), 2005; Family Memoirs, 2007. Recreations: architecture and history of the Border towers of Scotland; archaeology; family history and genealogy; Florence and the art and architecture of Tuscany; horology; heraldry; photography; gardening. Address: (h.) Telford House, Blairlogie, Stirling FK9 5PX.
E-mail: a.maxwellirving@tesco.net

May, Douglas James, LLB. Queen's Counsel, since 1989; b. 7.5.46, Edinburgh. Educ. George Heriot's; Edinburgh University. Advocate, 1971; Temporary Sheriff, 1990-99; Social Security Commissioner, Child Support Commissioner, since 1993; Parliamentary candidate (Conservative), Edinburgh East, 1974, Glasgow Cathcart, 1983. Recreations: golf (Captain: Scotland Universities Golfing Society, 1990-91, Merchants of Edinburgh Golf Club, 1997-99); photography (ARPS, 1997, FRPS, 2002, President, Edinburgh Photographic Society, 1996-99); travel.

May, Malcolm Stuart, BA, BD, STM, CQSW. Chief Officer, Dundee Voluntary Action, 1979-2002 (retired); b. 9.9.40, Isle of Shapinsay, Orkney; m., Alison Wood; 1 s.; 1 d. Educ. Kilmarnock Academy; The Gordon Schools, Huntly; Hamilton Academy; Queen's University, Belfast; Glasgow University; Union Theological Seminary, New York. Assistant Minister, The Old Kirk, West Pilton, Edinburgh, 1966-68; staff, Iona Community, Glasgow, 1968-72; social work training, 1972-73; Training Officer, Scottish Council for Voluntary Organisations, 1973-78. Member, Board of Management, Dundee College, 1989-2003; Non-Executive Director, Tayside Health Board, 1994-98. Recreations: reading; choral singing; hill-walking; woodwork. Address: (h.) 37 Campsie Drive, Milngavie G62 8HX; e-mail: malcolm.may@btopenworld.com

Mayhew, Dr. Peter Watts, BSc, PhD. Senior Conservation Manager, RSPB, since 1990; Commissioner, Deer Commission for Scotland, since 2005; b. 30.6.59, Glasgow; 2 d. Educ. Hutchesons' Grammar School; Glasgow University. Research Ornithologist, 1980-83; Head of Conservation, British Association for Shooting and Conservation, 1984-89. Chair, Capercaillie Biodiversity Action Plan Group. Recreations: mountaineering; travel; bird ringing. Address: (b.) RSPB, Etive House, Beechwood Park, Inverness IV2 3BW; T.-01463 228809; e-mail: pete.mayhew@rspb.org.uk

Mearns, Anne, MA (Hons), DipTP, MRTPI, MCMI, AssocCIPD, FRSA. Development Consultant; b. Glasgow. Educ. Hyndland Senior Secondary School; Glasgow University; Strathclyde University. Planning assistant, Coatbridge Burgh, 1969; Planner, Lanark County Council, 1969-73; Senior Planner (Research), Glasgow Corporation, 1973-75; Supervisory Planner (Policy Analysis), 1975-78, Assistant Chief, 1978-79, Chief Planner (Policy and Intelligence), 1979-87, City of Glasgow District Council Planning Department; Chief Corporate Planner, Town Clerk's Office, 1987-89, Depute Town Clerk (Corporate Policy Development), City of Glasgow District Council, 1989-94; Chief Executive, City of Aberdeen District Council, 1994-95; Chief Executive, Highlands of Scotland Tourist Board, 1995-97; Director, Hypertour, 1995-97; business adviser, 1997-2001; Director, The Scottish Parliament and Business Exchange, 2001-06. Member, Glasgow University General Council Business Committee, 1987-91; Member, Editorial Board, British Urban and Regional Information Systems Association, 1988-94; Member, Council, Glasgow and West of Scotland Institute of Public Administration, 1991-94; Member, Advisory Board, Graduate School of Environmental Studies, Strathclyde University, 1993-95; Chairperson, Forward Scotland, 2000-06; Trustee, Millennium Forest for Scotland Trust, 2002-06; Trustee, Clerk Maxwell Cancer Research Fund. Recreations: cerebral and cultural pursuits; community interests; clarsach. Address: (h.) 15 Springkell Gardens, Pollokshields, Glasgow G41 4BP; T.-0141-424 0069.

Meek, Professor Donald Eachann MacDonald, MA (Cantab), MA, PhD (Glas), FRHistS, FRSE. Professor of Scottish and Gaelic Studies, Edinburgh University, since 2002; Chairman, Gaelic Books Council, 2002-04; b. 16.5.49, Glasgow, brought up in Tiree; m., Rachel Jane Rogers; 2 d. Educ. Oban High School; Glasgow University; Emmanuel College, Cambridge. Lecturer, Senior Lecturer and Reader in Celtic, Edinburgh University, 1979-92; Professor of Celtic, Aberdeen University, 1993-2001. Assistant Editor, Historical Dictionary of Scottish Gaelic, Glasgow University, 1973-79; Honorary Secretary, Gaelic Society of Glasgow, 1974-79; Member, Gaelic Advisory Committee to Broadcasting Council for Scotland, 1976-78 and of Gaelic Panel, National Bible Society of Scotland, since 1978; President, Edinburgh and Lothians Baptist Association, 1992-93; Clerk and Treasurer, Board of Celtic Studies (Scotland), since 1994; Chief, Gaelic Society of Inverness, 1998, 1999; Chairman, Ministerial Advisory Group on Gaelic, Scottish Executive, 2001-02; Editor, Gaelic Bible, 1992 edition and later revisions; a General Editor, Dictionary of Scottish Church History and Theology, 1993; President, Scottish Church History Society, 2001-04. Publications: books include Mairi Mhor nan Oran, 1977, second edition 1998; The Campbell Collection of Gaelic Proverbs and Proverbial Sayings, 1978; Island Harvest: A History of Tiree Baptist Church, 1988; Sunshine and Shadow: the story of the Baptists of Mull, 1991; A Mind for Mission: essays (Editor), 1992; Tuath is Tighearna: Poetry of the Clearances and the Land Agitation (Editor), 1995; The Quest for Celtic Christianity, 2000; Caran an t-Saoghail: Anthology of Nineteenth-century Gaelic Poetry, 2003; The Kingdom of MacBrayne (Co-Author), 2006; Scottish Gaelic Studies, vols. 18, 19, 20, 21 (Editor); Gath, Vol. I - 4 (Co-editor); numerous articles on Gaelic and Highland themes. Recreations: getting to know the Highlands; watching CalMac; filling the wastepaper basket. Address: (b.) 27 George Square, Edinburgh EH8 9LD; T.-0131-650 4169; e-mail: d.e.meek@ed.ac.uk

Mehta, Phiroze Sorabji, BSc (Hons), BSc(Eng), MSc, CEng, FIMechE, FRSA, FHEA. Senior Lecturer in CAD, 1986-2005, AHOD Creative Technologies Division, 2001-02 (Retired); b. 9.10.44, Bombay; m., Margaret Jane Bowie; 2 s.; 1 d. Whessoe Ltd.: Design Engineer, 1970-75, Senior Design Engineer, 1975-78; Senior Design Engineer, Nuclear Design Department, Babcock Power Ltd., 1978-84; Senior Lecturer in Engineering Design, University of Central England, Birmingham, 1984-86; Glasgow Caledonian University, 1986-2005. Member, Organising Committee and University Representative Member, Conference on Education and Training in Finite Element Analysis; SQA Chief Moderator; Institution of Mechanical Engineers: Fellow, Professional Interview Panel, Chairman, Glasgow Panel; Academic Liaison Officer, Institution of Incorporated Engineers; Board Member, Scottish Qualifications Authority; Member, National Qualifications Committee; Director, SPTC, 1998-2000. Recreations: theatre; concerts; music. Address: (h.) 12 St. Leonards Road, Ayr KA7 2PT.

Meldrum, Angus Alexander, BSc, DIA. Chairman, Thistle Pub Company 3 plc, since 2006; Director, An Lochran (Glasgow Gaelic Arts Agency) Ltd., since 2006; Director, North British Trust Hotels Ltd., since 1999; The Patron, Benevolent Society of The Licensed Trade of Scotland, since 2005; Group Chairman, Belhaven Brewery Group plc, 2004-05 (Director, 2002-05); Managing Director, Tennent Caledonian Breweries Ltd., 1992-2001 (Director, since 1981); Chairman, Chrysalis Radio/Arrow Glasgow Ltd., 2003; b. 7.11.45, Stornoway; m., Anne-Marie; 1 s. Educ. Bayble School, Lewis; Kingussie School; Edinburgh University; Bath University Management School. Joined Bass plc, London, 1971; Tennent Caledonian Breweries Ltd., 1978; Brands Marketing Director, Bass Brewers Ltd., Burton-on-Trent, 1990-92; Director, Bass Ireland Ltd., 1981-95; Director, Tennents Ireland Ltd. (Dublin), 1981-95; Director, Bass Export Ltd., 1990-94; Director, Maclay's Brewery & Co. plc, Alloa, 1992-2002; Managing Director, J.G. Thomson Ltd. (Wines and Spirits Merchants), 1992-2001; President, Brewers Association of Scotland, 1992-94; Council Member, UK Brewers Society, 1992-94; Chairman, Scottish Licensed Trade Association, 1999-2000; Freeman, City of Glasgow, since 1982; Keeper of the Quaich, since 1992; Baron d'Honneur de Confrerie des Compagnons Goustevin de Normandie, since 2001; Scottish Licensed Trade Lifetime Achievement Award, 2001; Scottish

Advertising Industry Awards 2007 Special 21st Anniversary Award of Scotland's Best Marketeer Ever. Recreations: fishing; shooting; rugby; football; shinty; Scottish music; Gaelic culture. Address: (b.) Lochgreen Consultants, Lochgreen, Gryffe Road, Kilmacolm, Renfrewshire PA13 4BA; T.-01505 872609.

Meldrum, James, MA. Keeper of the Registers of Scotland; b. 9.8.52, Kirkintilloch. Educ. Lenzie Academy; Glasgow University. Administration Trainee/HEO (Admin), Scottish Office, 1973-79; Principal grade posts, Scottish Economic Planning Department, Scottish Development Department, Scottish Office Personnel Division, 1979-86; Deputy Director, Scottish Courts Administration, 1986-91; Head, Investment Assistance Division, Scottish Office Industry Department, 1991-94; Registrar General for Scotland, 1994-99; Director of Administrative Services, Scottish Executive, 1999-2002; Director of Business Management and Area Business Manager, Glasgow, Crown Offic and Procurator Fiscal Service, 2002-03. Address: (b.) Registers of Scotland, Meadowbank House, 153 London Road, Edinburgh EH8 7AU; T.-0131 659 6111.

Mele, Lorenzo, MA (Hons), BA (Hons). Artistic Director, 7:84 Theatre Company, since 2003; b. 21.2.67, Rome. Educ. Glasgow University; RSAMD. Director of two Fringe Firsts; founder and co-Artistic Director, MCT Theatre Company; active in Buddhist Society; winner of Pride Award, 2000. Recreations: walking my dog; supporting other Buddhists; trying to be a good neighbour. Address: (b.) 333 Woodlands Road, Glasgow G3 6NG; T.-0141 334 6686; e-mail: admin@784theatre.com

Melvin, John Robertson, LLB, Notary Public. Consultant Solicitor, Houghton Melvin Smith & Co, since 1998; Managing Director, Garioch Development Co. Ltd., since 1989; b. 8.8.56, Aberdeen; m., Susan; 2 s. Educ. Robert Gordon's College, Aberdeen; Aberdeen University. Apprentice Solicitor, Clark & Wallace, Aberdeen, 1976-78; Assistant Solicitor (various firms), 1978-84; Founding Partner, Houghton Melvin & Co, 1984-98. Recreations: golf; hill-walking. Address: (b.) 34 Duthie Terrace, Aberdeen AB10 7PQ; T.-01224 329300; e-mail: jrmelvin@btconnect.com

Mennie, William Patrick, BL, NP, IAC. MSI Consultant; Partner, Grigor & Young, Solicitors, Elgin and Forres, 1964-2004 (Senior Partner, from 1984); b. 11.10.37, Elgin; m., Patricia Leslie Bogie; 2 s.; 1 d. Educ. Elgin Academy; Edinburgh University. Solicitor, 1960; Honorary Sheriff at Elgin, since 1993; accredited by Law Society of Scotland as a specialist in agricultural law; Secretary, Malt Distillers Association of Scotland, 1970-2003. Recreations: game shooting and fishing. Address: (h.) Innesmill, Urquhart, Elgin; T.-01343 842643.

Menzies, Hon. Lord (Duncan A.Y. Menzies). Senator of the College of Justice, since 2001; b. 28.8.53, Edinburgh; m., Hilary Weston; 2 s. Educ. Edinburgh Academy; Cargilfield; Glenalmond (scholar); Wadham College, Oxford (scholar); Edinburgh University. Advocate, 1978; Standing Junior Counsel to The Admiralty, 1984-91; Queen's Counsel, 1991; accredited mediator, 1992; Temporary Sheriff, 1996-97; Advocate Depute, 1998-2000; Home Advocate Depute, 1998-2000; Chairman, Scottish Planning, Local Government and Environmental Bar Group, 1997-2001; Member, Faculty Council, 1997-2001; Parliamentary Candidate, Midlothian, 1983, Edinburgh Leith, 1987; founder, Scottish Wine Society. Recreations: shooting; golf; wines; planting trees. Address: (b.) Court of Session, Parliament House, Edinburgh; T.-0131-225 2595.

Menzies, Gordon, MA (Hons), DipEd. Independent Producer (retired Head of Educational Broadcasting, BBC Scotland); b. 30.7.27, Logierait, Perthshire; m., Charlotte; 2 s.; 1 d. Educ. Breadalbane Academy, Aberfeldy; Edinburgh University. Producer/Director, Who Are the Scots?, 1971, The Scottish Nation, 1972, The Chiel Amang Us, 1974, Ballad Folk, 1975, History Is My Witness, 1976, Play Golf with Peter Alliss, 1977, Scotch and Wry, 1978-79, Two Views of Burns, 1979, Barbara Dickson in Concert, 1981-84-86, The World of Golf, 1982, The Celts, 1987, Play Better Golf with Peter Alliss, 1989, Scotch and Wry Hogmanay, 1980-93; Editor, The Afternoon Show, 1981-85; Play Snooker with Dennis Taylor, 1990; Play Bridge with Zia, 1991; In Search of Scotland, 2001. Publications: Who Are the Scots?, 1971; The Scottish Nation, 1972; History Is My Witness, 1976; Play Golf, 1977; The World of Golf, 1982; Scotch and Wry, 1986; Double Scotch and Wry, 1988; Play Better Golf, 1989; In Search of Scotland, 2001; I. M. Jolly and Friends, 2004. Recreations: golf; snooker; curling; theatre. Address: (h.) 62 Gallowhill Avenue, Lenzie, Glasgow G66 4QD.

Menzies, Neil Graham Finlay, BSc. Corporate Adviser; b. 14.10.41, Meikleour; m., Lorna; 2 d. Educ. The John Lyon School, Harrow; University of St. Andrews. Voluntary Service Overseas, Nigeria, 1964-66; ICI, 1966-93, latterly Scottish Affairs Adviser. Scottish Adviser, Chemical Industries Association, 1993-2004; Non-Executive Director, Scottish Ambulance Service, 1995-99; Deputy Chairman, Scottish Water and Sewerage Customers Council, 1995-99; Member, Gas and Electricity Consumers Council (energywatch) 2000-05; Member, Balancing Settlement and Codes Panel (electricity market), 2002-05; Chairman, Water Industry Commissioner's Advisory Panel, 2002-04; Member, Scottish Rating and Valuation Council, 2001-02; Director, Royal Lyceum Theatre Company; Director, Scottish National Photography Centre; Public Member: Network Rail, 2007-10. Address: (b.) 13 Northumberland Street, Edinburgh EH3 6LL; T.-0131-557 4321; e-mail: Neil.Menzies@wwmail.co.uk

Merrylees, Andrew, RSA, BArch, DipTP, RSA, RIBA, FRIAS, FCSD, FRSA. Honorary Professor of Architecture, University of Dundee, since 1998; Consultant, Merrylees and Robertson, since 1997; Consultant, Hypostyle, since 2000; b. 13.10.33, Newmains; m., Maie Crawford; 2 s.; 1 d. Educ. Wishaw High School; University of Strathclyde. Sir Basil Spence, Glover and Ferguson: joined 1957, Associate, 1968, Partner, 1972; set up Andrew Merrylees Associates, 1985. Member: Advisory Council for the Arts in Scotland. RIBA Bronze Medal; Saltire Award; Civic Trust Award; Art in Architecture Award; RSA Gold Medal; SCONUL Award. Recreations: architecture; painting; cooking. Address: (b.) Quadrant, 17 Bernard Street, Edinburgh EH6 6PW; T.-0131-555 0688; e-mail: amerr@lineone.net

Meston, Professor Michael Charles, MA, LLB, JD. Emeritus Professor of Law, Professor of Scots Law, Aberdeen University, 1971-96; b. 13.12.32, Aberdeen; m., Dorothea Munro; 2 s. Educ. Robert Gordon's College, Aberdeen; Aberdeen University; Chicago University. Lecturer in Private Law, Glasgow University, 1959-64; Aberdeen University: Senior Lecturer in Comparative Law, 1964-68, Professor of Jurisprudence, 1968-71; Dean, Faculty of Law, 1970-73 and 1988-91; Honorary Sheriff, Grampian Highland and Islands, since 1972; Temporary Sheriff, 1993-99; Vice Principal, Aberdeen University, 1979-82; Trustee, National Museum of Antiquities of Scotland, 1982-85; Governor, Robert Gordon's College, Aberdeen, until 1997; Member, Grampian Health Board, 1985-91; Non-Executive Director, Aberdeen Royal Hospitals NHS Trust, 1992-97. Publications: The Succession (Scotland) Act 1964; The Matrimonial Homes

(Family Protection) (Scotland) Act 1981; The Scottish Legal Tradition, 1991; The Aberdeen Stylebook 1722, 2000; Meston's Succession Opinions, 2000. Recreations: golf; photography. Address: (h.) 4 Hamilton Place, Aberdeen AB15 4BH; T.-Aberdeen 641554; e-mail: mcmeston@corgarff.demon.co.uk

Michie of Gallanach, Baroness (Janet Ray Michie). MP (Lib. Dem.), Argyll and Bute, 1987-2001; b. 4.2.34; m., Dr. Iain Michie; 2 d.; 1 d. deceased. Educ. Aberdeen High School for Girls; Lansdowne House School, Edinburgh; Edinburgh School of Speech Therapy. MCST (Hons). Area Speech Therapist, Argyll and Clyde Health Board, 1977-87. Deputy Leader, Scottish Liberal Democrats; Liberal Spokeswoman on Transport and Rural Development, 1987-88; Liberal Democrat Spokeswoman on: Scotland, 1988-97, Women's Issues, 1988-94; Member, Select Committee on Scottish Affairs, 1992-97; Member, Chairmen's Panel, 1997-2001; Vice Chairman, Scottish Liberal Party, 1976-78; Chair, Scottish Liberal Democrats, 1992-93; Vice Chairperson, Parliamentary Group on Whisky Industry, 1990-01; Vice President, Royal College of Speech and Language Therapists, 1991-2001, re-elected, 2002; Member: An Comunn Gaidhealach, Scottish National Farmers' Union (SNFU), Scottish Crofting Foundation (SCF); Hon. Asso., National Council of Women of GB; Honorary President, Clyde Fishermen's Association; Life Peer. Recreations: golf; swimming; gardening; watching rugby. Address: (b.) House of Lords, London SW1A 0PW.

Michie, Professor David Alan Redpath, OBE, RSA, RGI, DA, FRSA, FFCS. Professor, Heriot Watt University, 1988-90; Head, School of Drawing and Painting, Edinburgh College of Art, 1982-90; b. 30.11.28, St. Raphael, France; m., Eileen Anderson Michie; 2 d. Educ. Hawick High School; Edinburgh College of Art. Travelling Scholarship, Italy, 1954-55; Lecturer, Grays School of Art, Aberdeen, 1957-61; Lecturer, Edinburgh College of Art, 1961 (Vice Principal, 1974-77). President, Society of Scottish Artists, 1961-63; Member: General Teaching Council for Scotland, 1975-80, Court, Heriot-Watt University, 1979-82, Council, British School at Rome, 1980-85, Museums and Galleries Commission, 1991-96, Royal West of England Academy, 1991-2000; Guthrie Award, RSA, 1964; David Cargill Prize, RGI, 1977; Lothian Region Award, 1977; Sir William Gillies Award, 1980; RGI Prize, 1990; Cornelissen Prize, RWA, 1992; one-man exhibitions, Mercury Gallery, London, nine times, 1966-99, Lothian Region Chambers, 1977, The Scottish Gallery, 1980, 1994, 1998, 2003, Loomshop Gallery, Lower Largo, 1981, 1987, Mercury Gallery, Edinburgh, 1986; Baarn and Amsterdam, 1991; Visiting Artist, University of the Arts, Belgrade, 1979; Visiting Professor, Faculty of Art Studio Department, UCLA, Santa Barbara, 1992. Address: (h.) 17 Gilmour Road, Edinburgh EH16 5NS.

Micklem, Rosalind, BA (Hons), PGCE, MPhil. National Director for Scotland, Equality and Human Rights Commission, since 2007; b. 7.6.56, Surrey. Educ. St. Paul's Girls' School, London; Oxford University; Leicester University; London University. Lecturer, North Oxfordshire Technical College, 1979-84; Education Officer, Northants and Hounslow, 1985-89; Vice Principal, Enfield College, 1989-95; Deputy Principal, Wirral Metropolitan College, 1995-97; Principal, Cardonald College, 1997-2007. Address: (b.) Equality and Human Rights Commission, The Optima Building, 58 Robertson Street, Glasgow G2 8DQ; e-mail: ros.micklem@equalityhumanrights.com

Middleton, David Fraser, MA. Head of Scotland Office, Ministry of Justice, since 2007; b. 23.6.56, Paisley; m., Diane Lamberton; 1 d. Educ. Paisley

Grammar School; Glasgow University. Joined Scottish Office as Administration Trainee, 1978; Private Secretary to Minister of State, Scottish Office, 1982-84; seconded to Cabinet Office, 1984; Principal, Scottish Office Finance Group, 1984-89; Director of Strategy, Whitfield Urban Partnership, 1989-91; Assistant Secretary, Housing, 1991-96; Assistant Secretary, Roads; Head of Personnel, 1997-99; Head of Local Government, Europe and External Relations Group, Department of Finance and Central Services, Scottish Executive, 1999-2002; Head of Food and Agriculture Group, Environment and Rural Affairs Department, Scottish Executive, 2002-06; Special Projects Officer, UHI (Millennium Institute), 2006-07 (on loan from Scottish Executive). Recreation: golf (Royal Musselburgh Golf Club). Address: (b.) Scotland Office, Dover House, Whitehall, London SW1A 2AU; T.-020-7270-6769; 0131-244-9006.

Middleton, Jeremy Richard Hunter, LLB, BD. Parish Minister, Davidson's Mains Parish Church, since 1988; b. 19.3.53, Kilbarchan; m., Susan (nee Hay); 3 s. Educ. Craigflower Preparatory School, Charterhouse; Old College, New College, Edinburgh. Address: (b.) 1 Quality Street, Edinburgh EH4 5BB; T.-0131 312 6282; e-mail: life@dmainschurch.plus.com

Midgley, Professor John Morton, OBE, BSc, MSc, PhD, CChem, FRSC, FRPharmS, FSP. Professor of Pharmaceutical and Medicinal Chemistry, Strathclyde University, since 1984 (Chairman and Head of Department, 1985-90), Emeritus Professor, since 1999, Research Professor, since 2000; b. 14.7.37, York; m., Jean Mary Tillyer; 2 s. Educ. Nunthorpe Grammar School, York; Manchester University; London University. Demonstrator, Manchester University, 1959-61; Assistant Lecturer, School of Pharmacy, London University, 1962-65; Research Associate, Massachusetts Institute of Technology, 1965-66; Lecturer, then Senior Lecturer, School of Pharmacy, London University, 1965-83; Visiting Professor, Universities of: Florida, 1978-89, Panjab, 1981, Lodz, 1985, Alexandria, 1987-88; Honorary Professor, China Pharmaceutical University, Nanjing, since 1987; Fellow, School of Pharmacy, London University, since 2002; Fellow, Royal Pharmaceutical Society of Great Britain, since 1984; Fellow, Royal Society of Chemistry, since 1988; Member: Committee on the Review of Medicines, 1984-92, British Pharmacopoeia Commission, 1984-2005 (Chairman: Committee C, 1984-2003, Committee L, 1991-2005, Committee B, 2002-05; Vice Chairman, 1990-2002), Committee on the Safety of Medicines, 1990-2002; Chairman, Chemistry, Pharmacy and Standards Sub-Committee, CSM, 1999-2002 (Vice Chairman, 1990-99); Member: External Advisory Panel, Committee on the Safety of Medicines, since 2002, European Panel of Experts on Human Medicines, since 1995, Council of Royal Pharmaceutical Society of GB, 1991-92, Science and Engineering Research Council Pharmacy Panel, 1985-90; UK Delegation to European Pharmacopoeia Commission, 1998-2005; Member, EPC Group of Experts, IOB, 1998-2004, Chairman, IOA, since 2001; Member, EPC Chairs of Chemical Groups Committee, since 2001; Member, USP Resolution 3 Advisory Panel; consultant to the pharmaceutical industry, USA, Japan, EU, since 1967. Recreations: fly fishing; fisheries management; training labradors; gardening; music; golf. Address: (h.) 116 Old Greenock Road, Bishopton, Renfrewshire PA7 5BB. E-mail: prof@jmidgley.freeserve.co.uk

Milburn, Professor George Henry William, PhD, CChem, FRSC, FBIM, Dr (h.c.), FRSA. Retired; Reseach Adviser/Research Professor, Napier University, 1998-99, Head, Department of Applied Chemical and Physical

Sciences, 1973-98; Adjunct Professor, University of South Florida, since 2000; Consultant, Lahti Polytechnic, Finland, 1998-2001; b. 25.11.34, Wallasey; m., Jean Muriel; 1 s.; 1 d. Educ. Wallasey Grammar School; Leeds University. Short service commission, Royal Corps of Signals, 1959-63; Staff Demonstrator, Leeds University, 1963-66; Research Fellow, Sydney University, 1967-68; Senior Scientific Officer, Agricultural Research Council, 1968-69; Lecturer, Plymouth Polytechnic, 1969-70; Senior Lecturer, Sheffield Polytechnic, 1970-73.Convener, Committee of Scottish University Heads of Chemistry Departments, 1994-97; Honorary Doctorate, Technical University, Budapest, 1988; Silver Star Laureate, Poland, 1996. Publications: more than 50 scientific publications including a textbook on crystal structure analysis. Recreations: golf; bridge; photography; guitar playing. Address: (h.) 9 Orchard Court, Longniddry, East Lothian; T.-01875 853228; e-mail: harry@milburnh.fsnet.co.uk

Mill, Douglas Russell, LLB, BA, MBA, DUniv, SSC, NP. Secretary and Chief Executive, Law Society of Scotland, since 1997; b. 3.1.57, Paisley; m., Christine; 2 s.; 1 d. Educ. Paisley Grammar School; Glasgow University. Former Depute Director, Centre for Professional Legal Studies, Strathclyde University; former Partner, MacFarlane Young & Co., Solicitors, Paisley. Publications: Successful Practice Management, 1992; Managing the Professional Partnership, 2000; Successful Law Firm Manager (Co-Author), 2000. Recreations: golf; rugby. Address: (b.) 26 Drumsheugh Gardens, Edinburgh EH3 7YR; T.-0131-226 7411.

Millan, Rt. Hon. Bruce, PC, CA. European Commissioner, 1989-95; b. 5.10.27, Dundee; m., Gwendoline May Fairey; 1 s.; 1 d. Educ. Harris Academy, Dundee. MP, Glasgow Craigton, 1959-83, Glasgow Govan, 1983-88; Parliamentary Secretary for the RAF, 1964-66; Parliamentary Secretary, Scottish Office, 1966-70; Minister of State, Scottish Office, 1974-76; Secretary of State for Scotland, 1976-79; Opposition Spokesman on Scottish Affairs, 1979-83. Address: (h.) 1 Torridon Avenue, Glasgow G41 5LA; T.-0141-427 6483.

Millan, Professor Charles Gordon, MA, PhD, FRSA, Officier Dans L'Ordre Des Palmes Académiques. Professor of French, Strathclyde University, since 1991; b. 25.9.46, Kirkcaldy; m., Margaret Anne Robbie; 1 s.; 1 d. Educ. Kirkcaldy High; Merrywood Grammar, Bristol; Edinburgh University. Temporary Lecturer, Edinburgh University, 1970-71; Teacher, Broughton High School, 1972-76; Strathclyde University, since 1976, Director, Languages for Business Unit, since 1990 (Languages for Export Award, 1994 and 2001), Chairman, Department of Modern Languages, 1994-98 and since 2000, Vice-Dean, Faculty of Arts and Social Sciences, 1995-98; Chair, University Council of Modern Languages (ScotCom), since 2001. Publications include: Pierre Louÿs ou le Culte de l'Amitié, 1979; Stéphane Mallarmé, Poésies (jointly), 1983; A Throw of the Dice: The Life of Stéphane Mallarmé, 1994; Documents Mallarmé, new series, I, 1998, II, 2000, III, 2003, IV, 2005; Situating Mallarmé, (Co-editor), 2000; Founding Editor, Les Cahiers Stéphane Mallarmé. Recreations: cinema; reading. Address: (b.) Livingstone Tower, Richmond Street, Glasgow G1 1XH; T.-0141-552 4400.

Millar, Professor Alan, MA, PhD, FRSE. Professor of Philosophy, Stirling University, since 1994; b. 14.12.47, Edinburgh; m., Rose-Mary Marchand; 1 s. Educ. Edinburgh University; Cambridge University. Stirling University: Lecturer in Philosophy, 1971, Senior Lecturer, 1991, Head, Department of Philosophy, 1988-94, 2003-06. Awarded Mind Association Research Fellowship, 1996-97; Visiting

Fellow, Clare Hall, Cambridge, 1997; appointed Fellow of the Royal Society of Edinburgh, 2005; Member, Editorial Board, Philosophical Quarterly, since 2002. Publications: Reasons and Experience, 1991; Reason and Nature (Co-Editor), 2002; Understanding People, 2004; articles in the philosophy of mind, epistemology, philosophy of religion, history of ethics. Recreations: reading; walking; films; cooking. Address: (b.) Stirling University, Stirling FK9 4LA; T.-01786 467555.

Millar, Ann Rangeley, MA (Hons), MSc. Assistant Director, Research Policy and Strategy Directorate, Scottish Higher Education Funding Council (Secondment, from 2004); Deputy Chief Researcher, Office of Chief Researcher, Scottish Executive Social Research, since 1993; b. 23.1.50, Yorkshire; m., Donald Iain Lamont Millar; 1 s. Educ. Perth Academy; Aberdeen University; Edinburgh University. Scottish Development Department: Research Officer, Population Research, 1973-75, Senior Research Officer, Urban Regeneration Research, 1976-78; Scottish Home and Health Department: Senior Research Officer, Criminological Research, 1979-86, Principal Research Officer, 1987-90, Principal Research Officer, Civil Law Research, 1991-93. Member, Economic and Social Research Council's Strategic Research Board. Recreations: travel; architecture. Address: (b.) Donaldson House, 97 Haymarket Terrace, Edinburgh EH12 5HD; e-mail: annmillar@sfc.uc.uk

Millar, Douglas Andrew Terris. Chief Executive, Lanarkshire Chamber of Commerce, since 2003; formerly Deputy Chief Executive, Glasgow Chamber of Commerce; Chairman, Chamber Pensions Limited, since 2001; Non-Executive Director, National Youth Orchestras of Scotland, since 2000; b. 18.6.55, Dunfermline. Educ. Queen Anne High School, Dunfermline; Aberdeen College of Commerce. Civil Servant, Scottish Office, 1972-97; Deputy Director, Scottish Chambers of Commerce, 1997-99; Non Executive Director, Scottish Television (Regional) Limited, 1998-2004. Fellow, Royal Society for the encouragement of Arts Manufacturers and Commerce (RSA); Elder, Dunfermline Abbey. Recreations: youth work; football. Address: (b.) Barncluith Business Centre, Townhead Street, Hamilton ML3 7DP; T.-01698 426882.

Millar, Professor Eileen Anne, MA, PhD, Cavaliere dell'Ordine al Merito della Repubblica Italiana. Stevenson Professor of Italian, University of Glasgow, 1992-2005, now Emeritus; Honorary Professorial Research Fellow, since 2005; b. Glasgow. Educ. Notre Dame High School, Glasgow; University of Glasgow. University of Glasgow: Lecturer, Department of Italian, 1968, Senior Lecturer, 1982. Publications: the Napoleonic period in Italian literature and Ignazio Silone. Recreations: music; travel; cooking. Address: 30 Torridon Avenue, Glasgow G41 5AU; T.-0141-427 5988.
E-mail: E.Millar@italian.arts.gla.ac.uk

Millar, Professor Graeme, OBE, BSc, FRPharmS. Scottish Food Standards Board Member, since 2005; Director, Dunfermline Building Society, since 2000; formerly Chairman, Scottish Consumer Council; Chairman, Company Net Ltd., 2002-03; Chairman, Common Services Agency, NHS Scotland, 1998-2004; Chairman, Edinburgh Sick Kids Friends Foundation, since 1999; Chairman, Scottish Construction Forum, since 2004; Director, Essentia Group Ltd., since 2003; Vice-Chairman, Quality Meat Scotland, 2003-05; b. 21.2.55; m., Fay; 3s. Educ. Boroughmuir Senior Secondary School; Heriot-Watt University. Vice-Chairman, Lothian Health Board, 1991-93; Non Executive Member/Director, Lothian Health Board,

1984-93; Chairman, Edinburgh Sick Children's NHS Trust, 1993-99; Executive Chairman, Scottish Pharmaceutical General Council, 1994-98; Managing Director, Graeme Millar Chemists Ltd., since 1979; Chairman, Scottish NHS Trust Chairman's Group, 1996-98; Chairman, Southern Scotland Electricity Consumers Board, 1996-2000; Chairman, Royal Pharmaceutical Society of Great Britain in Scotland, 1998-2000; Member, Advisory Committee on Borderline Substances, 1994-98; Secretary, Lothian NHS Endowment Investment Advisory Committee, 1994-99; Consultant with various pharmaceutical companies; Member, Merchant Company, Edinburgh; School Governor, Erskine Stewart's Melville. Recreations: golf at a mediocre standard; rugby; good company; good food; good wine.

Millar, Helen Jean, OBE, MA, FRSA. Deputy Lieutenant, City of Glasgow; Vice-Chairman, National Consumer Federation; Member, Water Customer Consultation Panel for S.W. Scotland; Chairman, Chief Scientist Office, Public Involvement Group; b. 10.10.31, Glasgow; 3 s.; 2 d. Educ. Craigholme School, Glasgow; Glasgow University. Chairman, Consumers in European Community Group, 1988-91; Chairman, Consumer's Committee for Scotland, 1980-89; Member and Vice-Chairman, Scottish Consumer Council, 1979-87; Chairman, Strathclyde Children's Panel, 1979-81; Member, Advisory Committee on Novel Foods, 1991-98; Member, Air Users Council, 1991-98; Chairman, Rail Passenger Committee for Scotland, 1996-2001; Vice-Chairman, New Glasgow Society, 1980-87; former Lecturer in charge, Children's Panel Training, Glasgow University; Founder Member, Board, Tron Theatre Club, Glasgow; Member, Multi Centre Research Ethics Committee for Scotland, 1997-2007. Recreations: theatre; arts in general; Glasgow; arguing. Address: (h.) 33 Aytoun Road, Glasgow G41; T.-0141-423 4152; e-mail: helen-millar@ecosse.net

Millar, Paul. Consul-General of the Czech Republic (Honorary), since 1996; b. 30.4.33, Brno, Czech Republic; m., Paula; 1 d. Educ. Mendel University, Brno. Agricultural advisory service; veterinary research; teaching, school of agriculture; Commonwealth Bureau of Animal Breeding and Genetics; Britbreed Ltd.; Fullwood CS. Publications: Mendelian Inheritance in Goats; Mendelian Inheritance in Cattle. Recreations: golf; gardening. Address: Consulate General of the Czech Republic, 12A Riselaw Crescent, Edinburgh EH10 6HL.
E-mail: paul.millar@blueyonder.co.uk

Miller, Professor Alan, BSc, PhD, CPhys, FInstP, FRSE, FIEEE (USA). Professor of Physics (Semiconductors) and Vice Principal (Research), St. Andrews University, since 1993; Professor of Physics and Electrical Engineering, University of Central Florida, 1989-93; b. 5.6.49, Dunfermline; m., Susan Linklater; 3 d. Educ. Gibraltar Grammar School; Edinburgh University; Bath University. Research Fellow, Heriot-Watt University, 1974-79; Visiting Assistant Professor, North Texas University, 1979-81; Senior Principal Scientific Officer, Royal Signals and Radar Establishment, Malvern, 1981-89; Professor of Physics and Electrical Engineering, University of Central Florida, 1989-2000; Editor, Optical and Quantum Electronics, and of Cambridge Studies in Modern Optics (series of monographs); Chair, Institute of Physics Semiconductor Physics Group; Past Chair, Committee of Scottish Professors of Physics; Past Chair, Scottish Chapter, Lasers and Electro-Optics Society; Past Chair, Royal Society of Edinburgh Physics Committee. Publications: Nonlinear Optics in Signal Processing (Editor); Nonlinear Optical Materials and Devices for Applications in Information Technology (Editor); Laser Sources and Applications (Editor); Semiconductor Quantum Optoelectronics, From

Quantum Physics to Smart Devices (Editor); Ultrafast phetonics (Editor); 180 research papers. Recreation: music. Address: (b.) School of Physics and Astronomy, North Haugh, St. Andrews KY16 9SS; T.-01334 463122.

Miller, Alan Douglas, LLB (Hons), DipLP. Part-time Sheriff; Consultant in Child Law and Youth Justice; Convener, Additional Support Needs Tribunal for Scotland; Deputy Chair, NHS Tribunal; b. 30.11.59, Edinburgh; m., Alison; 1 s.; 2 d. Educ. Stewart's/Melville College, Edinburgh; Edinburgh University. Assistant/Area Children's Reporter, Strathclyde, 1985-90; Regional Children's Reporter, Dumfries and Galloway, 1990-95; Principal Reporter, Scottish Children's Reporter Administration, 1995-2005. Non-Executive Director, Includem; Non-Executive Director, Linlithgow Young People's Project; Associate Member, Iona Community; Elder, Church of Scotland. Recreations: running; music; reading; family. Address (h.) 59 Avalon Gardens, Linlithgow, West Lothian EH49 7PL; T.-01506 844992; e-mail: alan@alandmiller.co.uk

Miller, Alexandra, MA, MSc. Director of Communications, National Library of Scotland, since 2004, b. Scotland; m., Colin Balfour. Educ. University of St. Andrews; Napier University. Communications posts with Spider Systems, Glasgow City Council, KPMG, the Scottish Arts Council, the Scottish Health Service and the Civil Service, 1975-91; Director of Corporate Affairs, Telewest plc, 1991-97; Director of Consultancy, Clearview Strategy, 1997-2004. Member, Chartered Institute of Marketing and the Chartered Institute of Public Relations; Member, BBC Broadcasting Council for Scotland, 2002-06; Member, BBC Audience Council Scotland, since 2006; Member, Executive Committee, Scottish Council for Development and Industry (SCDI), since 2004. Address: (b.) National Library of Scotland, George IV Bridge, Edinburgh EH1 1EW; T.-0131 623 3700; e-mail: a.miller@nls.uk

Miller, Professor Andrew, CBE, MA, BSc, PhD, DUniv (Stirling, Open University), FRSE, FIBiol. Principal and Vice-Chancellor, University of Stirling, 1994-2001; Emeritus Professor, since 2001; General Secretary, Royal Society of Edinburgh, 2001-05; Secretary and Treasurer, Carnegie Trust for the Universities of Scotland, since 2004; b. 15.2.36, Kelty, Fife; m., Rosemary S.H. Fyvie; 1 s.; 1 d. Educ. Beath High School; Edinburgh University. Assistant Lecturer in Chemistry, Edinburgh University, 1960-62; Postdoctoral Fellow, CSIRO, Melbourne, and Tutor in Chemistry, Ormond College, Melbourne University, 1962-65; Staff Scientist, MRC Laboratory of Molecular Biology, Cambridge, 1965-66; Lecturer in Molecular Biophysics, Oxford University and (from 1967) Fellow, Wolfson College, 1966-83 (Honorary Fellow, since 1995); on secondment as first Head, European Molecular Biology Laboratory, Grenoble Antenne, France, 1975-80; Professor of Biochemistry, Edinburgh University, 1984-94; Vice-Dean of Medicine, Edinburgh University, 1991-93; Vice-Principal, Edinburgh University, 1993-94. Committee Member: British Biophysical Society, 1972-74, SERC Synchrotron Radiation Facility Committee, 1979-82, Biological Sciences Committee, 1982-85, Neutron Beam Research Committee, 1982-85; Council Member, Institut Laue-Langevin, 1981-85; Member: MRC Joint Dental Committee, 1984-86, UGC Biological Sciences Committee, 1985-89; (part-time) Director of Research, European Synchrotron Radiation Facility, Grenoble, 1986-91; Member: Advisory Board, AFRC Food Research Institute, 1985, UFC Advisory Groups on Biological Sciences and Pre-clinical Medicine, 1989, Scientific Council, Scottish Knowledge plc, 1997-2002; Director, Scottish Knowledge plc, 1997-2002; Member, Minister of Education's Action Group on

Standards in Scottish Schools, 1997-99; Member, Council, Royal Society of Edinburgh, since 1997 (Convener, International Committee, 1999-2001, Chairman, RSE Foundation Scotland, since 2005); Member, UNESCO UK Science Committee, 2002-03; Adviser to Wellcome Trust on UK–French Synchrotron, 1999-2000; Member, Scottish Executive Science Strategy Group, 1999-2000; Interim Chief Executive, Cancer Research UK, 2001-02; Chairman, International Centre for Mathematical Sciences, Edinburgh, 2001-05; Member, Council, Open University, 2001-05; Deputy Chairman, Scottish Food Advisory Committee, 2003-05; Board Member, Food Standards Agency, 2003-05. Publications: Minerals in Biology (Co-Editor), 1986; over 180 research papers. Address: 5 Blackford Hill Grove, Edinburgh EH9 3HA.

Miller, Brian, DL, BSc (Hons). Rector, Dalziel High School, Motherwell, since 1990; b. 4.1.51, Glasgow; m., Margaret; 1 s.; 1 d. Educ. High School of Glasgow; Strathclyde University. Teacher of Mathematics, 1974-77; Assistant Principal Teacher, 1977-80; Principal Teacher, 1980-84; Assistant Head Teacher, Cranhill Secondary School, Glasgow, 1984-86; Depute Head Teacher, Stonelaw High School, Glasgow, 1986-90. Depute Lieutenant of Lanarkshire, since 2001. Recreation: bowls. Address: (b.) Crawford Street, Motherwell ML1 3AG; e-mail: bmiller@dalziel.n-lanark.sch.uk

Miller, Sheriff Colin Brown, LLB. Sheriff for South Strathclyde, Dumfries and Galloway, since 1991; b. 4.10.46, Paisley; m., Joan Elizabeth Blyth; 3 s. Educ. Paisley Grammar School; Glasgow University. Partner, McFadyen & Semple, Solicitors, Paisley, 1971-91; Council Member, Law Society of Scotland, 1983-91 (Convener, Conveyancing Committee, 1986-89; Convener, Judicial Procedure Committee, 1989-91; Chairman, Working Party on Rights of Audience in Supreme Courts, 1990-91); Dean, Faculty of Procurators in Paisley, 1991. Recreations: walking; photography; travel; railways; ships. Address: (b.) Ayr Sheriff Court, Wellington Square, Ayr; T.-01292 268474.

Miller, Sir Donald John, FREng, FRSE, BSc(Eng), DSc, DUniv, FIMechE, FIEE; b. 9.2.27, London; m., Fay G. Herriot; 1 s.; 2 d. Educ. Banchory Academy; Aberdeen University. Metropolitan-Vickers, 1947-53; British Electricity Authority, 1953-55; Preece Cardew & Rider (Consulting Engineers), 1955-66; Chief Engineer, North of Scotland Hydro-Electric Board, 1966-74; South of Scotland Electricity Board: Director of Engineering, 1974, appointed Deputy Chairman, 1979; Chairman, Scottish Power, 1982-92. Chairman, Power Division, IEE, 1977. Recreations: reading; gardening; walking; sailing. Address: (h.) Puldohran, Gryffe Road, Kilmacolm, Renfrewshire; T.-01505 873988.

Miller, Gordon, BSc. Rector, Blairgowrie High School, since 2007; b. 10.10.57, Glasgow; m., Julie Elizabeth; 1 s.; 1 d. Educ. High School of Glasgow; Strathclyde University. Assistant Teacher, Lochend Secondary School, Glasgow, 1980-85; Assistant Principal Teacher and Principal Teacher of Guidance, Lochgilphead High School, 1985-92; Assistant Rector, Carluke High School, 1992-96; Depute Rector, Crieff High School, 1996-99; Rector, Mearns Academy, 1999-2007. Council member, Headteachers' Association of Scotland, 2000-06; Treasurer, 2003-06. Recreations: golf; hill-walking. Address: (b.) Blairgowrie High School, Beeches Road, Blairgowrie PH10 6PW; T.-01250 873445.

Miller, Sheriff Ian Harper Lawson, MA, LLB. Sheriff of Glasgow and Strathkelvin at Glasgow, since 2001; b. 16.1.54, Aberdeen; m., Sheila Matthews Howie; 1 s.; 3 d. Educ. Robert Gordon's College, Aberdeen; Aberdeen University. Admitted as a Solicitor, 1980; Partner, Burnett & Reid, Solicitors, Aberdeen, 1986-91; Advocate, 1992;

Sheriff of Grampian, Highland and Islands at Aberdeen, 1998-2001. Recreations: reading; music. Address: (b.) Sheriff's Chambers, Sheriff Court of Glasgow and Strathkelvin, 1 Carlton Place, Glasgow G5 9DA; T.-0141-429 8888.

Miller, Rev. Ian Hunter, BA, BD. Minister, Bonhill, since 1975; b. 30.5.44, Johnstone; m., Joan Elizabeth Parr; 2 s. Educ. Johnstone High School; Glasgow University; Open University. Travel agent, latterly Branch Manager, A.T. Mays, 1962-69; Assistant Minister, Renfrew Old Kirk, 1974-75. Moderator, Dumbarton Presbytery, 1985-87; Past Chairman, Lomond and Argyll Division, NHS Argyll and Clyde; Vice-Chairman, West Dunbartonshire Health and Social Justice Committee. Recreations: golf; badminton; music; drama. Address: Bonhill Manse, 1 Glebe Gardens, Bonhill, Alexandria G83 9HR; T.-01389 753039.

Miller, Ian James, OBE, MA, LLB. Chairman, Mental Welfare Commission for Scotland, 2000-08; Member, National Appeal Panel for Entry to Health Boards' Pharmaceutical Lists, since 1997; Governor, Morrison's Academy, Crieff, 1998-2002; Member, Business Committee, University of Edinburgh General Council, 2001-05; Director, Edinburgh Healthcare NHS Trust, 1995-99; Trustee, Lothian Primary Care NHS Trust, 1999-2000; b. 21.10.38, Fraserburgh; m., Sheila Mary Hourston; 1 s.; 2 d. Educ. Fraserburgh Academy; Aberdeen University; Edinburgh University. Private legal practice, 1963-68; Senior Legal Assistant, Inverness County Council, 1968-70; Depute County Clerk, then County Clerk, Ross and Cromarty County Council, 1970-75; Chief Executive, Inverness District Council, 1975-77; Director of Law and Administration, Grampian Regional Council, 1977-84; Director, Kildonnan Investments Ltd., Aberdeen, 1984-87; Secretary and Academic Registrar, Napier University, Edinburgh, 1987-99. Recreations: golf; curling. Address: (h.) 80 Craiglockhart Road, Edinburgh EH14 1EP.

Miller, Dr Jack Elius, OBE, JP, OStJ, FRCGP; b. 7.3.18, Glasgow; m., Ida Warrens. Educ. Hillhead High School; Glasgow University. General Medical Practitioner in Glasgow (retired); Captain, Royal Army Medical Corps, 1944-46; Chairman (founder Member), Glasgow Marriage Guidance Council, 1956-61 (Hon. Vice-President, since 1961); Hon. Vice-President, Scottish Marriage Guidance Council, since 1967; Chairman: Scottish General Medical Services Committee, 1969-72, Association of Jewish Ex-Servicemen and Women of Scotland, 1952-61 and 1964-68; President, Glasgow Jewish Representative Council, 1969-72; Member, Council, BMA, 1964-81 (National Treasurer, 1972-81; Gold Medallist, 1982); Freeman, City of London; Member, Board of Deputies of British Jews, 1979-88; Vice-President, Prince and Princess of Wales Hospice, since 1981; Co-Chairman, Scottish Jewish Archives Committee, 1986-2001, President, since 2001; Chairman, Scottish Health Authorities Review of Priorities for the Eighties and Nineties, 1985-87. Publications: Glasgow Doctors' Handbook (three editions); Sharpen report. Recreations: travel; reading; communal affairs. Address: (h.) Westacres, 3 Westacres Road, Newton Mearns, Glasgow G77 6WW; T.-0141-616-5136.

Miller, James, CBE (1986), MA, CBIM. Chairman, 1970-99, Managing Director, 1970-91, The Miller Group Ltd. (formerly James Miller & Partners); Chairman, Royal Scottish National Orchestra, 1997-2002; b. 1.9.34, Edinburgh; m., 1, Kathleen Dewar (deceased); 2, Iris Lloyd-Webb; 1 s.; 3 d. Educ. Edinburgh Academy; Harrow School; Balliol College, Oxford. National Service, Royal Engineers. James Miller & Partners Ltd.: joined, 1958, appointed Director, 1960; Scottish Representative,

Advisory Committee to the Meteorological Services, 1980-92; Chairman, Federation of Civil Engineering Contractors, 1985-86, President, 1990-93; Director, British Linen Bank Ltd., 1983-99 (Chairman, 1997-99); Member, Scottish Advisory Board, British Petroleum, 1990-2001; Director, Bank of Scotland, 1993-2000; Deacon Convener, Incorporated Trades of Edinburgh, 1974-77; President, Edinburgh Chamber of Commerce, 1981-83; Assistant, 1982-85, Treasurer, 1990-92, Master, 1992-94, Merchant Company of Edinburgh; Chairman, Court, Heriot-Watt University, 1990-96. Recreation: shooting. Address: (h.) Alderwood, 49 Craigcrook Road, Edinburgh EH4 3PH; T.-0131-332 2222.

Miller, James Alexander, PhD, MBA, BSc (Hons), RN, FRSM, MHSM. Chief Executive, Royal College of Physicians and Surgeons of Glasgow, since 2005; b. 11.3.64, Bridge of Allan; m., Winnie Miller (nee Dekonski); 1 s.; 1 d. Educ. Alloa Academy; University of Edinburgh; Napier University; Abertay University. Student Nurse, North Lothian College of Nursing and Midwifery, 1983-86; various clinical and senior nurse roles in Edinburgh, 1986-92; West Lothian NHS Trust: Deputy Director of Nursing, 1992-94, Nurse Manager, 1994-98, General Manager, 1998-2001; General Manager, NHS Greater Glasgow, 2001-05. Publications: a number of peer reviewed manuscripts in journals. Recreations: golf; reading; music. Address: (h.) Tweeniehills, 33 Sandholes Road, Brookfield, Renfrewshire PA5 8UY; T.-01505 336057; e-mail: jamesm31@aol.com

Miller, James David Frederick, CBE, DUniv(Stirling, Paisley), MA (Cantab), CIMgt, FIPD, FRSA. Chairman, Wolverhampton and Dudley Breweries PLC, 1992-2001; Chairman, Fairbridge Scotland, 1998-2006; Vice-Chairman, Forth Valley Enterprise, 1996-2003; Director, J. and J. Denholm Ltd., 1997-2005; Chairman, Clackmannan College of FE, 2004-06; b. 5.1.35, Wolverhampton; m., Saffrey Blackett Oxley; 3 s. (1 deceased); 1 d. Educ. The Edinburgh Academy; Emmanuel College, Cambridge; London School of Economics. National Service, Argyll and Sutherland Highlanders (commissioned South Staffords); Council Member, Outward Bound Limited, 1985-95; Vice-Chairman, Royal Scottish National Orchestra; Director, Edinburgh Academy, 1985; Commissioner, Queen Victoria School, 1987-97; Governor, Scottish College of Textiles, 1989; Director, Edinburgh Military Tattoo Ltd., 1990-2000; Director, Scottish Life Assurance Company, 1995-2001; Chairman, Court, Stirling University, 1992-99; Chairman, SCOTVEC, 1992-96; Chairman, Scottish Examinations Board, 1994-96; Chairman, SQA (Scottish Qualifications Authority), 1996-2000. Recreations: gardening; golf; walking. Address: (h.) Blairuskin Lodge, Kinlochard, Aberfoyle, by Stirling FK8 3TP; T.-01877 387 249; e-mail: J.D.F.M@btinternet.com

Miller, Very Rev. John. Minister, Castlemilk East Parish, 1971-2007; Moderator, General Assembly, Church of Scotland, 2001-02; b. 11.11.41, Oxford; m., Mary; 3 c. Educ. Oxford University; Edinburgh University; Union Theological Seminary, New York; Teaching Certificate, Moray House College of Education. Assistant Minister, Richmond Craigmillar Church, Edinburgh, 1967-69. Recreation: cycling. Address: (b.) 98 Kirkcaldy Road, Glasgow G41 4LD; T.-0141 423 0221.

Miller, Keith Manson, CBE, D(Eng), BSc (Hons), DipMS. Chief Executive, Miller Group, since 1994; b. 19.3.49, Edinburgh. Educ. Loretto; Heriot-Watt University; Glasgow University. Recreations: sailing; skiing. Address: (b.) Miller Group Ltd., 2 Lochside View, Edinburgh Park, Edinburgh

EH12 9DH; T.-0870 336 5000.
E-mail: keith.miller@miller.co.uk

Miller, Professor Kenneth, LLB, LLM, PhD. Professor of Law, Strathclyde University, since 1992 (Vice Principal); b. 11.12.51, Paisley; m., Margaret Macleod. Educ. Paisley Grammar School; Strathclyde University; Queen's University, Canada. Lecturer in Law, then Senior Lecturer, Strathclyde University, 1975-91; Deputy General Editor, Stair Memorial Encyclopaedia of the Laws of Scotland, 1990-96; Editor, Juridical Review, since 2000; Deputy Chair, Central Arbitration Committee. Publications: Employment Law in Scotland (Co-Author); Law of Health and Safety at Work in Scotland; Employment Law – A Student Guide. Recreations: reading; golf; walking. Address: (b.) McCance Building, Strathclyde University, 16 Richmond Street, Glasgow G1 1XQ; T.-0141-552 4400.

Miller, Sir Ronald Andrew Baird, CBE (1985), CA, DSc, DUniv. Former Chairman, Dawson International PLC; b. 13.5.37, Edinburgh. Former Chairman, Court, Napier University.

Miller, Professor William L., MA, PhD, FBA, FRSA, FRSE. Edward Caird Professor of Politics, Glasgow University, since 1985; b. 12.8.43, Glasgow; m., Fiona Thomson; 2 s.; 1 d. Educ. Aberdeen Grammar School; Royal High School, Edinburgh; Edinburgh University; Newcastle University. Formerly Lecturer, Senior Lecturer and Professor, Strathclyde University; Visiting Professor, Virginia Tech., Blacksburg, Virginia, 1983-84; also taught at Universities of Essex and Cologne; frequent Contributor to Press and TV; Member, Editorial Board: Electoral Studies. Publications: Electoral Dynamics, 1977; The End of British Politics?, 1981; The Survey Method in the Social and Political Sciences, 1983; Elections and Voters, 1987; The Quality of Local Democracy, 1988; How Voters Change, 1990; Media and Voters, 1991; Alternatives to Freedom, 1995; Political Culture in Contemporary Britain, 1996; Values and Political Change in Postcommunist Europe, 1998; Models of Local Governance, 2000; A Culture of Corruption? 2001; Anglo-Scottish Relations from 1900 to Devolution and Beyond, 2005; Multicultural Nationalism: Islamophobia, Anglophobia and Devolution, 2006; The Open Economy and its Enemies - Public Opinion in East Asia and Eastern Europe, 2006. Address: (b.) Department of Politics, Glasgow University G12 8RT; T.-0141-330 5980.

Miller Smith, Charles. Chairman, Asia House, since 2007; b. 7.11.39; m. 1st, 1964, Dorothy Agnes Wilson Adams (d 1999); 1s.; 2d.; 2nd, 2004, Debjani Jash. Educ. Glasgow Academy; St Andrews University (MA). ACCA. Unilever: Financial Director, Vinyl Products, 1970-73; Head of Planning, 1974; Finance Director, Walls Meat Company, 1976; Vice-Chairman, Hindustan Lever, 1979-81; Speciality Chemicals Group, 1981; Chief Executive: PPF International, 1983, Quest International, 1986; Financial Director, Unilever Board, 1989; Executive, Unilever Foods, 1993-94; Imperial Chemical Industries: Director, 1994-2001, Chief Executive, 1995-99; Chairman, 1999-2001; Scottish Power plc: Dep. Chairman, 1999-2000, Chairman, 2000-07, Chairman, Advisory Board, since 2007; Non-Executive Director: Midland Bank, 1994-96, HSBC Holdings Plc, 1996-2001, Adviser, Goldman Sachs, 2002-05; Senior Advisor, Warburg Pincus, since 2005; Senior Adviser, RREEF Infrastructure, Deutsche Bank, since 2007; Senior Adviser, Defence Strategy & Solutions, since 2007; Director, Firstsource Solutions Ltd., since 2001; Member, Management Board MoD, 2002-07. Hon. LLD St Andrews, 1995. Recreations:

reading; walking. Address: (b.) ScottishPower, 1st Floor, 85 Buckingham Gate, London SW1E 6PD; T.-020-7651-2000. Club: National.

Millican, Douglas, Bcom, CA, AMCT. Finance and Regulation Director, Scottish Water, since 2007, Finance Director, 2002-07; b. 13.9.64, Edinburgh; m., Jane; 2 s.; 1 d. Educ. Edinburgh Academy; Edinburgh University. Price Waterhouse, 1986-90, 1990-93; East of Scotland Water: Financial Controller, 1996-2002; Commercial Director, 2000-02. Recreations: Church; skiing; cycling. Address: (b.) Scottish Water, Castle House, 6 Castle Drive, Dunfermline, Fife KY11 8GG; T.-01383 848465; e-mail: douglas.millican@scottishwater.co.uk

Milligan, Eric. Convener, Lothian and Borders Police Board, 2003-07; Lord Provost and Lord Lieutenant, City of Edinburgh, 1996-2003; b. 27.1.51, Edinburgh; m., Janis. Educ. Tynecastle High School; Napier College of Commerce and Technology. Former printer; Member (Labour), Edinburgh District Council, 1974-78; Lothian Regional Councillor, 1978-96 (Chairman, Finance Committee, 1980-82, 1986-90, Convener, 1990-96); President, COSLA, 1988-90; City of Edinburgh Councillor, since 1995 (Convener, 1995-96); JP, Edinburgh, 1996; awarded Chevalier, Ordre National du Mérite, 1996; honorary degree: Doctor of Business Administration, Napier University, 1999; Honorary Fellow, Royal College of Surgeons of Edinburgh, 2000; Honorary Degree: Doctor of the University, Heriot-Watt University, 2004. Address: (b.) City Chambers, High Street, Edinburgh EH1 1YJ; T-0131 200 2000.

Mills, Harold Hernshaw, CB, BSc, PhD. Chairman: Caledonian MacBrayne Ltd., 1999-2006, Edinburgh World Heritage Trust, 1999-2006, Land Trust; Board Member: Northlink Orkney and Shetland Ferries Ltd., Northlink Ferries Ltd.; Trustee, Scottish Maritime Museum; Board Member, Edinburgh City Centre Partnership Company, 2002-06; Trustee, The City of Adelaide Charitable Trust; b. 2.3.38, Greenock; m., Marion Elizabeth Beattie. Educ. Greenock High School; Glasgow University. Cancer Research Scientist, Roswell Park Memorial Institute, Buffalo, New York, 1962-64; Lecturer, Chemistry Department, Glasgow University, 1964-69; Principal, Scottish Home and Health Department, 1970-76; Assistant Secretary: Scottish Office, 1976-81, Privy Council Office, 1981-83, Scottish Development Department, 1983-84; Under Secretary, Scottish Development Department, 1984-88; Principal Finance Officer, Scottish Office, 1988-92; Secretary, Scottish Office Environment Department, 1992-95; Secretary and Head of Department, Scottish Office Development Department, 1995-98. Governor, Queen Margaret University College, 1998-2004; Director, Home in Scotland, 1998-2004 (Chairman, 2000-04); Director, Edinburgh City Centre Partnership, 2002-05; Director, Home Group, 2000-04; Director, Home Housing Trust, 2000-04. Address (h.) 21 Hatton Place, Edinburgh EH9 1UB.

Mills, Ian Thomas, BSc, MPhil. Arts/Education Consultant; b. 20.5.48, Hamilton; m., Margaret; 2 d. Educ. Dalziel High School, Motherwell; Glasgow University; Strathclyde University. Chemistry Teacher, Dalziel High School, Motherwell, 1970-75; Senior Housemaster, Lanark Grammar School, 1975-78; Assistant Head Teacher, then Depute Head Teacher, Carluke High School, 1978-85; Area Education Officer, Perth and Kinross, 1985-91; Assistant Director of Education, Tayside Regional Council, 1991-95; Director of Education and Leisure Services, East Dunbartonshire Council, 1995-2000; General Manager, National Youth Choir of Scotland, 2001-07. Administrator, Scottish International Piano Competition; Chairman, Scottish Amateur Music Association; Member, Making Music (Scotland) Committee; Member, Drake Music Project Board. Recreations: music; family-based activities;

Rotary. Address: 28 Kirkhouse Road, Blanefield G63 9BX; T.-07814989155; e-mail: ian@ian-mills.co.uk

Mills, Peter Rodney, BSc, MD, FRCP, FACP. Consultant Physician and Gastroenterologist, Western Infirmary, Glasgow, since 1988; b. 27.12.48, St. Albans; m., Hazel; 1 s.; 1 d. Educ. St. George's School, Harpenden; University of St. Andrews. Senior Registrar in Medicine/ Gastroenterology, Royal Infirmary, Glasgow, 1979; Visiting Assistant Professor, Yale University School of Medicine, 1983; Associate Professor, Division of Gastroenterology, Medical College of Virginia, 1985; Director of Medical Examinations, Royal College of Physicians and Surgeons of Glasgow, 2000-06; Chairman, Board for KBA in Gastroenterology, since 2007; President, Scottish Society of Gastroenterology, 2007-09. Publications: 120 papers in gastroenterology and liver journals. Recreations: golf; hillwalking. Address: (h.) 19 Kirklee Road, Glasgow G12 0RQ; T.-0141-339 8206. E-mail: p.r.mills@clinmed.gla.ac.uk

Mills, Thomas, BEd, CBiol, MIBiol, MIM. Head Teacher, St. Andrew's High School, Coatbridge, since 2005; Head Teacher, St. Patrick's High School, Coatbridge, 1996-2005; b. 17.2.47, Lennoxtown; m., Janice Alexis; 1 s.; 1 d. Educ. St. Mungo's Academy; St. Andrew's College; Paisley University. Teacher of Biology, John Bosco Secondary School, 1974-77; A.P.T., Biology, Lourdes Secondary School, 1977-83; Principal Teacher of Biology, Our Lady and St. Francis Secondary School, 1983-87; Assistant Head Teacher, Our Lady's High School, Motherwell, 1987-92; Depute Headteacher, John Ogilvie High School, Hamilton, 1992-96. Executive Member, Catholic Headteachers of Scotland, 1996-2005; Commissioner, Scottish Catholic Commission for Education, 1999-2005. Recreations: keep-fit; DIY; music; caravanning.

Milne, Colin McLeod, LLB. President, Employment Tribunals Scotland, since 2000; b. 14.3.47, Glasgow; 1 s.; 1 d. Educ. Kilmarnock Academy; Glasgow University. Partner, Wright Johnston & Mackenzie, Solicitors, Glasgow, until 1991; appointed Chairman of Industrial Tribunals, 1991, Regional Chairman, 1994. Address: (b.) Central Office of Employment Tribunals, Eagle Building, 215 Bothwell Street, Glasgow G2 7TS; T.-0141-204 0730.

Milne, James Smith, DL, CBE, DBA (Hon). Chairman and Managing Director, Balmoral Group Holdings Ltd., since 1980; b. 26.12.40, Aberdeen; m., Gillian; 2 s.; 2 d. Member, Executive Committee. SCDI; Chairman, Friends of Anchor Ari; Director of the Entrepreneurial Exchange; Member, Scottish Council Development and Industry's North-east committee. Recreations: field sports, family. Address: (b.) Balmoral Park, Loirston, Aberdeen; T.-01224 859000. E-mail: j.milne@balmoral.co.uk

Milne, Professor John Alexander, MBE, BA, BSc (Hons), PhD, FRSA. Chairman, Deer Commission for Scotland; Fellow, Macaulay Land Use Research Institute; b. 22.11.43, Edinburgh; m., Janet Erskine; 1 s. Educ. Edinburgh Academy; Edinburgh University; London University; Open University. Honorary Professor, University of Aberdeen; Editor, Grass and Forage Science. Address: (b.) Deer Commission for Scotland, Great Glen House, Leachkin Road, Inverness IV3 8NW; e-mail: john.milne@dcs.gov.uk

Milne, Professor Lorna Catherine, MA, PhD, Chevalier dans l'Ordre des Palmes Académiques. Professor of French, University of St. Andrews, since 2006, Dean of Arts, since 2006; b. 19.08.59, Stirling. Educ. Dollar Academy; St. Andrews; Auckland (New Zealand). HM Diplomatic Service, London and East Berlin, 1983-87; Doctoral Studies, 1987-91; Lecturer: Aston University, 1991-96, St. Andrews University, 1996-2001, Senior Lecturer, 2001-06. Publications: Author: L'Evangile Selon Michel, 1994, Patrick Chamoiseau: Espaces d'une ecriture antillaise, 2006; numerous scholarly articles. Address: (b.) University of St. Andrews, St. Andrews, Fife KY16 9AH; T.-01334 462159; e-mail: deanarts@st-andrews.ac.uk

Milne, Nanette Lilian Margaret, OBE, MBChB, FFARCS. MSP (Conservative), Northeast Region, since 2003; Conservative Spokesman on the Environment, since 2007, Spokesman on Health and Community Care, 2005-07; b. 27.4.42, Aberdeen; m., Dr. Alan D. Milne; 1 s.; 1 d. Educ. Aberdeen High School for Girls; University of Aberdeen. Various hospital posts (to registrar grade), 1965-73; career break, 1973-78; part-time medical research, 1978-92. Vice-chairman, Scottish Conservative Party, 1988-92; Aberdeen City Councillor, 1988-99; Director, Grampian Enterprise Ltd., 1992-98; Trustee, Aberdeen International Youth Festival; Member, Aberdeen University Court, 1996-2005. Recreations: the countryside (hill-walking, etc); skiing; golf; gardening. Address: Scottish Parliament, Holyrood, Edinburgh EH99 1SP; T.-0131-348 5652. E-mail: nanette.milne.msp@scottish.parliament.uk

Milne, Roy Stewart, BArch (Hons), RIBA, FRIAS. Director, Michael Laird Architects, since 2003; b. 17.12.48, Ormiston; m., Eleanor (nee Matheson); 2 s. Educ. Edinburgh Academy; Edinburgh University. Graduated in 1972 and emigrated to New Zealand, worked there as an architect, returning to UK in 1977; co-author of "The Care and Conservation of Georgian Houses", 1978; joined Michael Laird and Partners in 1977, becoming a partner in 1989. Address: (b.) Michael Laird Architects, 5 Forres Street, Edinburgh EH3 6DE; T.-0131 226 6991; e-mail: r.milne@michaellaird.co.uk

Milne, Simon Stephen, MBE, BSc, FRGS. Chief Executive, Scottish Wildlife Trust, since 2004; b. 30.1.59, Dundee; m., Francoise (ne Sevaux); 1 s.; 2 d. Educ. University of St. Andrews; Royal Naval College, Greenwich. Commissioned into Royal Marines, 1976; retired from Royal Marines in Rank of Lieutenant Colonel, 2000; Director, Sir Harold Hillier Gardens and Arboretum, 2000-04. Member, Scottish Executive's Ministerial Working Group for Aquaculture, since 2005; Member, Scottish Biodiversity Committee, since 2004. Recreations: ornithology; horticulture. Address: (b.) Scottish Wildlife Trust, Cramond House, Cramond Glebe Road, Edinburgh EH4 6NS.

Milton, Ian Murray, MCIM. Chairman, Milton Hotels Ltd.; Director, Nevis Range Development Company PLC; b. 25.7.45, Glasgow; m., Ann; 1 s.; 3 d. Educ. Lochaber High School; Scottish Hotel School, Glasgow. Began Milton Hotels with brother, 1965. Recreations: golf; skiing; computing. Address: (b.) Milton Hotels Ltd., 52 Stirling Business Centre, Wellgreen, Stirling FK8 2DZ; T.-01786 448330; e-mail: ian.milton@miltonhotels.com

Minett, Ross Jolyon, MSc, BSc (Hons). Campaigns Director, Advocates for Animals, formerly Director; Company Secretary, St. Andrew Animal Fund, since 2004. Educ. Ripon Grammar School; University of Edinburgh. BSc Ecological Science (Honours in Wildlife and Pest Management), 1991-95; MSc Applied Animal Behaviour and Animal Welfare, 1996-97; Information Officer -

Compassion in World Farming, 1998-99, Campaigns Officer, 1999-2000; Information Officer, Advocates for Animals, 2000-01, Campaigns Director, 2001-03. Recreations: walking my dogs; socialising with friends; DIY; photography. Address: (b) 10 Queensferry Street, Edinburgh EH2 4PG; T.-0131 225 6039, e mail; ross@advocatesforanimals.org

Minto, Brian J. L., OBE, CA, FRSA. Vice President, Scottish Fisheries Museum, Anstruther (Chairman, 1994-2005); Director, Dundee College, 1993-2005; b. 10.8.42, Lanark; m., Margot Morris; 1 s.; 1 d. Educ. Arbroath High School. Apprentice CA, 1959-64; Scottish Malt Distillers Ltd., 1967-70; MFPT Chartered Accountants, 1971-2004. Member: Scottish Business Education Council, 1982-85, Scottish Vocational Education Council, 1985-97, Scottish Qualifications Authority, 1997-2000, Scottish Further Education Funding Council, 1999-2001. Recreations: golf; walking; photography. Address: (h.) 3 Wester Leys, Hallyburton, Coupar Angus PH13 9JX.

Misra, Prem Chandra, BSc, MBB3, DPM (RCP&S, Edin and Glas), FRCPsych. Consultant Psychiatrist; Professor; b. 24.7.41, Lucknow, India; m., Sandhya; 1 s.; 2 d. Educ. KK Degree College and King George's Medical College, Lucknow, India; Lucknow University. Rotating Intern, King George's Medical College Hospital, Lucknow, 1967; Demonstrator, Department of Human Physiology, Lucknow University, 1967; Resident Senior House Officer, General Medicine and Geriatrics, Wigan and Leigh Group of Hospitals, 1968-69; Resident House Surgeon, General Surgery, Wigan Royal Infirmary, 1968-69; Resident House Physician, General Medicine, Whelley Hospital, Wigan, 1969-70; Resident Senior House Officer in Psychiatry, then Resident Registrar in Psychiatry, Bolton District General Hospital, 1970-73; Senior Psychiatric Registrar (Midland Area Consultant Training Scheme), Hollymoor Hospital, Birmingham, 1973-76; Consultant Psychiatrist, Solihull Area Health Authority, 1976; appointed Consultant Psychiatrist, Glasgow Royal Infirmary and Duke Street Hospital, 1976-2005; Consultant in Charge, Acorn Street Day Hospital, 1979-87; Deputy Physician Superintendent, Gartloch and Parkhead Hospitals, Glasgow, 1984-92. President, Indian Association of Strathclyde, since 1981; Member, Executive Committee: Strathclyde Community Relations Council, 1981-85, Scottish Council for Racial Equality, 1982-84; Member: Social and Welfare Committee, CRC, for Ethnic Groups and Vietnam Refugees, 1982-84; Board of Directors, Scottish Refugee Council, 1994-2000; Secretary, Division of Psychiatry, Eastern District of Glasgow, 1980-94; President, British Society of Medical and Dental Hypnosis (Scotland), 1987-89; Governor, Glasgow Caledonian University, 1998-2005; Lead Consultant of Royal College of Psychiatrists for Transcultural Psychiatry in Scotland; Member: Executive Committee, British Society of Research on Sex Education, International Scientific Committee on Sexuality and Handicap, International Advisory Board of Israel Society of Clinical and Experimental Hypnosis, International Committee of Sexologists, Society for the Advancement of Sexual Health; Executive Committee Member, European Society of Hypnosis; Justice of the Peace, 1980-2007; awarded Ludwika Bierkoskigo Medal by Polish Medical Association for "outstanding contributions in the prevention and treatment of disabilities"; "Robert Burns Award" by Indian Writers Association of Scotland; "Merit Award" by Greater Glasgow Health Council; and "Award of an Honour" by the Asian Federation of Sexology Mumbai, India. Publications: Modern Trends in Hypnosis; research papers. E-mail: prof.p.misra@firemail.co.uk

Mitchell, Rev. Alexander Bell, DipTechEd, BD. Minister, St. Blane's Church, Dunblane, since 2003; b. 28.6.49,

Baillieston; m., Elizabeth Brodie; 1 s.; 2 d. Educ. Uddingston Grammar School; New College, Edinburgh. Assistant Minister, Dunblane Cathedral, 1979-81; Minister, St Leonard's Church, Dunfermline, 1981-2003. Recreations: golf; hill-walking. Address: 49 Roman Way, Dunblane FK15 9DJ; T.-01786 822268.

Mitchell, David William, CBE. President, Scottish Conservative and Unionist Party, since 2004; Chairman, Scottish Conservative and Unionist Party, 2001-04; b. 4.1.33, Glasgow; m., Lynda Katherine Marion Guy; 1 d. Educ. Merchiston Castle School. Cmmnd (NS), RSF, 1950; Member, Board, Western General Hospital, 1965-72; President, Timber Trades Benevolent Society of UK, 1974; Member, Scottish Council, CBI, 1979-85; Director, Mallinson-Denny (Scotland), 1977-90; Hunter Timber Scotland, 1990-92; Joint Managing Director, M. & N. Norman (Timber) Ltd., 1992-96 (Non-Executive, 1996-98); President: Scottish Timber Trade Association, 1980-82, Scottish Conservative and Unionist Association, 1981-83; Member: Scottish Council (Development and Industry), 1984-95, Board of Cumbernauld New Town, 1985-97 (Chairman, 1987-97), Board of Management, Craighalbert Centre for Children with Motor Impairment, 1992-96; Treasurer, Scottish Conservative Party, 1990-93 and 1998-2001. Recreations: fishing; shooting; golf. Address: Old Mill House, Symington, Ayrshire KA1 5QL; T.-01563 830851.

Mitchell, Rev. Duncan Ross, BA (Hons), BD (Hons). Retired Minister, St. Andrews Church, West Kilbride; b. 5.5.42, Boddam, Aberdeenshire; m., Sandra Brown; 2 s.; 1 d. Educ. Hyndland Senior Secondary School, Glasgow; Strathclyde University; Glasgow University. Worked in insurance industry, four years; Minister, Craigmailen UF Church, Bo'ness, 1972-80; Convener, Assembly Youth Committee, UF Church, 1974-79; Member: Scottish Joint Committee on Religious Education, 1974-79, Multilateral Conversation in Scotland, 1976-79, Board of Social Responsibility, Church of Scotland, 1983-86; Ardrossan Presbytery: Convener, World Mission and Unity, 1984-88, Convener, Stewardship and Finance, 1988-91, Convener, Superintendence Committee, 1994-97; Convener, General Assembly Board of World Mission and Unity's Local Involvements Committee, and Executive Member of the Board, 1987-92; Church of Scotland Delegate to Council of Churches for Britain and Ireland Assembly; Moderator, Ardrossan Presbytery, 1992-93. Recreations: swimming; supporting Partick Thistle; writing poetry and short stories. Address: 11 Dunbar Gardens, Saltcoats; T.-01294 474575.

Mitchell, George Edward, CBE. Former Governor, Bank of Scotland; Executive Chairman, The Arkaga Fund; Chairman, The Malcolm Group; Non Executive Director, BUPA and Intrinsic Financial Services; b. 7.4.50, Edinburgh; m., Agnes; 3 d. Educ. Forrester High School, Edinburgh. Bank of Scotland, since 1966. Recreations: football; tennis; family.

Mitchell, Gordon K., DA, RSA, RSW, RGI. Artist; b. 16.11.52, Edinburgh; m., Deirdre; 1 s.; 3 d. Educ. Royal High School, Edinburgh College of Art. Former Art Teacher (Deputy Headmaster, St. Serf's School, 1986-89); elected: SSA, 1977, SAAC, 1990 (President, 1993-96), RSW, 1996, ARSA, 1998, RGI, 1998, RSA, 2005. Served on council of SSA, SAAC, RSW, SABA; Artist Convener, RGI, 2001-06; exhibited widely at home and abroad; work in public and private collections. Prizes and awards include: RSA Student Prize; Borders Biennial Competition; Scottish Drawing Competition; Mayfest Award; William Gillies Award; Scottish Amicable Prize; Scottish Provident Award; Whyte and Mackay Award; Dunfermline Building Society Award; RSA J. Murray Thompson Award; RSA Maude Gemmel Hutchison Award; Royal Bank of Scotland Award, RGI. Recreations: current affairs; golf. Address: (h.) 6

Learmonth Terrace, Edinburgh EH4 1PQ; T.-0131 332 3588; website: www.gordonmitchell.co.uk

Mitchell, Iain Grant, QC, LLB (Hons), FSA Scot, FRSA, FFCS. Queen's Counsel, since 1992; Temporary Sheriff, 1992-97; b. 15.11.51, Edinburgh. Educ. Perth Academy; Edinburgh University. Called to Scottish Bar, 1976; Past President, Diagnostic Society of Edinburgh; former Vice-President, Edinburgh University Conservative Association; Conservative candidate, Falkirk West, General Election, 1983, Kirkcaldy, General Election, 1987, Cumbernauld and Kilsyth, General Election, 1992, Dunfermline East, General Election, 1997, Edinburgh North and Leith, General Election, 2001, Dundee East, Scottish Parliament Election, 1999, Scotland, European Election, 1999, Falkirk West, Scottish Parliament Election, 2002; Honorary Secretary, Scottish Conservative and Unionist Association, 1993-98, Scottish Conservative and Unionist Party, 1998-2001; Chairman, North Queensferry Community Council; Chairman, North Queensferry Arts Trust; Reader, Church of Scotland; Chairman, Trust for an International Opera Theatre of Scotland; Chairman, Scottish Baroque Ensemble Ltd., 1999-2001; Member: Executive Committee of European Movement (Scottish Council), Committee, Perth Civic Trust, 1999-2002; Chairman, Perthshire Public Arts Trust; Trustee, Forth Bridge Memorial Public Arts Trust; Chairman, Faculty of Advocates IT Group; Chairman, Scottish Lawyers' European Group; Vice-Chairman, Scottish Society for Computers and Law; Editor, Scottish Parliament Law Review; Joint Editor, e-law Review. Recreations: music and the arts; photography; cinema; walking; history; travel; writing; finding enough hours in the day. Address: (b.) Advocates Library, Parliament House, High Street, Edinburgh; T.-0131-226 5071.

Mitchell, Ian Macaulay, BSc (Hons), MSc (Distinction). Deputy Director, Public Service Reform Policy, Scottish Government, since 2007; Director of Regeneration, Communities Scotland, 2003-07; b. 11.10.63, Dumfries; spouse, Elizabeth Riach; 1 s. Educ. Dumfries Academy; Heriot Watt University; Napier University. Planning Officer, Scottish Sports Council, 1987-88; Regional Development Co-ordinator, Lothian Regional Council, 1988-90; Senior Economic Policy Officer, Fife Regional Council, 1990-97; Team Leader, Corporate Policy, Fife Council, 1997-99; Head of Branch, Scottish Executive (Enterprise Networks; Local Government Constitution and Governance), 1999-2003. Former Member of Community Planning Task Force/Implementation Group. Recreations: hill walking; cycling; travel writing. Address: (b.) Public Service Reform and Efficient Government Division, Scottish Government, Room 3-H99, Victoria Quay, Edinburgh EH6 6QQ.

Mitchell, Sheriff James Kenneth, LLB. Sheriff of Glasgow and Strathkelvin, since 1985; b. 30.4.49, Glasgow; m., Frances Kane; 1 s. Educ. Paisley Grammar School; Glasgow University. Solicitor, 1972-78; Partner, Ross Harper and Murphy, 1975-78; admitted Faculty of Advocates, 1979. Council Member, Sheriffs' Association, 1998-2001; Member, Glasgow Sheriff Court Standing Advisory Committee, 1997-2000; Member, National Council, Victim Support Scotland, 2001-03; Member, Judicial Studies Committee, since 2005. Recreations: family; friends; football; films; fun. Address: (b.) Sheriff's Chambers, 1 Carlton Place, Glasgow G5 9DA; T.-0141-429 8888.

Mitchell, (Janet) Margaret, JP. Member (C), Central Scotland, Scottish Parliament, since 2003; b. 15.11.52, Coatbridge; m. (1978), Henry Thomson Mitchell. Educ. Coatbridge High School; Hamilton Teacher Training

College (DipEd); Open University (BA); Strathclyde University (LLB: DipLLP), Jordanhill College (Dip Media Studies); Primary School Teacher, Airdrie and Bothwell, 1974-93; Mem. and Cons. Gp. Leader, Hamilton DC, 1988-96; Non-Exec. Dir., Stonehouse and Hairmyres NHS Trust, 1993-97; Special Adviser to David McLetchie, MSP and James Douglas-Hamilton, MSP, 1999-2002; Scottish Cons. Justice Spokesman, 2003-07; Convener, Scottish Parliamentary Equal Opportunities Committee, 2007; Mem., Scottish Cons. Party Exec., 2002-03; Hon. Mem., Board of Advisers, ThinkScotland.org; Mem., Psoriasis Scotland Arthritis Link Volunteers, since 2004; JP South Lanarks, 1990. Recreations: music; cycling; photography. Address: Scottish Parliament, Edinburgh EH99 1SP; e-mail: margaret.mitchell.msp@scottish.parliament.uk

Mitchell, John, BSc. Head Teacher, Kilsyth Academy, 1985-2005; Board Member, SQA; Non-Executive Trustee of Lanarkshire Acute Hospitals Trust, 2001-04; b. 4.1.45, Kirkintilloch; m., Irene; 1 s.; 1 d. Educ. Lenzie Academy; Glasgow University; Jordanhill College. Teacher, North Kelvinside Secondary, Glasgow, 1968-70; Physics Teacher, Balfron High School, 1970-72; Bishopbriggs High School, 1972-79; Assistant Head Teacher, Kilsyth Academy, 1979-84; Depute Head Teacher, Knightswood Secondary, 1984-85. President, HAS, 1996. Address: (h.) 10 Blair Drive, Milton of Campsie; T.- 01360 310477.

Mitchell, (John) Angus (Macbeth), CB, CVO, MC, LLD(Hon), (Dundee), DUniv (Stirling). b. 25.8.24, Ootacamund, India; m., Ann Williamson; 2 s.; 2 d. Educ. Marlborough College; Brasenose College, Oxford. Royal Armoured Corps (Captain), 1943-46; Scottish Office, 1949-84; Principal Private Secretary to Secretary of State for Scotland, 1958-59; Under Secretary, Social Work Services Group, 1969-74; Secretary, Scottish Education Department, 1976-84. Order of Orange-Nassau, 1946; Chairman, Scottish Marriage Guidance Council, 1965-69; Vice-Convener, Scottish Council of Voluntary Organisations, 1986-91; Member, Commission for Local Authority Accounts in Scotland, 1985-89; Chairman of Court, Stirling University, 1984-92; Chairman, Scottish Action on Dementia, 1986-94; Member, Historic Buildings Council for Scotland, 1988-94; Trustee, Dementia Services Development Trust, 1988-2000. Publications: Scottish Office Ministers 1885-1985; Procedures for the Reorganisation of Schools in England, 1986; Monumental Inscriptions in SW Midlothian, 2004. Recreations: old Penguins; gravestones; family history. Address: (h.) 31/5 Kinnear Road, Edinburgh EH3 5PG; T.-0131 552 3454; e-mail: 31kinnear@googlemail.com

Mitchell, John Logan, QC, LLB (Hons). Queen's Counsel, since 1987; Advocate Depute, 1981-85; b. 23.6.47, Dumfries; m., Christine Brownlee Thomson; 1 s.; 1 d. Educ. Royal High School, Edinburgh; Edinburgh University. Called to Bar, 1974; Standing Junior Counsel to Forestry Commission; Standing Junior Counsel, Department of Agriculture and Fisheries. Past President, Royal High School F.P. Club. Recreations: running; golf. Address: (h.) 17 Braid Farm Road, Edinburgh; T.-031-447 8099.

Mitchell, Louise C., DL, MA. Director, Glasgow Royal Concert Hall, since 1996; b. London. Educ. Lady Margaret School, London; St. Andrews University; City University, London. Assistant Manager, Scottish Baroque Ensemble, 1979-81; Concerts Manager, London Sinfonietta, 1982-87; Assistant Director, Edinburgh International Festival, 1989-91; Music Programme Manager, Barbican Centre, 1992-94; Concerts Director, London Philharmonic Orchestra, 1994-96. Governor, RSAMD; Director, Prince and Princess of

Wales Hospice; Board Member, International Society for the Performing Arts; Vice Chair, British Association of Concert Halls. Recreations: travel; food and wine. Address: (b.) 2 Sauchiehall Street, Glasgow G2 3NY; T.-0141-353 8080.

Mitchell, Professor Neil James, PhD, MA, BA. Professor, Sixth Century Chair, Politics and International Relations, University of Aberdeen, since 2005; b. 19.9.53, London; 1 s.; 1 d. Educ. Sir Frederic Osborn School; Nottingham University; Indiana University, USA. Assistant Professor: Grinnell College, Iowa, USA, 1983, Iowa State University, USA, 1984-86; Professor and Chair, University of New Mexico, USA, 1986-2005. Publications: The Generous Corporation, 1989; The Conspicuous Corporation, 1997; Agents of Atrocity, 2004. Recreations: running; hillwalking; reading. Address: (b.) School of Social Science, Edward Wright Building, University of Aberdeen, Aberdeen AB24 3QY; T.-01224 273123; e-mail: n.mitchell@abdn.ac.uk

Mitchison, Professor John Murdoch, ScD, FRS, FRSE, Member Acad Europea. Professor Emeritus, Edinburgh University (Professor of Zoology, 1963-88); b. 11.6.22; m., Rosalind Mary Wrong (deceased); 1 s.; 3 d. Educ. Winchester College; Trinity College, Cambridge. Army Operational Research, 1941-46; Research Scholar, then Fellow, Trinity College, Cambridge, 1946-54; Lecturer, then Reader in Zoology, Edinburgh University, 1953-62; Member, Edinburgh University Court, 1971-74, 1985-88; Dean, Faculty of Science, 1984-85; Member: Academia Europaea, Scottish Marine Biological Association, 1961-67; Executive Committee Member, International Society for Cell Biology, 1964-72; Member: Biological Committee, SRC, 1972-75, Royal Commission on Environmental Pollution, 1974-79, Science Board, SRC, 1976-79, Working Group on Biological Manpower, DES, 1968-71, Advisory Committee on Safety of Nuclear Installations, Health and Safety Executive, 1981-84; President, British Society for Cell Biology, 1974-77. Publication: The Biology of the Cell Cycle. Address: (h.) Great Yew, Ormiston, East Lothian EH35 5NJ; T.-Pencaitland 340530.

Mitchison, Neil, MA, MBCS, CITP, CEng. European Commission Representative in Scotland, since 2006; b. 02.05.51; m., Aideen O'Malley; 3 s.; 2 d. Educ. Edinburgh Academy; Trinity College, Cambridge; Edinburgh University. Research Fellow, University of Sussex, 1978-79; Radio Producer, Presenter, and Journalist, BBC Highland, 1980-84; Computer Analyst and Research Project Manager, European Commission, 1985-93; Consultant Editor, Europe, BBC TV, 1993-94; Program Manager, Major Accident Hazards Bureau, European Commission, 1994-2002, Research Action Leader in Cyber Security, 2005-06. Vice President, Commission Scientifique "Risques Accidentels", INERIS (F), 1999-2006; President, Association for Go in Italy, 1999-2005; Parliamentary Candidate (Lib Dem), 1989, 1992, 1997 and 1999. Publications: Identity Theft a discussion paper, 2004; Accident Scenarios and Emergency Response, 1999; Guidelines on a Major Accident Prevention Policy and Safety Management System, 1998; Safety and Runaway Reactions, 1997; Safety Management Systems in the Process Industry, 1994. Address: (b.) 9 Alva Street, Edinburgh EH2 4PH; T.-0131 225 2058; e-mail: neil.mitchison@ec.europa.eu

Moffat, Alistair Murray, MA (Hons), MPhil. Journalist; Film Maker; b. 16.6.50, Kelso; m., Lindsay Thomas; 1 s.; 2 d. Educ. Kelso High School; St. Andrews University; Edinburgh University; London University. Ran Edinburgh Festival Fringe, 1976-81; Arts Correspondent/

Producer/Controller of Features/Director of Programmes, Scottish Television; Managing Director, Scottish Television Enterprises. Publications: The Edinburgh Fringe, 1978; Kelsae — A History of Kelso from Earliest Times, 1985; Remembering Charles Rennie Mackintosh, 1989; Arthur and the Lost Kingdoms, 1999; The Sea Kingdoms, 2001; The Borders, 2002; Homing, 2003; Heartland Images of the Scottish Borders, 2004; Before Scotland, 2005; Tyneside, 2005; East Lothian, 2006; "The Reivers", 2007; "Fife", 2007. Recreations: sleeping; supporting Kelso RFC. Address: (h.) The Henhouse, Selkirk TD7 5EY.

Moffat, Anne, RMN. Labour MP, East Lothian, since 2001; b. 30.3.58, Dunfermline; divorced; 1 s. Educ. Woodmill High School. Nursing sister; NEC, Cohse and Unison; former National President, Unison; former Ashford Borough Councillor; former Chair of Organisation, Labour Party; formerly on Labour Party NEC. Address: (b.) 65 High Street, Tranent, East Lothian EH33 1LN; T.-01875 614990.

Moffat, Douglas William John, LLB, WS. Partner, Tods Murray, LLP, since 1974; b. 3.10.47, Castle Douglas; 1 s.; 1 d. Educ. The Edinburgh Academy; Edinburgh University. Member: British Council of Shopping Centres, British Council of Offices, Investment Property Forum. Recreations: golf; squash; shooting; hillwalking. Address: (b.) Edinburgh Quay, 133 Fountainbridge, Edinburgh EH3 9AG; T.-0131 656 2000.

Moffett, Ian Weatherston, LLB (Hons), WS, NP. Partner, Anderson Strathern, since 2005; b. 25.4.50, Edinburgh; m., Jinty; 3 s. Educ. George Watsons Boys College, Edinburgh; Edinburgh University. Partner in Dundas & Wilson, 1977-2005; Non Executive Director, Registers of Scotland. Recreations: family; walking and country pursuits; golf; collecting books relating to Scottish History (particularly Speyside and Edinburgh). Address: (b.) 1 Rutland Court, Edinburgh EH3 8EY; T.-0131 270 7700. E-mail: ian.moffett@andersonstrathern.co.uk

Moignard, Professor Elizabeth Ann, MA, DPhil, FSA, FRSE. Professor of Classical Art and Archaeology, University of Glasgow, since 2000; Director, Institute for Art History, University of Glasgow, 1998-2004; Dean, Faculty of Arts, since 2005; b. 3.1.51, Poole; m., A.E. Yearling; 1 step-s.; 1 step-d. Educ. King's High School for Girls, Warwick; St. Hugh's College, Oxford University. Temporary Lecturer in Classics, University of Newcastle-upon-Tyne, 1977-78; University of Glasgow: Lecturer in Greek, 1978-93, Senior Lecturer in Classics, 1992-2000. Publications: Corpus Vasorum Antiquorum; Great Britain Fascicles 16 (National Museum of Scotland), 1989; 18 Glasgow Collections, 1997; 22 (Aberdeen University), 2006; Knossos, The North Cemetery, 1996. Recreations: music; collecting contemporary decorative art; crime fiction. Address: Faculty of Arts, University of Glasgow, Glasgow G12 8QQ; T.-0141-330 5253. E-mail: e.moignard@classics.arts.gla.ac.uk

Moir, Dorothy Carnegie, CBE, MB, ChB, MD, FFPHM, FRCP, MBA, LFHom. Chief Administrative Medical Officer/ Director of Public Health, Lanarkshire Health Board, since 1994; Honorary Senior Clinical Lecturer in Public Health, Aberdeen University; Honorary Senior Clinical Lecturer, Department of Public Health, Glasgow University; b. 27.3.42, Aberdeen; m., Alexander D. Moir; 3 s. Educ. Albyn School for Girls, Aberdeen; Aberdeen University. Research Fellow in Therapeutics and Pharmacology, 1966-69; Lecturer in Community Medicine, 1970-79; Community Medicine Specialist, Grampian

Health Board, 1979-88; Chief Administrative Medical Officer/Director of Public Health, Forth Valley Health Board, 1988-94. Address: (b.) 14 Beckford Street, Hamilton ML3 0TA; e-mail: dorothy.moir@lanarkshire.scot.nhs.uk

Moir, Mark Duncan, LLB, DipLP. Advocate, since 2000; b. 11.9.64, Edinburgh. Educ. Boroughmuir High School; Edinburgh University. Royal Air Force Police, 1983-92; Strathclyde Police, 1992-93. Address: (h.) Park Circus, Glasgow.

Mole, George Alexander (Sandy). Chairman: Scottish Borders Produce, since 2004, Coastal Grains Ltd., since 1998; President, National Farmers Union of Scotland, 1996-97; b. 7.6.43, Duns; m., Jean Mitchell; 1 s.; 2 d. Educ. St. Mary's, Melrose; Merchiston Castle. NFU of Scotland: President, Mid and East Berwick; Chairman, AFRC Cereal Consultative; Convener, Cereals Committee; Member: EEC Commission Cereals Advisory Committee, Home Grown Cereals Authority R. & D. Committee, Institute of Brewing Cereal Publicity. Recreations: golf; shooting. Address: Greenburn, Reston, Eyemouth TD14 5LP.

Mollison, Professor Denis, ScD. Professor of Applied Probability, Heriot-Watt University, 1986-2003, Professor Emeritus, since 2003; Trustee, John Muir Trust, since 1986 (Co-Founder,1983); b. 28.6.45, Carshalton; m., Jennifer Hutton; 1 s.; 3 d. Educ. Westminster School; Trinity College, Cambridge. Research Fellow, King's College, Cambridge, 1969; Lecturer in Statistics, Heriot-Watt University, 1973. Elected Member of Council, National Trust for Scotland, 1979-84, 1999-2004 and since 2005; Chairman, Mountain Bothies Association, 1978-94; Convener, Scottish Green Liberal Democrats, since 2001. Publications: research papers on epidemics, ecology and wave energy. Address: (h.) The Laigh House, Inveresk, Musselburgh EH21 7TD; T.-0131-665 2055; e-mail: d.mollison@ma.hw.ac.uk

Monaghan, Bernadette, MSc. Chief Executive, Apex Scotland, since 2002. Educ. Edinburgh University. Senior Manager, Sacro, 1998-2002. Member: Sentencing Commission for Scotland, Criminal Law Committee of the Law Society of Scotland; Secretary of the Edinburgh branch of SASO (Scottish Association for the Study of Offending). Address: (b.) Apex Scotland, 9 Great Stuart Street, Edinburgh EH3 7TP.

Monaghan, Professor Pat, FRSE. Professor of Animal Ecology, University of Glasgow, since 1997. Address: Environmental and Evolutionary Biology, Graham Kerr Building, University of Glasgow, Glasgow G12 8QQ; T.-0141-330 5968; e-mail: p.monaghan@bio.gla.ac.uk

Monckton, Professor Darren George, BSc, PhD. Professor of Human Genetics, University of Glasgow, since 2005; b. 28.8.66, Eastleigh. Educ. Wyvern Comprehensive, Fair Oak; University of Bath; University of Leicester. Postdoctoral Research Assistant, University of Leicester, 1992-93; Postdoctoral Research Fellow: Baylor College of Medicine, Houston, Texas, USA, 1993-95, UTMD Anderson Cancer Center, Houston, Texas, USA, 1995-96; University of Glasgow: Lecturer in Genetics, 1996-2000, Reader in Genetics, 2000-05. Muscular Dystrophy Association Neuromuscular Disease Research Fellow, 1993; Muscular Dystrophy Association Saunis Davis Jr. Neuromuscular Disease Named Research Fellow, 1994-96; Lister Institute Research Fellow, 1998-2003; Genetical Society Balfour Lecturer, 1999; Member of the Lister Institute of Preventive Medicine, since 2005; Leverhulme

Research Fellow, 2007-08; Tenovus (Scotland) Medal Lecturer, 2008; Scientific Meetings Officer for the UK Genetics Society, 2002-06; Chairman of the 4th International Myotonic Dystrophy Consortium Meeting, 2003. More than 50 journal articles, and book chapters published; more than 100 invited seminars and conference presentations. Recreations: fishing; football; wildlife and photography. Address: (b.) Institute of Biomedical and Life Sciences, University of Glasgow, Glasgow G12 8QQ; T.-0141 330 6213; e-mail: d.monckton@bio.gla.ac.uk

Mone, Rt. Rev. John Aloysius. Bishop Emeritus of Paisley; formerly Titular Bishop of Abercorn and Auxiliary Bishop of Glasgow; b. 22.6.29, Glasgow. Educ. Holyrood Secondary School; Seminaire St. Sulpice and Institut Catholique, Paris. Ordained Priest, 1952; Assistant: St. Ninian's, Knightswood, Glasgow, 1952-75, Our Lady and St. George, Glasgow, 1975-79; Parish Priest, St. Joseph's, Tollcross, Glasgow, 1979-84; Auxiliary Bishop in Glasgow, 1984-88; Bishop of Paisley, 1988-2004. Scottish President, Scottish Catholic Marriage Care; Chairman, Scottish Catholic International Aid Fund, 1975-77; President, Paisley Family Society; President, National Justice and Peace Commission, 1987-2004; President, National Social Care Commission, 1996-2004; President/Treasurer, Scottish Catholic International Aid Fund, 1985-2004. Address: 30 Esplanade, Greenock PA16 7RU.

Mone, Michelle, Founder and Co-Owner, MJM International Ltd., inventor of the Ultimo bra. World Young Business Achiever, 2000.

Monelle, Raymond, MA, BMus, PhD, ARCM. Writer on music; Honorary Professor, Edinburgh University; b. 19.8.37, Bristol; 2 d. Educ. Bristol Grammar School; Pembroke College, Oxford; Royal College of Music. Reviewer: The Independent. Publications: Linguistics and Semiotics in Music, 1992; The Sense of Music, 2000; The Musical Topic, 2006. Address: (h.) 80 Marchmont Road, Edinburgh EH9 1HR.

Monro, Stuart Kinnaird, OBE, BSc, PhD, CGeol, FGS, FHEA, FRSSA. Scientific Director, Our Dynamic Earth, since 1996; b. 3.3.47, Aberdeen; m., Shiela Monro, nee Wallace; 3 s.; 1 d. Educ. Aberdeen Academy; University of Aberdeen; University of Edinburgh. Appointed as Geologist to British Geological Survey (then, Institute of Geological Sciences), 1970; promoted to HSO in 1973, to SSO in 1975, and to Principal Geologist in 1986; retired from BGS, 2004. President: Edinburgh Geological Society, since 2005, Westmorland Geological Society, 1994-2005, Royal Scottish Society of Arts, 2002-05; Honorary Fellow, College of Science and Engineering, Edinburgh University, co-opted member of the University Court; Co-convenor of the Scottish Earth Science Education Forum (SESEF) and Chair of its Earth Science Trust; Member, Scottish Science Advisory Committee; Trustee, National Museums of Scotland; Non-executive Director of the Edinburgh International Science Festival; Honorary Geological Advisor to the John Muir Trust; Open University Tutor in Earth Sciences. Recreations: reading; travel; hill walking. Address: (h.) 34 Swanston Grove, Edinburgh EH10 7BW; T.-0131 445 4619; e-mail: skm3@tutor.open.ac.uk

Montagu-Smith, Group Captain Arthur, DL, RAF (Retd); b. 17.7.15; m., Elizabeth Hood Alexander (deceased); 1 s.; 1 d. Educ. Whitgift School; RAF Staff College. Commissioned RAF, 1935; Adjutant 99 Squadron, 1938-39; served Second World War, European Theatre, North Africa and Mediterranean; Flt. Cdr., 264 Squadron, 1940, and 221 Squadron, 1941; OC 248 Squadron, 1942-43;

Battle of Britain Gold Rosette, 1940; Battle of Atlantic, 1941; Mention-in-Despatches, 1942; Deputy Director, RAF Training, USA (Washington), 1944; OC 104 Wing, France, 1945; Hon. ADC, Governor, N.I., 1948-49; Air Adviser, New Delhi, 1949-50; RAF Representative, Chiefs of Staff Committee, UN, New York, 1951-53; HM Air Attache, Budapest, 1958 60; retired at own request, 1961; Regional Executive, Small Industries Council and Scottish Development Agency, 1962-80; Member, Elgin District Council, 1967-75; Member, Moray TAFA, 1961-68; Director, Elgin and Lossiemouth Harbour Company, 1966-90; Deputy Lieutenant, Morayshire, 1970-91; former Hon. County Representative, Moray and Nairn, RAF Benevolent Fund; Chairman, Elgin and Lossiemouth Scottish SPCA, 1971-82; Past President, Victoria League, Moray and Nairn; Past Chairman, Moray Association of Youth Clubs. Recreations: outdoor interests; travel; animal welfare. Address: (h.) Woodpark, by Lhanbryde, Elgin IV30 8LF; T.-0134 384 2220.

Monteith, Brian. MSP (Independent), Mid-Scotland and Fife, 1999-2007; former Conservative Spokesman on Finance, Local Government and Public Services (2003-05); Spokesman on Education, Arts, Culture and Sport, 1999-2003; m.; 2 s. International Public relations consultant; former National Chairman, Scottish Young Conservatives and Federation of Conservative Students; National Co-ordinator, No, No Campaign, Scottish devolution referendum.

Montgomerie, Colin, OBE (2005), MBE (1998); Professional golfer; b. 23.6.63; m. (1), Eimear, née Wilson (m dis 2006); 2 d.; 1 s.; m. (2), Gaynor Knowles. Amateur victories: Scottish Amateur Stroke-play Championship 1985, Scottish Amateur Championship 1987; tournament victories since turning professional in 1987: Portuguese Open 1989, Scandinavian Masters 1991, 1999 and 2001, Dutch Open 1993, Volvo Masters 1993 and 2002, Spanish Open 1994, English Open 1994, German Open 1994 and 1995, Trophee Lancome 1995, Dubai Desert Classic 1996, Irish Open 1996, 1997 and 2001, European Masters 1996, Sun City Million Dollar Challenge 1996, European Grand Prix 1997, King Hassan II Trophy 1997, World Cup (Individual) 1997, Andersen Consulting World Champion 1997, PGA Championship 1998, 1999 and 2000, German Masters 1998, British Masters 1998, Benson and Hedges International Open 1999, Standard Life Loch Lomond Invitational 1999, Int Open Munich 1999, World Matchplay Championships Wentworth 1999, French Open Paris 2000, Skins Game USA 2000, Ericsson Australian Masters 2001, TCL Classic 2002, Macau Open 2003, European Open Ireland 2007; US Open: third 1992, second 1994, 1997 and 2006; second, The Open, 2005; US PGA 1995 (second); Tournament Players Championship 1996 (second); team memb: Eisenhower Trophy (amateur) 1984 and 1986, Walker Cup (amateur) 1985 and 1987, Alfred Dunhill Cup 1988, 1991, 1992, 1993, 1994, 1995 (winners), 1996, 1997, 1998, 1999 and 2000, World Cup 1988, 1991, 1992, 1993, 1997, 1998 and 1999, Ryder Cup 1991, 1993, 1995 (winners), 1997 (winners), 1999, 2002 (winners), 2004 (winners) and 2006 (winners), UBS Cup 2003; Henry Cotton Rookie of the Year 1988, winner European Order of Merit 1993, 1994, 1995, 1996, 1997, 1998, 1999 and 2005. Recreations: motor cars; music; DIY. Address: (b.) IMG (London), McCormack House, Hogarth Business Park, Burlington Lane, Chiswick, London W4 2TH.

Montgomery, Sir (Basil Henry) David, 9th Bt, JP, DL. Lord Lieutenant, Perth and Kinross, 1995-2006; Chairman, Forestry Commission, 1979-89; b. 20.3.31.

Montgomery, Iona Allison Eleanor, BA (Hons), RSW. Artist; Lecturer (part-time): Edinburgh College of Art, since 1997, Grays School of Art, since 1994; b. 14.4.65, Glasgow. Educ. Boclair Academy; Glasgow School of Art; Tamarind Institute, University of New Mexico. Exhibited widely in UK, Europe, USA and Japan, since 1989; solo exhibitions in UK, Europe, USA; work in numerous public collections; Alexander Graham Munro Award, RSW, 1990; Lauder Award, 1991, Lady Artists Club Trust Award, 1992, Cross Trust Bursary, 1994, Glasgow District Council Bursary, 1995; elected, RSW, 1991. Recreations: walking; music; film; travel. Address: (h.) Flat 2/1, 171B Maryhill Road, Glasgow G20.

Montgomery, John, LLB (Hons). Sheriff at Ayr, since 2005; Solicitor, since 1976; b. 17.9.51, Kilwinning; m., Susan Wilson Templeton; 1 s.; 3 d. Educ. Ardrossan Academy; Glasgow University. Partner in Carruthers Curdie Sturrock & Co. Solicitors, Kilmarnock, 1980-2003; Temporary Sheriff, 1995-2000; Part-time Sheriff, 2001-03; Floating Sheriff, 2003-05. Recreations: gardening; walking; travel. Address: (b.) Sheriff Court, Wellington Square, Ayr KA7 1DR.

Montrose, 8th Duke of (James Graham), OStJ. Captain, Queen's Bodyguard for Scotland, since 2006, Member, since 1965; Member, House of Lords, since 1996, elected Hereditary Peer, 1999, Conservative Opposition Whip, since 2001, Opposition Spokesman for Scottish Affairs, since 2001; b. 6.4.35, Salisbury, Rhodesia; m., Catherine Elizabeth MacDonell Young; 2 s.; 1 d. Educ. Loretto. Farmer/Landowner; Member of Council, National Farmers Union of Scotland, 1981-86; Vice Chairman, Loch Lomond and Trossachs Working Party, 1991-93; President, Royal Highland and Agricultural Society, 1997-98; Chairman, Buchanan Community Council, 1982-93. Address: (b.) Montrose Estates Ltd., Buchanan Castle, Drymen, Glasgow G63 0AG; T.-01360 660307.

Moore, Douglas Thomas, Cert. Christian Studies (Glasgow). Auxiliary Minister, Maybole Parish Church, since 2003; Flight Information Services Officer, since 1995; b. 24.7.54, Glasgow; m., Margaret Lindsay; 2 s. Educ. Shawlands Academy. Air Traffic Control, since 1972; Reader, Church of Scotland, since 1998. Chaplain, Monkton and Prestwick Branch, British Legion, since 2000. Recreations: family; gardening. Address: (h.) 9 Midton Avenue, Prestwick, Ayrshire KA9 1PU; T.-01292 671352. E-mail: douglastmoore@hotmail.com

Moore, George, QC, LLB (Hons). Solicitor and Solicitor Advocate; Joint Senior Partner, HBM Sayers (formerly Hamilton Burns Moore) since 1973; b. 7.11.47, Kilmarnock; m., Ann Beattie; 2 s.; 1 d. Educ. High School of Glasgow; Glasgow University. Former Member, Glasgow and North Argyll Legal Aid Committee; former Reporter to Scottish Legal Aid Board; former part-time Chairman, Industrial Tribunals in Scotland; former Member, Sheriff Court Rules Council, 1987. Recreations: tennis; golf; windsurfing. Address: (b.) 13 Bath Street, Glasgow G2 1HY; T.-0141-353 2121.

Moore, Professor Johanna D., BS, MS, PhD, FRSE, FBCS, CITP. Professor, School of Informatics, Edinburgh University, since 1998; Director, Human Communication Research Centre, since 1998; b. 16.7.57, USA; m., Dr N. Goddard; 2 s. Educ. University of California at Los Angeles (UCLA). Graduate Research Assistant, then Teaching Assistant/Teaching Fellow, UCLA; University of Pittsburgh: Research Scientist, Learning Research and Development Centre, 1990-98, Assistant Professor of Computer Science and Intelligent Systems, 1990-96, Associate Professor of Linguistics, 1996-98, Associate Professor of Computer Science and Intelligent Systems, 1996-98, Director, Intelligent Systems Program, 1996-98. Publication: Participating in

Explanatory Dialogues: Interpreting and Responding to Questions in Context, 1995. Address: (b.) School of Informatics, Edinburgh University, 2 Buccleuch Place, Edinburgh EH8 9LW; T.-0131-651 1336.

Moore, Michael, MA, CA. MP (Liberal Democrat), Berwickshire, Roxburgh and Selkirk, since 2005, Tweeddale, Ettrick and Lauderdale, 1997-2005; UK Spokesman on Transport, 1999-2001, Spokesman on Scotland, 2001, Deputy Foreign Affairs Spokesman, 2001-05, Defence Spokesman, 2005-06, Foreign Affairs Spokesman, since 2006; Deputy Leader, Scottish Liberal Democrats, since 2002; b. 3.6.65; m., Alison Louise Hughes. Educ. Strathallan School; Jedburgh Grammar School; Edinburgh University. Manager, Corporate Finance practice, Coopers and Lybrand. Member, House of Commons Scottish Select Committee, 1997-99; Governor and Vice Chairman, Westminster Foundation for Democracy, 2002-05; Council Member, Royal Institute of International Affairs, since 2004; Parliamentary Visiting Fellow, St. Antony's College, Oxford, 2003-04. Recreations: jazz; films; walking; rugby. Address: (b.) House of Commons, London SW1A 0AA; e-mail: michaelmooremp@parliament.uk

Moorhouse, John Edwin, DL, FFCS. Trustee: Crichton Foundation, Columba 1400, Big Issue Foundation, The Frank Buttle Trust; Director: CTF Training, The Gordon Cook Conversations, 2025; Chairman: Grand Central Savings; b. 7.10.41; m., Susan; 2 s.; 2 d. Educ. Bridlington School. With Shell UK, 1963-94; Chief Executive, Scottish Business in the Community, 1990-98. DL, Edinburgh; Honorary Fellow, Institute of Contemporary Scotland, since 2001. Recreations: music; theatre. Address: (h.) Monybuie, Corsock, Castle Douglas DG7 3DY; T.-01644 440293; e-mail: john.moorhouse@btinternet.com

Moos, Khursheed Francis, OBE, MB, BS, BDS, FRCSEdin, FDS RCS (Eng, Edin), FDS RCPS (Glas). Consultant Oral and Maxillofacial Surgeon (retired); Honorary Professor, Glasgow University; b. 1.11.34, London; m., Katharine Addison; 2 s.; 1 d. Educ. Dulwich College; Guy's Hospital, London; Westminster Hospital. National Service, RADC, Lt., 1959, Capt., 1960; Registrar in Oral Surgery, Mount Vernon Hospital, Middlesex, 1966-67; Senior Registrar, Oral Surgery, University of Wales, Cardiff, 1967-69; Consultant Oral Surgeon, S. Warwicks and Coventry Hospitals, 1969-74; Consultant Oral and Maxillofacial Surgeon, Canniesburn Hospital, Glasgow, 1974-99; Dean, Dental Faculty, Royal College of Physicians and Surgeons of Glasgow, 1992-95; Chairman, Intercollegiate Examination Board in oral and maxillofacial surgery, 1995-98; Civilian Consultant to Royal Navy, since 1976; President: Cranio-facial Society of Great Britain, 1994-95, British Association of Oral and Maxillofacial Surgeons, 1991-92; Down Surgical Prize, 1988; Colyer Medal, Royal College of Surgeons of England, 1997; Indian Medical Association (UK): Chairman, Board of Directors, 1999-2000, President, 1998-99; Honorary Senior Research Fellow, Glasgow University, since 1999. Publications include contributions to books and various papers. Recreations: music; natural history; philately; Eastern philosophy; gardening. Address: (h.) 43 Colquhoun Street, Helensburgh G84 9JW; T.-01436 673232; e-mail: kmoos@udcf.gla.ac.uk

Moray, Earl of (Douglas John Moray Stuart), BA, FRICS; b. 13.2.28, Johannesburg; m., Malvina Dorothea Murray; 1 s.; 1 d. Educ. Hilton College, Natal; Trinity College, Cambridge. Address: (h.) Doune Park, Doune, Perthshire.

Morbey, Gillian, OBE, BA (Hons), RGN. Chief Executive Officer, Sense Scotland, since 1989; b. 11.6.53, Glasgow; m., Jeremy Morbey; 1 s.; 1 d. Educ. Williamwood High School; Strathclyde University. Nursing career within NHS;

first Development Officer, Sense Scotland, 1985. Past Chairperson, West of Scotland Branch, Scottish Association for the Deaf; Chairperson, Glasgow Council of Voluntary Services, 1994-97; Member, National Disability Council, 1998-2000. Winner of Ernst and Young Scottish Social Entrepreneur of the Year, 2005. Recreations: supporter of Worldwide Fund for Nature; reading; music; walking. Address: (b.) 43 Middlesex Street, Kinning Park, Glasgow G41 1EE; T.-0141 429 0294.

Morgan, Alasdair, MA, BA. MSP (SNP), South of Scotland, since 2003; MSP (SNP), Galloway and Upper Nithsdale, 1999-2003; MP (SNP), Galloway and Upper Nithsdale, 1997-2001; Deputy Presiding Officer, Scottish Parliament, since 2007; b. 21.4.45, Aberfeldy; m., Anne Gilfillan; 2 d. Educ. Breadalbane Academy, Aberfeldy; Glasgow University. SNP: National Treasurer, 1983-90, Senior Vice-Convener, 1990-91, National Secretary, 1992-97, Vice President, 1997-2004. Recreation: hill-walking. Address: (h.) Nether Cottage, Crocketford, Dumfries; e-mail: Alasdair.Morgan.msp@ scottish.parliament.uk

Morgan, Angela Rosalie, BA (Hons), CQSW, MSc (Econ). Chief Executive, Includem, since 2007; Director, Families Outside, since 2003; b. 28.02.58, Isleworth; m., John Short. Educ. Basingstoke High School for Girls; Sussex University; University of London. Resettlement Officer, MIND London, 1985-88; Scottish Association for Mental Health, 1988-2002 (latterly Deputy CE). National Advisory Body for Management of Offenders; Trustee, the Onward Trust. Recreations: reading; walking; birdwatching. Address: (b.) 23 Scotland Street, Glasgow G5 8NB; T.-0141 429 3492; e-mail: angela.morgan@includem.org.uk

Morgan, Diane, MA, BA. Writer and publisher; b. 12.2.36; m., David I Morgan; 1 s.; 1 d. Educ. Aberdeen High School for Girls; Aberdeen University; Cambridge University. Law Lecturer, RGIT; Founding Editor/Publisher, Leopard, 1974-88. Aberdeen Civic Society Award, 1982 and 2000. Publications: Archibald Simpson, Architect of Aberdeen (Co-Author), 1990; The Aberdeen Series: Footdee, 1993, Round About Mounthooly, 1995, The Spital, 1996, The Spital Lands: From Sunnyside to Pittodrie, 1997, Old Aberdeen, Vol. 1, 2000; A Monumental Business, 2001; The Woodside Story, 2003; Lost Aberdeen, 2004; Lost Aberdeen: The Outskirts, 2007. Recreations: book collecting; travel; French Foreign Legion history. Address: (b.) Denburn Books, 49 Waverley Place, Aberdeen, AB10 1XP; T.-01224 644492; e-mail: diane.morgan@btinternet.com

Morgan, Edwin (George), OBE, MA, Hon. DLitt (Loughborough, Glasgow, Edinburgh, St. Andrews, Heriot-Watt, Glasgow Caledonian), Hon.DUniv (Stirling, Waikato); Hon. MUniv (Open). Freelance Writer (Poet, Critic, Translator), since 1980; Emeritus Professor of English, Glasgow University, since 1980; b. 27.4.20, Glasgow. Educ. Rutherglen Academy; High School of Glasgow; Glasgow University. War Service, Royal Army Medical Corps, 1940-46; Glasgow University: Assistant Lecturer in English, 1947, Lecturer, 1950, Senior Lecturer, 1965, Reader, 1971, Titular Professor, 1975; Visiting Professor of English, Strathclyde University, 1987-90; Poet Laureate for Glasgow, 1999-2005; received Cholmondeley Award for Poets, 1968; Hungarian PEN Memorial Medal, 1972; Scottish Arts Council Book Awards, 1968, 1973, 1977, 1978, 1983, 1985, 1988, 1991, 1992; Saltire Society and Royal Bank Scottish Literary Award, 1983; Soros Translation Award (New York), 1985; Order of Merit, Republic of Hungary, 1997; Queen's Gold Medal for Poetry, 2000; Weidenfeld Translation Prize, 2001;

appointed National Poet for Scotland, 2004. Publications: (poetry): The Vision of Cathkin Braes, 1952, Beowulf, 1952, The Cape of Good Hope, 1955, Poems from Eugenio Montale, 1959, Sovpoems, 1961, Collins Albatross Book of Longer Poems (Editor), 1963, Starryveldt, 1965, Emergent Poems, 1967, Gnomes, 1968, The Second Life, 1968, Proverbfolder, 1969, Twelve Songs, 1970, The Horseman's Word, 1970, Scottish Poetry 1-6 (Co-Editor), 1966-72; Glasgow Sonnets, 1972, Wi the Haill Voice, 1972, The Whittrick, 1973, From Glasgow to Saturn, 1973, Fifty Renascence Love-Poems, 1975, Rites of Passage, 1976, The New Divan, 1977, Colour Poems, 1978, Platen: Selected Poems, 1978, Star Gate, 1979, Scottish Satirical Verse (Editor), 1980, Poems of Thirty Years, 1982, Grafts/Takes, 1983, Sonnets from Scotland, 1984, Selected Poems, 1985, From the Video Box, 1986, Themes on a Variation, 1988; Tales from Limerick Zoo, 1988; Collected Poems, 1990; Hold Hands Among the Atoms, 1991; Sweeping Out the Dark, 1994; Collected Translations, 1996; Virtual and Other Realities, 1997; Demon, 1999; New Selected Poems, 2000; Attila József, Sixty Poems, 2001; Cathures, 2002; Love and a Life, 2003; Tales from Baron Muncheusen, 2005; A Book of Lives, 2007; prose: Essays, 1974, East European Poets, 1976, Hugh MacDiarmid, 1976, Twentieth Century Scottish Classics, 1987; Nothing Not Giving Messages, 1990; Crossing the Border, 1990; Evening Will Come They Will Sew The Blue Sail, 1991; plays: The Apple-Tree, 1982; Master Peter Pathelin, 1983; Cyrano de Bergerac, 1992; Marlowe's Doctor Faustus (new version), 1999; Racine's Phaedra, 2000; AD, 2000. Address: (h.) Clarence Court, 234 Crow Road, Glasgow G11 7PD; T.-0141-357-7229.

Morgan, Professor Peter John, BSc, PhD, FIBiol, ChBiol, FRSE. Director and Chief Executive, Rowett Research Institute, Aberdeen, since 1999; b. 23.2.56, Armthorpe, Yorkshire; m.; Dr Denise Kelly; 1s.; 1d. Educ. Aylesbury Grammar School; Queen Mary College, London; University of Aberdeen; Imperial College, London. Recreations: music (classical and jazz); squash; swimming. Address; (b.) Rowett Research Institute, Greenburn Road, Bucksburn, Aberdeen; T.-01224 716663.

Morison, Hugh, CBE, MA, DipEd. Chief Executive, Scotch Whisky Association, 1994-2003; b. 22.11.43, Bognor Regis; m.; 2 d. Educ. Chichester High School for Boys; St. Catherine's College, Oxford. Assistant Principal, Scottish Home and Health Department, 1966-69; Private Secretary to Minister of State, Scottish Office, 1969-70; Principal: Scottish Education Department, 1971-73, Scottish Economic Planning Department, 1973-79 (seconded to Offshore Supplies Office, Department of Energy, 1974-75); Assistant Secretary, Scottish Economic Planning Department, 1979-82; Gwilym Gibbon Research Fellow, Nuffield College, Oxford, 1982-83; Assistant Secretary, Scottish Development Department, 1983-84; Under Secretary, Scottish Home and Health Department, 1984-88, Scottish Office Industry Department, 1988-93; Non-Executive Director, Weir Group PLC, 1988-93; Member, Health Appointments Advisory Committee (Scotland), 1995-2000; Member, Executive Committee, Barony Housing Association, since 1996, Convenor, since 2005; Chairman, Scottish Business and Biodiversity Group, 1999-2003; President, Confédération Européenne des Producteurs de Spiritueux, 2001-03; Chairman, Letterfearn Moorings Association, since 2001; Governor, UHI Millennium Institute, since 2004; Non-Executive Director, Praban na Linne Ltd., 2005-06. Publications: The Regeneration of Local Economies, 1987; Dauphine (Co-Author), 1991. Recreations: hill-walking; sailing; archaeology; literature.

Morrice, Graeme. Leader, West Lothian Council Labour Group; COSLA Executive Spokesperson for Resources and Capacity; b. 23.2.59, Edinburgh. Educ. Broxburn Academy; Napier University. Councillor,

West Lothian, since 1987. Recreations: music; art; literature. Address: (h.) 9 Tarbert Drive, Murieston Valley, Livingston EH54 9GZ; T.-01506 591630.

Morris of Balgonie & Eddergoll, Stuart Gordon Cathal, MStJ, DHM, FRSA, FSA Scot. Director, Balgonie Castle Enterprises, since 1985; Historian, Armorist and writer; b. 17.04.65, Aberfeldy, Perthshire. Educ. Bell Baxter High School; Elmwood College; Napier College; University of Birmingham. Director, Theobald-Hicks, Morris & Gifford, 2001-06. Matriculated Arms (Morris of Balgonie & Eddergoll, quartered with Stuart, formerly of Langlees), Court of the Lord Lyon, 1987; Member of the Venerable Order of St John of Jerusalem, 2003; Commander of the Order of Polonia Restituta, 1990; Companion of the Order of Malta, 2007; Freeman of the City of London, 2001; Liveryman, Worshipful Company of Meadmakers, 1982; FSA Scot, 1983; FRSA, 1990; Hon. Colonel, Commonwealth of Kentucky, 1999; Hon. Lieutenant Colonel and ADC. to the Governor of the State of Georgia, 1991; Founder Member: Heraldry Society of Scotland, Scottish Castles Association (Membership Secretary, since 1996, Secretary, 1998-2003, Chairman, 2003-05, Vice-Chairman, since 2005); Member of the Stewart Society (Council, 1998-2006); Vice-Chairman: Central Fife Group of the Order of St John, since 2007, Markinch Heritage Group, since 2007; Diploma of Honour, St. Andrew Association, Australia, 1994; Advance the Colors Award, Sons of Confederate Veterans, 2001; awarded 10th Anniversary Medal of the Albert Schweitzer Society of Austria, 1994. Recreations: heraldry; genealogy; history; history of highland dress; castles; portrait painting; archery. Address: Balgonie Castle, by Markinch, Fife KY7 6HQ; T.-01592 750 119; e-mail: sbalgonie@yahoo.co.uk; web: www.balgonie-castle.com

Morris, Alistair Lindsay, LLB, DipLP, WS NP. Solicitor; Chief Executive, Pagan Osborne; Director, St. Andrews Asset Managers Ltd.; b. 30.7.58, Dunfermline; m., Sandra Willins; 2 s. Educ. Queen Anne High School, Dunfermline; Aberdeen University. Council Member, Law Society of Scotland, since 1992, Convener, Insurance Committee, 1998-2001 and since 2004. Recreations: golf; motor sport; football; rugby. Address: (b.) 12 St. Catherine Street, Cupar, Fife KY15 4HH; T.-01334 653777.

Morris, Professor Andrew David, MBChB, MSc, MD, FRCPEdin, FRCPGlas, FRSE. Professor of Diabetic Medicine and Head of Planning and Development, College of Medicine, Dentistry and Nursing, Dundee University, since 2002; Chair, Scottish Diabetes Group (lead clinician for diabetes in Scotland), 2002-06; Chair, Translational Medicine Research Collaboration Steering Group, since 2006; b. 7.10.64; m., Elspeth Claire; 2 d.; 1 s. Educ. Robert Gordon's College, Aberdeen; Glasgow University. Undergraduate and research training, Glasgow University; since 1995, has co-ordinated the DARTS initiative (clinical network for people with diabetes in Tayside); Chair, Royal College of Edinburgh Diabetes Registry, 1998-2002; Chair, Health Technology Board for Scotland Topic Specific Group, 2001-2002; Member, Modernisation Board, NHS in Scotland, 2000-01; Member, Scottish Health Change Panel, 2002-05. Saltire Society Scottish Science Award, 2005. Recreations: golf; squash; family life. Address: (b.) University Department of Medicine, Ninewells Hospital and Medical School, Dundee DD1 9SY; T.-01382 632456.

Morris, Professor Christopher David, BA, DipEd, MIFA, FSA, FSA Scot, FRHistS, FRSA, FRSE. Professor of Archaeology, Glasgow University, 1990-2006, Vice-

Principal, 2000-06; Chair in Archaeology, UHI Millennium Institute, since 2007; b. 14.4.46, Preston. Educ. Queen Elizabeth's Grammar School, Blackburn; Durham University; Oxford University. Assistant Lecturer, Hockerill College of Education, Bishops Stortford, 1968-72; Lecturer, then Senior Lecturer in Archaeology, 1972-88, Reader in Viking Archaeology, 1989-90, Durham University. Member, Ancient Monuments Board for Scotland, 1990-2001; Royal Commissioner, Ancient and Historical Monuments of Scotland, since 2000. Recreations: classical music and opera; theatre; walking and fun runs. Address: (b.) Alexander Murray Building, HTC-UHI, High Street, Dingwall IV15 9HA.
E-mail: christopher.morris@uhi.ac.uk

Morris, Eleanor Smith, AB Arch Sci (Hons) (Harvard), MCP (U Penn), PhD (Edinburgh), MAICP, MRTPI. Town Planner and Trustee, Commonwealth Human Ecology Council, London, since 1998, Chair, Executive Committee (2008); Visiting Professor, Urban Planning and Sustainable Development, Clemson University, South Carolina, USA, 2003; NGO Delegate, UN World Urban Forum, Barcelona, Spain, 2004; 8th, 11th and 12th Commission on Sustainable Development, UN., New York, 1999, 2003 and 2004; Habitat (+5) UN General Assembly Special Session (UNGASS) 2001; Commonwealth Heads of Government Meeting, Durban, S.A., 1999; Abuja, Nigeria, 2003; Rapporteur, 16th Session UN Commission Human Settlements (Habitat), Nairobi, Kenya, 1997; b. 14.11.35, Washington DC, USA; m., James Shepherd Morris (deceased); 2 s.; 1 d. Educ. National Cathedral School for Girls, Washington DC; Germantown Friends School, Philadelphia, Pa; Harvard University; Universities of London, Pennsylvania, Edinburgh. Academic Director, Emerita MSc; Environmental Sustainability, Institute of Ecology and Resource Management and Centre for the Study of Environmental Change and Sustainability, Edinburgh University, 1996-98; Faculty Lecturer, Centre for Human Ecology, 1990-96; Lecturer/Course Director, Department of Urban Design and Regional Planning, University of Edinburgh, 1967-90; Lecturer/Course Director, Department of Architecture, Edinburgh University, 1960-67. Planning practice in Philadelphia City Planning Com., New Jersey and London (LCC public agencies); Trustee, Schulykill Center for Environmental Education, 1995-2001, 2003-09; Member, Advisory Board, National Museum for Women in Arts, since 1989; Past Chairman, Royal Town Planning Institute, Scotland, 1985-86; Member, Council, Executive and Buildings Committees, National Trust for Scotland, 1991-2005. Publications include: British Town Planning and Urban Design: Principles and Policies, 1997; "Berlin, London or Paris - A New Capital for Europe". Building a New Heritage in the New Europe, 1994. Recreations: piano; sailing. Address: (b.) Woodcote Park, Fala and Soutra, Midlothian EH37 5TG; T.-01875 833 789; e-mail: emorrischec@yahoo.co.uk

Morris, Sheriff John C., QC, LLB. Sheriff, South Strathclyde Dumfries and Galloway, at Airdrie, since 1998; b. 11.4.52. Educ. Allan Glen's School, Glasgow; Strathclyde University. Solicitor, 1975-85; called to Scottish Bar, 1985; Advocate Depute, 1989-92; called to English Bar, 1990; Temporary Sheriff, 1993-98; took silk, Scottish Bar, 1996. Chairman, Advocates Criminal Law Group, 1996-98; Member, Temporary Sheriffs Association Committee, 1994-98. Recreations: golf; bird-watching; walking; wine. Address: (b.) Airdrie Sheriff Court, Graham Street, Airdrie ML6 6EE; T.-01236 751 121.

Morris, Professor Richard Graham Michael, MA, DPhil, FRSE, FMedSci, FRS. Neuroscience, Edinburgh

University, (Professor, since 1993, Reader, 1989-93); b. 27.6.48, Worthing; m., Hilary Ann; 2 d. Educ. St. Albans, Washington DC; Marlborough College; Cambridge University; Sussex University. Addison Wheeler Fellow, Durham University, 1973-75; SSO, British Museum (Natural History), 1975-77; Researcher, BBC Television, 1977; Lecturer, St. Andrews University, 1977-86; MRC University Research Fellow, 1983-86. Member, MRC Neurosciences Grants Committee, 1981-85, MRC Neurosciences Board, 1993-98, Innovation Panel, 1997-2001, Strategy Development Group, 2000-04; Hon. Secretary, Experimental Psychological Society, 1985-89; Chairman: Brain Research Association, 1990-94, Sectional Committee for Medicine and Biomedical Sciences, Royal Society of Edinburgh, 1995-97; Member, Council, European Neuroscience Association, 1994-98; Member, Council, Royal Society of Edinburgh, Scottish Science Advisory Committee; President, Federation of European Neuroscience Societies; Fellow, Royal Society, Royal Society of Edinburgh, Academy of Medical Sciences, American Academy of Arts and Sciences, American Association for Advancement of Science; Chairman, Department of Neuroscience, Edinburgh University, 1998-2002; Head of Neurosciences and Mental Health, The Wellcome Trust, since 2007. Publications: academic papers and books. Recreation: sailing. Address: (b.) Centre for Cognitive and Neural Systems, Neuroscience, Edinburgh University, 1 George Square, Edinburgh EH8 9JZ; T.-0131-650 3518/4565.

Morris, Professor Robert John, BA, DPhil. Professor of Economic and Social History, Edinburgh University, since 1993; b. 12.10.43, Sheffield; m., Barbara; 1 s.; 1 d. Educ. Acklam Hall, Middlesbrough; Keble and Nuffield Colleges, Oxford. Lecturer, Senior Lecturer, then Professor, Economic and Social History, Edinburgh University, from 1968. Founding Editor, History and Computing; Convenor, Edinburgh University Press Committee; President, European Urban History Association, 2000-02. Recreations: planting apple trees and watching vegetables grow. Address: (b.) 55 George Square, Edinburgh EH8 9JU.

Morris, Very Rev. William James, KCVO, ChStJ, JP, BA, BD, PhD, LLD, DD, Hon. FRCP&SGlas, DLitt. Minister, Glasgow Cathedral, 1967-2005; Chaplain in Ordinary to The Queen in Scotland, 1969-96, Extra Chaplain, since 1996; Chairman, Iona Cathedral Trust, 1979-2005; Dean, Chapel Royal in Scotland, 1991-96; Chaplain to The Queen's Body Guard in Scotland (Royal Company of Archers), 1994-2007; b. 22.8.25, Cardiff; m., Jean Daveena Ogilvy Howie (see Jean Daveena Ogilvy Morris); 1 s. Educ. Cardiff High School; University of Wales (Cardiff and Aberystwyth); Edinburgh University. Ordained, 1951; Assistant, Canongate Kirk, Edinburgh, 1949-51; Minister: Barry Island and Cadoxton Presbyterian Church of Wales, 1951-53, St. David's, Buckhaven, 1953-57, Peterhead Old Parish Church, 1957-67; Chaplain, Peterhead Prison, 1963-67; Chaplain to Lord High Commissioner, 1975-76; Moderator, Deer Presbytery, 1965-66; Chaplain: Strathclyde Police, Glasgow Academy, 1970-2005, Trades House of Glasgow, 1967-2007; Member, Independent Broadcasting Authority, 1979-84 (Chairman, Scottish Advisory Committee); Member, Convocation, Strathclyde University; Honorary President, Glasgow Society of Social Service; Lord Provost's Award, 1996. Publication: A Walk Through Glasgow Cathedral, 1986; Amazing Graces, 2001. Recreation: living in hope. Address: (h.) 1 Whitehill Grove, Newton Mearns, Glasgow G77 5DA; T.-0141 639 6327.

Morrison, Sir Alexander Fraser, CBE, FRSA, BSc, CEng, FICE, MIHT, FScotvec, FCIOB. Director, Morrison

Construction Group Plc, 1970-2001 (Chairman, 1984-2000); Deputy Chairman, Clydesdale Bank Plc, 1999-2004 (Director, since 1994); b. 20.3.48, Dingwall; m., Patricia Janice Murphy; 1 s.; 2 d. Educ. Tain Royal Academy; Edinburgh University, Morrison Construction Group, since 1970; Managing Director, 1976-84. National Federation of Civil Engineering Contractors: Chairman, 1993-94, Vice President, 1994-96; Chairman, Highlands and Islands Enterprise, 1992-98; Vice President, Royal Highland and Agricultural Society of Scotland, 1995-96; Chairman, University of the Highlands and Islands Project, 1997-2000; Director, Aberforth Split Level Trust plc; Director, Chief Executives Organisation, since 2003; Chairman, Teasses Capital Ltd., since 2003; Chairman, Ramco Holdings Ltd., since 2005; winner, 1991 Scottish Business Achievement Award; Hon. Doctor of Technology: Napier University, 1995, Glasgow Caledonian University, 1997; Honorary Doctor, Open University, 2000; Council, St. Leonard's School, St Andrews, 1999-2007. Recreations: rugby; golf; skiing; opera; the countryside; theatre; art. Address: (b.) Teasses House, Ceres, Leven, Fife KY8 5PG.

Morrison, Rev. Alistair Hogarth, BTh, DipYCS. Minister, St. Mark's-Oldhall, Paisley, 1989-2004; b. 12.9.43, Glasgow; 1 s.; 1 d. Educ. Jordanhill College School; Aberdeen University; Jordanhill College of Education. City of Glasgow/Strathclyde Police, 1962-81 (resigned with rank of Inspector to train for Ministry); Minister, Elgin High Church, 1985-89. Strathclyde Medal for Bravery, 1976. Recreations: hill-walking; general fitness. Address: 92 St Leonard's Road, Ayr KA7 2PU; T.-01292 266021.

Morrison, Rev. Angus, MA, BD, PhD. Minister, St. Columba's Old Parish Church, Stornoway; Convener, Church of Scotland Mission and Discipleship Council, since 2005; Chaplain to the Queen in Scotland, since 2006; b. 30.8.53, Oban; m., Marion Jane Matheson; 3 s.; 1 d. Educ. Oban High School; Glasgow University; London University; Edinburgh University. Minister, Free Presbyterian Church of Scotland Oban Congregation, 1979-86, Edinburgh Congregation, 1986-89; Moderator, Southern Presbytery, Free Presbyterian Church, 1987-88; Minister, Associated Presbyterian Churches, Edinburgh, 1989-2000; Moderator, APC General Assembly, 1998-99. Contributor, Dictionary of Scottish Church History and Theology, 1993; Contributor, New Dictionary of National Biography; Contributor, Dizionario di Teologia Evangelica, 2007; Editor, Tolerance and Truth. The Spirit of the Age or the Spirit of God?, 2007; Moderator, Presbytery of Lewis, 2003-04; Chaplain to the Lord High Commissioner to the General Assembly of the Church of Scotland, 2005, 2006. Recreations: reading; walking; music. Address: (h.) St. Columba's Manse, Lewis Street, Stornoway, Isle of Lewis HS1 2JF.

Morrison, Colin Andrew, BA, MEd, DipM, FCIM, CertEd, FCIBS. Deputy Chief Executive and Director of Education, Chartered Institute of Bankers in Scotland; b. 14.10.61, Ellon; m., Stella Ross Ingram. Educ. Peterhead Academy; Robert Gordon's Institute of Technology; Aberdeen College of Education; Edinburgh University. Former Outdoor Pursuits Instructor and F.E. Lecturer/Senior Lecturer; Head of Business Studies, Stevenson College, 1990-91. Recreations: dinghy sailing; skiing. Address: (b.) 38b Drumsheugh Gardens, Edinburgh EH3 7SW; T.-0131-473 7777.

Morrison, David Ralston. Writer and Painter; b. 4.8.41, Glasgow; m., Edna May Wade; 1 s.; 1 d. Educ. Glasgow High School for Boys; Hamilton Academy; Strathclyde University. Librarian: Lanark County, Edinburgh College of Art, Caithness. Founded and ran Scotia Review, Wick Folk Club, Wick Festival of Poetry, Folk and Jazz; author of numerous books of poetry; edited Essays on Neil M. Gunn, Essays on Fionn MacColla; The Cutting Edge - Collected Poems, Poetry Salzbury, 2006. Recreations: walking; drystanedyking; reading; music. Address: (h.) 18 MacArthur Street, Wick KW1 5AX; T.-01955 603703; e-mail: ednadave@aol.com

Morrison, James, RSA, RSW, DA, DUniv (Stirling). Painter in oil and watercolour; b. 11.4.32, Glasgow; m., Dorothy McCormack; 1 s., 1 d. Educ. Hillhead High School; Glasgow School of Art. Taught part-time, 1955-58, won Torrance Memorial Prize, RGI, 1958; Visiting Artist, Hospitalfield, 1962-63; Council Member, SSA, 1964-67; staff, Duncan of Jordanstone College of Art, 1965-87; won Arts Council Travelling Scholarship to Greece, 1968; painting in various regions of France, 1976-82; numerous one-man exhibitions since 1956, in Scotland, London, Italy, France, West Germany, Canada; four works in private collection of Duke of Edinburgh and numerous other works in public and private collections; several group exhibitions since 1980 in UK and Europe; regular series of expeditions to paint in Africa (Botswana) and Canadian and Greenland High Arctic, since 1990. Publications: Aff the Squerr; Paris in Winter. Recreation: playing in a chamber music group. Address: (h.) Craigview House, Usan, Montrose, Angus; T.-Montrose 672639.

Morrison, Sheriff Nigel Murray Paton, QC. Sheriff of Lothian and Borders at Edinburgh, since 1996; b. 18.3.48, Paisley. Educ. Rannoch School. Called to the Bar of England and Wales, Inner Temple, 1972; admitted to Scottish Bar, 1975; Assistant Editor, Session Cases, 1976-82; Assistant Clerk, Rules Council, 1978-84; Clerk of Faculty, Faculty of Advocates, 1979-86; Standing Junior Counsel to Scottish Development Department (Planning), 1982-86; Temporary Sheriff, 1982-96; Chairman, Social Security Appeal Tribunals, 1982-91; Second (formerly Junior) Counsel to the Lord President of the Court of Session, 1984-89; First Counsel to the Lord President, 1989-96; Counsel to Secretary of State under Private Legislation Procedure (Scotland) Act 1936, 1986-96; QC, 1988; Chairman, Medical Appeal Tribunals, 1991-96; Trustee, National Library of Scotland, 1989-98; Director of Judicial Studies, 2000-04. Publications: Green's Annotated Rules of the Court of Session (Principal Editor); Stair Memorial Encyclopaedia of the Laws of Scotland (Contributor); Sentencing Practice (Editor). Recreations: music; riding; Scottish country dancing; being taken by his dogs for walks. Address: 27 Chambers Street, Edinburgh EH1 1LB; T.-0131-225 2525.

Morrison, Peter, MA, LLB. Singer (Baritone) entertainer and former solicitor; b. 14.8.40, Greenock; m., Irene McGrow; 1 s.; 1 d. Educ. Greenock Academy; Glasgow University. Local Authority (Paisley and Clydebank) legal departments, 1965-68; Private legal practice with Torrance Baird and Allan, Solicitors, Glasgow, 1968-77; own legal practice, 1977-96; consultant with Paton Farrell Solicitors, 1996-2000; now an associate with Adie Hunter, Solicitors, Glasgow; Choral scholar with Cecil Cope and Marjorie Blakeston; toured English Cathedrals, 1964/65 with choir; principal singer with University Cecilian Society for 6 years and also the University Choral society; started broadcasting with BBC in 1961 as a group singer and later as soloist; auditioned as soloist for BBC in 1967 and solo broadcasts and recitals thereafter; founder member of the John Currie Singers in 1968; first television series for BBC Scotland, 1971, continuing until 1979 and including Show of the North, Castles in the Air, Songs of Scotland, Something to Sing About (for BBC 2), This is Peter Morrison, 1977; other work includes Hogmanay shows, Friday Night is Music Night (radio), 1976-97, concerts in Royal Festival Hall, Albert Hall, Fairfield Halls, The Barbican Centre; television series for Channel 4 (Top Cs and Tiaras), STV and Grampian; innumerable theatre and concert performances in UK and abroad; entertained the Royal

Family at public occasions and private parties; many commercial CD recordings; immediate past President, Scottish Showbusiness Benevolent Fund; Honorary President: Glasgow Phoenix Choir, Arran Music and Drama Club. Recreations: golf; watching rugby, cricket and football; loves working with his children on stage whenever possible. E-mail: pmorrison1@toucansurf.com

Morrison, Rev. Roderick, MA, BD. Minister, Partick Gardner Street Church, Glasgow, since 1994; b. 3.7.43, Lochmaddy; m., Christina Ann MacDonald; 1 s.; 1 d. Educ. Lochportan Public School; Glasgow University and Trinity College. Assistant Minister, Drumchapel Old Parish Church, Glasgow, 1973-74; Minister: Carinish Parish Church, North Uist, 1974-81, High Church, Stornoway, Lewis, 1981-94. Recreations: sailing; fishing; shooting. Address: 148 Beechwood Drive, Broomhill, Glasgow G11 7DX; T.-0141-563 2638.

Morrison, William Garth, KT 2007, CBE, BA, CEng, MIEE. Lord-Lieutenant of East Lothian, since 2001; Farmer; President, Scottish Landowners Federation, 2001-03; Honorary President, Scottish Council, The Scout Association, since 2001; b. 8.4.43, Edinburgh; m., Gillian Cheetham; 2 s.; 1 d. Educ. Pangbourne College; Pembroke College, Cambridge. Service, Royal Navy, 1961-73, retiring with rank of Lt.; farming, since 1973; Member, Lothian Region Children's Panel, 1976-83 (Chairman, Midlothian/East Lothian Area Panel, 1978-81); Lamp of Lothian Trustee, 1978; Chairman, Lamp of Lothian Collegiate Trust, since 2001; Member: Lothian, Borders and Fife Committee, Prince's Trust, 1979, Lothian and Borders Committee, Prince's and Royal Jubilee Trusts, 1983-88, Society of High Constables of Holyroodhouse, 1979; Deputy Lieutenant, East Lothian, 1984-2001; Chief Scout, 1988-96; Member, World Scout Committee, 1992-2002; Chief Commissioner of Scotland, The Scout Association, 1981-88; Vice President, The Scout Association, since 1996; Member, Scottish Community Education Council, 1988-95; Chairman, East and Midlothian NHS Trust, 1993-97; Chairman, Royal Infirmary of Edinburgh NHS Trust, 1997-99; Chairman, Lothian Primary Care NHS Trust, 1999-2004; MacRobert Trustee, 1998, Chairman, 2007; SCEC Honorary Fellowship, 1995; Member, National Lottery Charities Board, 1995-99; S.E. Regional Chairman, Scottish Landowners Federation, 1996-2000; Vice President, Commonwealth Youth Exchange Council, since 1997. Recreations: golf; sailing; Scouting. Address: West Fenton, North Berwick, East Lothian; T.-01620 842154; e-mail: garth@westfenton.co.uk

Morrow, Martin Thomas, LLB (Hons), DipLP, NP. Solicitor Advocate; b. 2.7.64, Glasgow; m., Amanda Catherine; 1 s.; 2 d. Educ. St. Aloysius College, Glasgow; University of Strathclyde. Ian McCarry Solicitors, Glasgow, 1986-88; Levy, McRae, Solicitors, Glasgow, 1988-89; Blackadder, McMonagle, Solicitors, Falkirk, 1990-92; Principal, Milligan Telford and Morrow, Solicitors, since 1992. Member, Council, Law Society of Scotland, 1997-2001. Recreations:, golf; tennis. Address: 1 Cockburn Street, Falkirk FK1 1DJ; T.-01324 633221.

Morton, Earl of (John Charles Sholto Douglas). Farmer, since 1947; property consultant, since 1985; b. 19.3.27, Lyndhurst, Hampshire; m., Sheila Mary; 2 s.; 1 d. Educ. Malmesbury. Livestock farmer; estate owner; Chairman, Edinburgh Polo Club; Partner, Dalmahoy Farms. Lord of the Realm. Recreations: polo; swimming. Address: (b.) Dalmahoy Estate Office, Kirknewton, Midlothian EH27 8EB; T.-0131-333 1331.

Morton, Rev. Alasdair J., MA, BD, DipEd, DipRE, FEIS. Minister, Bowden linked with Newtown St. Boswells, 1991-2000; b. 8.6.34, Inverness; m., Gillian M. Richards; 2 s.; 2 d. Educ. Bell-Baxter School, Cupar; St. Andrews University; Hartford Theological Seminary. District Missionary/Minister, Zambia (Northern Rhodesia), 1960-65; Chaplain and Religious Education Lecturer, Malcolm Moffat Teachers' College, Serenje, Zambia, 1966-67; Principal, David Livingstone Teachers' College, Livingstone, Zambia, 1968-72; Minister, Greyfriars Parish Church, Dumfries, 1973-77; General Secretary, Department of Education, Church of Scotland, 1977-91. Recreations: choral singing; gardening. Address: 16 St Leonard's Road, Forres IV36 1DW; e-mail: alasgilmor@compuserve.com

Morton, Rev. Andrew Reyburn, MA, BD, DD. Alumni Officer, School of Divinity, Edinburgh University; b. 24.5.28, Kilmarnock; m., Marion Armstrong Chadwin; 2 s.; 2 d. Educ. Kilmarnock Academy; Glasgow University; Edinburgh University; Bonn University. Scottish Secretary, Student Christian Movement, 1953-56; Minister, Moncreiff Parish, East Kilbride, 1956-64; Chaplain, Edinburgh University, 1964-70; Warden, Wolfson Hall and Co-ordinating Warden, Halls of Residence, Glasgow University, 1970-74; Social Responsibility Secretary and, latterly, Secretary, Division of Community Affairs and Assistant General Secretary, British Council of Churches, 1974-81; Secretary, Inter-Church Relations Committee and Assistant Secretary, Overseas Council, subsequently Assistant Secretary, Board of World Mission and Unity, Church of Scotland, 1982-88; Deputy General Secretary, Board of World Mission and Unity, Church of Scotland, 1988-93; Associate Director, Centre for Theology and Public Issues, University of Edinburgh, 1994-2001; Secretary, Committee on Church and Nation, Church of Scotland, 1994-96. Recreation: walking. Address: (h.) 11 Oxford Terrace, Edinburgh, EH4 1PX; T.-0131-332 6592.

Morton, Elizabeth Stewart, NP, LicIPD, FIMgt. Depute Chief Executive/Executive Director of Corporate Support, East Ayrshire Council, since 2004; Solicitor; b. 21.8.56, Glasgow. Educ. Dalmellington High School; Ayr Academy; Glasgow University. Entered local government, 1974, as a legal apprentice; worked for Ayr County, Cunninghame District, Cumnock and Doon Valley District, Kyle and Carrick District; moved to Hamilton District as Chief Administrative Officer, 1990; Director of Administration and Legal Services, Kilmarnock and Loudoun District Council, 1993; Director of Law and Administration, Falkirk Council, 1995. Address: (b.) Council Headquarters, London Road, Kilmarnock KA3 7BU; T.-01563 576000.

Morton, Ellen, MA, BA. Board of Scottish Legal Aid, since 2002; Councillor for Helensburgh; Argyll and Bute, since 1999; b. 1.6.44, Clydebank; m., Gordon Morton; 1 s.; 3 d. Educ. Notre Dame High School, Dumbarton; Glasgow University; Strathclyde University. Teacher of English, 1966-94; Non-legal Member of Asylum and Immigration Tribunal (formerly Immigration and Asylum Tribunal), since 1996. Board Member of Helensburgh Partnership. Recreations: reading; family; travelling. Address: (h.) 18 Adelaide Street, Helensburgh G84 7DL; T.-01436-675500; e-mail: ellen.morton@clara.co.uk

Morton, Marion Armstrong, MA. Deputy Provost, City of Edinburgh, 1999-2003; Member (Labour), Edinburgh City Council, 1995-2003; b. 31.10.34, Glasgow; m., Rev. Dr. Andrew Reyburn Morton; 2 s.; 2 d. Educ. Hutchesons' Grammar School, Glasgow; University of Glasgow. Assistant Teacher of English, Eastwood Senior Secondary School, Renfrewshire, 1957-59; Waverley High School, Drumchapel, 1970-74; Head of English: Charles Edward

Brooke Grammar School, London, 1974-76, Rowan High School, London, 1976-82; Principal Teacher of English, Camelon High School, Falkirk, 1982-88. Chair, Edinburgh and Lothians Refugee Forum, 1999-2003; Member, Prison Visiting Committee, HMP Saughton, Edinburgh. Recreations: reading; theatre. Address: 11 Oxford Terrace, Edinburgh EH4 1PX; T.-0131-332 6592.

Morton, 'Uel (Samuel). Chief Executive, Quality Meat Scotland, since 2006. Formerly with United Farmers. Address: (b.) The Rural Centre, Ingliston, Newbridge EH28 8NZ; T.-0131 472 4040; e-mail: info@qmscotland.co.uk

Mosson, Lord Provost Alexander Francis. Lord Provost of the City of Glasgow, 1999-2003; Lord-Lieutenant, City of Glasgow, since 1999; Spokesperson for City Marketing and Events, Glasgow City Council; Chairman, Greater Glasgow and Clyde Valley Tourist Board, since 1999; b. 27.8.40, Glasgow; m., Maureen; 3 s.; 3 d. Educ. St Patrick's Primary School; St Patrick's Junior Secondary School; St Mungo's Academy. Served apprenticeship, Barclay Curles boiler shop and Alexander Stephen shipyard, Linthouse, as a plater; worked in insulating industry; then employed as an Industrial Appeals Organiser with British Red Cross Society, Scottish Branch; elected Councillor, 1984; former Deputy Lord Provost; former Vice Convener and Convener, Protective Services Committee; former Vice Convener of Personnel. Officer, Order of St. John, since 2000; Hon. Fellow of the Royal College of Physicians and Surgeons, 2003; Order of St. Christopher of Barga, 2004; Knight of the Holy Sepulchre of Jerusalem, September 2005; Freeman of the City of Bethlehem, 2004; Deputy Lord Lieutenant, 2004. Hon. LLD, Glasgow; Hon. LLD, Glasgow Caledonian; Hon. LLD, Strathclyde. Recreations: reading Scottish and Irish history; painting; watching football. Address: (h.) 1 Danes Drive, Glasgow G14 9HZ; T.-0141954 3360.

Mounfield, J. Hilary, OBE, MA (Hons). Convenor, Dementia Services Development Trust; Non-Executive Director, National Waiting Times Centre NHS Board; Chief Executive, Epilepsy Scotland, 1995-2005; Chair, European Committee of the International Bureau for Epilepsy, 2001-05; International Ambassador for Epilepsy; b. 19.7.41, Edinburgh; 2 s.; 1 d. Educ. Boroughmuir School; Edinburgh University. Research, Scottish Development Department and Ministry of Housing, 1963-66; teaching, London, 1973-84; fund-raising for charities, 1984-91; Appeals Director, Penumbra, 1991-95. Chair: ICFM, Scotland, 1993-95, Bighearted Scotland, 1993-96, Joint Epilepsy Council, 1998-2001; Convener, ACOSVO, 1997-2000; Chair, Voluntary Health Scotland, 2000-03; Founding Fellow, Institute of Contemporary Scotland. Recreations: reading; art; travel. E-mail: hilary.mounfield@blueyonder.co.uk

Moutinho, Professor Luiz, BA, MA, PhD, FCIM. Professor of Marketing and former Director, Doctoral Programme, Glasgow University School of Business and Management; b. 29.1.49, Lisbon. Held posts at: Cardiff Business School; University of Wales (Cardiff); Cleveland State University, Ohio; Northern Arizona University; California State University; Director, Doctoral Programmes, Confederation of Scottish Business Schools, 1987-89; Professor of Marketing, since 1989; appointed to Foundation Chair of Marketing, Glasgow University, 1996. Publications: 19 books, most recently Problems in Marketing, 2006. Address: (h.) Cragdarroch, Shore Road, Cove, G84 0NU; T.-01436 842851.

Mowat, Professor Norman Ashley George, MB, ChB, MRCP (UK), FRCP, FRCP (Edin), FRCP(Glas). Physician to the Queen in Scotland, since 2001; Professor of Medicine, Aberdeen University, since 2002; Consultant Physician and Gastroenterologist, Aberdeen Teaching Hospitals, since 1975; b. 11.4.43, Cullen; m., Kathleen Mary Cowie; 1 s.; 2 d. Educ. Fordyce Academy; Aberdeen University. House Officer, then Senior House Officer, then Registrar, Aberdeen Teaching Hospitals, 1966-72; Lecturer in Medicine, Aberdeen University, 1972-73; Lecturer in Gastroenterology and Research Associate, Medical College of St. Bartholomew's, London, 1973-75; Clinical Senior Lecturer in Medicine, Aberdeen University, 1975-2002. Formerly Visiting Physician to Shetland Islands; publications include Integrated Clinical Sciences: Gastroenterology (Co-Editor), 1985. Recreations: sailing; golf; soccer; reading; photography. Address: (h.) York House, York Place, Cullen, Buckie AB56 4UW; T.-01542 841346.

Muir, Ian Holstein, OBE, FSQA, MCIPD. Chairman, East Lothian Compact, since 2006; Chairman, ISEA (Independent Special Education Advice), 2002-05; Chairman, Jewel and Esk Valley College, 1995-2003; Board Member, Scottish Qualifications Authority, 1997-2001; Director, Association of Scottish Colleges, 1996-2001; Technology Management Consultant, 1995-2005; b. 14.3.37, Edinburgh; m., Pearl; 1 s. Educ. Knox Academy. Development Engineer, 1962-67; Chief Production Engineer, 1967, Manufacturing Manager, 1977-87; Company Systems Manager, 1987-89; Training and Education Manager, 1989-95. Chairman, Edinburgh Compact; Member, NTO Recognition Panel. Recreations: reading; crosswords and research. Address: Mavisbank, 46 Edinburgh Road, Tranent, East Lothian EH33 1AW; T.-01875 610444; e-mail: muirih@aol.com

Muir, Robert Douglas, MA (Hons), ACIB. Area Director, HIE Skye and Wester Ross; b. 28.8.54, Irvine; m., Nanette Thomson Buchanan; 2 s. Educ. Ardrossan Academy; Glasgow University; Tubingen Universitat. Chairman, Portree High School Parent Council. Recreations: history; travel; languages; music; following the fortunes of Kilmarnock F. C. Address: (b.) King's House, The Green, Portree, Isle of Skye IV51 9BS; T.-01478 612841; e-mail: robert.muir@hient.co.uk

Muir, Trevor, OBE. Chief Executive, Midlothian Council, since 1995; b. 10.7.49, Glasgow; m., Christine Ann; 1 s.; 1 d. Educ. High School of Glasgow; Langside College; Strathclyde University. Scottish Special Housing Association, 1973-77; City of Glasgow District Council, 1977-81; Director of Housing, City of Aberdeen District Council, 1981-87; Chief Executive, Midlothian District Council, 1987-96. Recreations: squash; family life. Address: (b.) Midlothian House, Buccleuch Street, Dalkeith, Midlothian EH22 1DJ.

Mulgrew, John, OBE, BSc. Chair, Learning and Teaching Scotland, since 2006; m., Anne. Educ. St. Mungo's Academy, Glasgow; University of Glasgow. Head Teacher, John Bosco Secondary School, Glasgow, 1976-81; held a number of senior posts within the education directorate in Strathclyde Regional Council, Depute Director of Education, 1993-95; Director of Education, East Ayrshire Council, 1995-2000; Executive Director of Educational and Social Services, East Ayrshire Council, 2000-06. Member, The Smith Group; serves on a great number of Boards and Advisory Committees including The Scottish Screen/Scottish Arts Council Joint Board. Address: (b.) Learning and Teaching Scotland, The Optima, 58 Robertson Street, Glasgow G2 8DU; T.-0141 282 5026; e-mail: j.mulgrew@ltscotland.org.uk

Mulholland, Francis, QC, LLB (Hons), MBA, DipLP, SSC, NP. Solicitor General for Scotland, since 2007;

Solicitor Advocate; b. 18.4.59, Coatbridge; m., Marie Elizabeth. Educ. Columba High School, Coatbridge; Aberdeen University; Edinburgh University. Trainee, Bird Semple & Crawford Herron, Solicitors, Glasgow, 1982-84; Procurator Fiscal Depute: Greenock, 1984-87, Glasgow, 1987-91; Solicitor, Crown Office, Edinburgh, 1991-96; Procurator Fiscal Depute, Edinburgh, 1996; Advocate Depute, 1997-99; Assistant Procurator Fiscal, Edinburgh, 1999-2002; Procurator Fiscal, Edinburgh, 2002-03; Senior Advocate Depute, 2003-06; Area Procurator Fiscal, Lothian and Borders, 2006-07. Recreations: football; golf; military history. Address: (b.) Crown Office, 25 Chambers Street, Edinburgh.

Mullen, Ian M., OBE, BSc, MRPharmS, DL. Consultant on healthcare and pharmaceutical issues; self-employed community pharmacist, since 1971; Chair, Forth Valley NHS Board, since 2002; Deputy Lieutenant, Stirling and Falkirk; b. 11.5.46, Stirling; m., Veronica Drummond; 2 s.; 1 d. Educ. St. Modan's High School, Stirling; Heriot-Watt University. Registered MPS, 1970; Chairman, Pharmaceutical General Council (Scotland), 1986-88; Vice-Chairman, National Pharmaceutical Consultative Committee, 1987-89; Member, UK Advisory Committee on Borderline Substances, 1986-89; Vice-Chairman, Forth Valley Health Board, 1989-91; Director, Common Services Agency of the NHS in Scotland, 1991-94, Vice-Chairman, 1993; Director, Central Scotland Chamber of Commerce, 1990-93; Chairman: St. Andrew's School Board, 1990-93, Falkirk and District Royal Infirmary NHS Trust, 1993-99, Scottish NHS Trust Chairmen's Group, 1998-2000, Forth Valley Acute Hospitals NHS Trust, 1999-2002, Scottish NHS Chairmen's Group, 2000-02, Scottish Health Matters (Communications Group), Urban Life Properties Ltd, since 2003; Member: Scottish Dental Practice Review Board, 1991-92, Shields Committee (NHS in Scotland), 1995-96. Recreations: walking; golf; watching football. Address: (h.) Burnside House, Kinkell Bridge, Auchterarder PH3 1EA; T.-01764 664 882; e-mail: ian.mullen@fvhb.scot.nhs.uk

Mullen, Professor Thomas John, LLB (Hons), Glasgow, LLM (Harvard). Professor and Head of Development, School of Law, University of Glasgow, since 2004; b. 26.01.59, Glasgow; m., Christine Hamilton; 1 s.; 1 d. Educ. St. Aloysius College, Glasgow; University of Glasgow; Harvard Law School. Legal Apprentice, Hughes Dowdall & Co, Glasgow, 1981-83; Solicitor (Scotland), since 1984; University of Glasgow: Lecturer in Public Law, 1983-92, Senior Lecturer in Public Law, 1992-2003. Special Adviser to House of Commons Select Committee on Scottish Affairs, 1996-97. Publications: Judicial Review in Scotland (Co-Author), 1996; Public Law in Scotland, eds (Co-Author), 2006. Recreations: reading; running; football; cooking. Address: (b.) School of Law, University of Glasgow G12 8QQ; T.-0141 330 4179; e-mail: t.mullen@law.gla.ac.uk

Mulligan, Margaret Mary, BA (Hons). MSP (Labour), Linlithgow, since 1999; Shadow Minister for Children and Early Years; Deputy Minister for Communities, 2003-04; Convenor, Education, Culture and Sport Committee, 1999-2001; b. 12.2.60, Liverpool; m., John; 2 s.; 1 d. Educ. Notre Dame High School; Manchester University. Retail and personnel management, 1981-86; Councillor, Edinburgh District Council, 1988-95 (Chair of Housing, 1992-97); Councillor, City of Edinburgh Council, 1995-99. Recreations: music; theatre; sport. Address: (b.) Scottish Parliament, Edinburgh EH99 1SP; T.-0131-348 5780.

Mumford, Colin John, BMedSci, DM, FRCP(E), DIMCRCS(Ed). Consultant Neurologist, Western General Hospital, Edinburgh and Royal Infirmary of Edinburgh, since 1996; b. 24.11.59, Liverpool. Educ. St. Margaret's High School, Liverpool; Nottingham University Medical School. Senior House Officer in Medicine, Newcastle upon Tyne teaching hospitals; Registrar in Neurology, Queen's Medical Centre, Nottingham and National Hospital for Neurology, London; Research Fellow, University of Cambridge; Senior Registrar in Neurology, Edinburgh teaching hospitals. Recreations: hillwalking; motorcycling. Address: (b.) Department of Clinical Neurosciences, Western General Hospital, Edinburgh EH4 2XU; T.-0131-537 1169.

Mundell, David Gordon, LLB (Hons), MBA, NP, WS. MP (Conservative), Dumfriesshire, Clydesdale and Tweeddale, since 2005; Chairman (interim), Scottish Conservative and Unionist Party; Shadow Secretary of State for Scotland, since 2005; MSP (C), South of Scotland, 1999-2005; b. 27.5.62, Dumfries; m., Lynda Carmichael; 2 s.; 1 d. Educ. Lockerbie Academy; Edinburgh University; Strathclyde University. Trainee Solicitor, Tindal Oatts, Glasgow, 1987-87; Solicitor, Maxwell Waddell, Glasgow, 1987-89; Commercial Lawyer, Biggart Baillie, Glasgow, 1989-91; Group Legal Adviser Scotland, BT, 1991-98; Head of National Affairs, BT Scotland, 1998-99. Recreations: family pursuits; travel. Address: House of Commons, London SW1A 0AA; T.-020 7219 4895; e-mail: mundelld@parliament.uk/

Mundell, John Weir. Chief Executive, Inverclyde Council, since 2006; formerly Corporate Director – Environment, East Dunbartonshire Council; b. Edinburgh; m., Karen; 3 s. Educ. Currie High School; Heriot-Watt University. Entered local government, 1974 (City of Edinburgh Corporation, then Commercial Manager, Lothian Regional Council); Head of Central Contracts, Central Regional Council, 1994-95. Recreations: karate; farming. Address: (b.) Municipal Buildings, Greenock PA15 1LY; T.-01475 712701.

Munn, Sir James, OBE, MA, DEd, LLD, DUniv; b. 27.7.20, Bridge of Allan; m., Muriel Jean Millar Moles; 1 d. (deceased). Educ. Stirling High School; Glasgow University. Indian Civil Service, 1941-48; various teaching appointments, Glasgow, 1949-57; Principal Teacher of Modern Languages, Falkirk High School, 1957-66 (Depute Rector, 1962-66); Principal Examiner in Modern Languages, Scottish Examination Board, 1965-66; Rector: Rutherglen Academy, 1966-70, Cathkin High School, 1970-83; Member, University Grants Committee, 1973-82; Member, Consultative Committee on the Curriculum, 1968-80, Chairman, 1980-87; Chairman, Committee to review the Structure of the Curriculum at S3 and S4, 1975-77; Member of Court, Strathclyde University, 1983-91; Manpower Services Commission/Training Commission Chairman for Scotland, 1984-88, Chairman, GB, 1987-88; University Commissioner, 1988-95. (h.) 4 Kincath Avenue, Rutherglen, Glasgow G73 4RP; T.-0141-634 4654.

Munn, Professor Pamela, OBE, MA, MLitt, CertEd. Professor of Curriculum Research, University of Edinburgh, since 1998; formerly Dean, Moray House School of Education; b. 31.3.49, Glasgow; m., Graham Hamilton Munn. Educ. Hermitage School, Helensburgh; Aberdeen University. Teacher of History, 1972-78; Research Fellow, Stirling University, 1979-84; Lecturer in Applied Research in Education, York University, 1984-86; Senior Research Officer, then Depute Director, Scottish Council for Research in Education, 1986-94; Professor of Curriculum Research, Moray House Institute of Education, 1994-98. Member, Scottish Consultative Council on the Curriculum; Fellowship, CIDREE, 1996; SCRE Silver Medal, 1984; Fellowship, SCRE, 2002; Chair, Education for Citizenship Review Group; Member, Discipline Task Group, Review of

Initial Teacher Education Group. Publications: The Changing Face of Education 14-16; Education in Scotland: policy and practice from pre-school to secondary, 1997; Parents and Schools: customers, managers or partners?, 1993; Alternatives to Exclusion from School, 2000. Recreations: hill-walking; gardening; reading, especially crime fiction. Address: (b.) Simon Laurie House, School of Education, University of Edinburgh, Holyrood Road, Edinburgh EH8 8AQ; T.-0131-651 6462.

Munro of Foulis, Hector William, MRICS. 31st Chief of Clan Munro; b. 20.2.50; m., Sarah Duckworth; 1 s.; 2 d. Educ. Oratory School; Royal Agricultural College, Cirencester. Farmer and Chartered Surveyor. Address: (h.) Foulis Mains, Evanton, Ross-shire.

Munro, Alexander, MB, ChB, ChM, FRCS. Consultant General Surgeon, Raigmore Hospital, Inverness, since 1978; Professor of Clinical Surgery, Aberdeen University, since 2002; b. 5.6.43, Ross and Cromarty; m., Maureen E. McCreath; 2 s.; 1 d. Educ. Fortrose Academy; Aberdeen University. Training in General Surgery at Registrar and Senior Registrar level, Aberdeen Hospitals, 1971-78; specialist training, St. Mark's Hospital, 1977. Recreation: gardening. Address: (h.) 23 Eriskay Road, Inverness; T.-Inverness 223804.

Munro, Professor Colin Roy, BA, LLB. Professor of Constitutional Law, Edinburgh University, since 1990 (Dean, Faculty of Law, 1992-94); b. 17.5.49, Aberdeen; m., Ruth Elizabeth Pratt; 1 s.; 1 d. Educ. Aberdeen Grammar School; Aberdeen University. Lecturer in Law, Birmingham University, 1971-72, Durham University, 1972-80; Senior Lecturer in Law, then Reader in Law, Essex University, 1980-85; Professor of Law, Manchester University, 1985-90; Chief Examiner, London University LLB (External) Degree, 1991-97; Member, Consultative Council, British Board of Film Classification, since 2000; Member, Advertising Advisory Committee, since 2005. Publications: Television, Censorship and the Law; Studies in Constitutional Law; Devolution and the Scotland Bill (Co-author); The Scotland Act 1998 (Co-author). Recreations: sport; cinema and theatre; real ale. Address: (b.) School of Law, Old College, South Bridge, Edinburgh EH8 9YL; T.-0131-650 2047.

Munro, Professor David Mackenzie, BSc, PhD, FRGS, FRSA, FSAScot. Director and Secretary, Royal Scottish Geographical Society, since 1996; Honorary Professor, Dundee University, since 2007; Member, Council, National Trust for Scotland; Chairman, Permanent Committee on Geographical Names for British Official Use; Chairman, UK Division of United Nations Group of Experts on Geographical Names; b. 28.5.50, Dundee. Educ. Daniel Stewart's College; Edinburgh Academy; Edinburgh University. Research Associate, then Research Fellow, Edinburgh University, 1979-96; Leader/Co Leader, Edinburgh University expeditions to Central America, 1981, 1986, 1988, 1991. Chairman, Michael Bruce Trust; Honorary President, Jules Verne Film Festival, Paris, 2001; Vice-President, 8th UN Conference on the Standardization of Geographical Names, 2002; Scotia Centenary Medal, 2005; Vice-Chairman, South Georgia Heritage Trust, 2006. Publications: Chambers World Gazetteer (Editor); Oxford Dictionary of the World (Editor); Gazetteer of the Baltic States; A World Record of Major Conflict Areas; Loch Leven and the River Leven – a Landscape Transformed; Consultant, Times Atlas of the World; Scotland: an Encyclopedia of Places and Landscapes; numerous articles and reports on land use in Central America. Recreations: walking; travel; exploring landscapes. Address: (b.) 40 George Street, Glasgow G1 1QE; T.-0141-552 3330.

Munro, Rev. David Peacock, MA, BD, STM. Minister, Bearsden North Church, 1967-96; Clerk, Presbytery of Dumbarton, 1986-2005; b. 7.9.29, Paisley; m., Jessie Scott McPherson; 3 d. Educ. Paisley Grammar School; Glasgow University; Union Theological Seminary, New York. Minister, Aberluthnott Parish Church, 1953-56, Castlehill Church, Ayr, 1956-67. Vice-Convener, General Assembly Council, 1988-90; Convener, 1990-95; Moderator, Dumbarton Presbytery, 1978-79; Chairman, General Assembly Board of Education, 1974-79; Convener, General Assembly Education Committee, 1981-85. Recreations: golf; gardening. Address: (h.) 14 Birch Road, Killearn, Glasgow G63 9SQ; T.-01360 550098.

Munro, Donnie, DA. Director of Development, Sabhal Mòr Ostaig; former Guitarist and Lead Singer, Runrig; b. Skye; m.; 3 children. Former Art Teacher, Inverness and Edinburgh; Rector, Edinburgh University, 1991-94; contested (Labour) Ross, Skye and Inverness West, 1999. Dr. HC, Edinburgh, 1994.

Munro, Jean Mary, BA (Hons), PhD. Vice President, Society of Antiquaries of Scotland, 2002-05; Chairman, Council, Scottish History Society, 1989-93; b. 2.12.23; m., Robert William Munro. Educ. London University; Edinburgh University. WRNS, 1944-47; freelance historical researcher; Member, Council, National Trust for Scotland, 1964-69 and 1987-92 (Executive, 1968-80); Chairman, Council, Scottish Genealogy Society, 1983-86 (Vice-President, since 1987); Chairman, Council, Scottish Local History Forum, 1984-88. Publications (as Jean Dunlop): the British Fisheries Society; the Clan Chisholm; the Clan Mackenzie; the Clan Gordon; the Scotts; the Clan Mackintosh; (with R.W. Munro): Tain through the Centuries; The Scrimgeours; The Acts of the Lords of the Isles. Recreations: reading; walking. Address: (h.) 15a Mansionhouse Road, Edinburgh EH9 1TZ; T.-0131-667 4601.

Munro, John Farquhar. MSP (Liberal Democrat), Ross, Skye and Inverness West, since 1999; Liberal Democrat Spokesperson for Gaelic and Culture; b. 26.8.34; m. Cecilia Robertson; 1 s.; 1 d. Educ. Plockton High School; Merchant Marine College, Sharpness. Former: crofter, manager in contracting company, merchant marine; ran own civil engineering company; Ross County Councillor, 1966-74; Skye and Lochalsh District Councillor, 1974-96 (Convener, 1984-95); Highland Regional Councillor, 1978-82 (Chair of Gaelic); Highland Unitary Councillor, 1995-99 (Leader, Liberal Democrats Group, Chair of Roads and Transport, Chair, Rail Network Partnership); Scottish Parliament: Member, Rural Affairs Committee, 1999-2000, Equal Opportunities Committee, 1999-2000; Member, Transport Committee, 2001, Member, Petitions Committee, since 2001, Member, Rural Development Committee, 2002; Former Board Member, Skye and Lochalsh Enterprise; Trustee, Gaelic College, Skye. Recreations: sailing; fishing; grandchildren; Gaelic language and culture (native speaker); church (Elder, Kintail Church of Scotland). Address: (b.) Scottish Parliament, Edinburgh EH99 1SP; T.-0131-348 5790.

Munro, John Forbes, OBE, FRCPEdin, FRCPGlas, FRCPLond, BA. B. 25.6.33, Edinburgh; m., Elizabeth Jean Durell Caird; 3 d. Educ. Edinburgh Academy; Chigwell School, Essex; Edinburgh University; Open University. Former Consultant Physician, Eastern General and Edenhall Hospitals and part-time Senior Lecturer, Edinburgh University; Registrar, Royal College of Physicians, Edinburgh, 1993-97. Recreations: art; gardening. Address: (h.) Backhill, Carberry, near Musselburgh, East Lothian; T.-0131-663 4935.

Munro, Rev. John P.L., MA, BD, PhD. Minister, Kinross Parish Church, since 1998; b. 11.5.47, Edinburgh; m., Pat Lawson; 1 s.; 1 d. Educ. Edinburgh Academy; Christ's College, Cambridge; Edinburgh University. Church of Scotland Chaplain, Stirling University, 1977-82; Lecturer, St. Paul's Theological College, Kenya, 1982-85; Minister, St. Vigeans and Knox's Church, Arbroath, 1986-90; Assistant Secretary, Church of Scotland Department of World Mission, 1990-98. Recreations: music; gliding. Address: (b.) 15 Station Road, Kinross KY13 8TG; T.- 01577 862952.

Munro, Rev. John Robert, DSD, BD. Minister, Edinburgh: Fairmilehead, since 1992; b. 23.11.48, Glasgow; m., Lillian Primrose; 1 d. Educ. Whitehill Senior Secondary, Glasgow; Royal Scottish Academy of Music and Drama, Edinburgh University. Assistant Minister, Palmerston Place, Edinburgh, 1975-76; Minister, St. Bernardo's, Stockbridge, Edinburgh, 1976-92. Various General Assembly Committees, 1978-2005; Ponton House Trust Presbytery Publicity Secretary. Recreation: golf. Address: (b.) 6 Braid Crescent, Edinburgh EH10 6AU; T.- 0131 446 9363; e-mail: revjohnmunro@hotmail.com

Munro, Kenneth Alexander, MA, FRSA. Convenor, Children in Scotland, 1999-2003; Chairman, Centre for Scottish Public Policy, 1997-2007; b. 17.12.36, Glasgow; m., Elizabeth Coats Forrest McCreanor; 2 d. Educ. Hutchesons' Boys' Grammar School; Glasgow University. Served, Intelligence Corps, 1955-57; family business, 1957-59; Scottish American Investment Company, 1963-66; Senior Research Officer, ETU, 1966-67; Secretary, Economic Development Committee, NEDO, 1967-69; Industrial Relations Manager, Ford Motor Co., 1969-74 (secondment to Pay Board, 1973-74); joined European Commission, 1974: Press Officer and Deputy Head of Office, London, 1982-88; Head of Representation in Scotland, 1988-98. Member (Labour), Brentwood DC, Essex, 1971-74; Member, Campaigning Committee, Queen Margaret University College, 1999-2003; Honorary Fellow, Faculty of Law, University of Edinburgh, since 1998; BP Advisory Board for Scotland, 1997-2003; Vice Chairman, John Smith Memorial Trust, 1994-2005; Vice-Chairman, John Smith Memorial Trust Advisory Board, 2005-07; Member, Equal Opportunities Advisory Committee for Scotland, 1993-2007; Member, Royal Commission on Reform of the House of Lords, 1999-2000; Chairman, European Movement Scottish Council, 2004-07, Vice Chairman, 2000-04, Honorary Secretary, 1991-2000; Parliamentary Candidate (Labour), West Aberdeenshire, General Election, 1964; Candidate (Labour), Lothian List, Scottish Parliament Election, 1999; Convener, Scotland in Europe, since 2000; Member, Council, Saltire Society, since 2003; Director, Our Europe, 2003-04; Chairman, International Committee, Saltire Society, 2005-07. Recreations: theatre; cinema; swimming; walking. Address: 23 Greenhill Gardens, Edinburgh EH10 4BL; T.-0131-447 2284.

Munro, Neil Kenneth, MA (Hons.) Editor, Times Educational Supplement Scotland, since 2001; b. 18.3.52, Stornoway; m., Eilish; 2 s. Educ. Nicolson Institute, Stornoway; Edinburgh University. Editor, West Highland Free Press, 1974-75; Reporter, Depute Editor, Times Educational Supplement Scotland, 1975-2001. Recreations: cycling; swimming; reading. Address: Thistle House, 21-23 Thistle Street, Edinburgh EH2 1DF; T.-0131-624 8333; e-mail: neil.munro@tes.co.uk

Murdoch, Professor Brian Oliver, BA, PhD, LittD, FRHistS, AMusTCL. Professor of German, Stirling University, since 1991; Emeritus, 2007; b. 26.6.44, London;

m., Ursula Irene Riffer; 1 s.; 1 d. Educ. Sir George Monoux Grammar School, London; Exeter University; Jesus College, Cambridge. Lecturer in German, Glasgow University; Assistant/Associate Professor of German, University of Illinois; Lecturer/Senior Lecturer in German, Stirling University; Visiting Fellow, Trinity Hall, Cambridge, 1989; Visiting Fellow and Waynflete Lecturer, Magdalen College, Oxford, 1994; Hulsean Lecturer in Divinity, University of Cambridge, 1997-98; Speaker's Lecturer in Biblical Studies, and Visiting Fellow of Oriel College, University of Oxford, 2000-02; author of a number of books and articles on medieval German and Celtic literature, also on literature of the World Wars. Recreations: jazz; numismatics; books. Address: (b.) German Department, Stirling University, Stirling FK9 4LA; T.- 01786 467546; e-mail: bom1@stir.ac.uk

Murdoch, Helen Elliot, MBA, FCIH, AIPD. Chief Executive, Hanover (Scotland) Housing Association Ltd., since 2007; Director, Housing & Care Services, 1995-2007; m., John Murdoch; 1 s. Professional Housing Management Trainee and other senior posts with SSHA (Scottish Special Housing Association), 1974-85; Area Housing Manager, Dunfermline District Council, 1985-95. Member and latterly Chair, Dunfermline Crossroads Scheme for 17 years; Member, various Scottish Government Working Parties; particular interest and experience in Strategic Management, Management of Change and Organisational Culture. Recreations: running; hill-walking; art. Address: 1 Dovecot Wynd, Mastertonhall, Dunfermline KY11 8SY; T.-0131 557 7420 (office); e-mail: hmurdoch@hsha.org.uk

Murdoch, Iain Campbell, MA, LLB, DipEd, BD. Minister, Cambuslang Old and Morningside Parish Church, Wishaw, since 1995; b. 16.10.50, Glasgow; m., Elizabeth Gibson; 1 s.; 1 d. Educ. Larchfield School, Helensburgh; Haileybury College, Hertford; Trinity College, Oxford; University of Edinburgh. Legal Apprentice, Simpson & Marwick WS, 1973-74; Economics Teacher, Brighton College, 1976-77; PT History, Keil School, 1977-79; Principal Teacher, General Studies, Rossall School, Fleetwood, 1979-89; Assistant Minister, Duddingston Kirk, Edinburgh, 1992-94; Founder Member and Present Advisor, MADE4U in ML2 (a charitable company making a difference in Wishaw). Parliamentary Candidate, SDP/Liberal Alliance, Wyre, 1983 and 1987; successful petitioner to Scottish Parliament, 2001-03; Member, Church of Scotland Task Force for Change. Recreation: hill walking. Address: (h.) 22, Coronation Street, Wishaw ML2 8LF; T.-01698-384235.
E-mail: iaincmurdoch@btopenworld.com

Murdoch, Professor Jim, MA, LLM. Professor of Public Law, Glasgow University, since 1998; b. 26.6.55, Hamilton. Educ. Strathaven Academy; Hutcheson's Grammar School; Glasgow University; University of California at Berkeley; Open University. Solicitor; Glasgow University: Lecturer; Senior Lecturer; Visiting Professor: University of Mainz; University of Hamburg; Professeur Stagière, Directorate of Human Rights, Council of Europe, Strasbourg. Publications: Reed and Murdoch, A Guide to Human Rights Law in Scotland (2nd Edition), 2007; The Protection of Liberty and Security of Person (2nd Edition), 2002; The Treatment of Prisoners: European Standards, 2006. Recreations: hill walking; foreign travel. Address: (b.) School of Law, Glasgow University, Glasgow, G12; T.-0141-330 4178.

Murdoch, Kirk, LLB, NP. Partner, McGrigors LLP, since 1982; Senior Partner Scotland, and Real Estate

Partner, McGrigors, Solicitors, since 2004; b. 7.3.55, Ayr; m., Julie; 2 s.; 1 d. Educ. Ayr Academy; Edinburgh University. McGrigor Donald: Apprentice, 1976, Legal Assistant, Partner, Real Estate, 1982, Head of Real Estate, 1992-97, Managing Partner, 1997-2002, Managing Partner Scotland and Real Estate Partner, 2002-04. Member, SCDI Executive Committee; Chairman, Managing Partner Forum (Scotland). Recreations: golf; rugby. Address: (b.) Pacific House, 70 Wellington Street, Glasgow G2 6SB; T.-0141-248-6677; e-mail: kirk.murdoch@mcgrigors.com

Mure, Kenneth Nisbet, QC. Advocate, Scotland, since 1975; Barrister, Grays Inn, since 1990; Fellow, Chartered Institute of Taxation, since 1981; b. 11.4.47, Glasgow. Educ. Cumbernauld JS School; Glasgow High School; Glasgow University. Address: (b.) Advocates' Library, Edinburgh.

Murie, John Andrew, MA, BSc, MBChB, MD, FRCS(Glas), FRCS(Edin). Consultant Vascular Surgeon, Edinburgh Royal Infirmary, since 1989; Editor, British Journal of Surgery, since 1989; b. 7.8.49, Airdrie. Educ. Airdrie Academy; Glasgow University. Clinical Reader in Surgery, Nuffield Department of Surgery, Oxford University, 1984-89; Hon. Consultant Surgeon, John Radcliffe Hospital, Oxford, 1984-89; Fellow, Green College, Oxford, 1984-89; Hon. Editorial Secretary, Association of Surgeons of Gt. Britain and Ireland, 1996-99, and Council Member, 1994-99; Clinical Director, General and Vascular Surgery, Edinburgh Royal Infirmary, 1995-2000; Hon. Senior Lecturer in Surgery, Edinburgh University, since 1989. Member of Council, Vascular Surgery Society of Gt. Britain and Ireland, 1998-2001; Member of Council, Royal College of Physicians and Surgeons of Glasgow, 1998-2006. Recreations: golf; running; reading; food and wine. Address: (b.) Department of Surgery, Royal Infirmary of Edinburgh, Edinburgh EH16 4SU; T.-0131 242 1059.

Murning, Lt. Col. Ian Henry, TD, LLB (Hons), LLM, DPA, FRICS, MCIArb. Partner, Ian H. Murning Associates, Chartered Surveyors, since 1994; Lecturer, Napier University, 1994-2007; Honorary Secretary, Royal Institution of Chartered Surveyors in Scotland, since 2007; Member, Investigation and Professional Conduct Enforcement Committee, Institute of Chartered Accountants of Scotland, since 2007; Member, Scottish Funding Council for Further and Higher Education, since 2005; Member, Scottish Further Education Funding Council, 2003-05; Chairman, Property and Capital Investment Committee, Scottish Funding Council, since 2005; b. 24.12.43, Chapelhall; m., Seona Jean Meiklejon; 1 s.; 2 d. Educ. Dalziel High School; Glasgow University; College of Estate Management; London University; Edinburgh University. Valuer, Stirling Valuation Office, Highlands and Islands; Office of Chief Valuer (Scotland); District Valuer, Dumfries and Galloway, 1988-94. Chairman, Royal Institution of Chartered Surveyors in Scotland, 1995-96; Member, General Council, Royal Institution of Chartered Surveyors, 1994-96; Commander, Royal Engineers (Home Defence), Army HQ Scotland, 1991-95; Commander, District Specialist Training Team, Army HQ Scotland, 1996-97; served with 52(L) Div/Dist Engrs (TA), 1963-67, Royal Monmouthshire Royal Engineers (Militia), 1967-68, 71 (Scottish) Engineer Regt (V), 1968-74; Member: Society of High Constables of Edinburgh, 1993, Merchant Company of Edinburgh, 1995, Territorial Auxiliary and Volunteer Reserve Association for the Lowlands, 1997; Governor, George Watson's College, since 2000. Address: (b.) 21 Redhall House Avenue, Edinburgh EH14 1JJ; T.-0131-443 8839.

Murphy, Jim. MP (Labour), East Renfrewshire (formerly Eastwood), since 1997; Minister for Europe, since 2007; b. 23.8.67, Glasgow; m.; 3 c. Educ. Bellarmine Secondary School, Glasgow; Milnerton High School, Cape Town. National President, National Union of Students, 1994-96; Special Projects Manager, Scottish Labour Party, 1996-97; PPS to Helen Liddell (Secretary of State for Scotland), 2001-02; Assistant Government Whip, 2002-05; Parliamentary Secretary, Cabinet Office, 2005-06; Minister of State for Employment and Welfare Reform, 2006-07. Recreations: football; cinema; reading. Address: 238 Ayr Road, Newton Mearns, East Renfrewshire G77 6AA.

Murphy, Peter Alexander, MA, MEd. Member (Labour), Angus Council, since 1999; Depute Provost (in Alliance Group), since May 2007; Rector, Whitfield High School, Dundee, 1976-93; b. 5.10.32, Aberdeen; m., Margaret Christie; 3 s.; 1 d. Educ. Aberdeen Grammar School; Aberdeen University. Assistant Principal Teacher of English, Aberdeen Grammar School, 1963-65; Principal Teacher of English, Summerhill Academy, Aberdeen, 1965-71; Head Teacher, Logie Secondary School, Dundee, 1971-76. Publications: Life and Times of Logie School (Co-Author); The Life of R.F. MacKenzie (A Prophet without Honour), 1999. Address: Ashlea, 44 Burnside Street, Carnoustie, Angus DD7 7HL; e-mail: cllrmurphy@angus.gov.uk

Murphy, Sean Francis, QC, MA (Hons), LLB, DipLP, PGCE. Sheriff of Glasgow and Strathkelvin, since 2007; b. 17.07.58, Glasgow; m., Honor; 1 s.; 2 d. Educ. St Aloysius College, Glasgow; University of St Andrews; Strathclyde University; Christ's and Notre Dame College of Education, Liverpool. Assistant Master of History, St Edmund Campion Upper School, Oxford, 1981-83 and St. Augustine's Upper School, Oxford, 1983-86; Messrs Ross Harper and Murphy, Glasgow: Trainee Solicitor, 1989-91, Court Assistant Solicitor, 1991; Visiting Lecturer in Law, Glasgow College of Technology, 1988-90; Advocate, 1992; Advocate Depute, 1991-2001; Standing Junior Counsel to the Scottish Executive, 2001-03; QC, 2003; Senior Advocate Depute, 2003-07. Secretary, Faculty of Advocates Criminal Lawyers Group, 1997-99; Committee Member, Scottish Medico-Legal Council, since 2006; Chairman, Glenmarnock Wheelers CC, 1994-2004. Recreations: cycling; reading; listening to radio drama and sitting patiently at Firhill. Address: (b.) Sheriff Court of Glasgow and Strathkelvin, 1 Carlton Place, Glasgow G5 9DA; T.-0141 429 8888. E-mail: sheriffsmurphy@scotcourts.gov.uk

Murray, Rt. Hon. Lord (Ronald King Murray), PC (1974), MA, LLB, Dr.h.c.(Edin). Senator of the College of Justice in Scotland, 1979-95; b. 15.6.22; m., Sheila Winifred Gamlin. Educ. George Watson's College; Edinburgh University; Jesus College, Oxford (Honorary Fellow, 1999). Advocate, 1953; QC, 1967; MP (Leith), 1970-79; Lord Advocate, 1974-79. Assessor, Edinburgh University Court, 1981-93 (Vice-Chairman, 1990-93). Recreations: sailing; astronomy. Address: (h.) 1 Inverleith Grove, Edinburgh EH3 5PB; T.-0131-551 5330.

Murray, Athol Laverick, PhD, MA, LLB, FRHistS, FSA Scot. Chairman, Scottish Records Association, 1997-2000; Vice-President, Society of Antiquaries of Scotland, 1989-92; Keeper of the Records of Scotland, 1985-90; b. 8.11.30, Tynemouth; m., Irene Joyce Cairns; 1 s.; 1 d. Educ. Lancaster Royal Grammar School; Jesus College, Cambridge; Edinburgh University. Research Assistant, Foreign Office, 1953; Scottish Record Office: Assistant Keeper, 1953-83, Deputy Keeper, 1983-84. Recreations: historical research; bowling. Address: (h.) 33 Inverleith

Gardens, Edinburgh EH3 5PR; T.-0131-552 4465; e-mail: atholmurray@hotmail.com

Murray, (Bridget) Jane, BA (Oxon), MA, PhD. Commissioner, Royal Commission on the Ancient and Historical Monuments of Scotland, since 1999; Chair, The Whithorn Trust, 2005-08; b. 25.7.37, Tunbridge Wells; m., John Murray, QC (Lord Dervaird); 3 s. Educ. Royal Tunbridge Wells County Grammar School for Girls; St Hugh's College, Oxford; Edinburgh University. Involved in various archaeological projects and organisations. Recreations: gardening; walking; architecture. Address: (h.) 4 Moray Place, Edinburgh EH3 6DS; T.-0131-225 1881.

Murray, Sir David Edward (KT 2007). Chairman, Murray International Holdings; Chairman, The Rangers Football Club plc; Founder, The Murray Foundation, 2007; Queen's Award for Voluntary Service, November 2006; b. 14.10.51, Ayr; 2 s. Educ. Fettes College; Broughton High School. Young Scottish Businessman of the Year, 1984; Hon. Doctorate, Heriot-Watt University, 1986; Chairman, UK 2000 (Scotland), 1987; Governor, Clifton Hall School, 1987. Recreations: sports sponsorship; collecting and producing wine, Chevalier du Tastevin - Clos de Vougeot, November 2006. Address: (b.) 9 Charlotte Square, Edinburgh EH2 4DR.

Murray, Diana Mary, MA (Cantab), FSA, FSAScot, MIFA. Secretary, Royal Commission on the Ancient and Historical Monuments of Scotland (RCAHMS), since 2004; b. 14.9.52, Birmingham; m., Robin F. Murray; 2 d. Educ. King Edward VI Camp Hill School for Girls, Birmingham; New Hall, Cambridge. RCAHMS: Research Assistant, 1976-83, Head of Recording Section, 1983-90, Curator, Archaeology Record, 1990-95, Curator Depute, National Monuments Record of Scotland (NMRS), 1995-2004. Chairman, Institute of Field Archaeologists, 1995-96; Council Member, National Trust for Scotland and Society of Antiquaries of London. Recreations: choral singing; gardening. Address: (b.) RCAHMS, John Sinclair House, 16 Bernard Terrace, Edinburgh EH8 9NX; T.-0131 662 1456; e-mail: diana.murray@rcahms.gov.uk

Murray, Duncan Law, LLB (Hons). Partner, Morton Fraser, Solicitors, since 2002; Part time Sheriff, 2006; b. 5.5.59; m., Ianthe Elizabeth Lee Craig; 2 s.; 1 d. Educ. Aberdeen Grammar School; Aberdeen University. Robson McLean Paterson: apprentice, 1980-82; Assistant, 1982-85; Partner, Robson McLean, 1985-2002. President, Law Society of Scotland, 2004-05. Recreations: golf; ski-ing; hill-walking; family. Club: Luffness New Golf. Address: (b.) Morton Fraser, 30/31 Queen Street, Edinburgh EH2 1JX; T.-0131 247 1000; Fax: 0131 247 1004. E-mail: duncan.murray@morton-fraser.com

Murray, Elaine Kildare, BSc (Hons). MSP (Labour), Dumfries since 1999; Deputy Minister for Tourism, Culture and Sport, 2001-03; b. 22.12.54, Hitchin, Herts; m., Jeff Leaver; 2 s.; 1 d. Educ. Mary Erskine School, Edinburgh; Edinburgh University; Cambridge University. Postdoctoral Research Fellow: Cavendish Laboratory, Cambridge, Royal Free Hospital, London; Senior Scientific Officer, Institute of Food Research, Reading; Associate Lecturer, Open University in Scotland. Recreations: family activities; reading; horseriding; keyboard. Address: Constituency Office, 5 Friars' Vennel, Dumfries DG1 2RQ; T.-01387 279205; e-mail: elaine.murray.msp@scottish.parliament.uk

Murray, Professor Gordon Cameron, BSc, BArch, MCIArb, RIBA, PPRIAS. Founding Partner, Gordon Murray & Dunlop Architects, since 1999; Professor of Architecture and Head of School, University of Strathclyde, since 2007; b. 26.7.52; m., Sharon Boyle; 2 d. Educ. University of Strathclyde. Assistant Architect:

Richard Moira, Betty Moira & James Wann, 1974; Department of Architecture and Related Services, 1975-77; Project Architect, Sinclair and Watt Architects, 1977-79; Partner: Cunningham Glass Murray Architects, 1987-92; Glass Murray Architects, 1992-99. External Examiner, University of Ulster, since 2004. President: Glasgow Inst. of Architects, 1998-2000; RIAS, 2003-05. Member, Board, Lighthouse Trust, since 2003. Publications: An Integrated Transport System for Greater Glasgow, 1977; (Co-Author); James Miller, Architect: a monograph, 1990; Challenging Contextualism: the work of gm and ad architects, 2002; Curious Rationalism, 2006; contributions to Herald, Scotsman, Architects' Journal, and Prospect. Recreations: cinema; art; saxophone; jazz; travel. Address: Breckenridge House, 274 Sauchiehall Street, Glasgow G2 3EH; T.-0141 331 2926; Fax: 0141 332 6790; e-mail: murraydunloparchitects.com

Murray, Gordon Lindsay Kevan. Partner, Murrays WS, Solicitors; Secretary, Royal Scottish National Orchestra Society Ltd.; Director, 1990-93, Secretary and Treasurer, The RSNO Foundation; b. 23.5.53, Glasgow; m., Susan Patricia; 1 s.; 3 d. Educ. Lenzie Academy; Edinburgh University. Address: (b.) 40 Castle Street, Edinburgh EH2 3BN; T.-0131-625 6625; e-mail: mail@murraysws.co.uk

Murray, Gregor Cumming, MA Hons (Oxon), MBA. Executive Director, Midlothian and East Lothian Chamber of Commerce, since 1998; Chairman, Business Environment Partnership, since 1997; b. 16.4.57, Edinburgh; m., Barbara (nee Parham); 3 s.; 2 d. Educ. George Watson's College; Newbattle Abbey, Trinity College, Oxford; Edinburgh University Management School. Career History: Bank of Scotland; Investors in Industry; Leith Enterprise Trust. Recreations: fly-fishing; golf; gardening; chess. Address: (b.) 42/3 Hardengreen Business Park, Dalkeith, Midlothian EH22 3NU; T.-0131-654-1234; e-mail: gm@met.org.uk

Murray, Rt. Rev. Ian, BA (Hons). Bishop of Argyll and The Isles, since 1999; b. 15.12.32, Lennoxtown. Educ. St. Ninian's High School, Kirkintilloch; St. Mary's College, Aberdeen; Royal Scots College, Valladolid; Open University. Ordained Priest, 1956; served: St. Mary's Cathedral, Edinburgh, St. Kenneth's Lochore, St. Columba's, Edinburgh; Vice-Rector, Royal Scots College, Valladolid, 1963-70; RC Chaplain, Stirling University, 1970-78; Parish Priest, St. Bride's Cowdenbeath, then St. Ninian's, Edinburgh; Rector, Royal Scots College, Valladolid, 1987; Parish Priest, Our Lady and St. Andrew's, Galashiels, 1994-96; appointed Parish Priest, St. Francis Xavier's, Falkirk, and Vicar-General, Archdiocese of St. Andrews and Edinburgh, 1996. Address: Bishop's House, Esplanade, Oban PA34 5AB.

Murray, Professor Isobel (Mary), MA, PhD. Writer and Critic; Honorary Research Professor in Modern Scottish Literature, Aberdeen University; Vice President, Association of Scottish Literary Studies; Associate Editor, New Oxford Dictionary of National Biography; b. 14.2.39, Alloa; m., Bob Tait. Educ. Dollar Academy; Edinburgh University. Assistant Lecturer, Lecturer, Senior Lecturer, Reader, Professor, Department of English, Aberdeen University; books include several editions of Oscar Wilde (most recently Oscar Wilde: The Major Works, 2000), introductions to new editions of J. MacDougall Hay's Gillespie, Ian MacPherson's Shepherds' Calendar, Robin Jenkins' Guests of War, Iain Crichton Smith's Consider the Lilies, George MacKay Brown's Magnus, and Jessie Kesson's Where the Apple Ripens; edited, Beyond This Limit: Selected Shorter Fiction of Naomi Mitchison; A Girl

Must Live: stories and poems by Naomi Mitchison; Ten Modern Scottish Novels (with Bob Tait), 1984; Scottish Writers Talking, 1996; Somewhere Beyond: A Jessie Kesson Companion; published Jessie Kesson: Writing Her Life, 2000 (National Library of Scotland/Saltire Society Research Book of the Year); Scottish Writers Talking 2, 2002; Scottish Writers Talking 3, 2006. Address: (b.) 5 St Machar Place, Old Aberdeen, Aberdeen AB24 3SF; T.-Aberdeen 491938.

Murray, Professor James, BSc, ARTC, CEng, FIMechE, FIEE, FIM. Vice Principal, Napier University, 1992-95, now Emeritus Professor; b. 25.7.30, Glasgow; m., Emily Lamb Beveridge (deceased); 1 s.; 1 d. Educ. Allan Glen's School, Glasgow; Glasgow University. Development Engineer, Ferranti Ltd., Edinburgh, 1952-62; Lecturer, Department of Mechanical Engineering, Heriot-Watt University, 1962-67; Head, Department of Production Engineering, Napier College, 1967-72; Head, Department of Industrial Studies, 1972-74; Assistant Principal and Dean, Faculty of Professional Studies, 1974-82; Assistant Principal/Dean, Faculty of Technology, 1982-92. Former Member, Council: SCOTEC, EITD, IProdE; Past Chairman, IProdE, Edinburgh Section and Scotland Region; Past Chairman: CEI Scotland, CNAA Engineering Board and Research Committee; former Member, Transport Tribunal, Scotland; former Governor, Moray House College of Education; former Member of Convocation, Heriot-Watt University; Trustee: National Museums of Scotland, 1997-2005, Scottish Maritime Museum, 2001-07; Elder, Church of Scotland, since 1957; former Chairman, Edinburgh Branch, Glasgow Graduates Association; President, Allan Glen's School Club, 1998-99. Publication: The History of Allan Glen's School and Allan Glen's School Club 1853-2003. Recreations: watching rugby; visiting museums; golf; gardening; studying light rail transport systems; opera. Address: (h.) 40 Elliot Road, Edinburgh EH14 1DZ.

Murray, John, BA (Hons), DipED, MEd. Headteacher, Harlaw Academy, since 1993; b. 2.2.52, Irvine; m., Margaret McLaughlin; 2 s.; 1 d. Educ. St. Michael's Academy, Kilwinning; Strathclyde University; Glasgow University; Stirling University. Teacher, Ardrossan Academy, 1975-78; Principal Teacher, St. Mungo's, Alloa, 1978-81; Principal Teacher, Lasswade High School, 1981-86; Assistant Rector, Woodmill High School, 1986-89; Depute Rector, Kirkcaldy High School, 1989-93. Recreations: family; football; golf. Address: (b.) 18 Albyn Place, Aberdeen AB10 1RG; T.-01224 589251.

Murray, Rev. John James, DipTH. Minister, Free Church of Scotland (Continuing); b. 11.9.34, Dornoch; m., Cynthia MacPhee; 1 s.; 1 d. Educ. Dornoch Academy; Edinburgh University; Free Church College. Caledonian Insurance Company, 1955-59; Assistant Editor, Banner of Truth Trust, 1960-73; Minister: Free High Church, Oban, 1978-89, St. Columba's Free Church, Edinburgh, 1989-2000, Edinburgh Free Church (Continuing), 2000-02, (retired 2002). Moderator, General Assembly, Free Church of Scotland (Continuing), 2003. Publications: Behind a Frowning Providence; The Life and Writings of John Marshall, 2005; Catch the Vision, 2007. Address: (h.) 7 Greenacres Way, Glasgow G53 7BG; T.-0141-620 3983. E-mail: johnmurray@fccontinuing.org

Murray, Leonard G., JP, KCHS, KGSJ, BL, SSC. Solicitor; former Senior Partner, Levy & McRae, Glasgow. Educ. St. Mungo's Academy, Glasgow; Glasgow University. After-dinner speaker; Wag of the Year, 2000. Recreations: golf; gardening. Address: (h.) 69 Campsie Drive, Milngavie, Glasgow G62 8HR; T.-0141 563 9624; e-mail: len.murray@ntlworld.com; website: lenmurray.co.uk

Murray, Professor Noreen Elizabeth, CBE, PhD, FRS, FRSE. Emeritus Professor, Institute of Cell and Molecular Biology, Edinburgh University; b. 26.2.35, Burnley; m., Kenneth Murray. Educ. Lancaster Girls' Grammar School; King's College, London; Birmingham University. Research Associate, Department of Biological Sciences, Stanford University, 1960-64; Research Fellow, Botany School, Cambridge, 1964-67; Edinburgh University: Member, MRC Molecular Genetics Unit, Department of Molecular Biology, 1968-74, Lecturer, then Senior Lecturer, Department of Molecular Biology, 1974-80; Group Leader, European Molecular Biology Laboratory, Heidelberg, 1980-82; rejoined Edinburgh University as Reader, 1982. Recreation: gardening. Address: (b.) Institute of Cell Biology, Edinburgh University, Mayfield Road, Edinburgh EH9 3JR; T.-0131-650 5374.

Murray, Norman Loch, BA, CA, FRSA. Chairman, Cairn Energy PLC; Director: Robert Wiseman Dairies PLC, Greene King PLC; b. 17.3.48, Kilmarnock; m., Pamela Anne Low; 2 s. Educ. George Watson's College; Heriot-Watt University; Harvard University Graduate School of Business Administration. Scottish & Newcastle Breweries PLC, 1971-73; Arthur Young, 1973-76; Peat Marwick Mitchell & Co. (Hong Kong), 1977-80; Royal Bank of Scotland PLC, 1980-85; Director, Charterhouse Development Capital Ltd., 1985-89; Chairman, Morgan Grenfell Private Equity Ltd.; Director, Morgan Grenfell & Co. Ltd.; Director, Morgan Grenfell Asset Management Ltd., 1989-98. Former directorships (non-executive): Bristow Helicopter Group Limited, Eurodollar (Holdings) Ltd., Taunton Cider plc, Glasgow Income Trust PLC, Penta Capital Partners Holdings Ltd; Institute of Chartered Accountants of Scotland: President, 2006-07, Member of Council, 1992-98; Chairman, British Venture Capital Association, 1997-98, of its Legal and Technical Committee, and member of Council, 1992-96; Governor and Chairman, Investment Committee, St. Columba's Hospice, 1999-2004; Chairman, Governing Council, George Watson's College, since 2004. Publication: Making Corporate Reports Valuable (Co-Author), 1988. Recreations: squash; golf; climbing; travel. Address: (b.) 50 Lothian Road, Edinburgh EH3 9BY.

Murray, Peter, LLB (Hons), DipLP. Partner, Ledingham Chalmers LLP, since 2002; b. 27.10.71, Edinburgh; m., Alison; 2 d. Educ. Easthampstead Park; Dunfermline High; Aberdeen University. Trainee/Assistant Solicitor, Clark & Wallace, Solicitors, 1984-87; Assistant Solicitor/Associate, Ledingham Chalmers, Solicitors, 1997-2002. Governor, Albyn School, Aberdeen; Burgess of The City of Aberdeen; Notary Public; Advocate in Aberdeen. Recreation: family. Address: (b.) Johnstone House, 52-54 Rose Street, Aberdeen AB10 1HA; T.-01224 408445; e-mail: peter.murray@ledinghamchalmers.com

Murray, Robert John, MSc, MCIBS. Vice President, COSLA; Leader, Angus Council, 1998-2007 (Deputy Leader, 1995-98); b. 3.2.51, Montrose; 1 s.; 1 d. Educ. Montrose Academy; University of Abertay, Dundee. Member, Tayside Regional Council, 1994-96; Board Member, NOSWA, 1999-2002; Member, North East of Scotland Water Customer Consultation Panel, 2003-06. Recreations: cycling; walking. Address: (h.) 8 Boechgrove, Monifieth DD5 4TE.

Murray, Roderick Macpherson, BA (Hons). Director, An Lanntair, since 1985; b. 31.3.56, Coll, Isle of Lewis. Educ. Back Junior Secondary School; Nicolson Institute, Stornoway; Glasgow School of Art. Recreations: cycling; chess; arts. Address: (b.) An Lanntair, Kenneth Street, Stornoway, Isle of Lewis HS1 2DS; T.-01851 703307; e-mail: roddy@lanntair.com

Murray, Professor T. Stuart, MD, PhD, FRCGP, FRCPEdin, FRCPGlas. West of Scotland Director of

Postgraduate General Practice Education, since 1985; Professor of General Practice, University of Glasgow, since 1992; b. 22.7.43, Muirkirk, Ayrshire; m., Anne Smith; 1 s.; 2 d. Educ. Muirkirk Junior Secondary School; Cumnock Academy; University of Glasgow. Early training in cardiology; entered general practice, 1971; Senior Lecturer in General Practice, 1977. Publication: Modified Essay Questions for the MRCGP Examination; Guide to Postgraduate Medical Education (Co-author). Recreations: travel; reading; sport. Address: (b.) NHS Education for Scotland, 3rd Floor, 2 Central Quay, 89 Hydepark Street, Glasgow G3 8BW; T.-0141-223 1456; e-mail: Stuart.Murray@nes.scot.nhs.uk

Murray, Thomas Kenneth, WS. Partner, Gillespie MacAndrew WS Solicitors, since 1983; b. 25.6.58, Edinburgh; m., Sophie Mackenzie; 3 d. Educ. Sedbergh School; Dundee University. Purse Bearer to Lord High Commissioner to Church of Scotland, since 2003; Chairman, British Hallmarking Council, since 2004. Chairman, Trefoil House. Recreations: fishing; golf. Address: 5 Atholl Crescent, Edinburgh EH3 8EJ; T.-0131 260 7501; e-mail: tom.murray@gillespiemacandrew.co.uk

Murray, William James Greig, MBBS, MS, FRCS(Ed), FRCS(Eng). Consultant Surgeon, Perth Royal Infirmary, since 1990; b. 19.10.51, Aberdeen; m., Pamela Jane Poole; 2 s. 2 d. Educ. Robert Gordon's College, Aberdeen; Dulwich College Preparatory School; Westminster School; Middlesex Hospital Medical School, London University. House Surgeon, Middlesex Hospital, 1975; Registrar, Surgery/Urology, King's College Hospital, 1982-87; Senior Registrar, University College Hospital, 1987-90. Recreations: golf; gardening; Scottish country dancing. Address: (b.) Perth Royal Infirmary, Perth PH1 1NX; T.-01738 623311.

Murray-Smith, Professor David James, MSc, PhD, CEng, FIEE, MInstMC. Emeritus Professor, Glasgow University; b. 20.10.41, Aberdeen; m., Effie Smith; 2 s. Educ. Aberdeen Grammar School; Aberdeen University; Glasgow University. Engineer, Inertial Systems Department, Ferranti Ltd., Edinburgh, 1964-65; Glasgow University: Assistant, Department of Electrical Engineering, 1965-67, Lecturer, 1967-77, Senior Lecturer, 1977-83, Reader, 1983-85, Professor of Engineering Systems and Control, 1985-2005, Dean, Faculty of Engineering, 1997-2001. Past Chairman, United Kingdom Simulation Council. Recreations: hill-walking; photography; strong interest in railways. Address: (b.) Department of Electronics and Electrical Engineering, Glasgow University, Glasgow G12 8QQ; T.-0141-330 5222.

Murray-Smith, Professor Roderick, BEng, PhD. Professor of Computing Science, Glasgow University, since 1999; Senior Researcher, Hamilton Institute, NUIM, Ireland, since 2002; b. 03.04.69, Glasgow; m., Sophie; 2 s. Educ. Bearsden Academy; Strathclyde University. Research Engineer, Daimler Benz Research, Berlin, Germany, 1990-97; Visiting Researcher, MIT, 1994-95; Research Fellow, Denmark Technical University, 1997-99. Publications: 3 edited books and a wide range of scientific papers. Address: (b.) Department of Computing Science, University of Glasgow; T.-0141 330 4984; e-mail: rod@dcs.gla.ac.uk

Murrell, Peter T. Chief Executive, Scottish National Party, since 2001; b. 8.12.64, Edinburgh. Educ. Craigmount High School, Edinburgh. Publicity Officer, Church of Scotland, 1984-87; Parliamentary Assistant to: Alex Salmond, MP,

1987-94, Allan Macartney, MEP, 1994-98; Head of Office, Ian Hudghton, MEP, 1998-99; Parliamentary Co-ordinator, SNP Westminster Group, 2000-01. Recreations: golf; cycling; walking. Address: (b.) 107 McDonald Road, Edinburgh EH7 4NW; T.-0131-525 8907; e-mail: peter.murrell@snp.org

Muscatelli, Professor Vito Antonio, MA (Hons), PhD, FRSE, AcSS, FRSA. Principal and Vice-Chancellor, Heriot-Watt University, since 2007; Daniel Jack Professor of Political Economy, Department of Economics, Glasgow University, 1992-2007; Vice Principal (Strategy and Advancement), 2004-07; b. 1.1.62, Bari, Italy; m., Elaine Flood; 1 s.; 1 d. Educ. High School of Glasgow; Glasgow University. Lecturer, Senior Lecturer, Glasgow University, 1984-92, Dean, Faculty of Social Sciences, 2000-04; Visiting Professor: University of Parma (Italy), 1989, Catholic University, Milan, 1991, 1997, University of Bari (Italy), since 1995; Editor, Scottish Journal of Political Economy, 1989-2003; Member, Editorial Advisory Board, International Review of Economics and Business, since 1995; Member, Advisory Panel of Economic Consultants to the Secretary of State for Scotland, 1998-99; Member, Council, Royal Economic Society, since 2002; Member, ESRC Research Grants Board, 2002-06; Hon. Fellow, Societa Italiana Degli Economisti, 1996; Fellow, Royal Society of Edinburgh, 2003; Academician, Learned Societies in the Social Sciences, 2004. Publications: Macroeconomic Theory and Stabilisation Policy (Co-author), 1988; Economic and Political Institutions in Economic Policy (Editor of volume), 1996; Monetary Policy, Fiscal Policies and Labour Markets: Macroeconomic Policymaking in the EMU, 2004; articles in journals. Recreations: music; literature; football; strategic games. Address: (b.) Heriot-Watt University, Edinburgh EH14 4AS; T.-0131 451 3360; e-mail: A.muscatelli@hw.ac.uk

Musson, John Nicholas Whitaker, MA (Oxon); b. 2.10.27; m., Ann Preist (deceased 2004); 1 s.; 3 d. Educ. Clifton College; Brasenose College, Oxford. Served as Guardsman and Lt., Lancashire Fusiliers, 1945-48; HM Colonial Administrative Service (later Overseas Civil Service) 1951-59 (District Officer, N. Nigeria); British Petroleum Co., London, 1959-61; Assistant Master and Housemaster, Canford School, Dorset, 1961-72; Warden, Glenalmond College, 1972-87; Scottish Division Chairman, Headmasters' Conference, 1981-83; Scottish Director, Independent Schools Careers Organisation, 1987-93; Governor, George Watson's College, Edinburgh, 1989-98; Governor, Clifton College, Bristol, since 1989; Director and Trustee, Scottish European Aid and Mercy Corps Europe, 1996-2000; Country Director, Bosnia/Herzegovina, for Mercy Corps/Scottish European Aid, 1998-99; Vice Chairman, Mercy Corps Scotland, 2000-07. Recreations: travel; art; Egyptology; swimming. Address: (h.) 47 Spylaw Road, Edinburgh EH10 5BP; T.-0131-337 0089.

Myles, Bob. Leader, Angus Council, since 2007. Address: (h.) Dalbog, Edzell, Brechin DD9 7UU; T.-01356 648265; e-mail: cllrmyles@angus.gov.uk

Myles, David Fairlie, CBE. Hill Farmer; Member, Angus District Council, 1984-96; b. 30.5.25, Cortachy, Kirriemuir; m., Janet I. Gall; 2 s.; 2 d. Educ. Brechin High School. Auctioneer's clerk, 1941-43; Royal Marines, 1943-46; Tenant Hill Farmer, since 1946; Director of auction company, 1963-81; Member, Transport Users Consultative Committee for Scotland, 1973-79; Council Member, NFU of Scotland, 1970-79 (Convener, Organisation and Publicity Committee, 1976-79); Member, Meat Promotion Executive, MLC, 1975-79; Chairman, North Angus and Mearns

Constituency Conservative Party, 1971-74; MP (Conservative), Banff, 1979-83; Joint Secretary, Backbench Conservative Agriculture Committee, 1979-83; Secretary, Backbench Conservative European Committee, 1980-83; Member: Select Committee on Agriculture and Select Committee on European Legislation, 1979-83, North of Scotland Hydro-Electric Board, 1985-89, Angus Tourist Board, 1984-92, Potato Marketing Board, 1988-97; Dean, Guildry of Brechin, 1993-94; Lord President, Court of Deans of Scotland, 1995-96; Session Clerk, Edzell-Lethnot Parish Church, 1996-2002; Elder, Edzell-Lethnot Parish Church. Recreations: curling; traditional Scottish fiddle music; works of Robert Burns. Address: (h.) The Gorse, Dunlappie Road, Edzell, Brechin DD9 7UB; T.-01356 648207.

Myskow, Lyndsey Morag, BSc, MB, ChB, DCH, DFFP. Principal in General Practice, since 1984; Honorary Senior Lecturer, Department of General Practice, University of Edinburgh, since 1999; Associate Specialist in Psychosexual Medicine, Royal Infirmary, since 2005; b. 28.10.55, Ilford, Essex; m., Derrick Wrenn. Educ. Linlithgow Academy; Edinburgh University Medical School. Recreations: cooking; exercise; cats. Address: (h.) 8 Magdala Crescent, Edinburgh EH12 5BE; T.-0131-337 1043; e-mail: lyndsey.myskow@lothian.scot.nhs.uk

N

Nagl, Hazel Anna, RSW, RGI, PAI. Artist/Painter (still life and landscape painter with a special interest in the Scottish garden); b. 2.11.53, Glasgow; m., James Geoffrey Keanie; 1 d. Educ. Glasgow School of Art. Exhibits on a regular basis throughout Scotland; RSW, 1988; PAI, 1995; SAAC 1994; RGI Stone Prize, 1987 and 1990; RGI Mackinlay Award, 1994; RGI Eastwood Publications Award, 1994; SAAC Prize, 1994; PAI Prize 1996 and 1998; 1st Prize, Laing Competition, 1999; RGI, 2000. Address: (h.) Lawmarnock House, Troon Drive, Bridge of Weir PA11 3HF.

Nairn, Nicholas Cameron Abel. Presenter, Landward, BBC Scotland, since 2007; Chef; Proprietor: Nairns Restaurant, Glasgow, 1997-2003, Nick Nairn Cook School, Port of Menteith, since 2000; Director, Taste of Scotland, 1996-2003; b. 12.1.59, Stirling; 1 d. Educ. McLaren High School, Callander. Merchant Navy, 1976-83. Presenter: Wild Harvest, BBC2, 1996, Ready Steady Cook, BBC2, since 1996, Celebrity Ready Steady Cook, Who'll Do the Pudding, BBC2, 1996-98, Wild Harvest Two, BBC2, 1996, Island Harvest, BBC1, 1997, Kitchen Invaders, BBC2, 2001, Back to Basics, Carlton TV, 2000, Cooking with History, BBC Radio Scotland, 2000, So You Think You're a Good Driver?, 2002, Nick Nairn and the Dinner Ladies, 2003, Great British Menu, BBC, 2006; Chef/Director, Braeval Restaurant, Aberfoyle, 1986-96; Hon. President, Drambuie Scottish Chefs National Cookery Centre, 1997-99; Chef/Consultant, Tesco; Winner, Scottish Field/Charles Heidsieck Scottish Restaurant of the Year, 1990; Good Food Guide County Restaurant of the Year, 1991; Macallan/Decanter Scottish Restaurant of the Year, 1992; Scottish Field/Bowmore Restaurant of the Year, 1992; STB Thistle Award for Contribution to Tourism through the Media; Glenfiddich Award for Contribution to Food and Drink, 2002; Winner, Glenfiddich Food and Drink Award, 2004 (Best Food and Drink programme for Nick Nairn and the dinner ladies); Winner: Scottish Chef of the Year, 1996, Jacob's Creek World Food Media Award - Silver Ladle for Best Television Show (Island Harvest), 1998; Member, Advisory Board, Scottish Chefs Association; Lifetime Achievement Award, SCA; Hon. President, Chefs' School; Member, Masterchefs of GB; Food Champion Consultant for the Scottish Executive Healthy Eating Campaign; Judge, Jacob's Creek World Food Media Awards, 2001, 2003, 2005; Doctor of Stirling University, 2007, in recognition of outstanding contribution to Scottish cuisine and work in promoting healthy eating; author of several books about cooking. Recreations: cycling; wind-surfing; wine; eating out; travel; Scottish art; fly fishing. Address: (b.) Nick Nairn Enterprise, Nick Nairn Cook School, Port of Menteith, Stirling FK8 3JZ; T.-01877 389 900; e-mail: info@nairnscookschool.com

Nanjiani, Shereen, MA (Hons). Presenter, Scotland Live, BBC Radio Scotland, since 2006; Journalist, Scottish Television, 1983-2006; b. 4.10.61, Elderslie. Educ. John Neilson High School, Paisley; Glasgow University. Joined STV as a trainee journalist, 1983; moved to reporting two years later; became presenter of Scotland Today, 1985; presented election programmes; presented, Secret Scotland documentary series; presented Scottish Politician of the Year Awards.

Napier, 14th Lord, and Ettrick, 5th Baron (Francis Nigel Napier), KCVO, DL. Treasurer to Princess Margaret, Countess of Snowdon, 1998-2002 (Private Secretary, Comptroller and Equerry, 1973-98); b. 5.12.30; m.; 2 s.; 2 d. Succeeded to title, 1987.

Napier, Brian William, MA, LLB, PhD, QC. Advocate (and barrister at the English bar), since 1996; Queen's Counsel, since 2002; b. 09.01.49, Dublin, Republic of Ireland; m., Elizabeth. Educ. George Watson's College, Edinburgh; University of Edinburgh; University of Cambridge. Lecturer and Teacher of Law, Queens' College, Cambridge, 1974-89; Professor of Law, Queen Mary College, University of London, 1989-96. Recreations: walking; music. Address: (b.) c/o Faculty of Advocates, Edinburgh EH1 1RF.

Nash, Professor Andrew Samuel, BVMS, PhD, CBiol, FIBiol, DipECVIM, MRCVS. Pro Vice-Principal, University of Glasgow, since 2008, Clerk of Senate, 2002-08, Vice-Principal (Learning and Teaching), 2002-04; b. 1.8.44, Birmingham; m., Rosemary Truscott Hamilton; 1 s.; 1 d. Educ. Judd School, Tonbridge; Glasgow University. General veterinary practice, Ilfracombe, 1967-72; House Physician, Glasgow University Veterinary School, 1973-75, then Lecturer/Senior Lecturer, 1975-92; Professor of Small Animal Medicine, Division of Small Animal Clinical Studies, Department of Veterinary Clinical Studies, Glasgow University Veterinary School, since 1992; Director of the Veterinary Hospital, 1993-96; Vice-Dean for Student Affairs, 1995-99; Director, Student Support Services, 1999-2001; Senate Assessor, University Court, 1999-2002; Royal College of Veterinary Surgeons Recognised Specialist in Small Animal Medicine, 1993-2002. Silver Medal in Veterinary Clinical Medicine, 1967; RSPCA Humane Award, 1970; Member, Board of Directors, Glasgow Dog and Cat Home, 1981-95; Hon. President, Scottish Cat Club, 1990-99; Member, Glasgow Presbytery, 1991-94; President, European Society of Veterinary Nephrology and Urology, 1992-94; Member, Board of Directors, Scottish Society for the Prevention of Cruelty to Animals, 1995-2003; author of more than 100 papers, articles, book chapters. Recreations: music; gardening; DIY; church work (church organist). Address: (b.) Senate Office, University of Glasgow, Glasgow G12 8QQ; T.-0141-330 4242; e-mail: A.Nash@admin.gla.ac.uk

Nash, Professor Anthony Aubrey, BSc, MSc, PhD, FMedSci, FRSE. Professor of Veterinary Pathology, Edinburgh University, since 1994; b. 6.3.49, Coalville; m., Marion Ellen Bazeley; 4 d. Educ. Nenbridge Secondary Modern School; Queen Elizabeth College, London University. Lecturer, Department of Pathology, Cambridge University, 1984; Visiting Investigator, Scripps Research Institute, La Jolla, USA, 1989; Professor and Head, Department of Veterinary Pathology, Edinburgh University, since 1994; Director, Centre for Infectious Diseases, Edinburgh University. Eleanor Roosevelt Cancer Fellowship, 1989-90. Recreations: family; gardening; football. Address: (b.) Veterinary Pathology, Summerhall, Edinburgh EH9 1QH; T.-0131-650 6164.

Nash, Derek Andrew, LLB, DipLegPrac, NP, WS. Partner, Lindsays WS, Solicitors, since 2003; b. 18.12.64, Glasgow; m., Anne; 1 s.; 1 d. Educ. Daniel Stewart's and Melville College, Edinburgh; University of Edinburgh. Training, Balfour and Manson, Solicitors, 1987-89; Orr MacQueen WS: Assistant, 1990-92, Associate, 1992-95, Partner, 1995-99; Partner, Skene Edwards WS, 1999-2003. Trustee, Heralds Trust. Recreations: golf; family; church; books; film. Address: (b.) Caledonian Exchange, 19A Canning Street, Edinburgh EH3 8HE; T.-0131 656 5734; e-mail: dan@lindsays.co.uk

Nash, Victoria Jane, BSc, PhD. Director for Scotland, Ofcom (Office of Communications), since 2004; b. 17.6.57, Northampton; m., Robin Campbell; 2 step d. Educ. Cheadle

Hulme School; Oxford Polytechnic; Stirling University. Senior Research Officer, Scottish Office Education Department, 1982-83; Project Co-ordinator, Scottish Council for Educational Technology, 1983-85; Policy Analyst, then Assistant Chief Executive, then Chief Executive, Fife Regional Council, 1985-96; Director, Scottish Water and Sewerage Customers Council, 1996-99; Chief Executive, East Dunbartonshire Council, 1999-2004. Board Member, Scottish Ballet and Forth Valley Health Board. Recreations: running; singing; swimming; cats. Address: (b.) Sutherland House, 149 St. Vincent Street, Glasgow G2 5NW; T.-0141 229 7400; e-mail: vicki.nash@ofcom.org.uk

Naumann, Laurie M. Freelance Social Policy Adviser; Director, Scottish Council for Single Homeless, 1978-99; b. 1943, Saffron Walden; m., Barbara; 2 s.; 3 d. Educ. Edinburgh, Gloucester and Nuremberg Rudolf Steiner; Leicester University. Furniture maker, Gloucestershire; Probation and After Care Officer, Leeds; Social Worker, Edinburgh; Council of Europe Social Fellowship to Finland to study services for the drunken offender, 1976; jointly won Rosemary Delbridge Memorial Trophy for influencing Parliament to legislate, 1983; Empathy Award for helping co-operation between state and voluntary sector in Hungary, 2002; on secondment to Scottish Office Social Work Services Inspectorate, 1992-95; Vice-Chair, Kingdom Housing Association; Board Member: Garvald Edinburgh, FEAT Enterprises and Grangemouth Enterprises; Member, Social Security Advisory Committee; Trustee, Voluntary Action Fund; Member, Polmont YOI Visiting Committee; Chair: Highland Housing and Community Care Trust, Refugee Survival Trust, Consultation and Involvement Trust Scotland. Recreations: travel; reading; walking; woodwork. Address: (h.) St. Ann's, Alexander III Street, Kinghorn, Fife KY3 9SD; T.-01592 890346.

Naylor, (Charles) John, OBE, MA, CCMI, FRSA. Chief Executive, Carnegie United Kingdom Trust, 1993-2003; b. 17.8.43, Newcastle upon Tyne; m., Margery Thomson; 2 s. Educ. Royal Grammar School, Newcastle upon Tyne; Clare College, Cambridge University. Director, YMCA National Centre, Lakeside, Cumbria, 1975-80; National Council of YMCAs: Deputy Secretary, 1980-82, National Secretary, 1982-93. Member and Chairman, YMCA European and World Committees, 1976-92; Chair, Association of Heads of Outdoor Education Centres, 1979-80; Chair, MSC and DES Working Party on Residential Experience and Unemployment, 1980-81; Member, National Advisory Council for Youth Service, 1985-88; Vice-Chairman, National Council for Voluntary Youth Services, 1985-88; Founding Convener, Scottish Grant-making Trusts' Group, 1994-97; Chairman, Brathay Exploration Group, 1995-2000, Trustee, 2000-06; Group Scout Leader, 82nd Inverleith (Cramond) Scouts, 1996-2003; Member, Development Grants Board, Scout Association (UK), since 2002, Chairman, since 2005; Member, Scottish Charity Law Review Commission, 2000-01; Big Lottery Fund (BLF) UK Board Member, 2004-06, Chair, Office of the Scottish Charity Regulator, 2006; Medical Research Scotland Board Member, 2005; Chair, BLF Voluntary and Community Funding Programme Scotland Committee; Chairman, BLF Scotland Young Peoples Fund; Treasurer and Trustee, The Tomorrow Project, since 2002. Publications: Guide to Scottish Grant-making Trusts; Writing Better Fund Raising Applications (Contributor); Charity Law and Change: British and German Perspectives (Contributor); contributions to other books and periodicals. Address: (b.) Orchard House, 25B Cramond Glebe Road, Edinburgh EH4 6NT; T.-0131 312 8956.

Neil, Alex., MA (Hons). MSP (SNP), Central Scotland, since 1999 (Co-Convener, European Committee; Convener,

Enterprise and Culture Committee, 2004-07, Chairman, Enterprise and Lifelong Learning Committee, 2000-03); Economic Consultant; b. 22.8.51, Irvine; m., Isabella Kerr; 1 s. Educ. Dalmellington High School; Ayr Academy; Dundee University. Scottish Research Officer, Labour Party, 1975; General Secretary, Scottish Labour Party (SLP), 1976; Marketing Manager, 1979-83; Director: Cumnock and Doon Enterprise Trust, 1983-87, Prince's Scottish Youth Business Trust, 1987-89; Chairman, Network Scotland Ltd., 1987-93; Policy Vice-Convener, Scottish National Party, 1994-2000. Recreations: family; reading; gardening; travel. Address: (h.) 26 Overmills Road, Ayr KA7 3LQ; T.-01292 286675.

Neil, Andrew Ferguson, MA (Hons), FRSA. Publisher, The Scotsman, Scotland on Sunday, Edinburgh Evening News, Scotsman.com, 1996-2006; Chief Executive: The Business, since 1999, The Spectator, since 2004, handbag.com, 2004-06; Presenter: This Week with Andrew Neil, BBC1, The Daily Politics, BBC2, Straight Talk, BBC News 24; Chairman: World Media Rights, since 2005, ITP Dubai, since 2006; Lord Rector, University of St. Andrews, 1999-2002; b. 21.5.49. Educ. Paisley Grammar School; Glasgow University. Conservative Research Department, 1971-72; Correspondent in Belfast, London, Washington, New York, for The Economist, 1973-82,UK Editor, London, 1982-83; Editor, Sunday Times, 1983-94; Chairman, Sky TV, 1988-90; Executive Editor, Fox News, New York, 1994; author of Full Disclosure (autobiography). Address: (b.) Glenburn Enterprises, PO Box 584, London SW7 3QY; T.-020 7581 1655; e-mail: afneil@aol.com

Neill, Gordon Webster McCash, DSO, SSC, FInstD. Solicitor and Notary Public; Honorary Sheriff; b. Arbroath; m., Margaret Mary Lamb; 1 s.; 1 d. Educ. Edinburgh Academy. Legal apprenticeship, 1937-39; Pilot, RAF, 1939-46 (DSO, French Croix de Guerres with silver gilt star and silver star); Partner, Neill & Gibb, SSC, 1947; Chairman, Dundee Area Board, British Law Insurance Co. Ltd., 1954; Principal, Neill & Mackintosh, SSC, 1967-89; Consultant, Thorntons WS, 1989-94; Past Chairman, Scottish Gliding Association and Angus Gliding Club Ltd.; Past President, Chamber of Commerce, Arbroath Rotary Club and Society of Solicitors and Procurators in Angus. Recreations: golf; walking; fishing. Address: (h.) 29 Duncan Avenue, Arbroath, Angus DD11 2DA; T.-01241 872221.

Neill, William Wilson, MA (Hons). Poet; b. 22.2.22, Prestwick; m., Doris Marie; 2 d. (by pr. m.). Educ. Ayr Academy; Edinburgh University. Served, RAF; won Sloane Verse Prize and Grierson Verse Prize while at Edinburgh University; Teacher; crowned Bard, Aviemore Mod, 1969; former Editor, Catalyst; former Editor, Lallans (Scots Language magazine); SAC Book Award, 1985; broadcasts, essays in Scotland's three tongues. Publications: Scotland's Castle, 1969; Poems, 1970; Four Points of a Saltire (Co-author), 1970; Despatches Home, 1972; Buile Shuibhne, 1974; Galloway Landscape: Poems, 1981; Cnu a Mogaill: Poems, 1983; Wild Places: Poems, 1985; Blossom, Berry, Fall: Poems 1986; Making Tracks: Poems, 1988; Straight Lines, 1992; Tales frae the Odyssey, 1992; Selected Poems, 1994; Tidsler, 1998; Stagioni, 1999; Caledonian Cramboclink, 2001; many poems in Gaelic, Scots and English magazines. Address: (h.) Burnside, Crossmichael, Castle Douglas DG7 3AP; T.-01556 670265.

Neilly, Gordon Joseph, BCom, CA. Chairman, Intelli Corporate Finance Limited, since 1999; b. 2.7.60, Irvine; spouse, Alison; 2 d. Educ. Auchenharvie Academy, Stevenston; Edinburgh University. Thomson McLintock

& Co., 1981-84; Ivory & Sime plc, 1984-97, latterly as Director Business Development; Partner, RMD Group plc, 1997-99 (sold to Deloitte & Touche, 1999, and rebranded Intelli). Scottish Finance Director of the Year, 1992; Scottish Corporate Financier of the Year, 1999. Recreations: driving; travelling; all sports. Address: (b.) 29 Rutland Square, Edinburgh, EH1 2BW; T.-0131-222 9400.

Neilson, Margaret Marion, MA (Hons), LLB, DipLP. Part-time Sheriff; Part-time Immigration Judge; Part-time Employment Judge; Part-time Chairman, Appeals Service Tribunals; formerly Partner, Balfour & Manson; b. Falkirk. Educ. Mary Erskine School, Edinburgh; Edinburgh University. Recreations: scuba diving; travel; hillwalking.

Nelson, Donald Bruce, BSc, MBA, PhD, FCMI. Academic Registrar and Deputy Secretary, University of Edinburgh, since 2004; b. 9.8.58, Stranraer; m., Christine Diane Thorburn; 1 s.; 1 d. Educ. Stranraer Academy; University of Glasgow; University of Edinburgh. HM Inspector of Taxes, 1983-84; University of Edinburgh: Administrative Officer, 1984-88, Faculty Officer, Faculty of Veterinary Medicine, 1988-90, Faculty Group Officer, Faculty of Science and Engineering, 1990-98, Director of Planning, 1998-2003, Director of Planning and Deputy Secretary, 2003-04; Director, Edinburgh University Press, 2001-03. Chairman, Edinburgh South Liberal Association, 1986-88; Treasurer, Edinburgh South Liberal Democrats, 1988-91; Member, The Association of University Teachers Administrative Staff Committee, 1991-97/Chairperson, 1994-97; Member, Association of University Administrators Executive Committee, since 2003/Vice-Chair and Chair-Elect, 2005-06/Chair, 2006-08; Member, Higher Education Senior Managers Forum, since 2006; Non-Executive Board Member, Student Awards Agency Scotland, 2007-10. Awarded Robbie Ewen Fellowship for University Administrators, 1997. Recreations: reading; listening to classical music; Stranraer Football Club. Address: (h.) 47 Beauchamp Road, Edinburgh EH16 6LU; T.-0131-664 3020; e-mail: d.b.nelson@ed.ac.uk

Nelson, (Peter) Frederick, BSc, CEng, MIEE. Electrical Systems Manager, RWE npower Technical Services Scotland; Chairman, Scottish Outdoor Recreation Network, since 2000; b. 2.9.52, Glasgow; m., (Caroline) Ann; 3 s. Educ. John Neilson; Strathclyde University. President, Scottish Canoe Association, 1980-90; Member, Commonwealth Games Council for Scotland, since 1982; Chairman, Scottish Sports Association, 1990-96; Member, Scottish Sports Council, 1990-98; Elder, Davidson's Mains Parish Church. Recreations: canoeing; cycling; DIY. Address: (h.) 11 Barnton Park Place, Edinburgh EH4 6ET.

Ness, James Iain, LLB, NP. Solicitor; Deputy Director, Professional Practice, Law Society of Scotland, since 2004; b. 5.7.57, Johannesburg; 1 s.; 1 d. Educ. Robert Gordon's, Aberdeen; Edinburgh University. Apprenticed, Connell & Connell, Edinburgh; Assistant, then Partner, then Senior Partner, Austins. Past President, Rotary Club of Dalbeattie; Board Member, Lawcare. Recreation: skiing. Address: (b.) 26 Drumsheugh Gardens, Edinburgh; T.-0131 226 7411.

Newall, Stephen Park, DL, Hon. LLD (Strathclyde). Deputy Lieutenant, Dunbartonshire, since 1985; b. 12.4.31, Bearsden, Dunbartonshire; m., Gay Sommerville Craig; 4 s.; 1 d. Educ. Loretto. Commissioned and served with Parachute Regiment, National Service, 1949-51; Sales Manager, A.P. Newall & Co., 1951-57; Managing Director, Bulten-Kanthal Stephen Newall Co. Ltd., 1957-80. Chairman: Epilepsy Association of Scotland, 1982-86; Finance Committee, University of Strathclyde, 1985-88; Council Member: Quarrier's Homes, 1983-88, Scottish Business School, 1983-85; Secretary of State for Scotland's Nominee on Court of Cranfield, 1985-92; Deacon Convener, Trades of Glasgow, 1983-84; Chairman, Court,

University of Strathclyde, 1988-93; Patron, University of Strathclyde Senior Studies Learning in Later Life, 2001-06. Recreations: farming; hill-walking; sailing; music. Address: (h.) Birchfield, East Burnside, Dollar, Clackmannanshire FK14 7AT; T.-01259 740106.

Newell, Professor Alan F., MBE, BSc, PhD, FIEE, CEng, FBCS, FRSE, ILTM, HonFCSLT. NCR Professor of Electronics and Microcomputer Systems, Dundee University, since 1980; Director, Dundee University Microcomputer Centre, since 1980; (Head, Department of Applied Computing, 1997-2002, Deputy Principal, 1993-95); Academic Leader, Queen Mother Research Centre for Information Technology to support older people, since 2003; b. 1.3.41, Birmingham; m., Margaret; 1 s.; 2 d. Educ. St. Philip's Grammar School; Birmingham University. Research Engineer, Standard Telecommunication Laboratories; Lecturer, Department of Electronics, Southampton University. Recreations: family life; skiing; sailing. Address: (b.) School of Computing, Dundee University, Dundee, DD1 4HN; T.-01382 384144.

Newlands, Rev. Professor George McLeod, MA, BD, PhD, DLitt, FRSA. Professor of Divinity, Glasgow University, 1986-2008; Principal, Trinity College, 1991-97, 2001-07; Dean, Faculty of Divinity, 1988-90; 12.7.41, Perth; m., Mary Elizabeth Wallace; 3 s. Educ. Perth Academy; Edinburgh University; Heidelberg University; Churchill College, Cambridge. Assistant Minister, Muirhouse, Edinburgh, 1969; Lecturer in Divinity, Glasgow University, 1969; University Lecturer in Divinity, Cambridge, 1973; Dean, Trinity Hall, Cambridge, 1982. Convener, Panel on Doctrine, Church of Scotland, 1995-99; Chairman, RAE 2008 Theology and Religious Studies. Publications: Hilary of Poitiers; Theology of the Love of God; The Church of God; Making Christian Decisions; God in Christian Perspective; Generosity and the Christian Future; John and Donald Baillie; The Transformative Imagination; Fifty Key Christian Thinkers; Traces of Liberality; Christ and Human Rights; Believing in the Text, Faith and Human Rights, The God of Love and Human Dignity: (Essays for George Newlands). Recreations: walking; music. Address: (b.) Faculty of Divinity, 4 The Square, Glasgow University, Glasgow G12 8QQ; e-mail: G.Newlands@arts.gla.ac.uk

Newlands, James Nichol, HNC, DipTechEd. Honorary Sheriff at Selkirk, since 1999; b. 20.11.37, Selkirk; m., Esther; 1 s.; 1 d. Educ. Selkirk High School; Napier University; Moray House College. Engineering Apprenticeship, 1952-58; National Service, KOSB, 1958-60; Engineering Industry, 1960-67; Lecturer, Galashiels College of FE, 1967-69; Teacher Training, Moray House, 1969-71; Teacher of Technical Education, Galashiels Academy, 1971-86; Principal Teacher of Technical Education, Selkirk High School, 1986-96; retired, 1996; Selkirk Provost, 1997-2001. Deacon of The Selkirk Incorporation of Hammermen, 1983-89, now a Life Member; serving on The Selkirk Silver Band Committee; served as a Reader on "The Borders Talking Newspaper" for 12 years, one of the founding members but now retired. Delivered the Address at The Redeswire Stone, Carter Bar, 2002; gave The Flodden Oration on Flodden Hill, 1999; delivered The Melrose Oration in Melrose Abbey, 2003; also The Trysten Tree Address in Kelso, 2004. Publications: author of "The History of The Selkirk Hammermen"; co-author of "The Flower of The Forest". Recreation: rugby supporter (captained Selkirk RFC, 1960-61). Address: (h.) 5 Mavis Bank, Selkirk TD7 4EA; T.-01750 20492.

Newman, Professor Simon Peter, BA, MA, MA, PhD, FRSA, FRHistS. Sir Denis Brogan Professor of American Studies, University of Glasgow, since 2002; Chairman, British Association for American Studies; b. 8.7.60, Basildon; m., Marina Moskowitz. Educ. St. Joseph's College, Ipswich; University of Nottingham; University of

Wisconsin; Princeton University. Assistant Professor of History, Northern Illinois University, 1991-97; Mellon Postdoctoral Fellow in the Humanities, University of Pennsylvania, 1994-95; Senior Lecturer in History, University of Glasgow, 1997-2002; Director, Andrew Hook Centre for American Studies, University of Glasgow, 1997-2002; Chairman, British Association for American Studies, since 2004. Philip A. Rollins Fellowship in History, Princeton University, 1989-90; Mellon Postdoctoral Fellowship in the Humanities, University of Pennsylvania, 1994-95; Resident Fellowship, Rockefeller Study and Conference Center, Bellagio, Italy, 1998; Coca Cola Fellowship, International Center for Jefferson Studies, Monticelle, Virginia, 2000; Member, Executive Committee, British Association for American Studies, 1999-2006; Chair, Scottish Association for the Study of America, 2001-03. Publications: Vue D'Amérique: La Révolution Française Jugée Par Les Américains (Co-editor), 1989; Parades and the Politics of the Street: Festive Culture in the Early American Republic, 1997; Embodied History: The Lives of the Poor in Early Philadelphia, 2003. Clubs: Reform Club. Recreations: long distance and cross country running; cooking. Address: (b.) Modern History, 1 University Gardens, University of Glasgow, Glasgow G12 8QQ; T.-0141-330 3585; e-mail:spn@arts.gla.ac.uk

Newton, Catriona Jane, BA, MA, FRSA. Director of Collection Development, National Library of Scotland, since 2003; b. 29.7.51, Glasgow; m., Professor Kenneth McMillan Newton; 1 s.; 2 d. Educ. Birkenhead High School; University College London; University of Sheffield. University of Liverpool, 1972-73; University of Dundee, 1974-79; University of St. Andrews, 1979-2000; National Library of Scotland, since 2000. Address: (b.) National Library of Scotland, George IV Bridge, Edinburgh EH1 1EW; T.-0131 623 3740; e-mail: c.newton@nls.uk

Ni, Professor Xiongwei, BSc, PhD, CEng, FIChemE, Professor of Process and Reaction Engineering, Heriot-Watt University, since 1999; b. 22.2.60, Beijing, China; m., Wendy Margaret Hogg; 1s.; 1d. Educ. Yan-Ting Primary and High School, Sichuan China; Chong-Qing University, Sichuan; Leeds University. Research Fellow, Edinburgh University, 1986-89; Research Associate, Cambridge University, 1989-91; Lecturer, Teeside University, 1991-94; Strathclyde University: Lecturer, 1994-96; Senior Lecturer, 1996-97; Senior Lecturer, Heriot-Watt University, 1997-99; Foxwell Memorial Award, Institute of Energy, 1985. Recreations: tennis; badminton; golf; bridge. Address: (b.) School of Engineering and Physical Sciences, Heriot-Watt University, Edinburgh, EH14 4AS; T.-0131-451 3781; e-mail: X.Ni@hw.ac.uk

Nicholls, Brian, BSc (Econ). Senior Business Consultant, Scottish Enterprise, 1991-98; Director, Scottish Opera, 1993-99; b. 21.9.28, London; m., Mary Elizabeth Harley; 1 s.; 2 d. Educ. Haberdashers' Aske's School; London University; Harvard Business School. George Wimpey Ltd., 1951-55; Constructors John Brown Ltd., 1955-75; Director, CJB Projects Ltd., 1972-75; Director, CJB Pipelines Ltd., 1974-75; Deputy Chairman, CJB Mohandessi Iran Ltd., 1974-75; Industrial Adviser to Secretary of State for Trade, 1975-78; Director: John Brown Engineering Ltd., 1978-91, John Brown Engineering Gas Turbines Ltd., 1978-91, Rugby Power Company Ltd., 1990-91; Vice President, John Brown Power Ltd., 1987-90; Member: Council, British Railway Export Group, 1976-78, British Overseas Trade Board, 1978; Vice Chairman, Scottish Council Development and Industry, 1991-98; Fellow, Scottish Council Development and Industry, 1998. Publications: Columnist for Jazz Journal, 1952-58; Editor: Jazz News, 1957-59. Deputy Chairman, National Jazz Federation, 1954-59.

Recreations: music; reading; walking. Address: (h.) Blairlogie Park, Blairlogie, by Stirling FK9 5PY; T.-01259 761497.

Nicholson, Sheriff Principal (Charles) Gordon (Brown), CBE, QC, MA, LLB. Temporary Judge of the Court of Session and High Court of Justiciary, since 2002; Sheriff Principal of Lothian and Borders, 1990-2002; b. 11.9.35, Edinburgh; m., Hazel Mary Nixon; 2 s. Educ. George Watson's College, Edinburgh; Edinburgh University. Admitted to Faculty of Advocates, 1961; Advocate Depute, 1968-70; Sheriff of Dumfries and Galloway, at Dumfries, 1970-76; Sheriff of Lothian and Borders, at Edinburgh, 1976-82; Honorary President, Victim Support Scotland, 1989-2005; Commissioner, Scottish Law Commission, 1982-89; Commissioner, Northern Lighthouse Board, 1990-2002 (Chairman, 1994-95). Publication: The Law and Practice of Sentencing in Scotland, 1981 (2nd edition, 1992); Sheriff Court Practice (Joint Editor) (2nd edition, 1998). Recreation: music. Address: (h.) Back O'Redfern, 24C Colinton Road, Edinburgh EH10 5EQ; T.-0131-447 4300; e-mail: g.nicholson199@btinternet.com

Nicholson, Professor Colin, BA. Professor of 18th Century and Modern Literature, University of Edinburgh, since 2000; b. 2.10.44, Wolverhampton; m., Elizabeth Wickes; 2 s.; 1 d. Educ. St. Chad's College; Leeds University. English Literature Department, University of Edinburgh: Lecturer, 1972, Senior Lecturer, 1990, Reader, 1994. Publications: Poem, Purpose and Place, 1992; Writing and the Rise of Finance, 1994; Edwin Morgan: Inventions of Modernity, 2002. Recreations: cycling; birdwatching. Address: (h.) 123 Trinity Road, Edinburgh EH5 3LB; T.-0131-552 3841; e-mail: elicens@staffmail.ed.ac.uk

Nicholson, Peter Alexander, LLB (Hons). Editor, Journal of the Law Society of Scotland, since 2004; Deputy Editor, 2003-04; Managing Editor, W. Green, The Scottish Law Publisher, 1989-2003; General Editor, Scots Law Times, 1985-2003; Scottish Editor, Current Law, 1985-96; General Editor, Greens Weekly Digest, 1986-2003; b. 22.5.58, Stirling; m., Morag Ann Fraser; 1 s.; 3 d. Educ. St. David's RC High School, Dalkeith; Edinburgh University. Admitted as Solicitor, 1981. Reporter and committee member, Client Relations Office, Law Society of Scotland. Lay Minister of the Eucharist. Recreations: choral singing; gardening; keeping fit. Address: (h.) 1 Frogston Gardens, Edinburgh EH10 7AF; T.-0131-445 1570.

Nicholson, Peter Duncan. Group Head of Human Resources, John Wood Group plc, since 2002; b. 22.06.56, Aberdeen; m., Dawn; 1 s.; 2 d. Educ. Robert Gordon's College, Aberdeen; Aberdeen College of Commerce. Apprentice Chartered Accountant, James Henry Reid, 1976-77; Bank Officer, Clydesdale Bank Ltd., 1977-80; District Accountant, Baker Production Services Ltd., 1980-82; Financial Accountant, Hunting Drilltech Ltd., 1982-85; Eastern Region Materials Manager, Eastman Teleco, 1985-93; Director, Human Resources, Baker Hughes Inteq, 1993-96; VP Human Resources, Smith International Inc (based in Houston, Texas), 1996-2002. Chairman, Scottish Business in the Community, Grampian; Non Executive Director: Scottish Business in the Community, Cornerstone Community Care. Recreations: golf; football; music; reading; war gaming. Address: (b.) John Wood House, Greenwell Road, Aberdeen AB12 3AX; T.-01224-851000; e-mail: peter.nicholson@woodgroup.com

Nickson of Renagour, Lord (David Wigley Nickson), KBE (1987), CBE (1981), DL, CBIM, FRSE. Life Peer; Chancellor, Glasgow Caledonian University, 1993-2002;

Vice Lieutenant, Stirling and Falkirk, 1997-2004 (Deputy Lieutenant, 1982-97);b. 27.11.29, Eton; m., Helen Louise Cockcraft; 3 d. Educ. Eton College; Royal Military Academy, Sandhurst. Commissioned, Coldstream Guards, 1949-54; William Collins: joined, 1954, Director, 1961-85, Joint Managing Director, 1967, Vice-Chairman, 1976-83, Group Managing Director, 1979-82; Director: Scottish United Investors plc, 1970-83, General Accident plc, 1971-98 (Deputy Chairman, 1993-98), Scottish & Newcastle Breweries plc, 1981-95 (Chairman, 1983-89), Radio Clyde Ltd., 1982-85, National Australia Bank Ltd., 1991-96, National Australian Group (UK) Ltd., 1993-98, Hambros PLC, 1989-98; Chairman, Clydesdale Bank, 1991-98 (Director, 1981-98); Chairman, Pan Books, 1982-83; Chairman, Scottish Enterprise, 1990-93 (SDA, 1988-90); President, CBI, 1986-88; Chairman, CBI in Scotland, 1979-81; Chairman, Countryside Commission for Scotland, 1983-86; Member: Scottish Industrial Development Advisory Board, 1975-80, Scottish Committee, Design Council, 1978-81, Scottish Economic Council, 1980-95, National Economic Development Council, 1985-88; Chairman, Atlantic Salmon Trust, 1988-95; Chairman, Senior Salaries Review Body, 1989-95; President, Association of District Salmon Fisheries Board, since 1996; Chairman, Secretary of State for Scotland's Scottish Salmon Strategy Task Force, 1995-97; Chairman, Scottish Advisory Committee, Imperial Cancer Research Fund, 1994-2001; Trustee: Princes Youth Business Trust, 1987-90, Princess Royal's Trust for Carers, 1990-94; Director, Countryside Alliance, 1998-2000; Captain of Queen's Bodyguard for Scotland (Royal Company of Archers); D.Univ, Stirling, 1986; Hon. DBA Napier Polytechnic, 1990; Honorary Fellow, Paisley College, 1992; Honorary Freeman, Fishmongers Company, 1999, Honorary Freeman, City of London, 1999. Recreations: fishing; bird-watching; the countryside. Address: (h.) The River House, Doune, Perthshire FK16 6DA; T.-01786 841614.

Nicol, Rev. Douglas Alexander Oag, MA, BD (Hons). Secretary, Church of Scotland Mission and Discipleship Council; b. 5.4.48, Dunfermline; m., Anne Wilson Gillespie; 2 s.; 1 d. Educ. Kirkcaldy High School; Edinburgh University; Glasgow University. Assistant Warden, St. Ninian's Centre, Crieff, 1972-76; Minister, Lochside, Dumfries, 1976-82; Minister, St. Columba, Kilmacolm, 1982-91. Chairman, Board of Directors, National Bible Society of Scotland, 1984-87; Convener, Board of National Mission, Church of Scotland, 1990-91; General Secretary, Church of Scotland Board of National Mission, 1991-2005. Recreations: family life and family history; travel; athletics. Address: (h.) 24 Corbiehill Avenue, Blackhall, Edinburgh EH4 5DR; T.-0131-336 1965.

Nicoll, Alan John, LLB, NP. Senior Partner, Laurie and Company Solicitors LLP, since 2002; b. 28.7.55, Aberdeen; m., Carole Jane Burtt; 2 s.; 2 d. Educ. Robert Gordon's College; University of Aberdeen. Served Apprenticeship at AC Morrison & Richards, 1976-78; Employed as Solicitor, Edmonds & Ledingham, 1978-80; Employed by John Laurie & Co, 1980-81, became a Partner in 1981. Chairman, Aberdeen Grammar School, School Board. Recreations: tennis; golf; skiing; hillwalking. Address: (b.) 17 Victoria Street, Aberdeen AB10 1UU; T.-01224 645085; e-mail: alan@laurieandco.co.uk

Nicoll, Andrew Ramsay, MA (Hons), MPhil, GradDipARM, RMSA. Keeper of The Scottish Catholic Archives, since 2003; b. 2.5.78, Dundee. Educ. Forfar Academy; University of Dundee; University College London. Address: (b.) Columba House, 16 Drummond Place, Edinburgh EH3 6PL; T.-0131 556 3661.

Nicolson, David M., CA. Chairman, Edinburgh City Centre Management Co.; Trustee Royal Botanic Gardens, Edinburgh; Vice Chairman, Quality Meat Scotland; b.

22.4.42, Edinburgh; m., Elizabeth Finlay Smith; 1 s.; 1 d. Educ. Royal High School, Edinburgh. Qualified as CA with Robertson & Maxtone Graham, Edinburgh, 1964; Peat Marwick Mitchell & Co., London, 1964-67; Partner, KPMG Edinburgh, 1968-97 (Managing Partner, 1988-96); Director, KPMG Asia Pacific, 1997-99. President: Edinburgh Junior Chamber of Commerce, 1975-76, Edinburgh Chamber of Commerce and Enterprise, 1994-96; former Member of Council, Institute of Chartered Accountants of Scotland. Recreations: golf; skiing; gardening. Address: (h.) Cluan House, Dunira, Comrie, Perthshire PH6 2JY; T.-01764 670849; e-mail: david.nicolson3@btinternet.com

Nicolson, Professor Donald James, BA, LLB, PhD. Professor of Law, Strathclyde University, since 2001; b. 1.6.61, Cape Town. Educ. Fish Hoek High School; University of Cape Town; Cambridge University. Temporary Lecturer, University of Cape Town, 1984; Lecturer, Reading University, 1989-92; Lecturer, Bristol University, 1992-2000. Publications: Professional Legal Ethics: Critical Interrogations, 1999; Feminist Perspectives on Criminal Law, 2000. Recreations: skiing; surfing; cycling; jazz; literature. Address: (b.) School of Law, Strathclyde University, 173 Stenhouse Building, 173 Cathedral Street, Glasgow G64 0RQ; T.-0141-548 3978.

Nicolson, John Alick (Jan); b. 26.9.45, Inverness; m., Effie; 1 s. Educ. Portree High School. Chairman, Skye and Lochalsh Enterprise, 1991-96; Board Member, Highlands and Islands Enterprise, 1996-98; Chairman, Hi-Screen Ltd., 1997-98; Director: Jansvans Ltd., Isle of Skye Renewables; Principal Partner, Jansport; Founder Member and Past Chairman, Isle of Skye Round Table. Recreations: collecting vintage vehicles. Address: (h.) Almondbank, Viewfield Road, Portree, Isle of Skye IV51 9EU; T.-01478 612696.

Nimmo, Rev. Peter William, BD, ThM. Minister of Old High St. Stephen's Parish Church, Inverness, since 2004; b. 19.1.66, Dumbarton; m., Katharina; 1 s.; 1 d. Educ. Vale of Leven Academy, Alexandria; Glasgow University; Princeton Theological Seminary, NJ, USA. Associate Minister, Currie Kirk, Edinburgh, 1996-98; Minister of High Carntyne Parish Church, Glasgow, 1998-2004. Address: 24 Damfield Road, Inverness IV2 3HU.

Nimmo, William, CBE, BArch, RIBA, FRIAS, FRSA. Senior Partner, William Nimmo & Partners, 1956-98, Consultant, since 1998; b. 1.4.29; m., Mae Morrison Hannah; 3 s.; 1 d. Educ. Wishaw High School; Mackintosh School of Architecture. Commissioned, Corps of Royal Engineers, 1954-55. Chairman, Braidwood Properties Ltd. Recreations: hill-walking; touring UK and Europe. Address: (h.) Auchenglen House, Braidwood, Carluke ML8 5PH; T.-01555 772021.

Nimmo Smith, Rt. Hon. Lord (William Austin Nimmo Smith), BA, LLB. Senator of the College of Justice, since 1996; b. 6.11.42, Edinburgh; m., Dr. Jennifer Nimmo Smith; 1 s.; 1 d. Educ. Eton; Balliol College, Oxford; Edinburgh University. Advocate, 1969; Standing Junior Counsel, Department of Employment, 1977-82; QC, 1982; Advocate Depute, 1983-86; Chairman, Medical Appeal Tribunals and Vaccine Damage Tribunals, 1986-91; part-time Member, Scottish Law Commission, 1988-96; Temporary Judge, Court of Session, 1995-96; Outer House, Court of Session, 1996-2005; Inner House, First Division, Court of Session, since 2005; Privy Counsellor, 2005; Chairman of Council, Cockburn Association (Edinburgh

Civic Trust), 1996-2001. Recreations: mountaineering; music. Address: (b.) Parliament House, Edinburgh EH1 1RQ.

Nisbet, James Barry Consitt, LLB. Stipendiary Magistrate, Glasgow, 1984-2007; b. 26.7.42, Forfar; m., Elizabeth McKenzie; 2 d. Educ. Forfar Academy; Edinburgh University. Legal Assistant, Warden Bruce & Co., WS, Edinburgh, 1967-68; Legal Assistant, then Junior Depute Town Clerk, then Depute Town Clerk, Perth City Council, 1968-75; Senior Depute Director of Administration, Perth and Kinross District Council, 1975-84. Head Server, St. Ninian's Episcopal Cathedral, Perth; Secretary-General, Scottish Guild of Servers. Recreations: transport, especially railways and tramways; archaeology; music; foreign travel; genealogy. Address: (b.) 12 Pitcullen Terrace, Perth PH2 7EQ.

Nisbet, Mary Sylvia. Secretary, Edinburgh Consumer Group, 1977-2002; Chairman, Morningside Community Council, 1995-2001; b. 28.7.37, Hampstead Heath, London; m., 1, Richard Cruickshanks Paterson (deceased); 2 s.; 2, James Bruce Hay Nisbet. Educ. Hornsey High School, London. Westminster Bank Ltd., 1954-55; GPO Continental Telephone Exchange, 1955-56; Scottish Widows Fund, 1957-61; freelance market research. Member, Edinburgh CAB Executive Committee, several years; Member, Post Officers Users' Council for Scotland, 1976-82; Member, Scottish Committee, Meat and Livestock Commission, 1990-95; Member, Executive, National Federation of Consumer Groups, 1992-97; Research/Survey work, Edinburgh Airport, 1982-98. Recreations: music; walking; crosswords. Address: (h.) 4/6 Belhaven Place, Edinburgh EH10 5JN; T.-0131-447 4148; e-mail: Brucemary.Nisbet@tesco.net

Nish, David. Group Finance Director, Standard Life plc; Non Executive Director, Northern Foods; b. 5.5.60, Glasgow; m., Caroline; 1 s.; 1 d. Educ. Paisley Grammar School; Glasgow University. Price Waterhouse: Graduate Trainee to Senior Manager, 1981-93, Partner, 1993-97; Deputy Finance Director, Scottish Power, 1997-99, Finance Director, 1999-2005, Executive Director, Infrostructure Division, 2005. Director, Royal Scottish National Orchestra. Recreations: trekking; golf; family; rugby.

Niven, Catharine, BSc, AMA, FSA(Scot). Curator, Inverness Museum and Art Gallery, since 1984; b. 23.9.52, Denbigh; m., Roger Niven. Educ. Loughton High School; Leicester University. Freelance archaeologist, working in Britain and Scandinavia; Keeper of Antiquities, Rotherham Museum, 1979-81; Assistant Curator (Archaeology), Inverness Museum and Art Gallery, 1981-84. Recreation: music. Address: (b.) Castle Wynd, Inverness IV2 3ED; T.-01463 237114.

Niven, Professor Catherine Ann (Kate), RGN, BScPsychol, PhD. Professor of Nursing and Midwifery Studies, Stirling University, since 1996; Director, The Chief Scientist's Unit for Nursing, Midwifery and Allied Health Professions Research, since 2000; b. 26.8.45 m.; 1 s.; 1 d. Educ. Notre Dame High School, Glasgow; Stirling University. Clinical posts in acute medicine and geriatrics, 1966-75; Teaching Assistant, Stirling University, 1980; Lecturer, Department of Psychology, Glasgow Polytechnic/Glasgow Caledonian University, 1983; Reader, 1993. Publications: Psychological Care for Families; The Health Psychology of Women (Co-Author); The Psychology of Reproduction, three volume series (Co-Author); numerous scientific papers. Recreations: gardening; having fun. Address: (b.) Iris

Murdoch Building, University of Stirling, Stirling FK9 4LA; T.-01786 466341.

Noakes, Rab. Director, Neon Productions Limited, since 1995; b. 13.5.47, St. Andrews; m., Stephanie Pordage. Educ. Bell Baxter Senior High School, Cupar, Fife. Minor Civil Service career in the MPNI working in Glasgow, Alloa and London, 1963-67; various labouring jobs including Flying Carpet Servicer, Guardbridge Paper Mill, 1967-69; in 1969 a summer of music residency in Denmark kick-started the ability to make a living from performing, writing, production and recording which continues to this day (15 albums and many songs recorded); in 1987 a contract with BBC culminated in the position of Head of Entertainment at BBC Radio Scotland; since setting up Neon Productions in 1995 thousands of hours have been provided for broadcast on radio and TV including a weekly show, Brand New Country, for BBC Radio Scotland; the company is also a record company and engages in music publishing. Council Member, SAC; Executive Committee, MU. Address: (b.) Studio Two, 19 Marine Crescent, Glasgow G51 1HD; T.-0141 429 6366; e-mail: mail@go2neon.com

Noble (or Nobail), Sir Iain, Bt. of Ardkinglas and Eilean Iarmain, OBE, MA. Entrepreneur and businessman; Founder and Chairman, Pràban na Linne Ltd ("The Gaelic Whiskies"), since 1979; Proprietor, Fearann Eilean Iarmain (estate management, Isle of Skye), since 1972; Chairman, Sir Iain Noble & Partners Ltd., Edinburgh; b. 8.9.35, Berlin. Educ. in China, Argentina and England; University College, Oxford. Scottish Council (Development and Industry), 1964-69; Co-founder and Joint Managing Director, Noble Grossart Ltd., Edinburgh, 1969-72; Founder and Chairman: Seaforth Maritime PLC, Aberdeen, 1972-77, Noble Group Ltd (Merchant Bankers), Edinburgh, 1980-2000; Founder and Director: Adam and Company plc, 1983-94; Director; Premium Trust PLC, 1993-2002; Chairman, Skye Bridge Ltd., 1994-96; Member, Edinburgh University Court, 1970-73; Founder, first Chairman and Trustee, Gaelic College of Sabhal Mor Ostaig, Skye, 1975-85; Trustee: National Museums of Scotland, 1986-90, NMS Charitable Trust, since 1990; Scotsman of the Year Award, 1982 (Knights Templar); President, Saltire Society, 1993-96; Founder and Chairman, Scots Australian Council, 1990-99; Keeper of the Quaich, since 2000; writer and lecturer on various topics. Editor, Sources of Finance, 1967-69; other interests: conservation; Gaelic traditions and music; cultural heritage; architecture; community development; Scottish politics. Recreations: deasbad, comhradh, orain is ceol le deagh chompanaich. Address: An Oifig, Eilean Iarmain, An t-Eilean Sgitheanach, IV43 8QR; T.-01471 833 266; 20 Great Stuart Street, Edinburgh EH3 7TN; T.-0131-220 2400; e-mail: Sir.Iain@eilean-iarmain.co.uk

Noble, Joseph Crawford, BSc, MRICS. Chief Executive, Scottish Enterprise Fife, since 2001; m., Anne; 1 s.; 1 d. Educ. Royal High School, Edinburgh; Heriot-Watt University. British Rail Property Board, 1980-87; City of Edinburgh District Council, 1984; Scottish Development Agency, 1985-89; Jones Lang Wootton, Chartered Surveyors, 1989-91. Board Member: Fife Environment Trust, Small Business Gateway, Fife, Next Steps Foundation. Recreations: sports including golf and football. Address: (b.) Kingdom House, Saltire Centre, Glenrothes; T.-01592 623000; e-mail: joe.noble@scotent.co.uk

Noble, Lillias Mary, BEd, MUniv (Open). Head of Learning Connections, Lifelong Learning Directorate, Directorate General Education, Scottish Government; b. 11.9.54, Vancouver. Educ. Larkhall Academy; Hamilton College of Education; Strathclyde University. Formerly

English and Guidance Teacher, Thurso High School, 1975-80; Wester Hailes Education Centre, 1980-84; Save the Children Fund, 1985-88; Director, LEAD Scotland, 1988-97; Education Adviser, Scottish Prison Service, 1997-2002; part-time Commissioner, 1992-98, and Vice Chairman, 1995-98, Mental Welfare Commission for Scotland. Recreation: climbing mountains. Address: (b.) Highlander House, 58 Waterloo Street, Glasgow G2 7DA; T.-0141 271 3710.

Noble, R. Ross, MA, FSA (Scot). Museum Curator, 1973-2003 (retired); Member, UNESCO Scotland Committee Network, since 2008; Member, Historic Environment Advisory Council for Scotland, since 2003; b. 9.6.42, Ayr; m., Jean; 1 s.; 1 d. Educ. Ardrossan Academy; Aberdeen University. Travelling Curator, Scottish Country Life Museums Trust, 1973-76; Curator, Highland Folk Museum and Regional (later Highland) Curator for the local authority's Museum Service, 1976-2003. Elected Fellow, Society of Antiquaries of Scotland, since 1982; Convenor, Scottish Country Life Museums Trust, 2000-07; Elected Director, Newtonmore Community Woodland and Development Trust, since 2003; Member: Museums Association, Scottish Vernacular Buildings Working Group, British Regional Furniture Society, Scottish History Society; Member and Past President, Society for Folk Life Studies. Publications include: The Cultural Impact of the Highland Clearances, BBC History On-Line, 2001; Earth Buildings in the Central Highlands: Research and Reconstruction. Medieval or Later Rural Settlements: 10 Years On, 2003; "Highland Vernacular Furniture and Context" in Furniture and Fittings in the Traditional Scottish Home, Scottish Vernacular Buildings Working Group, 2007. Recreations: walking; swimming; sailing; painting. Address: (h.) "Creageiro", Church Terrace, Newtonmore PH20 1DT; T.-01540 673392; e-mail: ross@creageiro.freeserve.co.uk

Noble, Timothy Peter, MA, MBA. Chairman: Palmaris Capital plc, Darnaway Venture Capital plc; Director: Scottish Friendly Assurance Society Ltd., Martin Energy Ltd.; b. 21.12.43; m., Elizabeth Mary Aitken; 2 s.; 1 d. Educ. University College, Oxford; Gray's Inn, London; INSEAD, Fontainebleau. Recreations: skiing; tennis; music; bridge; wine; astronomy; poetry. Address: (h.) Ardnahane, Barnton Avenue, Edinburgh; T.-0131-336 3565.

Noel-Paton, (Frederick) Ranald, BA, DBA (Hon). Chairman, Murray Global Return Trust plc, 2000-05 (Director, since 1998); b. 7.11.38, Bombay; m., Patricia Anne Stirling; 4 d. Educ. Rugby School; McGill University. Investment Analyst, Greenshields Inc., 1962-63; Management Trainee, United Biscuits, 1964; various posts, British United Airways Ltd., 1965-70; various senior executive posts, British Caledonian Airways, 1970-86 (General Manager, West Africa, 1975-79, General Manager, Far East, 1980-86, Director, Caledonian Far East Airways, 1984-86); Group Managing Director, John Menzies plc, 1986-97, Deputy Chairman, 1997-98; Chairman, Pacific Assets Trust plc, 1998-2004 (Director, 1986-2004); Director: General Accident plc, 1987-98, Royal Bank of Scotland Group, 1991-93, Macallan-Glenlivet plc, 1990-96. Recreations: fishing; walking; bird-watching; golf; the arts. Address: (h.) Pitcurran House, Abernethy, Perth PH2 9LH.

Normand, Andrew Campbell, LLB (Hons), DipLP. Partner, HBJ Gateley Wareing (formerly Henderson Boyd Jackson), since 1996; b. 4.12.62, Perth; m., Sheila; 3 s.; 1 d. Educ. Perth High School; Edinburgh University. Traineeship, Nightingale and Bell SSC, 1985-87; Assistant Solicitor, Gray Muirhead WS, 1991-96. WS Society; Committee Member, Edinburgh Headway Group. Recreations: jazz; piano. Address: (b.) Exchange Tower, 19 Canning Street, Edinburgh EH3 8EH; T.-0131 222 9847; e-mail: CNormand@hbj-gw.com

Normand, Sheriff Andrew Christie, CB, MA, LLB, LLM, SSC, FSAScot. Sheriff at Glasgow, since 2003; Crown Agent for Scotland, 1996-2003; b. 7.2.48, Edinburgh; m., Barbara Jean Smith; 2 d. Educ. George Watson's College, Edinburgh; Edinburgh University; Queen's University, Kingston, Ontario.

Norrie, Professor Kenneth McKenzie, LLB, DLP, PhD, FRSE. Professor and Head of the Law School, University of Strathclyde; b. 23.6.59, Dundee. Educ. Kirkton High School, Dundee; University of Dundee; University of Aberdeen. Lecturer in Law: University of Dundee, 1982-83, University of Aberdeen, 1983-90; Gastprofessor, Universität Regensburg, Germany, 1990; Senior Lecturer in Law, University of Strathclyde, 1990-95; Visiting Professor, University of Sydney, Australia, 1997. Publications: Parent and Child; Defamation; Trusts; Children's Hearings. Recreations: gardening; travel. Address: (b.) School of Law, University of Strathclyde, Stenhouse Building, 141 St James Road, Glasgow G4 0LT; T.-0141-548 3393.

Norris, Richard, BA (Hons). Director, Scottish Health Council, since 2005; b. 01.04.59, Luton; m., Morag; 2 d. Educ. Branston School, Lincolnshire; City of London Polytechnic. Postgraduate Student and Part Time Tutor in Politics, University of Edinburgh, 1996-90; Development Manager LCL (Print and Publicity), 1990-93; Chief Executive, Centre for Public Policy, 1993-97; Director of Policy, Scottish Association for Mental Health, 1997-2005. Address: (b.) Delta House, 50 West Nile Street, Glasgow G1 2NF; T.-0141 241 6308. E-mail: richard.norris@scottishhealthcouncil.org

Northesk, 14th Earl of (David John MacRae Carnegie); b. 3.11.54; m.; 3 d.; 1 s. (deceased). Educ. Eton; UCL. Succeeded to title, 1994; elected Member, House of Lords, since 1999.

Northrop, Alasdair, BA (Hons.). Editor, Scottish Business Insider, since 2000; Editor in Chief, Business7, since 2007; b. 23.5.57, Chalfont-St-Giles; 1 s. Educ. Leamington College for Boys; Middlesex Polytechnic. Reporter, Heart of England Newspapers, 1978-83; Sub Editor, Southern Evening Echo, Southampton, 1983-85; Deputy Editor, North Western Evening Mail, Barrow-in-Furness, 1985-89; Business Editor, Western Daily Press, Bristol, 1989-94; Business Editor, Manchester Evening News, 1994-2000. BT Business Journalist of the Year, 1996; BT North West Business Journalist of the Year, 1996. Recreations: theatre; music; walking; swimming; badminton; travelling. Address: (b.) 160 Dundee Street, Edinburgh EH11 1DQ; T.-0131-535 5512; e-mail: editor@insider.co.uk

Nutton, Richard William, MB, BS, MD, FRCS. Consultant Orthopaedic Surgeon, since 1987; Honorary Senior Lecturer, since 1989; b. 16.11.51, Halifax; m., Theresa Mary Turney; 2 s.; 1 d. Educ. Sedbergh School; Newcastle upon Tyne University. Special interest in knee and shoulder surgery. Recreations: fishing; shooting; golf; skiing; running. Address: (b.) Royal Infirmary of Edinburgh, Little France, Edinburgh; T.-0131-242 3493.

O

Ó Baoill, Professor Colm, MA, PhD, Professor of Celtic, Aberdeen University, since 1996; b. 22.9.38, Armagh, Ireland; m., Frances G. R.; 3 d. Educ. St. Patrick's College, Armagh; Queen's University of Belfast. Assistant Lecturer, Queen's University of Belfast, 1962; Aberdeen University: Lecturer, 1966, Senior Lecturer, 1980, retired 2003. Chief, Gaelic Society, Inverness, 1993. Address: (h.) 19 King's Crescent, Old Aberdeen AB24 3HJ; T.-01224 637064; e-mail: c.oboyle@abdn.ac.uk

O'Brien, Sir Frederick William Fitzgerald, QC, MA, LLB. Sheriff Principal, Lothian and Borders, 1978-89; Convener of Sheriffs Principal, 1972-89; b. 19.7.17, Edinburgh; m., Audrey Muriel Owen; 2 s.; 1 d. Educ. Royal High School, Edinburgh; Edinburgh University. Called to Scottish Bar, 1947; QC, 1960; Commissioner, Mental Welfare Commission, 1962-65; Senior Advocate Depute, Crown Office, 1964-65; Sheriff Principal, Caithness, Sutherland, Orkney and Shetland, 1965-75; Interim Sheriff Principal, Aberdeen, Kincardine and Banff, 1969-71; Sheriff Principal, North Strathclyde, 1975-78; Member: Scottish Medical Practices Committee, 1973-76, Scottish Records Advisory Council, 1974-83; Chairman, Sheriff Court Rules Council, 1975-81; Convener, General Council Business Committee, Edinburgh University, 1980-84; Past President, Royal High School FP Club (Honorary President, 1982-91); Chairman, Edinburgh Sir Walter Scott Club, 1989-92; Commissioner, Northern Lighthouse Board, 1965-89 (Chairman, 1983-84 and 1986-87). Recreations: music; golf (former captain, Scot. Bench and Bar Golfing Society). Address: (h.) 22 Arboretum Road, Edinburgh EH3 5PN; T.-0131-552 1923.

O'Brien, James Paul, MA (Hons), MEd, PhD, DipEdTech, FRSA. Vice-Dean, Moray House School of Education, Edinburgh University, since 1998; b. 23.4.50, Stirling; m., Elaine Margaret Kathleen Smith; 1 d. Educ. St. Mirin's Academy, Paisley; Glasgow University. Teacher, 1973-85; Lecturer, St. Andrew's College of Education, 1985-88, Director, 1988-93, Assistant Principal, 1992-93; Vice-Principal, Moray House Institute, 1993-98. Recreations: golf; music; reading. Address: (b.) Holyrood Campus, Holyrood Road, Edinburgh EH8 8AQ; T.-0131-651 6167.

O'Brien, Most Rev. Keith Michael Patrick, BSc, DipEd. Archbishop of St. Andrews and Edinburgh, since 1985; b. 17.3.38, Ballycastle, Northern Ireland. Educ. Saint Patrick's, Dumbarton; Holy Cross Academy, Edinburgh; Edinburgh University; St. Andrew's College, Drygrange; Moray House College of Education. Teacher, St. Columba's High School, Fife; Assistant Priest, Kilsyth, then Bathgate; Spiritual Director, St. Andrew's College, Drygrange; Rector, Blairs College, Aberdeen; ordained Archbishop by Cardinal Gray, 1985. Created Cardinal by Pope John Paul II on 21 October 2003; 2004: awarded Honorary Doctor of Laws, University of St. Francis Xavier, Antigonish, Nova Scotia; Honorary Doctor of Divinity, University of St. Andrews; Honorary Doctor of Divinity, University of Edinburgh. Recreations: music; walking. Address: Saint Bennet's, 42 Greenhill Gardens, Edinburgh EH10 4BJ.

O'Brien, Susan, BA (Hons), BPhil, LLB. Queen's Counsel, since 1998; Advocate, since 1987; b. 13.8.52, Edinburgh; m., Professor Peter Ross; 2 d. Educ. St George's School for Girls, Edinburgh; York University; Edinburgh University. Admitted Solicitor, 1980; Assistant Solicitor, Shepherd and Wedderburn, WS,

1980-86; Standing Junior Counsel to Registrar General, 1991, and to Home Office, 1992-97, and to Keeper of the Registers, 1998; Temporary Sheriff, 1995-99; part-time Chairman, Employment Tribunals, since 2000; Reporter to Scottish Legal Aid Board, 1999-2005; Chair, Caleb Ness Inquiry for Edinburgh and The Lothians Child Protection Committee, 2003; Chairman, Faculty Services Ltd., (and office bearer in the Faculty of Advocates), 2005-07. Address: (b.) Advocates' Library, Parliament Square, Edinburgh EH1 1RQ; T.-0131-226 5071.

O'Carroll, Derek, LLB (Hons), DipLP. Advocate; part-time Chairman, Social Security Appeals Tribunal, 1999-2007; former Convener, Scottish Legal Action Group; part-time Chairman, Private Rented Housing Panel for Scotland, 2002-07; part-time Chairman, Rent Assessment Panel for Scotland, 2002-07; part-time Chairman, Mental Health Tribunal for Scotland, since 2005; part-time Sheriff, since 2006; b. 20.1.60, St Albans. Educ. Cults Academy, Aberdeen; Edinburgh University. Citizens Rights Office, Edinburgh, 1982-85; Castlemilk Law Centre, Glasgow, 1985; Uludag University, Turkey, 1985-88; Transfert, Paris, 1988-90; Legal Services Agency, Glasgow, 1990-95; Govan Law Centre, Glasgow, 1995-99. Member, Scottish Legal Aid Board, 1998-2002; Director, Faculty Services Ltd., 2003-07; elected to Council of Faculty of Advocates, 2005-08; Director, Thistle Foundation, 2005-07. Recreations: good food and wine; swimming and keep-fit; travel. E-mail: derek.ocarroll@advocates.org.uk

O'Connor, Charlene, BSc, MSc. Board Member, Scottish Further Education Unit; formerly Senior Director, Skills and Learning, Scottish Enterprise; formerly Chief Executive, Scottish Enterprise Forth Valley; b. 16.8.61, Tranent, East Lothian; 1 s.; 1 d. Educ. Ross High School, Tranent; Napier University. Scottish National Blood Transfusion Service, Protein Fractionation Centre; G.D. Searle, High Wycombe, Bucks; Smith and Nephew Pharmaceuticals, Romford; Lothian and Edinburgh Enterprise. Recreations: gym; sailing; reading; cooking.

O'Donnell, Hugh. MSP (Liberal Democrat), Central Scotland, since 2007; b. 1.5.52. Address: (b.) Scottish Parliament, Edinburgh EH99 1SP.

O'Donnell, Laurie, MA (Hons), MEd. Director of Learning and Technology, Learning and Teaching Scotland, since 2005; b. 14.01.61, Edinburgh; m., Moira; 2 d. Educ. Our Lady's High School, Broxburn; University of Edinburgh. Teacher, School Manager, various posts, 1986-89; ICT Development Officer, Dundee City Council, 1999-2001; Learning and Teaching Scotland, 2001-08: Head of Future Learning and Teaching, Head of ICT Development, Director of ICT. Chair of Management Group, 'The Corner' Young People's Health Project, Dundee, 2004-07; Elected Member, Dundee District Council, 1992-96. Recreations: family; friends; golf; reading; movies and music. Address: (b.) Optima, Robertson Street, Glasgow G2 8DU; e-mail: l.odonnell@ltscotland.org.uk

O'Donovan, Professor Oliver Michael Timothy, MA, DPhil, FBA. Professor, Christian Ethics and Practical Theology, University of Edinburgh, since 2006; b. 28.06.45, Edgware, Middlesex; m., Joan Elizabeth Lockwood; 2 s. Educ. University College School, Hampstead; Balliol College, Oxford. Lecturer, Wycliffe Hall, Oxford, 1972-77; Assistant Professor, Wycliffe College, Toronto, 1977-82; Regius Professor of Moral and Pastoral Theology and Canon of Christ Church, Oxford,

1982-2006. Publications: Author: Resurrection and Moral Order, The Desire of The Nations, The Ways of Judgement. Address: (b.) New College, Mound Place, Edinburgh EH1 2LX; T.-0131-650-8953; e-mail: oliver.odonovan@ed.ac.uk

O'Dwyer, Professor Patrick Joseph, MCh, FRCSI, FRCSGlas. Professor of Surgery, Glasgow University, since 1998; Consultant Surgeon, Western Infirmary, Glasgow, since 1990; b. 24.7.52, Newport, Ireland; m., Marian; 3 s.; 1 d. Educ. Newport Vocational School; University College Cork. Trainee in Surgery, University Hospital, Cork, 1979-83; Research Fellow, Harvard Medical School, 1983-84; Clinical Fellow, Ohio State University, 1984-86; Lecturer in Surgery, University College Dublin, 1986-90; Senior Lecturer and Reader in Surgery, Glasgow University, 1990-98. Publications: 100 papers in journals. Recreations: music; hill-walking. Address: University Department of Surgery, Western Infirmary, Glasgow G11 6NT; T.-0141-211 2163.

O'Farrell, Rt. Rev. Mgr. Peter, BTh (Hons.). Priest, St. John of the Cross, Twechar; Prelate of Honour, since 1999; formerly Parish Priest, St. Matthew's, Bishopbriggs; b. 26.11.35, Wicklow, Ireland. Educ. CBS, Westland Row, Dublin; St. John's Seminary for the Clergy, Waterford, Ireland; Maynooth Pontifical University, Ireland. Ordained, Holy Trinity Cathedral, Waterford, Ireland; Assistant Priest: St. Aloysius, Springburn, Glasgow, 1962-73, St. Joseph's, Cumbernauld, 1973-80, St. Louise, Arden, Glasgow, 1980-90; Parish Priest: Our Lady and St. Margaret's, Kinning Park, Glasgow, 1990-95, St. Laurence's, Drumchapel, Glasgow, 1995-98. Tournaments Director, Clergy Golf, 20 years. Address: St. Matthews, St John of the Cross, Main Street, Twechar, Kilsyth G65 9TA; T.-01236 822263.

Ogg, Derek Andrew, LLB, FFCS. Queen's Counsel, since 1999; Advocate, since 1989; b. 19.9.54, Dunfermline. Educ. Dunfermline High School; Edinburgh University. Solicitor in private practice, 1980-89. Chairman, Institute of Chartered Accountants of Scotland Discipline Tribunal, since 2000; Chairman, Scottish AIDS Monitor Charitable Trust, 1983-94; Trustee, Waverly Care Trust (proprietors of Scotland's AIDS Hospice), since 1990. Member, Royal Philosophical Society of Glasgow. Recreations: hill-walking; classic cars; reading; music; occasional radio and TV commentator. Address: (h.) 18 Lanark Street, Glasgow G1 5PY; T.-0141-572 4843; e-mail: derekandrewogg@hotmail.com

Ogg, Fiona Marie, BSc (distinction), RGN. Chief Executive Officer, Advocates for Animals, since 2007; Company Secretary, St. Andrews Animal Fund, since 2007; b. 15.03.72, Kitwe, Zambia. Educ. Portobello High School; Queen Margaret University; Lothian College of Nursing, Midwifery and Health Visiting. Registered General Nurse, 1993-97; Planning Assistant, Heriot Watt University, 1997-98; Senior Campaigns Officer, Animal Offenders and The National Anti-Vivisection Society, 1999-2001; Campaigns Development Adviser, National Society for the Prevention of Cruelty to Children, 2001-04; (P/T) Communications and Emotional Intelligence Consultant, and NLP Trainer, 2003-07; Events Manager, Amnesty International UK, 2005; Forum Manager, Barnardo's/Heads Up Scotland, 2006-07. Recreations: enjoy beach/woodland walks; socialising; music and comedy; personal holistic development. Address: (b.) 10 Queensferry Street, Edinburgh EH12 4PG; T.-0131 225 6039; e-mail: fiona@advocatesforanimals.org

Ogilvy, Sir Francis (Gilbert Arthur), 14th Bt, ARICS. Chartered Surveyor; b. 22.4.69; m., Dorothy Margaret Stein; 3 s.; 1 d. Educ. Edinburgh Academy; Glenalmond College; Royal Agricultural College, Cirencester; BSc (Hons) (Reading). Address: (h.) Winton House, Pencaitland, East Lothian EH34 5AT.

Ogilvy, Julia Caroline, MA. Founder and Chairman, Project Scotland, since 2004; Non-Executive Director, LTSB Scotland, since 2004; b. 28.10.64, Cambridge; m., James Ogilvy; 1 s.; 1 d. Educ. Wycombe Abbey; University of St. Andrews. Marketing Manager, Garrard The Crown Jewellers, 1988-92; Managing Director, Hamilton and Inches, 1992-2003; Director: Columba 1400, since 2003, Atlantic Publishing, since 1996. Member of University Court, St Andrews, 1994-2002. 2001 Winner of Scottish Business Achievement Award (SABAAT); Scottish Businesswoman of the Year; Winner of Scottish Social Entrepreneur of the Year Award, 2007. Elder of Church of Scotland. Recreations: travel; books; church/religion. Address: (b.) Project Scotland, 49, Melville Street, Edinburgh EH3 7HL; T.-0131 226 0700; e-mail: juliaogilvy@btconnect.com

O'Grady, Sheriff Michael Gerard, QC, MA, LLB. Sheriff, Lothian and Borders, since 2007; Sheriff, Glasgow and Strathkelvin at Glasgow, 2000-07; b. 19.8.54, Glasgow; m., Sheena Margaret McDougall. Educ. St. Patrick's High School, Dumbarton; University of Glasgow. Solicitor, private practice (Ross Harper and Murphy, and Gordon McBain and O'Grady), 1977-88; called to the Bar, 1988; Advocate Depute, 1993-97; Standing Junior to Foreign and Commonwealth Office, 1997-98, QC, 1998; Temporary Judge, since 2004. Recreations: reading; music; guitar; travel. Address: (b.) Sheriffs' Chambers, Sheriff Court, Edinburgh.

Ogston, Professor Derek, CBE, MA, MD, PhD, DSc, MLitt, FRCPEdin, FRCP, FIBiol, FRSE, FRSA, BTh, Hon. LLD. Professor of Medicine, Aberdeen University, 1983-97 (Dean, Faculty of Medicine, 1984-87; Vice-Principal, 1987-97); Member, Court, Aberdeen University, 1998-2002; b. 31.5.32, Aberdeen; m., Cecilia Marie; 1 s.; 2 d. Educ. King's College School, Wimbledon; Aberdeen University. Aberdeen University: Lecturer in Medicine, 1962-69, Senior Lecturer in Medicine, 1969-75, MRC Travelling Fellow, 1967-68, Reader in Medicine, 1975-76, Regius Professor of Physiology, 1977-83. Member, Grampian Health Board, 1991-97 (Vice-Chairman, 1993-97); Member, General Medical Council, 1985-94. Publications: Haemostasis: Biochemistry, Physiology and Pathology (Joint Editor), 1977; The Physiology of Hemostasis, 1983; Antifibrinolytic Drugs: Chemistry, Pharmacology and Clinical Usage, 1984; Venous Thrombosis: Causation and Prediction, 1987; Life and Works of George Smith, RSA, 2000; George Leslie Hunter, 2002; Working Children (jointly), 2003; Leslie Hunter: Paintings of France and Italy, 2004; Children at School (jointly), 2005. Recreations: music; history of art; gardening. Address: (h.) 64 Rubislaw Den South, Aberdeen AB15 4AY; T.-Aberdeen 316587.

O'Hagan, Professor David, BSc, PhD, DSc, CChem, FRSC, FRSE. Professor and Head of Organic Chemistry, University of St. Andrews, since 2000; b. 29.9.61, Glasgow; m., Anne; 3 d. Educ. Holyrood Secondary School, Glasgow; Glasgow University; Southampton University. Postdoctoral research, Ohio State University, 1985-86; University of Durham: Demonstrator, 1986-88, Lecturer in Chemistry, 1988-99, Professor of Organic Chemistry, 1999-2000. Chairman, Editorial Board, Natural Product Reports, and Journal of Fluorine Chemistry; Chairman, RSC Fluorine Subject Group. Publication: The Polyketide Metabolites, 1991. Recreations: golf; walking; gardening.

Address: Millbank Park, 51 Millbank, Cupar, Fife KY15 5EA; T.-01334 650708; e-mail: dol@st-andrews.ac.uk

Oldfather, Irene, BA (Hons), MSc. MSP (Lab), Cunninghame South, since 1999; Chair, Cross Party Group on Alzheimers; Vice Chair, Cross Party Group on Tobacco Control; Vice President, Party European Socialists Committee of Regions; b. Glasgow. Educ. Strathclyde University; University of Arizona. Researcher, Dumbarton Council on Alcohol, 1976-77; Lecturer, University of Arizona, 1977-78; Research Officer, Strathclyde Regional Council, 1978-79; various posts, Glasgow District Council Housing Department, 1979-90; Political Researcher, Alex Smith MEP, 1990-98; writer and broadcaster on European affairs, 1994-98; part-time Lecturer, Paisley University, 1996-98; Councillor, North Ayrshire, 1995-99; Alternate Member, European Committee of the Regions; Chair, COSLA Task Group on EMU; Vice-Chair, West of Scotland European Consortium. Address: (b.) Sovereign House, Academy Road, Irvine KA12 8RL; T.-01294 313078.

Oldham, Professor John David, BSc, PhD. Head, Research and Development, SAC, since 2002; Professor of Animal Biology, SAC, since 1997; b. 20.7.49, Stockport; m., Catherine; 3 s. Educ. Cheadle Hulme School; Nottingham University. Post-doctoral Research Fellow, University of Alberta, 1973-74; Research Scientist, National Institute for Research in Dairying, 1974-84; Head, Animal Production Advisory and Development Department, Edinburgh School of Agriculture, 1984-90; SAC: Head, Genetics and Behavioural Sciences Department, 1990-97, Head, Animal Biology Division, 1997-2002. Secretary, The Nutrition Society, 1996-99; President, EAAP Nutrition Commission, 2000-03; Member, RAE Agriculture Panel; former Member, Editorial Board, British Journal of Nutrition, Animal Science. Sir John Hammond Memorial Prize, 1990; Saltire Society/Royal Bank of Scotland Scottish Science Award, 1995. Recreations: family, home and garden; walking; theatre; reading; music; sketching. Address: (b.) West Mains Road, Edinburgh EH9 3JG.

Oliver, Christopher William, BSc, MBBS, FRCS (Tr&Orth), FRCP, DMI, RCSEd. Consultant Trauma and Orthopaedic Surgeon, Royal Infirmary of Edinburgh, since 1997; Honorary Senior Lecturer, Orthopaedics, Edinburgh University, since 1997; b. 5.1.60, London; m., Josephine Hilton; 2 d. Educ. Romford Technical High School, London; University College Hospital, London. Basic surgical training, London and Harrow, 1985-89; Orthopaedic Registrar, York, Leeds, Harrogate, 1989-92; Research Fellow, Spinal Science, Middlesbrough, 1992-94; Senior Registrar, Oswestry and Stoke-on-Trent, 1994-96; Trauma Fellow, Harborview Hospital, Seattle, USA, 1996; Consultant Trauma Surgeon, John Radcliffe Hospital, Oxford, 1996-97. Member, Council, Royal College of Surgeons of Edinburgh, since 2002; Convener of Examinations, RCSEd, 2006-2009. Recreations: sailing; skiing; computers; motor-racing. Address: (b.) New Royal Infirmary Edinburgh, Old Dalkeith Road, Edinburgh EH16 4SU; T.-0131-242 3402. web: www.rcsed.ac.uk/fellows/cwoliver; e-mail: cwoliver@rcsed.ac.uk

O'Maolalaigh, Professor Roibeard, BA, MA, PhD. Professor of Gaelic, University of Glasgow, since 2005, Head of Department, Department of Celtic, since 2007; b. 05.07.66, Dublin, Ireland; m., Margaret Macleod; 4 s. Educ. Drimnagh Castle, CBS; University College, Dublin; University of Edinburgh. Career History: Lecturer, Department of Celtic, University of Edinburgh; Assistant Professor and Bibliographer, School of Celtic Studies,

Dublin Institute for Advanced Studies. Chairman, Gaelic Books Council. Address: (b.) Department of Celtic, University of Glasgow G12 8QQ; T.-0141-330-4222; e-mail: rom@celtic.arts.gla.ac.uk

O'Neill of Clackmannan, Lord (Martin (John) O'Neill), BA (Econ). MP (Labour), Ochil, 1997-2005 (Clackmannan, 1983-97, East Stirlingshire and Clackmannan, 1979-83); b. 6.1.45; m., Elaine Samuel; 2 s. Educ. Trinity Academy, Edinburgh; trades union and evening classes; Heriot-Watt University; Moray House College of Education. President, Scottish Union of Students, 1970-71; school teacher, 1974-79; Tutor, Open University, 1976-79. Member, Select Committee, Scottish Affairs, 1979-80; Opposition Spokesman, Scottish Affairs, 1980-84; Opposition Spokesman on Defence, 1984-88; Shadow Defence Secretary, 1988-92; Shadow Spokesman on Energy, 1992-95; Chair, Trade and Industry Select Committee, since 1995. Recreations: watching football; reading; listening to jazz; cinema. Address: (b.) House of Lords, London SW1; e-mail: oneillm@parliament.uk

O'Neil, Brian. Director of Human Resources, Historic Scotland, since 1997; b. 14.5.50, Edinburgh; m., Irene; 2 d. Educ. Gracemount Secondary School, Edinburgh. Joined Scottish Office, 1966; Head of Branch, Local Government Division, 1990-95. Recreations: golf; reading; gardening. Address: (b.) Historic Scotland, Longmore House, Salisbury Place, Edinburgh EH9 1SH; T.-0131-668 8667.

O'Neill, Mark William Robert, BA Hons, HDipEd, Grad. Cert. Mus. Studies. Head of Arts and Museums, Culture and Sport, Glasgow, since 2007; b. 10.11.56. Educ. University College, Cork; Leicester University; Getty Leadership Inst. Curator, Springburn Museum, 1985-90; Glasgow Museums, since 1990; Keeper of Social History, 1990-92; Senior Curator of History, 1992-97; Head, Curatorial Services, 1997-98; Head, Glasgow Museums, 1998-2005, Head of Arts and Museums, since 2005. FMA, 1997. Publications: numerous articles on philosophy and practice of museums. Recreations: classical music; fiction; psychology. Address: (b.) Glasgow Museums, Culture and Sport, Glasgow, 20 Trongate, Glasgow G1 5ES; T.-0141 287 0446; Fax: 0141 287 5151; e-mail: mark.o'neill@cs.glasgow.org

O'Neill, Dr William M., BSc, MB, BCh, BAO, FRCGP. General Medical Practitioner, Edinburgh; Scottish Secretary, British Medical Association, 2000-05; b. 4.5.52, Limerick. Educ. University College and St Vincent's Hospital, Dublin. Junior medical posts, St Vincent's Hospital and Mater Hospital, Dublin; Middlesex Hospital and St Thomas's Hospital, London; General Practitioner, Kensington, London, 1993-98; Consultant Senior Lecturer in Palliative Medicine, St Thomas's Hospital, London, 1991-93; Bristol Oncology Centre, 1993-95; Organisational Development Consultant, Primary Care Support Force, London, 1995-96; Science and Research Advisor, British Medical Association, London, 1996-2000. Address: (h.) 4 North East Circus Place, Edinburgh EH3 6SP.

O'Regan, Noel, BMus, MSc, DPhil. Senior Lecturer, Music, University of Edinburgh, since 1996; b. 27.12.49, Roscommon, Ireland. Educ. Gormanston College; University College Galway; University College Cork; Oxford University. Research Chemist, Pfizer Corporation, 1974-78; Teacher, Christian Brothers College, Cork, 1978-80; Lecturer in Music, University of Lancaster, 1984-85, University of Edinburgh, 1985-96. Chairman, Concerto Caledonia Board; Chairman, Georgian Concert Society;

Director, Edinburgh Renaissance Singers. Recreations: music; films; hillwalking; travelling. Address: (h.) 14 Rankeillor Street, Edinburgh EH8 9HY; T.-0131 667 7853; e-mail: n.o.regan@ed.ac.uk

O'Reilly, Denis St. John, MSc, MD, FRCP (Glas), FRCPath. Consultant Clinical Biochemist, Royal Infirmary, Glasgow, since 1984; Director, The Scottish Trace Element and Micronutrient Reference Laboratory; b. 30.3.51, Cork; m., Margaret M.P. Lucey; 2 s.; 1 d. Educ. Presentation Brothers College, Cork; University College, Cork; Birmingham University. Registrar, Queen Elizabeth Medical Centre, Birmingham, 1976-78; Senior Registrar, Bristol Royal Infirmary, 1978-84; Ainsworth Scholar-Research Fellow, Norsk Hydro Institute for Cancer Research, Oslo, 1982. Recreation: hill-walking. Address: (h.) 47 Strathblane Road, Milngavie G62 8HA.

O'Rourke, Daniel (Donny), MA, MPhil. Poet, journalist, film-maker, broadcaster, and teacher; b. 5.7.59, Port Glasgow. Educ. St. Mirin's Academy, Paisley; Glasgow University; Pembroke College, Cambridge. Vice President, European Youth Council, 1983-85; Chairman, Scottish Youth Council, 1982-84; Producer, BBC TV and Radio Scotland, 1984-86; Reporter, Scottish Television, 1986-87, Producer, 1987-92, Head of Arts, 1992-93, Head of Arts and Documentaries, 1993-94; Executive Producer, BBC Scotland, 1994-95; folk music reviewer, The Herald and New Statesman, 1985-90; Creative Writing Fellow, Glasgow University and Strathclyde University, 1995-97; Head of English and Media Studies, Department of Adult and Continuing Education, Glasgow University, 1996-98; Poet in Residence, Edinburgh International Book Festival, 1999; Columnist, Sunday Herald, 1999; Member, Manpower Services Commission Youth Training Board, 1982-84; Member, Scottish Community Education Council, 1981-84; Chairman of Judges, Scottish Writer of the Year Award, 1996, 1997; Director, Tron Theatre Company, 1993-95; Member, Editorial Board, "11/9"; Artistic Director, Reacquaintance Robert Burns in Glasgow (year-long celebration), 2000; theatre: The Kerrera Saga (with George Wyllie), 1998, On Your Nerve, A Wake for Frank O'Hara, 1996. Publications: Second City, 1991; Rooming Houses of America, 1993; Dream State, the new Scottish poets, 1994; chapter in Burns Now, 1994; Eftirs/Afters, 1996; The Waist Band and Other Poems, 1997; Modern Music, 1997; Ae Fond Kiss, 1999; Across the Water, 2000 (Co-Editor); New Writing Scotland anthologies – Some Kind of Embrace, 1997; The Glory Signs, 1998; Friends and Kangaroos, 1999; The Cleft in My Heart, 2008; Blame Yesterday, 2008; Still Waiting To Be Wise (CD, with Dave Whyte), 1999; On A Roll, 2001; poems in various anthologies and textbooks. Recreations: Italian food; playing guitar; Irish literature; Americana. Address: (h.) 63 Barrington Drive, Glasgow G4 9ES; e-mail: donny.orourke@btinternet.com

Ormiston, Linda, OBE (2001), MA, DRSAMD, Hon. DMus (St. Andrews). Singer — Mezzo Soprano; b. 15.1.48, Motherwell. Educ. Dalziel High School, Motherwell; Glasgow University; Royal Scottish Academy of Music and Drama; London Opera Centre. Has sung all over Britain, France, Belgium, Italy, Germany, Austria, Holland and Yugoslavia; has sung regularly at Scottish Opera, Opera North, and Glyndebourne; also well-known in lighter vein and as a member of The Music Box; recordings include Noyes Fludde, HMS Pinafore and Ruddigore with New Sadlers Wells Opera and Tell Me Pretty Maiden; has appeared at New York, Vancouver, Monte Carlo, Brussels and Tokyo; debut, Frankfurt Opera, 1993; debut, Salzburg Festival, 1994; debut, English National Opera, 1995. Recreations: playing the piano; skating; golf.

Ormond, Rupert Frank Guy, BA, MA, PhD. Chief Scientist, Save our Seas Foundation, since 2007; Director, University Marine Biological Station Millport, 1999-2006;

Senior Lecturer, London University, 1999-2006; Visiting Professor, Glasgow University, since 2000; b. 1.6.46, Bristol; m., Mauvis ne Gore; 2 s.; 1 d. Educ. Clifton College, Bristol; Peterhouse, Cambridge. Director, Marine Biological Station, Port Sudan, Sudan, 1972-74; Lecturer/Senior Lecturer, Biology Department, 1974-99, Director, Tropical Marine Research Unit, 1982-99, York University. District Councillor, Ryedale District Council, 1987-96; Member: North York Moors National Park Committee, 1995-96, Council, WWF Scotland, since 2000, Scottish Natural Heritage Scientific Advisory Committee, 2000-04. Publications include: Red Sea Coral Reefs (Co-author); Marine Biodiversity (Co-author). Recreations: natural history; travel; classical music. Address: (h.) 37 Main Street, Newton, West Lothian EH52 6QE.

O'Rourke, William, JP. Member, Glasgow City Council, since 1995; b. 11.10.39, Glasgow; m., Mary Gray; 4 s. 1 d. Educ. St. Gerard's Senior Secondary School. Former Member, Strathclyde Regional Council; President, Port Health Authorities. Recreations: politics; reading. Address: (b.) City Chambers, George Square, Glasgow G2 1DU; T.-0141-287 5803.

Orr, Joanne, BA (Hons), DipIndArch, MA, MBA. Chief Executive Officer, Museums Galleries Scotland, since 2004. Educ. Durham University Business School. Chair, UNESCO Scotland; UNESCO - UK Cultural Committee; ICOM - UK Board Member; Creative and Cultural Skills - Cultural Heritage Advisory Panel. Address: (b.) The Stack, Papermill Wynd, McDonald Road, Edinburgh EH7 4QL.

Orr, John Douglas, MB, ChB, MBA, FRCS(Edin). Consultant Paediatric Surgeon, Royal Hospital for Sick Children, Edinburgh, since 1984; b. 11.7.45, Edinburgh; m., Elizabeth Erica Yvonne Miklinska; 2 s.; 1 d. Educ. George Heriot's School, Edinburgh; High School, Dundee; University of St. Andrews; Stirling University. Formerly Medical Director, The Royal Hospital for Sick Children, Edinburgh and Associate Medical Director, University Hospitals Division - NHS Lothian. President, Royal College of Surgeons of Edinburgh, 2006-09. Recreations: golf; gardening. Address: (b.) Royal Hospital for Sick Children, Edinburgh EH9 1LF; Royal College of Surgeons of Edinburgh, Nicolson Street, Edinburgh EH8 9DW; T.-0131-527 1600; e-mail: President@rcsed.ac.uk

Orr-Ewing, Duncan Charles, BA, MRICS. Head of Species and Land Management, RSPB Scotland, since 1999; b. 19.01.64, Redhill; m., Caroline Louise; 1 d. Educ. Dr Challoner's Grammar School, Amersham, Bucks; Durham University. Chartered Surveyor, Humberts, Hatfield, Herts, 1986-91; Project Officer for Red Kite Reintroduction, RSPB Scotland, Inverness, 1991-94; Conservation Officer, Central Scotland, RSPB Scotland, Glasgow, 1994-99; Head of Species and Land Management, RSPB Scotland, Edinburgh, 1999-2008. Member of Scotland's Moorland Forum; Chair, Link Deer Task Force; Member, Central Scotland Raptor Study Group and Scottish Ornithologist's Club. Recreations: birdwatching; bird ringing; foreign travel. Address: (b.) RSPB Scotland, Dunedin House, 25 Ravelston Terrace, Edinburgh EH4 3TP; T.-0131 311 6500.
E-mail: duncan.orr-ewing@rspb.org.uk

Orr Ewing, Major Edward Stuart, DL, JP, CVO. Lord Lieutenant, Wigtown, 1989-2006; b. 28.9.31, London; m., 1, F.A.B. Farquhar (m. dissolved); 2, Diana Mary Waters; 1 s.; 2 d. Educ. Sherborne; RMCS, Shrivenham. Black Watch RHR, 1950-69 (Major); Farmer and Landowner, since 1964. Recreations: country sports; skiing; sailing; painting.

Orskov, Professor Egil Robert, OBE, BSc, PhD, DSc, FRSE. Director, International Feed Resource Unit, Macaulay Institute, since 2000, previously at Rowett Research Institute, 1990-2000; International Consultant, United Nations Organization, since 1980; b. 24.5.34, Denmark; m., Joan P.; 2 s.; 1 d. Post-doctoral work, USDA, Washington, 1966-67; Rowett Research Institute: Head, Sheep Section, 1967-75, Dairy Cattle Section, 1975-85, Head, Ruminant Nutrition, 1985-90. Honorary Professor: University of Aberdeen, Gadjah Mada University, Indonesia. Publications: five books; 550 papers. Recreations: music; travel; antique collector. Address: (b.) Macaulay Institute, Craigiebuckler, Aberdeen AB15 8QH; T.-01224 498243; e-mail: b.orskov@macaulay.ac.uk

Osborne, Rt. Hon. Lord (Kenneth Hilton Osborne), QC (Scot). Senator of the College of Justice, since 1990; b. 9.7.37. Advocate, 1962; QC, 1976; Chairman, Local Government Boundary Commission, 1990-2000.

Osborne, Sandra, MSc. MP (Labour), Ayr, Carrick and Cumnock, since 2005, Ayr, 1997-2005; b. 23.2.56; m., Alastair; 2 d. Educ. Camphill Senior Secondary School, Paisley; Anniesland College; Jordanhill College; Strathclyde University. Former community worker. Address: (b.) House of Commons, London SW1A 0AA.

O'Shea, Professor Sir Timothy Michael Martin, PhD, BSc. Principal and Vice-Chancellor, University of Edinburgh, since 2002; b. 28.3.49; m., Professor Eileen Scanlon; 2 s.; 2 d. Educ. Royal Liberty School, Havering; Sussex University; Leeds University. Open University: Founder, Computer Assisted Learning Research Group, 1978, Lecturer, 1980-82, Senior Lecturer, 1983-87, Institute of Educational Technology, Professor of IT and Education, 1987-97, Pro-Vice-Chancellor for QA and Research, 1994-97, Master, Birkbeck College and Professor of Information and Communication Technologies, 1998-2002, Provost, Gresham College, 2000-02, Pro-Vice-Chancellor, 2001-02, University of London. Address: University of Edinburgh, Old College, South Bridge, Edinburgh EH8 9YL.

Osler, Douglas Alexander, CB, KSG, MA (Hons). HM Senior Chief Inspector and Chief Executive, HM Inspectorate of Education, Scottish Executive, 1996-2002; Visiting Professor, Strathclyde University, 2002-05; b. 11.10.42, Edinburgh; m., Wendy I. Cochrane; 1 s.; 1 d. Educ. Royal High School, Edinburgh; Edinburgh University; Moray House College of Education. Assistant Teacher of History/Careers Master, Liberton Secondary School, Edinburgh, 1965-68; Principal Teacher of History, Dunfermline High School, 1968-74. English Speaking Union Fellowship to USA, 1966; International Visitor Program to USA, 1989; President, Standing International Conference of Inspectorates, 1999-2002; Interim Scottish Prisons Complaints Commissioner, 2003; Chair, Statutory Inquiry, Northern Ireland, 2004; led inquiry into Scottish Court Service, 2005; Chairman of Commissioners, South Eastern Education and Library Board, Northern Ireland, since 2006; Vice-Chairman, Royal Blind Asylum and School; Past President, Rotary Club of Edinburgh. Publications: Queen Margaret of Scotland; Sources for Modern Studies, Volumes 1 and 2.

O'Sullivan, Very Rev. Canon Basil, JCL. Parish Priest, Holy Family, Dunblane, since 1988; b. 1932, Fishguard. Educ. St. Finbarr's College, Cork; All Hallow's College, Dublin; Pontifical University of St. Gregory, Rome. Assistant Priest: St. Joseph's, Dundee, 1959-63, St. Andrew's Cathedral, Dundee, 1963-70; R.C. Chaplain, Dundee University, 1964-70; Parish Priest: St. John Vianney's, Alva, 1970-74, St. Columba's, Dundee, 1974-88. Canon of Dunkeld Chapter, since 1992. Judge of The Scottish Catholic Tribunal. Recreations: reading; gardening; walking. Address: (h.) St. Clare's, Claredon Place, Dunblane FK15 9HB; T.-01786 822146.

Oswald, Rev. John, BSc, BD, PhD. Interim Minister (North East Scotland); b. 10.10.47, Glasgow; m., Barbara R.; 1 s. Educ. Kelvinside Academy; Edinburgh University. Management posts, Nickerson Seed Specialists; Managing Director, David Bell Ltd., Penicuik; candidate for ministry; Assistant Minister, Eddleston linked with Peebles Old; Minister, Lorne and Lowland Parish Church, Campbeltown; Minister, Muthill with Trinity Gask and Kinkell. Recreations: tennis; gardening; reading. Address: 1 Woodlands Meadow, Rosemount, Blairgowrie PH10 6GZ.

Ouston, Hugh Anfield, MA (Hons), DipEd. Head of College, Robert Gordon's College, Aberdeen, since 2004; b. 4.4.52, Dundee; m., Yvonne; 2 s.; 2 d. Educ. Glenalmond School; Christ Church, University of Oxford. Teacher of History, North Berwick High School, 1977-84; Head of History, Beeslack High School, 1984-92; Assistant Head, Dunbar Grammar School, 1992-97; Deputy Principal, George Watson's College, 1997-2004. Recreations: birdwatching; gardening; hill walking; sailing; poetry. Address: (h.) Belhaven, 273 North Deeside Road, Milltimber, Aberdeen; T.-01224 733576; e-mail: h.ouston@rgc.aberdeen.sch.uk

Overend, Stuart John, BSc (Hons), CA, AMCT. Head of Operations, Private Equity Division, Aberdeen Asset Management PLC, since 1999; b. 16.4.70, Glasgow; m., Jennifer; 1 s.; 1 d. Educ. Williamwood High School; University of Strathclyde. KPMG, 1992-96; Clydesdale Bank Equity Ltd., 1996-99; holds various directorships. Chairman, Glasgow and West of Scotland ICAS Area Committee, 2002-06; Member, Council, Institute of Chartered Accountants of Scotland, 2002-06; Member, Legal and Technical Committee of the British Venture Capital Association. Recreations: rugby; golf. Address: (b.) 149 St. Vincent Street, Glasgow G2 5NW; T.-0141-306 7400; e-mail: stuart.overend@aberdeen-asset.com

Owen, Professor David Gareth, MA, BD (Hons), PhD, FICE, CEng. Professor Emeritus, Heriot-Watt University, since 2003 (Professor of Offshore Engineering, 1986-2003, Vice Principal, 1999-2001); b. 6.11.40, Brecon, Wales; m., Ann Valerie Wright; 2 d. Educ. Christ College, Brecon; Downing College, Cambridge. Graduate Engineer, John Laing & Son, London; Aerospace Engineer, Marconi Space and Defence Systems, Portsmouth; Lecturer in Civil Engineering, Heriot-Watt University; Visiting Professor, University of New Hampshire; Senior Lecturer, Department of Offshore Engineering, Heriot-Watt University. Recreations: music; travelling. Address: (h.) 7 Oak Lane, Edinburgh EH12 6XH; T.-0131-339 1740.

Owen, Olwyn, BA, MA, MIFA, FSA Scot. Secretary, Historic Environment Advisory Council for Scotland, since 2007; b. 28.05.55. Address: (b.) Longmore House, Salisbury Place, Edinburgh EH9 1SH; e-mail: olwyn.owen@scotland.gsi.gov.uk

Owens, Agnes. Author; b. 24.5.26, Milngavie; m., Patrick Owens; 2 s.; 4 d. Educ. Bearsden Academy. Worked in shops, factories and offices; came to writing by accident; author of Gentlemen of the West (Autumn Book Award, 1984), Like Birds in the Wilderness, A Working Mother,

People Like That, For the Love of Willie; short stories in Lean Tales, The Seven Deadly Sins and The Seven Cardinal Virtues, Bad Attitudes; wrote a play with Liz Lochhead which toured Scotland for three months. Recreations: walking; reading. Address: (h.) 21 Roy Young Avenue, Balloch, Dunbartonshire; T.-Alexandria 50921.

Owens, Mhairi. Head of Concern Worldwide Scotland, since 2004. Board Member, The Network of International Development Organisations in Scotland (NIDOS). Address: (b.) 40 St. Enoch Square, Glasgow G1 4DH; T.-0141 221 3610; e-mail: mhairi.owens@concern.net

P

Pacione, Professor Michael, MA, PhD, DSc. Professor of Geography, Strathclyde University, since 1990; b. 14.10.47, Dundee; m., Christine Hopper; 1 s.; 1 d. Educ. Lawside Academy, Dundee; Dundee University. Lecturer in Geography, Queens University, Belfast, 1973-75; Lecturer, Senior Lecturer, Reader, Strathclyde University, Glasgow, 1975-89; Visiting Professor, University of Guelph, 1984, and University of Vienna, 1995. Publications: 25 books and more than 125 academic research papers. Recreations: travel; photography; scuba diving. Address: (b.) Department of Geography, Strathclyde University, 50 Richmond Street, Glasgow G1 1XH; T.-0141-548 3793; e-mail: m.pacione@strath.ac.uk

Pack, Professor Donald Cecil, CBE, MA, DSc, CMath, FIMA, FEIS, FRSE. Emeritus Professor, Strathclyde University, since 1986; b. 14.4.20, Higham Ferrers; m., Constance Mary Gillam; 2 s.; 1 d. Educ. Wellingborough School; New College, Oxford. Ordnance Board, Cambridge, 1941-43; Armament Research Department, Ministry of Supply, Fort Halstead, 1943-46; Lecturer in Mathematics, St. Andrews University, 1947-52; Visiting Research Associate, Maryland University, 1951-52; Lecturer in Mathematics, Manchester University, 1952-53; Professor of Mathematics, Strathclyde University, 1953-82 (Vice-Principal, 1968-72); Honorary Professor, 1982-86; Member, various Government scientific boards and committees, 1952-84; Consultant, DERA Fort Halstead, Ministry of Defence, 1984-2001; Member, Defence Scientific Advisory Council, 1975-80; DERA Visiting Fellow, 1999; first Hon. Member, European Consortium for Mathematics in Industry, 1988; Chairman, Scottish Certificate of Education Examination Board, 1969-77; Chairman, Committee of Inquiry into Truancy and Indiscipline in Scottish Schools, 1974-77 ("Pack Report" published by HMSO, 1977); Hon. President, National Youth Orchestra of Scotland (Chairman, Steering Committee, 1978, Chairman, 1978-88); Member, Scottish Arts Council, 1980-85; Member, UK Committee for European Music Year 1985 and Chairman, Scotland Advisory Committee, 1983-86; Member: General Teaching Council for Scotland, 1966-73, Dunbartonshire Education Committee, 1960-66; Governor, Hamilton College of Education, 1976-81; Council Member, Royal Society of Edinburgh, 1960-63; Honorary Treasurer and Council Member, Institute of Mathematics and its Applications, 1964-72; Member: International Advisory Committee on Rarefied Gas Dynamics Symposia, 1976-88, British National Committee for Theoretical Mechanics, 1973-78, Council, Gesellschaft fuer angewandte Mathematik und Mechanik, 1977-83; Guest Professor: Technische Universitaet, Berlin, 1967, Bologna University and Politecnico di Milano, 1980, Technische Hochschule, Darmstadt, 1981; other visiting appointments, Warsaw University, 1977, Kaiserslautern University, 1980 and 1984. Past President: Edinburgh Mathematical Society, Glasgow Mathematical Association; Honorary President, Milngavie Music Club (President, 1983-93). Recreations: music; gardening; golf. Address: (h.) 18 Buchanan Drive, Bearsden, Glasgow G61 2EW; T.-0141-942 5764.

Pagan, Graeme Henry, MBE, BL, WS. Solicitor, Hosack & Sutherland, Oban, since 1960; Member, Solicitors Discipline Tribunal, 1995-2006; Honorary Sheriff of North Strathclyde at Oban, since 1988; b. 2.3.36, Cupar; m., Heather; 1 s.; 2 d. Educ. New Park, St. Andrews; Bedford School; Edinburgh University. Part-time Procurator Fiscal, Oban, 1970-79; Regional Organiser, Shelter Campaign for the Homeless, 1968-75; Chairman, Oban Housing Association, 1971-98; Founder Member, Oban Abbeyfield Society; Originator, Solicitors Will Aid; Convener, Argyll and Bute Scottish Liberal Democrats, 1991-2000; Director of Charity Companies Will Relief Scotland and Scottish International Relief. Publication: Memoirs: Once Bitten Twice Fined, 2004. Recreations: family; jazz; malt whisky; wandering in the Highlands on foot and bike. Address: (h.) Neaveton, Oban, Argyll; T.-01631 563737.

Page, Professor Alan Chisholm, LLB, PhD. Professor of Public Law, Dundee University, since 1985; b. 7.4.52, Broughty Ferry; m., Sheila Duffus; 1 s.; 1 d. Educ. Grove Academy; Edinburgh University. Lecturer in Law, University College, Cardiff, 1975-80; Senior Lecturer in Law, Dundee University, 1980-85; Head, Department of Law, 1980-95, 2005-06; Dean, School of Law, since 2006; Dean, Faculty of Law, 1986-89; SHEFC Lead Assessor in Law, 1995-96. Publications: Legislation; Investor Protection; The Executive in the Constitution. Recreation: mountaineering. Address: (h.) Westlands, Westfield Road, Cupar, Fife KY15 5DR.

Paget, Elspeth Mary, LLB (Hons), DipLP, TEP. Partner, Gillespie MacAndrew LLP, since 2005; b. 1960, Glasgow; 2 c. Educ. Wellington School, Ayr; University of Edinburgh. Traineeship with Alex Morison & Co., 1982-84; Assistant with AC Bennett & Fairweather WS, 1984-89; Partner, Bennett and Robertson, 1989-2005; Tutor in Private Client Course of The Diploma in Legal Practice, University of Edinburgh, 2002-06; Member, The Society of Trust and Estate Practitioners (STEP), since 2007. Address: (b.) 5 Atholl Crescent, Edinburgh EH3 8EJ; T.-0131 225 1677; e-mail: elspeth.paget@gillespie.macandrew.co.uk

Pagliari, Paul, MA. Director, Change and Corporate Services, Scottish Government, since 2006; Member, Employment Appeals Tribunal, since 2002; b. 31.03.60, Paisley. Educ. St. Aloysius College, Glasgow; Glasgow University. Career History: Human Resources: Ford Motor Company, then BT; Director Human Resources: Scottish Power, then Scottish Water, Director, Change and Corporate Services, Home Office. Recreations: tennis; skiing. Address: (b.) Room GE18, St Andrews House, Regent Road, Edinburgh; T.-0131 244 4624; e-mail: paul.pagliari@scotland.gsi.gov.uk

Paisley of Westerlea Duncan Wilson, FRSA, FSA Scot. Succeeded as 16th Head of the Name; 5th Laird of the Barony of Westerlea; Captain, Balgonie Castle; Ambassador (Overseas), Capability Scotland; Patron, Westerlea School, Edinburgh; Patron, Kagyu Samye Ling Monastery and Tibetan Centre, Eskdalemuir; b. 30.8.48, Woodcote; 3 d. Educ. Cannock House School; Westwood Regular Army, 1966-90 (Gordon Highlanders, RAOC) General List; King's Own Scottish Borderers, 1990-95; Regional Liaison Officer, Scottish Landowners' Federation, 1992-93; The Guild of Master Craftsmen: Assessment Officer (S.W. Scotland), 1993-96; Regional Manager and Trainer (W), 1996-2000; Chief Assessor (Scotland), since 2000; Director, Westerlea Trading; Chairman, Westerlea Trust; President, Scottish Tartans Society, 1997-2001; Director, Register of All Publicly known Tartans, 1997-2001; Freeman of Glasgow; Member, Incorporation of Weavers, Glasgow; Committee of the Heraldry Society of Scotland; Member, The Royal Celtic Society; Hon. Col. Legion of Frontiersmen, 2001-04. Recreations: hill-walking; Scottish domestic architecture; family history; gardening. Address: (h.) Rosebank, 21 California Road, Maddiston, Stirlingshire FK2 0NH; T./Fax-01324 710896; Mob: 07739 749038; e-mail: westerlea16th@yahoo.co.uk

Palfreyman, Professor John, BSc, DPhil, FIWSc. Head of the School of Contemporary Sciences and Depute Principal, University of Abertay Dundee; BioScientist; b. 30.7.51, Potters Bar; 2 d. Educ. Stationers' Company's School; London and Sussex Universities. Research

Biochemist, Royal Infirmary Glasgow; Research Fellow, MRC Institute of Virology, Glasgow; various posts: Dundee College of Technology, Dundee Institute of Technology, University of Abertay Dundee. Chair, Discovery STEM Space School; Board Member, Unicorn Preservation Society; Member, Mills Observatory Advisory Board. Recreations: theatre; photography; hill walking (Munro bagging). Address: (b.) School of Contemporary Sciences, University of Abertay Dundee, Bell Street, Dundee DD1 1HG; T.-01382 308640. E-mail: j.palfreyman@abertay.ac.uk

Panton, Jim. Chief Executive, Poppyscotland. Address: (b.) New Haig House, Logie Green Road, Edinburgh EH7 4HR.

Park, Ian Michael Scott, CBE, MA, LLB. Partner, Paull & Williamsons, Advocates, Aberdeen, 1961-91, Consultant thereafter; Member: Criminal Injuries Compensation Board, 1983-2000, Criminal Injuries Compensation Appeals Panel, 1996-2002; b. 7.4.38, Aberdeen; m., Elizabeth M.L. Struthers, BL, MBE; 2 s. Educ. Aberdeen Grammar School; Aberdeen University. Assistant to and subsequently Partner in Paull & Williamsons; Member, Society of Advocates in Aberdeen, since 1962, Treasurer, 1991-92, President, 1992-93; Sometime part-time Assistant, Department of Public Law, Aberdeen University; President, Law Society of Scotland, 1980-81 (Council Member, 1974-85); Chairman, Aberdeen Citizens Advice Bureau, 1962-84; Temporary Sheriff, 1976-84; Honorary Sheriff at Aberdeen, since 1996; part-time Chairman, Medical Appeals Tribunals, until 1996; frequent broadcaster on legal topics. Retired following diagnosis of Parkinsons Disease. Address: (h.) 46 Rubislaw Den South, Aberdeen AB15 4AY; T.-01224 313799.

Park, John William. MSP (Labour), Mid Scotland and Fife, since 2007; b. 14.9.73; m., Lisa; 2 d. Educ. Woodmill High School; Blacklaw Primary (both Dunfermline); Adam Smith College, Kirkcaldy; Carnegie College, Dunfermline. Rosyth Dockyard: Electrical Fitter, 1989-98, Trade Union Convenor, 1998-2001; AEEU, now AMICUS: Research Officer, 2001-02, National Industrial Campaigns Officer, 2002-03; Head of Employee Relations, Babcock Naval Services, 2003-04; Assistant Secretary, STUC, 2004-07. Address: (b.) Scottish Parliament, Edinburgh EH99 1SP; T.-0131 348 6754. E-mail: john.park.msp@scottish.parliament.uk

Park, Neil Ferguson, BSc, MBA. Managing Partner, Edgewood Consulting; Chairman, Scottish Sports Association; Director of Development, British Universities Sports Association; Director, Confederation of British Sport; b. 26.9.62, Gosport; m., Judith Frances; 1 s.; 1 d. Educ. Daniel Stewart's and Melville College, Edinburgh; Aberdeen University; Edinburgh University. Former General Manager, Scottish Athletics Limited; former Project Director, RGA Consulting; Lay Member, Sports Dispute Resolution Panel. Recreations: rugby; golf; roadrunning; writing. Address: (b.) 22 Craigcrook Road, Edinburgh EH4 3PG.

Parker, Anthony W. BA, MA, PhD, FHEA, FCS. Director, American Studies and Transatlantic Studies, University of Dundee, since 2000; Lecturer in History, University of Dundee, since 1996; b. 3.2.53, Little Rock, Arkansas, USA; m., Lisa Ann; 3 s. Educ. St. Andrews University; University of Georgia, Athens, Georgia, USA. Joined University of Dundee, 1996; Director, University Transatlantic Student Exchange Programme; Director of Administration and Undergraduate Programmes, Institute for Transatlantic, European and American Studies (ITEAS), since 2003; Consultant, Scottish Executive North American Strategy 2010 Group; External Academic Reviewer, National Museums of Scotland, Museum of Scotland International, 2001-2002; Convener, North American Studies Group, Scottish Confederation of University and Research Libraries, 1999-2006; Editor, Journal of Transatlantic Studies; Founding Member, Scottish Trans-Atlantic Relations Project; Council Member, Economic and Social History Society of Scotland; Fellow, Charles Warren Center for Studies in American History, Harvard University, International Seminar on the History of the Atlantic World, 1996. Publication: Scottish Highlanders in Colonial Georgia: the Recruitment, Emigration and Settlement in Darien, 1735–1748, 1997; numerous articles, book reviews, papers. Recreations: golf; more golf; rare books; antiques; photography; music; travel. Address: (b.) ITEAS, University of Dundee, Dundee DD1 4HN; T.-01382 345465; e-mail: a.w.parker@dundee.ac.uk

Parker, Cameron Holdsworth, CVO, OBE, DL, BSc. Lord Lieutenant of Renfrewshire, 1998-2007; b. 14.4.32, Dundee; m., Marlyne Honeyman; 3 s. Educ. Morrison's Academy, Crieff; Glasgow University. Managing Director, latterly also Chairman, John G. Kincaid & Co. Ltd., Greenock, 1967-80; Chairman and Chief Executive, Scott Lithgow Ltd., Port Glasgow, 1980-83; Board Member, British Shipbuilders, 1977-80, 1981-83; Chief Executive, Prosper Enginering Ltd., Irvine, 1983-84; Managing Director, Lithgows Limited, 1984-92, Vice-Chairman, 1992-97. Freeman, City of London; Liveryman, Worshipful Company of Shipwrights; Member, Council, CBI Scotland, 1986-92; Member, Argyll and Clyde Health Board, 1991-95; Board Member, Scottish Homes, 1992-96; Director, Clyde Shaw Ltd., 1992-94; Honorary President, Accord Hospice, 1998-2007; President, SSAFA Forces Help, Renfrewshire, 1998-2007; DUniv University of Paisley, 2003. Recreation: golf; gardening. Address: (h.) Heath House, Kilmacolm, Renfrewshire PA13 4PE; T.-01505 873197.

Parker, Colin. Chief Executive, Aberdeen Harbour Board, since 2006; b. 5.10.57, Manchester; m., Victoria Louise Walker; 2 d.; 1 s. Educ. HMS Conway Merchant Navy School; Liverpool Polytechnic. Merchant Navy Cadet and Officer, 1974-87; Aberdeen Harbour Board: Vessel Traffic Services Officer, 1987-90, Assistant Harbour Master, 1990-94, Harbour Master, 1994-2006. Board Member, Aberdeen and Grampian Chamber of Commerce, 2006. Council Member, British Ports Association, 2006; Chairman, Scottish Ports Committee of British Ports Association, 2002-06. Recreations: golf; badminton; walking; picture framing. Address: Harbour Office, 16 Regent Quay, Aberdeen AB11 5SS; T.-01224 597000.

Parker, Timothy Robert Walter, LLB. Depute Secretary to Church of Scotland General Trustees, since 1982; b. 7.10.44, Aberdeen; m., Janet Helen Nicol; 3 d. Educ. Trinity College, Glenalmond; Aberdeen University. Private practice as Solicitor, 1969-82. Formerly: Chairman, Lothian Primary Schools Chess League, Secretary, Lothian Federation of P.T.A.s. Recreations: bowling; walking; watching other sports; listening to music. Address: (h.) 35 Dudley Avenue, Edinburgh EH6 4PL; T.-0131-554 2076.

Parks, Rowan Wesley, MB, BCh, BAO, MD, FRCSI, FRCS(Edin). Reader in Surgery, University of Edinburgh, since 1999; Honorary Consultant Surgeon, Royal Infirmary of Edinburgh, since 1999; b. 5.3.66, Belfast; m., Janet Margaret; 2 s.; 2 d. Educ. Royal Belfast Academical Institution; Queen's University, Belfast. Research Fellow,

Queen's University, Belfast, 1994-96; Higher Surgical Trainee, Northern Ireland, 1996-98; Clinical Fellow, Edinburgh, 1998-99. Moynihan Medal, Association of Surgeons of Great Britain and Ireland; Millin Lecturer and Medal, Royal College of Surgeons of Ireland. Recreation: boating. Address: Department of Clinical and Surgical Sciences, Royal Infirmary of Edinburgh, Edinburgh EH16 4SA; T.-0131 242 3616; e-mail: R.W.Parks@ed.ac.uk

Parr, Professor John Brian, BSc (Econ), MA, PhD, AcSS. Professor of Regional and Urban Economics, Glasgow University, since 1989; b. 18.3.41, Epsom; m., Pamela Jean Harkins; 2 d. Educ. Henry Thornton School; London University; University of Washington. Instructor, University of Washington, 1966; Assistant Professor/Associate Professor, University of Pennsylvania, 1967-75; joined Glasgow University as Lecturer, 1975. Academician of the Academy of Learned Societies for the Social Sciences; Fellow of Regional Science Association International; Associate Editor, Journal of Regional Science, since 1979; Member, Board of Management, Urban Studies, since 1981; Member, Editorial Board, Review of Urban and Regional Development Studies, since 1995; Chairman, British-Irish Section, Regional Science Association International, 1981-85. Publications: numerous journal articles on urban and regional analysis; Christaller Central Place Structures (Co-Author); Regional Policy: Past Experience and New Directions (Co-Editor); Analysis of Regional Structure: Essays in Honour of August Lösch (Co-Editor); Market Centers and Retail Location (Co-Author). Address: (b.) Department of Urban Studies, Glasgow University, Glasgow G12 8QQ; T.-0141-339 8855, Ext. 4724/4121; e-mail: J.B.Parr@socsci.gla.ac.uk

Parratt, David Richmond, LLB (Hons), DipLP, NP, PhD, MCIArb, FSA Scot, FCS, FRSA. Advocate, since 1999; b. 13.2.70, Dundee; m., Margaret Sarah Thomson. Educ. Glasgow Academy; High School of Dundee; Aberdeen University; Edinburgh University. Solicitor, 1995-99; Tutor, Faculty of Law, Edinburgh University, 1996-98; Called to the Scottish Bar, 1999. Publication: "The Development and Use of Written Pleadings in Scots Civil Procedure" (Stair Society). Recreations: golf; skiing; antiquarian books. Address: (b.) Advocates' Library, Parliament House, Edinburgh EH1 1RF; T.-0131 226 5071; e-mail: dparratt@hotmail.com

Parratt, Emeritus Professor James Roy, MSc, PhD, DSc, MD (h.c.), DSc (med), FRCPath, DipRelStudies (Cantab), FRPharmS, FESC, FISHR, FIBiol, FRSE. Professor Emeritus, Strathclyde University, since 1998; b. 19.8.33, London; m., Pamela Joan Lyndon Marels; 2 s.; 1 d. Educ. St. Clement Danes Holborn Estate Grammar School; London University. Spent nine years in Nigeria as Head of Pharmacology, Nigerian School of Pharmacy, then in Physiology, University Medical School, Ibadan; joined Strathclyde University, 1967; appointed Reader, 1970; Personal Professor, Department of Physiology and Pharmacology, 1975-83; Professor of Cardiovascular Pharmacology, 1983-98; Research Professor, since 2001; Honorary Research Professor, Albert Szent-Gyorgy: Medical Faculty, University of Szeged, Hungary, since 1998; Head, Department of Physiology and Pharmacology, 1986-90. Chairman, Cardiac Muscle Research Group, 1980-83; Vice President, European Shock Society, 1995-98; Gold Medal, Szeged University, 1975; Honorary Member, Hungarian Pharmacological Society, 1983; Honorary Doctorate, Albert Szent-Gyorgi Medical University, Hungary, 1989; Gold J.E. Purkyne Honorary Medal, Academy of Sciences of Czech Republic, 1995; Sodalem honoris causa, Slovak Medical and Cardiological Societies, 1997; Honorary Member, Czech Cardiological Society, 1998; Honorary Citizen of the City of Winnipeg, 2001;

Chairman, Universities and Colleges Christian Fellowship, 1984-90; Chairman, Interserve Scotland, 2000-03; Leverhulme Trust Emeritus Fellow, 2001-03; Szent-Gyorgyi Fellow, Hungarian State Government, 2002-03; former Vice-Chairman, Scripture Union; Past Chairman, SUM Fellowship; Lay Preacher, Baptist Unions of Scotland and Great Britain; Honorary President, Baptist Lay Preachers Association of Scotland, 1985-90. Recreation: music. Address: (h.) 10 St. Germains, Bearsden, Glasgow G61 2RS; T.-0141-942 7164; (b.) Strathclyde Institute for Biomedical Sciences, 27 Taylor Street, Glasgow G4 0NR; T.-0141-548 2858; e-mail: pimjam.parratt@btinternet.com

Pasley, Anthony du Gard, FLI, FSGD, FSA Scot; Landscape Architect in private practice, since 1973; b. 10.8.29, Edinburgh. Educ. King's College School. Senior Associate, Sylvia Crowe and Associates, 1967-72; work has included major public projects but specialises in country gardens and estates in UK and Europe; has taught on courses at Kew Gardens, Wisley, Edinburgh and New York Botanic Gardens, Reading University, London University. Publications: Summer Flowers, 1977; The English Gardening School (Co-author), 1987; Garden and Landscape, 2004. Recreations: gardening; garden and architectural history; collecting books and paintings; opera. Address: Lodge Cottage, Ball Play Road, Moffat.

Patel of Dunkeld, Baron (Narendra Babubhai Patel). Chancellor, University of Dundee, since 2006; b. 1938, Tanzania; m., Dr. Helen Dally; 2 s.; 1 d. Educ. Harrow High School; St. Andrews University. Previously President, Royal College of Obstetrics and Gynaecologists; previously Chairman: Academy of Medicine, Royal College; Clinical Standards Board, Scotland, Quality Improvement Scotland; currently Chairman: National Patient Safety Agency, Stem Cell Oversight Committee, UK National Stem Cell Network; Member, Science and Technology Committee, since 1999; Patron of several charities; Fellow, Academy of Medical Science, Royal Society of Edinburgh; Hon. Dr. and Hon. Fellow, Universities and Colleges. Author of numerous publications on maternal/foetal medicine, epidemiology, obstetrics and gynaecology. Address: (b.) University of Dundee, Dundee DD1 4HN; T.-01382 632 959; e-mail: naren.patel@tuht.scot.nhs.uk

Paterson, Professor Alan Alexander, LLB (Hons), DPhil (Oxon), FRSA, FRSE. Solicitor. Professor of Law, Strathclyde University, since 1984; b. 5.6.47, Edinburgh; m., Alison Jane Ross Lowdon; 2 s.; 1 d. Educ. Edinburgh Academy; Edinburgh University; Pembroke College, Oxford. Research Associate, Oxford Centre for Socio-Legal Studies, 1972-73; Lecturer, Law Faculty, Edinburgh University, 1973-84; Visiting Professor, University of New Mexico Law School, 1982, 1986. Former Chairman: Committee of Heads of University Law Schools of the UK, Scottish Legal Action Group and British and Irish Legal Education and Technology Association; Chairman, Legal Services Group, Citizens Advice Scotland; Vice-Chair, Joint Standing Conference on Legal Education in Scotland; Member, Council, Law Society of Scotland; past President, Society of Legal Scholars; Member, Judicial Appointments Board, since 2002. Publications: The Law Lords, 1982; The Legal System of Scotland (Co-author), 1993; Law, Practice and Conduct for Solicitors (Co-author), 2006; Paths to Justice Scotland (Co-Author), 2001. Address: (b.) Centre for Professional Legal Studies, Strathclyde University Law School, 141 St James Road, Glasgow G4 0LT; T.-0141-548 3341; e-mail: prof.alan.paterson@strath.ac.uk

Paterson, Calum, BA, MBA, CA. Managing Director, Scottish Equity Partners, since 2000; b. 13.4.63, Edinburgh; m., Amanda McLean. Educ. Linlithgow Academy;

University of Strathclyde. Ernst and Young, 1985-88; Scottish Development Agency, 1988-91; Scottish Enterprise, 1991-2000. Recreation: various sports. Address: (b.) 17 Blythswood Square, Glasgow G2 4AD; T.-0141-273 4000.

Paterson, Professor David Maxwell, BSc, PhD. Head of the School of Biology, University of St. Andrews, Professor, Coastal Ecology, since 2000; b. 16.6.58, Dalry; m., Marie; 2 d. Educ. Royal High School, Edinburgh; University of Glasgow; University of Bath. Royal Society Research Fellow, University of Bristol, 1988; University of St. Andrews: Lecturer, 1993, Reader in Environmental Biology, 1996. Honorary Research Associate, Acadia University, Nova Scotia. Publications: Biostabilisation of Sediments (Joint Editor), 1994; Sedimentary Processes in the Intertidal Zone, (Joint Editor), 1998. Recreations: natural history; music; squash; family. Address: (h.) 22 Pinkerton Road, Crail, Fife KY10 3UB; T.-01333 450047; e-mail: d.paterson@st-and.ac.uk

Paterson, Dianne Elizabeth, LLB, NP. Managing Partner, Russel and Aitken, Solicitors, since 2006, Partner, since 1985; Non Executive Director of ESPC, since 2001; b. 8.1.58, Dundee; m., Dr. John W. Paterson. Educ. High School of Dundee; University of Aberdeen. Apprenticeship (Legal), Robson McLean and Paterson, 1979-81; Legal Assistant, Russel and Aitken, 1981-85. Credited for opening a property shop in The Royal Infirmary of Edinburgh (1988-2000); responsible for the launch of the 'Russel & Aitken Design Award'. Recreations: art; sculpture; opera; classical music. Address: (h.) 18 Clarendon Crescent, Edinburgh EH4 1PU; T.-0131 228 5500; (h.) 27 Rutland Square, Edinburgh EH1 2BU; e-mail: dianne.paterson@russelaitken.com

Paterson, Douglas McCallum, CBE, LLD, MA, MEd, DMS, DipM, MIM. Chief Executive, Aberdeen City Council, since 1995; b. 20.11.49, Macduff; m., Isobel Beaton; 2 d. Educ. Banff Academy; Aberdeen University; Robert Gordon University. John Wood Group, 1971-75; Grampian Regional Council: Teacher, 1976-81, Head Teacher, 1981-86, Advisor, 1986-90, Depute Director of Education, 1990-92, Senior Depute Director, 1992-94, Director of Education, 1994-95. Recreations: local history; fishing industry; music; walking; theatre. Address: (b.) Town House, Aberdeen; T.-01224 522500.

Paterson, George Matthew, CBE, BSc (Hons), PhD. Director, Food Standards Agency Scotland, since 2000; b. 16.3.42, Edinburgh; m., Patricia; 1 s.; 2 d. Educ. George Heriot's, Edinburgh; Edinburgh University. Postdoctoral Fellow, National Research Council of Canada, 1967-69; scientific and management posts in a variety of departments of Government of Canada, 1969-99. Recreations: tennis; golf. Address: (b.) St Magnus House, 25 Guild Street, Aberdeen; T.-01224 285102.

Paterson, Gil. MSP (SNP), West of Scotland, since 2007; b. 11.11.42, Glasgow. Address: (b.) Scottish Parliament, Edinburgh EH99 1SP; Constituency Office: Unit 21, 31 Clyde Street, Clydebank G81 1PF.

Paterson, Lt. Col. Howard Cecil, TD, FSA Scot. International Tourism Consultant and Artist; b. 16.3.20, Edinburgh; m., Isabelle Mary; 1 s. Educ. Daniel Stewart's College, Edinburgh; Edinburgh College of Art. Army, 1939-49; combat duties during War; personnel selection afterwards; Territorial Army, 1949-70; serves on Lowland Reserve Forces and Cadets Association; Founder Member,

Gunner Heritage Appeal; Member, City of Edinburgh Artillery Officers' Association; Member, Scottish Armed Forces Officers' Club; Assistant Personnel Manager, Jute Industries Ltd., Dundee, 1949-51; Organising Secretary, Scottish Country Industries Development Trust, 1951-66; Senior Director, Scottish Tourist Board, 1966-81. Chairman, Taste of Scotland Ltd., 1984-86; Vice-Chairman, John Buchan Society, 1990-95; Chairman, Trekking and Riding Society of Scotland, 1995-2003 (now Hon. President). Publications: Tourism in Scotland; Flavour of Edinburgh (with Catherine Brown). Recreations: fishing; shooting; riding; writing; drawing and painting; natural history; history. Address: (h.) Dovewood, West Linton, Peeblesshire, EH46 7DS; T.-01968 660346.

Paterson, Rev. John Love, MA, BD, STM. Minister Emeritus, St. Michael's Parish Church, Linlithgow, since 2003 (Minister, 1977-2003); Chaplain to The Queen, since 1996; b. 6.5.38, Ayr; m., Lorna Begg (see Lorna Marion Paterson). Educ. Ayr Academy; Glasgow University; Edinburgh University; Union Theological Seminary, New York. Minister: Presbyterian Church of East Africa, 1964-72, St. Andrew's, Nairobi, 1968-72; Chaplain, Stirling University, 1973-77. Moderator, West Lothian Presbytery, 1985. Recreations: gardening; Rotary. Address: 22 Waterfront Way, Stirling FK9 5GH; T.-01786 447165.

Paterson, Very Rev. John Munn Kirk, ACII, MA, BD, DD. Minister Emeritus, St. Paul's Church, Milngavie; b. 8.10.22, Leeds; m., Geraldine Lilian Parker; 2 s.; 1 d. Educ. Hillhead High School; Edinburgh University. Pilot, RAF, 1940-46; Insurance official, 1946-58; ordained Minister, Church of Scotland, 1964; Minister, St. John's Church, Bathgate, 1964-70; Minister, St. Paul's Church, Milngavie, 1970-87. Moderator, General Assembly, Church of Scotland, 1984-85; Life Member, Chartered Insurance Institute; Hon. Doctorate, Aberdeen University, 1986. Recreations: fishing; gardening. Address: (h.) 58 Orchard Drive, Edinburgh EH4 2DZ; T.-0131-332 5876.

Paterson, Lorna Marion, MA, Dip.Rel.Ed. General Secretary, Church of Scotland Guild, 1985-98; b. 26.1.38, Unst; m., Rev. John L. Paterson (qv). Educ. Inverurie Academy; Aberdeen University; Aberdeen College of Education. Teacher of English, History, Geography and Religious Education, 1960-62; Teacher of English, 1962-66; Administrative Assistant, Strathclyde University, 1966-68; Deputy Academic Registrar, then Education Administrator, Stirling University, 1968-79. Guider (Division Commissioner, West Lothian, 1982-85); Chairman, Linlithgow Arts Guild, 1999-2002; Elder, St. Michael's Parish Church, Linlithgow, 1995-2003; Vice Convener, Church of Scotland Parish Development Fund Committee, 2003-05; Member, Executive Committee, Scotland's Churches' Scheme, since 1999; Member, Scottish Women's Convention Steering Group (Convener, 2003-06). Recreations: singing; homemaking; reading; the arts; people. Address: (h.) Kirkmichael, 22 Waterfront Way, Stirling FK9 5GH; T.-01786 447165; e-mail: lornandian.paterson@virgin.net

Paterson, Wilma, DRSAM. Freelance Composer/Music Critic/Travel Writer; b. 23.4.44, Dundee; 1 s.; 1 d. Educ. Harris Academy; Royal Scottish Academy of Music. Composition study with Luigi Dallapiccola in Florence; writes chamber and incidental music; contributes to: The Scotsman, The Herald, The Lady, Sunday Times, Essentially America, Sunday Herald, etc. Publications: A Country Cup; Was Byron Anorexic?; Shoestring Gourmet; Flowers and Herbs of the Bible; Lord Byron's Relish; Salmon & Women, The Feminine Angle; Songs of Scotland (with Alasdair Gray). Address: Columbus Cottage, 39

Albert Street, Tayport, Fife DD6 9AT; T.-01382 552262; e-mail: WilmaMTPaterson@aol.com

Paterson-Brown, June, CBE, MBChB, JP, CVO. Lord Lieutenant, Roxburgh, Ettrick and Lauderdale, 1998-2007; b. 8.2.32, Edinburgh; m., Peter Neville Paterson-Brown (qv); 3 s.; 1 d. Educ. Esdaile School; Edinburgh University. Medical Officer, Family Planning and Well Woman's Clinics, 1959-85; Past Chairman: County of Roxburghshire Youth Committee, Roxburgh Duke of Edinburgh Award Committee; Scottish Chief Commissioner, Girl Guides Association, 1977-82; Non-Executive Director, Border Television plc, 1980-99; Vice-Chairman, Princes Trust, 1982-92 (Trustee, 1982-94); Chairman, Borders Region Children's Panel Advisory Committee, 1982-85; Chairman, Scottish Standing Conference of Voluntary Youth Organisations, 1983-85; Commonwealth Chief Commissioner, Girl Guides Association, 1985-90; Trustee, MacRobert Trusts, 1987-2002; Paul Harris Fellow, 1990; JP, since 1999. Recreations: golf; music; fishing; reading; grand-children. Address: (h.) Norwood, Hawick, Roxburghshire TD9 7HP; T.-01450 372352; e-mail: Pbnorwood@btinternet.com

Paterson-Brown, Peter Neville, MBChB, DObst RCOG. Medical Practitioner, retired; b. 23.3.31, Hawick; m., June Garden (see June Paterson-Brown); 3 s.; 1 d. Educ. Merchiston Castle School; Edinburgh University. Hon. Medical Adviser, Red Cross Scotland, 1981-94; Member, Scottish Committee, Medical Commission on Accident Prevention, 1978-91; Director, Children's Hospice Association Scotland, 1993-2000; Vice President, React, 1991-2001. Red Cross Badge of Honour, 1995. Publication: A Matter of Life or Death. Recreations: skiing; shooting; golf; fishing. Address: (h.) Norwood, Hawick, Roxburghshire; T.-01450 372352.

Paterson-Brown, Simon, MB BS, MPhil, MS, FRCS(Ed), FRCS Eng, FCS (HK). Consultant General Surgeon, Royal Infirmary, Edinburgh, since 1994; President-elect, Association of Upper Gastrointestinal Surgeons of Great Britain and Ireland; b. 6.2.58, Edinburgh; m., Dr Sheila Finnerty; 3 d. Educ. Trinity College, Glenalmond; St. Mary's Hospital Medical School, London. Senior Lecturer in Surgery, St. Mary's Hospital, London, 1993-94. Clinical Director, Department of Surgery, Royal Infirmary. Publications: Aids to Anatomy; Guide to Practical Procedures in Medicine and Surgery; Principles and Practice of Surgical Laparoscopy (Editor); Core Topics in General and Emergency Surgery (Editor). Recreations: music; skiing; golf; running. Address: Department of Surgery, Royal Infirmary, Edinburgh EH16 4SA; T.-0131 242 3645.

Paton, Alasdair Chalmers, BSc, CEng, FICE, FCIWEM. Chief Executive, Scottish Environment Protection Agency, 1995-2000; Retired Company Director; b. 28.11.44, Paisley; m., Zona G. Gill; 1 s.; 1 d. Educ. John Neilson Institution, Paisley; Glasgow University. Assistant Engineer, Clyde Port Authority, 1967-71; Assistant Engineer, DAFS, 1971-72; Senior Engineer, SDD, 1972-77; Engineer, Public Works Department, Hong Kong Government, 1977-80; Senior Engineer, then Principal Engineer, SDD, 1980-87; Deputy Chief Engineer, 1987-91; Director and Chief Engineer, Engineering, Water and Waste Directorate, Scottish Office Environment Department, 1991-95. Recreations: Rotary; sailing; golf. Address: (h.) Oriel House, Academy Square, Limekilns, Fife KY11 3HN; T.-01383 872218.

Paton, Hon. Lady (Ann Paton). Senator of the College of Justice, since 2000; m., Dr James Y. Paton. Educ. Laurel Bank School, Glasgow; Glasgow University (MA, LLB). Advocate, 1977; Standing Junior Counsel: Queen's and Lord Treasurer's Remembrancer, 1979, Office of Fair Trading in Scotland, 1981; QC (Scot),

1990; Advocate Depute, 1992-94. Director, Scottish Council of Law Reporting, 1995-2000; Member, Criminal Injuries Compensation Board, 1995-2000. Address: (b.) Parliament House, Edinburgh, EH1 1RQ.

Paton, Rev. Anne Shaw, BA, BD. Minister, East Kilbride Old Parish Church, since 2001; b. 10.11.63, Glasgow; m., Thomas Moan; 2 s. Educ. Vale of Leven Academy; Jordanhill College of Education; Glasgow University. Primary School Teacher, West Dunbartonshire. Address: 40 Maxwell Drive, The Village, East Kilbride G74 4HJ; T.-01355 220732; e-mail: annepaton@fsmail.net

Paton, David Romer, OBE, KStJ, DL. Chairman: Aberdeen Harbour Board, Aberdeen Foyer, Pitsligo Castle Trust, Friends of Grampian Stones, Order of St John (Aberdeen and North East), Prince's Scottish Youth Business Trust (Grampian), Scottish Traditional Skills Training Centre, The Mither Kirk Project, Whatever News Limited; Vice-Chairman, North East Scotland Preservation Trust; President: Grampian Houston Association, Aberdeen Civic Society; Director: Aberdeen and Grampian Chamber of Commerce, Aberdeen Foyer Services Ltd, Peacock Visual Arts; Trustee: Scottish Civic Trust, Aberdeen Tivoli Theatre Trust, Aberdeen University Development Trust, Old Aberdeen Heritage Trust; Council Member, National Trust for Scotland; Committee Member: Scottish Council for Development and Industry, SRPBA; Patron: Cancer Link Aberdeen and North (CLAN), UCAN, Touch of Tartan Ball; b. 5.3.35, Aberdeen; m., Juliette Burney; 2 s. Educ. Gordonstoun School; Keble College, Oxford. Chartered Surveyor in own practice; former Chairman: North East Scotland Preservation Trust, Association of Scottish Chambers of Commerce; former Chairman and President, Scottish Council for Development and Industry; Chairman: Royal Northern and University Club, Grampian Cancer Care Project, Grampian Epilepsy Association of Scotland Appeal, Grampian-Houston Association, Aberdeen Beyond 2000, Business Committee University Quincentenary Appeal Comitee, Don District Salmon Fishery Board; Past President, Aberdeen Chamber of Commerce; Burgess of Guild. FRICS; FSA Scot; HonDBA, Robert Gordon University. Recreations: fishing; conservation. Address: Grandhome, Danestone, Aberdeen AB22 8AR; T.-01224 722202.
E-mail: davidpaton@btconnect.com

Paton, Dr James Y., BSc, MBChB, MD, DCH, FRCPH, FRCP. Hon. Consultant Pediatrician, since 1989; Reader, Paediatric Respiratory Disease, Royal Hospital for Sick Children, Glasgow, since 2001; b. 8.12.51, Glasgow; m., Ann Paton. Educ. Jordanhill College School; Glasgow University. Publications: chapters and articles on Paediatric Respiratory Disease. Recreations: cycling; sailing. Address: (b.) Department of Child Health, RHSC, Yorkhill, Glasgow, G3; T.-0141-201 0238; e-mail: J.Y.Paton@clinmed.gla.ac.uk

Patrick, Bruce Robertson, BA, LLB, WS. Consultant, Maclay Murray & Spens, since 2003 (Partner, 1976-2003, Managing Partner, 1991-94, Senior Partner, 2000-03); Vice-Convenor, Law Society Company Law Committee, since 1990; b. 26.11.45, London; m., Hilary Jane Sutton; 1 s.; 2 d. Educ. Glasgow Academy; Edinburgh Academy; Exeter College, Oxford University; Edinburgh University. Apprentice, Mitchells Johnston, Solicitors, Glasgow, 1971-73; Assistant, Maclay Murray and Spens, Solicitors, 1973-75; Assistant, Coward Chance, Solicitors, London, 1975-76; Director, Dunedin Enterprise Investment Trust plc; Director, Scotland Yard Adventure Centre; Management Committee Member, Castle Rock Housing Association. Recreations: sailing; golf; hillwalking. Address: (b.)

Quartermile One, 15 Lauriston Place, Edinburgh EH3 9EP; T.-0131 228 7167.

Patterson, Lindy Ann, LLB (Hons), WS, ACIArb. Lawyer; Partner, Head of Construction, Dundas & Wilson; b. 12.9.58, Berwick-upon-Tweed. Educ. Eyemouth High School; Edinburgh University. Member, Scottish Building Contract Committee; Honorary Member of RICS; Scotland's first female Solicitor Advocate (May, 1993); former Member of number of Law Society Comittees and Commercial Court Consultative Committee; past Editor, Building Law and Development and Scottish Construction Law Review; Member, Building Standards Advisory Committee. Recreations: hill-walking; travel. Address: (b.) Saltire Court, Castle Terrace, Edinburgh.

Pattison, David Arnold, BSc, PhD. Best Value Inspector, Audit Commission, 2000-06 (retired); Hon. President, Scottish Youth Hostels Association; b. 9.2.41, Kilmarnock; m., Anne Ross Wilson; 2 s.; 1 d. Educ. Kilmarnock Academy; Glasgow University. Planning Assistant, Ayr County Council, 1963-64; PhD studies, Glasgow University, 1964-66; Planning Assistant, Dunbarton County Council, 1966-67; Lecturer, Strathclyde University, 1967-70; Head of Tourism, Highlands and Islands Development Board, 1970-81; Chief Executive, Scottish Tourist Board, 1981-85; Director Leisure and Tourism Consulting: Ernst & Young, 1985-89, Cobham Resource Consultants, 1989-96, Scott Wilson Resource Consultants, 1996-98; Director, David A. Pattison Associates, 1998-2000. External Examiner for postgraduate tourism courses, Strathclyde University, 1981-84. Recreations: reading; watching soccer and rugby; golf; gardening. Address: (h.) 7 Cramond Glebe Gardens, Cramond, Edinburgh EH4 6NZ.

Pattison, Rev. Kenneth John, MA, BD, STM. Minister, Kilmuir and Logie Easter, Ross-shire, 1996-2004; b. 22.4.41, Glasgow; m., Susan Jennifer Brierley Jenkins; 1 s.; 2 d. Educ. Lenzie Academy; Glasgow University; Union Theological Seminary, New York. Minister, Church of Central Africa Presbyterian, Malawi, 1967-77; Minister, Park Parish Church, Ardrossan, 1977-84; Chaplain, Glasgow Royal Infirmary, 1984-90; Associate Minister, St. Andrew's and St. George's, Edinburgh, 1990-96. Convener, Chaplaincies Committee, Church of Scotland, 1993-96. Recreations: gardening; family history. Address: (h.) 2 Castle Way, St. Madoes, Perthshire PH2 7NY; T.-01738 860340.

Patton, John. National Development Officer, Scottish League of Credit Unions, 2000-07; National President, Educational Institute of Scotland, 1999-2000; b. Derry, 1942; m., Elizabeth Scott; 3 c. Taught English in Northern Ireland, 1964-71; Press Officer, civil rights movement in Derry, 1968-70; taught in West Lothian, 1971-73, Zambia, 1973-76, Central Region, since 1976; Headteacher, Banchory Primary School, Tullibody, 1985-90, Craigbank Primary School, Sauchie, 1990-2000; fluent Irish Gaelic speaker. Recreations: Scottish and Irish traditional music. Address: 50 Fir Park, Tillicoultry FK13 6PJ; T.-01259 750530.

Pattullo, Sir (David) Bruce, Kt, CBE, BA, Hon. LLD (Aberdeen), DUniv (Stirling), Hon. DBA (Strathclyde), FRSE, FCIB (Scot). Governor, Bank of Scotland, 1991-98; Director (Non-Executive): British Linen Bank, 1977-98, Bank of Wales PLC, 1986-98, NWS Bank, 1986-98; b. 2.1.38, Edinburgh; m., Fiona Jane Nicholson; 3 s.; 1 d. Educ. Belhaven Hill School; Rugby; Hertford College, Oxford. National Service commission, Royal Scots (seconded to West Africa); joined Bank of Scotland, 1961; winner, first prize, Institute of Bankers in Scotland, 1964; Bank of Scotland: Manager, Investment Services Department, 1967-71, Deputy Manager, Bank of Scotland Finance Co. Ltd., 1971-73, Chief Executive, Group Merchant Banking Activities, 1973-78, Deputy Treasurer,

1978, Treasurer and General Manager, 1979-88, Director, 1980-98, Group Chief Executive and a Deputy Governor, Bank of Scotland, 1988-91. Chairman, Committee of Scottish Clearing Bankers, 1981–83 and 1987-89; Director, Standard Life Assurance Co., 1985-96; President, Institute of Bankers in Scotland, 1990-92. Recreations: tennis; hill-walking. Address: (h.) 6 Cammo Road, Edinburgh EH4 8EB.

Paul, Jeanette McIntosh, BSc, BArch (Hons), RIBA, ARIAS. Head of Postgraduate Studies for Duncan of Jordanstone College, University of Dundee, since 2007; Head of School of Design, University of Dundee, 2004-07; b. 27.10.56, Giffnock; m., Roderick. Educ. St. Denis School, Edinburgh; Duncan of Jordanstone College, University of Dundee. Assistant Architect, Sir Basil Spence Glover of Ferguson, Edinburgh, 1982-85; Project Architect, Andrew Merrylees Associates, Edinburgh, 1985-87; Senior Architect, Wilson of Wolmersley, Perth, 1987-88; University of Dundee: Lecturer in Interior and Environmental Design, 1988-2002, Senior Lecturer and Deputy Head, School of Design, 2002-04. President, Dundee Institute of Architects, 1999-2001; Board of Directors for WASPS (Workshop of Artists' Studio Provision Scotland Ltd.), since 1999; Joint Winner of The Scottish Design Award 2000 for best commercial/product design. Recreations: travelling; reading; dancing. Address: (b.) School of Design, Duncan of Jordanstone College, Perth Road, Dundee DD1 4HT; T.-01382 345290; e-mail: j.m.paul@dundee.ac.uk

Paul, Nigel Anthony Lewis, BSc (Chem), ACA. Director of Corporate Services, University of Edinburgh, since 2002; b. 4.11.53, Nuneaton, Warwickshire; m., Anne Rosalind Beasley; 2 d. Educ. King Henry VIII Grammar School, Coventry; Bristol University. Pannell Kerr Foster, Chartered Accountants, 1975-80; ICI PLC Agricultural Division, 1980-83: 1985-88); Britag Ltd., Chief Accountant, 1983-84; ICI Teesside Operations, 1989-93; ICI Chemicals and Polymers Group, Financial Controller, 1993-95; ICI International Halochemicals Business, Finance, Planning and IT Director, 1995-2002. Companies House, Non-Executive Director, since 2002; Edinburgh Research and Innovation Ltd., Chairman, since 2002; Edinburgh University Press, Trustee Director, since 2002; Edinburgh Technology Fund, Non-Executive Director, since 2003; Targeting Innovation Ltd., 2003-07; TMRI Ltd., since 2006; APUC Ltd., since 2007; Leadership Trust Tutor; Guest Lecturer, University of Manchester, 1997-2002. Recreations: music; performing arts; travel; reading. Address: (b.) University of Edinburgh, Charles Stewart House, 9-16 Chambers Street, Edinburgh EH1 1HT; T.-0131-650-9845; e-mail: nigel.paul@ed.ac.uk

Paxton, Professor Roland Arthur, MBE, MSc, PhD, HonDEng, CEng, FICE, FRSE, AMCST. Chairman, Institution of Civil Engineers Panel for Historical Engineering Works, 1990-2003, Vice Chairman, since 2003; Chairman, Historic Bridge and Infrastructure Awards, England and Wales, since 1998; Commissioner, Royal Commission on the Ancient and Historical Monuments of Scotland, 1992-2002; Hon. Professor, School of the Built Environment, Heriot-Watt University, since 1994; b. 29.6.32, Altrincham; m., Ann; 2 d. Educ. Altrincham Grammar School; Manchester College of Science and Technology; Heriot-Watt University. Cartographical surveyor, Ordnance Survey, 1953-55; Civil Engineer, Corporations of Sale, Manchester, Leicester, Edinburgh, and Lothian Regional Council, retiring as Senior Principal Engineer, 1959-90; Hon. Senior Research Fellow, Heriot Watt University, 1990-94. Chairman, Forth Bridges Visitor Centre Trust, since 1997; Secretary and Director, Laigh Milton Viaduct Conservation Project, 1992-99; Trustee, James Clerk Maxwell Foundation, since 1999; President, Edinburgh Bibliographical Society, 1992-95; Winner, Institution of Civil Engineers' Garth Watson Medal, 1999 and Carr Prize, 2001; Lecturer Award, Association for Preservation Technology International, 2000; American Society of Civil Engineers' History and Heritage Award, 2003; author of books and papers on technical innovation, conservation of structures, and historical engineering. Address: (b.) School of the Built Environment, Heriot-Watt University, Edinburgh EH14 4AS; T.-0131-449 5111.

Peacock, Professor Sir Alan Turner, Kt (1987), DSC (1945), MA (St. Andrews), HonDUniv (Stirling), Hon. DEcon (Zurich), Hon. DScEcon (Buckingham), HonDUniv (Brunel), HonDUniv (York), HonLLD (St. Andrews), HonLLD (Dundee), HonDSc (Edinburgh), Hon. Fellow (LSE), Lib Doc (Catania), Dr.h.c. (Lisbon), Laurea (h.c.) (Turin), FBA, FRSE. Honorary Research Professor in Public Finance, Edinburgh Business School, Heriot-Watt University, since 1985; b. 26.6.22, Ryton-on-Tyne; m., Margaret Martha Astell-Burt; 2 s.; 1 d. Educ. Grove Academy; Dundee High School; St. Andrews University. Royal Navy, 1942-45; Lecturer in Economics, St. Andrews, 1947-48; Lecturer, then Reader in Economics, London School of Economics, 1948-56; Professor of Economic Science, Edinburgh University, 1956-62; Professor of Economics, York University, 1962-78 (Deputy Vice Chancellor, 1963-69); Professor of Economics, University College, Buckingham, 1978-84; Principal, then Vice Chancellor, Buckingham University, 1980-84; Chief Economic Adviser, Department of Trade and Industry (on secondment), 1973-76. Member, Royal Commission on the Constitution, 1970-73; Member, Inquiry into Retirement Provision, 1983-85; SSRC Council, 1972-73; President, International Institute of Public Finance, 1966-69 (now Honorary President); Chairman, Committee on Financing the BBC, 1985-86; Chairman, Rowntree Inquiry on Takeovers, 1989-91; Executive Director, David Hume Institute, Edinburgh, 1985-91 (Honorary President, 2002-05); Chairman, Scottish Arts Council, 1986-92; Chairman, Academic Advisory Council, Institute of Economic Affairs, 1991-93; Head, UN Advisory Mission to Russia on Social Protection, 1992; Non-Executive Director, Macdonald Orr Ltd., 1991-98; Chairman, Hebrides Ensemble, 1994-99; Trustee, Policy Institute, since 2005; Scottish Free Enterprise Award, 1987; Keynes Lecturer, British Academy, 1994; Fellow, Accademia Nazionale dei Lincei, Rome; Royal Medal, Royal Society of Edinburgh, 2002. Publications: 30 books, over 200 articles on economics of public policy and of the arts. Recreations: attempting to write music; wine spotting. Address: (h.) 5/24 Oswald Road, Edinburgh EH9 2HE; T.-0131-667 5677; e-mail: pavone@blueyonder.co.uk

Peacock, Andrew John, BSc, MPhil, MD, FRCP. Honorary Professor, Glasgow University, since 2003; Consultant Physician (Respiratory), West Glasgow Hospitals, since 1990; Director, Scottish Pulmonary Vascular Unit; b. 13.11.49, Montreal; m., Jila Pezeshgi; 1 s.; 2 d. Educ. Westminster School; St. Bartholomew's Hospital Medical College, London University; Caius College, Cambridge University. Senior House Officer, St. Bartholomew's, Addenbrookes and Queen Square Hospitals; Registrar, Brompton Hospital; Senior Registrar, Southampton Hospitals; Research Fellow, University of Colorado; Visiting Scientist, National Heart and Lung Institute, London. Physiologist, 1993 British Expedition to Everest. Publication: Pulmonary Circulation: a handbook for clinicians. Recreations: anything to do with mountains; wine; tennis; golf. Address: (b.) Scottish Pulmonary Vascular Unit, Level 8, Western Infirmary, Glasgow, G11 6NT; T.-0141-211 6327.

Peacock, Professor John Andrew, MA, PhD, FRS, FRSE. Professor of Cosmology, Edinburgh University, since 1998; b. 27.3.56, Shaftesbury; m., Heather; 1 s.; 2 d. Educ. Cedars School, Leighton Buzzard; Jesus College, Cambridge. Research Astronomer, Royal Observatory, Edinburgh, 1981-92; Head of Research,

Royal Observatory, Edinburgh, 1992-98; UK representative, Anglo-Australian Telescope Board, 1995-2000. Publications: Cosmological Physics, 1999. Recreations: playing classical clarinet; hill walking. Address: (b.) Institute for Astronomy, Edinburgh University, Royal Observatory, Edinburgh, EH9 3HJ; T.-0131-668 8100; e-mail: jap@roe.ac.uk

Peacock, Peter James, CBE. MSP (Labour) Highlands and Islands, since 1999; Member, Rural Affairs and Environment Committee; formerly Minister for Education and Young People (2003-06); b. 27.2.52, Edinburgh; 2 s. Educ. Hawick High School; Jordanhill College of Education, Glasgow. Community Worker, Orkney Islands, 1973-75; former Area Officer, Highlands, Islands, Grampian, Scottish Association of Citizens Advice Bureaux; Member, Highland Regional Council, 1982-96; former Leader and Convener, Highland Council; formerly: Member, Highlands and Islands Convention, Honorary President, Scottish Library Association, Board Member, Centre for Highlands and Islands Policy Studies, Member, Scottish Natural Heritage, Non-Executive Director, Scottish Post Office Board, Member, Highland Area Committee, SCDI, Chairman, Scottish Library and Information Council, Vice-President, COSLA; Member, European Committee of the Regions, 1993-99; Chair, Commonwealth Education Ministers Conference, 2003; former Training, Organisation and Policy Consultant; Co-author, Vice-Chairman, subsequently Chairman of successful applicant group for Independent Local Radio franchise, Moray Firth. Recreations: ornithology; golf; watching rugby union. Address: (h.) 'Birchwood', IV2 7QR; T.-01667 460190.

Peaker, Professor Malcolm, FRS, DSc, HonDSc, PhD, FZS, FIBiol, FRSE. Non-executive Director, Edinburgh Instruments Ltd., since 2004; Director, Hannah Research Institute, Ayr, 1981-2003; Hannah Professor, Glasgow University, 1981-2003; b. 21.8.43, Stapleford, Nottingham; m., Stephanie Jane Large; 3 s. Educ. Henry Mellish Grammar School, Nottingham; Sheffield University, BSc Zoology; DSc; University of Hong Kong, SRC NATO Scholar; PhD. ARC Institute of Animal Physiology, 1968-78; Head, Department of Physiology, Hannah Research Institute, 1978-81. Chairman, London Zoo Board, 1992-93; Vice-President, Zoological Society of London, 1992-94; Member, Editorial Board: Journal of Dairy Science, 1975-78, International Zoo Yearbook, 1978-82, Journal of Endocrinology, 1981-91; Editor, British Journal of Herpetology, 1977-81; Munro Kerr Lecture, 1997; Raine Distinguished Visitor, University of Western Australia, 1998; 10th Edinburgh Centre for Rural Research/Royal Society of Edinburgh/Institute of Biology Annual Lecture, 2000; Distinguished Lecturer, University of Hong Kong 2002; Chairman, British Nutrition Foundation, 2002-04, Governor, since 1997; Member, Rank Prize Funds Advisory Committee on Nutrition, since 1997. Publications: Salt Glands in Birds and Reptiles, 1975; Avian Physiology (Editor), 1975; Comparative Aspects of Lactation (Editor), 1977; Physiological Strategies in Lactation (Co-Editor), 1984; Intercellular Signalling in the Mammary Gland (Editor), 1995; Biological Signalling and the Mammary Gland (Editor), 1997; papers. Recreations: vertebrate zoology; natural history; golf; grumbling about bureaucrats. Address: (b.) 13 Upper Crofts, Alloway, Ayr KA7 4QX.

Pearson of Rannoch, Lord (Malcolm Everard MacLaren Pearson). Life Peer; b. 20.7.42; m.; 3 d. Chairman, PWS Holdings plc; founded Rannoch Trust, 1984.

Pearson, Iain Clark, FCIBS. Consultant, The Royal Faculty of Procurators in Glasgow; retired senior banker; b. 13.5.45, Kilmarnock; m., Margaret Purdie; 1 s.; 1 d. Educ. Cumnock Academy. The Royal Bank of Scotland PLC: Senior Manager, Chester, 1986-89, Senior Manager, Glasgow West George Street, 1989-93, Regional Retail

Director (Glasgow and West of Scotland), 1993-95, Local Director (Corporate Banking), Glasgow and West of Scotland, 1995-98. 2005 President, New Cumnock Burns Club; 1989 President, Chartered Institute of Bankers, Chester and North Wales. Recreations: football; golf (St. Nicholas, Prestwick); reading. Address: (h.) 8, Bellevale Avenue, Ayr KA7 2RP; T.-01292 264236; e-mail: iain.pearson@tesco.net

Peat, Jeremy Alastair, BA, MSc, FRSA. Director, David Hume Institute, since 2005; Group Chief Economist, Royal Bank of Scotland, 1993-2005; Honorary Professor, Heriot-Watt University; Visiting Professor, Edinburgh University; Fellow, Industry and Parliament Trust; Council Member, Scottish Economic Society; Board of Governors, BBC, 2005-06; National Trustee for Scotland and Board Member, BBC Trust; Member, Competition Commission; Chair, BBC Pension Trust; Board Member, Signet Accreditation Society; National Governor for Scotland; b. 20.3.45, Haywards Heath; m., Philippa Ann; 2 d. Educ. St. Paul's School, London; Bristol University; University College London. Economic Assistant/Economic Adviser, Ministry of Overseas Development, 1969-77; Economic Adviser, Manpower Services Commission, 1978-80; Head, Employment Policy Unit, Ministry of Finance and Development Planning, Government of Botswana, 1980-84; Economic Adviser, HM Treasury, 1984-85; Senior Economic Adviser, Scottish Office, 1985-93. Hon. LLD, Aberdeen; Fellow, Chartered Institute of Bankers; Fellow, Royal Society of Edinburgh. Recreations: walking; reading; tennis; listening to music; golf.

Peattie, Cathy. MSP (Labour), Falkirk East, since 1999; Deputy Convener, Transport Infrastructure and Climate Change Committee; Convener, cross-party groups on: Carers, Culture and Media; Women, Asthma, Men's Violence against Women and Children. Former Convenor, Council of Voluntary Service Scotland; former Chair, Scottish Labour Women's Committee; President, The Scottish Parliament's Burns Club. Address: (b.) Scottish Parliament, Edinburgh EH99 1SP; T.-0131-348 5747; Constituency Office, 5 Kerse Road, Grangemouth; T.-01324 666026; e-mail: mail@cathypeattiemsp.org.uk; web: www.cathypeattiemsp.org.uk

Peden, Professor George Cameron, MA, DPhil, FRHistS, FRSE. Professor of History, Stirling University, since 1990; b. 16.2.43, Dundee; m., Alison Mary White; 3 s. Educ. Grove Academy, Broughty Ferry; Dundee University; Brasenose College, Oxford. Sub-Editor, Dundee Evening Telegraph, 1960-68; mature student, 1968-75; Tutorial Assistant, Department of Modern History, Dundee University, 1975-76; Temporary Lecturer, School of History, Leeds University, 1976-77; Lecturer in Economic and Social History, then Reader in Economic History, Bristol University, 1977-90; Visiting Fellow: All Souls College, Oxford, 1988-89, St. Catherine's College, Oxford, 2002. Publications: British Rearmament and the Treasury 1932-39, 1979; British Economic and Social Policy: Lloyd George to Margaret Thatcher, 1985; Keynes, The Treasury and British Economic Policy, 1988; The Treasury and British Public Policy, 1906-1959, 2000; Keynes and his Critics: Treasury Responses to the Keynesian Revolution, 1925-46 (Editor), 2004; The Transformation of Scotland: The Economy, since 1700 (Co-Editor), 2005; Arms, Economics and British Strategy: From Dreadnoughts to Hydrogen Bombs, 2007. Recreation: hill-walking. Address: (h.) Ardvurich, Leny Feus, Callander FK17 8AS; T.-01877 30488; e-mail: georgepeden@stir.ac.uk

Peggie, Robert Galloway Emslie, CBE, DUniv, FCCA. Chairman, Board, Edinburgh College of Art, 1998-99; Chairman, Local Government Staff Commission for Scotland, 1994-97; b. 5.1.29, Bo'ness; 1 s.; 1 d. Educ. Lasswade High School. Trainee Accountant, 1946-52; Accountant in industry, 1952-57; Edinburgh Corporation, 1957-72: O. and M. Officer, Assistant City Chamberlain, Deputy City Chamberlain, Reorganisation Steering Committee; Chief Executive, Lothian Regional Council, 1974-86; Commissioner (Ombudsman) for Local Administration in Scotland, 1986-94. Former Member, Court, Heriot-Watt University (Convener, Finance Committee); Governor, Edinburgh College of Art; former Trustee, Lloyds TSB Foundation. Recreation: golf. Address: 9A Napier Road, Edinburgh EH10 5AZ; T.-0131-229 6775.

Pelham Burn, Angus Maitland, LLD, JP, DL. Director, Bank of Scotland, 1977-2000, Chairman, North of Scotland Board, 1973-2001; Chairman, Aberdeen Airport Consultative Committee, since 1986; Director, Dana Petroleum plc, since 1999; b. 13.12.31, London; m., Anne; 4 d. Educ. Harrow; North of Scotland College of Agriculture. Hudson's Bay Company, 1951-58; Wolf Bounty Officer (Ontario), 1956-59; Company Director, since 1958; Chairman, Scottish Provident, 1995-98; Chairman, Aberdeen Asset Management PLC (formerly, Aberdeen Trust PLC), 1992-2000; Director, Abtrust Scotland Investment Company, 1989-96; Member, Kincardine County Council, 1967-75 (Vice Convener, 1973-75); Member, Grampian Regional Council, 1974-94; Member, Accounts Commission for Scotland, 1980-94 (Deputy Chairman, 1987-94); Director, Aberdeen Association for Prevention of Cruelty to Animals, 1975-95 (Chairman, 1984-89); former Chairman, Order of St. John (Aberdeen) Ltd.; Council Member, Winston Churchill Memorial Trust, 1984-94; Member, Queen's Bodyguard for Scotland (Royal Company of Archers), since 1968; Vice Lord Lieutenant, Kincardineshire, 1978-99, Deputy Lieutenant, since 1999; Governor, Lathallan School, 2001-04; Honorary Degree of Doctor of Law, (Robert Gordon University), 1996. Recreations: gardening; wildlife photography. Address: The Kennels Cottage, Dess, Aboyne, Aberdeenshire AB34 5AY.

Pelly, Frances, RSA. Sculptor; b. 21.7.47, Edinburgh. Educ. Morrison's Academy, Crieff; Duncan of Jordanstone College of Art, Dundee. Part-time lecturing, Dundee, 1974-78; full-time lecturing, Grays School of Art, Aberdeen, 1979-83. Recreations: riding; wildlife; gardening. Address: Quoyblackie, Rendall, Orkney KW17 2HA; T.-01856 751464.

Peltenburg, Professor Edgar, BA, PhD, FSA. Professor of Archaeology, Edinburgh University, since 1993; Director, Lemba Archaeological Research Centre, Cyprus, since 1985; b. 28.5.42, Montreal; 3 s.; 1 d. Educ. D'Arcy McGee, Montreal; Birmingham University. Lecturer in Archaeology and Resident Staff Tutor in Argyll, Glasgow University, 1969-78; Edinburgh University: Lecturer in Near Eastern Archaeology, 1978-88, Reader in Archaeology, 1988-93. Member of many committees, including UK Higher Education Funding Council's Research Assessment sub-Panel for Archaeology. Publications include: The Burrell Collection: Western Asiatic Antiquities, 1991. Address: (b.) School of History, Classics and Archaeology, University of Edinburgh, Old High School, Edinburgh EH1 1LT; T.-0131-650 2379.

Pender, Sheriff David James, LLB (Hons). Sheriff of North Strathclyde, since 1995; b. 7.9.49, Glasgow; m., Elizabeth; 2 s.; 2 d. Educ. Queen's Park Senior Secondary School, Glasgow; Edinburgh University. Partner,

MacArthur Stewart, Solicitors, Oban, 1977. Recreations: reading; travel; bridge. Address: (b.) Sheriff Courthouse, St. James Street, Paisley; T.-0141-887 5291.

Pender, Professor Gareth, BSc, PhD, CEng, FICE, FCIWEM. Professor of Environmental Engineering, Heriot-Watt University, since 2000, Director of Research; b. 24.1.60, Helensburgh; m., Isobel McNaught Connell; 2 s.; 1 d. Educ. Vale of Leven Academy; University of Strathclyde. Civil Engineer, Crouch and Hogg, Consulting Engineers, 1984-89; Lecturer, University of Glasgow, 1989-2000. Recreations: golf; skiing. Address: (b.) School of the Built Environment, Heriot-Watt University, Edinburgh EH14 4AS; T.-0131-451 3312; e-mail: g.pender@hw.ac.uk

Pengelley, Gerald Simon Horatio, BA, PGCE. Rector, Morrison's Academy, since 2004; b. 28.7.55, Bradford; m., Louise Watney; 3 s. Educ. Repton School; Bristol University; University of London Institute of Education. Teacher of History, Abingdon School, 1979-85; Head of History, Strathallan School, 1985-92; Deputy Headmaster and Director of Studies, Rossall School, 1992-2004. Recreations: history; fine art; gardening; sailing; mountaineering. Address: (b.) Morrison's Academy, Ferntower Road, Crieff, Perthshire PH7 3AN; T.-01764 653885.

Penman, David Roland, DA (Edin), DipTP (Edin), FRTPI (rtd.), ARIAS (rtd.), FSAScot. Reporter, Scottish Executive Inquiry Reporters' Unit, 1994-2002; b. 6.6.36, Manchester; m., Tamara Scott; 2 s.; 1 d. Educ. George Watson's Boys' College, Edinburgh; Edinburgh College of Art. Assistant Architect, private practices, 1960-67; Partner, Bamber Hall & Partners, Edinburgh, 1967-71; Depute County Planning Officer, Argyll County Council, 1971-73; County Planning Officer, Perth & Kinross Joint County Council, 1973-75; Director of Planning, Perth and Kinross District Council, 1975-94. Chairman, RTPI Scotland, 1984, Member of Council, 1978-85; President, Dundee Institute of Architects, 1988, Member of Council, 1980-90; Chairman, Scottish Urban Archaeological Trust, 1990-2003; formerly: Chairman, Duncan of Jordanstone College of Art, Vice-Chairman, Scottish Conservation Projects Trust, Director, Action Environment Ltd., Council Member, National Trust for Scotland. Recreations: hill-walking; art galleries; theatre; DIY; Scots history; fiddle-playing. Address: (h.) 6 Arthurstone Gardens, by Meigle, Perthshire PH12 8QY; T.-01828 640801.

Penman, Ian Douglas, BSc (Hons), MD, FRCP(Edin). Consultant Gastroenterologist, Western General Hospital, Edinburgh, since 1997; part-time Senior Lecturer, University of Edinburgh, since 1997; b. 2.2.64, Ayr; m., Jacqueline Patricia Kellaway; 1 s.; 1 d. Educ. Ayr Academy; University of Glasgow. Advanced Fellow, Medical University, South Carolina, USA, 1997-98. T.-0131-537 1758; e-mail: ian.penman@luht.scot.nhs.uk

Pennington, Professor (Thomas) Hugh, MB BS, PhD, Hon. DSc (Lancaster, Strathclyde, Aberdeen, Hull), FRCPath, FRCPEdin, FRSA, FMedSci, FRSE. Professor of Bacteriology Emeritus, University of Aberdeen; b. 19.4.38, Edgware, Middlesex; m., Carolyn Ingram Beattie; 2 d. Educ. Lancaster Royal Grammar School; St. Thomas's Hospital Medical School, London University. House appointments, St. Thomas's Hospital, 1962-63; Assistant Lecturer in Medical Microbiology, St. Thomas's Hospital Medical School, 1963-67; Postdoctoral Fellow, University of Wisconsin (Madison), 1967-68; Lecturer then Senior Lecturer in Virology, University of Glasgow, 1969-79;

Dean of Medicine University of Aberdeen, 1987-92; Professor of Bacteriology, Aberdeen University, 1979-2003; Governor, Rowett Research Institute, 1980-88, and 1996-2003; Member, Board of Directors, Moredun Research Institute, 2002-06; Chair, Expert Group on 1996 E.coli Outbreak in Central Scotland; Member: BBC Broadcasting Council for Scotland, 2000-05 (Vice Chair, 2003-05); Member, Scottish Food Advisory Committee of the Food Standards Agency, 2000-05; Member, Advisory Council of Campaign for Science and Engineering in the UK; Member, Technical Advisory Group, World Food Program; President, Society for General Microbiology, 2003-06; Chair, Public Inquiry into 2005 South Wales E. coli Outbreak; Caroline Walker Trust Consumer Advocate Award, 1997; Royal Institute of Public Health John Kershaw Memorial Prize, 1998; Thomas Graham Medal, Royal Glasgow Philosophical Society, 2001; Observer Food Monthly Hall of Fame Winner, 2005; Royal Scottish Society of Arts, Silver Medal, 2001, Keith Prize, 2006. Publications: When Food Kills, 2003; papers, articles and book chapters on viruses and bacteria, particularly their molecular epidemiology, and on food safety; contributor, London Review of Books; Editorial Consultant, The Lancet. Recreations: collecting books; dipterology. Address: (b.) Polwarth Building, University of Aberdeen, Aberdeen AB25 2ZD; e-mail: mmb036@abdn.ac.uk

Penrose, Rt. Hon. Lord (George William Penrose), PC, MA, LLB, LLD, DUniv, CA. Senator of the College of Justice, 1990-2005; b. 2.6.38, Port Glasgow; m., Wendy Margaret Ralph Cooper; 1 s.; 2 d. Educ. Port Glasgow High School; Greenock High School; University of Glasgow. Advocate, 1964; QC, 1978; Procurator to General Assembly of the Church of Scotland, 1984-90; Advocate Depute, 1987-88; Home Advocate Depute, 1989-90; Judge, First Division, Inner House, Court of Session, 2001-05; PC, 2001; Equitable Life Inquiry Reporter, 2004. Recreation: walking. Address: (b.) Supreme Courts, Parliament Square, Edinburgh.

Pentland, Brian, BSc, MB, ChB, FRCPE, FRCSLT. Consultant Neurologist in Rehabilitation Medicine, since 1982; Senior Lecturer in Rehabilitation Studies, Edinburgh University, since 1983; b. 24.6.49, Glasgow; m., Gillian Mary Duggua; 4 s. Educ. Liberton High School, Edinburgh; Edinburgh University. Junior hospital appointments in Edinburgh, Cumbria and Dundee; formerly Lecturer in Neurology in Edinburgh. Honorary Professor, Queen Margaret University, Edinburgh, 2005. Recreation: hill-walking. Address: (b.) Astley Ainslie Hospital, Grange Loan, Edinburgh EH9 2HL; T.-0131-537 9039.

Peppé, William Lawrence Tosco, OBE, JP, DL; b. 25.11.37, India; m., Deirdre Eva Preston Wakefield; 3 s. Educ. Wellington College; King's College, Cambridge. Naval Officer, 1955-91 – Commander. Vice Lord Lieutenant, Ross and Cromarty, Skye and Lochalsh, 2005; Hon. Sheriff, Portree and Lochmaddy Courts, 2007; Chairman, Skye and Lochalsh Access Forum, 2007. Recreation: country. Address: Glendrynoch Lodge, Carbost, Isle of Skye IV47 8SX; T.-01478 640218; e-mail: peppe@glendrynoch.co.uk

Pepper, Simon Richard, OBE, BSc, MSc. Rector, University of St. Andrews, since 2005; Director, WWF Scotland, 1985-2005; Member, Forestry Commission National Committee for Scotland, since 2003; Member, Cabinet Sub-committee on Sustainable Scotland, 2004-07; Member, Deer Commission for Scotland, since 2005; b. 27.9.47, Worthing; m., Moray; 2 s.; 3 d. Educ. Aberdeen University; University College London. Quelea Project, Chad, Central Africa, 1972-73; Country Parks Officer,

Essex County Council, 1973-79; Director, Cultullich Holiday Courses, Aberfeldy, 1979-85. Vice Convenor, Millennium Forest for Scotland, 1995-2001; Member, Secretary of State's Advisory Group on Sustainable Development, 1994-99. Rowing blue, Aberdeen University, Scottish Champion VIIIs, 1971; British University Champion Pairs, 1971. Recreations: enjoying the wild; managing sheep and native woodland of 42 hectare holding. Address: (h.) Upper Brae of Cultullich, Aberfeldy PH15 2EN.

Percy, Professor John Pitkeathly (Ian), CBE, LLD, CA, FRSA. Former Senior Partner, Grant Thornton, London and Scotland; Chairman, Queen Margaret University, since 2004; Non-Executive Director: The Weir Group PLC, Ricardo PLC, CALA Group Ltd; Deputy Chairman, The Weir Group PLC, since 2005; Deputy Chairman, Ricardo PLC, since 2005; former Chairman: The Accounts Commission, Audit Scotland, Kiln PLC (retired 2005), Companies House (retired 2006); b. 16.1.42, Southport; m., Sheila; 2 d. Educ. Edinburgh Academy; Edinburgh University. Managing Partner, Grant Thornton, London, 1981-88; Honorary Professor of Accounting, Aberdeen University, 1988. Freeman, City of London; Member, British Academy of Experts; Elder, St. Cuthbert's Church of Scotland; President, Institute of Chartered Accountants of Scotland, 1990-91. Recreations: golf; fishing. Address: (h.) 4 Westbank, Easter Park Drive, Edinburgh EH4 6SL.

Perman, Ray., BA Hons (Mod Hist), MBA. Chairman, Access to Finance Expert Group (formerly Small Business Investment Taskforce), since 2005; b. 1947, London; m., Fay Young; 3 s. Educ. University of St. Andrews; Open University; University of Edinburgh. Journalist: The Times, the Financial Times; Deputy Editor, the Sunday Standard, 1969-83; Insider Publications Ltd: Managing Director, 1983-94, Chairman, 1994-96, Director, 1996-99; Development Director, Caledonian Publishing plc, 1994-96; Director, GJWS Ltd, 1997-99; Chief Executive, Scottish Financial Enterprise, 1999-2003. Chairman, Inner Ear Ltd, since 2000; Member of the Court, Heriot-Watt University, since 2003; Board Member, Scottish Enterprise, since 2004; Chairman, Social Investment Scotland, since 2001; Chairman, Good Practice Ltd, since 2005. Board Member, Council for Entrepreneurial Finance, 1998-2001; Member of the Advisory Council of the Scottish Economic Policy Network, 2001-04; Member of the Scottish Economic Statistics Consultants Group, 2000-04; Visiting Lecturer in media management, State University of Saratov, Russia, 1997-2002; Trustee of the Advanced Management Foundation, 1999-2003 (a charitable trust promoting executive management education); Trustee of the Stewart Ivory Foundation, since 2001 (a charitable trust promoting financial education); Chairman of Worldwide Fund for Nature (WWF) Scottish Advisory Council, 1998-2004; Member of the UK Board of Trustees of the WWF, 2001-04. Recreations: painting; playing the blues; play bass in a blues band; planting trees. Address: 14 East Claremont Street, Edinburgh EH7 4JP; T.-0131 556 4646; mobile: 07971 164315; e-mail: ray.perman@btinternet.com

Perrie, Walter, MA, MPhil. Poet; b. 5.6.49, Lanarkshire. Educ. Hamilton Academy; Edinburgh and Stirling Universities. Publications: Books: Poem on a Winter Night, 1976; A Lamentation for the Children (SAC book award 1978), 1978; By Moon and Sun, 1980; Out of Conflict: Essays on Literature and Ideas, 1982; Concerning the Dragon (Poems), 1984; Roads that Move: a Journey through eastern Europe, 1991; From Milady's Wood and Other Poems, 1997; Caravanserai (poems), 2004; Decagon: Selected Poems, 1995-2005 (selected and edited with an introduction by John Herdman), 2005; Rhapsody of the Red Cliff (Poems), 2005; As Far as Thales: Beginning Philosophy, 2006; The King of France is Bald: Philosophy and Meaning, 2007; Twelve Fables of La Fontaine Made Owre intil Scots, 2007; Editing: Co Founding editor of Chapman, 1969-75; Guest editor, double issue of Lines Review on Canadian Literature, 1986; Managing editor, Margin, an international quarterly of the arts, 1986-91; presently Joint Editor of Fras - Scottish literary journal, since 2004. Fellowships: Scottish-Canadian exchange fellowship, 1984-85 (based at UBC Vancouver); University of Stirling writer-in-residence, 1991; Strathkelvin District creative writing fellow, 1992-93. Address: (h.) 10 Croft Place, Dunning, Perthshire PH2 0SB.

Perry, John Scott (Jack), BSc (Pure Sci), PGDip (Accountancy). Chief Executive, Scottish Enterprise, since 2004; b. 23.11.54; m., Lydia; 1 s.; 2 d. Educ. Glasgow University; Strathclyde University. CA (ICAS), 1979; Certified Public Accountant (USA), 1985; Ernst & Young, 1976-2003: Managing Partner, Glasgow, 1995-2003; Regional Industry Leader, Technol. Communications and Entertainment, Scotland and NI, 1999-2003. Chairman, CBI Scotland, 2001-03 (Member, Council, since 1996); Chairman, Regional Chairmen, Member, President's Committee, CBI. Former Member, Ministerial Task Force on Economic Forums. Visiting Tutor, Leadership Trust. Recreations: golf; skiing; reading; current affairs. Clubs: Glasgow Academical; Royal and Ancient Golf; Western Gailes Golf. Address: (b.) Scottish Enterprise, 150 Broomielaw, Atlantic Quay, Glasgow G2 8LU; T.-0141 228 2421; Fax: 0141 228 2040. E-mail: Jack.Perry@scotent.co.uk

Perth, 9th Earl of (John Eric Drummond); b. 1935. Succeeded to title, 2002.

Pertwee, Professor Roger Guy, MA, DPhil, DSc. Professor of Neuropharmacology, University of Aberdeen, since 1999; Director of Pharmacology, GW Pharmaceuticals, since 2002; b. 21.9.42, Wembley; m., Teresa Bronagh; 1 s. Educ. Eastbourne College; Christ Church, Oxford. International Cannabinoid Research Society: International Secretary, since 1991, President, 1997-98 and 2007-08; First Chairman, International Association for Cannabis as Medicine, 2005-07; Honorary Senior Research Fellow, Rowett Research Institute, since 1992; Visiting Professor, University of Hertfordshire, since 2000; Mechoulam Award for Outstanding Contributions to Cannabinoid Research, 2002. Author of numerous papers on cannabinoids (http://isihighlycited.com/). Address: School of Medical Sciences, Institute of Medical Sciences, University of Aberdeen, Foresterhill, Aberdeen AB25 2ZD; T.-01224 555740; e-mail: rgp@abdn.ac.uk

Peterken, Laurence Edwin, CBE, MA. Consultant; Member, Criminal Injuries Compensation Appeal Panel, 1997-2006; b. 2.10.31, London; m., 1, Hanne Birgithe Von Der Recke (deceased); 1 s.; 1 d.; 2, Margaret Raynal Blair; 1 s.; 1 d. Educ. Harrow School (Scholar); Peterhouse, Cambridge (Scholar). Pilot Officer, RAF Regt., Adjt. No. 20 LAA Sqdn., 1950-52; Service Divisional Manager, Hotpoint Ltd., 1961-63; Commercial Director, then Managing Director, British Domestic Appliances Ltd., 1963-68; Director, British Printing Corporation Ltd., 1969-73; Managing Director, Fashion Multiple Division, Debenhams Ltd., 1974-76; Management Auditor, 1976-77; Controller, Operational Services, GLC, 1977-85; President, GLC Chief Officers' Guild, 1983-85; Acting Director, Royal Festival Hall, 1985; General Manager, Greater Glasgow Health Board, 1986-93; Director, Special Projects, NHS in Scotland, 1993-96; Member, Scottish Committee, Council for Music in Hospitals, 1996-2007; Trustee, The Rodolfus Choir, since 1998; Lay Panel Member, Conduct and Competence Committee, Nursing and Midwifery Council, since 2004; Lay Panel Member, Disciplinary Committee, Chartered Institute of Management Accountants, since 2005. Recreations: music; cycling. Address: (h.) Carlston, Kilbarchan Road, Bridge of Weir PA11 3EG.

Peterson, George Sholto, NP. Solicitor and Notary Public, since 1956; Honorary Sheriff, since 1982; b. 18.9.27, Lerwick; m., Dorothy Hilda Spence; 2 s.; 4 d. Educ. Lerwick Central Public School; Edinburgh University. Secretary, The Shetland Trust, 1971-2002; Consultant, formerly Senior Partner, Tait & Peterson, Solicitors and Estate Agents, Lerwick; Dean, Faculty of Solicitors in Shetland, 1982-98; Honorary Pastor, Ebenezer Church, Lerwick. Recreations: studying theology; Diploma in Christian Studies, Aberdeen University (2006); reading. Address: (b.) Bank of Scotland Buildings, Lerwick, Shetland; T.-01595 693010; e-mail: info@tait-peterson.co.uk

Pethrick, Professor Richard Arthur, BSc, PhD, DSc, FRSC, FRSE, FIMMM. Professor in Chemistry, Strathclyde University, since 1983 (Head of Department, 1992-2005); b. 26.10.42; m., Joan Knowles Hume; 1 s. Educ. North Gloucestershire College, Cheltenham; London University; Salford University. Editor: British Polymer Journal, Polymer Yearbook, Polymer International, International Journal of Polymer Materials; Journal of Adhesion Science and Technology; Member, Polymer Committee, European Science Foundation; Member, Committee, MACRO Group, 1979-84; Member, SERC Polymer Materials Committee, since 1994; Elder, Merrylea Church of Scotland. Address: (b.) Department of Pure and Applied Chemistry, University of Strathclyde, Thomas Graham Building, Cathedral Street, Glasgow G1 1XL.

Petrie, Ian Duncan, MA, BD. Minister, St. Andrew's Church, Dundee, since 1986; b. 28.04.44, Arbroath; m., Marion; 3 s.; 1 d. Educ. Arbroath High; Dundee High; Edinburgh University, New College. Probationer Assistant, West St. Nicholas, Aberdeen, then Ordained Assistant, 1969-71; Minister, Westwood Parish, East Kilbride, 1971-86. Publications: Parish the Thought; To be Frank; Arthur's Seat. Recreations: walking; reading; playing golf badly. Address: 77 Blackness Avenue, Dundee DD1 2JN (Church of Scotland Manse); T.-01382 641695; e-mail: petrieduncan@aol.com

Petrie, Murray, FRICS. Chair, Operating Division, NHS Tayside; b. 8.6.46, Keith; m., Jennifer; 3 s. Educ. High School of Dundee. Consultant Chartered Surveyor. Vice Chair, NHS Tayside; Former Director, Maggie Centre (Dundee). Chairman, Tayside Primary Care NHS Trust, 1999-2004; Former Chair, Perth and Kinross Health and Social Care Co-operative. Recreations: rugby; golf; travelling. Address: (h.) Craigard, 6 Guthrie Terrace, Barnhill, Dundee DD5 2QX; T.-01382 776180.

Pettegree, Professor Andrew David Mark, FRHS. Professor of Modern History, St Andrews University, since 1998, Head of School of History; b. 16.9.57, Rhyl; m., Jane Ryan; 2 d. Educ. Oundle School; Oxford University (BA Hons). Schmidt Scholarship, 1980 (MA, DPhil, 1983); research scholarship, University of Hamburg, 1982-84; Research Fellow, Peterhouse, Cambridge; became Lecturer, St Andrews University, 1986; Reader, 1994; Director, St Andrews Reformation Studies Institute, 1993; Literary Director, Royal Historical Society, 1998. Publications include: Foreign Protestant Communities in Sixteenth Century London; Emden and the Dutch Revolt. Exile and the Development of Reformed Protestantism, 1992; The Early Reformation in Europe, 1992; Calvinism in Europe, 1540-1610 (Co-Editor); The Reformation of the Parishes. The Ministry and the Reformation in Town and Country, 1993; Calvinism in Europe, 1540-1620 (Co-Editor); Marian Protestantism. Six Studies, 1996; The Reformation World, 2000, Europe in the Sixteenth Century, 2001. Recreations: golf; tennis. Address: (b.) Reformation Institute, 69 South Street, St Andrews KY16 9AL; T.-01334 462903.

Pettigrew, Colin William, LLB (Hons). Floating Sheriff of North Strathclyde at Paisley, since 2002; b. 19.6.57, Glasgow; m., Linda; 1 s.; 1 d. Educ. The High School of Glasgow; The University of Glasgow. Assistant Court Solicitor, McClure, Naismith, Brodie and Co., Glasgow, 1980-82; Litigation Partner, Borland Johnston and Orr, Glasgow, then Borland Montgomerie Keyden, Glasgow, then TJ & WA Dykes, Hamilton, 1982-2002; Temporary Sheriff, 1999; Part Time Sheriff, 2001-02. Church of Scotland Elder. Recreations: rugby; golf; gardening and travel. Address: (b.) Sheriff Court House, St. James Street, Paisley; T.-0141-887-5291.
E-mail: sheriffcpettigrew@scotcourts.gov.uk

Phelps, Professor Alan David Reginald, MA, DPhil, CPhys, FInstP, FRSE. Professor, Physics, Strathclyde University, since 1993 (Head of Department, 1998-2001); b. 2.6.44, Basingstoke; m., Susan Helen Marshall; 1 d. Educ. Haverfordwest Grammar School; King's College, Cambridge; University College, Oxford. Research Associate, National Academy of Sciences (USA), 1972-73; Research Officer, Oxford University, 1973-78; Lecturer, then Senior Lecturer, then Reader in Physics, Strathclyde University, 1978-93, Deputy Head of Department, 1993-98. Chairman, Plasma Physics Group, Institute of Physics, 1995-97. Publications: 200 research papers and reports. Recreations: hill-walking; country pursuits. Address: (b.) Department of Physics, John Anderson Building, Strathclyde University, Glasgow G4 0NG; T.-0141-548 3166; e-mail: a.d.r.phelps@strath.ac.uk

Philip, Rt. Hon. Lord (Alexander Morrison). Senator of the College of Justice, since 1996; b. 3.8.42, Aberdeen; m., Shona Mary Macrae; 3 s. Educ. Glasgow High School; St. Andrews University; Glasgow University. Solicitor, 1967-72; Advocate, 1973; Advocate Depute, 1982-85; QC, 1984; Chairman, Medical Appeal Tribunals, 1988-92; Chairman, Scottish Land Court, 1993-96; President, Lands Tribunal for Scotland, 1993-96; Privy Counsellor, 2005. Recreations: piping; golf. Address: (b.) Parliament House, Edinburgh EH1 1RQ; T.-0131-225 2595.

Phillips, Hamish Andrew, BSc, MB, BChir, MRCP(UK), MSc, FRCR, MD. Consultant Clinical Oncologist, Edinburgh Cancer Centre, since 1999; Honorary Clinical Senior Lecturer, University of Edinburgh, since 2002; b. 30.3.62, Hitchin, Herts; m., Nicola Clare Chapman; 1 s.; 2 d. Educ. Fettes College; University of St. Andrews; Trinity Hall, University of Cambridge. SHO in Medicine, Dundee and Leicester; Registrar, Research Registrar then Senior Registrar, Department of Clinical Oncology, Western General Hospital, Edinburgh. Recreations: golf; walking; cooking. Address: (b.) Department of Clinical Oncology, Edinburgh Cancer Centre, Western General Hospital, Edinburgh.

Pia, Paul Dominic, LLB (Hons), WS, NP. Senior Partner, Burness (formerly W. & J. Burness WS), since 1974; b. 29.3.47, Edinburgh; m., Anne Christine Argent; 3 d. Educ. Holy Cross Academy, Edinburgh; Edinburgh University; University of Perugia. Law apprentice, Lindsays WS, 1968-

70; admitted as Solicitor and member of Society of Writers to HM Signet, 1971; Solicitor, W. & J. Burness WS, 1971-74; Associate Member, American Bar Association; Fellow, The Institute of Directors; Member, Scottish North American Business Council; Chairman, The Big Issue Foundation, Scotland; Trustee, Dewar Arts Awards; Chairman, Japan Society of Scotland, 1996-2000. Publications: Care Diligence and Skill (handbook for directors). Recreations: hill-walking; travel; foreign languages. Address: (b.) 50 Lothian Road, Edinburgh; T.-0131 473 6106; (h.) Lauriston, 67 Woodford Park, Edinburgh; T.-0131 441 7051.
E-mail: paul.pia@burness.co.uk

Pickard, Willis Ritchie Sturrock, MA, LLD, DEd; b. 21.5.41, Dunfermline; m., Ann Marie nee MacNeil; 2 d. Educ. Daniel Stewart's College; St. Andrews University. The Scotsman: Sub-editor, 1963-72, Leader writer, 1967-72, Features Editor, 1972-77; Editor, Times Educational Supplement Scotland, 1977-2001. Liberal Candidate, East Fife, 1970, 1974. Member, Scottish Arts Council; Chairman, Book Trust Scotland; Rector, Aberdeen University, 1988-90; Chairman, Scottish Liberal Club, since 2004; President, Edinburgh Pentlands Liberal Democrats; Trustee, National Library of Scotland, since 2005; Chairman, Theatre Objektiv; Fellow, Scottish Vocational Education Council. Recreations: reading; history research. Address: (h.) 13 Lockharton Gardens, Edinburgh EH14 1AU; T.-0131 443 7755.
E-mail: willis.pickard@btinternet.com

Pickering, Professor Martin John, BA, PhD, FRSE. Professor of The Psychology of Language and Communication, University of Edinburgh, since 2003; b. 02.06.66, London; m., Elizabeth; 1 s.; 2 d. Educ. City of London University; University of Durham; University of Edinburgh. Science and Engineering Research Council Postdoctoral Fellow, 1990-92; British Academy Postdoctoral Fellow, 1992-95; Glasgow University: Lecturer, 1995-99, Reader, 1999; Reader, Edinburgh University, 2000-03; British Academy Research Readership, 2005-07. Broadbent Lecturer, British Psychological Society, 2006. Publications: Associate Editor, Psychological Science, since 2007; over 70 journal papers. Recreation: entertaining my children. Address: (b.) Department of Psychology, University of Edinburgh, 7 George Square, Edinburgh EH8 9JZ; T.-0131 650 3447; e-mail: martin.pickering@ed.ac.uk

Pickett, Professor James, BSc (Econ), MLit. Professor Emeritus, Strathclyde University, since 1995; b. 7.6.29, Greenock; m., Janet Clelland; 1 s.; 3 d. Educ. Greenock Academy; School of Economics, Dundee; Edinburgh University; Glasgow University; University of Paris. Statistician, Dominion Bureau of Statistics, Canada, 1957-59; Lecturer, Senior Lecturer, Professor and Director, Livingstone Institute of Overseas Development, Strathclyde University, 1961-95; Visiting Professor, University of Saskatchewan, 1962-63; Special Economic Adviser, UN Economic Commision for Africa, 1965-68; Economic Adviser, African Development Bank, 1987-89; UN Chief Economic Adviser to Ethiopian Government, 1992-95; Consultant to British, Canadian and Ghanian Governments, UN, OECD; author and editor, seven books and numerous papers; FRSA; sometime President, Scottish Union of Students. Recreations: hill-walking; listening to music; photography; computing; long-suffering support of Greenock Morton F.C. Address: (h.) 18/4 Harbourside, Kip Village, Inverkip PA16 0BF; T.-01475 631046; e-mail: james.pickett1@btinternet.com

Pieri, Frank, LLB. Sheriff of South Strathclyde, Dumfries and Galloway, since 2005; b. 10.8.54, Glasgow; m., Dorothy Telfer; 2 d. Educ. St. Aloysius College, Glasgow; Glasgow University. Solicitor, 1976-93; Advocate at Scottish Bar, since 1994; Full Time Immigration

Adjudicator, 2000-04; Part Time Sheriff, 2004. Council Member: Scottish Law Agents Society, 1991-93, Council of Immigration Judges, 2003. Recreations: ambling; American crime fiction; Partick Thistle; opera. Address: (b.) Hamilton Sheriff Court, Beckford Street, Hamilton ML3 0BT; T.-01698 282957.
E-mail: sherifffpieri@scotcourts.gov.uk

Pighills, (Christopher) David, MA. Chairman, Pitlochry Festival Theatre, since 2000; Board Member, New Park Educational Trust, since 2007; former Chairman, Board of Governors, Strathallan School; b. 27.11.37, Bradford. Educ. Rydal School; Cambridge University. Fettes College, 1960-75; Headmaster, Strathallan School, 1975-93. Recreations: shooting; gardening; golf. Address: Donlellan, Foss, by Pitlochry PH16 5NQ; T.-01882 634232; e-mail: davidpighills@freeola.com

Pike, (Kathryn) Lorna, MA (Hons). Project Co-ordinator, Faclair na Gàidhlig, since 2003; b. 8.8.56, Fort William. Educ. Lochaber High School, Fort William; Edinburgh University. Editor, Concise Scots Dictionary, 1979-83; Dictionary of the Older Scottish Tongue: Assistant Editor, 1984-86, Editor, 1986-2001; Editor, Scottish National Dictionary Association, 2001-02; Research Officer, Feasibility Study, Institute for the Languages of Scotland, 2001-02; Senior Editor, Scottish Language Dictionaries, 2002-04. Recreations: riding; photography; handicrafts. Address: (b.) Sabhal Mòr Ostaig, Sleat, Isle of Skye IV44 8RQ; T.-01471 888 273.

Pilcher, Rosamunde, OBE. Author; b. 22.9.24, Lelant, Cornwall. Began publishing short stories in Woman and Home, 1945; since then has published hundreds of short stories. Novels include Sleeping Tiger, Under Gemini, Wild Mountain Thyme, The Carousel, Voices in Summer, The Shell Seekers, September, The Blue Bedroom, Flowers in the Rain, Coming Home, Winter Solstice; play: The Dashing White Sergeant. Address: (h.) Penrowan, Longforgan, Perthshire; T.- Dundee 360393.

Pinder, Christopher John, BA, DipLib, MLib, FCILIP. Director of Learning Information Services, Napier University, since 1999; b. 27.12.50, Blackpool. Educ. Wolverhampton Grammar School; University of Wolverhampton; University of Wales (Aberystwyth). Assistant Librarian: Lancashire County Library, 1974-76, Bristol Polytechnic, 1976-80; Systems Librarian, Bristol Polytechnic, 1980-84, Head of Reader Services, 1984-86; Depute Librarian, Napier University, 1986-99. Publications: various professional journal articles; book: "Providing Customer Oriented Services in Academic Libraries", 1996 - Joint Editor. Recreation: photography. Address: (b.) Craiglockhart Campus, Napier University, Edinburgh EH14 1DJ; T.-0131 455 4270; e-mail: c.pinder@napier.ac.uk

Pinder, Susan, OBE, MBA. Principal and Chief Executive, James Watt College, since 2008; b. 28.12.51, Tadcaster; m., Tony; 1 s. Educ. Selby Grammar School. Twenty-five years' experience in further education. Member, Board, Scotland's Colleges and Riverside Inverclyde; Convener of the ASC's Principals' Forum. Recreations: reading; gardening; travel. Address: James Watt College, Finnart Street, Greenock PA16 8HF; T.-01475 553001; e-mail: spinder@jameswatt.ac.uk

Piper, Professor Ronald Allen, BA, BD, PhD. University Vice-Principal (Teaching), St Andrews University, since 2003; Professor of Christian Origins, St. Andrews University, since 1997; b. 1948, U.S.A.; m., Faith Woodhouse; 1 d. Educ. Pomona College, Claremont, California; London University. Lecturer in New Testament Studies, Aberdeen University, 1979-80; Lecturer in New Testament Language and Literature, St. Andrews University, 1980-92, Reader in New Testament, 1992-97,

Principal, St. Mary's College, St. Andrews University, 1992-2001, Head, School of Divinity, 1992-2001. Secretary, British New Testament Society, 1990-93; Assistant Secretary, Studiorum Novi Testamenti Societas, since 2000. Publications: Wisdom in the Q-Tradition, 1989; The Gospel Behind the Gospels, 1995; numerous journal articles. Address: (b.) St. Mary's College, St. Andrews KY16 9JU; T.-01334 462850.

Pippard, Professor Martin John, BSc, MB, ChB, FRCPath, FRCP. Professor of Haematology, Dundee University, since 1989; Honorary Consultant Haematologist, NHS Tayside, since 1989; Dean of the School of Medicine, since 2007; b. 16.1.48, London; m., Grace Elizabeth; 2 s.; 1 d. Educ. Buckhurst Hill County High School; Birmingham University. House Physician and House Surgeon, 1972-73; Senior Medical House Officer, 1973-75; Research Fellow, Nuffield Department of Clinical Medicine, Oxford, 1975-78; MRC Travelling Research Fellow, University of Washington, Seattle, 1978-80; Wellcome Trust Research Fellow and Clinical Lecturer, Nuffield Department of Clinical Medicine, 1980-83; Consultant Haematologist, MRC Clinical Research Centre and Northwick Park Hospital, 1983-88. Recreations. gardening; hill-walking. Address: (b.) School of Medicine, Ninewells Hospital and Medical School, Dundee DD1 9SY; T.-01382 660111; e-mail: m.j.pippard@dundee.ac.uk

Pitcaithly, Mary, OBE, LLB, NP. Chief Executive, Falkirk Council, since 1998; b. 17.7.56, Falkirk; 1 d. Educ. Falkirk High; Edinburgh University. Depute Director, Law and Administration, Falkirk District Council, 1989-95; Assistant Chief Executive, Falkirk Council, 1995-98. Address: (b.) Municipal Buildings, Falkirk; T.-01324 506002.

Pitches, Sally Jane, LLB, NP. Executive Director, Girlguiding Scotland, since 1997; b. 5.6.57, Edinburgh. Educ. Currie High School; Strathclyde University. Solicitor, private practice, Edinburgh. Founding President, Edinburgh Breakfast Rotary Club; Senator, Junior Chamber International. Recreations: cookery; bridge; travel. Address: (b.) 16 Coates Crescent, Edinburgh; T.-0131-226 4511.

Pittilo, Professor Robert Michael, BSc, PhD, CBiol, FIBiol, FIBMS, FRSH, FLS, FRSA. Principal and Vice-Chancellor, The Robert Gordon University, since 2005; b. 7.10.54, Edinburgh; m., Dr Carol Blow. Educ. Kelvinside Academy, Glasgow; University of Strathclyde; North East London Polytechnic. Electron Microscopist, Glasgow Royal Infirmary, 1976-77; Electron Microscopist, University of Strathclyde, 1977-78; Agriculture Research Council Research Assistant, North East London Polytechnic, 1978-80; Post Doctoral Research Assistant, Department of Histopathology, Middlesex Hospital Medical School, 1981-85; Honorary Research Associate, Middlesex Hospital Medical School, 1985-94; Lecturer, then Senior Lecturer, then Reader in Biomedical Sciences, Kingston University, 1985-91; Professor of Biomedical Sciences and Head of Life Sciences, Kingston University, 1992-94; Dean of Faculty of Health and Social Care Sciences, Kingston University and St. George's Hospital Medical School (University of London), 1995-2001; Pro Vice-Chancellor, University of Hertfordshire, 2001-05. Trustee, Prince's Foundation for Integrated Health, since 2003; Non-Executive Director, Bedfordshire and Hertfordshire Strategic Health Authority, 2002-05; Chair, Department of Health Regulatory Working Group for Herbal Medicine, 2002-03; Chair, Department of Health Regulatory Group for Acupuncture, Traditional Chinese Medicine and Herbal Medicine, since 2006; Member, Universities Scotland Executive and Convenor, Learning and Teaching

Committee, since 2006; Non-Executive Director, Scottish Enterprise (Grampian), since 2006; Non-Executive Director, Scottish Traditional Skills Centre, since 2006; Board Member, Quality Assurance Agency (QAA) for Higher Education and QAA (Scotland), since 2006; Member, North East Committee for the Scottish Council for Industry and Development, since 2006. Various publications on parasitology and atherosclerosis. Recreations: hill walking; photography; clay shooting; cinema; music. Address: (b.) The Robert Gordon University, Schoolhill, Aberdeen AB10 1FR; T.-01224 262001; e-mail: R.M.Pittilo@rgu.ac.uk

Pittock, Professor Murray G.H., MA, DPhil, DLitt, FEA, FRSA, FRHistS, FSAScot, FRSE. Bradley Professor of English Literature, University of Glasgow; formerly Professor of Scottish and Romantic Literature, Manchester University, 2003-07; Professor in Literature, Strathclyde University, 1996-2003; Co-Editor, Scottish Studies Review; b. 5.1.62; m., Anne Grace Thornton Martin; 2 d. Educ. Aberdeen Grammar School; Glasgow University; Balliol College, Oxford (Snell Exhibitioner). Lecturer, then Reader, Edinburgh University, 1989-96. Associate Editor, New Dictionary of National Biography; Member, Strathclyde University Court, 1998-2000; President, Scottish Committee of Professors of English; Royal Society of Edinburgh BP Humanities Research Prize, 1992-94; British Academy Chatterton Lecturer in Poetry, 2002; Founding Director, Glasgow-Strathclyde School of Scottish Studies; Deputy Head, Arts, University of Manchester, 2004-06. Publications: The Invention of Scotland, 1991; Spectrum of Decadence, 1993; Poetry and Jacobite Politics in Eighteenth-Century Britain and Ireland, 1994; The Myth of the Jacobite Clans, 1995; Inventing and Resisting Britain, 1997; Jacobitism, 1998; Celtic Identity and the British Image, 1999; Scottish Nationality, 2001; A New History of Scotland, 2003; The Edinburgh History of Scottish Literature (co-editor), 2006; The Reception of Sir Walter Scott in Europe, 2007; James Boswell, 2007. Address: (h.) 10 Oban Drive, Glasgow.

Placido, Professor Francis, BSc, PhD, FInstP, FSAS, FION. Professor, University of the West of Scotland, since 1999; Director, Thin Film Centre; b. 29.9.46, Dalkeith; m., Dorothy Charlotte Torrance; 2 d. Educ. Dalkeith High School; University of Edinburgh. Demonstrator, University of Edinburgh, 1972-77; Paisley College of Technology: Lecturer, 1977-89, Reader in Physics, 1989-99. John Logie Baird Award for Innovation, 1998. Recreations: food and wine; painting. Address: (b.) Thin Film Centre, University of the West of Scotland, High Street, Paisley PA1 2BE; T.-0141-848 3610; e-mail: frank.placido@uws.ac.uk

Pollmann, Professor Karla Friedel Lore, MA, MD, PhD, Drhabil. Professor of Classics, St Andrews University, since 2000; b. 21.10.63, Tuebingen. Educ. Universities of Tuebingen, Munich, Bochum; Newnham College, Cambridge. Alexander-von-Humboldt Fellow, University College London, 1993-95; Lecturer, St Andrews University, 1995; Visiting Scholar, Green College, UBC, Vancouver, 1998; Institute for Advanced Study, Princeton, 1999; Charter Fellow, Wolfson College, Oxford, 1999-2000; NIAS Fellow, 2003-04; Cecil and Ida Green Visiting Professor, Green College, UBC, Vancouver, 2006; Visiting Professor, Theology, University of Aarhus, 2007. Publications: books and articles on early Christian poetry, Augustine, Latin epic and satire, double standards. Recreations: singing; walking; reading. Address: (b.) School of Classics, St Andrews University, St Andrews KY16 9AL.

Pollock, Sheriff Alexander, MA (Oxon), LLB. Sheriff of Grampian, Highland and Islands, at Inverness, since 2005; b. 21.7.44, Glasgow; m., Verena Francesca Gertraud Alice Ursula Critchley; 1 s.; 1 d. Educ. Rutherglen Academy; Glasgow Academy; Brasenose College, Oxford; Edinburgh

University; University for Foreigners, Perugia. Partner, Bonar Mackenzie & Kermack, WS, 1971-73; called to Scottish Bar, 1973; Conservative candidate: West Lothian, General Election, February 1974, Moray and Nairn, General Election, October 1974; MP, Moray and Nairn, 1979-83, Moray, 1983-87; Parliamentary Private Secretary to Secretary of State for Scotland, 1982-86; PPS to Secretary of State for Defence, 1986-87; Advocate Depute, 1990-91; Sheriff (Floating) of Tayside, Central and Fife, at Stirling, 1991-93; Sheriff of Grampian, Highland and Islands, at Aberdeen and Stonehaven, 1993-2001; Sheriff of Grampian, Highland and Islands, at Inverness and Portree, 2001-05. Member, Queen's Bodyguard for Scotland (Royal Company of Archers), since 1984. Recreations: walking; music. Address: (h.) Drumdarrach, Forres, Moray.

Pollock, Thomas Alexander Jackson, BArch, RIBA, FRIAS. Senior Partner, The Pollock Hammond Partnership, Architects; b. 7.10.48, Newbridge, Midlothian; m., Clare Gregory; 1 d. Educ. George Watson's College, Edinburgh; Middlebury College, Vermont, USA; University of Edinburgh. Michael Laird and Partners, Edinburgh, 1973-78; William A. Cadell Architects, Linlithgow, 1978-91 (Partner, 1982-91); Pollock Hammond Partnership, since 1991. Member, Conservation Committee, RIAS; Member, Cases Panel, Architectural Heritage Society of Scotland; Trustee, Clan Menzies Charitable Trust; former Chairman, Linlithgow Festival Trust. Recreations: travel; antiques; the arts. Address: (h.) Beinn Castle House, 293 High Street, Linlithgow EH49 7AT; T.-01506 844417; e-mail: mail@pollockhammondarchitects.co.uk

Polson, Michael Buchanan, LLB (Hons), DipLP, MBA. Head of Corporate, Dundas & Wilson, since 2003, Partner, since 1995; b. 8.7.64, Edinburgh; m., Alison; 1 s.; 2 d. Educ. Anderson High School, Shetland; University of Edinburgh; Edinburgh University Management School. Trainee, Dundas & Wilson, 1987-89, Assistant, 1989-90; Associate, Ashurst, 1990; Senior Solicitor, Dundas & Wilson, 1991-92, Associate, 1992-95. Recreations: most sports including golf, tennis and football. Address: (b.) Saltire Court, 20 Castle Terrace, Edinburgh EH1 2EN; T.-0131 200 7347; e-mail: michael.polson@dundas-wilson.com

Ponsonby, Bernard Joseph. Political Editor, STV, since 2000, Reporter/Presenter, since 1990; b. Glasgow. Educ. Trinity High School, Rutherglen; Strathclyde University. Researcher to Rt. Hon. Dr Dickson Mabon, 1987; Press Officer, Scottish Liberal Democrats, 1988-89; party's first Parliamentary candidate, Glasgow Govan, 1988; PR and Media Consultant, freelance Reporter for BBC Radio Scotland, 1989-90; Principal Presenter of political, election, and by-election programmes, Scottish Television, 1994-2004; presented Platform, since 1996, Scottish Voices, Scottish Questions, Trial by Night; Producer of political documentaries: The Salmond Years (2000), The Dewar Years (2001) and The Road to Holyrood (2004). Publication: Donald Dewar: Scotland's first First Minister (contributor). Recreations: golf; Celtic Football Club. Address: (b.) STV, Pacific Quay, Glasgow G51 1PQ; e-mail: bernard.ponsonby@stv.tv

Ponton, Professor John Wylie, BSc, PhD, FIChemE, FEng. Professor of Chemical Engineering, Edinburgh University, since 1989; b. 2.5.43, Edinburgh; m., Katherine Jane Victoria Eachus. Educ. Melville College, Edinburgh; Edinburgh University. Recreations: engineering; amateur radio; music. Address: (b.) Department of Chemical Engineering, Edinburgh University, EH9 3JL; T.-0131-650 4860; e-mail: jack@ecosse.org

Poole, Anna I., MA. Advocate; Singer; b. 11.8.70, Craigtoun; m., Richard J.M. Sweet; 1 d.; 1 s. Educ. Madras College, St Andrews; Oxford University. Qualified as a Solicitor of the Supreme Court of England and Wales, 1996; then as a Scottish Solicitor with Brodies, WS, 1997; called to Scottish Bar, 1998. Recreations: music; walking; reading. Address: (h.) 7 Warriston Crescent, Edinburgh EH3 5LA.

Poole, Sheriff Isobel Anne, LLB. Part Time Sheriff, since 2007; Sheriff of Lothian and Borders (retired 2007); b. 9.12.41, Oxford. Educ. Oxford High School for Girls (GDST); Edinburgh University. Advocate. Chair, The Edinburgh Sir Walter Scott Club, 2005-07. Recreations: country; arts; gardens; friends. Address: (b.) Sheriffs' Chambers, Sheriff Court, Edinburgh.

Poon, Professor Wilson, MA (Cantab), PhD (Cantab), FInstP, CPhys, FRSE. Professor of Condensed Matter Physics, Edinburgh University, since 1999, Director of Research Strategy, School of Physics, since 2006; Engineering and Physical Sciences Research Council (EPSRC) Senior Research Fellow, 2007-2012; b. 26.9.62, Hong Kong; m., Heidi Lau; 1 s.; 1 d. Educ. St Paul's Co-educational College, Hong Kong; Rugby School; Peterhouse and St. John's College, Cambridge. Research Fellow, St Edmund's College, Cambridge, 1986-88; Lecturer, Department of Applied Physics, Portsmouth Polytechnic, 1989; Edinburgh University: Lecturer, 1990-97; Senior Lecturer, 1997-99. Member, Doctrine Committee, Scottish Episcopal Church, since 2003. Recreation: piano. Address: (b.) School of Physics, Edinburgh University, Mayfield Road, Edinburgh, EH9 3JZ; T.-0131-650 5297; e-mail: w.poon@ed.ac.uk

Porteous, Brian William, BSc (Hons), FILAM, DipRM. Director of Culture, Sport and Lifestyle, Genesis Consulting, since 2001; b. 6.2.51, Falkirk; m., Shena; 3 s. Educ. Falkirk High School; St. Andrews University; Moray House College of Education; Loughborough University. Joined Scottish Sports Council as Development Officer, 1979, appointed Director of Operations, 1989; Depute Director, Cultural and Leisure Services and Parks and Recreation, Glasgow City Council, 1994-2001. Honorary Secretary, British Orienteering Federation, 1974-76; President, Scottish Orienteering Association, 1996-2000; Member, Board, SportsCoach UK, since 2002; Council Member, International Orienteering Federation, since 2004. Publication: Orienteering, 1979. Recreations: golf; orienteering; amateur opera/musicals; caravanning. Address: (h.) Croft House, 2 Spoker's Loan, Balfron, Glasgow G63 0PA; T.(b.)-0845 345 3355.

Porter, Professor David, RIBA, RIAS. Head, Mackintosh School of Architecture, Glasgow School of Art, since 2000; Director, Living Cities; b. 12.6.46, Cambridge; m., Elspeth Clements; 1 s.; 1 d. Educ. University College, London. Partner, Clements and Porter Architects, 1979-86; Visiting Tutor: Bristol University and Canterbury College of Art, 1979-83, Architectural Association and Bartlett School of Architecture, 1983-85; Partner, Neave Brown David Porter Architects, 1986-93; Director of Studies, School of Architecture, University of East London, 1993-98; Visiting Professor, School of Architecture, Aarhus, Denmark, 1996-98; Director of Education, The Prince's Foundation, 1998-2000. Address: (b.) 167 Renfrew Street, Glasgow G3 6RQ; T.-0141-353 4651.

Potter, Christina Ann, MBA, MBCS. Principal, Dundee College, since 2007; b. 19.8.53, Newcastle upon Tyne; m., Tom Potter; 2 s. Educ. Glenrothes High School; Warwick University. Computer Operator, Royal Bank of Scotland, 1969-72; Computer Support Executive, ICL, 1972-83; Systems Analyst, ISTEL,

1983-84; Computer Lecturer, Tile Hill College, Coventry, 1984-95; Vice Principal, Warwickshire College, 1995-97; Principal, Elmwood College, Cupar, 1997-2007. Member, Court, St. Andrews University. Recreations: walking; reading; theatre. Address: (b.) Dundee College, Kingsway Campus, Old Glamis Road, Dundee DD3 8LE; T.-01382 834834.

Pounder, Professor Derrick John, MB, ChB, FRCPA, FFPathRCPI, FCAP, FRCPath, FHKCPath, FFFLM. Professor of Forensic Medicine, Dundee University, since 1987; b. 25.2.49, Pontypridd; m., Georgina Kelly; 1 s.; 2 d. Educ. Pontypridd Boys' Grammar; Birmingham University. Senior Lecturer (Forensic Pathology), University of Adelaide; Deputy Chief Medical Examiner, Edmonton, Alberta, and Associate Professor, Universities of Alberta and Calgary, 1985-87. Board Member, UN Voluntary Fund for Victims of Torture; Freeman of Llantrisant; Member, Bonnetmakers of Dundee. Recreations: photography; medieval architecture; almost lost causes. Address: (b.) Department of Forensic Medicine, Dundee University, Dundee DD1 4HN; T.-01382 388020; e-mail: d.j.pounder@dundee.ac.uk

Power, Professor Michael John, BSc, MSc, DPhil, CClinPsychol. Professor of Clinical Psychology, Edinburgh University, since 1995; b. 10.8.54, London; m., Lorna Champion; 2 s.; 1 d. Educ. St Philip's Grammar School, Birmingham; University College London; Sussex University; Birmingham University. Clinical Psychologist, Guy's Hospital, London, 1982-84; Research Scientist, MRC, 1984-88; Lecturer in Clinical Psychology, Institute of Psychiatry, Maudsley Hospital, 1989-90; Senior Lecturer in Clinical Psychology, Royal Holloway, London University, 1990-94; Research Scientist, World Health Organisation, Geneva, 1994-95. Consultant Clinical Psychologist, Royal Edinburgh Hospital. Publications: Cognition and Emotion: From Order to Disorder (Co-author); Adult Psychological Problems (Co-author). Recreations: travel; literature; tennis; cinema. Address: (b.) Section of Clinical and Health Psychology, Medical School, Teviot Place, Edinburgh EH8 9AG; T.-0131 651 3943.

Prag, Thomas Gregory Andrew, MA, FCIM. Media Consultant; elected to Highland Council as Liberal Democrat, 2007; b. 2.1.47, London; m., Angela; 3 s. Educ. Westminster School; Brasenose College, Oxford. Joined BBC, 1968, as Studio Manager; Producer, BBC Radio Oxford; Programme Organiser, BBC Radio Highland; first Chief Executive, Moray Firth Radio, 1981, then Managing Director, then Chairman until 2001. Past President, Inverness and District Chamber of Commerce; Chairman, Media Support Solutions; Member, Board of Governors, UHI Millennium Institute; Board Member, Inverness Harbour Trust; Fellow, Radio Academy; Chair, Ofcom Advisory Committee Scotland; Belmont Eden Court Theatre. Recreations: good intentions towards restoration of 1950 Daimler; keeping clock collection wound; family; growing vegetables; chasing deer off vegetables. Address: Windrush, Easter Muckovie, Inverness IV2 5BN; e-mail: thomas@prags.co.uk

Press, Professor Jeffrey Ian, BA (Hons) (Spanish), BA (Hons) (Russian), PhD. Established Professor in Russian (Comparative Linguistics), St. Andrews University, since 1995; b. 23.3.47, Oldham; m., Marie-Christine Morris; 1 s.; 1 d. Educ. Hulme Grammar School, Oldham; London University. Lecturer in Russian, Queen Mary College, London University, 1970-79, SSEES and Queen Mary College, 1979-87, Senior Lecturer, 1987-89; Professor of Slavonic and Comparative Linguistics, London University,

1990-95. Publications: books on Russian, Breton, Slavonic languages, Ukrainian and Lithuanian linguistics. Recreations: astronomy; photography; walking; learning languages. Address: (b.) St. Andrews University, St. Andrews KY16 9AL; T.-01334 463631; e-mail: jip@st-andrews.ac.uk

Preston, David Michael, LLB, NP. Solicitor, since 1976; President, Law Society of Scotland, 2002-03; b. 26.8.52, Glasgow; m., Sheila Elizabeth; 2 s. Educ. Hillhead High School; Dundee University. Part-time Depute Procurator Fiscal, 1976-79; Clerk to General Commissioners of Income Tax, since 1976; Registrar, Episcopal Diocese of Argyll and the Isles, since 1977; Partner, Hosack and Sutherland, since 1978; Member, Council, Law Society of Scotland, since 1990 (Convenor: Update Committee, 1992-96, Remuneration Committee, 1996-99, Services Committee, 1999-2000, Professional Practice, 2000-01, Vice President, 2001-02, President, 2002-03). Past Chairman and first Hon. President, Oban Round Table; Chairman, Oban Youth and Community Association, since 1980; Commodore, Oban Sailing Club, 1992-93; Secretary, Atlantis Leisure, 1991-2001. Recreations: sailing; skiing; rugby spectating; golf. Address: (h.) Westbank, Duncraggan Road, Oban; T.-01631 563228.

Preston, Ian Mathieson Hamilton, CBE, BSc, PhD, FEng, MInstP, FIEE, Hon. FCIWEM. Chartered Engineer; b. 18.7.32, Bournemouth; m., Sheila Hope Pringle; 2 s. Educ. Kilmarnock Academy; Glasgow University. University Assistant Lecturer, 1957-59; joined SSEB as Assistant Reactor Physicist, 1959; various appointments until Chief Engineer, Generation Design and Construction Division, 1972; Director General, Central Electricity Generating Board, Generation Development and Construction Division, 1977-83; Deputy Chairman, South of Scotland Electricity Board, 1983-90; Chief Executive, Scottish Power, 1990-95. Non-Executive Director: Deutsche (Scotland), 1996-2002, Hub Power Co. (Pakistan), 1995-99, Kot Addu Power Co. (Pakistan), 1996-99, Mining Scotland Ltd., 1995-98, East of Scotland Water Authority, 1995-98; Chairman, Motherwell Bridge Holdings, 1995-2001; President, Scottish Council Development and Industry, 1997-2000. Address: 10 Cameron Crescent, Carmunnock, Glasgow G76 9DX.

Price, Barclay. Director, Arts and Business Scotland, since 2001; b. 26.7.45, Glasgow; m., Fiona Dick. Educ. Hillhead High School. Head of Development, Crafts Council; Administrator, Hoxton Hall Community Theatre; Visual Arts Subsidy Officer, Arts Council of GB; Officer, Clydesdale Bank; Depute Director (Planning and Development), Scottish Arts Council. Address: (b.) 6 Randolph Crescent, Edinburgh EH3 7TH; T.-0131-220 2499; e-mail: barclay.price@AandB.org.uk

Price, Professor David Brendan, BA(Hons), MBBChir, MA, DRCOG, FPCert, MRCGP. General Practice Airways Group Professor of Primary Care Respiratory Medicine, since 2000; b. 28.10.60, Slough; m., Dr Daryl Freeman; 2 s.; 2 d. Educ. Slough Grammar School; University of Cambridge. Paediatric Registrar, Australia, 1988-89; GP, 1999-2000; Chairman, Norwich Vocational Training Scheme, 1990-95; Director, Thorpe Respiratory Research, since 1998; Research Director, General Practice Airways Group, since 2000. Recreations: skiing; scuba diving; horse riding. Address: Department of General Practice and Primary Care, University of Aberdeen, Westburn Road, Aberdeen AB25 2AY; e-mail: d.price@abdn.ac.uk

Price, Professor Nicholas Charles, MA, DPhil (Oxon). Professor of Protein Science, Glasgow University, since

2000; b. 12.8.46, Stafford; m., Margaret Hazel Price; 1s.; 2d. Educ. King Edward VI Grammar School, Stafford; Merton College, Oxford; St John's College, Oxford. Stirling University: Lecturer, 1974-77; Senior Lecturer, 1977 -88; Reader, 1988-94; Professor of Biochemistry, 1994-2000. Publications: 3 books; 200 papers. Recreations; running; fundraising. Address: (b.) Joseph Black Building, Glasgow University, G12; T.-0141-330 2889.

Pride, Professor Stephen James, BSc, PhD, FRSE. Professor of Mathematics, Glasgow University, since 1992 (Reader in Mathematics, 1987-92); b. 8.1.49, Melbourne. Educ. Hampton High School, Melbourne; Monash University, Melbourne; Australian National University, Canberra. Research Fellow, Open University, 1974-78; Temporary Lecturer in Mathematics, King's College, London University, 1978-79; Lecturer in Mathematics, Glasgow University, 1979-87. Member, Editorial Board, London Mathematical Society, 1989-99; Member, Editorial Board, Semigroup Forum, since 2004; Member, Editorial Board, International Electronic Journal of Algebra, since 2006; Member, Mathematics College, Engineering and Physical Sciences Research Council, 1997-99; Member, Commonwealth Scholarship Commission Panel of Advisers, 2001-06. Publications: more than 78 articles on algebra (mainly group theory and theoretical computer science). Recreations: cycling; travelling; cinema; music. Address: (b.) Department of Mathematics, University of Glasgow, University Gardens, Glasgow G12 8QW; T.-0141 330 6528.

Priest, Professor Eric Ronald, BSc, MSc, PhD, FRSE, FRS. Wardlaw Professor, since 2002, Gregory Professor of Mathematics, St. Andrews University, since 1997, formerly Professor of Theoretical Solar Physics; b. 7.11.43, Birmingham; m., Clare Wilson; 3 s.; 1 d. Educ. King Edward VI School, Birmingham; Nottingham University; Leeds University. St. Andrews University: Lecturer in Applied Mathematics, 1968, Reader, 1977; SERC Senior Fellow, 1992-97. Elected Member, Norwegian Academy of Sciences and Letters, 1994; Chair, PPARC Astronomy Committee, 1998-2001; Chair, RSE Mathematics Committee, 1996-1998; Member, HEFC Research Assessment Exercise Committee, 1992, 1996, 2007; Chair, RSE Physics Committee, 2007-2010; Hale Prize, American Astronomical Society, 2002. Recreations: bridge; walking; singing; swingnastics; children. Address: (b.) Mathematics and Statistics Department, St. Andrews University, St. Andrews KY16 9SS; T.-01334 463709.

Pringle, Mike. MSP (LD), Edinburgh South, since 2003; b. 25.12.45, Zambia; m.; 2 s. Address: (b.) Scottish Parliament, Edinburgh EH99 1SP; T.-0131 348 5788.

Prior, Alan, BSc (Hons), MLitt, MRTPI, ILTM. Dean, Arts, Humanities and Social Sciences, Heriot-Watt University, 2004-07, Deputy Head, School of the Built Environment, since 2002; b. 21.12.51, Edinburgh; m., Brenda; 2 d. Educ. Portobello High School, Edinburgh; Heriot-Watt University; Glasgow University. Assistant Planning Officer, Perth and Kinross District Council, 1975-77; Senior/Principal Planning Officer, East Kilbride District Council, 1977-85; Lecturer/Senior Lecturer, Edinburgh College of Art, 1985-95; Head, School of Planning and Housing, Edinburgh College of Art, 1996-2002. Publication: joint editor, "Introduction to Planning Practice", 2000. Recreation: hill walking. Address: (b.) School of the Built Environment, Heriot-Watt University, Edinburgh EH14 4AS; T.-0131-451-4404; e-mail: a.prior@hw.ac.uk

Pritchard, Professor Duncan Henry, BA, MLitt, PhD. Professor of Philosophy, University of Edinburgh, since 2007; b. 30.01.74, Wolverhampton; m., Mandi; 2 s. Educ. University of St. Andrews. University of Stirling: Lecturer, 2000-02, Leverhulme Fellow, 2002-04, Reader, 2004-06, Professor, 2006-07. Publications: books include: Epistemic Luck; What Is This Thing Called Knowledge? Prizes include a 2007 Philip Leverhulme Prize. Address: (b.) Department of Philosophy, University of Edinburgh, Edinburgh EH8 9JX; T.-0131-651 1734; e-mail: duncan.pritchard@ed.ac.uk

Pritchard, Kenneth William, OBE, BL, WS. Secretary, Law Society of Scotland, 1976-97; Temporary Sheriff, 1995-99, Part-time Sheriff, 2000-03; b. 14.11.33, London; Honorary Sheriff, Dundee; m., Gretta Murray; 2 s.; 1 d. Educ. Dundee High School; Fettes College; St. Andrews University. National Service, Argyll and Sutherland Highlanders, 1955-57; 2nd Lt., 1956; TA, 1957-62 (Captain); joined J. & J. Scrimgeour, Solicitors, Dundee, 1957; Captain, DHSFPRFC, 1959-62; Senior Partner, 1970-76; Member: Sheriff Court Rules Council, 1973-76, Lord Dunpark's Committee considering Reparation upon Criminal Conviction, 1973-77; Hon. Visiting Professor, Law School, Strathclyde University; Hon. Member, Law Institute of Victoria, 1985; Hon. Member, Law Society of New Zealand, 1987; Hon. Member, Faculty of Procurators and Solicitors in Dundee; Member, University Court of Dundee, 1989-93; President, Dundee High School Old Boys Club, 1975-76. Recreation: golf. Address: (h.) 22/4 Kinellan Road, Edinburgh EH12 6ES; T.-0131-337 4294.

Prosser, Rt. Hon. Lord (William David Prosser), QC, MA (Oxon), LLB, HonFRIAS, PC. Senator of the College of Justice in Scotland and Lord of Session, 1986-2001; b. 23.11.34, Edinburgh; m., Vanessa Lindsay Prosser (qv); 2 s.; 2 d. Educ. Edinburgh Academy; Corpus Christi College, Oxford; Edinburgh University. Advocate, 1962; Queen's Counsel, 1974; Vice-Dean, Faculty of Advocates, 1979-83; Dean of Faculty, 1983-86. Chairman, Royal Lyceum Theatre Company, 1987-92; Chairman, Scottish Historic Buildings Trust, 1988-98; Chairman, Royal Fine Art Commission for Scotland, 1990-95; Chairman, Scottish Architectural Education Trust; Chairman, Chamber Group of Scotland, 1993-98; Trustee, Franco-British Council; Member, Board of Governors, UHI Millennium Institute; Officier, Ordre des Arts et des Lettres (France). Address: 7 Randolph Crescent, Edinburgh EH3 7TH; T.-0131-225 2709.

Prosser, (Leslie) Charles, DFA, DAEd. Consultant on quality of plans designing development, since 2005; Secretary, Royal Fine Art Commission For Scotland, 1976-2005; b. 27.10.39, Harrogate; m., Coral; 1 s.; 2 d. Educ. Bath Academy of Art at Corsham Court; Slade School of Fine Art, London University. Assistant Lecturer in Fine Art, Blackpool School of Art, 1962-64; Fine Art research, Royal Academy, Stockholm, 1964-65; Lecturer in Fine Art, Leeds/Jacob Kramer College of Art, 1965-76; research in Art Education, Leeds University, 1974-75. Leverhulme European Arts Research Award, 1964; FRSA, 1997; Hon. FRIAS, 1997, Hon. MRTPI, 2002. Recreations: snowboarding and hill-walking. Address: (h.) 28 Mayfield Terrace, Edinburgh EH9 1RZ; T.-0131-668 1141; e-mail: charles@quoplans.com

Prosser, Vanessa Lindsay, SRCN, SCM, AMSPAR. Chairman of Council, Queen's Nursing Institute, Scotland, 1994-2002; b. 7.11.39, Dairsie, Fife; m., William David Prosser (qv); 2 s.; 2 d. Educ. St Leonards School, St Andrews. Medical Receptionist/Secretary, 1980-2007. Lothian Health Council, 1984-88; Lothian Research Ethics Committee, since 1989; Scotland's Gardens Scheme, 1996-2002. Recreations: France. Address: (h.) 7 Randolph Crescent, Edinburgh, EH3 7TH; T.-0131-225 2709.

Proudfoot, Edwina Valmai Windram, MA, DipEd, FSA, FSA Scot, MIFA. Archaeologist; Director, St. Andrews Heritage Services, since 1988; Honorary Research Fellow, St. Andrews University, 1985-97; b. 9.3.35, Dover; m., Professor V. Bruce Proudfoot (qv); 2 s. Educ. Invergordon Academy; Inverness Royal Academy; Edinburgh University. Lecturer (including Adult Education) in Archaeology, since 1959; director of excavations, numerous projects; Editor, Discovery and Excavation in Scotland, 1977-90; President, Council for Scottish Archaeology, 1983-89; Founder, first Chairman, Tayside and Fife Archaeological Committee, 1975-82; Member, Ancient Monuments Board for Scotland, 1986-97; Chairman, St. Andrews Preservation Trust, 1988-93; Council Member, National Trust for Scotland, 1984-89, 1993-97, 1999-2004; Chairman, NTS Central, Fife and Tayside Committee, 1998-2000; Member, Executive Committee, NTS, 1994-2004; Honorary Vice-President, Buteshire Natural History Society, since 1999; Chairman, E. Fife Members Centre, NTS, 2000-04; Chairman, Scottish Church Heritage Research, since 2000. Recreations: gardening; music; walking. Address: 12 Wardlaw Gardens, St. Andrews, KY16 9DW; T.-01334 473293.

Proudfoot, Professor V. Bruce, OBE, BA, PhD, FSA, FRSE, FRSGS, FSA Scot. Vice-President, Royal Scottish Geographical Society, since 1993; Emeritus Professor of Geography, St. Andrews University; b. 24.9.30, Belfast; m., Edwina Valmai Windram Field; 2 s. Educ. Royal Belfast Academical Institution; Queen's University, Belfast. Research Officer, Nuffield Quaternary Research Unit, Queen's University, Belfast, 1954-58; Lecturer in Geography: Queen's University, Belfast, 1958-59, Durham University, 1959-67; Hatfield College, Durham: Tutor, 1960-63, Librarian, 1963-65; Visiting Fellow, University of Auckland and Commonwealth Visiting Fellow, Australia, 1966; Alberta University, Edmonton: Associate Professor, 1967-70, Professor, 1970-74; Co-ordinator, Socio-Economic Opportunity Studies and Staff Consultant, Alberta Human Resources Research Council, 1971-72; Professor of Geography, St. Andrews University, 1974-93. Royal Society of Edinburgh: Convener, Earth Sciences Committee, 1983-85, Vice-President, 1985-88, Convener, Grants Committee, 1988-91, General Secretary, 1991-96, Bicentenary Medal, 1997; Chairman, Society for Landscape Studies, 1979-83; Vice-President, Society of Antiquaries of Scotland, 1982-85; President, Section H, BAAS, 1985; Chairman, Rural Geography Study Group, Institute of British Geographers, 1980-84; Chairman of Council, 1993-99, Chairman of Dundee Centre, 1993-99, Royal Scottish Geographical Society; Hon. President, Scottish Association of Geography Teachers, 1982-84; Trustee, National Museum of Antiquities of Scotland, 1982-85; Hon. Treasurer, East Fife Members' Centre, National Trust for Scotland, 2002-08. Recreation: gardening. Address: (h.) Westgate, 12 Wardlaw Gardens, St. Andrews KY16 9DW; T.-01334 473293.

Provan, James Lyal Clark. Member, South East Region, European Parliament, 1999-2004, Member, South Downs West, 1994-99; Vice President, European Parliament, 1999-2004; Chairman, EP Tourism Group, 1997-2004; Chairman, EP Conciliation Committee with Council of Ministers, 1999-2003; Chairman, Rowett Research Institute, Aberdeen, 1991-99 (Board Member, 1990-2005); Non-Executive Director, CNH Global N.V. and New Holland (Holdings), N.V., 1994-2007; Farmer; b. 19.12.36, Glenfarg, Perthshire; m., Roweena Adele Lewis; 2 s.; 1 d. Educ. Ardvreck School, Crieff; Oundle School, Northants; Royal Agricultural College, Cirencester. National Farmers Union of Scotland: Area President, Kinross, 1965, Fife and Kinross, 1971; Tayside Regional Councillor, 1978-81; Member, Tay River Purification Board, 1978-81; Member (Conservative), European Parliament, NE Scotland, 1979-89; European Democratic (Conservative) Spokesman on Agriculture and Fisheries, 1981-87; Questor of European Parliament, 1987-89; former Executive Director, Scottish Financial Enterprise (1990-93); Chairman, McIntosh of Dyce Ltd., McIntosh Donald Ltd., 1989-94; Member, Agriculture and Food Research Council, 1990-94; Member, Lloyds of London, since 1984. Recreations: country pursuits; sailing; flying; politics; agriculture. Address: Summerfield, Glenfarg, Perthshire PH2 9QD; e-mail: jlcprovan@aol.com

Purcell, Steven John, JP. Leader, Glasgow City Council, since 2005; b. 19.9.72, Glasgow. Educ. St Thomas Aquinas Secondary School. Elected to Glasgow City Council, 1995; Convener, Property Services, 1997-99; Convener, Development and Regeneration Services, 1999-2003; Convener, Education Services Committee, 2003-2005. Member, Scottish Enterprise Glasgow Board; Chair, Glasgow and Clyde Valley Community Planning Partnership. Recreations: history; music; football. Address; (b.) City Chambers, Glasgow, G2 1DU.
E-mail: steven.purcell@councillors.glasgow.gov.uk

Purser, John Whitley, MA, PhD. Composer and Lecturer; Poet, Playwright, Musicologist, and Broadcaster; b. 10.2.42, Glasgow; 1 s.; 1 d. Educ. Fettes College; Glasgow University; Royal Scottish Academy of Music and Drama. Manager, Scottish Music Information Centre, 1985-87; Research Fellow, Sabhal Mòr Ostaig, since 2006; compositions include two operas, numerous orchestral and chamber works; three books of poetry, The Counting Stick, A Share of the Wind and Amoretti; six radio plays and two radio series, A Change of Tune and Scotland's Music; music history: Is the Red Light On?, Scotland's Music; literary criticism: The Literary Works of Jack B. Yeats; awards: McVitie Scottish Writer of the Year, 1992; Glenfiddich Living Scotland Award, 1991; Giles Cooper Award, 1992; New York International Radio Festival Gold Medal, 1992; Sony Gold Medal, 1993; Oliver Brown Award, 1993; Scottish Heritage Award, 1993; Hon. Life Member, Saltire Society, 1993. Recreations: numerous. Address: (b.) 3 Drinan, Elgol, Isle of Skye IV49 9BG; T.-01471 866262.

Purves, David, BSc, PhD. Environmental Biochemist; Playwright; b. 9.4.24, Selkirk; m., Lilian Rosemary; 3 s. Educ. Galashiels Academy; Edinburgh University. Head, Trace Element Department, Edinburgh School of Agriculture, 1956-82; Supervisor, Central Analytical Department, 1982-87; author of Trace Element Contamination of the Environment, 1985; poetry collections: Thrawart Threipins, 1976, Herts Bluid, 1995; many poems in Scots published including renderings in Scots of over 100 ancient Chinese poems; Fringe First play, The Puddok an the Princess, produced, 1985 and rendering in Scots of Macbeth published, 1992; 12 professional productions of plays in Scots; Joint Editor, Mak It New, anthology of 21 years of writing in Lallans, 1995; Editor, Lallans, 1987-95; author of A Scots Grammar, 1997 (revised, extended edition, 2002); Past Preses, Scots Language Society. Address: (h.) 8 Strathmond Road, Edinburgh EH4 8AD; T.-0131-339 7929; e-mail: david.purves@blueyonder.co.uk

Purvis, Jeremy. MSP (Liberal Democrat), Tweeddale, Ettrick and Lauderdale, since 2003; b. 15.1.74, Berwick-upon-Tweed. Educ. Berwick-upon-Tweed High School; Brunel University. Research Assistant to Sir David Steel, 1993; Parliamentary Assistant: Liberal International, 1994, ELDR Group, European Parliament, 1995; Personal Assistant to Sir David Steel, subsequently Lord Steel of

Aikwood, 1996-1998; GJW Scotland, 1998-2001; Company Director, McEwan Purvis, 2001-03. Member, Finance Committee, Scottish Parliament, 2003-05, Justice 2 Committee, 2005-07, Education, Lifelong Learning and Culture Committee, since 2007; Member, Board, Broomhill Day Centre; Member, European Movement, Scottish Council; Member, Amnesty International; Patron, Scottish HART. Recreations: classic cars; painting. Address: Scottish Parliament, Edinburgh EH99 1SP; T.-01896 663656; e-mail: jeremy.purvis.msp@scottish.parliament.uk

Purvis, John Robert, CBE, MA (Hons). Member for Scotland, European Parliament, since 1999 (Member, Industry, Research and Energy Committee; Vice-Chairman, Economic and Monetary Affairs Committee); International Business Consultant (Managing Partner, Purvis & Co.), since 1973; Director, European Utilities Trust PLC, 1994-2007; Chairman, Kingdom FM Radio Ltd., since 1997; Chairman, Belgrave Capital Management Ltd., since 1999; b. 6.7.38, St. Andrews; m., Louise Spears Durham; 1 s.; 2 d. Educ. Glenalmond; St. Andrews University. 2nd Lt., Scots Guards, 1956-58; First National City Bank (Citibank NA), London, New York City, Milan, 1962-69; Treasurer, Noble Grossart Ltd., Edinburgh, 1969-73; Director and Secretary, Brigton Farms Ltd., 1969-86; Managing Director, Founder, Owner, Gilmerton Management Services Ltd., 1973-92; Director: James River UK Holdings Ltd., 1984-95, Jamont NV, 1994-95; Member, European Parliament, Mid Scotland and Fife, 1979-84 (Deputy Chief Whip, Group Spokesman on Monetary Affairs, Energy, Research and Technology; Vice Chairman, European Parliament Delegation to the Gulf States); Chairman, IBA Scottish Advisory Committee, 1985-89; Member for Scotland, IBA, 1985-89; Member of Council, St. Leonards School, St. Andrews, 1981-89; Chairman, Economic Affairs Committee, Scottish Conservative and Unionist Association, 1986-97, Vice-President of Association, 1987-89; Member, Scottish Advisory Committee on Telecommunications, 1990-97; Director: Curtis Fine Papers Ltd., 1995-2001, Crown Vantage Ltd., 1995-2001. Recreations: Italy and Scotland. Address: PO Box 29222, St. Andrews KY16 8WL; T.-01334 475830.

Pusey, Professor Peter Nicholas, MA, PhD, FRS, FRSE. Professor of Physics, Edinburgh University, since 1991; b. 30.12.42, Oxford; m., Elizabeth Nind; 2 d. Educ. St Edward's School, Oxford; Cambridge University; University of Pittsburgh, USA. Post-doctoral Fellow, IBM, New York, 1969-72; Royal Signals and Radar Establishment (now QinetiQ), Malvern, 1972-91 (Grade 6 from 1980); Head, Department of Physics and Astronomy, Edinburgh University, 1994-97 and 2000-03. Publications: numerous in scientific literature. Address: (b.) School of Physics, Edinburgh University, Mayfield Road, Edinburgh, EH9 3JZ, T.-0131-650 5255; e-mail: pusey@ed.ac.uk

Pyle, Sheriff Derek Colin Wilson, LLB (Hons), NP, WS. Sheriff of Grampian, Highland and Islands at Inverness, since 2005; Sheriff of Tayside Central and Fife, 2000-05; b. 15.10.52, Cambridge; m., Jean Blackwood Baillie; 5 s.; 1 d. Educ. Royal High School, Edinburgh; Edinburgh University. Solicitor, since 1976; Partner, Wilson Pyle & Co., WS, 1980-89; Partner, Henderson Boyd Jackson, WS, 1989-99; Solicitor Advocate, since 1994. Formerly Fiscal to Law Society of Scotland; former Council Member, WS Society. Recreations: golf; hill-walking; painting house. Address: (b.) Sheriff's Chambers, The Castle, Inverness; T.-01463 230782.

Pyper, Mark Christopher Spring-Rice, BA. Principal, Gordonstoun Schools, since 1999 (Headmaster, Gordonstoun School, 1990-99); b. 13.8.47, Seaford; m., Jennifer L.; 1 s.; 2 d. Educ. Winchester College; Oxford University; London University. Assistant Master, Stoke Brunswick School, East Grinstead, 1966-68; Assistant Master, then Joint Headmaster, St. Wilfrid's School, Seaford, 1969-79; Registrar, Housemaster, then Deputy Headmaster, Sevenoaks School, 1979-90; Director, Sevenoaks Summer Festival, 1979-90. Address: (h.) Headmaster's House, Gordonstoun School, Elgin IV30 5RF; T.-01343 837807.

Q

Queensberry, 12th Marquess of (David Harrington Angus Douglas); b. 19.12.29. Educ. Eton. Professor of Ceramics, Royal College of Art, 1959-83; succeeded to title, 1954.

Quickfall, Julia Anne, MSc, BNurs, SRN, DN, HVCert, MIHM. Nurse Director, Queen's Nursing Institute Scotland, since 2003; b. 8.8.52, Melton Mowbray; m., Michael Quickfall; 3 s. Educ. King Edward VII Upper School, Melton Mowbray; University of Manchester; University of Edinburgh. Staff Nurse, St. Mary's Hospital, Manchester, 1974-75; Health Visitor: Stockport, 1975-78, St. Helen's and Knowsley, 1978-80, various GP practices in Edinburgh, 1987-95; Audit and Research Facilitator, 1995-97; Team Coordinator, Homeless Nursing Service, Edinburgh, 1997-2001; Asylum Seeker Project Facilitator, 2001-03. Appointed Member of Nursing and Midwifery Council Reference Panel, 2002; Travel Fellowship (Scottish Executive Health Department), 2002; Asylum Seeker Health Issues. Post Graduate PhD student researching cultural competence. Recreation: gardening. Address: (b.) 31 Castle Terrace, Edinburgh EH1 2EL; T.-0131 229 2333; e-mail: julia.quickfall@qnis.org.uk

Quigley, Elizabeth, MA (Hons). Correspondent, BBC Scotland, since 1999; b. 30.10.71, Glasgow. Educ. Lenzie Academy; St Andrews University. Reporter, The Scotsman, 1995-96; Reporter, Scotland on Sunday, 1996-97; Scottish Daily Mail, from 1997: Political Reporter/Acting Features Editor/Feature Writer. Address: (b.) BBC Scotland, The Tun, Holyrood Road, Edinburgh EH8 8PJ; T.-0131-248 4215.

Quinault, Francis Charles, BSc, PhD, FRSAMD. Retired Director of Learning and Teaching Quality, St. Andrews University (formerly Hebdomadar, Assistant Principal for External Affairs and Senior Lecturer in Psychology); Chairman, Byre Theatre; b. 8.5.43, London; m., Wendy Ann Horton; 1 s.; 2 d. Educ. Dulwich College; St. Catharine's College, Cambridge; Bristol University. Ford Foundation Scholar, Oslo University, 1969-70. Member, National Committee for the Training of University Teachers, 1981-87; Academic Board, RSAMD, 2004-07; Hon. Treasurer, The Kate Kennedy Trust; President, St. Andrews Business Club. Recreations: acting; singing; hill-walking. Address: (b.) University of St. Andrews, 91 North Street, St. Andrews KY16 9AJ; T.-01334 462141; 5 Hope Street, St. Andrews KY16 9HJ; T.-01334 474560; e-mail: fcq@st-and.ac.uk

Quinn, Brian, MA (Hons), MA (Econ), PhD, CBE, FCIBS. Chairman, Brian Quinn Consultancy, since 1996; Non-Executive Director, Genworth Finance Mortgage Insurance (2005); Non-Executive Director, Qatar Finance Centre Regulatory Authority, since 2006; b. 18.11.36, Glasgow; m., Mary Bradley; 2 s.; 1 d. Educ. St. Gerards Senior Secretary, Glasgow; University of Glasgow; University of Manchester; Cornell University (USA). International Monetary Fund, 1964-70; Staff member, Bank of England, 1970-88; Executive Director, Bank of England, 1988-96; Acting Deputy Governor (1995); Chairman, Nomura Bank International, 1996-99; Non-Executive Director, Bankgesellschaft Berlin UK Ltd., 1996-2002; Non-Executive Director, Surnitomo-Mitsui Bank Ltd. (2003); Non-Executive Director: Celtic plc, 1996-2007, Britannic Asset Management, 1998-2004; Chairman, Celtic plc, 2000-07; Non-Executive Director, Genwork Finance Mortgage Insurance Ltd., since 2004; Non-Executive Director, Qatar Finance Regulatory Authority, since 2006. Chairman, Supervisory Committee of EC Governors/European Monetary Institute; Honorary Professor of Economics and Finance, Glasgow University; Member: Basel Committee of Bank Supervisors, Advisory Committee, Toronto Centre, Advisory Board, The Financial Regulator; Advisor: The World Bank, The International Monetary Fund; Member, Advisory Board, Beatson Translational Research Centre, Glasgow University. Various articles and chapters in books published. Recreations: watching football; fishing; golf; reading; pilates. Address: (h./b.) 14, Homewood Road, St. Albans AL1 4BH; T.-01727-853900; e-mail: bqconns@aol.com

Quirk, Lesley Helen, CLJ, MCMI. Managing Partner, Quirk & Company, Business & Management Development Consultants, since 1985; b. Tarbert, Harris; m., Norman Linton Quirk (qv); 4 s. Educ. St George's School, Edinburgh. Appointed first Women's Business Adviser in Scotland, 1988; Independent Assessor for Public Appointments, 2001-07. UK Woman of Achievement, 1999; Scottish Businesswoman of the Year, 2001; Arts & Business UK Individual of the Year, 2004; Commander, Order of St Lazarus of Jerusalem, 2001; Hon. Lady Taverner, 1985. Recreations: family; DIY; sailing. Address: (h.) Glencleland House, Aberfoyle FK8 3TJ.

Quirk, Norman Linton, CA, CLJ. Chairman, Scottish Chamber of Commerce, since 2007; Managing Director, SAGA 105.2 fm, 2004-07; Executive Director, Scottish Ballet, 2000-2004, Vice Chairman and Managing Director, 1998-2000; Partner, Quirk & Co., business and management consultancy, since 1991; President, Glasgow Chamber of Commerce; b. 28.7.47, Glasgow; m., Lesley Helen Quirk (qv); 2 s.; 2 step-s. Educ. Dulwich College. Apprentice CA, 1965-71; Accountant/Office Manager, Thom Decorators, Coatbridge, 1971-74; Chief Accountant, Radio Clyde, Glasgow, 1974-84; Assistant Director, Institute of CAs of Scotland, 1985-87; Regional Controller, Joint Monitoring Unit, 1988-91; Managing Director, Scot FM, 1996. Chairman, Independent Radio Group of Scotland, 1996-2000; President, Glasgow Chamber of Commerce, 2006-08; Director, Scottish Chamber of Commerce, 2006; Community Councillor, Strathord Ward, 2000-06; Member, Incorporation of Hammermen; Director and Treasurer, Scottish Society for Autism; Director, Mull Theatre; Lord's Taverner; Commander, Order of St Lazarus of Jerusalem. Recreations: scuba diving; working with arts organisations. Address: (h.) Glencleland House, Aberfoyle FK8 3JJ; T.-01877 387210; e-mail: norman@quirk.co.uk

R

Racey, Professor Paul Adrian, MA, PhD, DSc, FIBiol, FRSE. Regius Professor of Natural History, Aberdeen University, since 1993 (Professor of Zoology, 1985-93); b. 7.5.44, Wisbech, Cambridgeshire; m., Anna Priscilla Notcutt; 3 s. Educ. Ratcliffe College, Leicester; Downing College, Cambridge. Rothamsted Experimental Station, Harpenden, 1965-66; Zoological Society of London, 1966-70; Unit of Reproductive Biology, Liverpool University, 1970-73; joined Department of Zoology, Aberdeen University, 1973. Recreations: riding; sailing; skiing. Address: (b.) School of Biological Sciences, Aberdeen University, Aberdeen AB24 2TZ; T.-01224 272858; e-mail: p.racey@abdn.ac.uk

Radcke, Ingo Heinrich. Consul General of the Federal Republic of Germany; Consul General for Scotland, Northumberland, Cumbria, Tyne and Wear, Durham, since 2003; b. 4.11.46, Copenhagen; m., Irmhild; 3 s.; 1 d. Educ. Kiel University; University of Lausanne; Edinburgh University. Traineeship, Federation of German Industries, London, 1973-74; Diplomatic School, Foreign Office, Bonn, 1976-78; German Embassy, Canberra, 1978-81; Foreign Office, Bonn, 1981-84; Ministry of Defence, Bonn, 1984-87; Foreign Office, Bonn, 1987-90; German Embassy, The Hague, 1990-92; Foreign Office, Bonn, 1992-97; Consul General, Apenrade, Denmark, 1997-2000; German Embassy, Madrid, 2000-03. Address: (b.) 16 Eglinton Crescent, Edinburgh EH12 5DG; T.-0131-337 2323; e-mail: german.consulate@btconnect.com

Radcliffe, Nicholas John, BSc (Double Hons), PhD. Director, Stochastic Solutions Limited, since 2007; Visiting Professor, Maths and Statistics, Edinburgh University, since 1995; b. 31.07.65, London; m., Morag Radcliffe; 1 s. Educ. Sir Frederic Osborn School; Univ. of Sussex; Edinburgh Univ. Manager, Information Systems Group, Edinburgh Parallel Computing Centre, University of Edinburgh, 1990-95; Technical Director, Quadstone Limited, 1995-2007; Advisor: Scottish Equity Partners, since 2000, Fluidinfo Limited, since 2006. Publication: Sustainability: A Systems Approach (Co-Author), 1996. Blog: The Scientific Marketer (http://scientificmarketer.com). Recreations: guitar/music; literature; film; golf. Address: (h.) 44 Braehead Road, Edinburgh EH4 6BB; T.-07713 787 602; e-mail: njr@stochasticsolutions.com

Rae, Barbara Davis, CBE. Painter and Printmaker; b. 10.12.43, Falkirk; 1 s. Educ. Morrisons Academy, Crieff; Edinburgh College of Art. Travelling scholarship, France and Spain, 1966; elected RSW, 1975; President, SSA, 1983; Scottish Arts Council grant, 1985; Hunting Group prize-winner, 1991; elected RSA, 1992; elected RA, 1996; study painting, South Africa, 1996; study visit, Arizona desert, 1998; doctorate, Napier University, 1999; various solo exhibitions in London, Edinburgh and internationally; work in many public collections. Hon. Fellowship, Royal College of Art, London; Hon. DLitt, Aberdeen University, 2003. Recreation: travel.

Rae, Sheriff Rita Emilia Anna, QC, LLB (Hons). Sheriff of Glasgow and Strathkelvin, since 1997. Educ. St. Patrick's High School, Coatbridge; Edinburgh University. Apprentice, Biggart, Lumsden & Co., Glasgow, 1972-74; Assistant Solicitor: Balfour & Manson, Edinburgh, 1974, Biggart, Baillie & Gifford, Glasgow, 1974-76; Solicitor and Partner, Ross Harper & Murphy, Glasgow, 1976-81; Former Tutor, Advocacy and Pleading, Strathclyde

University; Advocate, 1982; Queen's Counsel, 1992. Temporary High Court Judge, since 2004; Member, Sentencing Commission for Scotland, 2003-06; Vice Chair, Parole Board for Scotland, 2005-07, Member, since 2001; Member, Sacro; Life Member, Scottish Association for the Study of Delinquency, Chair, Glasgow Branch, since 2002. Recreations: piano; theatre; driving; walking; opera; music; Italy; gardening.

Rae, Scott Alexander, LLB (Hons), WS, NP, TEP. Partner, Morton Fraser WS, Edinburgh, since 1970; b. 17.12.44, Edinburgh; m., Annabel Riach; 3 s. Educ. Daniel Stewarts College, Edinburgh; Edinburgh University. Sometime Tutor and Course Leader, Edinburgh University; Law Society of Scotland Examiner in Taxation and Chairman, Board of Examiners. Member, VAT Tribunal (Scotland); Clerk, Incorporated Trades of Edinburgh; Member, International Academy of Estate and Trust Law; past Collector, Society of Writers to the Signet; Law Society of Scotland: Convener, Trust Law Committee, past Convener, Tax Law Committee, Charities Committee. Director, Harmeny Education Trust Ltd.; Director, Scottish Language Dictionaries Ltd; Trustee, John Watson's Trust; Nancy Ovens Trust and other charities. Address: (b.) 30-31 Queen Street, Edinburgh EH2 1JX; T.-0131-247 1000.

Rae, Simon Scott, LLB (Hons), DipLP, NP. Head of Corporate, DLA Piper Scotland (Partner), since 2004; b. 28.12.72, Edinburgh. Educ. George Watson's College, Edinburgh; Strathclyde University, Glasgow. Dundas & Wilson CS, Edinburgh, 1995-98; Clifford Chance, London, 1998-2004. Address: (b.) Rutland Square, Edinburgh (c/o DLA Piper); T.-0131-242-5085.
E-mail: simon.rae@dlapiper.com

Raeburn, James B., FCIS. Director, Scottish Print Employers Federation and Scottish Newspaper Publishers' Association, 1984-2007; Director, Scottish Daily Newspaper Society, since 1996; b. 18.3.47, Jedburgh; m., Rosemary Bisset; 2 d. Educ. Hawick High School. Edinburgh Corporation, 1964-69; Roxburgh County Council, 1969-71; Electrical Contractors' Association of Scotland, 1972-83 (Secretary, 1975-83). Director: Press Standards Board of Finance Ltd., since 1990 (Secretary and Treasurer, since 2003), Advertising Standards Board of Finance Ltd., since 1998, National Council for the Training of Journalists, 1993-2006, Publishing National Training Organisation Ltd., 2000-03. Recreation: golf. Address: (b.) 21 Lansdowne Crescent, Edinburgh EH12 5EH; T.-0131 535 1064.

Raeburn, Sheriff Susan Adiel Ogilvie, LLB, QC. Sheriff of Glasgow and Strathkelvin, since 1993; b. 23.4.54, Ellon. Educ. St. Margaret's School for Girls, Aberdeen; Edinburgh University. Admitted, Faculty of Advocates, 1977; took silk, 1991; part-time Chairman, Social Security Appeal Tribunals, 1986-91; Temporary Sheriff, 1988-92; part-time Chairman, Medical Appeal Tribunals, 1992-93; Reporter to Scottish Legal Aid Board, 1990-93. Recreations: the arts; travel. Address: (b.) Sheriff Court, P.O. Box 23, 1 Carlton Place, Glasgow G5 9DA; T.-0141-429 8888.

Raffe, Professor David James, BA, BPhil. Professor of Sociology of Education, University of Edinburgh, since 1992; Director of Research, School of Education, since 2002; b., 5.5.51, Felixstowe; m., Shirley; 1 s.; 1 d. Educ. The Leys School, Cambridge; New College and Nuffield College, Oxford University. Centre for Educational Sociology, University of Edinburgh: Research Fellow, 1975-79, Deputy Director, 1979-86, Director, 1987-91; Lecturer in Education, 1979-85, Reader in Education, 1985-

92. Publications: Reconstructions of Secondary Education, 1983; Fourteen to Eighteen, 1984; Education and the Youth Labour Market, 1988; British Baccalaureat, 1990; Part-time Higher Education, 1998; Policy Making and Policy Learning in 14-19 Education, 2007. Address: (b.) St. John's Land, Holyrood Road, Edinburgh EH8 8AQ.

Rafferty, John, LLB (Hons), FSI. Director, F & C Private Equity Trust PLC; Chairman, Burness, 1997-2004 (Partner, since 1977); Honorary consul for Canada in Scotland; b. 30.6.51, St Andrews. Educ. Edinburgh Academy; Edinburgh University. Burness: Apprentice Solicitor, 1973-75; Assistant Solicitor, 1975-77. Recreations: gardening; hill-walking; countryside. Address: (b.) 50 Lothian Road, Edinburgh EH3 9WJ; T.-0131-473 6000.

Rainey, John Bruce, BSc, MB, ChB, ChM, FRCSEdin. Consultant Surgeon, Borders General Hospital, Melrose and Western General Hospital, Edinburgh, since 2002; Honorary Senior Lecturer in Surgery, Edinburgh University, since 1988; Lead cancer clinician and Associate Medical Director, Border Health, since 2006; b. 10.5.52, Belfast; m., Dr. Linda Margaret King; 2 s.; 1 d. Educ. Royal Belfast Academical Institution; Edinburgh University. Trained in general surgery; Examiner in surgery and accident and emergency medicine for Royal College of Surgeons of Edinburgh. Aris and Gale Lecturer, Royal College of Surgeons of England, 1985. Recreations: family; sport; history and military history. Address: (h.) 144/7 Whitehouse Loan, Edinburgh EH9 2AN; T.-0131 447 8773.

Raison, Jeremy, BA (Hons). Artistic Director, Citizens Theatre, since 2003; b. 13.3.61, Tadworth; m., Sharon Mackenzie; 2 d. Educ. Bristol University. Associate Director, Traverse Theatre, 1986-87; Director (on attachment), National Theatre Studio, 1988; Artistic Director, Chester Gateway Theatre, 1993-97. TMA Award for Special Achievement in Regional Theatre; BBC Young Playwrights Award. Recreations: skiing; reading; writing. Address: Citizens Theatre, Gorbals, Glasgow G5 9DS; T.-0141-429 5561; e-mail: info@citz.co.uk

Raistrick, Evlyn, MA. Chairman, Scottish Hockey Union, 1992-96; Tournament Director: Atlanta Olympics, 1996, Commonwealth Games, Manchester, 2002; b. 13.8.42, Edinburgh; m., David William; 3 s. Educ. Boroughmuir School; Edinburgh University. Maths Teacher, Liberton High, 1964-72. Member, Scottish Sports Council, 1993-2001; Vice-Chairman, Executive, Scottish Sports Association, 1993-2001. Recreations: hockey; squash; golf. Address; (h.) Seton Mains House, Longniddry, East Lothian EH32 0PG.

Ralston, Professor Ian Beith McLaren, MA, PhD, FRSE, FSA, FSA Scot, MIFA. Professor of Archaeology, University of Edinburgh, since 1998; Chair, CFA Archaeology Ltd., since 2000; Vice-President, Society of Antiquaries of Scotland, since 2007; Chair, Standing Committee for Archaeology - the Universities, since 2007; b. 11.11.50, Edinburgh; m., Sandra Webb; 1 s.; 1 d. Educ. Edinburgh Academy; Edinburgh University. Aberdeen University: Research Fellow in Archaeology, 1974-77, Lecturer in Geography/ Archaeology, 1977-85; University of Edinburgh: Lecturer in Archaeology, 1985-90, Senior Lecturer in Archaeology, 1990-98. Honorary Chair, Institute of Field Archaeologists, 1991-92; Chair, Treasure Trove Advisory Panel, since 2004; President, Council for Scottish Archaeology, 1996-2000. Publications: Archaeological Resource Management in the United Kingdom – an introduction (Co-editor), 2 edn., 2006; The

Archaeology of Britain – an Introduction from the Upper Palaeolithic to the Industrial Revolution, (Co-editor), 1999; Scotland after the Ice Age (Co-editor), 2003; Celtic Fortifications (2006); books on French archaeology; exhibition catalogues; papers. Recreation: walking. Address: (b.) 12 Infirmary Street, Edinburgh EH1 1LT; T.-0131-650 2370; e-mail: ian.ralston@ed.ac.uk; web: www.ianralston.co.uk

Ralston, Professor Stuart Hamilton, MBChB, MRCP(UK), MD, FRCP(Glas), FRCP(Edin), FMedSci, FRSE. Professor of Rheumatology, University of Edinburgh; b. 24.10.55, Glasgow; m., Janet Thomson; 2 s.; 2 d. Educ. Allan Glen's School, Glasgow; Glasgow University. Junior House Officer, Glasgow Royal Infirmary, 1978-79; Senior House Officer, Falkirk and District Royal Infirmary and Aberdeen Teaching Hospitals, 1979-81; Registrar, General Medicine, Glasgow Royal Infirmary, 1981-84; Senior Registrar, Glasgow Royal Infirmary and Southern General Hospital, Glasgow, 1984-87; Locum Consultant Physician, Stobhill Hospital, Glasgow, 1989; Wellcome Senior Research Fellow and Honorary Consultant Physician, Northern General Hospital, Edinburgh, 1989-91; Senior Lecturer, Medicine and Therapeutics, Aberdeen University and Honorary Consultant Physician, Aberdeen Royal Hospitals NHS Trust, 1991-94, Reader, 1994-99; Director, Institute of Medical Science, University of Aberdeen; Professor of Medicine and Bone Metabolism, University of Aberdeen, 1999-2005. President, European Calcified Tissues Society, 1997-2005; Board Member, International Bone and Mineral Society, since 2001; Examiner, Royal College of Physicians of Edinburgh, since 1996; Scientific Advisor to: National Association for Relief of Paget's Disease, since 1997, National Osteoporosis Society, since 1997. Recreations: mountaineering; snowboarding. Address: (b.) Rheumatic Diseases Unit, Western General Hospital, Edinburgh EH4 2XU. E-mail: stuart.ralston@ed.ac.uk

Ramage, Alan W., CBE. Formerly Keeper of the Registers of Scotland; b. 4.12.43, Edinburgh; m., Fiona Lesslie. Educ. Boroughmuir School, Edinburgh. Recreations: keeping fit; reading. Address: (h.) 12 St Fillan's Terrace, Edinburgh EH10 4NH; T.-0131 447 8463.

Rampling, Professor Roy, PhD, MSc, BSc, DIC, ARCS, MBBS, FRCR, FRCP. Professor of Neuro-Oncology, University of Glasgow, since 2000; b. 13.9.46, Malta; m., Susan Bonham-Carter; 2 s.; 1 d. Educ. Clacton County High School; Imperial College, London; University College, London. University of Glasgow: Senior Lecturer, Radiation Oncology, 1987-97, Reader, 1997-2000. Address: Beatson Oncology Centre, Western Infirmary, Glasgow G11 6NT; T.-0141-211 2627; e-mail: r.rampling@udcf.gla.ac.uk

Ramsay, Rev. (Alexander) Malcolm, BA, LLB, DipMin. Parish Minister, Pitlochry (Church of Scotland), since 1998; b. 4.3.57, Livingstone, N. Rhodesia (now Zambia); m., Cati Balfour Paul; 1 d.; 1 s. Educ. Merchiston Castle School, Edinburgh; St. John's College, Cambridge; Edinburgh University. Solicitor, 1982-83; ordained Minister of Church of Scotland, 1986; Parish Minister of Bargrennan linked with Monigaff, Wigtownshire, 1987-93; Mission Partner of Church of Scotland teaching Theology in Presbyterian Church of Guatemala, 1994-98. Recreations: cycling; poetry. Address: (h.) Moulin Manse, Pitlochry, Perthshire PH16 5EP.

Ramsay, Major General Charles Alexander, CB, OBE. Landowner; b. 12.10.36, North Berwick; m. (1967), Hon. Mary MacAndrew; 2 s.; 2 d. Educ. Eton; Sandhurst.

Commissioned Royal Scots Greys, 1956; Staff College, Canada, 1967-68; Commanded Royal Scots Dragoon Guards, 1977-79; Commander 12th Armoured Brigade, 1980-82; Dep DMO MOD, 1983-84; GOC Eastern District, 1984-87; Director General, Army Organisation and Territorial Army, 1987-89; Chairman, Cockburns of Leith Ltd., 1993-2004; Director, John Menzies Plc, 1990-2004, Grey Horse Properties Ltd., Edinburgh Military Tattoo Ltd., 1991-2007; Colonel, The Royal Scots Dragoon Guards, 1992-98; Member, Royal Company of Archers (Queen's Bodyguard for Scotland). Recreations: field sports; equitation; travel. Address: (h.) Bughtrig, Coldstream, Berwickshire TD12 4JP; T.-01890 840678.

Randall, Rev. David James, MA, BD, ThM. Minister, Church of Scotland, Macduff, since 1971; b. 5.6.45, Edinburgh; m., Nan Wardlaw; 3 s.; 1 d.; 6 grandchildren. Educ. George Heriot's School; Edinburgh University; Princeton Theological Seminary. Recreations: jogging; reading. Address: The Manse, Macduff AB45 3QL; T.-01261 832316; e-mail: djrandall479@btinternet.com

Randall, Rev. David Steven, BA, BD. Minister, Bo'ness Old Kirk (Church of Scotland), since 2003; b. 28.1.71, Edinburgh; m., Linnea; 2 s.; 2 d. Educ. Banff Academy; Robert Gordon University; University of Aberdeen. Provision of Accounting Services to North Sea Oil Industry, Andersen Consulting (now known as Accenture), 1993-99; Parish Minister, The Church of Scotland, since 2002. Recreations: football; squash; current affairs; reading. Address: (b.) 10 Dundas Street, Bo'ness EH51 0DG; T.-01506 822206; e-mail: dsrandall@blueyonder.co.uk

Randall, John Norman, BA, MPhil. Chairman, The Islands Book Trust, since 2002; b. 1.8.45, Bromley, Kent; 1 s.; 1 d. Educ. Bromley Grammar School; Bristol University; Glasgow University. Department of Economic Affairs; Scottish Office; Assistant Secretary, Countryside and Natural Heritage Unit, Scottish Office Agriculture, Environment and Fisheries Department, 1995-99; Registrar General for Scotland, 1999-2003. Recreation: hill-walking. Address: (h.) 31 Lemreway, South Lochs, Isle of Lewis; T.-01851 880365.

Rankin, Professor Andrew C., BSc, MBChB, MD, MRCP, FRCP. Professor, Medical Cardiology, University of Glasgow, since 2006; Reader, Glasgow Royal Infirmary, 2002-06; b. 15.6.52, Larkhall; m., Clare Fitzsimons; 3 s. Educ. Hamilton Academy; Glasgow University. Registrar, Medical Cardiology, 1980; Lecturer, 1984, then Senior Lecturer, 1993, Medical Cardiology. Hon. Consultant Cardiologist, Glasgow Royal Infirmary, since 1993. Address; (b.) Department of Medical Cardiology, Glasgow Royal Infirmary, Glasgow; T.-0141-211 4833.

Rankin, Professor David W.H., MA, PhD, FRSC, CChem, FRSE. Professor of Structural Chemistry, Edinburgh University, since 1989; b. 8.6.45, Birkenhead; m., Stella M. Thomas; 3 s.; 1 d. Educ. Birkenhead School; King's College, Cambridge. Edinburgh University: ICI Research Fellow, 1969, Demonstrator, 1971, Lecturer, 1973, Reader, 1980, Professor, 1989. Publication: Structural Methods in Inorganic Chemistry. Address: (b.) School of Chemistry, Edinburgh University, West Mains Road, Edinburgh EH9 3JJ; T.-0131-650 4728.

Rankin, Ian, OBE. Novelist; b. 1960, Fife; m.; 2 s. Educ. Edinburgh University. Has been employed as grape-picker, swine-herd, taxman, alcohol researcher, hi-fi journalist and punk musician; creator of the Inspector Rebus novels; first Rebus novel, Knots and Crosses, 1987; this series now translated into 25 languages; elected Hawthornden Fellow; former winner, Chandler-Fulbright Award; two CWA "Daggers"; 1997 CWA Macallan Gold Dagger for fiction for Black and Blue; Mystery Writers of America Edgar Award for best novel: Resurrection Men, 2005; awarded the CWA Cartier Diamond Dagger for lifetime's achievement in crime writing; 1999 Alumnus of the Year, Edinburgh University; Honorary Doctorate: University of Abertay Dundee, University of St. Andrews, University of Edinburgh. Address: c/o Curtis Brown Ltd, Haymarket House, 28-29 Haymarket, London SW1Y 4SP.

Ransford, Tessa, OBE, HonDUniv (Paisley), MA, DipEd, FICS, FCHE. Poet; b. 8.7.38, Bombay; 1 s.; 3 d. Educ. St. Leonard's School, St. Andrews; Edinburgh University; Craiglockhart College of Education. Publicity Department, Oxford University Press, 1958; in Pakistan as wife of missionary, 1960-68; Assistant to the Director, Scottish Institute of Adult Education, 1982-83; founder, Scottish Poetry Library, Director, 1984-99. Editor, Lines Review, 1988-98; books of poetry: Poetry of Persons, 1975, While It Is Yet Day, 1976, Light of the Mind, 1980, Fools and Angels, 1984; Shadows from the Greater Hill, 1987; A Dancing Innocence, 1988; Seven Valleys, 1991; Medusa Dozen and other poems, 1994; Scottish Selection, 1998; When It Works It Feels Like Play, 1998; Indian Selection, 2000; Natural Selection, 2001; Noteworthy Selection, 2002; The Nightingale Question, translations from five poets from Saxony, 2004; Shades of Green, 2005 (shortlisted for the Eco-Creativity Award, 2006); Sonnet Selection, 2007; first prize, Jubilee poetry competition, Scottish Association for the Speaking of Verse, 1974; Scottish Arts Council Book Award, 1980; Howard Sergeant Award for services to poetry, 1989; Honorary Member: The Saltire Society, 1993, Scottish Library Association, 1999; Heritage Society of Scotland Annual Award, 1996; Society of Authors Travelling Scholarship, 2001; Writing Fellow, Royal Literary Fund, since 2001; Committee Member, Scottish International PEN; Initiator, Callum Macdonald Memorial Award for pamphlet poetry publishing; Chair, Edinburgh Book Fringe. Recreation: grandchildren. Address: (h.) 31 Royal Park Terrace, Edinburgh EH8 8JA; T.-0131-661 1277; e-mail: wisdomfield@talk21.com; web: www.wisdomfield.com

Rapport, Professor Nigel Julian, BA, MA, PhD, FRSA, FRSE. Professor of Anthropological and Philosophical Studies, St. Andrews University, since 1996; b. 8.11.56, Cardiff; m., Elizabeth J.A. Munro; 1 s.; 1 d. Educ. Clifton College, Bristol; Cambridge University; Manchester University. Research Fellow and Associate, Institute of Social and Economic Research, Memorial University of Newfoundland, 1983-87; Lecturer, Blaustein Institute for Desert Research, Ben-Gurion University of the Negev, Israel, 1988; Lecturer, Department of Social Anthropology, Manchester University, 1989; joined St. Andrews University as Lecturer, 1993. Hon. Secretary, Association of Social Anthropologists of the UK and Commonwealth, 1994-98; President, Anthropology and Archaeology Section, British Association for the Advancement of Science, 2000-01; Canada Research Chair in Globalization, Citizenship and Justice, 2004-07; 1996 Royal Society of Edinburgh prize lectureship in the humanities, 1996; Royal Anthropological Institute, Curl Essay Prize, 1996. Publications: Talking Violence: an anthropological interpretation of conversation in the city, 1987; Diverse World-Views in an English Village, 1993; The Prose and the Passion: anthropology, literature and the writing of E.M. Forster, 1994; Questions of Consciousness (Co-editor), 1995; Transcendent Individual, towards a literary and liberal anthropology, 1997; Migrants of Identity: Perceptions of Home in a World of Movement (Co-editor),

1998; Social and Cultural Anthropology: The Key Concepts, 2000; British Subjects – An Anthropology of Britain (Editor), 2002; The Trouble With Community – Anthropological Reflections on Movement, Identity and Collectivity, 2002; I am Dynamite: an alternative anthropology of power, 2003; Science, Democracy and The Open Society (Editor), 2006. Recreations: travel; sport; literature. Address: (b.) Department of Social Anthropology, St. Andrews University, St. Andrews KY16 9AL; T.-01334 462977.

Ratter, Drew, BA (Hons). Chairman, Crofters Commission; Crofter, since 1984; Shetland Councillor, since 1994; Crofters Commissioner/Board Member, since 1999; Board Member, Highlands and Islands Enterprise, since 2002; b. 28.3.52, Lerwick; m., Vivienne; 1 s.; 2 d. Educ. Anderson Educational Institute; University of Sussex; Massachusetts University; Edinburgh University. Scottish Crofters Union; Writer; Journalist, since 1984; Marketing Group, 1987-93; Shetland Enterprise Board Member, 1990-2002; Council Member, Scottish Consumer Council, since 2002. Recreations: reading; thinking. Address: (b.) Crofters Commission, 4-6 Castle Wynd, Inverness IV2 3EQ; e-mail: drew.ratter@shetland.gov.uk

Ratter, James Alexander, BSc, PhD, FRSE, FRGS. Retired; Senior Principal Scientific Officer, Head of Tropical Biology, Royal Botanic Garden, Edinburgh, 1987-99; b. 15.2.34, Cambridge; m., Pamela Joan Allsop. Educ. Liverpool College; University of Liverpool. University Demonstrator, University of Liverpool, 1958-60; Botanist, Royal Botanic Garden, Edinburgh: Scientific Officer, 1960-64, Senior Scientific Officer, 1964-69, Principal Scientific Officer, 1969-87; Visiting Professor (Co-Founder, Ecology Department), University of Brasilia, 1976-77; Co-Leader of Biodiversity Survey, Anglo-Brazilian Maracá Rainforest Project (INPA/Royal Geographical Society/SEMA), 1987-88. Specialist Adviser, HOC Environment Committee, Climatological and Environmental Effects of Rainforest Destruction, Session 1989-90 and 1990-91; Honorary Citizen, Municipality of Nova Xavantina, Mato Grosso, Brazil, 1997; Fellow, Brazilian Academy of Sciences, 1999; awarded Grand Cross, National Order of Scientific Merit, by President of the Republic of Brazil, 2000; Dr Hon. Causa, University of Brasilia, 2005. Recreations: field botany; Portuguese language; ornithology. Publications: Maracá: Rainforest Island (Co-Author), 1993; Maracá: The Biodiversity and Environment of an Amazonian Rainforest (Co-Author and Editor), 1998. Address: (b.) Royal Botanic Garden, 20A Inverleith Row, Edinburgh EH3 5LR; e-mail: j.ratter@rbge.org.uk

Raven, Hugh J. E. Member, UK Sustainable Development Commission, since 2004; Member of Board, Scottish Natural Heritage, 2004-07; Environment Adviser, Esmee Fairbairn Foundation, since 2000; Director, Soil Association Scotland, since 2006; Consultant; b. 20.4.61, London; m., Jane Smart-Smith; 2 d. Educ. various schools; Harper Adams Agricultural College; University of Kent at Canterbury. Policy Strategist for the British Overseas Aid Group (a coalition of Oxfam, Christian Aid, Save the Children (UK), CAFOD and ActionAid), 1996; Convenor of the UK Government Green Globe Task Force, 1997-99; Advisor on Rural Policy to Environment Minister Michael Meacher MP, 1999-2000. Director of Ardtornish Estate, Morvern, Argyll, since 1996. Councillor, Royal Borough of Kensington and Chelsea, 1990-94; Member of the BBC Rural and Agricultural Affairs Advisory Committee, 1994-97; Member of the UK Executive Committee of the British American Project, 1996-98; Trustee of the Soil Association, 1992-99; Chair of SERA, the environmental affiliate of the Labour Party, 1997-99; Chair, Lochaber and District Fisheries Trust, 1995-2002; Trustee of the Royal Society

for the Protection of Birds, 1997-2002; 1999, 2001 and 2003: Parliamentary Candidate, Scottish Labour Party, Argyll and Bute. Recreations: gardening badly; angling; sailing; idleness. Address: (h.) Kinlochaline Castle, Morvern, Oban, Argyll PA34 5UZ; e-mail: hugh@kinlochaline.co.uk

Reader, Professor Keith Anthony, MA (Cantab), BPhil, DPhil (Oxon), Chevalier dans l'Ordre des Palmes Académiques. Professor of Modern French, Glasgow University, since 2000; b. 20.12.45, Tunbridge Wells. Educ. Ifield Grammar School, Crawley, Sussex; Downing College, Cambridge; St John's College, Oxford. Lecturer, Caen University, France, 1970-71; Lecturer, Ecole Normale Supérieure, Paris, 1971-73; Lecturer, Manchester Polytechnic, 1973-74; Lecturer/Reader/Professor, Kingston Polytechnic/University, 1974-95; Professor of French, Newcastle University, 1995-2000; Member, Executive Committee, Society for French Studies, 1984-87; Editorial Board, Modern and Contemporary France, 1991-96; Treasurer, University Council of Modern Languages, 1996-2000; Editorial Board, French Studies, since 2005. Publications include: Régis Debray, 1995; Robert Bresson, 2000; The Papin Sisters (Co-author), 2001; The Abject Object, 2006. Address: (b.) Modern Languages Building, Glasgow University; T.-0141-330 3660.

Reay, 14th Lord (Hugh William Mackay); b. 19.7.37; m.; 2 d.; 2 s., 1 d. by pr. m. Educ. Eton; Christ Church. Succeeded to title, 1963; Member, European Parliament, 1973-79; Parliamentary Under Secretary of State, Department of Trade and Industry, 1991-92.

Reed, Hon. Lord (Robert John Reed). Senator of the College of Justice, since 1998; b. 7.9.56, Edinburgh; m., Jane Mylne; 2 d. Educ. George Watson's College, Edinburgh; Edinburgh University (LLB, 1st class Hons); Balliol College, Oxford (DPhil). Standing Junior Counsel: Scottish Education Department, 1988-89, Scottish Office Home and Health Department, 1989-95; called to English Bar, 1991; QC, 1995; Advocate Depute, 1996-98; ad hoc Judge of the European Court of Human Rights, 1999; Expert Adviser, EU/Council of Europe Joint Initiative with Turkey, 2002-04; Member, Advisory Board, British Institute of International and Comparative Law, 2001-05; Chairman, Franco-British Judicial Co-operation Committee, since 2005; President, EU Forum of Judges for the Environment, 2006-07; Member, UN Task Force on Access to Justice, since 2006; Convener, Children in Scotland, since 2006; Hon. Professor, Glasgow Caledonian University, since 2005, University of Glasgow, since 2006. Recreation: music. Address: (b.) Court of Session, Parliament House, Edinburgh EH1 1RQ.

Reed, Gavin Barras, BA. Chairman, Maclay Group plc; b. 13.11.34, Newcastle upon Tyne; m. Muriel Joyce; 1 s.; 3 d. Educ. Eton; Trinity College, Cambridge. National Service, Fleet Air Arm; joined The Newcastle Breweries, 1958; Vice-Chairman, Scottish & Newcastle plc, 1991-94; Chairman, John Menzies plc, 1997-2002. Director: Hamilton and Inches Ltd. (Chairman), Burtonwood Brewery plc, 1996-2005. Recreation: shooting. Address (h.) Broadgate, West Woodburn, Northumberland NE48 2RN.

Reed, Malcolm Christopher, CBE, MA, DPhil, FCIT, FIHT, FRSA, CIES. Chief Executive, Transport Scotland; b. 24.11.44, Cardigan, Wales; 2 d. Educ. Royal Grammar School, Newcastle upon Tyne; St Catherine's College, Oxford; Nuffield College, Oxford.

Assistant, Bodleian Library, Oxford; Lecturer, Glasgow University; Researcher/Associate Director, Planning Exchange, Glasgow; Planner, Chief Public Transport Co-ordinator, Greater Glasgow Passenger Transport Executive; Chief Policy Planner/Senior Executive Officer, Strathclyde Regional Council; Assistant Chief Executive, Strathclyde Regional Council; Director General, Strathclyde Passenger Transport Executive. Recreations: hill walking; listening to music; travel. Address: (b.) Buchanan House, 58 Port Dundas Road, Glasgow G4 0HF.
E-mail: chiefexecutive@transportscotland.gsi.gov.uk

Reed, Professor Peter, BA, RIBA, FRIAS, FSAScot. Emeritus Professor, Strathclyde University; b. 31.1.33, Hayes, Middlesex; m., Keow Chim Lim; 2 d. Educ. Southall Grammar School; Manchester University (State Scholar); Open University. Commissioned Officer, RAF, 1960-61; Assistant Lecturer, University of Hong Kong, 1961-64; Architect in practice, Malaysia, 1964-70; joined Strathclyde University Department of Architecture and Building Science as Lecturer, 1970; Professor of Architecture, 1986; Dean, Faculty of Engineering, 1988-90; Vice-Principal Elect, 1990-92; Vice-Principal, 1992-94. Secretary, Kilsyth Civic Trust, 1975-80; Chairman, Kilsyth Community Council, 1975-78; GIA Council, 1982-84; ARCUK Board of Education, 1985-95; Governor, Glasgow School of Art, 1982-94; Director, Glasgow West Conservation Trust, 1990-2000, Convener, 1996-2000; Chairman, Council, Charles Rennie Mackintosh Society, 1991-94. Publications include Glasgow: The Forming of the City (Editor). Recreations: opera; cricket. Address: 67 Dowanside Road, Glasgow G12 9DL; T.-0141-334 1356.

Reeks, David Robin, TD, DL, BSc(Eng). Vice Lord Lieutenant of Lanarkshire; b. 15.6.35, Parkstone; m., Kathleen Veronica Stephens; 1 s.; 1 d. Educ. Canford School; London University. Rig Engineer, UKAEA Dounreay, 1962-67; Senior Engineer, SSEB, 1967-90; Reactor Thermal Performance Engineer, Scottish Nuclear Ltd., 1990-94. Committee Member and Volunteer Convoy Leader, Edinburgh Direct Aid to Bosnia; TA Royal Engineers/Royal Corps of Transport, 1962-90. Recreations: hill-walking; Scottish country dancing. Address: 3 Cedar Place, Strathaven, Lanarkshire ML10 6DW; T.-01357 521695; e-mail: d-reeks@ukonline.co.uk

Rees, Alan Tait, MBE, MA (Cantab), CQSW; b. 4.8.31, Shanghai, China; m., Alison Margaret; 2 s.; 2 d. Educ. Kingswood School, Bath; Gonville and Caius College, Cambridge; London School of Economics; University College, Swansea. Community Development Officer, Tanzania; Lecturer in Youth and Community Studies, Moray House College; Organising Secretary, Board for Information in Youth and Community Service, Scotland; Senior Community Development Officer, Council of Social Service for Wales; Assistant Director, Edinburgh Voluntary Organisations' Council, retired 1993; Chair, Scotland Yard Adventure Centre, Edinburgh, 1986-98; Chair, Handicabs (Lothian), 1997-2001; Secretary and Treasurer, Scottish Accessible Transport Alliance; Member, Mobility and Access Committee for Scotland; Treasurer, Scottish Branch, International Play Association (IPA); Company Secretary, Scottish Alliance for Children's Rights. Recreations: gardening; painting and printmaking. Address: (h.) 20 Seaforth Drive, Edinburgh EH4 2BZ; T.-0131-315 3006.

Rees, Jennifer Linda, BSc, PhD, FRSS, MCMI, FHEA. Vice Principal (Academic Quality and Customer Service), Napier University, since 2006; b. 2.7.51, Edinburgh; m., Richard; 1 s.; 1 d. Educ. Edinburgh University; Bradford University. Operational Research Analyst, then Statistical Quality Control Manager, Scottish & Newcastle Breweries Ltd.; Lecturer, Department of Business Studies, Edinburgh University; Head, Department of Management Studies, Scottish College of Textiles; Assistant Principal (Academic), Bell College of Technology; Executive Director, Glasgow Caledonian University. Recreations: skiing; theatre; walking. Address: (b.) Napier University, Craighouse Campus, Edinburgh EH10 5LG.

Rees, Professor Jonathan, BMedSci, MBBS, FRCP, FRCPE, FMedSci. Grant Chair of Dermatology, University of Edinburgh, since 2000; b. 10.10.57, Cardiff; 2 d. Educ. St. Illtyd's College, Cardiff. Trained in internal medicine, Newcastle upon Tyne; trained in dermatology, Vienna and Newcastle-upon-Tyne; trained in molecular genetics, Newcastle-upon-Tyne and Strasbourg; Professor of Dermatology, University of Newcastle, 1992-2000. President, European Society for Dermatology Research. Recreation: changing research fields. Address: (b.) Department of Dermatology, University of Edinburgh, Lauriston Building, Lauriston Place, Edinburgh EH3 9HA; T.-0131-536 2041; e-mail: jonathan.rees@ed.ac.uk

Reese, Professor Jason Meredith, DPhil, FInstP, FIMechE, FRSE. Weir Professor of Thermodynamics and Fluid Mechanics, University of Strathclyde, since 2003; b. 24.6.67, London; m., Dr Alexandra Shepard. Educ. St. Paul's School, London; Imperial College, London; University of Oxford. Lecturer in Engineering, University of Aberdeen, 1996-2000; Lecturer in Mechanical Engineering and ExxonMobil Fellow, King's College London, 2001-03; Co-Founder, Brinker Technology Ltd., Aberdeen (Pipeline Leak Sealing and Detection Company), 2002. Philip Leverhulme Prize for Engineering, The Leverhulme Trust (2003); 36th Bruce Preller Prize Lectureship, Royal Society of Edinburgh (2004); MacRobert Award Finalist, Royal Academy of Engineering (2006). Recreations: playing the piano; conversation; byzantine history. Address: (b.) Department of Mechanical Engineering, University of Strathclyde, James Weir Building, Glasgow G1 1XJ; T.-0141 548 3131; e-mail: jason.reese@strath.ac.uk

Reeve, Bill, BSc (Hons) Dunelm, MBA, CEng, MIMechE. Director, Rail Delivery, Transport Scotland, since 2005; b. 22.08.64, Redruth; m., Helen Redican; 2 s. Educ. Hove County Grammar; Brighton, Hove and Sussex VIth Form College; St. Chad's College, Durham; Strathclyde Graduate Business School. Career History: Rolling Stock Maintenance Engineer, British Rail, then Rail Freight Investment Manager; Rail Freight Business Development Manager, EWS Ltd.; Director, Project Sponsorship, Strategic Rail Authority. Board Member, Railway Division of Institution of Mechanical Engineers. Recreations: time with family; sailing; international rail travel. Address: (b.) Buchanan House, 58 Port Dundas Road, Glasgow G4 0HF; T.-0141 272 7420.
E-mail: bill.reeve@transportscotland.gsi.gov.uk

Reeves, Philip Thomas Langford, RSA, PPRSW, RE, RGI, ARCA. Artist; b. 7.7.31, Cheltenham; m., Christine MacLaren (deceased); 1 d. Educ. Naunton Park School, Cheltenham; Cheltenham School of Art; Royal College of Art, London. Lecturer in Graphic Design, Glasgow School of Art, 1954-70, Head of Printmaking, 1970-91. Address: (h.) 13 Hamilton Drive, Glasgow G12 8DN; T.-0141-339 0720.

Reid, Alan, MP. Liberal Democrat MP, Argyll and Bute, since 2001; b. 7.8.54. Educ. Prestwick Academy;

Ayr Academy; Strathclyde University. Maths Teacher, 1976-77; Computer Programmer, 1977-85; Computer Project Manager, Glasgow University, 1985-2001. Address: (b.) House of Commons, London SW1A 0AA.

Reid, Allan William, MBChB, FRCR, FRCP. Consultant Radiologist: Glasgow Royal Infirmary, since 1989, Ross Hall Hospital, since 1991; Clinical Director of Imaging, Glasgow Royal Infirmary, since 1996; b. 20.6.58, Glasgow. Educ. Glasgow Academy; University of Glasgow. Recreations: photography; swimming; golf. Address: (b.) Department of Radiology, Glasgow Royal Infirmary, Glasgow G31 2ER; T.-0141-211 4783; e-mail: allan.reid@nhs.net

Reid, Professor Colin Turriff, MA, LLB. Professor of Environmental Law, Dundee University, since 1995 and Dean of the Faculty of Law and Accountancy, 2004-06; b. 10.6.58, Aberdeen; m., M. Anne Palin; 2 d. Educ. Robert Gordon's College, Aberdeen; University College, Oxford; Gonville and Caius College, Cambridge. Lecturer in Public Law, Aberdeen University, 1980-90; Senior Lecturer in Law, Dundee University, 1991-95. Publications: Nature Conservation Law; Environmental Law in Scotland (Editor); A Guide to the Scotland Act 1998 (Co-Author). Recreations: cricket; hockey. Address: (b.) School of Law, Dundee University, Dundee DD1 4HN; T.-01382 384461.

Reid, Derek Donald, MA. Chairman, Harris Tweed Textiles Ltd; various directorships of small companies; Visiting Professor of Tourism, Abertay University, since 2000; Governor, Pitlochry Theatre; b. 30.11.44, Aberdeen; m., Janice Anne Reid; 1 s.; 1 d. Educ. Inverurie Academy; Aberdeen University; Robert Gordon University. Cadbury-Schweppes, 1968-85 (latterly Divisional Director); founding Director/Owner, Premier Brands, 1985-90; Chief Executive, Scottish Tourist Board, 1994-96. Former Deputy Chairman, Sea Fish Industry Authority; former Deputy Chairman: Scotland The Brand; Honorary Doctorate, Business Administration, Robert Gordon University; Fellow, George Thomas Society. Recreations: golf; fishing; modern art; fine food/wine. Address: Broomhill, Kinclaven, Stanley, Perth PH1 4QL; T.-01250-883209.

Reid, Donald Bremner, MA, LLB. Chairman, Mitchells Roberton, since 1997; b. 1.3.51, Glasgow; m., Moira Ruth Wilson; 2 s. Educ. Jordanhill College School; University of Glasgow. Solicitor, 1975; Mitchells Johnston Hill and Hoggan: joined 1976, Partner, 1978, firm amalgamated to form Mitchells Roberton, 1985; Tutor, then Senior Tutor and Lecturer (part-time), University of Glasgow, 1980-99; Expert Witness. Secretary, Children 1st, Glasgow, 1979-99. Recreations: theatre; reading; drinking coffee and reading newspapers; France. Address: (b.) George House, 36 North Hanover Street, Glasgow G1 2AD; T.-0141-552 3422; e-mail: dbr@mitchells-roberton.co.uk

Reid, Professor Gavin Clydesdale, MA, MSc, PhD, FRSA, FFCS. Professor of Economics, St. Andrews University, since 1991; Founder/Director, Centre for Research into Industry, Enterprise, Finance and the Firm (CRIEFF), since 1991; Visiting Professor in Accounting and Finance, University of Strathclyde, since 2007; b. 25.8.46, Glasgow; 2 s.; 2 d. Educ. Lyndhurst Prep School; Frimley and Camberley Grammar School; Aberdeen University (Stephen Scholar); Southampton University; Edinburgh University. Lecturer, Senior Lecturer, Reader in Economics, Edinburgh University, 1971-91; Visiting Associate Professor: Queen's University, Ontario, 1981-82; Denver University, Colorado, 1984; Visiting Scholar, Darwin College, Cambridge, 1987-88; Visiting Professor,

University of Nice, 1998; Leverhulme Trust Research Fellowship, 1989-90; Nuffield Foundation Social Science Research Fellowship, 1997-98. Editorial Board: Scottish Journal of Political Economy, 1986-98, Small Business Economics, since 1997, Venture Capital, since 1998; Member, Council, Scottish Economic Society, 1990-2002, President, 1999-2002; Research Fellow, EIM Business and Policy Research, Rotterdam, since 2002; Chairman, Network of Industrial Economists, 1997-2001; Member, Economic Council, Britain in Europe, 2002-04; Chair, Scottish Institute for Enterprise Research Forum, 2002-03; National Conference of University Professors, President, 2003-06, Vice-President, 2002-03, Member, Council, since 1999; President, Institute of Contemporary Scotland, 2005-06; Chairman, ESRC Seminars in Accounting, Finance and Economics, since 2006. Publications: The Kinked Demand Curve Analysis of Oligopoly, 1981; Theories of Industrial Organization, 1987; The Small Entrepreneurial Firm (Co-author), 1988; Classical Economic Growth, 1989; Small Business Enterprise, 1993; Profiles in Small Business (Co-author), 1993; Venture Capital Investment, 1998; Information System Development in the Small Firm (Co-author), 2000; The Foundations of Small Business Enterprise, 2007; Risk Appraisal and Venture Capital in High Technology New Ventures (Co-Author), 2008. Recreations: music; reading; running; badminton; poetry; horse riding. Address: (h.) 23 South Street, St. Andrews KY16 9QS; T.-01334 472932.

Reid, Rt. Hon. George, MA, PC (2004). Stevenson Professor, University of Glasgow, since 2007; MSP (Elected SNP, but no political allegiance as Presiding Officer), Ochil, 2003-07; Presiding Officer and Convener of Parliamentary Bureau and Corporate Body, Scottish Parliament, 2003-07; MSP (SNP), Mid-Scotland and Fife, and Deputy Presiding Officer, 1999-2003; b. 4.6.39, Tullibody; m., Daphne Ann; 2 d. Educ. Dollar Academy; St Andrews University. Reporter, Daily Express; Reporter, Scottish Television; Producer, Granada Television; Head of News and Current Affairs, Scottish Television; Presenter, BBC; Director of Public Affairs, International Red Cross. MP, Clackmannan and East Stirlingshire, 1974-79; Member, Parliamentary Assembly of the Council of Europe, 1975-79; Trustee, Culture and Sport Glasgow and Edinburgh International Tattoo, since 2007; Honorary doctorates, Universities of St. Andrews, Queen Margaret and Edinburgh.

Reid, Harry William, BA (Hons), Dr hc (Edinburgh), DUniv (Glasgow), FRSA. Writer; Commissioning Consultant, Saint Andrew Press; former Editor, The Herald; b. 23.9.47, Glasgow; m., Julie Davidson (qv); 1 d. Educ. Aberdeen Grammar School; Fettes College; Oxford University. The Scotsman: Education Correspondent, 1973-77, Features Editor, 1977-81; Sports Editor, Sunday Standard, 1981-82; Executive Editor, Glasgow Herald, 1982-83, Deputy Editor, 1983-97; Chairman, Scottish Editors' Committee, 1999-2001. Visiting Fellow, Faculty of Divinity, Edinburgh University, 2001-02; Governor, Fettes College, since 2002. Publication: Dear Country: a quest for England, 1992; Outside Verdict: An Old Kirk in a New Scotland, 2002; The Final Whistle? Scottish Football: The Best and Worst of Times, 2005; Deadline: The Story of the Scottish Press, 2006. Recreations: reading; walking; supporting Aberdeen Football Club. Address: 12 Comely Bank, Edinburgh EH4 1AN; T.-0131-332 6690; e-mail: harry.reid@virgin.net

Reid, Heather M.M., OBE, BSc (Hons), MSc, CPhys, MInstP, FRMS. Weather Forecaster, Met Office, since 1993; BBC Scotland Weather Forecaster, since 1994; b. 6.7.69, Paisley. Educ. Camphill High School, Paisley;

Edinburgh University. Joined Met Office to work in satellite image research; became forecaster at Glasgow Weather Centre; now known as "Heather the Weather" to viewers. Past-Chair, Institute of Physics in Scotland, 1999-2001; active involvement in Edinburgh Science Festival, Techfest, and promoting the public understanding of science. Recreations: apart from lecturing and giving talks in spare time – watch cricket; hill-walking. Address: (b.) Glasgow Weather Centre, 220 St. Vincent Street, Glasgow G2 5QD; T.-0141-248 3451.

Reid, Hugh Watt, MBE, BVM&S, DipTVM, PhD, MRCVS. Transmissible Spongiform Encephallopathy Research Co-ordinator, Moredun Research Institute, since 2002; b. 23.6.42, Edinburgh; m., Irene Elisabeth; 1 s.; 2 d. Educ. George Watson's College, Edinburgh; Glasgow Academy; Aberdeen Grammar School; University of Edinburgh. Moredun Research Institute: Veterinary Research Officer, 1968-74, Principal Veterinary Research Officer, 1974-90, Head, Virology Division, 1990-2002. Member, Board of Directors, Vet Aid; previously office bearer: Association of Veterinary Teachers and Research Workers, Veterinary Deer Society, Edinburgh South Liberal Party. Publications: 150 papers/book chapters. Recreations: gardening; cycling; walking. Address: Pentlands Science Park, Bush Loan, Penicuik EH26 0PZ; T.-0131-445 5111.

Reid, Professor Ian Cameron, MB, ChB, BMedBiol, PhD, MRCPsych. Professor of Psychiatry, Aberdeen University, since 2003; b. 13.10.60, Dunfermline; m., Isla; 1 d. Educ. Dollar Academy; Aberdeen University; Edinburgh University. Lecturer in Mental Health, Aberdeen University; Research Fellow, Department of Pharmacology, then Lecturer in Psychiatry, Edinburgh University; Senior Lecturer in Mental Health, Aberdeen University; Professor in Psychiatry, Dundee University; presently Head of Department of Mental Health, University of Aberdeen. Recreation: curry. Address: (b.) Royal Cornhill Hospital, Aberdeen.

Reid, Professor J.S. Grant, BSc, PhD. Professor of Plant Biochemistry, Stirling University, 1994-2003, now Emeritus; b. 27.3.42, Huntly; m., Mary E. Edwards; 1 s.; 2 d. Educ. Gordon Schools, Huntly; Aberdeen University. Lecturer, University of Fribourg, Switzerland, 1970-73; Lecturer in Biochemistry, Stirling University, 1974-78; Visiting Associate Professor, University of Calgary, 1977-78; Senior Lecturer, then Reader, Stirling University, 1978-94; Visiting Professor, Unilever Research Laboratories, Netherlands, 1988. Address: (b.) School of Biological and Environmental Sciences, Stirling University, Stirling FK9 4LA; T.-01786 467762; e-mail: j.s.g.reid@stir.ac.uk

Reid, James Gordon, LLB (Hons), FCIArb. Queen's Counsel (Scotland), since 1993; Chairman (Part-time), VAT and Duties Tribunals, since 1997; Deputy Special Commissioner for Income Tax, since 1997; Temporary Judge of the Court of Session, since 2002; b. 24.7.52, Edinburgh; m., Hannah Hogg Hopkins; 2 s.; 1 d. Educ. Melville College, Edinburgh; Edinburgh University. Solicitor, 1976-80; Advocate, 1980-93; Standing Junior Counsel, Scottish Office Environment Department, 1986-93; admitted as Barrister, Inner Temple, 1991. Recreations: tennis; golf. Address: (h.) Blebo House, by St. Andrews, Fife KY15 5TZ.

Reid, Jimmy. Journalist and Broadcaster; b. 1932. Former Engineer; prominent in campaign to save Upper Clyde Shipbuilders; former Convener of Shop Stewards, AUEW; former (Communist) Member, Clydebank Town Council; former Member, Labour Party (contested Dundee East,

General Election, 1979); Member, SNP, since 2005; Rector, Glasgow University, 1971-74; Founder, Seven Days magazine; Columnist, The Herald, Glasgow; Honorary Fellow, Institute of Contemporary Scotland, since 2003.

Reid, Rt. Hon. John, PC, PhD. MP (Labour), Airdrie and Shotts, since 2005, Hamilton North and Bellshill, 1997-2005, Motherwell North, 1987-97; Secretary of State for the Home Department, 2006-07; b. 8.5.47, Bellshill; m., 1, Catherine McGowan (deceased), 2, Carine Adler; 2 s. Educ. St. Patrick's Senior Secondary School, Coatbridge; Stirling University. Scottish Research Officer, Labour Party, 1979-83; Political Adviser to Rt. Hon. Neil Kinnock, 1983-85; Scottish Organiser, Trade Unionists for Labour, 1986-87; Armed Forces Minister, 1997-98; Minister of Transport, 1998-99; Secretary of State for Scotland, 1999-2001; Secretary of State for Northern Ireland, 2001; Party Chair and Minister without Portolio, 2001-02; Leader of the Commons and President of the Council, 2002; Secretary of State for Health, 2003-05; Secretary of State for Defence, 2005-06. Recreations: crosswords; football; reading. Address: (b.) House of Commons, Westminster, London; Parliamentary Advice Office, 115 Graham Street, Airdrie ML6 6DE; T.-01236 748777; Fax: 01236 748666; e-mail: reidj@parliament.uk

Reid, Professor John Low, OBE, MA, DM, FRCP, FRSE. Regius Professor of Medicine, University of Glasgow, since 1989; Consultant Physician, Western Infirmary, Glasgow, since 1989; b. 1.10.43, Glasgow; m., Randa; 1 s.; 1 d. Educ. Kelvinside Academy; Fettes College; Magdalen College, Oxford University. Clinical and research posts, Royal Postgraduate Medical School, London and National Institutes of Health, Bethesda, USA; Regius Chair of Materia Medica, University of Glasgow, 1978-89. Publication: Lecture Notes in Clinical Pharmacology. Editor, Handbook of Hypertension. Recreations: outdoors; gardening; opera. Address: (h.) 5 Princes Terrace, Glasgow G12 9JW; T.-0141-211 2886.

Reid, Professor Kenneth Gilbert Cameron, CBE (2005), MA, LLB, WS, FRSE. Professor of Property Law, Edinburgh University, since 1994; Law Commissioner for Scotland, 1995-2005; b. 25.3.54, Glasgow; m., Elspeth Christie; 2 s.; 1 d. Educ. Loretto; St. John's College, Cambridge; Edinburgh University. Admitted as a Solicitor, 1980; Lecturer in Law, Edinburgh University, 1980. Author of numerous books and papers on the law of property. Recreation: classical music. Address: (b.) School of Law, Old College, South Bridge, Edinburgh EH8 9YL; T.-0131-650 2015.

Reid, Melanie Frances, MA (Hons). Writer and Columnist, The Times, since 2007; Senior Assistant Editor and Columnist, The Herald, 2001-07; b. 13.4.57, Barnet; m., Clifford Martin; 1 s.; divorced; m., David McNeil. Educ. Ormskirk Grammar School; Edinburgh University. The Scotsman: Graduate Trainee, 1980-82, Woman's Editor, 1983-87; Sunday Mail: Woman's Editor, 1987-2000, Associate Editor, 2000; Columnist, The Express, 2000. Member, Carnegie Commission for Rural Community Development, since 2004. Recreations: family; walking; doing bad dressage. Address: (b.) The Times, 124 Portman Street, Glasgow G41 1EJ; T.-0141-420-5296.

Reid, Seona Elizabeth, BA, HonDArt, HonDLitt, FRSA. Director, Glasgow School of Art, since 1999; Honorary Professor; b. 21.1.50, Paisley. Educ. Park School, Glasgow; Strathclyde University; Liverpool University. Business Manager, Theatre Royal, Lincoln, 1972-73; Press Officer, Northern Dance Theatre, Manchester, 1973-76; PRO, Ballet

Rambert, London, 1976-79; freelance arts consultant, 1979-81; Director, Shape, London, 1981-87; Assistant Director, Greater London Arts, 1987-90; Director, Scottish Arts Council, 1990-99. Board Member, Cove Park; Member: Knowledge and Evaluation Committee, Arts and Humanities Research Council, British Council Scottish Committee. Recreations: walking; travel; the arts. Address: (b.) 167 Renfrew Street, Glasgow G3 6RQ, T.-0141-353 4500.

Reid, Professor Stuart William John, BVMS, PhD, DVM, DipECVPH, FRSE, MRCVS. Professor, Comparative Epidemiology and Informatics, University of Glasgow and University of Strathclyde, since 1997; Dean of Faculty of Veterinary Medicine, University of Glasgow, since 2005; Visiting Professor, University of Sydney, since 2002; b. 30.5.64, Carlisle; partner Kathryn M.G. Knox; 2 d. Educ. Austin Friars School, Carlisle; University of Glasgow. Veterinary Surgeon, Insch, Aberdeenshire, 1987-88; University of Glasgow: Research Student, 1988-92, Researcher, 1992-96; Visiting Scholar, Cornell University, USA, 1995-97. Pfizer Academic Award, 1996; Trustee, Donkey Sanctuary, 1997; Trustee, Austin Friars St. Monicas, since 2001. T.-0141 330 5701; e-mail: dean@vet.gla.ac.uk

Reid, William James, CLJ, ACII, FBIBA. Managing Partner, Reid Enterprise; Director of Corporate Business - Scotland Landau Manson Ltd.; Hon. Vice-President, Children 1st; b. 18.9.32, Edinburgh; m., Patricia; 2 s. Educ. George Heriot's School. Director, Collins Halden & Co. Ltd., 1960-68, Joint Managing Director, 1968-72, Chairman and Chief Executive, 1972-78; Director, Halden McQuaker & Co. Ltd., Glasgow, 1964-73; Director, Collins Halden & Burnett Ltd., Aberdeen, 1962-74; Director, Hogg Robinson Ltd., London, 1978-84; Chief Executive, Hogg Robinson (Scotland) Ltd., 1978-84; Chairman and Chief Executive: Collins Halden (Scotland) Ltd., 1984-90, Heath Collins Halden (Scotland) Ltd., 1990-92, C.E. Heath (Scotland) Ltd., 1990-92; Chairman: City Business Venue (Scotland) Ltd., 1992-98, Reid Enterprise Ltd., 1992-99, Nickleby (Scotland) Ltd., 1995-98, Hubert Mitchell, 2000-03; President, Insurance Society of Edinburgh, 1978-79; Chairman, Corporation of Insurance Brokers Scotland, 1969-70; Member, National Council, Corporation of Insurance Brokers, 1968-71; Freeman of the City of London; Commander, Order of St. Lazarus. Address: (h.) 33/10 Murrayfield Road, Edinburgh EH12 6EP; T.-0131-337 1220.

Reid, Sir William Kennedy, KCB, MA, LLD (Aberdeen and Reading), FRCPEd, FRSE; b. 15.2.31, Aberdeen; m., Ann Campbell; 2 s.; 1 d. Educ. Robert Gordon's College; George Watson's College; Edinburgh University; Trinity College, Cambridge. Civil Servant, 1956-89, Department of Education and Science, Cabinet Office, Scottish Office; Member, Council on Tribunals and Its Scottish Committee, 1990-96; Member, Commission for Local Administration in England, 1990-96; Member, Commission for Local Administration in Wales, 1990-96. A Director, International Ombudsman Institute, 1992-96; Parliamentary Commissioner for Administration (Ombudsman), 1990-97; Health Service Commissioner for England, Scotland, Wales, 1990-97; Chairman, Mental Welfare Commission for Scotland, 1997-2000; Chairman, Advisory Committee on Distinction Awards, 1997-2000; Queen Elizabeth the Queen Mother Fellow, Nuffield Trust, 1998; Chairman of Council, St. George's School for Girls, 1997-2003; Hon. D. Litt (Napier), 1998; Hon. FRCSEd, 2002. Recreations: verse; hill-walking. Address: (h.) Darroch House, 9/1 East Suffolk Park, Edinburgh EH16 5PL.

Reilly, Eddie. Scottish Secretary, Public and Commercial Union (PCS), since 1999; STUC General Council, since 1999; b. 31.5.51, Baillieston; m., Susan Tymms; 1 s.; 1 d. Educ. St. Patrick's High School,

Coatbridge; Aberdeen University; Stirling University. Scottish Secretary, SCPS, 1978-85; Deputy General Secretary: SCPS, 1985-88, NUCPS, 1988-96, PTC, 1996-98, PCS, 1999; STUC General Council, 1981-85. Recreation: Glasgow Celtic supporter. Address: (b.) PCS, Glenorchy House, 20 Union Street, Edinburgh EH1 3LR; T.-0131-556-0407; e-mail: eddie.reilly@pcs.org.uk

Reiter, Nicholas Keith, AMRSC, BSc (Hons) (Econ), BSc (Hons) (Chem). Chief Executive, Crofters Commission; formerly Director, Deer Commission for Scotland; m., 10.12.52, London; m., Cindie Katrina Denning; 1 s.; 1 d. Educ. Lycee Francais de Londres; London School of Economics. Department to the Environment, 1976-87; Head of Policy, Westminster City Council, 1987-89; Director, Environmental Services, Ross and Cromarty District Council, 1989-96; Head of Policy, The Highland Council, 1996-98; Chief Executive, Shetland Islands Council, 1998-99. Recreations: hill walking; sea kayak; sailing; cycling; Open University. Address: (b.) Castle Wynd, Inverness IV2 3EQ.

Reith, David Stewart, LLB, NP, WS. Partner and Management Board/Chairman, Lindsays WS, Solicitors, Edinburgh, since 1976; b. 15.4.51, Edinburgh; m., Elizabeth Julia Hawkins; 1 s.; 1 d. Educ. Edinburgh Academy; Fettes College; Aberdeen University. Law Society of Scotland Accredited Charity Law Specialist; Scottish Legal Awards Partner of the Year, 2007. Member, Scottish Charities Finance Directors Group; Director: Lindsays Ltd., Alba Conservation Trust, The Glasite Meeting House Trust, Scottish Historic Buildings Trust, Cockburn Conservation Trust; Secretary: Edinburgh and Lothians Greenspace Trust, Ponton House Trust, Queensberry House Trust, Marisbank House Trust; Clerk, Incorporation of Cordiners; Honorary Solicitor, Architectural Heritage Society of Scotland; Cockburn Association. Recreations: hill walking; wine. Address: (h.) Woodside House, Gladsmuir, East Lothian EH33 2AL.

Reith, Sheriff Fiona Lennox, LLB, QC, WS, FSA Scot. Sheriff of Lothian and Borders at Edinburgh, since 2007; b. 17.7.55, Ipswich. Educ. Perth Academy; Aberdeen University. Solicitor, Edinburgh, 1979-82; admitted to W.S. Society, 1982; devilled, 1982-83; admitted to Faculty of Advocates, 1983; Standing Junior Counsel in Scotland to Home Office, 1989-92; Advocate-Depute, 1992-95; Standing Junior Counsel, Scottish Office Environment Department, 1995-96; QC, 1996; Sheriff of Tayside, Central and Fife, at Perth, 1999-2000; Sheriff of Glasgow and Strathkelvin, 2000-07. Member, Scottish Legal Aid Board Civil Legal Aid Sub-Committee and Supreme Court Reporter, 1989-92; Member, Sheriff Court Rules Council, 1989-93; External Examiner in Professional Conduct, Faculty of Advocates, 2000-06; Member, Council of Sheriffs Association, 2003-06; Member, Criminal Courts' Rules Council, since 2004; Member, Parole Board for Scotland, 2005-07, Vice-Chairman, since 2008; Member, Lord Coulsfield's Civil Justice Advisory Group, 2004-05 (Report in relation to the Civil Justice System in Scotland, published November 2005). Recreations: walking; theatre; good food and wine; travel. Address: (b.) Sheriff's Chambers, Edinburgh Sheriff Court, 25 Chambers Street, Edinburgh EH1 1LB; T.-0131-225 2525.

Rennie, Allan, Editor, Sunday Mail, since 2000; b. 5.7.60, Stirling. Educ. Kilsyth Academy. Springburn Times; Johnstone Gazette; Stirling Observer; The Sun; Evening News, Daily Record. Recreation: golf. Address: One Central Quay, Glasgow G3 8DA; T.-0141-309 3403; e-mail: a.rennie@sundaymail.co.uk

Rennie, Archibald Louden, CB, LLD, FDSRCS(Eng); b. 4.6.24, Guardbridge, Fife; m., Kathleen Harkess; 4 s. Educ.

Madras College, St. Andrews; St. Andrews University. Experimental Officer, Minesweeping Research Division, 1944-47; joined Department of Health for Scotland, 1947; Private Secretary to Secretary of State for Scotland, 1962-63; Assistant Secretary, Scottish Home and Health Department, 1963-69; Registrar General for Scotland, 1969-73; Under Secretary, Scottish Economic Planning Department, 1973-77; Secretary, Scottish Home and Health Department, 1977-84. Vice-Chairman, Advisory Committee on Distinction Awards, 1985-94; Chancellor's Assessor, St. Andrews University, 1985-89; Member, Scottish Records Advisory Council, 1985-93; Member, Council on Tribunals, and its Scottish Committee, 1987-88; Trustee, Lockerbie Air Disaster Appeal, 1988-91; Chairman, Disciplined Services Pay Review Committee, Hong Kong, 1988; Chairman, Blacket Association, 1971-73; Commodore, Elie and Earlsferry S.C., 1992-94; Chairman, Elie Harbour Trust, 1993-99; Chairman, Elie and the Royal Burgh of Earlsferry Community Council, 2001-03. Recreations: Firth-watching; pottering; reading. Address: (h.) The Laigh House, South Street, Elie, Fife KY9 1DN; T.-01333 330741.

Rennie, Colin. Development Manager for Scotland, Fields in Trust (FIT), formerly National Playing Fields Association (NPFA), since 2005; Chairman, Claverhouse Group; b. 1956, Montrose, Angus; m., Alyson; 2 s. Educ. Dundee College; Kingsway Technical College. Career History: Westminster Parliamentary Adviser; Chairman: North of Scotland Water Authority, Dundee Partnership; Convenor, Economic Development, Dundee City Council; Journalist; Architectural Draughtsman. Vice Chairman, The Claverhouse Group; former SET Board Member; former Dundee and Angus Tourist Board Member. Recreations: hill walking; fly fishing; visiting historic buildings; sport. Address: (b.) Dewar House, Staffa Place, Dundee DD2 3SX; T.-01382 817427; e-mail: colin.rennie@npfa.org

Rennie, Professor Robert, LLB, PhD, FRSA. Partner, Harper MacLeod Solicitors, Glasgow, since 2001; Professor of Conveyancing, Glasgow University, since 1993; b. 30.6.47, Glasgow; m., Catherine Mary McGregor; 1 s.; 3 d. Educ. Lenzie Academy; Glasgow University. Apprentice then Legal Assistant, Bishop Milne Boyd & Co., Solicitors, Glasgow; joined Ballantyne & Copland as Legal Assistant, 1971, Partner, 1972-2001; Past Convener, Law Society of Scotland Conveyancing Committee; Board Member, Capability Scotland. Recreation: classical music. Address: (b.) Harper MacLeod, The Ca'd'oro, 45 Gordon Street, Glasgow G1 3PE.

Rennie, Willie. MP (Liberal Democrat), Dunfermline and Fife West, since 2006; Liberal Democrat Spokesperson for Defence; Member, Defence Select Committee; b. 27.9.67; m., Janet; 2 s. Educ. Paisley College. Chief Executive, Scottish Liberal Democrats and the Party's Chief of Staff, Scottish Parliament, 1997-2001; formerly adviser to Fife's Lib Dem Council Group; self-employed consultant, 2001-03; Account Director, McEwan Purvis, 2003-06. Recreations: road running; hill running. Address: (b.) House of Commons, London SW1A 0AA.

Rennilson, John Douglas, MA, MSc, MRTPI, MRICS, MCMI. Director of Planning and Development, The Highland Council, 1998-2008 (formerly Director of Planning); b. 12.2.47, Edinburgh; m., Susan M.; 1 s.; 1 d. Educ. George Watson's College, Edinburgh; Edinburgh University; University of Wales. Lanarkshire County Council, 1970-74, latterly as Senior Planning Officer; Suffolk County Council, 1974-84, latterly as Assistant County Planning Officer (Environment); County Planning Officer, North Yorkshire County Council, 1984-96. Member, Executive, County Planning Officers Society (Chairman, Committee 3, 1989-91, and from 1995); Chairman, Scottish Society of Directors of Planning, 2000-01; Member, Committee on Radioactive Waste Management, since 2007; External Examiner, University of Newcastle, 2000-03. Recreations: golf; Scottish country dancing; branch line railways. Address: (b.) Glenurquhart Road, Inverness IV3 5NX; e-mail: john.rennilson@highland.gov.uk

Renshaw, Professor Eric, BSc, ARCS, DipStats, MPhil, PhD, CStat, FRSE. Professor of Statistics, Strathclyde University, since 1991; b. 25.7.45, Preston; m., Anne Renshaw. Educ. Arnold School, Blackpool; Imperial College, London; Manchester University; Sussex University; Edinburgh University. Lecturer, then Senior Lecturer in Statistics, Edinburgh University, 1969-91. Publication: Modelling Biological Populations in Space and Time. Recreations: skiing; golf; hill-walking; photography. Address: (b.) Department of Statistics and Modelling Science, Livingstone Tower, Strathclyde University, 26 Richmond Street, Glasgow G1 1XH; T.-0141-548 3591.

Renwick, Helen Rachael (Rae), Diploma in Food and Nutrition, Cert Ed, MEd. Head Teacher, Rosshall Academy; b. 5.9.51, Dunfermline; m., Thomas Renwick; 1 s.; 1 d. Educ. Beath High School; Queen Margaret College. Teacher: Balwearie High School, 1972-74; Craigroyston Community High School, 1974-75; Assistant Principal Teacher, Craigroyston Community High School, 1975-79; Principal Teacher, Wester Hailes Education Centre, 1979-80; Principal Teacher, Broughton High School, 1981-90; Assistant Head, Castlebrae High, 1990-95; Depute Head, Broxburn Academy, 1995-2000. Recreations: gardening; golf; travel. Address: (b.) 131 Crookston Road, Glasgow G52 3PD; T.-0141-582 0200.

Renwick, Professor John Peter, MA, PhD, DLitt, FRHistS, Commandeur des Palmes Académiques. John Orr Professor of French, Edinburgh University, 1980-2006; Director, Centre de Recherches Francophones Belges, since 1995; b. 25.5.39, Gillingham; m., Claudette Gorse; 1 s.; 1 d. Educ. Gillingham Grammar School; St. Bartholomew's Grammar School, Newbury; St. Catherine's College, Oxford; Sorbonne; British Institute in Paris (Leverhulme Research Scholar). Assistant Lecturer, then Lecturer, Glasgow University, 1964-66; Fellow, Churchill College, Cambridge, 1966-72; Maitre de Conférences Associé, Départment de Francais, Université de Clermont-Ferrand, 1970-71, 1972-74; Professor of French, New University of Ulster, 1974-80 (Pro-Vice-Chancellor, 1978-80); Member, Editorial Committee, The Complete Works of Voltaire; Member, Executive Committee, Voltaire Foundation; Member, Editorial Committee, Moralia (Paris); General Secretary, Society of the Friends of the Institut Français d'Ecosse; President, Comité Consultatif, Institut Français d'Ecosse; Médaille de la Ville de Bort. Publications: La destinée posthume de Jean-Francois Marmontel, 1972; Marmontel, Mémoires, 1972; Marmontel, Voltaire and the Belisaire affair, 1974; Marmontel, Correspondence, 1974; Catalogue de la bibliotheque de Jean-Baptiste Massillon, 1977; Voltaire et Morangies, ou les Lumieres l'ont échappé belle, 1982; Chamfort devant la posterité, 1986; Catalogue de la Bibliotheque du Comte D'Espinchal, 1988; Language and Rhetoric of the French Revolution, 1990; Voltaire, La Guerre Civile de Genève, 1990; Catalogue de la Bibliotheque du College de L'Oratoire de Riom 1619-1792, 1997; Voltaire, Brutus, 1998; Voltaire, Les Guèbres, 1999; Voltaire, Traité sur la Tolérance, 1999 and 2000; L'Invitation au Voyage (Studies in Honour of Peter France), 2000; Jean-Francois Marmontel (1723-1799): Dix études,

2001; Voltaire, Histoire du parlement de Paris, 2005; Voltaire, Essai sur les Probabilités en fait de Justice; Nouvelles Probabilités, 2006; 60@ifecosse, 2006. Address: (b.) 60 George Square, Edinburgh EH8 9JU.

Reoch, Torquil, MA. Producer, BBC Newsnight Scotland, since 1999; b. 17.6.54, Glasgow; m., Christine; 1 s.; 2 d.; 2 g-s. Educ. George Watson's College, Edinburgh; Edinburgh University; Glasgow University. News Trainee, BBC London, 1979; Reporter, BBC Radio Scotland, 1980; Scotland Correspondent, TV-am, 1983; News Producer, BBC Scotland, 1985; Producer, European Business Channel, Zurich, 1989; Editor, Good Morning Scotland, 1991; News Operations Editor, BBC Scotland, 1997. Recreations: financing higher education; family; dog. Address: (b.) BBC Scotland, Pacific Quay, Glasgow; T.-0141 422 7722.

Rettie, James Philip, CBE, TD. Farmer; Partner, Rettie Farming Co.; Director, Rettie & Co.; b. 7.12.26, Dundee; m., 1, Helen Grant; 2, Diana Harvey; 2 s.; 1 d. Educ. Trinity College, Glenalmond. Royal Engineers, 1945-48. Chairman, Sea Fish Industry Authority, 1981-87; Chairman, William Low & Co. PLC, 1980-85. Hon. Colonel, 117 and 277 FDSQNS RE (V), 1983-89. Recreations: shooting; gardening; walking. Address: (h.) Hill House, Ballindean, Inchture, Perthshire PH14 9QS; T.-01828 686337.

Reynolds, Professor Siân, BA, MA, PhD, Chevalier dans l'ordre des Palmes academiques. Professor (now emerita) of French, Stirling University, since 1990; Translator; b. 28.7.40, Cardiff; m., Peter France; 3 d. Educ. Howell's School, Llandaff; St. Anne's College, Oxford. Lecturer and Senior Lecturer, Sussex University, 1974-89; Lecturer, Edinburgh University, 1989-90; President, UK Association for the Study of Modern and Contemporary France, 1993-99. Publications: Women, State and Revolution (Editor); Britannica's Typesetters; France Between the Wars, gender and politics; Contemporary French Cultural Studies (Joint Editor), 2000; co-editor, The Biographical Dictionary of Scottish Women, 2006; Paris-Edinburgh, 2007 (Author); translations include F. Braudel, The Mediterranean and novels by crime writer, Fred Vargas. Recreation: going to the pictures. Address: (h.) 10 Dryden Place, Edinburgh EH9 1RP.

Riach, Alan, BA (Cambridge), PhD (Glasgow). Professor and Chair, Department of Scottish Literature, University of Glasgow, since 2006, Head of Department, 2001-06; President, Association for Scottish Literary Studies, since 2006; b. 1.8.57, Airdrie; m., Rae; 2 s. Educ. Gravesend School for Boys, Gravesend, Kent; Churchill College, University of Cambridge, 1976-79: BA; Department of Scottish Literature, University of Glasgow, 1979-85: PhD. Freelance writing and teaching, Scotland, 1985-86; Post-Doctoral Research Fellow, Lecturer, Senior Lecturer, Associate Professor of English, University of Waikato, Hamilton, New Zealand, 1986-2000; Pro-Dean, Faculty of Arts and Social Sciences, University of Waikato, Hamilton, New Zealand, 2000. Over 30 appearances on radio and television in New Zealand, Australia and Scotland. Publications: Representing Scotland in Literature, Popular Culture and Iconography, 2005; Hugh MacDiarmid's Epic Poetry, 1991; The Poetry of Hugh MacDiarmid, 1999; Hugh MacDiarmid: The Collected Works (General Editor), since 1992 (15 volumes published to 2003); The Radical Imagination: Lectures and Talks by Wilson Harris (Co-Editor); Scotlands: Poets and the Nation (Co-Editor); contributions to over 20 books and numerous contributions to journals; books of poetry: For What It Is (Co-Author), 1988; This Folding Map (Poems 1978-1988), 1990; An Open Return, 1991; First and Last Songs, 1995; From the

Vision of Hell: An Extract of Dante, 1998, Clearances, 2001; contributor to other books of poetry. Address: (b.) Department of Scottish Literature, University of Glasgow, 7 University Gardens, Glasgow G12 8QH; T.-0141-330 6144; e-mail: A.Riach@scotlit.arts.gla.ac.uk

Rice, Professor C. Duncan, MA, PhD, FR3E, FRHistS, FRSA. Principal and Vice-Chancellor, Aberdeen University, since 1996; b. 20.10.42, Aberdeen; m., Susan Ilene (qv); 2 s.; 1 d. Educ. Aberdeen University; Edinburgh University. Lecturer, Aberdeen University, 1966-69; Assistant Professor of History, then Associate Professor of History, Yale University, New Haven, 1970-79; Professor of History, Hamilton College, Clinton, New York, 1979-85; Professor of History, Dean of Faculty of Arts and Sciences, New York University, 1985-94 (Vice-Chancellor, 1991-96). Board Member: Heritage Lottery Fund Committee for Scotland, UCEA, Rowett Research Institute; Chairman, CASE Europe. Publications: The Rise and Fall of Black Slavery; The Scots Abolitionists 1831-1961; various articles and reviews. Recreations: studio ceramics; contemporary literature. Address: (b.) Aberdeen University, King's College, Aberdeen; T.-01224 272134.

Rice, Susan, CBE, BA, MLitt, DBA (Hon), DHC (Hon), DLitt (Hon), DUniv (Hon), FCIBS, CCMI, FRSA, FRSE. Chief Executive, Lloyds TSB Scotland plc, since 2000; b. 7.3.46, Rhode Island, USA; m., Professor C. Duncan Rice (qv); 2 s.; 1 d. Educ. Wellesley College, Mass., USA; Aberdeen University. Hon. Degrees: Robert Gordon University, Edinburgh University, Heriot-Watt University, Paisley University, Glasgow University. Dean, Yale University, 1973-79; Staff Aide to President, Hamilton College, 1980-81; Dean of Students, Colgate University, 1981-86; Senior Vice President and Division Head, Natwest Bancorp, 1986-96; Head, Branch Banking, then Managing Director, Personal Banking, Bank of Scotland, 1997-2000. Chair: Edinburgh International Book Festival, Committee of Scottish Clearing Banks, Centre for Social Justice Research in Scotland; Senior Independent Director, Scottish and Southern Energy; Director: Charity Bank, Scotland Futures Forum, Scottish Business in the Community; Non-Executive Director, Court of the Bank of England. Recreations: opera; modern art; hillwalking. Address: (b.) Henry Duncan House, 120 George Street, Edinburgh EH2 4TS; T.-0131-260 0401.
E-mail: Susan.Rice@lloydstsb.co.uk

Richards, Professor David, MA (Cantab), MA (Lond), PhD (Cantab). Professor of English Studies, University of Stirling, since 2006, Director, Centre of Commonwealth Studies, since 2006; b. 15.09.53, Oldham; m., Susan; 1 s.; 1 d. Educ. Manchester Grammar School; Churchill College, Cambridge University. Lecturer, University of Birmingham, 1981-83; Senior Lecturer, University of Leeds, 1983-2002; Founding Director, The Ferguson Centre, Open University, 2002-06. Publication: Masks of Difference: Cultural Representations in Literature, Anthropology and Art, 1995. Recreations: art; sailing; travel. Address: (b.) Department of English Studies, University of Stirling, Stirling; T.-01786 467502; e-mail: david.richards@stir.ac.uk

Richards, Professor Randolph Harvey, MA, VetMB, PhD, MRCVS, FRSM, FIBiol, FRAgS. Director, Institute of Aquaculture, University of Stirling, since 1996; Roberts Morris Bray Professor of Aquatic Veterinary Studies, since 1991; Veterinary Adviser, Scottish Salmon Producers' Organisation, since 2006; Veterinary Adviser, Scottish Quality Salmon, 1999-2006 (Veterinary Adviser, Scottish Salmon Growers' Association, 1986-99); b. 4.3.48, London;

m., Jennifer Halley; 1 d. Educ. Grove Park Grammar School, Wrexham; Jesus College, Cambridge University; University of Stirling. University of Stirling: Deputy Director, Unit of Aquatic Pathobiology, 1976-79, Deputy Director, Institute of Aquaculture, 1979-96. Member, Veterinary Products Committee, Medicines Commission, 1992-2000. Publications: numerous papers on fish pathology in learned journals. Recreations: fine wine and food; shooting. Address: University of Stirling, Stirling FK9 4LA; T.-01786 467870; e-mail: r.h.richards@stir.ac.uk

Richardson, Emeritus Professor John Stuart, MA, DPhil, FRSE. Professor of Classics, Edinburgh University, 1987-2002, Emeritus Professor, since 2002; Dean, Faculty of Arts, and Provost, Faculty Group of Arts, Divinity and Music, 1992-97; Hon. Professor, Durham University, since 2003; Vice-President, Society for the Promotion of Roman Studies, since 2001, President, 1998-2001; b. 4.2.46, Ilkley; m., (1) Patricia Helen Robotham (deceased); (2) Joan McArthur Taylor; 2 s. Educ. Berkhamsted School; Trinity College, Oxford. Lecturer in Ancient History, Exeter College, 1969-72, St. Andrews University, 1972-87; Priest, Scottish Episcopal Church, since 1980; Anglican Chaplain, St. Andrews University, 1980-87; Team Priest, St. Columba's, Edinburgh, since 1987; Honorary Canon, St. Mary's Cathedral, Edinburgh, since 2000. Publications: Roman Provincial Administration, 1976; Hispaniae, 1986; The Romans in Spain, 1996; Appian: The Wars of the Romans in Iberia, 2000; papers on ancient history. Recreation: choral singing. Address: (h.) 29 Merchiston Avenue, Edinburgh EH10 4PH; T.-0131-228 3094.

Richardson, Professor Neville Vincent, BA, DPhil, MRSC, FInstP, FRSE. Professor of Physical Chemistry, University of St. Andrews, since 1998; b. 25.2.50, Tadcaster; m., Jennifer Margaret; 2 step-s.; 2 step-d. Educ. Oglethorpe Grammar School, Tadcaster; Jesus College University of Oxford. SRC Research Fellow, Chemistry Department, University of Birmingham, 1974-77; Research Assistant, Fritz-Haber Institute, Max Planck Society, 1974-77; University of Liverpool: Lecturer, Chemistry Department, 1979, Senior Lecturer, 1984, Professor, 1988, Director, Surface Science, IRC. Marlow Medal, Royal Society of Chemistry, 1984; British Vacuum Society Medal, 1996; Surface and Colloid Chemistry Prize, RSC, 2003. Recreations: hillwalking; rock and ice climbing; skiing; squash. Address: School of Chemistry, North Haugh, University of St. Andrews. St. Andrews, Fife KY16 9ST; T.-01334 462395; e-mail: nvr@st-and.ac.uk

Riches, Christopher Gabriel, BSc. Publishing Consultant, since 2006; b. 25.3.52, Oxford; m., Catherine Mary Gaunt; 3 s. Educ. Marlborough College; Manchester University. Copy Editor, Penguin Books, 1973-74; Oxford University Press: Science Education Editor, 1974-76, Publishing Manager, Hong Kong, 1976-81, Reference Editor, 1981-88; Publishing Manager, Collins Reference, Glasgow, 1989-94, Editorial Director, 1994-2006. Council Member, Scottish Publishers' Association, 1995-2003; Hon. Secretary, St. Mary's Episcopal Church, Aberfoyle, 1994-98; Chair, School Board, Killearn Primary School, 1997-99. Recreations: book collecting; gardening; walking. Address: (h.) Achadhu House, Main Street, Killearn G63 9RJ; T.-01360 550544; e-mail: cgriches@aol.com

Richmond, John Kennedy, JP, DL. Chairman, Glasgow Airport Consultative Committee, since 1979; b. 23.4.37, Glasgow; m., Elizabeth Margaret; 1 s.; 1 d. Educ. King's Park Secondary School. Conservative Member, Glasgow Corporation, 1963-75; Member, Glasgow District Council, 1975-84; Deputy Lord Provost, 1977-80; Conservative Group Leader, 1975-77. Recreations: tennis; music; travel.

Address: (h.) 32 Lochhead Avenue, Lochwinnoch, Renfrewshire PA12 4AW; T.-01505 843 193; e-mail: richmond32@tiscali.co.uk

Rickman, David Edwin, BCom (Hons). Director of Rules and Equipment Standards, The R & A, since 1996; b. 9.10.64, St. Andrews; m., Jennifer Mary Cameron; 3 d. Educ. Madras College, St. Andrews; Edinburgh University. Joined R. & A. staff, 1987; appointed Assistant Secretary (Rules), 1990. Recreations: sport, especially golf. Address: (b.) c/o The R & A, St. Andrews, Fife KY16 9JD; T.-01334 460000.

Rickman, Professor Geoffrey Edwin, MA, DPhil (Oxon), FBA, FRSE, FSA. Professor of Roman History, St. Andrews University, 1981-97; Master of the United College of St. Salvator and St. Leonard, 1992-96; Pro Vice Chancellor, 1996-97; b. 9.10.32, Cherat, India; m., Ann Rosemary Wilson; 1 s.; 1 d. Educ. Peter Symonds' School, Winchester; Brasenose College, Oxford. Junior Research Fellow, Queen's College, Oxford; St. Andrews University: Lecturer in Ancient History, Senior Lecturer, Professor; Visiting Fellow, Brasenose College, Oxford; Member, Institute for Advanced Study, Princeton, 1998; Council Member, Society for Promotion of Roman Studies; British School at Rome: Member, Faculty of Archaeology, History and Letters, (Chairman, 1984-87), Chairman, Council, 1997-2002, Hon. Fellow, 2002. Publications: Roman Granaries and Storebuildings, 1971; The Corn Supply of Ancient Rome, 1980. Recreations: opera; swimming. Address: (h.) 56 Hepburn Gardens, St. Andrews, Fife; T.-St. Andrews 472063.

Riddell, Roderick Michael. Secretary, The Black Watch and Director, Museum of The Black Watch (Royal Highland Regiment), since 2005; b. 5.5.54, Edinburgh; m., Jennifer Brown; 1 d.; 2 s. Educ. Loretto School; Royal Military Academy, Sandhurst. Commissioned into The Black Watch, 1973; Mentioned in Dispatches, 1995; Commanding Officer 3rd Battalion, The Black Watch, 1996-99; Retired in the rank of Lt. Col, 2005. Address: (b.) Balhousie Castle, Perth PH1 5HR; T.-0131-310-8530.

Riddell, Stuart Low. Executive Director, Member Services, ICAS (Institute of Chartered Accountants of Scotland), since 2007; b. 11.8.63, Glasgow; m., Alison; 1 s.; 2 d. Educ. Merchiston Castle School, Edinburgh. Director, Fast Forward Positive Lifestyles Ltd. Recreations: golf; tennis; travelling; reading. Address: (h.) 33 Bonaly Wester, Edinburgh EH13 0RQ; T.-0131 441 6090; e-mail: sriddell@icas.org.uk

Riddle, Gordon Stewart, MA. Principal and Chief Ranger, Culzean Country Park, 1976-2005 (Property Manager, Culzean Castle and Country Park, 2001-05, Country Park and Conservation Manager, 2004-05); retired; b. 2.10.47, Kelso; m., Rosemary Robb; 1 s.; 1 d. Educ. Kelso High School; Edinburgh University; Moray House College of Education. Biology and History Teacher, Lasswade High School, 1970-71; National Ranger Training Course, 1971-72; Ranger and Depute Principal, Culzean Country Park, 1972-75; National Park Service (USA) Training Course, 1978; Winston Churchill Travelling Fellowship, USA, 1981. Member, Royal Society for the Protection of Birds, Scottish Committee, 1995-99; Chairman, South Strathclyde Raptor Study Group, since 1994. 2005 George Waterstone Memorial Award for services to the National Trust for Scotland; Member, the Scottish Raptor Monitoring Group representing the Scottish Ornithologists' Club. Publications: The Kestrel; Seasons with the Kestrel. Recreations: sport; gardening; birds of prey; photography; hill-walking; music;

writing. Address: (h.) Roselea, 5 Maybole Road, Kirkmichael, Ayrshire KA19 7PQ; T.-01655 750335.

Riddle, Philip, BA, MA, MSc. Chief Executive, VisitScotland, since 2001; b. 6.5.52, Dunfermline; m., Catherine; 3 s. Educ. Dunfermline High School; Trinity Hall, University of Cambridge; University of Edinburgh. Head, Oil and Gas Trading, Brunei Shell Petroleum, Brunei, 1982-85; Business Development Manager, Africa, Shell International Gas, London, 1985-88; Assistant Area Co-ordinator, South America, Shell International, London, 1988-91; Managing Director, Shell Namibia, Windhoek, 1991-95; Regional Development Director, Shell South Africa, Capetown, 1994-95; Vice President, Shell LPG Europe, Paris, 1995-99; Chairman, Maximedia, Leith. Aftercare Counsellor, Prince's Scotland Youth Business Trust; Consul General for the Netherlands in Namibia, 1992-95. Recreations: skiing; diving; walking; making sense of Scotland. Address: (b.) VisitScotland, Ocean Point One, 94 Ocean Drive, Edinburgh EH6 6JH; T.-0131 472 2201; e-mail: philip.riddle@visitscotland.com

Riddoch, Lesley, BA (Hons). Runs Feisty Ltd. (an independent radio podcast and tv production company); Presenter, Lesley Riddoch Programme, BBC Radio Scotland, 1999-2005; b. 21.2.60, Wolverhampton; m., Chris Smith May. Educ. High School of Glasgow; Wadham College, Oxford; University College, Cardiff. Sabbatical President, Oxford University Students Union, 1980; Reporter, BBC Radio Scotland, 1985-88; Co-Presenter, Head On, 1988-90; Presenter, Speaking Out, 1990-94; The Scotsman: Assistant Editor, 1994-96, Associate Editor, 1996-97; Speaker, The People's Parliament, Channel 4, 1994-98; Presenter, You and Yours, BBC Radio 4, 1996-98; Presenter, Midnight Hour, BBC2, 1996-98; Presenter, Channel 4's Powerhouse, 1997-98; Founder and Director, Harpies and Quines (feminist magazine). Trustee, Isle of Eigg Trust, since 1993; Founder and Director, Worldwoman. Norman McEwen Award, 1992; Cosmopolitan Woman of the Year (Communications), 1992; Plain English Award, 1993; Sony Broadcaster of the Year, Silver Award, 2000, 2001. Recreations: playing pool; walking. Address: (h.) Crannach Ha', Fowlis Wester, Crieff PH7 3NL.

Rifkind, Rt. Hon Sir Malcolm Leslie, KCMG, QC, LLB, MSc. Secretary of State for Foreign and Commonwealth Affairs, 1995-97; Secretary of State for Defence, 1992-95; Secretary of State for Transport, 1990-92; Secretary of State for Scotland, 1986-90; MP (Conservative), Edinburgh Pentlands, 1974-97, Kensington and Chelsea, since 2005; President, Edinburgh University Development Trust, since 2002; director of several companies; b. 21.6.46, Edinburgh; m., Edith Amalia Steinberg; 1 s.; 1 d. Educ. George Watson's College, Edinburgh; Edinburgh University. Assistant Lecturer, University of Rhodesia, 1967-68; called to Scottish Bar, 1970; Opposition Front-Bench Spokesman on Scottish Affairs, 1975-76; Member, Select Committee on European Secondary Legislation, 1975-76; Chairman, Scottish Conservatives' Devolution Committee, 1976; Joint Secretary, Conservative Parliamentary Foreign and Commonwealth Affairs Committee, 1977-79; Member, Select Committee on Overseas Development, 1978-79; Parliamentary Under-Secretary of State, Scottish Office, 1979-82; Parliamentary Under-Secretary of State, Foreign and Commonwealth Office, 1982-83; Minister of State, Foreign and Commonwealth Office, 1983-86; Member, Queen's Bodyguard for Scotland (Royal Company of Archers).

Rigg, David, MA (Hons). Secretary to Court, University of the West of Scotland, since 2008; University Secretary:

University of Paisley, 2002-07, University of the West of Scotland, 2007; b. 15.3.48, Insch; m., Margaret Taylor Mechie; 1 s.; 1 d. Educ. Daniel Stewart's College, Edinburgh; West Calder High School; Dundee University. British Gas, 1971-73; Administrative Assistant, Strathclyde University, 1973-79; Assistant Secretary, Paisley College, 1979-87; Registrar and Depute Secretary, University of Paisley, 1987-2002. Recreations: Argyll; travel, theatre; Hibernian Football Club. Address: (b.) University of the West of Scotland, Paisley Campus, Paisley PA1 2BE.

Rigg, John Alexander, BA, MA, PhD (Cantab). Head of European Structural Funds Division, Scottish Government, since 2006; b. 16.11.54, Leeds; m., Angela Mary English; 1 s.; 1 d. Educ. Roundhay School, Leeds; Trinity College, Cambridge. Research Assistant, Queen Mary College, London University, 1981-82; Senior Economic Analyst, Henley Centre for Forecasting, London, 1982-85; Director, Henley Centre, 1986-92; Economic Adviser, Scottish Office, 1992-95; Senior Economic Adviser, Scottish Office/Scottish Executive 1995-2002; Head of Funding for Learners Division, Scottish Executive, 2002-06. Visiting Professor, Department of Economics, University of Strathclyde, 1999-2002. Recreations: cinema; cricket; family history; rugby league. Address: (b.) Scottish Government, Enterprise, Energy and Tourism Directorate, Meridian Court, 5 Cadogan Street, Glasgow G2 6AT; e-mail: John.Rigg@scotland.gsi.gov.uk

Rimer, Jennifer, BMusHon, LRAM, DipEd, FFCS. Headteacher, St. Mary's Music School, Edinburgh, since 1996; SQA Examiner, Setter and Marker, since 1978; b. 16.10.47, Kirkcaldy; m., David Rimer; 3 d. Educ. Buckhaven High School; Edinburgh University. Music Teacher, Newcastle, 1970-72; Principal Music Teacher, Lothian Region, 1972-77; St. Mary's Music School: Piano Teacher/Academic Music Teacher, 1982-93; Head of Guidance, Careers and Academic Music, 1993-95. Member, HAS; Governor, George Heriot's School; Director, Edinburgh Youth Orchestra. Recreations: family; reading; theatre; art; concerts; youth orchestras; piano; tennis; yoga; walking. Address: (b.) St. Mary's Music School, Coates Hall, 25 Grosvenor Crescent, Edinburgh EH12 5EL; T.-0131-538 7766; e-mail: info@st-marys-music-school.co.uk

Rintoul, Gordon, BSc, MSc, PhD, AMA. Director, National Museums of Scotland, since 2002; b. 29.5.55, Glasgow; m., Stephanie; 1 s. Educ. Allan Glen's School, Glasgow; University of Edinburgh; University of Manchester. Curator, Colour Museum, Bradford, 1984-87; Director, Catalyst, The Museum of the Chemical Industry, Widnes, 1987-98; Chief Executive, Sheffield Galleries and Museums Trust, 1998-2002. Member, Advocacy Committee, National Museum Directors Conference; Honorary Professor, University of Edinburgh. Recreations: running; reading; travelling. Address: (b.) Chambers Street, Edinburgh EH1 1JF; T.-0131-247 4260; e-mail: g.rintoul@nms.ac.uk

Risk, Sir Thomas Neilson, BL, LLD (Glasgow), Dr. h.c. (Edin), FRSE; b. 13.9.22, Glasgow; m., Suzanne Eiloart; 4 s. (1 dec.) Educ. Kelvinside Academy, Glasgow; Glasgow University. Flt. Lt., RAF, 1941-46; RAFVR, 1946-53; Partner, Maclay, Murray & Spens, Solicitors, 1950-81; Bank of Scotland: Director, 1971-77, Deputy Governor, 1977-81, Governor, 1981-91; Chairman, Standard Life Assurance Company, 1969-77; Director, Shell UK Ltd., 1983-92; Director, The Merchants Trust plc, 1973-94; Director, British Linen Bank Limited, 1977-91 (Governor, 1977-86); Director, Bank of Wales, 1986-91; Director, Howden Group, 1971-87; Chairman, Scottish Financial Enterprise, 1986-89; Director, Barclays Bank, 1983-85;

Member, Scottish Economic Planning Council, 1983-91; Member, National Economic Development Council, 1987-91; Member, Scottish Industrial Development Board, 1972-75; Chairman: Edinburgh International Festival Endowment Fund, 1989-97, University of Glasgow Trust, 1992-2004; Hon. President, Citizens Theatre, Glasgow, 1995-2002. Address: (h.) 29/31 Inverleith Place, Edinburgh EH3 5QD; T.-0131-552 0571.

Ritchie, Alastair Newton Bethune; b. 30.4.21, London; m., Isobel Sinclair; 1 s.; 1 d. Educ. Harrow School; Corpus Christi College, Cambridge; Stirling University. Scots Guards, 1940-58; campaign North-West Europe, 1944-45; wounded; mentioned in Despatches; active service, Malaya and Far East, 1947-49; Canadian Army Staff College, 1951; Assistant Military Attache, Canada, 1952-53; active service, Canal Zone, Egypt, 1954; retired as Major, 1958; Argyll and Sutherland Highlanders TA, 1966-68; Partner, Drunkie Farms, Callander, 1967-91; Partner, Sheppards and Chase, Stock and Money Brokers and Member, Stock Exchange, 1960-85; Member, Stirling District Council, 1977-90; Member, Queen's Bodyguard for Scotland (Royal Company of Archers), 1966; Deputy Lieutenant, Stirling and Falkirk, 1979. Recreations: gardening; fishing; music. Address: (h.) The Steading, Castle Grove, Callander, Perthshire FK17 8AZ; T.-01877 330078; e-mail: mail@ritchieanb.fsnet.co.uk

Ritchie, Andrew, BD, DMin. Minister, Craiglockhart Parish Church, Edinburgh, since 1991; Assistant Chaplain, Royal Hospital for Sick Children, 1996-2001; b. 17.4.52, Dunfermline; m., Sheila; 3 s.; 1 d. Educ. Queen Anne School, Dunfermline; Edinburgh University; New College; Columbia Theological Seminary, Georgia. Assistant Minister, Dundee Parish Church, 1983-84; Minister, Clarkston Parish Church, Airdrie, 1984-91; Convener, Parish Assistance Committee, 1988-90; Vice-Convener, Parish Reappraisal Committee, 1990-93; Convener, Field-Staff Committee, 1993-96; Convener, New Charge Development Committee, 1999-2003. Recreations: music; reading; walking. Address: (h.) 202 Colinton Road, Edinburgh EH14 1BP; T.-0131-443 2020.

Ritchie, Anna, OBE, BA, PhD, FSA, FSA Scot. Freelance archaeologist; b. 28.9.43, London; m., Graham Ritchie; 1 s.; 1 d. Educ. Woking Grammar School for Girls; University of Wales; Edinburgh University. Excavations on Neolithic, Pictish and Viking sites in Orkney; public and university lectures; archaeological research and writing; Vice-President, Society of Antiquaries of London, 1988-92; President, Society of Antiquaries of Scotland, 1990-93; Trustee: National Museums of Scotland, 1993-2003, British Museum, 1999-2004. Address: (h.) 11/13 Powderhall Rigg, Edinburgh EH7 4GG; T.-0131 556 1128.

Ritchie, Cameron, LLB. Area Procurator Fiscal, Fife, since 2002; Procurator Fiscal, Stirling and Alloa, 1996-2002; Solicitor Advocate; b. 25.9.52, Paisley; m., Hazel; 2 s. Educ. John Neilson Institution, Paisley; Glasgow University. Apprentice Solicitor, Wright and Crawford, Paisley, 1972-74; Procurator Fiscal Depute, Ayr, 1974-75, Glasgow, 1975-88; Senior Procurator Fiscal Depute, Hamilton, 1988-93; Assistant Procurator Fiscal, Dundee, 1993-96. Recreations: golf; rugby; watching cricket; military history. Address: (b.) Procurator Fiscal's Office, Kirkcaldy; T.-01592 268661.

Ritchie, Professor David Scarth, MA (Cantab), FRSE. Trustee and Director, James Clerk Maxwell Foundation; Trustee, Clerk Maxwell Cancer Research Fund; m., 1 Heather McLennan (deceased); 2 s.; 2 d.; 2, Astrid Ilfra

Chalmers Watson. Educ. Edinburgh Academy; Cambridge University; Royal Naval College, Greenwich. Lt., Royal Navy, 1944-47; Technical Director, Barr & Stroud Ltd., 1969-85; Chairman, Scottish Education Department survey on industrial liasion in Central Institutions, 1985-88. Governor, Paisley University, 1984-95; Visiting Professor in Management of Technological Innovation, Strathclyde University, 1986-94. Address: (h.) Southwood, Newbyth, East Linton EH40 3DU; T.-01620-860-211.

Ritchie, Gordon James Nixon, LLB, NP. Honorary Sheriff of Grampian Highland and Islands at Stonehaven, since 2004; Partner, Connons of Stonehaven, Solicitors, since 1980; Clerk to the Lieutenancy of Kincardineshire, since 1996; b. 2.5.52, Aberdeen; m., Isobel; 2 s.; 2 d. Educ. Mackie Academy; Aberdeen University. Director, Aberdeen Solicitors Property Centre, since 1998. Founder and Secretary, Stonehaven Heritage Society; Editor, Stonehaven of Old, Vols. 1 & 2; Chairman, Stonehaven Town Partnership. Recreations: rallying; motor sport; local history. Address: (h.) Brewlaw, Catterline, Stonehaven, Kincardineshire AB39 2TY; T.-01569 762971; e-mail: gordon.ritchie@connons.co.uk

Ritchie, Ian Cleland, CBE, FREng, FRSE, FBCS, CEng, BSc. Chairman: iomart plc, since 2008, CAS, since 2004, Scapa, since 2006, Caspian Learning, since 2007, Studio Arts School, since 2008; Board Director, Digital Bridges Ltd., 2000-07; Director: Scottish Enterprise, 2000-05, Scottish Funding Council, 2002-07; b. 29.6.50, Edinburgh; m., Barbara Allan Cowie (deceased); 1 s.; 1 d. Educ. West Calder High School; Heriot-Watt University. Development Manager, ICL, 1973-82; Founder and CEO, Office Workstations Ltd., Edinburgh and Seattle, 1984-92; Honorary Professor, Heriot-Watt University, since 1992; Chair: Voxar, 1995-2002, VIS, 1995-2000, Orbital Software PLC, 1995-2001, Active Navigation Ltd., 1997-2003, Interactive University, since 2001, Sonaptic Ltd., 2002-06, Computer Application Services, since 2005, Connect, since 2006, Scapa Ltd., since 2006; Director: Particle Physics and Astronomy Research Council, 1999-2002, Epic Group PLC, 1999-2005, Sonaptic Ltd., 2003-06, Interactive University Ltd, since 2003, Channel Four Television Corp, 2000-05, Dynamic Earth, since 2004; Chair, Scottish Software Federation, 1988-89; President, British Computer Society, 1998-99; Trustee: Bletchley Park, since 2000, SCRAN, 1996-2005, National Museums of Scotland, since 2002; Member, Scottish Funding Council, 2002-07. Recreations: travel; theatre; arts; web browsing. Address: Coppertop, Green Lane, Lasswade, EH18 1HE; T.-0131-663 9486. E-mail: iritchie@coppertop.co.uk

Ritchie, Ian Kristensen, MB, ChB, FRCS(Ed), FRCSEd(Orth). Consultant Orthopaedic Surgeon, Forth Valley Acute Hospitals Trust, since 1992; b. 2.1.53, Annebk, Syria; m., Alyson; 3 d. Educ. Gordon Schools, Huntly; University of Aberdeen. Medical Officer, Royal Navy, 1978-83; surgical and orthopaedic training, Aberdeen Royal Infirmary, 1983-91; Postgraduate Tutor, Stirling Royal Infirmary, 1999-2003. Member, Council, Royal College of Surgeons of Edinburgh, 2000-05, 2006-2010; Lead Clinician, Orthopaedic Dept., Forth Valley, 2007; Director, Surgical Training, Royal College of Surgeons of Edinburgh, 2003. Recreations: hillwalking; reading. Address: (h.) Department of Orthopaedic and Trauma Surgery, Stirling Royal Infirmary, Stirling FK8 2AU; T.-01786 434073; e-mail: ian.ritchie@fvah.scot.nhs.uk

Ritchie, John Douglas, CA, AMIMC. Principal, Barstow and Millar, CA, since 2002; b. 9.10.52, Edinburgh; m., Joan Moira. Educ. George Watson's College. Barstow & Millar,

CA, 1971-85 (Partner, 1978-85); Partner, Pannell Kerr Forster, 1985-98 (Chairman, Edinburgh office, 1993-97). Member, National Board for Nursing, Midwifery and Health Visiting for Scotland, 1988-93, Hon. Consultant, 1993-97; Partner, Whitelaw Wells, 1998-2002; Member, Board, Viewpoint Housing Association, 1991-2000, and since 2002; Trustee, Viewpoint Trust, since 1991; President, Rotary Club of Braids, 1991-92; Member, Morningside Christian Council, 1985-92; Member, Church of Scotland Board of Parish Education, 1994-99; Treasurer, Scottish Churches Open College, 1995-99; Member, Merchant Company of the City of Edinburgh, since 1985, Assistant, Master's Court, 1998-2001; Trustee, Merchant Company Widows' Fund, 1997-2002; Member, Board of Management, Edinburgh's Telford College, 1998-2001; Trustee, Bequest Fund for Ministers in Outlying Districts of the Church of Scotland, since 1994; Director, Association of Independent Accountants in Scotland, 1999-2002 (Chairman, 2001-02); Director, Scottish Love in Action, since 2001; Secretary and Treasurer, Douglas Hay Trust, since 2000; Governor, Melville College Trust, since 2001; Trustee, The Merchant Company Retirement Benefits Scheme, since 2005; Director, Jamaica Education Support, since 2005; Treasurer, Challenger Children's Fund, since 2006; Member, New College Financial Board, since 2007. Address: (b.) Midlothian Innovation Centre, Pentlandfield, Roslin, Midlothian EH25 9RE; T.-0131-440 9030.

Ritchie, Professor Lewis Duthie, OBE, BSc, MSc, MBChB, MD, FRCPEdin, FRCGP, FFPH, FBCS, CEng, CITP, DRCOG, FRSA, MREHIS. James Mackenzie Professor of General Practice, University of Aberdeen, since 1992; Principal General Practitioner, Peterhead Health Centre, since 1984; Honorary Consultant in Public Health Medicine, Grampian Health Board, since 1993; b. 26.6.52, Fraserburgh; m., Heather. Educ. Fraserburgh Academy; University of Aberdeen; University of Edinburgh. General practitioner vocational training, 1979-82, public health medicine vocational training, 1982-87; Lecturer in General Practice, University of Aberdeen, 1984-92; Consultant in Public Health Medicine, Grampian Health Board, 1987-92. Publications: Computers in Primary Care; Community Hospitals in Scotland: Promoting Progress; Developing Primary Care in Scotland; papers on computers, cardiovascular disease, cancer, community hospitals and immunisation. John Perry Prize, British Computer Society, 1991; Ian Stokoe Award, Royal College of General Practitioners, 1992; Blackwell Prize, University of Aberdeen, 1995; Richard Scott Lecture, 2007; Eric Elder Medal, Royal New Zealand College of General Practitioners, 2007. Recreations: church; art; classical music; naval history; walking. Address: (h.) Cramond, 79 Strichen Road, Fraserburgh AB43 9QJ; T.-01346 510191; e-mail: l.d.ritchie@abdn.ac.uk

Ritchie, Murray. Scottish Political Editor, The Herald, 1997-2004; b. 5.9.41, Dumfries; m.; 1 s.; 2 d. Educ. High School of Glasgow. Scottish Farmer, 1958-60; Dumfries and Galloway Standard, 1960-65; Scottish Daily Record, 1965-67; East African Standard, 1967-71; joined Glasgow Herald, 1971. Journalist of the Year, Fraser Press Awards, 1980. Publication: Scotland Reclaimed, 2000.

Ritson, Bruce, MD, FRCPsych, FRCP(Ed), DipPsych. Clinical Director and Consultant Psychiatrist, Royal Edinburgh Hospital; Senior Lecturer in Psychiatry, Edinburgh University; Consultant, Royal Edinburgh Hospital, 1972-2002; b. 20.3.37, Elgin; m., Eileen Carey; 1 s.; 1 d. Educ. Edinburgh Academy; Edinburgh University; Harvard University. Trained in medicine, Edinburgh; postgraduate training in psychiatry, Edinburgh, Harvard and California; Director, Sheffield Region Addiction Unit, 1968-71; World Health Organisation consultant; Chairman,

Scottish Intercollegiate group on alcohol; former Chairman, Howard League in Scotland; Vice President, Medical Council on Alcohol; former Chairman, Substance Misuse Faculty, Royal College of Psychiatrists; Chairman, Advisory Panel on Alcohol and Drugs; DVLA; Parole Board Member. Recreations: friends; squash; theatre. Address: (b.) Royal Edinburgh Hospital, Morningside Park, Edinburgh; T.-0131-667 1735.

Roach, Professor Gary Francis, OStJ, BSc, MSc, PhD, DSc, ScD, CMath. Professor of Mathematics, Strathclyde University, since 1979 (Dean, Faculty of Science, since 1982); b. 8.10.33, Penpedairheol, South Wales; m., Isabella Grace Willins Nicol. Educ. University College, South Wales and Monmouthshire; London University; Manchester University. RAF (Education Branch), Flying Officer, 1955-58; Research Mathematician, British Petroleum Co. Ltd., 1958-61; Lecturer, Manchester University Institute of Science and Technology, 1961-66; Visiting Professor, University of British Columbia, 1966-67; Strathclyde University: Lecturer, 1967-70, Senior Lecturer, 1970-71, Reader, 1971-79. Fellow, Royal Astronomical Society; Fellow, Institute of Mathematics and its Applications; Fellow, Royal Society of Arts; Fellow, Royal Society of Edinburgh; Past President, Edinburgh Mathematical Society; Deacon, Incorporation of Bonnetmakers and Dyers of Glasgow. Recreations: mountaineering; photography; philately; gardening; music. Address: (b.) Department of Mathematics, Strathclyde University, Livingstone Tower, 26 Richmond Street, Glasgow G1 1XH; T.-0141-552 4400, Ext. 3804.

Roads, Elizabeth Ann, MVO, FSA (Scot). Lyon Clerk and Keeper of the Records, since 1986; Carrick Pursuivant of Arms, since 1992; b. 5.7.51; m., Christopher George William Roads; 2 s.; 1 d. Educ. Lansdowne House School, Edinburgh; Cambridge College of Technology; Study Centre for Fine Art, London. Christie's, Art Auctioneers, 1971-74; Court of the Lord Lyon, since 1975; temporarily Linlithgow Pursuivant Extraordinary, 1987. Recreations: history; reading; countryside activities. Address: (b.) Court of the Lord Lyon, HM New Register House, Edinburgh EH1 3YT; T.-0131-556 7255.

Robb, Professor Emeritus Alan, DA, MA, RCA. Artist and Professor of Fine Art, Duncan of Jordanstone College of Art, Dundee (retired, 2007); Head, School of Fine Art, 1983-2003; b. 24.2.46, Glasgow; m., Cynthia J. Neilson; 1 s.; 1 d. Educ. Robert Gordon's College, Aberdeen; Grays School of Art; Royal College of Art. Assistant Art Master, Oundle School, 1972-75; Crawford School of Art, Cork: Lecturer in Painting, 1975-78, Head of Painting, 1978-80, Head of Fine Art, 1980-83. Member, Fine Art Panel, CNAA, 1985-87; Specialist Advisor, CNAA, 1987-89; Director, Wasps, 1984-94; Director, Art in Partnership, 1987-92; Director, British Health Care Arts Centre, 1988-93; Member, SHEFC Research Advisory Group, 1993-98; Advisor to Commonwealth Commission, 1998-2006; Member, Steering Group, National Association for Fine Art Education, 1988-2005; Lead Assessor for Fine Art, SHEFC Quality Assessment, 1995-96; first one-man exhibition, New 57 Gallery, 1973; Arts Council touring two-man exhibition, 1978-79; regularly exhibits in Scotland; solo exhibitions: In the Mind's Eye, 1996, True Knowledge, East West Gallery, London, 1997-99. Publications: Irish Contemporary Art, 1980; In the Mind's Eye, 1996; I Live Now, Academic Gallery, Utrecht, 1999; East-West London; The House of Miracles, 2005; Ayermanana Cuenca, Spain, 2006. Address: (b.) Duncan of Jordanstone College of Art, University of Dundee, Perth Road, Dundee DD1 4HT.

Robb, Andrew (Andy), BSc (Agric). Director/CAO, Rural Payments and Inspections Directorate, Scottish Government, since 2004; b. 23.2.48, New Galloway, Kirkcudbright. Educ. Oban High School; Edinburgh University. Assistant Inspector, DAFS, Ayr, 1970-77;

Inspector, DAFS, Lothian and Borders, 1977-82; Principal Inspector, DAFS, Glasgow, 1982-84; Principal Agricutural Officer, DAFS, Edinburgh, 1984-86; Assistant Chief Agricultural Officer, SOAEFD, 1986-2004. Recreations: golf; bridge; garden and curling. Address: (b.) Pentland House, 47 Robb's Loan, Edinburgh EH14 1TY; T.-0131-244 6029; e-mail: andy.robb@scotland.gsi.gov.uk

Roberton, Esther A., BA. Member, Press Complaints Commission, since 2007; Non-Executive Director, Scottish Council for Development and Industry; b. 24.6.56, Kirkcaldy; m., William J. Roberton; 2 s. Educ. Buckhaven High School; Edinburgh University. Played a leading role in the campaign to secure and shape Scotland's Parliament, 1994-99; Chair, NHS Fife, 2000-04; Chair, Scottish Further Education Funding Council, 1999-2005; Member of Court, University of Dundee. Address: (h.) 15 Pinewood Drive, Dalgety Bay KY11 9SP; e-mail: esther@roberton.uk.com

Roberts, Professor Bernard, BSc, PhD, FRAS, FRSE. Professor of Solar Magnetohydrodynamics, since 1994; b. 19.2.46, Cork; m., Margaret Patricia Cartlidge; 4 s. Educ. Bletchley Secondary Modern and Bletchley Grammar Schools; Hull University; Sheffield University. Lecturer in Applied Mathematics, St. Andrews University, 1971-87, Reader, 1987-94. Chairman, UK Solar Physics Community, 1992-98; Member, Theory Research Assessment Panel, UK Particle Physics and Astronomy Research Council, 1998-2001, Member, Solar System Science Advisory Panel, 2001-03. Recreations: hill-walking; five-a-side football. Address: (b.) Mathematical Institute, St. Andrews University, St. Andrews KY16 9SS; T.-01334 463716.

Roberts, Jacqueline Claire, MA (Hons), MSc, CQSW. Chief Executive, Care Commission, since 2001; B. 8.1.49, Market Harborough; m.; 2 children. Educ. Loughborough High School for Girls; Oxford University. Social Worker, Oxford and Lambeth, 1971-86; Lecturer in Social Work, University of Dundee, 1986-87; Project Head, Polepark Family Counselling Centre, Tayside Regional Council Social Work Department, and Course Director, Child Protection Training, Northern College, 1987-93; management posts, social work, Dundee, 1993-97; Director of Social Work, Dundee City Council, 1997-2001. Publications: Consequences of Child Abuse (Co-Author), 1982; many papers, reports and book chapters, especially on child abuse.

Roberts, James Graeme, MA, PhD, FRSA. Professor Emeritus, Aberdeen University; b. 7.11.42, Glasgow; m., Elizabeth Watson Milo Tucker; 2 s.; 2 d. Educ. Hutchesons' Boys' Grammar School, Glasgow; St. Andrews University; Aberdeen University. Aberdeen University: Assistant Lecturer in English, 1964, Lecturer in English, 1968, Senior Lecturer, 1985, Head, Department of English, 1993, Dean of Arts and Divinity and Vice Principal, 1996-2001, Member, University Court, 1981-89, 1995-2005, Vice Principal (Teaching and Learning), 2001-05. Senior Associate (Higher Education Academy), since 2006; Chair, Aberdeen Performing Arts; Chair, Scottish Museums Council, 2001-07; Elder, Ferryhill Parish Church, Aberdeen. Recreations: walking; swimming; music. Address: (h.) 17 Devanha Gardens, Aberdeen AB11 7UU; T.-01224 582217; e-mail: j.g.roberts@abdn.ac.uk

Roberts, Rev. Maurice Jonathon, BA, BD. Minister: Free Church of Scotland, since 1974, Inverness Greyfriars Free Church of Scotland, 1994-99, Inverness Free Church of Scotland (Continuing), since 2000; Editor, The Banner of Truth, 1988-2003; b. 8.3.38, Timperley; m., Alexandra Macleod; 1 d. Educ. Lymm Grammar School; Durham University; London University; Free Church College, Edinburgh. Schoolteacher. Publications: The Thought of God; Sanctification and Glorification; In Deep Valley of Truth (Korean language); The Christian's High Calling; Great God of Wonders; Can We Know God? Recreations: reading; walking. Address: 3 Abertarff Road, Inverness IV2 3NW; T.-01463 220701.

Roberts, Professor Richard Henry, BA (Lancaster), MA and BD (Cantab), PhD (Edin). Professor Emeritus of Religious Studies, Lancaster University, since 2002; Honorary Professor in Residence, University of Stirling, since 2002; b. 06.03.46, Manchester; m., Audrey; 1 s. Educ. William Hulme's Grammar School, Manchester; Universities of Lancaster, Cambridge, Edinburgh and Tübingen. Lecturer in Theology and Religious Studies, University of Leeds, 1975-76; Lecturer in Systematic Theology, University of Durham, 1976-89; Maurice B. Reckitt Research Fellow, University of Lancaster, 1988-91; Professor of Divinity, University of St. Andrews, 1991-95; Professor of Religious Studies, Lancaster University, 1995-2002. Pastoral and Spiritual Care Committee of the Church of Scotland; Member of the Church of the Holy Rude, Stirling. Publications: Hope and its Hieroglyph: A Critical Decipherment of Ernst Bloch's 'Principal of Hope', 1990; A Theology on Its Way: Essays on Karl Barth, 1992; The Recovery of Rhetoric: Persuasive Discourse and Disciplinarity in the Human Sciences (Co-Author), 1993; Religion and the Transformations of Capitalism: Comparative Responses, 1995; Nature Religion Today: Paganism in the Modern World (Co-Author), 1998; Time and Value (Co-Author), 1998; Religion, Theology and the Human Sciences, 2001/02. Currently researching and writing the book, Religion and Social Theory: A Critical Introduction. Recreations: Astanga yoga; mountain walking; singing and music (violoncello and flute). Address: (b.) School of Languages, Cultures and Religions, Pathfoot Building, University of Stirling, Stirling FK9 4LA; T.-077070 479586; e-mail: r.h.roberts@stir.ac.uk

Robertson of Port Ellen, Rt. Hon. Lord (George Islay MacNeill Robertson), KT, GCMG, HonFRSE, FRSA, MA, PC. Chairman, Cable and Wireless International, since 2006; Deputy Chairman, Cable and Wireless plc, 2004-06; Deputy Chairman, TNK-BP, since 2006; Secretary-General, NATO, 1999-2003; b. 12.4.46, Port Ellen, Islay; m., Sandra Wallace; 2 s.; 1 d. Educ. Dunoon Grammar School; Dundee University. Tayside Study Economics Group, 1968-69; Scottish Organiser, General, Municipal, Boilermakers Union, 1969-78; Chairman, Scottish Labour Party, 1977-78; Member, Scottish Executive, Labour Party, 1973-79, 1993-97; MP, Hamilton, 1978-97, Hamilton South, 1997-99; PPS to Secretary of State for Social Services, 1979; Opposition Spokesman on Scottish Affairs, 1979-80, on Defence, 1980-81, on Foreign and Commonwealth Affairs, 1981-93, on Scottish Affairs, 1993-97; Principal Spokesman on Europe, 1984-93; Member, Shadow Cabinet, 1993-97; Shadow Scottish Secretary, 1993-97; Secretary of State for Defence, 1997-99. Member of Board, Scottish Development Agency, 1976-78; Board of Governors, Scottish Police College, 1975-78; Vice Chairman, British Council, 1985-93; President, Royal Institute of International Affairs, since 2001; Elder Brother, Trinity House, since 2002. Chairman, John Smith Memorial Trust, since 2004; Board, Weir Group plc, since 2004; Adviser, The Cohen Group (USA), since 2004. Hon LLD (Dundee), 2000; Hon DSc (Cranfield), 2000; Hon LLD (Bradford), 2000; Hon LLD (St Andrews); DUniv (Paisley), 2006; Hon Doct (Baku State University, Azerbaijan), 2001; Hon. Regt. Colonel, London Scottish Regiment, 2000; Hon. FRSE, 2003; GCMG (2004); KT (2004). Publication: 'Islay and Jura - Photographs', Birlinn, 2006. Recreations: family; photography; golf. Address: (b.) House of Lords, London SW1A 0PW.

Robertson, Professor Alastair Harry Forbes, BS, MA, PhD, FRSE. Professor of Geology, Edinburgh

University, since 1996; b. 6.12.49, Edinburgh; m., Gillian Mary Robertson; 1 s.; 1 d. Educ. Edinburgh Academy; Edinburgh University; Leicester University. Demonstrator, Cambridge University, 1974-76; Lecturer in Oceanography, Edinburgh University. 1977-85; Academic Visitor, Stanford University. USA, 1985- 86; Reader, Geology, Edinburgh University, 1986 96; Member and Chairman, various national and international committees. Publications: numerous scientific papers. Recreations: outdoor activities; mountain walking; travel; music. Address: (b.) School of Geosciences, Grant Institute of Earth Science, Edinburgh University, West Mains Road, Edinburgh, EH9 3JW; T.- 0131-650 8546.

Robertson, Alistair John, BMedBiol (Hons), MB, ChB, FRCPath, MIAC, FRSA, FFCS. Clinical Group Director of Clinical Support Services, Tayside University Hospitals NHS Trust; Consultant Histopathologist, Tayside Health Board, since 1982; Honorary Senior Lecturer in Pathology, Dundee University, since 1982; b. 29.6.50, Aberdeen; m., Frances Elizabeth Smith. Educ. Aberdeen Grammar School; Aberdeen University. House Physician, Ninewells Hospital, Dundee, 1975; House Surgeon, Aberdeen Royal Infirmary, 1976; Senior House Officer in Pathology, Ninewells Hospital, 1976; Lecturer in Pathology, Ninewells Hospital, 1977; Consultant in Administrative Charge, Perth and Kinross Unit Laboratories, 1982; Clinical Director in Pathology, Dundee Teaching Hospitals NHS Trust, 1993. Recreations: golf; classical music; caravanning; philately; photography; theatre. Address: (b.) Pathology Department, Ninewells Hospital and Medical School, Dundee; T.- Dundee 660111; e-mail: alistair.robertson@nhs.net

Robertson, Andrew Ogilvie, OBE, LLB. Partner, T.C. Young, Solicitors, 1968-2006; Secretary, Erskine Hospital, 1976-2002, Vice Chairman, since 2006; Secretary, Princess Royal Trust for Carers, 1990-2006, Trustee, since 2006; Chairman, Lintel Trust (formerly Scottish Housing Association Charitable Trust), since 1991; Director, Scottish Building Society, since 1994, Chairman, 2003-06; Chairman, Greater Glasgow Primary Care NHS Trust, 1999-2004; Vice Chairman, Greater Glasgow and Clyde NHS Trust, since 2004; Governor, Sedbergh School, since 2000; Director, Special Olympics, National Summer Games Glasgow 2005 Ltd.; b. 30.6.43, Glasgow; m., Sheila Sturton; 2 s. Educ Glasgow Academy; Sedbergh School; Edinburgh University. Director, Merchants House of Glasgow, 1978-2006; Secretary, Clydeside Federation of Community Based Housing Associations, 1978-93; Secretary, The Briggait Company Ltd., 1982-88; Director, Glasgow Chamber of Commerce, 1982-93; Chairman, Post Office Users Council for Scotland, 1988-99; Chairman, Greater Glasgow Community and Mental Health Services NHS Trust, 1994-97; Chairman, Glasgow Royal Infirmary University NHS Trust, 1997-99. Recreations: climbing; swimming; sailing; fishing. Address: (b.) 7 West George Street, Glasgow G2 1BA; T.-0141-221 5562.

Robertson, Angus, MP (SNP), Moray, since 2001; SNP Group Leader in Westminster (Shadow Minister for Foreign Affairs and Defence); b. 28.9.69, London; partner: Carron R.G. Anderson. Educ. Broughton High School; University of Aberdeen. News Editor, Austrian Broadcasting Corporation, 1991-99; Reporter, BBC Austria, 1992-99; Contributor: National Public Radio, USA, Radio Telefis Eireann, Ireland, Deutsche Welle, Germany; Consultant, Communication Skills International, 1994-2001. SNP Spokesman for Foreign Affairs and Defence; Member, European Scrutiny Committee; Vice Chair, All Party Whisky Group; Vice Chair, All Party Offshore Oil and Gas Group; Member, All Party Fisheries Group. Recreations: sport (football, rugby, skiing, playing golf badly); films;

travel; music; books; history; socialising. Address: (b.) 9 Wards Road, Elgin, Moray IV30 1NL; T.-01343 551111; e-mail: robertsona@parliament.uk

Robertson, Rev. Charles, LVO, JP, MA. Locum Minister, St. Cuthbert's Parish Church, Edinburgh; Chaplain to The Queen, since 1991; b. 22.10.40, Glasgow; m., Allson Margaret Malloch; 1 s.; 2 d. Educ. Camphill School, Paisley; Edinburgh University. Assistant Minister, North Morningside Church, Edinburgh, 1964-65; Minister, Kiltearn, Ross and Cromarty, 1965-78. Secretary, Panel on Worship, General Assembly, 1982-95, Convener, since 1995; Church of Scotland Representative on Joint Liturgical Group, since 1984, and Chairman, 1994-2000; UK Representative, English Language Liturgical Consultation, 1996-99; Secretary, Committee to Revise the Church Hymnary, since 1995; Chaplain to Lord High Commissioner, 1990, 1991 and to Her Grace The Princess Royal, 1996; Chaplain to: High Constables and Guard of Honour, since 1993, Clan Donnachaidh Society, 1981-96, Elsie Inglis Memorial Maternity Hospital, 1982-89, New Club, since 1986, Moray House, 1986-98, University of Edinburgh at Moray House, since 1998, No. 2 (City of Edinburgh) Maritime HQ Unit RAAF, since 1987, Royal Scots Club, since 1998; President, Church Service Society, 1988-91 (Hon. President, since 1991); Chairman, Board, Queensberry House Hospital, 1989-96; Chairman, Queensberry House Trust, since 1996; Governor, St. Columba's Hospice, Edinburgh, since 1986; Lecturer in Church Praise, St. Colm's College, 1980-93; Member, Broadcasting Standards Council, 1988-91 and 1992-93; Member, Historic Buildings Council for Scotland, 1990-99; Trustee, Church Hymnary Trust, since 1987; Trustee, Edinburgh Old Town Trust, 1987-91; Trustee, Edinburgh Old Town Charitable Trust, since 1994; Member, Edinburgh World Heritage Trust, 1999-2000; Director, Ludus Baroque, since 2001, Chairman, 2005; Co-author, By Lamplight, 2000; edited Singing the Faith, 1990, and St Margaret Queen of Scotland and Her Chapel, 1994; Secretary of Committees which compiled Hymns for a Day, 1983, Songs of God's People, 1988, Worshipping Together, 1991, Clann ag Urnaigh, 1997, Common Ground, 1998; The Church Hymnary: Fourth Edition, 2005. Address: 5 Lothian Road, Edinburgh EH1 2EP.

Robertson, D. Bruce, OBE, MA. Director of Education, Learning & Leisure, Aberdeenshire Council, since 2007; b. 7.6.51, Ellon; m., Louise Robertson; 2 d. Educ. Inverurie Academy; Aberdeen University. Teacher/Principal Teacher/Depute Rector, Grampian Regional Council, 1974-91; Education Officer/Assistant Director, Education/Depute Director, Education, Grampian Regional Council, 1991-96; Head of Education, Aberdeenshire Council, 1996-98; Director of Education, Culture & Sport, Highland Council, 1998-2007. President, Association of Directors of Education; Chairman, Advisory Committee of Duke of Edinburgh's Award; COSLA Education Advisor. Recreations: golf; hill-walking. Address: (b.) Woodhill House, Westburn Road, Aberdeen AB16 5GB; T.-01224 665420.

Robertson, Donald Buchanan, QC, BL, FSA(Scot). Advocate; Temporary Judge, Court of Session, 1991-2002; b. 29.3.32, Ardnadam, Argyll; m., 1, Louise Charlotte Linthorst Homan, 2, Daphne Jean Black Kincaid; 1 s.; 1 d. Educ. Dunoon Grammar School; Glasgow University. Solicitor, 1954; National Service, 1954-56; Advocate, 1960; Standing Junior to Registrar of Restrictive Practices, 1970-73; Member, Sheriff Court Rules Council, 1972-75; Member, Royal Commission on Legal Services in Scotland, 1976-80; Member, Legal Aid Central Committee, 1982-85; Chairman, VAT Tribunal, 1978-85; Honorary Sheriff, Lothian and Peebles, since 1982; Member, Criminal

Injuries Compensation Board, 1986-2002. Recreations: shooting; Scottish history; genealogy; numismatics. Club: New Club Edinburgh. Address: (h.) 11 Grosvenor Crescent, Edinburgh EH12 5EL; Cranshaws Castle, by Duns, Berwickshire TD11 3SJ.

Robertson, Donald Sinclair MacPherson, BSc, MSc, MBA. Managing Director, Robertson Group, since 2004, Orkney Today, since 2004, Orkney Media Group, since 2007; Director, S & J D Robertson Property Ltd and Stanley Services Ltd, Falkland Islands, since 2004; b. 26.06.67, Kirkwall; m.1: 1 d.; 1 s.; m.2: Michelle; 1 d.; 2 s. Educ. Fettes College; Heriot-Watt University; University of Edinburgh; University of Edinburgh Management School. Director, Robertson Group, 1991-96; Self-Employed, 1996-98; Procter & Gamble, 1999-2002; Honorary Consul, Federal Republic of Germany, since 2007. Recreations: fly fishing; shooting. Address: (h.) Highbury, East Road, Kirkwall, Orkney KW15 1HZ; T.-01856 874782; e-mail: sinclair@sjdrobertson.co.uk

Robertson, Professor Edmund Frederick, BSc, MSc, PhD, FRSE. Professor of Mathematics, St. Andrews University, since 1995; b. 1.6.43, St. Andrews; m., Helena Francesca; 2 s. Educ. Madras College, St. Andrews; St. Andrews University; Warwick University. Lecturer in Pure Mathematics, then Senior Lecturer, St. Andrews University, 1968-95. Vice Chairman, Madras College Endowment Trust, since 1986; Member, Scottish Mathematical Council, 1997-2004; Governor, Morrison's Academy, 1999-2006; Chairman, GAP Council, since 2003; Chairman, British Mathematical Colloquium Scientific Committee, since 2005; Partnership Award, 1992; European Academic Software Award, 1994; American Computational Engineering and Science Award, 1995; Scientific American web site award, 2002; MERLOT award, 2002. Publications: 26 books; 100 papers. Recreations: history of mathematics; computers. Address: (b.) Mathematical Institute, North Haugh, St. Andrews KY16 9SS; T.-01334 463743.

Robertson, Frances, RMN, DipCouns, CertCounsSuper, DHyp, IPDCert. Clinical Nurse Specialist/Community Development, Hollybush House (Combat Stress), since 1998; b. 24.2.50, Clydebank; m., George; 2 d. Educ. Notre Dame High School; Glasgow North College of Nursing; Strathclyde University; Glasgow College of Commerce. Student Nurse, then Staff Nurse, Gartnavel Royal Hospital, 1968-73; Staff Nurse, then Ward Sister, Southern General Hospital, 1974-78; P/T Staff Nurse, then A/U Unit Sister (Night Duty), 1982-94; Manager, Drug Rehab Unit, Aberlour Child Care Trust, 1994-95; Clinical Care Co-ordinator, Alexandra Nursing Home, 1995-96; Senior Sister/Supervisor, Heatherbank Nursing Home, 1996-98. Counsellor, Counselling Supervisor and Trainer, Cruse Bereavement Care, 1988-95; Winston Churchill Fellow, 2002; Member, Mensa, 1990. Recreation: walking. Address: (b.) Hollybush House, Hollybush by Ayr KA6 7EA; T.-01292 561331.
E-mail: cshb01@combatstress.org.uk

Robertson, Iain Alasdair, CBE, LLB. Chairman, Scottish Legal Aid Board, since 2006; Chairman, Coal Liabilities Strategy Board, since 2006; Member, Accounts Commission, since 2003; Independent Member, DTI Legal Services Group Board, since 2004; b. 30.10.49, Perth; m., Judith Helen Stevenson; 2 s.; 1 d. Educ. Perth Academy; Aberdeen University. Qualified as a Solicitor, 1973; service at home and abroad with British Petroleum, 1975-90, latterly as BP America's Director of Acquisitions; Chief Executive, Highlands and Islands Enterprise, 1990-2000. Board Member, Scottish Tourist Board, 1993-95; Board Member, Locate in Scotland Supervisory Board, 1992-

2000; Board Member, Cairngorm Partnership, 1998-2000; Director, Quality Scotland, 1999-2000; Director, Development and Strategy, AWG plc, 2000-03. Recreations: skiing; sailing; music.

Robertson, James Downie, DA, RSA, RSW, RGI. Painter; b. 2.11.31, Cowdenbeath; m., Ursula Orr Crawford (2nd marriage); 2 step-s.; 1 step-d. Educ. Hillhead High School; Glasgow School of Art. Teacher, Keith Grammar School, Banffshire, 1957-58; Lecturer (part-time), Glasgow School of Art, 1959; elected RSW, 1962; Lecturer in Drawing and Painting, Glasgow School of Art, 1967; elected Associate, Royal Scottish Academy, 1974; Senior Lecturer, Drawing and Painting, Glasgow School of Art, 1975-96; Resident Painter, Glasgow School of Art, 1996-98; elected, RGI, 1980; elected, RSA, 1989; Visiting Lecturer: Michaelis School of Fine Art, Cape Town University, South Africa, 1970, Grays School of Art, Aberdeen, 1986, Duncan of Jordanstone College of Art, Dundee, 1986, Newcastle-upon-Tyne Polytechnic, 1986, Millersville University, Pennsylvania, USA, 1987. Cargill Award, RGI, 1971; May Marshall Brown Award, RSW, 1976; Sir William Gillies Award, RSW, 1981; Cargill Award, RGI, 1982; Shell Expro Award, 1985; Graham Munro Award, RSW, 1987; Scottish Amicable Award, RGI, 1989; Scottish Post Office Award, RSA, 1993. Many solo and group exhibitions, UK and abroad (most recently: Roger Billcliffe Gallery, Glasgow, solo exhibiton, 2000, New Academy Gallery, London, joint exhibition, 2001, Jorgensen Fine Art Gallery, solo exhibition, 2002); work in many public, corporate and private collections; retrospective show, Glasgow School of Art, 2000; one man show: Jorgensen Fine Art, Dublin, 2005, Roger Billcliffe Gallery, Glasgow, 2006. DLitt (Glasgow), 2001. Recreations: drawing; painting; reading. Address: (h.) Carruthmuir, by Kilbarchan, Renfrewshire PA10 2QA; T.-01505 613592.

Robertson, James Ian Summers, FRSE, MD, FRCPLond, FRCPGlas, BSc, MB, BS, FAHA, CBiol, FIBiol, MD (Hons. Causa) Free Univ. of Brussels, BA (Rose Bruford College). Board Member, Scottish Opera, since 1999; b. 5.3.28, Welbeck; m., Maureen Patricia; 1 s.; 2 d. Educ. Queen Elizabeth's Grammar School, Mansfield; St Mary's Hospital Medical School, London University. Senior Lecturer and Hon. Consultant Physician, St Mary's Hospital, London, 1964-67; Member of staff, MRC, and Hon. Consultant Physician, Western Infirmary, Glasgow, 1967-87; Senior Consultant, Cardiovascular Medicine, Janssen Research Foundation, Belgium, 1987-94; Visiting Professor of Medicine, Prince of Wales Hospital, Hong Kong, 1988-93; Past President, International Society of Hypertension; former Chairman, Scientific Council on Hypertension, International Society and Federation of Cardiology; Foundation President, British Hypertension Society; former Adviser, Cardiovascular Diseases, World Health Organisation; Cheadle Gold Medal, 1954; Jodh Gold Medal, 1979; Hall Lecturer, Cardiac Society, Australia and New Zealand, 1976; Corcoran Lecturer, American Heart Association, 1978; MSD International Award, 1980; Robert Tigerstedt Award, 1980; William Harvey Lecturer, 1983; Scott Heron Lecturer, Queen's University of Belfast, 1984; Franz Gross Memorial Lecturer, International Society of Hypertension, 1984; Honorary Fellowships: Cardiac Society of Australia and New Zealand; Portuguese Cardiac Society; Mexican Hypertension Society; Southern African Hypertension Society; Polish Cardiac Society; Venezuelan Society of Pharmacology; Taiwan Society of Internal Medicine; Distinguished Member Award, International Society of Hypertension, 2006; Chilean Society of Cardiology. Publications: articles on cardiology, hypertension, endocrinology, music criticism; books on hypertension and endocrinology. Recreations: literature; opera;

cricket. Address: (h.) Elmbank, Manse Road, Bowling, Glasgow G60 5AA; T.-01389 873121.

Robertson, James Roy, MBE, BSc, MBChB, FRCGP, FRCP. Principal, General Practice, Muirhouse Medical Group, since 1980; Reader, School of Clinical Sciences, University of Edinburgh; Apothecary to the Royal Household at Holyrood House Palace; b. 15.3.51, Edinburgh; m., Elizabeth; 3 s. Educ. Merchiston Castle School, Edinburgh; University of Edinburgh. Member, various national governmental committees and working parties on drug abuse issues, HIV and AIDS and alcohol problems; author of papers on these subjects. Publication: Management of Drug Users in the Community (Editor), 1998. Recreations: outdoor activities; travel; family. Address: Department of Community Health Sciences, West Richmond Street, Edinburgh. E-mail: roy.robertson@ed.ac.uk

Robertson, John. MP (Labour), Glasgow North West, since 2005, Glasgow Anniesland, 2000-05; PPS to Kim Howells as Minister of State, Foreign and Commonwealth Office; b. 17.4.52, Glasgow; m.; 3 c. Educ. Stow College, Glasgow. Before entering Parliament, worked for 31 years with BT as telephone engineer and local customer manager. Chair: APPG on Nigeria, APPG Music, Communications APPG, APPG Nuclear Energy; Secretary, Smoking and Health APPG; Secretary, Scottish PLP. Address: (b.) House of Commons, London, SW1A 0AA.

Robertson, John Davie Manson, CBE, DL, BL, FRSE, FRSA. Chairman, Robertson Group of Companies, since 1979; Director, Stanley Services Ltd., Falkland Islands, since 1987; Founder Chairman, Orkney Today, since 2003; Chairman, Orkney Media Group, since 2007; Chairman, Kirkway Ba' Committee, since 1977; Member, National Health Service Tribunal, since 1990; b. 6.11.29, Golspie; m., Elizabeth Amelia Macpherson; 2 s.; 2 d. Educ. Kirkwall Grammar School; Edinburgh University. Anglo-Iranian Oil Co. and BP, UK and Middle East, 1953-58. Honorary Sheriff, Grampian, Highland and Islands, since 1977; Honorary Vice Consul for Denmark, 1972-2004; Honorary Consul, Federal Republic of Germany, 1976-2007; Chairman: Children's Panel for Orkney, 1971-76, Highlands and Islands Savings Committee, 1975-78, Children's Panel, Orkney Advisory Committee, 1977-82, Orkney Health Board, 1983-91 (Vice Chairman, 1979-83), Scottish Health Management Efficiency Group (SCOTMEG), 1985-95, Highland Health Board, 1991-97, North of Scotland Water Authority, 1995-98, Scottish Health Boards Chairmen's Group, 1996-97 (Vice Chairman, 1995), Lloyds TSB Foundation for Scotland, 1997-99 (Trustee, 1989-99); Member: Board of Management, Orkney Hospitals, 1970-74, Highlands and Islands Development Consultative Council, 1989-91, Board Highlands and Islands Enterprise, 1990-95. OBE, 1978; CBE, 1993; DL, Sutherland, 1999, FRSE, 2000; FRSA, 1993; Hon FCIWEM, 1996; Royal Order of Knight of Dannebrog, 1982; Officer's Cross of the Order of Merit, 1986. Publications: Uppies and Doonies, 1967; An Orkney Anthology, 1991; The Kirkwall Ba', 2004; Spinningdale and its Mill, 1791-2000; The Island of Fara, 1739-2007. Recreations: fly fishing; shooting; history. Address: (h.) Spinningdale House, Spinningdale, Sutherland IV24 3AD; T.-01862 881 240.

Robertson, John Graeme, CIBiol, MIBiol, MCMI, FLS, FRSA. Director, Habitat Scotland, since 1980; Director, Global Islands Network, since 2002; b. 15.8.54, Edinburgh; m., Anne Christie; 1 s.; 1 d. Educ. Scotus Academy, Edinburgh. Co-ordinator, Environmental Resource Centre;

Co-ordinator, Friends of the Earth Scotland; Editor, Islander Magazine; Chief Executive, Island Web Consortium; Director, International Centre for Island Studies. Churchill Fellow, 1996; English Speaking Union William Thyne Scholar, 1999. Recreations: exercising his dogs; travel to islands worldwide. Address: 'Loch Imrich', Main Street, Newtonmore, Inverness-shire PH20 1DP; T.-01540 673 939; e-mail: graeme@globalislands.net

Robertson, John Shaw, MA, FFCS. Rector, Dollar Academy, since 1994; b. 7.4.50, Glasgow; m., Mary; 1 s.; 1 d. Educ. Jordanhill College School; Glasgow University. English Master, Housemaster, Assistant Headmaster, Stewart's Melville, Edinburgh, 1973-87; Deputy Rector, Dollar Academy, 1987-94; HMC Academic Policy Sub-Committee, 1997-2002; Member, HMC Membership Committee, since 2003, Chairman Membership, since 2007; Council Member, SCCC; Governor, Ardvreck School, 1998-2003; Chairman, Scottish Division, HMC, 2000. Publication: Stewart's Melville: the first Ten Years (Co-author). Recreations: cricket (Scottish); music (English); literature (international). Address: Dollar Academy, Dollar FK14 7DU; T.-01259 742511.

Robertson, Judith. Head of Oxfam in Scotland, since 2005. Address: (b.) 207 Bath Street, Glasgow G2 4HZ; T.-0845 900 5678.

Robertson, Sir Lewis, CBE, FRSE. Chairman, Carnegie Trust for the Universities of Scotland, 1990-2003; b. 28.11.22, Dundee; m., Elspeth Badenoch (deceased); 2 s.; 1 s. (deceased); 1 d. Educ. Trinity College, Glenalmond. Apprentice Chartered Accountant, 1939-42; RAF Intelligence (Bletchley), 1942-46; entered family textile business, 1946; appointed Managing Director, Robertson Industrial Textiles, 1954; first Managing Director, Scott & Robertson, 1965 (Chairman, 1968); resigned, 1970; Chief Executive, Grampian Holdings, Glasgow, 1971-76 (also Deputy Chairman, 1972-76); Non-Executive Director, Scottish & Newcastle Breweries, 1975-87; Chairman: Triplex Lloyd plc, 1982-90, Girobank Scotland, 1984-90, Borthwicks plc, 1985-89, Lilley plc, 1986-93, Havelock Europa plc, 1989-92, Stakis plc, 1991-95, Posteru Executive Group, 1991-96; Director, Whitman International, Geneva, 1987-90; Chairman, Scottish Board (and UK Council Member), British Institute of Management, 1981-83; Chairman, Eastern Regional Hospitals Board, 1960-70; Member, Committee of Enquiry into the Relationship of the Pharmaceutical Industry with the NHS, 1965-67; Member, Monopolies (later Monopolies and Mergers) Commission, 1969-76; Deputy Chairman and first Chief Executive, Scottish Development Agency, 1976-81; Member, Scottish Economic Council, 1977-83; Member, Restrictive Practices Court, 1983-97; Member, Scottish Post Office Board, 1984-90; Member, Court, Dundee University, 1967-70 (first Finance Chairman); Council Member, Scottish Business School, 1978-83; Chairman, Scottish Arts Council, and Member, Arts Council of GB, 1970-71; Chairman, Scottish Advisory Committee, British Council, 1978-87; Council Member, Scottish History Society, 1984-89; first Chairman, Policy Committee, Scottish Episcopal Church, 1974-76; Trustee, Foundation for the Study of Christianity and Society, 1983-89; Member, Advisory Board, Edinburgh Edition of the Waverley Novels, since 1986; Director, Friends of Royal Scottish Academy, 1986-95; Member, Board, British Executive Service Overseas (Chairman, Scotland), 1995-98; Royal Society of Edinburgh: Fellow, since 1978, Member, Council, 1992-2000, Treasurer, 1994-99, Bicentenary Medal; Chairman, Scottish Division, Imperial Society of Knights Bachelor, 1995-99; Director and Trustee, Advanced Management Programme Scotland, 1996-2003; Trustee and Vice-Patron, Scottish Council for Research in

Education, 1997-2002; Trustee, Scottish Cancer Foundation, 1999-2006; Trustee, Foundation for Skin Research, 1999-2004. Hon. LLD, Dundee University, 1971; Hon. Doctorate of Business Administration, Napier University, 1992; Hon. DUniv, Stirling, 1993; Hon. LLD, Aberdeen, 1999; Hon. DUniv, Glasgow, 2003; Hon. FRCSEdin, 1999; Lifetime Achievement Award, Society of Turnaround Practitioners, 2004. Recreations: foreign travel; computer use; music; list-making. Address: 29/5 Inverleith Place, Edinburgh EH3 5QD; T.-078 36281919.

Robertson, Professor Pamela, BA (Hons), FRSA, FRSE. Senior Curator, Hunterian Art Gallery, and Professor of Mackintosh Studies, Glasgow University. Educ. St George's School for Girls, Edinburgh; University College, London. Member, Historic Buildings Council for Scotland, 1998-2002; Chair, C.R. Mackintosh Society, 2003-06; Member, Reviewing Committee for the Export of Works of Art, since 2003; Governor, Glasgow School of Art, since 2006; winner, Iris Foundation Award for outstanding contributions to the decorative arts, Bard University, New York, 1997. Publications include: C.R. Mackintosh: the architectural papers, 1990; C.R. Mackintosh: Art is the Flower, 1994; The Chronycle, 2001; Doves and Dreams: The Art of Frances Macdonald and J. Herbert McNair, 2006. Recreations: good food and wine; good company. Address: (b.) Hunterian Art Gallery, Glasgow University, Glasgow G12 8QQ; T.-0141-330 5431. E-mail: p.robertson@museum.gla.ac.uk

Robertson, Professor Peter Kenneth John, BSc (Hons), DPhil, CSci, CChem, FRSC, CEng, FEI, FICI. Vice-Principal and Pro Vice-Chancellor (Research and Commercialisation), Robert Gordon University, since 2006; b. 5.6.64, Belfast; m., Dr Jeanette Robertson; 2 s. Educ. Royal Belfast Academical Institution; University of Ulster. Research Officer, Faraday Centre, Carlow, Ireland, 1989-90; Lecturer, Carlow Regional College, Ireland, 1990-91; Higher Scientific Officer, Industrial Research and Technology Unit, 1991-95; Lecturer, School of Applied Sciences, Robert Gordon University, 1995-2000, Professor of Energy and Environmental Engineering, 2000-06. Chairman, Committee, Scottish Branch Royal Society of Chemistry's Analytical Division; Chairman, North of Scotland Branch, British Association. Recreations: hill-walking; photography; golf (very badly). Address: (b.) Robert Gordon University, The Scott Sutherland Building, Garthdee Road, Aberdeen AB10 7QB; T.-01224 263750.

Robertson, Raymond Scott, MA. Director of Public Affairs, Halogen Communications, since 2002; Chairman, Scottish Conservative and Unionist Party, 1997-2001; b. 11.12.59, Hamilton. Educ. Garrion Academy, Wishaw; University of Glasgow; Jordanhill College of Education. Teacher of History and Modern Studies; MP, Aberdeen South, 1992-97; PPS, Northern Ireland Office, 1993-95; Minister for Education, Housing, Fisheries and Sport, Scottish Office, 1995-97. Recreations: watching football; playing squash; reading.

Robertson, Brigadier Sidney Park, MBE, TD, JP, DL, BCom. Director, S. & J.D. Robertson Group Ltd. (Chairman, 1965-79); Honorary Sheriff, Grampian, Highlands and Islands, since 1969; Vice Lord Lieutenant of Orkney, 1987-90; b. 12.3.14, Kirkwall; m., Elsa Miller Croy (deceased); 1 s.; 1 d. Educ. Kirkwall Grammar School; MIBS; Edinburgh University. Commissioned, Royal Artillery, 1940 (Despatches, NW Europe, 1945); managerial posts, Anglo-Iranian Oil Co., Middle East, 1946-51; Manager Operations/Sales, Southern Division,

Shell-Mex and BP, 1951-54; founder, Robertson firm, 1954; Major Commanding 861 (Independent) Light Anti-Aircraft Battery RA (Orkney and Zetland), TA, 1956-61; Lt. Col. Commanding Lovat Scouts, 1962-65; Brigadier, CRA 51st Highland Division, 1966-67; Vice Chairman, Orkney Islands Shipping Company, 1975-79; Chairman, Orkney Hospitals Board of Management/Orkney Health Board, 1965-79; DL, 1968; Honorary Vice-President, Royal British Legion Scotland, Highlands and Islands Area, since 1975; President, Royal British Legion Scotland, Kirkwall Branch, 1957-97; Chairman, RNLI, Kirkwall Station Committee, 1972-97 (President, since 1997); Honorary Colonel, 102 (Ulster and Scottish) Light Air Defence Regiment, Royal Artillery, 1975-80; Hon. Colonel Commandant, Royal Regiment of Artillery, 1977-80; Vice President, National Artillery Association, since 1977; Chairman, Royal Artillery Council of Scotland, 1980-84; Patron, North Ronaldsay Heritage Trust; Honorary President, Orkney Bn., Boys' Brigade; Vice-President, RNLI, since 1985; President, Villars Curling Club, 1978-80, 1986-88; Honorary President: Friends of St. Magnus Cathedral, since 1994, Orkney Family History Society, 1996-2005; Freedom of Orkney, 1990; Honorary Fellowship, Edinburgh University, since 1996; Hon DLitt, Napier University, 2002; Honorary President, Orkney Norway Friendship Association, 1999-2005; Honorary Life Vice President, Longhope Lifeboat Museum Trust, since 2002. Recreations: travel; hill-walking; angling. Address: (h.) Daisybank, Kirkwall, Orkney; T.-01856 87 2085.

Robertson, Sue, BA, MSocSci. Director, One Parent Families Scotland, since 1988; b. 12.7.50, Carlisle; divorced; 1 s.; 2 d. Educ. Penrith Queen Elizabeth Grammar School; Oxford University; Birmingham University. Senior Economic Assistant, Scottish Economic Planning Department, 1973-78; Co-ordinator, Scottish Women's Aid, 1978-83; Training Officer, Scottish Council for Single Parents, 1983-88. Recreations: hill-walking; cycling; reading. Address: (b.) 13 Gayfield Square, Edinburgh EH1 3NX; T.-0131-556 3899.

Robertson, William Nelson, CBE, MA, FCII. Member, Advisory Board, Scottish Amicable, 1997-2003; b. 14.12.33, Berwick upon Tweed; m., Sheila Catherine; 2 d. Educ. Berwick Grammar School; Edinburgh University. Joined General Accident, 1958: Deputy Chief General Manager, 1989-90, Group Chief Executive, 1990-95, Director, 1984-95. Board Member, Association of British Insurers, 1991-95; Director: Morrison Construction, 1995-2001, Scottish Community Foundation, 1996-99, Edinburgh New Tiger Investment Trust, 1996-2001, Alliance Trust, 1996-2002, Second Alliance Trust, 1996-2002. Member, Court, University of Abertay, Dundee, 1996-99. Recreations: hill-walking; gardening.

Robins, John F. Secretary and Campaigns Consultant, Animal Concern, since 1988; Managing Director, Ethical Promotions Ltd., since 1988; Secretary, Save Our Seals Fund, since 1996; Secretary, Animal Concern Advice Line, since 2001; b. 2.1.57, Glasgow; m., Mary E.; 1 s.; 1 d. Educ. St. Ninian's High School. Co-ordinator, Glasgow Energy Group, 1978-80; Company Secretary, Scottish Anti-Vivisection Society, since 1981; Green Party activist and candidate, 1978-81; Delegate, Anti-Nuclear Campaign, 1978-81; Vice-Chair, Friends of the Earth (Scotland) Ltd., 1981-82; Co-ordinator, Scottish Animal Rights Network, 1983-91; Co-ordinator, Save Scotland's Seals Funds, 1988-96. Recreation: catching up on lost sleep. Address: (b.) P.O. Box 5178, Dumbarton G82 5YJ; T.-01389 841639; e-mail: animals@jfrobins.force9.co.uk

Robinson, Christine Mary, MA, PhD, JP. Director, Scottish Language Dictionaries, since 2005; Director of Outreach and Administration, Scottish Language Dictionaries, 2004-05; Honorary Fellow, School of Philosophy, Psychology and Language Sciences, Edinburgh

University, since 2005; b. 26.4.47, Alyth, Perthshire; m., David Robinson; 2 d. Educ. Perth Academy; University of Edinburgh. Former Teacher of horse-riding, chemistry, biology and advanced writing skills; Part-time Tutor/Lecturer, Edinburgh University, since 1982; Lexicographic Bibliographer, Dictionary of The Older Scottish Tongue, 2000-02; Visiting Lecturer, UHI, since 2002; Outreach Officer, Scottish Language Dictionaries, 2003-04. Publications: co-author, Scotspeak, 2001; Get Set for English Language, 2002. Recreation: humanist celebrant. Address: (b.) Scottish Language Dictionaries, 27 George Square, Edinburgh EH8 9LD; T.-0131 650 4149; e-mail: mail@scotsdictionaries.org.uk

Robinson, Professor Olivia F., MA, PhD, FRSE, FRHistS. Professor Emeritus, University of Glasgow, since 2004; b. 22.11.38, Dublin, Ireland. Educ. Newton Manor, Swanage, Dorset; Lady Margaret Hall, Oxford University; Westfield, London University. Successively Lecturer, Senior Lecturer, Reader and Professor in Roman Law in The Law School of Glasgow University; Rice Visiting Professor in the University of Kansas, 1995. Publications: The Criminal Law of Ancient Rome, 1995; Ancient Rome: City Planning and Administration, 1992; Penal Practice and Penal Policy in Ancient Rome, 2007. Recreations: fishing; skiing; wine. Address: (b.) School of Law, University of Glasgow, Glasgow G12 8QQ; T.-(h.) 0141 339 4115; e-mail: ofr@law.gla.ac.uk

Robison, Shona. MSP (SNP), Dundee East, since 2003; MSP (SNP), North East Scotland, 1999-2003; Minister for Public Health, since 2007; formerly Shadow Minister for Health; b. 26.5.66, Redcar; m., Stewart Hosie; 1 d. Educ. Alva Academy; Glasgow University; Jordanhill College. Admin Officer, 1989-90; Community Worker, 1990-93; Home Care Organiser, 1993-97. Recreation: hill-walking. Address: (b.) 8 Old Glamis Road, Dundee DD3 8HP; T.-01382 623200.

Robson, Euan Macfarlane, BA, MSc, MICA. Chief Executive, Scottish Sustainable Energy Foundation, since 2007; former Scottish Manager, Gas Consumers' Council; b. 17.2.54, Northumberland; m., Valerie; 2 d. Educ. Trinity College, Glenalmond; Newcastle-upon-Tyne University; Strathclyde University. Teacher, 1976-79; Deputy Secretary, Gas Consumers' Northern Council, 1981-86. Member, Northumberland County Council, 1981-89; Honorary Alderman, Northumberland CC, since 1989; Liberal/SDP Alliance candidate, Hexham, 1983, 1987; Liberal Democrat Scottish Parliamentary spokesman on: Rural Affairs, 1998-99, Justice and Home Affairs, 1999-2001; MSP for Roxburgh and Berwickshire, 1999-2007; Deputy Minister for Parliamentary Business, 2001-03; Deputy Minister for Education and Young People, 2003-05; Convener, Scottish Liberal Democrat Parliamentary Party, 2005-07. River Tweed Commissioner, 1995-2001; author.

Robson, Godfrey, CB (2002), MA. Director, Lloyds TSB Scotland, since 2001; Chairman, Frontline Consultants, since 2003 (Director, since 2003); b. 5.11.46; m. (marr. diss.); 1 s. Educ. St. Joseph's College, Dumfries; Edinburgh University. Scottish Office: Civil Servant, 1970-2000, Under Secretary, Economic and Industrial Affairs, 1993-2000, Director of Health Policy, 2000-02; Founding Chairman, National Jubilee Hospital, Clydebank, 2002-03; Director and Trustee, Caledonia Youth, since 2003; Senior Policy Advisor, ICAP, Washington DC, since 2004. Recreations: walking; travel by other means; reading history. Address: 50 East Trinity Road, Edinburgh EH5 3EN; T.-0131 552 9519; Chemin sons Baye, 84110 Vaison la Romaine, France; T.-04 90 37 18 32.

Rochford, Professor Gerard, BA, BSc. Psychotherapist; published poet, editor; b. 17.12.32, Dorking; m., Anne Prime (dec.); 3 s.; 7 d. Educ. Worcester Royal Grammar School; Hull University; Oxford University. Medical Research Council, 1960-63; Lecturer in Psychology: Aberdeen University, 1963-67, Hong Kong University, 1967-70; Lecturer/Senior Lecturer, 1970-78, Professor of Social Work Studies, 1978-88, Aberdeen University. Member, Scottish Association of Psychoanalytical Psychotherapists. Recreations: family; friends. Address: (h.) 47 Waverley Place, Aberdeen; T.-Aberdeen 644873.

Roddick, Jeanne Nixon, BD (Hons). Minister of Greenbank Parish Church, Glasgow, since 2003; b. 16.05.55, Lennoxtown; m., Graham; 1 s.; 2 d. Educ. Bellahouston Academy; Glasgow University. Address: Greenbank Manse, 38 Eaglesham Road, Clarkston, Glasgow G76 7DJ; T.-0141 644 1395; e-mail: jeanne.roddick@ntlworld.com

Rodger of Earlsferry, Rt. Hon. Lord (Alan Ferguson Rodger), PC, QC, MA, LLB, DCL. Lord of Appeal in Ordinary; b. 18.9.44. Educ. Kelvinside Academy, Glasgow; Glasgow University; New College, Oxford. Fellow, New College, Oxford, 1970-72; Member, Faculty of Advocates, 1974; Clerk of Faculty, 1976-79; Advocate Depute, 1985-88; Home Advocate Depute, 1986-88; Member, Mental Welfare Commission for Scotland, 1981-84; UK Delegation to CCBE, 1984-89; Maccabaean Lecturer, British Academy, 1991; Solicitor General for Scotland, 1989-92; Lord Advocate, 1992-95; Judge of the Court of Session, 1995-96; Lord President and Lord Justice General, 1996-2001. Address: (b.) House of Lords, London SW1A 0PW.

Rodger, Professor Albert Alexander, BSc (Eng), PhD, CEng, FICE, FGS. Vice Principal and Head of College of Physical Sciences, Aberdeen University, since 2003; Professor of Civil Engineering, Aberdeen University, since 1997 (Dean, Faculty of Science and Engineering, 2001-03); b. 12.5.51, Greenock; m., Jane Helen; 2 d. Educ. Aberdeen University. Project Engineer, Cementation Research Ltd., London, 1977-79; Aberdeen University: Lecturer in Engineering, 1979-89, Senior Lecturer, 1989-95, Personal Professor, 1995-97. Winner: Award for Excellence, Aberdeen University, 1994, 1997 National John Logie Baird Award for Innovation, Halcrow Premium, Institution of Civil Engineers, 1997, Design Council Millennium Product Award, 1999, Silver Medal, Royal Academy of Engineering, 2000. Recreations: history of church architecture; photography; swimming. Address: College of Physical Sciences, University of Aberdeen, Fraser Noble Building, Aberdeen AB24 3UE; T.-01224 272081; e-mail: a.a.rodger@abdn.ac.uk

Rodger, John Glenn, BEd, MEd. Director of Education and Lifelong Learning, Scottish Borders Council, since 2002; b. 11.5.56, Largs; m., Mary; 2 s. Educ. Ardrossan Academy; Nonington College of Physical Education; University of Edinburgh. PE Teacher, Knox Academy; Assistant Principal Teacher of PE, Penicuik High School; Gracemount High School: Principal Teacher of PE, Assistant Headteacher; PA, Chair of Education Committee, Lothian Regional Council; Head of Pupil Support Services, City of Edinburgh Council. Recreations: keeping fit; reading. Address: (b.) Council HQ, Newton St. Boswells, Melrose TD6 0SA; T.-01835 825095; e-mail: grodger@scotborders.gov.uk

Rodger, Professor Richard, MA, PhD, AcSS. Professor of Economic and Social History, University of Edinburgh, since 2007; b. 01.10.47, Norfolk. Educ. George Heriot's

School, Edinburgh; University of Edinburgh. Lecturer in Economic History, University of Liverpool, 1972-79; Lecturer and Senior Lecturer in Economic and Social History, University of Leicester, 1979-99; Associate Professor of History, University of Kansas, 1982-83, 1987; Visiting Research Fellow, Center for the Humanities, University of Kanas, 1986-87; Director, Centre for Urban History, 1999-2006; Project Director, East Midlands Oral History Archive, 2000-07; Professor of Urban History, University of Leicester, 1999-2007. Awards: Elected Member, Academy of Social Sciences, 2004, Frank Watson Prize for Best Book in Scottish History, 2001-02, Plain English Society Crystal Mark for Software Made Simple series of books. Publications: 16 books including The Transformation of Edinburgh: Land, Property and Trust in the Nineteenth Century, 2001; pbk 2004; Housing the People: the 'Colonies' of Edinburgh, 1860-1950, 1999; Testimonies of the City: Identity, Community and Change in a Contemporary Urban World (Co-Author), 2007; Housing in Urban Britain, 1780-1914, 1995; Cities of Ideas: Civil Society and Urban Governance in Britain 1800-2000 (Co-Author), 2004. Recreations: cricket; long-distance paths; landscapes. Address: (b.) School of History, Classics and Archaeology, University of Edinburgh, 50 George Square, Edinburgh EH8 9JY.
E-mail: richard.rodger@ed.ac.uk

Rodger, Willie, ARSA, RGI, DA (Glas), DUniv (Stirling), RSA (2005). Artist in lino and woodcuts; b. 3.3.30, Kirkintilloch; m., Anne Charmian Henry; 2 s.; 2 d. Educ. Lenzie Academy; Glasgow School of Art. Visualiser, London advertising agency, 1953-54; Art Teacher, Lenzie Academy, 1955-68; Head, Art Department, Clydebank High School, 1968-87. Artist in Residence, Sussex University, 1971; Scottish Historical Playing Cards, 1975; Saltire Awards for Art in Architecture, 1984-89; work in permanent collections in Scotland and England; commissions: Enamel Mural Exhibition Station, Glasgow; illustrations and mural, Dallas Dhu Distillery, Forres; design, Stained Glass Windows, St Mary's Parish Church, Kirkintilloch; Street Banners, 200 anniversary, Union Street, Aberdeen; edition of Lino Cut Prints, P&O Ferries; illustrations, Finding Alba, Scottish Television; lino cut illustrations for The Colour of Black and White by Liz Lochhead, 2003; Images in Bronze for Kirkintilloch Town Trail, 2004; Exhibition, Willie Rodger & Family, 40th Anniversary of Stirling University, 2007. Publications: Scottish Historical Playing Cards; The Field of Thistles (Illustrator); Willie Rodger, Open Eye Gallery. Recreations: gardening; jazz. Address: Stenton, Bellevue Road, Kirkintilloch, Glasgow G66 1AP; T.-0141-776 2116.

Rodgers, Professor Eamonn Joseph, BA, MA, PhD. Emeritus Professor; Professor of Spanish and Latin American Studies, University of Strathclyde, 1990-2004; b. 4.6.41, Belfast; m., Valerie Ann Goodman; 2 s. Educ. St Mary's, Belfast; Queen's University, Belfast. Trinity College Dublin: Junior Lecturer in Spanish, 1964-66, Lecturer in Spanish, 1966-78, Senior Lecturer in Spanish, 1978-89. Publications: From Enlightenment to Realism: The Novels of Galdos, 1870-86, 1987; Encyclopedia of Contemporary Spanish Culture, 1999. Recreations: music; walking. Address: University of Strathclyde, 26 Richmond Street, Glasgow G1 1XH; e-mail: e.rodgers@strath.ac.uk

Rodgers, Shane Andrew, BSc (Hons) Arch, Dip AAS, RIBA, FRIAS. Architect, HRI-Architects, since 2006; Architect, since 1985; b. 12.2.60, Derby; 1 s.; 1 d. Educ. Thurso High School; Robert Gordon's Institute of Technology, Aberdeen. Architect, Sinclair MacDonald and Son, Thurso, 1985-91; Partner, Leet Rodgers Practice, Thurso, 1991-98, Principal, The Rodgers Practice, 1998-2005. Aberdeen Society of Architects

Silver Medal, 1984; Past President, Inverness Architectural Association; Member, Council, RIAS. Address: (b.) HRI-Architects, 17 Queensgate, Inverness IV1 1DF; T.-01463 240066.

Roe, Professor Nicholas Hugh, MA (Oxon), DPhil (Oxon). Professor of English Literature, St. Andrews University, since 1996; b. 14.12.55, Fareham; m., Dr. Susan Jane Stabler; 1 s. Educ. Royal Grammar School, High Wycombe; Trinity College, Oxford. Lecturer in English, Queen's University of Belfast, 1982-85; St. Andrews University: Lecturer in English, 1985-94, Reader in English, 1994-96; Visiting Professor, University of Sao Paulo, 1989; Leverhulme Research Fellow, 1994-95; Director, Coleridge Conference, since 1994; Trustee, Keats-Shelley Memorial Association; Editor, Romanticism (journal); initiator and Director, St. Andrews Poetry Festival ('Stanza'), 1986-92. Publications: Coleridge's Imagination, 1985; Wordsworth and Coleridge, The Radical Years, 1988; The Politics of Nature, 1992; Selected Poetry of William Wordsworth, 1992; Keats and History, 1995; Selected Poems of John Keats, 1995; John Keats and the Culture of Dissent, 1997; Samuel Taylor Coleridge and the Sciences of Life, 2001; Leigh Hunt: Life, Poetics, Politics, 2003; Fiery Heart: The First Life of Leigh Hunt, 2005. Recreation: France. Address: (b.) School of English, St. Andrews University, St. Andrews KY16 9AL; T.-01334 476161.

Roe, William Deas, BSc, FRSA. Chairman, Highlands and Islands Enterprise, since 2004; Chairman, Disability and Carers Service, DWP; Chairman, Rocket Science UK Ltd., since 2004; b. 9.7.47, Perth. Educ. St Modan's High School, Stirling; Edinburgh University. Director, Shelter; Director of Student Housing, Edinburgh University; Assistant Director, Scottish Council for Voluntary Organisations; Principal, William Roe Associates; Councillor, Edinburgh City and Lothian Region, 1978-84; Board Member, Training and Development Corporation, Maine, USA; National Champion, National Endowment for Science, Technology and Arts (NESTA), since 2005. Recreations: sailing; skiing; hill-walking; visual arts; music; travel. Address: (h.) 3A Northumberland Street, Edinburgh EH3 6LL; T.-07771 930880.

Roff, Professor William Robert, MA, PhD. Professor Emeritus, Columbia University, New York, since 1991; Hon. Fellow, Islamic and Middle Eastern Studies, University of Edinburgh, since 1992; b. 02.05.29, Glasgow; m., Susanne; 2 d. Educ. Hillhead High School; Harris Academy; University of New Zealand; Australia National University. Lecturer in History, Monash University, Australia; Lecturer/Senior Lecturer, University of Malaya; Associate Professor/Professor of History, Columbia University, New York. Publications: numerous books and articles on muslim social history. Recreations: parenting. Address: (h.) 29 Shore Street, Cellardyke, Fife KY10 3BD; T.-01333 312131; e-mail: william.roff@btinternet.com

Rogers, David A., MA, PhD. Head of Housing Supply and Markets Division, Scottish Government, since 2004. Educ. University of Oxford; University of Cambridge. Address: (b.) 1-H 91, Scottish Government, Victoria Quay, Edinburgh EH6 6QQ; T.-0131-244 5511.
E-mail: david.rogers@scotland.gsi.gov.uk

Rogers, Ian Hart. Chief Executive, Scottish Decorators Federation, since 1999; b. 11.6.52, Glasgow; m., Helen; 2 s. Educ. Bearsden Academy; Clydebank College. Began career with Daily Record and Sunday Mail Ltd.;

became Sales Manager/Director of roofing and housebuilding company; joined Scottish Building Employers Federation as HQ Secretary. Director, SCORE; Member, Scottish Advisory Committee, CITB. Recreations: golf; walking; reading. Address: (b.) Castlecraig Business Park, Players Road, Stirling FK7 7SH; T.-01786 448838; Fax: 01786 450451.

Rolfe, Mervyn James, CBE, DL, OStJ, MEd, MSc, FRSA, FSAScot, JP. Convener, Scottish Police Services Authority, since 2007; Chief Executive, Dundee and Tayside Chamber of Commerce, 2002-06; Depute Leader and Convener, Economic Development Committee, Dundee City Council, 1999-2003; Associate Lecturer, University of Abertay, Dundee, since 2000; b. 31.7.47, Wisbech; m., Christine; 1 s. Educ. Buckhaven High School; Dundee University; University of Abertay Dundee. Civil servant, until 1983; Co-ordinator, Dundee Resources Centre for the Unemployed, 1983-87; Vice-Chair, Dundee Trades Council, 1981-82; Leader, Labour Group, Tayside Regional Council, 1994-96; Convener, Tayside Education Committee, 1986-94; Lord Provost and Lord Lieutenant of Dundee, 1996-99; Member, Executive Committee, COSLA, 1990-96; Governor, Dundee (latterly Northern) College of Education, 1986-94; Member, Dundee University Court, 1986-2000; Member, Scottish Community Education Council, 1986-88; Member, General Teaching Council, 1986-95; Member, Dundee Heritage Trust, 1986-99; Executive Member, Campaign for a Scottish Assembly, 1989-91; Member, Scottish Committee for Staff Development in Education, 1987-91; Board Member, Scottish Enterprise, Tayside, 1991-96, and 1999-2003; Member, Scottish ESF Objective 3 Monitoring Committee, 1999-2002; Chair, Dundee City Developments Ltd., 1999-2003; Chair, East of Scotland European Consortium, 2000-03; Chair, Instep Initiatives Ltd., 2003-06; Director, ESEP Ltd., since 1999 and Chair, since 2000; Member, City of Discovery Campaign, 1996-2006 (Chair, 1996-2002); Vice-Chair, Unicorn Preservation Society, since 2002; Board Member, Angus and Dundee Tourist Board, 1999-2005; Director, Destination Dundee, since 2005; Director, Maggie's Centre Dundee, 2000-04 and now Chair; Member, Dundee Partnership Forum, 2000-06; Honorary Fellow, University of Abertay, Dundee; Honorary Colonel 2 (City of Dundee) signal squadron (v). Recreations: reading; travel. Address: (h.) 17 Mains Terrace, Dundee; T.-01382 450073; e-mail: mervynrolfe@aol.com

Rolfe, William David Ian, PhD, FRSE, FGS, FMA. Keeper of Geology, National Museums of Scotland, 1986-96; b. 24.1.36; m., Julia Mary Margaret Rayer; 2 d. Educ. Royal Liberty Grammar School, Romford; Birmingham University. Geology Curator, University Lecturer, then Senior Lecturer in Geology, Hunterian Museum, Glasgow University, 1962-81; Deputy Director, 1981-86. President, Geological Society of Glasgow, 1973-76; Editor, Scottish Journal of Geology, 1967-72; President, Edinburgh Geological Society, 1989-91; President, Palaeontological Association, 1992-94; President, Society for the History of Natural History, 1996-99. Recreations: visual arts; walking; music. Address: 4A Randolph Crescent, Edinburgh, EH3 7TH; T.-0131-226 2094.

Rolland, Dr. Lawrence Anderson Lyon, DA, PPRIBA, PPRIAS, FRSE, FRSA. Retired Senior Partner, Hurd Rolland Partnership; General Trustee, Church of Scotland, since 1979; Chairman, Court, University of Dundee, 1998-2004; former Member, Architects Registration Board, London, and Chairman, Education and Practise Advisory Group; Chairman, RIBA Education Fund Committee and Chairman of Trustees, RIBA Education Fund; Member, Board, NTS, since 2005; Governor, Donaldson College for the Deaf; b. 6.11.37, Leven; m., Mairi Melville; 2 s.; 2 d.

Educ. George Watson's Boys College; Duncan of Jordanstone College of Art. Entered father's practice, 1959; joined partnership with Ian Begg bringing L. A. Rolland and Partners and Robert Hurd and Partners together as one partnership; Architect for: The Queen's Hall, Edinburgh; restoration and redesign of Bank of Scotland Head Office; much housing in Fife's royal burghs; British Golf Museum, St Andrews; General Accident Life Assurance, York; Minshull Street Crown Courts, Manchester; winner of more than 20 awards and commendations from Saltire Society, Stone Federation, Concrete Society, Civic Trust, Europa Nostra, R.I.B.A. and Times Conservation Award. President, Royal Incorporation of Architects in Scotland, 1979-81; President, Royal Institute of British Architects, 1985-87; Founder Chairman, Scottish Construction Industry Group, 1979-81; Member, Building EDC NEDC, 1982-88; Chairman, Board of Governors, Duncan of Jordanstone College of Art, 1993-94. Recreations: music; fishing. Address: (b.) School House, Newburn, Fife KY8 6JE; e-mail: rolland@newburn.org.uk

Rollinson, Timothy John Denis, BSc (Edin). Director General and Deputy Chairman, Forestry Commission, since 2004; b. 6.11.53, London; m., Dominique Christine; 1 s.; 2 d. Educ. Chigwell School, Edinburgh University. Forestry Commission: District Officer, Kent, 1976-78; New Forest, 1978-81; Head of Growth and Yield Studies, 1981-88; Land Use Planning, 1988-90; Parliamentary and Policy, 1990-93; Secretary, 1994-97; Chief Conservator, England, 1997-2000; Head of Policy and Practice, 2000-03; Director, Forestry Group, 2003-04. Chair, Forest Research Co-ordination Committee, 2000-04; Chair, Global Partnership on Forest Landscape Restoration, since 2002. FICFor, 1995; FIAgrE, 2004; President, Institute of Chartered Foresters, 2000-02; Chartered Environmentalist, 2005; Vice-Chair, Wood for good, since 2004; Companion, Chartered Management Institute, 2006. Recreations: golf; swimming; cycling. Address: (b.) Forestry Commission, 231 Corstorphine Road, Edinburgh EH12 7AT; T.-0131 314 6424.

Rollo, 14th Lord (David Eric Howard Rollo); b. 1943. Succeeded to title, 1997.

Rooney, Alison, BSc Hons (Maths/Econ), MBA. University Secretary, Glasgow Caledonian University, since 1999, formerly Executive Director, Resources and Administration; b. 9.4.58, Milngavie; 1 d. Educ. Hutchesons' Girls Grammar School; University of Strathclyde. Oil Supply Management and Refinery Production Control, BP Oil (Grangemouth Refinery), 1979-84; Business Development and Urban Renewal, Scottish Development Agency, 1984-89; Director of Marketing and Public Relations, SCOTVEC (Scottish Vocational Education Council), 1989-95; Director of Finance, Business and Corporate Planning, Marketing and Public Relations and Internal Communications, Registers of Scotland (Trading Fund), 1995-99. Active Member of local school PTA. Recreations: sailing; golf; tennis; walking and managing 40 acre estate in spare time! Address: (b.) Glasgow Caledonian University, Britannia Building, Cowcaddens Road, Glasgow G4 0BA; e-mail: a.rooney@gcal.ac.uk

Rorke, Professor John, CBE, PhD, BSc, DEng, CEng, FIMechE, FRSE. Professor Emeritus, formerly Professor of Mechanical Engineering, Heriot-Watt University, 1980-88, and Vice-Principal, 1984-88; b. 2.9.23, Dumbarton; m., Jane Craig Buchanan; 2 d. Educ. Dumbarton Academy; Royal Technical College, Glasgow. Lecturer, Strathclyde University, 1946-51; Assistant to Engineering Director, Alexander Stephen & Sons Ltd., 1951-56; Technical

Manager, then General Manager and Engineering Director, William Denny & Bros. Ltd., 1956-63; Technical Director, then Sales Director, Managing Director and Chairman, Brown Bros. & Co. Ltd. and Chairman, John Hastie of Greenock Ltd., 1963-78; Managing Director, Vickers Offshore Group, 1978 (Director of Planning, Vickers PLC, 1979-80). President, Institution of Engineers and Shipbuilders in Scotland, 1985-87; Chairman, Institute of Offshore Engineering Group, 1990-94. Recreations: bridge; golf. Address: (h.) 3 Barnton Park Grove, Edinburgh; T.-0131-336 3044.

Rosborough, Linda, BSc, PhD. Deputy Director, Marine Strategy Division, Scottish Government, since 2008; Head, Common Agricultural Policy Management Division, Scottish Government, 2002-08. Former Lecturer in planning and environmental studies; former advisor to Environment Committee, House of Commons; worked on university funding, Scottish Office; set up Social Inclusion Division, Scottish Executive, 1999 (Head of Division, 1999-2002). Address: (b.) Scottish Government, Area GH93, Victoria Quay, Edinburgh EH6 6QQ; T.-0131-244-6944.

Rose, Dilys Lindsay, BA. Writer of fiction, poetry, drama, librettos, since 1980; b. 7.2.54, Glasgow; 2 d. Educ. Edinburgh University. Publications include: fiction: Our Lady of the Pickpockets, Red Tides, War Dolls, Pest Maiden; Lord of Illusions; poetry: Beauty is a Dangerous Thing, Madame Doubtfire's Dilemma, Lure; Bodywork. Winner, first Macallan/Scotland on Sunday short story competition, 1991; Hawthornden Fellow; RLS Memorial Award recipient, 1997; Society of Authors Travel Award; Canongate Prizewinner, 2000; UNESCO/World City of Literature Exchange Fellow, 2006; McCash poetry winner, 2006; web: dilysrose.com

Rose, Kenneth Charles, LLP (Hons), DipLP. Solicitor, Partner, Dundas & Wilson CS LLP, since 1995; b. 23.10.63, Montrose; m., Aileen; 1 s. Educ. Kelso High School; University of Edinburgh. Dundas & Wilson: Trainee, 1986-88, Assistant/Associate, 1988-95. Recreations: music; keep fit; football; rugby. Address: c/o Dundas & Wilson CS LLP, Saltire Court, 20 Castle Terrace, Edinburgh EH1 2EN; T.-0131 200 7348; e-mail: kenneth.rose@dundas-wilson.com

Rose, Professor Richard, BA, DPhil, FBA. Director and Professor of Public Policy, Centre for the Study of Public Policy, Aberdeen University, since 2005; b. 9.4.33; m., Rosemary J.; 2 s.; 1 d. Educ. Clayton High School, Missouri, USA; Johns Hopkins University; London School of Economics; Lincoln and Nuffield Colleges, Oxford University. Political public relations, Mississippi Valley, 1954-55; Reporter, St. Louis Post-Dispatch, 1955-57; Lecturer in Government, Manchester University, 1961-66; Professor of Politics, Strathclyde University, 1966-80; Director, Centre for the Study of Public Policy, 1980-2005; Consultant Psephologist, The Times, Independent Television, Daily Telegraph, STV, UTV, etc., since 1964; Scientific Adviser, Paul Lazarsfeld Society, Vienna, since 1991; American SSRC Fellow, Stanford University, 1967; Visiting Lecturer in Political Sociology, Cambridge University, 1967; Director, ISSC European Summer School, 1973; Secretary, Committee on Political Sociology, International Sociological Association, 1970-85; Founding Member, European Consortium for Political Research, 1970; Member: US/UK Fulbright Commission, 1971-75, Eisenhower Fellowship Programme, 1971; Guggenheim Foundation Fellow, 1974; Visiting Scholar: Woodrow Wilson International Centre, Washington DC, 1974, Brookings Institute, Washington DC, 1976, American Enterprise Institute, Washington, 1980, Fiscal Affairs Department, IMF, Washington, 1984; Visiting Professor, European University Institute, Florence, 1977, 1978; Visitor, Japan Foundation, 1984; Hinkley Professor, Johns Hopkins University, 1987; Guest Professor, Wissenschaftzentrum, Berlin, 1988-90, 2005-07, Central European University, Prague, 1992-95, Max Planck Institute, Berlin, 1996; Ransone Lecturer, University of Alabama, 1990; Consultant Chairman, NI Constitutional Convention, 1976; Home Office Working Party on Electoral Register, 1975-77; Co-Founder, British Politics Group, 1974; Convenor, Work Group on UK Politics, Political Studies Association, 1976-88; Member, Council, International Political Science Association, 1976-82; Keynote Speaker, Australian Institute of Political Science, Canberra, 1978; Technical Consultant: OECD, World Bank, Council of Europe, International IDEA UN agencies; Member, National Endowment for Democracy International Forum, since 1997; Member, Transparency International Research Advisory Panel, since 1998; Advisor, House of Commons Public Administration Committee, 2003; Director, ESRC (formerly SSRC) Research Programme, Growth of Government, 1982-86; Honorary Vice President, Political Studies Association, UK, 1986; Editor, Journal of Public Policy, since 1985 (Chairman, 1981-85); Foreign Member, Finnish Academy of Science and Letters, 1985; Fellow of the British Academy, 1992; Fellow, American Academy of Arts and Sciences, 1994; Robert Marjolin AMEX Prize in International Economics, 1992; Lasswell Award for Lifetime Achievement in Public Policy, USA, 1999; Political Studies Association Award for Lifetime Achievement, 2000; Honorary doctorate, Orebru University, Sweden, 2005. Publications: The British General Election of 1959 (Co-author), 1960; Must Labour Lose? (Co-author), 1960; Politics in England, 1964; Studies in British Politics (Editor), 1966; Influencing Voters, 1967; Policy Making in Britain (Editor), 1969; People in Politics, 1970; European Politics (Joint Editor), 1971; Governing Without Consensus — An Irish Perspective, 1971; International Almanack of Electoral History (Co-author), 1974; Electoral Behaviour — A Comparative Handbook (Editor), 1974; Lessons From America (Editor), 1974; The Problem of Party Government, 1974; The Management of Urban Change in Britain and Germany (Editor), 1974; Northern Ireland — A Time of Choice, 1976; Managing Presidential Objectives, 1976; The Dynamics of Public Policy (Editor), 1976; New Trends in British Politics (Joint Editor), 1977; Comparing Public Policies (Joint Editor), 1977; What is Governing? — Purpose and Policy in Washington, 1978; Elections Without Choice (Joint Editor), 1978; Can Government Go Bankrupt? (Co-author), 1978; Britain — Progress and Decline (Joint Editor), 1980; Do Parties Make a Difference?, 1980; Challenge to Governance (Editor), 1980; Electoral Participation (Editor), 1980; Presidents and Prime Ministers (Joint Editor), 1980; Understanding the United Kingdom, 1982; United Kingdom Facts (Co-author), 1982; The Territorial Dimension in United Kingdom Politics (Joint Editor), 1982; Fiscal Stress in Cities (Joint Editor), 1982; Understanding Big Government, 1984; The Nationwide Competition for Votes (Co-author), 1984; Public Employment in Western Nations, 1985; Voters Begin to Choose (Co-author), 1986; Patterns of Parliamentary Legislation (Co-author), 1986; The Welfare State East and West (Joint Editor), 1986; Ministers and Ministries, 1987; Taxation By Political Inertia (Co-author), 1987; The Post-Modern President — The White House Meets the World, 1988; Ordinary People in Public Policy, 1989; Training Without Trainers? (Co-author), 1990; The Loyalty of Voters (Co-author), 1990; Lesson-Drawing in Public Policy, 1993; Inheritance before Choice, 1994; What Is Europe?, 1996; How Russia Votes (Co-author), 1997; Democracy and its Alternatives (Co-author), 1998; A Society Transformed: Hungary in Time-Space Perspective, (Co-author), 1999; The International Encyclopedia of Elections (Editor), 2000; Prime Minister in a Shrinking World, 2001; Elections Without Order: Russia's

Challenge to Vladimir Putin (Co-author), 2002); Elections and Parties in New European Democracies (Co-author), 2003; Learning from Comparative Public Policy, 2005; Russia Transformed (Co-author), 2006. Recreations: architecture (historical, Britain; modern, America); music; writing. Address: (h,) 1 East Abercromby Street, Helensburgh G84 7SP.

Rosebery, 7th Earl of (Neil Archibald Primrose), DL; b. 11.2.29; m., Alison Mary Deirdre Reid; 1 s.; 4 d. Educ. Stowe; New College, Oxford. Succeeded to title, 1974. Address: (h.) Dalmeny House, South Queensferry, West Lothian.

Rosie, Elaine, BA, MIoH. Training and Development Manager, Shelter Scotland, since 2004; Board Member, Scottish Legal Aid Board, since 2005; b. 6.9.62; m., Paul Grice; 2 d. Educ. James Gillespie's High School; Stirling University. Management Trainee, City of Edinburgh Council Housing Dept., 1984-86; London and Quadrant Housing Trust: Housing Officer, 1986-87, Special Projects Officer, 1987-88, Senior Development Officer, 1989-91; Senior Development Officer, Whiteinch and Scotstoun Housing Association, 1991-92; Depute Director, Shelter Scotland, 1992-2000; Scottish Homelessness Advisory Service Manager, 2000-04. Homepoint National Advisory Committee, 1993-2006. Recreations: hill walking; reading; swimming. E-mail: rosie_elaine@yahoo.co.uk

Rosie, George. Freelance Writer and Broadcaster; b. 27.2.41, Edinburgh; m., Elizabeth Ann Burness; 2 s.; 1 d. Educ. Trinity Academy, Edinburgh; Edinburgh School of Architecture. Editor, Interior Design magazine, 1966-68; freelance magazine writer, 1968-76; Scottish Affairs Correspondent, Sunday Times, 1976-86; Reporter, Channel 4 TV series Down the Line, 1986-87, Scottish Eye, 1988; Reporter/Writer, The Englishing of Scotland, 1988, Selling Scotland, 1989; Scotching the Myth, 1990; Losing the Heid, 1991; Independence Day, 1996; Secret Scotland, 1997-98, Our Friends in the South, 1998; After Lockerbie (BAFTA Best Documentary winner, 1999); Our Friends in the South, 2000; Chief Braveheart, 2005; Editor, Observer Scotland, 1988-89; award winner, RSPB birds and countryside awards, 1988. Publications: British in Vietnam, 1970; Cromarty, 1975; The Ludwig Initiative, 1978; Hugh Miller, 1982; The Directory of International Terrorism, 1986; as contributor: Headlines, the Media in Scotland, 1978; Death's Enemy, the Pilgrimage of Victor Frankenstein, 2001 (fiction); Curious Scotland, 2004; Tyneside, 2005; Scottish Government Yearbook, 1982; Scotland, Multinationals and the Third World, 1982; World Offshore Oil and Gas Industry Report, 1987; stage plays: In Had To Be You, 1994; radio plays: The Parsi, 1992; Postcards from Shannon, 2000. Recreation: hill-walking. Address: (h.) 70 Comiston Drive, Edinburgh EH10 5QS; T.-0131-447 9660.

Ross, Rt. Hon. Lord (Donald MacArthur Ross), PC, MA, LLB. Lord Justice Clerk and President of the Second Division of the Court of Session, 1985-97; a Senator of the College of Justice, 1977-97; Chairman, Judicial Studies Committee, Scotland, 1997-2001; Lord High Commissioner to the General Assembly of the Church of Scotland, 1990 and 1991; b. 29.3.27, Dundee; m., Dorothy Margaret Annand (d. 2004); 2 d. Educ. High School of Dundee; Edinburgh University. Advocate, 1952; QC, 1964; Vice-Dean, Faculty of Advocates, 1967-73; Dean of Faculty, 1973-76; Sheriff Principal of Ayr and Bute, 1972-73; Member, Scottish Committee, Council of Tribunals, 1970-76; Member, Committee on Privacy, 1970; Deputy

Chairman, Boundary Commission for Scotland, 1977-85; Member, Court, Heriot-Watt University, 1978-90, Chairman, 1984-90; Member, Parole Board for Scotland, 1997-2002; Vice President, Royal Society of Edinburgh, 1999-2002 (Member, Council, 1997-99). Hon. LLD, Edinburgh, Dundee, Abertay Dundee, Aberdeen; Hon. DUniv, Heriot-Watt; FRSE. Recreation: gardening; walking; travel. Address: (h.) 7/1 Tipperlinn Road, Edinburgh EH10 5ET; T.-0131 447 6771.

Ross, Alastair Robertson, CStJ, DA, PGDip, RSA, RGI, FRBS, FSA Scot, FRSA, MBIM, Hon. FRIAS, DArts. Artist; Lecturer in Fine Art, Duncan of Jordanstone College University of Dundee, 1994-2003; b. 8.8.41, Perth; m., Kathryn Margaret Greig Wilson; 1 d. Educ. St. Mary's Episcopal School, Dunblane; McLaren High School, Callander; Duncan of Jordanstone College of Art, Dundee. SED Postgraduate Scholarship, 1965-66; Dickson Prize for Sculpture, 1962; Holokrome (Dundee) Sculpture Prize and Commission, 1962; SED Travelling Scholarship, 1963; Royal Scottish Academy Chalmers Bursary, 1964; Royal Scottish Academy Carnegie Travelling Scholarship, 1965; Duncan of Drumfork Scholarship, 1965; award winner, Paris Salon, 1967; Medaille de Bronze, Societe des Artistes Francais, 1968; Elected Associate of the Royal Society of British Sculptors, 1968; Professional Member, Society of Scottish Artists, 1969; Visiting Lecturer, Glasgow School of Art, 1974; Lecturer in Fine Art, Duncan of Jordanstone College of Art, Dundee, 1966-94; Honorary Lecturer, Dundee University, 1969-94; Visiting Lecturer, University of Texas, Arlington, USA, 1996; Medaille D'Argent and elected Membre Associe, Societe des Artistes Francais, 1970; Scottish Representative and Member, Council, Royal Society of British Sculptors, 1972-92; Elected Fellow of the Royal Society of British Sculptors, 1975; Elected Associate of Royal Scottish Academy, 1980; Sir Otto Beit Medal, Royal Society of British Sculptors, 1988; Member, RSA Alexander Naysmith Fund Committee, 1986-89; Member, RSA Spalding Fund Committee, 1986-89; Member, RSA Kinross Fund Committee, 1994-97 and since 2005; Freeman, City of London, 1989; Sir William Gillies Bequest Award, Royal Scottish Academy, 1989; Council Member, Society of Scottish Artists, 1972-75; Vice President, Royal Society of British Sculptors, 1988-90; Council Member, British School at Rome, 1990-96; Invited Tutor, School of Scottish Artists in Malta, 1991-93; Hon. Fellow, Royal Incorporation of Architects in Scotland, 1992; Member, Board of Directors, Workshop and Artists' Studio Provision Scotland Ltd., 1997-2004; Council Member, Royal Scottish Academy, 1998-2001; commissioned to design and sculpt Spirit of Scotland Awards, since 1998; exhibited work widely in UK and abroad; work in: Scottish Arts Council Collection, Perth Art Gallery and Museum, Dundee Education Authority Collection, Dundee Art Gallery and Museum, University of Abertay Dundee, University of St Andrews, University of Dundee, Royal Burgh of St Andrews, Blackness Primary School, Dundee (Dundee Public Arts Scheme), P & O Steam Navigation Company, Superliner "Aurora", Court of the Lord Lyon HM New Register House; Rank Xerox HQ, Bucks, RC Diocese of Dunkeld; private collections in Austria, Switzerland, Egypt, USA, Norway, Bahamas, Canada, Portugal, India, UK; awarded Personal Civic Reception by City of Dundee, 1999; Member, Saltire Society Arts and Crafts in Architecture Awards Adjudication Panel, 2001-05; Royal Scottish Academy representative, Trust for St. John's Kirk of Perth, 2001-05; Hon. Doctorate of Arts, University of Abertay Dundee; Elected RGI, 2004; Hon. Member, Perthshire Art Association, 2005; External Assessor to the JD Fergusson Arts Awards Trust for the Trust's 2006 Travel Award, 2005; Member, Montrose Heritage Trust Sculpture Commission Adjudication Panel, 2005; Royal Scottish Academician, 2005; Member, RSA General Purposes Committee, since 2005; Elected Librarian of the Royal

Scottish Academy, 2005; Awarded Reid Kerr College Sculpture Prize of Paisley Art Institute, 2006; Member, Board of Patrons, University of Abertay Dundee Foundation, since 2006. Recreations: genealogy; heraldry; travel. Address: (h.) Ravenscourt, 28 Albany Terrace, Dundee, DD3 6HS; T.-01382 224235.

Ross, Alexander (Sandy), LLB, CYCW. Chief Executive, Murrayfield Media, since 2007; Managing Director, International Development, STV, 2004-07; Managing Director, Scottish Television, 2000-04; b. 17.4.48, Grangemouth; m., Alison Fraser; 2 s.; 1 d. Educ. Grangemouth High School; Edinburgh University; Moray House College. Apprentice lawyer, 1971-73; Lecturer, Paisley College, 1974-75; Producer, Granada TV, 1978-86; Controller, Arts and Entertainment, Scottish Television, 1986-95; Deputy Chief Executive, Scottish Television Enterprises, 1995-97; Controller Regional Production, Scottish Media Group, 1997-2000. Member, Edinburgh Town Council, 1971-74; Member, Edinburgh District Council, 1974-78; President, Moray House Students Union, 1976; Chairman, BAFTA, Scotland. Recreations: golf; music; reading; watching football; member, Glen Golf Club, Haunted Major Golf Society, Prestonfield Golf Club, Edinburgh Corporation Golf Club, Rhodes Golf Club. Address: (h.) 7 Murrayfield Avenue, Edinburgh EH12 6AU; T.-0131-539 1192.
E-mail: sandy.ross@murrayfieldmedia.com

Ross, Rev. Andrew Christian, MA, BD, STM, PhD, FRHistS, DLitt. Honorary Fellow in Ecclesiastical History, Edinburgh University; b. 10.5.31, Millerhill, Lothian; m., I. Joyce Elder; 4 s.; 1 d. (deceased). Educ. Dalkeith High School; Edinburgh University; Union Theological Seminary, New York. RAF, 1952-54; Minister, Church of Central Africa Presbyterian (Malawi), 1958-65; Senior Lecturer in Ecclesiastical History, Edinburgh University, 1966 until retirement (Principal of New College and Dean, Faculty of Divinity, 1978-84). Chairman, Lands Tribunal of Nyasaland, then Malawi Government, 1963-65; Vice Chairman, National Tenders Board, Nyasaland, then Malawi Government, 1963-65. Member, University Court, 1971-73; Convener, Student Affairs Committee, 1977-83; Kerr Lecturer, Glasgow University, 1984; Lecturer, Assembly's College, Belfast, 1985; Visiting Professor, Yale University and Dartmouth College, 1992. Publications: John Philip: Missions, Race and Politics in South Africa; Vision Betrayed: the Jesuits in China and Japan; Blantyre Mission and the Development of Malawi; David Livingstone: Mission and Empire. Recreation: coaching and watching football. Address: (h.) 20 Forbes Road, Edinburgh EH10 4ED; T.-0131-228 8984.

Ross, David Craib Hinshaw, LLB (Hons), NP. Partner, Biggart Baillie, Solicitors, since 1977, Chairman and Senior Partner, since 2001; Director, Glasgow Chamber of Commerce, since 1996, President, 2002; Chairman, Scottish Chambers of Commerce, 2003-07; b. 14.1.48, Glasgow; m., Elizabeth Clark; 2 s.; 1 d. Educ. Kelvinside Academy, Glasgow; Trinity College, Glenalmond; University of Glasgow. Maclay Murray and Spens: Apprenticeship, 1970-72, Assistant, 1972-75; Assistant, Biggart Baillie and Gifford, 1975-77, Head of Corporate, 1997-2001. Director, Scottish Council Development and Industry, 2003-07; Chairman, Euro-American Lawyers Group, 1997-2002; Secretary, Loganair Ltd., since 1997; Member of Court, University of Glasgow, since 2004; Director, APUC Limited, since 2007. Recreations: rhododendrons; windsurfing. Address: (h.) Eastfield, 10 Ledcameroch Road, Bearsden, Glasgow G61 4AB; T.-0141-942 2569.

Ross, Colonel Donald Grant Ross, OBE, DL. Lord Lieutenant of Dunbartonshire, since 2007; Deputy Lieutenant of Dunbartonshire, 2004-07; m.; 3 c. Served in the Argyll and Sutherland Highlanders, 1965-96; Commandant: Garelochhead Army Training Area, 1996-

1998, Argyll and Sutherland Highlanders Battalion of the Army Cadet Force, 1998-2003. Deputy Chairman of the Southern Area Committee of Highland Reserve Forces and Cadets Association; member of the Executive Committee of Erskine Hospital. Formerly member of the Church of Scotland Committee on Chaplains to the Armed Forces.

Ross, Fiona, MA. Principal, Fettes Centre for Language and Culture, Fettes College, since 2006; former Director of Marketing and Strategy, Hawthorn-Edinburgh (Edinburgh School of English), former Vice-Principal and former Principal; Singer, Scottish traditional song (Lead Singer, Handsel); b. 16.4.65, Glasgow. Educ. Hyndland Secondary School; University of Glasgow. Taught English overseas; Marketing Manager, Basil Paterson College, 1989-92; Director of Administration and Marketing, Scripps College, California and International House, New York, 1992-95; Educational Marketing Consultant, 1995-97; Principal, Edinburgh Tutorial College, 1997-2000; Principal, Regent Edinburgh, 1997-2000; Principal, Aspect International Language Academy, 2000-01. Recreations: traditional music and song; walking; good food; travel; animals. Address: (h.) 2 The Causeway, Duddingston Village, Edinburgh EH15 3PZ; T.-0131-661 8068; e-mail: FRoss90346@aol.com

Ross, Helen Elizabeth, BA, MA (Oxon), PhD (Cantab), FBPsS, CPsychol, FRSE. Honorary Reader, Stirling University, since 1994; b. 2.12.35, London. Educ. South Hampstead High School; Somerville College, Oxford; Newnham College, Cambridge. Assistant Mistress, schools in London and Oxfordshire, 1959-61; Research Assistant and student, Psychological Laboratory, Cambridge University, 1961-65; Lecturer in Psychology: Hull University, 1965-68, Stirling University, 1969-72; Senior Lecturer in Psychology, Stirling University, 1972-83; Research Fellow, DFVLR Institute for Aerospace Medicine, Bonn, 1980-81; Leverhulme Fellowship, 1983-84; Reader in Psychology, Stirling University, 1983-94; Honorary Reader, Stirling University, since 1994. Member, S.E. Regional Board, Nature Conservancy Council for Scotland, 1991-92; Fellowship Secretary, Royal Society of Edinburgh, 1994-97. Publications: Behaviour and Perception in Strange Environments, 1974; E.H. Weber: The Sense of Touch (Co-translator), 1978; E.H. Weber on the Tactile Senses (Co-translator), 1996; The Mystery of the Moon Illusion (Co-author), 2002. Recreations: skiing; Gaelic (Cert HE, 2007); hill-walking; compleat Munroist, 1998; traditional music; Member, Shiftin Bobbins Ceilidh Band. Address: (b.) Department of Psychology, Stirling University, Stirling FK9 4LA; T.-01786 467647; e-mail: h.e.ross@stir.ac.uk

Ross, John Alexander, CBE, FRAgS. Chairman, Dumfries and Galloway NHS Board, since 2001; Chairman, Moredun Research Institute, 2002-04; Chairman, Moredun Foundation, 2004; b. 19.2.45, Stranraer; m., Alison Jean Darling; 2 s.; 1 d. Educ. George Watson's College, Edinburgh. NFU of Scotland: Convener, Hill Farming Sub-Committee, 1984-90, Wigtown Area President, 1985-86, Convener, Livestock Committee, 1987-90, Vice-President, 1986-90, President, 1990-96. Chairman, Stranraer School Council, 1980-89; Session Clerk, Portpatrick Parish Church, 1975-80; Director, Animal Diseases Research Association; Commissioner, Meat and Livestock Commission, 1996-2002; Chairman, Dumfries and Galloway Health Board, 1997-2000; Chairman, Dumfries and Galloway Primary Care NHS Trust, 2000-01; Director, NFU Mutual Insurance Society, since 1996. Recreations: golf; curling. Address: Upper Dinvin Farm, Portpatrick, Stranraer DG9 8TL.

Ross, Kate, BSc (Hons), MEd. Mountaineer, since 1963; b. 2.1.45, West Bromwich; m., Duncan Ross (deceased). Educ. West Bromwich Grammar School; University College of North Wales, Bangor. Part Time Instructor,

National Mountaineering Centre, Glenmore Lodge, 1966-69; Instructor, University College of North Wales, 1969-72; Senior Instructor, Benmore Centre for Outdoor Education, 1972-79; Teacher (Maths), Gourock, 1981-82; Teacher and Assistant Principal Teacher of Maths, Dunoon Grammar School, 1982-92; Principal Teacher of Maths, Gourock High School, 1992-95. Mountaineering Council of Scotland Executive, 1993-2002, Vice President, 1997-2001; Chair, Scottish Mountain Safety Group, 1998-2002; Mountain Leader, Training Scotland, since 1995, Vice Chair, 1996-99, Chair, 2002-05; Mountain Leader Training UK, 1995-2005, Vice Chair, 1998-2002; President, Ladies Scottish Climbing Club, 1997-2000. Recreations: mountaineering; ski-ing; reading. Address: (h.) Ardmhor, Hunter Street, Dunoon PA23 8DZ; T.-01369 706578.

Ross, Kenneth Alexander, LLB (Hons). Sheriff of South Strathclyde, Dumfries and Galloway at Dumfries, since 2000; President, Law Society of Scotland, 1994-95 (Vice-President, 1993-94); b. 21.4.49; m., Morag Laidlaw; 1 s.; 1 d. Educ. Hutcheson's Grammar School, Glasgow; Edinburgh University. President, Edinburgh University Union, 1970-71. Partner, Gillespie, Gifford & Brown (formerly McGowans), Solicitors, Dumfries, 1975-97; Temporary Sheriff, 1987-97; Sheriff of Lothian and Borders at Linlithgow, 1997-2000. Member, Scottish Legal Aid Board, since 2004; Member, Council, Law Society of Scotland, 1987-96. Contested General Elections (C): Kilmarnock, Feb. 1974, Galloway, Oct. 1974. Recreations: gardening; golf; curling; walking. Address: Slate Row, Auchencairn, Castle Douglas, Kirkcudbrightshire DG7 1QL.

Ross, Rev. Professor Kenneth Rankin, BA, BD (Hons), PhD. Secretary, Church of Scotland World Mission Council, since 1998; b. 31.5.58, Glasgow; m., Hester Ferguson Carmichael; 3 s. Educ. Kelvinside Academy, Glasgow; Edinburgh University. Ordained, 1982; Parish Minister, Unst, Shetland, 1982-88; Mission Partner, Board of World Mission, seconded to University of Malawi as Lecturer and latterly Professor of Theology, 1988-98; Member, International Association for Mission Studies, 1999; Honorary Secretary, Jubilee Scotland, since 2001; Chair, Towards 2010, since 2001; Chair, Interim Board, Scotland-Malawi Partnership, 2005-06. Publications: Church and Creed in Scotland, 1988; Gospel Ferment in Malawi, 1995; Here Comes Your King! Christ, Church and Nation in Malawi, 1998; Following Jesus and Fighting HIV/Aids, 2002. Recreations: hill-walking; reading; being on the island of Islay. Address: (b.) 121 George Street, Edinburgh EH2 4YN; T.- 0131-225 5722; e-mail: Kross@cofscotland.org.uk

Ross, Rev. Matthew Zachary, LLB, BD, MTh, FSAScot, FFCS. Executive Secretary, Church and Society Commission, Conference of European Churches, since 2003; Church of Scotland Minister, since 1998; b. 15.11.67, Dundee. Educ. Westminster School; Edinburgh University; Glasgow University. Research Assistant, House of Commons, 1990-91; Political Researcher, Scottish Liberal Democrats, 1992-93; Researcher, P.S. Public Affairs Consultants Ltd., Edinburgh, 1993-94; Probationer for the ministry, Duddingston Kirk, Edinburgh, 1996-98; Minister, Ceres and Springfield Parish Church, 1998-2003; Acting Depute Clerk, General Assembly of the Church of Scotland, 2002-03. Secretary, Scottish Church Society, 1999-2004; Member, Board of Practice and Procedure, and of Legal Questions Committee, General Assembly of Church of Scotland; Member, Board of Practice and Procedure, and of Legal Questions Committee, General Assembly, 1999-2003; Convener, World Mission Committee, St Andrews Presbytery, 2000-03; Member,

Policy Committee, Centre for Theology and Public Issues, Edinburgh University, 1996-99; former Secretary, United Nations Association, Edinburgh Branch. Recreations: history; architecture; travel (especially by rail); sharing laughter with friends. Address: (b.) Conference of European Churches, Rue Joseph II 174, B-1000 Brussels, Belgium.

Ross, Michael David, CBE, FFA, CCMI, FRSA. Non-Executive Director, Pearl Group (Chairman of Audit Committee); Member, Finance and Investment Committees, National Trust for Scotland; Chair, Customer Impact Panel, ABI; Non-Executive Director: BIIH Ltd., mform Ltd.; Chief Executive, Scottish Widows, 1991-2003; Deputy Group Chief Executive, Lloyds TSB Group, 2000-03; Former Chairman, Scottish Financial Enterprise; Former Chairman, ABI; b. 9.7.46, Edinburgh; m., Pamela Marquis Speakman. Joined Scottish Widows, 1964, as Trainee Actuary: Assistant General Manager, 1986-88, Appointed Actuary, 1988, General Manager (Finance), 1988-90, Deputy Managing Director, 1990-91. Publication: Transactions of Faculty of Actuaries. Recreations: golf; curling; skiing; gardening. Address: (b.) 69 Morrison Street, Edinburgh.

Ross, Neil Kilgour, MA, LLB. Partner, Grigor & Young, Solicitors, since 1989; b. 17.5.54, Sutton Coldfield; m., Kathleen Rae; 1 d. Educ. Inverurie Academy; Aberdeen University. Legal apprentice, Western Isles Islands Council, 1977-79; Legal Assistant, Angus District Council, 1979-82; Depute Director of Legal Services, Clerk of the Peace and Clerk to the Licensing Board, Western Isles Islands Council, 1982-85. Director, Moray Council on Addictions; Director, Moray Property Searchers Ltd.; contributor, Stair Memorial Encyclopedia; Member, Council, Law Society of Scotland, 1994-2003. Recreations: wine; gardening; cricket. Address: (b.) 1 North Street, Elgin IV30 1UA; T.-01343 544077; e-mail: neil@grigor-young.co.uk

Ross, Nicholas Julian, ARCM. Section Principal Clarinet, Orchestra of Scottish Opera, since 1992; b. 29.1.55, Orsett; divorced; 1 s.; 1 d. Educ. Oakham School; Royal Academy of Music, London. Freelance, two years; joined Scottish Opera as 2nd Clarinet, 1980. Recreation: cycling. Address: (h.) 22 Eskdale Street, Glasgow G42 8UD; T.-0141-423 1262.

Ross, Stuart, LLB, CA. Chief Executive, The Belhaven Group, since 1989; Non-Executive Chairman, Montpeliers (Edinburgh) Ltd., since 1998; Non-Executive Director, Dunfermline Building Society, since 2007; b. 2.7.48, Glasgow; 2 s.; 1 d. Educ. Jordanhill College School; Glasgow University. Managing Director, Belhaven Brewery Co. Ltd., 1980. Past President, Benevolent Licensed Trade of Scotland; Past President, Scottish Beer and Pub Association; Chairman, Scottish Licensed Trade Association. Recreations: skiing; golf; keep-fit; swimming; reading; sports. Address: 6/33 Portland Gardens, Edinburgh EH6 6NJ; T.-01368 869106.

Ross, Thomas Leonard, LLB, DipLP. Advocate, since 2000; b. 25.10.63, Glasgow; m., Alison Mary Laurie; 2 d. Educ. Penilee Secondary, Glasgow; Strathclyde University. Admitted as Solicitor, 1985; Solicitor Advocate, 1998; admitted to Bar, 2000. President, Glasgow Bar Association, 1995; Board Member, Legal Defence Union, 1996-97; Criminal Editor, Scolag, 1994-95. Recreations: Victoria and Rachael Ross; Rangers FC; wine. Address: (h.) 7 Buchlyvie Road, Ralston, Renfrewshire PA1 3AD; T.-0141-581 9375; e-mail: thomasross1@ntlworld.com

Ross, Lt-Col. Sir (Walter Hugh) Malcolm, GCVO 2005, (CVO 1994, KCVO, 1999), OBE (1988), DL (2003), JP (2006), CStJ (2007). Chairman, Westminster Group plc, since 2007; Master of the Household to TRH The Prince of Wales and The Duchess of Cornwall, since 2006; Extra Equerry to HM The Queen, since 1988; HM Lord-Lt Stewartry of Kirkudbright, since 2006; Member, Queen's Body Guard for Scotland, Royal Company of Archers, since 1981; Brigadier, 2003; b. 27.10.43; m., Susan; 2 d.; 1 s. Educ. Eton; RMA Sandhurst. Scots Guards, 1964-87; Management Auditor, The Royal Household, 1987-89; Secretary, Central Chancery of The Orders of Knighthood, 1989-90; Comptroller, Lord Chamberlain's Office, 1991-2006 (Assistant Comptroller, 1987-90). Freeman, City of London, 1994. Address: Netherhall, Bridge-of-Dee, Castle Douglas, Kirkcudbrightshire DG7 2AA.

Ross, William Charles Cameron, DPhil, BTech (Hons), PGCE, MInstP, CPhys. Principal, Orkney College, since 2002; b. 26.1.60, Woking, Surrey; m., Sonia; 3 s. Educ. Winston Churchill School, Woking, Surrey; Universities of Bradford, Leeds, York. Career History: Thornton Upper School, Bradford; Batley High School for Boys; Bradford College; Bournville College, Birmingham. Address: (b.) Orkney College, East Road, Kirkwall, Orkney KW15 1LX; T.-01856 569000; e-mail: bill.ross@orkney.uhi.ac.uk

Ross Stewart, David Andrew, OBE, BA (Cantab). b. 30.11.30, Edinburgh; m., Susan Olive Routh; 2 s. Educ. Rugby School; Cambridge University. Assistant General Manager, Alex. Cowan & Sons (NZ) Ltd., 1959-62; General Manager, Alex. Cowan & Sons (Stationery) Ltd., 1962-66; General Manager, Spicers (Stationery) Ltd., 1966-68; Managing Director, John Bartholomew & Son Ltd., 1968-89. Director, Lothian Investment Fund for Enterprise Ltd.; Hon. Fellow, University of Edinburgh; Fellow, Scottish Council (Development and Industry). Recreations: fishing; gardening. Address: (b.) 13 Blacket Place, Edinburgh EH9 1RN; T.-0131-667 3221.

Rothes, 22nd Earl of (James Malcolm David Leslie); b. 1958. Succeeded to title, 2005.

Rougvie, Alexander, BSc, MA. Director of Continuing Education, University of St. Andrews, since 1991; b. 17.06.47, Kirkcaldy; m., Ann; 1 s.; 3 d. Educ. Kirkcaldy High School; Heriot-Watt University. Various construction management posts in London and SE, 1970-75; Building Manager, 1975; Circle 33 Housing Trust Ltd., 1979-87; Senior, then Principal Lecturer, Polytechnic of Central London, 1987-91; Continuing Education Coordinator, then Director of Continuing Education, University of St. Andrews. Various Housing Association Committee Memberships, 1984-2004; currently Member, SUALL and Scottish Consortium for Learning Disability. Publication: "Project Evaluation and Development", 1987. Recreations: gliding; music; travel; DIY; constructive idleness. Address: (b.) St. Katharine's West, The Scores, St. Andrews KY16 9AX.

Rowallan, Lord (John Polson Cameron), ARICS. Director, Rowallan Holdings Ltd., Rowallan Activity Centre Ltd., Rowallan Asset Management; Chairman, Lochgoin Covenanters Trust; b. 8.3.47, Glasgow; m., Claire; 2 s.; 2 d; 1 steps.; 1 stepd. Educ. Eton College; Royal Agricultural College. Estate Agent, since 1969; Farmer, since 1974; Company Director, since 1989; Commentator, since 1986; Patron, Depression Alliance. Recreations: skiing; equestrianism. Address: (h.) Meiklemosside, Fenwick, Ayrshire KA3 6AY.

Rowley, Professor David Ian, MB, ChB, BMedBiol, MD, FRCS. Professor of Orthopaedic and Trauma Surgery, Dundee University, since 1988; Director of Education, Royal College of Surgeons of Edinburgh; Visiting Professor of Surgical Education, University of Edinburgh; b. 4.7.51, Dewsbury; m., Ingrid Ginette; 1 s.; 1 d. Educ. Wheelwright Grammar School, Dewsbury; Aberdeen University; Sheffield University. Lecturer in Orthopaedic Surgery, Sheffield University, 1981; Senior Lecturer in Orthopaedic Surgery, Manchester University, and Senior Lecturer in Orthopaedic Mechanics, Salford University, 1985-88. Orthopaedic Editor, Journal of Royal College of Surgeons of Edinburgh, 1993-98; Member, Council, RCSEd, 2003-08; Regional Advisor in Surgery, NE Region, Royal College of Surgeons of Edinburgh; Examiner, Royal College of Surgeons, Edinburgh; Fellow, Royal Colleges, Glasgow, England, ad eundum; Intercollegiate Board Examiner, Orthopaedics; Non-Executive Member, NHS Tayside. Recreations: gardening; reading history. Address: (h.) Marclann Cottage, Kellie Castle, Arbroath; T.-01241 876466.

Rowling, Joanne Kathleen (J.K.), OBE, BA. Writer; b. 31.7.65; m.; 1 s.; 1 d. Educ. Exeter University. Publications: Harry Potter and the Philosopher's Stone, 1997; Harry Potter and the Chamber of Secrets, 1998; Harry Potter and the Prisoner of Azkaban, 1999; Harry Potter and the Goblet of Fire, 2000; Harry Potter and the Order of the Phoenix, 2003; Harry Potter and the Half-Blood Prince, 2005; Harry Potter and the Deathly Hallows, 2007. Address: Christopher Little Literary Agency, Eel Brook Studios, 125 Moore Park Road, London SW6 4PS.

Rowlings, Professor Cherry, BA. Professor of Social Work, Stirling University, since 1991; Member, Scottish Social Services Council, 2001-07; b. 10.11.44, Bristol. Educ. Duncan House School, Bristol; York University; Oxford University. Social Worker, London Borough of Croydon; Team Leader, London Borough of Lewisham; Research Officer, Oxford University; Senior Research Fellow, Keele University; Lecturer/Senior Lecturer, Bristol University. Member, CCETSW Council and Scottish Committee, 1992-2001; Non-Executive Director, Forth Valley Primary Care NHS Trust, 1998-2001. Publications: on social work and services for older people and on social work education in Europe. Address: (b.) Department of Applied Social Science, Stirling University, Stirling FK9 4LA; T.-01786 467710.

Rowlinson, Professor Peter, MA, DPhil. Emeritus Professor of Mathematics, University of Stirling, since 2006; b. 23.10.44, Cambridge; m., Carolyn. Educ. Cambridgeshire High School; New College, Oxford. University of Stirling: Lecturer in Mathematics, 1969-92, Senior Lecturer in Mathematics, 1992-94, Reader in Mathematics, 1994-96, Professor of Mathematics, 1996-2006. Visiting Associate Professor of Mathematics, California Institute of Technology, 1975-76; President, Edinburgh Mathematical Society, 2003-05. Publications: Eigenspaces of Graphs (Co-author), 1997; Spectral Generalizations of Line Graphs (Co-author), 2004; journal articles. Address: Department of Computing Science and Mathematics, University of Stirling, Stirling FK9 4LA; T.-01786 467468.

Roxburghe, 10th Duke of (Guy David Innes-Ker), b. 18.11.54; m., 1, Lady Jane Meriel Grosvenor (m. diss.); 2 s.; 1 d.; 2, Virginia Mary Wynn-Williams; 1 s.; 1 d. Educ. Eton; Sandhurst; Magdalene College, Cambridge. Address: (h.) Floors Castle, Kelso.

Roy, Frank, BA. MP (Labour), Motherwell and Wishaw, since 1997; b. 29.8.58, Motherwell; m., Ellen Foy; 1 s.; 1 d. Educ. St Joseph's High School, Motherwell; Our Lady's High School, Motherwell; Motherwell College; Glasgow Caledonian University.

Ravenscraig steelworker, 1977-91; PPS to Helen Liddell, Deputy Secretary of State for Scotland, 1998-99; PPS to Dr John Reid, MP, Secretary of State for Scotland, 1999-2001; PPS to Helen Liddell, Secretary of State for Scotland, 2001; Government Whip, since 2005. Address: (b.) House of Commons, London SW1A 0AA; T.-0171-219 3000; e-mail: Royf@parliament.uk

Roy, Kenneth. Editor, The Scottish Review, since 1995; Director, Institute of Contemporary Scotland, since 2000; Director, Young Scotland Programme, since 2002, and Young United Kingdom Programme, since 2003; b. 26.3.45, Falkirk; m., Margaret; 2 s. Journalism and occasional publishing, 1962-72; broadcasting, 1972-82; publishing and occasional journalism, 1983-2003; Founder and Publisher, Who's Who in Scotland, 1985-2005. Critic of the Year, Scottish Press Awards, 1990, 1993; Columnist of the Year, British Press Awards, 1994; Past President, Auchinleck Boswell Society; Oliver Brown Award, 2002. Publications include: Travels in a Small Country, 1987; Conversations in a Small Country, 1989; The Closing Headlines (autobiography), 1993. Address: (b.) 66 John Finnie Street, Kilmarnock KA1 1BS; T.-01563 530830.

Roy, Lindsay Allan, CBE, BSc, FRSA. Headteacher, Kirkcaldy High School, since 2007; Rector, Inverkeithing High School, 1989-2007; b. 19.1.49, Perth; m., Irene Elizabeth Patterson; 2 s.; 1 d. Educ. Perth Academy; Edinburgh University. Assistant Rector, Kirkcaldy High School, 1983-86; Depute Rector, Glenwood High School, Glenrothes, 1986-89; Chairman, Modern Studies Association, 1976-79; Chairman, Modern Studies Panel, Scottish Examination Board, 1980-83; Member, Consultative Committee on the Curriculum Central Committee for Social Subjects, 1978-85; Chairman, Higher Still Group Awards Steering Committee, 1996-98; Member, Board of Management, Lauder College, 1998-2006 (Chairman of its Curriculum and Student Affairs Committee); past President, Headteachers' Association of Scotland; Associate Assessor, HMI Inspection of Schools, since 1997; Member, Scottish Credit and Qualifications Framework Joint Advisory Committee, since 2002; Member, National Qualifications Steering Group, since 2003. Recreation: angling. Address: (b.) Dunnikier Way, Kirkcaldy KY1 3LR; T.-01592-583-405.

Royan, Professor Bruce, BA (Hons), MBA, MBCS, FCLIP, FCMI, FRSA, FSA(Scot). Chief Executive, Concurrent Computing Ltd., since 2002; Visiting Professor, School of Creative Industries, Napier University, since 1997; b. 22.1.47, Luton; m., Ann Elizabeth Wilkins; 1 s.; 1 d. Educ. Dunstable Grammar School; North West Polytechnic; Glasgow University. Systems Development Manager, British Library, 1975-77; Head of Systems, National Library of Scotland, 1977-85; Director, Singapore Integrated Library Automation Service, 1985-88; Principal Consultant, Infologistix Ltd., 1988-98; Director of Information Services and University Librarian, Stirling University, 1989-96; Chief Executive, Scottish Cultural Resources Access Network, 1996-2002; Interim Director of Knowledge and Information, The Robert Gordon University, 2004-05. Secretary, Working Party on Access to the National Database, 1980-83; Member, Council, Library Association of Singapore, 1987-88; Convenor, Higher Education IT Directors in Scotland, 1991-93; Executive Chairman, Bath Information and Data Services, 1991-96; Councillor, The Library Association, 1994-99; Chair, National Datasets Steering Group, 1994-96; Board Member, Croydon Libraries Internet Project, 1995-96; Chair, Scottish Collaborative On Demand Publishing Enterprise, 1996-98; Councillor, Institute of Information Scientists, 1997-99; Member, Content Creation Task Group, New Opportunities Fund, 1998; Member, National Grid for Learning Scottish

Steering Group, 1998-2003; Chair, UK Metadata for Education Group, 2000-04; Chair, British Council Library and Information Advisory Committee, 2001-03; Member, Culture Online Steering Committee, 2001-03; Director, Virtual Hamilton Palace Trust, since 2003; Councillor, Chartered Institute of Library and Information Professionals, since 2006. Recreations: antique maps; travel. Address: (b.) Concurrent Computing Ltd., Bowmont Tower, Greenhill Gardens, Edinburgh EH10 4BL; e-mail: bruce.royan@concurrentcomputing.co.uk

Royle, Trevor Bridge, MA, FRSE. Author and Journalist; Associate Editor, Sunday Herald; b. 26.1.45, Mysore, India; m., Dr. Hannah Mary Rathbone; 3 s. Educ. Madras College, St. Andrews; Aberdeen University. Editor, William Blackwood & Sons Ltd.; Literature Director, Scottish Arts Council, 1971-79. Publications: We'll Support You Evermore: The Impertinent Saga of Scottish Fitba' (Co-Editor), 1976; Jock Tamson's Bairns (Editor), 1977; Precipitous City: The Story of Literary Edinburgh, 1980; A Diary of Edinburgh, 1981; Edinburgh, 1982; Death Before Dishonour: The True Story of Fighting Mac, 1982; The Macmillan Companion to Scottish Literature, 1983; James and Jim: The Biography of James Kennaway, 1983; The Kitchener Enigma, 1985; The Best Years of their Lives: The Post-War National Service Experience, 1986; War Report: The War Correspondents' View of Battle from the Crimea to the Falklands, 1987; The Last Days of the Raj, 1989; A Dictionary of Military Quotations, 1989; Anatomy of a Regiment, 1990; In Flanders Fields: Scottish poetry and prose of the First World War, 1990; Glubb Pasha, 1992; Mainstream Companion to Scottish Literature, 1993; Orde Wingate: Irregular Soldier, 1995; Winds of Change, 1996; Scottish War Stories (Editor), 1999; Crimea – The Great Crimean War, 1854–56, 1999; Civil War: the wars of the three kingdoms 1638-1660, 2004; Patton: Old Blood and Guts, 2005; The Flowers Of The Forest: Scotland And The First World War, 2006; The Royal Scots: A Concise History, 2006; The Black Watch: A Concise History, 2006; The Gordon Highlanders: A Concise History, 2007; The Royal Highland Fusilier: A Concise History, 2007; Queen's Own Highlanders: A Concise History, 2007; radio plays: Magnificat, 1984; Old Alliances, 1985; Foreigners, 1987; Huntingtower, 1988; A Man Flourishing, 1988; The Pavilion on the Links, 1991; The Suicide Club, 1992; Tunes of Glory, 1995; stage play: Buchan of Tweedsmuir, 1991. Recreations: watching rugby football; hill-walking. Address: (h.) 6 James Street, Edinburgh EH15 2DS; T.-0131 669 2116.

Ruckley, Professor Charles Vaughan, CBE, MB, ChM, FRCSEdin, FRCPEdin. Emeritus Professor of Vascular Surgery, Edinburgh University; former Consultant Surgeon, Royal Infirmary, Edinburgh; b. 14.5.34, Wallasey; m., Valerie Anne Brooks; 1 s.; 1 d. Educ. Wallasey Grammar School; Edinburgh University. Research Fellow, University of Colorado, 1967-68. Vascular Surgical Society, Great Britain and Ireland: President, 1993-94, Secretary/Treasurer; Chairman, Venous Forum, Royal Society of Medicine, 1997-99; Member, Association of Surgeons of Great Britain and Ireland. Recreations: angling; music; skiing. Address: (b.) 1 Mayfield Terrace, Edinburgh EH9 1RU; T.-0131-667 8678.

Rumbles, Michael John, MSc (Econ), BEd. MSP (Liberal Democrat), West Aberdeenshire and Kincardine, since 1999; b. 10.6.56, South Shields; m., Pauline; 2 s. Educ. St James' School, Hebburn; Durham University; University of Wales. Army Officer, 1979-94; Team Leader, Business Management, Aberdeen College, 1995-99. Convener, Standards Committee, Scottish Parliament, 1999-2003; Liberal Democrat Rural Affairs and Environment Spokesperson, since 2007. Address:

(b.) The Scottish Parliament, Edinburgh EH99 1SP; T.-0131-348 5798.

Rummery, Professor Kirstein, LLB (Hons), MA, PhD. Professor of Social Policy, University of Stirling, since 2007; b. 12.06.70, London; m., Simon Lippmann; 2 s.; 1 d. Educ. Vienna International School; University of Kent; University of Birmingham. Research Fellow in Social Policy, University of Birmingham, 1992-95; Research Fellow, NPCRDC, University of Manchester, 1995-2002, Lecturer in Social Policy, 2002-05, Senior Lecturer, 2005-07. Member, The Social Policy Association Executive Committee; Member of Board of Directors of Engender. Publications: Author of 'Disability, Citizenship and Community Care', 2002; Co-editor, 'Partnerships, New Labour and the Governance of Welfare', 2002; Co-editor, 'Women And New Labour', 2007; Co-editor, Local Policy Review. Recreations: choral singing; cycling; cooking. Address: (b.) Department of Applied Social Sciences, Colin Bell Building, University of Stirling FK9 4LA; T.-01786-467693; e-mail: kirstein.rummery@stir.ac.uk

Rundell, David Richard, BSc, MSc, FBCS, CEng, CStat, CITP. Director of University Information and Computing Services, Heriot-Watt University, since 1990; b. 5.9.48, Plymouth; divorced; 3 d.; 1 step-d. Educ. Harwich County High, Harwich, Essex; St. Andrews University; Heriot-Watt University. Statistician, Medical School, Edinburgh University, 1970-76; Applications Team, Regional Computing Centre, University of Bath, 1976-79; User Services Manager, Computer Centre, Heriot-Watt University, 1979-90. Address: (b.) Computer Centre, Heriot-Watt University, Riccarton, Edinburgh EH14 4AS; T.-0131-449 5111.

Rush, Christopher, MA (Hons). Writer; b. 23.11.44, St. Monans; m., Patricia Irene Boyd (deceased); 1 s.; 1 d.; re-married Anna Kurkina; 1 d. Educ. Waid Academy; Aberdeen University. Former Teacher, George Watson's College, Edinburgh. Has won four Scottish Arts Council bursaries, two SAC book awards, twice been short-listed for Scottish Book of the Year Award; shortlisted for McVitie Scottish Writer of the Year, 1988; Screenwriter, Venus Peter (based on own book). Publications include: Peace Comes Dropping Slow; A Resurrection of a Kind; A Twelvemonth and A Day; Two Christmas Stories; Into the Ebb; With Sharp Compassion; Venus Peter Saves the Whale; Last Lesson of the Afternoon; To Travel Hopefully: Journal of a Death Not Foretold; Hellfire and Herring; Will. Recreations: music; reading; running; the sea. Address: (h.) East Cottage, Newton of Wormiston, Crail, Fife KY10 3XH; T.-01333 451229.

Russell, Alan, Chief Executive, Fife Chamber of Commerce, since 2006; b. 16.3.52, Uddingston; m., Anne; 1 s.; 1 d. Educ. St. John's Grammar, Hamilton; Hamilton Academy; Coatbridge Technical College; Bell College; Stow College. Technical Apprenticeship with Honeywell in Newhouse, 1968; became a Production Engineer before moving to Sunbeam Electric in East Kilbride; Management Services Officer, Strathclyde Regional Council (1975); moved into Economic Development and managed the successful Employment Grants Scheme; held Senior Economic Development Management positions with Fife Regional Council and Fife Council until 2004; worked with Lloyds TSB for 15 months until December 2005. Chairman of Fife Export Club, 1990-96. Recreations: golf; reading (detective stories). Address: (b.) Wemyssfield House, Wemyssfield, Kirkcaldy, Fife KY1 1XN; T.-01592 201932; e-mail: alanrussell@fifechamber.co.uk

Russell, Sir (Alastair) Muir, KCB (2001), DL, FRSE, FInstP. Principal and Vice-Chancellor, University of Glasgow, since 2003; b. 9.1.49; m., Eileen Alison Mackay. Educ. High School of Glasgow; Glasgow University (BSc NatPhil). Joined Scottish Office, 1970; seconded as Secretary to Scottish Development Agency, 1975-76; Assistant Secretary, 1981; Principal Private Secretary to Secretary of State for Scotland, 1981-83; Under Secretary, 1990; seconded to Cabinet Office, 1990-92; Under Secretary (Housing), Scottish Office Environment Department, 1992-95; Deputy Secretary, 1995, Secretary and Head of Department, Scottish Office Agriculture, Environment and Fisheries Department, 1995-98; Permanent Under-Secretary of State, Scottish Office, 1998-99; Permanent Secretary, Scottish Executive, 1999-2003. Non-Executive Director, Stagecoach Holdings, 1992-95. Council Member, Edinburgh Festival Society, 2004. Director, UCAS, since 2005; Council Member, ACU, March 2006; Convener, Universities Scotland, 2006-08; Trustee, USS (Oct. 2007). FRSE, 2000; FInstP, 2003; DL, 2004; CCMI (CIMgt, 2001); Hon. LLD, Strathclyde, 2000; DUniv, Glasgow, 2001; Hon FRCPS (Glasg), 2005. Freeman, City of London 2006. Recreations: music; food; wine. Clubs: Royal Commonwealth Society, Caledonian, New (Edinburgh). Address: (b.) University of Glasgow, Glasgow G12 8QQ; T.-0141 330 5995, 4250.

Russell, Sheriff Albert Muir Galloway, CBE, QC, BA (Oxon), LLB. Sheriff, Grampian, Highland and Islands, at Aberdeen, 1971-91; b. 26.10.25, Edinburgh; m., Margaret Winifred Millar; 2 s.; 2 d. Educ. Edinburgh Academy; Wellington College; Brasenose College, Oxford; Edinburgh University. Lt., Scots Guards, 1944-47; Member, Faculty of Advocates, 1951; Standing Junior Counsel to Board of Trade, Department of Agriculture and Forestry Commission; QC (Scot), 1965; Vice Chairman, Board of Management, Southern Group of Hospitals, Edinburgh, 1966-70; Governor, Moray House College of Education, 1965-70. Recreations: golf; music. Address: (h.) Tulloch House, 1 Aultbea, Ross-shire IV22 2JB.

Russell, Emeritus Professor Elizabeth Mary, CBE, MD, DSc, DipSocMed, DObstRCOG, FFCM, FRCPGlas, FRCPEdin, MRCGP, FRSE. Emeritus Professor of Social Medicine, Aberdeen University; Hon. Consultant in Public Health Medicine, 1972-2001; b. 27.1.36, Preston. Educ. Marr College, Troon; Glasgow University. General practice until 1964; medical management and social medicine, 1964-72; academic public health and health services research, since 1972. Recreations: gardening; music; woodwork. Address: (b.) Kilburn, Inchgarth Road, Pitfodels, Aberdeen AB15 9NX; T.-01224 861216; e-mail: e.m.russell@abdn.ac.uk

Russell, Ian Gordon, BEd, PhD. Director, Elphinstone Institute, Aberdeen University, since 1999; b. 17.2.47, Aberdeen; m., Norma; 1 s. Educ. King's School, Ely; Nottingham High School; Sheffield City College of Education; Leeds University. Headteacher, Anston Greenlands School, Rotherham, 1986-99; fieldwork in folklore and ethnology, since 1969; broadcast, made films, lectured, in UK and USA; created archive of Village Carols; published widely on traditional singing, humour, and Christmas carols; Director, Village Carols; Director, Festival of Village Carols; Editor, Folk Music Journal, 1980-93; Director, North Atlantic Fiddle Convention. Recreations: singing and playing folk music; walking; Morris dancing; travel. Address: (b.) Elphinstone Institute, Aberdeen University, MacRobert Building, King's College, Aberdeen AB24 5UA; T.-01224 272386.

Russell, Rev. John, MA. Minister, Tillicoultry Parish Church, 1978-2000; b. 29.5.33, Glasgow; m., Sheila Spence; 2 s. Educ. Cathedral School, Bombay; High School of Glasgow; Glasgow University. Licensed by Glasgow Presbytery, 1957; ordained by United Church of Canada,

1959; Assistant Minister: Trinity United Church, Kitchener, Ontario, 1958-60, South Dalziel Church, Motherwell, 1960-62; Minister: Scots Church, Rotterdam, 1963-72, Southend Parish Church, Kintyre, 1972-78; Member of various General Assembly Committees, since 1972; Convener, General Assembly's Committee on Unions and Readjustments, 1987-90; Convener, Parish Reappraisal Committee, 1990-94; Vice Convener, Board of National Mission, 1994-95; Convener, Board of National Mission, 1995-96; Moderator, Presbytery of Stirling, 1993-94; Clerk, Presbytery of Dunkeld and Meigle, 2001. Recreations: travel; reading. Address: Kilblaan, Gladstone Terrace, Birnam, Dunkeld PH8 0DP; T.-01350 728896.

Russell, John Graham, FCIT. Chairman: John G. Russell (Transport) Ltd., since 1969, Fife Warehousing Ltd., since 1988, Ice Tech Freezers Ltd., since 2005, Carntyne Transport Co. Ltd., since 1970; Director: Freight Transport Association, since 1994, Alloa Warehousing, since 1988, Sutherland Professional Funding Ltd., since 2003, CBI Scotland Council; b. Edinburgh; m., Isobel Margaret Hogg; 2 s.; 2 d. Educ. Merchiston Castle School, Edinburgh. Address: (b.) Deanside Road, Hillington, Glasgow G52 4XB; T.-0141 810 8215.
E-mail: john.russell@johngrussell.co.uk

Russell, Laurie James, BSc, MPhil. Chief Executive, The Wise Group, since 2006; b. 8.8.51, Glasgow; m., Pam; 2 s. Educ. Glasgow University. Researcher, Planning Department, Strathclyde Regional Council, 1976-78; Area Co-ordinator, Faifley Initiative, Clydebank, 1978-84; Executive, Chief Executive's Department, Strathclyde Regional Council, 1984-87; PA to Chief Executive, Strathclyde Regional Council, 1987-89; Chief Executive, Strathclyde European Partnership, 1989-2006. Recreations: politics; European issues; music; golf. Address: (b.) The Wise Group, 72 Charlotte Street, Glasgow G1 5DW; T.-0141 314 1461.

Russell, Michael, MA, FRSA. MSP (SNP), South of Scotland, since 2007 (previously 1999-2003); Minister for Environment, since 2007; b. 9.8.53, Bromley; m. Cathleen Macaskill; 1 s. Educ. Marr College, Troon; Edinburgh University. Creative Producer, Church of Scotland, 1974-77; Director: Cinema Seire, Comhairle Nan Eilean, 1977-81, Celtic Film and TV Festival, 1981-83; Executive Director, Network Scotland Ltd., 1983-91; Director, Eiala Bhan Ltd., since 1991; Chief Executive, SNP, 1994-99. Active in various voluntary and arts bodies. Publications: author of 7 books, including 'The Next Big Thing', 2007. Recreations: cooking; tending my argyll garden. Address: (h.) Feorlan, Glendaruel, Argyll PA22 3AH; e-mail: feorlean@madasafish.com

Russell, Professor Ric William Lockerby, OBE, DA, ARSA, ARIDA, ARIAS, Architect, since 1970; Senior Partner, Nicoll Russell Studios, since 1982; b 12,8,47, Stockton-on-Tees; m., Irene Hill; 1 s.; 3 d. Educ. Dundee High School; Duncan of Jordanstone College of Art; University of Dundee. Robbie and Wellwood Architects (Partner, 1977); co-founded Nicoll Russell, 1982; architect and designer responsible for major civic buildings and civil engineering structures throughout Britain; has lectured and tutored at many universities throughout career. Commissioner, Royal Fine Arts Commission for Scotland, 1998-2004; Advisory Board Member, Architecture and Design Scotland, since 2004; Member, Student Awards Committee, Royal Incorporation of Architects in Scotland; Member, Housing Awards Panel, Saltire Society, since 2000; has received seven Royal Institute of British Architects awards and five Civic Trust awards. Recreations: drawing; music; DIY. Address: (b.) Nicoll Russell Studios,

111 King Street, Broughty Ferry, Dundee; T.-01382 778966; e-mail: ric@nrsarchitects.com

Russell, Shendl, DCE. President, Scottish Official Board of Highland Dancing; Head Teacher; b. 29.3.56, Ayr; m., Robert D. Harvey. Educ. Ayr Academy; Craigie College. Scottish Official Board of Highland Dancing. Delegate, South Africa, Australia; former Scottish champion. Recreations: dancing; football; rugby. Address: (h.) 3 Greenside Avenue, Prestwick KA9 2HB; T.-01292 478577.

Russell, Professor William Clelland, BSc, PhD, FRSE. Professor of Biochemistry, University of St. Andrews, 1984-95, now Emeritus Research Professor; b. 9.8.30, Glasgow; m. 1, Dorothy Ada Brown (deceased); 2, Margaret McDougall; 1 s.; 1 d. Educ. Allan Glens' School, Glasgow; University of Glasgow. Chemist, Royal Ordnance Factories, 1955-56; Research Chemist, J&P Coats, Paisley, 1956-59; Research Fellow: Virology Unit, University of Glasgow, 1959-63, Ontario Cancer Institute, Toronto, Canada, 1963-64; staff member, latterly Head of Virology Division, MRC at National Institute for Medical Research, London, 1964-84. Member: MRC Grants Committee, SHHD Biomedical Committee; Chair, Scientists for Labour, 1995-2005. Publications: over 140 scientific papers. Recreations: walking; music. Address: (h.) 84 Bow Butts, Crail, Anstruther KY10 3UT; T.-01333 450614; e-mail: wcr@st-andrews.ac.uk

Russell-Johnston, Lord (Russell Russell-Johnston), MA (Hons). MP (Liberal Democrat), Inverness, Nairn and Lochaber (formerly Inverness), 1964-97; b. 28.7.32, Edinburgh; m., Joan Graham Menzies; 3 s. Educ. Carbost Public School; Portree High School; Edinburgh University; Moray House College of Education. National Service: commissioned into Intelligence Corps and 2nd i/c British Intelligence Unit, Berlin, 1958-59; History Teacher, Liberton Secondary School, Edinburgh, 1961-63; Research Assistant, Scottish Liberal Party, 1963-64; Joint Parliamentary Adviser, Educational Institute of Scotland, 1964-70; Member, Royal Commission on Local Government in Scotland, 1966-69; Parliamentary Spokesman for Scottish National Federation for the Welfare of the Blind, 1967-97; Parliamentary Representative, Royal National Institute for the Blind, 1977-97; Member, Select Committee on Scottish Affairs, 1969; Parliamentary Adviser, Scottish Police Federation, 1971-75; Scottish Liberal Party: elected to Executive, 1961, and Organisation Committee, 1962, Vice Chairman, 1965, Chairman, 1970-74, Leader, 1974-88, President, 1988-94; Liberal Party Spokesman on Education, 1964-66, on Foreign Affairs, 1970-75 and 1979-85, on Scotland, 1970-73, 1975-83, 1985-88, on Devolution, 1975, on Defence, 1983-88; Member, House of Commons Committee on Privileges, 1988-92; Liberal Democrat Parliamentary Spokesman, Foreign and Commonwealth Affairs, 1988-89, European Affairs, 1988-94, East/West Relations, 1989-94, Central and Eastern Europe, 1994-97; Leader, Council of Europe Liberal Democrat and Reform Group, 1994-99 (Hon. President, Liberal Group, since 2002); President, Council of Europe Sub Committee on Youth and Sport, 1992-94; President, WEU Committee on Parliamentary and Public Relations, since 1995 (Vice President, since 2002); Chairman, Council of Europe Committee on Culture and Education, 1996-99; President, Parliamentary Assembly of the Council of Europe, 1999-2002; Vice President, Liberal International, since 1994; Member, European Parliament, 1973-75 and 1976-79; Vice President, European Liberal Group and Group Spokesman on Regional Policy, 1973-75; Vice President of the Parliament's Political Committee, 1976-79; Member, Assemblies of Western European Union and Council of Europe, 1984-85, and since 1987; President, Scottish Liberal Democrats, 1988-94; Deputy Leader,

Parliamentary Party, 1988-92; Vice President, ELDR, 1990-92. Created Knight Bachelor, 1985; Created Lord Russell-Johnston of Minginish in Highland, 1997. Address: House of Lords, London, SW1A 0PW.

Rust, James Hamilton, LLB, WS, NP. Partner, Morton Fraser Solicitors, since 1985; b. 22.7.58, Aberdeen; m., Janet Anne Ruddiman; 1 s.; 1 d. Educ. Aberdeen Grammar School; Loretto School; Aberdeen University. Legal Apprentice and Assistant, Esslemont & Cameron, Aberdeen, 1979-82; Legal Assistant, Morton Fraser Solicitors, 1982-85; Collector, Society of Writers to Her Majesty's Signet. Joint Session Clerk, Wardie Parish Church. Recreations: running; theatre; Scottish Country Dancing; outdoor pursuits. Address: (b.) 30-31 Queen Street, Edinburgh EH2 1JX; T.-0131-247-1013; e-mail: james.rust@morton-fraser.com

Rutherford, Henry Roan, PhD, MSc, BArch, RIBA, FRIAS, MRTPI. Director, Wren Rutherford Austin Smith Lord, since 1997; b. 30.11.46, Dunfermline; m., Alison Moira Peebles; 1 s.; 1 d. Educ. Bell Baxter High School, Cupar; Heriot-Watt University; University of Edinburgh; University of Glasgow. Irvine New Town Corporation: Conservation Officer, 1972, Architect, Housing Group, 1974, Principal Architect (Housing), 1978; Partner, Wren Rutherford Architects, 1997. Awarded Joint Best Architect in Scotland, 1996; three Civic Trust Awards; four Saltire Society Awards; four RIBA Awards Scotland, four RIAS Awards. Recreations: sailing; hillwalking. Address: (b.) 296 St Vincent Street, Glasgow G2 5RU; T.-0141 223 8500.

Rutherford, John Alexander, BCom, FCA. Chief Executive, Sea Fish Industry Authority, since 2002; b. 5.12.48, Sunderland; m., Judith Ann; 3 s. Educ. Fettes College, Edinburgh; Birmingham University. Career History: Cooper Bros & Co.; Procter & Gamble plc; West of England Farmers Ltd.; WMF Ltd.; Countrywide Farmers Ltd. Hon. Treasurer, Abbeyfields, Biggar. Recreations: Morgan Sports Car Club; the countryside. Address: (b.) Wyndales Cottage, Symington, Biggar ML12 6JU; T.-01899 308294; e-mail: jarutherford@btinternet.com

Rutherford, William Hay, MA, LLB. Advocate in Aberdeen, since 1949; Honorary Sheriff, Grampian, Highland and Islands, since 1974; b. 9.11.16, Forres; m., Dr. Jean Aitken Steel Wilson; 1 s.; 2 d. Educ. Forres Academy; Aberdeen University. Law Apprentice, James & George Collie, Advocates, Aberdeen, 1936-39; 51st Highland Division, Royal Signals, 1939-46 (taken prisoner, St. Valery, France, 1940; held prisoner, Stalag VIIIB, Upper Silesia, 1940-45); Legal Assistant, John Angus, Advocate, Aberdeen, 1946-61; Partner, Christie, Buthlay & Rutherford, Advocates, Aberdeen, 1962-78, Raeburn Christie & Co., 1978-87. President, Society of Advocates, Aberdeen, 1985-86; Session Clerk, Kirk of St. Nicholas (City Kirk of Aberdeen), 1954-97; President, Royal Northern Agricultural Society, 1980; Chairman (part-time), Industrial Tribunals (Scotland), 1981-88; holder of British Horse Society 1994 Horse Trials Award for outstanding service to the sport. Recreations: country walking and wildlife study. Address: 43 Thorngrove House, 500 Great Western Road, Mannofield, Aberdeen AB10 6PF; T.-01224 322657.

Ryan, Jack, DipComEd. Chief Executive, Crossroads Caring Scotland, since 1997; b. 9.6.61, Hamilton; m., Janine Barbour; 2 s. Educ. Hamilton Grammar School; Moray House, Edinburgh. Draughtsman, 1978-81; professional musician, 1981-83; Community Musician, Strathclyde Regional Council, 1983-88; Senior Development Officer, Govan Initiative Ltd., 1990-91; Project Manager, CAVOC Motherwell, 1991-92; Director, Govan Community Organisations Council, 1992-96; Lottery Officer, South Lanarkshire Council, 1997. Recreations: musician; computer programming; running/swimming; youth rugby coach. Address: (b.) 24 George Square, Glasgow; T.-0141-226 3793.

Ryan, Professor Kevin Martin, BSc (Hons), PhD. Professor, Faculty of Medicine, University of Glasgow, since 2007; Senior Group Leader, Beatson Institute for Cancer Research, Glasgow, since 2007; b. 14.06.70, Stoke-on-Trent; m., Justine Nicola Parrott; 2 s. Educ. Biddulph High School, Staffordshire; University of Liverpool; University of Glasgow. Pre-Doctoral Fellow, Beatson Institute for Cancer Research, 1995-96; Post-Doctoral Fellow, United States National Cancer Institute, Maryland, USA, 1996-2001; Group Leader and Head, Tumour Cell Death Laboratory, Beatson Institute for Cancer Research, 2001-07. Fellowships and Awards: Cancer Research UK Senior Fellow, since 2002; European Association for Cancer Research - Certificate of Merit, 2002. Recreations: swimming; hill-walking; travel; watching Liverpool FC and arguing about science in the bar. Address: (b.) Beatson Institute for Cancer Research, Garscube Estate, Switchback Road, Glasgow G61 1BD; T.-0141 330 3655; e-mail: k.ryan@beatson.gla.ac.uk

Rycroft, Philip John, BA (Hons), DPhil. Director-General Education, Scottish Government, since 2007, Head of Enterprise, Transport and Lifelong Learning Department, 2006-07; b. 22.5.61, Skipton; m., Kate; 2 s. Educ. Leys School, Cambridge; Wadham College, Oxford. Scottish Office, 1989-94 (Agriculture Department - Research Division; Private Secretary to Agriculture & Fisheries Minister; Head - European Central Support Unit; Head - Sea Fisheries Policy Branch); European Commission, 1995-96: Cabinet of Sir Leon Brittan, Vice President of The European Commission; Scottish Office, 1997-98: Head of Division - Agriculture, Environment & Fisheries Department (Agriculture and Rural Policy); Scottish Executive, 1999-2000: Deputy Head of Policy Unit; Scottish & Newcastle plc, 2001-02: Public Affairs Manager; Scottish Executive, 2003-05: Head of Schools Group. Recreation: triathlon. Address: (b.) Meridan Court, Cadogan Street, Glasgow.

Ryder, Jane, MA. Chief Executive, Office of the Scottish Charity Regulator (OSCR), since 2006. Educ. St. Andrews University. Qualified as a solicitor in both England and Scotland and for 11 years was a partner in a commercial firm in Edinburgh; became Director of the Scottish Museums Council, 1995; appointed by Scottish Ministers in 2003 to establish the Office of the Scottish Charity Regulator (OSCR). Author of various articles and the textbook Professional Conduct for Scottish Solicitors. Address: (b.) OSCR, 2nd Floor, Quadrant House, 9 Riverside Drive, Dundee DD1 4NY.

S

Salmon, Professor Trevor C., MA (Hons), MLitt, PhD, FRSA. Chair of International Relations and Jean Monnet Chair of European Integration, Aberdeen University, since 1996; Professor, College of Europe, since 1995; b. 7.9.48, Cambridge; m., June Veronica Miller; 1 d. Educ. Soham Grammar School; Aberdeen University; St. Andrews University. Lecturer, National Institute for Higher Education, Limerick, 1973-78; Lecturer in International Relations, then Senior Lecturer, St. Andrews University, 1978-90; Jean Monnet Professor of European Integration, St. Andrews University, 1990-95. Elder, Church of Scotland. Publications: Building European Union (Co-author); Understanding the European Union (Co-author); Issues in International Relations; Towards a European Army. Address: (b.) Department of Politics and International Relations, Edward Wright Building, Aberdeen University, Aberdeen AB24 3QY; T.-01224 272080; e-mail: t.c.salmon@abdn.ac.uk

Salmond, Alexander Elliot Anderson, MA (Hons). Economist; MSP (SNP), Gordon, since 2007; First Minister of Scotland, since 2007; MP (SNP), Banff and Buchan, since 1987; Leader, Scottish National Party, 1990-2000 and since 2004; MSP (SNP), Banff and Buchan, 1999-2001; b. 31.12.54, Linlithgow; m., Moira McGlashan. Educ. Linlithgow Academy; St. Andrews University. Vice-President; Federation of Student Nationalists, 1974-77, St. Andrews University SRC, 1977-78; Founder Member, SNP 79 Group, 1979; Assistant Agricultural and Fisheries Economist, DAFS, 1978-80; Economist, Royal Bank of Scotland, 1980-87. Hon. Vice-President, Scottish Centre for Economic and Social Research; former Member, Select Committee on Energy. Address: (b.) 84 North Street, Inverurie, Aberdeenshire AB51 4QX; T.-01467 670070; Scottish Parliament, Edinburgh EH99 1SP.

Saltoun, Lady (Flora Marjory). Peer of the Realm, since 1979; elected Member, House of Lords, since 1999; Chief of the Name of Fraser, since 1979; b. 18.10.30, Edinburgh; 3 d. Educ. St. Mary's School, Wantage. Address: House of Lords, London, SW1A 0PW.

Salvesen, Alastair Eric Hotson, MBA, CA, HRSA, FCIM, FCMI, FRSA, FSAS. Chairman, Dawnfresh Seafoods Ltd., since 1983 (Managing Director, 1981-93); Chairman, Silvertrout Ltd, 2004; b. 28.7.41; m., Elizabeth Evelyn; 1 s.; 1 d. Educ. Fettes; Cranfield; Chairman: Starfish Ltd., since 1986, Mull of Kintyre Seafoods, since 1988, Dovecot Studios Ltd., since 2001; Director: Praha Investment Holdings Ltd., since 1985, Richmond Foods plc, 1994-2003, New Ingliston Ltd., since 1995, Luing Cattle Society, 1996-99; President, Royal Highland and Agricultural Society of Scotland, 2001-02; Executive Member: UK Association of Frozen Food Producers, 1990-2003, British Frozen Foods Federation, since 1992 (President, 1995-97); Member, Council, Shellfish Association of GB, 2003; Governor: Fettes College Trust, since 1994, Donaldson Trust, since 1997, Compass School, since 1994 (Chairman, since 1996); Member, Queen's Bodyguard for Scotland (The Royal Company of Archers); Liveryman, Worshipful Company of Fishmongers; Chairman, Shellfish Committee, FDF, since 2007. Recreations: shooting; archery; farming; forestry; contemporary Scottish art. Address: Whitburgh, Pathhead, Midlothian EH37 5SR; T.-01875 320304; (b.) Dawnfresh Seafoods Ltd., Bothwell Park Industrial Estate, Uddingston, Lanarkshire G71 6LS: T.-01698 810008.

Salvesen, Robin Somervell, FBIM, Chevalier de Dannebrog 1st Class. Vice Lieutenant of East Lothian; Chairman, Bells Nautical Trust; Chairman, Theodore Salvesen Trust; Chairman, Thistle Trust; b. 4.5.35, Edinburgh; m., Sari; 3 s.; 4 d. Educ. Fettes College; Oxford University. The Royal Scots, Queen's Own Nigeria Regiment; TA, 7/9 Bn., The Royal Scots, 8/9 Bn., The Royal Scots 52 Lowland Volunteers; retired Major; Director, shipping companies, A.F. Henry & Macgregor, Christian Salvesen plc; Lloyds Register of Shipping, 1974-87; Chamber of Shipping, 1974-88; British Shipowners Association, 1984-99; Member, Lights Advisory Committee, 1987-2003; Member, East Lothian Council, 1965-68; Royal Danish Consul, 1972-87; Vice Convenor, Daniel Stewarts and Melville College, 1978-80; Governor, Fettes College, 1975-85; Chairman, Leith Nautical College, 1979-88; former Chairman, Association for the Protection of Rural Scotland; President, Edinburgh Area Scouts, since 1991; Member, Merchant Company of the City of Edinburgh (Assistant, 1977-80); Elder, Church of Scotland, St Mary's, Haddington. Recreations: archery, shooting. Address: Eaglescairnie House, Haddington, EH41.

Samson, George Carmichael, CompBCS, FFCS. Director, Central Services, Administration, Law Society of Scotland, since 1986; b. 17.12.46, Dundee; m., Irene; 1 d. Sidlaw Industries (Organisation and Methods), 1967-77; Divisional Systems Co ordinator, Watson & Philip PLC, 1977-86. Law Society of Scotland. Recreations: guitar; photography; golf. Address: (b.) 26 Drumsheugh Gardens, Edinburgh EH3 7YR; T.-0131-476 8142.
E-mail: georgesamson@lawscot.org.uk

Sanders, John, BA (Hons), DipCons. Architectural Conservator, since 1988; Simpson & Brown Architects, Edinburgh, since 1989; Buildings Conservation Partner, since 2000; b. 9.3.61; m., Susan. Educ. Central School of Art, London; Heriot Watt University. Assistant on Conservation Projects, Charlewood Curry Partnership, Newcastle-upon-Tyne, 1985-87. Interests in 19th Century Church Architecture. Address: (b.) St. Ninian's Manse, Quayside Street, Edinburgh EH6 6EJ; T.-0131 555 4678; e-mail: jsanders@simpsonandbrown.co.uk

Sanderson of Bowden, Lord (Charles Russell Sanderson), KB. Life Peer; Chairman, Scottish Mortgage and Trust, 1993-2003; Chairman, Hawick Cashmere Co., since 1991; Chairman, Clydesdale Bank, 1999-2004; President, Royal Highland Agricultural Society, 2002-03; Vice Lord Lieutenant, Roxburgh and Selkirk, since 2003; Director, Develica Deutschland plc; Director, Accsys plc, since 2007; b. 30.4.33, Melrose; m., Frances Elizabeth Macaulay; 1 s.; 1 s. deceased; 2 d. Educ. St. Mary's School, Melrose; Glenalmond College; Bradford University; Scottish College of Textiles. Commissioned, Royal Signals; Partner, Charles P. Sanderson, 1958-87; former Director, Johnston of Elgin, Illingworth Morris, Edinburgh Woollen Mills; former Chairman, Shires Investment PLC, Edinburgh Financial Trust, Scottish Pride Holdings; President, Scottish Conservative and Unionist Association, 1977-79; Chairman, National Union of Conservative and Unionist Associations Executive Committee, 1981-86; Minister of State, Scottish Office, 1987-90; Chairman, Scottish Conservative Party, 1990-93; Chairman, Scottish Peers Association, 1998-2000; Director: United Auctions Ltd., 1993-99, Watson and Philip PLC, 1993-99, Morrison Construction PLC, 1995-2001; Member, Board, Yorkshire Bank and National Australia Bank Europe, 1999-2004; Chairman, Eildon Housing Association, 1976-83; Member, Court, Napier University, 1994-2001; Chairman, Glenalmond Council, 1994-2000; Chairman, St Mary's School, Melrose, 1998-2004; Member, Court, Frameworker Knitters Company, since 2000; Under Warden, 2003-04; Upper Warden, since 2004; Master, 2005-06; DL. Recreations: golf; amateur dramatics; photography; fishing. Address: (h.) Becketts Field, Bowden, Melrose, Roxburgh, TD6 0ST.

Sanderson, Professor Jeffrey John, BSc, PhD, FInstP. Professor of Theoretical Plasma Physics, St. Andrews University, 1985-2000, Professor Emeritus, since 2001, Vice Principal, 2000, Proctor, 1997-2000; b. 25.4.37, Birmingham; m., Mirjana Adamovic; 1 s.; 1 d. Educ. George Dixon Grammar School, Birmingham; Birmingham University; Manchester University. Research Associate, Maryland University, 1961-64; Theoretical Physicist, English Electric Co., Whetstone, 1964-66; Lecturer, then Senior Lecturer, then Reader in Applied in Applied Mathematics, St. Andrews University, 1966-85; Visiting Professor, Department of Physics, College of William and Mary, USA, 1976-77. Publications: Plasma Dynamics (Co-author), 1969; Laser Plasma Interactions (Joint Editor), 1979; The Physics of Plasmas (Co-author), 2003. Recreations: chess; Scottish country dancing; golf; hill-walking; choral singing. Address: (h.) 17 Spottiswoode Gardens, St. Andrews KY16 8SA; T.-01334 473862; e-mail: jjs@st-and.ac.uk

Sanderson, William. Farmer; Honorary Treasurer, Royal Highland and Agricultural Society of Scotland; Chairman, Royal Highland and Agricultural Society of Scotland, 2002-04; Vice President, Dalkeith Agricultural Society; b. 9.3.38, Lanark; m., Netta; 4 d. Educ. Dalkeith High School. Past Chairman, South Midlothian and Lothians and Peeblesshire Young Farmers Clubs; Past Chairman, Dalkeith Agricultural Society; President, Royal Caledonian Curling Club, 1984-85; Honorary Life Member, Oxenfoord and Edinburgh Curling Clubs; Past President, Oxenfoord and Edinburgh Curling Clubs; Scottish Curling Champion, 1971 and 1978 (2nd, World Championship, 1971). Recreations: curling; exhibiting livestock. Address: (h.) Blackshiels Farm, Blackshiels, Pathhead, Midlothian; T.-01875 833288.

Sanderson, Very Rev. William Roy, MA, DD. Minister, Church of Scotland; Extra Chaplain to The Queen in Scotland, since 1977 (Chaplain-in-Ordinary, 1965-77); b. 23.9.07, Leith; m., Muriel Easton; 3 s.; 2 d. Educ. Fettes College; Oriel College, Oxford; New College, Edinburgh. Ordained, 1933; Assistant Minister, St. Giles' Cathedral, 1932-34; Minister: St. Andrew's, Lochgelly, 1935-39, The Barony of Glasgow, 1939-63, Stenton with Whittingehame, 1963-73; Moderator, Glasgow Presbytery, 1958 and Haddington and Dunbar Presbytery, 1972-74; Moderator, General Assembly, 1967; Chairman, Scottish Religious Advisory Committee, BBC, 1961-71; Member, Central Religious Advisory Committee, BBC and ITA, 1961-71; Governor, Fettes College, 1967-77; Honorary President, Church Service Society; President, New College Union, 1975. Hon. DD (Glasgow), 1959. Recreations: reading; walking. Address: (h.) 20 Craigleith View, Station Road, North Berwick, EH39 4BF.

Sandison, Bruce Macgregor. Writer and Journalist; b. 26.9.38, Edinburgh; m., Dorothy Ann Rhodes; 2 s.; 2 d. Educ. Royal High School, Edinburgh. Commissioned into Royal Army Service Corps, 1956-60; sometime poultry farmer and agricultural contractor; full-time writing, since 1981; Columnist (environment, game fishing, hill-walking), The Herald, The Scotsman; contributor, Tales of the Loch, Sporting Gentleman's Gentleman (series), Radio Scotland, Radio 4, Landward, BBC TV; Founding Chairman, The Salmon Farm Protest Group, 2002. Publications: The Trout Lochs of Scotland; The Sporting Gentleman's Gentleman; Game Fishing in Scotland; The Hillwalker's Guide to Scotland; The Heather Isles; Tales of the Loch; Long Walks with Little People; Trout and Salmon Rivers and Lochs of Scotland; Walk Scotland. Recreations: hill-walking; game fishing; photography; swimming; music; reading; chess; bridge. Address: Hysbackie, Tongue, by Lairg, IV27 4XJ; T.-01847 55 274; e-mail: bruce@hysbackie.freeserve.co.uk

Sanford, Professor Anthony John, BSc, PhD, FBPsS, FRSA, CPsychol. Professor of Psychology, Glasgow University, since 1982 (Head, Department of Psychology,

1983-86); b. 5.7.44, Birmingham; m., Alison Jane Sutherland Newlands; 1 s.; 2 d. Educ. Waverley Grammar School; Leeds University; Cambridge University. MRC Research Scholar, Applied Psychology Unit, Cambridge; Postdoctoral Research Fellow, then Lecturer in Psychology, Dundee University; Senior Lecturer, then Reader in Psychology, Glasgow University. Gifford Lecturer in Natural Theology, Glasgow, 1983. Publications: Understanding Written Language (Co-author); Models, Mind and Man; Cognition and Cognitive Psychology; The Mind of Man; Communicating Quantities (Co-author); The Nature and Limits of Human Understanding (Editor). Recreations: hill-walking; industrial archaeology; music; cooking. Address: (b.) Department of Psychology, Glasgow University, Glasgow; T.-0141-330 4058.

Sannella, Professor Donald Theodore, BS, MS, PhD. Professor of Computer Science, Edinburgh University, since 1998; b. 7.12.56, Boston USA; m., Monika-Jeannette Lekuse; 1 s.; 1 d. Educ. Yale University; University of California at Berkeley; Edinburgh University. Editor-in-Chief, Theoretical Computer Science, since 2000. Address: (b.) Laboratory for Foundations of Computer Science, School of Informatics, Edinburgh University, EH9 3JZ; T.-0131-650 5184; e-mail: dts@inf.ed.ac.uk

Sarwar, Mohammed. MP, Glasgow Central, since 2005, Glasgow Govan, 1997-2005; b. 18.8.52; m.; 3 s.; 1 d. Educ. University of Faisalabad. Director, United Wholesalers Ltd., 1983-97; former Glasgow City Councillor. Address: House of Commons, London SW1A 1AA.

Satsangi, Jack (Jyoti), BSc, MBBS, DPhil, FRCP(Edin), FRCP (UK). Professor of Gastroenterology, University of Edinburgh, since 2000; Consultant Physician, Western General Hospital, Edinburgh, since 2000; b. 8.5.63, Batley. Educ. Brentwood School, Essex; St. Thomas's Hospital, London; Worcester College, University of Oxford. University of Oxford: MRC Training Fellow, 1992-96, MRC Clinician Scientist, 1997-2000; Honorary Consultant Physician, John Radcliffe Hospital, Oxford, 1999-2000. Member, Committee, Medical Research Society; Association of Physicians of Great Britain and Ireland. Recreations: tennis; running; saxophone. Address: (b.) Gastrointestinal Unit, Molecular Medicine Centre, Western General Hospital, Edinburgh EH4 2XU; T.-0131 651 1807; e-mail: j.satsangi@ed.ac.uk

Saunders, Professor Alison Marilyn, BA, PhD. Carnegie Professor of French, Aberdeen University; b. 23.12.44, Darlington. Educ. Wimbledon High School GPDST; Durham University. Lectrice, the Sorbonne, 1968-69; Lecturer in French, Aberdeen University, 1970-85; Senior Lecturer in French, 1985-90. Recreations: swimming; gardening; DIY; cooking; antiquarian book-collecting. Address: (h.) 75 Dunbar Street, Old Aberdeen, Aberdeen AB24 3UA; T.-01224 494806.

Saunders, Ann Walker, BA, MCLIP. Director of Community Services, East Renfrewshire Council, since 1995; b. 12.8.52, Glasgow; m., Christopher Saunders; 1 s.; 2 d. Educ. Hutchesons' Grammar School, Glasgow; Strathclyde University, Glasgow. Director of Arts and Libraries, then Director of Leisure Services, Renfrew District Council, 1991-95. Recreations: reading; travelling. Address: (b.) Council Offices, Eastwood Park, Giffnock, G46 6UG; T.-0141-577 3096.
E-mail: ann.saunders@eastrenfrewshire.gov.uk

Saunders, Professor David Stanley, BSc, PhD, FIBiol, FRES, FRSE. Professor of Insect Physiology, Edinburgh University, 1990-99, now Emeritus Professor; b. 12.3.35, Pinner; m., Jean Margaret Comrie Doughty; 3 s. Educ. Pinner County Grammar School; King's College, London; London School of Hygiene and Tropical Medicine. Joined academic staff, Zoology Department, Edinburgh, 1958; Visiting Professor: Stanford University, California, 1971-72, North Carolina University, 1983. Publications: Insect Clocks; Introduction to Biological Rhythms. Recreations: cycling; gardening; photography. Address: (b.) Institute of Cell, Animal and Population Biology, West Mains Road, Edinburgh, EH9 3JT.

Saunders, Donald Goodbrand. Poet and Writer, since 1968; b. 16.7.49, Glasgow; m., Anne; 1 s. Educ. McLaren High School, Callander. Writer, mainly of poetry, for 30 years; published four books, as well as contributing to various Scottish and UK periodicals and anthologies; has received three Scottish Arts Council writers' bursaries. Publications include: The Glasgow Diary, 1984; Findrinny, 1990; Sour Gas and Crude, 1999. Address: (h.) 17 Jellicoe Avenue, Gartmore, FK8 3RQ; T.-01877 389 074.

Saunders, Professor William Philip, BDS, PhD, FDSRCS(Edin), FDSRCPS(Glas), FDSRCS(Eng), MRD, FHEA, FHKAM. Professor of Endodontology, University of Dundee, since 2000; Dean of Dentistry, since 2000; b. 12.10.48, Carlisle; 1 s.; 1 d. Educ. Maidstone Grammar School; Royal Dental Hospital of London. Dental Officer, RAF, 1970-75; general dental practice, 1975-81; Lecturer, Department of Conservative Dentistry, Dundee University, 1981-88; Senior Lecturer in Clinical Practice, Glasgow Dental Hospital and School, 1988-93; Professor in Clinical Dental Practice, Glasgow University, 1993-95, Professor of Endodontology, 1995-2000. Postgraduate Dental Hospital Tutor, Glasgow Dental Hospital, 1992-95; Editor, International Endodontic Journal, 1992-98; President, British Endodontic Society, 1997-98; Chairman, Association of Consultants and Specialists in Restorative Dentistry, 1999-2002; Dental Council, Royal College of Surgeons of Edinburgh, since 2000; Chairman, Speciality Advisory Board in Restorative Dentistry RCSEd, since 2006; President-elect, European Society of Endodontology; Chair, Council of Heads and Deans of Dental Schools, UK, since 2008. Publications: papers and chapters in books on endodontology and applied dental materials science. Recreations: ornithology; natural history; Scottish art; golf; endodontics. Address: (b.) University of Dundee Dental School, Park Place, Dundee DD1 4HN.

Savage, Rev. Gordon Matthew Alexander, MA, BD. Minister, Maxwelltown West Church, Dumfries, since 1984; Clerk, Presbytery of Dumfries and Kirkcudbright, since 1987; b. 25.8.51, Old Kilpatrick; m., Mairi Janet MacKenzie; 2 s. Educ. Glasgow Academy; Edinburgh University. Assistant Minister: Dyce Parish Church, 1975-76, Dunblane Cathedral, 1976-77; Minister, Almondbank-Tibbermore with Logiealmond, 1977-84; Junior Clerk, Presbytery of Perth, 1981-84. Recreations: reading; railways; Clyde steamers; music. Address: Maxwelltown West Manse, 11 Laurieknowe, Dumfries DG2 7AH; T.-01387 252929.

Savidge, Malcolm Kemp, MA (Hons), FRGU. UK Vice-President, United Nations Association, since 2003; MP (Labour), Aberdeen North, 1997-2005; b. 9.5.46, Redhill. Educ. Wallington County Grammar School, Surrey; University of Aberdeen; Aberdeen College of Education. Production/Stock Control and Computer Assistant, Bryans' Electronics Ltd., 1970-71; Mathematics Teacher, Greenwood Dale Secondary School, Nottingham, 1971; Mathematics and Religious and Social Education Teacher, Peterhead Academy, 1972-73; Mathematics Teacher, Kincorth Academy, Aberdeen, 1973-97. Member, Aberdeen City Council, 1980-96: Vice-Chair, Labour Group, 1980-88, Finance Convener, Policy Vice-Convener, Deputy

Leader, 1994-96; Governor, Robert Gordon's Institute of Technology, 1980-88; Governor, Aberdeen College of Education, 1980-87; JP, 1984-96; Fellow, Robert Gordon University, 1997. Recreations: exploring life; puzzles; reading; real ale; spectator sport.

Savill, Professor Sir John Stewart, BA, MBChB, PhD, FRCP, FRCPE, FASN, FMedSci, FRSE. Vice Principal and Head, College of Medicine and Veterinary Medicine, University of Edinburgh, since 2002; b. 25.4.57, London; m., Barbara; 2 s. Educ. Thames Valley Grammar School; University of Oxford; University of Sheffield. House Surgeon, House Physician and House Officer, Sheffield, 1981-83; Senior House Officer, General Medicine, University Hospital, Nottingham, 1983-84; Rotating Registrar in Renal and General Medicine, Ealing and Hammersmith, 1984-86; MRC Training Fellow and Honorary Senior Registrar, Royal Postgraduate Medical School, 1986-89; Senior Registrar, Renal and General Medicine, Hammersmith Hospital, 1989-90; Wellcome Trust Senior Research Fellow in Clinical Science, and Senior Lecturer, University of London, 1990-93; Professor in Medicine, Head, Division of Renal and Inflammatory Disease, University of Nottingham and Honorary Consultant Physician, University Hospital, Nottingham, 1993-98; Professor of Medicine, 1998-2006, Professor of Experimental Medicine and former Director, MRC/University of Edinburgh Centre for Inflammation Research and Honorary Consultant Physician, Royal Infirmary of Edinburgh, 1998-. Member, Medical Research Council; Governor, Health Foundation. Recreations: hockey; rugby; cricket; football; literature. Address: University of Edinburgh, Queen's Medical Research Institute, 47 Little France Crescent, Edinburgh EH16 4TJ; T.-0131 242 9313; e-mail: head.cmum@ed.ac.uk

Saville, Alan, BA, FSA, MIFA, FSA Scot. Archaeologist; Senior Curator, National Museums of Scotland, since 1989; Editor, European Journal of Archaeology, 2004-07; Vice-President, Society of Antiquaries of Scotland, 2003-06; b. 31.12.46, London; m., Annette Carruthers. Educ. Colfe's Grammar School, London; Birmingham University. Archaeological Research Assistant, Department of the Environment, London, 1972-74; Archaeologist, Cheltenham Art Gallery and Museum, 1974-76; Field Officer, Western Archaeological Trust, Bristol, 1976-85; Archaeological Consultant, Cheltenham, 1985-89; President, Council for Scottish Archaeology, 2001-03; Member, Ancient Monuments Board for Scotland, 2001-03. Treasurer, Society of Antiquaries of Scotland, 1992-2000; Chairman, The Lithic Studies Society, 1983-90; Conservation Co-ordinator, The Prehistoric Society, 1989-93; Joint Editor, Transactions of the Bristol and Gloucestershire Archaeological Society, 1983-89. Recreations: book collecting; cinema. Address: (b.) Archaeology Department, National Museums of Scotland, Chambers Street, Edinburgh EH1 1JF; T.-0131-247 4054; e-mail: a.saville@nms.ac.uk

Saxon, Professor David Harold, OBE, MA, DPhil, DSc, CPhys, FInstP, FRSE. Kelvin Professor of Physics, Glasgow University, since 1990; Dean, Physical Sciences, 2002-08; Head, Department of Physics and Astronomy, 1996-2001; b. 27.10.45, Stockport; m., Margaret Flitcroft; 1 s.; 1 d. Educ. Manchester Grammar School; Balliol College, Oxford; Jesus College, Oxford. Research Officer, Nuclear Physics Department, Oxford University, 1969-70; Research Associate, Columbia University, New York, 1970-73; Rutherford Appleton Laboratory, Oxon: Research Associate, 1974-75, Senior Scientific Officer, 1975-76, Principal Scientific Officer, 1976-89; Chairman, PPARC Particle Physics Committee, 1992-95; Member: Scientific Policy Committee, CERN, Geneva, 1993-98, External

Review Committee, CERN, Geneva, 2002, Physics Research Committee, DESY, Hamburg, 1993-99, Research Assessment Panel (Physics), 1996; PPARC Council Member and Chairman of panel on public understanding of science, 1997-2001; Chairman, governing committee, Scottish Universities Summer Schools in Physics, 1997-2003; CCLRC: Council Member, 2000-01 and 2005-07, Chairman, Particle Physics Users Advisory Committee, 1999-2004; Chairman, Institute of Physics in Scotland, 2003-05; Member, Council, Royal Society of Edinburgh, 2001-04; Research Awards Convener, Royal Society of Edinburgh, 2002-05; Member, Scientific Advisory Committee, University Trento (Italy), 2001-04; Member, International Union of Pure and Applied Physics Commission C11, 2006-08. Address: (b.) Faculty of Physical Sciences, Glasgow University, Glasgow, G12 8QQ; T.-0141-330 4673.

Scanlan, Michael. Solicitor; Senior Partner, Russells Gibson McCaffrey (formerly Russells) Solicitors, Glasgow, since 1982; Member, Judicial Appointments Board, Scotland; b. 6.6.46, Glasgow; m., Margaret; 1 s. Educ. St. Aloysius College, Glasgow; Glasgow University. T. F. Russell & Co.: Apprentice, 1965-70, Assistant, 1971-73, Partner, since 1973; Temporary Sheriff, 1986-96; President, Law Society of Scotland, 1999-2000; former Member, Glasgow and North Argyll Legal Aid Committee; former Lecturer, Evidence and Procedure, Strathclyde University; former External Examiner, Glasgow University; Honorary Member, Royal Faculty of Procurators in Glasgow. Recreations: golf; reading. Address: (h.) Willowfield, Kirkintilloch Road, Lenzie; T.-0141-777 7677.

Schaper, Professor Joachim Ludwig Wilhelm, PhD (Cantab), Habilitation (Tübingen). Professor and Chair in Hebrew, Old Testament and Early Jewish Studies, University of Aberdeen, since 2006; b. 19.03.65, Hanover, Germany; m., Dr. Marie-Luise Ehrenschwendtner; 1 d. Educ. Schiller Schule (Hanover, Germany); Universität Tübingen; University of Cambridge, Trinity College. PhD Cambridge, 1993; Habilitation Tübingen, 1999; Universität Tübingen, 1999-2005; Heisenberg-Fellow of The Deutsche Forschungsgemeinschaft, 2002-05; Reader in Old Testament, University of Aberdeen, 2005-06. Recreations: books; travel. Address: (b.) University of Aberdeen, School of Divinity, History and Philosophy, Aberdeen AB24 3UB; T.-01224-581678; e-mail: j.schaper@abdn.ac.uk

Schlesinger, Professor Philip Ronald, BA, PhD, DrHC, FRSE, FRSA, AcSS. Professor in Cultural Policy, University of Glasgow, since 2007; b. 31.8.48, Manchester; m., Sharon Joy Rose; 2 d. Educ. North Manchester Grammar School; Queen's College, Oxford; London School of Economics. University of Greenwich: Lecturer, 1974, Senior Lecturer, 1977, Principal Lecturer, 1981; Head, Division of Sociology, 1981-88, Professor of Sociology, 1987-89; Professor of Film and Media Studies, Stirling University, 1989-2006; Social Science Research Fellow, Nuffield Foundation, 1982-83; Jean Monnet Fellow, European University Institute, Florence, 1985-86; British-Hispanic Chair of Doctoral Studies, Complutense University of Madrid, 2000-01; Chair, Research Assessment Panel for Communication, Cultural and Media Studies, 1995-96 and 1999-2001; Visiting Professor of Media and Communication, University of Oslo, 1993-2004; Visiting Fellow, Maison des Sciences de l'Homme, Paris, 2002, 2005; Co-Editor, Media, Culture and Society, since 1982; Media Adviser, Know How Fund, 1994-98; Board Member, Scottish Screen, 1997-2004; Board Member, The Research Centre for Television and Interactivity, Glasgow, since 1998; Member, Film Education Working Group reporting to Department of Culture, Media and Sport, 1998-99; Member, Scottish Advisory Committee of Ofcom, since 2004. Publications: Putting "Reality" Together, 1978, 1987; Televising "Terrorism", 1983; Communicating Politics, 1986; Media, Culture and Society, 1986; Los Intelectuales en la Sociedad de la Informacion, 1987; Media, State and Nation, 1991; Women Viewing Violence, 1992; Culture and Power, 1992; Reporting Crime, 1994; European Transformations, 1994; International Media Research, 1997; European Communication Council Report, 1997; Men Viewing Violence, 1998; Consenting Adults?, 2000; Open Scotland?, 2001; Mediated Access, 2003; The SAGE Handbook of Media Research, 2004; The European Union and the Public Sphere, 2007. Recreations: the arts; walking; travel. Address: Centre for Cultural Policy Research, University of Glasgow, Glasgow G12 8QQ; T.-0141 330 3806.

Schlicke, Paul Van Waters, BA, PhD. Senior Lecturer in English, University of Aberdeen, since 1989; Director of Undergraduate Programmes, since 2005; b. 21.04.43, Charleston, South Carolina, USA; m., Judith Ross Napier; 2 s.; 1 d. Educ. Gonzaga Preparatory School, Spokane, Washington, USA; Stanford University; University of California, San Diego. Lecturer in English, University of Aberdeen, 1971-89. President: Dickens Society of America, 1994, International Dickens Fellowship, 2003-05; Chairman, Board of Trustees, Charles Dickens Museum, since 2005. Recreation: road running. Address: (b.) School of Language and Literature, University of Aberdeen, Aberdeen AB24 3UB; T.-01224 272642; e-mail: p.schlicke@abdn.ac.uk

Schmidt-Leukel, Professor Perry Horst, Dipl theol, MA, Dr theol, Dr theol habil. Professor of Systematic Theology and Religious Studies (Chair of World Religions for Peace), Glasgow University; b. 21.9.54, Bonn; m., Doris; 2 s. Educ. University of Munich. Assistant Professor, Senior Assistant Professor, University of Munich, 1987-2000. Member, Secretariat Board, European Network of Buddhist-Christian Studies. Recent publication: War and Peace in World Religions, 2004; Buddhism and Christianity in Dialogue, 2005; Buddhism, Christianity and the Question of Creation, 2006; Understanding Buddhism, 2006. Address: (b.) Glasgow University, Department of Theology and Religious Studies, 4 The Square, Glasgow G12 8QQ; T.-0141 330 2501.

Schofield, Rev. Melville Frederick, MA. Former Chaplain to Western General and Associated Hospitals, Edinburgh, (retired); b. 3.10.35, Glasgow; m., Christina Skirving Crookston. Educ. Irvine Royal Academy; Dalkeith High School; Edinburgh University and New College. Ordained Assistant, Bathgate High, 1960-61; Minister, Canal Street, Paisley, 1961-67; Minister, Laigh Kirk, Kilmarnock, 1967-88. Former Moderator, Presbytery of Irvine and Kilmarnock; former Moderator, Synod of Ayr; radio and TV broadcaster; Past President, No. 0 Kilmarnock Burns Club. Recreations: international Burns engagements; golf; after-dinner speaking. Address: (h.) 25 Rowantree Grove, Currie, Midlothian, EH14 5AT; T.-0131-449 4745; e-mail: afterate@hotmail.com

Scobbie, Andrew Alexander, BA (Hons), MCLIP. Librarian, Midlothian Council, since 1998; Member, Edinburgh City Council, 2000-07; b. 22.3.51, Edinburgh; m., Hazel; 1 s. Educ. Tynemouth High School; Newcastle-upon-Tyne Polytechnic; Loughborough Technical College. North Tyneside Libraries, 1973-85. Member, Police Board, Lothian and Borders Police; Director, WORKTRACK; Chair, Board, Edinburgh International Conference Centre; Director, EDI Group Ltd; Justice of the Peace. Recreations: reading; church bell-ringing. Address: (b.) Midlothian House, Buccleuch Street, Dalkeith EH22 1DN.

Scobie, Rev. Andrew John, MA, BD. Minister, Cardross Parish Church, since 1965; b. 9.7.35, Windygates; m., Elizabeth Jeannette; 1 s.; 1 d. Educ. Whitehill Senior

Secondary School, Glasgow; Glasgow University (Medal in Systematic Theology); Gottingen University; Tubingen University; Marburg University. Assistantship, New Kilpatrick Church, Bearsden; Moderator, Dumbarton Presbytery, 1973-74 and 1999-2000; Convener, General Assembly's Parish Education Committee, 1978-80; Convener, General Assembly's Panel on Worship, 1986-90; Member, Joint Liturgical Group, 1987-91; Vice-Convener, General Assembly's Artistic Matters Committee, 1995-98; Ecumenical Representative, Church of England General Synod, 1995-98; Chairman or Vice-Chairman, Cardross Community Council, since inception; Executive Member, Association of Scottish Community Councils, since 1998, President, 2003-06. Publications: Studies in the Historical Jesus (Translator); contributions to New Ways to Worship, 1980, Prayers for Sunday Services, 1980, Three Orders for Holy Communion, 1986, Songs of God's People, 1988; Worshipping Together, 1991; Common Order, 1994; Common Ground, 1998; CH4, 2005. Recreations: golf; photography; wine making; visual arts. Address: The Manse, Cardross, Dumbarton G82 5LB; T.-01389 841289; e-mail: ascobie55@cardross.dunbartonshire. co.uk

Scobie, William Galbraith, MB, ChB, FRCSEdin, FRCSGlas. Former Consultant Paediatric Surgeon, Lothian Health Board, now retired; part-time Senior Lecturer, Department of Clinical Surgery, Edinburgh University, 1971-92; Assistant Director, Edinburgh Postgraduate Board for Medicine, 1986-92; b. 13.10.36, Maybole; m., Elizabeth Caldwell Steel; 1 s.; 1 d. Educ. Carrick Academy, Maybole; Glasgow University. Registrar, General Surgery, Kilmarnock Infirmary; Senior Registrar, Royal Hospital for Sick Children, Glasgow; Senior Registrar, Hospital for Sick Children, London; Senior Paediatric Surgeon, Abu Dhabi, 1980-81. Recreations: fishing; golf; gardening; music. Address: (h.) 133 Caiyside, Fairmilehead, Edinburgh EH10 7HR; T.-0131-445 7404.

Scothorne, Richard Mark, MA, MPhil. Managing Director, Rocket Science UK Ltd.; b. 17.7.53, Glasgow; m., Dr. Sarah Gledhill; 1 s.; 1 d. Educ. Royal Grammar School, Newcastle upon Tyne; St. Catharine's College, Cambridge; Edinburgh University. Various posts in local government, 1977-86; Scottish Director, British Shipbuilders Enterprise Ltd., 1986-87; Economic Development Manager (Depute Director of Planning), Lothian Regional Council, 1987-92; Director, Partners in Economic Development Ltd., 1992-99; Director, Workforce One Ltd., 1999-2001. Specialist Adviser to Select Committee on Education and Employment, 1997-2000. Publication: The Vital Economy: integrating training and enterprise (Co-author), 1990. Recreations: hill-walking; mountain biking; Scottish art. Address: (h.) 71 Murrayfield Gardens, Edinburgh, EH12 6DL; T.-0131-337 5476.
E-mail: richard.scothorne@rocketsciencelab.co.uk

Scott, Alastair, BA. Travel writer, freelance photographer, and broadcaster; b. 19.3.54, Edinburgh; m., Sheena. Educ. Blairmore; Sedbergh; Stirling University. Travelled around the world, 1978-83; wrote three travel books, 1984-87 – Scot Free, A Scot Goes South, A Scot Returns; cycled 5,000 miles in E. Europe, 1987-88; wrote Tracks Across Alaska (800-mile sled dog journey), 1988-90; travelled Scotland, 1993-94, wrote Native Stranger; presented BBC film version of Native Stranger, 1995; worked on fiction, took up sailing, 1996-2002; sailed solo round Ireland; first novel, Stuffed Lives, published 2003. Recreations: reading; running; sailing; playing concertina. Address: Arroch, Kylerhea, Isle of Skye, IV42 8NH; T.-01599 522329; web: www.alastair-scott.com

Scott, Professor Alexander, MA, MSc, PhD. Professorial Fellow, Heriot-Watt University, since 1989; b. 7.3.45, Lerwick; m., Anne Elliot; 3 d. Educ. Anderson Educational Institute; Boroughmuir Secondary; Edinburgh University. Research Assistant, Edinburgh University, 1967-70;

Research Fellow, Heriot-Watt University, 1970-89; Director, The Polecon Co., 1972-89; External Examiner, CNAA, 1981-85; Member, Joint Working Party on Economics, Scottish Examination Board, 1989-90; Chairman, Southfield Housing Society, 1977-80; Executive Director, Edinburgh Business School, since 1997; Trustee, Edinburgh Quartet, 2000-06. Publications: four books and numerous papers. Recreations: hill-walking; swimming; classical guitar; woodworking. Address: (b.) Edinburgh Business School, Heriot-Watt University, Edinburgh; T.-0131-451 3090.

Scott, Professor Andrew George, BA. Professor of European Union Studies, University of Edinburgh, since 2002; b. 3.10.53, Lanark. Educ. Lanark Grammar School; Heriot-Watt University. Economist, Scottish Office, 1978-79; Lecturer, Department of Economics, Heriot-Watt University, 1979-92; Senior Lecturer, Faculty of Law, University of Edinburgh, 1992-2002. Published widely on economic and political aspects of European integration. Recreations: hillwalking; running; reading; music. Address: (b.) School of Law, University of Edinburgh, Old College, Edinburgh.

Scott, Angela, BA (Hons), CPFA. Head of CIPFA (Chartered Institute of Public Finance and Accountancy) in Scotland. Address: (b.) CIPFA in Scotland, Fettes Park, 2nd Floor, West Wing, 496 Ferry Road, Edinburgh EH5 2DL; T.-0131 559 3606; e-mail: angela.scott@cipfa.org

Scott, Eleanor, R., MB, ChB. MSP (Green), Highlands and Islands, 2003-07; Community Paediatrician, NHS Highland, since 1980; b. 23.7.51, Inverness; divorced; 1 s.; 1 d.; partner: Rob Gibson. Educ. Bearsden Academy; University of Glasgow. Junior hospital doctor posts, Inverness, Stirling, Elgin, 1974-78; Trainee, general practice, Nairn, 1979. Has stood for election at all levels, 1990-2001. Recreations: traditional music; gardening. Address: Tir nan Oran, 8 Culcairn Road, Evanton, Ross-shire IV16 9YT; T.-01349 830388; e-mail: Eleanorsco@aol.com

Scott, Esme (Lady Scott), CBE, WS, MA, LLB, NP; b. 7.1.32, Edinburgh; m., 1, Ian Macfarlane Walker (deceased); 1 s.; 2, Kenneth Bertram Adam Scott, KCVO, CMG; 1 step-s.; 1 step-d. Educ. St. George's School for Girls, Edinburgh; Edinburgh University. Lawyer; Vice Chairman, National Consumer Council, 1984-87; Chairman, Scottish Consumer Council, 1980-85; Member, Equal Opportunities Commission, 1985-90; Chair, Scottish Association of Citizens Advice Bureaux; Chair, Volunteer Development Scotland, 1989-92; Chair, The Volunteer Centre UK, 1993-95; Member, Securities and Investments Board, 1991-93; Member, Court, Edinburgh University, 1989-92; Member, Scottish Committee, Council on Tribunals, 1986-92; Member, Social Security Advisory Committee, 1990-96; Member, National Council for Voluntary Organisations Board, 1993-95. Address: (h.) 13 Clinton Road, Edinburgh EH9 2AW.

Scott, Professor Hamish, MA, PhD, FBA, FRHistS. Professor of International History, St Andrews University, since 2000; b. 12.7.46, Glasgow. Educ. George Heriot's School, Edinburgh; Edinburgh University; London School of Economics. Lecturer, Birmingham University, 1970-78; joined St Andrews University as Lecturer, 1979. Publications: as author: The Rise of the Great Powers 1648-1815, 1983; British Foreign Policy in the Age of the American Revolution, 1990; The Emergence of the Eastern Powers 1756-1775, 2001; The Birth of a Great Power System 1740-1815, 2005; as editor: Enlightened Absolutism, 1990; The

European Nobilities in the Seventeenth and Eighteenth Centuries, 1995; 2nd ed, 2007; Royal and Republican Sovereignty in Early Modern Europe, 1997; Cultures of Power in Europe during the eighteenth century, 2007. Recreations: classical music; hill-walking; watching sport. Address: (b.) School of History, St Andrews University, St Andrews KY16 9AL; T.-01334 462 900; e-mail: hms3@st-andrews.ac.uk

Scott, Hugh Johnstone, DA, CertEd. Writer; Columnist for the Press and Post newspaper, since 2003; Art tutor, Pitlochry Festival Theatre, 2004; b. Paisley; m., Mary (Margo) Smith Craig Hamilton; 1 s.; 1 d. Educ. Paisley Grammar School; Glasgow School of Art. Various jobs, then art school; art teacher, until 1984; full-time writing since 1984, including Writing Fellow, City of Aberdeen, 1991; Lecturer in Creative Writing, Glasgow University Adult and Continuing Education Department, since 1988, Art Tutor, since 1998; Tutor in Creative Writing; winner, Woman's Realm children's short story competition, 1982; winner, children's category, Whitbread Book of the Year, 1989, for Why Weeps the Brogan?; short-listed, Mcvitie's Prize, 1990; Tutor, Arvon Foundation Ltd., 1994; Writing guru for Writers' Forum magazine, since 2007. Recreations: weight training; exploring England; day-dreaming; reading, of course; painting.

Scott, Hugh Niall. Director of Communications, University of St. Andrews, since 2007; b. 27.02.61, Glasgow; m., Rosemary; 2 s.; 1 d. Educ. High School of Dundee; University of Aberdeen. Tea Boy, DC Thomson and Co, Dundee, 1980-82; Reporter, Courier and Advertiser, 1982-84; Medical Correspondent, Courier and Advertiser, Evening Telegraph, 1984-96; Director: Beattie Media, 1996, Dundee City of Discovery Campaign, 1996-2000, Press Office, University of St. Andrews, 2000-06. Recreations: golf; guitars; worked edges. Address: (b.) St. Katharine's West, The Scores, St. Andrews, Fife KY16 9AL; T.-01334 462244; e-mail: niall.scott@st-andrews.ac.uk

Scott, Ian Edward. Deputy Chief Executive and Director of Change, Scottish Court Service, 1995-2004; m., Maureen Ferrie; 1 s.; 1 d. Educ. Bellahouston Academy. Regional Sheriff Clerk, Lothian and Borders, 1992-95; Sheriff Clerk, Edinburgh, 1992-95; Sheriff Clerk of Chancery, 1992-95; Regional Sheriff Clerk, Glasgow and Strathkelvin, 1996-98; Regional Sheriff Clerk, North Strathclyde, 1997-98; Area Director West, 1998-2001. Hon. Member, Royal Faculty of Procurators, Glasgow. Recreations: amateur astronomy; rugby; making changes. Address: (h.) Meadowbank, Annandale Avenue, Lockerbie; T.-01576 203132.

Scott, Ian McGregor, LLB (Hons), DipFM. Advocate, since 1990; part-time Immigration Adjudicator, since 1998; b. 4.5.51, Glasgow; m., Ann Janetta Cameron; 1 s.; 1 d. Educ. Hamilton Academy; Glasgow University. Law apprentice, 1973-75; Solicitor in private practice, Glasgow, 1975-90. Secretary, Clyde Valley Mountaineering Club, 1980-97. Recreations: mountaineering; military history. Address: (b.) Advocates' Library, Parliament House, Edinburgh EH1 1RF; T.-0131-226 5071.

Scott, James Archibald, CB, LVO, FRSE, FScotVec, MA; b. 5.3.32, Palestine; m., Dr. Elizabeth Agnes Joyce Scott; 3 s.; 1 d. Educ. Dollar Academy; St. Andrews University; Queen's University of Ontario. RAF Pilot, 1954-56; Commonwealth Relations Office, 1956-65, serving in New Delhi and New York; Scottish Office, 1965; Private Secretary to Secretary of State for Scotland, 1969-71;

Secretary, Scottish Education Department, 1984-88; Secretary, Industry Department for Scotland, 1988-91; Chief Executive, Scottish Development Agency, 1991-92; Executive Director, Scottish Financial Enterprise, 1992-95; Director, Scottish Power plc, 1993-96; Director, Dumyat Investment Trust PLC, 1995-2000; Member of Court, Heriot-Watt University, 1995-2001. Recreations: flying; golf. Address: (h.) 38 Queen's Crescent, Edinburgh EH9 2BA; T.-0131-667 8417.
E-mail: james.scott1@blueyonder.co.uk

Scott, James David, BSc (Hons), DipEd. Rector, Perth High School, since 1998; b. 30.9.52, Brechin; m., Rosalind Walker; 1 s. Educ. Arbroath High School; University of Dundee; Dundee College of Education. Mathematics Teacher, Lawside Academy, Dundee, 1975-79; St. Saviour's High School, Dundee: Assistant Principal Teacher of Mathematics, 1979-84, Principal Teacher of Computing, 1984-86; Assistant Project Co-ordinator, TVEI Tayside, 1986-89; Depute Rector, Glenwood High School, Glenrothes, 1990-94; Rector, Graeme High School, Falkirk, 1994-98. Secretary, Computing Panel, Scottish Examinations Board, 1983-86; Member, SEB/CCC Higher Computing Joint Working Party, 1985-86; Member, National Advisory Committee on Curriculum Flexibility, 2002-03. Recreations: aviation; computing; geography; hillwalking; military history; reading. Address: (b.) Oakbank Road, Perth PH1 1HB; T.-01738 628271; e-mail: jscott@perthhigh.pkc.sch.uk

Scott, James Niall, LLB. Consultant, McGrigors (Partner, 1979-2007); b. 5.4.52, Glasgow; m., Judith; 2 s.; 2 d. Educ. Jordanhill College School; Aberdeen University. External Examiner, Glasgow University Law School, 1990-92; Managing Partner, McGrigor Donald, 1994-97; Chairman, KLegal and McGrigors, 2002-04; Executive Chairman, UK Fisheries Offshore Oil and Gas Legacy Trust Fund Limited; Chairman, St Aloysius' Charitable Fund; Chairman, Mark Scott Foundation; Director: Board of The Treasury Solicitor, Barcapel Foundation Ltd and JW Galloway Limited; Public Interest Member, Council of the Institute of Chartered Accountants of Scotland; Consultant, Blue Sky Experiences Limited. Recreations: swimming; golf; hill-walking. Address: 66 Langside Drive, Glasgow G43 2ST; T.-0141-637 8759; e-mail: jniallscott@btconnect.com

Scott, James Orrock, FCCA. Board Member, Angus, East of Scotland Housing Association, since 1988; Chairman and Board Member, Northern Housing Company Limited, since 2000; Treasurer, SHARP (Scottish Heart and Arterial Disease Risk Prevention), 1992-2005; b. 13.12.40, Dundee; m., Alva; 1 s. Educ. Grove Academy. Former Senior Partner, Henderson Loggie, Chartered Accountants. Past President, Scottish Branch Executive, Society of Certified Accountants; first President, Scottish Athletics Federation. Recreations: athletics; bowling. Address: (h.) 99 Monifieth Road, Broughty Ferry, Dundee DD5 2SL; T.-01382 731822.

Scott, Janys Margaret, QC, MA (Cantab). Called to bar, 1992, took silk, 2007; b. 28.8.53, Radcliffe; m., Revd Dr Kevin F. Scott; 2 s.; 1 d. Educ. Queen Elizabeth's Girls Grammar School, Barnet; Newnham College, Cambridge. Lecturer in Iraq, 1976-78; Solicitor, Oxford, 1978-86; Solicitor, Edinburgh, 1987-91; Honorary Lecturer, Dundee University, 1989-94. Convener, Scottish Child Law Centre, 1992-97; Chairman, Stepfamily Scotland, 1998-2002; Visiting Bye-Fellow, Newnham College, Cambridge, 2002; Chairman, BAAF Scottish Legal Group, since 2004; appointed Part-time Sheriff, 2005. Publication: Education Law in Scotland, 2003. Address: (b.)

Parliament House, Edinburgh EH1 1RF; T.-0131-226 5071.

Scott, John. MSP (Conservative), Ayr, since 2000; Member, Scottish Parliament Corporate Body; Deputy Convener, Petitions Committee; m., Charity (deceased); 1 s.; 1 d. Farming at Balkissock, Ayrshire, since 1973; Founder Director, Ayrshire Country Lamb Ltd., 1988-93; partner in family catering enterprises, 1986-2000; established Ayrshire Farmers' Markets, 1999; Convener, Hill Farming Committee, National Farmers' Union of Scotland, 1993-99; Chairman, Ayrshire and Arran Farming and Wildlife Advisory Group, 1993-99; Chairman, South of Scotland Regional Wool Committee, 1996-2000; JP; Elder, Ballantrae Church; Chairman, Scottish Area Committee, UK Conservative Countryside Forum, 1998-2000; Chairman, Ayrshire Farmers' Market, since 2000; Chairman, Scottish Association of Farmers' Markets, 2001-04; Council Member, Scottish Agricultural Society, 2004; Coopted Regional Adviser on South of Scotland Board, Moredun Foundation, 2004. Recreations: geology; curling; bridge; rugby. Address: (b.) 1 Wellington Square, Ayr KA7 1EN.

Scott, John Andrew Ross. Chairman, NHS Orkney, since 2008; Editor, Orkney Today, 2003-08; Leader, Scottish Borders Council, 2002-03; Member, since 1995 (Liberal Democrat Scottish Transport Spokesman, 1998-99); Honorary Provost of Hawick, 1999-2002; News Editor, Hawick News, 2001-02; b. 6.5.51, Hawick; 2 s.; 2 d. Educ. Hawick High School. Worked on father's farm, 1966-74; Journalist, Hawick News, 1977-78, Tweeddale Press Group, 1978-2002, Chief Reporter, Southern Reporter, 1986-2000; first SDP Member, Roxburgh District Council (1980-85) and Borders Regional Council; Chairman, Roxburgh District Licensing Board, 1984-85; first Chairman, Borders Area Party, SDP, 1981-84; Secretary, Roxburgh and Berwickshire Liberal Democrats, 1988-89, Vice Chairman, 1993-94; Chairman, Scottish Association of Direct Labour Organisations Highways Division, 1994-96; Chairman, South East Scotland Transport Partnership, 1998-2003; Chairman, COSLA Road Safety Task Group, 1999-2001; Chairman, South of Scotland Rural Partnership, 2003; Liberal Democrat Candidate, Dumfries, 2001; South of Scotland Liberal Democrat Candidate, 1999 and 2003. Publication: Beyond Tweedbank: The case for extending the Borders Rail Link to Hawick, 2004. Recreations: writing; music; walking. Address: (h.) Burnquay, Weyland Bay, St. Ola, Orkney KW15 1TD; T.-01856 888813.

Scott, John Dominic, LLB, DipLP. Partner, Capital Defence Lawyers, since 1991; Solicitor-Advocate, since 2001; b. 20.7.64, Glasgow. Educ. Holyrood Secondary School, Glasgow; Glasgow University. Trainee and Assistant, Hughes, Dowdall & Company, Glasgow, 1985-88 (qualified Solicitor, since 1987); joined Gilfedder & McInnes (now Capital Defence Lawyers), Edinburgh, 1988; Member, Executive Committee, Howard League for Penal Reform in Scotland, Chair, since 2006; President, Edinburgh Bar Association. Address: (b.) 34 Leith Walk, Edinburgh EH6 5AA, T. 0131-553 4333.

Scott, John Hamilton. Farmer; Lord-Lieutenant, Shetland; Chairman: Woolgrowers of Shetland Ltd., Shetland Trust, Belmont Trust; b. 30.11.36; m., Wendy Ronald; 1 s.; 1 d. President, Shetland NFU, 1976; Nature Conservancy Council Committee for Scotland, 1984-91; N.E. Scotland Board, Scottish Natural Heritage, 1992-97; Chairman, Shetland Crofting, Farming and Wildlife Advisory Group, 1984-94; Chairman: Shetland Arts Trust, 1994-98, Sail Shetland Ltd., 1996-2000. Recreations: hills; music; pruning. Address: (h.) Keldabister Banks, Bressay, Shetland, ZE2 9EL; T.-01595 820281.

Scott, Rev. John Miller, MA, BD, DD, FSA Scot. Minister, St. Andrew's Scots Memorial Church, Jerusalem,

1985-88; b. 14.8.22, Glasgow; m., Dorothy Helen Loraine Bushnell; 2 s.; 1 d. Educ. Hillhead High School; Glasgow University and Trinity College. War Service, Egypt, Italy, India, 1942-46; Assistant Minister, Barony of Glasgow, 1948-49; Minister: Baxter Park Parish, Dundee, 1949-54; High Kirk of Stevenston, 1954-63; Kirk of the Crown of Scotland (Crown Court Church, Westminster), 1963-85; Moderator, Presbytery of England, 1971, 1979; Moderator, Presbytery of Jerusalem, 1986-88; Chairman, Israel Council, 1986-88; various periods of service on General Assembly Committees; Representative, World Alliance of Reformed Churches, Ecumenical Patriarchate, Istanbul, 1988. President, Caledonian Society of London, 1983-84; instituted Kirking Service for Scottish MPs and peers, 1966; Member, UNA Religious Advisory Committee, 1983-85; Convener, St Andrews Council of Churches, 1997. Hon DD (Glasgow), 1986. Recreations: travel; historical research; reading; gardening. Address: (h.) St. Martins, 6 Trinity Place, St. Andrews KY16 8SG; T.-01334 479518; e-mail: millerscott@aol.com

Scott, Sir Kenneth Bertram Adam, KCVO, CMG. Extra Equerry to The Queen, since 1996; b. 23.1.31, Belfast; m., 1, Gay Smart (deceased); m., 2, Esme Scott (qv); 1 s.; 1 d.; 1 step. s. Educ. George Watson's College; Edinburgh University. HM Diplomatic Service, 1954-85; HM Ambassador to Yugoslavia, 1982-85; Assistant Private Secretary/Deputy Private Secretary to The Queen, 1985-96; Acting Chairman, Provisional Election Commission for Bosnia, 1996. Governor, George Watson's College, 1997-2002; Vice-President, Royal Overseas League; Trustee: Edinburgh University Development Trust, Hopetoun House Preservation Trust, 1997-2007. Recreations: travel; music; golf; gardening. Address: (h.) 13 Clinton Road, Edinburgh EH9 2AW; T.-0131-447 5191.

Scott, Michael M., OBE, BSc, DipEd, MIBiol, CIBiol. Self-employed natural history writer, consultant, broadcaster and conservationist; b. 10.5.51, Edinburgh; m., Sue Scott. Educ. George Heriot's School, Edinburgh; Madras College, St. Andrews; University of Aberdeen. Assistant Education Officer, Royal Zoological Society of Scotland, 1974-76; Scottish Field Officer, Wildlife Youth Service, World Wildlife Fund, 1976-80. Radio work includes: Nature, The Living World, Natural History Programme, Litmus Test, MacGregor's Gathering); Scottish Co-ordinator, Plantlife – The Wild Plant Charity, 1989-2004; Chair, Save the Cairngorms Campaign, 1990-94; Editor, Scottish Environment News, 1991-2001; Chair, Scottish Wildlife and Countryside Link, 1995-99; Deputy Chairman, Scottish Natural Heritage, 1999-2005. Publications: Young Oxford Book of Ecology, 1994 (Environment Prize for Children and Young People's Literature, Germany, 2001); Collins' Guide to Scottish Wild Flowers, 1995. Recreations: natural history; photography; travel; Runrig concerts. Address: Strome House, North Strome, Lochcarron, Ross-shire IV54 8YJ; T.-01520 722901; e-mail: MSStrome@aol.com

Scott, Major Nigel William, MBA, Dip BA & Couns., MIOD, MCMI. Business Development Consultant, Head of Coaching, Institute of Directors Scotland, since 2005; Managing Director: Dundern Ltd., since 2002, Munro Greenhouses, since 2007; b. 28.4.59, Wimbledon, Surrey; m., Catherine Joy Macnaughton; 1 s.; 1 d. Educ. Dollar Academy; Royal Military College Sandhurst; Glasgow Polytechnic. Commissioned, Argyll and Sutherland Highlanders (Princess Louise's), 1978; served in Hong Kong, N. Ireland, Cyprus, Falklands, N. America, UK; commanded D Company 3/51 Highland Volunteers (TA), 1990-93; worked in management consultancy: Taylor Clarke Partnership, 1989-91, PE International, 1991-92; Senior Partner, Scott Associates: organisation development,

1993-2003; Strategy Director, The Forward Training Partnership, 1997-98; Director, Dundern Limited: organisation and business development, since 2003. Chair, Kilmaurs Primary School Board, 2002-05; JP East Ayrshire District Court, 2003-05; Argyll and Sutherland Highlanders Regimental Museum Committee member; Chairman, Stirling Branch Scottish Veterans' Garden City Association; Scottish Amateur Swimming Association Judge. Recreations: shooting; gardening; swimming; sailing; DIY; music; reading. Address: (h.) 10 Alexandra Drive, Alloa FK10 2DQ; T.-01259 729299.
E-mail: n.w.scott@btinternet.com

Scott, Paul Henderson, CMG, MA, MLitt. Honorary Fellow, Glasgow University, since 1996; b. 7.11.20, Edinburgh; m., B.C. Sharpe; 1 s.; 1 d. Educ. Royal High School, Edinburgh; Edinburgh University. HM Forces, 1941-47 (Major, RA); HM Diplomatic Service in Foreign Office, Warsaw, La Paz, Havana, Montreal, Vienna, Milan, 1947-80. Convener, Advisory Council for the Arts in Scotland, 1981-97; Rector, Dundee University, 1989-92; Convener, Scottish Centre for Economic and Social Research, 1990-95; Vice-President, Scottish National Party, 1991-97; President, Scottish Centre, International PEN, 1992-97; President, Edinburgh Sir Walter Scott Club, 1996; President, Saltire Society, 1996-2002. Publications: 1707, The Union of Scotland and England, 1979; Walter Scott and Scotland, 1981; John Galt, 1985; The Age of MacDiarmid (Co-Editor), 1980; In Bed with an Elephant: The Scottish Experience, 1985; A Scottish Postbag (Co-Editor), 1986; The Thinking Nation, 1989; Towards Independence — essays on Scotland, 1991; Andrew Fletcher and the Treaty of Union, 1992; Scotland in Europe: a dialogue with a sceptical friend, 1992; Scotland: a Concise Cultural History (Editor), 1993; Defoe in Edinburgh and Other Papers, 1995; Scotland's Ruine (Co-Editor), 1995; Scotland: An Unwon Cause, 1997; Still in Bed with an Elephant, 1998; The Boasted Advantages, 1999; A Twentieth Century Life, 2002; The Saltoun Papers (Editor), 2003; Scotland Resurgent, 2003; Spirits of the Age (Editor), 2005; The Union of 1707; Why and How, 2006; The Age of Liberation, 2007. Recreation: skiing. Address: (h.) 33 Drumsheugh Gardens, Edinburgh, EH3 7RN; T.-0131-225 1038.

Scott, Primrose Smith, CA. Head of Quality Review, Institute of Chartered Accountants of Scotland, 1999-2002; Senior Partner, The McCabe Partnership, 1987-99; b. 21.9.40, Gorebridge. Educ. Ayr Academy. Trained with Stewart Gilmour, Ayr; qualified as CA 1963; joined Romanes & Munro, Edinburgh, 1964; progressed through manager ranks to Partner, Deloitte Haskins & Sells, 1981-87; set up own practice, Linlithgow, 1987; moved practice to Edinburgh, 1997. Member, Accounts Commission, 1988-92; Non-Executive Director: Dunfermline Building Society, 1990-2005, Northern Venture Trust plc, 1995; Director, Ecosse Unique, since 2004; Institute of Chartered Accountants of Scotland: Member, Council, 1988-95, first Convener, GP Committee, 1990, Vice President, 1992-94, President, 1994-95; Honorary Treasurer, Hospitality Industry Trust Scotland, 1994-2002; Trustee, New Lanark Conservation Trust, 2002-06; Commissioner, Queen Victoria School, Dunblane, 1998-2006; Treasurer, Age Concern Scotland, since 2003; Fellow, SCOTVEC, 1994. Recreation: walking her dogs. Address: (h.) The Cleugh, Redpath, Earlston TD4 6AD.

Scott, Sheriff Richard John Dinwoodie, MA, LLB. Sheriff of Lothian and Borders at Edinburgh, 1986-2004 (of Grampian, Highland and Islands, at Aberdeen and Stonehaven, 1977-86); President, Sheriffs' Association, 2002-04; Member, Parole Board for Scotland, since 2003; Convener, Additional Support Tribunals for Scotland, since

2005; b. 28.5.39, Manchester; m., Josephine Moretta Blake; 2 d. Educ. Edinburgh Academy; Edinburgh University. Lektor, Folkuniversitet of Sweden, 1960-61; admitted to Faculty of Advocates, 1965; Standing Junior Counsel, Ministry of Defence (Air), 1969; Parliamentary candidate, 1974; Honorary Reader, Aberdeen University, 1980-86; Chairman, Scottish Association for the Study of Delinquency, 1997-2001. Address: (b.) Sheriffs' Chambers, Sheriff Court House, Edinburgh, EH1 1LB; T.-031-225 2525.

Scott, Professor Roger Davidson, BSc, PhD, CPhys, FInstP, FRSE. Personal Professorship, University of Glasgow, 1994; Non-Executive Director, Nuclear Decommissioning Authority, since 2004; b. 17.12.41, Lerwick; m., Marion McCluckie; 2 s.; 1 d. Educ. Anderson Institute, Lerwick; Edinburgh University. Demonstrator, Edinburgh University, 1965-68; Lecturer, then Depute Director, then Director, SURRC, 1968-98; Recreations: watching football; walking; home maintenance. Address: (h.) 6 Downfield Gardens, Bothwell G71 8UW; T.-01698 854121.

Scott, Roy, JP, OStJ, KCLJ, CMLJ, MD, FRCS (Glas), FRCS (Edin), FSA (Scot), DL. Retired Urologist; Honorary Sheriff, South Strathclyde/Dumfries/Galloway; b. 17.7.35, Waterloo, Wishaw; m., Janette J.C.; 1 s.; 2 d. Educ. Wishaw High School; University of Glasgow. House Phys/Surgeon; Captain (Temp. Major), RAMC - Kenya, Aden; Surgical Junior posts, Stobhill/Royal Infirmary Glasgow; Consultant Urologist, Glasgow Royal; Hon. Clinical Senior Lecturer, University of Glasgow; Hon. Lecturer, Strathclyde University; Hon. Member, South Central Section, American Urological Society; Ext. Referee, University of Amman; Past Council Member, British Association Urological Surgeons. Author/Co-Author, several books; Member, Millennium and New Millennium Masters Arkansas Traveller. Ex Deacon Inc Tailors; Ex-Convener, Trades House Glasgow; Past-President, Sandyford Burns Club; I.P. Grand Master, Great Priory of Scotland. Recreations: fishing; Burns; gardening; music; boating. Address: (h.) Garrion, 27 Forest View, Kildrum, Cumbernauld G67 2DB.
E-mail: roy-janette@blueyonder.co.uk

Scott, Stephen R., LLB, WS. Partner, McClure Naismith, since 2000; Solicitor, since 1988; b. 16.10.64, Elgin; m., Jane; 1 s. Educ. Elgin Academy; Edinburgh University. McClure Naismith: Assistant, 1993-96, Associate, 1996-2000. Recreation: marathon running. T.-0131 272 8348; e-mail: sscott@mcclurenaismith.com

Scott, Tavish Hamilton, BA (Hons). MSP (Liberal Democrat), Shetland, since 1999; Deputy Minister for Finance, Public Services and Parliamentary Business, Scottish Executive, 2003-05; Minister for Transport, 2005-07; b. 6.5.66, Inverness; 2 s.; 1 d. Educ. Anderson High School, Lerwick; Napier College, Edinburgh (which became Napier University). Research Assistant to Jim Wallace, MP, 1989-90; Press Officer, Scottish Liberal Democrats, 1990-92; Owner/Manager, Keldabister Farm, Bressay, 1992-99; Shetland Islands Councillor, 1995-99; Chairman, Lerwick Harbour Trust, 1997-99. Recreations: football; golf; swimming; cinema; reading; current affairs. Address: (b.) 171 Commercial Street, Lerwick ZE1 0XH; T.-01595 690044; e-mail: tavish.scott.msp@scottish.parliament.uk

Scott, William, BSc, MSc, FRPharmS, DSc (Hon). Chief Pharmaceutical Officer, Scottish Government, since 1992; Honorary Professor, The Robert Gordon University,

Aberdeen, since 2004; b. 26.10.49, Bellshill; m., Catherine Muir Gilmour; 1 s.; 1 d. Educ. Wishaw High School; Heriot Watt University; Strathclyde University. Resident Pharmacist, Nottingham City Hospital, 1975-76; Staff Pharmacist, Eastern General Hospital, Edinburgh, 1976-79; Principal Pharmacist, Western General Hospital, Edinburgh, 1979-86; Chief Administrative Pharmaceutical Officer, Tayside Health Board, 1986-90; Deputy Chief Pharmacist, Scottish Office, 1990-92. Honorary Doctorate of Science, Robert Gordon University, 2006. Recreations: walking; reading. Address: (b.) St. Andrews House, Edinburgh; T.-0131-244 2518.

Scott-Dempster, Robert Andrew, LLB (Hons), WS. Partner, Gillespie Macandrew WS, since 2003 (Head of Rural Property Department); b. 30.4.67, Reading; m., Camilla; 2 s. Educ. Marlborough College; Edinburgh University. Captain, 1st Battalion The Black Watch, 1990-95; Associate, Murray Beith Murray WS, 1997-2002. Director, Atlantic Salmon Trust; Scottish Committee Member, Agricultural Law Association. Recreations: fishing; golf; climbing/hill walking; biography. Address: (b.) 5 Atholl Crescent, Edinburgh EH3 8EJ; T.-0131 225 1677.
E-mail: robert.scott.dempster@gillespie.macandrew.co.uk

Scott Moncrieff, John Kenneth, LLB, WS. Partner, Murray Beith Murray, WS, since 1978; b. 9.2.51, Edinburgh; m., Pilla; 1 s.; 2 d. Educ. Marlborough College; Edinburgh University. Honorary Consul to Monaco; Lecturer and Tutor, Edinburgh University. Board Member, Cheek by Jowl Theatre Co. and Theatre Babel; Clerk to the Abbey Court, Holyrood; Trustee, various charitable trusts and companies. Recreations: football; theatre; hillwalking. Address: (b.) 39 Castle Street, Edinburgh EH2 3BH; T.-0131-225 1200; e-mail: jscottmoncrieff@murraybeith.co.uk

Scouller, Glen, DA, RGI, RSW. Artist; b. 24.4.50, Glasgow; m., Carol Alison Marsh; 2 d. Educ. Eastbank Academy; Garthamlock Secondary; Glasgow School of Art; Hospitalfield College of Art, Arbroath. RSA Painting Award, 1972; W. O. Hutcheson Prize for Drawing, 1973; travelling scholarship, Greece, 1973; started teaching, Glasgow schools, 1974; started part-time tutoring, Glasgow School of Art, 1986; Lauder Award, Glasgow Art Club, 1987; Scottish Amicable Award, Royal Glasgow Institute of Fine Arts, 1987; David Cargill Award, Royal Glasgow Institute of Fine Arts, 2006; elected, RGI, 1989; painting full-time since 1989; elected, Royal Scottish Society of Painters in Watercolours, 1997; solo exhibitions: John D. Kelly Gallery, Glasgow, 1977, The Scottish Gallery, Edinburgh, 1980, Fine Art Society, Glasgow, 1985, 1988, Harbour Arts Centre, Irvine, 1986, Fine Art Society, Edinburgh, 1989, Portland Gallery, London, 1989, 1992, 1994, 1998, Macauley Gallery, Stenton, 1990, 1993, 1996, French Institute, Edinburgh, 1990, Open Eye Gallery, Edinburgh, 1992, 1994, 1997, 2000, 2002, 2007, Roger Billcliffe Fine Art, Glasgow, 1992, 1995, 1998, Everard Read Gallery, Johannesburg, 1997, 2000, 2001, 2006, 2007; Corrymella Scott Gallery, Newcastle-upon-Tyne, 1999, Lemon Street Gallery, Truro, 2002; Roger Billcliffe Gallery, Glasgow, 2003, 2007; The John Davies Gallery, Stow-on-the-Wold, 2004; Red Box Gallery, Newcastle upon Tyne, 2005; Henshelwood Gallery, Newcastle upon Tyne, 2005; Thompson's Marylebone, London, 2006; work in public, corporate and private collections, UK and abroad. Recreations: travel; music. Address: East Loudounhill Farm, Darvel KA17 0LU.
E-mail: glen.scouller@btinternet.com

Scrimgeour, John Beocher, MB, ChB, DObst, RCOG, FRCOG, FRCS(Edin), FRCP (Edin). Consultant Obstetrician and Gynaecologist, 1972-97, now retired; Honorary Senior Lecturer in Obstetrics and Gynaecology, Edinburgh University, 1972-97; Medical Director, Western General Hospitals Unit, Edinburgh, 1993-97; President, Edinburgh Obstetrical Society, 1996-97; Vice Chairman, Scottish Association of Trust Medical Directors, 1996-97; b. 22.1.39, Elgin; m., Joyce Morrin; 1 s.; 1 d. Educ. Hawick High School; Edinburgh University. General Practitioner, Edinburgh, 1963-65; Senior House Officer: Stirling Royal Infirmary, 1965, and Registrar, Eastern General Hospital, Edinburgh, 1966-69; Senior Registrar, Edinburgh Royal Infirmary, 1970-72; Senior Secretary, Edinburgh Obstetrical Society, 1980-85; Chairman, Area Division of Obstetrics and Gynaecology, 1984-88; Member, Council, Royal College of Obstetricians and Gynaecologists, 1976-81; Member, Gynaecological Visiting Society of Great Britain and Ireland, since 1979. Publication: Towards the Prevention of Fetal Malformation, 1978. Recreations: gardening; golf. Address: (h.) 16, Belgrave Crescent, Edinburgh EH4 3AJ; T.-0131-332-6480.

Scullion, Adrienne Clare, MA, PhD, FRSA, FRSE. James Arnott Chair of Drama, University of Glasgow, since 2005; b. Glasgow. Educ. University of Glasgow. Lecturer, Trinity College Dublin, 1992-93; British Academy Post Doctoral Fellow, University of Glasgow, 1993-96, Lecturer, then Senior Lecturer, from 1996. Member, Board of Directors, The Citizens' Theatre, Glasgow. Address: (b.) Department of Theatre, Film and Television Studies, University of Glasgow, Glasgow G12 8QQ; T.-0141 330 4677; e-mail: a.scullion@tfts.arts.gla.ac.uk

Seafield, Earl of; b. 20.3.39, London; m., Leila Refaat (2nd m.); 2 s. Educ. Eton; Cirencester Agricultural College. Recreation: countryside activities. Address: Old Cullen, Cullen, Buckie AB56 4XW; T.-01542 840221.

Sealey, Barry Edward, CBE, BA (Hons) (Cantab), CBIM. Director: Morago Ltd., Archangel Informal Investment Ltd., The Dundas Commercial Property (General Partner) Ltd., The Landmark Trustee Co. Ltd., EZD Ltd., CXR Biosciences Ltd., Lab 901 Ltd., and other companies; Chairman, Indigo Lighthouse Group Ltd.; b. 3.2.36, Bristol; m., Helen Martyn; 1 s.; 1 d. Educ. Dursley Grammar School; St. John's College, Cambridge. RAF, 1953-55. Joined Christian Salvesen as trainee, 1958; joined Board, Christian Salvesen PLC (responsible for Food Services Division), 1969; appointed Managing Director, 1981, Deputy Chairman and Managing Director, 1987; retired from Christian Salvesen, 1990. Address: (h.) 4 Castlelaw Road, Edinburgh, EH13 0DN; e-mail: bes@morago.co.uk

Searle, Rev. David Charles, MA, DipTh. Retired; Minister of the Church of Scotland, since 1965; Warden, Rutherford House, Edinburgh, 1993-2003; b. 14.11.37, Swansea; m., Lorna Christine Wilson; 2 s.; 1 d. Educ. Arbroath High School; St. Andrews University; London University; Aberdeen University. Teacher, 1961-64; Assistant Minister, St. Nicholas Church, Aberdeen, 1964-65; Minister: Newhills Parish Church, 1965-75, Larbert Old, 1975-85, Hamilton Road Presbyterian Church, Bangor, Co. Down, 1985-93; Contributor, Presbyterian Herald; Editor, Rutherford Journal of Church and Ministry. Publications: Be Strong in the Lord; Truth and Love in a Sexually Disordered World; The Ten Commandments; Through the Year with William Still. Recreations: sail-boarding; gardening; hill-walking; stick-making. Address: (h.) 12 Cairnie Road, Arbroath DD11 3DY; T.-01241 872794; e-mail: dcs@davidsearle.plus.com

Seaton, Professor Anthony, CBE, BA, MD (Cantab), DSc(hc) Aberdeen, FRCPLond, FRCPEdin, FFOM, FMedSci. Emeritus Professor, Aberdeen University; Hon. Consultant, Institute of Occupational Medicine, Edinburgh, since 2003; b. 20.8.38, London; m., Jillian Margaret Duke; 2 s. Educ. Rossall School, Fleetwood; King's College,

Cambridge; Liverpool University. Assistant Professor of Medicine, West Virginia University, 1969-71; Consultant Chest Physician, Cardiff, 1971-77; Director, Institute of Occupational Medicine, Edinburgh, 1978-90; Professor of Environmental and Occupational Medicine, Aberdeen University, 1988-2003; Editor, Thorax, 1977-82; Chairman, Department of Environment Expert Panel on Air Quality Standards, 1991-2002; President, British Thoracic Society, 1999; Member, Department of Health Committee on Medical Aspects of Air Pollution, 1991-2003; Member, Royal Society Working Group on nanoscience, 2003/04. Publications: books and papers on occupational and respiratory medicine. Recreations: keeping fit; opera; painting. Address: (h.) 8 Avon Grove, Cramond, Edinburgh, EH4 6RF; T.-031-336 5113.

Seckl, Professor Jonathan Robert, BSc, MB, BS, MRCP(UK), PhD, FRCPE, FMedSci, FRSE. Moncrieff-Arnott Professor of Molecular Medicine, Edinburgh University, since 1997; Professor of Endocrinology, 1996-97; Head, School of Molecular and Clinical Medicine, 2002-03; Director of Research, College of Medicine and Veterinary Medicine, since 2005; Chairman, Molecular Medicine Centre, 1996-2001; Member, Scottish Science Advisory Committee, since 2004; b. 15.8.56, London; m., Molly; 1 s.; 1 d. Educ. William Ellis School, London; University College Hospital Medical School, London. Sir Jules Thorn Research Fellow in Neuroendocrinology, Charing Cross and Westminster Medical School, 1984-87; Honorary Clinical Assistant, National Hospital for Nervous Diseases, London, 1984-87; Lecturer in Medicine, Edinburgh University, 1987-89; Wellcome Trust/Royal Society of Edinburgh Senior Clinical Research Fellow, 1989-96. Address: (b.) Queen's Medical Research Institute, 47 Little France Crescent, Edinburgh EH16 4TJ; T.-0131-242-6777; e-mail: j.seckl@ed.ac.uk

Secombes, Professor Christopher John, BSc, PhD, DSc, FIBiol, FRSE. Professor, School of Biological Sciences, University of Aberdeen, since 1997 (Head of School since 2002); Head, Scottish Fish Immunology Research Centre, University of Aberdeen, since 2001; b. 1.4.56, London; m., Karen Ruth; 2 s.; 1 d. Educ. Longdean School, Hemel Hempstead; University of Leeds; University of Hull. Department of Zoology, University of Aberdeen: Lecturer, 1984-91, Senior Lecturer, 1991-97, Head of Zoology, 2001-02, established Chair of Zoology, 2004. President, International Society for Developmental and Comparative Immunology, 2003-06; Adjunct Professor, University of Tromso, 2003-06. Editor, Fish and Shellfish Immunology; Member, Editorial Board: Developmental and Comparative Immunology, Veterinary Immunology and Immunopathology. Address: (b.) School of Biological Sciences, University of Aberdeen, Zoology Building, Tillydrone Avenue, Aberdeen AB24 2TZ; T.-01224 272872; e-mail: c.secombes@abdn.ac.uk

Sefton, Rev. Henry Reay, MA, BD, STM, PhD. Co-ordinator in Christian Studies, Aberdeen University, 1995-97; Chaplain, College of St Nicholas, Aberdeen, since 1989; b. 15.1.31, Pitsligo. Educ. Brechin High School; St. Andrews University; Glasgow University; Union Theological Seminary, New York. Assistant Minister, Glasgow Cathedral, 1957-58, St. Margaret's, Knightswood, Glasgow, 1958-61; Acting Chaplain, Hope Waddell Training Institution, Nigeria, 1959; Associate Minister, St. Mark's, Wishaw, 1962; Minister, Newbattle, 1962-66; Assistant Secretary, Church of Scotland Department of Education, 1966-72; Lecturer in Church History, Aberdeen University, 1972-90, Senior Lecturer, 1991-92; Master of Christ's College, Aberdeen, 1982-92; Alexander Robertson Lecturer, Glasgow University, 1995; Moderator, Aberdeen Presbytery, 1982-83, Synod of Grampian, 1991-92;

Convener, Church of Scotland Board of Education, 1987-91; Clerk, Aberdeen Presbytery, 1993-95; President: Scottish Church Society, 1988-91, Church Service Society, 1991-93; Chairman, Association of University Teachers (Scotland), 1982-84. Recreations: hill-walking; church architecture; stamp and coin collecting. Address: (h.) 25 Albury Place, Aberdeen, AB11 6TQ; T.-01224 572305.

Selkirk of Douglas, Rt. Hon. Lord (James Alexander Douglas-Hamilton), QC, PC, MA, LLB. Appointed Life Peer, 1997; MSP (Conservative), Lothians, 1999-2007; MP (Conservative), Edinburgh West, 1974-97; b. 31.7.42, Strathaven; m., (Priscilla) Susan (Susie) Buchan; 4 s. Educ. Eton; Balliol College, Oxford; Edinburgh University. Officer, TA 6/7 Bn. Cameronians Scottish Rifles, 1961-66, TAVR, 1971-74, Captain 2 Bn. Lowland Volunteers; Advocate, 1968-74; Councillor, Murrayfield-Crammond, 1972-74; Scottish Conservative Whip, 1977; a Lord Cmnr., HM Treasury, 1979-81, PPS to Malcolm Rifkind MP, at Foreign Office, later as Secretary of State for Scotland, 1983-87; Parliamentary Under Secretary of State: at the Scottish Office for Home Affairs and Environment, 1987-89; for Home Affairs and Environment, 1989-92 (with additional responsibility for local government finance 1989-90, and with additional responsibility for the arts in Scotland, 1990-92); for Education and Housing, Scottish Office, 1992-95; Minister of State for Home Affairs and Health, Scottish Office, 1995-97. Member, Scottish Select Committee Scottish Affairs 1981-83; Honorary Secretary: Conservative Parliamentary Constitutional Committee, Conservative Parliamentary Aviation Committee, 1983-87; Chairman, Scottish Parliamentary All-Party Penal Affairs Committee, 1983; Honorary President, Scottish Amateur Boxing Association, 1975-98; President: Royal Commonwealth Society (Scotland), 1979-87, Scottish National Council of UN Association, 1981-87; Member, Council, National Trust for Scotland, 1977-82; Honorary Air Commodore No. 2 (City of Edinburgh) Maritime Headquarters Unit and President International Rescue Corps, 1995; Honorary Air Commodore No. 603 (City of Edinburgh) Squadron, since 2000; Patron, Hope and Homes for Children (Chairman, Edinburgh Support Group, 2002-07, Vice Chairman, since 2007); President, Scottish Veterans Garden City Association Incorporated, since 2003; President, Trinity House Charity, 2007. Oxford Boxing Blue, 1961; President, Oxford University Conservative Association, 1963; President, Oxford Union, 1964. Publications: Motive For A Mission: The Story Behind Hess's Flight to Britain, 1971; The Air Battle for Malta: The Diaries of a Fighter Pilot, 1981; Roof of the World: Man's First Flight over Everest, 1983; The Truth about Rudolf Hess, 1993. Recreations: golf; forestry; debating; history; boxing. Address: House of Lords, London; Scottish Parliament, Edinburgh EH99 1SP.

Sellar, William David Hamilton, BA, LLB, FRHistS. Lord Lyon King of Arms, since 2008; Bute Pursuivant of Arms, 2001-08; Honorary Fellow, Faculty of Law, University of Edinburgh, since 1997; b. 27.2.41, Burnside, Glasgow; m., Susan Margaret Sainsbury; 4 s. Educ. Kelvinside Academy; Fettes College; St. Edmund Hall, Oxford; Edinburgh University. Solicitor; Legal Assessor and Depute Clerk of Court, Scottish Land Court, 1967-68; Lecturer, Senior Lecturer, Faculty of Law, University of Edinburgh, 1969-95. Secretary, Company of Scottish History Ltd., 1972-77; Literary Director, The Stair Society, 1979-84; President, Scottish Society for Northern Studies, 1984-87; Member, Ancient Monuments Board, 1991-97; Chairman of Council, Scottish History Society, 1998-2001; Vice-President, Society of Antiquaries of Scotland, 1999-2002; Chairman, Conference of Scottish Medievalists, 2000-03. Publications on Scots Law and Legal History, Highland History and Genealogy. Recreations: walking; island hopping; golf. Address: (b.) Court of The Lord Lyon, HM New Register House, Edinburgh EH1 3YT.

Sellers, Professor Susan Catherine, MA, DEA, PhD. Professor of English and Related Literature, St Andrews University, since 1998; b. 7.5.57, Lymington; m., Jeremy Thurlow; 1 s. Educ. British School, Brussels; Sorbonne, Paris. Senior Researcher, Ecole Normale Superieure, Paris, 1989-95; Reader, St Andrews University, 1995-98; Visiting Fellow, New Hall, Cambridge, 1994-95; Invited Fellow, St John's College, Oxford, Summer 1994; Leverhulme Research Fellow and Senior Visiting Scholar, Trinity College, Cambridge, 2001-02. Publications: Writing Differences; Delighting the Heart; Taking Reality by Surprise; Feminist Criticism: Theory and Practice; Language and Sexual Difference; Coming To Writing (translation); Three Steps on the Ladder of Writing (translation); The Semi-Transparent Envelope: Women Writing (Co-author); The Hélène Cixous Reader; Instead of Full Stops; Hélène Cixous: Authorship, Autobiography and Love; The Cambridge Companion to Virginia Woolf (Co-editor); Myth and Fairy Tale in Contemporary Women's Fiction; The Writing Notebooks of Hélène Cixons (Editor). Address: (b.) School of English, University of St. Andrews, Fife, KY16 9AL; T.-01334 462666.

Selway, Mark Wayne. Chief Executive, The Weir Group plc, since 2001; b. 2.6.59, Adelaide, Australia; m., Catherine; 2 s.; 1 d. Educ. Westminster School, South Australia. Britax Rainsford Pty Ltd: Marketing Manager, 1985-87, Marketing Director, 1987-88; President, Britax Rainsford Inc., 1989-95; Managing Director, Britax Rear Vision Systems, 1995-96; Executive Director and Managing Director, Automotive Components, Britax International plc, 1996-2000. Recreation: travel. Address: (b.) The Weir Group plc, Clydesdale Bank Exchange, 20 Waterloo Street, Glasgow G2 6DB; T.-0141-308 3700; e-mail: m.selway@weir.co.uk

Sempill, 21st Baron (James William Stuart Whitemore Sempill); b. 25.2.49; m.; 1 s.; 1 d. Educ. St Clare's Hall, Oxford. Succeeded to title, 1995; Company Director; contested (Conservative) Edinburgh North and Leith, Scottish Parliamentary election, 1999.

Semple, Colin Gordon, MA, MBChB, FRCP(Glas), FRCP(Ed), FRCP(London), MD. Consultant Physician, Southern General Hospital, Glasgow, since 1988; Honorary Clinical Senior Lecturer, Glasgow University, since 1988; b. 19.3.53, Glasgow; m., Elaine; 1 s.; 1 d. Educ. Loretto School; Brasenose College, Oxford; Glasgow University. General Physician with interest in diabetes and endocrinology and special interest in postgraduate medical education (Associate Postgraduate Dean); Deputy Medical Director, NHS Education Scotland; Chairman, General Medicine Specialist Advisory Committee, 1999-2003; Royal College of Physicians and Surgeons of Glasgow: Member, Council, 1986-90, Deputy Honorary Secretary, 1995-98, Honorary Secretary, 1998-2001, Vice-President, 2005-07. Recreations: golf; gardening; walking; curling.

Semple, David, WS, LLB, NP. Mediator, coach, business adviser; Director: Catalyst Mediation Ltd., Scottish Mediation Network, NICSCo Ltd.; formerly Partner and Chairman, Semple Fraser WS; b. 29.12.43, Glasgow; m., Jet; 2 s.; 1 d. Educ. Loretto School; Glasgow University. Partner, Bird Son & Semple, 1968-73; Bird Semple and Crawford Herron, 1973-88; Bird Semple Fyfe Ireland, 1988-90. President, Glasgow Chamber of Commerce, 1996-97; Chairman, Interactive Media Alliance Scotland, 1998-99. Recreations: golf; hill-walking; bagpipes. Address: (b.) 39 Kelvin Court, Great Western Road, Glasgow G12 0AE; T.-0141-357 4887; e-mail: david@catalystmediation.co.uk

Semple, Peter d'Almaine, DL, MD, FRCPGlas, FRCPEdin, FRCPLond. Consultant Physician and Chest Specialist, Inverclyde District, since 1979; b. 30.10.45, Glasgow; m., Judith Mairi Abercromby; 2 d. Educ. Belmont House; Loretto; Glasgow University. Consultant Physician, Inverclyde Royal Hospital, 1979; former Postgraduate Medical Tutor, Inverclyde District; Honorary Clinical Senior Lecturer, Glasgow University. Past Chairman, Medical Audit Sub-Committee, Scottish Office; Past President, Greenock and District Faculty of Medicine; Past Chairman, West of Scotland Branch, British Deer Society; Past Director, Medical Audit, and Property Convenor, Royal College of Physicians and Surgeons of Glasgow; Deputy Lieutenant, Renfrewshire; Chairman, Ardgowan Hospice. Recreations: field sports; gardening. Address: (h.) High Lunderston, Inverkip, PA16 0DU; T.-01475 522342.

Semple, Walter George, BL, DUniv, NP, ACI Arb. Solicitor; b. 7.5.42, Glasgow; m., Dr. Lena Ohrstrom; 3 d. Educ. Belmont House, Glasgow; Loretto School; Glasgow University. President, Glasgow Juridical Society, 1968; Tutor and Lecturer (part-time), Glasgow University, 1970-79; Council Member, Law Society of Scotland, 1976-80 and since 2003; Chairman, Scottish Lawyers European Group, 1978-81; Member, Commission Consultative des Barreaux Europeens, 1978-80, 1984-87; President, Association Internationale des Jeunes Avocats, 1983-84; Chairman, Scottish Branch, Institute of Arbitrators, 1989-91; Board Member, Union Internationale des Avocats, 1997-2001; Dean, Royal Faculty of Procurators in Glasgow, 1998-2001; President, Franco Scottish Business Club, 2000-01; Chairman, Campbell Lee plc; Trustee, John Muir Trust. Recreations: golf; fishing; skiing; music. Address: (h.) 79 Lancefield Quay, Glasgow G3 8HA.

Sewel, Lord (John Buttifant Sewel), CBE. Senior Vice-Principal, University of Aberdeen, 1999-2004; Parliamentary Under-Secretary of State, Scottish Office, 1997-99; b. 1946. Educ. Hanson Boys' Grammar School, Bradford; Durham University; University College Swansea; Aberdeen University. Councillor, Aberdeen City Council, 1974-84 (Leader of the Council, 1977-80); President, COSLA, 1982-84; Member, Accounts Commission for Scotland, 1987-96; Member, Scottish Constitutional Convention, 1994-95; successively Research Fellow, Lecturer, Senior Lecturer, Professor, Aberdeen University, from 1969; Dean, Faculty of Economic and Social Sciences, 1989-94; Vice Principal and Dean, Faculty of Social Sciences and Law, 1995-96; created Peer, 1996. Recreations: hill-walking; skiing; watching cricket. Address: House of Lords, London SW1.

Sewell, Professor John Isaac, PhD, DSc, CEng, FIEE, FIEEE. Emeritus Professor of Electronic Systems, since 2005; Professor of Electronic Systems, Glasgow University, 1985-2005 (Dean, Faculty of Engineering, 1990-93; Member, Court, 2000-04); b. 13.5.42, Kirkby Stephen; m., Ruth Alexandra Baxter; 1 d. Educ. Kirkby Stephen Grammar School; Durham University; Newcastle-upon-Tyne University. Lecturer, Senior Lecturer, Reader, Department of Electronic Engineering, Hull University, 1968-85. Publications: 148 papers. Recreations: swimming; climbing. Address: (h.) 16 Paterson Place, Bearsden, Glasgow, G61 4RU; T.-0141-586 5336; e-mail: Sewellmac@aol.com

Seymour-Jackson, Ralph, BA. Chief Executive, Student Loans Company, Glasgow, since 2003; b. 11.5.63; m., Angela; 2 c. Pilot, RAF, 1980-88; actuary, Norwich Union, 1988-92; Chief Executive, Scoplife Life Insurance Company, Athens, 1992-96; Group Corporate Development and Marketing Manager, Scottish Provident Institution, 1996-98; Head of UK Operations, Scottish Provident, 1998-2000; IT Director, Abbey National Finance and Investment Services, 2001-03. Address: (b.) 100 Bothwell Street, Glasgow G2 7JD.

Shanks, Duncan Faichney, RSA, RGI, RSW. Artist; b. 30.8.37, Airdrie; m., Una Brown Gordon. Educ. Uddingston

Grammar School; Glasgow School of Art. Part-time Lecturer, Glasgow School of Art, until 1979; now full-time painter; one-man shows: Stirling University, Scottish Gallery, Fine Art Society, Talbot Rice Art Gallery, Edinburgh University, Crawford Centre, Maclaurin Art Gallery, Glasgow School of Art, Fine Art Society, touring exhibition (Wales); taken part in shows of Scottish painting, London, 1986, Toulouse, Rio de Janeiro, 1985, Wales, 1988; Scottish Arts Council Award; Latimer and MacAulay Prizes, RSA; Torrance Award, Cargill Award, MacFarlane Charitable Trust Award, RGI; May Marshall Brown Award, RSW; The Lord Provost's Prize for painting (GOMA), 1996; tapestry commissioned by Coats Viyella, woven by Edinburgh Tapestry Company, presented to Glasgow Royal Concert Hall, 1991. Recreations: music; gardening.

Shanks, Melvyn D., BSc, DipEd, MInstP, CPhys, SQH. Principal, Belmont House School, since 2006; b. 15.7.62, Glasgow; m., Lynn; 2 s. Educ. The High School of Glasgow; University of Glasgow; University of Strathclyde. Teacher of Physics and Maths, The High School of Glasgow, 1985-90; Belmont House School: Head of Physics, 1990-97, Depute Head, 1997-2005. Recreation: member of the Salvation Army; music; golf; reading. Address: (b.) Belmont House School, Newton Mearns, Glasgow G77 5DU; T.-0141-639-2922; e-mail: admin@belmontschool.co.uk or melvyn@waitrose.com

Shanks, Rev. Norman James, MA, BD, DD; b. 15.7.42, Edinburgh; m., Ruth Osborne Douglas; 2 s.; 1 d. Educ. Stirling High School; St. Andrews University; Edinburgh University. Scottish Office, 1964-79; Chaplain, Edinburgh University, 1985-88; Lecturer in Practical Theology, Glasgow University, 1988-95; Leader, Iona Community, 1995-2002; Minister, Govan Old Parish Church, Glasgow, 2003-07. Convener, Acts Commission on Justice, Peace, Social and Moral Issues, 1991-95; Chairman, Edinburgh Council of Social Service, 1985-88; Chairman, Secretary of State's Advisory Committee on Travelling People, 1985-88; Convener, Church and Nation Committee, Church of Scotland, 1988-92; Moderator, Glasgow Presbytery, 2002-03; President, Scottish Churches Open College, 2001-03; Member, Broadcasting Council for Scotland, 1988-93; Member, Scottish Constitutional Convention, 1989-97; Central Committee of World Council of Churches, 1998-2006 (Moderator of WCC 9th Assembly Planning Committee, 2003-06); Member of Board of Christian Aid, 2000-05; HonDD, Glasgow University, 2005. Recreations: armchair cricket; occasional golf. Address: (h.) 1 Marchmont Terrace, Glasgow, G12 9LT; T.-0141-339 4421.

Shanks, Ronald Alan, LLB Hons (with options in French Law), DipLP, NP. Partner, HBJ Gateley Wareing (formerly Henderson Boyd Jackson), since 2006; b. 19.4.74, Aberdeen; m., Kathryn; 2 s. Educ. The Edinburgh Academy; Aberdeen University; L'Université Pierre Mendes France, Grenoble, France. Henderson Boyd Jackson WS: Trainee Solicitor, 1998-2000, Solicitor, 2000-05, Partner, 2005-06. Member: Law Society of Scotland, Law Society of England and Wales. Recreations: skiing; cycling; family. Address: (b.) Exchange Tower, 19 Canning Street, Edinburgh EH3 8EH; T.-0131 228 2400; e-mail: ashanks@hbj-gw.com

Shanks, Thomas Henry, MA, LLB. Solicitor (retired); Writer; Honorary Sheriff, Lanark, since 1982; Chairman, Lanark Tolbooth Heritage Centre Trust; Chairman, Appeals Service, 1985-2003; b. 22.10.30, Lanark; m., Marjorie A. Rendall; 1 s.; 1 d. (by pr. m.); 3 step s.; 1 step d. Educ. Lanark Grammar School; Glasgow University. Intelligence Corps (National Service), 1954-56. Depute Clerk of Peace,

County of Lanark, 1961-74; Chairman, Royal Burgh of Lanark Community Council, 1977-80 and 1983-86; Captain, Lanark Golf Club, 1962 and 2001; Lanark Lord Cornet, 1968. Recreations: golf; writing. Address: (h.) 5 Friarsfield Road, Lanark.

Sharp, Paul M., BSc, PhD, MRIA. Alan Robertson Chair of Genetics, University of Edinburgh, since 2007; b. 12.09.57, Heanor. Educ. University of Edinburgh. Lecturer, Associate Professor, Trinity College, University of Dublin, 1982-93; Professor of Genetics, University of Nottingham, 1993-2007. President, Society for Molecular Biology and Evolution, 2008. Address: (b.) Institute of Evolutionary Biology, University of Edinburgh, Kings Buildings, Edinburgh EH9 3JT; T.-0131-651-3684; e-mail: paul.sharp@ed.ac.uk

Sharp, Professor Peter Frederick, BSc, PhD, CPhys, CSci, FInstP, ARCP, FIPEM, FRSE. Professor of Medical Physics, University of Aberdeen; b. 13.8.47, Spalding; 2 s. Educ. Spalding Grammar School; Durham University; Aberdeen University. University of Aberdeen: Lecturer in Medical Physics, 1974-83, Senior Lecturer in Medical Physics, 1983-90. Honorary Sheriff, Stonehaven. Publication: Practical Nuclear Medicine (Editor). Address: (b.) Department of Biomedical Physics and Bioengineering, Foresterhill, Aberdeen AB25 2ZD; T.-01224 552499; e-mail: p.sharp@biomed.abdn.ac.uk

Sharwood Smith, Professor Michael Anthony, PhD, MA, DipAppLing. Professor of Languages, Heriot-Watt University, since 1999; b. 22.5.42, Cape Town, South Africa; m., Ewa Maria Wróblewska; 2 d. Educ. King's School, Canterbury; St Andrews University; Edinburgh University. English Teacher: Centre Pédagogique Regionale, Montpellier, France; British Centre, Sweden; British Council Senior Lecturer, Adam Mickiewicz University, Poznan, Poland; Senior Lecturer, Utrecht University, Netherlands. Founding Vice-President, European Second Language Association. Publications: over 100 on English linguistics, applied linguistics and second language acquisition; books include: Second Language Learning: Theoretical Foundations, 1994; Founding Editor, Second Language Research journal. Recreations: painting and drawing; music, trumpet and guitar; flight simulation. Address: Department of Languages and Intercultural Studies, Heriot-Watt University, Riccarton, Edinburgh, EH14 4AS; T.-0131-449 5111, ext. 4107.

Shaw, Rev. Alistair Neil, MA (Hons), BD (Hons). Minister, St. Paul's Parish Church, Johnstone, since 2003; b. 6.7.53, Kilbarchan; m., Brenda Bruce; 2 d. Educ. Paisley Grammar School; University of Glasgow. Minister: Relief Parish Church, Bourtreehill, Irvine, 1982-88, Laigh Kirk, Kilmarnock, 1988-99, Greenbank Parish Church, Clarkston, Glasgow, 1999-2002. Recreations: foreign travel; ancient history; swimming; cycling; walking. Address: 9 Stanley Drive, Brookfield, Johnstone, Renfrewshire PA5 8UF; T.-01505 320060; e-mail: ans2006@talktalk.net

Shaw, Rev. Professor Douglas William David, MA, LLB, BD, DD, WS. Professor of Divinity, St. Andrews University, 1979-91 (Dean, Faculty of Divinity, 1983-86, Principal, St. Mary's College, 1986-92; Minister, Church of Scotland, since 1960; b. 25.6.28, Edinburgh; m., Edinburgh Academy; Loretto; Ashbury College, Ottawa; St. John's College, Cambridge; Edinburgh University. Practised law as WS (Partner, Davidson and Syme, WS, Edinburgh), 1952-57; Assistant Minister, St. George's West Church, Edinburgh, 1960-63; Official Observer, Second Vatican

Council, Rome, 1962; Lecturer in Divinity, Edinburgh University, 1963-79; Principal, New College, and Dean, Faculty of Divinity, Edinburgh, 1973-78; Visiting Fellow, Fitzwilliam College, Cambridge, 1978; Visiting Lecturer, Virginia University, 1979. Publications. Who is God?, 1968; The Dissuaders, 1978, In Divers Manners (Editor), 1990; Dimensions, 1992; Theology in Scotland. Recreation: golf. Address: (h.) 4/13 Succoth Court, Edinburgh EH12 6BZ; T.-0131-337 2130; e-mail:DWilliamDShaw@aol.com

Shaw, Rev. Duncan, BD (Hons), MTh. Minister, St. John's, Bathgate, since 1978; b. 10.4.47, Blantyre; m., Margaret S. Moore; 2 s.; 1 d. Educ. St. John's Grammar School, Hamilton; Hamilton Academy; Trinity College, Glasgow University. Assistant Minister, Netherlee Parish Church, Glasgow, 1974-77. Clerk, West Lothian Presbytery, since 1982 (Moderator, 1989-90). Recreations: gardening; travel (in Scotland). Address: St. John's Parish Church Manse, Mid Street, Bathgate, EH48 1QD; T.-Bathgate 653146; e-mail: westlothian@cofscotland.org.uk

Shaw, Jo, BA (Cantab), LenDr (Brussels), FRSA, AcSS. Salvesen Chair, European Institutions, University of Edinburgh, since 2005; Senior Research Fellow, Federal Trust, London, since 2001; b. 17.09.61, Shipley; 1 s. Educ. Bradford Girls' Grammar School; Trinity College, Cambridge. Lecturer in Law, University of Exeter, 1984-90; Senior Lecturer in Law, Keele University, 1990-95; Professor of European Law and Director of The Centre for The Study of Law in Europe, University of Leeds, 1995-2001; Professor of European Law, University of Manchester, 2001-04. Author of many books and papers on European Union Law. Recreations: painting; swimming; walking. Address: (b.) School of Law, University of Edinburgh, Old College, South Bridge, Edinburgh EH8 9YL; T.-0131 650 9587; e-mail: jo.shaw@ed.ac.uk

Shaw, Professor Sir John Calman, CBE, KStJ, Dr hc, LLD, BL, FRSE, CA, FCMA. Former Governor, Bank of Scotland (1999-2001); b. 10.7.32, Perth; m., Shirley Botterill; 3 d. Educ. Strathallan; Edinburgh University. Qualified as Chartered Accountant, 1954; Partner, Graham, Smart & Annan, CA, Edinburgh, latterly Deloitte Haskins & Sells, 1960-1987; President, Institute of Chartered Accountants of Scotland, 1983-84; Johnstone Smith Professor of Accountancy, Glasgow University, 1977-83; Non-Executive Director, Bank of Scotland, 1990-2001, Deputy Governor, 1991-99. Director of various Investment Trusts and other companies (1982-2002); former Trustee, Scottish Science Trust and David Hume Institute; Receiver General, Priory of Scotland of Most Venerable Order of St. John, 1992-2002; Chairman, Scottish Higher Education Funding Council, 1992-98; Board Member, Scottish Enterprise, 1990-98; Deputy Chairman, Edinburgh Festival Society, 1990-2000; Executive Director, Scottish Financial Enterprise, 1986-90, later Chairman, 1995-99; author of various texts and publications on accountancy and corporate governance. Recreations: listening to music; walking; travel. Address: (b.) Tayhill, Brae Street, Dunkeld PH8 0BA.

Shaw, Mark Robert, BA, MA, DPhil, FRSE. Honorary Research Associate (Department of Natural Sciences), National Museums of Scotland, Keeper of Natural Sciences (formerly Geology and Zoology), 1996-2005; b. 11.5.45, Sutton Coldfield; m., Francesca Dennis Wilkinson; 2 d. Educ. Dartington Hall School; Oriel College, Oxford. Research Assistant (Entomology), Zoology Department, Manchester University, 1973-76; University Research Fellow, Reading University, 1977-80; Assistant Keeper, Department of Natural History, Royal Scottish Museum,

1980-83; Keeper of Natural History, National Museums of Scotland, 1983-96. Recreations: field entomology; family life. Address: (h.) 48 St. Albans Road, Edinburgh, EH9 2LU; T.-0131-667 0577; (b.) National Museums of Scotland, Chambers Street, Edinburgh EH1 1JF; T.-0131-247 4246; e-mail: m.shaw@nms.ac.uk

Shaw, Neil, BSc, BA (Hons). Head Teacher, Boclair Academy, since 2002; b. 30.12.53, Airdrie; m., Nan; 1 s.; 1 d. Educ. Airdrie Academy; University of Glasgow. Mathematics Teacher, Caldervale High School, Airdrie, 1977-87; Principal Teacher of Mathematics: Crookston Castle Secondary School, Glasgow, 1987-90, Carluke High School, 1990-93; Assistant Head Teacher, Boclair Academy, Bearsden, 1993-98; Head Teacher, Broxburn Academy, 1998-2002. Recreations: golf (Airdrie Golf Club); supporter of Airdrie United FC. Address: (b.) Inveroran Drive, Bearsden G61 2PL; T.-0141-943 0216; e-mail: nshaw@boclair.e-dunbarton.sch.uk

Shaw, Richard Wright, CBE, MA, FRSA. Principal and Vice Chancellor, University of Paisley, 1992-2001; b. 22.9.41, Preston; m., Susan Angela; 2 s. Educ. Lancaster Royal Grammar School; Sidney Sussex College, Cambridge. Assistant Lecturer in Management, then Lecturer in Economics, Leeds University, 1964-69; Lecturer in Economics, then Senior Lecturer, Stirling University, 1969-84; part-time Lecturer, Glasgow University, 1978-79; Visiting Lecturer, Newcastle University, NSW, 1982; Head, Department of Economics, Stirling University, 1982-84; Professor and Head, Department of Economics and Management, Paisley College, 1984-86, Vice Principal, 1986, Principal, 1987-92. Director, Renfrewshire Enterprise, 1992-2000; Member, Scottish Economic Council, 1995-98; Director, Higher Education Careers Service Unit, 1996-2001; Member, Board of Management, Reid Kerr College, 1993-2001; Member, Scottish Business Forum, 1998-99; Convener, Committee of Scottish Higher Education Principals, 1996-98; Member, Independent Review of Higher Education Pay and Conditions, 1998-99; Chairperson, Lead Scotland, 2001-07. Fellow, Scottish Vocational Education Council, since 1995; DUniv (Glasgow), 2001. Recreations: sketching and painting. Address: (b.) Drumbarns, 18 Old Doune Road, Dunblane FK15 9AG.

Shaw, Emeritus Professor Susan Angela, MA (Cantab), DUniv (Glasgow) 2004, FCIM. Former Vice-Principal, Strathclyde University (2000-04); Professor of Marketing; b. 1.6.43, Bristol; m., Richard Shaw; 2 s. Educ. Kingswood Grammar School, Bristol; Girton College, Cambridge. Marketing Executive, ICI Fibres; Lecturer, Senior Lecturer, Professor, Stirling University. Recreations: hill-walking; opera. Address: (b.) 18 Old Doune Road, Dunblane FK15 9AG.

Shaw-Stewart, Lady (Lucinda Victoria), DL. Deputy Lieutenant of Renfrewshire, 2007; b. 29.9.49, Harrogate; m., Sir Houston Shaw-Stewart Bt; 1 s. Educ. Cranborne Chase School; diploma from Study Centre for the History of the Fine and Decorative Arts. Freelance Lecturer in Fine and Decorative Arts, 1969-82; National Trust for Scotland: London Representative, 1978-82, Member, Council, 1983-88, Vice-President, 1994-2001. Trustee, Sir William Burrell's Trust, since 1992; Honorary Vice President, Ardgowan Hospice, Greenock; Member, Chatsworth House Trust, since 2002; Trustee, Royal Collection Trust, since 2005; Trustee, NADFAS, since 2005. Address: (h.) Ardgowan, Inverkip, Renfrewshire PA16 0DW; T.-01475 521226.

Shea, Michael Sinclair MacAuslan, CVO, DL, MA, PhD. Chairman: Hill Adamson Project, Executive Committee, Edinburgh Military Tattoo; Scottish Member, Independent Television Commission, 1996-2003; Chairman: Royal Lyceum Theatre, 1998-2004, Scottish National

Photographic Centre, since 2001; b. 10.5.38, Carluke; m., Mona Grec Stensen; 2 d. Educ. Lenzie Academy; Gordonstoun; Edinburgh University. Entered Foreign Office, 1963; seconded to Cabinet Office; Deputy Director General, British Information Services, New York; Press Secretary to the Queen; Head of Political and Government Affairs, Hanson PLC. Former Visiting Professor, Graduate School, Strathclyde University; Trustee, National Galleries of Scotland; Governor, Gordonstoun; Board Member, Murray Johnstone companies; Non-Executive Chairman, P&A Group; Non-Executive Chairman, NZN.; Vice-Chairman, Foundation for Skin Research; has published 25 books of fiction and non-fiction. Address: (b.) 1A Ramsay Garden, Edinburgh EH1 2NA; T.-0131-220 1456.

Shearer, David James Buchanan, BAcc, CA, FRSA. Chairman, Crest Nicholson plc; Senior Independent Director, Renold plc, SMG plc, Superglass Holdings plc; Non Executive Director, Aberdeen New Dawn Investment Trust plc and Mithras Investment Trust plc, since 2007; Non Executive Director, Scottish Financial Enterprise, since 2005; Advisory Board Member, Martin Currie Limited; Governor, The Glasgow School of Art, since 2004; Non Executive Director, HBOS plc, 2004-07; b. 24.3.59, Dumfries; partner, Virginia Braid. Educ. Eastwood High School, Glasgow; Glasgow University; Columbia Business School (Leadership Development Programme). Joined Deloitte & Touche (formerly Touche Ross & Co.), 1979; qualified CA, 1982; Partner, 1988; Partner in charge, Corporate Finance, 1992-99; National Corporate Finance Executive Member, 1992-99; Global Director of Corporate Finance, Deloitte Touche Tohmatsu, 1996-99; Senior Partner, Scotland & Northern Ireland, 1999-2003; UK Board Member, 1999-2003; UK Executive Group Member, 1999-2003. Recreations: heli-skiing; yachting; rugby; golf; art; wine. Address: (b.) 4 Westbourne Gardens, Glasgow G12 9XD; T.-0141 342 4243.
E-mail: djbshearer@btopenworld.com

Shearer, Patrick John, QPM, MA, LLB. Chief Constable, Dumfries and Galloway Constabulary, since 2007; President of the Association of Chief Police Officers in Scotland, since 2008, formerly Vice President (2007-08); m.; 1 s.; 1 d. Educ. Aberdeen University. Joined Grampian Police, 1983 and following service operations and Criminal Investigation, was appointed Assistant Chief Constable for Operations in 2001 and then Deputy Chief Constable in 2005. Address: (b.) Dumfries and Galloway Constabulary, Police Headquarters, Cornwall Mount, Dumfries DG1 1PZ; T.-01387 242201; e-mail: executive@dg.pnn.police.uk

Shedden, Fred, MA, LLB. Non Executive Director: iomart Group plc, since 2000, Murray International Trust plc, since 2000, Equitable Life Assurance Society, since 2002; Vice-Chair, Glasgow School of Art; Chairman, Halladale Group plc; b. 30.6.44, Edinburgh; m., Irene; 1 s.; 1 d. Educ. Arbroath High School; Aberdeen University. McGrigor Donald: Partner, 1971, Managing Partner, 1985-92, Senior Partner, 1993-2000. Director, Scottish Financial Enterprise, 1989-99; Director, Standard Life Assurance Society, 1992-99; Director, Scottish Metropolitan Property PLC, 1998-2000. Address: shedden@madasafish.com

Sheehan, Wendy Anne, LLB, DipLP, NP. Head of Family Law, Pagan Osborne, since 2006; Part time Sheriff, since 2005; b. 26.12.68, Glasgow. Educ. St. George's School for Girls; University of Aberdeen. Trainee, Assistant, Associate Solicitor, Russel and Aitken, Solicitors, 1990-96; Associate, Balfour and Manson, Solicitors, 1996-2000; Partner, MHD Solicitors, 2000-06. Former Chair, Couple Counselling Lothian; former Convener, CALM. Author for

Butterworths Family Law Service; various published articles on family law. Listed as leading family lawyer in both Chambers and Partners guide to the legal profession and The Legal 500. Address: (b.) Pagan Osborne, 55-56 Queen Street, Edinburgh EH2 3PA; T.-0771-892-1242; e-mail: wsheehan@pagan.co.uk

Sheldon, David Henry, LLB (Hons), DipLP. Advocate, since 1998; b. 22.4.65, Dundee. Educ. High School of Dundee; Aberdeen University. Admitted as Solicitor, 1990; Lecturer in Private Law, Edinburgh University, 1990-98; Associate Dean, Faculty of Law, Edinburgh University, 1994-97; admitted to Faculty of Advocates, 1998. Former Member, Criminal Court Rules Committee. Publications: Evidence: Cases and Materials, 1996; Scots Criminal Law, 2nd edition, 1997; The Laws of Scotland: Stair Memorial Encyclopaedia (Contributor). Recreations: rock climbing; triathlon; music; song; laughter and the love of friends. Address: (b.) Advocates' Library, Parliament House, Edinburgh EH1 1RF; T.-0131-667 2043.

Shepherd, Professor James, BSc, MB, ChB, PhD, FRCPath, FRCP (Glas), FMedSci, FRSE. Honorary Professor in Vascular Biodiversity, University of Glasgow, since 2006; b. 8.4.44, Motherwell; m., Janet Bulloch Kelly; 1 s.; 1 d. Educ. Hamilton Academy; Glasgow University. Lecturer, Glasgow University: Biochemistry, 1968-72, Pathological Biochemistry, 1972-77; Assistant Professor of Medicine, Baylor College of Medicine, Houston, Texas, 1976-77; Senior Lecturer in Pathological Biochemistry, Glasgow University, 1977-84; Visiting Professor of Medicine, Geneva University, 1984; Director, West of Scotland Coronary Prevention Study; Director, Prospective Study of Pravastation in the Elderly at Risk; Principal Investigator, Jupiter UK, since 2005; Chairman, European Atherosclerosis Society, 1993-96; Visiting Professor, The Cleveland Clinic, 1998; author of textbooks and papers on lipoprotein metabolism and heart disease prevention. Address: (b.) Department of Biochemistry, Royal Infirmary, Glasgow, G4 OSF; T.-0141 552 0689.

Shepherd, Robert Horne (Robbie), MBE, MUniv (Aberdeen). Freelance Broadcaster, since 1976, including over twenty-five years as presenter of BBC Radio Scotland's Take The Floor and Reel Blend; Journalist and Author, specialising in the Doric language; b. 30.4.36, Dunecht, Aberdeen; m., Agnes Margaret (Esma) (1961); 1 s. Educ. Robert Gordon's College, Aberdeen. Left school at 15 to work in accountant's office, eventually becoming ASCA; management accountant, fish firm, 13 years; self-employed accountant; full-time on radio, since 1984. Member, Friends of Elphinstone Institute, University of Aberdeen; Trustee, Buchan Heritage Society and Charles Murray Memorial Fund. Author on Books of the Doric. Received the Hamish Henderson Award for services to Traditional Music and inducted into the Hall of Fame - Scots Trad Music Awards, 2006. Recreations: gardening; traditional arts of Scotland, especially the use of the Doric tongue.

Sheridan, James. Labour MP, Paisley and Renfrewshire North, since 2005, West Renfrewshire, 2001-05; b. 24.11.52, Glasgow; m., Jean; 1 s.; 1 d. Educ. St Pius Secondary School. Trade union official, TGWU, 1999-2000; material handler, 1984-99; TGWU Convenor, Pilkington Optronics, 1985-99. Recreation: keep-fit activities. Address: (h.) 31 Park Glade, Erskine, Renfrewshire PA8 7HH.

Sheridan, Rt. Rev. Mgr. John. Prelate of Honour; Parish Priest, St. Paul's, Whiteinch, Glasgow, 1986-2000; b. 22.8.29, Clydebank. Educ. Holyrood Senior Secondary School, Glasgow; Campion House, Osterley; Royal Scots College, Valladolid, Spain. Ordained Priest, 1956; Curate in Glasgow, 1956-63; Spiritual Director, Royal Scots College,

Valladolid, Spain, 1963-69; Curate in Glasgow, 1969-84; Parish Priest, Our Lady and St. Margaret's, Kinning Park, 1984-86; Chancellor, Archdiocese of Glasgow, 1983-92. Scout Area Chaplain, Glasgow, 1960-63; Scout District Commissioner, N.E. and N.W.II Districts, Glasgow, 1970-78; National Scout Chaplain, 1978-94; Hon. Vice Chairman, Scottish Catholic Scout Advisory Council, 1995; awarded Scout Silver Acorn, 1987; Member, Muirkirk Enterprise Group, 2001. Recreations: golf; painting; caravanning. Address: St. Thomas', 79 Wellwood Street, Muirkirk, East Ayrshire KA18 3QU; T.-01290 660087.

Sheridan, Michael. Principal Solicitor, Sheridans, Glasgow, since 1974; Secretary, Scottish Law Agents Society, since 2004; b. 28.3.48, Glasgow; m., Carole; 3 s. Educ. St. Aloysius College, Glasgow; University of Glasgow. Solicitor at Dundee and Glasgow, since 1972; College and University Lecturer, 1974-2001; Joint Standing Committee on Legal Education, 1998-2001; Legally Qualified Chairman, The Appeals Service, since 2000. Recreations: hill walking; running; travel. Address: (b.) Scottish Law Agents Society, 166 Buchanan Street, Glasgow G1 2LW; T.-0141 332 3536; e-mail: secretary@slas.co.uk

Sheridan, Tommy. MSP (Solidarity), Glasgow, 2006-07 (Scottish Socialist, 1999-2006). Member, Glasgow City Council, 1992-2003; President, Anti Poll Tax Federation, 1989-92.

Sherrard, Mary Stephen, MBE, BA. National President, Woman's Guild, Church of Scotland, 1993-96; Representative on Women's National Commission, 1993-98; b. 22.4.23, Renfrew; m., Rev. John A. Sherrard; 2 s.; 1 d. Educ. Girls' High School, Glasgow; Open University. Journalist; service in W.R.N.S.; playgroup work; Citizens Advice Bureau work. Elder, Church of Scotland. Recreations: crosswords; writing; walking on holiday. Address: (h.) Fair Havens, 19 Provost Kay Park, Victoria Manor, Kirkcaldy KY1 2RD; T.-01592 642821.

Sherriff, Robert Mark, CBE, MSI, BA, DL. Stockbroker, since 1960; Chairman, Executive Committee, Erskine Hospital, 2000-05; Chairman, The MacRobert Trust Tarland, 1994-2006; Appointed Vice Lord Lieutenant, Stirling: Falkirk, 1995; b. 29.3.36, Kilmacolm; m., Margaret Fraser; 2 s.; 2 d. Educ. Cargilfield; Sedbergh; Trinity College, Cambridge. National Service, 1954-56; served with TA from 1956; joined R.C. Greig & Co., Stockbroker, Glasgow, 1959; became a Partner (now Director); former Vice Chairman, Greig Middleton & Co. Ltd., Glasgow; former Director, Gerrard Group PLC, London; former Vice Chairman, Scottish Building Society; retired as Chairman, Highland TAVR, 1996. Recreations: tennis; golf; shooting; skiing. Address: (h.) The Old Manse, Blairdrummond, by Stirling FK9 4UX

Shiach, Allan G., BA. Chairman, Macallan-Glenlivet PLC, 1979-96; Chairman, Scottish Film Council, 1991-97; Chairman, Scottish Film Production Fund, 1991-96; Chairman, Scottish Screen, 1996-98; b. Elgin; m., Kathleen Breck; 2 s.; 1 d. Educ. Gordonstoun School; McGill University, Montreal. Writer/Producer, since 1970; Writer/Co-Writer: Don't Look Now, The Girl from Petrovia, Daryl, Joseph Andrews, Castaway, The Witches, Cold Heaven, Regeneration, In Love and War, and other films; Member: Broadcasting Council for Scotland, 1988-91; Member, Council, Scotch Whisky Association, 1984-96; Chairman, Writers' Guild of G.B., 1989-91; Director, Rafford Films, since 1982; Director, Scottish Media Group plc, since 1993; Governor, British Film Institute, 1992-98.

Hon. Doctorate of Arts, Napier University (June, 2007); Hon. Doctorate Honoris Causa, Aberdeen University (November 2007). Freeman, City of London, 1988; e-mail: algscott@aol.com

Shiach, Sheriff Gordon Iain Wilson, MA, LLB, BA (Hons). Sheriff of Lothian and Borders, at Edinburgh, 1984-97, and at Peebles, 1996-97; Part-time Commissioner, Mental Welfare Commission for Scotland, 2001-05; b. 15.10.35, Elgin; m., Margaret Grant Smith; 2 d. (1 deceased). Educ. Lathallan; Gordonstoun; Edinburgh University; Open University; Rose Bruford College. Admitted Advocate, 1960; practised as Advocate, 1960-72; Sheriff of Fife and Kinross, later Tayside, Central and Fife, at Dunfermline, 1972-79; Sheriff of Lothian and Borders, at Linlithgow, 1979-84; Hon. Sheriff, Elgin, since 1986; Member: Council of Sheriffs' Association, 1989-95 (President, 1993-95); Standing Committee on Criminal Procedure, 1989-93; Board, Lothian Family Conciliation Service, 1989-93; Parole Board for Scotland, 1990-99 (Vice Chairman, 1995-99); Council, Faculty of Advocates, 1993-95; Shrieval Training Group, 1994-95; Review Group on Social Work National Standards for Throughcare, 1994-95; Chairman, The Scottish Society, 1992-93, The Edinburgh Sir Walter Scott Club, 1995-98. Recreations: walking; swimming; music; art; film; theatre.

Shields, Tom, BA. Journalist; b. 9.2.48, Glasgow; 1 s.; 1 d. Educ. Bellarmine Comprehensive; Lourdes Secondary School (no miracle); Strathclyde University. Journalist, Sunday Post; Diary Writer, The Herald, 1979-2002; Columnist, The Sunday Herald. Publications: Tom Shields' Diary; Tom Shields Too; Tom Shields Free at Last; Tom Shields Goes Forth; Just the Three Weeks in Provence (Co-author). Recreation: Celtic studies.

Shields, Tom, BSc (Eng). Managing Director, Kemfine UK Ltd., since 2005, previously Vice President, Avecia Fine Chemicals, and Vice President, Manufacturing and SHE, Avecia Holdings Ltd.; former Chairman, Scottish Enterprise Forth Valley; b. 5.2.51, Belfast; m., Patsy; 1 s.; 2 d. Educ. Ballygomartin School; Queen's University of Belfast. Worked for Unilever; ICI: joined as Design Engineer, 1977, worked in Manchester, NE England and Ayrshire; Zeneca Engineering: Chief Engineer, 1993, worked in USA, appointed Site Manager, Zeneca Grangemouth, 1996, then became part of management buyout to form Avecia, 1999. Board Member, Scottish Enterprise Forth Valley, 1999-2005; lead the spin off of Fine Chemicals from Avecia to form Kemfine UK. Recreations: baseball; skiing; theatre. Address: Kemfine Ltd., Earls Road, Grangemouth FK3 8XG; T.-01324 494530; e-mail: tom.shields@kemfine.co.uk

Shimmield, Professor Graham, FRSE, FIBiol. Director, Scottish Association for Marine Science and Dunstaffnage Marine Laboratory, since 1996; b. 1.12.58, Trinidad; 2 d. Educ. Wellington College, Berkshire; University of Durham; University of Edinburgh. Lecturer in Chemical Oceanography, 1985-95; Reader, University of Edinburgh, 1995-96; Deputy Director, Centre for Coastal and Marine Science, 1998-2000. Deputy Director, UHI Millennium Institute, since 1999; President, European Federation of Marine Science and Technology Societies, since 1999; Honorary Professor, University of St. Andrews, since 2000. Address: (b.) Dunstaffnage Marine Laboratory, Dunbeg, Oban, PA37 1QA; T.-01631 559000; e-mail: gbs@sams.ac.uk

Shinwell, Sir (Maurice) Adrian, Kt, DL, LLB, NP, MCIArb. Solicitor; Senior Partner, Kerr Barrie, Glasgow, since 1991; Deputy Lieutenant, Renfrewshire, since 1999; b. 27.2.51; m., Lesley McLean; 2 s.; 1 d. Educ. Hutchesons' Boys' Grammar School; Glasgow University. Admitted Solicitor, 1975; joined Kerr, Barrie & Duncan, 1976; Notary Public, since 1976; Tutor (part-time), Law Faculty, Glasgow University, 1980-84; Solicitor-Mediator, 1994-2004; Director: National Theatre of Scotland, Digital Animations Group plc, 2002-07, St. Leonards School, 2001-2004, Kerr Barrie Nominees Ltd. Scottish Conservative and Unionist Association: Member, Scottish Council, 1982-98; Chairman, Eastwood Association, 1982-85; Chairman, Cumbernauld and Kilsyth Association, 1989-91; Vice-President, 1989-92; President, 1992-94; Scottish Conservative and Unionist Party: Chairman, Candidates' Board, Member, Scottish Executive and Scottish Council, 1998-2000; Member, Central Advisory Committee on Justices of the Peace, 1996-99; Vice Chairman, Justices of the Peace Advisory Committee, East Renfrewshire, 2000-06. Address: (h.) Sarona, South Road, Busby, Glasgow, G76 8JB; T.-0141-221 6844.

Shirreffs, Jennifer Anne, DL, CStJ, BSc. Director, Aberdeen and NE Deaf Society, since 1984, Chairman, Board of Directors, 1992-2003; Deputy Lieutenant, City of Aberdeen, since 2005; b. 20.1.49, Aberdeen; m., Dr. Murdoch J. Shirreffs. Educ. Aberdeen High School for Girls; University of Aberdeen. PA to Rt. Hon. Jo Grimmond MP while Rector of Aberdeen University, 1971-72; Co-ordinator, Community Arts Projects, Rowntree Trust, 1972-73. Chairman, Aberdeen Centenary Committee, Royal Scottish Society for Prevention of Cruelty to Children (now Children First), 1983-85; Trustee, Aberdeen Gomel Trust (Aberdeen City Council), since 1990; Vice-Chairman, St. John's Association (Aberdeen) and Order Committee, since 1994; Elected Commander of the Association, 2004; Chairman, Friends of Scottish Ballet (Grampian), since 1989; Member, National Council of Friends of Scottish Ballet, 1989-2007; Member, National Merchandising Committee of Friends of Scottish Ballet, 1994-2007; Chairman, Trading Company of Scottish Ballet, 2000-07; Chairman, Friends of Aberdeen and NE Scotland Music School, since 1998; Director, Aberdeen Performing Arts running His Majesty's Theatre and Music Hall, since 2001; University of Aberdeen: Member, General Council Business Committee, since 1994, Chairman, Friends of the Elphinstone Institute, since 2006; Member and past president (2005-06) of Rotary Club of Aberdeen St. Machar; Member and past president (2006-07) of the Inner Wheel of Aberdeen St. Machar. Recreations: piano playing; philately; travel and languages; cooking and entertaining; visual and performing arts and music of all types. Address: (h.) 72 Gray Street, Aberdeen AB10 6JE; T.-01224-321998; e-mail: jennys72@hotmail.co.uk

Shirreffs, Murdoch John, MB, ChB, DObstRCOG, FRCGP, MFHom. General Medical Practitioner, Aberdeen, since 1974; Medical Hypnotherapist and Homoeopathic Specialist; Specialist in Charge, NHS Grampian Homeopathy Service; b. 25.5.47, Aberdeen; m., Jennifer McLeod. Educ. Aberdeen Grammar School; Aberdeen University. General Practice Trainer, 1977-99; Secretary, Grampian Division, British Medical Association, 1978-2005; former Member, BMA Scottish Council. Past President, North of Scotland Veterans' Hockey Club; Member, Scottish LX (over 60s) Veterans' Hockey Team; Burgess, Guild of City of Aberdeen, since 2001. Recreations: hockey; opera and classical music; big band jazz; DIY; gardening; food and wine; travel. Address: (h.) 72 Gray Street, Aberdeen, AB10 6JE; T.-01224 321998. E-mail: murdoch_and_jenny_shirreffs@msn.com

Short, Agnes Jean, BA (Hons), MLitt. Writer; b. Bradford, Yorkshire; m., Anthony Short (qv); 3 s.; 2 d. Educ.

Bradford Girls' Grammar School; Exeter University; Aberdeen University. Various secretarial, research and teaching jobs, both in UK and abroad; took up writing, 1966; 19 novels, most of which have a Scottish setting; also short stories and radio; Constable Award, 1976. Recreations: dog-walking; whisky-tasting; good food; small hills. Address: (h.) Khantore, Crathie, by Ballater, Aberdeenshire, AB35 5TJ.

Shucksmith, Professor Mark, MA, MSc, PhD. Professor of Planning, University of Newcastle upon Tyne, since 2005; Professor of Land Economy, University of Aberdeen, 1993-2004; Co-director, Arkleton Centre for Rural Development Research, University of Aberdeen, 1995-2004; Chair, Scottish Government's Committee of Inquiry on Crofting, 2007-08; Programme Adviser, Joseph Rowntree Foundation's Action in Rural Areas Programme, since 1997; Co-Director, Scottish Centre for Social Justice Research, 2001-04; Adviser, Rural Affairs Committee, Scottish Parliament, 2000-04; Board Member: The Countryside Agency, since 2005, Commission for Rural Communities, since 2006; Vice President, International Rural Sociological Association, 2004-08; Member, Affordable Rural Housing Commission, 2005-06; b. 25.8.53, London; m., Janet; 2 d. Educ. Sidney Sussex College, University of Cambridge. Department of Agricultural Economics, University of Newcastle upon Tyne, 1977-81; Lecturer then Senior Lecturer then Reader in Land Economy, University of Aberdeen, 1981-93. Former Vice-Chair, Rural Forum; Program Chair, XI World Rural Sociology Congress. Publications: several books, notably on social exclusion in rural areas, rural housing, agricultural restructuring; over 50 papers in learned journals. Recreations: music; hillwalking; reading. Address: (b.) School of Architecture, Planning and Landscape, University of Newcastle upon Tyne, NE1 7RU; T.-0191 222 6808.

Sibbald, Michael Robert, BA, MBA. Group Human Resources Director, Home Retail Group plc; b. 30.8.48, Edinburgh; m., Margaret; 2 s.; 1 d. Educ. George Heriot's School; Heriot-Watt University; Glasgow University. Lay Member, Employment Appeals Tribunal, since 2002; Non Executive Director: Whitehall Industry Group, since 2004, Shaw Associates, since 2007; Member, Advisory Council, Public Concern at Work, 2006. Recreations: reading; sports cars; athletics; football. Address: (h.) The Long House, Deanfoot Road, West Linton EH46 7DX; T.-01968 660569.

Sibbett, Professor Wilson, CBE, FRS, BSc, PhD. Wardlaw Professor of Natural Philosophy, St. Andrews University (Director of Research, 1994-2003, Chairman, Department of Physics and Astronomy, 1985-94); Chair, Scottish Science Advisory Committee, 2002-06; b. 15.3.48, Portglenone, N. Ireland; m., Barbara Anne Brown; 3 d. Educ. Ballymena Technical College; Queen's University, Belfast. Postdoctoral Research Fellow, Blackett Laboratory, Imperial College, London, 1973-76; Lecturer in Physics, then Reader, Imperial College, 1976-85. Fellow: Institute of Physics, Royal Society of Edinburgh, Royal Society (of London). Honorary Degrees: LLD (Dundee), DSc (Trinity College Dublin). Recreation: golf. Address: (b.) School of Physics and Astronomy, St. Andrews University, North Haugh, St. Andrews, KY16 9SS; T.-01334 463100.

Siddiqui, Professor Mona, MA, MIL, PhD, DLitt (Hons), FRSE, FRSA. Professor of Islamic Studies and Public Understanding, Glasgow University, since 2006; Director, Centre for the Study of Islam, Glasgow University, since 1998; b. 3.5.63, Karachi, Pakistan; m., Farhaj; 3 s. Educ. Salendine-Nook High School, Huddersfield; Leeds University; Manchester University. Lecturer in Arabic and

Islamic Studies: Manchester Metropolitan University, 1989-90, Glasgow Caledonian University, 1993, Glasgow University, 1995. Chair, BBC Scottish Religious Advisory Council, 2005; Member, BBC Central Religious Advisory Council, 2003; Contributor, Thought for the Day, BBC Scotland and Radio 4. Recreations: interior decorating; cooking; reading. Address: (b.) 4 The Square, University of Glasgow, Glasgow G12 8QQ; e-mail: msi@arts.gla.ac.uk

Sillars, James. Management consultant; Assistant Secretary-General, Arab-British Chamber of Commerce, 1993-2002; b. 4.10.37, Ayr; m., Margo MacDonald (qv); 1 s.; 3 d. Educ. Ayr Academy. Member, Ayr Town Council and Ayr County Council Education Committee, 1960s; Member, Western Regional Hospital Board, 1965-70; Head, Organisation Department, Scottish TUC, 1968-70; MP, South Ayrshire, 1970-79; Co-Founder, Scottish Labour Party, 1976; MP, Glasgow Govan, 1988-92.

Silver, Gillian M., LLB, NP. Partner, MacNeill and Critchley, Solicitors, Inverness, since 1983; b. 13.5.56, Aberdeen; m., Chris. Educ. Inverness Royal Academy; Edinburgh University. Member, Local Government Boundary Commission for Scotland, 1995-99; Past Chairman, Highland Solicitors Property Centre Ltd.; Past Chairman, Solicitors Property Centres Scotland; Senator, Junior Chamber International. Recreations: golf; curling; choral singing; running; theatre. Address: (h.) The Garden House, Kincurdie, Rosemarkie IV10 8SJ; T.-01381 621211.

Sim, Ian Allan, BSc, CA. Director, Johnston Smillie, Chartered Accountants; b. 2.8.48, Edinburgh; 2 s. Educ. Lochaber High School; Edinburgh University. Manager, Deloittes, Chartered Accountants, 1973-76; Johnston Smillie, Chartered Accountants, since 1977. Treasurer, St. George's West Church; Director, Leith FM; Trustee, Canine Concern. Recreations: swimming; music. Address: (b.) 2 Roseburn Terrace, Edinburgh EH12 6AW; T.-0131 317 7377.

Sime, Martin, MA. Director and Chief Executive, Scottish Council for Voluntary Organisations, since 1991; b. 23.9.53, Edinburgh. Educ. George Heriot's; St. Andrews University; Edinburgh University. Social and Economic History Researcher, 1976-78; Sheep Farmer, 1978-81; Freelance Researcher, 1982; Project Manager, Sprout Market Garden, 1983-85; Development/Principal Officer (Day Services), Scottish Association for Mental Health, then Director, 1985-91. Recreations: cinema; food; bridge. Address: (b.) Mansfield Traquair Centre, Mansfield Place, Edinburgh EH3 6BB.

Simmers, Graeme Maxwell, CBE, CA, DL; b. 2.5.35, Glasgow; m., Jennifer M.H. Roxburgh; 2 s.; 2 d. Educ. Glasgow Academy; Loretto School. Qualified CA, 1959; commissioned Royal Marines, 1959-61, Hon. Colonel, Royal Marines Reserve, 2000-06. Former Partner, Kidsons Simmers CA; Chairman, Scottish Highland Hotels Group Ltd., 1972-92; Member, Scottish Tourist Board, 1979-86; Chairman, HCBA (Scotland), 1984-86; Past Chairman, Board of Management, Member of National Executive, BHA; Elder and Treasurer, Killearn Kirk; Governor, Queen's College, Glasgow, 1989-93; Chairman, Scottish Sports Council, 1992-99; Non-Executive Director: Forth Valley Acute Hospitals Trust, 1993-2001, Forth Valley Health Board, since 2002; Past Chairman of Governors, Loretto School; Captain, Royal and Ancient Golf Club of St. Andrews, 2001-02 (Past Chairman, Championship Committee). OBE, 1982. Recreations: rugby; golf; skiing. Address: (h.) Kincaple, Boquhan, Balfron, near Glasgow, G63 ORW; T.-01360 440375.

Simmons, Professor John Edmund Leonard, BSc, PhD, CEng, FRSE, FIMechE, FIEE. Professor Emeritus, Heriot-Watt University, since 2007 (Professor of Mechanical Engineering, 1992, Dean of Engineering, 1999, Head, Department of Mechanical and Chemical Engineering, 1994, Vice-Principal, 2002-06, Acting Principal, 2006-07); Chairman, TechniTex Faraday Partnership, 2000-03; Chairman, Academic Standards Committee, Institution of Mechanical Engineers, since 2004; b. 24.9.47, Faversham; m., Anne; 2 s.; 2 d. Educ. Birmingham University; Cambridge University. Production Manager, Baker Perkins Chemical Machinery, Stoke on Trent, 1977-80; Design Manager, Vickers plc–Michell Bearings, Newcastle upon Tyne, 1981-84; Lecturer in Engineering, Durham University, 1984-91. Recreations: gardening; walking; travelling; cinema. Address: (b.) Heriot-Watt University, Edinburgh, EH14 4AS; T.-0131-451 3001; e-mail: j.simmons@hw.ac.uk

Simon, Shona M. W., MA, LLB, DipCG, DipLP. Vice-President, Employment Tribunals (Scotland), since 2004; Employment Tribunal Chairman, since 2002; b. 9.5.60, Greenock; m., Dr. E. J. Simon; 2 s. Educ. Greenock Academy; University of Edinburgh. Careers Adviser, 1984-88; Partner, Mackay Simon, Employment Lawyers, 1993-2002; Equal Opportunities Development Adviser, Scottish Parliament, 2001-02. Publications: joint author, Employment Law (textbook); joint Update Editor, Leslie: Employment Tribunal Practice in Scotland; joint Editor, Green's Employment Law Bulletin. Recreations: cooking; reading. Address: (b.) Employment Tribunal Office, 54-56 Melville Street, Edinburgh EH3 7HF; T.-0131 226 5584; e-mail: shona.simon@judiciary.gsi.gov.uk

Simpson, Alan Gordon, DL, MA (Oxon), CEng, MICE. Partner, W. A. Fairhurst and Partners, since 1989; Chairman, University of Stirling Court, since 2007; Chairman, National Youth Orchestra of Scotland, since 1998; b. 15.2.50, Edinburgh; m., Jan; 1 s.; 1 d. Educ. Rugby School; Magdalen College, Oxford. Brian Colquoun and Partners, 1972-78; W.A. Fairhurst and Partners, since 1979; Deputy Lieutenant, Stirling and Falkirk; Chairman, Glasgow and West of Scotland Branch of the Institution of Civil Engineers, 2006-07; Member, Council, Institution of Civil Engineers, 2000-03. Recreations: music; skiing; archery. Address: (h.) Arntomie, Port of Menteith, by Stirling; (b.) 225 Bath Street, Glasgow.

Simpson, Professor David, CBE, DrTech (Abertay), Dr BA (Napier), DSc (Heriot Watt), CEng, FIEE, FRSE, FRSA. Chairman, Simpson Research Ltd.; Director, Bookham Inc; Director, Conjunct Ltd.; Director, Environcom Ltd.; Chairman, MIMIV Ltd.; Co-Founder, Elvingston Science Centre; b. 23.11.26, Ceres, Fife; m., Janice Ann; 1 s.; 2 d. Educ. Bell Baxter School, Cupar, Fife; Abertay University; Stanford University. R. & D. Engineer, Marconi, 1952-56; Managing Director, Microcell Electronics, 1956-60; General Manager, Hughes Microelectronics, 1960-62; Managing Director, Hewlett Packard Ltd., 1962-70; President, Gould Inc, Chicago, 1976-88. Recreations: hill walking; wood carving. Address: (h.) Elvingston House, Tranent EH33 1EH; T.-01875 408025; e-mail: xia90@dial.pipex.com

Simpson, Professor Hugh Walter, MB, ChB, MD, PhD, FRCPath, FRCP(Glas). Emeritus Professor; Senior Research Fellow, University Department of Surgery, Glasgow University and Royal Infirmary; Head of Pathology, Glasgow Royal Infirmary, 1984-93; Honorary Visiting Professor, University of Minnesota, since 1970; b. 4.4.31, Ceres Fife; m., Myrtle Emslie (see Myrtle Simpson);

3 s.; 1 d. Educ. Bryanston; Edinburgh University. Leader of numerous expeditions to polar and tropical regions; 4,000 miles sledged in polar regions; awarded Polar Medal, Mungo Park and Pery Medals; Man of the Year, Greenland Radio, 1965; Gold Medal Lecture, Royal College of Surgeons of Edinburgh, 1995; Scientist of the Year Lecture, Little Rock, Arkansas, 1978. Founder Editor, International Journal of Chronobiology; Visiting Scientist, National Institute of Health, Washington, 1978-79. Publications: 164 scientific publications, especially on breast cancer. Recreation: skiing. Address: (h.) Farleiter, Kincraig PH21 1NU; T.-01540 651288.
E-mail: SimpsonHWSimpson@aol.com

Simpson, James, OBE, BArch, FRIAS, RIBA, FSA (Scot). Partner, Simpson & Brown Architects, since 1977; b. 27.7.44, Edinburgh; m., Ann Bunney; 2 d. Educ. Bellhaven Hill; Glenalmond; Edinburgh College of Art. Ian G Lindsay and Partners, Edinburgh, 1962-71; Feilden and Mawson, Norwich, 1972-75; Feilden and Mawson, Edinburgh, 1975-77; Simpson & Brown Architects, since 1977. Commissioner, Royal Commission on the Ancient and Historical Monuments of Scotland (RCAHMS); Member, UK Executive Committee of the International Council for Monuments & Sites (ICOMOS); Member, Conservation Architecture Group of the Royal Institute of British Architects (RIBA); Trustee: Scottish Lime Centre Trust, Scottish Historic Buildings Trust; Architectural Adviser, Scottish Redundant Churches Trust. Address: (b.) St. Ninian's Manse, Quayside Street, Edinburgh EH6 6EJ; T.-0131 555 4678.
E-mail: jsimpson@simpsonandbrown.co.uk

Simpson, Very Rev. James Alexander, BSc (Hons), BD, STM, DD. Chaplain to the Queen in Scotland; Moderator, General Assembly of the Church of Scotland, 1994; b. 9.3.34, Glasgow; m., Helen Gray McCorquodale; 3 s.; 2 d. Educ. Eastwood Secondary School; Glasgow University; Union Seminary, New York. Minister: Grahamston Church, Falkirk, 1960-66, St. John's Renfield, Glasgow, 1966-76; Minister, Dornoch Cathedral, 1976-97. Publications: There is a time to ....; Marriage Questions Today; Doubts are not Enough; Holy Wit; Laughter Lines; The Master Mind; Dornoch Cathedral; More Holy Wit; Keywords of Faith; All About Christmas; The Laugh Shall Be First; Life, Love and Laughter; A Funny Way of Being Serious. Recreations: golf; photography; writing. Address: Dornoch, Perth Road, Bankfoot, Perthshire PH1 4ED; T.-01738 787710.

Simpson, Rev. James Hamilton, BD, LLB. Minister, The Mount Kirk, 1965-2004; Chairman, Church of Scotland General Trustees, 2003-07; b. 29.6.36, Overtown; m., Moira W. Sellar; 2 s. Educ. Buckhaven High School; Edinburgh University; Glasgow University. Prison Chaplain, Greenock, 1971-81; Hospital Chaplain, Ravenscraig, 1983-2006. Recreations: sea fishing; boating; gardening; touring (especially Iberia). Address: (h.) 82, Harbourside, Kip Village, Inverkip PA16 0BF; T.-01475 520 582.

Simpson, John Douglas, BSc(Hons). Headteacher, Fortrose Academy, since 1989; b. 2.3.51, Kilbirnie; m., Linda; 2 s.; 2 d. Educ. Spier's School, Beith; Glasgow University. Teacher of Biology, 1975; Principal Teacher, 1979; Assistant Headteacher, Merksworth High School, Paisley, 1983; Depute Headteacher, Cowdenknowes High School, Greenock, 1985. Recreations: golf; snooker. Address: (b.) Fortrose Academy, Fortrose, Ross-shire; T.-01381 620310.

Simpson, Kenneth James, BMSc, MBChB (Hons), MSc, MD, PhD, FRCP(Edin). Senior Lecturer in Hepatology, University of Edinburgh, since 2000; Consultant Physician, Royal Infirmary, Edinburgh, since 1996; b. 11.8.60, Edinburgh; m., Rona; 2 s.; 1 d. Educ. Craigmount High School, Edinburgh; University of Dundee, University of

London; University of Edinburgh. House Physician and Surgeon, Ninewells Hospital, Dundee, 1983-84; Senior House Officer, Western Infirmary/Gartnavel General, Glasgow, 1984-86; MRC Clinical Scientist, Clinical Research Centre, Northwick Park, London, 1986-89; Medical Registrar, Guildford and Kings College Liver Unit, 1989-91; Lecturer in Medicine/Senior Registrar, University of Edinburgh, Royal Infirmary, 1991-95; MRC Travelling Fellow, University of Michigan, USA, 1995-96. Member, Scottish Transplant Group. Publications: contributor to Davidson's Textbook of Medicine and other textbooks on hepatology; scientific papers. Recreations: reading crime novels; running. Address: (b) Royal Infirmary of Edinburgh, Old Dalkeith Road, Edinburgh EH16 4SA; T.-0131-536 2248; e-mail: k.simpson@ed.ac.uk

Simpson, Professor Mary, MA, PhD. Professor Emeritus, University of Edinburgh, since 2006; b. 4.12.42, Inverurie; m., Thomas Hardy Simpson; 1 s.; 1 d. Educ. Aberdeen Academy; Aberdeen University. Assistant Experimental Officer, Torry Research Station, Aberdeen, 1959-65; Researcher in Education, then Professor of Educational Research, Northern College, 1976-99; Professor of Classroom Learning, Edinburgh University, 1999-2005. Independent Member, National Educational Development Groups for: Standard Grade, 1983-87, 5–14 Assessment, 1989-92, Higher Still, 1994-97, 5-14 Evaluation Programme, 1991-97. Member, Scottish Consultative Council on the Curriculum, 1991-2000; Director and Chairman, Cornerstone Community Care Ltd., 1979-2000. Address: (h.) 6 Osborne Terrace, Edinburgh EH12 5HG.

Simpson, Myrtle Lillias, DL. Author and Lecturer; former Member, Scottish Sports Council; Past Chairman, Scottish National Ski Council; b. 5.7.31, Aldershot; m., Professor Hugh Simpson (qv); 3 s.; 1 d. Educ. 19 schools (father in Army). Writer/Explorer; author of 12 books, including travel, biography, historical and children's; first woman to ski across Greenland; attempted to ski to North Pole (most northerly point reached by a woman unsupported); numerous journeys in polar regions on ski or canoe; exploration in China and Peru; Mungo Park Medal, Royal Scottish Geographical Society; Perrie Medal, Ski Club of Great Britain; former Editor, Avenue (University of Glasgow magazine). Recreations: climbing; skiing; canoeing. Address: (h.) Farletter, Kincraig, Inverness-shire PH21 1NU; T.-01540 651288.
E-mail: simpsonhwsimpson@ aol.com

Simpson, Philip James Dalrymple, LLB (Hons), LLM, DipLP. Advocate, since 2001; Barrister (England and Wales), since 2001; b. 23.2.73, Glasgow; m., Anna Louise Robertson; 1 d. Educ. Bearsden Academy; University of Aberdeen; University of Regensburg; University of Edinburgh. Legal Assistant to the Lord President, 1999-2000; freelance legal translator, since 2001; called to English Bar (Inner Temple), 2001. Publications: articles on Scots law and legal history. Recreations: opera; chess; European literature. Address: (b.) Advocates Library, Parliament House, Edinburgh EH1 1RF; Littleton Chambers, 3 King's Bench Walk North, London EC4Y 7HR; T.-0131-226 5071.
E-mail: philip.simpson@advocates.org.uk

Simpson, Dr. Richard John, MB ChB, MRCGP, FRCPsych, DSHEC. MSP (Labour), Mid Scotland and Fife, since 2007; Shadow Minister for Public Health, since 2007; b. 22.10.42, Edinburgh; m., Christine Margaret MacGregor; 2 s. Educ. Perth Academy; Trinity College, Glenalmond; Edinburgh University. Career History: President of Scottish Union of Students; Principal in General Practice; Psychiatrist and Honorary Professor,

Stirling University; MSP, Ochil Constituency and Deputy Justice Minister; Consultant Psychiatrist in Addictions. Chair, Council of Management, Strathcarron Hospice; Chair, Medical Group of Scottish BAAF. Publications: 40 peer reviewed medical papers; 3 chapters of books on psychiatry in general practice; benzodiazepines psychology in general practice. Recreations: golf; gardening; classical music. Address: (b.) Scottish Parliament, Edinburgh EH99 1SP; e-mail: richard.simpson.msp@scottish.parliament.uk

Simpson, Dr Sheila Anne, MBChB, DObsRCOG, DCH, BSc(Hons), MD. Clinical Geneticist; Associate Specialist, Medical Genetics, Medical School, Foresterhill, Aberdeen; b. 7.5.50, Aberdeen. Educ. Aberdeen High School for Girls; Aberdeen University. Founder Member, UK Huntington's Disease Prediction Consortium; Member, World Federation of Neurology HD Research Group; Chair, Grampian Research Ethics Committee. Publications: Secrets in the Genes (Contributor); Truth and the Child – 10 years on; papers on HD, ethics. Recreations: antiquarian books; reading. Address: (b.) Medical Genetics, Grampian University Hospitals, Foresterhill, Aberdeen AB25 2ZD; T.-01224 552120.

Sinclair, 18th Lord (Matthew Murray Kennedy St Clair); m., Laura Cicely Coode; 1 s.; b. 9.12.68. Succeeded to title, 2004. Address: Knocknalling, St. Johns Town of Dalry, Castle Douglas DG7 3JT.

Sinclair, Rev. Colin Andrew Macalister, BA (Hons), BD (Hons). Minister, Palmerston Place Church of Scotland, since 1996; b. 16.9.53, Glasgow; m., Ruth Mary Murray; 1 s.; 3 d. Educ. Glasgow Academy; Stirling University; Edinburgh University. Training Officer, Scripture Union, Zambia, 1974-77; Assistant Minister, Palmerston Place Church of Scotland, Edinburgh, 1980-82; Church of Scotland Minister, Newton on Ayr, 1982-88; General Director, Scripture Union Scotland, 1988-96. Chair, Scripture Union International Council. Recreations: family; reading; sport. Address: (b.) Annan House, 10 Palmerston Place, Edinburgh EH12 5AA.

Sinclair, Rev. David Ian, BSc, BD, PhD, DipSW. Secretary, Church and Society Council, Church of Scotland, since 2005; b. 23.1.55, Bridge of Allan; m., Elizabeth Mary Jones; 1 s.; 1 d. Educ. High School of Stirling; Aberdeen University; Bristol University; University College, Cardiff; Edinburgh University. President, Student Christian Movement of Britain and Ireland, 1975-76; Social Worker (Community Development), Livingston, 1980-84; Assistant Minister, Dunblane Cathedral, 1987-88; Minister, St Andrews Martyrs, 1990-99, with Boarhills and Dunino, from 1993; Secretary, Church and Nation Committee, Church of Scotland, 1999-2005. Recreations: photography; music; armchair sport. Address: (b.) 121 George Street, Edinburgh EH2 4YN; T.-0131-225 5722; e-mail: dsinclair@cofscotland.org.uk

Sinclair, Douglas, CBE. Chair, Scottish Consumer Council, since 2006; Member, Accounts Commission, since 2007; b. 28.1.46, Ellon; m., Mairi; 2 d. Educ. Inverness Royal Academy; Edinburgh University. Administrative Assistant, Midlothian CC, 1969-72; Administrative Officer, Barnardo's Scotland, 1972-75; Depute Director of Administration, then Director of Administration, Western Isles Islands Council, 1975-85; Chief Executive, Ross and Cromarty DC, 1985-90; Chief Executive, Central Regional Council, 1990-95; Chief Executive, Convention of Scottish Local Authorities (COSLA), 1995-99; Chief Executive, Fife Council, 1999-2006. Address: (h.) 1 Queens Road, Stirling, FK8 2QY.

Sinclair, Eric T.A., MA, DipEd. Education Consultant, since 2000; Owner, The School Timetable Company; b. 20.9.48, Edinburgh; m., Johanna Beckley; 3 c. Educ. Bell Baxter High School, Cupar; St. Andrews University; Edinburgh University; Moray House College. Taught, Teacher Training Colleges, Cameroon, Nigeria; Head of English, English High School, Istanbul; Head of English, St Joseph's College, Dumfries; Assistant Rector, Forres Academy; Depute Rector, Bridge of Don Academy; Rector: Kirkwall Grammar School, Aboyne Academy and Deeside Community Centre, Aberdeenshire. Recreations: walking; gardening; reading. Address: (h.) 38 Barclay Park, Aboyne; T.-013398 86199; e-mail: eric@school-timetable.co.uk

Sinclair, Fiona Jane, BSc (Hons), BArch, FRIAS, MAPS. Architect in private practice, since 1982 (own practice, since 1998); Member, Historic Buildings Council for Scotland, 1998-2003; b. 28.8.57, Glasgow; m., David N. Page. Educ. Hyndland Senior Secondary School, Glasgow; Hermitage Academy, Helensburgh; Strathclyde University. Michael and Sue Thornley, Architects, Glasgow, 1981-98; Fiona Sinclair Architect, since 1998 (specialising in restoration of historic buildings); part-time Design Tutor, Department of Architecture, Strathclyde University, 1998-2000. Honorary Secretary, Glasgow Institute of Architects, since 1992. Publications: Scotstyle – 150 Years of Scottish Architecture, 1984; North Clyde Estuary (Co-author), 1992. Recreations: architecture; rowing. Address: (h.) Gatehead, Formakin Estate, Bishopton PA7 5NX; T.-(b.) 0141-552 2766.

Sinclair, Gerard William, LLB (Hons), DipLP, NP. Chief Executive, Scottish Criminal Cases Review Commission, since 2003; b. 24.9.61, Bellshill; m., Helen; 1 s.; 3 d. Educ. Trinity High School, Cambuslang; Strathclyde University. Trainee and Legal Assistant, Ross Harper and Murphy, Glasgow, 1984-88; Senior Partner, Sinclair McCormick and Giusti Martin, Glasgow, 1988-2003. Part-Time Sheriff; former Member, Council, Law Society of Scotland. Address: (b.) 17 Renfield Street, Glasgow G2 5AH; T.-0141 270 7030.

Sinclair, Martin Fraser, MA, CA. Director, NESSCO Ltd., since 1982; former Senior Partner, Chiene & Tait, CA (retired 2005); b. 18.7.45, Greenock; m., Patricia Anne Ogilvy Smith; 1 s.; 2 d. Educ. Edinburgh Academy; Edinburgh University. Apprentice, Chiene & Tait, CA; qualified, 1970; Peat Marwick Mitchell & Co., Vancouver, 1970-73. President, Institute of Chartered Accountants Benevolent Association, 1983-84. Athletics Blue, Edinburgh University; Captain, Scottish Universities Athletics Team, 1969. Recreations: skiing; squash; orienteering. Address: (b.) 61 Dublin Street, Edinburgh EH3 6NL; T.-0131-667 4250.

Sinclair, Dr. Robert, DHC, MBA, MNI, MIMgt. Principal, Banff and Buchan College, since 2000; b. 21.2.55, Fraserburgh. Educ. Fraserburgh Academy; Glasgow College of Nautical Studies; University of Aberdeen. Merchant Navy (Master Mariner) and Offshore Oil Industry, 1973-88; Lecturer, Nautical Science, 1988-90; Head, Department of Nautical Studies, 1990-92; Principal, North Atlantic Fisheries College, 1992-94; Depute Principal, Banff and Buchan College of Further Education, 1995-2000. Recreations: swimming; sailing; cycling. Address: (b.) Henderson Road, Fraserburgh AB43 9WA; T.-01346 575777.

Sinha, Professor Brajraman Prasad, BSc, Dip. Building Science, PhD, DSc. Professor of Structural Engineering, Edinburgh University, 1999-2002; now Emeritus Professor; b. 20.12.36, Hazipur, India; m., Nageshwari Sinha; 2 s.; 1 d. Educ. Zila School,

Monghyr, India; Patna University; Liverpool University; Edinburgh University. Engineering Assistant, Patna University, 1957-59; Assistant Engineer, Bihar Electricity Board, 1959-60; Assistant Engineer, Department of Public Works, Bihar, 1960-63; Design Engineer, 1968-69; Edinburgh University: Demonstrator and Researcher, 1966-68; Research Fellow to Senior Lecturer, 1969-95; Reader, 1995-99; Visiting Professor, Bihar College of Engineering, 1984; Visiting Academic, Santa Catarina Florianopolis, Brazil, since 1991; Visiting Professor, Indian Institute of Science, 2000; Visiting Professor, University of Dresden, 2003, University of Ancona (Italy), 2002; Executive Director, International Masonry Engineering Council for Developing Countries, 1984-2004. Member: Lothian Racial Equality Council, since 1984, Chair, 2004-07; Member, Senate, Edinburgh University, 1984-2002; Chairman, Hindu Temple and Cultural Centre, Edinburgh, 1985-86; President, Indian Arts Council, 1994. Publications: Structural Masonry for Developing Countries (co-ed.), 1992; Re-inforced and Pre-stressed Masonry (contributor), 1989. Recreations: reading; overseas travel; photography; table tennis; writing. Address: (b.) Institute of Infrastructures and Environment, School of Engineering and Electronics, Edinburgh University, Kings' Buildings, Edinburgh EGH9 3JN; T.-0131-650 5726; e-mail: B.Sinha@ed.ac.uk

Siress, Cary, PhD, MArch, BArch. Architect, Zürich, New York, since 1991; Lecturer, Architecture Design, University of Edinburgh, since 2006; b. 19.12.61, Louisville, KY, USA; m., Alexandra Heese. Educ. University of Kentucky College of Architecture, Lexington, KY, USA; Instituto Universitario di Architettura di Venezia, Venice, Italy; Columbia University Graduate School of Architecture, Planning and Preservation, New York, USA; Swiss Federal Institute of Technology (ETH), Zürich, Switzerland. Biennale di Venezia, Venice, Italy, invited entries for international architecture exhibition: project for Ponte dell' Academia, project for Ca' Venier dei Leoni (Peggy Guggenheim Museum), 1985-86; Ross Feldman Architects, Lexington, KY, USA, Project Architect for new Christian Church of Kentucky Headquarters (built), 1986-91; Thomas Leeser (Peter Eisenman Architects), New York, NY, USA, Project Architect for Egger House (unbuilt), 1991; New York State Council of the Arts Stipend, New York, USA, competitive funding award for outstanding work of architects and artists, 1991-92; Ruoss/Siress Architects, Zürich, Switzerland, Principal Partner in private office with Silva Ruoss, 1992-99. Honorary Prize: Reconstruction of the Souks of Beirut International Design Competition, Beirut, Lebanon, 1994, Project Architect in international design competition (unbuilt). Burkard, Meyer, Steiger Architects SIA/BSA Baden, Switzerland, Project Architect, 1994-96; Project Architect in invited international design competition with Dieter Dietz and Urs Egg (unbuilt), 1998; commission for planning study for Adidas headquarters and master plan for 100 hectares of future development (unbuilt), 1999; Project Architect, Vogt Landscape and Architecture, Zürich, Switzerland, 2000-02; ARTE Basel International Art and Architecture Exhibition, Basel, Switzerland/Miami, Florida, USA, 2001 and 2002. Member, University of Edinburgh International Office Committee. Publications include: Inchoate: An Experiment in Architectural Education. Spain. (eds), 2003 (contributor); Archipelagos: A Manual for Peripheral Buenos Aires. Buenos Aires. (eds). Recreations: travel; writing; art; guitar; photography. Address: (h.) 37/4 London Street, Edinburgh EH3 6LX; T.-07775 646 033; e-mail: cary.siress@ed.ac.uk

Sischy, Judith, BA, MA, FRSA. Director, Scottish Council of Independent Schools, since 1990; b. 20.12.47, Halifax. Educ. Newcastle upon Tyne Church High School; Bristol University; University of Toronto. Previously: Teacher of Modern Languages, Toronto, Canada, Edinburgh, Senior Official, Edinburgh Merchant Company. Member: Scottish Qualifications Authority Advisory Council, Council of the General Teaching Council for Scotland; Past President, Edinburgh Rotary Club. Recreations: music; walking; keep fit; swimming. Address: (b.) 21 Melville Street, Edinburgh EH3 7PE; T.-0131-220 2106.

Skene, Charles Pirie, OBE, DBA, FBIPP, ARPS, FRSA. Chairman, Skene Group of companies; Visiting Professor of Entrepreneurship, Robert Gordon University; Holder of the Queen's Award for Enterprise Promotion, 2005; b. 30.4.35, Aberdeen; m., Alison; 1 s.; 2 d. Educ. Loretto. Past President of numerous organisations, including Aberdeen Chamber of Commerce and Association of Scottish Chambers of Commerce; Past Chairman: Industry Year 1986, Industry Matters 1987; Donor of the Annual Skene Aberdeen Festival Award, 1976-99; Past Chairman, CBI Education and Training Committee; Chairman, CBI (Scotland) Enterprise Group, 1994-96; Member, Task Force to investigate under-achievement in schools, 1996-97; initiated Skene Young Entrepreneur's Award, Scotland, 1986; Member, Scottish Executive's Review of Education for Work and Enterprise Group, 2001-02; endowed Chair of Entrepreneurship, The Robert Gordon University Centre for Entrepreneurship, 2001; Trustee: Photographic Arts and Science Foundation, Oklahoma City. Address: (b.) 23 Rubislaw Den North, Aberdeen, AB15 4AL; T.-01224 326221.

Skene, Robert Taylor, BSc, Head Teacher, Torry Academy, Aberdeen, since 1995; b. 28.12.50, Aberdeenshire; m., Jennifer; 2 s. Educ. Bankhead Academy; Robert Gordon Institute of Technology. Address: (b.) Torry Academy, Tullos Circle, Aberdeen, AB11 8HD; T.-01224 876733.

Slack, Rev. William G., DipTh. General Director, Baptist Union of Scotland, since 2003 (General Secretary, 1995-2003); b. 29.1.49, Edinburgh; m., Vivienne; 1 d. Educ. Trinity Academy, Edinburgh; Hamilton Academy; Baptist Theological College of Scotland. Minister, Ladywell, Livingston, 1974-82; Minister, International Baptist Church, Aberdeen, 1982-95. Recreations: philately; swimming; music. Address: (b.) 14 Aytoun Road, Glasgow, G41 5RT.

Slater, Professor Peter James Bramwell, BSc, PhD, DSc, FIBiol, FRSE. Kennedy Professor of Natural History, St. Andrews University, since 1984 (Head, School of Biological and Medical Sciences, 1992-97; Dean, Faculty of Science, 1998-2002); b. 26.12.42, Edinburgh; m., Elisabeth Vernon Smith; 2 s. Educ. Edinburgh Academy; Glenalmond; Edinburgh University. Demonstrator in Zoology, Edinburgh University, 1966-68; Lecturer in Biology, Sussex University, 1968-84. Secretary, Association for the Study of Animal Behaviour, 1973-78, President, 1986-89, Medallist, 2000; European Editor, Animal Behaviour, 1979-82; Editor, Advances in the Study of Behavior, 1990-2005. Recreations: walking; ornithology; music. Address: (b.) School of Biology, St. Andrews, Fife; T.-01334 463500.

Slavin, Rev. William J., MA, STL, CPsychol. Chaplain, Royal Hospital for Sick Children, Glasgow; b. 17.1.40, Bristol. Educ. Blairs College, Aberdeen; Scots College, Rome; Glasgow University. Assistant Priest, Broomhill, Glasgow, 1965-70; Educational Psychologist, Glasgow Child Guidance Service, 1970-75; Deputy Director, Jessore

Training Centre, Bangladesh, 1975-80; Secretary, RC Justice and Peace Commission, 1980-85; Co-ordinator, Scottish Drugs Forum, 1986-92; Parish Priest, St. Alphonsus, The Barras, Glasgow, 1992-97; Chair, Emmaus Glasgow, since 2001. Recreation: An rud Gaidhealach. Address: (h.) 33 Partick Bridge Street, Glasgow G11 6PQ; T.-0141-338 6794; e-mail: wllyslav@aol.com

Sleeman, Professor Derek Henry, BSc, PhD, FBCS, FRSE. Fellow of European Artificial Intelligence Coordinating Committee (2004); Professor of Computing Science, Aberdeen University, since 1986; b. 11.1.41, Penzance; m., Margaret G. Rankine; 1 d. Educ. Penzance Grammar School; King's College, London. Secretary, SS AISB, 1979-82; Academic Co-ordinator, European Network of Excellence in Machine Learning, 1992-95. Publications: 150 technical papers. Recreations: hill and coastal path-walking; photography. Address: (b.) Computing Science Department, King's College, Aberdeen University, Aberdeen AB24 3FX; T.-01224 272288.

Smail, Peter James, MA, BM, BCh, FRCP, DCH. Formerly Consultant Paediatrician, Royal Aberdeen Children's Hospital (1980-2004); b. 10.10.43, Harrow; m., Janice Lockhart; 3 s.; 1 d. Recreations: member, Edinburgh Festival Chorus. Address: 36 Ashley Gardens, Aberdeen AB10 6RQ.

Small, Christopher. Writer; b. 15.11.19, London; 3 d. Educ. Dartington Hall; Pembroke College, Oxford. Journalist and miscellaneous writer; Literary Editor and Dramatic Critic, Glasgow Herald, 1955-80. Publications:Ariel Like A Harpy: Shelley, Mary & Frankenstein; The Road to Miniluv: George Orwell, the State & God; The Printed Word. Recreation: gardening. Address: (h.) Park House, Isle of Lismore, Oban, Argyll PA34 5UN; T.-01631 760222.

Small, Emeritus Professor John Rankin, CBE, DLitt, BSc (Econ), FCCA, FCMA. Emeritus Professor, Department of Accountancy and Finance, Heriot-Watt University; b. 28.2.33, Dundee; m., Catherine Wood; 1 s.; 2 d. Educ. Harris Academy; Dundee School of Economics. Industry and commerce; Lecturer, Edinburgh University; Senior Lecturer, Glasgow University. Director of and Consultant to various organisations; President, Association of Chartered Certified Accountants, 1982-83; Vice-Principal, Heriot-Watt University, 1974-78, 1987-90, Deputy Principal, 1990-94. Chairman, Commission for Local Authority Accounts in Scotland, 1983-92; Chairman, National Appeal Panel for Entry to Pharmaceutical Lists (Scotland), 1987-95; Board Member, Scottish Homes, 1993-2002. Recreation: golf. Address: (h.) 39 Caiystane Terrace, Edinburgh EH10 6ST; T.-0131-445 2638.

Small, Stephen J., CQSW. Director, St Andrew's Children's Society Ltd., since 1996; b. 3.11.61, Edinburgh; m., Kay L. Anderson; 1 s.; 2 d. Educ. Holyrood RC High School, Edinburgh; Moray House College of Education. Social Worker, Humberside County Council, 1986-88; Social Worker, Lothian Regional Council (Midlothian District), 1988-95; Senior Social Worker, St Andrew's Children's Society Ltd., 1995-96. Address: (b.) 7 John's Place, Leith, Edinburgh EH6 7EL; T.-0131 454 3370; e-mail: ssmall@standrews-children.org.uk

Small, William Douglas, LLB, MPhil. Sheriff at Oban and Fort William, since 2001; b. 20.1.50, Edinburgh; m., Judith Lilian May Lee; 2 s. Educ. Melville College, Edinburgh; Aberdeen and Glasgow Universities.

Solicitor, 1974-77; Depute Procurator Fiscal at Aberdeen and Edinburgh, 1977-85; Advocate, 1985-2001; Temporary Sheriff, 1997-99. Chairman of Board of Directors for Family Mediation, Argyll and Bute; Director, Aged Christian Friend Society of Scotland. Recreations: vintage motor cycle (AJS) and car (MGB); woodworking; walking; music.

Smart, Ian Stewart, LLB, NP. Vice President, Law Society of Scotland; Solicitor, Partner, Ian S. Smart & Co., since 1991; b. 10.9.58, Paisley. Educ. Paisley Grammar School; Glasgow University. Solicitor and then Partner, Ross Harper & Murphy, 1980-91; Council Member, Law Society of Scotland, since 1997. Recreations: Labour Party activist; St Mirren. Address: (b.) 3 Annan House, Cumbernauld G67 1DP; T.-01236 731027.

Smart, John Dalziel Beveridge, JP. Lord Lieutenant, Kincardineshire, 1999-2007 (retired); b. 12.8.32, Edinburgh; m., Valerie Blaber; 2 s. Educ. Harrow; Administrative Staff College. 2nd Lt., Black Watch (RHR), Korea, 1952; PA to Chief of Staff, 1953. J. & J. Smart (Brechin) Ltd., 1953 (Director, 1954), Director, Don Brothers, Buist & Co. Ltd., 1964 (Managing Director, 1985; retired, 1987). Chairman, British Polyolefin Textiles Association, 1986-97; Member, St. Andrews Management Institute, 1989; Chairman, Scottish American Community Relations Committee, 1990-93; Dean, Guildry of Brechin, 1991-93; DL, Kincardineshire, 1993; Member, Queen's Bodyguard for Scotland, Royal Company of Archers. Recreation: countryside. Address: (h.) Kincardine, 9A The Glebe, Edzell, Brechin DD9 7SZ; T.-01356 648416; e-mail: smart@woodmyre.freeserve.co.uk

Smethurst, Emeritus Professor Colin, BA, BLitt, MA, Officier Palmes Academiques. Marshall Professor of French, Glasgow University, 1980-98; b. 3.8.37, Bedford; m., Claudine Rozenberg; 2 d. Educ. Slough Grammar School; Keble College, Oxford. Assistant Lecturer, Lecturer, Senior Lecturer in French, Liverpool University, 1962-80. President, Institut Francais d'Ecosse, 1989-96; Secretary, Association of University Professors of French, 1983-87; Visiting Professor, Sorbonne (Paris IV), 1998-99. Publications: Zola: Germinal; Chateaubriand: Atala, René; editions of Balzac novels; Chateaubriand: Ecrits politiques. Address: (h.) 6 Westbourne Crescent, Bearsden G61 4HD.

Smillie, Anne. Chief Executive, Scottish Badminton Union, since 1989; Executive Board Member, Badminton World Federation; b. 17.8.56, Glasgow. Educ. Victoria Drive Secondary School; Anniesland College. Joined Scottish Badminton Union, 1980; Director of major badminton events, including 1992 European Championships, 1994 World Team Championships, 1997 World Team and Individual Championships. Recreations: music; reading. Address: (h.) 55 Westerton Avenue, Westerton, Glasgow; T.-0141-942 9804.

Smillie, Carol. Television Presenter. Credits include: Wheel of Fortune; The Travel Show; Holiday; The National Lottery Live; The Big Breakfast; Hearts of Gold; Get It On; Smillie's People; Changing Rooms; Midweek National Lottery Live; Holiday Memories; Holiday Heaven; Summer Holiday; Star Secrets; Holiday Swaps; Dream Holiday Homes; Postcode Challenge.

Smith of Gilmorehill, Baroness (Elizabeth Margaret Smith), MA. Peer, House of Lords, since 1995; Deputy Lieutenant, City of Edinburgh; Non-Executive Director,

City Inn Ltd.; Chairman, Edinburgh Festival Fringe Society, since 1995; President, Scottish Opera; Council Member, Russo-British Chamber of Commerce; Trustee, 21st Century Trust; Governor, English Speaking Union; Trustee, John Smith Memorial Trust; Patron, University of Glasgow 2001 Campaign; b. 4.6.40, Ayr; m., Rt. Hon. John Smith, MP (deceased); 3 d. Educ. Hutchesons Girls Grammar School; Glasgow University. LLD, Glasgow University, 1998. Recreations: family; garden; the arts. Address: (b.) House of Lords, London, SW1A 0PW.

Smith, Agnes Houston, BL. Honorary Sheriff, Dundee, since 1990; b. 27.9.33, Prestwick; m., David Robert Smith; 3 d. Educ. Hutchesons' Girls Grammar School, Glasgow; Glasgow University. Solicitor in Paisley, Edinburgh and Dundee, 1955-92. President, Dundee Society of Glasgow University Graduates; Non-Executive Director, Dundee Healthcare NHS Trust, 1993-99. Recreations: golf; gardening; grannying. Address: (h.) Windyridge, Kellas, by Broughty Ferry DD5 3PQ; T.-01382 350475.

Smith, Sir Alan, Kt (1982), CBE (1976), DFC (1941) and Bar (1942), DL, JP. President, Dawson International plc, Kinross, since 1982; b. 14.3.17, South Shields; m., 1, Margaret Stewart Todd (deceased); 2, Alice Elizabeth Moncur; 3 s.; 2 d. Educ. Bede College, Sunderland. Self-employed, 1931-36; Unilever, 1936-39; RAF, 1939-45; Managing Director, Todd & Duncan Ltd., Kinross, 1946-60; Chairman and Chief Executive, Dawson International, Kinross, 1960-82. Chairman, Quayle Munro PLC, Edinburgh, 1982-93; Board Member, Scottish Development Agency, 1982-87; Kinross Burgh Councillor, 1952-65; Provost of Kinross, 1959-65; Tayside Regional Councillor, 1979-90; Financial Convenor, Tayside Region, 1980-86. Recreations: work; sailing. Address: (h.) Ardgairney House, Cleish, by Kinross; T.-01577 850265.

Smith, Emeritus Professor Alan Gordon Rae, MA, PhD, FRAS, FRHistS, FRSE. Professor of Early Modern History, Glasgow University, 1995-2002, now Emeritus Professor; b. 22.12.36, Glasgow; m., Isabel Robertson; 1 s.; 1 d. Educ. Glasgow High School; Glasgow University; University College, London. Research Fellow, Institute of Historical Research, London University, 1961-62; Assistant in History, 1962-64, then Lecturer, Glasgow University, 1964-75; Senior Lecturer in Modern History, 1975-85; Reader, 1985-92, Professor in Modern History, 1992-95; Review Editor, History (Journal of the Historical Association), 1984-87; Member, Council, Royal Historical Society, 1990-94; Member, Governing Board, Institute of Historical Research, London University, 1994-99 and since 2001. Publications: The Government of Elizabethan England, 1967; The New Europe, 1969; Science and Society in the Sixteenth and Seventeenth Centuries, 1972; Servant of the Cecils: The Life of Sir Michael Hickes, 1977; The Emergence of a Nation State: The Commonwealth of England 1529-1660, 1984; The Anonymous Life of William Cecil, Lord Burghley, 1990; The Last Years of Mary Queen of Scots, 1990; Tudor Government, 1990; William Cecil, Lord Burghley, Minister of Queen Elizabeth I, 1991. Recreation: watching sport. Address: (h.) Department of History, Glasgow University, Glasgow G12 8QQ; T.-0141 330 4509.

Smith, Allan Keppie. CBE, DUniv, BSc, FREng, CEng, FIMechE, FWeldI. Chairman, Railcare Ltd., 1995-2001; Managing Director, Facilities Management Division, Babcock International Group PLC, Rosyth Royal Dockyard, until 1997; b. 18.5.32. Joined Army for National Service, 1953; commissioned, REME, 1954; Babcock & Wilcox: joined as Graduate Trainee, 1955; appointed: Industrial Engineering Manager, Renfrew Works, 1965, Production

Director, Renfrew Works, 1974, Managing Director, Renfrew and Dumbarton Works, 1976; Managing Director, Babcock Thorn Limited and Chairman, Rosyth Royal Dockyard plc, 1986; Director, Babcock International Group PLC, 1989. Past President, Scottish Engineering; Past Chairman, Council of the Welding Institute; Honorary Doctor, University of Paisley; awarded Institute of Marketing Scottish Marketer of the Year, 1992. Address: (h.) The Forts, Hawes Brae, South Queensferry EH30 9TE; T.-0131-319 1668.

Smith, Hon. Lady (Anne Smith), QC. Senator of the College of Justice in Scotland; b. 1955; m.; 1 s.; 1 d. Educ. Edinburgh University. Admitted, Faculty of Advocates, 1980. Address: Parliament House, Parliament Square, Edinburgh EH1 1RQ.

Smith, Rt. Rev. Brian Arthur, Episcopal Bishop of Edinburgh, since 2001; b. 1943; m., Elizabeth Hutchinson; 2 d. Educ. George Heriot's School, Edinburgh; Edinburgh University; Fitzwilliam College, Cambridge; Jesus College, Cambridge; Westcott House, Cambridge. Curate, Cuddesdon, 1972-79; Tutor, Cuddesdon College, Oxford, 1972-75; Ripon College, Cuddesdon: Director of Studies, 1975-78, Senior Tutor, 1978-79; Director of Training, Diocese of Wakefield, 1979-87; Priest-in-Charge, St. John, Halifax, 1979-85; Honorary Canon, Wakefield Cathedral, 1981-87; Archdeacon of Craven, 1987-93; Bishop Suffragan, Tonbridge, 1993-2001. Recreations: reading; music; walking; browsing in junk shops. Address: Diocesan Centre, 21a Grosvenor Crescent, Edinburgh EH12 5EL; T.-0131-538 7044; e-mail: bishop@edinburgh.anglican.org

Smith, Caroline Anne Scott, MBChB, LLB, DipLP. Partner, Russel + Aitken LLP; b. 23.6.55, Edinburgh; 1 s.; 1 d. Educ. St Denis School, Edinburgh; Edinburgh University. Hospital doctor, 1979-82; Assistant, Warner & Co., Edinburgh, 1986-88; Morton, Fraser, Milligan, Edinburgh, 1988-93; Associate, Loudons, Edinburgh, 1993-94; Partner, Loudons, 1994-2001. Recreations: walking; reading; travelling. Address: 27 Rutland Square, Edinburgh; T.-0131-228 5500.
E-mail: caroline.smith@russelaitken.com

Smith, David Alexander, LLB. Chairman, Shepherd and Wedderburn, WS, since 1999; Partner, since 1974; b. 17.11.47, Dundee; m., Hon. Lady Anne Smith (qv); 1 s.; 1 d. Educ. Fettes College, Edinburgh; Edinburgh University. Joined Shepherd and Wedderburn as apprentice, 1969. Recreations: hockey; golf; skiing; walking; running; opera; classical music. T.-(b.) 0131-473 5292; e-mail: david.smith@shepwedd.co.uk

Smith, David Bruce Boyter, OBE, Drhc, MA, LLB, FRSA, FInstD. Director and Chief Executive, Dunfermline Building Society, 1987-2001; Vice Chairman, Scottish Opera, 2000-04; Past Chairman, Building Societies Association; b. 11.3.42, St. Andrews; m., Christine Anne; 1 s.; 1 d. Educ. High School, Dunfermline; Edinburgh University. Legal training, Balfour & Manson, Edinburgh; admitted Solicitor, 1968; Solicitor, Standard Life Assurance Co., 1969-73; Dunfermline Building Society: Secretary, 1974-81, General Manager (Admin.), 1981-86, Deputy Chief Executive, 1986. Past Chairman, Northern Association of Building Societies; Vice President, European Mortgage Federation; Chairman, NHBC (Scotland) and Board Member, NHBC (UK); Member, Scottish Conveyancing and Executry Services Board, 1996-2003; Deputy Chairman, Glenrothes Development Corporation, 1990-96; Chairman, Institute of Directors, Scottish Division, 1994-97; Director, Scottish Fisheries Museum,

1990-2007; former Vice Chairman of Court and Finance Convener, Edinburgh University; Chairman, University of Edinburgh Trust; Chairman, Carnegie Dunfermline & Hero Fund Trusts; Finance Convener, Carnegie UK Trust; Executive Committee, Carnegie Trust for Universities of Scotland. Recreations: golf; sailing; the arts. Address: (h.) 26 Donibristle Gardens, Dalgety Bay, Dunfermline KY11 9NQ; T.-01383 829994.

Smith, Sheriff David Buchanan, MA, LLB, FSAScot. Sheriff of North Strathclyde at Kilmarnock, 1975-2001; b. 31.10.36, Paisley; m., Hazel Mary Sinclair; 1 s.; 1 d. Educ. Paisley Grammar School; Glasgow University; Edinburgh University. Advocate, 1961; Standing Junior Counsel to Scottish Education Department, 1968-75; Tutor, Faculty of Law, Edinburgh University, 1964-72; Trustee, Scottish Curling Museum Trust, since 1980. President, Kilmarnock and District History Group; Trustee Scottish National Dictionary Association, 1994-2002; President, Ayr Curling Club, 1995-96; Treasurer, Sheriffs' Association, 1979-89, Council Member, 1998-2001; Council Member, Stair Society, since 1995, Vice Chairman of Council, since 1998; Member, Scottish Records Advisory Council, since 2000; President, Eglinton County Curling Game, 2000 04; Member, Advisory Committee, Scottish Language Dictionaries, since 2002. Publications: Curling: An Illustrated History, 1981; The Roaring Game: Memories of Scottish Curling, 1985; contributions to The Laws of Scotland: Stair Memorial Encyclopedia, Vol. 6; George Washington Wilson in Ayrshire, 1991; Contributor to Macphail: Sheriff Court Practice, 2nd Ed., 1998; Sport, Scotland and the Scots (Contributor), 2001; The Oxford Companion to Scottish History (Contributor), 2001. Recreations: Scotland — history and culture; curling; collecting curliana; music; architecture; grandchildren. Address: (h.) 72 South Beach, Troon, KA10 6EG; T.-01292 312130.

Smith, Sir David Cecil, Kt, MA, DPhil, FRS, FRSE. Principal and Vice-Chancellor, Edinburgh University, 1987-94; President, Wolfson College, Oxford, 1994-2000; m., Lesley Margaret Mollison Mutch; 2 s.; 1 d. Educ. St. Paul's School, London; Queen's College, Oxford. Browne Research Fellow, Queen's College, Oxford, 1956-59; Harkness Fellow, University of California, Berkeley, 1959-60; University Lecturer, Department of Agriculture, Oxford University, 1960-74; Fellow and Tutor, Wadham College, Oxford, 1964-74; Melville Wills Professor of Botany, Bristol University, 1974-80; Sibthorpian Professor of Rural Economy, Oxford University, 1980-87. President, British Lichen Society, 1972-74; President, British Mycological Society, 1980; President, Society for Experimental Biology, 1983-85; President, Scottish Association for Marine Science, 1993-2000; President, Linnean Society, 2000-03. Publication: The Biology of Symbiosis (Co-author), 1987. Address: 13 Abbotsford Park, Edinburgh EH10 5DZ; T.-0131-446 0230; e-mail: smithsymbiosis@aol.com

Smith, David Frederick, BSc (Hons), MSc, PGCE, PhD. Senior Lecturer in The History of Medicine, University of Aberdeen, since 2005; b. 14.02.54, Windsor; m., Lorna Macdonald; 2 d. Educ. Windsor Grammar School; Reading University; London University; Edinburgh University; Moray House College. Teacher, Lothian Regional Council, 1982-88; Research Officer, Moray House College, 1988-91; Wellcome Trust Research Fellow, Glasgow University, 1991-94; Wellcome University Award Holder, then Lecturer, Aberdeen University, 1994-2005. Chair of the Executive Committee of the Society for the Social History of Medicine, 1993-95; Convenor of The Provisional Committee of International Society for Cultural History, 2007-08. Publications: Nutrition in Britain, 1997; Food, Science, Policy and Regulation, 2000; Food Poisoning,

Policy and Politics, 2005. Recreations: Scottish Country Dancing; hill walking; caravaning; keeping chickens. Address: (b.) King's College, University of Aberdeen, School of Divinity, History and Philosophy, Crombie Annexe, Meston Walk, Old Aberdeen AB24 3FX; T.-01224 273676; e-mail: d.f.smith@abdn.ac.uk

Smith, Deborah Rebecca, BA (Hons), MA. Deputy Director and Head of International Division, Scottish Government, since 2007; b. 17.01.74. Educ. Hutchesons' Grammar School, Glasgow; University College, Durham; University of Bradford. Joined Scottish Office, 1997; Private Secretary to the Minister for Finance, 1999-2001; Team Leader, European Structural Funds Division, 2001-03; Project Leader, Performance and Innovation Unit, 2004-06; Head of Alcohol and Drugs Misuse, 2006-07. Recreations: travel; running; reading; scuba diving; walking. Address: (b.) The Scottish Government, 2H (North), Victoria Quay, Edinburgh EH6 6QQ; T.-0131 244 5504; e-mail: deborah.smith@scotland.gsi.gov.uk

Smith, Donald Alexander, MA, PhD. Director, Netherbow Arts Centre, 1983-2001; Curator, John Knox House, since 1989; Director, Scottish Storytelling Centre, since 1995; b. 15.2.56, Glasgow; m., Alison; 3 s.; 2 d. Educ. Stirling High School; Edinburgh University. Researcher, School of Scottish Studies, 1979-82. Chairperson, Scotland 97 (anniversaries of St. Ninian and St. Columba); Organiser, Scottish Churches Millennium Programme; Chair, Scottish National Theatre Working Party (SAC/Scottish Executive), 2000-01; Chair, Literature Forum for Scotland, 2002-06; Board Member, National Theatre of Scotland, 2004-07. Publications: The Scottish Stage, 1994; Edinburgh Old Town Pilgrims' Way, 1995; John Knox House: Gateway to Edinburgh's Old Town,1996; Celtic Travellers: Scotland in the Age of the Saints, 1997; History of Scottish Theatre, 1998; Storytelling Scotland: A Nation in Narrative, 2001; A Long Stride Shortens the Road: Poems 1979-2004, 2004; Some to Thorns, Some to Thistles, 2005; The English Spy, 2007. Address: (b.) Scottish Storytelling Centre: The Netherbow, 43-45 High Street, Edinburgh EH1 1SR; T.-0131-556 9579.

Smith, (Edward) Alistair, CBE, MA, PhD; b. 16.1.39, Aberdeen. Educ. Aberdeen Grammar School; Aberdeen University. Lecturer in Geography, Aberdeen University, 1963-88; President, Scottish Conservative and Unionist Association, 1979-81; Deputy Chairman, Scottish Conservative Party, 1981-86; Member, Grampian Health Board, 1983-91; Director, Aberdeen University Development Trust, 1982-90; Director, Aberdeen University International Office, 1990-2002; Board Member, SCOTVEC, 1989-93; Member, Committee for Scotland, Nature Conservancy Council, 1989-91; Member, N.E. Regional Committee, Nature Conservancy Council, 1991-92. Publications: Europe: A Geographical Survey of the Continent (Co-author), 1979; Scotland's Future Development (Contributor), 1983. Recreations: travel; photography; music. Address: (h.) 68A Beaconsfield Place, Aberdeen AB15 4AJ; T.-01224 642932; e-mail: aberdeensmith@aol.com

Smith, Elaine A., BA (Hons), DPSM. MSP (Labour), Coatbridge and Chryston, since 1999; b. 7.5.63, Coatbridge; m., James Vann Smith; 1 s. Educ. St Patrick's School, Coatbridge; Glasgow College; St Andrew's Teacher Training College. Teacher, 1986-87; supply teacher, 1987-88; local government officer, Monklands District Council, 1988-90, Highland Regional Council, 1990-97; Volunteer Development Scotland, 1997-98; supply teacher, 1999. Recreations: family; swimming; bowling; reading. Address: (b.) Unit

65, Fountain Business Centre, Coatbridge, Lanarkshire; T.-01236 449122.

Smith, Elaine Constance, BA. Actress; b. 2.8.58, Baillieston; m., Robert Morton; 2 d. Educ. Braidhurst High School, Motherwell; Royal Scottish Academy of Music and Drama; Moray House College of Education. Teacher of Speech and Drama, Firrhill High School, Edinburgh, 1979-82; joined 7:84 Theatre Company, 1982; moved to Wildcat Stage Productions, 1982; since 1986, worked with Borderline Theatre Co., Royal Lyceum, Dundee Rep., Tron Theatre, Traverse, Byre Theatre and Lead in King's Theatre, Glasgow panto, 1997-2004; TV work includes City Lights, Naked Video, Rab C Nesbitt and 2000 Acres of Sky; original cast member, The Steamie; Film work includes Women Talking Dirty, 16 Years of Alcohol and Nina's Heavenly Delights. Patron, Family Mediation, Zero Tolerance, Audio Description Film Fund, SNIP, Scottish Youth Theatre, Borderline Theatre and Byre Theatre; Manager, Crossan Communications. Hon. Doctorate, Dundee University; BA, Queen Margaret University, 2007; appointed to Broadcasting Commission by Scottish Government in 2007; Agent: Independent Theatre Group, London; Production company with husband (RPM Arts), since 1990. Recreations: swimming; tennis; reading.

Smith, Elinor, MCIBS. Member, NHS Greater Glasgow Board; Vice Chair, Scottish Health Innovations Ltd; Board Member, Scottish Prison Service; Chair, South Glasgow University NHS Hospitals Division, 1999-2005; b. Greenock; m., David; 1 d. Educ. Pollokshields Senior Secondary School; Glasgow Caledonian University. First woman in Bank of Scotland appointed as sole manager of branch; former Associate Director of Small Business Banking, Bank of Scotland; Board Member, Scottish Enterprise Glasgow. Recreations: sometimes placing a sacred cow in fear of its life. Address: (b.) Trust Headquarters, Southern General Hospital, 1345 Govan Road, Glasgow G51 4TF; T.-0141-201 4444.

Smith, Elizabeth Jane, MA (Hons), DipEd. MSP (Conservative), Mid Scotland and Fife, since 2007; b. 27.2.60, Edinburgh. Educ. George Watson's College; University of Edinburgh; Moray House College of Education. Teacher of Economics and Modern Studies, George Watson's College, 1983-98; Head of Chairman's Office, Conservative Central Office, Scotland, 1998-2003; Part Time Teacher and Political Consultant, 2003-07. Fellow Commoner, Corpus Christi College, Cambridge, 1992. Publications: History of George Watson's Ladies College, 2006; Outdoor Adventures, 2003. Recreations: cricket; hill-walking; photography; travel. Address: (b.) Scottish Parliament, Holyrood Road, Edinburgh EH99 1SP; T.-0131 348 6762.
E-mail: elizabeth.smith.msp@scottish.parliament.uk

Smith, Professor Francis William, MD, FFRRCSI, FRCSEd, FRCR, FRCPE, DipSpMed. Consultant Radiologist, Grampian University Hospitals, since 1979; Professor of Health Sciences, Robert Gordon University, since 1999; Clinical Professor of Radiology, University of Aberdeen, since 2005; b. 8.1.43, Colchester; m., Pamela; 1 s.; 1 d. Educ. Prince Edward School, Rhodesia; Aberdeen University. Consultant in Nuclear Medicine, Aberdeen Royal Infirmary, 1979-97; pioneered the use of MRI scanning and started the world's first clinical MRI diagnostic service, 1982; President, Society for Magnetic Resonance Imaging, 1982; Editor in Chief, Magnetic Resonance Imaging, 1983-93; winner, Barclay Medal, British Institute of Radiology, 1997. Honorary Club Doctor, Dundee United

FC, since 1996. Address: (h.) 7 Primrosehill Road, Cults, Aberdeen AB15 9ND; T.-01224 868745.

Smith, Gordon Duffield. Chief Executive, Scottish Football Association, since 2007; b. 29.12.54, Kilwinning. Former football player; played for Rangers and Brighton & Hove Albion FC; later worked as a football agent and BBC football pundit. Address: (b.) The Scottish Football Association, Hampden Park, Glasgow G42 9AY.

Smith, Gordon James, CBE, BA. Resident Director for Scotland, IBM, since 1997; Director, Dunfermline Building Society, since 2006; Director, DSL, since 2006; b. 17.12.47; m., Margaret McKenzie; 2 s.; 2 d. Educ. University of Stirling. IBM: joined 1970; various appointments, 1970-97; Chairman: Business Enterprise Trusts, 1996-99; CBI Scotland, 2003-05; Regional Chms Committee, CBI, 2005-March 2006. Board Member: Scottish Qualifications Authority, 2000-04; Young Enterprise Scotland, 2000-04; Trust Board, Scottish Chamber Orchestra, 2000-04. Recreations: golf; travel; cooking. Club: New (Edinburgh). Address: (b.) IBM, 21 St. Andrew Square, Edinburgh EH2 1AY; T.-0131 558 4311.

Smith, Professor Hamilton, BSc, PhD, CChem, FRSC, FRCPath, FRSE. Professor of Forensic Medicine (Toxicology), Glasgow University, 1987-99; b. 27.4.34, Stirling; m., Jacqueline Ann Spittal. Educ. Kilsyth Academy; Glasgow University. Glasgow University: MRC Fellow, 1960, Special Research Fellow, 1963, Lecturer in Forensic Medicine Department, 1964, Senior Lecturer, 1973, Reader, 1984. Publication: Glaister's Medical Jurisprudence and Toxicology, 13th edition. Recreations: golf (New Club, St. Andrews); gardening. Address: (b.) 1 Park Avenue, Kirkintilloch, Glasgow G66 1EX; T.-0141-776 2901.

Smith, Dr. Hilary, BD (Hons), DipMin, MTh, PhD. Minister, St. Giles' Cathedral, Edinburgh, since 2003. Educ. University of Edinburgh. Managing Director, Camellia Catering, 1981-84; HM Prison Chaplaincy Service, 1986-94; Development Officer, University of Edinburgh, 1994-96; Minister, Caddonfoot linked with Galashiels: St. Ninians, 1999-2003. 1992 James C. Blackie Memorial Prize, University of Edinburgh; Member, Review Committee, Parole Board of Scotland. Address: St. Giles Cathedral, High Street, Edinburgh; T.-0131 225 4363.

Smith, Iain, BA (Hons). MSP (Scottish Liberal Democrat), North East Fife, since 1999; Deputy Minister for Parliament, Scottish Executive, 1999-2000; Convener, Procedures Committee, Scottish Parliament, 2003-05, Convener, Education Committee, 2005-07, Member, Europe and External Relations Committee, since 2007; Liberal Democrat Shadow Minister for Europe, External Relations and Culture; b. 1.5.60, Gateside, Fife. Educ. Bell Baxter High School, Cupar; Newcastle upon Tyne University. Councillor, Fife Council, 1995-99 (Leader of Opposition and Lib Dem Group, 1995-99); Councillor, Fife Regional Council, 1982-95 (Leader of Opposition and Lib Dem Group, 1986-95). Chair, Scottish Liberal Democrat General Election Campaign, 2001, 2005 and 2007. Recreations: sport (mainly football and cricket); cinema; travel; reading. Address: (b.) Constituency Office, 16 Millgate, Cupar, Fife KY15 5EG; T.-01334 656361; Scottish Parliament, Edinburgh EH99 1SP; T.-0131-348 5817; e-mail: iain.smith.msp@scottish.parliament.uk or is@iainsmith.org

Smith, Professor Ian K., MA, MEd, DipEd. Dean of School of Education, University of Paisley, since 2003; Head of School of Education, University of Paisley, 2000-03; b. 28.7.53, Glasgow; m., Aileen; 1 s. Educ. Hutchesons' Boys' Grammar School, Glasgow; University of Glasgow. Teacher of History, Lanark Division, Strathclyde Region, 1976-82; Principal Teacher of History, Dunbarton Division, Strathclyde Region, 1982-89; Staff Development Trainer, Dunbarton Division, 1989; Secondary Assistant Headteacher Posts, including School Co-ordinator TVEI, Dunbarton Division, 1989-92; Senior Lecturer and PGCE (Secondary) Course Co ordinator, Craigie College of Education (subsequently Faculty of Education, University of Paisley), 1992-2000. Member: SOED National Steering Group on Training for Mentoring, 1994-95; GTCS Working Group on Partnership in Initial Teacher Education, 1996-97; National Working Group on Quality Assurance in Initial Teacher Education, 1999-2002; Scottish Teacher Education Committee, since 2000 (Chair, since 2005); Scottish Executive Induction Implementation Group, since 2001; Scottish Executive National Chartered Teacher Review Group, 2007; General Teaching Council for Scotland, as Universities Scotland Representative, since 2001; Convener, GTCS Education Committee, since 2005. Publications: various academic and professional conference presentations, papers and reports, including recently 'Models of Partnership in Programmes of Initial Teacher Education. A Systematic Review Commissioned by the General Teaching Council Scotland' (Co-Author), 2005; Convergence or Divergence? Initial Teacher Education in Scotland and England (Co-Author), 2006. Recreations: reading; exercise; travel. Address: (b.) School of Education, University of Paisley, University Campus, Beech Grove, Ayr KA8 0SR; T.-01292 886272.

Smith, James David, OBE, MA, LLB. Retired Solicitor; b. 27.10.19, Dumbarton; m., Margaret McGregor Grant; 2 s. Educ. Dumbarton Academy; Glasgow University. Commissioned Highland Light Infantry, 1940; Town Clerk, Dumbarton, 1951-67; Chief Executive, Corporation of Greenock, 1967-75; Visiting Lecturer in Law, Paisley College of Technology, 1976-87. Address: (h.) Craigellachie, Balmaha Road, Drymen G63 0BY; T.-01360 660484.

Smith, Professor Jeremy John, BA, MPhil, PhD, AKC, FEA, FRSE. Professor of English Philology, Glasgow University, since 2000; b. 18.10.55, Hampton Court; m., Dr Elaine P. Higgleton; 1 d. Educ. Kingston Grammar School, Kingston-upon-Thames; King's College, London; Jesus College, Oxford; Glasgow University. College Lecturer, Keble College, Oxford. 1978-79; Glasgow University: Lecturer, English Language, 1979-90; Senior Lecturer, 1990-96; Reader, 1996-2000. Publications: Sound Change and the History of English, 2007; Introduction to Middle English (Co-author), 2002; New Perspectives on Middle English Texts (ed. with S. Powell), 2000; Essentials of Early English, 1999; Historical Study of English, 1996; English of Chaucer (with M. L. Samuels), 1988. Recreations; hill walking; opera. Address: (b.) Department of English Language, Glasgow University, Glasgow, G12 8QQ; T.-0141-330 5684.

Smith, John, Alexander, OND (Agri). Member, Scottish Land Court, since 2006; Partner, WW Smith and Son (Farmers), since 1978; b. 14.2.59, Cardenden; m., Susan Mary Watson; 3 d. Educ. Dundee High School; North of Scotland College of Agriculture, Craibstone. Member, Scottish Agricultural Wages Board, 1998-2006; Chairman, NFU Scotland Legal and Technical Committee, 2000-05; Director, Royal Highland Educational Trust, 2001-06; Chairman, Lantranto Agricultural Crops Industry Group, 2001-06. Host Farmer and School Speaker for Royal Highland Educational Trust. Recreations: curling with Lundie and Auchterhouse Curling Club. Address: (h.) Balruddery Farm, Invergowrie, Dundee DD2 5LJ; T.-01382 580428.

Smith, John Allan Raymond, PhD, FRCSEd, FRCSEng, MBChB. Immediate Past President, Royal College of Surgeons of Edinburgh (2003-06); Consultant General Surgeon, Northern General Hospital, Sheffield; b. 24.11.42, Aberdeen; m., Valerie; 2 s.; 3 d. Educ. Boroughmuir School, Edinburgh; Edinburgh University. House Office, Royal Infirmary, Edinburgh; Short service commission, Royal Army Medical Corps; Qualified FRCSEngland, FRCSEdinburgh, 1972; Research and Higher Surgical Training, Dumfries and Galloway Royal Infirmary rotating to Aberdeen Royal Infirmary; Senior Lecturer/Honorary Consultant, University of Sheffield, 1978-85; NHS Consultant, Northern General Hospital, Sheffield, 1985-90; Council Member, Royal College of Surgeons of Edinburgh, since 1990; Chairman, Joint Committee Intercollegiate Examinations, 1998-2000; Chairman, Joint Committee of Higher Surgical Training, 2000-03; Vice President, Royal College of Surgeons of Edinburgh, 1997-2000. Publications: several books and contributions to chapters etc. on surgical infection, surgical shock, nutrition. Recreations: travel; skiing; cooking; wine; family. Address: (b.) Royal College of Surgeons of Edinburgh, Nicolson Street, Edinburgh EH8 9DW; T.-0131 527 1635; e-mail: jarsmith@btinternet.com

Smith, Rev. John Raymond, MA, BD. Minister, Morningside United Church, Edinburgh, since 1998; b. 12.4.47, Dumfries; m., Isabel Jean McKemmie; 3 d. Educ. Dumfries Academy; University of Edinburgh; University of Geneva. Minister, School Wynd Church, Paisley, 1973-82; World Mission Secretary, Congregational Union of Scotland, 1978-86, President, 1988-89; Minister, Oakshaw Trinity Church, Paisley, 1991-98; Moderator, Presbytery of Edinburgh, 2007-08. Chair, Scottish United Reformed and Congregational College; Member, Public Liaison Group, Royal College of Surgeons, Edinburgh. Recreations: walking; writing; travel. Address: (h.) 1 Midmar Avenue, Edinburgh EH10 6BS; T.-0131 447 8724; e-mail: jrs@blueyonder.co.uk

Smith, Professor Leslie Samuel, BSc, PhD. Professor of Computing Science, University of Stirling, since 2000; b. 3.10.52, Glasgow; m., Brigitte Beck-Woerner. Educ. Allan Glen's School; University of Glasgow. Started programming in 1974, and returned to University to study it properly in 1977; Lecturer, Glasgow University, 1980-83; joined Stirling University after a year as an independent consultant. Member, EPSRC College; Senior Member, IEEE; Member, Acoustical Society of America and Society for Neuroscience. Recreations: playing jazz piano. Address: (b.) Department of Computing Science and Mathematics, University of Stirling, Stirling FK9 4LA; T.-01786 467435; e-mail: lss@cs.stir.ac.uk

Smith, Professor Lorraine Nancy, BScN, MEd, PhD. Professor of Nursing, Glasgow University, since 1990 (Head of School, 1990-2001); b. 29.6.49, Ottawa; m., Christopher Murray Smith; 1 s.; 1 d. Educ. University of Ottawa; Manchester University. Appointed, Clinical and Biomedical Research Committee (Scotland), 1992-94; co opted to National Board of Scotland for Nursing, Midwifery and Health Visiting, 1997-2000; appointed, Clinical Standards Advisory Group (UK), 1994-99; Convenor, Royal College of Nursing Research Society (Scotland), 1999-2005; Chair, Work Group of European Nurse Researchers, 2004-07. Recreations: reading; bridge; golf; sailing. Address: (b.) 5 Huntly Gardens, Glasgow G12 9AS; T.-0141-330 5498; e-mail: l.n.smith@clinmed.gla.ac.uk

Smith, Margaret, MA. MSP (Liberal Democrat), Edinburgh West; b. 1961, Edinburgh; 1 s.; 1 d.; 3 step-sons. Civil partnership, 2006. Educ. Broughton High School;

Edinburgh University. Political organiser; Member, City of Edinburgh Council, 1995-99. Recreation: golf. Address: (b.) Scottish Parliament, Edinburgh EH99 1SP; T.-0131-348 5786.

Smith, Matt, OBE, JP. Scottish Secretary, UNISON, since 1993; President, STUC, 1999-2000; b. 4.2.52, Irvine; m., Eileen; 1 s.; 1 d. Educ. Stevenston High School; Ardrossan Academy. NALGO employee from 1973; Senior Scottish Officer/Scottish Organiser, 1981-93; STUC Treasurer; Member, STUC General Council; Employment Appeals Tribunal; Scottish Committee, Equal Opportunities Commission; Executive, Scottish Council Development and Industry; former Member, Committee on Church and Nation, Church of Scotland; Scottish Local Government Information Unit; Centre for Scottish Public Policy; Regional Development Forum. Former Member and Vice-Chair, Broadcasting Council for Scotland; served on: McIntosh Commission (Local Government and a Scottish Parliament), Scotland FORward, Scottish Constitutional Convention, Labour for a Scottish Parliament; Member: North Ayrshire Justice Committee, Ayrshire Economic Forum; former Stevenston Burgh Councillor; parliamentary candidate, Labour, 1979. Recreations: family; travel; gardening; music. Address: (b.) UNISON House, 14 West Campbell Street, Glasgow, G2 6RX; T.-0870 7777 006.

Smith, Nicholas Charlton, BArch, MPhil, MIOA, FRIAS, RIBA, HonFaPS. Partner, Charlton Smith Partnership, Carnoustie, since 1988; Acoustic Consultant and Architect; b. 26.8.46, Hucknall; m., Pamela Ann; 1 s.; 1 d. Educ. Southwell Minster School; Liverpool University; Nottingham University. Architectural practice, 1972-76; Lecturer, Dundee University School of Architecture, 1976-88; Executive Director, RIAS CPD Service, 1988-95; Founding Director, Association of Planning Supervisors (now Association for Project Safety), 1996-99. Recreations: fly fishing; walking; music/opera; reading; travel. Address: 9 Dalhousie Street, Carnoustie DD7 6EJ; T.-01241 859495; e-mail: acoustics@consult-csp.co.uk

Smith, Nigel R. Principal, VoxScot Referendum Consultants, since 2004; Managing Director, Brook Valley Valves Ltd., 1976-2004; b. 9.6.41, Girvan; m., Jody; 2 s.; 2 d. Educ. Dollar Academy. Staff and management appointments, Bowater Paper, Richard Costain, Rank Hovis McDougall. Member, Executive, Scottish Engineering Employers Association, 1985-90; Member, Broadcasting Council for Scotland, 1986-90; Member, BBC General Advisory Council, 1991-93; Member, Glasgow Development Agency, Strategy Review Panel, 1993-94; Member, Scottish Constitutional Commission, 1993-94; Chairman, Broadcasting for Scotland Campaign, 1993-97; Chairman, Scotland Forward Devolution Yes Campaign, 1997; Member, Bank of England Scottish Consultative Committee, 1993-2003; Chairman, British "No" euro campaign, 2002-04. Recreations: hill-walking; offshore sailing; music; reading, particularly biography. Address: (b.) VoxScot, 2 Crosshouse Road, Campsie Glen, Glasgow G66 7AD; T.-01360 311413.

Smith, Professor Paul Gerard, BSc, MSc, PhD, MCIWEM. Professor of Civil and Environmental Engineering, Paisley University, since 1994; b. 12.2.50, Windsor; m., Sheila Margaret Susanne Smith; 2 d. Educ. Nottingham High School; Birmingham University. Civil Engineer, Babtie Group, 1973-76; University of Strathclyde: Lecturer, Senior Lecturer, 1976-94; joined Paisley University, 1994; Head Department of Civil Engineering, 1996-2000; Editor-in-Chief, International Journal of Environmental Health Research, since 1990. Publications: 4 books; 70 research publications.

Recreations; hill-walking; travel. Address: (h.) Ythancraig, Milton, Aberfoyle, Stirling, FK8 3TF; T.-01877 382585.

Smith, Ralph Andrew, QC, LLB, DipLP. Advocate, since 1985; QC, since 1999; b. 22.3.61, Scotland; m., Lucy Moore Inglis; 1 s.; 1 d. Educ. Edinburgh Academy; Kelvinside Academy; Aberdeen University. Junior Counsel to Lord President, 1989-90; Standing Junior Counsel to Department of Environment, 1992-99; Advocate Depute (ad hoc). Recreation: field sports. Address: (h.) Castlemains, Gifford, East Lothian EH41 4PL.

Smith, Sir Robert Haldane, CA, FCIBS. Chairman, The Weir Group plc, since 2002; Chair of the Organising Committee of the 2014 Commonwealth Games in Glasgow, since 2008; Member, Council of Economic Advisors to First Minister of Scotland, since 2007; Chairman, Advisory Group to Scottish Government on young people not in education, employment or training, since 2006; Chairman, Scottish and Southern Energy, since 2005; Non-executive Director: Standard Bank Group, since 2003, Aegon UK Ltd., since 2002, 3i Group plc, since 2004; Member, Judicial Appointments Board for Scotland, since 2002; Chancellor, University of The West of Scotland, since 2003; Regent, Royal College of Surgeons, since 2002; Deputy Chairman, China Britain Business Council, since 2003; b. 8.8.44, Glasgow; m.; 2 d. Educ. Allan Glen's School. Robb Ferguson & Co., CA, 1963-68; qualified CA, 1968; ICFC (now 3i); Managing Director, National Commercial and Glyns Ltd., 1983-85; General Manager, Corporate Finance Division, Royal Bank of Scotland plc; Managing Director, Charterhouse Development Capital Ltd., and Executive Director, Charterhouse Bank Ltd., 1985-89; Morgan Grenfell Private Equity: CEO, 1989-96, Chairman, 1989-2001; Member, Group Executive Committee, Deutsche Bank, 1996-2000; Chief Executive, Morgan Grenfell Asset Management, 1996-99; Vice Chairman, Deutsche Asset Management, Deutsche Bank AG, 1999-2002. Non-executive Director: Tip Europe plc, 1987-89, Stakis plc, 1997-99 (Chairman, 1998-99), Bank of Scotland plc, 1998-2000, MFI Furniture Group plc, 1987-2000. Member, Financial Services Authority, 1997-2000; Member, Board, Financial Reporting Council, 2001-04; Member, Board of Trustees, British Council, 2002-05; Chairman, FRC Group on Audit Committees Combined Code; Trustee, National Museums of Scotland, 1985-2002 (Chairman, Board of Trustees, 1993-2002); President, British Association of Friends of Museums, 1995-2005; President, Institute of Chartered Accountants of Scotland, 1996-97; Commissioner, Museums and Galleries Commission, 1988-98 (Vice Chairman, 1997-98). Hon. Doctorates, Edinburgh University, 1999, Glasgow University, 2001, Paisley University, 2003. Publication: Managing Your Company's Finances. Address: (b.) 39 Palmerston Place, Edinburgh EH12 5AU; T.-0131-527 6010.

Smith, Sir Robert Hill, Bt. MP (Liberal Democrat), West Aberdeenshire and Kincardine, since 1997; Liberal Democrat Deputy Leader of the House of Commons, since 2007; b. 15.4.58; m., Fiona Cormack; 3 d. Educ. Merchant Taylors' School, Northwood; University of Aberdeen. Managed family estate; Member, Aberdeenshire Council, 1995-97; Liberal Democrat Spokesman on Transport and the Environment, 1997-99, Scottish Affairs Spokesman, 1999-2001; Member, Scottish Affairs Select Committee, 1999-2001; Liberal Democrat Deputy Chief Whip, 2001-06; Scottish Whip, 1999-2001, Energy Spokesman, 2005-06; Member: Trade and Industry Select Committee, 2001-06, Procedures Committee, since 2001, International

Development Committee, since 2007; Vice Chairman, All-party Group for the UK Offshore Oil and Gas Industry; Treasurer, House of Commons Yacht Club; Honorary Vice President of Energy Action Scotland. Address: (b.) Constituency Office, 6 Dee Street, Banchory AB31 5ST; T.-01330 820330; e-mail: bobsmith@cix.co.uk

Smith, Robert Lupton, OBE, FRICS. Vice-President, Association for the Protection of Rural Scotland, since 1993 (Director, 1981-93); Chartered Surveyor in private practice, 1954-96; b. 26.4.24, Cheadle Hulme; m.; 3 d. Educ. George Watson's College; College of Estate Management; Heriot-Watt College. Chairman, Scottish Junior Branch, RICS, 1952; Member, Scottish Executive Committee, RICS, 1952-60; elected, Edinburgh Town Council, 1962-74 and Edinburgh District Council, 1974-77; Governor, Edinburgh College of Art, 1963-89; fought European Election, 1979, as Liberal; Deputy Traffic Commissioner, 1974-78; Chairman, Good Neighbours Housing Association, 1984-87; Scottish Liberal Party: Chairman, Executive Committee, 1971-74, Chairman, 1974, President, 1976-82; Council Member, Royal Scottish Geographical Society, 1957-92; Chairman, A9 Highland Hosts Group, 1995-2000; Director, Cockburn Conservation Trust Ltd., 1976-90; Chairman, Logierait Bridge Co. Ltd., 1993-2003. Recreations: visiting Orkney; reading; looking at fine art. Address: (h.) Charleston, Dalguise, near Dunkeld, PH8 0JX; T.-01350 728968.

Smith, Ronald A., MA, FEIS. General Secretary, Educational Institute of Scotland, since 1995; Member, General Council, STUC, since 1995; President, Education International Pan European Structure, incorporating the European Trade Union Committee for Education, since 2006; b. 9.6.51, Lerwick; m., Mae; 1 s.; 1 d. Educ. Anderson Educational Institute; Aberdeen University; Aberdeen College of Education. Teacher of Latin, then A.P.T. of Latin, then Principal Teacher of Modern Studies, Broxburn Academy, 1973-88; Assistant Secretary, EIS, 1988-95. Address: (b.) 46 Moray Place, Edinburgh, EH3 6BH; e-mail: rsmith@eis.org.uk

Smith, Shona Houston, LLB (Hons), DipLP, NP. Partner, Balfour and Manson; b. 17.11.66, Glasgow. Admitted, Solicitor, 1991; specialised in family law since 1993; Board Member, Scottish Child Law Centre, 1996-99; former Chair and Treasurer of the Family Law Association; Treasurer, Scottish Collaborative Family Law Group. Address: (b.) 62 Frederick Street, Edinburgh EH2 1LS; T.-0131 200 1238; e-mail: shona.smith@balfour-manson.co.uk

Smith, Emeritus Professor Stanley Desmond, OBE, BSc, PhD, DSc, FRS, FRSE. Professor of Physics, Heriot-Watt University, 1970-96; Chairman, Edinburgh Instruments Ltd., since 1971; b. 3.3.31, Bristol; m., Gillian Anne Parish; 1 s.; 1 d. Educ. Cotham Grammar School; Bristol University; Reading University. SSO, RAE, Farnborough, 1956-58; Research Assistant, Department of Meteorology, Imperial College, London, 1958-59; Lecturer, then Reader, Reading University, 1960-70; Head, Department of Physics, Heriot-Watt University, 1970-96. Member: Advisory Council for Applied Research and Development, 1985-87, Advisory Council on Science and Technology, 1987-88, Defence Scientific Advisory Council, 1985-91, SERC Astronomy and Planetary Science and Engineering Boards, 1985-88, Council, Institute of Physics, 1984-87; Chairman, Scottish Optoelectronics Association, 1996-98. Recreations: tennis; skiing; mountaineering; golf; raising the temperature. Address: (b.) Edinburgh Instruments Ltd., 2 Bain Square, Livingston, EH54 7DQ; T.-01506 425300; e-mail: des.smith@edinst.com

Smith, Tommy, DUniv. Musician (tenor saxophone), Educator and Composer; b. 27.4.67, Edinburgh. Won best soloist and best group award, Edinburgh International Jazz Festival, aged 14; recorded his first albums as a leader, aged 15; signed to Blue Note Records, 1989; won British Jazz Award, 1989; hosted Jazz Types, BBC TV; began recording for Linn Records, 1993; founded Scottish National Jazz Orchestra, 1995; won BT British Jazz Award for Best Ensemble, ScotRail Award for most outstanding group performance, Arts Foundation/Barclays Bank jazz composition fellowship prize, 1996; has premiered four original saxophone concertos; Sound of Love album reached No. 20 in American Gavin Jazz Chart; started own record company, 2000; Honorary Fellow, Royal Incorporation of Architects of Scotland and Creative Scotland Award, 2000; Founder, The Tommy Smith Youth Jazz Orchestra, since 2002; Hamlet British Jazz Award for best tenor saxophonist, 2002; made youngest-ever Doctor of the University, Heriot-Watt University, 1999; 21 solo albums; currently conducting masterclasses in Europe, Americas and Asia. Recreations: cinema; cooking; camping; DIY; badminton; art and design; poetry; history; golf; movies. Address: (b.) c/o Spartacus Records Ltd., PO Box 3743, Lanark ML11 9WD.

Smith, Walter, OBE. Manager, Rangers Football Club, since 2007; National Coach, Scottish Football Association, 2004-2007; b. 24.2.48, Lanark. Joined Dundee United, 1966; joined Dumbarton, 1975; rejoined Dundee United, 1977, became Youth coach, then Assistant Manager; appointed coach of Scotland Under 18 team, 1978; became coach of the Under 21 team, then Assistant Manager for the Scotland World Cup team, 1986; joined Rangers in 1986 and became Manager in 1991; won the league in first six full seasons; won the Scottish Cup and League Cup three times each; became Manager of Everton in 1998 until 2002; Assistant to Manchester United in 2004. Address: Rangers Football Club, Edmiston House, 100 Edmiston Drive, Ibrox, Glasgow G51 2YX.

Smith, Professor William Ewen, BSc, DIC, PhD, DSc, FRSC, FRSE. Professor of Inorganic Chemistry, since 1987; b. 21.2.41, Glasgow; m., Frances Helen Williamson; 1 s.; 1 d. Educ. Hutchesons' Boys Grammar School; Strathclyde University. Visiting Scientist, Oak Ridge National Laboratory, 1965-67; SERC and ICI Fellow, University College, London, 1967-69; Lecturer, Reader, Professor, Strathclyde University, since 1969. Publications: 200 papers and reviews. Recreations: golf; sailing. Address: (b.) Department of Pure and Applied Chemistry, Strathclyde University, Glasgow, G1 1XL; T.-0141-552 4400.

Smith, William Wilson Campbell, MA (Cantab), LLB (Glas). Partner, Biggart Baillie, Solicitors, Glasgow and Edinburgh; b. 17.5.46, Glasgow; m., Elizabeth Margaret Richards; 2 d. Educ. Glasgow Academy; St. Catharine's College, Cambridge; Glasgow University. Qualified as a Solicitor, 1972; Assistant Solicitor, Herbert Smith & Co., London, 1972-73; Partner, Biggart Baillie, since 1974, Managing Partner, 1997-2003. Trustee: Lennoxlove Trust, 2000-04, Glassford Sheltered Housing Trust, 1991-2004; Member, Joint Insolvency Examination Board, 1986-95; Deacon, Incorporation of Barbers, Glasgow, 1989-90. Recreations: croquet; golf; barbershop singing. Address: (b.) Dalmore House, 310 St. Vincent Street, Glasgow, G2 5QR; T.-0141-228 8000.
E-mail: csmith@biggartbaillie.co.uk

Smout, Professor Thomas Christopher, CBE, MA, PhD, FRSE, FSA (Scot), FBA. HM Historiographer in Scotland; b. 19.12.33. Address: Chesterhill, Shore Road, Anstruther, Fife KY10 3DZ.

Smuga, George Muirhead Russell, MA (Hons), DipEd. Headteacher, Royal High School, Edinburgh, since 1998; b. 6.11.47, Broughty Ferry; 1 s.; 1 d. Educ. Kirkcaldy High School; Edinburgh University. Principal Teacher, Modern Studies, then Assistant Headteacher, Portobello High

School; Depute Headteacher, Beeslack High School; Headteacher, North Berwick High School and Manager Quality Assurance, East Lothian. Co-author of four modern studies textbooks. Recreations: hill-walking; supporting Hibernian F.C. Address: (b.) Royal High School, Edinburgh EH4 6JP; e-mail: George.Smyth@ royalhigh.edin.sch.uk

Smyth, Professor John Fletcher, MD, FRCPE, FRCP, FRCSE, FRCR, FRSE. Professor of Medical Oncology, since 1979, and Director of Cancer Research Centre, 2002-05, University of Edinburgh; Hon. Director, Cancer Research UK (formerly Imperial Cancer Research Fund) Medical Oncology Unit, now Clinical Cancer Research Centre, 1980-2005; President of the Federation of European Cancer Societies, 2005-07; b. 26.10.45; m., (1) Catherine Ellis; 2 d (marr. diss.); m., (2) Ann Cull; 2 step d. Educ. Bryanston School; Trinity College, Cambridge (BA, 1967, MA, 1971); St. Bartholomews Hospital (MB Chir 1970); MD Cantab, 1976; MSc London, 1975; MRCP, 1973. House Officer posts: St. Bartholomew's Hosp. and RPMS, London, 1970-72; Assistant Lecturer, Dept. of Med. Oncology, St. Bartholomew's Hospital, 1972-73; CRC Research Fellowship Inst. Cancer Res., 1973-75; MRC Travelling Fellowship, Nat. Cancer Inst., USA, 1975-76; Senior Lecturer, Inst. Cancer Research, 1976-79. Honorary Consultant Physician, Royal Marsden Hospital and Brompton Hospital, 1977-79; Lothian Health Board, since 1979; Visiting Professor of Medicine and Associate Director for Medical Research, University of Chicago, 1979. Member of Council: EORTC, 1990-97; UICC, 1990-94; President, European Society for Medical Oncology, 1991-93; Treasurer, Federation of European Cancer Societies, 1992-97. Editor-in-Chief, European Journal of Cancer, since 2000. Publications: contributions to various medical and scientific journals on cancer medicine, pharmacology, clinical and experimental cancer therapeutics. Recreations: flying and singing (sometimes simultaneously). Club: Athenaeum. Address: 18 Inverleith Avenue South, Edinburgh EH3 5QA; T.-0131 552 3775.

Snodgrass, Ian, OBE, BSc (Hons), DipTP. Chief Executive, North Ayrshire Council, since 2004; m., Ann. Educ. University of Glasgow; University of Strathclyde. Managing Director, Renfrew District Council, 1995-96; Director of Planning and Transport, Renfrewshire Council, 1996-2004. President, Rotary Club of Paisley, 2003/04. Address: (b.) Cunninghame House, Irvine KA12 8EE; T.-01294 324 124; e-mail: asproul@north-ayrshire.gov.uk

Snowdon, Leslie C., MA (Hons). Editor, Scotland on Sunday, since 2006; Editor, Sunday Times Scotland, 2003-06; b. 23.6.61, RAF Cosford; m., Fiona; 2 s.; 1 d. Educ. Annan Academy; Edinburgh University. Photographer, Dumfriesshire Newspapers, 1984-89; Photographer and Sub-Editor, Dumfries and Galloway Standard, 1989-94; Sub-Editor, Chief Political Sub-Editor, Chief Sports Sub, Deputy Sports Editor, The Scotsman, 1994-99; Sports Editor, Sunday Times Scotland, 1999-2000; Deputy Sports Editor, The Sunday Times, 2000-03. Address: (b.) 108 Holyrood Road, Edinburgh EH8 8AS; T.-0131 6208424.

Somerville, Shirley Ann, BA (Hons). MSP (SNP), Lothians, since 2007; b. 2.9.74; m., Myles. Educ. Kirkcaldy High School; Strathclyde University; Stirling University. Scottish National Party: Member, since 1990, Convener, Edinburgh Central branch. Contested Edinburgh Central constituency, 2007 Scottish Parliament election. Returned as replacement MSP for Lothians region on 5 September 2007. Member: Transport, Infrastructure and Climate Change, since 2007. Address: (b.) Scottish Parliament, Edinburgh EH99 1SP.

Soutar, David, MB, ChB, FRCS(Ed), FRCS(Glas), ChM. Consultant Plastic Surgeon, West of Scotland Regional Plastic Maxillofacial Surgery Unit, since 1981; Chairman, Division of Trauma and Related Services, North Glasgow

Universities NHS Trust, 2000-06; b. 19.12.47, Arbroath; m., Myra; 2 s.; 1 d. Educ. Ayr Academy; University of Aberdeen. General surgical training, Grampian Health Board; plastic surgery training, Aberdeen, Glasgow, Munich; Honorary Clinical Senior Lecturer, Glasgow University. Member, Council, British Association of Plastic Surgeons, 1988-92, 1994-2002 (President, 2001). Publications: four books; over 30 book chapters; over 70 articles. Recreations: music; gardening. Address: (b.) Canniesburn Plastic Surgery Unit, Jubilee Building, Glasgow Royal Infirmary, Glasgow G4 0SF; T.-0141-211 5776; e-mail: david.soutar@northglasgow.scot.nhs.uk

Souter, Brian, BA. Chief Executive, Stagecoach Group plc, since 2002 (Chairman, 1980-2002); b. 1954; m., Elizabeth McGoldrick; 3 s.; 1 d. Educ. Dundee University; University of Strathclyde. Address: (b.) 10 Dunkeld Road, Perth, PH1 5TW.

Souter, William Alexander, MBChB(Hons), FRCSEd. Consultant Orthopaedic Surgeon, Princess Margaret Rose Orthopaedic Hospital, Edinburgh, 1968-1997; b. 11.5.33, Cupar; m., Kathleen Bruce Georgeson Taylor; 1 s.; 2 d. Educ. Falkirk High School; George Watson's Boys' College, Edinburgh; Medical School, Edinburgh University. Registrar in Hand Surgery, Derbyshire Royal Infirmary, 1964; Senior Registrar, Orthopaedic Department, Edinburgh, 1965-68; Instructor in Orthopaedic Surgery, University of Washington, Seattle, 1967; Honorary Senior Lecturer in Orthopaedics, Edinburgh University, 1977-97; Visiting Professor, Bioengineering Department, Strathclyde University, 1985-88. Member, Council, British Orthopaedic Association, 1986-88 and 1993-95; Member, Council, Royal College of Surgeons of Edinburgh, 1988-98; Inaugural President, British Elbow and Shoulder Society, 1989-90; British Society for Surgery of the Hand: Member, Council, 1977-78, 1992-94, President, 1993; Chairman, Accreditation Committee, Federation of European Societies for Surgery of the Hand, 1992-96; European Rheumatoid Arthritis Surgical Society: Member, Executive Committee, 1979-81 and 1993-2001, President, 1995-99; President, Rheumatoid Arthritis Surgical Society, 1982 and 1998-2000; Honorary Member: British Society for Surgery of the Hand, 2001, Societe Francaise Chirurgie Orthopedique et Traumatologique, 1999, Netherlands Rheumatoid Arthritis Surgical Society, 2001, Spanish Society for Surgery of the Shoulder and Elbow, 1996, European Rheumatoid Arthritis Surgical Society, 2002, British Elbow and Shoulder Society, 2003. Recreations: gardening; music; hill-walking; photography; golf. Address: (h.) Old Mauricewood Mains, Penicuik, Midlothian EH26 0NJ; T.-01968 672609; e-mail: WASouter@ukgateway.net

Southwood, Ann, BA (Hons), DipCG, CertYCW. Principal, Newbattle Abbey College, since 2000; b. 25.5.54, York. Educ. Queen Anne Grammar School, York; Middlesex Polytechnic. National Development Officer, Scottish Executive, Adult Educational Guidance Initiative Scotland, 1994-98; Adult Guidance Manager, Career Development, Edinburgh and Lothian, 1995-2000. Recreations: music; sport; travel. Address: (b.) Newbattle Road, Dalkeith EH22 3LL; T.-0131 663 1921; e-mail: office@newbattleabbeycollege.ac.uk

Sparks, Professor Leigh, MA, PhD, FRSA. Professor of Retail Studies, Stirling University, since 1992; Dean, Faculty of Management, 1995-2000; b. 15.2.57, Bridgend, Wales; m., Janice Lewis. Educ. The Brynteg C.S.; Christ's College, Cambridge; St. David's University College, Wales. Researcher, Lecturer, Senior Lecturer, Professor, Institute for Retail Studies, Department of Marketing, Stirling University. Recreation: watching sport, especially rugby.

Address: (b.) Institute for Retail Studies, Stirling University, Stirling FK9 4LA; T.-01786 467384; e-mail: Leigh.Sparks@stir.ac.uk

Spaull, Alison Mary, BSc, PhD, MBA. Director, Chief Scientist Office, Scottish Government Health Directorates, since 1996; Chairman, Tayside Flow Technologies Ltd., since 2007; Board Member, Scottish Health Innovations Ltd.; Member, Court, Glasgow Caledonian University, 2000-07; Member, Albany Ventures Technical Advisory Board, 2001-07; b. 5.8.52, Ewell. Educ. Surbiton High School; Rosebery County Grammar School; Reading University. Resarcher, Rothamsted Experimental Station, 1976-85; Crop Protection Adviser, East of Scotland College of Agriculture, 1985-90; Technical Secretary, Scottish Agricultural College, 1990-93; Research and Development Manager, Scottish Agriculture College, 1993-95; Health Services Research Manager, Chief Scientist Office, Scottish Office Department of Health, 1996. English Speaking Union Thynne Scholar, 1988; Council Member, Association of Applied Biologists, 1987 and 1989-91. Recreations: gardening; walking; equestrianism; the arts. Address: (b.) St Andrew's House, Regent Road, Edinburgh.

Speakman, Professor John Roger, BSc, PhD, DSc. Professor of Zoology, Aberdeen University, since 1997, and Director, Institute of Biological and Environmental Sciences, since 2007; b. 29.11.58, Leigh; m., Mary Magdelene; 1 s.; 1 d. Educ. Leigh Grammar School; Stirling University. Lecturer, 1989, Senior Lecturer, 1993, Reader, 1995, Aberdeen University; Chairman, Aberdeen Centre for Energy Regulation and Obesity, since 1998; Royal Society Leverhulme Senior Research Fellow, 2000. Publication: Body Composition Analysis: A Handbook of Non-Invasive Methods, 2001. Address: (b.) Department of Zoology, Aberdeen University, Aberdeen AB24 2TZ; T.-01224 272879.

Spence, Professor Alan, MA. Professor of Creative Writing, University of Aberdeen, Artistic Director, WORD Festival; Writer (poet, playwright, novelist, short-story writer); b. 5.12.47, Glasgow; m., Janani (Margaret). Educ. Allan Glen's School, Glasgow; Glasgow University. Writer in Residence, Glasgow University, 1975-77, Deans Community School, 1978, Traverse Theatre, Edinburgh, 1983, City of Edinburgh, 1986-87, Edinburgh University, 1989-82, Aberdeen University, 1996-2001 (Professor in Creative Writing, since 2001); winner, People's Prize, 1991; Macallan/Scotland on Sunday Short Story competition, 1993; McVitie's Prize, 1996; TMA Drama Award, 1996; Glenfiddich Spirit of Scotland Award, 2006. Publications: poetry: ah!; Glasgow Zen; Seasons of the Heart; Clear Light; short stories: Its Colours They Are Fine, Stone Garden; novels: The Magic Flute, Way to Go, The Pure Land; plays: Sailmaker; Space Invaders; Changed Days. Recreations: meditation; running; playing flute. Address: (b.) Word - University of Aberdeen Writers Festival, Office of External Affairs, University of Aberdeen, King's College, Aberdeen AB24 3FX; T.-01224 273874; e-mail: word@abdn.ac.uk

Spence, Emeritus Professor Alastair Andrew, CBE, MD, FRCA, FRCP (Glas & Edin), FRCS (Ed & Eng), Hon FDS, RCS Eng. Professor of Anaesthetics, Edinburgh University, 1984-98, Professor Emeritus, since 1998; President, Royal College of Anaesthetists, 1991-94; b. 18.9.36, Glasgow; m., Maureen Isobel Aitchison; 2 s. Educ. Ayr Academy; Glasgow University. Professor and Head, University Department of Anaesthesia, Western Infirmary, Glasgow, 1969-84; Editor, British Journal of Anaesthesia, 1973-83

(Chairman of the Board and Trustee, 1983-93); Hunterian Professor, Royal College of Surgeons of England, 1974; Joseph Clover Lecturer, 1990; Lewis Wright Lecture, American Society of Anesthesiologists, 2006; Member, Advisory Committee on Distinction Awards, since 1992; Medical Director, Scottish Advisory Committee on Distinction Awards, 1996 2000 Recreations: golf; gardening. Address: (h.) Harewood, Kilmacolm, PA13 4HX; T.-01505 872962.

Spence, James William, KFO (Norway), RON (Netherlands), DL (Orkney), BSc, MNI, MICS. Master Mariner, since 1971; Shipbroker, since 1975; Company Director, since 1977; Honorary Sheriff, Grampian Highland and Islands (Kirkwall), since 2000; b. 19.1.45, St. Ola, Orkney; m., 1, Margaret Paplay Stevenson (deceased); 3 s. (one deceased); 2, Susan Mary Price. Educ. Leith Nautical College, Edinburgh; Robert Gordon's Institute of Technology, Aberdeen; University of Wales, Cardiff. Merchant Navy, 1961-74 (Member, Nautical Institute, 1972, Member, Royal Institute of Navigation, 1971); Micoperi SpA, 1974-75 (Temporary Assistant Site Co-ordinator on Scapa Flow Project); John Jolly (Shipbrokers, Stevedores, Shipping and Forwarding Agents) since 1975 (Manager, 1975, Junior Partner, 1976-77, Proprietor and Managing Director, since 1977). Vice-Consul for Norway, 1976, Consul, 1978; Vice-Consul for the Netherlands, 1978-94; Member, Kirkwall Community Council, 1978-82; Member, Orkney Pilotage Committee, 1979-88; Chairman, Kirkwall Port Employers' Association, 1979-87 (Member, since 1975); Chairman, RNLI, Kirkwall Lifeboat Station Branch Committee, 1997-2004 (Station Hon. Secretary, 1987-96, Deputy Launching Authority, 1976-87); Chairman, Pier Arts Centre Trust, 1989-91 (Trustee, 1980-91); Chairman, Association of Honorary Norwegian Consuls in the UK and Ireland, 1993-95. Recreations: oenology; equestrian matters; Orcadian history; vintage motoring. Address: (h.) Alton House, Kirkwall, Orkney KW15 1NA; T.-01856 872268.
E-mail: cons.kirkwall@johnjolly.co.uk

Spence, Professor John, ARCST, BSc, MEng, PhD, DSc, FREng, FRSE, FRSA, CEng, FIMechE. Professor Emeritus, Strathclyde University, since 2001, Trades House of Glasgow Professor of Mechanics of Materials, 1982-2001; b. 5.11.37, Chapelhall; m., Margaret Gray Hudson; 2 s. Educ. Airdrie Academy; Royal College of Science and Technology; Sheffield University. Engineering apprenticeship, Stewarts & Lloyds (now British Steel Corporation); Senior Engineer, then Head of Stress Analysis, Babcock & Wilcox Research Division; Strathclyde University: Lecturer, 1966, Senior Lecturer, Reader, Professor since 1979, Deputy Principal, Pro-Vice Principal and Vice Principal, 1994-2001; Acting Principal, Bell College, Hamilton, 2004/05. Served on many national committees: Past President, Institution of Mechanical Engineers; EPSRC; British Standards Institution; Engineering Professors Council; Engineering Council Senate and BER; Research Assessment Exercise Panel 30; Accreditation Board, Hong Kong Institution of Engineers; Scottish Higher Education Funding Council, Royal Academy of Engineering Council. Address: (b.) Department of Mechanical Engineering, Strathclyde University, 75 Montrose Street, Glasgow, G1 1XJ; T.-0141-548 4497/2324.

Spencely, John Despenser, CBE; b. 5.10.39, Westerham, England; m., Marilyn Anne Read; 1 d. (by pr. m.). Educ. Bryanston School; Cambridge University; Edinburgh University. Consultant Architect, Arbiter; former Member, Scottish Building Contract Committee; President: Edinburgh Architectural Association, 1984-86, Royal Incorporation of Architects in Scotland, 1989-91; former

Lay Member, Scottish Solicitors Discipline Tribunal; former Visiting Professor, Napier University; Freeman of the City of London. Recreations: sailing; reading. Address: (b.) 19A Carlton Terrace, Edinburgh EH7 5DD; T.-0131 556 7080.

Spencer, Professor Alec P., BA (Hons), MA. Director, Rehabilitation and Care, Scottish Prison Service, 2001-06; Honorary Professor, Department of Applied Social Science, University of Stirling, since 2005; Chair, Scottish Accreditation Panel for Offender Programmes; Chairman of Board of Directors, INCLUDEM; Chairman of Council of SASO (Scottish Association for Study of Offending); Assessor for Commissioner for Public Appointments in Scotland (OCPAS); b. 12.3.46, London; m., Joan; 2 s.; 1 d. Educ. Dame Alice Owen School; Keele University. Joined Scottish Prison Service, 1972, as Assistant Governor: Polmont Borstal, Perth Prison, Glenochil; Deputy Governor, Aberdeen Prison, 1978; Prison Department HQ, 1981; Warden, Glenochil D.C., 1983; Deputy Governor, Glenochil Complex, 1987; Governor, Dungavel Prison, 1989; Governor, Peterhead Prison, 1992; Operational Adviser, PFI prison project SPS HQ, 1996; Governor, Edinburgh Prison, 1996; Governor, Glenochil Prison and Young Offenders' Institution, 2000. Chairman, Scottish Forum on Prisons and Families, 1990-2000; Butler Trust Award, 1987; Editor, ASPG Journal, 1982-90; Chairman: Security Category Working Group, SPS, 2000, Review of Future Management of Sex Offenders, 2002; Hon. Senior Research Fellow, Dundee University, 1995-98; Research Associate, Centre for Law and Society, Edinburgh University, 1999-2004; Adviser, Scottish Parliament, Justice 2 Sub-Committee Inquiry into Justice System and sexual offenders against children, 2006; Chairman, Dollar Community Council, 1990-93. Publication: Working with Sex Offenders in Prisons and through Release to the Community, 1999. Recreations: music; walking; writing. Address: Oakburn, 92 The Ness, Dollar, Clackmannanshire FK14 7EB; T.-01259 743044.
E-mail: spencer@oakburn.co.uk

Spencer, Very Rev. Paul Francis, CP. Rector, Saint Mungo's, Glasgow, since 1996; Catholic Chaplain, Glasgow Caledonian University, since 2001; Provincial Consultor, Passionist Congregation, since 2004; b. 2.3.54. Educ. Saint Mungo's Academy, Glasgow; University College, Dublin; Milltown Institute, Dublin; Pontifical Gregorian University, Rome. Professed as Member of Passionist Congregation, 1977; Ordained Priest, 1980; Vicar, Saint Mungo's, Glasgow, 1981-86; Master of Novices, Cochin, India, 1986-87; post-graduate studies, Rome, 1987-89; Rector, Mission Anglophone de France, Paris, 1989-96; Provincial Consultor, Congregation of the Passion, 1992-2000; Postulator of the Cause of Canonisation of Elizabeth Prout CP, since 1994; Member, Historical Commission for the Cause of Ignatius Spencer CP, since 1993; awarded Cross Pro piis meritis, Sovereign Military Order of Malta, 1995; appointed Papal Delegate to a Federation of Italian Monasteries, 2004. Publications: To Heal the Broken-Hearted: The Life of Blessed Charles of Mount Argus, 1988; As a Seal upon your Heart: The Life of Saint Paul of the Cross, Founder of the Passionists, 1994. Recreation: music. Address: (h.) Saint Mungo's Retreat, 52 Parson Street, Glasgow G4 0RX; T.-0141-552 1823.

Spens, Michael Colin Barkley, MA. Headmaster, Fettes College, Edinburgh, since 1998; b. 22.9.50, Weybridge; m., Deborah Susan; 1 s.; 2 d. Educ. Marlborough College; Selwyn College, Cambridge. United Biscuits Plc, 1972-74; Radley College, Oxon, 1974-93 (Assistant Master, 1974-93, i/c Careers, 1974-84, Housemaster, 1984-93); Headmaster, Caldicott, Farnham Common, 1993-98. Recreations: golf; running; wood-turning;

bridge; geology; mountaineering; electronics. Address: (h.) Headmasters' Lodge, Fettes College, Edinburgh EH4 1QX; T.-0131-311 6701.

Spiers, Rev. John McLaren, LTh, MTh. Minister, Orchardhill Church, Giffnock, 1977-2004; b. 12.12.43, Edinburgh; m., Janet Diane Watson; 2 d. Educ. George Watson's College, Edinburgh; Glasgow University. Probationer Assistant, Drumchapel Old Parish Church, Glasgow, 1971-72; Minister, South Church, Barrhead, 1972-77; Convener, Board of World Mission, 1996-2000; Moderator, Presbytery of Glasgow, 2001-02. Recreations: music; art; family life; gardening. Address: 58 Woodlands Road, Glasgow G46 7JQ

Spilg, Walter Gerson Spence, MB, ChB (Hons), FRCPath, FRCPG. Consultant Pathologist, Victoria Infirmary, Glasgow, 1972-99, in Administrative Charge, 1986-99; Honorary Clinical Senior Lecturer, Glasgow University, since 1973; b. 27.10.37, Glasgow; m., Vivien Anne Burns; 1 s.; 2 d. Educ. Hutchesons' Boys' Grammar School, Glasgow; Glasgow University. Registrar in Pathology, Glasgow Royal Infirmary, 1965-68; Senior Registrar in Pathology, Victoria Infirmary, Glasgow, 1968-69; Lecturer in Pathology, Glasgow University (Western Infirmary), 1969-72. Former President, Caledonian Branch, Association of Clinical Pathologists; (Locum) Consultant Pathologist, Wishaw General Hospital, Lanarkshire. Recreation: bridge. Address: (h.) 4B Newton Court, Newton Mearns, Glasgow, G77 5QL.

Spratt, Col. Douglas Norman, CBE, TD, DL. Director, Cameo of Edinburgh, 1984-99; b. 18.9.20, Ramsgate; m., Margaret; 1 d (deceased). Educ. Sir Roger Manwood's Grammar School, Sandwich, Kent. Honorary Colonel 71 (Scottish) Engineer Regiment (V), 1976-90; Chairman, Lowland TAVR, 1980-84; President, Edinburgh Branch, Chartered Institute of Marketing; Chairman, Friends of the Reserve Forces Association, Scotland; Member, High Constables of Edinburgh; Deputy Lieutenant, City of Edinburgh, 1984-94; Associate Member of the Military Attaches London. Recreations: fishing; sailing. Address: (h.) 6 Fernielaw Avenue, Edinburgh, EH13 OEE; T.-0131-441 1962.

Spray, Dr. Christopher James, MBE, PhD, MA, MIEEM. Director of Environmental Science, Scottish Environment Protection Agency, since 2004; b. 11.7.53, Marlborough; m., Deborah; 3 s. Educ. Marlborough College, Wiltshire; St. John's College, Cambridge; Aberdeen University. Research Fellow in Zoology, Aberdeen University, 1978-84; Anglian Water Authority, Cambridge, 1984-89; National Rivers Authority, Anglian Region, 1989-91; Conservation Manager, then Environment Director, Northumbrian Water Limited, 1991-2004; President, Institute of Ecology and Environmental Management, 2004-06; Trustee of Wildfowl and Wetlands Trust, since 2003; Trustee, Freshwater Biological Association, since 2006; Council Member, RSPB, 1999-2003; Trustee of British Trust for Ornithology, 2001-03; Director of River Restoration Project, 1995-99; past Chairman of Tweed Forum; past Director, Industry and Nature Conservation Association. Board Member, Heritage Lottery Fund (NE) Committee, 2001-04; Member, Government's Advisory Committee on Releases to the Environment, 1999-2002; Member, England Biodiversity Group, 2002-04. Recreations: birdwatching; running; conservation; hill walking. Address: (b.) Scottish Environment Protection Agency, Corporate Office, Erskine Court, Castle Business Park, Stirling FK9 4TR; T.-01786-452563; e-mail: chris.spray@sepa.org.uk

Sprent, Professor Janet I., OBE, BSc, ARCS, PhD, DSc, FRSE. Emeritus Professor of Plant Biology, Dundee University; Member, Royal Commission on Environmental Pollution, since 2002; b. 10.1.34, Slough; m., Emeritus

Professor Peter Sprent. Educ. Slough High School; Imperial College, London; Tasmania University. Has spent 31 years at Dundee University; research focussed on nitrogen fixing legumes, both tree and crop species; currently involved in international collaboration, mainly in Africa and Brazil; Dean of Science and Engineering, 1987-89; Deputy Principal of the University, 1995-98. Council Member, NERC, 1991-95; Member, Scottish Higher Education Funding Council, 1992-96; Member, Joint Nature Conservation Committee, 1994-2000; Member, then Chairman, Board of Governors, Macaulay Land Use Research Institute, 1989-2001; Member, Board, Scottish Natural Heritage, 2001-07; Council Member, Scottish Association for Marine Science, since 2003; Hon. Research Fellow, Scottish Crop Research Institute. Publications: five books and over 200 chapters/papers. Recreations: research; hill-walking. Address: 32 Birkhill Avenue, Wormit, Fife DD6 8PW; T.-01382 541706; e-mail: jisprent@aol.com

Sprot of Haystoun, Lt.-Col. Aidan Mark, MC, JP. Landowner (Haystoun Estate) and Farmer, since 1965; b. 17.6.19, Lilliesleaf. Educ. Belhaven Hill; Stowe. Commissioned, Royal Scots Greys, 1940, served Palestine, 1941-42, Western Desert, 1942-43, Italy, 1943-44, NW Europe, 1944-45; continued serving with Regiment in Germany until 1952, Libya, Egypt and Jordan, 1952-55, UK, 1955-58, Germany, 1958-62; Adjutant, 1944-45; Commanding Officer, 1959-62; retired, 1962. County Councillor, Peeblesshire, 1963-75; DL (Peeblesshire), 1966-80; Lord Lieutenant, Tweeddale, 1980-94; Member, Queen's Bodyguard for Scotland (Royal Company of Archers), since 1950; County Director, Peeblesshire Branch, Red Cross, 1966-74; Patron, since 1983; Badge of Honour, British Red Cross Society, 1998; County Commissioner, Peeblesshire Scout Association, 1968-73; Chairman, 1975-80, President, 1980-94; President, Borders Area Scout Association, 1994-99; Scout Medal of Merit, 1994; Honorary Secretary, Royal Caledonian Hunt, 1964-74; President, Lowlands of Scotland TA&VRA, 1986-89; President, Lothian Federation of Boys' Clubs, 1989-96, now Hon. Vice-President; Honorary Freeman, Tweeddale District, 1994; Vice-President, Royal Highland and Agricultural Society of Scotland, 1986; Trustee, Royal Scottish Agricultural Benevolent Institution, 1989-98; Member, Church of Scotland Service Chaplains Committee, 1974-82 and 1985-92; Honorary President, Peebles Branch, Royal British Legion Scotland, since 1990; Honorary President, Tweeddale Society, since 1994; Honorary Member, Rotary Club of Peebles, since 1986. Publication: Swifter than Eagles (war memoirs). Recreations: country sports; motor cycle touring. Address: (h.) Crookston, by Peebles, EH45 9JQ; T.-01721 740209.

Sproul-Cran, Robert Scott, MA (Cantab), PhD. Managing Director, Northlight Productions Ltd., since 1991; Chief Executive, Tartan TV Ltd., 2000-07; b. 14.8.50; m., Elizabeth Ann; 3 s.; 1 d. Educ. Daniel Stewart's College; Pembroke College, Cambridge; Edinburgh University. Trainee, Phillips & Drew, Stockbrokers, London, 1971-72; Announcer, then Head of Presentation, BBC Radio Scotland, 1979-85; Radio Manager, BBC Aberdeen, 1986-90; Scottish Correspondent, BBC Daytime Television, 1990-91; freelance Graphic Designer and Underwater Photographer, since 1976; Director, Scotland the Brand marketing organisation, 2003-04; Winner, Scottish Corporate Communications Award, RTS Award for video graphics; directed "In Search of the Tartan Turban" which was nominated for an RTS award and won a BAFTA in the British Academy Children's Film and Television Awards, 2004; illustrated Maurice Lindsay's Glasgow; exhibited, Aberdeen Artists' annual exhibition. Publication: Thicker than Water (novel and screenplay). Recreations: oil painting; printmaking; windsurfing; sub aqua; playing bad rock guitar. Address: (b.) Northlight Productions Ltd.,

Sunert House, Sunert Road, Aberdeen AB13 0JQ; T.-01224 862244; web: www.northlight.tv

Spurway, Professor Neil Connell, MA, PhD. Emeritus Professor of Exercise Physiology, University of Glasgow and Chair, Science and Religion Forum; b. 22.8.36, Bradford; m., Alison Katherine Middleton; 3 s. Educ. The Grammar School, Falmouth, Cornwall; Jesus College, Cambridge University. Assistant, then Lecturer, then Senior Lecturer in Physiology, University of Glasgow, 1963-96, Professor of Exercise Physiology, 1996-2001. Chair, British Association of Sport and Exercise Sciences, 2000-02; Chair, Glasgow University Gifford Lectureships Committee, 1994-98; Member, Exercise Physiology Steering Group, BOA, 1991-2004; President, Royal Philosophical Society of Glasgow, 2003-05; Council Member and Journal Editor, European Society for Study of Science and Theology. Publications: Humanity, Environment and God; Genetics and Molecular Biology of Muscle Adaptation (Co-Author); many papers and textbook chapters. Recreations: sailing; philosophy; theatre. Address: 76 Fergus Drive, Glasgow G20 6AP; T.-0141-946 3336; e-mail: N.Spurway@bio.gla.ac.uk

Squire of Rubislaw, Romilly, OStJ, DA, FSAScot, FRSA, SHA. Heraldic Artist and Quondam Herald Painter in the Court of the Lord Lyon, Edinburgh, and the Office of the Chief Herald of Ireland, Dublin, since 1983; Heraldic consultant to a number of exiled Royal Houses; b. 3.4.53, Glasgow. Educ. High School of Glasgow; Glasgow School of Art, Jordanhill College. Taught at Seconary School level, 1976-83. Participant in the world's first Heraldic Artists Workshop, Ottawa, Canada, 1996; awarded the "Corel Prize" for excellence in Heraldic Art, 1996; Craft Member, Society of Heraldic Arts, 1999; Grand Officer of the Imperial Order of the Star of Ethiopia, 2000; Board Member and Fellow, Society of Scottish Armigers, USA, 2003. Served on the Committee of the Heraldry Society of Scotland, 1989-99 and since 2000, currently Chairman of the Society; appointed Deputy Secretary to the Standing Council of Scottish Chiefs, 1990, Hon. Secretary, since 2003. Publications include: Gem Pocket Tartans; Kings and Queens of Europe and Kings and Queens of Great Britain; The Collins Encyclopedia of the Clans and Families of Scotland; Clans and Tartans. Address: Studio 4, 30 Elbe Street, Leith, Edinburgh EH6 7HW; T.-0131 553 2232; e-mail: romilly.squire@virgin.net

Stacey, Valerie Elizabeth, QC, LLB (Hons). Queen's Counsel, since 1999; Vice Dean, Faculty of Advocates, since 2004; Member, Judicial Appointments Board for Scotland, 2005-07; Member, Sentencing Commission for Scotland, 2003-06; b. 25.5.54, Lanark; m., Andrew; 2 s. Educ. Elgin Academy; Edinburgh University. Solicitor, 1978; Advocate, 1987; Advocate Depute, 1993-96; Standing Junior Counsel, Home Office in Scotland, 1996-99; Temporary Sheriff, 1997-99. Recreation: listening to music. Address: (b.) Advocates Library, Parliament House, Edinburgh EH1 1RF; T.-0131-226 5071.

Stachura, Professor Peter Desmond, MA, PhD, DLitt, FRHistS. Professor of Modern European History, Stirling University, since 2002; Director, Centre for Research in Polish History, Stirling University; Member of the Editorial Advisory Board of the academic history periodical, Glaukopis (Warsaw); b. 2.8.44, Galashiels; m., Kay Higgins; 1 s.; 1 d. Educ. St. Mirin's Academy, Paisley; Glasgow University; East Anglia University. Research Fellow, Institut für Europäische Geschichte, Mainz, Germany, 1970-71; Stirling University: Lecturer in History, 1971-83, Reader, 1983-2002. Chairman (and Founder), The Polish Society, since 1996; Editor, Occasional Papers

Series, Centre for Research in Polish History, since 2001. Publications: Nazi Youth in the Weimar Republic, 1975; The Weimar Era and Hitler: a critical bibliography, 1977; The Shaping of the Nazi State (Editor), 1978; The German Youth Movement, 1900-1945, 1981; Gregor Strasser and the Rise of Nazism, 1983; The Nazi Machtergreifung (Editor), 1983; Unemployment and the Great Depression in Weimar Germany (Editor), 1986; The Weimar Republic and the Younger Proletariat: an economic and social analysis, 1989; Political Leaders in Weimar Germany: a biographical study, 1992; Themes of Modern Polish History (Editor), 1992; Poland Between the Wars, 1918-1939 (Editor), 1998; Poland in the Twentieth Century, 1999; Perspectives on Polish History (Editor), 2001; The Poles in Britain 1940-2000 (Editor), 2004; Poland, 1918-1945: An Interpretive and Documentary History of the Second Republic, 2004; The Warsaw Rising, 1944 (Editor), 2007. Recreations: supporting Celtic FC; discovering Poland; vexillology. Address: (h.) Ashcroft House, Chalton Road, Bridge of Allan, FK9 4EF; T.-01786 832793; e-mail: p.d.stachura@stir.ac.uk

Stafford, William, MCIWM, MREHIS. Executive Director of Neighbourhood Services, East Ayrshire Council, since 1995; b. 25.3.54, Galston; m., Margaret Ann; 1 s. Educ. Galston High School; Loudoun Academy; College of Food Technology, Glasgow. Ayr County Council, 1971-75; various posts in Environmental Health, Cumnock and Doon Valley District Council, 1975-95. Recreations: motor sport; gardening. Address: (b.) Council Headquarters, London Road, Kilmarnock; T.-01563 576023.

Stagg, Ronald Michael, BSc, MSc, PhD. Deputy CEO, Fisheries Research Services, Marine Laboratory, Aberdeen, since 2001; b. 13.7.53, Llanfairfechan; 1 s.; 2 d. Educ. Friars Grammar School, Bangor; University College of North Wales, Bangor; University of Aston in Birmingham; Exeter University. Post-doctoral Research Assistant, Exeter University; Lecturer in Marine Animal Physiology, Heriot-Watt University; Marine Laboratory, Aberdeen: Ecotoxicology Section Leader, UG7, 1988-97, Programme Manager, Aquaculture and Aquatic Animal Health, 1997-2001. Recreation: part-time farmer. Address: (b.) PO Box 101, Victoria Road, Aberdeen AB11 9DB; T.-01224 295321.

Stair, 14th Earl of (John David James Dalrymple); b. 4.9.61, Edinburgh. Army Officer, 1981-86; Land Owner/Manager, since 1989. Board Member, Dumfries and Galloway Enterprise; Board Member, Scottish Environment Protection Agency, West. Recreation: outdoor activities. Address: (b.) Stair Estates, Rephad, Stranraer DG9 8BX; T.-01776 702024.

Stalley, Professor Richard Frank, MA, BPhil. Professor of Ancient Philosophy, Glasgow University, since 1997; Head of Philosophy Department, 1990-93, 2001-04; b. 26.11.42, Leamington; m., Ellen May Ladd; 1 s.; 1 d. Educ. De Aston School; Worcester College, Oxford; Harvard University. Lecturer in Moral Philosophy, Glasgow University, 1968-84; Senior Lecturer in Philosophy, 1984-97. Publications include: An Introduction to Plato's Laws, 1983; Aristotle's Politics, 1995; many articles on ancient philosophy and on Scottish philosophy. Recreations: walking; opera. Address: (b.) Philosophy Department, Glasgow University, Glasgow G12 8QQ; T.-0141-330 5045.

Stanley, Kenneth Alan, LLB (Hons), NP, WS. Solicitor; Senior Partner, Aitken Nairn, WS, Edinburgh, since 2000 (Partner, since 1984); b. 31.7.57, Edinburgh; m., Fiona

Morag; 2 d. Educ. Boroughmuir High School; University of Edinburgh. Solicitor, 1981; Alston Nairn and Hogg, WS, later with W.G. Leechman, becoming Partner in both firms which amalgamated with Aitken Kinnear to become Aitken Nairn. Recreation: golf. Address: (b.) 7 Abercromby Place, Edinburgh EH3 6LA; T.-0131-556 6644; e-mail: kens@aitkennairn.co.uk

Stansfeld, John Raoul Wilmot, MBE, DL, MA (Oxon), FIFM. Director, Dunninald Estate Ltd., since 1990; b. 15.1.35, London; m., Rosalinde Rachel Buxton; 3 s. Educ. Eton; Christ Church, Oxford. Lt., Gordon Highlanders, 1954-58; Director, Joseph Johnston & Sons Ltd., 1962-2001; Chairman, North Esk District Salmon Fishery Board, 1967-80; Esk Fishery Board Committee, 1980-85; Vice Chairman, Association of Scottish District Salmon Fishery Boards, 1970-85; Director and Chairman, Montrose Chamber of Commerce, 1984-97; Editor, Salmon Net Magazine, 1978-85; Chairman, Scottish Fish Farmers Association, 1970-73; Secretary, Diocese of Brechin, 1968-76. Member, Royal Company of Archers (Queen's Bodyguard for Scotland). Recreations: reading; jigsaw puzzles; trees. Address: (h.) Dunninald, Montrose, Angus, DD10 9TD; T.-01674 674842.

Stark, Edi, MA (Hons), ALA. Broadcaster (BBC Radio Scotland), and journalist; b. Edinburgh; m., Gavin Stark; 1 s.; 1 d. Educ. Aberdeen University; RGIT. Community Librarian, Glasgow and Livingston; Northsound Radio, 1980-90. Won Gold for best speech programme in the UK and Silver and bronze for best speech broadcaster in the UK, national Sony Radio Academy awards. Recreations: conversation; food and drink; travel; reading; contemporary art.

Steedman, Professor Mark, BSc (Hons), PhD. Professor of Cognitive Science, Edinburgh University, since 1998; Director, Institute for Communicating and Collaborative Systems, since 1998; b. 18.9.46, Middlesex; m., Professor Bonnie Webber. Educ. Watford Boys Grammar School; University of Sussex; Edinburgh University. Research Associate, School of Artificial Intelligence, Edinburgh University, 1969-72; Research Fellow: Edinburgh University, 1972-73, University of Sussex. 1973-76; Lecturer, University of Warwick, 1976-82; Edinburgh University: Lecturer, 1983-86, Reader, 1986-88; University of Pennsylvania: Associate Professor, Computational Linguistics, 1989-92, Professor in Computer and Information Science, 1992-98. Joint Founding Editor, Language and Cognitive Processes, 1984-92; Senior Editor, Cognitive Science, 1997-99; Advisory Editor: Cognition, since 1980; Linguistics, 1979-92; Journal of Semantics, since 1985; Language and Cognitive Processes, since 1993. Publications: Surface Structure and Interpretation, Linguistic Inquiry Monograph 30, 1996; The Syntactic Process, 2000. Recreations: jazz; hill-climbing. Address: (b.) ICCS, 2 Buccleuch Place, Edinburgh, EH8 9LW; T.-0131-650 4631.

Steedman, Robert Russell, OBE, RSA, RIBA, FRIAS, ALI, DA, MLA. Former Partner, Morris and Steedman, Architects and Landscape Architects (retired); b. 3.1.29, Batu Gajah, Malaysia; m., 1, Susan Scott (m. diss.); 1 s.; 2 d.; 2, Martha Hamilton. Educ. Loretto School; School of Architecture, Edinburgh College of Art; Pennsylvania University. Governor, Edinburgh College of Art, 1974-86; Commissioner, Countryside Commission for Scotland, 1980-88; Chairman, Central Scotland Woodlands Project, 1984-88; Association for the Protection of Rural Scotland Award Panel, 1995-99; elected Associate, Royal Scottish Academy, 1973, Academician, 1979; Council Member,

RSA, 1981 (Deputy President, 1982-83, 1999-2000, Secretary, 1983-91); Commissioner, Royal Fine Art Commission for Scotland, 1983-96; former Member, Council, RIAS; Member, Council, National Trust for Scotland, 1999-2006; Trustee, St. Andrews Preservation Trust, since 2002; Trustee, Falkland Heritage Trust, since 2002; nine Civic Trust Awards, 1963-78; British Steel Award, 1971; RIBA Award for Scotland, 1974, 1989; European Heritage Medal, 1975; Association for the Protection of Rural Scotland, 1977, 1989; Borders Region Award, 1984; Honorary Degree, DLitt, University of St. Andrews, 2006. Address: (h.) Muir of Blebo, Blebocraigs, by Cupar, Fife KY15 5UG.

Steel of Aikwood, Rt. Hon. Lord (David Steel), KT, KBE, PC, DL. Presiding Officer, Scottish Parliament, 1999-2003; MP, Tweeddale, Ettrick and Lauderdale, 1983-97 (Roxburgh, Selkirk and Peebles, 1965-83); Leader, Liberal Party, 1976-88; b. 31.3.38, Kirkcaldy; m., Judith MacGregor; 2 s.; 1 d. Educ. Prince of Wales School, Nairobi; George Watson's College, Edinburgh; Edinburgh University (MA, LLB). Assistant Secretary, Scottish Liberal Party, 1962-64; Interviewer, BBC TV Scotland, 1964-65; Presenter, weekly religious programme, STV, 1966-67, for Granada, 1969, for BBC, 1971-76; Liberal Chief Whip, 1970-75; Sponsor, Private Member's Bill to reform law on abortion, 1966-67; President, Anti-Apartheid Movement of Great Britain, 1966-69; Chairman, Shelter, Scotland, 1969-73; Member, British Council of Churches, 1971-75; Rector, Edinburgh University, 1982-85; Chubb Fellow, Yale, 1987; Hon. DUniv (Stirling), 1991; DLitt, University of Buckingham, 1994; Hon. Doctorate, Heriot Watt University, Edinburgh, 1996; HonLLD, Edinburgh, 1997; HonLLD, Strathclyde, 2000; HonLLD, Aberdeen 2001; HonDr, Open University, 2002; HonLLD, St Andrews, 2003; Hon LLD, Glasgow Caledonian, 2004; awarded Freedom of Tweeddale, 1988, and Ettrick and Lauderdale, 1990; The Commander's Cross of the Order of Merit (Germany), 1992; Chevalièr du Legion D'Honneur (France), 2003; Knight of the Order of the Thistle, 2004; DL, 1989; contested Central Italy seat, European elections, 1989; President, Liberal International, 1994-96; former Vice President, Countryside Alliance. Publications: Boost for the Borders, 1964; Out of Control, 1968; No Entry, 1969; The Liberal Way Forward, 1975; Militant for the Reasonable Man, 1977; High Ground of Politics, 1979; A House Divided, 1980; Border Country (with Judy Steel), 1985; The Time Has Come (with David Owen), 1987; Mary Stuart's Scotland (with Judy Steel), 1987; Against Goliath (autobiography), 1989. Recreations: angling; vintage motoring. Address: (b.) House of Lords, London SW1A 0PW.

Steel, Professor Christopher Michael, BSc, MB, ChB, PhD, DSc, FRCPEdin, FRCPath, FRCSEdin, FRSE, FMedSci. Emeritus Professor in Medical Science, St. Andrews University (Professor, 1994-2004); b. 25.1.40, Buckhaven; m., Dr. Judith Margaret Spratt; 2 s.; 1 d. Educ. Prince of Wales School, Nairobi; George Watson's College, Edinburgh; Edinburgh University. House Physician/House Surgeon/ Resident/Senior House Officer, Edinburgh Teaching Hospitals; Graduate Research Fellow in Medicine, 1968; joined MRC staff, 1971; MRC Travelling Research Fellow, University of Nairobi, 1972-73; Assistant Director, MRC Human Genetics Unit, Edinburgh, 1979. Board Member: Scottish Cancer Foundation, Medical Research Scotland, Association for International Cancer Research; published over 200 scientific papers and book chapters; Member, Government Gene Therapy Advisory Committee, 1994-99. Recreations: golf; skiing; music; theatre. Address: (b.) Bute Medical Building, St. Andrews, KY16 9TS; T.-01334 463599.

Steel, David Robert, MA, DPhil. Chief Executive, NHS Quality Improvement Scotland, since 2003; b. 29.5.48, Oxford; m., Susan Elizabeth Easton; 1 s.; 1 d. Educ.

Birkenhead School; Jesus and Nuffield Colleges, Oxford. Lecturer in Public Administration, Exeter University, 1972-84; Assistant Director, National Association of Health Authorities, 1984-86; Secretary, Health Board Chairmen's and General Managers' Groups and SCOTMEG, 1986-90; NHS in Scotland: Director of Corporate Affairs, 1990-95, Head of Health Gain, 1995-99; Chief Executive, Clinical Standards Board for Scotland, 1999-2002. Address: (b.) Elliott House, 8–10 Hillside Crescent, Edinburgh EH7 5EA; T.-0131-623 4298.

Steele, Gordon Mark, DPhil, BSc. Director, Scotch Whisky Research Institute, since 1993; b. 26.2.54, Hessle, Yorkshire; m., Rosemary Everett. Educ. Dundee High School; Oxford University (St. Catherine's College); Aberdeen University. Research Assistant, Oxford University, Zoology Department, 1979-85; Higher Scientific Officer, NERC, Institute of Virology, Oxford, 1985-88; Research Scientist, PFIZER Ltd., UK and USA, Drug discovery and development, 1988-93. Freeman of the City of London and Liveryman of The Worshipful Company of Distillers; Lothian NHS Research Ethics Committee 01; Research Committee, ICBD, Heriot-Watt University, Research Committee, Chemistry Department. Recreations: fishing; cooking; hill walking; sailing. Address: (b.) The Scotch Whisky Research Institute, The Robertson Trust Building, Research Park North, Riccarton, Edinburgh EH14 4AP; T.-0131 449 8900; e-mail: gordon.steele@swri.co.uk

Steele, Professor Robert James Campbell, BSc, MB, ChB, MD, FRCSEd, FRCSEng, FCSHK. Professor of Surgery, Dundee University, since 1996; b. 5.3.52, Edinburgh; m., Susan Margaret Cachia; 1 s.; 2 d. Educ. Daniel Stewart's College, Edinburgh; Edinburgh University. Surgical training, Edinburgh, 1977-85; Lecturer in Surgery, Chinese University of Hong Kong, 1985-86; Lecturer in Surgery, Aberdeen University, 1986-90; Senior Lecturer and Reader in Surgery, Nottingham University, 1990-96. Publications in: breast cancer, gastrointestinal surgery and colorectal cancer. Recreations: music; Scottish country dancing; country sports. Address:(b.) Department of Surgery and Molecular Oncology, Ninewells Hospital, Dundee DD1 9SY; T.-01382 660111; e-mail: r.j.c.steele@dundee.ac.uk

Steer, Christopher Richard, BSc (Hons), MB, ChB, DCH, FRCPE, FRCPCH. Consultant Paediatrician; Lead Clinician; Hon. Senior Lecturer, Department of Child Life and Health, Edinburgh University; Hon. Senior Lecturer, Department of Biomedical Science, St. Andrews University; Hon. Senior Lecturer, Department of Child Life and Health, Dundee University; General Medical Council Examiner and Associate; Principal Regional Examiner, SE Scotland for Royal College of Paediatrics and Child Health; b. 30.5.47, Clearbrook, near Plymouth; m., Patricia Mary Lennox. Educ. St. Olaves and St. Saviours Grammar School, London; Edinburgh University. Fellow, Royal Medical Society. Publications: Textbook of Paediatrics (Contributor); Treatment of Neurological Disorders (Contributor). Recreation: our garden. Address: (b.) Paediatric Unit, Kirkcaldy Acute Hospitals NHS Trust, Victoria Hospital, Kirkcaldy, Fife; T.-01592 643355.

Stein, Sheriff Colin Norman Ralph, BA, LLB. Sheriff of Tayside, Central and Fife, at Arbroath, since 1991; b. 14.6.48, Glasgow; m., Dr Linda McNaught; 1 s. Educ. Glenalmond College; Durham University; Edinburgh University. Admitted Member, Faculty of Advocates, 1975; appointed Sheriff, 1991. Recreations: gardening; fishing. Address: Sheriff's Chambers, Sheriff Court, High Street, Arbroath DD11 1HL; T.-01241 876600.

Steiner, Eleanor Margaret, MB, ChB, DPH, MFCM, MRCGP, MICGP, FRSH, FFICS, FFPH. Formerly General Practitioner at Appin and Easdale, formerly Principal in general practice in Perthshire; Executive Member, Scottish Child Law Centre; Medical Member, Disability Appeals Tribunal; Medical Assessor, Social Security Appeal Tribunals; Aeromedical Doctor, St. John International Air Ambulance; Member, SACOT (Scottish Advisory Committee on Telecommunications); Member, DIEL (OFTEL Committee for Advice on Disabled and Elderly); Founder, National Society of Associate GPs; contributor and literary consultant to various publications; m., Mark Rudie Steiner (qv). Educ. Albyn School, Aberdeen; Aberdeen University. Surgical Assistant, Freiburg; worked in hospitals, Switzerland, Canada, USA; Departmental Medical Officer/Senior Medical Officer, Aberdeen City; Organiser, Family Planning Services, Aberdeen; Member, Rubella Working Party; Adviser, Aberdeen Telephone Samaritans; Assistant, Psychiatry, Murray Royal Hospital, Perth; Thesis: Mortality and Morbidity in Scottish Mountains; Contributor, Scientific Congress, Institute of Advanced Medical Sciences, Moscow; Member, "FATE" (Friends at the End). Recreations: sailing; hill-walking; international contacts. Address: (h.) Atlantic House, Ellenabeich, Isle of Seil, by Oban, Argyll, PA34 4RF; T.-01852 300 593.

Steiner, Mark Rudie, LLB, NP. Legal Consultant; former part-time Chairman, Social Security Appeal Tribunal and Disability Appeal Tribunal; former Scottish Representative, Consumers in the European Community Group; Member, Potato Marketing Board Consumer Liaison Committee; Member, National Pharmaceutical Consultative Committee Working Group on Quality Assurance; m., Dr. Eleanor Steiner, DPH, MFCM, MRCGP, MICGP; 1 s. Educ. Aberdeen University. Long-time international radio/TV commentator; Editor, Canadian Broadcasting Corporation, Toronto and Montreal; Editor, Swiss Broadcasting Corporation, Berne; Lecturer on Swiss affairs and advisor to Anglo-Swiss organisations and authorities; international war crimes investigator; Procurator Fiscal in Scotland; Partner and Director of various firms and companies; Past Chairman, Perth Community Relations Council; Delegate, Scottish Council for Racial Equality; neutral observer at various overseas political trials; contributor to various international journals; retired Principal, Goodman Steiner & Co., Defence Lawyers and Notaries in Central Scotland; former Member, Scottish Consumer Council. Publications: Alpine Legends of Switzerland; Nell of the Seas and various travel and children's books; Literary Consultant and Editor with Nevis International Books. Recreations: sailing; developing international exchanges. Address: (h.) Atlantic House, Ellenabeich, Isle of Seil, by Oban, Argyll, PA34 4RF; T.-Balvicar 300 593.

Stell, Geoffrey Percival, BA, FSA, FSA Scot. Honorary Lecturer in History, University of Stirling; Head of Architecture, Royal Commission on the Ancient and Historical Monuments of Scotland, 1991-2004; b. 21.11.44, Keighley; m., Evelyn Florence Burns; 1 s.; 1 d. Educ. Keighley Boys' Grammar School; Leeds University; Glasgow University. Historic Buildings Investigator, RCAHMS, 1969-91; sometime Chairman, Scottish Vernacular Buildings Working Group; sometime Chairman, Scottish Urban Archaeological Trust; sometime Vice-President, Council for Scottish Archaeology. Publications include: Dumfries and Galloway; Monuments of Industry (Co-author); Buildings of St. Kilda (Co-author); Loads and Roads in Scotland (Co-editor); The Scottish Medieval Town (Co-editor); Galloway, Land and Lordship (Co-Editor); Materials and Traditions in Scottish Building (Co-Editor); Scotland's Buildings (Co-editor); Lordship and Architecture in Medieval and Renaissance Scotland (Co-editor). Recreations: gardening; music; travel, particularly

in Scotland and France. Address: (h.) Beechmount, Borrowstoun, Bo'ness, West Lothian, EH51 9RS; T.-01506 510366; e-mail: gpstell@gmail.com

Stenning, Professor Keith, PhD. Personal Chair in Human Communication, University of Edinburgh, since 1997; b. 15.6.48, London; m., Lynn Michell; 2 s. Educ. High Wycombe Grammar School; University of Oxford. Lecturer in Psychology, Liverpool University, 1975-83; University of Edinburgh: Lecturer in Cognitive Science and Psychology, 1983-89, Senior Lecturer, 1989, Professorial Fellow, 1989-97, Founding Director, ESRC-funded Interdisciplinary Research Centre in Human Communication, 1989-98, Senior Research Fellow, ESRC, 1999-2000. Chair, Cognitive Science Society. Publication: Seeing Reason – Image and Language in Learning to Think, 2002. Recreation: sailing. Address: (b.) HCRC, 2 Buccleuch Place, Edinburgh EH8 9LW; T.-0131-650 4444; e-mail: k.stenning@ed.ac.uk

Stephen, Alex, FCCA. Chief Executive, Dundee City Council, since 1995; (Chief Executive, City of Dundee District Council, 1991-95); b. 17.9.48, Dundee; m., Joyce; 1 s.; 1 d. Local government since 1970. Recreation: voluntary work. Address: (b.) 21 City Square, Dundee; T.-01382 434201.

Stephen, David, FCIPD. Chief Executive, Student Awards Agency for Scotland, since 1999; b. 21.11.47, Aberdeen; m., Rosalyn Jane; 1 s.; 1 d. Educ. Aberdeen Grammar School; Aberdeen University. Various posts, Scottish Office, 1972-98; Assistant Director of Manpower, NHS Management Executive, 1988-92; Head of Personnel Policy, Scottish Office, 1992-98; Director of Operations, SAAS, 1998-99. Recreations: golf; reading; Scotch Malt Whisky Society. Address: (b.) Gyleview House, 3 Redheughs Rigg, Edinburgh EH12 9HH; T.-0131-244 5867.

Stephen, Rev. Donald Murray, TD, MA, BD, ThM. Minister, Marchmont St. Giles' Parish Church, Edinburgh, 1974-2001; Secretary, Church of Scotland Chaplains' Association, 1991-2007; b. 1.6.36, Dundee; m., Hilda Swan Henriksen (deceased); 2 s.; 1 d; m., 2, Marjorie Roberta Bennet. Educ. Brechin High School; Richmond Grammar School, Yorkshire; Edinburgh University; Princeton Theological Seminary. Assistant Minister, Westover Hills Presbyterian Church, Arkansas, 1962-64; Minister, Kirkoswald, 1964-74; Chaplain, TA, 1965-85 (attached to 4/5 Bn., RSF, 205 Scottish General Hospital, 2nd Bn., 52nd Lowland Volunteers); Convener, Committee on Chaplains to Her Majesty's Forces, General Assembly, 1985-89. Recreations: golf; curling. Address: 10 Hawkhead Crescent, Edinburgh EH16 6LR; T.-0131-658 1216; e-mail: DonaldMStephen@aol.com

Stephen, Sheriff Mhairi Margaret, BA, LLB. Sheriff of Lothian and Borders at Edinburgh, since 1997; b. 22.1.54, Falkirk. Educ. George Watson's Ladies College; Edinburgh University. Allan McDougall and Co., SSC, 1976-97 (Partner, 1981-97). Recreations: curling; golf; hill-walking; music. Address: Sheriff's Chambers, Sheriff Court, 27 Chambers Street, Edinburgh EH1 1LB; T.-0131-225 2525.

Stephen, Nicol, LLB, DipLP. MSP (Liberal Democrat), Aberdeen South, since 1999; Deputy First Minister, and Minister for Enterprise and Lifelong Learning, 2005-07; Deputy Minister for Education and Young People, 2000-03 (Deputy Minister for Enterprise and Lifelong Learning, 1999-2000); Minister for Transport, 2003-05;

b. 23.3.60, Aberdeen; m., Caris Doig; 2 s.; 2 d. Educ. Robert Gordon's College, Aberdeen; Aberdeen University; Edinburgh University. Trainee Solicitor, C. & P.H. Chalmers, 1981-83; Solicitor, Milne and Mackinnon, 1983-88; Senior Manager, Touche Ross Corporate Finance, 1988-91; Member, Grampian Regional Council, 1982-92 (Chair, Economic Development, 1986-91); MP, Kincardine and Deeside, 1991-92; Scottish Liberal Democrats: Parliamentary Spokesperson for Small Businesses, 1991-92, Treasurer, 1992-95, Health Spokesperson, 1995-97, Education Spokesperson, 1997-99, Scottish Party Leader, since 2005; Director, Project Management, management consultancy company, 1992-99; Chairman for Rail Electrification Aberdeen to Edinburgh (CREATE), 1988-92; Director, Grampian Enterprise, 1989-92. Recreation: golf. Address: 173 Crown Street, Aberdeen AB11 6JA.
E-mail: nicol.stephen.msp@scottish.parliament.uk

Stephen, Peter. Lord Provost, City of Aberdeen, since 2007. Address: (b.) Town House, Aberdeen AB10 1LP; T.-01224 522637.

Stephens, Professor Jonathan Paul, BA (Hons), MMus, PhD, PGCE. Director of Music and Head of Aesthetic Education, University of Aberdeen; b. 12.7.51, Redruth; m., Rhona Lucas; 1 s.; 2 d. Educ. Redruth Grammar School; University of Wales, Aberystwyth. Secondary and private teaching, Wales, 1973-77; Lecturer in Music, Hertfordshire College of Higher Education, 1977-82; Lecturer in Music, 1982-84, Co-ordinator for Music Education, 1983-88, Principal Lecturer and Deputy Head of Music, 1984-88, Bretton Hall College of Higher Education; Director of Music (1988-2001) and Head of Aesthetic Education (1991-2001); Northern College, then Aberdeen University, since 2001; Professor in music and music education, since 1993. Chair, ISME, Commission for Music in Schools and Teacher Training, 1988-92; Founder Member and British Representative, European Association for Music in Schools, 1990-2000, Scottish representative, since 2001; President, International Research Alliance of Institutions for Music Education, 1997-99; Board Member, ISME, 2000-04; Member, Music in Education Section Committee of Incorporated Society of Musicians (UK), 2002-05 and since 2007; Executive Committee of National Association of Youth Orchestras, since 2004; Editorial Board of International Journal of Music Education, since 2004; compositions have been widely performed; frequent lecturer, music and music education, national and international. Recreations: reading; writing; composing; walking; gardening. Address: (b.) School of Education, University of Aberdeen, MacRobert Building, King's College, Aberdeen AB24 5UA.

Stephenson, Professor Jill, MA, PhD. Professor of Modern German History, University of Edinburgh, since 2006; b. 17.01.44, Edinburgh; m., Dr. R. P. Stephenson (deceased). Educ. George Watson's Ladies' College; University of Edinburgh. Assistant Lecturer in Modern History, University of Glasgow, 1969-70; Lecturer in History, University of Edinburgh, 1970 (Senior Lecturer, 1984, Reader, 1991). Publications: Women in Nazi Society, 1975; The Nazi Organisation of Women, 1981; Women in Nazi Germany, 2001; Hitler's Home Front: Württemberg Under The Nazis, 2006. Recreations: gardening; food and wine; opera. Address: (b.) School of History, Classics and Archaeology, University of Edinburgh, Edinburgh; e-mail: j.stephenson@ed.ac.uk

Stephenson, Professor Roger Henry, BA (Hons), PhD. William Jacks Professor of German, Glasgow University, since 1994; Principal Investigator, AHRB Large Research Project on 'Ernst Cassirer', 2002-07;

Head, School of Modern Languages and Cultures, Glasgow University, 2000-03; Director, Centre for Intercultural Studies, Glasgow University, since 1992; b. 5.11.46, Liverpool; m., Hedy. Educ. Holt High School, Liverpool; University College London. Lecturer, German, Glasgow University, 1972; Fellow, Cornell University, NY, USA, 1979; Glasgow University: Senior Lecturer, German, 1989; Head, German Department, 1990-97; Vice President, UK and Irish Conference, University Teachers of German, 1997-98; President, Scottish Conference, University Teachers of German, since 2006; Visiting Professor: University of Zurich, 2005, University of Hamburg, 2007. Publications: Goethe's Wisdom Literature, 1983; Goethe's Maximem und Relexionen, 1986; Goethe's Conception of Knowledge and Science, 1995; Goethe (Co-Author), 2001; Friedrich Nietzsche and Weimar Classicism, 2005. Address: (b.) Department of German, Glasgow University, Glasgow, G12 8QL; T.-0141-330 4144.
E-mail: R.Stephenson@german.arts.gla.ac.uk

Stevely, Professor William Stewart, CBE, BSc, DPhil, DipEd, FIBiol. Former Principal and Vice Chancellor, The Robert Gordon University (1997-2005); Professor Emeritus, The Robert Gordon University; Chairman, UCAS, 2001-05 (Member, Board, since 2000); Convener, Universities Scotland, 2002-04; Board Member, Scottish University for Industry (SUFI), since 2004; Board Member, Scottish Agricultural College, since 2005; Chairman, Ayrshire and Arran Health Board, since 2006; b. 6.4.43, West Kilbride; m., Sheila Anne Stalker; 3 s.; 2 d. Educ. Ardrossan Academy; Glasgow University; Oxford University. Lecturer and Senior Lecturer in Biochemistry, Glasgow University, 1968-88; Professor and Head, Department of Biology, Paisley College, 1988-92; Vice Principal, Paisley University, 1992-97. Member, Scottish Higher Education Funding Council, 1994-97; Member, National Board for Nursing, Midwifery and Health Visiting for Scotland, 1993-2000; Board Member, Quality Assurance Agency for Higher Education, 1998-2002. Address: (b.) The Robert Gordon University, Schoolhill, Aberdeen, AB10 1FR; T.-01224 262001.

Steven, John Douglas, MB, ChB, FRCOG. Consultant Obstetrician and Gynaecologist, Stirling Royal Infirmary, since 1981; b. 20.4.46, Perth. Educ. Douglas Ewart High School, Newton Stewart; Edinburgh University. Registrar in Obstetrics and Gynaecology, Western General Hospital, Edinburgh; Senior Registrar, Obstetrics and Gynaecology, Ninewells Hospital, Dundee. Address: (b.) Stirling Royal Infirmary, Stirling, FK8 2AU; T.-01786 434000.

Stevens, Claire, BA (Hons), DipMgt (Open), MICFM (Cert), FRSA. Director–Scotland, Community Service Volunteers, since 1998; b. 26.7.58, Sudbury, Suffolk. Educ. Sudbury Girls High; Sudbury Upper School; University of Warwick. Strathclyde Regional Council, 1981-84; Basildon District Council, 1984-85; Shelter Scotland, 1985-89; Age Concern Scotland, 1989-92; Scottish Council for Single Homeless, 1992-96; The Prince's Trust, 1996-98. Member, Board: Association of Chief Officers of Scottish Voluntary Organisations, North Edinburgh Arts Centre, Benchtours Theatre Company. Address: (b.) Wellgate House, 200 Cowgate, Edinburgh EH1 1NQ; T.-0131-622 7766.

Stevens, Professor Paul John, BA (Cantab), MA, PhD. Professor of Petroleum Policy and Economics, Dundee University, since 1993; b. 30.4.47, Liverpool; m., Cassie Stevens; 1 s.; 1 d. Educ. Alsop High School, Liverpool; Clare College, Cambridge; London University. Assistant Professor, American University of Beirut, 1973-75; oil consultant, Beirut, 1975-77; Assistant Professor, American

University of Beirut, 1977-79; Lecturer in Economics, then Senior Lecturer, University of Surrey, 1979-93. Publications: numerous books and papers on oil and gas. Recreations: travel; food and drink; golf. Address: (b.) CEPMLP, Dundee University, Dundee, DD1 4HN; T.- 01382 344300.

Stevenson of Coddenham, Baron (Henry Dennistoun Stevenson), Kt (1998), CBE (1981). Governor, Bank of Scotland, since 2006; Chairman, HBOS plc, since 2001; non executive director: The Western Union Company, Culture and Sport Glasgow, Loudwater Partners Ltd; b. 19.7.45; m., Charlotte; 4 s. Educ. Glenalmond; King's College, Cambridge. Chairman: the House of Lords Appointments Commission, Aldeburgh Music Ltd. Address: (b.) Bank of Scotland, The Mound, Edinburgh EH1 1YZ.

Stevenson, Celia Margaret Stirton. Head of Inward Investment and Communications, Scottish Screen; b. Ballantrae; m., Charles William Forbes Judge; 2 s.; 1 d. Educ. Wellington School, Ayr; Edinburgh College of Art. Interior design business, 1970-80; Reporter/Presenter, West Sound, Ayr, 1981-84; Scottish Television: Reporter/Presenter, 1984-86, Promotions trailer-maker, 1987-89, Head of Programme Planning and Film Acquisition, 1990-95; Director, Scottish Screen Locations Ltd., 1995-97; Director of Locations, Scottish Screen, 1997-98. Board Member, British Film Commission, 1997-2000; Member, Steering Group, UK Film Commission Network, 1996-98. Recreations: cooking; reading; keeping fit; gardening. Address: (b.) 249 West George Street, Glasgow G2 4QE; e-mail: celia.stevenson@scottishscreen.com

Stevenson, Gerda. Actress, Singer, Writer, Book Illustrator, Director; b. 10.4.56, West Linton; m., Aonghas MacNeacail; 1 s. Educ. Peebles High School; Royal Academy of Dramatic Art, London (DDA, Vanbrugh Award). Has performed with 7:84 Theatre Co., Scottish Theatre Company, Royal Lyceum Theatre (Edinburgh), Traverse Theatre, Communicado, Monstrous Regiment, Victoria Theatre (Stoke on Trent), Contact Theatre (Manchester) and with Freefall at Lilian Baylis Theatre, London, and Birmingham Rep; directed Uncle Jesus for Edinburgh Festival Fringe; Assistant Director, Royal Lyceum, on Merchant of Venice and A Doll's House; Founder Member and Director, Stellar Quines Theatre Co.; TV work includes Clay, Smeddum and Greenden, Square Mile of Murder, Grey Granite, Horizon: Battered Baby, The Old Master, Taggart, Dr. Finlay, The Bill; films: The Stamp of Greatness, Tickets to the Zoo, Blue Black Permanent (BAFTA Scotland Best Film Actress Award, 1993), Braveheart; directed short film, An Iobairt, in Gaelic for BBC; extensive radio work includes title roles in Bride of Lammermoor and Catriona; adapted a number of works for radio, most recently The Heart of Midlothian by Sir Walter Scott for BBC Radio 4 (nominated for a Sony Award in 2008); freelance producer for Radio Scotland; wrote and illustrated children's book, The Candlemaker.

Stevenson, (James Alexander) Stewart. MSP (SNP), Banff and Buchan, since 2001; Minister for Transport, Infrastructure and Climate Change, since 2007; former Shadow Deputy Justice Minister; b. 15.10.46; m., Sandra Isabel Pirie. Educ. Bell Baxter School, Cupar; Aberdeen University. Director, Technology Innovation, Bank of Scotland, 1969-99; part-time Lecturer, School of Management, Heriot-Watt University, since 2001. Address: (b.) 17 Maiden Street, Peterhead, Aberdeenshire AB42 1EE.

Stevenson, Professor Jane Barbara, MA, PhD. Regius Professor of Humanity, University of Aberdeen, since 2007; b. 12.2.59, London; m., Peter Davidson. Educ. Haberdashers' Aske's School for Girls; Newnham College, Cambridge. Drapers' Research Fellow, Pembroke College,

Cambridge, 1985-88; Lecturer, Late Antique and Early Medieval History, University of Sheffield, 1988-95; Interdisciplinary Research Fellow (later Reader), University of Warwick, 1995-2000; Reader in Post-Classical Latin, University of Aberdeen, 2000-05, Professor of Latin, 2005-07. Publications: Edward Burra; Women Latin Poets; The Laterculus Malalianus and the School of Archbishop Theodore; Good Women; Astraea. Recreations: cooking; gardening. Address: (b.) Department of History, King's College, University of Aberdeen AB24 JFX; T.-01888 562244; e-mail: j.b.stevenson@abdn.ac.uk

Stevenson, Professor Randall, MA, MLitt, FEA. Professor of Twentieth-Century Literature, University of Edinburgh, since 2005; b. 25.6.53, Banff; m., Sarah Carpenter; 2 s.; 1 d. Educ. Hillhead High School, Glasgow; Edinburgh University; Linacre, Oxford. Assistant, then Principal Lecturer in English, Women Teachers' Training College, Birin-Kebbi, NW State Nigeria; Lecturer, then Senior Lecturer, then Reader in English, University of Edinburgh. Publications include: Oxford English Literary History vol. 12, 1960-2000, 2006; Twentieth Century Scottish Drama (Co-Author), 2000; Modernist Fiction, 1998; Scottish Theatre since the Seventies, ed (Co-Author), 1996. Recreations: running; tennis; football; hill walking; astronomy. Address: (b.) Department of English Literature, University of Edinburgh EH8 9JX; T.-0131 650 4288. E-mail: randall.stevenson@ed.ac.uk

Stevenson, Ronald, DUniv (Stirling), DMus (Aberdeen), LLD (Dundee), FRMCM, HonFRIAS. Composer and Pianist; Broadcaster; Author; b. 6.3.28, Blackburn; m., Marjorie Spedding; 1 s.; 2 d. Educ. Royal Manchester College of Music; Conservatorio Di Santa Cecilia, Rome. Senior Lecturer, Cape Town University, 1963-65; BBC Prom debut in own 2nd Piano Concerto, 1972; Aldeburgh Festival recital with Sir Peter Pears, 1973; Busoni documentary, BBC TV, 1974; BBC Radio Scotland extended series on the bagpipe, clarsach and fiddle music of Scotland, 1980-84; Artist in Residence: Melbourne University, 1980, University of W. Australia, 1982, Conservatory of Shanghai, 1985; York University, 1987; published and recorded compositions: Passacaglia for Piano, two Piano Concertos, Violin Concerto (commissioned and premiered by Menuhin), Prelude, Fugue and Fantasy for Piano, Prelude and Fugue for Organ, In Memoriam Robert Carver, St. Mary's May Songs, A Child's Garden of Verses (BBC commission), Voces Vagabundae, Salute to Nelson Mandela (march for brass band), Cello Concerto (RSNO commission), A Carlyle Suite (piano), Le Festin d'Alkan (piano), Ben Dorain, epic for double choir and double orchestra. Publications: Western Music; Alan Bush - a symposium; The Paderewski Paradox; Ronald Stevenson: A Biography by Malcolm McDonald, 1989; Ronald Stevenson: The Man and his Music, edited by Colin Scott-Sutherland, 2005; Ronald Stevenson Society. www.ronaldstevensonsociety.org.uk for catalogue and CD recordings. Recreations: hill-walking; reading poetry, biographies and politics. Address: (h.) Townfoot House, West Linton, Peeblesshire; T.-01968 660511.

Stevenson, Struan John Stirton. MEP for Scotland, since 1999; Vice President, EPP-ED (European People's Party-European Democrats) Group in the European Parliament, since 2005; b. 4.4.48, Ballantrae; m., Pat Stevenson; 2 s. Educ. Strathallan School; West of Scotland Agricultural College. Conservative Councillor, Kyle and Carrick District Council, 1970-92 (Leader of the Administration, 1986-88); Conservative Group Leader, COSLA, 1986-88; European Parliament: Chairman, Fisheries Committee, 2001-04; Conservative

Spokesman on Fisheries and Deputy Spokesman on Agriculture; Member, Employment and Social Affairs Committee. Hon. Doctor of Science, State Medical Academy, Kazakhstan, 2000; Honorary Citizen of Semipalatinsk, East Kazakhstan, 2004; Hon. Professor, Sakharim University, Semey, 2007; Awarded Order of 'Shapagat' (Mercy) by President of Kazakhstan, 2007. Publication: 'Crying Forever'- A Nuclear Diary, 2006, Russian Edition, 2007. Recreations: contemporary art; music; theatre; opera; poetry; hill-walking. Address: (b.) 83 Princes Street, Edinburgh EH2 2ER; T.-0131-247 6890; e-mail: struan.stevenson@europarl.europa.eu

Stevenson, William Trevor, CBE, DL, FCIT; b. 21.3.21, Peebles; m., Alison Wilson Roy. Educ. Edinburgh Academy. Apprentice Engineer, 1937-41; Engineer, 1941-45; entered family food manufacturing business, Cottage Rusks, 1945; Managing Director, 1948-54; Chairman, 1954-59; Chief Executive, Cottage Rusks Associates, 1965-69; Regional Director, Ranks Hovis McDougall, 1969-74; Director, various companies in food, engineering, hotel and aviation industries, since 1974; Chairman, Alex. Wilkie Ltd., 1977-90; founder Chairman, Gleneagles Hotels, 1981-83; Chairman, Scottish Transport Group, 1981-86; Master, Company of Merchants of City of Edinburgh, 1978-80; Vice President, Edinburgh Chamber of Commerce, 1983-87; Founder, World Elite Airways, 1987. Recreations: flying; sailing; curling.

Stewart, A.J. (Ada F. Kay). Playwright and Author; b. 5.3.29, Tottington, Lancashire. Educ. Grammar School, Fleetwood. ATS Scottish Command; first produced play, 1951; repertory actress, 1952-54; BBC TV Staff Writer/Editor/Adaptor, Central Script Section, 1956-59; returned to Scotland, 1959, as stage and TV writer; winner, BBC New Radio Play competition, 1956; The Man from Thermopylae, presented in Festival of Contemporary Drama, Rheydt, West Germany, 1959, as part of Edinburgh International Festival, 1965, and at Masquers' Theatre, Hollywood, 1972; first recipient, Wendy Wood Memorial Grant, 1982; Polish Gold Cross for achievements in literary field. Publications: Falcon - The Autobiography of His Grace, James the 4, King of Scots, 1970; Died 1513-Born 1929 - The Autobiography of A.J. Stewart, 1978; The Man from Thermopylae, 1981. Recreation: work. Address: (h.) 33 Howe Street, Edinburgh EH3 6TF.

Stewart, Alan David, MA (Hons), MIPR. Head of Broadcasting and Telecommunications (Scotland), Ofcom; b. 27.7.58, Falkirk; m., Christine; 2 s. Educ. Graeme High School, Falkirk; Glasgow University; Strathclyde University. Assistant Public Relations Officer, Cumbernauld Development Corporation, 1983-86; Press Officer, Strathclyde Regional Council, 1986-92; Principal Officer (Corporate Communications and Marketing), Lothian Regional Council, 1992-94. Recreations: hill-walking; cycling; supporting Falkirk FC. Address: (h.) 12 Heugh Street, Falkirk FK1 5QR; T.-01324 631997.

Stewart, Sheriff Alastair Lindsay, QC, BA (Oxon), LLB(Edin). Sheriff of Tayside, Central and Fife at Dundee, 1990-2004; Temporary Judge, Court of Session and High Court of Justiciary, since 1996; Honorary Professor, Department of Law, Dundee University, since 2001; Interim Sheriff Principal, Lothian and Borders and Glasgow and Strathkelvin, 2005; b. 28.11.38, Aberdeen; m., 1, Annabel Claire Stewart (m. diss.); 2 s.; 2, Sheila Anne Mackinnon. Educ. Edinburgh Academy; St. Edmund Hall, Oxford; Edinburgh University. Admitted to Faculty of Advocates, 1963; Tutor, Faculty of Law, Edinburgh University, 1963-73; Standing Junior Counsel to the Registrar of Restrictive Trading Agreements, 1968-70;

Advocate Depute, 1970-73; Sheriff of Lanarkshire (later South Strathclyde, Dumfries and Galloway) at Airdrie, 1973-79; Sheriff of Grampian, Highland and Islands at Aberdeen and Stonehaven, 1979-90. Chairman, Scottish Association of Family Conciliation Services, 1986-89; Editor, Scottish Civil Law Reports, 1992-95; Member, Judicial Studies Committee, 2000-03. Publications: Sheriff Court Practice (Contributor), 1988; The Scottish Criminal Courts in Action, 1990, 1997; Sheriff Court Practice (Joint General Editor and Contributor), 1998; Stair Memorial Encyclopedia of the Laws of Scotland: Evidence Reissue, 2006. Recreations: music; reading; walking. Address: (h.) 86 Albany Road, Broughty Ferry, Dundee DD5 1JQ; T.-01382 477580; e-mail: als281138@aol.com

Stewart, Alexander Donald, BA, LLB, WS, DL; b. 18.6.33, Edinburgh; m., Virginia Mary Washington; 1 s.; 5 d. Educ. Wellington College, Berkshire; Oxford University; Edinburgh University. Hon. Consul for Thailand in Scotland; DL, Perth and Kinross. Recreations: music; field sports. Address: (h.) Ardvorlich, Lochearnhead, Perthshire.

Stewart, Andrew Fleming, LLB (Hons). Advocate, since 1996; b. 12.9.63, Dundee; m., Lesley Katherine Dawson; 2 d. Educ. Perth High School; Edinburgh University. Solicitor: Clifford Chance, London, 1988-90, Tods Murray WS, Edinburgh, 1990-94; Legal Assistant to Lord President, Court of Session, 1994-95; Tutor, Law Faculty, University of Edinburgh, 1985-88 and since 1990; Lecturer (part-time), Université de Nancy 2, France, since 1993; Standing Junior Counsel, Department of Trade and Industry, since 2000; Clerk to Examiners, Faculty of Advocates, 2001-03; Clerk of Faculty of Advocates, since 2003. Member, Board of Practice and Procedure, Church of Scotland, 2001-05; Treasurer, Scottish Committee, Franco-British Lawyers Society, 1998-2001; Editor, Session Cases, since 2001. Recreations: golf; music. Address: Advocates Library, Parliament House, Edinburgh EH1 1RF; T.-0131-226 5071.

Stewart, Angus, QC, BA, LLB. Queen's Counsel; b. 14.12.46; m., Jennifer Margaret Stewart; 1 d. Educ. Edinburgh Academy; Balliol College, Oxford University; Edinburgh University. Called to the Scottish Bar, 1975; Trustee, National Library of Scotland, since 1994; Treasurer, E Boat International Offshore Class Association, since 1994; Keeper of the Advocates Library, 1994-2002; President of the Stewart Society, 2001-04; Senior Advocate Depute, since 2005. Address: (h.) Ann Street, Edinburgh, EH4 1PJ; T.-0131-332 4083.

Stewart, Professor Emeritus Averil M., BA, FCOT, TDip, FFCS. Emeritus Professor of Occupational Therapy; Head, Department of Occupational Therapy and Art Therapy, Queen Margaret University College, Edinburgh, 1986-2001; b. 7.4.43, Edinburgh; m., J. Gavin Stewart. Educ. Dunfermline High School. Member, Vice-Chairman and Chairman, Occupational Therapists Board, CPSM, 1980-92; Trustee, Dementia Services Development Centre, 1996-2004; Secretary, Scottish Arctic Club, since 1998. Recreations: wilderness travel; gardening. Address: (h.) 29 Highfield Crescent, Linlithgow EH49 7BG; e-mail: gaveril.stewart@virgin.net

Stewart, Sir Brian John, CBE, MSc, CA. Chairman, Scottish & Newcastle plc, since 2000; b. 9.4.45, Stirling; m., Shona (Seonaid); 2 s.; 1 d. Educ. Perth Academy; Edinburgh University. J. & R. Morrison, CA, Perth, 1962-67; Ethicon Ltd., 1969-76; joined Scottish & Newcastle plc, 1976; Corporate Development Director, 1985; Group Finance Director, 1988; Chief Executive, 1991; Director

(Non-Executive), Standard Life plc, 1993-2007, Chairman, 2003-07; Director (Non-Executive), Booker plc, 1993-99. Recreations: skiing; golf. Address: (b.) 28 St. Andrew Square, Edinburgh EH2 1AF; T.-0131-528 2000.

Stewart, David. MSP (Labour), Highlands and Islands, since 2007; b. 5.5.56. Address: (b.) Scottish Parliament, Edinburgh EH99 1SP.

Stewart, Douglas Fleming, MA, LLB, WS, FSA Scot. Partner, J. & F. Anderson, WS, 1961-92; Solicitor, Crown Estate Scotland, 1970-91; b. 22.5.27, Sydney; m., Catherine Coleman; 2 d. Educ. George Watson's College; Edinburgh University. RAF, 1945-48; Chairman, Commercial Union, Edinburgh Board, 1979-91, and its Scottish Advisory Committee, 1977-97. Member, Edinburgh University General Council Business Committee, 1961-69; Secretary/Treasurer, Stewart Society, 1968-87 (also Hon. Vice-President); Trustee, Church of Scotland Trust (former Chairman); Session Clerk, Braid Church, Edinburgh, 1979-91; President, Watsonian Club, 1989-90; Chairman, Comiston Probus Club, 1999; President, Braid Bowling Club, 2003; Royal Overseas League, Edinburgh Committee; Royal Scottish Society of Arts (Science and Technology), Council. Publications: The Story of Braid Church (Co-author); A Lawful Union, the annals of J & F Anderson, WS and Strathern & Blair, WS (Co-author). Recreations: astronomy; bowling; swimming. Address: (h.) Greenhill Court, 98/5 Whitehouse Loan, Edinburgh EH9 1BD; T.-0131-447 4887.

Stewart, George Girdwood, CB, MC, TD, BSc, FICFor, Hon. FLI; b. 12.12.19, Glasgow; m., Shelagh Jean Morven Murray (deceased); 1 s.; 1 d. Educ. Kelvinside Academy, Glasgow; Glasgow University; Edinburgh University. Royal Artillery, 1940-46 (mentioned in Despatches); Forestry Commission: District Officer, 1949-60, Assistant Conservator, 1960-67, Conservator (West Scotland), 1967-69, Commissioner, Forest and Estate Management, 1969-79. Commanding Officer, 278 (Lowland) Field Regiment RA (TA), 1956-59; President, Scottish Ski Club, 1971-75; Vice President, National Ski Federation of Great Britain and Chairman, Alpine Racing Committee, 1975-78; National Trust for Scotland: Member of Council, 1975-79, Representative, Branklyn Garden, 1980-84, Regional Representative, Central and Tayside, 1984-88; Forestry Consultant, 1989-93; Chairman, Scottish Wildlife Trust, 1981-87; Member, Countryside Commission for Scotland, 1981-88; Member, Environment Panel, British Railways Board, 1980-90; Cairngorm Estate Adviser to Highlands and Islands Enterprise, 1988-98; Associate Director, Oakwood Environmental, 1990-2003; Member, Cairngorm Recreation Trust, since 1986; President, Scottish National Ski Council, 1988-94, Hon. Vice-President, since 1997; Specialist Adviser to House of Lords Select Committee on EEC Forestry Policy, 1986; National Service to Sport Award, 1995; Member, British Veterans' Tennis Team, World Team Championships, 1999, 2001, 2002; International Tennis Federation Super Seniors World Individual Championships 2006, Winner Doubles; Fellow, Royal Society of Arts. Recreations: skiing; veterans' tennis; studying Scottish painting. Address: (h.) Stormont House, 11 Mansfield Road, Scone, Perth PH2 6SA; T.-01738 551815.

Stewart, Gillian Mary, CB, BA (Hons). Civil Service Fast Stream Assessor; Member, Barnardo's Council and Chair, Barnardo's Scottish Committee; Member, Edinburgh University Court; Chair, Waverley Care Aids Trust; Vice Chair, Families Outside; b. 2.6.45, Gosforth; 2 s. Educ. Blyth Grammar School; Durham University. Joined

Scottish Office, 1970, as Assistant Principal; posts held in Education, Social Work Services Group, Environment; Head of Group, Scottish Office Home Department, 1992-99; Head of Children and Young People's Group, Scottish Executive Education Department, 1999-2002. Recreations: swimming; walking; theatre; music; gardening. Address: 4 Grange Terrace, Edinburgh EH9 2LD; T.-0131 662 1500.

Stewart, Professor Graham George, BSc, PhD, DSc, FIBrew, FIBiol. Director, International Centre for Brewing and Distilling, 1994-2006; b. 22.3.42, Cardiff; m., Olga Leonara. Educ. Cathays High School, Cardiff; University College Cardiff; Bath University. Lecturer in Biochemistry, Portsmouth College of Technology, 1967-69; various technical positions, J. Labatt Ltd., Canada, 1969-94. Recreations: rugby; music; travel. Address: (b.) Heriot-Watt University, Riccarton, Edinburgh, EH14 4AS; T.-0131-451 3184.

Stewart, Dr. Ian James, BSc, PhD. Senior Lecturer in Human Morphology, University of Aberdeen, since 2000, Licensed Teacher of Anatomy, since 2000; Honorary Curator, Anatomy Museum, since 2000; b. 26.02.52, Glasgow; m., Patricia; 1 s.; 2 d. Educ. Trinity Academy, Edinburgh; St. Andrews University; Southampton University. Southampton University: Technician, 1974-76, Research Assistant, 1976-78, Research Fellow, 1978-79, Lecturer, 1979-2000; Visiting Senior Scientist, University of Guelph, Canada, June-Sept., 1988; "Professeur Invite", University of Tours, France, May-June, 1995. Recreation: smallholder. Address: (b.) Anatomy, School of Medicine, Marischal College, University of Aberdeen, Aberdeen AB10 1YS; T.-01224 274320; e-mail: i.stewart@abdn.ac.uk

Stewart, Ian James. Deputy Editor, The Scotsman, since 2004; Editor, Edinburgh Evening News, 2001-04; b. 4.8.60, Kingston-upon-Thames; m., Lesley; 1 s.; 1 d. Educ. Royal High School, Edinburgh; Napier College, Edinburgh. Royal Marines, 1979-82; Nottingham Evening Post, 1986-91; The Scotsman, 1991-98; Scottish Daily Mail, 1998-1999; Scotland on Sunday, 1999-2001. Recreations: mountain biking; reading; cigar smoking. Address: (b.) 108 Holyrood Road, Edinburgh; T.-0131 620 8626.

Stewart, James Blythe, MA, LLB, LLB, Advocate; b. 22.4.43, Methil. Educ. Buckhaven High School; University of Edinburgh. Research Assistant, Faculty of Law, University of St. Andrews, 1966-67; Heriot-Watt University: Assistant Lecturer in Law, 1967-69, Lecturer in Law, 1969-76, Senior Lecturer in Law, 1976-98; retired 1998. Historian, East Fife FC. Recreations: football spectating; bowls; golf. Address: (h.) 3 Comely Bank Terrace, Edinburgh EH4 1AT; T.-0131-332 8228.

Stewart, Rev. James Charles, MA, BD, STM. Minister, Kirk of St. Nicholas, Aberdeen (The City Kirk), 1980-2000; b. 29.3.33, Glasgow. Educ. Glasgow Academy; St. Andrews University; Union Theological Seminary, New York. Assistant Minister, St. John's Kirk of Perth, 1959-64; Minister: St. Andrew's Church, Drumchapel, 1964-74, East Parish Church of St. Nicholas, Aberdeen, 1974-80. Chairman, Aberdeen Endowments Trust; Honorary President, and Editor of 'The Record', of the Church Service Society; Governor, Robert Gordon's College. Address: 54 Murray Terrace, Aberdeen AB11 7SB; T.-01224 587071.

Stewart, John Barry Bingham, LVO, OBE, BA, CA. Past Chairman, Martin Currie Ltd.; b. 21.2.31, Edinburgh; m., Ailsa Margaret Crawford. Educ. The Leys School,

Cambridge; Magdalene College, Cambridge. Accountancy training, Edinburgh; worked in London, United States and Canada; joined Martin Currie, 1960. Recreations: fishing; shooting; golf.. Address: 18 Hope Terrace, Edinburgh EH9 2AR; T.-0131-447 1626.

Stewart, Sheriff John Hall, LLB. Sheriff of Strathclyde, Dumfries and Galloway, at Hamilton, since 1996, at Airdrie, 1985-96; b. 15.3.44, Bellshill; m., Marion MacCalman; 1 s.; 2 d. Educ. Airdrie Academy; St. Andrews University. Admitted Solicitor, 1971; Advocate, 1978; Past President, Uddingston RFC; Past President, Uddingston Cricket and Sports Club. Address: (b.) Sheriff Court House, Beckford Street, Hamilton, ML3 6AA.

Stewart, Rev. Norma Drummond, MA, MEd, DipTh, BD. Minister, Strathbungo Queen's Park Church, Glasgow, 1979-2000; Locum Tenens, Dennistoun Blackfriars, Glasgow, 2000-06; Part-time Chaplain, Glasgow Royal Infirmary, 2001-06; b. 20.5.36, Glasgow. Educ. Hyndland Secondary School, Glasgow; Glasgow University; Bible Training Institute, Glasgow; University of London (External); Trinity College, Glasgow; International Christian College, Glasgow. Teacher, Garrioch Secondary School, Glasgow, 1958-62; Missionary, Overseas Missionary Fellowship, West Malaysia, 1965-74; ordained to ministry, Church of Scotland, 1977; occasional Lecturer and Tutor in Old Testament; Participant in Congress on World Evangelisation, Manila, 1989; Member, Council of Christians and Jews. Recreation: Old Testament research; information technology. Address: 127 Nether Auldhouse Road, Glasgow G43 2YS; T.-0141 637 6956; e-mail: ndrummondstewart@hotmail.com

Stewart, Norman MacLeod, BL, SSC. Consultant, Allan, Black & McCaskie, Solicitors, Elgin 1997-99, Senior Partner, 1984-97; Chairman, Elgin and Lossiemouth Harbour Board, since 1993; President, Law Society of Scotland, 1985-86; b. 2.12.34, Lossiemouth; m., Mary Slater Campbell; 4 d. Educ. Elgin Academy; Edinburgh University. Training and Legal Assistant, Alex. Morison & Co., WS, Edinburgh, 1954-58; Legal Assistant: McLeod, Solicitor, Portsoy, 1958-59, Allan, Black & McCaskie, Solicitors, Elgin, 1959-61 (Partner, 1961-97); Council Member, Law Society of Scotland, 1976-87 (Convener, Public Relations Committee, 1979-81, and Professional Practice Committee, 1981-84). Past President, Elgin Rotary Club; Past Chairman, Moray Crime Prevention Panel; President, Edinburgh University Club of Moray, 1987-89. Recreations: walking; golf; music; Spanish culture. Address: (h.) Argyll Lodge, Lossiemouth, Moray; T.-0134381 3150.

Stewart, Patrick Loudon McIain, MBE, LLB, WS, DL. Consultant, Stewart Balfour & Sutherland, Solicitors, Campbeltown, Senior Partner, 1982-2000; Secretary, Clyde Fishermen's Association, since 1970; Vice Lord Lieutenant, Argyll and Bute; Honorary Sheriff at Campbeltown; b. 25.7.45, Campbeltown; m., Mary Anne McLellan; 1 s.; 1 d. Educ. Edinburgh Academy; Edinburgh University. Partner, Stewart Balfour & Sutherland, Campbeltown, 1970; former Executive Member, Scottish Fishermen's Federation; former Director, Scottish Fishermen's Organisation Ltd.; member of many Scottish fishing industry committees; Clerk, General Commissioners of Income Tax — Islay; A Vice President of The Marine Society & Sea Cadets; Cadet Forces Medal and two clasps; Non Executive Director, Clyde Marine Holdings Ltd; Chairman, Loch Fyne Oysters Employee Benefit Trust. Recreations: sailing; shooting; youth work. Address: Craigadam, Campbeltown, Argyll PA28 6EP; T.-01586 552161.

Stewart, Robert Armstrong, BA, DipTP, FRTPI, MCMI. Director of Environmental Services, The Moray Council (formerly Director, Economic Development and Planning); b. Stirling. Planning Assistant, Lanark County Council, 1968-69; Planner, Glasgow, 1969-70; Senior Assistant, then Group Leader: Development Control, West Lothian County, 1970 75; Depute Director: Planning, East Lothian District, 1975-79; Director of Planning and Development, Moray District Council. Address: (b.) Council Office, High Street, Elgin, IV30 1BX.

Stewart, Sir Robert Christie, KCVO, CBE, TD; Lord Lieutenant, Clackmannanshire, since 1994; b. 3.8.26, Dollar; m., Ann Grizel Cochrane; 3 s.; 2 d. Educ. Eton; University College, Oxford. Lt., Scots Guards, 1944-49; 7th Bn., Argyll and Sutherland Highlanders TA, 1951-66; Lt.-Col., 1963-66; Hon. Col., 1/51 Highland Volunteers, 1972-75; Landowner; Lord Lieutenant, Kinross-shire, 1966-74; Member, Perth and Kinross County Council, 1953-75; Chairman, Kinross County Council, 1963-73; Chairman and President, Board of Governors, East of Scotland College of Agriculture, 1970-83. Recreations: shooting; golf; the countryside. Address: (h.) Arndean, by Dollar, FK14 7NH; T.-01259 742527.

Stewart, Sir William, Kt, PhD, DSc, FRS, FRSE. Chairman, Health Protection Agency, since 2003, Shadow Chairman, 2002-03; Chairman, National Radiological Protection Board, since 2003; President, Royal Society of Edinburgh, 1999-2002; former President, British Association for the Advancement of Science; b. 7.6.35; 1 s. Educ. Bowmore Junior Secondary School; Dunoon Grammar School; Glasgow University. Dundee University: Boyd Baxter Professor of Biology, 1968-94, Vice-Principal, 1985-87; Secretary and Chief Executive, AFRC, 1988-90; Chief Scientific Adviser, Cabinet Office, 1990-95, and Head of Office of Science and Technology, 1992-95. Honorary degrees from universities: Aberdeen, Abertay, Dundee, Edinburgh, Glasgow, Napier, Paisley, Stirling.

Stewartby, Lord (Bernard Harold Ian Halley), RD, FBA, FRSE, PC, Kt, Baron, KStJ, LittD. Retired Banker; b. 10.8.35, London; m., The Hon. Deborah Buchan JP (qv); 1 s.; 2 d. Educ. Haileybury; Jesus College, Cambridge (Hon. Fellow 1994). Royal Navy (National Service), 1954-56; Director, Brown Shipley and Co. Ltd., Merchant Bankers, 1971-83; MP North Hertfordshire (Conservative), 1974-92; Under-Secretary of State for Defence, 1983; Economic Secretary to the Treasury, 1983-87; Minister of State for the Armed Forces, 1987-88; Deputy Secretary of State, Northern Ireland, 1988-89; Director, Financial Services Authority, 1992-97; Deputy Chairman, Standard Chartered plc, 1993-2004; Deputy Chairman, Amlin plc, 1995-2006; Author, The Scottish Coinage, 1955; President, Sir Halley Stewart Trust, since 2002; President, The Stewart Society, since 2007; Chairman, Treasure Valuation Committee, 1996-2001; Medallist, The Royal Numismatic Society, 1996. Recreations: history; tennis. Address: (h.) Broughton Green, Broughton, by Biggar ML12 6HQ.

Stewartby (The Lady), Deborah Charlotte, JP. Non-Executive Director, Scottish Opera, 2000-03, Scottish Ballet, since 2000; Council Member, John Buchan Society (grand-daughter of John Buchan), since 2001, Chairman, since 2006; b. 19.10.47, London; m., Rt. Hon. Lord Stewartby; 1 s.; 2 d. Senior Researcher, 1974-92 (P.A. of Ian Stewart, MP); Director of Appeals and Public Affairs, Bryson House, Belfast, 1991-98. Governor, Princess Helena College, 1986-99; President,

Howard Cottage Society, 1995-2007; Member, Scottish Borders Childrens' Panel, 2004; Scottish Trustee, Barnardo's, 2004-06. Recreations: performing arts; gardening. Address: (h.) Broughton Green, Broughton, by Biggar ML12 6HQ; T.-01899 830 362.

Stewart-Clark, Sir Jack, Bt. Member of European Parliament for East Sussex and Kent South, 1979-99; Vice President, European Parliament, 1992-97; b. 17.9.29, West Lothian; m., Lydia Loudon; 1 s.; 4 d. Educ. Eton; Balliol College, Oxford; Harvard Business School. Coldstream Guards, 1948-49; J. & P. Coats, 1952-70; Philips Industries, 1970-79 (Managing Director, Philips Electrical Ltd., 1970-74, Pye of Cambridge Ltd., 1974-79). Member, Queen's Bodyguard for Scotland, Royal Company of Archers. Publications: European Competition Law; Drugs Education, It's My Problem as Well. Recreations: golf; tennis; photography; classic cars. Address: (h.) Dundas Castle, South Queensferry, near Edinburgh, EH30 9SP; T.-0131-331 1114.

Stihler, Catherine Dalling, MA (Hons), MLitt. Member, European Parliament, since 1999; Deputy Leader of the European Parliamentary Labour Party (EPLP), since 2004; Health and Fisheries Spokeswoman, EPLP, 1999-2004; Regional Policy and Fisheries Spokeswoman, EPLP, since 2004; President, Public Health All-party Group, 2000-02; Member of the Regional Policy and Fisheries Committees, since 2004; b. 30.7.73, Bellshill; m., David. Educ. Coltness High School, Wishaw; St Andrews University. PA (Researcher) to Anne Begg, MP, 1997-99; Organiser for Central and Eastern European politicians' visits to Scotland, 1995-97; Member, Labour Party NEC, 1995-97, and Scottish Executive, 1993-95, 1997-99; Editor, Parliament Magazine. Publication: Women and the Military (Contributor). Recreations: reading; going to the gym; singing; films. Address: (b.) Constituency Office, 25 Church Street, Inverkeithing, Fife KY11 1LG; T.-01383 417799.

Stimson, Professor William Howard, BSc, PhD, CBiol, FIBiol, FWIF, FIoN, FRSE. Professor of Immunology, Strathclyde University, since 1981; Director: Solus Biologicals Ltd., WH Stimson and Associates, Viragen International Inc, Viragen (Scotland) Ltd., Viranative Ab, Institute of Nanotechnology; b. 2.11.43, Liverpool; m., Jean Scott Baird; 1 s.; 1 d. Educ. Prince of Wales School, Nairobi; St. Andrews University. Research Fellow, Department of Obstetrics and Gynaecology, Dundee University, 1970-72; Lecturer, then Senior Lecturer, Biochemistry Department, Strathclyde University, 1973-80. Holder, Glasgow Loving Cup, 1982-83; Member, Editorial Boards, four scientific journals; 205 scientific publications; 18 patents. Recreations: mechanical engineering; walking; golf. Address: (b.) Division of Immunology, Microbiology and Biochemistry, SIPBS, Strathclyde University, 27 Taylor Street, Glasgow G4 0NR; T.-0141-548 3729; e-mail: w.h.stimson@strath.ac.uk

Stirling of Garden, Col. Sir James, KCVO, CBE, TD, BA, FRICS. Lord Lieutenant of Stirling and Falkirk, 1983-2005; Chartered Surveyor; b. 8.9.30; m., Fiona; 2 s.; 2 d. Educ. Rugby; Trinity College, Cambridge. Partner, Ryden and Partners, 1962-89; Director, Scottish Widows Life Assurance Society, 1974-96. Chairman, Highland TAVRA, 1981-86, President, 1990-96; Director, Woolwich Building Society, 1975-95; Honorary Sheriff, Stirling, since 1996. Prior, Order of St. John, Scotland; Hon. Doctor, University of Stirling, 2004; Grand Cross of the Order of St. John, 2004. Address: (h.) Garden, Buchlyvie, Stirlingshire.

Stirling, John Boyd, WS. Clerk to HM Society of Writers to the Signet, since 2002; Solicitor Advocate, since 2005; Partner, Gillespie MacAndrew WS, since 2005; b. 8.3.68, Glasgow; m., Julie; 2 s. Educ. Glasgow Academy; Edinburgh University. Trainee, W & J Burness WS; Solicitor, Scottish Office, Assistant, then Partner, Bennett and Robertson (which merged with Gillespie MacAndrew). Recreations: fly fishing; wine. Address: (b.) 5 Atholl Crescent, Edinburgh EH3 8EJ; T.-0131 225 1677; e-mail: john.stirling@gillespiemacandrew.co.uk

Stobo, James, CBE, DL, FRAgS. Farmer; Chairman, Moredun Foundation for Animal Health and Welfare, 1994-2000; Director, New Park Management Ltd.; b. 9.12.34, Lanark; m., Pamela Elizabeth Mary Herriot (deceased); 1 s.; 2 d. Educ. Edinburgh Academy. Farming, since 1951; Past Chairman and President, Scottish Association of Young Farmers Clubs; Member, Home-Grown Cereals Authority, 1971-76; President, National Farmers' Union of Scotland, 1973-74; President, Animal Diseases Research Foundation, 1980-95; President, Longridge Towers School, since 2000, Chairman of Governors, 1982-2000; Chairman, Scottish Seed Potato Development Council, 1988-95; Director, John Hogarth Ltd., Kelso Mills; Vice-President, Royal Smithfield Club; Trustee, Queen Elizabeth Castle of Mey Trust, since 1996; Director, Castle and Gardens of Mey Ltd.; President, Aberdeen-Angus Cattle Society, 2001-02; Deputy Lieutenant, County of Berwick, 1987. Recreation: photography. Address: Nabdean, Berwick-upon-Tweed TD15 1SZ; T.-01289 386224.

Stockdale, Elizabeth Joan Noel, MB, ChB, DMRD, FRCR, FRCPCH, MBA. Consultant Radiologist, Royal Aberdeen Children's Hospital and Aberdeen Royal Infirmary, since 1980; Clinical Senior Lecturer, Aberdeen University, since 1980; m., Christopher Leo Stockdale; 2 s.; 1 d. Educ. Aberdeen University. House Surgeon, Aberdeen Royal Infirmary; Senior House Surgeon, Professorial Surgical Unit, Hospital for Sick Children, Great Ormond Street; Registrar, St. George's Hospital; Senior Registrar, Royal National Orthopaedic Hospital, Royal Marsden Hospital, Atkinson Morley's Hospital; Chairman, Grampian Division, BMA, 1995-97; Member, BMA Scottish Council and SCHMS, 1997-2000; Member, RCR Standing Scottish Committee, 1979-2001. Recreations: theatre; classical music; travel. Address: (h.) 1 Grant Road, Banchory, Kincardineshire AB31 5UW; T.-013302 823096.

Stoddart, Sheriff Charles Norman, LLB, LLM, PhD. Sheriff of Lothian and Borders at Edinburgh, since 1995; b. 4.4.48, Dunfermline; m., Anne Lees; 1 d. Educ. Dunfermline High School; Edinburgh University; McGill University, Montreal. Private practice as Solicitor, 1972-73; Lecturer in Scots Law, Edinburgh University, 1973-80; private practice, 1980-88; Sheriff of North Strathclyde at Paisley, 1988-95; Director of Judicial Studies in Scotland, 1997-2000; Member, MacLean Committee on Serious Violent and Sexual Offenders, 1999-2000; Member, The Sentencing Commission for Scotland, 2003-06; Member, Policy Group, Civil Courts Review, since 2007. Publications: (as Co-author) The Law and Practice of Legal Aid in Scotland; Cases and Materials on Criminal Law; Cases and Materials on Criminal Procedure; (as author) Criminal Warrants; Bible John. Recreations: music; sport. Address: (b.) Sheriff's Chambers, Sheriff Court, 27 Chambers Street, Edinburgh, EH1 1LB; T.-0131-225 2525.

Stone, Professor David, MD, FRCP, FFPHM, FRCPCH. Founding Director, Paediatric Epidemiology and Community Health Unit, Department of Child Health, Glasgow University, Professor, Glasgow University, since 2000; b. 13.5.49, Glasgow; 2 s.; 2 d. Educ. High School of Glasgow; Edinburgh University. Trained in general medicine and public health, Glasgow and London; Senior Lecturer in Epidemiology, Ben Gurion University of the Negev, Israel, 1985-2000; Senior Lecturer, Glasgow

University, since 1985. Recreations: music; dining; current affairs. Address: PEACH Unit, Yorkhill Hospital, Glasgow G3 8SJ; T.-0141-201 0178.

Stone, Professor Frederick Hope, OBE, MB, ChB, FRCP, FRCPsych, FRCPCH. Professor of Child and Adolescent Psychiatry, Glasgow University, 1977-86; Consultant Psychiatrist, Royal Hospital for Sick Children, Glasgow, since 1954; b. 11.9.21, Glasgow; m., Zelda Elston, MA; 2 s.; 1 d. Educ. Hillhead High School, Glasgow; Glasgow University. RAMC, 1945-48; Acting Director, Lasker Mental Hygiene Clinic, Hadassah, Jerusalem, 1952-54; World Health Organisation Visiting Consultant, 1960, 1964; Member, Kilbrandon Committee, 1963-65; Secretary-General, International Association of Child Psychiatry, 1962-66; Member, Houghton Committee on Adoption, 1968-72; Chairman, Scottish Division, Royal College of Psychiatrists, 1981-84; President, Young Minds; Chairman, Strathclyde Children's Panel Advisory Committee, 1988-94. Publications: "Child Psychiatry for Students" (Co-author), 1998; Juvenile Justice in Scotland (Co-author); "Youth Justice and Child Protection" (Co-editor), 2007. Address: (h.) Flat 3c, 2 Hutchison Court, Berryhill Road, Giffnock, Glasgow G46 7NN; T.-0141-638 7554.

Stone, James Hume Walter Miéville, MA, FRSA. MSP (Liberal Democrat), Caithness, Sutherland and Easter Ross, since 1999; freelance newspaper columnist and broadcaster, since 1991; b. 16.6.54, Edinburgh; m., Flora Kathleen Margaret Armstrong; 1 s.; 2 d. Educ. Tain Royal Academy; Gordonstoun School; St Andrews University. Cleaner, fish-gutter, stores clerk, 1977-81; Assistant Site Administrator/Site Administrator, Bechtel G.B. Ltd., 1981-84; Administration Manager, Odfjell Drilling and Consulting Co. Ltd., 1984-86; Director, Highland Fine Cheeses Ltd., 1986-94; Member, Ross and Cromarty District Council, 1986-96; Member, The Highland Council, 1995-99 (Vice-Chair, Finance). Member, Cromarty Firth Port Authority, 1998-2001; Liberal Democrat Spokesman for: Education and Children, 1999-2000, Highlands and Fishing, 2000-01, Equal Opportunities, since 2001, Finance, since 2002; Member, Holyrood Progress Group, since 2000; Trustee, Tain Museum Trust; Trustee, Tain Guildry Trust; Trustee, Highland Buildings Preservation Trust; Director, The Highland Festival, 1994-2000. Recreations: gardening; reading; music; butterflies and funghi. Address: (b.) Scottish Parliament, Edinburgh EH99 1SP; T.-0131-348 5789.

Stone, Professor Trevor W., BPharm, PhD, DSc, FBPharmacolS. Professor of Pharmacology, Glasgow University, since 1989; co-Director, PharmaLinks, since 2003; b. 7.10.47, Mexborough; m., (1) Anne Corina; divorced; m., (2) L. Gail Darlington. Educ. Mexborough Grammar School; London University; Aberdeen University. Lecturer in Physiology, Aberdeen University, 1970-77; Senior Lecturer/Reader in Neuroscience, then Professor of Neuroscience, London University, 1977-88. Editor, British Journal of Pharmacology, 1980-86. Publications. 360 scientific papers and 13 books; Microiontophoresis and Pressure Ejection, 1985; Purines: Basic and Clinical Aspects, 1991; Neuropharmacology, 1995; Pills, Potions and Poisons – How Drugs Work, 2000. Recreations: photography; snooker; music; working. Address: (b.) Department of Pharmacology, West Medical Building, Glasgow University, Glasgow G12; T.-0141-330 4481.

Stormonth Darling, Robin Andrew. Honorary Consul of Mexico, 1992-2006; b. 1.10.26, Fulmer, Bucks; m. (1), Susan Mary Clifford-Turner; 3 s.; 1 d.; (2), Carola Marion Erskine-Hill. Educ. Abberley Hall; Winchester College.

Fleet Air Arm, 1945; 9th Queen's Royal Lancers, 1946-54, ADC to GOC-in-C Scotland; Laing and Cruickshank, 1954-87 (Chairman, 1980-87); Director, British Motor Corporation (British Leyland), 1960-76; Member, Stock Exchange Council, 1978-86; Deputy Chairman, Take-over Panel, 1985-87; Director: London Scottish Bank, 1984-92, Mercantile House Holdings, 1984-87, Ptarmigan Investment Trust, 1993-2003; Chairman: Dumyat Investment Trust, 1995-2000, Intrinsic Portfolio Funds, 2000-03; Chairman, Capital Opportunities Trust PLC, 1994-2003. Recreations: shooting; skiing; flying; swimming. Address: (h.) Balvarran, Enochdhu, Blairgowrie PH10 7PA; T.-01250 881248.

Stott, Professor David James, MB, ChB, MD(Glas), FRCP(Glas), FRCP(Edin). Professor of Geriatric Medicine, Glasgow University, since 1994; b. 4.6.59, Rugby; m., Shiona; 1 s.; 1 d. Educ. Eastwood High School; Glasgow University. Trained in research methodology, MRC Blood Pressure Unit, 1982-84; Senior Lecturer (Honorary Consultant) in Geriatric Medicine, 1991-94. Recreations: golf; hill-walking; acoustic guitar. Address: (b.) Academic Section of Geriatric Medicine, Glasgow Royal Infirmary G31 2ER; T.-0141-211 4976.

Stove, Thomas William. Convener, Shetland Islands Council, 1999-2003; b. 17.7.35, Sandwick, Shetland; m., Alma; 2 d. Educ. Anderson Education Institute, Lerwick. Owner/Director, Televiradio (Shetland) Ltd., 1966-96; Member, Zetland County Council/Shetland Islands Council, 1970-78; Member, Lerwick Harbour Trust, 1980-96 (Chairman, 1983-96). Chairman, Shetland Branch, Multiple Sclerosis Society. Recreations: boating; walking; classic cars; DIY. Address: (h.) Nordaal, Sandwick, Shetland ZE2 9HP; T.-01950 431434.

Strachan, Gordon, OBE. Manager, Celtic Football Club, since 2005; b. 9.2.57, Edinburgh. Played for Dundee, 1974-77, Aberdeen, 1977-84 (won three Scottish League titles, three Scottish Cups, the European Cup Winners' Cup and the European Super Cup), Manchester United, 1984-89, Leeds United, 1989-95, Coventry City, 1995-97; Manager: Coventry City, 1996-2001, Southampton, 2001-04. Won 50 international caps for Scotland and is a member of the Scotland Football Hall of Fame. Manager of the Year, 2006; inaugural Scottish PFA Manager of the Year, 2007. FIFA/SOS Ambassador for Scotland. Address: Celtic Football Club, Celtic Park, Glasgow G40 3RE.

Strachan, Professor Hew Francis Anthony, MA, PhD, FRHistS, FRSE, HonDUniv (Paisley) 2005. Chichele Professor of the History of War and Fellow, All Souls College, University of Oxford, since 2002; Professor of Modern History, Glasgow University, 1992-2002 (Visiting Professor, since 2002); Director, Scottish Centre for War Studies, 1996-2002; Life Fellow, Corpus Christi College, Cambridge, since 1992; b. 1.9.49, Edinburgh; m., Pamela Dorothy Tennant (née Symes); 1 s.; 1 step s.; 2 d.; 1 step d. Educ. Rugby School; Corpus Christi College, Cambridge. Senior Lecturer, Department of War Studies and International Affairs, Royal Military Academy, Sandhurst, 1978-79; Research Fellow, Corpus Christi College, Cambridge, 1975-78; Fellow, Corpus Christi College since 1979: Tutor for Admissions, 1981-88, Director of Studies in History, 1986-92, Senior Tutor, 1987 and 1989-92. Governor, Rugby School, 1985-2007, and Stowe School, 1990-2002; DL (Tweedale), since 2006; Commonwealth War Graves Commission, since 2006; Member, Council, Society for Army Historical Research, 1980-95, Army Records Society, 1990-94, Council, National Army

Museum, 1994-2003; Joint Editor, War in History; Member, Queen's Bodyguard for Scotland (Royal Company of Archers); Visiting Professor, Royal Norwegian Air Force Academy, since 2000. Publications: British Military Uniforms; History of the Cambridge University Officers Training Corps; European Armies and the Conduct of War; Wellington's Legacy: the Reform of the British Army 1830-54; From Waterloo to Balaclava: Tactics, Technology, and the British Army 1815-1854 (Templer Medal, 1986); The Politics of the British Army (Westminster Medal, 1998); Oxford Illustrated History of the First World War (Editor), 1998; The British Army, Manpower and Society into the 21st Century (Editor), 2000; The First World War Vol. I: To Arms, 2001; The First World War: a new illustrated history, 2003; Big Wars and Small Wars (Editor), 2006; Clausewitz's on War: A Biography, 2007; Clausewitz in the 21st Century (Editor), 2007; numerous articles and reviews. Recreations: shooting; rugby football. Address: (b.) All Souls College, University of Oxford; (h.) Glenhighton, Broughton, Biggar ML12 6JF.

Strachan, Tony. Agent for Scotland, Bank of England, since 2003; m.; 2 c. Joined Bank of England, 1974: worked in Exchange Control Department, Pension Fund Administration Unit, International Division, Banking Supervision Division, became Technical Assistant to Director of the Bank, seconded to Take-over Panel for two years, worked in Bank's Business Finance Division, became Bank's Agent in Manchester, then first Agent for North West. Formerly: Governor, Manchester Metropolitan University, Member, Court, University of Salford, Director, Manchester Millennium Ltd., Member, Board, North West Industrial Development Board, Deputy Chairman, Museum of Science and Industry, Manchester. Address: (b.) Bank of England, Agency for Scotland, 19 St. Vincent Place, Glasgow G1 2DT; T.-0141-221 7972.

Strang, Archie. Chief Executive Officer, South Lanarkshire Council, since 2006 (Depute Chief Executive, 2002-06). Address: (b.) Council Offices, Almada Street, Hamilton ML3 0AA; T.-01698 454208.

Strang, David James Reid, QPM, BSc, MSc. Chief Constable, Lothian and Borders Police, since 2007; Chief Constable, Dumfries and Galloway Constabulary, 2001-07; b. 9.4.58, Glasgow; m., Dr Alison B. Strang; 1 s.; 2 d. Educ. Glasgow Academy; Loretto School; St Chad's College, Durham University; Birkbeck College, London University. Constable to Chief Superintendent, Metropolitan Police, 1980-98; Assistant Chief Constable, Lothian and Borders Police, 1998-2001. Address: (b.) Lothian and Borders Police, Force Headquarters, Fettes Avenue, Edinburgh EH4 1RB; T.-0131 311 3131.

Strang, Gavin Steel, BSc (Hons), DipAgriSci, PhD. MP (Labour), East Edinburgh, since 1970; b. 10.7.43, Dundee; m., Bettina Smith; 1 s. Educ. Morrison's Academy, Crieff; Edinburgh University. Parliamentary Under Secretary of State, Department of Energy, February to October, 1974; Parliamentary Secretary, Ministry of Agriculture, 1974-79; Principal Labour Agriculture Spokesman, 1992-97; Cabinet Minister with responsibility for Transport, 1997-98. Member of the Select Committee on the Environment, Food and Rural Affairs. Recreations: golf; swimming; the countryside. Address: (b.) House of Commons, Westminster, London; T.-0171-219 3000.

Strang, William Frank Gourlay, BA (Oxon). Head of Sea Fisheries (Conservation), Scottish Executive; b. 30.6.61, Glasgow; m., Eleanor Ann Munro-Faure; 1 d. Educ.

Loretto; St. Edmund Hall, Oxford. Administration Trainee, Ministry of Agriculture Fisheries and Food, 1984; Private Secretary to Permanent Secretary, 1987-88; Private Secretary to Parliamentary Secretary, 1988-89; Agricultural Attache, British Embassy, Paris, 1990-94; Principal Private Secretary to Minister of Agriculture, 1994-97; Secretary to the Forestry Commission, 1997-2003. Recreations: hill-walking; bagpipes; local church. Address: (b.) Pentland House, 47 Robb's Loan, Edinburgh EH14 1TY.

Strange, Rt. Revd. Mark. Bishop of Moray, Ross & Caithness, since 2007; m., Jane; 3 c. Most recently served as rector of Holy Trinity Church, Elgin and priest in charge of St Margaret's, Lossiemouth, St Michael's, Dufftown and St Margaret's, Aberlour; formerly canon of St Andrew's Cathedral, synod clerk of the diocese, and had a leading role in developing the church's youth network throughout Scotland and organising its annual youth week events. During his consecration, was given the historic Diocesan Crozier, the sign of a bishop's pastoral office, gifted to the diocese by Bishop Robert Eden in 1886, the year the cathedral was built. Also received the bishop's ring, a gift from a parish he served as curate, and a silver pectoral cross, a gift from his present parish.

Strang Steel, Sir (Fiennes) Michael, 3rd Bt, CBE. Member, Deer Commission for Scotland; b. 22.2.43; m., Sally Russell; 2 s.; 1 d. Educ. Eton. Retired Major, 17th/21st Lancers, 1962-80. Former Forestry Commissioner; DL. Address: (h.) Philiphaugh, Selkirk, TD7 5LX.

Strang Steel, Malcolm Graham, BA (Cantab), LLB, WS. Partner, Turcan Connell, WS, since 1997; Partner, W. & J. Burness, WS, 1973-97; b. 24.11.46, Selkirk; m., Margaret Philippa Scott; 1 s.; 1 d. Educ. Eton; Trinity College, Cambridge; Edinburgh University. Sometime Chairman, Albyn Housing Society Ltd., Scottish Dyslexia Trust; Member, Council, Law Society of Scotland, 1984-90; Secretary, Scottish Agricultural Arbiters and Valuers Association. Recreations: shooting; fishing; skiing; tennis; reading. Address: (b.) Princes Exchange, 1 Earl Grey Street, Edinburgh EH3 9EE; T.-0131-228 8111.

Strathclyde, Lord (Thomas Strathclyde), PC. Leader of the Opposition, House of Lords, since 1998; b. 22.2.60, Glasgow; m., Jane; 3 d. Educ. Wellington College; East Anglia University; University of Aix-en-Provence. Bain Clarkson, Insurance Brokers, 1982-88; Government Whip, 1988; Minister for Tourism, 1989; Minister for Agriculture and Fisheries, Scottish Office, 1990-92; Parliamentary Under Secretary of State, DoE, 1992-93; Minister of State, Department of Trade and Industry, 1993-94; Government Chief Whip, 1994-97; Opposition Chief Whip, 1997-98. Chairman, Strathclyde Commission on Restructuring the Scottish Conservative and Unionist Party, 1997-98. Address: (b.) House of Lords, London SW1; T.-020 7219 3236.

Strathmore and Kinghorne, 18th Earl of (Michael Fergus Bowes Lyon); b. 7.6.57; m. (1) (divorced 2004); 3 s. m. (2), Dr. Damaris Stuart-William; 1 s. President, Boys' Brigade, 1994-99; DL, Angus, since 1993. Address: Glamis Castle, Forfar, DD8 1QJ.

Straton, Timothy Duncan, TD, CA, CTA. B. 1.10.42, Edinburgh; m., Gladys Margaret George (deceased); 1 s.; 1 d. Educ. Edinburgh Academy. Hon. Treasurer, Trinity Bowling Club. Recreations: family; photography; golf;

bowls. Address: (h.) 32 Wardie Road, Edinburgh EH5 3LG; T.-0131 552 4062.

Street, Margaret Dobson, MBE, FSA Scot; b. 18.10.20, Hawick; m., Richard Andrew Rutherford Street (deceased); 2 s. Educ. Hawick High School; Alva Academy. Civil Servant, 1938-48; Ministry of Labour and National Service, 1938-47; Ministry of National Insurance (Inspectorate), 1947-48; voluntary work since 1948, apart from freelance writing on household and conservation topics; Honorary Secretary Leith Civic Trust, until 1997, Patron, since 1998; Convener, Friends of North Carr Lightship; Member, North East Fife District Council, North Carr Management Committee; Saltire Society Representative, Council, National Trust for Scotland, 1986-95; Secretary, Mungo Park Commemoration Committee; Trustee, Robert Hurd Memorial Fund; Appeal Convener, Wallace Statue, Lanark; Member, Steering Committee, Brownsbank; Appeal Convener, Wallace Statue, Dryburgh; Vice-Chairman, Saltire Society, 1983-94, Chairman, 1995-97; Saltire Society's Andrew Fletcher of Saltoun Award for services to Scotland, 1992; Honorary Member, Saltire Society, 1997. Recreations: promotion of Scottish cultural activity; conservation. Address: (h.) 115 Trinity Road, Edinburgh; T.-0131-552 2409.

Stretton, James, BA. Member, Court, Bank of England, 1998-2003; Chairman, BE Pension Fund Trustee Company, 2001-05; Rector's Assessor, Edinburgh University, 2003-06; Member, Franchise Board, Lloyds of London, since 2003; Deputy Chairman, Edinburgh International Festival; Chairman, The Wise Group, since 2002; Member, Disciplinary Board of the Actuarial Profession, 2004-06; b. 16.12.43, Peterborough; m., Isobel Robertson; 2 d. Educ. Laxton Grammar School, Oundle; Worcester College, Oxford. Joined Standard Life, 1965; Chief Executive, UK Operations, Standard Life, 1988-2001. Recreations: music; gardening; reading; golf. Address: (h.) 15 Letham Mains, Haddington EH41 4NW.

Stringer, Professor Joan Kathleen, CBE, BA, CertEd, PhD, CCMI, FRSA, FRSE, HonDLitt (Keele). Principal and Vice-Chancellor, Napier University, since 2003; Member: Executive Committee, Scottish Council Development and Industry, since 1998, Council, World Association for Co-operative Education, 1998-2003, Edinburgh International Festival Council, 1999-2005, Scottish Committee, British Council, since 2000, Judicial Appointments Board for Scotland, since 2002; Convenor, Scottish Council for Voluntary Organisations, 2002-07; b. 12.5.48, Stoke on Trent; m., Roel Mali. Educ. Portland House High School, Stoke on Trent; Stoke on Trent College of Art; Keele University. Assistant Principal, Robert Gordon University, 1991-96, having joined as Lecturer, 1980; Principal, Queen Margaret University College, Edinburgh, 1996-2002; Visiting Lecturer, Aberdeen University, 1984-86. Member: Joint University Council for Social and Public Administration, 1982-91, Royal Institute of Public Administration, 1984-91, Management Board, North of Scotland Consortium on Wider Access, 1988-92, Board of Management, Aberdeen College, 1992-96, Grampian Health Board, 1994-96, CVCP Commission on University Career Opportunities, 1995-2001, Scottish Committee, National Committee of Inquiry into Higher Education (The Dearing Committee), 1996-97, Human Fertilisation and Embryology Authority, 1996-99, Secretary of State's Consultative Steering Group and Financial Issues Advisory Group on the Scottish Parliament, 1998-99, Scottish Council for Postgraduate Medical and Dental Education, 1999-2002, Scottish Health Minister's Learning Together Strategy Implementation Group, 2000-01, Scottish European Structural Funds Forum, 2000-02, Department of Health's Working Group on the Modernisation of the SHO,

2000-02, Scottish Nursing and Midwifery Education Council Advisory Group, 2000-01, Institute of Directors, The British Chamber of Commerce; Auditor, Higher Education Quality Council, 1992-95; Commissioner (with responsibility for Scotland), Equal Opportunities Commission, 1995-2001; Chair, Northern Ireland Equality Commission Working Group, 1998-99; Vice Convener, Committee of Scottish Higher Education Principals, 1998-2002; Commissioner, Scottish Election Commission, 1999; Chair, Scottish Executive Strategic Group on Women, 2003; Member, Board: Higher Education Statistics Agency, since 2003, Quality Assurance Agency for Higher Education, 2002-06, Higher Education Careers Services Unit, since 2000. Publications: contributed articles in field of politics with particular reference to British Public Administration and employment and training policy. Recreations: music (especially opera); gardening; cats. Address: (b.) Craighouse Campus, 10 Craighouse Road, Edinburgh EH10 5LG.

Strudwick, Major General Mark Jeremy, CBE. Chief Executive, The Prince's Scottish Youth Business Trust, since 2000; b. 19.4.45; m., Janet Elizabeth Coleridge Vivers; 1 s.; 1 d. Educ. St. Edmund's School, Canterbury; Royal Military Academy, Sandhurst. Commissioned, The Royal Scots (The Royal Regiment), 1966 (Colonel, 1995-2005); served UK, BAOR, Cyprus, Canada, India, Northern Ireland (Despatches twice); Commanded, 1st Bn. The Royal Scots, 1984-87; Instructor, Staff College Camberley, 1987-88; Assistant Chief of Staff, G1/G4 HQ Northern Ireland 1988-90; Higher Command and Staff Course, 1989; Commanded, 3 Infantry Bde., 1990-91; NDC New Delhi, 1992; Deputy Military Secretary, Ministry of Defence, 1993-95; Director of Infantry, 1996-97; ADC to HM The Queen, 1996-97; General Officer Commanding, Army in Scotland, and Governor, Edinburgh Castle, 1997-2000; Colonel Commandant, The Scottish Division, 1997-2000. Member, Royal Company of Archers, Queen's Bodyguard for Scotland, since 1994 (Brigadier 2006); Commodore Infantry Sailing Association, 1997-2000; Her Majesty's Commissioner, Queen Victoria School, Dunblane, 1997-2000; Governor: Royal School, Bath, 1993-2000, Gordonstoun School, 1999-2007; Chairman, Scottish Veterans' Residences; Trustee, Historic Scotland Foundation, since 2001. Recreations: golf; shooting; sailing. Address: c/o The Prince's Scottish Youth Business Trust, 15 Exchange Place, Glasgow G1 3AN; T.-0141-248-4999; e-mail: mark.strudwick@psybt.org.uk

Struthers, Professor Allan, BSc, MD, FRCP, FESC. Professor of Cardiovascular Medicine and Therapeutics, Dundee University, since 2000; b. 14.8.52, Glasgow; m., Julia Diggens; 1 s.; 1 d. Educ. Hutchesons' Boys' Grammar School; Glasgow University. Junior posts, Glasgow teaching hospitals, 1977-82; Senior Medical Registrar, Royal Postgraduate Medical School and Hammersmith Hospital, London, 1983-85; Wellcome Senior Lecturer, Department of Clinical Pharmacology, Ninewells Hospital, 1985-92; Professor of Clinical Pharmacology, 1992-2000. Recreations: cycling; swimming; travel; opera. Address: Bech-na-Mara, 5 Riverview, Newport-on-Tay DD6 8QX; T. 01382 542697.

Stuart, Jamie; b. 10.9.20, Glasgow; widower; 2 d. Educ. Whitehill School, Glasgow. Flying Officer/Wireless Operator/Air Gunner, RAF, 1941-46; Actor/Social Worker/Evangelist; athlete: Scottish two-miles steeplechase champion, 1948. Publications: A Glasgow Bible; Will I Be Called An Author? Address: (h.) 436 Edinburgh Road, Glasgow G33 2PW; T.-0141-778 2437.

Stuart, John Forester, MA (Cantab). Secretary General, General Synod, Scottish Episcopal Church, since 1996; b. 26.5.59, Broughty Ferry; m., Sally Ann Bell; 2 s. Educ. Dundee High School; Daniel Stewart's and Melville

College; Queens' College Cambridge, College of Law, Guildford. Articled Clerk and subsequently Solicitor, Macfarlanes, London, 1982-86; Solicitor and subsequently Partner, J. & F. Anderson, Solicitors, Edinburgh (merged, 1992, to become Anderson Strathern), 1986-96. Recreations: music; walking; astronomy. Address: (b.) 21 Grosvenor Crescent, Edinburgh EH12 5EE; T.-0131-225 6357.

Stuart, Mhairi Ross, MA (Hons). Presenter, Scotland Live, BBC Scotland, since 2006, Presenter, Good Morning Scotland, 1999-2006; b. 8.12.67, Glasgow; m., Roderick Stuart. Educ. Cleveden Secondary School, Glasgow; Glasgow University. BBC, since 1991 (News Trainee/Producer/Presenter). BT Scotland Radio News Broadcaster of the Year, 1999. Recreations: sailing; skiing. Address: (b.) News Room, BBC Scotland, 40 Pacific Quay, Glasgow G51 1DZ.

Sturgeon, David, BL, MLitt. Registrar and Deputy Secretary, Heriot-Watt University, 1967-95; b. 10.12.35, Kilwinning; m., Nancy McDougall; 1 d.; 2 s. Educ. Dalry High School, Ayrshire (Blair Medallist, 1950); Glasgow University. National Service (RASC - War Office), 1957-59; Trainee Actuary, Scottish Widows Fund, 1959-61; Administrative Assistant, Royal College of Science and Technology (later, Strathclyde University), 1961-67. Secretary and Treasurer, Edinburgh Society of Glasgow University Graduates, 1971-2004; Hon. degree, Heriot-Watt University, 1996; Chairman, Dalry (Ayrshire) Burns Club, 2002. Recreations: golf; music (particularly Scottish country dance music). Address: (h.) 10 Dalhousie Road, Eskbank, Midlothian EH22 3AS; T.-0131-663 1059; e-mail: davidsturgeon35@hotmail.com

Sturgeon, Nicola, LLB (Hons), DipLP. MSP (SNP), Glasgow, since 1999; Deputy First Minister, and Health Secretary, since 2007; b. 19.7.70, Irvine. Educ. Greenwood Academy, Irvine; University of Glasgow. Trainee Solicitor, Glasgow, 1993-95; Solicitor, Stirling, 1995-97; Solicitor, Drumchapel Law Centre, Glasgow, 1997-99. Recreations: reading; theatre. Address: (b.) Scottish Parliament, Edinburgh EH99 1SP.

Sturrock, Professor John Garrow, QC, LLB (Hons), LLM, FRSA, MCIArb. Queen's Counsel, since 1999; Director of Training and Education, Faculty of Advocates, 1994-2002; Visiting Professor of Advocacy Skills and Conflict Resolution, Glasgow Graduate School of Law, since 1999; Managing Director, Core Consulting and Mediation Ltd., 1999-2004; Director, Core Mediation Ltd., since 2000; Chief Executive, Core Solutions Group Ltd., since 2004; b. 15.4.58, Stirling; m., Fiona Swanson; 2 s.; 1 d. Educ. Stirling High School; Waid Academy, Anstruther; Edinburgh University; University of Pennsylvania. Senior President, Edinburgh University Students' Association, 1980-81; apprentice Solicitor, 1981-83; qualified Solicitor, 1983-84; Harkness Fellow, US, 1984-85; Member, Faculty of Advocates, since 1986; Standing Junior Counsel to Department of Transport in Scotland, 1991-94; Member, Judicial Studies Committee in Scotland, 1997-2004; Member, Training Faculty, Centre for Dispute Resolution, since 1999; accredited Mediator, since 1996; Member, Joint Standing Committee on Legal Education, 1988-2005; Member, Advisory Board, Centre for Professional Legal Practice, Dundee University, since 1998; Assessor, Scottish Higher Education Funding Council, 1995-96; Elder, Mayfield-Salisbury Parish Church, since 1991. Recreations: family; golf; contemporary music; ships and the sea. Address: (h.) 22 Fountainhall Road, Edinburgh EH9 2LW; T.-0131-667 8256; e-mail: John.Sturrock@core-solutions.com

Sturrock, Julia, OBE, MA. Local Government Councillor, Dundee, 1988-2007; Board Member, Scottish Natural Heritage; b. 19.4.52, Exeter; m., George; 1 s.; 1 d. Educ. Mount St. Mary's, Exeter; University of Dundee; Strathclyde University; Dundee College of Education. Administration jobs in radio and theatre, 1974-75; Secondary school teacher of English, 1976-96; Councillor in Dundee District Council, then Dundee City Council (posts of responsibility included convenerships with an environmental remit as well as four years as leader of the council), 1988-2007; Member, SEPA East Board, 1995-2004; Honorary Fellow of Institute of Wastes Management, 2002; Chair, IRRI (International Resources and Recycling Institute). Address: 44 Albany Terrace, Dundee DD3 6HS; T.-01382 225107; e-mail: juliesturrock@hotmail.com

Sturrock, Professor Roger Davidson, MB, BS, MRCS, MD, FRCPLond, FRCPGlas. McLeod/ARC Professor of Rheumatology, Glasgow University, since 1990; b. 20.10.46, Dundee; m., Helen; 3 d. Educ. Llanelli Boys' Grammar School; Queen Mary's School, Basingstoke; London University. Senior Lecturer and Hon. Consultant, Westminster Medical School, 1977-79; Senior Lecturer in Medicine and Hon. Consultant, Centre for Rheumatic Diseases, Glasgow Royal Infirmary, 1979-90; President, British Society for Rheumatology, 1996-98; Chair, Board of Trustees, Arthritis Research Campaign, 1999-2006. Recreations: hill-walking; music; choral singing. Address: (b.) Centre for Rheumatic Diseases, Medicine – Division of Immunology, Infection and Inflammation, Royal Infirmary, QEB Level 3, 10 Alexandra Parade, Glasgow G31 2ER; T.-0141-211 4687; e-mail: r.d.sturrock@clinmed.gla.ac.uk

Subak-Sharpe, Emeritus Professor John Herbert, CBE, FInstBiol, BSc, PhD, FRSE. Professor Emeritus, Glasgow University and Honorary Senior Research Fellow in Virology, since 1994; Professor of Virology, Glasgow University, 1968-94; Honorary Director, MRC Virology Unit, Institute of Virology, Glasgow, 1968-94; b. 14.2.24, Vienna; m., (1953) Barbara Naomi Morris; 2 s.; 1 d. Educ. Humanistisches Gymnasium, Vienna (escaped from Vienna to the UK by Kinder transport, 1939); Birmingham University. Assistant Lecturer, Glasgow University, 1954-56; Member, ARC scientific staff, AVRI Pirbright, 1956-61; Visiting Fellow, California Institute of Technology, 1961; Member, MRC Experimental Virus Research Unit scientific staff, Glasgow, 1961-68; Visiting Professor, NIH, Bethesda, 1967-68. Visiting Fellow, Clare Hall, Cambridge, 1986; elected Member (Past Chairman, Course and Workshops Committee), EMBO, since 1969; Trustee (former Secretary and Vice-President), Genetical Society, 1971-99; Member, Genetic Manipulation Advisory Group, 1976-80; Chairman, MRC Training Awards Panel, 1986-89; Member, Governing Body, West of Scotland Oncological Organisation, since 1974, and Governing Body, Animal Virus Research Institute, Pirbright, 1986-88; Member, Scientific Advisory Group of Equine Virology Research Foundation, 1987-98; Member, Medical Research Council Cell Biology and Disorders Board, 1988-92; Biochemical Society CIBA Medal and Prize, 1993. Recreations: travel; bridge. Address: (h.) 63 Kelvin Court, Glasgow G12 0AG; T.-0141-339 1863.

Suckling, Professor Colin James, OBE, BSc, PhD, DSc, CChem, FRSC, FRSA, FRCPS (Glasg), HonFRCS (Edin), FRSE. Freeland Professor of Chemistry, Strathclyde University, since 1984; b. 24.3.47, Birkenhead; m., Catherine Mary Faulkner; 2 s.; 1 d. Educ. Quarry Bank High School, Liverpool; Liverpool University. Lecturer, Department of Pure and Applied Chemistry, Strathclyde University, 1972; Royal Society Smith and Nephew Senior Research Fellow, 1980; Dean, Faculty of Science, 1992-96; Deputy Principal, 1996-98; Pro-Vice Principal, 1998-2000; Vice Principal, 2000-02; Convener, RSE Chemistry Committee, 1989-91; Member of Council, RSE, 1989-92;

Member, General Teaching Council, 1993-95; Member, Board: Systems Level Integration Ltd., 1998-2000, Lanarkshire Technology and Innovation Centre, 1998-2000; Governor, Bell College of Technology, 1999-2007; Member of Court, University of Paisley (West of Scotland); Chairman, West of Scotland Schools Symphony Orchestra Board; Chairman, Scottish Advisory Committee on Distinction Awards, 2003-05; Member, Joint Committee on Higher Surgical Training, 2003-05; Member, Senate of Surgery, 2003-05. Publications: Chemistry Through Models (Co-author), 1978; Biological Chemistry (Co-author), 1980; Enzyme Chemistry, Impact and Applications (Co-author), 1984, 1989, 1998; 200 research publications. Recreations: music; horn playing. Address: (b.) Department of Pure and Applied Chemistry, Strathclyde Universtiy, 295 Cathedral Street Glasgow, G1 1XL; T.-0141-548 2271; e-mail: c.j.suckling@strath.ac.uk

Suganuma, Kenichi, Consul-General. Consulate General of Japan in Edinburgh, since 2007; b. Ankara, Turkey; m.; 1 d.; 1 s. Educ. Faculty of Law, University of Tokyo; Graduate School of Arts and Sciences, Harvard University. Enterered Ministry of Foreign Affairs (MOFA), Japan, 1978; Japanese Delegation to OECD, Paris, 1981; Assistant Director, North East Asia Division, MOFA, 1983; Deputy Director, Human Rights and Refugees Division, MOFA, 1985; Senior Political Advisor, UN Good Offices Mission in Afghanistan and Pakistan (secondment to UN), 1988; First Secretary, Embassy of Japan in Belgium, 1989; Senior Advisor to the Director for Policy Planning in Charge of the 1993 Tokyo G7 Summit Meeting, 1992; Director for Non-Proliferation, Arms Control and Scientific Affairs Bureau, MOFA, 1993; Director for International Energy, Economic Affairs Bureau, MOFA and Member of IEA Board of Governors, 1995; Director of OECD Division, Economic Affairs Bureau, MOFA and Vice-Chair of the Negotiations for the Multilateral Agreement on Investment, 1997; Counsellor, Permanent Mission of Japan to the International Organizations in Vienna, 1998; Minister, Head of the Economic Department, Embassy of Japan in Russia, 2000; Minister and Deputy Head of Mission, Embassy of Japan in Singapore, 2003; Deputy Assistant Vice-Minister (Crisis Management), MOFA, 2005; Deputy Director-General, Consular Affairs Bureau and Deputy Director-General for Global Issues, International Cooperation Bureau, MOFA, 2006. Recreations: music; swimming. Address: 2 Melville Crescent, Edinburgh EH3 7HW; T.-0131 225 4777.

Sughrue, Cindy, PhD, BA (Hons). Executive Producer, Scottish Ballet, since 2004; Head of Dance, Scottish Arts Council, 2001-04; b. 30.3.63, Boston, USA. Educ. Sheffield University; Boston University. Freelance teacher, lecturer, performer, 1981-90; Director, Collective Gallery, 1990-94; General Manager, Dance Base (National Centre for Dance), 1994-97; Senior Performing Arts Officer, Scottish Arts Council, 1997-2001. Marshall Scholar, 1985-88; Ruth Michaelis-Jena Ratcliff Prize, special commendation, 1993. Recreations: hill-walking; attending dance/performing arts; travel. Address: (b.) Scottish Ballet, 261-268 West Princes Street, Glasgow G4 9EE; T.-0141-331-2931; e-mail: cindy.sughrue@scottishballet.co.uk

Summers, Alan Andrew, LLB, BCL. Advocate, since 1994; Standing Junior Counsel to Scottish Executive, 2000-05; b. 27.8.64, Bridge of Allan; m., Rosemary Helen Craig; 1 s.; 4 d. Educ. Grove Academy, Broughty Ferry; University of Dundee; St. Catherine's College, University of Oxford. Lecturer, Department of Scots Law, University of Edinburgh; Solicitor. Recreation: spending time with his family; reading. Address: (b.) Advocates Library, Parliament House, Edinburgh EH1 1RF; T.-0131-226 5071; e-mail: Alanandrewsummers@fsmail.net

Summers, John P., OBE, FREHIS, FCIWM. Chief Executive, Keep Scotland Beautiful, since 1999; b. 22.12.46, Rhynie; m., Alison; 1 s.; 1 d. Educ. Aberdeen Academy; Napier College, Edinburgh. Environmental Health Officer, Aberdeenshire, 1972-79; Depute Director of Environmental Health, Banff and Buchan District Council, 1979-90; Director of Environmental Health, Moray District Council, 1990-94, Chief Executive, 1994-96; Director of Technical Services, Moray Council, 1996-99. Chairman, Scottish Waste Awareness Group. Recreations: reading; Scottish traditional music. Address: (b.) Islay House, Livilands Lane, Stirling FK8 2BG; T.-01786 471333; e-mail: ksb@ksbscotland.org.uk

Sunter, Thomas Lacey Murray, DL. Deputy Lieutenant, Fife; b. 14.8.41, Liverpool; m., Margaret; 3 d. Educ. Merchant Taylors School, Crosby; Royal Naval College, Dartmouth. Royal Navy, 1960-96, including command of HMS Scylla, 1984-86 and HMS Endurance, 1987-89; UN Treaty Inspector, Antarctica, 1987-89; Ministry of Defence, 1989-91; Commander, RN Forces Hong Kong, 1991-94; Naval Base Commander, Rosyth, 1994-96; Chairman, Eden River Associates. Recreations: golf; tennis; reading. Address: (h.) Kirklands Cottage, Saline, Fife.

Sutherland, Countess of (Elizabeth Millicent Sutherland). Chief of Clan Sutherland; b. 30.3.21; m., Charles Noel Janson; 2 s.; 1 s. (deceased); 1 d. Educ. Queen's College, London; abroad. Land Army, 1939-41; Laboratory Technician, Raigmore Hospital, Inverness, and St. Thomas's Hospital, London, 1941-45. Address: (h.) Dunrobin Castle, Sutherland; House of Tongue, Lairg, Sutherland.

Sutherland of Houndwood, Lord (Stewart Ross), KT, FBA, PRSE, MA. President, David Hume Institute, since 2005; Hon. President, Alzheimer Scotland, since 2002; Chairman, Scottish Care, since 2002; Chairman, YTL Education (UK), since 2003; Pro-Chancellor, University of London, since 2006; Chairman, Associated Board of the Royal Schools of Music, since 2006; Member, Editorial Advisory Board, Encyclopedia Britannica, since 2005; President, Royal Society of Edinburgh, 2002-05; President, Saltire Society, 2002-05; Provost, Gresham College, London, since 2002; Chairman, QPA, 2002-05; Principal and Vice-Chancellor, Edinburgh University, 1994-2002; b. 25.2.41, Aberdeen; m., Sheena Robertson; 1 s.; 2 d. Educ. Woodside School; Robert Gordon's College; Aberdeen University; Cambridge University. Assistant Lecturer, Philosophy, UCNW, 1965-68; Lecturer, Senior Lecturer, Reader, Stirling University, 1968-77; Professor, Philosophy of Religion, King's College, London, 1977-90 (Vice-Principal, 1981-85, Principal, 1985-90); Vice-Chancellor, London University, 1990-94, and HM Chief Inspector of Schools (England), 1992-94; Visiting Fellow, Australian National University, 1974; Chairman, Brit. Acad. Postgraduate Studentships, 1987-94; Member: Council for Science and Technology, 1993-2000, Hong Kong University Grants Com., 1995-2003, Higher Education Funding Council, England, 1996-2002; Director, NHP, 2001-05; Editor, Religious Studies, 1984-90; Chairman: Royal Commission on the Funding of Long-Term Care of the Elderly, 1997-99, Secretary of State's Committee on Appeal Procedures, 1994-96, Royal Institute of Philosophy, 1988-2006; President, Society for Study of Theology, 1985, 1986. Publications: several books and papers. Recreations: jazz; theatre; rough gardening. Address: (b.) House of Lords, Westminster, London SW1A 0PW; e-mail: sutherlands@parliament.uk

Sutherland, Alan D.A., MA (Hons), MBA, MA. Chief Executive, Water Industry Commission for Scotland, since 2005; b. 8.4.62, Glasgow; m., Olga; 1 s.; 1 d. Educ. Eastwood High School; St Andrews University; University of Pennsylvania. Management trainee, Lloyds Bank PLC, 1984-85; Stockbroker, Savory Milln, 1985-86; Robert Fleming & Company, investment bank, 1986-91; Management Consultant, Bain & Company, 1992-97; Managing Director, Wolverine CIS Ltd., 1997-99; Water Industry Commissioner for Scotland, 1999-2005. Recreations: theatre; restaurants; history. Address: (b.) Water Industry Commission for Scotland, Ochil House, Springkerse Business Park, Stirling FK7 7XE; e-mail: enquiries@watercommission.co.uk

Sutherland, Colin T., BSc (Hons). Head Teacher, North Berwick High School, since 1999; b. 21.11.55, Glasgow; m., Anne; 2s. Educ. Paisley Grammar School; Glasgow University. Teacher, Garnock Academy, Kilbirnie, 1978-80; Teacher, Assistant Principal Teacher, Principal Teacher (Guidance), Castlehead High School, Paisley, 1980-90; Assistant Head Teacher, Greenock High School, 1991-94; Depute Head Teacher, Port Glasgow High School, 1994-99; Children's Panel, 1986-90; Member, Council, Headteachers' Association of Scotland, since 1999 and Executive, since 2001; Ambassador for Girl Guiding, since 2004. Recreations: family activity; reading; walking; cycling. Address: (b.) North Berwick High School, Grange Road, North Berwick, EH39 4QS; T.-01620 894661; e-mail: csutherland@northberwickhigh.elcschool.org.uk

Sutherland, David I.M., CBE, MA, MEd, DLitt, DUniv, DPhil, FCCEAM, FCMI, FRSA. Registrar, The General Teaching Council for Scotland, 1985-2001; b. 22.1.38, Wick; m., Janet H. Webster; 2 s. Educ. Aberdeen Grammar School; Aberdeen University; University of Zurich. Teacher of Modern Languages, Aberdeen Grammar School, 1962-66; Lecturer in Education, Stranmillis College of Education, Belfast, 1966-69; Lecturer in Educational Psychology, Craigie College of Education, Ayr, 1969-72; Assistant Director of Education, Sutherland County Council, 1972-75; Divisional Education Officer (Inverness), then Depute Director of Education, Highland Regional Council, 1975-85. Chair, Teacher Support Scotland; Trustee, Gordon Cook Foundation; Member, Planning Group, Scottish Forum for Professional Ethics. Recreations: golf; walking; theatre; reading. Address: Hazelwood, 5 Bonnington Road, Peebles EH45 9HF; T.-01721 722232.

Sutherland, Sheriff David Oman, MA, LLB. Sheriff, Wick, Dornoch, Stornoway, Inverness, since 2001; b. 24.8.50, Inverness; m., Jean Diana; 3 s.; 1 d. Educ. Morrisons Academy, Crieff; University of Edinburgh. Balfour and Manson, Edinburgh, 1973-76; Macneill and Critchley, Inverness, 1977-79; Sutherland and Co., Inverness, 1979-2001. Recreations: golf; reading. Address: Sheriff Court House, Bridge Street, Wick; T.-01955 602846.

Sutherland, Elizabeth (Elizabeth Margaret Marshall). Writer; b. 24.8.26, Kemback, Cupar; m., Rev. John D. Marshall; 2 s.; 1 d. Educ. St. Leonard's Girls' School, St. Andrews; Edinburgh University. Social Worker for Scottish Episcopal Church, 1974-80; Curator, Groam House Museum, Rosemarkie, 1982-93; author of: Lent Term (Constable Trophy), 1973, The Seer of Kintail, 1974, Hannah Hereafter (Scottish Arts Council Book Award), 1976, The Eye of God, 1977, The Weeping Tree, 1980, Ravens and Black Rain: The Story of Highland Second Sight, 1985, The Gold Key and The Green Life, 1986; In Search of the Picts, 1994; Guide to the Pictish Stones, 1997; Five Euphemias: Women in Medieval Scotland, 1999; Lydia, Wife of Hugh Miller of Cromarty, 2002; The Bird of

Truth, 2006. Recreations: Highland history; Gaelic folklore; the Picts. Address: (h.) 17 Mackenzie Terrace, Rosemarkie, Ross-shire IV10 8UH; T.-Fortrose 620924.

Sutherland, Ian Douglas, FRICS, MCIArb. Partner, D.M. Hall & Son, Chartered Surveyors, 1975-2005, Managing Partner, 1992-2001; b. 23.10.45, Colombo, Ceylon; m., Kathryn Wallace (deceased); 1 s.; 1 d; m., (2) Dr Linda Gilmore. Educ. St. Bees School, Cumberland. Joined D.M. Hall & Son as Trainee Surveyor, 1965. Member, Company of Merchants of the City of Edinburgh. Address: (h.) 9 Rhodes Park, North Berwick, East Lothian EH39 5NA; T.-01620 893406.

Sutherland, Lesley Anne Keith, MA (Hons), MEd (Hons), MPhil. Assistant Director (Learning, Policy and Strategy), Scottish Funding Councils for Further and Higher Education, since 2000; b. Falkirk. Educ. Falkirk High School; University of Glasgow. Teacher of English as a foreign language, Italy, 1973-74, 1976-78; Research Officer, National Union of Students, Scotland, 1978-83; Education Officer, Scottish Vocational Education Council, 1983-88; Regional Industrial Organiser, Education and Equalities, TGWU, 1988-2000. Member, Board, Centre for Scottish Public Policy; Lay Member, Employment Tribunal Scotland; Member, Management Committee, Engender. Recreations: reading; foreign travel and languages; music and singing.

Suttie, Alan John, FCMI. Chief Executive, Fife Society for the Blind, since 1987; b. 27.3.52, Bournemouth; m., Janet Mary; 1s. Educ. Kingsleigh School; Shoreditch College, University of London. Voluntary service overseas, India; Royal Commonwealth Society for the Blind, India; Royal National Institute for the Blind, Rehabilitation Programme Manager; Chairman, RNIB's Direct Services Committee. Recreations: hill walking; photography. Address: (b.) Fife Sensory Impairment Centre, Wilson Avenue, Kirkaldy; T.-01592 583272; e-mail: alansuttie@hotmail.com

Sventek, Professor Joseph Sherman, FRSE, FIET, SMIEEE, PhD, BA. Professor of Communication Systems, University of Glasgow, since 2002; b. 29.01.52, Corry, PA, USA; m., Virginia; 2 s. Educ. University of Rochester; University of California. Career History: Member of Technical Staff, Comp. Sci. Res. Dept., Lawrence Berkeley Laboratory; Deputy Chief Architect, ANSA Project; Chief Architect, Dist. Comp. Program, Hewlett-Packard; Distinguished Engineer, HP Laboratories; Director, Agilent Laboratories Scotland; Professor, Dept. of Computing Science, University of Glasgow. Member of UK Computing Research Committee; Member of Computer Science Subpanel of 2008 Research Assessment Exercise. Recreations: running; swimming; brass ensemble. Address: (b.) University of Glasgow, Department of Computing Science, Sir Alwyn Williams Building, Glasgow G12 8QQ; T.-0141 330-8078; e-mail: joe@dcs.gla.ac.uk

Swainson, Charles P., MBChB, FRCPE. Consultant Renal Physician, since 1981; Medical Director, NHS Lothian, since 1998; b. 18.5.48, Gloucester; m., Marie Irwin; 1 s. Educ. St. Edward's School, Cheltenham; Edinburgh University. Senior Lecturer, Christchurch, NZ, 1981-86; Consultant Physician, Royal Infirmary of Edinburgh, since 1986. Member, Lothian Children's Panel, 1987-95. Recreations: wine; golf; skiing. Address: (b.) NHS Lothian, 148 Pleasance, Edinburgh EH8 9RS.

Swan, Iain Ruairidh Cameron, MD, FRCS(Edin). Senior Lecturer in Otolaryngology, Glasgow University, since 1986; Consultant Otologist, MRC Institute of Hearing Research, since 1986; Honorary Consultant Otolaryngologist, Glasgow Royal Infirmary, since 1986; b. 19.5.52, Motherwell; m., Helen Buchanan; 1 s.; 1 d. Educ. Glasgow Academy; Glasgow University. SHO/Registrar,

Glasgow, 1978-81; Clinical Research Fellow, MRC Institute of Hearing Research, 1981; Senior Registrar in Otolaryngology, Glasgow, 1981-86; clinical attachment, University of Tubingen, 1984-85. Examiner, Final Fellowship, Royal College of Surgeons of Edinburgh and Royal College of Physicians and Surgeons, Glasgow. Recreations: bridge; opera; mountain biking. Address: (b.) Department of Otolaryngology, Royal Infirmary, Glasgow G31 2ER; T.-0141-211 4695; e-mail: iain@ihr.gla.ac.uk

Swanson, Alexander James Grenville, MB, ChB, FRCS Edin. Consultant Orthopaedic Surgeon, 1980-2001; Honorary Senior Lecturer, University of Dundee, since 2001; b. 18.10.41, Ecclefechan; 2 s. Educ. Dingwall Academy; St. Andrews University. Postgraduate training: St. Andrews, 1967-68, Edinburgh, 1968-69, Glasgow, 1969-70, Edinburgh, 1970-74, Dunfermline, 1974-75; Lecturer, then Senior Lecturer and Honorary Consultant, Dundee University, 1975-83. Recreations: downhill skiing; cross-country skiing; travel. Address: (h.) 9 Roxburgh Terrace, Dundee DD2 1NX.

Swanson, Carol Barbara, MA, MSc, PhD, MRTPI, MIFA, FSA, FSAScot. Manager, West of Scotland Archaeology Service, since 1996; b. 2.12.51, Thurso; m., Ian Johnson. Educ. Thurso High School; Edinburgh University; Strathclyde University. Planner: Lanark County Council, 1974-75, Strathclyde Regional Council, 1975-85; Regional Archaeologist, Strathclyde Regional Council, 1985-96. Address: (b.) West of Scotland Archaeology Service, 20 India Street, Glasgow G2 4PF; T.-0141-287 8334; e-mail: carol.swanson@wosas.glasgow.gov.uk

Swanson, Kenneth M., BSc, PhD, JP, DL. Farmer; Vice Lord Lieutenant, Caithness, 1996-2005; Assistant Director, Technology, Dounreay Nuclear Power Development Establishment, 1986-91; b. 14.2.30, Canisbay, Caithness; m., Elspeth J.W. Paton; 2 s.; 1 d. Educ. Wick High School; St. Andrews University. Flying Officer, Pilot, RAF, 1952; Lecturer in Physics, University of Wales, 1955; joined UKAEA, Dounreay, on Fast Reactors, 1958; appointed JP, 1970; DL, Caithness, 1977; Chairman, Caithness Jobs Commission, 1988-98; Director, Caithness and Sutherland Local Enterprise Company, 1990-99 (Vice-Chairman, 1994-99); Member, N.W. Board, Scottish Natural Heritage, 1992-99; author of papers and patents on the development of plutonium fuels for electricity production. Address: Knockglass, Westfield, Thurso; T.-0184 787 1201.

Swanston, Professor Michael Timothy, MA (Cantab), PhD. Professor of Psychology, University of Abertay Dundee, 1995-2008, now Professor Emeritus (Vice-Principal, 2002-08, Depute Principal, 2000-02, Head, School of Social and Health Sciences, 1995-2002); b. 6.6.47, Bristol; m., Georgina Mary; 1 s.; 2 d. Educ. Rugby School; Cambridge University (Pembroke College). Psychologist, Army Personnel Research Establishment, 1969-72; Lecturer in Psychology, Dundee Institute of Technology, 1972-84; Reader in Psychology, 1984-95; Honorary Research Fellow, Dundee university, since 1989. Vice-Chairman, Elmwood College Board of Management, 2000-07; Director, Dundee Ice Arena, 2000-02; Director, Dundee Sensation Science Centre, since 2007. Publications: one book; 50 papers. Recreations: golf; gardening. Address: (b.) University of Abertay Dundee, Bell Street, Dundee DD1 1HG; e-mail: m.t.swanston@abertay.ac.uk

Swapp, George David, OBE, DL, MA (Hons), DipEd. Deputy Lieutenant, Kincardineshire, 1990-2006; Member Aberdeenshire Council, 1995-2007; b. 25.5.31, Labuan; m., Eva Jane MacNab; 2 s.; 2 d. Educ. Mackie Academy,

Stonehaven; Aberdeen University. RAF Staff College, graduate and directing staff, 1965-68; Ministry of Defence (Training Policy), 1971-74 and 1978-80; promoted Wing Commander, 1971; Board Chairman, RAF Officer and Aircrew Selection Centre, 1974-78; Head, RAF Officer Training Establishment, Bracknell, 1980-83; retired from RAF, 1983. Former Member, Grampian Regional Council, 1986-96; President, Stonehaven Branch, Royal British Legion; founder Member, Stonehaven Heritage Society; Dunnottar Woodland Park Association; Church Elder. Recreations: hill-walking; local history; travel; geography; protection and enhancement of amenities and woodlands. Address: (h.) 9 Urie Crescent, Stonehaven AB39 2DY; T.-Stonehaven 764124.

Sweeney, Brian Philip, QFSM, MA, MIFireE, HonPhD, DipEFEng. Chief Officer and Chief Executive, Strathclyde Fire and Rescue, since 2004; b. 14.7.61, Glasgow; m., Pamela; 3 s. Educ. Holyrood Academy; University of Coventry; Glasgow Caledonian University. Former Surveyor; joined Strathclyde Fire Brigade, 1981; served in Glasgow and was promoted on three occasions, becoming Station Officer in 1989; promoted to Divisional Commander in 1998, then Director of Operations in 2000, then Deputy Chief in 2003. Member: Institution of Fire Engineers, Chief Fire Officers Association. Recreations: reading and music. Address: (b.) Brigade HQ, Bothwell Road, Lanarkshire ML3 0EA; T.-01698 338240; e-mail: brian.sweeney@strathclydefire.org

Sweeney, Sister Dorothea, SND, MA (Hons), BA(Soc) (Hons), PhD. Consultant and former Vice Principal, St. Andrew's College, 1985-96; b. Glasgow. Educ. Notre Dame High School, Glasgow; Glasgow University; Notre Dame College of Education; Bedford College and LSE, London University; Strathclyde University. Assistant Teacher of English, Our Lady & St. Francis Secondary School, Glasgow, 1960-63; entered Congregation of Sisters of Notre Dame, Sussex, 1963; Assistant Teacher of English, Notre Dame High School, Southwark, London, 1966-67; Notre Dame College of Education, Bearsden: Lecturer, Department of Psychology, 1970-76, Senior Lecturer, Department of Educational Science, 1976-80, Assistant Principal, 1980-85. Member, Board of Governors, St. Andrew's College, 1980-96; Member, CNAA Inservice Education Board, 1982-87, Committee for Teacher Education, 1987-89, and Committee for Scotland, 1990-92; Member, National Inter-College Committee for Educational Research, 1982-89; Convener, School Boards, Headteacher Training, Steering Committee, 1988-89; School Boards Members Training, 1989-90; Training Consultant, National Staff Development & Appraisal Training, 1991-92; Myers-Briggs Qualified Trainer, since 1990; part-time Counsellor, since 1968 (MBACP (Snr Accred); Sabbatical Semester, Weston Jesuit School of Theology, Cambridge, Massachusetts, 1998. Recreations: creative writing; dance; music; art; sport; drama; technology.

Sweeney, Irene Elizabeth. Retired Members' Secretary, UNISON Scotland; Chairperson, Scottish Pensioners Forum, since 2002; Member, Council, Scottish Civic Forum; b. 29.3.40, Edinburgh; m., Andrew Sweeney (deceased); 2 s.; 1 d. Educ. Tynecastle Secondary School, Edinburgh. St. Cuthbert's Co-op; Ethicon Ltd.; United Wire Ltd.; Dental Practice Board. Recreations: reading; walking; aquafit. Address: (h.) 46 Garnock Court, Irvine KA12 8EP; T.-01294 270736; e-mail: irene.sweeney1@btinternet.com

Sweeney, Jim. Chief Executive, YouthLink Scotland, since 2006; b. 5.6.53; m., Elizabeth; 2 s. Educ. Jordanhill (Diploma in Youth and Community Work); Strathclyde University (Masters Degree). Worked in local government in Lanark and Ayr, including Community Learning and Development Manager, North Lanarkshire, 1996-2006. Current appointments: Board member, John Wheatly College, member of Duke of Edinburgh Scottish Advisory Committee, Interim Standards Council CLD, LLUK panel member, Vice Chair of Young Scot and Scotland's Learning Partnership. Recreations: golf; bowling; reading; travel; cooking; music. Address: (b.) Rosebery House, 9 Haymarket Terrace, Edinburgh EH12 5EZ; T.-0131 313 2488; e-mail: jsweeney@youthlink.co.uk

Sweeney, William John, DRSAM, ARAM. Head of Department, Music, University of Glasgow, since 2005; Composer, since 1974; b. 05.01.50, Glasgow; m., Susannah Conway; 1 s.; 1 d. Educ. Knightswood Academy; RSAMD; RAM. Teacher of Clarinet and Woodwind, Central Region, 1975-85; Performer, 1973-95; Lecturer, University of Glasgow, since 1997. National Executive Committee, Musicians Union, 1989-2004; Chair of EC, 2003; Creative Scotland Award, 2005. Recreations: reading; walking. Address: (h.) 4 Stonefield Avenue, Glasgow G12 0JF; T.-0141-579-4789; e-mail: bsweeney@music.gla.ac.uk

Swinborn, Albert Victor, MA, MEd. Headteacher, Portlethen Academy, since 1997; b. 24.9.52, Aberdeen; m., Patricia. Educ. Aberdeen Grammar School; Aberdeen University. Teacher of English: Lossiemouth High School, Inverurie Academy; Principal Teacher of English, Hilton Academy; Assistant Headteacher/Depute Headteacher, Westhill Academy. Recreations: travel; Aberdeen FC; Burmese cats. Address: (b.) Portlethen Academy, Bruntland Road, Portlethen, Aberdeen AB12 4QL; T.-01224 782174.

Swinburne, John. MSP (SSCUP), Central Scotland, 2003-07; Director, Motherwell Football Club, since 1999; b. 4.7.30, Throop, USA; m., Moira Baird; 3 s.; 1 d. Educ. Dalziel High School, Motherwell. Engineer, 1947-77; freelance journalist, 1977-79; Commercial Manager, Motherwell Football Club, 1980-2003; Founder and Leader of the Scottish Senior Citizens Party and the first ever Member of Parliament in the UK representing pensioners. Author of three books on Motherwell F.C. Recreation: football. Address: (h.) Meikle Corsehill House, Stewarton KA3 5JH; T.-07881 856078.

Swingler, Robert James, MD, FRCP (Edin., Lond.) Leader, Clinical Neurosciences, Department of Neurology, NHS Tayside Acute Services Division, Ninewells Hospital and Medical School, Dundee; b. 4.7.56, London; 1 s.; 3 d. Educ. Wandsworth School; Guy's Hospital, University of London. Lecturer in Neurology, University of Edinburgh, 1987-90; Senior Registrar, Neurology, Dundee Royal Infirmary, 1990-95; MRC Travelling Fellow, Harvard University, 1992-93. Recreations: photography; cinema. Address: (b.) NHS Tayside Acute Services Division, Ninewells Hospital and Medical School, Dundee DD1 9SY; T.-01382 660111; e-mail: robert.swingler@nhs.net

Swinney, John Ramsay, MA (Hons). MSP (SNP), North Tayside, since 1999; Cabinet Secretary for Finance and Sustainable Growth, since 2007; Shadow Minister for Finance and Public Service Reform, Scottish Parliament, 2005-07; Leader, Scottish National Party, 2000-04; Leader of the Opposition, Scottish Parliament, 2000-04; MP (SNP), North Tayside, 1997-2001; b. 13.4.64, Edinburgh; m., Elizabeth Quigley; 1 s.; 1 d. Educ. Forrester High School, Edinburgh; Edinburgh University. Research Officer, Scottish Coal Project, 1987-88; Senior Managing Consultant, Development Options Ltd., 1998-92; Strategic Planning Principal, Scottish Amicable, 1992-97. SNP Treasury Spokesman, 1995-99; Deputy Leader, Scottish

National Party, 1998-2000; Shadow Minister for Enterprise and Lifelong Learning, 1999-2000. Convener, Enterprise and Lifelong Learning Committee (Scottish Parliament), 1999-2000; Convener, European and External Relations Committee, 2004-05. Recreation: hill-walking. Address: (b.) 35 Perth Street, Blairgowrie PH10 6DL; T.-01250 876576.

Swinson, Jo. MP (Liberal Democrat), Dunbartonshire East, since 2005; Liberal Democrat Shadow Women and Equalities Minister; Chair, Liberal Democrats' Campaign for Gender Balance; b. 5.2.80. Educ. Douglas Academy, Milngavie; London School of Economics. Address: (b.) House of Commons, London SW1A 0AA.

Swinton, Major General Sir John, KCVO, OBE, JP. Lord Lieutenant, Berwickshire, 1989-2000; Queen's Bodyguard for Scotland (Royal Company of Archers), since 1977 (Captain, 2003-07); President, Borders Branch, SSAFA, 1993-2006; Trustee, Scottish National War Memorial, since 1988 (Chairman, since 1995); President, Berwickshire Civic Society, 1996-2005 (Chairman, 1982-96); Chairman, Berwickshire Recreation Sports Trust, 1997-2005; Trustee, The Scots at War Trust, since 1996; Trustee, Berwick Military Tattoo, 1996-2007; Patron, POWER, since 1995; b. 21.4.25, London; m., Judith Balfour Killen; 3 s.; 1 d. Educ. Harrow School. Enlisted Scots Guards, 1943; commissioned, 1944; served NW Europe (twice wounded); Malaya, 1948-51 (Despatches); ADC to Field Marshal Sir William Slim, Governor General of Australia, 1953-54; Regimental Adjutant, Scots Guards, 1960-62; Adjutant, RMA, Sandhurst, 1962-64; comd. 2nd Bn., Scots Guards, 1966-68; Lt.-Col. commanding Scots Guards, 1970-71; Commander, 4th Guards Armoured Brigade, BAOR, 1972-73; Brigadier, Lowlands and Commander, Edinburgh and Glasgow Garrisons, 1975-76; GOC London District and Major General comd. Household Division, 1976-79. Honorary Colonel, 2nd Bn., 52nd Lowland Volunteers, 1983-90; President, Lowland TA & VRA, 1992-96; National Chairman, Royal British Legion Scotland, 1986-89; Coordinator for Scotland, Duke of Edinburgh's Award 25th Anniversary Appeal, 1980 (Honorary Liaison Officer for the Borders, 1983-85); Chairman, Roxburgh and Berwickshire Conservative Association, 1983-85; Chairman, Thirlestane Castle Trust, 1984-90; Trustee, Army Museums Ogilby Trust, 1978-91; Council Member, Commonwealth Ex-Services League, 1984-98; Member, Central Advisory Committee on War Pensions, 1986-89; Chairman, St. Abbs Head National Nature Reserve Joint Management Committee, 1991-98; President, Royal Highland and Agricultural Society of Scotland, 1993-94; President, Berwickshire Naturalists Club, 1996-97; Chairman, Scottish National Motorsport Collection, 1998-2001. Address: (h.) Kimmerghame, Duns, Berwickshire; T.-01361 883277; e-mail: kimmerghame@amserve.com

Swinton, Professor John, PhD, BD, RMN, RNMH. Professor in Practical Theology and Pastoral Care, Aberdeen University, since 1997; Honorary Professor, Centre for Advanced Nursing, Aberdeen University, since 1999; b. 20.10.57; m., Alison; 2 s.; 3 d. Educ. Summerhill Academy, Aberdeen; Aberdeen University. Registered nurse, 1976-90; Aberdeen University, 1990-97; Lecturer in Practical Theology, Glasgow University, 1997. Address: (b.) School of Divinity, Religious Studies and Philosophy, King's College, Old Aberdeen, Aberdeen AB24 3UB; T.-01224 273224.

Sykes, Diana Antoinette, MA (Hons). Director, Fife Contemporary Art & Craft (formerly Crawford Arts Centre), since 1988; b. 12.9.59, Stirling. Educ. Stirling High

School; University of St. Andrews; University of Manchester; Sweet Briar College, USA. Chair, Scottish Arts Council Exhibitions Panel, 1995-97; Member, St. Andrews Youth Theatre Board, 1991 2001; Chair, Management Committee, Mobile Projects Association Scotland, 1986-88. Recreations: travel; arts and museums and heritage. Address: (b.) FCA & C, The Town Hall, Queen's Gardens, St. Andrews KY16 9TA; T.-01334 474610; e-mail: diana.sykes@fcac.co.uk

Syme, Peter William, MA, DipAfrSts. Director, The Open University in Scotland, since 1997; b. 27.1.50, Brechin. Educ. Brechin High School; Trinity College, Glenalmond; Trinity College, Cambridge; Edinburgh University. VSO, Nigeria, 1972-74; Department of Education and Science, London, 1975-89, including Private Secretary to Sir James Hamilton, Permanent Secretary, 1979-80; seconded to Edinburgh University, 1983-85; Secretary to Review of University Grants Committee, 1985-87; Regional Director, Open University, London, 1990-97. Recreations: travel; photography; Africa. Address: (b.) The Open University in Scotland, 10 Drumsheugh Gardens, Edinburgh EH3 7QJ; T.-0131-226 3851.

Symington, Rev. Alastair Henderson, MA, BD. Minister, Old Parish Church of Troon, since 1998; Chaplain to The Queen in Scotland, since 1996; b. 15.4.47, Edinburgh; m., Eileen Margaret Jenkins; 2 d. Educ. Daniel Stewart's College, Edinburgh; Edinburgh University; Tubingen University, West Germany. Assistant Minister, Wellington Church, Glasgow, 1971-72; Chaplain, RAF, 1972-76; Minister: Craiglockhart Parish Church, Edinburgh, 1976-85, New Kilpatrick Parish Church, Bearsden, 1985-98. Convener, Committee on Chaplains to HM Forces, 1989-93; Vice-Convener, Board of Practice and Procedure, 2002-05; Convener, Committee on Presbytery Boundaries, 1999-2004; Contributor, Scottish Liturgical Review. Publications: Westminster Church Sermons, 1984; Reader's Digest Family Guide to the Bible (Co-author), 1985; For God's Sake, Ask!, 1993. Recreations: golf; rugby; music; France; wines. Address: 85 Bentinck Drive, Troon KA10 6HZ; T.-01292 313644; e-mail: revahs@tiscali.co.uk

T

Tait, A. Margaret, BSc. General Council Assessor on Court of University of Edinburgh; Member, St. Margaret's Chapel Guild, Edinburgh Castle; Member, Egyptology Scotland, Royal Caledonian Horticultural Society and Royal Horticultural Society; Member, British Federation of Women Graduates; Member, Resolutions Committee of International Federation of University Women, Geneva; Member, National Appeal Panel for Pharmaceutical List; Member, Lothian Pharmacy Practice Committee; b. 8.10.44, Edinburgh; m., J. Haldane Tait; 1 d. Educ. George Watson's Ladies' College, Edinburgh; Edinburgh University; Jordanhill College of Education. Former Teacher of Mathematics, Bellahouston Academy, Glasgow; former Member, Lothian Children's Panel; former Honorary Secretary, Scottish Association of Children's Panels; former Chairman, Dean House Children's Home, Edinburgh; Volunteer, Edinburgh Citizens' Advice Bureau; formerly Secretary of State's Nominee to General Teaching Council; former Member, Scottish Legal Aid Board; former Member, Lothian Health Council; former Vice Chairman, Lothian Healthy Volunteers and Student Research Modules Ethics Committee. Recreations: golf; horticulture; Spanish; playing bridge. Address: (h.) 6 Ravelston House Park, Edinburgh EH4 3LU; T.-0131-332 6795.

Tait, Elizabeth Joyce, CBE, FRSE, PhD, BSc, FRSA. Scientific Adviser, ESRC Innogen Centre, Edinburgh University, since 2007; Director, ESRC Innogen Centre, Edinburgh University, 2002-07; b. 19.02.38, Edinburgh; m., Dr. Alec Tait; 1 s.; 2 d. Educ. Glasgow High School for Girls; Glasgow University; Cambridge University. Career History: Lecturer, then Senior Lecturer, Technology Faculty, Open University; Professor, Environmental and Technology Management, University of Strathclyde; Deputy Director, Research and Advisory Services, Scottish Natural Heritage; Director, Scottish Universities Policy Research and Advice Centre (SUPRA), Edinburgh University. Member, Board of Directors, Scottish Stem Cell Network; Member, Governing Council, Roslin Institute; Member, Scottish Science Advisory Committee. Recreations: gardening; hill walking. Address: (b.) Innogen Centre, Old Surgeons Hall, High School Yards, Edinburgh EH1 1LZ; T.-0131 650 9174; e-mail: joyce.tait@ed.ac.uk

Tait, Stuart R., LLB (Hons), DipLP (Aberdeen). Partner, Dundas & Wilson CS LLP, since 1995; b. 22.8.63, Edinburgh; separated; 1 s.; 1 d. Educ. Fettes College, Edinburgh; Aberdeen University. Trained at Dundas & Wilson, 1986-88; Seconded to Linklaters & Paines, London, 1990-91. Member, Investment Property Forum. Recreations: swimming; cycling; curling; travel. Address: (b.) Saltire Court, 20 Castle Terrace, Edinburgh EH1 2EN; T.-0131-228 8000; e-mail: stuart.tait@dundas-wilson.com

Tait, Rev. Thomas William, BD, RAFVR (Rtd). Parish Minister, Rattray, Blairgowrie, 1972-97; Corps Chaplain, Air Training Corps (UK), since 2002; b. 11.11.31, Dunfermline; m., Irene Pope; 1 s.; 2 d. Educ. Dunfermline High School; St. Colm's College, Edinburgh; Edinburgh University; Christ's College, Aberdeen; Aberdeen University. HQ Staff, Boys' Brigade, 1954-61; Missionary, Church of Scotland, South Arabia, 1962-67; ordained and inducted, 1972; Member, Assembly Council, 1984-88; Chaplain, 2519 (Strathmore) Squadron, Air Training Corps, since 1974; Chaplain, Dundee and Central Scotland Wing, ATC, 1978-96; Principal Chaplain, Scotland and Northern Ireland, Air Training Corps, 1996-2002; awarded Defence Council Letter of Appreciation for Services to Air Cadet Organisation, 1999; Chairman, Blairgowrie Schools Council, 1975-89; Member, Perth and Kinross Health Council, 1980-91 (Chairman, 1984-91); Chairman, Tayside Health Council, 1992-98; Chairman, Blairgowrie and District Branch, Royal British Legion Scotland, 1992-97, and Chaplain, Angus and Perthshire Area, 1994-99; commissioned RAFVR, 1977 (retired Flt. Lt., 1988); Moderator, Dunkeld and Meigle Presbytery, 1978; awarded Lord Lieutenant's Certificate for Meritorious Service to ATC, 1985; Member, Secretary of State's Consultative Panel on Registration of Nursing Homes and Private Hospitals, 1993-97; Member, Tayside Health Board Quality Monitoring Team, 1993-98; Member, Scottish Office Nursing Homes Standards Steering Group, 1994-97; Member, Chaplain's Committee, Air Cadet Council (UK), since 1996; Member, CRAG (Clinical Research and Audit Group), 1997-98; Member, Multi Research Ethics Committee for Scotland, 1997-2001; Convener, Scottish Association of Health Councils, 1997-98; Member, Advocacy Team, State Hospital, Carstairs, since 1998; Member, Air Cadet Council, since 2002; Member, Air Cadet Organisation Management Board, since 2005. Recreations: encouraging others to work in voluntary organisations; swimming; reading; overseas travel. Address: 20 Cedar Avenue, Blairgowrie, Perthshire; T.-01250 874833.

Tallach, Rev James Ross, MB, ChB. Free Presbyterian Minister, Raasay, since 1983; Assistant Clerk of Synod, since 2005; b. Tighnabruaich, Argyll; m., Mairi McCuish Martin; 2 d. Educ. Nicolson Institute, Stornoway; Aberdeen University. House jobs in surgery, medicine and obstetrics, Inverness, Aberdeen, and Bellshill, 1967-69; Medical Missionary, Mbuma, Zimbabwe, 1969-76; training for ministry, 1976-80; ordained medical missionery, Mbuma, 1980-83. Moderator of Synod, 1996; Clerk to Foreign Mission Committee of F.P. Church, since 1989; Convener, Church Home, Inverness, since 2001; Convener, Training of Ministry Committee, since 2004. Recreations: gardening; walking. Address: Free Presbyterian Manse, Raasay, Kyle, Ross-shire IV40 8PB; T.-01478 660216; e-mail: james.tallach@homecall.co.uk

Tankel, Henry I., OBE, MD, FRCSEdin, FRCSGlas. Chairman, Glasgow Jewish Housing Association, 1996-2001; Surgeon, Southern General Hospital, Glasgow, 1962-91; b. 14.1.26, Glasgow; m., Judith Woolfson; 2 s.; 2 d. Educ. High School of Glasgow; Glasgow University. Fulbright Scholar, 1954-55; President, Glasgow Jewish Representative Council, 1974-77; Chairman, Glasgow Hospital Medical Services Committee, 1974-79; Board of Science and Education, 1978-81; President, United Synagogues of Scotland, 1978-85; Treasurer, Scottish Committee for Hospital Medical Services, 1978-91; Member, National Panel of Specialists, 1978-82 and 1987-91; invited to address General Assembly of Church of Scotland, 1984; Chairman, Scottish Joint Consultants Committee, 1989-92; Member, Scottish Health Service Advisory Council, 1989-93; Non-Executive Director, Southern General Hospital NHS Trust, 1993-97; Chairman, Glasgow Board of Jewish Education, 1985-90. Recreations: walking; making model boats. Address: (h.) 26 Dalziel Drive, Glasgow G41 4PU; T.-0141-423 5830.

Tannahill, Andrew James, MB, ChB, MSc, FFPH, FRCP (Edin, Glasg). Head of Evidence for Action/Consultant in Public Health Medicine, NHS Health Scotland, since 2005; Honorary Clinical Senior Lecturer, Public Health, Glasgow University, since 2001; b. 28.4.54, Inchinnan; m., Carol Elizabeth Fyfe. Educ. John Neilson Institution, Paisley; Glasgow University; Edinburgh University. Lecturer in Pathology, Glasgow University; Senior Registrar in Community Medicine, Lothian Health Board/Honorary

Clinical Tutor, Edinburgh University; Regional Specialist in Community Medicine, East Anglian Regional Health Authority/Associate Lecturer, Cambridge University; Senior Lecturer in Public Health Medicine, Glasgow University/Honorary Consultant in Public Health Medicine, Greater Glasgow Health Board; Chief Executive, Health Education Board for Scotland/Visiting Professor, Glasgow University/Honorary Senior Lecturer, Dundee University/Honorary Fellow, Edinburgh University; Consultant in Public Health Medicine, then Interim Director of Public Health, NHS Argyll and Clyde/Honorary Clinical Senior Lecturer, University of Glasgow. Publications: Health Promotion: Models and Values (Co-author); contributor to Health Promotion: Disciplines and Diversity, Scotland's Health and Health Services, and Debates and Dilemmas in Promoting Health; papers on health education, prevention and health promotion. Recreations: countryside and bird-watching; music; theatre; photography; digital imaging; painting; reading. Address: (b.) NHS Health Scotland, Clifton House, Clifton Place, Glasgow G3 7LS.

Tanner, Professor (Kathleen) Elizabeth, FREng, FBSE, MA, DPhil, FIMMM, FIMechE, CEng, CSci. Professor of the Mechanics of Materials and Structures, University of Glasgow, since 2007; Adjunct (Visiting) Professor of Biomechanics and Biomaterials, Lund University, Sweden, since 1998; b. 20.3.57, Farnham. Educ. Wycombe Abbey; Lady Margaret Hall, Oxford. University of London: Research Assistant, Department of Materials, Queen Mary College, 1983-88; Advanced Research Fellow, Queen Mary and Westfield College, 1988-93, Lecturer, Department of Materials and IRC in Biomedical Materials, 1993-95, Reader in Biomaterials and Biomechanics, Department of Materials and IRC in Biomedical Materials, 1995-98; Co-Head of the Biomechanics Laboratory, Department of Orthopaedics, Lund University, Sweden, 1998-2001; Dean of Engineering, Queen Mary and Westfield College, University of London, 1999-2000, Professor of Biomedical Materials, Department of Materials, 1998-2007. Founder Member and First President (2000), UK Society for Biomaterials; Secretary of European Society for Biomaterials, since 2005. Recreations: riding; tennis; cookery; dressmaking. Address: (b.) James Watt South Building, University of Glasgow, Glasgow G12 8QQ; T.- 0141 330 3733; e-mail: e.tanner@eng.gla.ac.uk

Tanner, Susanne Lesley Murning, LLB (Hons), DipLP, MCIArb. Advocate, since 2000; b. 29.10.74, Stirling; m., David Henderson Tanner; 1 s. Educ. George Watson's College, Edinburgh; Edinburgh University. Solicitor, Burness Solicitors, Edinburgh, 1997-99; devilling, 1999-2000. Tutor, Law of Evidence, Edinburgh University, 1996-99; External Tutor and Examiner, Planning Law, College of Estate Management, Reading, since 2000; Part-time Lecturer, Evidence and Delict, Napier University, since 2006; Member of the Merchant Company of Edinburgh, since 2004; Committee Member, Scottish Lawyers' European Group, since 1998. Address: (b.) Advocates' Library, Parliament House, Parliament Square, Edinburgh EH1 1RF; T.-0131 226 5071.
E-mail: susannetanner@hotmail.com

Tasker, Moira, MA (Hons), MSc. Director, The Cockburn Association (The Edinburgh Civic Trust), since 2006; b. 1976, Perth. Educ. Bell Baxter High School, Cupar, Fife; University of Edinburgh; Heriot-Watt University. Member, Cross Party Group on Architecture and The Built Environment of Scottish Parliament. Recreations: travel; Russian culture; cooking. Address: (b.) Trunk's Close, 55 High Street, Edinburgh; T.-0131 557 8686; e-mail: director@cockburnassociation.org.uk

Tate, Professor Austin, BA (Hons), PhD, CEng, FAAAI, FBCS, FBIS, FRSE. Director, AIAI (Artificial Intelligence Applications Institute), since 1985; Chair in Knowledge-Based Systems, Edinburgh University, since 1995; Chief

Technical Officer, I-C2 Systems Ltd.; b. 12.5.51, Knottingley, West Yorkshire; m., Margaret. Educ. King's School, Pontefract; Lancaster University; Edinburgh University. Address: (b.) AIAI, University of Edinburgh, Appleton Tower, Crichton Street, Edinburgh EH8 9LE; T.- 0131-650 2732.

Tavener, Alan, MA, ARCO, ARCM. Director of Music, Strathclyde University, since 1980; Artistic Director, Cappella Nova, since 1982; b. 22.4.57, Weston-Super-Mare; m., Rebecca Jane Gibson. Educ. City of Bath Boys' School; Brasenose College, Oxford. Conducted several world premieres of choral works and several CDs of early, romantic and contemporary music. Recreations: architecture; Italy; Scottish country dancing; food and drink. Address: (b.) Strathclyde University, Livingstone Tower, Richmond Street, Glasgow G1 1XH; T.-0141-548 3444.

Tavener, Rebecca Jane. Soprano; Co-Artistic Director and Manager, Cappella Nova; b. 3.5.58, Trowbridge; m., Alan Tavener. Co-founded Cappella Nova, 1982; Concert Manager, Glasgow University, 1983-89; Founder and Director, Chorus International, 1990-94; founded Canty (medieval vocal ensemble), 1998; launched new early music consortium for Scotland, 1998; launched own recording label, ROTA, 1998. Recreations: Italophilia; retail therapy; gourmandising; reading history books. Address: (h.) 172 Hyndland Road, Glasgow G12 9HZ; T.- (b.) 0141-552 0634; e-mail: rebecca@cappella-nova.com

Taylor, Rev. Baker Stephen Covington, BA (Hons), BBS, MA, MDiv. Minister, Kirk of St. Nicholas Uniting, Aberdeen (The City Church), since 2005; b. 1.12.58, Kountze, Texas, United States; m., The Rev. Gillian R. Trew. Educ. Temple High School; Temple College, Texas; University of Texas; Abilene Christian University; Austin Presbyterian Theological Seminary. Associate Minister, University Avenue Church of Christ, Austin, 1984-85; Lecturer, Abilene Christian University, 1986-89; Minister: Lee Green United Reformed Church, London, 1990-2005, Geddes Place United Reformed Church, Bexleyheath, Kent, 1990-94, Bromley United Reformed Church, Kent, 1994-2005. Chairperson, Friends of The Kirk of St. Nicholas; Governor, Robert Gordon's College; Honorary Chaplain, University of Aberdeen; Associate Member, Iona Community; Church Service Society; Scottish Church Society. Recreations: numismatics; vexillology; Gaelic studies; archaeology. Address: (h.) The Manse, 12 Louisville Avenue, Aberdeen AB15 4TX; T.-01224 314318; e-mail: minister@kirk-of-st-nicholas.org.uk

Taylor, Brian, MA (Hons). Political Editor, BBC Scotland; b. 9.1.55, Dundee; m., Pamela Moira Niven; 2 s. Educ. High School of Dundee; St. Andrews University. Reporter, Press and Journal, Aberdeen, 1977-80; Lobby Correspondent, Thomson Regional Newspapers, Westminster, 1980-85; Reporter, BBC Scotland, Glasgow, 1985-86; Co-Presenter, Left, Right and Centre, BBC Scotland, 1986-88; Political Correspondent, BBC Scotland, 1988-90. Publication: The Scottish Parliament, 1999; Scotland's Parliament: Triumph and Disaster, 2002. Recreations: golf; theatre. Address: (b.) BBC Scotland, Pacific Quay, Glasgow G51 1DA.

Taylor, Elizabeth (Liz) Dewar, MA (Hons). Journalist and Author; b. 25.4.31, Newport, Fife; m., Adam McNeill Taylor (deceased); 1 s.; 3 d. Educ. Morgan Academy, Dundee; Galashiels Academy; King's College, Aberdeen. Reporter, Edinburgh Evening Dispatch, 1954-56; freelance stringer, Bombay, 1960-65; freelance journalist and broadcaster, since 1971. Publications include: Living with Loss; Bringing Up Children On Your Own; Living Alone; The Writing Business; 20th Century Antiques; also 25 books as Elisabeth McNeill. Recreations: gardening; crossword puzzles; bridge; Scrabble; cinema; horse-racing. Address: (h.) Cairnhill, Newstead, Melrose TD6 9DX; T.-0189682 2972.

Taylor, Rev. Howard, BSc (Hons), BD (Hons), MTh. Chaplain, Heriot-Watt University, since 1998; Minister, St. David's Church, Knightswood, Glasgow, 1986-98; Visiting Lecturer in Christianity and Modern Science and Christianity and Contemporary Thought, International Christian College, since 1989; Lecturer in Moral and Social Philosophy, and Philosophy of Science and Religion, Heriot-Watt University; Visiting Lecturer (Western Religion, Philosophy and Science), Shanghai University of Finance and Economics; b. 6.6.44, Stockport; m., Eleanor Clark; 3 s. Educ. Gravesend Technical School, Kent; Nottingham University; Edinburgh University. Maths and Physics Teacher, Malawi University; Missionary in Malawi (minister of town and rural African churches, theological teacher, teacher of African languages to missionaries); Minister, Toward and Innellan Churches, Argyll. Creator, Philosophy of Science and Religion course, Heriot-Watt University (prize-winner for good courses in science and religion, Center for Theology and Natural Sciences, Berkeley, California). Publications: Faith Seeks Understanding, 1980; Pray Today 1982/83, 1982; In Christ All Things Hold Together; The Delusion of Unbelief in a Scientific Age; Faith and Understanding; The Uniqueness of Christ in a Pluralist World, 1994; Is the New Testament the Source of Anti-Semitism?,1994; Human Rights - Its Culture and Moral Confusions! Recreations: hill walking; reading; classical music. Address: (b.) Chaplaincy Centre, Heriot-Watt University, Edinburgh EH14 4AS; T.-0131-451 4508; e-mail: H.G.Taylor@ hw.ac.uk

Taylor, Rev. Ian, BSc, MA, LTh, DipEd. Lecturer on music and the arts, broadcaster, opera director; b. 12.10.32, Dundee; m., Joy Coupar, LRAM; 2 s.; 1 d. Educ. Dundee High School; St. Andrews University; Durham University; Sheffield University; Edinburgh University. Teacher, Mathematics Department, Dundee High School; Lecturer in Mathematics, Bretton Hall College of Education; Senior Lecturer in Education, College of Ripon and York St. John; Assistant Minister, St. Giles' Cathedral, Edinburgh; Minister, Abdie & Dunbog and Newburgh, 1983-97; Moderator, Presbytery of St. Andrews, 1995-96; Secretary, History of Education Society, 1968-73; extensive work in adult education (appreciation of music and the arts); Director, Summer Schools in Music, St. Andrews University; numerous courses for St. Andrews, Edinburgh, Cambridge and Hull Universities and WEA; has played principal roles in opera and operetta; Director, Gilbert and Sullivan Society of Edinburgh, 1979-87; Director, Tayside Opera, 1999; compiled Theatre Music Quiz series, Radio Tay; presented own operetta, My Dear Gilbert...My Dear Sullivan, BBC; Writer of revues and documentary plays with music, including Tragic Queen (Mary Queen of Scots), St. Giles' Cathedral, Edinburgh Festival Fringe, 1982, and John Knox (Church of Scotland Video); President, East Neuk of Fife Probus Club, 2007-08. Publications: How to Produce Concert Versions of Gilbert Sullivan; The Gilbert and Sullivan Quiz Book; The Opera Lover's Quiz Book. Address: Lundie Cottage, Arncroach, Fife KY10 2RN; T.-01333 720 222.

Taylor, James, BL (Edin), NP. Honorary Sheriff, Airdrie; Retired Solicitor, since 1986; b. 22.9.18, Haddington; m., Janette. Educ. Haddington Primary/ Macmerry Primary and Preston Lodge Secondary Schools; Edinburgh University. Apprentice Solicitor: Rattray & Stevenson, Solicitors,

Haddington, 1935-37, Drummond & Frazer, WS, Edinburgh, 1937-38; Qualified as Solicitor, Rattray & Stevenson, 1938-41; Solicitor: J. & A. Hastie, SSC, Edinburgh, 1941-45, Town Clerk's Department, City of Edinburgh, 1945-46; Depute Town Clerk, Burgh of Airdrie, 1946, Town Clerk, 1946-75. Assessor with Glasgow Magistrates' Court, 1975-86. Recreation: angling. Address: (h.) 38 Etive Drive, Airdrie, North Lanarkshire ML6 9QL; T.-01236-762307.

Taylor, James Alastair, BSc, LLB. Sheriff Principal of Glasgow and Strathkelvin at Glasgow; b. 21.2.51, Inverness; m., Lesley Macleod; 2 s. Educ. Nairn Academy; Aberdeen University. Apprenticed to Brander & Cruickshank, Advocates in Aberdeen, 1975-77; apprenticed to, Assistant with, Lefevre & Co., Advocates in Aberdeen, 1977-78; Assistant, later Partner, A.C. Morrison & Richards, Advocates in Aberdeen, 1978-87; Partner and latterly Head of Litigation Department, McGrigor Donald, 1988-98; attained rights of audience in Supreme Courts in Scotland, 1993; Sheriff of Lothian and Borders at Edinburgh, 1998; Sheriff of Glasgow and Strathkelvin, 1999-2005. Designated one of the sheriffs to hear commercial actions, 1999. Publications: International Intellectual Property Litigation (Contributor); Sentencing Practice (Contributor); Macphail's Sheriff Court Practice, 3rd Edn (Contributor). Recreations: golf; music; good food and wine. Address: (b.) 1 Carlton Place, Glasgow G5 9DA; e-mail: sheriffp.jtaylor@scotcourts.gov.uk

Taylor, James Bradley, OBE. Managing Director, Stewarton House Ltd.; Board Member: Scottish Ballet, since 2005, Scottish Public Pensions Agency, since 2007; Chair, Scotland's Lighthouse Museum, since 2005; IoD Faculty Member, since 2005; Board Member, Borders 1996 Company, since 2006; Board Member, Mull of Kintyre Seatours, since 2004; Nautical Assessor to the Court of Session, since 1996; Freeman of the City of London; High Constable of the Port of Leith; Fellow of the Royal Institute of Navigation; b. 12.8.45, Paisley; m., Elizabeth Sherwood. Educ. George Watson's College, Edinburgh; Britannia Royal Naval College; Defence School of Languages; Royal Naval College Greenwich; Royal College of Defence Studies. Chief Executive, Northern Lighthouse Board, 1993-2006; Community Councillor, Eddleston, 1999-2005. Royal Navy, 1963-93; commanded: HM Submarines Grampus, 1974-75; Orpheus, 1975-77; Spartan, 1980-82; HM Ship London, 1989-90; Chief of Staff, Submarine Flotilla, 1990-92; Member, Royal College of Defence Studies, 1992. Recreations: country sports; history; music and dance; classic cars; travel. Address: Stewarton House Limited, Eddleston, Peebles EH45 8PP.

Taylor, Rt. Rev. John Mitchell, MA. Bishop of Glasgow and Galloway, retired 1998; now Honorary Assistant Bishop, Glasgow and Galloway b. 23.5.32, Aberdeen; m., Edna Elizabeth Maitland; 1 s.; 1 d. Educ. Banff Academy; Aberdeen University; Theological College, Edinburgh. Curate, St. Margaret's, Aberdeen; Rector: Holy Cross, Knightswood, Glasgow, St. Ninian's, Pollokshields, Glasgow, St. John the Evangelist, Dumfries; Canon, St. Mary's Cathedral, Glasgow. Recreations: angling; hill-walking; sketching; music. Address: (h.) 10 St Georges, Castle Douglas DG7 1LN.

Taylor, Malcolm John, TD, MA (Hons), FRICS, ACIArb. Chartered Surveyor/Land Agent; Director, Bell Ingram; b. 21.11.61, Glasgow; m., Helen McKay; 2 s.; 1 d. Educ. Dumfries Academy; Aberdeen University. Chairman, RICS in Scotland, 2004-05. Recreations: field sports; music; natural history. Address: (b.) Bell Ingram, Manor Street, Forfar; T.-01307 462516.

Taylor, Margie, MSc, MBA, FDSRCSEd, FDSRCPS(Glasg), HonMFPHM. Formerly Consultant in Dental Public Health, NHS Lanarkshire; Chief Dental Officer, Scottish Government, 1994-2007; Honorary Senior Lecturer, Glasgow University; Dundee University; b. Edinburgh. Educ. James Gillespie's High School for Girls; Edinburgh University; Heriot-Watt University. Formerly Chief Administrative Dental Officer, Fife Health Board, and Honorary Senior Lecturer, St. Andrews University. Board Member, Health Scotland; Past President, Royal Odonto-Chirurgical Society of Scotland. Recreations: calligraphy; golfing (badly); cooking. Address: (b.) Scottish Government, Room IR.08, St. Andrew's House, Regent Road, Edinburgh EH1 3DG.

Taylor, Martin, MBE, DUniv (Paisley). Guitarist/ Composer, since 1972; b. 20.10.56, Harlow, Essex; m., Elizabeth Kirk; 2 s. Educ. Passmores Comprehensive School, Harlow. Self-taught guitarist (began playing aged four); became professional musician at 15, touring UK, Europe and USA, solo recording debut, 1978 (for Wave Records); toured world with Stephane Grappelli, 1979-90; recorded eight solo albums for Linn Records, 1990s, becoming biggest selling British jazz recording artist in the UK; became first British jazz artist to sign recording contract with Sony Jazz (Columbia) in over 30 years; currently tours the world as solo artist and records and composes music for television and film. Founder, Kirkmichael International Guitar Festival; Founder, Guitars for Schools Programme. Best Guitarist, British Jazz Awards, eleven times; Grammy nomination, 1987; Gold Badge of Merit, British Academy of Composers and Songwriters, 1999; Freedom of the City of London, 1998; received the BBC Radio 2 "Heart of Jazz" Award in recognition of his career in music, 2007; presented with a Lifetime Achievement Award from the North Wales Jazz Guitar Festival for his "Contributuion to Jazz Guitar Worldwide", 2007. Publication: Kiss and Tell (autobiography), 1999. Recreations: horse racing; horse drawn gypsy wagons; collects vintage and rare American guitars and mandolins.

Taylor, Rt. Rev. Maurice, STD. Bishop Emeritus of Galloway, since 2004; Bishop of Galloway, 1981-2004; b. 5.5.26, Hamilton. Educ. St. Aloysius College, Glasgow; Our Lady's High School, Motherwell; Pontifical Gregorian University, Rome. Royal Army Medical Corps, UK, India, Egypt, 1944-47; Assistant Priest: St. Bartholomew's, Coatbridge, 1951-52, St. Bernadette's, Motherwell, 1954-55; Lecturer, St. Peter's College, Cardross, 1955-65; Rector, Royal Scots College, Spain, 1965-74; Parish Priest, Our Lady of Lourdes, East Kilbride, 1974-81. Vice President, Progressio (formerly Catholic Institute for International Relations). Publications: The Scots College in Spain, 1971; Guatemala, A Bishop's Journey, 1991; El Salvador: Portrait of a Parish, 1992; Opening Our Lives to the Saviour (Co-author), 1995; Listening at the Foot of the Cross (Co-author), 1996; Being a Bishop in Scotland, 2006. Address: 41 Overmills Road, Ayr KA7 3LH; T.-01292-285865.

Taylor, Michael Thomas, MA, MEd. Rector, Dyce Academy, Aberdeen, since 1980; b. 17.2.47, Newcastle upon Tyne; m., Sheena Robertson; 1 s.; 2 d. Educ. Rutherford Grammar School, Newcastle upon Tyne; Trinity College, Cambridge; Aberdeen University. Teacher of Chemistry, Cannock Grammar School, 1969-75; Ellon Academy: Principal Teacher of Guidance, 1975-76, Assistant Head Teacher, 1977-78, Depute Rector, 1978-80. Secretary, Newmachar Community Council. Recreations: hill-walking; music; sailing. Address: (h.) Loch-An-Eilein, Newmachar, Aberdeenshire AB21 OUQ; T.-01651 862234.

Taylor, Peter Cranbourne, MA, CA. Chairman, Scottish National Blood Transfusion Association, since 1995; b. 11.8.38, Yeovil; m., Lois Mary; 1s.; 1d Educ. Edinburgh University. Chartered Accountant/Partner: Romanes and Munro, Edinburgh, 1964-74; Deloitte Haskins and Sells, 1974-90; Coopers and Lybrand, 1990-95. Member, Scottish Dental Practice Board, 1991-2001. Recreations: country pursuits. Address: (h.) Totleywells House, Winchburgh, West Lothian, EH52 6QJ; T.-0131-319 2155.

Taylor, Professor Samuel Sorby Brittain, BA, PhD, Officier dans l'Ordre des Palmes Academiques. Professor of French, St. Andrews University, 1977-95, now Professor Emeritus; b. 20.9.30, Dore and Totley, Derbyshire; m., Agnes McCreadie Ewan (deceased 2007); 2 d. Educ. High Storrs Grammar School, Sheffield; Birmingham University; Paris University. Royal Navy, 1956-58 (Sub Lt., RNVR); Personnel Research Officer, Dunlop Rubber Co. ("Sickness-Absence in Rubber Industry"), 1958-60; Institut et Musee Voltaire, Geneva, 1960-63; St. Andrews University: Lecturer, 1963, Reader, 1972, Professor, 1977, retired 1995; Chairman, National Council for Modern Languages, 1981-85; Member, Executive Committee, Complete Works of Voltaire, 1970-85; Project Leader, Inter-University French Language Teaching Research and Development Project, 1980-88; Director, Nuffield Foundation project ("Nuffield French for science students"), 1991-99; Chairman, Scottish Joint Working Party for Standard Grade in Modern Languages, 1982-84. Publications: definitive text of Voltaire's Works, 1974; definitive iconography of Voltaire, continuing. Recreations: athletics timekeeping; photography; Liberal Democrats; Franco-Scottish Society (editor, annual Bulletin). Address: (h.) 11 Irvine Crescent, St. Andrews KY16 8LG; T.-01334 472588; e-mail: ssbt@st-andrews.ac.uk

Taylor, Scott, BA (Hons) Marketing. Chief Executive, Glasgow City Marketing Bureau, since 2004; b. 20.06.62, Manchester; m., Carol; 1 s.; 1 d. Educ. Clayton High School; University of Strathclyde. Has been general manager of three Glasgow city centre hotels, as well as brand manager for two of Forte Hotels' brands; joined Greater Glasgow & Clyde Valley Tourist Board in 1998 as Director-Convention Bureau, later becoming Director of Marketing, encompassing both Leisure and Discretionary Business Tourism; took over as Acting Chief Executive in July 2004, leading the integration of GG & CVTB into the new VisitScotland structure in April 2005; set up Glasgow City Marketing Bureau (GCMB) during 2004-05. Council Director of Glasgow Chamber of Commerce, is on its Board of Management, is Chair of its Tourism Retail and Leisure Group and Chair of the Glasgow Strategic Major Events Forum; has previously held a number of directorships in Glasgow and is a member of the Marketing Society. Recreations: travelling; hill walking in Scotland. Address: (b.) Glasgow City Marketing Bureau, 11 George Square, Glasgow G2 1DY; T.-0141 566 0809; e-mail: scott.taylor@seeglasgow.com

Taylor, William James, QC (Scotland), QC (England and Wales), MA, LLB, FRSA. Advocate, since 1971; Barrister, since 1990; b. 13.9.44, Nairn. Educ. Robert Gordon's College, Aberdeen; Aberdeen University. Standing Junior Counsel to DHSS, 1978-79, to Foreign and Commonwealth Office, 1979-86; Temporary Sheriff, 1997-99; Member, Criminal Injuries Compensation Board, 1997-2000; Member, Scottish Criminal Cases Review Commission, 1999-2004. Parliamentary candidate (Labour), West Edinburgh, February and October, 1974; Lothian Regional Councillor, 1973-84 (Secretary, Labour Group); Chairman, COSLA Protective Services Committee; Part-time Sheriff;

Chairman, Scottish Opera. Recreations: the arts; sailing; skiing; Scottish mountains; restoring a garden. Address: (b.) Parliament House, Parliament Square, Edinburgh EH1 1RF; T.-0131-556 0101; e-mail: william.taylor@wanadoo.fr

Teasdale, Sir Graham Michael, KB, MB, BS, FRCP, FRCSEdin, FRCSGlas, FRCSLond, FACSHon, FMedSci, FRSE. Professor and Head, Department of Neurosurgery, Glasgow University, 1981-2003; Consultant Neurosurgeon, Institute of Neurological Sciences, Glasgow, 1975-2003; President, Society of British Neurological Surgeons, 2000-02; b. 23.9.40, Spennymoor; m.; 3 s.; 3 d. Educ. Johnston Grammar School, Durham; Durham University. Postgraduate clinical training, Newcastle-upon-Tyne, London and Birmingham, 1963-69; Assistant Lecturer in Anatomy, Glasgow University, 1969-71; specialist training in surgery and neurosurgery, Southern General Hospital, Glasgow, 1971-75; Senior Lecturer, then Reader in Neurosurgery, Glasgow University, 1975-81. President, International Neurotrauma Society, 1993-2000; Chairman, European Brain Injury Consortium, 1995-2003; President, Section of Clinical Neurosciences, Royal Society of Medicine, 1998-99; President, Royal College of Physicians and Surgeons of Glasgow; Chairman of Board, NHS Quality Improvement Scotland, 2006-10. Address: Duchal Road, Kilmacolm PA13 4AY.

Templeton, Professor Allan, MBChB, MD (Hons), FRCOG, FRCP, FMedSci, FRCPE. Professor of Obstetrics and Gynaecology, University of Aberdeen, since 1985; President, Royal College of Obstetricians and Gynaecologists, 2004-07; b. 28.6.46, Glasgow.; m., Gillian Penney; 3 s.; 1 d. Educ. Aberdeen Grammar School; University of Aberdeen. Junior hospital posts, Aberdeen Royal Infirmary; Lecturer then Senior Lecturer, University of Edinburgh. Former Member, Human Fertilisation and Embryology Authority. Publications: books and scientific papers on human infertility. Recreation: mountaineering. Address: (b.) Department of Obstetrics and Gynaecology, University of Aberdeen, Aberdeen Maternity Hospital, Foresterhill, Aberdeen AB25 2ZD; T.-01224 550590; e-mail: allan.templeton@abdn.ac.uk

Tennant, David. Actor; b. 18.4.71, Bathgate, Lothian. Educ. RSAMD. Acted with the 7:84 Theatre Company; Theatre includes: Touchstone in As You Like It (RSC), 1996, Romeo in Romeo and Juliet (RSC), 2000, Antipholus of Syracuse in Comedy of Errors (RSC), 2000, Jeff in The Lobby Hero (Donmar Warhouse and New Ambassadors), 2002 (nominated Best Actor Laurence Olivier Theatre Awards, 2003); Television incl: Casanova in Casanova 2005, The Doctor in Doctor Who, 2006 (tenth Doctor); Films incl: Bright Young Things, 2003, Harry Potter and the Goblet of Fire, 2005. Address: (b.) c/o Independent Talent Group, Oxford House, 76 Oxford Street, London W1D 1BS.

Terry, Nicholas Graham, BSc (Econ), MSocSci, MPhil. Vice-Principal (Planning and Resources), University of Abertay Dundee, since 2005; b. 18.2.53, Bishop Auckland; m., Marietta Diciacca. Educ. Marlowe Hall School; Universities of Hull, Birmingham and Bath. Management Trainee and Budget Controller with Black & Decker and Cummins Diesel Engine Company, 1969-75; Full-Time Student, 1975-81; various academic posts with the Universities of Northumbria and Edinburgh, 1981-2000; Head of Dundee Business School, 2000-04; Depute Principal (Planning and Resources), University of Abertay Dundee, 2004-05. Non-Executive Director of several companies, including University Spin-Outs and Advanced Management Programme in Scotland Ltd. Recreation: classic cars.

Address: (b.) Bell Street, Dundee DD1 1HG; T.-01382 308016; e-mail: n.terry@abertay.co.uk

Thewliss, James, BSc (Hons). Head Teacher, Harris Academy, Dundee, since 1997; b. 24.4.53, Motherwell; m., Ann White; 1 s.; 1 d. Educ. Dalziel High School, Motherwell; Glasgow University. Geography Teacher, Braidhurst High School, Motherwell, 1976 -85; Principal Teacher, Geography, Perth High School, 1986-89; Assistant Rector, Perth High School, 1989-91; Assistant Head Teacher, Carluke High School, 1991-93; Depute Rector, Wallace High School, Stirling, 1993-97. Vice Convener, General Teaching Council Scotland. Recreations: supporting Motherwell Football Club; football purist. Address: (b.) Harris Academy, Perth Road, Dundee, DD2 1NL; T.-01382 435700; james.thewliss@dundeecity.gov.uk

Thin, Andrew, BSc (Hons), MBA, DipM. Chairman, Scottish Natural Heritage, since 2006; b. 21.1.59, Edinburgh; m., Frances Elizabeth; 1 s.; 1 d. Educ. Glenalmond College; Edinburgh University. Director, James Thin Booksellers, 1985-89; Team Leader, Highlands and Islands Development Board, 1989-91; Chief Executive, Caithness and Sutherland Enterprise, 1991-95. Chairman, John Muir Trust, 1997-2003; Board Member, Crofters Commission, 2001-06; Convener, Cairngorms National Park Authority, 2003-06. Recreations: long-distance running; canoeing; hill-walking. Address: (h.) Wester Aucherflow, by Munlochy, Ross-shire IV8 8PQ; T.-01463 811632; e-mail: andrew@thin.freeserve.co.uk

Thin, David Ainslie, BSc. Chairman, James Thin Ltd., 1992-2002; b. 9.7.33, Edinburgh; m., Elspeth J.M. Scott; 1 s.; 2 d. Educ. Edinburgh Academy; Loretto School; Edinburgh University. James Thin Ltd., 1957-2002; President, Booksellers Association of GB and Ireland, 1976-78; Chairman, Book Tokens Ltd., 1987-95. Recreations: golf; travelling; reading. Address: (h.) Balfour House, 21/1 East Suffolk Park, Edinburgh EH16 5PN; T.-0131-667 2725.

Thomaneck, Professor Jurgen Karl Albert, JP, MEd, Drphil. Professor in German, Aberdeen University, 1992-2001; Aberdeen City Councillor, 1996-2003 (Convener, Education and Leisure Committee, 1999-2003); b. 12.6.41, Germany; m., Guinevere Ronald; 2 d. Educ. Universities of Kiel, Tubingen, Aberdeen. Lecturer in German, Aberdeen University, since 1968. Grampian Regional Councillor, 1984-96; President, Aberdeen Trades Council, 1982-2001; Convenor, Grampian Joint Police Board, 1995-98; Board Member, Grampian Enterprise Ltd., until 1995; President, KIMO UK, 1996-2003; author/editor of 10 books, 15 contributions to books, 30 articles in learned journals, all in German studies. Recreation: football. Address: (h.) 17 Elm Place, Aberdeen AB25 3SN.

Thomas, Professor Michael James, OBE, OM (Poland), BSc, MBA, DBA, FCIM, FMRS. Emeritus Professor of Marketing, Strathclyde University; President, Market Research Society, 1999-2004; b. 15.7.33, m.; 1 s.; 1 d. Educ. University College London; Indiana University. Metal Box Co. Ltd., London, 1957-60; Syracuse University Management School, 1960-71; Lancaster University, 1972-86; appointed Professor of Marketing, Strathclyde University, 1987. Former National Chairman, Chartered Institute of Marketing. Recreation: ornithology. Address: (h.) 40 Crichton Road, Rothesay, Isle of Bute PA20 9JT; e-mail: michael.thomas@Mi8.com

Thompson, Professor Alan Eric, MA (Hons), PhD, FRSA, FSA(Scot). Emeritus Professor of the Economics of Government, Heriot-Watt University; b. 16.9.24; m., Mary Heather Long; 3 s.; 1 d. Educ. Kingston-upon-Hull Grammar School; Edinburgh University. Edinburgh

University: Assistant in Political Economy, 1952-53; Lecturer in Economics, 1953-59 and 1964-71; Professor of the Economics of Government, Heriot-Watt University, 1972-87; Parliamentary Labour candidate, Galloway, 1950, 1951; MP (Labour), Dunfermline, 1959-64; Member, Royal Fine Art Commission for Scotland, 1975-80; Chairman, Northern Offshore Maritime Resources Study, 1974-83; Governor, Newbattle Abbey College, 1975-85 (Chairman, 1980-83); Member, Local Government Boundaries Commission for Scotland, 1975-80; Member, Scottish Council for Adult Education in HM Forces, 1973-2000; BBC National Governor for Scotland, 1975-79; Governor, Leith Nautical College, 1981-85; Trustee, Bell's Nautical Trust, 1981-85; Parliamentary Adviser, Scottish Pharmaceutical General Council, 1984-2000. Publications: Development of Economic Doctrine (Co-author), 1980; articles in academic journals. Address: (h.) 11 Upper Gray Street, Edinburgh EH9 1SN; T.-0131-667 2140.

Thompson, Bruce Kevin, MA. Headmaster, Strathallan School, since 2000; b. 14.11.59, Bath; m., Fabienne; 2d. Educ. Newcastle High School; New College, Oxford University. Cheltenham College: Assistant Master, 1983-94; Head of Classics, 1986-94; Assistant Housemaster, 1990-94; Depute Rector, Dollar Academy, 1994-2000; Governor, Craigclowan School. Recreations: coaching rugby; rowing; weight training; music; literature. Address: (b.) Strathallan School, Forgandenny, Perth, PH2 9EG; T.-01738 815000.

Thompson, Dave George, Dip in Consumer Affairs, MTSI. MSP (SNP), Highlands and Islands, since 2007; b. 20.9.49, Lossiemouth; m., Veronica; 1 s.; 3 d. Educ. Lossiemouth High Secondary. Trading Standards Officer (TSO), Banff Moray & Nairn CC, 1971-73; Assistant Chief TSO, Ross & Cromarty County Council, 1973-75; Chief TSO, Comhairle nan Eilean Siar, 1975-83; Depute Director of Trading Standards, Highland Regional Council, 1983-86, Director of Trading Standards, 1986-95; Director of Protective Services, Highland Council, 1995-2001. Member of Church of Scotland; Member of GMB. Recreations: DIY; golf; bridge; football; hillwalking. Address: (h.) Balnafettack Farm House, Leachkin Road, Inverness IV3 8NL; T.-01463 729235.
E-mail: dave.thompson.msp@scottishparliament.uk

Thompson, Edward Henry, OBE, FCCA, FCMA. Chairman, Scottish Retail Consortium, 1998-2006; Chairman, Dundee United FC, since 2002; b. 16.7.40, Glasgow; m., Cath; 1 s.; 1 d. Educ. Hyndland Senior Secondary School, Glasgow. Office Manager/Company Secretary, Duthie Shaw; joined Watson & Philip plc, 1963, joined Board of the company, 1976, appointed Joint Managing Director; left, 1991, to form new company (Morning Noon and Night Ltd.). Director of Scottish Premier League. Recreations: football; second home in Spain. Address: (h.) 15 Norrie Street, Broughty Ferry, Dundee DD5 2SD; T.-01382 833166.

Thompson, Francis George, IEng, FIET, LCGI, FSA (Scot). Author of books on Highland subjects; retired Senior Lecturer, Lews Castle College, Stornoway; Chairman, Lewis Museum Trust; b. 29.3.31, Stornoway; m., Margaret Elaine Pullar; 1 s.; 3 d. Educ. Nicolson Institute, Stornoway. From 1946: supply maintenance electrician, technical writer, assistant publicity manager, lecturer; has held various offices within An Comann Gaidhealach, including editorship of Sruth, bilingual newspaper, 1967-71; books include: Harris and Lewis, 1999; Harris Tweed, 1969; Highlands and Islands, 1974; Crofting Years, 1998; Shell Guide to Northern Scotland, 1987; The Western Isles,

1988; The Supernatural Highlands, 1998. Recreation: writing! Address: Am Fasgadh, 5 Rathad na Muilne, Stornoway, Lewis; T.-01851 703812.

Thompson, Simon, BA (Politics and Economics), MBA. Chief Executive, Chartered Institute of Bankers in Scotland, since 2007. Educ. University of Newcastle-upon-Tyne; University of Edinburgh. Lived and worked in Poland and the Czech Republic from 1994 to 2000, teaching and then managing a series of international education and training businesses; managed the International Accounting Education Standards Board (IAESB), an independent standards-setting board established by the International Federation of Accountants (IFAC), developing and promoting International Education Standards for Professional Accountants; previously worked for the Association of Chartered Certified Accountants (ACCA), establishing ACCA in 25 countries in Central & Eastern Europe, and leading a number of EU and other donor-funded accounting education and reform programmes. Address: (b.) The Chartered Institute of Bankers in Scotland, Drumsheugh House, 38b Drumsheugh Gardens, Edinburgh EH3 7SW; T.-0131 473 7777.

Thomson, Craig, BA (Hons), MPhil, EdD, DipRSA. Principal, Adam Smith College, since 2005; Chair, Scotland's Colleges International; b. 1.5.52, London; m., Carol; 1 s.; 1 d. Educ. Larbert High School; Heriot-Watt University; Bath University; Sheffield University. Teacher: Lochaber High School; Thurso High School; private training and research consultant in Kuwait and England. Address: (b.) Adam Smith College, St. Brycedale Avenue, Kirkcaldy, Fife KY1 1EX; T.-01592 268591.

Thomson, David Mark, BA. Artistic Director/Chief Executive, Royal Lyceum Theatre, Edinburgh, since 2003; b. 26.4.64, Bellshill; 1 s.; 1 d. Educ. Caldervale High School, Airdrie; Strathclyde University. Arts worker, Maryhill Arts Centre, Glasgow; Assistant Director, Theatre Royal, Stratford East, London; Assistant Director, Royal Shakespeare Company; Associate Director, Nottingham Playhouse; Artistic Director, Brunton Theatre, Musselburgh. Author of four professionally produced plays for theatre; Fringe First Award. Recreation: music. Address: (b.) Royal Lyceum Theatre, Grindlay Street, Edinburgh EH3 9AX; T.-0131 248 4800.

Thomson, Professor Derick S., MA (Aberdeen), BA (Cantab), DLitt (Univ. of Wales), DLitt (Univ. of Aberdeen), DLitt (Univ. of Glasgow), FRSE, FBA. Professor of Celtic, Glasgow University, 1963-91; b. 5.8.21, Stornoway; m., Carol Galbraith; 5 s.; 1 d. Educ. Nicolson Institute, Stornoway; Aberdeen University; Cambridge University; University College of North Wales, Bangor. Taught at Edinburgh, Glasgow and Aberdeen Universities before returning to Glasgow as Professor, 1963; Chairman, Gaelic Books Council, 1968-91; Honorary President: Scottish Gaelic Texts Society, Saltire Society, Scottish Poetry Library; former Member, Scottish Arts Council; first recipient, Ossian Prize, 1974; author of numerous books and articles, including An Introduction to Gaelic Poetry, The Companion to Gaelic Scotland, European Poetry in Gaelic and collections of Gaelic poetry, including collected poems Creachadh na Clarsaich and Meall Garbh/Rugged Mountain; Editor, Gairm, 1952-2002. Address: (h.) 15 Struan Road, Cathcart, Glasgow G44 3AT; T.-0141-637 3704.

Thomson, Derrick. Managing Director, STV (North) Ltd. (formerly Grampian Television), since 1999; b. 7.3.63, Aberdeen; m., Fiona; 1 d. Educ. Kirkwall Grammar School; Golspie High School. General trainee, Cinecosse Productions, 1979; moved to Grampian, 1981, as a trainee technician; joined Central TV, 1983; became sound supervisor on a variety of high-profile productions, including worldwide documentaries; started own production business, 1989; re-joined Grampian, 1992, rising to Production Executive; moved to Scottish TV during merger, 1997, running external resources for Scottish and Grampian. Recreations: fly fishing; flying; art; photography; travel. Address: (b.) STV (North) Ltd., Television Centre, Craigshaw Business Park, West Tullos, Aberdeen AB12 3QH; T.-01224 848848

Thomson, Sir (Frederick Douglas) David, Bt, BA. Chairman, Britannia Steam Ship Insurance Association Limited, since 1986 (Director, since 1965); Chairman, Through Transport Marine Mutual Assurance Association (Bermuda) Ltd., since 1983 (Director, since 1973); Chairman, S.A. Meacock & Co. Ltd., since 1996; Chairman, The Investment Company plc, since 2004; Member, Royal Company of Archers (Queen's Bodyguard for Scotland); b. 14.2.40, Edinburgh; 2 s.; 1 d. Educ. Eton; University College, Oxford. Recreations: shooting; skiing; tennis. Address: (h.) Holylee, Walkerburn, Peeblesshire; T.-01896 870673.

Thomson, George Buchanan, FCIBS; b. 10.1.24, Glasgow; m., Margaret R.H. Campbell. Educ. Eastwood Secondary School. Joined Union Bank of Scotland, 1940; War Service, 1942-46 with RAF (Navigator, Bomber Command); held various banking appointments, 1947-86; retired as Assistant General Manager (Branch Administration, West), Bank of Scotland; Past President, Institute of Bankers in Scotland; Director and Chairman, Association for the Relief of Incurables; Lately Hon. Treasurer, Scottish Civic Trust; former Convener, Board of Stewardship and Finance, Church of Scotland; Director, Ian Skelly Holdings Ltd., 1986-89; Director, Clydesdale Development Company, 1988-95; Moderator, Dumbarton Presbytery, Church of Scotland, 2000-01. Recreations: curling; bowling. Address: (h.) Kingswood, 26 Waverley Avenue, Helensburgh G84 7JU; T.-01436 672915.

Thomson, Rev. Iain Urquhart. Minister, Parish of Skene, since 1972; b. 13.12.45, Dundee; m., Christine Freeland; 1 s.; 2 d. Educ. Harris Academy, Dundee; Inverness Royal Academy; Aberdeen University; Christ's College, Aberdeen. Assistant Minister, Castlehill Church, Ayr, 1970-72. Clerk, Presbytery of Gordon, 1988-2000; Clerk and Treasurer, Synod of Grampian Trusts Committee, since 1993. Recreations: golf; theatre. Address: The Manse, Kirkton of Skene, Westhill, Aberdeenshire AB32 6LX; T.-01224 743277.

Thomson, Professor James Alick, MA, PhD. Professor of Psychology, Strathclyde University, since 2000, Head of Department of Psychology; b. 9.12.51, Inverness; m., Dana O'Dwyer; 1 d. Educ. Inverness Royal Academy; Edinburgh University. Research Scholar, Uppsala University, Sweden, 1973; Post-doctoral Fellow, University of Paris, 1977-78; Strathclyde University: Lecturer, 1979-91, Senior Lecturer, 1992-94, Reader, 1995-99. Publications: The Facts About Child Pedestrian Accidents, 1991; Child Development and the Aims of Road Safety Education (Co-Author), 1996; Child Safety: Problem and Prevention from Pre-School to Adolescence (Co-Author), 1996; Kerbcraft: A Manual for Road Safety Professionals, 1997; Studies in Perception and Action V (Co-Editor), 1999; Crossroads: Smart Strategies for Novice Pedestrians, 2005; 80 scientific articles and government reports. Recreations: rock climbing; hillwalking; mountaineering; photography; travel; Gaelic language and literature. Address: (b.) Department of Psychology, Strathclyde University, 40 George Street, Glasgow G1 1QE; T.-0141-548 2572; e-mail: j.a.thomson@strath.ac.uk

Thomson, James Henry McArthur, CIOH. Chief Executive, Bield Housing Association Limited, since 2003;

b. 25.07.53, Scotland. Educ. Lenzie Academy. Career History: Professional Trainee; Assistant Housing Manager; Regional Housing Manager; Regional Director; Director of Management Services; Director of Housing and Care Services. Address: (b.) 79 Hopetoun Street, Edinburgh; T.-0131 273 4000; e-mail: j.thomson@bield.co.uk

Thomson, Sir John Adam, GCMG; b. 27.4.27, Bieldside, Aberdeen; m., 1, Elizabeth Anne McClure (deceased); 3 s.; 1 d.; 2, Judith Ogden Bullitt. Educ. Aberdeen University; Trinity College, Cambridge. Joined Foreign Office, 1950; seconded to Cabinet Office as Chief of Assessment Staff, 1968-71; Minister and Deputy Permanent Representative, NATO, 1972; Head of UK Delegation, MBFR Exploratory Talks, Vienna, 1973; Assistant Under Secretary for Defence and Disarmament, 1973-76; British High Commissioner in India, 1977-82; British Permanent Representative and Ambassador to UN, 1982-87; Principal Director, 21st Century Trust, 1987-90; Director, ANZ Grindlays, 1987-96; International Adviser, ANZ Grindleys Bank, 1996-98; Chairman, Felmings Emerging Markets Investment Trust, 1990-97; Chairman, Minority Rights Group, 1991-99; Director's Visitor, Institute for Advanced Studies, Princeton, 1995-96. Trustee, National Museums of Scotland, 1990-99; Member, Council, International Institute of Strategic Studies, 1987-96; Trustee, Indian National Trust for Art and Cultural Heritage; Research Affiliate, MIT, Cambridge, Massachusetts. Recreations: hill-walking; tennis.

Thomson, Professor Joseph McGeachy, LLB, FRSE, FRSA, HonFSALS. Commissioner, Scottish Law Commission, since 2000; b. 6.5.48, Campbeltown. Educ. Keil School, Dumbarton; Edinburgh University. Lecturer in Law, Birmingham University, 1970-74; Lecturer in Laws, King's College, London, 1974-84; Professor of Law, Strathclyde University, 1984-90; Regius Professor of Law, Glasgow University, 1991-2005. Recreations: opera; ballet; food and wine. Address: (h.) 27 Howe Street, Edinburgh EH3 6TF; T.-0131 652 3870.

Thomson, Lesley Ann. Director, Liddell Thomson Management Consultants; b. 11.2.59, Glasgow. Vice-Chair, Board, Scottish Ballet; Chair, Board, Arches Theatre, Glasgow. Address: (b.) 225 West George Street, Glasgow G2 2ND; T.-0141-221 5775.

Thomson, Malcolm George, QC, LLB. Practice at Scottish Bar, since 1974; Temporary Judge, Court of Session, since 2002; b. 6.4.50, Edinburgh; m., Susan Gordon (m. dissolved); 2 d. Educ. Edinburgh Academy; Edinburgh University. Standing Junior Counsel, Department of Agriculture and Fisheries and Forestry Commission, 1982-87; QC (Scotland), 1987; called to the Bar, Lincoln's Inn, 1991; Chairman, National Health Service Tribunal, Scotland, 1995-2005; Member, Scottish Legal Aid Board, 1998-2006; Editor, Scots Law Times Reports, 1989-99; Scottish Case Editor, Current Law, since 1977. Recreations: sailing; skiing. Address: (h.)12 Succoth Avenue, Edinburgh EH12 6BT; T.-0131-337 4911.

Thomson, Professor Neil Campbell, MBChB, MD, FRCPGlas, FRCLond. Professor of Respiratory Medicine, Glasgow University, since 2001; Consultant Respiratory Physician, since 1982; b. 3.4.48, Kilmarnock; m., Lorna Jean; 2 s.; 1 d. Educ. Speir's School, Beith; Glasgow University. Junior hospital doctor, Glasgow teaching hospitals, 1972-80; Research Fellow, McMaster University, Hamilton, Ontario, 1980-81; Consultant Respiratory Physician, Western Infirmary, since 1982; Honorary Professor, Glasgow

University, 1996-2001; Chair, British Lung Foundation Scientific Committee, 2001-2004; Member, Committee on Safety of Medicine, 1999-2001. Publications: Asthma and COPD: Basic Mechanisms and Clinical Management, 2002; Manual of Asthma Management (2nd edition), 2001. Recreations: reading; hill-walking. Address: (b.) Department of Respiratory Medicine, Western Infirmary, Glasgow; T.-0141-211 3241.

Thomson, Sheriff Nigel Ernest Drummond, CBE, MA, LLB. Sheriff of Lothian and Borders, at Edinburgh, 1976-96; b. 19.6.26, Aberdeen; m., Snjolaug Magnusson; 1 s.; 1 d. Educ. George Watson's Boys' College; St. Andrews University; Edinburgh University. Called to Scottish Bar, 1953; appointed Sheriff at Hamilton, 1966; Member, Scottish Arts Council, 1978 (Chairman, Music Committee, 1979-84). Honorary President, Strathaven Arts Guild; Honorary President, Scottish Association for Counselling, 1986-89; Vice President, British Association for Counselling, 1992-2002; Chairman, Edinburgh Youth Orchestra Society, 1986-92; Convenor, Council for Music in Hospitals in Scotland, 1992-2001; Honorary Texas Ranger, 1994. Recreations: music; woodwork; golf. Address: (h.) 50 Grange Road, Edinburgh; T.-0131-667 2166.

Thomson, Paul William, BSc (Hons), PhD, DipEd. Rector, Jordanhill School, Glasgow, since 1997; b. 25.7.57, Glasgow; m., Dr. Mary Thomson; 2 s. Educ. Dollar Academy; University of Glasgow. Teacher of Physics, Boclair Academy, 1983-87; Principal Teacher of Physics, Chryston High School, 1987-90; Assistant Head Teacher, Vale of Leven Academy, 1990-94; Depute Head Teacher, Hermitage Academy, 1994-97. Member, Board, Scottish Examinations Board, 1990-98; Member, Board, Scottish Qualifications Authority, 1997-2000; Member, SQA Advisory Council, since 2003; Member, General Convocation, University of Strathclyde, since 1997. Winner, Becta 'ICT in Practice Leadership Award', 2006. Recreations: tennis; golf. Address: (b.) 45 Chamberlain Road, Glasgow G13 1SP; T.-0141-576 2500; e-mail: PThomson@jordanhill.glasgow.sch.uk

Thomson, Rev. Peter David, MA, BD. Minister, Comrie with Dundurn, 1978-2004; b. 4.11.41, St. Andrews; m., Margaret Celia Murray; 1 s.; 1 d. Educ. Dundee High School; Edinburgh University; Glasgow University; Tubingen University. Minister, Balmaclellan with Kells, 1968-78; Moderator, Kirkcudbright Presbytery, 1974-75; Convener, Nomination Committee, General Assembly, 1982-85. Chairman, New Galloway and Kells Community Council, 1976-78; Moderator, Perth Presbytery, 1988-89. Recreations: haphazardly pursued interests in photography, wildlife, music, theology, current affairs. Address: 34 Queen Street, Perth PH2 0EJ.

Thomson, Professor Richard Ian, MA, DipHistArt (Oxon), MA, PhD, FRSE. Watson Gordon Professor of Fine Art, Edinburgh University, since 1996; Director, Visual Arts Research Institute, Edinburgh, 1999-2004; Trustee, National Galleries of Scotland; b. 1.3.53, Tenterden; m., Belinda Jane Greaves; 2 s. Educ. Dragon School, Oxford; Shrewsbury School; St. Catherine's College, Oxford; Courtauld Institute of Art, London University. Lecturer/Senior Lecturer/Reader, Manchester University, 1977-96; Curator or Co-Curator of several exhibitions: The Private Degas, 1987, Camille Pissarro: Impressionist Landscape and Rural Labour, 1990, Monet to Matisse, 1994; Seurat and the Bathers, 1997; Theo van Gogh, 1999; Monet: the Seine and the Sea 1878-1883, 2003; Toulouse-Lautrec and Montmartre, 2005; Degas, Sickert, Toulouse-Lautrec, 2005. Publications: Toulouse-Lautrec, 1977;

Seurat, 1985; Degas: The Nudes, 1988; Edgar Degas: Waiting, 1995; Framing France (Editor), 1998; Soil and Stone (Co-Editor), 2003; The Troubled Republic. Visual Culture and Social Debate in France, 1889-1900, 2004. Recreations: jazz; gardening. Address: (b.) History of Art, School of Arts, Culture and Environment, University of Edinburgh, 20 Chambers Street, Edinburgh EH1 1JZ; T.-0131-650 4124.

Thomson, Roy Hendry, KStJ, DL, MA (Hons). Past President, Scottish Liberal Democrats; President, Mental Health Aberdeen; Chairman, Friends of Aberdeen University Library; Past Chairman, Kaleidoscope, Aberdeen International Children's Festival; b. 27.8.32, Aberdeen; m., Nancy; 3 d. Educ. Aberdeen Grammar School; Aberdeen University. National Service, Gordon Highlanders, 1955-57; personnel and market research, Rowntree & Co. Ltd., 1957-60; Chairman/Director, family motor business, until 1986; former Director, The Scottish Ballet (Chairman, 1983-87); former Member, City of Aberdeen District Council; Past President: Rotary Club of Aberdeen, Mountain Rescue Association, Aberdeen; former Chairman, Scottish Liberal Democrats; former Marketing Director, Aberdeen International Youth Festival. Recreations: skiing; hill-walking. Address: (h.) 19 Westhill Grange, Westhill, Aberdeenshire AB32 6QJ; T.-Aberdeen 743858; e-mail: royhthomson@aol.com

Thomson, S. Kenneth, MHSM, DipHSM. Chief Executive, Yorkhill NHS Trust, 1997-2000; Conductor, Glasgow Gaelic Musical Association, since 1983; Board Member, National Waiting Times Special Health Board; Lay Member, Employment Tribunals; Lay Member, Royal Pharmaceutical Society of GB Investigating Committee, since 2007; b. 20.8.49, Campbeltown; m., Valerie Ferguson; 1 s.; 1 d. Educ. Keil School, Dumbarton. Administrative trainee, Scottish Health Service; various administrative and management posts, Glasgow and West of Scotland; Chief Executive, Law Hospital NHS Trust, 1997-2000. National Mod Gold Medallist, 1979. Recreations: opera; Gaelic language and culture; theatre; The Archers; swimming; composing and arranging music. Address: (h.) 14 Cleveden Drive, Glasgow G12 0SE; T.-0141-334 7773.

Thomson, Sir Thomas James, Kt (1991), CBE (1983), OBE (1978), MB, ChB, FRCPGlas, FRCPLond, FRCPEdin, FRCPIre. Chairman, Greater Glasgow Health Board, 1987-93; Member, Court, University of Strathclyde, 1992-97; b. 8.4.23, Airdrie; m., Jessie Smith Shotbolt; 2 s.; 1 d. Educ. Airdrie Academy; Glasgow University. Lecturer, Department of Materia Medica, Glasgow University, 1953-61; Postgraduate Adviser to Glasgow Northern Hospitals, 1961-80; Honorary Secretary, RCPSGlas, 1965-73; Secretary, Specialist Advisory Committee for General Internal Medicine for UK, 1970-74; Chairman: Medico-Pharmaceutical Forum, 1978-80 (Chairman, Education Advisory Board, 1979-83); Conference of Royal Colleges and Faculties in Scotland, 1982-85, National Medical Consultative Committee for Scotland, 1982-87; President, RCPSGlas, 1982-84; Hon.FACP, 1983; Hon. LLD, Glasgow University, 1988; DUniv, Strathclyde University, 1997. Publications: Dilling's Pharmacology (Co-Editor); Gastroenterology - an integrated course. Address: (h.) 1 Varna Road, Glasgow G14 9NE.

Thomson, Walter Nigel Jamieson, LLB, NP, WS. Partner, Robson McLean W.S.; b. 5.3.44, Galashiels; m., Susan; 1 d.; 2 s. by pr. m. Educ. George Watson's College, Edinburgh; Edinburgh University. Apprentice, McNeill and Sime W. S., 1969-71; Partner, McNeill and Sime W. S. and Kilgour McNeill and Sime, 1971-89. Musical Director,

JUBILO, an Edinburgh choir. Recreations: music; walking. Address: (b.) 28 Abercromby Place, Edinburgh; T.-0131-556 0556; e-mail: wt@robson-mclean.co.uk

Thomson, William P. L., OBE, MA, MUniv, DipEd; b. 9.5.33, Newmilns; m., Elizabeth Watson; 1 s.; 3 d. Educ. Dundee High School; St. Andrews University. Teacher of History and Geography/Deputy Head Teacher, Anderson High School, Shetland, 1958-71; Rector, Kirkwall Grammar School, Orkney, 1971-91; Historian. Honorary Sheriff. Publications: The Little General and the Rousay Crofters, 1981; Kelp-Making in Orkney, 1983; History of Orkney, 1987; Lord Henry Sinclair's 1492 Rental of Orkney, 1996; New History of Orkney, 2001. Address: (h.) South Manse, Burray, Orkney KW17 2SS; T.-01856 731330.

Thorburn, David John, LLB, FCIBS. Executive Director UK, Clydesdale Bank PLC, since 2002; b. 9.1.58, Glasgow; m., Maureen; 1 d. Educ. Hamilton Academy; Glasgow University; Harvard Business School. Clydesdale Bank PLC, 1978-83; TSB Group PLC, 1984-93; Clydesdale Bank PLC, since 1993. President, Chartered Institute of Bankers in Scotland; Director, Scottish Financial Enterprise; Vice Chairman, CBI Scotland. Address: (b.) Clydesdale Bank Exchange, 20 Waterloo Street, Glasgow G2 6DB.

Thornhill, Professor Christopher John, BA, MA (Cantab), PhD. Professor of European Political Thought, University of Glasgow, since 2006; b. 08.06.66, Shipley, West Yorkshire; 1 s.; 1 d. Educ. Oakbank Grammar School, Keighley; Bradford College; Cambridge University. Lecturer: University of Sussex, 1993-95; King's College London, 1995-2003; Reader, King's College London, 2003-04, Professor, 2004-05. Publications include: Political Theory in Modern Germany, 1999; Karl Jaspers: Politics and Metaphysics, 2002; Niklas Luhmann's Theory of Politics and Law (Co-Author), 2003; German Political Philosophy: The Metaphysics of Law, 2006. Recreations: classical music; hill-walking; travel; cricket. Address: (b.) Department of Politics, Adam Smith Building, University of Glasgow G12 8RT; T.-0141 330 5076; e-mail: c.thornhill@lbss.gla.ac.uk

Thornton, Philip John Roger, WS, MA, DipALP, NP. Senior Partner, Russel and Aitken, Solicitors, since 2003; b. 28.7.47, Prestbury; m., Alexandra Janet Taylor; 2 d. Educ. Manchester Grammar School; Edinburgh University. Assistant Solicitor, Cuthbertson, Riddle and Graham, WS, 1972-73, Russel and Aitken, WS, 1973-75; Partner, Russel and Aitken, since 1975. Tutor, Edinburgh University; Examiner, Society of Messengers at Arms and Sheriff Officers; Secretary, Edinburgh Family Planning Trust. Recreations: family holidays; art history; hill-walking; cinema; football; tennis. Address: (b.) 27 Rutland Square, Edinburgh EH1 2BU; T.-0131 228 5500.

Thurso, 3rd Viscount Sir (John Archibald Sinclair), BT. MP (Liberal Democrat), Caithness, Sutherland and Easter Ross, since 2001; b. 10.9.53; m.; 2 s.; 1 d. Educ. Eton. Chairman, Scrabster Harbour, 1997-2001; Non-Executive Director: Lochdhu Hotels, since 1975 (Chairman, since 1995), Sinclair Family Trust, since 1976 (Chairman, since 1995), Thurso Fisheries, since 1979 (Chairman, since 1995); Ulbster Holdings, since 1994 (Chairman, since 1994), Mossimans Ltd., 1998-2002; President, Academy of Food and Wine Service, since 1998. Address: Thurso East Mains, Thurso.

Tiefenbrun, Ivor Sigmund, MBE. Executive Chairman, Linn Products Ltd., Glasgow; b. 18.3.46, Glasgow; m., Evelyn Stella Balarksy; 2 s.; 1 d. Educ. Strathbungo Senior Secondary School; Strathclyde University (Sixties dropout). Worked overseas, 1971-73; founded Linn Products, 1973.

Chairman, Federation of British Audio, 1983-87; Council Member, Design Council, 1995-98; Founder Member, Entrepreneurial Exchange; Honorary Fellow, Glasgow School of Art, since 1999; Scottish Entrepreneur of the Year, 2001. Appointed Visiting Professor at Strathclyde University by the Department of Design, Manufacture and Engineering Management, 2004. Recreations: thinking; music; reading; sailing. Address: (b.) Linn Products Ltd., Glasgow Road, Waterfoot, Eaglesham, Glasgow G76 0EQ; T.-0141-307 7777; e-mail: ivor@linn.co.uk

Timmins, Professor Graham, BA, MPhil, PhD. Professor of Politics, University of Stirling, since 2006; Head of Department, Department of Politics, since 2002; b. 22.10.62, Swinton, Manchester; m., Sabine; 2 d. Educ. Two Trees Secondary School; Tameside Technical College; Portsmouth Polytechnic; University of Glasgow. University of Huddersfield: Lecturer in Politics, 1991-94, Senior Lecturer in Politics, 1994-2000, Head of History, Politics and Modern Languages, 1997-2000; Senior Lecturer in Politics, University of Stirling, 2000-06. Publications: Russia and Europe in the Twenty-First Century: An Uneasy Partnership (Co-Editor), 2007. Recreations: cycling; walking; canoeing. Address: (b.) University of Stirling, Department of Politics, Stirling FK9 4LA; T.-01786 467 568; e-mail: graham.timmins@stir.ac.uk

Timms, Peter. Chairman, Caledonian MacBrayne, since 2006. Member, Argyll and the Islands Enterprise Board. Address: (b.) CalMac Ferries Ltd., Ferry Terminal, Gourock PA19 1QP.

Tims, Robert Andrew John, MA. Headmaster, St Leonards School, St Andrews, since 2003; b. 26.5.52, Surrey; m., Heidi Lehmann. Educ. Eton; Jesus, Cambridge. Assistant Master, Abbs Cross School, Hornchurch, 1974-78; Assistant Master, 1978, Head of Year, 1984, Undermaster, 1989, Housemaster, 1995, Senior Master, 2002, Malvern College. Recreations: reading; music. Address: (b.) Headmaster's House, St Leonards School, St Andrews KY16 9QJ; T.-01334 472126.

Titterington, Professor (Donald) Michael, BSc, PhD, DipMathStat, FRSE. Professor of Statistics, Glasgow University, since 1988; b. 20.11.45, Marple, Cheshire; m., Mary Hourie Philp; 1 s. Educ. High School of Stirling; Edinburgh University; Cambridge University. Lecturer, then Senior Lecturer, then Titular Professor, Department of Statistics, Glasgow University, 1972-88; visiting appointments: Princeton University, 1978, State University of New York, 1980, Wisconsin University, 1982, Australian National University, 1982, 1994, 1995; Associate Editor, Biometrika, 1979-85, Annals of Statistics, 1983-85 and 1995-96, Journal, American Statistical Association, 1986-88 and 1991-96, and IEEE Transactions on Pattern Analysis and Machine Intelligence, 1994-96; Joint Editor, Journal of the Royal Statistical Society, Series B, 1986-89, and Statistical Science, 1992-94; Editor, Biometrika, 1996-2007; Council Member, Royal Statistical Society, 1987-92; elected Fellow, Institute of Mathematical Statistics, 1986; elected Member, International Statistical Institute, 1991; Royal Statistical Society Guy Medal in Silver, 2006. Publications: Statistical Analysis of Finite Mixture Distributions (Co-author); many journal articles. Recreation: being a father. Address: (b.) Department of Statistics, Glasgow University, Glasgow, G12 8QQ; T.-0141-330 5022.

Todd, Rev. Andrew Stewart, MA, BD, DD. Minister, St. Machar's Cathedral, Old Aberdeen, 1967-93; Extra Chaplain to The Queen in Scotland, since 1996 (Chaplain-in-Ordinary, 1991-96); b. 26.5.26, Alloa; m., Janet Agnes Brown Smith; 2 s.; 2 d. Educ. High School of Stirling; Edinburgh University; Basel University. Assistant Minister,

St. Cuthbert's, Edinburgh, 1951-52; Minister: Symington, Lanarkshire, 1952; North Leith, 1960; Member, Church Hymnary Revision Comittee, 1963-73; Convener, General Assembly's Committee on Public Worship and Aids to Devotion, 1974-78; Moderator, Aberdeen Presbytery, 1980-81; Convener, Panel on Doctrine, 1990-95; Member, Church Hymnary Trust; awarded Honorary Doctorate, Aberdeen University, 1982; translator of three theological books from German into English; Honorary President, Church Service Society; Honorary President, Scottish Church Society. Recreations: music; gardening. Address: (h.) Fentoun House, 11 Bedford Place, Alloa FK10 1LJ; T.-01259 212737.

Todd, Professor Janet, MA, PhD. Professor of English Literature, University of Aberdeen, since 2005; Honorary Fellow, Lucy Cavendish College, Cambridge, since 1999; b. Llandrindod; m., Derek Hughes; 1 s.; 1 d. Educ. Dr Williams' School, Dolgellau; Newnham College, Cambridge; University of Florida. Lecturer in English, University of Cape Coast, 1964-67, University of Florida, 1969-71; Assistant Professor of English, University of Puerto Rico, 1972-74; Assistant, Associate, Full Professor of English, Rutgers University, 1974-83; Fellow in English, Sidney Sussex College, 1983-90; Chair in English, University of East Anglia, 1990-2000; Francis Hutcheson Professor of English Literature, Glasgow University, 2000-04. Publications: many books, most recently Mary Wollstonecraft: a revolutionary life, 2000; Rebel Daughters: Ireland in Conflict 1798, 2003; ed. Cambridge edition of Jane Austen, 2005-08; Cambridge Introduction to Jane Austen, 2006; Death and the Maidens, 2007. Address: (b.) Department of English, University of Aberdeen, Aberdeen AB24 3FX.

Toft, Anthony Douglas, CBE, BSc, MD, FRCPE, FRCPGlas, FRCPLond, FRCPI, FACP(Hon), FRACP(Hon), FRCSE, FRCPC(Hon), FRCGP(Hon), FFPM (Hon), FFAEM (Hon), FCPS Pakistan (Hon), FCPS Bangladesh (Hon), FAM Singapore (Hon), MAM Malaysia (Hon). Consultant Physician, Royal Infirmary, Edinburgh, since 1978; Physician to the Queen in Scotland, since 1996; Chief Medical Officer, Scottish Equitable Life Assurance, since 1987; President, British Thyroid Association, 1996-99; Chairman, Professional and Linguistic Assessment Board, 1999-2006; President, Royal College of Physicians of Edinburgh, 1991-94; b. 29.10.44, Perth; m., Maureen Darling; 1 s.; 1 d. Educ. Perth Academy; Edinburgh University. Chairman, Collegiate Members' Committee, Royal College of Physicians of Edinburgh, 1978; Vice-President, Royal College of Physicians, 1989-91; Chairman, Scottish Royal Colleges, 1992-94; Chairman, Joint Committee of Higher Medical Training, 1993-96; Member, Health Appointments Advisory Committee, 1994-2000. Recreations: golf; gardening. Address: (h.) 41 Hermitage Gardens, Edinburgh EH10 6AZ; T.-0131-447 2221; e-mail: toft41@hotmail.com

Togneri, Martin, MA (Hons), MBA. Director and Dean, Caledonian Business School, Glasgow Caledonian University, since 2007; b. 27.4.56, Stirling; m., Kathleen; 2 s. Educ. St. Modan's High School, Stirling; University of Glasgow; University of Strathclyde. Burroughs Machines Ltd., 1978-80; University of Glasgow, 1980-83; Accounts Commission, 1983-84; Scottish Development Agency/Scottish Enterprise, 1984-98; Cadence Design Systems Inc., 1998-2000; Chief Executive, Scottish Development International, 2000-07. Address: (b.) Cowcaddens Road, Glasgow G4 0BA; T.-0141-331 3129; e-mail: martin.togneri@gcal.ac.uk

Tolley, David Anthony, MB, BS (Lond), FRCS, FRCSEdin, FRCPEdin. Consultant Urological Surgeon, Western General Hospital, Edinburgh, since 1980; Honorary Senior Lecturer, Department of Surgery/Urology,

Edinburgh University, since 1980; Director, Scottish Lithotriptor Centre; Honorary Treasurer, RCSEd; formerly Director of Standards, Royal College of Surgeons, Edinburgh; formerly President, European Intrarenal Surgery Society, European Association Academic Urologists; b. 29.11.47, Warrington; m., Judith Anne Finn; 3 s.; 1 d. Educ. Manchester Grammar School; Kings College Hospital Medical School, London University. House Surgeon and Physician, Kings College Hospital; Lecturer in Human Morphology, Southampton University; Lecturer in Anatomy and Fulbright Fellow, University of Texas at Houston; Surgical Registrar, Hammersmith and Ealing Hospitals, London; Senior Surgical Registrar (Urology), Kings College Hospital, London; Senior Urological Registrar, Yorkshire Regional Training Scheme. Previously Member: MRC Working Party on Urological Cancer; MRC Working Party on Superficial Bladder Cancer; Editorial Board, British Journal of Urology; Council, British Association of Urological Surgeons; Standing Commitee on Postgraduate Education; Board, Minimal Access Therapy Training Unit Scotland; Education Committee, Royal College of Surgeons of Edinburgh; Member, Specialty Advisory Committee in Urology; former President, British Society for Endourology; Past Chairman, Scottish Urological Oncology Group; formerly Chairman, Specialty Advisory Board in Urology, Royal College of Surgeons of Edinburgh; former Member, Council, Royal College of Surgeons of Edinburgh; formerly Chairman, Section of Endourology, British Association of Urological Surgeons; Examiner, Intercollegiate Board in Urology; Member, Board, European Society for Urotechnology; Member, Editorial Board, Journal of Endourology; Member, Editorial Board, Hungarian Endourology; Honorary Member, Romanian Society for Endourology; Honorary Member, Romanian Urological Association; Editor, Surgeons' News; Chairman, Quincentenary Board, Royal College of Surgeons Edinburgh. Address: (b.) Murrayfield Hospital, Corstorphine Road, Edinburgh; T.-0131-334 0363.

Tolson, Jim, BSc (Hons) Computer Networking. MSP (Liberal Democrat), Dunfermline West, since 2007; Shadow Minister for Communities and Sport; b. 26.5.65, Kirkcaldy; m., Alison. Educ. Ballingry Junior High School; Napier University, Edinburgh. Fitter/Turner, 1981-2000; Member, Dunfermline District Council, 1992-96; Member, Fife Council, 1995-2007. Local Government and Communities Committee. Recreations: gardening; music; reading; travel; motoring. Address: (b.) Scottish Parliament, Edinburgh EH99 1SP; Constituency Office: 2nd Floor, 1 High Street, Dunfermline KY12 7DL; T.-01383 841700; e-mail: jim.tolson.msp@scottish.parliament.uk

Tombs, Sebastian Martineau, BArch, DipArch (Cantab), FRIAS, RIBA, MCIArb. First Chief Executive, Architecture and Design Scotland, 2005; Secretary/Chief Executive, Royal Incorporation of Architects in Scotland, 1995-2005; b. 11.10.49, Sussex; m., Eva Heirman; 4 s.; 2 d. Educ. Bryanston; Cambridge University. RMJM, Edinburgh, 1975-76; Roland Wedgwood, Edinburgh, 1976-77; Fountainbridge Housing Association, Edinburgh, 1977-78; Housing Corporation, 1978-81; Edinburgh District Council Housing Department, 1982-86; Depute Secretary, RIAS, 1986-94; Founder and first Secretary, Scottish Ecological Design Association, 1991-94, Chairman, 1994-97. Founder and first Chairman, Association of Planning Supervisors, 1995-97; Scottish Liberal Democrat candidate, Edinburgh North and Leith, Scottish Parliament elections, 1999 and 2003, and General Election, 2001. Recreations: choral music; doggerel; sketching; designing cartograms; cycled backwards 58 miles from Edinburgh to Glasgow, June 2005. Address: (b.) Architecture and Design Scotland, Bakehouse Close, 146 Canongate, Edinburgh EH8 8DD; T.-0131 556 6699; Fax: 0131 556 6633; e-mail: info@ads.org.uk

Tomkins, Professor Adam, LLB (UEA), LLM (Lond). John Millar Professor of Public Law, University of Glasgow, since 2003; b. 28.06.69, Newbury; m., Lauren J. Apfel; 2 s. Educ. Gillingham School, Dorset; University of East Anglia; London School of Economics. Career History: Lecturer in Law, King's College London; Fellow and Tutor in Law, St. Catherine's College, Oxford. Publications: Author of: "The Constitution After Scott", 1998; "Public Law", 2003; "Our Republican Constitution", 2005; "European Union Law", 2006; "British Government and The Constitution", 2007. Recreations: whisky; Arsenal FC. Address: (b.) School of Law, University of Glasgow, Glasgow G12 8QQ; T.-0141 330 4180; e-mail: a.tomkins@law.gla.ac.uk

Tomkins, Patrick Lindsay, QPM, BA (Hons), RCDS. HM Chief Inspector of Constabulary for Scotland, since 2007; b. 20.8.60, Folkestone; m., Susan; 1 s.; 1 d. Educ. Hastings Grammar School; King's College, London; Royal College of Defence Studies. Sussex Police, 1979; Chief Superintendent, Metropolitan Police, 1993; Commander, Metropolitan Police, 1997; Assistant Inspector of Constabulary, 1999; Chief Constable, Lothian and Borders Police, 2002-07. Recreations: fly fishing; cycling; reading. Address: (b.) 1st Floor West, St. Andrews House, Regent Road, Edinburgh EH1 3DG; T.-0131 244 5614.

Tomlinson, Professor Alan, MSc, PhD, DSc, FCOptom, FAAO. Professor of Vision Science, Glasgow Caledonian University, since 1992; b. 18.3.44, Bolton; partner, Professor Daphne McCulloch; 1 s. Educ. Lampton Grammar School, North London; Bradford University; Manchester University Institute of Science and Technology. Fellowship, British Optical Association, 1966; Registration, General Optical Council, 1966; Lecturer, Ophthalmic Optics: Bradford University, 1967-68; UMIST, 1968-77; Director, Clinical Research, Wesley Jesson Inc, Chicago, USA, 1977-79 and 1983-86; Professor of Optometry: Indiana University, 1980-83, Southern California College of Optometry, 1986-91; Council Member, General Optical Council, since 1999; Member, British Universities Committee of Optometry, since 1992, Chair, 1997-99; Council Member, College of Optometry (UK), 1994-98; Member, Advisory Committee, American Academy of Optometry, 1993-98. Publications: Complications of Contact Lens Wear, 1992. Recreations: tennis; running; theatre; music. Address: (b.) Department of Vision Science, Glasgow Caledonian University, City Campus, Glasgow, G4 0BA; T.-0141-331 3380.

Toner, Mary Catherine, BEd (Hons), DPSE. Chief Executive, Scottish Marriage Care, since 1998; b. 14.5.46, Shotts; widow; 2 s. Educ. St. Andrew's College; Jordanhill College. Primary School Teacher, Glasgow and Lanarkshire, 1984-91; Head Teacher, St. Anthony's Primary School, West Lothian, 1991-94; Education Officer, Lothian Region and West Lothian, 1994-98. Former Counsellor, Supervisor, Tutor, Scottish Marriage Care. Recreations: travelling; reading; gardening. Address: (b.) 72 Waterloo Street, Glasgow G2 7DA; T.-0141-222 2166.

Topping, Professor Barry H.V., BSc, PhD, CEng, CMath, CITP, MBCS, MICE, MIStructE, MIMechE, FIMA. Emeritus Professor of Computational Mechanics, School of Engineering and Physical Sciences, Heriot-Watt University, Edinburgh (formerly Professor); Director, Computational Technology Solutions, Stirlingshire; Honorary Professor, University of Pecs, Hungary; b. 14.2.52, Manchester. Educ. Bedford Modern School; City University, London. Lecturer

in Civil Engineering, Edinburgh University, 1978-88; Von-Humboldt Research Fellow, Stuttgart University, 1986-87; Senior Lecturer, Heriot-Watt University, 1988-89, Reader, 1989-90, Professor of Structural Engineering, 1990-95. Co-Editor, Computers and Structures; Co-Editor, Advances in Engineering Software. Address: (b.) Dun Eaglais, Station Brae, Kippen, Stirlingshire FK8 3DY.

Torphichen, 15th Lord (James Andrew Douglas Sandilands); b. 27.8.46; m.; 4 d. Address: Calder House, Mid Calder, West Lothian.

Torrance, Very Rev. Professor Iain Richard, TD, MA, BD, DPhil, DD, DTheol, LHD, CorrFRSE. Professor in Patristics and Christian Ethics (Emeritus), University of Aberdeen, since 2004; Master of Christ's College, Aberdeen, 2001-04; Moderator, General Assembly, Church of Scotland, 2003-04; a Chaplain to The Queen in Scotland, since 2001; Co-Editor, Scottish Journal of Theology, since 1982; b. 13.1.49, Aberdeen; m., Morag Ann MacHugh; 1 s.; 1 d. Educ. Edinburgh Academy; Monkton Combe School, Bath; Edinburgh University; St. Andrews University; Oriel College, Oxford University. Minister, Northmavine, Shetland, 1982-85; Lecturer in New Testament and Christian Ethics, Queen's College, Birmingham, 1985-89; Lecturer in New Testament and Patristics, Birmingham University, 1989-93; Aberdeen University: Lecturer, 1993-97, Senior Lecturer in Divinity, 1997-99, Professor in Patristics and Christian Ethics, (Personal Chair), 1999-2004, Head, Department of Divinity with Religious Studies, 2000-01; Dean, Faculty of Arts and Divinity, 2001-03; Chaplain to the Moderator of the General Assembly, 1976; Member, International Dialogue between the Orthodox and the Reformed Churches, since 1992; Member, General Assembly's Panel on Doctrine, 1993-2002; Member, Ethics Committee, Grampian Health Board, 1996-2000; Hon. Secretary, Aberdeen A.U.T., 1995-98, Hon. President, 1998-99; Secretary, Society for the Study of Christian Ethics, 1995-98; Judge, Templeton (UK) Awards, 1994-99; TA Chaplain, 1982-97; ACF Chaplain, 1996-2000; Member, Academie Internationale des Sciences Religieuses, since 1997; Convener, General Assembly's Committee on Chaplains to HM Forces, 1998-2002; Senate Assessor to Aberdeen University Court, 1999-2003; Member, Committee of Highland TAVRA, 1999-2004; Member, QAA's Benchmarking Panel for Degrees in Theology and Religious Studies, 1999-2000; Select Preacher, University of Oxford, 2004; Free Burgess of the Burgh of Aberdeen, 2004; Friend for Life Award 2004, Equality Network, Scotland; Honorary Doctor of Divinity (St Andrews 2005; Aberdeen 2005); Honorary Doctor of Theology (Debrecen, 2006); Honorary Doctor of Humane Letters (King Coll, TN, 2007); Corresponding Fellow, Royal Society of Edinburgh, 2007. Publications: Christology after Chalcedon, 1988; Human Genetics: a Christian perspective (Co-author), 1995; Ethics and the Military Community, 1998; To Glorify God: Essays on Modern Reformed Liturgy (Co-Author), 1999; Bioethics for the New Millennium (Editor), 2000. Recreations: historical Scottish culture (buildings, literature, art). Address: (h.) 17 St Bernard's Crescent, Edinburgh EH4 1NR; T.-0131-315-3746; e-mail: irt@abdn.ac.uk

Torrance, Very Rev. Professor Thomas Forsyth, MBE, MA, BD, DrTheol, DLitt, DD, DrTeol, DTheol, DSc, FBA, FRSE. Emeritus Professor, Edinburgh University, since 1979; b. 30.8.13, Chengdu, Sichuan, China; m., Margaret Edith Spear; 2 s.; 1 d. Educ. Canadian School, Chengdu, China; Bellshill Academy, Lanarkshire; Edinburgh University; Basel University; Oriel College, Oxford. Minister: Alyth Barony Parish Church, 1940-47; served as Church of Scotland Chaplain, 1943-45; Minister, Beechgrove Parish Church, Aberdeen, 1947-50; Edinburgh

University: Professor of Church History, 1950-52, Professor of Christian Dogmatics, 1952-79; Templeton Prize, 1978; Moderator, General Assembly of the Church of Scotland, 1976-77. Cross of St. Mark, First Class, 1970; Protopresbyter of Greek Orthodox Church (Hon.), 1973; President, Academie Internationale des Sciences Religieuses, 1972-81. Publications: The Doctrine of Grace in the Apostolic Fathers, 1949; Calvin's Doctrine of Man, 1949; Royal Priesthood, 1955; Kingdom and Church, 1956; The School of Faith, 1959; Conflict and Agreement in the Church, 1959; Karl Barth: An Introduction to his Early Theology, 1962; Theology in Reconstruction, 1965; Theological Science, 1969 (Collins Prize); Space, Time and Incarnation, 1969; God and Rationality, 1971; Theology in Reconciliation, 1975; Space, Time and Resurrection, 1976; The Ground and Grammar of Theology, 1980; Christian Theology and Scientific Culture, 1980; Divine and Contingent Order, 1981; Reality and Evangelical Theology, 1982; Juridical and Physical Law, 1982; The Mediation of Christ, 1983; Transformation and Convergence in the Frame of Knowledge, 1984; Reality and Scientific Theology, 1985; The Trinitarian Faith, 1988; The Hermeneutics of John Calvin, 1988; Karl Barth: Biblical and Evangelical Theologian, 1990; Trinitarian Perspectives, 1993; Preaching Christ Today, 1993; Divine Meaning, 1995; The Christian Doctrine of God, 1995; Scottish Theology, 1996; The Person of Jesus Christ, 2000; The Doctrine of Jesus Christ, 2002; Theological and Natural Science, 2002. Founding Editor of Scottish Journal of Theology. Recreations: formerly golf, squash, fishing; now walking. Address: (h.) 37 Braid Farm Road, Edinburgh EH10 6LE; T.-0131-447 3224.

Tosh, Murray, MA. MSP (Conservative), West of Scotland, 2003-07, South of Scotland, 1999-2003 (Deputy Presiding Officer, Scottish Parliament, 2001-07); b. 1.9.50, Ayr; m., Christine (deceased); 2 s.; 1 d. Educ. Kilmarnock Academy; Glasgow University; Jordanhill College of Education. Principal Teacher of History, Kilwinning Academy, 1977, Belmont Academy, Ayr, 1984; Councillor, Kyle and Carrick District Council, 1987-96 (Convener of Housing, 1992-96); Chairman, Central Ayrshire Conservative and Unionist Association, 1980-83, Ayr Conservative and Unionist Association, 1985-90. Recreations: hill-walking; reading; some sports (spectator only). Address: (h.) 24/4 Lochend Close, Edinburgh EH8 8BL.

Toth, Emeritus Professor Akos George, Dr. Jur., PhD. Professor of Law, Strathclyde University, 1984-2001; Jean Monnet Chair of European Law, 1991-2001; b. 9.2.36, Mezotur, Hungary; m., Sarah Kurucz. Educ. Budapest University; Szeged University; Exeter University. Strathclyde University: Lecturer in Law, 1971-76, Senior Lecturer, 1976-82, Reader, 1982-84; British Academy Research Readership, 1993-95. Publications: Legal Protection of Individuals in the European Communities, 1978; The Oxford Encyclopaedia of European Community Law: Vol. I: 1990, Vol. II: 2005. Recreations: travel; music; opera; theatre; swimming; walking. Address: (b.) Strathclyde University, Law School, Level 3, Lord Hope Building, 141 St. James Road, Glasgow G4 0LT; T.-0141-548 3594; e-mail: toth@strath.ac.uk

Totten, Sheriff William John, LLB (Hons). Sheriff of Glasgow and Strathkelvin, since 1999; b. 11.9.54, Paisley; m., Shirley Ann Morrison; 1 s. Educ. John Neilson Institute, Paisley; Glasgow University. Apprentice, Tindal, Oatts and Rodger, Solicitors, 1977-79; admitted as Solicitor, 1979; Procurator Fiscal Service, 1979-83; Assistant, then Partner, Beltrami and Co., 1983-88; admitted to Faculty of Advocates, 1989; Advocate Depute, 1993-96. Address: (b.) Glasgow

Sheriff Court, 1 Carlton Place, Glasgow; T.-0141-429 8888.

Towndrow, Morag Stirling, MA (Hons), MEd. Headteacher, Barrhead High School, since 2002; b. 22.6.50, Glasgow; m., Peter; 2 s. Educ. Penicuik High School; University of Glasgow; Jordanhill College. Assistant Principal Teacher: Guidance, Claremont High School, East Kilbride, 1974-77, English, Kirkintilloch High School, 1986-90; Boclair Academy, Bearsden: Principal Teacher, English, 1990-94, Assistant Headteacher, 1994-99; Deputy Headteacher, Woodfarm High School, 1999-2002. Recreations: family; literature; Isle of Arran. Address: (b.) Aurs Road, Barrhead G78 2SJ; T.-0141-577 2100; e-mail: towndrowm@barrhead.e-renfrew.sch.uk

Townley, Professor Barbara, BA, MSc, PhD. Professor, Chair of Management Science, St. Andrews University; Director, Institute for Capitalising on Creativity; b. 9.10.54, Manchester. Educ. Worsley Wardley Grammar School; Lancaster University; London School of Economics. Lecturer: Lancaster University, 1983-85, University of Warwick Business School, 1985-90; Professor, Faculty of Business, University of Alberta, Canada, 1990-2000; Chair of Management and Organization, Edinburgh University, 2000-05. Publications: author of two books and many articles on management, organisation, performance measurement. Currently researching the creative industries. Recreation: travel. Address: (b.) Management School, Gateway, North Haugh, University of St Andrews, St Andrews, Fife KY16 9SS; T.-01334 462200.

Trainer, Emeritus Professor James, MA, PhD, DLitt. Professor of German, Stirling University, 1969-97 (Emeritus) (Deputy Principal, 1973-78, 1981-87, 1989-92); b. 2.3.32; m., Barbara Herta Reinhard (deceased); 2 s.; 1 d. Educ. St. Andrews University; Free University of Berlin. Lecturer in German, St. Andrews University, 1958-67; Visiting Professor, Yale University, 1964-65; Visiting Scholar, University of California at Santa Barbara, 1989; Vice-Convener, SUCE, 1987-94; Convener, SUCE Modern Languages Panel, 1979-86; Member, Inter University and Polytechnic Council, since 1983; Member, Scottish Examination Board, 1975-82; Chairman, SED Postgraduate Awards Committee, since 1989; Member, UK Fulbright Committee, 1985-93; Trustee, National Library of Scotland, 1986-91; Chairman, Scottish Conference of University Teachers of German, 1978-80; Member, National Academic Audit Unit; Member, SHEFCO Quality Assessment Committee; Member Overseas Research Students Awards Committee, CVCP; Governor, Morrison's Academy, Crieff, 1994-98. Recreations: music; cricket; translating. Address: (h.) 5 Pathfoot Avenue, Bridge of Allan FK9 4SA; T.-01786 833422; e-mail: jt4@stirling.ac.uk

Trainor, Professor Richard Hughes, BA, MA, DPhil, FRHistS, AcSS, FRSA, FKC. Principal and Professor of Social History, King's College London, since 2004; b. 31.12.48, New Jersey; m., Dr. Marguerite Wright Dupree; 1 s.; 1 d. Educ. Calvert Hall High School, Maryland; Brown University; Princeton University; Merton and Nuffield Colleges, Oxford University. Junior Research Fellow, Wolfson College, Oxford, 1977-79; Lecturer, Balliol College, Oxford, 1978-79; Glasgow University: Lecturer in Economic History, 1979-89, Senior Lecturer in Economic and Social History, 1989-95, Director, Design and Implementation of Software in History Project, 1985-89, Professor of Social History, 1995-2000, Co-Director, Computers in Teaching Initiative Centre for History, 1989-2000, Dean of Social Sciences, 1992-96, Vice-Principal, 1996-2000, Senior Vice-Principal, 1999-2000; Vice-Chancellor and Professor of Social History, Greenwich

University, 2000-04. Honorary Fellow, Trinity College of Music, since 2003; Honorary Fellow, Merton College, Oxford, since 2004; Rhodes Scholar; Chair, Advisory Council, Institute of Historical Research, since 2004; Honorary Secretary, Economic History Society, 1998-2004; President, Universities UK, since 2007; Convener, Steering Group, Universities UK/DfES Review of Student Services, 2002; Member, US/UK Fulbright Commission, since 2003; Council Member, Arts and Humanities Research Council, since 2006; Joint Editor, Scottish Economic and Social History, 1989-94. Publications: Black Country Elites: the exercise of authority in an industrialised area 1830-1900, 1993; University, City and State: the University of Glasgow since 1870 (Joint Author), 2000. Recreations: parenting; observing politics; tennis. Address: (h.) 45 Mitre Road, Glasgow G14 9LE; T.-0207 848 3434.

Trew, Professor Arthur Stewart, BSc, PhD. Professor of Computational Science, University of Edinburgh, since 2006, Director of EPCC, since 1997; b. 20.10.57, Belfast, Northern Ireland; m., Lesley Margaret Trew (nee Smart); 1 s.; 1 d. Educ. Royal Belfast Academical Institution; University of Edinburgh. Computing Officer, University of Edinburgh, 1983-85; Lecturer, Department of Clinical Sciences, Glasgow, 1985-86; Research Fellow, Department of Physics, Edinburgh, 1986-90; Programme Manager, EPCC, 1990-94, Executive Director, EPCC, 1994-97, Deputy Director, NESC, since 2001. Director, UoE HPCx Ltd. Recreations: running; cycling; hill walking. Address: (b.) EPCC, University of Edinburgh, James Clerk Maxwell Building, King's Buildings, Mayfield Road, Edinburgh; T.-0131 650 5025; e-mail: a.s.trew@ed.ac.uk

Trewavas, Professor Anthony James, BSc, PhD, FRS, FRSE, FRSA, FWIF, Academia Europea. Professor, Institute of Cell and Molecular Biology, Edinburgh University, since 1990; b. 17.6.39, London; m., Valerie; 1 s.; 2 d. Educ. Roan Grammar School; University College, London. Lecturer/Reader, Edinburgh University; Visiting Professor, Universities of Michigan State, Calgary, California (Davis), Bonn, Illinois, North Carolina, National University of Mexico; University of Milan. Publications: 210 scientific papers; two books. Recreations: music (particularly choral); reading. Address: (h.) Old Schoolhouse, Croft Street, Penicuik EH26 9DH; e-mail: Trewavas@ed.ac.uk

Trickett, Dr. Anthony Robert Trickett, MBE, MRCS, LRCP, DL. Lord Lieutenant for Orkney since 2007; m. Practiced in several hospitals in Manchester, 1964-66; Anatomy at University of Manchester, 1966-67; General Practitioner in Pembroke in Dyfed, 1967-73; Hoy and Walls, 1973-2000. Honorary Medical Advisor of Longhope Lifeboat, since 1973, and since 1995 its Honorary Secretary. Chairman of the Longhope Lifeboat Museum Trust, since 2000; Divisional Medical Advisor; Member of the Medical and Survival Committee of the Royal National Lifeboat Institution (RNLI) and received the Institution's Silver Badge in 1994 and the Gold Badge in 2004. Trustee of the Hoy Trust since 1984, becoming its chairman in 1992; Trustee of the Pickaquoy Centre in Kirkwall, since 2003; Director of Orkney Enterprise, 2000-06; Director of the Gable End Theatre in Hoy and is chairman of the Hoy Half Marathon. Deputy Lieutenant of Orkney, 1999-2005; Vice Lord Lieutenant, 2005-07.

Trotter, Alexander Richard, OStJ, JP, FRSA. Lord Lieutenant of Berwickshire, since 2000; Chairman, Thirlestane Castle Trust, 1996-2007; b. 20.2.39, London; m., Julia Henrietta Greenwell; 3 s. Educ. Eton College; City of London Technical College. Royal Scots Greys, 1958-68; Member, Berwickshire County Council, 1969-75 (Chairman, Roads Committee, 1974-75); Manager, Charterhall Estate and Farm, since 1969; Chairman, Meadowhead Ltd. (formerly Mortonhall Park Ltd.), since 1974; Director, Timber Growers' GB Ltd., 1977-82; Vice

Chairman, Border Grain Ltd., 1989-2003; Council Member, Scottish Landowners' Federation, 1975-2004 (President, 1996-2001, Chairman, Land Use Committee, 1975-78, Convener, 1982-85); Member, Department of Agriculture Working Party on the Agricultural Holding (Scotland) Legislation, 1981-82; Member, Nature Conservancy Council, and Chairman, Scottish Committee, 1985-90; Member, UK Committee for Euro Year of the Environment, 1986-88; Member, Scottish Tourist Board Graded Holiday Parks Overseeing Committee, since 1993; Brigadier, Queen's Bodyguard for Scotland (Royal Company of Archers). Recreations: skiing; golf; shooting. Address: Charterhall, Duns, Berwickshire, TD11 3RE; T.-01890 840210; e-mail: alex@charterhall.net

Troup, Gillian Elizabeth (Gill), BA, MA (Hons), MSc, MBA, MCMI. Deputy Principal, University of the West of Scotland, since 2007; Head of Higher Education and Learner Support, Scottish Executive, 2004-07; b. 22.12.55, Edinburgh. Educ. High School of Dundee; University of Edinburgh; University of Aberdeen; Open University; Glasgow Caledonian University. Contract Researcher/Research Supervisor, Medical School, University of Dundee, 1981-84; Researcher, Scottish Community Education Council, 1984-85; Education and Welfare Adviser, Edinburgh University Students' Association, 1985-90; Director of Student Affairs, City of London Polytechnic (London Metropolitan University), 1990-93; Head of Student Services, Glasgow Caledonian University, 1993-2002; Head of Further and Adult Education, Scottish Executive, 2002-04. Chair, YouthScotland, 1999-2006. Address: (b.) University of the West of Scotland, High Street, Paisley PA1 2BE; T.-0141 848 3100. E-mail: gill.troup@uws.ac.uk

Truman, Donald Ernest Samuel, BA, PhD, FIBiol, CBiol. Higher Education Consultant; b. 23.10.36, Leicester; m., Kathleen Ramsay; 1 s.; 1 d. Educ. Wyggeston School, Leicester; Clare College, Cambridge. NATO Research Fellow, Wenner-Grenn Institute, Stockholm, 1962-63; MRC Epigenetics Research Group, Edinburgh, 1963-72; Lecturer, Department of Genetics, Edinburgh University, 1972-78; Senior Lecturer, 1978-89, Head of Department, 1984-89, Director of Biology Teaching Unit, 1985-89; Vice-Dean and Vice-Provost, Faculty of Science and Engineering, 1989-98; Assistant Principal, Edinburgh University, 1998-2002; Aneurin Bevan Memorial Fellow, Government of India, 1978; Chairman, Edinburgh Centre for Rural Research, 1993-2002; Member, Council, Scottish Agricultural College, 1995-2002; Director, Edinburgh Technopole Company Ltd., 1996-2002; Member, Board of Directors, Edinburgh Lifelong Learning Partnership, 1999-2002. Publications: The Biochemistry of Cytodifferentiation, 1974; Differentiation in Vitro (Joint Editor), 1982; Stability and Switching in Cellular Differentiation, 1982; Coordinated Regulation of Gene Expression, 1986. Recreations: gardening; books; birds. Address: (h.) 36 Ladysmith Road, Edinburgh EH9 3EU.

Truscott, Ian, QC, LLB (Hons), LLM, PhD. Advocate; Barrister; Visiting Professor of Law, Strathclyde University, since 1998; Part-time Chairman, Employment Tribunal (England and Wales), since 2002; b. 7.11.49, Perth; m., Julia; 4 s. Educ. Perth Academy; Edinburgh University; Leeds University; Strathclyde University. Solicitor, 1973-87; Advocate, since 1988; Barrister, since 1995; QC, since 1997. Address: (b.) Advocates' Library, Parliament Square, Edinburgh; T.-0131-260 5697.

Tucker, Derek Alan. Editor, Press and Journal, Aberdeen, since 1992; b. 31.10.53, Liverpool; 1 s.; 1 d. Educ. Quarry Bank High School, Liverpool; Municipal Grammar School, Wolverhampton. Reporter/Chief Reporter/News Editor/Deputy Editor, Express and Star, Wolverhampton,

1972-92. Member, Press Complaints Commission, 1995-97 and since 2006; Member, Code of Practice Committee, 2002-05; Chairman, Editors' Committee, Scottish Daily Newspaper Society, 2003-04. Recreations: golf; travel; watching any sport not involving horses. Address; (b.) Lang Stracht, Mastrick, Aberdeen; T.-01224 690222.

Tucker, Professor John Barry, BA, MA, PhD, FRSE. Professor Emeritus, University of St. Andrews, since 2006, Professor of Cell Biology, 1990-2006; b. 17.3.41, Arundel; m., Janet Stephen Murray; 2 s. Educ. Queen Elizabeth Grammar School, Atherstone; Peterhouse, Cambridge (State Scholar and Kitchener National Memorial Scholar). Fulbright Travel Scholar and Research Associate, Department of Zoology, Indiana University, 1966-68; SERC Research Fellow, Department of Zoology, Cambridge, 1968-69; Lecturer in Zoology, St. Andrews University, 1969-79 (Chairman, Zoology Department, 1982-84); Reader in Zoology, 1979-90. Member: SERC Advisory Group II, 1977-80, SERC Molecular Biology and Genetics Sub-committee, 1986-89, Editorial Board of Journal of Embryology and Experimental Morphology, 1979-88. Recreations: cycling; hill-walking; tennis; reluctant gardener. Address: (b.) School of Biology, Bute Building, University of St. Andrews, St. Andrews, Fife KY16 9TS; T.-01334 463560; e-mail: jbt@st-and.ac.uk

Tudhope, James Mackenzie, CB, BL; b. 11.2.27, Glasgow; m., Margaret W. Kirkwood; 2 s. Educ. Dunoon Grammar School; Glasgow University. Army Service, 1945-48; Solicitor, 1951; private legal practice, 1951-55; Procurator Fiscal Depute, 1955; Senior Procurator Fiscal Depute, 1962; Assistant Procurator Fiscal, Glasgow, 1968-70; Procurator Fiscal: Kilmarnock 1970-73, Dumbarton, 1973-76; Regional Procurator Fiscal: South Strathclyde, Dumfries and Galloway, 1976-80, Glasgow and Strathkelvin, 1980-87. Member, Council, Law Society of Scotland, 1983-86; Honorary Sheriff, Kilmarnock, since 1989. Recreations (include): serendipity; worrying. Address: (h.) Point House, Dundonald Road, Kilmarnock;T.-01563 523727.

Turley, Mark John, BSc (Hons), MBA, MCIOH. Director, Services for Communities, since 2006; Director of Housing, City of Edinburgh Council, since 1996; Executive Director of Housing, City of Edinburgh District Council, since 1993; b. 25.6.60, Dudley. Educ. High Arcal Grammar School, Sedgley; Leicester University. Sheffield City Council, 1981-91; Head of Tenant Services, York City Council, 1991-93. Recreations: playing violin and guitar; reading. Address: (b.) Level C5, Waverley Court, 4 East Market Street, Edinburgh EH8 8BG; T.-0131-529 7325.

Turmeau, Professor William Arthur, CBE, FRSE, Dr. h.c. (Edinburgh University), Doctor of Education (Napier University), BSc, PhD, CEng, FIMechE. Chairman, Scottish Environment Protection Agency, 1995-99; Principal and Vice-Chancellor, Napier University, 1982-94; b. 19.9.29, London; m., Margaret Moar Burnett; 1 d. Educ. Stromness Academy, Orkney; Edinburgh University; Moray House College of Education; Heriot-Watt University. Royal Signals, 1947-49; Research Engineer, Northern Electric Co. Ltd., Montreal, 1952-54; Mechanical Engineer, USAF, Goose Bay, Labrador, 1954-56; Contracts Manager, Godfrey Engineering Co. Ltd., Montreal, 1956-61; Lecturer, Bristo Technical Institute, Edinburgh, 1962-64; Napier College: Lecturer and Senior Lecturer, 1964-68, Head, Department of Mechanical Engineering, 1968-75, Assistant Principal and Dean, Faculty of Technology, 1975-82. Member, IMechE Academic Standards Committee; Vice Chairman, ASH (Scotland). Recreations: modern jazz; Leonardo da Vinci. Address: (h.) 132 Victoria Street,

Stromness, Orkney KW16 3BU; T.-01856 850500; e-mail: profwaturmeau@aol.com

Turnbull, Wilson Mark, DipArch, MLA (Penn), MBCS, RIBA, FRIAS, FLI. Principal, Mark Turnbull Landscape Architect; Chairman and Director, Turnbull Jeffrey Partnership, Landscape Architects, 1999-2001 (Principal, 1982-98); Chairman and Director, Envision, since 1999; b. 1.4.43, Edinburgh. Educ. George Watson's; Edinburgh College of Art; University of Pennsylvania. Assistant Professor of Architecture, University of Southern California, 1970-74; Partner, W.J. Cairns and Partners, Environmental Consultants, 1974-82; Partner, Design Innovations Research, 1976-81; Council Member, Cockburn Association (Edinburgh Civic Trust), 1986-95; Commissioner, Countryside Commission for Scotland, 1988-92; Commissioner, Royal Fine Art Commission for Scotland, 1996-2005; Chairman, Edinburgh Greenbelt Initiative, 1988-91; Director, Edinburgh Greenbelt Trust, since 1991, Vice-Chairman, 1993-2002. Awards: Andrew Grant Travel Scholarships; Edinburgh Corporation Medal for Civic Design; Faculty Medal, Department of Landscape Architecture, University of Pennsylvania; Fulbright Scholarship. Recreation: sailing. Address: (b.) Creag an Tuirc House, Balquhidder, Perthshire FK19 8NY; T.-01877 384 728.

Turner, Professor Charles Michael R., BSc, PhD. Professor of Parasitology, University of Glasgow, since 2004, Head of Infection and Immunity, since 2006; b. 04.12.58, Lapford, Devon; m., Judith; 2 d. Educ. Queen Elizabeth Comprehensive, Crediton, Devon; Kings College London. Beit Memorial Fellow, Glasgow, 1986-89, Royal Society Research Fellow, 1989-97, Leverhulme Research Fellow, 2005-06, Assistant Dean, 2001-04. Interests in tropical infectious diseases, particularly African sleeping sickness. Recreations: fishing; Partick Thistle. Address: (b.) Glasgow Biomedical Research Centre, 120 University Place, University of Glasgow, Glasgow G12 8TA; T.-0141 330 6629; e-mail: m.turner@bio.gla.ac.uk

Turner, John R., MA, HonMA, MusB, FRCO. Organist and Director of Music, Glasgow Cathedral, since 1965; Lecturer, Royal Scottish Academy of Music, 1965-2007; Organist, Strathclyde University, since 1965; b. Halifax. Educ. Rugby; Jesus College, Cambridge. Recreations: reading; travel. Address: (h.) Binchester, 1 Cathkin Road, Rutherglen, Glasgow G73 4SE; T.-0141-634 7775.

Turner, Professor Kenneth John, BSc, PhD. Professor of Computing Science, Stirling University, since 1987; b. 21.2.49, Glasgow; m., Elizabeth Mary Christina; 2 s. Educ. Hutchesons' Boys Grammar School; Glasgow University; Edinburgh University. Data Communications Designer, International Computers Ltd., 1974-76; Senior Systems Analyst, Central Regional Council, 1976-77; Data Communications Consultant, International Computers Ltd., 1977-87. Recreations: choral singing; craft work; sailing. Address: (b.) Department of Computing Science and Mathematics, Stirling University, Stirling, FK9 4LA; T.-01786 467423.

Turner, William John, MSc, BSc (Hons), ILTM. Dean, Paisley Business School, formerly Associate Dean; b. 18.8.50, Willenhall; m., Rosemary; 2 s. Educ. Wednesfield Grammar School; London Business School; University of Bristol. Market Researcher, Market Analyst, Tioxide Group (subsidiary of ICI), 1973-78; Lecturer, then Senior Lecturer, then Associate Dean, University of Paisley (previously Paisley College), 1978 onwards; Secondment to "Scottish Higher Education Funding Council", 1996-98,

Senior Assessor (responsible for quality assessments in Universities in a range of subject areas). Member of Scottish Baptist College Committee. Recreations: Queens Park Baptist Church, Glasgow - range of activities and responsibilities. Address: (b.) Paisley Business School, University of Paisley, High Street, Paisley PA1 2BE; T.-0141 848 3360; e-mail: john.turner@paisley.ac.uk

Turok, Professor Ivan Nicholas, BSc, MSc, PhD, MRTPI. Professor of Urban Economic Development, Director of Research, Department of Urban Studies, Glasgow University, since 1996; b. 7.8.56, Cape Town; m., Elizabeth; 1 s.; 3 d. Educ. William Ellis School, London; Bristol University. Lecturer, Glasgow University, 1984-87; Senior Lecturer and Professor, Strathclyde University, 1987-96. Publications: over 100 articles and books. Recreations: African development; cycling; current affairs; visiting cities. Address: (b.) 25 Bute Gardens, Glasgow G12 8RS; T.-0141-330 6274; e-mail: I.Turok@socsci.gla.ac.uk

Twaddle, Alison Mary, MA. General Secretary, Church of Scotland Guild, since 1998; b. 25.1.50, Anston; m., Laurence Twaddle; 1 s.; 2 d. Educ. Broadway Grammar School, Barnsley; St Andrews University. Health Service administrator; translator; Europe Secretary, Board of World Mission; Information Officer, Church of Scotland Guild. Address: (b.) 121 George Street, Edinburgh EH2 4YN; T.-0131-225 5722.

Tweeddale, 14th Marquis of (Charles David Montagu Hay); b. 6.8.47; succeeded to title, 2005.

Twist, Benjamin. Theatre Director, since 1985; b. 17.4.62, London; m., Margaret Corr. Educ. Crown Woods Comprehensive School; University of Edinburgh. Freelance Director of Theatre, Music Theatre and Opera throughout Scotland, UK, Europe, North America and New Zealand; Artistic Director of Contact Theatre, Manchester, 1994-98. Member, SAC Capital Committee, 1999-2003; Chair, Scottish Arts Council Capital Committee, since 2003; Member, Scottish Arts Council, since 2003; Chair: SAC Capital Committee, 2003-07, SAC Lottery Committee, since 2007; Member: SAC, 2003-07, Joint Board of SAC and Scottish Screen, since 2007. Address: (b.) 12 Manor Place, Edinburgh EH3 7DD; e-mail: ben.twist@blueyonder.co.uk

Twist (nee Eaves), Rev. Lily Pamela, BSc (Physics/Maths), BTh, PGCE. Chair, Synod of Methodist Church in Scotland, since 2007; b. 3.7.50, Liverpool. Educ. Bristol University; Chester University (Northern Ordination Course). Physics educator. Recreations: pianist; educational travel; crafts. Address: Methodist Church Centre, Scottish Churches House, Dunblane FK15 0AJ; T.-01786 820295; e-mail: meth@scottishchurcheshouse.org

Tyre, Colin Jack, QC, LLB, DESU. Advocate, since 1987; b. 17.4.56, Dunoon; m., Elaine Patricia Carlin; 1 s.; 2 d. Educ. Dunoon Grammar School; Edinburgh University; Universite d'Aix Marseille. Lecturer in Scots Law, Edinburgh University, 1980-83; Tax Editor, CCH Editions Ltd., Bicester, 1983-86; Standing Junior Counsel to Scottish Office Environment Department in planning matters, 1995-98; President, Council of Bars and Law Societies of Europe, 2007; Member, UK Delegation to CCBE, 1999-2004; Head of Delegation, 2004; Scottish Law Commissioner (part-time), since 2003. Publications: CCH Inheritance Tax Reporter; contributor to Stair Memorial Encyclopaedia; Tax for Litigation Lawyers (Co-Author). Recreations: orienteering; golf; mountain walking; popular music. Address: (b.) Advocates' Library, 1 Parliament Square, Edinburgh; T.-0131-226 5071.

U

Ulph, Professor David Tregear, MA, BLitt, FRSA, FEEA. Professor of Economics, University of St. Andrews, since 2006, Head of School of Economics & Finance, since 2006; b. 26.10.46, Belshill; m.; Elizabeth Margaret; 2 d. Educ. Hutchesons Boys Grammar School; University of Glasgow; University of Oxford. Lecturer in Economics: University of Stirling, 1971-77, University College London, 1977-82; Reader in Economics, University College London, 1982-84; Professor of Economics, University of Bristol, 1984-91, Head of Department of Economics, 1984-87; Professor of Economics, University College London, 1992-2001, Head of Department of Economics, 1992-97, Executive Director, ESRC Centre for Economic Learning and Social Evolution, 1997-2001; Chief Economist and Director of Analysis & Research, Inland Revenue, 2001-04; Chief Economist and Director of Analysis, HM Revenue & Customs, 2004-06. Member: Economic Affairs Committee, ESRC, 1986-88, Research Grants Board, ESRC, 1993-98, Council of European Economic Association, 1991-94, Council of Royal Economic Society, 1995-99; Member of Editorial Board: Review of Economic Studies, 1981-90, Journal of Industrial Economics, 1986-88, European Economic Review, 1991-95. Recreations: bridge; cinema; travel; cooking. Address: (h.) Sealladh Mor, Bankhead Courtyard, Bankhead Farm, Peat Inn, Fife KY15 5LF; T.-01334 840393; e-mail: david@ulph.me.uk

Upton, Emeritus Professor Brian Geoffrey Johnson, BA, MA, DPhil, FRSE, FGS. Emeritus Professor of Petrology, Edinburgh University, since 1999; b. 2.3.33, London; m., Bodil Aalbaek Upton; 2 s.; 1 d. Educ. Reading School; St John's College, Oxford University. Geological Survey of Greenland, 1958-60; Fulbright Fellow, California Institute of Technology, 1961-62; Lecturer, Geology, Edinburgh University, 1962-72; Carnegie Fellow, Geophysical Laboratory, Washington, 1970-71; Edinburgh University: Reader in Geology, 1972-82; Professor of Petrology, 1982-99; Executive Editor, Journal of Petrology, 1983-94; Clough Medallist, Geological Society, Edinburgh, 2001. Recreations: painting; gardening; travel. Address: (b.) School of GeoSciences, Grant Institute, Edinburgh University, West Mains Road, Edinburgh, EH9 3JW; T.-0131-650 5110.

Uren, Neal Gordon, BSc (Hons), MB, ChB, MD (Hons), FRCP. Consultant Cardiologist, since 1997; b. 9.11.60, Kirkcaldy; m., Dr. Janet Murray; 2 s.; 1 d. Educ. Balwearie High School, Kirkcaldy; University of Edinburgh. House Officer, Edinburgh, 1984-85; Senior House Officer, Newcastle Teaching Hospitals, 1985-87; Hammersmith Hospital: Cardiology Registrar, 1988-89, Research Registrar, 1990-93; Senior Registrar, Leicester, 1993-97; Interventional Fellow, Stanford University Hospital, USA, 1995-96. Council Member, British Cardiovascular Society. Recreations: golf; guitar; travel. Address: New Royal Infirmary, Edinburgh EH16 4SA; T.-0131 242 1046; e-mail: neal.uren@luht.scot.nhs.uk

U'ren, William Graham, BSc (Hons), DipTP, FRTPI. Planning Support Manager, Dundas and Wilson CS, LLP; b. 28.12.46, Glasgow; m., Wendy; 2 d. Educ. Aberdeen Grammar School; Aberdeen University; Strathclyde University. Planning Assistant: Clackmannan County Council, 1970-72, Lanark County Council, 1972-75; Principal and Chief Planning Officer, Clydesdale District Council, 1975-82; Director of Planning and Technical Services, Clydesdale District Council, 1982-96;

Environment Services Manager, Planning and Economic Development, South Lanarkshire Council, 1996-97; Director, Royal Town Planning Institute in Scotland, 1997-2007. Past Chairman, Scottish Society of Directors of Planning; Director, Built Environment Forum Scotland; Chairman, Friends of New Lanark; Trustee of the Crichton Trust; Director, Planning Aid Scotland. Recreations: conservation; listening to music; travel; town-twinning; watching cricket and rugby; bird watching; philately. Address: (b.) 125 Hyndford Road, Lanark ML11 9AU.

Urquhart, Celia Margaret Lloyd, RGN, MBA, FCMI. Chief Executive, Coralyn Ltd; m., George MacFarlane Sinclair. Member, Merchants House, Glasgow; Member, Association of Trades House Ladies; Past Chairman, Court, Glasgow Caledonian University; formerly: Member, Board, Scottish Enterprise and Glasgow Chamber of Commerce; Member, Nursing Board for Scotland. Address: (b.) 35 Victoria Crescent Road, Glasgow G12 9DD.

Urquhart, Very Rev John. Parish Priest, St. Bernadette's, Larbert, since 1989; Founder and Former Chairman, Diocesan Heritage and Arts Group; b. 1.7.34, Bowhill, Fife. Educ. St. Ninian's, Bowhill; St. Columba's Cowdenbeath; Blairs College, Aberdeen; Scots College, Spain; St. Andrew's College, Drygrange. Assistant: St. Joseph's, Sighthill, Edinburgh, Our Lady and St. Andrew's, Galashiels; Chaplain, St. Mary's Balnakiel; Parish Priest: St. Paul's, Muirhouse, Edinburgh, St. Margaret's, Dunfermline. Address: 323 Main Street, Larbert FK5 4EU; T.-01324 553250.

Urquhart, Linda Hamilton, LLB, WS. Chief Executive, Morton Fraser, since 1999; b. 21.9.59, Edinburgh; m., David S Burns QC; 2 d. Educ. James Gillespie's High School; University of Edinburgh. Trainee Solicitor, Steedman Ramage WS, 1991-93; Morton Fraser: Solicitor, 1993-95, Partner, since 1995. Council Member, CBI Scotland (Vice Chair, since 2007); Board Member, Edinburgh and Lothians Board of The Prince's Trust, Scotland; Co-Editor, Greens Property Law Bulletin; Director, ESPC Limited, ESPC (UK) Limited and DCA Limited; Ambassador, Girlguiding UK. Recreations: sailing; skiing. Address: (b.) 30-31 Queen Street, Edinburgh EH2 1JX; T.-0131-247-1020; e-mail: linda.urquhart@morton-fraser.com

Usher, Professor John Richard, BSc (Hons), MSc, PhD, CMATH. Professor of Mathematics, Robert Gordon University, 1998-2001; b. 12.5.44, London; m., Sheila Mary McKendrick; 1 d. Educ. St. Nicholas Grammar School, London; Hull University; St Andrews University. Lecturer, Mathematics, Teesside Polytechnic, 1970-74; Senior Lecturer, Mathematics, Glasgow College of Technology, 1974-82; Head of School of Mathematics (later School of Computing and Mathematical Sciences), Robert Gordon University, 1983-92; Senior Lecturer, Mathematics, 1992-98; Scottish Branch Committee, IMA: Vice-Chairman, 1983-85, Chairman, 1985-88, Hon. Member, 1988 -89; Member, IMA Council, 1987-90; External examiner for various Universities; Examiner for SCOTEC; Moderator for SCOTVEC; Member, UCAS Scottish Higher Education Mathematical Sciences and Computing Panel; Lay Reader, St. Ternans, Scottish Episcopal Church, Muchalls. Recreations: reading; walking; theatre-going; concert-going; bridge. Address: 20 St. Crispin's Road, Newtonhill, Stonehaven, Kincardineshire AB39 3PS; e-mail: john.usher@homecall.co.uk

Usher, Professor Michael Barham, OBE, BSc, PhD, DUniv, CBiol, FIBiol, FRES, FRSE. Chief Scientist, Scottish Natural Heritage, 1991-2001, Leverhulme Emeritus Fellow, 2001-03; b. 19.11.41, Old Colwyn; m., Kathleen Fionna Munro; 1 s.; 1 d. Educ. Portsmouth Grammar School; Edinburgh University. Lecturer, Senior

Lecturer, Reader, Department of Biology, University of York, 1967-91; Adviser on termite research, British Technical Assistance to the Government of Ghana, 1971-73; research in Antarctic and Sub-Antarctic, 1980-81; Nature Conservancy Council for Scotland and Scottish Natural Heritage, Chief Scientific Adviser/Chief Scientist, 1991-2001; Honorary Professor: in Zoology, University of Aberdeen, in Environmental Science, University of Stirling, in Biological Sciences, University of Edinburgh. Trustee of Royal Botanic Garden Edinburgh and Woodland Trust. Publications: 240 scientific papers; 14 books. Recreations: walking; gardening; natural history photography; philately. Address: (b.) School of Biological and Environmental Sciences, University of Stirling, Stirling, FK9 4LA; e-mail: m.b.usher@stir.ac.uk

V

van der Kuyl, Professor Christiaan Richard David, FRSE, BSc (Hons). CEO, Scotland Online; Chairman, Tayforth Consulting Limited and 4J Studios Limited; b. 20.8.69, Dundee. Technology Entrepreneur; Chairman: Add Knowledge, Knowledge Limited; Member of Scottish Scientific Advisory Committee; Director, Schools Enterprise Scotland; Director, Sensation Science Centre, Dundee; Visiting Professor, Digital Entertainment, University of Abertay Dundee; Hon DBA, Napier University; Chairman, Campbell Hunter Creative Board, Kelvingrove Art Gallery, Glasgow; Member, Smith Group. Recreations: playing computer games; music; golf. Club: New Club. Address: (b.) Tayforth Consulting Limited, Seabraes, Perth Road, Dundee DD1 4LN; T.-01382 341027.

van Heyningen, Professor Simon, MA, PhD, FRSC, FIBiol. Vice-Principal and Director of Quality Enhancement, Edinburgh University, since 2002; Chair, Edinburgh Printmakers, since 2005; b. 17.12.43, London; m., Veronica Daniel; 1 s.; 1 d. Educ. Westminster School; King's College, Cambridge. Department of Chemistry, Northwestern University, Illinois, 1968-70; Department of Biochemistry, Oxford University, 1970-74; joined Department of Biochemistry, Edinburgh University, 1974. Chair, Quality Assurance Agency Benchmarking Group in Biosciences, 2000; Scottish Enhancement Theme on Assessment, 2004-06. Address: (b.) Old College, South Bridge, Edinburgh EH8 9YL; T.-0131-650 8238; e-mail: S.vanHeyningen@ed.ac.uk

van Heyningen, Veronica, MA, MS, DPhil, FRS, FRSE, FMedSci. Section Head, MRC Human Genetics Unit, Edinburgh, since 1977; b. 12.11.46, Hungary; m., Dr. Simon van Heyningen; 1 s.; 1 d. Educ. Humphrey Perkins School, Leicestershire; Girton College, Cambridge; Northwestern University, Illinois; Lady Margaret Hall, Oxford. Beit Memorial Fellow, 1973-76; Howard Hughes International Research Scholar, 1993-98; Honorary Professor, Edinburgh University, 1995; Hon. Treasurer, The Genetical Society, 1994-98; Trustee, National Museums of Scotland, 1994-2000; Member, Human Genetics Commission, 2000-05. Recreations: visiting museums; travel; talking to people. Address: (b.) MRC Human Genetics Unit, Edinburgh, EH4 2XU; T.-0131-467 8405.

Vannet, Sheriff Alfred Douglas, LLB, FRSA. Sheriff of South Strathclyde, Dumfries and Galloway at Airdrie, since 2001; All-Scotland floating Sheriff, 2000-01; b. 31.7.49, Dundee; m., Pauline Margaret Renfrew; 1 s.; 1 d. Educ. High School of Dundee; Dundee University. Procurator Fiscal Depute, Dundee, 1976-77; Procurator Fiscal Depute, then Senior Procurator Fiscal Depute, Glasgow, 1977-84; Assistant Solicitor, Crown Office, 1984-90; Deputy Crown Agent, 1990-94; Regional Procurator Fiscal, Grampian, Highland and Islands at Aberdeen, 1994-97; Regional Procurator Fiscal, Glasgow and Strathkelvin, 1997-99. Honorary Member, Royal Faculty of Procurators in Glasgow, since 1997. Recreations: music; walking; curling. Address: (b.) Airdrie Sheriff Court, Graham Street, Airdrie; e-mail: sheriff.advannet@scotcourts.gov.uk

Vardy, Professor Alan Edward, BSc, PhD, DSc, DEng, FREng, FRSE, EurIng, CEng, FICE, FASCE, FRSA. Research Professor in Civil Engineering, Dundee University, since 1995; Director, Dundee Tunnel Research, since 1995; b. 6.11.45, Sheffield; m., Susan Janet; 2 s.; 1 d. Educ. High Storrs Grammar School, Sheffield; Leeds University. Lecturer in Civil Engineering, Leeds University, 1972-75; Royal Society Warren Research Fellow, Cambridge University, 1975-79; Dundee University: Professor of Civil Engineering, 1979-95 (Deputy Principal, 1985-89, Vice-Principal, 1988-89); Director, Wolfson Bridge Research Unit, 1980-90; Royal Society/SERC Industrial Fellow, 1990-94; Director, Lightweight Structures Unit, 1998-2004. Address: Kirkton of Abernyte, Perthshire PH14 9SS; T.-01828 686241.

Varty, Professor E. Kenneth C., BA (Hons), PhD, DLitt, FSA, Chevalier dans l' Ordre des Palmes Academiques, Chevalier dans l' Ordre des Arts et des Lettres. Professor Emeritus and Hon. Professorial Research Fellow, Glasgow University, since 1996; Life Member, Clare Hall, Cambridge University, since 1984; b. 18.8.27, Derbyshire; m., Hedwig; 2 d. Educ. Bemrose School, Derby; Nottingham University. Assistant Lecturer, then Lecturer, French, University College of N. Staffs, 1953-61; Lecturer/Senior Lecturer, French, Leicester University, 1961-68; Stevenson Professor of French, Glasgow University, 1968-90; Dean, Faculty of Arts, Glasgow University, 1978-81; President, Alliance Française de Glasgow, 1982-89. Publications: Reynard, Renart, Renaert, 1999; Reynard the Fox, 2000. Recreations: travel; art galleries; museums; historic sites etc. Address: (h.) 4 Dundonald Road, Glasgow, G12 9LJ; T.-0141 339 1413.

Veal, Sheriff Kevin Anthony, KSG, KC*HS, LLB. Sheriff of Tayside Central and Fife at Forfar, since 1993; b. 16.9.46, Chesterfield; m., Monica Flynn; 2 s.; 2 d. Educ. Lawside Academy, Dundee; St. Andrews University. Partner, Burns Veal and Gillan, Dundee, 1971-93; Legal Aid Reporter, 1978-93; Temporary Sheriff, 1984-93; Tutor, Department of Law, Dundee University, 1978-85; Dean, Faculty of Procurators and Solicitors in Dundee, 1991-93. Musical Director, Cecilian Choir, Dundee, since 1975; Member, University Court, Abertay Dundee, since 1998; Member, Council, Sheriffs' Association, 2000-03; Honorary President, Dundee Operatic Society, since 2003. Recreations: organ and classical music; hill-walking. Address: (b.) Sheriff Courthouse, Market Street, Forfar DD8 3LA; T.-01307 462186.

Vermeulen, Rev. Chris, BTh (Rhodes), MA (Sheffield). Minister, Orchardhill Parish Church, Giffnock, since 2005; b. 19.1.61, Vanderbijlpark, South Africa; m., Elaine; 1 s.; 1 d. Educ. Vaal High School, Vanderbijlpark, South Africa; Rhodes University; Sheffield University. Formerly Minister, St. David's Presbyterian Church (Nigel, South Africa); moved to Scotland to study at Glasgow University while still ministering part time in the Falkirk area; called to Barrhead Congregational Church (now part of the United Reformed Church) and served as their minister for 6 years until 2000; moved to Manchester to become Research Fellow, Woodlands Project on a 5 year contract. Vice-Convenor, Glasgow Presbytery Mission Strategy. Co-Founder, the www.emergingchurch.info website; currently serves on the organising committee of the Euro Church Network (www.eurochurch.net); instrumental in bringing the Together in Missions Missional Leadership course to Scotland (www.missionalleadership.org.uk). Publication: "The Church Facing the Future". Address: Orchardhill Parish Church, 12 Church Road, Giffnock, Glasgow G46 6JR; e-mail: chris@orchardhill.org.uk

Vernon, Professor Richard Geoffrey, BSc, PhD, FIBiol. Honorary Fellow, Hannah Research Institute; b. 19.2.43, Maidstone; m., Mary Christine Cunliffe; 1 s.; 1 d. Educ.

Newcastle High School; Birmingham University. Research Fellow, University of Toronto, 1969-72; Senior Scientist then Head of Department, Hannah Research Institute, 1972-95; Head, Science Planning and Development and Head, Molecular Homeorhesis Group, Hannah Research Institute, 1995-2003; Hon. Lecturer, Glasgow University, 1985-2003; Visiting Professor, Department of Medicine, University of Liverpool, 2001-04; Honorary Senior Research Fellow, University of Glasgow, 2003-06; Treasurer, Scottish Ornithologists' Club; Council Member, Scottish Branch, Institute of Biology; Consultant Editor, Journal of Dairy Research, 1990-2003; Member, Editorial Board, British Journal of Nutrition, 1981-87, Domestic Animal Endocrinology (USA), 1992-95; Chairman, Scottish Section, Nutrition Society, 1989-91; Member, AFRC Animals Research Grants Board, 1991-94; Past President, Birmingham University Mountaineering Club; Chairman, Belmont Academy School Board, 1989-93. Publications: Physiological Strategies in Lactation (Co-editor); 250 scientific papers. Recreations: hill-walking; ornithology; bridge; photography. Address: (h.) 29 Knoll Park, Ayr, KA7 4RH; T.-01292 442195.

Vettese, Raymond John, DipEd, BA (Hons). Teacher and Writer; b. 1.11.50, Arbroath; m., Maureen Elizabeth. Educ. Montrose Academy; Dundee College of Education; Open University. Journalist, Montrose Review, 1968-72; student, 1972-75; barman, 1975-77; factory worker, 1977-78; clerical officer, 1978-85; teacher, since 1985 (supply teacher, 1997-2001); Library Assistant, 2001; Preses, Scots Language Society, 1991-94; William Soutar Fellowship, 1989-90; SAC Bursary, 1999. Publications: Four Scottish Poets, 1985; The Richt Noise, 1988 (Saltire Society Best First Book); A Keen New Air, 1995. Recreations: reading; music; cooking; chess. Address: (h.) 9 Tayock Avenue, Montrose, DD10 9AP; T.-01674 678943.

Vettriano, Jack, OBE. Painter. Early career in Scottish coalfields; received no formal tuition in art; first submitted works to Royal Scottish Academy, 1988; widely exhibited.

Vickerman, Professor Keith, BSc, PhD, DSc, FLS, FMedSci, FRSE, FRS. Regius Professor of Zoology, Glasgow University, 1984-98; Consultant Expert on Parasitic Diseases, World Health Organisation, 1973-98; b. 21.3.33, Huddersfield; m., Moira Dutton; 1 d. Educ. King James Grammar School, Almondbury; University College, London (Fellow, 1985). Wellcome Lecturer in Protozoology, University College, London, 1958-63; Tropical Research Fellow, Royal Society, 1963-68; Glasgow University: Reader in Zoology, 1968-74; Professor of Zoology, 1974-84, Head, Department of Zoology, 1979-85. Leeuwenhoek Lecturer, Royal Society, 1994; Linnean Society Gold Medal for contributions to science, 1996. Publications: The Protozoa (Co-author), 1967; many papers in scientific and medical journals. Recreations: drawing and painting; gardening. Address: (h.) 16 Mirrlees Drive, Glasgow G12 OSH.

Vickers, Lisa. US Consul General to Scotland, since 2006; b. 26.1.64, USA. Educ. University of the Pacific, CA; Durham University. Member, US Foreign Service, since 1990; Consular Officer, Embassy, Mexico City; Management Officer, Embassy, Suva Fiji; Consul, Embassy, Helsinki; American Citizen Services Chief, Embassy, Warsaw; Consul General, Embassy, Kyiv; Principal Officer, Merida. Address: (b.) 3 Regent Terrace, Edinburgh.

Vine, John, CBE, QPM, BA, MSc, FCIPD. Chief Constable, Tayside Police, since 2000; m.; 2 s.; 1 d.

Joined West Yorkshire Metropolitan Police, 1981; appointed Divisional Commander, Halifax; Head of Inspectorate, West Yorkshire, 1995; Assistant Chief Constable, Lancashire, 1996. Recreations: running; gardening; fishing; fell-walking; reading; politics. Address: (b.) PO Box 59, West Bell Street, Dundee, DD1 9JU; T.-01382 596003.
E-mail: mail@tayside.pnn.police.uk

Vousden, Karen Heather, BSc, PhD, FRSE, FRS, FMedSci. Director, Beatson Institute for Cancer Research, since 2002; b. 19.7.57, Gravesend; m., Robert Ludwig; 1 d. Educ. Gravesend School for Girls; Queen Mary College, London University. Head, Human Papillomavirus Group, Ludwig Institute for Cancer Research, St Mary's Hospital, 1987-95; Director, Molecular Virology and Carcinogenesis Laboratory, ABL Basic Research Program, USA, 1995-99; Chief, Regulation of Cell Growth Laboratory, National Cancer Institute, USA, 1999-2002. Recreation: hill-walking. Address; (b.) Beatson Institute for Cancer Research, Garscube Estate, Switchback Road, Bearsden, Glasgow G61 1BD; T.-0141 330 2424.

W

Waddell, Bruce. Editor, Daily Record; b. 18.3.59, Bo'ness, West Lothian; m., Catherine; 1 s. Educ. Graeme High School, Falkirk; Napier University. Reporter, Journal and Gazette, Linlithgow, 1977-87; News Sub-editor, The Scottish Sun, 1987-90; Deputy Editor, Sunday Scot, 1991; Marketing Executive, Murray International, 1991-92; Features Sub-editor, The Sun, 1992-93; Deputy Editor, The Scottish Sun, 1993-98; Editor, The Scottish Sun, 1998-2003. Recreations: golf; football; classic cars. Address: (b.) One Central Quay, Glasgow G3 8DA; T.-0141 309 3000.

Waddell, John MacLaren Ogilvie, LLB, WS. Chief Executive, Archangel Informal Investment Ltd.; b. 12.4.56, Inverness; m., Alice Emily Bain; 1 s.; 1 d. Educ. Inverness Royal Academy; George Watson's College; Edinburgh University. Qualified as a Solicitor, 1980. Address: (b.) 20 Rutland Square, Edinburgh EH1 2BB.

Waddell, Moray, BSc(Hons), MSc, CEng, MIEE, MIMechE, MCIBSE. Director of Engineering, Northern Lighthouse Board, since 2000; b. 22.3.64, Haddington; m., Susan Joan Tennant; 2 s. Educ. Dunbar Grammar School; Edinburgh University; Glasgow University. Trainee engineer, Property Services Agency; Engineer and Project Manager, Property Services Agency and Ministry of Defence. Recreations: sailing; motor sports. Address: (b.) 84 George Street, Edinburgh, EH2 3DA; T.-0131-473 3100.

Wade, Martyn John, BA, MLib, MCLIP, FRSA. National Librarian, National Library of Scotland, since 2002; b. 24.3.55, Birmingham; m., Anne. Educ. King Edward VI Grammar School, Birmingham; Newcastle upon Tyne Polytechnic; University of Wales, Aberystwyth. Area Library Officer, Cambridge, 1994-99; Head of Libraries, Information and Learning, Glasgow City Council, 1999-2002. Recreations: the arts; motorcycling; reading; cooking; walking. Address: (b.) National Library of Scotland, George IV Bridge, Edinburgh EH1 1EW; T.-0131-226 4531; e-mail: m.wade@nls.uk

Wade, Professor Nicholas James, BSc, PhD, FRSE. Professor of Visual Psychology, Dundee University, since 1991; b. 27.3.42, Retford, Nottinghamshire; m., Christine Whetton; 2 d. Educ. Queen Elizabeth's Grammar School, Mansfield; Edinburgh University; Monash University. Postdoctoral Research Fellow, Max-Planck Institute for Behavioural Physiology, Germany, 1969-70; Lecturer in Psychology, Dundee University, 1970-78, Reader, 1978-91. Publications: The Art and Science of Visual Illusions, 1982; Brewster and Wheatstone on Vision, 1983; Visual Allusions: Pictures of Perception, 1990; Visual Perception: an introduction, 1991; Psychologists in Word and Image, 1995; A Natural History of Vision, 1998; Purkinje's Vision: The Dawning of Neuroscience, 2001; Destined for Distinguished Oblivion. The Scientific Vision of William Charles Wells (1757–1817), 2003; Perception and Illusion: Historical Perspectives, 2005; The Moving Tablet of the Eye. The Origins of Modern Eye Movement Research, 2005; Insegne Ambiguë. Percorsi Obliqui tra Storia, Scienza e Arte, da Galileo a Magritte, 2007; Circles: Science, Sense and Symbol, 2007. Recreations: golf; cycling. Address: (h.) 36 Norwood, Newport-on-Tay, Fife DD6 8DW; T.-01382 543136.
E-mail: n.j.wade@dundee.ac.uk

Waigh, Professor Roger David, BPharm, PhD, DSc, CChem, FRSC. Professor of Medicinal Chemistry, Strathclyde University, since 1991; b. 8.8.44, Loughborough; m., Sally Joy Bembridge; 1 s.; 1 d. Educ. Sir George Monoux Grammar School, Walthamstow; Bath University. Lecturer, Strathclyde University, 1970-76; Lecturer, then Senior Lecturer, Manchester University, 1976-91. Recreations: bird-watching; golf; photography. Address: (b.) Strathclyde Institute of Pharmacy and Biomedical Sciences, 27 Taylor Street, Glasgow G4 ONR; T.-0141-548 4355.

Wake, Joseph Robert, MA, OPA; b. 16.5.42, Corbridge; 1 s.; 2 d. Educ. Royal Grammar School, Newcastle upon Tyne; Edinburgh University; Moray House College of Education. Teacher, Kirkcaldy High School, 1966-69, St. Modan's High School, Stirling, 1969-71; Principal Teacher of Modern Languages, Grangemouth High School, 1971-72; Head of Central Bureau for Educational Visits and Exchanges in Scotland, 1972-2002; International Education Adviser, British Council Scotland, 2002-07 (retired). Recreations: cricket; philately; Scottish dancing. Address: (h.) 4 Downie Grove, Edinburgh EH12 7AX; T.-0131 334 1523.

Wakefield, Peter, MA (Hons), MEd, PGCE, ILTM. Head of Department, University of Dundee, 2004-07; b. 17.8.54, Cardiff; m., Helen, 1 s.; 1 d. Educ. Barry Boys Comprehensive School; University of Dundee. Class Teacher, Chapel Park Primary School, 1977-85; Head Teacher, Liff Primary School, 1985-89; Northern College: Lecturer, 1989-95, Senior Lecturer, 1995-2001; Senior Lecturer, University of Dundee, 2001-04. Recreations: hill walking; cycling; angling. Address: (b.) University of Dundee, Gardyne Campus, Broughty Ferry, Dundee DD5 1NY; T.-01382 464317; e-mail: p.wakefield@dundee.ac.uk

Wakeford, Richard George, BSc. Director-General Environment, Scottish Government, since 2007, Head, Environment and Rural Affairs Department, 2005-07; b. 6.10.53; m., Susan Mary Beacham; 3 s. Educ. Chichester High School for Boys; King's College, London. Executive Officer, 1975-80, Assistant Private Secretary to Minister of State, 1979-80, DoE; HEO posts, DoE and Department of Transport, 1980-83; Department of the Environment: Private Secretary to Permanent Secretary, 1983-85; Planning Inspectorate, 1985; Development Control, 1985-87; Bill Manager, Water Privatisation, 1988-89; Principal, Environment White Paper Team, 1990; (last) Chief Executive, Crown Suppliers, 1991; Head of Development Plans and Policies, 1991-94; Assistant Secretary, Economic and Domestic Secretariat, Cabinet Office, 1994-96; Chief Executive: Countryside Commission, 1996-99, Countryside Agency, 1999-2004. UK Sustainable Development Commissioner, 2000-04. Non-executive Board Member, DEFRA, 2001-04. Mid Career Fellow, Princeton University, 1987-88. Publications: Speeding Planning Appeals, 1986; American Development Control: parallels and paradoxes from a British perspective, 1990. Recreations: gardening; photography; built and natural landscape. Address: (b.) Pentland House, 47 Robb's Loan, Edinburgh EH14 1TY; T.-0131 244 6021.

Walde, Professor Thomas W., LLM (Harvard), Dr.iur. Professor of International Economic, Natural Resources and Energy Law, University of Dundee, since 1991; b. 1949, Germany; 1 s. Educ. Universities of Heidelberg, Frankfurt and Harvard. Institute for International Economic Law, Frankfurt, 1975-80; U.N. Natural Resources and Energy Division, 1980-85; Adviser to Governments on mineral development policies, legislation, and contract negotiations; Interregional Advisor on Petroleum and Mineral Legislation, U.N. (D.T.C.D.); EC Jean Monnet Professor of European Economic and Energy Law; Editor, Journal of World Energy; Visiting Professor, Universite de Paris II - Pantheon; Fellow, European Centre for Policy Studies; Columbia University, International Investment Programme.

Corresponding Editor, International Legal Materials; Editor, CEPMCP On-line Journal; Associate Editor: Journal of World Trade, Journal of World Investment; frequent Mediator, Expert and Arbitration in international investment disputes; Member: Essex Court Chambers (London), ASIL, AIPN, BIICL, IBA, LCIA, DIS, IAIP. One of the 3 arbitrators from Scotland named in international surveys of the world's leading arbitrators; Euromoney nomination as one of the world's leading energy lawyers. Address: (b.) Park Place, Dundee DD1 4HN; T.-01382 344300.
Website: www.OGEL.org; www.cepmlp.org

Walker, Alan George Taylor, LLB Notary Public. Honorary Sheriff of North Strathclyde, Campbeltown, since 2004; Senior Partner, Stewart Balfour and Sutherland, since 1997; b. 20.6.44, Dumfries; m., Marlene; 2 s.; 1 d.; 1 stepson; 1 stepdaughter. Educ. Dumfries Academy; Glasgow University. Law Apprentice to long established firm of Moncrieff Warren Paterson and Co., Glasgow, 1965-67; qualified as Solicitor, 1967; assumed into Partnership, 1970; chose to leave Glasgow, 1975; Partner, Stewart Balfour and Sutherland, since 1976. Past Dean, Faculty of Solicitors, Campbeltown; Panel Member, Prince's Scottish Youth Business Trust; Committee Member, Glenbarr War Memorial Trust; Hon. President, Carradale Golf Club. Recreations: golf; boating; choral singing; past conductor, Carradale Gaelic Choir; presently Choirmaster, Lorne and Lowland Church, Campbeltown. Address: (h.) Ezel Cottage, Shore Road, Carradale, Campbeltown PA28 6SH; T.-01583 431 637; e-mail: walker872@btinternet.com

Walker, Professor Andrew Charles, BA, MSc, PhD, FInstP, FRSE, CPhys. Professor of Modern Optics, Heriot-Watt University, since 1988; Vice Principal; b. 24.6.48, Wembley; m., Margaret Elizabeth; 1 s.; 1 d. Educ. Kingsbury County Grammar School; Essex University. Postdoctoral Fellowship, National Research Council of Canada, 1972-74; SRC Research Fellowship, Essex University, 1974-75; Higher/Senior Scientific Officer, UKAEA Culham Laboratory, 1975-83; Lecturer/Reader, Heriot-Watt University, 1983-88. Honorary Secretary, Quantum Electronics Group, Institute of Physics, 1982-85; Chairman, Scottish Branch, Institute of Physics, 1993-95; Vice President, Royal Society of Edinburgh, 2001-04; Director, Edinburgh Business School; Fellowship Secretary, Royal Society of Edinburgh, since 2005. Recreations: music; sailing. Address: (b.) Heriot-Watt University, Edinburgh EH14 4AS; T.-0131-451 3036.

Walker, Audrey R., BA, MCLIP. Librarian, Turcan Connell, since 2006; b. 18.10.57, Glasgow. Educ. Clydebank High School; Robert Gordon University, Aberdeen. Library Assistant, 1975-80; Senior Library Assistant, Telford College, Edinburgh, 1980-84; Assistant Librarian: Scottish Office Library, 1987, Post-Graduate Medical Library, 1988-90, Advocates Library, 1990-94, Signet Library, 1994-2006. Chartered Institute of Library and Information Professionals in Scotland: Representative to CILIP Council, London; Organiser, Meadowbank National Track League. Recreations: cycling; reading; cross-stitch; cinema. Address: (b.) Turcan Connell, Princes Exchange, 1 Earl Grey Street, Edinburgh EH3 9EE; T.-0131 228 8111.

Walker, Professor Brian Robert, BSc, MB, ChB, MD, FRCPE. Professor of Endocrinology, University of Edinburgh, since 2001; b. 12.7.63, Glasgow; m., Dr Jane Walker; 2 s. Educ. Glasgow Academy; University of Edinburgh. University of Edinburgh: MRC Training Fellow, 1990-93, Lecturer in Medicine, 1993-96, British Heart Foundation Senior Research Fellow, 1996-2006. Address: (b.) Endocrinology Unit, Centre for Cardiovascular Science, Queen's Medical Research Institute, 47 Little France Crescent, Edinburgh EH16 4TJ; T.-0131 242 6770; e-mail: B.Walker@ed.ac.uk

Walker, Professor David Maxwell, CBE, QC, MA, PhD, LLD, Hon. LLD, FBA, FRSE, FRSA, FSA Scot. Regius Professor of Law, Glasgow University, 1958-90; Honorary Senior Research Fellow, since 1990; b. 9.4.20, Glasgow; m., Margaret Knox, OBE, MA. Educ. High School of Glasgow; Glasgow University; Edinburgh University; London University. HLI and Indian Army, 1939-46; Advocate, 1948; in practice, Scottish Bar, 1948-54; Professor of Jurisprudence, Glasgow University, 1954-58; Barrister (Middle Temple), 1957; QC (Scot), 1958; Dean, Faculty of Law, Glasgow University, 1956-59; Convener, School of Law, 1984-88. Chairman, High School of Glasgow Trust. Publications: Law of Damages in Scotland; The Scottish Legal System; Law of Delict in Scotland; Law of Civil Remedies in Scotland; Law of Prescription in Scotland; Law of Contracts in Scotland; Oxford Companion to Law; Principles of Scottish Private Law (four volumes); The Scottish Jurists; Stair's Institutions (Editor); Stair Tercentenary Studies (Editor); A Legal History of Scotland, (7 vols). Recreations: book collecting; Scottish history; motoring. Address: (h.) 1 Beaumont Gate, Glasgow G12 9EE; T.-0141-339 2802.

Walker, Emeritus Professor David Morrison, OBE, DA, FSA, FSA Scot, FRSE, HFRIAS, Hon. LLD (Dundee), Hon. DLitt (St Andrews). Honorary Professor of Art History, University of St. Andrews, 1994-2001, Emeritus Professor, since 2001; Chief Inspector of Historic Buildings, Scottish Office Environment Department, 1988-93; Manager, Dictionary of Scottish Architects research and database project, since 2002; b. 31.1.33, Dundee; m., Averil Mary Stewart McIlwraith (deceased); m. (2), Sheila Margaret Mould (2005); 1 s. Educ. Morgan Academy, Dundee; Dundee College of Art. Voluntary work for National Buildings Record, Edinburgh, 1952-56; National Service, Royal Engineers, 1956-58; Glasgow Education Authority, 1958-59; Dundee Education Authority, 1959-61; Historic Buildings Branch, Scottish Office: Senior Investigator of Historic Buildings, 1961-76, Principal Investigator of Historic Buildings, 1976-78; Principal Inspector of Historic Buildings, 1978-88. Alice Davis Hitchcock Medallion, 1970. Publications: Dundee Nineteenth Century Mansions, 1958; Architecture of Glasgow (Co-author), 1968 (revised and enlarged edition, 1987); Buildings of Scotland: Edinburgh (Co-author), 1984; Dundee: An Illustrated Introduction (Co-author), 1984; St. Andrew's House: an Edinburgh Controversy 1912-1939, 1989; Central Glasgow: an illustrated architectural guide (Co-author), 1989. Address: (h.) 22 Inverleith Row, Edinburgh EH3 5QH.

Walker, Donald George, MA (Hons). Sports Editor, The Scotsman, since 1998; b. 16.6.68, St. Andrews; 2 s. Educ. Kirkcaldy High School; University of Edinburgh. Trainee journalist, DC Thomson, Dundee, 1991; Reporter, Edinburgh and Lothians Post, 1992-93; Sub-Editor, Daily Mirror, London, 1993-97; Deputy Sports Editor, The Scotsman, 1997-98. Recreations: football and East Fife FC. E-mail: dwalker@scotsman.com

Walker, (Edward) Michael, CBE, FRICS. Chairman, Walker Group (Scotland) Ltd., Westerwood Ltd., and associated companies, since 1986 (Founder, 1969); Chairman, Lothian and Edinburgh Ltd. (LEEL), 1996-2000 (Director, since 1991); b. 12.4.41, Aberdeen; m., Flora

Margaret; 2 s.; 1 d. Educ. Aberdeen Grammar School. President, Edinburgh and District Master Builders Association, 1987 and 1996; Past President, Scottish House Builders Association; former Committee Member, NHBC (Scotland) Ltd., 1990-96; former Lord Dean of Guild, City of Edinburgh, 1992-96; Captain of Industry Award, Livingston Industrial and Commercial Association, 1987. Recreations: skiing; scuba diving; walking; reading. Address: (b.) Walker Group (Scotland) Ltd., Westerwood House, Royston Road, Deans Industrial Estate, Livingston, W. Lothian; T.-01506 413101.

Walker, Ernest John Munro, CBE. Former Chairman, now Senior Consultant to UEFA Stadia and Security Committee; b. 20.7.28, Glasgow; m., Anne; 1 s.; 2 d. Educ. Queen's Park Secondary School. Army (Royal Horse Artillery), 1946-48; Assistant Secretary, industrial textile company, 1948-58; Assistant Secretary, Scottish Football Association, 1958-77, Secretary, 1977-90; Chairman, Health Education Board for Scotland, 1990-94. Director, Euro-Sportring; Member, Football Work Permits Review Panel for Scotland; Hon. Life Member, Queen's Park Football Club; Member: National Trust for Scotland, Saltire Society; Vice-President, Newspaper Press Fund. Recreations: golf (past Captain, Haggs Castle GC); fishing; music; travel.

Walker, Professor Greg Mapley, BA, PhD, FRHS, FEA. Masson Professor of English Literature, University of Edinburgh, since 2007; b. 08.09.59, Coventry; m., Sharon; 2 s. Educ. Horndean School; Southampton University. Career History: British Academy Post-Doctoral Fellow, University of Southampton; Lecturer in English: University of Queensland, University of Buckingham, University of Leicester; Reader, and Professor of English, University of Leicester. Publications: author of books including, Writing Under Tyranny: English Literature and The Henrician Reformation, 2005. Recreations: dog lover; fan of progressive rock music; Nottingham Forest FC. Address: (b.) Department of English Literature, University of Edinburgh, Edinburgh EH8 9JX; T.-0131 650 3049; e-mail: greg.walker@ed.ac.uk

Walker, Rev. James Bernard, MA, BD, DPhil. Chaplain, St. Andrews University, since 1993; Associate Director, Student Support Services; b. 1946, Malawi; m., Sheila; 3 s. Educ. Hamilton Academy; Edinburgh University; Merton College, Oxford. Church of Scotland Minister: Mid Craigie linked with Wallacetown, Dundee, 1975-78, Old and St Paul's, Galashiels, 1978-87; Principal, The Queen's College, Birmingham, 1987-93; joined St. Andrews University in 1993. Publication: Israel — Covenant and Land, 1988. Recreations: hill-walking; tennis; golf. Address: 3A St. Mary's Place, St. Andrews KY16 9UY; T.-01334 462865.

Walker, Jane, MB, ChB, MRCP, FRCR. Consultant Radiologist, since 1995; b. 12.7.62, West Kirby; m., Brian Walker; 2 s. Educ. Birkenhead High School; Edinburgh University. House and Senior House Officer posts; trained in radiology, Edinburgh; specialised in obstetric and gynaecological radiology. Address: (b.) Ultrasound Department, Simpson Centre for Reproductive Health, Royal Infirmary, 51 Litle France Crescent, Edinburgh EH16 4SA; T.-0131-242 2801; e-mail: jane.walker@luht.scot.nhs.uk

Walker, Timothy Frederick. Principal, Glenmore Lodge, Aviemore (sportscotland), since 1995; b. 11.12.48, Stannington; m., Helen; 2 d. Royal Marines (Mountain and Arctic Warfare Cadre); Outward Bound, Eskdale; Joint Services Mountain Training Centre, Scotland; Tutor, Seneca College, Ontario, Canada; Instructional Officer, Scottish Sports Council. Publication: Cross Country Skiing. Chairman, BASI Nordic; Representative, Action of Churches Together in Scotland; Director, Aviemore and Cairngorms Destination Management Organisation; Trustee, Catherine Smith Memorial Trust; Member of Strategic Advisory Panel, Duke of Edinburgh's Award Scotland; Governor, Aiglon College, Villars, Switzerland. Recreations: all aspects of mountaineering; skiing. Address: (h.) Drumullie Steading, Boat of Garten, Inverness-shire PH24 3BX; T.-(b.) 01479 861 256; (h.) 01479 831 316.

Walker, Professor William Barclay, BSc, MSc. Professor of International Relations, University of St. Andrews, since 1996, Head, School of International Relations, 2003-06; b. 7.12.46, Longforgan; m., Carolyn Scott; 1 s. Educ. Shrewsbury School; Edinburgh University. Design Engineer, Ferranti Ltd., 1970-72; Research Fellow, Science Policy Research Unit, Sussex University, 1974-78; Research Fellow, Royal Institute of International Affairs, 1978-80; Science Policy Research Unit, Sussex University: Senior Fellow, 1981-92, Professorial Fellow and Director of Research, 1993-96; Member, Strategic Research Board, Economic and Social Research Council, 2002-06. Publications: Plutonium and Highly Enriched Uranium: World Inventories, Capabilities and Policies (Co-author), 1997; Unchartered Waters: The UK, Nuclear Weapons and the Scottish Question (Co-Author), 2001; Weapons of Mass Destruction and International Order, 2004. Recreations: piano-playing; running; ornithology. Address: (b.) School of International Relations, University of St. Andrews, St. Andrews KY16 9AX; T.-01334 462934.

Wallace, Archibald Duncan, MB, ChB. Medical Practitioner, Campbeltown, since 1950; Hon. Sheriff of North Strathclyde at Campbeltown, since 1980; b. 4.1.26, Glasgow; m., Rona B. MacLennan; 1 s.; 2 d. Educ. High School of Glasgow; Glasgow University. Sector Medical Officer, Argyll and Clyde Health Board, until 1988; Civilian MO to RAF Machrihanish, until 1988. Past Chairman, Campbeltown Branch, RNLI; Past President, Campbeltown Rotary Club; Past Captain, Machrihanish Golf Club. Recreations: golf; gardening. Address: (h.) Lilybank House, Low Askomil, Campbeltown; T.-01586 52658.

Wallace, Gavin, MA (Hons), PhD. Head of Literature, Scottish Arts Council, since 2002; b. 27.5.59, Willerby, England; partner: Pauline Jones; 2 s. Educ. Prestwick Academy; University of Edinburgh. Assistant Editor, Cencrastus, 1981-88; Visiting Lecturer in British Fiction, Shinwa Women's University, Kobe, Japan, 1988-90; Associate Lecturer in Literature/Humanities, Open University in Scotland, 1990-2001; freelance lecturer, journalist, researcher,broadcaster, 1991-97; Co-editor, Edinburgh Review, 1993-97; Literature Officer, Scottish Arts Council, 1997-2002. Publications: The Scottish Novel Since the 1970s (Co-editor), 1992; Scottish Theatre since the 1970s (Co-editor), 1996; numerous articles, essays and papers on 20th century Scottish literature and culture. Recreations: music; cinema; travel; cycling; cooking. Address: (b.) 12 Manor Place, Edinburgh EH3 7DD; T.-0131-226 6051; e-mail: gavin.wallace@scottisharts.org.uk

Wallace, Heather M., BSc, PhD, FRCPath, FBTS. Senior Lecturer, Department of Medicine and Therapeutics, Aberdeen University, since 1991; b. 10.6.54, Edinburgh; m., Dr R. John Wallace; 1 s.; 1 d. Educ. Hamilton Academy; Glasgow University; Aberdeen University. Aberdeen University: Postdoctoral Fellow, MRC, 1979-81, CRC, 1981-83; Wellcome

Lecturer, 1983; New Blood Lecturer, 1983-91, University Research Fellow, 1991-92. Recreations: golf; tennis; badminton. Address: (b.) Aberdeen University, Polwarth Building, Foresterhill, Aberdeen; T.-01224 552481; e-mail: h.m.wallace@abdn.ac.uk

Wallace, Iain Wilson, BSc (Hons), MB, ChB, MBA, FRCGP, DRCOG. Associate Medical Director, Women and Children's Directorate, NHS Greater Glasgow and Clyde, since 2006; b. 3.3.60; m., Jane; 2 d. Educ. Paisley Grammar School; University of Glasgow; University of Strathclyde. Recreations: travel; eating out; motor racing. Address: (b.) Royal Hospital for Sick Children, Dalnair Street, Glasgow G3 8SJ.
E-mail: iain.wallace@ggc.scot.nhs.uk

Wallace, Rev. James, MA, BD. Minister of Peebles: St. Andrews Leckie Church of Scotland, since 1983; NHS Spiritual Care, Chaplain, NHS Borders, since 2005; b. 8.9.46, Greenock; m., Marjorie; 1 s.; 2 d. Educ. Dunfermline High School; Edinburgh University; New College, Edinburgh. Assistant, Paisley Abbey, 1972-73; Minister of Lochcraig, Church of Scotland, Fife, 1973-83; Part-time Chaplain to Hay Lodge Hospital, 1983-2005. Recreations: rugby; music; reading. Address: Mansefield, Innerleithen Road, Peebles EH45 8BE; T.-01721 721749; e-mail: jimwallace@freeola.com

Wallace of Tankerness, Rt. Hon. Lord (James Robert Wallace), PC, QC, MA (Cantab), LLB (Edinburgh), Hon DLitt (Heriot-Watt). Created Life Peer, 2007; Hon. Professor, Institute of Petroleum Engineering, Heriot-Watt University, 2007; Board of St. Magnus Festival, 2007; MSP (Liberal Democrat), Orkney, 1999-2007; Deputy First Minister, 1999-2005; Minister for Justice, 1999-2003; Minister for Enterprise and Lifelong Learning, 2003-05; MP (Liberal Democrat, formerly Liberal), Orkney and Shetland, 1983-2001; Leader, Scottish Liberal Democrats, 1992-2005; Advocate, 1979; QC (Scot.), 1997; b. 25.8.54, Annan; m., Rosemary Janet Fraser; 2 d. Educ. Annan Academy; Downing College, Cambridge; Edinburgh University. Called to Scottish Bar, 1979; contested Dumfries, 1979, and South of Scotland Euro Constituency, 1979; Member, Scottish Liberal Party Executive, 1976-85 (Vice-Chairman, Policy, 1982-85); Honorary President, Scottish Young Liberals, 1984-85; Liberal Democrat Spokesman on Fisheries, 1988-97, and on Scotland, since 1992; jointly awarded Andrew Fletcher Award for services to Scotland, 1998. Publication: New Deal for Rural Scotland (Co-Editor), 1983. Recreations: golf; reading; travelling. Address: (h.) Northwood House, Tankerness, Orkney KW17 2QS; T.-01856 861383; e-mail: wallacej@parliament.uk

Wallace, John, OBE, MA, FRSAMD, FRAM, HonRCM. Principal, Royal Scottish Academy of Music and Drama, since 2002; b. Methilhill. Educ. Buckhaven High School; King's College, Cambridge; York University; Royal Academy of Music. Principal Trumpet, Philharmonia Orchestra, 1976-95; Principal Trumpet, London Sinfonietta, 1987-2001; founded The Wallace Collection (brass ensemble), 1986; Artistic Director of Brass, Royal Academy of Music, 1993-2001; has premiered new works by Peter Maxwell Davies, Harrison Birtwistle, H K Gruber, Malcolm Arnold, James MacMillan, Stuart MacRae, Mark Anthony Turnage and Jonathan Dove. Publication: Companion to Brass Instruments (Co-Editor), 1997. Address: (b.) RSAMD, 100 Renfrew Street, Glasgow G2 3DB.

Wallace, Rev. William Fitch, BDS, BD. Minister, Pulteneytown and Thrumster Church, since 1990; Convener, Church of Scotland Board of Ministry, 2002-03; b. 6.10.39, Falkirk; m., Jean Wyness Hill; 1 s.; 3 d. Educ. Allan Glen's School; Glasgow University; Edinburgh University. Minister, Wick St. Andrew's and Thrumster Church, 1974-90; former missionary dentist. Convener, Church of Scotland Board of Social Responsibility, 1993-97. Recreations: family; golf; gardening. Address: The Manse, Coronation Street, Wick KW1 5LS; T.-01955 603166.

Wallace, Professor William Villiers, MA, FRHistS. Director, Institute of Russian and East European Studies, Glasgow University, 1979-92, now Senior Research Fellow; Vice-President, Council for Education in World Citizenship, since 1996; b. 15.12.26, Glasgow; m., Gulli Fyfe; 2 s.; 1 d. Educ. Hutchesons' Boys' Grammar School; Glasgow University; London University. RNVR, 1944-47; appointments in History, Pittsburgh University, London University, Aberdeen University, Durham University, 1953-67; Professor of History, New University of Ulster, 1967-79; Dean of Social Sciences, University of Glasgow, 1989-92. President, Association of University Teachers, 1974-75, Chairman, Association of University Teachers (Scotland), 1986-88; Member of Council of Royal Institute of International Affairs and Chairman of Scottish Branch, 1984-89; Member of Scottish Committee of British Council, 1988-2000; Foreign Member, Russian Academy of Technological Sciences; Visiting Professor, Sunderland University, 1995-2000. Address: (b.) Department of Russian and East European Studies, Glasgow University, Hetherington Building, Bute Gardens, Glasgow G12 8RS; T.-0141-330 5585.

Walls, Professor Andrew Finlay, OBE, MA, BLitt, DD, FSA Scot. Honorary Professor, Edinburgh University, since 1987; Curator of Collections, Centre for the Study of Christianity in the Non-Western World, since 1996; Emeritus Professor, Religious Studies, University of Aberdeen; b. 21.4.28; m., Doreen Mary Harden; 1 s.; 1 d. Librarian, Tyndale House, Cambridge, 1952-57; Lecturer in Theology, Fourah Bay College, Sierra Leone, 1957-62; Head, Department of Religion, Nigeria University, 1962-65; Aberdeen University: Lecturer in Church History, 1966-69, Senior Lecturer, 1969, first Head, Department of Religious Studies, and Riddoch Lecturer in Comparative Religion, 1970, Reader, 1975, Professor of Religious Studies, 1979-85, Emeritus Professor, 1985; Director, Centre for the Study of Christianity in the Non-Western World, 1982-96; Visiting Professor of World Christianity, Yale University, 1988; Visiting Professor of Ecumenics and Mission, Princeton Theological Seminary, 1997-2001; Monrad Visiting Professor of World Christianity, Harvard University, 2000. Co-opted Member, Aberdeen Education Committee, 1971-74; Aberdeen City Councillor, 1974-80; Convener, Arts and Recreation, COSLA, 1978-80; Chairman, Council for Museums and Galleries in Scotland, 1978-81; Vice-Chairman, Committee of Area Museums Councils, 1980-81; Member, Williams Committee on the future of the national museums, 1979-82; Trustee, National Museum of Antiquities of Scotland, 1982-85; Member, Museums Advisory Board for Scotland, 1984-85; Trustee, National Museums of Scotland, 1985-87; Methodist Preacher; Past Chairman, Disablement Income Group, Scotland; President, British Association for the History of Religions, 1977-80; Secretary, Scottish Institute of Missionary Studies; Editor, Journal of Religion in Africa, 1967-86; Henry Martyn Lectures, Cambridge University, 1988; Margaret Harris Lectures, Dundee University, 1989; Annual Missiology Lecturer, Fuller Theological Seminary, 1996; Burns Lecturer, Otago University, New Zealand, 2000; Lowell Lecturer, Boston University, 2004; Bainton Lecturer, Yale Divinity School, 2004; Co-chair, Yale-Edinburgh Group on the History of the Missionary Movement; Emeritus Professor, Akrofi Christaller Memorial Centre, Ghana, 2003. Distinguished Career Award, American Society of Church History, 2007. Address: (h.) 58 Stanley Street, Aberdeen AB10 6UR; T.-01224 581929.

Walsh, Garry Michael, MSc, PhD, FIMLS. Reader, School of Medicine, University of Aberdeen, since 2004; b. 4.8.57, London; m., Catherine. Educ. St. James' School, London; Brunel University; London University. Medical Laboratory Scientific Officer, Histocompatability Testing Laboratory, Royal Postgraduate Medical School, London; academic research, Cardiothoracic Institute, Brompton Hospital, London; Visiting Fellow, Allergy Division, National Children's Hospital, Tokyo, Japan; postdoctoral position, University of Oxford; Senior Research Fellow/Honorary Lecturer, later Honorary Senior Lecturer, Department of Medicine and Therapeutics, University of Leciester Medical School; joined Aberdeen University, 1997 as Senior Lecturer. Scientific Advisor, UCB Institute of Allergy, Brussels; Member, MRC Advisory Board; Founding Editor of Therapeutics and Clinical Risk Management; Member of Editorial Board of Clinical and Experimental Allergy. Publications: over 100 papers and review articles in international scientific and medical journals). Recreations: hillwalking; golf; gastronome; motorocycling. Address: Department of Medicine and Therapeutics, Institute of Medical Sciences, University of Aberdeen, Foresterhill, Aberdeen AB25 2ZD; T.-01224 552786; e-mail: g.m.walsh@abdn.ac.uk

Walsh, Professor Timothy Simon, BSc (Hons), MBChB (Hons), FRCP, FRCA, MD, MSc. Consultant, Anaesthetics and Intensive Care, Edinburgh Royal Infirmary, since 1999; Professor, University of Edinburgh, since 1999; b. 17.1.64, Redhill, Surrey; m., Claire Doldon; 3 s. Educ. Trinity School, Croydon; University of Edinburgh. Trained in general medicine, anaesthetics and intensive care in South East Scotland; medical officer, rural South Africa, 1989-90; research, Scottish Liver Transplant Unit. Publications: 45 publications in area of critical care, since 2000. Address: Royal Infirmary of Edinburgh, Edinburgh EH3 9YW; T.-0131-536 1000.

Walton, Professor Henry John, MD, PhD, FRCPE, FRCPsych, DPM, Hon.MD. Physician; Emeritus Professor of Psychiatry and of International Medical Education, Edinburgh University; Hon. Fellow, College of Medicine, Edinburgh University; b. 15.2.24, South Africa; m., Sula Wolff. Educ. University of Cape Town; London University; Columbia University, NY; Edinburgh University. Registrar in Neurology and Psychiatry, University of Cape Town, 1946-54; Head, Department of Psychiatry, 1957-60; Senior Registrar, Maudsley Hospital, London, 1955-57; Senior Lecturer in Psychiatry, then Professor of Psychiatry, Edinburgh University, 1962-85; appointed Professor of International Medical Education, 1986; former Editor, Medical Education; President, Association for Medical Education in Europe, 1972-86, Hon. Life President, since 1986; Immediate Past-President, World Federation for Medical Education (Member, Executive Council); frequent Consultant to WHO; Member, Academies of Medicine of Argentina, Belgium and Poland; Member of Presidium, Albert Schweitzer World Academy of Medicine, Warsaw, 2003; Chairman, Board of Governors, Edinburgh Printmakers, 2000-04. Publications: as Editor: Small Group Psychotherapy, 1974; Dictionary of Psychiatry, 1985; as Co-Editor: Newer Developments in Assessing Clinical Competence, 1986; as Co-Author: Alcoholism, 1988; Report of the World Conference on Medical Education, 1988; Report on World Summit of Medical Education, 1993; International Medical Education in Graduate Prospects in a Changing World, 1998; as Contributor: Contemporary Psychiatry, 2001; International Encyclopaedia of the Social and Behavioural Sciences, 2001. Recreations: literature; visual arts, particularly Western painting and Chinese and Japanese art. Address: 38 Blacket Place, Edinburgh, EH9 1RL; T.-0131-667 7811.

Walton, Professor John Christopher, BSc, PhD, DSc, CChem, FRSC, FRSE. Research Professor of Chemistry, St. Andrews University, since 1997; b. 4.12.41, St. Albans;

m., Jane Lehman; 1 s.; 1 d. Educ. Watford Grammar School for Boys; Sheffield University. Assistant Lecturer: Queen's College, St. Andrews, 1966-67, Dundee University, 1967-69; Lecturer in Chemistry, United College, St. Andrews, 1969-80; Senior Lecturer, 1980-86, Reader, 1986-96. Elder, Seventh-day Adventist Church. Recreations: music; philosophy. Address: (b.) School of Chemistry, St. Andrews University, St. Andrews, Fife, KY16 9ST; T.-01334 463864.

Wannop, Professor Urlan Alistair, OBE, MA, MCD, MRTPI. Emeritus Professor of Urban and Regional Planning, Strathclyde University; b. 16.4.31, Newtown St. Boswells; 1 s.; 1 d. Educ. Aberdeen Grammar School; Edinburgh University; Liverpool University. Appointments in public and private practice, 1956-68; Team Leader, Coventry-Solihull-Warwickshire Sub-Regional Planning Study, 1968-71; Director, West Central Scotland Plan, 1972-74; Senior Deputy Director of Planning, Strathclyde Regional Council, 1975-81; Professor of Urban and Regional Planning, Strathclyde University, 1981-96. Member, Parliamentary Boundary Commission for Scotland, 1983-98. Address: (h.) 43 Lomond Street, Helensburgh G84 7ES; T.-01436 674622.

Ward, Professor Sir John Macqueen, CBE, CA, Companion, FRSE, CIEE, FRSA. Chairman, Scottish Enterprise; Chairman, European Assets Trust NV; Trustee, National Museums of Scotland; former Resident Director, Scotland and North of England, IBM United Kingdom Ltd; Professor, Heriot Watt University; former Chairman, Scottish Homes; former Chairman, Dunfermline Building Society; b. 1.8.40, Edinburgh; m., Barbara Macintosh; 1 s.; 3 d. Educ. Edinburgh Academy; Fettes College. Joined IBM UK Ltd. at Greenock plant, 1966; worked in France and UK; appointed European Director of Information Systems, 1975, and Havant Site Director, 1981. Past Chairman: SQA, Macfarlane Group, Queen Margaret University College, Governing Body, Scottish CBI, Scottish Post Office Board, Quality Scotland Foundation, Advisory Scottish Council for Education and Training Targets, Scottish Electronics Forum, Institute of Technology Management; former Director, Scottish Business in the Community; Honorary Doctorate, Napier University, Strathclyde University, Heriot-Watt University, Glasgow Caledonian University; Queen Margaret University College. Address: (b.) 5 Atlantic Quay, 150 Broomielaw, Glasgow G2 8LU; T.-0141 248 2700.

Ward, Professor Mark Gordon, BA. Professor of German Language and Literature, Glasgow University, since 1997; Director of Studies, Crichton Campus, since 1999; Principal Examiner, CSYS AH German, since 1987; b. 4.2.51, Hemel Hempstead; m., Janet Helen; 2 s. Educ. Leeds Grammar School; King's College, London University. Tutorial Research Scholar, Bedford College, London University, 1974-75; Lecturer, then Senior Lecturer, Department of German, Glasgow University, 1975-97; Dean, Faculty of Arts, 1995-99. Publications include: Theodor Storm: Der Schimmelreiter, 1988; Laughter, Comedy and Aesthetics: Kleist's Der Zerbrochne Krug, 1995; Perspectives on German Realism, 1998; Romantic Dreams, 1998; Theodor Storm – Erzählstrategien und Patriarchat, 1999. Recreations: music; gardening; sport. Address: (b.) University of Glasgow, Crichton Campus, Dumfries DG1 4ZL; T.-01387 702037; e-mail: mgw@arts.gla.ac.uk

Ward, Maxwell Colin Bernard, MA. Managing Director, The Independent Investment Trust, since 2000; Chairman: Scottish Equitable Policyholders' Trust, since 2004; Director, Aegon UK, since 1999; Chairman, Dunedin Income Growth Investment Trust, 2002-06; Director, Foreign and Colonial Investment Trust, since 2001; b. 22.8.49, Sherborne; m., Sarah Marsham; 2 s.; 2 d. Educ. Harrow; St. Catharine's, Cambridge. Baillie Gifford & Co.: Trainee, 1971-75, Partner, 1975-2000. Director: Scottish

Equitable Life Assurance Society, 1988-94, Scottish Equitable plc, 1995-99; Board Member, Capability Scotland. Recreations: tennis; squash; bridge; country pursuits. Address: (b.) 11 Charlotte Square, Edinburgh EH2 4DR; T.-0131-220 4167.

Ward Thompson, Professor Catharine J., BSc, DipLA, FLI, FRSA. Research Professor in Landscape Architecture and Director of OPENspace Research Centre, Edinburgh College of Art/Heriot Watt University, since 2002; Hon. Professor, University of Edinburgh, Arts, Culture and Environment, since 2007; b. 5.12.52; m., Henry Swift Thompson; 3 c. Educ. Holy Cross Convent, Chalfont St. Peter; Southampton University; Edinburgh University. Landscape Assistant/Landscape Architect/ Senior Landscape Architect, 1973-81; Lecturer and Studio Instructor, School of Landscape Architecture, Edinburgh College of Art, 1981-88; Head of School, 1989-2000; Director of Research, Environmental Studies, 2000-02; Consultant, Landscape Design and Research Unit, Heriot-Watt University, 1989-2005. Recreations: dance; gardening. Address: (h.) 11 Douglas Crescent, Edinburgh EH12 5BB; T.-0131-221 6176 (work).

Wardrop, James Arneil, DL, FCIBS, FUniv, FSA (Scot). Retired Banker; Deputy Lieutenant, Renfrewshire; Chairman, Peter Brough Bequest Fund; Chairman, Accord Hospice; Secretary, Society of Friends of Paisley Abbey; Governor, University of Paisley; Hon. Vice-Patron, Japan Society of Scotland; Hon. President, Paisley Art Institute; b. 19.4.40, Paisley. Educ. John Neilson Institution, Paisley. Joined National Bank of Scotland, by a process of mergers absorbed into Royal Bank of Scotland, Deputy Agent, San Francisco, 1978-81, Manager, International Division, 1981-94 - Edinburgh and Glasgow; Honorary Vice President, Ferguslie Cricket Club; Hon. President, T.S. Grenville, Sea Cadets, Paisley Unit; Elder, Paisley Abbey; Trustee, Miss Kibble's Trust; Director, Incorporated Glasgow Renfrewshire Society; Member, Committee, Scotland's Gardens Scheme, Renfrewshire and Inverclyde and National Committee; Member, Renfrewshire Valuation Appeal Panel; Past Deacon, Paisley Hammermen Society; Member of Executive, Paisley District Battalion, the Boys' Brigade; Lately Box Master, Old Weavers Incorporation, Paisley. Recreations: country pursuits; gardening; music. Address: (h.) Saint Kevins, Meikleriggs, Paisley, PA2 9PT; T.-0141-887 3627.

Wark, Kirsty, BA; b. 1955, Dumfries; m., Alan Clements; 1 s.; 1 d. Educ. Edinburgh University. Joined BBC as radio researcher, 1976; became radio producer, current affairs; produced and presented Seven Days, 1985; then concentrated on presenting (Reporting Scotland; Left, Right and Centre); General Election night coverage, 1987, 1992, 1997; BBC coverage, Scottish Parliamentary elections, 1999; Presenter, Breakfast Time, Edinburgh Nights; Presenter, The Late Show, 1990-93; Presenter, One Foot in the Past, 1993-99; joined Newsnight and Newsnight Review's team of presenters, 1993; Presenter, Restless Nation, Building a Nation; The Kirsty Wark Show; Lives Less Ordinary; Tales from Europe. Journalist of the Year, BAFTA Scotland, 1993; Best TV Presenter award, 1997; Scot of the Year, 1998; Scottish Insider Business Woman of the Year, 2002; former Council Member, Prince's Trust; Patron, Maggie's Centre; formed production company with husband in 1990. Recreations: family; tennis; swimming; cooking; beach-combing; reading. Address: (b.) Black Pepper Media Ltd., PO Box 26323, Ayr KA7 9AY; e-mail: info@blackpeppermedia.com web: www.blackpeppermedia.com

Warner of Craigenmaddie, Gerald, OStJ, MA, FSAScot. Author; Columnist, Scotland on Sunday, 1997-2007; Leader Writer, Scottish Daily Mail, since 1998; b. 22.3.45. Educ. St. Aloysius' College, Glasgow; Glasgow University. Vice-Chairman, Una Voce (International Latin Mass Federation),

Scotland, 1965-66; Administrative Assistant, Glasgow University, 1971-74; author and broadcaster, 1974-89; Diarist (under pseudonym Henry Cockburn), Sunday Times Scotland, 1989-95; columnist, 1992-95; Special Adviser to Secretary of State for Scotland, 1995-97. Council Member, 1745 Association, 1967-70; Member, Scottish Council of Monarchist League, 1969-71; Chairman, The Monday Club - Scotland, 1973-74; Secretary, Conservative Party's Scottish Policy Committee on Education, 1976-77; Parliamentary candidate, Hamilton, October 1974. Knight of Grace and Devotion, Sovereign Military Order of Malta, 1979; Knight, Jure Sanguinis, Sacred Military Constantinian Order of St. George, 1994; Knight of the Order of Merit of St. Joseph of Tuscany, 2005; Knight of the Order of St. Maurice and St. Lazarus, 2005. Publications: Homelands of the Clans, 1980; Being of Sound Mind, 1980; Tales of the Scottish Highlands, 1982; Conquering by Degrees, 1985; The Scottish Tory Party: A History, 1988; The Sacred Military Order of St. Stephen Pope and Martyr, 2005; Scotland's Ten Tomorrows (contributor), 2006. Recreations: literature; genealogy; Brummelliana. Address: 17 Huntly Gardens, Glasgow G12 9AT.

Warnock, Henry, BSc, CEng, MCIBSE, MIMechE. Chairman, Scottish Youth Theatre, since 1998; Director, Henderson Warnock, since 1993; b. 14.2.57, Glasgow; m., Felicity. Educ. Allan Glens School, Glasgow; University of Strathclyde. Design Engineer: IDC, Stratford-upon-Avon, DSSR, Glasgow; Senior Design Engineer: Building Design Partnership, Brian Ford Partnership. Director: Theatre Cryptic, Dancebase, Edinburgh. Recreations: travelling; rollerblading; music; film. Address: 38 New City Road, Glasgow G4 9JT; T.-0141-353 2444; e-mail: hwarnock@hendersonwarnock.com

Waterhouse, Professor Lorraine Alice Margaret, BA (Maths/Psych), MSW. Professor of Social Work, University of Edinburgh, since 1994, formerly Head of School, Social and Political Studies; b. 3.7.49, Toronto, Canada; m., J. D. Waterhouse; 1 s.; 1 d. Educ. St. Michaels, London, Ontario, Canada; University of Western Ontario, London, Canada. Social Worker, Royal Hospital for Sick Children, Dept. of Child and Family Psychiatry, Edinburgh, 1972-76; Lecturer, Social Work (Half-Time), University of Edinburgh, 1976-80; Senior Social Worker (Half-Time), Royal Hospital for Sick Children, Edinburgh, 1976-80; University of Edinburgh: Lecturer, Social Work (Half-Time), 1980-92, Lecturer, Social Policy (Quarter-Time), 1988-94, Senior Lecturer, Social Work (Part-Time), 1992-94. Member: Joint University Council (Social Work), 1994-2000, Editorial Board, Journal of Social Work, since 2001, Editorial Board, Journal of Child and Family Social Work, since 1996, Editorial Board, British Journal of Social Work, since 2004; Convenor, Enquire, Children in Scotland, 2000-03; Chair, Individual Employment Complaints Tribunals for Edinburgh City, since 1998. Address: (b.) University of Edinburgh, School of Social and Political Studies, Adam Ferguson Building, George Square, Edinburgh EH8 9LL; T.-0131 650 3913; e-mail: lorraine.waterhouse@ed.ac.uk

Waters, Donald Henry, OBE, CA. Director, Scottish Media Group, 1997-2005; Deputy Chairman and Chief Executive, Grampian Television PLC, 1993-97 (Chief Executive and Director, 1987-93); b. 17.12.37, Edinburgh; m., June Leslie Hutchison; 1 s.; 2 d. Educ. George Watson's, Edinburgh; Inverness Royal Academy. Director, John M. Henderson and Co. Ltd., 1972-75; Grampian Television PLC: Company Secretary, 1975, Director of Finance, 1979; Director: Scottish Television and Grampian Sales Ltd., 1980-97, Moray Firth Radio Ltd., 1982-97, Independent Television Publications Ltd., 1987-90,

Cablevision Scotland PLC, 1987-91; Chairman, Celtic Film and Television Association, 1994-96; Vice-Chairman, BAFTA Scotland; Visiting Professor of Film and Media Studies, Stirling University; Chairman, Police Dependant Trust for Grampian, 1992-96; Past Chairman, Royal Northern and University Club, Aberdeen, Chairman, Glenburnie Properties Ltd., 1993-97; Director: Central Scotland Radio Ltd. (Scot FM), 1994-96 (Chairman, 1995-96), GRT Bus Group PLC, 1994-96, British Linen Bank Ltd., 1995-99, Bank of Scotland North of Scotland Local Board, 1999-2001, Scottish Post Office Board, 1996-2001, Consignia Advisory Board for Scotland, 2001-03, Johnstons of Elgin Ltd., since 1999, Aberdeen Asset Management PLC, since 2000; Member, ITV Council and ITV Broadcast Board; Fellow, Royal Society of Arts; Council Member, CBI Scotland, 1994-2001; Council Member, Cinema and Television Benevolent Fund, 1987-99; Member, Royal Television Society, since 1988; Director, Aberdeen Royal Hospital NHS Trust, 1996-99; Chairman, New Royal Aberdeen Children's Hospital Project Steering Group; Member of Council, Aberdeen Chamber of Commerce, 1996-2003; Governor, Aberdeen University, 1998; Member, Grampian and Islands Family Trust, since 1988; Joint Chairman, Grampian Cancer Macmillan Appeal, 1999; Member of Council, SATRO; Burgess of Guild Assessor, 1997-2002. Address: (h.) Balquhidder, 141 North Deeside Road, Milltimber, Aberdeen AB13 0JS; T.-Aberdeen 867131; e-mail: donaldwaters@btinternet.com

Waters, Fergus Cameron. Director, Scottish Mining Museum, since 1996; b. 15.2.57, Tanzania; m., Alison Crawford. Educ. Rannoch School; Moray College of Further Education. Marketing Manager, Castlewynd Studios, 1984-88; Commercial and Marketing Manager, Ford and Etal Estates, 1988-94; General Manager, Hartlepool Historic Quay, 1994-96. Recreations: cycling; skiing; sailing. Address: (b.) Scottish Mining Museum, Lady Victoria Colliery, Newtongrange EH22 4QN; T.-0131-663 7519.
E-mail: enquiries@scottishminingmuseum.com

Watson of Invergowrie, Lord (Michael Goodall Watson), BA (Hons). MSP (Labour), Glasgow Cathcart, 1999-2005; Minister for Tourism, Culture and Sport, Scottish Executive, 2001-03; MP (Labour), Glasgow Central, 1989-97; b. 1.5.49, Cambuslang. Address: (b.) House of Lords, Westminster, London SW1A 0PW.

Watson, Alexander Bell, OBE, DL, MA, MEd, FCMI, FSA Scot, FRSA. Deputy Lieutenant for Angus, since 2007; Secretary, Society of Local Authority Chief Executives & Senior Managers (Scotland), since 2005; Chair of Angus College Board of Management, since 2005; Chair, Entitlement Card Project Group, Customer First, since 2005; Member of Board of NHS Tayside, since 2005; Executive Director of Young Scot, since 2005; Member, Scottish Funding Council (2006); Chief Executive, Angus Council, 1995-2005 (Chief Executive, Tayside Regional Council, 1995); Honorary Fellow, University of Abertay; b. 20.5.45, Airdrie; m., Jean; 3 s. Educ. Airdrie Academy; Glasgow University; Jordanhill College of Education. Teacher of Classics, Morrison's Academy, Crieff, 1968; Principal Teacher of Classics: Portree High School, 1971, McLaren High School, Callander, 1973; Assistant Director of Education: Central, 1975, Strathclyde, 1983; Senior Depute Director of Education, Central Regional Council, 1986; Director of Education, Tayside Regional Council, 1990-94. President, then General Secretary, Association of Directors of Education in Scotland, 1992-95; Chair, National Co-ordinating Committee on Staff Development of Teachers, 1994-95; Member, Board of Management, Angus College, since 1997; Hon. Secretary, Society of Local Authority Chief Executives and Senior Managers

(Scotland), 1997-2005; Chair, Scottish Advisory Committee, Duke of Edinburgh's Award Scheme, 1999-2003; Vice-Chairman, Young Scot, 2002-05; Vice-Chairman, Angus College Board of Management, 2003-05; Member, Carnegie Commission on Rural Community Development, since 2004. Recreations: music; reading; fishing; Scottish heritage; DIY. Address: (b.) SOLACE (Scotland), Dundee City Council, Floor 1, Podium Block, 28 Crichton Street, Dundee DD1 3RZ; T.-07707 255 003.

Watson, Alistair Gordon, LLB, DipLP, NP. Sheriff of North Strathclyde at Kilmarnock, since 2007; b. 1.7.59, Dundee; m., Susan; 1 s.; 2 d. Educ. High School of Dundee; University of Dundee. Procurator Fiscal Depute (1984-89); Partner in Cameron Pinkerton & Co, Solicitors, then Watson & Mackay, Solicitors, 1989-98; appointed Scotland's First Public Defender in 1998; Director of Public Defence Solicitors' Office, 1998-2005; All Scotland Floating Sheriff, at North Strathclyde, 2005-07. Recreations: family; photography. Address: (b.) Kilmarnock Sheriff Court, St Marnock Street, Kilmarnock KA1 1ED.

Watson, Dave, LLB. Unison Scottish Organiser (Policy), since 1999; b. 24.5.56, Liverpool; m., Maureen. Educ. Nower Hill High School; Stanmore College; University of Strathclyde. Leisure Management, London Borough Harrow, 1974-79; Organising Assistant, South Wales NALGO; Branch Organiser, Dorset NALGO, 1980-90; Regional Officer, Unison Scotland, 1990-99; Scottish Executive Health Department HR Strategy Implementation Manager (Secondment), 1999-2001. Secretary, Socialist Health Association; Scottish Labour Party Executive; Vice-Chair, Scottish Labour Party, 2007; Secretary, Scottish Trade Union Labour Party (STULP). Recreations: hillwalking; military history. Address: (b.) Unison House, 14 West Campbell Street, Glasgow G2 6RX; T.-0870 7777 006; e-mail: d.watson@unison.co.uk

Watson, Garry Sanderson, OBE, CA; b. 31.7.40, Glasgow; m., Elizabeth Ann; 4 d. Educ. Glasgow Academy. Hill Samuel Bank, 1969-91; Scottish Legal Services Ombudsman, 1994-2000; Advisor to Standards Committee, Scottish Parliament, 2000-01; Governor, Macaulay Land Use Research Institute, 1997-2004 (Vice-Chairman, 2003/04); Director, Business in the Community, 1985-88; Director, Braveheart Investment Group plc, since 2001 (Chairman, since 2003); Hon. Treasurer, National Association of Citizens' Advice Bureaux, 1986-91; Hon. Treasurer, Scottish Association of CAB, 1992-95; Director, Edinvar Housing Association, 1992-2003 (Chair, 1997-2001); Director, The Places for People Group, since 2003. Recreations: tennis; hill-walking; shooting. Address: (h.) Newlandburn House, Newlandrig, by Gorebridge, Midlothian, EH23 4NS; T.-01875 820939.

Watson, Professor George Alistair, BSc, MSc, PhD, FIMA, FRSE. Professor, Department of Mathematics, Dundee University, since 1988; b. 30.9.42, Aberfeldy; m., Hilary Mackay; 1 d. Educ. Breadalbane Academy; Edinburgh University; Australian National University. Demonstrator, Computer Unit, Edinburgh University, 1964-66; Dundee University: Research Fellow, then Lecturer, Mathematics Department, 1969-82; Senior Lecturer, Mathematical Sciences Department, 1982-84; Reader, Department of Mathematics and Computer Science, 1984-88. Recreation: gardening. Address: (h.) 7 Albany Road, Broughty Ferry, Dundee DD5 1NS; T.-01382 779473.

Watson, Professor George Joseph Bernard, BA, BLitt. Emeritus Professor, Irish Literature in the English

Language, Aberdeen University, formerly Director, Research Institute of Irish and Scottish Studies; b. 8.12.42, Portadown; m., Joanna King; 1 s.; 2 d. Educ. St Patrick's College, Armagh; Queen's University, Belfast; Wadham College, Oxford. Lecturer, Senior Lecturer, Reader, Professor, Department of English, Aberdeen University; Visiting Professor, Hamilton College, USA, 1985-86, Wake Forest University, USA, 1989; Andrew Mellon Fellow, National Humanities Center, USA, 2000-01; Director, Yeats International Summer School, Sligo, 1998-2000. Vice-Chair, British Association of Irish Studies, 1988-1992; Secretary, Irish-Scottish Academic Initiative, 1996-2000. Publications: Irish Identity and the Literary Revival, 1979; Drama, 1984; edited Yeats's Short Fiction, 1995. Recreations: football; golf; walking in mountains. Address: (b.) Aberdeen University, 19 College Bounds, Old Aberdeen, Aberdeen AB24 3UG; T.-01224 272196.

Watson, Professor John Francis, BSc, PhD, CEng, FIEE, SMIEEE. Dean, Faculty of Design and Technology, Robert Gordon University, since 2005; b. 3.1.55, Kirkcaldy; m., Patricia; 3 s. Educ. Kirkcaldy High School; Heriot Watt University. Development Engineer, GEC, 1977-81; RGIT: Lecturer, 1981-86, Senior Lecturer, 2003-06, Head, School of Engineering. Recreations: fly fishing; running and occasionally walking. Address: (b.) Faculty of Design and Technology, Robert Gordon University, Scott Sutherland Building, Garthdee Road, Aberdeen AB10 7QB; T.-01224 263500; e-mail: j.f.watson@rgu.ac.uk

Watson, John Matthew, BSc Astrophysics (Edin), MSc Astrophysics (London). Programme Director, Scotland, Amnesty International, since 2007; b. 30.6.69, Glasgow; m., Davina Shiell; 1 d. Educ. Holyrood Secondary, Glasgow; Edinburgh University; London University. Youth and Student Co-ordinator, CND; National Co-ordinator, SERA (Socialist Environment and Resources Association); Head of Scottish Campaigns, World Development Movement; Parliamentary Officer, Barnardo's. Address: (b.) Rosebery House, 9 Haymarket Terrace, Edinburgh EH12 5EZ; T.-0131 313 7012; e-mail: john.watson@amnesty.org.uk

Watson, Norma Anne, DCE, ACE, NFFC, FEIS, FRSA. Convener, General Teaching Council for Scotland, 1999-2007; Head Teacher, Kirkhill Nursery School, Broxburn, 1983-2007; b. Edinburgh; m., Christopher Simpson Watson. Educ. Broxburn Academy; Moray House College of Education. Vice-Convener, Educational Institute of Scotland Education Committee. Recreations: walking; reading. Address: (b.) General Teaching Council for Scotland, Clerwood House, 96 Clermiston Road, Edinburgh EH12 6UT; T.-0131 314 6000.

Watson, Peter, BA, LLB, SSC. Solicitor (Levy & McRae); b. 22.1.54, Greenock; m., Claire Watson; 2 d. Educ. Eastwood High School, Glasgow; Strathclyde University; Edinburgh University; Scandinavian Maritime Law Institute, Norway; Dundee Petroleum Law Institute. Qualified, 1981; Solicitor to the Supreme Courts; Notary Public; former Temporary Sheriff, now part-time Sheriff; Past President, Society of Solicitor Advocates; Hon. Vice-President and former Chairman, Association of Mediators; Visiting Professor, Nova University, Fort Lauderdale, Florida; Member, Steering Committee, and Negotiator, Piper Alpha Disaster Group; Secretary, Braer Disaster Group; Secretary, Lockerbie Air Disaster Group; former Official Collaborator, International Labour Organisation, Geneva; Member, Criminal Rules Council; Member, Board, Sports Law Centre, Anglia University; Honorary Citizen of Nashville, Tennessee; large media practice based in Glasgow. Publications: Civil Justice System in Britain; Crimes of War – The Antony Gecas Story; The Truth

Written in Blood; Dunblane – A Predictable Tragedy; DNA and the Criminal Trial; In Pursuit of Pan Am. Recreations: working out; drinking fine wine; golf. Address: (b.) Levy & McRae, 266 St. Vincent Street, Glasgow G2 5RL; T.-0141-307 2311.

Watson, Professor Roderick, MA, PhD, FRSE. Poet; Literary Critic and Writer; Professor in English, Stirling University; Director, Stirling Centre for Scottish Studies; b. 12.5.43, Aberdeen; m., Celia Hall Mackie; 1 s.; 1 d. Educ. Aberdeen Grammar School; Aberdeen University; Peterhouse, Cambridge. Lecturer in English, Victoria University, British Columbia, 1965-66; collections of poetry include Trio; True History on the Walls; Into The Blue Wavelengths. Other books include The Penguin Book of the Bicycle, MacDiarmid, The Poetry of Norman MacCaig, The Poetry of Scotland (Editor) and The Literature of Scotland (2 vols). Recreation: cycling; motor cycling. Address: (h.) 19 Millar Place, Stirling; T.-Stirling 475971.

Watt, David C., DipEd, BA, DPE, CYS. Scottish Director, Institute of Directors; author; m., Maggie. Board Member: Basketball Scotland, Scottish Gymnastics, Intellectual Assets Centre; former Scottish Partnership Manager, New Millennium Experience Company. Address: (b.) 29 Abercromby Place, Edinburgh EH3 6QE; T.-0131 557 5488.

Watt, Hamish, LLB, NP. Secretary/Treasurer, Montrose Chamber of Commerce, since 1984; b. 2.11.47; m., Sheena; 2 s. Educ. Forfar Academy; Dundee College; University of Dundee. Member of Montrose Port Authority; past Course Leader in Advocacy and Pleading, Dundee University. Recreations: reading; cycling; hill walking. Address: (b.) 55 High Street, Montrose DD10 8LR; T.-01674 671199; e-mail: hamish.watt@wattssolicitors.com

Watt, Jacqui, MA (Hons), MSc. Chief Executive, Scottish Federation of Housing Associations, since 2005; b. 29.1.63, Lerwick, Shetland. Educ. Anderson High School; Edinburgh and Bristol Universities. Set up a housing service in Shetland for the island's 2,500 tenants; Development Officer for a drugs project in South Wales; policy work with Cardiff City Council; set up one of the first Housing Consortia in Bath for people with learning and mental health problems; reorganised a collective women's organisation in London and this led to a Regional Manager post with Knightstone HA in Bristol; Gloucester City Council (Head of Housing DSO); returned to Scotland in 1999 as the Head of Housing Management for the City of Edinburgh Council; Executive Director, Community Services, Shetland (7 years). Recreations: swimming; dance, body work and music. Address: (b.) 4th Floor, Pegasus House, 375 West George Street, Glasgow G2 4LW; T.-0141 332 8113; e-mail: jwatt@sfha.co.uk

Watt, Jim, MBE (1980). Boxer; b. 18.7.48, Glasgow. Turned professional, 1968; British Lightweight Champion, 1972-73, 1975-77; European Lightweight Champion, 1977-79; World Lightweight Champion, 1979-81; four successful defences of World title; Freedom of Glasgow, 1981.

Watt, Karen, MA, MSc, ACIS. Director of Regulation and Inspection, Communities Scotland, since 2003; b. 5.7.64, Antrim; m., Dr Stephen Watt; 3 s. Educ. Antrim Grammar School; St Andrews University. Department of Social Security, 1987-91; Scottish Homes: Senior Planning

Analyst, 1991-96, Performance Auditor, 1996-98, Performance Audit Manager, 1998-2001; Head of Regulatory Policy and Information, Communities Scotland, 2001-03. Address: (b.) Highlander House, 58 Waterloo Street, Glasgow G2 7DA; T.-0141-305-4187; e-mail: karen.watt@communitiesscotland.gsi.gov.uk

Watt, Maureen. MSP (SNP), North East Scotland, since 2006; Minister for Schools and Skills, since 2007; b. 23.6.51, Aberdeen; m. Educ. Keith Grammar School; University of Strathclyde; University of Birmingham. Comprehensive School Teacher, Social Studies, Reading, Berkshire, 1974-76; Personnel Assistant, then Personnel Manager, Deutag Drilling (now part of the Abbot Group of Companies). Address: (b.) Scottish Parliament, Edinburgh EH99 1SP; Constituency Office: 825-827 Great Northern Road, Aberdeen AB24 2BR.

Watt, Professor Roger, BA (Cantab), PhD, FRSE. Professor of Psychology, Stirling University, since 1988; b. London; m., Helen; 2 s.; 1 d. Educ. St. Olaves School; Downing College, Cambridge. Formerly Scientist, MRC Applied Psychology Unit, Cambridge; expert witness, various including Cullen Inquiry and Ladbroke Grove Rail Crash. 2 books published. Recreation: trumpet player. Address: (b.) Department of Psychology, Stirling University, Stirling FK9 4LA; T.-01786 467640; e-mail: r.j.watt@stirling.ac.uk

Watters, Pat. President, Convention of Scottish Local Authorities, since 2001; b. 4.2.48, Glasgow; m., Marilyn; 1 s.; 1 d. Educ. Our Lady and St Margaret's School. Entered local government, Strathclyde Regional Council, 1982; Vice President, COSLA, 1999-2001; former COSLA Spokesperson for Personnel Resources and local government's Lead Negotiator; Chair, Scottish Strategy Forum for Local Authority Employees; Vice-Chair, Police Negotiating Board; Chair, PNB Chief Officers Committee; Member, South Lanarkshire Council, since 1995 (Chair of Corporate Resources). Address: (h.) 74 Juniper Avenue, East Kilbride G75 9JS; T.-0131 474 9200.

Watterson, Professor Andrew, BA, PhD, CFIOSH, FCR. Professor of Health, University of Stirling, since 2000; Director of Occupational and Enviromental Health Research Group, since 2000; b. 13.08.48. Lecturer in Health, Southampton University, 1980-92; Head of OSHU, NTU, 1992-94; Head of Department of Health, De Montfort University, Leicester and Professor of Occupational and Environmental Health, 1994-2000. Publications: author of 3 books, 1 edited book, 15 chapters in books and numerous peer reviewed papers in scientific and medical journals. Address: (b.) Occupational and Environmental Health Research Group, University of Stirling, Stirling FK9 4LA; e-mail: aew1@stir.ac.uk

Waugh, David, MLA, ARIBA, FLI, MRTPI, FRIAS. Architect; Landscape Architect; Planning Consultant; b. Scotland; m. Educ. Edinburgh College of Art, School of Architecture and School of Town Planning; University of Pennsylvania, School of Fine Arts, Department of Landscape Architecture. Sir Frank Mears and Partners: Consultant, Partner; Principal, David Waugh-Sir Frank Mears. Member: RIBA, RIAS, The Landscape Institute, RTPI; Awards and Commendations; Membership of Professional Committees. Recreations: travel; photography. Address: (b) 44 Northumberland Street, Edinburgh EH3 6JF.

Way of Plean, George Alexander, SBSt.J, LLB (Hons), FSAScot, FRSA, NP, SSC, Companion of the Order of Malta. Senior Litigation Partner, Beveridge and Kellas, SSC, since 1985; Procurator Fiscal to HM Court of Lord Lyon, since 2003; b. 22.5.56, Edinburgh; m., Rosemary Calder; 1 s. Educ. Boroughmuir School; University of Edinburgh. Apprenticed to W. F. M. Whitelaw, W. S.,

1978-80; Solicitor, Beveridge and Kellas, 1980-85. Secretary, Standing Council of Scottish Chiefs, 1984-2003; Member, Convention of the Baronage of Scotland; Past President, Society of Solicitors in the Supreme Courts; Member, Council, Law Society of Scotland, since 2001; Freeman, City of Glasgow, 1997. Publications: Collins Clans and Family Encyclopaedia (Editor-in-Chief); Homelands of the Clans; Everyday Scots Law; Scottish Clans and Tartans. Recreations: heraldry and orders of chivalry. Address: (b.) Hope Chambers, 52 Leith Walk, Leith, Edinburgh EH6 5HW; T.-0131-554 6321.

Weatherhead, Alexander Stewart, OBE, TD, MA, LLB. Retired Solicitor; formerly Senior Partner, Brechin Tindal Oatts (formerly Tindal Oatts), Solicitors, Glasgow (Partner, 1960-97, Consultant, 1997-98); b. 3.8.31, Edinburgh; m., Harriett Foye; 2 d. Educ. Glasgow Academy; Glasgow University. Royal Artillery, 1950-52; TA, 1952; Lt. Col. Commanding 277 (A&SH) Field Regiment, RA (TA), 1965-67, The Lowland Regiment, RA (T), 1967 and Glasgow and Strathclyde Universities OTC, 1970-73; Colonel, 1974; TAVR Colonel, Lowlands (West), 1974-76; ADC (TAVR) to The Queen, 1977-81; Honorary Colonel, Glasgow and Strathclyde Universities OTC, 1982-98; Member, Lowlands RFCA, since 1967, Chairman, 1990-93; Member, Royal Artillery Council for Scotland, 1972 (Vice Chairman, 1996-2001); Council Member, Law Society of Scotland, 1971-84 (Honorary Vice-President, 1983-84); Member, Royal Commission on Legal Services in Scotland, 1976-80; Council Member, Society for Computers and Law, 1973-86, Honorary Member, since 1986 (Chairman, 1981-84); Temporary Sheriff, 1985-92; Member, Royal Faculty of Procurators in Glasgow, since 1960 (Dean, 1991-95, Hon. Member, 1997); Director, Glasgow Chamber of Commerce, 1991-95; Member, Research Ethics Committee, Glasgow Royal Infirmary, 1999-2006; Member, Medical Research Ethics Committee, Scotland (B), 2005-06; Member, Incorporation of Weavers of Glasgow, since 1949; Commodore, Royal Western Yacht Club, 1995-98. Recreations: tennis; sailing; reading; music. Address: (h.) 52 Partickhill Road, Glasgow G11 5AB; T.-0141-334 6277.

Weaver, C. Giles H., FCA, MBA. Proprietor, Greywalls Hotel, Gullane, since 1976; Chairman, Kenmore European Industrial Fund Ltd.; Chair, Helical Bar PLC; Chairman, Charter European Trust PLC; b. 4.4.46; m., Rosamund B. Mayhew; 2 s.; 2 d. Educ. Eton College; London Business School. Ernst & Young, 1966-70; London Business School, 1971-73; Jessel Securities/Berry Wiggins, 1973-76; Director, Ivory & Sime plc, 1976-86; Managing Director Pensions, Prudential Portfolio Managers, 1986-90; Murray Johnstone Ltd.: CIO, 1990-93, Managing Director, 1993-99, Chairman, 1999-2000. Trustee, Lutyens Trust; Director: Aberdeen Asset Management plc, James Finlay Ltd.; Chair, New Club Edinburgh. Recreations: golf; bridge; skiing; stalking. Address: (b.) Greywalls, Gullane, East Lothian EH31 2EG; T.-01620 842144.

Weaver, Professor Lawrence Trevelyan, MA, MB BChir, DObstRCOG, DCH, MD, FRCP, FRCPGlas, FRCPCH, FRSA, DSc. Honorary Consultant Paediatrician, Royal Hospital for Sick Children, Yorkhill, Glasgow, since 1994; Samson Gemmell Professor of Child Health, University of Glasgow, since 1996; b. 13.10.48; m., Camilla Simmons; 1 s.; 1 d. Educ. Clifton College, Bristol; Corpus Christi College, Cambridge University; St. Thomas's Hospital Medical School. General professional training Newcastle University Hospitals; MRC Training Fellow, Dunn Nutritional Laboratory and Honorary Senior Registrar, Department of Paediatrics, Addenbrooke's Hospital, Cambridge, 1984-86; Clinical Research Fellow and Fulbright Scholar, Harvard Medical School Departments of Pediatric Gastroenterology and Nutrition, Children's

Hospital and Massachusetts General Hospital, Boston, 1987-88; Member, MRC Scientific Staff, Dunn Nutrition Laboratory and Honorary Consultant Paediatrician, Addenbrooke's Hospital and University of Cambridge, 1988-94; Reader in Human Nutrition, University of Glasgow, 1994-96. Address: Department of Child Health, Royal Hospital for Sick Children, Yorkhill, Glasgow G3 8SJ; T.-0141-201 0236.

Weaver, Professor Richard Young. Professor Emeritus, University of Glasgow; Visiting Professor, Hunter Centre for Entrepreneurship, University of Strathclyde; b. 9.10.45, Glasgow; m., Linda; 2 s. Educ. University of Strathclyde. Management Consultant, since 1980; Managing Director, 1984-94. Member, Royal Society of Edinburgh Enterprise Fellowship Committee, 1997; Member, UK Committee on Enterprise, 1987. Recreations: music; reading. Address: (b.) University of Glasgow, University Avenue, Glasgow G12 8QQ; e-mail: profweaver@mac.com

Webb, Professor David John, MD, DSc, FRCP, FRCPE, FRSE, FESC, FFPM, FMedSci, FBPharmacolS. Christison Professor of Therapeutics and Clinical Pharmacology, Clinical Pharmacology Unit and Research Centre, Edinburgh University, since 1995; Head, University Department of Medical Sciences, Western General Hospital, Edinburgh, 1998-2001; Leader, Wellcome Trust Cardiovascular Research Initiative, 1998-2001; Head, Centre for Research in Cardiovascular Science, Edinburgh University, 1997-2004; Director, Clinical Research Centre and Honorary Consultant Physician, Western General Hospital, Edinburgh, since 1990; Chair, UK Committee Heads and Professors of Clinical Pharmacology and Therapeutics, 2004; b. 1.9.53, Greenwich; m., Dr. Margaret Jane Cullen; 3 s. Educ. Dulwich College, London; London University: Royal London Hospital. Junior hospital appointments, 1977-79; Medical Registrar, Royal London rotation, 1979-82; MRC Research Fellow, MRC Blood Pressure Unit, Glasgow, and Honorary Lecturer, Glasgow University, 1982-85; Lecturer in Pharmacology and Clinical Pharmacology, St. George's Hospital Medical School, London, and Honorary Medical Senior Registrar, St. George's Hospital, London, 1985-89; Senior Lecturer in Medicine, Edinburgh University. Member, British Hypertension Society, since 1991; Member, MRC Scientific Advisory Board, since 1996; Member, Wellcome Trust Physiology and Pharmacology Panel, 1997-2000; Chairman, British Heart Foundation Project Grants Committee, since 2004; Member, Multi-Centre Research Ethics Committee for Scotland, 1997-2000; Honorary Trustee and Joint Research Director, High Blood Pressure Foundation and Endocrine Research Trust, since 1991; Chairman, Symposium Committee, Royal College of Physicians, Edinburgh, since 1998; Chairman, Lothian Drug and Therapeutics Committee, 1998-2004; Chairman, Committee on Clinical Pharmacology, Royal College of Physicians, London, 1999-2000; Member, Association of Clinical Professors of Medicine and of Association of Physicians of Great Britain and Ireland; Chair, New Drugs Committee, 2001-05; Chair, Scottish Medicines Consortium, since 2005; Vice-President, Royal College of Physicians of Edinburgh, since 2006; EACPT Executive Committee, since 2005; International Union of Basic and Clinical Pharmacology (IUPHAR) Executive Committee, since 2005; Adviser in Clinical Pharmacology and Therapeutics, Scottish Executive Health Department. Recreations: opera; bridge; summer and winter mountaineering. Address: (h.) 75 Great King Street, Edinburgh EH3 6RN; e-mail: d.j.webb@ed.ac.uk

Webb, Professor Jeffrey R.L., BSc, DPhil, FRSE. Professor of Mathematics, Glasgow University, since 1987 (Reader, 1982-87); b. 19.12.45, Stourport-on-Severn; m.,

Angela Millard; 1 s.; 1 d. Educ. King Charles I School, Kidderminster; Sussex University. Royal Society European Programme Fellowship, 1970-71; Science Research Council Fellowship, Sussex University, 1971-73; Lecturer in Mathematics, Glasgow University, 1973-78 and 1979-82; Visiting Associate Professor, Indiana University, 1978-79; Visiting Professor, Tulane University, New Orleans, 1982. Editorial Boards: Nonlinear Analysis, Glasgow Mathematical Journal, Fixed point theory and its applications; Editorial Adviser, London Mathematical Society. Recreations: chess; books; listening to music. Address: (b.) Mathematics Department, Glasgow University, Glasgow G12 8QW; T.-0141-330 5181.

Webster, Andrew George, LLB (Hons), DipLP, FRSA. Advocate, since 1992; b. 20.7.67, Wick; m., Sheila Mairead; 2 d. Educ. Wick High School; University of Aberdeen. Standing Junior Counsel to: Ministry of Defence (Air Force), 1997-2000, Ministry of Defence, since 2000. Address: (b.) Advocates' Library, Parliament House, Edinburgh EH1 1RF; T.-0131-226 5071.

Webster, Jack (John Barron), MUniv. Author and Journalist; b. 8.7.31, Maud, Aberdeenshire; m., Eden Keith; 3 s. Educ. Maud School; Peterhead Academy; Robert Gordon's College, Aberdeen. Reporter, Turriff Advertiser; Reporter/Sub Editor, Aberdeen Press & Journal/Evening Express; Chief Sub-Editor, Scottish Sunday Express; Feature Writer, Scottish Daily Express; Feature Writer, Sunday Standard; Columnist, The Herald. Columnist of the Year, 1996; Speaker of the Year, 1996. Publications: The Dons, 1978; A Grain of Truth, 1981; Gordon Strachan, 1984; Another Grain of Truth, 1988; 'Tis Better to Travel, 1989; Alistair MacLean (biography), 1991; Famous Ships of the Clyde, 1993; The Flying Scots, 1994; The Express Years, 1994; In the Driving Seat, 1996; The Herald Years, 1996; From Dali to Burrell, 1997; Webster's World, 1997; The Reo Stakis Story, 1999; The Auld Hoose: The Story of Robert Gordon's College, 2005; Jack Webster's Aberdeen, 2007; television films: The Roup, 1985; As Time Goes By, 1987; Northern Lights, 1989; Webster Goes West, 1991; John Brown: The Man Who Drew a Legend, 1994; Walking Back to Happiness, 1996; video film: The Glory of Gothenburg, 1993; stage play: The Life of Grassic Gibbon, 2007. Address: (b.) 58 Netherhill Avenue, Glasgow G44 3XG; T.-0141-637 6437.
E-mail: jack@jackwebster.fsnet.co.uk

Webster, Professor John Bainbridge, MA, PhD, DD, FRSE. Professor of Systematic Theology, Aberdeen University, since 2003; b. 20.6.55, Mansfield. Educ. Bradford Grammar School; Cambridge University. Chaplain and Tutor, St John's College, Durham, 1982-86; Professor of Systematic Theology, Wycliffe College, University of Toronto, 1986-96; Lady Margaret Professor of Divinity, University of Oxford, 1996-2003. Publications: Eberhard Jungel; Barth's Ethics of Reconciliation; Barth's Moral Theology; Barth; Word and Church; Holiness; Holy Scripture; Confessing God; Barth's Earlier Theology. Address: (b.) King's College, Aberdeen University, Aberdeen AB24 3UB.

Webster, Professor Nigel Robert, BSc, MB, ChB, PhD, FRCA, FRCPEdin, FRCSEdin. Professor of Anaesthesia and Intensive Care, Aberdeen University, since 1994; b. 14.6.53, Walsall; m., Diana C.S. Webster; 1 s.; 2 d. Educ. Edward Shelley High School, Walsall; Leeds University. Member, scientific staff/Consultant, Clinical Research Centre, Northwick Park Hospital, Harrow; Consultant in Anaesthesia and Intensive Care, St. James's University Hospital, Leeds. Address: (b.) Institute of Medical Sciences, Foresterhill, Aberdeen AB25 2ZD; T.-01224 681818.

Webster, Professor Robin Gordon Maclennan, OBE, MA (Cantab), MA (Arch), RIBA, FRIAS, ARSA. Emeritus Professor of Architecture, Scott Sutherland School of Architecture, The Robert Gordon University, Aberdeen; Partner, CameronWebster architects, since 2005; Senior Partner, Robin Webster & Associates, Aberdeen, 1984-2004; b. 24.12.39, Glasgow; m., Katherine S. Crichton (deceased); 1 s.; 2 d. Educ. Glasgow Academy; Rugby School; St. John's College, Cambridge; University College London. Assistant, Gillespie Kidd & Coia, Architects, Glasgow, 1963-64; National Building Agency, London, 1965-67; Senior Partner, Spence and Webster, Architects, 1972-84; Lecturer, Bartlett School of Architecture, 1969-74; Visiting Lecturer, Washington University, St. Louis, 1975, Cambridge University, 1976-77, and Mackintosh School, Glasgow School of Art, 1978-84. Winner, New Parliamentary Building Competition, Westminster, 1972; 1st prize, New York Waterfront Competition, 1988; Winner, 1997 Sellic library competition for University of Edinburgh; Chairman, Association of Scottish Schools of Architecture, 1986-90; President, Aberdeen Society of Architects, 1989-91; Commissioner, Royal Fine Art Commission for Scotland, 1992-98; Treasurer, Glasgow City Heritage Trust, since 2006. Recreations: looking and drawing. Address: (h.) 7 Walmer Crescent, Glasgow G51 1AT; T.-0141 427 4494; e-mail: robin.webster@mac.com

Weighton, Rev. Gillian Elizabeth, BD (Hons), CertMin, STM. Parish Minister, Bridge of Allan Parish Church, since 2004; University of Stirling Chaplain, since 2006; b. 5.4.67, Bellshill; m., Alister Weighton. Educ. Earnock High School, Hamilton; St. Andrews and Glasgow Universities; Union Theological Seminary, New York. Minister, St. James Parish Church, Ayr, 1992-2004; Part-Time Chaplain: Ayr Hospital, 1994-97, University of Paisley (Craigie Campus), 1997-99. Member, Committee on Chaplains in Forces in Church of Scotland. Recreations: cycling; walking; swimming; theatre; reading; music; photography. Address: (h.) 29 Keir Street, Bridge of Allan FK9 4QJ; T.-01786 832753; e-mail: gillweighton@aol.com

Weir, Viscount (William Kenneth James Weir), BA, Hon. DEng (Glasgow), Hon. FEng. Director, The Weir Group PLC, 1966-99 (Chairman, 1983-99); Director and former Vice-Chairman, St. James' Place Capital plc; Chairman, Balfour Beatty plc, 1996-2003 (Deputy Chairman, 1992-96, Director, since 1977); Chairman, CP Ships Ltd., 2001-04; Director, Canadian Pacific Railway Co., 1989-2004; Chairman, Major British Exporters; b. 9.11.33, Glasgow; m., 1, Diana MacDougall (m. diss.); 2, Jacqueline Mary Marr (m. diss.); 3, Marina Sevastopoulo; 2 s.; 1 d. Educ. Eton; Trinity College, Cambridge. Member, London Advisory Committee, Hongkong and Shanghai Banking Corporation, 1980-92; Deputy Chairman, Charterhouse J. Rothschild PLC, 1983-85; Member, Court, Bank of England, 1972-84; Co-Chairman, RIT and Northern PLC, 1982-83; Director, 1970, Chairman, 1975-82, Great Northern Investment Trust Ltd.; Member, Scottish Economic Council, 1972-85; Director, British Steel Corporation, 1972-76; Chairman, Patrons of National Galleries of Scotland, 1984-95; Member, Queen's Bodyguard for Scotland (Royal Company of Archers). Recreations: shooting; golf; fishing. Address: (h.) Rodinghead, Mauchline, Ayrshire.

Weir, Professor Alexander Douglas, MA, MEd, FRSA. Professor of Education, Strathclyde University, 1993-2007; b. 2.9.42, Falkirk; m., Alison Marion Cook; 1 s.; 1 d. Educ. Falkirk High School; Edinburgh University. Lecturer, Falkirk College of Technology, 1965-67; Senior Research Officer, Scottish Council for Research in Education, 1967-74; Lecturer, Glasgow University, 1974-79; Director, Scottish Vocational Preparation Unit, 1979-85; Director,

Vocational Initiatives Unit, Glasgow University, 1985-88; Director of Research, Jordanhill College of Education, 1988-91, Assistant Principal, 1991-93; Vice Dean (Research), 1993-97, Dean, 1997-2001, Faculty of Education, Strathclyde University. Member, National Executive, Boys' Brigade, 1976-84; Chair, Strathclyde Regional Conference of Voluntary Youth Organisations, 1991-94; Vice-Convener, General Teaching Council for Scotland, 2001-05; Board Member, Learning and Teaching Scotland, since 2004; author of five books and 100 articles. Recreations: walking; the arts. Address: (b.) Faculty of Education, Strathclyde University, Southbrae Drive, Glasgow G13 1PP; T.-0141-950 3395.

Weir, Michael, LLB, NP. SNP MP, Angus, since 2001; b. 24.3.57, Arbroath; m., Anne; 2 d. Educ. Arbroath High School; Aberdeen University. Myers and Wills, Montrose, 1979-81; Charles Wood and Son, Kirkcaldy, 1982-83; Myers and Wills, Montrose, 1983-84; J. & D.G. Shiell, Brechin, 1984-2001. Dean of Society of Procurators and Solicitors in Angus, 2001; Member: Trade and Industry Select Committee, Speakers Chairman's Panel. Address: (b.) 16 Brothock Bridge, Arbroath DD11 1NG; T.-01241 874522.

Welbury, Professor Richard, MB, BS, BDS, PhD, FDSRCS, FDSRCPS, FRCPCH. Professor of Paediatric Dentistry, Glasgow University, since 2001; Deputy Head of Dental School, Glasgow; b. 16.8.54, Morpeth; m., Tracey; 1 s.; 3 d. Educ. Wrekin College, Wellington; Newcastle upon Tyne Dental and Medical Schools. MRC Research Associate, Dental School, Newcastle upon Tyne, 1985-88; Lecturer, then Consultant in Paediatric Dentistry, Dental School, Newcastle upon Tyne, 1988-2001. Chairman, SAC in Paediatric Dentistry, 2003-06; President, European Academy of Paediatric Dentistry, 2006-08; Past President, British Society for Paediatric Dentistry. Publication: Paediatric Dentistry (textbook). Recreations: golf; hill-walking; rugby union. Address: (b.) Dental Hospital and School, 378 Sauchiehall Street, Glasgow G2 3JZ; T.-0141 211 9665.

Welch, Dr. Dorothy Ann, BSc, PhD. College Registrar, University of Edinburgh, since 2001; b. 1.3.60, University of Edinburgh, since 2001; b. 1.3.60, Dundee; m., Alan Welch; 1 s.; 1 d. Educ. University of Edinburgh; University of Cambridge. Career History: Lecturer in Chemistry, Heriot-Watt University; Computing Officer, University of Edinburgh; Director of Scottish Wider Access Programme; Administration, University of Edinburgh. Address: (h.) 48 Cluny Gardens, Edinburgh EH10 6BN; e-mail: d.welch@ed.ac.uk

Weller, Professor David Paul, MBBS, MPH, PHD, FRACGP, MRCGP, FAFPHM. James Mackenzie Professor of General Practice, Edinburgh University, since 2000; b. 21.7.59, Adelaide; m., Dr Belinda Weller; 1 s.; 2 d. Educ. Prince Alfred College, Adelaide; University of Adelaide. Training and working in family medicine, UK and Australia, 1984-90; PhD studies, 1991-94; Senior Lecturer, Department of General Practice, Flinders University of South Australia, 1995-99. Board Member, Lothian Primary Care Trust, Scottish Cancer Foundation. Recreations: running; hill-walking; piano. Address: (h.) 24/2 Fettes Row, Edinburgh EH3 6RH; T.-0131-557-8464.

Weller, Richard, MD, FRCP (Ed). Senior Lecturer, Dermatology, University of Edinburgh, since 2002; b. 21.7.62, Münster, Germany; m., Dr Julie Gallagher. Educ. Malvern College; St. Thomas' Hospital, London University.

General medical training, England and Australia, 1987-92; dermatology training: St. John's Institute of Dermatology, London, 1993, Aberdeen Royal Infirmary, 1994-96; Lecturer, Dermatology, Edinburgh Royal Infirmary, 1996-98; Visiting Research Fellow: Immunbiologie Abteilung, HHU, Düsseldorf, 1999, Department of Surgery, University of Pittsburgh, USA, 2000-01. Recreations: mountaineering; sailing. Address: (h.) 24/2 Fettes Row, Edinburgh EH3 6RH; T.-0131-557-8464; e-mail: r.weller@ed.ac.uk

Welsh, Andrew Paton, MA (Hons), DipEd, DipFrench (Open). MSP (SNP), Angus, since 1999, Member, Scottish Parliament Corporate Body, 1999-2006; Convener, Audit Committee, 1999-2003; Deputy Convener, Local Government and Transport Committee, 2003-04; Member, Scottish Commission for Public Accounts; National Vice-President, SNP, 1987-2004; Deputy Convener, Audit Committee, 2004-07; Convener, Finance Committee, since 2007; Member, Audit Committee, since 2007; MP (SNP), Angus, 1997-2001 (MP, Angus East, 1987-97); b. 9.4.44, Glasgow; m., Sheena Margaret Cannon (see Sheena Margaret Welsh); 1 d. Educ. Govan High School; Glasgow University. Member, Stirling District Council, 1974; MP (SNP), South Angus, 1974-79; SNP Parliamentary Spokesman on Housing, 1974-78 and 1987-2001, Self-Employed and Small Businesses, 1975-79 and 1987-97, Agriculture, 1975-79 and 1987-97, Education, 1997-2001; Parliamentary Chief Whip, 1977-79 and 1987-99; Member, Select Committee on Members' Interests, 1989-92; Member, House of Commons Chairmen's Panel, 1997-2001; Member, Scottish Affairs Committee, 1992-2001; SNP Executive Vice Chairman for Administration, 1979-83, for Local Government, 1984-87; Parliamentary candidate, East Angus, 1983; Member, Church and Nation Committee, Church of Scotland, 1984-85; Member, Dundee University Court, 1984-87; Provost, Angus District Council, 1984-87; Convener, Cross Party Tartan Day Group, since 2005; Trustee, National Prayer Breakfast for Scotland; Trustee, Scottish Bible Society. Recreations: music; horse riding; languages. Address: (h.) Montquhir, Carmyllie, Arbroath; T.-01241 860317; e-mail: Andrew.Welsh.msp@ scottish.parliament.uk

Welsh, Ian, MA (Hons), MA, DPSE, FRSA. Chief Executive, Momentum Scotland, since 2001; Director of UK Services, Rehab Group, since 2007; b. Prestwick; m., Elizabeth; 2 s. Educ. Prestwick Academy; Ayr Academy; University of Glasgow. Former professional footballer, Kilmarnock FC; Teacher (former Deputy Head Teacher, Auchinleck Academy); formerly Director, Human Resources and Public Affairs, Prestwick International Airport; Chief Executive, Kilmarnock FC, 1997-2001. Former Member, Kyle and Carrick District Council, then South Ayrshire Council; former MSP; former Governor, Craigie College of Education; former Chair, North Ayrshire Partnership; former Chair, Scottish Advisory Committee of the Voluntary Sector National Training Organisation; Board Member: Borderline Theatre Company, The Space Place, Irvine Bay Urban Regeneration Company, Borderline Theatre Company, Space Unlimited; Chair: Ayr United Football Academy, Ayrshire Business in the Community; Governor, University of the West of Scotland. Address: (b.) Momentum Head Office, The Stables, Carlton Court, Glasgow G5 9JP; T.-0141-221-2333.

Wemyss and March, Earl of (Francis David Charteris), KT (1966), Hon. LLD (St. Andrews), Hon. DUniv (Edinburgh), JP, BA. Chief of family Charteris; Lord Lieutenant, East Lothian, 1967-87; b. 19.1.12, London; m., Mavis Lynette Gordon Murray (deceased); 1 s.; 1 d.; 1 s. (deceased); 1 d. (deceased); 2, Shelagh Kennedy. Educ. Eton; Balliol College, Oxford. Commissioned, Lovat Scouts (TA), 1932-44; Basutoland Administrative Service, 1937-

44; War Service, African Auxiliary Pioneer Corps, Middle East, 1941-44; Chairman, Council, National Trust for Scotland, 1947-67 (President, 1967-91, President Emeritus, 1991); Chairman, Scottish Churches Council, 1964-71; Chairman, Royal Commission on Ancient and Historical Monuments of Scotland, 1949-84; Vice-President, Marie Curie Memorial Foundation; President, Royal Scottish Geographical Society, 1958-62; President, National Bible Society of Scotland, 1960-83; Lieutenant, Queen's Bodyguard for Scotland (Royal Company of Archers). Recreations: countryside and conservation. Address: (h.) Gosford House, Longniddry, East Lothian EH32 0PX; T.-01875 870200.

West, Peter William Alan, OBE, DL, MA, DUniv, DPhil. Secretary to the University, Strathclyde University, since 1990; b. 16.3.49, Edinburgh; m., Margaret Clark; 1 s.; 1 d. Educ. Edinburgh Academy; St. Andrews University. Administrator, Edinburgh University, 1972-77; Assistant Secretary, Leeds University, 1977-83; Deputy Registrar, Strathclyde University, 1983-89. Convener, Malawi Millennium Project; Chair, Scotland/Malawi Partnership; Doctor (honoris causa), University of Rostov-on-Don, Russia; Doctor (honoris causa), University of Malawi; Deputy Lieutenant of the City of Glasgow; Honorary Fellowship, Bell College, Hamilton. Awarded the OBE for services to HE in Scotland and Malawi in the Queen's Birthday Honours, 2006. Recreations: reading; drinking wine; supporting the leading football teams of Scotland (Hibernian) and Africa (the Flames of Malawi) through thick and thin. Address: (b.) Strathclyde University, McCance Building, 16 Richmond Street, Glasgow G1 1XQ; T.-0141-548 2001.

Whaling, Rev. Professor Frank, BA, MA, PhD, ThD, FSAM, FRAS, FABI, FWLA, FIBA, FICS, FWIA. Emeritus Professor of the Study of Religion, Edinburgh University; Methodist Minister; b. 5.2.34, Pontefract; m., Norma S.H.; 1 s.; 1 d. Educ. Kings School, Pontefract; Christ's College, Cambridge; Wesley House, Cambridge; Harvard University. Methodist Minister, Birmingham Central Hall, 1960-62, Faizabad and Banaras, North India, 1962-66, Eastbourne, 1966-69; Teaching Fellow, Harvard University, 1972-73; appointed Lecturer, Study of Religion, Edinburgh University, 1973. Theyer Honor Award, Harvard; Maitland Award, Cambridge; various Reseach Awards; Chair, Scottish Churches China Group, 1985-93; Chair, Edinburgh Inter-Faith Association, 1989-99, President, since 1999; Director, Edinburgh Cancer Help Centre, 1987-91; Chair, Scottish Inter-Faith Symposium, 1987-94; Consultant, World Without Hunger (charity); BBC, Paulist Press, International Inter-Faith Council; Alistair Hardy Trust; Encyclopedia of World Spirituality (26 vols); Chair, Edinburgh International Centre for World Spiritualities, 1999; Executive Director, Scottish Inter-Faith Council, 2002-05. Council Member, SHAP Working Party on Religion in Education, Religious Education Movement in Scotland. Visiting Lecturer and Professor, USA, China, South Africa, India, England; Hon. Life Fellow, British Association for the Study of Religion; ICS Scot of the Year, 2007. Publications: over 100 papers, over 200 reviews; books written and/or edited: An Approach to Dialogue: Hinduism and Christianity, 1966; The Rise of the Religious Significance of Rama, 1980; John and Charles Wesley, 1981; The World's Religious Traditions: Current Perspectives in Religious Studies, 1984; Contemporary Approaches to the Study of Religion: Vol. I, 1984, Vol. II, 1985; Christian Theology and World Religions, 1986; Religion in Today's World, 1987; Compassion Through Understanding, 1990; Dictionary of Beliefs and Religions, 1992; The World: How It Came Into Being and our Responsibility for It, 1994; Theory and Method in Religious Studies, 1995;

Christian Prayer for Today, 2002; General Editor: (9 vol) Understanding Religion, since 2002. Recreations: music; art; sport; inter-faith activities. Address: (h.) 21 Gillespie Road, Edinburgh EH13 0NW; T.-0131-441 2112.

Whatley, Professor Christopher Allan, BA, PhD, FRHistS, FRSE. Professor of Scottish History, Dundee University, Vice-Principal and Head, College of Arts and Social Sciences, since 2006 (Dean, Faculty of Arts and Social Sciences, 2002-06, Head, Department of History, 1995-2002); b. 29.5.48, Birmingham; 1 s.; 1 d. Educ. Bearsden Academy; Strathclyde University. Lecturer, Ayr College, 1975-79, Dundee University, 1979-88, St. Andrews University, 1988-92, Dundee University, 1992-94; Senior Lecturer, 1994. Editor, Scottish Economic and Social History, 1995-99; Chairman, SCCC Review Group, Scottish History in the Curriculum; Consultant Editor, Scotland's Story; Chair, Scottish Historical Review Trust, 2002-06; Director, Dundee University Press, since 2003; Board member, Dundee Repertory Theatre, since 2007. Publications: The Scottish Salt Industry, 1570-1850; Onwards from Osnaburgs: the rise and progress of a Scottish textile company; Bought and Sold for English Gold?: explaining the union of 1707; The Manufacture of Scottish History (Co-editor); The Life and Times of Dundee (Co-author); The Remaking of Juteopolis: Dundee 1891-1991 (Editor); John Galt (Editor); The Industrial Revolution in Scotland; Modern Scottish History, 1707 to the Present (Co-editor); Scottish Society 1707-1830: Beyond Jacobitism, Towards Industrialisation; Victorian Dundee: Image and Realities (Co-editor); The Scots and the Union. Address: (h.) Tayfield Cottage, 51 Main Street, Longforgan, by Dundee DD2 5EW; T.-01382 360794; e-mail: c.a.whatley@dundee.ac.uk

Wheater, Professor Roger John, OBE, DUniv, CBiol, FIBiol, FRSA, FRSGS (Hon), FRZSS (Hon), FRSE. President, Scottish Wildlife Trust, since 2006; Chairman, National Trust for Scotland, 2000-05; Director, Royal Zoological Society of Scotland, 1972-98; Honorary Professor, Edinburgh University, since 1993; b. 24.11.33, Brighton; m., Jean Ord Troup; 1 s.; 1 d. Educ. Brighton, Hove and Sussex Grammar School; Brighton Technical College. Commissioned, Royal Sussex Regiment, 1953; served Gold Coast Regiment, 1953-54; 4/5th Bn., Royal Sussex Regiment (TA), 1954-56; Colonial Police, Uganda, 1956-61; Chief Warden, Murchison Falls National Park, 1961-70; Director, Uganda National Parks, 1970-72; Member, Co-ordinating Committee, Nuffield Unit of Tropical Animal Ecology; Member, Board of Governors, Mweka College of Wildlife Management, Tanzania; Director, National Park Lodges Ltd.; Member, Uganda National Research Council; Vice Chairman, Uganda Tourist Association; Council Member, 1980, and President, 1988-91, International Union of Directors of Zoological Gardens; Chairman, Federation of Zoological Gardens of Great Britain and Ireland, 1993-96; Chairman, Anthropoid Ape Advisory Panel, 1977-91; Member, International Zoo Year Book Editorial Board, 1987-99; President, Association of British Wild Animal Keepers, 1984-99; Chairman, Membership and Licensing Committee, 1984-91; Chairman, Working Party on Zoo Licensing Act, 1981-84; Council Member, Zoological Society of London, 1991-92, 1995-99, 2002-03, Vice President, 1999; Chairman, Whipsnade Wild Animal Park, 1999-2002; Vice-President, World Pheasant Association, since 1994; Trustee, Gorilla Organisation, since 1995; Chairman, European Association of Zoos and Aquaria, 1994-97; Member of Council, National Trust for Scotland, 1973-78, and 2000-05, Executive Committee, 1982-87, and 2000-05; Chairman, Cammo Estate Advisory Committee, 1980-95; ESU William Thyne Scholar, 1975 (Trustee, Thyne Scholarship, since 1997); Assessor, Council, Scottish Wildlife Trust, 1973-92; Consultant, World Tourist Organisation (United Nations), since 1980; Member, Secretary of State for Scotland's Working Group on Environmental Education, 1990-94; Board Member, Scottish Natural Heritage, 1995-99 (Deputy Chairman, 1997-99); Chairman, Access Forum, 1996-2000; Founder Patron, Dynamic Earth, Trustee, since 1999, Vice-Chairman, Edinburgh Branch, English Speaking Union, 1977-81; President, Edinburgh Special Mobile Angling Club, 1982-86; President, Cockburn Trout Angling Club, since 1997; Trustee, Tweed Foundation, since 2006; Chairman, Tourism and Environment Forum, 1999-2003; Chairman, Heather Trust, 1999-2002; Deputy Chairman, Zoo Forum, 1999-2002; Vice-President, European Network of National Heritage Organisations, 2000-05. Recreations: country pursuits; painting; gardening. Address: (h.) 17 Kirklands, Innerleithen, Borders EH44 6NA; T.-01896-830403; e-mail: roger.wheater@btinternet.com

Wheatley, Professor Denys N., BSc, PhD, DSc, MD (h.c.) multi, CIBiol, FIBiol, FRCPath. Visiting Professor of Physiology, Wayne State Medical School, Detroit; Professor, Semmelweis Medical University; Foreign Member, Ukrainian Academy of Medical Sciences; Director, "BioMEdES; Secretary General, International Federation for Cell Biology, since 2002; Chief Scientific Officer, Bio-Cancer Treatments International; formerly at the Dept. of Pathology, University of Aberdeen; b. 18.3.40, Ascot; m., Pamela; 2 d. Educ. Windsor Grammar School; King's College, University of London. Research Fellow, Aberdeen University, 1964-67; MRC Travelling Fellow/USPHS Fellow, 1967-70; 1970 onwards: Lecturer, Senior Lecturer, Reader, Cell Pathology, Aberdeen University. Director and Vice-Chairman, Enterprise Music Scotland. Publications include: Cell Growth and Division; The Centriole: a central enigma of cell biology; Editor: Cell Biology International, Cancer Cell International, Theoretical Biology and Medical Modelling, Oncology News. Recreations: cello; piano; swimming; painting. Address: (h.) Leggat House, Keithhall, Inverurie AB51 0XL; T.-01467-670280.

Wheatley, The Right Hon. Lord (John Francis Wheatley), PC, QC, BL. Senator, College of Justice, since 2000; b. 9.5.41, Edinburgh; m., Bronwen Catherine Fraser; 2 s. Educ. Mount St. Mary's College, Derbyshire; Edinburgh University. Called to Scottish Bar, 1966; Standing Counsel to Scottish Development Department, 1968-74; Advocate Depute, 1974-78; Sheriff, Perthshire and Kinross-shire, at Perth, 1980-98; Temporary High Court Judge, 1992; Sheriff Principal of Tayside Central and Fife, 1998-2000. Member, Parole Board, 2000-03; Chairman, Judicial Studies Committee, 2000-06. Recreations: music; gardening. Address: Braefoot Farmhouse, Fossoway, Kinross-shire.

Wheeler, Sir (Harry) Anthony, Kt (1988), OBE, PPRSA, Hon. RA, Hon. RHA, Hon. RGI, Hon. DDes, Hon. RBS, PPRIAS, FRIBA, FRSA, BArch, MRTPI(rtd), DipTP. Founder, Wheeler & Sproson, Architects and Town Planners, Edinburgh and Kirkcaldy; Hon. President, Saltire Society, since 1995; b. 7.11.19, Stranraer; m., Dorothy Jean Campbell; 1 d. Educ. Stranraer High School; Glasgow School of Architecture; Strathclyde University. War Service, Royal Artillery, 1939-46; John Keppie Scholar and Sir Rowand Anderson Studentship, RIBA Grissell Medallist, Neale Bursar; Assistant to City Architect, Oxford, to Sir Herbert Baker & Scott, London; Senior Architect, Glenrothes Development Corporation; began private practice in Fife; Senior Lecturer, Dundee School of Architecture, 1952-58; Saltire Awards and Commendations (22), Civic Trust Awards and Commendations (12); Trustee, Scottish Civic Trust, 1970-83; Member, Royal Fine Art Commission for Scotland, 1967-85; President, Royal Scottish Academy, 1983-90. Recreations: sketching and water colours; fishing; music; drama; gardens. Address: (h.) 31/6 Kinnear Road, Edinburgh EH3 5PG.

Wheeler, Professor Simon Jonathan, MA, DPhil, CEng, MICE. Cormack Professor of Civil Engineering, Glasgow University, since 1996, Head of Department of Civil Engineering, since 2005; b. 30.4.58, Warlingham, Surrey; m., Noelle Patricia O'Rourke; 1 s.; 2 d. Educ. Whitehaven Grammar School; St. John's College, Cambridge; Balliol College, Oxford. University Lecturer in Soil Mechanics, Queen's University of Belfast, 1984-88; Lecturer in Soil Mechanics, Sheffield University, 1988-92; Lecturer in Civil Engineering, Oxford University, and Fellow of Keble College, Oxford, 1992-95. Recreation: mountaineering. Address: (b.) Department of Civil Engineering, Rankine Building, Glasgow G12 8LT; T.-0141-330 5202.

White, Iain, BSc (Hons), MEd, MIBiol, CBiol. Head Teacher, Govan High School, Glasgow, since 1994; b. 2.2.54, Greenock; m., Gail. Educ. Greenock High School; Glasgow University. Biology Teacher, then Principal Biology Teacher, Cowdenknowes High School, Greenock, 1977-87; Assistant Rector, Rothesay Academy, 1987-92; Depute Head Teacher, Port Glasgow High School, 1992-94. Past Captain, Greenock Golf Club. Recreations: golf; skiing; travel; watching football; Robert Burns; after-dinner speaking. Address: (b.) Govan High School, 12 Ardnish Street, Glasgow G51 4NB; T.-0141-582-0090; e-mail: IWhite@govanhigh.glasgow.sch.uk

White, Sandra. MSP (SNP), Glasgow, since 1999; b. 17.8.51, Glasgow; m.; 3 c. Educ. Garthamlock Secondary School; Glasgow College; Cardonald College. Former Councillor; Press Officer, William Wallace Society. Recreations: reading; walking; meeting people. Address: (b.) Scottish Parliament, Edinburgh EH99 1SP.

White, Professor Stephen Leonard, MA, PhD, DPhil, LittD, FRSE. Bryce Professor of Politics, Glasgow University, since 1991; b. 1.7.45, Dublin; m., Ishbel MacPhie; 1 s. Educ. St. Andrew's College, Dublin; Trinity College, Dublin; Glasgow University; Wolfson College, Oxford. Lecturer in Politics, Glasgow University, 1971-85, Reader, 1985-91. President, British Association for Slavonic and East European Studies, 1994-97; Chief Editor, Journal of Communist Studies and Transition Politics. Publications include: Political Culture and Soviet Politics, 1979; Britain and the Bolshevik Revolution, 1980; Origins of Detente, 1986; The Bolshevik Poster, 1988; After Gorbachev, 1993; Russia Goes Dry, 1996; How Russia Votes (with others), 1997; Values and Political Change in Postcommunist Europe (with others), 1998; Russia's New Politics, 2000; The Soviet Elite from Lenin to Gorbachev (Co-author), 2000; Putin's Russia and the Enlarged Europe (with others), 2006. Address: (h.) 11 Hamilton Drive, Glasgow G12 8DN; T.-0141-334 9541.

Whitefield, Gavin, CPFA, DPA. Chief Executive, North Lanarkshire Council, since 2000; b. 7.2.56; m., Grace; 2 d. Educ. Lanark Grammar School; Bell College, Hamilton. Audit Assistant, Exchequer and Audit Department, Civil Service, 1974-76; Clydesdale District Council: Assistant Auditor, 1976-84, Computer Development Officer, 1984-86, Principal Housing Officer (Finance and Administration), 1986-89; Assistant Director of Housing (Finance and Administration), Motherwell District Council, 1989-95; Director of Housing and Property Services, North Lanarkshire Council, 1995-2000. Chair, SOLACE Scotland. Recreations: hill-walking; football. Address: (b.) P.O. Box 14, Civic Centre, Motherwell ML1 1TW; T.-01698 302252.

Whitefield, Karen. MSP (Labour), Airdrie and Shotts, since 1999; b. 8.1.70, Bellshill. Educ. Calderhead High School, Shotts; Glasgow Caledonian University. Civil

servant, Benefits Agency, 1991-92; PA to Rachel Squire, MP, 1992-99. Congressional Intern on Capitol Hill, 1990. Recreations: swimming; reading; travel. Address: (b.) 3 Sandvale Place, Shotts ML7 5EF; T.-01501 822200.
E-mail: karen.whitefield.msp@scottish.parliament.uk

Whiten, Professor (David) Andrew, BSc, PhD, FBPS, AcSS, FRSE, FBA. Professor of Evolutionary and Developmental Psychology, St. Andrews University, since 1997, Wardlaw Professor of Psychology, since 2000; Royal Society Leverhulme Trust Senior Research Fellow, 2006-07; b. 20.4.48, Grimsby; m., Dr. Susie Challoner; 2 d. Educ. Wintringham School, Grimsby; Sheffield University; Bristol University; Oxford University. Research Fellow, Oxford University, 1972-75; Lecturer, then Reader, St. Andrews University, 1975-97; Visiting Professor, Zurich University, 1992, Emory University, 1996; Delwart International Scientific Prize, 2001; Rivers Memorial Medal, Royal Anthropological Institute of Great Britain and Ireland, 2007. Publications: see http://culture.st-and.ac.uk/whiten. Recreations: painting; walking; wildlife; good-lifing. Address: (b.) School of Psychology, St. Andrews University, St. Andrews KY16 9JU; e-mail: a.whiten@st-and.ac.uk

Whitley, Elizabeth Young, MA. Writer; great granny and "old crone", since 1996; Hon. Vice President, Scottish Covenanters Memorials Association; b. 26.12.15, Glasgow; m., Rev. Harry Whitley (dec.); 5s. (1 dec.); 2d. Educ. Laurelbank School, Glasgow; Glasgow University; Perugia, Italy; London School of Economics. Freelance writer and voluntary social worker since schooldays; writer for BBC radio for many years, Scots Home Service, World Service; Writer: The Bulletin, Glasgow Herald, Scots Magazine; weekly radio programme, Music For You; weekly columnist, Scottish Daily Express; ran girls' clubs and mixed clubs in Port Glasgow, Partick; Chairman, Clubs' Advisory Committee, 1959-59; Member, Faversham Committee report on A.I.D.; Member, Pilkington Committee on Broadcasting; Prospective Parliamentary Candidate, SNP, against Sir Alec Douglas Home (saved deposit). Publications: Plain Mr Knox, (biography of John Knox), 1966; The Two Kingdoms, (following research into the Covenanters). Recreations: gardening; reading; listening to silence. Address: (h.) The Glebe, Southwick, Dumfries, DG2 8AR; T.-01387 780276.

Whitley, Rev. Laurence Arthur Brown, MA, BD, PhD. Minister, Glasgow Cathedral (St Mungo or High), since 2007; Minister, Montrose Old (now Old and St Andrew's) Parish, 1985-2007; (Busby East with West, 1975-85); b. 19.9.49, Port Glasgow; m., Catherine MacLean MacFadyen; 1 s.; 1 d. Educ. Edinburgh Academy; Edinburgh University; St. Andrews University. Assistant Minister, St. Andrews, Dundee, 1974-75. Parliamentary candidate (SNP), Dumfriesshire, February and October, 1974. Recreation: enkenotopomachetikosis. Address: (h.) 23 Laurel Park Close, Glasgow G13 1RD; T.-0141-954-0216; e-mail: labwhitley@btinternet.com

Whittemore, Professor Colin Trengove, BSc, PhD, DSc, NDA, CBiol, FIBiol, FRSE. Professor of Agriculture and Rural Economy, Edinburgh University, 1990-2007; Head, Institute of Ecology and Resource Management, Edinburgh University, 1991-2001; now Postgraduate Dean, College of Science and Engineering; b. 16.7.42, Chester; m., Chris; 1 s.; 3 d. Educ. Rydal School; Newcastle-upon-Tyne University. Lecturer in Agriculture, Edinburgh University and Head, Animal Production, Advisory and Development, Edinburgh School of Agriculture; Professor of Animal

Production, Head, Animal Division, Edinburgh School of Agriculture; Head, Department of Agriculture, Edinburgh University. Sir John Hammond Memorial Prize for scientific contribution to an understanding of nutrition and growth; President, British Society of Animal Science, 1998; Royal Agricultural Society of England Gold Medal for research; Mignini Oscar; David Black Award. Publications: author of over 200 research papers and five text books of animal sciences. Recreations: skiing; riding. Address: (h.) 17, Fergusson View, West Linton, Peeblesshire EH46 7DJ.

Whitton, David. MSP (Labour), Strathkelvin and Bearsden, since 2007; b. 22.4.52. Address: (b.) Scottish Parliament, Edinburgh EH99 1SP.

Whitty, Niall Richard, MA, LLB, FRSE. General Editor, Stair Memorial Encyclopaedia, since 2000; Visiting Professor, Edinburgh University School of Law, since 2000; b. 28.10.37, Malaya; m., Elke M.M. Gillis; 3 s.; 1 d. Educ. Morrison's Academy, Crieff; St Andrews University; Edinburgh University. Apprenticeship, 1963-65; private practice, 1965-66; Member, legal staff, Scottish Office Solicitor's office, 1967-71; legal staff, Scottish Law Commission, 1971-94; Commissioner, Scottish Law Commission, 1995-2000. Recreations: gardening; piping; legal history. Address: (h.) St Martins, Victoria Road, Haddington EH41 4DJ; T.-0162 082 2234.

Whyte, Professor Iain Boyd, BA, MPhil, MA, PhD, FRSE, FRSA. Professor of Architectural History, Department of Architecture, Edinburgh University, since 1996; b. 6.3.47, Bexley; m., Deborah Smart; 1 s.; 1 d. Educ. St Dunstan's College; Nottingham University; Cornell University; Cambridge University; Leeds University. Lecturer, then Reader, then Professor of Architectural History, Edinburgh University; External Examiner: Courtauld Institute of Art, National University of Singapore, University College London. Getty Scholar, 1989-90; Getty Grant Program Senior Scholar, 1998-2000; Visiting Senior Program Officer, Getty Grant Program, 2002-04; Trustee, National Galleries of Scotland, 1998-2002; Member, Selection Committee, 23rd Council of Europe exhibition, 1995-96; Director, VARIE (Visual Arts Research Institute Edinburgh), since 2002; extensive publications on architectural and art history. Recreations: music; rowing. Address: (b.) Department of Architecture, 20 Chambers Street, Edinburgh EH1 1JZ; T.-0131-650 2322.

Whyte, Rev. James, BD, DipCE. Parish Minister, Fairlie, Ayrshire, since 1999; b. 26.4.46, Glasgow; m., Norma Isabella West; 1 s.; 2 d. Educ. Glasgow; Jordanhill College; Glasgow University. Trained as planning engineer; studied community education (Glasgow and Boston, Mass., USA); Community Organiser with Lamp of Lothian Collegiate Trust, Haddington; Organiser of Community Education, Dumbarton, 1971-73; Assistant Principal Community Education Officer, Renfrew Division, Strathclyde Region, 1973-77; entered ministry, Church of Scotland, 1977; Assistant Minister: Barrhead Arthurlie, 1977-78, St. Marks, Oldhall, Paisley, 1978-80; Minister: Coupar Angus Abbey, 1981-87, Broom, Newton Mearns, 1987-2006. Recreations: gardening; reading. Address: Manse of Fairlie, KA29 0ER; T.-01475 568 342.

Whyte, Robert, MB, ChB, FRCPsych, DPM. Consultant Psychotherapist, Carswell House, Glasgow, 1979-2000; b. 1.6.41, Edinburgh; m., Susan Frances Milburn; 1 s.; 1 d. Educ. George Heriot's, Edinburgh; St Andrews University. House Officer in Surgery, Arbroath Infirmary, 1966; House Officer in Medicine, Falkirk and District Royal Infirmary,

1967; Trainee in Psychiatry, Dundee Psychiatric Services, 1967-73; Consultant Psychiatrist, Duke Street Hospital, Glasgow, 1973. Past Chairman, Scottish Association of Psychoanalytical Psychotherapists. Address: (h.) Waverley, 70 East Kilbride Road, Busby, Glasgow G76 8HU; T.-0141-644 1639.

Wickham-Jones, Caroline R., MA, MIFA, FSA, FSA Scot, FFCS. Archaeologist; b. 25.4.55, Middlesborough; 1 s. Educ. Teesside High School; Edinburgh University. Freelance archaeologist, author and broadcaster with research interests in early (postglacial) settlement of Scotland, stone tools, landscape history, and the preservation of the cultural heritage; Member, Sustainable Development Panel; Trustee, Orkney Archaeological Trust; former Council Member, National Trust for Scotland; Council Member, Institute of Field Archaeologists, 1986-90; former Secretary, Society of Antiquaries of Scotland; former Trustee, John Muir Trust; Livery Woman of the City of London (Skinners Company). Presenter, Orky-ology for BBC Radio Orkney. Publications: Scotland's First Settlers; Arthurs Seat and Holyrood Park, a Visitor's Guide; Orkney, an Historical Guide; The Landscape of Scotland, a hidden history; Between the Wind and the Water, World Heritage Orkney. Recreations: travel; wilderness walking; socialising. Address: (h.) Cassie, St. Ola, Orkney KW15 1TP; e-mail: c.wickham-jones@mesolithic.co.uk

Wiercigroch, Professor Marian, MEng, ScD, CMath, FIMA. Professor of Applied Dynamics and Director, Centre for Applied Dynamics, Aberdeen University; b. 14.7.60, Poland. Educ. Silesian University of Technology, Poland. Research Fellow, Aberdeen University, 1990-91; Lecturer, Silesian University of Technology, 1992-93; Senior Fulbright Fellow, University of Delaware, USA, 1994; Lecturer, then Senior Lecturer, then Reader, Aberdeen University, 1994-2002, Professor of Engineering, 2002-06; Sixth Century Chair in Applied Dynamics, since 2006. Recreations: Alpine skiing; tennis; hill-walking. Address: (b.) Centre for Applied Dynamics Research, School of Engineering, Aberdeen University AB24 3UE.

Wightman, John Watt, CVO, CBE, RD, MA, LLB, WS. Chairman, Morton Fraser Partnership, 1988-99; Solicitor to H. M. The Queen in Scotland, 1984-99; Chairman, Craig & Rose PLC, 1993-2000; b. 20.11.33, Leith; m., Isla Macleod; 1 s.; 2 d. Educ. Daniel Stewart's College; St. Andrews University; Edinburgh University. Morton Fraser Partnership, 1960-99 (Partner, then Finance Director). Commodore, Royal Naval Reserve, 1982-85; Chairman, Lowland TAVRA, 1992-95; Elder, St. George's West Church; Trustee: Earl Haig Fund for Scotland, 1999-2004, Douglas Haig Memorial Homes. Recreations: sailing; fishing; ornithology. Address: 58 Trinity Road, Edinburgh EH5 3HT; T.-0131 551 6128.

Wilcox, Christine Alison, BA (Hons), ALA. Librarian, S.S.C. Library, Edinburgh, since 1991; b. 18.7.63, New Zealand; m., Michael Wilcox; 2 s.; 1 d. Educ. South Wilts Grammar School, Salisbury; Manchester Polytechnic Library School. Assistant Librarian, Barlow Lyde and Barlow Gilbert, Solicitors, London, 1984-86; Librarian, Beaumont and Son, Solicitors, London, 1986-89; posting to Bahrain accompanying husband, 1989-91. Secretary, Scottish Law Librarians Group, 1993-95. Publications: Directory of Legal Libraries in Scotland; Union List of Periodical and Law Report Holdings in Scotland. Recreations: needlework; hill-walking. Address: (b.) S.S.C. Library, 11 Parliament Square, Edinburgh EH1 1RF; T.-0131-225 6268; e-mail: christine@ssclibrary.co.uk

Wild, John Robin, JP, BDS, DPD, FDSRCS(Edin), DGDP. Chairman, District Courts Association, 2002-04; Chief Dental Officer, Department of Health, 1997-2000; Consultant in Dental Public Health, NHS Dumfries and Galloway, 2005-07; b. 12.9.41, Scarborough; m., Eleanor

Daphne Kerr; 1 s.; 2 d. Educ. Sedbergh School; Edinburgh University; Dundee University. General Dental Practitioner, Scarborough, 1965-71; Dental Officer, East Lothian, 1971-74;Chief Administrative Dental Officer, Borders Health Board, 1974-87; Regional Dental Postgraduate Adviser, S.E. Regional Committee for Postgraduate Medical Education, 1982-87; Deputy Chief Dental Officer, 1987-93, then Chief Dental Officer and Director of Dental Services for the NHS in Scotland, 1993-97, Scottish Office Department of Health; Hon. Senior Lecturer, Dundee Dental School, since 1993; JP for District of Ettrick and Lauderdale, since 1982; Past Chairman, Scottish Council, British Dental Association; Vice President, Commonwealth Dental Association, 1997-2003; President, Council of European Chief Dental Officers, 1999-2000; Chairman, Scottish Borders Justices Committee, 2000-05; Member, Judicial Council for Scotland, since 2007. Recreations: vintage cars (restoration and driving); music; gardening. Address: (h.) Braehead House, St. Boswells, Roxburghshire; T.-01835 823203.

Wilkin, Andrew, BA, MA, MCIL. Senior Lecturer in Italian Studies, University of Strathclyde, since 1986; b. 30.5.44, Farnborough; m., Gaynor Carole Gray; 1 s.; 1 d. (also 1 s.; 1 d. by pr. m.). Educ. Royal Naval School, Malta; University of Manchester; Open University. Assistant Lecturer, then Lecturer in Italian Studies, University of Strathclyde, 1967-86; Associate Dean, Faculty of Arts and Social Sciences, 1986-93; Course Director, BA European Studies, 1989-97. Governor, Craigie College of Education, 1985-91; Editor, Tuttitalia, 1992-97; Member, Modern Languages Panel, UCAS Scotland, 1993-2000. Publications: Harrap's Italian Verbs (Compiler), 1990, 2002; G. Verga, Little Novels of Sicily (Editor), 1973; 25 Years Emancipation? – Women in Switzerland 1971-96 (Co-Editor), 1997. Invested Cavaliere dell'Ordine al Merito della Repubblica Italiana, 1975; Elder, St. David's Memorial Park Church, Kirkintilloch. Recreations: travel; reading; Scottish History; supporting Partick Thistle F. C. Address: (b.) Department of Modern Languages, University of Strathclyde, Glasgow G1 1XH; T.-0141-548 3914; e-mail: andrew.wilkin@strath.ac.uk

Wilkins, Emeritus Professor Malcolm Barrett, BSc, PhD, DSc, AKC, FRSE. Regius Professor of Botany, Glasgow University, 1970-2000, now Emeritus Professor (Dean, Faculty of Science, 1985-88; Member, University Court, 1993-97); b.27.2.33, Cardiff; m., Mary Patricia Maltby; 1 s.; 1 d. (deceased). Educ. Monkton House School, Cardiff; King's College, London University. Lecturer in Botany, King's College, London, 1958-64; Lecturer in Biology, then Professor of Biology, East Anglia University, 1964-67; Professor of Plant Physiology, Nottingham University, 1967-70. Rockefeller Foundation Fellow, Yale University, 1961-62; Corporation Research Fellow, Harvard University, 1962-63; Darwin Lecturer, British Association for the Advancement of Science, 1967; elected Corresponding (Honorary) Member, American Society of Plant Physiologists, 1984; Chairman, Life Science Working Group, European Space Agency, 1987-89; Trustee, Royal Botanic Garden, Edinburgh, 1990-99, Chairman, 1994-99; Vice President, Royal Society of Edinburgh, 1994-97; Member, Advisory Council, Scottish Agricultural College, since 1992. Recreations: fishing; model engineering. Address: (h.) 5 Hughenden Drive, Glasgow G12 9XS; T.-0141-334 8079.

Wilkinson, Sheriff Alexander Birrell, QC, MA, LLB. Sheriff of Lothian and Borders at Edinburgh, 1996-2001; Sheriff of Glasgow and Strathkelvin at Glasgow, 1991-96; Temporary Judge, Court of Session, 1993-2003; b. 2.2.32, Perth; m., Wendy Imogen Barrett; 1 s.; 1 d. Educ. Perth Academy; St. Andrews University; Edinburgh University. Advocate, 1959; practised at Scottish Bar, 1959-69; Lecturer in Scots Law, Edinburgh University, 1965-69; Sheriff of Stirling, Dunbarton and Clackmannan, at Stirling and Alloa, 1969-72; Professor of Private Law, Dundee University, 1972-86 (Dean, Faculty of Law, 1974-76 and 1986); Sheriff of Tayside, Central and Fife at Falkirk, 1986-91; a Chairman, Industrial Tribunals (Scotland), 1972-86; Chancellor, Dioceses of Brechin, 1980-98, and of Argyll and the Isles, 1985-98, Scottish Episcopal Church; a Director, Scottish Episcopal Church Nominees Ltd., since 2004 and a Trustee of the General Synod of the Scottish Episcopal Church, since 2005; Chairman, Scottish Marriage Guidance Council, 1974-77; Chairman, Legal Services Group, Scottish Association of CAB, 1979-83; President, The Sheriffs' Association, 1997-2000. Publications: Gloag and Henderson's Introduction to the Law of Scotland, 8th and 9th editions (Co-editor); The Scottish Law of Evidence; The Law of Parent and Child in Scotland (Co-author); Macphail's Sheriff Court Practice, 2nd Edition (Contributor). Recreations: collecting books and pictures; reading; travel.

Wilkinson, Professor John Eric, BSc, MEd, PhD, CPsychol, FRSA. Professor of Education, Glasgow University, since 1998; Deputy Dean, Faculty of Education, 2001-05; b. 22.5.44, Lancashire; 2 s.; 1 d. Educ. Accrington Grammar School; St Andrews University; Dundee University; Glasgow University. Assistant Master, Brockehurst Sixth Form College, 1968-70; Research Assistant, Nottingham University, 1970-72; Glasgow University: Lecturer, Education, 1973-91; Senior Lecturer, 1991-98; Head of Department, 1995-99; Visiting Professor, Taipei Municipal University of Education, ROC, 2006. Publications: numerous journal articles, a book, and book chapters. Recreations: art collecting; ballet appreciation; swimming. Address: (b.) Department of Educational Studies, Glasgow University; (h.) Flat 4, 17 Crown Terrace, Glasgow, G12 9ES.

Wilkinson, Professor Paul, MA. Emeritus Professor of International Relations, St. Andrews University; Chairman of the Advisory Board, Centre for the Study of Terrorism and Political Violence, St. Andrews University; Writer on conflict and terrorism; b. 9.5.37, Harrow, Middlesex; m., Susan; 2 s.; 1 d. Educ. John Lyon School; University College, Swansea; University of Wales. RAF, 1959-65; Assistant Lecturer in Politics, University College, Cardiff, 1966-68; University of Wales: Lecturer, 1968-75, Senior Lecturer, 1975-77, Reader in Politics, 1978-79; Professor of International Relations, Aberdeen University, 1979-89; Editor, Terrorism and Political Violence, 1989-2006; Member, Editorial Board, Security Handbook, Social Intelligence, Violence and Aggression, Studies in Conflict and Terrorism, Risk Management: An International Journal; Editor, Key Concepts in International Relations; Scottish Free Enterprise Award, 1982; Honorary Fellow, University College, Swansea, 1986; Special Consultant, CBS America, 1989-90, BBC, since 1989; Aviation Security Adviser to IFAPA, 1988; Safety Adviser, World Tourism and Travel Council; FRSA, 1995; Visiting Fellow, Trinity Hall, Cambridge, 1997-98; Special Adviser, House of Commons Select Committee on Defence, since 2001. Publications: Social Movement, 1971; Political Terrorism, 1974; Terrorism and the Liberal State, 1986 (revised edition); The New Fascists, 1983; Terrorism: Theory and Practice (Co-author), 1979; British Perspectives on Terrorism (Editor), 1981; Contemporary Research on Terrorism (Joint Editor), 1987; Technology and Terrorism (Editor), 1994; Terrorism: British Perspectives (Editor), 1993; Research Report for Inquiry into Legislation Against Terrorism, Vol. II, 1996; Aviation Terrorism and Security (Joint Editor); Terrorism Versus Democracy: The Liberal State Response, 2006 (revised edition); Addressing the New International Terrorism (Co-author), 2003; International Relations: a very short introduction, 2007; Homeland Security in the UK (Editor), 2007. Recreations: modern art; poetry; walking. Address: (b.) School of International Relations, St. Andrews University, St. Andrews KY16 9AL; T.-01334 462900.

Will, David Houston, CBE, BL. Honorary Vice-President, FIFA, since 2007; Chairman, FIFA Ticketing Sub-Committee, 2010 FIFA World Cup, South Africa; b. 20.11.36, Glasgow; m., Margaret; 2 d. Educ. Brechin High School; Edinburgh University. Chairman, Brechin City FC, 1966-91; appointed to SFA Council, 1970; President, SFA, 1984-89; Vice-President, UEFA, 1986-90; Vice-President, FIFA, 1990-2007. Recreations: golf; curling. Address: (h.) Ingledene, 13 Latch Road, Brechin, Angus; T.-01356 622273.

Willetts, Professor Brian Benjamin, MA, PhD, CEng, FICE, FRSE. Professor Emeritus of Engineering, Aberdeen University; b. 12.6.36, Old Hill; m., Patricia Margaret Jones; 1 s.; 1 d. Educ. King Edward VI School, Stourbridge; Emmanuel College, Cambridge. Assistant Engineer, City of Birmingham, 1959-61; Executive Engineer, Government of Northern Nigeria, 1961-63; Lecturer/Senior Lecturer, Lanchester Polytechnic, 1963-66; Aberdeen University: Lecturer/Senior Lecturer, 1967-85, Professor of Civil Engineering, 1985-2001. Address: (h.) Grove, 24 Broomlands, Kelso, Roxburghshire TD5 7PR; T.-01573 225968.

Williams, Brian Owen, MD, HonDSc, FRCP. President, Royal College of Physicians and Surgeons of Glasgow, since 2006; Consultant Geriatrician, since 1982; b. 27.02.47, Glasgow; m., Martha; 2 d. Educ. Kings Park Secondary, Glasgow; University of Glasgow. Trained in General Medicine and Geriatric Medicine; President: British Geriatric Society, 1998-2000, European Union Geriatric Medicine Society, 1998-2000. Honorary Professor, University of Glasgow, since 2007. Publications: book chapters and original papers on medicine of old age. Recreations: gardening; theatre; literature. Address: (h.) 15 Thorn Drive, High Burnside, Glasgow G73 4RH; T.-0141 634 4480; e-mail: b.williams4@btinternet.com

Williams, Craig David, MA (Hons), PGDJ. Editor, Newsnight Scotland, BBC, since 2001; b. 9.8.71, Edinburgh; m., Pauline McLean; 1 s. Educ. Royal High School, Edinburgh; University of Edinburgh; Strathclyde University. Reporter: Border Telegraph, 1994-95, Radio Borders, 1995-96, Radio Forth, 1996-97; Producer, BBC Scotland News and Current Affairs, 1997-2000; Media Correspondent, Business am, 2000-01. Address: (b.) BBC Scotland, Zone 4.14, 40 Pacific Quay, Glasgow G51 1DA; T.-0141-338 3440; e-mail: craig.williams@bbc.co.uk

Williams, Professor Jeffrey Graham, BSc, PhD, FRSE. Professor of Developmental Biology, Dundee University, since 1998; Wellcome Trust Principal Research Fellow; b. 5.11.48, Tredegar; m., Dr Natalia Zhukovskaya; 2 s.; 2 d. Educ. Abertillery Grammar School; Kings College, London. Harkness Fellow/Postdoctoral Fellow, MIT (Boston, USA), 1973-75; Staff Scientist, ICRF, 1975-94; Jodrell Professor of Anatomy, UCL, 1994-98. Member, CRC Scientific Committee, 1992-94; Member, MRC Molecular and Cellular Medicine Board, since 1998. Recreations: squash; golf; guitar. Address: (b.) College of Life Sciences, MSI/WTB/JBC Complex, University of Dundee, Dundee DD1 5EH; T.-01382 385823.

Williams, Professor Morgan Howard, BSc Hons, PhD, DSc, CEng, FBCS, FRSA. Professor of Computer Science, Heriot-Watt University, since 1980 (Head of Department, 1980-88 and 2002-03); b. 15.12.44, Durban; 2 s. Educ. Grey High School, Port Elizabeth; Rhodes University, Grahamstown. Physicist in Antarctic Expedition, 1968-69; Rhodes University: Lecturer in Computer Science, 1970-72,

Senior Lecturer, 1972-77, Professor and Head of Department, 1977-80. Address: School of Mathematical and Computer Sciences, Heriot-Watt University, Riccarton, Edinburgh EH14 4AS; T.-0131-451 3430.

Williams, Roger Bevan, PhD, BMus, FRCO, FTCL, ARCM, PGCE, FGMS. Conductor, Composer, Musician; Master of Chapel and Ceremonial Music, University of Aberdeen, since 2006; Head, Music Department, University of Aberdeen, 1988-2006; b. 30.8.43, Swansea; m., Ann Therese Brennan; 1 s.; m., Katherine Ellen Smith; 2 s.; 1 d. Educ. Mirfield Grammar School, Yorkshire; Huddersfield School of Music; University College, Cardiff; Goldsmiths' College, University of London; King's College, Cambridge. Assistant Organist, Holy Trinity Church, Brompton, 1971; Lecturer, 1971, Director, 1973-75, Chiswick Music Centre; Organist, St. Patrick's Church, Soho, 1973; Musical Director, Sacred Heart Church, Wimbledon, 1975; Lecturer, West London Institute, 1975-78; Organist, Our Lady of Victories, Kensington, 1978-97; Lecturer, University of Aberdeen, 1978-88; Chorus Master, SNO Chorus, 1984-88; Harpsichordist, Aberdeen Sinfonietta, since 1988; first recording of Arne's Six Organ Concertos, 1988; Music at Castle Fraser: catalogue, 1995, CDs, 1997; numerous compositions, editions, catalogues of music holdings in North East Scotland. Recreations: board games; cooking; gardening. Address: (h.) The Old Hall, Barthol Chapel, Oldmeldrum, Inverurie AB51 8TD; T.-01651 806634.

Williams, Tommy, JP. Social Worker, since 1980; Member, Renfrewshire Council (Depute Leader of Council and Convenor, Community and Family Care Board); b. 28.8.52, Paisley; m., Margaret; 1 d. Educ. St. Mirin's Academy, Paisley; Notre Dame College of Education, Bearsden. Social Worker, Glasgow; UNISON Convener, Strathclyde Social Work Stewards, 1991-96; Member, Argyll and Clyde Health Board, 2001-06; Member, Greater Glasgow and Clyde Health Board; Chair, Renfrewshire Community Health Partnership; Chair, North Strathclyde Community Justice Authority; Chair, Renfrewshire Leisure Ltd., since 2003; Chair, Paisley and Renfrewshire North Labour Party. Recreation: supporting Celtic. Address: 83 Arkleston Road, Paisley PA1 3TS; T.-0141-887 6465.

Williamson, Andrew Grant, LLB, DipLP, NP. Partner, McClure Naismith, Edinburgh, since 2004; b. 10.10.67, Nottingham; partner: Katrina Mitchell; 2 s. Educ. Ashville College, Harrogate; Aberdeen University. Training, Murray Beith & Murray, 1989-92; Secondment, Harvis Trien & Beck, New York; Solicitor: Maclay Murray & Spens, 1992-93, Burness, 1993-96; Stockbroker, Peel Hunt, 1996-98; Partner, Henderson Boyd Jackson, 1998-2002; Partner and Head of Corporate, Edinburgh, DLA, 2002-04. Director: Craigmillar Development & Enterprise Limited, Cre8te Limited. Recreations: reading; golf; films; tidying up after toddler son. Address: (b.) 3 Ponton Street, Edinburgh EH3 9QQ; T.-0131 272 8378. E-mail: awilliamson@mcclurenaismith.com

Williamson, (Andrew) Peter, MSc, HDip, MHCIMA. Managing Director, NMS Enterprises Ltd., since 2003; Director, Visitor Operations, National Museums Scotland; b. 23.9.63, Edinburgh; m., Jennifer; 2 s.; 1 d. Educ. George Watson's College; Napier University. Walt Disney Company, 1984-85; Sheraton International Hotel Company, 1986-93; Whitbread Hotel Company (Marriott Hotels UK), 1995-2002. Member: Edinburgh Tourism Action Group (ETAG), Unique Venues of Edinburgh (UVE). Recreations: golf; reading; travelling. Address: (b.) National Museums Scotland, Chambers Street, Edinburgh EH1 1JF; T.-0131 247 4365; e-mail: p.williamson@nms.ac.uk

Williamson, Rev. Colin Raymond, LLB, BD. Minister, The Stewartry of Strathearn, since 2000; b.

20.1.42, Belfast, Northern Ireland; m., Arlene; 1 s.; 2 d. Educ. Dumbarton Academy; University of Glasgow; University of Edinburgh. Assistant, The Auld Kirk of Ayr (St. John The Baptist), 1971-72; Minister: Auchencairn with Rerrick, 1972-78, Leith St. Pauls, 1978-84, Aberdalgie and Dupplin with Forteviot, 1984-2000. Convener, The General Assembly's Panel on Worship, 1980-84; Chaplain: Forth Division RNR, 1980-91, HMP Perth, 1991-2001. Recreations: guitar playing; vintage tractors; rural life. Address: The Manse, Aberdalgie, Perth PH2 0QD; T.-01738 625854; e-mail: office@stewartryofstrathearn.com.uk

Williamson, Raymond MacLeod, MA, LLB, FRSA, FRSAMD. Solicitor, since 1968; Part-time Employment Judge; b. 24.12.42, Glasgow; m., Brenda; 1 s.; 1 d. Educ. High School of Glasgow; Glasgow University. Partner, MacRoberts Solicitors, Glasgow and Edinburgh, 1971-2006. Secretary, High School of Glasgow Educational Trust; Governor, High School of Glasgow; Chairman, National Youth Choir of Scotland; Chairman, Scottish International Piano Competition; Chairman, Royal Scottish National Orchestra, 1985-91; Governor, Royal Scottish Academy of Music and Drama, 1990-2002; Chairman, Children's Music Foundation in Scotland, 1994-2000; Dean, Royal Faculty of Procurators in Glasgow, 2001/04; President, Glasgow High School Club, 2003/04. Recreation: music. Address: (h.) 11 Islay Drive, Newton Mearns, Glasgow G77 6UD; T.-0141-639 4133.

Wilson of Tillyorn, Baron (David Clive Wilson), KT, GCMG, MA (Oxon), PhD, FRSE. Life Peer (1992). Master of Peterhouse, Cambridge, since 2002; Chancellor, Aberdeen University, since 1997; Deputy Vice-Chancellor, Cambridge University, since 2005; Member, Council, Glenalmond College, 1994-2005 (Chairman, 2000-05); President, Bhutan Society of the UK, since 1993; President, Hong Kong Society and Hong Kong Association, since 1994; Registrar, Order of St. Michael and St. George, since 2001; Vice-President, Royal Scottish Geographical Society, since 1998; Member, Board, Martin Currie Pacific Trust, 1993-2003; Trustee, Carnegie Trust for the Universities of Scotland, since 2000; Member, Prime Minister's Advisory Committee on Business Appointments, since 2000; b. 14.2.34, Alloa; m., Natasha Helen Mary Alexander; 2 s. Educ. Trinity College, Glenalmond; Keble College, Oxford. Entered Foreign Service, 1958; Third Secretary, Vientiane, 1959-60; language student, Hong Kong, 1960-62; Second, later First Secretary, Peking, 1963-65; FCO, 1965-68; resigned, 1968; Editor, China Quarterly, 1968-74; Visiting Scholar, Columbia University, New York, 1972; rejoined Diplomatic Service, 1974; Cabinet Office, 1974-77; Political Adviser, Hong Kong, 1977-81; Head, S. European Department, FCO, 1981-84; Assistant Under Secretary of State, FCO, 1984-87; Governor of Hong Kong, 1987-92. Member, Governing Body, School of Oriental and African Studies, 1992-97; Member, Council, CBI Scotland, 1993-2000; Chairman, Scottish and Southern Energy plc (formerly Scottish Hydro Electric), 1993-2000; Chairman, Scottish Committee, British Council, 1993-2002; Trustee, Scotland's Churches Scheme, 1999-2002; Chairman, Scottish Peers Association, 2000-02 (Vice-Chairman, 1998-2000); Chairman, Trustees, National Museums of Scotland, 2002-06 (Trustee since 1999); Hon.LLD (Aberdeen); Hon.DLitt (Sydney); Hon.DLitt (Abertay, Dundee); Hon. LLD, Chinese University, Hong Kong; Hon.DLitt (Hong Kong); KStJ. Recreations: mountaineering; reading. Address: (b.) Peterhouse, Cambridge CB2 1RD; (ho.) 64 Great King Street, Edinburgh EH3 6QY.

Wilson, Alan Oliver Arneil, MB, ChB, DPM, FRCPsych, FFCS. Former consultant in private practice, Murrayfield Hospital, Edinburgh (now retired); Member, Executive Group of Board of Directors, and First President, World Association for Psychosocial Rehabilitation; Consultant (in Scotland), Ex-Services Mental Welfare Society; b. 4.1.30,

Douglas; m., Dr. Fiona Margaret Davidson; 3 s. Educ. Biggar High School; Edinburgh University. RAMC, 1953-55; psychiatric post, Stobhill General Hospital, Glasgow, and Garlands Hospital, Carlisle, 1955-63; Consultant Psychiatrist and Deputy Physician Superintendent, St. George's Hospital, Morpeth, 1963-77; Consultant Psychiatrist, Bangour Hospitals, 1977-89; former Member, Clinical Teaching Staff, Faculty of Medicine, Edinburgh University; Clinical Lecturer, University of Newcastle upon Tyne. Chairman, Group for Study of Rehabilitation and Community Care, Scottish Division, RCPsych. V.M. Bekhterev Medal awarded by Bekhterev Psychoneurological Research Institute, St. Petersburg; Gálfi Béla Award for services to Hungarian Psychosocial Rehabilitation; Member, Founding Group, Morpeth Northumbrian Gathering; former Hibernian FC footballer. Recreations: golf; music; guitar; blethering. Address: (h.) 1, Croft Wynd, Milnathort, Perth and Kinross KY13 9GH; T.-01577 864477.

Wilson, Allan. MSP (Labour), Cunninghame North, 1999-2007; Deputy Minister for Enterprise and Lifelong Learning, 2004-07; b. 1954, Glasgow; m.; 2 s. Educ. Spiers School, Beith. Former Head of Higher Education (Scotland), UNISON. Recreation: football. Address: (h.) 44 Stoneyholm Road, Kilbirnie, Ayrshire KA25 7JS.

Wilson, Bill. MSP (SNP), West of Scotland, since 2007; b. 11.12.63. Address: Scottish Parliament, Edinburgh EH99 1SP.

Wilson, Brian, PC, MA (Hons), FSA (Scot). Chairman, Airtricity UK, since 2005; Director: Celtic plc, since 2005, AMEC Nuclear, since 2005, Interregnum plc, since 2006; Prime Minister's Special Representative on Overseas Trade, 2003-05; MP (Labour), Cunninghame North, 1987-2005; former Minister for Energy and Industry, Department of Trade and Industry; b. 13.12.48, Dunoon; m., Joni Buchanan; 2 s.; 1 d. Educ. Dunoon Grammar School; Dundee University; University College, Cardiff. Journalist; Publisher and Founding Editor, West Highland Free Press; Contributor to The Guardian, Glasgow Herald, etc.; first winner, Nicholas Tomalin Memorial Award for Journalism; contested Ross and Cromarty, Oct., 1974, Inverness, 1979, Western Isles, 1983; front-bench spokesman on Scottish Home Affairs etc., 1988-92, Transport, 1992-94 and 1995-96, Trade and Industry, 1994-95; Minister of State, Scottish Office (Education, Industry and Highland and Islands), 1997-98; Minister for Trade, Department of Trade and Industry, 1998-99; Minister of State for Scotland, 1999-2001; Minister of State, Foreign and Commonwealth Office, 2001. Visiting Professor, Glasgow Caledonian University, since 2007.

Wilson, Brian, OBE, LLB. Deputy Chairman, Local Government Boundary Commission for Scotland, since 1999; b. 20.2.46, Perth; m., Isobel Esson; 3 d. Educ. Buckie High School; Aberdeen University. Various posts with Marks & Spencer, Banff County Council, Inverness County Council and Banff and Buchan District Council; Chief Executive, Inverness District Council, 1978-95; Depute Chief Executive, The Highland Council, 1995-98. Chairman, Ness Fishery Conservation Trust. Recreations: fishing; walking; painting; computing; cutting hedges. Address: (h.) 11 Lochardil Place, Inverness IV2 4LN; T.-01463 237454.

Wilson, Carolyn Ann Buchanan, LLB (Hons), DipLP, NP. Partner, CCW LLP, since 2003; Partner, Pagan Osborne, 2003/03; b. 6.10.64, Paisley; divorced; 2 s.; 1 d. Educ. Hutchesons' Grammar School, Glasgow; Strathclyde University; Edinburgh University. Trainee, Morton Fraser & Milligan (WS); Assistant in Residential Conveyancing, Dundas & Wilson CS; Commercial Property Assistant, Maclay Murray & Spens; In-House Lawyer, Mitsubishi Finance International; Commercial Property Assistant,

Dundas & Wilson; Part-time Commercial Property Associate, Rollo Davidson McFarlane. Recreations: exercise classes; tennis; cooking; standing on sidelines of rugby; football and any other childrens sporting activities. Address: (h.) 40 Charlotte Square, Edinburgh EH2 4QH; T.-0131-220-3334; e-mail: carolyn.wilson@ccwlegal.co.uk

Wilson, Colin Alexander Megaw, LLB (Hons). First Scottish Parliamentary Counsel, since 2006; b. 4.1.52, Aberdeen; m., Mandy Esca Clay; 1 s., 1 d. Educ. High School of Glasgow; Edinburgh University. Admitted as a Solicitor, 1975; Assistant Solicitor, then Partner, Archibald Campbell & Harley, WS, Edinburgh, 1975-79; Assistant Legal Secretary to Lord Advocate, 1979-99, and until 1993 Assistant, then Depute, Parliamentary Draftsman for Scotland; Scottish Parliamentary Counsel, 1993-2006. Recreations: hill-walking; cycling; choral singing; family. Address: (b.) Office of the Scottish Parliamentary Counsel, Victoria Quay, Edinburgh EH6 6QQ; T.-0131-244 1670; e-mail: colin.wilson@scotland.gsi.gov.uk

Wilson, Donald, BA (Hons), MSc, TQ (Secondary); b. 4.12.59, Selkirk. Educ. Galashiels Academy; University of Stirling; The City University, London; Moray House College of Education, Edinburgh. Teacher of Computing, since 1984; Adult Education Tutor, since 1984; Acting Senior Teacher, ICT, 1997-99; Curriculum Development Officer, ICT, 1999-2001. Labour Councillor, City of Edinburgh Council, since 1999; Bailie of City of Edinburgh Council, since 2007; Labour Group Spokesperson for Smart City, since 2007; Member, Gorgie Dalry Partnership, since 1993, Member, Gorgie Dalry Community Council, since 1987; Member, Board: Edinburgh Technology Transfer Centre, since 1999, International Center for the Mathematical Sciences, since 1999; Chair, Transnational Demos Project, since 2001; Executive Member for Smart City, 2006-07; Executive Member for Education & Care Standards, 2005-06; Executive Member for Modernising Government, 2003-05; Vice-Chair, Edinburgh International Science Festival, since 2007, Chair, 1999-2007; Member, Edinburgh Science Foundation, since 2007, Chair, 1999-2007; Chair, Edinburgh Convention Bureaux, 2003-05, Vice-Chair, 2005-06; Chair, City of Edinburgh Council, Smart City & ICT Sounding Board, 2000-07; Member, Edinburgh & Lothians Tourist Board, 1999-2005, Chair, 2003-05; Chair, Edinburgh & Lothians Area Tourism Partnership, 2005-06; Chair, MPI-PEC Conference Host Committee, 2003-04; Vice Convener, Economic Development Committee, City of Edinburgh Council, 1999-2000; Convener, Children & Young People Scrutiny Panel, 2000-01; Member, Board, EDI, 1999-2007; Convener, Local Development Committee Conveners, City of Edinburgh Council, 2002-07; Convener, Scrutiny Panel Conveners, City of Edinburgh Council, 2002-06. Recreations: film; opera; sci-fi; computers. Address: (h.) 20 Stenhouse Mill Lane, Edinburgh EH11 3LR; T.-0131-443 5716; e-mail: donald.wilson@edinburgh.gov.uk

Wilson, Gerald R., CB, MA, FRSE, DUniv. Special Adviser, Royal Bank of Scotland Group; b. 7.9.39, Edinburgh; m., Margaret (deceased); 1 s.; 1 d. Educ. Holy Cross Academy; Edinburgh University. Assistant Principal, Scottish Home and Health Department, 1961-65; Private Secretary, Minister of State for Scotland, 1965-66; Principal, Scottish Home and Health Department, 1966-72; Private Secretary to Lord Privy Seal, 1972-74, to Minister of State, Civil Service Department, 1974; Assistant Secretary, Scottish Economic Planning Department, 1974-77; Counsellor, Office of the UK Permanent Representative to the Economic Communities, Brussels, 1977-82; Assistant Secretary, Scottish Office, 1982-84; Under Secretary, Industry Department for Scotland, 1984-88; Secretary, Scottish Office Education and Industry Department, 1988-99, Scottish Executive Enterprise and Lifelong Learning Department, 1999; Member, Court, Strathclyde University, since 1999, Deputy Convener, since 2004; Member, Board:

Royal Scottish National Orchestra, 2000-06 (Vice Chairman, since 2002); ICL (Scotland), 2000-02; Fairbridge in Scotland, Chairman, since 2006; St Andrew's Children's Society; Chairman, Scottish European Educational Trust, since 2006; Governor, George Watson's College, Edinburgh, since 2000; Chairman, Scottish Biomedical Foundation Ltd., 1999-2004. Recreation: music. Address: (b.) 4 Inverleith Avenue South, Edinburgh EH3 5QA.

Wilson, Professor Gordon McAndrew, MA, PhD, FRSA. Chair, East Ayrshire Community Health Partnership, since 2005; b. 4.12.39, Glasgow; m., Alison Rosemary Cook; 2 s.; 1 d. Educ. Eastwood Secondary School; Glasgow University; Jordanhill College of Education. Teacher of History and Modern Studies: Eastwood Secondary School, 1963-65, Eastwood High School, 1965-67; Lecturer in Social Studies, Hamilton College of Education, 1967-73 (Head of Department, 1973-81); Principal Lecturer in Inservice Education, then Assistant Principal, Jordanhill College of Education, 1981-88; Principal, Craigie College of Education, 1988-93; Assistant Principal and Director of University Campus Ayr, Paisley University, 1993-99, now Emeritus Professor. Chairman, South Ayrshire Hospitals NHS Trust, 1997-99; Chairman, Ayrshire and Arran Acute Hospitals NHS Trust, 1999-2004; Non-Executive Board Member, NHS Ayrshire and Arran, 1999-2007; President, Ayrshire Chamber of Commerce and Industry, 2002-04; Chair, Seascape (South Ayrshire Escape from Homelessness), since 2004; Chair, Friends of Maclaurin Galleries, Ayr, since 2005. Recreations: reading; gardening; walking; music. Address: (h.) 51 Greenfield Avenue, Alloway, Ayr KA7 4NX; T.-01292 443889.

Wilson, Helen Frances, DA, RSW, RGI, PAI. Artist; b. 25.7.54, Paisley; 1 d. Educ. John Neilson High School, Paisley; Glasgow School of Art. Drawings and paintings in public and private collections; awards and prizes include: Cargill Travelling Scholarship (Colonsay and Italy), 1976; First Prize, Scottish Drawing Competition, 1997; elected: RGI, 1984, RSW, 1997. Recreations: working with pre-school children; watching theatre, ballet, pantomime and people. Address: (h.) 1 Partickhill Road, Glasgow; T.-0141-339 5827.

Wilson, Ian Matthew, CB, MA. b. 12.12.26, Edinburgh; m., 1, Anne Chalmers (deceased); 3 s.; 2, Joyce Town. Educ. George Watson's College; Edinburgh University. Assistant Principal, Scottish Home Department, 1950; Private Secretary to Permanent Under Secretary of State, Scottish Office, 1953-55; Principal, Scottish Home Department, 1955; Assistant Secretary: Scottish Education Department, 1963, Scottish Home and Health Department, 1971; Assistant Under Secretary of State, Scottish Office, 1974-77; Under Secretary, Scottish Education Department, 1977-86; Secretary of Commissions for Scotland, 1987-92. Member, RSAMD Governing Body, 1992-2000; President, University of Edinburgh Graduates' Association, 1995-97; Director, Scottish International Piano Competition, 1997-2004. Address: (h.) 47 Braid Hills Road, Edinburgh EH10 6LD; T.-0131-447 1802.

Wilson, James Wiseman, OBE, OStJ. Director, Barcapel Foundation, since 1970; b. 31.5.33, Glasgow; m., Valerie Grant; 1 s.; 3 d. Educ. Trinity College, Glenalmond; Harvard Business School. Marketing Director, Scottish Animal Products, 1959-63; Sales Director, then Managing Director, then Chairman, Robert Wilson & Sons (1849) Ltd., 1964-85. National Trust for Scotland: Member of Council, 1977-82 and 1984-89, President, Ayrshire Members' Centre; Honorary President, Skelmorlie Golf Club and Irvine Pipe Band; won Aims of Industry Free Enterprise Award (Scotland), 1980. Recreations: golf;

backgammon; skiing; bridge; travelling. Address: (h.) Skelmorlie Castle, Skelmorlie, Ayrshire PA17 5EY; T.-01475 521127.

Wilson, Janette Sylvia, LLB, NP. Solicitor of the Church of Scotland and Law Agent to the General Assembly, since 1995; b. 15.1.51, Inverness; m., Stuart Ronald Wilson. Educ. Inverness Royal Academy; Edinburgh University. Law Apprentice, then Assistant, Dundas & Wilson, CS, Edinburgh, 1973-77; Assistant, then Partner, Ross Harper & Murphy, Edinburgh, 1977-81; Depute Solicitor, Church of Scotland, 1981-95. Member, Council of the Law Society of Scotland (Convener, Conveyancing Committee, Member, Professional Conduct and In-House Lawyers Group Committees); Secretary, Scottish Churches Committee; Secretary, Dr Neil's Garden Trust. Recreations: keeping fit; reading; gardening. Address: (b.) 121 George Street, Edinburgh; T.-0131-225 5722.

Wilson, John G., MA. MSP (SNP), Central Scotland, since 2007; Director, Scottish Low Pay Unit, 2001-07; b. 28.11.56, Falkirk; m., Frances M. McGlinchey; 1 d. Educ. Camelon High School; Glasgow University. Coachbuilder, 1972-82; Project Co-ordinator, Castlemilk Housing Involvement Project, 1987-94; Director, Glasgow Council of Tenants Associations, 1994-97; The Poverty Alliance: Senior Economic Development Officer, 1998-99, Fieldwork Manager, 1999-2001. Falkirk District Councillor, 1980-82; SNP Parliamentary candidate, Hamilton South, 2001, 2003; Westminster Candidate, 2005, Lanark and Hamilton East. Recreations: Tai Chi; archery; National Trust; Historic Scotland; RSPB. Address: (b.) Scottish Parliament, Edinburgh EH99 1SP; T.-0131-348 6684.

Wilson, Lena, BA, MBA. Chief Operating Officer, Scottish Enterprise, since 2000; b. 13.2.64, Paisley. Educ. St Andrews High School, East Kilbride; Glasgow Caledonian University; Strathclyde University. Production and quality management, electronics industry, 1985-89; Manager, Locate in Scotland, 1989-94; Deputy Chief Executive, Scottish Enterprise Forth Valley, 1994-98; Senior Advisor, World Bank, Washington DC, 1998-2000. Board Member, Prince's Scottish Youth Business Trust; Member, Strategic Board, scottishathletics; Tartan Clef Foundation member. Recreations: keeping fit; travel; cinema; theatre; music; socialising. Address: (b.) Scottish Enterprise, 150 Broomielaw, Atlantic Quay, Glasgow G2 8LU; T.-0141-228 2904.

Wilson, Les. Documentary Producer/Director, since 1980; Director, Caledonia TV Ltd., since 1992; b. 17.7.49, Glasgow; m., Adrienne Cochrane (marr. diss., 2006); 2 d. Educ. Grove Academy, Broughty Ferry. Trainee Journalist, 1969-70; hippy trail, 1970-71; Reporter, Greenock Telegraph, 1972-73; Reporter, STV, 1973-78; Editor, STV political programme, Ways and Means, 1979-80; Producer/Director, STV, 1981-92. Winner, Celtic Film Festival Award, 1991; BAFTA Scotland and British Telecom Factual/Current Affairs awards, 1997; British Telecom Factual/Current Affairs award, 1998. Publication: Scotland's War (Co-author), 1995. Recreation: Islay – the island, its people, its malts. Address: (b.) 147 Bath Street, Glasgow G2 4SQ; T.-0141-564 9100.

Wilson, Professor Lindsay, BA, DipEd, PhD, CPsychol. Professor of Psychology, University of Stirling, since 1998; b. 24.6.51, Aberdeen; m., Jean; 2 s. Educ. Biggar High School; University of Stirling; University of Edinburgh. Research Fellow, Max Planck Institute for Psychiatry, Munich, 1979-80; University of Stirling: Medical Research Council Training Fellow, 1980-83, Lecturer then Senior Lecturer, 1983-98, Head, Department of Psychology, 1995-2001. Recreations: sailing; hillwalking. Address: (b.) Department of Psychology, University of Stirling, Stirling FK9 4LA; T.-01786 467640.

Wilson, Monica Anne, BA, DipPCT. Director, CHANGE (Men Learning to End Their Violence to Women) Ltd., since 1997; Counsellor in Primary Care, since 1997; b. 4.3.51, Arundel; m., Keith Stewart; 1 step-d. Educ. Our Lady of Sion School, Worthing; Stirling University; Edinburgh University; Strathclyde University. Research Assistant, Stirling University, 1975-78; Research Officer, Scottish Consumer Council, 1978-80; Research Fellow, Edinburgh University, 1980-82; Research and Development Officer, Forth Valley Health Board, 1985-89; Joint Co-ordinator, CHANGE Project, 1989-96. Publication: Men Who Are Violent to Women (Co-Author), 1997; Trustee, Respect (National Association for Perpetrator Programmes and Associated Services). Recreations: gardening; DIY; sailing; music. Address: (b.) 4-6 South Lumley Street, Grangemouth FK3 8BT; T.-01324 485595; e-mail: monica@changeweb.org.uk

Wilson, Peter Liddell, BSc, MA, FCMI, FCIPD. Secretary, Heriot-Watt University, since 1991; b. 8.12.42, Douglas; m., Joy Janet Gibson; 2 d. Educ. Lanark Grammar School; Glasgow University; Birkbeck College, London University. Mathematics Teacher, Lanark Grammar School, 1964-67; Royal Navy (Instructor Lieutenant), 1967-70; Army (Royal Army Educational Corps), 1970-90: Commander Education, 1st Armoured Division (Lt. Col.), 1983-85, SOI Education HQ BAOR (Lt. Col.), 1986-88, MOD (Resettlement) (Colonel), 1988-90. Chairman, Edinburgh Conference Centre, since 1991. Received The Royal Norwegian Order of Merit, 1994. Recreations: golf; jogging; hill-walking; theatre. Address: (b.) Heriot-Watt University, Edinburgh EH14 4AS; T.-0131-451 3364.

Wilson, Peter M., QPM, LLB. Chief Constable, Fife Constabulary, since 2001; b. 24.8.53, Edinburgh; m.; 1 s.; 1 d. Educ. George Watson's College; Edinburgh University; Cambridge University (Diploma in Applied Criminology). Joined Edinburgh City Police, 1973; Lothians and Borders Police, 1975-97; Grampian Police, 1997-2001; HM Inspectorate of Constabulary, 2001. Recreation: golf. Address: (b.) Detroit Road, Glenrothes KY6 2RJ; T.-01592 418411.

Wilson, Robert Gordon, BL, LLD. Retired Solicitor; b. 16.4.38, Glasgow; m., Edith M. Hassall; 2 d. Educ. Douglas High School for Boys; Edinburgh University. National Secretary, SNP, 1963-71; MP, Dundee East, 1974-87; Scottish National Party: Chairman and National Convener, 1979-90, Vice-President, 1992-97; Rector, Dundee University, 1983-86; Member, Court, University of Abertay Dundee 1992-96; Member, Church and Nation Committee, Church of Scotland, 2000-03; Director, Age Concern Dundee Ltd., 2001-05; Temp. Chairman, Couple Counselling Tayside, 2006. Recreations: reading; sailing. Address: (h.) 48 Monifieth Road, Dundee DD5 2RX.

Wilson, Robert (Robin) Wight, DL, CA. Chairman, Quarriers, 1997-2004; b. 14.1.37, Glasgow; m., Jean; 2 s.; 1 d. Educ. Glenalmond School. Qualified as accountant, 1960; National Service, Royal Navy, 1960-61; Partner, Touche Ross and Co. (now Deloitte and Touche), 1965-94; retired, 1994; took up numerous directorships; Chairman, Ridings Sawmills Ltd., 1989-2005; member of various church, sport and school committees. Recreations: previously hockey and squash; now golf; travel. Address: (h.) Rossall, Gryffe Road, Kilmacolm, Renfrewshire, PA13 4AZ; T.-01505-872671.

Wilson, Roy. General Manager, Pitlochry Festival Theatre, 1961-95, Art Exhibitions Director, 1995-2004; b. St. Andrews. Educ. Burgh School and Madras College, St. Andrews. Proprietor, grocer's business, St. Andrews, 1953-58; Assistant Manager, Pitlochry Festival Theatre, 1958-61. Winner David K. Thomson Award, 1995, in recognition of his contribution to Pitlochry Festival Theatre. Recreations: plays and theatre in general; most forms of classical music, with particular interest in choral singing; listening to records; reading; art and antiques. Address: (h.) Bruach Lane, Pitlochry, Perthshire PH16 5DG; T.-Pitlochry 472897.

Wilson, Thomas Black, OBE, BSc (Hons), CEng, MBCS, FRSA. Principal, Glasgow Metropolitan College, since 2004; Principal, Glasgow College of Building and Printing, 1989-2004; Chair, Learning + Teaching Scotland, 2000-06; b. 23.12.43, Airdrie; m., Barbara Smith; 1 s.; 1 d. Educ. Cumnock Academy; Glasgow University; Jordanhill College. Principal Teacher, Prestwick Academy, 1969-74; Head, Computing Department, Ayr College, 1974-84; Depute Principal: Barmulloch College, Glasgow, 1984-86, Cardonald College, Glasgow, 1986-89. Member, Scottish Central Committee (Mathematics), 1975-82; Chair, Glasgow Telecolleges Network, 1994-2001; Member, Digital Task Force Scotland, 1999-2001; Member, National Grid for Learning Steering Group, 1999-2004; Chair, Scottish Council for Educational Technology, 1999-2000 (Governor, 1994-2000); Hon. Professor, Glasgow Caledonian University, since 1995. Recreations: reading; writing; music. Address: (b.) 60 North Hanover Street, Glasgow G1 2BP; T.-0141-566 6222.

Wilson, Valerie, BA, MSc, EdD. Hon. Senior Research Fellow, SCRE Centre, University of Glasgow, since 2004; Director, Scottish Council for Research in Education (Glasgow University), 1999-2004; b. Lancashire; m., 3 s. Educ. Cowley Girls' Grammar School; Hull University; Edinburgh University; Sheffield University. Teacher in various secondary schools, 1966-72; Tutor, Edinburgh University Centre for Continuing Education, 1978-85; Principal Consultant, International Training Services Ltd., 1986-90; Director, Stirling University Management Development Unit, 1991-94; Programme Manger, SCRE, 1994-97; Principal Researcher, Scottish Office Educational Research Unit, 1997-99. Publications: numerous research reports, articles and conference papers. Recreations: hill walking; gardening; reading group. Address: (b.) Faculty of Education, University of Glasgow, 11 Eldon Street, Glasgow G3 6NH; T.-0141-330-1968; e-mail: valerie.wilson@ scre.ac.uk

Windsor, Malcolm L., PhD, FRSC, OBE. Secretary, North Atlantic Salmon Conservation Organization, since 1984; b. 12.4.38, Bristol; m., Sally; 2 d. Educ. Cotham Grammar School, Bristol; Bristol University. Researcher, University of California, 1965-67; fisheries research, Humber Laboratory, Hull, 1967-75; Fisheries Adviser to Chief Scientist, Ministry of Agriculture and Fisheries, London, 1975-84. Secretary, Duddingston Village Conservation Society. Publication: book on fishery products. Recreations: local conservation work; jazz; walking. Address: (b.) 11 Rutland Square, Edinburgh EH1 2AS; T.-0131-228 2551; e-mail: hq@nasco.int

Windsor, Col. Rodney Francis Maurice, CBE, DL. Farmer; b. 22.2.25, Redhill; m., Deirdre Chichester (deceased); m. Angela Stainton; 2 s.; 1 d. Educ. Tonbridge School. Enlisted Royal Armoured Corps, 1943; commissioned The Queen's Bays, 1944-52; Captain, 1949;

ADC to CINC and High Commissioner Austria, 1949-50; served in North Irish Horse (TA), 1959-67; Lt. Col. Commanding, 1964-67; Colonel TA N. Ireland, 1967-71; ADC (TA) to HM The Queen, 1970-75; Member, Highland TA Association, 1971-77; Member, Banff and Buchan District Valuation Appeal Committee, 1982-96 (Chairman, 1989-96); Deputy Lieutenant:, Co. Antrim, 1967-97, Aberdeenshire, since 1989; Hon. President, Turiff Branch, Royal British Legion Scotland, since 1997; Member, Aberdeen Committee, Scottish Veterans Garden City Association, since 1993. Recreations: field sports; golf. Address: (h.) Mains of Warthill, Meikle Wartle, Inverurie, Aberdeenshire AB51 5AJ; T.-01651 821273.

Winn, Professor Philip, BA, PhD. Professor of Psychology and Dean of the Faculty of Science, University of St. Andrews; b. 31.10.54, Hull; m., Jane E. Burrows; 2 s.; 1 d. Educ. Isleworth Grammar School; University of Hull. Research Scientist, Institute of Neurology, 1979-80; Pinsent-Darwin Student in Mental Pathology, University of Cambridge, 1980-83; on Faculty, University of St. Andrews, since 1984. Recreations: cooking; music; literature; football; cycling. Address: (b.) School of Psychology, University of St. Andrews, St. Mary's College, South Street, St. Andrews, Fife KY16 9JP; T.-01334 362067; e-mail: pw@st-andrews.ac.uk

Winney, Robin John, MB, ChB, FRCPEdin. Retired Consultant Renal Physician, Edinburgh Royal Infirmary; b. 8.5.44, Dunfermline. Educ. Dunfermline High School; Edinburgh University. Recreations: badminton; curling. Address: (h.) 74 Lanark Road West, Currie, Midlothian EH14 5JZ.

Winstanley, Charles, TD, JP, MBA, DBA, DL. Chairman, NHS Lothian, since 2007; Member, Asylum and Immigration Tribunal, since 2003; b. 6.3.52, London; m., Columbine (separated); 1 s.; 1 d. Educ. Wellington College; RMA Sandhurst; Brunel University; Henley Management College. Justice of the Peace, since 1993; Member, National Consumer Council for Postal Services, since 2002; Chairman, Norfolk Probation Board, 2001-06; Panel Chairman, General Medical Council, 2000-07; Non Executive Director, Norfolk and Norwich University Hospital Trust, 1999-2006. Deputy Lieutenant, Greater London, 1997-2007. Recreations: fly fishing; sailing; motorcycling. Address: (h.) Roundel End, Stevenson, Haddington, East Lothian EH41 4PU; T.-07836 752352. E-mail: cjwinstanley@aol.com

Wisden, Professor William, MA, PhD (Cantab). Professor of Neuroscience, University of Aberdeen, since 2005; b. 28.01.64, Shoreham-by-Sea; m., Bianca; 1 d. Educ. King's Manor Comprehensive School, Shoreham-by-Sea; Cambridge University, Fitzwilliam College. EMBO Long-term fellowship, University of Heidelberg Germany; Group Leader; MRC Laboratory of Molecular Biology, Cambridge, 1993-2000, Clinical Neurology Department, University of Heidelberg, Germany, 2001-05. Research Interests: neurobiology, how the brain stores motor memories. Recreations: running; walking; gardening. Address: (h.) Institute of Medical Sciences, University of Aberdeen, Fosterhill, Aberdeen AB25 2ZD; T.-01224-551941; e-mail: w.wisden@abdn.ac.uk

Wiseman, Alan William. Director and Chairman, Robert Wiseman Dairies, since 1979; National Dairy Council, Scottish Dairy Association; b. 20.8.50, Giffnock. Educ. Duncanrig Senior Secondary School, East Kilbride. Left school to be one of his father's milkmen, 1967; has been a milkman ever since. Scottish Businessman of the Year,

1992; Scottish Business Achievement Award, 1994; Fellow, Royal Agricultural Society. Recreations: golf; shooting. Address: (b.) Cadzow House, High Parks Farm, Hamilton.

Wishart, Colin Fraser, DA, RIBA, FRIAS, SSA. Chartered Architect; Principal, Freespace Architecture, since 2002; Visiting Teaching Fellow, Duncan of Jordanstone College, University of Dundee, since 1997; Honorary Fellow, The School of Arts, Culture and Environment, The University of Edinburgh, since 2004; Professional Member, Society of Scottish Artists, since 1990; architectural photographer; b. 20.8.47, Dundee; divorced. Educ. Grove Academy; Duncan of Jordanstone College of Art. Architect, Thoms and Wilkie, Chartered Architects, Dundee, 1972-73; Senior Architect, City of Dundee Corporation, 1973-90; Principal Architect, City of Dundee Council, 1990-96; Partner, Battledown Studio, Natural Architecture, 1996-2002. Past President, Dundee Institute of Architects; Director, The Art Extraordinary Trust. Recreations: photography; fine art; music; poetry. Address: 3 Bruce's Wynd, Pittenweem KY10 2NR; T.-01333 310 589; e-mail: colinform@hotmail.co.uk

Wishart, Gordon. Editor, Evening Telegraph, Dundee, since 2005; b. 1.3.47; wife deceased; 2 s. Educ. Morgan Academy, Dundee. Joined DC Thomson in 1966; after short spell on Courier and Advertiser moved to Sports Desk on Evening Telegraph; later transferred to subbing, then Chief Sub, Production Editor and Deputy Editor. Recreation: watching football. Address: Evening Telegraph, 80 Kingsway East, Dundee DD4 8SL; T.-01382 223131; e-mail: newsdesk@eveningtelegraph.co.uk

Wishart, Professor Jennifer Grant, MA, PhD, CPsychol, FRSE. Professor of Developmental Disabilities in Childhood, University of Edinburgh, since 1998; b. 9.5.48, Dundee; m., Thomas Arrol. Educ. Harris Academy, Dundee; University of Edinburgh. Research Psychologist, University of Edinburgh, 1970-96 (Research Associate, 1970-79, Research Fellow, 1979-90, Senior Research Fellow, 1990-95, Reader, 1995-96); first Scottish Chair in Special Education, Moray House Institute of Education, Heriot-Watt University, 1996-98. Advisor to Scottish, UK and European Down's Syndrome Associations, International Society on Early Intervention, National Down Syndrome Foundation (Canada) and other charities. Publications: numerous papers/chapters in psychology/education/medical journals and textbooks. Recreations: wine/food; English pointers. Address: Moray House School of Education, Holyrood Road, Edinburgh EH8 8AQ; T.-0131-651 6099; e-mail: J.Wishart@ed.ac.uk

Wishart, Peter. MP (SNP), Perth and North Perthshire, since 2005, North Tayside, 2001-05; SNP Westminster: Chief Whip, 2001-07, Spokesperson for Culture, Media and Sport, since 2001, Spokesperson for Transport, 2001-05, Spokesperson for International Development, since 2005; b. 9.3.62; 1 s. Educ. Moray House College of Education. Community worker, 1984-85; musician with Runrig, 1985-2001. Address: (b.) 35 Perth Street, Blairgowrie, Perthshire PH10 6DL; 15 Princes Street, Perth PH2 8NG.

Wishart, Robert Charles, BSocSc, DipTP. Chief Statistician, Scottish Government, since 1999; b. 14.8.52, Dunfermline; m., Kathy Somers; 1 s. Educ. Dunfermline High School; Birmingham University; Strathclyde University. Planning Department, Lanarkshire County Council, 1973-75; Strathclyde Regional Council, 1975-96, latterly Senior Executive Officer (Social Policy Research and Information); Depute Head of Social Policy, Glasgow City Council, 1996-99. Address: (b.) Scottish Government, 3R01 St. Andrew's House, Regent Road, Edinburgh EH1 3DG; T.-0131-244 0302.

Wishart, Ruth. Columnist, The Herald; Broadcaster, BBC Radio, since 1989; b. Glasgow; m., Rod McLeod. Educ. Eastwood Senior Secondary School. Trustee, National Galleries of Scotland; Chair, Dewar Arts Awards; Chair, Theatre Cryptic. Contact: ruth@kilcreggan.demon.co.uk

Wiszniewski, Adrian, BA (Hons). Artist/Designer; b. 31.3.58, Glasgow; m., Diane Foley; 2 s.; 1 d. Educ. Mackintosh School of Architecture, Glasgow School of Art. Around 40 solo exhibitions throughout the world, since 1983; commissions include: two large paintings for Liverpool Anglican Cathedral 1996, Gallery of Modern Art, Glasgow, 1996, Millennium Tower, Hamilton, 1997-98; work purchased by museums worldwide including Tate Gallery, London and MOMA, New York. New York Design Award for designs of six rugs in collaboration with Edinburgh Tapestry Workshop; has created limited edition books. Recreations: looking at pictures; cinema; family.

Withers, Professor Charles William John, BSc, PhD, FBA, FRSE, FRHistS, FRGS, FRSA, Member, Academea Europaea. Professor of Geography, Edinburgh University, since 1994; b. 6.12.54, Edinburgh; m., Anne; 2 s.; 1 d. Educ. Daniel Stewart's College, Edinburgh; St. Andrews University; Cambridge University. Publications: author of 12 books, 100 academic articles. Recreations: reading; hill-walking. Address: (b.) Institute of Geography, Edinburgh University, Drummond Street, Edinburgh; T.-0131-650 2559.

Withers, James. Chief Executive, NFU Scotland, since 2008, Deputy Chief Executive, 2005-08. Address: (b.) NFU Scotland, Rural Centre, West Mains, Ingliston, Newbridge, Midlothian EH28 8LT; T.-0131 472 4000.

Withers, John Alexander (Jack), FCIL. Writer; b. Glasgow; m., Beate (Bea) Haertel. Educ. North Kelvinside School; Jordanhill College of Education (Youth and Community Diploma). Left school at 14; worked in garage, electrical industry, labouring, National Service, unemployment, razor-blade salesman; long periods abroad, wandering, wondering, working: France, FRG, Italy, Scandinavia, Spain, North Africa; youth worker; freelance writer; ski instructor; librarian; performance poet; Scottish republican and radical; plays for radio, TV, theatre; James Kennoway Screenplay Award (shared); Scottish Arts Council Awards; short stories published in numerous journals in UK, Denmark and West Germany; Editor, Two Tongues — Two Cities; books: Glasgow Limbo, A Real Glasgow Archipelago, Balancing on a Barbed Wire Fence, Hijack. Address: (h.) Flat 6/2, 6 Kirklee Gate, Glasgow G12 0SZ.

Witney, Eur. Ing. Professor Brian David, BSc, MSc, PhD, NDA, NDAgrE, CEng, CEnv, FIMechE, Hon.FIAgrE, MemASABE, FFCS. Director, Land Technology Ltd., since 1995; Hon. Professor of Agricultural Engineering, Edinburgh University, since 1989; Professor of Terramechanics, Scottish Agricultural College, Edinburgh, 1994-95; b. 8.6.38, Edinburgh; m., Maureen M.I. Donnelly; 1 s.; 2 d. Educ. Daniel Stewart's College, Edinburgh; Edinburgh University; Durham University; Newcastle University. Senior Research Associate, Newcastle upon Tyne University, 1962-66; Research Fellow, US Army

Research Office, Duke Univ., 1966-67; Senior Scientific Officer, Military Engineering Experimental Establishment, Christchurch, 1967-70; Head, Agricultural Engineering Department, East of Scotland College of Agriculture, Edinburgh, 1970-86; Director, Scottish Centre of Agricultural Engineering, 1987-95, and Vice-Dean, Scottish Agricultural College, 1990-95. President, Institution of Agricultural Engineers, 1988-90; President, European Society of Agricultural Engineers, 1993-94; Managing Editor, Landwards, 1996-2007; Managing Editor, Land Technology, 1994-96; Editor and Chairman, Editorial Board, Journal of Agricultural Engineering Research, 1998-2001, Biosystems Engineering, 2002-07; Chairman, Douglas Bomford Trust, 1998-2003. EurAgEng Award for services to agricultural engineering, 2000. Publication: Choosing and Using Farm Machines. Address: (b.) Land Technology Ltd., 33 South Barnton Avenue, Edinburgh EH4 6AN; T.-0131-336 3129.

Wittet, Ian, MA, CA. Managing Director, Coburn Blair, since 1997; b. 25.2.46, London; m., Roselyne; 4 s.; 3 d. Educ. Ampleforth College; Downing College, Cambridge. Trained John M. Geoghegan, CA, 1967-71; Peat Marwick Mitchell, Paris, 1971-72; Slater Walker, Paris, 1972-73; John M. Geoghegan, 1974-75; ASA International, 1975-2003 (Partner, 1977-86; Director, 1986-88; Managing Director, 1988-2001; Chairman, 2001-03). Honorary Consul for Turkey. Recreations: swimming; golf; bridge; travel. Address: (h.) 7 Belford Park, Edinburgh EH4 3DP; T.-0131 221 6590; e-mail: iwittet@coburnblair.co.uk

Woldman, Ethne. Chief Executive, Jewish Care Scotland, since 1996; b. 27.3.45, Glasgow; m., Harold; 1 s.; 2 d. Educ. Hutchesons' Grammar School, University of Strathclyde. Research Assistant and Research Officer, University of Glasgow; Research Officer, Ayr County Council; Principal Officer, Research, Strathclyde Regional Council; Principal Officer, Community Care; Trustee, Targu Mures Trust; Delegate, Glasgow Jewish Representative Council. Recreations: walking; voluntary work; theatre. Address: (b.) May Terrace, Giffnock, Glasgow G46 6LD; T.-0141 620 1800; e-mail: admin@jcarescot.org.uk

Wolf, Professor Charles Roland, BSc, PhD, FRSE, FMedSci, FSA, FBTS. Director, Dundee University Biomedical Research Centre, since 1992; Honorary Director, CR-UK Molecular Pharmacology Unit, Dundee, since 1992; Founder and Chief Scientific Officer, CXR Biosciences Ltd., since 2001; b. 26.2.49, Sedgefield; m., Helga Loth; 1 s.; 1 d. Educ. Surrey University. Royal Society Fellow, Institute for Physiological Chemistry, University of Searland, W. Germany 1976-77; Visiting Fellow, National Institute of Environmental Health Sciences, North Carolina, 1977-80; Visiting Scientist, ICI Central Toxicology Laboratories, Macclesfield, 1980-81; Head Scientist, Biochemistry Section, Institute of Toxicology, Mainz, W. Germany, 1981-82; Head, ICRF Molecular Pharmacology Group, Edinburgh University, 1982-92. Gerhard Zbinden Award, 2001. Publications; Molecular Genetics of Drug Resistance (Co-Editor), 1997; numerous scientific papers. Recreations: weaving; piano playing; gardening; hiking; poetry. Address: (b.) Biomedical Research Centre, Level 5, Ninewells Hospital and Medical School, Dundee DD1 9SY; T.-01382 632621.

Wolfe, William Cuthbertson, CA. Member, National Council, Scottish National Party, since 1991; Trustee, Comann Each nan Eilean (Eriskay Pony Society), since 2003; b. 22.2.24; 2 s.; 2 d. Educ. Bathgate Academy; George Watson's College, Edinburgh. Army Service, 1942-47, NW Europe and Far East; Air OP Pilot. Hon. Publications Treasurer, Saltire Society, 1953-60; Scout County Commissioner, West Lothian, 1960-64; Hon. President (Rector), Students' Association, Heriot-Watt University, 1966-69; contested (SNP) West Lothian, 1962, 1964, 1966, 1970, Feb. and Oct. 1974, 1979, North Edinburgh, Nov. 1973; Chairman, SNP, 1969-79, President, 1980-82; Treasurer, Scottish CND, 1982-85; Secretary, Scottish Poetry Library, 1985-91; Member, Forestry Commission's National Committee for Scotland, 1974-87; Vice-Chair, Scottish CND, 2002-06. Publication: Scotland Lives.

Wong, Emeritus Professor Henry H.Y., BSc, PhD, DIC, CEng, FRAeS, DUniv. Emeritus Professor, Department of Aeronautics and Fluid Mechanics, Glasgow University; Senior Research Fellow, since 1987; Adviser to the Guangdong Higher Education Bureau, China, since 1985; Adviser to Glasgow University on Chinese Affairs, since 1986; Chair Professor, Nanjing University of Aeronautics and Astronautics, since 1987; "Concurrent" Professor, National University of Defense Technology, Changsha, since 1989; b. 23.5.22, Hong Kong; m., Joan Anstey; 2 s.; 1 d. Educ. St. Stephen College, Hong Kong; Jiao-Tong University, Shanghai; Imperial College, London; Glasgow University. Assistant Lecturer, Jiao-Tong University, 1947-48; Engineer, Armstrong Siddeley, 1949; Structural Engineer, Hunting Percival Aircraft, 1949-51; Senior Structural Engineer, de Havilland Aircraft, 1952-57; Senior Lecturer, Hatfield Polytechnic, 1957-59; Lecturer, Senior Lecturer, then Reader in Aeronautics and Fluid Mechanics, Glasgow University, from 1960; Economic and Technological Consultant to Shantou Special Economic Zone, China, since 1988. Former Treasurer and Vice-Chairman, Kilmardinny Music Circle; Chairman, Glasgow Summer School, 1979-95; Consulting Editor, Contemporary Who's Who, American Biographical Institute, since 2002; City of Glasgow Lord Provost's Award, 1988. Recreations: reading; music; painting; swimming. Address: (h.) 77 Antonine Road, Bearsden, Glasgow; T.-0141-942 8346.

Wood, Alex, BA (Hons), MLitt, MEd. Principal and Head Teacher, Wester Hailes Education Centre, since 2000; b. 17.11.50, Dundee; m., Frances Kinnear; 2 d. Educ. Paisley Grammar School; New University of Ulster; Moray House College of Education; Stirling University. English Teacher, Craigroyston High School, 1973-75; Community Worker, Pilton Central Association, 1975-77; Remedial Teacher, Craigroyston High School, 1977-79; Principal Teacher, Learning Support, Craigroyston High School, 1979-90; Head of Centre, Millburn, Bathgate, 1990-96; Head Teacher, Kaimes School, 1996-99; Special Schools and Social Inclusion Manager, Edinburgh Education Department, 1999-2000. Member of Editorial Advisory Panel and contributor to SecEd; contributor to The Spire (programme of Brechin City FC); columnist, TESS. Edinburgh District Councillor, Pilton Ward, 1980-87; Parliamentary Candidate, Dumfriesshire, 1979; Parliamentary Candidate, West Edinburgh, 1984. Recreations: genealogy; horse-riding; reading. Address: (b.) 5 Murrayburn Drive, Edinburgh; T.-0131-442 2201; e-mail: alex.wood@whec.edin.sch.uk

Wood, Brian James, JP, BSc (Hons), FRSA. Rector, Hazlehead Academy, Aberdeen, since 1993; Honorary Sheriff at Stonehaven; b. 6.12.49, Banff; m., Doreen A. Petrie; 1 s.; 1 d. Educ. Banff Academy; Aberdeen Academy; Aberdeen University; Aberdeen College of Education. Teacher of Physics, George Heriot's School, Edinburgh, 1972-75; Mackie Academy, 1975-89, latterly as Depute Rector; Rector, Mearns Academy, 1989-93. Chairman, Justices of the Peace for Kincardine and

Deeside; Member, Chairmen of Justices Committee for Scotland; Elder, Church of Scotland. Recreations: sport; reading; music; travel; theatre; DIY. Address: (h.) 13 Edinview Gardens, Stonehaven; T.-01569 763888; e-mail: bwood@hazacad.org.uk

Wood, Graham Allan, MBChB, BDS, FDSRCPS, FRSC(Ed), FDSRCS(Ed), FDSRCS(Eng). Consultant Oral and Maxillofacial Surgeon, Southern General Hospital, Glasgow, since 1995; Vice Dean, Faculty of Dental Surgery, Royal College of Physicians and Surgeons of Glasgow, since 2004; Honorary Clincial Senior Lecturer, University of Glasgow, since 1995; Clinical Professor, University of Texas, USA, 1990-2000; b. 15.8.46, Glasgow; m., Lindsay Balfour; 1 s.; 1 d. Educ. Hillhead High School, Glasgow; University of Glasgow; University of Dundee. General dental practice, Glasgow, 1968-70; House Officer, Senior House Officer, Registrar, dental specialties, Glasgow Dental Hospital, Glasgow Victoria Infirmary and Canniesburn Hospital, 1970-72; Dental Surgeon, Grenfell Mission, Labrador, Canada, 1972-73; House Officer (plastic surgery), Dundee Royal Infirmary, 1978; Senior Registrar (oral and maxillofacial surgery), North Wales, 1979-83; Consultant, Oral and Maxillofacial Surgeon, North Wales, 1983-95. Fellow, International Association of Oral and Maxillofacial Surgeons; Fellow, British Association of Oral and Maxillofacial Surgeons. Recreations: hillwalking; golf; sailing; skiing. Address: (h.) Abbotsford, Broomknowe Road, Kilmacolm PA13 4HX; T.-01505 873954; e-mail: Graham.Wood@sgh.scot.nhs.uk

Wood, Sir Ian Clark, CBE (1982), LLD, BSc, DBA, DTech, CBIM, FCIB, FRSE. Chairman and Chief Executive, John Wood Group PLC, 1967-2006, Chairman, since 2007; Chairman, J.W. Holdings, since 1982; Chancellor, Robert Gordon University, since 2004; b. 21.7.42, Aberdeen; m., Helen Macrae; 3 s. Educ. Robert Gordon's College, Aberdeen; Aberdeen University. Joined family business, John Wood & Sons, 1964; Chairman, Scottish Enterprise Board, 1997-2000; Fellow, Royal Society of Arts; Grampian Industrialist of the Year, 1978; Young Scottish Businessman of the Year, 1979; Scottish Free Enterprise Award, 1985; Scottish Business Achievement Award Trust — joint winner, 1992, corporate elite leadership award services category; Hon. LLD, 1984; Hon. DBA, 1998; HonDTech, 2002; Corporate Elite "World Player" Award, 1996; Scottish Business Insider Ambassador for Scotland, 2001; Fellow: Scottish Vocational Educational Council, Scottish Qualifications Authority; Business Achievement Award, Business Insider, 2002; Entrepreneurial Exchange Hall of Fame, 2002; Business Insider/PWC Scotland PLC Awards, CEO of the Year, 2003; Glenfiddich Spirit of Scotland Award for Business, 2003; Member, SeaFar Group. Recreations: tennis; family; art. Address: (b.) John Wood Group PLC, John Wood House, Greenwell Road, East Tullos, Aberdeen; T.-01224 851000.

Wood, Jane Frances. Head of Corporate Affairs, Alliance Boots, Scotland, since 1999; b. 11.4.62, Oxford; m., Christopher Wood; 1 s.; 1 d. Educ. Madras College; Napier University. Marketing Manager, Scottish and Newcastle, 1987-89; Marketing Director, The Guinea Group, 1989-97; Director of Communications, GJW Public Affairs Europe, 1997-99. Chair, Fusion Assets; Board Director, Edinburgh City Centre Management; Board Director, Scottish Business in the Community; Council Member, CBI Scotland; Chair, North Lanarkshire Regeneration Company; Vice-Chair, Scottish Retail Consortium. Address: (h.) Port Lodge, 7 High Street, Dunbar, East Lothian EH42 1EA; T.-01368 865265; e-mail: jane.wood@allianceboots.com

Wood, Professor Robert Anderson, BSc, MB, ChB, FRCPEdin and Glas, FRCSEdin, FRCPsych. Her Majesty's Inspector of Anatomy for Scotland, since 2007; Postgraduate Medical Dean and Professor of Clinical Medicine, Aberdeen University, 1992-99; Member, Criminal Injuries Compensation Panel; Member, Advocates Discipline Tribunal; Member, Client Relations Committee, Law Society of Scotland; b. 26.5.39, Edinburgh; m., Dr. Sheila Pirie; 1 s.; 3 d. Educ. Edinburgh Academy; Edinburgh University. Consultant Physician, Perth Royal Infirmary, 1972-92; Deputy Director of Postgraduate Medical Education, Dundee University, 1985-91; Dean, RCPE, 1992-95, Councillor, 1990-92, Treasurer, 1999-2003, Trustee, since 2004; Director, MDDUS, since 2004, previously Member of Council, 1992-2004; Member, Harveian Society (President, 1998-99). Member, Royal and Ancient, Blairgowrie, Elie and Craigie Hill golf clubs. Address: (h.) Ballomill House, Abernethy, Perthshire.

Wood, Robert Bruce, LLB (Hons), LLM. Chairman, Morton Fraser LLP, since 1998; b. 2.10.51, Dunfermline; m., Agnes; 2 s.; 1 d. Educ. Madras College, St. Andrews; University of Edinburgh; University of California (Berkeley). Partner, Morton Fraser, since 1977. Past Chairman, Interlaw - International Association of Law Firms; Part-time Lecturer, School of Law, University of Edinburgh, 1979-89. Publications: Location: Leasing of Moveables (Butterworths: Stair Memorial Encyclopaedia of Law of Scotland); Scottish Section of Salinger: Factoring, 2006. Recreations: golf; mediaeval history. Address: (b.) 30-31 Queen Street, Edinburgh EH2 1JX; e-mail: bruce.wood@morton.fraser.com

Woodroffe, Wing Commander Richard John, MBE. Veolia Water Nevis, since 2007; b. 12.6.50, Newmarket; m., Elizabeth Clare; 3 s. Educ. Khormaksar, Changi, Rutlish and King Alfred's (Wantage) Grammar Schools; North Berkshire College. Purser Officer, P&O Lines Ltd., 1968; joined RAF, 1971: Pilot Officer, RAF St. Athan, 1972, Deputy Officer Commanding Accounts Flight, RAF Benson, 1973-74, Officer Commanding Personnel Services Flight, RAF Saxa Vord, 1974-75, promoted to Flying Officer, 1974, Operations Wing Adjutant and No. 3 (F) Squadron Intelligence Officer, RAF Germany Harrier Force, 1976-78, promoted to Flight Lieutenant, 1978, Officer Commanding Administration Flight, RAF Saxa Vord, 1979, Aide-de-Camp to Air Officer Commanding-in-Chief, Headquarters RAF Strike Command, 1980-82, Works Services and Airfield Survival Measures Project Officer, RAF Kinloss, 1982-84, promoted to Squadron Leader, 1984, College Secretariat 1 and College Press Liaison Officer, RAF College, Cranwell, 1984-86, Officer Commanding Personnel Management Squadron, RAF Bruggen, 1986-88, promoted to Wing Commander, 1988, assumed command of Administration Wing, RAF Leuchars, Fife, 1988-91, Air Member for Personnel's Management Planner and Briefer, MOD, 1991-93, Chairman of Boards, Officer and Aircrew Selection Centre, Cranwell then Deputy President, Ground Boards, 1993-96; posted to NATO HQ Allied Forces Central, 1996-2001; General Secretary, Royal British Legion Scotland, 2001-04; Thames Water Nevis, 2004-07. Recreations: sub-aqua; fishing; flytying; rough shooting; social golf; rugby. Club: The Royal Air Force. Address: Pitreavie Court, Dunfermline; T.-01383 749630.

Woods, (Adrien) Charles, MA. Visiting Professor, University of Strathclyde, European Policies Research Centre; formerly Senior Director, Strategy and Chief Economist, Scottish Enterprise; b. 22.9.55, London. Educ. St. Andrews University. Various posts, Scottish Development Agency, 1981-91; Scottish Enterprise: Director, Policy and Planning, 1991-92, Director, Operations, 1992-94; Chief Executive, Scotland Europa, 1994-97. Recreations: golf; cycling. E-mail: charlie.woods3@btinternet.com

Woods, Professor Kevin James, BSc, PhD, MIHM HonMFPH. Director-General Health, Scottish Government, since 2007, Head, Health Department, 2005-07; Chief

Executive, NHS Scotland, since 2005; Chief Executive, North Central London SHA, 2004-05; Director, Health Policy, Avon, Gloucestershire and Wiltshire SHA, 2004; William R. Lindsay Professor of Health Policy and Economic Evaluation, University of Glasgow, 2000-03; Chair, SAMH, 2000-03; b. 9.2.53, Sale; m., Helen Denise; 3 d. Educ. Sale County Grammar School; Queen Mary College, London University. Lecturer in Health Care, Queen Mary College and London Hospital Medical College, 1979-85; Consumer and Operational Research Officer/Deputy District General Manager, North Derbyshire Health Authority, 1985-89; District General Manager, Chester Health Authority, 1990; Regional Director of Corporate Planning/Regional General Manager, Trent Regional Health Authority, 1991-94; Director of Strategy and Performance Management, NHS Management Executive, Scottish Executive, 1995-2000. Hon. Fellow, Health Services Management Unit, Manchester University, 1990-99. Recreations: running; golf; soccer. Address: (b.) St. Andrew's House, Regent Road, Edinburgh EH1 3DG.

Woods, Professor Philip John, BSc, PhD, CPhys, FInstP. Professor of Nuclear Physics, Edinburgh University, since 2000, Head of Institute for Physics, since 2005; b. 25.6.61, Lincoln; m., Colette; 1 s.; 1 d. Educ. City Comprehensive School, Lincoln; Manchester University. Research Fellow, Birmingham University; Lecturer, then Reader, Edinburgh University, 1988-2000. Recreation: overseas travel. Address: (b.) Department of Physics and Astronomy, Edinburgh University, Edinburgh EH9 3JZ; T.-0131-650 5283.

Woods, Simon, BA, MA (Cantab). Chief Executive, Royal Scottish National Orchestra, since 2005; b. 4.9.63, Kingston upon Thames; m., Karin Brookes; 1 s.; 1 d. Educ. Kings College School, Wimbledon; Clare College, Cambridge. London Philarmonic Orchestra, 1987-88; EMI Classics, Producer, 1988-97; Vice-President, Philadelphia Orchestra, 1997-2004; President, New Jersey Symphony, 2004-05. Address: (b.) 73 Claremont Street, Glasgow G3 7JB.

Woolhouse, Professor Mark Edward John, OBE, MA, MSc, PhD, FRSE. Chair of Infectious Disease Epidemiology, University of Edinburgh, since 1997; b. 25.4.59, Shrewsbury; m., Dr. Francisca Mutapi; 1 d. Educ. Tiffin School, Kingston, Surrey; New College, University of Oxford; University of York; Queen's University, Canada. Research Fellow: University of Zimbabwe, 1985-86; Imperial College, London, 1986-89, University of Oxford, 1989-97. Recreations: walking; fly-fishing. Address: (b.) Centre for Infectious Diseases, University of Edinburgh, Ashworth Laboratories, King's Buildings, West Mains Road, Edinburgh EH9 3JT; T.-0131 650 5456.

Woollins, Professor John Derek, BSc, PhD, FRSE, FRSC, CChem. Professor (Chemistry), Head of School, Chemistry, St Andrews University, since 1999; b. 18.8.55, Cleethorpes; m., Alexandra Martha Zoya; 3 s.; 1 d. Educ. Cleethorpes Grammar School; University of East Anglia. University of British Columbia; Michigan State University; Leeds University; Imperial College, London; Professor, Loughborough University. Publications include: (books) Non Metal Rings, Cages, Clusters; Inorganic Experiments; 400 papers. Recreations: skiing; travel. Address: (b.) Department of Chemistry, St Andrews University, St Andrews KY16 9ST; T.-01334 463861.

Woolman, The Hon. Lord (Stephen Woolman), QC, LLB. Senator of the College of Justice in Scotland, since 2008; Advocate, since 1987; b. 16.5.53, Edinburgh; m.,

Dr Helen Mackinnon; 2 d. Educ. George Heriot's School; Aberdeen University. Lecturer in Law, Edinburgh University, 1978-87; QC, 1998; Advocate Depute, 1999-2002. Publication: Contract (3rd edition), 2001. Keeper of the Advocates Library, since 2004. Recreation: cinema. Address: (b.) Advocates' Library, Parliament House, Edinburgh EH1 1RF.

Wooton, Professor Ian, MA, MA, MPhil, PhD, FRSA. Professor of Economics, Strathclyde University, since 2003; Research Fellow, Centre for Economic Policy Research, London, since 1994; b. 4.4.57, Kirkcaldy; 1 s.; 1 d. Educ. Kirkcaldy High School; St. Andrews University; Columbia University, New York. Associate Professor of Economics, University of Western Ontario, London, Canada, 1982-95; Bonar-Macfie Professor of Economics, Glasgow University, 1995-2003. Recreations: travel; architecture; calligraphy. Address: (b.) Department of Economics, Strathclyde University, Sir William Duncan Building, 130 Rottenrow, Glasgow G4 0GE; T.-0141 548 3580; (h.) Flat 2B, 67 Cleveden Road, Glasgow G12 0JN; T.-0141-357 0277.

Worden, John Leonard, MA (Hons), MSc, MIPD. Dean, International Strategy and Operations, Napier University; Dean, Napier University Business School, 1996-2006; b. 19.12.49, London; m., Morag; 2 s.; 2 d. Educ. Apsley Grammar; Dundee University; Leicester University. Trainee Housing Manager, Dundee Corporation, 1974; Assistant Training Officer, Tayside Regional Council, 1975; Senior Personnel Practitioner, Tayside Regional Council, 1978; Personnel Manager, Veeder Root Ltd., 1980; Lecturer, Human Resource Management, Glasgow Caledonian University, 1981; Senior Lecturer, Napier University, 1984; Associate Head/Director of Management Development Unit, Napier University, 1990; Independent Chairman, Midlothian Council Job Evaluation Appeals Committee; Honorary Professor, Shandong University of Economics; PR China Adviser, China EU Association; Director, China EU DRC. Recreations: hill-walking; literature; football. Address: (b.) Napier University, Craiglockhart Campus, Edinburgh; T.-0131 455 4500.

Worthington, Tony, BA, MEd. Member, International Development Committee, since 1999; International Development Consultant, since 2005; Chair, Advisory Group, Natural Resources Institute, since 2005; Director, African Chapters Parliamentary Network on World Bank, since 2005; b. 11.10.41, Hertfordshire; m., Angela; 1 s.; 1 d. Educ. City School, Lincoln; London School of Economics; York University; Glasgow University. MP (Labour), Clydebank and Milngavie, 1987-2005; Parliamentary Under Secretary of State, Northern Ireland Office, 1997-98. Recreation: gardening. Address: (h.) 24 Cleddans Crescent, Hardgate, Clydebank; T.-01389 873195.
E-mail: tony@tonyworthington.com

Wray, Professor David, MD (Hons), BDS, MB, ChB, FDSRCPS, FDSRCS (Edin), FMedSci. Professor of Oral Medicine, Glasgow University, since 1993 (Dean, Dental School, 2000-05); Hon. Consultant, Greater Glasgow and Clyde Health Board, since 1993; Clinical Director, Glasgow Dental Hospital, since 2004; b. 3.1.51, Carshalton; m., Alyson P.M. Wray; 4 s.; 1 d. Educ. Uddingston Grammar School; Glasgow University. Fogarty Fellow, N.I.H. Bethesda, USA, 1979-81; Wellcome Research Fellow, Royal Dental, London, 1982; Senior Lecturer, Edinburgh University, 1983-92. Recreations: golf; curling; skiing. Address: (h.) 125 Dowanhill Street, Glasgow G12 9DN; e-mail: d.wray@dental.gla.ac.uk

Wright, Alex, ILTM, AIWSc, BSc, MA, PhD, FFCS. Lecturer in Scottish Politics, University of Dundee, since 1998; Independent Assessor for Ministerial appointments to public bodies in Scotland, since 2002; b. 4.1.52, Perth.

Educ. Aldenham School; University of Dundee. Army reservist, Royal Signals and Royal Wiltshire Yeomanry, 1975-82. Management posts, Meyer International plc, 1972-90; Research Fellow, University of Dundee, 1997-98; Visiting Research Fellow, Institute for Advanced Studies in the Humanities, University of Edinburgh, 2002; Academic Fellow, Hansard Society, 2007. Member, Institute of Welsh Affairs; Member, Scottish Consumer Council, 1998-2002; Member, Study of Parliament Group, 2003. Publications: Scotland: The Challenge of Devolution (Editor and Contributing Author), 2000; Who Governs Scotland?, 2005; contributions to: Region Building, 1995, EMU – An Expanding Europe and the World, 1998, Europe United, The United Kingdom Disunited, 2000; Scotland in Europe – Independence or Federalism?, 2001; The Internationalisation of Scottish Politics, 2003; Westminster, Devolution and the EU, 2004. Recreations: Scottish cuisine; bird watching; walking and thinking. Address: (b.) Department of Politics, University of Dundee, Dundee DD1 4HN; T.-01382 344594; e-mail: a.wright@dundee.ac.uk

Wright, Andrew Paul Kilding, OBE, BArch, RIBA, PPRIAS, FRSA, FSA Scot, FFCS. Chartered Architect and Heritage Consultant; Partner, Law & Dunbar-Nasmith, 1981-2001; b. 11.2.47, Walsall; m., Jean Patricia; 1 s.; 2 d. Educ. Queen Mary's Grammar School, Walsall; Liverpool University School of Architecture. Practising architect, since 1972; President, Inverness Architectural Association, 1986-88; External Examiner, Robert Gordon University, 1990-2003; Council, Royal Institute of British Architects, 1988-94 and 1995-97; President, Royal Incorporation of Architects in Scotland, 1995-97 (Member, Council, RIAS, 1985-94, 1995-99); Diocesan Architect, Diocese of Moray, Ross and Caithness, 1989-98; Consultant Architect to National Trust for Scotland for Mar Lodge Estate, 1995-99; Board Director, Glasgow 1999 Festival Company, 1996-2003; Member, Ancient Monuments Board for Scotland, 1996-2003; Commissioner, Royal Fine Art Commission for Scotland, 1997-2005; Hon. Adviser, Scottish Redundant Churches Trust, since 1996; Member, Church of Scotland Committee on Artistic Matters, 1999-2005; Trustee, Clan MacKenzie Charitable Trust, since 1998; Architectural Adviser, Holyrood Progress Group, Scottish Parliament, 2000-04; Conservation Adviser to Highland Buildings Preservation Trust, since 2001; Conservation Advisory Panel to Hopetoun House Preservation Trust, 1997-2007; Member, Historic Environment Advisory Council for Scotland, since 2003, Vice-Chair, 2003-06; Member, National Trust for Scotland Conservation Committee, since 2007; Member, Post Completion Advisory Group, Holyrood Building Project, 2004-06; Member, Built Environment Advisory Group, North Highland Initiative, since 2006. Recreations: music; railway history; fishing. Address: (b.) 16 Moy House Court, Forres IV36 2NZ; T.-01309 676655.

Wright, Bill, RSW, RGI, PAI, DA. Painter; b. 1.9.31, Glasgow; m., Anne Elizabeth; 3 d. Educ. Hyndland Secondary School; Glasgow School of Art. Work in several public and private collections in Norway, USA, Germany, Switzerland, Sarajavo, Saudi Arabia, Belgium; included in exhibitions in Wales, Poland, Germany, Norway, Yugoslavia, Netherlands; elected: RSW, 1977, RGI, 1990, PAI, 1995; formerly Adviser in Art, Strathclyde Regional Council; formerly Lecturer, Scottish Arts Council; President, Scottish Artists Benevolent Society. Recreations: opera; gardening; lobster fishing. Address: (h.) Old Lagalgarve Cottage, Bellochantuy, Argyll PA28 6QE; T.-01586 820372.

Wright, Charlotte, BA (Hons). Area Director, Lochaber Enterprise, since 2004; b. 6.2.63, Lincoln; m., David Wilson; 1 d. Educ. Hookergate School; Sunderland University. Various senior posts, NHS, South Tyneside, 1987-95; Partner, Lime Tree Gallery, 1995-97; Development Manager, Lochaber Enterprise, 1997-99; Head of Business and Community Development, Lochaber Enterprise, 1999-2003; Acting Chief Executive, Lochaber Enterprise, 2002-04. Recreations: running; walking in the Scottish hills. Address: (b.) St. Mary's House, Gordon Square, Fort William PH33 6DY; T.-01397 704326; e-mail: c.wright@hient.co.uk

Wright, Professor Crispin James Garth, MA, PhD, FBA, BPhil, DLitt, FRSE. Professor of Logic and Metaphysics, St. Andrews University, since 1978; Leverhulme Personal Research Professor, 1998-2003; Bishop Wardlaw Professor, since 1997; Global Distinguished Professor, New York University, since 2002; b. 21.12.42, Bagshot, Surrey; m., Catherine; 2 s. Educ. Birkenhead School; Trinity College, Cambridge. Junior Research Fellow, Trinity College, Oxford, 1967-69; Fellow/Research Fellow, All Souls College, Oxford, 1969-78. Publications: Wittgenstein on the Foundations of Mathematics, 1980; Frege's Conception of Numbers as Objects, 1983; Realism, Meaning and Truth, 1986; Truth and Objectivity, 1992; The Reason's Proper Study (Co-author), 2001; Saving the Differences, 2003. Recreations: mountaineering; gardening; travel. Address: (b.) Department of Logic and Metaphysics, St. Andrews University, St. Andrews KY16 9AL.

Wright, David John, MB, BS, FRCA, FRCPE. Consultant Anaesthetist, Western General Hospital, Edinburgh, 1979-2005; b. 13.4.44, Oswestry; m., Bronwen; 2 s.; 1 d. Educ. Bristol Grammar School; St. Bartholomew's Hospital Medical College, London. Honorary Editor, Scottish Society of the History of Medicine. Address: (h.) 20 Lennox Row, Edinburgh EH5 3JW; T.-0131-552 3439; e-mail: dr.david.wright@virgin.net

Wright, Rev. David Livingston, MA, BD, FFCS. Minister of Religion, Church of Scotland, since 1957; b. 18.5.30, Aberdeen; m., Margaret Brown; 1 d.; 2 s. Educ. Robert Gordon's College, Aberdeen; King's College, Aberdeen University. Organist and choirmaster, 1946-54; Minister: Cockenzie Chalmers Memorial, 1957-64, Forfar Lowson Memorial, 1964-71, Hawick Old, 1971-85, linked with Teviothead, 1972, Stornoway St Columba's Old Parish, 1985-98. Former Moderator of Presbytery and served on Assembly committees; former Chairman, Scottish Reformation Society and National Church Association. Publications: The Meaning of the Lord's Day; Reformed Book of Common Order (Contributor); Reformed and Evangelical (Editor); The Difference Christ Makes; Preaching the Word. Recreations: walking the dog; reading; playing piano and organ. Address: (h.) 84 Wyvis Drive, Nairn IV12 4TP; T.-01667 451613.

Wright, Professor Eric George, BSc, PhD, CBiol, MIBiol, FRCPath, FRSE. Professor of Experimental Haematology, University of Dundee, since 1999; b. 11.1.49, Wolverhampton. Educ. Wolverhampton Grammar School; Sussex University, Manchester University. WHO Research Fellow, Sloan Kettering Cancer Center, New York; Research Fellow, Paterson Institute for Cancer Research, Manchester; Lecturer in Cellular Pathology, University of St. Andrews; senior scientific positions, Medical Research Council Radiation and Genome Stability Unit, Harwell; Honorary Professor, Brunel University, University of Reading. David Anderson-Berry Medal, Royal Society of Edinburgh, 1999; Member, UK Department of Health Committee on Medical Effects of Radiation in the Environment; Member of Steering Committee, Academic Clinical Oncology and Radiobiology Research Network.

Publications: 150 scientific papers. Recreations: music; gardening; hillwalking. Address: (b.) University of Dundee, Department of Molecular and Cellular Pathology, Ninewells Hospital and Medical School, Dundee DD1 9SY; T.-01382 632169, e-mail: o.g.wright@dundee.ac.uk

Wright, George Gordon. Publisher and Photographer; b. 25.6.42, Edinburgh; m., Carmen Ilie; 1 s. Educ. Darroch Secondary School; Heriot Watt College. Started publishing as a hobby, 1969; left printing trade, 1973, to develop own publishing company; founder Member, Scottish General Publishers Association; Past Chairman, Scottish Young Publishers Society; Oliver Brown Award, 1994; Secretary/Treasurer, 200 Burns Club, since 1991. Photographic Exhibitions: The Netherbow, 1979; National Library of Scotland, 2001. Publications: MacDiarmid: An Illustrated Biography, 1977; A Guide to the Royal Mile, 1979; Orkney From Old Photographs, 1981; A Guide to Holyrood Park and Arthur's Seat, 1987. Recreations: history of Edinburgh; photography; jazz. Address: (h.) 25 Mayfield Road, Edinburgh EH9 2NQ; T.-0131-667 1300.

Wright, Rev. Kenyon Edward, CBE, MA, BA, BSc, MTh, DLitt. Convener, Vision 21; Director, Kairos; Consultant on Justice and Peace to ACTS (Action of Churches Together in Scotland); Canon Emeritus and Companion of the Order of the Cross of Nails, Coventry Cathedral; Fellow and Executive Member, Scottish Council (Development and Industry); b. 31.8.32, Paisley; m., Betty Robinson; 3 d. Educ. Paisley Grammar School; Glasgow University; Cambridge University. Missionary in India, 1955-70; Director, Ecumenical Social and Industrial Institute, Durgapur, India, 1963-70; Director, Urban Ministry, Coventry Cathedral, 1970-74; Canon Residentiary and Director of International Ministry, Coventry Cathedral, 1974-81; General Secretary, Scottish Churches Council and Director, Scottish Churches House, 1981-90; former Chair, Executive, Scottish Constitutional Convention; Member, Consultative Steering Group on the Scottish Parliament. Recreations: reading; walking; travel; living life to the full. Address: 1 Churchill Close, Ettington, Stratford CV37 7SP; T.-01789-740356; e-mail: kenyonwright@aol.com

Wright, Malcolm Robert, MHSM, DipHSM. Chief Executive, NHS Education for Scotland; b. 1.9.57, Blyth; m., Hilary; 1 s.; 1 d. Educ. Kings School, Tynemouth; Penicuik High School. Hospital Manager, Great Ormond Street, London, 1989-92; Unit General Manager, Lothian Health Board, 1992-94; Chief Executive, Edinburgh and Sick Children's NHS Trust, 1994-99; Chief Executive, Dumfries and Galloway Acute and Maternity Hospitals NHS Trust, 1999-2001; Chief Executive, Dumfries and Galloway Health Board, 2001-04. Non-Executive Director, Scottish Leadership Foundation; Chair, Children and Young People's Health Support Group; Chair, IHM Scotland, 2007. Recreations: cycling; reading. Address: (b.) Thistle House, 91 Haymarket Terrace, Edinburgh EH12 5HE; T.-0131 313 8030; e-mail: malcolm.wright@nes.scot.nhs.uk

Wright, Philip, BSc, CEng, MICE, Hon.FCIWEM. Deputy Director, Climate Change Division, Scottish Government, since 2007; b. 15.4.49, Edinburgh; m., Anne Margaret; 3 d. Educ. St. Anthony's Secondary School; Tynecastle Secondary School; Heriot Watt University. Civil Engineer, Edinburgh Corporation, 1971-75, Lothian Regional Council, 1975-82; joined Scottish Office as Senior Civil Engineer, 1982; Assistant Chief Engineer, 1991; Head, European Environment and Engineering Unit, and Chief Water Engineer, 1997. Head of Climate Change and Air Division, 2007. Chairman, Scotland and Northern Ireland Forum for Environmental Research; Director, Foundation for Water Research; Member, Environment Advisory

Group, Ofgem. Recreations: football; golf; walking. Address: (b.) Victoria Quay, Edinburgh EH6 6QQ; T.-0131-244 0193.

Wright, Professor Robert Edward, BA, MA, PhD, FRSA, FFCS, ILTM, AcSS. Professor of Economics, University of Strathclyde, since 2005; b. 28.4.58, Trenton, Ontario, Canada. Educ. Trenton High School; University of Western Ontario; University of Stockholm; INED, Paris; University of Michigan. Research Fellow, Birkbeck College, London University, 1987; Lecturer/Senior Lecturer in Economics, University of Glasgow, 1991-95; Professor of Economics, University of Stirling, 1995-2005. Recreation: mountaineering. Address: (b.) Department of Economics, Sir William Duncan Building, 130 Rottenrow, Glasgow G4 0GE; T.-0141 548 3861.

Wright, Timothy Edward, BA. Chief Executive, Edinburgh University Press, since 1998; b. 17.2.60; m., Michaela Hoskier; 2 s.; 2 d. Educ. St. Edmund's School, Canterbury; Sunderland Polytechnic. Longman Publishing Group: European Sales Manager, 1984-90, International Sales Director, 1990-94; Sales and Marketing Director, Churchill Livingstone Publishers, 1994-98; Council Member, UK Publishers Association, since 2007; Chairman, Independent Publishers Guild, since 2006 (Director, 2001-05); Member: Book Development Council of Publishers Association, 1994-98, Scottish Arts Council Arts Project Committee, 1999-2002, International Board, Publishers Association, 2002-07; Council Academic and Professional Publishers; Director, St. Mary's Music School, Edinburgh, 2000-04. Recreations: shooting; fishing; cricket; classical music. Clubs: MCC, Farmers'. Address: 23 The Causeway, Duddington Village, Edinburgh EH15 3QA; T.-0131 620 0335.
E-mail: timothy.wright@eup.ed.ac.uk

Wunsch, Nigel John, BA. Principal Route Planner, Network Rail; b. 21.5.58, Bellshill; m., Linda. Educ. St. Aloysius College; Dundee College of Technology. Various local management jobs, ScotRail, 1981-91; resource planning, ScotRail, 1991-94; timetable planning, Railtrack, 1994-98. Recreations: amateur theatre. Address: (b.) Buchanan House, 58 Port Dundas Road, Glasgow; T.-0141-555 4022.

Wyke, John Anthony, MA, PhD, VetMB, HonFRCVS, FRSE, FMedSci. Chairman, Scottish Cancer Foundation, since 2002; Emeritus Professor, Glasgow University; b. 5.4.42, Cleethorpes. Educ. Dulwich College; Cambridge University; Glasgow University; London University. Leukemia Society of America Fellow, Universities of Washington and Southern California, 1970-72; Staff Scientist, Imperial Cancer Research Fund, 1972-85; Assistant Director of Research, 1985-87; Director, Beatson Institute for Cancer Research, 1987-2002. Address: (b.) c/o Beatson Institute for Cancer Research, Garscube Estate, Switchback Road, Glasgow G61 1BD; e-mail: j.wyke@beatson.gla.ac.uk

Wylie, Rev. William Andrew, MA; b. 17.5.27, London; m., Jennifer Barclay Mack; 4 d. by pr. m. Educ. Glasgow Academy; Glasgow University and Trinity College. Royal Navy, 1944-47; Chaplain, Clyde Division, RNVR, 1954-59; Minister: Stepps, 1953-59, Scots Kirk, Lausanne, 1959-67; General Secretary, Scottish Churches Council, 1967-71; Minister, St. Andrew's and St. George's, Edinburgh, 1972-85; Chaplain, Inverclyde Industrial Mission, 1985-86; Chaplain to the offshore oil industry, 1986-91; founded Prioritas Consultants, 1991; elected Burgess of Aberdeen,

1990; Co-Founder and Chairman, Lausanne International School, 1962-67; Chairman of Governors, Aiglon College, Switzerland, 1984-91 (Hon. Chaplain, 1991); Governor, Fettes College, 1978-85; Hon. Fellow, Energy Institute; Hon. Citizen, Indianapolis, 1970. Publication: Just Being There. Recreations: gardening; writing; music; labradors; not playing golf. Address: (h.) Wellrose Cottage, Peat Inn, Fife KY15 5LH; T.-01334 840600.

Wyllie, George, MBE. Artist; b. 1921, Glasgow. Installations; performances; events; best known for "paper boat" installation and exhibition, Glasgow, Liverpool, London and New York, 1989-90; Visiting Lecturer, Glasgow School of Art; Associate, Royal Scottish Academy; Hon. DLitt, Strathclyde University, Glasgow; Honorary Fellow, Institute of Contemporary Scotland, since 2003.

Wyllie, Gordon Malcolm, SBStJ, LLB, DUniv (Glasgow), FSA Scot, NP, TEP, FFCS, WS. Partner, Biggart Baillie, Solicitors; Clerk to General Commissioners of Inland Revenue, Glasgow North and South Divisions; b. Newton Mearns. Educ. Dunoon Grammar School; Glasgow University. Honorary Treasurer, Edinburgh Summer School in Ancient Greek, 1975-99; Director, Bailford Trustees Ltd.; Chairman, Britannia Panopticon Music Hall Trust, 1997-2005; Convener, Scottish Grant-Making Trusts Group, since 2006; Regional Chairman, Action Medical Research; Member, Council, Friends at the End, 2000-02; Chairman, Edinburgh Subscription Ball Committee; Freeman of Glasgow; Deacon, Incorporation of Hammermen of Edinburgh, 1996-99; Preses, Grand Antiquity Society of Glasgow, 2000-01; Boxmaster, Convenery of Trades of Edinburgh, 2000-03; Deacon Convener, Trades of Edinburgh, 2003-06; Clerk to the Trades House of Glasgow, 1987-2004; Governor, Trades Maiden Hospital of Edinburgh; Chairman, Edinburgh West End Community Council, since 2005; Deacon, Inc. of Bonnetmakers and Dyers of Edinburgh, 2003-08; wrote Scottish contribution to International Bar Association's International Dictionary of Succession Terms; Elder, Glasgow Cathedral, since 2005; Member, Succession Committee of the Law Society of Scotland, since 2005 and the European Commission's Group of Experts on Succession and Wills in the EU. Recreations: music; history and the arts generally; country walks; foreign travel. Address: (b.) 310 St. Vincent Street, Glasgow; T.-0141-228 8000.

Wyllie, Very Rev. Dr. Hugh Rutherford, MA, Hon.DD (Aberdeen), FCIBS. Minister, Old Parish Church of Hamilton, 1981-2000; Moderator, General Assembly of the Church of Scotland, 1992-93; Lay Member, Scottish Executive's Working Party, General Medical Practitioners, 2000-02; b. 11.10.34, Glasgow; m., Eileen E. Cameron, MA; 2 d. Educ. Shawlands Academy; Hutchesons' Grammar School, Glasgow. Union Bank of Scotland, 1951-53; RAF, 1953-55; Glasgow University, 1956-62; Assistant Minister, Glasgow Cathedral, 1962-65; Minister, Dunbeth Church, Coatbridge, 1965-72; Minister, Cathcart South Church, Glasgow, 1972-81; Moderator, Presbytery of Hamilton, 1989-90, Convener, Business Committee, 1991-95; President, Hamilton Burns Club, 1990; founder Member, Hamilton Centre for Information for the Unemployed, 1983; introduced Dial-a-Fact on drugs and alcohol, 1986; established Hamilton Church History Project, 1984-87; Convener, General Assembly's Stewardship and Budget Committee, 1978-83; Convener, Stewardship and Finance Board, 1983-86; Convener, Assembly Council, 1987-91; Member, Board of Nomination to Church Chairs, 1985-91 and 1993-99; Member, General Assembly's Board of Practice and Procedure, 1991-95; Member, Board of Communication,

1999-2003; Non-Executive Director, Lanarkshire Health Care NHS Trust, 1995-99, Vice-Chairman, 1996-99; Trustee, Lanarkshire Primary Care NHS Trust, 1999-2001; Dr William Barclay Memorial Lecturer, 1994; admitted as Hon. Freeman, District of Hamilton, 1992; elected Member, Council, Scout Association, 1993-2003; Master, Hamilton Hospital, 1982-2000; Chaplain: Royal British Legion, Hamilton, 1981-2001, Lanarkshire Burma Star Association, 1983-2001, Q Division, Strathclyde Police, 1984-2001; George and Thomas Hutcheson Award, 2002. Recreations: gardening; DIY. Address: 18 Chantinghall Road, Hamilton ML3 8NP.

Wyllie, James Hogarth, BA, MA. Reader in International Relations, Aberdeen University and Director, Conflict and Security Studies Programme; b. 7.3.51, Dumfries; m., Claire Helen Beaton; 2 s. Educ. Sanquhar Academy; Dumfries Academy; Stirling University; Lancaster University. Research Officer, Ministry of Defence, 1974-75; Tutor in Politics, Durham University, 1975-77; Lecturer in Politics, University of East Anglia, 1977-79; freelance journalism; frequent current affairs comment and analysis, BBC Radio; Commonwealth Fellow, University of Calgary, 1988; International Affairs Analyst, Grampian Television, 1989-94; Specialist Correspondent, Jane's Intelligence Review, 1992-98. Publications: Influence of British Arms; European Security in the Nuclear Age; Economist Pocket Guide to Defence (Co-author); International Politics since 1945 (Contributor); European Security in the New Political Environment. Address: (b.) Department of Politics and International Relations, Aberdeen University, Aberdeen AB24 3QY; T.-01224 272725; e-mail: j.h.wyllie@abdn.ac.uk

Wynd, Andrew H. D., DipSocWk, CQSW, MIOD. Chief Executive, Scottish Spina Bifida Association. Address: (b.) The Dan Young Building, 6 Craighalbert Way, Cumbernauld, Glasgow G68 0LS; T.-01236 794500; e-mail: chiefexec@ssba.org.uk

Y

Yarrow, Sir Eric Grant, MBE, DL, CEng, MRINA, FRSE. Chairman, Clydesdale Bank PLC, 1985-91 (Director, since 1962); Director, National Australia Bank Ltd., 1987-91; b. 23.4.20, Glasgow; m., 1, Rosemary Ann Young (deceased); 1 s. (deceased); 2, Annette Elizabeth Francoise Steven (m. diss.); 3 s.; 3, Joan Botting; 3 step d. Educ. Marlborough College; Glasgow University. Served engineering apprenticeship, G. & J. Weir, 1938-39; Royal Engineers, 1939-45; served Burma, 1942-45 (Major, RE, 1945); Yarrow & Co. Ltd. (later Yarrow PLC): Assistant Manager, 1946, Director, 1948, Managing Director, 1958-67, Chairman, 1962-85, President, 1985-87; Director, Standard Life Assurance Company, 1958-91; Chairman, Princess Louise Scottish Hospital, Erskine, 1980-86, Hon. President, since 1986; President, Scottish Convalescent Home for Children, 1957-70; Council Member, Royal Institution of Naval Architects, since 1957 (Vice President, 1965, Honorary Vice President, 1972); Member, General Committee, Lloyd's Register of Shipping, 1960-89; Deacon, Incorporation of Hammermen in Glasgow, 1961-62; Chairman, Yarrow (Shipbuilders) Ltd., 1962-79; Officer (Brother), Order of St. John, since 1965; Deputy Lieutenant, County of Renfrewshire, 1970-96; Prime Warden, Worshipful Company of Shipwrights, 1970-71; Council Member, Institute of Directors, 1983-90; President, Smeatonian Society of Civil Engineers, 1983-84; President, The Marlburian Club, 1984; President, Scottish Area, Burma Star Association, since 1990; Vice President, Royal Highland and Agricultural Society for Scotland, 1990. Address: (h.) Craigrowan, Kilmacolm PA13 4PD; T.-01505 872067; e-mail: egyarrow@aol.com

Yates, Keith, BSc (Hons), OBE. Chief Executive, Stirling Council, since 1995; b. 13.3.48, Preston; m., Aileen; 1 s.; 2 d. Educ. Preston Grammar School; Sheffield University; Liverpool University. Consultant, Peat Marwick Kates, 1971; Planning Officer, Oxfordshire County Council, 1972; Consultant, Colin Buchanan and Partners, 1973; Planning Officer, Scottish Office, 1974; Group Leader, Regional Report, Strathclyde Regional Council, 1975; senior executive posts, Strathclyde Regional Council, 1980-91; Assistant Chief Executive, Central Regional Council, 1991-95. Recreations: reading; current affairs; running; hillwalking (treble Munroist). Address: (b.) Viewforth, Stirling FK8 2ET; T.-01786 443320.

Young, Professor Archie, BSc, MBChB, MD, FRCP (Glas), FRCP (Lond), FRCP (Edin). Professor of Geriatric Medicine, University of Edinburgh, since 1998; b. 19.9.46, Glasgow; 1 s.; 1 d. Educ. High School of Glasgow. Training posts, Glasgow, London, Oxford; Consultant/Honorary Consultant posts: Oxford Rehabilitation Research Unit, University of Oxford, Royal Free Hospital and Medical School, London; Professor of Geriatric Medicine, Royal Free Hospital Medical School. Recreations: physical. Address: (b.) Geriatric Medicine Unit, University of Edinburgh, Edinburgh Royal Infirmary, Little France Crescent, Edinburgh EH16 4SA.

Young, Chick. Football Correspondent, BBC Television and Radio, since 1988; b. 4.5.51, Glasgow. Educ. Glasgow High School; Bellahouston Academy, Glasgow. Daily Record, 1969-72; Carrick Herald, Girvan, 1972; Irvine Herald, 1972-73; Charles Buchan's Football Monthly, London, 1973-74; Editor, Scottish Football magazine, 1974-75; Scottish Daily News, 1975; Scottish Daily Express, 1976; Evening Times, Glasgow, 1977-88; Radio Clyde, 1977-95; BBC, since 1988; Sunday People, 1988-89;

Scotland on Sunday, 1989-91; Columnist, Daily Star, since 1996; Columnist, Daily Express, since 2004; Columnist, BBC website, since 2002. Fraser Award, Young Journalist of the Year, 1973; British Provincial Sports Journalist of the Year, 1987; Sony Award, British Sports Broadcaster of the Year (Bronze), 1997; Scottish Sports Journalist of the Year Runner-up, 1997 and 2002; RTS Provincial Sports Reporter of the Year, 2000. Publications: Rebirth of the Blues; Mo. Address: (b.) BBC TV Sport, 40 Pacific Quay, Glasgow G51 1DA; T.-0141-338 2622. E-mail: chick.young@bbc.co.uk

Young, Professor Daniel Greer, MB, ChB, FRCSEdin, FRCSGlas, DTM&H. Former Professor of Paediatric Surgery, Glasgow University, now Honorary Senior Research Fellow; former President, British Association of Paediatric Surgeons; b. Skipness, Argyll; m., Agnes Gilchrist Donald; 1 s.; 1 d. Educ. Wishaw High School; Glasgow University. Resident Assistant Surgeon, Hospital for Sick Children, London; Senior Lecturer, Institute of Child Health, London University; Honorary Consultant Surgeon, Hospital for Sick Children, London, and Queen Elizabeth Hospital, Hackney, London; Senior Lecturer and Head, Department of Surgical Paediatrics, Glasgow University, Honorary Consultant Surgeon (retired), Royal Hospital for Sick Children and Stobhill General Hospital, Glasgow; Honorary Senior Research Fellow, Department of Surgical Paediatrics. Past President, Royal Medico-Chirurgical Society of Glasgow; Honorary President, Scottish Spina Bifida Association; Member of Council, Royal College of Physicians and Surgeons; Past Chairman, Intercollegiate Board in Paediatric Surgery; Past Chairman, National Paramedic Training Board, Scottish Ambulance Service; former Member, Professional Advisory Group, Scottish Ambulance Service; Past Chairman, West of Scotland Surgical Association; Honorary Member: British Association of Paediatric Surgeons, Hungarian Paediatric Surgical Association, South African Paediatric Surgical Association, American Surgical Paediatric Association, Polish Association of Paediatric Surgeons, Egyptian Paediatric Surgical Association; Trustee, Society for Research into Hydrocephalus and Spina Bifida; Denis Browne Gold Medal, 1999. Recreations: curling; gardening. Address: (b.) Department of Paediatric Surgery, Royal Hospital for Sick Children, Yorkhill, Glasgow G3 8SJ; T.-0141-201 0572.

Young, John Henderson, OBE, DL, FCMI. Justice of the Peace, 1968-2007; Chairman, Association of Former MSPs; MSP (Conservative), West of Scotland, 1999-2003 (retired); Member, Scottish Parliament Corporate Body, 1999-2003; Deputy Convener, National Galleries Bills Committee, 2003; Deputy Lieutenant of Glasgow, since 1981; Chairman, Association of Scottish Conservative Councillors, 1991-94, Hon. President, since 1994; Member, SPTA, 1996-99; Member, Scottish Parliament Animal Welfare Committee, since 1999; Local Government Commissioner, Rifkind Policy Commission, 1998; Scottish Conservative Transport Spokesman, 1998; Member, Strathclyde Passenger Transport Authority; Member, Commonwealth Parliamentary Delegation of the Scottish Parliament to Quebec, Canada, 2002; b. 21.12.30, Glasgow; m., Doris Paterson (deceased); 1 s. Educ. Hillhead High School, Glasgow; Scottish College of Commerce. RAF, 1949-51. Councillor, Glasgow Corporation, 1964-73; Glasgow District Council, 1974-96, City of Glasgow Council, 1996-99; Police Judge, 1971-72; Bailie/Magistrate of Glasgow on four occasions; Leader, Glasgow City Council, 1977-79, Leader of the Opposition, 1979-80, 1988-92, from 1996-98 (City of Glasgow Council); former Chairman/Vice-Chairman, Council committees; Parliamentary candidate (Conservative), Rutherglen, 1966, Cathcart, 1992, Eastwood, 1999; former Chairman, Cathcart Conservatives; Chairman, Glasgow Euro Constituency,

1987-91; Export Manager, Teacher's Whisky; Public Relations Consultant; former Vice-Chairman, Scottish Pakistani Association; Secretary, Scottish/South African Society, 1986-88; Governor, Hutcheson's Educational Trust, 1991-97; Member, Glasgow Sports Promotion Council; Life Member, Merchants House of Glasgow; Kentucky Colonel, 1984; Hon. Don Cossack (Russia), 1989; Lord Provost's Award, 1989. Publication: A History of Cathcart Conservative Association, 1918-93. Recreations: meeting people; history; reading; animal welfare. Address: (h.) 4 Deanwood Avenue, Netherlee, Glasgow G44 3RJ; T.-0141-637 9535.

Young, John Maclennan, OBE. Farmer, since 1949; Hon. Sheriff, Grampian, Highlands and Islands, since 1995; JP for Caithness, 1970-99; b. 6.6.33, Thurso. Educ. Thurso Miller Academy. Member, Caithness County Council, 1961-75 (Chairman, Housing Committee, 1968-73, Chairman, Planning Committee, 1973-75); Member, Highland Regional Council, 1974-90 (Chairman, Roads and Transport Committee, 1978-90); Member, The Highland Council, 1995-99; Provost of Caithness, 1995-99; Member, Caithness District Council, 1974-96 (Convener of the Council, 1974-96); President, Caithness Area Executive Commitee, NFU of Scotland, 1963 and 1964; Chairman, Scrabster Harbour Trust, 2001-03; Chairman, Wick Airport Consultative Committee, 1990-2002. Address: (b.) Sordale, Halkirk, Caithness KW12 6XB; T.-01847 831228.

Young, Laurence Mitchell, MBE (1998). Director, Discovery Award Association, since 1995; b. 2.7.27, Dundee; m., Margaret Thomson Fawns; 1 s.; 1 d. Educ. Stobswell Junior Secondary School; Dundee Training College. Early career in building industry; military service, King's Own Scottish Borderers, 1945-48; joined Stobswell Boys' School, 1956; Technical Teacher, 1956-67, Special Assistant, 1967-73; Principal Teacher of Guidance, Craigie High School, Dundee, 1973-87; retired, 1987; involved with Duke of Edinburgh Award, since 1964: Group Scheme Leader to Stobswell Boys' School, 1964-73, Group Leader, Craigie High School, 1973-87, Duke of Edinburgh Counsellor and Advisor for Dundee, 1969-92, Secretary/Treasurer, Dundee District Award Co-ordination Committee, since 1974; Co-Founder, Tay Award, 1985-96; Founder Member, Discovery Award, since 1987: Group Leader, Pilot Group, 1987-89, Chairman, Dundee Group, 1989-93; Chairman, Association Steering Group, 1993-95; Elder, Church of Scotland, since 1968. Recreations: family; people. Address: (h.) 124 Tweed Crescent, Menzieshill, Dundee DD2 4DS; T.-01382 641800.

Young, Mark Richard, BSc, PhD, FRES, FIBiol, CBiol. Senior Lecturer, Aberdeen University, since 1989; b. 27.10.48, Worcester; m., Jennifer Elizabeth Tully; 1 s.; 1 d. Educ. Kings School, Worcester; Birmingham University. Lecturer, Aberdeen University, 1973-89; Director of Teaching, School of Biological Sciences, since 2004; Academic Director, Centre for Learning and Teaching, since 2007. Member, North Board, Scottish Environment Protection Agency, 1996-2002; Member, Advisory Committee on SSSIS, since 1998. Recreations: natural history; walking; ball sports; visiting Hebridean islands. Address: (b.) School of Biological Sciences, University of Aberdeen, Tillydrone Avenue, Aberdeen AB24 2TZ; T.-01224 272863; e-mail: m.young@abdn.ac.uk

Young, Neil J., BArch, DipArch. Development Consultant and Co. Director, 1989-2005; b. 13.8.53, Glasgow; m., May; 1 s.; 1 d. Educ. Speir's School, Beith; Glasgow University; Mackintosh School of Architecture. Senior Partner, Young and Gault Architects, 1989-2005;

Director: Neima Ltd; Loch Lomond Leisure Ltd; The Haven Kilmacolm; Mission Scotland; Foundation Totai; Consultant to HBC Vision Ltd; Compass Christian Centre Glenshee; Glasgow City Mission; Scripture Union; Mission Networker with Baptist Union of Scotland. Recreations: church; charities; travel. Address: (b.) 1 Robinsfield, Bardowie, Milngavie G62 6ER.

Young, Raymond Kennedy, CBE, BArch (Hons), FRIAS. Chairman, Architecture and Design Scotland, since 2004; b. 23.1.46; m., Jean; 3 s. Educ. University of Strathclyde. Project Architect, ASSIST/University of Strathclyde, 1971-74; Housing Corporation, 1974-89 (Director, Scotland); Director, North, and Director Research and Innovation, Scottish Homes, 1989-97; self-employed, since 1997. Hon. Senior Research Fellow, Department of Urban Studies, University of Glasgow, since 1997; Member, UK Sustainable Development Commission, 2000-04; Visiting Professor, Department of Architecture, University of Strathclyde, since 2006. Publications: general professional publications. Recreations: theatre; music listening!; no sports. Address: Bakehouse Close, 146 Canongate, Edinburgh EH8 8DD; T.-0131 556 6699; Fax: 0131 556 6633; e-mail: info@ads.org.uk

Young, Rona Macdonald, BD, DipEd. Minister of Crosshouse Parish Church, since 1991; Minister of New Cumnock Parish Church, since 2001 (Church returned to Full Status in 2004); b. 4.5.50, Giffnock, Glasgow; m., Thomas C. Young; 2 d. Educ. Marr College, Troon; Craigie College, Ayr; Glasgow University. Primary School Teacher, Bentinck Primary, Kilmarnock, 1971-75; Minister of Crosshouse Parish Church, 1991-2001 (Church returned to Full Status in 1996). Recreation: reading. Address: (h. and b.) 37 Castle, New Cumnock, Cumnock, Ayrshire KA18 4AG; T.-01290 338296. E-mail: revronyoung@hotmail.com

Young, Professor Stephen, BCom, MSc. Professor, Department of Management, Glasgow University, since 2006; b. 20.8.44, Berwick upon Tweed; 1 s.; 1 d. Educ. Berwick Grammar School; Liverpool University; Newcastle University. Economist, Government of Tanzania, 1966-68; Head, International Economics, Milk Marketing Board, 1969-73; Lecturer/Senior Lecturer, Paisley College of Technology, 1973-79; Senior Lecturer/Professor, Strathclyde University, 1980-2005. Recreations: mountaineering (Munrost 3410); cycling; running. Address: (h.) 42 Brierie Gardens, Crosslee, Johnstone PA6 7BZ; T.-01505 615554.

Young, Sheriff Principal Sir Stephen Stewart Templeton, QC, 3rd Bt. Sheriff Principal of Grampian, Highland and Islands, since 2001; b. 24.5.47; m.; 2 s. Educ. Rugby; Trinity College, Oxford; Edinburgh University. Sheriff, Glasgow and Strathkelvin, 1984; Sheriff of North Strathclyde at Greenock, 1984-2001. Address: (b.) Sheriff Court House, Castle Street, Aberdeen AB10 1WP.

Young, William Smith Geates, LLB (Hons), NP. Managing Partner, Brechin Tindal Oatts, since 1997; b. 21.12.55, Girvan; m., Margot Glanville Jones. Educ. Girvan Academy; Glasgow University. Joined Tindal Oatts & Rodger, 1978; admitted as Solicitor, 1980; Managing Partner, Tindal Oatts, 1993. SFA Class 1 Referee List, 1990-2005; FIFA List of International Linesmen, 1992, 1993; FIFA List of International Referees, 1994-2000. Daily Mail Sports Columnist. Recreations: football; golf; after-dinner speaking. Address: (b.) 48 St. Vincent Street, Glasgow G2 5HS; T.-0141-221 8012; e-mail: wsgy@bto.co.uk

Younger, John David Bingham, LVO, JP. Lord-Lieutenant of Tweeddale, since 1994; b. 20.5.39, Doune; m., Anne Rosaleen Logan; 1 s.; 2 d. Educ. Eton College;

Royal Military Academy, Sandhurst. Argyll and Sutherland Highlanders, 1957-69; Scottish and Newcastle Breweries, 1969-79; Founder and Managing Director, Broughton Brewery Ltd., 1979-95; Director, Broughton Ales, 1995-96. Deputy Lieutenant, Tweeddale, 1987, Vice Lord-Lieutenant, 1992. Chairman, Board of Governors, Belhaven Hill School Trust, 1988; Chairman, Scottish Borders Tourist Board, 1989; Member, A&SH Regimental Trust and Committee, 1985; Member, Queen's Bodyguard for Scotland (Royal Company of Archers) since 1969, Secretary, 1993-2007, Brigadier, 2002; Vice President, RHASS, 1994; River Tweed Commissioner, 2002; President: Lowland Reserve Forces and Cadets Association, since 2006, SSAFA Forces Help (Borders), since 2006, Peebles County Cricket Club, since 2006. Recreation: the countryside. Address: (h.) Glenkirk, Broughton, Peeblesshire ML12 6JF; T.-01899 830570.

Younger, Sheriff Robert Edward Gilmour, MA, LLB. Sheriff of Tayside, Central and Fife, at Stirling, 1992-2004 (retired), Stirling and Alloa, 1987-92; b. 25.9.40, Stirling; m., Helen Jane Hayes; 1 s.; 1 d. Educ, Winchester; New College, Oxford; Edinburgh University; Glasgow University. Advocate, 1968-79; Sheriff of Glasgow and Strathkelvin, at Glasgow, 1979-82, and of Tayside, Central and Fife, at Stirling and Falkirk, 1982-87. Recreation:wondering. Address: (h.) Old Leckie, Gargunnock, Stirling; T.-01786 860213.

Younger, Susan Emma, LLB, DipLP, WS, NP. Partner and Head of Banking, Morton Fraser, since 2002; b. 12.4.64, Morpeth; m., Michael Younger; 3 d. Educ. St. Margarets, Newington, Edinburgh; Aberdeen University. Traineeship, Bonar Mackenzie, 1987-89; Assistant, Shepherd and Wedderburn, 1989-90; Associate, Anderson Strathern, 1990-2002. Tutor for Professional Competency Course for WS Society. Recreations: skiing; cooking; piano and my 3 beautiful children. Address: (b.) 30/31 Queen Street, Edinburgh EH2 1JX; T.-0131-247-1204; e-mail: susan.younger@morton-fraser.com

Youngson, Professor George Gray, MB, ChB, PhD, FRCSEdin. Consultant Surgeon, Royal Aberdeen Children's Hospital, since 1985; Honorary Professor of Paediatric Surgery, Aberdeen University, since 1999; b. 13.5.49, Glasgow; m., Sandra Jean Lister; 1 s.; 2 d. Educ. Buckhaven High School; Aberdeen University. House Officer to Professor George Smith, 1973; Research Fellow, 1975; Registrar in General Surgery, 1975-77; Senior Resident in Cardiac and Thoracic Surgery, University Hospital, London, Ontario, 1979; Lecturer in Clinical Surgery, Aberdeen University, 1981; Clinical Fellow, Paediatric Surgery, Hospital for Sick Children, Toronto, 1983; Lecturer in Surgical Paediatrics and Transplantation, Aberdeen University, 1984; Regional Advisor, Examiner and Member of Council, Royal College of Surgeons of Edinburgh. Recreations: sport (tennis, golf and squash); music (piobaireachd, guitar). Address: (h.) Birken Lodge, Bieldside, Aberdeen.

Z

Zealley, Andrew King, MB, ChB, FRCP, FRCPsych, DPM. Former Deputy Chairman, The State Hospitals Board for Scotland; former Consultant Psychiatrist, Lothian Health Board and Honorary Senior Lecturer, Edinburgh University; b. 28.10.35, Stockton-on-Tees; m., Dr. Helen Elizabeth Zealley (qv); 1 s.; 1 d. Educ. Sherborne School; Edinburgh University. Chairman, Lothian Area Medical Committee, 1978-88; Chairman, Lothian Research Ethics Committee, 1988-2004; Physician Superintendent, Royal Edinburgh Hospital, 1984-94; Medical Director, Edinburgh Healthcare NHS Trust, 1994-96. Publications include: Companion to Psychiatric Studies, 6th edition (Co-editor). Recreations: running; sailing; skiing. Address: (h.) Viewfield House, Tipperlinn Road, Edinburgh EH10 5ET; T.-0131-447 5545; e-mail: andrewzealley@hotmail.com

Zealley, Helen Elizabeth, OBE, MD, FRCPE, FFPH. Non-Executive Member, NHS Health Scotland, since 2003; Non-Executive Member, Scottish Environment Protection Agency, since 2006; Chief Administrative Medical Officer and Director of Public Health, Lothian Health Board, 1988-2000; Honorary Senior Lecturer, Edinburgh University, 1988-2000; b. 10.6.40; m., Dr. Andrew Zealley (qv); 1 s.; 1 d. Educ. St. Albans High School; Edinburgh University. Former Member, Council, Royal College of Physicians, Edinburgh; former Member, Board, Faculty of Public Health Medicine; Vice President, MedAct; former Member, Court, Edinburgh University; Trustee, Waverley Care, since 2001; Chair, Board, Friends of the Earth, Scotland, since 2003. Recreations: family and home; sailing; skiing. Address: (b.) 12 Tipperlinn Road, Edinburgh EH10 5ET; T.-0131-447 5545.

Zhao, Professor Min, MD, PhD. Professor, School of Medical Sciences, University of Aberdeen, since 2004; Honorary Consultant, Department of Ophthalmology, NHS Grampian, since 2006; b. 07.03.63, Dali, China; m., Linxia Liang; 1 s.; 1 d. Educ. The 3rd Military Medical University. Research Fellow: Research Institute of Surgery, China, 1991-94, University College London, 1994-95; Department of Biomedical Sciences, University of Aberdeen: Postdoctoral Fellow, 1995-99, Lecturer, 1999-2002, Senior Lecturer, 2002-04. Have expertise in wound healing research; published in Nature, PNAS, Physiological Review etc. Address: (b.) School of Medical Sciences, University of Aberdeen, Aberdeen AB25 2ZD; T.-01224 555732; e-mail: m.zhao@abdn.ac.uk